INFORMATION
PLEASE
ALMANAC®
ATLAS & YEARBOOK

44TH EDITION

HOUGHTON MIFFLIN COMPANY BOSTON

1991

Executive Editor
Otto Johnson
Associate Editor
Vera Dailey
Contributing Editors
Arthur Reed, Jr. (Current Events)
William E. Bruno (World Countries)
Dennis M. Lyons (Sports)
Staff
Manuscript Editors:
Lori S. Elkins and
Arthur Vidro
Maps
Maps copyright © Hammond Incorporated.
Requests for map use should be sent to Hammond Incorporated, Maplewood, New Jersey 07040.

The Information Please Almanac invites comments and suggestions from readers. Because of the many letters received, however, it is not possible to respond personally to every correspondent. Nevertheless, all suggestions are most welcome, and the editors will consider them carefully. (Information Please Almanac does not rule on bets or wagers.)

ISBN (Hardcover): 55132–3
ISBN (Paperback): 55133–1
ISSN: 0073–7860

Previous editions of INFORMATION PLEASE were published in 1989, 1988, 1987, 1986, 1985, and 1984 by Houghton Mifflin Company, in 1982 by A&W Publishing Company, and in 1981, 1980, and 1979 by Simon & Schuster, in 1978 and 1977 by Information Please Publishing, Inc., and from 1947–1976 by Dan Golenpaul Associates.

Copies of Information Please Almanac may be ordered directly by mail from:
Customer Service Department
Houghton Mifflin Company
Burlington, Ma 01803
Phone toll-free, (800) 225-3362 for price and shipping information. In Massachusetts phone: 272-1500.

INFORMATION PLEASE ALMANAC®
Editorial Office
Houghton Mifflin Company
215 Park Avenue South
New York, N.Y. 10003

PROFILE OF THE UNITED STATES

This Profile was created by the editors of *Information Please* from many data sources. Most figures are approximate. For additional details about the United States, please refer to the appropriate sections of the *Information Please Almanac*. NOTE: Figures given are latest available at presstime.

GEOGRAPHY

Number of states: 50
Land area (1990): 3,615,100 sq. mi. Share of world land area (1990): 6.2%
Northernmost point: Point Barrow, Alaska
Easternmost point: West Quoddy Head, Maine
Southernmost point: Ka Lae (South Cape), Hawaii
Westernmost point: Pochnoi Point, Alaska
Geographic center: in Butte County, S.D. (44″ 58′ N. lat., 103° 46′ W. long.)

POPULATION

Total (July 1990): 251,400,000
Center of population (1980): 1/4 mile west of De-Soto in Jefferson County, Mo.
Males (1988): 120,203,000
Females (1988) 126,126,000
White persons (1988): 207,748,000
Black and other persons (1988): 38,582,000
Breakdown by age groups (1988):
    Under 5 years: 18,456,000
    5-14 years: 34,655,000
    15-24 years: 37,622,000
    25-64 years: 125,231,000
    65 and over: 30,367,000
Centenarians (est. July 1989): 61,000; (proj. 2000): over 100,000; (proj. 2080): 1,440,000
Median age (1989): males, 31.6; females, 33.8
Rural population (1988): 56,390,000
Metropolitan population (1988): 189,413,000
Families (March 1989): 65,837,000
Average family size (March 1989): 3.16
Home ownership (1987): 58,164,000
Married couples (March 1989): 52,924,000
Unmarried couples (1989): 2,764,000
Single parents (March 1988): female, 6,273,000; male, 1,047,000
Widows (March 1989): 11,495,000
Widowers (March 1989): 2,282,000

VITAL STATISTICS

Births (1989, provisional): 4,021,000
Deaths (1989, provisional): 2,155,000
Marriages (1989, provisional): 2,404,000
Divorces (1989, provisional): 1,163,000
Infant mortality rate (est. 1988): 10/1,000
Legal abortions (1988): 1,590,750
Life expectancy (1986): white men, 72; white women, 78.8; black men, 65.2; black women, 73.5

CIVILIAN LABOR FORCE

Males (1988): 66,927,000 (94.5% employed)
Females (1988): 54,742,000 (94.4% employed)
Teenagers 16-19 (1988): 8,031,000 (84.7% employed)
Self-employed (1988): 9,917,000; 1,398,000 in agriculture; 8,519,000 in nonagriculture

INCOME AND CREDIT

Gross National Product (1989): $5,233,300,000,000
Personal income per capita (1988): $16,489
Median family income (1989): $32,448
Individual shareholders (1985): 47,040,000
Number below poverty level (1988): white, 20,765,000; black and other minorities, 11,113,000
Credit market debt outstanding (1988): $11,415,000,000,000
Mortgage debt outstanding (1988): $3,254,000,000,000
Consumer credit outstanding (1989): $727,600,000,000

EDUCATION

Public elementary and secondary pupils (proj. 1990): 40,772,000
Public elementary and secondary classroom teachers (proj. fall 1990): 2,401,000 (approx. 70.5% female, 29.5% male)
College enrollment, public and private (proj. 1990): 12,935,000
Money spent on elementary and secondary education (proj. 1990-1991): $212,900,000,000

CONVENIENCES

Households with microwaves (1987): 61%
Radio stations (AM and FM, 1988): 9,087
Television stations (Jan. 1988): 1,362
Registered automobiles (est. 1989): 144,375,000
Households with telephones (March 1989): 93%
Newspaper circulation (English language morning and evening, Sept. 30, 1989): 62,649,218
Cable TV subscribers (1989): 47,800,000
Total TV homes (est. Jan. 1, 1989): 90,000,000
Homes with VCRs (Feb. 1989): 58,000,000
Personal computers used at home (1988): 22,380,000

CRIME

Total arrests (est. 1989): 14,340,900; males, 86.2%; females, 13.8%; under 18, 16.1%
Child neglect and abuse cases (1987): 2,025,200
Prisoners under sentence of death (1988): 2,124
Law enforcement officers killed (1988): 155
Total murder victims (1989): 18,954
Households touched by crime (1988 prelim.): 22,844,000 (24.6%)
Violent crimes (1988): 1,566,000
Thefts (1988): 7,706,000

CONTENTS

SPECIAL SECTIONS

ASTRONOMY 326
AWARDS 706, 985, 986
AVIATION 354

BUSINESS AND ECONOMY 42

CALENDAR AND HOLIDAYS 576
CONSUMER'S RESOURCE GUIDE 588
COUNTRIES OF THE WORLD 152
CROSSWORD PUZZLE GUIDE 513
CURRENT EVENTS 974

DISASTERS, GREAT 383
DRUGS AND DRUG ABUSE 443

EDUCATION 833
ELECTIONS 34
ENERGY 361
ENVIRONMENT 563
ENTERTAINMENT AND CULTURE 736

FIRST AID 78

GEOGRAPHY 457

HEADLINE HISTORY 95

INDEX 7
INVENTIONS AND TECHNOLOGY 549

LAW ENFORCEMENT AND CRIME 823

MEDIA 297

MILITARY 304

NUTRITION AND HEALTH 80

PERSONAL FINANCE 411
PEOPLE.............................677, 899
POSTAGE 989

RELIGION 375

SCIENCE 529
SCIENCE AND LEARNING 534
SOCIAL SECURITY AND AGING 426
SPACE 316
SPORTS 863
STRUCTURES 129

TAXES 70
TOLL-FREE NUMBERS 596
TRAVEL 391

UNITED NATIONS 293
U.S. HISTORY AND GOVERNMENT 611
U.S. STATES AND CITIES 745
U.S. STATISTICS 790

WEATHER AND CLIMATE 664
WHERE TO FIND OUT MORE 441
WEIGHTS AND MEASURES 366
WORLD STATISTICS 137
WRITER'S GUIDE 436

YEAR IN PICTURES 497

SPECIAL FEATURES

DRUGS & DRUG ABUSE 443
Vital information on the history, use, and abuse of legal and illegal drugs and their effects. Provides sources of help and information.

PERSONAL FINANCE 411
How to make wise investment decisions: The new CDs, how to buy insurance, bonds, a home, including tax saving tips and more.

SOCIAL SECURITY & AGING 426
Up-to-date facts you need to know about the Social Security system, how to apply, your benefits, Medicare, and the supplementary income program.

LAW ENFORCEMENT & CRIME 823
The latest data on crime rates, arrests, recidi-

vism, drug offenders, profiles of felons, child abuse, and much more.

SCIENCE & LEARNING 534
The most important scientific theories and discoveries from the 15th century to the present. With illustrations and biographies.

THE YEAR IN PICTURES 497
Photo highlights of news events that made headlines in 1990

INVENTIONS & TECHNOLOGY 549
An illustrated chronology of the world's important technological discoveries and achievements from the invention of printing to the present.

SPECIAL ARTICLES

ASTRONOMY

Exploring Other Worlds and Protecting This
One: The Connection by Carl Sagan **326**
A Lesson in Astronomy U.S. Naval Observa-
tory **352**

AGING

Can America Learn for Tomorrow From the
Aging of Japan Today? by Barry Robinson
426
The Social Security System: Safe and Sound
by Gwendolyn S. King **435**

BUSINESS

Facing the "Totally New and Dynamic" An interview with Peter Drucker **42**

CONSUMERS

Telemarketing Travel Fraud Federal Trade
Commission **588**

CRIME

Recidivism of Prisoners Bureau of Justice Statistics **823**

CURRENT EVENTS

Crisis in the Persian Gulf by Arthur P. Reed,
Jr. **976**
The Changing Face of Europe by Arthur P.
Reed, Jr. **974**

DRUGS

Past and Present Cocaine Epidemics by Constance Holden **451**

ENERGY

The Fuels of The Future Consumer Reports
361

ENVIRONMENT

Pollution Knows No Boundaries by Sharon
Begley **563**
1990 Environmental Quality Index by National Wildlife Federation **565**

HEALTH

Focus on Microwave Food Packaging by Dixie
Farley **80**
The Four Main Food Poisoners **82**
Cancer Risks You Can Avoid **84**
Understanding AIDS **85**
Dietary Guidelines For Americans **88**

PERSONAL FINANCE

The ABCs of the New CDs by Carole Gould
411
Investing in U.S., Municipal, and Corporate
Bonds by Neal Ochsner **412**
A Guide to Life Insurance by Virginia Apple-
garth **415**
Making Bank Deposits **417**
Reducing Your Tax Bill for Two-Income Cou-
ples by Candace E. Trunzo **419**
Qualifying for a Mortgage—How Much Can
You Afford? by Kenneth R. Harney **420**

SCIENCE

The Human Genome Project by James D. Watson **529**

SPACE

Why Mars Should Be Earth's Next Goal by
Oleg Borisov **316**

U.S. STATISTICS

How We're Changing U.S. Bureau of the Census **790**

TAXES

The Federal Income Tax by Touche Ross **70**

TRAVEL

When You Need Help, Call the Citizen's Emergency Center Bureau of Consular Affairs
391
Health Hints for the International Traveler
398
Countries Requiring AIDS Testing For Entry
(Chart) **401**

PROFILE OF THE WORLD

GEOGRAPHY

Total area: 510,072,000 sq km; (196,887,792 sq. mi.); 361, 132,000 sq km (139,396,952 sq mi.) (70.8%) is water and 148,940,000 sq km (57,490,840 sq mi.) (29.2%) is land

Comparative area: land area about 16 times the size of the U.S.

Land boundaries: 442,000 km (274,482 mi.)

Coastline: 359,000 km (222,939 mi.)

Maritime claims:
Contiguous zone: generally 24 nm, but varies from 4 nm to 24 nm
Continental shelf: generally 200 nm, but some are 200 meters in depth
Exclusive fishing zone: most are 200 nm, but varies from 12 nm to 200 nm
Extended economic zone: 200 nm, only Madagascar claims 150 nm
Territorial sea: generally 12 nm, but varies from 3 nm to 200 nm

Disputes: 13 international land boundary disputes—Argentina-Uruguay, Bangladesh-India, Brazil-Paraguay, Brazil-Uruguay, Cambodia-Vietnam, China-India, China-U.S.S.R., Ecuador-Peru, El Salvador-Honduras, French Guiana-Suriname, Guyana-Suriname, Guyana-Venezuela, Qatar-UAE

Climate: two large areas of polar climates separated by two rather narrow temperate zones from a wide equatorial band of tropical to subtropical climates

Terrain: highest elevation is Mt. Everest at 8,848 meters (29, 108 ft) and lowest elevation is the Dead Sea at 392 meters (1,290 ft) below sea level; greatest ocean depth is the Marianas Trench at 10,924 meters (35,839 ft)

Natural resources: the oceans represent the last major frontier for the discovery and development of natural resources

Land use: 10% arable land; 1% permanent crops; 24% meadows and pastures; 31% forest and woodland; 34% other; includes 1.6% irrigated

Environment: large areas subject to severe weather (tropical cyclones), natural disasters (earthquakes, landslides, tsunamis, volcanic eruptions), industrial disasters, pollution (air, water, acid rain, toxic substances), loss of vegetation (overgrazing, deforestation, desertification), loss of wildlife resources, soil degradation, soil depletion, erosion

PEOPLE

Population: 5,316,644,000 (July 1990), growth rate 1.7% (1990)

Birth rate: 27 births/1,000 population (1990)

Death rate: 9 deaths/1,000 population (1990)

Infant mortality rate: 70 deaths/1,000 live births (1990)

Life expectancy at birth: 60 years male, 64 years female (1990)

Total fertility rate: 3.4 children born/woman (1990)

This section is reprinted from *The World Factbook, 1990,* published by the Directorate of Intelligence of the Central Intelligence Agency. Metric conversions by *Information Please Almanac.*

Literacy: 77% men; 66% women (1980)

Labor force: 1,939,000,000 (1984)

GOVERNMENT

Administrative divisions: 246 nations, dependencies, and geographic entities

Legal system: varies among each of the entities; 160 are parties to the United Nations International Court of Justice (ICJ) or World Court

Diplomatic representation: there are 157 members of the U.N.

ECONOMY

Overview: In 1989 the World economy grew at an estimated 3.0%, somewhat lower than the estimated 3.4% for 1988. The technologically advanced areas—North America, Japan, and Western Europe—together account for 65% of the gross world product (GWP) of $20.3 trillion; these developed areas grew in the aggregate at 3.5%. In contrast, the Communist (Second World) countries typically grew at between 0% and 2%, accounting for 23% of GWP. Experience in the developing countries continued mixed, with the newly industrializing countries generally maintaining their rapid growth, and many others struggling with debt, inflation, and inadequate investment. The year 1989 ended with remarkable political upheavals in the Communist countries, which presumably will dislocate economic production still further. The addition of nearly 100 million people a year to an already overcrowded globe will exacerbate the problems of pollution, desertification, underemployment, and poverty throughout the 1990s.

GWP (gross world product): $20.3 trillion, per capita $3,870; real growth rate 3.0% (1989 est.)

Inflation rate (consumer prices): 5% (1989 est.)

Exports: $2,694 billion (f.o.b. 1988); *commodities*—n.a.; *partners*—in value, about 70% of exports from industrial countries

Imports: $2,750 billion (c.i.f. 1988); *commodities*—n.a.; *partners*—in value, about 75% of imports by the industrial countries

External debt: $1,008 billion for less developed countries (1988 est.)

Industrial production: growth rate 5% (1989 est.)

Electricity: 2,838,680,000 kW capacity; 11,222,029 million kWh produced, 2,140 kWh per capita (1989)

Industries: chemicals, energy, machinery, electronics, metals, mining, textiles, food processing

Agriculture: cereals (wheat, maize, rice), sugar, livestock products, tropical crops, fruit, vegetables, fish

DEFENSE FORCES

Branches: ground, maritime, and air forces at all levels of technology

Military manpower: 29.15 million persons in the defense forces of the World (1987)

Defense expenditures: 5.4% of GWP, or $1.1 trillion (1989 est.)

COMPREHENSIVE INDEX

A

Abacus, 561
Abbreviations:
  Degrees, Academic, 863
  Postal, 992
  Weights and measures, 366–74
Abidjan, Ivory Coast, 215
ABSCAM, 123
Absolute zero, 366, 370, 373, 562
Abortions, 122, 123, 125, 127, 143, 816
Abu Dhabi, United Arab Emirates, 275
Academic costume, 863
Academy Awards, 713–15
Acadia, 105
Acadia National Park, 571
Accidents:
  Aircraft accidents, 355, 387–88
  Deaths from, 383–90, 817–18
  Fires and explosions, 384–85
  Motor vehicle, 817–18
  Railroad accidents, 388, 818
  Shipwrecks, 386
  Rates, 817, 818
  See also Disasters
Accra, Ghana, 199
Acid rain, 563, 564
Aconcagua Peak, 155, 468
Acre, 367, 368, 369
Acropolis, 97, 129
ACTION, 648
Actium, Battle of, 98
Actors, actresses:
  Awards for, 713–15, 729, 985
  Famous, 677–705
Adams, John, 650
  See also Headline History; Presidents (U.S.)
Adams, John Quincy, 651
  See also Headline History; Presidents (U.S.)
Adams National Historic Site, 573
Adding machine, 561
Addis Ababa, Ethiopia, 187
Address, forms of, 439–40
Aden, Yemen, 288
Adenauer, Konrad, 198, 677
Administration, Office of, 647
Admirals (U.S.), 304
  First, 128
Adrenaline, isolation of, 561
Adriatic Sea, 153, 214, 252, 288
Advent (season), 585, 586
Advertising, 59
  Expenditures, 59
  Leading agencies, 59
Aegean Islands, 200
Aegean Sea, 200, 273
Aerial combat, first, 355
Aerial photographers, first, 354
Afars and Issas. See Djibouti
Afghanistan, 123, 152, 261
  See also Countries
AFL-CIO, 120, 599
Africa, 465
  Explorations and discoveries, 457
  Map, 488–89
  Population, 140
  Portuguese territory, 249
  Southernmost point, 257
  See also Continents; Countries
Agate (measure), 369
Age:
  Arrests by, 825, 826
  At first marriage, 811
  Death rates by, 819, 821–22
  Life expectancy by, 142, 821
  Of unmarried mothers, 814

Population by, 141, 792–93, 796
School enrollment by, 833
Age limits:
  Driving licenses, 832
  School attendance, 834
Agencies (U.N.), 295–96
Agencies (U.S.), 648, 649
Aggtelek Cavern, 475
Agincourt, Battle of, 101
Aging
  See Social Security & Aging
Agnew, Spiro T., 630
  Resignation, 122, 660
Agriculture:
  Animals on farms, 60
  Economic statistics, 46, 60, 61
  Employment, 51, 54, 58
  Farm laborers, 51, 54, 58
  History, 556
  Income, 60
  Production by state, 60
  See also Food
Agriculture, U.S. Dept. of, 647
  Secretaries of, 640–43
AIDS, 85–87, 125
  Approved medicines, 86
  Cases, 86
  Clinical trials, 87
  Hot line, 87, 596
  Testing, 87, 401
Air (atmosphere), 335, 348
Air distances, cities, 407–10
Air Force, U.S., 305
  See also Armed Forces
Air Force, U.S. Department of:
  Secretary of, 647
Air Force Academy, U.S., 306
Airlines:
  First scheduled passenger service, 356
  Freight, 65
  Passenger traffic, 358
  Pilots, 358
  See also Travel
Airmail, 989, 991
  Firsts, 128, 355
  International, 991
  Priority mail, 989
  Stamps for, 990
Airplanes:
  Accidents, 387–88
  Exports and imports, 69
  Fastest, 359
  Invention, 354–55
  Passenger traffic, 358
  Pilots, 358
  Records, 360
Air pollution, 566
Airports, world's busiest, 358
Air transport company, first, 354
Akkadian civilization, 95, 97
Alabama, 745
  See also States of U.S.
Alabama–Coosa River, 478
Alamo, Battle of the, 107, 769
Aland Islands, 189
Alaska, 745–46
  Bought, 108, 746, 806
  Discovered, 105, 458, 746
  Gold Rush, 746
  Maps, 481–82
  Mountain peaks, 478
  National parks, 571, 572
  Oil, 746
  Volcanoes, 459, 746
  See also States of U.S.
Albania, 152, 153
  See also Countries
Alberta, Canada, 168, 169
Albuquerque, New Mexico, 778
  See also Cities (U.S.)
Alcohol. See Liquor

Alcohol abuse, 448, 455–56
Aldrin, Edwin E., Jr., 121, 324
Aleutian Islands, 106, 459
  Maps, 492, 496
Alexander the Great, 97, 152, 185, 210, 457, 677
Alexandria, Egypt, 184
Alexandria, Pharos of, 129
Alfred the Great, 99, 276
Algeria, 120, 153
  War of Independence, 119, 190
  See also Countries
Alhambra, 130
Ali, Muhammad (Cassius Clay), 899, 917
Aliens, in U.S., 808
Allende, Salvador, 172
Alliance for Progress, 120
All Saints' Day, 584
All-Star Game, Baseball, 951–52
Alpha Centauri, 332
Alps, 157, 190, 214, 267, 288
  Tunnels under, 134**
Altamaha–Ocmulgee River, 478
Altamira Cave, 475
Altiplano, 162
Altitude records, aircraft, 360
Altitudes. See Elevations
Aluminum:
  As element, 531
  Manufacture, electrolytic, 554
Amazon River, 163, 175, 458, 471
Amendments to Constitution, 618–22
  Civil rights, 618–22
  Right to bear arms, 618
  Search and seizure, 618
American Academy and Institute of Arts and Letters, 600
American Federation of Labor, 120, 599
American folklore, 644
American History. See United States History
American Independent Party, 637
American Indians. See Indians
American League. See Baseball; Football
American Red Cross, 608
American Revolution. See Revolutionary War
American Samoa, 774
American's Creed, The, 626
America's Cup, 946
Amish. See Mennonites
Amman, Jordan, 218
Ampere, 366, 369, 370
Amphetamines, 449, 452
Amphibians, endangered, 568
Amsterdam, Netherlands, 236
Amsterdam-Rhine Canal, 136
Amu Darya River, 472
Amur River, 173, 259, 471
Amusement. See Recreation
Ancient empires, 97
  Map, 96
Ancient history, events, 95–127
Andaman Islands, 206
Andaman Sea, 469
Andes, 155, 172, 175, 245, 468–69
Andorra, 153, 154
Andropov, Yuri V., 123, 124, 261, 262
Anesthetic, first use of, 561
Angel Falls, 472
Angkor Wat, 130
Angola, 154, 249
  See also Countries
Angstrom, 367, 369
Anguilla, 280
Animals:
  Classification, 561
  Endangered species, 566–68

7

Farm, 60, 61
Gestation, incubation, longevity, 570
Group terminology, 570
Names of, 569
Speed of, 570
State animals, 745–73
Ankara, Turkey, 273
Annapolis, Md., 755, 756
Naval Academy, 305–06, 756
Anniversaries, wedding, 528
Antananarivo, Madagascar, 226
Antarctica, 458, 463, 465
Australian Antarctic Territory, 157
British Antarctic Territory, 280
Exploration, 114, 458
Falkland Islands, 281
First flight over, 356
French Antarctica, 194
Icecap, 575
Ross Dependency, 238
Volcanoes, 463
Antarctic Circle, 458, 583
Anthem, National, 624
Antibiotics, 561
Anti-Comintern Treaty, 117, 197, 217
Antietam, Battle of, 108
Antigua, 155
Antigua and Barbuda, 154, 155
See also Countries
Antimony, 531
Antiparos Cavern, 475
Antipodes Islands, 238
Antiseptic, 561
Antitoxin, diphtheria, 561
Antoinette Perry Awards, 729
Antwerp, Belgium, 159
Anzio beachhead, 117
Apalachicola-Chattahoochee River, 478
Apartheid, 257
Apennine Mountains, 214, 252, 267
Apennine Tunnel, 134
Aphelion, 328, 350, 582
Apia, Western Samoa, 287
Apollo flights, 324–25
Apollo/Soyuz Test Project, 122, 325
Apothecaries fluid measure, 367
Apothecaries weight, 367
Appalachian Trail, 575
Appendicitis, 817
Appleseed, Johnny, 644
Appomattox surrender, 108, 771
Aqaba, Gulf of, 185, 213
Aquino, Benigno, 123, 246
Aquino, Corazon C., 124, 127, 246
Arabia, explored, 457
See specific Arab countries for other data
Arabian Desert, 474
Arab-Israeli wars, 118, 120–23, 185, 210, 218, 223, 253, 268, 273
See also Egypt; Israel; Jordan; Lebanon; Saudi Arabia; Syria
Arab League, 151, 210, 221, 253, 273, 275, 288
Arabs, 99
Aral Lake, 470
Arbor Day, 585
Archery, 878
Architecture. See Structures
Arctic Area: 458
Exploration, 458
First polar flight, 356
Icecap, 575
Arctic Circle, 583
Arctic Ocean, 469
Ardennes, 160
Area:
Cities of U.S., 778–87
Continents, 465
Countries, 137–38, 152–292
Deserts, 474
Formulas for, 372
Islands, 473–74
Lakes, 470–71, 575

Measure of, 366–68
Oceans, seas, 469, 575
States of U.S., 745–73
U.S. and territories, 792, 806
U.S. growth, 792, 806
Map, 805
World, 465
Argentina, 120, 123, 155, 156
Volcanoes, 462
See also Countries
Aristotle, 97, 678
Arithmetic. See Mathematics
Arizona, 746
See also States of U.S.
Arkansas, 746–47
See also States of U.S.
Arkansas River, 458, 472, 478
Arlington National Cemetery, 574, 627, 630
Armada, Spanish, 103, 263, 277
Armed Forces (U.S.), 304–08, 312–15
Defense expenditures, 61–63
History, 304–05
Joint Chiefs of Staff, 647
Medal of Honor, 315
Military interventions, 312
Officers, 304
Ranks, 304
Service academies, 305–07
Spending for, 62–63
Strength, 315
Veterans' benefits, 309–10
War casualties, 307, 311
Women, 118
See also Defense; Selective Service; Veterans
Armenia, U.S.S.R., 260
Armenian Massacre, 114
Armistice Day, 585
Arms Control and Disarmament Agency, U.S., 649
Armstrong, Neil A., 121, 324
Army, U.S. Department of the, 304
Expenditures, 62–63
Secretary of, 647
See also Armed Forces
Arrests, 824–26
See also Law enforcement; Crime
"Arsenal of the Nation," 748
Arsenic, 531
Arson, arrests for, 825–26
Art:
Glossary and Movements, 737–38
See individual artists listed in People section
Artemis, Temple of, 129
Arthur, Chester A., 655
See also Headline History; Presidents (U.S.)
Articles of Confederation, 626
Artificial Respiration, 79
Art Ross Trophy, 904
Arts and the Humanities, National Foundation on the, 648
Arts and Letters, American Academy and Institute of, 600
Aruba, 237
Asama, Mount, 459
Ascension Day, 584, 586
Ascension Island, 282
Ashmore Islands, 157
Ash Wednesday, 583, 586
Asia, 459, 465
Exploration and discoveries, 457
Map, 492–93
Population, 140
See also Continents; Countries
Assassinations, attempts, 644
See also Chronology
Assault, 825–26, 828–29
Assistance, public, 64
Associations, 599–610
Sports organizations, 931
Assyrian Empire, 95, 97, 210
Asteroids, 345

Astronauts, 128, 322–25
See also Space Exploration
Astronomical unit, 329, 369
Astronomy, 326–53
Asteroids, 345
Atmosphere, 335, 348
Auroras, 347
Comets, 345–46
Conjunctions, 349–50
Constants, 329
Constellations, 347
Eclipses, 350
Hubble Space Telescope, 322, 348
Measures, 329, 369, 370
Meteors and meteorites, 346
Moon, 331–32, 349–50
Phenomena (1991), 349–50
Planets, 332–45
Radio telescopes, 348
Seasons, 335, 576, 582–83
Stars, 328–29, 332, 348
Sun, 329, 349–50
Supernovas, 329
Telescopes, 348
Terms, 328–29
Universal time, 349
Zodiac, 347
See also Space Exploration
Asunción, Paraguay, 244
Aswan Dam, 132–33, 185, 470
See also High Aswan Dam
Atacama Desert, 172, 474
Athens, Greece, 97, 200
See also Cities (world)
Athletes. See Sports Personalities
Atlanta, Ga., 108, 750, 778
See also Cities (U.S.)
Atlantic Charter, 117
Atlantic Ocean, 469
Hurricanes, 667–69
Islands, 473–74
U.S. coastline, 479
Volcanoes, 462
Atlas Mountains, 233
Atmosphere, 335, 348
Water in, 575
Atom bomb, 117–18
Dropped on Japan, 117, 217
Atomic energy, 545
Atomic Energy Agency, International, 295
Atomic numbers, 531–32
Atomic Theory, 561
Atomic weights, 531–32
Atonement, Day of, 584, 586
Attila the Hun, 98, 678
Attlee, Clement, 278, 678
Attorneys General:
State, 745–73
United States, 639–43, 647
Auckland Islands, 238
Augustus, Emperor, 98, 678
Auroras, 347–48
Austerlitz, Battle of, 106
Austin, Tex., 769, 778
See also Cities (U.S.)
Australasia. See Oceania
Australia, 156, 157, 458
Explored, 458
Islands of, 157, 474
Map, 495
See also Continents; Countries
Australian Antarctic Territory, 157
Australian Desert, 156, 474
Austria, 117, 157
See also Countries
Authors: See Awards; People
Automobiles:
Accident deaths, 817–18
Drunken driving arrests, 825–26
Economic statistics, 66–67
Exports and imports, 67, 69
Industry, hours and wages, 55
Inventions, 558
Mileage, 365
Registrations, 66, 67, 365

Sales, 67
Services, 47
  State laws, 832
  Theft statistics: 825–26, 828–29
  U.S. production, 66
  World production, 148
  See also Motor Vehicles
Auto racing, 947–49
Autumn (1991), 576
Avalanches, 383
Average, mathematical, 374
Aviation, 354–60
  Accidents, 387–88
  Airports, world's busiest, 358
  Firsts, 354–58
  Helicopter records, 358
  International Civil Aviation
    Organization, 295
  Inventions, 354–60, 560
  Pilots, 358
  Records, 360
  Traffic (passengers, freight), 65,
    358
  Women, 355, 357–58
  World records, 360
  See also Airlines; airplanes
Avoirdupois weight, 367
Awards, 706–35, 985–86
  Academy Awards (Oscars), 713–15
  American Library Association, 730
  Antoinette Perry, 729
  Baseball Hall of Fame, 763, 952–53
  Bollingen (poetry), 730
  Broadcasting, 717, 731
  Christopher, 735
  Cy Young, 963
  du Pont-Columbia, 731
  Emmy, 985
  Fermi, 727
  Grammy Awards, 732
  Hart Trophy, 903–04
  Heisman Trophy, 881
  Kennedy Center Honors, 735
  Medal of Freedom, 733–35
  Miss America, 744, 985
  Most Valuable Player, baseball, 963
  Most Valuable Player, basketball,
    896
  Most Valuable Player, hockey,
    903–04
  Music, 727, 732
  National Book Awards, 730
  National Book Critics Circle Awards,
    730
  National Society of Film Critics, 717
  New York Drama Critics', 728–29
  Nobel Prizes, 706–12, 986
  Obies, 730
  Peabody, 717
  Presidential Medal of Freedom,
    733–35
  Pulitzer Prizes, 718–27
  Rookie of the Year, baseball, 964
  Sigma Delta Chi. *See* Society of
    Professional Journalists
  Society of Professional Journalists,
    731
  Sullivan, 944
  Tony, 729
Axel Heiberg, 474
Axis Powers, 117
Ayatollah Khomeini, 123, 209
Azerbaijan, U.S.S.R., 260
Azores, 248
Azov, Sea of, 469
Aztecs, 101, 231
Azuma, 459

B

Babbage, Charles, 107, 540, 555,
  561
Babylon, Hanging Gardens, 97, 129
Babylonian Empire, 97, 210
Bach, Johann Sebastian, 678

Bacteria, 95, 561
Baffin Bay, discovered, 458
Baffin Island, 473
Baghdad, Iraq, 210
Bagnell Dam, 759
Bahá' i Faith, 375
Bahamas, 158
  See also Countries
Bahrain, 158
  See also Countries
Baikal, Lake, 470
Bakelite, 554
Baker Island, 774
Bakke case, 122
Balance of payments, 68
Balaton, Lake, 204
Balearic Islands, 263
Bale (weight), 369
Balfour Declaration, 112, 212
Balkans, 250, 289
Balkan Wars, 110
Balloons:
  Flights, 354, 356–58
  Invention, 354
Ball-point pen, 562
Baltic Sea, 469
Baltimore, Md., 755–56, 778
  See also Cities (U.S.)
Bamako, Mali, 228
Bandar Seri Begawan, Brunei, 164
Bangkok, Thailand, 270
  See also Cities (world)
Bangladesh, 158–59, 207, 242
  See also Countries
Bangui, Central African Republic, 171
Banjul, Gambia, 195
Bank of North America, 128
Banks and banking:
  Deposits, 417–18
  Firsts, 128
  Largest, 49, 50
Banks (island), 474
Barbados, 159
  See also Countries
Barbiturates, 448–49
Barbuda. *See* Antigua and Barbuda
Barometer, 561
Baseball, 951–71
  All-Star Game, 951–52
  American League averages, 967–68
  Attendance records, 966
  Batting statistics, 954, 958, 959,
    960–61, 964
  Club standings, 958, 967
  Cy Young Award, 963
  Hall of Fame, 763, 931, 952–53
  History, 951
  Home run statistics, 954, 958, 959,
    960, 965, 966
  Individual all–time records, 965–66
  Measurements, standard, 973
  Most Valuable Players, 963
  National League averages, 968
  No-hit and perfect games, 954
  Pennant winners, 961–62
  Pitching statistics, 954, 958,
    964–65, 967, 968
  Records, 954, 958, 964–66
  Rookie of the Year, 964
  World Series records and standing,
    955–58
  World Series, 1990, 970
Baseball Hall of Fame, 763, 952–53
Basketball, 876, 891–98
  College, 891–94
  History, 891
  Measurements, standard, 973
  Most Valuable Players, 896
  Olympic Games, 876
  Professional, 894–98
Bassatere, St. Kitts–Nevis, 251
Bastille Day, 106
Basutoland. *See* Lesotho
Bataan surrender (1942), 117
Battlefields, National, 571, 573
Battle of Hastings, 99, 277

Battles. *See* specific battles
Bay of Pigs, 120, 178
Beaumount–Port Arthur Canal, 136
Bechuanaland. *See* Botswana
Bedloe's Island, 628
Beef, food value, 90
Beethoven, Ludwig von, 106, 679
Begin, Menachem, 123, 186, 213
Beijing, China, 127, 173
  See also Peking
Beirut, Lebanon, 214, 222, 223
Belfast, Northern Ireland, 279
Belgian Congo. *See* Zaire
Belgium, 159–60
  See also Countries
Belgrade, Yugoslavia, 288
  See also Cities (world)
Belize, 160
  See also Countries
Bell, Alexander Graham, 109, 557,
  679
Belmont Stakes, 922–24
Belmopan, Belize, 160
Benelux, 198, 226
Benin, 161
  See also Countries
Bentsen, Lloyd, 40
Bering Sea, 469
Bering Strait, 458
Berlin, Congress of, 109
Berlin, East, 195, 198
Berlin, Germany, 198–99
  Airlift (1948), 118, 198
  East Berlin uprising (1953), 119,
    198
  Wall (1961), 120, 127, 198–99
  World War II, 117
  See also Cities (world)
Berlin, Treaty of (1899), 774
Bermuda, 280
  See also Countries
Bern, Switzerland, 267
Bessarabia, 250, 260
Bessemer converter, 553
Bhutan, 161–62
  See also Countries
Biafra, 121, 240
Biathlon, 867
Bible, 101, 103
  Books of the, 382
  Old Testament, 95, 97, 382, 521,
    522
Bicentennial, 122
Bicycles:
  Deaths from collisions with motor
    vehicles, 818
  Invention, 561
  See also Cycling
Bifocal lens, 561
Big Bend National Park, 571
Bikini Atoll, 120, 776
Bill of Rights, 106, 618, 619
Bills (Congressional):
  How a bill becomes a law, 638–39
  Procedure, 614, 638–39
Bills (money), 374
Billy the Kid, 644
Biographies:
  Of U.S. Presidents, 650–63
  Pulitzer Prizes for, 725–26
  See also People
Bioko (formerly Fernando Po), 187
Biotechnology, 533
Birds:
  Endangered species, 567
  State birds, 745–73
Birmingham, Alabama, 745
Birmingham, England, 275
Birth dates, place of, People,
  677–705
Birth rates, 143, 813–15
Birthstones, 593
Births (U.S.):
  Age of mother, 814
  Live, 813–15
  To unmarried women, 814

Bismarck, Otto von, 197, 679
Bissau, Guinea–Bissau, 202
Black Death, 101, 277
Black Friday, 108
Black Hills, 768
Black hole, 328
Black Hole of Calcutta, 105
"Black Moon," 332
Blackout, Northeast, 121
Black Rock Desert, 474
Black Sea, 259, 469
Blacks in U.S.:
  Births, birth rates, 814–15
  Elected officials, 41, 127
  Employment, 54, 57
  Population statistics, 792–93, 796,
    806, 809
  School enrollment, 833
  See also Civil rights; Nonwhite
    persons; Racial statistics; Racial
    violence; Slavery
Blanc, Mont, 134, 190
Blood, circulation of, 561
Blue Grotto, 475
Blue Nile, 188
Board foot (measure), 369
Bobsledding, 867
Boers, 107, 110, 257
Boer War, 110, 257, 278
Bogotá, Colombia, 175
Bohemia, 180
Bohr, Niels Henrick David, 542, 543,
  544, 679, 707
Boiling points:
  Elements, 531–32
  Water, 373
Bolivia, 162
  See also Countries
Bolsheviks, 112, 260
Bolt (measure), 369
Bolts and screws, 371
Bombay, India, 206
  See also Cities (world)
Bonaire, 237
Bonaparte, Napoleon, 106, 107, 190,
  191, 679
Bonds, 412–15
Bonn, West Germany, 196, 198
Books:
  Awards, 723–27, 730, 735
  Notable (1989), 736
  Reference, 302–03
Boone, Daniel, 644, 679, 754
Booth, John Wilkes, 108, 644, 654,
  679
Bophuthatswana, 257, 258
  See also Countries
Boquerón (volcano), 462
Borneo (island), 208, 227, 473
  Brunei, 164, 208
Boron, 531
Boroughs, New York City, 783, 802
Bosnia, 289
Boston, Mass., 756, 778, 779
  Fire (1872), 384
  See also Cities (U.S.)
Boston Massacre, 103
Boston Tea Party, 103, 756
Botanic garden, first, 128
Botswana, 162–63
  See also Countries
Boulder Dam. *See* Hoover Dam
Bounty, H.M.S., 106, 282
Bourbon Kings of France, 190, 191
Bowl games (football), 879–81
Bowling, 906–07
  Measurements, standard, 973
Boxer Rebellion, 110, 173, 312
Boxing, 876–77, 917–21
  Amateur, 973
  Bare–knuckle, 917
  Heavyweight champion fights,
    917–18
  History, 917
  Louis, Joe, 917
  Measurements, standard, 973

Olympic Games, 876–77
  Professional, 917–21
  Titleholders, 917–21
  World championship fights, 917–21
Boyne, Battle of the, 105
Boy Scouts of America, 110, 601
Brahmaputra River, 159, 206, 471
Braille, 561
Brandt, Willy, 198, 680
Brazil, 163–64, 458
  See also Countries
Brazos River, 478
Brazzaville, Congo, 176
Bread, food value, 89, 93
Brest–Litovsk, Treaty of, 260
Bretton Woods Conference, 118
Brezhnev, Leonid, 123, 261, 680
Bridges, 135–36
Bridgetown, Barbados, 159
British Columbia, Canada, 168, 169
British Commonwealth. *See*
  Commonwealth of Nations
British Guiana. *See* Guyana
British Honduras. *See* Belize
British Indian Ocean Territory, 280
British Museum, 130
British New Guinea. *See* Papua, New
  Guinea
British Open Champions, 943
British Solomon Islands. *See* Solomon
  Islands
British thermal unit, 369
British Virgin Islands, 280–81
Broadcasting awards, 717, 731
Broad jump. *See* Track and Field
Broadway theater, longest runs, 743
Brodie, Steve, 644
Bronx, The, 783, 802
Bronx Zoo, 569
Brooklyn, 783, 802
Brooklyn Bridge, 109, 135, 553
Brown, John, 108, 680
Brown v. Board of Education, 119
Brunei, 164
  See also Countries
Brussels, Belgium, 159
  See also Cities (world)
Bryan, William Jennings, 109, 680
  Presidential candidate, 636
  Secretary of State, 641
Bryce Canyon National Park, 571
Btu, 369, 373
Buchanan, James, 653
  See also Headline History; Presidents
    (U.S.)
Bucharest, Romania, 249
  See also Cities (world)
Budapest, Hungary, 204, 205
  See also Cities (world)
Buddha, Gautama, 97, 378–79, 687
Buddhism, 97, 98, 99, 378–79
  Followers, 375–76
Budget, Federal, 53, 61, 62–63, 64
Budget, Office of Management and,
  647
Budget. *See* Expenditures; Revenue
Buenos Aires, Argentina, 155
  See also Cities (world)
Buffalo, N.Y., 779
  See also Cities (U.S.)
Buffalo Bill, 644, 680
Buildings:
  New construction (U.S.), 46
  Notable skyscrapers (U.S.), 133–34
  Structures, famous, 129–36
Bujumbura, Burundi, 166
Bulganin, Nikolai A., 119, 261
Bulgaria, 162
  See also Countries
Bulge, Battle of the, 117
Bullet, 561
Bunyan, Paul, 644
Bull Run, Battle of, 108, 628
Buran, Soviet Space Shuttle, 325
Burger, Warren E., 645
Burgesses, House of, 128

Burglary, 825, 826, 828, 829
Burkina Faso, 165
  See also Countries
Burma. *See* Myanmar
Burns, treatment of, 78
Burr, Aaron, 106, 629, 634, 680
Burundi, 166
  See also Countries
Buses, 66, 67, 69, 365
  Economic statistics, 66, 67
Bush, George, 40, 126, 629, 630,
  663
Business, economy, 42–69
  Investments, foreign, in U.S.
    businesses, 68
  Largest, 48–49
  Retail sales, 47
  See also Retail trade; Wholesale
    trade; Industry
Busing to achieve school integration,
  121
Butter:
  Cholesterol and fat, 91
  Economic statistics, 61
Byelorussia, U.S.S.R., 259, 260
Byrd, Richard E., 114, 356, 681
Byzantine architecture, 129
Byzantium, 97, 98

C

Cabinets (U.S.), 639–43
  First woman member, 128
  Salaries, 41
Cable television, 743
Caesar, Julius, 98, 190, 681
Cairo, Egypt, 184, 186
  See also Cities (world)
Cairo Conference, 117
Calcium, 531
Calcutta, India, 206
  See also Cities (world)
Calder Trophy, 904
Calendar, 576–87
  Chinese, 586
  History, 580–81
  Islamic, 586
  Names of days and months, 582
  Perpetual, 578–79
  Sports, 864
  Three–year (1990–92), 576–77
Calgary, Alberta, Canada, 168
Calhoun, John C., 634, 681
California, 747
  Gold Rush, 107, 747
  Mountain peaks, 478
  Volcanoes, 459
  See also States of U.S.
Californium, 531
Calvin, John, 102, 681
Cambodia, 119, 121, 123, 166
  See also Countries
Cambrian Mountains, 275
Cambrian Period, 530
Camera, 109, 558
Cameroon, 167
  See also Countries
Camp Fire, Inc., 601
Canada, 168–70
  Economy, 168
  Geography, 168
  Government, 168
  History, 169–70
  Latitude and longitude, 477
  Map, 484
  Population, 168
  Provinces, 168
  Territories, 168
  Time zones, 582
  See also Countries
Canadian River, 478
Canals, 136
Canary Islands, 263, 388, 462
Cancer, 84, 85, 93, 817
Cancer, Tropic of, 583

Candela, 366
Canoe racing, 878
Canton Island, 774, 775
Canyonlands, National Park, 571
Cape Horn, 172, 458
Cape of Good Hope, 257, 457
Capetian Dynasty, 99, 190, 191
Cape Town, South Africa, 256
  See also Cities (world)
Cape Verde, 170, 462
  See also Countries
Capitalization, rules for, 436
Capital punishment, first state to
  abolish, 128
  See also Executions
Capitals, foreign, 152–292
Capitals of states, 745–73
Capitals of U.S.:
  Early capitals, 762, 766
  Washington, D.C., 787
Capitol, U.S., 627
Capone, Al, 114
Capri, 475
Capricorn, Tropic of, 583
Caracas, Venezuela, 285
  See also Cities (world)
Carat (measure), 369–70
Cardiovascular disease, 817
Caribbean area:
  Islands, 459, 474
  Map, 485
  Volcanoes, 462
  See also specific countries
Caribbean Sea, 469, 474
  Map, 485
Carloadings, railroad, 65
Carlsbad Caverns, 475, 571
Carnival season, 583
Caroline Islands, 776
  Map, 495
Carolingian Dynasty, 190, 191
Carpathian Mountains, 247, 249
Carter, Jimmy (James E., Jr.), 661
  See also Headline History; Presidents
  (U.S.)
Carthage, 95, 97, 98, 99
Cartoons:
  Awards for, 719
  First colored, 128
Casablanca, Morocco, 232
Casablanca Conference, 117
Caspian Sea, 209, 259, 469, 470
Castries, St. Lucia, 251
Castro, Fidel, 120, 177–79, 681
Casualties, war, 307, 311
Caterpillar Club, 356
Cathedrals, 129–30
Catholic churches, 375–76
  See also Roman Catholic Church
Cattle, 60
Caucasus, 259, 459
Cavaliers, 103
Caves, caverns, 475
Cayman Islands, 281
CEA, 647
Celebes, 208, 473
Celestial Sphere: 352–53
Cells, theory, 546
Celluloid:
  Discovery, 554
  First commercial production, 554
Celsius (Centigrade) scale, 366, 370,
  373
Cemeteries, National, 574
  Arlington, 574, 627, 630
Cenozoic Era, 531
Census. *See* Population
Centigrade (Celsius) scale, 366, 370,
  373
Central African Republic, 171
  See also Countries
Central America, 459
  Map, 485
  Volcanoes, 462
  See also specific countries
Central Intelligence Agency, 647

Central Powers, 112
Cerebrovascular diseases, 817
Cermak, Anton J., 117, 644
Certified mail, 990
Ceylon. *See* Sri Lanka
CFCs (chlorofluorocarbons), 563,
  564, 565
Chaco, 155, 244
Chad, 171–72
  See also Countries
Chad, Lake, 171, 470
Chain (measure), 367, 370
Challenger (space shuttle), 124, 323,
  387
Chamberlain, Neville, 278, 681
Channel Islands, 281
Charlemagne, 99, 190, 191, 196,
  681
Charles I of England, 103, 276, 755,
  763, 767
Charlotte, N.C., 763, 779
  See also Cities (U.S.)
Cheese:
  Cholesterol and fat, 90
  Economic statistics, 61
Chemicals, 45, 55, 69
Chemistry:
  Discoveries and theories, 561–62
  Elements, 531–32
  Nobel Prizes for, 709–10, 986
Chernenko, Konstantin U., 124, 261,
  262
Chesapeake Bay, 755
Chernobyl nuclear accident, 125,
  262, 385
Chess, 972
Chiang Kai-shek, 117, 174, 682
Chicago, Ill., 752, 779
  Climate, 664
  Fire (1871), 109, 384
  St. Valentine's Day Massacre, 114
  See also Cities (U.S.)
Chickens:
  Cholesterol and fat, 90
  Economic statistics, 60, 61
  Incubation and longevity, 570
Children:
  Abuse and neglect, 829
  Birth statistics, 143, 813–15
  Births to unmarried women, 814
  Death statistics, 143, 817, 819,
  820, 821
  Education statistics, 833–36
  Life expectancy, 142, 820–22
  Number of, 796
  Runaways, 825, 826
Children's Crusade, 101
Chile, 172–73
  Volcanoes, 462
  See also Countries
China, 118, 121, 173–75
  Boxer Rebellion, 120, 173, 312
  Great Wall, 108, 130, 173
  History, 173–75
  Japan and, 109, 114, 117, 173,
  174, 217
  Map, 492–93
  Ming dynasty, 101, 103, 173
  Nuclear weapons testing, 121, 174
  Provinces and regions, 174
  Structures, 130
  U.S. and, 175
  Yuan dynasty, 101, 173
  See also Countries; Headline History
China (Taiwan) *See* Taiwan
China Sea, 469
"China seat" (U.N.), 121, 174, 269
Chinese in U.S.:
  Births, birth rates, 815
  See also Nonwhite persons
Chinese-Japanese War (1894–95),
  109, 173, 217
Cholesterol, 89–91
Chlorofluorocarbons (CFCs), 563,
  564, 565

Chou En-lai. *See* Zhou Enlai
Christ. *See* Jesus Christ
Christian holidays, 583–84
Christianity, 98, 99, 375–77
  Roman Empire, 98, 376
  World membership, 375
  See also Religion; Roman Catholic
  Church
Christian Science, 377
Christmas, 576, 585
Christmas Island, 157, 255
Christopher Awards, 735
Chromium, 531
Chromosphere, 331
Chronology:
  For 1990, 975–986
  4500 B.C.–A.D. 1989, 95–127
  Major developments in science, 534
  Space Age, 321–22
Churches (buildings):
  Famous, 129–30
  In largest cities, 778–87
Churches (organizations), 375–77
  See also Religion
Churchill, Sir Winston, 117, 118,
  278, 682
Church of England, 102, 277
CIA, 647
Cimarron River, 478
Cimmerian civilization, 97
Cincinnati, Ohio, 764, 779
  See also Cities (U.S.)
CIO, 120
Circular measure, 367, 372, 373
Circumference, formula for, 372
Ciskei, 258
Cities (Canadian):
  Latitude and longitude, 477
  Time of day, 477
Cities (U.S.), 778–89
  Bridges, 135–36
  Buildings, notable skyscrapers,
  133–34
  Chambers of Commerce, 778–87
  Climate, 664–65
  Commissions, councils, 789
  Consumer Price Index, 43
  Crime rates, 829
  Distances between, 405–08
  Government statistics, 789
  Latitudes and longitudes, 477
  Mayors, managers, 778–87, 789
  Newspapers, 297–301
  Officials, terms and salaries, 789
  Police departments, 827
  Population figures:
    Largest, 778–88
    Largest by state, 745–73
    1970–80 (table), 798–804
  Population growth, 798–804
  Ports, 65
  Time of day, 477
  Tunnels, 134
  Zoos, 568, 569
  See also specific cities
Cities (world):
  Bridges, 135–36
  Distances between, 409–10
  Largest, by country, 152–292
  Large (table), 138–39
  Population, 138–39, 152–292
  Latitudes and longitudes, 467
  Southernmost, 172
  Time of day, 467
  Tunnels, 134
  Zoos, 568
  See also specific cities
City managers, 778–86, 789
Civilian labor force, 53, 56
Civil rights:
  Bill of rights, 618–19
  Emancipation Proclamation, 624–25
  Fourteenth Amendment, 108, 619
  Other Constitutional provisions, 617,
  619–22
Civil Rights, Commission on, 649

Civil Service Commission, U.S., 109
  See also Office of Personnel
    Management
Civil time, 349, 582
Civil War, American, 108, 307
  Confederate States, 108, 625
  Gettysburg Address, 625
Civil War, English, 103, 277
Civil War, Russian, 112, 260
Civil War, Spanish, 117, 263
Clark, Charles Joseph, 169, 170
Clay, Cassius. *See* Ali, Muhammad
Clay, Henry, 107, 634, 651, 682
Cleopatra, 98, 185
Cleveland, Grover, 655
  See also Headline History; Presidents
    (U.S.)
Cleveland, Ohio, 764, 779
  See also Cities (U.S.)
Climate. *See* Weather
Clocks, pendulum, 561
Clothing:
  Economic statistics, 45, 55, 69
  Industry, hours and wages, 55
  Price indexes, 43
Cloture rule, 638
Coal, 69
  Economic statistics, 56, 69,
    146–47
  Industry, hours and wages, 56
  World production, 146–47
Coast Guard, U.S., 305, 306
Coast Guard Academy, U.S., 306
Coastline of U.S., 479
Cobalt, 531
Cocaine, facts on, 451–52
Cochise, 746
Cocoa, 61, 69
Cocos (Keeling) Islands, 255
Code of Hammurabi, 95
C.O.D. mail, 990
Cody, William F., 644, 682
Coffee, 61, 69
Coins. *See* Money
Collect-on-delivery mail, 990
College graduates, 834
Colleges and Universities, 837–62
  Accredited, 837–62
  Endowments, 836
  Enrollments, 833, 837–62
  Firsts, 128
  Faculty salaries, 836
  Graduates, 834
  Libraries, 835
  United States, 837–62
Colombia, 175–76
  Volcanoes, 462
  See also Countries
Colombo, Sri Lanka, 263
  See also Sri Jayewardenapura Kotte
Colonial Williamsburg, 771
Colorado, 747–48
  Mountain peaks, 478
  See also States of U.S.
Colorado Desert, 474
Colorado River (Colorado-Mexico),
  457, 472, 478
Colorado River (Texas), 478
  Hoover Dam, 131, 760
Colorado Springs, Colo., 748
  Air Force Academy, U.S., 306
Colors, state, 745–73
Colosseum (Rome), 98, 129
Colossus at Rhodes, 129
Columbia River, 472, 478, 771
  Grand Coulee Dam, 132, 771
Columbia (space shuttle), 123, 325
Columbus, Christopher, 101, 201,
  216, 272, 457, 458, 682
Columbus, Ohio, 764, 779–80
  See also Cities (U.S.)
Columbus Day, 584
Colville River, 478
Combustion, nature of, 561
Comets, 345–46
Cominform, 118

Comintern, 112, 118
Commerce. *See* Foreign trade;
  Interstate Commerce
Commerce, U.S. Dept. of, 647
  Secretaries of, 641–43
Commissions, city, 789
Committees:
  Congressional, 38–39
  National, 633
Commodities, Producer Price Index,
  45
Common Market, 120, 122
  See also European Economic
    Community
Commonwealth of Nations, 151, 203,
  206, 227, 229, 265, 272, 291
Commonwealth, Puritan, 276–77
Commune, Revolutionary, 106
Communicable diseases, 817
Communications:
  FCC, 648
  Industry, hours and wages, 56
  ITU, 295
  See also specific type of
    communication
Communism, 107, 112
Communist Internationals, 109, 112
Communist Manifesto, 107
Communist Party (U.S.S.R.), 261
Community, European Economic,
  120, 263, 278
Como, Lake, 117, 214
Comoros, 176
  Volcanoes, 462
  See also Countries
Composers:
  Awards, 727, 735
  See also People; Entertainment and
    Culture
Compressed natural gas, 362
Computer, inventions, 555, 561
Comstock Lode, 760
Conakry, Guinea, 202
Conditioned reflex, 561
Confederate Memorial Day, 585
Confederate States, 108, 625
  Flag, 628
  Secession, readmission dates, 625
Confucianism, 379
  Number of followers, 375
Confucius, 97, 173, 379, 682
Congo, 176–77
  See also Countries
Congo, Democratic Republic of the.
  See Zaire
Congo River, 177, 289, 457, 471
Congresses, Continental, 103,
  611–12, 626
Congress of Industrial Organizations,
  120
Congress of Vienna, 107, 157, 190
Congress (U.S.), 34–39
  Adjournment, 614
  Assembling time, 614, 621
  Committees, 38–39
  Compensation and privileges, 614
  Constitutional provisions, 613–22
  First sessions, 626
  First women members, 128
  Legislative powers, 614, 620, 621,
    638
  Powers and duties, 613–15
  Salary of members, 41, 614
  See also House of Representatives;
    Senate
Conjunctions (planetary), 349–50
Connecticut, 748
  See also States of U.S.
Connecticut River, 478, 748
Constantinople, 101, 102, 200,
  273
  See also Istanbul
Constellations, 347
Constitutions (state):
  Dates adopted, 745–73
  First, 128, 748

Constitution (U.S.), 106, 613–22,
  766
  Amendment procedure, 617
  Amendments, 618–22
  Drafting of, 613
  Ratification, 613, 618, 626
  Supremacy of, 617
Consumer Price Index, 43, 144
Consumer Product Safety
  Commission, 648
Consumers:
  Complaints, 595
  Credit, 44
  Metric conversion tables, 371, 373
  Price indexes, 43
  Toll–free numbers, 596–98
  Travel fraud, 588–89
Continental Congresses, 103,
  611–12, 626
Continental Divide, 476, 759
Construction industry, 46, 59
Continental Drift, 332, 458
Continents, 458–59
  Area, 465
  Elevations, 465
  Explorations, discoveries, 457–58
  Maps, 481–96
  Populations, 140, 465
  Religions, 375
  See also specific continents
Controllers (of states), 745–73
Conventions, National, 632–33
Converter, Bessemer, 553
Cook Islands, 238
Coolidge, Calvin, 657
  See also Headline History; Presidents
    (U.S.)
Copenhagen, Denmark, 181
  See also Cities (world)
Copper, 531
Coptic Christians, 184, 188, 377
Copyrights, 589–91
Coral Sea Islands, 157
Core (of the Earth), 332
Corn:
  Economic statistics, 60, 147–48
  World production, 147–48
Corona of sun, 331
Corporations:
  Profits, 52
  Taxes, 78, 80
Corpus Christi (holiday), 586
Corregidor, 117
Corruption, public, prosecutions for,
  826
Corsica, 190, 214
Cortés, Hernando, 102, 231, 457,
  682
Cosmetics, 561
Cosmology, 330
Cosmonauts, 322–25
Costa Rica, 177
  See also Countries
Cost of living, international, 144
Cotopaxi, 462
Cotton, 60
Cotton Bowl, 880
Council of Economic Advisors, 647
Council of Nicaea, 98, 376
Council of Trent, 102, 580
Council on Environmental Quality,
  647
Councils, city, 789
Counterfeiting, 825, 826, 828
Counties (per state), 745–73
Countries of world, 151–292
  Agriculture, 147–48, 152–292
  Areas, 137–38, 152–292
  Birth rates, 143
  Capitals, 152–292
  Cities, large, 138–39, 152–292
  Death rates, 143
  Economic conditions, 152–292
  Explorations and discoveries of
    selected areas, 457–58
  Foreign trade, 150, 152–292

Governments, 152–292
History, 152–292
Holidays, 587
Immigration to U.S., 807
Industry, 152–292
Languages, 152–292
Life expectancy, 142
Maps, 481–96
Monetary units, 152–292
Natural features, 152–292
Petroleum production, 146–47, 364
Political parties, 152–292
Population densities, 152–292
Populations, 140, 152–292, 465
Population (table), 137–38
Premiers, prime ministers, 152–292
Presidents, 152–292
Rulers, 152–292
Structures, 129–36
U.N. members, 293
U.S. interventions in, 312
World Wars I and II, 112–17, 311
Zoos, 568
See also Geography (world); History
  (world)
Couples, unmarried, by sex and age,
  810
Court, International, 295
Courts (federal), 616–17, 645–46
  See also Supreme Court
Courts (state), 776–77
Cows:
  Economic statistics, 60
  Gestation and longevity, 570
  See also Cattle
"Coxey's Army," 109
CPI, 43
Crack, facts on, 452
CRAF/Cassini Mission, 319–20
Crater Lake National Park, 459, 571
Craters, meteorite, 346
Cream:
  Cholesterol and fat, 91
  Economic statistics, 61
Credit, consumer, 44
Creeds:
  American's, The, 626
  Nicene, 98, 376
Cretaceous Period, 530
Crete, 95, 97, 99, 200, 459
Crime:
  Assassinations and attempts, 644
  Corruption, prosecutions for, 826
  Rates, 829
  Statistics, 823–31
  Trial rights, 617–19
Crimean War, 108, 273, 278
Croatia, 289
Crockett, Davy, 107, 644, 683
Cromwell, Oliver, 103, 276, 277,
  683
Crossbow, 561
Crossword puzzle guide, 513–28
Crucifixion of Christ, 98, 376
Crusades, 101
Crust (of the Earth), 332
Cuba, 177–79
  Bay of Pigs invasion, 120, 178
  Island, 474
  Missile crisis, 120, 178, 261, 658
  Refugees, 179
  See also Countries
Cubic measure, 366–67
Cubit (measure), 370
Cultural Revolution, 175
Cumberland River, 478
Cuneiform, 95
Curaçao, 237
Curfew law arrests, 825–26
Curie, Marie, 110, 542, 683, 707,
  709
Curie, Pierre, 110, 683, 707
Curling (sport), 913
Currency. *See* Money
Current events, chronology of 1990,
  975–86

Custer, Gen. George, 109, 683, 759,
  764
Custer's Last Stand, 109, 759
Customs, declarations, 392–93
Cycling, 878
Cyclotron, 114, 561
Cyprus, 179, 200, 274
  Greek–Turkish crisis, 179, 274
  See also Countries
Cy Young Award, 963
Czechoslovakia, 117–18, 180–81
  Warsaw Pact invasion of, 121, 180
  See also Countries

D

Dahomey. *See* Benin
Dairy products:
  Cholesterol and fats, 90, 91
  Economic statistics, 61, 69
Dakar, Senegal, 253
Dalai Lama, 120, 707
Dallas, Tex., 121, 644, 659, 664,
  769, 780
  See also Cities (U.S.)
Damascus, Syria, 268
Damavend, Mount, 209
Dams, 131–32
Danube River, 157, 165, 180, 196,
  204, 250, 288, 471
Dardanelles, 112, 273
Dare, Virginia, 128, 763
Dar es Salaam, Tanzania, 269
Darling River, 472
Darrow, Clarence, 114, 683
Darwin, Charles, 108, 546, 547, 561,
  683
Dasht-e-Kavir Desert, 474
Dasht-e-Lut Desert, 474
Date line, 582
Davis, Jefferson, 108, 585, 683
Davis Cup, 932, 936
Daylight Savings Time, 576
Days:
  Names of, 582
  Sidereal and solar, 329, 581
D-Day, 117
Dead Sea, 212
Death dates of, People, 677–705
Death penalty, 122, 831
Deaths and death rates, 143, 817–19
  Accidental, 817–18
  Countries, 143
  Diseases, 817
  In disasters, 383–90
  Motor vehicle, 817, 818
  War casualties, 307, 311
Deaths in 1989–90, 987–88
Death Valley, 474–76, 572, 747
Debs, Eugene V., 109, 636, 683
Debts, National, 45, 62–63
Decathlon. *See* Track and Field
Decibel, 370
Decimals, fractions, 372
Declaration of Independence,
  611–12, 766
Decoration Day. *See* Memorial Day
Deerfield Massacre, 105
Defense, U.S. Dept. of, 647
  Expenditures, 61, 62–63
  Secretaries of, 642–43
  See also Armed Forces (U.S.)
de Gaulle, Charles, 120, 190, 191,
  684
Degrees, academic, 863
  First for women, 128
Delaware, 749
  See also States of U.S.
Delaware River, 478
Democratic Party:
  Members of Congress, 34–37
  National Committee chairmen, 633
  National conventions, 109–110,
    124, 126, 633
  Senate floor leaders, 39

Denali National Park, 571, 746
Deng, Xiaoping, 122, 127, 174, 175
Denmark, 181–82
  See also Countries
Densities of Population:
  United States, 792–97
  World, 152–292, 465
Denver, Colo., 664, 747, 780
  See also Cities (U.S.)
Depression (1930s), 114
Desegregation in schools, 119–21
Deserts, 474
Detroit, Mich., 757, 780
  See also Cities (U.S.)
Deuterium, 561
Devil's Hole, 475
Devonian Period, 530
Devon Island, 474
Dhaka, Bangladesh, 158
Diabetes mellitus, 817
Diamond mine (Arkansas), 747
Diamonds, 108, 257, 593
Diesel engine, 109
Dietary allowances, recommended
  daily, 93, 94
Dinaric Alps, 288
Diphtheria, 817
  Antitoxin, 561
Diplomatic personnel, 396–98
Directory, French, 106, 191
Dirigibles, 354
  Firsts, 354
Disability benefits, 309
Disasters, 383–90
  Aircraft accidents, 384, 387–88
  Avalanches, 383–84
  Earthquakes, 383
  Explosions, 383–84, 390
  Fires, 383–84
  Floods, 383–84
  Nuclear power plant accidents, 385
  Railroad accidents, 384, 386, 388
  Shipwrecks, 384, 386
  Space, 387
  Storms, 384, 386, 667–68
  Tidal waves, 383–84
  Volcanic eruptions, 383
  Wartime, 390
Discoveries:
  Chemical elements, 531–32
  Geographical, 457, 458
  Scientific, 534–48, 561–62
Discus throw. *See* Track and Field
Diseases:
  AIDS, 85–87
  Cardiovascular, 817
  Communicable, 817
  Deaths from, 817
  Medical discoveries, 561–62
  Sexually transmitted, 87
  Tropical, 292
Distance:
  Airplane records, 360
  Between cities, 405–10
Distilled spirits. *See* Liquor
District of Columbia, 749, 787
  See also Washington, D.C.
Diving. *See* Swimming
"Divorce capitals," 760
Divorce statistics, 809
Djibouti, Republic of, 182
  See also Countries
DNA, 548, 561, 711
Dnieper River, 259, 472
Doctors (physicians), first woman,
  128
Dodecanese Islands, 200
Dominica, 183
  See also Countries
Dominican Republic, 183
  U.S. interventions in, 183, 312
  See also Countries
Don River, 259, 472
Draft evaders, 122
Drama. *See* Theater
Dram (measure), 367

Dred Scott case, 108
Dreyfus, Alfred, 109, 684
Drivers:
  Accidents, 817–18
  Arrests for drunkenness, 825, 826
  State laws, 832
Dropouts, high school, 833
Drug Control Policy, National Office of, 647
Drugs & Drug Abuse: 443–56
  Alcohol, 448, 455–56
  Cannabis, 446, 453–54
  Cocaine and crack, 446, 448, 449, 450, 451–52
  Depressants, 446, 448
  Drug uses and effects, 446
  Economic statistics, 69
  Hallucinogens, 446, 448, 450, 454
  Hotline (toll–free), 597
  In colleges, 448
  In high schools, 450, 452
  Narcotics, 443–50
  Sources of help, 456
  Stimulants, 446, 448, 450
  Tobacco, 448, 456
  See also Narcotics
Drunkenness, arrests for, 825, 826
Dry measure, 367
Duarte, José Napoleón, 187
Dublin, Ireland, 211, 212
  See also Cities (world)
Dukakis, Michael S., 40, 126
Dunkerque evacuation, 117
Duomo (Florence), 130
Durable goods, 45, 59
  See also individual items
Dynamite, 108, 553
Dynamo, 552
Dutch East Indies. See Indonesia
Dutch Guiana. See Suriname

E

Earhart, Amelia, 114, 117, 357, 685
Earth (planet), 95, 332–33, 335
  Astronomical constants, 329
  Geological periods, 530–31
  Life on, 95, 530–31
  Origin, 95, 332
  See also Planets; World
Earthquakes, 110, 126, 127, 383, 384, 466
East China Sea, 469
East Germany. See Germany, East
Eastern Front (World War I), 112
Eastern Orthodox churches, 375–77
Easter Island, 172
Easter Rebellion, 61, 211
Easter Sunday, 584, 586
Ebert, Friedrich, 197
Eclipses, 350
Economic Advisers, Council of, 647
Economic and Social Council, U.N., 294–95
Economics, Nobel Prize for, 712, 986
Economic statistics (U.S.), 43–69, 144–45, 147–50
Economic statistics (world), 69, 144–50
Economy:
  U.S., 42–69
  World, 144–50
Ecuador, 184
  Volcanoes, 462
  See also Countries
Ecumenical Councils, 120, 284, 376, 377
  Council of Nicaea, 98, 376
  Council of Trent, 102
  Vatican Council I, 377
  Vatican Council II, 120, 123, 284, 377
Eddy, Mary Baker, 685
Eden, Anthony, Sir, 119, 278, 685
Edict of Nantes, 102, 105

Edinburgh, Scotland, 275
Edison, Thomas A., 109, 552, 558, 685
Education, 833–63
  Attendance laws, 834
  College costs, 837–62
  Employment, payrolls, 61
  Enrollments, 833, 837–62
  Expenditures, college, 835
  Federal aid, 835
  Graduates, 834
  Prayer in schools, 120
  School statistics, 833–36
  Service academies, 305–07
  Supreme Court school decisions, 109, 119, 122
  Teachers, 836
  Veterans' benefits, 309–10
  See also Colleges & Universities
Education, Department of, 648
  Secretaries, 643
Edward VIII, 117, 276
Eggs:
  Cholesterol and fat, 90
  Economic statistics, 61, 69
Egypt, Arab Republic of, 119, 184–86
  Israel and, 120–23, 185, 213–14
  Maps, 488, 494
  Pyramids, 129
  Suez Canal, 120, 136, 185, 186, 213
  See also Arab–Israeli wars; Countries
Egyptian Empire, 95, 97
  Mythology, 528
  Structures, 129
Eiffel Tower, 130
Einstein, Albert, 110, 117, 542, 543, 544, 561, 685, 707
  Theorem, 372, 543, 561
Eire. See Ireland (Republic)
Eisenhower, Dwight D., 658
  See also Headline History; Presidents (U.S.)
Eisenhower Doctrine, 120, 658
Elbe River, 180, 195, 196
Elbert, Mount, 478
Election Day, 576, 584, 586
Elections, presidential, 40, 634–37
  Election results, 1789–1988, 634–37
Electoral College, 619, 621, 632
  Voting, 40, 632, 634–37, 638
Electrical appliances and equipment, 47
Electricity:
  Economic statistics, 43
  Electric current, 366
  Hydroelectric plants, 133
  Hydroelectric power, 133
  Inventions and discoveries, 362, 558, 561–62
  Nuclear power, 363
  Nuclear power plants, 363–64
Electrocution, first, 128
Electromagnet, 561
Electron microscope, 562
Electrons, 561
Elementary schools, 833, 835
Elements, chemical, 531–32
Elevations:
  Cities of U.S., 778–87
  Continents, 465
  Deserts, 474
  Extremes of U.S., 475
  Mountain peaks, 468–69
  States of U.S., 476
  Volcanoes, 459, 462, 463
Elizabeth I, Queen, 102, 103, 276, 277
Elizabeth II, Queen, 129, 275, 277, 278
Elks (BPOE), 601
Ellesmere Island, 473
Ellice Islands. See Tuvalu
Ell (measure), 370

El Paso, Tex., 769, 780
  See also Cities (U.S.)
El Salvador, 123, 186, 187
  Volcanoes, 462
  See also Countries
Emancipation Proclamation, 624–25
Embezzlement arrests, 825, 826, 828
Emmy Awards, 985
Empire, Second (French), 107, 190, 191
Empires, Ancient, 95–127
Empire State Building, 133
Employment, 44, 51, 53, 54, 55, 56, 58, 59
  Average weekly earnings, 55, 56
  By race, occupation, 54
  Government, 61
  Labor force, 51, 53, 54, 57, 58, 778–87
  Taxes, 71
  Unemployment, 59, 145, 778–87
  Unions, 51
  Women, 53, 54, 56, 58
  See also Labor
Endangered species, 566–68
Enderbury Island, 774, 775
Energy, 361–65, 552
  Compressed natural gas, 362
  Consumption, 146–47, 365
  Electricity, 362
  Ethanol, 362
  Fuels of the future, 361–62
  Gasoline, 361
  Methanol, 361–62
  Solar–hydrogen, 362
  World production, 146–47
Energy, U.S. Department of, 648
  Secretaries, 643
Enewetak (Eniwetok) Atoll, 119, 776
Engels, Friedrich, 107, 685
Engine:
  Diesel, 552
  Steam, 552
England, 275–79
  Area, population, 277
  Rulers, 276
  Structures, 130
  See also United Kingdom
Enlightenment, The, 105
Enrollment, school. See Education
Entebbe, 122
Entente Cordiale, 110
Entertainment and culture, 736–44
  Art movements, 737–38
  Motion pictures, 744
  Music, 739–40
  Orchestras, symphony, 736
  Plays, 743
Environment, 563–75
  Acid rain, 563, 564
  Chlorofluorocarbons (CFCs), 563, 564, 565
  Endangered species, 566–68
  Forests, 566
  Greenhouse warming, 564–65
  National Park System, 571–75
  Ozone depletion, 564
  Pollution, 565–66
  Quality index, 565, 566
  Soil erosion, 566
  World's water supply, 575
Environmental Protection Agency, 648
Environmental Quality, Council on, 647
EPA, 648
Epiphany, 583
Episcopal Church, 122
"E pluribus unum," 626
Equal Employment Opportunity Commission, 648
Equatorial Guinea, 187
  See also Countries
Equestrian Events, 878
Equinox(es), 335, 580–81, 583

Equipment expenditures, 46
Ericson, Leif, 99, 169, 457, 685
Erie, Lake, 470
 Battle of, 107, 764
Erie Canal, 752, 762
Eritrea, Ethiopia, 188
Eros (asteroid), 345
Espionage, 124, 125
 American convicted of spying, 124, 125
Estate & gift taxes, 71, 73–74
Estonia, 117, 260
Ethanol, 362
Ether (anesthetic), 107, 561
Ethiopia, 117, 187, 188, 215
 See also Countries
Etna, Mount, 214, 462
Etruscans, 97
Euclid, 97, 561, 685
Euphrates River, 95, 210, 472
Eurasia, 459
Europe, 459, 465
 Explorations and discoveries, 457
 Map, 490–91
 Population, 140
 See also Continents; Countries
European Economic Community, 68, 120, 151, 263, 278
European Recovery Program, 118
Everest, Mount, 119, 236, 465, 468
Everglades National Park, 571, 750
Evolution, human, 95
Evolution, theory of, 108, 114, 545, 546, 561
 Scopes trial, 114
Executions:
 First electrocution, 128
 Methods by state, 831
 See also Capital punishment
Executive Departments and Agencies, 647–49
Exosphere, 335
Expectation of life, 142, 820–22
Expenditures:
 Advertising, 59
 Education, 835
 Federal government, 53, 61, 62–63, 64
 Gross national product, 45
 Plant and equipment, 46
 State governments, 776, 777
Explorations, 457, 458
Explorer (satellite), 120, 348
Explosions, 384–85
Explosives (inventions), 553, 554
Export–Import Bank, 649
Exports:
 United States, 67, 69, 150
 Value by country, 150
Express Mail, 989
Extradition between states, 617

F

Faeroe Islands, 182
Fahrenheit scale, 366, 373
Fairs and Expositions. *See* World's Fairs
Falkland Islands, 123, 155, 279, 281
Fall (1991), 576
Falling bodies:
 Formulas for, 372
 Law of, 372, 535, 561
Families:
 Characteristics, 812–13
 Income, 44, 46, 812–13
 Of U.S. Presidents, 631
 Statistics, 44, 46, 811, 812–13
Famous People, 677–705
 Sports Personalities, 899–902
 See also Awards; Headline History
Far East:
 Map, 492–93
 See also individual countries
Faraday, Michael, 539–40, 541, 685

Farm Credit Administration, 648
Farm Index, 46
Farms. *See* Agriculture
Farragut, David G., Adm., 108, 128
Fascists, 112, 215
Fats and oils, 61, 69, 89–91
Fat Tuesday. *See* Shrove Tuesday
FBI, 122, 123, 647
FCA, 648
FDIC, 648
Feasts, Jewish, 584–86
FEC, 648
Federal budget, 53, 61, 62–63, 64
 Foreign assistance, 53
 Public debt, 45, 62–63
 Social welfare expenditure, 53, 64
Federal Bureau of Investigation, 122, 123, 647
Federal Communications Commission, 648
Federal Courts, 616, 617, 645, 646
 See also Supreme Court
Federal Deposit Insurance Corporation, 648
Federal Election Campaign Act, 122
Federal Election Commission, 648
Federal Energy Administration. *See* Department of Energy
Federal Government. *See* United States Government
Federalist papers, 651
Federalist Party, 629, 634, 650
Federal Maritime Commission, 648
Federal Mediation and Conciliation Service, 648
Federal Power Commission. *See* Department of Energy
Federal Reserve Board, 648
Federal Reserve System, 110, 648
Federal Trade Commission, 110, 648
Fencing, 878, 921
Fermentation, 561
Fermi, Enrico, 118, 544, 552, 685, 708, 727
Fernando Po, Equatorial Guinea. *See* Bioko
Fertilizers, 69
Festival of Lights, 585, 586
Fibers, man–made, 554
Fiction, awards for, 723, 724, 730
Fifth Republic (French), 120, 190, 191
Figure skating, 865, 867, 913
Fiji, 188, 189
 See also Countries
Filament, tungsten, 558
Filibusters, 638
Fillmore, Millard, 653
 See also Headline History; Presidents (U.S.)
Films. *See* Motion pictures
Fingal's Cave, 475
Finland, 189
 See also Countries
Firearms:
 As murder weapons, 828, 829
 Inventions, 549, 555
"Fireballs," 346
Fireman, 61
Fires:
 Arson arrests, 825, 826
 Famous, 384–85
First Aid, 78–79
First Fruits, Feast of, 584, 586
Firsts:
 In America, 128
 In aviation, 354–60
Fish:
 Economic statistics, 69
 Endangered species, 568
 Fat and cholesterol, 90
Fishing (sport), record catches, 910–11
Five and ten-cent store, first, 128
Flag (Confederate), 628
Flag Day, 584

Flag (U.S.), 628
 Pledge to, 628
Fleming, Sir Alexander, 114, 548, 561, 686, 711
Flights:
 First, 354–60
 Orbital, 261, 324–25
 Records, 360
Floods, 383–84
 The Johnstown Flood, 109, 384
Floor Leaders of Senate, 39
Florence, Italy, 101, 214
Florida, 457, 749
 See also States of U.S.
Flour, economic statistics, 61, 69
Flowers:
 State, 745–73
FMCS, 648
FM radio stations, 778–87
Folklore, American, 644
Food:
 Content:
  Cholesterol, 89–91
  Fat, 89–91
  Fiber, 89, 93
  Sodium, 89, 91
 Economic statistics, 55, 60, 61, 69
 Industry, hours and wages, 55
 Microwaveable, 80–81
 Poisons, 82, 83
 Price indexes, 43
 Recommended daily dietary allowances, 93, 94
 U.S. consumption, 61
 See also Agriculture
Food and Agriculture Organization, U.N., 295
Food-choking, treatment of, 78
Football, 879–90
 American Conference champions, 887
 American League champions, 887
 Bowl games, 879–81
 College, 879–84
 Hall of Fame, 882–84, 887–88, 931
 Heisman Memorial Trophy, 881
 History, 879
 National Conference champions, 886–87
 National Football League, 126, 885–90
 National League champions, 886
 Nicknames of clubs, 884–85
 Professional, 884–90
 Records, professional, 889–90
 Stadiums, 884–85
 Standard measurements, 973
 Super Bowl, 885–86
Ford, Gerald R., 122, 660, 661
 Assassination attempts, 122, 644
 See also Headline History; Presidents (U.S.)
Ford, Henry, 110, 558, 686
Foreign aid (U.S.), 53, 63
Foreign embassies, 393–96
Foreign mail. *See* International mail
Foreign trade (U.S.), 67, 68, 69
Foreign trade (world):
 By country, 150, 152–292
 Exports–imports table, 150
Foreign words and phrases, 440–42
Forests:
 Resources of countries, 152–292
 State forests, 745–73
Forgery, 825, 826, 828
Formosa. *See* Taiwan
Forms of address, 439–40
Formulas, math, physics, 372
Fort Dodge, 753
Fort Sumter, Battle of, 108, 767
Fort Ticonderoga, 763, 770
Fort Worth, Tex., 769, 780, 781
 See also Cities (U.S.)
Fountain pen, 562
Four Freedoms, 118

Four Noble Truths, 379
Fourth of July, 584
Fractions, decimals, 372
France, 189–94
  NATO, 190
  Rulers (table), 191
  Structures, 130
  See also Countries
Franco, Francisco, 117, 263, 686
Franco-Prussian War, 108, 190
Frankfurt, West Germany, 196
Franklin, Benjamin, 538, 561, 611, 626, 686
Fraternity, first, 128
"Freedom March," 745
Freedom of the press, 103, 105, 618
Freedoms, Constitutional, 618–22
Freetown, Sierra Leone, 254
Freezing point of water, 370
Freight ton (measure), 370
Freight traffic, 65
FRELIMO, 234
French and Indian War, 105, 752, 757, 758, 764, 768, 770, 772
French Guiana, 192
French Polynesia, 193
French Revolution, 106, 190
French Somaliland. *See* Djibouti
French Southern and Antarctic Lands, 194
French Sudan. *See* Mali
French Territory of the Afars and Issas. *See* Djibouti
Freud, Sigmund, 110, 112, 562, 686
Friendly Islands, 271
Friends (Quakers), 377
Fritchie, Barbara, 644
Frost bite, treatment of, 79
FRS, 648
Fruit:
  Economic statistics, 61
  Fiber content, 93
FTC, 648
Fuel, 45, 69, 361–62
  Compressed natural gas, 362
  Electricity, 362
  Ethanol, 362
  Gasoline, 361
  Methanol, 361–62
  See also specific fuels
Fuel consumption, motor vehicle, 365
Fujiyama, 217, 459
Funafuti, Tuvalu, 274
"Fundamental Orders," 748
Fur, 69
Furniture:
  Economic statistics, 45, 47, 55
  Industry, hours and wages, 55

G

Gabon, 194–95
  See also Countries
Gadsden Purchase, 746, 762, 806
Gagarin, Yuri A., 120, 261, 324
Galápagos Islands, 184, 458
Galilee, Sea of, 212
Galaxy, 328, 331
Galileo, 103, 328, 535, 561, 686
Gambia, 195
  See also Countries
Gambia River, 195, 457
Gambier Island, 193
Gambling, 232–33, 760, 761, 825, 826
Gandhi, Indira, 124, 207, 686
Gandhi, Mohandas K., 118, 207, 686
Ganges River, 159, 206, 472
"Gang of Four," 122, 175
Garfield, James A., 644, 655
  Assassination, 109, 644, 655
  See also Headline History; Presidents (U.S.)
Gas, natural, manufactured, 69
Gasoline service stations, 47

Gasoline, motor vehicle, 361, 365
Gator Bowl, 880–81
GATT, 295
Gaza Strip, 121, 185, 213
Gemini flights, 322, 324
Gemstones, 593
General Agreement on Tariffs and Trade (GATT), 295
General Assembly, U.N., 294
General Service Administration, 648
General Sherman Tree, 747
Generals (U.S.), 304
Generator, electric, 552
Genes, 548
Geneva, Lake, 267
Geneva, Switzerland, 112, 267
Geneva Conference (1954), 119
Genghis Khan, 99, 152, 687
Genocide, 114
Genome, 529
Geographic centers:
  Of states, 745–73
  Of United States, 475
Geographic literacy, 480
Geographic Society, National, 603
Geography:
  Caves and caverns, 475
  Coastline of U.S., 479
  Continental Divide, 476
  Continents, 457–59, 465, 481–96
  Deserts, 474
  Elevations, 465
  Explorations, discoveries, 457, 458
  Islands, 473, 474
  Lakes, 470–71
  Map section, 481–96
  Mountain peaks, 468–69
  National Parks, 571–75
  Oceans, seas, 469
  Of countries, 152–292
  Rivers, 471, 472, 478–80
  United States, 475–80
  Volcanoes, 459–63
   Map, 460, 461
  Waterfalls, 472, 473
  World, 457–75
Geological periods, 530–31
Geometric formulas, 372
Geometry, 561
Georgetown, Guyana, 203
Georgia, 750
  See also States of U.S.
Georgia, U.S.S.R., 260
Germany:
  History, 196–99
  Nazi regime, 114, 117, 197
  Rulers (table), 197
  World War I, 112, 197
  World War II, 117, 198
  Zoos, 568
  See also Germany, East; Germany, West
Germany, East, 195–97
  See also Countries
Germany, West, 118, 196–99
  See also Countries
Geronimo, 109, 687, 746, 762
Gestation periods, animals, 570
Gettysburg Address, 625
Gettysburg, Battle of, 108, 625, 766
Ghana, 199
  See also Countries
Ghent, Treaty of, 107, 651
Gibraltar, 281
  Border reopened, 124
Gift taxes, federal, 71, 73–74
Gilbert Islands, 219, 238
  See also Kiribati
Giotto probes, 322
Girl Scouts of U.S.A., 604
Giscard d'Estaing, Valéry, 191, 192
Glacier National Park, 571, 759
Glasgow, Scotland, 275
  See also Cities (world)
Glass, economic statistics, 69
Glenn, John H., Jr., 34, 120, 324

Glossaries:
  Art movements, 737–38
  Weather, 670
GNP, 45
Gobi Desert, 173, 474
Gods and goddesses, 523–28
Godwin Austen, Mount (K–2), 468
Golan Heights, 121, 185, 213, 268
Gold:
  As element, 531
  Karat (measure of purity), 370, 374
  Standard, 109
Gold Coast: *See* Ghana
Golden Gate Bridge, 135, 747
Golden Temple (India), 124, 207
Gold Rush:
  Alaska, 746
  California, 107, 747
Golf, 941–44
  British Open Champions, 943
  Earnings, 944
  History, 941
  Masters Tournament winners, 941
  Standard measurements, 973
  U.S. Amateur Champions, 942, 943
  U.S. Open Champions, 941–42, 943
  U.S. P.G.A. Champions, 942
Good Friday, 584, 586
Gorbachev, Mikhail S., 124, 126, 127, 261, 262, 687
Gorky, U.S.S.R., 259
Gospels, 98, 376
Gothic architecture, 130
Goths, 98
Gotland, Sweden, 266
Government, U.S. *See* United States Government
Government employment, 61
Governments (foreign), 152–292
  Heads of state, 152–292
Governors of states, 37, 745–73
  First woman, 114, 128, 773
  Puerto Rico, 773
  Terms and salaries, 776, 777
  U.S. Territories, 773–75
Graduates, high school, college, 834
Grain, 69
  Food values, 89, 93
  See also specific grains
Gram (measure), 366, 369, 371, 373
Grammy Awards, 732
Grand Canyon National Park, 571
Grand Coulee Dam, 132, 133, 771
  Hydroelectric plant, 133, 771
Grand Prix (of auto racing), 948
Grand Teton National Park, 571
Grant, Ulysses S., 108, 654
  See also Headline History; Presidents (U.S.)
Grants for education, 835
Graves, Presidential, 630
Gravitation, law of, 536, 561
Great Arabian Desert, 474
Great Australian Desert, 474
Great Bear Lake, 470
Great Britain (country). *See* United Kingdom
Great Britain (island), 473
Great gross (measure), 370
Great Lakes, 470
Great Salt Lake, 107, 471, 769
Great Salt Lake Desert, 474
Great Seal of U.S., 626
Great Slave Lake, 470
Great Smoky Mountains National Park, 571, 763, 769
Great Sphinx of Egypt, 95, 129
Great Wall of China, 98, 173, 130
Greece, 200
  See also Countries
Greece, ancient, 95, 96, 97, 200, 523–27, 865
  Mythology, 523–27
  Persian Wars, 97
  Structures, 129

Greenback Party, 635
Greenland, 99, 182, 457–59, 473
Green Mountain Boys, 770
Green River (Ky.), 478
Green River (Wyoming–Utah), 478
Greenhouse effect, 327, 564, 565
Greenwich time, 582
Gregorian calendar, 580–81
Grenada, 200–01
  U.S. military intervention, 123, 201, 312
  See also Countries
Gromyko, Andrei A., 262, 688
Gross (measure), 370
Gross National Product, 45, 152–292
GSA, 648
Guadalcanal, 255
Guadalupe Mountains National Park, 571, 769
Guadeloupe, 192
Guam, 774, 776
Guatemala, 201
  Volcanoes, 462
  See also Countries
Guernsey, 281
Guevara, Ché, 162, 178
Guiana, British. *See* Guyana
Guiana, Dutch. *See* Suriname
Guiana, French, 192
Guinea, Portuguese. *See* Guinea–Bissau
Guinea, Spanish. *See* Equatorial Guinea
Guinea-Bissau, 202
  See also Countries
Guinea (republic), 202
  See also Countries
Gulf of Mexico, 231, 469
Gulf of Tonkin Resolution, 119, 121
Gunpowder, 561
Guns. *See* Firearms
Gunter's chain (measure), 367, 370
Gupta, 98
Gutenberg, Johannes, 549, 562, 688
Guyana, 203
  See also Countries
Gymnastics, 878, 972, 976
Gyrocompass, 561
Gyroscope, 561

H

Hague, The, The Netherlands, 236
Hague Conventions, 110
Hailstone, largest, 670
Haile Selassie, 188, 688
Hainan Island, 173
Haiti, 106, 203
  Duvalier, Jean–Claude, 124, 203
  U.S. intervention in, 203, 312
  See also Countries
Haleakala National Park, 571
Halicarnassus, Mausoleum at, 129
Halley's Comet, 125, 345, 346, 537
Hall of Fame:
  Baseball, 763, 931, 952–53
  Football, 882–84, 931
Halloween, 584
Hambletonian, 939
Hamburg, West Germany, 196
Hamilton, Alexander, 106, 639, 650, 651, 688
Hammarskjöld, Dag, 119, 290, 294, 688
Hammer throw. *See* Track and Field
Hammurabi, Code of, 95
Handball, 950
Hand (measure), 370
Hanging as death penalty, 831
Hanging Gardens, 97, 129
Hannibal, 98, 688
Hanoi, Vietnam, 119, 286
Hanover, House of, 276
Hanukkah, 585, 586
Hapsburg, House of, 157, 204

Harare (formerly Salisbury), Zimbabwe, 291
Harding, Warren G., 656, 657
  See also Headline History; Presidents (U.S.)
Hardware, 47
Harness racing, 938–40
Harpers Ferry raid, 108
Harrison, Benjamin, 655
  See also Headline History; Presidents (U.S.)
Harrison, William Henry, 652
  See also Headline History; Presidents (U.S.)
Hart Trophy, 903–04
Harvard University, 128
Harvest, Feast of, 584, 586
Hashemite Kingdom. *See* Jordan
Hastings, Battle of, 99, 277
Havana, Cuba, 178
Hawaii, 105, 750
  Maps, 482, 495
  U.S. military action in, 312
  Volcanoes, 462, 465, 751
  See also States of U.S.
Hawaii Volcanoes National Park, 571, 751
Hayes, Rutherford B., 654, 655
  See also Headline History, Presidents (U.S.)
Haymarket Riots, 109
Headline History, 95, 127
Health, Education, and Welfare, U.S. Dept. of, 642–43, 648
  Secretaries of, 642–43
  See also Health and Human Services, Dept. of; Education, Dept. of
Health and Human Services, Dept. of, 647, 648
  Secretaries of, 643
Health care, 80–94
  AIDS cases, 86
  AIDS clinical trials, 87
  Approved AIDS medicines, 86
Heard Island, 157
Heart, human:
  Disease, 83, 84, 817
  First artificial (1966, 1982), 121, 123
  Transplants, 121
Heat cramps, treatment of, 79
Heat exhaustion, treatment of, 79
Heath, Edward, 278
Heat stroke, treatment of, 79
Hebrew Pentecost, 584, 586
Hebrides, 275
Hectare, 368
Hegira (Hijra), 99, 378
Heimlich Maneuver, 78
Heisman Memorial Trophy, 881
Helicopters:
  First flights, 354, 357, 358
  Records, 358
  Invention, 354, 560
Helium, 531
  Discovered on sun, 561
  First use in balloon, 356
Helmholtz, Hermann von, 541, 546
Helsinki, Finland, 189
Heredity, 108, 547, 561
Hermitage, The (Andrew Jackson's home), 630, 769
Heroin, 445, 446, 448, 449, 450
Hertz (measure), 370
Herzegovina, 289
Hides, 45, 69
High Aswan Dam, 132, 133, 185, 470
Highest points, U.S., 476
High jump. *See* Track and Field
High schools, 833, 834, 835
  Graduates, 834
Highways, road mileages, 405–06
Hijackings, 122, 126
Hijra. *See* Hegira
Hillary, Sir Edmund, 119, 689
Himalayas, 206, 208, 468–69

Hindenburg, Paul von, 197, 704
Hindenburg (zeppelin), 387
Hinduism, 378
  Number of followers, 375
Hindu Kush range, 152
Hirohito, Emperor, 126, 217, 689
Hiroshima, Japan:
  Atomic bombing, 117, 217
Hispanics. *See* Spanish origin, persons of
Hispaniola, 183, 203, 474
Historical parks and sites, 571–74
History, headline, 95–127
History books, awards for, 724–25, 735
History (U.S.). *See* United States History
History (world), 95–127, 152–292
  Ancient empires, 95–98
  Chronology for 1990, 975–86
  Discoveries, 457, 458
  Explorations, 457, 458
  Headline History, 95–127
  Seven Wonders, 129
  See also Chronology
Hitler, Adolf, 112, 114, 117, 197, 689
Hittite civilization, 95, 97
Ho Chi Minh, 119, 286
Ho Chi Minh City, Vietnam, 286
Hockey, ice, 867, 903–06
  Amateur champions, 867
  History, 903
  N.H.L. Trophy winners, 903–05
  Professional, 903–06
  Standard measurements, 973
Hogshead (measure), 370
Hokkaido, 217, 474
Holidays, 576, 583–84
  Calendar, 576, 583–85, 586
  National, by country, 587
  Religious, 583–85, 586
Holland. *See* Netherlands
Holocaust, 114
  Buchenwald liberation anniversary, 124
Holocene Period, 531
Holy Roman Empire, 99, 102, 196
Holy Saturday, 586
Homer, 95, 689
Home run records, 954, 958, 959, 960, 965, 966
Homestake Mine, 768
Homestead Strike, 109
Homicide. *See* Murder
Honduras, 204
  See also Countries
Honduras, British. *See* Belize
Hong Kong, 175, 281–82
Honolulu, Hawaii, 781
  See also Cities (U.S.)
Honshu, Japan, 217, 473
Hood, Mount, 459, 476, 766
Hoover, Herbert, 657
  See also Headline History; Presidents (U.S.)
Hoover Dam, 131, 470, 760
  Lake Mead, 575, 760
Horn, Cape, 172, 458
Horsepower, 370
Horse racing, 922–24
  Belmont Stakes, 922–24
  History, 922
  Kentucky Derby, 109, 754, 922–24
  Preakness Stakes, 922–24
  Triple Crown, 922–24
  See also Harness Racing
Hostages, American, 123, 125, 209
Hotels, hours and wages, 56
"Hot Line," 120–21
Hot Springs National Park, 571, 747
Households, 46, 56, 812–13
House of Burgesses, 128
House of Representatives (U.S.), 35–37, 613–14
  Apportionment, 613, 620

Committees, 38–39
Eligibility, 613
First woman member, 128
Shooting on floor of, 119
Speakers, 39
See also Congress (U.S.)
Housing:
Construction, 46
Economic statistics, 43, 46
Housing and Urban Development, U.S.
Dept. of, 648
Secretaries of, 643
Houston, Tex., 769, 781
See also Cities (U.S.)
Houston Canal, 136
Howland Island, 774
Hsi River (Si Kiang). *See* Xi Jiang
Huang Ho, 173, 471
Hubble, Edwin Powell, 348, 544, 545
Hudson Bay, 169, 458, 469
Hudson River, 458, 762
Hudson's Bay Company, 169
Huguenots, 102, 105
Humidity, relative, 674–76
Humphrey, Hubert H., 630
"Hundred Days," 107
Hundred Years' War, 101, 190, 277
Hungary, 204–05
1956 uprisings, 120, 205
See also Countries
Huns. *See* Mongols
Huron, Lake, 168, 470, 757
Hus, Jan, 101, 180
Hurricanes, 667–70
Hussein, King, 218, 288, 690
Hyde Park, N.Y. (F.D.R.), 630, 763
Hydroelectric plants, 133
Hydrogen, 531
First use in balloon, 354
Hydrogen, heavy, 114, 561
Hydrogen bomb, 118, 261

ICC, 648
Icecaps, Arctic, Antarctic, 575
Ice Cave, 475
Ice hockey. *See* Hockey
Iceland, 99, 205–06, 457, 459
Island, 474
Volcanoes, 462
See also Countries
Ice skating. *See* Figure skating; Speed
skating
Idaho, 751
See also States of U.S.
Ikhnaton, 95
"Iliad," 95
Illinois, 751, 752
See also States of U.S.
Illinois River, 478
IMF, 295
Immigration statistics, 807, 808
Impeachments, 126, 613, 614, 616,
644, 645
Andrew Johnson, 645, 654
Richard Nixon, 122, 660
Imperial gallon, 368
Imports:
United States, 69, 150
Value by country, 150
Inca Empire, 101, 102, 162, 172,
184, 245
Income:
By occupation, 44, 55, 56
Family, 44, 46
Farm income, 61
Household, 44, 46
National income, 52
Per capita, 43, 52, 778–87
See also Revenue; Salaries; Wages
Income tax (federal), 62–63, 77–81
Collections, 62, 71
Established, 70, 108, 620
Incubation periods, animals, 570

Independence, Declaration of,
611–12
Independence Day, 584
Independence Hall, 627, 766
India, 105, 108, 118, 159, 206–08,
242, 278
Sikh rebellion, 124, 207
Structures, 130
See also Countries
Indiana, 752
See also States of U.S.
Indianapolis, Ind., 752, 781
See also Cities (U.S.)
Indianapolis "500," 947–48
Indian Ocean, 469
Islands, 473, 474
Volcanoes, 462
Indians (American):
Births and birth rates, 815
Population of reservations, 808
Reservations, 746, 808
Individual retirement accounts, 419
Indochina. *See* Cambodia; Laos;
Vietnam
Indonesia, 208
Volcanoes, 462
See also Countries
Indus River, 206, 242, 471
Industrial Revolution, 105, 551
Industry:
Employment, 54, 59
Foreign countries, 146–50
Hours and wages, 55, 56
Plant and equipment costs, 46
Production indexes, 45
See also individual industries
Infantile paralysis. *See* Poliomyelitis
Infant mortality, 817, 819, 820, 821
Influenza, 112, 817
Information Agency, U.S., 649
Information bureaus, sports, 931
"Information Please" quiz show, 128
Ingathering, Feast of, 584, 586
Inini, 192
Inquisition, 101, 103, 535
Insulin, 122, 561, 711
Insurance:
Life insurance, 46
Unemployment, 591, 592
Insured mail, 990
Intelligence testing, 561
Interest:
Public debt, 62–63
Interior, U.S. Dept. of, 647
Secretaries of, 639–43
Internal Revenue Service. *See* Taxes
International affairs, news events,
1990. *See* Current Events
International Atomic Energy Agency,
295
International Bank, 295
International Civil Aviation
Organization, 295
International Court, 295
International Date Line, 582
International Development
Association, 295
International Development
Cooperation Agency, U.S., 649
International Finance Corp., 295
International Labor Organization, 296
International mail, 991
International Maritime Organization,
296
International Monetary Fund, 118,
295
International organizations, U.S.
contributions to, 63
Internationals, 109, 112
International System of Units,
366–69
International Telecommunication
Union, 296
International Trade Commission, U.S.,
649
Interplanetary probes, 321–22

Interstate commerce, 65
Interstate Commerce Commission,
648
Inventions and discoveries, 561–62
Inventions & Technology, 549–62
Iolani Palace, 751
Ionian Islands, 200
Ionosphere, 335
Iowa, 752, 753
See also States of U.S.
IRA (Irish Republic Army), 123, 124,
126, 212, 280
Iran, 123, 209–10
Hostage crisis, 123, 209
Map, 494
Shah of, 123, 209
War with Iraq, 123, 210, 211
See also Countries; News events
Iran-Contra affair, 125, 126
Iraq, 123, 210–11
Israel and, 210
Map, 494
War with Iran, 123, 210, 211
See also Countries; News events
Ireland, Northern, 212, 275,
279–80
See also United Kingdom
Ireland (island), 474
Ireland (republic), 112, 211–12
See also Countries
Irish Republican Army, 123, 124,
212, 279
Iron:
As element, 532
Economic statistics, 55, 69
"Iron Curtain," 118
Irrawaddy River, 234, 472
Irtish River, 471
Islam, 378, 586
Number of Moslems, 375
Islamabad, Pakistan, 242
Islands, 473, 474
See also specific islands
Isle of Man, 282
Isle Royale National Park, 571
Isotopes of elements, 531–32, 561
Israel, 212–14
Balfour Declaration, 112, 212
Entebbe rescue, 122
Independence (1948), 118, 213
Invasion of Lebanon, 123, 213, 223
Map, 494
Wars with Arabs, 118, 120–23,
185, 210, 213, 218
See also Countries; Headline History
Israel, ancient, 95, 212, 375–76
Istanbul, Turkey, 273
See also Constantinople
Italy, 214, 215
Structures, 129–36
Volcanoes, 462
World War I, 112
World War II, 117
See also Countries; Roman Empire
Ivory Coast, 215, 216
See also Countries
Iwo Jima, 459

Jackson, Andrew, 651, 652
See also Headline History; Presidents
(U.S.)
Jackson, Miss., 758
Jackson, Jesse, Rev., 690
Jacksonville, Fla., 749, 781
See also Cities (U.S.)
Jack the Ripper, 109
Jakarta, Indonesia, 208
Jamaica, 216
See also Countries
James, Jesse, 644, 690
James River, 478
Jamestown, Va., 103, 458, 771
Jammu, 207

Japan, 216–18, 457
China and, 109, 114, 117, 173, 217
Islands, 217, 473, 474
Russia and, 110, 217, 260
Volcanoes, 217, 459
War trial, 118
World War I, 112
World War II, 117, 118
World War II peace treaty, 119, 217
See also Countries
Japanese in U.S.:
Births and birth rates, 815
See also Nonwhite persons
Japan Sea, 217, 469
Japurá River, 472
Jarvis Island, 774
Java, 208, 473
See also Indonesia
Javelin throw. *See* Track and Field
Jefferson Awards, 731
Jefferson, Thomas, 106, 611, 650, 651
Birthday, 585
See also Headline History; Presidents (U.S.)
Jehovah's Witnesses, 377
Jenolan Caves, 475
Jersey (island), 281
Jerusalem, 95, 97, 98, 99, 101, 212, 218, 375–76
Jesus Christ, 98, 376
Jet propulsion:
First use in aviation, 357, 560
Invention, 552
Jewelry:
Birthstones, 593
Jewish holidays, 583–84
Jewish New Year, 584, 586
Jews. *See* Judaism
Jihad, 101
Joan of Arc, 101, 690
Jobs. *See* Employment
Jockeys. *See* Horse racing
Johnson, Andrew, 645, 654
Impeachment, 645, 654
See also Headline History; Presidents (U.S.)
Johnson, Lyndon B., 659
See also Headline History; Presidents (U.S.)
Johnston Atoll, 775
Johnstown flood (1889), 109, 384
Joint Chiefs of Staff, 647
Jones, Casey, 644
Jordan (kingdom), 218
Israel and, 218
See also Countries
Journalism awards, 718–23, 731
Juan Fernández Islands, 172
Judaism, 375–76
Congregations, 376
Followers, 375
Holidays, 583–86
Women clergy approved, 124
Judiciary, U.S.:
Act of 1789, 128
Constitutional provisions, 616, 617
See also Supreme Court
Judo, 878
Julian Calendar, 580, 581
Jupiter (planet), 318, 331, 333, 337–38
Space probe, 318
See also Planets
Jura Mountains, 267, 530
Jurassic Period, 530
Jury trial, 617, 618, 619
Justice, U.S. Department of, 647
Attorneys General, 639–43
Justices. *See* Supreme Court
Justinian Code, 98–99
Justinian I (the Great), 98–99
Jutland, Battle of, 112

K

Kabul, Afghanistan, 126, 152
Kalahari Desert, 474
Kamchatka, 459
Kampala, Uganda, 274
Kampuchea. *See* Cambodia
Kanawha-New River, 478
Kansas, 753
See also States of U.S.
Kansas City, Mo., 664, 758, 781
See also Cities (U.S.)
Kansas-Nebraska Act, 108
Karafuto. *See* Sakjalin
Kara Kum Desert, 474
Karat (measure), 370, 374
Kariba Lake, 470
Katanga (now Shaba), 290
Kashmir, 207, 242
Katmandu, Nepal, 236
Kazakhstan, U.S.S.R., 260
Kellogg-Briand Pact, 114
Kelvin (scale), 366, 370
Kennedy, Cape. *See* Cape Canaveral
Kennedy, Edward M., 34, 38, 121
Kennedy, Jacqueline. *See* Onassis, Jacqueline
Kennedy, John F., 120, 121, 644, 658, 659
Death, 121, 644, 659
Warren Report, 121
See also Headline History; Presidents (U.S.)
Kennedy, Robert F., 121, 642, 644
Kennedy Center Honors, 735
Kennedy International Airport, 358, 763
Kennedy Space Center, 750
Kent's Cavern, 475
Kent State University, 121, 123
Kentucky, 754
See also States of U.S.
Kentucky Derby, 109, 754, 922–24
Kenya, 219
See also Countries
Kepler, Johannes, 103, 328, 345, 534, 535, 691
Key, Francis Scott, 624, 691
Kharkov, U.S.S.R., 259
Khartoum, Sudan, 109, 264
Khmer Republic. *See* Cambodia
Khomeini, Ayatollah, 123, 126, 127, 209
Khrushchev, Nikita, 120, 261, 659, 691
Kiel Canal, 136
Kiev, U.S.S.R., 259, 260
Kigali, Rwanda, 250
Kilauea, 462
Kilogram, 366, 369, 373
Kilometer, 366, 368, 371, 373
Kindergarten, 833
King, Rev. Martin Luther, Jr., 120, 121, 644, 691
Kingman Reef, 775
Kings:
Of England, 276
Of France, 191
Of Judah and Israel, 523
Of Prussia, 197
Of Russia, 261
Kings Canyon National Park, 572
Kingston, Jamaica, 216
Kingstown, St. Vincent and the Grenadines, 251
Kinshasa, Zaire, 289
Kirghizia, U.S.S.R., 260
Kiribati, 219
See also Countries
Kissinger, Henry A., 174, 186, 213, 286, 643, 691, 706
Kitty Hawk, N.C., 110, 354, 763
Kiwanis International, 605
Kjólen Mountains, 266

Knights of Columbus, 605
Knights of Pythias, 605
Knot (measure), 370
Know-Nothing Party, 637
Knox, John, 102, 691
Kohoutek (comet), 345
Koran (Qur'an), 378
Korea, North, 219–20
See also Countries; Korean War
Korea, South, 220, 221
See also Countries; Korean War
Korean Airlines Incident (1983), 123
Korean War, 118, 220, 312
Casualtites, U.S., 307
Unknown Soldier of, 627
Kosciusko, Mount, 156
Kosygin, Alexei N., 261
Krakatau, 383, 462
Kremlin (structure), 129–30
K-2 (Mount Godwin Austen), 468
Kuala Lumpur, Malaysia, 227
Kublai Khan, 101, 173, 232, 691
Ku Klux Klan, 112
Kunlun Mountains, 173
Kuomintang, 174, 269
Kurile Islands, 217, 260, 459
Kuskokwim River, 478
Kuwait, 221, 222
See also Countries
Ky, Nguyen Cao. *See* Nguyen Cao Ky
Kyushu (island), 217, 474
Kyzyl Kum Desert, 474

L

Labor:
Civilian labor force, 51, 53, 58, 59, 778–87
ILO, 296
NLRB, 648
Statistics, 54, 57, 58, 59, 61
Unions, leading, 51
See also Employment
Labor, U.S. Department of, 647
Secretaries of, 641–43
Labor Day, 576, 584, 586
Labrador, 169, 457
Laccadive Islands, 206
Lacrosse, 949
Lady Byng Trophy, 904
Lagos, Nigeria, 240
Lakes, 470–71
Total volume, 575
See also specific lakes
Lakeshores, National, 571, 574
"Lame Duck" Amendment, 621
Lamp, electric incandescent, 558
Lancaster, House of, 276
Land:
Area of cities, 778–87
Area of countries, 137–38, 152–292
Area of states, 745–73
World area, 465
Land rushes, 765
Languages:
Use by country, 152–292
Laos, 222
See also Countries
Lao-Tse, 97, 173, 380, 692
La Paz, Bolivia, 162
See also Cities (world)
Larceny, 825, 826, 828, 829
Largest businesses, 1989, 48–49
Laser, 555
Lassen Peak, 459, 747
Lassen Volcanic National Park, 572
Lateran Treaty, 114, 284
Latin America:
Alliance for Progress, 120
Maps, 485–87
Population, 140
See also specific countries
Latitudes of cities, 467, 477
Latvia, 117, 260

Laundries, hours, wages, 56
Lausanne, Switzerland, 267
Law, codes of, 95, 99, 106
Law, first unconstitutional, 128
Law enforcement, 823–32
  Corruption, prosecutions for, 826
  Officers killed, 827
  Prisoners under death sentence, 831
  See also Crime; Arrests
Laws. *See* Bills (Congressional)
Lawyers:
  First woman, 128
Lead, 532
League (measure), 370
League of Nations, 112, 117, 118, 197, 267
Leaning Tower of Pisa, 130
Leather:
  Economic statistics, 45, 55
  Industry, hours and wages, 55
Lebanon, 123, 213, 222–24
  Civil War, 223
  Israeli Invasion, 123, 223
  U.S. military action in, 223, 312
  See also Countries
Lee, Robert E., 108, 585, 692
Leeward Islands. *See* British Virgin Islands; Montserrat
Legal holidays, 585
Legends, American folklore, 644
Legionnaire's disease, 122
Legislatures (state), 776, 777
  Only unicameral, 760, 777
Legislatures (world), 152–292
  Oldest, 205
Lena River, 259, 471
Lend-Lease, 118
Length, units of, 366–70
  Metric System, 366–70
Lenin, Vladimir, 112, 260, 261, 692
Leningrad, U.S.S.R., 259, 260
  See also Cities (World)
Lens, bifocal, 561
Lent, 583
Leonardo da Vinci, 102, 683
Leopold-Loeb case, 114
Lesbos, 200
Lesotho, 224
  See also Countries
Lesser Antilles, volcanoes, 462
Letters:
  Complaint letters, 595
  Forms of address, 439–40
  Postal regulations, 989–92
Lewis and Clark expedition, 106, 458, 751, 753, 764, 765, 768, 771
Lexington-Concord, Battle of, 103, 756
Liberia, 224–25
  See also Countries
Liberty, Statue of, 109, 628, 763
Liberty Bell, 627, 766
Libraries, 737, 835
  College and university, 835
  First circulating, 128
  U.S. public, 737
Libreville, Gabon, 194
Libya, 125, 225
  See also Countries
Libyan Desert, 474
Licenses:
  Drivers' licenses, 832
  Pilots' certificates, 358
Lidice, Czechoslovakia, 117
Lie, Trygve, 294
Liechtenstein, 225
  See also Countries
Life expectancy, 142, 820–22
Life insurance, 46, 415–17
Life on earth, 95, 530–31
Light:
  Discoveries, 562
  Velocity of, 329, 562

"Lighthouse of the Mediterranean," 462
Lightning rod, 562
Light–year, 329, 370
Lilongwe, Malawi, 227
Lima, Peru, 245
  See also Cities (world)
Lincoln, Abraham, 644, 653, 654, 752
  Assassination, 108, 644, 654
  Emancipation Proclamation, 624–25
  Gettysburg Address, 625
  Home, 752
  Lincoln–Douglas debates, 108
  See also Headline History; Presidents (U.S.)
Lincoln's Birthday, 583
Lindbergh, Charles A., 114, 356, 692
Lindbergh kidnapping, 114
Linear measure, 366–69
Linotype machine, 562
Lions Clubs, 606
Lipari Islands, 462
Liquid measure, 367, 368, 369, 371, 373
Liquor:
  Economic statistics, 47, 69
  Effects, 89, 93
  Law violations, 825, 826
  Moderation in use of, 89
  Taxes, 71
  See also Prohibition
Lisbon, Portugal, 248
  Earthquake (1755), 105, 383
  See also Cities (world)
Liter, 366, 368, 369, 371, 373
Literature:
  Authors. *See* Awards; People
  Prizes for, 707, 723, 724, 730, 735, 986
Lithium, 532
Lithography, 562
Lithuania, 117, 260
Little Big Horn, Battle of, 109, 759
Little Brown Jug, 939
Little Missouri River, 478
"Little White House," 750
Livestock, 60, 61
Loans:
  Educational loans, 835
  VA loans, 309
Locarno Conferences, 114
Locomotive, 559
Logan, Mount, 168
Logarithm, 562
Lomé, Togo, 271
London, England, 275
  Fire (1666), 105, 384
  Great Plague, 105
  Structures, 130
  See also Cities (world)
London, Tower of, 130
Long, Huey P., 117, 644, 693
Long Beach, Calif., 781, 782
  See also Cities (U.S.)
Longevity, animal, 570
Long Island, Battle of, 103
Longitude of cities, 467, 477
Loom, 562
Lord's prayer, 120
Los Angeles, Calif., 664, 747, 782
  See also Cities (U.S.)
Lots, Feast of, 583, 586
Louisiana, 754, 755
  See also States of U.S.
Louisiana Purchase, 106, 107, 651, 747, 751, 753, 754, 757, 758, 764, 765, 768, 773, 806
Louisiana Superdome, 131
Louis, Joe, 900, 917
Louis XVI, 106, 191
Louisville, Ky., 754
  See also Cities (U.S.)
Louvre, 130
Lowest points, U.S., 475, 476
LSD, 446, 448, 455

Luanda, Angola, 154
Luge (sport), 867
Lumber and wood:
  Economic statistics, 45, 47, 55, 69
  Industry, hours and wages, 55
  See also Forests
Lunar flights, 320–22
Lunar probes, 321–23
Lunation, 580
Luray Cavern, 475
Lusaka, Zambia, 290
Lusitania, 112
Luther, Martin, 102, 197, 377, 693
Lutherans, 125, 377
Luxembourg, 225
  See also Countries
Luzon, Philippines, 246, 474
Lydian civilization, 97

M

Macao, 149
MacArthur, Douglas, 114, 118, 217, 220, 693
Maccabean revolt, 98
MacDonald, Ramsay, 278, 693
Macedonia, 200, 289
Machine gun, 562
Machinery:
  Economic statistics, 45, 47, 69
  Industry, hours and wages, 55
  Inventions, 561–62
Machu Picchu, Peru, 99
Mackenzie River, 168, 458, 471
Mackinac Straits Bridge, 135
Macmillan, Harold, 278, 693
Madagascar, 226–27, 473
  See also Countries
Madeira, Portugal, 248
Madeira River, 471
Madison, James, 651
  See also Headline History; Presidents (U.S.)
Madrid, Spain, 262
  See also Cities (world)
Magazines, 297
Magellan, Ferdinand, 102, 246, 458, 693
Maggiore, Lake, 214, 267
Magna Carta, 101, 277
Magnesium, 532
Magnum (measure), 370
Mahabharata, 378
Mail:
  Air–mail route, first, 128
  Postal regulations, 989–92
Maine, 755
  See also States of U.S.
Maine (battleship), 109, 178
Majorca, 263
Malabo, Equatorial Guinea, 187
Malagasy, 226
Malawi, 227
  See also Countries
Malaya. *See* Malaysia
Malay Archipelago, 208
Malaysia, 227
  See also Countries
Malcolm X, 121
Maldives, 228
  See also Countries
Malé, Maldives, 228
Malenkov, Georgi M., 119, 260, 261
Mali, 228–29
  See also Countries
Mali Empire, 101
Malta, 229
  See also Countries
Mammals:
  Age of, 531
  Endangered, 567
Mammoth Cave, 475, 572, 754
Man, Isle of, 282
Management and Budget, Office of, 647

Managerial workers, 54
Managua, Nicaragua, 238
Manama, Bahrain, 158
Manchu Dynasty, 103, 110, 173, 217
Manchukuo, 174, 217
Manchuria, 114, 174, 217
Manganese, 532
Manhattan, 762, 783, 802
Manhattan Project, 118
Manila, Philippines, 246
  See also Cities (world)
Manitoba, 168, 169
Manned space flights, 322–25
Manslaughter, 825, 826
Mantle (of the Earth), 332
Manufacturing. See Industry
Mao Tse-tung. See Mao Zedong
Mao Zedong, 174, 693
Maps, 481–96
  Ancient empires, 96
  Expansion of the United States, 805
  Germany attack on Soviet Russia, 115
  Moslem world, 100
  Pacific Theater, 116
  Partition of Africa, 1914, 111
  Territorial changes after W.W. I, 113
  U.S. during Revolution, 104
  World time zones, 493
Maputo, Mozambique, 233
Marathon, Battle of, 97
Marconi, Guglielmo, 109, 694
Marco Polo, 101, 457, 698
Mardi Gras, 583
Margarine, 61, 91
Mariana Islands, 776
Marie Antoinette, 106, 694
Marijuana, 449, 450, 454
Marine Corps, U.S., 304, 305
  Actions, 110, 114, 120–22, 123, 184, 239, 312
  Commandant of, 647
  See also Armed Forces
Mariner space probes, 319, 321
Marne, Battles of the, 112
Marquesas Islands, 193
Marriage statistics, 809–11, 812–13
Mars (planet), 331, 333, 336–37
  Space probes, 321–22
  See also Planets
Marshall, John, 645, 694
Marshall Islands, 776
Marshall Plan, 118, 658
Martinique, 192, 193
  Mount Pelée, 462
Martin Luther King Day, 583
Mary, Queen of Scots, 103, 694
Marx, Karl, 107, 108, 694
Maryland, 755, 756
  See also States of U.S.
Maseru, Lesotho, 224
Mason and Dixon's Line, 476
Mass:
  Chemical elements, 531–32
  Metric System, 366
Massachusetts, 756
  See also States of U.S.
Mass–energy theorem, 372, 543
Massive, Mount, 478
Masters Tournment (golf), 941
Match, 562
Maternal mortality, 817
Mathematics:
  Averages, 374
  Decimals and fractions, 372
  Formulas, 372
  Mean and median, 374
  Metric and U.S. equivalents, 366–69
  Prefixes and multiples, 372
  Prime numbers, 374
Matter-energy theorem, 372, 543
Mauna Kea, 462, 465, 476, 751
Mauna Loa, 462, 751
Maundy Thursday, 586

Mauritania, 229–30
  See also Countries
Mauritius, 230
  See also Countries
Maximilian, Emperor, 108, 231, 694
Maxwell, James Clerk, 541–42, 694
Mayaguez incident, 122
Mayflower Compact, 623
Mayflower (ship), 103, 623
Mayors, U.S., 778–87, 789
Mayotte, 193
Mbabane, Swaziland, 265
McCarthy (Joseph) hearings, 119
McDonald Islands, 157
McHenry, Fort, 107, 624
McKinley, Mount, 465, 469, 475, 476, 478, 571
McKinley, William, 644, 655
  See also Headline History; Presidents (U.S.)
McNary Dam, 766
Mean and median, 374
Measles, 817
Measurement ton, 370
Measures, weights, 366–73
  Capacities and volumes, 367–68
  Conversion factors, 373
  Cooking, 371
Meat:
  Economic statistics, 61, 69, 149
  Fat and cholesterol, 90
  World production, 149
Mecca, Saudi Arabia, 99, 125, 252, 378
Medal of Freedom, 733–35
Medal of Honor, 315
Mede civilization, 97
Media, 297–301
  Magazines, 297
  Newspapers, 297–301
Mediation and Conciliation Service, Federal, 648
Mediation Board, National, 648
Medical care, economic statistics, 43
Medicare, 121
Medicine:
  Discoveries, 561–62
  Nobel Prizes for, 710–11, 986
Medina, Saudi Arabia, 99, 253, 378
Mediterranean Sea, 469
  Volcanoes, 462
"Mein Kampf" (Hitler), 114
Mekong River, 286, 471
Melting points, of elements, 531–32
Melville Island, 474
Memorial Day, 584
Memorial Day, Confederate, 585
Memorials, National, 571, 574
Memphis, Tenn., 768, 782
  See also Cities (U.S.)
Mendelevium, 532
Mendelian Law, 547, 562
Mennonites, 377
Merced River, waterfalls, 472, 473
Merchant Marine Academy, U.S., 306–07
Mercury (element), 532
Mercury (planet), 331, 333, 335
  Flights, 320–22
  See also Planets
Mercury, Project, 320–22
Mercury-vapor lamp, 560
Meredith, James H., 120
Merrimac (ship), 108
Mesabi Range, 757
Mesa Verde National Park, 572, 748
Mesopause, 335
Mesopotamia, 97, 98, 210
Mesopotamian Empire, 95, 97
Mesosphere, 335
Mesozoic Era, 530
Metals:
  As elements, 531–32
  Economic statistics, 45, 69

Industry, hours and wages, 55
Mineral wealth in countries, 152–292
Meteors and meteorites, 346
  Showers, 346
Meter (measure), 366–68, 373
Methadone, 446
Methanol, 361
Methodists, Methodism, 106, 377
Metric System, 366–69, 371, 373
  Conversion tables, 371, 373
Metropolitan areas, 793–96
Metropolitan Opera, 109
Mexican Cession, 107, 231
Mexican War, 107, 231, 307, 746, 748, 760, 762, 769, 773
Mexico, 95, 97, 98, 107, 230–31
  Conquest of, 102, 231, 457
  Map, 485
  Revolution, 110
  U.S. military actions in, 110, 231, 312
  Volcanoes, 462
  See also Countries
Mexico, Gulf of, 469
Mexico City, Mexico, 230
  See also Cities (world)
Miami, Fla., 664, 782
  See also Cities (U.S.)
Michigan, 756, 757
  See also States of U.S.
Michigan, Lake, 458, 470, 752, 757
Micronesia, 776
Microscope, compound, 562
Microwave ovens, 80–81
Middle East:
  Arab–Israeli conflicts, 118, 120–23, 185, 212–14, 218, 223, 268
  Map, 494
Midway Islands, 775
Mileage:
  U.S. cities, between, 405–08
  World cities, between, 409–10
Mile records:
  Race horses (harness), 938, 939
  Runners, 927–28
Military. See National defense; Armed Forces
Military Academy, U.S., 305, 763
Military forces. See Armed Forces
Military interventions, U.S., 312
Military Parks, National, 571, 573
Military strength, U.S., 313, 315
Milk:
  Cholesterol and fat, 90
  Economic statistics, 61
Milk River, 478
Milky Way, 328, 331
Milwaukee, Wis., 772, 782
  See also Cities (U.S.)
Mindanao, Philippines, 246, 474
Mindszenty, Jozsef Cardinal, 205
Minerals. See Coal; Metals
Minerals:
  Dietary allowances, 94
Ming Dynasty, 101, 103, 173
Mining:
  Hours and wages, 56
  Union, 51
Minneapolis, Minn., 757, 782
  See also Cities (U.S.)
Minnesota, 757, 758
  See also States of U.S.
Minoan culture, 95, 97
Minority Presidents, 638
Minsk, Byelorussia, U.S.S.R., 259, 260
Minutemen, 756
Miquelon. See St. Pierre
Mir (space station), 323, 324, 325
Mississippi, 758
  See also States of U.S.
Mississippi-Missouri-Red Rock River, 471, 479
Mississippi River, 457, 458, 471, 479, 754, 758

Missouri, 758, 759
See also States of U.S.
Missouri (battleship), 117
Missouri Compromise, 107, 651, 758
Missouri-Red Rock River, 479
Missouri River, 471, 479
Mistletoe, 585
Mitterrand, François, 189, 191, 192
Mmabatho, Bophuthatswana, 258
Mobile-Alabama-Coosa River, 479
Mobile homes, 46
Modified Mercalli Intensity Scale, 466
Mogadishu, Somalia, 256
Mohammed, 99, 253, 378, 695
Mojave Desert, 474
Moldavia, U.S.S.R., 260
Mole (measure), 366
Moluccas Islands, 208
Monaco, 231–32
See also Countries
Mondale, Walter F., 630
Monetary Fund, International, 118, 295
Money:
Designs of U.S. bills, 374
Of countries, 152–292
Portraits on U.S. bills, 374
Money orders, postal, 990
Mongolia, 232, 457
See also Countries
Mongols, 98, 101, 173, 259, 260
Monitor (ship), 108
"Monkey Trial," 114
Monroe, James, 651
See also Headline History; Presidents (U.S.)
Monroe Doctrine, 107, 623, 651
Monrovia, Liberia, 224
Montana, 759
See also State of U.S.
Mont Blanc, 134, 190
Mont Blanc Tunnel, 134
Monte Carlo, Monaco, 232
Montenegro, 289
Montevideo, Uruguay, 283
See also Cities (world)
Months:
Birthstones for, 593
Name derivations, 582
Monticello, Va., 651, 771
Montreal, Quebec, Canada, 168, 170
Montserrat, 282
"Monumental Mountain," 475
Monuments, National, 571, 572–73
Moon, 331–32
Apollo program, 324–25
Eclipses, 350
First manned landing, 121, 322, 324
Lunar probes, 321–22
Perigee and apogee, 349–50
Phases, 349–50
Phenomena, 349–50
Moons of planets, 328, 331, 336, 337–38, 340, 341–42, 343–44
Moors, 101
Moravia, 180
Mormons, 107, 377, 769
Moro, Aldo, 122
Morocco, 232–33
See also Countries
Moroni, Comoros, 176
Morse, Samuel F. B., 107, 557, 695
Mortality. See Deaths
Mortgages: 420–25
Tax advantages of, 419
Terminology, 425
Moscow, U.S.S.R., 259–61
See also Cities (world)
Moses, 95
Moslem architecture, 130
Most Valuable Player:
Baseball, 963
Basketball, 896
Hockey, 903–04

"Mother of Presidents," 770, 771
Motion pictures:
Awards, 713–15, 735
Income from, 744
Inventions, 558–59
Stars, 677–705, 713–15
Top-grossing, 744
Top rentals of 1989, 744
Motorcycle, 558
Motor vehicles:
Accident deaths, 817–18
Economic statistics, 66–67
Fuel consumption, 365
Registration, 66, 365
State laws, 832
Theft, 825, 826, 828, 829
See also Automobiles; Buses
Mottoes:
National, 630
State, 745–73
Mountains:
United States, 469, 476, 478
World, 468–69
See also names of mountains; Volcanoes
Mount McKinley National Park. See Denali National Park
Mount Rainier National Park, 572, 771
Mount Vernon, Va., 630, 650, 771
Movies. See Motion pictures
Mozambique, 233–34, 249
See also Countries
Mozart, Wolfgang Amadeus, 105, 696
Mubarak, Hosni, 184–86
Mulroney, Brian, 124, 168, 169, 170
Munich, West Germany, 196
Beer Hall Putsch (1923), 112
Munich Conference (1938), 117, 180, 197
Murder, 825, 826, 828, 829
Murray River, 472
Muscat, Oman, 241
Museums, first science museum, 128
Music:
Classical, 732, 739, 740
Popular, 732, 739, 740
Pulitzer Prize for, 727
U.S. symphony orchestras, 736
Muslims. See Islam
Mussolini, Benito, 112, 117, 215, 696
Myanmar, 166, 234
See also Countries
Mythology:
Egyptian, 528
Greek, 523–27
Norse, 527, 528
Roman, 523–27

N

NAACP, 607
Nagasaki, Japan, 117, 217
Nairobi, Kenya, 219
Names:
Animal, 569
Days, 582
Months, 582
Old Testament, 521, 522
States, origins of, 745–73
Namibia, 234–35
See also Countries
Nantes, Edict of, 102, 105
Napoleon Bonaparte. See Bonaparte, Napoleon
Napoleonic Code, 106
Napoleonic Wars, 106, 190, 260, 278
Narcotics:
Cocaine and crack, 446, 450, 451–52
Violations, arrests for, 391, 825, 826, 828

NASA, 648
NASCAR, 948, 949
Nashville-Davidson, Tenn., 768, 783
See also Cities (U.S.)
Nassau, Bahamas, 158
Nasser, Gamal Abdel, 185, 213, 253, 288, 696
National Aeronautics and Space Administration, 648
National Anthem, 624
National Basketball Association, 894–98
National Capital Parks, 571, 574
National Cemeteries, 574
Arlington, 574, 627, 630
National Committees, 633
National Conventions, 632, 633
National debt, 45, 62–63
Interest, 62–63
Validity, 620
National defense:
Spending for, 44, 53, 61, 62–63
National Foundation on the Arts and Humanities, 648
National Guard, The, 308
National Historical Parks, 571, 572
National Historic Sites, 571, 573–74
National Hockey League, 903–06, 931
National income, 52
National Labor Relations Board, 648
National League. See Baseball; Football
National Mediation Board, 648
National Park System, 571–75
National Parkways, 571, 574
National Republican Party, 634
National Scenic Riverways, 571, 574
National Science Foundation, 648
National Security Council, 647
National Society of Film Critics Awards, 717
National Transportation Safety Board, 648
National Zoo, 569
NATO. See North Atlantic Treaty Organization
Natural features (of countries), 152–292
See also Geography
Naturalization statistics, 808
Natural resources:
Countries, 152–292
States of U.S., 745–73
Nauru, 235
See also Countries
Nautilus (submarine), 119
Naval Academy, U.S., 305–06, 756
Navy (U.S.), 106, 304
Expenditures, 62–63
First admiral, 128
Secretaries of, 639–43, 647
See also Armed Forces
Nazis, 114, 117, 118, 120, 197
N'Djamena, Chad, 171
Neanderthal, 95
"Neap tides," 332
Near East, map, 494
Nebraska, 759, 760
Kansas–Nebraska Act, 108
See also States of U.S.
Nebuchadnezzar, 97, 129
Negev Desert, 212
Negroes. See Blacks
Nehru, Jawaharlal, 207, 696
Nelson River, 472
Neosho River, 479
Nepal, 235
See also Countries
Neptune (planet), 331, 333, 342
See also Planets
Neptunium, 532, 562
Netherlands, 236–37
See also Countries
Netherlands Antilles, 237
Networks, TV, 742

Neutron, discovery of, 562
Nevada, 760
    See also States of U.S.
Nevis, 257
New Amsterdam, 105, 762
Newark, N.J., 761, 783
    See also Cities (U.S.)
New Brunswick, 168, 169
New Caledonia, 193, 194
"New Colossus, The," 628
New Cornelia Tailings, 132, 746
New Deal, 117, 657, 658
New Delhi, India, 206
Newfoundland, Canada, 105, 168, 474
New Freedom, 656
"New Frontier," 658
New Guinea. *See* Papua New Guinea
New Hampshire, 760, 761
    See also States of U.S.
New Hebrides. *See* Vanuatu
New Jersey, 761
    See also States of U.S.
New Mexico, 761, 762
    See also States of U.S.
New Orleans, 665, 754, 783
    See also Cities (U.S.)
New Orleans, Battle of, 107, 754
News:
    Chronology (4500 B.C. to A.D. 1989), 95–127
    Current Events, 974–86
    Deaths in 1989–90, 987–88
Newspapers, 297–301
    Awards, 718–27, 731
    Firsts, 128
    Oldest still published, 748
    Postal rates, 989
Newsreel, first, 128
Newton, Isaac, 105, 536, 537, 561, 696
Newton (measure), 366
New Year, Jewish, 584, 586
New Year's Day, 583
New York City, 762, 783, 802
    Boroughs, 783, 802
    Bridges, 135
    Buildings and structures, 130–31, 133–34
    Climate, 665
    Kennedy Airport, 358, 763
    Statue of Liberty, 628, 763
    Tunnels, 134
    Tweed Ring, 108
    U.N. Headquarters, 763
    World's Fairs, 117, 743
    See also Cities (U.S.)
New York Drama Critics' Circle Awards, 728–29
New York (State), 762, 763
    See also States of U.S.
New Zealand, 237–38
    First visited, 458
    Volcanoes, 459
    See also Countries
Niagara Falls, 473, 763
Niamey, Niger, 239
Nicaea, Council of, 98, 376
Nicaragua, 238–39
    U.S. military actions in, 239, 312
    Volcanoes, 462
    See also Countries
Nicene Creed, 98, 376
Nickel (element), 532
Nicknames:
    Football teams, 884
    States (U.S.), 747–73
Nicobar Islands, 206
Nicosia, Cyprus, 179
Niger, 239–40
    See also Countries
Nigeria, 240
    See also Countries
Niger River, 239, 471
Nile River, 185, 264, 471
    High Aswan Dam, 132, 133, 185

Niobrara River, 479
Nirvana, 379
Nitroglycerin, 553
Niue (island), 238
Nixon, Richard M., 659, 660
    Resignation, 122, 660
    See also Headline History; Presidents (U.S.)
NLRB, 648
Noatak River, 479
Nobel, Alfred, 108, 109, 542, 553, 696, 706
Nobel Prizes, 109, 542, 706–12, 986
    For 1990, 986
Nonfiction (general), awards for, 726–27, 730, 735
Nonwhite persons in U.S.:
    Deaths and death rates, 819, 820, 821–22
    Life expectancy, 820–22
    Population statistics, 792–93, 796, 806, 808
    See also Chinese; Indians; Japanese; Blacks in U.S.
Norfolk Island, 157
Normandy, House of, 276
Normandy Invasion, 117
Norris Trophy, 904
North America, 459, 465
    Explorations, discoveries, 457, 458
    Maps, 481–85
    Population, 140
    See also Continents; Countries
North Atlantic Treaty Organization, 118, 119, 151
    France and, 190
    Turkey and, 274
North Canadian River, 479
North Carolina, 763
    See also States of U.S.
North Cascades National Park, 572
North Dakota, 763, 764
    See also States of U.S.
Northeast Passage, 458
Northern Ireland, 212, 275, 279–80
    See also United Kingdom
"Northern lights," 347
Northern Rhodesia. *See* Zambia
North Island (New Zealand), 238, 473
North Platte River, 479
North Pole, 110, 458
    Flights over, 356, 357
    Reached, 110, 458
North Sea, 160, 181, 196, 236, 241, 276, 469
Northwest Passage, 458, 765
Northwest Territories, 168, 169
Norway, 240–41
    See also Countries
Notre-Dame de Paris, 130
Nouakchott, Mauritania, 229
Nova Scotia, 168, 169, 457
Novelists. *See* Awards; People
NRC, 648
NSF, 648
Nubian Desert, 474
Nuclear fission, 543, 544, 562
Nuclear physics, discoveries and theories, 544, 562
Nuclear power plants, 363–64
    Accidents, 123, 125, 385
    United States, 363–64
Nuclear-proliferation agreement, 122
Nuclear reactors, 363–64
Nuclear Regulatory Commission, 648
Nuclear weapons, 313, 314
    Offensive nuclear missiles, 313, 314
    Testing, 118–21
Nuclear Winter, 327
Nuku'alofa, Tonga, 271
Numbers:
    Decimals and fractions, 372

Prime, 374
Roman, 374
Nuremberg laws, 114
Nuremberg war crimes trial, 114, 118
Nutrition, 80–94
    Contents of foods, 88–91, 93
    Dietary allowances, 93, 94
    Dietary guidelines, 88, 89
Nuts, food value, 89
Nyasa, Lake, 470
Nyasaland. *See* Malawi
Nylon, 554

O

Oakland, Calif., 747, 783
    See also Cities (U.S.)
OAS. *See* Organization of American States
Oaths:
    Constitutional, 616, 618
    Presidential, 616
Oberlin College, 128
Obie Awards, 730
Ob River, 471
Occupational Safety and Health Review Commission, 649
Oceania, 459, 465
    Countries, 465
    Elevations, 465
    Explorations and discoveries, 458
    Population, 140, 465
    Religions, 375
    Entries under Continents *may also apply*
Ocean liners. *See* Steamships
Oceans, 469
    Volume of, 575
Odd Fellows, Independent Order of, 607
Oder-Neisse Line, 198
Odessa, U.S.S.R., 259
"Odyssey," 95
Office of Personnel Management, 649
Offices, Executive, 647–49
Ohio, 764, 765
    See also States of U.S.
Ohio-Allegheny River, 472, 479
Ohio River, 479
Ohm, 370
Ohm's Law, 540, 562
Oil (petroleum):
    Crude production, 146–47, 364
    Economic statistics, 55, 69, 146–47
    Exports by country of destination, 365
    First well in U.S., 128
    Imported directly from OPEC countries, 365
    Industry, hours and wages, 55
    Spill, Exxon Valdez, 126
    World production, 146–47, 364
Oils, fats: 61, 69, 89–91
    Food value, 91
O.K. Corral, 746
Okhotsk Sea, 469
Okinawa, 217
Oklahoma, 765
    See also States of U.S.
Oklahoma City, Okla., 765, 783, 784
    See also Cities (U.S.)
Öland, 266
Old North Church, 756
Old Testament names, 521, 522
Olympic Games, 865–78
    History, sites, 95, 110, 865
    Munich Massacre, 122
    1984 Games, 124, 262
    1988 Games, 865–78
Olympic National Park, 572
Omaha, Neb., 759, 760, 784
    See also Cities (U.S.)

Oman, 241–42
See also Countries
Onassis, Aristotle, 232, 697
Onassis, Jacqueline, 631, 658, 697
Ontario, Canada, 168
Ontario, Lake, 470
OPEC, 253, 365
Opium, 444, 446
Opium War, 107
OPM, 649
Orange Bowl, 880
Orange River, 472
Orbits:
    Comets, 345–46
    Minor planets (asteroids), 345
    Moon, 331–32
    Planets, 328, 332–45
Orchestras, symphony, 736
Ordovician Period, 530
Oregon, 765, 766
    Volcanoes, 459
    See also States of U.S.
Organization of American States, 118, 151, 173
    Dominican Republic and, 184
Organization of Petroleum Exporting Countries, 151, 253, 365
Organizations, 599–610
    Sports, 931
Orinoco River, 175, 472
Orkney Islands, 276
Orthodox churches, 99, 375–77, 586
Osage River, 479, 759
Oscars (awards), 713–15
Oslo, Norway, 240
Oswald, Lee Harvey, 121, 644, 659
Ottawa, Ontario, Canada, 168, 170
Ottoman Turks, 268, 273
Ouachita River, 479
Ouagadougou, Burkina Faso, 165
Outer Mongolia. See Mongolia
Owen Falls Lake, 470
Ozark Mountains, 759
Ozone, discovery of, 562
Ozonosphere, 326, 335, 564

P

Pacific Islands (U.S.), 776
Pacific Ocean, 469
    Discovery, 457
    Islands, 473, 474
    Map, 495
    "Ring of Fire," 459–62
    U.S. coastline, 479
    Volcanoes, 459, 462
    See also Oceania
Pacts. See Treaties
Pagodas, 130
Painted Desert, 474
Painters. See People
Pakistan, 118, 159, 207, 242–43
    See also Countries
Palau Islands, 776
Paleozoic Era, 530
Palestine, 97, 212
Palestine Liberation Organization, 123, 213, 218, 223
Palm Sunday, 583–84, 586
Pamir Mountain Range, 468–69
Panama, 122, 243–44
    U.S. military action in, 127, 312
    See also Countries
Panama Canal, 110, 122, 244, 136
    Treaties, 122, 243
Panama City, Panama, 243
Panay (gunboat), 117
Pancake Tuesday, 583
Panel quiz radio show, first, 128
Panmunjom, North Korea, 221
Pantheon, Rome, 129
Papal States, 273
Papeete, French Polynesia, 193
Paper:
    Economic statistics, 45, 55, 69

Industry, hours and wages, 55
    Invention of, 562
Paper currency, portraits on, 374
Papua New Guinea, 244, 473
    First visited, 458
    See also Countries
Parachute, 562
Parachuting:
    Caterpillar Club, 356
    First jump, 354
Paraguay, 244–45
    See also Countries
Paraguay River, 163, 244, 472
Paramaribo, Suriname, 265
Paraná River, 163, 244, 471
Parcel post, 989
Parícutin, 462
Paris, France: 189, 190
    Structures, 130
    World War I, 112
    World War II, 117, 190
Paris, Peace of (1783), 103
Paris, Treaty of (1898), 109
Paris, Treaty of (1947), 118, 205
Parks:
    Affiliated areas, 575
    City-owned, 778–87
    National Park System, 571–75
    State parks, 745–73
Parliament (Great Britain), 101, 103, 106, 114, 276, 277
Parsec (measure), 329, 370
Parties, political (world), 152–292
Pasover, 584, 586
Passports and Customs, 392–93
Pasteur, Louis, 108, 546, 547, 561, 697
Patagonia, 155
Patents, 593
Paulo Afonso Falls, 163
Peace Corps, 649
Peace Prizes, Nobel, 706, 986
Peace River, 472
Peak Cavern, 475
Pearl Harbor attack, 117, 118, 217, 750
Peary, Robert E., 110, 458, 697
Pedestrian deaths, 818
Pee Dee–Yadkin River, 479
Peking, China, 130, 173
    Structures, 130
    See also Beijing; Cities (world)
Pelée, Mount, 462
Peloponnesian War, 97
Penicillin, 114, 561, 711
Pennsylvania, 106
    See also States of U.S.
Pennyweight, 367
Pensions:
    Veterans, 310
Pentagon, 647
Pentagon Papers, 119
Pentathlon, 873, 878
Pentecost, 584, 586
Pentecost, Hebrew, 584, 586
People, 677–705
    See also Current Events
People's Party (Populists), 635, 636
Per capita income:
    By states, 52
    Countries, 152–292
Pérez de Cuéllar, Javier, 294
Performers. See People
Pericles, 97
Perihelion, 328, 349, 582
Periodic law, 562
Periodic table, 562
Permian Period, 530
Perón, Juan D., 120, 155, 697
Perpetual calendar, 578–79
Persia, ancient, 97
Persia, modern. See Iran
Persian Gulf States. See United Arab Emirates
Personal Finance, 411–25
    Bank deposits, 417–18

Bonds, 412–15
    Certificates of deposit, 411–12
    401(k) Plans, 420
    IRAs, 419
    Life insurance, 415–17
    Mortgages, 420–25
    SEPs, 420
    Taxes, 419–20
Peru, 245, 458
    See also Countries
Petition, right of, 618
Petrified Forest National Park, 572
Petroleum. See Oil
P.G.A. Champions, 942
Pharos of Alexandria, 129
Philadelphia, Pa., 106, 766, 784
    Continental Congresses, 626
    Liberty Bell, 627, 766
    See also Cities (U.S.)
Philippines, 123, 124, 246–47
    Marcos, Ferdinand, 123, 124, 246
    Tydings–McDuffie Act, 246
    U.S. Territory, 806
    Volcanoes, 459
    See also Countries
Philosophers. See People
Phnom Penh, Cambodia, 123, 166
Phoenician Empire, 95, 97
Phoenix, Ariz., 625, 746, 784
    See also Cities (U.S.)
Phoenix Islands, 219, 774
Phonographs:
    Invention, 109
    Records, 740
Photography:
    Awards, 719–20, 731
    Equipment, 69
    First aerial, 354
    Inventions, 109, 557
Photosphere, 331
Phrygian civilization, 97
Physical Fitness, President's Council on, 649
Physics:
    Inventions, discoveries, and theories, 539–45, 561–62
    Nobel Prizes for, 707–09, 986
Pi (measure), 370, 372
Pica (measure), 370
Pierce, Franklin, 653
    See also Headline History; Presidents (U.S.)
Pigs, Bay of, 120, 178
Pikes Peak, 478, 748
Pilcomayo River, 472
Pilgrims, 103, 756
Pilots, number of, 358
Pindus Mountains, 200
Pioneer probes, 320–22
Pipe (measure), 370
Pisa, Leaning Tower of, 130
Pitcairn Island, 106, 282
Pittsburgh, Pa., 766, 784
    See also Cities (U.S.)
Pizarro, Francisco, 102, 184, 245, 263, 458, 698
Plague, 99, 101, 105, 277
Planck, Max, 542, 698, 707
Planets, 328, 333–44, 351
    Conjunctions, 349–50
    Exploration of, 321–22
    Minor planets (asteroids), 334, 345
    Moons of, 336–44, 349–50
    Origin of, 328
    See also Space Exploration; Astronomy
Plantagenet, House of, 276, 277
Plants, classification of, 561
Plastics:
    Economic statistics, 69
    Inventions and discoveries, 554
Plata River, 163, 283
Plate-tectonics theory, 465
Plato, 97, 698
Plays, longest Broadway runs, 743
Playwrights. See People; Theater

Pledge to flag, 628
Pleistocene Period, 531
PLO, 123, 213, 218, 223
  Achille Lauro hijacked, 124
Plow, 562
Pluto (planet), 333, 344
  See also Planets
Plutonium, 532, 562
Plymouth Colony, 103, 756
Plymouth Rock, 103
Pneumonia, 817
Pocket veto, 639
Poetry, awards for, 726, 730
Poets. *See* People; Awards
Poets Laureate:
  Of England, 717
  Of the United States, 729
Point Four program, 118
Point (measure), 370
Poisons, food 82, 83
Poisons, treatment of, 78
Poland, 105, 106, 112, 117, 120,
  247–48
  Poznan uprising (1956), 120
  Solidarity Union, 247
  Workers strikes, 248
  World War II (1939), 117, 197,
  247
  See also Countries
Polar flights, 356, 357
Pole vault. *See* Track and Field
Policemen, statistics, 827
Policy Development, White House
  Office of, 647
Poliomyelitis:
  Vaccines, 119, 562
Political parties (U.S.). *See* specific
  parties
Political parties (world), 152–292
Polk, James K., 652, 653
  See also Headline History; Presidents
  (U.S.)
Poll tax, 622
Pollution: 563–65, 566
  Air, 566
  Water, 566
Polo, Marco, 101, 457, 698
Pol Pot, 123, 166, 287
Polymerization, 554
Polynesia, French, 193
Pompeii, 383, 462
Pompidou, Georges, 191, 192
Pontiffs, Roman Catholic, 380–82
Pony Express, 759
Popes, 380–82
  John Paul I, 122, 284, 382
  John Paul II, 122, 123, 127, 284,
  382
  John XXIII, 120, 284, 382
  Paul VI, 120, 122, 284, 382
Popocatépetl, 462
Population (U.S.), 792–804, 806,
  809
  Age, by, 778–87, 792–93, 796,
  808
  Black, 778–87, 792–93, 796, 806,
  808, 809
  Census required by Constitution,
  613
  Census years, 792
  Cities:
    Largest, 778–88
    Largest of each state, 745–73
    1970–1980, 798–804
  Civilian labor force, 51, 53, 54
  Colonial estimates, 792
  Densities (1790–1980), 792, 797
  Family groups, 811, 812–13
  Female, 792–93, 796
  Foreign-born, 792–93, 807, 808
  Growth, 792–804
  Households, 811
  Indians on reservations, 808
  Male, 792–93, 796
  Marital status, 810, 811
  Married couples, 811

Metropolitan areas, 793–96
Nativity, 792–93
Poverty level, persons below, 808
Projections, 809
Race, 778–87, 792–93, 796, 806,
  808
Sex, 792–93, 796
Shifts, 797
65 and over, 778–87, 792–93,
  796
Spanish origin, 778–87, 796, 806,
  808
States, 1790–1980, 797
Territories, 773–75, 806
Total, 806
Urban, 793–96, 798–804
Working population, 51, 53, 54, 58
Population (world), 137–41, 465
  Cities, by country, 152–292
  Cities, large (table), 138–39
  Continents, 140, 465
  Countries (table), 137–38
  Countries, 137–38, 152–292
  Densities, 138–39, 152–292, 465
Populists. *See* People's Party
Porcupine River, 479
Port Arthur, Kwantung, China, 110
Port-au-Français, French Southern and
  Antarctic Lands, 194
Port-au-Prince, Haiti, 203
Portland, Ore., 784, 785
  See also Cities (U.S.)
Port Louis, Mauritius, 230
Port Moresby, Papua New Guinea,
  244
Port-of-Spain, Trinidad and Tobago,
  272
Porto-Novo, Benin, 161
Portraits on U.S. currency, 374
Ports, U.S., commerce at, 65
Portsmouth, Treaty of, 110, 761
Portugal, 248–49
  See also Countries
Portuguese Guinea. *See*
  Guinea–Bissau
Portuguese West Africa. *See* Angola
Positron, 562
Post, Wiley, 357, 698
Postal regulations, 989–92
Postal Service, U.S., 106, 649,
  989–92
  Employment, 61
  Rates, 989–92
Postal Union, Universal, 295
Postcards, 989
Postmasters General, 639–43
Post Office Department. *See* Postal
  Service
Postojna Grotto, 475
Potatoes, economic statistics, 60, 61
Potomac River, 479, 787
Potsdam Conference, 117, 118
Poultry:
  Cholesterol and fat, 90
  Economic statistics, 60, 61
Poverty level, persons below, 808
Powder River, 479
Power failure of 1965, 121
Power loom, 562
Poznan, Poland, uprising, 120
Prague, Czechoslovakia, 180
  See also Cities (world)
Praia, Cape Verde, 170
Preakness Stakes, 922–24
Precipitation, 664–65
Premiers and Prime Ministers:
  Canada, 169
  Countries, 152–292
  Great Britain, 278
  Soviet Union, 261
Presbyterian churches, 102, 377
Presidential candidates, 634–35
  First woman, 128
Presidential elections, 634–37
Presidential Medal of Freedom,
  733–35

Presidential oath, 616
"Presidents, Mother of," 770, 771
President's Council on Physical
  Fitness and Sports, 649
Presidents (foreign), 152–292
  France, 191, 192
  Germany, 197
Presidents (U.S.), 629–30, 639–43,
  650–63
  Assassinations and attempts, 644
  Biographies, 650–63
  Burial places, 630
  Cabinets, 639–43
  Constitutional provisions, 615–16
  Continental Congresses, 626
  Election procedure, 615–16, 619,
  632–33
  Elections, 40, 634–35
  Families, 631
  Minority Presidents, 638
  Powers, duties, 615–16
  Mount Rushmore carvings, 768
  National Historic Sites, 573
  Nomination, 631–32
  Oath of Office, 616
  Portraits on currency, 374
  Qualifications, 615
  Religious affiliations, 629
  Salary, 41, 616
  Succession to, 616, 621, 622, 623
  Tabulated data, 629
  Term of office, 615, 621
  Wives and children, 631
  See also entries under Presidential
Press, freedom of, 103, 105, 618
Price Indexes:
  Consumer, 43
  GNP deflator, 45
  Producer, 45
Prime Ministers. *See* Premiers
Prime numbers, 374
Prince Edward Island, 168, 169
Prince of Wales, 277
Prince of Wales Trophy, 904
Príncipe, 252
Printing:
  Economic statistics, 55
  Industry, hours and wages, 55
  Inventions, 549, 562
  Measures, 369, 370
  See also Publishing
Priority mail. *See* Airmail
Private schools, 833, 836, 837–62
Prizes. *See* Awards
Probes, lunar, deep space, 321–22
Production indexes, U.S. industries,
  45
  See also kind of industry or product
Professional Golfers Association
  Champions, 942
Professional personnel, 54
Programming, information, 562
Progressive Party (1912, 1924,
  1948), 636
Prohibition, 112, 117, 620, 621
Promontory Summit, 769
Propeller, screw, 562
Prostitution, arrests for, 825, 826
Protestantism, 102, 377
  Protestants, number of, 375, 376
  Reformation, 102, 197, 377
Proton, 562
Prudhoe Bay, Alaska, 746
Prussia, 197
  Kings of, 197
Psychoanalysis, 562
Public assistance, 64
Public schools, 833, 835, 836,
  837–62
Public utilities, 363
  Employment, 59
  Hours and wages, 56
  Largest companies, 49
Publishing:
  Magazines, 297
  Newspapers, 297–301

Notable books, 1989, 736
Printed matter, 69
Pueblo (ship), 121
Puerto Rico, 773, 774
    Execution methods, 831
    Holidays, 585
Pulitzer Prizes, 718–27
Pullman strike, 109
Pulsars, 328
Punctuation rules, 437–39
Punic Wars, 97, 98
Punjab, 207, 242, 457
Pupils. *See* Students
Purim, 583, 586
Puritan Commonwealth, 277
Purús River, 471
Pyongyang, North Korea, 118, 219
Pyramids of Egypt, 129

Q

Qaddafi, Muammar el, 172, 225, 265
Qatar, 249
    See also Countries
Quakers. *See* Friends
Quayle, Dan, 40
Quantum theory, 542, 543, 562
Quart, 367, 368, 369, 373
Quasars, 328, 330
Quebec, Canada, 168
Quebec, Que., Canada, 168
    See also Cities (world)
Queensberry Rules, 917
Queens (NYC), 783, 802
Queens of England, 276
Quintal (measure), 370
Quintuplets, Dionne (1934), 117
Quire, 370
Quisling, Maj. Vidkun, 241
Quito, Ecuador, 184
Quiz show, first panel, 128
Qur'an. *See* Koran

R

Rabies, 562
Racial statistics:
    Births and birth rates, 815
    Crime, 826, 831
    Deaths and death rates, 819
    Employment, 54, 59
    Family characteristics, 811, 812–13
    Population, 792–93, 796, 808, 809
    School enrollment, 833
Racial violence (U.S.), 121
Racing. *See* kind of racing
Radar, 560
Radiation, neutron-induced, 562
Radio:
    Awards, 717, 731
    Inventions, 559, 560
    Stations in U.S. cities, 778–87
Radioactivity, 109, 562
Radiocarbon dating, 562
Radio telescopes, 348
Railroad Retirement Board, 649
Railroads:
    Accidents; deaths, 384, 388, 818
    Economic statistics, 65
    Firsts, 128
    Freight, 65
Railroad tunnels, 134
Rainfall, greatest, 666
Rainier, Mount, 459, 476, 478, 771
Ramakrishna, 378
Ramayana, 378
Ranger space probes, 320
Rangoon, Burma. *See* Yangon, Myanmar
Rape, 825, 826, 829
Reactors, nuclear, 363, 385
Reagan, Ronald, 644, 662
    Assassination attempt, 123, 644, 662

Bitburg Cemetery visit, 124
    See also Headline History; Presidents (U.S.)
Ream (measure), 370
Reaper, 556
Recommended Daily Dietary Allowances, 93, 94
Reconstruction, 109
Reconstruction Finance Corporation (1932), 114
Records, aviation, 359, 360
Records, phonograph, 740
Records, sports. *See* specific sports
Recreation:
    Government employment, 61
Recreation Areas, National, 571, 574–75
Red Cross, American, 608
Red Desert (An Nafud), 474
Red Guards (1966), 171
Red River (N.M.–La.), 479
Red Rock River, 471, 479
Red Sea, 469
Redwood National Park, 572
Reference books, 302–03
Reformation, 102, 196–7, 376, 377
Registered mail, 989–90
Reichstag fire, 114
Reign of Terror (1793–94), 106
Rejoicing of the Law, 584, 586
Relativity theories, 110, 543, 562
Religion, 375–82
    Churches in U.S., 376
    Churches in U.S. cities, 778–87
    Colleges, affiliation with, 837–62
    Freedom of religion, 618
    Holidays, 583–585
    Popes, 380–82
    Practice by country, 152–292
    World faiths, 375–80
    See also specific religions and churches
Religious affiliations:
    Presidents, 629
    Supreme Court Justices, 645, 646
Renaissance, 101, 102
    Architecture, 130
Rent, 43
Reparations (World War I), 112
Reporting, awards, 720–23
Representatives. *See* House of Representatives
Reptiles, Age of, 530
Reptiles, endangered, 567
Republic, oldest, 252
Republican Party:
    Founding, 108
    Members of Congress, 34–37
    National Committee chairmen, 633
    National conventions, 124, 126, 631–32, 633
    Senate floor leaders, 39
Republican River, 479
Reservations, Indian, 746, 808
Residence requirements, for voting, 637
Resources, world, by country, 152–292
Retail Trade:
    Hours and wages, 56
    Sales, 47
Retirement:
    401(k) plans 420
    See also Social Security & Aging
Réunion, 193, 462
Revenue:
    Bills for raising, 614
    National, 53, 62
Revolutionary War, American, 103, 105
    Casualties, 307
    Continental Congresses, 611–12, 626
    Declaration of Independence, 611–12
Revolver, 555

Reykjavik, Iceland, 205
    See also Cities (world)
Rhine River, 190, 196, 236, 267
Rhode Island, 766, 767
    See also States (U.S.)
Rhodes, Cecil, 291, 699
Rhodes, Colossus at, 129
Rhodesia. *See* Zambia; Zimbabwe
Rhodope Mountains, 165
Rhône River, 190, 267
Ribbon Falls, 472
Rice:
    Economic statistics, 69, 147–48
    World production, 147–48
Richmond (NYC). *See* Staten Island
Richter Magnitude Scale, 466
Ride, Sally K., 123, 128
"Ring of Fire," 459–62, 465
Rio de Janeiro, Brazil, 163
    See also Cities (world)
Rio de la Plata, 283
Rio Grande, 471, 479
Río Muni, 187
Riots. *See* Racial violence
Rivers:
    Dams, 131–32
    Total volume, 575
    U.S., 131–32, 478–80
    World, 131–32, 471, 472
Riyadh, Saudi Arabia, 252
Roads:
    Mileages, 405–06
Roanoke Island, 763
Roanoke River, 479, 763
Robbery, 825, 826, 828, 829
Rockefeller Center, 130
Rocket engine flight, first, 356
Rocky Mountain National Park, 572
Rodeo, 924
Roentgen, Wilhelm Konrad, 109, 542, 548, 562, 699, 707
Roentgen (measure), 370
Roller bearing, 562
Roman Catholic Church, 123, 375, 377
    Council of Nicaea, 98, 376
    Council of Trent, 102
    Great Schism, 101
    Inquisition, 101, 103
    Membership, 375–76
    Popes, 284, 377, 380–82
    Vatican, 130, 284
    Vatican Council I, 377
    Vatican Council II, 120, 284, 377
Roman Empire, 97, 98, 214
    Mythology, 523–27
    Structures, 129
Romanesque architecture, 130
Romania, 249–50
    See also Countries
Roman numerals, 374
Rome, Italy, 214
    Founded, 95
    Structures, 129–30
    World War II, 117
    See also Cities (world)
Rookie of the year (baseball), 964
Roosevelt, Eleanor, 631, 657, 699
Roosevelt, Franklin D., 644, 657
    See also Headline History; Presidents (U.S.)
Roosevelt, Theodore, 644, 655, 656, 706
    See also Headline History; Presidents (U.S.)
Roosevelt's (FDR) Birthday, 585
Roseau, Dominica, 183
Rose Bowl, 879–80
Rosenberg trial, 119
Roses, Wars of the, 101, 277
Rosh Hashana, 584, 586
Ross, Betsy, 628, 644
Ross Dependency, 238
Ross Trophy, 904
Rotary International, 608
Rough Riders, 656

Rowing, 878, 937
Rubber:
  Economic statistics, 69
  Vulcanized, 553
Ruby, Jack (1963), 121, 644, 659
Rulers of countries, 152–292
Rumania. *See* Romania
Running. *See* Track and Field
Rupert's Land, 169
Rushmore, Mount, 768
Russia:
  History, 259–62
  Kremlin (structure), 129–30
  Revolution, 112, 260
  Rulers, 261
  Structures, 129–30
  World War I, 112, 260
  World War II, 117, 260
  See also Countries; Soviet Union
Russo-Finnish War, 117, 189, 260
Russo-Japanese War, 110, 217, 260,
  656
  Treaty signed in Portsmouth, N.H.,
  110, 761
Russo-Turkish War, 109, 273
Rwanda, 250–51
  See also Countries
Ryukyu Islands, 217

S

Sabah, Malaysia, 164, 227
Sabine River, 479
Sabin vaccine, 562
Sacco-Vanzetti case, 112
Sacramento, Calif., 785
Sacramento River, 479
Sadat, Anwar el-, 123, 185, 186,
  213, 700
Sagamore Hill National Historic Site,
  574
Sahara, 153, 225, 233, 272, 457,
  474
Saigon, Vietnam. *See* Ho Chi Minh
  City
St. Bartholomew Massacre, 102
St. Christopher–Nevis. *See* St. Kitts
  and Nevis
St. Croix, V.I., 775
St. Francis River, 479
St. George's, Grenada, 200
St. Helena, 107, 282
St. Helens, Mount, 459, 771
St. John, V.I., 775
St. John the Divine, Cathedral of,
  130–31
St. John's, Antigua and Barbuda, 155
St. Kitts and Nevis, 251
  See also Countries
St. Lawrence River, 168, 457, 471
St. Lawrence Seaway, 120, 136,
  763
St. Louis, Mo., 758, 785
  See also Cities (U.S.)
St. Lucia, 251
  See also Countries
St. Mark's Cathedral, 129
St. Mihiel, Battle of, 112
St. Patrick's Cathedral, 131
St. Patrick's Day, 583
St. Paul, Minn., 757
  See also Cities (U.S.)
St. Peter, Basilica of, 102, 130
St. Petersburg, Russia. *See* Leningrad
St. Pierre and Miquelon, 193
St. Thomas, V.I., 775
St. Valentine's Day, 583
St. Valentine's Day Massacre, 114
St. Vincent and the Grenadines,
  251–52
  See also Countries
Saipan, 776
Sakhalin, 474
Sakigake probes, 322
Salamis, Battle of, 97

Salaries:
  Federal government, 41
  Industrial wages, 56
  National income and, 52
  State governments, 776, 777
Sales, retail and wholesale, 47
Sales taxes:
  State, 83
Sales workers, 54
Salisbury, Zimbabwe. *See* Harare
Salk vaccine, 119, 562
Salmon River, 479
SALT. *See* Strategic Arms Limitation
  Talks
Salvador, El. *See* El Salvador
Salvation Army, 608
Salween River, 472
Samoa, American, 774
Samoa, Western, 287, 288
Samoan archipelago, 462
Samos, 200
San'a', Yemen 288
San Antonio, Tex. 769, 785
  See also Cities (U.S.)
San Diego, Calif., 747, 785
  See also Cities (U.S.)
Sandinista guerrillas, 239
Sandwich Islands, 750
San Francisco, Calif., 747, 785
  Bridges, 135
  Climate, 665
  Earthquake (1906), 110, 384
  See also Cities (U.S.)
San Jacinto, Battle of, 107, 769
San Joaquin River, 479
San Jose, Calif., 747, 785, 786
  See also Cities (U.S.)
San José, Costa Rica, 177
San Juan River, 479
San Marino, 252
  See also Countries
San Salvador, El Salvador, 186
San Stefano, Treaty of, 109
Santa Claus, 585
Santee-Wateree-Catawba River, 480
Santiago, Chile, 172
Santiago de Cuba, 178
Santo Domingo, Dominican Rep., 183
São Francisco River, 163, 471
São Tomé and Principe, 252
  See also Countries
Saratoga, Battle of, 103
Sarawak, Malaysia, 164, 208, 227
Sardinia, 99, 214
Saskatchewan, Canada, 168, 169
Saskatchewan River, 472
Satellites, scientific, 120, 345
Satellites (moons), 335, 336,
  337–38, 340, 341–42, 343–44
  Orbits defined, 328
"Saturday Night Massacre," 122
Saturn (planet), 319, 331, 333, 337
  See also Planets
Saudi Arabia, 252–53
  See also Countries
Sault Ste. Marie Canal, 136, 757
Savings bank, first in U.S., 128
Saxe-Coburg, House of, 276
Saxon kings, 276
SBA, 649
Scenic Riverways, National, 571, 574
Scarlet fever, 817
Scenic Trail, National, 571, 575
Schism, Great, 101
Schmidt, Helmut, 198
Schools:
  And Supreme Court, 119–21
  First public, 128
  Statistics, 833–36
  See also Colleges and universities;
  Education
Schuman Plan (1951), 119
Science, 529–33, 534–48
  Chemical elements, 531–32
  Fermi Award, 727
  High energy physics, 533

Inventions, discoveries, and theories,
  561–62
  Metric System, 366–69, 371, 373
  Nobel Prizes, 707–12, 986
  Superconducting super collider, 533
  UNESCO, 295
  Weights and measures, 366–74
  See also Astronomy; Atomic energy;
  Chemistry; Mathematics; Medicine;
  Physics
Science and Technology, Office of,
  647
Science Foundation, National, 648
Scopes evolution trial, 114
Score (measure), 370
Scotland, 105, 275, 277
  See also United Kingdom
Scott, Dred, 108
Screw propeller, 556, 562
Scythian civilization, 97
Seafood, food value, 90, 97
Seal of U.S., Great, 626
Sears Tower, 133
Seas, 469
  Total volume, 575
Seashores, National, 571, 574
Seasons, 335, 576, 582
SEATO. *See* Southeast Asia Treaty
  Organization
Seattle, Wash., 665, 771, 786
  See also Cities (U.S.)
SEC, 649
Second International, 109
Secondary schools, 833, 834, 835
Secretaries-General (U.N.), 294
Securities and Exchange Commission,
  649
Security Council, National, 647
Security Council, U.N., 294
Seine River, 190
Selassie, Haile, *See* Haile Selassie
Selective Service System, 117, 649
Seljuk Turks, 101
Senate (U.S.), 34–35, 38, 613–14
  Birthdates of members, 34–35
  Committees, 38
  Eligibility, 613
  First woman member, 128
  Floor leaders, 39
  Impeachment cases, 613–14
  See also Congress (U.S.)
Senegal, 253–54
  See also Countries
Seoul, South Korea, 220
  See also Cities (world)
Sepoy Mutiny, 108, 206
Sequoia National Park, 572, 747
Serbia, 289
Service academies, 305–07
Service industries, employment, 59
SETI, 353
Seven Cities of Gold, 746
Seven Weeks' War, 108
Seven Years' War, 105, 169
Seven Wonders of World, 129
Seward, William, 585, 640, 644, 746
"Seward's Folly," 746
Sexes, distribution by:
  Arrests, 825
  Colleges, 834
  Death rates, 819, 820, 821–22
  Degrees received, 834
  Employment, 44, 57, 58
  Graduates, 834
  Life expectancy, 820–22
  Marriage statistics, 810, 811
  Population in U.S., 796
  Ratio of men to women, 792–93
Sex offenses, arrests for, 825, 826,
  828
Seychelles, 254
Shaba, Zaire, 290
Shah of Iran, 123, 209
Shang Dynasty, 95
Shanghai, China, 173, 174
  See also Cities (world)

Shannon River, 211
Shasta, Mount, 459, 478
Shatt-al-Arab, 210, 472
Shemini Atseret, 586
Shavuot, 584, 586
Shenandoah National Park, 572, 771
Shenandoah (dirigible), 387
Shepard, Alan B., Jr., 120, 322, 324
Sherman Antitrust Act, 109
Shetland Islands, 276, 457
Shikoku, 217
Shintoism, 379–80
  Number of followers, 375
Ship canals, 136
Shipping, commerce, 65
Ships. See Steamships
Shipwrecks, famous, 384, 386
Shock, treatment of, 78–79
Shooting, death rates from, 828
Shooting (sport), 971
"Shooting stars," 346
Shoreline of U.S., 479
Shot-put. See Track and Field
Shrove Tuesday, 583, 586
Siam. See Thailand
Siberia, 259
Sicily, 99, 110, 214
  Volcanoes, 462
Sidereal time, 329, 581
Sierra Leone, 254–55, 457
  See also Countries
Sihanouk, Norodom, 166
Sikh Rebellion (India), 124, 207
Sikkim, 208
Silurian Period, 530
Simhat Torah, 584, 586
Simplon Tunnel, 134
Sinai Peninsula, 120, 121, 185, 213
Singapore, 117, 228, 255
  See also Countries
Singers. See People
Singing Cave, 475
Single persons, 810
Sino-Japanese War, 109
Sirhan, Sirhan Bishara, 121, 644
Sistine Chapel, 102, 130
Six-day War, 121, 213
  See also Arab–Israeli wars
Skating, ice, 865–66, 867, 913
Skiing, 866–67, 908–09
  Olympic Games, 866–67
  U.S. Championships, 908–09
  World Cup, 908
Skylab, 324–25
Skyscrapers:
  First, 128
  In U.S., 133–34
Slavery:
  Abolished in British Empire, 107
  Dred Scott case, 108
  Emancipation Proclamation, 624–25
  First slaves to America, 102
  First slaves to United States, 128,
    771
  First state to forbid, 770
  Importation barred, 106
  Kansas–Nebraska Act, 108
  Prohibited in U.S., 619
Small Business Administration, 649
Smallpox and vaccination against,
  106
Smoky Hill River, 480
Snake River, 480
Snowdon, Mount, 276
Snowfall, greatest, 666
Snyder-Gray case, 114
Soccer, 936, 945–46
Social Security & Aging, 426–35
  in Japan, 426–28
  Medicare, 434–35
  Social Security Act, 429–33
Socialist parties (U.S.), 636
Societies and associations, 599–610
Society Islands, 193
Socrates, 97, 701
Sofia, Bulgaria, 164

Softball, 950
Solar–hydrogen fuel, 362
Solar system, 329, 334, 535, 562
Solar time, 329, 581
Solomon Islands, 255–56
Solstice, 335
Somalia, 256
  See also Countries
Somaliland, French. See Djibouti
Somme, Battle of the, 112
Somoza Debayle, Gen. Anastasio,
  123, 239
Songs, state, 745–73
"Sooners," 765
Sophocles, 97, 701
Sorority, first, 128
Sound:
  First flight faster than, 357
  Speed of, 370, 372
Sources, reference, 302–03
South Africa, Rep. of, 125, 256–59
  See also Countries
South America, 459, 465
  Explorations, discoveries, 458
  Map, 486–87
  Southernmost point, 172
  See also Continents; Countries
South Carolina, 767
  See also States of U.S.
South China Sea, 469
South Dakota, 767, 768
  See also States of U.S.
Southeast Asia, map, 492–93
Southeast Asia Treaty Organization,
  treaty signed, 119
Southeast Asia War. See Vietnam War
Southern Alps, 238
Southern and Antarctic Lands, 194
Southern Cameroons. See Nigeria
"Southern lights," 347
Southern Rhodesia. See Zimbabwe
Southern Yemen. See Yemen
  (People's Democratic Republic of)
South Georgia Island, 281
South Island (New Zealand), 238,
  473
South Manchurian Railway, 174
South Orkney Islands, 281
South Platte River, 480
South Pole:
  First flight over, 356
  Reached, 110, 458
South Shetland Islands, 281
South-West Africa. See Namibia
Soviet Union, 259–62
  Afghanistan invasion, 123, 152,
    261
  Area, elevations, and population
    density, 465
  Constitution, 261
  Germany, nonaggression pact with
    (1939), 117, 260
  Government, 259
  Hydrogen bomb, 119, 120, 261
  Korean Airlines incident, 123
  Map, 491–92
  Moscow Summer Olympics, 261
  Nuclear forces, 314
  Nuclear weapons testing, 118
  Population, 140
  Rulers, 261
  Space programs, 126, 316–17,
    321–22, 323–24
  World War II, 117, 260
  See also Countries; Russia
Soyuz flights, 323, 324
Space exploration, 316–25, 326–53
  Accidents, 387
  Astronauts, 324–25
  Cassini mission, 319–20
  Chronology of unmanned probes,
    321–22
  First manned space station, 322
  Galileo project, 318, 322
  Magellan, 320, 322
  Manned flights, 324–25

Mars observer, 319
Moon landings and explorations,
  320–22
Scientific satellites (U.S.), 321–22
Soviet space program, 316–17,
  323, 325
Space shuttle, 124, 322–23
Space station Freedom, 318
Ulysses, 318–19
See also Astronomy
Spain, 95, 99, 102, 103, 105, 106,
  108, 109, 114, 262–63
  See also Countries
Span (measure), 370
Spanish-American War, 109, 110,
  178, 307
Spanish Armada, 103, 263, 277
Spanish Civil War, 117, 263
Spanish origin, persons of:
  Population, 796, 806, 808
Spanish Succession, War of the, 105
Sparta, 97
Spartacus, 98
Speakers of the House, 39
Special-delivery mail, 990
Specific gravity of elements, 531–32
Spectrum, 562
Speech, freedom of, 618
Speed:
  Of falling body, 535
  Of light, 329, 562
  Of sound, 370, 372
Speed records, airplanes, 360
Speed records, sports. See individual
  sports
Speed skating, 866, 867, 912
Spermatozoa, 562
Sphinx, Great, 95, 129
Spinning inventions, 562
Spiral nebula, 328
Spirit of St. Louis (plane), 356
Spitsbergen, 241, 458
Sports, 864–973
  Calendar, 864
  Measurements, standard, 973
  Olympic Games, 865–78
  Organizations and information
    bureaus, 931
  Personalities, 899–902
  See also individual sports
Spring (1991), 576
"Spring tides," 332
Sputnik I (satellite), 120, 261
Square (measure), 370
Sri Jayewardenapura Kotte, Sri Lanka,
  263
Sri Lanka, 263–64, 474
  See also Countries
Stadiums, Football, 884
Stalin, Joseph, 113, 117, 118, 119,
  260, 261, 701
Stalingrad, Battle of, 117
Stamp Act, 103
Stamps, postage, 128, 990
  United Nations, 992
Standard time, 582
Stanley Cup, 903, 905
Stars, 328–29, 332
  Brightest, 332
  Constellations, 332
  Twinkling of, 348
"Star-Spangled Banner," 624
"Stars," of entertainment, 677–705
START. See Strategic Arms Reduction
  Talks
State, Secretaries of (states),
  745–73
State, U.S. Department of, 647
  Secretaries of, 639–43
Staten Island, 783, 802
  See also New York City
States, Confederate, 625
States of U.S., 745–77
  Agricultural production, 60
  Areas, 745–73
  Births and birth rates, 815

Coastlines, 479
Congress members, 34–37
Constitutional provisions, 615, 617
Deaths and death rates, 818
Education, 834
Elections, presidential, 40
Execution methods, 831
Firsts, 128
Government employment, 61
Government statistics, 776, 777
Governors, 37, 745–73
Highest court members, term and salary, 776, 777
Holidays, 585
Motor vehicle deaths, 818
Motor vehicle laws, 832
Motor vehicle registrations, 66
Newspapers, 301
Per capita personal income, 52
Per capita tax burden by, 76
Population, 745–73, 797, 806
Procedure for admitting new states, 617
Representatives, 35–37
School attendance laws, 834
Senators, 34–35
Taxes. *See* Taxes
Tax Freedom Day, by 76
Thirteen original, 613
Tourism offices, 402–04
Unemployment benefits, 592
Voting qualifications, 637
States' rights, 615, 617, 619
States' Rights Democratic Party, 636
Statue of Liberty, 109, 628, 763
Steam engine, 105, 551, 552
Steamship, 556
Steamships, disasters, 386
Steel, 55, 69, 149
    World consumption, 149
    World production, 149
Stock-car racing, 948, 949
Stockholm, Sweden, 266
    See also Cities (world)
Stock market, 47, 48, 50
    50 leading stocks, 50
    50 most active stocks, 47
    Shareholders, 47, 48
    Stock exchange seat sales, 48
Stone (measure), 370
Stonehenge, 95
Stone Mountain, 750
Stores, retail. *See* Retail trade
Storms, 383, 384, 667–69
Strategic Arms Limitation Talks, 123, 261
Strategic Arms Reduction Talks, 261, 262
Stratopause, 335
Stratosphere, 335
Stratosphere, first flight into, 356
Strikes (labor), 58, 125, 126
    First strike in U.S., 128
Stromboli, 462
Structures:
    Bridges, 135–36
    Canals, 136
    Dams, 131–32
    Famous, 129–36
    Seven Wonders, 129
    Skyscrapers, U.S., 133–34
    Tunnels, 134
Stuart, House of, 276
Students:
    College and professional, 833, 837–62
    Elementary and secondary school, 833
Submarines, 110
    Disasters, 384, 387
    First atomic-powered, 119
Subways, first in U.S., 128
Sucre, Bolivia, 162
Sudan, 264–65, 457
    See also Countries

Suez Canal, 108, 120, 136, 185, 186, 213
    Egypt seizes (1956), 120, 185
Suffrage. *See* Voting
Suffragettes, 110
Sugar:
    Economic statistics, 61, 69
    Moderation in use of, 89
Sugar Bowl (football), 880
Suisei probes, 322
Sukarno, 208
Sukkot, 584, 586
Suleiman I, 102
Sulfa drugs, 562
Sullivan Award, 944
Sumatra, 208, 473
    Volcanoes, 462
Sumerian civilization, 95, 97
Summer (1991), 576
Sun, 328, 329
    Eclipses, 350
    Phenomena, 349–50
    Seasons, 582–83
    Time based on, 581–82
Sungari River, 472
Sun spots, 329
Sun Yat-sen, 110, 173, 702
Super Bowl, 885–86
Superconductors, 533
Superior, Lake, 168, 470, 757
Superdome, 131
Supernovas, 329
Supersonic aircraft, 357
Supreme Court (U.S.):
    Constitutional provisions, 616, 617
    First law declared unconstitutional, 128
    First woman member, 123, 128
    Justices, 121, 123, 125, 645, 646
    Major decisions (1954–89), 119–21, 123–27
    Salaries, 41
Supreme Courts, state, 776, 777
Surgery, first antiseptic, 108
Suribachi, Mount, 459
Suriname, 265
    See also Countries
Surveying measures, 367
Surveyor probes, 320
Susquehanna River, 480
Sutter's Mill, 747
Suva, Fiji, 188
Svendrup Islands, 169
Swains Islands, 774
Swaziland, 265–66
    See also Countries
Sweden, 266–67
    See also Countries
Sweets, food value, 91
Swimming, 873–76, 878, 914–16
    Olympic Games, 873–76, 878
Switzerland, 267
    See also Countries
Sydney, Australia, 156
    See also Cities (world)
Symbols: chemical elements, 531–32
Symphony orchestras, 736
Synodic month, 329
Syphilis, 817
    Wassermann test, 562
Syria, 210, 212, 267–68
    Israel and, 213, 223, 268
    Map, 494
    See also Countries

T

Tabernacles, Feast of, 584, 586
Tabloid newspaper, first, 128
Tadzhikistan, U.S.S.R. 260
Taft, William Howard, 645, 656
    See also Headline History; Presidents (U.S.)
Tahiti, 193
Taipei, Taiwan, 268–69

Taiwan (Republic of China), 268–69
    Map, 495
Taj Mahal, 130
Takla Makan Desert, 474
Talmud, 376
Tamerlane, 152, 702
Tananarive, Madagascar. *See* Antananarivo
Tanana River, 480
Tanganyika. *See* Tanzania
Tanganyika, Lake, 457, 470
T'ang Dynasty, 173
Tannenberg, Battle of, 112
Tanzania, 269–70
    See also Countries
Taoism, 97, 380
Tarawa, 219
Tarbela Dam, 132
Tasmania, 156, 458, 474
Taxes, 70–77
    Constitutional provisions for, 614, 615, 620, 622
    Corporation taxes, federal, 71, 73
    Corporation taxes, state, 73, 77
    Estate taxes, federal, 71, 73–74
    Excise, 71
    Franchise taxes, state, 73
    Gift taxes, federal, 71, 73–74
    Income tax, federal, 70–73
    Income tax, history, 70
    Individual returns, 73
    Internal Revenue Service, 70–71
    Personal income 78–79, 419–20
    Sales and use taxes, state, 77
    State and local, paid by city dwellers, 75
Taylor, Zachary, 653
    See also Headline History; Presidents (U.S.)
Tea, 69
Teachers, 836
Teapot Dome, 113, 657
Tegucigalpa, Honduras, 204
Teheran, Iran, 209
    See also Cities (world)
Teheran Conference (1943), 117
Tektites, 346
Tel Aviv, Israel, 212
Telegraph:
    Invention, 557
    Trans–Atlantic cable, 107, 557
Telephones:
    Economic statistics, 56
    Toll–free numbers, 596–98
    Invention, 109, 557
Telescope:
    Hubble Space, 347
    Invention, 549
    Optical, radio, 348
    Very large, 348
Television:
    Awards, 717, 731, 735, 985
    Cable, 743
    Color, 119
    Inventions, 114, 559
    Miniseries, 741
    Networks, 742
    News shows, 731, 741
    Prime time, 742, 743
    Soap operas, 741
    Sports shows, 741
    Stations in cities, 778–87
    Syndicated programs, 741
    Viewing, 741–43
Temperatures:
    International, 403
    In U.S. cities, 664–65
    Scales, 366, 370, 373
    U.S. extremes, 666, 671, 673, 674
    World extremes, 666
Tenerife, Canary Islands, 388, 462
Tennessee, 768, 769
    See also States of U.S.
Tennessee River, 480
Tennessee Valley Authority, 649, 769

Tennis, 932–36
  Earnings, 936
  History, 932
  Standard measurements, 973
Terrorism, 109, 122, 123, 124, 126, 179, 213, 223, 225, 280, 284
Teotihuacan, Mexico, 97
Territorial expansion of U.S., 806
  Map, 805
Territories of U.S., 773–76
  Areas, 773–75, 806
  Execution methods, 831
  Population, 773–75, 806
Tertiary Period, 531
Teutonic Knights, 247
Texas, 769
  War of Independence, 107, 769
  See also States of U.S.
Textiles, economic statistics, 45, 55, 69
Thailand, 270–71
  See also Countries
Thames River, 276
Thanksgiving Day, 585, 586
Thant, U, 290, 294
Thar Desert, 474
Thatcher, Margaret, 123, 124, 275, 278, 280
Theater:
  Awards, 724, 728–29
  Celebrities of, 677–705
  First vaudeville, 128
  Longest Broadway runs, 743
Theft, 825, 826, 828, 829
Theories, scientific, 561–62
Therm (measure), 370
Thermodynamics, 540, 541
Thermometer:
  Invention, 562
  Scales, 370, 373, 562
Thermopause, 335
Thermopylae, Battles of, 97, 98
Thermosphere, 315
Thimphu, Bhutan, 161
Thieu, Nguyen Van, 119, 286
Third Estate, 106
Third International, 112
"Third World," 289
Thirty Years' War, 103, 197, 266
Thohoyandou, Venda, 259
Three Mile Island, 123, 385
Tibet, 173, 174, 457
Tidal shoreline of U.S., 479
Tidal waves, 383, 670
Tides, 332
Tien-Pamir Mountains, 259
Tien Shan Mountains, 173
Tierra del Fuego, 172, 474
Tigris River, 95, 210, 472
Time:
  Kinds of, 581–82
  Universal and civil, 349, 581–82
Time of day, cities, 467, 477
Time zones, 581–82
  World (Map), 493
Timor, 208, 249
Tin, 532
Tinian (island), 776
Tippecanoe, 652, 752
Tirana, Albania, 152
Tires, pneumatic, 109
Titanic (ship), 110, 386
Titicaca, Lake, 162, 470
Tito, Marshal, 118, 289, 703
Tobacco:
  Abuse of, 456
  Economic statistics, 55, 60, 69
  In Connecticut, 748
  Taxes, 71, 77
Tobago. See Trinidad and Tobago
Tocantins River, 472
Togo, 271
  See also Countries
Tojo, Hideki (1948), 118
Tokelau Island, 238

Tokyo, Japan, 103, 216
  See also Cities (world)
Toledo, Ohio, 764, 786
  See also Cities (U.S.)
Tomb of the Unknown Soldier, 627
Tombigbee River, 480
Ton:
  Gross or long, 369, 373
  Metric, 366, 369, 373
  Net or short, 369, 373
Tonga, 271–72
  See also Countries
Tony Awards, 729
Torah, 376, 584
Tornadoes, 669, 670
Toronto, Ont., Canada, 168
Toulouse, France, 190
Tourist information. See Travel
Tours, Battle of, 99
Tower of London, 130
Township (measure), 370
Toys and games, 69
Track and Field, 868–73, 925–30
  Athletics Congress National Championships, 929
  History, 925
  History of mile run, 927
  Indoor records, 928–30
  Olympic Games, 868–73
  N.C.A.A. championships 930
  Outdoor records, 928, 929, 930
  Pole vault, 929
Tractor, invented, 556, 562
Trade. See Foreign trade; Interstate Commerce
Trade Commission, Federal, 648
Trade Commission, U.S. International, 649
Trademarks, 592
Trade Negotiations, Office of U.S. Trade Representative, 647
Trade unions. See Unions, labor
Trafalgar, Battle of, 106
Trains. See Railroads
Trans-Alaska Pipeline, 746
Transarctic flight, first, 355–56
Transatlantic flights, 356, 357
Transcontinental flights, 355–57
Transistor, 560
Transkei, 258
  See also Countries
Transpacific flight, 357
Transportation:
  Accident death rates, 817–18
  Economic statistics, 65–66
  Employment, 59
  Freight traffic, 65
  Fuel consumption, 365
  Industry, hours and wages, 56
  Inventions, 556–560, 561
  See also kinds of transportation
Transportation, U.S. Department of, 648
  Secretaries of, 643
Transportation equipment, 45, 69
Travel, 391–410
  AIDS testing, 401
  Air distances between cities, 407–10
  Diplomatic personnel, 396–98
  Emergencies, 391
  Foreign embassies, 393–96
  Health hints abroad, 398–400
  Information sources, 402–04
  Mileage, motor vehicle, 365
  Mileages between cities, 405–10
  Passports and Customs, 392–93
  Telemarketing fraud, 588, 589
  Traveler warnings, 404
Treason defined, 617
Treasurers (of states), 745–73
Treasury, U.S. Dept. of, 647
  Secretaries, 639–43
Trees, State, 745–73
Triangle Shirtwaist Factory fire, 110
Triassic Period, 530

Trieste, 215, 289
Trinidad and Tobago, 272
  See also Countries
Trinity River, 480
Trinity Sunday, 586
Triple Alliance, 109
Triple Crown (horse racing), 922–24
Triple jump. See Track and Field
Tripoli, Libya, 225
Tristan da Cunha, 282
Trojan War, 95
Tropical storms, 669
Tropical year, 329
Tropic of Cancer, 583
Tropic of Capricorn, 583
Tropopause, 335
Troposphere, 335
Trotsky, Leon, 112, 114, 117, 260, 703
Trotting. See Harness racing
Troy, ancient, 95
Troy weight, 367
Trucks and trucking, 65, 66, 67, 365
Trucial States. See United Arab Emirates
Trudeau, Pierre E., 169, 703
Truman, Harry S., 644, 657, 658
  See also Headline History; Presidents (U.S.)
Truman Doctrine, 118, 658
Trusteeship Council, U.N., 295
Trusteeships, U.N., 295, 776
Trust Territory of Pacific Islands, 295, 776
Tuberculosis, 109, 817
Tucson, Ariz., 786
  See also Cities (U.S.)
Tudor, House of, 276
Tugela Falls, 472
Tulsa, Okla., 765, 786
  See also Cities (U.S.)
Tungsten filament, 558
Tunis, Tunisia, 272
Tunisia, 272
  See also Countries
Tun (measure), 370
Tunnels, 134
Turbojet, first flight, 357
Turkey, 273–74
  See also Countries
Turkish-Russian War, 109, 273
Turkmenistan, U.S.S.R., 260
Turks and Caicos Islands, 282–83
Turner, John, 169, 170
Turner, Nat, 107
Tuskegee Institute, 745
Tutankhamen, 95
Tutu, Rev. Desmond, 125, 706
Tuvalu, 274
  See also Countries
TVA, 649, 769
Tweed Ring, 109
Twelfth Night, 583
Tydings-McDuffie Act (1934), 246
Tyler, John, 652
  See also Headline History; Presidents (U.S.)
Typhoid fever, 817

U

Uganda, 274–75
  See also Countries
Ukraine, U.S.S.R., 260
  See also Soviet Union
Ulan Bator, Mongolia, 232
Ulbricht, Walter, 197, 198
Ulster, Northern Ireland, 279
Umtala, Transkei, 258
Uncertainty principle, 562
Uncle Sam, 644
Unemployment, 57, 58, 59, 145
  Insurance, 591, 592
UNESCO, 295
Union Islands. See Tokelau Island

Union Labor Party, 635
Union of Soviet Socialist Republics.
See Soviet Union
Unions, labor, 51
Unitarianism, 377
United Arab Emirates, 275
See also Countries
United Automobile Workers, 51
United Kingdom, 275–83
Map, 490
Prime Ministers, 278
Rulers, 276
Zoos, 568
See also Countries
United Nations, 293–96
Agencies, 295–96
Charter, 294
"China seat," 121, 174, 269
Economic and Social Council,
294–95
Established, 118
Events, 118, 121
General Assembly, 294
International Court, 295
Member nations, 293
Principal organs, 294–95
Secretariat, 294
Security Council, 294
Stamps, 992
Trusteeship Council, 295
Trust territories, 244, 295, 776
U.S. contributions to, 63
United Nations Educational, Scientific,
and Cultural Organization, 295
United States, 283
Aliens admitted, 807, 808
Area, 806
Armed forces, 304–15
Balance of payments, 68
Birth statistics, 813, 814–15
Bridges, 135–36
Businesses, foreign investments in, 68
Canals, 136
Church memberships, 376
Climate extremes, 666
Coastline, 479
Colleges, 837–62
Crime statistics, 823–31
Dams, 131–32
Death statistics, 817–19
Disasters, 383–90
District Courts, 828
Divorce statistics, 809
Economic statistics, 43–69
Education statistics, 833–36
Exports, 67, 69, 150
Extreme points, 475
Fairs and Expositions, 743
Family statistics, 44, 46, 811,
812–13
Flag, 628
Geography, 475–80
Growth, 806
Highest points, 476
Holidays, 583–85
Immigration, 807, 808
Imports, 69, 150
Labor force, 51, 53, 54, 778–87
Largest cities, 778–88
Latitudes and longitudes, 477
Libraries, 737
Life expectancy in, 820–22
Lowest points, 476
Magazines, 297
Maps, 104, 482–83, 672, 805
Marriage statistics, 809–811, 812
Mileages between cities, 405–08
Motor vehicle laws, 832
National Anthem, 624
National Park System, 571–75
Naturalization statistics, 808
Newspapers, 297–301
Passports and customs, 392–93
Population, 792–809
For detailed listing, see Population
(U.S.)

Postal regulations, 989–92
Profile, 3
Skyscrapers, 133–34
Societies and associations, 599–610
State tourism offices, 402–04
Symphony orchestras, 736
Territories, 773–76, 806
Travel information, 402–04
Tunnels, 134
Universities, 837–62
Weather and climate, 664–76
Zoos, 568, 569
See also Cities (U.S.); Countries of
the World; Foreign trade;
Interstate commerce; States (U.S.);
U.S. Government; U.S. History
United States Government:
Armed forces, 304–15
Cabinet, 639–43
Congress. See Congress (U.S.)
Constitution, 613–22
Employment, 61
Executive Departments, 647–49
Expenditures and receipts, 53, 61,
62–63
Federal budget, 53, 62
Foreign aid, 53, 63
Great Seal, 626
Independent agencies, 648, 649
Judicial powers, 616, 617
National Park System, 571–75
Presidents, 629–30, 650–63
Salaries of officials, 41
Supreme Court, 616, 617, 645,
646
Unemployment insurance, 591, 592
Veterans' benefits, 309
Voting qualifications, 620, 622
See also individual entries elsewhere
in index for more extensive listing
United States History:
Armed services, 304–05
Articles of Confederation, 626
Assassinations and attempts, 644
Atlantic Charter (1941), 117
Cabinets, 639–43
Chronology, 103
Civil War, 108
Colonization, 103
Constitution, 613–22
Continental Congresses, 103, 626
Declaration of Independence,
611–12
Disasters, 383–90
Discoveries and explorations, 457,
458
Elections, presidential, 40, 634–37
Emancipation Proclamation, 624–25
Firsts, 128
Flag, 628
Gettysburg Address, 625
Historical events, 102–27
Impeachments, 644, 645
Mason and Dixon's Line, 476
Mayflower Compact, 622
Military interventions, 312
Minority Presidents, 638
Monroe Doctrine, 623
National Committee chairmen, 633
Presidents, 629, 650–63
Pulitzer Prizes for, 724–25
Revolutionary War period, 103
Speakers of the House, 39
"Star-Spangled Banner," 624
Statue of Liberty, 628
Territorial expansion, 806
Unknown soldiers, 627
War casualties, 307, 311
See also names of wars
White House, 571, 574, 622
Worst marine disaster, 386
Universal Postal Union, 296
Universal time, 349
Universe, origin of, 328
Universities, United States, 837–62
See also Colleges

Unknown Soldier, Tomb of the, 627
Unleavened Bread, Feast of, 584,
586
Upanishads, 378
Upper Volta. See Burkina Faso
Ural Mountains, 259
Ural River, 472
Uranium:
As element, 532
Uranus (planet), 331, 333, 340, 342
See also Planets
Urey, Harold, 114, 561, 703, 709
Uruguay, 283–84
See also Countries
Uruguay River, 283
Utah, 769, 770
See also States of U.S.
U-2 incident (1960), 120
Uzbekistan, U.S.S.R. 260

VA, 648
Vaccination:
Polio, 562
Smallpox, 539, 562
Vacuum tube, 559
Vaduz, Liechtenstein, 225
Valentine's Day, 583
Valentine's Day Massacre, 114
Valetta, Malta, 229
Valley Forge, Pa., 103, 766
Valois, House of, 191
Van Allen Belt, 348, 562
Van Buren, Martin, 652
See also Headline History; Presidents
(U.S.)
Vancouver, B.C., Canada, 168
Vandalism arrests, 825, 826
Vandals, 98
Vanuatu, 284
See also Countries
Vatican City State, 284, 285
See also Countries; Roman Catholic
Church
Vatican Council I, 377
Vatican Council II, 120, 284, 377
Vatican (structures), 130
Vaudeville theater, first, 128
Vedas, 378
V-E Day (1945), 117
Vegetables:
Economic statistics, 61, 69
Fiber, 93
Venda, 259
Venera probes, 321
Venezuela, 285
See also Countries
Venus (planet), 331, 333, 335
Space probes, 320–22
See also Planets
Verdun, Battle of, 112
Vermont, 770
See also States of U.S.
Vernal Equinox, 580–81
Verrazano-Narrows Bridge, 135
Versailles, Palace of, 103, 197, 130
Versailles, Treaty of, 112, 117, 197
Vesuvius, Mount, 383, 462
Veterans:
Benefits, 309–10
Education, 309–10
March (1932), 114
Veterans Affairs, Department of, 648
Veterans' Day, 576, 585
Veto power, 614, 638
Vezina Trophy, 904
Vice-Presidential Candidates:
First woman, 128
Vice Presidents (U.S.):
As Acting President, 622
Election procedure, 615–16, 619
List of, 629–30
Nomination, 632
Powers and duties, 613

Salary, 41
Succession to Presidency, 616, 621, 622, 623
Term of office, 621
Much of what applies to Presidents (U.S.) *also applies to Vice Presidents*
Vichy, France, 191, 192, 286
Vicksburg, Battle of, 108
Victoria, Lake, 269, 274, 470
Victoria, Queen, 107, 109, 110, 276, 278
Victoria, Seychelles, 254
Victoria Falls, 457, 473
Victoria (island), 473
Vientiane, Laos, 222
Vienna, Austria, 157
Vienna, Congress of, 107, 157, 190
Viet Cong, 119, 286
Vietnam, 119, 222, 286, 287
See also Countries; Chronology
Vietnam War, 119, 286, 312
Casualties, U.S., 307
Unknown Serviceman of, 627
See also Cambodia; Chronology; Laos, Thailand
Viking probes, 320, 321
Vikings, 99, 181, 241
Vila, Vanuatu, 284
Vinson Massif, 465
Virginia, 770, 771
See also States of U.S.
Virginia Beach, Va., 770, 786
Virgin Islands, British, 280
Virgin Islands, U.S., 112, 775
Virgin Islands National Park, 572
Vitamins:
Dietary allowances, 93, 94
Discoveries, 562
V-J Day (1945), 117, 118
Volcanoes, 383, 459–63, 465
Famous eruptions, 383
Islands, 462
Principal types, 463
"Ring of Fire," 459–62
Volga River, 259, 471
Hydroelectric plants on, 133
Lakes, 470
Volleyball, 971
Volume:
Formulas for, 372
Measure of, 366, 367, 368–73
Voskhod flights, 323, 324
Vostok flights, 323, 324
Voting:
18–year-olds, 121, 622
Presidential elections, 40, 41, 634–37
Qualification by state, 637
Rights, 621, 622
Unusual voting results, 638
Women's suffrage, 112, 128, 621
Voyager probes, 124, 127, 320–21
Voyageurs National Park, 572

W

Wabash River, 480
Wages, hours:
Industrial, 55
National income and, 52
See also Income
Wake Island, 775, 776
Waldheim, Kurt, 124, 125, 157, 294
Wales, 275
See also United Kingdom
Wales, Prince of, 277
Walesa, Lech, 127, 247–48, 706
Walking. *See* Track and Field
Wallace, George, 121, 644
Wallis and Futuna Islands, 194
Wall of China, 98, 130, 173
Wall Street:
Inside traders' scandal, 125

War, U.S. Department of, Secretaries of, 639–43
War casualties, 307, 311
War crimes, 114, 118, 125, 126
War of 1812, 107, 307
Warren, Earl, 645
Warren Report (1965), 121
Wars. *See* individual wars
Warsaw Pact, 119–20, 151
Warsaw, Poland, 247
See also Cities (world)
Warsaw Ghetto, 114
Warsaw Treaty Organization, 205, 247, 250, 261
Wars of the Roses, 101, 277
Wartime disasters, 390
War trials (1946), 118
Washington, D.C., 106, 107, 787
Bonus march (1932), 114
Civil rights rally (1963), 120
Climate, 665
Twenty–third Amendment, 621, 622
White House, 571, 574, 622
See also Cities (U.S.); *much information under* States *also applies to Washington, D.C.*
Washington, George, 103, 106, 650
See also Headline History; Presidents (U.S.)
Washington, Mount, 476
Washington Birthplace National Monument, 573
Washington Monument, 627
Washington's Birthday, 583
Washington (state), 771
Mountains and volcanoes, 459
See also States of U.S.
Washita River, 480
Wasserman Test, 562
Water:
Boiling and freezing points, 373
World supply, 575
Waterfalls, 472, 473
Watergate, 122, 660
Waterloo, Battle of, 107, 197, 278
Waterways, traffic on, 65
Watt (measure), 370
Watt, James, 105, 551, 704
Watts riots (1965, 1966), 121
Watusi, 166
Weapons, 825, 826, 828, 829
Weather and climate, 384, 664–76
Disastrous storms, 383, 384, 667, 669
Glossary, 670
Hail, hailstones, 670
Humidity, relative, 674–76
Hurricanes, 667–69, 670
Of U.S. cities, 664–65
Tornadoes, 669, 670
Tropical storms, 669
World extremes, 666
Weaving cloth, 562
Wedding anniversaries, 528
Weight, desirable, 92
Weightlifting, 878, 946
Weights, atomic, 531
Weights, measures, 366–74
Capacities, volumes, 366–70
Conversion factors, 373
Welfare. *See* Public Assistance
Weimar Republic, 197
Wellington, New Zealand, 237
Western Samoa, 287, 288
See also Countries
West Germany. *See* Germany, West
West Indies:
Discovery, 457
Map, 485
Volcanoes, 462
See also specific islands
West Irian, 208
Westminster Abbey, 130
West Point (U.S. Military Academy), 305, 763

West Virginia, 771, 772
See also States of U.S.
Wheat, 60, 147–48
World production, 147–48
Wheat flour. *See* Flour
Wheel, 562
Where to find out more, 302–03
Whig Party (U.S.), 635, 652, 653
Whipple theory, 345
Whiskey Rebellion, 106
White House, 571, 574, 622
White River, 480
Whitney, Mount, 476, 478, 747
Whitsunday, 584
WHO, 295
Wholesale trade:
Employment, 59
Hours and wages, 56
Price indexes, 45
Sales, 47
Whooping cough, 817
Williamsburg, Va., 771
William the Conqueror, 99, 276, 277
William II, Kaiser, 197
Wilson, Harold, 278, 705
Wilson, Woodrow, 656
See also Headline History; Presidents (U.S.)
Wimbledon champions, 934–35
Wind Cave National Park, 475, 572
Wind chill factor, 665
Windhoek, Namibia, 235
Windmill, 562
Windsor, House of, 276
Wind velocities of hurricanes, 667–69
Windward Islands. *See* St. Lucia; St. Vincent and the Grenadines
Winnie Mae (plane), 357
Winter (1991), 576
Winnipeg, Lake, 470
WIPO, 295
Wisconsin, 772, 773
See also States of U.S.
Wisconsin River, 480
Wives of Presidents, 631
WMO, 295
Wollaston Islands, 172
Women:
Armed forces, 118
Arrests, 825
Death rates, 819
Earnings, 44, 46, 56, 57
Education, 56, 834
Employment, 53, 54, 56, 57, 58
Families maintained by, 56, 811
Famous, 677–705
Firsts, 127, 128, 354, 357
Heads of families, 56, 811
In labor force, 53, 54, 56, 58
Life expectancy, 142, 820, 821–22
Marriage statistics, 809, 810
Mothers, 814
Mothers employed, 54
Number, 796
Political firsts, 126
Presidents' wives, 631
Ratio of men to women, 792–93
Suffrage, 112, 128, 621
Wonders of the World, Seven, 129
Wood pulp, 45, 69
Wood. See Lumber and wood
Woolworth Building, 134
Working population, 51, 53, 54, 56, 57, 58
World:
Air distances, 409–10
Area, 465
Bridges, 135–36
Canals, 136
Caves, caverns, 475
Climate extremes, 666
Consumer Price Indexes, 144
Countries of, 152–292
Dams, 131–32
Deserts, 474

Disasters, 383–90
Economy, 144–50
Education, expenditure, 145
Elevations, 465
Explorations, discoveries, 457,
    458
Geography. *See* Geography (world)
Highest mountain peaks, 468–69
History. *See* History (world)
Hydroelectric plants, 133
Islands, 473, 474
Lakes, 470–71
Map, 496
Population. *See* Population (world)
Profile, 6
Religion, 375–80
Rivers, 471, 472
Seven Wonders of the, 129
Statistics, 137–50
Structures, famous, 129–36
Tunnels, 134
Unemployment, 145
Volcanoes, 459–63
Waterfalls, 472, 473
Water supply, 575
Zoos, 568
    See also Cities (world); Countries;
    Earth; Governments (foreign)
World Bank (IBRD), 118, 295
World Court, International Court of
    Justice, 125, 295
World Cup, Soccer, 945
World Health Organization,
    295
World History, 95–127,
    152–292
World Intellectual Property
    Organization (WIPO), 295
World Map, Time zones, 493
World Meteorological Organization,
    295
World Series: 1903–89, 955–57
    1990 Games, 970
    Records and standing, 955–58
World's Fairs, 743
    Chicago:
        Century of Progress International
            Exposition (1933–34), 743
        World's Columbia Exposition
            (1893), 743
    Knoxville, Tenn. (1982), 743
    New York:
        Crystal Palace Exposition (1853),
            743
        Peace Through Understanding
            (1964–65), 743

World of Tomorrow (1939–40),
    117, 743
    Spokane (1974), 743
World Time Zones, 582
    Map, 493
World Trade Center, 131,
    133
World War I, 112
    Casualties, 307, 311
    Unknown Soldier of, 627
World War II, 117
    Casualties, 307, 311
    Chronology, 117
    Declarations of war (U.S.),
        117
    Treaties, 118
    Unknown Soldier of, 627
    See also involved countries
Wrangell, Mount, 459, 478
Wrestling, 878, 940
Wright, Orville and Wilbur, 354,
    705
Writers. *See* People
Writer's Guide, 436–42
    Capitalization, 436
    Punctuation, 437–39
Wyandotte Cave, 475, 752
Wyoming, 773
    See also States of U.S.

X

Xavier, St. Francis, 457
Xenon (element), 532
Xerography, 560
Xhosa, 258
X-rays, 109, 542, 548, 562

Y

Yachting, 878, 946
Yalta Conference, 117, 118
Yangon, Myanmar, 234
    See also Cities (World)
Yangtze Kiang, 173, 471
Yaoundé, Cameroon, 167
Yasukuni, 379
Year in Pictures, The, 497–512
Year, defined, 581
Yellow River, 173, 471
Yellowstone National Park, 572, 759,
    773
Yellowstone River, 480
Yemen Arab Republic, 288

Yemen, People's Democratic Republic
    of, 288
Yemen, Republic of 288
    See also Countries
Yenisei River, 259, 471
Yogurt, 90
Yoga, 378
Yom Kippur, 584, 586
York, House of, 276
Yorktown, Battle of, 103, 771
Yosemite National Park, 572,
    747
Yosemite, waterfalls, 472, 473
Young, Brigham, 107, 705
Young Men's Christian Association,
    610
Young Women's Christian
    Association, 610
Yugoslavia, 288, 289
    See also Countries
Yukon River, 471, 480
Yukon Territory, 168, 169

Z

Zaire, 120, 289, 290
    U.N. action, 290
    See also Countries
Zama, Battle of, 98
Zambezi River, 291, 457, 472
    Kariba Dam, 291, 470
Zambia, 290, 291
    See also Countries
Zanzibar. *See* Tanzania
Zenger, John Peter, 105, 705
Zeppelin:
    First Flight, 354
Zero, 562
Zeus, statue of, 129
Zhou Enlai, 174, 705
Zhujiang River, 173
Zimbabwe, 291, 292
    Kariba Dam, 291, 470
    See also Countries
Zinc, 532
Zionism, 213
Zion National Park, 572
ZIP codes, 798–804
Zodiac, 347
Zoological gardens, 568
Zoos, American, 568, 569
Zugspitze (peak), 196
Zwelitsha, Ciskei, 258
Zwingli, Ulrich, 102

ELECTIONS

The Hundredth and Second Congress

Election returns as of 9:00 a.m. Thursday Nov. 8, 1990

The Senate

Senior Senator is listed first. The dates in the first column indicate period of service. The date given in parentheses after the Senator's name is year of birth. All terms are for six years and expire in January. Mailing address of Senators: The Senate, Washington, D.C. 20510.

ALABAMA
1979–97 Howell T. Heflin (D) (1921)
1987–93 Richard C. Shelby (D) (1934)
ALASKA
1968–97 Ted Stevens (R) (1923)
1981–93 Frank H. Murkowski (R) (1933)
ARIZONA
1977–95 Dennis DeConcini (D) (1937)
1987–93 John McCain (R) (1936)
ARKANSAS
1975–93 Dale Bumpers (D) (1925)
1979–97 David H. Pryor (D) (1934)
CALIFORNIA
1969–93 Alan Cranston (D) (1914)
1983–95 Pete Wilson (R) (1933)
COLORADO
1979–93 Timothy E. Wirth (D) (1939)
1991–97 Hank Brown (R) (1940)
CONNECTICUT
1981–93 Christopher J. Dodd (D) (1944)
1989–95 Joseph I. Lieberman (D) (1942)
DELAWARE
1971–95 William V. Roth, Jr. (R) (1921)
1973–97 Joseph R. Biden, Jr. (D) (1942)
FLORIDA
1987–93 Bob Graham (D) (1936)
1989–95 Connie Mack III (R) (1940)
GEORGIA
1972–97 Sam Nunn (D) (1938)
1987–93 Wyche Fowler, Jr. (D) (1940)
HAWAII
1963–93 Daniel K. Inouye (D) (1924)
1990–95 Daniel K. Akaka (D) (1924)
IDAHO
1981–93 Steven D. Symms (R) (1938)
1991–97 Larry E. Craig (R) (1945)
ILLINOIS
1981–93 Alan J. Dixon (D) (1927)
1985–97 Paul Simon (D) (1928)
INDIANA
1977–95 Richard G. Lugar (R) (1932)
1989–97 Daniel R. Coats (R) (1943)
IOWA
1981–93 Charles E. Grassley (R) (1933)
1985–97 Tom Harkin (D) (1939)
KANSAS
1969–93 Robert J. Dole (R) (1923)
1978–97 Nancy Landon Kassebaum (R) (1932)
KENTUCKY
1974–93 Wendell H. Ford (D) (1924)
1985–97 Mitch McConnell (R) (1942)
LOUISIANA
1972–97 J. Bennett Johnston (D) (1932)
1987–93 John B. Breaux (D) (1944)
MAINE
1979–97 William S. Cohen (R) (1940)
1980–95 George J. Mitchell (D) (1933)
MARYLAND
1977–95 Paul Sarbanes (D) (1933)
1987–93 Barbara A. Mikulski (D) (1936)
MASSACHUSETTS
1962–95 Edward M. Kennedy (D) (1932)
1985–97 John F. Kerry (D) (1943)
MICHIGAN
1976–95 Donald W. Riegle, Jr. (D) (1938)
1979–97 Carl Levin (D) (1934)

MINNESOTA
1978–95 David F. Durenberger (R) (1934)
1991–97 Paul Wellstone (D)[1]
MISSISSIPPI
1978–97 Thad Cochran (R) (1937)
1989–95 Trent Lott (R) (1941)
MISSOURI
1976–95 John C. Danforth (R) (1936)
1987–93 Christopher S. (Kit) Bond (R) (1939)
MONTANA
1978–97 Max Baucus (D) (1941)
1989–95 Conrad Burns (R) (1935)
NEBRASKA
1979–97 James Exon (D) (1921)
1989–95 Robert Kerrey (D) (1943)
NEVADA
1987–93 Harry M. Reid (D) (1939)
1989–95 Dick Bryan (D) (1937)
NEW HAMPSHIRE
1980–93 Warren B. Rudman (R) (1930)
1991–97 Robert C. Smith (R) (1941)
NEW JERSEY
1979–97 Bill Bradley (D) (1943)
1982–95 Frank R. Lautenberg (D) (1924)
NEW MEXICO
1973–97 Pete V. Domenici (R) (1932)
1983–95 Jeff Bingaman (D) (1943)
NEW YORK
1977–95 Daniel P. Moynihan (D) (1927)
1981–93 Alfonse M. D'Amato (R) (1937)
NORTH CAROLINA
1973–97 Jesse Helms (R) (1921)
1986–93 Terry Sanford (D) (1917)
NORTH DAKOTA
1960–95 Quentin N. Burdick (D) (1908)
1987–93 Kent Conrad (D) (1948)
OHIO
1974–93 John H. Glenn, Jr. (D) (1921)
1976–95 Howard M. Metzenbaum (D) (1917)
OKLAHOMA
1979–97 David L. Boren (D) (1941)
1981–93 Don Nickles (R) (1948)
OREGON
1967–97 Mark O. Hatfield (R) (1922)
1969–93 Bob Packwood (R) (1932)
PENNSYLVANIA
1977–95 John Heinz (R) (1938)
1981–93 Arlen Specter (R) (1930)
RHODE ISLAND
1961–97 Claiborne Pell (D) (1918)
1976–95 John H. Chafee (R) (1922)
SOUTH CAROLINA
1956–97 Strom Thurmond (R) (1902)
1966–93 Ernest F. Hollings (D) (1922)
SOUTH DAKOTA
1979–97 Larry Pressler (R) (1942)
1987–93 Thomas A. Daschle (D) (1947)
TENNESSEE
1977–95 James R. Sasser (D) (1936)
1985–97 Albert Gore (D) (1948)
TEXAS
1971–95 Lloyd M. Bentsen (D) (1921)
1985–97 Phil Gramm (R) (1942)
UTAH
1974–93 E.J. (Jake) Garn (R) (1932)
1977–95 Orrin G. Hatch (R) (1934)

1. Birthdate unknown at press time.

VERMONT
1975–93 Patrick J. Leahy (D) (1940)
1989–95 James M. Jeffords (R) (1934)
VIRGINIA
1979–97 John W. Warner (R) (1927)
1989–95 Charles Robb (D) (1939)
WASHINGTON
1987–93 Brock Adams (D) (1927)
1989–95 Slade Gorton (R) (1928)

WEST VIRGINIA
1959–95 Robert C. Byrd (D) (1918)
1985–97 John D. (Jay) Rockefeller IV (D) (1937)
WISCONSIN
1981–93 Robert W. Kasten, Jr. (R) (1942)
1989–95 Herbert Kohl (D) (1935)
WYOMING
1977–95 Malcolm Wallop (R) (1933)
1979–97 Alan K. Simpson (R) (1931)

The House of Representatives

The numerals indicate the Congressional Districts of the states; the designation AL means At Large. All terms end January 1993. Mailing address of Representatives: House of Representatives, Washington, D.C. 20515.

ALABAMA
(7 Representatives)
1. H.L. (Sonny) Callahan (R)
2. William Dickinson (R)
3. Glenn Browder (D)
4. Tom Bevill (D)
5. Bud Cramer (D)
6. Ben Erdreich (D)
7. Claude Harris (D)

ALASKA
(1 Representative)
AL Don Young (R)

ARIZONA
(5 Representatives)
1. John Rhodes (R)
2. Morris Udall (D)
3. Bob Stump (R)
4. Jon Kyl (R)
5. Jim Kolbe (R)

ARKANSAS
(4 Representatives)
1. Bill Alexander (D)
2. Ray Thornton (D)
3. John Hammerschmidt (R)
4. Beryl Anthony (D)

CALIFORNIA
(45 Representatives)
1. Frank Riggs (R)
2. Wally Herger (R)
3. Bob Matsui (D)
4. Vic Fazio (D)
5. Nancy Pelosi (D)
6. Barbara Boxer (D)
7. George Miller (D)
8. Ron Dellums (D)
9. Pete Stark (D)
10. Don Edwards (D)
11. Tom Lantos (D)
12. Tom Campbell (R)
13. Norm Mineta (D)
14. John Doolittle (D)
15. Gary Condit (D)
16. Leon Panetta (D)
17. Cal Dooley (D)
18. Richard Lehman (D)
19. Robert Lagomarsino (R)
20. Bill Thomas (R)
21. Elton Gallegly (R)
22. Carlos Moorhead (R)
23. Tony Beilenson (D)
24. Henry Waxman (D)
25. Edward Roybal (D)
26. Howard Berman (D)
27. Mel Levine (D)
28. Julian Dixon (D)
29. Maxine Waters (D)
30. Marty Martinez (D)
31. Mervyn Dymally (D)
32. Glenn Anderson (D)
33. David Dreier (R)
34. Esteban Torres (D)
35. Jerry Lewis (R)
36. George Brown (D)
37. Al McCandless (R)
38. Robert Dornan (R)
39. William Dannemeyer (R)
40. Christopher Cox (R)
41. Bill Lowery (R)
42. Dana Rohrabacher (R)
43. Ron Packard (R)
44. Randall Cunningham (R)
45. Duncan Hunter (R)

COLORADO
(6 Representatives)
1. Pat Schroeder (D)
2. David Skaggs (D)
3. Ben Campbell (D)
4. Wayne Allard (R)
5. Joel Hefley (R)
6. Dan Schaefer (R)

CONNECTICUT
(6 Representatives)
1. Barbara Kennelly (D)
2. Sam Gejdenson (D)
3. Rosa DeLauro (D)
4. Christopher Shays (R)
5. Gary Franks (R)
6. Nancy Johnson (R)

DELAWARE
(1 Representative)
AL Tom Carper (D)

FLORIDA
(19 Representatives)
1. Earl Hutto (D)
2. Pete Peterson (D)
3. Charles Bennett (D)
4. Craig James (R)
5. Bill McCollum (R)
6. Cliff Stearns (R)
7. Sam Gibbons (D)
8. Bill Young (R)
9. Mike Bilirakis (R)
10. Andy Ireland (R)
11. Jim Bacchus (D)
12. Tom Lewis (R)
13. Porter Goss (R)
14. Harry Johnston (D)
15. Clay Shaw (R)
16. Larry Smith (D)
17. Bill Lehman (D)
18. Ileana Ros-Lehtinen (R)
19. Dante Fascell (D)

GEORGIA
(10 Representatives)
1. Lindsay Thomas (D)
2. Charles Hatcher (D)
3. Richard Ray (D)
4. Ben Jones (D)
5. John Lewis (D)
6. Newt Gingrich (R)
7. George Darden (D)
8. Roy Rowland (D)
9. Ed Jenkins (D)
10. Doug Barnard (D)

HAWAII
(2 Representatives)
1. Neil Abercrombie (D)
2. Patsy Mink (D)

IDAHO
(2 Representatives)
1. Larry LaRocco (D)
2. Richard Stallings (D)

ILLINOIS
(22 Representatives)
1. Charles Hayes (D)
2. Gus Savage (D)
3. Marty Russo (D)
4. George Sangmeister (D)
5. William Lipinski (D)
6. Henry Hyde (R)
7. Cardiss Collins (D)
8. Dan Rostenkowski (D)
9. Sid Yates (D)
10. John Porter (R)
11. Frank Annunzio (D)
12. Philip Crane (R)
13. Harris Fawell (R)
14. Dennis Hastert (R)
15. Edward Madigan (R)
16. John Cox, Jr. (D)
17. Lane Evans (D)
18. Bob Michel (R)
19. Terry Bruce (D)
20. Richard Durbin (D)
21. Jerry Costello (D)
22. Glenn Poshard (D)

INDIANA
(10 Representatives)
1. Peter Visclosky (D)
2. Phil Sharp (D)
3. Tim Roemer (D)
4. Jill Long (D)
5. Jim Jontz (D)
6. Dan Burton (R)
7. John Myers (R)
8. Frank McCloskey (D)
9. Lee Hamilton (D)
10. Andy Jacobs (D)

IOWA
(6 Representatives)
1. Jim Leach (R)
2. Jim Nussel (R)
3. Dave Nagle (D)
4. Neal Smith (D)
5. James Ross Lightfoot (R)
6. Fred Grandy (R)

KANSAS
(5 Representatives)
1. Pat Roberts (R)
2. Jim Slattery (D)

3. Jan Meyers (R)
4. Dan Glickman (D)
5. Richard Nichols (R)

KENTUCKY
(7 Representatives)
1. Carroll Hubbard (D)
2. Bill Natcher (D)
3. Romano Mazzoli (D)
4. Jim Bunning (R)
5. Harold Rogers (R)
6. Larry Hopkins (R)
7. Carl Perkins (D)

LOUISIANA
(8 Representatives)
1. Robert Livingston (R)
2. William J. Jefferson (D)
3. Bill Tauzin (D)
4. Jim McCrery (R)
5. Jerry Huckaby (D)
6. Richard Baker (R)
7. Jimmy Hayes (D)
8. Clyde Holloway (R)

MAINE
(2 Representatives)
1. Tom Andrews (D)
2. Olympia Snowe (R)

MARYLAND
(8 Representatives)
1. Wayne Gilchrest (R)
2. Helen Bentley (R)
3. Benjamin Cardin (D)
4. Tom McMillen (D)
5. Steny Hoyer (D)
6. Beverly Byron (D)
7. Kweisi Mfume (D)
8. Connie Morella (R)

MASSACHUSETTS
(11 Representatives)
1. Silvio Conte (R)
2. Richard Neal (D)
3. Joseph Early (D)
4. Barney Frank (D)
5. Chester Atkins (D)
6. Nick Mavroules (D)
7. Ed Markey (D)
8. Joseph Kennedy (D)
9. Joe Moakley (D)
10. Gerry Studds (D)
11. Brian Donnelly (D)

MICHIGAN
(18 Representatives)
1. John Conyers, Jr. (D)
2. Carl D. Pursell (R)
3. Howard Wolpe (D)
4. Fred Upton (R)
5. Paul Henry (R)
6. Bob Carr (D)
7. Dale Kildee (D)
8. Bob Traxler (D)
9. Guy Vander Jagt (R)
10. David Camp (R)
11. Bob Davis (R)
12. David Bonior (D)
13. Barbara-Rose Collins (D)
14. Dennis Hertel (D)
15. William Ford (D)
16. John Dingell (D)
17. Sander Levin (D)
18. William Broomfield (R)

MINNESOTA
(8 Representatives)
1. Tim Penny (D)
2. Vin Weber (R)
3. Jim Ramstad (R)
4. Bruce Vento (D)
5. Martin Sabo (D)
6. Gerry Sikorski (D)
7. Collin Peterson (D)
8. James Oberstar (D)

MISSISSIPPI
(5 Representatives)
1. Jamie Whitten (D)
2. Mike Espy (D)
3. Sonny Montgomery (D)
4. Mike Parker (D)
5. Gene Taylor (D)

MISSOURI
(9 Representatives)
1. William Clay (D)
2. Joan Horn (D)
3. Richard Gephardt (D)
4. Ike Skelton (D)
5. Alan Wheat (D)
6. Tom Coleman (R)
7. Mel Hancock (R)
8. Bill Emerson (R)
9. Harold Volkmer (D)

MONTANA
(2 Representatives)
1. Pat Williams (D)
2. Ron Marlenee (R)

NEBRASKA
(3 Representatives)
1. Douglas Bereuter (R)
2. Peter Hoagland (D)
3. Bill Barrett (R)

NEVADA
(2 Representatives)
1. Jim Bilbray (D)
2. Barbara Vucanovich (R)

NEW HAMPSHIRE
(2 Representatives)
1. Bill Zeliff (R)
2. Dick Swett (D)

NEW JERSEY
(14 Representatives)
1. Robert Andrews (D)
2. Bill Hughes (D)
3. Frank Pallone (D)
4. Chris Smith (R)
5. Marge Roukema (R)
6. Bernard Dwyer (D)
7. Matthew Rinaldo (R)
8. Robert Roe (D)
9. Robert Torricelli (D)
10. Donald Payne (D)
11. Dean Gallo (R)
12. Richard Zimmer (R)
13. Jim Saxton (R)
14. Frank Guarini (D)

NEW MEXICO
(3 Representatives)
1. Steve Schiff (R)
2. Joseph Skeen (R)
3. Bill Richardson (D)

NEW YORK
(34 Representatives)
1. George Hochbrueckner (D)
2. Tom Downey (D)
3. Robert Mrazek (D)
4. Norman Lent (R)
5. Raymond McGrath (R)
6. Floyd Flake (D)
7. Gary Ackerman (D)
8. Jim Scheuer (D)
9. Thomas Manton (D)
10. Charles Schumer (D)
11. Edolphus Towns (D)
12. Major Owens (D)
13. Stephen Solarz (D)
14. Susan Molinari (R)
15. William Green (R)
16. Charles Rangel (D)
17. Ted Weiss (D)
18. Jose Serrano (D)

19. Eliot Engel (D)
20. Nita Lowey (D)
21. Hamilton Fish, Jr. (R)
22. Benjamin Gilman (R)
23. Michael McNulty (D)
24. Gerald Solomon (R)
25. Sherwood Boehlert (R)
26. David O'B. Martin (R)
27. Jim Walsh (R)
28. Matt McHugh (D)
29. Frank Horton (R)
30. Louise Slaughter (D)
31. Bill Paxon (R)
32. John LaFalce (D)
33. Henry Nowak (D)
34. Amory Houghton (R)

NORTH CAROLINA
(11 Representatives)
1. Walter Jones (D)
2. Tim Valentine (D)
3. Martin Lancaster (D)
4. David Price (D)
5. Stephen Neal (D)
6. Howard Coble (R)
7. Charlie Rose (D)
8. Bill Hefner (D)
9. Alex McMillan (R)
10. Cass Ballenger (R)
11. Charles Taylor (R)

NORTH DAKOTA
(1 Representative)
AL Byron Dorgan (D)

OHIO
(21 Representatives)
1. Charles Luken (D)
2. Willis Gradison, Jr. (R)
3. Tony Hall (D)
4. Michael Oxley (R)
5. Paul Gillmor (R)
6. Bob McEwen (R)
7. David Hobson (R)
8. John Boehner (R)
9. Marcy Kaptur (D)
10. Clarence Miller (R)
11. Dennis Eckart (D)
12. John Kasich (R)
13. Don Pease (D)
14. Tom Sawyer (D)
15. Chalmers Wylie (R)
16. Ralph Regula (R)
17. James Traficant (D)
18. Doug Applegate (D)
19. Ed Feighan (D)
20. Mary Rose Oakar (D)
21. Louis Stokes (D)

OKLAHOMA
(6 Representatives)
1. Jim Inhofe (R)
2. Mike Synar (D)
3. Bill Brewster (D)
4. Dave McCurdy (D)
5. Mickey Edwards (R)
6. Glenn English (D)

OREGON
(5 Representatives)
1. Les Aucoin (D)
2. Bob Smith (R)
3. Ron Wyden (D)
4. Peter Defazio (D)
5. Mike Kopetski (D)

PENNSYLVANIA
(23 Representatives)
1. Tom Foglietta (D)
2. Bill Gray (D)
3. Robert Borski (D)

4. Joe Kolter (D)
5. Richard Schulze (R)
6. Gus Yatron (D)
7. Curt Weldon (R)
8. Peter Kostmayer (D)
9. E.G. Shuster (R)
10. Joseph McDade (R)
11. Paul Kanjorski (D)
12. John Murtha (D)
13. Lawrence Coughlin (R)
14. William Coyne (D)
15. Don Ritter (R)
16. Robert Walker (R)
17. George Gekas (R)
18. Rick Santorum (R)
19. William Goodling (R)
20. Joe Gaydos (D)
21. Tom Ridge (R)
22. Austin Murphy (D)
23. William Clinger, Jr. (R)

RHODE ISLAND
(2 Representatives)
1. Ron Machtley (R)
2. Jack Reed (D)

SOUTH CAROLINA
(6 Representatives)
1. Arthur Ravenel (R)
2. Floyd Spence (R)
3. Butler Derrick (D)
4. Liz Patterson (D)
5. John Spratt (D)
6. Robin Tallon (D)

SOUTH DAKOTA
(1 Representative)
AL Tim Johnson (D)

TENNESSEE
(9 Representatives)
1. James Quillen (R)
2. Jimmy Duncan (R)
3. Marilyn Lloyd (D)

4. Jim Cooper (D)
5. Bob Clement (D)
6. Bart Gordon (D)
7. Don Sundquist (R)
8. John Tanner (D)
9. Harold Ford (D)

TEXAS
(27 Representatives)
1. Jim Chapman (D)
2. Charlie Wilson (D)
3. Steven Bartlett (R)
4. Ralph Hall (D)
5. John Bryant (D)
6. Joe Barton (R)
7. William Archer (R)
8. Jack Fields (R)
9. Jack Brooks (D)
10. J.J. Pickle (D)
11. Chet Edwards (D)
12. Pete Geren (D)
13. Bill Sarpalius (D)
14. Greg Laughlin (D)
15. Kika de la Garza (D)
16. Ron Coleman (D)
17. Charles Stenholm (D)
18. Craig Washington (D)
19. Larry Combest (R)
20. Henry Gonzalez (D)
21. Lamar Smith (R)
22. Tom DeLay (R)
23. Albert Bustamante (D)
24. Martin Frost (D)
25. Mike Andrews (D)
26. Dick Armey (R)
27. Solomon Ortiz (D)

UTAH
(3 Representatives)
1. James Hansen (R)
2. Wayne Owens (D)
3. Bill Orton (D)

VERMONT
(1 Representative)
AL Bernie Sanders (Ind)

VIRGINIA
(10 Representatives)
1. Herb Bateman (R)
2. Owen Pickett (D)
3. Thomas Bliley (R)
4. Norman Sisisky (D)
5. L.F. Payne (D)
6. Jim Olin (D)
7. French Slaughter (R)
8. Jim Moran (D)
9. Frederick Boucher (D)
10. Frank Wolf (R)

WASHINGTON
(8 Representatives)
1. John Miller (R)
2. Al Swift (D)
3. Jolene Unsoeld (D)
4. Sid Morrison (R)
5. Tom Foley (D)
6. Norm Dicks (D)
7. Jim McDermott (D)
8. Rod Chandler (R)

WEST VIRGINIA
(4 Representatives)
1. Alan Mollohan (D)
2. Harley Staggers (D)
3. Bob Wise (D)
4. Nick Rahall (D)

WISCONSIN
(9 Representatives)
1. Les Aspin (D)
2. Scott Klug (R)
3. Steve Gunderson (R)
4. Jerry Kleczka (D)
5. Jim Moody (D)
6. Thomas Petri (R)
7. Dave Obey (D)
8. Toby Roth (R)
9. James Sensenbrenner (R)

WYOMING
(1 Representative)
AL Craig Thomas (R)

The Governors of the Fifty States

State	Governor	Current term[1]	State	Governor	Current term[1]
Ala.	Guy Hunt (R)	1991–95	Mont.	Stanley Stephens (R)	1989–93
Alaska	Tony Knowles (D)	1990–94[2]	Neb.	Ben Nelson (D)	1991–95
Ariz.	Fife Symington (R)	1991–95	Nev.	Bob Miller (D)	1991–95
Ark.	Bill Clinton (D)	1991–95	N.H.	Judd Gregg (R)	1991–93
Calif.	Pete Wilson (R)	1991–95	N.J.	James J. Florio (D)	1990–94
Colo.	Roy Romer (D)	1991–95	N.M.	Bruce King (D)	1991–95
Conn.	Lowell P. Weicker Jr. (Ind.)	1991–95	N.Y.	Mario M. Cuomo (D)	1991–95
Del.	Michael Castle (R)	1989–93	N.C.	James G. Martin (R)	1989–93
Fla.	Lawton Chiles (D)	1991–95	N.D.	George A. Sinner (D)	1989–93
Ga.	Zell Miller (D)	1991–95	Ohio	George Voinovich (R)	1991–95
Hawaii	John Waihee (D)	1990–94[2]	Okla.	David Walters (D)	1991–95
Idaho	Cecil D. Andrus (D)	1991–95	Ore.	Barbara Roberts (D)	1991–95
Ill.	Jim Edgar (R)	1991–95	Pa.	Robert P. Casey (D)	1991–95
Ind.	B. Evan Bayh III (R)	1989–93	R.I.	Bruce G. Sundlun (D)	1991–93
Iowa	Terry E. Branstad (R)	1991–95	S.C.	Carroll A. Campbell, Jr. (R)	1991–95
Kan.	Joan Finney (D)	1991–95	S.D.	George S. Mickelson (R)	1991–95
Ky.	Wallace Wilkinson (D)	1987–91[2]	Tenn.	Ned McWherter (D)	1991–95
La.	Charles (Buddy) Roemer (D)	1988–92[3]	Tex.	Ann Richards (D)	1991–95
Me.	John R. McKernan, Jr. (R)	1991–95	Utah	Norman H. Bangerter (R)	1989–93
Md.	William Donald Schaefer (D)	1991–95	Vt.	Richard Snelling (R)	1991–93
Mass.	William F. Weld (R)	1991–95	Va.	L. Douglas Wilder (D)	1990–94
Mich.	John Engler (R)	1991–95	Wash.	Booth Gardner (D)	1989–93
Minn.	Jon Grunseth (R)	1991–95	W. Va.	Gaston Caperton (D)	1989–93
Miss.	Ray Mabus (D)	1988–92	Wis.	Tommy G. Thompson (R)	1991–95
Mo.	John D. Ashcroft (R)	1989–93	Wyo.	Mike Sullivan (D)	1991–95

1. Except where indicated, all terms begin in January. 2. December. 3. March.

Senate and House Standing Committees, 101st Congress

Committees of the Senate

Agriculture, Nutrition, and Forestry (19 members)
Chairman: Patrick J. Leahy (Vt.)
Ranking Rep.: Richard G. Luger (Ind.)
Appropriations (29 members)
Chairman: Robert C. Byrd (W.Va.)
Ranking Rep.: Mark O. Hatfield (Ore.)
Armed Services (19 members)
Chairman: Sam Nunn (Ga.)
Ranking Rep.: John Warner (Va.)
Banking, Housing, and Urban Affairs (21 members)
Chairman: Donald W. Riegle (Mich.)
Ranking Rep.: E. J. (Jake) Garn (Utah)
Budget (23 members)
Chairman: James R. Sasser (Tenn.)
Ranking Rep.: Pete V. Domenici (N.M.)
Commerce, Science, and Transportation
(20 members)
Chairman: Ernest F. Hollings (S.C.)
Ranking Rep.: John C. Danforth (Mo.)
Energy and Natural Resources (19 members)
Chairman: J. Bennett Johnston (La.)
Ranking Rep.: James A. McClure (Idaho)
Environment and Public Works (16 members)
Chairman: Quentin N. Burdick (N.D.)
Ranking Rep.: John H. Chafee (R.I.)
Finance (20 members)
Chairman: Lloyd M. Bentsen (Texas)
Ranking Rep.: Bob Packwood (Ore.)
Foreign Relations (19 members)
Chairman: Claiborne Pell (R.I.)
Ranking Rep.: Jesse Helms (N.C.)
Governmental Affairs (14 members)
Chairman: John Glenn (Ohio)
Ranking Rep.: William V. Roth, Jr. (Del.)
Judiciary (14 members)
Chairman: Joseph R. Biden, Jr. (Del)
Ranking Rep.: Strom Thurmond (S.C.)
Labor and Human Resources (16 members)
Chairman: Edward M. Kennedy (Mass.)
Ranking Rep.: Orrin G. Hatch (Utah)
Rules and Administration (16 members)
Chairman: Wendell H. Ford (Ky.)
Ranking Rep.: Ted Stevens (Alas.)
Small Business (19 members)
Chairman: Dale Bumpers (Ark.)
Ranking Rep.: Rudy Boschwitz (Minn.)
Veterans' Affairs (11 members)
Chairman: Alan Cranston (Calif.)
Ranking Rep: Frank H. Murkowski (Alas.)

Select and Special Committees

Aging (19 members)
Chairman: David H. Pryor (Ark.)
Ranking Rep.: John Heinz (Pa.)
Ethics (6 members)
Chairman: Howell T. Heflin (Ala.)
Ranking Rep.: Warren Rudman (N.H.)
Indian Affairs (8 members)
Chairman: Daniel K. Inouye (Hawaii)
Ranking Rep.: Frank H. Murkowski (Alas.)
Intelligence (15 members)
Chairman: David L. Boren (Okla.)
Ranking Rep.: William S. Cohen (Me.)

Committees of the House

Agriculture (43 members)
Chairman: E. (Kika) de la Garza (Texas)
Ranking Rep.: Edward R. Madigan (Ill.)

Appropriations (57 members)
Chairman: Jamie L. Whitten (Miss.)
Ranking Rep.: Silvio O. Conte (Mass.)
Armed Services (52 members)
Chairman: Les Aspin (Wis.)
Ranking Rep.: William L. Dickinson (Ala.)
Banking, Finance, and Urban Affairs (52 members)
Chairman: Henry B. Gonzalez (Texas)
Ranking Rep.: Chalmers P. Wylie (Ohio)
Budget (36 members)
Chairman: Leon E. Panetta (Calif.)
Ranking Rep.: Bill Frenzel (Minn.)
District of Columbia (11 members)
Chairman: Ronald V. Dellums (Calif.)
Ranking Rep.: Stanford E. Parris (Va.)
Education and Labor (35 members)
Chairman: Augustus F. Hawkins (Calif.)
Ranking Rep.: William F. Goodling (Pa.)
Energy and Commerce (43 members)
Chairman: John D. Dingell (Mich.)
Ranking Rep.: Norman Lent (N.Y.)
Foreign Affairs (45 members)
Chairman: Dante B. Fascell (Fla.)
Ranking Rep.: William S. Broomfield (Mich.)
Government Operations (39 members)
Chairman: John Conyers, Jr. (Mich.)
Ranking Rep.: Frank Horton (N.Y.)
House Administration (20 members)
Chairman: Frank Annunzio (Ill.)
Ranking Rep.: Newt Gingrich (Ga.)
Interior and Insular Affairs (41 members)
Chairman: Morris K. Udall (Ariz.)
Ranking Rep.: Don Young (Alas.)
Judiciary (35 members)
Chairman: Jack Brooks (Texas)
Ranking Rep.: Hamilton Fish, Jr. (N.Y.)
Merchant Marine and Fisheries (43 members)
Chairman: Walter B. Jones (N.C.)
Ranking Rep.: Robert W. Davis (Mich.)
Post Office and Civil Service (21 members)
Chairman: William D. Ford (Mich.)
Ranking Rep.: Benjamin Gilman (N.Y.)
Public Works and Transportation (51 members)
Chairman: Glenn Anderson (Calif.)
Ranking Rep.: John P. Hammerschmidt (Ark.)
Rules (13 members)
Chairman: Vacant
Ranking Rep.: James H. Quillen (Tenn.)
Science, Space, and Technology (48 members)
Chairman: Robert A. Roe (N.J.)
Ranking Rep.: Robert S. Walker (Pa.)
Small Business (43 members)
Chairman: John J. LaFalce (N.Y.)
Ranking Rep.: Joseph M. McDade (Pa.)
Standards of Official Conduct (12 members)
Chairman: Julian C. Dixon (Calif.)
Ranking Rep.: John T. Myers (Ind.)
Veterans' Affairs (34 members)
Chairman: G. V. (Sonny) Montgomery (Miss.)
Ranking Rep.: Bob Stump (Ariz.)
Ways and Means (36 members)
Chairman: Dan Rostenkowski (Ill.)
Ranking Rep.: William Archer (Texas)

Select Committees

Aging (62 members)
Chairman: Edward Roybal (Calif.)
Ranking Rep.: Matthew J. Rinaldo (N.J.)

Children, Youth, and Families (30 members)
Chairman: George Miller (Calif.)
Ranking Rep.: Thomas Bliley (Va.)
Hunger (25 members)
Chairman: Vacant
Ranking Rep.: William Emerson (Mo.)

Intelligence (20 members)
Chairman: Anthony C. Beilenson (Calif.)
Ranking Rep.: Henry Hyde (Ill.)
Narcotics Abuse and Control (27 members)
Chairman: Charles B. Rangel (N.Y.)
Ranking Rep.: Lawrence Coughlin (Pa.)

Speakers of the House of Representatives

Dates served	Congress	Name and state	Dates served	Congress	Name and state
1789–1791	1	Frederick A. C. Muhlenberg (Pa.)	1863–1869	38–40	Schuyler Colfax (Ind.)
1791–1793	2	Jonathan Trumbull (Conn.)	1869–1869	40	Theodore M. Pomeroy (N.Y.)[5]
1793–1795	3	Frederick A. C. Muhlenberg (Pa.)	1869–1875	41–43	James G. Blaine (Me.)
1795–1799	4–5	Jonathan Dayton (N.J.)[1]	1875–1876	44	Michael C. Kerr (Ind.)[6]
1799–1801	6	Theodore Sedgwick (Mass.)	1876–1881	44–46	Samuel J. Randall (Pa.)
1801–1807	7–9	Nathaniel Macon (N.C.)	1881–1883	47	J. Warren Keifer (Ohio)
1807–1811	10–11	Joseph B. Varnum (Mass.)	1883–1889	48–50	John G. Carlisle (Ky.)
1811–1814	12–13	Henry Clay (Ky.)[2]	1889–1891	51	Thomas B. Reed (Me.)
1814–1815	13	Langdon Cheves (S.C.)	1891–1895	52–53	Charles F. Crisp (Ga.)
1815–1820	14–16	Henry Clay (Ky.)[3]	1895–1899	54–55	Thomas B. Reed (Me.)
1820–1821	16	John W. Taylor (N.Y.)	1899–1903	56–57	David B. Henderson (Iowa)
1821–1823	17	Philip P. Barbour (Va.)	1903–1911	58–61	Joseph G. Cannon (Ill.)
1823–1825	18	Henry Clay (Ky.)	1911–1919	62–65	Champ Clark (Mo.)
1825–1827	19	John W. Taylor (N.Y.)	1919–1925	66–68	Frederick H. Gillett (Mass.)
1827–1834	20–23	Andrew Stevenson (Va.)[4]	1925–1931	69–71	Nicholas Longworth (Ohio)
1834–1835	23	John Bell (Tenn.)	1931–1933	72	John N. Garner (Tex.)
1835–1839	24–25	James K. Polk (Tenn.)	1933–1934	73	Henry T. Rainey (Ill.)[7]
1839–1841	26	Robert M. T. Hunter (Va.)	1935–1936	74	Joseph W. Byrns (Tenn.)[8]
1841–1843	27	John White (Ky.)	1936–1940	74–76	William B. Bankhead (Ala.)[9]
1843–1845	28	John W. Jones (Va.)	1940–1947	76–79	Sam Rayburn (Tex.)
1845–1847	29	John W. Davis (Ind.)	1947–1949	80	Joseph W. Martin, Jr. (Mass.)
1847–1849	30	Robert C. Winthrop (Mass.)	1949–1953	81–82	Sam Rayburn (Tex.)
1849–1851	31	Howell Cobb (Ga.)	1953–1955	83	Joseph W. Martin, Jr. (Mass.)
1851–1855	32–33	Linn Boyd (Ky.)	1955–1961	84–87	Sam Rayburn (Tex.)[10]
1855–1857	34	Nathaniel P. Banks (Mass.)	1962–1971	87–91	John W. McCormack (Mass.)[11]
1857–1859	35	James L. Orr (S.C.)	1971–1977	92–94	Carl Albert (Okla.)[12]
1859–1861	36	Wm. Pennington (N.J.)	1977–1987	95–99	Thomas P. O'Neill, Jr. (Mass.)[13]
1861–1863	37	Galusha A. Grow (Pa.)	1987–1989	100–101	James C. Wright, Jr. (Tex.)[14]
			1989–	101–	Thomas S. Foley (Wash.)

1. George Dent (Md.) was elected Speaker pro tempore for April 20 and May 28, 1798. 2. Resigned during second session of 13th Congress. 3. Resigned between first and second sessions of 16th Congress. 4. Resigned during first session of 23rd Congress. 5. Elected Speaker and served the day of adjournment. 6. Died between first and second sessions of 44th Congress. During first session, there were two Speakers pro tempore: Samuel S. Cox (N.Y.), appointed for Feb. 17, May 12, and June 19, 1876, and Milton Sayler (Ohio), appointed for June 4, 1876. 7. Died in 1934 after adjournment of second session of 73rd Congress. 8. Died during second session of 74th Congress. 9. Died during third session of 76th Congress. 10. Died between first and second sessions of 87th Congress. 11. Not a candidate in 1970 election. 12. Not a candidate in 1976 election. 13. Not a candidate in 1986 election. 14. Resigned during first session of 101st Congress. *Source: Congressional Directory.*

Floor Leaders of the Senate

Democratic	Republican
Gilbert M. Hitchcock, Neb. (Min. 1919–20)	Charles Curtis, Kan. (Maj. 1925–29)
Oscar W. Underwood, Ala. (Min. 1920–23)	James E. Watson, Ind. (Maj. 1929–33)
Joseph T. Robinson, Ark. (Min. 1923–33, Maj. 1933–37)	Charles L. McNary, Ore. (Min. 1933–44)
Alben W. Barkley, Ky. (Maj. 1937–46, Min. 1947–48)	Wallace H. White, Jr., Me. (Min. 1944–47, Maj. 1947–48)
Scott W. Lucas, Ill. (Maj. 1949–50)	Kenneth S. Wherry, Neb. (Min. 1949–51)
Ernest W. McFarland, Ariz. (Maj. 1951–52)	Styles Bridges, N. H. (Min. 1951–52)
Lyndon B. Johnson, Tex. (Min. 1953–54, Maj. 1955–60)	Robert A. Taft, Ohio (Maj. 1953)
Mike Mansfield, Mont. (Maj. 1961–77)	William F. Knowland, Calif. (Maj. 1953–54, Min. 1955–58)
Robert C. Byrd, W. Va. (Maj. 1977–81, Min. 1981–86, Maj. 1987–88)	Everett M. Dirksen, Ill. (Min. 1959–69)
George John Mitchell, Me. (Maj. 1989–)	Hugh Scott, Pa. (Min. 1969–1977)
	Howard H. Baker, Jr., Tenn. (Min. 1977–81, Maj. 1981–84)
	Robert J. Dole, Kan. (Maj. 1985–86, Min. 1987–)

NOTE: Min. = Minority Leader; Maj. = Majority Leader. *Source:* United States Senate, Secretary for the Majority.

Presidential Election of 1988

Principal Candidates for President and Vice President
Republican: George H. Bush; J. Danforth Quayle
Democratic: Michael S. Dukakis; Lloyd Bentsen

State	Total	*Bush* Rep.	Per-cent	*Dukakis* Dem.	Per-cent	Plurality	Electoral vote R	Electoral vote D
Alabama	1,378,476	815,576	59.17	549,506	39.86	266,070	9	—
Alaska	200,116	119,251	59.59	72,584	36.27	46,667	3	—
Arizona	1,171,873	702,541	59.95	454,029	38.74	248,512	7	—
Arkansas	827,738	466,578	56.37	349,237	42.19	117,341	6	—
California	9,887,065	5,054,917	51.13	4,702,233	47.56	352,684	47	—
Colorado	1,372,394	728,177	53.06	621,453	45.28	106,724	8	—
Connecticut	1,443,394	750,241	51.98	676,584	46.87	73,657	8	—
Delaware	249,891	139,639	55.88	108,647	43.48	30,992	3	—
D.C.	192,877	27,590	14.30	159,407	82.65	131,817	—	3
Florida	4,302,313	2,618,885	60.87	1,656,701	38.51	962,184	21	—
Georgia	1,809,672	1,081,331	59.75	714,792	39.50	366,539	12	—
Hawaii	354,461	158,625	44.75	192,364	54.27	33,739	—	4
Idaho	408,968	253,881	62.08	147,272	36.01	106,609	4	—
Illinois	4,559,120	2,310,939	50.69	2,215,940	48.60	94,999	24	—
Indiana	2,168,621	1,297,763	59.84	860,643	39.69	437,120	12	—
Iowa	1,225,614	545,355	44.50	670,557	54.71	125,202	—	8
Kansas	993,044	554,049	55.79	422,636	42.56	131,413	7	—
Kentucky	1,322,517	734,281	55.52	580,368	43.88	153,913	9	—
Louisiana	1,628,202	883,702	54.27	717,460	44.06	166,242	10	—
Maine	555,035	307,131	55.34	243,569	43.88	63,562	4	—
Maryland	1,714,358	876,167	51.11	826,304	48.20	49,863	10	—
Massachusetts	2,632,805	1,194,635	45.38	1,401,415	53.23	206,780	—	13
Michigan	3,669,163	1,965,486	53.57	1,675,783	45.67	289,703	20	—
Minnesota	2,096,790	962,337	45.90	1,109,471	52.91	147,134	—	10
Mississippi	931,527	557,890	59.89	363,921	39.07	193,969	7	—
Missouri	2,093,713	1,084,953	51.82	1,001,619	47.84	83,334	11	—
Montana	365,674	190,412	52.07	168,936	46.20	21,476	4	—
Nebraska	661,465	397,956	60.16	259,235	39.19	138,721	5	—
Nevada	350,067	206,040	58.86	132,738	37.92	73,302	4	—
New Hampshire	451,074	281,537	62.41	163,696	36.29	117,841	4	—
New Jersey	3,099,553	1,743,192	56.24	1,320,352	42.60	422,840	16	—
New Mexico	521,287	270,341	51.86	244,497	46.90	25,844	5	—
New York[1]	6,485,683	3,081,871	47.52	3,347,882	51.62	266,011	—	36
North Carolina	2,134,370	1,237,258	57.97	890,167	41.71	347,091	13	—
North Dakota	297,261	166,559	56.03	127,739	42.97	38,820	3	—
Ohio	4,393,699	2,416,549	55.00	1,939,629	44.15	476,920	23	—
Oklahoma	1,171,036	678,367	57.93	483,423	41.28	194,944	8	—
Oregon	1,201,694	560,126	46.61	616,206	51.28	56,080	—	7
Pennsylvania	4,536,251	2,300,087	50.70	2,194,944	48.39	105,143	25	—
Rhode Island	404,620	177,761	43.93	225,123	55.64	47,362	—	4
South Carolina	986,009	606,443	61.50	370,554	37.58	235,889	8	—
South Dakota	312,991	165,415	52.85	145,560	46.51	19,855	3	—
Tennessee	1,636,250	947,233	57.89	679,794	41.55	267,439	11	—
Texas	5,427,410	3,036,829	55.95	2,352,748	43.35	684,081	29	—
Utah	647,008	428,442	66.22	207,343	32.05	221,099	5	—
Vermont	243,328	124,331	51.10	115,775	47.58	8,556	3	—
Virginia	2,191,609	1,309,162	59.74	859,799	39.23	449,363	12	—
Washington	1,865,253	903,835	48.46	933,516	50.05	29,681	—	10
West Virginia	653,311	310,065	47.46	341,016	52.20	30,951	—	6
Wisconsin	2,191,608	1,047,499	47.80	1,126,794	51.41	79,295	—	11
Wyoming	176,551	106,867	60.53	67,113	38.01	39,754	3	—
Total	**91,594,809**	**48,886,097**	**53.37**	**41,809,074**	**45.65**	**7,077,023**	**426**	**112**

1. Bush figure is combined Republican and Conservative Party votes; Dukakis figure is combined Democratic and Liberal Party votes. NATIONAL TOTALS OF OTHER CANDIDATES FOR PRESIDENT: Ronald E. Paul, Libertarian, 432,179; Lenora B. Fulani, New Alliance, 217,219; David Duke, Populist, 47,047; Eugene J. McCarthy, Consumer, 30,905; James C. Griffin, American Independent; 27,818; Lyndon H. LaRouche, National Economic, 25,562; William A. Marra, Right to Life, 20,504; Ed Winn, Workers League, 18,693; James Mac Warren, Socialist Workers, 15,604; Herbert Lewin, Peace & Freedom, 10,370; Earl Dodge, Prohibition, 8,002; Larry Holmes, Workers World, 7,846; Willa Kenoyer, Socialist, 3,882; Delmar Dennis, American, 3,475; Jack Herer, GrassRoots, 1,949; Louie G. Youngkeit, Independent, 372; John G. Martin, Third World Assembly, 236; write-ins and None of the Above, 27,975. *Source: Federal Elections 88*, Federal Election Commission.

Black Elected Officials

Year	U.S. and State Legislatures[1]	City and County Offices[2]	Law Enforcement[3]	Education[4]	Total
1970 (Feb.)	182	715	213	362	1,472
1975 (Apr.)	299	1,878	387	939	3,503
1977 (July)	316	2,497	447	1,051	4,311
1978 (July)	316	2,595	454	1,138	4,503
1979 (July)	315	2,647	486	1,136	4,584
1980 (July)	326	2,832	526	1,206	4,890
1981 (July)	343	2,863	549	1,259	5,014
1982 (July)	342	2,951	563	1,259	5,115
1983 (July)	366	3,197	607	1,369	5,559
1984 (Jan.)	396	3,259	636	1,363	5,654
1985 (Jan.)	407	3,517	661	1,431	6,016[5]
1986 (Jan.)	420	3,824	676	1,504	6,424[5]
1987 (Jan.)	440	3,966	728	1,547	6,681
1988 (July)	436	4,105	738	1,550	6,829
1989 (Jan.)	448	4,406	759	1,612	7,225
1990 (Jan.)	447	4,499	769	1,655	7,370

1. Includes elected State administrators and governors. 2. County commissioners and councilmen, mayors, vice mayors, aldermen, regional officials, and other. 3. Judges, magistrates, constables, marshals, sheriffs, justices of the peace, and other. 4. Members of State education agencies, college boards, school boards, and other. 5. Includes Black elected officials in the Virgin Islands. *Source:* Joint Center for Political and Economic Studies, Washington, D.C., *Black Elected Officials: A National Roster,* Copyright.

Annual Salaries of Federal Officials

President of the U.S.	$200,000[1]	Senators	$101,900
Vice President of the U.S.	160,600	Representatives	125,100
Cabinet members	138,900	President Pro Tempore of Senate	113,400
Under secretaries of executive departments	115,300	Majority and Minority Leader of the Senate	113,400
Deputy Secretaries of State, Defense, Treasury	125,100	Majority and Minority Leader of the House	138,900
Deputy Attorney General	125,100	Speaker of the House	160,600
Secretaries of the Army, Navy, Air Force	125,100	Chief Justice of the United States	160,600
		Associate Justices of the Supreme Court	153,600

1. Plus taxable $50,000 for expenses and a nontaxable sum (not to exceed $100,000 a year) for travel expenses. 2. Plus taxable $10,000 for expenses. NOTE: All salaries shown above are taxable. Data are as of January 1991. *Source:* Office of Personnel Management.

Characteristics of Voters in 1988 Presidential Election
(in thousands)

Characteristic	Persons of voting age	Persons reporting they voted		Persons reporting they did not vote	Characteristic	Persons of voting age	Persons reporting they voted		Persons reporting they did not vote
		Total	Percent				Total	Percent	
Male	84,531	47,704	56.4	36,826	North and West	117,373	69,129	58.9	48,243
Female	93,568	54,519	58.3	39,048	South	60,725	33,094	54.5	27,631
White	152,848	90,357	59.1	62,492	Education				
Black	19,692	10,144	51.5	9,548	8 years or less	19,145	7,025	36.7	12,120
Spanish origin[1]	12,893	3,710	28.8	9,183	9-11 years	21,052	8,698	41.3	12,354
Age: 18-20	10,742	3,570	33.2	7,172	12 years	70,033	38,328	54.7	31,706
21-24	14,827	5,684	38.3	9,142	13-15 years	34,264	22,090	64.5	12,174
25-34	42,677	20,468	48.0	22,210	16 or more	33,604	26,083	77.6	7,521
35-44	35,186	21,550	61.2	13,636	Employed	113,836	66,510	58.4	47,327
45-54	24,277	16,170	66.6	8,107	Unemployed	5,809	2,243	38.6	3,565
55-64	21,585	14,964	69.3	6,621	Not in labor force	58,453	33,471	57.3	24,983
65-74	17,578	12,840	73.0	4,738	Total	178,098	102,224	57.4	75,875
75 and over	11,226	6,978	62.2	4,248					

1. Persons of Spanish origin may be of any race. *Source:* Department of Commerce, Bureau of Commerce, Bureau of the Census, *Current Population Survey,* November 1988.

Business & Economy

Facing the "Totally New and Dynamic"

An interview with Peter Drucker by Edward Reingold

Q. In the remaining years of the 20th century . . .

A. We are already deep in the new century, a century that is fundamentally different from the one we still assume we live in. Although most everyone has a sense of deep unease with prevailing political and economic policies, whether in the U.S. or Japan or West Germany or England or Eastern Europe. Things somehow don't fit, and there is a clear sign that while we don't yet see the new [era], we know the old one is no longer right, no longer congruent. For 500 years the century mark has been almost irrelevant; the new century has always begun at least 25 years earlier.

Q. What kind of new century are we in, then?

A. In this 21st century world of dynamic political change, the significant thing is that we are in a post-business society. Business is still very important, and greed is as universal as ever; but the values of people are no longer business values, they are professional values. Most people are no longer part of the business society; they are part of the knowledge society. If you go back to when your father was born and mine, knowledge was an ornament, a luxury—and now it is the very center. We worry if the kids don't do as well in math tests as others. No earlier civilization would have dreamed of paying any attention to something like this. The greatest changes in our society are going to be in education.

Q. This is a result of advanced technology, is it not?

A. Every major change in educational technology changes not only how we learn but also what we learn. Just as the printed book totally changed the curriculum of the schools, so are the computer and tape recorder and video. The printed book is primarily a tool for adults. The new tools are for children; they fit the way children learn best. We now know how to make the accumulated wisdom of the human race relevant again. We should know that the old approach to education is theoretical and unsound. We still believe that teaching and learning are two sides of the same coin, but we ought to realize that they are not; one learns a subject, and one teaches a person. The process is increasingly going to shift to self-teaching on the basis of new technology because we now have these self-teaching tools.

Q. You call this a post-business society, but predatory takeovers and greenmail are still with us.

A. Yes. There is an old proverb that says if you don't have gravediggers you need vultures. And with management of large corporations being accountable to no one for the past 30 years, you need vultures. The vultures are the raiders who have come to clean up. But the cost to society of the hostile takeover is extremely high. It totally demoralizes a company, and above all it demoralizes middle management, the people who actually do the work.

Q. But don't you think there can be reasonable benefits even from a hostile takeover?

A. Let me say there is absolutely no doubt that a good many of these conglomerates need to be unbundled, need to be split up. Many managements have been building empires without economic justification, just for the sake, well, partly of having a big company, and partly for the sake of dealmaking. I will tell you a secret: dealmaking beats working. Dealmaking is exciting and fun, and working is grubby. Running anything is primarily an enormous amount of grubby detail work and very little excitement, so dealmaking is kind of romantic, sexy. That's why you have deals that make no sense. There's also another rule that says if you can't run this business, buy another one. There are a lot of companies around that need to be restructured and split up, that never had a justification for being.

Q. Then what are the implications for U.S. business competing in the world economy in the new century?

A. For a hundred years, we have had basically a European-based American foreign policy. Now the world economy is moving very fast toward regions rather than nations. The Soviet empire is unraveling. In North America the only question is whether Mexico will join in; Canada has basically already integrated with the U.S.

In Asia one of the big question marks is whether the Japanese will succeed—they are certainly trying—in creating a Far Eastern trading bloc that would include Korea, Taiwan, Singapore, Hong Kong and, I think, Thailand. The question is whether China will go along. After all, the old Japanese co-prosperity sphere basically was built around the development potential of the coastal cities of Shanghai and Canton.

Q. So the world of the 21st century is split into competing trading groups: Europe, North America and Asia?

A. Yes, and the activities of three big trading blocs will have political consequences. I think we are already in the midst of this, and the pattern is not going to be fair trade or protectionism but reciprocity.

Q. That's a bad word to the Japanese.

A. Very bad, and quite rightfully so. Reciprocity is a two-way street, and that is not the Japanese way of doing business. It is a threat to them. But in some ways Japanese industry is way ahead of the government.

Q. You mean by exporting manufacturing to the U.S. and the E.C.?

A. Yes. For example, those big car-carrying ships landing in San Pedro or Rotterdam are going to be as obsolete as the steam locomotive.

Peter Drucker consults on corporate management worldwide. This interview Copyright 1990 The Time Inc. Magazine Company. Reprinted by permission.

Q. How do you envision the new living patterns in the years ahead?

A. The city as we know it is obsolete. It is a 19th century product based on our 19th century ability to move people. Moving ideas and information then was more difficult, and the great inventions of the 19th century were the streetcar and the post office. Today we have an incredible ability to move ideas and information, but the movement of people is grinding to a standstill.

Q. And what happens to cities? Do they become ghost towns?

A. I don't think you can foretell the shape of the city of tomorrow, but what you can say is that the city of the 19th century reached its pinnacle, its apogee, in the 20th, in the 1980s, with an enormous building boom all over the world. This also happened in the great cathedral-building era a millennium ago. But nobody would build a monastery for 600 Benedictine monks anymore. I think we have seen the last outburst of the city as we know it.

Q. Then what will we do in the cities?

A. I don't know what the function of the city will be. Look, the medieval cathedral functioned more as a town cultural center, school and governmental center than as a church most of the year. Nobody lived in Chartres. I do not see our cities as ghost towns so much as a congeries of ghettos—the city is already becoming a place where only the very rich, the very young, and the very poor live. The middle class works in the city but doesn't live there. Those enormous central offices we have built in the post-World War II period are, I think, very largely going to be counterproductive. The clerical work will move out. Our largest single pool of labor in the years ahead will be older people and part-time employees, and they aren't going to commute four hours to work. This is soon going to be a problem all over the world.

Q. Do you think we and our institutions are ready to cope with what you call "new Realities?"

A. Many are still stuck in the world of 1960. What we face now is totally new and dynamic—and we are quite unprepared for it. ☐

Consumer Price Indexes

(1982-84 = 100)

Year	All items	En- ergy	Food	Shel- ter	Apparel[1]	Trans- porta- tion	Medical care	Fuel oil	Electric- ity	Utility (gas)	Tele- phone	Com- modi- ties
1960	29.6	22.4	30.0	25.2	45.7	29.8	22.3	13.5	29.9	17.6	58.3	33.6
1970	38.8	25.5	39.2	35.5	59.2	37.5	34.0	16.5	31.8	19.6	58.7	41.7
1975	53.8	42.1	59.8	48.8	72.5	50.1	47.5	34.9	50.0	31.1	71.7	58.2
1980	82.4	86.0	86.8	81.0	90.9	83.1	74.9	87.7	75.8	65.7	77.7	86.0
1987	113.6	88.6	113.5	121.3	110.6	105.4	130.1	75.8	110.0	95.1	116.5	107.7
1988	118.3	89.3	118.2	127.1	115.4	108.7	138.6	75.8	111.5	94.5	116.0	111.5

1. Includes upkeep. *Source: Statistical Abstract of the United States 1989.*

Consumer Price Index for All Urban Consumers

(1982-84 = 100)

Group	March 1990	March 1989	Group	March 1990	March 1989
All items	128.7	122.3	Fuel oil, coal, bottled gas	91.5	81.5
Food	131.5	123.5	House operation[1]	112.8	110.5
Alcoholic beverages	127.8	121.8	House furnishings	106.9	105.1
Apparel and upkeep	125.4	119.3	Transportation	116.8	111.9
Men's and boys' apparel	119.3	115.9	Medical care	158.7	146.1
Women's and girls' apparel	126.8	119.4	Personal care	129.0	123.6
Footwear	116.9	114.1	Tobacco products	175.1	159.2
Housing, total	126.8	121.5	Entertainment	130.9	124.7
Rent	136.5	131.1	Personal and educational		
Gas and electricity	107.9	104.8	expenses	166.3	154.6

1. Combines house furnishings and operation. *Source:* Department of Labor, Bureau of Labor Statistics.

Per Capita Personal Income

Year	Amount	Year	Amount	Year	Amount	Year	Amount	Year	Amount
1935	$474	1965	$2,773	1975	$5,851	1980	$9,910	1985	$13,896
1945	1,223	1970	3,893	1976	6,402	1981	10,949	1986	14,597
1950	1,501	1972	4,493	1977	7,043	1982	11,480	1987	15,471
1955	1,881	1973	4,980	1978	7,729	1983	12,098	1988	16,491
1960	2,219	1974	5,428	1979	8,638	1984	13,114	1989[1]	17,567

1. Preliminary. *Source:* Department of Commerce, Bureau of Economic Analysis.

Total Family Income
(figures in percent)

	White			Black			Hispanic[1]		
Income range	1988	1985	1975	1988	1985	1975	1988	1985	1975
Families (thousands)[2]	56,492	54,991	49,873	7,409	6,921	5,586	4,823	4,206	2,499
Under $5,000	3.0	3.3	2.2	11.9	11.6	6.9	8.4	7.0	5.6
$5,000 to $9,999	5.5	6.5	6.3	15.4	16.8	18.3	11.9	15.6	13.8
$10,000 to $14,999	8.1	8.5	8.8	13.6	12.8	14.7	13.6	14.0	14.9
$15,000 to $24,999	17.7	18.8	19.7	19.7	21.8	23.2	22.2	22.6	25.3
$25,000 to $34,999	17.4	18.2	20.5	13.4	14.4	16.4	16.5	16.5	19.4
$35,000 to $49,999	21.0	20.6	22.7	13.3	13.1	13.7	15.5	13.5	14.1
$50,000 to $74,999	17.6	16.0	14.3	9.3	7.6	5.8	8.3	8.6	5.4
$75,000 to $99,999	5.6	4.7	3.3	2.0	1.3	0.8	2.3	1.5	0.9
$100,000 and over	4.2	3.3	2.1	1.3	0.6	0.3	1.3	0.8	0.6
Median income	$33,915	$32,051	$31,374	$19,329	$18,455	$19,304	$21,769	$20,919	$21,002

1. Persons of Hispanic origin may be of any race. 2. As of March 1989. *Source:* Department of Commerce, Bureau of the Census.

Median Weekly Earnings of Full-Time Workers by Occupation and Sex

	Men		Women		Total	
Occupation	Number of workers (in thousands)	Median weekly earnings	Number of workers (in thousands)	Median weekly earnings	Number of workers (in thousands)	Median weekly earnings
Managerial and prof. specialty	12,419	$717	10,526	$491	22,945	$595
Executive, admin, and managerial	6,653	737	4,781	442	11,434	595
Professional specialty	5,766	696	5,745	493	11,511	594
Technical, sales, and admin. support	9,416	489	16,010	323	25,425	368
Technicians and related support	1,660	549	1,337	415	2,997	485
Sales occupations	4,614	491	3,487	287	8,102	393
Administrative support, incl. clerical	3,141	439	11,186	322	14,327	340
Service occupations	4,204	322	4,531	222	8,735	262
Private household	9	(1)	263	158	272	158
Protective service	1,494	468	233	442	1,727	463
Service, except private household and protective	2,701	274	4,034	223	6,735	240
Precision production, craft, and repair	10,378	480	915	313	11,293	466
Mechanics and repairers	3,674	475	176	396	3,851	471
Construction trades	3,743	465	67	(1)	3,810	462
Other precision production, craft, and repair	2,960	498	672	297	3,632	466
Operators, fabricators, and laborers	11,340	378	3,811	256	15,151	336
Machine operators, assemblers, and inspectors	4,487	393	2,914	253	7,401	323
Transportation and material moving occupations	3,887	417	202	307	4,090	412
Handlers, equipment cleaners, helpers, and laborers	2,965	304	695	257	3,661	295
Farming, forestry, and fishing	1,114	258	160	207	1,274	246

1. Data not shown where base is less than 100,000. NOTE: Figures are for the fourth quarter of 1989. *Source:* U.S. Department of Labor, Bureau of Labor Statistics, "Employment and Earnings," January 1990.

Consumer Credit
(installment credit outstanding; in billions of dollars, seasonally adjusted)

Holder	1989	1988	1987	1986	1985	1984	1980	1975
Commercial banks	343.9	324.8	287.2	266.8	245.1	211.6	147.0	82.9
Finance companies	140.8	146.2	141.1	134.7	111.9	89.9	62.2	32.7
Credit unions	90.9	88.3	81.0	77.1	72.7	66.1	44.0	25.7
Retailers[1]	42.6	48.3	46.0	43.3	42.9	40.9	28.7	18.2
Other[2]	61.2	67.1	64.4	59.9	53.8	40.9	20.1	9.2
Total[3]	727.6	674.7	619.8	581.8	526.5	449.5	302.1	168.7

1. Excludes 30-day charge credit held by retailers, oil and gas companies, and travel and entertainment companies. 2. Includes mutual savings banks, savings and loan associations, and gasoline companies. 3. Beginning 1989, outstanding balances of pools upon which securities have been issued; these balances are no longer on the balance sheets for the loan originators. Data are *not* available historically. *Source:* Federal Reserve Bulletin.

The Public Debt

Year	Gross debt Amount (in millions)	Per capita	Year	Gross debt Amount (in millions)	Per capita
1800 (Jan. 1)	$ 83	$ 15.87	1950	$256,087 [1]	$1,688.30
1860 (June 30)	65	2.06	1955	272,807 [1]	1,650.63
1865	2,678	75.01	1960	284,093 [1]	1,572.31
1900	1,263	16.60	1965	313,819 [1]	1,612.70
1920	24,299	228.23	1970	370,094 [1]	1,807.09
1925	20,516	177.12	1975	533,189	2,496.90
1930	16,185	131.51	1980	907,701	3,969.55
1935	28,701	225.55	1985	1,823,103	7,598.51
1940	42,968	325.23	1988	2,602,338	10,534.42
1945	258,682	1,848.60	1989	2,857,431	11,452.12

1. Adjusted to exclude issues to the International Monetary Fund and other international lending institutions to conform to the budget presentation. *Source:* Department of the Treasury, Financial Management Service.

Gross National Product or Expenditure[1]
(in billions)

Item	1989	1988	1987	1986	1985	1980	1970	1960	1950
Gross national product	$5,234.0	$4,880.6	$4,524.3	$4,231.6	$4,014.9	$2,732.0	$1,015.5	515.3	288.3
GNP in constant (1982) dollars	4,144.1	4,024.4	3,853.7	3,717.9	3,618.7	3,187.1	2,416.2	1,665.3	1,203.7
Personal consumption expenditures	3,471.1	3,235.1	3,010.8	2,797.4	2,629.0	1,732.6	640.0	330.7	192.1
Durable goods	473.2	455.2	421.0	406.0	372.2	219.3	85.7	43.5	30.8
Nondurable goods	1,123.4	1,052.3	998.1	942.0	911.2	681.4	270.3	153.2	98.2
Services	1,874.4	1,727.6	1,591.7	1,449.5	1,345.6	831.9	284.0	134.0	63.2
Gross private domestic investment	773.4	750.3	699.9	659.4	643.1	437.0	148.8	78.2	55.1
Residential structures	234.6	232.4	226.4	217.3	188.8	122.5	40.5	26.3	20.5
Nonresidential structures	511.7	487.2	444.3	435.2	442.9	322.8	105.2	48.8	27.8
Producers' durable equipment	366.7	346.8	307.3	299.5	303.0	n.a.	n.a.	n.a.	n.a.
Change in business inventories	27.1	30.6	29.3	6.9	11.3	−8.3	3.1	3.1	6.8
Net export of goods and services	−47.1	−73.7	−112.6	−97.4	−78.0	32.1	8.5	5.9	2.2
Government purchases	1,036.6	968.9	926.1	872.2	820.8	530.3	218.2	100.6	38.8
Federal	403.2	381.3	381.6	366.5	355.2	208.1	98.8	54.4	19.1
National defense	302.2	298.0	294.8	277.8	259.1	142.7	76.8	45.3	14.3
Other	101.1	83.3	86.8	88.7	96.1	65.4	22.0	9.1	4.8
State and local	633.4	587.6	544.5	505.7	465.6	322.2	119.4	46.1	19.8

1. Current dollars except as noted. NOTE: n.a. = not available. *Source:* Department of Commerce, Bureau of Economic Analysis.

Producer Price Indexes by Major Commodity Groups
(1982 = 100)

Commodity	1989	1988	1985	1980	1975	1970
All commodities	112.2	106.9	103.2	89.8	58.4	38.1
Farm products	110.7	104.9	95.1	102.9	77.0	45.8
Processed foods and feeds	117.8	112.7	103.5	95.9	72.6	44.6
Textile products and apparel	112.3	109.2	102.9	89.7	67.4	52.4
Hides, skins, and leather products	136.3	131.4	108.9	94.7	56.5	42.0
Fuels and related products and power	72.9	66.7	91.4	82.8	35.4	15.3
Chemicals and allied products	123.1	116.3	103.7	89.0	62.0	35.0
Rubber and plastic products	112.6	109.3	101.9	90.1	62.2	44.9
Lumber and wood products	126.7	118.9	106.6	101.5	62.1	39.9
Pulp, paper, and allied products	137.8	130.4	113.3	86.3	59.0	37.5
Metals and metal products	124.1	118.7	104.4	95.0	61.5	38.7
Machinery and equipment	117.4	113.2	107.2	86.0	57.9	40.0
Furniture and household durables	116.9	113.1	107.1	90.7	67.5	51.9
Nonmetallic mineral products	112.6	111.2	108.6	88.4	54.4	35.3
Transportation equipment	117.7	114.3	107.9	82.9	56.7	41.9
Miscellaneous products	n.a.	120.2	109.4	93.6	53.4	39.8

NOTE: n.a. = not available. *Source:* Department of Commerce, Bureau of Economic Analysis.

Weekly Earnings of Full-Time Women Workers

Major occupation group	1989 weekly earnings	% Men's weekly earnings
Managerial and professional specialty	$488	70.4
Executive, administrative, and managerial	458	65.6
Professional specialty	506	73.5
Technical, sales, and administrative support	317	66.0
Technicians and related support	403	74.9
Sales occupations	278	57.1
Administrative support, including clerical	316	75.1
Service occupations	218	71.2
Precision production, craft, and repair	311	66.3
Operators, fabricators, and laborers	252	68.9
Machine operators, assemblers, and inspectors	251	66.2
Transportation and material moving	307	75.2
Handlers, equipment cleaners, helpers, and laborers	241	81.1
Farming, forestry, and fishing	211	83.7
Total; all occupations	**328**	**70.1**

1. Median usual weekly earnings. Half the workers earn more and half the workers usually earn less each week. *Source:* U.S. Department of Labor, Bureau of Labor Statistics.

Median Family Income
(in current dollars)

Year	Income	Percent change	Year	Income	Percent change
1970	$ 9,867	—	1984	25,948	5.1
1975	13,719	—	1985	27,144	5.0
1980	21,023	6.9	1986	28,236	4.0
1981	22,388	6.5	1987	29,744	5.3
1982	23,433	4.7	1988	30,992	4.0
1983	24,580	4.9	1989	32,448	4.5

Source: U.S. Department of Labor, Bureau of Labor Statistics, *Employment and Earnings.*

Expenditures for New Plant and Equipment[1]
(in billions of dollars)

Year	Manufacturing	Transportation[2]	Total nonmanufacturing	Total
1950	$7.73	$2.87	$18.08	$25.81
1955	12.50	3.10	24.58	37.08
1960	16.36	3.54	32.63	48.99
1965	25.41	5.66	45.39	70.79
1970	36.99	7.17	69.16	106.15
1975	53.66	9.95	108.95	162.60
1980	112.33	16.60	202.15	314.47
1983	116.20	13.97	227.15	343.35
1984	138.82	16.52	260.16	398.99
1985	153.48	18.02	278.46	431.94
1986	142.69	18.80	284.54	427.23
1987	145.90	18.85	294.77	440.66
1988	166.32	21.34	317.17	483.48
1989	184.54	24.59	347.50	532.04

1. Data exclude agriculture. 2. Transportation is included in total nonmanufacturing. NOTE: This series was revised in June 1990. *Source:* Department of Commerce, Bureau of the Census.

New Housing Starts[1] and Mobile Homes Shipped
(in thousands)

Year	No. of units started	Year	No. of units started	Year	Mobile homes shipped
1900	189	1970	1,469	1965	216
1910	387	1975	1,171	1970	401
1920	247	1980	1,313	1975	213
1925	937	1981	1,100	1980	222
1930	330	1982	1,072	1982	240
1935	221	1983	1,712	1983	296
1940	603	1984	1,756	1984	295
1945	326	1985	1,745	1985	284
1950	1,952	1986	1,807	1986	244
1955	1,646	1987	1,623	1987	233
1960[1]	1,296	1988[2]	1,488	1988	218
1965	1,510	1989	1,376	1989	198

1. Prior to 1960, starts limited to nonfarm housing; from 1960 on, figures include farm housing. 2. As of 1988 data for housing starts no longer includes public housing starts and only includes private housing starts. *Sources:* Department of Commerce, Housing Construction Statistics, 1900–1965, and Construction Reports, Housing Starts, 1970–83, Manufactured Housing Institute, 1965–76; National Conference of States on Building Codes and Standards.

Life Insurance in Force
(in millions of dollars)

As of Dec. 31	Ordinary	Group	Industrial	Credit	Total
1915	$16,650	$100	$4,279	—	$21,029
1930	78,756	9,801	17,693	$ 73	106,413
1945	101,550	22,172	27,675	365	151,762
1950	149,071	47,793	33,415	3,844	234,168
1955	216,812	101,345	39,682	14,493	373,332
1960	341,881	175,903	39,563	29,101	586,448
1965	499,638	308,078	39,818	53,020	900,554
1970	734,730	551,357	38,644	77,392	1,402,123
1980	1,760,474	1,579,355	35,994	165,215	3,541,038
1985	3,247,289	2,561,595	28,250	215,973	6,053,107
1988	4,511,608	3,232,080	25,456	251,015	8,020,159
1989	4,939,964	3,469,498	24,446	260,107	8,694,015

Source: American Council of Life Insurance.

Farm Indexes
(1977 - 100)

Year	Prices paid by farmers[1]	Prices rec'd by farmers[2]	Ratio
1950	37	56	151
1955	40	51	128
1960	44	52	118
1965	49	54	115
1970	56	60	109
1975	90	101	113
1980	138	134	97
1985	162	128	79
1988	169	138	82
1989	177	147	83

1. Commodities, interest, and taxes and wage rates. 2. All crops and livestock. *Source:* Department of Agriculture, National Agricultural Statistics Service.

Estimated Annual Retail and Wholesale Sales by Kind of Business

(in millions of dollars)

Kind of business	1989	1988	Kind of business	1989	1988
Retail trade, total	1,733,654	1,650,005	Furniture and home furnishings	29,601	29,163
Building materials, hardware, garden supply, and mobile home dealers	93,018	91,206	Lumber and other construction materials	58,632	58,901
Automotive dealers	377,690	371,573	Electrical goods	111,228	101,578
Furniture, home furnishings, and equipment stores	90,016	85,395	Hardware, plumbing, heating, and supplies	43,419	42,903
General merchandise group stores	202,570	191,800	Machinery, equipment, supplies	262,167	225,408
Food stores	349,269	326,504	Scrap and waste materials	(s)	(s)
Gasoline service stations	115,534	107,906	Nondurable goods, total	888,234	826,743
Apparel and accessory stores	91,227	84,865	Total, (excluding farm-product raw materials)		
Eating and drinking places	173,527	165,511	Paper and paper products	50,741	46,554
Drug and proprietary stores	61,104	57,444	Drugs, drug proprietaries, and druggists' sundries	43,968	39,274
Liquor stores	20,009	19,605	Apparel, piece goods, & notions	57,989	51,862
Merchant wholesale trade, total	1,748,194	1,622,115	Groceries and related products	242,802	228,128
Total (excluding farm-product raw materials)			Beer, wine, distilled alcoholic beverages	42,201	42,055
Durable goods, total	859,960	795,372	Miscellaneous nondurable goods	136,124	130,714
Motor vehicles and automotive parts and supplies	164,975	164,538	Tobacco and tobacco products	(s)	(s)

NOTE: (S) = does not meet publication standards. *Source:* Department of Commerce, Bureau of the Census.

Shareholders in Public Corporations

Characteristic	1985	1983	1981	1980	1975	1970	1965
Individual shareholders (thousands)	47,040	42,360	32,260	30,200	25,270	30,850	20,120
Owners of shares listed on New York Stock Exchange (thousands)	25,263	26,029	25,504[1]	23,804	17,950	18,290	12,430
Adult shareowner incidence in population	1 in 4	1 in 4	1 in 5	1 in 5	1 in 6	1 in 4	1 in 6
Median household income	$36,800	$33,200	$29,200	$27,750	$19,000	$13,500	$9,500
Adult shareowners with household income: under $10,000 (thousands)	2,151	1,460	2,164	1,742	3,420	8,170	10,080
$10,000 and over (thousands)	40,999	36,261	26,913	25,715	19,970	20,130	8,410
Adult female shareowners (thousands)	22,509	20,385	14,154	13,696	11,750	14,290	9,430
Adult male shareowners (thousands)	22,484	19,226	15,785	14,196	11,630	14,340	9,060
Median age	44	45	46	46	53	48	49

NOTE: Latest figures available. 1. Adjusted. *Source:* New York Stock Exchange.

50 Most Active Stocks in 1989

Stock	Share volume	Stock	Share volume	Stock	Share volume
American Tel. & Tel. (1)	387,071,700	AMR Corporation	179,635,800	Pan Am Corporation	147,650,200
Int'l Business Machines (2)	336,983,600	Phillips Petroleum (20)	179,386,300	Boeing Company	146,857,900
Texaco Inc. (7)	305,679,500	McDonald's Corporation	176,981,004	Mobil Corporation (39)	146,270,200
General Electric (3)	304,873,400	BankAmerica Corporation	176,971,500	K mart Corporation	143,287,300
Exxon Corporation (6)	271,395,700	Upjohn Company (40)	173,497,500	SmithKline Beckman[3]	142,327,300
Union Carbide (11)	253,104,000	Chevron Corporation	173,086,700	Pacific Telesis	140,833,300
Morris (Philip) (31)	242,535,300	Unisys Corporation (41)	169,350,300	Navistar International (26)	140,506,500
Eastman Kodak (14)	231,648,700	Merck & Co.	163,051,600	Chase Manhattan Corporation	137,288,300
USX Corporation (36)	229,107,800	Paramount Communications[2]	159,325,400	Occidental Petroleum (4)	137,130,000
Ford Motor (10)	216,632,900	Baxter International (22)	156,295,600	Chrysler Corporation (37)	136,907,200
Warner Communications	216,349,000	Sears, Roebuck (23)	155,363,000	Avon Products	135,399,100
General Motors (17)	210,943,900	Digital Equipment (19)	155,241,400	Anheuser-Busch Companies	132,193,200
American Express (15)	206,478,600	Federal National Mortgage	153,035,600	PepsiCo, Inc.	131,995,000
Citicorp (29)	203,063,100	Dow Chemical (38)	151,642,800	Amoco Corporation	130,934,900
Texas Utilities (18)	190,561,200	Computer Associates International	150,448,800	Compaq Computer	130,523,200
Bristol-Myers Squibb[1]	190,060,300			Marion Merrell Dow[4]	130,299,900
Burlington Resources	181,194,700	Syntex Corporation	148,674,900	Coca-Cola Company (43)	129,779,000

NOTE: 1988 ranking in parentheses, if among top 50. 1. Formerly Bristol-Myers Co. 2. Formerly Gulf + Western. 3. Delisted in July. 4. Formerly Marion Laboratories. *Source:* New York Stock Exchange.

Geographic Distribution of Shareowners of Public Corporations
(in thousands)

State	1985	1983	1981	1980	State	1985	1983	1981	1980
Alabama	483	424	339	319	Montana	112	107	85	74
Alaska	160	114	77	88	Nebraska	286	255	207	193
Arizona	575	513	382	364	Nevada	168	156	118	109
Arkansas	311	246	200	178	New Hampshire	203	167	124	112
California	6,006	5,367	4,016	3,525	New Jersey	1,905	1,675	1,228	1,176
Colorado	695	598	445	407	New Mexico	221	183	154	133
Connecticut	946	835	611	560	New York	4,954	4,695	3,357	3,177
Delaware	142	122	89	87	North Carolina	963	822	660	639
D.C.	211	193	137	131	North Dakota	117	93	71	65
Florida	2,343	2,056	1,366	1,272	Ohio	1,939	1,884	1,513	1,466
Georgia	1,000	804	606	570	Oklahoma	515	452	345	285
Hawaii	256	234	174	175	Oregon	441	389	331	314
Idaho	158	136	101	98	Pennsylvania	2,139	2,071	1,615	1,521
Illinois	2,565	2,468	1,924	1,866	Rhode Island	206	188	138	130
Indiana	856	751	682	674	South Carolina	406	361	296	282
Iowa	442	427	361	357	South Dakota	103	91	70	69
Kansas	400	352	305	260	Tennessee	665	614	460	428
Kentucky	462	392	324	325	Texas	3,061	2,606	1,898	1,720
Louisiana	633	568	440	397	Utah	276	246	185	176
Maine	188	165	127	123	Vermont	92	86	62	57
Maryland	936	879	644	602	Virginia	1,204	987	739	678
Massachusetts	1,477	1,292	991	941	Washington	847	805	620	571
Michigan	1,786	1,672	1,385	1,349	West Virginia	257	251	209	209
Minnesota	794	681	544	514	Wisconsin	851	779	640	619
Mississippi	251	220	179	169	Wyoming	94	92	70	59
Missouri	939	796	616	587	**Total**	**47,040**	**42,360**	**32,260**	**30,200**

New York Stock Exchange Seat Sales for Cash, 1989

	Price				Price		
Month	High	Low	Number	Month	High	Low	Number
January	$640,000	625,000	2	July	$550,000	$515,000	2
February	650,000	—	1	August	—	—	0
March	675,000	600,000	3	September	525,000	500,000	2
April	550,000	—	1	October	500,000	436,000	5
May	530,000	500,000	4	November	470,000	440,000	2
June	550,000	—	1	December	430,000	420,000	5

NOTE: In addition, there were six private seat sales, ranging from a high of $650,000 and a low of $500,000; one EX—OTR sale for $525,000 and one EX—OTR private sale. *Source:* New York Stock Exchange.

Largest Businesses, 1989
(in millions of dollars)
Source: FORTUNE 500 and SERVICE 500 © 1990 The Time Inc. Magazine Company. All rights reserved.

50 LARGEST INDUSTRIAL CORPORATIONS

	Sales	Assets
General Motors	126,974.3	173,297.1
Ford Motor	96,932.6	160,893.3
Exxon	86,656.0	83,219.0
Int'l Business Machines	63,438.0	77,734.0
General Electric	55,264.0	128,344.0
Mobil	50,976.0	39,080.0
Philip Morris	39,069.0	38,528.0
Chrysler	36,156.0	51,038.0
E.I. Du Pont de Nemours	35,209.0	34,715.0
Texaco	32,416.0	25,636.0
Chevron	29,443.0	33,884.0
Amoco	24,214.0	30,430.0
Shell Oil	21,703.0	27,599.0
Procter & Gamble	21,689.0	16,351.0
Boeing	20,276.0	13,278.0
Occidental Petroleum	20,068.0	20,741.0
United Technologies	19,765.5	14,598.2
Eastman Kodak	18,398.0	23,652.0
USX	17,755.0	17,500.0
Dow Chemical	17,730.0	22,166.0
Xerox	17,635.0	30,088.0
Atlantic Richfield	15,905.0	22,261.0
Pepsico	15,419.6	15,126.7
RJR Nabisco Holdings	15,224.0	36,412.0
McDonnell Douglas	14,995.0	13,397.0
Tenneco	14,439.0	17,381.0
Digital Equipment	12,866.0	10,667.8
Westinghouse Electric	12,844.0	20,314.0
Rockwell International	12,633.1	8,938.8
Phillips Petroleum	12,492.0	11,256.0
Allied-Signal	12,021.0	10,132.0
Minnesota Mining & Mfg.	11,990.0	9,776.0
Hewlett-Packard	11,899.0	10,075.0
Sara Lee	11,738.3	6,522.7

International Paper	11,378.0	11,582.0
Conagra	11,340.4	4,278.2
Aluminum Co. of America	11,161.5	11,540.6
Caterpillar	11,126.0	10,926.0
Goodyear Tire & Rubber	11,044.7	8,460.3
Unocal	10,417.0	9,257.0
Georgia-Pacific	10,171.0	7,056.0
Weyerhaeuser	10,105.6	15,976.0
Unisys	10,096.9	10,751.0
General Dynamics	10,053.2	6,548.6
Lockheed	9,932.0	6,792.0
Sun	9,927.0	8,699.0
Johnson & Johnson	9,844.0	7,919.0
Motorola	9,620.0	7,686.0
Anheuser-Busch	9,481.3	9,025.7
Bristol-Myers Squibb	9,422.0	8,497.0

25 LARGEST RETAILING COMPANIES

	Sales	Assets
Sears Roebuck	53,912.9	86,971.6
K Mart	29,557.0	13,145.0
Wal-Mart Stores	25,921.8	8,198.5
American Stores	22,004.2	7,398.0
Kroger	19,087.8	4,242.0
J.C. Penney	16,405.0	12,698.0
Safeway Stores	14,324.6	4,538.0
Dayton Hudson	13,644.7	6,683.7
May Department Stores	12,043.0	7,802.0
Great Atlantic & Pacific Tea	10,072.7	2,640.4
Winn-Dixie Stores	9,151.1	1,575.1
Woolworth	8,820.0	3,907.0
Southland	8,421.3	3,438.8
Melville	7,554.0	3,031.8
Albertson's	7,422.7	1,862.7
R.H. Macy	6,974.1	6,560.7
Supermarkets General Hold.	6,298.7	2,556.5
McDonald's	6,142.0	9,175.0
Walgreen	5,395.5	1,681.1
Publix Super Markets	5,386.2	1,307.2
Vons Cos.	5,222.2	1,654.6
Price	5,033.4	1,116.8
Federated Department Stores	4,867.2	6,572.2
Toys "R" US	4,787.8	3,074.7
Food Lion	4,717.1	1,281.7

10 LARGEST TRANSPORTATION COMPANIES

	Operating revenues	Assets
United Parcel Service	12,380.7	7,888.1
AMR	10,589.5	10,877.4
UAL	9,914.5	7,206.7
Delta Air Lines	8,089.5	6,484.0
CSX	7,821.0	12,298.0
Texas Air	6,768.7	7,656.1
Union Pacific	6,590.0	12,459.0
NWA	6,553.8	5,337.4
USAir Group	6,257.3	6,069.0
Federal Express	5,183.3	5,293.4

10 LARGEST DIVERSIFIED FINANCIAL COMPANIES

	Assets	Revenues
American Express	130,855.0	25,047.0
Federal Nat'l Mortgage Ass'n	124,314.8	11,497.0
Salomon	118,250.0	8,999.0
Aetna Life & Casualty	87,099.0	19,671.4
Merrill Lynch	63,942.3	11,855.4
CIGNA	57,779.0	15,654.0
Travelers	56,563.0	12,523.0
Morgan Stanley Group	53,275.5	5,831.0
American International Group	46,142.9	14,150.0

10 LARGEST LIFE INSURANCE COMPANIES

	Assets	Premium and annuity income
Prudential of America	129,118.1	21,535.2
Metropolitan Life	98,740.3	15,183.1
Equitable Life Assurance	52,511.9	4,620.1
AETNA Life	52,022.6	8,642.6
Teachers Insurance & Annuity	44,374.1	3,198.0
New York Life	37,302.4	6,428.1
Connecticut General Life	33,991.2	2,513.6
Travelers	32,087.5	5,169.3
John Hancock Mutual Life	30,924.8	6,017.6
Northwestern Mutual Life	28,500.0	3,751.9

10 LARGEST COMMERCIAL BANKS

	Assets	Deposits
Citicorp	230,643.0	137,922.0
Chase Manhattan Corp.	107,369.0	69,073.0
BankAmerica Corp.	98,764.0	81,186.0
J.P. Morgan & Co.	88,964.0	39,158.0
Security Pacific Corp.	83,943.0	52,630.0
Chemical Banking Corp.	71,513.0	50,151.0
NCNB Corp.	66,190.8	48,576.3
Manufacturers Hanover Corp.	60,479.0	41,994.0
First Interstate Bancorp	59,051.4	46,467.7
Bankers Trust New York Corp.	55,658.4	26,220.1

10 LARGEST UTILITIES

	Assets	Operating revenues
GTE	31,986.5	17,541.4
Bellsouth	30,049.8	13,996.3
Bell Atlantic	26,219.7	11,448.6
NYNEX	25,909.0	13,210.6
US West	25,425.9	9,690.6
Pacific Gas & Electric	21,352.0	8,719.5
Pacific Telesis Group	21,194.0	9,593.0
Southwestern Bell	21,160.5	8,729.8
Southern	20,086.0	7,520.0
American Information Tech.	19,833.0	10,211.3

New Business Concerns and Business Failures

Formations and Failures	1988[1]	1987	1986	1985	1984	1983	1982	1980
Business formations								
Index, net formations (1967 = 100)	124.1	121.2	120.4	120.9	121.3	117.5	116.4	129.9
New Incorporations (1,000)	68.2	68.5	702	663	635	602	566	534
Failures, number (1,000)	57.1	61.2	61.6	57.1	52.0	31.3	24.9	11.7
Rate per 10,000 concerns	98	102	120	115	107	110	88	42

1. Preliminary. *Sources:* U.S. Bureau of Economic Analysis and Dun & Bradstreet Corporation.

50 Leading Stocks in Market Value

Stock	Market value (millions)	Listed shares (millions)	Stock	Market value (millions)	Listed shares (millions)
Exxon Corp.	$90,862	1,812.7	Southwestern Bell	19,219	300.9
General Electric	59,760	926.5	Minnesota Mining & Manufacturing	18,792	236.0
International Business Machines	54,679	579.4	NYNEX Corp.	18,617	204.6
American Telephone & Telegraph	48,953	1,075.9	PepsiCo, Inc.	18,402	287.5
Morris (Philip)	39,032	934.9	American Home Products	18,142	168.8
Merck & Co.	35,303	455.5	American Int'l Group	17,971	173.6
Coca-Cola Co.	32,317	418.3	Texaco Inc.	16,183	274.3
Bristol-Myers Squibb	29,280	522.9	Waste Management	16,104	460.1
du Pont de Nemours	28,318	230.2	U S WEST	15,482	193.2
BellSouth Corporation	28,139	486.2	Eastman Kodak	15,363	373.6
Amoco Corp.	28,088	514.2	Abbott Laboratories	15,321	225.3
Mobil Corporation	27,296	435.9	Disney (Walt)	15,266	136.3
General Motors	26,546	628.3	Schlumberger Ltd.	14,908	303.5
Wal-Mart Stores	25,256	566.0	American Express	14,653	420.1
GTE Corp.	24,615	351.6	Sears, Roebuck	14,628	384.9
Atlantic Richfield	24,286	217.6	McDonald's Corp.	14,514	417.7
Procter & Gamble	23,953	340.4	Royal Dutch Petroleum	14,334	185.5
Dow Chemical	23,267	327.1	Boeing Co.	13,796	232.9
Chevron Corp.	23,178	342.1	Westinghouse Electric	13,623	184.1
Johnson & Johnson	22,780	383.7	Anheuser-Busch	12,844	333.6
Bell Atlantic	22,222	199.7	Berkshire Hathaway	11,930	1.4
Pacific Telesis	21,804	432.8	Warner Communications	11,839	185.4
American Information Technologies (Ameritech)	19,979	293.8	BCE Inc.	11,815	301.0
			Seagrams Co.	11,780	128.7
Ford Motor	19,726	452.2	Pfizer Inc.	11,498	165.4
Eli Lilly	19,307	282.9	**Total**	**$1,175,970**	**19,489.2**

NOTE: As of Dec. 31, 1989. *Source:* New York Stock Exchange.

Top 50 Banks in the World

Bank	Country	Deposits (U.S. dollars)	Bank	Country	Deposits (U.S. dollars)
Dai-Ichi Kangyo Bank Ltd., Tokyo	Japan	403,386,126,193 [1]	Swiss Bank Corp., Basle	Switzerland	123,539,256,000 [1]
Sumitomo Bank Ltd., Osaka	Japan	368,167,430,610 [1]	Toyo Trust & Banking Co. Ltd., Toyo	Japan	117,492,324,355 [2]
Fuji Bank, Ltd., Tokyo	Japan	362,575,295,833 [1]	Union Bank of Switzerland, Zurich	Switzerland	114,096,403,656 [2]
Mitsubishi Bank Ltd., Tokyo	Japan	359,960,178,697 [1]	Nippon Credit Bank, Ltd., Tokyo	Japan	113,890,048,045 [1]
Sanwa Bank Ltd., Osaka	Japan	353,692,139,934 [1]	Commerzbank, Frankfurt	Germany	113,016,860,000 [1]
Industrial Bank of Japan, Ltd., Tokyo	Japan	256,905,555,665 [1]	Deutsche Genossenschaftsbank, Frankfurt	Germany	109,354,031,874 [1]
Credit Agricole Mutuel, Paris	France	242,311,948,300 [1]	Istituto Bancario San Paolo di Torino, Turin	Italy	107,663,678,274 [1]
Banque Nationale de Paris	France	231,769,484,000 [1]	Banco do Brasil, Brasilia	Brazil	105,195,166,384 [2]
Tokai Bank Ltd., Nagoya	Japan	227,738,519,511 [1]	Banca Nazionale del Lavoro, Rome	Italy	104,489,637,000 [1]
Norinchukin Bank, Tokyo	Japan	219,773,041,914	Westdeutsche Landesbank Girozen-trale, Duesseldorf	Germany	104,324,980,000 [1]
Mitsubishi Trust & Banking Corp., Tokyo	Japan	213,485,098,466 [2]	Bayerische Vereinsbank, Munich	Germany	102,306,000,000 [1]
Credit Lyonnais, Paris	France	211,005,505,000 [1]	Midland Bank Plc, London	United Kingdom	100,591,190,000 [1]
Barclays Bank Plc, London	United Kingdom	205,461,760,000 [1]	Saitama Bank Ltd., Urawa	Japan	98,665,555,088 [1]
Mitsui Bank, Ltd., Tokyo	Japan	203,291,465,903 [1]	Kyowa Bank, Ltd., Tokyo	Japan	97,910,617,239 [1]
Deutsche Bank, Frankfurt	Germany	202,607,135,750 [1]	Amsterdam-Rotterdam Bank, Amsterdam	Netherlands	94,173,280,000 [1]
Bank of Tokyo, Ltd.	Japan	200,547,845,630 [1]	Lloyds Bank Plc, London	United Kingdom	92,642,620,000 [1]
Sumitomo Trust & Banking Co., Ltd., Osaka	Japan	190,943,020,692 [2]	Algemene Bank Nederland, Amsterdam	Netherlands	90,747,368,000 [1]
National Westminster Bank Plc, London	United Kingdom	187,064,290,000 [1]	Rabobank Nederland, Utrecht	Netherlands	90,352,796,000 [1]
Mitsui Trust & Banking Co., Ltd., Tokyo	Japan	182,629,635,615 [2]	Bayerische Hypotheken-und Wechsel-Bank, Munich	Germany	89,902,700,011 [1]
Societe Generale, Paris	France	176,019,715,000 [1]	Credit Suisse, Zurich	Switzerland	89,115,552,000 [1]
Long-Term Credit Bank of Japan, Ltd., Tokyo	Japan	174,240,317,152 [2]	Banca Commerciale Italiana, Milan	Italy	88,809,129,900 [1]
Taiyo Kobe Bank, Ltd., Kobe	Japan	172,977,970,205 [2]	Royal Bank of Canada, Montreal	Canada	88,573,064,592 [1]
Yasuda Trust & Banking Co. Ltd., Tokyo	Japan	157,813,185,014 [1]	Bank of America NT&SA, San Francisco	United States	85,340,000,000
Citibank NA, New York	United States	157,772,000,000			
Daiwa Bank, Ltd., Osaka	Japan	155,494,965,279 [2]			
Dresdner Bank, Frankfurt	Germany	145,666,029,692 [1]			
Hongkong and Shanghai Banking Corp., Hong Kong	Hong Kong	132,835,072,000 [1]			

NOTE: As of Dec. 31, 1989. 1. Consolidated data. 2. Data are not consolidated for affiliates more than 50% owned. *Source:* American Banker, July 26, 1990. Reprinted by permission of American Banker/Bond Buyer.

National Labor Organizations With Membership Over 100,000

Members[1]	Union
943,582	Automobile, Aerospace and Agricultural Implement Workers of America, International Union, United
135,000	Bakery, Confectionery, and Tobacco Workers International Union
105,000	Boilermakers, Iron Ship Builders, Blacksmiths, Forgers and Helpers, International Brotherhood of
106,275	Bricklayers and Allied Craftsmen, International Union of
140,000	Bridge, Structural and Ornamental Iron Workers, International Association of
609,000	Carpenters and Joiners of America, United Brotherhood of
272,000	Clothing and Textile Workers Union, Amalgamated
700,000	Communications Workers of America
2,000,000	Education Association, National (Ind.)
845,000	Electrical Workers, International Brotherhood of
180,000	Electronic, Electrical, Salaried, Machine and Furniture Workers, International Union of
180,000	Fire Fighters, International Association of
1,235,000	Food and Commercial Workers International Union, United
210,000	Government Employees, American Federation of
185,585	Graphic Communications International Union
301,300	Hotel Employees and Restaurant Employees International Union
570,000	Laborers' International Union of North America
175,000	Ladies' Garment Workers' Union, International
315,000	Letter Carriers, National Association of
767,000	Machinists and Aerospace Workers, International Association of
171,000	Mine Workers of America, United (Ind.)
197,000	Nurses' Association, American (Ind.)
125,000	Office and Professional Employees International Union
100,000	Oil, Chemical and Atomic Workers International Union
360,000	Operating Engineers, International Union of
133,000	Painters and Allied Trades of the United States and Canada, International Brotherhood of*
232,000	Paper Workers International Union, United
325,000	Plumbing and Pipe Fitting Industry of the United States and Canada, United Association of Journeymen and Apprentices of the*
330,000	Postal Workers Union, American
180,000	Retail, Wholesale, and Department Store Union
100,000	Rubber, Cork, Linoleum, and Plastic Workers of America, United
925,000	Service Employees International Union
147,000	Sheet Metal Workers' International Association
1,250,000	State, County and Municipal Employees of America, American Federation of
655,000	Steelworkers of America, United
715,000	Teachers, American Federation of
1,700,000	Teamsters, Chauffeurs, Warehousemen and Helpers of America, International Brotherhood of
165,000	Transit Union, Amalgamated
200,000	Transportation ● Communications International Union
100,000	Transportation Union, United

*Did not reply. NOTE: Figures are most recent available.

Persons in the Labor Force

Year	Labor force[1] Number (thousands)	% working-age population	Percent of labor force in[2] Farm occupation	Nonfarm occupation	Year	Labor force[1] Number (thousands)	% working-age population	Percent of labor force in[2] Farm occupation	Nonfarm occupation
1830	3,932	45.5	70.5	29.5	1910	37,371	52.2	31.0	69.0
1840	5,420	46.6	68.6	31.4	1920	42,434	51.3	27.0	73.0
1850	7,697	46.8	63.7	36.3	1930	48,830	49.5	21.4	78.6
1860	10,533	47.0	58.9	41.1	1940	52,789	52.2	17.4	82.6
1870	12,925	45.8	53.0	47.0	1950	60,054	53.5	11.6	88.4
1880	17,392	47.3	49.4	50.6	1960	69,877	55.3	6.0	94.0
1890	23,318	49.2	42.6	57.4	1970	82,049	58.2	3.1	96.9
1900	29,073	50.2	37.5	62.5	1980	106,085	62.0	2.2	97.8

1. For 1830 to 1930, the data relate to the population and gainful workers at ages 10 and over. For 1940 to 1960, the data relate to the population and labor force at ages 14 and over; for 1970 and 1980, the data relate to the population and labor force at age 16 and over. For 1940 to 1980, the data include the Armed Forces. 2. The farm and nonfarm percentages relate only to the experienced civilian labor force. *Source:* Department of Commerce, Bureau of the Census.

Corporate Profits[1]
(in billions of dollars)

Item	1990[2]	1989	1988	1987	1985	1980	1975	1970
Domestic industries	237.9	253.5	285.0	222.3	190.8	161.9	107.6	62.4
Financial	26.2	27.3	35.7	30.1	21.0	26.9	11.8	12.1
Nonfinancial	211.7	226.2	249.3	192.1	169.7	134.9	95.8	50.2
Manufacturing	80.5	86.9	98.4	96.8	73.0	72.9	52.6	26.6
Wholesale and retail trade	38.4	39.1	40.1	42.8	49.7	23.6	21.3	9.5
Other	40.2	36.0	36.0	17.6	14.0	38.4	21.9	14.1
Rest of world	51.8	47.8	43.7	36.4	31.8	29.9	13.0	6.5
Total	289.7	301.3	328.6	258.7	222.6	191.7	120.6	68.9

1. Corporate profits with inventory valuation adjustment. 2. Preliminary. *Source:* U.S. Bureau of Economic Analysis, *Survey of Current Business.*

National Income by Type
(in billions of dollars)

Type of share	1989	1988	1985	1980	1975	1970	1965	1960	1950
National income	$4,266.5	$3,968.4	$3,222.3	$2,121.4	$1,215.0	$800.5	$564.3	$414.5	$241.1
Compensation of employees	3,144.4	2,904.7	2,368.2	1,596.5	931.1	603.9	393.8	294.2	154.6
Wages and salaries	2,631.1	2,436.9	1,965.8	1,343.6	805.9	542.0	358.9	270.8	146.8
Supplements to wages and salaries	513.3	467.8	402.4	252.9	125.2	61.9	35.0	23.4	7.8
Proprietors' income[1][2]	352.1	324.5	254.4	130.6	87.0	66.9	57.3	46.2	37.5
Business and professional	305.9	288.2	225.2	107.2	63.5	50.0	42.4	34.2	24.0
Farm	46.2	36.3	29.2	23.4	23.5	16.9	14.8	12.0	13.5
Rental income of persons	7.9[1]	19.3[1]	7.6[1]	31.8	22.4	23.9	19.0	15.8	9.4
Corporate profits[1][2]	272.0	328.4	280.7	182.7	95.9	69.4	76.1	49.9	37.7
Net interest	460.8	391.5	311.4	179.8	78.6	36.4	18.2	8.4	2.0

1. Includes capital consumption adjustment. 2. Includes inventory valuation adjustment. *Source:* Department of Commerce, Bureau of Economic Analysis.

Per Capita Personal Income by States

State	1989[1]	1988	1987	1980	State	1989[1]	1988	1987	1980
Alabama	$13,679	$12,845	$12,038	$7,465	Montana	$13,852	$12,896	$12,330	$8,342
Alaska	21,173	19,042	18,438	13,007	Nebraska	15,360	14,783	14,123	8,895
Arizona	15,881	15,000	14,340	8,854	Nevada	18,827	17,521	16,374	10,848
Arkansas	12,984	12,212	11,431	7,113	New Hampshire	20,251	19,230	17,933	9,150
California	19,740	18,757	17,773	11,021	New Jersey	23,764	22,146	20,343	10,966
Colorado	17,494	16,465	15,678	10,143	New Mexico	13,191	12,469	11,892	7,940
Connecticut	24,604	23,039	21,256	11,532	New York	20,540	19,261	17,921	10,179
Delaware	19,116	17,693	16,433	10,059	North Carolina	15,221	14,293	13,327	7,780
D.C.	23,436	21,471	19,498	12,251	North Dakota	13,261	12,764	12,829	8,642
Florida	17,694	16,603	15,591	9,246	Ohio	16,499	15,530	14,579	9,399
Georgia	16,188	15,273	14,382	8,021	Oklahoma	14,151	13,355	12,569	9,018
Hawaii	18,306	16,775	15,557	10,129	Oregon	15,785	14,876	13,890	9,309
Idaho	13,762	12,596	11,790	8,105	Pennsylvania	17,422	16,224	15,182	9,353
Illinois	18,858	17,588	16,396	10,454	Rhode Island	18,061	16,846	15,649	9,227
Indiana	16,005	14,856	13,937	8,914	South Carolina	13,616	12,934	12,074	7,392
Iowa	15,524	14,680	14,014	9,226	South Dakota	13,244	12,741	12,401	7,800
Kansas	16,182	15,736	15,085	9,880	Tennessee	14,765	13,859	12,962	7,711
Kentucky	13,777	12,830	12,008	7,679	Texas	15,483	14,592	13,843	9,439
Louisiana	13,041	12,298	11,509	8,412	Utah	13,027	12,180	11,521	7,671
Maine	16,310	15,088	13,988	7,760	Vermont	16,399	15,303	14,280	7,957
Maryland	21,020	19,565	18,242	10,394	Virginia	18,970	17,671	16,544	9,413
Massachusetts	22,196	20,834	19,153	10,103	Washington	17,640	16,452	15,633	10,256
Michigan	17,745	16,544	15,544	9,801	West Virginia	12,529	11,696	11,001	7,764
Minnesota	17,746	16,649	15,784	9,673	Wisconsin	16,759	15,625	14,762	9,364
Mississippi	11,835	11,123	10,318	6,573	Wyoming	14,135	13,634	12,865	11,018
Missouri	16,431	15,458	14,630	8,812	United States	17,567	16,491	15,471	9,494

1. Preliminary. *Source:* U.S. Department of Commerce, Bureau of Economic Analysis, *Survey of Current Business.*

The Federal Budget—Receipts and Outlays
(in billions of dollars)

Description	1991[1]	1990[1]	1989	Description	1991[1]	1990[1]	1989
RECEIPTS BY SOURCE				Commerce & housing credit	17.8	20.3	27.7
Individual income taxes	528.5	489.4	445.7	Transportation	30.7	29.2	27.6
Corporate income taxes	129.7	112.0	103.6	Community development	8.1	8.8	5.4
Social insurance taxes				Education	40.6	37.6	36.7
and contributions	421.4	385.4	359.4	Health	64.4	57.8	48.4
Excise taxes	37.6	36.2	34.1	Medicare	104.2	96.6	85.0
Estate and gift taxes	9.8	9.3	8.7	Income security	140.8	146.6	136.0
Customs duties	18.6	16.8	16.3	Social security	264.7	248.5	232.5
Miscellaneous receipts	24.6	24.4	22.8	Veterans benefits	30.6	28.9	30.1
Total budget receipts	**1,170.2**	**1,073.5**	**990.7**	Administration of justice	12.8	10.5	9.4
OUTLAYS BY FUNCTION				General government	11.0	10.6	9.1
National Defense	306.5	296.4	303.6	Net interest	173.7	175.6	169.1
International affairs	17.9	14.6	9.6	Allowances	0.1	—	—
Gen. science	15.2	14.1	12.8	Undistributed receipts	−38.4	−36.5	−37.2
Energy	4.6	3.2	3.7	**Total outlays**	**1,241.0**	**1,194.8**	**1,142.6**
Natural resources	18.1	17.5	16.2	**Total deficit**	**−70.8**	**−121.3**	**−151.9**
Agriculture	17.6	14.6	16.9				

1. Estimated. NOTE: The fiscal year is from Oct. 1 to Sept. 30. *Source:* Executive Office of the President, Office of Management and Budget.

Foreign Assistance
(in millions of dollars)

	Non-military programs			Military programs		
Calendar years	Net new grants	Net new credits	Net other assistance	Net grants	Net credits	Total net assistance[1]
1945–1950[2]	$18,413	$8,086	—	$ 1,525	—	$28,023
1956–60	8,291	1,462	2,226	13,269	42	25,290
1966–70	8,808	9,238	−564	13,296	192	30,970
1971–75	12,939	5,479	−725	16,940	2,044	36,677
1976–80	14,277	10,919	−286	5,662	6,959	37,531
1981-1985	29,025	7,071	−2	9,295	10,836	56,226
1986	7,898	302	5	4,125	1,212	13,543
1987	7,408	−2,657	−27	3,131	334	8,189
1988	7,469	195	−36	3,576	−4,205	6,999
1989	7,552	−296	−9	3,411	−1,924	8,733
Total postwar period	**141,923**	**45,885**	**1,699**	**95,811**	**15,482**	**300,800**

1. Excludes investment in international nonmonetary financial institutions of $19,622 million. 2. Includes transactions after V-J Day (Sept. 2, 1945). NOTE: Detail may not add to total due to rounding. *Source:* Department of Commerce, Bureau of Economic Analysis.

Women in the Civilian Labor Force
(16 years of age and over; in thousands)

Labor force status	1989	1988	1987	1986	1985	1984
In the labor force:	56,030	54,742	53,658	52,413	51,050	49,709
16 to 19 years of age	3,818	3,872	3,875	3,824	3,767	3,810
20 years and over	52,212	50,870	49,783	48,589	47,283	45,900
Employed	53,027	51,696	50,334	48,706	47,259	45,915
16 to 19 years of age	3,282	3,313	3,260	3,149	3,105	3,122
20 years and over	49,745	48,383	47,075	45,557	44,154	42,793
Unemployed	3,003	3,046	3,324	3,707	3,791	3,794
16 to 19 years of age	536	558	616	675	661	687
20 years and over	2,467	2,488	2,709	3,032	3,129	3,107
Not in the labor force:	41,601	42,014	42,195	42,376	42,686	43,068
Women as percent of labor force	45.2	45.0	44.8	44.5	44.2	43.8
Total civilian noninstitutional population	97,630	96,756	95,853	94,789	93,736	92,778

Source: Department of Labor, Bureau of Labor Statistics, annual averages.

Employed Persons 16 Years and Over, by Race and Major Occupational Groups
(number in thousands)

	1989		1988	
Race and occupational group	Number	Percent distri- bution	Number	Percent distri- bution
WHITE				
Managerial and professional specialty	27,459	27.0	26,408	26.5
Executive, administrative, & managerial	13,555	13.3	13,022	13.0
Professional specialty	13,903	13.7	13,386	13.4
Technical, sales, & administrative support	31,619	31.1	31,178	31.2
Technicians & related support	3,125	3.1	3,019	3.0
Sales occupations	12,741	12.5	12,495	12.5
Administrative support, including clerical	15,752	15.5	15,664	15.7
Service occupations	12,237	12.0	12,105	12.1
Precision production, craft, and repair	12,369	12.2	12,305	12.3
Operators, fabricators, and laborers	14,752	14.5	14,665	14.7
Farming, forestry, fishing	3,149	3.1	3,150	3.2
Total	**101,584**	**100.0**	**99,812**	**100.0**
BLACK				
Managerial and professional specialty	1,862	15.6	1,794	15.4
Executive, administrative, & managerial	840	7.0	789	6.8
Professional specialty	1,022	8.5	1,005	8.6
Technical, sales, & administrative support	3,346	28.0	3,239	27.8
Technicians & related support	347	2.9	329	2.8
Sales occupations	906	7.6	839	7.2
Administrative support, including clerical	2,094	17.5	2,071	17.8
Service occupations	2,731	22.9	2,698	23.1
Precision production, craft, and repair	1,089	9.1	1,029	8.8
Operators, fabricators, and laborers	2,714	22.7	2,672	22.9
Farming, forestry, and fishing	210	1.8	226	1.9
Total	**11,953**	**100.0**	**11,658**	**100.0**

Source: Department of Labor, Bureau of Labor Statistics.

Mothers Participating in Labor Force
(figures in percentage)

	Mothers with children		
Year	Under 18 years	6 to 17 years	Under 6 years[1]
1955	27.0	38.4	18.2
1965	35.0	45.7	25.3
1975	47.4	54.8	38.9
1980	56.6	64.4	46.6
1981	58.1	65.5	48.9
1982	58.5	65.8	49.9
1983	58.9	66.3	50.5
1984	60.5	68.2	52.1
1985	62.1	69.9	53.5
1986	62.8	70.4	54.4
1987	64.7	72.0	56.7
1988	65.0	73.3	56.1

1. May also have older children. NOTE: For 1950 and 1955 data are for April; for 1965 and 1975–88, data are for March. *Source:* Department of Labor, Bureau of Labor Statistics. NOTE: Data are most recent available.

Women in the Labor Force

Year	Number[1] (thousands)	% Female population aged 16 and over[1]	% of Labor force population aged 16 and over[1]
1900	5,319	18.8	18.3
1910	7,445	21.5	19.9
1920	8,637	21.4	20.4
1930	10,752	22.0	22.0
1940	12,845	25.4	24.3
1950	18,408	33.9	29.0
1960[2]	23,268	37.8	32.5
1970	31,580	43.4	37.2
1980	45,611	51.6	42.0
1987	53,818	56.1	44.3
1988	54,904	56.6	44.5
1989	56,198	57.5	44.8

1. For 1900–1930, data relate to population and labor force aged 10 and over; for 1940, to population and labor force aged 14 and over; beginning 1950, to population and labor force aged 16 and over. 2. Beginning in 1960, figures include Alaska and Hawaii. *Sources:* Department of Commerce, Bureau of the Census, and Department of Labor, Bureau of Labor Statistics.

Persons Below the Poverty Level, 1960-1988

(in thousands)

Year	All persons	White	Black	Spanish origin[1]	Year	All persons	White	Black	Spanish origin[1]
1960	39,851	28,309	—	—	1979	26,072	17,214	8,050	2,921
1970	25,420	17,484	7,548	—	1980	29,272	19,699	8,579	3,491
1971	25,559	17,780	7,396	—	1981	31,822	21,553	9,173	3,713
1972	24,460	16,203	7,710	—	1982	34,398	23,517	9,697	4,301
1973	22,973	15,142	7,388	2,366	1983	35,303	23,984	9,882	4,633
1974	23,370	15,736	7,182	2,575	1984	33,700	22,955	9,490	4,806
1975	25,877	17,770	7,545	2,991	1985	33,064	22,860	8,926	5,236
1976	24,975	16,713	7,595	2,783	1986	32,370	22,183	8,983	5,117
1977	24,720	16,416	7,726	2,700	1987	32,546	21,409	9,683	5,470
1978	24,497	16,259	7,625	2,607	1988	63,743	51,202	9,864	7,003

1. Persons of Spanish origin may be of any race. *Source:* U.S. Department of Commerce, Bureau of the Census.

Manufacturing Industries—Gross Average Weekly Earnings and Hours Worked

Industry	1989 Earnings	1989 Hours worked	1988 Earnings	1988 Hours worked	1985 Earnings	1985 Hours worked	1980 Earnings	1980 Hours worked	1975 Earnings	1975 Hours worked	1970 Earnings	1970 Hours worked
All manufacturing	$429.27	41.0	$417.99	41.1	$385.56	40.5	$288.62	39.7	$189.51	39.4	$133.73	39.8
Durable goods	457.60	41.6	447.26	41.8	415.71	41.2	310.78	40.1	205.09	39.9	143.07	40.3
Primary metal industries	531.48	43.0	529.74	43.6	484.72	41.5	391.78	40.1	246.80	40.0	159.17	40.5
Iron and steel foundries	474.99	42.6	478.73	43.6	429.62	40.8	328.00	40.0	220.99	40.4	151.03	40.6
Nonferrous foundries	406.70	41.5	403.50	41.9	388.74	41.8	291.27	39.9	190.03	39.1	138.16	39.7
Fabricated metal products	438.05	41.6	428.03	41.8	398.96	41.3	300.98	40.4	201.60	40.0	143.67	40.7
Hardware, cutlery, hand tools	429.08	41.1	421.64	41.5	396.42	40.7	275.89	39.3	187.07	39.3	132.33	40.1
Other hardware	440.37	40.7	437.60	41.4	385.40	41.3	195.42	39.4	133.46	40.2		
Structural metal products	408.70	41.2	391.41	40.9	369.00	41.0	291.85	40.2	202.61	40.2	142.61	40.4
Electric and electronic equipment	423.50	40.8	415.33	41.0	384.48	40.6	276.21	39.8	180.91	39.5	130.54	39.8
Machinery, except electrical	480.82	42.4	467.32	42.6	427.04	41.5	328.00	41.0	219.22	40.9	154.95	41.1
Transportation equipment	580.88	42.4	570.47	42.7	542.72	42.7	379.61	40.6	242.61	40.3	163.22	40.3
Motor vehicles and equipment	615.47	43.1	612.05	43.5	584.64	43.5	394.00	40.0	262.68	40.6	170.07	40.3
Lumber and wood products	355.29	40.1	346.58	40.3	326.36	39.8	252.18	38.5	167.35	39.1	117.51	39.7
Furniture and fixtures	325.88	39.5	312.05	39.4	283.29	39.4	209.17	38.1	142.13	37.9	108.58	39.2
Nondurable goods	391.55	40.2	378.68	40.2	342.86	39.5	255.45	39.0	168.78	38.8	120.43	39.1
Textile mill products	314.88	41.0	302.91	41.1	266.39	39.7	203.31	40.1	133.28	39.2	97.76	39.9
Apparel and other textile products	234.95	37.0	225.09	36.9	208.00	36.3	161.42	35.4	111.97	35.1	84.37	35.3
Leather and leather products	249.38	37.9	235.50	37.5	217.09	37.3	169.09	36.7	120.80	37.4	92.63	37.2
Food and kindred products	379.73	40.7	368.04	40.4	341.60	40.0	271.95	39.7	184.17	40.3	127.98	40.5
Tobacco manufactures	593.28	38.6	579.49	39.8	448.26	37.2	294.89	38.1	171.38	38.0	110.00	37.8
Paper and allied products	516.57	43.3	502.85	43.2	466.34	43.1	330.85	42.2	207.58	41.6	144.14	41.9
Printing and publishing	410.89	37.8	400.14	38.0	365.31	37.7	279.36	37.1	198.32	37.0	147.78	37.7
Chemicals and allied products	553.74	42.4	535.94	42.3	484.78	41.9	344.45	41.5	219.63	40.9	153.50	41.6
Petroleum and allied products	683.99	44.3	668.22	44.4	603.72	43.0	422.18	41.8	267.07	41.6	182.76	42.7

Source: Department of Labor, Bureau of Labor Statistics.

Nonmanufacturing Industries—Gross Average Weekly Earnings and Hours Worked

Industry	1989 Earnings	1989 Hours worked	1988 Earnings	1988 Hours worked	1985 Earnings	1985 Hours worked	1975 Earnings	1975 Hours worked	1970 Earnings	1970 Hours worked
Bituminous coal and lignite mining	$696.78	43.0	675.11	42.4	$630.77	41.4	$284.53	39.2 [2]	$186.41	40.8
Metal mining	585.08	42.8	557.94	42.3	547.24	40.9	250.72	42.3	165.68	42.7
Nonmetallic minerals	513.91	45.6	498.49	45.4	451.68	44.5	213.09	43.4	155.11	44.7
Telephone communications	561.15	40.9	555.90	41.3	512.52	41.1	221.18	38.4	131.60	39.4
Radio and TV broadcasting	424.86	35.2	412.49	35.9	381.39	37.1	214.50	39.0	147.45	38.2
Electric, gas, and sanitary services	619.28	41.9	594.46	41.6	534.59	41.7	246.79	41.2	172.64	41.5
Local and suburban transportation	369.02	38.4	350.49	38.6	309.85	38.3	196.89	40.1	142.30	42.1
Wholesale trade	395.48	38.1	377.95	38.1	358.36	38.7	188.75	38.6	137.60	40.0
Retail trade	189.01	28.9	183.62	29.1	177.31	29.7	108.22	32.4	82.47	33.8
Hotels, tourist courts, motels	206.82	31.1	199.68	31.2	176.90	30.5	89.64	31.9	68.16	34.6
Laundries and dry cleaning plants	225.04	34.2	216.83	34.2	198.70	34.2	106.05	35.0	77.47	35.7
General building contracting	471.24	37.4	454.41	37.4	414.78	37.1	254.88	36.0	184.40	36.3

Source: Department of Labor, Bureau of Labor Statistics.

Median Income Comparisons of Year-Round Workers by Educational Attainment 1988

(persons 25 years and over)

Years of school completed	Median income Women	Median income Men	Income gap in dollars	Women's income as a percent of men's	Percent men's income exceeded women's
Elementary school:					
Less than 8 years	n.a.	n.a.	n.a.	n.a.	n.a.
8 years	n.a.	n.a.	n.a.	n.a.	n.a.
High School:					
1 to 3 years	$6,295	$14,067	$7,772	45	123
4 years	9,748	21,186	11,438	46	117
College:					
1 to 3 years	13,367	25,397	12,030	53	90
4 years	18,415	32,328	13,913	57	76

Source: Department of Commerce, Bureau of the Census. NOTE: Data are latest available. n.a. = not available.

Characteristics of Households With Female Householder, 1988

Characteristics	Number of households	Income bracket	Number of households
All female householders	28,293,000	3 persons	40,084,000
MARITAL STATUS		4 persons or more	3,960,000
Married, husband present	3,061,000	**RELATED CHILDREN UNDER 18**	
Married, husband absent	2,768,000	No related children	19,653,000
Widowed	9,628,000	1 or more related children	8,640,000
Divorced	6,527,000	**TOTAL HOUSEHOLD INCOME[2]**	
Single (never married)	6,310,000	Under $2,500	1,194,000
RACE AND SPANISH ORIGIN		$2,500 to $4,999	2,920,000
OF HOUSEHOLDER		$5,000 to $7,499	3,694,000
White	22,542,000	$7,500 to $9,999	2,561,000
Black	5,136,000	$10,000 to $14,999	4,066,000
Spanish origin[1]	1,832,000	$15,000 to $24,999	5,660,000
SIZE OF HOUSEHOLD		$25,000 to $49,000	6,182,000
1 person	13,101,000	$50,000 and over	2,017,000
2 persons	7,149,000	Median income	14,600
		Mean income	20,532

1. Persons of Spanish origin may be of any race. 2. Income during previous calendar year. *Source:* Department of Commerce, Bureau of the Census.

Unemployment by Marital Status, Sex, and Race[1]

Marital status and race	Men Number	Men Unemployment rate	Women Number	Women Unemployment rate
White, 16 years and over	2,636,000	4.5	2,135,000	4.5
Married, spouse present	1,044,000	2.8	947,000	3.5
Widowed, divorced, or separated	329,000	5.6	454,000	5.1
Single (never married)	1,263,000	8.1	734,000	6.4
Black, 16 years and over	773,000	11.5	772,000	11.4
Married, spouse present	184,000	5.8	153,000	6.3
Widowed, divorced, or separated	106,000	10.7	187,000	9.6
Single (never married)	483,000	18.8	432,000	17.7
Total, 16 years and over	3,525,000	5.2	3,003,000	5.4
Married, spouse present	1,276,000	3.0	1,145,000	3.7
Widowed, divorced, or separated	448,000	6.3	656,000	5.9
Single (never married)	1,801,000	9.6	1,202,000	8.4

1. 1989 Annual Averages. *Source:* U.S. Department of Labor, Bureau of Labor Statistics.

Earnings Distribution of Year-Round, Full-Time Workers, by Sex, 1988

(persons 15 years old and over as of March 1988)

Earnings group	Number Women	Number Men	Distribution (percent) Women	Distribution (percent) Men	Likelihood of a woman in each earnings group (percent)[1]
$2,499 or less	492,000	569,000	1.6	1.2	1.3
$2,500 to $4,999	467,000	371,000	1.5	0.8	1.9
$5,000 to $7,499	1,373,000	1,146,000	4.4	2.4	1.8
$7,500 to $9,999	2,280,000	1,467,000	7.3	3.0	2.4
$10,000 to $14,999	6,959,000	5,330,000	22.3	11.0	2.0
$15,000 to $19,999	6,631,000	6,314,000	21.2	13.1	1.6
$20,000 to $24,999	4,943,000	6,488,000	15.8	13.4	1.2
$25,000 to $49,999	7,397,000	20,299,000	23.7	42.0	0.6
$50,000 and over	695,000	6,303,000	2.2	13.1	0.2
Total	31,237,000	48,285,000	100.0	100.0	—

Figures obtained by dividing percentages for women by percentages for men. Figures may not add to totals because of rounding.
Source: Department of Commerce, Bureau of the Census.

Comparison of Median Earnings of Year-Round, Full-Time Workers 15 Years and Over, by Sex, 1960 to 1988

Year	Median earnings Women	Median earnings Men	Earnings gap in current dollars	Women's earnings as a percent of men's	Percent men's earnings exceeded women's	Earnings gap in constant 1988 dollars
1960	$3,257	$5,368	$2,111	60.7	64.8	$8,437
1965	3,828	6,388	2,560	60.0	66.9	9,614
1970	5,323	8,966	3,643	59.4	68.4	11,107
1975	7,504	12,758	5,254	58.8	70.0	11,553
1980	11,197	18,612	7,415	60.2	66.2	10,646
1981	12,001	20,260	8,259	59.2	68.8	10,749
1982	13,014	21,077	8,063	61.7	62.0	9,884
1983	13,915	21,881	7,966	63.6	57.2	9,462
1984	14,780	23,218	8,438	63.7	57.1	9,607
1985	15,624	24,195	8,571	64.7	54.9	9,423
1986	16,232	25,256	9,024	64.3	55.6	9,740
1987	16,909	26,008	9,099	65.0	53.8	9,475
1988	17,606	26,656	9,050	66.0	51.4	9,050

Source: Department of Commerce, Bureau of the Census.

Occupations of Employed Women

(16 years of age and over. Figures are percentage)

Occupations	1989[1]	1988[1]	1987[1]	1986[1]	1985[1]	1984[1]	1983[1]
Managerial and professional	25.9	25.2	24.4	23.7	23.4	22.5	21.9
Technical, sales, administrative support	44.2	44.6	45.1	45.6	45.5	45.6	45.8
Service occupations	17.7	17.9	18.1	18.3	18.5	18.7	18.9
Precision production, craft and repair	2.2	2.3	2.3	2.4	2.4	2.4	2.3
Operators, fabricators, laborers	8.9	8.9	9.0	8.9	9.1	9.6	9.7
Farming, forestry, fishing	1.1	1.1	1.1	1.1	1.2	1.2	1.3

1. Annual averages. NOTE: Details may not add up to totals because of rounding. *Source:* Department of Labor.

Employed and Unemployed Workers by Full- and Part-Time Status, Sex, and Age: 1970 to 1989

(In thousands)

	1989	1988	1987	1986	1985	1980	1975	1970
Total 16 yr and over								
Employed	117,342	114,968	112,440	109,597	107,150	99,303	85,846	78,678
Full time	97,369	95,214	92,957	90,529	88,535	82,564	71,585	66,752
Part time	19,973	19,754	19,483	19,069	18,615	16,742	14,260	11,924
Unemployed	6,528	6,701	7,425	8,237	8,312	7,637	7,929	4,093
Full time	5,211	5,357	5,979	6,708	6,793	6,269	6,523	3,206
Part time	1,317	1,343	1,446	1,529	1,519	1,369	1,408	889
Men, 20 yr and over								
Employed	60,837	59,781	58,726	57,569	56,562	53,101	48,018	45,581
Full time	56,386	55,353	54,381	53,317	52,425	49,699	45,051	43,138
Part time	4,451	4,427	4,345	4,252	4,137	3,403	2,966	2,444
Unemployed	2,867	2,987	3,369	3,751	3,715	3,353	3,476	1,638
Full time	2,651	2,778	3,147	3,508	3,479	3,167	3,255	1,502
Part time	215	209	222	243	236	186	223	137
Women, 20 yr. and over								
Employed	49,745	48,383	47,074	45,556	44,154	38,492	30,726	26,952
Full time	38,408	37,299	36,121	34,812	33,604	29,391	23,242	20,654
Part time	11,337	11,084	10,953	10,744	10,550	9,102	7,484	6,297
Unemployed	2,467	2,487	2,709	3,032	3,129	2,615	2,684	1,349
Full time	1,963	1,987	2,178	2,468	2,536	2,135	2,210	1,077
Part time	504	500	530	565	593	480	474	271
Both sexes 16–19 yr.								
Employed	6,759	6,805	6,640	6,472	6,434	7,710	7,104	6,144
Full time	2,574	2,562	2,454	2,400	2,507	3,474	3,292	2,960
Part time	4,185	4,243	4,185	4,073	3,927	4,237	3,810	3,183
Unemployed	1,194	1,226	1,347	1,454	1,468	1,669	1,767	1,106
Full time	596	592	653	733	777	966	1,057	626
Part time	598	634	694	721	690	701	709	480

Source: U.S. Dept. of Labor, Bureau of Labor Statistics.

Work Stoppages Involving 1,000 Workers or More[1]

Year	Work stoppages	Workers involved (thousands)	Man-days idle (thousands)	Year	Work stoppages	Workers involved (thousands)	Man-days idle (thousands)
1950	424	1,698	30,390	1981	145	729	16,908
1955	363	2,055	21,180	1982	96	656	9,061
1960	222	896	13,260	1983	81	909	17,461
1965	268	999	15,140	1984	68	391	8,499
1970	381	2,468	52,761	1985	61	584	7,079
1975	235	965	17,563	1986	72	900	11,861
1978	219	1,006	23,774	1987	46	174	4,456
1979	235	1,021	20,409	1988	40	118	4,381
1980	187	795	20,844	1989	51	452	16,996

1. The number of stoppages and workers relate to stoppages that began in the year. Days of idleness include all stoppages in effect. Workers are counted more than once if they were involved in more than one stoppage during the year. *Source:* U.S. Department of Labor. Bureau of Labor Statistics, *Monthly Labor Review. July 1990.*

Leading Advertising Agencies in World Billings

(in thousands of dollars)

Agency	1989	1988
Saatchi & Saatchi Advertising	$5,176,351 [2]	$4,584,436 [2]
McCann-Erickson	4,632,105 [2]	4,335,116 [1]
J. Walter Thompson	4,407,500 [2]	3,857,000
Ogilvy & Mather Worldwide	4,167,752 [2]	3,482,638 [2]
Backer Spielvogel Bates Worldwide	4,166,504 [2]	3,804,784 [2]
Young & Rubicam [3]	4,137,000 [2]	3,578,300 [2]
FCB-Publicis	4,122,000 [2]	3,900,000 [2]
Lintas: Worldwide	3,795,662 [2]	3,469,000 [2]
D'Arcy Masius Benton & Bowles	3,408,656	2,991,557 [1]
Leo Burnett Co.	3,245,464	2,865,087

1. Restated 1988 billings. 2. Estimated. 3. Excludes HDM. *Source: Ad Week Magazine,* Top 30 Worldwide Agencies, March 12, 1990 edition. Copyright © Ad Week Magazine Network 1990. All rights reserved.

Unemployment Rate, 1989

Race and age	Women [1]	Men [1]
All races:	5.4	5.2
16 to 19 years	14.0	15.9
20 years and over	4.7	4.5
White	4.5	4.5
16 to 19 years	11.5	13.7
20 years and over	4.0	3.9
Minority races:	10.0	10.0
16 to 19 years	28.7	29.2
20 years and over	8.7	8.7

1. Annual averages. *Source:* Bureau of Labor Statistics, Department of Labor.

Unemployment Rate in the Civilian Labor Force

Year	Unemployment Rate	Year	Unemployment Rate
1920	5.2	1976	7.7
1922	6.7	1978	6.0
1924	5.0	1980	7.1
1926	1.8	1981	7.6
1928	4.2	1982	9.7
1930	8.7	1983	9.6
1932	23.6	1984	7.5
1934	21.7	1985	7.2
1936	16.9	1986	7.0
1938	19.0	1987	6.2
1940	14.6	1988	5.4
1942	4.7	1989	5.2
1944	1.2	Jan.	5.4
1946	3.9	Feb.	5.1
1948	3.8	March	5.0
1950	5.3	April	5.3
1952	3.0	May	5.1
1954	5.5	June	5.2
1956	4.1	July	5.2
1958	6.8	Aug.	5.2
1960	5.5	Sept.	5.3
1962	5.5	Oct.	5.2
1964	5.2	Nov.	5.3
1966	3.8	Dec.	5.3
1968	3.6	1990	
1970	4.9	Jan.	5.2
1972	5.6	Feb.	5.2
1974	5.6	March	5.1
		April	5.3

NOTE: Estimates prior to 1940 are based on sources other than direct enumeration. *Source:* Department of Labor, Bureau of Labor Statistics.

Employment and Unemployment

(in millions of persons)

Category	1990 [2]	1989	1988	1985	1980	1975	1970	1950	1945	1932	1929
EMPLOYMENT STATUS [1]											
Civilian noninstitutional population	187.7	186.4	184.6	178.2	167.7	153.2	137.1	105.0	94.1	—	—
Civilian labor force	124.9	123.9	121.7	115.5	106.9	93.8	82.8	62.2	53.9	—	—
Civilian labor force participation rate	66.5	66.5	65.9	64.8	63.8	61.2	60.4	59.2	57.2	—	—
Employed	118.1	117.3	115.0	107.2	99.3	85.8	78.7	58.9	52.8	38.9	47.6
Employment-population ratio	62.9	63.0	62.3	60.1	59.2	56.1	57.4	56.1	56.1	—	—
Agriculture	3.1	3.2	3.2	3.2	3.4	3.4	3.5	7.2	8.6	10.2	10.5
Nonagricultural industries	115.0	114.1	111.8	104.0	95.9	82.4	75.2	51.8	44.2	28.8	37.2
Unemployed	6.8	6.5	6.7	8.3	7.6	7.9	4.1	3.3	1.0	12.1	1.6
Unemployment rate	5.4	5.3	5.5	7.2	7.1	8.5	4.9	5.3	1.9	23.6	3.2
Not in labor force	62.8	62.5	62.9	62.7	60.8	59.4	54.3	42.8	40.2	—	—
INDUSTRY											
Total nonagricultural employment	110.5	108.6	105.6	97.5	90.4	76.9	70.9	45.2	40.4	23.6	31.3
Goods-producing industries	25.5	25.6	25.2	24.9	25.7	22.6	23.6	18.5	17.5	8.6	13.3
Mining	0.7	0.7	0.7	0.9	1.0	0.8	0.6	0.9	0.8	0.7	1.1
Construction	5.3	5.3	5.1	4.7	4.3	3.5	3.6	2.4	1.1	1.0	1.5
Manufacturing: Durable goods	11.3	11.5	11.4	11.5	12.2	10.7	11.2	8.1	9.1	—	—
Nondurable goods	8.0	8.1	8.0	7.8	8.1	7.6	8.2	7.1	6.5	—	—
Services-producing industries	85.0	82.9	80.3	72.7	64.7	54.3	47.3	26.7	22.9	15.0	18.0
Transportation and public utilities	5.9	5.7	5.5	5.2	5.1	4.5	4.5	4.0	3.9	2.8	3.9
Trade, Wholesale	6.3	6.2	6.0	5.7	5.3	4.4	4.0	2.6	1.9	—	—
Retail	19.8	19.6	19.1	17.4	15.0	12.6	11.0	6.8	5.4	—	—
Finance, insurance, and real estate	6.9	6.8	6.7	6.0	5.2	4.2	3.6	1.9	1.5	1.3	1.5
Services	27.8	26.9	25.6	22.0	17.9	13.9	11.5	5.4	4.2	2.9	3.4
Federal government	3.2	3.0	3.0	2.9	2.9	2.7	2.7	1.9	2.8	0.6	0.5
State and local government	15.1	14.7	14.4	13.5	13.4	11.9	9.8	4.1	3.1	2.7	2.5

1. For 1929–45, figures on employment status relate to persons 14 years and over; beginning in 1950, 16 years and over.
2. As of April; seasonally adjusted; industry data are preliminary. *Source:* Bureau of Labor Statistics.

Livestock on Farms (in thousands)

Type	1990	1989	1988	1985	1980	1975	1970	1965	1960	1950
Cattle[1]	99,337	99,180	99,622	109,582	111,242	132,028	112,369	109,000	96,236	77,963
Dairy cows[1]	10,149	10,212	11,116	10,311	10,758	11,220	13,303	16,981	19,527	23,853
Sheep[1]	11,368	10,858	10,945	10,716	12,699	14,515	20,423	25,127	33,170	29,826
Swine[2]	53,852	55,469	54,384	54,073	67,318	54,693	57,046	56,106	59,026	58,937
Chickens[2]	5,717,111	5,462,359	5,221,248	4,689,973	4,201,706	3,173,820	3,220,085	2,535,141	1,976,737	535,266
Turkeys[3]	260,230	242,421	240,438	185,427	165,243	124,165	116,139	105,914	84,458	44,134

1. As of Jan. 1. 2. As of Jan. 1 the previous year for 1945–60 and Dec. 1 for 1965–90. 3. Turkeys 1975–90 as of Dec. 1 the previous year. *Source:* Department of Agriculture, Statistical Reporting Service, Economic Research Service.

Agricultural Output by States, 1989 Crops

State	Corn (1,000 bu)	Wheat (1,000 bu)	Cotton (1,000 ba[1])	Potatoes (1,000 cwt)	Tobacco (1,000 lb)	Cattle[2] (1,000 head)	Swine[3] (1,000 head)
Alabama	14,580	6,600	390.0	2,571	—	1,780	300
Alaska	—	—	—	—	—	8.2	0.7
Arizona	1,885	10,722	1,115.0	1,827	—	830	100
Arkansas	7,076	52,800	850.0	—	—	1,750	710
California	27,200	52,605	2,688.0	17,991	—	4,900	140
Colorado	134,850	62,100	—	22,587	—	2,900	230
Connecticut	—	—	—	66	2,781	76	6.2
Delaware	13,300	3,108	—	1,152	—	31	32
Florida	5,920	1,885	34.0	8,304	18,200	1,925	140
Georgia	52,250	22,400	350.0	—	87,000	1,450	1,200
Hawaii	—	—	—	—	—	205	39
Idaho	6,250	91,420	—	102,475	—	1,660	72
Illinois	1,322,250	105,020	—	858	—	1,950	5,700
Indiana	691,600	51,920	—	960	13,237	1,300	4,350
Iowa	1,445,500	3,290	—	270	—	4,700	13,500
Kansas	155,000	213,600	1.0	—	—	5,700	1,450
Kentucky	136,880	22,500	—	—	398,835	2,420	975
Louisiana	12,540	10,850	875.0	27	—	1,100	55
Maine	—	—	—	22,000	—	116	9.3
Maryland	44,000	8,600	—	315	10,625	315	180
Massachusetts	—	—	—	600	669	71	33
Michigan	222,610	33,920	—	9,200	—	1,225	1,260
Minnesota	700,000	102,504	—	15,750	—	2,650	4,450
Mississippi	9,800	15,300	1,560.0	—	—	1,390	180
Missouri	219,840	86,950	269.0	—	5,350	4,500	2,700
Montana	320	145,030	—	2,228	—	2,350	220
Nebraska	852,000	55,350	—	3,126	—	5,800	4,200
Nevada	—	1,200	—	2,600	—	570	14
New Hampshire	—	—	—	—	—	46	8.7
New Jersey	7,242	1,365	—	888	—	70	30
New Mexico	9,765	3,200	122.0	4,025	—	1,380	25
New York	53,010	5,850	—	6,628	—	1,540	124
North Carolina	88,350	21,420	140.0	2,310	541,550	900	2,570
North Dakota	34,875	242,320	—	15,070	—	1,750	280
Ohio	342,200	62,730	—	1,462	17,100	1,680	2,080
Oklahoma	9,204	153,900	180.0	—	—	5,300	230
Oregon	3,520	53,835	—	23,308	—	1,400	90
Pennsylvania	98,880	7,955	—	4,715	19,200	1,890	975
Rhode Island	—	—	—	300	—	7	5.9
South Carolina	30,940	17,835	155.0	—	102,480	590	430
South Dakota	190,800	83,080	—	1,980	—	3,380	1,720
Tennessee	56,710	18,900	473.0	60	89,889	2,325	700
Texas	148,400	60,000	3,028.0	3,408	—	13,400	500
Utah	2,640	5,950	—	1,495	—	800	27
Vermont	—	—	—	—	—	297	5.7
Virginia	40,150	12,650	3.3	1,440	95,778	1,700	450
Washington	15,750	110,610	—	64.310	—	1,330	56
West Virginia	4,370	516	—	—	2,040	490	32
Wisconsin	310,800	9,320	—	23,460	9,445	4,170	1,250
Wyoming	3,895	4,708	—	578	—	1,220	16
U.S. Total	7,527,152	2,035,818	12,233.3	370,344	1,414,179	99,337	53,852

1. 480-lb net-weight bales. 2. Number on farms as of Jan. 1, 1990. 3. Number on farms as of Dec. 1, 1989. *Source:* Department of Agriculture, Statistical Reporting Service.

Farm Income
(in millions of dollars)

Year	Cash receipts from marketings		Government payments	Total cash income
	Crops	Livestock, livestock products		
1925	5,545	5,476	—	11,021
1930	3,868	5,187	—	9,055
1935	2,977	4,143	$573	7,693
1940	3,469	4,913	723	9,105
1945	9,655	12,008	742	22,405
1950	12,356	16,105	283	28,764
1955	13,523	15,967	229	29,842
1960	15,023	18,989	703	34,958
1965	17,479	21,886	2,463	42,215
1970	20,977	29,532	3,717	54,768
1975	45,813	43,089	807	90,707
1980	71,746	67,991	1,285	143,295
1982	72,338	70,257	3,492	150,620
1984[1]	69,471	72,968	8,431	155,253
1985[1]	74,290	69,845	7,705	156,882
1986[1]	64,005	71,534	11,814	152,473
1987[1]	63,751	75,717	16,747	162,023
1988	72,569	78,862	14,480	171,579

1. Figures revised. 2. Includes items not listed. *Source:* Department of Agriculture, Economic Research Service. NOTE: Figures are latest available.

Per Capita Consumption of Principal Foods[1]

Food	1989	1988	1987
Red meat[2]	111.3	115.1	113.3
Poultry	60.5	57.1	55.3
Fish and shellfish (edible weight)	15.7	15.0	15.5
Eggs	29.7	31.0	32.1
Fluid milk and cream[3]	230.3	233.4	237.4
Ice cream	16.0	17.2	18.3
Cheese (excluding cottage)	23.7	23.6	24.0
Butter (actual weight)	4.3	4.5	4.6
Margarine (actual weight)	10.1	10.2	10.5
Total fats and oils	60.7	62.7	62.7
Selected fresh fruits (farm weight)	n.a.	94.4	96.9
Peanuts (shelled)	7.1	6.8	6.4
Selected fresh vegetable	101.9	98.7	95.4
White potatoes[4]	123.3	123.5	125.4
Sugar (refined)	62.2	62.0	62.4
Corn sweeteners (dry weight)	69.7	69.6	68.6
Flour and cereal products	167.5	171.8	170.2
Soft drinks (gal)	32.0	31.7	30.5
Coffee bean equivalent	10.2	10.2	10.2
Cocoa (chocolate liquor equivalent)	5.0	4.9	4.8

1. As of August 1990. Except where noted, consumption is from commercial sources and is in terms of retail weight. 2. Boneless, trimmed equivalent. 3. Includes milk and cream produced and consumed on farms. 4. Farm-weight equivalent of fresh and processed use. n.a. = not available.

Government Employment and Payrolls

Year and function	Employees (in thousands)				October payrolls (in millions)			
	Total	Federal[1]	State	Local	Total	Federal[1]	State	Local
1940	4,474	1,128	3,346		$566	177	$389	
1945	6,677	3,496	3,181		1,059	591	468	
1950	6,402	2,117	1,057	3,228	1,528	613	218	696
1955	7,432	2,378	1,199	3,855	2,265	846	326	1,093
1960	8,808	2,421	1,527	4,860	3,333	1,118	524	1,691
1965	10,589	2,588	2,028	5,973	4,884	1,484	849	2,551
1970	13,028	2,881	2,755	7,392	8,334	2,428	1,612	4,294
1975	14,973	2,890	3,271	8,813	13,224	3,584	2,653	6,987
1979	15,971	2,869	3,699	9,403	18,077	4,728	3,869	9,480
1980	16,213	2,898	3,753	9,562	19,935	5,205	4,285	10,445
1981	15,968	2,865	3,726	9,377	21,193	5,239	4,668	11,287
1982	15,841	2,848	3,744	9,249	23,173	5,959	5,022	12,192
1983	16,034	2,875	3,816	9,344	24,525	6,302	5,346	12,878
1984	16,436	2,942	3,898	9,595	26,904	7,137	5,815	13,952
1985	16,690	3,021	3,984	9,685	28,945	7,580	6,329	15,036
1986	16,933	3,019	4,068	9,846	30,670	7,561	6,810	12,298
1987	17,281	3,091	4,115	10,076	32,382	7,924	7,298	17,160
1988, total	17,588	3,112	4,236	10,240	34,203	7,976	7,842	18,385
National defense and international relations	1,060	1,060	(2)	(2)	2,749	2,749	(2)	(2)
Postal service	834	834	(2)	(2)	2,050	2,050	(2)	(2)
Education	7,525	14	1,854	5,656	13,161	37	2,929	10,195
Instructional employees	4,249	n.a.	570	3,679	9,241	n.a.	1,347	7,893
Highways	559	4	253	302	1,060	15	527	518
Health and Hospitals	1,694	263	705	726	3,245	634	1,370	1,240
Police protection	803	79	85	640	1,849	240	214	1,396
Local fire protection	340	(2)	(2)	340	664	(2)	(2)	664
Sewerage & sanitation	230	n.a.	1	229	438	n.a.	3	435
Parks & recreation	314	24	38	252	401	55	55	291
Natural resources	422	227	159	37	958	611	294	53
Financial administration	483	143	138	203	916	314	283	319
All other	3,324	464	1,003	1,855	6,712	1,271	2,167	3,274

1. Civilians only. 2. Not applicable. NOTE: n.a. = not available. Detail may not add to totals because of rounding. *Source:* Department of Commerce, Bureau of the Census.

Receipts and Outlays of the Federal Government

(in millions of dollars)

From 1789 to 1842, the federal fiscal year ended Dec. 31; from 1844 to 1976, on June 30; and beginning 1977, on Sept. 30.

		Receipts				
		Internal revenue		Miscel-		
Year	Customs (including tonnage tax)[1]	Income and profits tax	Other	laneous taxes and receipts	Total receipts	Net receipts[2]
1789–1791	$ 4	—	—	—	$ 4	$ 4
1800	9	—	$ −1	$ 1	11	11
1810	9	—	—	1	9	9
1820	15	—	—	3	18	18
1830	22	—	—	3	25	25
1840	14	—	—	6	20	20
1850	40	—	—	4	44	44
1860	53	—	—	3	56	56
1865	85	—	209	39	334	334
1870	195	—	185	32	411	411
1880	187	—	124	23	334	334
1890	230	—	143	31	403	403
1900	233	—	295	39	567	567
1910	334	—	290	52	675	675
1915	210	$ 80	335	72	698	683
1929	602	2,331	607	493	4,033	3,862
1933	251	746	858	225	2,080	1,997
1939	319	2,189	2,972	188	5,668	4,979
1943	324	16,094	6,050	934	23,402	21,947
1944	431	34,655	7,030	3,325	45,441	43,563
1945	355	35,173	8,729	3,494	47,750	44,362
1950	423	28,263	11,186	1,439	41,311	36,422
1956[4]	705	56,639	20,564	389	78,297	74,547
1960	1,123	67,151	28,266	1,190	97,730	92,492
1965	1,478	79,792	39,996	1,598	122,863	116,833
1970	2,494	138,689	65,276	3,424	209,883	193,743
1975	3,782	202,146	108,371	6,711	321,010	280,997
1980	7,482	359,927	192,436	12,797	572,641	520,050
1985	12,079	474,074	311,092	18,576	815,821	733,996
1986	13,323	412,102	323,779	19,887	(5)	769,091
1987	15,085	476,483	343,268	19,307	(5)	854,143
1988	16,198	495,376	377,469	19,909	(5)	908,953
1989	16,334	549,273	402,200	22,800	(5)	990,691

	Outlays					
Year	Department of Defense (Army, 1789–1950)	Department of the Navy	Interest on public debt	All other	Net outlays[3]	Surplus (+) or deficit (−)
1789–1791	$ 1	—	$ 2	$ 1	$ 4	—
1800	3	$ 3	3	1	11	—
1810	2	2	3	1	8	$ +1
1820	3	4	5	6	18	—
1830	5	3	2	5	15	+10
1840	7	6	—	11	24	−4
1850	9	8	4	18	40	+4
1860	16	12	3	32	63	−7
1865	1,031	123	77	66	1,298	−964
1870	58	22	129	101	310	+101
1880	38	14	96	120	268	+66
1890	45	22	36	215	318	+85
1900	135	56	40	290	521	+46
1910	190	123	21	359	694	−19
1915	202	142	23	379	746	−63
1929	426	365	678	1,658	3,127	+734
1933	435	349	689	3,125	4,598	−2,602

			Outlays			
Year	Department of Defense (Army, 1789–1950)	Department of the Navy	Interest on public debt	All other	Net outlays[3]	Surplus (+) or deficit (−)
1939	695	673	941	6,533	8,841	−3,862
1943	42,526	20,888	1,808	14,146	79,368	−57,420
1944	49,438	26,538	2,609	16,401	94,986	−51,423
1945	50,490	30,047	3,617	14,149	98,303	−53,941
1950	5,789	4,130	5,750	23,875	39,544	−3,122
1956[4]	35,693	—	6,787	27,981	70,460	+4,087
1960	43,969	—	9,180	39,075	92,223	+269
1965	47,179	—	11,346	59,904	118,430	−1,596
1970	78,360	—	19,304	98,924	196,588	−2,845
1975	87,471	—	32,665	205,969	326,105	−45,108
1980	136,138	—	74,860	368,013	579,011	−58,961
1985	244,054	—	178,945	513,810	936,809	−202,813
1986	273,369	—	135,284	581,136	989,789	−220,698
1987	282,016	—	138,519	581,612	1,002,147	−148,004
1988	290,349	—	151,711	621,995	1,064,055	−155,102
1989	303,600	—	169,100	649,943	1,142,643	−123,785

1. Beginning 1933, tonnage tax is included in "Other receipts." 2. Net receipts equal total receipts less (a) appropriations to federal old-age and survivors' insurance trust fund beginning fiscal year 1939 and (b) refunds of receipts beginning fiscal year 1933. 3. Includes Air Force 1950–65 (in millions): 1950—$3,521; 1956—$16,750; 1960—$19,065; 1965—$18,471. 4. Beginning 1956, computed on unified budget concepts; not strictly comparable with preceding figures. 5. Net receipts are now the total receipts. Public Law 99-177 moved two social security trust funds off-budget. *Source:* Department of the Treasury, Financial Management Service, and *Budget of the United States Government Fiscal Year 1991.* NOTE: Totals figures may not add to totals because of rounding of some items.

Contributions to International Organizations

(for fiscal year 1989 in millions of dollars)

Organization	Amount[1]
United Nations and Specialized Agencies	
United Nations	$ 144.86
Food and Agriculture Organization	25.00
International Atomic Energy Agency	35.16
International Civil Aviation Organization	7.37
International Labor Organization	27.59
International Telecommunication Union	4.92
United Nations Industrial Development Organization	12.67
World Health Organization	65.35
World Meteorological Organization	6.07
Others (7 Programs, less than $1 million)	3.21
Peacekeeping Forces	
United Nations Force in Cyprus	7.31
United Nations Disengagement Observer Force (UNDOF) and UNIFIL	29.00
Multinational Force and Observers	24.38
Inter-American Organizations	
Organization of American States	32.97
Inter-American Institute for Cooperation on Agriculture	10.85
Inter-American Tropical Tuna Commission	2.68
Pan American Health Organization	32.06
Others (4 Programs, less than $1 million)	.58
Regional Organizations	
NATO Civilian Headquarters (and MBFR)	23.21
Organization for Economic Cooperation and Development	33.98
Others (3 Programs, less than $1 million)	1.34
Other International Organizations	
Customs Cooperation Council	2.17
General Agreement on Tariffs and Trade	6.38

Organization	Amount[1]
International Agency for Research on Cancer	1.05
International Institute for Cotton	1.42
Others (35 Programs, less than $1 million)	5.74
Special Voluntary Programs	
Consultative Group on International Agricultural Research	40.00
International Atomic Energy Agency Technical Assistance Fund	21.83[2]
International Fund for Agricultural Development	2.50
International Organization for Migration	6.17
OAS Special Development Assistance Fund	4.00
OAS Special Multilateral Fund (Education and Science)	4.75
OAS Special Projects Fund (Mar del Plata)	1.00
PAHO Special Health Promotion Funds	10.00
United Nations Children's Fund	60.00
United Nations Development Program	108.00
United Nations Environment Program	9.50
U.N. Capital Development Fund	1.50
U.N./FAO World Food Program	171.20[3]
U.N. Fund for Drug Abuse Control	1.05
U.N. High Commissioner for Refugees Program:	
Regular Programs (4)	102.53
Special Programs (12)	23.23
United Nations Relief and Works Agency:	
Regular Program	61.30
Special Emergency Programs	2.00
WHO Special Programs	20.00
WMO Voluntary Cooperation Program	1.96
Others (10 Programs, less than $1 million)	3.93
Total U.S. Contributions	$1,203.77

1. Estimated. 2. Includes cash, commodities and services, and $7.55 million for the Safeguards Program and other non-proliferation activities. 3. Includes cash, commodities and services, and $69.9 million for the International Emergency Food Reserve.

Social Welfare Expenditures Under Public Programs
(in millions of dollars)

Year and source of funds	Social insur-ance	Public aid	Health and medical pro-grams[1]	Veter-ans' pro-grams	Edu-cation	Hous-ing	Other social welfare	All health and medical care[2]	Total social welfare	Total social welfare as: Percent of gross national product	Percent of total gov't outlays
FEDERAL											
1960	14,307	2,117	1,737	5,367	868	144	417	2,918	24,957	5.0	28.1
1970	45,246	9,649	4,775	8,952	5,876	582	2,259	16,600	77,337	8.1	40.1
1975	99,715	27,205	8,513	16,570	8,629	2,541	4,264	34,645	167,436	11.5	53.8
1980	191,162	48,666	12,886	21,254	13,452	6,608	8,786	68,989	303,276	11.5	53.2
1981	224,574	55,946	13,596	23,229	13,372	6,045	7,304	80,505	344,066	11.6	54.0
1982	250,551	52,485	14,598	24,463	11,917	7,176	6,500	90,776	367,691	12.0	52.5
1983	274,212	55,895	15,594	25,561	12,397	8,087	7,046	100,274	398,792	12.0	51.9
1984	288,743	58,480	16,622	25,970	13,010	10,226	7,349	103,927	420,399	11.3	50.2
1985	313,108	61,985	18,630	26,704	13,796	11,088	7,548	118,955	452,860	11.5	47.8
1986	326,588	65,615	19,926	27,072	15,022	10,164	7,977	125,730	472,364	11.3	47.6
1987	345,082	69,233	22,219	27,641	16,054	11,110	8,504	143,020	499,844	11.0	50.4
STATE AND LOCAL											
1960	4,999	1,984	2,727	112	16,758	33	723	3,478	27,337	5.5	60.1
1970	9,446	6,839	5,132	127	44,970	120	1,886	8,791	68,519	7.1	64.0
1975	23,298	14,122	9,195	449	72,234	631	2,683	17,847	122,612	8.4	63.7
1980	38,592	23,133	14,771	212	107,597	601	4,813	31,309	189,720	7.2	66.5
1981	42,821	26,477	17,124	212	114,773	688	4,679	36,327	206,774	7.0	63.1
1982	52,481	28,367	19,195	245	121,957	778	5,154	40,738	228,178	7.4	62.6
1983	56,846	29,935	20,382	265	129,416	1,003	5,438	42,854	243,285	7.3	60.1
1984	52,378	32,206	20,383	301	139,046	1,306	5,946	44,540	251,569	6.8	58.9
1985	59,420	34,792	22,430	338	152,622	1,540	6,398	48,587	277,540	7.0	59.0
1986	63,816	37,464	24,408	373	163,495	1,872	6,728	53,884	298,158	7.1	58.2
1987	69,941	41,462	25,400	410	188,486	2,129	6,773	60,566	344,601	7.4	59.6
TOTAL											
1960	19,307	4,101	4,464	5,479	17,626	177	1,139	6,395	52,293	10.5	38.4
1970	54,691	16,488	9,907	9,078	50,846	701	4,145	25,391	145,856	15.2	48.2
1975	123,013	41,326	17,708	17,019	80,863	3,172	6,947	52,492	290,047	20.0	57.4
1980	229,754	71,799	27,657	21,466	121,050	7,210	13,599	100,298	492,534	18.7	57.4
1981	267,395	82,424	30,720	23,441	128,145	6,734	11,983	116,832	550,841	18.6	56.9
1982	303,033	80,852	33,793	24,708	133,874	7,954	11,654	131,514	595,869	19.4	55.7
1983	331,058	85,830	35,976	25,826	141,813	9,090	12,484	143,128	642,077	19.3	54.5
1984	341,120	90,685	37,006	26,275	152,056	11,532	13,295	148,467	671,969	18.2	52.8
1985	372,529	96,777	41,060	27,042	166,418	12,627	13,946	167,542	730,399	18.5	51.2
1986	390,404	103,079	44,334	27,445	178,518	12,036	14,705	179,614	770,522	18.4	47.9
1987	415,023	110,695	47,619	28,051	204,540	13,240	15,278	203,586	834,446	18.4	53.5
PERCENT OF TOTAL, BY TYPE											
1960	36.9	7.8	8.5	10.5	33.7	0.3	2.2	12.2	100.0	(3)	(3)
1970	37.5	11.3	6.7	6.2	34.9	0.5	3.0	17.2	100.0	(3)	(3)
1975	42.4	14.2	6.1	5.9	27.9	1.1	2.4	18.1	100.0	(3)	(3)
1980	46.6	14.6	5.6	4.4	24.6	1.5	2.8	20.4	100.0	(3)	(3)
1984	50.9	13.4	5.6	3.9	22.6	1.5	2.0	23.1	100.0	(3)	(3)
1985	51.0	13.2	5.6	3.7	22.8	1.7	1.9	22.9	100.0	(3)	(3)
1986	50.7	13.4	5.8	3.6	23.2	1.6	1.9	23.3	100.0	(3)	(3)
1987	49.7	13.3	5.7	3.4	24.5	1.6	1.8	24.4	100.0	(3)	(3)
FEDERAL PERCENT OF TOTAL											
1960	74.1	51.6	38.9	98.0	4.9	81.2	36.6	45.6	47.7	(3)	(3)
1970	82.7	58.5	48.2	98.6	11.6	82.9	54.5	65.4	53.0	(3)	(3)
1975	81.1	65.8	48.1	97.4	10.7	80.1	61.4	66.0	57.7	(3)	(3)
1980	83.2	67.8	46.6	99.0	11.1	91.7	64.6	68.8	61.6	(3)	(3)
1984	84.7	64.2	43.6	99.0	8.5	87.4	54.7	70.0	62.4	(3)	(3)
1985	84.0	64.0	45.4	98.8	8.3	87.8	54.1	71.0	62.0	(3)	(3)
1986	83.6	63.5	44.9	98.6	8.4	84.4	54.2	70.0	61.3	(3)	(3)
1987	83.1	62.5	46.7	98.5	7.8	83.9	55.7	70.3	59.9	(3)	(3)

1. Excludes program parts of social insurance, public aid, veterans, and other social welfare. 2. Combines health and medical programs with medical services provided in connection with social insurance, public aid, veterans, and other social welfare programs. 3. Not applicable. NOTE: Figures are latest available. *Source:* Department of Health and Human Services. *Social Security Bulletin,* November 1989 and earlier issues.

Domestic Freight Traffic by Major Carriers
(in millions of ton-miles)[1]

Year	Railroads Ton-miles	Railroads % of total	Inland waterways[2] Ton-miles	Inland waterways[2] % of total	Motor trucks Ton-miles	Motor trucks % of total	Oil pipelines Ton-miles	Oil pipelines % of total	Air carriers Ton-miles	Air carriers % of total
1940	379,201	61.3	118,057	19.1	62,043	10.0	59,277	9.6	14	—
1945	690,809	67.3	142,737	13.9	66,948	6.5	126,530	12.3	91	—
1950	596,940	56.2	163,344	15.4	172,860	16.3	129,175	12.1	318	—
1955	631,385	49.5	216,508	17.0	223,254	17.5	203,244	16.0	481	—
1960	579,130	44.1	220,253	16.8	285,483	21.7	228,626	17.4	778	—
1965	708,700	43.3	262,421	16.0	359,218	21.9	306,393	18.7	1,910	0.1
1970	771,168	39.8	318,560	16.4	412,000	21.3	431,000	22.3	3,274	0.2
1975	759,000	36.7	342,210	16.5	454,000	22.0	507,300	24.6	3,732	0.2
1980	932,000	37.2	420,000	16.9	567,000	22.6	588,000	23.1	4,528	0.2
1982	810,000	35.8	351,000	15.5	525,000	23.2	571,000	25.3	4,476	0.2
1983	841,000	36.0	359,000	15.4	575,000	24.6	556,000	23.8	5,870	0.3
1985	895,000	36.4	382,000	15.6	610,000	24.9	564,000	22.9	6,080	0.2
1986	889,000	35.5	393,000	15.7	634,000	25.4	578,000	23.1	7,100	0.3
1987	972,000	36.8	411,000	15.6	661,000	25.1	587,000	22.2	8,670	0.3
1988	1,028,000	37.0	438,000	15.8	699,000	25.1	605,000	21.8	9,300	0.3
1989[3]	1,048,000	37.3	444,000	15.8	712,000	25.3	597,000	21.2	9,820	0.35

1. Mail and express included, except railroads for 1970. 2. Rivers, canals, and domestic traffic on Great Lakes. 3. Preliminary. *Source:* For 1987 on, *Transportation in America, 8th Edition,* Eno Foundation for Transportation.

Tonnage Handled by Principal U.S. Ports
(Over 10 million tons annually; in thousands of tons)

Port	1988	1987	Port	1988	1987
New Orleans	175,501	167,917	Tacoma Harbor, Wash.	20,668	17,129
New York	155,062	154,536	Boston, Port of	20,641	19,829
Houston	124,887	112,546	Richmond, Calif.	18,913	21,431
Valdez Harbor, Alaska	107,145	106,867	Seattle	18,646	18,552
Baton Rouge, La.	78,857	73,401	Huntington, W.Va.	17,701	18,772
Corpus Christi, Texas	57,932	53,539	Lorain Harbor, Ohio	17,475	14,372
Tampa Harbor, Fla.	50,252	44,303	Indiana Harbor, Ind.	16,643	13,335
Norfolk Harbor, Va.	46,872	39,993	Jacksonville, Fla.	15,806	13,483
Long Beach, Calif.	46,560	45,898	Detroit	15,331	14,129
Los Angeles, Calif.	45,214	40,460	Freeport, Texas	15,138	13,980
Texas City, Texas	42,747	37,233	Toledo Harbor, Ohio	14,742	16,211
Baltimore Harbor, Md.	41,926	37,488	Cleveland	14,551	13,914
Duluth-Superior, Minn.	40,002	36,462	Port Everglades, Fla.	14,207	14,045
Philadelphia	37,827	37,336	Savannah, Ga.	13,981	13,201
Lake Charles, La.	37,312	31,730	Anacortes, Wash.	13,638	13,687
Mobile, Ala.	36,476	32,384	San Juan, P.R.	13,503	13,452
Pittsburgh	34,373	28,840	Galveston, Texas	12,355	8,684
Portland, Ore.	31,971	26,812	Presque Isle, Mich.	11,433	9,333
Beaumont, Texas	31,947	29,758	Cincinnati, Ohio	11,243	11,995
Marcus Hook, Pa.	29,815	28,154	Honolulu, Hawaii	10,655	9,737
St. Louis (Metropolitan)	29,011	27,571	Ashtabula, Ohio	10,335	8,888
Pascagoula, Miss.	28,528	27,824	Conneaut Harbor, Ohio	10,220	7,047
Port Arthur, Texas	23,801	20,615	Calcite, Mich.	10,205	8,159
Chicago	22,894	20,705	Memphis, Tenn.	10,200	11,220
Paulsboro, N.J.	22,004	17,936	Oakland, Calif.	10,140	9,212
Newport News, Va.	21,391	19,624			

Source: Department of the Army, Corps of Engineers.

Annual Railroad Carloadings

Year	Total	Year	Total	Year	Total	Year	Total
1930	30,173,000	1955	32,761,707[1]	1980	22,223,000[1]	1985	19,501,242[1]
1935	22,015,000	1960	27,886,950[1]	1981	21,342,987[1]	1986	19,588,666[1]
1940	36,358,000	1965	28,344,381[1]	1982	18,584,760[1]	1987	20,602,204[1]
1945	41,918,000	1970	27,015,020[1]	1983	19,013,250[1]	1988	22,599,993[1]
1950	38,903,000	1975	22,929,843[1]	1984	20,945,536[1]	1989	21,226,015

[1]Only Class 1 railroads. *Source:* Association of American Railroads.

Estimated Motor Vehicle Registration, 1989

(in thousands; including publicly owned vehicles)

State	Autos[1]	Trucks and buses	Motor-cycles	Total	State	Autos[1]	Trucks and buses	Motor-cycles	Total
Alabama	3,065	1,010	48	4,075	Montana	438	295	26	733
Alaska	233	134	8	367	Nebraska	886	454	27	1,340
Arizona	1,993	792	81	2,785	Nevada	589	246	19	835
Arkansas	835	601	14	1,436	New Hampshire	774	202	39	976
California	16,799	4,858	628	21,657	New Jersey	5,384	510	97	5,894
Colorado	2,132	800	102	2,932	New Mexico	773	474	34	1,247
Connecticut	2,535	160	54	2,695	New York	8,861	1,323	208	10,184
Delaware	407	122	9	529	North Carolina	3,698	1,503	56	5,201
Dist. of Col.	252	16	2	268	North Dakota	388	274	23	662
Florida	9,014	2,364	184	11,378	Ohio	7,129	1,691	244	8,820
Georgia	3,802	1,583	75	5,385	Oklahoma	1,682	899	62	2,581
Hawaii	626	93	17	719	Oregon	1,815	552	70	2,367
Idaho	609	344	43	953	Pennsylvania	6,354	1,568	177	7,922
Illinois	6,579	1,512	245	8,091	Rhode Island	566	121	23	687
Indiana	3,115	1,150	104	4,265	South Carolina	1,849	625	28	2,474
Iowa	1,848	765	179	2,613	South Dakota	420	287	30	707
Kansas	1,543	694	74	2,237	Tennessee	3,509	873	53	4,382
Kentucky	1,887	954	33	2,841	Texas	8,523	4,042	197	12,565
Louisiana	1,986	998	34	2,984	Utah	807	381	27	1,188
Maine	770	218	39	988	Vermont	347	126	18	473
Maryland	2,908	631	60	3,539	Virginia	3,637	1,092	61	4,729
Massachusetts	3,292	499	58	3,791	Washington	2,883	1,192	130	4,075
Michigan	5,637	1,656	200	7,293	West Virginia	932	389	17	1,321
Minnesota	2,553	714	117	3,267	Wisconsin	3,290	753	197	4,043
Mississippi	1,377	434	25	1,811	Wyoming	291	200	20	491
Missouri	2,753	1,120	60	3,873	**Total**	**144,375**	**44,294**	**4,376**	**188,669**

1. Includes taxicabs. NOTE: Figures are latest available. *Source:* Department of Transportation, Federal Highway Administration.

Passenger Car Production by Make

Companies and models	1989	1988	1985	1980	1975	1970
American Motors Corporation	—	—	109,919	164,725	323,704	276,127
Chrysler Corporation						
Plymouth	258,847	313,700	369,487	293,342	443,550	699,031
Dodge	453,428	511,133	482,388	263,169	354,482	405,699
Chrysler	203,624	248,012	414,193	82,463	102,940	158,614
Imperial	—	—	—	—	1,930	10,111
Total	**915,899**	**1,072,845**	**1,266,068**	**638,974**	**902,902**	**1,273,455**
Ford Motor Company						
Ford	1,165,886	1,304,819	1,098,627	929,627	1,301,414	1,647,918
Mercury	297,678	293,766	374,446	324,528	405,104	310,463
Lincoln	213,517	207,156	163,077	52,793	101,520	58,771
Total	**1,677,081**	**1,805,741**	**1,636,150**	**1,306,948**	**1,808,038**	**2,017,152**
General Motors Corporation						
Chevrolet	1,196,953	1,381,967	1,691,254	1,737,336	1,687,091	1,504,614
Pontiac	732,177	806,356	702,617	556,429	523,469	422,212
Oldsmobile	520,981	562,920	1,168,982	783,225	654,342	439,632
Buick	470,052	484,851	1,001,461	783,575	535,820	459,931
Cadillac	293,589	265,030	322,765	203,991	278,404	152,859
Total	**3,213,752**	**3,501,124**	**4,887,079**	**4,064,556**	**3,679,126**	**2,979,248**
Checker Motors Corporation				3,197	3,181	4,146
Volkswagen of America	—	35,998	96,458	197,106		
Honda	362,274	366,354	238,159	145,337		
Mazda	216,501	163,289				
Nissan	115,584	109,897	43,810	—	—	—
Toyota	231,279	55,480				
Industry total	**6,823,097**	**7,110,728**	**8,184,821**	**6,375,506**	**6,716,951**	**6,550,128**

Source: Motor Vehicle Manufacturers Association of the United States.

Motor Vehicle Data

	1988	1987	1980	1970	1960
U.S. passenger cars and taxis registered (thousands)	141,252	137,208	121,724	89,280	61,671
Total mileage of U.S. passenger cars (millions)	1,429,297	1,355,330	1,111,596	916,700	588,083
Total fuel consumption of U.S. passenger cars (millions of gallons)	71,654	70,573	71,883	67,820	41,169
World registration of cars, trucks, and buses (thousands)	539,790	515,386	411,113	246,368	126,955
U.S. registration of cars, trucks, and buses (thousands)	184,397	179,044	155,796	108,418	73,858
U.S. share of world registration of cars, trucks, and buses	34.2%	34.7%	37.9%	44.0%	58.2%

Source: Motor Vehicle Manufacturers Association of the U.S.

Domestic Motor Vehicles Sales
(in thousands)

Type of Vehicle	1988	1987	1986	1985	1984	1983	1980	1975
Passenger Cars								
Passenger car factory sales	7,105	7,085	7,516	8,002	7,621	6,739	6,400	6,713
Passenger car (new) retail sales[1]	10,626	10,278	11,460	11,042	10,390	9,182	8,979	8,640
Domestic[2]	7,526	7,081	8,215	8,205	7,952	6,795	6,581	7,050
Subcompact[3]	1,019	1,101	1,325	1,297	2,322	1,776	1,604	700
Compact[3]	2,781	2,388	2,461	2,563	1,336	1,110	1,659	2,336
Standard[3]	1,722	1,565	1,888	1,882	1,817	1,825	1,358	1,956
Intermediate[3]	2,017	2,026	2,540	2,464	2,484	2,071	1,957	2,058
Imports[4]	3,100	3,197	3,245	2,838	2,439	2,387	2,398	1,587
Trucks								
Truck and bus factory sales	4,121	3,821	3,393	3,357	3,075	2,414	1,667	2,272
Truck and bus retail sales[5]	4,608	4,174	4,031	3,984	3,538	2,709	2,232	2,351
Light duty (up to 14,000 GVW)[6]	4,273	3,885	3,766	3,700	3,261	2,521	1,964	2,076
Med. duty (14,000-26,000 GVW)[6]	83	55	51	53	61	48	92	169
Heavy duty (over 26,000 GVW)[6]	251	234	214	231	216	141	176	106
Motorcycles								
Motorcycles (new) retail sales[7]	710	935	1,045	1,260	1,305	1,185	1,070	940
All-terrain vehicles	290	395	465	550	550	425	n.a.	n.a.
All-terrain vehicle imports	209	320	498	683	635	430	n.a.	n.a.
Motorcycle imports total[8]	287	318	550	733	441	540	1,120	948

1. Based on data from U.S. Dept. of Commerce. 2. Includes domestic models produced in Canada and Mexico. 3. Beginning 1980, cars produced in U.S. by foreign manufacturers are included. 4. Excludes domestic models produced in Canada. 5. Excludes motorcoaches and light-duty imports from foreign manufacturers. Includes imports sold by franchised dealers of U.S. manufacturers. Starting in 1986 includes sales of trucks over 10,000 lbs. GVW by foreign manufacturers. 6. Gross vehicle weight (fully loaded vehicles). 7. Estimates by Motorcycle Industry Council Inc., Costa Mesa, Calif. Includes all-terrain vehicles and scooters. Excludes mopeds/motorized bicycles. 8. *Source:* Motorcycle Industry Council Inc. Data from U.S. Dept. of Commerce. Excludes mopeds/motorized bicycles and all-terrain vehicles. NOTE: n.a. = not available. *Source: Statistical Abstract of the United States 1990.*

Domestic and Export Factory Sales of Motor Vehicles
(in thousands)

	From plants in United States								
	Passenger cars			Motor trucks and buses			Total motor vehicles		
Year	Total	Domestic	Exports	Total	Domestic	Exports	Total	Domestic	Exports
1970	6,547	6,187	360	1,692	1,566	126	8,239	7,753	486
1975	6,713	6,073	640	2,272	2,003	269	8,985	8,076	909
1980	6,400	5,840	560	1,667	1,464	203	8,067	7,304	763
1984	7,621	7,030	591	3,075	2,884	191	10,696	9,914	782
1985	8,002	7,337	665	3,357	3,126	231	11,359	10,463	896
1986	7,516	6,869	647	3,393	3,130	263	10,909	9,999	910
1987	7,085	6,487	598	3,821	3,509	312	10,906	9,996	910
1988	7,105	6,437	668	4,120	3,795	325	11,225	10,232	993
1989	6,807	6,181	626	4,062	3,752	310	10,869	9,933	936

Source: Motor Vehicle Manufacturers Association of the U.S.

U.S. Direct Investment in EEC Countries, 1989

(in millions of dollars)

Countries	All industries	Petroleum	Manufacturing	Wholesale	Banking	Finance & Insurance	Services	Other industries
Belgium	$8,290	$502	$4,407	$1,945	$ 335	$ 796	$ 267	$ 38
Denmark	1,246	(¹)	288	482	42	226	(¹)	(¹)
France	14,747	1,050	9,490	2,531	211	872	275	318
Germany, Federal Republic of	23,059	2,600	14,430	1,285	1,456	2,515	−46	820
Greece	265	(¹)	91	49	27	(¹)	29	(¹)
Ireland	6,237	−28	5,082	18	7	1,160	6	−8
Italy	10,634	574	6,830	1,417	281	1,055	189	288
Luxembourg	904	5	543	6	253	97	0	0
Netherlands	17,168	1,907	7,541	2,471	177	3,798	1,088	185
Portugal	612	50	230	147	131	(¹)	(¹)	8
Spain	6,002	98	3,865	915	681	28	295	119
United Kingdom	60,810	10,063	22,097	2,464	2,884	20,599	1,748	955
Total	$149,975	$17,034	$74,893	$13,730	$6,486	$31,177	$3,929	$2,726

1. Suppressed to avoid disclosure of data of individual companies. *Source: Survey of Current Business*, June 1990.

Balance of International Payments

(in billions of dollars)

Item	1989	1988	1987	1985	1980	1975	1970	1965	1960
Exports of goods, services, and income	$603.2	$533.4	$432.1	$366.0	$343.2	$157.9	$68.4	$42.7	$30.5
Merchandise, adjusted, excluding military	360.5	319.2	250.3	214.4	224.0	107.1	42.5	26.5	19.7
Transfers under U.S. military agency sales contracts	8.3	10.0	11.2	9.0	8.2	3.9	1.5	0.8	0.3
Receipts of income on U.S. investments abroad	127.5	107.8	104.7	90.0	75.9	25.4	11.8	7.4	4.6
Other services	106.9	92.7	79.9	45.0	36.5	19.3	9.9	6.4	4.3
Imports of goods and services	−689.5	−641.7	−575.6	−461.2	−333.9	−132.6	−60.0	−32.8	−23.7
Merchandise, adjusted, excluding military	−475.3	−446.5	−409.8	−339.0	−249.3	−98.0	−39.9	−21.5	−14.8
Direct defense expenditures	−14.6	−14.6	−14.1	−12.0	−10.7	−4.8	4.9	−3.0	−3.1
Payments of income on foreign assets in U.S.	−128.4	−105.5	−82.4	−65.0	−43.2	−12.6	−5.5	−2.1	−1.2
Other services	−80.0	−75.0	−69.3	−46.0	−30.7	−17.2	−9.8	−6.2	−4.6
Unilateral transfers, excluding military grants, net	−14.7	−14.6	−14.2	−15.0	−7.0	−4.6	−3.3	−2.9	−2.3
U.S. Government assets abroad, net	1.2	−3.0	1.0	−2.8	−5.2	−3.5	−1.6	−1.6	−1.1
U.S. private assets abroad, net	−102.9	−81.5	−86.4	−26.0	−71.5	−35.4	−10.2	−5.3	−5.1
U.S. assets abroad, net	−127.0	−84.2	−62.9	−27.7	−86.1	−39.7	−9.3	−5.7	−4.1
Foreign assets in U.S., net	214.6	219.3	218.0	127.1	50.3	15.6	6.4	0.7	2.3
Statistical discrepancy	22.4	−10.6	1.9	23.0	29.6	5.5	−0.2	−0.5	−1.0
Balance on goods, services, and income	−95.3	−113.8	−147.7	−106.8	9.5	25.2	8.5	10.0	6.9
Balance on current account	−110.0	−126.5	−143.7	−118.0	3.7	18.4	2.4	5.4	2.8

NOTE: — denotes debits. *Source:* Department of Commerce, Bureau of Economic Analysis.

Foreign Investors in U.S. Business Enterprises

	Number				Investment outlays (millions of dollars)			
	1989¹	1988	1987	1986	1989¹	1988	1987	1986
Investments, total	1,101	1,424	978	1,040	$64,565	$72,692	$40,310	$39,177
Acquisitions	645	869	543	555	55,822	64,855	33,933	31,450
Establishments	456	555	435	485	8,743	7,837	6,377	7,728
Investors, total	1,240	1,542	1,051	1,121	64,565	72,692	40,310	39,177
Foreign direct investors	539	566	480	476	20,429	18,569	11,773	8,602
U.S. affilates	701	976	571	645	44,136	54,123	28,536	30,575

1. Figures are preliminary. *Source:* U.S. Department of Commerce, *Survey of Current Business*, May 1990.

Imports of Leading Commodities
(value in millions of dollars)

Commodity	1989	1988
Food and agricultural commodities	**$16,583.9**	**$16,118.6**
Animal feeds	283.0	218.6
Cocoa	732.5	877.4
Coffee	2,272.1	2,340.8
Corn	55.7	18.3
Cotton, raw	3.3	1.0
Dairy products, eggs	442.8	400.8
Fish	2,137.1	2,003.0
Furskins, undressed	118.0	156.8
Hides and skins, undressed	98.5	102.6
Live animals	875.4	752.3
Meat and preparations	2,565.3	2,737.0
Oils and fats, animal	0.4	8.7
Oils and fat, vegetable	657.8	798.6
Rice	62.1	57.7
Soybeans	23.9	16.9
Sugar	611.1	442.1
Tobacco, unmanufactured	650.5	444.6
Vegetables and fruits	4,936.6	4,677.1
Wheat	57.8	64.3
Machinery and transport equipment	**132,355.4**	**126,073.9**
Airplanes	2,803.8	2,641.6
Airplane parts	2,939.7	2,759.3
Cars and trucks	52,983.7	54,441.7
Parts	15,268.8	14,765.1
Spacecraft and parts	80.6	63.1
General industrial machinery	14,470.4	12,821.7
Metalworking machinery	3,880.1	3,310.2
Office machinery	25,679.3	22,523.0
Power generating machinery	14,249.0	12,748.2
Manufactured goods	**113,862.3**	**107,563.6**
Artwork and antiques	2,171.0	2,045.1
Chemicals—fertilizers	999.1	1,027.2
Chemicals—medicinal, pharmaceutical	2,085.8	1,867.7
Chemicals—organic and inorganic	10,273.1	10,566.2
Clothing and footwear	32,952.5	29,452.1
Gem diamonds	4,357.6	4,292.5
Glass	791.1	783.3
Iron and steel mill products	9,400.6	10,228.5
Metal manufactures	6,387.6	4,741.4
Paper, paperboard and articles	8,549.3	8,393.0
Photographic apparatus and supplies	3,423.4	2,898.2
Plastic articles	3,007.2	4,074.3
Pottery	1,245.6	1,321.1
Printed matter	1,618.8	1,584.7
Rubber articles	915.6	(X)
Scientific instruments and parts	5,845.7	5,170.8
Textile yarns, fabrics, and articles	6,094.0	6,338.9
Tires and tubes, automotive	2,392.3	2,032.9
Toys, games and sporting goods	8,409.3	6,714.1
Watches, clocks and parts	909.0	1,896.8
Wood manufactures	2,033.7	2,134.8
Mineral fuels and related products	**51,459.5**	**40,689.1**
Coal	74.4	25.5
Natural gas	1,761.2	1,877.1
Petroleum and petroleum products	49,623.9	38,786.5
Crude materials excluding agricultural products	**10,482.1**	**9,262.8**
Cork, wood and lumber	3,521.2	3,307.6
Pulp and waste paper	3,077.6	2,685.4
Metal ores, scrap	3,883.3	3,269.8
Tobacco excluding agricultural, beverages	**1,639.7**	**1,537.2**
Cigarettes	48.8	36.2
Distilled alcoholic beverages	1,590.9	1,501.0
All others	**146,542.90**	**139,707.1**
Total	**472,925.8**	**440,952.3**

Exports of Leading Commodities
(value in millions of dollars)

Commodity	1989	1988
Food and agricultural commodities	**$35,621.0**	**$34,122.70**
Animal feeds	2,964.6	3,398.2
Cocoa	14.5	14.1
Coffee	11.8	42.7
Corn	6,690.2	5,189.7
Cotton, raw	2,249.6	1,959.8
Dairy products, eggs	439.2	493.1
Fish	1,407.1	1,361.8
Furskins, undressed	155.3	188.3
Hides and skins, undressed	1,567.0	1,634.0
Live animals	490.5	602.2
Meat and preparations	2,819.0	2,426.5
Oils and fats, animal	37.6	530.1
Oils and fats, vegetable	743.0	867.6
Rice	969.7	798.5
Soybeans	3,997.4	4,889.2
Sugar	2.8	100.3
Tobacco, unmanufactured	1,340.6	1,253.2
Vegetables and fruits	3,808.5	3,487.6
Wheat	5,912.6	4,884.8
Machinery and transport equipment	**100,094.4**	**91,727.8**
Airplanes	14,321.9	12,045.7
Airplane parts	8,781.6	7,372.0
Cars and trucks	11,904.5	11,228.0
Parts	11,504.0	12,235.0
Spacecraft and parts	534.1	534.2
General industrial machinery	13,095.5	10,485.8
Metalworking machinery	2,603.1	1,918.7
Office machinery	23,183.8	23,129.2
Power generating machinery	14,165.9	12,779.2
Manufactured goods	**63,853.9**	**54,839.6**
Artwork and antiques	1,619.8	976.2
Chemicals—fertilizers	2,820.7	2,523.8
Chemicals—medicinal, pharmaceutical	3,659.9	3,931.8
Chemicals—organic and inorganic	14,927.9	12,944.2
Clothing and footwear	2,455.5	1,812.8
Gem diamonds	1,086.7	909.6
Glass	808.9	717.5
Iron and steel mill products	3,166.6	2,019.2
Metal manufactures	3,763.5	3,292.3
Paper paperboard and articles	4,194.9	3,846.6
Photographic apparatus and supplies	2,480.9	2,281.3
Plastic articles	1,449.0	2,070.7
Pottery	63.7	57.7
Printed matter	2,640.0	1,914.1
Rubber articles	493.9	(X)
Scientific instruments and parts	10,923.8	8,889.4
Textile yarns, fabrics, and articles	3,897.3	3,643.7
Tires and tubes, automotive	699.8	771.0
Toys, games and sporting goods	1,514.9	1,269.3
Watches, clocks and parts	165.2	124.0
Wood manufactures	1,021.0	844.4
Mineral fuels and related products	**9,408.5**	**7,865.0**
Coal	4,242.1	3,957.5
Natural gas	226.6	215.0
Petroleum and petroleum products	4,939.8	3,692.5
Crude material excluding agricultural products	**14,621.0**	**12,387.4**
Cork, wood, lumber	4,965.2	4,373.1
Pulp and waste paper	4,342.9	3,718.8
Metal ores, scrap	5,312.9	4,295.5
Tobacco excluding agricultural, beverages	**3,596.0**	**2,810.5**
Cigarettes	3,369.2	2,651.4
Distilled alcoholic beverages	226.8	159.1
All other	**137,155.9**	**117,899.1**
Total	**364,349.8**	**322,426.4**

Source: Department of Commerce, Bureau of the Census, Foreign Trade Division.

TAXES

History of the Income Tax in the United States

Source: Deloitte & Touche

The nation had few taxes in its early history. From 1791 to 1802, the United States Government was supported by internal taxes on distilled spirits, carriages, refined sugar, tobacco and snuff, property sold at auction, corporate bonds, and slaves. The high cost of the War of 1812 brought about the nation's first sales taxes on gold, silverware, jewelry, and watches. In 1817, however, Congress did away with all internal taxes, relying on tariffs on imported goods to provide sufficient funds for running the Government.

In 1862, in order to support the Civil War effort, Congress enacted the nation's first income tax law. It was a forerunner of our modern income tax in that it was based on the principles of graduated, or progressive, taxation and of withholding income at the source. During the Civil War, a person earning from $600 to $10,000 per year paid tax at the rate of 3%. Those with incomes of more than $10,000 paid taxes at a higher rate. Additional sales and excise taxes were added, and an "inheritance" tax also made its debut. In 1866, internal revenue collections reached their highest point in the nation's 90-year history—more than $310 million, an amount not reached again until 1911.

The Act of 1862 established the office of Commissioner of Internal Revenue. The Commissioner was given the power to assess, levy, and collect taxes, and the right to enforce the tax laws through seizure of property and income and through prosecution. His powers and authority remain very much the same today.

In 1868, Congress again focused its taxation efforts on tobacco and distilled spirits and eliminated the income tax in 1872. It had a short-lived revival in 1894 and 1895. In the latter year, the U.S. Supreme Court decided that the income tax was unconstitutional because it was not apportioned among the states in conformity with the Constitution.

By 1913, with the 16th Amendment to the Constitution, the income tax had become a permanent fixture of the U.S. tax system. The amendment gave Congress legal authority to tax income and resulted in a revenue law that taxed incomes of both individuals and corporations. In fiscal year 1918, annual internal revenue collections for the first time passed the billion-dollar mark, rising to $5.4 billion by 1920. With the advent of World War II, employment increased, as did tax collections—to $7.3 billion. The withholding tax on wages was introduced in 1943 and was instrumental in increasing the number of taxpayers to 60 million and tax collections to $43 billion by 1945.

In 1981, Congress enacted the largest tax cut in U.S. history, approximately $750 billion over six years. The tax reduction, however, was offset by two tax acts, in 1982 and 1984, which attempted to raise approximately $265 billion.

On Oct. 22, 1986, President Reagan signed into law one of the most far-reaching reforms of the United States tax system since the adoption of the income tax. The Tax Reform Act of 1986, as it was called, attempted to be revenue neutral by increasing business taxes and correspondingly decreasing individual taxes by approximately $120 billion over a five-year period.

The President signed the Technical and Miscellaneous Revenue Act of 1988 (TAMRA) on November 10, 1988. In addition to providing a number of substantive provisions, TAMRA also provided technical corrections for both the Tax Reform Acts of 1984 and 1986.

Internal Revenue Service

The Internal Revenue Service (IRS), a bureau of the U.S. Treasury Department, is the federal agency charged with the administration of the tax laws passed by Congress. The IRS functions through a national office in Washington, 7 regional offices, 63 district offices, and 10 service centers.

Operations involving most taxpayers are carried out in the district offices and service centers. District offices are organized into Resources Management, Examination, Collection, Taxpayer Service, Employee Plans and Exempt Organizations, and Criminal Investigation. All tax returns are filed with the service centers, where the IRS computer operations are located.

IRS service centers are processing an ever increasing number of returns and documents. In 1989 the number of returns and supplemental documents processed totaled 199.6 million. This represented a 2.9% increase over 1988.

Prior to 1987, all tax return processing was performed by hand. This process was time consuming and costly. In an attempt to improve the speed and efficiency of the manual processing procedure, the IRS began testing an electronic return filing system beginning with the filing of 1985 returns.

The two most significant results of the test were that refunds for the electronically filed returns were issued more quickly and the tax processing error rate was significantly lower when compared to paper returns.

Electronic filing of individual income tax returns with refunds became an operational program in selected areas for the 1987 processing year. In 1989, the IRS expanded the program to 48 district offices with 9,435 preparers, software firms, and communication firms transmitting 1.2 million returns. The remaining 15 districts will be added in the 1990 filing season.

In its continuing effort of expanding the electronic filing of individual income tax returns, the IRS began accepting Non-resident Alien Returns (Form 1040 NR) for electronic filing in 1989.

Internal Revenue Service

	1989	1988	1987	1986	1985	1970
U.S. population (in thousands)	248,777	246,329	244,344	241,995	239,714	204,878
Number of IRS employees	114,758	114,873	102,188	95,880	92,254	68,683
Cost to govt. of collecting						
$100 in taxes	$0.51	$0.54	$0.49	$0.49	$0.48	$0.45
Tax per capita	$4,073.22	$3,792.15	$3,627.22	$3,232.51	$3,098.99	$955.31
Collections by principal sources (in thousands of dollars)						
Total IRS collections	$1,013,322,133	$935,106,594	$886,290,590	$782,251,812	$742,871,541	$195,722,096
Income and profits taxes						
Individual	515,731,504	473,666,566	465,452,486	416,568,384	396,659,558	103,651,585
Corporation	117,014,564	109,682,554	102,858,985	80,441,620	77,412,769	35,036,983
Employment taxes	345,625,586	318,038,990	277,000,469	244,374,767	225,214,568	37,449,188
Estate and gift taxes	8,973,146	7,784,445	7,667,670	7,194,956	6,579,703	3,680,076
Alcohol taxes	NOTE 4	NOTE 4	11,097,677	5,647,485	5,398,100	4,746,382
Tobacco taxes	NOTE 4	NOTE 4	NOTE 2	4,607,845	4,483,193	2,094,212
Manufacturers' excise taxes	NOTE 3	NOTE 3	10,221,574	9,927,742	10,020,574	6,683,061
All other taxes	25,977,333	25,934,040	11,991,729	13,489,014	17,103,077	2,380,609

NOTE: For fiscal year ending September 30th. NOTE 2: Alcohol and tobacco tax collections are included in the "All other taxes" amount. NOTE 3: Manufacturers' excise taxes are included in the "All other taxes" amount. NOTE 4: Alcohol and tobacco tax collections are now collected and reported by the Bureau of Alcohol, Tobacco, and Firearms.

Auditing Tax Returns

Most taxpayers' contacts with the IRS arise through the auditing of their tax returns. The Service has been empowered by Congress to inquire about all persons who may be liable for any tax and to obtain for review the books and/or records pertinent to those taxpayers' returns. A wide-ranging audit operation is carried out in the 63 district offices by 16,323 field agents and 3,255 office auditors.

Selecting Returns for Audit

The primary method used by the IRS in selecting returns for audits is a computer program that measures the probability of tax error in each return. The data base (established by an in-depth audit of randomly selected returns in various income categories) consists of approximately 200–250 individual items of information taken from each return. These 200–250 variables individually or in combination are weighted as relative indicators of potential tax change. Returns are then scored according to the weights given the combinations of variables as they appear on each return. The higher the score, the greater the tax change potential. Other returns are selected for examination on the basis of claims for refund, multi-year audits, related return audits, and other audits initiated by the IRS as a result of informants' information, special compliance programs, and the information document matching program.

In 1989, the IRS recommended additional tax and penalties on 837,423 returns, totaling $21 billion.

The Appeals Process

The IRS attempts to resolve tax disputes through an administrative appeals system. Taxpayers who, after audit of their tax returns, disagree with a proposed change in their tax liabilities are entitled to an independent review of their cases. Taxpayers are able to seek an immediate, informal appeal with the Appeals Office. If, however, the dispute arises from a field audit and the amount in question exceeds $10,000, a taxpayer must submit a written protest. Alternatively, the taxpayer can wait for the examiner's report and then request consideration by the Appeals Office and file a protest if necessary. Taxpayers may represent themselves or be represented by an attorney, accountant, or any other advisor authorized to practice before the IRS. Taxpayers can forego their right to the above process and await receipt of a deficiency notice. At this juncture, taxpayers can either (1) not pay the deficiency and petition the Tax Court by a required deadline or (2) pay the deficiency and file a claim for refund with the District Director's office. If the claim is not allowed, a suit for refund may be brought either in the District Court or the Claims Court within a specified period.

Federal Individual Income Tax

The Federal individual income tax is levied on the world-wide income of U.S. citizens and resident aliens and on certain types of U.S. source income of non-residents. For a non-itemizer, "tax table income" is adjusted gross income (*see* below) less $2,050 for each personal exemption and the standard deduction (*see* below). If a taxpayer itemizes, tax table income is adjusted gross income minus total itemized deductions and personal exemptions. Previous law provided 5 tax brackets, with a top rate of 38.5 percent. For the 1990 tax year, there are only 2 tax brackets, 15% and 28%. In addition there is a 5% surtax for high-income taxpayers.

Tax Brackets—1990 Taxable Income

Joint Return	Single Taxpayer	Rate
$0-$32,450	$0-$19,450	15%
32,451-78,400	19,451-47,050	28%
78,401-162,770[1]	47,051-97,620[1]	33%
162,771[1] and up	97,621[1] and up	28%

1. Increase this figure by $11,480 for each personal exemption.

Who Must File a Return[1]

You must file a return if you are:	and your gross income is at least:
Single (legally separated, divorced, or married living apart from spouse with dependent child) and are under 65	$5,300
Single (legally separated, divorced, or married living apart from spouse with dependent child) and are 65 or older	$6,100
A person who can be claimed as a dependent on your parent's return, and who has taxable dividends, interest, or other unearned income	$500
Head of household under age 65	$6,800
Head of household over age 65	$7,600
Married, filing jointly, living together at end of year (or at date of death of spouse), and both are under 65	$9,550
Married, filing jointly, living together at end of year (or at date of death of spouse), and one is 65 or older	$10,200
Married, filing jointly, living together at end of year (or at date of death of spouse), and both are 65 or older	$10,850
Married, filing separate return, or married but not living together at end of year	$2,050
A person with income from sources within U.S. possessions	$2,050
Self-employed and your net earnings from self-employment were at least $400	
A person who received any advance earned income credit payments from their employer during the year	
A person who owes minimum tax, individual retirement arrangement tax, investment credit recapture tax or social security tax on unreported tips	

1. In 1990.

Adjusted Gross Income

Gross income consists of wages and salaries, unemployment compensation, tips and gratuities, interest, dividends, annuities, rents and royalties, up to 1/2 of Social Security Benefits if the recipient's income exceeds a base amount, and certain other types of income. Among the items excluded from gross income, and thus not subject to tax, are public assistance benefits and interest on exempt securities (mostly state and local bonds).

Adjusted gross income is determined by subtracting from gross income: alimony paid, penalties on early withdrawal of savings, payments to an I.R.A. (reduced proportionately based upon adjusted gross income levels if taxpayer is an active participant in an employer maintained retirement plan), payments to a Keogh retirement plan and self-employed health insurance payments (25% limit). Employee business expenses and job related moving expenses are now treated as itemized deductions.

Itemized Deductions

Taxpayers may itemize deductions or take the standard deduction. The standard deduction replaces the zero bracket amount. The standard deduction amounts for 1990 are as follows: Married filing jointly and surviving spouses $5,450; Heads of household $4,750; Single $3,250; and Married filing separate returns $2,725. Taxpayers who are age 65 or over or are blind are entitled to an additional standard deduction of $800 for single taxpayers and $650 for a married taxpayer.

In itemizing deductions, the following are major items that may be deducted in 1990: state and local income and property taxes, charitable contributions, employee moving expenses, medical expenses (exceeding 7.5% of adjusted gross income), casualty losses (only the amount over the $100 floor which exceeds 10% of adjusted gross income), interest payments (only 10% of personal interest payments are deductible) and miscellaneous deductions (deductible only to the extent by which cumulatively they exceed 2% of adjusted gross income).

Personal Exemptions

Personal exemptions are available to the taxpayer for himself, his spouse, and his dependents. The 1990 amount is $2,050 for each individual. Under the 1986 act, no exemption is allowed a taxpayer who can be claimed as a dependent on another taxpayer's return. Additional personal exemptions for taxpayers age 65 or over or blind have been eliminated.

Credits

Taxpayers can reduce their income tax liability by claiming the benefit of certain tax credits. Each dollar of tax credit offsets a dollar of tax liability. The following are a few of the available tax credits:

Certain lower-income households with dependent children may claim an Earned Income Credit of up to $953.40 on $6,810 of earned income. This maximum credit will be reduced if earned income or adjusted gross income exceeds $10,730, and the credit will be zero for families with incomes over $20,264. The earned income credit is a refundable credit.

A credit for Child and Dependent Care Expenses is available for amounts paid to care for a child or other dependent so that the taxpayer can work. The credit is between 20% and 30% (depending on adjusted gross income) of up to $2,400 of employment-related expenses for one qualifying child or dependent and up to $4,800 of expenses for two or more qualifying individuals.

The elderly and those under 65 who are retired under total disability may be entitled to a credit of up to $750 (if single) or $1,125 (if married and filing jointly). No credit is available if the taxpayer is single and has adjusted gross income of $17,500 or more, or $5,000 or more in nontaxable Social Security benefits. Similarly, the credit is unavailable to a married couple if their adjusted gross income exceeds $25,000 or if their nontaxable Social Security benefits equal or exceed $7,500.

Other tax credits available to taxpayers include the targeted jobs credit. This credit is due to expire on October 1, 1990 unless Congress extends the expiration date.

Federal Income Tax Comparisons

Taxes at Selected Rate Brackets After Standard Deductions and Personal Exemptions[1]

Adjusted gross income	Single return listing no dependents				Joint return listing two dependents			
	1990	1989	1988	1975	1990	1989	1988	1975
$ 10,000	$ 705	$ 735	$ 758	$ 1,506	$ −953[2]	$ −910[2]	$ −700[2]	$ 829
20,000	2,205	2,235	2,258	4,153	926	1,020	1,080	2,860
30,000	4,388	4,561	4,694	8,018	2,453	2,520	2,580	5,804
40,000	7,188	7,361	7,494	12,765	3,953	4,020	4,080	9,668
50,000	9,988	10,161	10,389	18,360	5,960	6,272	6,549	14,260

1. For comparison purposes, tax rate schedules were used. 2. Refund based on earned income credit for families with dependent children.

Federal Corporation Taxes

Corporations are taxed under a graduated tax rate structure as shown in the chart. For tax years beginning on or after July 1, 1987, the benefits of the lower rates are phased out for corporations with taxable income between $100,000 and $335,000 and totally eliminated for corporations with income equal to or in excess of $335,000.

If the corporation qualifies, it may elect to be an S corporation. If it makes this election, the corporation will not (with certain exceptions) pay corporate tax on its income. Its income is instead passed through and taxed to its shareholders. There are several requirements a corporation must meet to qualify as an S corporation including having 35 or fewer shareholders, and having only one class of stock.

Tax Years Beginning on or After July 1, 1987

Taxable income	Tax rate
$0–$50,000	15%
$50,001–75,000	25
75,001–100,000	34
100,000–335,000	39
335,001 and up	34

State Corporation Income and Franchise Taxes

All states but Nevada, South Dakota, Texas, Washington, and Wyoming impose a tax on corporation net income. The majority of states impose the tax at flat rates ranging from 2.35% to 15%. Several states have adopted a graduated basis of rates for corporations.

Nearly all states follow the federal law in defining net income. However, many states provide for varying exclusions and adjustments.

A state is empowered to tax all of the net income of its domestic corporations. With regard to non-resident corporations, however, it may only tax the net income on business carried on within its boundaries. Corporations are, therefore, required to apportion their incomes among the states where they do business and pay a tax to each of these states. Nearly all states provide an apportionment to their domestic corporations, too, in order that they not be unduly burdened.

Several states tax unincorporated businesses separately.

Federal Estate and Gift Taxes

A Federal Estate Tax Return must be filed for the estate of every U.S. citizen or resident whose gross estate, if the decedent died in 1990, exceeds $600,000. An estate tax return must also be filed for the estate of a non-resident, if the value of his gross estate in the U.S. is more than $60,000 at the date of death. The estate tax return is due nine months after the date of death of the decedent, but a reasonable extension of time to file may be obtained for good reason. Tax due is to be paid when the return is filed. The executor of an estate with an interest in closely held business that comprises at least 35% of the adjusted gross estate may pay estate tax attributable to the business in from two to ten equal annual installments. In such a case, a 5-year extension for the payment of estate taxes may be exercised for that portion of the tax attributable to a closely held business.

Under the unified federal estate and gift tax structure, individuals who made taxable gifts during the calendar year are required to file a gift tax return by April 15 of the following year.

A unified credit of $192,800 (during 1990) is available to offset both estate and gift taxes. Any part of the credit used to offset gift taxes is not available to offset estate taxes. As a result, although they are still taxable as gifts, lifetime transfers no longer cushion the impact of progressive estate tax rates. Lifetime transfers and transfers made at death are cumulated for estate tax rate purposes.

Gift taxes are computed by applying the uniform rate schedule to lifetime taxable transfers (after deducting the unified credit) and subtracting the taxes payable for prior taxable periods. In general, estate taxes are computed by applying the uniform rate schedule to cumulated transfers and subtracting the gift taxes paid. An appropriate adjustment is made for taxes on lifetime transfers—such as certain gifts within three years of death—in a decedent's estate.

Among the deductions allowed in computing the amount of the estate subject to tax are funeral expenditures, administrative costs, claims and bequests to religious, charitable, and fraternal organizations or government welfare agencies, and state inheritance taxes. For transfers made after 1981 during life or death, there is an unlimited marital deduction.

An annual gift tax exclusion is provided that permits tax-free gifts to each donee of $10,000 for each year. A husband and wife who agree to treat gifts to third persons as joint gifts can exclude up to $20,000 a year to each donee. An unlimited exclusion for medical expenses and school tuition paid for the benefit of any donee is also available.

Federal Estate and Gift Taxes
Unified Rate Schedule, 1990[1]

If the net amount is:		Tentative tax is:		
From	To	Tax +	%	On excess over
$ 0	$ 10,000	$ 0	18	$ 0
10,001	20,000	1,800	20	10,000
20,001	40,000	3,800	22	20,000
40,001	60,000	8,200	24	40,000
60,001	80,000	13,000	26	60,000
80,001	100,000	18,200	28	80,000
100,001	150,000	23,800	30	100,000
150,001	250,000	38,800	32	150,000
250,001	500,000	70,800	34	250,000
500,001	750,000	155,800	37	500,000
750,001	1,000,000	248,300	39	750,000
1,000,001	1,250,000	345,800	41	1,000,000
1,250,001	1,500,000	448,300	43	1,250,000
1,500,001	2,000,000	555,800	45	1,500,000
2,000,001	2,500,000	780,800	49	2,000,000
2,500,001	3,000,000	1,025,800	53	2,500,000
3,000,001 and up	—	1,290,800	55	3,000,000

1. The estate and gift tax rates are combined in the single rate schedule effective for the estates of decedents dying, and for gifts made, after Dec. 31, 1976.

Recent Legislation

On December 19, 1989, the President signed into law the Revenue Reconciliation Act of 1989 (the "Act"). Changes imposed by the Act include:

Internal Revenue Code Section 89 Repealed

Code Section 89, which provided nondiscrimination and qualification rules for employee benefit plans, was repealed. Prior law nondiscrimination rules were reinstated.

Limitation on Corporate Net Operating Loss Carrybacks

The Act significantly curtailed the ability of a C corporation to obtain refunds of prior year's taxes due to a net operating loss carryback. The carryback is now limited where the losses are generated by interest deductions attributable to certain corporate equity-reducing transactions ("CERT").

Who Shoulders the U.S. Federal Income Tax Burden?

The top earning half of the population continues to pay well over 90% of the Federal individual tax bill, according to Tax Foundation analysis of the most recent 1988 tax return data. Data from 1988 reflect the first year for which most provisions of the Tax Reform Act of 1986 (TRA'86) were fully implemented. Despite all the major tax legislation witnessed over the past decade, the share of individual income taxes paid by the top earning half of America's taxpayers has varied less than two percent—from a low of 92.6% in 1982 to a high of 94.5% in 1988.

The average tax payment of the top ten percent of earners in 1988 was $21,573, 88% higher than in 1979. While this group of only 11 million earners paid well over half the total income taxes in 1988, their adjusted gross income ranged down to $58,368, not exactly "fat cat" status. It still takes millions of middle and upper-middle income taxpayers to pay the bulk of the total income tax bill.

The data also noted that the 110 million returns filed for tax year 1988 reported a sharp increase in adjusted gross income of over $323 billion, largely due to the repeal or limitation of a number of income exclusions and adjustments by the new law. □

State and Local Taxes Paid by a Family of Four in Selected Large Cities, 1988

City	Total Taxes Paid by Gross Family Income Level			Percent of Income by Income Level		
	$25,000	$50,000	$75,000	$25,000	$50,000	$75,000
Albuquerque, NM	1,898	3,944	6,296	7.6	7.9	8.4
Atlanta, GA	2,107	4,403	7,014	8.4	8.8	9.4
Baltimore, MD	2,809	5,712	8,594	11.2	11.4	11.5
Bridgeport, CT	2,188	3,653	6,033	8.8	7.3	8.0
Burlington, VT	2,015	4,055	6,653	8.1	8.1	8.9
Charleston, WV	2,097	4,134	7,166	8.4	8.3	9.6
Charlotte, NC	2,255	4,539	6,815	9.0	9.1	9.1
Chicago, IL	2,031	3,913	5,762	8.1	7.8	7.7
Cleveland, OH	2,508	5,256	8,148	10.0	10.5	10.9
Columbia, SC	2,131	4,540	7,394	8.5	9.1	9.9
Des Moines, IA	2,640	5,444	8,451	10.6	10.9	11.3
Detroit, MI	3,002	6,068	9,236	12.0	12.1	12.3
Honolulu, HI	2,522	5,299	8,054	10.1	10.6	10.7
Indianapolis, IN	2,239	3,943	6,299	9.0	7.9	8.4
Jackson, MS	1,921	3,863	6,556	7.7	7.7	8.7
Louisville, KY	2,193	4,417	6,586	8.8	8.8	8.8
Memphis, TN	1,890	3,163	4,522	7.6	6.3	6.0
Milwaukee, WI	3,425	7,299	11,044	13.7	14.6	14.7
Newark, NJ	2,751	5,572	8,542	11.0	11.1	11.4
New York City, NY	2,465	6,393	10,151	9.9	12.8	13.5
Norfolk, VA	2,327	4,444	7,258	9.3	8.9	9.7
Omaha, NE	2,241	4,257	7,002	9.0	8.5	9.3
Philadelphia, PA	3,073	5,781	8,356	12.3	11.6	11.1
Portland, ME	1,966	4,890	8,482	7.9	9.8	11.3
Portland, OR	3,332	7,018	10,973	13.3	14.0	14.6
Providence, RI	2,614	4,986	8,297	10.5	10.0	11.1
St. Louis, MO	2,076	3,969	6,090	8.3	7.9	8.1
Salt Lake City, UT	2,285	4,771	7,254	9.1	9.5	9.7
Sioux Falls, SD	2,337	4,052	5,724	9.3	8.1	7.6
Washington, DC	2,514	5,427	8,557	10.1	10.9	11.4

NOTE: Data based on average family of four (one wage earner, wife or husband, and two school age children) owning their own home and living in a city where taxes apply. Comprises State and local sales, income, auto, and real estate taxes. *Source:* Government of the District of Columbia, Department of Finance and Revenue, *Tax Rates and Tax Burdens in the District of Columbia: a Nationwide Comparison.*

Labor Firsts in America

Source: U.S. Department of Labor.

The first . . .

Labor organization was formed by the Boston shoemakers and coopers guilds, which obtained a three-year charter (1648).

Women's labor organization was established by maidservants in New York City to protest abuses they suffered from their mistresses' husbands (1734).

National labor union that still exists today is the International Typographical Union (1850).

Union of federal employees was formed by New York City letter carriers (1863).

State to create a permanent agency to mediate labor disputes was New York (1886).

Federal arbitration law was passed (1888).

State to study occupational safety was Massachusetts (1850), which also passed the first legislation requiring factory safeguards (1877) and factory inspections (1879).

Pension was established by the Plymouth Colony for disabled soldiers (1638).

Federal government pension was established to assist wounded and disabled Revolutionary soldiers (1776).

Private pension plan offered by a company was established by the American Express Company (1875).

State law restricting child labor was in Massachusetts. It states that no child under the age of 15 shall work in "manufacturing establishments" unless the child attended school for at least three of the 12 months preceding any year of employment (1836).

Dispute that may be labeled a strike occurred in Jamestown, Va., as Polish workers protested against being denied the right to vote (1619).

Criminal prosecution of strikers came after a strike of cartmen in New York City (1677).

Strike of national importance occurred when railroad workers on several eastern and midwestern lines struck to protest wage cuts (1877).

National general strike, and the first designated "May Day" strike, occurred when approximately 340,000 workers demonstrated for an eight-hour day in several cities (1886).

Massive strike by federal employees was by postal workers (1970).

Fixed wage rates were set by the governor of Virginia and the Council of London Company (1621).

States to have equal pay legislation for women were Michigan and Montana (1919).

Minimum wage of 25 cents per hour was established by the Fair Labor Standards Act (1938).

Anti-discrimination law against women was in Illinois (1872).

Per Capita Tax Burden by State
Fiscal Years 1989-1991

State	Per capita burden 1991	Per capita burden 1990	Per capita burden 1989	State	Per capita burden 1991	Per capita burden 1990	Per capita burden 1989
Alabama	$ 3,298	$ 3,037	$ 2,821	Montana	$ 3,300	$ 3,024	$ 2,807
Alaska	5,164	4,891	4,667	Nebraska	3,871	3,545	3,277
Arizona	3,697	3,483	3,309	Nevada	4,606	4,364	4,159
Arkansas	3,122	2,863	2,655	New Hampshire	5,374	5,014	4,703
California	4,921	4,600	4,331	New Jersey	6,776	6,239	5,780
Colorado	4,202	3,905	3,660	New Mexico	3,105	2,890	2,719
Connecticut	7,358	6,768	6,252	New York	5,647	5,178	4,779
Delaware	5,344	4,953	4,629	North Carolina	3,747	3,469	3,237
Dist. of Columbia	6,326	5,770	5,292	North Dakota	3,366	3,086	2,862
Florida	4,391	4,127	3,908	Ohio	4,366	3,997	3,689
Georgia	3,912	3,646	3,424	Oklahoma	3,438	3,173	2,959
Hawaii	4,354	4,044	3,781	Oregon	3,995	3,678	3,423
Idaho	3,137	2,891	2,698	Pennsylvania	4,569	4,189	3,873
Illinois	5,166	4,738	4,375	Rhode Island	4,906	4,517	4,193
Indiana	4,032	3,693	3,409	South Carolina	3,280	3,040	2,843
Iowa	3,886	3,541	3,261	South Dakota	3,179	2,919	2,709
Kansas	4,236	3,899	3,623	Tennessee	3,711	3,424	3,183
Kentucky	3,280	3,008	2,783	Texas	3,870	3,619	3,410
Louisiana	3,230	2,952	2,725	Utah	2,934	2,731	2,568
Maine	3,909	3,607	3,358	Vermont	4,065	3,761	3,511
Maryland	5,456	5,046	4,694	Virginia	4,681	4,341	4,052
Massachusetts	6,076	5,577	5,149	Washington	4,462	4,146	3,886
Michigan	4,695	4,298	3,966	West Virginia	3,026	2,758	2,541
Minnesota	4,561	4,200	3,902	Wisconsin	4,139	3,803	3,529
Mississippi	2,668	2,451	2,276	Wyoming	3,730	3,429	3,189
Missouri	4,159	3,823	3,544	**U.S. Total**	**$ 4,511**	**$ 4,170**	**$ 3,884**

Source: Tax Foundation, based on Fiscal Year 1991 Budget of the U.S.

Tax Freedom Day[1] by State
Calendar Year 1990

State	Tax Freedom Day	Number of days	Rank	State	Tax Freedom Day	Number of days	Rank
Alabama	April 29	119	34	Montana	April 26	116	44
Alaska	May 9	129	8	Nebraska	April 25	115	46
Arizona	May 4	124	19	Nevada	May 3	123	24
Arkansas	April 25	115	45	New Hampshire	April 19	109	51
California	May 4	124	17	New Jersey	May 9	129	9
Colorado	April 27	117	40	New Mexico	May 10	130	7
Connecticut	May 12	132	5	New York	May 23	143	2
Delaware	May 18	138	3	North Carolina	May 2	122	25
Dist. of Columbia	May 23	143	1	North Dakota	April 27	117	41
Florida	May 2	122	26	Ohio	May 4	124	18
Georgia	April 29	119	37	Oklahoma	May 5	125	16
Hawaii	May 17	137	4	Oregon	April 25	115	47
Idaho	April 24	114	48	Pennsylvania	May 6	126	13
Illinois	May 5	125	14	Rhode Island	May 7	127	12
Indiana	April 27	117	42	South Carolina	May 3	123	22
Iowa	April 26	116	43	South Dakota	April 19	109	50
Kansas	May 2	122	27	Tennessee	April 29	119	36
Kentucky	April 29	119	35	Texas	April 28	118	39
Louisiana	May 2	122	28	Utah	April 28	118	38
Maine	May 3	123	23	Vermont	April 30	120	30
Maryland	May 12	132	6	Virginia	April 30	120	33
Massachusetts	May 8	128	10	Washington	May 5	125	15
Michigan	May 3	123	20	West Virginia	April 30	120	31
Minnesota	May 8	128	11	Wisconsin	May 3	123	21
Mississippi	April 20	110	49	Wyoming	April 30	120	32
Missouri	May 1	121	29	**U.S. Total**	**May 5**	**125**	**—**

1. Tax Freedom Day is the day on which the American taxpayer will have earned enough money to pay his 1990 total taxes.
Source: Tax Foundation.

Major State Taxes and Rates
as of July 15, 1990

State	Income taxes Corporate	Income taxes Individual	General Sales and Use Tax	Gasoline Tax (per gallon)	Cigarette Tax (per pack of 20)	Property Tax
Alabama	5%[F]	2 to 5%[F]	4%[a]	11 cents	16.5 cents	X
Arizona	9.3[F]	3.8 to 7[F]	5[a]	17[b]	15[b]	X
Arkansas	1 to 6	1 to 7	4[a]	13.5	21	X
California	9.3[c]	1 to 9.3[c]	5[a, d]	9[b]	35	X
Colorado	5 to 5.3[d]	5[c]	3[a]	20[b]	20	X
Connecticut	11.5[e, f]	1 to 14[g]	8	22[b]	40	X
District of Columbia	10[f]	6 to 9.5	6	18	17	X
Georgia	6	1 to 6	4[a]	7.5 + 3% of retail	12	X
Hawaii	4.4 to 6.4	2 to 10	4[a]	19.8 to 27.5	40% of wholesale	
Idaho	8	2 to 8.2	5	18	18	X
Illinois	4.8[h]	3	6.25[a]	19	30	X
Indiana	3.4[i]	3.4	5	15	15.5	X
Iowa	6 to 12[F, j]	.4 to 9.98[F, c]	4[a]	20	31	
Kansas	4.5[f]	3.65 to 8.75[k]	4.25[a]	16[b]	24	X
Kentucky	3 to 7.25	2 to 6[F]	6[a]	15[l]	3	X
Louisiana	4 to 8[F]	2 to 6[F]	4[a]	20	16	X
Maine	3.5 to 8.93	2 to 8.5	5	17	31[b]	X
Maryland	7	2 to 5	5	18.5	13	X
Massachusetts	9.5[m]	5.95[n]	5	17[b]	26	X
Michigan	2.35	4.6	4	15	25	X
Minnesota	9.5[b, c]	6 to 8.5[o]	6[a]	20	38	X
Mississippi	3 to 5	3 to 5	6	18[d]	18	X
Missouri	5 to 6.5[F, e]	1.5 to 6[F]	4.225[a, d]	11	13	X
Nebraska	5.17 to 7.24[b]	2 to 5.9[b]	5[a]	21.9[l]	27	X
New Jersey	9[f]	2 to 7	7	10.5	40	X
New Mexico	4.8 to 7.6	1.8 to 8.5	5	16	15	X
New York	9[c, f]	4 to 7.875[d, p]	4[a]	8	39	X
North Carolina	7	6 to 7	3[a]	21.5	2	X
North Dakota	3 to 10.5[F, c]	2.67 to 12[F, q]	5	17	30[d]	X
Ohio	5.1 to 8.9	.743 to 6.9	5[a]	20	18	X
Oklahoma	6	.5 to 10[F, k]	4.5[a]	16	23	
Pennsylvania	8.5	2.1	6[a]	12	18	X
Rhode Island	9	22.96% of modified Federal Income tax	7[d]	20[l]	37	X
South Carolina	5	3 to 7[d]	5[a]	16	7	X
Tennessee	6	6[g]	5.5[a]	20	13	
Utah	5	2.55 to 7.2[F]	5[a]	19	23	X
Vermont	5.5 to 8.25	28% of Federal income tax[d]	4	15[d]	17	X
Virginia	6	2 to 5.75	3.5[a]	17.5	2.5	X
West Virginia	9.3[d]	3 to 6.5[c]	6	15.5	17	X
Wisconsin	7.9	4.9 to 6.93	5[a]	21.5[l]	30[e]	X
Florida	5.5[c]	These 7 states have no individual income tax	6[a]	4[r]	33.9	X
Nevada	These 5 states have no corporate income tax		5.75[a]	18	35[d]	X
South Dakota			4[a]	18	23	
Texas			6.25[a]	15	41	
Washington			6.5[a]	22[b, l]	34[d]	X
Wyoming			3[a]	9[l]	12	X
Alaska	1 to 9.4	These 5 states have no general sales tax		8	29	X
Delaware	8.7	3.2 to 7.7[F]		16[b]	14[b]	
Montana	6.75[f, s]	2 to 11[F]		20	18	X
New Hampshire	8	5[g]		16	25	X
Oregon	6.6	5 to 9[F]		18[b]	28	X

X. Indicates state levies a property tax. F. Allows federal income tax as a deduction. a. Local taxes are additional. b. Future increases scheduled under current law. c. Alternative minimum tax is imposed. d. Future reductions scheduled under current law. e. Alternative methods of calculation may be required. f. Corporate surtax is imposed, Connecticut—20%, District of Columbia—5%, Kansas—2.25%, New Jersey—.375%, New York—15%, Montana—5%. g. In Connecticut, New Hampshire, and Tennessee, rates apply to income from dividends and interest. Capital gains are taxed at 7% in Connecticut. h. Additional 2.5% personal property replacement tax imposed. i. A supplemental net income tax is imposed at 4.5%. j. Franchise tax is 5% of taxable net income. k. In Kansas and Oklahoma, the higher rates apply to taxpayers deducting Federal income tax. l. Tax rate is periodically adjusted administratively. m. Excise tax is imposed equal to the greater of $456. n. Tax of 12% on income derived from interest, dividends, and capital gains. o. Additional tax is imposed on income over specified levels, varying with filing status. p. Qualified taxpayers may elect to pay alternative taxes at varying rates. q. Optional tax of 14% of taxpayers federal income tax liability. r. In addition, Florida imposes a 6.9 cent sales tax on gasoline. s. 7% rate for corporations using water's edge apportionment. *Source:* Compiled by Tax Foundation from survey of state revenue offices and data reported by Commerce Clearing House through June 15, 1990.

FIRST AID

Information Please Almanac is not responsible and assumes no responsibility for any action undertaken by anyone utilizing the first aid procedures which follow.

The Heimlich Maneuver[1]

Food-Choking

What to look for: Victim cannot speak or breathe; turns blue; collapses.

To perform the Heimlich Maneuver when the victim is standing or sitting:

1. Stand behind the victim and wrap your arms around his waist.
2. Place the thumb side of your fist against the victim's abdomen, slightly above the navel and below the rib cage.
3. Grasp your fist with the other hand and press your fist into the victim's abdomen with a quick upward thrust. Repeat as often as necessary.
4. If the victim is sitting, stand behind the victim's chair and perform the maneuver in the same manner.
5. After the food is dislodged, have the victim seen by a doctor.

When the victim has collapsed and cannot be lifted:

1. Lay the victim on his back.
2. Face the victim and kneel astride his hips.
3. With one hand on top of the other, place the heel of your bottom hand on the abdomen slightly above the navel and below the rib cage.
4. Press into the victim's abdomen with a quick upward thrust.
5. Should the victim vomit, quickly place him on his side and wipe out his mouth to prevent aspira-

tion (drawing of vomit into the throat).
6. After the food is dislodged, have the victim seen by a doctor.
NOTE: If you start to choke when alone and help is not available, an attempt should be made to self-administer this maneuver.

Burns[2]

First Degree: Signs/Symptoms—reddened skin. **Treatment**—Immerse quickly in cold water or apply ice until pain stops.

Second Degree: Signs/Symptoms—reddened skin, blisters. **Treatment**—(1) Cut away loose clothing. (2) Cover with several layers of cold moist dressings or, if limb is involved, immerse in cold water for relief of pain. (3) Treat for shock.

Third Degree: Signs/Symtoms—skin destroyed, tissues damaged, charring. **Treatment**—(1) Cut away loose clothing (do not remove clothing adhered to skin). (2) Cover with several layers of sterile, cold, moist dressings for relief of pain and to stop burning action. (3) Treat for shock.

Poisons[2]

Treatment—(1) Dilute by drinking large quantities of water. (2) Induce vomiting except when poison is corrosive or a petroleum product. (3) Call the poison control center or a doctor.

Shock[2]

Shock may accompany any serious injury: blood loss, breathing impairment, heart failure, burns. Shock can kill—treat as soon as possible and con-

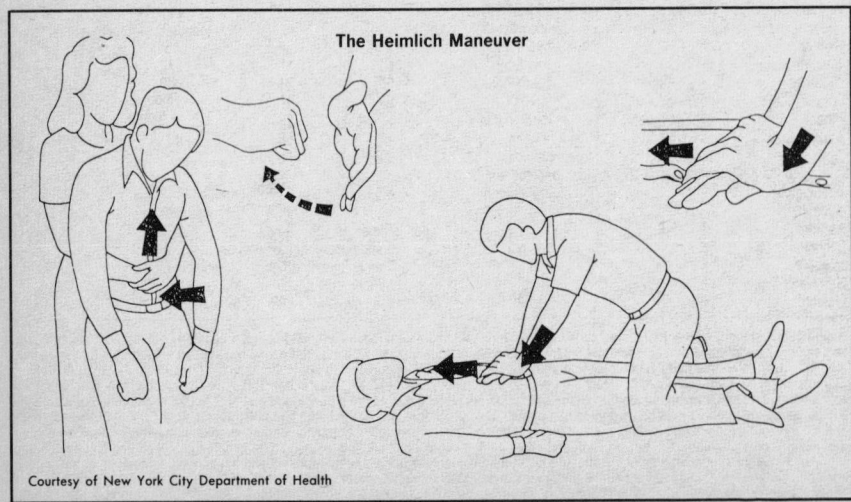

The Heimlich Maneuver

Courtesy of New York City Department of Health

tinue until medical aid is available.

Signs/Symptoms—(1) Shallow breathing. (2) Rapid and weak pulse. (3) Nausea, collapse, vomiting. (4) Shivering. (5) Pale, moist skin. (6) Mental confusion. (7) Drooping eyelids, dilated pupils.

Treatment—(1) Establish and maintain an open airway. (2) Control bleeding. (3) Keep victim lying down. Exception: Head and chest injuries, heart attack, stroke, sun stroke. If no spine injury, victim may be more comfortable and breathe better in a semi-reclining position. If in doubt, keep the victim flat. Elevate the feet unless injury would be aggravated. Maintain normal body temperature. Place blankets under and over victim.

Frostbite[2]

Most frequently frostbitten: toes, fingers, nose, and ears. It is caused by exposure to cold.

Signs/Symptoms—(1) Skin becomes pale or a grayish-yellow color. (2) Parts feel cold and numb. (3) Frozen parts feel doughy.

Treatment—(1) Until victim can be brought inside, he should be wrapped in woolen cloth and kept dry. (2) Do not rub, chafe, or manipulate frostbitten parts. (3) Bring victim indoors. (4) Place in warm water (102° to 105°) and make sure it remains warm. Test water by pouring on inner surface of your forearm. Never thaw if the victim has to go back out into the cold which may cause the affected area to be refrozen. (5) Do not use hot water bottles or a heat lamp, and do not place victim near a hot stove. (6) Do not allow victim to walk if feet are affected. (7) Once thawed, have victim gently exercise parts. (8) For serious frostbite, seek medical aid for thawing because pain will be intense and tissue damage extensive.

Heat Cramps[2]

Affects people who work or do strenous exercises in a hot environment. To prevent it, such people should drink large amounts of cool water and add a pinch of salt to each glass of water

Signs/Symptoms—(1) Painful muscle cramps in legs and abdomen. (2) Faintness. (3) Profuse perspiration.

Treatment—(1) Move victim to a cool place. (2) Give him sips of salted drinking water (one teaspoon of salt to one quart of water). (3) Apply manual pressure to the cramped muscle.

Heat Exhaustion[2]

Signs/Symptoms—(1) Pale and clammy skin. (2) Profuse perspiration. (3) Rapid and shallow breathing. (4) Weakness, dizziness, and headache.

Treatment—(1) Care for victim as if he were in shock. (2) Remove victim to a cool area, do not allow chilling. (3) If body gets too cold, cover victim.

Heat Stroke[2]

Signs/Symptoms—(1) Face is red and flushed. (2) Victim becomes rapidly unconscious. (3) Skin is hot and dry with no perspiration.

Treatment—(1) Lay victim down with head and shoulders raised. (2) Reduce the high body temperature as quickly as possible. (3) Apply cold applications to the body and head. (4) Use ice and fan if

available. (5) Watch for signs of shock and treat accordingly. (6) Get medical aid as soon as possible.

Artificial Respiration[3]

(Mouth-to-Mouth Breathing—In Cases Like Drowning, Electric Shock or Smoke Inhalation.)

There is need for help in breathing when breathing movements stop or lips, tongue, and fingernails become blue. When in doubt, apply artificial respiration until you get medical help. No harm can result from its use and delay may cost the patient his life. Start immediately. Seconds count. Clear mouth and throat of any obstructions with your fingers.

For Adults: Place patient on back with face up.

Lift the chin and tilt the head back. If air passage is still closed, pull chin up by placing fingers behind the angles of the lower jaw and pushing forward.

Take deep breath, place you mouth over patient's mouth, making leak-proof seal.

Pinch patient's nostrils closed.

Blow into patient's mouth until you see his chest rise.

—OR—

Take deep breath, place your mouth over patient's nose, making leak-proof seal.

Seal patient's mouth with your hand.

Blow into patient's nose until you see his chest rise.

Remove your mouth and let patient exhale.

Repeat about 12 times a minute. (If the patient's stomach rises markedly, exert moderate hand pressure on the stomach just below the rib cage to keep it from inflating.)

For Infants and Small Children: Place your mouth over patient's mouth and nose. Blow into mouth and nose until you see patient's chest rise normally.

Repeat 20 to 30 times per minute. (Don't exaggerate the tilted position of an infant's head.)

NOTE: For emergency treatment of heart attack, cardiopulmonary resuscitation (CPR) is recommended. Instruction in CPR can be obtained through local health organizations or schools.

Sources: 1. New York City Department of Health. NOTE: Heimlich Maneuver, T.M. Pending. 2. *First Aid,* Mining Enforcement and Safety Administration, U.S. Department of the Interior. 3. *Health Emergency Chart,* Council on Family Health.

NUTRITION & HEALTH

Focus on Microwave Food Packaging

By Dixie Farley

Sales of microwave-packaged foods are expected to reach $3 billion by 1992, up from $900 million in 1987 and $53 million in 1983. To capture this expanding market, industry has devised numerous packaging innovations. For instance, microwave-absorbing "heat susceptors" induce high temperatures to provide popcorn in a jiffy or brown and crisp pizza and other foods, and plastic "dual-ovenables" are prepared for use in either the conventional or microwave oven.

But the way FDA sees it, the revolutionary technologies producing these niceties were applied before the agency's regulations were ready for them. Although both types of packaging may be manufactured with components that comply with various food additive requirements, FDA has not evaluated the safety of all these materials at temperatures above 300 degrees Fahrenheit. Yet, heat susceptors sometimes exceed 500° F, and dual-oven plastic trays in conventional ovens are usually used at 350° F to 400° F.

FDA's Center for Food Safety and Applied Nutrition (CFSAN) has no information to show a health risk. The center is concerned, however, that such high temperature use of these materials may cause packaging components such as adhesives, polymers, paper, and paperboard—known as indirect food additives—to migrate into food at excessive levels.

Indirect Additive Safety

The agency has been regulating indirect food additives since 1958, with the result that most of these regulations predate the technologies behind microwave heat-susceptor and dual-ovenable packaging. Because FDA could not foresee the extreme heat produced by these innovations, it did not initially specify temperature for migration testing of many indirect additives. In September 1988, FDA issued new recommendations for migration testing protocols, including those for high heat applications.

A Possible Problem?

The food-contact surface of heat-susceptor packaging is usually a metalized polyethylene terephthalate (PET) film laminated to paperboard with adhesive. This metalized film absorbs the microwave energy in the oven and, with most of the microwaves absorbed, the package becomes a little "frying pan" that actively participates in the cooking. (*See* "What Makes the Microwave Run?")

Initial CFSAN studies indicated that the PET film is not a protective barrier between the food and the outer packaging and that the PET itself contributes migrants to the food. Three minutes of microwave heating with susceptors caused more than 70 percent of PET components, called oligomers, to migrate into the corn oil used in the studies to simulate food. Six minutes' heating caused 95 percent migration.

Because susceptors help cook the food, they're known as active packaging. Only a small percentage of microwave packages use susceptors. The vast majority use passive materials, which are transparent to microwaves; the waves pass through the materials to cook the food. These materials are heated solely from the cooking food, so they don't get much hotter than the food.

Still, even some passive packaging, such as dual-ovenables, will produce migration at high temperatures. When CFSAN laboratory personnel heated PET-containing dual-oven trays in a conventional oven at 350° F—following package instructions—they detected migration of the oligomer constituents at levels similar to those found with susceptors. Such migration is possible because foods must be cooked in conventional ovens for a longer time than in microwave ovens and because many conventional ovens heat higher than the temperature setting. (For example, an oven set at 350° F could in fact be heating at 400° F.)

Migration from the packages may turn out to be harmless. But CFSAN as yet doesn't have enough safety data to evaluate uses at these high temperatures.

In response, the Society of the Plastics Industry and the National Food Processors Association jointly sponsored a committee to obtain the information and to work with the American Society for Testing and Materials to develop standardized tests for susceptor packaging.

On Sept. 8, 1989, CFSAN published a notice in the *Federal Register* specifying the data industry is required to provide and the deadlines for these submissions. CFSAN will use the information to make decisions about amending indirect food additive regulations.

Members of the food-packaging industry had claimed CFSAN's use of corn oil simulant rather than food in the laboratory tests did not represent actual use conditions. So, during the spring and summer of 1989, CFSAN chemists developed analytical methods to measure the extent of migration of heat-susceptor packaging components into food. They tested different kinds of susceptors and looked at pizza, popcorn, waffles, and breaded products such as fish sticks. In a meeting with the industry's ad hoc committee on Sept. 25, CFSAN released findings about one sample—french fried potatoes: 5 to 7 parts per million (ppm) of PET oligomers and 15 ppm of diethylene glycol dibenzoate (an adhesive component) had migrated from the film to the food. Though that was only one example, it showed that susceptors used under high heat conditions can cause migration and demonstrated that CFSAN now has test methods to show this actually occurs in food.

While current reports to CFSAN show no health

This article was condensed from "Keeping Up with the Microwave Revolution," by Dixie Farley, *FDA Consumer*, March 1990. Dixie Farley is a staff writer for *FDA Consumer*.

hazard due to substances migrating from heat-susceptor and dual-ovenable packaging, the center will continue working with industry to obtain more conclusive safety information. CFSAN also has contracted with an outside firm to examine migration of packaging components into food.

What Makes the Microwave Run?

Microwaves are a form of electrical and magnetic energy moving through space. They are useful in cooking because they're absorbed by foods but reflected by metal and because they pass through glass, paper, plastic, and similar materials.

Produced by a magnetron electron tube, microwaves bounce about inside the metal oven until absorbed by food. They cause food molecules such as water, a very efficient microwave absorber, to vibrate and thus produce heat to cook the food. That's why foods high in water content, such as fresh vegetables, can be cooked more quickly than other foods. Microwaved foods retain more vitamins and minerals than foods cooked other ways because microwaving takes less time and doesn't require much additional water.

Though microwaves produce heat directly in the food, they really don't cook food from the inside out, says Joanne Barron, who heads the television acoustic and microwave products branch at FDA's Center for Devices and Radiological Health. "With thick foods like roasts," she says, "microwaves generally cook only about an inch of the outer layers. The heat is then slowly conducted inward, cooking along the way."

An area of a food where there is increased moisture will heat more quickly than other areas. So, when heating up a jelly roll, for instance, it's a good idea to let the food stand after cooking for a minute or two until the heat disperses throughout. To promote uniform cooking, recipes for the microwave usually include directions such as "turn the food midway through cooking" and "cover and let stand after cooking."

As a rule, it's not good to use metal pans made for conventional ovens or aluminum foil because the reflected microwaves cause uneven cooking and could even damage the oven. However, some new metal cookware is specially configured for use in microwave ovens. Barron says these pans are safe, provided instructions for use are carefully followed.

Some oven models have a protector on the magnetron tube to allow use of a small amount of metal, such as meat skewers or strips of foil over chicken wings and legs. The instructions that come with each microwave oven tell what kinds of containers to use and how to test for suitability for use.

Microwave oven output, also given in an oven's packaging literature, can vary from 200 watts to around 750 watts—the bigger the oven, the greater the output tends to be. Ovens with fewer watts take longer to cook—sometimes as much as 30 percent more time. Some microwave-packaged foods are labeled with heating directions by wattage.

The Campbell Microwave Institute suggests the following test for gauging output:

• Fill a glass measuring cup with exactly 1 cup of tap water.
• Microwave, uncovered, on "high" until water begins to boil.

If boiling occurs in:	wattage is:
less than 3 minutes	600 to 700
3 to 4 minutes	500 to 600
more than 4 minutes	less than 500 watts

How Safe is Your Oven?

Properly used, a microwave oven is extremely safe. Under authority of the Radiation Control for Health and Safety Act, FDA's Center for Devices and Radiological Health ensures that microwave ovens made after 1971 meet a radiation safety standard requiring:

• two independent interlock systems to stop microwave production the moment the latch is released or the door is opened
• a monitoring system to stop the oven if either or both of the interlocks fail.

The standard limits microwave leakage to 5 milliwatts per square centimeter (mW/cm^2) at about 2 inches from the oven—a very low level of exposure. (Medical applications use up to 1,000 mW/cm^2 without apparent ill effects.) FDA tests have shown that *actual* microwave emission is under 2 mW/cm^2.

Moreover, exposure decreases dramatically with distance. Someone 20 inches from the oven would receive only about one one-hundredth of the radiation as a person 2 inches away. There is no radiation residue after microwave production stops. The whirring noise some ovens make after the door is opened is the fan and has nothing to do with radiation.

To make sure the standard is met, FDA tests microwave ovens in manufacturing plants and its own laboratories. According to Joanne Barron, chief of CDRH's television acoustic and microwave products branch, recent tests by state health officials, FDA field inspectors, and laboratory analysts from the Winchester Engineering and Analytical Center in Massachusetts have very rarely detected an oven that emits leakage above the standard.

To be sure radiation levels from a microwave oven remain as low as possible, consumers can take these steps:

• Don't use an oven if an object is caught in the door or if the door doesn't close firmly or is otherwise damaged. If you have an older model oven with a soft mesh door gasket, check for deterioration, which would require servicing.
• If you suspect excessive microwave leakage, contact the manufacturer, a reputable servicing firm, the local state health department, or the nearest FDA office. FDA has found the inexpensive home microwave-testing devices that are available to be generally inaccurate.
• Don't operate an empty oven if the instruction manual warns against this. In some ovens, the magnetron tube can be damaged by unabsorbed energy.
• If there are signs of rusting inside the oven, have the oven repaired.
• Clean the door and oven cavity—the outer edge, too—with water and mild detergent. Do not use abrasives such as scouring pads.
• Follow the manufacturer's instruction manual for recommended operating procedures and safety precautions.
• Be sure children who use the microwave can do so safely.

There previously was concern that electromagnetic emissions from a microwave oven could interfere with a heart pacemaker. Modern pacemakers are shielded against such interference, but some older models may still be adversely affected by proximity to a microwave oven. If in doubt, check with your doctor. □

The Four Main Food Poisoners

Source: U.S. Department of Agriculture, Food Safety and Inspection Service.

It's important to know the difference between organisms that cause foods to spoil—to rot or turn bad—and those that can cause food poisoning.

A major difference is the temperatures the two types like. Most food poisoning bacteria like room temperatures (around 60° to 90° F). They don't grow at low refrigerator temperatures. By "grow" we mean that bacteria divide, multiplying in number.

But food spoilage organisms—like some bacteria, and yeasts, and molds—can grow at lower temperatures. Even when food is in the refrigerator at temperatures as low as 40° F, these spoilage agents can continue to reproduce.

While it's hard to be grateful for them, most food spoilage organisms at least make themselves known. The food looks or smells awful. That's a help—you know to throw it out.

Unfortunately, the bacteria that commonly cause food poisoning—with its mild-to-severe intestinal flu-like symptoms—are not nearly so obvious.

Most of them can't be seen, smelled, or tasted. The smartest way to handle the food poisoners is to make life so hard they can't multiply enough to cause trouble.

Staphylococcus Aureus

Staphylococcus aureus is the scientific name for a small, round organism that is a leading cause of food poisoning.

We literally carry staph with us all of the time. It lives in our noses and on our skin. You can find it in concentrated form in boils, pimples, and other skin infections.

When transmitted to food, usually by handling, staph starts growing. At warm temperatures—100° F is ideal—certain types of staph multiply rapidly and produce a toxin or poison that makes people sick.

Staph symptoms? Nausea, vomiting, and diarrhea usually appear 2 to 6 hours after eating staph-infected food, and last a day or two. The illness is usually not too serious in healthy people.

While cooking kills most bacteria, the staph toxin is not destroyed by ordinary cooking. So you must be very careful in handling food to prevent staph from growing enough to produce toxin.

Don't let prepared foods—particularly starchy foods, cooked and cured meats, cheese and meat salads—sit out at room temperature over 2 hours. Staph is often associated with these foods.

Salmonella

Salmonella—which appears as short, thin rods under the microscope—is another major cause of food poisoning in this country.

Actually, salmonella is the name used for some 2,000 closely related bacteria that cause more severe flu-like symptoms than staph—diarrhea, vomiting, fever. Infants and young children, the ill, and the elderly may be seriously affected. Symptoms normally appear 12 to 36 hours after eating, and may last 2 to 7 days.

Salmonella continually cycles through the environment in the intestinal tracts of people and animals.

The bacteria are often found in raw or undercooked foods, such as poultry, eggs, and meat. Unpasteurized milk can also contain salmonella.

Control is a simple matter, though, because thorough cooking kills salmonella.

Perfringens

Perfringens, full name *Clostridium perfringens,* ranks third as a cause of food poisoning. It, too, is present throughout the environment—in the soil, the intestines of animals and humans, and in sewage.

Perfringens differs from staph and salmonella, however, in two ways. First, it's anaerobic, which means it grows only where there is little or no oxygen. Second, it produces two kinds of cells.

The normal perfringens cell is the unpleasant one—it produces the poison which makes you sick. But perfringens has a spore cell too, which can survive circumstances that knock out the normal cells.

These spores are tricky, because at temperatures between 70° and 120° F, they can become normal cells again, multiplying quickly to disease-causing levels.

Perfringens shows its ugly side—usually diarrhea and gas pains—some 8 to 24 hours after consumption. While the symptoms often end within a day, people with certain medical conditions—ulcer patients, for instance—can be seriously affected.

Called the "cafeteria germ" because it often strikes food served in quantity and left for long periods on a steam table or at room temperature, perfringens is often found in cooked beef, turkey, gravy, dressing, stews, and casseroles.

Special attention to refrigeration, which keeps perfringens from growing, and dividing large portions into small dishes for serving are the best hedges against perfringens. Dividing buffet foods into several small dishes exposes more of the food to the air, thus reducing the anaerobic conditions perfringens likes.

Botulism

Botulism, while very rare, is the deadly food poisoning caused by *Clostridium botulinum.* Although it needs just the right conditions to develop, botulism is clearly a danger because the spores are always around in soil and water.

Like perfringens, the botulinum bacteria—rod-shaped under the microscope—grow best in anaerobic (reduced oxygen) conditions. Since the canning process forces air out of food, the botulinum bacteria may find improperly canned foods a good place to grow.

Low-acid vegetables such as green beans, corn, beets, and peas, which may have picked up botulinum spores from the soil, are at risk. The risk is greater if they are home-canned, and safe canning procedures have not been followed precisely.

Like the perfringens spore, the botulinum spore is tough. While high cooking temperatures will kill the normal botulinum cell, it takes still higher temperatures to kill the spore. That's why canning is done with a pressure canner. If the spores are not killed in the canning process, they can become normal cells again and produce the deadly poison.

If you eat botulinum-contaminated food, symptoms will develop in 12 to 48 hours. The poison attacks the nervous system, causing double vision, droopy eyelids, trouble swallowing, and difficult breathing. Without treatment, a patient can die of suffocation—the nerves no longer stimulate breathing.

There is an antitoxin, which has reduced the number of deaths from botulism, but patients may still suffer nerve damage, and recovery is often slow.

To avoid botulism, carefully examine any canned food, especially home-canned food, which looks suspicious. Danger signs are milky liquids (that should be clear) surrounding vegetables, cracked jars, loose lids, and swollen cans or lids.

Don't use canned goods showing any of these signs. *Don't even taste them!* Even a very small amount of botulinum toxin can be highly dangerous.

Throw suspect canned goods away, carefully. You don't want animals, children, or anyone else who might rummage through the trash to get ill. Wrap the cans in plastic, then in heavy paper bags, for deposit in a secure trash can. □

Heart Disease Leading Killer of Americans

Source: American Heart Association, © 1989. Latest data available.

What's the number one killer in America? Millions of people believe it's cancer. Cardiovascular disease holds that deadly distinction.

FACT: In 1987 heart and blood pressure diseases killed nearly one million Americans, almost as many as cancer, accidents, pneumonia, influenza, and all other causes of death combined.

FACT: Almost one in two Americans dies of cardiovascular disease.

FACT: Of the current U.S. population of about 243 million, nearly 67 million people—more than one in four Americans—suffer some form of cardiovascular disease.

Make no mistake. Cancer and other diseases are a real threat. But let's put things in perspective. In 1987 about 477,000 Americans died of cancer. In the same year, more than 13,000 Americans died of AIDS. That's tragic, but the tragedy is compounded if Americans focus on these diseases and neglect a disease that claims more than twice as many victims. Cardiovascular diseases are killers.

Cardiovascular diseases may be discounted, in part, because they're perceived as diseases of the elderly. But that's an over-simplification, because about 180,000 Americans under age 65 die from cardiovascular diseases every year.

Modifying a methodology developed by the Centers for Disease Control to include data for people under age 75, "Total Cardiovascular Disease" accounted for 4,950,000 years of potential life lost in 1986, followed by cancer (4,330,000) and injuries (3,150,000).

Cardiovascular diseases demand attention. Too many people are dying. And many deaths may be preventable—by lowering blood pressure, stopping smoking, reducing the amount of cholesterol in the blood, knowing the warning signs of heart disease. Education is vital.

Death rates from heart attack, stroke and other cardiovascular diseases *are* declining. Advances in medical treatment and healthier lifestyles in recent years have undoubtedly contributed. But there's still a long way to go and no time for complacency. Because someone dies—from cardiovascular disease—every 32 seconds.

Heart Attack—Signals and Action
Know the warning signals of a heart attack:
● Uncomfortable pressure, fullness, squeezing or pain in the center of the chest lasting two minutes or longer.

  ● Pain spreading to the shoulders, neck or arms.

  ● Severe pain, lightheadedness, fainting, sweating, nausea or shortness of breath.

Not all these warning signs occur in every heart attack. If some start to occur, however, don't wait. Get help immediately!

Know what to do in an emergency:
  ● Find out which area hospitals have 24-hour emergency cardiac care.

  ● Determine (in advance) the hospital or medical facility nearest your home and office, and tell your family and friends to call this facility in an emergency.

  ● Keep a list of emergency rescue service numbers next to the telephone and in your pocket, wallet or purse.

  ● If you have chest discomfort that lasts two minutes or longer, call the emergency rescue service.

  ● If you can get to a hospital faster by going yourself and not waiting for an ambulance, have someone drive you there.

Be a Heart Saver:
  ● If you're with someone experiencing the signs of a heart attack—and the warning signs last two minutes or longer—act immediately.

  ● Expect a "denial." It's normal for someone with chest discomfort to deny the possibility of something as serious as a heart attack. But don't take "no" for an answer. Insist on taking prompt action.

  ● Call the emergency service, or

  ● Take the person to the nearest hospital emergency room that offers 24-hour emergency cardiac care.

  ● Give CPR (mouth-to-mouth breathing and chest compression) if it's necessary and you're properly trained. □

Women and Heart Disease

Source: American Heart Association.

  ● Heart attack is the No. 1 killer of American women. One in nine women from the ages of 45 to 64 has some form of cardiovascular disease, and the ratio climbs to one in three at age 65 and beyond.

  ● Approximately 247,000 of the more than 520,000 heart attack deaths that occur each year happen to women.

  ● More than 90,000 women die each year of stroke.

  ● All heart and blood vessel diseases combined claim nearly 500,000 women's lives each year, compared with fewer than 220,000 deaths for all forms of cancer.

  ● Women who have heart attacks are twice as likely as men to die within the first few weeks.

  ● Thirty-nine percent of women die within a year after a heart attack compared with 31 percent of men.

• Among U. S. women, aged 18 to 74, 25 percent of whites and 39 percent of blacks have high blood pressure.

• The age-adjusted death rate for coronary heart disease is 22 percent higher for black women than for white women, and the death rate for stroke is 75 percent higher.

• From ages 35 to 74, the death rate from heart attack among black women is one and one-half times that of white women and three times that of women of other races. After age 75, death rates for white women are higher.

• About 22 million American women smoke, making their risk of heart attack two to six times that of a non-smoker.

• Recent studies also show that women smokers who use oral contraceptives are up to 39 more times likely to have a heart attack and up to 22 times more likely to have a stroke than women who don't smoke or use birth control pills.

• Close to one-third of all American adult women have cholesterol levels that put them at increased risk of developing heart disease. If the cholesterol level is over 240 milligrams per deciliter (mg/dl), the risk of heart disease is twice what it would be if the level is below the desirable level of 200 mg/dl.

• Individuals who weigh 30 percent or more of their desirable weight are more likely to develop heart disease and stroke, even if they have no other risk factors.

• The risk of heart attack in women with diabetes is more than double that of non-diabetic women. □

Cancer Risks You Can Avoid

Source: National Cancer Institute, National Institutes of Health.

What is Cancer?

Cancer is really a group of diseases. There are more than 100 different types of cancer, but they all are a disease of some of the body's cells.

Healthy cells that make up the body's tissues grow, divide, and replace themselves in an orderly way. This process keeps the body in good repair. Sometimes, however, normal cells lose their ability to limit and direct their growth. They divide too rapidly and grow without any order. Too much tissue is produced, or *tumors* begin to form. Tumors can be either *benign* or *malignant.*

Benign tumors are not cancer. They do not spread to other parts of the body and they are seldom a threat to life. Often, benign tumors can be removed by surgery, and they are not likely to return.

Malignant tumors are cancer. They can invade and destroy nearby tissue and organs. Cancer cells also spread, or *metastasize,* to other parts of the body, and form new tumors.

Because cancer can spread, it is important for the doctor to find out as early as possible if a tumor is present and if it is cancer. As soon as a diagnosis is made, treatment can begin.

Signs and Symptoms of Cancer

Cancer and other illnesses often cause a number of problems you can watch for. The most common warning signs of cancer are:

Change in bowel or bladder habits;

A sore that does not heal;

Unusual bleeding or discharge;

Thickening or lump in the breast or elsewhere;

Indigestion or difficulty swallowing;

Obvious change in a wart or mole;

Nagging cough or hoarseness.

These signs and symptoms can be caused by cancer or by a number of other problems. They are *not* a sure sign of cancer. However, it is important to see a doctor if any problem lasts as long as 2 weeks. Don't wait for symptoms to become painful; pain is not an early sign of cancer.

Preventing Cancer

By choosing a lifestyle that avoids certain risks, you can help protect yourself from developing cancer. Many cancers are linked to factors that you can control.

Tobacco—Smoking and using tobacco in any form has been directly linked to cancer. Overall, smoking causes 30 percent of all cancer deaths. The risk of developing lung cancer is 10 times greater for smokers than for nonsmokers. The amount of risk from smoking depends on the number and type of cigarettes you smoke, how long you have been smoking, and how deeply you inhale. Smokers are also more likely to develop cancers of the mouth, throat, *esophagus,* pancreas, and bladder. And now there is emerging evidence that smoking can also cause cancer of the stomach and cervix.

The use of "smokeless" tobacco (chewing tobacco and oral snuff) increases the risk of cancer of the mouth and *pharynx.* Once you quit smoking or using smokeless tobacco, your risk of developing cancer begins to decrease right away.

Diet—What you eat may affect your chances of developing cancer. Scientists think there is a link between a high-fat diet and some cancers, particularly those of the breast, colon, *endometrium,* and prostate. Obesity is thought to be linked with increased death rates for cancers of the prostate, pancreas, breast, and ovary. Still other studies point to an increased risk of getting stomach cancer for those who frequently eat pickled, cured, and smoked foods. The National Cancer Institute believes that eating a well-balanced diet can reduce the risk of getting cancer. Americans should eat more high-fiber foods (such as whole-grain cereals and fruits and vegetables) and less fatty foods.

Sunlight—Repeated exposure to sunlight increases the risk of skin cancer, especially if you have fair skin or freckle easily. In fact, ultraviolet radiation from the sun is the main cause of skin cancer, which is the most common cancer in the United States. Ultraviolet rays are strongest from 11 a.m. to 2 p.m. during the summer, so that is when risk is greatest. Protective clothing, such as a hat and long sleeves, can help block out the sun's harmful rays. You can also use sunscreens to help protect yourself. Sunscreens with a number 15 on the label means most of the sun's harmful rays will be blocked out.

Alcohol—Drinking large amounts of alcohol (one or two drinks a day is considered moderate) is associated with cancers of the mouth, throat, esophagus, and liver. People who smoke cigarettes and drink alcohol have an especially high risk of getting cancers of the mouth and esophagus.

X-rays—Large doses of radiation increase cancer risk. Although individual x-rays expose you to very little radiation, repeated exposure can be harmful. Therefore, it is a good idea to avoid unnecessary x-rays. It's best to talk about the need for each x-ray with your doctor or dentist. If you do need an x-ray, ask if shields can be used to protect other parts of your body.

Industrial Agents and Chemicals—Being exposed to some industrial agents or chemicals increases cancer risk. Industrial agents cause damage by acting alone or together with another cancer-causing agent found in the workplace or with cigarette smoke. For example, inhaling asbestos fibers increases the risk of lung disease and cancer. This risk is especially high for workers who smoke. You should follow work and safety rules to avoid coming in contact with such dangerous materials.

Being exposed to large amounts of household solvent cleaners, cleaning fluids, and paint thinners should be avoided. Some chemicals are especially dangerous if inhaled in high concentrations, particularly in areas that are not well ventilated. In addition, inhaling or swallowing lawn and garden chemicals increases cancer risk. Follow label instructions carefully when using pesticides, fungicides, and other chemicals. Such chemicals should not come in contact with toys or other household items.

Hormones—Taking *estrogen* to relieve menopausal symptoms (such as hot flashes) has been associated with higher-than-average rates of cancer of the uterus. Numerous studies also have examined the relationship between oral contraceptives (the pill) and a variety of female cancers. Recent studies report that taking the pill does not increase a woman's chance of getting breast cancer. Also, pill users appear to have a lower-than-average risk of cancers of the endometrium and ovary. However, some researchers believe that there may be a higher risk of cancer of the cervix among pill users. Women taking hormones (either estrogens or oral contraceptives) should discuss the benefits and risks with their doctor.

Unavoidable Risks

Certain risk factors for cancer cannot be controlled, but people at high risk can help protect themselves by getting regular checkups. Some groups that have a higher-than-average risk of developing cancer are described below.

(1) Individuals who have close relatives with *melanoma* or cancer of the breast or colon. A small number of these cancers tends to occur more often in some families. If a close relative has been affected by one of these cancers, you should tell your doctor and be sure to have regular checkups to detect early problems.

(2) Persons who have had x-ray treatment to the head or neck when they were children or young adults. Exposure to these x-ray treatments may result in *thyroid* tumors, which have been associated with radiation given for an enlarged *thymus* gland, enlarged tonsils and *adenoids,* whooping cough, ringworm of the scalp, acne, and other head and neck conditions. Most thyroid tumors are not cancer. If thyroid cancer does develop, it usually can be cured. If you have had such x-rays, you should have a doctor examine your throat and neck every 1 or 2 years.

(3) Daughters and sons whose mothers took a drug called diethylstilbestrol (DES) to prevent miscarriages while they were pregnant with them. DES and some similar drugs given to mothers during pregnancy have been linked to certain unusual tissue formations in the vagina and cervix of their daughters. DES also has caused a rare type of vaginal and cervical cancer in a small number of exposed daughters. Women who took DES and DES-type drugs during pregnancy may themselves have a moderately increased risk of developing breast cancer. DES-exposed daughters and mothers should have examinations at least once a year that include pelvic and breast exams and Pap tests.

No link with cancer due to DES exposure before birth has been found in boys and men. However, there may be an increase in certain reproductive and urinary system problems in DES-exposed sons, who should also be examined regularly by a doctor. □

Understanding AIDS

The Acquired Immune Deficiency Syndrome, or AIDS, was first reported in the United States in mid-1981. The total AIDS cases in the United States (including U.S. territories) as of May 31, 1990, were 136,204, and of these cases, 83,145 deaths were reported, says the Center for Disease Control in Atlanta. According to World Health Organization projections in June 1990, there will be 5-6 million new cases of AIDS by the year 2000 and 15-20 million HIV infected. It is estimated that 700,000 people worldwide have AIDS, and that at least 8 million are infected with the HIV virus.

AIDS is characterized by a defect in natural immunity against disease. People who have AIDS are vulnerable to serious illnesses which would not be a threat to anyone whose immune system was functioning normally. These illnesses are referred to as "opportunistic" infections or diseases: in AIDS patients the most common of these are Pneumocystis carinii pneumonia (PCP), a parasitic infection of the lungs; and a type of cancer known as Kaposi's sarcoma (KS). Other opportunistic infections include unusually severe infections with yeast, cytomegalovirus, herpes virus, and parasites such as Toxoplasma or Cryptosporidia. Milder infections with these organisms do not suggest immune deficiency.

AIDS is caused by a virus usually known as human immunodeficiency virus, or HIV. Symptoms of full-blown AIDS include a persistent cough, fever, and difficulty in breathing. Multiple purplish blotches and bumps on the skin may indicate Kaposi's sarcoma. The virus can also cause brain damage.

People infected with the virus can have a wide range of symptoms—from none to mild to severe. At least a fourth to a half of those infected will de-

AIDS Cases Reported to World Health Organization

Continent	1981[1]	1982	1983	1984	1985	1986	1987	1988	1989	1990	Total
Africa	0	3	14	82	686	3,272	9,900	18,792	8,748	21	41,518
Americas	376	1,096	3,238	6,461	12,249	20,151	31,077	36,771	31,867	3,873	147,159
Asia	1	2	8	7	31	56	120	151	212	0	588
Europe	39	74	270	649	1,651	3,338	6,501	9,259	9,589	211	31,581
Oceania	0	1	6	45	126	242	402	538	534	0	1,894
Total	416	1,176	3,536	7,244	14,743	27,059	48,000	65,511	50,950	4,105	222,740

1. Includes cases reported prior to 1981. Data as of February 1990.

velop AIDS within four to ten years. Many experts think the percentage will be much higher.

AIDS is spread by sexual contact, needle sharing, or less commonly through transfused blood or its components. The risk of infection with the virus is increased by having multiple sexual partners, either homosexual or heterosexual, and sharing of needles among those using illicit drugs. The occurrence of the syndrome in hemophilia patients and persons receiving transfusions provides evidence for transmission through blood. It may be transmitted from infected mother to infant before, during, or shortly after birth (probably through breast milk).

Scientists have discovered how AIDS infects brain cells and have identified genes that affect the AIDS virus. But efforts to devise a treatment or vaccine are complicated by the fact that AIDS is caused by two, perhaps three, similar viruses, and that the virus mutates frequently.

With no cure in sight, prudence could save thousands of people in the U.S. who have yet to be ex-

Approved AIDS Medicines

Drug name	Company	Indication	U.S. Development status
Bactrim™[1] Trimethoprim and Sulfamethoxazole	Hoffmann-La Roche (Nutley, NJ)	PCP treatment	Approved
Cytovene® Ganciclovir (IV)	Syntex (Palo Alto, CA)	CMV retinitis	Approved
Daraprim®[1] Pyrimethamine	Burroughs Wellcome (Rsch. Triangle Park, NC)	toxoplasmosis treatment	Approved
Diflucan Fluconazole	Pfizer (New York, NY)	cryptococcal meningitis, candidiasis	Approved
Intron RA[1] Interferon-alpha 2b	Schering-Plough (Madison, NJ)	Kaposi's sarcoma	Approved
NebuPent® Aerosol Pentamidine Isethionate	Fujisawa Pharmaceutical (Deerfield, IL)	PCP prophylaxis	Approved (Orphan Drug)
Pentam® 300 IM & IV Pentamidine Isethionate	Fujisawa Pharmaceutical (Deerfield, IL)	PCP treatment	Approved
Retrovir® Zidovudine; AZT	Burroughs Wellcome (Rsch. Triangle Park, NC)	HIV positive asymptomatic and symptomatic (ARC, AIDS), pediatric and adult	Approved
Roferon®-A[1] Interferon alfa-2a	Hoffmann-La Roche (Nutley, NJ)	Kaposi's sarcoma	Approved
Septra®[1] Trimethoprim and Sulfamethoxazole	Burroughs Wellcome (Rsch. Triangle Park, NC)	PCP treatment	Approved
Zovirax® Acyclovir	Burroughs Wellcome (Rsch. Triangle Park, NC)	herpes zoster/simplex	Approved

1. Denotes medicine has been approved by the FDA for other conditions. **NOTE:** The latest survey of AIDS medicines in development by the Pharmaceutical Manufacturers Association shows that 77 medicines and combination therapies are being developed by 40 companies to treat AIDS and related disorders. **GLOSSARY: ARC**—AIDS-related complex. **candidiasis**—A fungal infection, usually of the moist cutaneous areas of the body, including the skin, mouth, esophagus (**candida esophagitis**), and respiratory tract. **CMV**—Cytomegalovirus. An opportunistic infection that can cause blindness and be fatal in AIDS patients. **cryptococcal meningitis**—A fungal infection that affects the three membranes (meninges) surrounding the brain and spinal cord. Symptoms include severe headache, vertigo, nausea, anorexia, sight disorders and mental deterioration. **Herpes zoster/simplex**—Three strains of the herpes virus often occur in AIDS patients: **Herpes simplex virus I (HSV I),** which causes cold sores or fever blisters on the mouth or around the eyes, can be transmitted to the genital region. The latent virus can reactivate to produce infection by stress, trauma, other infections, or suppression of the immune system. **Herpes simplex II (HSV II)** causes painful sores of the anus or gentials which may lie dormant in nerve tissue and can be reactivated to produce the sores. **Herpes varicella zoster virus (HVZ)** may appear in adulthood as a result of having had chicken pox (caused by the varicella virus) as a child. Herpes zoster, also called shingles, consists of very painful blisters on the skin and follows nerve pathways. **Kaposi's sarcoma**—A rare malignant skin tumor that occurs in some AIDS patients. It can be accompanied by fever, enlarged lymph nodes and gastro-intestinal problems. **PCP**—Pneumocystis carinii pneumonia. A severe lung infection found in nearly 80 percent of all AIDS patients at some time during the course of the disease and a major cause of death. **toxoplasmosis**—A disease due to infection with the protozoa *Toxoplasma gondii,* frequently causing focal encephalitis (inflammation of the brain). It may also involve the heart, lung, adrenal glands, pancreas and testis. *Source:* Pharmaceutical Manufacturers Association. Data as of August 20, 1990.

posed to the virus. Their fate will depend less on science than on the ability of large numbers of human beings to change their behavior in the face of growing danger. Experts believe that couples who have had a totally monogamous relationship for the past decade are safe. A negative blood test would be near-certain evidence of safety.

People who should be tested for AIDS include gay men and intravenous drug users, their sex partners, and anyone who has had several sex partners, if their sexual history is unknown, during any one of the last five years. Anyone who tests positive should see a physician immediately for a medical evaluation. Persons testing positive should inform their sex partners and should use a condom during sex. They should not donate blood, body organs, other tissue or sperm, nor should they share toothbrushes, razors, or other implements that could become contaminated with blood.

Information about where to go for confidential testing for the presence of the AIDS virus is provided by local and state health departments. There is a National AIDS Hot Line: (800) 342-2437 for recorded information about AIDS, or (800) 433-0366 for specific questions. □

Helping a Person With AIDS

No one will require more support and more love than your friend with AIDS. Feel free to offer what you can, without fear of becoming infected. You need to take precautions such as wearing rubber gloves only when blood is present.

If you don't know anyone with AIDS, but you'd still like to offer a helping hand, become a volunteer. You can be sure your help will be appreciated by a person with AIDS.

This might mean dropping by a supermarket to pick up groceries or just being there to talk. Above all, keep an upbeat attitude. It will help you and everyone face the disease more comfortably.

Blood Supply Grows Safer

Studies by the American Red Cross and U.S. Centers for Disease Control indicate the risk of contracting AIDS through blood transfusions was about 1 in 28,000 for the average transfusion in 1987. The studies further showed that the chance that an AIDS-contaminated unit of blood will get through screening tests is decreasing by more than 30 percent a year.

Also a study of 693,000 blood donors in Washington, D.C., found 284 who tested positive for the antibody to the AIDS virus (HIV). Following the HIV-positive donors during a 42-month study, researchers concluded that a small number of persons infected with the AIDS virus continued to donate blood in spite of attempts to stop them, including giving them literature explaining risks and recommending voluntary self-exclusion.

Another study examined the risk of exposure to AIDS through blood transfusions. Approximately 2.5 percent of Americans with AIDS—12,000 people, according to CDC—became infected through blood transfusions before HIV testing of the nation's blood supply began in March of 1985. The study concluded that over 95 percent of people who received infected blood became HIV-positive, with the number reaching approximately 49 percent within seven years. The risk for contracting AIDS from a transfusion of infected blood was highest when the blood donor developed AIDS

soon after donation, the study reported. *(Source: FDA Consumer.)* □

AIDS Clinical Trials

A federal AIDS Clinical Trials Information Service has been established to provide current information, free of charge, about AIDS drug testing. Dial 1-800-TRIALS-A Monday through Friday from 9:00 a.m. to 7:00 p.m. E.S.T.

Among the services, callers may request to speak with a Spanish-speaking health specialist or may obtain computer printouts from searches of the clinical trials database. The service is confidential.

The service is part of a coordinated AIDS Public Health Service information effort. It is sponsored by the National Institute of Allergy and Infectious Diseases, in cooperation with the Centers for Disease Control, which sponsors the National AIDS Clearinghouse. The service complements a database on all AIDS therapies in clinical trials developed by the Food and Drug Administration. Plans are under way to make all this information available through the National Library of Medicine's on-line services. *(Source:* The National Foundation for Infectious Diseases.) □

Cuba Quarantines AIDS Patients

Cuba is the only country in the world to require both mandatory testing of its population for the AIDS virus and the mandatory quarantining of its AIDS patients.

Those who test positive are sent to the government quarantine center in Havana where they are kept apart from the rest of the population. □

Sexually Transmitted Diseases

According to the National Institute of Allergy and Infectious Diseases (NIAID), sexually transmitted diseases (STDs) are a growing public health problem. More than 20 infectious agents are transmitted by sexual means and the STDs they cause are associated with a wide variety of acute and chronic health problems. The economic impact alone is estimated to be billions of dollars annually in the United States.

The National Institute of Allergy and Infectious Diseases created a STD branch in 1989 to direct research at prevention and control of STDs and their complications.

A few U.S. statistics put STDs in perspective:

● More than 4 million Americans are newly infected each year with *Clamydia*.

● About 2 million new cases of gonorrhea occur each year.

● About 1 million American women develop pelvic inflammatory disease.

● Approximately 500,000 new cases of genital herpes are identified each year, and it is estimated that 30 million Americans are affected by this painful, recurrent, and currently incurable disease.

● Genital warts are caused by the human papillomavirus (HPV), and about a million new cases are diagnosed each year.

● Syphilis, one of the world's oldest known STDs, has decreased in some populations but risen in others. In 1987, the largest single-year increase in cases of primary and secondary syphilis in more than a quarter of a century was reported with increases predominating among heterosexual men and women, particularly among blacks and hispanics. The incidence of congenital syphilis increased more than 20% to 10.5 cases per 100,000 live births. □

Dietary Guidelines for Americans

Source: FDA Consumer.

The "Dietary Guidelines for Americans" were made public in September 1985 by the U.S. Department of Agriculture and the Department of Health and Human Services. They are intended to provide healthy Americans with sensible, uncomplicated guidance on the kinds of foods they should be eating. Basically, their advice to Americans is: concentrate on eating a balanced and varied diet that provides the nutrients essential to good health, increase consumption of starch and fiber, but reduce fat, sugar, sodium, and alcohol.

The guidelines differ little from those announced by USDA and HHS in 1980. The advisory committee concluded that no recent nutrition research was persuasive enough to warrant any major changes. Not enough is known to describe an "ideal" diet for every individual because nutrition needs vary according to a person's sex, age, health, body size, and other factors. So the guidelines are aimed at those Americans who are in good health. They do not apply to people with diseases or conditions that affect nutritional needs.

More than 40 different nutrients—in the form of vitamins, minerals, amino acids (from proteins), essential fatty acids (from fats and oils), and calories from carbohydrates, fats, and proteins—are needed for good health. However, no one can be expected to keep track of all of them. Instead, most people generally can expect to satisfy their nutritional requirements by eating a variety of foods.

The guidelines do not suggest specific goals for such substances as fats and dietary fiber because of the need for more research. Instead, the guidelines state that "for the U.S. population as a whole, increasing starch and fiber in our diets and reducing calories (primarily from fats, sugars, and alcohol) is sensible. These suggestions are especially appropriate for people who have other risk factors for chronic diseases, such as a family history of obesity, premature heart disease, diabetes, high blood pressure, high blood cholesterol levels, or for those who use tobacco, particularly cigarette smokers."

Here are the guidelines and the rationale for each of them:

Eat a variety of foods

Most foods have more than one nutrient, but no single food provides all the essential nutrients. That is achieved by eating a balanced, varied diet that emphasizes the major food groups—fruits and vegetables; cereals and other foods made from grains; dairy products; and meats, fish, poultry, eggs, and dry beans and peas.

For example, dairy products such as milk are a source of protein, fats, sugar, vitamin A, riboflavin and other B vitamins, calcium, phosphorus, and other nutrients. But they provide little iron. Meat provides protein, several B vitamins, iron and zinc but little calcium. Vitamins A and C, folic acid, fiber, and various minerals are obtained from fruit and vegetables. Whole-grain and enriched breads, cereals, and other grain products provide B vitamins, iron, protein, and fiber.

Although there are some exceptions, a varied diet based on these food groups will satisfy the nutrient requirements of most healthy individuals without the need for supplements. "There are no known advantages and some potential harm in consuming excessive amounts of any nutrient," the guidelines stress. "Large dose supplements of any nutrient should be avoided. You will rarely need to take vitamin or mineral supplements if you eat a variety of foods."

However, there are some exceptions. Iron supplements often are needed by women in their childbearing years. Pregnant and breast-feeding women have an increased need for certain nutrients, notably iron, folic acid, vitamin A, and calcium. Infants also have special nutritional needs. Breast-feeding is recommended for the first three to six months because infants absorb nutrients from breast milk better than cow's milk. Breast milk also contains substances that provide immunity to some diseases until the infant's body is able to produce these substances itself.

After three to six months, babies can start taking solid foods. Prolonged breast- or bottle-feeding without solid foods or iron supplements can result in iron deficiency, the guidelines point out. Flavoring baby foods with salt and sugar is also discouraged.

Elderly people also have to be extra careful about getting enough of all the essential nutrients because many older people eat less. The guidelines stress meals based on the basic food groups and a reduction in the consumption of fats, oils, sugars, sweets, alcohol, and other foods that are high in calories but low in other nutrients. Some elderly men and women who take certain medications that affect nutrient intake also may require supplements. Such supplements, however, should be taken only under the guidance of a physician.

Maintain a Desirable Weight

Experts estimate that one-third or more of all adult Americans are overweight and that, at any given time, more than 20 million Americans are resorting to diets to shed excess weight. Obesity is a major health concern in the United States, for it increases the risk of such chronic diseases as high blood pressure, heart disease, stroke, and diabetes.

Although many Americans keep searching for easy paths to losing weight, most such efforts are doomed to failure, in the view of most nutrition experts. Losing weight and not regaining it, the guidelines suggest, means eating foods high in nutritional value but with fewer calories, getting more exercise, and shedding weight at a sensible, gradual rate, a pound or two each week.

The guidelines warn that diets of less than 800 calories a day can be hazardous and should be followed only under medical supervision. Severely restricted, low-calorie diets make it extremely difficult to obtain the nutrients essential to maintaining good health, and they can have adverse effects. The guidelines warned: "Some people have developed kidney stones, disturbing psychological changes, and other complications while following such diets. A few people have died suddenly and without warning."

Frequent use of laxatives, induced vomiting, and other extreme measures should not be used to lose weight, according to the guidelines. Such actions can cause imbalances that can lead to irregular heartbeats and even death.

The emphasis should be on keeping body weight

at a reasonable level for one's sex, age, and height.

Severe weight loss—below what is recommended—also is discouraged. Some people have suffered nutrient deficiencies, infertility, hair loss, skin changes, cold intolerance, severe constipation, psychiatric disturbances, and other complications from excessive weight losses. A doctor should be seen about any sudden, unexplained loss of weight.

Avoid Too Much Fat, Saturated Fat, and Cholesterol

The American diet generally is high in fat and cholesterol compared to some countries, and Americans tend to have high blood cholesterol levels. High blood cholesterol is one of the risk factors for heart attack. Nutritionists lack enough research data to make specific recommendations about how much fat and cholesterol the general public should eat, but the guidelines urge a sensible reduction in total fat—especially saturated fat—and cholesterol.

Among the suggested ways of doing this is to trim excess fat off meats and to eat lean meat, fish, poultry, and dry beans and peas as protein sources; use low-fat dairy products; eat moderate amounts of eggs and organ meats; limit intake of foods high in saturated fat, such as butter, cream, heavily hydrogenated fats, shortenings, and foods with palm and coconut oils; and broil or bake, rather than fry, foods.

The effect of diet on blood cholesterol levels varies among individuals. Some people—for reasons not completely understood—can eat foods high in saturated fat and cholesterol and maintain reasonable blood cholesterol levels, while others on low-fat, low-cholesterol diets still end up with high cholesterol levels. Heredity is believed to play a role. Acknowledging the controversy over what recommendations would be appropriate for the general public, the guidelines state that it would be "sensible" for Americans to reduce their daily consumption of fat. This is especially appropriate, the guidelines say, for individuals who have other cardiovascular risk factors, such as smoking or family histories of premature heart disease, high blood pressure, and diabetes. The guidelines do not suggest complete avoidance of any foods, because many foods that contain fat and cholesterol also provide high-quality protein and many essential vitamins and minerals.

Eat Foods With Adequate Starch and Fiber

The guidelines favor a moderate increase in consumption of fiber-containing foods. The American diet generally is low in fiber, yet there is evidence that fiber can help reduce chronic constipation, diverticular disease, and some types of "irritable bowel." Fruits, whole-grain breads and cereals, vegetables, dry beans and peas, and nuts are good sources of starch and fiber.

Carbohydrates and fat are major sources of energy (calories). If Americans cut back on fat consumption, energy needs can still be met from carbohydrates, especially the complex carbohydrates. "Carbohydrates are especially helpful in weight reduction diets, because, ounce for ounce, they contain about half as many calories as fats do," the guidelines said.

Simple carbohydrates like sugar provide calories but little other nutritional benefit. In contrast, complex carbohydrates—such as starch in bread and other grain products, beans, peas, nuts, seeds, fruits, and vegetables—contain other essential nutrients. Also, eating more foods with complex carbohydrates adds dietary fiber.

(Dietary fiber describes parts of plant foods that generally are not digestible by humans. Foods differ in the kinds of fiber they contain. Wheat bran has several kinds of fiber and has laxative properties but does not affect blood cholesterol levels. Other kinds of fiber have no laxative effects but seem to reduce blood cholesterol.)

Although in recent years there have been studies suggesting that the risk of colon cancer is greater among those with low-fiber diets, the guidelines state that more research is needed before definitive judgments can be made.

Avoid Too Much Sugar

It is not necessary to avoid eating simple sugars. It would, in fact, be difficult, because sugars are naturally present in many foods and are added to many processed products, usually in the form of sucrose, glucose, maltose, dextrose, lactose, fructose, corn sweeteners, honey and syrups. The major health concern with excess sugar consumption is tooth decay, especially when sugars (and starches, as well) are consumed between meals. The guidelines discourage eating sweets between meals. The guidelines also restate the age-old advice about proper dental hygiene, brushing after meals, drinking fluoridated water, and using fluoridated toothpastes and mouth rinses.

Avoid Too Much Sodium

Sodium is essential to the human body, but most Americans consume far more than they need, especially from table salt (which is 40 percent sodium). An intake of 1,100 to 3,300 milligrams a day is generally recommended. Salt is not the only source, for a wide variety of sodium compounds is used in many processed foods and beverages. The principal concern with high sodium consumption is for people with hypertension (high blood pressure) and those who may be susceptible to it.

If You Drink Alcoholic Beverages, Do So In Moderation

In urging moderate use of alcohol, the guidelines also support the national effort to discourage drinking and driving. From a nutritional standpoint, alcohol is high in calories but provides virtually no other nutritional benefit. The guidelines note that one or two standard-sized drinks daily appear to cause no harm in healthy adults.

Overweight people should be aware that alcohol adds calories. Heavy drinkers especially can suffer appetite loss, and this can lead to nutritional deficiencies and other health problems, such as cirrhosis of the liver and some types of cancer.

Pregnant women are advised by the National Institute of Alcohol Abuse and Alcoholism to refrain from drinking alcohol because excessive consumption may cause birth defects or other problems during pregnancy. The level of consumption at which risks to an unborn child occur has not been established, the guidelines declare. □

Fat, Cholesterol, and Your Health

For the U.S. population as a whole, it is sensible to reduce daily intake of total fat, saturated fat, and cholesterol. Why? High blood cholesterol levels increase the risk of heart disease and the blood cholesterol level of many Americans is undesirably high. Eating a diet high in fat—especially saturated fatty acids and cholesterol—causes elevated blood cholesterol levels in many people.

For many, high blood cholesterol levels can be reduced by eating diets lower in saturated fatty acids and cholesterol. However, some people can eat diets high in total fat, saturated fatty acids, and cholesterol and still maintain normal blood cholesterol. Others have high blood cholesterol levels even on lowfat, low-cholesterol diets.

For adults, blood cholesterol is considered to be high if it measures more than 200 to 240 milligrams of cholesterol per deciliter of blood, depending on age. Ask your doctor to check your blood cholesterol.

Fat and Cholesterol

Fat is the most concentrated source of food energy (calories). Each gram of fat supplies about 9 calories, compared with about 4 calories per gram of protein or carbohydrate and 7 calories per gram of alcohol. In addition to providing energy, fat aids in the absorption of certain vitamins. Some fats provide linoleic acid, an essential fatty acid which is needed by everyone in small amounts.

Butter, margarine, shortening, and oil are obvious sources of fat. Well-marbled meats, poultry skin, whole milk, cheese, ice cream, nuts, seeds, salad dressings, and some baked products also provide a lot of fat.

Cholesterol is a fat-like substance found in the body cells of humans and animals. Cholesterol is needed to form hormones, cell membranes, and other body substances. The body is able to make the cholesterol it needs for these functions. Cholesterol is not needed in the diet.

Cholesterol is present in all animal tissues—meat, poultry, and fish—in milk and milk products, and in egg yolks. Both the lean and fat of meats and the meat and skin of poultry contain cholesterol. Cholesterol is *not* found in foods of plant origin such as fruits, vegetables, grains, nuts, seeds, and dry beans and peas.

Fatty Acids are the basic chemical units in fat. They may be either "saturated," "monounsaturated," or "polyunsaturated." All dietary fats are made up of *mixtures* of these fatty acid types.

Saturated fatty acids are found in largest proportions in fats of animal origin. These include the fats in whole milk, cream, cheese, butter, meat, and poultry. Saturated fatty acids are also found in large amounts in some vegetable oils, including coconut and palm.

Monounsaturated fatty acids are found in fats of

Meat, Poultry, Fish

		Total fat grams	Saturated fatty acids grams	Cholesterol milligrams
Beef arm, roasted:				
Lean and fat	3 oz.	16	8	80
Lean only	3 oz.	6	3	77
Ground beef, cooked:				
Regular	3 oz. patty	17	7	77
Lean	3 oz. patty	15	6	80
Pork rib, roasted:				
Lean and fat	3 oz.	20	7	69
Lean only	3 oz.	12	4	67
Beef liver, fried	3 oz.	9	2	372
Chicken, light and dark meat, roasted:				
With skin	3 oz.	12	3	75
Without skin	3 oz.	6	2	76
Halibut fillets, broiled, with margarine	3 oz.	6	1	48
Tuna salad	1/2 cup	10	2	40
Crabs, hard-shell, steamed	2 med.	2	0	96
Dry beans, cooked	1/2 cup	1	trace	0
Peanut butter	2 tbsp.	16	2	0
Egg, large, cooked	1 yolk	6	2	274
	1 white	trace	0	0

Source: USDA, Human Nutrition Information Service.

Milk, Cheese, Yogurt

		Total fat grams	Saturated fatty acids grams	Cholesterol milligrams
Milk:				
Whole	1 cup	8	5	33
2% fat	1 cup	5	3	18
Skim	1 cup	1	trace	5
Buttermilk	1 cup	2	1	9
Yogurt:				
Lowfat plain	8 oz. carton	4	2	14
Lowfat fruit-flavored	8-oz. carton	2	2	10
Cottage cheese:				
Creamed	1 cup	9	6	31
Lowfat	1 cup	4	3	19
Cheese:				
Natural Cheddar	1 oz.	9	6	30
Mozzarella, part skim milk	1 oz.	5	3	15
Process American	1 oz.	9	6	27
Macaroni and cheese	3/4 cup	17	7	32
Vanilla ice cream	1/2 cup	7	4	30
Vanilla ice milk	1/2 cup	3	2	9

Source: USDA, Human Nutrition Information Service.

both plant and animal origin. Olive oil and peanut oil are the most common examples of fat with mostly monounsaturated fatty acids. Also, most margarines and hydrogenated vegetable shortenings tend to be high in monounsaturated fatty acids.

Polyunsaturated fatty acids are found in largest proportions in fats of plant origin. Sunflower, corn, soybean, cottonseed, and safflower oils are vegetable fats that usually contain a high proportion of polyunsaturated fatty acids. Some fish are also sources of polyunsaturated fatty acids.

NOTE: *All* fats, whether they contain mainly saturated fatty acids, monounsaturated fatty acids, or polyunsaturated fatty acids, provide the same number of calories. □

New FDA Sulfite Proposal

FDA has proposed that sulfites in many canned, frozen, dehydrated, and other commercially prepared foods be generally recognized as safe (GRAS) within certain levels and that manufacturers must declare on food labels levels of sulfites greater than 10 parts per million.

The term sulfites refers to six sulfur-based chemicals that have been used for many years as preservatives, as antioxidants to prevent discoloration, and as disinfection agents for food containers, among other uses.

The new proposal would establish limits on sulfite levels and require that stores selling products such as dried fruit and shrimp in bulk would have to use counter signs, cards, or other displays stating that the bulk products have been treated with sulfites.

A small minority of people are sulfite-sensitive and may suffer adverse reactions ranging from hives, nausea and diarrhea to shortness of breath and even death.

In 1986, the FDA banned the use of sulfites on fresh fruits and vegetables, particularly those

Fats and Sweets

		Total fat grams	Saturated fatty acids grams	Cholesterol milligrams
Butter	1 tbsp.	11	7	31
Margarine:				
Soft	1 tbsp.	11	2	0
Stick	1 tbsp.	11	2	0
Vegetable oil (corn)	1 tbsp.	14	2	0
Salad dressing:				
Mayonnaise	1 tbsp.	11	2	8
Mayonnaise-type	1 tbsp.	5	1	4
Italian, low-calorie	1 tbsp.	trace	trace	0
Italian	1 tbsp.	9	1	0
Cream:				
Sour	1 tbsp.	3	2	5
Light (table)	1 tbsp.	3	2	10
Nondairy, frozen	1 tbsp.	2	1	0
Cream cheese	1 oz. (2 tbsp.)	10	6	31
Cake, frosted, devil's food	1/12 8"-layer	11	5	50
Brownie	1 brownie	6	1	18
Pie, apple	1/6 pie	18	5	2

Source: USDA, Human Nutrition Information Service.

served at salad bars, and in 1987 proposed banning their use on fresh, pre-cut potatoes and processed potato products that are served or sold unpackaged or unlabled to consumers. The FDA decided that these unlabeled items were a risk for those sensitive to sulfites. □

Facts on Sodium

What is sodium?

Sodium is a mineral that occurs naturally in some foods and is added to many foods and beverages. Most of the sodium in the American diet comes from table salt, which is 40% sodium and 60% chloride. One teaspoon of salt contains about 2,000 milligrams of sodium.

Why Is Sodium Important?

Sodium attracts water into the blood vessels and helps maintain normal blood volume and blood pressure. Sodium is also needed for the normal function of nerves and muscles.

How Much Sodium Do I Need?

Although some sodium is essential to your health, you need very little. The National Research Council of the National Academy of Sciences suggests that a "safe and adequate" range of sodium intake per day is about 1,100 to 3,300 milligrams for

adults. This is well below the amount that most American adults consume.

Sodium in Processed Foods

Most of the sodium in processed foods is added to preserve and/or flavor them. Salt is the major source of sodium added to these foods. It is added to most canned and some frozen vegetables, smoked and cured meats, pickles, and sauerkraut. Salt is used in most cheeses, sauces, soups, salad dressings, and in many breakfast cereals. Sodium is also found in many other ingredients used in food processing. Examples of sodium-containing ingredients, and their uses in foods are: baking powder—leavening agent; baking soda—leavening agent; monosodium glutamate—flavor enhancer; sodium benzoate—preservative; sodium caseinate—thickener and binder; sodium citrate—buffer, used to control acidity in soft drinks and fruit drinks; sodium nitrate—curing agent in meat, provides color, prevents botulism (a food poisoning); sodium phosphate—emulsifier, stabilizer, buffer; sodium propionate—mold inhibitor; sodium saccharin—artificial sweetener.

About Condiments

Watch out for commercially prepared condiments, sauces, and seasonings when preparing and serving foods for you and your family. Many, like those that follow, are high in sodium: onion salt, celery salt, garlic salt, seasoned salt, meat tenderizer, bouillon, baking powder, baking soda, monosodium glutamate (msg), soy sauce, steak sauce, barbecue sauce, catsup, mustard, Worcestershire sauce, salad dressings, pickles, chili sauce, relish.

The link between salt and sodium may be a little hard to understand at first. If you remember that

Salt-Sodium Conversions

1/4 tsp. salt = 500 mg sodium
1/2 tsp. salt = 1,000 mg sodium
3/4 tsp. salt = 1,500 mg sodium
1 tsp. salt = 2,000 mg sodium

1 teaspoon of salt provides 2,000 milligrams of sodium, however, you can estimate the amount of sodium that you add to foods during cooking and preparation, or even at the table.

Height and Weight Tables for Longevity

Please note that the tables are not used for underwriting and do not necessarily indicate the weights that reduce the likelihood of illness. Nor are the weights those that optimize job performance or at which a person looks the best. It also does not mean that people have a license to gain. It simply indicates that many people may have fewer pounds to lose.

According to Metropolitan Life, for the greatest longevity people should aim for the weights shown on the new tables. The company no longer labels these weights "ideal" or "desirable" because these adjectives mean different things to different people.

How to Determine Your Body Frame

In order to use these tables, you need to know your body frame. Here's how to make a simple approximation of your frame size:

Extend your arm and bend the forearm upward at a 90-degree angle. Keep the fingers straight and turn the inside of your wrist away from the body. Place the thumb and index finger of your other hand on the two prominent bones on *either side* of your elbow. Measure the space between your fingers against a ruler or a tape measure.* Compare the measurements on the following tables.

These tables list the elbow measurements for medium-framed men and women of various heights. Measurements lower than those listed indicate you have a small frame and higher measurements indicate a large frame.

*For the most accurate measurement, have your physician measure your elbow breadth with a caliper.

Men

Height in 1-in. heels	Elbow breadth
5 ft 2 in.-5 ft 3 in.	2 1/2 in.-2 7/8 in.
5 ft 4 in.-5 ft 7 in.	2 5/8 in.-2 7/8 in.
5 ft 8 in.-5 ft 11 in.	2 3/4 in.-3 in.
6 ft 0 in.-6 ft 3 in.	2 3/4 in.-3 1/8 in.
6 ft 4 in.	2 7/8 in.-3 1/4 in.

Women

Height in 1-in. heels	Elbow breadth
4 ft 10 in.-4 ft. 11 in.	2 1/4 in.-2 1/2 in.
5 ft 0 in.-5 ft 3 in.	2 1/4 in.-2 1/2 in.
5 ft 4 in.-5 ft 7 in.	2 3/8 in.-2 5/8 in.
5 ft 8 in.-5 ft 11 in.	2 3/8 in.-2 5/8 in.
6 ft 0 in.	2 1/2 in.-2 3/4 in.

Metropolitan's Height and Weight Tables for Longevity

MEN[1]					WOMEN[2]				
Height Feet Inches		Small frame	Medium frame	Large frame	Height Feet Inches		Small frame	Medium frame	Large frame
5	2	128-134	131-141	138-150	4	10	102-111	109-121	118-131
5	3	130-136	133-143	140-153	4	11	103-113	111-123	120-134
5	4	132-138	135-145	142-156	5	0	104-115	113-126	122-137
5	5	134-140	137-148	144-160	5	1	106-118	115-129	125-140
5	6	136-142	139-151	146-164	5	2	108-121	118-132	128-143
5	7	138-145	142-154	149-168	5	3	111-124	121-135	131-147
5	8	140-148	145-157	152-172	5	4	114-127	124-138	134-151
5	9	142-151	148-160	155-176	5	5	117-130	127-141	137-155
5	10	144-154	151-163	158-180	5	6	120-133	130-144	140-159
5	11	146-157	154-166	161-184	5	7	123-136	133-147	143-163
6	0	149-160	157-170	164-188	5	8	126-139	136-159	146-167
6	1	152-164	160-174	168-192	5	9	129-142	139-153	149-170
6	2	155-168	164-178	172-197	5	10	132-145	142-156	152-173
6	3	158-172	167-182	176-202	5	11	135-148	145-159	155-176
6	4	162-176	171-187	181-207	6	0	138-151	148-162	158-179

1. Weights at ages 25-59 based on lowest mortality. Weight in pounds according to frame (in indoor clothing weighing 5 lb., shoes with 1 in. heels). 2. Weights at ages 25-59 based on lowest mortality. Weight in pounds according to frame (in indoor clothing weighing 3 lb., shoes with 1-in. heels). *Source of basic data: 1979 Build Study,* Society of American and Association of Life Insurance Medical Directors of America, 1980.

Facts on Fiber

Dietary fiber is the parts of plants that humans can't digest.

There are several types of fiber, such as cellulose, pectin, lignin, and gums. Plants differ in the types and amounts of fiber they contain.

Different types of fiber function differently in the body. It is important to eat a variety of plant foods to benefit from effects of different kinds of fiber.

Some kinds of fiber have a laxative effect, producing softer, bulkier stools and more rapid movement of wastes through the intestine. Fiber is helpful in preventing and treating constipation and diverticular disease.

The possible benefits of dietary fiber for colon cancer, heart disease, diabetes, and obesity are being studied. Whether such benefits exist is not yet known.

It is not clear exactly how much and what types of fiber we need in our diets daily. However, for most Americans, a moderate increase in dietary fiber by eating more fiber-containing foods like those listed on this page is desirable.

There is no reason to take fiber supplements or to add fiber to foods that already contain it.

Some fiber foods are: whole-grain breads; whole-grain breakfast cereals; whole-wheat pasta; vegetables, especially with edible skins, stems, seeds; dry beans and peas; whole fruits, especially with edible skins or seeds; nuts and seeds.

What Are Whole Grains?

Whole grains are products that contain the entire grain, or all the grain that is edible. They include the bran and germ portions which contain most of the fiber, vitamins, and minerals, as well as the starchy endosperm.

Some examples are whole wheat, cracked wheat, bulgur, oatmeal, whole cornmeal, popcorn, brown rice, whole rye, and scotch barley.

High Fiber Food Sources

(4 grams or more per serving)

Food source	Serving
Breads and cereals	
All Bran*	1/3 cup-1 oz
Bran Buds*	1/3 cup-1 oz
Bran Chex	2/3 cup-1 oz
Corn bran	2/3 cup-1 oz
Cracklin' Bran	1/3 cup-1 oz
100% Bran*	1/2 cup-1 oz
Raisin Bran	3/4 cup-1 oz
Bran, unsweetened*	1/4 cup
Wheat germ, toasted, plain	1/4 cup-1 oz
Legumes (Cooked portions)	
Kidney beans	1/2 cup
Lima beans	1/2 cup
Navy beans	1/2 cup
Pinto beans	1/2 cup
White beans	1/2 cup
Fruits	
Blackberries	1/2 cup
Dried prunes	3

*Indicates foods that have 6 or more grams of fiber per serving. Source: National Cancer Institute.

Whole wheat doesn't have to mean bread or cereal. Try these: brown rice, corn tortillas, unbuttered popcorn, scotch barley—in soups, tabbouleh—a bulgar wheat salad, whole-wheat pasta.

Alcohol Facts

About two-thirds of Americans 18 or older drink alcoholic beverages, and about three-quarters of students in the 10th and 12th grades also indulge. Long-term alcohol abuse lops 10 years or so off the lifespan and prematurely ages the brain by about the same.

Recommended Daily Dietary Allowances[1]

Designed for the maintenance of good nutrition of practically all healthy persons in the U.S. (revised 1989)

Category	Age (years) or Condition	Weight[2] (kg)	Weight[2] (lb)	Height[2] (cm)	Height[2] (in)	Protein (g)	Fat-Soluble Vitamins — Vitamin A (μg RE)[3]	Vitamin D (μg)[4]	Vitamin E (mg α-TE)[5]	Vitamin K (μg)
Infants	0.0–0.5	6	13	60	24	13	375	7.5[4]	3	5
	0.5–1.0	9	20	71	28	14	375	10	4	10
Children	1–3	13	29	90	35	16	400	10	6	15
	4–6	20	44	112	44	24	500	10	7	20
	7–10	28	62	132	52	28	700	10	7	30
Males	11–14	45	99	157	62	45	1,000	10	10	45
	15–18	66	145	176	69	59	1,000	10	10	65
	19–24	72	160	177	70	58	1,000	10	10	70
	25–50	79	174	176	70	63	1,000	5	10	80
	51+	77	170	173	68	63	1,000	5	10	80
Females	11–14	46	101	157	62	46	800	10	8	45
	15–18	55	120	163	64	44	800	10	8	55
	19–24	58	128	164	65	46	800	10	8	60
	25–50	63	138	163	64	50	800	5	8	65
	51+	65	143	160	63	50	800	5	8	65
Pregnant						60	800	10	10	65
Lactating	1st 6 months					65	1,300	10	12	65
	2nd 6 months					62	1,200	10	11	65

Category	Age (years) or Condition	Weight[2] (kg)	Weight[2] (lb)	Height[2] (cm)	Height[2] (in)	Vita-min C (mg)	Thia-min (mg)	Ribo-flavin (mg)	Niacin (mg NE)[6]	Vita-min B$_6$ (mg)	Fo-late (µg)	Vita-min B$_{12}$ (µg)
									Water-Soluble Vitamins			
Infants	0.0–0.5	6	13	60	24	30	0.3	0.4	5	0.3	25	0.3
	0.5–1.0	9	20	71	28	35	0.4	0.5	6	0.6	35	0.5
Children	1–3	13	29	90	35	40	0.7	0.8	9	1.0	50	0.7
	4–6	20	44	112	44	45	0.9	1.1	12	1.1	75	1.0
	7–10	28	62	132	52	45	1.0	1.2	13	1.4	100	1.4
Males	11–14	45	99	157	62	50	1.3	1.5	17	1.7	150	2.0
	15–18	66	145	176	69	60	1.5	1.8	20	2.0	200	2.0
	19–24	72	160	177	70	60	1.5	1.7	19	2.0	200	2.0
	25–50	79	174	176	70	60	1.5	1.7	19	2.0	200	2.0
	51+	77	170	173	68	60	1.2	1.4	15	2.0	200	2.0
Females	11–14	46	101	157	62	50	1.1	1.3	15	1.4	150	2.0
	15–18	55	120	163	64	60	1.1	1.3	15	1.5	180	2.0
	19–24	58	128	164	65	60	1.1	1.3	15	1.6	180	2.0
	25–50	63	138	163	64	60	1.1	1.3	15	1.6	180	2.0
	51+	65	143	160	63	60	1.0	1.2	13	1.6	180	2.0
Pregnant						70	1.5	1.6	17	2.2	400	2.2
Lactating	1st 6 months					95	1.6	1.8	20	2.1	280	2.6
	2nd 6 months					90	1.6	1.7	20	2.1	260	2.6

Category	Age (years) or Condition	Weight[2] (kg)	Weight[2] (lb)	Height[2] (cm)	Height[2] (in)	Cal-cium (mg)	Phos-phorus (mg)	Mag-nesium (mg)	Iron (mg)	Zinc (mg)	Iodine (µg)	Sele-nium (µg)
								Minerals				
Infants	0.0–0.5	6	13	60	24	400	300	40	6	5	40	10
	0.5–1.0	9	20	71	28	600	500	60	10	5	50	15
Children	1–3	13	29	90	35	800	800	80	10	10	70	20
	4–6	20	44	112	44	800	800	120	10	10	90	20
	7–10	28	62	132	52	800	800	170	10	10	120	30
Males	11–14	45	99	157	62	1,200	1,200	270	12	15	150	40
	15–18	66	145	176	69	1,200	1,200	400	12	15	150	50
	19–24	72	160	177	70	1,200	1,200	350	10	15	150	70
	25–50	79	174	176	70	800	800	350	10	15	150	70
	51+	77	170	173	68	800	800	350	10	15	150	70
Females	11–14	46	101	157	62	1,200	1,200	280	15	12	150	45
	15–18	55	120	163	64	1,200	1,200	300	15	12	150	50
	19–24	58	128	164	65	1,200	1,200	280	15	12	150	55
	25–50	63	138	163	64	800	800	280	15	12	150	55
	51+	65	143	160	63	800	800	280	10	12	150	55
Pregnant						1,200	1,200	320	30	15	175	65
Lactating	1st 6 months					1,200	1,200	355	15	19	200	75
	2nd 6 months					1,200	1,200	340	15	16	200	75

1. The allowances, expressed as average daily intakes over time, are intended to provide for individual variations among most normal persons as they live in the United States under usual environmental stresses. Diets should be based on a variety of common foods in order to provide other nutrients for which human requirements have been less well defined. 2. Weights and heights of Reference Adults are actual medians for the U.S. population of the designated age, as reported by NHANES II. The median weights and heights of those under 19 years of age were taken from Hamill et al. (1979) (pages 16-17). The use of these figures does not imply that the height-to-weight ratios are ideal. 3. Retinol equivalents. 1 retinol equivalent = 1 µg retinol or 6 µg β-carotene. 4. As cholecalciferol. 10 µg cholecalciferol = 400 ɪᴜ of vitamin D. 5. α-Tocopherol equivalents. 1 mg d-α tocopherol = 1 α-ᴛᴇ. See text for variation in allowances and calculation of vitamin E activity of the diet as α-tocopherol equivalents. 6. 1 ɴᴇ (niacin equivalent) is equal to 1 mg of niacin or 60 mg of dietary tryptophhan. *Source: Recommended Dietary Allowances*, © 1989 by the National Academy of Sciences, National Academy Press, Washington, D.C.

Recognizing the *Real* Whole Wheat

All whole-wheat bread is brown, but not all brown bread is whole wheat.

By law, bread that is labeled "whole wheat" must be made from 100 percent whole-wheat flour. "Wheat bread" may be made from varying proportions of enriched white flour and whole-wheat flour. The type of flour present in the largest amount is listed first on the ingredient label. Sometimes a dark color is provided by caramel coloring, also listed on the label.

The milling of the wheat to produce white flour results in the loss of nutrients as the bran and germ are removed. Enrichment replaces four important nutrients: iron, thiamin, riboflavin, and niacin. But flours made from the whole grain contain more of other nutrients, such as folic acid, vitamin B$_6$, vitamin E, phosphorus, magnesium, and zinc, than enriched white flour.

You don't have to switch to whole-wheat bread to increase your intake of whole grains.

Many products on the market are made of a mixture of whole-grain flours and enriched flour.

HEADLINE HISTORY

In any broad overview of history, arbitrary compartmentalization of facts is self-defeating (and makes locating interrelated people, places, and things that much harder). Therefore, Headline History is designed as a "timeline"—a chronology that highlights both the march of time and interesting, sometimes surprising, juxtapositions.

Also see related sections of *Information Please,* particularly Inventions and Discoveries, Countries of the World, etc.

B.C.
Before Christ or Before Common Era (B.C.E.)

5 billion B.C. Planet Earth formed.
3 billion B.C. First signs of primeval life (bacteria and blue-green algae) appear in oceans.
600 million B.C. Earliest date to which fossils can be traced.
1.7 million B.C. First discernible hominids (*Australopithecus* and *Homo habilis*). Early hunters and food-gatherers.
500,000 B.C. *Homo erectus* (crude chopping tools).
70,000 B.C. Neanderthal man (use of fire and advanced tools).
35,000 B.C. Neanderthal man being replaced by later groups of *Homo sapiens* (i.e. Cro-Magnon man, etc.).
18,000 B.C. Cro-Magnons being replaced by later cultures.
15,000 B.C. Migrations across Bering Straits into the Americas.
10,000 B.C. Semi-permanent agricultural settlements in Old World.
10,000–4,000 B.C. Development of settlements into cities and development of skills such as the wheel, pottery and improved methods of cultivation in Mesopotamia and elsewhere.

NOTE: For futher information on the geographic development in Earth's prehistory, see the Science section.

4500–3000 B.C. Sumerians in the Tigris and Euphrates valleys develop a city-state civilization; first phonetic writing (**c.3500 B.C.**). Egyptian agriculture develops. Western Europe is neolithic, without metals or written records. Earliest recorded date in Egyptian calendar (**4241 B.C.**). First year of Jewish calendar (**3760 B.C.**). Copper used by Egyptians and Sumerians.
3000–2000 B.C. Pharaonic rule begins in Egypt. Cheops, 4th dynasty (**2700–2675 B.C.**). The Great Sphinx of Giza. Earliest Egyptian mummies. Papyrus. Phoenician settlements on coast of what is now Syria and Lebanon. Semitic tribes settle in Assyria. Sargon, first Akkadian king, builds Mesopotamian empire. The Gilgamesh epic (**c.3000 B.C.**). Abraham leaves Ur (**c.2000 B.C.**). Systematic astronomy in Egypt, Babylon, India, China.
2000–1500 B.C. Hyksos invaders drive Egyptians from Lower Egypt (**17th century B.C.**). Amosis I frees Egypt from Hyksos (**c.1600 B.C.**). Assyrians rise to power—cities of Ashur and Nineveh. Twenty-four-character alphabet in Egypt. Israelites enslaved in Egypt. Cuneiform inscriptions used by Hittites. Peak of Minoan culture on Isle of Crete—earliest form of written Greek. Hammurabi, king of Babylon, develops oldest existing code of laws (**18th century B.C.**). In Britain, Stonehenge erected on some unknown astronomical rationale.
1500–1000 B.C. Ikhnaton develops monotheistic religion in Egypt (**c.1375 B.C.**). His successor, Tutankhamen, returns to earlier gods. Moses leads Israelites out of Egypt into Canaan—Ten Commandments. Greeks destroy Troy (**c.1193 B.C.**). End of Greek civilization in Mycenae with invasion of Dorians. Chinese civilization develops under Shang dynasty. Olmec civilization in Mexico—stone monuments; picture writing.
1000–900 B.C. Solomon succeeds King David, builds Jerusalem temple. After Solomon's death, kingdom divided into Israel and Judah. Hebrew elders begin to write Old Testament books of Bible. Phoenicians colonize Spain with settlement at Cadiz.
900–800 B.C. Phoenicians establish Carthage (**c.810 B.C.**). The *Iliad* and the *Odyssey,* perhaps composed by Greek poet Homer.
800–700 B.C. Prophets Amos, Hosea, Isaiah. First recorded Olympic games (**776 B.C.**). Legendary founding of Rome by Romulus (**753 B.C.**). Assyrian

Brontosaur

Moses

Egyptian chariots
(1500 B.C.)

95

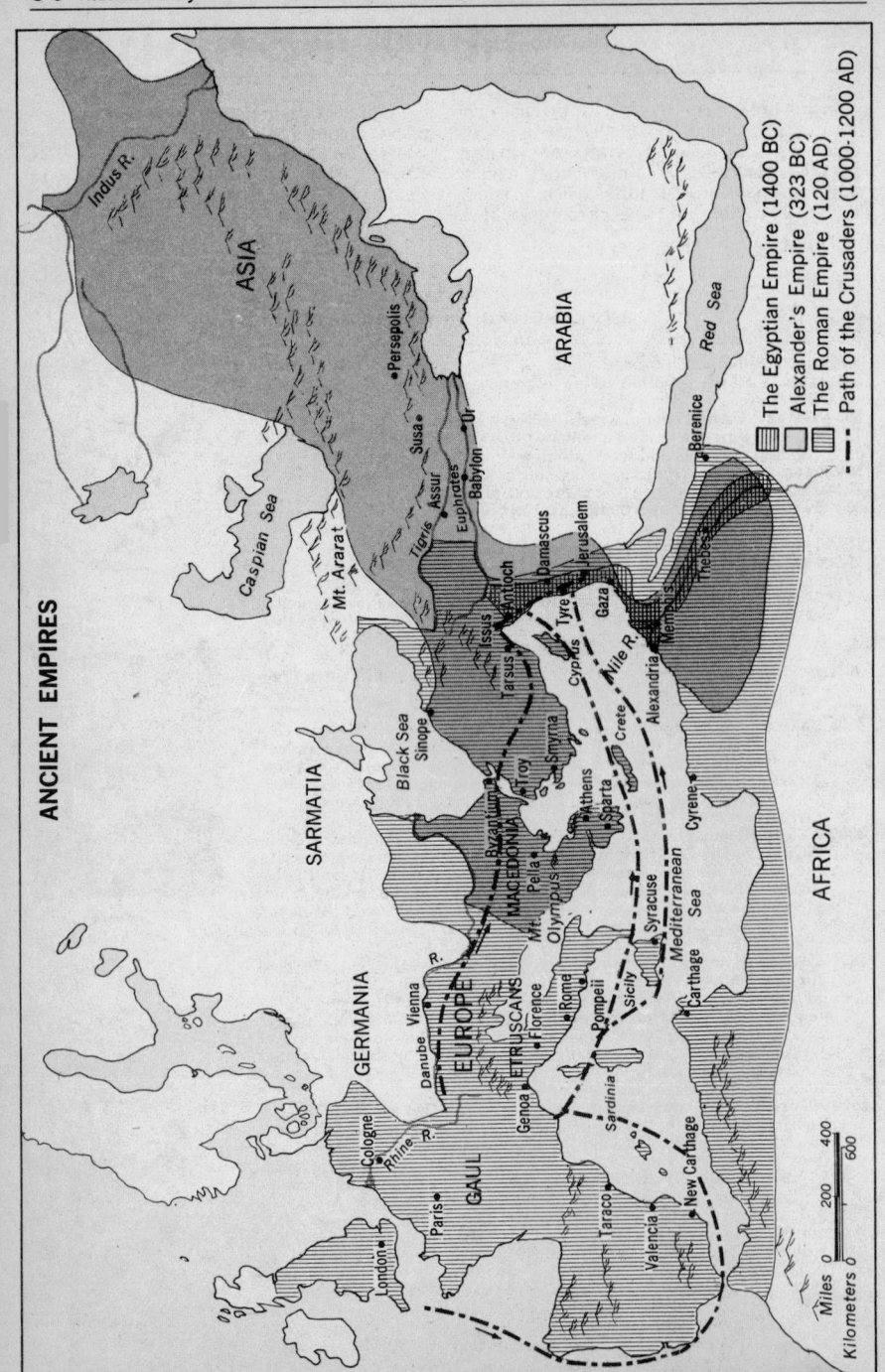

ANCIENT EMPIRES

The Egyptian Empire (1400 BC)
Alexander's Empire (323 BC)
The Roman Empire (120 AD)
Path of the Crusaders (1000-1200 AD)

Some Ancient Civilizations

Name	Approximate dates	Location	Major cities
Akkadian	2350–2230 **B.C.**	Mesopotamia, parts of Syria, Asia Minor, Iran	Akkad, Ur, Erich
Assyrian	1800–889 **B.C.**	Mesopotamia, Syria	Assur, Nineveh, Calah
Babylonian	1728–1686 **B.C.** (old) 625–539 **B.C.** (new)	Mesopotamia, Syria, Palestine	Babylon
Cimmerian	750–500 **B.C.**	Caucasus, northern Asia Minor	—
Egyptian	2850–715 **B.C.**	Nile valley	Thebes, Memphis, Tanis
Etruscan	900–396 **B.C.**	Northern Italy	—
Greek	900–200 **B.C.**	Greece	Athens, Sparta, Thebes, Mycenae, Corinth
Hittite	1640–1200 **B.C.**	Asia Minor, Syria	Hattusas, Nesa
Lydian	700–547 **B.C.**	Western Asia Minor	Sardis, Miletus
Mede	835–550 **B.C.**	Iran	Media
Minoan	3000–1100 **B.C.**	Crete	Knossos
Persian	559-330 **B.C.**	Iran, Asia Minor, Syria	Persepolis, Pasargadae
Phoenician	1100–332 **B.C.**	Palestine (colonies: Gibraltar, Carthage Sardinia)	Tyre, Sidon, Byblos
Phrygian	1000–547 **B.C.**	Central Asia Minor	Gordion
Roman	500 **B.C.–A.D.** 300	Italy, Mediterranean region, Asia Minor, western Europe	Rome, Byzantium
Scythian	800–300 **B.C.**	Caucasus	—
Sumerian	3200–2360 **B.C.**	Mesopotamia	Ur, Nippur

king Sargon II conquers Hittites, Chaldeans, Samaria (end of Kingdom of Israel). Earliest written music. Chariots introduced into Italy by Etruscans.

700–600 B.C. End of Assyrian Empire (**616 B.C.**)—Nineveh destroyed by Chaldeans (Neo-Babylonians) and Medes (**612 B.C.**). Founding of Byzantium by Greeks (c.**660 B.C.**). Building of the Acropolis in Athens. Solon, Greek lawgiver (**640–560 B.C.**). Sappho of Lesbos, Greek poetess, Lao-Tse, Chinese philosopher and founder of Taoism (born c.**604 B.C.**).

600–500 B.C. Babylonian king Nebuchadnezzar builds empire, destroys Jerusalem (**586 B.C.**). Babylonian Captivity of the Jews (starting **587 B.C.**). Hanging Gardens of Babylon. Cyrus the Great of Persia creates great empire, conquers Babylon (**539 B.C.**), frees the Jews. Athenian democracy develops. Aeschylus, Greek dramatist (**525–465 B.C.**). Confucius (**551–479 B.C.**) develops philosophy-religion in China. Buddha (**563–483 B.C.**) founds Buddhism in India.

500–400 B.C. Greeks defeat Persians: battles of Marathon (**490 B.C.**), Thermopylae (**480 B.C.**), Salamis (**480 B.C.**). Peloponnesian Wars between Athens and Sparta (**431–404 B.C.**)—Sparta victorious. Pericles comes to power in Athens (**462 B.C.**). Flowering of Greek culture during the Age of Pericles (**450–400 B.C.**). Sophocles, Greek dramatist (**496–c.406 B.C.**). Hippocrates, Greek "Father of Medicine" (born **460 B.C.**). Xerxes I, king of Persia (rules **485–465 B.C.**).

400–300 B.C. Pentateuch—first five books of the Old Testament evolve in final form. Philip of Macedon assassinated (**336 B.C.**) after conquering Greece; succeeded by son, Alexander the Great (**356–323 B.C.**), who destroys Thebes (**335 B.C.**), conquers Tyre and Jerusalem (**332 B.C.**), occupies Babylon (**330 B.C.**), invades India, and dies in Babylon. His empire is divided among his generals; one of them, Seleucis I, establishes Middle East empire with capitals at Antioch (Syria) and Seleucia (in Iraq). Trial and execution of Greek philosopher Socrates (**399 B.C.**). Dialogues recorded by his student, Plato. Euclid's work on geometry (**323 B.C.**). Aristotle, Greek philosopher (**384–322 B.C.**). Demosthenes, Greek orator (**384–322 B.C.**). Praxiteles, Greek sculptor (**400–330 B.C.**).

300–251 B.C. First Punic War (**264–241 B.C.**): Rome defeats the Carthaginians and begins its domination of the Mediterranean. Temple of the Sun at Teotihuacan, Mexico (c.**300 B.C.**). Invention of Mayan calendar in

Confucius (551-479 B.C.)

Plato (427?-347 B.C.)

**Archimedes
(287-212 B.C.)**

Yucatán—more exact than older calendars. First Roman gladiatorial games (264 **B.C.**). Archimedes, Greek mathematician (287–212 **B.C.**).

250–201 B.C. Second Punic War (219–201 **B.C.**): Hannibal, Carthaginian general (246–142 **B.C.**), crosses the Alps (218 **B.C.**), reaches gates of Rome (211 **B.C.**), retreats, and is defeated by Scipio Africanus at Zama (202 **B.C.**). Great Wall of China built (c.215 **B.C.**).

200–151 B.C. Romans defeat Seleucid King Antiochus III at Thermopylae (191 **B.C.**)—beginning of Roman world domination. Maccabean revolt against Seleucids (167 **B.C.**).

150–101 B.C. Third Punic War (149–146 **B.C.**): Rome destroys Carthage, killing 450,000 and enslaving the remaining 50,000 inhabitants. Roman armies conquer Macedonia, Greece, Anatolia, Balearic Islands, and southern France. Venus de Milo (c.140 **B.C.**). Cicero, Roman orator (106–43 **B.C.**).

100–51 B.C. Julius Caesar (100–44 **B.C.**) invades Britain (55 **B.C.**) and conquers Gaul (France) (c.50 **B.C.**). Spartacus leads slave revolt against Rome (71 **B.C.**). Romans conquer Seleucid empire. Roman general Pompey conquers Jerusalem (63 **B.C.**). Cleopatra on Egyptian throne (51–31 **B.C.**). Chinese develop use of paper (c.100 **B.C.**). Virgil, Roman poet (70–19 **B.C.**). Horace, Roman poet (65–8 **B.C.**).

50–1 B.C. Caesar crosses Rubicon to fight Pompey (50 **B.C.**). Herod made Roman governor of Judea (47 **B.C.**). Caesar murdered (44 **B.C.**). Caesar's nephew, Octavian, defeats Mark Antony and Cleopatra at Battle of Actium (31 **B.C.**), and establishes Roman empire as Emperor Augustus—rules 27 **B.C.**—**A.D.** 14. Birth of Jesus Christ (variously given from 4 **B.C.** to **A.D.** 7). Ovid, Roman poet (43 **B.C.**—**A.D.** 18).

A.D.

The Christian or Common Era (C.E.)

**Jesus Christ
(4? B.C.-29? A.D.)**

1–49 After Augustus, Tiberius becomes emperor (dies, 37), succeeded by Caligula (assassinated, 41), who is followed by Claudius. Crucifixion of Jesus (probably 30). Han dynasty in China founded by Emperor Kuang Wu Ti. Buddhism introduced to China.

50–99 Claudius poisoned (54), succeeded by Nero (commits suicide, 68). Missionary journeys of Paul the Apostle (34–60). Jews revolt against Rome; Jerusalem destroyed (70). Roman persecutions of Christians begin (64). Colosseum built in Rome (71–80). Trajan (rules 98–116); Roman empire extends to Mesopotamia, Arabia, Balkans. First Gospels of St. Mark, St. John, St. Matthew.

100–149 Hadrian rules Rome (117–138); codifies Roman law, establishes postal system, builds wall between England and Scotland. Jews revolt under Bar Kokhba (122–135); final *Diaspora* (dispersion) of Jews begins.

150–199 Marcus Aurelius (rules Rome 161–180). Oldest Mayan temples in Central America (c.200)., Mayan civilization develops writing, astronomy, mathematics.

200–249 Goths invade Asia Minor (c.220). Roman persecutions of Christians increase. Persian (Sassanid) empire re-established. End of Chinese Han dynasty.

250–299 Increasing invasions of the Roman empire by Franks and Goths. Buddhism spreads in China.

300–349 Constantine the Great (rules 312–337) reunites eastern and western Roman empires, with new capital (Constantinople) on site of Byzantium (330); issues Edict of Milan legalizing Christianity (313); becomes a Christian on his deathbed (337). Council of Nicaea (325) defines orthodox Christian doctrine. First Gupta dynasty in India (c.320).

350–399 Huns (Mongols) invade Europe (c.360). Theodosius the Great (rules 392–395)—last emperor of a united Roman empire. Roman empire permanently divided in 395: western empire ruled from Rome; eastern empire ruled from Constantinople.

400–449 Western Roman empire disintegrates under weak emperors. Alaric, king of the Visigoths, sacks Rome (410). Attila, Hun chieftain, attacks Roman provinces (433). St. Patrick returns to Ireland (432). St. Augustine's *City of God* (411).

450–499 Vandals destroy Rome (455). Western Roman empire ends as Odoacer, German chieftain, overthrows last Roman emperor, Romulus Augustulus, and becomes king of Italy (476). Ostrogothic kingdom of Italy established by Theodoric the Great (493). Clovis, ruler of the Franks, is converted to Christianity (496). First schism between western and eastern churches (484). Peak of Mayan culture in Mexico (c.460).

500–549 Eastern and western churches reconciled (519). Justinian I, the

Great (483–565), becomes Byzantine emperor (527), issues his first code of civil laws (529), conquers North Africa, Italy, and part of Spain. Plague spreads through Europe (from 542). Arthur, semi-legendary king of the Britons (killed, c.537). Boëthius, Roman scholar (executed, 524).

550–599 Beginnings of European silk industry after Justinian's missionaries smuggle silkworms out of China (553). Mohammed, founder of Islam (570–632). Buddhism in Japan (c.560). St. Augustine of Canterbury brings Christianity to Britain (597). After killing about half the population, plague in Europe subsides (594).

600–649 Mohammed flees from Mecca to Medina (the *Hegira*); first year of the Muslim calendar (622). Muslim empire grows (634). Arabs conquer Jerusalem (637), destroy Alexandrian library (641), conquer Persians (641). Fatima, Mohammed's daughter (606–632).

650–699 Arabs attack North Africa (670), destroy Carthage (697). Venerable Bede, English monk (672–735).

700–749 Arab empire extends from Lisbon to China (by 716). Charles Martel, Frankish leader, defeats Arabs at Tours/Poitiers, halting Arab advance in Europe (732). Charlemagne (742–814).

750–799 Caliph Harun al-Rashid rules Arab empire (786–809): the "golden age" of Arab culture. Vikings begin attacks on Britain (790), land in Ireland (795). Charlemagne becomes king of the Franks (771). City of Machu Picchu flourishes in Peru.

800–849 Charlemagne (Charles the Great) crowned first Holy Roman Emperor in Rome (800). Arabs conquer Crete, Sicily, and Sardinia (826–827). Charlemagne dies (814), succeeded by his son, Louis the Pious, who divides France among his sons (817).

850–899 Norsemen attack as far south as the Mediterranean but are repulsed (859), discover Iceland (861). Alfred the Great becomes king of Britain (871), defeats Danish invaders (878). Russian nation founded by Vikings under Prince Rurik, establishing capital at Novgorod (855–879).

900–949 Vikings discover Greenland (c.900). Arab Spain under Abd ar-Rahman III becomes center of learning (912–961).

950–999 Eric the Red establishes first Viking colony in Greenland (982). Mieczyslaw I becomes first ruler of Poland (960). Hugh Capet elected King of France in 987; Capetian dynasty to rule until 1328. Musical notation systematized (c.990). Vikings and Danes attack Britain (988–999). Holy Roman Empire founded by Otto I, King of Germany since 936, crowned by Pope John XII in 962.

11th century A.D.

c.1000 Hungary and Scandinavia converted to Christianity. Viking raider Leif Ericson discovers North America, calls it *Vinland.* Chinese invent gunpowder. *Beowulf*, Old English epic.

1009 Moslems destroy Holy Sepulchre in Jerusalem.

1013 Danes control England. Canute takes throne (1016), conquers Norway (1028), dies (1035); kingdom divided among his sons: Harold Harefoot (England), Sweyn (Norway), Hardecanute (Denmark).

1040 Macbeth murders Duncan, king of Scotland.

1053 Robert Guiscard, Norman invader, establishes kingdom in Italy, conquers Sicily (1072).

1054 Final separation between Eastern (Orthodox) and Western (Roman) churches.

1055 Seljuk Turks, Asian nomads, move west, capture Baghdad, Armenia (1064), Syria, and Palestine (1075).

1066 William of Normandy invades England, defeats last Saxon king, Harold II, at Battle of Hastings, crowned William I of England ("the Conqueror").

1073 Emergence of strong papacy when Gregory VII is elected. Conflict with English and French kings and German emperors will continue throughout medieval period.

1095 (*See* special material on "The Crusades.")

12th century A.D.

1150–67 Universities of Paris and Oxford founded in France and England.

1162 Thomas à Becket named Archbishop of Canterbury, murdered by Henry II's men (1170). Troubadours (wandering minstrels) glorify romantic concepts of feudalism.

1189 Richard I ("the Lionhearted") succeeds Henry II in England, killed in France (1199), succeeded by King John.

13th century A.D.

1211 Genghis Khan invades China, captures Peking (1214), conquers Persia (1218), invades Russia (1223), dies (1227).

**Viking Discovery
of Greenland (c.900)**

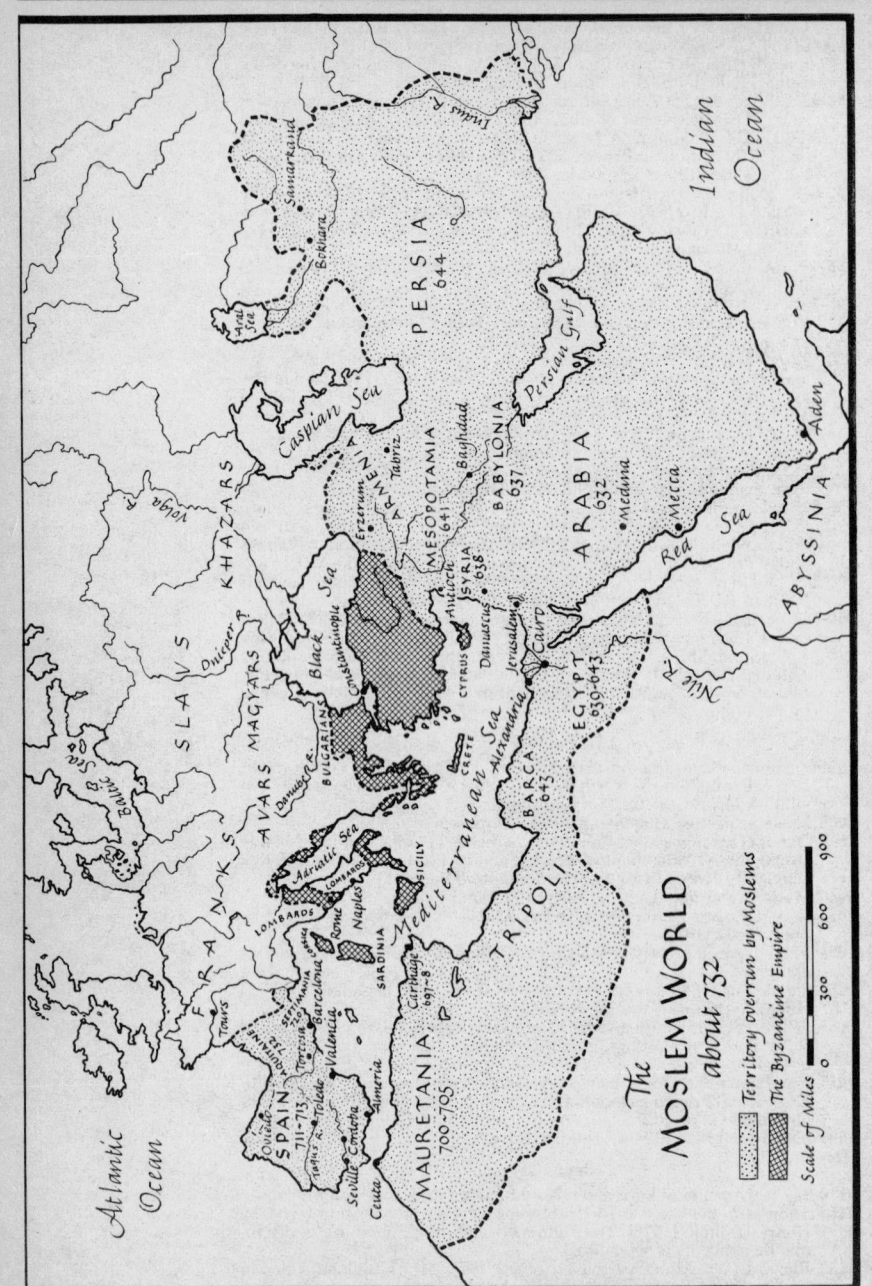

The
MOSLEM WORLD
about 732

Territory overrun by Moslems

The Byzantine Empire

Scale of Miles

0   300   600   900

1215 King John forced by barons to sign Magna Carta at Runneymede, limiting royal power.

1233 The Inquisition begins as Pope Gregory IX assigns Dominicans responsibility for combatting heresy. Torture used (**1252**). Ferdinand and Isabella establish Spanish Inquisition (**1478**). Tourquemada, Grand Inquisitor, forces conversion or expulsion of Spanish Jews (**1492**). Forced conversion of Moors (**1499**). Inquisition in Portugal (**1531**). First Protestants burned at the stake in Spain (**1543**). Spanish Inquisition abolished (**1834**).

1241 Mongols defeat Germans in Silesia, invade Poland and Hungary, withdraw from Europe after Ughetai, Mongol leader, dies.

1251 Kublai Khan governs China, becomes ruler of Mongols (**1259**), establishes Yuan dynasty in China (**1280**), invades Burma (**1287**), dies (**1294**).

1271 Marco Polo of Venice travels to China, in court of Kublai Khan (**1275–1292**), returns to Genoa (**1295**) and writes *Travels*.

1295 English King Edward I summons the Model Parliament.

John Wycliffe
(1320-1384)

14th century A.D.

1312-37 Mali Empire reaches its height in Africa under King Mansa Musa.

1337-1453 Hundred Years' War—English and French kings fight for control of France.

c.1325 The beginning of the Renaissance in Italy: writers Dante, Petrarch, Boccaccio; painter Giotto. Development of *No* drama in Japan. Aztecs establish capital on site of modern Mexico City. Peak of Moslem culture in Spain. Small cannon in use.

1347-1351 At least 25 million people die in Europe's "Black Death" (bubonic plague).

1368 Ming dynasty begins in China.

1376-82 John Wycliffe, pre-Reformation religious reformer and followers translate Latin Bible into English.

1378 The Great Schism (to 1417)—rival popes in Rome and Avignon, France, fight for control of Roman Catholic Church.

c.1387 Chaucer's *Canterbury Tales*.

15th century A.D.

1415 Henry V defeats French at Agincourt. Jan Hus, Bohemian preacher and follower of Wycliffe, burned at stake in Constance as heretic.

1418-60 Portugal's Prince Henry the Navigator sponsors exploration of Africa's coast.

Joan of Arc
(1412-1431)

1428 Joan of Arc leads French against English, captured by Burgundians (**1430**) and turned over to the English, burned at the stake as a witch after ecclesiastical trial (**1431**).

1438 Inca rule in Peru.

1450 Florence becomes center of Renaissance arts and learning under the Medicis.

1453 Turks conquer Constantinople, end of the Byzantine empire. Hundred Years' War between France and England ends.

1455 The Wars of the Roses, civil wars between rival noble factions, begin in England (to 1485). Having invented printing with movable type at Mainz, Germany, Johann Gutenberg completes first Bible.

1462 Ivan the Great rules Russia until 1505 as first czar; ends payment of tribute to Mongols.

1492 Moors conquered in Spain by troops of Ferdinand and Isabella. Columbus discovers Caribbean islands, returns to Spain (**1493**). Second voyage to Dominica, Jamaica, Puerto Rico (**1493–1496**). Third voyage to Orinoco (**1498**). Fourth voyage to Honduras and Panama (**1502–1504**).

1497 Vasco da Gama sails around Africa and discovers sea route to India (**1498**). Establishes Portuguese colony in India (**1502**). John Cabot, employed by England, reaches and explores Canadian coast. Michelangelo's *Bacchus* sculpture.

Christopher Columbus
(1451-1506)

THE CRUSADES (1096–1291)

In 1095 at Council of Clermont, Pope Urban II calls for war to rescue Holy Land from Moslem infidels. *First Crusade* (1096)—about 500,000 peasants led by Peter the Hermit prove so troublesome that Byzantine Emperor Alexius ships them to Asia Minor; only 25,000 survive return after massacre by Seljuk Turks. Followed by organized army, led by nobility, which reaches Constantinople (1097), conquers Jerusalem (1099), Acre (1104), establishes Latin Kingdom protected by Knights of St. John the Hospitaller (1100), and Knights Templar (1123). Seljuk Turks start series of counterattacks (1144). *Second Crusade* (1146) led by King Louis VIII of France and Emperor Conrad III. Crusaders perish in Asia Minor (1147).

Saladin controls Egypt (1171), unites Islam in Holy War (*Jihad*) against Christians, recaptures Jerusalem (1187). *Third Crusade* (1189) under kings of France, England, and Germany fails to reduce Saladin's power. *Fourth Crusade* (1200–1204)—French knights sack Greek Christian Constantinople, establish Latin empire in Byzantium. Greeks reestablish Orthodox faith (1262).

Children's Crusade (1212)—Only 1 of 30,000 French children and about 200 of 20,000 German children survive to return home. Other Crusades—against Egypt (1217), *Sixth* (1228), *Seventh* (1248), *Eighth* (1270). Mamelukes conquer Acre; end of the Crusades (1291).

**Michelangelo Buonarreti
(1475-1564)**

**Martin Luther
(1483-1546)**

**Anthony Van Dyck
(1599-1641)**

16th century A.D.

1501 First black slaves in America brought to Spanish colony of Santo Domingo.

c.1503 Leonardo da Vinci paints the *Mona Lisa*.

1506 St. Peter's Church started in Rome; designed and decorated by such artists and architects as Bramante, Michelangelo, da Vinci, Raphael, and Bernini before its completion in **1626.**

1509 Henry VIII ascends English throne. Michelangelo paints the ceiling of the Sistine Chapel.

1517 Turks conquer Egypt, control Arabia. Martin Luther posts his 95 theses denouncing church abuses on church door in Wittenberg—start of the Reformation in Germany.

1519 Ulrich Zwingli begins Reformation in Switzerland. Hernando Cortes conquers Mexico for Spain. Charles I of Spain is chosen Holy Roman Emperor Charles V. Portuguese explorer Fernando Magellan sets out to circumnavigate the globe.

1520 Luther excommunicated by Pope Leo X. Suleiman I ("the Magnificent") becomes Sultan of Turkey, invades Hungary (1521), Rhodes (1522), attacks Austria (1529), annexes Hungary (1541), Tripoli (1551), makes peace with Persia (1553), destroys Spanish fleet (1560), dies (1566). Magellan reaches the Pacific, is killed by Philippine natives (1521). One of his ships under Juan Sebastián del Cano continues around the world, reaches Spain (1522).

1524 Verrazano, sailing under the French flag, explores the New England coast and New York Bay.

1527 Troops of the Holy Roman Empire attack Rome, imprison Pope Clement VII—the end of the Italian Renaissance. Castiglione writes *The Courtier*. The Medici expelled from Florence.

1532 Pizarro marches from Panama to Peru, kills the Inca chieftain, Atahualpa, of Peru (1533). Machiavelli's *Prince* published posthumously.

1535 Reformation begins as Henry VIII makes himself head of English Church after being excommunicated by Pope. Sir Thomas More executed as traitor for refusal to acknowledge king's religious authority. Jacques Cartier sails up the St. Lawrence River, basis of French claims to Canada.

1536 Henry VIII executes second wife, Anne Boleyn. John Calvin establishes Presbyterian form of Protestantism in Switzerland, writes *Institutes of the Christian Religion*. Danish and Norwegian Reformations. Michelangelo's *Last Judgment*.

1541 John Knox leads Reformation in Scotland, establishes Presbyterian church (1560).

1543 Publication of *On the Revolution of Heavenly Bodies* by Polish scholar Nicolaus Copernicus—giving his theory that the earth revolves around the sun.

1545 Council of Trent to meet intermittently until 1563 to define Catholic dogma and doctrine, reiterate papal authority.

1547 Ivan IV ("the Terrible") crowned as Czar of Russia, begins conquest of Astrakhan and Kazan (1552), battles nobles (boyars) for power (1564), kills his son (1580), dies, and is succeeded by a son who gives power to Boris Godunov (1584).

1553 Roman Catholicism restored in England by Queen Mary I, who rules until 1558. Religious radical Michael Servetus burned as heretic in Geneva by order of John Calvin.

1554 Benvenuto Cellini completes the bronze *Perseus*.

1556 Akbar the Great becomes Mogul emperor of India, conquers Afghanistan (1581), continues wars of conquest (until 1605).

1558 Queen Elizabeth I ascends the throne (rules to 1603). Restores Protestantism, establishes state Church of England (Anglicanism). Renaissance will reach height in England—Shakespeare, Marlowe, Spenser.

1561 Persecution of Huguenots in France stopped by Edict of Orleans. French religious wars begin again with massacre of Huguenots at Vassy. St. Bartholomew's Day Massacre—thousands of Huguenots murdered (1572). Amnesty granted (1573). Persecution continues periodically until Edict of Nantes (1598) gives Huguenots religious freedom (until 1685).

1568 Protestant Netherlands revolts against Catholic Spain; independence will be acknowledged by Spain in 1648. High point of Dutch Renaissance—painters Rubens, Van Dyck, Hals, and Rembrandt.

1570 Japan permits visits of foreign ships. Queen Elizabeth I excommunicated by Pope. Turks attack Cyprus and war on Venice. Turkish fleet defeated at Battle of Lepanto by Spanish and Italian fleets (1571). Peace of Constantinople (1572) ends Turkish attacks on Europe.

1580 Francis Drake returns to England after circumnavigating the globe. Knighted by Queen Elizabeth I (**1581**). Montaigne's *Essays* published.
1583 William of Orange rules The Netherlands; assassinated on orders of Philip II of Spain (**1584**).
1587 Mary, Queen of Scots, executed for treason by order of Queen Elizabeth I. Monteverdi's *First Book of Madrigals.*
1588 Defeat of the Spanish Armada by English. Henry, King of Navarre and Protestant leader, recognized as Henry IV, first Bourbon king of France. Converts to Roman Catholicism in 1593 in attempt to end religious wars.
1590 Henry IV enters Paris, wars on Spain (**1595**), marries Marie de Medici (**1600**), assassinated (**1610**). Spenser's *The Faerie Queen,* El Greco's *St. Jerome.* Galileo's experiments with falling objects.
1598 Boris Godunov becomes Russian Czar. Tycho Brahe describes his astronomical experiments.

Francis Bacon (1561-1626)

17th century A.D.

1600 Giordano Bruno burned as a heretic. Ieyasu rules Japan, moves capital to Edo (Tokyo). Shakespeare's *Hamlet* begins his most productive decade. English East India Company established to develop overseas trade.
1607 Jamestown, Virginia, established—first permanent English colony on American mainland.
1609 Samuel de Champlain establishes French colony of Quebec.
1611 Gustavus Adolphus elected King of Sweden. King James Version of the Bible published in England. Rubens paints his *Descent from the Cross.*
1614 John Napier discovers logarithms.
1618 Start of the Thirty Years' War (to **1648**)—Protestant revolt against Catholic oppression; Denmark, Sweden, and France will invade Germany in later phases of war. Kepler proposes his Third Law of planetary motion.
1620 Pilgrims, after three-month voyage in *Mayflower,* land at Plymouth Rock. Francis Bacon's *Novum Organum.*
1633 Inquisition forces Galileo to recant his belief in Copernican theory.
1642 English Civil War. Cavaliers, supporters of Charles I, against Roundheads, parliamentary forces. Oliver Cromwell defeats Royalists (**1646**). Parliament demands reforms. Charles I offers concessions, brought to trial (**1648**), beheaded (**1649**). Cromwell becomes Lord Protector (**1653**). Rembrandt paints his *Night Watch.*
1644 End of Ming Dynasty in China—Manchus come to power. Descartes' *Principles of Philosophy.* John Milton's *Areopagitica* on the freedom of the press.
1648 End of the Thirty Years' War. German population about half of what it was in **1618** because of war and pestilence.
1658 Cromwell dies; his son, Richard, resigns and Puritan government collapses.
1660 English Parliament calls for the restoration of the monarchy; invites Charles II to return from France.
1661 Charles II is crowned King of England. Louis XIV begins personal rule as absolute monarch; starts to build Versailles.

Giordano Bruno (1548-1600)

George Washington (1732-1799)

THE FOUNDING OF THE AMERICAN NATION

Colonization of America begins: Jamestown, Va. (**1607**); Pilgrims in Plymouth (**1620**); Massachusetts Bay Colony (**1630**) New Netherland founded by Dutch West India Company (**1623**), captured by English (**1664**). Delaware established by Swedish trading company (**1638**), absorbed later by Penn family. Proprietorships by royal grants to Lord Baltimore (Maryland, **1632**); Captain John Mason (New Hampshire, **1635**); Sir William Berkeley and Sir George Carteret (New Jersey, **1663**); friends of Charles II (the Carolinas, **1663**); William Penn (Pennsylvania, **1682**); James Oglethorpe and others (Georgia, **1732**).

Increasing conflict between colonists and Britain on western frontier because of royal edict limiting western expansion (**1763**), and regulation of colonial trade and increased taxation of colonies (Writs of Assistance allow search for illegal shipments, **1761**; Sugar Act, **1764**; Currency Act, **1764**; Stamp Act, **1765**; Quartering Act, **1765**; Duty Act, **1767**.) Boston Massacre (**1770**). Lord North attempts conciliation (**1770**). Boston Tea Party (**1773**), followed by punitive measures passed by Parliament—the "Intolerable Acts."

First Continental Congress (**1774**) sends "Declaration of Rights and Grievances" to king, urges colonies to form Continental Association. Paul Revere's Ride and Lexington and Concord battle between Massachusetts minutemen and British (**1775**).

Second Continental Congress (**1775**), while sending "olive branch" to the king, begins to raise army, appoints Washington commander-in-chief, and seeks alliance with France. Some colonial legislatures urge their delegates to vote for independence. Declaration of Independence (July 4, **1776**).

Major Battles of the Revolutionary War: *Long Island:* Howe defeats Putnam's division of Washington's Army in Brooklyn Heights, but Americans escape across East River (**1776**). *Trenton and Princeton:* Washington defeats Hessians at Trenton. British at Princeton, winters at Morristown (**1776–77**). Howe winters in Philadelphia; Washington at Valley Forge (**1777–78**). Burgoyne surrenders British army to General Gates at *Saratoga* (**1777**).

France recognizes American independence (**1778**). The War moves south: Savannah captured by British (**1778**); Charleston occupied (**1780**); Americans fight successful guerrilla actions under Marion, Pickens, and Sumter. In the West, George Rogers Clark attacks Forts Kaskaskia and Vincennes (**1778–1779**), defeating British in the region. Cornwallis surrenders at *Yorktown,* Virginia (Oct. 19, **1781**). By **1782**, Britain is eager for peace because of conflicts with European nations. *Peace of Paris* (**1783**): Britain recognizes American independence.

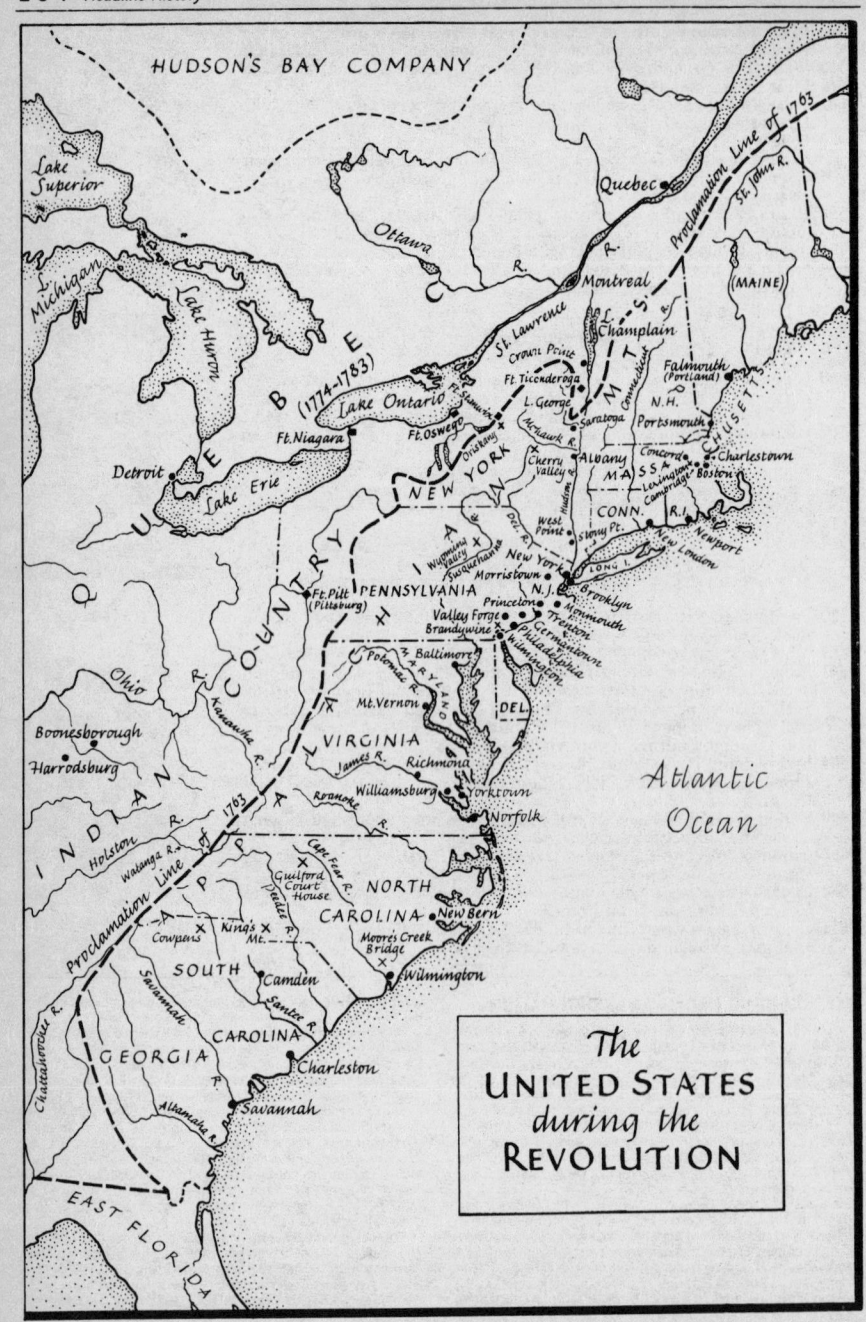

The
UNITED STATES
during the
REVOLUTION

1664 British take New Amsterdam from the Dutch. English limit "Nonconformity" with re-established Anglican Church. Isaac Newton's experiments with gravity.

1665 Great Plague in London kills 75,000.

1666 Great Fire of London. Molière's *Misanthrope.*

1683 War of European powers against the Turks (to 1699). Vienna withstands three-month Turkish siege; high point of Turkish advance in Europe.

1685 James II succeeds Charles II in England, calls for freedom of conscience (1687). Protestants fear restoration of Catholicism and demand "Glorious Revolution." William of Orange invited to England and James II escapes to France (1688). William III and his wife, Mary, crowned. In France, Edict of Nantes of 1598, granting freedom of worship to Huguenots (French Protestants), is revoked by Louis XIV; thousands of Protestants flee.

1689 Peter the Great becomes Czar of Russia—attempts to westernize nation and build Russia as a military power. Defeats Charles XII of Sweden at Poltava (1709). Beginning of the French and Indian Wars (to 1763), campaigns in America linked to a series of wars between France and England for domination of Europe.

1690 William III of England defeats former King James II and Irish rebels at Battle of the Boyne in Ireland. John Locke's *Human Understanding.*

**John Locke
(1632-1704)**

18th century A.D.

1701 War of the Spanish Succession begins—the last of Louis XIV's wars for domination of the continent. The Peace of Utrecht (1714) will end the conflict and mark the rise of the British Empire. Called Queen Anne's War in America, it ends with the British taking New Foundland, Acadia, and Hudson's Bay Territory from France, and Gibraltar and Minorca from Spain.

1704 Deerfield (Conn.) Massacre of English colonists by French and Indians. Bach's first cantata. Jonathan Swift's *Tale of a Tub. Boston News Letter*—first newspaper in America.

1707 United Kingdom of Great Britain formed—England, Wales, and Scotland joined by parliamentary Act of Union.

1729 J. S. Bach's *St. Matthew Passion.* Isaac Newton's *Principia* translated from Latin into English.

1735 John Peter Zenger, New York editor, acquitted of libel in New York, establishing press freedom.

1740 Capt. Vitus Bering, Dane employed by Russia, discovers Alaska.

1746 British defeat Scots under Stuart Pretender Prince Charles at Culloden Moor. Last battle fought on British soil.

1751 Publication of the *Encyclopédie* begins in France, the "bible" of the Enlightenment.

1755 Samuel Johnson's *Dictionary* first published. Great earthquake in Lisbon, Portugal—over 60,000 die.

1756 Seven Years' War (French and Indian War in America) (to 1763), in which Britain and Prussia defeat France, Spain, Austria, and Russia. France loses North American colonies; Spain cedes Florida to Britain in exchange for Cuba. In India, over 100 British prisoners die in "Black Hole of Calcutta."

1757 Beginning of British Empire in India as Robert Clive, British commander, defeats Nawab of Bengal at Plassey.

1759 British capture Quebec from French. Voltaire's *Candide.* Haydn's *Symphony No. 1.*

1762 Catherine II ("the Great") becomes Czarina of Russia. J. J. Rousseau's *Social Contract.* Mozart tours Europe as six-year-old prodigy.

1765 James Watt invents the steam engine.

1769 Sir William Arkwright patents a spinning machine—an early step in the Industrial Revolution.

1772 Joseph Priestley and Daniel Rutherford independently discover nitrogen. Partition of Poland—in 1772, 1793, and 1795, Austria, Prussia, and Russia divide land and people of Poland, end its independence.

1775 The American Revolution (*see* "The Founding of the American Nation"). Priestley discovers hydrochloric and sulfuric acids.

1776 Adam Smith's *Wealth of Nations.* Edward Gibbon's *Decline and Fall of the Roman Empire.* Thomas Paine's *Common Sense.* Fragonard's *Washerwoman.* Mozart's *Haffner Serenade.*

1778 Capt. James Cook discovers Hawaii. Franz Mesmer uses hypnotism.

1781 Immanuel Kant's *Critique of Pure Reason.* Herschel discovers Uranus.

1783 End of Revolutionary War (*see* special material on "The Founding of

**Catherine II
(1729-1796)**

**Napoleon Bonaparte
(1769-1821)**

the American Nation"). William Blake's poems. Beethoven's first printed works.

1784 Crimea annexed by Russia. John Wesley's *Deed of Declaration*, the basic work of Methodism.

1785 Russians settle Aleutian Islands.

1787 The Constitution of the United States signed. Lavoisier's work on chemical nomenclature. Mozart's *Don Giovanni*.

1788 French *Parlement* presents grievances to Louis XVI who agrees to convening of Estates-General in **1789**—not called since **1613**. Goethe's *Egmont*. Laplace's *Laws of the Planetary System*.

1789 French Revolution (*see* special material on the "French Revolution"). In U.S., George Washington elected President with all 69 votes of the Electoral College, takes oath of office in New York City. Vice President: John Adams. Secretary of State: Thomas Jefferson. Secretary of Treasury: Alexander Hamilton.

1790 H.M.S. *Bounty* mutineers settle on Pitcairn Island. Aloisio Galvani experiments on electrical stimulation of the muscles. Philadelphia temporary capital of U.S. as Congress votes to establish new capital on Potomac. U.S. population about 3,929,000, including 698,000 slaves. Lavoisier formulates *Table of 31 chemical elements.*

1791 U.S. Bill of Rights ratified. Boswell's *Life of Johnson*.

1794 Kosciusko's uprising in Poland quelled by the Russians. In U.S., Whiskey Rebellion in Pennsylvania as farmers object to liquor taxes. U.S. Navy and Post Office Department established.

1796 Napoleon Bonaparte, French general, defeats Austrians. In the U.S., Washington's Farewell Address **(Sept. 17)**; John Adams elected President; Thomas Jefferson, Vice President. Edward Jenner introduces smallpox vaccination.

1798 Napoleon extends French conquests to Rome and Egypt.

1799 Napoleon leads coup that overthrows Directory, becomes First Consul—one of three who rule France.

19th century A.D.

1800 Napoleon conquers Italy, firmly establishes himself as First Consul in France. In the U.S., Federal Government moves to Washington. Robert Owen's social reforms in England. William Herschel discovers infrared rays. Alessandro Volta produces electricity.

1801 Austria makes temporary peace with France. United Kingdom of Great Britain and Ireland established with one monarch and one parliament; Catholics excluded from voting.

1803 U.S. negotiates Louisiana Purchase from France: For $15 million, U.S. doubles its domain, increasing its territory by 827,000 sq. mi. (2,144,500 sq km), from Mississippi River to Rockies and from Gulf of Mexico to British North America.

1804 Haiti declares independence from France; first black nation to gain freedom from European colonial rule. Napoleon proclaims himself emperor of France, systematizes French law under *Code Napoleon*. In the U.S., Alexander Hamilton is mortally wounded in duel with Aaron Burr. Lewis and Clark expedition begins exploration of what is now northwestern U.S.

1805 Lord Nelson defeats the French-Spanish fleets in the Battle of Trafalgar. Napoleon victorious over Austrian and Russian forces at the Battle of Austerlitz.

1807 Robert Fulton makes first successful steamboat trip on *Clermont* between New York City and Albany.

1808 French armies occupy Rome and Spain, extending Napoleon's empire. Britain begins aiding Spanish guerrillas against Napoleon in Peninsular War. In the U.S., Congress bars importation of slaves. Beethoven's *Fifth* and *Sixth Symphonies* performed.

1812 Napoleon's Grand Army invades Russia in June. Forced to retreat in winter, most of Napoleon's 600,000 men are lost. In the U.S., war with

**Thomas Jefferson
(1743-1826)**

**Alexander Hamilton
(1755-1804)**

FRENCH REVOLUTION (1789-1799)

Revolution begins when Third Estate (Commons) delegates swear not to disband until France has a constitution. Paris mob storms Bastille, symbol of royal power **(July 14, 1789)**. National Assembly votes for Constitution, Declaration of the Rights of Man, a limited monarchy, and other reforms **(1789-90)**. Legislative Assembly elected, Revolutionary Commune formed, and French Republic proclaimed **(1792)**. War of the First Coalition—Austria, Prussia, Britain, Netherlands, and Spain fight to restore French nobility **(1792-97)**. Start of series of wars between France and European powers that will last, almost without interruption, for 23 years. Louis XVI and Marie Antoinette executed. Committee of Public Safety begins Reign of Terror as political control measure. Interfactional rivalry leads to mass killings. Danton and Robespierre executed. Third French Constitution sets up Directory government **(1795)**.

Britain declared over freedom of the seas for U.S. vessels. U.S.S. *Constitution* sinks British frigate. (*See* special material on the "War of 1812.")

1814 French defeated by allies (Britain, Austria, Russia, Prussia, Sweden, and Portugal) in War of Liberation. Napoleon exiled to Elba, off Italian coast. Bourbon King Louis XVIII takes French throne. George Stephenson builds first practical steam locomotive.

1815 Napoleon returns: "Hundred Days" begin. Napoleon defeated by Wellington at Waterloo, banished again to St. Helena in South Atlantic. Congress of Vienna: victorious allies change the map of Europe.

1817 Simón Bolívar establishes independent Venezuela, as Spain loses hold on South American countries. Bolívar named President of Colombia (**1819**). Peru, Guatemala, Panama, and Santo Domingo proclaim independence from Spain (**1821**).

1820 Missouri Compromise—Missouri admitted as slave state but slavery barred in rest of Louisiana Purchase north of 36°30′ N.

1822 Greeks proclaim a republic and independence from Turkey. Turks invade Greece. Russia declares war on Turkey (**1828**). Greece also aided by France and Britain. War ends and Turks recognize Greek independence (**1829**). Brazil becomes independent of Portugal. Schubert's *Eighth Symphony* ("The Unfinished").

1823 U.S. Monroe Doctrine warns European nations not to interfere in Western Hemisphere.

1824 Mexico becomes a republic, three years after declaring independence from Spain. Beethoven's *Ninth Symphony.*

1825 First passenger-carrying railroad in England.

1830 French invade Algeria. Louis Philippe becomes "Citizen King" as revolution forces Charles X to abdicate. Mormon church formed in U.S. by Joseph Smith.

1831 Polish revolt against Russia fails. Belgium separates from the Netherlands. In U.S., Nat Turner leads unsuccessful slave rebellion.

1833 Slavery abolished in British Empire.

1834 Charles Babbage invents "analytical engine," precursor of computer. McCormick patents reaper.

1836 Boer farmers start "Great Trek"—Natal, Transvaal, and Orange Free State founded in South Africa. Mexican army besieges Texans in Alamo. Entire garrison, including Davy Crockett and Jim Bowie, wiped out. Texans gain independence from Mexico after winning Battle of San Jacinto. Dicken's *Pickwick Papers.*

1837 Victoria becomes Queen of Great Britain. Mob kills Elijah P. Lovejoy, Illinois abolitionist publisher.

1839 First Opium War (to **1842**) between Britain and China, over importation of drug into China.

1840 Lower and Upper Canada united.

1841 U.S. President Harrison dies (**April 4**) one month after inauguration; John Tyler becomes first Vice President to succeed to Presidency.

1844 Democratic convention calls for annexation of Texas and acquisition of Oregon ("Fifty-four-forty-or-fight"). Five Chinese ports opened to U.S. ships. Samuel F. B. Morse patents telegraph.

1845 Congress adopts joint resolution for annexation of Texas.

1846 Failure of potato crop causes famine in Ireland. U.S. declares war on Mexico. California and New Mexico annexed by U.S. Brigham Young leads Mormons to Great Salt Lake. W.T. Morton uses ether as anesthetic. Sewing machine patented by Elias Howe.

1848 Revolt in Paris: Louis Philippe abdicates; Louis Napoleon elected President of French Republic. Revolutions in Vienna, Venice, Berlin, Milan, Rome, and Warsaw. Put down by royal troops in **1848–49**. U.S.-Mexico War ends; Mexico cedes claims to Texas, California, Arizona, New Mexico, Utah, Nevada. U.S. treaty with Britain sets Oregon Territory boundary at 49th parallel. Karl Marx and Friedrich Engels' *Communist Manifesto.*

1849 California gold rush begins.

1850 Henry Clay opens great debate on slavery, warns South against secession.

1851 Herman Melville's *Moby Dick.* Harriet Beecher Stowe's *Uncle Tom's Cabin.*

1852 South African Republic established. Louis Napoleon proclaims himself Napoleon III ("Second Empire").

Charles Dickens
(1812-1870)

Henry Clay
(1777-1852)

WAR OF 1812

British interference with American trade, impressment of American seamen, and "War Hawks" drive for western expansion lead to war. American attacks on Canada foiled; U.S. Commodore Perry wins battle of Lake Erie (**1813**). British capture and burn Washington (**1814**) but fail to take Fort McHenry at Baltimore. Andrew Jackson repulses assault on New Orleans after treaty of Ghent ends war (**1815**). War settles little but strengthens U.S. as independent nation.

**Dred Scott
(1795?-1858)**

1853 Crimean War begins as Turkey declares war on Russia. Commodore Perry reaches Tokyo.

1854 Britain and France join Turkey in war on Russia. In U.S., Kansas-Nebraska Act permits local option on slavery; rioting and bloodshed. Japanese allow American trade. Antislavery men in Michigan form Republican Party. Tennyson's *Charge of the Light Brigade.* Thoreau's *Walden.*

1855 Armed clashes in Kansas between pro- and anti-slavery forces. Florence Nightingale nurses wounded in Crimea. Walt Whitman's *Leaves of Grass.*

1856 Flaubert's *Madame Bovary.*

1857 Supreme Court, in Dred Scott decision, rules that a slave is not a citizen. Financial crisis in Europe and U.S. Great Mutiny (Sepoy Rebellion) begins in India. India placed under crown rule as a result.

1858 Pro-slavery constitution rejected in Kansas. Abraham Lincoln makes strong antislavery speech in Springfield, Ill.: ". . . this Government cannot endure permanently half slave and half free." Lincoln-Douglas debates. First trans-Atlantic telegraph cable completed by Cyrus W. Field.

1859 John Brown raids Harpers Ferry; is captured and hanged. Work begins on Suez Canal. Unification of Italy starts under leadership of Count Cavour, Sardinian premier. Joined by France in war against Austria. Edward Fitzgerald's *Rubaiyat of Omar Khayyam.* Charles Darwin's *Origin of Species.* J. S. Mill's *On Liberty*

1861 U.S. Civil War begins as attempts at compromise fail (*see* special material on "The Civil War"). Congress creates Colorado, Dakota, and Nevada territories; adopts income tax; Lincoln inaugurated. Serfs emancipated in Russia. Pasteur's theory of germs. Independent Kingdom of Italy proclaimed under Sardinian King Victor Emmanuel II.

**Abraham Lincoln
(1809-1865)**

1863 French capture Mexico City; proclaim Archduke Maximilian of Austria emperor.

1865 Lincoln fatally shot at Ford's Theater by John Wilkes Booth. Vice President Johnson sworn as successor. Booth caught and dies of gunshot wounds; four conspirators are hanged. Joseph Lister begins antiseptic surgery. Gregor Mendel's Law of Heredity. Lewis Carroll's *Alice's Adventures in Wonderland.*

1866 Alfred Nobel invents dynamite (patented in Britain 1867). Seven Weeks' War: Austria defeated by Prussia and Italy.

1867 Austria-Hungary Dual Monarchy established. French leave Mexico; Maximilian executed. Dominion of Canada established. U.S. buys Alaska from Russia for $7,200,000. South African diamond field discovered. Volume I of Marx's *Das Kapital.* Strauss's *Blue Danube.*

1868 Revolution in Spain; Queen Isabella deposed, flees to France. In U.S., Fourteenth Amendment giving civil rights to blacks is ratified. Georgia under military government after legislature expels blacks.

**Ulysses S. Grant
(1822-1885)**

1869 First U.S. transcontinental rail route completed. James Fisk and Jay Gould attempt to control gold market causes Black Friday panic. Suez Canal opened. Mendeleev's periodic table of elements.

1870 Franco-Prussian War (to 1871): Napoleon III capitulates at Sedan. Revolt in Paris; Third Republic proclaimed.

THE CIVIL WAR
(The War Between the States or the War of the Rebellion)

Apart from the matter of slavery, the Civil War arose out of both the economic and political rivalry between an agrarian South and an industrial North and the issue of the right of states to secede from the Union.

1861 After South Carolina secedes **(Dec. 20, 1860),** Mississippi, Florida, Alabama, Georgia, Louisiana, and Texas follow, forming the Confederate States of America, with Jefferson Davis as president **(Jan.-March).** War begins as Confederates fire on Fort Sumter **(April 12).** Lincoln calls for 75,000 volunteers. Southern ports blockaded by superior Union naval forces. Virginia, Arkansas, Tennessee, and North Carolina secede to complete 11-state Confederacy. Union army advancing on Richmond repulsed at first Battle of Bull Run **(July).**

1862 Edwin M. Stanton named Secretary of War **(Jan.).** Grant wins first important Union victory in West, at Fort Donelson; Nashville falls **(Feb.).** Ironclads, Union's *Monitor* and Confederate's *Virginia (Merrimac)* duel at Hampton Roads **(March).** New Orleans falls to Union fleet under Farragut; city occupied **(April).** Grant's army escapes defeat at Shiloh. Memphis falls as Union gunboats control upper Mississippi **(June).** Confederate general Robert E. Lee victorious at second Battle of Bull Run **(Aug.).** Union army under McClellan halts Lee's attack on Washington in the Battle of Antietam **(Sept.).** Lincoln removes McClellan for lack of aggressiveness. Burnside's drive on Richmond fails at Fredericksburg **(Dec.).** Union forces under Rosecrans chase Bragg through Tennessee; battle of Murfreesboro **(Oct.-Jan. 1863).**

1863 Lee defeats Hooker at Chancellorsville; "Stonewall" Jackson, Confederate general, dies **(May).** Confederate invasion of Pennsylvania stopped at Gettysburg by George Meade—Lee loses 20,000 men—the greatest battle of the War **(July).** It and the Union victory at Vicksburg mark the war's turning point. Union general George H. Thomas, the "Rock of Chickamauga," holds Bragg's forces on Georgia-Tennessee border **(Sept.).** Sherman, Hooker, and Thomas drive Bragg back to Georgia. Tennessee restored to the Union **(Nov.).**

1864 Ulysses S. Grant named commander-in-chief of Union forces **(March).** In the Wilderness campaign, Grant forces Lee's Army of Northern Virginia back toward Richmond **(May-June).** Sherman's Atlanta campaign and "march to the sea" **(May-Sept.).** Farragut's victory at Mobile Bay **(Aug.).** Hood's Confederate army defeated at Nashville. Sherman takes Savannah **(Dec.).**

1865 Sheridan defeats Confederates at Five Forks; Confederates evacuate Richmond **(April).** On **April 9,** Lee surrenders to Grant at Appomattox.

1871 France surrenders Alsace-Lorraine to Germany; war ends. German Empire proclaimed with Prussian King as Kaiser Wilhelm I. Fighting with Apaches begins in American West. Boss Tweed corruption exposed in New York. The Chicago Fire, with 250 deaths and $196-million damage. Stanley meets Livingston in Africa.

1872 Congress gives amnesty to most Confederates. Jules Verne's *Around the World in 80 Days.*

1873 Economic crisis in Europe. U.S. establishes gold standard.

1875 First Kentucky Derby.

1876 Sioux kill Gen. George A. Custer and 264 troopers at Little Big Horn River. Alexander Graham Bell patents the telephone.

1877 After Presidential election of 1876, Electoral Commission gives disputed Electoral College votes to Rutherford B. Hayes despite Tilden's popular majority. Russo-Turkish war (ends in 1878 with power of Turkey in Europe broken). Reconstruction ends in the American South. Thomas Edison patents phonograph.

1878 Congress of Berlin revises Treaty of San Stefano ending Russo-Turkish War; makes extensive redivision of southeastern Europe. First commercial telephone exchange opened in New Haven, Conn.

1880 U.S.-China treaty allows U.S. to restrict immigration of Chinese labor.

1881 President Garfield fatally shot by assassin; Vice President Arthur succeeds him. Charles J. Guiteau convicted and executed (in 1882).

Geronimo (1829-1909)

1882 Terrorism in Ireland after land evictions. Britain invades and conquers Egypt. Germany, Austria, and Italy form Triple Alliance. In U.S., Congress adopts Chinese Exclusion Act. Rockefeller's Standard Oil Trust is first industrial monopoly. In Berlin, Robert Koch announces discovery of tuberculosis germ.

1883 Congress creates Civil Service Commission. Brooklyn Bridge and Metropolitan Opera House completed.

1885 British Gen. Charles G. "Chinese" Gordon killed at Khartoum in Egyptian Sudan.

1886 Bombing at Haymarket Square, Chicago, kills seven policemen and injures many others. Eight alleged anarchists accused—three imprisoned, one commits suicide, four hanged. (In 1893, Illinois Governor Altgeld, critical of trial, pardons three survivors.) Statue of Liberty dedicated. Geronimo, Apache Indian chief, surrenders.

1887 Queen Victoria's Golden Jubilee. Sir Arthur Conan Doyle's first Sherlock Holmes story, "A Study in Scarlet."

Samuel Clemens (Mark Twain) (1835-1910)

1888 Historic March blizzard in Northeast U.S.—many perish, property damage exceeds $25 million. George Eastman's box camera (the Kodak). J.B. Dunlop invents pneumatic tire. Jack the Ripper murders in London.

1889 Second (Socialist) International founded in Paris. Indian Territory in Oklahoma opened to settlement. Thousands die in Johnstown, Pa., flood. Mark Twain's *A Connecticut Yankee in King Arthur's Court.*

1890 Congress votes Sherman Antitrust Act. Sitting Bull killed in Sioux uprising.

1892 Battle between steel strikers and Pinkerton guards at Homestead, Pa.; union defeated after militia intervenes. Silver mine strikers in Idaho fight non-union workers; U.S. troops dispatched. Diesel engine patented.

1894 Sino-Japanese War begins (ends in 1895 with China's defeat). In France, Capt. Alfred Dreyfus convicted on false treason charge (pardoned in 1906). In U.S., Jacob S. Coxey of Ohio leads "Coxey's Army" of unemployed on Washington. Eugene V. Debs calls general strike of rail workers to support Pullman Company strikers; strike broken, Debs jailed for six months. Thomas A. Edison's kinetoscope given first public showing in New York City.

1895 X-rays discovered by German physicist, Wilhelm Roentgen.

1896 Supreme Court's *Plessy v. Ferguson* decision—"separate but equal" doctrine. Alfred Nobel's will establishes prizes for peace, science, and literature. Marconi receives first wireless patent in Britain. William Jennings Bryan delivers "Cross of Gold" speech at Democratic Convention

Thomas A. Edison (1847-1931)

SPANISH-AMERICAN WAR (1898–1899)

War fires stoked by "jingo journalism" as American people support Cuban rebels against Spain. American business sees economic gain in Cuban trade and resources and American power zones in Latin America. Outstanding events: Submarine mine explodes U.S. battleship *Maine* in Havana Harbor (**Feb. 15**); 260 killed; responsibility never fixed. Congress declares independence of Cuba (**April 19**). Spain declares war on U.S. (**Apr. 24**); Congress (**Apr. 25**) formally declares nation has been at war with Spain since Apr. 21. Commodore George Dewey wins seven-hour battle of Manila Bay (**May 1**). Spanish fleet destroyed off Santiago, Cuba (**July 3**); city surrenders (**July 17**). Treaty of Paris (ratified by Senate 1899) ends war. U.S. given Guam and Puerto Rico and agrees to pay Spain $20 million for Philippines. Cuba independent of Spain; under U.S. military control for three years until **May 20, 1902**. Yellow fever is eradicated and political reforms achieved.

Marie Curie
(1867–1934)

Theodore Roosevelt
(1858–1919)

Albert Einstein
(1879-1955)

in Chicago. First modern Olympic games held in Athens, Greece.

1898 Chinese "Boxers," anti-foreign organization, established. They stage uprisings against Europeans in 1900; U.S. and other Western troops relieve Peking legations. Spanish-American War (*see* special material on the "Spanish-American War"). Pierre and Marie Curie discover radium and polonium.

1899 Boer War (or South African War). Conflict between British and Boers (descendants of Dutch settlers of South Africa). Causes rooted in longstanding territorial disputes and in friction over political rights for English and other "uitlanders" following 1886 discovery of vast gold deposits in Transvaal. (British victorious as war ends in 1902.) Casualties: 5,774 British dead, about 4,000 Boers. Union of South Africa established in 1908 as confederation of colonies; becomes British dominion in 1910.

20th century A.D.

1900 Hurricane ravages Galveston, Tex.; 6,000 drown. Sigmund Freud's *The Interpretation of Dreams.*

1901 Queen Victoria dies; succeeded by son, Edward VII. As President McKinley begins second term, he is shot fatally by anarchist Leon Czolgosz. Theodore Roosevelt sworn in as successor.

1902 Enrico Caruso's first gramophone recording.

1903 Wright brothers, Orville and Wilbur, fly first powered, controlled, heavier-than-air plane at Kitty Hawk, N.C. Henry Ford organizes Ford Motor Company.

1904 Russo-Japanese War—competition for Korea and Manchuria: In 1905, Port Arthur surrenders to Japanese and Russia suffers other defeats; President Roosevelt mediates Treaty of Portsmouth, N.H., ending war with concessions for Japan. *Entente Cordiale:* Britain and France settle their international differences. General theory of radioactivity by Rutherford and Soddy. New York City subway opened.

1905 General strike in Russia; first workers' soviet set up in St. Petersburg. Sailors on battleship *Potemkin* mutiny; reforms including first Duma (parliament) established by Czar's "October Manifesto." Albert Einstein's special theory of relativity and other key theories in physics. Franz Lehar's *Merry Widow.*

1906 San Francisco earthquake and three-day fire; 500 dead. Roald Amundsen, Norwegian explorer, fixes magnetic North Pole.

1907 Second Hague Peace Conference, of 46 nations, adopts 10 conventions on rules of war. Financial panic of 1907 in U.S.

1908 Earthquake kills 150,000 in southern Italy and Sicily. U.S. Supreme Court, in Danbury Hatters' case, outlaws secondary union boycotts.

1909 North Pole reached by American explorers Robert E. Peary and Matthew Henson.

1910 Boy Scouts of America incorporated.

1911 First use of aircraft as offensive weapon in Turkish-Italian War. Italy defeats Turks and annexes Tripoli and Libya. Chinese Republic proclaimed after revolution overthrows Manchu dynasty. Sun Yat-sen named president. Mexican Revolution: Porfirio Díaz, president since 1877, replaced by Francisco Madero. Triangle Shirtwaist Company fire in New York; 145 killed. Richard Strauss's *Der Rosenkavalier.* Irving Berlin's *Alexander's Ragtime Band.* Amundsen reaches South Pole.

1912 Balkan Wars (1912–13) resulting from territorial disputes: Turkey defeated by alliance of Bulgaria, Serbia, Greece, and Montenegro; London peace treaty (1913) partitions most of European Turkey among the victors. In second war (1913), Bulgaria attacks Serbia and Greece and is defeated after Romania intervenes and Turks recapture Adrianople. *Titanic* sinks on maiden voyage; over 1,500 drown.

1913 Suffragettes demonstrate in London. Garment workers strike in New York and Boston; win pay raise and shorter hours. Sixteenth Amendment (income tax) and 17th (popular election of U.S. senators) adopted. Bill creating U.S. Federal Reserve System becomes law. Stravinsky's *The Rite of Spring.*

1914 World War I begins (*see* special material on "World War I"). Panama Canal officially opened. Congress sets up Federal Trade Commission, passes Clayton Antitrust Act. U.S. Marines occupy Veracruz, Mexico, intervening in civil war to protect American interests.

1915 U.S. protests German submarine actions and British blockade of Germany. U.S. banks lend $500 million to France and Britain. D. W. Griffith's film *Birth of a Nation.* Albert Einstein's *General Theory of Relativity.*

1916 Congress expands armed forces. Tom Mooney arrested for San Francisco bombing (pardoned in 1939). Pershing fails in raid into Mexico in

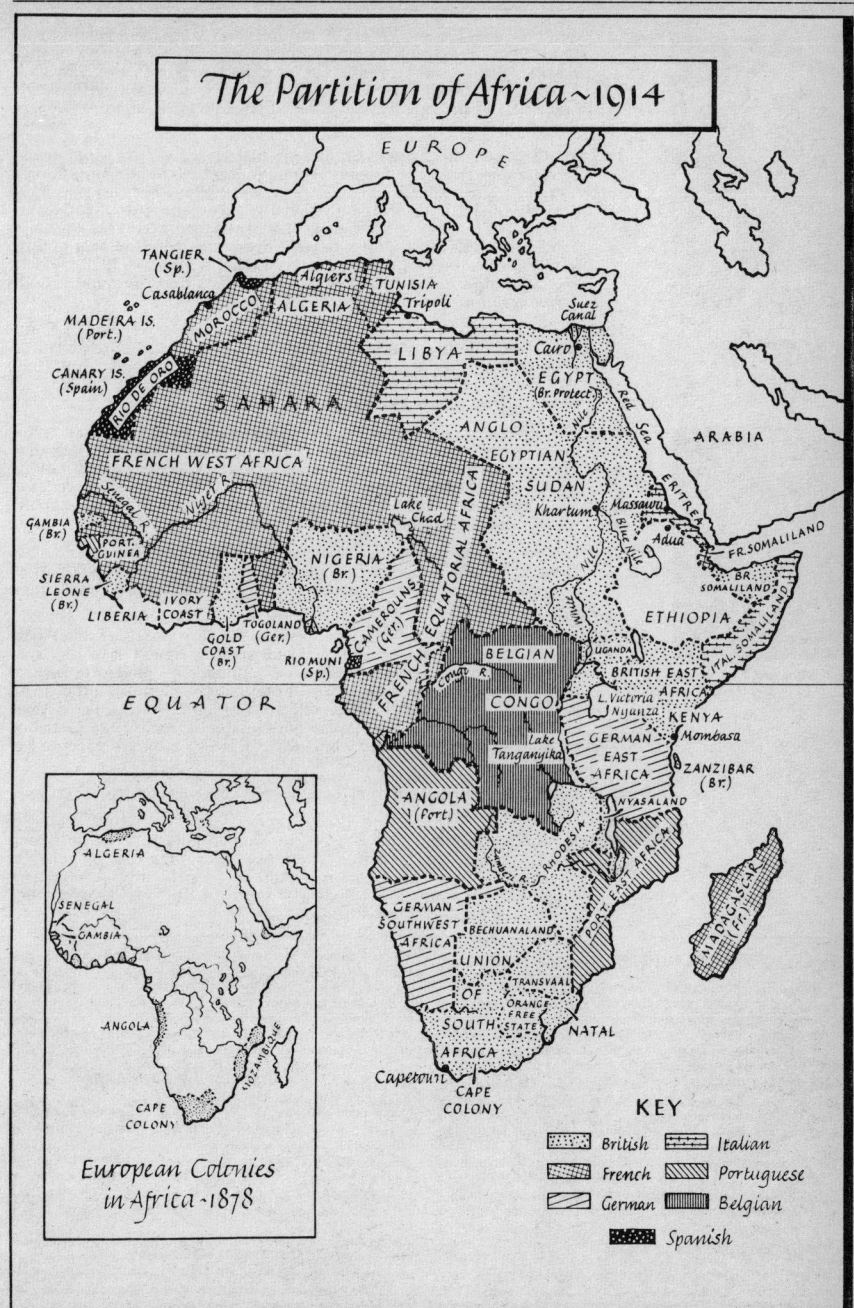

The Partition of Africa ~ 1914

EUROPE

TANGIER (Sp.)
Casablanca
MADEIRA IS. (Port.)
Algiers
TUNISIA
Tripoli
Suez Canal
MOROCCO
ALGERIA
CANARY IS. (Spain)
RIO DE ORO
SAHARA
LIBYA
Cairo
EGYPT (Br. Protect)
ARABIA
FRENCH WEST AFRICA
ANGLO EGYPTIAN SUDAN
Khartum
Massawa
Red Sea
ERITREA
GAMBIA (Br.)
PORT. GUINEA
Senegal
Niger
Lake Chad
Blue Nile
Adua
FR. SOMALILAND
SIERRA LEONE (Br.)
LIBERIA
IVORY COAST
GOLD COAST (Br.)
TOGOLAND (Ger.)
NIGERIA (Br.)
RIO MUNI (Sp.)
CAMEROONS (Ger.)
FRENCH EQUATORIAL AFRICA
BR. SOMALILAND
ETHIOPIA
ITAL. SOMALILAND
EQUATOR
Congo R.
BELGIAN CONGO
Lake Tanganyika
UGANDA
BRITISH EAST AFRICA
L. Victoria Nyanza
KENYA
Mombasa
GERMAN EAST AFRICA
ZANZIBAR (Br.)
ANGOLA (Port.)
NYASALAND
RHODESIA
PORT. EAST AFRICA
MADAGASCAR (Fr.)
GERMAN SOUTHWEST AFRICA
BECHUANALAND
MOZAMBIQUE
UNION OF SOUTH AFRICA
TRANSVAAL
ORANGE FREE STATE
NATAL
Capetown
CAPE COLONY

ALGERIA
SENEGAL
GAMBIA
ANGOLA
MOZAMBIQUE
CAPE COLONY

European Colonies in Africa ~ 1878

KEY

British		Italian
French		Portuguese
German		Belgian
Spanish		

**Vladimir Lenin
(1870-1924)**

**Woodrow Wilson
(1856-1924)**

quest of rebel Pancho Villa. U.S. buys Virgin Islands from Denmark for $25 million. President Wilson re-elected with "he kept us out of war" slogan. "Black Tom" explosion at munitions dock in Jersey City, N.J., $40,000,000 damages; traced to German saboteurs. Margaret Sanger opens first birth control clinic. Easter Rebellion in Ireland put down by British troops.

1917 First U.S. combat troops in France as U.S. declares war (**April 6**). Russian Revolution—climax of long unrest under czars. February Revolution—Czar forced to abdicate, liberal government created. Kerensky becomes prime minister and forms provisional government (**July**). In October Revolution, Bolsheviks seize power in armed coup d'état led by Lenin and Trotsky. Kerensky flees. Revolutionaries execute the czar and his family (**1918**). Reds set up Third International in Moscow (**1919**). Balfour Declaration promises Jewish homeland in Palestine. Sigmund Freud's *Introduction to Psychoanalysis.*

1918 Russian Civil War between Reds (Bolsheviks) and Whites (anti-Bolsheviks); Reds win in **1920**. Allied troops (U.S., British, French) intervene (**March**); leave in **1919**. Japanese hold Vladivostok until **1922**. World-wide influenza epidemic strikes; by **1920**, nearly 20 million are dead. In U.S. alone, 500,000 perish.

1919 Third International (Comintern) establishes Soviet control over international Communist movements. Paris peace conference. Versailles Treaty, incorporating Wilson's draft Covenant of League of Nations, signed by Allies and Germany; rejected by U.S. Senate. Congress formally ends war in **1921**. Eighteenth (Prohibition) Amendment adopted. Alcock and Brown make first trans-Atlantic non-stop flight.

1920 League of Nations holds first meeting at Geneva, Switzerland. U.S. Dept. of Justice "red hunt" nets thousands of radicals; aliens deported. Women's suffrage (19th) amendment ratified. First Agatha Christie mystery. Sinclair Lewis's *Main Street.*

1921 Reparations Commission fixes German liability at 132 billion gold marks. German inflation begins. Major treaties signed at Washington Disarmament Conference limit naval tonnage and pledge to respect territorial integrity of China. Irish Free State formed in southern Ireland as self-governing dominion of British Empire. In U.S., Nicola Sacco and Bartolomeo Vanzetti, Italian-born anarchists, convicted of armed robbery murder; case stirs world-wide protests; they are executed in 1927.

1922 Mussolini marches on Rome; forms Fascist government. Irish Free State officially proclaimed.

1923 Adolf Hitler's "Beer Hall Putsch" in Munich fails; in **1924** he is sentenced to five years in prison where he writes *Mein Kampf;* released after eight months. Occupation of Ruhr by French and Belgian troops to enforce reparations payments. Widespread Ku Klux Klan violence in U.S. George Gershwin's *Rhapsody in Blue.*

WORLD WAR I (1914-1918)

Imperial, territorial, and economic rivalries lead to the "Great War" between the Central Powers (Austria-Hungary, Germany, Bulgaria, and Turkey) and the Allies (U.S., Britain, France, Russia, Belgium, Serbia, Greece, Romania, Montenegro, Portugal, Italy, Japan). About 10 million combatants killed, 20 million wounded.

1914 Austrian Archduke Francis Ferdinand and wife assassinated in Sarajevo by Serbian nationalist, Gavrilo Princip (**June 28**). Austria declares war on Serbia (**July 28**). Germany declares war on Russia (**Aug. 1**), on France (**Aug. 3**), invades Belgium (**Aug. 4**). Britain declares war on Germany (**Aug. 4**). Germans defeat Russians in Battle of Tannenberg on Eastern Front (**Aug.**). First Battle of the Marne (**Sept.**). German drive stopped 25 miles from Paris. By end of year, war on the Western Front is "positional" in the trenches.

1915 German submarine blockade of Great Britain begins (**Feb.**). Dardanelles Campaign—British land in Turkey (**April**), withdraw from Gallipoli (**Dec. to Jan. 1916**). Germans use gas at second Battle of Ypres (**April–May**). *Lusitania* sunk by German submarine—1,198 lost, including 128 Americans (**May 7**). On Eastern Front, German and Austrian "great offensive" conquers all of Poland and Lithuania; Russians lose 1 million men (by **Sept. 6**). "Great Fall Offensive" by Allies results in little change from 1914 (**Sept.–Oct.**). Britain and France declare war on Bulgaria (**Oct. 14**).

1916 Battle of Verdun—Germans and French each lose about 350,000 men (**Feb.**). Extended submarine warfare begins (**March**). British-German sea battle of Jutland (**May**); British lose more ships, but German fleet never ventures forth again. On Eastern front, the Brusilov offensive demoralizes Russians, costs them 1 million men (**June–Sept.**). Battle of the Somme—British lose over 400,000; French, 200,000; Germans, about 450,000; all with no strategic results (**July–Nov.**). Romania declares war on Austria-Hungary (**Aug. 27**). Bucharest captured (**Dec.**).

1917 U.S. declares war on Germany (**April 6**). Submarine warfare at peak (**April**). On Italian Front, Battle of Caporetto—Italians retreat, losing 600,000 prisoners and deserters (**Oct.–Dec.**). On Western Front, Battles of Arras, Champagne, Ypres (third battle), etc. First large British tank attack (**Nov.**). U.S. declares war on Austria-Hungary (**Dec. 7**). Armistice between new Russian Bolshevik government and Germans (**Dec. 15**).

1918 Great offensive by Germans (**March–June**). Americans' first important battle role at Château-Thierry—as they and French stop German advance (**June**). Second Battle of the Marne (**July–Aug.**)—start of Allied offensive at Amiens, St. Mihiel, etc. Battles of the Argonne and Ypres panic German leadership (**Sept.–Oct.**). British offensive in Palestine (**Sept.**). Germans ask for armistice (**Oct. 4**). British armistice with Turkey (**Oct.**). German Kaiser abdicates (**Nov.**). Hostilities cease on Western Front (**Nov. 11**).

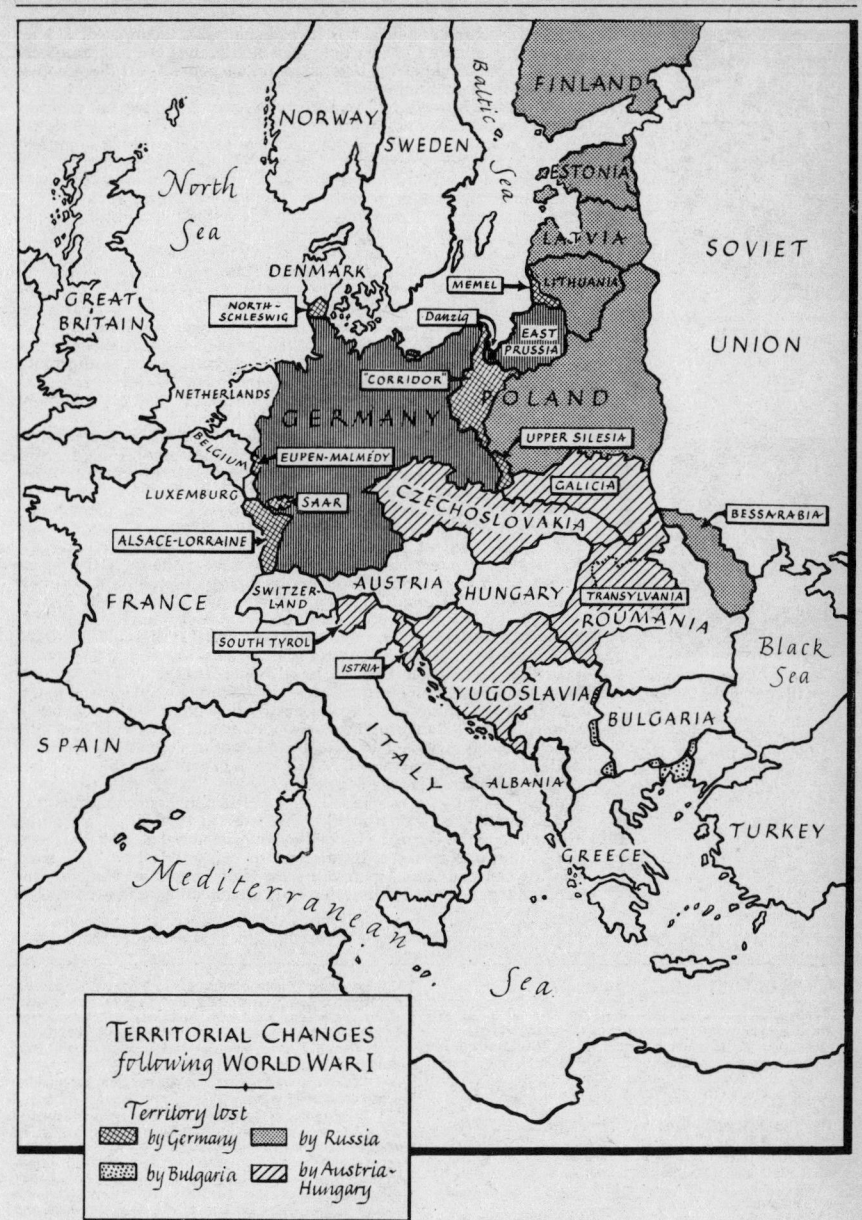

TERRITORIAL CHANGES
following WORLD WAR I

Territory lost

by Germany	by Russia
by Bulgaria	by Austria-Hungary

1924 Death of Lenin; Stalin wins power struggle, rules as Soviet dictator until
death in 1953. Italian Fascists murder Socialist leader Giacomo Matte-
otti. Interior Secretary Albert B. Fall and oilmen Harry Sinclair and Edward L. Doheny are charged with conspiracy and bribery in the Teapot
Dome scandal, involving fraudulent leases of naval oil reserves. In 1931,
Fall is sentenced to year in prison; Doheny and Sinclair acquitted of

Charles A. Lindbergh (1902-1974)

Herbert C. Hoover (1874-1964)

bribery. Nathan Leopold and Richard Loeb convicted in "thrill killing" of Bobby Franks in Chicago; defended by Clarence Darrow; sentenced to life imprisonment. (Loeb killed by fellow convict in 1936; Leopold paroled in 1958, dies in 1971.)

1925 Nellie Tayloe Ross elected governor of Wyoming; first woman governor elected in U.S. Locarno conferences seek to secure European peace by mutual guarantees. John T. Scopes convicted and fined for teaching evolution in a public school in Tennessee "Monkey Trial"; sentence set aside. John Logie Baird, Scottish inventor, transmits human features by television. Adolf Hitler publishes Volume I of *Mein Kampf.*

1926 General strike in Britain brings nation's activities to standstill. U.S. marines dispatched to Nicaragua during revolt; they remain until 1933. Gertrude Ederle of U.S. is first woman to swim English Channel.

1927 German economy collapses. Socialists riot in Vienna; general strike follows acquittal of Nazis for political murder. Trotsky expelled from Russian Communist Party. Charles A. Lindbergh flies first successful solo non-stop flight from New York to Paris. Ruth Snyder and Judd Gray convicted of murder of Albert Snyder; they are executed at Sing Sing prison in 1928. *The Jazz Singer,* with Al Jolson, first part-talking motion picture.

1928 Kellogg-Briand Pact, outlawing war, signed in Paris by 65 nations. Alexander Fleming discovers penicillin. Richard E. Byrd starts expedition to Antarctic; returns in 1930.

1929 Trotsky expelled from U.S.S.R. Lateran Treaty establishes independent Vatican City. In U.S., stock market prices collapse, with U.S. securities losing $26 billion—first phase of Depression and world economic crisis. St. Valentine's Day gangland massacre in Chicago.

1930 Britain, U.S., Japan, France, and Italy sign naval disarmament treaty. Nazis gain in German elections. Cyclotron developed by Ernest O. Lawrence, U.S. physicist.

1931 Spain becomes a republic with overthrow of King Alfonso XIII. German industrialists finance 800,000-strong Nazi party. British parliament enacts statute of Westminster, legalizing dominion equality with Britain. Mukden Incident begins Japanese occupation of Manchuria. In U.S., Hoover proposes one-year moratorium of war debts. Harold C. Urey discovers heavy hydrogen. Gangster Al Capone sentenced to 11 years in prison for tax evasion (freed in 1939; dies in 1947).

1932 Nazis lead in German elections with 230 Reichstag seats. Famine in U.S.S.R. In U.S., Congress sets up Reconstruction Finance Corporation to stimulate economy. Veterans march on Washington—most leave after Senate rejects payment of cash bonuses; others removed by troops under Douglas MacArthur. U.S. protests Japanese aggression in Manchuria. Amelia Earhart is first woman to fly Atlantic solo. Charles A. Lindbergh's baby son kidnapped, killed. (Bruno Richard Hauptmann arrested in 1934, convicted in 1935, executed in 1936.)

1933 Hitler appointed German chancellor, gets dictatorial powers. Reichstag fire in Berlin; Nazi terror begins. (*See* special material on "The Holocaust.") Germany and Japan withdraw from League of Nations. Giuseppe Zangara executed for attempted assassination of President-elect

---

THE HOLOCAUST (1933-1945)

"Holocaust" is the term describing the Nazi annihilation of about 6 million Jews (two thirds of the pre-World War II European Jewish population), including 4,500,000 from Russia, Poland, and the Baltic; 750,000 from Hungary and Romania; 290,000 from Germany and Austria; 105,000 from The Netherlands; 90,000 from France; 54,000 from Greece, etc.

The Holocaust was unique in its being *genocide*—the systematic destruction of a people solely because of religion, race, ethnicity, nationality, or homosexuality—on an unmatched scale. Along with the Jews, another 9 to 10 million people—Gypsies, Slavs (Poles, Ukrainians, and Belorussians)—were exterminated.

The only comparable act of genocide in modern times was launched in April 1915, when an estimated 600,000 Armenians were massacred by the Turks.

1933 Hitler named German Chancellor **(Jan.).** Dachau, first concentration camp, established **(March).** Boycotts against Jews begin **(April).**

1935 Anti-Semitic Nuremberg Laws passed by Reichstag **(Sept.).**

1937 Buchenwald concentration camp opens **(July).**

1938 Extension of anti-Semitic laws to Austria after annexation **(March).** *Kristallnacht* (Night of Broken Glass)—anti-Semitic riots in Germany and Austria **(Nov. 9).** 26,000 Jews sent to concentration camps; Jewish children expelled from schools **(Nov.).** Expropriation of Jewish property and businesses **(Dec.).**

1940 As war continues, Nazi acts against Jews extended to German-conquered areas.

1941 Deportation of German Jews begins; massacres of Jews in Odessa and Kiev—68,000 killed **(Nov.);** in Riga and Vilna—almost 60,000 killed **(Dec.).**

1942 Unified Jewish resistance in ghettos begins **(Jan.).** 300,000 Jews from Warsaw Ghetto deported to Treblinka death camp **(July).**

1943 Warsaw Ghetto uprisings **(Jan.** and **April);** Ghetto exterminated **(May).**

1944 476,000 Hungarian Jews sent to Auschwitz **(May-June).** D-day **(June 6).** Soviet Army liberates Maidanek death camp **(July).** Nazis try to hide evidence of death camps **(Nov.).**

1945 Americans liberate Buchenwald and British liberate Bergen-Belsen camps **(April).** Nuremberg War Crimes Trial **(Nov. 1945 to Oct. 1946).**

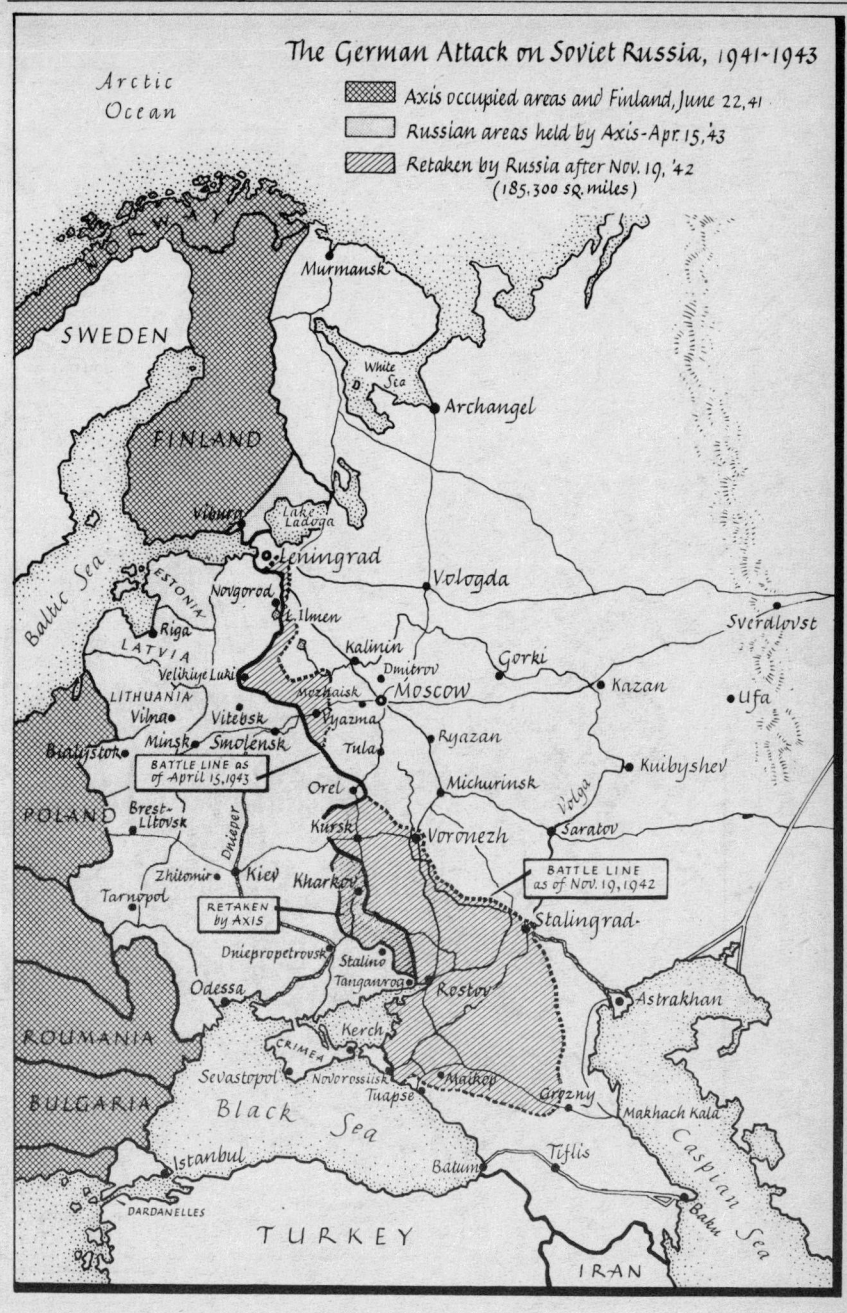

The German Attack on Soviet Russia, 1941-1943

- ▨ Axis occupied areas and Finland, June 22, 41
- ▢ Russian areas held by Axis - Apr. 15, 43
- ▨ Retaken by Russia after Nov. 19, '42
  (185,300 sq. miles)

Arctic Ocean

SWEDEN

FINLAND

Murmansk

White Sea

Archangel

Viipuri

Lake Ladoga

Leningrad

Novgorod

L. Ilmen

Vologda

Sverdlovsk

Baltic Sea

ESTONIA

Riga

LATVIA

Velikiye Luki

Kalinin

Dmitrov

Gorki

Kazan

Ufa

LITHUANIA

Vilna

Mozhaisk

MOSCOW

Vitebsk

Vyazma

Minsk

Smolensk

Tula

Ryazan

Kuibyshev

Bialystok

BATTLE LINE as of April 15, 1943

Orel

Michurinsk

Volga

POLAND

Dnieper

Kursk

Voronezh

Saratov

Brest-Litovsk

Zhitomir

Kiev

Kharkov

BATTLE LINE as of Nov. 19, 1942

Tarnopol

RETAKEN by AXIS

Dniepropetrovsk

Stalino

Stalingrad

Odessa

Taganrog

Rostov

Astrakhan

Kerch

ROUMANIA

CRIMEA

Sevastopol

Novorossiisk

Maikop

Grozny

BULGARIA

Tuapse

Makhach Kala

Black Sea

Istanbul

Batum

Tiflis

Caspian Sea

DARDANELLES

Baku

T U R K E Y

I R A N

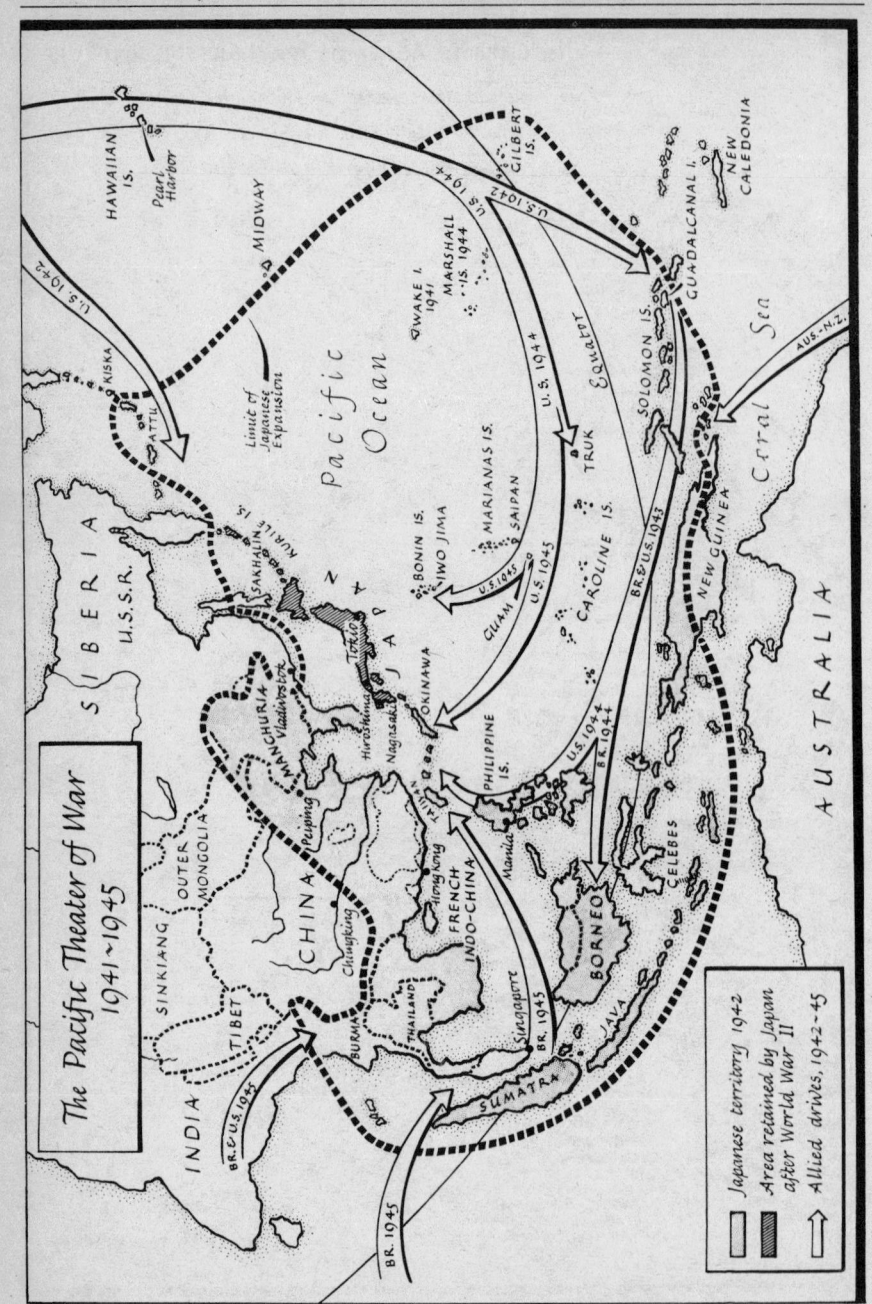

The Pacific Theater of War 1941~1945

Roosevelt in which Chicago Mayor Cermak is fatally shot. Roosevelt inaugurated ("the only thing we have to fear is fear itself"); launches New Deal. Prohibition repealed. U.S.S.R. recognized by U.S.

1934 Chancellor Dollfuss of Austria assassinated by Nazis. Hitler becomes Führer. U.S.S.R. admitted to League of Nations. Dionne sisters, first quintuplets to survive beyond infancy, born in Canada.

1935 Saar incorporated into Germany after plebiscite. Nazis repudiate Versailles Treaty, introduce compulsory military service. Mussolini invades Ethiopia; League of Nations invokes sanctions. Roosevelt opens second phase of New Deal in U.S., calling for social security, better housing, equitable taxation, and farm assistance. Huey Long assassinated in Louisiana.

1936 Germans occupy Rhineland. Italy annexes Ethiopia. Rome-Berlin Axis proclaimed (Japan to join in 1940). Trotsky exiled to Mexico. King George V dies; succeeded by son, Edward VIII, who soon abdicated to marry American-born divorcée, and is succeeded by brother, George VI. Spanish civil war begins. (Franco's fascist forces defeat Loyalist forces by 1939, when Madrid falls.) War between China and Japan begins, to continue through World War II. Japan and Germany sign anti-Comintern pact; joined by Italy in 1937.

**Amelia Earhart
(1898-1937)**

1937 Hitler repudiates war guilt clause of Versailles Treaty; continues to build German power. Italy withdraws from League of Nations. U.S. gunboat *Panay* sunk by Japanese in Yangtze River. Japan invades China, conquers most of coastal area. Amelia Earhart lost somewhere in Pacific on round-the-world flight.

1938 Hitler marches into Austria; political and geographical union of Germany and Austria proclaimed. Munich Pact—Britain, France, and Italy agree to let Germany partition Czechoslovakia. Douglas "Wrong-Way" Corrigan flies from New York to Dublin.

1939 Germany occupies Bohemia and Moravia; renounces pacts with Poland and England and concludes 10-year non-aggression pact with U.S.S.R. Russo-Finnish War begins; Finns to lose one-tenth of territory in 1940 peace treaty. World War II begins (*see* special material on "World War II"). In U.S., Roosevelt submits $1,319-million defense budget, proclaims U.S. neutrality, and declares limited emergency. Einstein writes FDR about feasibility of atomic bomb. New York World's Fair opens.

1940 Trotsky assassinated in Mexico. Estonia, Latvia, and Lithuania annexed by U.S.S.R. U.S. trades 50 destroyers for leases on British bases in Western Hemisphere. Selective Service Act signed.

WORLD WAR II (1939-1945)

Axis powers (Germany, Italy, Japan, Hungary, Romania, Bulgaria) *vs.* Allies (U.S., Britain, France, U.S.S.R., Australia, Belgium, Brazil, Canada, China, Denmark, Greece, Netherlands, New Zealand, Norway, Poland, South Africa, Yugoslavia).

1939 Germany invades Poland and annexes Danzig; Britain and France give Hitler ultimatum **(Sept. 1)**, declare war **(Sept. 3)**. Disabled German pocket battleship *Admiral Graf Spee* blown up off Montevideo, Uruguay, on Hitler's orders **(Dec. 17)**. Limited activity ("Sitzkrieg") on Western Front.

1940 Nazis invade Netherlands, Belgium, and Luxembourg **(May 10)**. Chamberlain resigns as Prime Minister; Churchill takes over **(May 10)**. Germans cross French frontier **(May 12)** using air/tank/infantry "Blitzkrieg" tactics. Dunkerque evacuation—about 335,000 out of 400,000 Allied soldiers rescued from Belgium by British civilian and naval craft **(May 26–June 3)**. Italy declares war on France and Britain; invades France **(June 10)**. Germans enter Paris; city undefended **(June 14)**. France and Germany sign armistice at Compiègne **(June 22)**. Nazis bomb Coventry, England **(Nov. 14)**.

1941 Germans launch attacks in Balkans. Yugoslavia surrenders—General Mihajlovic continues guerrilla warfare; Tito leads left-wing guerrillas **(April 17)**. Nazi tanks enter Athens; remnants of British Army quit Greece **(April 27)**. Hitler attacks Russia **(June 22)**. Atlantic Charter—FDR and Churchill agree on war aims **(Aug. 14)**. Japanese attacks on Pearl Harbor, Philippines, Guam force U.S. into war; U.S. Pacific fleet crippled **(Dec. 7)**. U.S. and Britain declare war on Japan. Germany and Italy declare war on U.S.; Congress declares war on those countries **(Dec. 11)**.

1942 British surrender Singapore to Japanese **(Feb. 15)**. U.S. forces on Bataan peninsula in Philippines surrender **(April 9)**. U.S. and Filipino troops on Corregidor island in Manila Bay surrender to Japanese **(May 6)**. Village of Lidice in Czechoslovakia razed by Nazis **(June 10)**. U.S. and Britain

land in French North Africa **(Nov. 8)**.

1943 Casablanca Conference—Churchill and FDR agree on unconditional surrender goal **(Jan. 14–24)**. German 6th Army surrenders at Stalingrad—turning point of war in Russia **(Feb. 1–2)**. Remnants of Nazis trapped on Cape Bon, ending war in Africa **(May 12)**. Mussolini deposed; Badoglio named premier **(July 25)**. Allied troops land on Italian mainland after conquest of Sicily **(Sept. 3)**. Italy surrenders **(Sept. 8)**. Nazis seize Rome **(Sept. 10)**. Cairo Conference: FDR, Churchill, Chiang Kai-shek pledge defeat of Japan, free Korea **(Nov. 22–26)**. Teheran Conference: FDR, Churchill, Stalin agree on invasion plans **(Nov. 28–Dec. 1)**.

1944 U.S. and British troops land at Anzio on west Italian coast and hold beachhead **(Jan. 22)**. U.S. and British troops enter Rome **(June 4)**. D-Day—Allies launch Normandy invasion **(June 6)**. Hitler wounded in bomb plot **(July 20)**. Paris liberated **(Aug. 25)**. Athens freed by Allies **(Oct. 13)**. Americans invade Philippines **(Oct. 20)**. Germans launch counteroffensive in Belgium—Battle of Bulge **(Dec. 16)**.

1945 Yalta Agreement signed by FDR, Churchill, Stalin—establishes basis for occupation of Germany, returns to Soviet Union lands taken by Germany and Japan; U.S.S.R. agrees to friendship pact with China **(Feb. 11)**. Mussolini killed at Lake Como **(April 28)**. Admiral Doenitz takes command in Germany; suicide of Hitler announced **(May 1)**. Berlin falls **(May 2)**. V-E Day—Germany signs unconditional surrender terms at Rheims **(May 7)**. Potsdam Conference—Truman, Churchill, Atlee (after **July 28**), Stalin establish council of foreign ministers to prepare peace treaties; plan German postwar government and reparations **(July 17–Aug. 2)**. A-bomb blasts Hiroshima **(Aug. 6)**. U.S.S.R. declares war on Japan **(Aug. 8)**. Nagasaki hit by A-bomb **(Aug. 9)**. Japan surrenders **(Aug. 14)**. V-J Day—Japanese sign surrender terms aboard battleship *Missouri* **(Sept. 2)**.

D-Day, June 6, 1944

**Winston Churchill,
Franklin D. Roosevelt,
and Joseph V. Stalin
at Yalta**

**Harry S. Truman
(1884–1972)**

1941 Japanese surprise attack on U.S. fleet at Pearl Harbor brings U.S. into World War II. Manhattan Project (atomic bomb research) begins. Roosevelt enunciates "four freedoms," signs lend-lease act, declares national emergency, promises aid to U.S.S.R.

1942 Declaration of United Nations signed in Washington. Women's military services established. Enrico Fermi achieves nuclear chain reaction. Japanese and persons of Japanese ancestry moved inland from Pacific Coast. Coconut Grove nightclub fire in Boston kills 491.

1943 President freezes prices, salaries, and wages to prevent inflation. Income tax withholding introduced.

1944 G.I. Bill of Rights enacted. Bretton Woods Conference creates International Monetary Fund and World Bank. Dumbarton Oaks Conference—U.S., British Commonwealth, and U.S.S.R. propose establishment of United Nations.

1945 Yalta Conference (Roosevelt, Churchill, Stalin) plans final defeat of Germany (**Feb.**). Germany surrenders (**May 7**). San Francisco Conference establishes U.N. (**April–June**). FDR dies (April 12). Potsdam Conference (Truman, Churchill, Stalin) establishes basis of German reconstruction (**July–Aug**). Japan surrenders (**Sept. 2**).

1946 First meeting of U.N. General Assembly opens in London (**Jan. 10**). League of Nations dissolved (**April**). Italy abolishes monarchy (**June**). Verdict in Nuremberg war trial: 12 Nazi leaders (including 1 tried in absentia) sentenced to hang; 7 imprisoned; 3 acquitted (**Oct. 1**). Goering commits suicide a few hours before 10 other Nazis are executed (**Oct. 15**). Winston Churchill's "Iron Curtain" speech warns of Soviet expansion.

1947 Britain nationalizes coal mines (**Jan. 1**). Peace treaties for Italy, Romania, Bulgaria, Hungary, Finland signed in Paris (**Feb. 10**). Soviet Union rejects U.S. plan for U.N. atomic-energy control (**March 4**). Truman Doctrine proposed—the first significant U.S. attempt to "contain" communist expansion (**March 12**). Marshall Plan for European recovery proposed—a coordinated program to help European nations recover from ravages of war (**June**). (By 1951, this "European Recovery Program" had cost $11 billion.) India and Pakistan gain independence from Britain (**Aug. 15**). Cominform (Communist Information Bureau) founded under Soviet auspices to rebuild contacts among European Communist parties, missing since dissolution of Comintern in 1943 (**Sept.**). (Yugoslav party expelled in 1948 and Cominform disbanded in 1956.)

1948 Gandhi assassinated in New Delhi by Hindu fanatic (**Jan. 30**). Communists seize power in Czechoslovakia (**Feb. 23–25**). Burma and Ceylon granted independence by Britain. Organization of American States (OAS) Charter signed at Bogotá, Colombia (**April 30**). Nation of Israel proclaimed; British end Mandate at midnight; Arab armies attack (**May 14**). Berlin airlift begins (**June 21**); ends May 12, 1949. Stalin and Tito break (**June 28**). Independent Republic of Korea is proclaimed, following election supervised by U.N. (**Aug. 15**). Verdict in Japanese war trial: Tojo and six others sentenced to hang (hanged Dec. 23); 18 imprisoned (**Nov. 12**). United States of Indonesia established as Dutch and Indonesians settled conflict (**Dec. 27**). Alger Hiss, former U.S. State Department official, indicted on perjury charges after denying passing secret documents to communist spy ring. Convicted in second trial (1950) and sentenced to five-year prison term.

1949 Cease-fire in Palestine (**Jan. 7**). Truman proposes Point Four Program to help world's backward areas (**Jan. 20**). Israel signs armistice with Egypt (**Feb. 24**). Start of North Atlantic Treaty Organization (NATO)—treaty signed by 12 nations (**April 4**). German Federal Republic (West Germany) established (**Sept. 21**). Truman discloses Soviet Union has set off atomic explosion (**Sept. 23**). Communist People's Republic of China formally proclaimed by Chairman Mao Zedong (**Oct. 1**).

1950 Truman orders development of hydrogen bomb (**Jan. 31**). Korean War (*see* special material on the "Korean War"). Assassination attempt on

KOREAN WAR (1950–1953)

1950 North Korean Communist forces invade South Korea (June 25). U.N. calls for cease-fire and asks U.N. members to assist South Korea (June 27). Truman orders U.S. forces into Korea (June 27). North Koreans capture Seoul (June 28). Gen. Douglas MacArthur designated commander of unified U.N. forces (July 8). Pusan Beachhead—U.N. forces counterattack and capture Seoul (Aug.–Sept.), capture Pyongyang, North Korean capital (Oct.). Chinese Communists enter war (**Oct. 26**), force U.N. retreat toward 39th parallel (**Dec.**).

1951 Gen. Matthew B. Ridgeway replaces MacArthur after he threatens Chinese with massive retaliation (**April 11**). Armistice negotiations (**July**) continue with interruptions until **June 1953.**

1953 Armistice signed (**June 26**). Chinese troops withdraw from North Korea (**Oct. 26, 1958**), but over 200 violations of armistice noted to **1959.**

President Truman by Puerto Rican nationalists (**Nov. 1**). Brink's robbery in Boston; almost $3 million stolen (**Jan. 17**).

1951 Six nations agree to Schuman Plan to pool European coal and steel (**March 19**)—in effect **Feb. 10, 1953**. Julius and Ethel Rosenberg sentenced to death for passing atomic secrets to Russians (**March**). Japanese peace treaty signed in San Francisco by 49 nations (**Sept. 8**). Color television introduced in U.S.

1952 George VI dies; his daughter becomes Elizabeth II (**Feb. 6**). NATO conference approves European army (**Feb.**). AEC announces "satisfactory" experiments in hydrogen-weapons research; eyewitnesses tell of blasts near Enewetak (**Nov.**).

1953 Gen. Dwight D. Eisenhower inaugurated President of United States (**Jan. 20**). Stalin dies (**March 5**). Malenkov becomes Soviet Premier; Beria, Minister of Interior; Molotov, Foreign Minister (**March 6**). Dag Hammarskjold begins term as U.N. Secretary-General (**April 10**). Edmund Hillary, of New Zealand, and Tenzing Norkay, of Nepal, reach top of Mt. Everest (**May 29**). East Berliners rise against Communist rule; quelled by tanks (**June 17**). Egypt becomes republic ruled by military junta (**June 18**). Julius and Ethel Rosenberg executed in Sing Sing prison (**June 19**). Korean armistice signed (**July 27**). Moscow announces explosion of hydrogen bomb (**Aug. 20**).

Dwight D. Eisenhower
(1890–1969)

1954 First atomic submarine *Nautilus*, launched (**Jan. 21**). Five U.S. Congressmen shot on floot of House as Puerto Rican nationalists fire from spectators' gallery; all five recover (**March 1**). Army *vs.* McCarthy inquiry—Senate subcommittee report blames both sides (**Apr. 22–June 17**). Dien Bien Phu, French military outpost in Vietnam, falls to Vietminh army (**May 7**). (*see* special material on the "Vietnam War.") U.S. Supreme Court (in *Brown* v. *Board of Education of Topeka*) unanimously bans racial segregation in public schools (**May 17**). Eisenhower launches world atomic pool without Soviet Union (**Sept. 6**). Eight-nation Southeast Asia defense treaty (SEATO) signed at Manila (**Sept. 8**). West Germany is granted sovereignty, admitted to NATO and Western European Union (**Oct. 23**). Dr. Jonas Salk starts innoculating children against polio. Algerian War of Independence against France begins (**Nov.**); France struggles to maintain colonial rule until 1962 when it agrees to Algeria's independence.

Joseph Stalin
(1879–1953)

1955 Nikolai A. Bulganin becomes Soviet Premier, replacing Malenkov (**Feb. 8**). Churchill resigns; Anthony Eden succeeds him (**April 6**). Federal Republic of West Germany becomes a sovereign state (**May 5**). Warsaw

---

VIETNAM WAR (1950–1975)

U.S., South Vietnam, and Allies versus North Vietnam and National Liberation Front (Viet Cong). Outstanding events:

1950 President Truman sends 35-man military advisory group to aid French fighting to maintain colonial power in Vietnam.

1954 After defeat of French at Dienbienphu, Geneva Agreements (**July**) provide for withdrawal of French and Vietminh to either side of demarcation zone (DMZ) pending reunification elections, which are never held. Presidents Eisenhower and Kennedy (from 1954 onward) send civilian advisors and, later, military personnel to train South Vietnamese.

1960 Communists from National Liberation Front in South.

1963 Ngo Dinh Diem, South Vietnam's premier, slain in coup (**Nov. 1**).

1961–1963 U.S. military advisors rise from 2,000 to 15,000.

1964 North Vietnamese torpedo boats reportedly attack U.S. destroyers in Gulf of Tonkin (**Aug. 2**). President Johnson orders retaliatory air strikes. Congress approves Gulf of Tonkin resolution (**Aug. 7**) authorizing President to take necessary steps to "maintain peace."

1965 U.S. planes begin combat missions over South Vietnam. In **June**, 23,000 American advisors committed to combat. By end of year over 184,000 U.S. troops in area.

1966 B-52s bomb DMZ, reportedly used by North Vietnam for entry into South (**July 31**).

1967 South Vietnam National Assembly approves election of Nguyen Van Thieu as President (**Oct. 21**).

1968 U.S. has almost 525,000 men in Vietnam. In Tet offensive (**Jan.–Feb.**), Viet Cong guerrillas attack Saigon, Hue, and some provincial capitals. President Johnson orders halt to U.S. bombardment of North Vietnam (**Oct. 31**). Saigon and N.L.F. join U.S. and North Vietnam in Paris peace talks.

1969 President Nixon announces Vietnam peace offer (**May 14**)—begins troop withdrawals (**June**). Viet Cong forms Provisional Revolutionary Government. U.S. Senate calls for curb on commitments (**June 25**). Ho Chi Minh, 79, North Vietnam president, dies (**Sept. 3**); collective leadership chosen. Some 6,000 U.S. troops pulled back from Thailand and 1,000 marines from Vietnam (announced **Sept. 30**). Massive demonstrations in U.S. protest or support war policies (**Oct. 15**).

1970 Nixon announces sending of troops to Cambodia (**April 30**). Last U.S. troops removed from Cambodia (**June 29**).

1971 Congress bars use of combat troops, but not air power, in Laos and Cambodia (**Jan. 1**). South Vietnamese troops, with U.S. air cover, fail in Laos thrust. Many American ground forces withdrawn from Vietnam combat. *New York Times* publishes Pentagon papers, classified material on expansion of war (**June**).

1972 Nixon responds to North Vietnamese drive across DMZ by ordering mining of North Vietnam ports and heavy bombing of Hanoi-Haiphong area (**April 1**). Nixon orders "Christmas bombing" of north to get North Vietnamese back to conference table (**Dec.**).

1973 President orders halt to offensive operations in North Vietnam (**Jan. 15**). Representatives of North and South Vietnam, U.S., and N.L.F. sign peace pacts in Paris, ending longest war in U.S. history (**Jan. 27**). Last American troops departed in their entirety (**March 29**).

1974 Both sides accuse each other of frequent violations of cease-fire agreement.

1975 Full-scale warfare resumes. Communists victorious (**April 30**). South Vietnam Premier Nguyen Van Thieu resigns (**April 21**). U.S. Marine Embassy guards and U.S. civilians and dependents evacuated (**April 30**). More than 140,000 Vietnamese refugees leave by air and sea, many to settle in U.S. Provisional Revolutionary Government takes control (**June 6**).

1976 Election of National Assembly paves way for reunification of North and South.

Yuri A. Gagarin
(1934-1968)

Pact, east European mutual defense agreement, signed (**May 14**). Argentina ousts Perón (**Sept. 19**). President Eisenhower suffers coronary thrombosis in Denver (**Sept. 24**). Martin Luther King, Jr., leads black boycott of Montgomery, Ala., bus system (**Dec. 1**); desegregated service begun (**Dec. 21**). AFL and CIO become one organization—AFL-CIO (**Dec. 5**).

1956 Nikita Khrushchev, First Secretary of U.S.S.R. Communist Party, denounces Stalin's excesses (**Feb. 24**). First aerial H-bomb tested over Namu islet, Bikini Atoll—10 million tons TNT equivalent (**May 21**). Worker's uprising against Communist rule in Poznan, Poland, is crushed (**June 28–30**). Egypt takes control of Suez Canal (**July 26**). Israel launches attack on Egypt's Sinai peninsula and drives toward Suez Canal (**Oct. 29**). British and French invade Egypt at Port Said (**Nov. 5**). Cease-fire forced by U.S. pressure stops British, French, and Israeli advance (**Nov. 6**). Revolt starts in Hungary—Soviet troops and tanks crush anti-Communist rebellion (**Nov.**).

1957 Eisenhower Doctrine calls for aid to Mideast countries which resist armed aggression from Communist-controlled nations (**Jan. 5**). Eisenhower sends troops to Little Rock, Ark., to quell mob and protect school integration (**Sept. 24**). Russians launch *Sputnik I*, first earth-orbiting satellite—the Space Age begins (**Oct. 4**).

1958 Army's Jupiter-C rocket fires first U.S. earth satellite, *Explorer I*, into orbit (**Jan. 31**). Egypt and Syria merge into United Arab Republic (**Feb. 1**). European Economic Community (Common Market) established by Rome Treaty becomes effective **Jan. 1, 1958**. Khrushchev becomes Premier of Soviet Union as Bulganin resigns (**Mar. 27**). Gen. Charles de Gaulle becomes French premier (**June 1**), remaining in power until **1969**. New French constitution adopted (**Sept. 28**), de Gaulle elected president of 5th Republic (**Dec. 21**). Eisenhower orders U.S. Marines into Lebanon at request of President Chamoun, who fears overthrow (**July 15**).

1959 Cuban President Batista resigns and flees—Castro takes over (**Jan. 1**). Tibet's Dalai Lama escapes to India (**Mar. 31**). St. Lawrence Seaway opens, allowing ocean ships to reach Midwest (**April 25**).

1960 American U-2 spy plane, piloted by Francis Gary Powers, shot down over Russia (**May 1**). Khrushchev kills Paris summit conference because of U-2 (**May 16**). Powers sentenced to prison for 10 years (**Aug. 19**)—freed in **February 1962** in exchange for Soviet spy. Top Nazi murderer of Jews, Adolf Eichmann, captured by Israelis in Argentina (**May 23**)—executed in Israel in 1962. Communist China and Soviet Union split in conflict over Communist ideology. Belgium starts to break up its African colonial empire, gives independence to Belgian Congo (Zaire) on **June 30**. Cuba begins confiscation of $770 million of U.S. property (**Aug. 7**).

Fidel Castro
(Aug. 13, 1926)

1961 U.S. breaks diplomatic relations with Cuba (**Jan. 3**). John F. Kennedy inaugurated President of U.S. (**Jan. 20**). Kennedy proposes Alliance for Progress—10-year plan to raise Latin American living standards (**Mar. 13**). Moscow announces putting first man in orbit around earth, Maj. Yuri A. Gagarin (**April 12**). Cuba invaded at Bay of Pigs by an estimated 1,200 anti-Castro exiles aided by U.S.; invasion crushed (**April 17**). First U.S. spaceman, Navy Cmdr. Alan B. Shepard, Jr., rockets 116.5 miles up in 302-mile trip (**May 5**). Virgil Grissom becomes second American astronaut, making 118-mile-high, 303-mile-long rocket flight over Atlantic (**July 21**). Gherman Stepanovich Titov is launched in Soviet spaceship *Vostok II:* makes 17 1/2 orbits in 25 hours, covering 434,960 miles before landing safely (**Aug. 6**). East Germans erect Berlin Wall between East and West Berlin to halt flood of refugees (**Aug. 13**). U.S.S.R. fires 50-megaton hydrogen bomb, biggest explosion in history (**Oct. 29**).

1962 Lt. Col. John H. Glenn, Jr., is first American to orbit earth—three times in 4 hr 55 min (**Feb. 20**). Adolf Eichmann hanged in Israel for his part in Nazi extermination of six million Jews (**May 31**). France transfers sovereignty to new republic of Algeria (**July 3**). Cuban missile crisis—U.S.S.R. to build missile bases in Cuba; Kennedy orders Cuban blockade, lifts blockade after Russians back down (**Aug.–Nov.**). James H. Meredith, escorted by Federal marshals, registers in University of Mississippi (**Oct. 1**). Pope John XXIII opens Second Vatican Council (**Oct. 11**)—Council holds four sessions, finally closing Dec. 8, 1965. Cuba releases 1,113 prisoners of 1961 invasion attempt (**Dec. 24**).

1963 France and West Germany sign treaty of cooperation ending four centuries of conflict (**Jan. 22**). Pope John XXIII dies (**June 3**)—succeeded June 21 by Cardinal Montini, who becomes Paul VI. U.S. Supreme Court rules no locality may require recitation of Lord's Prayer or Bible verses in public schools (**June 17**). Civil rights rally held by 200,000 blacks and whites in Washington, D.C. (**Aug. 28**). Washington-to-Moscow "hot line" communications link opens, designed to reduce risk of accidental war (**Aug. 30**). President Kennedy shot and killed by sniper in Dallas, Tex. Lyndon B. Johnson becomes President same day (**Nov. 22**). Lee Harvey Oswald, accused assassin of President Kennedy, is shot and killed by Jack Ruby, Dallas nightclub owner (**Nov. 24**).

1964 U.S. Supreme Court rules that Congressional districts should be roughly equal in population (**Feb. 17**). Jack Ruby convicted of murder in slaying of Lee Harvey Oswald; sentenced to death by Dallas jury (**March 14**)—conviction reversed **Oct. 5, 1966**; Ruby dies **Jan. 3, 1967**, before second trial can be held. Three civil rights workers—Schwerner, Goodman, and Cheney—murdered in Mississippi (**June**). Twenty-one arrests result in trial and conviction of seven by Federal jury. President's Commission on the Assassination of President Kennedy issues Warren Report concluding that Lee Harvey Oswald acted alone.

John F. Kennedy
(1917-1963)

1965 Rev. Dr. Martin Luther King, Jr., and more than 2,600 other blacks arrested in Selma, Ala., during three-day demonstrations against voter-registration rules (**Feb. 1**). Malcolm X, black-nationalist leader, shot to death at Harlem rally in New York City (**Feb. 21**). U.S. Marines land in Dominican Republic as fighting persists between rebels and Dominican army (**April 28**). Medicare, senior citizens' government medical assistance program, begins (**July 1**). Blacks riot for six days in Watts section of Los Angeles: 34 dead, over 1,000 injured, nearly 4,000 arrested, fire damage put at $175 million (**Aug. 11–16**). Power failure in Ontario plant blacks out parts of eight northeastern states of U.S. and two provinces of southeastern Canada (**Nov. 9**).

1966 Black teen-agers riot in Watts, Los Angeles; two men killed and at least 25 injured (**March 15**). Michael E. De Bakey implants artificial heart in human for first time at Houston hospital; plastic device functions and patient lives (**April 21**).

1967 Three Apollo astronauts—Col. Virgil I. Grissom, Col. Edward White II, and Lt. Cmdr. Roger B. Chaffee—killed in spacecraft fire during simulated launch (**Jan. 27**). Israeli and Arab forces battle; six-day war ends with Israel occupying Sinai Peninsula, Golan Heights, Gaza Strip, and east bank of Suez Canal (**June 5**). Red China announces explosion of its first hydrogen bomb (**June 17**). Racial violence in Detroit; 7,000 National Guardsmen aid police after night of rioting. Similar outbreaks occur in New York City's Spanish Harlem, Rochester, N.Y., Birmingham, Ala., and New Britain, Conn. (**July 23**). Thurgood Marshall sworn in as first black U.S. Supreme Court justice (**Oct. 2**). Dr. Christian N. Barnard and team of South African surgeons perform world's first successful human heart transplant (**Dec. 3**)—patient dies 18 days later.

Lyndon B. Johnson
(1908–1973)

1968 North Korea seizes U.S. Navy ship *Pueblo*; holds 83 on board as spies (**Jan. 23**). President Johnson announces he will not seek or accept presidential renomination (**March 31**). Martin Luther King, Jr., civil rights leader, is slain in Memphis (**April 4**)—James Earl Ray, indicted in murder, captured in London on **June 8**. In 1969 Ray pleads guilty and is sentenced to 99 years. Sen. Robert F. Kennedy is shot and critically wounded in Los Angeles hotel after winning California primary (**June 5**)—dies **June 6**. Sirhan B. Sirhan convicted 1969. Czechoslovakia is invaded by Russians and Warsaw Pact forces to crush liberal regime (**Aug. 20**).

1969 Richard M. Nixon is inaugurated 37th President of the U.S. (**Jan. 20**). Apollo 11 astronauts—Neil A. Armstrong, Edwin E. Aldrin, Jr., and Michael Collins—take man's first walk on moon (**July 20**). Sen. Edward M. Kennedy pleads guilty to leaving scene of fatal accident at Chappaquiddick, Mass. (**July 18**) in which Mary Jo Kopechne was drowned—gets two-month suspended sentence (**July 25**).

Martin Luther King, Jr.
(1929-1968)

1970 Biafra surrenders after 32-month fight for independence from Nigeria (**Jan. 12**). Rhodesia severs last tie with British Crown and declares itself a racially segregated republic (**March 1**). Four students at Kent State University in Ohio slain by National Guardsmen at demonstration protesting April 30 incursion into Cambodia (**May 4**). Senate repeals Gulf of Tonkin resolution (**June 24**).

1971 Supreme Court rules unanimously that busing of students may be ordered to achieve racial desegregation (**April 20**). Anti-war militants attempt to disrupt government business in Washington (**May 3**)—police and military units arrest as many as 12,000; most are later released. Twenty-sixth Amendment to U.S. Constitution lowers voting age to 18. U.N. seats Communist China and expels Nationalist China (**Oct. 25**).

1972 President Nixon makes unprecedented eight-day visit to Communist China (**Feb.**). Britain takes over direct rule of Northern Ireland in bid for peace (**March 24**). Gov. George C. Wallace of Alabama is shot by Arthur H. Bremer at Laurel, Md., political rally (**May 15**). Five men are apprehended by police in attempt to bug Democratic National Commit-

Richard M. Nixon
(Jan. 9, 1913)

tee headquarters in Washington D.C.'s Watergate complex—start of the Watergate scandal (**June 17**). Supreme Court rules that death penalty is unconstitutional (**June 29**). Eleven Israeli athletes at Olympic Games in Munich are killed after eight members of an Arab terrorist group invade Olympic Village; five guerrillas and one policeman are also killed (**Sept. 5**).

1973 Great Britain, Ireland, and Denmark enter European Common Market (**Jan. 1**). Nixon, on national TV, accepts responsibility, but not blame, for Watergate; accepts resignations of advisers H. R. Haldeman and John D. Ehrlichman, fires John W. Dean III as counsel. (**April 30**). Greek military junta abolishes monarchy and proclaims republic (**June 1**). U.S. bombing of Cambodia ends, marking official halt to 12 years of combat activity in Southeast Asia (**Aug. 15**). Fourth and biggest Arab-Israeli War begins as Egyptian and Syrian forces attack Israel as Jews mark Yom Kippur, holiest day in their calendar. (**Oct. 6**). Spiro T. Agnew resigns as Vice President and then, in Federal Court in Baltimore, pleads no contest to charges of evasion of income taxes on $29,500 he received in 1967, while Governor of Maryland. He is fined $10,000 and put on three years' probation (**Oct. 10**). In the "Saturday Night Massacre," Nixon fires special Watergate prosecutor Archibald Cox and Deputy Attorney General William D. Ruckelshaus; Attorney General Elliot L. Richardson resigns (**Oct. 20**). Egypt and Israel sign U.S.-sponsored ceasefire accord (**Nov. 11**).

1974 Patricia Hearst, 19-year-old daughter of publisher Randolph Hearst, kidnapped by Symbionese Liberation Army. (**Feb. 5**). House Judiciary Committee adopts three articles of impeachment charging President Nixon with obstruction of justice, failure to uphold laws, and refusal to produce material subpoenaed by the committee (**July 30**). Richard M. Nixon announces he will resign the next day, the first President to do so (**Aug. 8**). Vice President Gerald R. Ford of Michigan is sworn in as 38th President of the U.S. (**Aug. 9**). Ford grants "full, free, and absolute pardon" to ex-President Nixon (**Sept. 8**).

1975 John N. Mitchell, H. R. Haldeman, John D. Ehrlichman, and Robert C. Mardian found guilty of Watergate cover-up. Mitchell, Haldeman, and Ehrlichman are sentenced on Feb. 21 to 30 months-8 years in jail and Mardian to 10 months-3 years (**Jan. 1**). American merchant ship *Mayaguez*, seized by Cambodian forces, is rescued in operation by U.S. Navy and Marines, 38 of whom are killed (**May 15**). *Apollo* and *Soyuz* spacecraft take off for U.S.-Soviet link-up in space (**July 15**). President Ford escapes assassination attempt in Sacramento, Calif., (**Sept. 5**). President Ford escapes second assassination attempt in 17 days. (**Sept. 22**).

1976 Supreme Court rules that blacks and other minorities are entitled to retroactive job seniority (**March 24**). Ford signs Federal Election Campaign Act (**May 11**). Supreme Court rules that death penalty is not inherently cruel or unusual and is a constitutionally acceptable form of punishment (**July 3**). Nation celebrates Bicentennial (**July 4**). Israeli airborne commandos attack Uganda's Entebbe Airport and free 103 hostages held by pro-Palestinian hijackers of Air France plane; one Israeli and several Ugandan soldiers killed in raid (**July 4**). Mysterious disease that eventually claims 29 lives strikes American Legion convention in Philadelphia (**Aug. 4**). Jimmy Carter elected U.S. President (**Nov. 2**).

1977 First woman Episcopal priest ordained (**Jan. 1**). Scientists identify previously unknown bacterium as cause of mysterious "legionnaire's disease" (**Jan. 18**). Carter pardons Vietnam draft evaders (**Jan. 21**). Scientists report using bacteria in lab to make insulin (**May 23**). Supreme Court rules that states are not required to spend Medicaid funds on elective abortions (**June 20**). Deng Xiaoping, purged Chinese leader, restored to power as "Gang of Four" is expelled from Communist Party (**July 22**). Nuclear-proliferation pact, curbing spread of nuclear weapons, signed by 15 countries, including U.S. and U.S.S.R. (**Sept. 21**).

Viking I and II
(Launched 1975)

1978 President chooses Federal Appeals Court Judge William H. Webster as F.B.I. Director (**Jan. 19**). Rhodesia's Prime Minister Ian D. Smith and three black leaders agree on transfer to black majority rule (**Feb. 15**). Former Italian Premier Aldo Moro kidnapped by left-wing terrorists, who kill five bodyguards (**March 16**); he is found slain (**May 9**). U.S. Senate approves Panama Canal neutrality treaty (**March 16**); votes treaty to turn canal over to Panama by year 2000 (**April 18**). Californians in referendum approve Proposition 13 for nearly 60% slash in property tax revenues (**June 6**). Supreme Court, in Bakke case, bars quota systems in college admissions but affirms constitutionality of programs giving advantage to minorities (**June 28**). Pope Paul VI, dead at 80, mourned (**Aug. 6**); new Pope, John Paul I, 65, dies unexpectedly after 34 days in office (**Sept. 28**); succeeded by Karol Cardinal Wojtyla of Poland as John Paul II (**Oct. 16**). "Framework for Peace" in Middle East signed by

Voyager I and II
(Launched 1977)

Egypt's President Anwar el-Sadat and Israel Premier Menachem Begin after 13-day conference at Camp David led by President Carter (**Sept. 17**).

1979 Oil spills pollute ocean waters in Atlantic and Gulf of Mexico (**Jan. 1, June 8, July 21**). Ohio agrees to pay $675,000 to families of dead and injured in Kent State University shootings (**Jan. 4**). Vietnam and Cambodian insurgents it backs announce fall of Phnom Penh, Cambodian capital, and collapse of Pol Pot regime (**Jan. 7**). Shah leaves Iran after year of turmoil (**Jan. 16**); revolutionary forces under Moslem leader, Ayatollah Ruhollah Khomeini, take over (**Feb. 1** et seq.). Conservatives win British election; Margaret Thatcher new Prime Minister (**March 28**). Nuclear power plant accident at Three Mile Island, Pa., releases radioactivity (**March 28**). Carter and Brezhnev sign SALT II agreement (**June 14**). Nicaraguan President Gen. Anastasio Somoza Debayle resigns and flees to Miami (**July 17**); Sandinistas form government (**July 19**). Earl Mountbatten of Burma, 79, British World War II hero, and three others killed by blast on fishing boat off Irish coast (**Aug. 27**); two I.R.A. members accused (**Aug. 30**). Iranian militants seize U.S. Embassy in Teheran and hold hostages (**Nov. 4**). Soviet invasion of Afghanistan stirs world protests (**Dec. 27**).

Margaret Thatcher
(Oct. 13, 1925)

1980 Six U.S. Embassy aides escape from Iran with Canadian help (**Jan. 29**). F.B.I.'s undercover operation "Abscam" (for Arab scam) implicates public officials (**Feb. 2**). U.S. breaks diplomatic ties with Iran (**April 7**). Eight U.S. servicemen are killed and five are injured as helicopter and cargo plane collide in abortive desert raid to rescue American hostages in Teheran (**April 25**). Supreme Court upholds limits on Federal aid for abortions (**June 30**). Shah of Iran dies at 60 (**July 27**). Anastasio Somoza Debayle, ousted Nicaragua ruler, and two aides assassinated in Asunción, Paraguay capital (**Sept. 17**). Iraq troops hold 90 square miles of Iran after invasion (**Sept. 19**). Ronald Reagan elected President in Republican sweep (**Nov. 4**). Three U.S. nuns and lay worker found shot in El Salvador (**Dec. 4**). John Lennon of Beatles shot dead in New York City (**Dec. 8**).

Sally K. Ride
(May 26, 1951)

1981 U.S.-Iran agreement frees 52 hostages held in Teheran since Nov. 4, 1979 (**Jan. 18**); hostages welcomed back in U.S. (**Jan. 25**). Ronald Reagan takes oath as 40th President (**Jan. 20**). President Reagan wounded by gunman, with press secretary and two law-enforcement officers (**March 30**). Pope John Paul II wounded by gunman (**May 14**). Supreme Court rules, 4-4, that former President Nixon and three top aides may be required to pay monetary damages for unconstitutional wiretap of home telephone of former national security aide (**June 22**). Reagan nominates Judge Sandra Day O'Connor, 51, of Arizona as first woman on Supreme Court (**July 7**). More than 110 die in collapse of aerial walkways in lobby of Hyatt Regency Hotel in Kansas City; 188 injured (**July 18**). Air controllers strike, disrupting flights (**Aug. 3**); Government dismisses strikers (**Aug. 11**).

1982 British overcome Argentina in Falklands war (**April 2-June 15**). Israel invades Lebanon in attack on P.L.O. (**June 4**). John W. Hinckley, Jr. found not guilty because of insanity in shooting of President Reagan (**June 21**). Alexander M. Haig, Jr. resigns as Secretary of State (**June 25**). Equal rights amendment fails ratification (**June 30**). Lebanese Christian Phalangists kill hundreds of people in two Palestinian refugee camps in West Beirut (**Sept. 15**). Princess Grace, 52, dies of injuries when car plunges off mountain road; daughter, Stephanie, 17, suffers serious injuries (**Sept. 14**). Leonid I. Brezhnev, Soviet leader, dies at 75 (**Nov. 10**). Yuri V. Andropov, 68, chosen as successor (**Nov. 15**). Artificial heart implanted for first time in Dr. Barney B. Clark, 61, at University of Utah Medical Center in Salt Lake City (**Dec. 2**); Barney Clark dies (**March 23, 1983**).

1983 Pope John Paul II signs new Roman Catholic code incorporating changes brought about by Second Vatican Council (**Jan. 25**). Second space shuttle, *Challenger*, makes successful maiden voyage, which includes the first U.S. space walk in nine years (**April 4**). U.S. Supreme Court declares many local abortion restrictions unconstitutional (**June 15**). Sally K. Ride, 32, first U.S. woman astronaut in space as a crew member aboard space shuttle *Challenger* (**June 18**). U.S. admits shielding former Nazi Gestapo chief, Klaus Barbie, 69, the "butcher of Lyons," wanted in France for war crimes (**Aug. 15**). Benigno S. Aquino, Jr., 50, political rival of Philippines President Marcos, slain in Manila (**Aug. 21**). South Korean Boeing 747 jetliner bound for Seoul apparently strays into Soviet airspace and is shot down by a Soviet SU-15 fighter after it had tracked the airliner for two hours; all 269 aboard are killed, including 61 Americans (**Aug. 30**). Terrorist explosion kills 237 U.S. Marines in Beirut (**Oct. 23**). U.S. and Caribbean allies invade Grenada (**Oct. 25**).

Space Shuttle Columbia
(Launched April 12, 1981)

**Indira Gandhi
(1917-1984)**

**Ronald W. Reagan
(Feb. 6, 1911)**

**Mikhail S. Gorbachev
(March 2, 1931)**

1984 Bell System broken up (**Jan. 1**). France gets first deliveries of Soviet natural gas (**Jan. 1**). Syria frees captured U.S. Navy pilot, Lieut. Robert C. Goodman, Jr. (**Jan. 3**). U.S. and Vatican exchange diplomats after 116-year hiatus (**Jan. 10**). Reagan orders U.S. Marines withdrawn from Beirut international peacekeeping force (**Feb. 7**). Yuri V. Andropov dies at 69; Konstantin U. Chernenko, 72, named Soviet Union leader (**Feb. 9**). Italy and Vatican agree to end Roman Catholicism as state religion (**Feb. 18**). Reagan ends U.S. role in Beirut by relieving Sixth Fleet from peacekeeping force (**March 30**). First baby born from frozen embryo in Australia (**April 10**). Congress rebukes President Reagan on use of federal funds for mining Nicaraguan harbors (**April 10**). Gunman fires from Libyan Embassy into London crowd, killing British policewoman (**April 17**). Soviet Union withdraws from summer Olympic games in U.S., and other bloc nations follow (**May 7 et seq.**). World Court rules against U.S. on mining of Nicaraguan harbors (**May 10**). Federal judge finds U.S. negligent in 1950 atomic tests (**May 10**). José Napoleón Duarte, moderate, elected president of El Salvador (**May 11**). Three hundred slain as Indian Army occupies Sikh Golden Temple in Amritsar (**June 6**). Thirty-ninth Democratic National Convention, in San Francisco, nominates Walter F. Mondale and Geraldine A. Ferraro (**July 16–19**). Thirty-third Republican National Convention, at Dallas, renominates President Reagan and Vice President Bush (**Aug. 20–25**). Brian Mulroney and Conservative party win Canadian election in landslide (**Sept. 4**). British Prime Minister Margaret Thatcher nearly killed by I.R.A. assassination attempt (**Oct. 12**). Indian Prime Minister Indira Gandhi assassinated by two Sikh bodyguards; 1,000 killed in anti-Sikh riots; son Rajiv succeeds her (**Oct. 31**). President Reagan re-elected in landslide with 59% of vote (**Nov. 7**). Toxic gas leaks from Union Carbide plant in Bhopal, India, killing 2,000 and injuring 150,000 (**Dec. 3**).

1985 Two thousand refugee Ethiopian Jews perish in Sudan (**Jan. 18**). Ronald Reagan, 73, takes oath for second term as 40th President (**Jan. 20**). New Zealand bars U.S. ship when Washington refuses to say whether she carries nuclear arms (**Feb. 4**). Border of Gibraltar reopened under Spain-Britain agreement (**Feb. 5**). Worldwide Conservative Rabbinical Assembly approves women in clergy (**Feb. 14**). General Westmoreland settles libel action against CBS (**Feb. 18**). Prime Minister Margaret Thatcher addresses Congress, endorsing Reagan's policies (**Feb. 20**). Kidnapped U.S. drug agent and his pilot slain in Mexico (**March 6**). U.S.S.R. leader Chernenko dies at 73 and is replaced by Mikhail Gorbachev, 54 (**March 11**). Secretary of Labor Raymond J. Donovan, facing New York fraud trial, resigns; first sitting Cabinet member to be indicted (**March 15**). Tens of thousands mark 40th anniversary of liberation of Buchenwald death camp (**April 13**). Reagan target of wide attacks by Jewish leaders and others over visit to Bitburg Cemetery, West Germany, where SS troops are buried (**April 18 et seq. May 5**). Two Shiite Moslem gunmen capture TWA airliner with 133 aboard, 104 of them Americans (**June 14**); 39 remaining hostages freed in Beirut (**June 30**). Supreme Court, 5-4, bars public school teachers from parochial schools (**July 1**). Arthur James Walker, 50, retired naval officer, convicted by federal judge of participating in Soviet spy ring (**Aug. 9**). Thousands dead in Mexico earthquake (**Sept. 19**). P.L.O. terrorists hijack *Achille Lauro,* Italian cruise ship, with 80 passengers, plus crew (**Oct. 7**); American, Leon Klinghoffer, killed (**Oct. 8**). Italian government toppled by political crisis over hijacking of *Achille Lauro* (**Oct. 16**). John A. Walker and son, Michael I. Walker, 22, sentenced in Navy espionage case (**Oct. 28**). Volcano eruption leaves 25,000 dead and missing in Colombia (**Nov. 14**). Reagan and Gorbachev meet at summit (**Nov. 19**); agree to step up arms control talks and renew cultural contacts (**Nov. 21**). Terrorists seize Egyptian Boeing 737 airliner after takeoff from Athens (**Nov. 23**); 59 dead as Egyptian forces storm plane on Malta (**Nov. 24**). U.S. budget-balancing bill enacted (**Dec. 12**). Newfoundland plane crash kills 248 U.S. soldiers (**Dec. 12**). Terrorists kill 19 at Rome and Vienna airports (**Dec. 30**).

1986 Spain and Portugal join Common Market (**Jan. 1**). President freezes Libyan assets in U.S. (**Jan. 8**). Supreme Court bars racial bias in trial jury selection (**Jan. 14**). Britain and France plan Channel tunnel (**Jan. 20**). *Voyager 2* spacecraft reports secrets of Uranus (**Jan. 26**). Space shuttle *Challenger* explodes after launch at Cape Canaveral, Fla., killing all seven aboard (**Jan. 28**). Haiti President Jean-Claude Duvalier flees to France (**Feb. 7**). President Marcos flees Philippines after ruling 20 years, as newly elected Corazon Aquino succeeds him (**Feb. 26**). Prime Minister Olaf Palme of Sweden shot dead (**Feb. 28**). Kurt Waldheim service as Nazi army officer revealed (**March 3**). Leo M. Frank, Georgia lynching victim, pardoned posthumously on killing charge (**March 11**). Union Carbide agrees to settlement with victims of Bhopal gas leak in India

(March 22). Two scientific teams report finding AIDS viruses (March 26). Halley's Comet yields information on return visit (April 10). U.S. planes attack Libyan "terrorist centers" (April 14). Desmond Tutu elected Archbishop in South Africa (April 14). Three hostages slain in Lebanon in reprisal for bombing of Libya (April 17). Major nuclear accident at Soviet Union's Chernobyl power station alarms world (April 28 et seq.). Ex-Navy analyst, Jonathan Jay Pollard, 31, guilty as spy for Israel (June 4). Supreme Court reaffirms abortion rights (June 11). Millions of blacks strike in South Africa on anniversary of 1976 Soweto uprising (June 16). World Court rules U.S. broke international law in mining Nicaraguan waters (June 27). Supreme Court voids automatic provisions of budget-balancing law (July 7). Jerry A. Whitworth, ex-Navy radioman, convicted as spy (July 24). Moslem captors release Rev. Lawrence Martin Jenco (July 26). Senate Judiciary Committee approves William H. Rehnquist to be Chief Justice of U.S. (Aug. 14). Mexican police torture U.S. narcotics agent (Aug. 14). House votes arms appropriations bill rejecting Administration's "star wars" policy (Aug. 15). Volcano gas from lake bottom kills 1,500 in Cameroon (Aug. 25). Three Lutheran church groups in U.S. set to merge (Aug. 29). Nicholas Daniloff, correspondent for *U.S. News & World Report,* detained in Moscow on espionage charges (Aug. 30); released and allowed to leave Soviet Union (Sept. 29). Congress overrides Reagan veto of stiff sanctions against South Africa (Sept. 29 and Oct. 2). Congress approves immigration bill barring hiring of illegal aliens, with amnesty provision (Oct. 17). Reagan signs $11.7-billion budget reduction measure (Oct. 21). He approves sweeping revision of U.S. tax code (Oct. 22). Democrats triumph in elections, gaining eight seats to win Senate majority (Nov. 4). Secret initiative to send arms to Iran revealed (Nov. 6 et seq.); Reagan denies exchanging arms for hostages and halts arms sales (Nov. 19); diversion of funds from arms sales to Nicaraguan contras revealed (Nov. 25). Walkers, father and son, sentenced in naval spy ring (Nov. 6). Soviet lifts ban on Andrei D. Sakharov, rights activist (Dec. 19). Hotel fire kills 96 in Puerto Rico (Dec. 31).

Corazon C. Aquino
(Jan. 25, 1933)

1987 William Buckley, U.S. hostage in Lebanon, reported slain (Jan. 20). U.S. charges three Wall Street traders with making millions in illegal inside trading (Feb. 12). French sentence Georges Ibrahim Abdallah, Lebanese terrorist, to life in two killings (Feb. 28). Reagan admits "mistake" in Iran-Contra affair (March 4). Appeals Court reverses $2-million libel judgment against Washington Post (March 13). F.D.A. approves drug AZT for treating AIDS victims (March 20). South Africa outlaws protests to win freedom for detainees (April 11). Reagan imposes 100% retaliatory tariff on many Japanese imports (April 17). Argentine army blocks antigovernment rebellion (April 17). Gene-altered bacteria tested in experiment to aid agriculture (April 24). U.S. puts Austrian President Kurt Waldheim on list of those banned from country (April 27). Nicaraguan rebels kill Benjamin Ernest Linder, 27, American volunteer worker (April 28). Quebec accepts Canadian constitution as "distinct society" (May 1). Supreme Court rules Rotary clubs must admit women (May 4). Thousands of aliens seek legal status under new amnesty law (May 5). First Soviet ship attacked in Persian Gulf (May 8). Ulster police slay nine attackers in police station battle (May 8). Three-way heart transplant performed (May 12). Soviet launches world's most powerful rocket (May 16). Iraqi missiles kill 37 in attack on U.S. frigate *Stark* in Persian Gulf (May 17); Iraqi president apologizes (May 18). Former Labor Secretary Raymond J. Donovan acquitted in construction fraud (May 25). Lebanon's Prime Minister Rashid Karami, 55, assassinated (June 1). Three U.S. agencies investigate charges of fraud against TV evangelical PTL Ministry (June 10). Prime Minister Thatcher wins rare third term in Britain (June 11). Robert B. Anderson, 77, former Treasury Secretary, sentenced for tax evasion (June 25). Supreme Court Justice Lewis F. Powell, Jr., retires (June 26). Klaus Barbie, 73, Gestapo wartime chief in Lyons, sentenced to life by French court for war crimes (July 4). Marine Lieut. Col. Oliver L. North tells Congressional inquiry higher officials approved his secret Iran-Contra operations (July 7–10). Admiral John M. Poindexter, former National Security Adviser, testifies he authorized use of Iran arms sale profits to aid Contras (July 15–22). Portugal gets majority government (July 19). Secretary of State George P. Shultz testifies he was deceived repeatedly on Iran-Contra affair (July 23–24). India and Sri Lanka sign pact to end four years of ethnic violence (July 29). Soviet sentences three Chernobyl officials for safety violations in nuclear disaster (July 29). Defense Secretary Caspar W. Weinberger tells inquiry of official deception and intrigue (July 31, Aug. 3). Hundreds killed in clashes at Moslem holy site of Mecca (Aug. 1). Five regional presidents agree on peace accord for Central America (Aug. 7).

Kurt Waldheim
(Dec. 21, 1918)

**George H. Bush
(June 12, 1924)**

Reagan says Iran arms-Contra policy went astray and accepts responsibility (**Aug. 12**). Charles Glass, ABC correspondent, escapes from Beirut kidnappers (**Aug. 18**). Jewels retrieved from wreckage of liner *Titanic* (**Aug. 20**). Ceremonies in Philadelphia celebrate 200th year of U.S. Constitution (**Sept. 17**). National Football League players strike (**Sept. 23**); walkout ends without new contract (**Oct. 15**). Severe earthquake strikes Los Angeles, leaving 100 injured and six dead (**Oct. 1**). Senate, 58-42, rejects Robert H. Bork as Supreme Court Justice (**Oct. 23**).

1988 U.S. and Canada reach free-trade agreement (**Jan. 2**). Supreme Court, 5-3, backs public school officials' power to censor student activities (**Jan. 13**). Leslie F. Manigat, former professor, elected Haiti president (**Jan. 24**). Lyn Nofziger, former Reagan advisor, convicted of violating Federal ethics law (**Feb. 11**). Palestinian gunman, Ibrahim Mohammed Khaled, sentenced to 30 years for part in 1985 Rome airport attack (**Feb. 12**). Marine Lieut. Col. William R. Higgins abducted in Lebanon (**Feb. 17**). Nine killed in Soviet plane hijacking (**March 10**). Robert C. McFarlane, former National Security Adviser, pleads guilty in Iran-Contra case (**March 11**). First U.S. black archbishop chosen to head Atlanta archdiocese (**March 15**). Irish mobs kill two British soldiers (**March 19**). Congress overrides Reagan veto of civil rights bill (**March 22**). Arizona Gov. Evan Mecham removed from office after impeachment trial (**April 4**). Gunmen hijack Kuwaiti airliner (**April 5 et seq.**). Khalil al-Wazir, P.L.O. official, assassinated in Tunisia (**April 16**). Supreme Court upholds taxation of municipal bonds (**April 20**). Israel court dooms John Demjanjuk, 68, "Ivan the Terrible," for Nazi war crimes (**April 25**). Reagan-Gorbachev summit in Moscow ends without major results (**May 29 et seq.**). Million blacks start three-day protest strike in South Africa (**June 6**). Soviet court clears executed Bolsheviks (**June 13**). Supreme Court rules against private-club membership restrictions (**June 20**). Justices, in rebuff to Reagan, uphold special-prosecutor law (**June 29**). U.S. Navy ship shoots down Iranian airliner in Persian Gulf, mistaking it for jet fighter; 290 killed (**July 3**). Terrorists kill nine tourists on Aegean cruise (**July 11**). Democratic convention nominates Gov. Michael Dukakis of Massachusetts for President and Texas Senator Lloyd Bentsen for Vice President (**July 17 et seq.**). Flash floods kill thousands in China (**Aug. 2**). Reagan signs sweeping measure aimed at unfair trading (**Aug. 3**). Reagan signs law to compensate interned Japanese-Americans (**Aug. 10**). Republicans nominate Vice President George Bush for President and Indiana Senator Dan Quayle for Vice President (**Aug. 15 et seq.**). Plane blast kills Pakistan President Mohammad Zia ul-Haq (**Aug. 17**). I.R.A. bomb kills eight British soldiers in Ulster (**Aug. 20**). More than 40 killed as three jets collide in midair in air show at West German base (**Aug. 28**). Michael K. Deaver, Reagan friend, sentenced for lying about lobbying (**Sept. 23**). Gorbachev named Soviet President (**Oct. 1**). Foes defeat Pinochet in Chile's Presidential plebiscite (**Oct. 5**). U.S. and Philippines sign military-base treaty (**Oct. 17**). Computer "virus" disrupts network. Computer science graduate student blamed (**Nov. 2 et seq.**). Republicans sweep 40 states in election. Vice President Bush beats Gov. Michael S. Dukakis (**Nov. 8**). Independent Palestine proclaimed by Yasir Arafat, P.L.O. chairman, recognizes Israel, at least implicitly, for first time (**Nov. 15**). Soviet space shuttle *Buran* succeeds in debut completing two orbits (**Nov. 15**). Soviet legislature approves political restructuring and new national legislature (**Dec. 1**). Benazir Bhutto, first Islamic woman Prime Minister, chosen to lead Pakistan's government (**Dec. 1**). Earthquake in Soviet Armenia kills 25,000, injures 15,000, and leaves at least 400,000 homeless (**Dec. 7**). Two Soviet astronauts set record for staying in space 366 days (**Dec. 21**). Pan-Am 747 explodes from terrorist bomb and crashes in Lockerbie, Scotland, killing all 259 aboard and 11 on ground (**Dec. 21**).

1989 U.S. planes shoot down two Libyan fighters over international waters in Mediterranean that displayed "clear hostile intent" (**Jan. 4**). Emperor Hirohito of Japan dead at 87 (**Jan. 7**). George Herbert Walker Bush inaugurated as 41st U.S. President (**Jan. 20**). South Africa's President P.W. Botha, 73, resigns as head of long-governing Nationalist Party (**Feb. 2**). Soviet troops complete withdrawal from Kabul (**Feb. 5**). Congress rejects 51% pay increase proposed by Federal panel (**Feb. 7**). Ronald H. Brown is first black to be elected chairman of the Democratic National Committee (**Feb. 10**). Iran's Ayatollah Khomeini declares author Salman Rushdie's book "The Satanic Verses" offensive and sentences him and his publishers to death (**Feb. 14**). Nearly 90% of Eastern Airlines planes are grounded as pilots and flight attendants support machinists' strike (**March 4**). Senate vote of 53-47 rejects Bush nominee, John Tower, for Secretary of Defense (**March 9**). Ruptured tanker Exxon *Valdez* sends 11 million gallons of crude oil into Alaska's Prince William Sound

(March 24). Is worst U.S. oil spill. Thousands rally for abortion rights in Washington, D.C., and urge Supreme Court to keep abortion "safe and legal" (April 9). Stadium crush kills 94 and injures 170 during soccer match in Sheffield, England (April 15). Blast in a 16-inch gun turret kills 42 on Battleship *Iowa* (April 19). Tens of thousands of Chinese students take over Beijing's central square in rally for democracy (April 19 et seq.). Shuttle *Atlantis* launches *Magellan* spacecraft for flight to Venus (May 4). More than one million Chinese demonstrators in Beijing put pressure on Government for more democracy. Crowds demand resignations of Deng Xiaoping, senior leader, and Prime Minister Li Peng. Chaos spreads across nation (mid-May et seq.). Mikhail S. Gorbachev named Soviet President (May 25). U.S. jury convicts Oliver L. North of crimes stemming from role as covert agent to aid Contras (May 4). House Speaker Jim Wright resigns in the aftermath of his investigation by the House Ethics Committee (May 31). Thousands killed as Chinese troops crack down on pro-democracy in Beijing. Chinese leaders take hard line toward demonstrators and arrests and wave of executions begin (June 4 et seq.). Iranian leader, Ayatollah Khomeini, 87, is buried (June 6). U.S. Government suspends high-level meetings with Chinese Government (June 20). Supreme Court, 5-4, gives states right to impose new restrictions on abortions, stopping short of overturning 1973 Roe vs. Wade decision that established that right (July 3). President Bush visits Poland and Hungary and offers economic aid (July 9-12). Lebanese Shiite Muslim terrorists report hanging of Lieut. Col. William R. Higgins, taken hostage in 1988 (July 31). Congress approves $166-billion savings and loan industry rescue (Aug. 5). Kristin M. Baker is the first female to become First Captain of the West Point Corps of Cadets (Aug. 8). Army Gen. Colin L. Powell is first black to become Chairman of Joint Chiefs of Staff (Aug. 9). P.W. Botha quits as South Africa's President (Aug. 14). *Voyager 2* spacecraft speeds by Neptune after making startling discoveries about planet and its moons (Aug. 29). Hurricane Hugo devastates Caribbean islands to South Carolina (Sept. 18). Coup to overthrow Panamanian dictator, Manuel Noriega, fails (Oct. 3). TV evangelist Jim Bakker is convicted of 24 counts of fraud and conspiracy (Oct. 5). Earthquake measuring 7.1 on Richter scale hits Northern California, killing 61 and leaving thousands homeless (Oct. 17). Space Shuttle *Atlantis* launches Galileo spacecraft on its trip to Jupiter (Oct. 18). Senate rejects constitutional amendment to outlaw desecrating the American flag (Oct. 19). Bush administration and Congress compromise on raising the minimum wage to $3.80 in 1990 and $4.25 in 1991 (Oct. 31). L. Douglas Wilder, Democrat, is elected as first black governor of Virginia (Nov. 7). New York City elects David N. Dinkins, Democrat, its first black mayor (Nov. 7). Deng Xiaoping resigns from China's leadership after 65-year political career (Nov. 9). After 28 years, Berlin Wall is open to West and thousands of jubilant East Germans flood West Berlin and West Germany (Nov. 11). Lech Walesa, founder of Poland's Solidarity movement, addresses joint session of U.S. Congress (Nov. 15). Lebanon's President, René Moawad, is assassinated by car bomb after seventeen days in office (Nov. 22). Czech Parliament ends Communists' dominant role in Czechoslovakian society and promises free elections (Nov. 30). Pope John Paul II and Soviet leader Mikhail Gorbachev hold talk at Vatican City (Dec. 1). President Bush and Gorbachev hold shipboard summit off Malta (Dec. 2-3). A military coup to overthrow Philippine President Corazon Aquino is defeated (Dec. 7). Brent Scowcroft, U.S. National Security Advisor, visits China to mend relations after attacks on pro-democracy protesters (Dec. 9). Romanian uprising overthrows Communist Government (Dec. 15 et seq.). President Ceausescu and wife are executed by army. (Dec. 25). U.S. troops invade Panama, seeking capture of Gen. Manuel Noriega (Dec. 20). Noriega takes refuge in Vatican Embassy; resistance to U.S. collapses (Dec. 24).

L. Douglas Wilder
(Jan. 17, 1931)

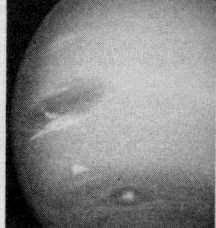

Neptune seen from
Voyager 2

PICTURE CREDITS. The following credits list the names of organizations and individuals who have contributed illustrations to HEADLINE HISTORY. The editors wish to thank all of them for their assistance. The credits are arranged alphabetically by picture source, then picture title and page number in HEADLINE HISTORY. Credits: AIP Niels Bohr Library, **Marie Curie** and **Albert Einstein**, p. 110; British Information Services, **Margaret Thatcher**, p. 123; Embassy of The Philippines, **Corazon C. Aquino**, p. 125; Harry S. Truman Library, **Harry S. Truman**, p. 118; John Fitzgerald Kennedy Library, Boston, **John F. Kennedy**, p. 121; Matthew Kalmenott, **Brontosaur**, p. 95; NASA Photos, **Charles A. Lindbergh**, p. 114, **Voyager and Viking**, p. 122, **Space Shuttle Columbia**, p. 123; **Sally K. Ride**, p. 123; National Portrait Gallery, Smithsonian Institution, **Theodore Roosevelt**, p. 110; Novosti Photos, **Vladimir Lenin**, p. 112; **Yuri A. Gagarin**, p. 120; **Mikhail S. Gorbachev**, p. 124; The Library of Congress Picture Collection, **Christopher Columbus**, p. 101, **Dred Scott**, p. 108, **Geronimo**, p. 109, **Woodrow Wilson**, p. 112, **Herbert C. Hoover**, p. 114, **Amelia Earhart**, p. 117, **Dwight D. Eisenhower**, p. 119, **Lyndon B. Johnson**, p. 121, **Richard M. Nixon**, p. 122; The Permanent Mission of India to the U.N., **Indira Gandhi**, p. 124; Republican National Committee, **Ronald W. Reagan**, p. 124, **George H. Bush**, p. 126; U.S. Army Photos, **D-Day, Yalta Conference**, p. 118, **Joseph Stalin**, p. 119; AP/Wide World Photos, Inc., **Martin Luther King, Jr.**, p. 121, U.N. Photo, **Fidel Castro**, p. 120, U.N. Photo by D. Burnett, **Kurt Waldheim**, p. 125. MAP CREDITS: Maps on pp. 100, 104, 111, 113, 115, and 116 from *An Encyclopedia of World History*, by William L. Langer, The Fifth Edition, Copyright 1940, 1948, 1952, and © 1967, 1972 by Houghton Mifflin Company. Reprinted by permission of Houghton Mifflin Company.

Firsts in America

This selection is based on our editorial judgment. Other sources may list different firsts.

Admiral in U.S. Navy: David Glasgow Farragut, 1866.

Air-mail route, first transcontinental: Between New York City and San Francisco, 1920.

Assembly, representative: House of Burgesses, founded in Virginia, 1619.

Bank established: Bank of North America, Philadelphia, 1781.

Birth in America to English parents: Virginia Dare, born Roanoke Island, N.C., 1587.

Botanic garden: Established by John Bartram in Philadelphia, 1728 and is still in existence in its original location.

Cartoon, colored: "The Yellow Kid," by Richard Outcault, in *New York World*, 1895.

College: Harvard, founded 1636.

College to confer degrees on women: Oberlin (Ohio) College, 1841.

College to establish coeducation: Oberlin (Ohio) College, 1833.

Electrocution of a criminal: William Kemmler in Auburn Prison, Auburn, N.Y., Aug. 6, 1890.

Five and Ten Cents Store: Founded by Frank Woolworth, Utica, N.Y., 1879 (moved to Lancaster, Pa., same year).

Fraternity: Phi Beta Kappa; founded Dec. 5, 1776, at College of William and Mary.

Law to be declared unconstitutional by U.S. Supreme Court: Judiciary Act of 1789. Case: *Marbury v. Madison*, 1803.

Library, circulating: Philadelphia, 1731.

Newspaper, illustrated daily: *New York Daily Graphic*, 1873.

Newspaper published daily: *Pennsylvania Packet and General Advertiser*, Philadelphia, Sept., 1784.

Newspaper published over a continuous period: *The Boston News-Letter*, April, 1704.

Newsreel: Pathé Frères of Paris, in 1910, circulated a weekly issue of their *Pathé Journal*.

Oil well, commercial: Titusville, Pa., 1859.

Panel quiz show on radio: *Information Please*, May 17, 1938.

Postage stamps issued: 1847.

Public School: Boston Latin School, Boston, 1635.

Railroad, transcontinental: Central Pacific and Union Pacific railroads, joined at Promontory, Utah, May 10, 1869.

Savings bank: The Provident Institute for Savings, Boston, 1816.

Science museum: Founded by Charleston (S.C.) Library Society, 1773.

Skyscraper: Home Insurance Co., Chicago, 1885 (10 floors, 2 added later).

Slaves brought into America: At Jamestown, Va., 1619, from a Dutch ship.

Sorority: Kappa Alpha Theta, at De Pauw University, 1870.

State to abolish capital punishment: Michigan, 1847.

State to enter Union after original 13: Vermont, 1791.

Steam-heated building: Eastern Hotel, Boston, 1845.

Steam railroad (carried passengers and freight): Baltimore & Ohio, 1830.

Strike on record by union: Journeymen Printers, New York City, 1776.

Subway: Opened in Boston, 1897.

"Tabloid" picture newspaper: *The Illustrated Daily News* (now *The Daily News*), New York City, 1919.

Vaudeville theater: Gaiety Museum, Boston, 1883.

Woman astronaut to ride in space: Dr. Sally K. Ride, 1983.

Woman astronaut to walk in space: Dr. Kathryn D. Sullivan, 1984.

Woman cabinet member: Frances Perkins, Secretary of Labor, 1933.

Woman candidate for President: Victoria Claflin Woodhull, nominated by National Woman's Suffrage Assn. on ticket of Nation Radical Reformers, 1872.

Woman candidate for Vice-President: Geraldine A. Ferraro, nominated by a major party on ticket of the Democratic Party, 1984.

Woman doctor of medicine: Elizabeth Blackwell; M.D. from Geneva Medical College of Western New York, 1849.

Woman elected governor of a state: Mrs. Nellie Tayloe Ross, Wyoming, 1925.

Woman elected to U.S. Senate: Mrs. Hattie Caraway, Arkansas; elected Nov., 1932.

Woman graduate of law school: Mrs. Ada H. Kepley, Union College of Law, Chicago, 1870.

Woman member of U.S. House of Representatives: Jeannette Rankin; elected Nov., 1916.

Woman member of U.S. Senate: Mrs. Rebecca Latimer Felton of Georgia; appointed Oct. 3, 1922.

Woman member of U.S. Supreme Court: Mrs. Sandra Day O'Connor; appointed July 1981.

Woman suffrage granted: Wyoming Territory, 1869.

Written constitution: *Fundamental Orders of Connecticut*, 1639.

STRUCTURES

The Seven Wonders of the World

(Not all classical writers list the same items as the Seven Wonders, but most of them agree on the following.)

The Pyramids of Egypt. A group of three pyramids, *Khufu, Khafra,* and *Menkaura* at Giza, outside modern Cairo, is often called the first wonder of the world. The largest pyramid, built by Khufu (Cheops), a king of the fourth Dynasty, had an original estimated height of 482 ft (now approximately 450 ft). The base has sides 755 ft long. It contains 2,300,000 blocks; the average weight of each is 2.5 tons. Estimated date of construction is 2800 B.C. Of all the Seven Wonders, the pyramids alone survive.

Hanging Gardens of Babylon. Often listed as the second wonder, these gardens were supposedly built by Nebuchadnezzar about 600 B.C. to please his queen, Amuhia. They are also associated with the mythical Assyrian Queen, Semiramis. Archeologists surmise that the gardens were laid out atop a vaulted building, with provisions for raising water. The terraces were said to rise from 75 to 300 ft.
    The Walls of Babylon, also built by Nebuchadnezzar, are sometimes referred to as the second (or the seventh) wonder instead of the Hanging Gardens.

Statue of Zeus (Jupiter) at Olympia. The work of Phidias (5th century B.C.), this colossal figure in gold and ivory was reputedly 40 ft high. All trace of it is lost, except for reproductions on coins.

Temple of Artemis (Diana) at Ephesus. A beautiful structure, begun about 350 B.C. in honor of a non-Hellenic goddess who later became identified with the Greek goddess of the same name. The temple, with Ionic columns 60 ft high, was destroyed by invading Goths in A.D. 262.

Mausoleum at Halicarnassus. This famous monument was erected by Queen Artemisia in memory of her husband, King Mausolus of Caria in Asia Minor, who died in 353 B.C. Some remains of the structure are in the British Museum. This shrine is the source of the modern word "mausoleum."

Colossus at Rhodes. This bronze statue of Helios (Apollo), about 105 ft high, was the work of the sculptor Chares, who reputedly labored for 12 years before completing it in 280 B.C. It was destroyed during an earthquake in 224 B.C.

Pharos of Alexandria. The seventh wonder was the Pharos (lighthouse) of Alexandria, built by Sostratus of Cnidus during the 3rd century B.C. on the island of Pharos off the coast of Egypt. It was destroyed by an earthquake in the 13th century.

Famous Structures

Ancient

The *Great Sphinx of Egypt,* one of the wonders of ancient Egyptian architecture, adjoins the pyramids of Giza and has a length of 240 ft. It was built in the 4th dynasty.
    Other Egyptian buildings of note include the *Temples of Karnak* and *Edfu* and the *Tombs at Beni Hassan.*
    The *Parthenon of Greece,* built on the Acropolis in Athens, was the chief temple to the goddess Athena. It was believed to have been completed by 438 B.C. The present temple remained intact until the 5th century A.D. Today, though the Parthenon is in ruins, its majestic proportions are still discernible.
    Other great structures of ancient Greece were the *Temples at Paestum* (about 540 and 420 B.C.); the *Temple of Poseidon* (about 460 B.C.); the *Temple of Apollo* at Corinth (about 540 B.C.); the *Temple of Apollo* at Bassae (about 450–420 B.C.); the famous *Erechtheum* atop the Acropolis (about 421–405 B.C.); the *Temple of Athena Niké* at Athens (about 426 B.C.); the *Olympieum* at Athens (174 B.C.–A.D. 131); the *Athenian Treasury* at Delphi (about 515 B.C.); the *Propylaea* of the Acropolis at Athens (437–432 B.C.); the *Theater of Dionysus* at Athens (about 350–325 B.C.); the *House of Cleopatra* at Delos (138 B.C.) and the *Theater* at Epidaurus (about 325 B.C.).
    The *Colosseum (Flavian Amphitheater)* of *Rome,* the largest and most famous of the Roman amphitheaters, was opened for use A.D. 80. Elliptical in shape, it consisted of three stories and an upper gallery, rebuilt in stone in its present form in the third century A.D. Its seats rise in tiers, which in turn are buttressed by concrete vaults and stone piers. It could seat between 40,000 and 50,000 spectators. It was principally used for gladiatorial combat.
    The *Pantheon* at Rome, begun by Agrippa in 27 B.C. as a temple, was rebuilt in its present circular form by Hadrian (A.D. 110–25). Literally the Pantheon was intended as a temple of "all the gods." It is remarkable for its perfect preservation today, and it has served continuously for 20 centuries as a place of worship.
    Famous Roman arches include the *Arch of Constantine* (about A.D. 315) and the *Arch of Titus* (about A.D. 80).

Later European

St. *Mark's Cathedral* in Venice (1063–67), one of the great examples of Byzantine architecture, was begun in the 9th century. Partly destroyed by fire in 976, it was later rebuilt as a Byzantine edifice.
    Other famous Byzantine examples of architecture are St. *Sophia* in Istanbul (A.D. 532–37); *San Vitale* in Ravenna (542); St. *Paul's Outside the Walls,* Rome (5th century); the *Kremlin* baptism

and marriage church, Moscow (begun in 1397); and *St. Lorenzo Outside the Walls*, Rome, begun in 588.

The *Cathedral Group* at Pisa (1067–1173), one of the most celebrated groups of structures built in Romanesque-style, consists of the cathedral, the cathedral's baptistery, and the *Leaning Tower*. This trio forms a group by itself in the northwest corner of the city. The cathedral and baptistery are built in varicolored marble. The campanile *(Leaning Tower)* is 179 ft. high and leans more than 16 ft out of the perpendicular. There is little reason to believe that the architects intended to have the tower lean.

Other examples of Romanesque architecture include the *Vézelay Abbey* in France (1130); the *Church of Notre-Dame-du-Port* at Clermont-Ferrand in France (1100); the *Church of San Zeno* (begun in 1138) at Verona, and *Durham Cathedral* in England.

The *Alhambra* (1248–1354), located in Granada, Spain, is universally esteemed as one of the greatest masterpieces of Moslem architecture. Designed as a palace and fortress for the Moorish monarchs of Granada, it is surrounded by a heavily fortified wall more than a mile in perimeter. The location of the Alhambra in the Sierra Nevada provides a magnificent setting for this jewel of Moorish Spain.

The *Tower of London* is a group of buildings and towers covering 13 acres along the north bank of the Thames. The central *White Tower*, begun in 1078 during the reign of William the Conqueror, was originally a fortress and royal residence, but was later used as a prison. The *Bloody Tower* is associated with Anne Boleyn and other notables.

Westminster Abbey, in London, was begun in 1045 and completed in 1065. It was rebuilt and enlarged in 1245–50.

Notre-Dame de Paris (begun in 1163), one of the great examples of Gothic architecture, is a twin-towered church with a steeple over the crossing and immense flying buttresses supporting the masonry at the rear of the church.

Other famous Gothic structures are *Chartres Cathedral* (12th century); *Sainte Chapelle*, Paris (1246–48); *Laon Cathedral*, France (1160–1205); *Reims Cathedral* (about 1210–50; rebuilt after its almost complete destruction in World War I); *Rouen Cathedral* (13th–16th centuries); *Amiens Cathedral* (1218–69); *Beauvais Cathedral* (begun 1247); *Salisbury Cathedral* (1220–60); *York Minster* or the *Cathedral of St. Peter* (begun in the 7th century); *Milan Cathedral* (begun 1386); and *Cologne Cathedral* (13th–19th centuries); badly damaged in World War II.

The Duomo (cathedral) in Florence was founded in 1298, completed by Brunelleschi and consecrated in 1436. The oval-shaped dome dominates the entire structure.

The *Vatican* is a group of buildings in Rome comprising the official residence of the Pope. The *Basilica of St. Peter*, the largest church in the Christian world, was begun in 1450. The *Sistine Chapel*, begun in 1473, is noted for the art masterpieces of Michelangelo, Botticelli, and others. The *Basilica of the Savior* (known as *St. John Lateran*) is the first-ranking Catholic Church in the world, for it is the cathedral of the Pope.

Other examples of Renaissance architecture are the *Palazzo Riccardi*, the *Palazzo Pitti* and the *Palazzo Strozzi* in Florence; the *Farnese Palace* in Rome; *Palazzo Grimani* (completed about 1550) in Venice; the *Escorial* (1563–93) near Madrid; the *Town Hall* of Seville (1527–32); the *Louvre*, Paris;

the *Château* at Blois, France; *St. Paul's Cathedral*, London (1675–1710; badly damaged in World War II); the *École Militaire*, Paris (1752); the *Pazzi Chapel*, Florence, designed by Brunelleschi (1429); the Palace of *Fontainebleau* and the *Château de Chambord* in France.

The *Palace of Versailles*, containing the famous Hall of Mirrors, was built during the reign of Louis XIV and served as the royal palace until 1793.

Outstanding European buildings of the 18th and 19th centuries are the *Superga* at Turin, the *Hôtel-Dieu* in Lyons, the *Belvedere Palace* at Vienna, the *Royal Palace* of Stockholm, the *Opera House* of Paris (1863–75); the *Bank of England*, the *British Museum*, the *University of London*, and the *Houses of Parliament*, all in London; the *Panthéon*, the *Church of the Madeleine*, the *Bourse*, and the *Palais de Justice* in Paris.

The *Eiffel Tower*, in Paris, was built for the Exposition of 1889 by Alexandre Eiffel. It is 984 ft high.[1]

1. 1,056 ft, including the television tower.

Asiatic and African

The *Taj Mahal* (1632–50), at Agra, India, built by Shah Jahan as a tomb for his wife, is considered by some as the most perfect example of the Mogul style and by others as the most beautiful building in the world. Four slim white minarets flank the building, which is topped by a white dome; the entire structure is of marble.

Other examples of Indian architecture are the temples at Benares and Tanjore.

Among famed Moslem edifices are the *Dome of the Rock* or *Mosque of Omar*, Jerusalem (A.D. 691); the *Citadel* (1166), and the *Tombs of the Mamelukes* (15th century), in Cairo; the *Tomb of Humayun* in Delhi; the *Blue Mosque* (1468) at Tabriz, and the *Tamerlane Mausoleum* at Samarkand.

Angkor Wat, outside the city of Angkor Thom, Cambodia, is one of the most beautiful examples of Cambodian or Khmer architecture. The sanctuary was built during the 12th century.

Great Wall of China (228 B.C.?), designed specifically as a defense against nomadic tribes, has large watch towers which could be called buildings. It was erected by Emperor Ch'in Shih Huang Ti and is 1,400 miles long. Built mainly of earth and stone, it varies in height between 18 and 30 ft.

Typical of Chinese architecture are the pagodas or temple towers. Among some of the better-known pagodas are the *Great Pagoda of the Wild Geese* at Sian (founded in 652); *Nan t'a* (11th century) at Fang Shan; the *Pagoda of Sung Yueh Ssu* (A.D. 523) at Sung Shan, Honan.

Other well-known Chinese buildings are the *Drum Tower* (1273), the *Three Great Halls* in the Purple Forbidden City (1627), *Buddha's Perfume Tower* (19th century), the *Porcelain Pagoda*, and the *Summer Palace*, all at Peking.

United States

Rockefeller Center, in New York City, extends from 5th Ave. to the Avenue of the Americas between 48th and 52nd Sts. (and halfway to 7th Ave. between 47th and 51st Sts.). It occupies more than 22 acres and has 19 buildings.

The Cathedral of St. John the Divine, at 112th St. and Amsterdam Ave. in New York City, was begun in 1892 and is now in the final stages of completion. When completed, it will be the largest cathedral in the world: 601 ft long, 146 ft wide at the nave, 320 ft wide at the transept. The east end is designed in Romanesque-Byzantine style, and the nave and west end are Gothic.

St. Patrick's Cathedral, at Fifth Ave. and 50th St. in New York City, has a seating capacity of 2,500. The nave was opened in 1877, and the cathedral was dedicated in 1879.

Louisiana Superdome, in New Orleans, is the largest arena in the history of mankind. The main area can accommodate up to 95,000 people. It is the world's largest steel-constructed room. Unobstructed by posts, it covers 13 acres and reaches 27 stories at its peak.

World Trade Center, in New York City, was dedicated in 1973. Its twin towers are 110 stories high (1,350 ft), and the complex contains over 9 million sq ft of office space. A restaurant is on the 107th floor of the North Tower.

World's Highest Dams

Name	River, Country or State	Structural height		Gross reservoir capacity		Year completed
		feet	meters	thousands of acre feet	millions of cubic meters	
Rogun	Vakhsh, U.S.S.R.	1066	325	9,404	11,600	1985
Nurek	Vakhsh, U.S.S.R.	984	300	8,512	10,500	1980
Grande Dixence	Dixence, Switzerland	935	285	324	400	1962
Inguri	Inguri, U.S.S.R.	892	272	801	1,100	1984
Chicoasén	Grijalva, Mexico	869	265	1,346	1,660	1981
Vaiont	Vaiont, Italy	869	265	137	169	1961
Tehri	Bhagirathi, India	856	261	2,869	3,540	UC
Kinshau	Tons, India	830	253	1,946	2,400	1985
Guavio	Orinoco, Colombia	820	250	811	1,000	1989
Mica	Columbia, Canada	794	242	20,000	24,670	1972
Sayano-Shushensk	Yenisei, U.S.S.R.	794	242	25,353	31,300	1980
Mihoesti	Aries, Romania	794	242	5	6	1983
Chivor	Batá, Colombia	778	237	661	815	1975
Mauvoisin	Drance de Bagnes, Switzerland	777	237	146	180	1957
Oroville	Feather, California	770	235	3,538	4,299	1968
Chirkey	Sulak, U.S.S.R.	764	233	2,252	2,780	1977
Bhakra	Sutlej, India	741	226	8,002	9,870	1963
El Cajón	Humuya, Honduras	741	226	4,580	5,650	1984
Hoover	Colorado, Arizona/Nevada	726	221	28,500	35,154	1936
Contra	Verzasca, Switzerland	722	220	70	86	1965
Dabaklamm	Dorferbach, Austria	722	220	191	235	UC
Mratinje	Piva, Yugoslavia	722	220	713	880	1973
Dworshak	N. Fk. Clearwater, Idaho	717	219	3,453	4,259	1974
Glen Canyon	Colorado, Arizona	710	216	27,000	33,304	1964
Toktogul	Naryn, U.S.S.R.	705	215	15,800	19,500	1978
Daniel Johnson	Manicouagan, Canada	703	214	115,000	141,852	1968
San Roque	Agno, Philippines	689	210	803	990	UC
Luzzone	Brenno di Luzzone, Switzerland	682	208	71	87	1963
Keban	Firat, Turkey	679	207	25,110	31,000	1974
Dez	Dez, Abi, Iran	666	203	2,707	3,340	1963
Almendra	Tormes, Spain	662	202	2,148	2,649	1970
Kölnbrein	Malta, Austria	656	200	166	205	1977
Kārūn	Karun, Iran	656	200	2,351	2,900	1976
Altinkaya	Kizil Irmak, Turkey	640	195	4,672	5,763	1986
New Bullards Bar	No. Yuba, California	637	194	960	1,184	1968
Lakhwar	Yamuna, India	630	192	470	580	1985
New Melones	Stanislaus, California	625	191	2,400	2,960	1979
Itaipu	Paraná, Brazil/Paraguay	623	190	23,510	29,000	1982
Kurobe 4	Kurobe, Japan	610	186	162	199	1964
Swift	Lewis, Washington	610	186	756	932	1958
Mossyrock	Cowlitz, Washington	607	185	1,300	1,603	1968
Oymopinar	Manavgat, Turkey	607	185	251	310	1983
Atatürk	Firat, Turkey	604	184	39,482	48,700	UC
Shasta	Sacramento, California	602	183	4,550	5,612	1945
Bennett WAC	Peace, Canada	600	183	57,006	70,309	1967
Karakaya	Firat, Turkey	591	180	7,767	9,580	1986
Tignes	Isère, France	591	180	186	230	1952
Amir Kabir (Karad)	Karadj, Iran	591	180	166	205	1962
Tachien	Tachia, Taiwan	591	180	188	232	1974
Dartmouth	Mitta-Mitta, Australia	591	180	3,243	4,000	1978
Özköy	Gediz, Turkey	591	180	762	940	1983
Emosson	Barberine, Switzerland	590	180	184	225	1974
Zillergründl	Ziller, Austria	590	180	73	90	1986
Los Leones	Los Leones, Chile	587	179	86	106	1986
New Don Pedro	Tuolumne, California	585	178	2,030	2,504	1971
Alpa-Gera	Cormor, Italy	584	178	53	65	1965

Name	River, country, or state	Structural height		Gross reservoir capacity		Year completed
		feet	meters	Thousands of acre feet	millions of cubic meters	
Kopperston Tailings 3	Jones Branch, West Virginia	580	177	—	—	1963
Takase	Takase, Japan	577	176	62	76	1979
Nader Shah	Marun, Iran	574	175	1,313	1,620	1978
Hasan Ugurlu	Yesil Irmak, Turkey	574	175	874	1,078	1980
Pauti-Mazar	Mazar, Ecuador	540	165	405	500	1984
Hungry Horse	S.Fk., Flathead, Montana	564	172	3,470	4,280	1953
Longyangxia	Huanghe, China	564	172	20,025	24,700	1983
Cabora Bassa	Zambezi, Mozambique	561	171	51,075	63,000	1974
Maqarin	Yarmuk, Jordan	561	171	259	320	1987
Amaluza	Paute, Ecuador	558	170	81	100	1982
Idikki	Periyar, India	554	169	1,618	1,996	1974
Charvak	Chirchik, U.S.S.R.	552	168	1,620	2,000	1970
Gura Apelor Retezat	Riul Mare, Romania	552	168	182	225	1980
Grand Coulee	Columbia, Washington	550	168	9,390	11,582	1942
Boruca	Terraba, Costa Rica	548	167	12,128	14,960	UC
Vidraru	Arges, Romania	545	166	380	465	1965
Kremasta (King Paul)	Achelōus, Greece	541	165	3,850	4,750	1965

NOTE: UC = under construction. *Source:* Department of the Interior, Bureau of Reclamation and *International Water Power and Dam Construction.*

World's Largest Dams

Dam	Location	Volume (thousands)		Year completed
		Cubic meters	Cubic yards	
New Cornelia Tailings	Arizona	209,500	274,015	1973
Pati (Chapetón)	Argentina	200,000	261,590	UC
Tarbela	Pakistan	121,720	159,203	1976
Fort Peck	Montana	96,049	125,628	1940
Atatürk	Turkey	84,500	110,522	UC
Yacyretá-Apipe	Paraguay/Argentina	81,000	105,944	UC
Guri (Raul Leoni)	Venezuela	78,000	102,014	1986
Rogun	U.S.S.R.	75,500	98,750	1985
Oahe	South Dakota	70,339	92,000	1963
Mangla	Pakistan	65,651	85,872	1967
Gardiner	Canada	65,440	85,592	1968
Afsluitdijk	Netherlands	63,400	82,927	1932
Oroville	California	59,639	78,008	1968
San Luis	California	59,405	77,700	1967
Nurek	U.S.S.R.	58,000	75,861	1980
Garrison	North Dakota	50,843	66,500	1956
Cochiti	New Mexico	48,052	62,850	1975
Tabka (Thawra)	Syria	46,000	60,168	1976
Bennett W.A.C.	Canada	43,733	57,201	1967
Tucurui	Brazil	43,000	56,242	1984
Boruca	Costa Rica	43,000	56,242	UC
High Aswan (Sadd-el-Aali)	Egypt	43,000	56,242	1970
San Roque	Philippines	43,000	56,242	UC
Kiev	U.S.S.R.	42,841	56,034	1964
Dantiwada Left Embankment	India	41,040	53,680	1965
Saratov	U.S.S.R.	40,400	52,843	1967
Mission Tailings 2	Arizona	40,088	52,435	1973
Fort Randall	South Dakota	38,227	50,000	1953
Kanev	U.S.S.R.	37,860	49,520	1976
Mosul	Iraq	36,000	47,086	1982
Kakhovka	U.S.S.R.	35,640	46,617	1955
Itumbiara	Brazil	35,600	46,563	1980
Lauwerszee	Netherlands	35,575	46,532	1969
Beas	India	35,418	46,325	1974
Oosterschelde	Netherlands	35,000	45,778	1986

NOTE: UC = under construction. *Source:* Department of the Interior, Bureau of Reclamation and *International Water Power and Dam Construction.*

World's Largest Hydroelectric Plants

Name of dam	Location	Rated capacity (MW) Present	Rated capacity (MW) Ultimate	Year of initial operation
Itaipu	Brazil/Paraguay	1,400	12,600	1984
Grand Coulee	Washington	6,480	10,080	1942
Guri (Raul Leoni)	Venezuela	2,800	10,060	1968
Tucuruí	Brazil	—	7,500	1985
Sayano-Shushensk	U.S.S.R.	—	6,400	1980
Krasnoyarsk	U.S.S.R.	6,096	6,096	1968
Corpus-Posadas	Argentina/Paraguay	—	6,000	UC
LaGrande 2	Canada	5,328	5,328	1982
Churchill Falls	Canada	5,225	5,225	1971
Bratsk	U.S.S.R.	4,100	4,600	1964
Ust'—Ilimsk	U.S.S.R.	3,675	4,500	1974
Cabora Bassa	Mozambique	2,075	4,150	1974
Yacyretá-Apipe	Argentina/Paraguay	—	4,050	UC
Rogun	U.S.S.R.	—	3,600	1985
Paulo Afonso	Brazil	3,409	3,409	1954
Salto Santiago	Brazil	1,332	3,333	1980
Pati (Chapetón)	Argentina	—	3,300	UC
Brumley Gap	Virginia	3,200	3,200	1973
Ilha Solteira	Brazil	3,200	3,200	1973
Inga I	Zaire	360	2,820	1974
Gezhouba	China	965	2,715	1981
John Day	Oregon/Washington	2,160	2,700	1969
Nurek	U.S.S.R.	900	2,700	1976
Revelstoke	Canada	900	2,700	1984
São Simao	Brazil	2,680	2,680	1979
LaGrande 4	Canada	2,637	2,637	1984
Mica	Canada	1,736	2,610	1976
Volgograd—22nd Congress	U.S.S.R.	2,560	2,560	1958
Fos do Areia	Brazil	2,511	2,511	1983
Itaparica	Brazil	—	2,500	1985
Bennett W.A.C.	Canada	2,116	2,416	1969
Chicoasén	Mexico	—	2,400	1980
Atatürk	Turkey	—	2,400	UC
LaGrande 3	Canada	2,310	2,310	1982
Volga—V.I. Lenin	U.S.S.R.	2,300	2,300	1955
Iron Gates I	Romania/Yugoslavia	2,300	2,300	1970
Iron Gates II	Romania/Yugoslavia	270	2,160	1983
Bath County	Virginia	—	2,100	1985
High Aswan (Saad-el-Aali)	Egypt	2,100	2,100	1967
Tarbela	Pakistan	1,400	2,100	1977
Piedra del Aquila	Argentina	—	2,100	UC
Itumbiara	Brazil	2,080	2,080	1980
Chief Joseph	Washington	2,069	2,069	1956
McNary	Oregon	980	2,030	1954
Green River	North Carolina	—	2,000	1980
Tehri	India	—	2,000	UC
Cornwall	New York	—	2,000	1978
Ludington	Michigan	1,979	1,979	1973
Robert Moses—Niagara	New York	1,950	1,950	1961
Salto Grande	Argentina/Uruguay	—	1,890	1979

Note: MW = Megawatts, UC = under construction. *Source:* Department of the Interior, Bureau of Reclamation and *International Water Power and Dam Construction.*

Notable U.S. Skyscrapers

City	Building	Stories	Height ft	Height m	City	Building	Stories	Height ft	Height m
Chicago	Sears Tower	110	1,454	443	Chicago	John Hancock Center	100	1,127	343
New York	World Trade Center	110	1,377	419	New York	Chrysler	77	1,046	319
New York	Empire State	102	1,250	381	Los Angeles	First Interstate World Center	73	1,017	310
Chicago	AMOCO	80	1,136	346	Houston	Texas	75	1,002	305

City	Building	Floors	ft	m
Houston	Allied Bank	71	985	300
Chicago	311 South Wacker Drive	65	969	295
New York	American International	66	952	290
Philadelphia	One Liberty Place	62	945	288
Seattle	Columbia Seafirst Center	76	943	287
New York	Citicorp Center	59	915	279
New York	40 Wall Tower	71	900	274
Chicago	Two Prudential Center	64	900	274
Philadelphia	Mellon Bank Center	56	880	268
Chicago	Water Tower Place	74	859	262
Los Angeles	First Interstate Bank	62	858	261
San Francisco	Transamerica Pyramid	61	853	260
Chicago	First National Bank	60	851	259
New York	RCA	70	850	259
Philadelphia	Two Liberty Place	52	845	257
Pittsburgh	USX Tower	64	841	256
Atlanta	One Atlantic Center	50	825	251
New York	Chase Manhattan	60	813	248
New York	Pan Am	59	808	246
New York	Woolworth	55	792	241
Boston	John Hancock Tower	60	790	241
San Francisco	Bank of America	52	779	237
Minneapolis	IDS Tower	57	775	236
New York	One Liberty Plaza	54	775	236
New York	One Penn Plaza	57	774	236
Minneapolis	Norwest Center	57	772	235
Miami	Southeast Financial Centre	55	765	233
Atlanta	Peachtree Plaza	73	754	230
New York	Exxon	54	750	229
Boston	Prudential Tower	52	750	229
Detroit	Detroit Plaza Hotel	73	747	228
Dallas	First Interstate Bank Tower	60	744	227
Los Angeles	Security Pacific Plaza	55	743	226
Los Angeles	Wells Fargo Center	54	743	227
New York	One Astor Plaza	54	730	222
Houston	Gulf Tower	52	725	221
New York	Marine Midland	52	724	221
Los Angeles	Mitsui (North Tower) Fudosan Tower	52	716	218
Pittsburgh	One Mellon Bank Center	54	715	218
Houston	One Shell Plaza	50	714	218
Indianapolis	Banc One Center Tower	51	711	216
Dallas	Renaissance Tower	56	710	216
Cleveland	Terminal Tower	52	708	216
New York	Union Carbide	52	707	215
New York	General Motors	50	705	215
Seattle	AT&T Gateway Tower	62	702	214
New York	Metropolitan Life	50	700	213
Philadelphia	Blue Cross Tower	50	700	213

NOTE: Height does not include TV towers and antennas. *Source: Information Please* questionnaires.

Notable Tunnels

Name	Location	Length mi.	Length km	Year completed
Railroad, excluding subways				
Seikan	Tsugara Strait, Japan	33.1	53.3	1983
Simplon (I and II)	Alps, Switzerland-Italy	12.3	19.8	1906 & 1922
Apennine	Bologna-Florence, Italy	11.5	18.5	1934
St. Gotthard	Swiss Alps	9.3	14.9	1881
Lötschberg	Swiss Alps	9.1	14.6	1911
Mont Cénis	French Alps	8.5[1]	13.7	1871
New Cascade	Cascade Mountains, Washington	7.8	12.6	1929
Vosges	Vosges, France	7.0	11.3	1940
Arlberg	Austrian Alps	6.3	10.1	1884
Moffat	Rocky Mountains, Colorado	6.2	9.9	1928
Shimuzu	Shimuzu, Japan	6.1	9.8	1931
Rimutaka	Wairarapa, New Zealand	5.5	8.9	1955
Vehicular				
St. Gotthard	Alps, Switzerland	10.2	16.4	1980
Mt. Blanc	Alps, France-Italy	7.5	12.1	1965
Mt. Ena	Japan Alps, Japan	5.3	8.5	1976[2]
Great St. Bernard	Alps, Switzerland-Italy	3.4	5.5	1964
Mount Royal	Montreal, Canada	3.2	5.1	1918
Lincoln	Hudson River, New York-New Jersey	2.5	4.0	1937
Queensway Road	Mersey River, Liverpool, England	2.2	3.5	1934
Brooklyn-Battery	East River, New York City	2.1	3.4	1950
Holland	Hudson River, New York-New Jersey	1.7	2.7	1927
Fort McHenry	Baltimore, Maryland	1.7	2.7	1985
Hampton Roads	Norfolk, Virginia	1.4	2.3	1957
Queens-Midtown	East River, New York City	1.3	2.1	1940
Liberty Tubes	Pittsburgh, Pennsylvania	1.2	1.9	1923
Baltimore Harbor	Baltimore, Maryland	1.2	1.9	1957
Allegheny Tunnels	Pennsylvania Turnpike	1.2	1.9	1940[3]

1. Lengthened to its present 8.5 miles in 1881. 2. Parallel tunnel begun in 1976. 3. Parallel tunnel built in 1965, twin tunnel in 1966. NOTE: UC = under construction. *Source:* American Society of Civil Engineers and International Bridge, Tunnel & Turnpike Association.

Notable Modern Bridges

Name	Location	Length of main span, ft	m	Year completed
Suspension				
Humber	Hull, Britain	4,626	1,410	1981
Verrazano-Narrows	Lower New York Bay	4,260	1,298	1964
Golden Gate	San Francisco Bay	4,200	1,280	1937
Mackinac Straits	Michigan	3,800	1,158	1957
Bosporus	Istanbul	3,524	1,074	1973
George Washington	Hudson River at New York City	3,500	1,067	1931
Ponte 25 de Abril	Tagus River at Lisbon	3,323	1,013	1966
Forth Road	Queensferry, Scotland	3,300	1,006	1964
Severn	Severn River at Beachley, England	3,240	988	1966
Tacoma Narrows	Puget Sound at Tacoma, Wash.	2,800	853	1950
Kanmon Strait	Kyushu-Honshu, Japan	2,336	712	1973
Angostura	Orinoco River at Ciudad Bolivar, Venezuela	2,336	712	1967
Transbay (twin spans)	San Francisco Bay	2,310	704	1936
Bronx-Whitestone	East River, New York City	2,300	701	1939
Pierre Laporte	St. Lawrence River at Quebec, Canada	2,190	668	1970
Delaware Memorial (twin bridges)	Delaware River near Wilmington, Del.	2,150	655	1951, 1968
Seaway Skyway	St. Lawrence River at Ogdensburg, N.Y.	2,150	655	1960
Gas Pipe Line	Atchafalaya River, Louisiana	2,000	610	1951
Walt Whitman	Delaware River at Philadelphia	2,000	610	1957
Tancarville	Seine River at Tancarville, France	1,995	608	1959
Lillebaelt	Lillebaelt Strait, Denmark	1,969	600	1970
Ambassador International	Detroit River at Detroit	1,850	564	1929
Throgs Neck	East River, New York City	1,800	549	1961
Benjamin Franklin	Delaware River at Philadelphia	1,750	533	1926
Skjomen	Narvik, Norway	1,722	525	1972
Kvalsund	Hammerfest, Norway	1,722	525	1977
Kleve-Emmerich	Rhine River at Emmerich, West Germany	1,640	500	1965
Bear Mountain	Hudson River at Peekskill, N.Y.	1,632	497	1924
Wm. Preston Lane, Jr., Memorial (twin bridges)	Near Annapolis, Md.	1,600	488	1952, 1973
Williamsburg	East River, New York City	1,600	488	1903
Newport	Narragansett Bay at Newport, R.I.	1,600	488	1969
Brooklyn	East River, New York City	1,595	486	1883
Cantilever				
Quebec Railway	St. Lawrence River at Quebec, Canada	1,800	549	1917
Forth Railway (twin spans)	Queensferry, Scotland	1,710	521	1890
Minato Ohashi	Osaka, Japan	1,673	510	1974
Commodore John Barry	Chester, Pa.	1,644	501	1974
Greater New Orleans (twin spans)	Mississippi River, Louisiana	1,576	480	1958
Howrah	Hooghly River at Calcutta	1,500	457	1943
Transbay Bridge	San Francisco Bay	1,400	427	1936
Baton Rouge	Mississippi River, Louisiana	1,235	376	1968
Tappan Zee	Hudson River at Tarrytown, N.Y.	1,212	369	1955
Longview	Columbia River at Longview, Wash.	1,200	366	1930
Patapsco River	Baltimore Outer Harbor Crossing	1,200	366	1976
Queensboro	East River, New York City	1,182	360	1909
Steel Arch				
New River Gorge	Fayetteville, W. Va.	1,700	518	1977
Bayonne	Kill Van Kull at Bayonne, N.J.	1,675	510	1931
Sydney Harbor	Sydney, Australia	1,670	509	1932
Fremont	Portland, Ore.	1,255	383	1973
Zdákov	Vltava River, Czechoslovakia	1,244	380	1967
Port Mann	Fraser River at Vancouver, British Columbia	1,200	366	1964
Thatcher Ferry	Panama Canal, Panama	1,128	344	1962
Laviolette	St. Lawrence River, Trois Rivieres, Quebec	1,100	335	1967
Runcorn-Widnes	Mersey River, England	1,082	330	1961
Birchenough	Sabi River at Fort Victoria, Rhodesia	1,080	329	1935

Name	Location	Length of main span, ft	Length of main span, m	Year completed
Cable-Stayed				
Annacis	Vancouver, B.C., Canada	1525	465	1986
Yokohama-ko-odan	Kanagawa, Japan	1509	460	UC
Second Hooghly	Calcutta, India	1500	457	UC
Chao Phya	Thailand	1476	450	1986
Barrios de Luna	Spain	1444	440	1983
Iwaguroshima	Kagawa, Japan	1378	420	UC
Shizakuishishima	Kagawa, Japan	1378	420	UC
Meiko Nishi	Aichi, Japan	1329	405	1985
St. Nazaire	Loire River, St. Nazaire, France	1325	404	1975
Rande	Rande, Spain	1312	400	1977
Dame Point	Jacksonville, Florida, U.S.A.	1300	396	1988
Houston Ship Channel	Baytown, Texas	1250	381	UC
Hale Boggs Memorial	Luling, Louisiana, U.S.A.	1222	373	1983
Dusseldorf Flehe	West Germany	1207	368	1979
Tjörn	Sweden	1200	366	1981
Sunshine Skyway	Tampa, Florida, U.S.A.	1200	366	1987
Continuous Truss				
Astoria	Columbia River at Astoria, Oregon	1,232	376	1966
Oshima	Oshima Island, Japan	1,066	325	1976
Croton Reservoir	Croton, N.Y.	1,052	321	1970
Tenmon	Kumamoto, Japan	984	300	1966
Kuronoseto	Nagashima-Kyushu, Japan	984	300	1974
Ravenswood	Ohio River, Ravenswood, W. Va.	902	275	1981
Dubuque	Mississippi River at Dubuque, Iowa	845	258	1943
Braga Memorial	Taunton River at Somerset, Mass.	840	256	1966
Graf Spee	Germany	839	256	1936
Cooper River	Charleston, S.C.	945	288	UC
Concrete Arch				
Jesse H. Jones Memorial	Houston Ship Channel, Texas	1,500	455	1982
KRK	Zagreb, Yugoslavia	1,280	390	1979
Gladesville	Parramatta River at Sydney, Australia	1,000	305	1964
Amizade	Paraná River at Foz do Iguassu, Brazil	951	290	1964
Arrábida	Porto, Portugal	886	270	1963
Sandö	Angerman River at Kramfors, Sweden	866	264	1943
Shibenik	Krka River, Yugoslavia	808	246	1966
Fiumarella	Catanzaro, Italy	758	231	1961
Zaporozhe	Old Dnepr River, U.S.S.R.	748	228	1952
Novi Sad	Danube River, Yugoslavia	692	211	1961

1. Concrete bridge. NOTE: UC = under construction. *Source: Encyclopaedia Britannica,* American Society of Civil Engineers, and Bridge Division, Federal Highway Administration.

Famous Ship Canals

Name	Location	Length (miles)[1]	Width (feet)	Depth (feet)	Locks	Year opened
Albert	Belgium	80.0	53.0	16.5	6	1939
Amsterdam-Rhine	Netherlands	45.0	164.0	41.0	3	1952
Beaumont-Port Arthur	United States	40.0	200.0	34.0	—	1916
Chesapeake and Delaware	United States	19.0	250.0	27.0	—	1927
Houston	United States	50.0	[2]	40.0	—	1914
Kiel (Nord-Ostsee Kanal)	Germany	61.3	144.0	36.0	4	1895
Panama	Canal Zone	50.7	110.0	41.0	12	1914
St. Lawrence Seaway	U.S. and Canada	2,400.0 [3]	([4])	—	—	1959
Montreal to Prescott	U.S. and Canada	11.5	80.0	30.0	7	1959
Welland	Canada	27.5	80.0	27.0	8	1931
Sault Ste. Marie	Canada	1.2	60.0	16.8	1	1895
Sault Ste. Marie	United States	1.6	80.0	25.0	4	1915
Suez	Egypt	100.6 [5]	197.0	36.0	—	1869

1. Statute miles. 2. 300-400 feet. 3. From Montreal to Duluth. 4. 442–550 feet; there are 11.5 miles of locks, 80 feet wide and 30 feet deep. 5. From Port Said lighthouse to entrance channel in Suez roads. *Source:* American Society of Civil Engineers.

WORLD STATISTICS

Area and Population by Country
Mid-1990 Estimates

Country	Area[1]	Population
Afghanistan	249,999	15,900,000
Albania	11,100	3,300,000
Algeria	919,591	25,600,000
Angola	481,351	8,500,000
Antigua and Barbuda	171	100,000
Argentina	1,068,297	32,300,000
Australia	2,967,894	17,100,000
Austria	32,374	7,600,000
Bahamas	5,380	200,000
Bahrain	240	500,000
Bangladesh	55,598	114,800,000
Barbados	166	300,000
Belgium	11,749	9,900,000
Belize	8,867	200,000
Benin	43,483	4,700,000
Bhutan	18,147	1,600,000
Bolivia	424,162	7,300,000
Botswana	231,804	1,200,000
Brazil	3,286,472	150,400,000
Brunei	2,226	300,000
Bulgaria	42,823	8,900,000
Burkina Faso	105,869	9,100,000
Burundi	10,747	5,600,000
Cambodia	69,880	7,000,000
Cameroon	183,568	11,100,000
Canada	3,851,790	26,600,000
Cape Verde	1,557	400,000
Central African Republic	240,534	2,900,000
Chad	495,753	5,000,000
Chile	292,257	13,200,000
China, People's Republic of	3,705,390	1,119,900,000
Colombia	439,735	31,800,000
Comoros	694	500,000
Congo	132,046	2,200,000
Costa Rica	19,575	3,000,000
Cuba	42,803	10,600,000
Cyprus	3,572	700,000
Czechoslovakia	49,370	15,700,000
Denmark	16,629	5,100,000
Dijibouti	8,494	400,000
Dominica	290	100,000
Dominican Republic	18,816	7,200,000
Ecuador	109,483	10,700,000
Egypt	386,660	54,700,000
El Salvador	8,124	5,300,000
Equatorial Guinea	10,830	400,000
Ethiopia	471,776	51,700,000
Fiji	7,055	800,000
Finland	130,119	5,000,000
France	211,207	56,400,000
Gabon	103,346	1,200,000
Gambia	4,361	900,000
Germany, East	41,826	16,300,000
Germany, West	95,976	63,200,000
Ghana	92,099	15,000,000
Greece	50,944	10,100,000
Grenada	133	100,000
Guatemala	42,042	9,200,000
Guinea	94,927	7,300,000
Guinea-Bissau	13,948	1,000,000
Guyana	83,000	800,000
Haiti	10,714	6,500,000
Honduras	43,277	5,100,000
Hungary	35,919	10,600,000
Iceland	39,768	300,000
India	1,269,340	853,400,000
Indonesia	735,355	189,400,000
Iran	636,293	55,600,000
Iraq	167,924	18,800,000
Ireland	27,136	3,500,000
Israel	8,019	4,600,000
Italy	116,303	57,700,000
Ivory Coast	322,460	12,600,000
Jamaica	4,243	2,400,000
Japan	143,750	123,600,000
Jordan	37,737	4,100,000
Kenya	224,960	24,600,000
Korea, North	46,540	21,300,000
Korea, South	38,025	42,800,000
Kuwait	6,880	2,100,000
Laos	91,429	4,000,000
Lebanon	4,015	3,300,000
Lesotho	11,720	1,800,000
Liberia	43,000	2,600,000
Libya	679,359	4,200,000
Luxembourg	998	400,000
Madagascar	226,657	12,000,000
Malawi	45,747	9,200,000
Malaysia	127,316	17,900,000
Maldives	115	200,000
Mali	478,764	8,100,000
Malta	122	400,000
Mauritania	397,954	2,000,000
Mauritius	790	1,100,000
Mexico	761,601	88,600,000
Mongolia	604,247	2,200,000
Morocco	172,413	25,600,000
Mozambique	309,494	15,700,000
Myanmar	261,220	41,300,000
Namibia	318,261	1,500,000
Nepal	54,362	19,100,000
Netherlands	14,405	14,900,000
New Zealand	103,736	3,300,000
Nicaragua	50,193	3,900,000
Niger	489,189	7,900,000
Nigeria	356,667	118,800,000
Norway	125,181	4,200,000
Oman	82,030	1,500,000
Pakistan	310,403	114,600,000
Panama	29,761	2,400,000
Papua New Guinea	178,259	4,000,000
Paraguay	157,047	4,300,000
Peru	496,222	21,900,000
Philippines	115,830	66,100,000
Poland	120,725	37,800,000
Portugal	35,553	10,400,000
Qatar	4,247	500,000
Romania	91,699	23,300,000
Rwanda	10,169	7,300,000
St. Lucia	238	200,000
St. Vincent and the Grenadines	150	100,000
Saudi Arabia	829,996	15,000,000
Senegal	75,750	7,400,000
Sierra Leone	27,699	4,200,000

Country	Area[1]	Population	Country	Area[1]	Population
Singapore	224	2,700,000	Tunisia	63,170	8,100,000
Solomon Islands	10,983	300,000	Turkey	301,381	56,700,000
Somalia	246,200	8,400,000	Uganda	91,134	18,000,000
South Africa	471,443	39,600,000	U.S.S.R.	8,649,496	291,000,000
Spain	194,896	39,400,000	United Arab Emirates	32,278	1,600,000
Sri Lanka	25,332	17,200,000	United Kingdom	94,525	57,400,000
Sudan	967,495	25,200,000	United States	3,615,105	251,400,000
Suriname	63,037	400,000	Uruguay	68,037	3,000,000
Swaziland	6,704	800,000	Vanuatu	5,700	200,000
Sweden	173,731	8,500,000	Venezuela	352,143	19,600,000
Switzerland	15,941	6,700,000	Vietnam	127,243	70,200,000
Syria	71,498	12,600,000	Western Samoa	1,097	200,000
Taiwan	13,885	20,200,000	Yemen[2]	203,849	9,800,000
Tanzania	364,898	26,000,000	Yugoslavia	98,766	23,800,000
Thailand	198,456	55,700,000	Zaire	905,563	36,600,000
Togo	21,927	3,700,000	Zambia	290,584	8,100,000
Trinidad and Tobago	1,981	1,300,000	Zimbabwe	150,803	9,700,000

1. Square miles. 2. People's Democratic Republic of Yemen and Yemen Arab Republic united in 1990. *Source: 1990 World Population Data Sheet,* Population Reference Bureau, Inc., Washington, D.C.

World's Largest Cities With 2 Million or More Population by Rank (Estimated Mid-Year Population in Thousands)

Rank in 1989	City	1989	1990	1995	2000	Area (square miles)	Density 1989 (pop. per square mile)
1.	Tokyo-Yokohama, Japan	26,640	26,952	28,447	29,971	1,089	24,463
2.	Mexico City, Mexico	19,478	20,207	23,913	27,872	522	37,314
3.	Sao Paulo, Brazil	17,376	18,052	21,539	25,354	451	38,528
4.	Seoul, South Korea	15,716	16,268	19,065	21,976	342	45,953
5.	New York, United States	14,618	14,622	14,638	14,648	1,274	11,473
6.	Osaka-Kobe-Kyoto, Japan	13,777	13,826	14,060	14,287	495	27,833
7.	Bombay, India	11,428	11,777	13,532	15,357	95	120,299
8.	Calcutta, India	11,413	11,663	12,885	14,088	209	54,607
9.	Buenos Aires, Argentina	11,360	11,518	12,232	12,911	535	21,233
10.	Rio de Janeiro, Brazil	11,153	11,428	12,786	14,169	260	42,894
11.	Moscow, Soviet Union	10,278	10,367	10,769	11,121	379	27,117
12.	Los Angeles, United States	9,974	10,060	10,414	10,714	1,110	8,985
13.	Cairo, Egypt	9,585	9,851	11,155	12,512	104	92,168
14.	Manila, Philippines	9,584	9,880	11,342	12,846	188	50,978
15.	Jakarta, Indonesia	9,275	9,588	11,151	12,804	76	122,033
16.	London, United Kingdom	9,222	9,170	8,897	8,574	874	10,551
17.	Tehran, Iran	8,915	9,354	11,681	14,251	112	79,594
18.	Paris, France	8,693	8,709	8,764	8,803	432	20,123
19.	Delhi, India	8,156	8,475	10,105	11,849	138	59,102
20.	Essen, West Germany	7,499	7,474	7,364	7,239	704	10,653
21.	Karachi, Pakistan	7,417	7,711	9,350	11,299	190	39,038
22.	Lagos, Nigeria	7,264	7,602	9,799	12,528	56	129,705
23.	Shanghai, China	6,837	6,873	7,194	7,540	78	87,659
24.	Chicago, United States	6,523	6,526	6,541	6,568	762	8,560
25.	Lima, Peru	6,335	6,578	7,853	9,241	120	54,789
26.	Taipei, Taiwan	6,308	6,513	7,477	8,516	138	45,710
27.	Istanbul, Turkey	6,230	6,461	7,624	8,875	165	37,760
28.	Beijing, China	5,710	5,736	5,865	5,993	151	37,816
29.	Bangkok, Thailand	5,623	5,791	6,657	7,587	102	55,126
30.	Hong Kong, Hong Kong	5,607	5,656	5,841	5,956	20	28,036
31.	Madras, India	5,582	5,743	6,550	7,384	115	48,541
32.	Bogota, Colombia	5,501	5,710	6,801	7,935	79	69,638
33.	Santiago, Chile	5,154	5,275	5,812	6,294	128	40,269
34.	Tianjin, China	4,767	4,804	5,041	5,298	49	97,291
35.	Milan, Italy	4,727	4,738	4,795	4,839	344	13,741
36.	Nagoya, Japan	4,678	4,736	5,017	5,303	307	15,236
37.	Pusan, South Korea	4,659	4,838	5,748	6,700	54	86,284
38.	Leningrad, Soviet Union	4,653	4,667	4,694	4,738	139	33,474
39.	Bangalore, India	4,410	4,612	5,644	6,764	50	88,191
40.	Madrid, Spain	4,391	4,451	4,772	5,104	66	66,527

Rank in 1989	City	1989	1990	1995	2000	Area (square miles)	Density 1989 (pop. per square mile)
41.	Shenyang, China	4,215	4,248	4,457	4,684	39	108,080
42.	Barcelona, Spain	4,101	4,163	4,492	4,834	87	47,138
43.	Lahore, Pakistan	4,101	4,236	4,986	5,864	57	71,949
44.	Manchester, United Kingdom	4,069	4,050	3,949	3,827	357	11,397
45.	Dhaka, Bangladesh	4,016	4,224	5,296	6,492	32	125,511
46.	Philadelphia, United States	4,011	4,007	3,988	3,979	471	8,515
47.	San Francisco, United States	3,924	3,958	4,104	4,214	428	9,167
48.	Baghdad, Iraq	3,813	3,941	4,566	5,239	97	39,304
49.	Ho Chi Minh City, Vietnam	3,562	3,645	4,064	4,481	31	114,914
50.	Belo Horizonte, Brazil	3,549	3,683	4,373	5,125	79	44,922
51.	Sydney, Australia	3,491	3,515	3,619	3,708	338	10,328
52.	Ahmadabad, India	3,476	3,595	4,200	4,837	32	108,618
53.	Hyderabad, India	3,448	3,563	4,149	4,765	88	39,180
54.	Athens, Greece	3,423	3,468	3,670	3,866	116	29,511
55.	Kinshasa, Zaire	3,403	3,575	4,520	5,646	57	59,704
56.	Miami, United States	3,359	3,421	3,679	3,894	448	7,498
57.	Guangzhou, China	3,313	3,330	3,485	3,652	79	41,942
58.	Surabaya, Indonesia	3,155	3,205	3,428	3,632	43	73,368
59.	Guadalajara, Mexico	3,148	3,262	3,839	4,451	78	40,364
60.	Caracas, Venezuela	3,148	3,188	3,338	3,435	54	58,296
61.	Wuhan, China	3,144	3,169	3,325	3,495	65	48,376
62.	Toronto, Canada	3,080	3,108	3,296	3,296	154	20,001
63.	Greater Berlin, Germany	3,024	3,022	3,018	3,006	274	11,036
64.	Detroit, United States	3,022	2,995	2,865	2,735	468	6,457
65.	Rome, Italy	3,005	3,021	3,079	3,129	69	43,556
66.	Naples, Italy	2,940	2,960	3,051	3,134	62	47,424
67.	Porto Alegre, Brazil	2,912	3,015	3,541	4,109	231	12,608
68.	Melbourne, Australia	2,896	2,907	2,946	2,968	327	8,856
69.	Montreal, Canada	2,882	2,896	2,996	3,071	164	17,572
70.	Alexandria, Egypt	2,850	2,899	3,114	3,304	35	81,420
71.	Casablanca, Morocco	2,807	2,891	3,327	3,795	35	80,202
72.	Rangoon, Burma	2,760	2,813	3,075	3,332	47	58,724
73.	Monterrey, Mexico	2,730	2,837	3,385	3,974	77	35,448
74.	Kiev, Soviet Union	2,700	2,751	2,983	3,237	62	43,548
75.	Dallas, United States	2,689	2,743	2,972	3,257	419	6,418
76.	Ankara, Turkey	2,687	2,782	3,263	3,777	55	48,852
77.	Singapore, Singapore	2,666	2,695	2,816	2,913	78	34,185
78.	Harbin, China	2,598	2,618	2,747	2,887	30	86,591
79.	Washington, United States	2,529	2,547	2,637	2,707	357	7,082
80.	Boston, United States	2,473	2,475	2,480	2,485	303	8,162
81.	Taegu, South Korea	2,413	2,529	3,201	4,051	(n.a.)	(n.a.)
82.	Lisbon, Portugal	2,366	2,396	2,551	2,717	(n.a.)	(n.a.)
83.	Poona, India	2,351	2,447	2,987	3,647	(n.a.)	(n.a.)
84.	Chengdu, China	2,331	2,349	2,465	2,591	25	93,242
85.	Tashkent, Soviet Union	2,313	2,365	2,640	2,947	(n.a.)	(n.a.)
86.	Budapest, Hungary	2,300	2,301	2,313	2,335	138	16,666
87.	Chongqing, China	2,284	2,339	2,632	2,961	(n.a.)	(n.a.)
88.	Vienna, Austria	2,282	2,313	2,474	2,647	(n.a.)	(n.a.)
89.	Houston, United States	2,258	2,298	2,456	2,651	310	7,284
90.	Birmingham, United Kingdom	2,178	2,170	2,130	2,078	223	9,768
91.	Bucharest, Romania	2,139	2,150	2,214	2,271	52	41,132
92.	Salvador, Brazil	2,123	2,209	2,694	3,286	(n.a.)	(n.a.)
93.	Havana, Cuba	2,087	2,109	2,218	2,333	(n.a.)	(n.a.)
94.	Kanpur, India	2,024	2,076	2,356	2,673	(n.a.)	(n.a.)

Source: U.S. Bureau of the Census, 1989, International Data Base. NOTE: For this table cities are defined as population clusters of continuous built-up area with a population density of at least 5,000 persons per square mile. The boundary of the city was determined by examining detailed maps of each city in conjunction with the most recent official population statistics. Exclaves of areas exceeding the minimum population density were added to the city if the intervening gap was less than one mile. To the extent practical, nonresidential areas such as parks, airports, industrial complexes, and water were excluded from the area reported for each city, thus making the population density reflective of the concentrations in the residential portions of the city. By using a consistent definition for the city, it is possible to make comparisons of the cities on the basis of total population, area, and population density.

Political and administrative boundaries were disregarded in determining the population of a city. Berlin includes both East and West Berlin, as well as population from East Germany. Detroit includes Windsor, Canada.

The population of each city was projected based on the proportion each city was of its country total at the time of the last two censuses and projected country populations (U.S. Bureau of the Census 1989). The area expansion of the city was not projected, hence density figures are valid only for 1989.

Population figures for the nine cities with (n.a.) in the area and density columns were derived by a less precise method, not involving the use of detailed maps. In addition, three other cities (Abidjan, Ivory Coast; Khartoum, Sudan; and Medan, Indonesia) were estimated to have at least 2,000,000 inhabitants as of midyear 1989. However, projections for these cities could not be prepared because the apparent growth rates indicate that data are not comparable. Thirty-four other cities are projected to have at least 2,000,000 inhabitants by midyear 2000.

Estimates of World Population by Regions

				Estimated population in millions				
Year	North America[1]	Latin America[2]	Europe[3]	U.S.S.R.	Asia[4]	Africa	Oceania	World total
1650	1	7	103	([5])	257	100	2	470
1750	1	10	144	([5])	437	100	2	694
1850	26	33	274	([5])	656	100	2	1,091
1900	81	63	423	([5])	857	141	6	1,571
1950	166	164	392	180	1,380	219	13	2,513
1960	199	215	425	214	1,683	275	16	3,027
1970	226	283	460	244	2,091	354	19	3,678
1980	252	365	484	266	2,618	472	23	4,478
1984	262	398	491	275	2,785	532	24	4,766
1985	264	410	492	278	2,831	566	24	4,865
1986	267	419	493	280	2,876	583	25	4,942
1987	270	421	495	284	2,930	601	25	5,026
1988	272	429	497	286	2,995	623	26	5,128
1989	275	438	499	289	3,061	646	26	5,234
1990	278	447	501	291	3,116	661	27	5,321

1. U.S. (including Alaska and Hawaii), Bermuda, Canada, Greenland, and St. Pierre and Miquelon. 2. Mexico, Central and South America, and Caribbean Islands. 3. Includes Russia 1650–1900. 4. Excludes Russia (U.S.S.R.). 5. Included in Europe. NOTE: From 1930 on European Turkey included in Asia not Europe. *Sources:* W.F. Willcox, 1650–1900; United Nations, 1930–70. United States Department of Commerce, Bureau of the Census, 1984; *1986-1990 World Population Data Sheet*, Population Reference Bureau, Inc., Washington, D.C.

World's 20 Most Populous Countries: 1990 and 2100

	1990			2100	
Rank	Country	Population	Rank	Country	Population
1.	China	1,119,900,000	1.	India	1,631,800,000
2.	India	853,400,000	2.	China	1,571,400,000
3.	USSR	291,000,000	3.	Nigeria	508,800,000
4.	United States	251,400,000	4.	USSR	375,900,000
5.	Indonesia	189,400,000	5.	Indonesia	356,300,000
6.	Brazil	150,400,000	6.	Pakistan	315,800,000
7.	Japan	123,600,000	7.	United States	308,700,000
8.	Nigeria	118,800,000	8.	Bangladesh	297,100,000
9.	Bangladesh	114,800,000	9.	Brazil	293,200,000
10.	Pakistan	114,600,000	10.	Mexico	195,500,000
11.	Mexico	88,600,000	11.	Ethiopia	173,300,000
12.	Vietnam	70,200,000	12.	Vietnam	168,100,000
13.	Philippines	66,100,000	13.	Iran	163,800,000
14.	Germany, West	63,200,000	14.	Zaire	138,900,000
15.	Italy	57,700,000	15.	Japan	127,900,000
16.	United Kingdom	57,400,000	16.	Philippines	125,100,000
17.	Turkey	56,700,000	17.	Tanzania	119,600,000
18.	France	56,400,000	18.	Kenya	116,400,000
19.	Thailand	55,700,000	19.	Burma	111,700,000
20.	Iran	55,600,000	20.	Egypt	110,500,000

Sources: 1990 World Population Data Sheet of the Population Reference Bureau, Inc; *2100,* World Bank.

The Changing Family Internationally

Far-reaching changes are occurring in family structures and household living arrangements in the developed countries. Families are becoming smaller, and household composition patterns over the past several decades have been away from the traditional nuclear family and toward more single-parent households, more persons living alone, and more couples living together out of wedlock. The one-person household has become the fastest growing type.

Scandinavian countries have been the paceset-ters in the development of many of the non-traditional forms of family living, especially births outside of wedlock and cohabitation outside of legal marriage. Women in these societies also have the highest rates of labor force participation.

Japan is the most traditional society of those studied, with very low rates of divorce and births out of wedlock and the highest proportion of married-couple households. But even in Japan, family patterns are changing: sharp drops in fertility have led to much smaller families.

World Population by Age Group, 1989, and Projections, 2000

(In percent. Covers countries with 10 million or more population in 1989)

Country	1989 Under 5 years old	1989 5 to 14 years old	1989 15 to 64 years old	1989 65 years old and over	2000 Under 5 years old	2000 5 to 14 years old	2000 15 to 64 years old	2000 65 years old and over
Afghanistan	16.8	26.5	54.1	2.6	16.0	25.9	55.3	2.8
Algeria	16.9	27.4	52.3	3.4	13.7	25.9	56.7	3.6
Argentina	9.9	20.0	61.1	9.0	9.1	17.4	63.6	9.8
Australia	7.6	14.9	66.6	10.9	7.1	14.4	66.8	11.6
Bangladesh	17.0	27.9	51.9	3.3	14.8	25.3	56.6	3.2
Brazil	12.4	23.6	59.9	4.1	10.3	20.2	64.3	5.2
Burma	14.3	24.0	57.7	3.9	12.6	23.2	59.9	4.3
Cameroon	17.1	26.8	53.0	3.1	16.3	26.2	54.5	3.1
Canada	7.2	13.8	67.7	11.3	5.9	13.1	68.0	13.1
Chile	10.3	19.8	64.0	6.0	8.8	17.8	66.4	7.1
China: Mainland	9.8	17.4	67.2	5.6	8.5	18.3	66.2	7.1
Taiwan	8.3	19.4	66.4	5.9	6.9	14.4	70.5	8.2
Colombia	12.5	22.1	61.9	3.5	9.9	20.7	64.9	4.4
Cuba	8.1	14.8	68.5	8.6	6.9	14.9	68.5	9.7
Czechoslovakia	7.0	16.3	65.0	11.6	7.2	13.5	67.3	12.1
East Germany	6.7	13.1	67.3	13.0	5.8	12.7	67.8	13.7
Ecuador	14.1	25.5	56.6	3.7	11.8	22.5	61.5	4.2
Egypt	15.1	25.3	56.2	3.4	13.4	24.0	58.7	3.8
Ethiopia	17.9	28.1	51.3	2.6	17.9	27.5	51.8	2.8
France	6.8	13.4	66.1	13.7	6.0	12.9	65.5	15.6
Ghana	18.8	25.5	52.7	3.0	17.8	28.4	50.8	3.0
Greece	5.9	13.9	66.5	13.8	5.7	11.5	65.3	17.5
Hungary	5.9	14.7	66.3	13.1	6.7	12.2	67.1	14.0
India	13.4	23.1	60.0	3.4	11.2	21.6	63.1	4.1
Indonesia	13.0	24.3	59.9	2.8	10.5	20.8	64.4	4.2
Iran	18.0	26.6	51.9	3.4	16.6	27.5	51.9	4.0
Iraq	18.8	28.9	49.0	3.2	18.0	28.6	50.4	3.0
Italy	5.3	12.0	68.4	14.3	5.9	11.1	66.3	16.7
Ivory Coast	18.6	27.6	51.8	2.0	18.3	28.0	51.4	2.3
Japan	5.7	13.3	69.4	11.6	6.3	11.1	66.5	16.1
Kenya	21.4	30.1	46.4	2.1	20.2	30.5	47.2	2.1
Madagascar	19.0	27.2	50.4	3.4	18.2	28.2	50.4	3.1
Malaysia	12.5	22.8	60.9	3.8	10.2	20.5	65.0	4.3
Mexico	13.8	25.1	57.0	4.1	12.3	22.6	60.4	4.7
Morocco	15.2	25.8	55.0	4.0	13.1	24.0	58.5	4.4
Mozambique	18.0	26.8	52.8	2.5	17.4	27.3	52.7	2.6
Nepal	16.6	26.9	53.7	2.8	15.3	25.4	56.3	3.0
Netherlands	6.1	12.1	69.0	12.8	6.0	12.2	67.7	14.1
Nigeria	18.0	26.9	53.1	2.0	17.8	26.9	52.6	2.7
North Korea	13.7	23.8	58.6	3.9	11.3	22.3	61.7	4.7
Pakistan	17.2	26.0	52.8	4.0	16.5	26.2	53.4	3.9
Peru	13.4	25.2	57.7	3.7	10.9	21.4	63.2	4.5
Philippines	15.5	25.2	56.0	3.3	14.1	24.7	57.4	3.8
Poland	8.4	17.2	64.6	9.8	6.8	14.8	66.9	11.6
Portugal	7.0	15.0	65.8	12.2	6.6	13.5	66.2	13.8
Romania	7.6	16.1	66.1	10.2	7.3	14.7	65.5	12.6
Saudi Arabia	15.9	21.5	60.7	1.9	15.6	24.7	57.0	2.7
South Africa	15.3	24.6	56.2	3.9	14.8	24.7	56.4	4.0
South Korea	9.7	18.5	67.2	4.5	8.6	17.0	68.4	5.9
Soviet Union	9.3	16.8	64.7	9.3	7.9	16.3	64.4	11.5
Spain	6.3	14.9	65.9	12.9	6.4	12.5	65.6	15.5
Sri Lanka	10.5	21.9	62.5	5.0	9.2	17.9	66.8	6.2
Sudan	18.3	27.1	51.5	3.1	16.9	27.3	52.7	3.2
Syria	19.0	28.6	49.4	3.0	18.4	28.5	50.0	3.0
Tanzania	19.8	28.4	48.8	2.9	19.3	28.8	49.2	2.7
Thailand	9.7	21.7	64.5	4.1	8.3	16.6	69.6	5.5
Turkey	13.4	23.7	58.5	4.4	11.2	21.7	61.9	5.2
Uganda	19.6	28.4	49.7	2.3	19.1	28.9	49.8	2.2
United Kingdom	6.6	12.2	65.7	15.6	5.9	13.0	65.7	15.4
United States	7.5	14.1	66.0	12.4	6.4	13.9	66.8	12.9
Venezuela	14.1	24.4	57.9	3.6	12.0	22.5	61.1	4.4
Vietnam	15.0	24.9	56.5	3.7	12.9	24.0	58.9	4.3
West Germany	5.1	9.7	69.8	15.4	5.4	10.9	66.7	17.1
Yugoslavia	7.5	15.6	67.7	9.1	6.7	13.9	66.8	12.5
Zaire	18.2	27.5	51.5	2.8	17.4	27.6	52.3	2.8

Source: U.S. Bureau of the Census, *World Population Profile: 1989*.

Expectation of Life by Age and Sex for Selected Countries

Country	Period	Males						Females					
		0	1	10	20	40	60	0	1	10	20	40	60
NORTH AMERICA													
U.S.	1986	71.30	71.10	62.40	52.80	34.50	18.00	78.30	78.00	69.20	59.40	40.20	22.50
Canada	1984-1986	73.00	72.63	63.86	54.25	35.46	18.39	79.78	79.35	70.55	60.74	41.30	23.27
Mexico	1979	62.10	—	—	—	—	—	66.00	—	—	—	—	—
Trinidad & Tobago	1980-1985	66.88	67.34	58.97	49.39	31.13	15.84	71.62	71.64	63.18	53.44	34.55	18.42
CENTRAL AND SOUTH AMERICA													
Brazil[4]	1985-1990	62.30	—	—	—	—	—	67.60	—	—	—	—	—
Chile	1985-1990	68.05	68.43	59.87	50.27	32.30	16.84	75.05	75.29	66.69	56.93	37.81	20.58
Costa Rica[4]	1985-1990	72.41	—	—	—	—	—	77.04	—	—	—	—	—
Ecuador[2]	1985	63.39	67.12	60.43	51.16	33.57	17.76	67.59	70.64	63.09	54.51	36.32	19.43
Guatemala	1979-1980	55.11	59.09	54.38	45.55	30.56	16.57	59.43	62.98	58.74	49.79	33.01	17.50
Panama[3]	1980-1985	69.20	70.16	62.37	53.01	35.02	18.55	72.85	73.60	65.71	56.17	37.56	20.28
Peru	1980-1985	56.77	62.32	57.21	48.13	30.97	15.41	66.50	65.67	60.48	51.34	33.82	17.07
Uruguay	1984-1986	68.43	69.67	61.03	51.40	32.68	16.65	74.88	75.89	67.24	57.46	38.27	21.01
Venezuela	1985	66.68	68.45	60.31	50.92	33.07	17.30	72.80	74.16	65.90	56.23	37.31	20.30
EUROPE													
Austria	1987	71.53	71.31	62.50	52.88	34.24	17.62	78.13	77.82	69.00	59.16	39.74	21.58
Belgium	1979-1982	70.04	69.99	61.26	51.64	32.98	16.26	76.79	76.61	67.88	58.08	38.82	20.93
Cyprus	1983-1987	73.90	73.91	65.14	55.47	36.48	19.27	77.82	77.61	68.85	58.99	39.43	21.12
Czechoslovakia	1985	67.25	67.33	58.57	48.88	30.22	14.63	74.71	74.58	65.80	55.95	36.51	18.74
Denmark[5]	1986-1987	71.80	71.40	62.60	52.90	34.10	17.40	77.60	77.20	68.40	58.50	39.10	21.70
Finland	1986	70.49	69.98	61.12	51.42	32.87	16.66	78.72	78.08	69.19	59.33	39.94	21.62
France	1987	72.03	71.69	62.91	53.24	34.76	18.41	80.27	79.79	70.99	61.16	41.84	23.67
Germany, East[6]	1986-1987	69.73	69.45	60.70	51.01	32.29	15.91	75.74	75.32	66.54	56.70	37.33	19.44
Germany, West[6]	1985-1987	71.81	71.52	62.73	53.01	34.07	17.26	78.37	77.97	69.15	59.30	39.87	21.72
Greece	1980	72.15	72.82	64.13	54.48	35.58	18.17	76.35	76.78	68.24	58.43	38.95	20.63
Hungary	1987	65.67	65.99	57.24	47.54	29.36	14.83	73.74	73.83	65.05	55.22	36.11	18.94
Ireland	1980-1982	70.14	69.94	61.25	51.58	32.63	15.90	75.62	75.35	66.58	56.75	37.26	19.54
Italy	1983	71.43	71.37	62.58	52.92	33.90	17.04	78.14	77.99	69.19	59.34	38.83	21.54
Netherlands	1985-1986	72.95	72.64	63.84	54.08	34.86	17.48	79.55	79.12	70.29	60.43	40.94	22.75
Norway	1987	72.75	72.42	63.66	53.96	35.08	17.94	79.55	79.16	70.32	60.47	40.93	22.70
Poland	1987	66.81	67.11	58.39	48.71	30.38	15.27	75.20	75.32	66.54	56.69	37.35	19.77
Portugal	1979-1982	68.35	69.10	60.66	51.31	33.09	16.74	75.20	75.72	67.17	57.46	38.27	20.29
Spain	1980-1982	72.52	72.54	63.88	54.20	35.35	18.39	78.61	78.44	69.73	59.91	40.46	22.13
Sweden	1987	74.16	73.66	64.80	55.06	36.12	18.73	80.15	79.60	70.73	60.86	41.39	23.07
Switzerland	1986-1987	73.80	73.40	64.60	54.90	36.20	18.80	80.50	80.00	71.20	61.40	42.00	23.50
U.S.S.R.	1985-1986	64.15	65.03	56.94	47.39	29.73	15.14	73.27	73.93	65.80	56.05	37.00	19.64
United Kingdom	1984-1987	71.22	71.49	62.70	52.97	33.82	16.69	77.51	77.15	68.34	58.48	38.99	21.09
England and Wales	1983-1985	71.80	71.58	62.79	53.07	33.89	16.75	77.74	77.40	68.59	58.74	39.24	21.36
Northern Ireland	1983	69.25	69.30	60.57	50.93	32.13	15.62	75.65	75.40	66.63	56.80	37.44	19.09
Scotland	1985	70.05	69.76	60.97	51.27	32.26	15.68	75.83	75.49	66.71	56.86	37.45	19.90
Yugoslavia	1984-1985	68.13	—	60.39	50.97	32.54	16.93	73.55	—	66.27	56.47	37.59	20.35
ASIA													
Bangladesh	1984	54.90	62.40	58.80	49.80	31.90	16.20	54.70	60.30	57.80	49.30	32.10	16.00
India	1976-1980	52.50	58.60	54.80	45.80	28.30	14.10	52.10	58.60	56.60	47.80	31.20	15.90
Iran	1976	55.75	60.78	53.87	45.19	29.19	14.58	55.04	60.14	54.38	44.97	30.47	15.39
Israel[7]	1985	73.53	73.48	64.74	55.04	35.94	18.70	76.99	76.85	68.09	58.25	38.75	20.54
Japan[8]	1987	75.61	75.01	66.25	56.50	37.35	19.94	81.39	80.76	71.94	62.05	42.54	24.00
Korea, South	1978-1979	62.70	63.73	55.62	46.21	28.13	12.74	69.07	71.02	63.46	53.86	35.04	17.87
Pakistan	1976-1978	59.04	66.46	61.34	52.30	34.77	19.25	59.20	65.58	60.68	51.98	35.23	19.27
Sri Lanka	1981	67.78	68.99	60.99	51.64	33.19	17.74	71.66	72.67	64.75	55.36	36.96	19.57
Syria	1976-1979	63.77	66.92	59.88	50.69	32.74	16.16	64.70	67.06	60.14	50.90	32.84	16.23
AFRICA													
Egypt[4]	1985-1990	59.29	—	—	—	—	—	61.97	—	—	—	—	—
Kenya[4]	1985-1990	56.50	—	—	—	—	—	60.46	—	—	—	—	—
South Africa	1985-1990	57.51	—	—	—	—	—	63.48	—	—	—	—	—
OCEANIA													
Australia[9]	1986	72.77	72.50	63.74	54.13	35.39	18.10	79.13	78.74	69.94	60.13	40.71	22.54
New Zealand	1986-1988	71.03	70.94	62.24	52.75	34.09	17.12	77.27	77.02	68.27	58.50	39.21	21.47

Table heading note: Average future lifetime in years at stated age

1. Provisional. 2. Excluding nomadic Indian tribes. 3. Excluding tribal Indian population. 4. Estimates prepared by the Population Division of the United Nations. 5. Excluding data for Faeroe Islands and Greenland. 6. Including relevant data relating to Berlin. No separate data have been supplied. 7. Including data for East Jerusalem and Israeli residents in certain other territories under occupation by Israeli military forces since June 1967. 8. Japanese nationals in Japan only. 9. Excluding full-blooded aborigines. NOTE: Figures are latest available as of August 1990. *Source:* United Nations *Demographic Yearbook, 1988.*

Crude Birth and Death Rates for Selected Countries
(per 1,000 population)

Country	Birth rates					Death rates				
	1988	1987	1985	1980	1975	1988	1987	1985	1980	1975
Australia	14.9	15.0	15.7	15.3	16.9	7.2	7.2	7.5	7.4	7.9
Austria	11.6	11.4	11.6	12.0	12.5	11.0	11.2	11.9	12.2	12.8
Belgium	n.a.	11.9	11.5	12.7	12.2	n.a.	10.7	11.2	11.6	12.2
Canada	14.5	14.4	14.8	15.4	15.8	7.3	7.2	7.2	7.2	7.4
Cuba	18.1	17.4	18.0	14.1	n.a.	6.5	6.3	6.4	5.7	n.a.
Czechoslovakia	13.8	13.8	14.5	16.4	19.6	11.4	11.5	11.8	12.1	11.5
Denmark	11.5	11.0	10.6	11.2	14.2	11.5	11.3	11.4	10.9	10.1
Finland	12.8	12.0	12.8	13.1	13.9	9.9	9.7	9.8	9.3	9.3
France	13.8	13.8	13.9	14.8	14.1	9.4	9.5	10.1	10.2	10.6
Germany, East	12.9	13.6	13.7	14.6	10.8	12.8	12.9	13.5	14.2	14.3
Germany, West	11.0	10.5	9.6	10.0	9.7	11.2	11.2	11.5	11.6	12.1
Greece	10.7	10.6	11.7	15.4	15.7	9.3	9.5	9.4	9.1	8.9
Hong Kong	13.3	12.4	14.0	16.9	n.a.	4.9	4.8	4.6	5.1	n.a.
Hungary	11.7	11.9	12.2	13.9	18.4	13.2	13.4	13.9	13.6	12.4
Ireland	15.3	16.6	17.6	21.9	21.5	8.9	8.8	9.4	9.7	10.6
Israel	22.6	22.7	23.5	24.1	28.2	6.6	6.7	6.6	6.7	7.1
Italy	9.9	9.6	10.1	11.2	14.8	9.3	9.3	9.5	9.7	9.9
Japan	10.7	11.1	11.9	13.7	17.2	6.5	6.2	6.2	6.2	6.4
Luxembourg	12.1	11.5	11.2	11.5	11.2	10.0	10.9	11.0	11.5	12.2
Malta	15.8	15.9	16.8	16.0	18.3	7.8	8.4	8.5	8.8	8.8
Mauritius	19.9	19.3	18.8	27.0	25.1	6.5	6.5	6.8	7.2	8.1
Mexico	n.a.	n.a.	34.1	35.3	37.5	n.a.	n.a..	5.3	6.2	7.2
Netherlands	12.6	12.7	12.3	12.8	13.0	8.4	8.3	8.5	8.1	8.3
New Zealand	n.a.	16.8	15.6	n.a.	18.4	n.a.	8.4	8.4	n.a.	8.1
Norway	13.7	13.0	12.3	12.5	14.1	10.8	10.7	10.7	10.1	9.9
Panama	24.8	25.7	26.6	26.8	32.3	n.a.	n.a.	n.a.	n.a.	n.a.
Poland	15.5	16.1	18.2	19.5	18.9	9.8	10.0	10.3	9.8	8.7
Portugal	11.9	12.0	12.8	16.4	19.1	9.6	9.3	9.6	9.9	10.4
Singapore	20.0	16.8	16.6	17.3	17.8	5.2	5.0	5.2	5.2	5.1
Spain	n.a.	n.a.	11.7	16.1	19.1	n.a.	n.a.	8.0	7.7	8.2
Sweden	13.3	12.5	11.8	11.7	12.6	11.4	11.1	11.3	11.0	10.8
Switzerland	12.2	11.8	11.6	11.3	12.3	9.2	9.2	9.2	9.2	8.7
Tunisia	27.5	n.a.	31.3	35.2	36.6	n.a.	n.a.	n.a.	n.a.	n.a.
United Kingdom	13.8	13.6	13.3	13.5	12.5	11.4	11.2	11.8	11.8	11.9
United States	15.9	15.7	15.7	16.2	14.0	8.8	8.7	8.7	8.9	8.9
Yugoslavia	15.0	15.3	15.9	17.0	18.2	9.0	9.2	9.1	9.0	8.7

NOTE: n.a. = not available. *Source:* United Nations, *Monthly Bulletin of Statistics,* May 1990.

Legal Abortions in Selected Countries, 1979–1987

Country	1979	1980	1981	1982	1983	1984	1985	1986	1987
Bulgaria	147,888	155,876	152,370	147,791	134,165	131,140	132,041	134,686	—
Canada	65,043	65,751	65,053	66,254	61,750	62,291	60,956	62,406	—
Cuba	106,549	103,974	108,559	126,745	116,956	139,588	138,671	160,926	—
Czechoslovakia	94,486	100,170	103,517	107,638	108,662	113,802	119,325	124,188	158,451
Denmark	23,193	23,334	22,779	21,462	20,791	20,742	19,919	20,067	20,830
Finland	15,849	15,037	14,120	13,861	13,360	13,645	13,832	13,310	—
France	156,810	171,218	180,695	181,122	182,862	180,789	173,335	166,797	161,036
Germany, West	82,788	87,702	87,353	91,064	86,529	86,298	83,538	84,274	88,540
Greece	137	117	109	—	220	193	180[1]	—	—
Hungary	80,767	80,882	78,421	78,682	78,599	82,191	81,970	83,586	84,547
Iceland	556	523	597	613	687	—	—	—	—
India	—	346,327	388,405	500,624	492,696	561,033	583,704	—	—
Israel	15,925	14,708	14,514	16,829	15,593	18,948	18,406	17,469	—
Italy	187,752	207,644	216,755	231,308	231,061	228,377	210,192	196,969	—
Netherlands	—	—	20,897	20,187	19,700	18,700[1]	17,300[1]	—	—
New Zealand	—	5,945	6,758	6,903	7,198	7,275	7,130	8,056	8,789
Norway	14,456	13,531	13,845	13,496	13,646	14,070	14,599	15,474	15,422
Poland	220,431	133,835	130,070	141,177	130,980	132,844	135,564	129,720	122,536
Singapore	16,999	18,219	18,890	15,548	19,100	22,190	23,512	21,374	—
Sweden	34,709	34,887	33,294	32,604	31,014	30,755	30,838	33,090	34,707
United Kingdom	128,365	136,782	171,455	171,417	170,620	179,102	180,983	157,168	165,542
United States	—	—	—	1,573,920[2]	—	1,577,180[2]	1,588,550[2]	—	1,559,110[2]

1. Provisional. 2 Figures are from The Alan Guttmacher Institute. NOTE: Data latest available as of August 1990. *Source:* United Nations, *Demographic Yearbook, 1988.*

Cost of Living of United Nations Personnel in Selected Cities as Reflected by Index of Retail Prices, 1989

(New York City, December 1989 = 100)

City	Index	City	Index	City	Index
Abu Dhabi	80 [1]	Dar es Salaam	75 [1]	Nassau	108
Addis Ababa	86 [1]	Geneva	117	New Delhi	70
Algiers	90 [1]	Guatemala City	76	Panama City	78
Amman	74	The Hague	94	Paris	100
Ankara	63	Helsinki	116	Port-au-Prince	89
Athens	77	Islamabad	67	Quito	64
Baghdad	128 [1]	Jakarta	86	Rabat	77
Bangkok	70	Kabul	105	Rome	98
Beirut	71	Kathmandu	50	Roseau	90
Belgrade	83	Kingston	62	San Salvador	70
Bogota	81	Kinshasa	86 [1]	Santiago	61
Bonn	108	La Paz	59	Seoul	110
Brazzaville	95 [1]	Lagos	78 [1]	Sofia	68
Brussels	90	Lima	77	Sydney	85
Budapest	49	London	96	Tokyo	129
Buenos Aires	65	Madrid	102	Tripoli	112 [1]
Cairo	83	Managua	65	Tunis	67
Caracas	79	Manila	73	Valetta	71
Colombo	65	Mexico City	70	Vienna	103
Copenhagen	107	Montevideo	77	Warsaw	36
Dhaka	66	Montreal	89	Washington, D.C.	91
Dakar	95	Nairobi	65	Yangon	92

1. Calculated on the basis of cost of Government or subsidized housing which is normally lower than prevailing rentals. *Source:* United Nations, *Monthly Bulletin of Statistics, March 1990.*

Consumer Price Indexes for Selected Countries

(1982-84 = 100)

Country	Total[1]		Food[2]		Clothing		Housing[3]		Transportation	
	1988	1980	1988	1980	1988	1980	1988	1980	1988	1980
Australia	143.3	75.8	140.5	78.2	144.7	82.0	146.8	75.0	n.a.	n.a.
Austria	113.8	85.3	111.1	87.3	115.1	91.3	112.2	82.3	113.9	84.1
Canada	123.2	76.1	121.4	80.2	119.1	85.4	121.1	74.7	119.3	70.6
France	124.2	72.3	121.3	71.4	136.7	75.7	121.5	70.3	124.3	71.9
Germany, West	106.2	86.7	102.8	87.8	109.6	88.6	104.9	85.5	104.2	85.7
Italy	141.9	64.0	136.7	66.3	151.6	65.2	138.1	61.9	135.1	63.1
Japan	105.7	90.9	104.3	91.4	114.1	90.1	112.7	90.7	101.9	92.2
Netherlands	105.8	85.9	101.9	88.3	103.2	91.2	105.9	80.8	108.2	85.2
Sweden	133.4	75.8	139.2	69.1	119.9	84.1	130.1	76.6	n.a.	n.a.
United Kingdom	125.6	78.5	118.9	82.2	113.0	96.3	132.2	74.9	119.4	79.9
United States	118.3	82.4	118.2	86.8	115.4	90.9	118.5	81.1	108.7	83.1

1. Includes other items not shown separately. 2. Restaurant meals, alcohol, and tobacco are included for some countries, excluded for others. 3. Includes shelter, utilities, and household furnishings and operations. However, actual coverage and measurements vary significantly from country to country. NOTE: n.a. = not available. *Source:* United States Department of Labor, Bureau of Labor Statistics. From *Statistical Abstract of the United States 1990.*

Labor Force Participation Rates by Sex[1]

Country	Female				Male				Females as percent of total labor force			
	1988	1987	1985	1980	1988	1987	1985	1980	1988	1987	1985	1980
Canada	52.6	50.9	48.5	46.2	70.9	70.1	68.7	73.0	43.8	43.2	42.7	39.7
France	n.a.	39.7	39.7	40.0	n.a.	61.1	62.2	68.6	n.a.	42.0	41.6	39.4
Germany, West	n.a.	36.6 [2]	35.5	36.7	n.a.	64.1 [2]	63.7	68.9	39.6 [2]	39.4 [2]	38.9	38.0
Italy	28.9 [2]	28.6 [2]	27.8	27.9	61.9 [2]	61.6 [2]	62.5	66.0	33.9 [2]	33.6	32.7	31.7
Japan	46.6	46.2	46.3	45.7	75.0	74.9	75.9	77.9	39.7	39.6	39.3	38.4
Sweden	62.2 [2]	61.6	59.7	58.0	71.5 [2]	71.0	70.5	73.6	47.9 [2]	47.7	47.1	45.1
United Kingdom	47.3 [2]	45.9 [2]	44.4 [2]	44.8	69.7 [2]	68.2 [2]	68.0 [2]	72.8	42.5 [2]	42.4 [2]	41.7 [2]	40.4
United States	53.4	52.5	50.4	47.7	72.0	71.5	70.9	72.0	45.0	44.8	44.1	42.4

1. Labor force of all ages as percent of population, 15–64 years old. 2. Preliminary. n.a. = not available. *Source: Statistical Abstract of the United States 1990.*

Unemployment Figures for Selected Countries: 1984-1989

(In thousands except for percentages)

Country	1989 No.	1989 %	1988 No.	1988 %	1987 No.	1987 %	1986 No.	1986 %	1985 No.	1985 %	1984 No.	1984 %
Australia	509.1	6.2	576.2	7.2	628.8	8.1	609.9	8.1	601.6	8.3	642.1	9.0
Austria[1]	149.2	5.0	158.6	5.3	164.5	5.6	152.0	5.2	139.5	4.8	130.5	4.5
Belgium[1 2 8]	419.3	n.a.	459.4	10.9	500.8	11.9	516.8	12.3	557.4	13.5	595.0	14.4
Canada	1,018.0	7.5	1,047.0	7.8	1,167.0	8.9	1,236.0	9.6	1,327.9	10.5	1,399.0	11.3
Chile	249.8	n.a.	285.8	8.1	343.6	7.9	374.3	8.8	273.4	17.0	285.0	18.4
Cyprus[1]	6.2	n.a.	7.4	n.a.	8.7	3.4	9.2	3.7	8.3	3.3	8.0	3.3
Denmark[1]	264.9	9.4	243.9	8.7	219.4	8.0	217.3	8.0	247.8	9.2	276.3	10.3
Finland[3]	89.0	3.5	116.0	4.5	130.0	5.1	140.0	5.4	163.2	6.3	158.0	6.2
Germany, West[1]	2,032.0	7.9	2,236.6	8.7	2,232.5	8.9	2,228.0	9.0	2,304.0	9.3	2,265.6	9.1
Hong-Kong	30.0	1.1	37.9	1.4	47.5	1.7	76.3	2.8	83.6	3.2	101.0	3.9
Ireland[4]	231.6	17.9	241.4	18.6	247.3	19.0	236.4	18.2	230.6	17.7	214.2	16.2
Israel[5]	n.a.	n.a.	100.0	6.4	90.0	6.1	104.0	7.1	97.0	6.7	85.0	5.9
Italy	2,865.0	12.0	2,885.0	12.0	2,832.0	12.0	2,611.0	11.1	2,471.0	10.6	2,391.0	10.4
Japan[3]	1,420.0	2.3	1,550.0	2.5	1,730.0	2.9	1,670.0	2.8	1,564.3	2.6	1,600.0	2.7
Korea[3]	459.0	2.6	435.0	2.5	519.0	3.1	611.0	3.8	619.0	4.0	567.0	3.8
Netherlands[1 6]	390.0	n.a.	682.2	n.a.	685.5	11.5	710.7	12.0	761.0	15.6	822.4	17.6
Norway	106.0	3.8	69.3	3.2	45.0	2.1	40.0	1.9	51.0	2.5	61.0	3.0
Philippines[7]	n.a.	n.a.	n.a.	n.a.	2,085.0	n.a.	1,438.0	6.4	1,316.0	6.1	1,231.0	6.1
Portugal	232.8	5.0	262.2	5.7	319.6	7.1	381.6	8.4	384.7	8.5	381.0	8.3
Puerto Rico[8]	n.a.	n.a.	158.0	15.0	171.0	16.8	188.0	18.9	211.0	21.8	198.0	20.7
Sweden	61.0	1.4	72.0	1.6	84.0	1.9	117.0	2.1	125.0	2.8	136.0	3.1
Switzerland[1 9]	17.5	0.6	22.2	0.7	24.7	0.8	25.7	0.8	30.3	1.0	35.2	1.1
United Kingdom[1 10]	1,800.5	6.4	2,370.4	8.4	2,953.4	10.6	3,289.1	11.9	3,271.2	13.5	3,159.8	13.1
United States	6,528.0	5.3	6,701.0	5.5	7,425.0	6.2	8,237.0	7.0	8,312.0	7.2	8,539.0	7.5
Yugoslavia[1]	1,201.2	14.9	1,131.8	14.1	1,080.6	13.6	1,086.7	13.9	1,040.0	13.8	974.8	13.3

1. Employment office statistics. All others labor force sample surveys unless otherwise indicated. 2. Scope of series revised as of 1985. 3. Scope of series revised as of 1986. 4. Excluding agriculture, fishing and private domestic services. 5. Including persons who did not work in the country during the previous 12 months. 6. Based on labor force sample surveys beginning 1988 and scope of series revised. 7. Average of less than 12 months. 8. Excluding people temporarily laid off. 9. Scope of series revised as of 1984. 10. Excluding persons temporarily laid off. Excluding adult students registered for vacation employment. NOTE: n.a.= not available. Source: United Nations, Monthly Bulletin of Statistics, July 1990.

Public Expenditure for Education for Selected Countries

Country	Year	Percent of total expenditure	Percent of GNP	Country	Year	Percent of total expenditure	Percent of GNP
Algeria	1987	27.8	9.8	Mexico	1987	n.a.	3.4
Argentina	1987	8.9[2]	1.9[2]	Morocco	1987	25.5	8.3
Australia	1986	12.6	5.8	Nepal	1985	10.8	2.8
Bangladesh	1986	10.5[2]	2.2[2]	Netherlands	1985	16.4	6.8
Brazil	1986	17.7	4.5	Nigeria	1986	12.0[6]	1.4[6]
Canada	1987	15.4	7.2	Philippines	1987	n.a.	2.0
Chile	1987	n.a.	3.6	Poland	1987	12.5	4.4
China	1985	n.a.	2.7	Portugal	1987	n.a.	4.5[2]
Czechoslovakia	1987	8.0	n.a.	Romania	1985	n.a.	2.1
Egypt	1987	n.a.	5.5	Soviet Union	1987	n.a.	7.3[4]
Ethiopia	1986	9.9	4.2	Spain	1987	n.a.	3.2
France	1986	n.a.	5.7[3]	Tanzania	1987	9.7	4.1
Germany, E.	1987	5.4[5]	5.1[45]	Thailand	1987	17.9	3.6
Germany, W.	1986	9.2	4.4	Turkey	1987	n.a.	1.7[1]
Hungary	1987	6.3	5.6	UK	1986	n.a.	5.0
India	1986	n.a.	3.4	US	1985	n.a.	6.7[7]
Indonesia	1981	9.3	2.0	Venezuela	1985	21.3	5.4
Italy	1986	8.6[2]	4.0[2]	Yugoslavia	1986	n.a.	3.8
Japan	1986	17.7	5.0	Zaire	1980	32.3[5]	3.4[5]
Korea, S.	1987	26.6	4.2	Zimbabwe	1986	16.2	8.5

1. Expenditure on third-level education is not included. 2. Ministry of Education expenditures only. 3. Metropolitan France only. 4. Percent of net material product. 5. Current expenditures only. 6. Federal government expenditures only. 7. Data refer to total public and private expenditures on education. n.a. = not available. NOTE: Expenditure includes both capital and current expenditures on public education and subsidized private education except as noted above. Source: United Nations Educational, Scientific and Cultural Organization, Paris, France, Statistical Yearbook (Copyright). From Statistical Abstract of the United States 1990.

Energy, Petroleum, and Coal, by Country

Country	Energy consumed[1] (coal equiv.) Total (mil. metric tons) 1987	1980	Per capita (kilograms) 1987	1980	Electric energy production[2] (bil. kwh) 1987	1980	Crude petroleum production[3] (mil. metric tons) 1987	1980	Coal production[4] (mil. metric tons) 1987	1980
Algeria	33.3	24.8	1,441	1,327	13.4	7.1	33.1	47.4	(Z)[5]	(Z)
Argentina	59.5	49.3	1,912	1,746	52.2	39.7	22.0	25.3	.4	.4
Australia[6]	110.6	91.2	6,845	6,195	132.2	96.1	25.1	18.9	147.8	72.5
Austria	30.1	30.5	4,018	4,058	50.2	42.0	1.1	1.5	(Z)	(Z)
Bahrain	6.8	4.4	14,680	12,651	3.0	1.7	2.0	2.4	n.a.	n.a.
Bangladesh	6.9	3.8	64	44	5.9	2.7	(Z)	(Z)	(X)	(X)
Belgium	55.1	59.1	5,560	5,997	62.4	53.6	(X)	(X)	4.4[7]	6.3
Brazil	108.5	92.5	767	763	202.3	139.5	28.5	9.1	6.9	5.2
Bulgaria	53.1	47.3	5,912	5,254	43.5	34.8	.3[5]	.3[5]	.2	.3
Canada	256.5	254.2	9,915	10,547	496.3	377.5	75.2	70.4	32.7	20.2
Chile	11.8	11.4	938	1,025	15.6	11.8	1.3	1.6	1.6	1.0
China	800.8	562.8	749	571	497.3	300.6	134.1	105.9	928.0	595.8
Colombia	24.5	23.8	817	923	35.4	22.9	19.4	6.5	14.6	4.9
Cuba	14.5	13.6	1,442	1,394	13.6	9.9	.9	.3	(X)	(X)
Czechoslovakia	98.2	97.4	6,311	6,364	85.8	72.7	.1	.1	25.7[7]	28.3[7]
Denmark	27.4	26.9	5,346	5,254	29.4	27.1	4.6	.3	(X)	(X)
Ecuador	6.2	5.7	627	708	5.7	3.4	8.9	10.4	n.a.	(NA)
Egypt	33.8	20.1	674	488	32.5	18.9	45.2	29.4	(X)	(X)
Ethiopia	1.2	.9	28	27	.8	.7	(X)	(X)	n.a.	(NA)
Finland	28.1	26.4	5,692	5,514	53.5[8]	38.7[8]	(X)	(X)	(X)	(X)
France[9]	206.9	237.3	3,720	4,409	356.2[8]	246.4[8]	3.2	1.2	16.3[7]	20.2[7]
Germany, East	131.3	121.8	7,891	7,276	114.2	98.8	(Z)	(Z)	(Z)	(Z)
Germany, West	342.0	359.4	5,624	5,829	415.8	368.8	3.8[10]	4.6	82.4	94.5
Greece	24.5	20.1	2,452	2,088	30.1	22.7	1.1	(Z)	(X)	(X)
Hong Kong	10.6	7.3	1,891	1,448	23.8	12.6	n.a.	(NA)	(X)	(X)
Hungary	40.5	40.6	3,819	3,787	29.7	23.9	1.9	2.0	2.4[7]	3.1[7]
India	220.5	139.4	275	202	217.5	119.3	30.1	9.4	177.0	109.1
Indonesia	47.2	34.7	274	230	34.8	14.2	64.6	77.6	1.7	.3
Iran[11]	65.9	45.7	1,285	1,177	37.9	22.4	113.4	72.7	1.2[5]	.9[5]
Iraq	12.5	10.7	735	807	22.9	11.4	101.8	130.1	n.a.	(NA)
Ireland	12.5	11.1	3,462	3,268	12.6	10.9	(X)	(X)	(Z)	.1
Israel	12.2	8.8	2,794	2,273	17.5	12.5	(X)	(Z)	(X)	(X)
Italy[12]	204.4	174.9	3,570	3,112	198.3	185.7	3.9	1.8	(Z)	(Z)[5]
Japan	456.1	434.8	3,741	3,726	699.0	577.5	.6[5]	.4	13.0	18.0
Korea, North	57.9	48.5	2,708	2,713	50.2	35.0	(X)	(X)	39.5[5]	36.0[5]
Korea, South	74.2	52.3	1,760	1,373	80.3	40.1	(X)	(X)	24.3	18.6
Kuwait[13]	17.1	6.9	9,191	5,019	18.4	9.4	61.4	84.1	n.a.	n.a.
Libya	11.0	7.3	3,023	2,456	14.3	4.8	46.8	88.3	(X)	(X)
Malaysia	20.8	12.2	1,283	882	17.4	10.2	24.3	13.2	(X)	(X)
Mexico	140.9	118.6	1,697	1,709	104.8[8]	67.0[8]	132.1	99.9	11.1	7.0
Morocco	7.8	6.4	336	319	7.1	4.9	(Z)[5]	(Z)	.8	.7
Myanmar	2.7	2.2	68	62	2.3	1.3	1.0	1.6	(Z)	(Z)
Netherlands	106.0	93.0	7,265	6,543	68.4	64.8	4.3	1.3	(Z)[5][14]	(Z)
New Zealand[18]	12.7	10.0	3,858	3,152	27.0	22.0	1.3	.3	2.1[5]	2.0
Nigeria	16.9	11.0	166	136	9.9	7.2	62.1	104.2	.1[5]	.2
Norway[15]	28.3	26.3	6,782	6,423	103.8	84.1	47.8	24.6	.4	.3
Pakistan	27.8	16.6	250	191	33.5	15.3	2.0	.5	2.4	1.5
Peru	11.7	12.0	564	693	14.2	9.8	8.8	9.6	.2[5]	.1[5]
Philippines	15.4	16.7	265	346	23.9	17.9	.3	.5	1.2	.3
Poland	181.5	176.8	4,810	4,935	145.8	121.9	.1	.3	193.0	193.1
Portugal	13.6	11.2	1,329	1,153	20.1	15.3	(X)	(X)	.3	.2
Romania	106.1	100.0	4,624	4,505	73.1	67.5	10.2[5]	11.5	8.8[5]	8.1
Saudi Arabia[13]	79.4	25.3	6,322	2,745	37.1	18.9	198.1	495.9	n.a.	n.a.
South Africa[16]	107.6	90.2	2,816	2,751	122.5	90.4	(X)	(X)	177.3	116.6
Soviet Union	1,867.2	1,473.1	6,634	5,549	1,664.9	1,293.9	624.0	603.2	519.1	492.9
Spain	81.9	88.4	2,106	2,359	133.2	110.5	1.6	1.6	14.5[7]	13.1[7]
Sudan	1.5	1.5	64	82	1.1	1.0	(X)	(X)	(X)	(X)
Sweden	41.8	44.5	5,004	5,376	146.6	96.7	(Z)	(Z)	(Z)	(Z)
Switzerland[17]	24.8	23.3	3,794	3,636	57.0[8]	48.1[8]	(X)	(X)	(X)	(X)
Syria	11.5	7.3	1,025	835	7.2	3.8	12.2	8.3	(X)	(X)
Taiwan[19]	n.a.	37.9	n.a.	2,127	n.a.	42.0	n.a.	.2	(X)	2.6
Tanzania	.9	.8	38	44	.9	.7	(X)	(X)	(Z)	(Z)
Thailand	26.3	17.3	493	372	30.0	15.1	1.0	(Z)	(Z)	(Z)
Trinidad and Tobago	7.1	7.5	5,770	6,992	3.3	2.0	8.1	11.0	n.a.	n.a.

Country	Energy consumed[1] (coal equiv.) Total (mil. metric tons)		Per capita (kilograms)		Electric energy production[2] (bil. kwh)		Crude petroleum production[3] (mil. metric tons)		Coal production[4] (mil. metric tons)	
	1987	1980	1987	1980	1987	1980	1987	1980	1987	1980
Tunisia	5.0	4.1	651	639	4.5	2.8	5.0	5.6	(X)	(X)
Turkey	52.4	31.9	998	718	44.4	23.3	2.6	2.3	3.5	3.6
United Arab Emirates	27.4	16.8	18,832	17,188	13.1	6.3	72.1	82.8	n.a.	n.a.
United Kingdom	290.8	271.0	5,107	4,850	300.2	284.9	117.6	78.9	104.4[7]	130.1[7]
United States	2,322.9	2,364.5	9,542	10,386	2,686[8]	2,354	418.6	424.2	761.1	710.4
Venezuela	55.1	49.0	3,018	3,140	54.7	35.9	95.5	114.8	.1	(Z)
Vietnam	7.4	6.6	118	122	5.3	3.8	n.a.	n.a.	5.6	5.2
Yugoslavia	56.7	48.0	2,423	2,152	80.8	59.4	3.9	4.2	.4	.4
Zaire	2.1	2.0	64	69	5.3	4.2	1.3[5]	1.0	(Z)[5]	.1
Zambia	1.9	2.3	248	403	8.5[8]	9.2	(X)	(X)	.5	.6
World, total	9,653.6	8,544.3	1,921	1,919	10,467	8,247	2,787	2,979	3,334	2,728

n.a. = not available. X = Not applicable. Z = Less than 50,000 metric tons. 1. Based on apparent consumption of coal, lignite, petroleum products, natural gas, and hydro, nuclear, and geothermal electricity. 2. Comprises production by utilities generating primarily for public use, and production by industrial establishments generating primarily for own use. Relates to production at generating centers, including station use and transmission losses. 3. Includes shale oil, but excludes natural gasoline. 4. Excludes lignite and brown coal, except as noted. 5. United Nations Statistical Office estimate. 6. For year ending June 30 of year shown. 7. Includes slurries. 8. Net production, i.e. excluding station use. 9. Includes Monaco. 10. Includes inputs other than crude petroleum and natural gas liquids. 11. For year ending March 20 of year shown. 12. Includes San Marino. 13. Includes share of production and consumption in the Neutral Zone. 14. Includes patent fuel and hard coal briquettes. 15. Includes Svalbard and Jan Mayen Islands. 16. Includes Botswana, Lesotho, Namibia, and Swaziland. 17. Includes Liechtenstein. 18. For year ending March 31 for year shown. 19. *Source:* U.S. Bureau of the Census. Data from Republic of China publications. *Source:* Except as noted, Statistical Office of the United Nations, New York, N.Y., *Energy Statistics Yearbook, 1986* (copyright). From: *Statistical Abstract of the United States, 1990.*

Wheat, Rice, and Corn—Production for Selected Countries

(in thousands of metric tons)

Country	Wheat			Rice			Corn		
	1986	1985	1984	1986	1985	1984	1986	1985	1984
Argentina	8,900	8,700	13,220	405	410	476	12,400	11,530	9,500
Australia	17,356	16,127	18,666	687	864	632	228	291	238
Belgium[2]	1,265[1]	1,215	1,330	n.a.	n.a.	n.a.	58[1]	90[1]	53
Brazil	5,433	4,323	1,983	10,399	9,019	9,027	20,510	22,020	21,164
Canada	31,850	24,252	21,199	n.a.	n.a.	n.a.	6,694	7,472	7,024
China: Mainland[3]	89,002	85,812	87,817	177,000	171,417	181,193	65,560	64,056	73,600
Egypt	1,929	1,872	1,815	2,450[1]	2,310	2,236	3,801[1]	3,982[1]	3,170
France	26,587	28,890	32,977	60	62	36	10,792	12,409	10,493
Germany, West	10,406	9,866	10,223	n.a.	n.a.	n.a.	1,302	1,204	1,026
Greece	2,200	1,789	2,308	102	103	92	2,070	1,948	2,091
Hungary	5,803	6,578	7,392	44	38	33	7,214	6,818	6,686
India	46,885	44,069	45,476	90,000	96,306	87,553	8,000	6,890	8,442
Indonesia	n.a.	n.a.	.n.a.	39,275	39,033	38,136	5,767	4,330	5,288
Iran	7,128	6,661	5,500[3]	1,569	1,523	1,600	50[3]	50[1]	50[1]
Iraq	1,100[1]	1,406	471	145[1]	149	109	36[1]	41	30
Italy	9,070	8,516	10,057	1,082	1,123	1,009	6,560	6,309	6,672
Japan	876	874	741	14,559	14,578	14,848	1	2	2
Korea, South	5[1]	11	17	7,790	7,855	7,970	113	132	133
Mexico	4,772	5,207	4,505	523	809	484	12,154	13,957	12,910
Myanmar	246	206	214	15,000[3]	15,219	14,255	350[3]	323	303
Pakistan	13,923	11,703	10,882	5,241	4,437	4,973	1,067	1,009	1,028
Soviet Union	92,300	78,100	68,600	2,600	2,570	2,720	12,500	14,400	13,600
Sweden	1,714	1,338	1,776	n.a.	n.a.	n.a.	n.a.	n.a.	n.a.
Thailand	n.a.	n.a.	n.a.	19,100	20,264	19,905	4,197	4,934	4,226
United Kingdom	13,874	12,046	14,970	n.a.	n.a.	n.a.	1[3]	1[3]	1[3]
United States	56,792	65,999	70,618	6,097	6,120	6,296	209,632	225,478	194,928
Vietnam	n.a.	n.a.	n.a.	16,197	15,875	15,506	600[1]	600	525
Yugoslavia	4,776	4,859	5,595	48	36	36	12,502	9,896	11,312
World, total	535,842	506,034	516,457	475,533	474,728	470,284	480,609	488,325	452,753

1. Unofficial figure. 2. Includes Luxembourg. 3. FAO estimate. NOTES: Rice data cover rough and paddy. Data for each country pertain to the calendar year in which all or most of the crop was harvested. n.a. = not available. *Source:* Food and Agriculture Organization of the United Nations, Rome, Italy, 1986. *FAO Production Yearbook, vol. 40* (copyright). From: *Statistical Abstract of the United States, 1990.*

Wheat, Rice and Corn Exports and Imports, 1985-1987

(in thousands of metric tons. Countries listed are the 10 leading exporters or importers in 1987)

Exporters	1985	1986	1987	Importers	1985	1986	1987
WHEAT				**WHEAT**			
United States	24,810	24,555	30,638	Soviet Union	20,309	15,745	18,097
Canada	17,007	15,957	22,140	China: Mainland	6,135	6,883	14,050
Australia	15,704	16,109	14,789	Japan	5,510	5,620	5,476
France	16,943	13,367	14,220	Egypt	4,524	4,329	5,162
Argentina	9,583	4,021	4,197	Italy	4,534	5,259	4,617
United Kingdom	1,886	3,987	4,122	South Korea	2,986	3,449	4,121
West Germany	1,045	2,143	2,262	Iran	2,144	1,908	3,600
Soviet Union	1,250	1,181	1,480	Iraq	2,096	2,185	2,900
Hungary	2,002	1,670	1,281	Brazil	4,041	2,255	2,749
Sweden	626	466	691	Poland	1,703	1,662	2,343
RICE				**RICE**			
Thailand	4,062	4,524	4,443	Iran	539	493	800
United States	1,940	2,392	2,472	Soviet Union	321	493	599
Pakistan	719	1,316	1,240	China: Mainland	213	326	559
China: Mainland	1,046	1,123	1,202	Iraq	500	550	524
Italy	727	676	610	Vietnam	422	500	450
Myanmar	452	636	486	Ivory Coast	342	361	401
India	250	200	350	Nigeria	356	320	400
North Korea	200	200	225	Saudi Arabia	428	375	381
Uruguay	242	270	204	Hong Kong	378	368	373
Australia	341	178	186	Senegal	336	378	307
CORN				**CORN**			
United States	44,033	27,099	40,906	Japan	14,225	14,653	16,504
France	4,456	5,799	6,305	Soviet Union	16,600	7,236	9,238
Argentina	7,069	7,411	3,963	China: Mainland	3,108	3,659	5,249
China: Mainland	6,338	5,642	3,917	South Korea	3,406	3,671	4,566
South Africa	400	1,800	2,350	Mexico	1,726	1,704	3,603
Thailand	2,752	3,981	1,628	Egypt	1,907	2,028	2,200
Yugoslavia	900	1,798	1,166	Netherlands	2,374	1,977	1,760
Belgium-Luxembourg	656	364	604	Belgium-Luxembourg	1,930	1,466	1,729
Spain	2	60	459	United Kingdom	1,455	1,482	1,471
Greece	209	580	368	Malaysia	1,182	1,204	1,302

—Represents or rounds to zero. *Source:* U.S. Dept. of Agriculture, Economic Research Service. Data from Food and Agriculture Organization of the United Nations, Rome, Italy, *FOA Trade Yearbook*. From *Statistical Abstract of the United States 1990.*

Passenger Car Production[1]

(in thousands, monthly averages)

Country	1988	1987	1986	1985	1984	1983	1982
Argentina[2]	—	—	11.7	9.6	11.9	11.0	9.2
Australia[2]	26.2	25.2	26.5	31.8	28.4	30.3	31.3
Austria	0.6	0.6	0.6	0.6	0.6	0.5	0.6
Brazil[2]	32.9	33.1	39.9	38.3	55.5	57.1	57.2
Canada	84.0	—	88.4	89.6	86.1	80.9	67.3
Czechoslovakia	13.7	14.5	15.4	15.2	15.0	14.9	14.5
France	261.5	248.5	227.7	232.0	242.5	269.0	257.2
Germany, East	18.2	18.1	18.2	17.5	16.8	15.7	15.2
Germany, West	359.1	361.7	356.1	347.1	315.3	322.9	314.3
India	14.5	12.9	10.8	7.8	7.3	5.7	5.3
Italy	157.0	142.7	136.9	112.8	119.7	116.3	108.0
Japan	683.3	657.6	650.9	637.1	589.4	596.0	573.5
Korea, South[2]	72.3	64.8	38.1	21.8	13.9	10.7	8.3
Mexico[2]	—	19.0	16.5	23.8	20.6	17.8	27.0
Netherlands	10.0	10.4	9.9	9.0	9.1	8.9	7.6
Poland	24.5	24.5	24.2	23.6	23.2	22.4	19.0
Romania	—	—	10.3	11.2	10.4	7.5	8.7
Spain	131.3	119.3	108.2	101.4	94.8	92.5	78.7
Sweden	—	—	34.6	33.4	26.2	31.2	26.9
U.S.S.R.	—	108.3	109.9	111.0	110.6	109.6	108.9
United Kingdom	102.2	95.2	84.9	87.3	75.8	87.1	74.0
United States[3]	592.1	590.4	626.3	666.8	635.2	565.1	422.8
Yugoslavia	25.8[2]	25.8[2]	17.5	19.1	15.6	14.0	13.2

1. Vehicles built on imported chassis or assembled from imported parts are excluded except for those countries marked. 2. Including assembly. 3. Factory sales. *Source:* United Nations, *Monthly Bulletin of Statistics, January 1990.*

Meat—Production by Country
(in thousands of metric tons)

Country	1980	1985	1987, est.	Country	1980	1985	1987, est.
Argentina	3,220	3,077	2,951	Mexico	2,044	2,289	2,125
Australia[1]	2,332	2,086	2,373	Poland	2,397	2,192	2,502
Brazil	3,115	3,045	3,003	Soviet Union	12,698	14,050	15,210
China	12,664	18,443	20,136	United Kingdom	2,305	2,419	2,440
France	3,823	3,733	3,853	United States	17,680	17,874	17,564
Italy	2,305	2,462	2,413	West Germany	4,759	4,845	5,095
Japan	1,893	2,087	2,155	**World, total**	104,535	115,537	119,724

1. Year ending June 30. NOTE: Covers beef and veal (incl. buffalo meat), pork (incl. bacon and ham), and mutton and lamb (incl. goat meat). Refers to meat from animals slaughtered within the national boundaries irrespective of origin of animals, and relates to commercial and farm slaughter. In terms of carcass weight. Excludes lard, tallow, and edible offals. NOTE: Data are most recent available. *Source:* Statistical Office of the United Nations, New York, NY, *Statistical Yearbook.* (Copyright.) From: *Statistical Abstract of the United States 1990.*

Crude Steel Production and Consumption

	Production (mil. metric tons)			Consumption					
				Total (mil. metric tons)			Per capita (kilograms)		
Country	1987	1986	1985	1987	1986	1985	1987	1986	1985
Argentina	3.6	3.1	2.7	3.0	n.a.	n.a.	95	n.a.	n.a.
Australia	6.1	6.7	6.3[1]	5.8	5.8	5.8	354	363	366
Austria	0.2	0.2	0.3	1.7	2.1	1.8	229	274	235
Bangladesh	0.1	0.1	0.1	0.5	0.3	0.5	5	3	5
Belgium	9.8	9.7	10.7	2.5	0.7	2.8[2]	244	64	275[2]
Brazil	12.0	11.3	11.4	14.0	n.a.	n.a.	99	n.a.	n.a.
Bulgaria	3.0	3.0	2.9	3.4	2.3	3.0	381	258	336
Canada	14.6	14.0	13.4	13.0	11.4	11.9	507	443	471
China: Mainland	56.3	52.2	46.8	69.7	66.2	66.6	64	64	63
Czechoslovakia	15.4	15.1	15.0	11.0	10.3	11.0	703	665	709
France	17.7	17.6	18.8	14.4	14.2	14.2	259	257	258
Germany, East	8.2	8.0	7.9	9.7	4.1	9.5	581	249	574
Germany, West	35.9	36.7	40.1	28.0	28.1	29.3	457	460	481
Greece	0.9	0.9	1.0	1.9	1.7	1.6	189	175	164
India	12.0	11.3	11.0	16.0	n.a.	n.a.	20	n.a.	n.a.
Italy	22.7	22.7	23.7	22.8	20.6	20.7	397	360	362
Japan	97.9	97.6	104.4	71.0	60.3	66.7	582	496	553
Korea, North	6.5	6.5	6.5	6.8	9.2	8.4	316	441	413
Korea, South	2.6	4.1	4.9	13.0	n.a.	n.a.	308	n.a.	n.a.
Mexico	7.0	6.9	7.2	7.6	8.1	8.3	93	102	105
Netherlands	1.8	3.0	3.4	3.9	3.7	4.4	263	254	305
Nigeria	0.2	0.2	0.3	0.8	0.5	0.9	8	5	9
Poland	15.6	15.7	14.8	15.9	15.0	15.2	422	400	409
Romania	13.9	13.5	13.0	n.a.	10.4	10.9	n.a.	451	480
South Africa	8.9	8.0	8.5	6.3	n.a.	n.a.	164	n.a.	n.a.
Soviet Union	161.9	160.6	154.7	164.6	n.a.	n.a.	582	n.a.	n.a.
Spain	11.5	12.0	14.6	8.3	8.0	9.9	214	208	257
Sweden	4.7	4.7	4.8	3.5	3.4	3.2	421	406	384
Turkey	7.0	6.0	4.7	7.7	n.a.	n.a.	149	n.a.	n.a.
United Kingdom	17.2	14.5	15.5	14.7	12.9	14.4	259	227	254
United States	80.9	74.0	80.1[3]	102.9	89.3	107.3	417	370	448
Venezuela	3.7	3.4	3.1	4.1	3.7	3.2	227	208	186
Yugoslavia	1.9	2.0	2.0	4.0	5.1	5.1	170	218	221
World	681.1	665.0	673.5	n.a.	n.a.	n.a.	n.a.	n.a.	n.a.

1. Year ending June 30. 2. Luxembourg included with Belgium. 3. Excludes steel for castings made in foundries operated by companies not producing ingots. n.a. = not available. NOTE: Production data cover both ingots and steel for castings and exclude wrought (puddled) iron. Consumption data represent apparent consumption (i.e. production plus imports minus exports) and do not take into account changes in stock. *Source:* Statistical Office of the United Nations, New York, NY, *Statistical Yearbook.* (Copyright.) From *Statistical Abstract of the United States 1990.* NOTE: Figures are latest available.

Quinoa—Wonder Grain for the 1990s

More than 500 years ago the Incas fed a thriving civilization with a crop they believed had magical powers. Today health-conscious consumers worldwide have discovered the magic is simple nutrition. Quinoa (pronounced keen-wha) has become a key source of income and food for Ecuadorean villagers since CARE helped reintroduce the crop several years ago. *Source: CARE World Report.*

Value of Exports and Imports
(in millions of U.S. dollars)

Country	Exports[1]	Imports[1]	Country	Exports[1]	Imports[1]
Afghanistan	$433[2]	$900[2]	Libya	$8,766[3]	$4,723[3]
Algeria	8,186[3]	7,029[3]	Madagascar	274[2]	364[2]
Argentina	9,135[2]	5,322[2]	Malawi	268	503
Australia	36,923	40,030	Malaysia	25,080	22,558
Austria	32,429	38,873	Mali	251[2]	513[2]
Bahamas	2,545[3]	3,233[3]	Malta	714[2]	1,354[2]
Bahrain	2,689	2,866	Mauritania	428[3]	235[3]
Bangladesh	1,305	2,729[2]	Mauritius	979[2]	1,286[2]
Barbados	186	673	Mexico	20,658[2]	18,954[2]
Belgium-Luxembourg	101,261	99,675	Morocco	3,603[2]	4,772[2]
Benin	167[4]	288[4]	Myanmar	215	191
Bolivia	597[2]	595[2]	Netherlands	107,877	104,266
Brazil	34,392	18,281	New Zealand	8,867	8,781
Bulgaria	17,223[2]	16,582[2]	Nicaragua	300[3]	923[3]
Burkina Faso	142[2]	489[2]	Nigeria	7,383[3]	3,917[3]
Burundi	78	179	Norway	27,061	23,676
Cameroon	924[2]	1,271[2]	Oman	3,933	2,255
Canada	116,013	113,975	Pakistan	4,642	7,119
Cape Verde	3[2]	106[2]	Panama	280[2]	795[2]
Central African Republic	131[5]	252[5]	Papua-New Guinea	1,281	1,535
Chile	7,048[2]	4,924[2]	Paraguay	607[2]	555[2]
Colombia	4,873[2]	4,564[2]	Peru	2,672[2]	2,556[2]
Congo	673[5]	528[5]	Phillippines	7,747	10,732
Costa Rica	1,362	1,743	Poland	13,155	10,085
Cuba	5,518[2]	7,579[2]	Portugal	12,669	18,886
Cyprus	810	2,281	Qatar	3,541[6]	1,139[6]
Czechoslovakia	14,455	14,277	Romania	12,543[3]	10,590[3]
Denmark	26,913	27,744	Rwanda	130[3]	357[3]
Dominican Republic	892[2]	1,840[2]	Saudi Arabia	23,737[2]	21,784[2]
Ecuador	2,165	1,714	Senegal	606[3]	1,023[3]
Egypt	8,150	23,527	Sierra Leone	137	189
El Salvador	566[2]	1,049[2]	Singapore	44,678	49,676
Ethiopia	446[2]	1,075[2]	Solomon Islands	64[3]	79[3]
Fiji	416	694	Somalia	104[3]	132[3]
Finland	23,289	24,570	Spain	44,424	71,429
France	178,846	192,484	Sri Lanka	1,554	2,109
Gabon	1,271[5]	866[5]	Sudan	509[2]	1,060[2]
Gambia	40[3]	127[3]	Suriname	301[3]	294[3]
Germany, East	32,206[2]	31,129[2]	Sweden	51,545	48,897
Germany, West	343,195	271,175	Switzerland	51,549	58,221
Ghana	1,014[2]	907[2]	Syria	3,006	2,046
Greece	5,307[2]	12,015[2]	Tanzania	276[2]	823[2]
Guatemala	323	404	Thailand	15,952[2]	20,285[2]
Guyana	207[6]	255[6]	Togo	242[2]	487[2]
Haiti	200[2]	344[2]	Tonga	9	54
Honduras	782[3]	903[3]	Trinidad	1,404[2]	1,123[2]
Hungary	9,584	8,803	Tunisia	3,027	4,378
Iceland	1,409	1,396	Turkey	7,952	11,065
India	15,982	18,998	Uganda	386[4]	—[4]
Indonesia	19,218[2]	13,249[2]	U.S.S.R.	109,212	114,550
Iran	20,247[7]	18,296[7]	United Arab Emirates	15,837[5]	5,838[5]
Iraq	9,785[7]	6,636[7]	U.K.	152,447	197,728
Ireland	20,974	17,564	U.S.	364,080	487,900
Israel	10,318	12,706	Uruguay	1,405[2]	1,177[2]
Italy	138,503	152,913	Vanuatu	20[2]	71[2]
Ivory Coast	3,110[3]	2,241[3]	Venezuela	8,475[2]	11,476[2]
Jamaica	967	1,801	Western Samoa	12	67
Japan	275,173	210,840	Yemen, Democratic	81[2]	653[2]
Jordan	926	2,119	Yemen, Arab	31[3]	887[3]
Kenya	1,071[2]	1,993[2]	Yugoslavia	13,363	14,802
Korea, South	62,375	61,448	Zaire	1,120[2]	764[2]
Kuwait	7,161[2]	5,565[2]	Zambia	1,178[2]	839[2]
Liberia	382[3]	308[3]	Zimbabwe	1,419[2]	1,046[2]

1. 1989 unless otherwise indicated. 2. 1988. 3. 1987. 4. 1984. 5. 1986. 6. 1985. 7. 1983 *Source:* United Nations, *Monthly Bulletin of Statistics,* July 1990.

Countries of the World by Groupings

KEY

1—Member of the Organization of American States (OAS)
2—Member of the Organization of African Unity (OAU)
3—Member of the Organization of Petroleum Exporting Countries (OPEC)
4—Member of the North Atlantic Treaty Organization (NATO)
5—Member of the Association of Southeast Asian Nations (ASEAN)
6—African States associated with EEC (EAMA)
7—Member of the Arab League
8—Member of the Warsaw Pact
9—Member of the European Economic Community (EEC)
10—Member of the European Free Trade Association (EFTA)
11—Member of British Commonwealth of Nations
12—Member of the Economic Community of West African States (ECOWAS)
13—Member of the Organization for Economic Cooperation and Development (OECD)
14—Member of Inter-American Treaty of Reciprocal Assistance (Rio Pact)
15—Member of the Nonaligned Movement

NORTH AMERICA

Canada: 4, 11, 13
Mexico: 1, 14
United States: 1, 4, 13, 14

SOUTH AMERICA

Argentina: 1, 14, 15
Bolivia: 1, 14, 15
Brazil: 1, 14
Chile: 1, 14
Colombia: 1, 14
Ecuador: 1, 3, 14, 15
Guyana: 11, 15
Paraguay: 1, 14
Peru: 1, 14, 15
Suriname: 1, 15
Uruguay: 1, 14
Venezuela: 1, 3, 14

CENTRAL AMERICA

Belize: 11, 15
Costa Rica: 1, 14
El Salvador: 1, 14
Guatemala: 1, 14
Honduras: 1, 14
Nicaragua: 1, 14, 15
Panama: 1, 14, 15

CARIBBEAN REGION

Antigua and Barbuda: 11
Bahamas: 11
Barbados: 1, 11, 15
Cuba: 15
Dominica: 1, 11
Dominican Republic: 1, 14
Grenada: 1, 11, 15
Haiti: 1, 14
Jamaica: 1, 11, 15
St. Kitts and Nevis: 1, 11
St. Lucia: 1, 11, 15
St. Vincent and the Grenadines: 11
Trinidad and Tobago: 1, 11, 14, 15

EUROPE

Albania
Andorra
Austria: 10, 13
Belgium: 4, 9, 13
Bulgaria: 8
Cyprus: 11
Czechoslovakia: 8
Denmark: 4, 9, 13
Finland: 10 (assoc. mem.), 13
France: 4, 9, 13
Germany, East: 8
Germany, West: 4, 9, 13
Greece: 4, 9, 13
Hungary: 8
Iceland: 4, 10, 13
Ireland: 9, 13
Italy: 4, 9, 13
Liechtenstein
Luxembourg: 4, 9, 13
Malta: 11, 15
Monaco
Netherlands: 4, 9, 13
Norway: 4, 10, 13
Poland: 8
Portugal: 4, 9, 10, 13
Romania: 8
San Marino
Spain: 4, 9, 13
Sweden: 10, 13
Switzerland, 10, 13
U.S.S.R.: 8
United Kingdom: 4, 9, 11, 13
Vatican City State
Yugoslavia: 15

MIDDLE EAST

Bahrain: 7, 15
Iran: 3, 15
Iraq: 3, 7, 15
Israel: 15
Jordan: 7, 15
Kuwait: 3, 7, 15
Lebanon: 7, 15
Oman: 7, 15
Qatar: 3, 7, 15
Saudi Arabia: 3, 7, 15
Syria: 7, 15
Turkey: 4, 9 (assoc. mem.), 13
United Arab Emirates: 3, 7, 15
Yemen: 7, 15

FAR EAST

China, People's Republic of
China, Republic of
Japan: 13
Korea, North: 15
Korea, South
Mongolia
Philippines: 5

SOUTHEAST ASIA

Brunei: 11
Cambodia
Indonesia: 3, 5, 15
Laos: 15
Malaysia: 5, 11, 15
Singapore: 5, 11, 15
Thailand: 5
Vietnam: 15

SOUTH ASIA

Afghanistan: 15
Bangladesh: 11, 15
Bhutan: 15
India: 11, 15
Maldives: 11, 15
Myanmar
Nepal: 15
Pakistan: 15
Sri Lanka: 11, 15

OCEANIA

Australia: 11, 13
Fiji: 11
Kiribati: 11
Nauru: 11[1]
New Zealand: 11, 13
Papua New Guinea: 11
Solomon Islands: 11
Tonga: 11
Tuvalu: 11[1]
Vanuatu (New Hebrides) 11
Western Samoa: 11

AFRICA

Algeria: 2, 3, 7, 15
Angola: 2, 15
Benin: 2, 12, 15
Bophuthatswana
Botswana: 2, 11, 15
Burkina Faso: 2, 6, 15
Burundi: 2, 15
Cameroon: 2, 6, 15
Cape Verde: 2, 15
Central African Republic: 2, 15
Chad: 2, 15
Comoro Islands: 2, 15
Congo: 2, 15
Djibouti: 2, 7, 15
Egypt: 2, 15
Equatorial Guinea: 2, 15
Ethiopia: 2, 15
Gabon: 2, 3, 15
Gambia: 2, 11, 12, 15
Ghana: 2, 11, 12, 15
Guinea: 2, 12, 15
Guinea-Bissau: 2, 15
Ivory Coast: 2, 12, 15
Kenya: 2, 11, 15
Lesotho: 2, 11, 15
Liberia: 2, 12, 15
Libya: 2, 3, 7, 15
Madagascar: 2, 15
Malawi: 6, 11, 15
Mali: 2, 12, 15
Mauritania: 2, 7, 15
Mauritius: 2, 11, 15
Morocco: 6, 7, 15
Mozambique: 2, 15
Niger: 6, 12, 15
Nigeria: 2, 3, 11, 12, 15
Rwanda: 2, 15
São Tomé and Príncipe: 2, 15
Senegal: 2, 6, 12, 15
Seychelles: 2, 11, 15
Sierra Leone: 2, 11, 12, 15
Somalia: 2, 6, 7, 15
South Africa, Rep. of: 15
Sudan: 2, 7, 15
Swaziland: 2, 11, 15
Tanzania: 2, 11, 15
Togo: 2, 6, 12, 15
Transkei
Tunisia: 2, 7, 15
Uganda: 2, 11, 15
Venda
Zaire: 2, 6, 15
Zambia: 2, 11, 15
Zimbabwe: 2, 11, 15

1. Special status.

COUNTRIES OF THE WORLD

(For late reports, see Current Events of 1990)

AFGHANISTAN

Republic of Afghanistan
President: Lt. Gen. Najibullah (1986)
Area: 250,000 sq mi. (647,500 sq km)
Population (est. mid-1990): 15,900,000 (Average annual rate of natural increase: 2.6%)
Density per square mile: 59
Capital: Kabul
Largest cities (est. 1983): Kabul, 750,000; Kandahar, 225,000; Herat, 150,000
Monetary unit: Afghani
Languages: Pushtu and Dari Persian (both official)
Religion: Islam (Sunni, 74%; Shiite, 25%; other 1%)
National name: Jamhouri Afghanistan
Literacy rate: 12%
Economic summary: Gross domestic product (1988): $3.1 billion, $220 per capita. Average annual growth rate (1976–79): 2.5%. Arable land: 12%; labor force: 4,980,000; principal products: wheat, cotton, fruits, nuts, wool. Labor force in industry: 10.2%; major products: carpets and textiles. Natural resources: natural gas, oil, coal, copper, sulfur, lead, zinc, iron, salt, precious and semi-precious stones. Exports: fresh and dried fruits, nuts, natural gas, carpets. Imports: petroleum products and food supplies. Major trading partners: U.S.S.R., Soviet bloc countries, Japan, and China.

Geography. Afghanistan, approximately the size of Texas, lies wedged between the U.S.S.R., China, Pakistan, and Iran. The country is split east to west by the Hindu Kush mountain range, rising in the east to heights of 24,000 feet (7,315 m). With the exception of the southwest, most of the country is covered by high snow-capped mountains and is traversed by deep valleys.

Government. A Marxist "people's republic" was created by Noor Taraki's coup of April 27, 1978. In May 1986, Lt. Gen. Najibullah, head of the secret police, became general secretary of the Central Committee of the People's Democratic Party of Afghanistan, replacing Babrak Karmal. Najibullah became President in Nov. 1986.

History. Darius I and Alexander the Great were the first conquerors to use Afghanistan as the gateway to India. Islamic conquerors arrived in the 7th century and Genghis Khan and Tamerlane followed in the 13th and 14th centuries.

In the 19th century, Afghanistan became a battleground in the rivalry of imperial Britain and Czarist Russia for the control of Central Asia. The Afghan Wars (1838–42 and 1878–81) fought against the British by Dost Mohammed and his son and grandson ended in defeat.

Afghanistan regained autonomy by the Anglo-Russian agreement of 1907 and full independence by the Treaty of Rawalpindi in 1919. Emir Amanullah founded the kingdom in 1926.

Taraki's attempts to create a Marxist state with Soviet aid brought armed resistance from conservative Muslim opposition.

Taraki was succeeded by Prime Minister Hafizullah Amin. Amin was replaced by Babrak Karmal, who had called for Soviet troops under a mutual defense treaty. Pakistan and other Moslem nations called for a U.N. Security Council session and charged that Amin had been executed on Dec. 27 by Soviet troops already present in Kabul. The Council's call for immediate withdrawal of Soviet troops was vetoed by the U.S.S.R. on Jan. 8, 1980.

The Soviet invasion was met with unanticipated fierce resistance from the Afghan population, resulting in a bloody war. Soviet troops were estimated by Western sources to number about 110,000 in Afghanistan. Pitted against the Soviets' bombers, helicopter gunships, heavy artillery and mechanized infantry were upward of 90,000 Afghan tribesmen who called themselves "mujahedeen," or "holy warriors." In the early fighting, many of the guerrillas were armed only with flintlock rifles, but later they acquired more modern weapons, including rockets that they used to attack Soviet installations.

Soviet saturation bombing has demolished many villages in several regions of the country. The nation's population was reported to have shrunk by as much as one third, with at least four million having fled to Iran or Pakistan and up to one million killed in the war.

In April 1988, the U.S.S.R., U.S.A., Afghanistan, and Pakistan signed accords calling for an end to outside aid to the warring factions, in return for Soviet withdrawal by 1989. This took place in February of that year but the U.S. and the U.S.S.R. have continued to aid the warring Communist and mujahedeen factions.

ALBANIA

People's Socialist Republic of Albania
President of Presidium: Ramiz Alia (1982)
Premier: Adil Carcani (1982)
Area: 11,100 sq mi. (28,748 sq km)
Population (est. mid-1990): 3,300,000 (average annual rate of natural increase: 2.0%)
Density per square mile: 287
Capital and largest city (est. 1983): Tirana, 206,100
Monetary unit: Lek
Language: Albanian, Greek
Religions: nonreligious, 55%; Islam, 21%; atheist, 19%, Christian, 5%
National name: Republika Popullore Socialiste e Shqipërisë
Literacy rate 75%
Economic summary: Gross national product (1986 est.): $2.7–$2.9 billion. Average annual growth rate (1970–78): 4.2%. Per capita income (1986 est.): $930. Arable land: 21%; labor force: 1,500,000 (1987); principal products: wheat, corn, potatoes, sugar beets, cotton, tobacco. Labor force in industry: 40%; major products: textiles, timber, construction materials, fuels, semi-processed minerals. Exports: minerals, metals, fuels, foodstuffs, agricultural materials. Imports: machinery, equipment, and spare parts, minerals, metals, fuels, construction materials, foodstuffs. Major trading partners: Greece, Yugoslavia, Czechoslovakia, Poland, Hungary, Bulgaria, Romania, W. and E. Germany, France, Italy

Geography. Albania is situated on the eastern shore of the Adriatic Sea, with Yugoslavia to the north and east and Greece to the south. Slightly larger than Maryland, it is a mountainous country, mostly over 3,000 feet (914 m) above sea level, with a narrow, marshy coastal plain crossed by several rivers. The centers of population are contained in the interior mountain plateaus and basins.

Government. Albania is ruled by the Albanian Workers (Communist) Party, headed by a Politburo which hands down all policy decisions. President Ramiz Alia became First Secretary of the party and the Politburo upon the death in 1985 of Enver Hoxha, who wielded absolute power for four decades.

History. Albania proclaimed its independence on Nov. 28, 1912, after a history of Roman, Byzantine, and Turkish domination.

Largely agricultural, Albania is one of the poorest countries in Europe. A battlefield in World War I, after the war it became a republic in which a conservative Moslem landlord, Ahmed Zogu, proclaimed himself President in 1925, and then proclaimed himself King Zog I in a monarchy in 1928. He ruled until Italy annexed Albania in 1939. Communist guerrillas under Enver Hoxha seized power in 1944, near the end of World War II.

His regime closed all of the nation's 2,169 churches and mosques in 1967 in a move to make Albania "the first atheist state in the world."

Hoxha died on April 11, 1985, at the age of 78. His successor as Communist party chief was Ramiz Alia, 59, who had been President since 1982.

ALGERIA

Democratic and Popular Republic of Algeria
President: Chadli Bendjedid (1979)
Prime Minister: Hamrouche Mouloud (1989)
Area: 919,595 sq mi. (2,381,751 sq km)
Population (est. mid-1990): 25,600,000 (average annual rate of natural increase: 31%)
Density per square mile: 27
Capital: Algiers
Largest cities (est. 1987): Algiers, 1,483,000; Oran, 590,000; Constantine, 438,000; Annaba, 310,000
Monetary unit: Dinar
Languages: Arabic (official), French, Berber
Religion: Islam (Sunni)
National name: République Algérienne Democratique et Populaire—El Djemhouria El Djazaïria Demokratia Echaabia
Literacy rate 80%
Economic summary: Gross domestic product (est. 1986): $59 billion, $2,645 per capita. Real growth rate: 2%. Arable land: 3%; labor force: 3,700,000; principal products: wheat, barley, oats, wine, citrus fruits, olives, livestock. Labor force in industry: 40%; major products: petroleum, gas, petrochemicals, fertilizers, iron and steel, textiles, transport equipment. Natural resources: petroleum, natural gas, iron ore, phosphates, lead, zinc, mercury, uranium. Exports: petroleum and gas, iron, wine, phosphates. Imports: food, capital and consumer goods. Major trading partners: U.S., West Germany, France, Italy, Belgium, Netherlands, Canada.

Geography. Nearly four times the size of Texas, Algeria is bordered on the west by Morocco and on the east by Tunisia and Libya. To the south are Mauritania, Mali, and Niger. Low plains cover small areas near the Mediterranean coast, with 68% of the country a plateau between 2,625 and 5,250 feet (800 and 1,600 m) above sea level. The highest point is Mount Tahat in the Sahara, which rises 9,850 feet (3,000 m).

Government. Algeria is governed by the President, whose term runs for 5 years. A new Constitution was approved on Feb. 23, 1989.

A National Popular Assembly of 295 members exercises legislative power, serving for a five-year term. The National Liberation Front, which led the struggle for independence from France, is the only legal party.

History. As ancient Numidia, Algeria became a Roman colony at the close of the Punic Wars (145 B.C.). Conquered by the Vandals about A.D. 440, it fell from a high state of civilization to virtual barbarism, from which it partly recovered after invasion by the Moslems about 650.

In 1492 the Moors and Jews, who had been expelled from Spain, settled in Algeria. Falling under Turkish control in 1518, Algiers served for three centuries as the headquarters of the Barbary pirates. The French took Algeria in 1830 and made it a part of France in 1848.

On July 5, 1962, Algeria was proclaimed independent. In October 1963, Ahmed Ben Bella was elected President. He began to nationalize foreign holdings and aroused opposition. He was overthrown in a military coup on June 19, 1965, by Col. Houari Boumediène, who suspended the Constitution and sought to restore financial stability.

Boumediène died in December 1978 after a long illness. Chadli Bendjedid, Secretary-General of the National Liberation Front, took the presidency in a smooth transition of power. On July 4, 1979, he released from house arrest former President Ahmed Ben Bella, who had been confined for 14 years since his overthrow.

Algeria, chosen by Iran to represent it in negotiations in November 1980 with the United States, was able to secure the eventual release of 52 Americans who had been held hostage in the U.S. Embassy in Teheran. The hostages were flown to Algiers on Jan. 20, 1981, and turned over to U.S. custody, ending 444 days in captivity.

ANDORRA

Principality of Andorra
Episcopal Co-Prince: Msgr. Joan Martí y Alanis, Bishop of Seo de Urgel, Spain
French Co-Prince: François Mitterrand, President of France (1981)
First Syndic: Francesc Cerqueda Pasquet (1982)
Area: 175 sq mi. (453 sq km)
Population (est. 1990): 49,974 (average annual growth rate: 2.2%)
Density per square mile: 282
Capital (est. 1986): Andorra la Vella, 15,639
Monetary units: French franc and Spanish peseta

Languages: Catalán (official); French, Spanish
Religion: Roman Catholic
National names: Les Vallées d'Andorre-Valls d'Andorra
Literacy rate 100%
Economic summary: Arable land: 2%; labor force: NA; principal products: oats, barley, cattle, sheep. Major products: tobacco products and electric power; tourism. Natural resources: water power, mineral water. Major trading partners: Spain and France.

Geography. Andorra lies high in the Pyrenees Mountains on the French-Spanish border. The country is drained by the Valira River.

Government. A General Council of 28 members, elected for four years, chooses the First Syndic and Second Syndic. In 1976 the Andorran Democratic Party, the principality's first political party, was formed.

History. An autonomous and semi-independent co-principality, Andorra has been under the joint suzerainty of the French state and the Spanish bishops of Urgel since 1278.

ANGOLA

People's Republic of Angola
President: José Eduardo dos Santos (1979)
Area: 481,350 sq mi. (1,246,700 sq km)
Population (est. mid-1989): 8,500,000 (average annual rate of natural increase: 3%)
Density per square mile: 18
Capital and largest city (est. 1983): Luanda, 525,000
Monetary unit: Kwanza
Languages: Bantu, Portuguese (official)
Religions: Roman Catholic, 69%; Protestant, 20%; traditional, 10%
Literacy rate: 20%
Economic summary: Gross domestic product (1987 est.): $4.7 billion. $600 per capita; stagnant growth. Arable land: 2%. Labor force: 2,783,000; Labor force in industry: 15%. Principal agricultural products: coffee, sisal, corn, cotton, sugar, tobacco, bananas, cassava. Major industrial products: oil, diamonds, processed fish, tobacco, textiles, cement, processed food and sugar, brewing. Natural resources: diamonds, gold, iron, oil. Exports: oil, coffee, diamonds, fish and fish products, iron ore, timber, corn. Imports: machinery and electrical equipment, bulk iron, steel and metals, textiles, clothing, food. Major trading partners: Brazil, U.S.S.R., Cuba, Portugal, U.S.

Geography. Angola, more than three times the size of California, extends for more than 1,000 miles (1,-609 km) along the South Atlantic in southwestern Africa. Zaire is to the north and east; Zambia to the east, and South-West Africa (Namibia) to the south. A plateau averaging 6,000 feet (1,829 m) above sea level rises abruptly from the coastal lowlands. Nearly all the land is desert or savanna, with hardwood forests in the northeast.

Government. A Marxist "people's republic" is the recognized government, but large areas in the east and south are held by the Union for the Total Independence of Angola (Unita), led by Jonas Savimbi. President José Eduardo dos Santos heads the only official party, the Popular Movement for the Liberation of Angola-Workers Party. The Popular Movement won out over Savimbi's group and a third element in an internal struggle after Portugal granted its former colony independence on Nov. 11, 1975. Elections promised at the time of independence have never taken place, and the government relies heavily on Soviet support and Cuban troops, while Savimbi receives aid from South Africa and the U.S.

History. Discovered by the Portuguese navigator Diego Cao in 1482, Angola became a link in trade with India and the Far East. Later it was a major source of slaves for Portugal's New World colony of Brazil. Development of the interior began after the Treaty of Berlin in 1885 fixed the colony's borders, and British and Portuguese investment pushed mining, railways, and agriculture.

Following World War II, independence movements began but were sternly suppressed by military force. The April revolution of 1974 brought about a reversal of Portugal's policy, and the next year President Francisco da Costa Gomes signed an agreement to grant independence to Angola. The plan called for election of a constituent assembly and a settlement of differences by the MPLA and the National Front for the Liberation of Angola (FNLA) and the National Union for the Total Independence of Angola (UNITA).

The Organization of African Unity, recognized the MPLA government led by Agostinho Neto on Feb. 11, 1976, and the People's Republic of Angola became the 47th member of the organization.

Although militarily victorious, Neto's regime had yet to consolidate its power in opposition strongholds in the east and south.

In March 1977 and May 1978, Zairean refugees in Angola invaded Zaire's Shaba Province, bringing charges by Zairean President Mobutu Sese Seko that the unsucessful invasions were Soviet-backed with Angolan help. Angola, the U.S.S.R., and Cuba denied complicity.

Neto died in Moscow of cancer on Sept. 10, 1979. The Planning Minister, José Eduardo dos Santos, was named President.

The South-West Africa People's Organization, or Swapo, the guerrillas fighting for the independence of the disputed territory south of Angola also known as Namibia, fought from bases in Angola and the South African armed forces also maintained troops there both to fight the SWAPO guerrillas and to assist the UNITA guerrillas against Angolan and Cuban troops.

In February 1986, President Reagan, following a repeal of an earlier ban on military aid to Joseph Savimbi's UNITA rebels, resumed military aid.

In December 1988, Angola, Cuba, and South Africa signed agreements calling for Cuban withdrawal from Angola and South African withdrawal from Namibia by July 1991 and independence for Namibia.

ANTIGUA AND BARBUDA

Sovereign: Queen Elizabeth II
Governor-General: Sir Wilfred E. Jacobs (1981)
Prime Minister: Vere C. Bird, Sr. (1981)
Area: 170 sq mi. (442 sq km)
Population (est. mid-1990): 100,000 (average annual growth rate: 1%)

Density per square mile: 377
Capital and largest city (est. 1983): St. John's, 30,000
Monetary unit: East Caribbean dollar
Language: English
Religions: Anglican and Roman Catholic
Literacy rate: 90%
Member of Commonwealth of Nations
Economic summary: Gross national product (1987): $215 million. Average annual growth rate (1983–86): 7.5%. Per capita income (1986): $1,750. Arable land: 18%; Labor force: 30,000; Labor force in industry: 7% (1983); principal product: cotton. Major industry: tourism. Exports: clothing, rum, lobsters. Imports: fuel, food, machinery. Major trading partners: U.K., U.S.

Geography. Antigua, the larger of the two main islands located 295 miles (420 km) south-southeast of San Juan, P.R., is low-lying except for a range of hills in the south that rise to their highest point at Boggy Peak (1,330 ft; 405 m). As a result of its relative flatness, Antigua suffers from cyclical drought, despite a mean annual rainfall of 44 inches. Barbuda is a coral island, well-wooded.

Government. Executive power is held by the Cabinet, presided over by Prime Minister Vere C. Bird, Sr. A 17-member Parliament is elected by universal suffrage. The Antigua Labour Party, led by Prime Minister Bird, holds 15 seats and the remaining two are held by an independent member, H. Frank, and the United National Democratic Party.

History. Antigua was discovered by Christopher Columbus in 1493 and named for the Church of Santa Maria la Antigua in Seville. Colonized by Britain in 1632, it joined the West Indies Federation in 1958. With the breakup of the Federation, it became one of the West Indies Associated States in 1967, self-governing in internal affairs. Full independence was granted Nov. 1, 1981.

ARGENTINA

Argentine Republic
President: Carlos S. Menem (1989)
Area: 1,072,067 sq mi. (2,776,654 sq km)
Population (est. mid-1990): 32,300,000 (average annual rate of natural increase: 1.3%)
Density per square mile: 30
Capital: Buenos Aires
Largest cities (est. 1983): Buenos Aires, 3,000,000; Córdoba, 1,000,000; Rosario, 950,000; La Plata, 450,000; San Miguel de Tucumán, 400,000
Monetary unit: Austral
Language: Spanish
Religion: Predominantly Roman Catholic
National name: República Argentina
Literacy rate 94%
Economic summary: Gross national product (1987): $74.3 billion; $2,360 per capita; real growth rate: 2%. Arable land: 9%; labor force: 10,900,000; principal products: grains, oilseeds, livestock products. Labor force in industry: 31%; major products: processed foods, motor vehicles, consumer durables, textiles, chemicals. Natural resources: minerals, lead, zinc, tin, copper, iron, manganese, oil, uranium. Exports: meats, corn, wheat, wool, hides and industrial products (durables, textiles, airplanes etc.). Imports: machinery, fuel and lubricating oils, iron and steel, chemical products. Major trading partners: U.S., Brazil, Italy, West Germany, Netherlands, Soviet Union, France, Bolivia.

Geography. With an area slightly less than one third of the United States and second in South America only to its eastern neighbor, Brazil, in size and population, Argentina is a plain, rising from the Atlantic to the Chilean border and the towering Andes peaks. Aconcagua (23,034 ft.; 7,021 m) is the highest peak in the world outside Asia. It is bordered also by Bolivia and Paraguay on the north, and by Uruguay on the east.

The northern area is the swampy and partly wooded Gran Chaco, bordering on Bolivia and Paraguay. South of that are the rolling, fertile pampas, rich for agriculture and grazing and supporting most of the population. Next southward is Patagonia, a region of cool, arid steppes with some wooded and fertile sections.

Government. Argentina is a federal union of 22 provinces, one national territory, and the Federal District. Under the Constitution of 1853 (restored by a Constituent National Convention in 1957), the President and Vice President are elected every six years by popular vote through an electoral college. The President appoints his Cabinet. The Vice President presides over the Senate but has no other powers. The Congress consists of two houses: a 46-member Senate and a 254-member Chamber of Deputies.

History. Discovered in 1516 by Juan Díaz de Solis, Argentina developed slowly under Spanish colonial rule. Buenos Aires was settled in 1580; the cattle industry was thriving as early as 1600.

Invading British forces were expelled in 1806–07, and when Napoleon conquered Spain, the Argentinians set up their own government in the name of the Spanish King in 1810. On July 9, 1816, independence was formally declared.

As in World War I, Argentina proclaimed neutrality at the outbreak of World War II, but in the closing phase declared war on the Axis on March 27, 1945, and became a founding member of the United Nations. Juan D. Perón, an army colonel, emerged as the strongman of the postwar era, winning the Presidential elections of 1946 and 1951.

Opposition to Perón's increasing authoritarianism, led to a coup by the armed forces that sent Perón into exile in 1955. Argentina entered a long period of military dictatorships with brief intervals of constitutional government.

The former dictator returned to power in 1973 and his wife was elected Vice-President.

After Peron's death in 1974, his widow became the hemisphere's first woman chief of state, but was deposed in 1976 by a military junta.

In December 1981, Lt. Gen. Leopoldo Galtieri, commander of the army, was named president.

On April 2, 1982, Galtieri landed thousands of troops on the Falkland Islands on and reclaimed the Malvinas, their Spanish name, as national territory. By May 21, 5,000 British marines and paratroops landed from the British armada, and regained control of the islands.

Galtieri resigned three days after the surrender of the island garrison on June 14. Maj. Gen. Reynaldo Bignone, took office as President on July 1. Civilian rule was promised by early 1984 and on July 16 Bignone lifted the six-year ban on political parties.

In the presidential election of October 1983, Raúl Alfonsín, leader of the middle-class Radical Civic Union, handed the Peronist Party its first defeat since its founding.

Among the enormous problems facing Alfonsín

after eight years of mismanagement under military rule was a $45-billion foreign debt, the developing world's third largest. In some circles, fears were voiced that the new civilian government might repudiate the debt, triggering a wholesale repudiation by debtor countries that could bring on a worldwide financial collapse. But after cliff-hanging negotiations with American, European, and Japanese banks representing the country's private creditors, the Alfonsín government agreed on June 29, 1984, to pay $350 million in overdue interest and was moving toward austerity measures.

With the arrears mounting at the rate of $150 million a month, the debt to foreign creditors mounted to $48 billion by mid-1985, and more than $1 billion was past due. On June 11, the Alfonsin government reached agreement with the International Monetary Fund on an austerity program designed to put Argentina into a position to pay its way internationally and keep current with its debt obligations. The agreement opened the door for up to $1.2 billion of new loans to Argentina. A key requirement of the pact was that inflation, which had been running at 1,010%, be brought down to 150% by April 1986.

Three days later, on June 14, President Alfonsin announced an "economy of war" to bring the inflation rate down. The program combined the creation of a new currency—the austral, meaning southern—to replace the peso, wage and price controls and a halt to the government's deficit spending. In April 1986, the austral was devalued to spur exports.

Twin economic problems of growing unemployment and quadruple-digit inflation led to a Peronist victory in the elections of May 1989. Inflation of food prices led to riots that induced Alfonsin to step down in June 1989, six months early, in favor of the Peronist, Carlos Menem.

AUSTRALIA

Commonwealth of Australia
Sovereign: Queen Elizabeth II
Governor-General: William Hayden (1989)
Prime Minister: Robert J. L. Hawke (1983)
Area: 2,966,150 sq mi. (7,682,300 sq km)
Population (est. mid-1990): 17,100,000 (average annual rate of natural increase: 0.8%)
Density per square mile: 6
Capital (est. 1988): Canberra, 297,300
Largest cities (1988 for metropolitan area): Sydney, 3,596,000; Melbourne, 3,002,300; Brisbane, 1,240,-300; Adelaide, 1,023,700; Perth, 1,118,800
Monetary unit: Australian dollar
Language: English
Religions: Roman Catholic, 28%; Anglican, 28%; Uniting Church (combined Methodist-Presbyterian), 14%
Literacy rate: 99.%
Member of Commonwealth of Nations
Economic summary: Gross national product (1987): $202.2 billion, $12,580 per capita; average annual real growth rate (1986): 1.25% Arable land: 6%; labor force: 6% (1986); principal products: wool, meat, cereals, sugar, sheep, cattle, dairy products. Labor force: 7,700,-

000; Labor force in manufacturing and industry: 16.2% (1987); major products: machinery, motor vehicles, iron and steel, chemicals. Natural resources: iron ore, bauxite, zinc, lead, tin, coal, oil, gas, copper, nickel, uranium. Exports: wheat, wool, coal. Imports: meat; iron ore; capital equipment. Major trading partners: Japan, U.S., U.K., New Zealand, West Germany, ASEAN.

Geography. The continent of Australia, with the island state of Tasmania, is approximately equal in area to the United States (excluding Alaska and Hawaii), and is nearly 50% larger than Europe (excluding the U.S.S.R.).

Mountain ranges run from north to south along the east coast, reaching their highest point in Mount Kosciusko (7,308 ft; 2,228 m). The western half of the continent is occupied by a desert plateau that rises into barren, rolling hills near the west coast. It includes the Great Victoria Desert to the south and the Great Sandy Desert to the north. The Great Barrier Reef, extending about 1,245 miles (2,000 km), lies along the northeast coast.

The island of Tasmania (26,178 sq mi.; 67,800 sq km) is off the southeastern coast.

Government. The Federal Parliament consists of a bicameral legislature. The House of Representatives has 148 members elected for three years by popular vote. The Senate has 76 members elected by popular vote for six years. One half of the Senate is elected every three years. Voting is compulsory at 18. Supreme federal judicial power is vested in the High Court of Australia in the Federal Courts, and in the State Courts invested by Parliament with Federal jurisdiction. The High Court consists of seven justices, appointed by the Governor-General in Council. Each of the states has its own judicial system.

History. Dutch, Portuguese, and Spanish ships sighted Australia in the 17th century; the Dutch landed at the Gulf of Carpentaria in 1606. Australia was called New Holland, Botany Bay, and New South Wales until about 1820.

Captain James Cook, in 1770, claimed possession for Great Britain. A British penal colony was set up at what is now Sydney, then Port Jackson, in 1788, and about 161,000 transported English convicts were settled there until the system was suspended in 1839.

Free settlers established six colonies: New South Wales (1786), Tasmania (then Van Diemen's Land) (1825), Western Australia (1829), South Australia (1834), Victoria (1851), and Queensland (1859).

The six colonies became states and in 1901 federated into the Commonwealth of Australia with a Constitution that incorporated British parliamentary tradition and U.S. federal experience. Australia became known for liberal legislation: free compulsory education, protected trade unionism with industrial conciliation and arbitration, the "Australian" ballot facilitating selection, the secret ballot, women's suffrage, maternity allowances, and sickness and old age pensions.

In the election of 1983, Robert Hawke, head of the Labor Party, became Prime Minister. The Labor government was reelected in a Federal election in December 1984.

By mid-1982, however, world recession was slowing the resources boom. Low resource prices were an issue in the election of 1987 but Hawke was able secure re-election on a platform of diversifying the economy.

Australian External Territories

Norfolk Island (13 sq mi.; 36.3 sq km) was placed under Australian administration in 1914. Population in 1988 was about 1,800.

The Ashmore and Cartier Islands (.8 sq mi.), situated in the Indian Ocean off the northwest coast of Australia, came under Australian administration in 1934. In 1938 the islands were annexed to the Northern Territory. On the attainment of self-government by the Northern Territory in 1978, the islands which are uninhabited were retained as Commonwealth Territory.

The Australian Antarctic Territory (2,360,000 sq mi.; 6,112,400 sq km), comprises all the islands and territories, other than Adélie Land, situated south of lat. 60° S and lying between long. 160° to 45° E. It came under Australian administration in 1936.

Heard Island and the McDonald Islands (158 sq mi.; 409.2 sq km), lying in the sub-Antarctic, were placed under Australian administration in 1947. The islands are uninhabited.

Christmas Island (52 sq mi.; 134.7 sq km) is situated in the Indian Ocean. It came under Australian administration in 1958. Population in 1988 was about 2,000.

Coral Sea Islands (400,000 sq mi.; 1,036,000 sq km, but only a few sq mi. of land) became a territory of Australia in 1969. There is no permanent population on the islands.

AUSTRIA

Republic of Austria
President: Kurt Waldheim (1986)
Chancellor: Franz Vranitzky (1986)
Area: 32,375 sq mi. (83,851 sq km)
Population (est. mid-1990): 7,600,000 (average annual rate of natural increase: 0.1%)
Density per square mile: 235
Capital: Vienna
Largest cities (est. 1983): Vienna, 1,550,000; Graz, 240,000; Linz, 200,000; Salzburg, 135,000; Innsbruck, 115,000; Klagenfurt, 85,000
Monetary unit: Schilling
Language: German
Religion: Roman Catholic, 89%
Literacy rate: 98%
National name: Republik Österreich
Economic summary: Gross domestic product (1987): $118.1 billion; $15,573 per capita; 1.3% real growth rate. Arable land: 6%. Labor force: 7,700,000 (1987); Labor force in industry and manufacturing: 6.1%; principal agricultural products: livestock, forest products, grains, sugar beets, potatoes; principal products: iron and steel, chemicals, machinery, paper and pulp. Natural resources: iron ore, petroleum, timber, magnesite, aluminum, coal, lignite, cement, copper, hydropower. Exports: iron and steel products, timber, paper, textiles, electrotechnical machines, chemical products. Imports: machinery, chemicals, foodstuffs, textiles and clothing, petroleum. Major trading partners: West Germany, Italy, Switzerland, U.S., Eastern Europe.

Geography. Slightly smaller than Maine, Austria includes much of the mountainous territory of the eastern Alps (about 75% of the area). The country contains many snowfields, glaciers, and snow-capped peaks, the highest being the Grossglockner (12,530 ft; 3,819 m). The Danube is the principal river. Forests and woodlands cover about 40% of the land area.

Almost at the heart of Europe, Austria has as its neighbors Italy, Switzerland, West Germany, Czechoslovakia, Hungary, Yugoslavia, and Liechtenstein.

Government. Austria is a federal republic composed of nine provinces (Bundesländer), including Vienna. The President is elected by the people for a term of six years. The bicameral legislature consists of the Bundesrat, with 58 members chosen by the provincial assemblies, and the Nationalrat, with 183 members popularly elected for four years. Presidency of the Bundesrat revolves every six months, going to the provinces in alphabetical order.

History. Settled in prehistoric times, the Central European land that is now Austria was overrun in pre-Roman times by various tribes, including the Celts. Charlemagne conquered the area in 788 and encouraged colonization and Christianity. In 1252, Ottokar, King of Bohemia, gained possession, only to lose the territories to Rudolf of Hapsburg in 1278. Thereafter, until World War I, Austria's history was largely that of its ruling house, the Hapsburgs.

Austria emerged from the Congress of Vienna in 1815 as the Continent's dominant power. The *Ausgleich* of 1867 provided for a dual sovereignty, the empire of Austria and the kingdom of Hungary, under Francis Joseph I, who ruled until his death on Nov. 21, 1916. He was succeeded by his grandnephew, Charles I.

During World War I, Austria-Hungary was one of the Central Powers with Germany, Bulgaria, and Turkey, and the conflict left the country in political chaos and economic ruin. Austria, shorn of Hungary, was proclaimed a republic in 1918, and the monarchy was dissolved in 1919.

A parliamentary democracy was set up by the Constitution of Nov. 10, 1920. To check the power of Nazis advocating union with Germany, Chancellor Engelbert Dolfuss in 1933 established a dictatorship, but was assassinated by the Nazis on July 25, 1934. Kurt von Schuschnigg, his successor, struggled to keep Austria independent but on March 12, 1938, German troops occupied the country, and Hitler proclaimed its *Anschluss* (union) with Germany, annexing it to the Third Reich.

After World War II, the U.S. and Britain declared the Austrians a "liberated" people. But the Russians prolonged the occupation. Finally Austria concluded a state treaty with the U.S.S.R. and the other occupying powers and regained its independence on May 15, 1955. The second Austrian republic, established Dec. 19, 1945, on the basis of the 1920 Constitution (amended in 1929), was declared by the federal parliament to be permanently neutral.

Vienna has since become a headquarters for several international organizations such as OPEC.

On June 8, 1986, former UN Secretary-General Kurt Waldheim was elected to the ceremonial office of President in a campaign marked by controversy over his alleged links to Nazi war-crimes in Yugoslavia.

In the summer of 1990, a four-year boycott by European heads of state was broken when Czechoslovakia's President Vaclav Havel visited Waldheim seeking economic aid and investment.

BAHAMAS

Commonwealth of the Bahamas
Sovereign: Queen Elizabeth II
Governor-General: Sir Henry M. Taylor (1988)
Prime Minister: Lynden O. Pindling (1967)
Area: 5,380 sq mi. (13,939 sq km)
Population (est. mid-1990): 200,000 (average annual rate of natural increase, 1990, 1%)
Density per square mile: 46
Capital and largest city (est. 1984 for metropolitan area): Nassau, 139,000
Monetary unit: Bahamian dollar
Language: English
Religions: Baptist, 29%; Anglican, 23%; Roman Catholic, 23%; Methodist, 7%
Literacy rate: 95%
Member of Commonwealth of Nations
Economic summary: Gross domestic product (1987 est.): $2.3 billion; $9,632 per capita; 4.4% real growth rate. Labor force: 132,600; Principal agricultural products: fruits, vegetables. Major industrial products: fish, refined petroleum, pharmaceutical products; tourism. Natural resources: salt, aragonite. Exports: lobster, fish, pharmaceuticals, cement, rum. Imports: foodstuffs, manufactured goods, fuels. Major trading partners: U.S., U.K., Nigeria, Canada.

Geography. The Bahamas are an archipelago of about 700 islands and 2,400 uninhabited islets and cays lying 50 miles off the east coast of Florida. They extend from northwest to southeast for about 760 miles (1,223 km). Only 22 of the islands are inhabited; the most important is New Providence (80 sq mi.; 207 sq km), on which Nassau is situated. Other islands include Grand Bahama, Abaco, Eleuthera, Andros, Cat Island, San Salvador (or Watling's Island), Exuma, Long Island, Crooked Island, Acklins Island, Mayaguana, and Inagua.

The islands are mainly flat, few rising above 200 feet (61 m). There are no fresh water streams. There are several large brackish lakes on several islands including Inagua and New Providence.

Government. The Bahamas moved toward greater autonomy in 1968 after the overwhelming victory in general elections of the Progressive Liberal Party, led by Prime Minister Lynden O. Pindling. The black leader's party won 29 seats in the House of Assembly to only 7 for the predominantly white United Bahamians, who had controlled the islands for decades before Pindling became Premier in 1967.

With its new mandate from the 85%-black population, Pindling's government negotiated a new Constitution with Britain under which the colony became the Commonwealth of the Bahama Islands in 1969. On July 10, 1973, The Bahamas became an independent nation as the Commonwealth of the Bahamas. The islands established diplomatic relations with Cuba in 1974.

In the 1982 election, Pindling's Progressive Liberal Party won 32 of 43 seats in Parliament; the Free National Movement, 11.

In the 1987 election, Pindling's Progressive Liberal Party won 31 of 49 seats in Parliament; the Free National Movement, 16.

History. The islands were reached by Columbus in October 1492, and were a favorite pirate area in the early 18th century. The Bahamas were a crown colony from 1717 until they were granted internal self-government in 1964.

BAHRAIN

State of Bahrain
Emir: Sheik Isa ibn-Sulman al-Khalifa (1961)
Prime Minister: Sheik Khalifa bin Sulman al-Khalifa (1970)
Area: 240 sq mi. (620 sq km)
Population (est. mid-1990): 500,000 (average annual rate of natural increase: 2.3%)
Density per square mile: 1,968.5
Capital (est. 1982): Manama, 150,000
Monetary unit: Bahrain dinar
Languages: Arabic (official), English
Religion: Islam
Literacy rate : 40%
Economic summary: Gross domestic product (1987): $3.5 billion, $7,550 per capita; real growth rate (1988): 0%. Labor force (1982): 140,000; labor force in industry and commerce: 85%; principal products: eggs, vegetables, fruits; major products: oil, aluminum, fish. Natural resources: oil, fish. Exports: oil, natural gas, aluminum, fish. Imports: machinery, oil-industry equipment, motor vehicles, foodstuffs. Major trading partners: Saudi Arabia, U.S., U.K., Japan.

Geography. Bahrain is an archipelago in the Persian Gulf off the coast of Saudi Arabia. The islands for the most part are level expanses of sand and rock.

Government. A new Constitution was approved in 1973. It created the first elected parliament in the country's history. Called the National Council, it consisted of 30 members elected by male citizens for four-year terms, plus up to 16 Cabinet ministers as ex-officio members. In August 1975, the Amir dissolved the National Council.

History. A sheikdom that passed from the Persians to the al-Khalifa family from Arabia in 1782, Bahrain became, by treaty, a British protectorate in 1820. It has become a major Middle Eastern oil center and, through use of oil revenues, is one of the most developed of the Persian Gulf sheikdoms. The Emir, Sheik Isa ibn-Sulman al-Khalifa, who succeeded to the post in 1961, is a member of the original ruling family. Bahrain announced its independence on Aug. 14, 1971.

BANGLADESH

People's Republic of Bangladesh
President: H. M. Ershad (1983)
Vice President: Moudud Ahmed (1989)
Area: 55,598 sq mi. (143,998 sq km)
Population (est. mid-1990): 114,800,000 (average annual rate of natural increase: 2.8%)
Density per square mile: 2,063
Capital and largest city (est 1986): Dhaka, 4,470,000
Monetary unit: Taka
Principal languages: Bengali (official), English
Religions: Islam, (official) 83%; Hindu, 16%
Literacy rate: 29%
Member of Commonwealth of Nations
Economic summary: Gross domestic product (1988): $18.1 billion, $170 per capita; −2.9% real growth rate. Arable land: 67%; principal products: rice, jute, tea, sugar, wheat. Labor force: 35,100,000, 11% in industry and commerce; major industrial products: jute goods, textiles, leather, sugar, fertilizer, paper, pharmaceuticals. Natural resources: natural gas. Exports: jute goods, jute, tea,

leather, garments. Imports: food grains, fuels, raw cotton, fertilizer, manufactured goods. Major trading partners: U.S., Japan, Singapore, U.K., China, India.

Geography. Bangladesh, on the northern coast of the Bay of Bengal, is surrounded by India, with a small common border with Burma in the southeast. It is approximately the size of Wisconsin. The country is low-lying riverine land traversed by the many branches and tributaries of the Ganges and Brahmaputra rivers. Elevations averages less than 600 feet (183 m) above sea level. Tropical monsoons and frequent floods and cyclones inflict heavy damage in the delta region.

Government. On Oct. 15, 1986, Ershad was elected President, in an election boycotted by the opposition, for a five-year term. Martial law ended in November. Parliamentary elections held in March 1988, though boycotted by the opposition and much of the population, gave Ershad's Jatiya Party 250 of 300 seats.

History. The former East Pakistan was part of imperial British India until Britain withdrew in 1947. The two Pakistans were united by religion (Islam), but their peoples were separated by culture, physical features, and 1,000 miles of Indian territory. Bangladesh consists primarily of East Bengal (West Bengal is part of India and its people are primarily Hindu) plus the Sylhet district of the Indian state of Assam. For almost 25 years after independence from Britain, its history was as part of Pakistan (*see* Pakistan).

The East Pakistanis unsuccessfully sought greater autonomy from West Pakistan. The first general elections in Pakistani history, in December 1970, saw virtually all 171 seats of the region (out of 300 for both East and West Pakistan) go to Sheik Mujibur Rahman's Awami League.

Attempts to write an all-Pakistan Constitution to replace the military regime of Gen. Yahya Khan failed. Yahya put down a revolt in March 1971. An estimated one million Bengalis were killed in the fighting or later slaughtered. Ten million more took refuge in India.

In December 1971, India invaded East Pakistan, routed the West Pakistani occupation forces, and created Bangladesh. In February 1974, Pakistan agreed to recognize the independence of Bangladesh.

On March 24, 1982, Gen. Hossain Mohammad Ershad, army chief of staff, took control in a bloodless coup. Ershad assumed the office of President in 1983.

BARBADOS

Sovereign: Queen Elizabeth II
Governor-General: Dame Nita Barrow (June 1990)
Prime Minister: L. Erskine Sandiford (1987)
Area: 166 sq. mi. (431 sq km)
Population (est. mid-1990): 300,000; growth rate: .5%.
Density per square mile: 1,560
Capital and largest city (est. 1988): Bridgetown, 102,000
Monetary unit: Barbados dollar
Language: English

Religions: Anglican, 70%; Methodist, 9%; Roman Catholic, 4%
Literacy rate: 99%
Member of Commonwealth of Nations
Economic summary: Gross domestic product (1987 est.): $1.4 billion, $5,405 per capita, .6% real growth rate. Arable land: 77%; principal products: sugar cane, subsistence foods. Labor force: 112,300; 37% services and government. Major industrial products: light manufactures, sugar milling, tourism. Exports: sugar and sugar cane byproducts, clothing, electrical parts. Imports: foodstuffs, machinery, manufactured goods. Major trading partners: U.S., Caribbean nations, U.K., Canada.

Geography. An island in the Atlantic about 300 miles (483 km) north of Venezuela, Barbados is only 21 miles long (34 km) and 14 miles across (23 km) at its widest point. It is circled by fine beaches and narrow coastal plains. The highest point is Mount Hillaby (1,105 ft; 337 m) in the north central area.

Government. The Barbados legislature dates from 1627. It is bicameral, with a Senate of 21 appointed members and an Assembly of 27 elected members.

The major political parties are the Democratic Labor Party (20 seats in Assembly), led by Prime Minister L. Erskine Sandiford; Barbados Labor Party (3 seats), led by Henry Deb. Forde and National Democratic Party (4 seats) led by Richie Haynes.

History. Barbados, with a population 90% black, was settled by the British in 1627. It became a crown colony in 1885. It was a member of the Federation of the West Indies from 1958 to 1962. Britain granted the colony independence on Nov. 30, 1966, and it became a parliamentary democracy.

While retaining membership in the Commonwealth of Nations and economic ties with Britain, Barbados seeks broader economic and political relations with Western Hemisphere countries. Diplomatic ties with Cuba were established in 1972.

BELGIUM

Kingdom of Belgium
Sovereign: King Baudouin I (1951)
Premier: Wilfried Martens (1981)
Area: 11,781 sq mi. (30,513 sq km)
Population (est. mid-1990): 9,900,000 (average annual rate of natural increase: .2%)
Density per square mile: 843
Capital: Brussels
Largest cities (est. 1987): Brussels, 970,346; Antwerp, 479,748; Ghent, 233,856; Charleroi, 209,395; Liège, 200,891; Bruges, 117,755
Monetary Unit: Belgian franc
Languages: Flemish, 57%; French, 32%; bilingual (Brussels), 10%; German, 0.7%.
Religion: Roman Catholic, 75%
National name: Royaume de Belgique—Koninkrijk van België
Literacy rate: 98%
Economic summary: Gross national product (1988 est.): $155 billion, $15,690 per capita; 2.9% real growth rate. Arable land: 24%; principal products: livestock, poultry, grain, sugar beets, flax, tobacco, potatoes, vegetables, fruits. Labor force: 4,000,000; 37% in industry; major products: fabricated metal, iron and steel, machinery, textiles, chemicals, food processing. Exports: (Belg.-Luxembourg Econ. Union) iron

and steel products, chemicals, pharmaceuticals, textile products. Imports: (Belg.-Luxembourg Econ. Union) nonelectrical machinery, motor vehicles, textiles, chemicals, fuels. Major trading partners: West Germany, France, Netherlands, U.K., U.S., Italy.

Geography. A neighbor of France, West Germany, the Netherlands, and Luxembourg, Belgium has about 40 miles of seacoast on the North Sea at the Strait of Dover. In area, it is approximately the size of Maryland. The northern third of the country is a plain extending eastward from the seacoast. North of the Sambre and Meuse Rivers is a low plateau; to the south lies the heavily wooded Ardennes plateau, attaining an elevation of about 2,300 feet (700 m).

The Schelde River, which rises in France and flows through Belgium, emptying into the Schelde estuaries, enables Antwerp to be an ocean port.

Government. Belgium, a parliamentary democracy under a constitutional monarch, consists of nine provinces. Its bicameral legislature has a Senate, with its 181 members elected for four years—106 by general election, 50 by provincial councillors and 25 by the Senate itself. The 212-member Chamber of Representatives is directly elected for four years by proportional representation. There is universal suffrage, and those who do not vote are fined.

Belgium joined the North Atlantic Alliance in 1949 and is a member of the European Community. NATO and the European Community have their headquarters in Brussels.

The sovereign, Baudouin I, was born Sept. 7, 1930, the son of King Leopold III and Queen Astrid. He became King on July 17, 1951, after the abdication of his father. He married Doña Fabiola de Mora y Aragón on Dec. 15, 1960. Since he has no children, his brother, Prince Albert, is heir to the throne.

History. Belgium occupies part of the Roman province of Belgica, named after the Belgae, a people of ancient Gaul. The area was conquered by Julius Caesar in 57–50 B.C., then was overrun by the Franks in the 5th century. It was part of Charlemagne's empire in the 8th century, then in the next century was absorbed into Lotharingia and later into the Duchy of Lower Lorraine. In the 12th century it was partitioned into the Duchies of Brabant and Luxembourg, the Bishopric of Liège, and the domain of the Count of Hainaut, which included Flanders.

In the 16th century, Belgium, with most of the area of the Low Countries, passed to the Duchy of Burgundy and was the marriage portion of Archduke Maximilian of Hapsburg and the inheritance of his grandson, Charles V, who incorporated it into his empire. Then, in 1555, they were united with Spain.

By the treaty of Utrecht in 1713, the country's sovereignty passed to Austria. During the wars that followed the French Revolution, Belgium was occupied and later annexed to France. But with the downfall of Napoleon, the Congress of Vienna in 1815 gave the country to the Netherlands. The Belgians revolted in 1830 and declared their independence.

Germany's invasion of Belgium in 1914 set off World War I. The Treaty of Versailles (1919) gave the areas of Eupen, Malmédy, and Moresnet to Belgium. Leopold III succeeded Albert, King during World War I, in 1934. In World War II, Belgium was overwhelmed by Nazi Germany, and Leopold III was made prisoner. When he attempted to return in 1950, Socialists and Liberals revolted. He abdicated July 16, 1951, and his son, Baudouin, became King the next day.

Despite the increasingly strong divisions between the French- and Flemish-speaking communities, a Christian Democrat-Liberal coalition that took office in December 1981 came close to setting a record for longevity among the 32 governments that had ruled Belgium since World War II. Headed by Prime Minister Wilfried Martens—the fifth government he had led since 1979—it survived several serious political challenges, including the implementation of an unpopular economic austerity program in 1983 and the deployment of NATO cruise missiles in March 1985.

Strife between French and Flemish speakers almost toppled the government in 1986 and 1987. Elections in Dec. 1987 saw Marten's coalition barely holding on in the face of a resurgent Socialist opposition.

BELIZE

Sovereign: Queen Elizabeth II
Governor-General: Dame Minita Gordon (1981)
Prime Minister: George Price (1989)
Area: 8,867 sq mi. (22,965 sq km)
Population (est. mid-1990): 200,000 (average annual rate of natural increase: 3.1%)
Density per sq mi.: 17
Capital (1989): Belmopan, 8,000
Largest city (1989): Belize City, 70,000
Monetary unit: Belize dollar
Languages: English (official) and Spanish, Maya, Carib
Religions: Roman Catholic, 62%; Anglican, 12%; Methodist, 6%; Baha'i, 2.5%
Literacy rate: 93%
Member of Commonwealth of Nations
Economic summary: Gross domestic product (1987): $247 million, $1,438 per capita, 6.5% real growth rate (1988 est.). Arable land: 2%; principal products: sugar cane, citrus fruits, corn, molasses, rice, bananas, livestock. Labor force: 51,500; 10.3% in manufacturing; major products: timber, processed foods, furniture, rum, soap. Natural resource: timber. Exports: sugar, molasses, clothing, lumber, citrus fruits, fish. Imports: fuels, transportation equipment, foodstuffs, textiles, machinery. Major trading partners: U.S., U.K., Trinidad and Tobago, Canada.

Geography. Belize (formerly British Honduras) is situated on the Caribbean Sea south of Mexico and east and north of Guatemala. In area, it is about the size of New Hampshire. Most of the country is heavily forested with various hardwoods. Mangrove swamps and cays along the coast give way to hills and mountains in the interior. The highest point is Victoria Peak, 3,681 feet (1,122 m).

Government. Formerly the colony of British Honduras, Belize became a fully independent commonwealth on Sept. 21, 1981, after having been self-governing since 1964. Executive power is nominally wielded by Queen Elizabeth II through an appointed Governor-General but effective power is held by the Prime Minister, who is responsible to a 28-member parliament elected by universal suffrage.

History. Once a part of the Mayan empire, the area was deserted until British timber cutters began exploiting valuable hardwoods in the 17th century. Efforts by Spain to dislodge British settlers, including a major naval attack in 1798, were defeated. The territory was formally named a British colony in 1862 but administered by the Governor of Jamaica until 1884.

Guatemala has long made claims to the territory and refused to recognize Britain's efforts to grant independence to Belize. Fear of Guatemala caused many inhabitants to oppose independence until a tentative agreement was reached between Britain, Belize, and Guatemala in March 1981 that would offer access to the Caribbean through Belizean territory for Guatemala. The agreement broke down, however, and 1,600 British troops remained to protect the new state after the flag-raising ceremony on Sept. 21, 1981.

BENIN

Republic of Benin
Interim Prime Minister: Nicephore Soglo (1990)
Area: 43,483 sq mi. (112,622 sq km)
Population (est. mid-1990): 4,700,000 (average annual rate of natural increase: 3.2%)
Density per square mile: 107
Capital (est. 1984): Porto-Novo, 208,000
Largest city (est. 1982): Cotonou, 490,000
Monetary unit: Franc CFA
Ethnic groups: Fons and Adjas, Baribas, Yorubas, Mahis
Languages: French, African languages
Religions: indigenous, 70%; Christian, 15%; Islam, 15%
National name: Republique Populaire du Benin
Literacy rate (1981): 20%
Economic summary: Gross domestic product (1986 est.): $1.4 billion. $340 per capita; real growth rate (1986 est.): −0.2%. Arable land: 2%; principal products: oil palms, peanuts, cotton, coffee, tobacco, corn, rice, livestock, fish. Labor force: 51,500; less than 2% industry. Major industrial products: processed palm oil, palm kernel oil, textiles, beverages. Natural resources: low-grade iron ore, limestone, some offshore oil. Exports: palm and agricultural products. Imports: clothing, consumer goods, lumber, fuels, foodstuffs, machinery, transportation equipment. Major trading partners: France and other Western European countries.

Geography. This West African nation on the Gulf of Guinea, between Togo on the west and Nigeria on the east, is about the size of Tennessee. It is bounded also by Burkina Faso and Niger on the north. The land consists of a narrow coastal strip that rises to a swampy, forested plateau and then to highlands in the north. A hot and humid climate blankets the entire country.

Government. The change in name from Dahomey to Benin was announced by President Mathieu Kerekou on November 30, 1975. Benin commemorates an African kingdom that flourished in the 17th century. At the same time, Kerekou announced the formation of a political organization, the Party of the People's Revolution of Benin, to mark the first anniversary of his declaration of a "new society" guided by Marxist-Leninist princi-

ples. Kérékou repudiated Marxism-Leninism in 1989.

History. One of the smallest and most densely populated states in Africa, Benin was annexed by the French in 1893. The area was incorporated into French West Africa in 1904. It became an autonomous republic within the French Community in 1958, and on Aug. 1, 1960, was granted its independence within the Community.

Gen. Christophe Soglo deposed the first president, Hubert Maga, in an army coup in 1963. He dismissed the civilian government in 1965, proclaiming himself chief of state. A group of young army officers seized power in December 1967, deposing Soglo. They promulgated a new Constitution in 1968.

In December 1969, Benin had its fifth coup of the decade, with the army again taking power. In May 1970, a three-man presidential commission was created to take over the government. The commission had a six-year term; each member serves as president for two years. Maga turned over power as scheduled to Justin Ahomadegbe in May 1972, but six months later yet another army coup ousted the triumvirate and installed Lt. Col. Mathieu Kerekou as President. He stepped down in 1990. He was replaced by Nicephore Soglo who will head an interim government until after elections in March 1991.

BHUTAN

Kingdom of Bhutan
Ruler: King Jigme Singye Wangchuk (1972)
Area: 18,000 sq mi. (46,620 sq km)
Population (est. mid-1990): 1,600,000 (average annual rate of natural increase: 2.1%)
Density per square mile: 85
Capital (est. 1984): Thimphu, 30,000
Monetary unit: Ngultrum
Language: Dzongkha
Religions: Buddhist, 75%; Hindu, 25%
National name: Druk-yul
Literacy rate: 15%
Economic summary: Gross domestic product (1987): $252 million, $170 per capita, 14% real growth rate. Arable land: 2%. Labor force in agriculture: 95%; principal products: rice, barley, wheat, potatoes, fruit. Major industrial product: cement. Natural resources: timber, hydroelectric power. Exports: fruits and vegetables, timber, coal, cement. Imports: fuels, machinery, vehicles. Major trading partner: India.

Geography. Mountainous Bhutan, half the size of Indiana, is situated on the southeast slope of the Himalayas, bordered on the north and east by Tibet and on the south and west by India. The landscape consists of a succession of lofty and rugged mountains running generally from north to south and separated by deep valleys. In the north, towering peaks reach a height of 24,000 feet (7,315 m).

Government. Bhutan is a constitutional monarchy. The King rules with a Council of Ministers and a Royal Advisory Council. There is a National Assembly (Parliament), which meets semiannually, but no political parties.

History. British troops invaded the country in 1865 and negotiated an agreement under which Britain undertook to pay an annual allowance to Bhutan on condition of good behavior. A treaty with India in 1949 increased this subsidy and placed Bhutan's foreign affairs under Indian control.

In the 1960s, Bhutan undertook modernization, abolishing slavery and the caste system, emancipating women and enacting land reform. In 1985, Bhutan made its first diplomatic links with non-Asian countries.

BOLIVIA

Republic of Bolivia
President: Jaime Paz Zamora (1989)
Area: 424,162 sq mi. (1,098,581 sq km)
Population (est. mid-1990): 7,300,000 (average annual rate of natural increase: 2.6%).
Density per square mile: 17
Judicial capital (est. 1985): Sucre, 86,609
Administrative capital (est. 1985): La Paz, 992,592
Largest cities (est. 1985): Santa Cruz, 441,717; Cochabamba, 317,251; Oruro, 178,393
Monetary unit: Boliviano
Languages: Spanish, Quechua, Aymara
Religion: Roman Catholic, 94%; others, 3%
National name: República de Bolivia
Literacy rate: 63%
Economic summary: Gross national product (1987): $4.6 billion, $680 per capita, 2.4% real growth rate. Arable land: 3%. Labor force in agriculture: 50%; principal products: potatoes, corn, rice, sugar cane, bananas, coffee. Labor force in industry: 19%; major products: refined petroleum, processed foods, tin, textiles, clothing. Natural resources: petroleum, natural gas, tin, lead, zinc, copper, tungsten, bismuth, antimony, gold, sulfur, silver, iron ore. Exports: tin, lead, zinc, silver, antimony, coffee, sugar, cotton, soya beans, leather, citrus, natural gas. Imports: foodstuffs, chemicals, capital goods, pharmaceuticals, transport equipment. Major trading partners: U.S., Argentina, U.K., Brazil, Netherlands.

Geography. Landlocked Bolivia, equal in size to California and Texas combined, lies to the west of Brazil. Its other neighbors are Peru and Chile on the west and Argentina and Paraguay on the south.

The country is a low alluvial plain throughout 60% of its area toward the east, drained by the Amazon and Plata river systems. The western part, enclosed by two chains of the Andes, is a great plateau—the Altiplano, with an average altitude of 12,000 feet (3,658 m). More than 80% of the population lives on the plateau, which also contains La Paz. At an altitude of 11,910 feet (3,630 m), it is the highest capital city in the world.

Lake Titicaca, half the size of Lake Ontario, is one of the highest large lakes in the world, at an altitude of 12,507 feet (3,812 m). Islands in the lake hold ruins of the ancient Incas.

Government. President Victor Paz Estenssoro was inaugurated on Aug. 7, 1985, after the Congress, at a raucous session, chose him over Hugo Banzer, the candidate who had received the most votes in a popular election on July 14. Banzer won 28.6% of the 1.7 million votes tallied and Paz won 26.4%. Under the Constitution, if no Presidential candidate receives 50% of the vote, Congress chooses between the top two vote-getters.

History. Famous since Spanish colonial days for its mineral wealth, modern Bolivia was once a part of the ancient Incan Empire. After the Spaniards defeated the Incas in the 16th century, Bolivia's predominantly Indian population was reduced to slavery. The country won its independence in 1825 and was named after Simón Bolívar, the famed liberator.

Since 1825 Bolivia has had more than 60 revolutions, 70 Presidents, and 11 Constitutions.

Harassed by internal strife, Bolivia lost great slices of territory to three neighbor nations. Several thousand square miles and its outlet to the Pacific were taken by Chile after the War of the Pacific (1879–84). In 1903 a piece of Bolivia's Acre province, rich in rubber, was ceded to Brazil. And in 1938, after a war with Paraguay, Bolivia gave up claim to nearly 100,000 square miles of the Gran Chaco.

In 1965 a guerrilla movement mounted from Cuba and headed by Maj. Ernesto (Ché) Guevara began a revolutionary war. With the aid of U.S. military advisers, the Bolivian army, helped by the peasants, smashed the guerrilla movement, wounding and capturing Guevara on Oct. 8, 1967, and shooting him to death the next day.

Faltering steps toward restoration of civilian government were halted abruptly on July 17, 1980, when Gen. Luis Garcia Meza Tejada seized power. A series of military leaders followed before the military moved, in 1982, to return the government to civilian rule. Hernán Siles Zuazo was inaugurated President on Oct. 10, 1982.

Under Siles' left-of-center government, the country was regularly shut down by work stoppages, the bulk of Bolivia's natural resources—natural gas, gold, lithium, potassium and tungsten—were either sold on the black market or left in the ground, the country had the lowest per-capita income in South America, and inflation approached 3,000 percent. In 1985, the 73-year-old Siles decided he was unable to carry on and quit a year early.

No candidate won a majority in the elections in 1985 and Victor Paz Estenssoro, 77, was picked by Congress to become President. During his administration, inflation continued to rise and the currency collapsed. Drastic economic measures were taken toward the end of the year, including a wage freeze and a cutback of government price subsidies, which lowered the inflation rate to about 276%. The economy showed signs of growth in 1987, for the first time since 1980.

BOPHUTHATSWANA

See South Africa

BOTSWANA

Republic of Botswana
President: Quett K. Masire (1980)
Area: 231,800 sq mi. (600,360 sq km)
Population (est. mid-1990): 1,200,000 (average annual rate of natural increase: 2.9%)
Density per square mile: 5
Capital and largest city (est. 1984): Gaborone, 79,000

Monetary unit: Pula
Languages: English, Setswana
Religions: Christian, 48%; traditional, 49%
Member of Commonwealth of Nations
Literacy rate: 59%
Economic summary: Gross domestic product (1987): $1.5 billion, $1,310 per capita, 8.4% real growth rate (FY1988). Arable land: 2%; principal products: livestock, sorghum, corn, millet, cowpeas, beans. Labor force: 400,-000; 163,000 formal sector employees, most others involved in cattle raising and subsistence agriculture. Major industrial products: diamonds, copper, nickel, salt, soda ash, potash, coal, frozen beef; tourism. Natural resources: diamonds, copper, nickel, salt, soda ash, potash, coal, natural gas. Exports: diamonds, cattle, animal products, copper, nickel. Imports: foodstuffs, vehicles, textiles, petroleum products. Major trading partners: South Africa, U.K., U.S., Switzerland.

Geography. Twice the size of Arizona, Botswana is in south central Africa, bounded by South-West Africa, Zambia, Zimbabwe, and South Africa. Most of the country is near-desert, with the Kalahari occupying the western part of the country. The eastern part is hilly, with salt lakes in the north.

Government. The Botswana Constitution provides, in addition to the unicameral National Assembly, for a House of Chiefs, which has a voice on bills affecting tribal affairs. There is universal suffrage.

The major political parties are the Democratic Party (29 of 34 elective seats in 36-man Legislative Assembly), led by President Quett Masire; National Front (4 seats), led by Kenneth Koma; People's Party (1 seat), led by Kenneth Nkhwa.

History. Botswana is the land of the Batawana tribes, which, when threatened by the Boers in Transvaal, asked Britain in 1885 to establish a protectorate over the country, then known as Bechuanaland. In 1961, Britain granted a Constitution to the country. Self-government began in 1965, and on Sept. 30, 1966, the country became independent. Since 1975, it has been an associate member of the European Common Market.

BRAZIL

Federative Republic of Brazil
President: Fernando Collor de Mello (1990)
Area: 3,286,470 sq mi. (8,511,957 sq km)
Population (est. mid-1990): 150,400,000 (average annual rate of natural increase: 1.9%)
Density per square mile: 45
Capital: Brasília, (est. 1985) 1,576,657
Largest cities (est. 1985): São Paulo, 10,099,086; Rio de Janeiro, 5,615,149; Salvador, 1,811,367; Belo Horizonte, 2,122,073; Recife, 1,289,627; Porto Alegre, 1,275,483
Monetary unit: Cruzado
Language: Portuguese
Religion: Roman Catholic, 88%; Protestant, 6%
National name: República Federativa de Brasil
Literacy rate: 74%
Economic summary: Gross national product (1987): $313 billion, $2,130 per capita, 2.9% real growth rate. Arable land: 7%; principal products: coffee, sugar cane, oranges, cocoa, soybeans, tobacco, cattle. Labor force (1988 est.): 57,000,000; 25% in industry; major industrial products: steel, chemicals, petrochemicals, machinery, motor vehicles, cement, lumber. Natural resources: iron ore, manganese, bauxite, nickel, other industrial metals, hydropower, timber. Exports: coffee, iron ore, soybeans, sugar, beef, transport equipment, footwear, orange juice. Imports: wheat, copper, petroleum, machinery, chemicals, pharmaceuticals. Major trading partners: U.S., West Germany, Japan, Saudi Arabia.

Geography. Brazil covers nearly half of South America, extends 2,965 miles (4,772 km) north-south, 2,691 miles (4,331 km), east-west, and borders every nation on the continent except Chile and Ecuador. It is the fifth largest country in the world, ranking after the U.S.S.R., Canada, China, and the U.S.

More than a third of Brazil is drained by the Amazon and its more than 200 tributaries. The Amazon is navigable for ocean steamers to Iquitos, Peru, 2,300 miles (3,700 km) upstream. Southern Brazil is drained by the Plata system—the Paraguay, Uruguay, and Paraná Rivers. The most important stream entirely within Brazil is the São Francisco, navigable for 1,000 miles (1,903 km), but broken near its mouth by the 275-foot (84 m) Paulo Afonso Falls.

Government. The military took control in 1964, ousting the last elected civilian President and installing a series of military men (with the Congress ratifying the junta's choice). Election of a civilian President by the 686-member electoral college took place in January 1985.

A new constitution in 1988 provided for the president to be elected for a five-year term through direct, compulsory and secret suffrage. The National Congress maintains a bicameral structure—a Senate, whose members serve eight-year terms, and a Chamber of Deputies, elected for four-year terms.

History. Brazil is the only Latin American nation deriving its language and culture from Portugal. Adm. Pedro Alvares Cabral claimed the territory for the Portuguese in 1500. He brought to Portugal a cargo of wood, pau-brasil, from which the land received its name. Portugal began colonization in 1532 and made the area a royal colony in 1549.

During the Napoleonic wars, King João VI, then Prince Regent, fled the country in 1807 in advance of the French armies and in 1808 set up his court in Rio de Janeiro. João was drawn home in 1820 by a revolution, leaving his son as Regent. When Portugal sought to reduce Brazil again to colonial status, the prince declared Brazil's independence on Sept. 7, 1822, and became Pedro I, Emperor of Brazil.

Harassed by his parliament, Pedro I abdicated in 1831 in favor of his five-year-old son, who became Emperor in 1840 as Pedro II. The son was a popular monarch, but discontent built up and, in 1889, following a military revolt, he had to abdicate. Although a republic was proclaimed, Brazil was under two military dictatorships during the next four years. A revolt permitted a gradual return to stability under civilian Presidents.

The President during World War I, Wenceslau Braz, cooperated with the Allies and declared war on Germany.

In World War II, Brazil cooperated with the Western Allies, welcoming Allied air bases, patrolling the South Atlantic, and joining the invasion of Italy after declaring war on the Axis.

Gen. João Baptista de Oliveira Figueiredo, became President in 1979 and pledged a return to democracy in 1985.

The electoral college's choice of Tancredo Neves on Jan. 15, 1985, as the first civilian President since 1964 brought a nationwide wave of optimism, but the 75-year-old President-elect was hospitalized and underwent a series of intestinal operations. The civilian government was inaugurated on schedule on March 15, but only Neves' Vice Presidential running mate, José Sarney, was sworn in, and he was widely distrusted because he had previously been a member of the governing military regime's political party. When Neves died on April 21, Sarney became President.

Congressional elections in Nov. 1986 gave pro-Sarney candidates a large majority.

Economically, Brazil's $93-billion foreign debt was the Third World's largest, and inflation reached a staggering 229% annual rate in 1984, almost double the 115% rate in 1983. But tough austerity measures imposed by the International Monetary Fund appeared to be taking hold and, by mid-1984, Brazilian economists said the country's recession had ended and Brazil was on the road to recovery.

In 1985 the GNP increased by 8.3% and in February 1986, President Sarney announced an across-the-board price and wage freeze that failed to stop a resurgence of inflation to about 600%. Collor's plan to deal with inflation has so far consisted of freezing most of the money in circulation and lowering tariffs to force prices of domestic goods down.

Government. Sultan Haji Hassanal Bolkiah is ruler of the state, a former British protectorate which became fully sovereign and independent on New Year's Day, 1984, presiding over a Privy Council and Council of Ministers appointed by himself. The Constitution provides for a three-tiered system of indirect elections, but the last elections were held in 1965. The only known opposition leader is in exile. In 1985, the Brunei National Democratic Party (BDNP) was formed but was dissolved by the sultan in 1988.

History. Brunei (pronounced broon-eye) was a powerful state from the 16th to the 19th century, ruling over the northern part of Borneo and adjacent island chains. But it fell into decay and lost Sarawak in 1841, becoming a British protectorate in 1888 and a British dependency in 1905.

The Sultan regained control over internal affairs in 1959, but Britain retained responsibility for the state's defense and foreign affairs until the end of 1983, when the sultanate became fully independent.

Sultain Bolkiah was crowned in 1968 at the age of 22, succeeding his father, Sir Omar Ali Saifuddin, who had abdicated. During his reign, exploitation of the rich Seria oilfield has made the sultanate wealthy. The majority of the population lives in and around the capital, situated on the Brunei River nine miles from its mouth.

BRUNEI DARUSSALAM

State of Brunei Darussalam
Sultan: Haji Hassanal Bolkiah
Area: 2,226 sq mi. (5,765 sq km)
Population (est. mid-1990): 300,000 (annual rate of natural increase: 2.5%)
Density per square mile: 115
Capital and largest city (est. 1987): Bandar Seri Begawan, 56,300
Monetary unit: Brunei dollar
Ethnic groups: Malay, 68.6%; Chinese, 18%; Europeans and Indians, 7%; other, 5.4%
Languages: Malay (official), Chinese, English
Religions: Islam (official religion), 60%; Christian, 8%; Buddhist and local, 32%
Literacy rate: 45%
Member of Commonwealth of Nations, ASEAN, UN, OIC
Economic summary: Gross domestic product (1987): $3.1 billion, $13,360 per capita. Arable land: 1%; principle agricultural products: fruit, rice, pepper. Labor force: 68,128; 50.4% in production of oil, natural gas and construction. major industrial products: crude petroleum, liquified natural gas. Natural resources: petroleum, natural gas, timber. Exports: crude petroleum, liquified natural gas. Imports: machinery, transport equipment, manufactured goods, foodstuffs. Major trading partners: Japan, U.S., U.K., Singapore, South Korea.

Geography. About the size of Delaware, Brunei is an independent sultanate on the northwest coast of the island of Borneo in the South China Sea, wedged between the Malaysian states of Sabah and Sarawak. Three quarters of the thinly populated country is covered with tropical rain forest; there are rich oil and gas deposits.

BULGARIA

People's Republic of Bulgaria
President:: Zhelgu Zhelev (1990)
Prime Minister (Chairman of Council of Ministers): Andrei Lukanov (1990)
Area: 42,823 sq mi. (110,912 sq km)
Population (est. mid-1990): 8,900,000 (average annual rate of natural increase: 0.1%)
Density per square mile: 210.2
Capital: Sofia
Largest cities (est. 1986): Sofia, 1,114,962; Plovdiv, 342,-131; Varna, 302,211; Ruse, 183,746; Burgas, 182,570
Monetary unit: Lev
Language: Bulgarian
Religions: atheist, 65%; Eastern Orthodox, 27%; Muslim, 8%
National name: Narodna Republika Bulgariya
Literacy rate: 98%
Economic summary: Gross national product (1988): $67.6 billion, $7,540 per capita, 1.8% real growth rate. Arable land: 34%; principal products: grains, tobacco, fruits, vegetables. Labor force: 4,300,000, 33% in industry; major products: processed agricultural products, machinery, electronics, chemicals. Natural resources: metals, minerals, timber. Exports: machinery and transport equipment, fuels, minerals, raw materials, agricultural products. Imports: machinery and transportation equipment, fuels, raw materials, metals, agricultural raw materials. Major trading partners: U.S.S.R., Soviet bloc countries.

Geography. Two mountain ranges and two great valleys mark the topography of Bulgaria, a country the size of Tennessee. Situated on the Black Sea in the eastern part of the Balkan peninsula, it shares borders with Yugoslavia, Romania, Greece, and Turkey. The Balkan belt crosses the center of the country, almost due east-west, rising to a height of 7,800 feet (2,377 m). The Rhodope range breaks off from the Balkans in the west, curves, and then straightens out to run nearly parallel along the southern border. Between the two ranges, is the valley of the Maritsa, Bulgaria's principal river. Between the Balkan range and the Danube, which forms most of the northern boundary with Romania, is the Danubian tableland.

Southern Dobruja, a fertile region of 2,900 square miles (7,511 sq km), below the Danube delta, is an area of low hills, fens, and sandy steppes.

Government. The present Constitution has been in effect since May 18, 1971. The National Assembly, consisting of 400 members elected for five-year terms, is the governing body. It elects the State Council and the Council of Ministers.

History. The first Bulgarians, a tribe of wild horsemen akin to the Huns, crossed the Danube from the north in A.D. 679 and subjugated the Slavic population of Moesia. They adopted a Slav dialect and Slavic customs and twice conquered most of the Balkan peninsula between 893 and 1280. After the Serbs subjected their kingdom in 1330, the Bulgars gradually fell prey to the Turks, and from 1396 to 1878 Bulgaria was a Turkish province. In 1878, Russia forced Turkey to give the country its independence; but the European powers, fearing that Bulgaria might become a Russian dependency, intervened. By the Treaty of Berlin in 1878, Bulgaria became autonomous under Turkish sovereignty.

In 1887, Prince Ferdinand of Saxe-Coburg-Gotha was elected ruler of Bulgaria; on Oct. 5, 1908, he declared the country independent and took the title of Tsar.

Bulgaria joined Germany in World War I and lost. On Oct. 3, 1918, Tsar Ferdinand abdicated in favor of his son, Tsar Boris III. Boris assumed dictatorial powers in 1934–35. When Hitler awarded Bulgaria southern Dobruja, taken from Romania in 1940, Boris joined the Nazis in war the next year and occupied parts of Yugoslavia and Greece. Later the Germans tried to force Boris to send his troops against the Russians. Boris resisted and died under mysterious circumstances on Aug. 28, 1943.

Simeon II, infant son of Boris, became nominal ruler under a regency. Russia declared war on Bulgaria on Sept. 5, 1944. An armistice was agreed to three days later, after Bulgaria had declared war on Germany. Russian troops streamed in the next day and under an informal armistice a coalition "Fatherland Front" cabinet was set up under Kimon Georgiev.

A Soviet-style people's Republic was established in 1947 and Bulgaria acquired the reputation of being the most slavishly loyal to Moscow of all the East European Communist countries. An Italian prosecutor's report in 1984 charged that Bulgaria, possibly with Soviet support, master-minded the 1981 attempt by Turkish gunman Mehmet Ali Agea to assassinate Pope John Paul II.

Zhikov resigned in 1989 after 35 years in power. His successor, Peter Mladenov, purged the Politburo, ended the Communist monopoly on power and held free elections in May 1990 that led to a surprising victory for the Communists, renamed the Bulgarian Socialist Party. Mladenov was forced to resign in July 1990.

BURKINA FASO

President of the Popular Front: Blaise Compaore (1987)
Area: 105,870 sq mi. (274,200 sq km)
Population (est. mid-1990): 9,100,000 (average annual rate of natural increase: 3.2%)
Density per square mile: 82
Capital and largest city (est. 1985): Ouagadougou, 442,000
Monetary unit: Franc CFA
Ethnic groups: Mossis, Bobos, Lobis, Fulanis
Languages: French, Moré, Dioula, Fulani
Religions: Animist, 65%; Islam, 25%; Roman Catholic, 10%
National name: Burkina Faso
Literacy rate: 13%
Economic summary: Gross domestic product (1986): $1.32 billion, $160 per capita, 10% real growth rate. Arable land: 10%. Labor force in agriculture: 82%; principal products: millet, sorghum, corn, rice, livestock, peanuts, sugar cane, cotton. Major industrial products: processed agricultural products, light industrial items, brick, brewed products. Natural resources: manganese, limestone, marble, gold, uranium, bauxite, copper. Exports: livestock, peanuts, cotton. Imports: textiles, food and consumer goods, transport equipment, machinery, fuels. Major trading partners: Ivory Coast, France, Ghana, Western European nations.

Geography. Slightly larger than Colorado, Burkina Faso, formerly known as Upper Volta, is a landlocked country in West Africa. Its neighbors are the Ivory Coast, Mali, Niger, Benin, Togo, and Ghana. The country consists of extensive plains, low hills, high savannas, and a desert area in the north.

Government. The former French colony has been governed by a series of military leaders since a coup in November 1980 overthrew the last elected president. All political parties were banned.

History. The country, called Upper Volta by the French, consists chiefly of the lands of the Mossi Empire, where France established a protectorate over the Kingdom of Ouagadougou in 1897. Upper Volta became a separate colony in 1919, was partitioned among Niger, the Sudan, and the Ivory Coast in 1933 and was reconstituted in 1947. An autonomous republic within the French Community, it became independent on Aug. 5, 1960.

President Maurice Yameogo was deposed on Jan. 3, 1966, by a military coup led by Col. Sangoulé Lamizana, who dissolved the National Assembly and suspended the Constitution. A new Constitution was adopted later that year and a new Assembly was elected. However, dissension within the Volta Democratic Union, the major party, led to renewed military rule. Constitutional rule returned in 1978 with the election of an Assembly and a presidential vote in June in which Gen. Lamizana won by a narrow margin over three other candidates.

On Nov. 25, 1980, there was a bloodless coup which placed Gen. Lamizana under house arrest. Col. Sayé Zerbo took charge as the President of the Military Committee of Reform for National Progress. Maj. Jean-Baptiste Ouedraogo toppled Zerbo in another coup on Nov. 7, 1982. Captain Thomas Sankara, in turn, deposed Ouedraogo a year later. His government changed the country's name on Aug. 3, 1984, to Burkina Faso (the "land of upright men") to sever ties with its colonial past. He was overthrown and killed by Blaise Compaore in 1987.

BURMA

See Myanmar

BURUNDI

Republic of Burundi
President: Maj. Pierre Buyoya (1987)
Prime Minister: Adrien Sibomana (1988)
Area: 10,747 sq mi. (27,834 sq km)
Population (est. mid-1990): 5,600,000 (average annual rate of natural increase: 3.2%)
Density per square mile: 508
Capital and largest city (1986): Bujumbura, 272,600
Monetary unit: Burundi franc
Languages: Kirundi (official), French
Religions: Roman Catholic, 62%; Protestant, 5%; indigenous, 32%
National name: Republika Y'Uburundi
Literacy rate: 30%
Economic summary: Gross domestic product (1986): $1.3 billion, $239 per capita; 4% real growth rate. Arable land: 43%; Principal agricultural products: coffee, tea, cotton, bananas, sorghum. Labor force: 1,900,000 (1983 est.); 93% in agriculture. Major industrial products: light consumer goods. Natural resources: nickel, kaolin, gold, unexploited copper and platinum deposits. Exports: coffee, tea, cotton, hides and skins. Imports: textiles, food, transport equipment, petroleum products. Major trading partners: U.S., Western Europe, Finland.

Geography. Wedged among Tanzania, Zaire, and Rwanda in east central Africa, Burundi occupies a high plateau divided by several deep valleys. It is equal in size to Maryland.

Government. Legislative and executive power is vested in the president.

Burundi's first Constitution, approved July 11, 1974, placed UPRONA (Unity and National Progress), the only political party, in control of national policy.

History. Burundi was once part of German East Africa. An integrated society developed among the Watusi, a tall, warlike people and nomad cattle raisers, and the Bahutu, a Bantu people, who were subject farmers. Belgium won a League of Nations mandate in 1923, and subsequently Burundi, with Rwanda, was transferred to the status of a United Nations trust territory.

In 1962, Burundi gained independence and became a kingdom under Mwami Mwambutsa IV. His son deposed him in 1966 to rule as Ntaré V.

Premier Micombero overthrew the Mwami, a few months later, installing himself as president.

One of Africa's worst tribal wars, which became genocide, occurred in Burundi in April 1972, following the return of Ntare V. He was given a safe-conduct promise in writing by President Micombero but was "judged and immediately executed" by the Burundi leader. His return was apparently attended by an invasion of exiles of Burundi's Hutu tribe. Whether Hutus living in Burundi joined the invasion is unclear, but after it failed, the victorious Tutsis proceeded to massacre some 100,000 persons in six weeks, with possibly 100,000 more slain by summer.

On Nov. 1, 1976, a military coup led by Lt. Col. Jean-Baptiste Bagaza ousted Micombero, who was serving his second term. Bagaza assumed the presidency Nov. 3, suspended the Constitution, and announced that a 30-member Supreme Revolutionary Council would be the governing body.

Bagaza was elected head of the only legal political party in 1979 and re-elected to a second five-year term as party chieftain in 1984, but was overthrown in 1987.

CAMBODIA

People's Republic of Kampuchea
President: Heng Samrin (1979)
Prime Minister: Hun Sen (1985)
Area: 69,884 sq mi. (181,000 sq km)
Population (est. mid-1990): 7,000,000 (average annual rate of natural increase: 2.2%)
Density per square mile: 98
Capital and largest city (est. 1980 for metropolitan area): Phnom Penh, 500,000
Monetary unit: Riel
Ethnic groups: Khmer, 90%; Chinese, 5%; other minorities 5%
Languages: Khmer (official), French
Religion: Theravada Buddhist, 5% others
Literacy rate: 48%
Economic summary: Gross domestic product (1984): $570 million, $90 per capita. Arable land: 16%. Principal agricultural products: rice, rubber, corn. Labor force: 3,300,000; 74% in agriculture. Major industrial products: fish, wood and wood products, milled rice, rubber, cement. Natural resources: timber, gemstones, iron ore, manganese, phosphate. Exports: natural rubber, rice, pepper, wood. Imports: foodstuffs, fuel, machinery. Major trading partners: Vietnam, U.S.S.R., Eastern Europe, Japan, India.

Geography. Situated on the Indochinese peninsula, Cambodia is bordered by Thailand and Laos on the north and Vietnam on the east and south. The Gulf of Siam is off the western coast. The country, the size of Missouri, consists chiefly of a large alluvial plain ringed in by mountains and on the east by the Mekong River. The plain is centered on Lake Tonle Sap, which is a natural storage basin of the Mekong.

Government. A bloodless coup toppled Prince Sihanouk in 1970. It was led by Lon Nol and Prince Sisowath Sirik Matak, Sihanouk's cousin. Sihanouk moved to Peking to head a government-in-exile. On Oct. 9, 1970, Lon Nol proclaimed himself President.

The Lon Nol regime was overthrown in April 1975 by Pol Pot, a leader of the Communist Khmer Rouge forces, who instituted a xenophobic reign of terror. Pol Pot was in turn ousted on Jan. 8, 1979, by Vietnamese forces. A new government led by Heng Samrin was installed.

History. Cambodia came under Khmer rule about A.D. 600. Under the Khmers, magnificent temples were built at Angkor. The Khmer kingdom once ruled over most of Southeast Asia, but attacks by the Thai and the Vietnamese almost annihilated the empire until the French joined Cambodia, Laos, and Vietnam into French Indochina.

Under Norodom Sihanouk, enthroned in 1941, and particularly under Japanese occupation during World War II, nationalism revived. After the ouster of the Japanese, the Cambodians sought independence, but the French returned in 1946, granting the country a Constitution in 1947 and independence within the French Union in 1949. Sihanouk won full military control during the French-Indochinese War in 1953. He abdicated in 1955 in favor of his parents, remaining head of the government, and when his father died in 1960, became chief of state without returning to the throne. In 1963, he sought a guarantee of Cambodia's neutrality from all parties to the Vietnam War.

On March 18, 1970, while Sihanouk was abroad trying to get North Vietnamese and the Vietcong out of border sanctuaries near Vietnam, anti-Vietnamese riots occurred, and Sihanouk was overthrown.

North Vietnamese and Vietcong units in border sanctuaries began moving deeper into Cambodia, threatening rapid overthrow of the new regime headed by Lon Nol. President Nixon sent South Vietnamese and U.S. troops across the border on April 30. U.S. ground forces, limited to 30-kilometer penetration, withdrew by June 30.

The Vietnam peace agreement of 1973 stipulated withdrawal of foreign forces from Cambodia, but fighting continued between Hanoi-backed insurgents and U.S.-supplied government troops. U.S. air support for the government forces was ended by Congress on Aug. 15, 1973.

Fighting reached a quick climax early in 1975, as government troops fell back in bitter fighting, Lon Nol fled by air April 1, leaving the government under the interim control of Premier Long Boret. On April 16, the government's capitulation ended the five-year war, but not the travails of war-ravaged Cambodia.

A new Constitution was proclaimed in December 1975, establishing a 250-member People's Assembly, a State Presidium headed by Pol Pot, and a Supreme Judicial Tribunal. Samphan replaced Sihanouk as head of state in April 1976, and the former monarch became a virtual prisoner until freed by Pol Pot in 1979.

In the next two years, from 2 million to 4 million Cambodians are estimated to have died under the brutality of the Pol Pot regime. Border clashes with Vietnam developed into a Vietnamese invasion and by the end of 1978 the Pol Pot government appeared to be collapsing.

Despite the capture of Phnom Penh on Jan. 8, fighting continued in isolated areas. Retreating Pol Pot forces and refugees totaling 40,000 were driven into Thailand by May.

At a meeting in Kuala Lumpur, Malaysia, on June 22, 1982, Sihanouk formed an alliance with Son Sann, his former prime minister, and Khieu Samphan, Pol Pot's representative, to oppose the Heng Samrin regime installed in Phnom Penh by the Vietnamese.

While Sihanouk remained in exile, about 9,000 noncommunist troops loyal to him and another 15,000 under Son Sann joined about 35,000 communist Pol Pot forces fighting the 170,000 Vietnamese troops supporting the Heng Samrin government. The Cambodian insurgents suffered a major defeat in March 1985 when Vietnamese forces overran their camps in Cambodia and forced them into Thailand. Resistance forces were able to switch to hit-and-run tactics and operate effectively inside the country.

The Vietnamese plan to withdraw by early 1990 has led to negotiations to have a political settlement in place by then. The main issues are the level of inclusion of the Khmer Rouge, with their record of atrocities, in any new government, the organization and powers of the interim government pending new elections and the role of the United Nations in the transition.

CAMEROON

Republic of Cameroon
President: Paul Biya (1982)
Area: 183,569 sq mi. (475,442 sq km)
Population (est. mid-1990): 11,100,000 (average annual rate of natural increase: 2.6%)
Density per square mile: 59
Capital: Yaoundé
Largest cities (est. 1985): Douala, 852,700; Yaoundé, 583,500
Monetary unit: Franc CFA
Languages: French and English (both official); Foulbé, Bamiléke, Ewondo, Donala, Mungaka, Bassa
Religions: Roman Catholic, 35%; Animist, 12%; Islam, 35%; Protestant, 18%
National name: République du Cameroun
Literacy rate: 65%
Economic summary: Gross domestic product (1987): $12.3 billion; $1,190 per capita; .6% real growth rate. Arable land: 13%. principal products: coffee, cocoa, timber, corn, peanuts. Labor force in agriculture: 74.4%. Major products: crude oil, small manufacturing, consumer goods, aluminum. Natural resources: timber, some oil, bauxite, hydropower potential. Exports: cocoa, coffee, timber, aluminum, petroleum. Imports: consumer goods, machinery, food, beverages, tobacco, fuel. Major trading partners: France, U.S., Western European nations.

Geography. Cameroon is a West African nation on the Gulf of Guinea, bordered by Nigeria, Chad, the Central African Republic, the Congo, Equatorial Guinea, and Gabon. It is nearly twice the size of Oregon.

The interior consists of a high plateau, rising to 4,500 feet (1,372 m), with the land descending to a lower, densely wooded plateau and then to swamps and plains along the coast. Mount Cameroon (13,350 ft.; 4,069 m), near the coast, is the highest elevation in the country. The main rivers are the Benue, Nyong, and Sanaga.

Government. After a 1972 plebiscite, a unitary nation was formed out of East and West Cameroon to replace the former Federal Republic. A Constitution was adopted, providing for election of a president every five years and of a 120-seat National Assembly (later increased to 180), whose nominal five-year term can be extended or shortened by the president. The Cameroon People's Democratic Movement is the only political party.

History. The Republic of Cameroon is inhabited by Hamitic and Semitic peoples in the north, where Islam is the principal religion, and by Bantu peoples in the central and southern regions, where native animism prevails. The tribes were conquered by many invaders.

The land escaped colonial rule until 1884, when treaties with tribal chiefs brought the area under German domination. After World War I, the League of Nations gave the French a mandate over 80% of the area, and the British 20% adjacent to Nigeria. After World War II, when the country came under a U.N. trusteeship in 1946, self-government was granted, and the Cameroun People's Union emerged as the dominant party by campaigning for reunification of French and British Cameroon and for independence. Accused of being under Communist control, it waged a campaign of revolutionary terror from 1955 to 1958, when it was crushed. In British Cameroon, unification was pressed also by the leading party, the

Kamerun National Democratic Party, led by John Foncha.

France set up Cameroun as an autonomous state in 1957, and the next year its legislative assembly voted for independence by 1960. In 1959 a fully autonomous government of Cameroun was formed under Ahmadou Ahidjo. Cameroun became an independent republic on Jan. 1, 1960, adopted a Constitution in a referendum in February, and chose a National Assembly in April. The Assembly elected Ahidjo president. A federal Constitution was approved in 1961, and the Federal Republic of Cameroon came into being in October, headed by Ahidjo and Foncha.

CANADA

Sovereign: Queen Elizabeth II
Governor General: Ramon Hnatyshyn (1990)
Prime Minister: Brian Mulroney (1984)
Area: 3,851,809 sq mi. (9,976,186 sq km)
Population (est. mid-1990): 26,600,000 (average annual rate of natural increase: 0.7%)
Density per square mile: 7
Capital: Ottawa, Ont.
Largest cities (1986 census; metropolitan areas): Toronto, 3,427,168; Montreal, 2,921,357; Vancouver, 1,380,-729; Ottawa, 819,263; Edmonton, 785,465; Calgary, 671,326; Winnipeg, 625,304; Quebec, 603,627; Hamilton, 557,029; St. Catherines-Niagara, 343,258
Monetary Unit: Canadian dollar
Languages: English, French
Religions: Roman Catholic, 46%; Protestant, 41%; no religion, 7%; Eastern Orthodox, 2%; Jewish, 1%; other, 1.3%
Literacy rate: 99%
Economic Summary: Gross national product (1988): $471.5 billion, $18,070 per capita, 4.1% real growth rate. Arable land: 5%. Principal products; wheat, barley, oats, livestock. Labor force: 13,380,000; 75% in manufacturing. Major industrial products; transportation equipment, petroleum, chemicals, wood products. Exports: wheat, petroleum, lumber and wood products, ores, motor vehicles. Imports: electronic equipment, chemicals. Major trading partners: U.S., Japan, U.K., U.S.S.R., West Germany.

Geography. Covering most of the northern part of the North American continent and with an area larger than that of the United States, Canada has an extremely varied topography. In the east the mountainous maritime provinces have an irregular coast line on the Gulf of St. Lawrence and the Atlantic. The St. Lawrence plain, covering most of southern Quebec and Ontario, and the interior continental plain, covering southern Manitoba and Saskatchewan and most of Alberta, are the principal cultivable areas. They are separated by a forested plateau rising from lakes Superior and Huron.

Westward toward the Pacific, most of British Columbia, Yukon, and part of western Alberta are covered by parallel mountain ranges including the Rockies. The Pacific border of the coast range is ragged with fiords and channels. The highest point in Canada is Mount Logan (19,850 ft; 6,050 m), which is in the Yukon.

Canada has an abundance of large and small lakes. In addition to the Great Lakes on the U.S.

border, there are 9 others that are more than 100 miles long (161 km) and 35 that are more than 50 miles long (80 km).

The two principal river systems are the Mackenzie and the St. Lawrence. The St. Lawrence, with its tributaries, is navigable for over 1,900 miles (3,058 km).

Government. Canada, a self-governing member of the Commonwealth of Nations, is a federation of 10 provinces (Alberta, British Columbia, Manitoba, New Brunswick, Newfoundland, Nova Scotia, Ontario, Prince Edward Island, Quebec, and Saskatchewan) and two territories (Northwest Territories and Yukon) whose powers were spelled out in the British North America Act of 1867. With the passing of the Constitution Act of 1981, the act and the Constitutional amending power were transferred from the British government to Canada so that the Canadian Constitution is now entirely in the hands of the Canadians.

Actually the Governor General acts only with the advice of the Canadian Prime Minister and the Cabinet, who also sit in the federal Parliament. The Parliament has two houses: a Senate of 104 members appointed for life, and a House of Commons of 295 members apportioned according to provincial population. Elections are held at least every five years or whenever the party in power is voted down in the House of Commons or considers it expedient to appeal to the people. The Prime Minister is the leader of the majority party in the House of Commons—or, if no single party holds a majority, the leader of the party able to command the support of a majority of members of the House. Laws must be passed by both houses of Parliament and signed by the Governor General in the Queen's name.

The 10 provincial governments are nominally headed by Lieutenant Governors appointed by the federal government, but the executive power in each actually is vested in a Cabinet headed by a Premier, who is leader of the majority party. The provincial legislatures are composed of one-house assemblies whose members are elected for four-year terms. They are known as Legislative Assemblies, except in Newfoundland, where it is the House of Assembly, and in Quebec, where it is the National Assembly.

The judicial system consists of a Supreme Court in Ottawa (established in 1875), with appellate jurisdiction, and a Supreme Court in each province, as well as county courts with limited jurisdiction in

Population by Provinces and Territories

Province	1981 (Census)	1983 (June Estimate)
Alberta	2,237,724	2,352,300
British Columbia	2,744,467	2,825,000
Manitoba	1,026,241	1,046,300
New Brunswick	696,403	706,600
Newfoundland	567,681	576,200
Nova Scotia	847,442	859,300
Ontario	8,625,107	8,816,000
Prince Edward Island	122,506	123,900
Quebec	6,438,403	6,514,900
Saskatchewan	968,313	992,000
Northwest Territories	45,741	48,600
Yukon Territory	23,153	22,200
Total	**24,343,181**	**24,883,400**

Source: Statistics Canada.

Canadian Governors General and Prime Ministers Since 1867

Term of office	Governor General	Term	Prime Minister	Party
1867–1868	Viscount Monck[1]	1867–1873	Sir John A. MacDonald	Conservative
1869–1872	Baron Lisgar	1873–1878	Alexander Mackenzie	Liberal
1872–1878	Earl of Dufferin	1878–1891	Sir John A. MacDonald	Conservative
1878–1883	Marquess of Lorne	1891–1892	Sir John J. C. Abbott	Conservative
1883–1888	Marquess of Lansdowne	1892–1894	Sir John S. D. Thompson	Conservative
1888–1893	Baron Stanley of Preston	1894–1896	Sir Mackenzie Bowell	Conservative
1893–1898	Earl of Aberdeen	1896	Sir Charles Tupper	Conservative
1898–1904	Earl of Minto	1896–1911	Sir Wilfrid Laurier	Liberal
1904–1911	Earl Grey	1911–1917	Sir Robert L. Borden	Conservative
1911–1916	Duke of Connaught	1917–1920	Sir Robert L. Borden	Unionist
1916–1921	Duke of Devonshire	1920–1921	Arthur Meighen	Unionist
1921–1926	Baron Byng of Vimy	1921–1926	W. L. Mackenzie King	Liberal
1926–1931	Viscount Willingdon	1926	Arthur Meighen	Conservative
1931–1935	Earl of Bessborough	1926–1930	W. L. Mackenzie King	Liberal
1935–1940	Baron Tweedsmuir	1930–1935	Richard B. Bennett	Conservative
1940–1946	Earl of Athlone	1935–1948	W. L. Mackenzie King	Liberal
1946–1952	Viscount Alexander	1948–1957	Louis S. St. Laurent	Liberal
1952–1959	Vincent Massey	1957–1963	John G. Diefenbaker	Conservative
1959–1967	George P. Vanier	1963–1968	Lester B. Pearson	Liberal
1967–1973	Roland Michener	1968–1979	Pierre Elliott Trudeau	Liberal
1974–1979	Jules Léger	1979–1980	Charles Joseph Clark	Conservative
1979–1984	Edward R. Schreyer	1980–1984	Pierre Elliott Trudeau	Liberal
1984–	Jeanne Sauvé	1984–1984	John Turner	Liberal
		1984–	Brian Mulroney	Conservative

1. Became Governor General of British North America in 1861.

most of the provinces. The Governor General in Council appoints these judges.

History. The Norse explorer Leif Ericson probably reached the shores of Canada (Labrador or Nova Scotia) in A.D. 1000, but the history of the white man in the country actually began in 1497, when John Cabot, an Italian in the service of Henry VII of England, reached Newfoundland or Nova Scotia. Canada was taken for France in 1534 by Jacques Cartier. The actual settlement of New France, as it was then called, began in 1604 at Port Royal in what is now Nova Scotia; in 1608, Quebec was founded. France's colonization efforts were not very successful, but French explorers by the end of the 17th century had penetrated beyond the Great Lakes to the western prairies and south along the Mississippi to the Gulf of Mexico. Meanwhile, the English Hudson's Bay Company had been established in 1670. Because of the valuable fisheries and fur trade, a conflict developed between the French and English; in 1713, Newfoundland, Hudson Bay, and Nova Scotia (Acadia) were lost to England.

During the Seven Years' War (1756–63), England extended its conquest, and the British Maj. Gen. James Wolfe won his famous victory over Gen. Louis Montcalm outside Quebec on Sept. 13, 1759. The Treaty of Paris in 1763 gave England control.

At that time the population of Canada was almost entirely French, but in the next few decades, thousands of British colonists emigrated to Canada from the British Isles and from the American colonies. In 1849, the right of Canada to self-government was recognized. By the British North America Act of 1867, the Dominion of Canada was created through the confederation of Upper and Lower Canada, Nova Scotia, and New Brunswick. Prince Edward Island joined the Dominion in 1873.

In 1869 Canada purchased from the Hudson's Bay Company the vast middle west (Rupert's Land) from which the provinces of Manitoba (1870), Alberta, and Saskatchewan (1905) were later formed. In 1871, British Columbia joined the Dominion. The country was linked from coast to coast in 1885 by the Canadian Pacific Railway.

During the formative years between 1866 and 1896, the Conservative Party, led by Sir John A. MacDonald, governed the country, except during the years 1873–78. In 1896, the Liberal Party took over and, under Sir Wilfrid Laurier, an eminent French Canadian, ruled until 1911.

By the Statute of Westminster in 1931 the British Dominions, including Canada, were formally declared to be partner nations with Britain, "equal in status, in no way subordinate to each other," and bound together only by allegiance to a common Crown.

Newfoundland became Canada's 10th province on March 31, 1949, following a plebiscite. Canada includes two territories—the Yukon Territory, the area north of British Columbia and east of Alaska, and the Northwest Territories, including all of Canada north of 60° north latitude except Yukon and the northernmost sections of Quebec and Newfoundland. This area includes all of the Arctic north of the mainland, Norway having recognized Canadian sovereignty over the Svendrup Islands in the Arctic in 1931.

The Liberal Party, led by William Lyon Mackenzie King, dominated Canadian politics from 1921 until 1957, when it was succeeded by the Progressive Conservatives. The Liberals, under the leadership of Lester B. Pearson, returned to power in 1963. Pearson remained Prime Minister until 1968, when he retired and was replaced by a former law professor, Pierre Elliott Trudeau. Trudeau maintained Canada's defensive alliance with the United States, but began moving toward a more independent policy in world affairs.

Trudeau set about creating what he termed a "just society," stressing domestic reforms. His election was considered in part a response to the most serious problem confronting the country, the division between French- and English-speaking Canadians, which had led to a separatist movement in the predominantly French province of Quebec. Trudeau, himself a French Canadian, supported programs for bilingualism and an increased measure of provincial autonomy, although he would not tolerate the idea of separatism. In 1974, the provincial government voted to make French the official language of Quebec.

Conflicts over the law establishing French as the dominant language in Quebec, particularly in schooling, kept separatism as a national issue, but by-elections in 1977 produced easy victories for Trudeau's ruling Liberals in four Quebec seats in the national legislature.

Economic problems appeared to take precedence over politics in 1978, as the Sun Life Assurance Company of Canada, the nation's largest insurance firm, announced that it would move its headquarters from Montreal to Toronto. Many businesses had left the province earlier, but Sun Life was the first to cite the language law as the reason for its departure.

Despite Trudeau's removal of price and wage controls in 1978, continuing inflation and a high rate of unemployment caused him to delay elections until May 22, 1979. The delay gave Trudeau no advantage—the Progressive Conservatives under Charles Joseph Clark defeated the Liberals everywhere except in Quebec, New Brunswick, and Newfoundland.

Clark took office as the head of Canada's fifth minority government in the last 20 years.

His government collapsed after only six months when a motion to defeat the Tory budget carried by 139-133 on Dec. 13, 1979. On the same day, the Quebec law making French the exclusive official language of the province—an issue which had been expected to provide Clark's first major internal test—was voided by the Canadian Supreme Court.

In national elections Feb. 18, 1980, the resurgent Liberals under Trudeau scored an unexpectedly big victory, winning 146 seats (147 when a vacancy was filled a month later), while the Conservatives fell from 136 to 103 and the New Democrats won 32 seats.

Resolving a dispute that had occupied Trudeau since the beginning of his tenure, Queen Elizabeth II, in Ottawa on April 17, 1982, signed the Constitution Act, cutting the last legal tie between Canada and Britain. Since 1867, the British North America Act required British Parliament approval for any Canadian constitutional change.

The new charter was approved by the federal House of Commons, 246–24, on Dec. 2, 1981, and by a 59–23 vote of the Senate six days later. The Constitution retains Queen Elizabeth as Queen of Canada and keeps Canada's membership in the Commonwealth.

Ending an era, Trudeau retired on June 30, 1984, after 16 years as prime minister, except for the nine-month interruption in 1979–80.

His successor as Liberal Party leader and Prime Minister, John N. Turner, called an early election for a new Parliament after polls showed the Liberals had made a big comeback from the last months of Trudeau's term, despite Canada's continuing recession and 11.2% unemployment, the highest in 40 years.

In the national election on Sept. 4, 1984, the Progressive Conservative Party scored an overwhelming victory, fundamentally changing the country's political landscape. The Conservatives, led by Brian Mulroney, a 45-year-old corporate lawyer, won the highest political majority in Canadian history, Mulroney was sworn in as Canada's 18th Prime Minister on Sept. 17.

The dominant foreign issue was a free-trade pact with the U.S., a treaty bitterly opposed by the Liberal and New Democratic parties. The conflict led to elections in Nov. 1988 that solidly re-elected Mulroney and gave him a mandate to proceed with the agreement.

The issue of separatist sentiments in French-speaking Quebec flared up again in 1990 with the failure of the Meech Lake accord. The accord was designed to ease the Quebecers' fear of losing their identity within the English-speaking majority by giving Quebec constitutional status as a "distinct society."

CAPE VERDE

Republic of Cape Verde
President: Aristides Pereira (1975)
Premier: Maj. Pedro Pires (1975)
Area: 1,557 sq mi. (4,033 sq km)
Population: (est. mid-1990): 400,000 (average annual rate of natural increase: 2.8%)
Density per square mile: 237
Capital (est. 1982): Praia, 37,676
Largest city (est. 1982): Mindelo, 50,000
Monetary unit: Cape Verde escudo
Language: Portuguese, Criuolo
Religion: Roman Catholic fused with indigenous beliefs, 98%
National name: República de Cabo Verde
Literacy rate: 37%
Economic summary: Gross national product (1987): $136 million; $400 per capita; $5.8% real growth rate. Arable land: 9%. Labor force in agriculture: 57%. Principal agricultural products: bananas, corn, sugar cane, beans. Major industry: fishing, salt mining. Natural resources: salt, siliceous rock. Exports: fish, textiles, bananas, salt. Imports: machinery, petroleum products, corn, rice. Major trading partners: Portugal, U.K., Japan, Angola, Zaire.

Geography: Cape Verde, only slightly larger than Rhode Island, is an archipelago in the Atlantic 385 miles (620 km) west of Dakar, Senegal.

The islands are divided into two groups: Barlavento in the north, comprising Santo Antão (291 sq mi.; 754 sq km), Boa Vista (240 sq mi.; 622 sq km), São Nicolau (132 sq mi.; 342 sq km), São Vicente (88 sq mi.; 246 sq km), Sal (83 sq mi.; 298 sq km), and Santa Luzia (13 sq mi.; 34 sq km); and Sotavento in the south, consisting of São Tiago (383 sq mi.; 992 sq km), Fogo (184 sq mi.; 477 sq km), Maio (103 sq mi.; 267 sq km), and Brava (25 sq mi.; 65 sq km). The islands are mostly mountainous, with the land deeply scarred by erosion. There is an active volcano on Fogo.

Government. The islands became independent on July 5, 1975, under an agreement negotiated with Portugal in 1974. The 56-member National Assembly chose Aristides Pereira as President and Maj.

Pedro Pires as Premier. All members of the Assembly belong to the African Party for the Independence of Portuguese Guinea and Cape Verde, then the only party that entered candidates in the election. It is committed to union with Guinea-Bissau, another former Portuguese colony.

History. Uninhabited upon their discovery in 1456, the Cape Verde islands became part of the Portuguese empire in 1495. A majority of their modern inhabitants are of mixed Portuguese and African ancestry. A coaling station developed during the 19th century on the island of São Vicente has grown in recent years to an oil and gasoline storage depot for ships and aircraft.

CENTRAL AFRICAN REPUBLIC

Head of Government: Gen. André Kolingba (1981)
Area: 241,313 sq mi. (625,000 sq km)
Population (est. mid-1990): 2,900,000 (average annual rate of natural increase: 2.5%)
Density per square mile: 12
Capital and largest city (est. 1985): Bangui, 473,000
Monetary unit: Franc CFA
Ethnic groups: Mandja-Baya, Banda, Mbaka, Azande, Yakoma, Mbanziri, Sango
Languages: French (official) and Sango
Religions: Protestant and Roman Catholic with animist influence, 40%; indigenous, 24%; Islam, 15%; other, 11%
National name: République Centrafricaine
Literacy rate: 33%
Economic summary: Gross domestic product (1987): $1,106 million; $410 per capita; 1.4% real growth rate. Arable land: 3%; principal products: cotton, coffee, peanuts, food crops, livestock. Labor force (1986 est.): 775,413; 85% in agriculture. Major industrial products: timber, textiles, soap, cigarettes, diamonds, processed food, brewed beverages. Natural resources: diamonds, uranium, timber. Exports: diamonds, cotton, timber, coffee. Imports: machinery and electrical equipment, petroleum products, textiles. Major trading partners: France, Japan, U.S., Western Europe, Algeria, Yugoslavia.

Geography. Situated about 500 miles north (805 km) of the equator, the Central African Republic is a landlocked nation bordered by Cameroon, Chad, the Sudan, Zaire, and the Congo. Twice the size of New Mexico, it is covered by tropical forests in the south and semidesert land in the east. The Ubangi and Shari are the largest of many rivers.

Government. On Dec. 4, 1976, the Central African Republic became the Central African Empire. Marshal Jean-Bédel Bokassa, who had ruled the republic since he took power in a military coup Dec. 31, 1965, was declared Emperor Bokassa I. He was overthrown in a coup on Sept. 20, 1979. Former President David Dacko, returned to power and changed the country's name back to the Central African Republic. An army coup on Sept. 1, 1981, deposed Dacko and suspended the Constitution and all political parties. A Military Committee of National Redress was set up to run the country. A new constitution was enacted on Nov. 21, 1986 that extended Kolingba's term another six years and allowed for parliamentary elections in which the Centrafrican Democratic Assembly would be the only party.

History. As the colony of Ubangi-Shari, what is now the Central African Republic was united with Chad in 1905 and joined with Gabon and the Middle Congo in French Equatorial Africa in 1910. After World War II a rebellion in 1946 forced the French to grant self-government. In 1958 the territory voted to become an autonomous republic within the French Community, but on Aug. 13, 1960, President David Dacko proclaimed the republic's independence from France.

Dacko undertook to move the country into Peking's orbit, but was overthrown in a coup on Dec. 31, 1965, by the then Col. Jean-Bédel Bokassa, Army Chief of Staff. In August 1977, the U.S. State Department protested the Emperor's jailing of American and British newsmen.

Bokassa staged an elaborate coronation ceremony on the first anniversary of the Empire. The cost of the ceremony was one fourth of the annual foreign-exchange earnings of the country.

CHAD

Republic of Chad
President: Hissen Habré (1982)
Area: 495,752 sq mi. (1,284,000 sq km)
Population (est. mid-1990): 5,000,000 (average annual rate of natural increase, 2.5%)
Density per square mile: 10
Capital and largest city (est. 1986): N'djamena, 511,700
Monetary unit: Franc CFA
Ethnic groups: Baguirmiens, Kanembous, Saras, Massas, Arabs, Toubous, Goranes
Languages: French and Arabic (official), many tribal languages
Religions: Islam, 44%; Christian, 33%; traditional, 23%
National name: République du Tchad
Literacy rate: 17%
Economic summary: Gross domestic product (1986 est.): $818 billion; $160 per capita; real growth rate: -2.0%. Arable land: 2%; principal agricultural products: cotton, cattle, sugar, subsistence crops. Labor force in agriculture: 85%. Major products: livestock and livestock products, beer, food processing, textiles, cigarettes. Natural resources: petroleum, unexploited uranium, kaolin. Exports: cotton, livestock and animal products, fish. Imports: food, motor vehicles and parts, petroleum products, machinery, cement, textiles. Major trading partners: France, Nigeria, and central African countries.

Geography. A landlocked country in north central Africa, Chad is about 85% the size of Alaska. Its neighbors are Niger, Libya, the Sudan, the Central African Republic, Cameroon, and Nigeria.

Lake Chad, from which the country gets its name, lies on the western border with Niger and Nigeria. In the north is a desert that runs into the Sahara.

Government. Hissen Habré became president of Chad on June 7, 1982, by overthrowing Goukouni Oueddei.

History. Chad was absorbed into the colony of French Equatorial Africa, as part of Ubangi-Shari, in 1910. France began the country's development after 1920, when it became a separate colony. In

1946, French Equatorial Africa was admitted to the French Union. By referendum in 1958 the Chad territory became an autonomous republic within the French Union.

An independence movement led by the first Premier and President, François (later Ngarta) Tombalbaye, achieved complete independence on Aug. 11, 1960.

Tombalbaye was killed in the 1975 coup and was succeeded by Gen. Félix Malloum, who faced a Libyan-financed rebel movement throughout his tenure in office. A ceasefire backed by Libya, Niger, and the Sudan early in 1978 failed to end the fighting, and French military aid was increased.

Nine rival groups meeting in Lagos, Nigeria, in March 1979 agreed to form a provisional government headed by Goukouni Oueddei, a former rebel leader. Fighting broke out again in Chad in March 1980, when Defense Minister Hissen Habré challenged Goukouni and seized the capital. By the year's end, Libyan troops supporting Goukouni recaptured N'djamena, and Libyan President Muammar el-Qaddafi, in January 1981, proposed a merger of Chad with Libya.

The Libyan merger proposal was rejected and Libyan troops withdrew from Chad but in 1983 poured back into the barren northern part of the country in support of Goukouni. France, in turn, sent troops into southern Chad in support of Habré.

A Qaddafi-Goukouni break in Nov. 1986 led to the defection of his troops. Government troops then launched an offensive in early 1987 that drove the Libyans out of most of the country.

CHILE

Republic of Chile

President: Patricio Aylwin (1990)
Area: 292,132 sq mi. (756,622 sq km)
Population (est. mid-1990): 13,200,000 (average annual rate of natural increase: 1.7%)
Density per square mile: 44
Capital: Santiago
Largest cities (est. 1986): Santiago, 4,804,200; Valparaíso, 277,900; Concepción, 292,700; Antofagasta, 203,100; Talcahuano, 229,500; Temuco, 215,400
Monetary unit: Peso
Language: Spanish
Religion: Roman Catholic, 89%; Protestant, 11%; small Jewish and Muslim populations.
National name: República de Chile
Literacy rate: 96%
Economic summary: Gross domestic product (1988): $19.4 billion; $1,520 per capita; 6.8% real growth rate. Arable land: 2%; principal products: wheat, corn, sugar beets, vegetables, wine, livestock. Labor force: 85% in agriculture. Major industrial products: processed fish, transportation equipment, iron and steel, pulp, paper. Natural resources: copper, timber, iron ore, nitrates. Exports: copper, iron ore, paper and wood products, fruits. Imports: sugar, wheat, vehicles, petroleum, capital goods. Major trading partners: U.S., Japan, West Germany, Brazil, Argentina, Venezuela, France.

Geography. Situated south of Peru and west of Bolivia and Argentina, Chile fills a narrow 1,800-mile

(2,897 km) strip between the Andes and the Pacific. Its area is nearly twice that of Montana.

One third of Chile is covered by the towering ranges of the Andes. In the north is the mineral-rich Atacama Desert, between the coastal mountains and the Andes. In the center is a 700-mile-long (1,127 km) valley, thickly populated, between the Andes and the coastal plateau. In the south, the Andes border on the ocean.

At the southern tip of Chile's mainland is Punta Arenas, the southernmost city in the world, and beyond that lies the Strait of Magellan and Tierra del Fuego, an island divided between Chile and Argentina. The southernmost point of South America is Cape Horn, a 1,390-foot (424-m) rock on Horn Island in the Wollaston group, which belongs to Chile.

The Juan Fernández Islands, in the South Pacific about 400 miles (644 km) west of the mainland, and Easter Island, about 2,000 miles (3,219 km) west, are Chilean possessions.

Government. Under the 1980 Constitution, the President serves a four-year term. There is a bicameral legislature which opened its first session in 1990.

History. Chile was originally under the control of the Incas in the north and the fierce Araucanian people in the south. In 1541, a Spaniard, Pedro de Valdivia, founded Santiago. Chile won its independence from Spain in 1818 under Bernardo O'Higgins and an Argentinian, José de San Martin. O'Higgins, dictator until 1823, laid the foundations of the modern state with a two-party system and a centralized government.

The dictator from 1830 to 1837, Diego Portales, fought a war with Peru in 1836–39 that expanded Chilean territory. The Conservatives were in power from 1831 to 1861. Then the Liberals, winning a share of power for the next 30 years, disestablished the church and limited presidential power. Chile fought the War of the Pacific with Peru and Bolivia from 1879 to 1883, winning Antofagasta, Bolivia's only outlet to the sea, and extensive areas from Peru. A revolt in 1890 led by Jorge Montt overthrew, in 1891, José Balmaceda and established a parliamentary dictatorship that existed until a new Constitution was adopted in 1925. Industrialization began before World War I and led to the formation of Marxist groups.

Juan Antonio Ríos, President during World War II, was originally pro-Nazi but in 1944 led his country into the war on the side of the U.S.

A small abortive army uprising in 1969 raised fear of military intervention to prevent a Marxist, Salvador Allende Gossens, from taking office after his election to the presidency on Sept. 4, 1970, with 36.3% of the vote in a three-way battle. Dr. Allende was the first President in a non-Communist country freely elected on a Marxist-Leninist program.

Allende quickly established relations with Cuba and the People's Republic of China and nationalized several American companies.

Allende's overthrow and death in an army assault on the presidential palace in September 1973 ended a 46-year era of constitutional government in Chile, which had boasted the longest such record in Latin America.

The takeover was led by a four-man junta headed by Army Chief of Staff Augusto Pinochet Ugarte, who assumed the office of President.

Committed to "exterminate Marxism," the junta embarked on a right-wing dictatorship. It suspended parliament, banned political activity, and broke relations with Cuba.

The Human Rights Commission of the Organization of American States charged the junta with "most grave violations" of basic liberties. In July, Chile denied entry to a U.N. investigatory panel. On June 9, 1978, the government reversed that policy to permit the U.N. Human Rights Commission to send an investigative mission to Chile.

In 1977, Pinochet, in a speech marking his fourth year in power, promised elections by 1985 if conditions warranted. Earlier, he had abolished DINA, the secret police, and decreed an amnesty for political prisoners, an action Amnesty International said might affect only 200–400 of some 1,500 political prisoners.

Pinochet was inaugurated on March 11, 1981, for an eight-year term as President, at the end of which, according to the Constitution adopted six months earlier, the junta would nominate a civilian as successor, although Pinochet announced that he might serve another eight-year term. The 1989 plebiscite resulted in a defeat for Pinochet. He stepped down in January 1990 in favor of Patricio Aylwin who was be elected Dec. 1989.

CHINA

People's Republic of China
President: Gen. Yang Shangkun (1988)
Premier: Li Peng (1987)
Area: 3,691,521 sq mi. (9,561,000 sq km)[1]
Population (est. mid-1990): 1,119,900,000 (average rate of natural increase: 1.4%)
Density per square mile: 298
Capital: Beijing
Largest cities (est. 1983): Shanghai, 11,940,000; Beijing (Peking) 9,330,000; Tianjin (Tientsin) 7,850,000; Canton, 6,840,000; Wuhan, 5,940,000; Shenyang (Mukden), 5,210,000; Nanjing (Nanking), 4,560,000; Chongqing (Chungking), 3,890,000; Harbin; 3,730,000
Monetary unit: Yuan
Languages: Chinese, (Mandarin, Cantonese, and local dialects)
Religions: Non-religious, 59%; folk religions, 20%; atheist, 12%
National name: Zhonghua Renmin Gongheguo
Literacy rate: 76.5%
Economic summary: Gross national product (1988); $350 billion; $320 per capita; 11% real growth rate. Arable land: 10%; principal products: rice, wheat, grains, cotton. Labor force: 513,000,000; 61.1% in agriculture. Major industrial products: iron and steel, textiles, armaments, petroleum. Natural resources: coal, natural gas, limestone, marble, metals, hydropower potential. Exports: agricultural products, oil, minerals, metals, manufactured goods. Imports: grains, chemical fertilizer, steel, industrial raw materials, machinery and equipment. Major trading partners: Japan, Hong Kong, U.S., West Germany, Singapore, Canada, U.S.S.R., Italy.

1. Including Manchuria and Tibet.

Geography. China, which occupies the eastern part of Asia, is slightly larger in area than the U.S. Its coastline is roughly a semicircle. The greater part of the country is mountainous, and only in the lower reaches of the Yellow and Yangtze Rivers are there extensive low plains.

The principal mountain ranges are the Tien Shan, to the northwest; the Kunlun chain, running south of the Taklimakan and Gobi Deserts; and the Trans-Himalaya, connecting the Kunlun with the borders of China and Tibet. Manchuria is largely an undulating plain connected with the north China plain by a narrow lowland corridor. Inner Mongolia contains the relatively fertile southern and eastern portions of the Gobi. The large island of Hainan (13,500 sq mi.; 34,380 sq km) lies off the southern coast.

Hydrographically, China proper consists of three great river systems. The northern part of the country is drained by the Yellow River (Huang Ho), 2,109 miles long (5,464 km) and mostly unnavigable. The central part is drained by the Chang Jiang (Yangtze Kiang), the third longest river in the world 2,432 miles (6,300 km). The Zhujiang (Si Kiang) in the south is 848 miles long (2,197 km) and navigable for a considerable distance. In addition, the Amur (1,144 sq mi.; 2,965 km) forms part of the northeastern boundary.

Government. With 2,978 deputies, elected for four-year terms by universal suffrage, the National People's Congress is the chief legislative organ. A State Council has the executive authority. The Congress elects the Premier and Deputy Premiers. All ministries are under the State Council, headed by the Premier.

The Communist Party controls the government.

History. By 2000 B.C.; the Chinese were living in the Huang Ho basin, and they had achieved an advanced stage of civilization by 1200 B.C. The great philosophers Lao-tse, Confucius Mo Ti, and Mencius lived during the Chou dynasty (1122–249 B.C.). The warring feudal states were first united under Emperor Ch'in Shih Huang Ti, during whose reign (246–210 B.C.) work was begun on the Great Wall. Under the Han dynasty (206 B.C.–A.D. 220), China prospered and traded with the West.

In the T'ang dynasty (618–907), often called the golden age of Chinese history, painting, sculpture, and poetry flourished, and printing made its earliest known appearance.

The Mings, last of the native rulers (1368–1644), overthrew the Mongol, or Yuan, dynasty (1280–1368) established by Kublai Khan. The Mings in turn were overthrown in 1644 by invaders from the north, the Manchus.

China closely restricted foreign activities, and by the end of the 18th century only Canton and the Portuguese port of Macao were open to European merchants. Following the Anglo-Chinese War of 1839–42, however, several treaty ports were opened, and Hong Kong was ceded to Britain. Treaties signed after further hostilities (1856–60) weakened Chinese sovereignty and removed foreigners from Chinese jurisdiction. The disastrous Chinese-Japanese War of 1894–95 was followed by a scramble for Chinese concessions by European powers, leading to the Boxer Rebellion (1900), suppressed by an international force.

The death of the Empress Dowager Tzu Hsi in 1908 and the accession of the infant Emperor Hsüan T'ung (Pu-Yi) were followed by a nationwide rebellion led by Dr. Sun Yat-sen, who became first President of the Provisional Chinese Republic in 1911. The Manchus abdicated on Feb. 12, 1912. Dr. Sun resigned in favor of Yuan Shih-k'ai, who suppressed the republicans but was forced by a se-

Provinces and Regions of China

Name	Area (sq mi.)	Area (sq km)	Capital
Provinces			
Anhui (Anhwei)	54,015	139,900	Hefei (Hofei)
Fujian (Fukien)	47,529	123,100	Fuzhou (Fukien)
Gansu (Kansu)	137,104	355,100	Lanzhou (Lanchow)
Guangdong (Kwangtung)	89,344	231,400	Canton
Guizhou (Kweichow)	67,181	174,000	Guiyang (Kweiyang)
Hebei (Hopei)	81,479	211,030	Shijiazhuang (Shitikiachwang)
Heilongjiang (Heilungkiang)[1]	178,996	463,600	Harbin
Henan (Honan)	64,479	167,000	Zhengzhou (Chengchow)
Hubei (Hupeh)	72,394	187,500	Wuhan
Hunan	81,274	210,500	Changsha
Jiangsu (Kiangsu)	40,927	106,000	Nanjing (Nanking)
Jiangxi (Kiangsi)	63,629	164,800	Nanchang
Jilin (Kirin)[1]	72,201	187,000	Changchun
Liaoning[1]	53,301	138,050	Shenyang
Quinghai (Chinghai)	278,378	721,000	Xining (Sining)
Shaanxi (Shensi)	75,598	195,800	Xian (Sian)
Shandong (Shantung)	59,189	153,300	Jinan (Tsinan)
Shanxi (Shansi)	60,656	157,100	Taiyuan
Sichuan (Szechwan)	219,691	569,000	Chengdu (Chengtu)
Yunnan	168,417	436,200	Kunming
Zhejiang (Chekiang)	39,305	101,800	Hangzhou (Hangchow)
Autonomous Region			
Guangxi Zhuang (Kwangsi Chuang)	85,096	220,400	Nanning
Nei Monggol (Inner Mongolia)[1]	454,633	1,177,500	Hohhot (Huhehot)
Ningxia Hui	30,039	77,800	Yinchuan (Yinchwan)
Xinjiang Uygur (Sinkiang Uighur)[1]	635,829	1,646,800	Urumqi (Urumchi)
Xizang (Tibet)	471,660	1,221,600	Lhasa

1. Together constitute (with Taiwan) what has been traditionally known as Outer China, the remaining territory forming the historical China Proper. NOTE: Names are in Pinyin, with conventional spelling in parentheses.

rious rising in 1915–16 to abandon his intention of declaring himself Emperor. Yuan's death in June 1916 was followed by years of civil war between rival militarists and Dr. Sun's republicans.

Nationalist forces, led by Gen. Chiang Kai-shek and with the advice of Communist experts, soon occupied most of China, setting up a Kuomintang regime in 1928. Internal strife continued, however, and Chiang broke with the Communists.

An alleged explosion on the South Manchurian Railway on Sept. 18, 1931, brought invasion of Manchuria by Japanese forces, who installed the last Manchu Emperor, Henry Pu-Yi, as nominal ruler of the puppet state of "Manchukuo." Japanese efforts to take China's northern provinces in July 1937 were resisted by Chiang, who meanwhile had succeeded in uniting most of China behind him. Within two years, however, Japan seized most of the ports and railways. The Kuomintang government retreated first to Hankow and then to Chungking, while the Japanese set up a puppet government at Nanking headed by Wang Jingwei.

Japan's surrender in 1945 touched off civil war between Nationalist forces under Chiang and Communist forces led by Mao Zedong, the party chairman. Despite U. S. aid, the Chiang forces were overcome by the Maoists, backed by the Soviet bloc, and were expelled from the mainland. The Mao regime, established in Peking as the new capital, proclaimed the People's Republic of China on Oct. 1, 1949, with Zhou Enlai as Premier.

After the Korean War began in June 1950, China led the Communist bloc in supporting North Korea, and on Nov. 26, 1950, the Mao regime intervened openly.

In 1958, Mao undertook the "Great Leap Forward" campaign, which combined the establishment of rural communes with a crash program of village industrialization. These efforts also failed, causing Mao to lose influence to Liu Shaoqi, who became President in 1959, to Premier Zhou, and to Party Secretary Deng Xiaoping.

China exploded its first atomic (fission) bomb in 1964 and produced a fusion bomb in 1967.

Mao moved to Shanghai, and from that base he and his supporters waged what they called a Cultural Revolution. In the spring of 1966 the Mao group formed Red Guard units dominated by youths and students, closing the schools to free the students for agitation.

The Red Guards campaigned against "old ideas, old culture, old habits, and old customs." Often they were no more than uncontrolled mobs, and brutality was frequent. Early in 1967 efforts were made to restore control. The Red Guards were urged to return home. Schools started opening.

Persistent overtures by the Nixon Administration resulted in the dramatic announcement in July that Henry Kissinger, President Richard M. Nixon's national security adviser, had secretly visited Peking and reached agreement on a visit by the President to China.

The movement toward reconciliation, which signaled the end of the U.S. containment policy toward China, provided irresistible momentum for Chinese admission to the U.N. Despite U.S. opposition to expelling Taiwan (Nationalist China), the world body overwhelmingly ousted Chiang in seating Peking.

President Nixon went to Peking for a week early

in 1972, meeting Mao as well as Zhou. The summit ended with a historic communiqué on February 28, in which both nations promised to work toward improved relations.

In 1973, the U.S. and China agreed to set up "liaison offices" in each other's capitals, which constituted de facto diplomatic relations. Full diplomatic relations were barred by China as long as the U.S. continued to recognize Nationalist China.

On Jan. 8, 1976, Zhou died. His successor, Vice Premier Deng Xiaoping was supplanted within a month by Hua Guofeng, former Minister of Public Security. Hua became permanent Premier in April. In October he was named successor to Mao as Chairman of the Communist Party.

After Mao died on Sept. 10, a campaign against his widow, Jiang Qing, and three of her "radical" colleagues began. The "Gang of Four" was denounced for having undermined the party, the government, and the economy.

Jiang was brought to trial in 1980 and sentenced on Jan. 25, 1981, to die within two years unless she showed repentance, in which case she would be imprisoned for life.

At the Central Committee meeting of 1977, Deng was reinstated as Deputy Premier, Chief of Staff of the Army, and member of the Central Committee of the Politburo.

At the same time, Jiang Qing, Wang Hongwen, Zhang Chunqiao, and Yao Wenyuan—the notorious "Gang of Four"—were removed from all official posts and banished from the party.

In May 1978, expulsion of ethnic Chinese by Vietnam produced an open rupture. Peking sided with Cambodia in the border fighting that flared between Vietnam and Cambodia, charging Hanoi with aggression.

On Aug. 12, 1978, China and Japan signed a treaty of peace and friendship. Peking and Washington then announced that they would open full diplomatic relations on Jan. 1, 1979 and the Carter Administration abrogated the Taiwan defense treaty. Deputy Premier Deng sealed the agreement with a visit to the United States that coincided with the opening of embassies in both capitals on March 1.

On Deng's return from the U.S. Chinese troops invaded Vietnam to avenge alleged violations of Chinese territory. The action was seen as a reaction to Vietnam's invasion of Cambodia.

The first People's Congress in five years confirmed Zhao Ziyang, an economic planner, as Premier replacing Hua Guofeng, who had held the post since 1976.

After the Central Committee meeting of June 27–29, 1981, Hu Yaobang, a Deng protégé, was elevated to the party chairmanship, replacing Hua Guofeng. Deng became chairman of the military commission of the central committee, giving him control over the army. The committee's 215 members concluded the session with a statement holding Mao Zedong responsible for the "grave blunder" of the Cultural Revolution.

On June 18, 1983, the Chinese Parliament elected Li Xiannian, an economics and financial specialist, as the first national president since 1969. Previously an outspoken critic of the United States, he was the official host when President Reagan visited China in April 1984.

Under Deng Xiaoping's leadership, meanwhile, China's Communist ideaology was almost totally reinterpreted and sweeping economic changes were set in motion in the early 1980s. The Chinese scrapped the personality cult that idolized Mao Zedong, muted Mao's old call for class struggle and exportation of the Communist revolution, and imported Western technology and management techniques to replace the Marxist tenets that retarded modernization.

Also under Deng's leadership, the Chinese Communists worked out an arrangement with Britain for the future of Hong Kong after 1997. The flag of China will be raised but the territory will retain its present social, economic and legal system.

The removal of Hu Yaobang as party chairman in January 1987 was a sign of a hard-line resurgence. He was replaced by former Premier Zhao Ziyang. Conflict between hard-liners and moderates continued and reached a violent climax in 1989. Student demonstrations calling for accelerated liberalization were crushed by military force in June, resulting in several hundred deaths. This was followed by a purge of moderates, including party leader Zhao Ziyang, who was replaced with Jiang Zemin.

COLOMBIA

Republic of Colombia
President: César Gaviria Trujillo (1990)
Population (est. mid-1990): 31,800,000 (average annual rate of natural increase, 2.0%)
Density per square mile: 71
Capital: Bogotá
Largest cities (est. 1985): Bogotá, 4,208,000; Medellín, 2,069,000; Cali, 1,654,000; Barranquilla, 1,120,000; Bucaramanga, 545,000; Cartagena, 530,000
Monetary unit: Peso
Language: Spanish
Religion: Roman Catholic
National name: República de Colombia
Literacy rate (1985): 88%
Economic summary: Gross domestic product (est. 1987): $33 billion; $1,140 per capita; 5.4% real growth rate. Arable land: 4%; principal products: coffee, bananas, rice, corn, sugar cane, cotton, tobacco, sorghum. Labor force: 11,000,000; 21% in industry; major products: textiles, processed food, beverages, chemicals, cement. Natural resources: petroleum, natural gas, coal, iron ore, nickel, gold, silver. Exports: coffee, fuel oil, cotton, bananas. Imports: machinery, electrical equipment, chemical products, metals and metal products, transportation equipment. Major trading partners: U.S., West Germany, Japan, Venezuela, Netherlands, Brazil.

Geography. Colombia, in the northwestern part of South America, is the only country on that continent that borders on both the Atlantic and Pacific Oceans. It is nearly equal to the combined areas of California and Texas.

Through the western half of the country, three Andean ranges run north and south, merging into one at the Ecuadorean border. The eastern half is a low, jungle-covered plain, drained by spurs of the Amazon and Orinoco, inhabited mostly by isolated, tropical-forest Indian tribes. The fertile plateau and valley of the eastern range are the most densely populated parts of the country.

Government. Colombia's President, who appoints his own Cabinet, serves for a four-year term. The Senate, the upper house of Congress, has 114 members elected for four years by direct vote. The House of Representatives of 199 members is directly elected for four years.

History. Spaniards in 1510 founded Darien, the first permanent European settlement on the American mainland. In 1538 the Spaniards established the colony of New Granada, the area's name until 1861. After a 14-year struggle, in which Simón Bolívar's Venezuelan troops won the battle of Boyacá in Colombia on Aug. 7, 1819, independence was attained in 1824. Bolívar united Colombia, Venezuela, Panama, and Ecuador in the Republic of Greater Colombia (1819–30), but lost Venezuela and Ecuador to separatists. Bolívar's Vice President, Francisco de Paula Santander, founded the Liberal Party as the Federalists while Bolívar established the Conservatives as the Centralists.

Santander's presidency (1832–36) re-established order, but later periods of Liberal dominance (1849–57 and 1861–80), when the Liberals sought to disestablish the Roman Catholic Church, were marked by insurrection and even civil war. Rafael Nuñez, in a 15-year-presidency, restored the power of the central government and the church, which led in 1899 to a bloody civil war and the loss in 1903 of Panama over ratification of a lease to the U.S. of the Canal Zone. For 21 years, until 1930, the Conservatives held power as revolutionary pressures built up.

The Liberal administrations of Enrique Olaya Herrera and Alfonso López (1930–38) were marked by social reforms that failed to solve the country's problems, and in 1946, insurrection and banditry broke out, claiming hundreds of thousands of lives by 1958. Laureano Gómez (1950–53); the Army Chief of Staff, Gen. Gustavo Rojas Pinilla (1953–56), and a military junta (1956–57) sought to curb disorder by repression.

Subsequent presidents were Alberto Lleras Calmargo (1957–62); Guillermo León Valencia (1962–66); Carlos Lleras Restrepo (1966–70); Misael Pastrana Borrero (1970–74); and Alfonso López Michelson (1974–78).

Julio César Turbay Ayala, Liberal Party candidate in 1978, won a narrow victory—approximately 140,000 of a total of nearly 2.5 million votes—over the Conservative Party candidate. The Liberals also retained control of both the Senate and House.

Government efforts to stamp out the Movement of April 19 (M-19), an urban guerrilla organization, intensified in 1981 with the capture of some of the leaders. A general amnesty offered to the organization failed to bring an end to the movement. In 1986 three of its leaders were killed in separate gun battles. The Liberals won a solid majority in 1982, but a party split enabled Belisario Betancur Cuartas, the Conservative candidate, to win the presidency on May 31. After his inauguration, he ended the state of siege that had existed almost continuously for 34 years and renewed the general amnesty of 1981.

In May 1986, the liberal Virgilio Barco Vargas was elected by a record-breaking margin.

COMOROS

Federal Islamic Republic of the Comoros
President: Said Mohammed Djohar (1989)
Area: 690 sq mi. (1,787 sq km)
Population (est. 1990): 500,000 (average annual rate of natural increase: 3.4%)
Density per square mile: 640
Capital and largest city (est. 1980): Moroni (on Grande Comoro), 20,000
Monetary unit: Franc CFA
Languages: French, Arabic
Religions: Islam, 86%; Roman Catholic, 14%.
National name: République Fédéral Islamique des Comores
Literacy rate (1981): 15%
Economic summary: Gross national product (1986): $163 million, $390 per capita; real growth rate 2.1%. Arable land: 35%. Labor force: 140,000 (1982); 80% in agriculture. Principal agricultural products: perfume essences, copra, coconuts, cloves, vanilla, cinnamon, yams; major industrial products: perfume distillations. Exports: perfume essences, vanilla, copra, cloves. Imports: foodstuffs, fuels, chemicals, cotton textiles, cement. Major trading partners: France, Kenya, Pakistan, West Germany, Reunion, China.

Geography. The Comoros Islands—Grande Comoro, Anjouan, Mohéli, and Mayotte (which retains ties to France)—are an archipelago of volcanic origin in the Indian Ocean between Mozambique and Madagascar.

Government. A coup by foreign mercenaries on May 13, 1978, deposed President Ali Soilih, who had held power since 1975. A "political and military directorate" headed by Ahmed Abdallah Abderemane and Mohammed Ahmed governed until the adoption of a constitution on Oct. 1 ushered in a republic. With the resignation of Ahmed two days later, Abdallah became president.

History. Under French rule since 1886, the Comoros declared themselves independent July 6, 1975. However, Mayotte, with a Christian majority, voted against joining the other, mainly Islamic, islands, in the move to independence and remains French.

A month after independence, Justice Minister Ali Soilih staged a coup with the help of mercenaries, overthrowing the new nation's first president, Ahmed Abdallah. He was overthrown on May 13, 1978, when a small boatload of French mercenaries, some of whom had aided him three years earlier, seized government headquarters. These mercenaries assassinated Abdallah in a coup attempt in 1989. They were forced to leave by French military pressure.

CONGO

People's Republic of the Congo
President: Col. Denis Sassou-Nguessou (1979)
Prime Minister: Alphonse Poaty-Sovchlaty (1989)
Area: 132,046 sq mi. (342,000 sq km)
Population (est. mid-1990): 2,200,000 (average annual rate of natural increase: 3.3%)
Density per sq mile: 16.7
Capital and largest city (est. 1984): Brazzaville, 595,102
Monetary unit: Franc CFA
Ethnic groups: Kongo, Teke, Boubangi
Languages: French, Lingala, Kokongo
Religions: traditional, 42%; Christian, 50%; Muslim, 2%
National name: République Populaire du Congo
Literacy rate: 80%
Economic summary: Gross domestic product (1987): $2.2

billion; $1,060 per capita; real growth rate −5.2%. Arable land: 2%. Principal agricultural products: sugar cane, bananas, coffee, cocoa, peanuts. Labor force: 79,100; 75% in agriculture. Major industrial products: refined oil, cigarettes, cement, beverages, milled sugar. Natural resources: wood, potash, petroleum, natural gas. Exports: oil, lumber, tobacco, wood, coffee. Imports: machinery, transportation equipment, manufactured consumer goods, iron and steel, foodstuffs. Major trading partners: France, U.S., Italy, Spain, Brazil, West Germany.

Geography. The Congo is situated in west Central Africa astride the Equator. It borders on Gabon, Cameroon, the Central African Republic, Zaire, and the Angola exclave of Cabinda, with a short stretch of coast on the South Atlantic. Its area is nearly three times that of Pennsylvania.

Most of the inland is tropical rain forest, drained by tributaries of the Zaire (Congo) River, which flows south along the eastern border with Zaire to Stanley Pool. The narrow coastal plain rises to highlands separated from the inland plateaus by the 200-mile-wide Niari River Valley, which gives passage to the coast.

Government. Since the coup of September 1968 the country has been governed by a military regime. The Congolese Labor Party is the only party.

History. The inhabitants of the former French Congo, mainly Bantu peoples with Pygmies in the north, were subjects of several kingdoms in earlier times.

The Frenchman Pierre Savorgnan de Brazza signed a treaty with Makoko, ruler of the Bateke people, in 1880, which established French control. The area, with Gabon and Ubangi-Shari, was constituted the colony of French Equatorial Africa in 1910. It joined Chad in supporting the Free French cause in World War II. The Congo proclaimed its independence without leaving the French Community in 1960.

Maj. Marien Ngouabi, head of the National Council of the Revolution, took power as president on Jan. 1, 1969. He was sworn in for a second five-year term in 1975. A visit to Moscow by Ngouabi in March ended with the signing of a Soviet-Congolese economic and technical aid pact.

A four-man commando squad assassinated Ngouabi in Brazzaville on March 18, 1977. Five days later the assassination of Émile Cardinal Biayenda, Archbishop of Brazzaville, was announced. Former President Alphonse Massamba-Débat, accused of plotting both deaths, was executed.

Col. Joachim Yhombi-Opango, Army Chief of Staff, assumed the presidency on April 4. In June, the new government agreed to resume diplomatic relations with the U.S., ending a 12-year rift. Yombhi-Opango resigned on Feb. 4, 1979, and was replaced by Col. Denis Sassou-Neguessou.

Capital and largest city (est. 1984): San José, 278,500
Monetary unit: Colón
Language: Spanish
Religion: Roman Catholic
National name: República de Costa Rica
Literacy rate (1984): 93%
Economic summary: Gross domestic product (1987): $4.3 billion; $1,529 per capita; 3% real growth rate. Arable land: 6%; principal products: bananas, coffee, sugar cane, rice, corn, livestock. Labor force: 868,300; 35.1% in industry and commerce; major products: processed foods, textiles and clothing, construction materials, fertilizer. Natural resource: timber, hydropower potential. Exports: coffee, bananas, beef, sugar, cocoa. Imports: manufactured products, machinery, chemicals, foodstuffs, fuels, fertilizer. Major trading partners: U.S., Central American countries, West Germany, Japan.

Geography. This Central American country lies between Nicaragua to the north and Panama to the south. Its area slightly exceeds that of Vermont and New Hampshire combined.

Most of Costa Rica is tableland, from 3,000 to 6,000 feet (914 to 1,829 m) above sea level. Cocos Island (10 sq mi.; 26 sq km), about 300 miles (483 km) off the Pacific Coast, is under Costa Rican sovereignty.

Government. Under the 1949 Constitution, the president and the one-house Legislative Assembly of 57 members are elected for terms of four years.

The army was abolished in 1949. There is a civil guard and a rural guard.

History. Costa Rica was inhabited by 25,000 Indians when Columbus discovered it and probably named it in 1502. Few of the Indians survived the Spanish conquest, which began in 1563. The region was administered as a Spanish province. Costa Rica achieved independence in 1821 but was absorbed for two years by Agustín de Iturbide in his Mexican Empire. It was established as a republic in 1848.

Except for the military dictatorship of Tomás Guardia from 1870 to 1882, Costa Rica has enjoyed one of the most democratic governments in Latin America.

Rodrigo Carazo Odio, leader of a four-party coalition called the Unity Party, won the presidency in February 1978. His tenure was marked by a disastrous decline in the economy, which forced postponement of foreign debt payments at the end of 1981. Luis Alberto Monge Álvarez, a former union organizer and cofounder of the National Liberation Party, swept to victory in the Feb. 7, 1982, national elections.

On Feb. 2, 1986, Oscar Arias Sanchez won the national elections on a neutralist platform, defeating Rafael Angel Calderon, who was a stronger supporter of U.S. policies in Central America. Arias initiated a policy of preventing contra usage of Costa Rican territory.

COSTA RICA

Republic of Costa Rica
President: Rafuel Angel Calderón (1990)
Area: 19,652 sq mi. (50,898 sq km)
Population (est. mid-1990): 3,000,000 (average annual rate of natural increase: 2.5%)
Density per square mile: 151

CUBA

Republic of Cuba
President: Fidel Castro Ruz (1976)
Area: 44,218 sq mi. (114,524 sq km)
Population (est. mid-1990): 10,600,000 (average annual rate of natural increase: 1.2%)
Density per square mile: 236

Capital: Havana
Largest cities (est. 1986): Havana, 2,013,746; Santiago de Cuba, 358,764; Camagüey, 260,782; Holguin, 194,728; Santa Clara, 178,278
Monetary unit: Peso
Language: Spanish
Religion: Roman Catholic, 40%; non-religious, 49%; atheist, 6%
National name: República de Cuba
Literacy rate: 96%
Economic summary: Gross national product (in 1974 dollars): $18.7 billion, $1,800 per capita; 2.3% real growth rate (1989). Arable land: 23%; principal products: sugar, tobacco, coffee, rice, fruits. Labor force: 3,300,000; 29% in industry; major products: processed sugar and tobacco, refined oil products, textiles, chemicals, processed food, metals, light consumer products. Natural resources: metals, primarily nickel, timber. Exports: coffee, sugar, nickel, shellfish, tobacco. Imports: capital goods, industrial raw materials, petroleum, foodstuffs. Major trading partners: U.S.S.R., other Communist bloc countries, Spain, Japan.

Geography. The largest island of the West Indies group (equal in area to Pennsylvania), Cuba is also the westernmost—just west of Hispaniola (Haiti and the Dominican Republic), and 90 miles (145 km) south of Key West, Fla., at the entrance to the Gulf of Mexico.

The island is mountainous in the southeast and south central area (Sierra Maestra). Elsewhere it is flat or rolling.

Government. Since 1976, elections have been held every five years to elect the National Assembly, which in turn elects the 31-member Council of States, its President, First Vice-President, five Vice-Presidents, and Secretary. Fidel Castro is President of the Council of State and of the government and First Secretary of the Communist Party of Cuba, the only political party.

History. Arawak Indians inhabiting Cuba when Columbus discovered the island in 1492 died off from diseases brought by sailors and settlers. By 1511, Spaniards under Diego Velásquez were founding settlements that served as bases for Spanish exploration. Cuba soon after served as an assembly point for treasure looted by the conquistadores, attracting French and English pirates.

Black slaves and free laborers were imported to work sugar and tobacco plantations, and waves of chiefly Spanish immigrants maintained a European character in the island's culture. Early slave rebellions and conflicts between colonials and Spanish rulers laid the foundation for an independence movement that turned into open warfare from 1867 to 1878. The poet, José Marti, in 1895 led the struggle that finally ended Spanish rule, thanks largely to U.S. intervention in 1898 after the sinking of the battleship *Maine* in Havana harbor.

A treaty in 1899 made Cuba an independent republic under U.S. protection. The U.S. occupation, which ended in 1902, suppressed yellow fever and brought large American investment. From 1906 to 1909, Washington invoked the Platt Amendment to the treaty, which gave it the right to intervene in order to suppress any revolt. U.S. troops came back in 1912 and again in 1917 to restore order. The Platt Amendment was abrogated in 1934.

Fulgencio Batista, an army sergeant, led a revolt in 1934 that overthrew the regime of President Gerado Machado.

Batista's Cuba was a police state. Corrupt officials took payoffs from American gamblers who operated casinos, demanded bribes from Cubans for various public services and enriched themselves with raids on the public treasury. Dissenters were murdered and their bodies dumped in gutters.

Fidel Castro Ruz, a hulking, bearded attorney in his 30s, landed in Cuba on Christmas Day 1956 with a band of 12 fellow revolutionaries, evaded Batista's soldiers, and set up headquarters in the jungled hills of the Sierra Maestra range. By 1958 his force had grown to about 2,000 guerrillas, for the most part young and middle class. Castro's brother, Raul, and Ernesto (Ché) Guevara, an Argentine physician, were his top lieutenants. Businessmen and landowners who opposed the Batista regime gave financial support to the rebels. The United States, meanwhile, cut off arms shipments to Batista's army.

The beginning of the end for Batista came when the rebels routed 3,000 government troops and captured Santa Clara, capital of Las Villas province 150 miles from Havana, and a trainload of Batista reinforcements refused to get out of their railroad cars. On New Year's Day 1959, Batista flew to exile in the Dominican Republic and Castro took over the government. Crowds cheered the revolutionaries on their seven-day march to the capital.

The United States initially welcomed what looked like the prospect for a democratic Cuba, but a rude awakening came within a few months when Castro established military tribunals for political opponents, jailed hundreds, and began to veer leftward. Castro disavowed Cuba's 1952 military pact with the United States. He confiscated U.S. investments in banks and industries and seized large U.S. landholdings, turning them first into collective farms and then into Soviet-type state farms. The United States broke relations with Cuba on Jan. 3, 1961. Castro thereupon forged an alliance with the Soviet Union.

From the ranks of the Cuban exiles who had fled to the United States, the Central Intelligence Agency· recruited and trained an expeditionary force, numbering less than 2,000 men, to invade Cuba, with the expectation that the invasion would spark an uprising of the Cuban populace against Castro. The invasion was planned under the Eisenhower administration and President John F. Kennedy gave the go-ahead for it in the first months of his administration, but rejected a CIA proposal for U.S. planes to provide air support. The landing at the Bay of Pigs on April 17, 1961, was a fiasco. Not only did the invaders fail to receive any support from the populace, but Castro's tanks and artillery made short work of the small force.

A Soviet attempt to change the global power balance by installing in Cuba medium-range missiles—capable of striking targets in the United States with nuclear warheads—provoked a crisis between the superpowers in 1962 that had the potential of touching off World War III. After a visit to Moscow by Cuba's war minister, Raul Castro, work began secretly on the missile launching sites.

Denouncing the Soviets for "deliberate deception," President Kennedy on Oct. 22 announced that the U.S. navy would enforce a "quarantine" of shipping to Cuba and search Soviet bloc ships to prevent the missiles themselves from reaching the island. After six days of tough public statements on both sides and secret diplomacy, Soviet Premier Nikita Khrushchev on Oct. 28 ordered the missile sites dismantled, crated and shipped back to the Soviet Union, in return for a U.S. pledge not to attack Cuba. Limited diplomatic ties were reestablished on Sept. 1, 1977.

Emigration increased dramatically after April 1, 1980, when Castro, irritated by the granting of asylum to would-be refugees by the Peruvian embassy in Havana, removed guards and allowed 10,000 Cubans to swarm into the embassy grounds.

As an airlift began taking the refugees to Costa Rica, Castro opened the port of Mariel to a "freedom flotilla" of ships and yachts from the United States, many of them owned or chartered by Cuban-Americans to bring out relatives. More than 125,000 Cubans poured out of Mariel in a mass exodus. It wasn't until after they had reached the United States that it was discovered that the regime had opened prisons and mental hospitals to permit criminals, homosexuals and others unwanted in Cuba to join the refugees.

For most of President Ronald Reagan's first term, U.S.-Cuban relations were frozen, with Secretary of State Alexander Haig calling Havana the "source" of troubles in Central America. But late in 1984, an agreement was reached between the two countries. Cuba would take back more than 2,700 Cubans who had come to the United States in the Mariel exodus but were not eligible to stay in the country under U.S. immigration law because of criminal or psychiatric disqualification. The United States, in exchange, would reinstitute regular immigration for Cubans to the United States. Castro cancelled it when the U.S. began the Radio Marti broadcasts in May 1985 to bring a non-Communist view to the Cuban people.

As the first step in the accord, 23 Cuban aliens were moved from Atlanta Federal Penitentiary on Feb. 21, 1985 and flown to Havana.

After a machinegun attack by leftist rebels in June 1985 killed 13 diners—including six Americans—at an outdoor cafe in El Salvador, President Reagan listed Cuba with Iran, Libya, North Korea and Nicaragua in what he called "a confederation of terrorist states".

In January 1987, the U.S. withdrew its chief of mission when Cuba excluded him from diplomatic functions.

CYPRUS

Republic of Cyprus
President: Dr. George Vassiliou (1988)
Area: 3,572 sq mi (9,251 sq km)
Population (est. mid-1990): 700,000 (average annual rate of natural increase: 1.0%)
Density per square mile: 195
Capital and largest city: Nicosia, 123,298
Monetary unit: Cyprus pound
Languages: Greek, Turkish, English
Religions: Greek Orthodox, 82%; Islam, 18%
National name: Kypriaki Dimokratia—Kibris Cumhuriyeti
Member of Commonwealth of Nations
Literacy rate (1981): 89%
Economic summary: Gross domestic product (1987): $3.7 billion; $5,670 per capita; 7.2% real growth rate. Arable

land: 40%; principal products: vine products, citrus, potatoes, other vegetables. Labor force: 251,406 (in Greek area); 33% in industry; major products: beverages, footwear, clothing, cement, asbestos mining. Natural resources: copper, asbestos, gypsum, building stone, marble, clay, salt. Exports: food and beverage, clothing, machinery. Imports: manufactured goods, machinery and transportation equipment, petroleum products, foodstuffs. Major trading partners: U.K., Lebanon, Italy, Turkey, Arab countries, Japan, West Germany.

Geography. The third largest island in the Mediterranean (one and one half times the size of Delaware), Cyprus lies off the southern coast of Turkey and the western shore of Syria. Most of the country consists of a wide plain lying between two mountain ranges that cross the island. The highest peak is Mount Olympus at 6,406 feet (1,953 m).

Government. Under the republic's Constitution, for the protection of the Turkish minority the vice president as well as three of the 10 Cabinet ministers must be from the Turkish community, while the House of Representatives is elected by each community separately, 70% Greek Cypriote and 30% Turkish Cypriote representatives.

The Greek and Turkish communities are self-governing in questions of religion, education, and culture. Other governmental matters are under the jurisdiction of the central government. Each community is entitled to a Communal Chamber.

The Greek Communal Chamber, which had 23 members, was abolished in 1965 and its function was absorbed by the Ministry of Education. The Turkish Communal Chamber, however, has continued to function.

History. Cyprus was the site of early Phoenician and Greek colonies. For centuries its rule passed through many hands. It fell to the Turks in 1571, and a large Turkish colony settled on the island.

In World War I, on the outbreak of hostilities with Turkey, Britain annexed the island. It was declared a crown colony in 1925.

For centuries the Greek population, regarding Greece as its mother country, has sought self-determination and reunion with it *(enosis)*. The resulting quarrel with Turkey threatened NATO. Cyprus became an independent nation on Aug. 16, 1960, with Britain, Greece, and Turkey as guarantor powers.

Archbishop Makarios, president since 1959, was overthrown July 15, 1974, by a military coup led by the Cypriot National Guard. The new regime named Nikos Giorgiades Sampson as president and Bishop Gennadios as head of the Cypriot Church to replace Makarios. The rebels were led by rightist Greek officers who supported *enosis*.

Diplomacy failed to resolve the crisis. Turkey invaded Cyprus by sea and air July 20, 1974, asserting its right to protect the Turkish Cypriote minority.

Geneva talks involving Greece, Turkey, Britain, and the two Cypriote factions failed in mid-August, and the Turks subsequently gained control of 40% of the island. Greece made no armed response to the superior Turkish force, but bitterly suspended military participation in the NATO alliance.

The tension continued after Makarios returned to become President on Dec. 7, 1974. He offered self-government to the Turkish minority, but rejected any solution "involving transfer of populations and amounting to partition of Cyprus."

Turkish Cypriots proclaimed a separate state

under Rauf Denktash in the northern part of the island in Nov. 1983, and proposed a "biregional federation."

Makarios died on Aug. 3, 1977, and Spyros Kyprianou was elected to serve the remainder of his term. Kyprianou was subsequently re-elected in 1978 and 1983.

Kyprianou's victory in the legislative elections on December 8, 1985, was seen as a vote of support for his hard-line approach to reunification talks, which remained deadlocked, support that dwindled enough by 1988 for George Vassiliou to defeat Kyprianou. Vassiliou has conducted some informal talks with Denktask, leader of the Turkish Cypriots.

CZECHOSLOVAKIA

Czech and Slovak Federal Republic
President: Václav Havel (1989)
Premier: Marian Calfa (1989)
Area: 49,374 sq mi. (127,896 sq km)
Population (est. mid-1990): 15,700,000 (average annual rate of natural increase: 0.2%)
Density per square mile: 317
Capital: Prague
Largest cities (est. 1989): Prague, 1,206,098; Bratislava, 429,743; Brno, 388,084; Ostrova, 329,587; Kosice, 229,175
Monetary unit: Koruna
Languages: Czech, Slovak, Hungarian
Religions: Roman Catholic, 67%; atheist, 20%; Czechoslovak Church, 4%
National name: Ceskoslovenská Socialistická Republika
Literacy rate (1981): 100%
Economic summary: Gross national product (1988): $158.2 billion; $10,130 per capita; 1.4% real growth rate. Arable land: 40%; principal products: wheat, rye, oats, corn, barley, potatoes, sugar beets, hogs, cattle, horses. Labor force: 8,200,000 (1987); 36.9% in industry; major products: iron and steel, machinery and equipment, cement, textiles, motor vehicles, armaments, chemicals, ceramics. Natural resources: coal/coke, timber, lignite, uranium, magnesite. Exports: machinery, chemicals, vehicles, consumer goods. Imports: machinery, equipment, fuels, raw materials, food, consumer goods. Major trading partners: U.S.S.R. and Soviet bloc, Yugoslavia, West Germany, Austria

Geography. Czechoslovakia lies in central Europe, a neighbor of East and West Germany, Poland, the U.S.S.R., Hungary, and Austria. It is equal in size to New York State. The principal rivers—the Elbe, Danube, Oder, and Moldau—are vital commercially to this landlocked country, for both waterborne commerce and agriculture, which flourishes in fertile valleys irrigated by these rivers and their tributaries.

Government. Since 1969 the supreme organ of the state has been the Federal Assembly, which has two equal chambers: the Chamber of People, with 150 deputies, and the Chamber of Nations, with 150 deputies (75 from the Czech Socialist Republic and 75 from the Slovak Socialist Republic). The chief executive is the President, who is elected by the Federal Assembly for a two-year term. The Premier and his Cabinet are appointed by the President but are responsible to the Federal Assembly. The leader of the Czechoslovak Communist Party is General Secretary Ladislav Adamec.

History. Probably about the 5th century A.D., Slavic tribes from the Vistula basin settled in the region of modern Czechoslovakia. Slovakia came under Magyar domination. The Czechs founded the kingdom of Bohemia, the Premyslide dynasty, which ruled Bohemia and Moravia from the 10th to the 16th century. One of the Bohemian kings, Charles IV, Holy Roman Emperor, made Prague an imperial capital and a center of Latin scholarship. The Hussite movement founded by Jan Hus (1369?–1415) linked the Slavs to the Reformation and revived Czech nationalism, previously under German domination. A Hapsburg, Ferdinand I, ascended the throne in 1526. The Czechs rebelled in 1618. Defeated in 1620, they were ruled for the next 300 years as part of the Austrian Empire.

In World War I, Czech and Slovak patriots, notably Thomas G. Masaryk and Milan Stefanik, promoted Czech-Slovak independence from abroad while their followers fought against the Central Powers. On Oct. 28, 1918, Czechoslovakia proclaimed itself a republic. Shortly thereafter Masaryk was unanimously elected first President.

Hitler provoked the country's German minority in the Sudetenland to agitate for autonomy. At the Munich Conference on Sept. 30, 1938, France and the U.K., seeking to avoid World War II, agreed that the Nazis could take the Sudetenland. Dr. Eduard Beneš, who had succeeded Masaryk, resigned on Oct. 5, 1938, and fled to London. Czechoslovakia became a state within the German orbit and was known as Czecho-Slovakia. In March 1939, the Nazis occupied the country.

Soon after Czechoslovakia was liberated in World War II and the government returned in April 1945, it was obliged to cede Ruthenia to the U.S.S.R. In 1946, a Communist, Klement Gottwald, formed a six-party coalition Cabinet. Pressure from Moscow increased until Feb. 23–25, 1948, when the Communists seized complete control in a coup. Following constituent assembly elections in which the Communists and their allies were unopposed, a new Constitution was adopted.

The "people's democracy" was converted into a "socialist" state by a new Constitution adopted June 11, 1960.

After the death of Stalin and the relaxing of Soviet controls, Czechoslovakia witnessed a nationalist awakening. In 1968 conservative Stalinists were driven from power and replaced by more liberal, reform-minded Communists.

Soviet military maneuvers on Czechoslovak soil in May 1968 were followed in July by a meeting of the U.S.S.R. with Poland, Bulgaria, East Germany, and Hungary in Warsaw that demanded an accounting, which Prague refused. Czechoslovak-Soviet talks on Czechoslovak territory, at Cierna, in late July led to an accord. But the Russians charged that the Czechoslovaks had reneged on pledges to modify their policies, and on Aug. 20–21, troops of the five powers, estimated at 600,000, executed a lightning invasion and occupation.

Soviet secret police seized the top Czechoslovak leadership and detained it for several days in Moscow. But Soviet efforts to establish a puppet regime failed. President Ludvik Svoboda negotiated an accord providing for a gradual troop withdrawal in return for "normalization" of political policy.

Czechoslovakia signed a new friendship treaty with the U.S.S.R. that codified the "Brezhnev doctrine," under which Russia can invade any Eastern

European socialist nation that threatens to leave the satellite camp.

One of the most vigorous of the Eastern European groups formed to support human rights in the wake of the 1975 Helsinki Conference on Security and Cooperation in Europe was the Czech "Charter 77," an association of 240 intellectuals who signed a New Year manifesto protesting the suppression of freedom. Detentions of the signers began immediately, and a second manifesto appeared on January 8 with 300 signatures condemning the official reaction to the first.

Anti-government demonstrations reached a head in 1990 when the brutal suppression of a protest on November 17 led to massive popular protests against the Husak regime. Members of the opposition formed the Civic Forum, which pushed for democratization. Marian Colfa became the country's first non-Communist Premier since 1948. Opposition leader Vaclav Havel was elected President on December 29. Opposition groups won a majority in both legislative chambers in the elections of June 1990.

DENMARK

Kingdom of Denmark

Sovereign: Queen Margrethe II (1972)
Premier: Poul Schlüter (1982)
Area: 16,631 sq mi. (43,075 sq km)[1]
Population (est. mid-1990): 5,100,000 (average annual rate of natural increase: 0.0%)
Density per square mile: 309
Capital: Copenhagen
Largest cities (est. 1985): Copenhagen, 1,358,540; Aarhus, 252,071; Odense, 171,468; Alborg, 154,750
Monetary unit: Krone
Language: Danish, small German-speaking minority
Religion: Lutheran (established)
National name: Kongeriget Danmark
Literacy rate: 100%
Economic summary: Gross domestic product (1987): $101.3 billion; $19,780 per capita; real growth rate −1.1%. Arable land: 61%; principal products: meat, dairy products, fish, grains. Labor force: 2,860,000; 18.4% in manufacturing; major products; industrial and construction equipment, electronics, chemicals, textiles. Natural resources: oil, zinc, lead, coal, molybdenum, cryolite, uranium. Exports: meat and dairy products, fish, industrial machinery, textiles and clothing, chemical products, transportation equipment. Imports: industrial raw materials, fuel, machinery and equipment, transport equipment, petroleum, chemicals. Major trading partners: West Germany, Sweden, U.K., U.S., Norway.

1. Excluding Faeroe Islands and Greenland.

Geography. Smallest of the Scandinavian countries (half the size of Maine), Denmark occupies the Jutland peninsula, which extends north from Germany between the tips of Norway and Sweden. To the west is the North Sea and to the east the Baltic.

The country also consists of several Baltic islands; the two largest are Sjaelland, the site of Copenhagen, and Fyn. The narrow waters off the north coast are called the Skagerrak and those off the east, the Kattegat.

Government. Denmark has been a constitutional monarchy since 1849. Legislative power is held jointly by the Sovereign and parliament. The Constitution of 1953 provides for a unicameral parliament called the Folketing, consisting of 179 popularly elected members who serve for four years. The Cabinet is presided over by the Sovereign, who appoints the Prime Minister.

The Sovereign, Queen Margrethe II, was born April 16, 1940, and became Queen—the first in Denmark's history—Jan. 15, 1972, the day after her father, King Frederik IX, died at 72 in the 25th year of his reign. Margrethe was the eldest of his three daughters (by Princess Ingrid of Sweden). The nation's Constitution was amended in 1953 to permit her to succeed her father in the absence of a male heir to the throne. (Denmark was ruled six centuries ago by Margrethe I, but she was never crowned Queen since there was no female right of succession.)

History. Denmark emerged with establishment of the Norwegian dynasty of the Ynglinger in Jutland at the end of the 8th century. Danish mariners played a major role in the raids of the Vikings, or Norsemen, on Western Europe and particularly England. The country was Christianized by St. Ansgar and Harald Blaatand (Bluetooth)—the first Christian king—in the 10th century. Harald's son, Sweyn, conquered England in 1013. His son, Canute the Great, who reigned from 1014 to 1035, united Denmark, England, and Norway under his rule; the southern tip of Sweden was part of Denmark until the 17th century. On Canute's death, civil war tore the country until Waldemar I (1157–82) re-established Danish hegemony over the north.

In 1282, the nobles won the Great Charter, and Eric V was forced to share power with parliament and a Council of Nobles. Waldemar IV (1340–75) restored Danish power, checked only by the Hanseatic League of north German cities allied with ports from Holland to Poland. His daughter, Margrethe, in 1397 united under her rule Denmark, Norway, and Sweden. But Sweden later achieved autonomy and in 1523, under Gustavus I, independence.

Denmark supported Napoleon, for which it was punished at the Congress of Vienna in 1815 by the loss of Norway to Sweden. In 1864, Bismarck, together with the Austrians, made war on the little country as an initial step in the unification of Germany. Denmark was neutral in World War I.

In 1940, Denmark was invaded by the Nazis. King Christian X reluctantly cautioned his countrymen to accept the occupation, but there was widespread resistance against the Nazis. In 1944, Iceland declared its independence from Denmark, ending a union that had existed since 1380.

Liberated by British troops in May 1945, the country staged a fast recovery in both agriculture and manufacturing and was a leader in liberalizing trade. It joined the United Nations in 1945 and NATO in 1949.

The Social Democrats largely ran Denmark after the war but were ousted in 1973 in an election dominated by protests against high taxes. A minority government was formed by the Liberal Democrats, with their leader, Poul Hartling, as Premier. After losing a vote of confidence in January 1975, Hartling resigned and was succeeded by Anker Jørgensen, a Social Democrat who was Premier in 1972–73.

Disputes over economic policy led to elections in 1981 that led to Poul Schülter coming to power in early 1982. Further disputes over his pro-NATO posture led to elections in May, 1988 that marginally confirmed his position, despite previous losses in the general election of Sept., 1987.

Outlying Territories of Denmark

FAEROE ISLANDS

Status: Autonomous part of Denmark
Lagmand (President): Jogran Sundstein (1989)
Area: 540 sq mi. (1,399 sq km)
Population (1989): 47,283 (average annual growth rate: .9%)
Density per square mile: 87
Capital (est. 1982): Thorshavn, 12,750
Monetary unit: Faeroese krone
Literacy rate: 99%
Economic summary: Gross domestic product (1986): $773 million; $16,800 per capita. Arable land: 2%; principal agricultural products: sheep and cattle. Labor force: 17,585, largely engaged in fishing manufacturing, transportation and commerce. Major industrial product: fish. Exports: fish and fish products. Imports: machinery and transport equipment, foodstuffs, petroleum and petroleum products. Major trading partners: Denmark, U.S., U.K., West Germany

This group of 18 islands, lying in the North Atlantic about 200 miles (322 km) northwest of the Shetland Islands, joined Denmark in 1386 and has since been part of the Danish kingdom. The islands were occupied by British troops during World War II, after the German occupation of Denmark.

The Faeroes have home rule under a bill enacted in 1948; they also have two representatives in the Danish Folketing.

GREENLAND

Status: Autonomous part of Denmark
Premier: Jonathan Motzfeldt (1983)
Area: 840,000 sq mi. (incl. 708,069 sq mi. covered by icecap) (2,175,600 sq km)
Population (1989): 55,415 (growth rate: 12%)
Capital (est. 1982): Godthaab, 10,000
Monetary unit: Krone
Literacy rate: 99%
Economic summary: Gross national product (1985): $374 million; $7,000 per capita; 0% real growth rate. Arable land: 0%; principal agricultural products: hay, sheep, garden produce. Labor force: 22,800, largely engaged in fishing, hunting, sheep breeding. Major industries: mining, slaughtering, fishing, sealing. Natural resources: metals, cryolite, iron ore, coal, uranium, fish. Exports: fish and fish products, metalic ores and concentrates. Imports: petroleum and petroleum products, machinery and transport equipment, foodstuffs. Major trading partners: Denmark, U.S., Finland, West Germany, U.K.

Greenland, the world's largest island, was colonized in 985–86 by Eric the Red. Danish sovereignty, which covered only the west coast, was extended over the whole island in 1917. In 1941 the U.S. signed an agreement with the Danish minister in Washington, placing it under U.S. protection during World War II but maintaining Danish sovereignty. A definitive agreement for the joint defense of Greenland within the framework of NATO was signed in 1951. A large U.S. air base at Thule in the far north was completed in 1953.

Under 1953 amendments to the Danish Constitution, Greenland became part of Denmark, with two representatives in the Danish Folketing. On May 1, 1979, Greenland gained home rule, with its own local parliament (Landsting), replacing the Greenland Provincial Council.

In February 1982, Greenlanders voted to withdraw from the European Community, which they had joined as part of Denmark in 1973. Danish Premier Anker Jørgensen said he would support the request, but with reluctance.

Greenland is the world's only source of natural cryolite, important in making aluminum.

DJIBOUTI

Republic of Djibouti
President: Hassan Gouled Aptidon (1977)
Prime Minister: Barkat Gourad Hamadou (1978)
Area: 8,490 sq mi. (22,000 sq km)
Population (est. mid-1990): 400,000 (average annual rate of natural increase: 3.0%)
Density per square mile: 46
Capital (est. 1980): Djibouti, 200,000
Monetary unit: Djibouti franc
Languages: Arabic, French, Afar, Somali, Issa
Religions: Islam (Sunni), 94%; Christian, 6%
National name: Jumhouriyya Djibouti
Literacy rate: 20%
Economic summary: Gross domestic product (1986): $333 million, $1,067 per capita; real growth rate −.7%. Arable land: 0%; principal agricultural products: goats, sheep, camels. Labor force: NA. Industries: port and maritime support, construction. Exports: hides, cattle, coffee (in transit from Ethiopia). Imports: machinery, transport equipment, foodstuffs. Major trading partners: France, Ethiopia, Japan, Belgium, U.K., Saudi Arabia, Yemen

Geography. Djibouti lies in northeastern Africa on the Gulf of Aden at the southern entrance to the Red Sea. It borders on Ethiopia and Somalia. The country, the size of Massachusetts, is mainly a stony desert, with scattered plateaus and highlands.

Government. On May 8, 1977, the population of the French Territory of the Afars and Issas voted by more than 98% for independence. Voters also approved a 65-member interim Constituent Assembly. France transferred sovereignty to the new nation of Djibouti on June 27. Later in the year it became a member of the Organization of African Unity and the Arab League. The People's Progress Assembly is the only legal political party.

History. The territory that is now Djibouti was acquired by France between 1843 and 1886 by treaties with the Somali sultans. Small, arid, and sparsely populated, Djibouti is important chiefly because of the capital city's port, the terminal of the Djibouti-Addis Ababa railway that carries 60% of Ethiopia's foreign trade.

Originally known as French Somaliland, the colony voted in 1958 and 1967 to remain under French rule. It was renamed the Territory of the Afars and Issas in 1967 and took the name of its capital city on attaining independence.

Somali rebels in Ethiopia's Ogaden Province cut the railway to Djibouti in June 1977 and there was fear that the new nation might be absorbed by Somalia. In July 1980, Djibouti granted base rights to United States ships and planes in exchange for undisclosed amounts of aid.

DOMINICA

Commonwealth of Dominica
President: Sir Clarence Seignoret (1985)
Prime Minister: Mary Eugenia Charles (1980)
Area: 290 sq mi. (751 sq km)
Population: (est. mid-1990): 100,000 (average annual rate of natural increase: 2.1%)
Density per square mile: 287
Capital and largest city (est. 1981): Roseau, 20,000
Monetary unit: East Caribbean dollar
Languages: English and French patois
Religions: Roman Catholic, Anglican, Methodist
Member of Commonwealth of Nations
Literacy rate: 80%
Economic summary: Gross national product (1987): $124.5 billion; $1,320 per capita; 4.6% real growth rate. Arable land: 9%; principal products: bananas, citrus fruits, coconuts, cocoa. Labor force: 25,000; 32% in industry and commerce (1984). Major industries: agricultural processing; tourism. Exports: bananas, lime juice, cocoa, coconut oil, soap. Imports: machinery and equipment, foodstuffs, manufactured goods, chemicals. Major trading partners: U.K., Caribbean countries, U.S.

Geography. Dominica is an island of the Lesser Antilles in the Caribbean south of Guadeloupe and north of Martinique.

Government. Dominica is a republic, with a president elected by the House of Assembly as head of state and a prime minister appointed by the president on the advice of the Assembly. The Freedom Party (11 of 21 seats in the Assembly) is led by Prime Minister Mary Eugenia Charles. The Opposition United Workers Party holds six seats and the United Dominica Labor Party holds four seats.

History. Discovered by Columbus in 1493, Dominica was claimed by Britain and France until 1815, when Britain asserted sovereignty. Dominica, along with other Windward Isles, became a self-governing member of the West Indies Associated States in free association with Britain in 1967.

Full independence was granted on Nov. 3, 1978, and the first Prime Minister, Patrick R. John, declared a socialist course for the new republic.

Dissatisfaction over the slow pace of reconstruction after Hurricane David struck the island in September 1979 brought a landslide victory for the opposition Freedom Party in July 1980. The vote gave the prime ministership to Mary Eugenia Charles, a strong advocate of free enterprise. The Freedom Party won again in 1985 elections, giving Miss Charles a second five-year term as prime minister.

DOMINICAN REPUBLIC

President: Joaquin Balaguer (1986)
Area: 18,704 sq mi. (48,442 sq km)
Population (est. mid-1990): 7,200,000 (average annual rate of natural increase: 2.5%)
Density per square mile: 373
Capital: Santo Domingo
Largest cities (est. 1983): Santo Domingo, 1,410,000; Santiago de los Caballeros, 285,000
Monetary unit: Peso
Language: Spanish
Religion: Roman Catholic
National name: República Dominicana
Literacy rate: 74%
Economic summary: Gross domestic product (1987 est.): $5.6 billion, $800 per capita; 8.1% real growth rate. Arable land: 23%; principal products: sugar cane, coffee, cocoa, tobacco, bananas, corn. Labor force: 2,300,000– 2,600,000; 18% in industry; major products: processed sugar, textiles, nickel, silver, and gold mining. Natural resources: nickel, bauxite, gold, silver. Exports: sugar, nickel, coffee, tobacco, gold, cocoa. Imports: foodstuffs, petroleum, industrial raw materials, capital equipment. Major trading partners: U.S., Venezuela, Mexico.

Geography. The Dominican Republic in the West Indies, occupies the eastern two thirds of the island of Hispaniola, which it shares with Haiti. Its area equals that of Vermont and New Hampshire combined.

Crossed from northwest to southeast by a mountain range with elevations exceeding 10,000 feet (3,048 m), the country has fertile, well-watered land in the north and east, where nearly two thirds of the population lives. The southwest part is arid and has poor soil, except around Santo Domingo.

Government. The president is elected by direct vote every four years. Legislative powers rest with a Senate and a Chamber of Deputies, both elected by direct vote, also for four years. All citizens must vote when they reach 18 years of age, or even earlier if they are married.

History. The Dominican Republic was discovered by Columbus in 1492. He named it La Española, and his son, Diego, was its first viceroy. The capital, Santo Domingo, founded in 1496, is the oldest European settlement in the Western Hemisphere. Spain ceded the colony to France in 1795, and Haitian blacks under Toussaint L'Ouverture conquered it in 1801.

In 1808 the people revolted and the next year captured Santo Domingo, setting up the first republic. Spain regained title to the colony in 1814. In 1821 the people overthrew Spanish rule, but in 1822 they were reconquered by the Haitians. They revolted again in 1844, threw out the Haitians, and established the Dominican Republic, headed by Pedro Santana. Uprisings and Haitian attacks led Santana to make the country a province of Spain from 1861 to 1865. The U.S. Senate refused to ratify a treaty of annexation. Disorder continued until the dictatorship of Ulíses Heureaux; in 1916, when disorder broke out again, the U.S. sent in a contingent of marines, who remained until 1934.

A sergeant in the Dominican army trained by the marines, Rafaél Leonides Trujillo Molina, overthrew Horacio Vásquez in 1930 and established a dictatorship that lasted until his assassination 31 years later.

A new Constitution was adopted in 1962, and the first free elections since 1924 put Juan Bosch, a leftist leader, in office. A planned program of reforms with U.S. support was cut off by a right-wing military coup that replaced Bosch with a civilian triumvirate.

Leftists rebelled April 24, 1965, and President Lyndon Johnson sent in marines and troops. After an OAS ceasefire request May 6, a compromise installed Hector Garcia-Godoy as provisional president. Joaquin Balaguer won in free elections in 1966 against Bosch, and a peacekeeping force of 9,000 U.S. troops and 2,000 from other countries withdrew. Balaguer restored political and economic stability.

Balaguer's longtime support for free elections faltered in May 1978, when the army suspended the counting of ballots as he trailed in a fourth-term bid. After a warning from President Jimmy Carter, however, Balaguer accepted the victory of Antonio Guzmán of the opposition Dominican Revolutionary Party.

Salvador Jorge Blanco of the Dominican Revolutionary Party was elected President on May 16, 1982, defeating Balaguer and Bosch. Austerity measures imposed by the International Monetary Fund, including sharply higher prices for food and gasoline, provoked rioting in the spring of 1984 that left more than 50 dead.

Saying he feared they would provoke "some kind of revolution," Blanco dragged his feet about putting into effect further IMF demands for higher prices and taxes and devaluation of the peso, and came within weeks of defaulting on several big loans.

Balaguer was elected President in May 1986 and aimed economic policy at diversifying the economy. On April 30, 1987, Blanco asked for political asylum in Venezuela after charges of corruption during his term were levelled against him.

ECUADOR

Republic of Ecuador
President: Rodrigo Borja Cevallos (1988)
Area: 109,484 sq mi. (270,670 sq km)
Population (est. mid-1990): 10,700,000 (average annual rate of natural increase: 2.5%)
Density per square mile: 95
Capital: Quito
Largest cities (est. 1987): Guayaquil, 1,572,615; Quito, 1,137,705; Cuenca, 201,490
Monetary unit: Sucre
Languages: Spanish, Quéchua
Religion: Roman Catholic, 95%
National name: República del Ecuador
Literacy rate: 85%
Economic summary: Gross domestic product (1986). $9.4 billion; $940 per capita; 5% real growth rate. Arable land: 6%; principal products: bananas, cocoa, coffee, sugar cane, fruits, corn, potatoes, rice. Labor force: 2,800,000; 13% in manufacturing; major products: processed foods, textiles, fish, petroleum. Natural resources: petroleum, fish, silver, gold. Exports: petroleum, shrimp, bananas, coffee, cocoa, fish products. Imports: agricultural and industrial machinery, industrial raw materials, foodstuffs, chemical products, transportation and communication equipment. Major trading partners: U.S., EEC, Brazil, Chile, Japan.

Geography. Ecuador, equal in area to Nevada, is in the northwest part of South America fronting on the Pacific. To the north is Colombia and to the east and south is Peru. Two high and parallel ranges of the Andes, traversing the country from north to south, are topped by tall volcanic peaks. The high-est is Chimborazo at 20,577 feet (6,272 m).

The Galápagos Islands (or Colón Archipelago) (3,029 sq mi.; 7,845 sq km) in the Pacific Ocean about 600 miles (966 km) west of the South American mainland, became part of Ecuador in 1832.

Government. A 1978 Constitution returned Ecuador to civilian government after eight years of military rule. The President is elected to a term of four years and a House of Representatives of 71 members is popularly elected for the same period.

History. The tribes in the northern highlands of Ecuador formed the Kingdom of Quito around A.D. 1000. It was absorbed, by conquest and marriage, into the Inca Empire. Pizarro conquered the land in 1532, and through the 17th century a thriving colony was built by exploitation of the Indians. The first revolt against Spain occurred in 1809. Ecuador then joined Venezuela, Colombia, and Panama in a confederacy known as Greater Colombia.

On the collapse of this union in 1830, Ecuador became independent. Subsequent history was one of revolts and dictatorships; it had 48 presidents during the first 131 years of the republic. Conservatives ruled until the Revolution of 1895 ushered in nearly a half century of Radical Liberal rule, during which the church was disestablished and freedom of worship, speech, and press was introduced.

A three-man military junta which had taken power in a 1976 coup, agreed to a free presidential election on July 16, 1978. Jaime Roldós Aguilera won the runoff on April 29, 1979.

The 40-year-old President died in the crash of a small plane May 24, 1981. Vice President Osvaldo Hurtado Larrea became President. León Febres Cordero, was installed President in August 1984. Combined opposition parties won a majority in the 71-member Congress large enough to block significant action, a majority increased in the June 1986 elections.

Problems with the military plagued Febres in 1986-87, and he faced two rebellions.

In 1988, Rodrigo Borja was elected President. He was also able to form a coalition in the House, confirming a leftward shift in the government and promising smoother executive-legislative relations.

EGYPT

Arab Republic of Egypt
President: Hosni Mubarak (1981)
Premier: Dr. Atef Sedki (1986)
Area: 386,900 sq. mi. (1,002,000 sq km)
Population (est. mid-1990): 54,700,000 (average annual rate of natural increase: 2.9%)
Density per square mile: 142
Capital: Cairo
Largest cities (est. 1987): Cairo, 12,560,000; **(1986 est.):** Alexandria, 2,893,000; Giza, 1,670,800; Shubra el Khema, 533,300; El Mahalla el Kubra, 385,300
Monetary unit: Egyptian pound
Language: Arabic
Religions: Islam, 93%; Christian (mostly Copt), 7%
Literacy rate: 43%
Economic summary: Gross national product (1987): $25.6 billion; $490 per capita; .5% real growth rate. Arable

land: 3%; principal products: cotton, wheat, rice, corn. Labor force: 15,000,000; 20% in privately owned services and manufacturing; major products: textiles, processed foods, chemicals, fertilizer, petroleum and petroleum products. Natural resources: iron ore, phosphates, petroleum, gypsum. Exports: cotton, petroleum, cement. Imports: foodstuffs, machinery, fertilizers, woods. Major trading partners: U.S., Western Europe, Japan, Eastern Europe.

Geography. Egypt, at the northeast corner of Africa on the Mediterranean Sea, is bordered on the west by Libya, on the south by the Sudan, and on the east by the Red Sea and Israel. It is nearly one and one half times the size of Texas.

The historic Nile flows through the eastern third of the country. On either side of the Nile valley are desert plateaus, spotted with oases. In the north, toward the Mediterranean, plateaus are low, while south of Cairo they rise to a maximum of 1,015 feet (309 m) above sea level. At the head of the Red Sea is the Sinai Peninsula, between the Suez Canal and Israel.

Navigable throughout its course in Egypt, the Nile is used largely as a means of cheap transport for heavy goods. The principal port is Alexandria.

The Nile delta starts 100 miles (161 km) south of the Mediterranean and fans out to a sea front of 155 miles between the cities of Alexandria and Port Said. From Cairo north, the Nile branches into many streams, the principal ones being the Damietta and the Rosetta.

Except for a narrow belt along the Mediterranean, Egypt lies in an almost rainless area, in which high daytime temperatures fall quickly at night.

Government. Executive power is held by the President, who is elected every six years and can appoint one or more Vice Presidents.

The National Democratic Party, led by President Hosni Mubarak, is the dominant political party. Elections on April 6, 1987 confirmed its huge majority (348 of 448 seats). There is also a three-party alliance, that includes the Muslim Brotherhood, that forms the main opposition (60 seats). The New Wafd is the third largest party (35 seats).

History. Egyptian history dates back to about 4000 B.C., when the kingdoms of upper and lower Egypt, already highly civilized, were united. Egypt's "Golden Age" coincided with the 18th and 19th dynasties (16th to 13th centuries B.C.), during which the empire was established. Persia conquered Egypt in 525 B.C.; Alexander the Great subdued it in 332 B.C.; and then the dynasty of the Ptolemies ruled the land until 30 B.C., when Cleopatra, last of the line, committed suicide and Egypt became a Roman province. From 641 to 1517 the Arab caliphs ruled Egypt, and then the Turks took it for their Ottoman Empire.

Napoleon's armies occupied the country from 1798 to 1801. In 1805, Mohammed Ali, leader of a band of Albanian soldiers, became Pasha of Egypt. After completion of the Suez Canal in 1869, the French and British took increasing interest in Egypt.

British troops occupied Egypt in 1882, and British resident agents became its actual administrators, though it remained under nominal Turkish sovereignty. In 1914, this fiction was ended, and Egypt became a protectorate of Britain.

Egyptian nationalism forced Britain to declare Egypt an independent, sovereign state on Feb. 28, 1922, although the British reserved rights for the protection of the Suez Canal and the defense of Egypt. In 1936, by an Anglo-Egyptian treaty of alliance, all British troops and officials were to be withdrawn, except from the Suez Canal Zone. When World War II started, Egypt remained neutral. British imperial troops finally ended the Nazi threat to Suez in 1942 in the battle of El Alamein, west of Alexandria.

In 1951, Egypt abrogated the 1936 treaty and the 1899 Anglo-Egyptian condominium of the Sudan (*See* Sudan). Rioting and attacks on British troops in the Suez Canal Zone followed, reaching a climax in January 1952. The army, led by Gen. Mohammed Naguib, seized power on July 23, 1952. Three days later, King Farouk abdicated in favor of his infant son. The monarchy was abolished and a republic proclaimed on June 18, 1953, with Naguib holding the posts of Provisional President and Premier. He relinquished the latter in 1954 to Gamal Abdel Nasser, leader of the ruling military junta. Naguib was deposed seven months later and Nasser confirmed as President in a referendum on June 23, 1956.

Nasser's policies embroiled his country in continual conflict. In 1956, the U.S. and Britain withdrew their pledges of financial aid for the building of the Aswan High Dam. In reply, Nasser nationalized the Suez Canal and expelled British oil and embassy officials. Israel, barred from the Canal and exasperated by terrorist raids, invaded the Gaza Strip and the Sinai Peninsula. Britain and France, after demanding Egyptian evacuation of the Canal Zone, attacked Egypt on Oct. 31, 1956. Worldwide pressure forced Britain, France, and Israel to halt the hostilities. A U.N. emergency force occupied the Canal Zone, and all troops were evacuated in the spring of 1957.

On Feb. 1, 1958, Egypt and Syria formed the United Arab Republic, which was joined by Yemen in an association known as the United Arab States. However, Syria withdrew from the United Arab Republic in 1961 and Egypt dissolved its ties with Yemen in the United Arab States.

On June 5, 1967, Israel invaded the Sinai Peninsula, the East Bank of the Jordan River, and the zone around the Gulf of Aqaba. A U.N. ceasefire on June 10 saved the Arabs from complete rout.

Nasser declared the 1967 cease-fire void along the Canal in April 1969 and began a war of attrition. The U.S. peace plan of June 19, 1970, resulted in Egypt's agreement to reinstate the cease-fire for at least three months, (from August) and to accept Israel's existence within "recognized and secure" frontiers that might emerge from U.N.-mediated talks. In return, Israel accepted the principle of withdrawing from occupied territories.

Then, on Sept. 28, 1970, Nasser died, at 52, of a heart attack. The new President was Anwar el-Sadat, an associate of Nasser and a former newspaper editor.

The Aswan High Dam, whose financing by the U.S.S.R. was its first step into Egypt, was completed and dedicated in January 1971.

In July 1972, Sadat ordered the expulsion of Soviet "advisors and experts" from Egypt because the Russians had not provided the sophisticated weapons he felt were needed to retake territory lost to Israel in 1967.

The fourth Arab-Israeli war broke out Oct. 6, 1973, while Israelis were commemorating Yom Kippur, the Jewish high holy day. Egypt swept deep into the Sinai, while Syria strove to throw Israel off the Golan Heights.

A U.N.-sponsored truce was accepted on October 22. In January 1974, both sides agreed to a settlement negotiated by U.S. Secretary of State Henry A. Kissinger that gave Egypt a narrow strip along the entire Sinai bank of the Suez Canal. In June, President Nixon made the first visit by a U.S. President to Egypt and full diplomatic relations were established. The Suez Canal was cleared and reopened on June 5, 1975.

Kissinger pursued "shuttle diplomacy" between Cairo and Jerusalem to extend areas of agreement. Israel yielded on three points—the possession of the Mitla and Giddi passes in the Sinai and the Abu Rudeis oil field in the peninsula—and both sides committed themselves to annual renewal of the U.N. peacekeeping force in the Sinai.

In the most audacious act of his career, Sadat flew to Jerusalem at the invitation of Prime Minister Menachem Begin and pleaded before Israel's Knesset on Nov. 20, 1977, for a permanent peace settlement. The Arab world reacted with fury—only Morocco, Tunisia, Sudan, and Oman approved.

Egypt and Israel signed a formal peace treaty on March 26, 1979. The pact ended 30 years of war and established diplomatic and commercial relations.

Egyptian and Israeli officials met in the Sinai desert on April 26, 1979, to implement the peace treaty calling for the phased withdrawal of occupation forces from the peninsula. By mid-1980, two thirds of the Sinai was transferred, but progress here was not matched—the negotiation of Arab autonomy in the Gaza Strip and the West Bank.

Sadat halted further talks in August 1980 because of continued Israeli settlement of the West Bank. On October 6 1981, Sadat was assassinated by extremist Muslim soldiers at a parade in Cairo. Vice President Hosni Mubarak, a former Air Force chief of staff, was confirmed by the parliament as president the next day.

Although feared unrest in Egypt did not occur in the wake of the assassination, and Israel completed the return of the Sinai to Egyptian control on April 25, 1982, Mubarak was unable to revive the autonomy talks. Israel's invasion of Lebanon in June imposed a new strain on him, and brought a marked cooling in Egyptian-Israeli relations, but not a disavowal of the peace treaty.

During 1985, pressures by Moslem fundamentalists to implement Islamic law in Egypt increased. In response, the government began putting all mosques under control of the minister for religious endowments. In July, authorities arrested at least 45 fundamentalists including Sheik Hafez Salama, the fundamentalist cleric spearheading the campaign for immediate application of *sharia*, the Islamic legal code dating back 1,300 years.

In February 1986, a riot by the security forces had to be quelled by the army; an incident that underscored Mubarak's dependence on the army in the face of growing Islamic fundamentalism and increasing discontent with the failing economy.

Suez Canal. The Suez Canal, in Egyptian territory between the Arabian Desert and the Sinai Peninsula, is an artificial waterway about 100 miles (161 km) long between Port Said on the Mediterranean and Suez on the Red Sea. Construction work, directed by the French engineer Ferdinand de Lesseps, was begun April 25, 1859, and the Canal was opened Nov. 17, 1869. The cost was 432,807,882 francs. The concession was held by an Egyptian joint stock company, *Compagnie Universelle du Canal Maritime de Suez*, in which the British government held 353,504 out of a total of 800,000 shares. The concession was to expire Nov. 17, 1968, but the company was nationalized July 26, 1956, by unilateral action of the Egyptian government.

The Canal was closed in June 1967 after the Arab-Israeli conflict. With the help of the U.S. Navy, work was begun on clearing the Canal in 1974, after the cease-fire ending the Arab-Israeli war. It was reopened to traffic June 5, 1975.

EL SALVADOR

Republic of El Salvador
President: Alfredo Cristiani (1989)
Area: 8,260 sq mi. (21,393 sq km)
Population (est. mid-1990): 5,300,000 (average annual rate of natural increase: 2.7%)
Density per square mile: 620
Capital: San Salvador
Largest cities (est. 1985): San Salvador, 459,902; Santa Ana, 137,879; Mejicanos, 91,465; San Miguel, 88,520
Monetary unit: Colón
Language: Spanish
Religion: Roman Catholic
National name: República de El Salvador
Literacy rate: 69%
Economic summary: Gross domestic product (1988): $4.1 billion; $780 per capita; 1% real growth rate. Arable land: 27%; principal products: coffee, cotton, corn, sugar, rice, sorghum. Labor force: 1,700,000; 16% in manufacturing; major products: processed foods, clothing and textiles, petroleum products. Natural resources: hydro- and geothermal power, crude oil. Exports: coffee, cotton, sugar, shrimp. Imports: machinery, automotive vehicles, petroleum, foodstuffs, fertilizer. Major trading partners: U.S., Guatemala, Japan, West Germany, Mexico, Costa Rica, Venezuela.

Geography. Situated on the Pacific coast of Central America, El Salvador has Guatemala to the west and Honduras to the north and east. It is the smallest of the Central American countries, its area equal to that of Massachusetts, and the only one without an Atlantic coastline.

Most of the country is a fertile volcanic plateau about 2,000 feet (607 m) high. There are some active volcanoes and many scenic crater lakes.

Government. A new Constitution enacted in 1983 vests executive power in a President elected for a nonrenewable, five-year term, and legislative power in a 60-member National Assembly elected by universal suffrage and proportional representation. Judicial power is vested in a Supreme Court, composed of a President and eleven magistrates elected by the Assembly, and subordinate courts.

History. Pedro de Alvarado, a lieutenant of Cortés, conquered El Salvador in 1525. El Salvador, with the other countries of Central America, declared its independence from Spain on Sept. 15, 1821, and was part of a federation of Central American states until that union was dissolved in 1838. Its independent career for decades thereafter was marked by numerous revolutions and wars against other Central American republics.

On Oct. 15, 1979, a junta deposed the President, Gen. Carlos Humberto Romero, seeking to halt increasingly violent clashes between leftist and rightist forces.

On Dec. 4, 1980, three American nuns and an American lay worker were killed in an ambush near San Salvador, causing the Carter Administration to suspend all aid pending an investigation. The naming of José Napoleón Duarte, a moderate civilian, as head of the governing junta brought a resumption of U.S. aid.

Defying guerrilla threats, voters on March 28, 1982, elected a rightist majority to a constituent assembly that dismissed Duarte and replaced him with a centrist physician, Dr. Alvaro Alfredo Magaña. The rightist majority repealed the laws permitting expropriation of land, and critics charged that the land-reform program begun under Duarte was dead. Even though fighting continued, with reports of government violations of human rights, the Reagan Administration asked certification of El Salvador's eligibility for resumed foreign aid, and this was approved by Congress.

In an election closely monitored by American and other foreign observers, Duarte was elected President in May 1984.

Duarte's Christian Democratic Party scored an unexpected electoral triumph in national legislative and municipal elections held in March 1985, a winning majority in the new National Assembly. The rightist parties that had been dominant in the previous Constituent Assembly demanded that the vote be nullified, but the army high command rejected their assertion the voting had been fraudulent. The army's refusal to support the rightists was interpreted as a turning point in El Salvador's struggle for political stability.

At the same time, U.S. officials said that while the rebels still were far from being defeated, there had been marked improvement in the effectiveness of government troops in the civil war against antigovernment guerrillas that has been waged mainly in the countryside. The rebels responded by initiating a campaign of urban terror; killing and kidnapping pro-government figures. In 1986, Duarte called for a new round of talks with the rebels. This was seen as an attempt to revive a popularity that was falling due to his perceived failure to improve the economy, implement promised social programs or end the war. These broke down in September. Duarte's inability to find solutions led to the right-wing ARENA party controlling half the seats in the National Assembly, in the elections of March, 1988. The decisive victory of Alfredo Christiani, the ARENA candidate for president, gives the rightwing party effective control of the country, given their political control of most of the municipalities.

EQUATORIAL GUINEA

Republic of Equatorial Guinea
President: Col. Teodoro Obiang Nguema Mbasogo (1979)
Prime Minister: Capt. Cristino Seriche Bioko
Area: 10,830 sq mi. (28,051 sq km)
Population (mid-1990): 400,000 (average annual rate of natural increase: 2.6%)

Density per square mile: 33
Capital and largest city (est. 1983): Malabo, 37,500
Monetary unit: CFA Franc
Languages: Spanish, pidgin English, Fang, Bubi, N'Dowe
Religions: Roman Catholic, Protestant, traditional
National name: República de Guinea Ecuatorial
Literacy rate: 55%
Economic summary: Gross national product (1986): $75 million, $300 per capita. Arable land: 5%; principal products: cocoa, wood, coffee; rice, yams. Natural resource: wood, crude oil. Exports: cocoa, wood, coffee. Imports: foodstuffs, textiles, machinery. Major trading partner: Spain

Geography. Equatorial Guinea, formerly Spanish Guinea, consists of Rio Muni (10,045 sq mi.; 26,117 sq km), on the western coast of Africa, and several islands in the Gulf of Guinea, the largest of which is Bioko (formerly Fernando Po) (785 sq mi.; 2,033 sq km). The other islands are Annobón, Corisco, Elobey Grande, and Elobey Chico. The total area is twice that of Connecticut.

Government. The Constitution of 1973 was suspended after a coup on Aug. 3, 1979. A Supreme Military Council, headed by the president, exercises all power. Political parties were banned until Aug. 1987.

History. Fernando Po and Annobón came under Spanish control in 1778. From 1827 to 1844, with Spanish consent, Britain administered Fernando Po, but in the latter year Spain reclaimed the island. Río Muni was given to Spain in 1885 by the Treaty of Berlin.

Negotiations with Spain led to independence on Oct. 12, 1968.

In 1969, anti-Spanish incidents in Río Muni, including the tearing down of a Spanish flag by national troops, caused 5,000 Spanish residents to flee for their safety, and diplomatic relations between the two nations became strained. A month later, President Masie Nguema Biyogo Negue Ndong charged that a coup had been attempted against him. He seized dictatorial powers and arrested 80 opposition politicians and even several of his Cabinet ministers and the secretary of the National Assembly.

A coup on Aug. 3, 1979, deposed Masie, and a junta led by Lieut. Col. Teodoro Obiang Nguema Mbasogo took over the government. Obiang expelled Soviet technicians and reinstated cooperation with Spain.

ETHIOPIA

People's Democratic Republic of Ethiopia
President: Mengistu Haile Mariam (1987)
Prime Minister: Hailu Yemenu (1989)
Area: 472,432 sq mi. (1,223,600 sq km)
Population (est. mid-1990): 51,700,000 (average annual rate of natural increase: 2%)
Density per square mile: 105
Capital: Addis Ababa
Largest cities (est. 1984): Addis Ababa, 1,423,111; Asmara, 275,385
Monetary unit: Birr
Languages: Amharic (official), Galligna, Tigrigna
Religions: Ethiopian Orthodox, 40%; Islam, 35%; traditional, 15%
Literacy rate: 35%

Economic summary: Gross domestic product (FY87 est.): $5.7 billion; $130 per capita; 3.4% real growth rate. Arable land: 12%; principal products: coffee, barley, wheat, corn, sugar cane, cotton, oilseeds, livestock. Major industrial products: cement, cotton textiles, refined sugar, processed foods, refined oil. Natural resources: potash, salt, gold, platinum, copper. Exports: coffee, hides and skins, oilseeds. Imports: petroleum, foodstuffs. Major trading partners: U.S.S.R., U.S., W. Germany, Italy, Japan, Djibouti, South Yemen.

Geography. Ethiopia is in east central Africa, bordered on the west by the Sudan, the east by Somalia and Djibouti, the south by Kenya, and the north by the Red Sea. It is nearly three times the size of California.

Over its main plateau land, Ethiopia has several high mountains, the highest of which is Ras Dashan at 15,158 feet (4,620 m). The Blue Nile, or Abbai, rises in the northwest and flows in a great semicircle east, south, and northwest before entering the Sudan. Its chief reservoir, Lake Tana, lies in the northwestern part of the plateau.

Government. On Feb. 22, 1987, a new constitution came into effect. It establishes a Communist civilian government with a national assembly, the Shengo, which elected Mengistu as president for a five-year term. The Workers Party of Ethiopia is the only party.

History. Black Africa's oldest state, Ethiopia can trace 2,000 years of recorded history. Its now deposed royal line claimed descent from King Menelik I, traditionally believed to have been the son of the Queen of Sheba and King Solomon. The present nation is a consolidation of smaller kingdoms that owed feudal allegiance to the Ethiopian Emperor.

Hamitic peoples migrated to Ethiopia from Asia Minor in prehistoric times. Semitic traders from Arabia penetrated the region in the 7th century B.C. Its Red Sea ports were important to the Roman and Byzantine Empires. Coptic Christianity came to the country in A.D. 341, and a variant of that communion became Ethiopia's state religion.

Ancient Ethiopia reached its peak in the 5th century, then was isolated by the rise of Islam and weakened by feudal wars. Modern Ethiopia emerged under Emperor Menelik II, who established its independence by routing an Italian invasion in 1896. He expanded Ethiopia by conquest.

Disorders that followed Menelik's death brought his daughter to the throne in 1917, with his cousin, Tafari Makonnen, as Regent, heir presumptive, and strongman. When the Empress died in 1930, Tafari was crowned Emperor Haile Selassie I.

As Regent, Haile Selassie outlawed slavery. As Emperor, he worked for centralization of his diffuse realm, in which 70 languages are spoken, and for moderate reform. In 1931, he granted a Constitution, revised in 1955, that created a parliament with an appointed Senate and an elected Chamber of Deputies, and a system of courts. But basic power remained with the Emperor.

Bent on colonial empire, fascist Italy invaded Ethiopia on Oct. 3, 1935, forcing Haile Selassie into exile in May 1936. Ethiopia was annexed to Eritrea, then an Italian colony, and Italian Somaliland to form Italian East Africa, losing its independence for the first time in recorded history. In 1941, British troops routed the Italians, and Haile Selassie returned to Addis Ababa.

Deep discontent erupted in the fall of 1973. A long drought had caused famine that killed 100,000 peasants and drove thousands of others to cities, where food was scarce and inflation was rampant. Charges of mismanagement of drought relief sparked riots in Addis Ababa in 1974, and unpaid troops in Asmara, capital of Eritrea, mutinied to protest conditions.

In August 1974, the Armed Forces Committee nationalized Haile Selassie's palace and estates and directed him not to leave Addis Ababa. On Sept. 12, 1974, he was deposed after nearly 58 years as Regent and Emperor. The 82-year-old "Lion of Judah" was placed under guard. Parliament was dissolved and the Constitution suspended.

On Aug. 27, 1975, Haile Selassie died in a small apartment in his former Addis Ababa palace where he had been treated as a state prisoner. He was 83.

Lt. Col. Mengistu Haile Mariam was named head of state Feb. 2, 1977, to replace Brig. Gen. Teferi Benti, who was killed in a factional fight of the Dirgue after having ruled since 1974. The government was losing its fight to hold Eritrea and in the southeastern region of Ogaden, Somali guerrillas backed by Somali regular forces threatened the ancient city of Harar. In October, the U.S.S.R. announced it would end military aid to Somalia and henceforth back its new ally, Ethiopia. This, together with the intervention of Cuban troops in Ogaden, turned the tide for Mengistu. By March 1978, the badly beaten Somalis had retreated to their homeland. This brought an end to large-scale fighting with Somalia, but border skirmishing continued intermittently.

The Marxist government still had not quelled the Eritrean secessionists in the north by 1988. In addition, a secessionist struggle was going on in Tigre, the province adjoining Eritrea. By mid-1990, Eritreans had taken the whole province except the provincial capital, Asmara.

A Communist regime was formally proclaimed on Sept. 10, 1984, with Mengistu as party leader.

FIJI

President: Ratu Sir Penaia Ganilau (1987)
Prime Minister: Ratu Sir Kamisese Mara (1987)
Area: 7,078 sq mi. (18,333 sq km)
Population (est. mid-1990): 800,000 (average annual rate of natural increase: 2.2%)
Density per square mile: 98.9
Capital (1985): Suva (on Viti Levu), 75,000
Monetary unit: Fiji dollar
Languages: Fijian, Hindustani, English
Religions: Christian, 50%; Hindu, 41%; Islam, 8%
Literacy rate (1985): 80%
Economic summary: Gross domestic product (1987): $1.2 billion; $1,680 per capita; real growth rate −11.2%. Arable land: 8%; principal products: sugar, copra, rice, ginger. Labor force: 176,000; 60% subsistence agriculture; 40% wage earners. Major industrial products: refined sugar, gold, lumber. Natural resources: timber, fish, gold, copper. Exports: sugar, copra. Imports: foodstuffs, machinery, manufactured goods, fuels, chemicals. Major trading partners: U.K., Australia, Japan, New Zealand

Geography. Fiji consists of more than 330 islands in the southwestern Pacific Ocean about 1,960 miles (3,152 km) from Sydney, Australia. The two largest islands are Viti Levu (4,109 sq mi.; 10,642 sq km) and Vanua Levu (2,242 sq mi.; 5,807 sq km). The island of Rotuma (18 sq mi.; 47 sq km), about 400 miles to the north, is a dependency of Fiji. Overall, Fiji is nearly as large as New Jersey.

The largest islands in the group are mountainous and volcanic, with the tallest peak being Mount Victoria (4,341 ft; 1,323 m) on Viti Levu. The islands in the south have dense forests on the windward side and grasslands on the leeward.

Government. An April, 1987, election brought the newly formed Fijian Labor Party to power. Riots by ethnic Fijians against the Indian-dominated government sparked coups by the Fijian-dominated army in May, 1987 and Sept., 1987. The new government is structured to preserve Fijian control.

History. In 1874, an offer of cession by the Fijian chiefs was accepted, and Fiji was proclaimed a possession and dependency of the British Crown.

During World War II, the archipelago was an important air and naval station on the route from the U.S. and Hawaii to Australia and New Zealand.

Fiji became independent on Oct. 10, 1970. The next year it joined the five-island South Pacific Forum, which intends to become a permanent regional group to promote collective diplomacy of the newly independent members. The Forum also includes Western Samoa, Tonga, Nauru, and the self-governing segments of the Cook Islands.

In Oct., 1987, Brig. Gen. Sitiveni Rabuka, the coup leader, declared Fiji a republic and removed it from the British Commonwealth.

FINLAND

Republic of Finland
President: Mauno H. Koivisto (1982)
Premier: Harri Holkeri (1987)
Area: 130,119 sq mi. (337,009 sq km)
Population (est. mid-1990): 5,000,000 (average annual rate of natural increase: 0.3%)
Density per square mile: 38
Capital: Helsinki
Largest cities (est. 1987): Helsinki, 487,749; Tampere, 170,097; Espoo, 162,106; Turku, 160,974
Monetary unit: Markka
Languages: Finnish, Swedish
Religions: Lutheran, 90%; Eastern Orthodox, 1%
National name: Suomen Tasavalta—Republiken Finland
Literacy rate: almost 100%
Economic summary: Gross national product (1987): $87.7 billion; $17,780 per capita; 3.6% real growth rate. Arable land: 8%; principal products: dairy and meat products, cereals, sugar beets, potatoes. Labor force: 2,570,000; 22.9% mining and manufacturing; major products: metal manufactures, forestry and wood products, refined copper, ships, electronics. Natural resource: timber. Exports: timber, paper and pulp, ships, machinery, iron and steel, clothing, footwear. Imports: petroleum and petroleum products, chemicals, transportation equipment, machinery, textile yarns, foodstuffs, fodder grain. Major trading partners: W. Germany, Sweden, U.S.S.R., U.K., U.S.

Geography. Finland stretches 700 miles (1,127 km) from the Gulf of Finland on the south to Soviet Petsamo, north of the Arctic Circle. The U.S.S.R. extends along the entire eastern frontier while Norway is on her northern border and Sweden lies on her western border. In area, Finland is three times the size of Ohio.

Off the southwest coast are the Aland Islands, controlling the entrance to the Gulf of Bothnia. Finland has more than 200,000 lakes.

The Swedish-populated Aland Islands (581 sq mi.; 1,505 sq km) have an autonomous status under a law passed in 1921.

Government. The president, chosen for six years by the popularly elected Electoral College of 301 members, appoints the Cabinet. The one-chamber Diet, the Eduskunta, consists of 200 members elected for four-year terms by proportional representation.

History. At the end of the 7th century, the Finns came to Finland from their Volga settlements, taking the country from the Lapps, who retreated northward. The Finns' repeated raids on the Scandinavian coast impelled Eric IX, the Swedish King, to conquer the country in 1157 and bring it into contact with Western Christendom. By 1809 the whole of Finland was conquered by Alexander I of Russia, who set up Finland as a Grand Duchy.

The first period of Russification (1809–1905) resulted in a lessening of the powers of the Finnish Diet. The Russian language was made official, and the Finnish military system was superseded by the Russian. The pace of Russification was intensified from 1908 to 1914. When Russian control was weakened as a consequence of the March Revolution of 1917, the Diet on July 20, 1917, proclaimed Finland's independence, which became complete on Dec. 6, 1917.

Finland rejected Soviet territorial demands, and the U.S.S.R. attacked on Nov. 30, 1939. The Finns made an amazing stand of three months and finally capitulated, ceding 16,000 square miles (41,440 sq km) to the U.S.S.R. Under German pressure, the Finns joined the Nazis against Russia in 1941, but were defeated again and ceded the Petsamo area to the U.S.S.R. In 1948, a 20-year treaty of friendship and mutual assistance was signed by the two nations and renewed for another 20 years in 1970.

After 25 years in office, President Urho K. Kekkonen resigned in October 1981 because of ill health. Premier Mauno Koivisto, leader of the Social Democratic Party, was elected President on Jan. 26, 1982, winning decisively over a conservative rival with support from Finnish Communists. On Feb. 17, Kalevi Sorsa, a Social Democrat, took office as Premier, heading the same center-left coalition Koivisto had led but elections on Mar. 16, 1987 brought the conservative National Coalition Party into the government.

FRANCE

French Republic
President: François Mitterrand (1981)
Premier: Michel Rocard (1988)
Area: 211,208 sq mi. (547,026 sq km)
Population (est. mid-1990): 56,400,000 (average annual rate of natural increase: 0.4%)
Density per square mile: 266
Capital: Paris

Largest cities (est. 1983): Paris, 2,150,000; **(1982 est.):** Marseilles, 868,435; Lyons, 410,455; Toulouse, 344, 917; Nice, 331,165; Nantes, 237,789; Strasbourg, 247, 068; Bordeaux, 201,965
Monetary unit: Franc
Language: French, declining regional dialects
Religion (est.): Roman Catholic, 76%
National name: République Française
Literacy rate (1981): 99%
Economic summary: Gross national product (1988): $939.2 billion; $16,800 per capita; 2.3 % real growth rate. Arable land: 32%; principal products: cereals, feed grains, livestock and dairy products, wine, fruits, vegetables, potatoes. Labor force: 24,170,000; 31.3% industry; major products: chemicals, automobiles, processed foods, iron and steel, aircraft, textiles, clothing. Natural resources: coal, iron ore, bauxite, fish, forests. Exports: textiles and clothing, chemicals, machinery and transport equipment, agricultural products. Imports: machinery, crude petroleum, chemicals, agricultural products. Major trading partners: West Germany, Italy, U.S., Belgium-Luxembourg, U.K., Netherlands.

Geography. France (80% the size of Texas) is second in size to the U.S.S.R. among Europe's nations. In the Alps near the Italian and Swiss borders is Europe's highest point—Mont Blanc (15,781 ft; 4,810 m). The forest-covered Vosges Mountains are in the northeast, and the Pyrenees are along the Spanish border.

Except for extreme northern France, which is part of the Flanders plain, the country may be described as four river basins and a plateau. Three of the streams flow west—the Seine into the English Channel, the Loire into the Atlantic, and the Garonne into the Bay of Biscay. The Rhône flows south into the Mediterranean. For about 100 miles (161 km), the Rhine is France's eastern border.

West of the Rhône and northeast of the Garonne lies the central plateau, covering about 15% of France's area and rising to a maximum elevation of 6,188 feet (1,886 m). In the Mediterranean, about 115 miles (185 km) east-southeast of Nice, is Corsica (3,367 sq mi.; 8,721 sq km).

Government. The president is elected for seven years by universal suffrage. He appoints the premier, and the Cabinet is responsible to Parliament. The president has the right to dissolve the National Assembly or to ask Parliament for reconsideration of a law. The Parliament consists of two houses: the National Assembly and the Senate.

History. The history of France, as distinct from ancient Gaul, begins with the Treaty of Verdun (843), dividing the territories corresponding roughly to France, Germany, and Italy among the three grandsons of Charlemagne. Julius Caesar had conquered part of Gaul in 57–52 B.C., and it remained Roman until Franks invaded it in the 5th century.

Charles the Bald, inheritor of *Francia Occidentalis,* founded the Carolingian dynasty, which ruled over a kingdom increasingly feudalized. By 987, the crown passed to Hugh Capet, a princeling who controlled only the Ile-de-France, the region surrounding Paris. For 350 years, an unbroken Capetian line added to its domain and consolidated royal authority until the accession in 1328 of Philip VI, first of the Valois line. France was then the most powerful nation in Europe, with a population of 15 million.

The missing pieces in Philip's domain were the French provinces still held by the Plantagenet kings of England, who also claimed the French crown. Beginning in 1338, the Hundred Years' War eventually settled the contest. English longbows defeated French armored knights at Crécy (1346) and the English also won the second landmark battle at Agincourt (1415), but the final victory went to the French at Castillon (1453).

Absolute monarchy reached its apogee in the reign of Louis XIV (1643–1715), the Sun King, whose brilliant court was the center of the Western world.

Revolution plunged France into a blood bath beginning in 1789 and ending with a new authoritarianism under Napoleon Bonaparte, who had successfully defended the infant republic from foreign attack and then made himself First Consul in 1799 and Emperor in 1804.

The Congress of Vienna (1815) sought to restore the pre-Napoleonic order in the person of Louis XVIII, but industrialization and the middle class, both fostered under Napoleon, built pressure for change, and a revolution in 1848 drove Louis Phillipe, last of the Bourbons, into exile.

A second republic elected as its president Prince Louis Napoleon, a nephew of Napoleon I, who declared the Second Empire in 1852 and took the throne as Napoleon III. His opposition to the rising power of Prussia ignited the Franco-Prussian War (1870–71), ending in his defeat and abdication.

A new France emerged from World War I as the continent's dominant power. But four years of hostile occupation had reduced northeast France to ruins. The postwar Third Republic was plagued by political instability and economic chaos.

From 1919, French foreign policy aimed at keeping Germany weak through a system of alliances, but it failed to halt the rise of Adolf Hitler and the Nazi war machine. On May 10, 1940, mechanized Nazi troops attacked, and, as they approached Paris, Italy joined with Germany. The Germans marched into an undefended Paris and Marshal Henri Philippe Pétain signed an armistice June 22. France was split into an occupied north and an unoccupied south, the latter becoming a totalitarian state with Pétain as its chief.

Allied armies liberated France in August 1944. The French Committee of National Liberation, formed in Algiers in 1943, established a provisional government in Paris headed by Gen. Charles de Gaulle. The Fourth Republic was born Dec. 24, 1946.

The Empire became the French Union; the National Assembly was strengthened and the presidency weakened; and France joined the North Atlantic Treaty Organization. A war against communist insurgents in Indochina was abandoned after the defeat at Dien Bien Phu. A new rebellion in Algeria threatened a military coup, and on June 1, 1958, the Assembly invited de Gaulle to return as premier with extraordinary powers. He drafted a new Constitution for a Fifth Republic, adopted Sept. 28, which strengthened the presidency and reduced legislative power. He was elected president Dec. 21.

De Gaulle took France out of the NATO military command in 1967 and expelled all foreign-controlled troops from the country. He later went on to attempt to achieve a long-cherished plan of regional reform. This, however, aroused wide opposition. He decided to stake his fate on a referendum. At the voting in April 1969, the electorate defeated the plan.

Rulers of France

Name	Born	Ruled[1]
CAROLINGIAN DYNASTY		
Pepin the Short	c. 714	751–768
Charlemagne[2]	742	768–814
Louis I the Debonair[3]	778	814–840
Charles I the Bald[4]	823	840–877
Louis II the Stammerer	846	877–879
Louis III[5]	c. 863	879–882
Carloman[5]	?	879–884
Charles II the Fat[6]	839	884–887
Eudes (Odo), Count of Paris	?	888–898
Charles III the Simple[8]	879	893–923[9]
Robert I[10]	c. 865	922–923
Rudolf (Raoul), Duke of Burgundy	?	923–936
Louis IV d'Outremer	c. 921	936–954
Lothair	941	954–986
Louis V the Sluggard	c. 967	986–987
CAPETIAN DYNASTY		
Hugh Capet	c. 940	987–996
Robert II the Pious[11]	c. 970	996–1031
Henry I	1008	1031–1060
Philip I	1052	1060–1108
Louis VI the Fat	1081	1108–1137
Louis VII the Young	c.1121	1137–1180
Philip II (Philip Augustus)	1165	1180–1223
Louis VIII the Lion	1187	1223–1226
Louis IX (St. Louis)	1214	1226–1270
Philip III the Bold	1245	1270–1285
Philip IV the Fair	1268	1285–1314
Louis X the Quarreler	1289	1314–1316
John I[12]	1316	1316
Philip V the Tall	1294	1316–1322
Charles IV the Fair	1294	1322–1328
HOUSE OF VALOIS		
Philip VI	1293	1328–1350
John II the Good	1319	1350–1364
Charles V the Wise	1337	1364–1380
Charles VI the Well-Beloved	1368	1380–1422
Charles VII	1403	1422–1461
Louis XI	1423	1461–1483
Charles VIII	1470	1483–1498
Louis XII the Father of the People	1462	1498–1515
Francis I	1494	1515–1547
Henry II	1519	1547–1559
Francis II	1544	1559–1560
Charles IX	1550	1560–1574
Henry III	1551	1574–1589
HOUSE OF BOURBON		
Henry IV of Navarre	1553	1589–1610
Louis XIII	1601	1610–1643
Louis XIV the Great	1638	1643–1715
Louis XV the Well-Beloved	1710	1715–1774
Louis XVI	1754	1774–1792[13]
Louis XVII (Louis Charles de France)[14]	1785	1793–1795

Name	Born	Ruled[1]
FIRST REPUBLIC		
National Convention	—	1792–1795
Directory (Directoire)	—	1795–1799
CONSULATE		
Napoleon Bonaparte[15]	1769	1799–1804
FIRST EMPIRE		
Napoleon I	1769	1804–1815[16]
RESTORATION OF HOUSE OF BOURBON		
Louis XVIII le Désiré	1755	1814–1824
Charles X	1757	1824–1830[17]
BOURBON-ORLEANS LINE		
Louis Philippe ("Citizen King")	1773	1830–1848[18]
SECOND REPUBLIC		
Louis Napoleon[19]	1808	1848–1852
SECOND EMPIRE		
Napoleon III (Louis Napoleon)	1808	1852–1870[20]
THIRD REPUBLIC (PRESIDENTS)		
Louis Adolphe Thiers	1797	1871–1873
Marie E. P. M. de MacMahon	1808	1873–1879
François P. J. Grévy	1807	1879–1887
Sadi Carnot	1837	1887–1894
Jean Casimir-Périer	1847	1894–1895
François Félix Faure	1841	1895–1899
Émile Loubet	1838	1899–1906
Clement Armand Fallières	1841	1906–1913
Raymond Poincaré	1860	1913–1920
Paul E. L. Deschanel	1856	1920–1920
Alexandre Millerand	1859	1920–1924
Gaston Doumergue	1863	1924–1931
Paul Doumer	1857	1931–1932
Albert Lebrun	1871	1932–1940
VICHY GOVERNMENT (CHIEF OF STATE)		
Henri Philippe Pétain	1856	1940–1944
PROVISIQNAL GOVERNMENT (PRESIDENTS)		
Charles de Gaulle	1890	1944–1946
Félix Gouin	1884	1946–1946
Georges Bidault	1899	1946–1947
FOURTH REPUBLIC (PRESIDENTS)		
Vincent Auriol	1884	1947–1954
René Coty	1882	1954–1959
FIFTH REPUBLIC (PRESIDENTS)		
Charles de Gaulle	1890	1959–1969
Georges Pompidou	1911	1969–1974
Valéry Giscard d'Estaing	1926	1974–1981
François Mitterrand	1916	1981–

1. For Kings and Emperors through the Second Empire, year of end of rule is also that of death, unless otherwise indicated. 2. Crowned Emperor of the West in 800. His brother, Carloman, ruled as King of the Eastern Franks from 768 until his death in 771. 3. Holy Roman Emperor 814–840. 4. Holy Roman Emperor 875–877 as Charles II. 5. Ruled jointly 879–882. 6. Holy Roman Emperor 881–887 as Charles III. 7. Died 888. 8. King 893–898 in opposition to Eudes. 9. Died 929. 10. Not counted in regular line of Kings of France by some authorities. Elected by nobles but killed in Battle of Soissons. 11. Sometimes called Robert I. 12. Posthumous son of Louis X; lived for only five days. 13. Executed 1793. 14. Titular King only. He died in prison according to official reports, but many pretenders appeared during the Bourbon restoration. 15. As First Consul, Napoleon held the power of government. In 1804, he became Emperor. 16. Abdicated first time June 1814. Re-entered Paris March 1815, after escape from Elba; Louis XVIII fled to Ghent. Abdicated second time June 1815. He named as his successor his son, Napoleon II, who was not acceptable to the Allies. He died 1821. 17. Died 1836. 18. Died 1850. 19. President; became Emperor in 1852. 20. Died 1873.

His successor Georges Pompidou continued the de Gaulle policies of seeking to expand France's influence in the Mideast and Africa, selling arms to South Africa (despite the U.N. embargo), to Libya, and to Greece, and in 1971 he endorsed British entry into the Common Market.

Pompidou died of cancer in April 1974 and the special election to choose a successor was won by Valéry Giscard d'Estaing.

Socialist François Mitterrand attained a stunning victory in the May 10, 1981, Presidential election over the Gaullist alliance that had held power since 1958.

The victors immediately moved to carry out campaign pledges to nationalize major industries, halt nuclear testing, suspend nuclear power plant construction, and impose new taxes on the rich. On Feb. 11, 1982, the nationalization bills became law.

The Socialists' policies during Mitterrand's first two years created a 12% inflation rate, a huge trade deficit, and devaluations of the franc. In early 1983, Mitterand, embarked on an austerity program to control inflation and reduce the trade deficit. He increased taxes and slashed government spending. A halt in economic growth, declining purchasing power for the average Frenchman, and an increase in unemployment to 10% followed. Mitterrand sank lower and lower in the opinion polls.

In mid-1984, Mitterrand moved toward the political center. He appointed a new Premier, Laurent Fabius who ended the Socialist-Communist coalition. He proposed cuts that would reduce the French worker's income and social security taxes by 5 to 8%. Mitterrand promised further tax cuts.

In March, 1986, a center-right coalition led by Jacques Chirac won a slim majority in legislative elections. Chirac became Premier initiating a period of "co-habitation" between him and the Socialist President, Mitterrand, a cooperation marked by sparring over Chirac's plan to denationalize major industries and effect a harder line on security issues and on New Caledonia.

Mitterrand's decisive re-election in May, 1987, led to Chirac being replaced as Premier by Michel Rocard, a Socialist. Mitterrand called legislative elections for June, 1987 that gave the Socialists a plurality.

Overseas Departments

Overseas Departments elect representatives to the National Assembly, and the same administrative organization as that of mainland France applies to them.

FRENCH GUIANA (including ININI)

Status: Overseas Department
Prefect: Jacques Dewatre (1986)
Area: 35,126 sq mi. (90,976 sq km)
Population (est. mid 1990): 94,702 (average annual growth rate: 3.2%)
Capital (est. 1982): Cayenne, 37,097
Monetary unit: Franc
Language: French
Religion: Roman Catholic
Literacy rate: 82%
Economic summary: Gross domestic product (1982): $210 million; $3,230 per capita. Arable land: NEGL%; principal agricultural products: rice, corn, manioc, cocoa, bananas, sugar cane. Labor force: 23,265; 21.2% in industry; major industrial products: timber, rum, rosewood essence, gold mining, processed shrimp. Natural resources: bauxite, timber, cinnabar, low-grade iron ore. Exports: shrimp, timber, rum, rosewood essence. Imports: food, consumer and producer goods, petroleum. Major trading partners: U.S., France, Trinidad, Japan.

French Guiana, lying north of Brazil and east of Suriname on the northeast coast of South America, was first settled in 1604. Penal settlements, embracing the area around the mouth of the Maroni River and the Iles du Salut (including Devil's Island), were founded in 1852; they have since been abolished.

During World War II, French Guiana at first adhered to the Vichy government, but the Free French took over in 1943. French Guiana accepted in 1958 the new Constitution of the French Fifth Republic and remained an Overseas Department of the French Republic.

GUADELOUPE

Status: Overseas Department
Prefect: Yves Bonnet (1986)
Area: 687 sq mi. (1,779 sq km)
Population (est. mid-1990): 300,000 (average annual growth rate: 1.4%)
Capital (est. 1983): Basse-Terre, 35,000
Largest city (est. 1982): Pointe-à-Pitre, 50,000
Monetary unit: Franc
Language: French, Creole patois
Religions: Roman Catholic
Literacy rate: over 70%
Economic summary: Gross domestic product (1984): $998 million; $3,630 per capita; 15.7% real growth rate (Aug. '79–'80). Arable land: 18%; principal agricultural products: sugar cane, bananas, rum, tobacco. Labor force: 120,000; 25.8% industry. Major industries: construction, public works, sugar, rum, tourism. Exports: sugar, fruits and vegetables, bananas. Imports: foodstuffs, clothing, consumer goods, petroleum. Major trading partner: France.

Guadeloupe, in the West Indies about 300 miles (483 km) southeast of Puerto Rico, was discovered by Columbus in 1493. It consists of the twin islands of Basse-Terre and Grande-Terre and five dependencies—Marie-Galante, Les Saintes, La Désirade, St. Barthélemy, and the northern half of St. Martin. The volcano Soufrière (4,813 ft; 1,467 m), also called La Grande Soufrière, is the highest point on Guadeloupe. Violent activity in 1976 and 1977 caused thousands to flee their homes.

French colonization began in 1635. In 1958, Guadeloupe voted in favor of the new Constitution of the French Fifth Republic and remained an Overseas Department of the French Republic.

MARTINIQUE

Status: Overseas Department
Prefect: Edouard LaCroix (1986)
Area: 431 sq mi. (1,116 sq km)
Population (est. mid-1990): 300,000 (average annual growth rate: 1.3%)
Capital (est. 1984): Fort-de-France, 97,814
Monetary unit: Franc

Languages: French, Creole patois
Religion: Roman Catholic
Literacy rate (1981): 70%
Economic summary: Gross domestic product (1984): $1.3 billion, $3.650 per capita. Average annual growth rate (1970–79): 4.3%. Arable land: 10%; principal agricultural products: sugar cane, bananas, rum, pineapples. Labor force: 100,000; 31.7% in service industry. Major industries: sugar, rum, refined oil, cement, tourism. Natural resource: fish. Exports: bananas, refined petroleum products, rum, sugar, pineapples. Imports: foodstuffs, clothing and other consumer goods, petroleum products, construction materials. Major trading partners: France, U.S.

Martinique, lying in the Lesser Antilles about 300 miles (483 km) northeast of Venezuela, was probably discovered by Columbus in 1502 and was taken for France in 1635. Following the Franco-German armistice of 1940, it had a semiautonomous status until 1943, when authority was relinquished to the Free French. The area, administered by a Prefect assisted by an elected council, is represented in the French Parliament. In 1958, Martinique voted in favor of the new Constitution of the French Fifth Republic and remained an Overseas Department of the French Republic.

RÉUNION

Status: Overseas Department
Prefect: Jean Anciaux (1986)
Area: 970 sq mi. (2,510 sq km)
Population (est. mid-1989): 565,548 (average annual growth rate, 1.5%)
Capital (est. 1986): Saint-Denis, 109,072
Monetary unit: Franc
Languages: French, Creole
Religion: Roman Catholic
Economic summary: Gross domestic product (1985): $2.4 billion; $4,290 per capita. Arable land: 20%; principal agricultural products: rum, vanilla, bananas, perfume plants. Major industrial products: rum, cigarettes, processed sugar. Exports: sugar, perfume essences, rum, molasses. Imports: manufactured goods, foodstuffs, beverages, machinery and transportation equipment, petroleum products. Major trading partners: France, Mauritius.

Discovered by Portuguese navigators in the 16th century, the island of Réunion, then uninhabited, was taken as a French possession in 1642. It is located about 450 miles (724 km) east of Madagascar, in the Indian Ocean. In 1958, Réunion approved the Constitution of the Fifth French Republic and remained an Overseas Department of the French Republic.

ST. PIERRE AND MIQUELON

Status: Overseas Department
Prefect: Bernard Leurguin (1986)
Area: 93 sq mi. (242 sq km)
Population (est. 1989): 6,303; .4% growth rate.
Capital (est. 1981): Saint Pierre, 5,800
Economic summary: Major industries: fishing, canneries. Exports: fish, pelts. Imports: food, petroleum. Major trading partners: Canada, France, U.S., U.K., Portugal.

The sole remnant of the French colonial empire in North America, these islands were first occupied by the French in 1604. Their only importance arises from proximity to the Grand Banks, located 10 miles south of Newfoundland, making them the center of the French Atlantic cod fisheries. On July 19, 1976, the islands became an Overseas Department of the French Republic.

Overseas Territories

Overseas Territories are comparable to Departments, except that their administrative organization includes a locally-elected government.

FRENCH POLYNESIA

Status: Overseas Territory
High Commissioner: Bernard Gerard (1986)
Area: 1,544 sq mi. (4,000 sq km)
Population (mid-1990): 200,000 (average annual growth rate: 2.5%)
Monetary unit: Pacific financial community franc
Language: French
Religions: Protestant, 47%; Roman Catholic, 40%
Capital (est. 1983): Papeete (on Tahiti), 23,496
Economic summary: Gross national product (1983): $1.3 billion. Average annual growth rate (1970–78): 2.8%. Per capita income (1983): $7,620. Principal agricultural product: copra. Major industries: tourism, maintenance of French nuclear test base. Exports: coconut products, mother of pearl, vanilla. Imports: fuels, foodstuffs, equipment. Major trading partners: France, U.S.

The term French Polynesia is applied to the scattered French possessions in the South Pacific—Mangareva (Gambier), Makatea, the Marquesas Islands, Rapa, Rurutu, Rimatara, the Society Islands, the Tuamotu Archipelago, Tubuai, Raivavae, and the island of Clipperton—which were organized into a single colony in 1903. There are 120 islands, of which 25 are uninhabited.

The High Commissioner is assisted by a Council of Government and a popularly elected Territorial Assembly. The principal and most populous island—Tahiti, in the Society group—was claimed as French in 1768. In 1958, French Polynesia voted in favor of the new Constitution of the French Fifth Republic and remained an Overseas Territory of the French Republic. The natives are mostly Maoris.

The Pacific Nuclear Test Center on the atoll of Mururoa, 744 miles (1,200 km) from Tahiti, was completed in 1966.

MAYOTTE

Status: Territorial collectivity
Prefect: Guy DuPuis (1986)
Area: 146 sq mi. (378 sq km)
Population (est. 1985): 66,282
Capital (est. 1985): Dzaoudzi, 5,675
Principal products: vanilla, essential oils, copra

The most populous of the Comoro Islands in the Indian Ocean, with a Christian majority, Mayotte voted in 1974 and 1976 against joining the other, predominantly Moslem islands, in declaring themselves independent. It continues to retain its ties to France.

NEW CALEDONIA AND DEPENDENCIES

Status: Overseas Territory
High Commissioner: Ferdinand Wibaux (1986)

Area: 7,374 sq mi. (19,103 sq km)[1]
Population (mid-1990): 200,000 (average annual growth rate: 1.9%)
Capital (est. 1983): Nouméa, 60,112
Monetary unit: Pacific financial community franc
Languages: French, Melanesian and Polynesian dialects
Religion: Christian
Literacy rate: Not known
Economic summary: Gross national product (1983): $1.21 billion. Average annual growth rate (1970–78): −4.9%. Per capita income (1983): $8,050. Principal agricultural products: coffee, copra, beef, wheat, vegetables. Major industrial product: nickel. Natural resources: nickel, chromite, iron ore. Exports: nickel, chrome. Imports: mineral fuels, machinery, transport equipment, foodstuffs. Major trading partners: France, Japan, U.S., Australia.

1. Including dependencies.

New Caledonia (6,466 sq mi.; 16,747 sq km), about 1,070 miles (1,722 km) northeast of Sydney, Australia, was discovered by Capt. James Cook in 1774 and annexed by France in 1853. The government also administers the Isle of Pines, the Loyalty Islands (Uvéa, Lifu, and Maré), the Belep Islands, the Huon Island group, and Chesterfield Islands.

The natives are Melanesians; about one third of the population is white and one fifth Indochinese and Javanese. The French National Assembly on July 31, 1984, voted a bill into law that granted internal autonomy to New Caledonia and opened the way to possible eventual independence. This touched off ethnic tensions and violence between the natives and the European settlers, with the natives demanding full independence and sovereignty while the settlers wanted to remain part of France. In June, 1988, France resumed direct administration of the territory and promised a referendum on self-determination in 1998. This was agreed to by organizations representing the natives and the French settlers.

SOUTHERN AND ANTARCTIC LANDS

Status: Overseas Territory
Administrator: Claude Pieri
Area: 3,004 sq mi. (7,781 sq km, excluding Adélie Land)
Capital: Port-au-Français

This territory is uninhabited except for the personnel of scientific bases. It consists of Adélie Land (166,752 sq mi.; 431,888 sq km) on the Antarctic mainland and the following islands in the southern Indian Ocean: the Kerguelen and Crozet archipelagos and the islands of Saint-Paul and New Amsterdam.

WALLIS AND FUTUNA ISLANDS

Status: Overseas Territory
Administrator Superior: Jacques Le Henaff (1988)
Area: 106 sq mi. (274 sq km)
Population (July 1989): 14,575
Capital (1980): Wallis (on Uvea), 600

The two islands groups in the South Pacific between Fiji and Samoa were settled by French missionaries at the beginning of the 19th century. A protectorate was established in the 1880s. Following a referendum by the Polynesian inhabitants, the status was changed to that of an Overseas Territory in 1961.

GABON

Gabonese Republic
President: Omar Bongo (1967)
Premier: Oye Mba Casimir (1990)
Area: 103,346 sq mi. (267,667 sq km)
Population (est. mid-1990): 1,200,000 (average annual rate of natural increase: 2.2%)
Density per square mile: 11
Capital and largest city (est. 1983): Libreville, 257,000
Monetary unit: Franc CFA
Ethnic groups: Bateke, Obamba, Bakota, Shake, Pongwés, Adumas, Chiras, Punu, and Lumbu
Languages: French (official) and Bantu dialects
Religions: Roman Catholic, 65%, Protestant, 19%
National name: République Gabonaise
Member of French Community
Literacy rate: 65%
Economic summary: Gross national product (1986): $3.4 billion; $3,300 per capita; real growth rate −2%. Arable land: 1%; principal products: sugar cane, coffee, wood, palm oil, rice, bananas, peanuts. Labor force: 120,000 salaried; 30% in industry and commerce; major products: petroleum, natural gas, processed wood, manganese, uranium. Natural resources: wood, petroleum, iron ore, manganese, uranium. Exports: crude petroleum, wood and wood products, minerals. Imports: mining and road-building machinery, electrical equipment, foodstuffs, textiles, transport vehicles. Major trading partners: France, U.S., West Germany.

Geography. This West African land with the Atlantic as its western border is also bounded by Equatorial Guinea, Cameroon, and the Congo. Its area is slightly less than Kentucky's.

From mangrove swamps on the coast, the land becomes divided plateaus in the north and east and mountains in the north. Most of the country is covered by a dense tropical forest.

Government. The president is elected for a seven-year term. Legislative powers are exercised by a National Assembly, which is elected for a seven-year term. After his conversion to Islam in 1973, President Bongo changed his given name, Albert Bernard, to Omar. The Parti Démocratique Gabonais (all National Assembly seats) is led by President Bongo. He was re-elected without opposition in 1973 and in 1980.

History. Little is known of Gabon's history, even in oral tradition, but Pygmies are believed to be the original inhabitants. Now there are many tribal groups in the country, the largest being the Fang people who constitute a third of the population.

Gabon was first visited by the Portuguese navigator Diego Cam in the 15th century. In 1839, the French founded their first settlement on the left bank of the Gabon Estuary and gradually occupied the hinterland during the second half of the 19th century. It was organized as a French territory in 1888 and became an autonomous republic within the French Union after World War II and an independent republic on Aug. 17, 1960.

Immense resources in oil, uranium, manganese, and iron help give Gabon's inhabitants a per capita annual income of $2,890, one of the highest in black Africa. To speed exploitation of a billion-ton iron ore reserve in the Belinga-Mekambo region, the government began work in 1969 on a 350-mile railroad leading from the coast into the area. The project was initiated by President León Mba, who died in 1967, and has been continued by his hand-picked successor, Omar Bongo.

In 1974, Bongo negotiated 60% control of an iron-ore venture half-owned by the Bethlehem Steel Corp. In October of that year, he visited Peking and concluded an economic and technical agreement with China.

GAMBIA

Republic of the Gambia
President: Sir Dawda K. Jawara (1970)
Area: 4,093 sq mi. (10,600 sq km)
Population (est. mid-1990): 900,000 (average annual rate of natural increase: 2.6%)
Density per square mile: 191
Capital (est. 1983): Banjul, 44,188
Monetary unit: Dalasi
Languages: Native tongues, English (official)
Religions: Islam, 90%, Christian, 9%, traditional, 1%
Member of Commonwealth of Nations
Literacy rate: 12%
Economic summary: Gross domestic product (FY88): $145 million; $180 per capita; 5.4% real growth rate. Arable land: 16%; principal products: peanuts, rice, palm kernels. Labor force: 400,000; 18.9% in industry, commerce and services. Major industrial products: processed peanuts. Natural resources: fish. Exports: peanuts and peanut products, fish. Imports: textiles, foodstuffs, tobacco, machinery, petroleum products. Major trading partners: U.S., EEC, Africa.

Geography. Situated on the Atlantic coast in westernmost Africa and surrounded on three sides by Senegal, Gambia is twice the size of Delaware. The Gambia River flows for 200 miles (322 km) through Gambia on its way to the Atlantic. The country, the smallest on the continent, averages only 20 miles (32 km) in width.

Government. The president's five-year term is linked to the 35-member unicameral House of Representatives, from which he appoints his Cabinet members and the vice president.

The major political party is the People's Progressive Party (27 seats in House of Representatives), led by President Jawara.

History. During the 17th century, Gambia was settled by various companies of English merchants. Slavery was the chief source of revenue until it was abolished in 1807. Gambia became a crown colony in 1843 and an independent nation within the Commonwealth of Nations on Feb. 18, 1965.

Full independence was approved in a 1970 referendum, and on April 24 of that year Gambia proclaimed itself a republic.

President Dawda K. Jawara won overwhelming re-election to his fifth term on May 5, 1982, in a vote that was also seen as an endorsement of his proposal for a confederation with Senegal.

GERMANY, EAST

German Democratic Republic
Acting Head of State: Dr. Sabine Bergmann-Pohl (1990)
Chairman of Council of Ministers: Lothar de Maiziere
Area: 41,767 sq mi. (108,177 sq km)[1]
Population (est. mid-1990): 16,300,000 (average annual growth rate: 0.0%)
Density per square mile: 397.4
Capital: Berlin (eastern sector)
Largest cities (est. 1986): East Berlin, 1,215,586; Leipzig, 553,660; Dresden, 519,769; Karl-Marx Stadt, 315,452; Magdeburg, 288,965; Rostock, 238,011
Monetary unit: Mark of the Deutsche Demokratische Republik
Language: German
Religions: Protestant, 53%; Roman Catholic, 8%
National name: Deutsche Demokratische Republik
Literacy rate: 100%
Economic summary: Gross national product (1988): $207.2 billion; $12,500 per capita; 1.8% real growth rate. Arable land: 45%; principal products: grains, potatoes, sugar beets, meat and dairy products. Labor force: 8,960,000; 37.5% in industry; major products: steel, chemicals, machinery, electrical and precision engineering products. Natural resources: brown coal, potash, bauxite. Exports: machinery and equipment, chemical products, textiles, clothing. Imports: raw materials, fuels, agricultural products, machinery and equipment. Major trading partners: U.S.S.R., Soviet bloc, West Germany.

1. Including East Berlin (156 square miles), which has been incorporated into the German Democratic Republic.

Geography. East Germany lies on the Baltic Sea with Poland to the east and Czechoslovakia to the south. The border with West Germany is roughly a line running south from Lübeck for about 250 miles. The main river is the Elbe, which flows from Dresden in the southeast to the North Sea in the northwest. The Oder and Neisse Rivers form the border with Poland. Most of the country, which is the size of Tennessee, is situated in the north German plain.

Government. East Germany is a multi-party, Democratic Socialist state. Elections scheduled for Dec. 2, 1990, will determine the government of the new unified Germany.

History. (For history before 1945, *see* Germany, West.) The area now occupied by East Germany, as well as adjacent areas in Eastern Europe, consists of Mecklenburg, Brandenburg, Lusatia, Saxony, and Thuringia. Soviet armies conquered the five territories by 1945. In the division of 1945 they were allotted to the U.S.S.R. Soviet forces created a State controlled by the secret police with a single party, the Socialist Unity (Communist) Party. The Russians appropriated East German plants to restore their war-ravaged industry.

When the Federal Republic of Germany was established in West Germany, the East German states adopted a more centralized constitution for the Democratic Republic of Germany, and it was put into effect on Oct. 7, 1949. The U.S.S.R. thereupon dissolved its occupation zone, but Soviet troops remained. The Western Allies declared that the East German Republic was a Soviet creation undertaken without self-determination and refused to recognize it. It was recognized only within the Soviet bloc.

By 1973, normal relations were established between East and West Germany and the two states entered the United Nations.

The 25-year diplomatic hiatus between East Germany and the U.S. ended Sept. 4, 1974, with the establishment of formal relations.

Chairman of the Council of State Erich Honecker gave strong backing to the Soviet Union's stern policy toward Poland as the workers' demand for democratic rights advanced in 1980 and 1981.

On Oct. 28, 1980, he closed the border, which had been open between the two states for 10 years, permitting only certified relatives or invited friends to visit. Five million Poles had visited East Germany in the previous year, largely to find cheaper and more abundant consumer goods.

In February 1981, Honecker, in a surprise gesture, declared at his party's 16th Congress that German reunification might eventually be possible, something the Communist regime had ruled out 10 years earlier. He also eased border restrictions on exchanges with West Germany imposed a few months before, and made a long-delayed, long-planned milestone visit to West Germany in Sept. 1987.

The temporary incapacitation of Honecker with a gall-bladder attack in mid-1989 sparked a mass exodus from the country and protests. These led to a lifting of exit restrictions and Honecker's resignation and, later, of the whole Politburo.

The new government allowed multi-party elections which were won by the newly-formed Christian Democrats. International and inter-German negotiations on reunification began in early 1990. A social and economic merger became effective on July 1, 1990, and included the adoption of the West German mark as the East German currency. Reunification with West Germany took place in October 1990, and East Germany ceased to exist. Political unification will be completed with the holding of all-German elections in December 1990. (*See* Current Events for later details.*)

GERMANY, WEST

Federal Republic of Germany
President: Richard von Weizsäcker (1984)
Chancellor: Helmut Kohl (1982)
Area: 96,010 sq mi. (248,667 sq km)[1]
Population (mid-1990): 63,200,000. (average annual growth rate: −0%)
Density per square mile: 640
Capital (est. 1985): Bonn, 292,600
Largest cities (1986): Hamburg, 1,575,700; Munich, 1, 269,400; Cologne, 914,000; Essen, 617,700; Frankfurt, 593,400; Dortmund, 569,800; Dusseldorf, 561,200; Stuttgart, 564,200; Bremen, 524,700; Hannover, 506, 400; West Berlin, 2,014,100 (1987 census)
Monetary unit: Deutsche Mark
Language: German
Religions: Protestant, 49%; Roman Catholic, 45%
National name: Bundesrepublik Deutschland
Literacy rate: 99%
Economic summary: Gross national product (1988): $1,120 billion; $18,370 per capita; 3.6% real growth rate. Arable land: 30%; principal products: grains, potatoes, sugar beets. Labor force: 27,790,000; 41.6% in industry; major products: chemicals, machinery, vehicles. Natural resources: iron ore, timber, coal. Exports: machines and machine tools, chemicals, motor vehicles, iron and steel products. Imports: manufactured and agricultural products, raw materials, fuels. Major trading partners: France, Netherlands, Belgium-Luxembourg, Italy, U.S., U.K.

1. Excluding West Berlin (184 square miles with 1986 population of 1,879,000).

Geography. The Federal Republic of Germany occupies the western half of the central European area historically regarded as German. This was the part of Germany occupied by the United States, Britain, and France after World War II, when the eastern half of prewar Germany was split roughly between a Soviet-occupied zone, which became the present German Democratic Republic, and an area annexed by Poland.

West Germany's neighbors are France, Belgium, Luxembourg, and the Netherlands on the west, Switzerland and Austria on the south, Czechoslovakia and East Germany on the east, and Denmark on the north.

The northern plain, the central hill country, and the southern mountain district constitute the main physical divisions of West Germany, which is slightly smaller than Oregon. The Bavarian plateau in the southwest averages 1,600 feet (488 m) above sea level, but it reaches 9,721 feet (2,962 m) in the Zugspitze Mountains, the highest point in the country.

Important navigable rivers are the Danube, rising in the Black Forest and flowing east across Bavaria into Austria, and the Rhine, which rises in Switzerland and flows across the Netherlands in two channels to the North Sea and is navigable by ocean-going and coastal vessels as far as Cologne. The Elbe, which also empties into the North Sea, is navigable within Germany for smaller vessels. The Weser, flowing into the North Sea, and the Main and Mosel (Moselle), both tributaries of the Rhine, are also important.

Government. Under the Constitution of May 23, 1949, the Federal Republic was established as a parliamentary democracy. The Parliament consists of the Bundesrat, an upper chamber representing and appointed by the 10 Länder, or states (plus West Berlin), and the Bundestag, a lower house elected for four years by universal suffrage. Each house has non-voting representatives from West Berlin. A federal assembly composed of Bundestag deputies and deputies from the state parliaments elects the President of the Republic for a five-year term; the Bundestag alone chooses the Chancellor, or Prime Minister. Each of the Länder and West Berlin have a legislature popularly elected for a four-year or five-year term.

The major political parties are the Christian Democratic Union-Christian Social Union (223 of 497 seats in the Bundestag), led by Chancellor Helmut Kohl; Social Democratic Party (186 seats) led by Hans-Jochen Vogel; and the Free Democratic Party (46 seats), led by Otto Count Larbsdorff, the Greens (42 seats). Kohl's government is a coalition with the Free Democrats.

History. Immediately before the Christian era, when the Roman Empire had pushed its frontier to the Rhine, what is now Germany was inhabited by several tribes believed to have migrated from Central Asia between the 6th and 4th centuries B.C. One of these tribes, the Franks, attained supremacy in western Europe under Charlemagne, who was crowned Holy Roman Emperor A.D. 800. By the Treaty of Verdun (843), Charlemagne's lands east of the Rhine were ceded to the German Prince Louis. Additional territory acquired by the Treaty of Mersen (870) gave Germany approximately the area it maintained throughout the Middle Ages. For several centuries after Otto the Great was crowned King in 936, the German rulers were also usually heads of the Holy Roman Empire.

Relations between state and church were changed by the Reformation, which began with

Rulers of Germany and Prussia

Name	Born	Ruled[1]	Name	Born	Ruled[1]
KINGS OF PRUSSIA			**GERMAN FEDERAL REPUBLIC**		
Frederick I[2]	1657	1701–1713	**(WEST) (PRESIDENTS)**		
Frederick William I	1688	1713–1740	Theodor Heuss	1884	1949–1959[9]
Frederick II the Great	1712	1740–1786	Heinrich Luebke	1895	1959–1969[8]
Frederick William II	1744	1786–1797	Gustav Heinemann[10]	1899	1969–1974
Frederick William III	1770	1797–1840	Walter Scheel	1919	1974–1979
Frederick William IV	1795	1840–1861	Karl Carstens	1914	1979–1984
William I	1797	1861–1871[3]	Richard von Weizsäcker	1920	1984–
EMPERORS OF GERMANY			**GERMAN DEMOCRATIC REPUBLIC**		
William I	1797	1871–1888	**(EAST)**		
Frederick III	1831	1888–1888	Wilhelm Pieck[5]	1876	1949–1960
William II	1859	1888–1918[4]	Walter Ulbricht[11]	1893	1960–1973
			Willi Stoph[12]	1914	1973–1976
HEADS OF THE REICH			Erich Honecker[12]	1912	1976–1989
Friedrich Ebert[5]	1871	1919–1925	Egon Krenz[12]		1989–
Paul von Hindenburg[5]	1847	1925–1934	Manfred Gerlach[12]		1989–1990
Adolf Hitler[6 7]	1889	1934–1945	Sabine Bergman-Pohl[12]		1990–
Karl Doenitz[6]	1891	1945–1945			

1. Year of end of rule is also that of death, unless otherwise indicated. 2. Was Elector of Brandenburg (1688–1701) as Frederick III. 3. Became Emperor of Germany in 1871. 4. Died 1941. 5. President. 6. Führer. 7. Named Chancellor by President Hindenburg in 1933. 8. Died 1972. 9. Died 1963. 10. Died 1976. 11. Chairman of Council of State. Died 1973. 12. Chairman of Council of State.

Martin Luther's 95 theses, and came to a head in 1547, when Charles V scattered the forces of the Protestant League at Mühlberg. Freedom of worship was guaranteed by the Peace of Augsburg (1555), but a Counter Reformation took place later, and a dispute over the succession to the Bohemian throne brought on the Thirty Years' War (1618–48), which devastated Germany and left the empire divided into hundreds of small principalities virtually independent of the Emperor.

Meanwhile, Prussia was developing into a state of considerable strength. Frederick the Great (1740–86) reorganized the Prussian army and defeated Maria Theresa of Austria in a struggle over Silesia. After the defeat of Napoleon at Waterloo (1815), the struggle between Austria and Prussia for supremacy in Germany continued, reaching its climax in the defeat of Austria in the Seven Weeks' War (1866) and the formation of the Prussian-dominated North German Confederation (1867).

The architect of German unity was Otto von Bismarck, a conservative, monarchist, and militaristic Prussian Junker who had no use for "empty phrasemaking and constitutions." From 1862 until his retirement in 1890 he dominated not only the German but also the entire European scene. He unified all Germany in a series of three wars against Denmark (1864), Austria (1866), and France (1870–71), which many historians believe were instigated and promoted by Bismarck in his zeal to build a nation through "blood and iron."

On Jan. 18, 1871, King Wilhelm I of Prussia was proclaimed German Emperor in the Hall of Mirrors at Versailles. The North German Confederation, created in 1867, was abolished, and the Second German Reich, consisting of the North and South German states, was born. With a powerful army, an efficient bureaucracy, and a loyal bourgeoisie, Chancellor Bismarck consolidated a powerful centralized state.

Wilhelm II dismissed Bismarck in 1890 and embarked upon a "New Course," stressing an intensified colonialism and a powerful navy. His chaotic foreign policy culminated in the diplomatic isolation of Germany and the disastrous defeat in World War I (1914–18).

The Second German Empire collapsed following the defeat of the German armies in 1918, the naval mutiny at Kiel, and the flight of the Kaiser to the Netherlands on November 10. The Social Democrats, led by Friedrich Ebert and Philipp Scheidemann, crushed the Communists and established a moderate republic with Ebert as President.

The Weimar Constitution of 1919 provided for a President to be elected for seven years by universal suffrage and a bicameral legislature, consisting of the Reichsrat, representing the states, and the Reichstag, representing the people. It contained a model Bill of Rights. It was weakened, however, by a provision that enabled the President to rule by decree.

President Ebert died Feb. 28, 1925, and on April 26, Field Marshal Paul von Hindenburg was elected president.

The mass of Germans regarded the Weimar Republic as a child of defeat, imposed upon a Germany whose legitimate aspirations to world leadership had been thwarted by a world conspiracy. Added to this were a crippling currency debacle, a tremendous burden of reparations, and acute economic distress.

Adolf Hitler, an Austrian war veteran and a fanatical nationalist, fanned discontent by promising a Greater Germany, abrogation of the Treaty of Versailles, restoration of Germany's lost colonies, and destruction of the Jews. When the Social Democrats and the Communists refused to combine against the Nazi threat, President Hindenburg made Hitler chancellor on Jan. 30, 1933.

With the death of Hindenburg on Aug. 2, 1934, Hitler repudiated the Treaty of Versailles and began full-scale rearmament. In 1935 he withdrew Germany from the League of Nations, and the next year he reoccupied the Rhineland and signed the anti-Comintern pact with Japan, at the same time strengthening relations with Italy. Austria was annexed in March 1938. By the Munich agreement in September 1938 he gained the Czech Sudetenland, and in violation of this agreement he completed the dismemberment of Czechoslovakia in March 1939. But his invasion of Poland on Sept. 1,

1939, precipitated World War II.

On May 8, 1945, Germany surrendered unconditionally to Allied and Soviet military commanders, and on June 5 the four-nation Allied Control Council became the *de facto* government of Germany. (For details of World War II, *see* Headline History.)

At the Berlin (or Potsdam) Conference (July 17–Aug. 2, 1945) President Truman, Premier Stalin, and Prime Minister Clement Attlee of Britain set forth the guiding principles of the Allied Control Council. They were Germany's complete disarmament and demilitarization, destruction of its war potential, rigid control of industry, and decentralization of the political and economic structure. Pending final determination of territorial questions at a peace conference, the three victors agreed in principle to the ultimate transfer of the city of Königsberg (now Kaliningrad) and its adjacent area to the U.S.S.R. and to the administration by Poland of former German territories lying generally east of the Oder-Neisse Line.

For purposes of control Germany was divided in 1945 into four national occupation zones, each headed by a Military Governor.

The Western powers were unable to agree with the U.S.S.R. on any fundamental issue. Work of the Allied Control Council was hamstrung by repeated Soviet vetoes; and finally, on March 20, 1948, Russia walked out of the Council. Meanwhile, the U.S. and Britain had taken steps to merge their zones economically (Bizone); and on May 31, 1948, the U.S., Britain, France, and the Benelux countries agreed to set up a German state comprising the three Western Zones.

The U.S.S.R. reacted by clamping a blockade on all ground communications between the Western Zones and Berlin, an enclave in the Soviet Zone. The Western Allies countered by organizing a gigantic airlift to fly supplies into the beleaguered city, assigning 60,000 men to it. The U.S.S.R. was finally forced to lift the blockade on May 12, 1949.

The Federal Republic of Germany was proclaimed on May 23, 1949, with its capital at Bonn. In free elections, West German voters gave a majority in the Constituent Assembly to the Christian Democrats, with the Social Democrats largely making up the opposition. Konrad Adenauer became chancellor, and Theodor Heuss of the Free Democrats was elected first president.

Agreements in Paris in 1954 giving the Federal Republic full independence and complete sovereignty came into force on May 5, 1955. Under it, West Germany and Italy became members of the Brussels treaty organization created in 1948 and renamed the Western European Union. West Germany also became a member of NATO. In 1955 the U.S.S.R. recognized the Federal Republic. The Saar territory, under an agreement between France and West Germany, held a plebiscite and despite economic links to France voted to rejoin West Germany. It became a state of West Germany on Jan. 1, 1957.

In 1963, Chancellor Adenauer concluded a treaty of mutual cooperation and friendship with France and then retired. He was succeeded by his chief inner-party critic, Ludwig Erhard, who was followed in 1966 by Kurt Georg Kiesinger. He, in turn, was succeeded in 1969 by Willy Brandt, former mayor of West Berlin.

The division between West Germany and East Germany was intensified when the Communists erected the Berlin Wall in 1961. In 1968, the East German Communist leader, Walter Ulbricht, imposed restrictions on West German movements into West Berlin. The Soviet-bloc invasion of Czechoslovakia in August 1968 added to the tension.

A treaty with the U.S.S.R. was signed in Moscow in August 1970 in which force was renounced and respect for the "territorial integrity" of present European states declared.

Three months later, West Germany signed a similar treaty with Poland, renouncing force and setting Poland's western border as the Oder-Neisse Line. It subsequently resumed formal relations with Czechoslovakia in a pact that "voided" the Munich treaty that gave Nazi Germany the Sudetenland.

Both German states were admitted to the United Nations in 1973.

Brandt, winner of a Nobel Peace Prize for his foreign policies, was forced to resign in 1974 when an East German spy was discovered to be one of his top staff members. Succeeding him was a moderate Social Democrat, Helmut Schmidt.

Helmut Schmidt, Brandt's successor as chancellor, staunchly backed U.S. military strategy in Europe nevertheless, staking his political fate on the strategy of placing U.S. nuclear missiles in Germany unless the Soviet Union reduced its arsenal of intermediate missiles.

The chancellor also strongly opposed nuclear freeze proposals and won 2-1 support for his stand at the convention of Social Democrats in April. The Free Democrats then deserted the Socialists after losing ground in local elections and joined with the Christian Democrats to unseat Schmidt and install Helmut Kohl as chancellor in 1982.

Kohl's tenure has seen a dwindling of the nuclear freeze issue after the deployment of the U.S. missiles. U.S.-Soviet negotiations in 1987 produced a treaty setting up the removal of medium- and short-range missiles from Europe. An economic upswing in 1986 led to Kohl's re-election.

The fall of the Communist government in East Germany left only Soviet objections to German reunification to be dealt with. This was resolved in July 1990. Soviet objections to a reunified Germany belonging to NATO were dropped in return for German promises to reduce their military and engage in wide-ranging economic cooperation with the Soviet Union.

BERLIN

Status: West Berlin: State of West Germany; East Berlin: capital of East Germany
Governing Mayor, West Berlin: Walter Momper (SDP) (1989)
Mayor, East Berlin: Tino Schwierzina (1990)
Area: 340 square miles (West Berlin, 184; East Berlin, 156)
Population (est. 1986): 3,094,600 (West Berlin, 1,879,-000; East Berlin, 1,215,600)

Berlin, the capital of prewar Germany, lay entirely within the borders of East Germany. After the war, the city was occupied by the forces of the U.S., Britain, France, and the U.S.S.R. The three western sectors, known as West Berlin, contain 55% of the area and 60% of the population.

West Berlin is a state of the Federal Republic of Germany, but supreme authority remains in the hands of the three Western powers in accordance with postwar agreements. This will change when German reunification is completed. The government is composed of the governing mayor, the 11-

member Senate (his Cabinet), and the House of Representatives, a popularly elected legislative body that elects the governing mayor and the Senate.

East Berlin is governed by a City Assembly elected by Communist Party members, and a Magistrate (City Council) chosen by the Assembly and headed by the mayor. In violation of the Four Power Agreements, the Soviet Sector was incorporated into the German Democratic Republic and became the capital of that country.

Major anti-Communist riots broke out in East Berlin in June 1953 and, on Aug. 13, 1961, the Soviet Sector was sealed off by a Communist-built wall, 26 1/2 miles (43 km) long, running through the city. It was built to stem the flood of refugees seeking freedom in the West, 200,000 having fled in 1961 before the wall was erected.

On Nov. 9, 1989, several weeks after the resignation of East Germany's long-time Communist leader, Erich Honecker, the wall's designer and chief defender, the East German government opened its borders to the West and allowed thousands of its citizens to pass freely through the Berlin Wall. They were cheered and greeted by thousands of West Berliners, and many of the jubilant newcomers celebrated their new freedom by climbing on top of the hated wall.

The following day, East German troops began dismantling parts of the wall. It was ironic that this wall was built to keep the citizens from leaving and, 28 years later, it was being dismantled for the same reason.

On Nov. 22, new passages were opened at the north and south of the Brandenburg Gate in an emotional ceremony attended by Chancellor Helmut Kohl of West Germany and Chancellor Hans Modrow of East Germany. The opening of the Brandenburg Gate climaxed the ending of the barriers that had divided the German people since the end of World War II. By the end of the year the entire wall, including Checkpoint Charlie,[1] had been removed.

Pollsters have found that most West Germans want Berlin to be the capital of the future united Germany. However, several politicians in the Federal Republic would like Bonn to remain the capital, with others suggesting that both cities share the governmental and bureaucratic role.

1. The border crossing point in the American sector of Berlin reserved for non-Germans traveling to the eastern half of the city. All border checks were abolished and all streets that were blocked by the former walled sections of the city were reopened.

GHANA

Republic of Ghana

Chairman of Provisional National Defense Council: Flight Lt. Jerry John Rawlings (1981)
Area: 92,100 sq mi. (238,537 sq km)
Population (est. mid-1990): 15,000,000 (average annual rate of natural increase: 3.1%)
Density per square mile: 158
Capital: Accra
Largest cities (est. 1984): Accra, 859,600; Kumasi, 348,900; Tamale, 136,800
Monetary unit: Cedi
Languages: English (official), Native tongues (Brong Ahafo, Twi, Fanti, Ga, Ewe, Dagbani)
Religions: Christian 40–50%; Islam 10–20%, and Animist
Literacy rate: 45% (in English)
Member of Commonwealth of Nations
Economic summary: Gross national product (1986 est.):

$5.7 billion; $410 per capita; 5.3% real growth rate. Arable land: 5%; principal products: cocoa, coconuts, coffee, cassava, yams, rice, rubber. Labor force: 3,700,000; 18.7% in industry; major products: mining products, cocoa products, aluminum. Natural resources: gold, diamonds, bauxite, manganese, timber, fish. Exports: cocoa beans and products, gold, timber, manganese ore. Imports: textiles and manufactured goods, food, fuels, transport equipment. Major trading partners: U.K., U.S., Nigeria, U.S.S.R., Switzerland, Netherlands.

Geography. A West African country bordering on the Gulf of Guinea, Ghana has the Ivory Coast to the west, Burkina Faso to the north, and Togo to the east. It compares in size to Oregon.

The coastal belt, extending about 270 miles (435 km), is sandy, marshy, and generally exposed. Behind it is a gradually widening grass strip. The forested plateau region to the north is broken by ridges and hills. The largest river is the Volta.

Government. Ghana returned to military rule after two years of constitutional government when Flight Lt. Jerry Rawlings, who led a coup in 1979 and stepped down voluntarily, seized power on Dec. 31, 1981. Rawlings heads a Provisional National Defense Council, which exercises all power.

History. Created an independent country on March 6, 1957, Ghana is the former British colony of the Gold Coast. The area was first seen by Portuguese traders in 1470. They were followed by the English (1553), the Dutch (1595), and the Swedes (1640). British rule over the Gold Coast began in 1820, but it was not until after quelling the severe resistance of the Ashanti in 1901 that it was firmly established. British Togoland, formerly a colony of Germany, was incorporated into Ghana by referendum in 1956. As the result of a plebiscite, Ghana became a republic on July 1, 1960.

Premier Kwame Nkrumah attempted to take leadership of the Pan-African Movement, holding the All-African People's Congress in his capital, Accra, in 1958 and organizing the Union of African States with Guinea and Mali in 1961. But he oriented his country toward the Soviet Union and China and built an autocratic rule over all aspects of Ghanaian life.

In February 1966, while Nkrumah was visiting Peking and Hanoi, he was deposed by a military coup led by Gen. Emmanuel K. Kotoka.

A series of military coups followed and on June 4, 1979, Flight Lieutenant Jerry Rawlings overthrew Lt. Gen. Frederick Akuffo's military rule on June 4, 1979. Rawlings permitted the election of a civilian president to go ahead as scheduled the following month, and Hilla Limann, candidate of the People's National Party, took office. Charging the civilian government with corruption and repression, Rawlings staged another coup on Dec. 31, 1981. As chairman of the Provisional National Defense Council, Rawlings instituted an austerity program and reduced budget deficits.

On July 11, 1985, a relative of Rawlings, Michael Agbotui Soussoudis, 39, and Sharon M. Scranage, 29, who had been a low-level clerk in the Central Intelligence Agency station in the West African country, were arrested in the United States on espionage charges. Reagan Administration officials said the American woman had given Soussoudis, her Ghanian lover, information about the agency's operations in Ghana and that as a result, at least one CIA informant had been murdered and the CIA feared reprisals would be taken by the Rawlings government against as many as 10 others.

GREECE

Hellenic Republic
President: Constantine Karamanlis (1990)
Premier: Constantine Mitsotakis (1990)
Area: 50,961 sq mi. (131,990 sq km)
Population (est. mid-1990): 10,100,000 (average annual rate of natural increase: 0.2%)
Density per square mile: 197
Capital: Athens
Largest cities (1981 census): Athens, 3,027,000; Salonika, 706,000; Patras, 150,000; Larissa, 102,000; Heraklion, 111,000; Volos, 107,000.
Monetary unit: Drachma
Language: Greek
Religion: Greek Orthodox
National name: Elliniki Dimokratia
Literacy rate: 95%
Economic summary: Gross national product (1986): $46.6 billion; $4,670 per capita; 0% real growth rate. Arable land: 23%; principal products: grains, fruits, vegetables, olives, olive oil, tobacco, cotton, livestock, dairy products. Labor force: 3,860,000; 20% in manufacturing and mining; major products: textiles, chemicals, food processing. Natural resources: bauxite, iron, forests. Exports: fruits, textiles, tobacco. Imports: machinery and automotive equipment, petroleum, consumer goods, chemicals, foodstuffs. Major trading partners: West Germany, Netherlands, Italy, France, Saudi Arabia, U.S.A., U.K.

Geography. Greece, on the Mediterranean Sea, is the southernmost country on the Balkan Peninsula in southern Europe. It is bordered on the north by Albania, Yugoslavia, and Bulgaria; on the west by the Ionian Sea; and on the east by the Aegean Sea and Turkey. It is slightly smaller than Alabama.

North central Greece, Epirus, and western Macedonia all are mountainous. The main chain of the Pindus Mountains rises to 9,000 feet (2,743 m) in places, separating Epirus from the plains of Thessaly. Mt. Olympus, rising to 9,570 feet (2,909 m) in the north near the Aegean Sea, is the highest point in the country. Greek Thrace is mostly a lowland region separated from European Turkey by the lower Evros River.

Among the many islands are the Ionian group off the west coast; the Cyclades group to the southeast; other islands in the eastern Aegean, including the Dodecanese Islands, Euboea, Lesbos, Samos, and Chios; and Crete, the fourth largest Mediterranean island.

Government. A referendum in December 1974, five months after the collapse of a military dictatorship, ended the Greek monarchy and established a republic. Ceremonial executive power is held by the president; the Premier heads the government and is responsible to a 300-member unicameral Parliament.

History. Greece, with a recorded history going back to 766 B.C., reached the peak of its glory in the 5th century B.C., and by the middle of the 2nd century B.C., it had declined to the status of a Roman province. It remained within the Eastern Roman Empire until Constantinople fell to the Crusaders in 1204.

In 1453, the Turks took Constantinople, and by 1460 Greece was a Turkish province. The insurrection made famous by the poet Lord Byron broke out in 1821, and in 1827 Greece won independence with sovereignty guaranteed by Britain, France, and Russia.

The protecting powers chose Prince Otto of Bavaria as the first king of modern Greece in 1832 to reign over an area only slightly larger than the Peloponnese Peninsula. Chiefly under the next king, George I, chosen by the protecting powers in 1863, Greece acquired much of its present territory. During his 57-year reign, a period in which he encouraged parliamentary democracy, Thessaly, Epirus, Macedonia, Crete, and most of the Aegean islands were added from the disintegrating Turkish empire. An unsuccessful war against Turkey after World War I brought down the monarchy, to be replaced by a republic in 1923.

Two military dictatorships and a financial crisis brought George II back from exile, but only until 1941, when Italian and German invaders defeated tough Greek resistance. After British and Greek troops liberated the country in October 1944, Communist guerrillas staged a long campaign in which the government received U.S. aid under the Truman Doctrine, the predecessor of the Marshall Plan.

A military junta seized power in April 1967, sending young King Constantine II into exile December 14. Col. George Papadopoulos, as premier, converted the government to republican form in 1973 and as President ended martial law. He was moving to restore democracy when he was ousted in November of that year by his military colleagues. The regime of the "colonels," which had tortured its opponents and scoffed at human rights, resigned July 23, 1974, after having bungled an attempt to seize Cyprus.

Former Premier Karamanlis returned from exile to become premier of Greece's first civilian government since 1967.

On Jan. 1, 1981, Greece became the 10th member of the European Community. On Oct. 18, the first Socialist government in Greek history won power, and Andreas Papandreou became the new Premier.

Double-digit inflation and scandals in the Socialist government led to them losing their majority in the elections of June 1989. The opposition New Democracy Party did not gain a majority, however, leading to the creation of a NDP-Communist coalition that will initiate an investigation of the scandals and then call new elections. Later elections led to a Conservative majority.

GRENADA

State of Grenada
Sovereign: Queen Elizabeth II
Governor General: Paul Scoon (1978)
Prime Minister: Nicholas Braithwaite (1990)
Area: 133 sq mi. (344 sq km)
Population (est. mid-1990): 100,000 (average annual growth rate, 3%)
Density per square mile: 751.9
Capital and largest city (est. 1981): St. George's, 4,800
Monetary unit: East Caribbean dollar
Ethnic groups: Caribs and Indians
Language: English
Religions: Roman Catholic, 64%; Anglican, 21%
Member of Commonwealth of Nations
Literacy rate: 85%
Economic summary: Gross domestic product (1987 est.): $118.7 million; $1,400 per capita; 6% real growth rate.

Arable land: 15%; principal products: spices, cocoa, bananas. Exports: nutmeg, cocoa beans, bananas, mace. Imports: foodstuffs, machinery, building materials. Labor force: 36,000; 31% in services. Major trading partners: U.K., Trinidad, U.S.

Geography. Grenada (the first "a" is pronounced as in "gray") is the most southerly of the Windward Islands, about 100 miles (161 km) from the South American coast. It is a volcanic island traversed by a mountain range, the highest peak of which is Mount St. Catherine (2,756 ft.; 840 m).

Government. A Governor-General represents the sovereign, Elizabeth II. The Prime Minister is the head of government, chosen by a 15-member House of Representatives elected by universal suffrage every five years.

History. Grenada was discovered by Columbus in 1498. After more than 200 years of British rule, most recently as part of the West Indies Associated States, it became independent Feb. 7, 1974, with Eric M. Gairy as Prime Minister.

Prime Minister Maurice Bishop, a protégé of Cuba's President Castro, was killed in a military coup on Oct. 19, 1983. At the request of five members of the Organization of Eastern Caribbean States, President Reagan ordered an invasion of Grenada on Oct. 25 involving over 1,900 U.S. troops and a small military force from Barbados, Dominica, Jamaica, St. Lucia, and St. Vincent. The troops met strong resistance from Cuban military personnel on the island. Reagan said he ordered the invasion to protect some 1,000 American citizens on the island, and to help restore democratic institutions in that country. A centrist coalition led by Herbert A. Blaize, a 66-year-old lawyer, won 14 of the 15 seats in Parliament in an election in December 1984, and Blaize became Prime Minister.

GUATEMALA

Republic of Guatemala
President: Marco Vinicio Cerezo Arévalo (1986)[1]
Area: 42,042 sq mi. (108,889 sq km)
Population (est. mid-1990): 9,200,000 (average annual rate of natural increase: 3.1%)
Density per square mile: 213
Capital and largest city (est. 1982): Guatemala City, 1,250,000
Monetary unit: Quetzal
Languages: Spanish, Indian dialects
Religion: Roman Catholic, Protestant, Mayan.
National name: República de Guatemala
Literacy rate (1983): 51%
Economic summary: Gross domestic product (1987 est.): $9.6 billion; $1,110 per capita; 2% real growth rate. Arable land: 12%; principal products: corn, beans, coffee, cotton, cattle, sugar, bananas, fruits and vegetables, timber. Labor force: 2,500,000; 14% in manufacturing; principal products: prepared foods, textiles, construction materials, tires, pharmaceuticals. Natural resources: nickel, timber, shrimp. Exports: coffee, cotton, sugar, fruits and vegetables, bananas. Imports: manufactured products, machinery, transportation equipment, chemicals, fuels. Major trading partners: U.S., Central American nations, Caribbean, Mexico.

1. Elections in Dec. 1990.

Geography. The northernmost of the Central American nations, Guatemala is the size of Tennessee. Its neighbors are Mexico on the north, west, and east and Belize, Honduras, and El Salvador on the east. The country consists of two main regions—the cool highlands with the heaviest population and the tropical area along the Pacific and Caribbean coasts. The principal mountain range rises to the highest elevation in Central America and contains many volcanic peaks. Volcanic eruptions are frequent.

The Petén region in the north contains important resources and archaeological sites of the Mayan civilization.

Government. On December 8, 1985, Marco Vinicio Cerezo Arévalo, a left-of-center Christian Democrat, won in elections that were generally free from military interference. A 100-seat Congress was also elected.

Both the President and the Congress are elected for five-year terms and the President may not be re-elected.

History. Once the site of the ancient Mayan civilization, Guatemala, conquered by Spain in 1524, set itself up as a republic in 1839. From 1898 to 1920, the dictator Manuel Estrada Cabrera ran the country, and from 1931 to 1944, Gen. Jorge Ubico Castaneda was the strongman. In 1944 the National Assembly elected Gen. Federico Ponce president, but he was overthrown in October. In December, Dr. Juan José Arévalo was elected as the head of a leftist regime that continued to press its reform program. Jacobo Arbenz Guzmán, administration candidate with leftist leanings, won the 1950 elections.

Arbenz expropriated the large estates, including plantations of the United Fruit Company. With covert U.S. backing, a revolt was led by Col. Carlos Castillo Armas, and Arbenz took refuge in Mexico. Castillo Armas became president but was assassinated in 1957. Constitutional government was restored in 1958, and Gen. Miguel Ydigoras Fuentes was elected president.

A wave of terrorism, by left and right, began in 1967, and in August 1968 U.S. Ambassador John Gordon Mein was killed when he resisted kidnappers. Fear of anarchy led to the election in 1970 of Army Chief of Staff Carlos Araña Osorio, who had put down a rural guerrilla movement at the cost of nearly 3,000 lives. Araña, surprisingly, pledged social reforms when he took office. Another military candidate, Gen. Kjell Laugerud, won the presidency in 1974 amid renewed political violence.

The administration of Gen. Romeo Lucas Garcia, elected president in 1978, ended in a coup by a three-man military junta on March 23, 1982. Lucas Garcia was charged by Amnesty International with responsibility for at least 5,000 political murders in a reign of brutality and corruption that brought a cutoff of U.S. military aid in 1978. Hopes for improvement under the junta faded when Gen. José Efraín Ríos Montt took sole power in June.

President Oscar Mejía Victores, another general, seized power from Rios Montt in an August 1983 coup and pledged to turn over power to an elected civilian President in 1985. A constituent assembly was elected on July 1, 1984, to write a new Constitution.

Attempts by President Cerezo to improve social programs and raise taxes on the wealth have been hampered by right-wing opposition and military coup attempts.

GUINEA

Republic of Guinea
President: Brig. Gen. Lansana Conté (1984)
Area: 94,925 sq mi. (245,857 sq km)
Population (est. mid-1990): 7,300,000 (average annual rate of natural increase: 2.5%)
Density per square mile: 69
Capital and largest city (est. 1983): Conakry, 656,000
Monetary unit: Guinean franc
Languages: French (official), native tongues (Malinké, Susu, Fulani)
Religions: Islam, 85%; 10% Christian, 5% indigenous
National name: République de Guinée
Literacy rate: 28%
Economic summary: Gross national product (1987): $1.7 billion, $270 per capita; real growth rate (1987 est.): 5.9%. Arable land: 6%. Principal agricultural products: rice, cassava, millet, corn, coffee, bananas, pineapples. Labor force: 2,400,000 (1983); 11% in industry and commerce. Major industrial products: bauxite, alumina, light manufactured and processed goods, diamonds. Natural resources: bauxite, iron ore, diamonds, gold, water power. Exports: bauxite, alumina, pineapples, bananas, coffee. Imports: petroleum, machinery, transport equipment, foodstuffs, textiles. Major trading partners: U.S., U.S.S.R., France, W. Germany, Italy.

Geography. Guinea, in West Africa on the Atlantic, is also bordered by Guinea-Bissau, Senegal, Mali, the Ivory Coast, Liberia, and Sierra Leone. Slightly smaller than Oregon, the country consists of a coastal plain, a mountainous region, a savanna interior, and a forest area in the Guinea Highlands. The highest peak is Mount Nimba at about 6,000 feet (1,829 m).

Government. Military government headed by President Lansana Conté, who promoted himself from colonel to brigadier general after a 1984 coup.

History. Previously part of French West Africa, Guinea achieved independence by rejecting the new French Constitution, and on Oct. 2, 1958, became an independent state with Sékou Touré as president. Touré led the country into being the first avowedly Marxist state in Africa. Diplomatic relations with France were suspended in 1965, with the Soviet Union replacing France as the country's chief source of economic and technical assistance.

In 1966, when a Ghanaian military coup deposed Kwame Nkrumah as President, Touré welcomed him to Guinea and declared him joint president and party leader. The titles proved to be only honorary.

Touré accused Ghana of being an American imperialist puppet, and the U.S. Embassy in his capital, Conakry, was sacked. However, relations with the United States were soon restored.

Prosperity came in 1960 after the start of exploitation of bauxite deposits. Touré was re-elected to a seven-year term in 1974 and again in 1981.

After 26 years as President, Touré died in the United States in March 1984, following surgery. A week later, a military regime headed by Col. Lansana Conté took power with a promise not to shed any more blood after Touré's harsh rule. Conté became President and his co-conspirator in the coup, Col. Diara Traoré, became Prime Minister, but Conté later demoted Traoré to Education Minister.

Traoré tried to seize power on July 4, 1985, while Conté was out of the country, but his attempted coup was crushed by troops loyal to Conté.

GUINEA-BISSAU

Republic of Guinea-Bissau
President of the Council of State: João Bernardo Vieira (1980)
Area: 13,948 sq mi. (36,125 sq km)
Population (est. mid-1990): 1,000,000 (average annual rate of natural increase: 2.1%)
Density per square mile: 69
Capital and largest city (est. 1980): Bissau, 110,000
Monetary unit: Guinea-Bissau peso
Language: Portugese Criolo, African languages
Religions: traditional, 65%; Islam, 30%; Christian, 5%
National name: República da Guiné-Bissau
Literacy rate: 9%
Economic summary: Gross national product (1986): $168 million; $170 per capita; real growth rate –.6%. Arable land: 9%; principal products: palm oil, root crops, rice, coconuts, peanuts. Labor force: n.a. Major industries: food processing, beer, soft drinks. Natural resources: potential bauxite deposits; fish and timber. Exports: peanuts, coconuts, shrimp, fish, wood. Imports: foodstuffs, manufactured goods, fuels, transportation equipment. Major trading partners: Portugal, Spain, and other Eur. countries.

Geography. A neighbor of Senegal and Guinea in West Africa, on the Atlantic coast, Guinea-Bissau is about half the size of South Carolina.

The country is a low-lying coastal region of swamps, rain forests, and mangrove-covered wetlands, with about 25 islands off the coast. The Bijagos archipelago extends 30 miles (48 km) out to sea. Internal communications depend mainly on deep estuaries and meandering rivers, since there are no railroads. Bissau, the capital, is the main port.

Government. After the overthrow of Louis Cabral in November 1980, the nine-member Council of the Revolution formed an interm government. In 1982, they formed a new government consisting of the President, 2 Vice-Presidents, 18 ministers and 10 state secretaries.

History. Guinea-Bissau was discovered in 1446 by the Portuguese Nuno Tristao, and colonists in the Cape Verde Islands obtained trading rights in the territory. In 1879 the connection with the Cape Verde Islands was broken. Early in the 1900s the Portuguese managed to pacify some tribesmen, although resistance to colonial rule remained.

The African Party for the Independence of Guinea-Bissau and Cape Verde was founded in 1956 and several years later began guerrilla warfare that grew increasingly effective. By 1974 the rebels controlled most of the countryside, where they formed a government that was soon recognized by scores of countries. The military coup in Portugal in April 1974 brightened the prospects for freedom, and in August the Lisbon government signed an agreement granting independence to the province as of Sept. 10. The new republic took the name Guinea-Bissau. Its government was immediately recognized by the United States.

In November 1980, Prémier João Bernardo Vieira headed a coup that deposed Luis Cabral, President since 1974. A Revolutionary Council assumed the powers of government, with Vieira as its head.

GUYANA

Cooperative Republic of Guyana
President: Desmond Hoyte (1985)
Area: 83,000 sq mi. (214,969 sq km)
Population (est. mid-1990): 800,000 (average annual rate of natural increase: 1.9%)
Density per square mile: 9
Capital and largest city (est. 1981): Georgetown, 200,000
Monetary unit: Guyana dollar
Languages: English (official), Hindi, Urdu, Creole
Religions: Hindu, 34%; Protestant, 18%; Islam, 9%; Roman Catholic, 18%; Anglican, 16%
Member of Commonwealth of Nations
Literacy rate: 86%
Economic summary: Gross domestic product (1987): $344 million; $450 per capita; .7% real growth rate. Arable land: 3%; principal products: sugar, rice. Labor force: 268,000; 44.5% industry and commerce; major products: bauxite, alumina. Natural resources: bauxite, gold, diamonds, hardwood timber, shrimp. Exports: sugar, bauxite, alumina, rice, timber. Imports: fuels, machinery. Major trading partners: U.K., U.S., Trinidad, Venezuela.

Geography. Guyana is situated on the northern coast of South America east of Venezuela, west of Suriname, and north of Brazil. The country consists of a low coastal area and the Guiana Highlands in the south. There is an extensive north-south network of rivers. Guyana is the size of Idaho.

Government. Guyana, formerly British Guiana, proclaimed itself a republic on Feb. 23, 1970, ending its tie with Britain while remaining in the Commonwealth.

Guyana has a unicameral legislature, the National Assembly, with 53 members directly elected for five-year terms and 12 elected by local councils. A 24-member Cabinet is headed by the President.

History. British Guiana won internal self-government in 1952. The next year the People's Progressive Party, headed by Cheddi B. Jagan, an East Indian dentist, won the elections and Jagan became Prime Minister. British authorities deposed him for alleged Communist connections. A coalition ousted Jagan in 1964, installing a moderate Socialist, Forbes Burnham, a black, as Prime Minister. On May 26, 1966, the country became an independent member of the Commonwealth and resumed its traditional name, Guyana.

After ruling Guyana for 21 years, Burnham died on Aug. 6 1985, in a Guyana hospital after a throat operation. Desmond Hoyte, the country's Prime Minister succeeded him under the Guyanese constitution.

HAITI

Republic of Haiti
President: Ertha Pascal-Trovillot (1990)
Area: 10,714 sq mi. (27,750 sq km)
Population (est. mid-1990): 6,500,000 (average annual rate of natural increase: 2.2%)
Density per square mile: 596
Capital and largest city (est. 1984): Port-au-Prince, city, 461,464; urban area, 738,342
Monetary unit: Gourde
Languages: French, Creole
Religion: Roman Catholic, 80%; Baptist, 10%

National name: République d'Haïti
Literacy rate: 23%
Economic summary: Gross domestic product (FY 1987 est.): $2.2 billion; $360 per capita; .5% real growth rate. Arable land: 20%; principal products: coffee, sugar cane, corn, sorghum. Labor force: 2,300,000; 9% in industry; major products: refined sugar, textiles, flour, cement, light assembly products. Natural resource: bauxite. Exports: coffee, light industrial products, sugar, cocoa, sisal. Imports: consumer goods, foodstuffs, industrial equipment, petroleum products. Major trading partner: U.S.

Geography. Haiti, in the West Indies, occupies the western third of the island of Hispaniola, which it shares with the Dominican Republic. About the size of Maryland, Haiti is two thirds mountainous, with the rest of the country marked by great valleys, extensive plateaus, and small plains. The most densely populated region is the Cul-de-Sac plain near Port-au-Prince.

History. Discovered by Columbus, who landed at Môle Saint Nicolas on Dec. 6, 1492, Haiti in 1697 became a French possession known as Saint Domingue. An insurrection among a slave population of 500,000 in 1791 ended with a declaration of independence by Pierre-Dominique Toussaint l'Ouverture in 1801. Napoleon Bonaparte suppressed the independence movement, but it eventually triumphed in 1804 under Jean-Jacques Dessalines, who gave the new nation the aboriginal name Haiti.

Its prosperity dissipated in internal strife as well as disputes with neighboring Santo Domingo during a succession of 19th-century dictatorships, a bankrupt Haiti accepted a U.S. customs receivership from 1905 to 1941. Direct U.S. rule from 1915 to 1934 brought a measure of stability and a population growth that made Haiti the most densely populated nation in the hemisphere.

In 1949, after four years of democratic rule by President Dumarsais Estimé, dictatorship returned under Gen. Paul Magloire, who was succeeded by François Duvalier in 1957.

Duvalier established a dictatorship based on secret police, known as the "Ton-ton Macoutes," who gunned down opponents of the regime. Duvalier's son, Jean-Claude, or "Baby Doc," succeeded his father in 1971 as ruler of the poorest nation in the Western Hemisphere.

Government. There is a provisional government compromised of a President and a Council of State. However, its power is limited by the state of near-anarchy in Haiti. Duvalier fled the country in February, 1986 after strong unrest. His Chief of Staff, Lt. Gen. Henri Namphy, established a governing council with himself as head. A new constitution was enacted in March, 1987. The army stopped the first scheduled elections in November and army-sponsored elections led to the election of Leslie Manigat in Jan., 1988. He was overthrown in June 1988 in a military coup led by Namphy, after the former attempted to dismiss him. He was in turn overthrown by Lt. Gen. Prosper Avril.

The ruling council that took power upon the exile of Duvalier was criticized for the inclusion of former Duvalier aides.

Anti-government protests aginst the Avril governments crackdown on opposition leaders forced Avril to resign. Ertha-Trovillot, a former Supreme Court Justice, became President in March 1990.

HONDURAS

Republic of Honduras
President: Rafael L. Callejas (1990)
Area: 43,277 sq mi. (112,088 sq km)
Population (est. mid-1990): 5,100,000 (average annual rate of natural increase: 3.1%)
Density per square mile: 115
Capital and largest city (1985): Tegucigalpa, 571,400
Monetary unit: Lempira
Languages: Spanish, some Indian dialects, English in Bay Islands Department
Religion: Roman Catholic
National name: República de Honduras
Literacy rate: 56%
Economic summary: Gross domestic product (1987): $4 billion; $840 per capita; 4.2% real growth rate. Arable land: 14%; principal products: bananas, coffee, sugar cane, seafood, citrus, tobacco. Labor force: 1,300,000; 9% in manufacturing; major industrial products: processed agricultural products, textiles and clothing, wood products. Natural resources: timber, gold, silver, lead, zinc, antimony. Exports: bananas, coffee, lumber, meat, petroleum products, tobacco, sugar, shrimp and lobster. Imports: manufactured goods, machinery, transportation equipment, chemicals, petroleum. Major trading partners: U.S., Caribbean countries, Western Europe, Japan, Latin America.

Geography. Honduras, in the north central part of Central America, has a 400-mile (644-km) Caribbean coastline and a 40-mile (64-km) Pacific frontage. Its neighbors are Guatemala to the west, El Salvador to the south, and Nicaragua to the east. Honduras is slightly larger than Tennessee.

Generally mountainous, the country is marked by fertile plateaus, river valleys, and narrow coastal plains.

Government. The President serves a four-year term. There is a 134-member National Congress.

History. Columbus discovered Honduras on his last voyage in 1502. Honduras, with four other countries of Central America, declared its independence from Spain in 1821 and was part of a federation of Central American states until 1838. In that year it seceded from the federation and became a completely independent country.

U.S. Marines intervened in 1903 and 1923. In 1931, 1932, and 1937, major revolutions were crushed by force.

In July 1969, El Salvador invaded Honduras after Honduran landowners had deported several thousand Salvadorans. The fighting left 1,000 dead and tens of thousands homeless. By threatening economic sanctions and military intervention, the OAS induced El Salvador to withdraw.

Although parliamentary democracy returned with the election of Roberto Suazo Córdova as President in 1982 after a decade of military rule, Honduras faced severe economic problems and tensions along its border with Nicaragua. "Contra" rebels, waging a guerrilla war against the Sandinista regime in Nicaragua, used Honduras as a training and staging area. At the same time, the United States used Honduras as a site for military exercises and built bases to train both Honduran and Salvadoran troops. Honduras received $1 billion in U.S. economic and military aid from 1982–87.

HUNGARY

Republic of Hungary
Interim President: Arpad Goncz (1990)
Premier: Miklós Németh (1988)
Area: 35,919 sq mi. (93,030 sq km)
Population (est. mid-1990): 10,600,000 (average annual rate of natural increase: −0.2%)
Density per square mile: 294
Capital: Budapest
Largest cities (est. 1986): Budapest, 2,076,000; Miskolc, 211,700; Debrecen, 211,800; Szeged, 182,100; Pécs, 177,100
Monetary unit: Forint
Language: Magyar
Religions: Roman Catholic, 67%; Protestant, 25%; atheist, 7%
National name: Magyar Köztársaság
Literacy rate: 99%
Economic summary: Gross national product (1988): $91.8 billion; $8,670 per capita; 1.1% real growth rate. Arable land: 54%; principal products: corn, wheat, potatoes, sugar beets, vegetables, wine grapes, fruits. Labor force: 4,860,000; 31.4% in industry; major products: steel, chemicals, pharmaceuticals, textiles, transport equipment. Natural resources: some bauxite and iron. Exports: machinery and tools, industrial and consumer goods, raw materials. Imports: machinery, raw materials. Major trading partners: U.S.S.R., Warsaw Pact countries, West Germany, Yugoslavia, Austria, and Italy.

Geography. This central European country the size of Indiana is bordered by Austria to the west, Czechoslovakia to the north, the U.S.S.R. and Romania to the east, and Yugoslavia to the south.

Most of Hungary is a fertile, rolling plain lying east of the Danube River and drained by the Danube and Tisza rivers. In the extreme northwest is the Little Hungarian Plain. South of that area is Lake Balaton (250 sq mi.; 648 sq km).

Government. Hungary is a People's Republic with legislative power vested in the unicameral National Assembly, whose 352 members are elected directly for four-year terms. The National Assembly elects the President. The supreme body of state power is the 21-member Presidential Council elected by the National Assembly. The supreme administrative body is the Council of Ministers, headed by the Premier.

The major political parties are the Socialist Party, the Hungarian Democratic Forum, the Young Democrats, the Alliance of Free Democrats and the Social Democrats.

History. About 2,000 years ago, Hungary was part of the Roman provinces of Pannonia and Dacia. In A.D. 896 it was invaded by the Magyars, who founded a kingdom. Christianity was accepted during the reign of Stephen I (St. Stephen) (997–1038).

The peak of Hungary's great period of medieval power came during the reign of Louis I the Great (1342–82), whose dominions touched the Baltic, Black, and Mediterranean seas.

War with the Turks broke out in 1389, and for more than 100 years the Turks advanced through the Balkans. When the Turks smashed a Hungarian army in 1526, western and northern Hungary accepted Hapsburg rule to escape Turkish occupation. Transylvania became independent under Hungarian princes. Intermittent war with the Turks was waged until a peace treaty was signed in 1699.

After the suppression of the 1848 revolt against Hapsburg rule, led by Louis Kossuth, the dual monarchy of Austria-Hungary was set up in 1867.

The dual monarchy was defeated with the other Central Powers in World War I. After a short-lived republic in 1918, the chaotic Communist rule of 1919 under Béla Kun ended with the Romanians occupying Budapest on Aug. 4, 1919. When the Romanians left, Adm. Nicholas Horthy entered the capital with a national army. The Treaty of Trianon of June 4, 1920, cost Hungary 68% of its land and 58% of its population. Meanwhile, the National Assembly had restored the legal continuity of the old monarchy; and, on March 1, 1920, Horthy was elected Regent.

Following the German invasion of Russia on June 22, 1941, Hungary joined the attack against the Soviet Union, but the war was not popular and Hungarian troops were almost entirely withdrawn from the eastern front by May 1943. German occupation troops set up a puppet government after Horthy's appeal for an armistice with advancing Soviet troops on Oct. 15, 1944, had resulted in his overthrow. The German regime soon fled the capital, however, and on December 23 a provisional government was formed in Soviet-occupied eastern Hungary. On Jan. 20, 1945, it signed an armistice in Moscow. Early the next year, the National Assembly approved a constitutional law abolishing the thousand-year-old monarchy and establishing a republic.

By the Treaty of Paris (1947), Hungary had to give up all territory it had acquired since 1937 and to pay $300 million reparations to the U.S.S.R., Czechoslovakia, and Yugoslavia. In 1948 the Communist Party, with the support of Soviet troops seized control. Hungary was proclaimed a People's Republic and one-party state in 1949. Industry was nationalized, the land collectivized into state farms, and the opposition terrorized by the secret police.

The terror, modeled after that of the U.S.S.R., reached its height with the trial of Jozsef Cardinal Mindszenty, Roman Catholic primate. He confessed to fantastic charges under duress of drugs or brainwashing and was sentenced to life imprisonment in 1949. Protests were voiced in all parts of the world.

On Oct. 23, 1956, anti-Communist revolution broke out in Budapest. To cope with it, the Communists set up a coalition government and called former Premier Imre Nagy back to head it. But he and most of his ministers were swept by the logic of events into the anti-Communist opposition, and he declared Hungary a neutral power, withdrawing from the Warsaw Treaty and appealing to the United Nations for help.

One of his ministers, János Kádár, established a counter-regime and asked the U.S.S.R. to send in military power. Soviet troops and tanks suppressed the revolution in bloody fighting after 190,000 people had fled the country and Mindszenty, freed from jail, had taken refuge in the U.S. Embassy.

Kádár was succeeded as Premier, but not party secretary, by Gyula Kallai in 1965. Continuing his program of national reconciliation, Kádár emptied prisons, reformed the secret police, and eased travel restrictions.

Hungary developed the reputation of being the freest East European state.

After 15 years' asylum in the U.S. Embassy, Mindszenty, under an agreement between the Vatican and the Hungarian regime, was allowed to travel into exile to Rome in 1971. In a move applauded by Kádár, Pope Paul VI removed Mindszenty from his honorary post as Primate of Hungary in 1974. The Cardinal died in Vienna in 1975.

Relations with the U.S. improved in 1972 when World War II debt claims between the two nations were settled. On Jan. 6, 1978, the U.S. returned to Hungary, over anti-Communist protests, the 977-year-old crown of St. Stephen, held at Fort Knox since World War II.

A reform movement in the late-1980s led to the disbanding of the party militia, the withdrawal of political cells from factories and offices, and free multi-party elections. The new Parliament elected Arpad Goncz, who had been jailed for his role in the 1956 uprising, as interim President.

ICELAND

Republic of Iceland

President: Mrs. Vigdis Finnbogadottir (1980)
Prime Minister: Steingrimur Hermannsson (1988)
Area: 39,709 sq mi. (102,846 sq km)
Population (est. mid-1990): 300,000 (average annual rate of natural increase: 1.1%)
Density per square mile: 6.0
Capital and largest city (1988): Reykjavik, 95,799
Monetary unit: M.N. króna
Language: Icelandic
Religion: Evangelical Lutheran
National name: Lydveldid Island
Literacy rate: 99.9%
Economic summary: Gross domestic product (1987): $5.3 billion; $21,660 per capita; 6.6% real growth rate. Arable land: NEGL%; principal agricultural products: livestock, hay, fodder, cheese. Labor force: 122,280; 55.4% in commerce, finance and services; major products: processed aluminum, fish. Natural resources: fish, diatomite, hydroelectric and geothermal power. Exports: fish, animal products, aluminum. Imports: petroleum products, machinery and transportation equipment, food, textiles. Major trading partners: U.S., U.S.S.R., Western European countries.

1. Including some offshore islands.

Geography. Iceland, an island about the size of Kentucky, lies in the north Atlantic Ocean east of Greenland and just touches the Arctic Circle. It is one of the most volcanic regions in the world.

Small fresh-water lakes are to be found throughout the island, and there are many natural phenomena, including hot springs, geysers, sulfur beds, canyons, waterfalls, and swift rivers. More than 13% of the area is covered by snowfields and glaciers, and most of the people live in the 7% of the island comprising fertile coastlands.

Government. The president is elected for four years by popular vote. Executive power resides in the prime minister and his Cabinet. The Althing (Parliament) is composed of 63 members in two houses. They elect 22 of themselves to constitute the Upper House, the remaining 41 representing the Lower House.

History. Iceland was first settled shortly before 900, mainly by Norse. A Constitution drawn up about 930 created a form of democracy and provided for an Althing, or General Assembly.

In 1262–64, Iceland came under Norwegian rule and passed to ultimate Danish control through the formation of the Union of Kalmar in 1483. In 1874, Icelanders obtained their own Constitution. In 1918, Denmark recognized Iceland as a separate state with unlimited sovereignty but still nominally under the Danish king.

On June 17, 1944, after a popular referendum, the Althing proclaimed Iceland an independent republic.

The British occupied Iceland in 1940, immediately after the German invasion of Denmark. In 1942, the U.S. took over the burden of protection. Iceland refused to abandon its neutrality in World War II and thus forfeited charter membership in the United Nations, but it cooperated with the Allies throughout the conflict. Iceland joined the North Atlantic Treaty Organization in 1949.

Iceland unilaterally extended its territorial waters from 12 to 50 nautical miles in 1972, precipitating a running dispute with Britain known as the "cod war." Icelandic warships harassed British trawlers, which then received aid from British gunboats; some trawlers were shelled, and Icelandic and British warships collided in 1973. The World Court ruled in 1974 that the 50-mile limit could not be applied unilaterally, but Iceland rejected the ruling.

An agreement calling for registration of all British trawlers fishing within 200 miles of Iceland and a 24-hour time limit on incursions was finally reached in 1976.

INDIA

Republic of India
President: Ramaswamy Venkataraman (1987)
Prime Minister: Vishwanath Pratap Sinuh (1989)
Area: 1,229,737 sq mi. (3,185,019 sq km)
Population (est. mid-1990): 853,400,000 (average annual rate of natural increase: 2.1%)
Density per square mile: 658
Capital (1980 census): New Delhi, 619,417
Largest cities (1981 est.): Calcutta, 9,194,018; Greater Bombay, 8,243,405; Delhi, 5,729,283; Madras, 4,289,347; Bangalore, 2,921,751; Ahmedabad, 2,548,-057; Kanpur, 1,639,064
Monetary unit: Rupee
Principal languages; Hindi (official), English (official), Bengali, Gujarati, Kashmiri, Malayalam, Marathi, Oriya, Punjabi, Tamil, Telugu, Urdu, Kannada, Assamese (all recognized by the Constitution)
Religions: Hindu, 83%; Islam, 11%; Christian, 3%; Sikh, 2%
National name: Bharat
Literacy rate: 36%
Member of Commonwealth of Nations
Economic summary: Gross national product (1987): $231 billion; $290 per capita; 1.2% real growth rate. Arable land: 55%; principal products: rice, wheat, oilseeds, cotton, tea, opium poppy (for pharmaceuticals). Labor force: 284,400,000; 67% in agriculture. Major industrial products: jute, processed food, steel, machinery, transport machinery, cement. Natural resources: iron ore, coal, manganese, mica, bauxite, limestone, textiles. Exports: diamonds, iron goods, textiles and clothing, tea, crude oil. Imports: machinery and transport equipment, petroleum, edible oils, fertilizers. Major trading partners: U.S., U.S. S.R., Japan, Saudi Arabia, U.K.

Geography. One third the area of the United States, the Republic of India occupies most of the subcontinent of India in south Asia. It borders on China in the northeast. Other neighbors are Pakistan on the west, Nepal and Bhutan on the north, and Burma and Bangladesh on the east.

The country contains a large part of the great Indo-Gangetic plain, which extends from the Bay of Bengal on the east to the Afghan frontier on the Arabian Sea on the west. This plain is the richest and most densely settled part of the subcontinent. Another distinct natural region is the Deccan, a plateau of 2,000 to 3,000 feet (610 to 914 m) in elevation, occupying the southern portion of the subcontinent.

Forming a part of the republic are several groups of islands—the Laccadives (14 islands) in the Arabian Sea and the Andamans (204 islands) and the Nicobars (19 islands) in the Bay of Bengal.

India's three great river systems, all rising in the Himalayas, have extensive deltas. The Ganges flows south and then east for 1,540 miles (2,478 km) across the northern plain to the Bay of Bengal; part of its delta, which begins 220 miles (354 km) from the sea, is within the republic. The Indus, starting in Tibet, flows northwest for several hundred miles in the Kashmir before turning southwest toward the Arabian Sea; it is important for irrigation in Pakistan. The Brahmaputra, also rising in Tibet, flows eastward, first through India and then south into Bangladesh and the Bay of Bengal.

Government. India is a federal republic. It is also a member of the Commonwealth of Nations, a status defined at the 1949 London Conference of Prime Ministers, by which India recognizes Queen as head of the Commonwealth. Under the Constitution effective Jan. 26, 1950, India has a parliamentary type of government.

The constitutional head of the state is the President, who is elected every five years. He is advised by the Prime Minister and a Cabinet based on a majority of the bicameral Parliament, which consists of a Council of States (Rajya Sabha), representing the constituent units of the republic and a House of the People (Lok Sabha), elected every five years by universal suffrage.

History. The Aryans, or Hindus, who invaded India between 2400 and 1500 B.C. from the northwest found a land already well civilized. Buddhism was founded in the 6th century B.C. and spread through northern India.

In 1526, Moslem invaders founded the great Mogul empire, centered on Delhi, which lasted, at least in name, until 1857. Akbar the Great (1542–1605) strengthened this empire and became the ruler of a greater portion of India than had ever before acknowledged the suzerainty of one man. The long reign of his great-grandson, Aurangzeb (1658–1707), represents both the culmination of Mogul power and the beginning of its decay.

Vasco da Gama, the Portuguese explorer, visited India first in 1498, and for the next 100 years the Portuguese had a virtual monopoly on trade with the subcontinent. Meanwhile, the English founded the East India Company, which set up its first factory at Surat in 1612 and began expanding its influence, fighting the Indian rulers and the French, Dutch, and Portuguese traders simultaneously.

Bombay, taken from the Portuguese, became the seat of English rule in 1687. The defeat of French and Islamic armies by Lord Clive in the decade ending in 1760 laid the foundation of the British Empire in India. From then until 1858, when the administration of India was formally transferred to the British Crown following the Sepoy Mutiny of native troops in 1857, the East India Company suppressed native uprisings and extended British rule.

After World War I, in which the Indian states sent more than 6 million troops to fight beside the Allies, Indian nationalist unrest rose to new heights under the leadership of a little Hindu lawyer, Mohandas K. Gandhi, called Mahatma Gandhi. His tactics called for nonviolent revolts against British authority. He soon became the leading spirit of the All-India Congress Party, which was the spearhead of revolt. In 1919 the British gave added responsibility to Indian officials, and in 1935 India was given a federal form of government and a measure of self-rule.

In 1942, with the Japanese pressing hard on the eastern borders of India, the British War Cabinet tried and failed to reach a political settlement with nationalist leaders. The Congress Party took the position that the British must quit India. In 1942, fearing mass civil disobedience, the government of India carried out widespread arrests of Congress leaders, including Gandhi.

Gandhi was released in 1944 and negotiations for a settlement were resumed. Finally, in February 1947, the Labor government announced its determination to transfer power to "responsible Indian hands" by June 1948 even if a Constitution had not been worked out.

Lord Mountbatten as Viceroy, by June 1947, achieved agreement on the partitioning of India along religious lines and on the splitting of the provinces of Bengal and the Punjab, which the Moslems had claimed.

The Indian Independence Act, passed quickly by the British Parliament, received royal assent on July 18, 1947, and on August 15 the Indian Empire passed into history.

Jawaharlal Nehru, leader of the Congress Party, was made Prime Minister. Before an exchange of populations could be arranged, bloody riots occurred among the communal groups, and armed conflict broke out over rival claims to the princely state of Jammu and Kashmir. Peace was restored only with the greatest difficulty. In 1949 a Constitution, along the lines of the U.S. Constitution, was approved making India a sovereign republic. Under a federal structure the states were organized on linguistic lines.

The dominance of the Congress Party contributed to stability. In 1956 the republic absorbed the former French settlements. Five years later, it forcibly annexed the Portuguese enclaves of Goa, Damao, and Diu.

Nehru died in 1964. His successor, Lal Bahadur Shastri, died on Jan. 10, 1966. Nehru's daughter, Indira Gandhi, became Prime Minister, and she continued his policy of nonalignment.

In 1971 the Pakistani Army moved in to quash the independence movement in East Pakistan that was supported by clandestine aid from India, and some 10 million Bengali refugees poured across the border into India, creating social, economic, and health problems. After numerous border incidents, India invaded East Pakistan and in two weeks forced the surrender of the Pakistani army. East Pakistan was established as an independent state and renamed Bangladesh.

In the summer of 1975, the world's largest democracy veered suddenly toward authoritarianism when a judge in Allahabad, Mrs. Gandhi's home constituency, found her landslide victory in the 1971 elections invalid because civil servants had illegally aided her campaign. Amid demands for her resignation, Mrs. Gandhi decreed a state of emergency on June 26 and ordered mass arrests of her critics, including all opposition party leaders except the Communists.

In 1976, India and Pakistan formally renewed diplomatic relations.

Despite strong opposition to her repressive measures and particularly the resentment against compulsory birth control programs, Mrs. Gandhi in 1977 announced parliamentary elections for March. At the same time, she freed most political prisoners.

The landslide victory of Morarji R. Desai unseated Mrs. Gandhi and also defeated a bid for office by her son, Sanjay.

Mrs. Gandhi staged a spectacular comeback in the elections of January 1980.

In 1984, Mrs. Gandhi ordered the Indian Army to root out a band of Sikh holy men and gunmen who were using the holiest shrine of the Sikh religion, the Golden Temple in Amritsar, as a base for terrorist raids in a violent campaign for greater political autonomy in the strategic Punjab border state. As many as 1,000 people were reported killed in the June 5–6 battle, including Jarnall Singh Bhindranwale, the Khomeini-like militant leader, and 93 soldiers. The perceived sacrilege to the Golden Temple kindled outrage among many of India's 14 million Sikhs and brought a spasm of mutinies and desertions by Sikh officers and soldiers in the army.

On Oct. 31, 1984, Mrs. Gandhi was assassinated by two men identified by police as Sikh members of her bodyguard. The ruling Congress I Party chose her second son, Rajiv Gandhi, to succeed her as Prime Minister.

On July 24, Rajiv Gandhi and moderate Sikh leaders agreed on a package of steps to ease Sikh hostility toward the government and end the turmoil in the state of Punjab. A key element called for a change in the Punjab boundaries to increase the Sikh population within the state and give it greater political influence. Prime Minister Gandhi also yielded to demands for more lenient treatment of Sikhs arrested in riots over the last three years. Violence continued unabated with about 1,000 people being killed in 1986 and the first half of 1987 and Gandhi established direct rule on May 11, 1987, dissolving the local government.

Native States. Most of the 560-odd native states and subdivisions of pre-1947 India acceded to the new nation, and the central government pursued a vigorous policy of integration. This took three forms: merger into adjacent provinces, conversion into centrally administered areas, and grouping into unions of states. Finally, under a controversial reorganization plan effective Nov. 1, 1956, the unions of states were abolished and merged into adjacent states, and India became a union of 15 states and 8 centrally administered areas. A 16th state was added in 1962, and in 1966, the Punjab was partitioned into two states.

Resolution of the territorial dispute over Kashmir grew out of peace negotiations following the two-week India-Pakistan war of 1971. After sporadic skirmishing, an accord reached July 3, 1972, committed both powers to withdraw troops from a temporary cease-fire line after the border was fixed. Agreement on the border was reached Dec. 7, 1972.

In April 1975, the Indian Parliament voted to make the 300-year-old kingdom of Sikkim a full-fledged Indian state, and the annexation took effect May 16.

Situated in the Himalayas, Sikkim was a virtual dependency of Tibet until the early 19th century. Under an 1890 treaty between China and Great Britain, it became a British protectorate, and was made an Indian protectorate after Britain quit the subcontinent.

INDONESIA

Republic of Indonesia
President: Suharto (1969)[1]
Area: 735,268 sq mi. (1,904,344 sq km)[2]
Population (est. mid-1990): 189,400,000 (average annual rate of natural increase: 1.8%)
Density per square mile: 251
Capital: Jakarta
Largest cities (est. 1983): Jakarta, 7,636,000; Surabaja, 2,289,000; Bandung, 1,602,000; Medan, 1,966,000; Semarang, 1,269,000
Monetary unit: Rupiah
Languages: Bahasa Indonesia (official), Dutch, English, and more than 60 regional languages
Religions: Islam, 87%; Christian, 10%; Hindu Buddhist, 3%
National name: Republik Indonesia
Literacy rate: 64%
Economic summary: Gross national product (1987): $69 billion; $880 per capita; 3.8% real growth rate. Arable land: 8%; principal products: rice, cassava, sugarcane, rubber, coffee. Labor force: 67,000,000; 10% in manufacturing; major products: oil, textiles, food and beverages, light manufactures, cement, fertilizer, rubber. Natural resources: oil, timber, nickel, natural gas, tin, bauxite, copper. Exports: petroleum and liquid natural gas, timber, rubber, coffee, tin. Imports: rice, wheat, textiles, chemicals, machinery, transport equipment, iron and steel. Major trading partners: Japan, U.S., Singapore, Saudi Arabia, West Germany.

1. General Suharto served as Acting President of Indonesia from 1967 to 1969. 2. Includes West Irian (former Netherlands New Guinea), renamed Irian Jaya in March 1973 (159,355 sq mi.; 412,731 sq km), and former Portuguese Timor (5,763 sq mi.; 14,925 sq km), annexed in 1976.

Geography. Indonesia is part of the Malay archipelago in Southeast Asia with an area nearly three times that of Texas. It consists of the islands of Sumatra, Java, Madura, Borneo (except Sarawak and Brunei in the north), the Celebes, the Moluccas, Irian Jaya, and about 30 smaller archipelagos, totaling 13,677 islands, of which about 6,000 are inhabited. Its neighbor to the north is Malaysia and to the east Papua New Guinea.

A backbone of mountain ranges extends throughout the main islands of the archipelago. Earthquakes are frequent, and there are many active volcanoes.

Government. The President is elected by the People's Consultative Assembly, whose 1000 members include the functioning legislative arm, the 500-member House of Representatives. Meeting at least once every five years, the Assembly has broad policy functions. The House, 100 of whose members are appointed by the President, meets at least once annually. General Suharto was elected unopposed to a fifth five-year term in 1988.

History. Indonesia is inhabited by Malayan and Papuan peoples ranging from the more advanced Javanese and Balinese to the more primitive Dyaks of Borneo. Invasions from China and India contributed Chinese and Indian admixtures.

During the first few centuries of the Christian era, most of the islands came under the influence of Hindu priests and traders, who spread their culture and religion. Moslem invasions began in the 13th century, and most of the area was Moslem by the 15th. Portuguese traders arrived early in the 16th century but were ousted by the Dutch about 1595. After Napoleon subjugated the Netherlands homeland in 1811, the British seized the islands but returned them to the Dutch in 1816. In 1922 the islands were made an integral part of the Netherlands kingdom.

During World War II, Indonesia was under Japanese military occupation with nominal native self-government. When the Japanese surrendered to the Allies, President Sukarno and Mohammed Hatta, his Vice President, proclaimed Indonesian independence from the Dutch on Aug. 17, 1945. Allied troops—mostly British Indian troops—fought the nationalists until the arrival of Dutch troops. In November 1946, the Dutch and the Indonesians reached a draft agreement contemplating formation of a Netherlands-Indonesian Union, but differences in interpretation resulted in more fighting between Dutch and Indonesian forces.

On Nov. 2, 1949, Dutch and Indonesian leaders agreed upon the terms of union. The transfer of sovereignty took place at Amsterdam on Dec. 27, 1949. In February 1956 Indonesia abrogated the Union with the Netherlands and in August 1956 repudiated its debt to the Netherlands. In 1963, Netherlands New Guinea was transferred to Indonesia and renamed West Irian. In 1973 it became Irian Jaya.

Hatta and Sukarno, the co-fathers of Indonesian independence, split after it was achieved over Sukarno's concept of "guided democracy." Under Sukarno, the country's leading political figure for almost a half century, the Indonesian Communist Party gradually gained increasing influence.

After an attempted coup was put down by General Suharto, the army chief of staff, and officers loyal to him, thousands of Communist suspects were sought out and killed all over the country. Suharto took over the reins of government, gradually eased Sukarno out of office, and took full power in 1967.

Suharto permitted national elections, which moved the nation back to representative government. He also ended hostilities with Malaysia. Under President Suharto, Indonesia has been strongly anticommunist. It also has been politically stable and has made progress in economic development.

Indonesia invaded the former Portuguese half of the island of Timor in 1975, and annexed the territory in 1976. On a visit to Jakarta in July 1984, Secretary of State George P. Shultz expressed concern about reports of human rights abuses being carried out by Indonesian forces in East Timor. More than 100,000 Timorese, a sixth of the mostly Catholic population, were reported to have died from famine, disease, and fighting since the annexation.

IRAN

Islamic Republic of Iran
President: Hashemi Rafsanjani (1989)
Area: 636,293 sq mi. (1,648,000 sq km)
Population (est. mid-1990): 55,600,000 (average annual rate of natural increase: 3.6%)
Density per square mile: 85
Capital: Teheran
Largest cities (est. 1986): Teheran, 6,037,658; Isfahan, 1,422,308; Mashed, 2,038,388; Tabriz, 1,566,932
Monetary unit: Rial
Languages: Farsi (Persian), Kurdish, Arabic
Religions: Shi'ite Moslem, 93%; Sunni Moslem, 5%
Literacy rate: 48%
Economic summary: Gross national product (1988): $93.5 billion; $1,800 per capita; real growth rate −2%. Arable land: 8%; principal products: wheat, barley, rice, sugar beets, cotton, dates, raisins, sheep, goats. Labor force: 15,400,000; 21% in manufacturing; major products: crude and refined oil, textiles, cement, processed foods, steel and copper fabrication. Natural resources: oil, gas, iron, copper. Exports: petroleum, carpets. Imports: machinery, military supplies, foodstuffs, pharmaceuticals. Major trading partners: Japan, West Germany, Netherlands, U.K., Italy, Spain, Turkey.

Geography. Iran, a Middle Eastern country south of the Caspian Sea and north of the Persian Gulf, is three times the size of Arizona. It shares borders with Iraq, Turkey, the U.S.S.R., Afghanistan, and Pakistan.

In general, the country is a plateau averaging 4,000 feet (1,219 m) in elevation. There are also maritime lowlands along the Persian Gulf and the Caspian Sea. The Elburz Mountains in the north rise to 18,603 feet (5,670 m) at Mt. Damavend. From northwest to southeast, the country is crossed by a desert 800 miles (1,287 km) long.

Government. The Pahlavi dynasty was overthrown on Feb. 11, 1979, by followers of the Ayatollah Ruhollah Khomeini. After a referendum endorsed the establishment of a republic, Khomeini drafted a Constitution calling for a President to be popularly elected every four years, an appointed Prime Minister, and a unicameral National Consultative Assembly, popularly elected every four years. A constitutional amendment in 1989 eliminated the post of Prime Minister.

Khomeini also instituted a Revolutionary Council to insure the adherence to Islamic principles in all phases of Iranian life. The Council formally handed over its powers to the Assembly after the organization of the legislature in July 1980, but continued to exercise power behind the scenes.

History. Oil-rich Iran was called Persia before 1935. Its key location blocks the lower land gate to Asia and also stands in the way of traditional Russian ambitions for access to the Indian Ocean. After periods of Assyrian, Median, and Achaemenidian rule, Persia became a powerful empire under Cyrus the Great, reaching from the Indus to the Nile at its zenith in 525 B.C. It fell to Alexander in 331–30 B.C. and to the Seleucids in 312–02 B.C., and a native Persian regime arose about 130 B.C. Another Persian regime arose about A.D. 224, but it fell to the Arabs in 637. In the 12th century, the Mongols took their turn ruling Persia, and in the early part of the 18th century, the Turks occupied the country.

An Anglo-Russian convention of 1907 divided Persia into two spheres of influence. British attempts to impose a protectorate over the entire country were defeated in 1919. Two years later, Gen. Reza Pahlavi seized the government and was elected hereditary Shah in 1925. Subsequently he did much to modernize the country and abolished all foreign extraterritorial rights.

Increased pro-Axis activity led to Anglo-Russian occupation of Iran in 1941 and deposition of the Shah in favor of his son, Mohammed Reza Pahlavi.

Ali Razmara became premier in 1950 and pledged to restore efficient and honest government, but he was assassinated after less than nine months in office and Mohammed Mossadegh took over. Mossadegh was ousted in August 1953, by Fazollah Zahedi, whom the Shah had named premier.

Opposition to the Shah spread, despite the imposition of martial law in September 1978, and massive demonstrations demanded the return of the exiled Ayatollah Ruhollah Khomeini. Riots and strikes continued despite the appointment of an opposition leader, Shahpur Bakhtiar, as premier on Dec. 29. The Shah and his family left Iran on Jan. 16, 1979, for a "vacation," leaving power in the hands of a regency council.

Khomeini returned on Feb. 1 to a nation in turmoil as military units loyal to the Shah continued to support Bakhtiar and clashed with revolutionaries. Khomeini appointed Mehdi Bazargan as premier of the provisional government and in two days of fighting, revolutionaries forced the military to capitulate on Feb. 11.

The new government began a program of nationalization of insurance companies, banks, and industries both locally and foreign-owned. Oil production fell amid the political confusion.

Khomeini, ignoring opposition, proceeded with his plans for revitalizing Islamic traditions. He urged women to return to the veil, or chador; banned alcohol and mixed bathing, and prohibited music from radio and television broadcasting, declaring it to be "no different from opium."

Revolutionary militants invaded the U.S. Embassy in Teheran on Nov. 4, 1979, seized staff members as hostages, and precipitated an international crisis.

Khomeini refused all appeals, even a unanimous vote by the U.N. Security Council demanding immediate release of the hostages.

Iranian hostility toward Washington was reinforced by the Carter administration's economic boycott and deportation order against Iranian students in the U.S., the break in diplomatic relations and ultimately an aborted U.S. raid in April aimed at rescuing the hostages.

As the first anniversary of the embassy seizure neared, Khomeini and his followers insisted on their original conditions: guarantee by the U.S. not to interfere in Iran's affairs, cancellation of U.S. damage claims against Iran, release of $8 billion in frozen Iranian assets, an apology, and the return of the assets held by the former imperial family.

These conditions were largely met and the 52 American hostages were released on Jan. 20, ending 444 days in captivity.

From the release of the hostages onward, President Bani-Sadr and the conservative clerics of the dominant Islamic Republican Party clashed with growing frequency. He was stripped of his command of the armed forces by Khomeini on June 6 and ousted as President on June 22. On July 24, Prime Minister Mohammed Ali Rajai was elected overwhelmingly to the Presidency.

Rajai and Prime Minister Mohammed Javad Bahonar were killed on Aug. 30 by a bomb in Bahonar's office. Hojatolislam Mohammed Ali Khamenei, a clergyman, leader of the Islamic Republican Party and spokesman for Khomeini, was elected President on Oct. 2, 1981.

The sporadic war with Iraq regained momentum in 1982, as Iran launched an offensive in March and regained much of the border area occupied by Iraq in late 1980. Khomeini rejected Iraqi bids for a truce, insisting that Iraq's President Saddam Hussein must leave office first.

Iran continued to be at war with Iraq well into 1988. Although Iraq expressed its willingness to cease fighting, Iran stated that it would not stop the war until Iraq agreed to make payment for war damages to Iran, and punish the Iraqi government leaders involved in the conflict. The fighting, spread into the Persian Gulf in 1984, with Iraq attacking tankers loading at Iran's Kharg Island, and Iran striking back at tankers calling at Saudi Arabia and the smaller, oil-rich Arab Gulf states. The latter has led to clashes with the U.S. Navy.

On July 20, 1988, Khomeini, after a series of Iranian military reverses, agreed to cease-fire negotiations with Iraq. A cease-fire went into effect Aug. 20, 1988.

Khomeini died in June 1989. He was replaced as the supreme religious leader by President Ali Khamenei.

IRAQ

Republic of Iraq
President: Saddam Hussein (1979)
Area: 167,920 sq mi. (434,913,000 sq km)
Population (est. mid-1990): 18,800,000 (average annual rate of natural increase: 3.9%)
Density per square mile: 108
Capital: Baghdad
Largest cities (est. 1985): Baghdad, 4,648,609; Basra, 616,700; Mosul, 570,926
Monetary unit: Iraqi dinar
Languages: Arabic (official) and Kurdish
Religions: Islam, 97%; Christian, 3%
National name: Al Jumhouriya Al Iraqia
Literacy rate: about 55%
Economic summary: Gross national product (1988): $34 billion, $1,950 per capita; 0% real growth rate. Arable land: 12%; principal products: dates, livestock, wheat, barley, sugarcane, rice. Labor force: 3,500,000 (1980); 28% in industry; major products: petroleum, shoes, beer, textiles. Natural resources: oil, natural gas, gypsum, sulfur. Exports: petroleum, foodstuffs. Imports: manufactured goods, machinery, chemicals, livestock. Major trading partners: France, Italy, Japan, West Germany, Brazil, U.K., U.S., Turkey, Soviet bloc.

Geography. Iraq, a triangle of mountains, desert, and fertile river valley, is bounded on the east by Iran, on the north by Turkey, the west by Syria and Jordan, and the south by Saudi Arabia and Kuwait. It is twice the size of Idaho.

The country has arid desertland west of the Euphrates, a broad central valley between the Euphrates and Tigris, and mountains in the northeast. The fertile lower valley is formed by the delta of the two rivers, which join about 120 miles (193 km) from the head of the Persian Gulf. The gulf coastline is 26 miles (42 km) long. The only port for seagoing vessels is Basra, which is on the Shatt-al-Arab River near the head of the Persian Gulf.

Government. Since the coup d'etat of July 1968, Iraq has been governed by the Arab Ba'ath Socialist Party through a Council of Command of the Revolution headed by the President. There is also a Council of Ministers headed by the President.

History. From earliest times Iraq was known as Mesopotamia—the land between the rivers—for it embraces a large part of the alluvial plains of the Tigris and Euphrates.

An advanced civilization existed by 4000 B.C. Sometime after 2000 B.C. the land became the center of the ancient Babylonian and Assyrian empires. It was conquered by Cyrus the Great of Persia in 538 B.C., and by Alexander in 331 B.C. After an Arab conquest in A.D. 637–40, Baghdad became capital of the ruling caliphate. The country was cruelly pillaged by the Mongols in 1258, and during the 16th, 17th, and 18th centuries was the object of repeated Turkish-Persian competition.

Nominal Turkish suzerainty imposed in 1638 was replaced by direct Turkish rule in 1831. In World War I, an Anglo-Indian force occupied most of the country, and Britain was given a mandate over the area in 1920. The British recognized Iraq as a kingdom in 1922 and terminated the mandate in 1932 when Iraq was admitted to the League of Nations. In World War II, Iraq generally adhered to its 1930 treaty of alliance with Britain, but in 1941, British troops were compelled to put down a pro-Axis revolt led by Premier Rashid Ali.

Iraq became a charter member of the Arab League in 1945, and Iraqi troops took part in the Arab invasion of Palestine in 1948.

Faisal II, born on May 2, 1935, succeeded his father, Ghazi I, who was killed in an automobile accident on April 4, 1939. Faisal and his uncle, Crown Prince Abdul-Ilah, were assassinated in August 1958 in a swift revolutionary coup that brought to power a military junta headed by Abdul Karem Kassim. Kassim, in turn, was overthrown and killed in a coup staged March 8, 1963, by the Ba'ath Socialist Party.

Abdel Salam Arif, a leader in the 1958 coup, staged another coup in November 1963, driving the Ba'ath members of the revolutionary council from power. He adopted a new constitution in 1964. In 1966, he, two Cabinet members, and other supporters died in a helicopter crash. His brother, Gen. Abdel Rahman Arif, assumed the presidency, crushed the opposition, and won an indefinite extension of his term in 1967. His regime was ousted in July 1968 by a junta led by Maj. Gen. Ahmed Hassan al-Bakr.

A long-standing dispute over control of the Shatt al-Arab waterway between Iraq and Iran broke into full-scale war on Sept. 20, 1980. Iraqi planes attacked Iranian airfields and the Abadan refinery, and Iraqi ground forces moved into Iran.

Despite the smaller size of its armed forces, Iraq took and held the initiative by seizing Abadan and Khurramshahr together with substantial Iranian territory by December and beating back Iranian counterattacks in January. Peace efforts by the Islamic nations, the nonaligned, and the United Nations failed as 1981 wore on and the war stagnated. In 1982, the Iraqis fell back to their own country and dug themselves in behind sandbagged defensive fortifications. With massive firepower, they turned back wave after wave of attacking Iranian troops and revolutionary guards, many of them in their teens. From the beginning of the war in September 1980 to September 1984, foreign military analysts estimated that more than 100,000 Iranians and perhaps 50,000 Iraqis had been killed.

The Iraqis clearly wanted to end the war, but the Iranians refused. In March of 1985, Iraq apparently won the largest battle of the long war, crushing a major Iranian offensive in the southern marshes in a week of heavy fighting that killed an estimated 30,000 Iranians and perhaps 10,000 Iraqis.

In February 1986, Iranian forces gained on two fronts; on the Fao peninsula in the south and in the northern mountains, but Iraq retook most of the lost ground in 1988 and the war continued a stalemate. In August, Iraq and Iran agreed to hold direct talks after a ceasefire takes effect.

In July 1990, President Hussein claimed that Kuwait was flooding world markets with oil and forcing down prices. A mediation attempt by Arab leaders failed, and on Aug. 2, 1990, over this and territorial claims, Iraqi troops invaded Kuwait and set up a puppet government. (*See* Current Events for later details.)

IRELAND

President: Patrick J. Hillery (1976)
Taoiseach (Prime Minister): Charles J. Haughey (1987)
Area: 26,600 sq mi. (68,394 sq km)
Population (est. mid-1990): 3,500,000 (average annual rate of natural increase: 0.6%)
Density per square mile: 131
Capital: Dublin
Largest cities (est. 1982): Dublin, 550,000; Cork, 140,000; Limerick, 60,000
Monetary unit: Irish pound (punt)
Languages: Irish, English
Religions: Roman Catholic, 94%; Protestant, 5%
National name: Eire
Literacy rate: 99%
Economic summary: Gross national product (1988): $30.6 billion; $8,640 per capita; .9% real growth rate. Arable land: 14%; principal products: cattle and dairy products, pigs, poultry and eggs, sheep and wool, horses, barley, sugar beets. Labor force: 1,301,667; 21.4% in manufacturing and construction; major products: processed foods, metals and engineering, electronics, beverages and tobacco, chemicals. Natural resources: zinc, lead, natural gas, barite, copper, gypsum, limestone, dolomite, peat, silver. Exports: livestock, dairy products, machinery, chemicals, processed foods, data processing equipment, raw materials and minerals. Imports: grains, petroleum products, machinery, chemicals, textile yarn, cereals. Major trading partners: U.K., Western European countries, U.S.

Geography. Ireland is situated in the Atlantic Ocean and separated from Britain by the Irish Sea. Half the size of Arkansas, it occupies the entire island except for the six counties which make up Northern Ireland.

Ireland resembles a basin—a central plain rimmed with mountains, except in the Dublin region. The mountains are low, with the highest peak, Carrantuohill in County Kerry, rising to 3,415 feet (1,041 m).

The principal river is the Shannon, which begins in the north central area, flows south and southwest for about 240 miles (386 km), and empties into the Atlantic.

Government. Ireland is a parliamentary democracy. The National Parliament (Oireachtas) consists of the president and two Houses, the House of Representatives (Dáil Éireann) and the Senate (Seanad Éireann), whose members serve for a maximum term of five years. The House of Representatives has 166 members elected by proportional representation; the Senate has 60 members of whom 11 are nominated by the prime minister, 6 by the universities and the remaining 43 from various vocational panels. The prime minister (Taoiseach), who is the head of government, is appointed by the president on the nomination of the House of Representatives, to which he is responsible.

History. In the Stone and Bronze Ages, Ireland was inhabited by Picts in the north and a people called the Erainn in the south, the same stock, apparently, as in all the isles before the Anglo-Saxon invasion of Britain. About the fourth century B.C., tall, red-haired Celts arrived from Gaul or Galicia. They subdued and assimilated the inhabitants and established a Gaelic civilization.

By the beginning of the Christian Era, Ireland was divided into five kingdoms—Ulster, Connacht, Leinster, Meath, and Munster. St. Patrick introduced Christianity in 432 and the country developed into a center of Gaelic and Latin learning. Irish monasteries, the equivalent of universities, attracted intellectuals as well as the pious and sent out missionaries to many parts of Europe and, some believe, to North America.

Norse depredations along the coasts, starting in 795, ended in 1014 with Norse defeat at the Battle of Clontarf by forces under Brian Boru. In the 12th century, the Pope gave all Ireland to the English Crown as a papal fief. In 1171, Henry II of England was acknowledged "Lord of Ireland," but local sectional rule continued for centuries, and English control over the whole island was not reasonably absolute until the 17th century. By the Act of Union (1801), England and Ireland became the "United Kingdom of Great Britain and Ireland."

A steady decline in the Irish economy followed in the next decades. The population had reached 8.25 million when the great potato famine of 1846–48 took many lives and drove millions to emigrate to America. By 1921 it was down to 4.3 million.

In the meantime, anti-British agitation continued along with demands for Irish home rule. The advent of World War I delayed the institution of home rule and resulted in the Easter Rebellion in Dublin (April 24–29, 1916), in which Irish nationalists unsuccessfully attempted to throw off British rule. Guerrilla warfare against British forces followed proclamation of a republic by the rebels in 1919.

The Irish Free State was established as a dominion on Dec. 6, 1922, with the six northern counties as part of the United Kingdom. Ireland was neutral in World War II.

In 1948, Éamon de Valera, American-born leader of the Sinn Fein, who had won establishment of the Free State in 1921 in negotiations with Britain's David Lloyd George, was defeated by John A. Costello, who demanded final independence from Britain. The Republic of Ireland was proclaimed on April 18, 1949. It withdrew from the Commonwealth but in 1955 entered the

United Nations. Since 1949 the prime concern of successive governments has been economic development.

Through the 1960s, two antagonistic currents dominated Irish politics. One sought to bind the wounds of the rebellion and civil war. The other was the effort of the outlawed extremist Irish Republican Army to bring Northern Ireland into the republic. Despite public sympathy for unification of Ireland, the Dublin government dealt rigorously with IRA guerrillas caught inside the republic's borders.

In the elections of June 11, 1981, Garret M. D. FitzGerald, leader of the Fine Gael, was elected Prime Minister by 81 to 78 with the support of 15 Labor Party members and one independent Socialist added to his own party's 65 members. Other independents abstained, among them Kieran Doherty, a prisoner in Northern Ireland's Maze Prison, who with another prisoner had won election to the Southern Parliament (the Republic's Constitution extends citizenship to anyone born in Northern Ireland). Doherty died after a hunger strike on Aug. 3, one of nine Maze prisoners to do so.

FitzGerald resigned Jan. 27, 1982, after his presentation of an austerity budget aroused the opposition of independents who had backed him previously. Former Prime Minister Haughey was sworn in on March 9 and presented a budget with nearly a $1 billion deficit, with additional public spending aimed at stimulating the lagging economy. FitzGerald was re-elected Prime Minister on Dec. 14, 1982 but was unable to solve the problem of unemployment and the elections of 1987 brought Haughey back into power on March 10.

ISRAEL

State of Israel
President: Chaim Herzog (1988)
Prime Minister: Yitzhak Shamir (1988) (term ends Nov., 1992)
Area: 8,020 sq mi. (20,772 sq km)
Population (est. mid-1989): 4,371,478[1] (average annual rate of natural increase: 1.6%)
Density per square mile: 559
Capital: Jerusalem[2]
Largest cities (est. 1986): Jerusalem, 468,400[3]; Tel Aviv, 320,300; Haifa, 223,400
Monetary unit: Shekel
Languages: Hebrew, Arabic, English
Religions: Jewish, 82%, Islam, 14%, Christian, 2.3%, Druze and others, 1.7%
National name: Medinat Yisra'el
Literacy rate: 92%
Economic summary: Gross national product (1988): $36 billion; $8,400 per capita; 1% real growth rate. Arable land: 17%; principal products: citrus and other fruits, vegetables, beef, dairy and poultry products. Labor force: 1,400,000 (1984 est.); 22.8% in industry, mining and manufacturing; major products: processed foods, cut diamonds, clothing and textiles, chemicals, metal products, transport and electrical equipment, plastics. Natural resources: sulfur, rock salt, phosphates, potash, bromine. Exports: polished diamonds, citrus and other fruits, clothing and textiles, processed foods, high technology products, computerized medical equipment, military hardware, fertilizer and chemical products. Imports: rough diamonds, chemicals, oil, machinery, iron and steel, cereals, textiles, vehicles, ships. Major trading partners: U.S., West Germany, U.K., Switzerland, France, Italy, Belgium, Luxembourg.

1. Includes West Bank, Gaza Strip, East Jerusalem. 2. Not recognized by U.S. which recognizes Tel Aviv. 3. Includes East Jerusalem.

Geography. Israel, slightly smaller than Massachusetts, lies at the eastern end of the Mediterranean Sea. It is bordered by Egypt on the west, Syria and Jordan on the east, and Lebanon on the north.

Northern Israel is largely a plateau traversed from north to south by mountains and broken by great depressions, also running from north to south.

The maritime plain of Israel is remarkably fertile. The southern Negev region, which comprises almost half the total area, is largely a wide desert steppe area. The National Water Project irrigation scheme is now transforming it into fertile land. The Jordan, the only important river, flows from the north through Lake Hule (Waters of Merom) and Lake Kinneret (Sea of Galilee or Sea of Tiberias), finally entering the Dead Sea, 1,290 feet (393 m) below sea level. This "sea," which is actually a salt lake (394 sq mi.; 1,020 sq km), has no outlet, its water balance being maintained by evaporation.

Government. Israel, which does not have a written constitution, has a republican form of government headed by a president elected for a five-year term by the Knesset. He may serve no more than two terms. The Knesset has 120 members elected by universal suffrage under proportional representation for four years. The government is administered by the Cabinet, which is headed by the prime minister.

The Knesset decided in June 1950 that Israel would acquire a constitution gradually through the years by the enactment of fundamental laws. Israel grants automatic citizenship to every Jew who desires to settle within its borders, subject to control of the Knesset.

History. Palestine, cradle of two great religions and homeland of the modern state of Israel, was known to the ancient Hebrews as the "Land of Canaan." Palestine's name derives from the Philistines, a people who occupied the southern coastal part of the country in the 12th century B.C.

A Hebrew kingdom established in 1000 B.C. was later split into the kingdoms of Judah and Israel; they were subsequently invaded by Assyrians, Babylonians, Egyptians, Persians, Macedonians, Romans, and Byzantines. The Arabs took Palestine from the Byzantine Empire A.D. 634–40. With the exception of a Frankish Crusader kingdom from 1099 to 1187, Palestine remained under Moslem rule until the 20th century (Turkish rule from 1516), when British forces under Gen. Sir Edmund Allenby defeated the Turks and captured Jerusalem Dec. 9, 1917. The League of Nations granted Britain a mandate to govern Palestine, effective in 1923.

Jewish colonies—Jews from Russia established one as early as 1882—multiplied after Theodor Herzl's 1897 call for a Jewish state. The Zionist movement received official approval with the publication of a letter Nov. 2, 1917, from Arthur Balfour, British Foreign Secretary, to Lord Rothschild, a British Jewish leader. Balfour promised support for the establishment of a Jewish homeland in Palestine on the understanding that the civil and religious rights of non-Jewish Palestinians would be safeguarded.

A 1937 British proposal called for an Arab and a Jewish state separated by a mandated area incorporating Jerusalem and Nazareth. Arabs opposed this, demanding a single state with minority rights for Jews, and a 1939 British White Paper retreated, offering instead a single state with further Jewish immigration to be limited to 75,000. Although the White Paper satisfied neither side, further discussion ended on the outbreak of World War II, when the Jewish population stood at nearly 500,000, or 30% of the total. Illegal and legal immigration during the war brought the Jewish population to 678,000 in 1946, compared with 1,269,000 Arabs. Unable to reach a compromise, Britain turned the problem over to the United Nations in 1947, which on November 29 voted for partition—despite strong Arab opposition.

Britain did not help implement the U.N. decision and withdrew on expiration of its mandate May 14, 1948. Zionists had already seized control of areas designated as Jewish, and, on the day of British departure, the Jewish National Council proclaimed the State of Israel.

U.S. recognition came within hours. The next day, Jordanian and Egyptian forces invaded the new nation. At the cease-fire Jan. 7, 1949, Israel increased its original territory by 50%, taking western Galilee, a broad corridor through central Palestine to Jerusalem, and part of modern Jerusalem. (In April 1950, Jordan annexed areas of eastern and central Palestine that had been designated for an Arab state, together with the old city of Jerusalem).

Chaim Weizmann and David Ben-Gurion became Israel's first president and prime minister. The new government was admitted to the U.N. May 11, 1949.

The next clash with Arab neighbors came when Egypt nationalized the Suez Canal in 1956 and barred Israeli shipping. Coordinating with an Anglo-French force, Israeli troops seized the Gaza Strip and drove through the Sinai to the east bank of the Suez Canal, but withdrew under U.S. and U.N. pressure. In 1967, Israel threatened retaliation against Syrian border raids, and Syria asked Egyptian aid. Egypt demanded the removal of U.N. peace-keeping forces from Suez, staged a national mobilization, closed the Gulf of Aqaba, and moved troops into the Sinai. Starting with simultaneous air attacks against Syrian, Jordanian, and Egyptian air bases on June 5, Israel during a six-day war totally defeated its Arab enemies. Expanding its territory by 200%, Israel at the cease-fire held the Golan Heights, the West Bank of the Jordan River, the Old City, and all of the Sinai and the east bank of the Suez Canal.

Israel insisted that Jerusalem remain a unified city and that peace negotiations be conducted directly, something the Arab states had refused to do because it would constitute a recognition of their Jewish neighbor.

Egypt's President Gamal Abdel Nasser renounced the 1967 cease-fire in 1969 and began a "war of attrition" against Israel, firing Soviet artillery at Israeli forces on the east bank of the canal. Nasser died of a heart attack on Sept. 28, 1970, and was succeeded by Anwar el-Sadat.

In the face of Israeli reluctance even to discuss the return of occupied territories, the fourth Mideast war erupted Oct. 6, 1973, with a surprise Egyptian and Syrian assault on the Jewish high holy day of Yom Kippur. Initial Arab gains were reversed

when a cease-fire took effect two weeks later, but Israel suffered heavy losses in manpower.

U.S. Secretary of State Henry A. Kissinger arranged a disengagement of forces on both the Egyptian and Syrian fronts. Geneva talks, aimed at a lasting peace, foundered, however, when Israel balked at inclusion of the Palestine Liberation Organization, a group increasingly active in terrorism directed against Israel.

A second-stage Sinai withdrawal signed by Israel and Egypt in September 1975 required Israel to give up the strategic Mitla and Gidi passes and to return the captured Abu Rudeis oil fields. Egypt guaranteed passage of Israeli cargoes through the reopened Suez Canal, and both sides renounced force in the settlement of disputes. Two hundred U.S. civilian technicians were stationed in a widened U.N. buffer zone to monitor and warn either side of truce violations.

A dramatic breakthrough in the tortuous history of Mideast peace efforts occurred Nov. 9, 1977, when Egypt's President Sadat declared his willingness to go anywhere to talk peace. Prime Minister Menachem Begin on Nov. 15 extended an invitation to the Egyptian leader to address the Knesset. Sadat's arrival in Israel four days later raised worldwide hopes. But optimism ebbed even before Begin was invited to Ismailia by Sadat, December 25–26.

An Israeli peace plan unveiled by Begin on his return, and approved by the Knesset, offered to end military administration in the West Bank and the Gaza Strip, with a degree of Arab self-rule but no relinquishment of sovereignty by Israel. Sadat severed talks on Jan. 18 and, despite U.S. condemnation, Begin approved new West Bank settlements by Israelis.

A PLO raid on Israel's coast on March 11, 1978, killed 30 civilians and provoked a full-scale invasion of southern Lebanon by Israel three days later to attack PLO bases. Israel withdrew three months later, turning over strongpoints to Lebanese Christian militia wherever possible rather than to a U.N. peacekeeping force installed in the area.

On March 14, 1979, after a visit by Carter, the Knesset approved a final peace treaty, and 12 days later Begin and Sadat signed the document, together with Carter, in a White House ceremony. Israel began its withdrawal from the Sinai on May 25 by handing over the coastal town of El Arish and the two countries opened their border on May 29.

One of the most difficult periods in Israel's history began with a confrontation with Syria over the placing by Syria of Soviet surface-to-air missiles in the Bekaa Valley of Lebanon in April 1981. President Reagan dispatched Philip C. Habib to prevent a clash. While Habib was seeking a settlement, Begin ordered a bombing raid against an Iraqi nuclear reactor on June 7, invoking the theory of preemptive self-defense because he said Iraq was planning to make nuclear weapons to attack Israel.

Although Israel withdrew its last settlers from the Sinai in April 1982 and agreed to a Sinai "peace patrol" composed of troops from four West European nations, the fragile peace engineered by Habib in Lebanon was shattered on June 9 by a massive Israeli assault on southern Lebanon. The attack was in retaliation for what Israel charged was a PLO attack that critically wounded the Israeli ambassador to London six days earlier.

Israeli armor swept through UNIFIL lines in southern Lebanon, destroyed PLO strongholds in Tyre and Sidon, and reached the suburbs of Beirut on June 10. As Israeli troops ringed Moslem East Beirut, where 5,000 PLO guerrillas were believed trapped, Habib sought to negotiate a safe exit for them.

A U.S.-mediated accord between Lebanon and Israel, signed on May 17, 1983, provided for Israeli withdrawal from Lebanon. Israeli withdrawal was conditioned on withdrawal of Syrian troops from the Bekaa Valley, however, and the Syrians refused to leave. Israel eventually withdrew its troops from the Beirut area, but kept them in southern Lebanon. Lebanon, under pressure from Syria, canceled the accord in March 1984.

Prime Minister Begin resigned on Sept. 15, 1983. On Oct. 10, Likud Party stalwart Yitzhak Shamir was elected Prime Minister.

After a close election, the two major parties worked out a carefully balanced power-sharing agreement and the Knesset, on Sept. 14, 1984 approved a national unity government including both the Labor Alignment and the Likud bloc.

By the anniversary of the invasion of Lebanon in June of 1985, Israel had withdrawn most—but not all—of its troops from the country. Israeli combat units left, but military advisers remained in a security zone along Israel's northern frontier.

The Peres government decided in May to exchange 1,150 Palestinian prisoners—including terrorists—for three Israeli soldiers who had been held since the Lebanon war by the Popular Front for the Liberation of Palestine. Another development dividing Israelis was the verdict by a three-judge court on July 10 convicting three Jewish settlers of murder and 12 others of different violent crimes against Arabs.

In one hopeful development, the coalition government declared an economic emergency on July 1 and imposed sweeping austerity measures intended to break the country's 260% inflation. Key elements were an 18.8% devaluation of the shekel, price increases in most government-subsidized products as gasoline, dismissal of 9,000 government employees, government spending cuts and a wage and price freeze. By the end of Peres' term in October, 1986, the shekel had been revalued and stabilized and inflation was down to less than 20%.

Differences in the approach to take to peace talks started to strain the government in 1987.

In Dec. 1987, riots by Gazan Palestinians led to the current general uprising throughout the occupied territories which consists of low-level violence and civil disobedience. As a consequence, in 1988 the PLO formally declared an independent state. Also, in response to their ostensible recognition of Israel in that year, the U.S. established low-level diplomatic contacts with the PLO.

A deadlock in the elections of Dec. 1988 led to a continuation of the Likud-Labor national unity government. This collapsed in 1990, leading to Shamir forming a right-wing coalition that included the religious parties.

ITALY

Italian Republic
President: Francesco Cossiga (1985)
Premier: Giulio Andreotti (1989)
Area: 116,500 sq mi. (301,278 sq km)
Population (est. mid-1990): 57,700,000 (average annual rate of natural increase: .1%)

Density per square mile: 495
Capital: Rome
Largest cities (1984): Rome, 2,826,733; Milan, 1,535,-722; Naples, 1,206,955; Turin, 1,049,997; Genoa, 738,099; Palermo, 716,149; Bologna, 442,307; Florence, 435,698; Catania, 377,707; Bari, 368,216.
Monetary unit: Lira
Language: Italian
Religion: Roman Catholic, almost 100%
National name: Repubblica Italiana
Literacy rate: 93%
Economic summary: Gross national product (1989): $861.3 billion; $14,953 per capita; 34% real growth rate. Arable land: 32%; principal products: grapes, olives, citrus fruits, vegetables, wheat, corn. Labor force: 23,-670,000; 37.9% in industry; major products: machinery, autos, textiles, shoes, chemicals. Natural resources: mercury, potash, sulfur, fish, gas, marble. Exports: Engineering, chemicals, textiles, metals, shoes, food. Imports: engineering, chemicals, food, metals. Major trading partners: West Germany, France, United States, United Kingdom, Switzerland.

Geography. Italy is a long peninsula shaped like a boot bounded on the west by the Tyrrhenian Sea and on the east by the Adriatic. Slightly larger than Arizona, it has for neighbors France, Switzerland, Austria, and Yugoslavia.

Approximately 600 of Italy's 708 miles (1,139 km) of length are in the long peninsula that projects into the Mediterranean from the fertile basin of the Po River. The Apennine Mountains, branching off from the Alps between Nice and Genoa, form the peninsula's backbone, and rise to a maximum height of 9,560 feet (2,912 m) at the Gran Sasso d'Italia (Corno). The Alps form Italy's northern boundary.

Several islands form part of Italy. Sicily (9,926 sq mi.; 25,708 sq km) lies off the toe of the boot, across the Strait of Messina, with a steep and rockbound northern coast and gentler slopes to the sea in the west and south. Mount Etna, an active volcano, rises to 10,741 feet (3,274 m), and most of Sicily is more than 500 feet (3,274 m) in elevation. Sixty-two miles (100 km) southwest of Sicily lies Pantelleria (45 sq mi.; 117 sq km), and south of that are Lampedusa and Linosa. Sardinia (9,301 sq mi.; 24,-090 sq km), which is just south of Corsica and about 125 miles (200 km) west of the mainland, is mountainous, stony, and unproductive.

Italy has many northern lakes, lying below the snow-covered peaks of the Alps. The largest are Garda (143 sq mi.; 370 sq km), Maggiore (83 sq mi.; 215 sq km), and Como (55 sq mi.; 142 sq km).

The Po, the principal river, flows from the Alps on Italy's western border and crosses the Lombard plain to the Adriatic.

Government. The president is elected for a term of seven years by Parliament in joint session with regional representatives. The president nominates the premier and, upon the premier's recommendations, the members of the Cabinet. Parliament is composed of two houses: a Senate with 315 elective members and a Chamber of Deputies of 630 members elected by the people for a five-year term.

History. Until A.D. 476, when the German Odoacer became head of the Roman Empire in the west, the history of Italy was largely the history of Rome. From A.D. 800 on, the Holy Roman Emperors, Popes, Normans, and Saracens all vied for control over various segments of the Italian peninsula. Numerous city states, such as Venice and Genoa, and many small principalities flourished in the late Middle Ages.

In 1713, after the War of the Spanish Succession, Milan, Naples, and Sardinia were handed over to Austria, which lost some of its Italian territories in 1735. After 1800, Italy was unified by Napoleon, who crowned himself King of Italy in 1805; but with the Congress of Vienna in 1815, Austria once again became the dominant power in Italy.

Austrian armies crushed Italian uprisings in 1820-1821, and 1831. In the 1830s Giuseppe Mazzini, brilliant liberal nationalist, organized the Risorgimento (Resurrection), which laid the foundation for Italian unity.

Disappointed Italian patriots looked to the House of Savoy for leadership. Count Camille di Cavour (1810–61), Premier of Sardinia in 1852 and the architect of a united Italy, joined England and France in the Crimean War (1853–56), and in 1859, helped France in a war against Austria, thereby obtaining Lombardy. By plebiscite in 1860, Modena, Parma, Tuscany, and the Romagna voted to join Sardinia. In 1860, Giuseppe Garibaldi conquered Sicily and Naples and turned them over to Sardinia. Victor Emmanuel II, King of Sardinia, was proclaimed King of Italy in 1861.

Allied with Germany and Austria-Hungary in the Triple Alliance of 1882, Italy declared its neutrality upon the outbreak of World War I on the ground that Germany had embarked upon an offensive war. In 1915, Italy entered the war on the side of the Allies.

Benito (Il Duce) Mussolini, a former Socialist, organized discontented Italians in 1919 into the Fascist Party to "rescue Italy from Bolshevism." He led his Black Shirts in a march on Rome and, on Oct. 28, 1922, became premier. He transformed Italy into a dictatorship, embarking on an expansionist foreign policy with the invasion and annexation of Ethiopia in 1935 and allying himself with Adolf Hitler in the Rome-Berlin Axis in 1936. He was executed by Partisans on April 28, 1945 at Dongo on Lake Como.

Following the overthrow of Mussolini's dictatorship and the armistice with the Allies (Sept. 3, 1943), Italy joined the war against Germany as a co-belligerent. King Victor Emmanuel III abdicated May 9, 1946, and left the country after having installed his son as King Humbert II. A plebiscite rejected monarchy, however, and on June 13, King Humbert followed his father into exile.

The peace treaty of Sept. 15, 1947, required Italian renunciation of all claims in Ethiopia and Greece and the cession of the Dodecanese to Greece and of five small Alpine areas to France. Much of the Istrian Peninsula, including Fiume and Pola, went to Yugoslavia.

The Trieste area west of the new Yugoslav territory was made a free territory (until 1954, when the city and a 90-square-mile zone were transferred to Italy and the rest to Yugoslavia).

Scandal brought the long reign of the Christian Democrats to an end when Italy's 40th premier since World War II, Arnaldo Forlani, was forced to resign in the wake of disclosure that many high-ranking Christian Democrats and civil servants belonged to a secret Masonic lodge known as "P-2."

When the Socialists deserted the coalition, Forlani was forced to resign on May 26, 1981, leaving to Giovanni Spadolini of the small Republican Party the task of forming a new government. He was succeeded by Amintore Fanfani, a Christian Democrat, the following year. Bettino Craxi, a Socialist, became Premier in 1983.

Craxi was forced to resign on June 27, 1986 following the loss of a key secret-ballot vote in Parliament. After a month of political wrangling, Craxi was able to form a new government on condition that his term end in March, 1987.

Disputes over who Craxi's successor would be led to general elections in June, 1987 in which the Socialists and the Christian Democrats gained at the expense of the Communists and the smaller parties. Giovanni Goria, a Christian Democrat, became the new Premier. Budget disputes led to Goria being replaced by Ciriaco De Mita in April, 1988.

IVORY COAST

Republic of Côte d'Ivoire
President: Félix Houphouët-Boigny (1960)
Area: 124,502 sq mi. (322,462 sq km)
Population (est. mid-1989): 11,619,099 (average annual rate of natural increase: 3.8%)
Density per square mile: 97
Capital: Yamoussoukro[1]
Monetary unit: Franc CFA
Ethnic groups: 60 different groups: principals are Baoule, Bete, Senoufou, Malinke, Agni
Languages: French and African languages (Diaula esp.)
Religions: folk beliefs, 44%; Christian, 32%; Islam, 24%
National name: République de la Côte d'Ivoire
Literacy rate: 35%
Economic summary: Gross domestic product (1987): $10.3 billion; $960 per capita; real growth rate −2.7%. Arable land: 9%; Labor force in agriculture: 85%; principal products: coffee, cocoa, sugar, corn, cotton. Major industrial products: food, cement, bananas, pineapples. Natural resources: diamonds, iron ore, oil refining, auto assembly, textiles, timber. Exports: coffee, cocoa, tropical woods. Imports: raw materials, consumer goods, fuels. Major trading partners: France, U.S., Western European countries, Nigeria.

1. Not recognized by U.S. which recognizes Abidjan.

Geography. The Ivory Coast, in western Africa on the Gulf of Guinea, is a little larger than New Mexico. Its neighbors are Liberia, Guinea, Mali, Burkina Faso, and Ghana.

The country consists of a coastal strip in the south, dense forests in the interior, and savannas in the north. Rainfall is heavy, especially along the coast.

Government. The government is headed by a President who is elected every five years by popular vote, together with a National Assembly of 175 members.

The Parti Démocratique de la Côte d'Ivoire, a member of the Rassemblement Démocratique Africain, is the only political party.

History. The Ivory Coast attracted both French and Portuguese merchants in the 15th century. French traders set up establishments early in the 19th century, and in 1842, the French obtained territorial concessions from local tribes, gradually extending their influence along the coast and inland. The area was organized as a territory in 1893, became an autonomous republic in the French Union after World War II, and achieved independence on Aug. 7, 1960.

The Ivory Coast formed a customs union in 1959 with Dahomey (Benin), Niger, and Burkina Faso. The country is one of the most prosperous and stable in West Africa.

JAMAICA

Sovereign: Queen Elizabeth II
Governor-General: Sir Florizel Glasspole (1973)
Prime Minister: Michael Manley (1989)
Area: 4,411 sq mi. (11,424 sq km)
Population (est. mid-1990): 2,400,000 (average annual rate of natural increase: 1.7%)
Density per square mile: 586
Capital and largest city (est. 1982): Kingston, 104,000
Monetary unit: Jamaican dollar
Language: English
Religions: Protestant, 71%; Roman Catholic, 10%; Rastafarian, 7%
Member of Commonwealth of Nations
Literacy rate: 76%
Economic summary: Gross domestic product (1987): $2.9 billion; $1,160 per capita; 5% real growth rate. Arable land: 19%; principal products: sugar cane, citrus fruits, bananas, spices, coconuts, coffee, cocoa. Labor force: 728,700; 28% in industry and commerce; major products: bauxite, textiles, processed foods, light manufactures. Natural resources: bauxite, gypsum. Exports: alumina, bauxite, sugar, clothing, citrus fruits, rum, cocoa. Imports: fuels, machinery, transport and electrical equipment, food, fertilizer. Major trading partners: U.S., U.K., Netherlands Antilles, Venezuela.

Geography. Jamaica is an island in the West Indies, 90 miles (145 km) south of Cuba and 100 miles (161 km) west of Haiti. It is a little smaller than Connecticut.

The island is made up of a plateau and the Blue Mountains, a group of volcanic hills, in the east. Blue Mountain (7,402 ft.; 2,256 m) is the tallest peak.

Government. The legislature is a 60-member House of Representatives elected by universal suffrage and an appointed Senate of 21 members. The Prime Minister is appointed by the Governor-General and must, in the Governor-General's opinion, be the person best able to command the confidence of a majority of the members of the House of Representatives.

History. Jamaica was inhabited by Arawak Indians when Columbus discovered it in 1494 and named it St. Iago. It remained under Spanish rule until 1655, then became a British possession. The island prospered from wealth brought by buccaneers to their base, Port Royal, the capital, until the city disappeared in the sea in 1692 after an earthquake. The Arawaks died off from disease and exploitation, and slaves, mostly black, were imported to work sugar plantations. Abolition of the slave trade (1807), emancipation of the slaves (1833), and a gradual drop in sugar prices led to depressed economic conditions that resulted in an uprising in 1865.

The following year Jamaica's status was changed to that of a colony, and conditions improved considerably. Introduction of banana cultivation made the island less dependent on the sugar crop for its well-being.

On May 5, 1953, Jamaica attained internal autonomy, and in 1958 it led in organizing the West Indies Federation. This effort at Caribbean unification failed. A nationalist labor leader, Sir Alexander Bustamente, led a campaign for withdrawal from the Federation. As the result of a popular referendum in 1961, Jamaica became independent on Aug. 6, 1962.

Michael Manley became Prime Minister in 1972 and initiated a socialist program and in 1977, the government bought 51% of the Kaiser and Reynolds bauxite operations.

The Labor Party defeated Manley's People's National Party in 1980 and its capitalist-oriented leader, Edward P.G. Seaga, became Prime Minister. He instituted measures to encourage private investment.

Like other Caribbean countries, Jamaica was hard-hit by the 1981–82 recession. By 1984, austerity measures that Seaga instituted in the hope of bringing the economy back into balance included elimination of government subsidies. Devaluation of the Jamaican dollar made Jamaican products more competitive on the world market and Jamaica achieved record growth in tourism and agriculture. Manufacturing also grew. But at the same time, the cost of many foods went up 50% to 75% and thousands of Jamaicans fell deeper into poverty.

The PNP decisively won local elections in mid-July, 1987, signaling a weakening in Seaga's position. In 1989, Manley swept back into power with a clear-cut victory. He indicated that he would pursue more centrist policies than he did in his previous administration.

JAPAN

Emperor: Akihito (1989)
Prime Minister: Toshiki Kaifu (1989)
Area: 143,574 sq mi. (371,857 sq km)
Population (est. mid-1990): 123,600,000 (average annual rate of natural increase: 6%)
Density per square mile: 857
Capital: Tokyo
Largest cities (est. 1986): Tokyo, 8,354,615; Yokohama, 2,992,926; Osaka, 2,636,249; Nagoya, 2,116,381; Sapporo, 1,542,979; Kyoto, 1,479,218; Kobe, 1,410,000; Fukuoka, 1,160,440; Kitakyusho, 1,056,402; Kawasaki, 1,088,624
Monetary unit: Yen
Language: Japanese
Religions: Shintoist, Buddhist
National name: Nippon
Literacy rate (1981): 99%
Economic summary: Gross national product (1988): $1,843 billion; $15,030 per capita; 4.8% real growth rate. Arable land: 13%; principal products: rice, vegetables, fruits, sugar. Labor force: 60,290,000; 33% in manufacturing; major products: machinery and equipment, metals and metal products, textiles, autos, consumer electronics, chemicals, electrical and electronic equipment. Natural resource: fish. Exports: machinery and equipment, automobiles, metals and metal products, textiles. Imports: fossil fuels, metal ore, raw materials, foodstuffs, machinery and equipment. Major trading partners: U.S., Middle East, Western Europe, Indonesia, China, Australia, Canada, South Korea, Taiwan

Geography. An archipelago extending more than

1,744 miles (2,790 km) from northeast to southwest in the Pacific, Japan is separated from the east coast of Asia by the Sea of Japan. It is approximately the size of Montana.

Japan's four main islands are Honshu, Hokkaido, Kyushu, and Shikoku. The Ryukyu chain to the southwest was U.S.-occupied and the Kuriles to the northeast are Russian-occupied. The surface of the main islands consists largely of mountains separated by narrow valleys. There are about 60 more or less active volcanoes, of which the best-known is Mount Aso. Mount Fuji, seen on postcards, is not active.

Government. Japan's Constitution, promulgated on Nov. 3, 1946, replaced the Meiji Constitution of 1889. The 1946 Constitution, sponsored by the U.S. during its occupation of Japan, brought fundamental changes to the Japanese political system, including the abandonment of the Emperor's divine rights. The Diet (Parliament) consists of a House of Representatives of 511 members, elected for four years, and a House of Councilors of 252 members, half of whom are elected every three years for six-year terms. Executive power is vested in the Cabinet, which is headed by a Prime Minister, nominated by the Diet from its members.

On Jan. 7, 1989, Emperor Hirohito, Japan's longest-reigning monarch died and was succeed by his son, Akihito (born 1933). He was married in 1959 to Michiko Shoda (the first time a crown prince married a commoner). They have two sons, Hiro and Aya, and a daughter, Nori.

History. A series of legends attributes creation of Japan to the sun goddess, from whom the later emperors were allegedly descended. The first of them was Jimmu Tenno, supposed to have ascended the throne in 660 B.C.

Recorded Japanese history begins with the first contact with China in the 5th century A.D. Japan was then divided into strong feudal states, all nominally under the Emperor, but with real power often held by a court minister or clan. In 1185, Yoritomo, chief of the Minamoto clan, was designated Shogun (Generalissimo) with the administration of the islands under his control. A dual government system—Shogun and Emperor—continued until 1867.

First contact with the West came about 1542, when a Portuguese ship off course arrived in Japanese waters. Portuguese, traders, Jesuit missionaries, and Spanish, Dutch, and English traders followed. Suspicious of Christianity and of Portuguese support of a local Japanese revolt, the shoguns prohibited all trade with foreign countries; only a Dutch trading post at Nagasaki was permitted. Western attempts to renew trading relations failed until 1853, when Commodore Matthew Perry sailed an American fleet into Tokyo Bay.

Japan now quickly made the transition from a medieval to a modern power. Feudalism was abolished and industrialization was speeded. An imperial army was established with conscription. The shogun system was abolished in 1868 by Emperor Meiji, and parliamentary government was established in 1889. After a brief war with China in 1894–95, Japan acquired Formosa (Taiwan), the Pescadores Islands, and part of southern Manchuria. China also recognized the independence of Korea (Chosen), which Japan later annexed (1910).

In 1904–05, Japan defeated Russia in the Russo-Japanese War, gaining the territory of southern Sakhalin (Karafuto) and Russia's port and rail rights in Manchuria. In World War I Japan seized Germany's Pacific islands and leased areas in China. The Treaty of Versailles then awarded it a mandate over the islands.

At the Washington Conference of 1921–22, Japan agreed to respect Chinese national integrity. The series of Japanese aggressions that was to lead to the nation's downfall began in 1931 with the invasion of Manchuria. The following year, Japan set up this area as a puppet state, "Manchukuo," under Emperor Henry Pu-Yi, last of China's Manchu dynasty. On Nov. 25, 1936, Japan joined the Axis by signing the anti-Comintern pact. The invasion of China came the next year and the Pearl Harbor attack on the U.S. on Dec. 7, 1941.

(For details of World War II (1939–45), *see* Headline History.)

Japan surrendered formally on Sept. 2, 1945, aboard the battleship *Missouri* in Tokyo Bay after atomic bombs had hit Hiroshima and Nagasaki. Southern Sakhalin and the Kurile Islands reverted to the U.S.S.R., and Formosa (Taiwan) and Manchuria to China. The Pacific islands remained under U.S. occupation. General of the Army Douglas MacArthur was appointed Supreme Commander for the Allied Powers on Aug. 14, 1945.

A new Japanese Constitution went into effect in 1947. In 1949, many of the responsibilities of government were returned to the Japanese. Full sovereignty was granted to Japan by the Japanese Peace Treaty in 1951.

The treaty took effect on April 28, 1952, when Japan returned to full status as a nation. It was admitted into the United Nations in 1958.

Following the visit of Prime Minister Eisaku Sato to Washington in 1969, the U.S. agreed to return Okinawa and other Ryukyu Islands to Japan in 1972, and both nations renewed the security treaty in 1970.

When President Nixon opened a dialogue with Peking in 1972, Prime Minister Kakuei Tanaka, who succeeded Sato in 1972, quickly established diplomatic relations with the mainland Chinese and severed ties with Formosa.

Announcement on June 19, 1981 that Japan's gross national product grew at a rate of nearly 5% for the fiscal year ending March 31 brought new demands for increased imports of manufactured goods by Japan, which international trade experts charged was still creating barriers against trade despite repeated promises by Tokyo to relax such restrictions.

The same figure was agreed to by Japan for the following year, and for the first time, Japanese automobile exports declined for the 12-month period ending March 31, 1982. In an effort to remove non-tariff trade barriers, which U.S. businessmen held responsible for their inability to increase sales in Japan, the Suzuki government appointed a special ombudsman with authority to cut red tape.

Under continued U.S. prodding, Tokyo announced an increase in defense spending with the 1987 budget reaching the target figure of 1% of the gross national product.

Suzuki was defeated in 1982 by Yasuhiro Nakasone who is considered pro-Western and better relations with the United States have ensued. Despite some opposition to his pro-Western policies in general, his Liberal Democratic party won decisively in the elections of July 7, 1986 and he was granted another year beyond his four-year limit which would have expired in October, 1986. Noboru Takeshita succeeded him in November 1987.

In 1989, an influence-peddling scandal shook the LDP and led to Takeshita's resignation. He was succeeded by Sousuke Uno, who also resigned in scandal.

JORDAN

The Hashemite Kingdom of Jordan
Ruler: King Hussein I (1952)
Prime Minister and Minister of Defense: Mudar Badran (1989)
Area: 37,297 sq mi. (96,599 sq km)[1]
Population (est. mid-1990): 4,100,000[1] (average annual rate of natural increase: 3.5%)
Density per square mile: 105
Capital: Amman
Largest cities (est. 1986): Amman, 972,000; Zarka, 392, 220; Irbid, 271,000; Salt, 134,100
Monetary unit: Jordanian dinar
Languages: Arabic, English
Religions: Islam (Sunni), 95%; Christian, 5%
National name: Al Mamlaka al Urduniya al Hashemiyah
Literacy rate: 75%
Economic summary: Gross national product (1990): $4.9 billion; $1,780 per capita; 2.1% real growth rate (1986). Arable land: 4%; principal products: wheat, fruits, vegetables, olive oil. Labor force: 550,000; 20% in manufacturing and mining; major products: phosphate, refined petroleum products, cement. Natural resources: phosphate, potash. Exports: phosphates, fruits, and vegetables, foodstuffs, fertilizer. Imports: petroleum products, textiles, capital goods, motor vehicles, foodstuffs. Major trading partners: U.S., Japan, Saudi Arabia, Iraq, U.K., W. Germany.

---

1. Includes territory occupied by Israel in 1967 war.

Geography. The Middle East kingdom of Jordan is bordered on the west by Israel and the Dead Sea, on the north by Syria, on the east by Iraq, and on the south Saudi Arabia. It is comparable in size to Indiana.

Arid hills and mountains make up most of the country. The southern section of the Jordan River flows through the country.

Government. Jordan is a constitutional monarchy with a bicameral parliament.

The upper house consists of 40 members appointed by the king and the lower house is composed of 80 members elected by popular vote. The Constitution guarantees freedom of religion, speech, press, association, and private property.

All political parties were banned in 1957.

History. In biblical times, the country that is now Jordan contained the lands of Edom, Moab, Ammon, and Bashan. In A.D. 106 it became part of the Roman province of Arabia and in 633–36 was conquered by the Arabs.

Taken from the Turks by the British in World War I, Jordan (formerly known as Transjordan) was separated from the Palestine mandate in 1920, and in 1921, placed under the rule of Abdullah ibn Hussein.

In 1923, Britain recognized Jordan's independence, subject to the mandate. In 1946, grateful for

Jordan's loyalty in World War II, Britain abolished the mandate. That part of Palestine occupied by Jordanian troops was formally incorporated by action of the Jordanian Parliament in 1950.

King Abdullah was assassinated in 1951. His son Talal was deposed as mentally ill the next year. Talal's son Hussein, born Nov. 14, 1935, succeeded him.

From the beginning of his reign, Hussein had to steer a careful course between his powerful neighbor to the west, Israel, and rising Arab nationalism, frequently a direct threat to this throne. Riots erupted when he joined the Central Treaty Organization (the Baghdad Pact) in 1955, and he incurred further unpopularity when Britain, France, and Israel attacked the Suez Canal in 1956, forcing him to place his army under nominal command of the United Arab Republic of Egypt and Syria.

The 1961 breakup of the UAR eased Arab national pressure on Hussein, who was the first to recognize Syria after it reclaimed its independence. Jordan was swept into the 1967 Arab-Israeli war, however, and lost the old city of Jerusalem and all of its territory west of the Jordan river, the West Bank. Embittered Palestinian guerrilla forces virtually took over sections of Jordan in the aftermath of defeat, and open warfare broke out between the Palestinians and government forces in 1970.

Despite intervention of Syrian tanks, Hussein's Bedouin army defeated the Palestinians, suffering heavy casualties. A U.S. military alert and Israeli armor massed on the Golan Heights contributed psychological weight, but the Jordanians alone drove out the Syrians and invited the departure of 12,000 Iraqui troops who had been in the country since the 1967 war. Ignoring protests from other Arab states, Hussein by mid-1971 crushed Palestinian strength in Jordan and shifted the problem to Lebanon, where many of the guerrillas had fled.

In October 1974, Hussein concurred in an Arab summit resolution calling for an independent Palestinian state and endorsing the Palestine Liberation Organization as the "sole legitimate representative of the Palestinian people." This apparent reversal of policy changed with the growing disillusion of Arab states with the P.L.O., however, and by 1977 Hussein referred again to the unity of people on both banks of the Jordan.

As Egypt and Israel neared final agreement on a peace treaty early in 1979, Hussein met with Yassir Arafat, the PLO leader, on March 17 and issued a joint statement of opposition. Although the U.S. pressed Jordan to break Arab ranks on the issue, Hussein elected to side with the great majority, cutting ties with Cairo and joining the boycott against Egypt.

On June 15, 1978, Hussein, who had celebrated his 25th anniversary on the throne, married his fourth wife, Elizabeth Halaby, 26, daughter of the former president of Pan American World Airways.

In September 1980, Jordan declared itself with Iraq in its conflict with Iran and, despite threats from Syria, opened ports to war shipments for Iraq.

In April 1983, Jordan rejected the American-sponsored Palestine peace plan.

An attempt to enlist Arafat in a new peace process collapsed in early 1986. Hussein then began a rapproachment with President Assad of Syria.

In 1988, Hussein formally renounced all claims to the West Bank, thus implicitly acknowledging Palestinian claims to statehood and torpedoing USA-sponsored efforts at a Palestinian confederation with Jordan.

KAMPUCHEA
See Cambodia

KENYA
Republic of Kenya
President: Daniel arap Moi (1978)
Area: 224,960 sq mi. (582,646 sq km)
Population (est. mid-1990): 24,600,000 (average annual rate of natural increase: 3.8%)
Density per square mile: 107
Capital: Nairobi
Largest cities (est. 1985): Nairobi, 1,000,000; Mombasa, 700,000
Monetary unit: Kenyan shilling
Languages: English (official), Swahili (national), and several other languages spoken by 40 ethnic groups
Religions: Protestant, 38%; Roman Catholic, 28%; traditional, 26%; Islam, 6%
Literacy rate: 59%
Member of Commonwealth of Nations
National name: Jamhuri ya Kenya
Economic summary: Gross domestic product (1987): $8.1 billion; $370 per capita; 4.8% real growth rate. Arable land: 3%; principal products: coffee, sisal, tea, pyrethrum, cotton, livestock. Labor force: 7,400,000; 14% in industry and commerce; major products: textiles, processed foods, consumer goods, refined oil. Natural resources: gold, limestone, minerals, wildlife. Exports: coffee, tea, foodstuffs, refined petroleum. Imports: machinery, transport equipment, crude oil, iron and steel products. Major trading partners: Western European countries, Japan, U.S., Uganda, U.K., Rwanda, Middle East.

Geography. Kenya lies on the equator in east central Africa on the coast of the Indian Ocean. It is twice the size of Nevada. Kenya's neighbors are Tanzania, Uganda, the Sudan, Ethiopia, and Somalia.

In the north, the land is arid; the southwestern corner is in the fertile Lake Victoria Basin; and a length of the eastern depression of Great Rift Valley separates western highlands from those that rise from the lowland coastal strip. Large game reserves have been developed.

Government. Under its Constitution Kenya has a one-house National Assembly of 188 members, elected for five years by universal suffrage and 12 nominated and 2 ex-officio, for a total of 202. Since 1969, the president has been chosen by a general election.

The Kenya African National Union (KANU), led by the president, is the only political party allowed.

President Jomo Kenyatta died in his sleep on Aug. 22, 1978. Vice President Daniel arap Moi was elected to succeed him on Oct. 10.

History. Kenya, formerly a British colony and protectorate, was made a crown colony in 1920. The whites' domination of the rich plateau area, the White Highlands, long regarded by the Kikiyu people as their territory, was a factor leading to native terrorism, called the Mau Mau movement, in 1952. In 1954 the British began preparing the territory for African rule and independence. In 1961 Jomo Kenyatta was freed from banishment to become leader of the Kenya African National Union.

Internal self-government was granted in 1963; Kenya became independent on Dec. 12, 1963, with Kenyatta the first president.

Moi's tenure has been marked by a consolidation of power which has included the harassment of political opponents, the banning of secret ballots, and his declaration that KANU was more powerful than the Assembly or the courts.

KIRIBATI
Republic of Kiribati
President: Ieremia Tabai (1979)
Area: 277 sq mi. (717 sq km)
Population (est. 1989): 68,828 (average annual growth rate: 1.5%)
Density per square mile: 245
Capital (1985): Tarawa, 21,393
Monetary unit: Australian dollar
Language: English
Religions: Roman Catholic, 48%; Protestant, 45%
Member of Commonwealth of Nations
Literacy rate: 90%
Economic summary: Gross domestic product (1987): $24.7 million; $370 per capita; .5% real growth rate. Arable land: NEGL%: Principal agricultural products: copra, vegetables. Exports: fish, copra. Imports: foodstuffs, fuel, transportation equipment. Major trading partners: New Zealand, Australia, Japan, American Samoa, Western Europe.

Geography. Kiribati, formerly the Gilbert Islands, consists of three widely separated main groups of Southwest Pacific islands, the Gilberts on the equator, the Phoenix Islands to the east, and the Line Islands further east. Ocean Island, producer of phosphates until it was mined out in 1981, is also included in the two million square miles of ocean, which give Kiribati an important fishery resource.

Government. The president holds executive power. The legislature consists of a House Assembly with 39 members.

History. A British protectorate since 1892, the Gilbert and Ellice Islands became a colony in 1915–16. The two island groups were separated in 1975 and given internal self-government.

Tarawa and others of the Gilbert group were occupied by Japan during World War II. Tarawa was the site of one of the bloodiest battles in U.S. Marine Corps history when Marines landed in November 1943 to dislodge the Japanese defenders.

Princess Anne, representing Queen Elizabeth II, presented the independence documents to the new government on July 12, 1979.

KOREA, NORTH
Democratic People's Republic of Korea
President: Marshal Kim Il Sung (1972)
Premier: Yong Hyong Muk (1989)
Area: 46,768 sq mi. (121,129 sq km)
Population (est. mid-1990): 21,300,000 (average annual rate of natural increase: 2.1%)
Density per square mile: 484
Capital and largest city (est. 1982): Pyongyang, 1,500,-000
Monetary unit: Won
Language: Korean
Religions: atheist, 68%; traditional, 16%
National name: Choson Minjujuui Inmin Konghwaguk

Literacy rate: 95% (est.)
Economic summary: Gross national product (1988): $20 billion; $910 per capita. Arable land: 18%; principal products: corn, rice, vegetables. Labor force: 6,100,000; 52% nonagricultural; Major industrial products: machines, electric power, chemicals, textiles, fertilizers, metallurgical products. Natural resources: coal, iron ore, hydroelectric power. Exports: minerals, chemical and metallurgical products. Imports: machinery and equipment, petroleum, foodstuffs, coking coal. Major trading partners: U.S.S.R., China, Japan.

Geography. Korea is a 600-mile (966 km) peninsula jutting from Manchuria and China (and a small portion of the U.S.S.R.) into the Sea of Japan and the Yellow Sea off eastern Asia. North Korea occupies an area slightly smaller than Pennsylvania north of the 38th parallel.

The country is almost completely covered by a series of north-south mountain ranges separated by narrow valleys. The Yalu River forms part of the northern border with Manchuria.

Government. The elected Supreme People's Assembly, as the chief organ of government, chooses a Presidium and a Cabinet. The Cabinet, which exercises executive authority, is subject to approval by the Assembly and the Presidium.

The Korean Workers (Communist) Party, led by President Kim Il Sung, is the only political party.

History. According to myth, Korea was founded in 2333 B.C. by Tangun. In the 17th century, it became a vassal of China and was isolated from all but Chinese influence and contact until 1876, when Japan forced Korea to negotiate a commercial treaty, opening the land to the U. S. and Europe. Japan achieved control as the result of its war with China (1894–95) and with Russia (1904–05) and annexed Korea in 1910. Japan developed the country but never won over the Korean nationalists.

After the Japanese surrender in 1945, the country was divided into two occupation zones, the U.S.S.R. north of and the U.S. south of the 38th parallel. When the cold war developed between the U.S. and U.S.S.R., trade between the zones was cut off. In 1948, the division between the zones was made permanent with the establishment of separate regimes in the north and south. By mid-1949, the U.S. and U.S.S.R. withdrew all troops. The Democratic People's Republic of Korea (North Korea) was established on May 1, 1948. The Communist Party, headed by Kim Il Sung, was established in power.

On June 25, 1950, the North Korean army launched a surprise attack on South Korea. On June 26, the U.N. Security Council condemned the invasion as aggression and ordered withdrawal of the invading forces. On June 27, President Harry S. Truman ordered air and naval units into action to enforce the U.N. order. The British government did the same, and soon a multinational U.N. command was set up to aid the South Koreans. The North Korean invaders took Seoul and pushed the South Koreans into the southeast corner of their country.

Gen. Douglas MacArthur, U.N. commander, made an amphibious landing at Inchon on September 15 behind the North Korean lines, which resulted in the complete rout of the North Korean army. The U.N. forces drove north across the 38th parallel, approaching the Yalu River. Then Communist China entered the war, forcing the U.N. forces into headlong retreat. Seoul was lost again, then regained; ultimately the war stabilized near the 38th parallel but dragged on for two years while the belligerents negotiated. An armistice was agreed to on July 27, 1953.

President Carter, visiting Seoul from June 29 to July 1, 1979, proposed that the U.S., North Korea, and South Korea meet "to promote dialogue and reduce tensions in the area," possibly leading to re-unification of the two Koreas. Pyongyang's official party newspaper rejected the proposal, saying the North favors reunification talks but without the "alien interference" of the U.S.

Kim again rejected as a "foolish burlesque" an invitation on Jan. 12, 1981, by South Korea's military chief, Chun Doo Hwan, to hold reunification talks in Seoul. Kim refused again when Chun repeated the invitation on March 3 during his inauguration as President of the Southern republic.

In July 1990, North and South Korea signed a historic agreement to meet in September and discuss the easing of political and military confrontations.

KOREA, SOUTH

Republic of Korea
President: Roh Tae Woo (1987)
Premier: Kang Young Hoon (1988)
Area: 38,031 sq mi. (98,500 sq km)
Population (est. mid-1990): 42,100,000 (average annual rate of natural increase: 2.1%)
Density per square mile: 133
Capital: Seoul
Largest cities (est. 1985): Seoul, 9,900,000; Pusan, 3,650,000; Taegu, 2,000,000; Inchon, 1,600,000
Monetary unit: Won
Language: Korean
Religions: Buddhist, 19%; Protestant, 16%; Roman Catholic, 5%
National name: Taehan Min'guk
Literacy rate: 95%
Economic summary: Gross national product (1988): $171 billion; $4,045 per capita; 12% real growth rate. Arable land: 21%; principal products: rice, barley. Labor force: 16,900,000; 27% in mining and manufacturing; major products: clothing and textiles, processed foods, chemical fertilizers, chemicals, automobiles, steel, electronics equipment. Natural resources: iron and copper ore, tungsten, graphite, limestone, coal, gold, silver. Exports: Textiles, automobiles, electric and electronics, ships, and steel. Imports: oil, grains, chemicals, machinery, electronics. Major trading partners: U.S., Japan.

Geography. Slightly larger than Indiana, South Korea lies below the 38th parallel on the Korean peninsula. It is mountainous in the east; in the west and south are many harbors on the mainland and offshore islands.

Government. Constitutional amendments enacted in Sept. 1987 called for direct election of a President, who would be limited to a single five-year term, and increased the powers of the National Assembly *vis a vis* the President.

The National Assembly was expanded from 276 to 299 seats, filled by proportional representation.

History. South Korea came into being in the aftermath of World War II as the result of a 1945 agreement making the 38th parallel the boundary between a northern zone occupied by the U.S.S.R.

and a southern zone occupied by U.S. forces. (For details, *see* North Korea.)

Elections were held in the U.S. zone in 1948 for a national assembly, which adopted a republican Constitution and elected Syngman Rhee president. The new republic was proclaimed on August 15 and was recognized as the legal government of Korea by the U.N. on Dec. 12, 1948.

On June 25, 1950, South Korea was attacked by North Korean Communist forces. U.S. armed intervention was ordered on June 27 by President Harry S. Truman, and on the same day the U.N. invoked military sanctions against North Korea. Gen. Douglas MacArthur was named commander of the U.N. forces. U.S. and South Korean troops fought a heroic holding action but, by the first week of August, they had been forced back to a 4,000-square-mile beachhead in southeast Korea.

There they stood off superior North Korean forces until September 15, when a major U.N. amphibious attack was launched far behind the Communist lines at Inchon, port of Seoul. By September 30, U.N. forces were in complete control of South Korea. They then invaded North Korea and were nearing the Manchurian and Siberian borders when several hundred thousand Chinese Communist troops entered the conflict in late October. U.N. forces were then forced to retreat below the 38th parallel.

On May 24, 1951, U.N. forces recrossed the parallel and had made important new inroads into North Korea when truce negotiations began on July 10. An armistice was finally signed at Panmunjom on July 27, 1953, leaving a devastated Korea in need of large-scale rehabilitation.

The U.S. and South Korea signed a mutual-defense treaty on Oct. 1, 1953.

Rhee, president since 1948, resigned in 1960 in the face of rising disorders. PoSun Yun was elected to succeed him, but political instability continued. In 1961, Gen. Park Chung Hee took power and subsequently built up the country. The U.S. stepped up military aid, building up South Korea's armed forces to 600,000 men. The South Koreans sent 50,000 troops to Vietnam, at U.S. expense.

Park's assassination on Oct. 26, 1979, by Kim Jae Kyu, head of the Korean Central Intelligence Agency, brought a liberalizing trend as Choi Kyu Hah, the new President, freed imprisoned dissidents. The release of opposition leader Kim Dae jung in February 1980 generated anti-government demonstrations that turned into riots by May. Choi resigned on Aug. 16. Chun Doo Wha, head of a military Special Committee for National Security Measures, was the sole candidate as the electoral college confirmed him as President on Aug. 27.

Elected to a full seven-year term on Feb. 11, Chun had visited Washington on Feb. 2 to receive President Reagan's assurance that U.S. troops would remain in South Korea.

Debate over the Presidential succession in 1988 was the main dispute in 1986-87 with Chun wanting election by the electoral college and the opposition demanding a direct popular vote, charging that Chun could manipulate the college. On April 13, 1987, Chun declared a close on the debate but when, in June, he appointed Roh Toe Woo, the DJP chairman as his successor, violent protests broke out. Roh, and later, Chun, agreed that direct elections should be held. A split in the opposition led to Roh's election on Dec. 16, 1987, with 36.6% of the vote.

Legislative elections deprived Roh's DJP of its Assembly majority in April, 1988. Roh declared his

willingness to share leadership posts with the opposition.

In July 1990, North Korea agreed to meet in September and discuss the easing of political and military confrontations.

KUWAIT

State of Kuwait

Emir: Sheik Jaber al-Ahmad al-Sabah[1] (1977)
Prime Minister: Sheik Sa'ad Abdullah al-Salim[1] (1978)
Area: 6,880 sq mi. (17,820 sq km)
Population (est. mid-1990): 2,100,000 (average annual rate of natural increase: 2.5%)
Density per square mile: 304
Capital (est. 1980): Kuwait, 60,525
Largest city (est. 1980): Hawalli, 152,402
Monetary unit: Kuwaiti dinar
Languages: Arabic and English
Religions: Islam
National name: Dawlat al Kuwayt
Literacy rate: about 71%
Economic summary: Gross domestic product (1988): $19.1 billion; $10,410 per capita; 4% real growth rate. Labor force: 566,000 (1986); 45% in services. Major products: crude and refined oil, fertilizer, chemicals, building materials, shrimp. Natural resources: petroleum, fish, shrimp. Exports: crude and refined petroleum, shrimp. Imports: foodstuffs, automobiles, building materials, machinery, textiles. Major trading partners: U.S., Japan, Italy, Netherlands, Iraq, W. Germany.

1. In exile.

Geography. Kuwait is situated northeast of Saudi Arabia at the northern end of the Persian Gulf, south of Iraq. It is slightly larger than Hawaii. The low-lying land is mainly sandy and barren.

Government. Sheik Jaber al-Ahmad al-Sabah rules as Emir of Kuwait and appoints the Prime Minister, who appoints his Cabinet (Council of Ministers). The National Assembly was suspended on July 3, 1986. There are no political parties in Kuwait.

History. Kuwait obtained British protection in 1897 when the Sheik feared that the Turks would take over the area. In 1961, Britain ended the protectorate, giving Kuwait independence, but agreed to give military aid on request. Iraq immediately threatened to occupy the area and Sheik Sabah al-Salem al-Sabah called in British troops in 1961. Soon afterward the Arab League sent in troops, replacing the British. The prize was oil.

Oil was discovered in the 1930s. Kuwait proved to have 20% of the world's known oil resources. It has been a major producer since 1946, the world's second largest oil exporter. The Sheik, who gets half the profits, devotes most of them to the education, welfare, and modernization of his kingdom. In 1966, Sheik Sabah designated a relative, Jaber al-Ahmad al-Sabah, as his successor.

By 1968, the sheikdom had established a model welfare state, and it sought to establish dominance among the sheikdoms and emirates of the Persian Gulf.

A worldwide decline in the price of oil reduced Kuwait's oil income from $18.4 billion in 1980 to only $9 billion in 1983. During the same period Kuwait's support for Iraq in its war with Iran sparked terrorist attacks in Kuwait by radical Shiite Moslem supporters of Iran's Ayatollah Khomeini. The risk of Iranian attack prompted Kuwait to obtain U.S. protection for its tankers in 1987.

In May 1985, a suicide bomber drove into the motorcade of Sheik Jaber al-Ahmad al-Sabah, the ruler. The Sheik escaped with minor cuts and bruises.

In July 1990, Iraq President Hussein blamed Kuwait for falling oil prices. After a failed Arab mediation attempt to solve the dispute peacefully, Iraq invaded Kuwait on Aug. 1, 1990, and set up a pro-Iraqi provisional government. (*See* Current Events for later details.)

LAOS

Lao People's Democratic Republic
President (acting): Phuomi Vongvichit (1986)
Chairman of the Council of Ministers: Kaysone Phomvihane (1975)
Area: 91,429 sq mi. (236,800 sq km)
Population (est. mid-1990): 4,000,000 (average annual rate of natural increase: 2.5%)
Density per square mile: 43
Capital and largest city (est. 1984): Vientiane, 200,000
Monetary unit: Kip
Languages: Lao (official), French, English
Religions: Buddhist, 58%; tribal, 34%
Literacy rate: 85%
Economic summary: Gross domestic product: (1987) $551 million; $140 per capita; 2.2% real growth rate. Arable land: 4%; principal products: rice, corn, vegetables. Labor force: 1–1.5 million; 85–90% in agriculture. Major industrial products: tin, timber, tobacco, textiles, electric power. Natural resources: tin, timber, hydroelectric power. Exports: electric power, forest products, tin concentrates, coffee. Imports: rice, foodstuffs, petroleum products, machinery, transport equipment. Major trading partners: Thailand, Malaysia, Vietnam, China, Japan, France, Vietnam

Geography. A landlocked nation in Southeast Asia occupying the northwestern portion of the Indochinese peninsula, Laos is surrounded by China, Vietnam, Cambodia, Thailand, and Burma. It is twice the size of Pennsylvania.

Laos is a mountainous country, especially in the north, where peaks rise above 8,000 feet (2,438 m). Dense forests cover the northern and eastern areas. The Mekong River, which forms the boundary with Burma and Thailand, flows entirely through the country for 300 miles (483 km) of its course.

Government. Laos is a people's democratic republic with executive power in the hands of the premier. The monarchy was abolished Dec. 2, 1975, when the Pathet Lao ousted a coalition government and King Sisavang Vatthana abdicated. The King was appointed "Supreme Adviser" to the President, the former Prince Souphanouvong. Former Prince Souvanna Phouma, Premier since 1962, was made an "adviser" to the government. The Lao People's Revolutionary Party (Pathet Lao), led by Chairman Kaysone Phomvihane, is the only political party.

History. Laos became a French protectorate in 1893, and the territory was incorporated into the union of Indochina. A strong nationalist movement developed during World War II, but France reestablished control in 1946 and made the King of Luang Prabang constitutional monarch of all Laos. France granted semiautonomy in 1949 and then,

spurred by the Viet Minh rebellion in Vietnam, full independence within the French Union in 1950. In 1951, Prince Souphanouvong organized the Pathet Lao, a Communist independence movement, in North Vietnam. The Viet Minh in 1953 established the Pathet Lao in power at Samneua. Viet Minh and Pathet Lao forces invaded central Laos, and civil war resulted.

By the Geneva agreements of 1954 and an armistice of 1955, two northern provinces were given the Pathet Lao, the royal regime the rest. Full sovereignty was given the kingdom by the Paris agreements of Dec. 29, 1954. In 1957, Prince Souvanna Phouma, the royal Premier, and the Pathet Lao leader, Prince Souphanouvong, the Premier's half-brother, agreed to reestablishment of a unified government, with Pathet Lao participation and integration of Pathet Lao forces into the royal army. The agreement broke down in 1959, and armed conflict broke out again.

In 1960, the struggle became three-way as Gen. Phoumi Nosavan, controlling the bulk of the royal army, set up in the south a pro-Western revolutionary government headed by Prince Boun Gum. General Phoumi took Vientiane in December, driving Souvanna Phouma into exile in Cambodia. The Soviet bloc supported Souvanna Phouma. In 1961, a cease-fire was arranged and the three princes agreed to a coalition government headed by Souvanna Phouma.

But North Vietnam, the U.S. (in the form of Central Intelligence Agency personnel), and China remained active in Laos after the settlement. North Vietnam used a supply line (Ho Chi Minh trail) running down the mountain valleys of eastern Laos into Cambodia and South Vietnam, particularly after the U.S.-South Vietnamese incursion into Cambodia in 1970 stopped supplies via Cambodian seaports.

An agreement, reached in 1973 revived coalition government. The Communist Pathet Lao seized complete power in 1975, installing Souphanouvong as president and Kaysone Phomvihane as premier. Since then other parties and political groups have been moribund and most of their leaders have fled the country.

In July 1985, Laos agreed to help the United States search for U.S. servicemen missing since the Indochina war.

In 1985, border clashes between Laos and Thailand intensified, with over 120 skirmishes reported in 1984 and 1985.

LEBANON

Republic of Lebanon
President: Elias Hrawi (1989)
Premier: Dr. Salim El Hoss (1989)
Area: 4,015 sq mi. (10,400 sq km)
Population (est. mid-1990): 3,300,000 (average annual rate of natural increase: 2.1%)
Density per square mile: 822
Capital: Beirut
Largest cities (est. 1989): Beirut, 500,000; Tripoli, 300,-000
Monetary unit: Lebanese pound
Languages: Arabic (official), French, English
Religions: Islam, approx. 50% (3 sects); Christian, approx. 50% (13 sects)
National name: Al-Joumhouriya al-Lubnaniya
Literacy rate: 75%
Economic summary: Gross domestic product (1985): $1.8 billion. Per capita income: n.a. Arable land: 21%; princi-

pal products: fruits, wheat, corn, barley, potatoes, tobacco, olives, onions. Labor force: 650,000; 79% in industry, commerce and services; major products: processed foods, textiles, cement, chemicals, refined oil. Exports: fruits, vegetables, textiles. Imports: metals, machinery, foodstuffs. Major trading partners: U.S., Western European and Arab countries.

Geography. Lebanon lies at the eastern end of the Mediterranean Sea north of Israel and west of Syria. It is four fifths the size of Connecticut.

The Lebanon Mountains, which parallel the coast on the west, cover most of the country, while on the eastern border is the Anti-Lebanon range. Between the two lies the Bekaa Valley, the principal agricultural area.

Government. Lebanon is governed by a President, elected by Parliament for a six-year term, and a Cabinet of Ministers appointed by the President but responsible to Parliament.

Parliament has 99 members elected for a four-year term by universal suffrage and chosen by proportional division of religious groups.

History. After World War I, France was given a League of Nations mandate over Lebanon and its neighbor Syria, which together had previously been a single political unit in the Ottoman Empire. France divided them in 1920 into separate colonial administrations, drawing a border that separated predominantly Moslem Syria from the kaleidoscope of religious communities in Lebanon in which Maronite Christians were then dominant. After 20 years of the French mandate regime, Lebanon's independence was proclaimed on Nov. 26, 1941, but full independence came in stages. Under an agreement between representatives of Lebanon and the French National Committee of Liberation, most of the powers exercised by France were transferred to the Lebanese government on Jan. 1, 1944. The evacuation of French troops was completed in 1946.

Civil war broke out in 1958, with Moslem factions led by Kamal Jumblat and Saeb Salam rising in insurrection against the Lebanese government headed by President Camille Chamoun, a Maronite Christian. At Chamoun's request, President Eisenhower on July 15 sent U.S. troops to reestablish the government's authority.

Clan warfare between various factions in Lebanon goes back centuries. The hodgepodge includes Maronite Christians, who since independence have dominated the government; Sunni Moslems, who have prospered in business and shared political power; the Druse, a secretive Islamic splinter group; and at the bottom of the heap until recently, Shiite Moslems.

A new—and bloodier—Lebanese civil war that broke out in 1975 resulted in the addition of still another ingredient in the brew—the Syrians. In the fighting between Lebanese factions, 40,000 Lebanese were estimated to have been killed and 100,000 wounded between March 1975 and November 1976. At that point, a Syrian-dominated Arab Deterrent Force intervened and brought large-scale fighting to a halt.

Palestinian guerrillas staging raids on Israel from Lebanese territory drew punitive Israeli raids on Lebanon, and two large-scale Israeli invasions. The Israelis withdrew in June after the U.N. Security Council created a 6,000-man peacekeeping force for the area, called UNIFIL. As they departed, the Israelis turned their strongpoints over to a Christian militia that they had organized, instead of to the U.N. force.

The second Israeli invasion came on June 6, 1982, and this time it was a total one. It was in response to an assassination attempt by Palestinian terrorists on the Israeli ambassador in London.

A U.S. special envoy, Philip C. Habib, negotiated the dispersal of most of the PLO to other Arab nations and Israel pulled back some of its forces. The violence seemed to have come to an end when, on Sept. 14, Bashir Gemayel, the 34-year-old President-elect, was killed by a bomb that destroyed the headquarters of his Christian Phalangist Party.

The day after Gemayel's assassination, Israeli troops moved into west Beirut in force. On Sept. 17 it was revealed that Christian militiamen had massacred hundreds of Palestinians in two refugee camps but Israel denied responsibility.

On Sept. 20, Amin Gemayel, older brother of Bashir Gemayel, was elected President by the parliament.

The massacre in the refugee camps prompted the return of a multinational peacekeeping force composed of U.S. Marines and British, French, and Italian soldiers. Their mandate was to support the central Lebanese government, but they soon found themselves drawn into the struggle for power between different Lebanese factions. During their stay in Lebanon, 260 U.S. Marines and about 60 French soldiers were killed, most of them in suicide bombings of the Marine and French Army compounds on Oct. 23, 1983. The multinational force left in the spring of 1984.

During 1984, Israeli troops remained in southern Lebanon and Syrian troops remained in the Bekaa Valley. By the third anniversary of the invasion, June 6, 1985, all Israeli troops had withdrawn except for several hundred "advisers" to a Christian militia trained and armed by the Israelis.

During 1985, the long-deprived Shiites shouldered aside the traditional urban upper class of Sunni oligarchs as the dominant Moslem faction in west Beirut. The more extremist Shiite factions such as Hizbullah (Party of God), inspired by Iran's Ayatollah Ruhollah Khomeini, wanted to establish an Iranian-style religious state in Lebanon and were virulently anti-Israel and anti-U.S. They later defeated the moderate Amal Faction of the Shiites in Beirut's southern suburbs in 1988. Hizbullah has conducted hit-and-run warfare against the Christian militia and its Israeli advisers in southern Lebanon.

Events since the Israeli withdrawal included Shiite-PLO fighting resulting from PLO attempts to reestablish its old power base in areas now held by Shiite militia.

In July 1986, Syrian observers took position in Beirut to monitor a peacekeeping agreement. The agreement broke down and fighting between Shiite and Druze militia in West Beirut became so intense that Syrian troops moved in force in February 1987, suppressing militia resistance.

Amin Gemayel's Presidency expired on Sept. 23, 1988. The impossibility of setting up elections led Gemayel to designate a government under army chief Gen. Michael Aoun. Aoun's government was rejected by Prime Minister Selim al-Hoss who established a rival government in Muslim West Beirut.

In October 1989, Lebanese Christian and Moslem deputies approved a tentative peace accord and the new National Assembly selected a President. Christian leader Aoun, charging that the accord didn't place enough pressure on the Syrians to withdraw, refused to recognize the new government.

LESOTHO

Kingdom of Lesotho
Sovereign: King Moshoeshoe II (1966)
Chairman, Military Council: Maj. Gen. Justin Lekhanya (1986)
Area: 11,720 sq mi. (30,355 sq km)
Population (est. mid-1990): 1,800,000 (average annual rate of natural increase: 2.8%)
Density per square mile: 147
Capital and largest city (est. 1983): Maseru, 70,000
Monetary unit: Loti
Languages: English and Sesotho (official); also Zulu and Xhosa
Religions: Roman Catholic, 44%; Lesotho Evangelical Church, 30%; Anglican, 12%
Member of Commonwealth of Nations
Literacy rate: 65%
Economic summary: Gross domestic product (1988 est.): $408 million; $245 per capita; 7.3% real growth rate. Arable land: 10%; principal products: corn, wheat, sorghum, barley. Labor force: 689,000; 86.2% in subsistence agriculture. Natural resources: diamonds. Exports: wool, mohair, wheat, cattle, diamonds, hides and skins. Imports: foodstuffs, building materials, clothing, vehicles, machinery. Major trading partner: South Africa.

Geography. Mountainous Lesotho, the size of Maryland, is surrounded by the Republic of South Africa in the east central part of that country except for short borders on the east and south with two discontinuous units of the Republic of Transkei. The Drakensberg Mountains in the east are Lesotho's principal chain. Elsewhere the region consists of rocky tableland.

Government. In January, 1986, following an economic crisis caused by a South African blockade, the military overthrew Chief Johnathan and established a Military Council and a Council of Ministers that would exercise a policy less tolerant of anti-apartheid activists within its borders.

The King has also been given greater powers.

History. Lesotho (formerly Basutoland) was constituted a native state under British protection by a treaty signed with the native chief Moshesh in 1843. It was annexed to Cape Colony in 1871, but in 1884 it was restored to direct control by the Crown.

The colony of Basutoland became the independent nation of Lesotho on Oct. 4, 1966.

In the 1970 elections, Ntsu Mokhehle, head of the Basutoland Congress Party, claimed a victory, but Jonathan declared a state of emergency, suspended the Constitution, and arrested Mokhehle. The major issue in the election was relations with South Africa, with Jonathan for close ties to the surrounding white nation, while Mokhehle was for a more independent policy. Jonathan jailed 45 opposition politicians, declared the King had "technically abdicated" by siding with the opposition party, exiled him to the Netherlands, and named his Queen and her seven-year-old son as Regent.

The King returned after a compromise with Jonathan in which the new Constitution would name him head of state but forbid his participation in politics.

LIBERIA

Republic of Liberia
President: Gen. Samuel K. Doe (1980)
Area: 43,000 sq mi. (111,370 sq km)
Population (est. mid-1990): 2,600,000 (average annual rate of natural increase: 3.2%)
Density per square mile: 58
Capital and largest city (est. 1984): Monrovia, 425,000
Monetary unit: Liberian dollar
Languages: English (official) and tribal dialects
Religions: traditional, 75%; Christian, 10%; Islam, 15%
Literacy rate: 20%
Economic summary: Gross domestic product (1987): $973 million; $410 per capita; 1.7% real growth rate. Arable land: 1%; principal products: rubber, rice, palm oil, cassava, coffee, cocoa. Labor force: 510,000; 4.5% in industry and commerce; major products: iron ore, diamonds, processed rubber, processed food, construction materials. Natural resources: iron ore, rubber, timber, diamonds. Exports: iron ore, rubber, timber, diamonds. Imports: machinery, petroleum products, transport equipment, foodstuffs. Major trading partners: U.S., West Germany, Netherlands, Italy, Belgium.

Geography. Lying on the Atlantic in the southern part of West Africa, Liberia is bordered by Sierra Leone, Guinea, and the Ivory Coast. It is comparable in size to Tennessee.

Most of the country is a plateau covered by dense tropical forests, which thrive under an annual rainfall of about 160 inches a year.

Government. Since April 25, 1980, Liberia had been under military rule by the 17-member People's Redemptive Council, which suspended the Constitution after overthrowing the civilian government. On July 22, 1984, the Council was replaced with an interim, appointed National Assembly in a step toward return of civilian rule.

History. Liberia was founded in 1822 as a result of the efforts of the American Colonization Society to settle freed American slaves in West Africa. In 1847, it became the Free and Independent Republic of Liberia.

The government of Africa's first republic was modeled after that of the United States, and Joseph J. Roberts of Virginia was elected the first president. He laid the foundations of a modern state and initiated efforts, never too successful but pursued for more than a century, to bring the aboriginal inhabitants of the territory to the level of the emigrants. The English-speaking descendants of U.S. blacks, known as Americo-Liberians, were the intellectual and ruling class. The indigenous inhabitants, divided, constitute 99% of the population.

After 1920, considerable progress was made toward opening up the interior, a process that was spurred in 1951 by the establishment of a 43-mile (69-km) railroad to the Bomi Hills from Monrovia.

In July 1971, while serving his sixth term as president, William V. S. Tubman died following surgery and was succeeded by his long-time associate, Vice President William R. Tolbert, Jr.

Tolbert was ousted in a military coup carried out April 12, 1980, by army enlisted men led by Master Sgt. Samuel K. Doe. Tolbert and 27 other high officials were executed. Doe and his colleagues based their action on the grievances of "native" Liberians against corruption and misrule by the Americo-Liberians who had ruled the country since its founding.

In November 1985, an attempted coup against Doe following a disputed re-election, was bloodily put down and the coup leader, a former associate of Doe's, was executed.

A rebellion led by Charles Taylor, a former Doe aide, started in December 1989 and, by mid-July 1990, had taken most of Liberia's key population and economic centers and surrounded the capital.

LIBYA

Socialist People's Libyan Arab Jamahiriya
Head of State: Col. Muammar el-Qaddafi (1969)
Secretary-General of the General People's Committee:
  Omar Mustafa el-Montassir (1987)
Area: 679,536 sq mi. (1,759,998 sq km)
Population (est. mid-1990): 4,200,000 (average annual
  rate of natural increase: 3.1%)
Density per square mile: 6
Capital: Tripoli
Largest cities (est. 1980): Tripoli, 587,400; Benghazi,
  267,700
Monetary unit: Libyan dinar
Language: Arabic
Religion: Islam
National name: Al-Jumhuria al-Arabia al-Libya
Literacy rate: 50%
Economic summary: Gross national product (1988): ca.
  $20 billion, $5,410 per capita; real growth rate: 0%.
  Arable land: 1%; principal products: wheat, barley, olives,
  dates, citrus fruits, peanuts. Labor force: 1,000,000;
  31% in industry; major products: petroleum, processed
  foods, textiles, handicrafts. Natural resources: petroleum,
  natural gas. Export: petroleum. Imports: machinery,
  foodstuffs, manufactured goods. Major trading partners:
  Italy, West Germany, U.K., France, Spain, Japan.

Geography. Libya stretches along the northeastern coast of Africa between Tunisia and Algeria on the west and Egypt on the east; to the south are the Sudan, Chad, and Niger. It is one sixth larger than Alaska.

A greater part of the country lies within the Sahara. Along the Mediterranean coast and farther inland is arable plateau land.

Government. In a bloodless coup d'etat on Sept. 1, 1969, the military seized power in Libya. King Idris I, who had ruled since 1951, was deposed and the Libyan Arab Republic proclaimed. The official name was changed in 1977 to the Socialist People's Libyan Arab Jamahiriya. The Revolutionary Council that had governed since the coup was renamed the General Secretariat of the General People's Congress. The Arab Socialist Union Organization is the only political party.

History. Libya was a part of the Turkish dominions from the 16th century until 1911. Following the outbreak of hostilities between Italy and Turkey in that year, Italian troops occupied Tripoli; Italian sovereignty was recognized in 1912.

Libya was the scene of much desert fighting during World War II. After the fall of Tripoli on Jan. 23, 1943, it came under Allied administration. In 1949, the U.N. voted that Libya should become independent by 1952.

Discovery of oil in the Libyan Desert promised financial stability and funds for economic development.

The Reagan Administration, accusing Libya of supporting international terrorism, closed the Libyan embassy in Washington on May 6, 1981. After talks with Libyan officials in July, the U.S. concluded that no improvement in relations was possible, although U.S. oil companies remained active in Libya and 2,000 U.S. citizens continued to work there.

On Aug. 19, 1981, two U.S. Navy F-14's shot down two Soviet-made SU-22's of the Libyan air force that had attacked them in air space above the Gulf of Sidra, claimed by Libya but held to be international by the U.S. In December, Washington asserted that Libyan "hit squads" had been dispatched to the U.S. and security was drastically tightened around President Reagan and other officials. Reagan requested remaining American citizens to leave Libya and nearly all did by Dec. 15. When the Mobil Oil Company abandoned its operations in April 1982, only four U.S. firms were still in Libya, using Libyan or third-country personnel.

Qaddafi's troops also supported rebels in Chad but suffered major military reverses in 1987.

In December 1985, Qaddafi lauded as "heroic" a terrorist attack on Rome and Vienna airports that killed 20 people.

On March 24, 1986, U.S. and Libyan forces skirmished in the Gulf of Sidra, with two Libyan patrol boats being sunk.

On April 14, after a Libyan-backed attack on a West Berlin disco in which two people, including an American serviceman, were killed, Reagan ordered an air raid on Libyan military installations.

LIECHTENSTEIN

Principality of Liechtenstein
Ruler: Prince Hans Adam (1989)
Prime Minister: Hans Brunhart (1978)
Area: 61 sq mi. (157 sq km)
Population (mid-1989): 28,074 (average annual growth
  rate: 0.8%)
Density per square mile: 459.0
Capital and largest city (est. 1986): Vaduz, 4,920
Monetary unit: Swiss franc
Language: German
Religions: Roman Catholic, 86%; Protestant, 9%
Literacy rate: 100%
Economic summary: Gross national product: $405 million;
  $15,000 per capita (1984). Arable land: 25%; Labor
  force in agriculture: 4%; principal products: livestock,
  vegetables, corn, wheat, potatoes, grapes. Labor force:
  12,258; 54.4% in industry, trade and building; major
  products: high-technology products, building equipment,
  food products, machinery, industrial goods. Natural
  resources: timber, hydroelectric power, salt. Exports:
  manufactured metal products, machines and instruments,
  chemical products. Imports: raw materials, machinery,
  processed foods and goods. Major trading partners:
  Switzerland and other Western European countries.

Geography. Tiny Liechtenstein, not quite as large as Washington, D.C., lies on the east bank of the Rhine River south of Lake Constance between Austria and Switzerland. It consists of low valley land and Alpine peaks. Falknis (8,401 ft; 2,561 m) and Naatkopf (8,432 ft; 2,570 m) are the tallest.

Government. The Constitution of 1921, amended in 1972, provides for a legislature, the Landtag, of 25 members elected by direct male suffrage.

History. Founded in 1719, Liechtenstein was a member of the German Confederation from 1815 to 1866, when it became an independent principality. It abolished its army in 1868 and has managed to stay neutral and undamaged in all European wars since then. In a referendum on July 1, 1984, male voters granted women the right to vote, a victory for Prince Hans Adam.

LUXEMBOURG

Grand Duchy of Luxembourg
Ruler: Grand Duke Jean (1964)
Premier: Jacques Santer (1984)
Area: 999 sq mi. (2,586 sq km)
Population (est. mid-1990): 400,000 (average annual rate of natural increase: 0.2%)
Density per square mile: 379
Capital and largest city (est. 1982): Luxembourg, 80,000
Monetary unit: Luxembourg franc
Languages: Luxermbourgish, French, German
Religion: Mainly Roman Catholic
National name: Grand-Duché de Luxembourg
Literacy rate: 100%
Economic summary: Gross national product (1988 est.): $4.9 billion; $13,380 per capita; 3% real growth rate. Arable land: 24%; principal products: livestock, dairy products, wine. Labor force: 161,000; 24.7% in industry; major products: banking, steel, plastics, synthetic fibers. Natural resource: Iron ore. Exports: steel, plastics, chemicals, textiles. Imports: machinery, chemicals, consumer goods. Major trading partners: European Common Market countries.

Geography. Luxembourg is a neighbor of Belgium on the west, West Germany on the east, and France on the south. The Ardennes Mountains extend from Belgium into the northern section of Luxembourg.

Government. Luxembourg's unicameral legislature, the Chamber of Deputies, consists of 59 members elected for five years.

History. Sigefroi, Count of Ardennes, an offspring of Charlemagne, was Luxembourg's first sovereign ruler. In 1060, the country came under the rule of the House of Luxembourg. From the 15th to the 18th century, Spain, France, and Austria held it in turn. The Congress of Vienna in 1815 made it a Grand Duchy and gave it to William I, King of the Netherlands. In 1839 the Treaty of London ceded the western part of Luxembourg to Belgium.

The eastern part, continuing in personal union with the Netherlands and a member of the German Confederation, became autonomous in 1848 and a neutral territory by decision of the London Conference of 1867, governed by its Grand Duke. Germany occupied the duchy in World Wars I and II. Allied troops liberated the enclave in 1944.

In 1961, Prince Jean, son and heir of Grand Duchess Charlotte, was made head of state, acting for his mother. She abdicated in 1964, and Prince Jean became Grand Duke. Grand Duchess Charlotte died in 1985.

By a customs union between Belgium and Luxembourg, which came into force on May 1, 1922, to last for 50 years, customs frontiers between the two countries were abolished. On Jan. 1, 1948, a customs union with Belgium and the Netherlands (Benelux) came into existence. On Feb. 3, 1958, it became an economic union.

MADAGASCAR

Democratic Republic of Madagascar
President and Head of State: Didier Ratsiraka (1975)
Prime Minister: Lt. Col. Victor Ramahatra (1988)
Area: 226,660 sq mi. (587,050 sq km)
Population (est. mid-1990): 12,000,000 (average annual rate of natural increase: 3.2%)
Density per square mile: 51
Capital and largest city (est. 1983): Antananarivo, 700,000
Monetary unit: Malagasy franc
Languages: Malagasy, French
Ethnic groups: Merina (or Hova), Betsimisaraka, Betsileo, Tsimihety, Antaisaka, Sakalava, Antandroy
Religions: traditional, 47%; Roman Catholic, 26%; Protestant, 23%; Islam, 2%
National name: Repoblika Demokratika Malagasy
Literacy rate: 53%
Economic summary: Gross domestic product (1987): $2.1 billion; $195 per capita; 1.4% real growth rate. Arable land: 4%; principal products: rice, livestock, coffee, vanilla, sugar, cloves, cotton, sisal, peanuts, tobacco. Labor force: 4,900,000; 90% in subsistence agriculture. Major industrial products: processed food, textiles, assembled automobiles, soap, mining products. Natural resources: graphite, chromium, ilmenite, semiprecious stones. Exports: coffee, cloves, vanilla, graphite, cotton products. Imports: consumer goods, foodstuffs, crude petroleum. Major trading partners: France, U.S., U.S.S.R., Indonesia.

Geography. Madagascar lies in the Indian Ocean off the southeast coast of Africa opposite Mozambique. The world's fourth-largest island, it is twice the size of Arizona. The country's low-lying coastal area gives way to a central plateau. The once densely wooded interior has largely been cut down.

Government. The Constitution of Dec. 30, 1975, approved by referendum following a military coup, provides for direct election by universal suffrage of a president for a seven-year term, a Supreme Council of the Revolution as a policy-making body, a unicameral People's National Assembly of 137 members (elected for five-year terms), and a military Committee for Development. The new constitution followed a period of martial rule that began with the suspension of the republic's original bicameral legislature in 1972.

History. The present population is of black and Malay stock, with perhaps some Polynesian, called Malagasy. The French took over a protectorate in 1885, and then in 1894–95 ended the monarchy, exiling Queen Rànavàlona III to Algiers. A colonial administration was set up, to which the Comoro Islands were attached in 1908, and other territories later. In World War II, the British occupied Madagascar, which retained ties to Vichy France.

An autonomous republic within the French Community since 1958, Madagascar became an independent member of the Community in 1960. In

May 1973, an army coup led by Maj. Gen. Gabriel Ramanantsoa ousted Philibert Tsiranana, president since 1959.

With unemployment and inflation both high, Ramanantsoa resigned Feb. 5, 1975. His leftist-leaning successor, Interior Minister Richard Ratsimandrava, an Army lieutenant colonel, was killed six days later by a machine-gun ambush in Antananarivo, the capital.

The government was subsequently taken over by a 18-member Supreme Council of the Revolution, which ruled by modified martial law and suspended political party activities.

On June 15, 1975, Comdr. Didier Ratsiraka was named President. He announced that he would follow a socialist course and, after nationalizing banks and insurance companies, declared all mineral resources nationalized.

with the Arab slavers in 1887–89. After Britain annexed the Nyasaland territory in 1891, making it a protectorate in 1892, Sir Harry Johnstone, the first high commissioner, using Royal Navy gunboats, wiped out the slavers.

Nyasaland became the independent nation of Malawi on July 6, 1964. Two years later, it became a republic within the Commonwealth of Nations.

Dr. Hastings K. Banda, Malawi's first Prime Minister, became its first President. He pledged to follow a policy of "discretionary nonalignment." Banda alienated much of black Africa by maintaining good relations with South Africa. He argued that his landlocked country had to rely on South Africa for access to the sea and trade.

MALAWI

Republic of Malawi
President: Hastings Kamuzu Banda (1966)
Area: 45,747 sq mi. (118,484 sq km)
Population (est. mid-1990): 9,200,000 (average annual rate of natural increase: 3.4%)
Density per square mile: 168.3
Capital (est. 1986): Lilongwe, 202,900
Largest city (est. 1986): Blantyre, 378,100
Monetary unit: Kwacha
Languages: English and Chichewa (National); also Tombuka
Religions: Christian, 57%; traditional, 19%; Islam, 16%
Member of Commonwealth of Nations
Literacy rate: 25%
Economic summary: Gross domestic product (1986): $1.2 billion; $170 per capita; growth rate: −0.3%. Arable land: 25%; principal products: tobacco, tea, sugar, corn, peanuts. Labor force: 428,000 wage earners; 16% in manufacturing; major products: food, beverages, tobacco, textiles, processed wood, consumer goods. Natural resource: limestone. Exports: tobacco, sugar, tea. Imports: machinery, transport equipment, building and construction materials, fuel. Major trading partners: U.K., U.S., Japan, West Germany, South Africa.

Geography. Malawi is a landlocked country the size of Pennsylvania in southeastern Africa, surrounded by Mozambique, Zambia, and Tanzania. Lake Malawi, formerly Lake Nyasa, occupies most of the country's eastern border. The north-south Rift Valley is flanked by mountain ranges and high plateau areas.

Government. Under a Constitution that came into effect on July 6, 1966, the president is the sole head of state; there is neither a prime minister nor a vice president. The National Assembly has 107 members.

There is only one national party—the Malawi Congress Party led by President Hastings K. Banda, who was designated President for life in 1970.

History. The first European to make extensive explorations in the area was David Livingstone in the 1850s and 1860s. In 1884, Cecil Rhodes's British South African Company received a charter to develop the country. The company came into conflict

MALAYSIA

Paramount Ruler: Azlan Muhibuddin Shah, Sultan of Perak (1989)
Prime Minister: D.S. Mahathir Bin Mohamed (1981)
Area: 128,328 sq mi. (332,370 sq km)
Population (est. mid-1990): 17,900,000 (average annual rate of natural increase: 2.5%)
Density per square mile: 137
Capital: Kuala Lumpur
Largest cities (est. 1980 by U.N.): Kuala Lumpur, 1,000,-000; George Town (Pinang), 300,000; Ipoh, 275,000
Monetary unit: Ringgit
Languages: Malay (official), Chinese, Tamil, English
Religions: Islam, (official), 53%; Buddhist, 17%; Chinese folk religions, 12%; Hindu, 7%; Christian, 6%
Member of Commonwealth of Nations
Literacy rate: 65%
Economic summary: Gross domestic product (1988 est.): $34.3 billion; $2,092 per capita; 7.4% real growth rate. Arable land: 3%; principal products: rice, rubber, palm products. Labor force: 6,090,000; 14.6% in manufacturing. Major industrial products: processed rubber, timber, and palm oil, tin, petroleum, light manufactures, electronics equipment. Natural resources: tin, oil, copper, timber. Exports: natural rubber, palm oil, tin, timber, petroleum. Imports: machinery, transport equipment, chemicals. Major trading partners: Japan, Singapore, U.S., Western European countries.

Geography. Malaysia is at the southern end of the Malay Peninsula in southeast Asia. The nation also includes Sabah and Sarawak on the island of Borneo to the southeast. Its area slightly exceeds that of New Mexico.

Most of Malaysia is covered by dense jungle and swamps, with a mountain range running the length of the peninsula. Extensive forests provide ebony, sandalwood, teak, and other woods.

Government. Malaysia is a sovereign constitutional monarchy within the Commonwealth of Nations. The Paramount Ruler is elected for a five-year term by the hereditary rulers of the states from among themselves. He is advised by the prime minister and his cabinet. There is a bicameral legislature. The Senate, whose role is comparable more to that of the British House of Lords than to the U.S. Senate, has 68 members, partly appointed by the Paramount Ruler to represent minority and special interests, and partly elected by the legislative assemblies of the various states.

The House of Representatives, is made up of 180

members, who are elected for five-year terms.

History. Malaysia came into existence on Sept. 16, 1963, as a federation of Malaya, Singapore, Sabah (North Borneo), and Sarawak. In 1965, Singapore withdrew from the federation. Since 1966, the 11 states of former Malaya have been known as West Malaysia, and Sabah and Sarawak have been known as East Malaysia.

The Union of Malaya was established April 1, 1946, being formed from the Federated Malay States of Negri Sembilan, Pahang, Perak, and Selangor; the Unfederated Malay States of Johore, Kedah, Kelantan, Perlis, and Trengganu; and two of the Straits Settlements—Malacca and Penang. The Malay states had been brought under British administration during the late 19th and early 20th centuries.

It became the Federation of Malaya on Feb. 1, 1948, and the Federation attained full independence within the Commonwealth of Nations in 1957.

Sabah, constituting the extreme northern portion of the island of Borneo, was a British protectorate administered under charter by the British North Borneo Company from 1881 to 1946, when it assumed the status of a colony. It was occupied by Japanese troops from 1942 to 1945.

Sarawak extends along the northwestern coast of Borneo for about 500 miles (805 km). In 1841, part of the present territory was granted by the Sultan of Brunei to Sir James Brooke. Sarawak continued to be ruled by members of the Brooke family until the Japanese occupation.

From 1963, when Malaysia became independent, it was the target of guerrilla infiltration from Indonesia, but beat off invasion attempts. In 1966, when Sukarno fell and the Communist Party was liquidated in Indonesia, hostilities ended.

In the late 1960s, the country was torn by communal rioting directed against Chinese and Indians, who controlled a disproportionate share of the country's wealth. Beginning in 1968, the government moved to achieve greater economic balance through a rural development program.

Malaysia felt the impact of the "boat people" fleeing Vietnam early in 1978. Because the refugees were mostly ethnic Chinese, the government was apprehensive about any increase of a minority that previously had been the source of internal conflict in the country. In April 1988, it announced that starting in April 1989 it would accept no more refugees.

In April 1987, Prime Minister Mahathir barely fended off a challenge that would have removed him as head of his party.

MALDIVES

Republic of Maldives
President: Maumoon Abdul Gayoom (1978)
Area: 115 sq mi. (298 sq km)
Population (est. mid-1990): 200,000 (average annual rate of natural increase: 3.7%)
Density per square mile: 1,822
Capital and largest city (est. 1985): Malé, 53,800
Monetary unit: Maldivian rufiyaa
Language: Divehi
Religion: Islam
Literacy rate: 94%
Economic summary: Gross domestic product (1987): $69.7

million; $440 per capita; 9% real growth rate. Arable land: 10%. Principal agricultural products: coconuts, tropical fruits. Labor force: 66,000; 80% in fishing. Major products: fish, processed coconuts, bananas. Natural resource: fish, coconuts. Export: fish, clothing, ambergris. Imports: rice, wheat, sugar, petroleum products. Major trading partners: Sri Lanka, Singapore, U.S., Thailand, U.K.

Geography. The Republic of Maldives is a group of atolls in the Indian Ocean about 417 miles (671 km) southwest of Sri Lanka. Its 1,300 coral islets stretch over an area of 35,200 square miles (90,000 sq km).

Government. The 9-member Cabinet is headed by the president. The Majlis (Parliament) is a unicameral legislature consisting of 48 members. Eight of these are appointed by the president. The others are elected for five-year terms, 2 from the capital island of Malé and 2 from each of the 19 administrative atolls.

There are no political parties in the Maldives.

History. The Maldives (formerly called the Maldive Islands) are inhabited by an Islamic seafaring people. Originally the islands were under the suzerainty of Ceylon. They came under British protection in 1887 and were a dependency of the then colony of Ceylon until 1948. The independence agreement with Britain was signed July 26, 1965.

For centuries a sultanate, the islands adopted a republican form of government in 1952, but the sultanate was restored in 1954. In 1968, however, as the result of a referendum, a republic was again established in the islands.

Ibrahim Nasir, president since 1968, was removed from office by the Majlis in November 1978 and replaced by Maumoon Abdul Cayoom. A national referendum confirmed the new leader.

MALI

Republic of Mali
President of the Republic: Gen. Moussa Traoré (1969)
Area: 478,819 sq mi. (1,240,142 sq km)
Population (est. mid-1990): 8,100,000 (average annual rate of natural increase: 3%)
Density per square mile: 19
Capital and largest city (est. 1981): Bamako, 750,000
Monetary unit: Franc CFA
Ethnic groups: Bambara, Peul, Soninke, Malinke, Songhai, Dogon, Senoufo, Minianka, Berbers, and Moors
Languages: French (official), African languages
Religions: Islam, 90%; traditional, 9%; Christian, 1%
National name: République de Mali
Literacy rate: 10%
Economic summary: Gross domestic product (1986): $1.7 billion; $180 per capita; 9.6% real growth rate. Arable land: 2%; Principal agricultural products: millet, sorghum, corn, rice, sugar, cotton, peanuts, livestock. Labor force: 3,100,000; 80% in agriculture. Major industrial products: consumer goods, phosphates, gold, fish. Natural resources: bauxite, iron ore, maganese, phosphate, salt, limestone, gold. Exports: livestock, peanuts, dried fish, cotton, skins. Imports: textiles, vehicles, petroleum products, machinery, sugar, cereals. Major trading partners: Western Europe; also U.S.S.R., and China.

Geography. Most of Mali, in West Africa, lies in the Sahara. A landlocked country four fifths the size of

Alaska, it is bordered by Guinea, Senegal, Mauritania, Algeria, Niger, Burkina Faso, and the Ivory Coast.

The only fertile area is in the south, where the Niger and Senegal Rivers provide irrigation.

Government. The army overthrew the government on Nov. 19, 1968, and formed a provisional government. The Military Committee of National Liberation consists of 14 members and forms the decision-making body.

In late 1969 an attempted coup was foiled, and Lt. Moussa Traoré, president of the Military Committee took over as chief of state and later as head of government, ousting Capt. Yoro Diakité as Premier.

The Malian People's Democratic Union, established in 1976, is the only political party.

History. Subjugated by France by the end of the 19th century, this area became a colony in 1904 (named French Sudan in 1920) and in 1946 became part of the French Union. On June 20, 1960, it became independent and, under the name of Sudanese Republic, was federated with the Republic of Senegal in the Mali Federation. However, Senegal seceded from the Federation on Aug. 20, 1960, and the Sudanese Republic then changed its name to the Republic of Mali on September 22.

In the 1960s, Mali concentrated on economic development, continuing to accept aid from both Soviet bloc and Western nations, as well as international agencies. In the late 1960s, it began retreating from close ties with China. But a purge of conservative opponents brought greater power to President Modibo Keita, and in 1968 the influence of the Chinese and their Malian sympathizers increased. By a treaty signed in Peking in 1968, China agreed to help build a railroad from Mali to Guinea, providing Mali with vital access to the sea.

Mali, with Mauritania, the Ivory Coast, Senegal, Dahomey (Benin), Niger, and Burkina Faso signed a treaty establishing the Economic Community for West Africa.

A six-year sub-Sahara drought devastated Mali before disastrously heavy rains began in 1974. Emergency shipments from a dozen nations and international organizations helped alleviate a famine that affected 1.8 million Malians and killed thousands.

Mali and Burkina Faso fought a brief border war from December 25 to 29, 1985.

Economic summary: Gross domestic product (1987): $1.6 billion; $4,310 per capita; 6% real growth rate. Arable land: 38%; principal products: potatoes, wheat, barley, citrus, vegetables, hogs, poultry. Labor force: 125,674; 24% in manufacturing; major products: textiles, wine, beer, processed foods, plastics, electronic equipment. Natural resources: limestone, salt. Exports: textiles, yarns, manufactured goods, ships, printed matter, electronic products. Imports: manufactured goods, machinery, transport equipment. Major trading partners: West Germany, U.K., Italy.

Geography. The five Maltese islands—with a combined land area smaller than Philadelphia—are in the Mediterranean about 60 miles (97 km) south of the southeastern tip of Sicily.

Government. The government is headed by a Prime Minister, responsible to a 69-member House of Representatives elected by universal suffrage.

The major political parties are the Nationalists (35 of 69 seats in the House,) led by Prime Minister Edward Fenech Adami; Malta Labor Party (34 seats), led by Carmelo Mifsud Bonnici.

History. The strategic importance of Malta was recognized by the Phoenicians, who occupied it, as did in their turn the Greeks, Carthaginians, and Romans. The apostle Paul was shipwrecked there in A.D. 58.

The Knights of St. John (Malta), who obtained the three habitable Maltese islands of Malta, Gozo, and Comino from Charles V in 1530, reached their highest fame when they withstood an attack by superior Turkish forces in 1565.

Napoleon seized Malta in 1798, but the French forces were ousted by British troops the next year, and British rule was confirmed by the Treaty of Paris in 1814.

Malta was heavily attacked by German and Italian aircraft during World War II, but was never invaded by the Axis.

Malta became an independent nation on Sept. 21, 1964, and a republic Dec. 13, 1974, but remained in the British Commonwealth. The Governor-General, Sir Anthony Mamo, was sworn in as first president and Dom Mintoff became prime minister.

After 13 years in office, Mintoff resigned as Prime Minister on Dec. 22, 1984, giving way to chosen successor, Carmelo Mifsud Bonnici, who had been Senior Deputy Prime Minister. Fenech Adami's election ended 16 years of Labor rule.

MALTA

Republic of Malta
President: Dr. Vincent Tabone (1989)
Prime Minister: Edward Fenech Adami (1987)
Area: 122 sq mi. (316 sq km)
Population (est. mid-1990): 400,000 (average annual rate of natural increase: 0.8%)
Density per square mile: 2,833
Capital (est. 1987): Valetta, 9,300
Largest city (est. 1987): Birkirkara, 20,300
Monetary unit: Maltese lira
Languages: Maltese and English
Religion: Roman Catholic
National name: Repubblika Ta Malta
Member of Commonwealth of Nations
Literacy rate: 83%

MAURITANIA

Islamic Republic of Mauritania
Chief of State and Head of Government: Col. Maaouye Ould Sidi Ahmed Taya (1984)
Area: 397,953 sq mi. (1,030,700 sq km)
Population (est. mid-1990): 2,000,000 (average annual rate of natural increase: 2.7%)
Density per square mile: 5.3
Capital and largest city (est. 1981): Nouakchott, 175,000
Monetary unit: Ouguyia
Ethnic groups: Moors, Black/moor mix, 70%; Blacks, 30%.
Languages: Arabic and French
Religion: Islam
National name: République Islamique de Mauritanie

Literacy rate: 17%
Economic summary: Gross domestic product: $843 million; $440 per capita; 2.7% real growth rate. Arable land: 1%; Principal agricultural products: livestock, millet, maize, wheat, dates, rice. Labor force: 465,000 (1981 est.); 45,000 wage earners; 14% in industry and commerce. Major industrial products: iron ore, processed fish. Natural resources: copper, iron ore, gypsum, fish. Exports: iron ore, fish, copper. Imports: foodstuffs, petroleum, capital goods. Major trading partners: France, Western Europe, Senegal, U.S.

Geography. Mauritania, three times the size of Arizona, is situated in northwest Africa with about 350 miles (592 km) of coastline on the Atlantic Ocean. It is bordered by Morocco on the north, Algeria and Mali on the east, and Senegal on the south.

The country is mostly desert, with the exception of the fertile Senegal River valley in the south and grazing land in the north.

Government. An Army coup on July 10, 1978, deposed Moktar Ould Daddah, who had been President since Mauritania's independence in 1960. President Mohammed Khouna Ould Haidala, who seized power in the 1978 coup, was in turn deposed in a Dec. 12, 1984, coup by army chief of staff Maaouye Ould Sidi Ahmed Taya, who assumed the title of President.

History. Mauritania was first explored by the Portuguese. The French organized the area as a territory in 1904.

Mauritania became an independent nation on Nov. 28, 1960, and was admitted to the United Nations in 1961 over the strenuous opposition of Morocco, which claimed the territory. With Moors, Arabs, Berbers, and blacks frequently in conflict, the government in the late 1960s sought to make Arab culture dominant to unify the land.

Mauritania acquired administrative control of the southern part of the former Spanish Sahara when the colonial administration withdrew in 1975, under an agreement with Morocco and Spain. Mauritanian troops moved into the territory but encountered resistance from the Polisario Front, a Saharan independence movement backed by Algeria. The task of trying to pacify the area proved a heavy burden. Mauritania signed a peace agreement with the Polisario insurgents in August 1979, withdrew from the territory and renounced territorial claims.

Increased military spending and rising casualties in Western Sahara contributed to the discontent that brought down the civilian government of Ould Daddah in 1978. A succession of military rulers has followed.

MAURITIUS

Sovereign: Queen Elizabeth II
Governor-General: Sir Veerasamy Ringadoo (1986)
Prime Minister: Aneerood Jugnauth (1982)
Area: 787 sq mi. (2,040 sq km)
Population (est. mid-1990): 1,100,000 (average annual rate of natural increase: 1.3%)
Density per square mile: 1,419
Capital and largest city (est. 1980): Port Louis, 155,000
Monetary unit: Mauritian rupee
Languages: English (official), French, Creole, Hindi, Urdu, Chinese

Religions: Hindu, 52%, Roman Catholic, 26%; Islam, 13%
Member of Commonwealth of Nations
Literacy rate: 83%
Economic summary: Gross domestic product (1987 est.): $1.3 billion; $1,280 per capita; 5.4% real growth rate (FY87 est). Arable land: 54%; principal products: sugar cane, tea. Labor force: 335,000; 22% in manufacturing; major products: processed sugar and tea, molasses, rum, textiles. Natural resources: fish. Exports: sugar, tea, textiles. Imports: foodstuffs, manufactured goods. Major trading partners: U.K., France, S. Africa, U.S.

Geography. Mauritius is a mountainous island in the Indian Ocean east of Madagascar.

Government. Mauritius is a member of the British Commonwealth, with Queen Elizabeth II as head of state. She is represented by a governor-general, who chooses the prime minister from the unicameral Legislative Assembly. The Legislative Assembly has 70 members, 62 of whom are elected by direct suffrage. The remaining 8 are chosen from among the unsuccessful candidates.

History. Mauritius was seized from France by British troops in 1810 and ceded to Britain by the Treaty of Paris in 1814. Until 1903, Mauritius and the Seychelles were administered as a single colony. The colony of Mauritius became an independent nation on March 12, 1968.

The nation has an Indian majority, descendants of laborers imported from India to work the sugar plantations after the abolition of slavery in 1834. The native blacks speak French and are Roman Catholics.

The Labor Party government of Sir Seewoosagur Ramgoolam, who had ruled Mauritius since independence, was toppled in a 1982 election by the Movement Militant Mauricien, which had campaigned for recovery of Diego Garcia island, separated from Mauritius during the colonial period and leased by Britain to the United States for a naval base. But an Alliance Party coalition, including the Labor Party, regained power at the end of 1983 and brought back Ramgoolam as Prime Minister. He was succeeded by Aneerood Jugnauth of his party in 1982.

MEXICO

United Mexican States
President: Carlos Salinas de Gortari (1988)
Area: 761,600 sq mi. (1,972,547 sq km)
Population (est. mid-1990): 88,600,000 (average annual rate of natural increase: 2.4%)
Density per square mile: 40
Capital: Federal District (Mexico City)
Largest cities (1989): Federal District, 19,479,000; Guadalajara, 3,186,500; Monterey, 2,858,800; Puebla, 1,707,000; Leon, 1,006,700
Monetary unit: Peso
Languages: Spanish, Indian languages
Religion: Mostly Roman Catholic
Official name: Estados Unidos Mexicanos
Literacy rate: 88%
Economic summary: Gross domestic product (1987): $135.9 billion; $1,640 per capita; 1.4% real growth

rate. Arable land: 12%;principal products: corn, cotton, sugar cane, fruits, sorghum, wheat, frijol, soybeans, milled rice, barley, cartamo. Labor force: 26,100,000 (1988); 12.8% in manufacturing; major products: processed foods, chemicals, basic metals and metal products, petroleum. Natural resources: petroleum, silver, copper, gold, lead, zinc, natural gas, timber. Exports: cotton, shrimp, cattle and meat, coffee, machinery, petroleum, plastic materials, silver ingots, fruits and vegetables. Imports: machinery, equipment, industrial vehicles, intermediate goods. Major trading partners: U.S., Japan, Western European countries.

Geography. The United States' neighbor to the south, Mexico is about one fifth its size. Baja California in the west, an 800-mile (1,287-km) peninsula, forms the Gulf of California. In the east are the Gulf of Mexico and the Bay of Campeche, which is formed by Mexico's other peninsula, the Yucatán.

The center of Mexico is a great, high plateau, open to the north, with mountain chains on east and west and with ocean-front lowlands lying outside of them.

Government. The President, who is popularly elected for six years and is ineligible to succeed himself, governs with a Cabinet of secretaries. Congress has two houses—a 400-member Chamber of Deputies, elected for three years, and a 64-member Senate, elected for six years.

Each of the 31 states has considerable autonomy, with a popularly elected governor, a legislature, and a local judiciary. The President of Mexico appoints the mayor of the Federal District.

History. At least two civilized races—the Mayas and later the Toltecs—preceded the wealthy Aztec empire, conquered in 1519–21 by the Spanish under Hernando Cortés. Spain ruled for the next 300 years until 1810 (the date was Sept. 16 and is now celebrated as Independence Day), when the Mexicans first revolted. They continued the struggle and finally won independence in 1821.

From 1821 to 1877, there were two emperors, several dictators, and enough presidents and provisional executives to make a new government on the average of every nine months. Mexico lost Texas (1836), and after defeat in the war with the U.S. (1846–48) it lost the area comprising the present states of California, Nevada, and Utah, most of Arizona and New Mexico, and parts of Wyoming and Colorado.

In 1855, the Indian patriot Benito Juárez began a series of liberal reforms, including the disestablishment of the Catholic Church, which had acquired vast property. A subsequent civil war was interrupted by the French invasion of Mexico (1861), the crowning of Maximilian of Austria as Emperor (1864), and then his overthrow and execution by forces under Juárez, who again became President in 1867.

The years after the fall of the dictator Porfirio Diaz (1877–80 and 1884–1911) were marked by bloody political-military strife and trouble with the U.S., culminating in the punitive expedition into northern Mexico (1916–17) in unsuccessful pursuit of the revolutionary Pancho Villa. Since a brief period of civil war in 1920, Mexico has enjoyed a period of gradual agricultural, political, and social reforms. Relations with the U.S. were again disturbed in 1938 when all foreign oil wells were expropri-

ated. Agreement on compensation was finally reached in 1941.

The last year of José López Portillo's presidency was shadowed by economic problems caused by falling oil prices.

Miguel de la Madrid Hurtado, candidate of the ruling Partido Revolucionario Institucional, won the July 4 election for a six-year term.

During 1983 and 1984, Mexico suffered its worst financial crisis in 50 years, leading to critically high unemployment and an inability to pay its foreign debt. The collapse of oil prices in 1986 cut into Mexico's export earnings and worsened the situation.

In an election held on July 7, 1985, the ruling Institutional Party declared it had won all seven contested governorships and an overwhelming majority in the national Chamber of Deputies. Accusations of vote fraud by the ruling party intensified after state elections in 1986 in which it claimed a victory amidst reports of election irregularities such as ballot stuffing.

Although the PRI's candidate, Carlos Salinas de Gortari, won the presidential election, the opposition parties on the left and the right showed unprecedented strength. This continued in mid-1989 when the ruling PRI acknowledged an unprecedented defeat in a gubernatorial election.

MONACO

Principality of Monaco
Ruler: Prince Rainier III (1949)
Minister of State: Jean Ausseil (1986)
Area: 0.73 sq mi. (465 acres)
Population (1989): 28,188 (average annual growth rate: .9%)
Density per square mile: 38,356.2
Capital: Monaco-Ville
Monetary unit: French franc
Languages: French, Monégasque, Italian
Religion: Roman Catholic
National name: Principauté de Monaco
Literacy rate: 99%

Geography. Monaco is a tiny, hilly wedge driven into the French Mediterranean coast nine miles east of Nice.

Government. Prince Albert of Monaco gave the principality a Constitution in 1911, creating a National Council of 18 members popularly elected for five years. The head of government is the Minister of State.

Prince Rainier III, born May 31, 1923, succeeded his grandfather, Louis II, on the latter's death, May 9, 1949. Rainier was married April 18, 1956, to Grace Kelly, U.S. actress. A daughter, Princess Caroline Louise Marguerite, was born on Jan. 23, 1957 (married to Philippe Junot June 28, 1978 and divorced in 1980; married to Stefano Casiraghi Dec. 29, 1983, and gave birth to a son, Andrea Albert, June 9, 1984); a son, Prince Albert Louis Pierre, on March 14, 1958; and Princess Stéphanie Marie Elisabeth, on Feb. 1, 1965. Princess Grace died Sept. 14, 1982, of injuries received the day before when the car she was driving went off the road near Monte Carlo. She was 52. Her daughter Stéphanie suffered neck injuries.

The special significance attached to the birth of descendants to Prince Rainier stems from a clause in the Treaty of July 17, 1919, between France and Monaco stipulating that in the event of vacancy of the Crown, the Monégasque territory would become an autonomous state under a French protectorate.

The National and Democratic Union (all 18 seats in National Council), led by Auguste Medecin, is the only political party.

History. The Phoenicians, and after them the Greeks, had a temple on the Monacan headland honoring Hercules. From *Monoikos*, the Greek surname for this mythological strong man, the principality took its name. After being independent for 800 years, Monaco was annexed to France in 1793 and was placed under Sardinia's protection in 1815. In 1861, it went under French guardianship but continued to be independent.

By a treaty in 1918, France stipulated that the French government be given a veto over the succession to the throne.

Monaco is a little land of pleasure with a tourist business that runs as high as 1.5 million visitors a year. It had popular gaming tables as early as 1856. Five years later, a 50-year concession to operate the games was granted to François Blanc, of Bad Homburg. This concession passed into the hands of a private company in 1898.

Monaco's practice of providing a tax shelter for French businessmen resulted in a dispute between the countries. When Rainier refused to end the practice, France retaliated with a customs tax. In 1967, Rainier took control of the Société des Bains de Mer, operator of the famous Monte Carlo gambling casino, in a program to increase hotel and convention space. He paid $8 million to Greek shipping magnate Aristotle Onassis for his shares.

MONGOLIA

Mongolian People's Republic
Chairman of Presidium of the Great People's Khural (President): Punsalmaagiyn Ochirbat (1990)
Chairman of Council of Ministers (Premier): Sharavyn Gunjaadarj (1990)
Area: 604,250 sq mi. (1,565,000 sq km)
Population (est. mid-1990): 2,200,000 (average annual rate of natural increase: 2.8%)
Density per square mile: 4
Capital and largest city (est. 1985): Ulan Bator, 488,200
Monetary unit: Tugrik
Language: Mongolian
Religion: Lamaistic Buddhism
National name: Bugd Nairamdakh Mongol Ard Uls
Literacy rate: about 90%
Economic summary: Gross domestic product (1985 est.): $1.7 billion; $880 per capita (1985 est.); 3.6% real growth rate. Arable land: 1%. Principal agricultural products: livestock, wheat, oats, barley. Major industrial products: animal products, building materials, coal. Natural resources: coal, copper, molybdenum. Exports: livestock, animal products, wool, nonferrous metals.

Imports: machinery and equipment, clothing, petroleum. Major trading partners: U.S.S.R. and Soviet bloc countries.

Geography. Mongolia lies in eastern Asia between Soviet Siberia on the north and China on the south. It is slightly larger than Alaska.

The productive regions of Mongolia—a tableland ranging from 3,000 to 5,000 feet (914 to 1,524 m) in elevation—are in the north, which is well drained by numerous rivers, including the Hovd, Onon, Selenga, and Tula.

Much of the Gobi Desert falls within Mongolia.

Government. The Mongolian People's Republic is a socialist state. The highest organ of state power is the Great People's Khural (Parliament), which is elected for a term of four years and is convened once a year. The Great People's Khural elects the Presidium, which consists of a chairman, two vice chairmen, a secretary, and six members. The Council of Ministers is set up by the Great People's Khural and consists of a chairman, vice chairmen, and ministers.

The Mongolian People's Revolutionary Party, is led by Gombojavyn Ochirbat. In 1990, the Mongolian Communist Party gave up its constitutional monopoly on power.

History. The Mongolian People's Republic, formerly known as Outer Mongolia, is a Soviet satellite. It contains the original homeland of the historic Mongols, whose power reached its zenith during the 13th century under Kublai Khan. The area accepted Manchu rule in 1689, but after the Chinese Revolution of 1911 and the fall of the Manchus in 1912, the northern Mongol princes expelled the Chinese officials and declared independence under the Khutukhtu, or "Living Buddha."

In 1921, Soviet troops entered the country and facilitated the establishment of a republic by Mongolian revolutionaries in 1924 after the death of the last Living Buddha. China, meanwhile, continued to claim Outer Mongolia but was unable to back the claim with any strength. Under the 1945 Chinese-Russian Treaty, China agreed to give up Outer Mongolia, which, after a plebiscite, became a nominally independent country.

Allied with the U.S.S.R. in its dispute with China, Mongolia has mobilized troops along its borders since 1968 when the two powers became involved in border clashes on the Kazakh-Sinkiang frontier to the west and on the Amur and Ussuri Rivers. A 20-year treaty of friendship and cooperation, signed in 1966, entitled Mongolia to call upon the U.S.S.R. for military aid in the event of invasion.

MOROCCO

Kingdom of Morocco
Ruler: King Hassan II (1961)
Prime Minister: Azzedine Laraki (1986)
Area: 172,413 sq mi. (446,550 sq km)
Population (est. mid-1990): 25,600,000 (average annual rate of natural increase: 2.6%)
Density per square mile: 149
Capital: Rabat
Largest cities: Casablanca, 3,500,000; Rabat-Sale, 1,000,000; Fez, 600,000; Marrakesh, 500,000; Laayoune, 100,000
Monetary unit: Dirham

Languages: Arabic, French, Berber dialects, Spanish
Religions: Islam, Christian, Jewish
National name: al-Mamlaka al-Maghrebia
Literacy rate: 35%
Economic summary: Gross domestic product (1987): $18 billion; $740 per capita; 1.5% real growth rate. Arable land: 18%; products: barley, wheat, citrus fruits, vegetables. Labor force: 7,400,000; 15% in industry; major products: textiles, chemicals. Natural resources: phosphates, lead, manganese, fisheries. Exports: phosphates, citrus fruits, vegetables, canned fruits and vegetables, canned fish, carpets. Imports: capital goods, fuels, foodstuffs, iron and steel. Major trading partners: France, West Germany, Italy, Spain, Japan, U.S.

Geography. Morocco, about one tenth larger than California, is just south of Spain across the Strait of Gibraltar and looks out on the Atlantic from the northwest shoulder of Africa. Algeria is to the east and Mauritania to the south.

On the Atlantic coast there is a fertile plain. The Mediterranean coast is mountainous. The Atlas Mountains, running northeastward from the south to the Algerian frontier, average 11,000 feet (3,353 m) in elevation.

Government. The King, after suspending the 1962 Constitution and dissolving Parliament in 1965, promulgated a new Constitution in 1972. He continued to rule by decree until June 3, 1977, when the first free elections since 1962 took place. The 306-member Chamber of Deputies has 204 elected seats, with the balance chosen by local councils and groups.

History. Morocco was once the home of the Berbers, who helped the Arabs invade Spain in A.D. 711 and then revolted against them and gradually won control of large areas of Spain for a time after 739.

The country was ruled successively by various native dynasties and maintained regular commercial relations with Europe, even during the 17th and 18th centuries when it was the headquarters of the famous Salé pirates. In the 19th century, there were frequent clashes with the French and Spanish. Finally, in 1904, France and Spain divided Morocco into zones of French and Spanish influence, and these were established as protectorates in 1912.

Meanwhile, Morocco had become the object of big-power rivalry, which almost led to a European war in 1905 when Germany attempted to gain a foothold in the rich mineral country. By terms of the Algeciras Conference (1906), Morocco was internationalized economically, and France's privileges were limited.

The Tangier Statute, concluded by Britain, France, and Spain in 1923, created an international zone at the port of Tangier, permanently neutralized and demilitarized. In World War II, Spain occupied the zone, ostensibly to ensure order, but was forced to withdraw in 1945.

Sultan Mohammed V was deposed by the French in 1953 and replaced by his uncle, but nationalist agitation forced his return in 1955. On his death on Feb. 26, 1961, his son, Hassan, became King.

France and Spain recognized the independence and sovereignty of Morocco in 1956. Later the same year, the Tangier international zone was abolished.

In 1975, tens of thousands of Moroccans crossed the border into Spanish Sahara to back their government's contention that the northern part of the territory was historically part of Morocco. At the same time, Mauritania occupied the southern half of the territory in defiance of Spanish threats to resist such a takeover. Abandoning its commitment to self-determination for the territory, Spain withdrew, and only Algeria protested.

When Mauritania signed a peace treaty with the Algerian-backed Polisario Front in August 1979, Morocco occupied and assumed administrative control of the southern part of the Western Sahara, in addition to the northern part it already occupied. Under pressure from other African leaders, Hassan agreed in mid-1981 to a cease-fire with a referendum under international supervision to decide the fate of the Sahara territory, but the referendum was never carried out.

King Hassan, startled the Reagan Administration in mid-August 1984 by signing a treaty of union with Col. Muammar el-Qaddafi, the Libyan leader.

The Moroccans described the treaty as the culmination of a process in which Libya had withdrawn its support for the Polisario in the Western Sahara, and Morocco had agreed to refrain from sending troops to help the French in Chad.

King Hassan became the second Arab leader to meet with an Israeli leader when, on July 21, 1986, Israeli Prime Minister Shimon Peres came to Morocco. Libyan criticism of the meeting led to King Hassan's abrogation of the treaty with Libya.

MOZAMBIQUE

People's Republic of Mozambique
President: Joaquim Chissano (1986)
Prime Minister: Dr. Mario Machungo (1986)
Area: 303,073 sq mi. (799,380 sq. km.)
Population (est. mid-1990): 15,700,000 (average annual rate of natural increase: 2.7%)
Density per square mile: 49
Capital and largest city (est. mid-1986): Maputo, 882,800
Monetary unit: Metical
Languages: Portuguese (official), Bantu languages
Religions: traditional, 60%; Christian, 30%; Islam, 10%
National name: República Popular de Moçambique
Literacy rate: 17%
Economic summary: Gross national product (1987 est.): $500 million; per capita less than $100; 4% real growth rate. Arable land: 4%. Principal agricultural products: cotton, cashew nuts, sugar, tea, copra, peanuts. Labor force: 90% in agriculture. Major products: processed foods, petroleum products, beverages, textiles, tobacco. Natural resources: bauxite, coal, iron ore, copper, diamonds. Exports: cashew nuts, cotton, sugar, shrimp, petroleum products, tea, copra, prawns, citrus, textiles. Imports: refined petroleum, machinery, vehicles, consumer goods, arms. Major trading partners: U.S., Western Europe, Eastern Europe, U.S.S.R.

Geography. Mozambique stretches for 1,535 miles (2,470 km) along Africa's southeast coast. It is nearly twice the size of California. Tanzania is to the north; Malawi, Zambia, and Zimbabwe to the west; and South Africa and Swaziland to the south.

The country is generally a low-lying plateau broken up by 25 sizable rivers that flow into the Indian Ocean. The largest is the Zambezi; which provides access to central Africa. The principal ports are Maputo and Beira, which is the port for Zimbabwe.

Government. After having been under Portuguese colonial rule for 470 years, Mozambique became independent on June 25, 1975. It is a Marxist state. The first President, Samora Moises Machel, headed the National Front for the Liberation of Mozambique (FRELIMO) in its 10-year guerrilla war for independence. He died in a plane crash on Oct. 19, 1986 and was succeeded by his Foreign Minister, Joaquim Chissano.

History. Mozambique was discovered by Vasco da Gama in 1498, although the Arabs had penetrated into the area as early as the 10th century. It was first colonized in 1505, and by 1510, the Portuguese had control of all the former Arab sultanates on the east African coast.

FRELIMO was organized in 1963. Guerrilla activity had become so extensive by 1973 that Portugal was forced to dispatch 40,000 troops to fight the rebels. A cease-fire was signed in September 1974, when Portugal agreed to grant Mozambique independence.

On Jan. 25, 1985, Mozambique's celebration of a decade of independence from Portugal was not a happy one. The government was locked in a five-year-old, stalemated, paralyzing war with anti-government guerrillas, known as the MNR, backed by the white minority government in South Africa. At the same time, like those in much of eastern Africa, the peasants who make up most of the population suffered from the consequences of four years of drought, with thousands reported starving.

MYANMAR

Union of Myanmar
Head of State (Chairman): Gen. Saw Maung (1988)
Area: 261,220 sq mi. (676,560 sq km)
Population (est. mid-1990): 41,300,000 (average annual rate of natural increase: 2%)
Density per square mile: 156
Capital: Yangon
Largest cities (est. 1983): Yangon, 2,458,712; Mandalay, 532,895; Moulmein, 219,991; Bassein, 144,092
Monetary unit: Kyat
Language: Burmese, minority languages
Religions: Buddhist, 89%; Christian, 5%; Islam, 3%
National name: Pyidaungsu Myanmar Naingngandau
Literacy rate: 78%
Economic summary: Gross domestic product (FY 1988): $9.3 billion; $230 per capita; 2.2% real growth rate. Arable land: 15%; principal products: legumes, sugar cane, corn, rice, peanuts. Labor force: 15,800,000; 13.7% in industry; major products: textiles, footwear, processed agricultural products, wood and wood products, refined petroleum. Natural resources: timber, nickel, cobalt, copper, gold, precious stones, crude oil and natural gas. Exports: rice, teak, beans, ores. Imports: machinery, transportation and construction equipment, manufactured goods. Major trading partners: Singapore, West Germany, U.K., Japan, Singapore.

Geography. Myanmar occupies the northwest portion of the Indochinese peninsula. India lies to the northwest and China to the northeast. Bangladesh, Laos, and Thailand are also neighbors. The Bay of Bengal touches the southwestern coast.

Slightly smaller than Texas, the country is divided into three natural regions: the Arakan Yoma, a long, narrow mountain range forming the barrier between Myanmar and India; the Shan Plateau in the east, extending southward into Tenasserim; and the Central Basin, running down to the flat fertile delta of the Irrawaddy in the south. This delta contains a network of intercommunicating canals and nine principal river mouths.

Government. On March 2, 1962, the government of U Nu was overthrown and replaced by a Revolutionary Council, which assumed all power in the state. Gen. U Ne Win, as chairman of the Revolutionary Council, became the chief executive. In 1972, Ne Win and his colleagues resigned their military titles. In 1974, Ne Win dissolved the Revolutionary Council and became President under the new Constitution. He voluntarily relinquished the presidency on Nov. 9, 1981.

History. In 1612, the British East India Company sent agents to Burma, but the Burmese long resisted efforts of British traders, and Dutch and Portuguese as well, to establish posts on the Bay of Bengal. By the Anglo-Burmese War in 1824–26 and two following wars, the British East India Company expanded to the whole of Burma by 1886. Burma was annexed to India. It became a separate colony in 1937.

During World War II, Burma was a key battleground; the 800-mile Burma Road was the Allies' vital supply line to China. The Japanese invaded the country in December 1941, and by May 1942 had occupied most of it, cutting the Burma Road. After one of the most difficult campaigns of the war, Allied forces liberated most of Burma prior to the Japanese surrender in August 1945.

Burma became independent on Jan. 4, 1948. In 1951 and 1952 the Socialists achieved power, and Burma became the first Asian country to introduce social legislation.

In 1968, after the government had made headway against the Communist and separatist rebels, the military regime adopted a policy of strict nonalignment and followed "the Burmese Way" to socialism. But the insurgents continued active.

In July 1988, Ne Win announced his resignation from the Burmese Socialist Program Party (BSPP), the only legal political party, effectively retiring from politics.

He was succeeded by U Sein Lwin who was forced out of office by widespread protests in August. Former Attorney General U Maung Maung was subsequently named President on August 19. Unrest continued and the civilian government was overthrown in Sept. 1988 by a military junta led by General Saw Maung, an associate of U Ne Win. He changed the name of the party to the National Unity Party.

The new government held elections in May 1990 and the opposition National League for Democracy won in a landslide despite its leaders being in jail or under house arrest.

NAMIBIA

President: Sam Nujoma (1990)
Status: Independent Country
Area: 318,261 sq mi. (824,296 sq km)
Population (mid-1990): 1,500,000 (average annual growth rate: 3.2%)
Density per square mile: 2
Administrator-General: Louis Pienaar (1986)

Capital (est. 1980): Windhoek, 85,000
Summer capital (est. 1980): Swakopmund, 17,500
Monetary unit: South African rand
National name: Suidwes-Afrika/Namibië; South-West
Africa/Namibia
Literacy rate: 100% whites/28% non-whites
Economic summary: Gross national product (1986): $1.25
billion; $1,060 per capita; 3.5% real growth rate. Arable
land: 1%; principal products: corn, millet, sorghum,
livestock. Labor force: 500,000; 19% in industry and
commerce; major products: canned meat, dairy products,
tanned leather, textiles, clothing. Natural resources:
diamonds, copper, lead, zinc, uranium, fish. Exports:
diamonds, copper, lead, zinc, beef cattle, karakul pelts.
Imports: construction materials, fertilizer, grain,
foodstuffs. Major trading partner: South Africa.

Geography. Namibia, bounded on the north by Angola and Zambia and on the east by Botswana and
South Africa, was discovered by the Portuguese explorer Diaz in the late 15th century. It is for the
most part a portion of the high plateau of southern
Africa with a general elevation of from 3,000 to
4,000 feet.

Government: Namibia became independent in
1990 after its new constitution was ratified. A
multi-party democracy with an independent judiciary was established.

History. The territory became a German colony in
1884 but was taken by South African forces in
1915, becoming a South African mandate by the
terms of the Treaty of Versailles in 1920.

South Africa's application for incorporation of
the territory was rejected by the U.N. General Assembly in 1946 and South Africa was invited to prepare a trusteeship agreement instead. By a law
passed in 1949, however, the territory was brought
into much closer association with South Africa—including representation in its Parliament.

In 1969, South Africa extended its laws to the
mandate over the objection of the U.N., particularly its black African members. When South Africa
refused to withdraw them, the Security Council
condemned it.

Under a 1974 Security Council resolution, South
Africa was required to begin the transfer of power
to the Namibians by May 30, 1975, or face U.N. action, but 10 days before the deadline Prime Minister Balthazar J. Vorster rejected U.N. supervision.
He said, however, that his government was prepared to negotiate Namibian independence, but
not with the South-West African People's Organization, the principal black separatist group. Meanwhile, the all-white legislature of South-West Africa eased several laws on apartheid in public
places.

Despite international opposition, the Turnhalle
Conference in Windhoek drafted a constitution to
organize an interim government based on racial divisions, a proposal overwhelmingly endorsed by
white voters in the territory in 1977. At the urging
of ambassadors of the five Western members of the
Security Council—the U.S., Britain, France, West
Germany, and Canada—South Africa on June 11
announced rejection of the Turnhalle constitution
and acceptance of the Western proposal to include
the South-West Africa People's Organization
(SWAPO) in negotiations.

Although negotiations continued between South
Africa, the western powers, neighboring black African states, and internal political groups, there was
still no agreement on a final independence plan. A
new round of talks aimed at resolving the 18-year-
old conflict ended in a stalemate on July 25, 1984.
Dr. Willie van Niekerk, South Africa's Administrator-General in the territory, met in the remote
Cape Verde Islands with leaders of the insurgents,
including SWAPO leader Sam Nujoma, to "explore
the possibilities of bringing about a cessation of violent and armed activities in South-West Africa."

As policemen wielding riot sticks charged demonstrators in a black, South-West Africa township,
South Africa handed over limited powers to a new,
multiracial administration in the former German
colony on June 17, 1985. Installation of the new
government ended South Africa's direct rule, but
South Africa retained an effective veto over the
new government's decisions along with responsibility for the territory's defense and foreign policy,
and South Africa's efforts to quell the insurgents
seeking independence continued.

An agreement between South Africa, Angola
and Cuba arranged for elections for a Constituent
Assembly in Nov. 1989 to establish a new government. SWAPO won 57% of the vote, a majority but
not enough to dictate a constitution unilaterally. In
February 1990, SWAPO leader Sam Nujoma was
elected President and took office when Namibia
became independent on March 21, 1990.

NAURU

Republic of Nauru
President and Head Chief: Kenos Aroi (1989)
Area: 8.2 sq mi. (21 sq km)
Population (mid-1989): 9,053 (average annual growth rate:
1.7%)
Density per square mile: 1,086
Capital: Yaren
Monetary unit: Australian dollar
Languages: Nauruan and English
Religions: Protestant, 58%; Roman Catholic, 24%;
Confucian and Taoist, 8%
Special relationship within the Commonwealth of Nations
Literacy rate: 99%
Economic summary: Gross national product (1985): more
than $160 million; $20,000 per capita. Major industrial
products: phosphates. Natural resources: phosphates.
Exports: phosphates. Imports: foodstuffs, fuel, machinery.
Major trading partners: Australia, New Zealand, U.K.,
Japan.

Geography. Nauru (pronounced NAH oo roo) is an
island in the Pacific just south of the equator, about
2,500 miles (4,023 km) southwest of Honolulu.

Government. Legislative power is invested in a
popularly elected 18-member Parliament, which
elects the President from among its members. Executive power rests with the President, who is assisted by a five-member Cabinet.

History. Nauru was annexed by Germany in 1888.
It was placed under joint Australian, New Zealand,
and British mandate after World War I, and in 1947
it became a U.N. trusteeship administered by the
same three powers. On Jan. 31, 1968, Nauru became an independent republic.

NEPAL

Kingdom of Nepal
Ruler: King Birendra Bir Bikram Shah Deva (1972)
Prime Minister: Krishna Prasad Bhattarai (1990)
Area: 54,463 sq. mi. (141,059 sq km)
Population (mid-1990): 19,100,000 (average annual rate of natural growth: 2.5%)
Density per square mile: 344
Capital and largest city (est. 1980): Katmandu, 400,000
Monetary unit: Nepalese rupee
Languages: Nepali (official), Newari, Bhutia, Maithali
Religions: Hindu, 90%; Buddhist, 5%; Islam, 3%
Literacy rate: 23%
Economic summary: Gross domestic product (FY88): $3.1 billion; $170 per capita; 7.1% real growth rate. Arable land: 17%. Labor force in agriculture: 93%; principal products: rice, maize, wheat, millet, jute, sugar cane, oilseed, potatoes. Labor force in industry: 2%; major products: sugar, lumber, jute, cigarettes, cement. Natural resources: water, timber, hydroelectric potential. Exports: rice and food products, jute, and timber. Imports: textiles, manufactured goods, construction materials, fuel. Major trading partners: India, Japan.

Geography. A landlocked country the size of Arkansas, lying between India and the Tibetan Autonomous Region of China, Nepal contains Mount Everest (29,108 ft.; 8,872 m), the tallest mountain in the world. Along its southern border, Nepal has a strip of level land that is partly forested, partly cultivated. North of that is the slope of the main section of the Himalayan range, including Everest and many other peaks higher than 20,000 feet (6,096 m).

Government. A new Constitution promulgated by King Mahendra in 1962 provided for a unicameral legislature called the National Panchayat. A multiparty system was introduced in April 1990. There is a coalition government consisting of members of Nepali Congress, United Leftist Front, and independents, headed by the Prime Minister.

History. The Kingdom of Nepal was unified in 1768 by King Prithwi Narayan Shah. A commercial treaty was signed with Britain in 1792, and in 1816, after more than a year's hostilities, the Nepalese agreed to allow British residents to live in Katmandu, the capital. In 1923, Britain recognized the absolute independence of Nepal. Between 1846 and 1951, the country was ruled by the Rana family, which always held the office of prime minister. In 1951, however, the King took over all power and proclaimed a constitutional monarchy.

Mahendra Bir Bikram Shah became King in 1955. After Mahendra, who had ruled since 1955, died of a heart attack in 1972, Prince Birendra, at 26, succeeded to the throne.

In the first election in 22 years, on May 2, 1980, voters approved the continued autocratic rule by the King with the advice of a partyless Parliament. The King, however, permitted the election of a new legislature, in May 1986, to which the Prime Minister and Cabinet are responsible.

A dispute with India over the renewal of a trade and transit treaty led to India closing most of the border crossings, causing severe economic disruption.

In 1990, pro-democracy movement forced King Birendra to lift the ban on political parties and appoint an opposition leader to head an interim government as Prime Minister.

THE NETHERLANDS

Kingdom of the Netherlands
Sovereign: Queen Beatrix (1980)
Premier: Ruud Lubbers (1982)
Area: 16,041 sq. mi. (41,548 sq. km.)
Population (est. mid-1990): 14,900,000 (average annual rate of natural increase: 0.4%)
Density per square mile: 1,031
Capital: Amsterdam; seat of government: The Hague
Largest cities: Amsterdam, 694,656; Rotterdam, 576,218; 's-Gravenhage, 444,000; Utrecht, 230,738; Endhoven, 191,500
Monetary unit: Guilder
Language: Dutch
Religions: Roman Catholic, 36%; Dutch Reformed, 19%; unaffiliated, 27%
National name: Koninkrijk der Nederlanden
Literacy rate: 99%
Economic summary: Gross domestic product (1988): $223.3 billion; $15,170 per capita; 4% real growth rate. Arable land; 25%; principal products: wheat, barley, sugar beets, potatoes, meat and dairy products. Labor force: 5,300,000; 28.2% in manufacturing and construction; major products: metal fabrication, textiles, chemicals, electronic equipment, petroleum, fishing. Exports: foodstuffs, machinery, natural gas, chemicals, petroleum products, textiles. Imports: machinery, crude petroleum, chemicals, textiles, mineral ores. Major trading partners: West Germany, Belgium, France, U.K., U.S.

Geography. The Netherlands, on the coast of the North Sea, has West Germany to the east and Belgium to the south. It is twice the size of New Jersey.

Part of the great plain of north and west Europe, the Netherlands has maximum dimensions of 190 by 160 miles (360 by 257 km) and is low and flat except in Limburg in the southeast, where some hills rise to 300 feet (92 m). About half the country's area is below sea level, making the famous Dutch dikes a requisite to the use of much land. Reclamation of land from the sea through dikes has continued through recent times.

All drainage reaches the North Sea, and the principal rivers—Rhine, Maas (Meuse), and Schelde—have their sources outside the country. The Rhine is the most heavily used waterway in Europe.

Government. The Netherlands and its former colony of the Netherlands Antilles form the Kingdom of the Netherlands.

The Netherlands is a constitutional monarchy with a bicameral Parliament. The Upper Chamber has 75 members elected for six years by representative bodies of the provinces, half of the members retiring every three years. The Lower Chamber has 150 members elected by universal suffrage for four years. The two Chambers have the right of investigation and interpellation; the Lower Chamber can initiate legislation and amend bills.

The Sovereign, Queen Beatrix Wilhelmina Armgard, born Jan. 31, 1938, was married on March 10, 1966, to Claus von Amsberg, a former West German diplomat. The marriage drew public criticism because of the bridegroom's service in the German army during World War II. In 1967, Beatrix gave birth to a son, Willem-Alexander Claus George Ferdinand, the first male heir to the throne since 1884. She also has two other sons, Johan Friso Bernhard Christian David, born in 1968, and Constantijn Christof Frederik Aschwin, born the next year.

History. Julius Caesar found the low-lying Netherlands inhabited by Germanic tribes—the Nervii, Frisii, and Batavi. The Batavi on the Roman frontier did not submit to Rome's rule until 13 B.C., and then only as allies.

A part of Charlemagne's empire in the 8th and 9th centuries A.D., the area later passed into the hands of Burgundy and the Austrian Hapsburgs, and finally in the 16th century came under Spanish rule.

When Philip II of Spain suppressed political liberties and the growing Protestant movement in the Netherlands, a revolt led by William of Orange broke out in 1568. Under the Union if Utrecht (1579), the seven northern provinces became the Republic of the United Netherlands.

The Dutch East India Company was established in 1602, and by the end of the 17th century Holland was one of the great sea and colonial powers of Europe.

The nation's independence was not completely established until after the Thirty Years' War (1618–48), after which the country's rise as a commercial and maritime power began. In 1814, all the provinces of Holland and Belgium were merged into one kingdom, but in 1830 the southern provinces broke away to form the Kingdom of Belgium. A liberal Constitution was adopted by the Netherlands in 1848.

In spite of its neutrality in World War II, the Netherlands was invaded by the Nazis in May 1940, and the East Indies were later taken by the Japanese. The nation was liberated in May 1945. In 1948, after a reign of 50 years, Queen Wilhelmina resigned and was succeeded by her daughter Juliana.

In 1949, after a four-year war, the Netherlands granted independence to the East Indies, which became the Republic of Indonesia. In 1963, it turned over the western half of New Guinea to the new nation, ending 300 years of Dutch presence in Asia. Attainment of independence by Suriname on Nov. 25, 1975, left the Dutch Antilles as the Netherlands' only overseas territory.

Prime Minister Van Agt lost his narrow majority in elections on May 26, 1981, in which the major issue was the deployment of U.S. cruise missiles on Dutch soil. Public opposition to the missiles forced the Netherlands, along with Belgium, to reverse its position in 1982 despite the Prime Minister's personal support for the NATO decision to deploy the new weapons in Western Europe. Van Agt lost his centrist coalition in May 1982 in a dispute over economic policy, and was succeeded by Ruud Lubber as Premier. Lubber announced on November 1, 1985 to accept the deployment of the U.S. missiles.

Netherlands Autonomous Country

NETHERLANDS ANTILLES

Status: Part of the Kingdom of the Netherlands
Governor: Mr. J. M. Saleh (1990)
Premier: Maria Liberia Peters
Area: 313 sq mi. (800 sq km)
Population (mid-1990): 200,000 (average annual growth rate: 1.3%)
Capital (est. 1978): Willemstad, 152,000
Literacy rate: 95%
Economic summary: Gross national product (1985): $1.2

billion; $6,460 per capita; −2.1% real growth rate. Arable land: 8%. Principal agricultural products: pigs, goats. Labor force: 89,000; 28% industry and commerce (1983). Major industries: oil refining, tourism. Natural resource: phosphate. Export: petroleum. Import: petroleum. Major trading partners: U.S., Venezuela.

Geography. The Netherlands Antilles comprise two groups of Caribbean islands 500 miles (805 km) apart: one, about 40 miles (64 km) off the Venezuelan coast, consists of Curaçao (173 sq mi.; 448 sq km), Bonaire (95 sq mi.; 246 sq km), the other, lying to the northeast, consists of three small islands with a total area of 34 square miles (88 sq km).
Government. There is a constitutional government formed by the Governor and Cabinet and an elected Legislative Council. The area has complete autonomy in domestic affairs.

ARUBA

Status: Part of the Kingdom of the Netherlands
Governor: F. B. Tromp
Prime Minister: J. H. A. Eman
Area: 75 sq mi. (193 sq km)
Population: (est. mid-1988): 62,322 (average annual growth rate: 0.29%)
Capital: (1986): Oranjestad, 19,800
Literacy rate: 95%
Economic summary: Gross national product (1986): $378 million. Real growth rate (1986): −31%. Per capita income, $6,100. Little agriculture. Major industries: tourism, light manufacturing (tobacco, beverages, consumer goods.

Geography. Aruba, an island slightly larger than Washington D.C., lies 18 miles (28.9 km) off the coast of Venezuela in the southern Caribbean.
Government. The governmental structure comprises the Governor, appointed by the Queen for a term of six years; the Legislature consisting of 21 members elected by universal suffrage for terms not exceeding four years; and the Council of Ministers, presided over by the Prime Minister, which holds executive power.

NEW ZEALAND

Sovereign: Queen Elizabeth II
Governor-General: Sir Paul Reeves (1985)
Prime Minister: Geoffrey Palmer (1989)
Area: 103,884 sq mi. (269,062 sq km) (excluding dependencies)
Population (est. mid-1990): 3,300,000 (average annual growth rate: 0.8%)
Density per square mile: 33
Capital: Wellington
Largest cities (est. 1988): Auckland, 324,400; Wellington, 829,000; Christchurch, 299,400
Monetary unit: New Zealand dollar
Languages: English, Maori
Religions: Church of England, 26%; Presbyterian, 17%; Roman Catholic, 14%
Member of Commonwealth of Nations
Literacy rate: 99.5%
Economic summary: Gross domestic product (FY88) $27.9 billion; $8,390 per capita; real growth rate −.2%. Arable land: 2%; principal products: wool, meat, dairy products, livestock. Labor force: 1,591,900: 19.8% in manu-

facturing; major products: processed foods, textiles, machinery, transport equipment, wood and paper products, financial services. Natural resources: forests, coal, gold. Exports: meat, dairy products, wool. Imports: machinery, minerals, chemicals, consumer goods. Major trading partners: Japan, Australia, U.K., U.S.

Geography. New Zealand, about 1,250 miles (2,012 km) east of Australia, consists of two main islands and a number of smaller, outlying islands so scattered that they range from the tropical to the antarctic. The country is the size of Colorado.

New Zealand's two main components are North Island and South Island, separated by Cook Strait, which varies from 16 to 190 miles (26 to 396 km) in width. North Island (44,281 sq mi.; 114,688 sq km) is 515 miles (829 km) long and volcanic in its south-central part. This area contains many hot springs and beautiful geysers. South Island (58,093 sq mi.; 150,461 sq km) has the Southern Alps along its west coast, with Mount Cook (12,349 ft; 3,764 m) the highest point.

The largest of the outlying islands are the Auckland Islands (234 sq mi.; 606 sq km), Campbell Island (44 sq mi.; 114 sq km), the Antipodes Islands (24 sq mi.; 62 sq km), and the Kermadec Islands (13 sq mi.; 34 sq km).

Government. New Zealand was granted self-government in 1852, a full parliamentary system and ministries in 1856, and dominion status in 1907. The Queen is represented by a Governor-General, and the Cabinet is responsible to a unicameral Parliament of 97 members, who are elected by popular vote for three years.

History. New Zealand was discovered and named in 1642 by Abel Tasman, a Dutch navigator. Captain James Cook explored the islands in 1769. In 1840, Britain formally annexed them.

From the first, the country has been in the forefront in instituting social welfare legislation. It adopted old age pensions (1898); a national child welfare program (1907); social security for the aged, widows, and orphans, along with family benefit payments; minimum wages; a 40-hour week and unemployment and health insurance (1938); and socialized medicine (1941).

The New Zealand Labor Party, headed by David Lange, swept Sir Robert Muldoon's conservative National Party from power in a parliamentary election on July 14, 1984. Lange's campaign promise to ban American nuclear-powered and nuclear-armed naval vessels from New Zealand waters provoked a crisis in the 33-year-old Anzus alliance of the United States, Australia and New Zealand. After New Zealand refused to let a U.S. warship make a port call on the ground it might be carrying nuclear weapons, Secretary of State George P. Shultz on July 17, 1985, accused New Zealand of undermining the U.S. nuclear deterrent and weakening its own security.

Cook Islands and Overseas Territories

The Cook Islands (93 sq mi.; 241 sq km) were placed under New Zealand administration in 1901. They achieved self-governing status in association with New Zealand in 1965. Population in 1978 was about 19,600. The seat of government is on Rarotonga Island.

The island's chief exports are citrus juice, clothing, canned fruit, and pineapple juice. Nearly all of the trade is with New Zealand.

Niue (100 sq mi.; 259 sq km) was formerly administered as part of the Cook Islands. It was placed under separate New Zealand administration in 1901 and achieved self-governing status in association with New Zealand in 1974. The capital is Alofi. Population in 1980 was about 3,300.

Niue exports passion fruit, copra, plaited ware, honey, and limes. Its principal trading partner is New Zealand.

The Ross Dependency (160,000 sq mi.; 414,400 sq km), an Antarctic region, was placed under New Zealand administration in 1923.

Tokelau (4 sq mi.; 10 sq km) was formerly administered as part of the Gilbert and Ellice Islands colony. It was placed under New Zealand administration in 1925. Its population is about 1,600.

NICARAGUA

Republic of Nicaragua
President: Violeta Barrios de Chamorra (1990)
Area: 50,180 sq mi. (130,000 sq km)
Population (mid-1990): 3,900,000 (average annual rate of natural increase: 3.3%)
Density per square mile: 70
Capital and largest city (est. 1985): Managua, 682,111
Monetary unit: Cordoba
Language: Spanish
Religion: Roman Catholic, 91%
National name: República de Nicaragua
Literacy rate: 87%
Economic summary: Gross domestic product (1990): $2.1 billion; $610 per capita; real growth rate −8% (1988). Arable land: 9%; principal products: cotton, coffee, sugar cane, rice, corn, beans, cattle. Labor force: 1,086,000; 13% in industry (1986); major products: processed foods, chemicals, metal products, clothing and textiles, beverages, footware. Natural resources: timber, fisheries. Exports: coffee, cotton, seafood, bananas, food and nonfood agricultural products. Imports: machinery, chemicals and pharmaceuticals, transport equipment, clothing, petroleum. Major trading partners: Mexico, West Germany, Japan, France, Cuba, Central America, Caribbean.

Geography. Largest but most sparsely populated of the Central American nations, Nicaragua borders on Honduras to the north and Costa Rica to the south. It is slightly larger than New York State.

Nicaragua is mountainous in the west, with fertile valleys. A plateau slopes eastward toward the Caribbean.

Two big lakes—Nicaragua, about 100 miles long (161 km), and Managua, about 38 miles long (61 km)—are connected by the Tipitapa River. The Pacific coast is volcanic and very fertile. The Caribbean coast, swampy and indented, is aptly called the "Mosquito Coast."

Government. After an election on Nov. 4, 1984, Daniel Ortega began a six-year term as President on Jan. 10, 1985. He was defeated in general elections held in Feb. 1990, by Violeta Chamorro.

History. Nicaragua, which established independence in 1838, was first visited by the Spaniards in 1522. The chief of the country's leading Indian tribe at that time was called Nicaragua, from whom the nation derived its name. A U.S. naval force intervened in 1909 after two American citizens had been executed, and a few U.S. Marines were kept in the country from 1912 to 1925. The Bryan-Chamorro Treaty of 1916 (terminated in 1970) gave the U.S. an option on a canal route through Nicaragua, and naval bases. Disorder after the 1924 elections brought in the marines again.

A guerrilla leader, Gen. César Augusto Sandino, began fighting the occupation force in 1927. He fought the U.S. troops until their withdrawal in 1933. They trained Gen. Anastasio (Tacho) Somoza García to head a National Guard. In 1934, Somoza assassinated Sandino and overthrew the Liberal President Juan Batista Sacassa, establishing a military dictatorship with himself as president. He spurred the economic development of the country, meanwhile enriching his family through estates in the countryside and investments in air and shipping lines. On his assassination in 1956, he was succeeded by his son Luis, who alternated with trusted family friends in the presidency until his death in 1967. Another son, Maj. Gen. Anastasio Somoza Debayle, became President in 1967.

Sandinista guerrillas, leftists who took their name from Gen. Sandino, launched an offensive in May 1979.

After seven weeks of fighting, Somoza fled the country on July 17, 1979. The Sandinistas assumed power on July 19, promising to maintain a mixed economy, a non-aligned foreign policy, and a pluralist political system. However, the prominence of Cuban President Fidel Castro at the celebration of the first anniversary of the revolution and a five-year delay in holding elections increased debate over the true political color of the Sandinistas.

On Jan. 23, 1981, the Reagan Administration suspended U.S. aid, charging that Nicaragua, with the aid of Cuba and the Soviet Union, was supplying arms to rebels in El Salvador. The Sandinistas denied the charges. Later that year, Nicaraguan guerrillas known as "contras," began a war to overthrow the Sandinistas.

The elections were finally held on Nov. 4, 1984, with Daniel Ortega Saavedra, the Sandinista junta coordinator, winning 63% of the votes cast for President. He began a six-year term on Jan. 10, 1985.

Meanwhile, the war between the Sandinistas and the U.S.-backed contras continued, and on Feb. 21, 1985, President Reagan denounced the Sandinista regime and said his objective was to "remove it in the sense of its present structure." On May 1, Reagan ordered an embargo on U.S. trade with Nicaragua, telling Congress that the policies and actions of the Sandinistas constituted a threat to U.S. security.

In October 1985, Nicaragua suspended civil liberties and in June 1986, Congress voted $100 million in aid, military and non-military, to the contras.

The war intensified in 1986-87, with the resupplied contras establishing themselves inside the country. Negotiations sponsored by the Contadora (neutral Latin American) nations, but a peace plan

sponsored by Arias, the Costa Rican president, led to a treaty signed by the Central American leaders in August 1987, that called for an end to outside aid to guerrillas and negotiations between hostile parties. Congress later cut off military aid to the contras. Although the two sides agreed to a cease-fire in March, 1988, further negotiations were inconclusive.

In 1989, an accord established a one-year advance in general elections to Feb. 1990. It also called for easing press restrictions and the release of political prisoners and the disbanding of the contras.

Violetta Chamorro, owner of the opposition paper *La Prensa*, led a broad anti-Sandinista coalition to victory in the presidential and legislative elections, ending 11 years of Sandinista rule.

NIGER

Republic of Niger
Chief of State: Brigadier Ali Saibou (1987)
Area: 489,206 sq mi. (1,267,044 sq km)
Population (est. mid-1990): 7,900,000 (average annual rate of natural increase: 3%)
Density per square mile: 15
Capital and largest city (est. 1983): Niamey, 399,100
Monetary unit: Franc CFA
Ethnic groups: Hausa, 54%; Djerma and Songhai, 24%; Peul, 11%
Languages: French (official); Hausa, Songhai; Arabic
Religions: Islam, 80%; Animist and Christian, 20%
National name: République du Niger
Literacy rate: 21%
Economic summary: Gross domestic product (1987 est.): $2.2 billion; $310 per capita; —.7% real growth rate. Arable land: 3%; principal products: peanuts, cotton, livestock, millet, sorghum, bananas, rice. Labor force: 2,500,000 (1982); 90% in agriculture. Major industrial products: uranium, cement, bricks, light industrial products. Natural resources: uranium, coal, iron ore. Exports: uranium, peanuts, livestock, hides, skins. Imports: fuels, machinery, transport equipment, foodstuffs, consumer goods. Major trading partners: France, Nigeria, Japan, Algeria, U.S.

Geography. Niger, in West Africa's Sahara region, is four fifths the size of Alaska. It is surrounded by Mali, Algeria, Libya, Chad, Nigeria, Benin, and Burkina Faso.

The Niger River in the southwest flows through the country's only fertile area. Elsewhere the land is semiarid.

Government. After a military coup on April 15, 1974, Gen. Seyni Kountché suspended the Constitution and instituted rule by decree. Previously, the President was elected by direct universal suffrage for a five-year term and a National House of Assembly of 50 members was elected for the same term. He died on Nov. 10, 1987, and Col. Saibou, his Chief of Staff, succeeded him.

The Parti Progressiste Nigérien-Rassemblement Démocratique Africain, the only political party, was dissolved in 1974.

History. Niger was incorporated into French West Africa in 1896. There were frequent rebellions, but when order was restored in 1922, the French made the area a colony. In 1958, the voters approved the French Constitution and voted to make the territory an autonomous republic within the French Community. The republic adopted a Constitution in 1959 and the next year withdrew from the Community, proclaiming its independence.

The 1974 army coup ousted President Hamani Diori, who had held office since 1960. He was charged with having mishandled relief for the terrible drought that had devastated Niger and five neighboring sub-Saharan nations for several years. An estimated 2 million people were starving in Niger, but 200,000 tons of imported food, half U.S.-supplied, substantially ended famine conditions by the year's end. The new President, Lt. Col. Seyni Kountché, Chief of Staff of the army, installed a 12-man military government. A predominantly civilian government was formed by Kountché in 1976.

NIGERIA

Federal Republic of Nigeria
President: Gen. Ibrahim Badamasi Babangida (1985)
Area: 356,700 sq mi. (923,853 sq km)
Population (mid-1990): 118,800,000 (average annual rate of natural increase: 3%)
Density per square mile: 323
Capital: Lagos
Largest cities (est. 1983): Lagos, 1,097,000; Ibadan, 1,060,000; Ogbomosho, 527,400; Kano, 487,100
Monetary unit: Naira
Languages: English (official) Hausa, Yoruba, Ibo
Religions: Islam, 47%; Christian, 34%; Animist, 18%
Member of Commonwealth of Nations
Literacy rate: 30%
Economic summary: Gross domestic product (1987): $78 billion; $720 per capita; real growth rate −2.6%. Arable land: 31%; principal products: peanuts, cotton, cocoa, grains, fish, yams, cassava, livestock. Labor force: $45–50 million (1984 est.); 19% in industry; major products: crude oil, natural gas, coal, tin, processed rubber, cotton, petroleum, hides, textiles, cement, chemicals. Natural resources: petroleum, tin, columbite, iron ore, coal, limestone, timber. Exports: oil, cocoa, palm products, rubber, timber, tin. Imports: machinery and transport equipment, manufactured goods, chemicals, wheat. Major trading partners: U.K., Western European countries, U.S.

Geography. Nigeria, one third larger than Texas and black Africa's most populous nation, is situated on the Gulf of Guinea in West Africa. Its neighbors are Benin, Niger, Cameroon, and Chad.

The lower course of the Niger River flows south through the western part of the country into the Gulf of Guinea. Swamps and mangrove forests border the southern coast; inland are hardwood forests.

Government. After 12 years of military rule, a new Constitution re-established democratic government in 1979, but it lasted four years. The military again took over from the democratically elected civilian government on Dec. 31, 1983. The arms of the military government include an Armed Forces Ruling Council, a National Council of State, and National Council of Ministers. The various ministers make up the Federal Executive Council. There are state military governors.

History. Between 1879 and 1914, private colonial developments by the British, with reorganizations of the Crown's interest in the region, resulted in the formation of Nigeria as it exists today. During World War I, native troops of the West African frontier force joined with French forces to defeat the German garrison in the Cameroons.

Nigeria became independent on Oct. 1, 1960.

Organized as a loose federation of self-governing states, the independent nation faced an overwhelming task of unifying a country with 250 ethnic and linguistic groups.

Rioting broke out again in 1966, the military commander was seized, and Col. Yakubu Gowon took power. Also in that year, the Moslem Hausas in the north massacred the predominantly Christian Ibos in the east, many of whom had been driven from the north. Thousands of Ibos took refuge in the Eastern Region. The military government there asked Ibos to return to the region and, in May 1967, the assembly voted to secede from the federation and set up the Republic of Biafra. Civil war broke out.

In January 1970, after 31 months of civil war, Biafra surrendered to the federal government.

Gowon's nine-year rule was ended in 1975 by a bloodless coup that made Army Brigadier Muritala Rufai Mohammed the new chief of state. Mohammed was assassinated the next year 1976 by a group of seven young officers, who failed to seize control of the government.

The return of civilian leadership was established with the election of Alhaji Shehu Shagari, as president in 1979.

A coup on December 31, 1983, restored military rule. The military regime headed by Maj. Gen. Mohammed Buhari was overthrown in a bloodless coup on Aug. 27, 1985, led by Maj. Gen. Ibrahim Babangida, who proclaimed himself president.

NORWAY

Kingdom of Norway
Sovereign: King Olav V (1957)
Prime Minister: Jan P. Syse (1989)
Area: 125,049 sq mi. (323,877 sq km)
Population (1990): 4,200,000 (average annual growth rate: 0.3%)
Density per square mile: 34
Capital: Oslo
Largest cities (1988): Oslo, 450,308; Bergen, 209,912; Trondheim, 135,542; Stavanger, 96,316
Monetary unit: Krone
Language: Norwegian
Religion: Evangelical Lutheran (state), 88%
National name: Kongeriket Norge
Literacy rate: 100%
Economic summary: Gross domestic product (1987): $82.6 billion; $19,768 per capita; 1.3% real growth rate. Arable land: 3%; principal products: dairy products, livestock, grain, potatoes, furs, wool. Labor force: 2,128,-000; 17.2% in mining and manufacturing; major products: oil and gas, fish, pulp and paper, ships, aluminum, iron, steel, nickel, fertilizers, transportation equipment, hydroelectric power, petrochemicals. Natural resources: fish, timber, hydroelectric power, ores, oil, gas. Exports: oil, natural gas, fish products, chemicals, pulp and paper, aluminum. Imports: machinery, motor vehicles,

foodstuffs, iron and steel, textiles and clothing. Major trading partners: U.K., Sweden, West Germany, U.S., Denmark, Netherlands.

Geography. Norway is situated in the western part of the Scandinavian peninsula. It extends about 1,100 miles (1,770 km) from the North Sea along the Norwegian Sea to more than 300 miles (483 km) above the Arctic Circle, the farthest north of any European country. It is slightly larger than New Mexico. Sweden borders on most of the eastern frontier, with Finland and the U.S.S.R. in the northeast.

Nearly 70% of Norway is uninhabitable and covered by mountains, glaciers, moors, and rivers. The hundreds of deep fiords that cut into the coastline give Norway an overall oceanfront of more than 12,000 miles (19,312 km). Nearly 50,000 islands off the coast form a breakwater and make a safe coastal shipping channel.

Government. Norway is a constitutional hereditary monarchy. Executive power is vested in the King together with a Cabinet, or Council of State, consisting of a Prime Minister and at least seven other members. The Storting, or Parliament, is composed of 165 members elected by the people under proportional representation. The Storting discusses and votes on political and financial questions, but divides itself into two sections (Lagting and Odelsting) to discuss and pass on legislative matters. The King cannot dissolve the Storting before the expiration of its term.

The sovereign is Olav V, born July 2, 1903, only son of Haakon VII and Princess Maud (1869–1938), third daughter of Edward VII of England. He succeeded to the throne on the death of his father Sept. 20, 1957. He married Princess Märtha of Sweden (1901–1954) on March 21, 1929. Their children are Princess Ragnhild Alexandra (born 1930), Princess Astrid (born 1932), and Crown Prince Harald (born 1937). In 1968, the Crown Prince married Sonja Haraldsen, a commoner.

History. Norwegians, like the Danes and Swedes, are of Teutonic origin. The Norsemen, also known as Vikings, ravaged the coasts of northwestern Europe from the 8th to the 11th century.

In 1815, Norway fell under the control of Sweden. The union of Norway, inhabited by fishermen, sailors, merchants, and peasants, and Sweden, an aristocratic country of large estates and tenant farmers, was not a happy one, but it lasted for nearly a century. In 1905, the Norwegian Parliament arranged a peaceful separation and invited a Danish prince to the Norwegian throne—King Haakon VII. A treaty with Sweden provided that all disputes be settled by arbitration and that no fortifications be erected on the common frontier.

When World War I broke out, Norway joined with Sweden and Denmark in a decision to remain neutral and to cooperate in the joint interest of the three countries. In World War II, Norway was invaded by the Germans on April 9, 1940. It resisted for two months before the Nazis took over complete control. King Haakon and his government fled to London, where they established a government-in-exile. Maj. Vidkun Quisling, whose name is now synonymous with traitor or fifth columnist, was the most notorious Norwegian collaborator with the Nazis. He was executed by the Norwegians on Oct. 24, 1945.

Despite severe losses in the war, Norway recovered quickly. The country led the world in social experimentation. A neighbor of the U.S.S.R., Norway sought to retain good relations with the Soviet Union without losing its identity with the West. It entered the North Atlantic Treaty Organization in 1949.

Verification of U.S. and Soviet oil strikes in separated areas of Norway's sector of the North Sea bottom led the Storting in 1975 to impose stiff tax and royalty rates on concession holders. Following discovery of a North Sea field expected to produce 900,000 barrels a day by 1984, Parliament in 1976 approved establishment of a national refining and distributing company to market petroleum products at home and abroad.

Dependencies of Norway

Svalbard (24,208 sq mi.; 62,700 sq km), in the Arctic Ocean about 360 miles north of Norway, consists of the Spitsbergen group and several smaller islands, including Bear Island, Hope Island, King Charles Land, and White Island (or Gillis Land). It came under Norwegian administration in 1925. The population in 1986 was 3,942 of which 1,387 were Norwegians.

Bouvet Island (23 sq mi.; 60 sq km), in the South Atlantic about 1,600 miles south-southwest of the Cape of Good Hope, came under Norwegian administration in 1928.

Jan Mayen Island (147 sq mi.; 380 sq km), in the Arctic Ocean between Norway and Greenland, came under Norwegian administration in 1929.

Peter I Island (96 sq mi.; 249 sq km), lying off Antarctica in the Bellinghausen Sea, came under Norwegian administration in 1931.

Queen Maud Land, a section of Antarctica, came under Norwegian administration in 1939.

OMAN

Sultanate of Oman
Sultan: Qabus Bin Said (1970)
Area: 82,030 sq mi. (212,458 sq km)[i]
Population (mid-1990): 1,500,000 (average annual rate of natural increase: 3.3%)
Density per square mile: 17
Capital and largest city (est. 1981): Muscat, 70,000
Monetary unit: Omani rial
Language: Arabic (official); also English and Indian languages
Religion: Islam, 86%
National name: Saltonat Uman
Literacy rate: 20%
Economic summary: Gross domestic product (1987 est.): $7.5 billion; $6,110 per capita; 3.6% real growth rate. Principal agricultural products: dates, fruit, cereal, livestock. Labor force: 430,000; 60% in agriculture. Major industries: petroleum drilling, fishing, construction. Natural resources: oil, marble, copper, limestone. Exports: oil. Imports: machinery and transport equipment, food, mineral fuels. Major trading partners: U.K., U.S., China, Japan, Korea, Thailand.

1. Excluding the Kuria Muria Islands.

Geography. Oman is a 1,000-mile-long (1,700-km)

coastal plain at the southeastern tip of the Arabian peninsula lying on the Arabian Sea and the Gulf of Oman. The interior is a plateau. The country is the size of Kansas.

Government. The Sultan of Oman (formerly called Muscat and Oman), an absolute monarch, is assisted by a council of ministers, six specialized councils, a consultative council and personal advisers.

There are no political parties.

History. Although Oman is an independent state under the rule of the Sultan, it has been under British protection since the early 19th century.

Muscat, the capital of the geographical area known as Oman, was occupied by the Portuguese from 1508 to 1648. Then it fell to Persian princes and later was regained by the Sultan.

The Kuria Muria Islands, formerly part of Aden, were given to Oman by the British in 1967.

In a palace coup on July 23, 1970, the Sultan, Sa'id bin Taimur, who had ruled since 1932, was overthrown by his son, who promised to establish a modern government and use new-found wealth to aid the people of this very isolated state.

PAKISTAN

Islamic Republic of Pakistan
President: Gulam Ishaq Khan (1988)
Caretaker Prime Minister: Ghulam Mustafa Jatoi (1990)
Area: 310,400 sq mi. (803,936 sq km)[1]
Population (mid-1990): 114,600,000 (average annual growth rate: 3%)
Density per square mile: 356
Capital (1981 census): Islamabad, 201,000
Largest cities (1981 census for metropolitan area): Karachi, 5,208,100; Lahore, 2,952,700; Faisalabad, (Lyallpur) 1,920,000; Rawalpindi, 920,000; Hyderabad, 795,000
Monetary unit: Pakistan rupee
Principal languages: Urdu (national), English (official), Punjabi, Sindhi, Pashtu, and Baluchi
Religions: Islam, 97%; Hindu, Christian, Buddhist, Parsi
Literacy rate: 26%
Economic summary: Gross national product (FY88): $39.4 billion; $370 per capita; 4.9% real growth rate. Arable land: 26%; principal products: wheat, rice, cotton, sugarcane. Labor force: 28,900,000; 13% in mining and manufacturing; major products: cotton textiles, processed foods, tobacco, chemicals, natural gas. Natural resources: natural gas, limited petroleum, iron ore. Exports: raw and manufactured cotton, rice, carpets, leather, fish. Imports: food grains, edible oil, crude oil, machinery, chemicals, transport equipment. Major trading partners: U.S., U.K., West Germany, Saudi Arabia, Japan.

1. Excluding Kashmir and Jammu. 2. Does not include about 3 million refugees from Afghanistan.

Geography. Pakistan is situated in the western part of the Indian subcontinent, with Afghanistan and Iran on the west, India on the east, and the Arabian Sea on the south.

Nearly twice the size of California, Pakistan consists of towering mountains, including the Hindu Kush in the west, a desert area in the east, the Punjab plains in the north, and an expanse of alluvial plains. The 1,000-mile-long (1,609 km) Indus River flows through the country from the Kashmir to the Arabian Sea.

Government. Pakistan is a federal republic with a bicameral legislature.

History. Pakistan was one of the two original successor states to British India. For almost 25 years following independence in 1947, it consisted of two separate regions East and West Pakistan, but now comprises only the western sector. It consists of Sind, Baluchistan, the former North-West Frontier Province, western Punjab, the princely state of Bahawalpur, and several other smaller native states.

The British became the dominant power in the region in 1797 following Lord Clive's military victory, but rebellious tribes kept the northwest in turmoil. In the northeast, the formation of the Moslem League in 1906 estranged the Moslems from the Hindus. In 1930, the league, led by Mohammed Ali Jinnah, demanded creation of a Moslem state wherever Moslems were in the majority. He supported Britain during the war. Afterward, the league received almost a unanimous Moslem vote in 1946 and Britain agreed to the formation of Pakistan as a separate dominion.

Pakistan was proclaimed a republic March 23, 1956. Iskander Mirza, then Governor General, was elected Provisional President and H. S. Suhrawardy became the first non-Moslem League Prime Minister.

The election of 1970 set the stage for civil war when Sheik Muuibur told East Pakistanis to stop paying taxes to the central government. West Pakistan troops moved in and fighting began. The independent state of Bangladesh, or Bengali nation, was proclaimed March 26, 1971.

The intervention of Indian troops protected the new state and brought President Yahya Kahn down. Bhutto took over and accepted Bangladesh as an independent entity.

Diplomatically, 1976 saw the resumption of formal relations between India and Pakistan.

Pakistan's first elections under civilian rule took place in March 1977 and provoked bitter opposition protest when Bhutto's party was declared to have won 155 of the 200 elected seats in the 216-member National Assembly. A rising tide of violent protest and political deadlock led to a military takeover on July 5. Gen. Mohammed Zia ul-Haq became Chief Martial Law Administrator.

Bhutto was tried and convicted for the 1974 murder of a political opponent, and despite worldwide protests was executed on April 4, 1979, touching off riots by his supporters. Zia declared himself President on Sept. 16, 1978, a month after Fazel Elahi Chaudhry left office upon the completion of his 5-year term.

A measure of representative government was restored with the election of a new National Assembly in February 1985, although leaders of opposition parties were banned from the election and it was unclear what powers Zia would yield to the legislature.

On December 30, 1985, Zia ended martial law. In May 1988, Zia deposed Prime Minister Mohammed Junejo and dissolved the National Assembly on the grounds that they had not moved quickly enough to establish Islamic law or deal with ethnic *strife.*

On August 19, 1988, President Zia was killed in a midair explosion of a Pakistani Air Force plane.

Elections at the end of 1988 brought longtime Zia opponent Benazir Bhutto, daughter of Zulfikar Bhutto, into office as Prime Minister.

In August 1990, Pakistan's President dismissed

Prime Minister Bhutto on charges of corruption and incompetence. He dissolved parliament and promised new elections in October.

PANAMA

Republic of Panama

President: Guillermo Endara Galimany (1990)
Area: 29,761 sq mi. (77,082 sq km)
Population (mid-1990): 2,400,000 (average annual rate of natural increase: 2.2%)
Density per square mile: 80
Capital and largest city (est. 1987): Panama City, 440,-000
Monetary unit: Balboa
Language: Spanish (official); many bilingual in English
Religions: Roman Catholic, 89%; Protestant, 6%
National name: República de Panamá
Literacy rate: 90%
Economic summary: Gross domestic product (1988): $4.2 billion; $1,830 per capita; real growth rate −15 to −20%. Arable land: 6%; principal products: bananas, corn, sugar, rice, coffee. Labor force: 770,472 (1987); 10.5% in manufacturing and mining; major industrial products: refined petroleum, sugar. Natural resources: copper, mahogany, shrimp. Exports: bananas, refined petroleum, sugar, shrimp, coffee. Imports: petroleum, manufactured goods, machinery and transportation equipment, food. Major trading partners: U.S., Central America and the Caribbean, Western Europe, Mexico, Japan.

Geography. The southernmost of the Central American nations, Panama is south of Costa Rica and north of Colombia. The Panama Canal bisects the isthmus at its narrowest and lowest point, allowing passage from the Caribbean Sea to the Pacific Ocean.

Panama is slightly smaller than South Carolina. It is marked by a chain of volcanic mountains in the west, moderate hills in the interior, and a low range on the east coast. There are extensive forests in the fertile Caribbean area.

Government. In 1972, a new Constitution was approved by a new 505-seat National Assembly of Community Representatives (corregidores), which was created in the first election in five years. The Charter provides for indirect election of the President by the Assembly for a six-year term.

History. Visited by Columbus in 1502 on his fourth voyage and explored by Balboa in 1513, Panama was the principal transshipment point for Spanish treasure and supplies to and from South and Central America in colonial days. In 1821, when Central America revolted against Spain, Panama joined Colombia, which already had declared its independence. For the next 82 years, Panama attempted unsuccessfully to break away from Colombia. After U. S. proposals for canal rights over the narrow isthmus had been rejected by Colombia, Panama proclaimed its independence with U.S. backing in 1903.

For canal rights in perpetuity, the U.S. paid Panama $10 million and agreed to pay $250,000 each year, increased to $430,000 after devaluation of the U.S. dollar in 1933 and was further increased under a revised treaty signed in 1955. In exchange, the U.S. got the Canal Zone—a 10-mile-wide strip across the isthmus—and a considerable degree of influence in Panama's affairs.

In 1968, Dr. Arnulfo Arias was elected President for the third time in three decades. And for the third time, he was thrown out of office by the military. A two-man junta, Col. José M. Pinilla and Col. Bolívar Urrutia, took control. They were ousted by Gen. Omar Torrijos Herrera, who named a new junta, with Demetrio Lakas Bahas as President.

Panama and the U.S. agreed in 1974 to negotiate the eventual reversion of the canal to Panama, despite strongly expressed opposition in the U.S. Congress. The texts of two treaties—one governing the transfer of the canal and the other guaranteeing its neutrality after transfer—were negotiated by August 1977 and were signed by Pres. Omar Torrijos Herara and President Carter in Washington on September 7. A Panamanian referendum approved the treaties by more than two thirds on October 23, but further changes were insisted upon by the U.S. Senate.

The principal change was a reservation specifying that despite the neutrality treaty's specification that only Panama shall maintain forces in its territory after transfer of the canal Dec. 31, 1999, the U.S. should have the right to use military force to keep the canal operating if it should become obstructed. The Senate approved the treaties in March-April, 1978. On June 16, Carter and Torrijos exchanged instruments of ratification in Panama City.

The basic treaty provides an increase from $2.3 million a year in royalties to $10 million a year during the transition period, with an additional annual payment of $10 million if it can be obtained from tolls. It also requires the use of more Panamanians as canal employees in the interim and pledges the U.S. not to pursue the development of another canal without the agreement of Panama.

The death of Torrijos in a plane crash on July 31, 1981, left a power vacuum. President Aristides Royo, named by Torrijos in 1978 to a six-year term, clashed with the leadership of the National Guard and was unable to harmonize factions within the ruling Democratic Revolutionary Party. On July 30, 1982, Royo resigned in favor of Vice President Ricardo de la Espriella.

Nicolas Ardito Barletta, Panama's first directly elected President in 16 years, was inaugurated on Oct. 11, 1984, for a five-year term. He lacked the necessary support to solve the country's economic crisis and resigned September 28, 1985. He was replaced by Vice President Eric Arturo Delvalle.

In June, 1986, reports surfaced that the behind-the-scenes strongman, Gen. Manuel Noriega, was involved in drug trafficking and the murder of an opposition leader. In 1987, Noriega was accused by his ex-Chief of Staff of assassinating Torrijos in 1981. He was indicted in the U.S. for drug trafficking but when Delvalle attempted to fire him, he forced the National Assembly to replace Delvalle with Manuel Solis Palma. Despite protests and U.S. economic sanctions, Noriega remains in power.

The crisis continued when Noreiga called presidential elections for when the current term expires. Despite massive fraud by Noreiga, the opposition seemed headed to a landslide. Noreiga annulled the elections and suppressed protests by the opposition.

In December 1989, the Assembly named Noriega the "maximum leader" and declared the U.S. and Panama to be in a state of war. A further series of incidents led to a U.S. invasion overthrowing Noriega, who was brought to the U.S. to stand trial for drug trafficking. Guillermo Endora, who probably would have won the election suppressed by Noriega, was instated as President.

Panama Canal. First conceived by the Spaniards in 1524, when King Charles V of Spain ordered a survey of a waterway across the Isthmus, a construction concession was granted by the Colombian government in 1878 to St. Lucien N. B. Wyse, representing a French company. Two years later, the French Canal Company, inspired by Ferdinand de Lesseps, began construction of what was to have been a sea-level canal. The effort ended in bankruptcy nine years later and the United States ultimately paid the French $40 million for their rights and assets.

The U.S. project, built on territory controlled by the United States, and calling for the creation of an interior lake connected to both oceans by locks, got under way in 1904. Completed in 1914, the Canal is 40.27 miles long and lifts ships 85 feet above sea level through a series of three locks on the Pacific and Atlantic sides. Enlarged in later years, each lock now measures 1,000 feet in length, 110 feet in width, and 40 feet in depth of water.

PAPUA NEW GUINEA

Sovereign: Queen Elizabeth II
Governor General: Sir Kingsford Dibela (1983)
Prime Minister: Rabbie Namaliu (1988)
Area: 178,704 sq mi. (462,840 sq km)
Population (mid-1990): 4,000,000 (average annual rate of natural increase: 2.7%)
Density per square mile: 22
Capital and largest city (est. 1986): Port Moresby, 145,-000
Monetary unit: Kina
Languages: English, Melanesian pidgin, Hiri Motu, and 717 distinct native languages
Religions: over half Christian, remainder indigenous.
Member of Commonwealth of Nations
Literacy rate: 32%
Economic summary: Gross domestic product (1987 est.): $2.93 billion; $745 per capita; 2.9% real growth rate. Principal products: coffee, copra, palm oil, cocoa, tea, coconuts. Labor force: 1,660,000; 732,806 salaried; 9% industry and commerce. Major industrial products: coconut oil, plywood, wood chips, gold, silver. Natural resources: copper, gold, silver, timber, natural gas. Exports: gold, copper, coffee and cocoa beans, copra, timber. Imports: food, machinery, transport equipment, fuels. Major trading partners: Australia, U.K., Japan, West Germany, Singapore.

Geography. Papua New Guinea occupies the eastern half of the island of New Guinea, just north of Australia, and many outlying islands. The Indonesian province of Irian Jaya is to the west. To the north and east are the islands of Manus, New Britain, New Ireland, and Bougainville, all part of Papua New Guinea.

Papua New Guinea is about one tenth larger than California. Its mountainous interior has only recently been explored. The high-plateau climate is temperate, in contrast to the tropical climate of the coastal plains. Two major rivers, the Sepik and the Fly, are navigable for shallow-draft vessels.

Government. Papua New Guinea attained independence Sept. 16, 1975, ending a United Nations trusteeship under the administration of Australia. Parliamentary democracy was established by a Constitution that invests power in a 109-member national legislature.

History. The eastern half of New Guinea was first visited by Spanish and Portuguese explorers in the 16th century, but a permanent European presence was not established until 1884, when Germany declared a protectorate over the northern coast and Britain took similar action in the south. Both nations formally annexed their protectorates and, in 1901, Britain transferred its rights to a newly independent Australia. Australian troops invaded German New Guinea in World War I and retained control under a League of Nations mandate that eventually became a United Nations trusteeship, incorporating a territorial government in the southern region, known as Papua.

Australia granted limited home rule in 1951 and, in 1964, organized elections for the first House of Assembly. Autonomy in internal affairs came nine years later.

PARAGUAY

Republic of Paraguay
President: Gen. Andres Rodriguez (1989)
Area: 157,047 sq mi. (406,752 sq km)
Population (mid-1990): 4,300,000 (average annual rate of natural increase: 2.8%)
Density per square mile: 26
Capital and largest city (est. 1985): Asunción, 477,000
Monetary unit: Guaraní
Languages: Spanish (official), Guaraní
Religion: Roman Catholic (official)
National name: República del Paraguay
Literacy rate: 84%
Economic summary: Gross domestic product (1987): $7.4 billion; $1,740 per capita; 3% real growth rate. Arable land: 20%; principal products: soybeans, cotton, hides, sweet potatoes, tobacco, corn, rice, sugar cane. Labor force: 1,300,000; 34% in industry and commerce; major products: packed meats, crushed oilseeds, beverages, textiles, light consumer goods, cement. Natural resources: Copper, gold and silver, iron ore, coal, timber, fish. Exports: cotton, soybeans, meat products, tobacco, timber, coffee, hides. Imports: fuels and lubricants, machinery and motors, motor vehicles, beverages, tobacco, foodstuffs. Major trading partners: Argentina, Brazil, West Germany, U.S., Netherlands, Switzerland, Algeria

Geography. California-size Paraguay is surrounded by Brazil, Bolivia, and Argentina in south central South America. Eastern Paraguay, between the Paraná and Paraguay Rivers, is upland country with the thickest population settled on the grassy slope that inclines toward the Paraguay River. The greater part of the Chaco region to the west is covered with marshes, lagoons, dense forests, and jungles.

Government. The President is elected by popular vote for five years. The legislature is bicameral, consisting of a Senate of 30 members and a Chamber of Representatives of 60 members. There is also a Council of State, whose members are nominated by the government.

History. In 1526 and again in 1529, Sebastian Cabot explored Paraguay when he sailed up the Paraná and Paraguay Rivers. From 1608 until their expulsion from the Spanish dominions in 1767, the Jesuits maintained an extensive establishment in the south and east of Paraguay. In 1811, Paraguay revolted against Spanish rule and became a nominal republic under two Consuls.

Actually, Paraguay was governed by three dictators during the first 60 years of independence. The third, Francisco López, waged war against Brazil and Argentina in 1865–70, a conflict in which the male population was almost wiped out. A new Constitution in 1870, designed to prevent dictatorships and internal strife, failed to do so, and not until 1912 did a period of comparative economic and political stability begin.

After World War II, politics became particularly unstable.

Stroessner ruled under a state of siege until 1965, when the dictatorship was relaxed and exiles returned. The Constitution was revised in 1967 to permit Stroessner to be re-elected.

Although oil exploration begun by U.S. companies in the Chaco boreal in 1974 has been fruitless, Paraguay found prosperity in another form of energy when construction started in 1978 on the Itaipu Dam on the Parana River as a joint Paraguayan-Brazilian project. The largest hydroelectric development in the world when completed, Itaipu will generate 12.6 megawatts of electricity, surpassing the U.S. Grand Coulee Dam.

The Stroessner regime was criticized by the U.S. State Department during the Carter administration as a violator of human rights, but unlike Argentina and Uruguay, Paraguay did not suffer cuts in U.S. military aid. The criticism is credited with having reduced the number of political prisoners to a "few hundred."

The government was forced to devalue the guarani as a condition for IMF help for the ailing economy.

Stroessner was overthrown by an army leader, Gen. Andres Rodriguez, in 1989. Rodriguez won in Paraguay's first multi-candidate elections in decades. He has promised to hand over power to an elected civilian successor in 1993.

PERU

Republic of Peru
President: Alberto Fujimori (1990)
Premier: Armando Villanueva (1988)
Area: 496,222 sq mi. (1,285,216 sq km)
Population (mid-1990): 21,900,000 (average annual rate of natural increase: 2.4%)
Density per square mile: 43
Capital: Lima
Largest cities (est. 1987): Lima, 5,330,800; Arequipa, 572,000; Callao, 545,000; Trujillo, 476,000; Chiclayo, 379,000
Monetary unit: Inti
Languages: Spanish, Quéchua, Aymara, and other native languages
Religion: Roman Catholic
National name: República del Perú
Literacy rate: est. 80%
Economic summary: Gross domestic product (1988): $19.6 billion; $920 per capita; real growth rate −8.4%. Arable land: 3%; principal products: wheat, potatoes, beans, rice, sugar, cotton, coffee. Labor force: 6,800,000 (1986); 19% in industry; major products: processed minerals, fish meal, refined petroleum, textiles. Natural resources: silver, gold, iron, copper, fish, petroleum, timber. Exports: copper, fish products, cotton, sugar, coffee, lead, silver, zinc, wool, oil, iron ore. Imports: machinery, foodstuffs, chemicals, pharmaceuticals. Major trading partners: U.S., Japan, Western European, and Latin American countries.

Geography. Peru, in western South America, extends for nearly 1,500 miles (2,414 km) along the Pacific Ocean. Colombia and Ecuador are to the north, Brazil and Bolivia to the east, and Chile to the south.

Five sixths the size of Alaska, Peru is divided by the Andes Mountains into three sharply differentiated zones. To the west is the coastline, much of it arid, extending 50 to 100 miles (80 to 160 km) inland. The mountain area, with peaks over 20,000 feet (6,096 m), lofty plateaus, and deep valleys, lies centrally. Beyond the mountains to the east is the heavily forested slope leading to the Amazonian plains.

Government. The President, elected by universal suffrage for a five-year term, holds executive power. A Senate of 60 members and a Chamber of Deputies of 180 members, both elected for five-year terms, share legislative power.

History. Peru was once part of the great Incan empire and later the major vice-royalty of Spanish South America. It was conquered in 1531–33 by Francisco Pizarro. On July 28, 1821, Peru proclaimed its independence, but the Spanish were not finally defeated until 1824. For a hundred years thereafter, revolutions were frequent, and a new war was fought with Spain in 1864–66.

Peru emerged from 20 years of dictatorship in 1945 with the inauguration of President José Luis Bustamante y Rivero after the first free election in many decades. But he served for only three years and was succeeded in turn by Gen. Manual A. Odria, Manuel Prado y Ugarteche, and Fernando Belaúnde Terry. On Oct. 3, 1968, Belaúnde was overthrown by Gen. Juan Velasco Alvarado.

Velasco nationalized the nation's second biggest bank and turned two large newspapers over to Marxists in 1970, but he also allowed a new agreement with a copper-mining consortium of four American firms.

In 1975, Velasco was replaced in a bloodless coup by his Premier, Gen. Francisco Morales Bermudez, who promised to restore civilian government. In elections held on May 18, 1980, Belaunde Terry, the last previous civilian President and the candidate of the conservative parties that have traditionally ruled Peru, was elected President again. By the end of his five-year term in 1985, the country was in the midst of acute economic and social crisis.

But Peru's fragile democracy survived this period of stress and when he left office in 1985 Belaunde Terry was the first elected President to turn over power to a constitutionally elected successor since 1945. Alan Garcia Pérez, a 36-year-old Social Democrat, was inaugurated President on July 28, 1985. In his inaugural address, he said Peru would limit payments on its foreign debt to no more than 10% of its export earnings, instead of the terms demanded by the International Monetary Fund.

The savage war with the Sendero Luminoso guerrillas, a Maoist group, continued unabated with much of Peru remaining under military control.

THE PHILIPPINES

Republic of the Philippines
President: Corazon C. Aquino (1986)
Vice President: Salvador H. Laurel (1986)
Area: 115,830 sq mi. (300,000 sq km)
Population (mid-1990): 66,100,000 (average annual rate of natural increase: 2.6%)
Density per square mile: 560
Capital: Manila
Largest cities (est. 1984): Manila, 1,728,400[1]; Quezon City, 1,326,000; Cebu, 552,200
Monetary unit: Peso
Languages: Filipino (based on Tagalog), English; regional languages: Tagalog, Ilocano, Cebuano, others
Religions: Roman Catholic, 85%; Islam, 4%; Aglipayan (Independent Philippine Christian), 4%; Protestant, 3%
National name: Republika ng Pilipinas
Literacy rate: 88%
Economic summary: Gross domestic product (1987): $33.6 billion; $546 per capita; 5% real growth rate. Arable land: 26%; principal products: rice, corn, coconuts, sugar cane, bananas, tobacco. Labor force: 22,889,000; 20% in industry and commerce; major products: textiles, pharmaceuticals, chemicals, food processing, electronics assembly. Natural resources: forests, metallic and non-metallic minerals. Exports: electronic equipment, coconut products, sugar, logs and lumber, copper concentrates, bananas, garments, nickel. Imports: petroleum, industrial equipment, wheat. Major trading partners: U.S., Japan.

1. Metropolitan area population is 7,500,000.

Geography. The Philippine Islands are an archipelago of over 7,000 islands lying about 500 miles (805 km) off the southeast coast of Asia. The overall land area is comparable to that of Arizona. The northernmost island, Y'Ami, is 65 miles (105 km) from Taiwan, while the southernmost, Saluag, is 40 miles (64 km) east of Borneo.

Only about 7% of the islands are larger than one square mile, and only one third have names. The largest are Luzon in the north (40,420 sq mi.; 104,-687 sq km), Mindanao in the south (36,537 sq mi.; 94,631 sq km), Samar (5,124 sq mi.; 13,271 sq km).

The islands are of volcanic origin, with the larger ones crossed by mountain ranges. The highest peak is Mount Apo (9,690 ft; 2,954 m) on Mindanao.

Government. On February 2, 1987, the Filipino people voted for a new Constitution that established a 24-seat Senate and a 250-seat House of Representatives and gave President Aquino a six-year term. It limits the powers of the President, who can't be re-elected.

History. Fernando Magellan, the Portuguese navigator in the service of Spain, discovered the Philippines in 1521. Twenty-one years later, a Spanish exploration party named the group of islands in honor of Prince Philip, later Philip II of Spain. Spain retained possession of the islands for the next 350 years.

The Philippines were ceded to the U.S. in 1899 by the Treaty of Paris after the Spanish-American War. Meanwhile, the Filipinos, led by Emilio Aguinaldo, had declared their independence. They continued guerrilla warfare against U.S. troops until the capture of Aguinaldo in 1901. By 1902, peace was established except among the Moros.

The first U.S. civilian Governor-General was William Howard Taft (1901–04). The Jones Law (1916) provided for the establishment of a Philippine Legislature composed of an elective Senate and House

of Representatives. The Tydings-McDuffie Act (1934) provided for a transitional period until 1946, at which time the Philippines would become completely independent.

Under a Constitution approved by the people of the Philippines in 1935, the Commonwealth of the Philippines came into being, with Manuel Quezon y Molina as president.

On Dec. 8, 1941, the Philippines were invaded by Japanese troops. Following the fall of Bataan and Corregidor, Quezon established a government-in-exile, which he headed until his death in 1944. He was succeeded by Vice President Sergio Osmeña.

U.S. forces led by Gen. Douglas MacArthur reinvaded the Philippines in October 1944 and, after the liberation of Manila in February 1945, Osmeña re-established the government.

The Philippines achieved full independence on July 4, 1946. Manual A. Roxas y Acuña was elected first president. Subsequent presidents have been Elpidio Quirino (1948–53), Ramón Magsaysay (1953–57), Carlos P. García (1957–61), Diosdado Macapagal (1961–65), Ferdinand E. Marcos (1965–86).

The Philippines was one on six nations criticized by the U.S. State Department for human-rights violations in a report made public in 1977, although the department recommended continuing aid because of the importance of U.S. bases in the Philippines.

Marcos, who had freed the last of the national leaders still in detention, former Senator Benigno S. Aquino, Jr., in 1980 and permitted him to go to the United States, ended eight years of martial law on January 17, 1981.

Despite having been warned by First Lady Imelda Marcos that he risked being killed if he came back, opposition leader Aquino returned to the Philippines from self-exile on Aug. 21, 1983. He was shot to death as he was being escorted from his plane by military police at Manila International Airport. The government contended the assassin was a small-time hoodlum allegedly hired by communists, who was in turn shot dead by Filipino troops, but there was widespread suspicion that the Marcos government was involved in the murder.

The assassination sparked huge anti-government rallies and violent clashes between demonstrators and police, which continued intermittently through most of 1984, and helped the fragmented opposition parties score substantial gains in the May 14, 1984, elections for a National Assembly with greater power than a previous interim parliament.

On Jan. 23, 1985, one of Marcos' closest associates, Gen. Fabian C. Ver, the armed forces chief of staff, and 25 others were charged with the 1983 assassination of Aquino. Their trial dragged on through most of the year, with defense attorneys charging the evidence against Ver and the other defendants was fabricated.

In an attempt to re-secure American support, Marcos set Presidential elections for Feb. 7, 1986. After Ver's acquittal, and with the support of the Catholic church, Corazon Aquino, widow of Benigno Aquino, declared her candidacy. Marcos was declared the winner but the vote was widely considered to be rigged and anti-Marcos protests continued. The defection of Defense Minister Juan Enrile and Lt. Gen. Fidel Ramos signaled an end of military support for Marcos, who fled into exile in the U.S. on Feb. 25, 1986.

The Aquino government survived coup attempts by Marcos supporters and other right-wing elements including one, in November, by Enrile. Legislative elections on May 11, 1987, gave pro-Aquino candidates a large majority.

The growth of the Communist insurgency in the Philippines remains a matter of increasing concern, both in Manila and Washington.

POLAND

Republic of Poland
President: Gen. Wojciech Jaruzelski (1988)
Prime Minister: Tadeusz Mazowiecki (1989)
Area: 120,727 sq mi. (312,683 sq km)
Population (mid-1990): 37,800,000 (average annual rate of natural increase: .6%)
Density per square mile: 316
Capital: Warsaw
Largest cities (est. 1986): Warsaw, 1,659,400; Lodz, 847,900; Krakow, 740,100; Wrocław, 637,200; Poznan, 575,100; Gdansk, 464,600; Szczecin, 392,300
Monetary unit: Zloty
Language: Polish
Religions: Roman Catholic.
National name: Rzeczpospolita Polska
Literacy rate: 98%
Economic summary: Gross national product (1988): $276.3 billion; $7,280 per capita; 2.1% real growth rate. Arable land: 48%; principal products: grains, sugar beets, potatoes, hogs and other livestock. Labor force: 18,630,000 (1987); 44% in industry and commerce; major products: iron and steel, chemicals, textiles, processed foods, transport equipment. Natural resources: coal, sulfur, copper, natural gas. Exports: coal, machinery and equipment, chemicals, industrial products. Imports: machinery and equipment, fuels, raw materials, agricultural and food products. Major trading partners: Communist bloc countries, U.K., Italy, U.S., West Germany, France.

Geography. Poland, a country the size of New Mexico in north central Europe, borders on East Germany to the west, Czechoslovakia to the south, and the U.S.S.R. to the east. In the north is the Baltic Sea.

Most of the country is a plain with no natural boundaries except the Carpathian Mountains in the south and the Oder and Neisse Rivers in the east. Other major rivers, which are important to commerce, are the Vistula, Warta, and Bug.

Government. The 1952 Constitution describes Poland as a people's republic. The supreme organ of state authority is the Sejm (Parliament), which is composed of 460 members elected for four years. A 100-seat Senate was established in 1989.

History. Little is known about Polish history before the 11th century, when King Boleslaus I (the Brave) ruled over Bohemia, Saxony, and Moravia. Meanwhile, the Teutonic knights of Prussia conquered part of Poland and barred the latter's access to the Baltic. The knights were defeated by Wladislaus II at Tannenberg in 1410 and became Polish vassals, and Poland regained a Baltic shoreline. Poland reached the peak of power between the 14th and 16th centuries, scoring military successes against the Russians and Turks. In 1683, John III

(John Sobieski) turned back the Turkish tide at Vienna.

An elective monarchy failed to produce strong central authority, and Prussia, and Austria were able to carry out a first partition of the country in 1772, a second in 1792, and a third in 1795. For more than a century thereafter, there was no Polish state, but the Poles never ceased their efforts to regain their independence.

Poland was formally reconstituted in November 1918, with Marshal Josef Pilsudski as Chief of State. In 1919, Ignace Paderewski, the famous pianist and patriot, became the first premier. In 1926, Pilsudski seized complete power in a coup and ruled dictatorially until his death on May 12, 1935, when he was succeeded by Marshal Edward Smigly-Rydz.

Despite a 10-year nonaggression pact signed in 1934, Hitler attacked Poland on Sept. 1, 1939. Russian troops invaded from the east on September 17, and on September 28 a German-Russian agreement divided Poland between Russia and Germany. Wladyslaw Raczkiewicz formed a government-in-exile in France, which moved to London after France's defeat in 1940.

All of Poland was occupied by Germany after the Nazi attack on the U.S.S.R. in June 1941.

The legal Polish government soon fell out with the Russians, and, in 1944, a Communist-dominated Polish Committee of National Liberation received Soviet recognition. Moving to Lublin after that city's liberation, it proclaimed itself the Provisional Government of Poland. Some former members of the Polish government in London joined with the Lublin government to form the Polish Government of National Unity, which Britain and the U.S. recognized.

On Aug. 2, 1945, in Berlin, President Harry S. Truman, Joseph Stalin and Prime Minister Clement Attlee of Britain established a new *de facto* western frontier for Poland along the Oder and Neisse Rivers. (The border was finally agreed to by West Germany in a nonagression pact signed Dec. 7, 1970.) On Aug. 16, 1945, the U.S.S.R. and Poland signed a treaty delimiting the Soviet-Polish frontier. Under these agreements, Poland was shifted westward. In the east it lost 69,860 square miles (180,934 sq km) with 10,772,000 inhabitants; in the west it gained (subject to final peace-conference approval) 38,986 square miles (100,973 sq km) with a prewar population of 8,621,000.

A New Constitution in 1952 made Poland a "people's democracy" of the Soviet type. In 1955, Poland, became a member of the Warsaw Treaty Organization, and its foreign policy became identical with that of the U.S.S.R. The government undertook persecution of the Roman Catholic Church as a remaining source of opposition.

Wladyslaw Gomulka was elected leader of the United Workers (Communist) Party in 1956. He denounced the Stalinist terror, ousted many Stalinists, and improved relations with the church. Most collective farms were dissolved, and the press became freer.

A strike that began in shipyards and spread to other industries in August 1980 produced a stunning victory for workers when the economically hard-pressed government accepted for the first time in a Marxist state the right of workers to organize in independent unions.

Led by Solidarity, a free union founded by Lech

Walesa, workers launched a drive for liberty and improved conditions. A national strike for a five-day week in January 1981 led to the dismissal of Premier Pinkowski and the naming of the fourth Premier in less than a year, Gen. Wojciech Jaruzelski.

Antistrike legislation was approved on Dec. 2 and martial law declared on Dec. 13, when Walesa and other Solidarity leaders were arrested. Ten days later, President Reagan ordered sanctions against the Polish government, stopping food shipments and cutting commercial air traffic. The sanctions were lifted in early 1987.

Despite demands for declaring Poland in default, Congress in February authorized payment of $3.5 million in interest charges to U.S. banks that had given loans to Poland for food purchases.

Martial law was formally ended in 1984 but the government retained emergency powers. On July 21, 1984, the Parliament marked the 40th anniversary of Communist rule in Poland by enacting an amnesty bill authorizing the release of 652 political prisoners—virtually all except for those charged with high treason, espionage, and sabotage—and 35,000 common criminals. On September 10, 1986, the government freed all 225 remaining political prisoners.

The abduction and murder in October 1984 of a pro-Solidarity, Roman Catholic priest, the Rev. Jerzy Popieluszko, jolted the government as no other event had since the start of the Solidarity movement in 1980. After a 25-day trial before a five-judge tribunal, four state security policemen were convicted on Feb. 7, 1985, and sentenced to prison terms of 14 to 25 years for the murder.

Increasing opposition to the government because of the failing economy led to a new wave of strikes in 1988. Unable to totally quell the dissent, it relegalized Solidarity and allowed them to compete in elections.

Solidarity won a stunning victory, taking almost all the seats in the Senate and all of the 169 seats they were allowed to contest in the Sejm. This has given them substantial influence in the new government.

PORTUGAL

Republic of Portugal
President: Mario Soares (1986)
Prime Minister: Anibal Cavaco Silva (1987)
Area: 35,550 sq mi. (92,075 sq km)
Population (mid-1990): 10,400,000 (average annual rate of natural increase: 0.2%)
Density per square mile: 293
Capital: Lisbon
Largest cities (est. 1985): Lisbon, 827,800; Opporto, 344,500
Monetary unit: Escudo
Language: Portuguese
Religion: Roman Catholic 97%, 1% Protestant, 2% other.
National name: República Portuguesa
Literacy rate: 80%
Economic summary: Gross domestic product (1987): $33.5 billion; $3,250 per capita; 5% real growth rate. Arable land: 32%; principal products: grains, potatoes, olives, wine grapes. Labor force: 4,580,000; 34% in industry; major products: textiles, footwear, wood pulp, paper, cork, metal products, refined oil, chemicals, canned fish, wine. Natural resources: fish, cork, tungsten, iron ore. Exports: cotton, textiles, cork and cork products, canned fish, wine, timber and timber products, resin. Imports: petroleum, cotton, foodgrains, industrial machinery, iron and steel, chemicals. Major trading partners: Western European countries, U.S.

Geography. Portugal occupies the western part of the Iberian Peninsula, bordering on the Atlantic Ocean to the west and Spain to the north and east. It is slightly smaller than Indiana.

The country is crossed by many small rivers, and also by three large ones that rise in Spain, flow into the Atlantic, and divide the country into three geographic areas. The Minho River, part of the northern boundary, cuts through a mountainous area that extends south to the vicinity of the Douro River. South of the Douro, the mountains slope to the plains about the Tejo River. The remaining division is the southern one of Alentejo.

The Azores, stretching over 340 miles (547 km) in the Atlantic, consist of nine islands divided into three groups, with a total area of 902 square miles (2,335 sq km). The nearest continental land is Cape da Roca, Portugal, about 900 miles (1,448 km) to the east. The Azores are an important station on Atlantic air routes, and Britain and the U.S. established air bases there during World War II.

Madeira, consisting of two inhabited islands, Madeira and Porto Santo, and two groups of uninhabited islands, lies in the Atlantic about 535 miles (861 km) southwest of Lisbon. The Madeiras are 307 square miles (796 sq km) in area.

Government. The Constitution of 1976, revised in 1982, provides for popular election of a President for a five-year term and for a legislature, the Assembly of the Republic, for four years.

History. Portugal was a part of Spain until it won its independence in the middle of the 12th century. King John I (1385–1433) unified his country at the expense of the Castilians and the Moors of Morocco. The expansion of Portugal was brilliantly coordinated by John's son, Prince Henry the Navigator. In 1488, Bartolomew Diaz reached the Cape of Good Hope, proving that the Far East was accessible by sea. In 1498, Vasco da Gama reached the west coast of India. By the middle of the 16th century, the Portuguese Empire was in West and East Africa, Brazil, Persia, Indochina, and Malaya.

In 1581, Philip II of Spain invaded Portugal and held it for 60 years, precipitating a catastrophic decline of Portuguese commerce. Courageous and shrewd explorers, the Portuguese proved to be inefficient and corrupt colonizers. By the time the Portuguese dynasty was restored in 1640, Dutch, English, and French competitors began to seize the lion's share of the world's colonies and commerce. Portugal retained Angola and Mozambique in Africa, and Brazil (until 1822).

The corrupt King Carlos, who ascended the throne in 1889, made Joao Franco the Premier with dictatorial power in 1906. In 1908, Carlos and his heir were shot dead on the streets of Lisbon. The new King, Manoel II, was driven from the throne in the Revolution of 1910 and Portugal became a French-style republic.

Traditionally friendly to Britain, Portugal fought in World War I on the Allied side in Africa as well as on the Western Front. Weak postwar governments and a revolution in 1926 brought Antonio Oliveira Salazar to power. He kept Portugal neutral in World War II but gave the Allies naval and air bases after 1943.

Portugal lost the tiny remnants of its Indian empire—Goa, Daman, and Diu—to Indian military occupation in 1961, the year an insurrection broke out in Angola. For the next 13 years, Salazar, who died in 1970, and his successor, Marcello Caetano, fought independence movements amid growing world criticism. Leftists in the armed forces, weary of a losing battle, launched a successful revolution on April 25, 1974.

In 1980, President General Antonia Ramalho Eanes won a second four-year term with 57% of the popular vote.

In late 1985, a PSP-PSD split ended the Soares coalition government. Cavaco Silva, an advocate of free-market economics, was the Social Democratic candidate. His party emerged with a plurality, unseating the Socialists.

In July, 1987, the governing Social Democratic Party was swept back into office with 50.22% of the popular vote, giving Portugal its first majority Government since democracy was restored in 1974.

Portuguese Overseas Territory

After the April 1974 revolution, the military junta moved to grant independence to the territories, beginning with Portuguese Guinea in September 1974, which became the Republic of Guinea-Bissau.

Mozambique and Angcla followed, leaving only Portuguese Timor and Macao of the former empire. Despite Lisbon's objections, Indonesia annexed Timor.

MACAO

Status: Territory
Governor: Carlos Melancia (1987)
Area: 6 sq mi. (15.5 sq km)
Population (mid-1990): 500,000 (average annual growth rate: 1.5%)
Capital (1970 census): Macao, 241,413
Monetary unit: Patacá
Literacy rate (1981): 99% (excluding Chinese)
Economic summary: Gross domestic product (1987 est.): $2.0 billion, $4,350 per capita; real growth rate (1987 est.): 8%. Principal agricultural products: rice and vegetables. Major industrial products: clothing, textiles, plastics, furniture. Exports: textiles and clothing. Imports: raw materials, foodstuffs. Major trading partners: Hong Kong, China, U.S., West Germany, France.

Macao comprises the peninsula of Macao and the two small islands of Taipa and Colôane on the South China coast, about 35 miles (53 km) from Hong Kong. Established by the Portuguese in 1557, it is the oldest European outpost in the China trade, but Portugal's sovereign rights to the port were not recognized by China until 1887. The port has been eclipsed in importance by Hong Kong, but it is still a busy distribution center and also has an important fishing industry. Portugal will return Macao to China in 1999.

QATAR

State of Qatar
Emir: Sheikh Khalifa bin Hamad al-Thani (1972)
Area: 4,000 sq mi. (11,437 sq km)
Population (mid-1990): 500,000 (average annual rate of natural increase: 2.3%)
Density per square mile: 103
Capital (est. 1981): Doha, 190,000
Monetary unit: Qatari riyal
Language: Arabic; English is also widely spoken
Religion: Islam, 94%; Christian, 6%
Literacy rate: 70%
Economic summary: Gross national product (1987): $5.4 billion; $17,070 per capita; 9% real growth rate. Labor force: 104,000. Major industrial product: oil. Natural resources: oil, gas. Export: oil. Major trading partners: Japan, U.K., W. Germany, France, India.

Geography. Qatar occupies a small peninsula that extends into the Persian Gulf from the east side of the Arabian Peninsula. Saudi Arabia is to the west and the United Arab Emirates to the south. The country is mainly barren.

Government. Qatar, one of the Arabian Gulf states, lies between Bahrain and United Arab Emirates. For a long time, it was under Turkish protection, but in 1916, the Emir accepted British protection. After the discovery of oil in the 1940s and its exploitation in the 1950s and 1960s, political unrest spread to the sheikhdoms. Qatar declared its independence in 1971. The next year the current Sheikh, Khalifa bin Hamad al-Thani, ousted his cousin in a bloodless coup.

ROMANIA

Socialist Republic of Romania
President: Ion Iliescu (1990)
Premier: Petre Roman
Area: 91,700 sq mi. (237,500 sq km)
Population (mid-1990): 23,300,000 (average annual rate of natural increase: 0.5%)
Density per square mile: 250.8
Capital: Bucharest
Largest cities (est. July 1, 1986): Bucharest, 2,014,359 (1987); Brasov, 351,493; Constanta, 327,676; Timisoara, 325,272; Iasi, 313,060; Cluj-Napoca, 310,017; Galati, 295,372 .
Monetary unit: Leu
Languages: Romanian, Magyar
Religions: Romanian Orthodox, 80%; Roman Catholic, 6%; 4% others
National name: Republica Socialista România
Literacy rate: 98%
Economic summary: Gross national product (1988): $151.3 billion; $6,570 per capita; 2.1% real growth rate. Arable land: 43%; principal products: corn, wheat, livestock. Labor force: 10,690,000; 34% in industry; major products: steel, cement, metal production and processing, chemicals, food processing, textiles. Natural resources: oil, timber, natural gas, coal. Exports: machinery, minerals and metals, foodstuffs, lumber, fuel, manufactures. Imports: machinery, minerals, fuels, agricultural products, consumer goods. Major trading partners: U.S.S.R., East Germany, West Germany, Iran, Egypt, Italy.

Geography. A country in southeastern Europe slightly smaller than Oregon, Romania is bordered on the west by Hungary and Yugoslavia, on the north and east by the U.S.S.R., on the east by the Black Sea, and on the south by Bulgaria.

The Carpathian Mountains divide Romania's upper half from north to south and connect near the center of the country with the Transylvanian Alps, running east and west.

North and west of these ranges lies the Transylvanian plateau, and to the south and east are the plains of Moldavia and Walachia. In its last 190 miles (306 km), the Danube River flows through Romania only. It enters the Black Sea in northern Dobruja, just south of the border with the Soviet Union.

Government. After the overthrow of Nicolae Ceausescu's Communist government at the end of 1989, an interim-government headed by the Front for National Salvation took power and proclaimed its commitment to establishing a multi-party democracy in the nation.

History. Most of Romania was the Roman province of Dacia from about A.D. 100 to 271. From the 6th to the 12th century, wave after wave of barbarian conquerors overran the native Daco-Roman population. By the 16th century, the main Romanian principalities of Moldavia and Walachia had become satellites within the Ottoman Empire, although they retained much independence. After the Russo-Turkish War of 1828–29, they became Russian protectorates. The nation became a kingdom in 1881 after the Congress of Berlin.

King Ferdinand ascended the throne in 1914. At the start of World War I, Romania proclaimed its neutrality, but later joined the Allied side and in 1916 declared war on the Central Powers. The armistice of Nov. 11, 1918, gave Romania vast territories from Russia and the Austro-Hungarian Empire.

The gains of World War I, making Romania the largest Balkan state, included Bessarabia, Transylvania, and Bukovina. The Banat, a Hungarian area, was divided with Yugoslavia.

In 1925, Crown Prince Carol renounced his rights to the throne, and when King Ferdinand died in 1927, Carol's son, Michael (Mihai) became King under a regency. However, Carol returned from exile in 1930, was crowned King Carol II, and gradually became a powerful political force in the country. In 1938, he abolished the democratic Constitution of 1923.

In 1940, the country was reorganized along Fascist lines, and the Fascist Iron Guard became the nucleus of the new totalitarian party. On June 27, the Soviet Union occupied Bessarabia and northern Bukovina. By the Axis-dictated Vienna Award of 1940, two fifths of Transylvania went to Hungary, after which Carol dissolved Parliament and granted the new premier, Ion Antonescu, full power. He abdicated and again went into exile.

Romania subsequently signed the Axis Pact on Nov. 23, 1940, and the following June joined in Germany's attack on the Soviet Union, reoccupying Bessarabia. Following the invasion of Romania by the Red Army in August 1944, King Michael led a coup that ousted the Antonescu government. An armistice with the Soviet Union was signed in Moscow on Sept. 12, 1944.

A Communist-dominated government bloc won elections in 1946, Michael abdicated on Dec. 30, 1947, and Romania became a "people's republic." In 1955, Romania joined the Warsaw Treaty Organization and the United Nations. A decade later, with the adoption of a new Constitution emphasizing national autonomy, and especially after Nicolae Ceausescu came to power in 1967, Bucharest became an increasingly dissident voice in the Soviet bloc. Despite his liberal international record, at home Ceausescu harshly suppressed dissidents calling for freedom of expression in the wake of the Helsinki agreements.

An army-assisted rebellion in Dec. 1989 led to Ceausescu's overthrow. He was tried and executed. Elections in May 1990 led to the head of the interim government, Ion Iliescu, being elected President.

RWANDA

Republic of Rwanda
President: Maj. Gen. Juvénal Habyarimana (1973)
Area: 10,169 sq mi. (26,338 sq km)
Population (mid-1990): 7,300,000 (average annual rate of natural increase: 3.4%)
Density per square mile: 687
Capital and largest city (est. 1981): Kigali, 155,000
Monetary unit: Rwanda franc
Languages: Kinyarwanda and French
Religions: Roman Catholic, 56%; Protestant, 12%; Islam, 9%; Animist, 23%
National name: Republulika y'u Rwanda
Literacy rate: 54%
Economic summary: Gross domestic product (1987): $2.3 billion; $340 per capita; real growth rate −2.8%. Arable land: 29%; principal products: coffee, tea, bananas, yams, beans. Labor force in industry: 2%; major products: processed foods, light consumer goods, minerals. Natural resources: cassiterite, wolfram. Exports: coffee, tea, tungsten, tin, pyrethrum, hides, and skins. Imports: textiles, foodstuffs, machinery, and equipment. Major trading partners: Belgium, West Germany, Kenya, Japan, France, U.S.

Geography. Rwanda, in east central Africa, is surrounded by Zaire, Uganda, Tanzania, and Burundi. It is slightly smaller than Maryland.

Steep mountains and deep valleys cover most of the country. Lake Kivu in the northwest, at an altitude of 4,829 feet (1,472 m) is the highest lake in Africa. Extending north of it are the Virunga Mountains, which include Volcan Karisimbi (14,-187 ft.; 4,324 m), Rwanda's highest point.

Government. Grégoire Kayibanda was President from 1962 until he was overthrown in a bloodless coup on July 5, 1973, by the military led by Gen. Juvénal Habyarimana.

In a plebiscite in December 1978, Habyarimana was elected to a five-year term as president and a new constitution adopted that provides for an elected Assembly and a single official party, the National Revolutionary Development Movement.

History. Rwanda, which was part of German East Africa, was first visited by European explorers in 1854. During World War I, it was occupied in 1916 by Belgian troops. After the war, it became a Belgian League of Nations mandate, along with Burundi, under the name of Ruanda-Urundi. The mandate was made a U.N. trust territory in 1946. Until the Belgian Congo achieved independence in 1960, Ruanda-Urundi was administered as part of that colony.

Ruanda became the independent nation of Rwanda on July 1, 1962.

ST. KITTS AND NEVIS

Federation of St. Kitts and Nevis
Sovereign: Queen Elizabeth II
Governor General: Sir Clement Athelston Arrindell (1985)
Prime Minister: Kennedy Alphonse Simmonds (1980)
Area: St. Kitts 65 sq mi. (169 sq km); Nevis 35 sq mi. (93 sq km)
Total population (mid-1990): 40,000 (average annual rate of natural increase: 1.3%)
Capital: Basseterre (on St. Kitts), 19,000
Largest town on Nevis: Charlestown, 1,771
Monetary unit: East Caribbean dollar
Economic summary: Gross domestic product (1986): $83 million; $2,210 per capita; 4.6% real growth rate. Arable land: 22%. Principal agricultural products: sugar, cotton. Labor force: 20,000 (1981). Major industries: tourism, sugar processing, salt extraction. Exports: sugar, molasses. Imports: foodstuffs, manufactured goods. Major trading partners: U.S., U.K., Japan, Trinidad.

St. Christopher-Nevis, preferably St. Kitts and Nevis, was formerly part of the West Indies Associated States which were established in 1967 and consisted of Antigua and St. Kitts-Nevis-Anguilla of the Leeward Islands, and Dominica, Grenada, St. Lucia, and St. Vincent of the Windward Islands. Statehood for St. Vincent was held up until 1969 because of local political uncertainties. (Grenada, became independent in 1974, Dominica in 1978, St. Lucia and St. Vincent in 1979, and Antigua (known as Antigua and Barbuda) in 1981.) Anguilla's association with St. Christopher-Nevis ended in 1980.

Two members of the Leeward group—the British Virgin Islands and Montserrat—did not become Associated States.

St. Christopher-Nevis, now St. Kitts and Nevis, became independent on September 19, 1983.

ST. LUCIA

Sovereign: Queen Elizabeth II
Governor-General: (acting) Stanislaus A. James (1989)
Prime Minister: John Compton (1982)
Area: 238 sq mi. (616 sq km)
Population (mid-1990): 200,000 (average annual rate of natural increase: 2.2%)
Density per square mile: 627
Capital (est. 1972): Castries, 45,000
Monetary unit: East Caribbean dollar
Languages: English and patois
Religions: Roman Catholic, 91%; Protestant, 7%; Anglican, 3%
Member of Commonwealth of Nations
Literacy rate: 78%
Economic summary: Gross domestic product (1987): $166.1 million; $1,250 per capita; 2.1% real growth rate. Arable land: 8%; principal products: bananas, coconuts, sugar, cocoa, spices. Major industrial products: clothing, assembled electronics, beverages. Exports: bananas, cocoa. Imports: foodstuffs, machinery and equipment, fertilizers, petroleum products. Major trading partners: U.K., U.S., Caribbean countries.

Geography. One of the Windward Isles of the Eastern Caribbean, St. Lucia lies just south of Martinique. It is of volcanic origin. A chain of wooded mountains runs from north to south, and from them flow many streams into fertile valleys.

Government. A Governor-General represents the sovereign, Queen Elizabeth II. A Prime Minister is head of government, chosen by a 17-member House of Assembly elected by universal suffrage for a maximum term of· five years.

History. Discovered by Spain in 1503 and ruled by Spain and then France, St. Lucia became a British territory in 1803. With other Windward Isles, St. Lucia was granted home rule in 1967 as one of the West Indies Associated States. On Feb. 22, 1979, St. Lucia achieved full independence in ceremonies boycotted by the opposition St. Lucia Labor Party, which had advocated a referendum before cutting ties with Britain.

Unrest and a strike by civil servants forced Prime Minister John Compton to hold elections in July, in which his United Workers Party lost its majority for the first time in 15 years.

A Labor Party government was ousted in turn by Compton and his followers, in elections in May 1982.

Formerly dependent on a single crop, bananas, St. Lucia has sought to lower its chronic unemployment and payments deficit. The government provided tax incentives to a U.S. corporation, Amerada Hess, to facilitate location of a $150-million oil refinery and transshipment terminal on the island.

ST. VINCENT AND THE GRENADINES

Sovereign: Queen Elizabeth II
Governor-General: David Jack (1989)
Prime Minister: James Mitchell (1984)
Area: 150 sq mi. (389 sq km)
Population (mid-1990): 100,000 (average annual rate of natural increase: 1.9%)
Density per square mile: 700
Capital and largest city (est. 1984): Kingstown, 18,378
Monetary unit: East Caribbean dollar
Language: English, some French patois
Religions: Anglican, 47%; Methodist, 28%; Roman Catholic, 13%
Member of Commonwealth of Nations
Literacy rate: 85%
Economic summary: Gross domestic product (1986): $94.6 million; $900 per capita; 2.7% real growth rate. Arable land: 38%; principal products: bananas, arrowroot, coconuts. Labor Force: 67,000 (1984 est.). Major industry: food processing. Exports: bananas, arrowroot, copra. Imports: foodstuffs, machinery and equipment, chemicals, fuels, clothing. Major trading partners: U.K., U.S., Canada, Caribbean nations.

Geography. St. Vincent, chief island of the chain, is 18 miles (29 km) long and 11 miles (18 km) wide. One of the Windward Islands in the Lesser Antilles, it is 100 miles (161 km) west of Barbados. The island is mountainous and well forested. The Grenadines, a chain of nearly 600 islets with a total area of only 17 square miles (27 sq km), extend for 60 miles (96 km) from northeast to southwest between St. Vincent and Grenada, southernmost of the Windwards.

St. Vincent is dominated by the volcano La Soufrière, part of a volcanic range running north and south, which rises to 4,048 feet (1,234 m). The volcano erupted over a 10-day period in April 1979, causing the evacuation of the northern two thirds of the island. (There is also a volcano of the same name on Basse-Terre, Guadeloupe, which became violently active in 1976 and 1977.)

Government. A Governor-General represents the sovereign, Queen Elizabeth II. A Prime Minister, elected by a 13-member unicameral legislature, holds executive power.

History. Discovered by Columbus in 1498, and alternately claimed by Britain and France, St. Vincent became a British colony by the Treaty of Paris in 1783. The islands won home rule in 1969 as part of the West Indies Associated States and achieved full independence Oct. 26, 1979. Prime Minister Milton Cato's government quelled a brief rebellion Dec. 8, 1979 attributed to economic problems following the eruption of La Soufrière in April, 1979. Unlike a 1902 eruption which killed 2,000, there was no loss of life but widespread losses to agriculture.

SAN MARINO

Most Serene Republic of San Marino
Co-Regents: Two selected every six months by Grand and General Council
Area: 23.6 sq mi. (62 sq km)
Population (mid-1989): 22,980 (average annual growth rate: 0.6%)
Density per square mile: 974.6
Capital and largest city (est. 1982 for metropolitan area): San Marino, 4,500
Monetary unit: Italian lira
Language: Italian
Religion: Roman Catholic
National name: Repubblica di San Marino
Literacy rate: 98%
Economic summary: Gross national product: NA. Arable land: 17%; principal products: wheat and other grains, grapes, fruits, vegetables. Labor force: approx. 4,300. Major industrial products: textiles, paper, leather, cement and other building materials. Exports: building stone, lime, chestnuts, wheat, hides, baked goods. Imports: manufactured consumer goods. Major trading partner: Italy.

Geography: One tenth the size of New York City, San Marino is surrounded by Italy. It is situated in the Apennines, a little inland from the Adriatic Sea near Rimini.

Government. The country is governed by two co-regents. Executive power is exercised by ten ministers. In 1959, the Grand Council granted women the vote.

History. According to tradition, San Marino was founded about A.D. 350 and had good luck for centuries in staying out of the many wars and feuds on the Italian peninsula. It is the oldest republic in the world.

A person born in San Marino remains a citizen and can vote no matter where he lives.

SÃO TOMÉ AND PRÍNCIPE

Democratic Republic of São Tomé and Principe
President: Manuel Pinto da Costa (1975)
Prime Minister: Celestino Rocha da Costa (1988)
Area: 370 sq mi. (958 sq km)
Population (mid-1990): 100,000 (average annual growth rate: 2.7%)
Density per square mile: 326
Capital and largest city (est. 1984): São Tomé, 34,997
Monetary unit: Dobra
Language: Portuguese
Religions: Roman Catholic, Evangelical Protestant, Seventh-Day Adventist
Literacy rate: 54%
Economic summary: Gross domestic product (1986): $37.9 million; $340 per capita; 1.8% annual growth rate. Arable land: 1%. Principal agricultural products: cocoa, copra, coconuts, palm oil, coffee, bananas. Labor force: 21,096 (1981): mostly in subsistence agriculture. Major industrial products: shirts, soap, beer, processed fish and shrimp. Exports: cocoa, coffee, copra, palm oil. Imports: foodstuffs, textiles, machinery, electrical equipment, fuels, lubricants. Major trading partners: Netherlands, Portugal, East Germany, West Germany, U.S.

Geography. The tiny volcanic islands of São Tomé and Príncipe lie in the Gulf of Guinea about 150 miles (240 km) off West Africa. São Tomé (about 330 sq mi.; 859 sq km) is covered by a dense mountainous jungle, out of which have been carved large plantations. Príncipe (about 40 sq. mi.; 142 sq km) consists of jagged mountains. Other islands in the republic are Pedras Tinhosas and Rolas.

Government. The Constitution grants supreme power to a People's Assembly composed of members elected for four years. The Assembly chooses the President of the republic from candidates named by the Movement for the Liberation of São Tomé and Príncipe, the only legal party.

History. São Tomé and Príncipe were discovered by Portuguese navigators in 1471 and settled by the end of the century. Intensive cultivation by slave labor made the islands a major producer of sugar during the 17th century but output declined until the introduction of coffee and cacao in the 19th century brought new prosperity. The island of São Tomé was the world's largest producer of cacao in 1908 and the crop is still the most important. An exile liberation movement was formed in 1953 after Portuguese landowners quelled labor riots by killing several hundred African workers.

The Portuguese revolution of 1974 brought the end of the overseas empire and the new Lisbon government transferred power to the liberation movement on July 12, 1975. Most of the 4,000 Portuguese inhabitants departed during the transition period.

SAUDI ARABIA

Kingdom of Saudi Arabia
Ruler and Prime Minister: King Fahd bin 'Abdulaziz (1982)
Area: 865,000 sq mi. (2,250,070 sq km)
Population (mid-1990): 15,000,000 (average annual rate of natural increase: 3.4%)
Density per square mile: 18
Capital: Riyadh
Largest cities (est. 1980): Jeddah, 1,500,000; Riyadh, 1,250,000; Mecca, 750,000
Monetary unit: Riyal

Language: Arabic
Religion: Islam
National name: Al-Mamlaka al-'Arabiya as-Sa'udiya
Literacy rate: 52%
Economic summary: Gross domestic product (1988): $74 billion; $5,480 per capita; 5.2% real growth rate. Arable land: 1%; principal products: dates, grains, livestock. Labor force: 4,200,000; 28% in industry and oil; major products: petroleum, cement, plastic products, steel. Natural resource: oil. Exports: petroleum and petroleum products, wheat. Imports: manufactured goods, transport equipment, construction materials, processed food. Major trading partners: U.S., Western European countries, Japan, West Germany, Bahrain.

Geography. Saudi Arabia occupies most of the Arabian Peninsula, with the Red Sea and the Gulf of Aqaba to the west, the Arabian Gulf to the east. Neighboring countries are Jordan, Iraq, Kuwait, Qatar, the United Arab Emirates, the Sultanate of Oman, and Yemen.

A narrow coastal plain on the Red Sea rims a mountain range that spans the length of the western coastline. These mountains gradually rise in elevation from north to south. East of these mountains is a massive plateau which slopes gently downward toward the Arabian Gulf. Part of this plateau is covered by the world's largest sand desert, the Rub Al-Khali, or Empty Quarter. Saudi Arabia's oil region lies primarily along the Arabian Gulf.

Government. Saudi Arabia is a monarchy based on the Sharia (Islamic law), as revealed in the Koran (the holy book) and the Hadith (teachings and sayings of the prophet Mohammed). A Council of Ministers was formed in 1953, which acts as a Cabinet under the leadership of the King. There are 21 Ministries.

Royal and ministerial decrees account for most of the promulgated legislation, treaties, and conventions. There are no political parties.

History. Mohammed united the Arabs in the 7th century, and his followers, led by the caliphs, founded a great empire, with its capital at Medina. Later, the caliphate capital was transferred to Damascus and then Baghdad, but Arabia retained its importance because of the holy cities of Mecca and Medina. In the 16th and 17th centuries, the Turks established at least nominal rule over much of Arabia, and in the middle of the 18th century, it was divided into separate principalities.

The Kingdom of Saudi Arabia is almost entirely the creation of King Ibn Saud (1882–1953). A descendant of earlier Wahabi rulers, he seized Riyadh, the capital of Nejd, in 1901 and set himself up as leader of the Arab nationalist movement. By 1906 he had established Wahabi dominance in Nejd. He conquered Hejaz in 1924–25, consolidating it and Nejd into a dual kingdom in 1926. In 1932, Hejaz and Nejd became a single kingdom, which was officially named Saudi Arabia. A year later the region of Asir was incorporated into the kingdom.

Oil was discovered in 1936, and commercial production began during World War II. Saudi Arabia was neutral until nearly the end of the war, but it was permitted to be a charter member of the United Nations. The country joined the Arab League in 1945 and took part in the 1948–49 war against Israel.

On Ibn Saud's death in 1953, his eldest son, Saud, began an 11-year reign marked by an increasing hostility toward the radical Arabism of Egypt's Gamal Abdel Nasser. In 1964, the ailing Saud was deposed and replaced by the Premier, Crown Prince Faisal, who gave vocal support but no military help to Egypt in the 1967 Mideast war.

Faisal's assassination by a deranged kinsman in 1975 shook the Middle East, but failed to alter his kingdom's course. His successor was his brother, Prince Khalid. Khalid gave influential support to Egypt during negotiations on Israeli withdrawal from the Sinai desert.

King Khalid died of a heart attack June 13, 1982, and was succeeded by his half-brother, Prince Fahd bin 'Abdulaziz, 60, who had exercised the real power throughout Khalid's reign. King Fahd, a pro-Western modernist, chose his 58-year-old half-brother, Abdullah, as Crown Prince.

Saudi Arabia and the smaller, oil-rich Arab states on the Persian Gulf, fearful that they might become Ayatollah Ruhollah Khomeini's next targets if Iran conquered Iraq, made large financial contributions to the Iraqi war effort. They began being dragged into the conflict themselves in the spring of 1984, when Iraq and Iran extended their ground war to attacks on Gulf shipping. First, Iraq attacked tankers loading at Iran's Kharg Island terminal with air-to-ground missiles, then Iran struck back at tankers calling at Saudi Arabia and other Arab countries.

President Reagan ordered the sale, at the end of May, of 400 Stinger antiaircraft missiles to Saudi Arabia. Shortly afterward, Saudi fighter planes shot down two Iranian planes as they approached a foreign tanker over the Gulf. The Saudis were directed to the targets by a U.S. Air Force AWAC plane.

At the same time, cheating by other members of the Organization of Petroleum Exporting Countries, competition from nonmember oil producers, and conservation efforts by consuming nations combined to drive down the world price of oil. Saudi Arabia has one-third of all known oil reserves, but falling demand and rising production outside OPEC combined to reduce its oil revenues from $120 billion in 1980 to $43 billion in 1984 to less the $25 billion in 1985, threatening the country with domestic unrest and undermining its influence in the Gulf area.

Saudi Arabia broke relations with Iran in April 1988 over the issues of riots by Iranian pilgrims in Mecca in July, 1987 and Iranian naval attacks on Saudi vessels in the Persian Gulf.

Following the invasion of Kuwait in August 1990, Saudi Arabia allowed the U.S. to station military forces there ("Operation Desert Shield") to defend its territory against possible Iraqi invasion. (*See* Current Events.)

SENEGAL

Republic of Senegal
President: Abdou Diouf (1981)
Area: 75,954 sq mi. (196,722 sq km)
Population (mid-1990): 7,400,000 (average annual rate of natural increase: 2.7%)
Density per square mile: 95
Capital and largest city (est. 1982): Dakar, 975,000
Monetary unit: Franc CFA
Ethnic groups: Wolofs, Sereres, Peuls, Tukulers, and others
Languages: French (official); Wolof, Serer, other ethnic dialects

Religions: Islam, 91%; indigenous, 6%; Christian, 2%
National name: République du Sénégal
Literacy rate: 23%
Economic summary: Gross national product (1987): $2 billion; $290 per capita; 4.2% real growth rate. Arable land: 27%; principal products: peanuts, millet, corn, rice, sorghum. Labor force: 2,509,000; 77% subsistence agriculture workers. Major industrial products: processed food, phosphates, refined petroleum, peanut oil, fertilizer, cement, and fish. Natural resources: fish, phosphate, iron ore. Exports: peanuts, phosphate rock, canned fish. Imports: foodstuffs, consumer goods, machinery, transport equipment, petroleum. Major trading partners: France, Western European countries, African neighbors.

Geography. The capital of Senegal, Dakar, is the westernmost point in Africa. The country, slightly smaller than South Dakota, surrounds Gambia on three sides and is bordered on the north by Mauritania, on the east by Mali, and on the south by Guinea and Guinea-Bissau.

Senegal is mainly a low-lying country, with a semidesert area in the north and northeast and forests in the southwest. The largest rivers include the Senegal in the north and the Casamance in the south tropical climate region.

Government. There is a National Assembly of 120 members, elected every five years. There is universal suffrage and a constitutional guarantee of equality before the law.

History. The Portuguese had some stations on the banks of the Senegal River in the 15th century, and the first French settlement was made at Saint-Louis about 1650. The British took parts of Senegal at various times, but the French gained possession in 1840 and organized the Sudan as a territory in 1904. In 1946, together with other parts of French West Africa, Senegal became part of the French Union. On June 20, 1960, it became an independent republic federated with the Sudanese Republic in the Mali Federation, from which it withdrew two months later.

In 1973, Senegal joined with six other states to create the West African Economic Community.

SEYCHELLES

Republic of Seychelles
President: France-Albert René (1977)
Area: 175 sq mi. (453 sq km)
Population (mid-1990): 100,000 (average annual rate of natural increase: 1.7%)
Density per square mile: 629
Capital: Victoria, 24,000
Monetary unit: Seychelles rupee
Languages: English and French (official); Creole
Religions: Roman Catholic, 90%; Anglican, 8%
Member of Commonwealth of Nations
Literacy rate: 65%
Economic summary: Gross domestic product (1986): $192 million; $2,924 per capita; 1.4% real growth rate. Arable land: 4%; principal products: vanilla, copra, cinnamon. Labor force: 27,700; 31% in industry and commerce; major products: processed copra and vanilla, coconut oil. Exports: cinnamon, vanilla, copra. Imports: food, tobacco, manufactured goods, machinery, petroleum products,

textiles, transport equipment. Major trading partners: U.K., Bahrain, Japan, Pakistan, Reunion, South Africa.

Geography. Seychelles consists of an archipelago of about 100 islands in the Indian Ocean northeast of Madagascar. The principal islands are Mahé (55 sq mi.; 142 sq km), Praslin (15 sq mi.; 38 sq km), and La Digue (4 sq mi.; 10 sq km). The Aldabra, Farquhar, and Desroches groups are included in the territory of the republic.

Government. Seized from France by Britain in 1810, the Seychelles Islands remained a colony until June 29, 1976. The state is an independent republic within the Commonwealth.

On June 5, 1977, Prime Minister Albert René ousted the islands' first President, James Mancham, suspending the Constitution and the 25-member National Assembly. Mancham, whose "lavish spending" and flamboyance were cited by René in seizing power, charged that Soviet influence was at work. The new president denied this and, while more left than his predecessor, pledged to keep the Seychelles in the nonaligned group of countries.

An unsuccessful attempted coup against René attracted international attention when a group of 50 South African mercenaries posing as rugby players attacked the Victoria airport on Nov. 25, 1981. They caused extensive damage before they hijacked an Air India plane and returned to South Africa, where all but five were freed. Only after widespread international protest did the Pretoria government, which denied any responsibility for the attack, reverse the decision and order all the mercenaries tried as hijackers.

SIERRA LEONE

Republic of Sierra Leone
President: Maj. Gen. Joseph Saidu Momoh (1985)
Area: 27,700 sq mi. (71,740 sq km)
Population (mid-1990): 4,200,000 (average annual rate of natural increase: 2.5%)
Density per square mile: 143.2
Capital and largest city (est. 1985): Freetown, 500,000
Monetary unit: Leone
Languages: English (official), Mende, Temne, Krio
Religions: Islam, 30%; indigenous, 30%; Christian, 10%; other, 30%
Member of Commonwealth of Nations
Literacy rate: 24%
Economic summary: Gross domestic product (FY87): $965 million, $247 per capita; real growth rate (FY87): 1.8%. Arable land: 23%; principal products: coffee, cocoa, ginger, rice. Labor force: 1,500,000; 19% in industry; major products: diamonds, bauxite, rutile, beverages, cigarettes, construction goods. Natural resources: diamonds, bauxite, iron ore. Exports: diamonds, iron ore, palm kernels, cocoa, coffee. Imports: food, petroleum products, chemicals, machinery. Major trading partners: U.K., U.S., Western European countries, Japan.

Geography. Sierra Leone, on the Atlantic Ocean in West Africa, is half the size of Illinois. Guinea, in the north and east, and Liberia, in the south, are its neighbors.

Mangrove swamps lie along the coast, with wooded hills and a plateau in the interior. The eastern region is mountainous.

Government. Sierra Leone became an independent nation on April 27, 1961, and declared itself a republic on April 19, 1971.

Sierra Leone became a one party state under the aegis of the All People's Congress Party in April 1978.

History. The coastal area of Sierra Leone was ceded to English settlers in 1788 as a home for blacks discharged from the British armed forces and also for runaway slaves who had found asylum in London. The British protectorate over the hinterland was proclaimed in 1896.

After elections in 1967, the British Governor-General replaced Sir Albert Margai, head of SLPP, which had held power since independence, with Dr. Stevens, head of APC, as prime minister. The Army took over the government; then another coup in April 1968 restored civilian rule and put the military leaders in jail.

A coup attempt early in 1971 by the army commander was apparently foiled by loyal army officers, but the then Prime Minister Stevens called in troops of neighboring Guinea's army, under a 1970 mutual defense pact, to guard his residence. After perfunctorily blaming the U.S. for the coup attempt, Stevens switched Governors-General, changed the Constitution, and ended up with a republic, of which he was first president. He was accused of taking "sweeping dictatorial powers," but was re-elected in 1978. Dr. Stevens' picked successor, Major-General Joseph Saidu Momoh was elected unopposed on Oct. 1, 1985.

SINGAPORE

Republic of Singapore
Prime Minister: Lee Kuan Yew (1959)
Area: 220 sq mi. (570 sq km)
Population (mid-1990): 2,700,000 (average annual rate of natural increase: 1.5%)
Density per square mile: 11,972
Capital (est. mid-1988): Singapore, 2,600,000
Monetary unit: Singapore dollar
Languages: Malay, Chinese (Mandarin), Tamil, English
Religions: Islam, Christian, Buddhist, Hindu, Taoist
Member of Commonwealth of Nations
Literacy rate: 86%
Economic summary: Gross domestic product (1988 est.): $23.7 billion; $8,870 per capita; 10.9% real growth rate. Arable land: 4%; principal products: poultry, hogs, vegetables, fruits. Labor force: 1,250,000; 25.5% in manufacturing; major industries: petroleum refining, ship repair, rubber processing, electronics, financial services, biotechnology. Exports: petroleum products, rubber, manufactured goods, electronics. Imports: capital equipment, manufactured goods, petroleum. Major trading partners: U.S., Japan, Malaysia, Hong Kong, Saudi Arabia, West Germany, China, Thailand.

Geography. The Republic of Singapore consists of the main island of Singapore, off the southern tip of the Malay Peninsula between the South China Sea and the Indian Ocean, and 54 nearby islands.

There are extensive mangrove swamps extending inland from the coast, which is broken by many inlets.

Government. There is a Cabinet, headed by the Prime Minister, and a Parliament of 79 members elected by universal suffrage.

The People's Action Party, led by Prime Minister Lee Kuan Yew, is the ruling political party in Parliament, holding all but two seats.

History. Singapore, founded in 1819 by Sir Stamford Raffles, became a separate crown colony of Britain in 1946, when the former colony of the Straits Settlements was dissolved. The other two settlements—Penang and Malacca—were transferred to the Union of Malaya, and the small island of Labuan was transferred to North Borneo. The Cocos (or Keeling) Islands were transferred to Australia in 1955 and Christmas Island in 1958.

Singapore attained full internal self-government in 1959. On Sept. 16, 1963, it joined Malaya, Sabah (North Borneo), and Sarawak in the Federation of Malaysia. It withdrew from the Federation on Aug. 9, 1965, and proclaimed itself a republic the next month.

SOLOMON ISLANDS

Sovereign: Queen Elizabeth II
Governor-General: Sir George Lepping (1988)
Prime Minister: Solomon Mamaloni (1989)
Area: 11,500 sq mi. (29,785 sq km)
Population (mid-1990): 300,000 (average annual rate of natural increase: 3.5%)
Density per square mile: 29
Capital and largest city (est. 1986): Honiara (on Guadalcanal), 30,499
Monetary unit: Solomon Islands dollar
Languages: English, Pidgin, 70 other languages and dialects
Religions: Anglican; Roman Catholic; South Seas Evangelical; other Protestant
Member of British Commonwealth
Literacy rate: 60%
Economic summary: Gross domestic product (1987): $141.3 million; $469 per capita; −4.6% real growth rate. Arable land: 1%. Principal agricultural products: copra, palm oil, rice, cocoa, yams, pigs. Labor force: 23,448; 7% in construction, manufacturing and mining. Major industrial products: processed fish, timber, jute, soap, canned meat, handicrafts. Natural resources: fish, timber, gold, bauxite. Exports: fish, timber, copra, palm oil. Imports: machinery and transport equipment, foodstuffs, fuel, manufactured goods. Major trading partners: Japan, Australia, U.K.

Geography. Lying east of New Guinea, this island nation consists of the southern islands of the Solomon group: Guadalcanal, Malaita, Santa Isabel, San Cristóbal, Choiseul, New Georgia, and numerous smaller islands.

Government. After 85 years of British rule, the Solomons achieved independence July 7, 1978. The Crown is represented by a Governor-General and legislative power is vested in a unicameral legislature of 38 members, led by the Prime Minister.

History. Discovered in 1567 by Alvaro de Mendana, the Solomons were not visited again for about 200 years. In 1886, Great Britain and Germany divided the islands between them. In 1914, Australian forces took over the German islands and the Solomons became an Australian mandate in 1920. In World War II, most of the islands were occupied by the Japanese. American forces landed on Guadalcanal on Aug. 7, 1942. The islands were the scene of several important U.S. naval and military victories. They are still largely undeveloped, with only 60 miles of paved road and fewer than 2,500 motor vehicles.

SOMALIA

Somali Democratic Republic
President: Maj. Gen. Mohamed Siad Barre (1969)
Prime Minister: Lt. Gen. Muhammad Ali Samator (1987)
Area: 246,199 sq mi. (637,655 sq km)
Population (mid-1990): 8,400,000 (average annual rate of natural increase: 3.1%)
Density per square mile: 34
Capital and largest city (est. 1982): Mogadishu, 700,000
Monetary unit: Somali shilling
Language: Somali (official), Arabic, English, Italian
Religion: Islam (Sunni)
National name: Al Jumhouriya As-Somalya al-Dimocradia
Literacy rate: 60%
Economic summary: Gross domestic product (1987): $1.5 billion; $190 per capita; 1.5% real growth rate. Arable land: 2%; principal products: livestock, bananas, sorghum, cereals, sugar cane, maize. Labor force: 2,200,000; very few are skilled laborers; a few small industries: sugar refining, textiles, petroleum refining. Natural resources: uranium. Exports: livestock, skins and hides, bananas. Imports: textiles, cereals, construction materials and equipment, machinery, petroleum products, transport equipment. Major trading partners: Saudi Arabia, Italy, U.S.

Geography. Somalia, situated in the Horn of Africa, lies along the Gulf of Aden and the Indian Ocean. It is bounded by Djibouti in the northwest, Ethiopia in the west, and Kenya in the southwest. In area it is slightly smaller than Texas.

Generally arid and barren, Somalia has two chief rivers, the Shebelle and the Juba.

Government. Maj. Gen. Mohamed Siad Barre took power on Oct. 21, 1969, in a coup that established a Supreme Revolutionary Council as the governing body, replacing a parliamentary government. On July 1, 1976, Barre dissolved the Council, naming its members to the Somali Socialist Party, organized that day as the nation's only legal political party. In December 1979, a 171-member People's Assembly was elected under a new Constitution adopted in August. The Assembly confirmed Barre as President for a six-year term. He was re-elected in 1986.

History. From the 7th to the 10th century, Arab and Persian trading posts were established along the coast of present-day Somalia. Nomadic tribes occupied the interior, occasionally pushing into Ethiopian territory. In the 16th century, Turkish rule extended to the northern coast and the Sultans of Zanzibar gained control in the south.

After British occupation of Aden in 1839, the Somali coast became its source of food. The French established a coaling station in 1862 at the site of Djibouti and the Italians planted a settlement in

Eritrea. Egypt, which for a time claimed Turkish rights in the area, was succeeded by Britain. By 1920, a British protectorate and an Italian protectorate occupied what is now Somalia. The British ruled the entire area after 1941, with Italy returning in 1950 to serve as United Nations trustee for its former territory.

In mid-1960, Britain and Italy granted independence to their respective sectors, enabling the two to join as the Republic of Somalia on July 1. Somalia broke diplomatic relations with Britain in 1963 when the British granted the Somali-populated Northern Frontier District of Kenya to the Republic of Kenya.

On Oct. 15, 1969, President Abdi Rashid Ali Shermarke was assassinated and the army seized power, dissolving the legislature and arresting all government leaders. Maj. Gen. Mohamed Siad Barre, as President of a renamed Somali Democratic Republic, leaned heavily toward the U.S.S.R.

In 1977, Somalia openly backed rebels in the easternmost area of Ethiopia, the Ogaden desert, which had been seized by Ethiopia at the turn of the century.

Somalia acknowledged defeat in an eight-month war against the Ethiopians, having lost much of its 32,000-man army and most of its tanks and planes. In March 1978, the U.S. agreed to supply $7 million in food over six months, in addition to $6 million in emergency food relief provided in December. The U.S. refused to consider weapons sales, however, unless Somalia gave up all claims to northern Kenya, the Ogaden, and the Republic of Djibouti, all once claimed as "Greater Somalia." Barre refused to do this.

A U.S. announcement on Jan. 9, 1980, that bases for U.S. ships and planes in the Indian Ocean would be sought in Somalia, Oman, and Kenya, brought a request from Somalia for $1 billion worth of modern arms and an equal amount of economic aid. In August, an agreement was signed giving the U.S. use of military bases in Somalia in return for $25 million in military aid in 1981 and more in subsequent years. In 1988, guerrillas in the north went on the offensive and threatened the northern regional capital.

SOUTH AFRICA

Republic of South Africa
President: F.W. de Klerk (1989)
Area: 471,440 sq mi. (1,221,030 sq km)
Population (mid-1990): 39,600,000 (average annual rate of natural increase: 2.7%)
Density per square mile: 82.1
Administrative capital: Pretoria
Legislative capital: Cape Town
Judicial capital: Bloemfontein
Largest cities (est. 1985): Johannesburg, 1,609,000; Cape Town, 1,912,000; Durban, 1,000,000; Pretoria, 823,000.
Monetary unit: Rand
Languages: English, Afrikaans (official); Xhosa, Zulu, other African tongues
Religions (1984): Dutch Reformed, 40%; Anglican, 11%; Roman Catholic, 8%; other Christian, 25%
National name: Republic of South Africa
Literacy rate: 99% (whites), 60-70% blacks (govt. est.)
Economic summary: Gross domestic product (1987): $81

billion; $2,360 per capita; 2.6% real growth rate. Arable land: 10%; principal products: corn, wool, wheat, sugar cane, tobacco, citrus fruits. Labor force: 11,000,000; 29% in industry and commerce; major products: gold, coal, diamonds, assembled automobiles, machinery, textiles, iron and steel, chemicals, fertilizer. Natural resources: gold, diamonds, platinum, uranium, coal, iron ore, asbestos, manganese. Exports: gold, wool, diamonds, corn, uranium, sugar, fruits, hides and skins, asbestos, fish products. Imports: motor vehicle parts, machinery, metals, petroleum products, chemicals, textiles. Major trading partners: U.S., West Germany, Japan, U.K., African nations.

Geography. South Africa, on the continent's southern tip, is washed by the Atlantic Ocean on the west and by the Indian Ocean on the south and east. Its neighbors are Namibia in the northwest, Zimbabwe and Botswana in the north, and Mozambique and Swaziland in the northeast. The kingdom of Lesotho forms an enclave within the southeastern part of South Africa. Bophuthatswana, Transkei, Ciskei, and Venda are independent states within South Africa, which occupies an area nearly three times that of California.

The country has a high interior plateau, or veld, nearly half of which averages 4,000 feet (1,219 m) in elevation.

There are no important mountain ranges, although the Great Escarpment, separating the veld from the coastal plain, rises to over 11,000 feet (3,350 m) in the Drakensberg Mountains in the east. The principal river is the Orange, rising in Lesotho and flowing westward for 1,300 miles (2,092 km) to the Atlantic.

The southernmost point of Africa is Cape Agulhas, located in Cape Province about 100 miles (161 km) southeast of the Cape of Good Hope.

Government. A new Constitution in 1984 created a new office of Executive State President, with potentially authoritarian powers. Pieter W. Botha, Prime Minister since 1978, was sworn in as President on Sept. 14, 1984. The President has the power to act at his own discretion (e.g. appoint cabinet members) as well as power that has to be exercised in consultation with the cabinet (e.g. declare war, ratify treaties).

The new Constitution brought whites, Indians, and coloreds (mixed-race) into a racially divided Parliament made up of three separate chambers for different racial groups. It provides for selection of the President by an Electoral College made up of representatives from the three chambers.

Ten "Bantustans," or black homelands, have unicameral legislatures elected by black voters.

History. The Dutch East India Company landed the first settlers on the Cape of Good Hope in 1652, launching a colony that by the end of the 18th century numbered only about 15,000. Known as Boers or Afrikaners, speaking a Dutch dialect known as Afrikaans, the settlers as early as 1795 tried to establish an independent republic.

After occupying the Cape Colony in that year, Britain took permanent possession in 1814 at the end of the Napoleonic wars, bringing in 5,000 settlers. Anglicization of government and the freeing of slaves in 1833 drove about 12,000 Afrikaners to make the "great trek" north and east into African tribal territory, where they established the republics of the Transvaal and the Orange Free State.

The discovery of diamonds in 1867 and gold nine years later brought an influx of "outlanders" into

the republics and spurred Cecil Rhodes to plot annexation. Rhodes's scheme of sparking an "outlander" rebellion to which an armed party under Leander Starr Jameson would ride to the rescue misfired in 1895, forcing Rhodes to resign as prime minister of the Cape colony. What British expansionists called the "inevitable" war with the Boers eventually broke out on Oct. 11, 1899.

The defeat of the Boers in 1902 led in 1910 to the Union of South Africa, composed of four provinces, the two former republics and the old Cape and Natal colonies. Louis Botha, a Boer, became the first Prime Minister.

Jan Christiaan Smuts brought the nation into World War II on the Allied side against Nationalist opposition, and South Africa became a charter member of the United Nations in 1945, but refused to sign the Universal Declaration of Human Rights. Apartheid—racial separation—dominated domestic politics as the Nationalists gained power and imposed greater restrictions on Bantus, Coloreds, and Asians.

Afrikaner hostility to Britain triumphed in 1961 with the declaration on May 31 of the Republic of South Africa and the severing of ties with the Commonwealth. Nationalist Prime Minister H. F. Verwoerd's government in 1963 asserted the power to restrict freedom of those who opposed rigid racial laws. Three years later, amid increasing racial tension and criticism from the outside world, Verwoerd was assassinated. His Nationalist successor, Balthazar J. Vorster, launched a campaign of conciliation toward conservative black African states, offering development loans and trade concessions.

A scandal led to Vorster's resignation on June 4, 1978. Pieter W. Botha succeeded him as Prime Minister, and became President on Sept. 14, 1984.

South Africa's policy of apartheid—or racial separation—excluded the country's black majority from participation in the country's government and kept blacks at the bottom rung of the economic ladder. Protests against apartheid by militant blacks, beginning in the latter half of 1984, led to a state of emergency being declared twice. The first, on July 20, 1985, covered 36 cities and towns and gave the police powers to make arrests without warrants and to detain people indefinitely. The second, declared on June 12, 1986, covered the whole nation. It gave the police a similar extension of powers and banned "subversive" press reports. It was extended for another year in June 1988.

Elections on May 7, 1987 increased the power of Botha's Nationalist party while enabling the far-right Conservative Party to replace the liberal Progressives as the official opposition. The results of the whites-only vote indicated a strong conservative reaction against Botha's policy of limited reform.

A stroke led Botha to step down as leader of his party in 1989 in favor of Frederick de Klerk. De Klerk has accelerated the pace of reform. He unbanned the African National Congress, the principal anti-apartheid organization, and released Nelson Mandela, the ANC deputy chief, after 27 1/2 years imprisonment. Negotiations between the government and the ANC have commenced.

BOPHUTHATSWANA

Republic of Bophuthatswana
President: Kgosi Lucas Mangope (1977)
Area: 15,573 sq mi. (40,333 sq km)
Population (est. 1988): 1,300,000 (average annual growth rate: 2.8%)

Density per square mile: 83.5
Capital: Mmabatho
Largest city (est. 1987): Mabopane, 100,000
Monetary unit: South African rand
Languages: Setswana, English, Afrikaans
Religions: Methodist, Lutheran, Anglican, Presbyterian,
Dutch Reformed, Roman Catholic, A.M.E.

Geography. Bophuthatswana consists of seven discontinuous areas within the boundaries of South Africa. Most of them share a common border with Botswana.
Government. The republic has a 108-member Legislative Assembly, three quarters of whom are elected and the others appointed. President Mangope's Democratic Party is the majority party.
History. Bophuthatswana was given independence by South Africa on Dec. 6, 1977, following Transkei as the second "homeland" to be established by Pretoria. The new state and Transkei are recognized only by South Africa and each other.

Mangope, as chief minister in the pre-independence period, sought linkage of the six units into a consolidated area, but was unable to achieve his objective. A second issue, the citizenship of Tswanas in South Africa who wished to remain South African nationals, was settled by enabling them to have citizenship in South African homelands not yet independent.

About two thirds of the population of Bophuthatswana live permanently or as migrants in white areas of South Africa.
Economy. Bophuthatswana is richer than many other South African homelands, as it has more than half of the republic's platinum deposits. All foreign trade is included with South Africa's, and it is economically dependent at present on that country.

CISKEI

Republic of Ciskei
President: Chief Lennox Leslie Wongama Sebe (1981)
Area: 3,282 sq mi. (8,500 sq km)
Population (est. 1982): 675,000
Density per square mile: 205.7
Capital (est. 1980): Zwelitsha, 30,750
Largest city (est. 1981): Mdantsane, 159,000
Monetary unit: South African rand
Languages: Xhosa (official) and English
Religions: Methodist, Lutheran, Anglican, and Bantu
Christian

Geography. Ciskei is surrounded by South Africa on three sides, with the Indian Ocean on the south. From a subtropical coastal strip, the land rises through grasslands to the mountainous escarpment that edges the South African interior plateau.
Government. Legislative power is vested in a National Assembly with 22 elected seats. Thirty-three hereditary chiefs complete the membership of the Assembly. The President holds executive power. South Africa's State President retains the power to legislate by proclamation and has veto power over the budget. The Ciskei National Independence Party holds all elective seats in the Assembly.
History. Oral tradition ascribes the origin of the Cape Nguni peoples to the central lakes area of Africa. They arrived in what is now Ciskei in the mid-17th century. White settlers from the Cape Colony first entered the territory a century later, but the Dutch East India Colony sought unsuccessfully to discourage white penetration. Nine wars between whites and the inhabitants, by now known as Xhosas, occurred between 1779 and 1878.

A Ciskeian territorial authority was established in 1961, with 84 chiefs and an executive council exercising limited self-government. In 1972, 20 elected members were added to the legislative assembly and a chief minister and six cabinet members elected by the assembly to function as an executive.

A proposed Constitution was approved by referendum on Oct. 30, 1980, and independence ceremonies held on Dec. 4. No government outside South Africa recognized the new state.
Economy. A subsistence agricultural economy has been superseded by commuter and migratory labor, which accounted for 64% of national income in 1977. There is some light industry and a potential for exploitation of limestone and other minerals.

TRANSKEI

Republic of Transkei
President: Chief Tutor N. Ndamase (1986)
Head of Military Council: Maj. Gen. Bantu Holomisa (1987)
Area: 15,831 sq mi. (41,002 sq km)
Population (est. 1986): 3,609,962 (growth rate: 2.2%)
Density per square mile: 151.6
Capital (est. 1989): Umtala, 57,796
Monetary unit: South African rand
Languages: English, Xhosa, Southern Sotho
Religions: Christian, 66%; tribal, 24%
Economic summary: Gross domestic product: $150 million.
Per capita income: $86. Principal agricultural products:
tea, corn, sorghum, dry beans. Major industrial products:
timber, textiles. Natural resource: timber. Exports: timber,
tea, sacks. Imports: foodstuffs, machines, equipment.
Major trading partner: South Africa.

Geography. Transkei occupies three discontinuous enclaves within southeast South Africa that add up to twice the size of Massachusetts. It has a 270-mile (435 km) coastline on the Indian Ocean. The capital, Umtala, is connected by rail to the South African port of East London, 100 miles (161 km) to the southwest.
Government. Transkei was granted independence by South Africa as of Oct. 26, 1976. A constitution called for organization of a parliament composed of 77 chiefs and 75 elected members, with a ceremonial president and executive power in the hands of a prime minister.

The Organization of African States and the chairman of the United Nations Special Committee Against Apartheid denounced the new state as a sham and urged governments not to recognize it.
History. British rule was established over the Transkei region between 1866 and 1894, and the Transkeian Territories were formed in 1903. Under the Native Land Act of 1913, the Territories were reserved for black occupation. In 1963, Transkei was given internal self-government and a legislature that elected Paramount Chief Kaiser Matanzima as Chief Minister, a post he retained in elections in 1968 and 1973. Instability led to a coup in Dec. 1987.
Economy. Some 60% of Transkei is cultivated, producing corn, wheat, beans, and sorghum. Grazing is important. Some light industry has been established.

VENDA

Republic of Venda
Chairman of the Council of National Unity: Col. Gabriel Mutheiwana Ramushwana (1990)
Area: 2,510 sq mi. (6,500 sq km)
Population (est. 1982): 400,000 (average annual growth rate: 2.4%)
Density per square mile: 214.5
Capital: Thohoyandou
Largest town (est. 1980): Makearela, 2,500
Monetary unit: South African rand
Languages: Venda, English, Afrikaans
Religions: Christian, tribal
Economic summary: Gross domestic product: $156 million. Per capita income: $312. Principal agricultural products: meat, tea, fruit, sisal, corn. Major industrial products: timber, graphite, magnetite.

Geography. Venda is composed of two noncontiguous territories in northeast South Africa with a total area of about half that of Connecticut. It is mountainous but fertile, well-watered land, with a climate ranging from tropical to subtropical.

Government. The third of South Africa's homelands to be granted independence, Venda became a separate republic on Sept. 13, 1979, unrecognized by any government other than South Africa and its sister homelands, Transkei and Bophuthatswana. The President is popularly elected. An 84-seat legislature is half elected, half appointed.

History. The first European reached Venda in 1816, but the isolation of the area prevented its involvement in the wars of the 19th century between blacks and whites and with other tribes. Venda came under South African administration after the Boer War in 1902. Limited home rule was granted in 1962. Chief Patrick R. Mphephu, leader of one of the 27 tribes that historically made up the Venda nation, became Chief Minister of the interim government in 1973 and President upon independence in 1979. There has been a military regime in power since April 5, 1990.

SOVIET UNION

Union of Soviet Socialist Republics
President: Mikhail S. Gorbachev (1990)
Chairman of Council of Ministers (Premier): Nikolai I. Ryzhkov (1985)
Area: 8,649,489 sq mi. (22,402,200 sq km)
Population (est. mid-1989): 289,000,000 (average annual rate of natural increase: 1.0%)
Density per square mile: 33
Capital: Moscow
Largest cities (est. 1986): Moscow, 8,714,000; Leningrad, 4,904,000; Kiev, 2,495,000; Tashkent, 2,077,000; Baku, 1,722,000; Kharkov, 1,567,000; Minsk, 1,510,-000; Gorky, 1,409,000; Novosibirsk, 1,405,000; Sverdlovsk, 1,315,000; Kuibyshev, 1,267,000; Dnepropetrovsk, 1,166,000; Tbilisi, 1,174,000; Odessa, 1,132,000; Yerevan, 1,148,000; Omsk, 1,122,-000; Chelyabinsk, 1,107,000; Donetsk, 1,081,000
Monetary unit: Ruble
Languages: Russian, Ukranian, Uzbek, Byelorussian, Kazak, Tatar
Religions: Russian Orthodox (predominant), Islam, Roman Catholic, Jewish, Lutheran, atheist
National name: Soyuz Sovyetskikh Sotsialisticheskikh Respublik
Literacy rate: 99%

Economic summary: Gross national product (1988): $2,500 billion; $8,700 per capita; 1.5% real growth rate. Arable land: 10%; principal products: wheat, rye, corn, oats, potatoes, sugar beets, cotton and flax, cattle, pigs, sheep. Labor force: 151,000,000 civilians; 78% in industry; major products: ferrous and nonferrous metals, fuels and power, building materials, chemicals, machinery. Natural resources: fossil fuels, water power, timber, manganese, lead, zinc, nickel, mercury, potash, phosphate. Exports: petroleum and petroleum products, natural gas, machinery and equipment, manufactured goods. Imports: grain, machinery and equipment, foodstuffs, raw materials, consumer manufactures. Major trading partners: 67%, E. European countries; 22%, Western industrialized countries; 11% less developed countries.

Geography. The U.S.S.R. is the largest unbroken political unit in the world, occupying more than one seventh of the land surface of the globe. The greater part of its territory is a vast plain stretching from eastern Europe to the Pacific Ocean. This plain, relieved only occasionally by low mountain ranges (notably the Urals), consists of three zones running east and west: the frozen marshy tundra of the Arctic; the more temperate forest belt; and the steppes or prairies to the south, which in southern Soviet Asia become sandy deserts.

The topography is more varied in the south, particularly in the Caucasus between the Caspian and Black Seas, and in the Tien-Pamir mountain system bordering Afghanistan, Sinkiang, and Mongolia. Mountains (Stanovoi and Kolyma) and great rivers (Amur, Yenisei, Lena) also break up the sweep of the plain in Siberia.

In the west, the major rivers are the Volga, Dnieper, Don, Kama, and Southern Bug.

Government. The creation of a new supreme legislature—the 2,250-member Congress of Peoples Deputies—was approved at the 19th Communist Party Conference which opened on June 28, 1988. The new representative body has 1,500 members elected from territorial and national districts, and 750 deputies elected at the congresses or plenary sessions of governing bodies of party, trade union, cooperative, women, and other officially recognized organizations. All the deputies are elected for a five-year term. The first elections were held in March 1989. The Congress meets semi-annually to decide important constitutional, political, and socioeconomic issues. Although it elected Gorbachev as President in 1990, further Presidential elections are to be held by direct popular vote.

The Congress of Peoples Deputies elects from its members, a small (542) standing government body—the bicameral Supreme Soviet which considers and decides all legislative, administrative, and monitoring questions. It reports to the Congress of People Deputies.

In addition, the administrative Council of Ministers carries out the daily operations of the government.

History. Tradition says the Viking Rurik came to Russia in A.D. 862 and founded the first Russian dynasty in Novgorod. The various tribes were united by the spread of Christianity in the 10th and 11th centuries; Vladimir "the Saint" was converted in 988. During the 11th century, the grand dukes of Kiev held such centralizing power as existed. In 1240, Kiev was destroyed by the Mongols, and the Russian territory was split into numerous smaller dukedoms, early dukes of Moscow extended their dominions through their office of tribute collector for the Mongols.

Republics of the U.S.S.R.

Republic and capital	Area sq mi.	Population est. 1986 (thousands)
Russian S.F.S.R. (Moscow)	6,593,391	144,000
Ukraine (Kiev)	233,089	50,900
Kazakhstan (Alma-Ata)	1,064,092	16,000
Byelorussia (Minsk)	80,154	10,000
Uzbekistan (Tashkent)	158,069	18,500
Georgia (Tbilsi)	26,872	5,271
Azerbaijan (Baku)	33,475	6,700
Lithuania[1] (Vilnius)	25,174	3,600
Moldavia (Kishinev)	13,012	4,100
Latvia[1] (Riga)	24,595	2,600
Kirghizia (Frunze)	76,641	4,000
Tadzhikistan (Duschambe)	55,019	4,600
Armenia (Erevan)	11,506	3,343
Turkmenistan (Ashkhabad)	188,417	3,200
Estonia[1] (Tallinn)	17,413	1,542

1. Soviet jurisdiction not recognized by the United States.

In the late 15th century, Duke Ivan III acquired Novgorod and Tver and threw off the Mongol yoke. Ivan IV, the Terrible (1533–84), first Muscovite Tsar, is considered to have founded the Russian state. He crushed the power of rival princes and boyars (great landowners), but Russia remained largely medieval until the reign of Peter the Great (1689–1725), grandson of the first Romanov Tsar, Michael (1613–45). Peter made extensive reforms aimed at westernization and, through his defeat of Charles XII of Sweden at the Battle of Poltava in 1709, he extended Russia's boundaries to the west.

Catherine the Great (1762–96) continued Peter's westernization program and also expanded Russian territory, acquiring the Crimea and part of Poland. During the reign of Alexander I (1801–25), Napoleon's attempt to subdue Russia was defeated (1812–13), and new territory was gained, including Finland (1809) and Bessarabia (1812). Alexander originated the Holy Alliance, which for a time crushed Europe's rising liberal movement.

Alexander II (1855–81) pushed Russia's borders to the Pacific and into central Asia. Serfdom was abolished in 1861, but heavy restrictions were imposed on the emancipated class. Revolutionary strikes following Russia's defeat in the war with Japan forced Nicholas II (1894–1917) to grant a representative national body (Duma), elected by narrowly limited suffrage. It met for the first time in 1906, little influencing Nicholas in his reactionary course.

World War I demonstrated tsarist corruption and inefficiency and only patriotism held the poorly equipped army together for a time. Disorders broke out in Petrograd (now Leningrad) in March 1917, and defection of the Petrograd garrison launched the revolution. Nicholas II was forced to abdicate on March 15, 1917, and he and his family were killed by revolutionists on July 16, 1918.

A provisional government under the successive premierships of Prince Lvov and a moderate, Alexander Kerensky, lost ground to the radical, or Bolshevik, wing of the Socialist Democratic Labor Party. On Nov. 7, 1917, the Bolshevik revolution, engineered by N. Lenin[1] and Leon Trotsky, overthrew the Kerensky government and authority was vested in a Council of People's Commissars, with Lenin as Premier.

The humiliating Treaty of Brest-Litovsk (March 3, 1918) concluded the war with Germany, but civil war and foreign intervention delayed Communist control of all Russia until 1920. A brief war with Poland in 1920 resulted in Russian defeat.

The Union of Soviet Socialist Republics was established as a federation on Dec. 30, 1922.

The death of Lenin on Jan. 21, 1924, precipitated an intraparty struggle between Joseph Stalin, General Secretary of the party, and Trotsky, who favored swifter socialization at home and fomentation of revolution abroad. Trotsky was dismissed as Commissar of War in 1925 and banished from the Soviet Union in 1929. He was murdered in Mexico City on Aug. 21, 1940, by a political agent.

Stalin further consolidated his power by a series of purges in the late 1930s, liquidating prominent party leaders and military officers. Stalin assumed the premiership May 6, 1941.

Soviet foreign policy, at first friendly toward Germany and antagonistic toward Britain and France and then, after Hitler's rise to power in 1933, becoming anti-Fascist and pro-League of Nations, took an abrupt turn on Aug. 24, 1939, with the signing of a nonaggression pact with Nazi Germany. The next month, Moscow joined in the German attack on Poland, seizing territory later incorporated into the Ukrainian and Byelorussian S.S.R.'s. The war with Finland, 1939–40, added territory to the Karelian S.S.R. set up March 31, 1940; the annexation of Bessarabia and Bukovina from Romania became part of the new Moldavian S.S.R. on Aug. 2, 1940; and the annexation of the Baltic republics of Estonia, Latvia, and Lithuania in June 1940 (still unrecognized by the U.S.) created the 14th, 15th, and 16th Soviet Republics. (The number of so-called "Union" republics was reduced to 15 in 1956 when the Karelian S.S.R. became one of the 20 Autonomous Soviet Socialist Republics based on ethnic groups.)

The Soviet-German collaboration ended abruptly with a lightning attack by Hitler on June 22, 1941, which seized 500,000 square miles of Russian territory before Soviet defenses, aided by U.S. and British arms, could halt it. The Soviet resurgence at Stalingrad from November 1942 to February 1943 marked the turning point in a long battle, ending in the final offensive of January 1945.

Then, after denouncing a 1941 nonaggression pact with Japan in April 1945, when Allied forces were nearing victory in the Pacific, the Soviet Union declared war on Japan on Aug. 8, 1945, and quickly occupied Manchuria, Karafuto, and the Kurile islands.

The U.S.S.R. built a cordon of Communist states running from Poland in the north to Albania and Bulgaria in the south, including East Germany, Czechoslovakia, Hungary, and Romania, composed of the territories Soviet troops occupied at the war's end. With its Eastern front solidified, the Soviet Union launched a political offensive against the non-Communist West, moving first to block the Western access to Berlin. The Western powers countered with an airlift, completed unification of West Germany, and organized the defense of Western Europe in the North Atlantic Treaty Organization.

Stalin died on March 6, 1953, and was succeeded the next day by G. M. Malenkov as Premier. His chief rivals for power—Lavrenti P. Beria (chief of

1. N. Lenin was the pseudonym taken by Vladimir Ilich Ulyanov. It is sometimes given as Nikolai Lenin or V. Lenin.

Rulers of Russia Since 1533

Name	Born	Ruled[1]	Name	Born	Ruled[1]
Ivan IV the Terrible	1530	1533–1584	Alexander II	1818	1855–1881
Theodore I	1557	1584–1598	Alexander III	1845	1881–1894
Boris Godunov	c.1551	1598–1605	Nicholas II	1868	1894–1917[7]
Theodore II	1589	1605–1605			
Demetrius I[2]	?	1605–1606	**PROVISIONAL GOVERNMENT**		
Basil IV Shuiski	?	1606–1610[3]	**(PREMIERS)**		
"Time of Troubles"	—	1610–1613	Prince Georgi Lvov	1861	1917–1917
Michael Romanov	1596	1613–1645	Alexander Kerensky	1881	1917–1917
Alexis I	1629	1645–1676			
Theodore III	1656	1676–1682	**POLITICAL LEADERS**		
Ivan V[4]	1666	1682–1689[5]	N. Lenin	1870	1917–1924
Peter I the Great[4]	1672	1682–1725	Aleksei Rykov	1881	1924–1930
Catherine I	c.1684	1725–1727	Vyacheslav Molotov	1890	1930–1941
Peter II	1715	1727–1730	Joseph Stalin[8]	1879	1941–1953
Anna	1693	1730–1740	Georgi M. Malenkov	1902	1953–1955
Ivan VI	1740	1740–1741[6]	Nikolai A. Bulganin	1895	1955–1958
Elizabeth	1709	1741–1762	Nikita S. Khrushchev	1894	1958–1964
Peter III	1728	1762–1762	Leonid I. Brezhnev	1906	1964–1982
Catherine II the Great	1729	1762–1796	Yuri V. Andropov	1914	1982–1984
Paul I	1754	1796–1801	Konstantin U. Chernenko	1912	1984–1985
Alexander I	1777	1801–1825	Mikhail S. Gorbachev	1931	1985–
Nicholas I	1796	1825–1855			

1. For Tsars through Nicholas II, year of end of rule is also that of death, unless otherwise indicated. 2. Also known as Pseudo-Demetrius. 3. Died 1612. 4. Ruled jointly until 1689, when Ivan was deposed. 5. Died 1696. 6. Died 1764. 7. Killed 1918. 8. General Secretary of Communist Party, 1924–53.

the secret police), Nikolai A. Bulganin, and Lazar M. Kaganovich—were named first deputies. Beria was purged in July and executed on Dec. 23, 1953.

The new power in the Kremlin was Nikita S. Khrushchev, First Secretary of the party.

Khrushchev formalized the Eastern European system into a Council for Mutual Economic Assistance (Comecon) and a Warsaw Pact Treaty Organization as a counterweight to NATO.

In its technological race with the U.S., the Soviet Union exploded a hydrogen bomb in 1953, developed an intercontinental ballistic missile by 1957, sent the first satellite into space (Sputnik I) in 1957, and put Yuri Gagarin in the first orbital flight around the earth in 1961.

Khrushchev's downfall stemmed from his decision to place Soviet nuclear missiles in Cuba and then, when challenged by the U.S., backing down and removing the weapons. He was also blamed for the ideological break with China after 1963.

Khrushchev was forced into retirement on Oct. 15, 1964, and was replaced by Leonid I. Brezhnev as First Secretary of the Party and Aleksei N. Kosygin as Premier.

President Nixon visited the U.S.S.R. for summit talks in May 1972, concluding agreements on strategic-arms limitation and a declaration of principles on future U.S.-Soviet relations.

Presidents Gerald R. Ford and Brezhnev met in Vladivostok in November 1974 and reached tentative agreements to be incorporated into a treaty at the Geneva SALT talks in 1975. They proposed a ceiling of 2,400 ICBM's for each side, of which no more than 1,320 could have MIRV's.

President Carter, actively pursuing both human rights and disarmament, joined with the Soviet Union in September 1977 to declare that the SALT I accord, which would have expired Oct. 1 without further action, be maintained in effect while the two sides sought a new agreement (SALT II).

Brezhnev's 1977 election to the presidency followed publication of a new Constitution supplanting the one adopted in 1936. It specified the dominance of the Communist Party, previously unstated.

Carter and the ailing Brezhnev signed the SALT II treaty in Vienna on June 18, 1979, setting ceilings on each nation's arsenal of intercontinental ballistic missiles. Doubts about Senate ratification grew, and became a certainty on Dec. 27, when Soviet troops invaded Afghanistan. Despite protests from the Moslem and Western worlds, Moscow insisted that Afghan President Hafizullah Amin had asked for aid in quelling a rebellion.

In the face of evidence that Amin had been liquidated by Soviet advisers before the troops arrived, the Soviet Union vetoed a Security Council resolution on Jan. 7, 1980, that called for a withdrawal. Carter ordered a freeze on grain exports and high-technology equipment.

On Jan. 20, Carter called for a world boycott of the Summer Olympic Games scheduled for Moscow. The boycott, less than complete, nevertheless marred the first Olympics to be held in Moscow as the United States, Canada, Japan, and to a partial extent all the western allies except France and Italy shunned the event.

The Soviet Union maintained a stony defense in the face of criticism from Western Europe and the U.S., and a summit meeting of 37 Islamic nations that unanimously condemned the "imperialist invasion" of Afghanistan.

Despite the tension between Moscow and Washington, Strategic Arms Reduction Talks (START) began in Geneva between U.S. and Soviet delegations in mid-1982. Negotiations on intermediate missile reduction also continued in Geneva.

On November 10, 1982, Soviet radio and television announced the death of Leonid Brezhnev. Yuri V. Andropov, who formerly headed the

K.G.B., was chosen to succeed Brezhnev as General Secretary. By mid-June 1983, Andropov had assumed all of Brezhnev's three titles.

The Soviet Union broke off both the START talks and the parallel negotiations on European-based missiles in November 1983 in protest against the deployment of medium-range U.S. missiles in Western Europe.

After months of illness, Andropov died in February 1984. Konstantin U. Chernenko, a 72-year-old party stalwart who had been close to Brezhnev, succeeded him as General Secretary and, by mid-April, had also assumed the title of President. In the months following Chernenko's assumption of power, the Kremlin took on a hostile mood toward the West of a kind rarely seen since the height of the cold war 30 years before. Led by Moscow, all the Soviet bloc countries except Romania boycotted the 1984 Summer Olympic Games in Los Angeles—tit-for-tat for the U.S.-led boycott of the 1980 Moscow Games, in the view of most observers.

After 13 months in office, Chernenko died on March 10, 1985. He had been ill much of the time and left only a minor imprint on Soviet history.

Chosen to succeed him as Soviet leader was Mikhail S. Gorbachev, at 54 the youngest man to take charge of the Soviet Union since Stalin. Under Gorbachev, the Soviet Union began its long-awaited shift to a new generation of leadership. Unlike his immediate predecessors, Gorbachev did not also assume the title of President but wielded power from the post of party General Secretary. In a surprise move, Gorbachev elevated Andrei Gromyko, 75, for 28 years the Soviet Union's stony-faced Foreign Minister, to the largely ceremonial post of President. He installed a younger man with no experience in foreign affairs, Eduard Shevardnadze, 57, as Foreign Minister.

A new round of U.S. Soviet arms reduction negotiations began in Geneva in March 1985, this time involving three types of weapons systems—strategic, or long-range, missiles and bombers; medium-range systems in Europe, and space-based systems. In the new talks, the two sides differed sharply on how to approach the three-part negotiations, with the United States putting the focus on cuts in land-based weapons while the Soviet Union made curbing space weapons its first priority.

After months of quiet negotiations, Reagan and Gorbachev agreed to meet in Geneva on Nov. 19-20,1985—the 11th postwar meeting between the leaders of the two superpowers. Expectations for concrete results were low because the Geneva arms talks appeared to be at an impasse, with both sides repeating old slogans.

The Soviet Union took much criticism in early 1986 over the April 24 meltdown at the Chernobyl nuclear plant and its reluctance to give out any information on the accident.

In October, 1986, a potential agreement on strategic weapons reduction broke down over Soviet insistence that SDI be terminated as the price of such an agreement, but by Dec., 1987 the superpowers signed an accord eliminating medium-range missiles in Europe at the Reagan-Gorbachev summit in Washington.

In June 1987, Gorbachev obtained the support of the Central Committee for proposals that would loosen some government controls over the economy and in June, 1988, an unusually open party conference approved several resolutions for changes in the structure of the Soviet system.

These included a shift of some power from the Party to local soviets, a ten-year limit on the terms of elected government and party officials, and an alteration in the office of the President to give it real power in domestic and foreign policy. Gorbachev was elected President in 1989. The elections to the Congress were the first competitive elections in the Soviet Union since 1917. Dissident candidates won a surprisingly large minority although pro-Government deputies maintained a strong lock on the Supreme Soviet.

Glasnost took a new turn when Lithuania declared its independence. The central government responded with an economic blockade. After a stalemate, Lithuania suspended, but didn't revoke, its declaration in return for a lifting of the blockade.

The possible beginning of the fragmentation of the Communist party took place when Boris Yeltsin, leader of the Russian S.S.R. who urges faster reform, left the Communist party along with other radicals.

SPAIN

Kingdom of Spain
Ruler: King Juan Carlos I (1975)
Prime Minister: Felipe González Márquez (1982)
Area: 194,885 sq mi. (504,750 km²)[1]
Population (mid-1990): 39,400,000 (average annual growth rate: 0.3%)
Density per square mile: 201
Capital: Madrid
Largest cities (est. 1987): Madrid, 3,158,800; Barcelona, 1,752,627; Valencia, 774,748; Seville, 645,817
Monetary unit: Peseta
Languages: Spanish, Basque, Catalan, Galician
Religion: Roman Catholic
National name: Reino de España
Literacy rate: 97%
Economic summary: Gross national product (1987): $288.3 billion; $7,390 per capita; 5.5% real growth rate. Arable land: 31%; principal products: cereals, vegetables, citrus fruits, wine, olives and olive oil, livestock. Labor force: 14,200,000; 24% in industry; major products: processed foods, textiles, footwear, petrochemicals, steel, automobiles, ships. Natural resources: coal, lignite, water power, uranium, mercury, pyrites, fluorospar, gypsum, iron ore, zinc, lead, tungsten, copper. Exports: fresh fruits, iron and steel products, textiles, footwear, automobiles, fruits and vegetables, wine. Imports: machinery and transportation equipment, chemicals, fuels, automobiles, iron, steel. Major trading partners: Western European nations, U.S., Middle Eastern countries.

1. Including the Balearic and Canary Islands.

Geography. Spain occupies 85% of the Iberian Peninsula in southwestern Europe, which it shares with Portugal; France is to the northeast, separated by the Pyrenees. The Bay of Biscay lies to the north, the Atlantic Ocean to the west, and the Mediterranean Sea to the south and east: Africa is less than 10 miles (16 km) south at the Strait of Gibraltar.

A broad central plateau slopes to the south and east, crossed by a series of mountain ranges and river valleys.

Principal rivers are the Ebro in the northeast, the Tajo in the central region, and the Guadalquivir in the south.

Off Spain's east coast in the Mediterranean are the Balearic Islands (1,936 sq mi.; 5,014 sq km), the largest of which is Majorca. Sixty miles (97 km) west of Africa are the Canary Islands (2,808 sq mi.; 7,273 sq km).

Government. King Juan Carlos I (born Jan. 5, 1938) succeeded Generalissimo Francisco Franco Bahamonde as Chief of State Nov. 27, 1975.

The Cortes, or Parliament, consists of a Chamber of Deputies of 350 members and a Senate of 208, all elected by universal suffrage. The new Cortes, replacing one that was largely appointed or elected by special constituencies, was organized under a constitution adopted by referendum Dec. 6, 1978.

History. Spain, originally inhabited by Celts, Iberians and Basques, became a part of the Roman Empire in 206 B.C., when it was conquered by Scipio Africanus. In A.D. 412, the barbarian Visigothic leader Ataulf crossed the Pyrenees and ruled Spain, first in the name of the Roman emperor and then independently. In 711, the Moslems under Tariq entered Spain from Africa and within a few years completed the subjugation of the country. In 732, the Franks, led by Charles Martel, defeated the Moslems near Poitiers, thus preventing the further expansion of Islam in southern Europe. Internal dissension of Spanish Islam invited a steady Christian conquest from the north.

Aragon and Castile were the most important Spanish states from the 12th to the 15th century, consolidated by the marriage of Ferdinand II and Isabella I in 1469. The last Moslem stronghold, Granada, was captured in 1492. Roman Catholicism was established as the official state religion and the Jews (1492) and the Moslems (1502) expelled.

In the era of exploration, discovery, and colonization, Spain amassed tremendous wealth and a vast colonial empire through the conquest of Peru by Pizarro (1532–33) and of Mexico by Cortés (1519–21). The Spanish Hapsburg monarchy became for a time the most powerful in the world.

In 1588, Philip II sent his Invincible Armada to invade England, but its destruction cost Spain its supremacy on the seas and paved the way for England's colonization of America. Spain then sank rapidly to the status of a second-rate power and never again played a major role in European politics. Its colonial empire in the Americas and the Philippines vanished in wars and revolutions during the 18th and 19th centuries.

In World War I, Spain maintained a position of neutrality. In 1923, Gen. Miguel Primo de Rivera became dictator. In 1930, King Alfonso XIII revoked the dictatorship, but a strong antimonarchist and republican movement led to his leaving Spain in 1931. The new Constitution declared Spain a workers' republic, broke up the large estates, separated church and state, and secularized the schools. The elections held in 1936 returned a strong Popular Front majority, with Manuel Azaña as President.

On July 18, 1936, a conservative army officer in Morocco, Francisco Franco Bahamonde, led a mutiny against the government. The civil war that followed lasted three years and cost the lives of nearly a million people. Franco was aided by Fascist Italy and Nazi Germany, while Soviet Russia helped the Loyalist side. Several hundred leftist Americans served in the Abraham Lincoln Brigade on the side of the republic. The war ended when Franco took Madrid on March 28, 1939.

Franco became head of the state, national chief of the Falange Party (the governing party), and Premier and Caudillo (leader). In a referendum in 1947, the Spanish people approved a Franco-drafted succession law declaring Spain a monarchy again. Franco, however, continued as Chief of State.

In 1969, Franco and the Cortes designated Prince Juan Carlos Alfonso Victor María de Borbón (who married Princess Sophia of Greece on May 14, 1962) to become King of Spain when the provisional government headed by Franco came to an end. He is the grandson of Alfonso XIII and the son of Don Juan, pretender to the throne.

Franco died of a heart attack on Nov. 20, 1975, after more than a year of ill health, and Juan Carlos was proclaimed King seven days later.

Over strong rightist opposition, the government legalized the Communist Party in advance of the 1977 elections. Premier Adolfo Suaraz Gonzalez's Union of the Democratic Center, a coalition of a dozen centrist and rightist parties, claimed 34.3% of the popular vote in the election.

Under pressure from Catalonian and Basque nationalists, Suárez granted home rule to these regions in 1979, but centrists backed by him did poorly in the 1980 elections for local assemblies in the two areas. Economic problems persisted, along with new incidents of terrorism, and Suárez resigned on Jan. 29, 1981 and was succeded by Leopoldo Calvo Sotelo.

With the overwhelming election of Prime Minister Felipe González Márquez and his Spanish Socialist Workers Party in the Oct. 20, 1982, parliamentary elections, the Franco past was finally buried. The thrust of Gonzalez, a pragmatic moderate, was to modernize rather than radicalize Spain. As promised, the Socialists did not carry out widespread nationalization of private industry, but did seek to nationalize the high-tension power grid.

A treaty admitting Spain, along with Portugal, to the European Economic Community took effect on Jan. 1, 1986. Later that year, in June, Spain voted to remain in NATO, but outside of its military command and Gonzalez's Socialists retained their majority in national elections.

SRI LANKA

Democratic Socialist Republic of Sri Lanka
President: Ranasinghe Premadasa (1988)
Prime Minister: Hondoval D. B. Wijetunga (1989)
Area: 25,332 sq mi. (65,610 sq km)
Population (mid-1990): 17,200,000 (average annual rate of natural increase: 1.5%)
Density per square mile: 666
Capital: Sri Jayewardenepura Kotte (Colombo)
Largest cities (est. 1984): Colombo, 664,000; Dehiwela, 188,000; Moratuwa, 138,000; Jaffna, 138,000
Monetary unit: Sri Lanka rupee
Languages: Sinhala, Tamil, English
Religions: Buddhist, 69%; Hindu, 15%; Islam, 8%; Christian, 8%
Member of Commonwealth of Nations
Literacy rate: 87%
Economic summary: Gross domestic product (1987): $6.04 billion; $370 per capita; 1.5% real growth rate. Arable land: 16%; principal products: tea, coconuts, rubber, rice,

spices. Labor force: 6,600,000; 13.3% in mining and manufacturing; major products: consumer goods, textiles, chemicals, paper and paper products. Natural resources: limestone, graphite, gems. Exports: textiles, tea, rubber, petroleum products, gems and jewelry. Imports: petroleum, machinery, transport equipment, sugar. Major trading partners: Egypt, Iraq, Saudi Arabia, U.S., U.K., West Germany, Japan, Singapore, India.

Geography. An island in the Indian Ocean off the southeast tip of India, Sri Lanka is about half the size of Alabama. Most of the land is flat and rolling; mountains in the south central region rise to over 8,000 feet (2,438 m).

Government. Ceylon became an independent country in 1948 after British rule and reverted to the traditional name (resplendent island) on May 22, 1972. A new Constitution was adopted in 1978, replacing that of 1972.

The new Constitution set up the National State Assembly, a 168-member unicameral legislature that serves for six years unless dissolved earlier.

History. Following Portuguese and Dutch rule, Ceylon became an English crown colony in 1798. The British developed coffee, tea, and rubber plantations and granted six Constitutions between 1798 and 1924. The Constitution of 1931 gave a large measure of self-government.

Ceylon became a self-governing dominion of the Commonwealth of Nations in 1948.

Presidential elections were held in December 1982, and won by J.R. Jayewardene.

Tension between the Tamil minority and the Sinhalese majority continued to build and erupted in bloody violence in 1983 that has grown worse since. There are about 2.6 million Tamils in Sri Lanka, while the Sinhalese make up about three-quarters of the 17-million population. Tamil extremists are fighting for a separate nation.

Negotiations broke down in late 1986. A string of Tamil atrocities in early 1987 brought on a government offensive in May-June against guerilla base areas. Although it was largely successful, the increased intensity of the civil war dimmed hopes for a settlement.

An accord signed in July, 1987, between Jayewardene and Prime Minister Gandhi of India called for: the disarming of Tamil militants, amnesty for Tamil guerrillas, Tamil and English to share official status with Sinhala, greater political autonomy for Tamil-dominated areas, the closure of Tamil bases in India and an Indian peacekeeping force to help guarantee the accord. This led to fighting between Indian troops and Tamils in the north and violence by extreme Sinhala nationalists in the south. The Indian troops were withdrawn at the end of 1989.

SUDAN

Republic of the Sudan
Prime Minister: Brig. Omar Hassam Ahmed Bashir (1989)
Area: 967,491 sq mi. (2,505,802 sq km)
Population (mid-1990): 25,200,000 (average annual rate of natural increase: 2.9%)
Density per square mile: 25

Capital: Khartoum
Largest cities (est. 1988): Khartoum, 817,000; Omdurman, 527,000; Port Sudan, 207,000
Monetary unit: Sudanese pound
Languages: Arabic, English, tribal dialects
Religions: Islam, 73%; Animist, 18%; Christian, 9%
National name: Jamhuryat es-Sudan
Literacy rate: 20%
Economic summary: Gross national product (FY87): $8.5 billion; $340 per capita; 6% real growth rate (FY88 est.). Arable land: 5%; principal products: cotton, peanuts, sesame seeds, gum arabic, sorghum, wheat, beans, barley. Labor force: 6,500,000; 10% in industry and commerce; major products: cement, textiles, pharmaceuticals, shoes, processed foods. Natural resources: some iron ore, copper, chrome, industrial metals. Exports: cotton, peanuts, gum arabic, groundnuts. Imports: textiles, petroleum products, vehicles, tea, wheat. Major trading partners: U.K., West Germany, Saudi Arabia, U.S., Netherlands, France.

Geography. The Sudan, in northeast Africa, is the largest country on the continent, measuring about one fourth the size of the United States. Its neighbors are Chad and the Central African Republic on the west, Egypt and Libya on the north, Ethiopia on the east, and Kenya, Uganda, and Zaire on the south. The Red Sea washes about 500 miles of the eastern coast.

The country extends from north to south about 1,200 miles (1,931 km) and west to east about 1,000 miles (1,609 km). The northern region is a continuation of the Libyan Desert. The southern region is fertile, abundantly watered, and, in places, heavily forested. It is traversed from north to south by the Nile, all of whose great tributaries are partly or entirely within its borders.

Government. A multi-party democracy was established. Elections were held in April, 1986.

The three main parties in the 264-seat Parliament are the National Islamic Front (51 seats), Umma (99 seats) and the Democratic Unionist Party (63 seats). They formed a consensus government in May 1988.

History. The early history of the Sudan (known as the Anglo-Egyptian Sudan between 1898 and 1955) is linked with that of Nubia, where a powerful local kingdom was formed in Roman times with its capital at Dongola. After conversion to Christianity in the 6th century, it joined with Ethiopia and resisted Mohammedanization until the 14th century. Thereafter the area was broken up into many small states until 1820–22, when it was conquered by Mohammed Ali, Pasha of Egypt. Egyptian forces were evacuated during the Mahdist revolt (1881–98), but the Sudan was reconquered by the Anglo-Egyptian expeditions of 1896–98, and in 1899 became an Anglo-Egyptian condominium, which was reaffirmed by the Anglo-Egyptian treaty of 1936.

Egypt and Britain agreed in 1953 to grant self-government to the Sudan under an appointed Governor-General. An all-Sudanese Parliament was elected in November-December 1953, and an all-Sudanese government was formed. In December 1955, the Parliament declared the independence of the Sudan, which, with the approval of Britain and Egypt, was proclaimed on Jan. 1, 1956.

In October 1969, Maj. Gen. Gaafar Mohamed Nimeiri, the president of the Council for the Revolution, took over as prime minister. He was elected the nation's first president in 1971.

In 1976, a third coup was attempted against Nimeiri. Nimeiri accused President Muammar el Qaddafi of Libya of having instigated the attempt and broke relations with Libya.

On April 6, 1985, while out of the country on visits to the United States and Egypt, Nimeiri lost power in the same way he gained it 16 years previously—by a military coup headed by his Defense Minister, Gen. Abdel Rahman Siwar el-Dahab.

Among the problems that the new government faced were a debilitating civil war with rebels in the south of the country, other sectarian and tribal conflicts, and the famine that affected more than four million Sudanese.

The government's inability to cope with the war led to disaffections within the army and a military coup in June 1989. The new leader, Brigadier Bashir, dissolved the constitution, parliament and all political parties.

SURINAME

Republic of Suriname
President: Ramsewak Shankar (1988)
Vice President and Prime Minister: Henck Aaron (1988)
Area: 63,251 sq mi. (163,820 sq km)
Population (mid-1990): 400,000 (average annual rate of natural increase: 2%)
Density per square mile: 6.3
Capital and largest city (est. 1982): Paramaribo, 100,000
Monetary unit: Suriname guilder
Languages: Dutch, Surinamese (lingua franca), English also widely spoken
Religions: Protestant, Roman Catholic, Hindu, Islam
Literacy rate: 65%
Economic summary: Gross domestic product (1987): $1.19 billion; $2,800 per capita; real growth rate −8.4%. Arable land: NEGL %; principal products: rice. Labor force: 104,000 (1984); major products: aluminum, alumina, processed foods, lumber. Natural resources: bauxite, iron ore, timber, fish, shrimp. Exports: bauxite, alumina, aluminum, rice, shrimp, lumber and wood products. Imports: capital equipment, petroleum, iron and steel, cotton, flour, meat, dairy products. Major trading partners: U.S., Trinidad, Netherlands, Norway.

Geography. Suriname lies on the northeast coast of South America, with Guyana to the west, French Guiana to the east, and Brazil to the south. It is about one tenth larger than Michigan. The principal rivers are the Corantijn on the Guyana border, the Marowijne in the east, and the Suriname, on which the capital city of Paramaribo is situated. The Tumuc-Humac Mountains are on the border with Brazil.
Government. Suriname, formerly known as Dutch Guiana, became an independent republic on Nov. 25, 1975. Elections in November 1987 gave the Front for Democracy and Development coalition an overwhelming majority in the 51-seat National Assembly. The coalition elected Shankar and Aaron as President and Vice-President in January, 1988.

A draft constitution approved in September, 1987, gave the military a continuing behind-the-scenes role in the government.

History. England established the first European settlement on the Suriname River in 1650 but transferred sovereignty to the Dutch in 1667 in the Treaty of Breda, by which the British acquired New York. Colonization was confined to a narrow coastal strip, and until the abolition of slavery in 1863, African slaves furnished the labor for the plantation economy. After 1870, laborers were imported from British India and the Dutch East Indies.

In 1948, the colony was integrated into the Kingdom of the Netherlands and two years later was granted full home rule in other than foreign affairs and defense. After race rioting over unemployment and inflation, the Netherlands offered complete independence in 1973. Henck A. E. Aaron, leader of a coalition of Creole (Surinamese of African descent) parties, advocated independence, while Jaggernath Lachmon, leader of the Surinamese of East Indian descent, urged delay.

Aaron retained power in the first post-independence elections in 1977. He had promised early elections when Army sergeants and a lieutenant staged a coup on Feb. 25 and installed a civilian, Dr. Henk R. Chin A Sen, as Prime Minister. A subsequent military intervention made Henk Chin A Sen president, abolishing the legislature and instituting a military government.

In mid-1986, Ronnie Brunswijk, a former army private, began a guerilla insurgency in eastern Suriname. A peace treaty was signed between him and the government in 1989.

SWAZILAND

Kingdom of Swaziland
Ruler: King Mswati III (1986)
Prime Minister: Obed Dlamihi (1989)
Area: 6,704 sq mi. (17,363 sq km)
Population (mid-1989): 800,000 (average annual rate of natural increase: 3.1%)
Density per square mile: 114
Capital (est. 1986): Mbabane, 40,000
Monetary unit: Lilangeni
Languages: English and Swazi (official)
Religions: Christian, 77%; Animist, 27%
Member of Commonwealth of Nations
Literacy rate (1985): 68%
Economic summary: Gross national product (1987 est.): $539 million; $750 per capita; .7% real growth rate. Arable land: 8%; principal products: corn, livestock, sugar cane, citrus fruits, cotton, rice, pineapples. Labor force: 195,000; about 92,000 wage earners with 14% in manufacturing; major products: milled sugar, ginned cotton, processed meat and wood. Natural resources: asbestos, diamonds. Exports: sugar, wood products, iron ore, asbestos, citrus fruits, cotton. Imports: motor vehicles, fuels and lubricants, foodstuffs, chemicals. Major trading partners: South Africa, U.K., U.S.

Geography. Swaziland, 85% the size of New Jersey, is surrounded by South Africa and Mozambique. The country consists of a high veld in the west and a series of plateaus descending from 6,000 feet (1,829 m) to a low veld of 1,500 feet (457 m).
Government. In 1967, a new Constitution established King Sobhuza II as head of state and provided for an Assembly of 24 members elected by universal suffrage, together with a Senate of 12

members—half appointed by the Assembly and half by the King. In 1973, the King renounced the Constitution, suspended political parties, and took total power for himself. In 1977, he replaced the Parliament with an assembly of tribal leaders. The Parliament reconvened in 1979.

History. Bantu peoples migrated southwest to the area of Mozambique in the 16th century. A number of clans broke away from the main body in the 18th century and settled in Swaziland. In the 19th century they organized as a tribe, partly because they were in constant conflict with the Zulu. Their ruler, Mswazi, applied to the British in the 1840s for help against the Zulu. The British and the Transvaal governments guaranteed the independence of Swaziland in 1881.

South Africa held Swaziland as a protectorate from 1894 to 1899, but after the Boer War, in 1902, Swaziland was transferred to British administration. The Paramount Chief was recognized as the native authority in 1941.

In 1963, the territory was constituted a protectorate, and on Sept. 6, 1968, it became the independent nation of Swaziland.

King Sobhuza died in August 1982.

SWEDEN

Kingdom of Sweden
Sovereign: King Carl XVI Gustaf (1973)
Prime Minister: Ingvar Carlsson (1986)
Area: 173,800 sq mi. (449,964 sq km)
Population (mid-1990): 8,500,000 (average annual rate of natural increase: 0.2%)
Density per square mile: 49
Capital: Stockholm
Largest cities (est. 1986): Stockholm, 1,435,000; Göteborg, 704,000; Malmö, 458,000
Monetary unit: Krona
Language: Swedish
Religion: Swedish Lutheran, 95%
National name: Konungariket Sverige
Literacy rate: 99.5%
Economic summary: Gross national product (1987): $116.5 billion; $13,897 per capita; 3.1% real growth rate. Arable land: 7%. Principal agricultural products: dairy products, grains, sugar beets, potatoes, wood. Labor force: 4,390,000; 22% in mining and manufacturing; major products: machinery, instruments, metal products, automobiles. Natural resources: forests, iron ore, hydroelectric power, unmined uranium. Exports: machinery, motor vehicles, wood pulp, paper products, iron and steel products. Imports: machinery, petroleum, yarns, foodstuffs, iron and steel, chemicals. Major trading partners: Norway, West Germany, U.K., Denmark, Finland, U.S.

Geography. Sweden occupies the eastern part of the Scandinavian peninsula, with Norway to the west, Finland and the Gulf of Bothnia to the east, and Denmark and the Baltic Sea in the south. It is one tenth larger than California.

The country slopes eastward and southward from the Kjólen Mountains along the Norwegian border, where the peak elevation is Kebnekaise at 6,965 feet (2,123 m) in Lapland. In the north are mountains and many lakes. To the south and east are central lowlands and south of them are fertile areas of forest, valley, and plain.

Along Sweden's rocky coast, chopped up by bays and inlets, are many islands, the largest of which are Gotland and Oland.

Government. Sweden is a constitutional monarchy. Under the 1975 Constitution, the Riksdag is the sole governing body. The prime minister is the political chief executive.

In 1967, agreement was reached on part of a new Constitution after 13 years of work. It provided for a single-house Riksdag of 350 members (later amended to 349 seats) to replace the 104-year old bicameral Riksdag. The members are popularly elected for three years. Ninety-two present members of the Riksdag are women.

The King, Carl XVI Gustaf, was born April 30, 1946, and succeeded to the throne Sept. 19, 1973, on the death at 90 of his grandfather, Gustaf VI Adolf. Carl Gustaf was married on June 19, 1976, to Silvia Sommerlath, a West German commoner. They have three children: Princess Victoria, born July 14, 1977; Prince Carl Philip, born May 13, 1979; and Princess Madeleine, born June 10, 1982. Under the new Act of Succession, effective Jan. 1, 1980, the first child of the reigning monarch, regardless of sex, is heir to the throne.

History. The earliest historical mention of Sweden is found in Tacitus' *Germania,* where reference is made to the powerful king and strong fleet of the Suiones. Toward the end of the 10th century, Olaf Sköttkonung established a Christian stronghold in Sweden. Around 1400, an attempt was made to unite the northern nations into one kingdom, but this led to bitter strife between the Danes and the Swedes.

In 1520, the Danish King, Christian II, conquered Sweden and in the "Stockholm Bloodbath" put leading Swedish personalities to death. Gustavus Vasa (1523–60) broke away from Denmark and fashioned the modern Swedish state.

Sweden played a leading role in the second phase (1630–35) of the Thirty Years' War (1618–48). By the Treaty of Westphalia (1648), Sweden obtained western Pomerania and some neighboring territory on the Baltic. In 1700, a coalition of Russia, Poland, and Denmark united against Sweden and by the Peace of Nystad (1721) forced it to relinquish Livonia, Ingria, Estonia, and parts of Finland.

Sweden emerged from the Napoleonic Wars with the acquisition of Norway from Denmark and with a new royal dynasty stemming from Marshal Jean Bernadotte of France, who became King Charles XIV (1818–44). The artificial union between Sweden and Norway led to an uneasy relationship, and the union was finally dissolved in 1905.

Sweden maintained a position of neutrality in both World Wars.

An elaborate structure of welfare legislation, imitated by many larger nations, began with the establishment of old-age pensions in 1911. Economic prosperity based on its neutralist policy enabled Sweden, together with Norway, to pioneer in public health, housing, and job security programs.

Forty-four years of Socialist government were ended in 1976 with the election of a conservative coalition headed by Thorbjörn Fälldin, a 50-year-old sheep farmer.

Fälldin resigned on Oct. 5, 1978, when his conservative parties partners demanded less restrictions on nuclear power, and his successor, Ola Ullsten, resigned a year later after failing to achieve a consensus on the issue. Returned to office by his co-alition partners, Fälldin said he would follow the course directed by a national referendum. On March 23, 1980, voters backed the development of 12 nuclear plants and use of them for at least 25 years to supply 40% of national energy needs while the search for alternative sources continued.

Olof Palme and the Socialists were returned to power in the election of 1982.

In February 1986, Palme was killed by an unknown assailant. His death shocked the world.

SWITZERLAND

Swiss Confederation
President: Jean-Pascal Delamuraz (1989)
Vice President: Arnold Koller (1989)
Area: 15,941 sq mi. (41,288 sq km)
Population (mid-1990): 6,700,000 (average annual rate of natural increase: 0.3%)
Density per square mile: 414.0
Capital: Bern
Largest cities (est. 1988): Zurich, 346,879; Basel, 171,-574; Geneva, 161,473; Bern, 136,292; Lausanne, 124,022
Monetary unit: Swiss franc
Languages: German, 65%; French, 18%; Italian, 10%; Romansch, 1%
Religions: Roman Catholic, 48%; Protestant, 44%
National name: Schweiz/Suisse/Svizzera/Svizra
Literacy rate: 99.5%
Economic summary: Gross national product (1988): $111.3 billion; $16,900 per capita; 2.6% real growth rate. Arable land: 10%; principal products: cheese and other dairy products, livestock, fruits, grains, wine. Labor force: 3,050,000; 39% in industry and crafts; major products: watches and clocks, precision instruments, machinery, chemicals, pharmaceuticals, textiles, generators, turbines. Natural resources: water power, timber, salt. Exports: electrical machinery, chemicals, precision instruments, textiles, foodstuffs, textile yarns, dyestuffs, chemicals. Imports: transport equipment, metals and metal products, foodstuffs, chemicals, textile yarns. Major trading partners: West Germany, France, U.S., Italy, U.K., Japan

Geography. Switzerland, in central Europe, is the land of the Alps. Its tallest peak is the Dufourspitze at 15,203 feet (4,634 m) on the Swiss side of the Italian border, one of 10 summits of the Monte Rose massif in the Apennines. The tallest peak in all of the Alps, Mont Blanc (15,771 ft; 4,807 m), is actually in France.

Most of Switzerland comprises a mountainous plateau bordered by the great bulk of the Alps on the south and by the Jura Mountains on the northwest. About one fourth of the total area is covered by mountains and glaciers.

The country's largest lakes—Geneva, Constance (Bodensee), and Maggiore—straddle the French, German-Austrian, and Italian borders, respectively.

The Rhine, navigable from Basel to the North Sea, is the principal inland waterway. Other rivers are the Aare and the Rhône.

Switzerland, twice the size of New Jersey, is surrounded by France, West Germany, Austria, Liechtenstein, and Italy.

Government. The Swiss Confederation consists of 23 sovereign cantons, of which three are divided into six half-cantons. Federal authority is vested in a bicameral legislature. The Ständerat, or State Council, consists of 46 members, two from each canton. The lower house, the Nationalrat, or National Council, has 200 deputies, elected for four-year terms.

Executive authority rests with the Bundesrat, or Federal Council, consisting of seven members chosen by parliament. The parliament elects the President, who serves for one year and is succeeded by the Vice President. The federal government regulates foreign policy, railroads, postal service, and the national mint. Each canton reserves for itself important local powers.

A constitutional amendment adopted in 1971 by referendum gave women the vote in federal elections and the right to hold federal office. An equal rights amendment was passed in a national referendum June 14, 1981, barring discrimination against women under canton as well as federal law.

History. Called Helvetia in ancient times, Switzerland in the Middle Ages was a league of cantons of the Holy Roman Empire. Fashioned around the nucleus of three German forest districts of Schwyz, Uri, and Unterwalden, the Swiss Confederation slowly added new cantons. In 1648 the Treaty of Westphalia gave Switzerland its independence from the Holy Roman Empire.

French revolutionary troops occupied the country in 1798 and named it the Helvetic Republic, but Napoleon in 1803 restored its federal government. By 1815, the French- and Italian-speaking peoples of Switzerland had been granted political equality.

In 1815, the Congress of Vienna guaranteed the neutrality and recognized the independence of Switzerland. In the revolutionary period of 1847, the Catholic cantons seceded and organized a separate union called the *Sonderbund.* In 1848 the new Swiss Constitution established a union modeled upon that of the U.S. The Federal Constitution of 1874 established a strong central government while maintaining large powers of control in each canton.

National unity and political conservatism grew as the country prospered from its neutrality. Its banking system became the world's leading repository for international accounts. Strict neutrality was its policy in World Wars I and II. Geneva was the seat of the League of Nations (later the European headquarters of the United Nations) and of a number of international organizations.

In 1971, the Swiss Supreme Court ruled that Swiss banks must show U.S. tax officials records of U.S. citizens suspected of tax fraud, thus significantly modifying a 1934 law that had seemed to forbid any bank disclosures.

SYRIA

Syrian Arab Republic
President: Hafez al-Assad (1971)
Premier: Mahmoud al-Zubi (1987)
Area: 71,498 sq mi. (185,180 sq km)
Population (mid-1990): 12,600,000 (average annual

rate of natural increase: 3.8%)
Density per square mile: 169
Capital: Damascus
Largest cities (est. 1987): Damascus, 1,292,000; Aleppo, 1,216,000; Homs, 431,000; Hama, 214,000; Latakia, 241,000
Monetary unit: Syrian pound
Language: Arabic
Religions: Islam, 90%; Christian, 10%
National name: Al-Jamhouriya al Arabiya As-Souriya
Literacy rate: 55%
Economic summary: Gross domestic product (1985): $20.3 billion, $1,962 per capita; 5.6% real growth rate. Arable land: 28%; principal products: Cotton, wheat, barley, tobacco, sheep, goats. Labor force: 2,400,000; 32% in industry; major products: textiles, cement, petroleum, processed food. Natural resources: chrome, manganese, asphalt, iron ore, rock salt, phosphate, oil, natural gas. Exports: petroleum, textiles, tobacco. Imports: machinery and metal products, fuels, foodstuffs. Major trading partners: Italy, Romania, U.S.S.R., U.S., Iran, Libya, France, West Germany.

Geography. Slightly larger than North Dakota, Syria lies at the eastern end of the Mediterranean Sea. It is bordered by Lebanon and Israel on the west, Turkey on the north, Iraq on the east, and Jordan on the south.

Coastal Syria is a narrow plain, in back of which is a range of coastal mountains, and still farther inland a steppe area. In the east is the Syrian Desert, and in the south is the Jebel Druze Range. The highest point in Syria is Mount Hermon (9,232 ft; 2,814 m) on the Lebanese border.

Government. Syria's first permanent Constitution was approved in 1973, replacing a provisional charter that had been in force for 10 years. It provided for an elected People's Council as the legislature.

In the first election in 10 years, in 1973, the Ba'ath Arab Socialist Party of President Hafez al-Assad, running on a unified National Progressive ticket with the Communist and Socialist parties, won 70% of the vote and a commensurate proportion of the seats in the People's Assembly. In 1977 and 1981 elections, the ruling Ba'athists won by similar margins.

History. Ancient Syria was conquered by Egypt about 1500 B.C., and after that by Hebrews, Assyrians, Chaldeans, Persians, and Greeks. From 64 B.C. until the Arab conquest in A.D. 636, it was part of the Roman Empire except during brief periods. The Arabs made it a trade center for their extensive empire, but it suffered severely from the Mongol invasion in 1260 and fell to the Ottoman Turks in 1516. Syria remained a Turkish province until World War I.

A secret Anglo-French pact of 1916 put Syria in the French zone of influence. The League of Nations gave France a mandate over Syria after World War I, but the French were forced to put down several nationalist uprisings. In 1930, France recognized Syria as an independent republic, but still subject to the mandate. After nationalist demonstrations in 1939, the French High Commissioner suspended the Syrian Constitution. In 1941, British and Free French forces invaded Syria to eliminate Vichy control. During the rest of World War II, Syria was an Allied base.

Again in 1945, nationalist demonstrations broke into actual fighting, and British troops had to restore order. Syrian forces met a series of reverses while participating in the Arab invasion of Palestine in 1948. In 1958, Egypt and Syria formed the United Arab Republic, with Gamal Abdel Nasser of Egypt as President. However, Syria became independent again on Sept. 29, 1961, following a revolution.

In the war of 1967, Israel quickly vanquished the Syrian army. Before acceding to the U.N. ceasefire, the Israeli forces took over control of the fortified Golan Heights commanding the Sea of Galilee.

Syria joined Egypt in attacking Israel in October 1973 in the fourth Arab-Israeli war, but was pushed back from initial successes on the Golan Heights to end up losing more land. However, in the settlement worked out by U.S. Secretary of State Henry A. Kissinger in 1974, the Syrians recovered all the territory lost in 1973 and a token amount of territory, including the deserted town of Quneitra, lost in 1967.

Syrian troops, in Lebanon since 1976 as part of an Arab peacekeeping force whose other members subsequently departed, intervened increasingly during 1980 and 1981 on the side of Moslem Lebanese in their clashes with Christian militants supported by Israel. When Israeli jets shot down Syrian helicopters operating in Lebanon in April 1981, Syria moved Soviet-built surface-to-air (SAM 6) missiles into Lebanon's Bekaa Valley. Israel demanded that the missiles be removed because they violated a 1976 understanding between the governments. The demand, backed up by bombing raids, prompted the Reagan Administration to send veteran diplomat Philip C. Habib as a special envoy to avert a new conflict between the nations.

Habib's carefully engineered cease-fire was shattered by a new Israeli invasion in June 1982, when Israeli aircraft bombed Bekaa Valley missile sites, claiming to destroy all of them along with 25 Syrian planes that had sought to defend the sites. On the ground, Syrian army units were driven back by Israeli armor along the Lebanese coast. The Syrians, who were equipped with Soviet weapons, were outfought everywhere by U.S.-equipped Israelis.

Nevertheless, while the Israelis overran most of the rest of Lebanon, the Syrians retained their positions in the Bekaa Valley. Over the next three years, as the Israelis gradually withdrew their forces, the Syrians remained. As the various Lebanese factions fought each other, the Syrians became the dominant force in the country, both militarily and politically.

The extent of Syrian influence in Lebanaon was demonstrated dramatically after Lebanese Shiite extremists hijacked a TWA airliner from Athens to Beirut on June 14, 1985. President al-Assad played the key role in delicate, many-sided negotiations that obtained the release of the 39 American hostages from the plane 17 days later.

TAIWAN

Republic of China
President: Lee Teng-hui (1988)
Premier: Lee Huan (1989)
Area: 13,895 sq mi. (35,988 sq km)
Population (mid-1990): 20,200,000 (average annual rate of natural increase: 1.2%)
Density per square mile: 1,604
Capital: Taipei

Largest cities (est. 1986): Taipei, 2,507,620; Kaohsiung, 1,302,849; Taichung, 674,936; Tainan, 639,888; Chilung (Keelung), 351,524
Monetary unit: New Taiwan dollar
Languages: Chinese (Mandarin) and various dialects
Religions: Chinese Folk, 49%; Buddhist, 43%; Christian, 7%
Literacy rate: 92%
Economic summary: Gross national product (1986): $72.8 billion. Real growth rate (1985-7): 8.0%. Per capita income (1986): $3,750. Land used for agriculture: 30%; labor force: 20%; principal products: rice, yams, sugar cane, bananas, pineapples, citrus fruits. Labor force in industry: 42%; major products: textiles, clothing, chemicals, processed foods, electronic equipment, cement, ships, plywood. Natural resources: coal, natural gas, limestone, marble. Exports: textiles, electrical machinery, plywood. Imports: machinery, basic metals, crude oil, chemicals. Major trading partners: U.S., Japan, Saudi Arabia.

Geography. The Republic of China today consists of the island of Taiwan, an island 100 miles (161 km) off the Asian mainland in the Pacific; two offshore islands, Quemoy and Matsu; and the nearby islets of the Pescadores chain. It is slightly larger than the combined areas of Massachusetts and Connecticut.

Taiwan is divided by a central mountain range that runs from north to south, rising sharply on the east coast and descending gradually to a broad western plain, where cultivation is concentrated.

Government. The President and the Vice President are elected by the National Assembly for a term of six years. There are five major governing bodies called Yuans: Executive, Legislative, Judicial, Control, and Examination. Taiwan's internal affairs are administered by the Taiwan Provincial Government under the supervision of the Provincial Assembly, which is popularly elected.

The majority and ruling party is the Kuomintang (KMT) (Nationalist Party) led by President Lee Teng-hui. The main opposition party is the Democratic Progressive Party (DPP).

History. Taiwan was inhabited by aborigines of Malayan descent when Chinese from the areas now designated as Fukien and Kwangtung began settling it beginning in the 7th century, becoming the majority.

The Portuguese explored the area in 1590, naming it The Beautiful (Formosa). In 1624 the Dutch set up forts in the south, the Spanish in the North. The Dutch threw out the Spanish in 1641 and controlled the island until 1661, when the Chinese General Koxinga took it over, established an independent kingdom, and expelled the Dutch. The Manchus seized the island in 1683 and held it until 1895, when it passed to Japan after the first Sino-Japanese War. Japan developed and exploited it, and it was heavily bombed by American planes during World War II, after which it was restored to China.

After the defeat of its armies on the mainland, the Nationalist Government of Generalissimo Chiang Kai-shek retreated to Taiwan in December 1949. With only 15% of the population consisting of the 1949 immigrants, Chiang dominated the island, maintaining a 600,000-man army in the hope of eventually recovering the mainland. Japan renounced its claim to the island by the San Francisco Peace Treaty of 1951.

By stationing a fleet in the Strait of Formosa the U.S. prevented a mainland invasion in 1953.

The "China seat" in the U.N., which the Nationalists held with U.S. help for over two decades was lost in October 1971, when the People's Republic of China was admitted and Taiwan ousted by the world body.

Chiang died at 87 of a heart attack on April 5, 1975. His son, Chiang Ching-kuo, continued as Premier and dominant power in the Taipei regime. He assumed the presidency in 1978, and Sun Yun-hsuan became Premier.

President Carter's announcement that the U.S. would recognize only the People's Republic of China after Jan. 1, 1979, and that the U.S. defense treaty with the Nationalists would end aroused protests in Taiwan and in the U.S. Congress. Against Carter's wishes, Congress, in a bill governing future relations with Taiwan, guaranteed U.S. action in the event of an attack on the island. The legislation also provided for the continuation of trade and other relations through an American Institute in Taipei, housed in the former American Embassy.

Although the U.S. had assured Taiwan of continuing arms aid, a communiqué on Aug. 17, 1982, signed by Washington and Peking and promising a gradual reduction of such aid, cast a shadow over Taiwan. The striking success of the DPP in legislative elections in December 1986 marked a slight loosening of the KMT's hold on power.

TANZANIA

United Republic of Tanzania
President: Ali Hassan Mwinyi (1985)
Prime Minister: Joseph Warioba (1985)
Area: 364,900 sq mi. (945,087 sq km)[1]
Population (mid-1990): 26,000,000 (average annual rate of natural increase: 3.7%)
Density per square mile: 72
Capital and largest city (est. 1984): Dar es Salaam, 1,-400,000
Monetary unit: Tanzanian shilling
Languages: Swahili, English, local languages
Religions: Christian, 33%; Islam, 33%; Animist, 33%
Member of Commonwealth of Nations
Literacy rate: 85%
Economic summary: Gross domestic product (FY87): $4.96 billion; $258 per capita; 3.9% real growth rate. Arable land: 5%; Principal products: coconuts, maize, rice, wheat, cotton, coffee, sisal cashew nuts, pyrethrum, cloves. Labor force: 732,200; 10% in industry and commerce (1986 est.). Major industrial products: textiles, light manufactures, refined oil, processed agricultural products, diamonds, cement, fertilizer. Natural resources: hydroelectric potential, unexploited iron and coal. Exports: coffee, cotton, sisal, diamonds, cloves, cashew nuts. Imports: manufactured goods, textiles, machinery and transport equipment, crude oil, foodstuffs. Major trading partners: West Germany, U.K., U.S., Iran.

1. Including Zanzibar.

Geography. Tanzania is in East Africa on the Indian Ocean. To the north are Uganda and Kenya; to the west, Burundi, Rwanda, and Zaire; and to the south, Mozambique, Zambia, and Malawi. Its area is three times that of New Mexico.

Tanzania contains three of Africa's best-known lakes—Victoria in the north, Tanganyika in the west, and Nyasa in the south. Mount Kilimanjaro in the north, 19,340 feet (5,895 m), is the highest point on the continent.

Government. Under the republican form of government, Tanzania has a President elected by universal suffrage who appoints the Cabinet ministers. The 244-member National Assembly is composed of 119 elected members from the mainland, 50 elected from Zanzibar, 10 members appointed by the President (from both Tanganyika and Zanzibar), 5 national members (elected by the National Assembly after nomination by various national institutions), 20 members elected by Zanzibar's House of Representatives, 25 Regional Commissioners sitting as *ex officio* members, and 15 seats reserved for women (elected by the National Assembly).

The Tanganyika African National Union, the only authorized party on the mainland, and the Afro-Shirazi Party, the only party in Zanzibar and Pemba, merged in 1977 as the Revolutionary Party (Chama Cha Mapinduzi) and elected Julius K. Nyerere as its head.

History. Arab traders first began to colonize the area in A.D. 700. Portuguese explorers reached the coastal regions in 1500 and held some control until the 17th century, when the Sultan of Oman took power. With what are now Burundi and Rwanda, Tanganyika became the colony of German East Africa in 1885. After World War I, it was administered by Britain under a League of Nations mandate and later as a U.N. trust territory.

Although not mentioned in old histories until the 12th century, Zanzibar was believed always to have had connections with southern Arabia. The Portuguese made it one of their tributaries in 1503 and later established a trading post, but they were driven out by Arabs from Oman in 1698. Zanzibar was declared independent of Oman in 1861 and, in 1890, it became a British protectorate.

Tanganyika became independent on Dec. 9, 1961; Zanzibar, on Dec. 10, 1963. On April 26, 1964, the two nations merged into the United Republic of Tanganyika and Zanzibar. The name was changed to Tanzania six months later.

An invasion by Ugandan troops in November 1978 was followed by a counterattack in January 1979, in which 5,000 Tanzanian troops were joined by 3,000 Ugandan exiles opposed to President Idi Amin. Within a month, full-scale war developed.

Nyerere kept troops in Uganda in open support of former Ugandan President Milton Obote, despite protests from opposition groups, until the national elections in December 1980. Although Obote asked that the Tanzanians remain after his victory in order to control guerrilla resistance, Nyerere ordered their withdrawal in May 1981, citing the $1-million-a-month drain on his precarious finances.

In November 1985, Nyerere stepped down as President. Ali Hassan Mwinyi, his Vice-President, succeeded him. Nyerere remained chariman of the party.

THAILAND

Kingdom of Thailand
Ruler: King Bhumibol Adulyadej (1946)
Prime Minister: Maj. General Chatichai Choonharan (1988)
Area: 198,455 sq mi. (514,000 sq km)
Population (mid-1990): 55,700,000 (average annual rate

of natural increase: 1.5%)
Density per square mile: 280
Capital and largest city (est. 1984): Bangkok, 5,174,682
Monetary unit: Baht
Languages: Thai (Siamese), Chinese, English
Religions: Buddhist, 95%; Islam, 4%
National name: Thailand
Literacy rate (1985): 85.5%
Economic summary: Gross national product (1988 est.): $52.2 billion; $965 per capita; 11% real growth rate. Arable land: 34%; principal products: rice, rubber, corn, tapioca, sugar, coconuts. Labor force: 26,000,000; 11% in industry and commerce; major products: processed food, textiles, wood, cement, tin, tungsten, jewelry. Natural resources: fish, natural gas, forests, fluorite, tin, tungsten. Exports: rice, tapioca, sugar, rubber, tin, textiles, jewelry. Imports: machinery and transport equipment, fertilizer, crude oil, fuels and lubricants, base metals, chemicals. Major trading partners: Japan, U.S., Singapore, Malaysia, Netherlands, U.K., Hong Kong, W. Germany.

Geography. Thailand occupies the western half of the Indochinese peninsula and the northern two thirds of the Malay peninsula in southeast Asia. Its neighbors are Myanmar on the north and west, Laos on the north and northeast, Cambodia on the east, and Malaysia on the south. Thailand is about the size of France.

Most of the population is supported in the fertile central alluvial plain, which is drained by the Chao Phraya River and its tributaries.

Government. King Bhumibol Adulyadej, who was born Dec. 5, 1927, second son of Prince Mahidol of Songkhla, succeeded to the throne on June 9, 1946, when his brother, King Ananda Mahidol, died of a gunshot wound. He was married on April 28, 1950, to Queen Sirikit; their son, Vajiralongkorn, born July 28, 1952, is the Crown Prince.

Thailand is a constitutional monarchy with a 357-member Parliament.

History. The Thais first began moving down into their present homeland from the Asian continent in the 6th century A.D. and by the end of the 13th century ruled most of the western portion. During the next 400 years, the Thais fought sporadically with the Cambodians and the Burmese. The British obtained recognition of paramount interest in Thailand in 1824, and in 1896 an Anglo-French accord guaranteed the independence of Thailand.

A coup in 1932 changed the absolute monarchy into a representative government with universal suffrage. After five hours of token resistance on Dec. 8, 1941, Thailand yielded to Japanese occupation and became one of the springboards in World War II for the Japanese campaign against Malaya.

After the fall of its pro-Japanese puppet government in July 1944, Thailand pursued a policy of passive resistance against the Japanese, and after the Japanese surrender, Thailand repudiated the declaration of war it had been forced to make against Britain and the U.S. in 1942.

Thailand's major problem in the late 1960s was suppressing guerrilla action by Communist invaders in the north.

Although Thailand had received $2 billion in U.S. economic and military aid since 1950 and had sent troops (paid by the U.S.) to Vietnam while permitting U.S. bomber bases on its territory, the collapse of South Vietnam and Cambodia in the spring of 1975 brought rapid changes in the country's diplomatic posture.

At the Thai government's insistence, the U.S. agreed to withdraw all 23,000 U.S. military personnel remaining in Thailand by March 1976. Diplomatic relations with China were established in 1975. Meanwhile, overtures toward an accommodation with the new regime in South Vietnam were initiated.

After three years of civilian government ended with a military coup on Oct. 6, 1976, Thailand reverted to military rule. Political parties, banned after the coup, gained limited freedom in 1980. The same year, the National Assembly elected Gen. Prem Tinsulanonda as prime minister. General elections on April 18, 1983, and July 27, 1986 resulted in Prem continuing as prime minister over a coalition government.

Refugees from Laos, Cambodia, and Vietnam flooded into Thailand in 1978 and 1979, and despite efforts by the United States and other Western countries to resettle them, a total of 130,000 Laotian and Vietnamese refugees were living in camps along the Cambodian border in mid-1980. A drive by Vietnamese occupation forces on western Cambodian areas loyal to the Pol Pot government, culminating in invasions of Thai territory in late June, drove an estimated 100,000 Cambodians across the line as refugees, adding to the 200,000 of their countrymen already in Thailand. The total of 430,000 were being fed by United Nations and church relief organizations but the Thai government complained of the burden of their presence.

The Vietnamese incursions, notwithstanding Hanoi's claim that the troops were only seeking guerrillas hidden in the refugee camps, prompted a Thai appeal to Washington for military aid. In July, 35 reconditioned tanks and other weapons were flown to Thailand.

On April 3, 1981, a military coup against the Prem government failed. Another coup attempt on Sept. 9, 1985, was crushed by loyal troops after 10 hours of fighting in Bangkok. Four persons were killed and about 60 wounded.

General elections in 1988 led to Prem stepping down in favor of Chatichai Choonharan.

TOGO

Republic of Togo
President: Gen. Gnassingbé Eyadema (1967)
Area: 21,925 sq mi. (56,785 sq km)
Population (mid-1990): 3,700,000 (average annual rate of natural increase: 3.6%)
Density per square mile: 157
Capital and largest city (est. 1982): Lomé, 285,000
Monetary unit: Franc CFA
Languages: Ewé, Mina (south), Kabyé, Cotocoli (north), French (official), and many dialects
Religions: Animist, 46%; Christian, 37%; Islam, 17%
National name: République Togolaise
Literacy rate: 18%
Economic summary: Gross domestic product (1987 est.): $1.3 billion; $390 per capita; 3.8% real growth rate. Arable land: 25%; principal products: yams, manioc, millet, sorghum, cocoa, coffee, peanuts. Labor force: 78% in agriculture. Major products: phosphate, textiles, processed food. Natural resources: marble, phosphate, limestone. Exports: phosphate, cocoa, coffee. Imports: consumer goods, fuels, machinery, foodstuffs. Major trading partners: France, U.K., Japan, Netherlands, W. Germany.

Geography. Togo, twice the size of Maryland, is on the south coast of West Africa bordering on Ghana to the west, Burkina Faso to the north and Benin to the east.

The Gulf of Guinea coastline, only 32 miles long (51 km), is low and sandy. The only port is at Lomé. The Togo hills traverse the central section.

Government. The government of Nicolas Grunitzky was overthrown in a bloodless coup on Jan. 13, 1967, led by Lt. Col. Etienne Eyadema (now Gen. Gnassingbé Eyadema). A National Reconciliation Committee was set up to rule the country. In April, however, Eyadema dissolved the Committee and took over as President. In December 1979, a 67-member National Assembly was voted in by national referendum. The Assembly of the Togolese People is the only political party.

History. Freed slaves from Brazil were the first traders to settle in Togo. Established as a German colony (Togoland) in 1884, the area was split between the British and the French as League of Nations mandates after World War I and subsequently administered as U. N. trusteeships. The British portion voted for incorporation with Ghana.

Togo became independent on April 27, 1960. Sylvanus Olympio, its first President, was assassinated in 1963 and succeeded by Nicolas Grunitzky.

TONGA

Kingdom of Tonga
Sovereign: King Taufa'ahau Tupou IV (1965)
Prime Minister: Prince Fatafehi Tu'ipelehake (1965)
Area: 290 sq mi. (751 sq km)
Population (mid 1989): 100,465 (average annual growth rate: 0.8%)
Density per square mile: 344
Capital (est. 1986): Nuku'alofa, 28,899
Monetary unit: Pa'anga
Languages: Tongan, English
Religions: Free Wesleyan, 47%; Roman Catholic, 16%; Free Church of Tonga, 14%; Mormon, 9%; Church of Tonga, 9%
Member of Commonwealth of Nations
Literacy rate: 95%
Economic summary: Gross national product (FY87): $65.8 million; $670 per capita; 3% real growth rate. Arable land: 25%; principal products: vanilla, coffee, ginger, black pepper, coconuts, bananas, copra. Labor force: 70% in agriculture. Major industrial products: copra, desiccated coconut. Natural resources: fish. Exports: copra, coconut products, bananas. Imports: manufactures, foodstuffs, machinery, petroleum. Major trading partners: New Zealand, Australia, Fiji, U.K.

Geography. Situated east of the Fiji Islands in the South Pacific, Tonga (also called the Friendly Islands) consists of some 150 islands, of which 36 are inhabited.

Most of the islands contain active volcanic craters; others are coral atolls.

Government. Tonga is a constitutional monarchy. Executive authority is vested in the Sovereign, a Privy Council, and a Cabinet headed by the Prime Minister. Legislative authority is vested in the Legislative Assembly.

History. The present dynasty of Tonga was founded in 1831 by Taufa'ahau Tupou, who took the name George I. He consolidated the kingdom by conquest and in 1875 granted a Constitution.

In 1900, his great-grandson, George II, signed a treaty of friendship with Britain, and the country became a British protected state. The treaty was revised in 1959.

Queen Salote Tupou reigned from 1918 to 1964 and was succeeded by her son, who became King Taufa'ahau Tupou IV.

Tonga became independent on June 4, 1970.

TRANSKEI

See South Africa

TRINIDAD AND TOBAGO

Republic of Trinidad and Tobago
President: Noor Hassanali (1987)
Prime Minister: A.N.R. Robinson (1986)
Area: 1,980 sq mi. (5,128 sq km)
Population (mid-1990): 1,300,000 (average annual rate of natural increase: 2.0%)
Density per square mile: 628
Capital and largest city (est. 1981): Port-of-Spain, 125,-000
Monetary unit: Trinidad and Tobago dollar
Languages: English (official); Hindi, French, Spanish
Religions: Christian, 64%; Hindu, 25%; Islam, 6%
Member of Commonwealth of Nations
Literacy rate: 95%
Economic summary: Gross domestic product (FY 1987): $65.8 million; $670 per capita; 3% real growth rate. Arable land: 25%; principal products: sugar cane, cocoa, coffee, citrus. Labor force: 70% in agriculture. Major industrial products: petroleum, processed food, cement; tourism. Natural resources: petroleum. Exports: petroleum, ammonia, fertilizer. Imports: chemicals, foodstuffs, machinery and equipment. Major trading partners: U.S., Caribbean, Western Europe.

Geography. Trinidad and Tobago lies in the Caribbean Sea off the northeast coast of Venezuela. The area of the two islands is slightly less than that of Delaware.

Trinidad, the larger, is mainly flat and rolling, with mountains in the north that reach a height of 3,085 feet (940 m) at Mount Aripo. Tobago is heavily forested with hardwood trees.

Government. The legislature consists of a 24-member Senate and a 36-member House of Representatives.

The political parties are the National Alliance for Reconstruction, led by Prime Minister A.N.R. Robinson (33 seats in the House of Representatives); People's National Movement (3 seats).

History. Trinidad was discovered by Columbus in 1498 and remained in Spanish possession, despite raids by other European nations, until it capitulated to the British in 1797 during a war between Britain and Spain.

Trinidad was ceded to Britain in 1802, and in 1899 it was united with Tobago as a colony. From 1958 to 1962, Trinidad and Tobago was a part of the West Indies Federation, and on Aug, 31, 1962, it became independent.

On Aug. 1, 1976, Trinidad and Tobago cut its ties with Britain and became a republic, remaining within the Commonwealth and recognizing Queen Elizabeth II only as head of that organization.

TUNISIA

Republic of Tunisia
President: Gen. Zine al-Abidine Ben Ali (1987)
Prime Minister: Hamed Karoui (1989)
Area: 63,379 sq mi. (164,152 sq km)
Population (mid-1990): 8,100,000 (average annual rate of natural increase: 2%)
Density per square mile: 125
Capital and largest city (est. 1981): Tunis, 600,000
Monetary unit: Tunisian dinar
Languages: Arabic, French
Religion: Islam (Sunni): 99.4%
National name: Al-Joumhouria Attunisia
Literacy rate: 64%
Economic summary: Gross domestic product (1987 est.): $9.6 billion, $1,270 per capita; 5.8% real growth rate. Arable land: 20%; principal products: wheat, olives, citrus fruits, grapes, dates. Labor force: 2,250,000; 32% in agriculture. Major industrial products: crude oil, olive oil, textiles, and leather, chemical fertilizers, petroleum. Natural resources: oil, phosphates, iron ore, lead, zinc. Exports: petroleum, phosphates, textiles. Imports: machinery and equipment, consumer goods, foodstuffs. Major trading partners: France, West Germany, Italy, U.S.

Geography. Tunisia, at the northernmost bulge of Africa, thrusts out toward Sicily to mark the division between the eastern and western Mediterranean Sea. Twice the size of South Carolina, it is bordered on the west by Algeria and by Libya on the south.

Coastal plains on the east rise to a north-south escarpment which slopes gently to the west. Saharan in the south, Tunisia is more mountainous in the north, where the Atlas range continues from Algeria.

Government. Executive power is vested by the Constitution in the president, elected for five years and eligible for re-election to two additional terms. Legislative power is vested in a House of Deputies elected by universal suffrage.

In 1975, the National Assembly amended the Constitution to make Habib Bourguiba president for life. At 71, Bourguiba was re-elected to a fourth five-year term when he ran unopposed in 1974. He was deposed by Gen. Zine Ben Ali in 1987. Ben Ali was elected to a five-year term in April 1989.

History. Tunisia was settled by the Phoenicians and Carthaginians in ancient times. Except for an interval of Vandal conquest in A.D. 439–533, it was part of the Roman Empire until the Arab conquest of 648–69. It was ruled by various Arab and Berber dynasties until the Turks took it in 1570–74. French troops occupied the country in 1881, and the Bey signed a treaty acknowledging a French protectorate.

Nationalist agitation forced France to grant internal autonomy to Tunisia in 1955 and to recognize Tunisian independence and sovereignty in 1956. The Constituent Assembly deposed the Bey on July 25, 1957, declared Tunisia a republic, and elected Habib Bourguiba as president.

Bourguiba maintained a pro-Western foreign policy that earned him enemies. Tunisia refused to break relations with the U.S. during the Israeli-Arab war in June 1967.

Tunisia ended its traditionally neutral role in the Arab world when it joined with the majority of Arab League members to condemn Egypt for concluding a peace treaty with Israel. The Tunisian capital was offered as the temporary headquarters of the League, following the expulsion of Egypt.

Developments in 1986-87 were characterized by a consolidation of power by the 84-year-old Bourguiba and his failure to arrange for a successor. This issue was settled when the then-Prime Minister, Gen. Ben Ali, deposed Bourguiba on the grounds that the latter's "senility and lingering illness" rendered him unfit to rule. Ben Ali succeeded him as per the Constitution and promised democratic reforms.

TURKEY

Republic of Turkey
President: Turgut Ozal (1989)
Prime Minister: Vildirim Akbulut (1989)
Area: 300,947 sq mi. (incl. 9,121 in Europe) (779,452 sq km)
Population (mid-1990): 56,700,000 (average annual rate of natural increase: 2.1%)
Density per square mile: 184
Capital: Ankara
Largest cities (1985 census): Istanbul, 5,858,558; Ankara, 3,462,880; Izmir, 2,316,843; Adana, 1,757,102; Bursa, 1,327,762; Gaziantep, 953,859
Monetary unit: Turkish Lira
Language: Turkish
Religion: Islam (Sunni), 99.2%
National name: Türkiye Cumhuriyeti
Literacy rate: 80%
Economic summary: Gross domestic product (est. 1987): $62.6 billion; $1,180 per capita; 7.9% real growth rate. Arable land: 30%; principal products: cotton, tobacco, cereals, sugar beets, fruits, nuts. Labor force: 18,800,-000; 14% in industry; major products: textiles, coal, minerals, processed foods, steel, petroleum. Natural resources: coal, chromite, copper, boron, oil. Exports: cotton, tobacco, fruits, nuts, livestock products, textiles. Imports: crude oil, machinery, transport equipment, metals, mineral fuels, fertilizer, chemicals. Major trading partners: West Germany, Iraq, France, Italy, U.S.S.R., U.S., U.K., Iran, Japan.

Geography. Turkey is at the northeastern end of the Mediterranean Sea in southeast Europe and southwest Asia. To the north is the Black Sea and to the west the Aegean Sea. Its neighbors are Greece and Bulgaria to the west, the U.S.S.R. to the north, Iran to the east, and Syria and Iraq to the south. Overall, it is a little larger than Texas.

The Dardanelles, the Sea of Marmara, and the Bosporus divide the country.

Turkey in Europe comprises an area about equal to the state of Massachusetts. It is hilly country drained by the Maritsa River and its tributaries.

Turkey in Asia, or Anatolia, about the size of Texas, is roughly a rectangle in shape with its short sides on the east and west. Its center is a treeless plateau rimmed by mountains.

Government. The President is elected by the Grand National Assembly for a seven-year term and is not eligible for re-election.

In a military coup on Sept. 12, 1980, led by Gen. Kenan Evren, the Chief of General Staff, Premier Süleyman Demirel was ousted, the Grand National Assembly dissolved and the Constitution suspended. Demirel, former Premier Bülent Ecevit, and some 100 legislators and political figures were detained, but later released. Martial law was declared and all political parties were dissolved. New elections were held in 1983 and a new Assembly was established.

The Prime Minister and his Council of Ministers hold the executive power although the President has the right to veto legislation.

History. The Ottoman Turks first appeared in the early 13th century in Anatolia, subjugating Turkish and Mongol bands pressing against the eastern borders of Byzantium. They gradually spread through the Near East and Balkans, capturing Constantinople in 1453 and storming the gates of Vienna two centuries later. At its height, the Ottoman Empire stretched from the Persian Gulf to western Algeria.

Defeat of the Turkish navy at Lepanto by the Holy League in 1571 and failure of the siege of Vienna heralded the decline of Turkish power. By the 18th century, Russia was seeking to establish itself as the protector of Christians in Turkey's Balkan territories. Russian ambitions were checked by Britain and France in the Crimean War (1854–56), but the Russo-Turkish War (1877–78) gave Bulgaria virtual independence and Romania and Serbia liberation from their nominal allegiance to the Sultan.

Turkish weakness stimulated a revolt of young liberals known as the Young Turks in 1909. They forced Sultan Abdul Hamid to grant a constitution and install a liberal government. Reforms were no barrier to further defeats, however, in a war with Italy (1911–12) and the Balkan Wars (1912–13). Under the influence of German military advisors, Turkey signed a secret alliance with Germany on Aug. 2, 1914, that led to a declaration of war by the Allied powers and the ultimate humiliation of the occupation of Turkish territory by Greek and other Allied troops.

In 1919, the new Nationalist movement, headed by Mustafa Kemal, was organized to resist the Allied occupation and, in 1920, a National Assembly elected him President of both the Assembly and the government. Under his leadership, the Greeks were driven out of Smyrna, and other Allied forces were withdrawn.

The present Turkish boundaries (with the exception of Alexandretta, ceded to Turkey by France in 1939) were fixed by the Treaty of Lausanne (1923) and later negotiations. The caliphate and sultanate were separated, and the sultanate was abolished in 1922. On Oct. 29, 1923, Turkey formally became a republic, with Mustafa Kemal, who took the name Kemal Atatürk, as its first President. The caliphate was abolished in 1924, and Atatürk proceeded to carry out an extensive program of reform, modernization, and industrialization.

Gen. Ismet Inönü was elected to succeed Atatürk in 1938 and was re-elected in 1939, 1943, and 1946. Defeated in 1950, he was succeeded by Celâl Bayar. In 1939, a mutual assistance pact was concluded with Britain and France. Neutral during most of World War II Turkey, on Feb. 23, 1945, declared war on Germany and Japan, but took no active part in the conflict.

Turkey became a full member of NATO in 1952.

Turkey invaded Cyprus by sea and air July 20, 1974, following the failure of diplomatic efforts to resolve the crisis caused by the ouster of Archbishop Makarios.

Talks in Geneva involving Greece, Turkey, Britain, and Greek Cypriot and Turkish Cypriot leaders brokers down in mid-August. Turkey unilaterally announced a cease-fire August 16, after having gained control of 40% of the island. Turkish Cypriots established their own state in the north on Feb. 13, 1975.

U.S.-Turkish relations, excellent for a generation, were seriously damaged when Congress voted to end arms sales to Turkey in 1975 because arms the U.S. had supplied for mutual defense had been used in the invasion of Cyprus.

In July 1975, after a 30-day warning, Turkey took over control of all the U.S. installations except the big joint defense base at Incirlik, which it reserved for "NATO tasks alone."

The establishment of military government in September 1980 stopped the slide toward anarchy and brought some improvement in the economy. The military regime was criticized, however, for suppression of human rights.

A Constituent Assembly, consisting of the six-member National Security Council and members appointed by them, drafted a new Constitution that was approved by an overwhelming (91.5%) majority of the voters in a Nov. 6, 1982, referendum. Prime Minister Turgut Özal's Motherland Party came to power in parliamentary elections held in late 1983. Özal was re-elected in November 1987.

TUVALU

Sovereign: Queen Elizabeth II
Governor-General: Tupua Leupena (1986)
Prime Minister: Bikenibeu Paeniv (1989)
Area: 10 sq mi. (26 sq km)
Population (mid-1989): 8,624 (average annual growth rate: 1.7%)
Density per square mile: 848
Capital and largest city (est. 1981): Funafuti, 2,500
Monetary unit: Australian dollar
Languages: Tuvaluan, English
Member of the Commonwealth of Nations
Literacy rate: 50%
Economic summary: Gross national product (1984): $4 million. Per capita income (1984): $450. Principal agricultural products: copra and coconuts. Export: copra. Imports: food and fuels. Major trading partners: Australia, U.K., Fiji, New Zealand.

Geography. Formerly the Ellice Islands, Tuvalu consists of nine small islands scattered over 500,000 square miles of the western Pacific, just south of the equator.

Government. Official executive power is vested in a Governor-General, representing the Queen, who is appointed by her on the recommendation of the Tuvalu government. Actual executive power lies with a Prime Minister, who is responsible to a House of Assembly composed of eight elected members.

History. The Ellice Islands became a British protectorate in 1892 and were annexed by Britain in 1915–16 as part of the Gilbert and Ellice Islands Colony. The Ellice Islands were separated in 1975, given home rule, and renamed Tuvalu. Full independence was granted on Sept. 30, 1978.

UGANDA

Republic of Uganda
President: Yoweri Musevni (1986)
Prime Minister: Dr. Samson Kiseka (1986)
Area: 91,343 sq mi. (236,880 sq km)
Population (mid-1990): 18,000,000 (average annual rate of natural increase: 3.6%)
Density per square mile: 187
Capital and largest city (est. 1980): Kampala, 458,000
Monetary unit: Ugandan shilling
Languages: English (official), Swahili, Luganda, Ateso, Luo
Religions: Christian, 63%; Islam, 16%
Member of Commonwealth of Nations
Literacy rate: 52%
Economic summary: Gross domestic product (1987 est.): $3.6 billion; $220 per capita; 2.9% real growth rate. Arable land: 23%; principal products: coffee, tea, cotton, sugar. Labor force: 4,500,000 (est.); 94% in subsistence activities. Major industrial products: sugar, beer, tobacco, cotton textiles, cement. Natural resources: copper, cobalt, limestone, salt. Exports: coffee, cotton. Imports: petroleum products, machinery, transport equipment, metals, food. Major trading partners: U.S., U.K., Kenya, Spain.

Geography. Uganda, twice the size of Pennsylvania, is in east Africa. It is bordered on the west by Zaire, on the north by the Sudan, on the east by Kenya, and on the south by Tanzania and Rwanda.

The country, which lies across the Equator, is divided into three main areas—swampy lowlands, a fertile plateau with wooded hills, and a desert region. Lake Victoria forms part of the southern border.

Government. The country has been run by the National Reistance Movement (NRM) since January, 1986.

History. Uganda was first visited by European explorers as well as Arab traders in 1844. An Anglo-German agreement of 1890 declared it to be in the British sphere of influence in Africa, and the Imperial British East Africa Company was chartered to develop the area. The company did not prosper financially, and in 1894 a British protectorate was proclaimed.

Uganda became independent on Oct. 9, 1962.

Sir Edward Mutesa was elected the first President and Milton Obote the first Prime Minister of the newly independent country. With the help of a young army officer, Col. Idi Amin, Prime Minister Obote seized control of the government from President Mutesa four years later.

On Jan. 25, 1971, Col. Amin deposed President Obote. Obote went into exile in Tanzania. Amin expelled Asian residents and launched a reign of terror against Ugandan opponents, torturing and killing tens of thousands. In 1976, he had himself proclaimed President for Life. In 1977, Amnesty International estimated that 300,000 may have died under his rule, including church leaders and recalcitrant cabinet ministers.

After Amin held military exercises on the Tanzanian border, angering Tanzania's President Julius Nyerere, a combined force of Tanzanian troops and Ugandan exiles loyal to former President Obote invaded Uganda and chased Amin into exile.

After a series of interim administrations, President Obote led his People's Congress Party to victory in 1980 elections that opponents charged were rigged.

Obote continued Amin's human rights abuses. The U.S. reported in August 1984 that the abuses included large-scale massacres.

On July, 27, 1985, army troops staged a coup taking over the government. Obote fled into exile. The military regime installed Gen. Tito Okello as chief of state.

The National Resistance Army (NRA), an anti-Obote group led by Yoweri Musevni, kept fighting after being excluded from the new regime. They seized Kampala on January 29, 1986, and Musevni was declared President but strife still continues in the nothern part of the country.

UNION OF SOVIET SOCIALIST REPUBLICS

See Soviet Union

UNITED ARAB EMIRATES

President: Sheikh Zayed Bin Sultan Al-Nahayan (1971)
Prime Minister: Sheik Rashid Bin Said al-Maktoum (1979)
Area: 32,000 sq mi. (82,880 sq km)
Population (mid-1990): 1,600,000 (average annual rate of natural increase: 1.9%)
Density per square mile: 53
Capital and largest city (est. 1981): Abu Dhabi, 225,000
Monetary unit: Dirham
Language: Arabic; Farsi and English widely spoken
Religion: Islam (Sunni, 80%; Shiite, 20%)
Literacy rate: 68%
Economic summary: Gross national product (1987 est.): $22 billion, $11,900 per capita; real growth rate (1987 est.): 3.0%. Arable land: NEGL%; principal products: vegetables, dates, tobacco, fruit. Labor force: 580,000 (1986 est.); 85% in industry and commerce; major products: fish, light manufactures, petroleum, construction materials. Natural resources: oil. Exports: petroleum, dates, fish. Imports: consumer goods, food. Major trading partners: Japan, Western Europe, U.S.

Geography. The United Arab Emirates, in the eastern part of the Arabian Peninsula, extends along part of the Gulf of Oman and the southern coast of the Persian Gulf. The nation is the size of Maine. Its neighbors are Saudi Arabia in the west and south, Qatar in the north, and Oman in the east. Most of the land is barren and sandy.

Government. The United Arab Emirates was formed in 1971 by seven emirates known as the Trucial States—Abu Dhabi (the largest), Dubai, Sharjah, Ajman, Fujairah, Ras al Khaimah and Umm al-Qaiwain.

The loose federation allows joint policies in foreign relations, defense, and development, with each member state keeping its internal local system of government headed by its own ruler. A 40-member legislature consists of eight seats each for Abu Dhabi and Dubai, six seats each for Ras al Khaimah and Sharjah, and four each for the others. It is a member of the Arab League.

History. Originally the area was inhabited by a seafaring people who were converted to Islam in the seventh century. Later, a dissident sect, the Carmathians, established a powerful sheikdom, and its army conquered Mecca. After the sheikdom disintegrated, its people became pirates.

Threatening the sultanate of Muscat and Oman early in the 19th century, the pirates provoked the intervention of the British, who in 1820 enforced a partial truce and in 1853 a permanent truce. Thus what had been called the Pirate Coast was renamed the Trucial Coast.

UNITED KINGDOM

United Kingdom of Great Britain and Northern Ireland
Sovereign: Queen Elizabeth II (1952)
Prime Minister: Margaret Thatcher (1979)
Area: 94,247 sq mi. (244,100 sq km)
Population (mid-1990): 57,400,000 (average annual rate of natural increase: 0.2%)
Density per square mile: 606
Capital: London, England
Largest cities (est. 1990): London, 9,170,000; Manchester, 4,050,000; Birmingham, 2,170,000; **(est. mid. 1987)** Glasgow, 715,621; Leeds, 709,000; Sheffield, 532,300; Liverpool, 476,000; Bradford, 462,500; Edinburgh, 438,232; Bristol, 384,400
Monetary unit: Pound sterling (£)
Languages: English, Welsh, Scots Gaelic
Religions: Church of England (established church); Church of Wales (disestablished); Church of Scotland (established church—Presbyterian); Church of Ireland (disestablished); Roman Catholic; Methodist; Congregational; Baptist; Jewish
Literacy rate: 99.5%
Economic summary: Gross national product (1988): $758.4 billion; $13,329 per capita; 3.8% real growth rate. Arable land: 29%; principal products: wheat, barley, potatoes, sugar beets, livestock, dairy products. Labor force: 28,200,000; 23.4% in manufacturing and construction. Major industrial products: machinery and transport equipment, metals, processed food, paper, textiles, chemicals, clothing. Natural resources: coal, oil, gas. Exports: machinery, transport equipment, chemicals, petroleum. Imports: foodstuffs, petroleum, machinery, chemicals, crude materials. Major trading partners: Western European nations, U.S.

Geography. The United Kingdom, consisting of England, Wales, Scotland, and Northern Ireland, is twice the size of New York State. England, in the southeast part of the British Isles, is separated from Scotland on the north by the granite Cheviot Hills; from them the Pennine chain of uplands extends south through the center of England, reaching its highest point in the Lake District in the northwest. To the west along the border of Wales—a land of steep hills and valleys—are the Cambrian Mountains, while the Cotswolds, a range of hills in

Rulers of England and Great Britain

Name	Born	Ruled[1]	Name	Born	Ruled[1]
SAXONS[2]			**HOUSE OF YORK**		
Egbert[3]	c.775	828–839	Edward IV	1442	1461–1483[5]
Ethelwulf	?	839–858	Edward V	1470	1483–1483
Ethelbald	?	858–860	Richard III	1452	1483–1485
Ethelbert	?	860–866			
Ethelred I	?	866–871	**HOUSE OF TUDOR**		
Alfred the Great	849	871–899	Henry VII	1457	1485–1509
Edward the Elder	c.870	899–924	Henry VIII	1491	1509–1547
Athelstan	895	924–939	Edward VI	1537	1547–1553
Edmund I the Deed-doer	921	939–946	Jane (Lady Jane Grey)[6]	1537	1553–1553
Edred	c.925	946–955	Mary I ("Bloody Mary")	1516	1553–1558
Edwy the Fair	c.943	955–959	Elizabeth I	1533	1558–1603
Edgar the Peaceful	943	959–975			
Edward the Martyr	c.962	975–979	**HOUSE OF STUART**		
Ethelred II the Unready	968	979–1016	James I[7]	1566	1603–1625
Edmund II Ironside	c.993	1016–1016	Charles I	1600	1625–1649
DANES			**COMMONWEALTH**		
Canute	995	1016–1035	Council of State	—	1649–1653
Harold I Harefoot	c.1016	1035–1040	Oliver Cromwell[8]	1599	1653–1658
Hardecanute	c.1018	1040–1042	Richard Cromwell[8]	1626	1658–1659[9]
SAXONS			**RESTORATION OF HOUSE OF**		
Edward the Confessor	c.1004	1042–1066	**STUART**		
Harold II	c.1020	1066–1066	Charles II	1630	1660–1685
			James II	1633	1685–1688[10]
HOUSE OF NORMANDY			William III[11]	1650	1689–1702
William I the Conqueror	1027	1066–1087	Mary II[11]	1662	1689–1694
William II Rufus	c.1056	1087–1100	Anne	1665	1702–1714
Henry I Beauclerc	1068	1100–1135			
Stephen of Boulogne	c.1100	1135–1154	**HOUSE OF HANOVER**		
			George I	1660	1714–1727
HOUSE OF PLANTAGENET			George II	1683	1727–1760
Henry II	1133	1154–1189	George III	1738	1760–1820
Richard I Coeur de Lion	1157	1189–1199	George IV	1762	1820–1830
John Lackland	1167	1199–1216	William IV	1765	1830–1837
Henry III	1207	1216–1272	Victoria	1819	1837–1901
Edward I Longshanks	1239	1272–1307			
Edward II	1284	1307–1327	**HOUSE OF SAXE-COBURG[12]**		
Edward III	1312	1327–1377	Edward VII	1841	1901–1910
Richard II	1367	1377–1399[4]			
			HOUSE OF WINDSOR[12]		
HOUSE OF LANCASTER			George V	1865	1910–1936
Henry IV Bolingbroke	1367	1399–1413	Edward VIII	1894	1936–1936[13]
Henry V	1387	1413–1422	George VI	1895	1936–1952
Henry VI	1421	1422–1461[5]	Elizabeth II	1926	1952–

1. Year of end of rule is also that of death, unless otherwise indicated. 2. Dates for Saxon kings are still subject of controversy. 3. Became King of West Saxons in 802; considered (from 828) first King of all England. 4. Died 1400. 5. Henry VI reigned again briefly 1470–71. 6. Nominal Queen for 9 days; not counted as Queen by some authorities. She was beheaded in 1554. 7. Ruled in Scotland as James VI (1567–1625). 8. Lord Protector. 9. Died 1712. 10. Died 1701. 11. Joint rulers (1689–1694). 12. Name changed from Saxe-Coburg to Windsor in 1917. 13. Was known after his abdication as the Duke of Windsor, died 1972.

Gloucestershire, extend into the surrounding shires.

The remainder of England is plain land, though not necessarily flat, with the rocky sand-topped moors in the southwest, the rolling downs in the south and southeast, and the reclaimed marshes of the low-lying fens in the east central districts.

Scotland is divided into three physical regions—the Highlands, the Central Lowlands, containing two-thirds of the population, and the Southern Uplands. The western Highland coast is intersected throughout by long, narrow sea-lochs, or fiords. Scotland also includes the Outer and Inner Hebrides and other islands off the west coast and the

Orkney and Shetland Islands off the north coast.

Wales is generally hilly; the Snowdon range in the northern part culminates in Mount Snowdon (3,560 ft, 1,085 m), highest in both England and Wales.

Important rivers flowing into the North Sea are the Thames, Humber, Tees, and Tyne. In the west are the Severn and Wye, which empty into the Bristol Channel and are navigable, as are the Mersey and Ribble.

Government. The United Kingdom is a constitutional monarchy, with a Queen and a Parliament that has two houses: the House of Lords with about

830 hereditary peers, 26 spiritual peers, about 270 life peers and peeresses, and 9 law-lords, who are hereditary, or life, peers, and the House of Commons, which has 650 popularly elected members. Supreme legislative power is vested in Parliament, which sits for five years unless sooner dissolved.

The executive power of the Crown is exercised by the Cabinet, headed by the Prime Minister. The latter, normally the head of the party commanding a majority in the House of Commons, is appointed by the Sovereign, with whose consent he or she in turn appoints the rest of the Cabinet. All ministers must be members of one or the other house of Parliament; they are individually and collectively responsible to the Crown and Parliament. The Cabinet proposes bills and arranges the business of Parliament, but it depends entirely on the votes in the House of Commons. The Lords cannot hold up "money" bills, but they can delay other bills for a maximum of one year.

By the Act of Union (1707), the Scottish Parliament was assimilated with that of England, and Scotland is now represented in Commons by 71 members. The Secretary of State for Scotland, a member of the Cabinet, is responsible for the administration of Scottish affairs.

Ruler. Queen Elizabeth II, born April 21, 1926, elder daughter of King George VI and Queen Elizabeth, succeeded to the throne on the death of her father on Feb. 6, 1952; married Nov. 20, 1947, to Prince Philip, Duke of Edinburgh, born June 10, 1921; their children are Prince Charles[1] (heir presumptive), born Nov. 14, 1948; Princess Anne, born Aug. 15, 1950; Prince Andrew, born Feb. 19, 1960; and Prince Edward, born March 10, 1964. The Queen's sister is Princess Margaret, born Aug. 21, 1930. Prince William Arthur Philip Louis, son of the Prince and Princess of Wales and second in line to the throne, was born June 21, 1982. A second son, Prince Henry Charles Albert David, was born Sept. 15, 1984, and is third in line.

History. Roman invasions of the 1st century B.C. brought Britain into contact with the Continent. When the Roman legions withdrew in the 5th century A.D., Britain fell easy prey to the invading hordes of Angles, Saxons, and Jutes from Scandinavia and the Low Countries. Seven large kingdoms were established, and the original Britons were forced into Wales and Scotland. It was not until the 10th century that the country finally became united under the kings of Wessex. Following the death of Edward the Confessor (1066), a dispute about the succession arose, and William, Duke of Normandy, invaded England, defeating the Saxon King, Harold II, at the Battle of Hastings (1066). The Norman conquest introduced Norman law and feudalism.

The reign of Henry II (1154–89), first of the Plantagenets, saw an increasing centralization of royal power at the expense of the nobles, but in 1215 John (1199–1216) was forced to sign the Magna Carta, which awarded the people, especially the nobles, certain basic rights. Edward I (1272–1307)

1. The title Prince of Wales, which is not inherited, was conferred on Prince Charles by his mother on July 26, 1958. The investiture ceremony took place on July 1, 1969. The previous Prince of Wales was Prince Edward Albert, who held the title from 1911 to 1936 before he became Edward VIII.

Area and Population of United Kingdom

Subdivision	Area sq mi	Area sq km	Population (est. mid-1987)
England and Wales	58,381	151,207	50,243,000
Scotland	30,414	78,772	5,112,000
Northern Ireland	5,452	14,121	1,575,200
Total	**94,247**	**244,100**	**56,930,200**

continued the conquest of Ireland, reduced Wales to subjection and made some gains in Scotland. In 1314, however, English forces led by Edward II were ousted from Scotland after the Battle of Bannockburn. The late 13th and early 14th centuries saw the development of a separate House of Commons with tax-raising powers.

Edward III's claim to the throne of France led to the Hundred Years' War (1338–1453) and the loss of almost all the large English territory in France. In England, the great poverty and discontent caused by the war were intensified by the Black Death, a plague that reduced the population by about one third. The Wars of the Roses (1455-85), a struggle for the throne between the House of York and the House of Lancaster, ended in the victory of Henry Tudor (Henry VII) at Bosworth Field (1485).

During the reign of Henry VIII (1509–47), the Church in England asserted its independence from the Roman Catholic Church. Under Edward VI and Mary, the two extremes of religious fanaticism were reached, and it remained for Henry's daughter, Elizabeth I (1558-1603), to set up the Church of England on a moderate basis. In 1588, the Spanish Armada, a fleet sent out by Catholic King Philip II of Spain, was defeated by the English and destroyed during a storm. During Elizabeth's reign, England became a world power.

Elizabeth's heir was a Stuart—James VI of Scotland—who joined the two crowns as James I (1603–25). The Stuart kings incurred large debts and were forced either to depend on Parliament for taxes or to raise money by illegal means. In 1642, war broke out between Charles I and a large segment of the Parliament; Charles was defeated and executed in 1649, and the monarchy was then abolished. After the death in 1658 of Oliver Cromwell, the Lord Protector, the Puritan Commonwealth fell to pieces and Charles II was placed on the throne in 1660. The struggle between the King and Parliament continued, but Charles II knew when to compromise. His brother, James II (1685-88), possessed none of his ability and was ousted by the Revolution of 1688, which confirmed the primacy of Parliament. James's daughter, Mary, and her husband, William of Orange, were now the rulers.

Queen Anne's reign (1702–14) was marked by the Duke of Marlborough's victories over France at Blenheim, Oudenarde, and Malplaquet in the War of the Spanish Succession. England and Scotland meanwhile were joined by the Act of Union (1707). Upon the death of Anne, the distant claims of the elector of Hanover were recognized, and he became King of Great Britain and Ireland as George I.

The unwillingness of the Hanoverian kings to

British Prime Ministers Since 1770

Name	Term	Name	Term
Lord North (Tory)	1770–1782	Marquis of Salisbury (Conservative)	1886–1892
Marquis of Rockingham (Whig)	1782–1782	William E. Gladstone (Liberal)	1892–1894
Earl of Shelburne (Whig)	1782–1783	Earl of Rosebery (Liberal)	1894–1895
Duke of Portland (Coalition)	1783–1783	Marquis of Salisbury (Conservative)	1895–1902
William Pitt, the Younger (Tory)	1783–1801	Earl Balfour (Conservative)	1902–1905
Henry Addington (Tory)	1801–1804	Sir H. Campbell-Bannerman (Liberal)	1905–1908
William Pitt, the Younger (Tory)	1804–1806	Herbert H. Asquith (Liberal)	1908–1915
Baron Grenville (Whig)	1806–1807	Herbert H. Asquith (Coalition)	1915–1916
Duke of Portland (Tory)	1807–1809	David Lloyd George (Coalition)	1916–1922
Spencer Perceval (Tory)	1809–1812	Andrew Bonar Law (Conservative)	1922–1923
Earl of Liverpool (Tory)	1812–1827	Stanley Baldwin (Conservative)	1923–1924
George Canning (Tory)	1827–1827	James Ramsay MacDonald (Labor)	1924–1924
Viscount Goderich (Tory)	1827–1828	Stanley Baldwin (Conservative)	1924–1929
Duke of Wellington (Tory)	1828–1830	James Ramsay MacDonald (Labor)	1929–1931
Earl Grey (Whig)	1830–1834	James Ramsay MacDonald (Coalition)	1931–1935
Viscount Melbourne (Whig)	1834–1834	Stanley Baldwin (Coalition)	1935–1937
Sir Robert Peel (Tory)	1834–1835	Neville Chamberlain (Coalition)	1937–1940
Viscount Melbourne (Whig)	1835–1841	Winston Churchill (Coalition)	1940–1945
Sir Robert Peel (Tory)	1841–1846	Clement R. Attlee (Labor)	1945–1951
Earl Russell (Whig)	1846–1852	Sir Winston Churchill (Conservative)	1951–1955
Earl of Derby (Tory)	1852–1852	Sir Anthony Eden (Conservative)	1955–1957
Earl of Aberdeen (Coalition)	1852–1855	Harold Macmillan (Conservative)	1957–1963
Viscount Palmerston (Liberal)	1855–1858	Sir Alec Frederick Douglas-Home	
Earl of Derby (Conservative)	1858–1859	(Conservative)	1963–1964
Viscount Palmerston (Liberal)	1859–1865	Harold Wilson (Labor)	1964–1970
Earl Russell (Liberal)	1865–1866	Edward Heath (Conservative)	1970–1974
Earl of Derby (Conservative)	1866–1868	Harold Wilson (Labor)	1974–1976
Benjamin Disraeli (Conservative)	1868–1868	James Callaghan (Labor)	1976–1979
William E. Gladstone (Liberal)	1868–1874	Margaret Thatcher (Conservative)	1979–
Benjamin Disraeli (Conservative)	1874–1880		
William E. Gladstone (Liberal)	1880–1885		
Marquis of Salisbury (Conservative)	1885–1886		
William E. Gladstone (Liberal)	1886–1886		

rule resulted in the formation by the royal ministers of a Cabinet, headed by a Prime Minister, which directed all public business. Abroad, the constant wars with France expanded the British Empire all over the globe, particularly in North America and India. This imperial growth was checked by the revolt of the American colonies (1775–81).

Struggles with France broke out again in 1793 and during the Napoleonic Wars, which ended at Waterloo in (1815).

The Victorian era, named after Queen Victoria (1837–1901), saw the growth of a democratic system of government that had begun with the Reform Bill of 1832. The two important wars in Victoria's reign were the Crimean War against Russia (1853–56) and the Boer War (1899–1902), the latter enormously extending Britain's influence in Africa.

Increasing uneasiness at home and abroad marked the reign of Edward VII (1901–10). Within four years after the accession of George V in 1910, Britain entered World War I when Germany invaded Belgium. The nation was led by coalition Cabinets, headed first by Herbert Asquith and then, starting in 1916, by the Welsh statesman David Lloyd George. Postwar labor unrest culminated in the general strike of 1926.

King Edward VIII succeeded to the throne on Jan. 20, 1936, at his father's death, but abdicated on Dec. 11, 1936 (in order to marry an American divorcee, Wallis Warfield Simpson) in favor of his brother, who became George VI.

The efforts of Prime Minister Neville Chamberlain to stem the rising threat of Nazism in Germany failed with the German invasion of Poland on Sept. 1, 1939, which was followed by Britain's entry into World War II on September 3. Allied reverses in the spring of 1940 led to Chamberlain's resignation and the formation of another coalition war Cabinet by the Conservative leader, Winston Churchill, who led Britain through most of World War II. Churchill resigned shortly after V-E Day, May 7, 1945, but then formed a "caretaker" government that remained in office until after the parliamentary elections in July, which the Labor Party won overwhelmingly. The government formed by Clement R. Attlee began a moderate socialist program.

For details of World War II (1939–45), see Headline History.

In 1951, Churchill again became Prime Minister at the head of a Conservative government. George VI died Feb. 6, 1952, and was succeeded by his daughter Elizabeth II.

Churchill stepped down in 1955 in favor of Sir Anthony Eden, who resigned on grounds of ill health in 1957, and was succeeded by Harold Macmillan and Sir Alec Douglas-Home. In 1964, Harold Wilson led the Labor Party to victory.

A lagging economy brought the Conservatives back to power in 1970. Prime Minister Edward Heath won Britain's admission to the European Community.

Margaret Thatcher became Britain's first woman Prime Minister as the Conservatives won 339 seats on May 3, 1979.

An Argentine invasion of the Falkland Islands on April 2, 1982, involved Britain in a war 8,000 miles from the home islands. Although Argentina had long claimed the Falklands, known as the Malvinas in Spanish, negotiations were in progress until a month before the invasion. The Thatcher government responded to the invasion with a 40-ship task force, which sailed from Portsmouth on April 5. U.S. efforts to settle the dispute failed and United Nations efforts collapsed as the Argentine military government ignored Security Council resolutions calling for a withdrawal of its forces.

When more than 11,000 Argentine troops on the Falklands surrendered on June 14, 1982, Mrs. Thatcher declared her intention to garrison the islands indefinitely, together with a naval presence.

The military victory bolstered Conservative fortunes at least temporarily, but economic problems continued for the government. Unemployment had risen to a record 2.91 million by mid-June.

In the general election of June 9, 1983, Prime Minister Thatcher and her Conservative party won a landslide victory over the Laborites and other opponents. The Tories seized 58 seats in the House of Commons, giving the Labor party its worst defeat since 1922.

Although there were continuing economic problems and foreign policy disputes, an upswing in the economy in 1986-87 led Thatcher to call elections for June 11 in which she won a near-unprecedented third consecutive term.

NORTHERN IRELAND

Status: Part of United Kingdom
Secretary of State: Thomas Jeremy King
Area: 5,452 sq mi. (14,121 sq km)
Population (est. mid-1987): 1,575,200
Density per square mile: 279.7
Capital and largest city (est. mid-1987): Belfast, 303,800
Monetary unit: British pound sterling
Languages: English, Gaelic
Religions: Roman Catholic, 28%; Presbyterian, 22.9%; Church of Ireland, 19%; Methodist, 4%

Geography. Northern Ireland comprises the counties of Antrim, Armagh, Down, Fermanagh, Londonderry, and Tyrone, which make up predominantly Protestant Ulster and form the northern part of the island of Ireland, westernmost of the British Isles. It is slightly larger than Connecticut.
Government. Northern Ireland is an integral part of the United Kingdom (it has 12 representatives in the British House of Commons), but under the terms of the government of Ireland Act in 1920, it had a semiautonomous government. But in 1972, after three years of internal strife which resulted in over 400 dead and thousands injured, Britain suspended the Ulster parliament. The Ulster counties became governed directly from London after an attempt to return certain powers to an elected Assembly in Belfast.

The Northern Ireland Assembly was dissolved in 1975 and a Constitutional Convention was elected to write a Constitution acceptable to Protestants and Catholics. The convention failed to reach agreement and closed down the next year.
History. Ulster was part of Catholic Ireland until

the reign of Elizabeth I (1558–1603) when, after crushing three Irish rebellions, the crown confiscated lands in Ireland and settled in Ulster the Scot Presbyterians who became rooted there. Another rebellion in 1641–51, crushed as brutally by Oliver Cromwell, resulted in the settlement of Anglican Englishmen in Ulster. Subsequent political policy favoring Protestants and disadvantaging Catholics encouraged further settlement in Northern Ireland.

But the North did not separate from the South until William Gladstone presented in 1886 his proposal for home rule in Ireland as a means of settling the Irish Question. The Protestants in the North, although they had grievances like the Catholics in the South, feared domination by the Catholic majority. Industry, moreover, was concentrated in the north and dependent on the British market.

When World War I began, civil war threatened between the regions. Northern Ireland, however, did not become a political entity until the six counties accepted the Home Rule Bill of 1920. This set up a semiautonomous Parliament in Belfast and a Crown-appointed Governor advised by a Cabinet of the Prime Minister and eight ministers, as well as a 12-member representation in the House of Commons in London.

As the Republic of Ireland gained its sovereignty, relations improved between North and South, although the Irish Republican Army, outlawed in recent years, continued the struggle to end the partition of Ireland. In 1966–69, communal rioting and street fighting between Protestants and Catholics occurred in Londonderry, fomented by extremist nationalist Protestants, who feared the Catholics might attain a local majority, and by Catholics demonstrating for civil rights.

Rioting, terrorism, and sniping killed more than 2,200 people from 1969 through 1984 and the religious communities, Catholic and Protestant, became hostile armed camps. British troops were brought in to separate them but themselves became a target of Catholics.

In 1973, a new British charter created a 78-member Assembly elected by proportional representation that gave more weight to Catholic strength. It created a Province Executive with committee chairmen of the Assembly heading all government departments except law enforcement, which remained under London's control. Assembly elections in 1973 produced a majority for the new Constitution that included Catholic assemblymen.

Ulster's leaders agreed in 1973 to create an 11-member Executive Body with six seats assigned to Unionists (Protestants) and four to members of Catholic parties. Unionist leader Brian Faulkner headed the Executive. Also agreed to was a Council of Ireland, with 14 seats evenly divided between Dublin and Belfast, which could act only by unanimous vote.

Although the Council lacked real authority, its creation sparked a general strike by Protestant extremists in 1974. The two-week strike caused Faulkner's resignation from the Executive and resumption of direct rule from London.

In April 1974, London instituted a new program that responded to some Catholic grievances, but assigned more British troops to cut off movement of arms and munitions to Ulster's violence-racked cities.

Violence continued unabated, with new heights reached early in 1976 when the British government announced the end of special privileges for political prisoners in Northern Ireland. British Prime Minister James Callaghan visited Belfast in July and pledged that Ulster would remain part of the United Kingdom unless a clear majority wished to separate.

In October 1977, the 1976 Nobel Prize for Peace was awarded to Mairead Corrigan and Betty Williams for their campaign for peace in Northern Ireland. Intermittent violence continued, however, and on Aug. 27, 1979, an I.R.A. bomb killed Earl Mountbatten as he was sailing off southern Ireland.

New talks aimed at a restoration of home rule in Northern Ireland began and quickly ended in January 1980. In May, Mrs. Thatcher met with the new Prime Minister of the Irish Republic, Charles Haughey, but she insisted that the future of Ulster must be decided only by its people and the British Parliament. Haughey declared that an internal solution "cannot and will not succeed."

Civil disturbances reached new heights in the summer of 1981 as Irish nationalist prisoners went on hunger strikes in Maze Prison to attain their demands for "political" status.

Ten nationalists died before the strike ended in August as families of fasters asked that they be fed.

On November 15, 1985, Mrs. Thatcher signed an agreement with Irish Prime Minister Garrett Fitzgerald giving Ireland a consultative role in the affairs of Northern Ireland. It was met with intense disapproval by the Ulster Unionists.

Dependencies of the United Kingdom

ANGUILLA

Status: Dependency
Governor: B. G. Canty (1989)
Area: 35 sq mi. (91 sq km)
Population (1988): 6,875
Monetary unit: East Caribbean dollar
Literacy: 80%

Anguilla was originally part of the West Indies Associated States as a component of St. Kitts-Nevis-Anguilla.

In 1967, Anguilla declared its independence from the St. Kitts-Nevis-Anguilla federation. Britain however, did not recognize this action. In February 1969, Anguilla voted to cut all ties with Britain and become an independent republic. In March, Britain landed troops on the island and, on March 30, a truce was signed. In July 1971, Anguilla became a dependency of Britain and two months later Britain ordered the withdrawal of all its troops.

A new Constitution for Anguilla, effective in February 1976, provides for separate administration and a government of elected representatives. The Associated State of St. Kitts-Nevis-Anguilla ended Dec. 19, 1980.

BERMUDA

Status: Self-governing dependency
Governor: Sir Desmond Langley (1988)
Premier: John Swan (1982)
Area: 20 sq mi. (52 sq km)
Population (mid-1989): 58,238 (average annual growth rate: 0.2%)
Capital (est. 1985): Hamilton, 1,700
Monetary unit: Bermuda dollar
Literacy rate: 98%
Economic summary: Gross domestic product (FY87): $1.28 billion; $22,050 per capita; 2.7% real growth rate. Arable land: 0%. Principal agricultrual products: bananas, vegetables, citrus fruits, dairy products. Labor force: 32,000; 47% clerical and in services. Major industrial products: structural concrete, paints, perfumes, furniture. Natural resource: limestone. Exports: semi-tropical produce, light manufactures. Imports: foodstuffs, fuel, machinery. Major trading partners: U.S., U.K., Canada.

Bermuda is an archipelago of about 360 small islands, 580 miles (934 km) east of North Carolina. The largest is (Great) Bermuda, or Long Island. Discovered by Juan de Bermúdez, a shipwrecked Spaniard, early in the 16th century, the islands were settled in 1612 by an offshoot of the Virginia Company and became a crown colony in 1684.

In 1940, sites on the islands were leased for 99 years to the U.S. for air and navy bases. Bermuda is also the headquarters of the West Indies and Atlantic squadron of the Royal Navy.

In 1968, Bermuda was granted a new Constitution, its first Prime Minister, and autonomy, except for foreign relations, defense, and internal security. The predominantly white United Bermuda Party has retained power in four elections against the opposition—the black-led Progressive Laborites—although Bermuda's population is 60% black. Serious rioting occurred in December 1977 after two blacks were hanged for a series of murders, including the 1973 assassination of the Governor, Sir Richard Sharples, and British troops were summoned to restore order.

BRITISH ANTARCTIC TERRITORY

Status: Dependency
High Commissioner: William Hugh Fullerton (1988)
Area: 500,000 sq mi. (1,395,000 sq km)
Population (1986): no permanent residents

The British Antarctic Territory consists of the South Shetland Islands, South Orkney Islands, and nearby Graham Land on the Antarctic continent, largely uninhabited. They are dependencies of the British crown colony of the Falkland Islands but received a separate administration in 1962, being governed by a British-appointed High Commissioner who is Governor of the Falklands.

BRITISH INDIAN OCEAN TERRITORY

Status: Dependency
Commissioner: R. Edis
Administrator: R. Crompton
Administrative headquarters: Victoria, Seychelles
Area: 85 sq mi, (220 sq km)

This dependency, consisting of the Chagos Archipelago and other small island groups, was formed in 1965 by agreement with Mauritius and the Seychelles. There is no permanent civilian population in the territory.

BRITISH VIRGIN ISLANDS

Status: Dependency
Governor: Mark Herdman (1986)

Area: 59 sq mi. (153 sq km)
Population (mid-1989): 12,124 (growth rate: 1.1%)
Capital (est. 1986): Road Town (on Tortola): 2,479
Monetary unit: U.S. dollar

Some 36 islands in the Caribbean Sea northeast of Puerto Rico and west of the Leeward Islands, the British Virgin Islands are economically interdependent with the U.S. Virgin Islands to the south. They were formerly part of the administration of the Leeward Islands. They received a separate administration in 1956 as a crown colony. In 1967 a new Constitution was promulgated that provided for a ministerial system of government headed by the Governor. The principal islands are Tortola, Virgin Gorda, Anegada and Jost Van Dyke.

CAYMAN ISLANDS

Status: Dependency
Governor: Alan James Scott
Area: 100 sq mi. (259 sq km)
Population (mid-1989): 23,768 (growth rate: 3.1%)
Capital (est. 1988): George Town (on Grand Cayman), 11,000
Monetary unit: Cayman Islands dollar

This dependency consists of three islands—Grand Cayman (76 sq mi; 197 sq km), Cayman Brac (22 sq mi; 57 sq km), and Little Cayman (20 sq mi; 52 sq km)—situated about 180 miles (290 km) northwest of Jamaica. They were dependencies of Jamaica until 1959, when they became a unit territory within the Federation of the West Indies. In 1962, upon the dissolution of the Federation, the Cayman Islands became a British dependency.

The islands' chief export is turtle products.

CHANNEL ISLANDS

Status: Crown dependencies
Lieutenant Governor of Jersey: Adm. Sir William Pillar (1985)
Lieutenant Governor of Guernsey: Sir Alexander Boswell (1985)
Area: 120 sq mi. (311 sq km)
Population (1988): 133,960
Capital of Jersey: St. Helier
Capital of Guernsey: St. Peter Port
Monetary units: Guernsey pound; Jersey pound

This group of islands, lying in the English Channel off the northwest coast of France, is the only portion of the Duchy of Normandy belonging to the English Crown, to which it has been attached since the conquest of 1066. It was the only British possession occupied by Germany during World War II.

For purposes of government, the islands are divided into the Bailiwick of Jersey (45 sq mi.; 117 sq km) and the Bailiwick of Guernsey (30 sq mi.; 78 sq km), including Alderney (3 sq mi.; 7.8 sq km); Sark (2 sq mi.; 5.2 sq km), Herm, Jethou, etc. The islands are administered according to their own laws and customs by local governments. Acts of Parliament in London are not binding on the islands unless they are specifically mentioned. The Queen is represented in each Bailiwick by a Lieutenant Governor.

FALKLAND ISLANDS AND DEPENDENCIES

Status: Dependency
Governor: William Hugh Fullerton (1988)
Acting Chief Executive: R. Sampson
Area: 4,700 sq mi. (12,173 sq km)
Population (mid-1989): 1,943 (growth rate: .5%)
Capital (est. 1986): Stanley (on East Falkland), 1,231
Monetary unit: Falkland Island pound

This sparsely inhabited dependency consists of a group of islands in the South Atlantic, about 250 miles (402 km) east of the South American mainland. The largest islands are East Falkland and West Falkland. Dependencies are South Georgia Island (1,450 sq mi.; 3,756 sq km), the South Sandwich Islands, and other islets. Three former dependencies—Graham Land, the South Shetland Islands, and the South Orkney Islands—were established as a new British dependency, the British Antarctic Territory, in 1962.

The chief industry is sheep raising and, apart from the production of wool, hides and skins, and tallow, there are no known resources. The whaling industry is carried on from South Georgia Island.

The chief export is wool.

GIBRALTAR

Status: Self-governing dependency
Governor: Sir Peter Terry
Chief Minister: J. Bossano
Area: 2.25 sq mi. (5.8 sq km)
Population (1989): 29,528 (growth rate: .2%)
Monetary unit: Gibraltar pound
Literacy rate: 99%
Economic summary: Gross national product (FY85 est.): $129 million. Exports: re-exports of tobacco, petroleum, wine. Imports: manufactured goods, fuels, foodstuffs. Major trading partners: U.K., Morocco, Portugal, Netherlands.

Gibraltar, at the south end of the Iberian Peninsula, is a rocky promonotory commanding the western entrance to the Mediterranean. Aside from its strategic importance, it is also a free port, naval base, and coaling station. It was captured by the Arabs crossing from Africa into Spain in A.D. 711. In the 15th century, it passed to the Moorish ruler of Granada and later became Spanish. It was captured by an Anglo-Dutch force in 1704 during the War of the Spanish Succession and passed to Great Britain by the Treaty of Utrecht in 1713. Most of the inhabitants of Gibraltar are of Spanish, Italian, and Maltese descent.

Spanish efforts to recover Gibraltar culminated in a referendum in 1967 in which the residents voted overwhelmingly to retain their link with Britain. Spain sealed Gibraltar's land border in 1969 and did not open communications until April 1980, after the two governments had agreed to solve their dispute in keeping with a United Nations resolution calling for restoration of the "Rock" to Spain.

HONG KONG

Status: Dependency
Governor: Sir David Wilson (1987)
Area: 398 sq mi. (1,031 sq km)
Population (mid-1990): 5,800,000 (average annual rate of natural increase: 0.8%)

Density per square mile: 14,218
Capital (1976 census): Victoria (Hong Kong Island), 501,-700
Monetary unit: Hong Kong dollar
Literacy rate: 75%
Economic summary: Gross domestic product (1987): $46.2 billion; $8,260 per capita; 13.6% real growth rate. Arable land: 7%; principal products: vegetables, rice, dairy products. Labor force: 2,640,000; 35.8% in manufacturing; major industrial products: textiles, clothing, toys, transistor radios, watches, electronic components. Exports: clothing, textiles, toys, watches, transistor radios, electronic components. Imports: raw materials, consumer goods, food. Major trading partners: U.S., U.K., Japan, West Germany, China, Taiwan.

The crown colony of Hong Kong comprises the island of Hong Kong (32 sq mi.; 83 sq km), Stonecutters' Island, Kowloon Peninsula, and the New Territories on the adjoining mainland. The island of Hong Kong, located at the mouth of the Pearl River about 90 miles (145 km) southeast of Canton, was ceded to Britain in 1841.

Stonecutters' Island and Kowloon were annexed in 1860, and the New Territories, which are mainly agricultural lands, were leased from China in 1898 for 99 years. Hong Kong was attacked by Japanese troops Dec. 7, 1941, and surrendered the following Christmas. It remained under Japanese occupation until August 1945.

After two years of painstaking negotiation, authorities of Britain and the People's Republic of China agreed in 1984 that Hong Kong would return to Chinese sovereignty on June 30, 1997, when Britain's lease on the New Territories expires. They also agreed that the vibrant capitalist enclave on China's coast would retain its status as a free port and its social, economic, and legal system as a special administrative region of China. Current laws will remain basically unchanged.

Under a unique "One Country, Two Systems" arrangement, the Chinese government promised that Hong Kong's lifestyle would remain unchanged for 50 years, and that freedoms of speech, press, assembly, association, travel, right to strike and religious belief would be guaranteed by law. However, the chief executive and some of the legislature will be appointed by Beijing.

Hong Kong will continue to have its own finances and issue its own travel documents, and Peking will not levy taxes.

The crackdown by hard-liners in China has led to apprehension that Hong Kong's autonomy won't be respected.

ISLE OF MAN

Status: Self-Governing Crown Dependency
Lieutenant Governor: Maj. Gen. Laurence A.W. New
Area: 227 sq mi. (588 sq km)
Population (mid-1989): 64,728 (growth rate: .2%)
Capital (1986): Douglas, 20,368
Monetary unit: Isle of Man pound

Situated in the Irish Sea, equidistant from Scotland, Ireland, and England, the Isle of Man is administered according to its own laws by a government composed of the Lieutenant Governor, a Legislative Council, and a House of Keys, one of the most ancient legislative assemblies in the world.

The chief exports are beef and lamb, fish, and livestock.

LEEWARD ISLANDS

See British Virgin Islands; Montserrat

MONTSERRAT

Status: Dependency
Governor: Christopher John Turner (1987)
Area: 38 sq mi. (98 sq km)
Population (mid-1989): 12,428 (growth rate: .3%)
Capital (est. 1988): Plymouth, 3,000
Monetary unit: East Caribbean dollar

The island of Montserrat is in the Lesser Antilles of the West Indies. Until 1956, it was a division of the Leeward Islands. It did not join the West Indies Associated States established in 1967.

The chief exports are cattle, potatoes, cotton, lint, recapped tires, mangoes, and tomatoes.

PITCAIRN ISLAND

Status: Dependency
Governor: R. A. C. Byatt
Island Magistrate: B. Young
Area: 1.75 sq mi. (4.5 sq km)
Population (mid-1989): 68 (growth rate: 0%)
Capital: Adamstown

Pitcairn Island, in the South Pacific about midway between Australia and South America, consists of the island of Pitcairn and the three uninhabited islands of Henderson, Duicie, and Oeno. The island of Pitcairn was settled in 1790 by British mutineers from the ship *Bounty*, commanded by Capt. William Bligh. It was annexed as a British colony in 1838. Overpopulation forced removal of the settlement to Norfolk Island in 1856, but about 40 persons soon returned.

The colony is governed by a 10-member Council presided over by the Island Magistrate, who is elected for a three-year term.

ST. HELENA

Status: Dependency
Governor: Robert F. Stimson (1988)
Area: 120 sq mi. (310 sq km)
Population (mid-1989): 7,200 (growth rate: .6%)
Capital (1987): Jamestown, 1,330
Monetary unit: Pound sterling

St. Helena is a volcanic island in the South Atlantic about 1,100 miles (1,770 km) from the west coast of Africa. It is famous as the place of exile of Napoleon (1815–21).

It was taken for England in 1659 by the East India Company and was brought under the direct government of the Crown in 1834.

St. Helena has two dependencies: Ascension (34 sq mi.; 88 sq km), an island about 700 miles (1,127 km) northwest of St. Helena; and Tristan da Cunha (40 sq mi.; 104 sq km), a group of six islands about 1,500 miles (2,414 km) south-southwest of St. Helena.

TURKS AND CAICOS ISLANDS

Status: Dependency
Governor: Michael Bradley (1987)

Area: 193 sq mi. (500 sq km)
Population (mid-1989): 9,531 (growth rate: 2.4%)
Capital (est. 1988): Grand Turk, 3,146
Monetary unit: U.S. dollar

These two groups of islands are situated at the southeast end of the Bahamas. The principal islands in the Turks group are Grand Turk and Salt Cay; the principal ones in the Caicos group are South Caicos, East Caicos, Middle (or Grand) Caicos, North Caicos, Providenciales, and West Caicos.

The Turks and Caicos Islands were dependencies of Jamaica until 1959, when they became a unit territory within the Federation of the West Indies. In 1962, when Jamaica became independent, the Turks and Caicos became a British crown colony. The present Constitution has been in force since 1969.

Chief exports in 1974 were crayfish (73%) and conch (25%).

VIRGIN ISLANDS
See British Virgin Islands

UNITED STATES
The United States of America
President: George Bush (1989)
Area: 3,540,939 sq mi. (9,171,032 sq km)
Population (mid-1990): 251,400,000 (average annual rate of natural increase: 0.8%)
Density per square mile: 69
Capital (1988 est.): Washington, D.C., 617,000
Largest cities (1988 est.): New York, 7,352,700; Los Angeles, 3,352,710; Chicago, 2,977,520; Houston, 1,698,090; Philadelphia, 1,647,000; San Diego, 1,070,310; Detroit, 1,035,920
Monetary unit: Dollar
Language: predominantly English, sizable Spanish-speaking minority
Religions: Protestant (78.7 million members); Roman Catholic (52.3 million members); Jewish (5.8 million members)
Literacy rate: 96%
Economic summary: Gross national product (1988): $4,862; $19,800 per capita; 3.8% real growth rate. Arable land: 20%; principal products: corn, wheat, barley, oats, sugar, potatoes, soybeans, fruits, beef, veal, pork. Labor force: 122,000,000. Major industrial products: petroleum products, fertilizers, cement, pig iron and steel, plastics and resins, newsprint, motor vehicles, machinery, natural gas, electricity. Natural resources: coal, oil, water power, copper, gold, silver, minerals, timber. Exports: machinery, chemicals, aircrafts, military equipment, cereals, motor vehicles, grains. Imports: crude and partly refined petroleum, machinery, automobiles. Major trading partners: Canada, Japan, United Kingdom, West Germany, Mexico, Saudi Arabia.

Government. The president is elected for a four-year term and may be re-elected only once. In 1989, the bicameral Congress consisted of the 100-member Senate (55 Democrats, 45 Republicans), elected to a six-year term with one-third of the seats becoming vacant every two years, and the 435-member House of Representatives (257 Democrats, 176 Republicans),[1] elected every two years. The minimum voting age is 18.

1. As of July 1990 there were 2 vacant House seats.

URUGUAY
Oriental Republic of Uruguay
President: Luis Alberto Lacalle (1990)
Area: 68,040 sq mi. (176,224 sq km)
Population (mid-1990): 3,000,000 (average annual rate of natural increase: 0.8%)
Density per square mile: 44
Capital and largest city (est. 1982): Montevideo, 1,325,000
Monetary unit: Peso
Language: Spanish
Religion: Roman Catholic, 60%
National name: Republica Oriental del Uruguay
Literacy rate: 96%
Economic summary: Gross domestic product (1988 est.): $7.5 billion, $2,530 per capita; 1% real growth rate. Arable land: 8%; principal products: livestock, grains, sugar. Labor force: 1,300,000; 19% in manufacturing; major products: processed meats, wool and hides, textiles, shoes, handbags and leather wearing apparel, cement, refined petroleum. Natural resources: hydroelectric power potential. Exports: meat, hides, wool, textiles. Imports: crude petroleum, transportation equipment, chemicals, machinery, metals. Major trading partners: U.S., Brazil, Argentina, Nigeria, Western Europe.

Geography. Uruguay, on the east coast of South America south of Brazil and east of Argentina, is comparable in size to the State of Washington.

The country consists of a low, rolling plain in the south and a low plateau in the north. It has a 120-mile (193 km) Atlantic shore line, a 235-mile (378 km) frontage on the Rio de la Plata, and 270 miles (435 km) on the Uruguay River, its western boundary.

Government. After elections in November 1984, Julio Maria Sanguinetti was inaugurated as President on March 1, 1985, ending 12 years of military rule. Under the Constitution, Presidents serve a single five-year term. The bicameral Congress, dissolved by the military in 1973, also was restored in 1985.

History. Juan Díaz de Solis, a Spaniard, discovered Uruguay in 1516, but the Portuguese were first to settle it when they founded Colonia in 1680. After a long struggle, Spain wrested the country from Portugal in 1778. Uruguay revolted against Spain in 1811, only to be conquered in 1817 by the Portuguese from Brazil. Independence was reasserted with Argentine help in 1825, and the republic was set up in 1828.

Independence, however, did not restore order, and a revolt in 1836 touched off nearly 50 years of factional strife, with occasional armed intervention from Argentina and Brazil.

Uruguay, made prosperous by meat and wool exports, founded a welfare state early in the 20th century. A decline began in the 1950s as successive governments struggled to maintain a large bureaucracy and costly social benefits. Economic stagnation and political frustration followed.

A military coup ousted the civilian government in 1973. The military dictatorship that followed used fear and terror to demoralize the population, taking thousands of political prisoners, probably the highest proportion of citizens jailed for political reasons anywhere in the world.

Under the generals, the country's worst economic crisis in decades produced 66% inflation,

30% unemployment and a foreign debt of $5 billion. Per capita income sank to $1,100.

After ruling for 12 years, the military regime permitted election of a civilian government in November 1984 and relinquished rule in March 1985.

VANUATU

Republic of Vanuatu
President: Fred Timakata (1989)
Prime Minister: Fr. Walter Lini (1980)
Area: 5,700 sq mi. (14,763 sq km)
Population (mid-1990): 200,000 (average annual rate of natural increase: 3.2%)
Density per square mile: 28
Capital (est. 1987): Port Vila, 15,100
Monetary unit: Vatu
Religions: Presbyterian, 47%; Roman Catholic, 15%; Anglican, 15%; other Christian, 10%; Animist, 9%
Literacy rate: 10-20%
Economic Summary: Gross domestic product (1986): $84 million, $580 per capita; real growth rate (1986): –1.0%. Arable land: 1%. Principal agricultural products: copra, cocoa, coffee. Exports: copra, cocoa, coffee, frozen fish. Imports: food, machinery. Major trading partners: France, New Zealand, Japan, Australia, Netherlands.

Geography. Formerly known as the New Hebrides, Vanuatu is an archipelago of some 80 islands lying between New Caledonia and Fiji in the South Pacific. Largest of the islands is Espiritu Santo (875 sq mi.; 2,266 sq km); others are Efate, Malekula, Malo, Pentecost, and Tanna. The population is largely Melanesian of mixed blood.

Government. The constitution by which Vanuatu achieved independence on July 30, 1980, vests executive authority in a President, elected by an electoral college for a five-year term. A unicameral legislature of 39 members exercises legislative power.

History. The islands were discovered by Pedro Fernandes de Queiros of Portugal in 1606 and were charted and named by the British navigator James Cook in 1774. Conflicting British and French interests were resolved by a joint naval commission that administered the islands from 1887. A condominium government was established in 1906.

The islands' plantation economy, based on imported Vietnamese labor, was prosperous until the 1920s, when markets for its products declined. The New Hebrides escaped Japanese occupation in World War II and the French population was among the first to support the Gaullist Free French movement.

A brief rebellion by French settlers and plantation workers on Espiritu Santo led by Jimmy Stevens in May 1980 threatened the scheduled independence of the islands. Britain sent a company of Royal Marines and France a contingent of 50 policemen to quell the revolt, which the new government said was financed by the Phoenix Foundation, a right-wing U.S. group. With the British and French forces replaced by soldiers from Papua New Guinea, independence ceremonies took place on July 30. The next month it was reported that Stevens had been arrested and the revolt quelled.

VATICAN CITY STATE

Ruler: Pope John Paul II (1978)
Area: 0.17 sq mi. (0.44 sq km)
Population (mid-1989): 755
Density per square mile: 4,424
Monetary unit: Lira
Languages: Latin and Italian
Religion: Roman Catholic
National name: Stato della Città del Vaticano

Geography. The Vatican City State is situated on the Vatican hill, on the right bank of the Tiber River, within the commune of Rome.

Government. The Pope has full legal, executive, and judicial powers. Executive power over the area is in the hands of a Commission of Cardinals appointed by the Pope. The College of Cardinals is the Pope's chief advisory body, and upon his death the cardinals elect his successor for life. The cardinals themselves are created for life by the Pope.

In the Vatican the central administration of the Roman Catholic Church throughout the world (Holy See) is carried on by the Secretariat of State, nine Congregations, three tribunals, twelve councils, and five offices. In its diplomatic relations, the Holy See is represented by the Papal Secretary of State.

History. The Vatican City State, sovereign and independent, is the survivor of the papal states that in 1859 comprised an area of some 17,000 square miles (44,030 sq km). During the struggle for Italian unification, from 1860 to 1870, most of this area became part of Italy.

By an Italian law of May 13, 1871, the temporal power of the Pope was abrogated, and the territory of the Papacy was confined to the Vatican and Lateran palaces and the villa of Castel Gandolfo. The Popes consistently refused to recognize this arrangement and, by the Lateran Treaty of Feb. 11, 1929, between the Vatican and the Kingdom of Italy, the exclusive dominion and sovereign jurisdiction of the Holy See over the city of the Vatican was again recognized, thus restoring the Pope's temporal authority over the area.

The first session of Ecumenical Council Vatican II was opened by John XXIII on Oct. 11, 1962, to plan and set policies for the modernization of the Roman Catholic Church. Pope Paul VI continued the Council, opening the second session on Sept. 29, 1963.

On Aug. 26, 1978, Cardinal Albino Luciani was chosen by the College of Cardinals to succeed Paul VI, who had died of a heart attack on Aug. 6. The new Pope, who took the name John Paul I, was born on Oct. 17, 1912, at Forno di Canale in Italy.

(For a listing of all the Popes, *see* the Index.)

Only 34 days after his election, John Paul I died of a heart attack, ending the shortest reign in 373 years. On Oct. 16, Cardinal Karol Wojtyla, 58, was chosen Pope and took the name John Paul II.

A visit to the Irish Republic and to the United States in September and October 1979, followed by a 12-nation African tour in May 1980 and a visit in July to Brazil, the most populous Catholic nation, further established John Paul's image as a "people's" Pope. On May 13, 1981, a Turkish terrorist shot the Pope in St. Peter's Square, the first assassination attempt against the Pontiff in modern times.

Mehmet Ali Agca was sentenced on July 22 to life imprisonment by an Italian Court.

The Pontiff traveled to Britain and Argentina in 1982. He also made a visit to Poland.

On June 3, 1985, the Vatican and Italy ratified a new church-state treaty, known as a concordat, replacing the Lateran Pact of 1929. The new accord affirmed the independence of Vatican City but ended a number of privileges the Catholic Church had in Italy, including its status as the state religion. The treaty ended Rome's status as a "sacred city."

VENEZUELA

Republic of Venezuela
President: Carlos Andrés Pérez (1989)
Area: 352,143 sq mi. (912,050 sq km)
Population (mid-1990): 19,600,000 (average annual rate of natural increase: 2.3%)
Density per square mile: 54
Capital: Caracas
Largest cities (est. 1981 for metropolitan area): Caracas, 3,000,000; Maracaibo, 890,000; Valencia, 616,000; Barquisimento, 498,000
Monetary unit: Bolivar
Language: Spanish, Indian dialects in interior
Religion: Roman Catholic
National name: Republica de Venezuela
Literacy rate: 88.4%
Economic summary: Gross domestic product (1988): $47.3 billion; $2,520 per capita; 4.2% real growth rate. Arable land: 3%; principal products: rice, coffee, corn, sugar, bananas, dairy and meat products. Labor force: 5,800,-000; 28% in industry; principal products: refined petroleum products, iron and steel, paper products, cement, textiles, transport equipment. Natural resources: petroleum, natural gas, iron ore, hydroelectric power. Exports: petroleum, iron ore. Imports: industrial machinery and equipment, manufactures, chemicals, foodstuffs. Major trading partners: U.S., Canada, Japan, Netherlands, Antilles, W. Germany.

Geography. Venezuela, a third larger than Texas, occupies most of the northern coast of South America on the Caribbean Sea. It is bordered by Colombia to the west, Guyana to the east, and Brazil to the south.

Mountain systems break Venezuela into four distinct areas: (1) the Maracaibo lowlands; (2) the mountainous region in the north and northwest; (3) the Orinoco basin, with the llanos (vast grass-covered plains) on its northern border and great forest areas in the south and southeast; (4) the Guiana Highlands, south of the Orinoco, accounting for nearly half the national territory. About 80% of Venezuela is drained by the Orinoco and its tributaries.

Government. Venezuela is a federal republic consisting of 20 states, the Federal District, two territories and 72 islands in the Caribbean. There is a bicameral Congress, the 50 members of the Senate and the 201 members of the Chamber of Deputies being elected by popular vote to five-year terms.

The President is also elected for five years. He must be a Venezuelan by birth and over 30 years old. He is not eligible for re-election until 10 years after the end of his term.

History. Columbus discovered Venezuela on his third voyage in 1498. A subsequent Spanish explorer gave the country its name, meaning "Little Venice." There were no important settlements until Caracas was founded in 1567. Simón Bolívar, who led the liberation of much of the continent from Spain, was born in Caracas in 1783. With Bolívar taking part, Venezuela was one of the first South American colonies to revolt against Spain, in 1810, but it was not until 1821 that independence was won. Federated at first with Colombia and Ecuador, the country set up a republic in 1830 and then sank for many decades into a condition of revolt, dictatorship, and corruption.

From 1908 to 1935, Gen. Juan Vicente Gómez ruled tyrannically, picking satellites to alternate with him in the presidential palace. Thereafter, there was a struggle between democratic forces and those backing a return to strong-man rule. Dr. Rómulo Betancourt and the liberal Acción Democrática Party won a majority of seats in a constituent assembly to draft a new Constitution in 1946. A well-known writer, Rómulo Gallegos, candidate of Betancourt's party, easily won the presidential election of 1947. But, the army ousted Gallegos the next year and instituted a military junta.

The country overthrew the dictatorship in 1958 and thereafter enjoyed democratic government. Rafael Caldera Rodríguez, President from 1969 to 1974, legalized the Communist Party and established diplomatic relations with Moscow.

Venezuela and neighboring Guyana in 1970 called a 12-year moratorium on their border dispute (Venezuela claimed 50,000 square miles of Guyana's 83,000). In 1974, President Carlos Andrés Perez took office.

In 1976, Venezuela nationalized 21 oil companies, mostly subsidiaries of U.S. firms, offering compensation of $1.28 billion. Oil income in that year was $9.9 billion, and although production decreased 2.2%, revenue remained at the same level in 1977 because of higher prices, largely financing an ambitious social welfare program.

Despite difficulties at home, Pérez continued to play an active foreign role in extending economic aid to Latin neighbors, in backing the human-rights policy of President Carter, and in supporting Carter's return of the Panama Canal to Panama.

Opposition Christian Democrats capitalized on Pérez's domestic problems to elect Luis Herrera Campíns President in Venezuela's fifth consecutive free election, on Dec. 3, 1978.

Herrera Campins at first supported U.S. policy in Central America, lining up behind the government of El Salvador but he later shifted toward a "political solution" that would include the insurgents. In March 1982, he assailed Reagan's policy as "interventionist."

When the Falklands war broke out, Venezuela became one of the most vigorous advocates of the Argentine cause and one of the sharpest critics of the U.S. decision to back Britain.

Jaime Lusinchi of the Democratic Action party won the country's sixth consecutive free election, on Dec. 4, 1983, and was inaugurated President in March 1984. In 1985, he reached a debt-rescheduling agreement with Venezuela's creditors for its $21-billion debt.

VIETNAM

Socialist Republic of Vietnam
President: Vo Chi Cong (1987)
Premier: Do Muoi (1988)
Area: 127,246 sq mi. (329,566 sq km)
Population (mid-1990): 70,200,000 (average annual rate of natural increase: 2.5%)
Density per square mile: 525
Capital: Hanoi
Largest cities (est. 1979): Ho Chi Minh City (Saigon),[1] 3,450,000; Hanoi, 2,600,000; Haiphong, 1,280,000; (est. 1973); Da Nang, 492,200; Nha Trang, 216,200; Qui Nho'n, 213,750; Hué 209,000
Monetary unit: Dong
Languages: Vietnamese (official), French, English, Khmer, Chinese
Religions: Buddhist, Roman Catholic, Islam, Taoist, Confucian, Animist
National name: Công Hòa Xa Hôi Chú Nghia Viêt Nam
Literacy rate: 78%
Economic summary: Gross national product (1987): $12.6 billion; $198 per capita; 2.1% real growth rate. Arable land: 22%; principal products: rice, rubber, fruits and vegetables, corn, sugar cane, fish. Labor force: 32,900,-000 (1987). Major industrial products: processed foods, textiles, cement, chemical fertilizers, glass, tires. Natural resources: phosphates, forests, coal. Exports: agricultural products, coal, minerals. Imports: petroleum, steel products, railroad equipment, chemicals, medicines, raw cotton, fertilizer, grain. Major trading partners: U.S.S.R., Singapore, Japan, Eastern Europe.

1. Includes suburb of Cholon.

Geography. Vietnam occupies the eastern and southern part of the Indochinese peninsula in Southeast Asia, with the South China Sea along its entire coast. China is to the north and Laos and Cambodia to the west. Long and narrow on a north-south axis, Vietnam is about twice the size of Arizona.

The Mekong River delta lies in the south and the Red River delta in the north. Heavily forested mountain and plateau regions make up most of the country.

Government. Less than a year after the capitulation of the former Republic of Vietnam (South Vietnam) on April 30, 1975, a joint National Assembly convened with 249 deputies representing the North and 243 representing the South. The Assembly set July 2, 1976, as the official reunification date. Hanoi became the capital, with North Vietnamese President Ton Duc Thang becoming President of the new Socialist Republic of Vietnam and North Vietnamese Premier Pham Van Dong becoming its head of government. By 1981, the National Assembly had increased to 496 members. Truong Chinh succeeded Thang in 1981.

Dang Cong san Vietnam (Communist Party), led by General Secretary Nguyen Van Linh, is the ruling political party. There are also the Socialist Party and the Democratic Party.

History. The Vietnamese are descendants of Mongoloid nomads from China and migrants from Indonesia. They recognized Chinese suzerainty until the 15th century, an era of nationalistic expansion, when Cambodians were pushed out of the southern area of what is now Vietnam.

A century later, the Portuguese were the first Europeans to enter the area. France established its influence early in the 19th century and within 80 years conquered the three regions into which the country was then divided—Cochin-China in the south, Annam in the center, and Tonkin in the north.

France first unified Vietnam in 1887, when a single governor-generalship was created, followed by the first physical links between north and south—a rail and road system. Even at the beginning of World War II, however, there were internal differences among the three regions.

Japan took over military bases in Vietnam in 1940 and a pro-Vichy French administration remained until 1945. A veteran Communist leader, Ho Chi Minh, organized an independence movement known as the Vietminh to exploit a confused situation. At the end of the war, Ho's followers seized Hanoi and declared a short-lived republic, which ended with the arrival of French forces in 1946.

Paris proposed a unified government within the French Union under the former Annamite emperor, Bao Dai. Cochin-China and Annam accepted the proposal, and Bao Dai was proclaimed emperor of all Vietnam in 1949. Ho and the Vietminh withheld support, and the revolution in China gave them the outside help needed for a war of resistance against French and Vietnamese troops armed largely by the U.S.

A bitter defeat at Dien Bien Phu in northwest Vietnam on May 5, 1954, broke the French military campaign and brought the division of Vietnam at the conference of Geneva that year.

In the new South, Ngo Dinh Diem, Premier under Bao Dai, deposed the monarch in 1955 and established a republic with himself as President. Diem used strong U.S. backing to create an authoritarian regime that suppressed all opposition but could not eradicate the Northern-supplied Communist Viet Cong.

Skirmishing grew into a full-scale war, with escalating U.S. involvement. A military coup, U.S.-inspired in the view of many, ousted Diem Nov. 1, 1963, and a kaleidoscope of military governments followed. The most savage fighting of the war occurred in early 1968, during the Tet holidays.

Although the Viet Cong failed to overthrow the Saigon government, U.S. public reaction to the apparently endless war forced a limitation of U.S. troops to 550,000 and a new emphasis on shifting the burden of further combat to the South Vietnamese. Ho Chi Minh's death on Sept. 3, 1969, brought a quadrumvirate to replace him but no flagging in Northern will to fight.

U.S. bombing and invasion of Cambodia in the summer of 1970—an effort to destroy Viet Cong bases in the neighboring state—marked the end of major U.S. participation in the fighting. Most American ground troops were withdrawn from combat by mid-1971 as heavy bombing of the Ho Chi Minh trail from North Vietnam appeared to cut the supply of men and matériel to the South.

Secret negotiations for peace by Secretary of State Henry A. Kissinger with North Vietnamese officials during 1972 after heavy bombing of Hanoi and Haiphong brought the two sides near agreement in October. When the Northerners demanded the removal of the South's President Nguyen Van Thieu as their price, President Nixon ordered the "Christmas bombing" of the North. The conference resumed and a peace settlement was signed in Paris on Jan. 27, 1973. It called for release of all U.S. prisoners, withdrawal of U.S. forces, limitation of both sides' forces inside South Vietnam, and a commitment to peaceful reunification.

Despite Chinese and Soviet endorsement, the agreement foundered. U.S. bombing of Communist-held areas in Cambodia was halted by Congress in August 1973, and in the following year Communist action in South Vietnam increased.

An armored attack across the 17th parallel in January 1975 panicked the South Vietnamese army and brought the invasion within 40 miles of Saigon by April 9. Thieu resigned on April 21 and fled, to be replaced by Vice President Tran Van Huong, who quit a week later, turning over the office to Gen. Duong Van Minh. "Big Minh" surrendered Saigon on April 30, ending a war that took 1.3 million Vietnamese and 56,000 American lives, at the cost of $141 billion in U.S. aid.

On May 3, 1977, the U.S. and Vietnam opened negotiations in Paris to normalize relations. One of the first results was the withdrawal of U.S. opposition to Vietnamese membership in the United Nations, formalized in the Security Council on July 20. Two major issues remained to be settled, however: the return of the bodies of some 2,500 U.S. servicemen missing in the war and the claim by Hanoi that former President Nixon had promised reconstruction aid under the 1973 agreement. Negotiations failed to resolve these issues.

The new year also brought an intensification of border clashes between Vietnam and Cambodia and accusations by China that Chinese residents of Vietnam were being subjected to persecution. Peking cut off all aid and withdrew 800 technicians.

By June, 133,000 ethnic Chinese were reported to have fled Vietnam, and a year later as many as 500,000 of the 1.8 million Vietnamese of Chinese ancestry were believed to have escaped.

Half of them had gone by land or sea to China. Tens of thousands more had survived boat passage to Thailand, Malaysia, Indonesia, or Hong Kong. U.S. officials said 100,000 may have died. Survivors said they had paid up to $5,000 in bribes to leave Vietnam, and U.S. and British officials charged Hanoi with a deliberate extortion policy.

Hanoi was undoubtedly preoccupied with a continuing war in Cambodia, where 60,000 Vietnamese troops were aiding the Heng Samrin regime in suppressing the last forces of the pro-Chinese Pol Pot regime. In early 1979, Vietnam was conducting a two-front war, defending its northern border against a Chinese invasion and at the same time supporting its army in Cambodia.

Despite Hanoi's claims of total victory, resistance in Cambodia continued through 1984. Vietnam's second conflict, on its border with China, also flared sporadically.

The Hanoi government agreed in July 1984 to resume technical talks with U.S. officials on the possible whereabouts of the 2,490 Americans still listed as missing, most of them believed dead. In August 1985, the North Vietnamese turned over to an American team 26 numbered crates described as containing the remains of 26 U.S. servicemen.

Economic troubles continued, with the government seeking to reschedule its $1.4-billion foreign hard-currency debt, owed mainly to Japan and the International Monetary Fund. In late 1987, a shuffle of the Vietnamese Politburo brought in new leaders who are expected to slightly relax the government grip on the economy and crack down on corruption within the party.

The exodus of the Vietnamese boat people also continued, despite a growing tendency by passing ships not to help the Vietnamese fleeing their country by boat.

In 1988, Vietnam also began limited troop withdrawals from Laos and Cambodia. The government has undertaken to withdraw completely from Cambodia by mid-1990.

(For a Vietnam War chronology, see Headline History.)

WESTERN SAMOA

Independent State of Western Samoa

Head of State: Malietoa Tanumafili II (1962)
Prime Minister: Tofilau Eti Alesana (1988)
Area: 1,093 sq mi. (2,831 sq km)
Population (mid-1990): 200,000 (average annual growth rate: 2.8%)
Density per square mile: 183
Capital and largest city (1980): Apia, 33,400
Monetary unit: Tala
Languages: Samoan and English
Religions: Congregational, 50%; Roman Catholic, 22%; Methodist, 16%
National name: Samoa i Sisifo
Member of Commonwealth of Nations
Literacy rate: 90%
Economic summary: Gross domestic product (1987 est.): $100 million; $570 per capita; 1% real growth rate. Arable land: 19%; principal products: copra, cocoa, bananas, timber. Labor force: 37,000; 22,000 employed in agriculture (1963 est.). Major industrial products: timber, light industrial products. Natural resource: timber. Exports: copra, cocoa, bananas, timber. Imports: food, manufactured goods, machinery. Major trading partners: New Zealand, Australia, U.S., Fiji, Japan

Geography. Western Samoa, the size of Rhode Island, is in the South Pacific Ocean about 2,200 miles (3,540 km) south of Hawaii midway to Sydney, Australia, and about 800 miles (1,287 km) northeast of Fiji. The larger islands in the Samoan chain are mountainous and of volcanic origin. There is little level land except in the coastal areas, where most cultivation takes place.

Government. Western Samoa has a 47-member Legislature, consisting mainly of the titleholders (chiefs) of family groups, with two members elected by universal suffrage to represent those not belonging to such groups. When the present Head of State dies, successors will be elected by the Legislature for five-year terms.

History. The Samoan islands were discovered in the 18th century and visited by Dutch and French traders. Toward the end of the 19th century, conflicting interests of the U.S., Britain, and Germany resulted in a treaty signed in 1899. It recognized the paramount interests of the U.S. in those islands east of 171° west longitude (American Samoa) and Germany's interests in the other islands (Western Samoa); the British withdrew in return for recognition of their rights in Tonga and the Solomons.

New Zealand occupied Western Samoa in 1914, and was granted a League of Nations mandate. In 1947, the islands became a U.N. trust territory administered by New Zealand.

Western Samoa became independent on Jan. 1, 1962.

REPUBLIC OF YEMEN

President: Ali Abdullah Salen
Vice President: Ali Salem al-Baidh
Area: 203,850 sq mi. (527,970 sq km)
Population (est. mid-1990): 9,800,000 (average annual rate of natural increase: 3.3%)
Capital and largest city: San'a', 427,185
Monetary unit: Both Dinar and Rial
Language: Arabic
Religion: Islam (Sunni and Shite)
Literacy rate: 20%
Economic summary: Gross national product (North Yemen) 1987: $4.5 billion, $690 per capita; real growth rate 4.8 %; Gross national product (South Yemen) 1986: $1.01 billion. $480 per capita, real growth rate 6.6%; Principal agricultural products: wheat, sorghum, cattle, sheep, cotton, fruits, coffee, dates. Principal industrial products: crude and refined oil, textiles, leather goods, handicrafts, salt, fish meal; Exports: cotton, coffee, hides, vegetables, dried fish; Imports: textiles, manufactured consumer goods, foodstuffs, sugar, grain, flour. Major trading partners: UK, France, Japan, Saudi Arabia, Australia, UAE.

Geography: Formerly known as the states of Yemen and the Yemen Arab Republic, the Republic of Yemen occupies the southwestern tip of the Arabian Peninsula on the Red Sea opposite Ethiopia, and extends along the southern part of the Arabian Peninsula on the Gulf of Aden and the Indian Ocean. Saudi Arabia is to the north and Oman is to the east. The country is about the size of France.

It has a 700-mile (1,130-km) narrow coastal plain in the south that gives way to a mountainous region and then a plateau area. Some of the interior highlands in the west attain a height of 12,000 feet (3,660 m).
Government: Parliamentary. There is a five-man ruling Presidential Council consisting of the President, Vice-President, and three other members. They are Salem Saleh Mohammed, the former deputy to the new vice-president, Abdel-Karim al-Arshi, former speaker of Yemen's parliament, and Abdel-Aziz Abdulghani, former Prime Minister of the Yemen Arab Republic. Elections are planned for the end of 1992.
History. The history of Yemen dates back to the Minaean kingdom (1200-650 B.C.). It accepted Islam in A.D. 628, and in the 10th century came under the control of the Rassite dynasty of the Zaidi sect. The Turks occupied the area from 1538 to 1630 and from 1849 to 1918. The sovereign status of Yemen was confirmed by treaties signed with Saudi Arabia and Britain in 1934.

Yemen joined the Arab League in 1945 and established diplomatic relations with the U.S. in 1946.

In 1962, a military revolt of elements favoring President Gamal Abdel Nasser of Egypt broke out. A ruling junta proclaimed a republic, and Yemen became an international battleground, with Egypt and the U.S.S.R. supporting the revolutionaries, and King Saud of Saudi Arabia and King Hussein of Jordan the royalists. The civil war continued until the war between the Arab states and Israel broke out in June 1967. Nasser had to pull out many of his troops and agree to a cease-fire and withdrawal of foreign forces. The war finally ended with the defeat of the royalists in mid-1969.

The People's Republic of Southern Yemen was established Nov. 30, 1967, when Britain granted independence to the Federation of South Arabia.

This Federation consisted of the state (once the colony) of Aden and 16 of the 20 states of the Protectorate of South Arabia (once the Aden Protectorate). The four states of the Protectorate that did not join the Federation later became part of Southern Yemen.

The Republic of Yemen was established on May 23, 1990 when pro-western Yemen and Marxist Yemen Arab Republic merged after 300 years of separation to form the new nation. The union had been approved by both governments in November 1989.

The new president, Ali Abdullah Salen of Yemen was elected by the parliaments of both countries. The parliaments also chose South Yemen's Ali Salem al-Baidh, secretary general of the ruling socialist party to be the new vice-president.

In 1984, the Hunt Oil Co. of Dallas discovered oil in North Yemen, the first time it had been found in the desolate Arab state, one of the world's poorest nations. Construction of a pipeline began in 1986 and exports began in 1988. The new government hopes that additional oil reserves will be found in the south.

YUGOSLAVIA

Socialist Federal Republic of Yugoslavia
President: Janez Drnovšek (1989)
President of Federal Executive Council (Premier): Ante Marković (1989)
Area: 98,766 sq mi. (255,804 sq km)
Population (mid-1990): 23,800,000 (average annual rate of natural increase: 0.6%)
Density per square mile: 240
Capital: Belgrade
Largest cities (est. 1982): Belgrade, 1,250,000; Zagreb, 765,000; Skopje, 505,000; Sarajevo, 450,000; Ljubljana, 255,000; Split, 200,000
Monetary unit: Dinar
Languages: Serbo-Croatian, Slovene, Macedonian (all official)
Religions: Eastern Orthodox, 50%; Roman Catholic, 30%; Islam, 10%
National name: Socijalisticka Federativna Republika Jugoslavija
Literacy rate: 90%
Economic summary: Gross national product (1988): $154.1 billion, $6,540 per capita; .1% real growth rate. Arable land: 28%; principal products: corn, wheat, tobacco, sugar beets. Labor force: 9,600,000; 27% in mining and manufacturing; major products: wood, processed food, nonferrous metals, machinery, textiles. Natural resources: coal, timber, copper, iron, lead, zinc, bauxite. Exports: leather goods, textiles, machinery. Imports: machinery, chemicals, iron, and steel. Major trading partners: U.S.S.R., West Germany, Italy, U.S., Czechoslovakia.

Geography. Yugoslavia fronts on the eastern coast of the Adriatic Sea opposite Italy. Its neighbors are Austria, Italy, and Hungary to the north, Romania and Bulgaria to the east, and Greece and Albania to the south. It is slightly larger than Wyoming.

About half of Yugoslavia is mountainous. In the north, the Dinaric Alps rise abruptly from the sea and progress eastward as a barren limestone plateau called the Karst. Montenegro is a jumbled mass of mountains, containing also some grassy slopes and fertile river valleys. Southern Serbia, too, is mountainous. A rich plain in the north and northeast, drained by the Danube, is the most fertile area of the country.

Government. Yugoslavia is a federal republic composed of six socialist republics—Serbia (which includes the provinces of Vojvodina and Kosovo), Croatia, Slovenia, Bosnia-Herzegovina, Macedonia, and Montenegro. Actual administration is carried on by the Federal Executive Council and its secretaries.

The League of Communists and the Socialist Alliance of the Working People are the major political parties.

History. Yugoslavia was formed Dec. 4, 1918, from the patchwork of Balkan states and territories where World War I began with the assassination of Archduke Ferdinand of Austria at Sarajevo on June 28, 1914. The new Kingdom of Serbs, Croats, and Slovenes included the former kingdoms of Serbia and Montenegro; Bosnia-Herzegovina, previously administered jointly by Austria and Hungary; Croatia-Slavonia, a semi-autonomous region of Hungary, and Dalmatia, formerly administered by Austria. King Peter I of Serbia became the first monarch, his son acting as Regent until his accession as Alexander I on Aug. 16, 1921.

Croatian demands for a federal state forced Alexander to assume dictatorial powers in 1929 and to change the country's name to Yugoslavia. Serbian dominance continued despite his efforts, amid the resentment of other regions. A Macedonian associated with Croatian dissidents assassinated Alexander in Marseilles, France, on Oct. 9, 1934, and his cousin, Prince Paul, became Regent for the King's son, Prince Peter.

Paul's pro-Axis policy brought Yugoslavia to sign the Axis Pact on March 25, 1941, and opponents overthrew the government two days later. On April 6 the Nazis occupied the country, and the young King and his government fled. Two guerrilla armies —the Chetniks under Draza Mihajlovic supporting the monarchy and the Partisans under Tito (Josip Broz) leaning toward the U.S.S.R.—fought the Nazis for the duration of the war. In 1943, Tito established an Executive National Committee of Liberation to function as a provisional government.

Tito won the election held in the fall of 1945, as monarchists boycotted the vote. A new Assembly abolished the monarchy and proclaimed the Federal People's Republic of Yugoslavia, with Tito as Prime Minister.

Ruthlessly eliminating opposition, the Tito government executed Mihajlovic in 1946. With Soviet aid, Tito annexed the greater part of Italian Istria under the 1947 peace treaty with Italy but failed in his claim to the key port of Trieste. Zone B of the former free territory of Trieste went to Yugoslavia in 1954.

Tito broke with the Soviet bloc in 1948 and Yugoslavia has since followed a middle road, combining orthodox Communist control of politics and general overall economic policy with a varying degree of freedom in the arts, travel, and individual enterprise. Tito, who became President in 1953 and President for life under a revised Constitution adopted in 1963, has played a major part in the creation of a "non-aligned" group of states, the so-called "third world."

The Marshal supported his one-time Soviet mentors in their quarrel with Communist China, but even though he imprisoned the writer Mihajlo Mihajlov and other dissenters at home, he criticized Soviet repression of Czecholovakia in 1968.

Tito's death on May 4, 1980, three days before his 88th birthday, removed from the scene the last World War II leader. A rotating presidency designed to avoid internal dissension was put into effect immediately, and the feared clash of Yugoslavia's multiple nationalities and regions appeared to have been averted. A collective presidency, rotated annually among the six republics and two autonomous provinces of the federal republic, continued to govern according to a constitutional change made in 1974.

Demonstrations by ethnic Albanians in Kosovo for freedom from Serb rule were met with a forcible response from Serb authorities under the direction of Serb leader Slobodan Miloslovic. Miloslovic has mobilized Serb sentiment not only against the Albanians but also against the central government, raising the spectre of further divisiveness within Yugoslavia. In 1990, elections in the states of Croatia and Slovenia were won by parties advocating greater autonomy.

ZAIRE

Republic of Zaire
President: Mobutu Sese Seko (1965)
Prime Minister: Kengo Wa Dondo (1988)
Area: 905,365 sq mi. (2,344,885 sq km)
Population (mid-1990): 36,600,000 (average annual rate of natural increase: 3.3%)
Density per square mile: 38
Capital: Kinshasa
Largest cities (est. 1984): Kinshasa, 2,653,558; Lubumbashi, 543,268; Mbuji-Mayi, 423,363; Kananga, 290,898
Monetary unit: Zaire
Languages: French (official), English, Bantu dialects, mainly Swahili, Lingala, Ishiluba, and Kikongo
Religions: Roman Catholic 48%, Protestant 29%, Islam 10%; syncretic and traditional, 10%
Ethnic groups: Bantu, Sudanese, Nilotics, Pygmies, Hamites
National name: République du Zaïre
Literacy rate: 55% male, 37% female
Economic summary: Gross domestic product (1987): $5 billion; $170 per capita; 2.5% real growth rate. Arable land: 3%; principal products: coffee, palm oil, rubber, sugar, cotton, cocoa, bananas, plantains, vegetables, fruits. Labor force: 15,000,000; 13% in industry. Major industrial products: processed and unprocessed minerals, consumer goods. Natural resources: copper, cobalt, zinc, industrial diamonds, manganese, tin, gold, silver, bauxite, iron, coal, crude oil, 13% of world hydroelectric potential. Exports: copper, cobalt, diamonds, petroleum, coffee. Imports: consumer goods, foodstuffs, mining and other machinery, transport equipment. Major trading partners: Belgium, France, U.S., West Germany.

Geography. Zaire is situated in west central Africa and is bordered by the Congo, the Central African Republic, the Sudan, Uganda, Rwanda, Burundi, Tanzania, Zambia, Angola, and the Atlantic Ocean. It is one quarter the size of the U.S.

The principal rivers are the Ubangi and Bomu in the north and the Zaire (Congo) in the west, which flows into the Atlantic. The entire length of Lake Tanganyika lies along the eastern border with Tanzania and Burundi.

Government. Under the Constitution approved by referendum in 1967 and amended in 1974, the third Constitution since 1960, the president and a unicameral Legislature are elected by universal suffrage for five-year terms.

In 1971, the government proclaimed that the Democratic Republic of the Congo would be known as the Republic of Zaire, since the Congo River's name had been changed to the Zaire. In addition, President Joseph D. Mobutu took the name Mobutu Sese Seko and Katanga Province became Shaba.

There is only one political party: the Popular Movement of the Revolution, led by President Mobutu. However, in April 1990, Mobutu lifted the ban on opposition parties and promised that elections would be held in April, 1991.

History. Formerly the Belgian Congo, this territory was inhabited by ancient Negrito peoples (Pygmies), who were pushed into the mountains by Bantu and Nilotic invaders. The American correspondent Henry M. Stanley navigated the Congo River in 1877 and opened the interior to exploration. Commissioned by King Leopold II of the Belgians, Stanley made treaties with native chiefs that enabled the King to obtain personal title to the territory at the Berlin Conference of 1885.

Criticism of forced labor under royal exploitation prompted Belgium to take over administration of the Congo, which remained a colony until agitation for independence forced Brussels to grant freedom on June 30, 1960. Moise Tshombe, Premier of the then Katanga Province seceded from the new republic on July 11, and another mining province, South Kasai, followed. Belgium sent paratroopers to quell the civil war, and with President Joseph Kasavubu and Premier Patrice Lumumba of the national government in conflict, the United Nations flew in a peacekeeping force.

Kasavubu staged an army coup in 1960 and handed Lumumba over to the Katangan forces. A U.N. investigating commission found that Lumumba had been killed by a Belgian mercenary in the presence of Tshombe. Dag Hammarskjold, U.N. Secretary-General, died in a plane crash en route to a peace conference with Tshombe on Sept. 17, 1961.

U.N. Secretary-General U Thant submitted a national reconciliation plan in 1962 that Tshombe rejected. Tshombe's troops fired on the U.N. force in December, and in the ensuing conflict Tshombe capitulated on Jan. 14, 1963. The peacekeeping force withdrew, and, in a complete about-face, Kasavubu named Tshombe Premier to fight a spreading rebellion. Tshombe used foreign mercenaries and, with the help of Belgian paratroops airlifted by U.S. planes, defeated the most serious opposition, a Communist-backed regime in the northeast.

Kasavubu abruptly dismissed Tshombe in 1965 and was himself ousted by Gen. Joseph-Desiré Mobutu, Army Chief of Staff. The new President nationalized the Union Minière, the Belgian copper mining enterprise that had been a dominant force in the Congo since colonial days. The plane carrying the exiled Tshombe was hijacked in 1967 and he was held prisoner in Algeria until his death from a heart attack was announced June 29, 1969.

Mobutu eliminated opposition to win election in 1970 to a term of seven years, which was renewed in a 1977 election. He invited U.S., South African, and Japanese investment to replace Belgian interests. In 1975, he nationalized much of the economy, barred religious instruction in schools, and decreed the adoption of African names.

On March 8, 1977, invaders from Angola calling themselves the Congolese National Liberation Front pushed into Shaba and threatened the important mining center of Kolwezi. France and Bel-

gium responded to Mobutu's pleas for help with weapons, but the U.S. gave only nonmilitary supplies.

In April, France flew 1,500 Moroccan troops to Shaba to defeat the invaders, who were, Mobutu charged, Soviet-inspired, and Cuban-led. U.S. intelligence sources, however, confirmed Soviet and Cuban denials of any participation and identified the rebels as former Katanga gendarmes who had fled to Angola after their 1963 defeat.

On May 15, 1978, a new assault from Angola resulted in the capture of Kolwezi and the death of 100 whites and 300 blacks. In this second invasion, France and Belgium intervened directly as 1,000 Foreign Legion paratroopers repelled the Katangese and 1,750 Belgian soldiers helped evacuate 2,000 Europeans. The U.S. supplied 18 air transports for both the troop movement and the evacuation. This time President Carter himself backed Mobutu's renewed assertions of Soviet-Cuban participation.

In 1984 and 1985, Zaire and Angola signed bilateral agreements aimed at improved relations, including an agreement not to support rebels in each other's country.

ZAMBIA

Republic of Zambia
President: Kenneth D. Kaunda (1964)
Prime Minister: Gen. Malimba Masheke (1989)
Area: 290,586 sq mi. (752,618 sq km)
Population (mid-1990): 8,100,000 (average annual rate of natural increase: 3.8%)
Density per square mile: 28
Capital: Lusaka
Largest cities (est. 1982): Lusaka, 650,000; Kitwe, 345,000; Ndola, 325,000; Chingola, 195,000
Monetary unit: Kwacha
Languages: English and local dialects
Religions: Animist, Roman Catholic, Protestant.
Member of Commonwealth of Nations
Literacy rate: 55.5%
Economic summary: Gross domestic product (1987): $2 billion; $240 per capita; real growth rate −.2%. Arable land: 7%; principal products: corn, tobacco, fruits, sugar cane. Labor force: 2,455,000; 6% in mining, manufacturing and construction; major products: copper, cobalt, chemicals, zinc, fertilizers. Natural resources: copper, zinc, lead, cobalt, coal. Exports: copper, zinc, lead, cobalt, tobacco. Imports: manufactured goods, machinery and transport equipment, foodstuffs. Major trading partners: Western Europe, Japan, South Africa, U.S.

Geography. Zambia, a landlocked country in south central Africa, is about one tenth larger than Texas. It is surrounded by Angola, Zaire, Tanzania, Malawi, Mozambique, Zimbabwe, Botswana, and Namibia (formerly South-West Africa). The country is mostly a plateau that rises to 8,000 feet (2,434 m) in the east.

Government. Zambia (formerly Northern Rhodesia) is governed by a president, elected by universal suffrage, and a Legislative Assembly, consisting of 125 members elected by universal suffrage and up to 10 additional members nominated by the president.

In 1972, the Assembly passed a law making the ruling United National Independence Party, led by

President Kenneth D. Kaunda, the only legal political party.

History. Empire builder Cecil Rhodes obtained mining concessions in 1889 from King Lewanika of the Barotse and sent settlers to the area soon thereafter. It was ruled by the British South Africa Company, which he established, until 1924, when the British government took over the administration.

From 1953 to 1964, Northern Rhodesia was federated with Southern Rhodesia and Nyasaland in the Federation of Rhodesia and Nyasaland. On Oct. 24, 1964, Northern Rhodesia became the independent nation of Zambia.

Kenneth Kaunda, the first president, kept Zambia within the Commonwealth of Nations. The country's economy, dependent on copper exports, was threatened when Rhodesia declared its independence from British rule in 1965 and defied U.N. sanctions, which Zambia supported, an action that deprived Zambia of its trade route through Rhodesia. The U.S., Britain, and Canada organized an airlift in 1966 to ship gasoline into Zambia. In 1967, Britain agreed to finance new trade routes for Zambia.

Kaunda visited China in 1967, and China later agreed to finance a 1,000-mile railroad from the copper fields to Dar es Salaam in Tanzania. A pipeline was opened in 1968 from Ndola in Zambia's copper belt to the Indian Ocean at Dar es Salaam, ending the three-year oil drought.

In 1969, Kaunda announced the nationalization of the foreign copper-mining industry, with Zambia to take 51% (over $1 billion, estimated), and an agreement was reached with the companies on payment. He then announced a similar takeover of foreign oil producers.

Zambia suffered heavy damage from bombing raids by the former Rhodesian air force on Zimbabwean guerrilla bases and on its transportation links. These actions, combined with falling prices for copper and cobalt, forced Kaunda to declare a state of economic austerity in January 1981.

A strike by copper-belt workers, in 1981, directed partly against cuts in consumer subsidies and partly at UNIP, the regime's single party, brought a quick victory for the workers after they shut down production. In February, Kaunda installed a new Prime Minister and a new party chief, both more acceptable to the powerful copper-belt unions, and in April, UNIP readmitted union leaders who had been expelled at the time of the strike.

ZIMBABWE

Republic of Zimbabwe
Executive President: Robert Mugabe (1987)
Area: 150,699 sq mi. (390,308 sq km)
Population (mid-1990): 9,700,000 (average annual rate of natural increase: 3.2%)
Density per square mile: 67
Capital: Harare
Largest cities (est. 1983 for metropolitan area): Harare, 681,000; Bulawayo, 429,000
Monetary unit: Zimbabwean dollar
Languages: English (official), Ndebele, Shona
Religions: Christian, 25%; Animist 24%; Syncretic 50%
Literacy rate: 77%
Economic summary: Gross domestic product (1988 est.): $5.5 billion; $540 per capita; 6% real growth rate.

Arable land: 7%; principal agricultural products: tobacco, corn, sugar, tea, cotton, livestock. Labor force: 3,100,-000; 10% in mining, manufacturing and construction; major products: steel, textiles, chemicals, vehicles, gold, copper. Natural resources: gold, copper, chrome, nickel, tin, asbestos. Exports: gold, tobacco, asbestos, copper, meat, chrome, nickel, corn, sugar. Imports: machinery, petroleum products, transport equipment. Major trading partners: South Africa, UK

Geography. Zimbabwe, a landlocked country in south central Africa, is slightly smaller than California. It is bordered by Botswana on the west, Zambia on the north, Mozambique on the east, and South Africa on the south.

A high veld up to 6,000 feet (1,829 m) crosses the country from northeast to southwest. This is flanked by a somewhat lower veld that contains ranching country. Tropical forests that yield hardwoods lie in the southeast.

In the north, on the border with Zambia, is the 175-mile-long (128-m) Kariba Lake, formed by the Kariba Dam across the Zambezi River. It is the site of one of the world's largest hydroelectric projects.

Government. An amendment to the Constitution in October, 1987 created the position of Executive President that would combine Presidential and Prime Ministerial functions. Prime Minister Mugabe was the sole candidate and was elected to this post December 30. On December 22, the long negotiated ZANU-ZAPU merger was promulgated with ZAPU head Joshua Nkomo becoming a Vice President of the renamed ZANU(PF). In August, 1987, the Parliament voted to abolish the 20 whites-only seats that had existed since 1980. The remaining 80 members selected replacements who were obliged to support Mugabe's ZANU party.

In March, 1990, a constitutional amendment adopted a 150-seat unilateral legislature (House of Assembly) in place of the old bicameral one.

History. Zimbabwe was colonized by Cecil Rhodes's British South Africa Company at the end of the 19th century. In 1923, European settlers voted to become the self-governing British colony of Southern Rhodesia rather than merge with the Union of South Africa. After a brief federation with Northern Rhodesia and Nyasaland in the post-World War II period, Southern Rhodesia chose to remain a colony when its two partners voted for independence in 1963.

On Nov. 11, 1965, the white-minority government of Rhodesia unilaterally declared its independence from Britain.

In 1967, the U.N. imposed mandatory sanctions against Rhodesia. The country moved slowly toward meeting the demands of black Africans. The white-minority regime of Prime Minister Ian Smith withstood British pressure, economic sanctions, guerrilla attacks, and a right-wing assault.

On March 1, 1970, Rhodesia formally proclaimed itself a republic, and within the month nine nations, including the U.S., closed their consulates there.

Heightened guerrilla war and a withdrawal of South African military aid—particularly helicopters—marked the beginning of the collapse of Smith's 11 years of resistance in the spring of 1976. Under pressure from South Africa, Smith agreed with the U.S. that majority rule should come within two years.

In the fall, Smith met with black nationalist leaders in Geneva. The meeting broke up six weeks later when the Rhodesian Premier insisted that whites must retain control of the police and armed forces during the transition to majority rule. A British proposal called for Britons to take over these powers.

Divisions between Rhodesian blacks—Bishop Abel Muzorewa of the African National Congress and Ndabaningi Sithole as moderates versus Robert Mugabe and Joshua Nkomo of the Patriotic Front as advocates of guerrilla force—sharpened in 1977 and no agreement was reached. In July, with white residents leaving in increasing numbers and the economy showing the strain of war, Smith rejected outside mediation and called for general elections in order to work out an "internal solution" of the transfer of power.

On March 3, 1978, Smith, Muzorewa, Sithole, and Chief Jeremiah Chirau signed an agreement to transfer power to the black majority by Dec. 31, 1978. They constituted themselves an Executive Council, with chairmanship rotating but Smith retaining the title of Prime Minister. Blacks were named to each cabinet ministry, serving as co-ministers with the whites already holding these posts. African nations and the Patriotic Front leaders immediately denounced the action, but Western governments were more reserved, although none granted recognition to the new regime.

White voters ratified a new constitution on Jan. 30, 1979, enfranchising all blacks, establishing a black majority Senate and Assembly, and changing the country's name to Zimbabwe Rhodesia. A general election on April 24 gave Muzorewa's party 67.3% of the vote.

Muzorewa agreed to negotiate with Mugabe and Nkomo in British-sponsored talks beginning Sept. 9. By December, all parties accepted a new draft constitution, a cease-fire, and a period of British ad-ministration pending a general election.

In voting completed on Feb. 29, 1980, Mugabe's ZANU-Patriotic Front party won 57 of the 80 Assembly seats reserved for blacks. Nkomo's ZAPU-Patriotic Front party won 20 seats and Muzorewa's United African National Council only three. In an earlier vote on Feb. 14, the Rhodesian Front won all 20 seats reserved for whites in the Assembly.

At a ceremony on April 18, Prince Charles of Britain handed to President-elect Rev. Canaan Banana the symbols of independence. Mugabe, a Marxist, had already pledged his support for continuation of the existing free-market economy.

On April 18, 1980, Britain formally recognized the independence of Zimbabwe.

In January 1981, Mugabe dismissed Nkomo as Home Minister and his onetime rival left the government in protest. At the same time, the Prime Minister discharged Edgar Z. Tekere, Manpower and Planning Minister, who had been tried and acquitted of the murder of a white farmer.

Mugabe survived both tests and scored an unprecedented triumph when, in response to his appeal for economic aid, Western nations pledged $1.8 billion for the next three years.

The 1985 harvest was good in Zimbabwe and the country could feed itself. But political turmoil and civil strife continued. In what Western analysts viewed as a free and fair election, President Mugabe's African National Union increased its sizeable majority in the House of Assembly but Mugabe was frustrated because it did not win the 70 seats he sought to cement one-party rule. After the election, Mugabe cracked down on Nkomo's ZAPU-Patriotic Front party.

In April 1990, Mugabe was re-elected and his ZANU(PF) party given virtual unanimity in the Assembly.

(For late reports, see Current Events of 1990)

Global Report on Tropical Diseases

According to a recent World Health Organization report, almost a half billion people—nearly one person in ten—are now suffering from tropical diseases and support for major new research and control initiatives is needed to curb a worsening situation.

WHO estimates for the number of people infected, some with more than one disease are: malaria, 270 million; schistosomiasis, 200 million; lymphatic filariasis, the cause of elephantiasis, 90 million; Chagas disease, 16 to 18 million; onchocerciasis (river blindness), 17 million; leishmaniasis, 12 million; leprosy, 10 to 12 million; African sleeping sickness, 25,000 new cases a year. More than 90 percent of the malaria carriers live in sub-Saharan Africa.

Some 2.1 billion people—almost half the world's population—are at risk for malaria, living in areas where the disease is common; 1.6 billion are at risk for leprosy; more than 900 million for lymphatic filariasis; 600 million for schistosomiasis; 350 million for leishmaniasis; 90 million risk Chagas disease; another 90 million risk river blindness; 50 million risk African sleeping sickness.

Most people with tropical diseases are in Africa. The whole population of the Continent—500 million people—is at risk from at least one tropical disease. Eighty percent of the African population—400 million—live in areas where little has been done to control malaria transmission and where the problem remains virtually unchanged or is worsening. The most rampant diseases in Africa are malaria, schistosomiasis, river blindness, and African sleeping sickness.

Asia is estimated to have more than 100 million cases of tropical diseases per year. The most serious diseases are malaria, schistosomiasis, and filariasis. In Central and South America, more than 35 million people are infected. There, the most serious diseases are Chagas, schistosomiasis, and malaria.

Even Europe is not free of tropical diseases. Leishmaniasis is still endemic in all countries around the Mediterranean including Southern France, Greece, Israel, Italy, Portugal, Soviet Union and Spain. Turkey suffered a major epidemic of malaria during the 1970s, associated with an important irrigation project, and still reports cases of malaria and leishmaniasis.

Business travelers and tourists often import tropical diseases, especially malaria. For example, the United Kingdom reported more than 1,700 cases of imported malaria in 1989; Switzerland reported more than 300 in 1988, with two cases transmitted near Geneva airport. Airport malaria has become a frequent phenomenon in Europe. In the United States of America, about 1,000 cases of imported malaria are diagnosed each year. Local transmission has occasionally been reported, particularly in California and Texas. □

UNITED NATIONS

The 159 Members of the United Nations

Country	Joined U.N.[1]	Country	Joined U.N.[1]	Country	Joined U.N.[1]
Afghanistan	1946	Germany, East	1973	Oman	1971
Albania	1955	Germany, West	1973	Pakistan	1947
Algeria	1962	Ghana	1957	Panama	1945
Angola	1976	Greece	1945	Papua New Guinea	1975
Antigua and Barbuda	1981	Grenada	1974	Paraguay	1945
Argentina	1945	Guatemala	1945	Peru	1945
Australia	1945	Guinea	1958	Philippines	1945
Austria	1955	Guinea-Bissau	1974	Poland	1945
Bahamas	1973	Guyana	1966	Portugal	1955
Bahrain	1971	Haiti	1945	Qatar	1971
Bangladesh	1974	Honduras	1945	Romania	1955
Barbados	1966	Hungary	1955	Rwanda	1962
Belgium	1945	Iceland	1946	St. Kitts and Nevis	1983
Belize	1981	India	1945	St. Lucia	1979
Benin	1960	Indonesia	1950	St. Vincent and the Grenadines	1980
Bhutan	1971	Iran	1945	São Tomé and Príncipe	1975
Bolivia	1945	Iraq	1945	Saudi Arabia	1945
Botswana	1966	Ireland	1955	Senegal	1960
Brazil	1945	Israel	1949	Seychelles	1976
Brunei	1984	Italy	1955	Sierra Leone	1961
Bulgaria	1955	Ivory Coast	1960	Singapore	1965
Burkina Faso	1960	Jamaica	1962	Solomon Islands	1978
Burundi	1962	Japan	1956	Somalia	1960
Byelorussian S.S.R.	1945	Jordan	1955	South Africa	1945
Cambodia	1955	Kenya	1963	Spain	1955
Cameroon	1960	Kuwait	1963	Sri Lanka	1955
Canada	1945	Laos	1955	Sudan	1956
Cape Verde	1975	Lebanon	1945	Suriname	1975
Central African Republic	1960	Lesotho	1966	Swaziland	1968
Chad	1960	Liberia	1945	Sweden	1946
Chile	1945	Libya	1955	Syria	1945
China[2]	1945	Luxembourg	1945	Tanzania	1961
Colombia	1945	Madagascar	1960	Thailand	1946
Comoros	1975	Malawi	1964	Togo	1960
Congo	1960	Malaysia	1957	Trinidad and Tobago	1962
Costa Rica	1945	Maldives	1965	Tunisia	1956
Cuba	1945	Mali	1960	Turkey	1945
Cyprus	1960	Malta	1964	Uganda	1962
Czechoslovakia	1945	Mauritania	1961	Ukrainian S.S.R.	1945
Denmark	1945	Mauritius	1968	U.S.S.R.	1945
Djibouti	1977	Mexico	1945	United Arab Emirates	1971
Dominica	1978	Mongolia	1961	United Kingdom	1945
Dominican Republic	1945	Morocco	1956	United States	1945
Ecuador	1945	Mozambique	1975	Uruguay	1945
Egypt	1945	Myanmar	1948	Vanuatu	1981
El Salvador	1945	Namibia	1990	Venezuela	1945
Equatorial Guinea	1968	Nepal	1955	Vietnam	1977
Ethiopia	1945	Netherlands	1945	Western Samoa	1976
Fiji	1970	New Zealand	1945	Yemen, Republic of	1947
Finland	1955	Nicaragua	1945	Yugoslavia	1945
France	1945	Niger	1960	Zaire	1960
Gabon	1960	Nigeria	1960	Zambia	1964
Gambia	1965	Norway	1945	Zimbabwe	1980

1. The U.N. officially came into existence on Oct. 24, 1945. 2. On Oct. 25, 1971, the U.N. voted membership to the People's Republic of China, which replaced the Republic of China (Taiwan) in the world body.

Six Official Languages Used by U.N.

There are six official working languages recognized by the United Nations. They are Chinese, English, French, Russian, and Spanish, which have been in use since the world body was organized, and Arabic, which was added by the General Assembly in 1973 and by the Security Council in 1982.

Preamble of the United Nations Charter

The Charter of the United Nations was adopted at the San Francisco Conference of 1945. The complete text may be obtained by writing to the United Nations Sales Section, United Nations, New York, N.Y. 10017, and enclosing $1.

We the peoples of the United Nations determined to save succeeding generations from the scourge of war, which twice in our lifetime has brought untold sorrow to mankind, and

To reaffirm faith in fundamental human rights, in the dignity and worth of the human person, in the equal rights of men and women and of nations large and small, and

To establish conditions under which justice and respect for the obligations arising from treaties and other sources of international law can be maintained, and

To promote social progress and better standards of life in larger freedom, and for these ends

To practice tolerance and live together in peace with one another as good neighbors, and

To unite our strength to maintain international peace and security, and

To insure, by the acceptance of principles and the institution of methods, that armed force shall not be used, save in the common interest, and

To employ international machinery for the promotion of the economic and social advancement of all peoples, have resolved to combine our efforts to accomplish these aims.

Accordingly, our respective Governments, through representatives assembled in the city of San Francisco, who have exhibited their full powers found to be in good and due form, have agreed to the present Charter of the United Nations and do hereby establish an international organization to be known as the United Nations.

Principal Organs of the United Nations

Secretariat

This is the directorate on U.N. operations, apart from political decisions. All members contribute to its upkeep. Its staff of over 6,000 specialists is recruited from member nations on the basis of as wide a geographical distribution as possible. The staff works under the Secretary-General, whom it assists and advises.

Secretaries-General

Javier Pérez de Cuéllar, Peru, Jan. 1, 1982.
Kurt Waldheim, Austria, Jan. 1, 1972, to Dec. 31, 1981.
U Thant, Burma, Nov. 3, 1961, to Dec. 31, 1971.
Dag Hammarskjöld, Sweden, April 11, 1953, to Sept. 17, 1961.
Trygve Lie, Norway, Feb. 1, 1946, to April 10, 1953.

General Assembly

The General Assembly is the world's forum for discussing matters affecting world peace and security, and for making recommendations concerning them. It has no power of its own to enforce decisions.

The Assembly is composed of the 51 original member nations and those admitted since, a total of 159. Each nation has one vote. On important questions including international peace and security, a two-thirds majority of those present and voting is required. Decisions on other questions are made by a simple majority.

The Assembly's agenda can be as broad as the Charter. It can make recommendations to member nations, the Security Council, or both. Emphasis is given on questions relating to international peace and security brought before it by any member, the Security Council, or nonmembers.

The Assembly also maintains a broad program of international cooperation in economic, social, cultural, educational, and health fields, and for assisting in human rights and freedoms.

Among other duties, the Assembly has functions relating to the trusteeship system, and considers and approves the U.N. Budget. Every member contributes to operating expenses according to its means.

Security Council

The Security Council is the primary instrument for establishing and maintaining international peace. Its main purpose is to prevent war by settling disputes between nations.

Under the Charter, the Council is permitted to dispatch a U.N. force to stop aggression. All member nations undertake to make available armed forces, assistance, and facilities to maintain international peace and security.

Any member may bring a dispute before the Security Council or the General Assembly. Any nonmember may do so if it accepts the charter obligations of pacific settlement.

The Security Council has 15 members. There are five permanent members: the United States, the Soviet Union, Britain, France, and China; and 10 temporary members elected by the General Assembly for two-year terms, from five different regions of the world.

Voting on procedural matters requires a nine-vote majority to carry. However, on questions of substance, the vote of each of the five permanent members is required.

Current temporary members are (term expires Dec. 31, 1990): Canada, Colombia, Ethiopia, Finland, and Malaysia; (term expires Dec. 31, 1991): Cuba, Democratic Yemen, Ivory Coast, Romania, and Zaire.

Economic and Social Council

This council is composed of 54 members elected by the General Assembly to 3-year terms. It works closely with the General Assembly as a link with groups formed within the U.N. to help peoples in such fields as education, health, and human rights. It insures that there is no overlapping and sets up commissions to deal with economic conditions and collect facts and figures on conditions over the world. It issues studies and reports and may make recommendations to the Assembly and specialized agencies.

Functional Commissions

Statistical Commission; Population Commission; Commission for Social Development; Commission on Human Rights; Commission on the Status of Women; Commission on Narcotic Drugs.

Regional Commissions

Economic Commission for Europe (ECE); Economic and Social Commission for Asia and the Pacific (ESCAP); Economic Commission for Latin America and the Caribbean (ECLAC); Economic Commission for Africa (ECA); Economic and Social Commission for Western Asia (ESCWA).

Trusteeship Council

This council supervises territories administered by various nations and placed under an international trusteeship system by the United Nations. Each nation is charged with developing the self-government of the territory and preserving and advancing the cultural, political, economic, and other forms of welfare of the people.

The Trusteeship Council is currently composed of 5 members: 1 member—the United States—that administers a trust territory, and 4 members—China, France, the Soviet Union, and the United Kingdom—that are permanent members of the Security Council but do not administer trust territories.

The following countries ceased to be administering members because of the independence of territories they had administered: Italy and France in 1960, Belgium in 1962, New Zealand and the United Kingdom in 1968 and Australia in 1975. France and the U.K. became nonadministering members.

As of December 1985, there was only one trust territory: the Trust Territory of the Pacific Islands (administered by the United States).

International Court of Justice

The International Court of Justice sits at The Hague, the Netherlands. Its 15-judge bench was established to hear disputes among states, which must agree to accept its verdicts. Its judges, charged with administering justice under international law, deal with cases ranging from disputes over territory to those concerning rights of passage.

Following are the members of the Court and the years in which their terms expire on Feb. 5:

President: Jose Maria Ruda, Argentina (1991)
Vice President: Keba Mbaye, Senegal V.P. (1991)
Robert Y. Jennings, United Kingdom (1991)
Gilbert Guillaume, France (1991)
Raghunandan Swarup Pathak, India (1991)
Taslim Olawale Elias, Nigeria (1994)
Jens Evensen, Norway (1994)
Ni Zhengyu, China (1994)
Manfred Lachs, Poland (1994)
Shigeru Oda, Japan (1994)
Roberto Ago, Italy (1997)
Mohamed Shahabuddeen, Guyana (1997)
Stephen Schwebel, United States (1997)
Mohammed Bedjaoui, Algeria (1997)
Nikolai Tarassov, U.S.S.R. (1997)

Agencies of the United Nations

INTL. ATOMIC ENERGY AGENCY (IAEA)

Established: Statute for IAEA, approved on Oct. 26, 1956, at a conference held at U.N. Headquarters, New York, came into force on July 29, 1957. The Agency is under the aegis of the U.N., but unlike the following, it is not a specialized agency.

Purpose: To promote the peaceful uses of atomic energy; to ensure that assistance provided by it or at its request or under its supervision or control is not used in such a way as to further any military purpose.

Headquarters: Vienna International Center, P.O. Box 100, A-1400 Vienna, Austria

FOOD AND AGRICULTURE ORGANIZATION OF THE UNITED NATIONS (FAO)

Established: October 16, 1945, when constitution became effective.

Purpose: To raise nutrition levels and living standards; to secure improvements in production and distribution of food and agricultural products.

Headquarters: Via delle Terme di Caracalla, 00100, Rome, Italy.

GENERAL AGREEMENT ON TARIFFS AND TRADE (GATT)

Established: Jan. 1, 1948.

Purpose: An International Trade Organization (ITO) was originally planned. Although this agency has not materialized, some of its objectives have been embodied in an international commercial treaty, the General Agreement on Tariffs and Trade. Its purpose is to sponsor trade negotiations.

Headquarters: Centre William Rappard, 154 Rue de Lausanne, 1211, Geneva 21, Switzerland.

INTERNATIONAL BANK FOR RECONSTRUCTION AND DEVELOPMENT (IBRD) (WORLD BANK)

Established: December 27, 1945, when Articles of Agreement drawn up at Bretton Woods Conference in July 1944 came into force. Began operations on June 25, 1946.

Purpose: To assist in reconstruction and development of economies of members by facilitating capital investment and by making loans to governments and furnishing technical advice.

Headquarters: 1818 H St., N.W., Washington, D.C. 20433.

INTL. CIVIL AVIATION ORGANIZATION (ICAO)

Established: April 4, 1947, after working as a provisional organization since June 1945.

Purpose: To study problems of international civil aviation; to establish international standards and regulations; to promote safety measures, uniform regulations for operation, simpler procedures at international borders, and the use of new technical methods and equipment. It has evolved standards for meteorological services, traffic control, communications, radio beacons and ranges, search and rescue organization, and other facilities. It has brought about much simplification of customs, immigration, and public health regulations as they apply to international air transport. It drafts international air law conventions, and is concerned with economic aspects of air travel.

Headquarters: International Aviation Square, 1000 Sherbrooke St. West, Montreal, Quebec, H3A 2R2, Canada.

INTL. DEVELOPMENT ASSOCIATION (IDA)

Established: Sept. 24, 1960. An affiliate of the World Bank, IDA has the same officers and staff as the Bank.

Purpose: To further economic development of its members by providing finance on terms which bear less heavily on balance of payments of members than those of conventional loans.

Headquarters: 1818 H St., N.W., Washington, D.C. 20433.

INTERNATIONAL FINANCE CORPORATION (IFC)

Established: Charter of IFC came into force on July 20, 1956. Although IFC is affiliated with the World Bank, it is a separate legal entity, and its funds are entirely separate from those of the Bank. However, membership in the Corporation is open only to Bank members.

Purpose: To further economic development by encouraging the growth of productive private enterprise in its member countries, particularly in the less developed areas; to invest in productive private enterprises in association with private investors, without government guarantee of repayment where sufficient private capital is not available on reasonable terms; to serve as a clearing house to bring together investment opportunities, private capital (both foreign and domestic), and experienced management.

Headquarters: 1818 H St., N.W., Washington, D.C. 20433.

INTERNATIONAL FUND FOR AGRICULTURAL DEVELOPMENT (IFAD)

Established: June 18, 1976. Began operations in December 1977.

Purpose: To mobilize additional funds for agricultural and rural development in developing countries through projects and programs directly benefiting the poorest rural populations.

Headquarters: 107 Via del Serafico, 00142, Rome, Italy.

INTERNATIONAL LABOR ORGANIZATION (ILO)

Established: April 11, 1919, when constitution was adopted as Part XIII of Treaty of Versailles. Became specialized agency of U.N. in 1946.

Purpose: To contribute to establishment of lasting peace by promoting social justice; to improve labor conditions and living standards through international action; to promote economic and social stability. The U.S. withdrew from the ILO in 1977 and resumed membership in 1980.

Headquarters: 4, route des Morillons, CH-1211 Geneva 22, Switzerland.

INTERNATIONAL MARITIME ORGANIZATION (IMO)

Established: March 17, 1958.

Purpose: To give advisory and consultative help to promote international cooperation in maritime navigation and to encourage the highest standards of safety and navigation. Its aim is to bring about a uniform system of measuring ship tonnage; systems now vary widely in different parts of the world. Other activities include cooperation with other U.N. agencies on matters affecting the maritime field.

Headquarters: 4 Albert Embankment, London SE 1 7SR England.

INTERNATIONAL MONETARY FUND (IMF)

Established: Dec. 27, 1945, when Articles of Agreement drawn up at Bretton Woods Conference in July 1944 came into force. Fund began operations on March 1, 1947.

Purpose: To promote international monetary cooperation and expansion of international trade; to promote exchange stability; to assist in establishment of multilateral system of payments in respect of currency transactions between members.

Headquarters: 700 19th St., N.W., Washington, D.C. 20431.

INTERNATIONAL TELECOMMUNICATION UNION (ITU)

Established: 1865. Became specialized agency of U.N. in 1947.

Purpose: To extend technical assistance to help members keep up with present day telecommunication needs; to standardize communications equipment and procedures; to lower costs. It also works for orderly sharing of radio frequencies and

makes studies and recommendations to benefit its members.

Headquarters: Place des Nations, 1211 Geneva 20, Switzerland.

UNITED NATIONS EDUCATIONAL, SCIENTIFIC, AND CULTURAL ORGANIZATION (UNESCO)

Established: Nov. 4, 1946, when twentieth signatory to constitution deposited instrument of acceptance with government of U.K.

Purpose: To promote collaboration among nations through education, science, and culture in order to further justice, rule of law, and human rights and freedoms without distinction of race, sex, language, or religion.

Headquarters: UNESCO House. Place de Fontenoy, 7e, Paris, France.

UNITED NATIONS INDUSTRIAL DEVELOPMENT ORGANIZATION (UNIDO)

Established: Nov. 17, 1966. Became specialized agency of the U.N. in 1985.

Purpose: To promote and accelerate the industrialization of the developing countries.

Headquarters: UNIDO, Vienna International Centre, P.O. Box 300, A-1400 Vienna, Austria.

UNIVERSAL POSTAL UNION (UPU)

Established: Oct. 9, 1874. Became specialized agency of U.N. in 1947.

Purpose: To facilitate reciprocal exchange of correspondence by uniform procedures by all UPU members; to help governments modernize and speed up mailing procedures.

Headquarters: Weltpoststrasse 4, Berne, Switzerland.

WORLD HEALTH ORGANIZATION (WHO)

Established: April 7, 1948, when 26 members of the U.N. had accepted its constitution, adopted July 22, 1946, by the International Health Conference in New York City.

Purpose: To aid attainment by all people of highest possible level of health.

Headquarters: 20 Avenue Appia, 1211 Geneva 27, Switzerland.

WORLD INTELLECTUAL PROPERTY ORGANIZATION (WIPO)

Established: April 26, 1970, when its Convention came into force. Originated as International Bureau of Paris Union (1883) and Berne Union (1886), later succeeded by United International Bureau for the Protection of Intellectual Property (BIRPI). Became a specialized agency of the U.N. in December 1974.

Purpose: To promote legal protection of intellectual property, including artistic and scientific works, artistic performances, sound recordings, broadcasts, inventions, trademarks, industrial designs, and commercial names.

Headquarters: 34 Chemin des Colombettes, 1211 Geneva 20, Switzerland.

WORLD METEOROLOGICAL ORGANIZATION (WMO)

Established: March 23, 1950, succeeding the International Meteorological Organization, a nongovernmental organization founded in 1878.

Purpose: To promote international exchange of weather reports and maximum standardization of observations; to help developing countries establish weather services for their own economic needs; to fill gaps in observation stations; to promote meteorological investigations affecting jet aircraft, satellites, energy resources, etc.

Headquarters: 41 Avenue Giuseppe Motta, Geneva, Switzerland.

MEDIA

Leading Magazines: United States and Canada

Magazine	Circulation[1]	Magazine	Circulation[1]
American Health—Fitness of Body and Mind	1,000,689	Omni	925,436
Better Homes and Gardens	8,005,311	1,001 Home Ideas	1,603,099
Bon Appetit	1,355,404	Outdoor Life	1,507,529
Business Week (North America)	889,535	Parents Magazine	1,752,697
Car and Driver	934,377	Penthouse	1,830,823
Changing Times, The Kiplinger Magazine	1,300,153	People Weekly	3,270,835
Chatelaine	965,609	Playboy	3,421,203
Consumers Digest	813,373	Popular Mechanics	1,650,693
Cosmopolitan	2,702,125	Popular Photography	927,388
Country Home	963,081	Popular Science	1,818,403
Country Living	1,801,414	Practical Homeowner	759,857
Discover	1,053,034	Prevention	3,134,914
Ebony	1,791,976	Psychology Today	887,770
Elle	826,336	Reader's Digest	16,343,599
Essence	851,034	Reader's Digest (Canadian English Edition)	1,323,348
Family Circle	5,461,786	Redbook	3,901,419
The Family Handyman	1,382,547	Rolling Stone	1,216,781
Field & Stream	2,015,577	Self	1,213,314
Food & Wine	823,530	Seventeen	1,766,161
Glamour	2,224,135	Smithsonian	2,342,443
Globe	1,329,413	Soap Opera Digest	1,466,014
Golf Digest	1,363,907	Southern Living	2,318,841
Golf Magazine	1,091,379	Sport	960,066
Good Housekeeping	5,152,245	Sports Illustrated	3,424,393
Gourmet	807,377	Star	3,588,753
Health	1,088,696	Sunset, The Magazine of Western Living	1,393,015
Home Magazine	925,335	'Teen	1,100,237
Home Mechanix	1,209,395	Time	4,339,029
Homeowner	791,310	Travel & Leisure	1,115,328
Hot Rod	911,667	True Story	1,150,844
House Beautiful	939,735	TV Guide	15,867,750
Jet	860,671	TV Guide (Canada)	820,158
Ladies Home Journal	5,038,297	U.S. News & World Report	2,209,996
Life	1,749,723	US	1,365,892
Mademoiselle	1,162,206	Victoria	793,790
McCall's	5,088,686	Vogue	1,247,920
Money	1,834,618	Weekly World News	848,767
Motor Trend	818,021	Weight Watchers Magazine	1,007,755
Nation's Business	858,228	Woman's Day	4,705,288
National Enquirer	4,100,740	The Workbasket	1,295,578
National Examiner	893,956	Workbench	909,119
National Geographic Magazine	10,890,660	Working Woman	909,201
New Woman	1,390,830	Yankee	1,002,781
Newsweek	3,180,011	YM	967,249

1. Average total paid circulation for the six-month period ending December 31, 1987. The table lists magazines with combined newsstand and subscription circulation of over 750,000. *Source:* Audit Bureau of Circulations. Publishers' Statements for six-month period ending December 31, 1988.

Major U.S. Daily Newspapers[1]

City and newspaper	Net paid circulation			
	Morning[2]	All-Day[2]	Evening[2]	Sunday
Akron, Ohio: *Beacon Journal*	153,683		—	221,258
Albany, N.Y.: *Times-Union* (M & S)	105,306		—	168,915
Albuquerque, N.M.: *Journal* (M & S); *Tribune* (E)	121,396[4]		40,987[4]	154,646[4]
Allentown, Pa.: *Call* (M & S)	137,634			183,325
Amarillo, Tex.: *News* (M); *Globe-Times* (E); *News-Globe* (S)	42,809		22,153[3]	75,389
Asbury Park, N.J.: *Press*	—		149,820	218,684
Atlanta: *Constitution* (M); *Journal* (E); *Journal and Constitution* (S)	310,434		194,938	682,001
Atlantic City, N.J.: *Press*	79,376		—	97,785

City and newspaper	Net paid circulation			
	Morning[2]	All-Day[2]	Evening[2]	Sunday
Augusta, Ga.: *Chronicle* (M); *Herald* (E);				
Chronicle—Herald (S)	67,656[3]		12,436[3]	92,960
Austin, Tex.: *American-Statesman*	176,517		—	223,257
Bakersfield, Calif.: *Californian*	83,423[4]		—	93,165[4]
Baltimore: *Sun*	233,539[3]		167,637[3]	494,067
Bangor, Me.: *News*	78,222[3]		—	94,648[5]
Baton Rouge, La.: *Advocate* (M & S); *State-Times* (E)	79,490[3]		27,442[3]	133,505
Bergen County (Hackensack), N.J.; *Record*	—		161,546[4]	230,070[4]
Beaumont, Tex.: *Enterprise*	69,238		—	84,697
Binghamton, N.Y.: *Press & Sun-Bulletin* (M & S)	70,413		—	92,140
Birmingham, Ala.: *Post-Herald* (M); *News* (E & S)	64,532[3]		173,947[3]	212,698
Boston: *Globe*	522,981[3]		—	787,858
Herald	370,752[3]		—	253,233
Christian Science Monitor	115,499[3]		—	—
Bridgeport, Conn.: *Telegram* (M); *Post* (E); *Sunday Post*	18,352[3]		55,977[3]	89,838
Buffalo, N.Y.: *News*	—	315,732[3]	—	380,610
Camden, N.J.: *Courier-Post*	—		103,295[4]	103,671[4]
Canton, Ohio: *Repository*	—		57,447[4]	75,669[4]
Cedar Rapids, Iowa: *Gazette*	71,328		—	83,148
Charleston, S.C.: *News & Courier* (M);				
Evening Post; News & Courier Post (S)	81,633[3]		35,253[3]	123,610
Charleston, W. Va.: *Gazette* (M); *Mail* (E);				
Gazette-Mail (S)	55,172		50,624	105,126
Charlotte, N.C.: *Observer*	232,018		—	292,004
Chattanooga, Tenn.: *Times* (M); *News-Free Press* (E & S)	46,737		55,428	108,348
Chicago: *Tribune*	740,713[3]		—	1,141,455
Sun-Times	532,678[3]		—	566,808
Daily Herald (M); *Sunday Herald*	91,696		—	90,580
Cincinnati: *Enquirer* (M & S); *Post* (E)	198,828		106,440	344,313
Cleveland: *Plain Dealer*	438,066[3]		—	561,150
Colorado Springs, Colo.: *Gazette Telegraph*	103,645		—	117,161
Columbia, S.C.: *State*	144,995		—	170,714
Columbus, Ohio: *Dispatch*	252,363		—	386.936
Corpus Christi, Tex.: *Caller* (M); *Caller-Times* (S)	68,136[4]		—	90,204[4]
Dallas: *News*	378,116[6]		—	565,164
Times-Herald	—	222,519	—	332,449
Wall Street Journal (Southwest edition)	198,554[3]		—	—
Davenport, Iowa: *Quad City Times*	—	56,573[3]	—	82,513
Dayton, Ohio: *News*	181,172		—	232,059
Daytona Beach, Fla.: *News-Journal*	97,214		—	113,405
Denver: *Post*	246,837		—	408,544
Rocky Mountain News	364,790		—	415,322
Des Moines, Iowa: *Register*	208,457		—	349,015
Detroit: *Free Press* (M); *News* (E);				
News & Free Press (S)	639,767[37]		526,147[37]	1,270,420[37]
Duluth, Minn.: *News-Tribune*	61,224		—	84,630
Erie, Pa.: *News* (M); *Times* (E); *Times-News* (S)	30,782[3]		40,842[3]	103,247
El Paso, Tex.: *Times* (M & S); *Herald-Post* (E)	62,725[4]		29,205[4]	99,500[4]
Eugene, Ore.: *Register-Guard*	73,468		—	77,187
Evansville, Ind.: *Courier* (M); *Press* (E); *Courier & Press* (S)	63,245		35,825	117,197
Fayetteville, N.C.: *Times* (M); *Observer* (E);				
Observer-Times (S)	30,482[34]		41,016[34]	77,148[34]
Flint, Mich.: *Journal*	—		108,805[3]	125,394
Fort Lauderdale, Fla.: *Sun-Sentinel* (M); *News* (E);				
News & Sun-Sentinel (S)	257,091[3]		14,483[3]	350,211
Fort Myers, Fla.: *News-Press*	97,560		—	125,586
Fort Wayne, Ind.: *Journal-Gazette* (M & S); *News-Sentinel* (E)	63,200		56,024	137,011
Fort Worth: *Star-Telegram*	160,038[3]		97,214[3]	333,955
Fresno, Calif.: *Bee*	148,491[4]		—	181,065[4]
Gary, Ind.: *Post-Tribune*	74,365		—	87,873
Grand Rapids, Mich.: *Press*	—		141,700	185,027
Green Bay, Wis.: *Press-Gazette*	—		57,488	81,961
Greensboro, N.C.: *News & Record*	116,613		—	131,398
Greensburg, Pa.: *Tribune-Review*	51,821		—	82,155
Greenville, S.C.: *News* (M); *Piedmont* (E); *News & Piedmont* (S)	88,088[3]		25,726[3]	134,497
Harrisburg, Pa.: *Patriot* (M); *Evening News;*				
Sunday Patriot-News	57,094[3]		50,331[3]	172,429
Hartford, Conn.: *Courant*	230,358		—	316,792

City and newspaper	Net paid circulation			
	Morning[2]	All-Day[2]	Evening[2]	Sunday
Honolulu: *Advertiser* (M); *Star-Bulletin* (E);				
Star-Bulletin & Advertiser (S)	102,515[4]		91,658[4]	203,281[4]
Houston: *Chronicle*	—	449,755	—	620,752
Post	328,869		—	371,634
Huntsville, Ala.: *News* (M); *Times* (E & S)	16,385[3]		58,101[3]	78,640
Indianapolis: *Star* (M & S); *News* (E)	226,170		102,730	404,112
Jackson, Miss.: *Clarion-Ledger*	102,124[3]		—	123,101
Jacksonville, Fla.: *Times-Union*	179,009[3]		—	243,809
Kalamazoo, Mich.: *Gazette*			66,531	82,280
Kansas City, Mo.: *Times* (M); *Star* (E & S)	275,665[8]		157,255[8]	417,286
Knoxville, Tenn.: *Journal* (E); *News-Sentinel* (M & S)	103,722		41,651	170,378
Lakeland, Fla.: *Ledger*	86,981[4]		—	105,441[4]
Lancaster, Pa.: *Intelligencer-Journal* (M); *New Era* (E);				
News (S)	44,399[4]		54,687[4]	104,357[4]
Lansing, Mich.: *State-Journal*	70,083		—	91,986
Las Vegas, Nev.: *Review-Journal*	—	134,371[3]	—	168,162
Sun	55,665		—	59,219
Lexington, Ky.: *Herald-Leader*	125,435		—	157,254
Lincoln, Neb.: *Star* (M); *Journal* (E); *Journal & Star* (S)	39,192		42,575	82,590
Little Rock, Ark.: *Gazette*	136,925[9]		—	221,594
Democrat	129,010		—	220,014
Long Beach, Calif.: *Press-Telegram*	130,055[3]		4,016[3]	155,386
Long Island (Melville), N.Y.: *Newsday*	—	711,264[3]	—	713,779
Los Angeles: *Times*	1,210,077		—	1,504,540
News	202,384		—	214,205
Louisville, Ky.: *Courier-Journal*	235,698		—	326,259
Lubbock, Tex.: *Avalanche-Journal*	67,232		—	75,182
Macon, Ga.: *Telegraph and News*	73,983		—	102,439
Madison, Wis.: *State Journal* (M & S); *Capital Times* (E)	82,412[3]		26,337[3]	153,643
Melbourne, Fla.: *Today*	82,799		—	112,285
Memphis, Tenn.: *Commercial Appeal*	216,758		—	293,004
Miami, Fla.: *Herald*	443,216		—	551,027
Middletown, N.Y.: *Times Herald-Record* (M); *Record* (S)	83,356[4]		—	97,324[4]
Milwaukee: *Sentinel* (M); *Journal* (E & S)	173,829[3]		276,280[3]	502,637
Minneapolis: *Star & Tribune*	410,226		—	663,063
Mobile, Ala.: *Register* (M); *Press* (E); *Press-Register* (S)	58,603[34]		43,380[34]	110,749[4]
Modesto, Calif.: *Bee*	81,522[4]		—	91,416[4]
Montgomery, Ala. *Advertiser* (M); *Journal* (E);				
Journal & Advertiser (S)	50,200[3]		15,090[3]	77,687
Naperville, Ill.: *Wall Street Journal* (Midwest edition)	529,823[3]		—	—
Nashville, Tenn.: *Tennessean* (M & S); *Banner* (E)	129,136		61,684	264,663
New Haven, Conn.: *Register*	105,144		—	139,714
New Orleans: *Times-Picayune*	—	281,919[4]	—	334,313[4]
New York: *News*	1,180,139[3]		—	896,189
Times	1,149,683[3]			1,706,013
Post	504,720[3]		—	161,551
Wall Street Journal (Eastern edition)	805,089[3]		—	—
National edition	1,935,866[3]		—	—
Women's Wear Daily				
Newark, N.J.: *Star-Ledger*	470,045[34]		—	687,054[4]
Newport News—Hampton, Va.: *Press* (M & S); *Times Herald* (E)	79,077[34]		26,367[34]	118,464[4]
Norfolk-Portsmouth-Virginia Beach-Chesapeake, Va.:	151,251[34]		79,012[34]	236,886[4]
Virginian-Pilot (M); *Ledger-Star* (E);				
Virginian-Pilot/Ledger-Star (S)				
Oakland, Calif.: *Tribune* (M & S)	n.a.			n.a.
Oklahoma City: *Oklahoman* (M & S)	225,861		—	322,717
Omaha, Neb.: *World-Herald*	123,540[3]		96,989[3]	286,935
Orange County (Santa Ana), Calif.: *Register*	—	349,019[3]	—	402,060
Orlando, Fla.: *Sentinel*	—	285,024	—	387,505
Palo Alto, Calif.: *Wall Street Journal* (Western edition)	402,400[3]		—	—
Peninsula Times Tribune	—		43,735	46,147
Peoria, Ill.: *Journal Star*	—	91,532[3]		115,172
Philadelphia: *Inquirer* (M & S); *Daily News* (E)	522,020[3]		235,828[3]	994,539
Phoenix, Ariz.: *Republic* (M & S); *Gazette* (E)	382,952[4]		98,911[4]	581,386[4]

City and newspaper	Net paid circulation			
	Morning[2]	All-Day[2]	Evening[2]	Sunday
Pittsburgh: *Post-Gazette, Sun-Telegraph* (M); *Press* (E & S)	165,371[3]		228,232[3]	557,563
Pontiac, Mich.: *Oakland Press*	—	76,170	—	83,639
Portland, Me.: *Press-Herald* (M); *Express* (E)	60,447[3][10]		23,772[3][10]	—
Maine Sunday Telegram	—		—	142,302
Portland, Or.: *Oregonian*	—	332,250[3]	—	428,095
Providence, R.I.: *Journal Bulletin;* Journal (S)	—	203,099[3]	—	263,884
Quincy, Mass.: *Patriot-Ledger*	—		90,912[3][4]	102,701[4][11]
Raleigh, N.C.: *News & Observer* (M & S)	155,684[4]		—	188,913[4]
Reading, Pa.: *Times* (M); *Eagle* (E & S)	45,678[3]		32,009[3]	113,302
Reno, Nev.: *Gazette Journal*	64,942		—	79,459
Richmond, Va.: *Times-Dispatch* (M & S); *News-Leader* (E)	143,167		104,265	255,260
Riverside, Calif.: *Press-Enterprise* (M & S)	156,508		—	164,748
Roanoke, Va.: *Times & World-News*	82,924[3]		40,094[3]	126,774
Rochester, N.Y.: *Democrat & Chronicle* (M & S); *Times-Union* (E)	129,352[3]		86,767[3]	259,431
Rockford, Ill.: *Register Star*	72,976		—	87,097
Sacramento, Calif.: *Bee*	263,412[4]		—	322,870[4]
Union	n.a.			n.a.
St. Louis: *Post-Dispatch*	376,286[3]		—	561,585
St. Paul: *Pioneer Press*	—	197,265[3]	—	257,725
St. Petersburg, Fla.: *Times*	381,277[4]		—	494,018[4]
Salt Lake City, Utah: *Tribune* (M & S);	112,630		—	143,705
Deseret News (E & S)	—		62,418	69,279
San Antonio: *Express News*	—	183,958	—	271,038
Light	—	178,122	—	253,672
San Bernardino, Calif.: *Sun*	88,817		—	100,193
San Diego, Calif.: *Union* (M & S); *Tribune* (E)	271,131[4]		117,623[4]	443,788[4]
San Francisco: *Chronicle* (M); *Examiner* (E);				
Examiner & Chronicle (S)	569,257[3]		140,704[3]	713,172
San Gabriel Valley, Calif.: *Tribune* (M); *Tribune-News* (S)	63,742		—	83,383
San Jose, Calif.: *Mercury-News*	—	281,369[3]	—	334,284
Santa Rosa, Calif.: *Press Democrat*	89,838		—	97,234
Sarasota, Fla.: *Herald-Tribune* (M & S)	139,036[4]		—	167,569[4]
Seattle: *Post-Intelligencer* (M); *Times* (E); combined (S)	201,505[4]		233,855[3]	512,010
Shreveport, La.: *Times* (M & S); *Journal* (E)	77,137[4]		18,152[4]	105,122[4]
Savannah, Ga.: *News* (M & S); *Press* (E)	53,456[3]		18,374[3]	77,280
South Bend-Mishawaka, Ind.: *Tribune*	—		91,355	129,862
Spokane, Wash.: *Spokesman-Review* (M & S); *Chronicle* (E)	97,928[3]		24,829[3]	144,571
Springfield, Ill.: *State Journal-Register*	69,260		—	77,778
Springfield, Mass.: *Union News; Republican* (S)	—	112,180	—	157,840
Springfield, Mo.: *News-Leader*	60,882		—	101,176
Staten Island, N.Y.: *Advance* (E&S)	—		75,648	89,507
Syracuse, N.Y.: *Post-Standard* (M); *Herald-Journal* (E);	85,189		92,661	223,450
Herald-American (S)				
Tacoma, Wash.: *News-Tribune*	118,152		—	133,844
Tallahassee, Fla.: *Democrat*	60,637		—	75,516
Tampa, Fla.: *Tribune* (M); *Tribune & Times* (S)	309,638[4]		—	407,225[4]
Toledo, Ohio: *Blade*	—		154,365	218,219
Trenton, N.J.: *Times* (M&S)	76,897		—	90,659
Trentonian (M & S)	69,004		—	63,810
Tucson, Ariz.: *Star* (M & S); *Citizen* (E)	94,565[4]		53,508[4]	176,049[4]
Tulsa, Okla.: *World* (M & S); *Tribune* (E)	128,139[4]		67,704[4]	244,042[4]
Walnut Creek, Calif.: *Contra Costa Times*	89,092		—	99,145
Washington, D.C.: *Post*	824,282[3]		—	1,154,420
Times	n.a.			
USA Today	1,387,233[9]		—	—
West Palm Beach, Fla.: *Post*	190,172[3]		—	234,897
Wichita, Kan.: *Eagle-Beacon*	121,730		—	196,686
Wilmington, Del.: *News Journal*	—	119,315[4]	—	138,134[4]
Winston-Salem, N.C.: *Journal*	95,110		—	106,635
Worcester, Mass.: *Telegram Gazette; Telegraph* (S)	—	117,399[3]	—	136,632
Youngstown, Ohio: *Vindicator*	—		89,541[4]	135,607[4]

1. Listing is of cities in which any one edition of a newspaper exceeds an average net paid circulation of 75,000; newspapers of smaller circulation in those cities are also included. 2. Unless otherwise indicated, figures are average Monday-through-Saturday circulation for six-month period ending March 31, 1990. 3. Average Monday-through-Friday circulation. 4. Three-month average for period ending March 31, 1990. 5. Week-end edition. 6. Monday-Thursday, Saturday. 7. (11-27-89 to 3-31-90) 8. (10-1-89 to 2-28-90) 9. Average Monday through Thursday circulation. 10. (12-3-89 to 3-31-90) 11. Saturday edition. n.a. = not available.

English Language Daily and Sunday U.S. Newspapers

(number of newspapers as of Feb. 1, 1990; circulation as reported for Sept. 30, 1989)

State	Morning papers and circulation		Evening papers and circulation		Total M and E and circulation		Sunday papers and circulation	
Alabama	15	304,150	12	457,096	27	761,246	20	754,203
Alaska	3	66,476	4	58,739	7	125,215	4	143,631
Arizona	6	471,908	13	252,867	19	724,775	11	794,154
Arkansas	8	364,029	25	206,960	32	570,989	17	664,761
California	51	4,946,669	70	1,697,980	119	6,644,649	67	6,768,207
Colorado	10	814,391	17	155,841	27	970,232	11	1,145,752
Connecticut[1]	11	574,854	14	291,913	23	866,767	11	829,345
Delaware	2	84,316	1	60,071	2	144,387	2	169,425
D.C.	2	880,540	0	0	2	880,540	1	1,126,123
Florida[1]	31	2,811,306	15	292,034	45	3,103,340	35	3,801,850
Georgia	14	690,420	22	464,974	36	1,155,394	18	1,270,141
Hawaii	2	106,209	4	139,232	6	245,441	5	261,528
Idaho	6	115,732	6	90,776	12	206,508	8	221,738
Illinois[1]	15	1,803,311	56	800,820	70	2,604,131	27	2,781,299
Indiana	13	635,484	60	906,787	73	1,542,271	21	1,354,567
Iowa[1]	11	431,251	27	301,933	37	733,184	10	732,581
Kansas	7	277,939	39	257,958	46	535,897	17	492,029
Kentucky	6	419,638	17	240,640	23	660,278	12	667,802
Louisiana[1]	13	474,984	16	301,873	28	776,857	21	885,443
Maine	5	231,837	3	54,453	8	286,290	2	185,641
Maryland	8	430,283	6	282,202	14	712,485	7	666,128
Massachusetts[1]	7	1,215,556	37	853,692	42	2,069,248	13	1,758,652
Michigan[1]	12	1,117,883	42	1,422,960	52	2,540,843	21	2,562,401
Minnesota[1]	11	658,004	15	289,559	25	947,563	13	1,136,083
Mississippi	6	209,869	16	190,015	22	399,884	14	376,951
Missouri	9	815,123	36	436,519	45	1,251,642	19	1,329,135
Montana	5	138,460	6	49,645	11	188,105	7	190,443
Nebraska	4	190,308	15	278,659	19	468,967	7	437,472
Nevada[1]	4	188,893	5	91,010	8	279,903	4	310,475
New Hampshire	2	76,861	8	150,078	10	226,939	0	151,702
New Jersey[1]	11	1,058,524	12	601,303	22	1,659,827	17	1,892,692
New Mexico	3	151,951	16	160,960	19	312,911	13	283,228
New York[1]	25	6,118,411	48	1,381,940	71	7,500,351	37	5,736,074
North Carolina	12	841,013	42	605,938	54	1,446,951	31	1,402,757
North Dakota	5	135,884	5	50,255	10	186,139	7	182,921
Ohio[1]	11	1,336,193	76	1,413,004	87	2,749,197	33	2,867,634
Oklahoma	10	432,243	39	308,344	49	740,587	41	880,826
Oregon[1]	5	301,973	16	352,732	20	654,705	10	674,478
Pennsylvania[1]	38	1,810,551	56	1,489,596	93	3,300,147	30	3,181,734
Rhode Island	1	102,098	6	193,088	7	295,186	3	307,527
South Carolina	10	526,447	7	131,680	17	658,127	13	705,745
South Dakota	4	102,935	8	64,115	12	167,050	4	135,389
Tennessee[1]	9	563,641	20	401,229	28	964,870	16	1,073,203
Texas[1]	35	2,362,704	73	1,253,662	104	3,616,366	95	4,579,308
Utah	1	109,423	5	175,304	6	284,727	6	326,038
Vermont	4	96,337	4	33,080	8	129,417	3	100,325
Virginia[1][2]	16	1,988,368	20	515,432	34	2,503,800	15	966,140
Washington[1]	9	534,754	18	630,930	26	1,165,684	15	1,168,483
West Virginia	9	246,068	14	193,667	23	439,735	10	393,749
Wisconsin	7	327,090	29	826,939	36	1,154,029	15	1,107,560
Wyoming	6	65,724	4	29,718	10	95,442	4	72,677
Totals	**530**	**40,759,016**	**1,125**	**21,890,202**	**1,626**	**62,649,218**	**847**	**62,008,154**
Total U.S., Sept. 30, 1988	520	40,452,815	1,141	22,242,001	1,642	62,694,816	840	61,474,189
Total U.S., Sept. 30, 1987	511	39,123,807	1,166	23,702,466	1,645	62,826,273	820	60,111,863
Total U.S., Sept. 30, 1986	499	37,441,125	1,188	25,060,911	1,657	62,502,036	802	58,924,518
Total U.S., Sept. 30, 1985	482	36,361,561	1,220	26,404,671	1,676	62,766,232	798	58,825,978
Total U.S., Sept. 30, 1984	458	35,424,418	1,257	27,657,322	1,688	63,081,740	783	57,573,979
Total U.S., Sept. 30, 1983	446	33,842,142	1,284	28,802,461	1,701	62,644,603	722	56,747,436
Total U.S., Sept. 30, 1982	434	33,174,087	1,310	29,313,090	1,711	62,487,177	768	56,260,764
Total U.S., Sept. 30, 1981	408	30,552,316	1,352	30,878,429	1,730	61,430,745	755	55,180,004
Total U.S., Sept. 30, 1980	387	29,414,036	1,388	32,787,804	1,745	62,201,840	736	54,676,173

1. "All-day" newspapers are listed in morning and evening columns but only once in the total, and their circulations are divided between morning and evening figures. Adjustments have been made in state and U.S. total figures. 2. Includes nationally circulated daily. Circulation counted only in the state indicated. *Source: Editor and Publisher International Yearbook, 1990.*

See the Entertainment and Culture section for additional Media information.

WHERE TO FIND OUT MORE

Reference Books and Other Sources

This cannot be a record of all the thousands of available sources of information. Nevertheless, these selected references will enable the reader to locate additional facts about many subjects covered in the *Information Please Almanac*. The editors have chosen sources that they believe will be helpful to the general reader.

General References

Encyclopedias are a unique category, since they attempt to cover most subjects quite thoroughly. The most valuable multivolume encyclopedias are the **Encyclopaedia Britannica** and the **Encyclopedia Americana**. Useful one-volume encyclopedias are the **New Columbia Encyclopedia** and the **Random House Encyclopedia**.

Dictionaries and similar "word books" are also unique: **The American Heritage Dictionary, Second College Edition**, containing 200,000 definitions and specialized usage guidance; **The American Heritage Illustrated Encyclopedic Dictionary**, containing 180,000 entries, 275 boxed encyclopedic features, and 175 colored maps of the world; **Webster's Third New International Dictionary, Unabridged**; **Webster's II New Riverside University Dictionary**, containing 200,000 definitions plus hundreds of word history paragraphs; and the multivolume **Oxford English Dictionary**, providing definitions in historical order. **Roget's II The New Thesaurus**, containing thousands of synonyms grouped according to meaning, assists writers in choosing just the right word. The quick reference set—**The Word Book II** (over 40,000 words spelled and divided), **The Right Word II** (a concise thesaurus), and **The Written Word II** (a concise guide to writing, style, and usage)—are based on **The American Heritage Dictionary** and are intended for the busy reader needing information fast. Two excellent books of quotations are **Bartlett's Familiar Quotations** and **The Oxford Dictionary of Quotations**.

There are a number of useful atlases: the **New York Times Atlas of the World**, a number of historical atlases (Penguin Books), **Oxford Economic Atlas of the World**, **Rand McNally Cosmopolitan World Atlas: New Census Edition**, and **Atlas of the Historical Geography of the United States** (Greenwood). Many contemporary road atlases of the United States and foreign countries are also available.

A source of information on virtually all subjects is the United States Government Printing Office (GPO). For information, write: Superintendent of Documents, Washington, D.C. 20402.

For help on any subject, consult: **Subject Guide to Books in Print**, **The New York Times Index**, and the **Reader's Guide to Periodical Literature** in your library.

Specific References

AIDS Answer Book (Network Publishers)
America Votes (Congressional Quarterly, Inc.)
American Indian, Reference Encyclopedia of the (B. Klein Publications)

American Revolution, The (American Heritage)
Anatomy, Gray's (Saunders)
Antiques and Collectibles Price List, the Kovels' (Crown)
Architectural & Building Technology, Dictionary of (Elsevier)
Architecture, Encyclopedia of World (VanNostrand Reinhold)
Art, History of (Prentice-Hall)
Art, Oxford Companion to (Oxford University Press)
Art, Who's Who in American (R.R. Bowker)
Art Directory, American (R.R. Bowker)
Associations, Encyclopedia of (Gale Research Co.)
Astronomy, Peterson First Guide (Houghton Mifflin)
Authors, 1000–1900, European (H.W. Wilson)
Authors, Twentieth Century (H.W. Wilson)
Automobile Facts and Figures (Kallman)
Automotive Yearbook (Wards Communication)
Ballet & Modern Dance: A Concise History (Princeton Book Co.)
Banking and Finance, Encyclopedia of (Bankers Publishing Co.)
Baseball Encyclopedia (Macmillan)
Biographical Dictionary, Chambers (Cambridge University Press)
Biography Yearbook, Current (H.W. Wilson)
Birds, Field Guide to the, Peterson Field Guide Series (Houghton Mifflin)
Black Americans, Who's Who Among (Who's Who Among Black Americans, Inc.)
Book Review Digest, 1905– (H.W. Wilson)
Catholic Encyclopedia, New (Publishers Guild)
Chemistry, Encyclopedia of (VanNostrand Rinehold)
Chemistry, Lange's Handbook of, 13th Edition (McGraw Hill)
Christian Church, Oxford Dictionary of the (Oxford University Press)
Citizens Band: Radio Rules and Regulations (AMECO)
College Cost Book, 1986-87, The (The College Board)
Composers, Great 1300–1900 (H.W. Wilson)
Composers Since 1900 (H.W. Wilson)
Computer Science and Technology, Encyclopedia of (Dekker)
Computer Software (W.H. Freeman)
Computer Terms, Dictionary of (Barron)
Condo and Co-op Information Book, Complete (Houghton Mifflin)
Congressional Quarterly Almanac (Congressional Quarterly, Inc.)
Consumer Reports (Consumers Union)
Costume, The Dictionary of (Scribners)
Drama As You Like It (DOK Publications)
Cultural Literacy, The Dictionary of (Houghton Mifflin)
Drama, 20th Century, England, Ireland, the United States (Random House)
Ecology Information and Organizations, Guide to (H.W. Wilson)
Energy Factbook (McGraw-Hill)

Environmental Progress and Challenges: EPA's Update (Government Printing Office)
Environmental Science (Saunders College Publishing)
Europa Year Book (Gale Research Co.)
Fact Books, The Rand McNally (Rand)
Facts, Famous First (H.W. Wilson)
Facts on File (Facts on File, Inc.)
Film: A Reference Guide (Greenwood)
(Film) Guide to Movies on Video-cassette (Consumers Reports)
(Finance) Touche Ross Guide to Personal Financial Management (Prentice-Hall)
American Recipe Collection (Fell.)
Football Made Easy (Jonathan David)
Games, Book of (Jazz Press)
Gardening, Encyclopedia of (Houghton Mifflin)
Gardening, Taylor's Pocket Guides (Houghton Mifflin)
Geography, Dictionary of (Penguin Books)
Government Manual, U.S. (U.S. Office of the Federal Register, Government Printing Office)
History, Album of American (Scribner's)
History, Dictionary of American (Rowman)
History, Documents of American (Prentice-Hall)
History, Encyclopedia of Latin-American (Greenwood)
History, Encyclopedia of World (Houghton Mifflin)
Hockey, the Illustrated History: An Official Publication of the National Hockey League (Doubleday)
How the World Works, A Guide to Science's Greatest Discoveries (Quill/William Morrow)
Infomania, The Guide to Essential Electronic Services (Houghton Mifflin Company)
Islam, Dictionary of (Orient Book Distributors)
Jazz in the Seventies, Encyclopedia of (Horizon)
Jewish Concepts, Encyclopedia of (Hebrew Publishers)
Legal Word Book, The (Houghton Mifflin)
Libraries, World Guide to (K. G. Saur)
Library Directory, American (R.R. Bowker)
Literary Market Place (R. R. Bowker)
Literature, Oxford Companion to American (Oxford University Press)
Literature, Oxford Companion to Classical (Oxford University Press)
Literature, Oxford Companion to English (Oxford University Press)
(Literature) Reader's Adviser: A Layman's Guide to Literature (R.R. Bowker)
Literature, Reader's Encyclopedia of American (T.Y. Crowell)
Medical Encyclopedia, Home (Fawcett)
Medical & Health Sciences Word Book (Houghton Mifflin)
Museums (Princeton Archway)
Music and Musicians, Handbook of American (Da Capo)
Music, Concise Oxford Dictionary of (Oxford University Press)
Music, Harvard Dictionary of (Harvard University Press)
Musical Terms, Dictionary of (Gordon Press)
Mystery Writers, Twentieth Century Crime and (St. Martin's Press)
Mythology (Little, Brown and Co.)
National Park Guide (Rand McNally)
New Nations: A Student Handbook (Shoe String)
Numismatics Fireside Companion, Vol. 2 (Bowers & Merena)
Occupational Outlook Handbook (U.S. Bureau of Labor Statistics, Government Printing Office)
Operas, New Milton Cross Complete Stories of the Great (Doubleday)

Physics (Wiley)
Pocket Data Book, U.S.A. (U.S. Department of Commerce, Bureau of the Census, Government Printing Office)
Poetry, Granger's Index to (Columbia University Press)
Politics, Almanac of American (Barone & Co.)
Politics, Who's Who in American (R.R. Bowker)
Pop/Rock, Dictionary of American (Schirmer Books)
Prescription & Non-Prescription Drugs, Complete Guide to (HP Books)
Radon, A Citizen's Guide to (Government Printing Office)
Religions, The Facts on File Dictionary of (Facts on File)
Robert's Rules of Order Revised (Morrow & Co.)
Science, American Men and Women of (R.R. Bowker)
Science and Technology, Asimov's Biographical Encyclopedia of (Doubleday)
Scientific Encyclopedia, VanNostrand's (VanNostrand Reinhold)
Secondary Schools, Guide to Independent 1986-87 (Peterson's Guides)
Secretary's Handbook, The Professional (Houghton Mifflin)
Shakespeare, The Riverside (Houghton Mifflin)
Ships, Boats, & Vessels, Illustrated Encyclopedia of (Overlook Press)
Social Security Handbook (USGPO)
Stamp Collecting for Beginners (Wilshire)
Stars and Planets, Field Guide to the (Houghton Mifflin)
States, Book of the (Council of State Governments)
Statesman's Year-Book (St. Martin's)
Theater, Oxford Companion to the (Oxford University Press)
Performing Arts Information (KSU)
(Travel) The Birnbaum Guides (Houghton Mifflin)
United Nations, Demographic Yearbook (Unipub)
United Nations, Statistical Yearbook of the (Unipub)
United States, Historical Statistics of the Colonial Times to 1970 (Revisionist Press)
United States, Statistical Abstract of the (U.S. Department of Commerce, Bureau of the Census, Government Printing Office)
Vitamin Book: A No-Nonsense Consumer Guide (Bantam)
Washington Information Directory (Congressional Quarterly, Inc.)
The Way Things Work (Houghton Mifflin)
Who's Who in America (Marquis)
Wines, Dictionary of American (Morrow)
Women, Notable American (Harvard University Press)
World War I (American Heritage)
World War II (American Heritage)
Writer's Market (Writers Digest)
Zip Code and Post Office Directory, National (U.S. Postal Service, Government Printing Office)

See the full range of publications of Dun & Bradstreet and Standard & Poor's for corporate financial and stockholder information.

For detailed information on American colleges and universities, see the many publications of the American Council on Education.

Also see many other specialized Who's Who volumes not listed here for biographies of famous people in many fields.

MILITARY

Highest Ranking Officers in the Armed Forces

ARMY[1]
Generals; Colin L. Powell, Chairman of the Joint Chiefs of Staff; Carl E. Vuono, Chief of Staff; Robert RisCassi, Vice Chief of Staff; John R. Galvin, Supreme Allied Commander, Europe and Commander-in-Chief, U.S. European Command; Edwin H. Burba, Jr.; John W. Foss; James J. Lindsay; Louis C. Menetrey; Crosbie E. Saint; H. Norman Schwartzkopf; Maxwell R. Thurman; William G.T. Tuttle, Jr.

AIR FORCE
Generals: John T. Chain, Michael J. Dugan, Monroe W. Hatch, Jr., Hansford T. Johnson, Donald J. Kutyna; James P. McCarthy, Charles C. McDonald, Merrill A. McPeak, Robert D. Russ, John A. Shaud, Larry D. Welch, Ronald W. Yates.

NAVY
Admirals: Frank B. Kelso II, Chief of Naval Operations; Huntington Hardisty; Powell F. Carter, Jr.; David E. Jeremiah; Leon A. Edney; Bruce DeMars; James R. Hogg; Jonathan T. Howe.

MARINE CORPS
Generals: Alfred M. Gray, Commandant of the Marine Corps; Joseph J. Went, Assistant Commandant of the Marine Corps and Chief of Staff.
Lieutenant Generals: Ernest T. Cook, Jr., William G. Carson, Jr., William R. Etnyre, Charles H. Pitman, Carl E. Mundy, Jr., Norman H. Smith, Robert F. Milligan, John R. Dailey.

Gen. Colin Luther Powell

Four-star Army general Colin Powell became the 12th chairman of the Joint Chiefs of Staff on Oct. 3, 1989, and is the first black American to hold the nation's highest military honor. U.S. Army Photo.

1. On March 15, 1978, George Washington, the commander of the Continental Army in the American Revolution and our first President, was promoted posthumously to the newly-created rank of General of the Armies of the United States. Congress authorized this title to make it clear that Washington is the Army's senior general. *Source:* Department of Defense.

COAST GUARD
Admiral: Adm. J. William Kime, Commandant.
Vice Admirals: Vice Adm. Martin H. Daniell, Jr., Vice Commandant; Vice Adm. Howard B. Thorsen, Commander Atlantic Area; Vice Adm. A. Bruce Beren, Commander Pacific Area.

History of the Armed Services

Source: Department of Defense.

U.S. Army

On June 14, 1775, the Continental Congress "adopted" the New England Armies—a mixed force of volunteers besieging the British in Boston—appointing a committee to draft "Rules and regulations for the government of the Army" and voting to raise 10 rifle companies as a reinforcement. The next day, it appointed Washington commander-in-chief of the "Continental forces to be raised for the defense of liberty," and he took command at Boston on July 3, 1775. The Continental Army that fought the Revolution was our first national military organization, and hence the Army is the senior service. After the war, the army was radically reduced but enough survived to form a small Regular Army of about 700 men under the Constitution, a nucleus for expansion in the 1790s to successfully meet threats from the Indians and

from France. From these humble beginnings, the U.S. Army has developed, normally expanding rapidly by absorbing citizen soldiers in wartime and contracting just as rapidly after each war.

U.S. Navy

The antecedents of the U.S. Navy go back to September 1775, when Gen. Washington commissioned 7 schooners and brigantines to prey on British supply vessels bound for the Colonies or Canada. On Oct. 13, 1775, a resolve of the Continental Congress called for the purchase of 2 vessels for the purpose of intercepting enemy transports. With its passage a Naval Committee of 7 men was formed, and they rapidly obtained passage of legislation calling for procurement of additional vessels. The Continental Navy was supplemented by privateers and ships operated as state navies, but soon after the British surrender it was disestablished.

In 1794, because of dissatisfaction with the payment of tribute to the Barbary pirates, Congress authorized construction of 6 frigates. The first, *United States,* was launched May 10, 1797, but the Navy still remained under the control of the Secretary of War until April 1798, when the Navy Department was created under the Secretary of the Navy with Cabinet rank.

U.S. Air Force

Until creation of the National Military Establishment in September 1947, which united the services under one department, military aviation was a part of the U.S. Army. In the Army, aeronautical operations came under the Signal Corps from 1907 to 1918, when the Army Air Service was established. In 1926, the Army Air Corps came into being and remained until 1941, when the Army Air Forces succeeded it as the Army's air arm. On Sept. 18, 1947, the U.S. Air Force was established as an independent military service under the National Military Establishment. At that time, the name "Army Air Forces" was abolished.

U.S. Coast Guard

Our country's oldest continuous seagoing service, the U.S. Coast Guard, traces its history back to 1790, when the first Congress authorized the construction of ten vessels for the collection of revenue. Known first as the Revenue Marine, and later as the Revenue Cutter Service, the Coast Guard received its present name in 1915 under an act of Congress combining the Revenue Cutter Service with the Life-Saving Service. In 1939, the Lighthouse Service was also consolidated with this unit. The Bureau of Marine Inspection and Navigation was transferred temporarily to the Coast Guard in 1942, permanently in 1946. Through its antecedents, the Coast Guard is one of the oldest organizations under the federal government and, until the Navy Department was established in 1798, served as the only U.S. armed force afloat. In times of peace, it operates under the Department of Transportation, serving as the nation's primary agency for promoting marine safety and enforcing federal maritime laws. In times of war, or on direction of the President, it is attached to the Navy Department.

U.S. Marine Corps

Founded in 1775 and observing its official birthday on Nov. 10, the U.S. Marine Corps was developed to serve on land, on sea, and in the air.

Marines have fought in every U.S. war. From an initial two battalions in the Revolution, the Corps reached a peak strength of six divisions and five aircraft wings in World War II. Its present strength is three active divisions and aircraft wings and a Reserve division/aircraft wing team. In 1947, the National Security Act set Marine Corps strength at not less than three divisions and three aircraft wings.

Service Academies

U.S. Military Academy

Source: U.S. Military Academy.

Established in 1802 by an act of Congress, the U.S. Military Academy is located on the west bank of the Hudson River some 50 miles north of New York City. To gain admission a candidate must first secure a nomination from an authorized source. These sources are:

Congressional

Representatives
Senators
Other: Vice Presidential
    District of Columbia
    Puerto Rico
    Am. Samoa, Guam, Virgin Is.

Military-Service-Connected Nominations (Each Class)

Presidential
Enlisted members of Army
Enlisted members of Army Reserve/
    National Guard
Sons and daughters of deceased and disabled
    veterans (approximately)
Honor military, naval schools
    and ROTC
Sons and daughters of persons awarded the
    Medal of Honor

Any number of applicants can meet the requirements for a *nomination* in these categories. *Appointments* (offers of admission), however, can only be made to the number of applicants shown above. Candidates may be nominated for vacancies during the year preceding the day of admission, which occurs in early July. The best time to apply is during the junior year in high school.

Candidates must be citizens of the U.S., be unmarried, be at least 17 but not yet 22 years old on July 1 of the year admitted, have a secondary-school education or its equivalent, and be able to meet the academic, medical, and physical aptitude requirements. Academic qualification is determined by an analysis of entire scholastic record, and performance on either the American College Testing (ACT) Assessment Program Test or the College Entrance Examination Board Scholastic Aptitude Test (SAT). Entrance requirements and procedures for appointment are described in the Admissions Bulletin, available without charge from Admissions, U.S. Military Academy, West Point, N.Y. 10996-1797.

Cadets are members of the Regular Army. As such they receive full scholarships and annual salaries from which they pay for their uniforms, textbooks, and incidental expenses. Upon successful completion of the four-year course, the graduate receives the degree of Bachelor of Science and is commissioned a second lieutenant in the Regular Army with a requirement to serve as an officer for a minimum of five years.

U.S. Naval Academy

Source: U.S. Naval Academy.

The Naval School, established in 1845 at Fort Severn, Annapolis, Md., was renamed the U.S. Naval Academy in 1850. A four-year course was adopted a year later.

The Superintendent is a rear admiral. A civilian academic dean heads the academic program. A captain heads the 4,525-man Brigade of Midshipmen and military, professional, and physical training. The faculty is half military and half civilian.

Graduates are awarded the Bachelor of Science or Bachelor of Science in Engineering and are commissioned as officers in the U.S. Navy or Marine Corps.

Midshipmen are nominated for an appointment from several official sources, which are summarized below. The numbers represent the total each nominator may have at the academy at any one time. Five each from the Vice President, U.S. Senators, U.S. Representatives, the delegate from Washington, D.C., and the Resident Commissioner of Puerto Rico. Delegates from Guam and the Virgin Islands nominate two each, with one each from the Governor of Puerto Rico, the delegate from American Samoa, and the Office of the Administrator of the Panama Canal Commission.

Annual nominations are from several other sources: Presidential nominations for 100 sons and daughters of career military personnel; 85 each from the regular Navy and Marine corps, and the Navy and Marine Corps reserve; 20 from NROTC/NJROTC/MCJROTC and Honor Military and Naval schools; 65 sons and daughters of disabled veterans or POWs, 600 qualified alternates; and an unlimited number of sons and daughters of Medal of Honor recipients.

To have basic eligibility for admission, candidates must be citizens of the U.S., of good moral character, at least 17 and not more than 22 years of age on July 1 of their entering year, and unmarried.

In order to be considered for admission, a candidate must obtain a nomination from one of the sources of appointments listed above. The Admissions Board at the Naval Academy examines the candidate's school record, College Board or ACT scores, recommendations from school officials, extracurricular activities, and evidence from other sources concerning his or her character, leadership potential, academic preparation, and physical fitness. Qualification for admission is based on all of the above factors.

Tuition, board, lodging, and medical and dental care are provided. Midshipmen receive over $500 a month for books, uniforms, and personal needs.

For general information or answers to specific questions, write: Superintendent, U.S. Naval Academy, (Attention: Candidate Guidance), Annapolis, Md. 21402-5018.

U.S. Air Force Academy

Source: U.S. Air Force Academy.

The bill establishing the Air Force Academy was signed by President Eisenhower on April 1, 1954. The first class of 306 cadets was sworn in on July 11, 1955, at Lowry Air Force Base, Denver, the Academy's temporary location. The Cadet Wing moved into the Academy's permanent home north of Colorado Springs, Colorado, in 1958.

Cadets receive four years of academic, military, and physical education to prepare them for leadership as officers in the Air Force. The Academy is authorized a total of 4,400 cadets. Each new class averages 1,400. The candidates for the Academy must be at least 17 but less than 22 on July 1 of the year for which they enter the Academy, must be a United States citizen, never married, and be able to meet the mental and physical requirements. A candidate is required to take the following examinations and tests: (1) the Service Academies' Qualifying Medical Examination; (2) either the American College Testing (ACT) Assessment Program test or the College Entrance Examination Board Scholastic Aptitude Test (SAT); and (3) a Physical Aptitude Examination.

Each new cadet must deposit $1,000 at the time of admission to the Academy, otherwise cadets receive their entire education at government expense and, in addition, are paid more than $500 per month base pay. From this sum, they pay for their uniforms, textbooks, tailoring, laundry, entertainment tickets, etc. Upon completion of the four-year program, leading to a Bachelor of Science degree, a cadet who meets the qualifications is commissioned a second lieutenant in the U.S. Air Force. Nearly 70 percent enter pilot or navigator training. For details on admissions, write: Director of Cadet Admissions (RRS), HQ USAF Academy, Colorado Springs, CO 80840-5651.

U.S. Coast Guard Academy

Source: U.S. Coast Guard Academy.

The U.S. Coast Guard Academy, New London, Conn., was founded on July 31, 1876, to serve as the "School of Instruction" for the Revenue Cutter Service, predecessor to the Coast Guard.

The J.C. Dobbin, a converted schooner, housed the first Coast Guard Academy, and was succeeded in 1878 by the barque Chase, a ship built for cadet training. First winter quarters were in a sail loft at New Bedford, Mass. The school was moved in 1900 to Curtis Bay, Md., to provide a more technical education, and in 1910 was moved back to New England to Fort Trumbull, New London, Conn. In 1932 the Academy moved to its present location in New London.

The Academy today offers a four-year curriculum for the professional and academic training of cadets, which leads to a Bachelor of Science degree and a commission as ensign in the Coast Guard.

Cadets receive appointment through nationwide competition, which includes either the December administration of the College Entrance Examination Board tests, or the American College Testing (ACT) Program tests. Applications must be submitted to the Coast Guard not later than December 15 and to the College Entrance Examination Board, 30 days prior to the tests.

Women were admitted to the Coast Guard Academy for the first time during 1976 as members of the Class of 1980. Candidates must be between 17 and 22 years of age, physically sound, and unmarried. They must agree to remain unmarried until graduation and to serve at least five years on active duty. Cadets receive one-half of an Ensign's base pay per year to cover their uniform and incidental expenses and are furnished their rations and quarters. Applications may be made to Director of Admissions, U.S. Coast Guard Academy, New London, Conn. 06320.

U.S. Merchant Marine Academy

Source: U.S. Merchant Marine Academy.

The U.S. Merchant Marine Academy, situated at Kings Point, N.Y., on the north shore of Long Island, was dedicated Sept. 30, 1943. It is maintained by the Department of Transportation under direction of the Maritime Administration.

The Academy has a complement of approximately 840 men and women representing every state, D.C., the Canal Zone, Puerto Rico, Guam,

American Samoa, and the Virgin Islands. It is also authorized to admit up to 12 candidates from the Western Hemisphere and 30 other foreign students at any one time.

Candidates are nominated by Senators and members of the House of Representatives. Nominations to the Academy are governed by a state and territory quota system based on population and the results of the College Entrance Examination Board tests.

A candidate must be a citizen not less than 17 and not yet 22 years of age by July 1 of the year in which admission is sought. Fifteen high school credits, including 3 units in mathematics (from al-gebra, geometry and/or trigonometry), 1 unit in science (physics or chemistry) and 3 in English are required.

The course is four years and includes one year of practical training aboard a merchant ship. Study includes marine engineering, navigation, satellite navigation and communications, electricity, ship construction, naval science and tactics, economics, business, languages, history, etc.

Upon completion of the course of study, a graduate receives a Bachelor of Science degree, a license as a merchant marine deck or engineering officer, and a commission as an Ensign in the Naval Reserve.

U.S. Casualties in Major Wars

War	Branch of service	Numbers engaged	Battle deaths	Other deaths	Total deaths	Wounds not mortal	Total casualties[1]
Revolutionary War	Army	n.a.	4,044	n.a.	n.a.	6,004	n.a.
1775 to 1783	Navy	n.a.	342	n.a.	n.a.	114	n.a.
	Marines	n.a.	49	n.a.	n.a.	70	n.a.
	Total	**n.a.**	**4,435**	**n.a.**	**n.a.**	**6,188**	**n.a.**
War of 1812	Army	n.a.	1,950	n.a.	n.a.	4,000	n.a.
1812 to 1815	Navy	n.a.	265	n.a.	n.a.	439	n.a.
	Marines	n.a.	45	n.a.	n.a.	66	n.a.
	Total	**286,730**	**2,260**	**n.a.**	**n.a.**	**4,505**	**n.a.**
Mexican War	Army	n.a.	1,721	11,550	13,271	4,102	17,373
1846 to 1848	Navy	n.a.	1	n.a.	n.a.	3	n.a.
	Marines	n.a.	11	n.a.	n.a.	47	n.a.
	Total	**78,718**	**1,733**	**n.a.**	**n.a.**	**4,152**	**n.a.**
Civil War[2]	Army	2,128,948	138,154	221,374	359,528	280,040	639,568
1861 to 1865	Navy	84,415	2,112	2,411	4,523	1,710	6,233
	Marines		148	312	460	131	591
	Total	**2,213,363**	**140,414**	**224,097**	**364,511**	**281,881**	**646,392**
Spanish-American War	Army	280,564	369	2,061	2,430	1,594	4,024
1898	Navy	22,875	10	0	10	47	57
	Marines	3,321	6	0	6	21	27
	Total	**306,760**	**385**	**2,061**	**2,446**	**1,662**	**4,108**
World War I	Army	4,057,101	50,510	55,868	106,378	193,663	300,041
1917 to 1918	Navy	599,051	431	6,856	7,287	819	8,106
	Marines	78,839	2,461	390	2,851	9,520	12,371
	Total	**4,734,991**	**53,402**	**63,114**	**116,516**	**204,002**	**320,518**
World War II	Army[3]	11,260,000	234,874	83,400	318,274	565,861	884,135
1941 to 1946	Navy	4,183,466	36,950	25,664	62,614	37,778	100,392
	Marines	669,100	19,733	4,778	24,511	67,207	91,718
	Total	**16,112,566**	**291,557**	**113,842**	**405,399**	**670,846**	**1,076,245**
Korean War	Army	2,834,000	27,704	9,429	37,133	77,596	114,729
1950 to 1953	Navy	1,177,000	458	4,043	4,501	1,576	6,077
	Marines	424,000	4,267	1,261	5,528	23,744	29,272
	Air Force	1,285,000	1,200	5,884	7,084	368	7,452
	Total	**5,720,000**	**33,629**	**20,617**	**54,246**	**103,284**	**157,530**
War in Southeast Asia[4]	Army[5]	4,386,000	30,904	7,270	38,174	96,802	134,976
	Navy[5]	1,842,000	1,634	916	2,552	4,178	6,730
	Marines	794,000	13,079	1,750	14,829	51,392	66,221
	Air Force	1,740,000	1,765	815	2,580	931	3,511
	Total	**8,744,000**	**47,382**	**10,753**	**58,135**	**153,303**	**211,438**

1. Excludes captured or interned and missing in action who were subsequently returned to military control. 2. Union forces only. Totals should probably be somewhat larger as data or disposition of prisoners are far from complete. Final Confederate deaths, based on incomplete returns, were 133,821, to which should be added 26,000–31,000 personnel who died in Union prisons. 3. Army data include Air Force. 4. As of Nov. 11, 1986. 5. Includes a small number of Coast Guard of which 5 were battle deaths. NOTE: All data are subject to revision. For wars before World War I, information represents best data from available records. However, due to incomplete records and possible difference in usage of terminology, reporting systems, etc., figures should be considered estimates. n.a. = not available. *Source:* Department of Defense.

The National Guard

Source: Departments of the Army and the Air Force, National Guard Bureau.

The National Guard of the U.S. originated in 1636 with the Old North, South and East Regiments of the Colonial Militia in Massachusetts Bay Colony. It is the oldest military force in the country. Guardmembers have served this country at home and overseas in every major conflict in which the U.S. has been involved.

At the close of Fiscal Year '89, the Army National Guard had 456,960 people, ranking it the eleventh largest army in the world. In that same time period, the Air National Guard had 116,000 people, ranking the air "arm" of the National Guard as the fifth largest Air Force in the world.

In peacetime, the National Guard is commanded by the governors of the respective states/territories and may be called to state active duty by the governor to assist in state emergencies, disasters, and civil disturbances. During a war or national emergency, the National Guard may be called to active duty by the President or Congress. The National Guard serves as the primary source of augmentation for the Army and the Air Force.

The Army Guard operated in fiscal year 1989 with $5.5 billion, the Air Guard $3.2 billion. Although a substantial portion of National Guard funding comes from the federal government, the respective states and territories provide fiscal support in such areas as state missions, recruiting and training administration, armory construction, and funding for state-salaried employees.

The Army National Guard is made up of 3,000 units located in 2,600 communities throughout the 50 states, Puerto Rico, Guam, the Virgin Islands and the District of Columbia.

The Army National Guard provides roughly 43% of the total Army's combat capability and approximately 20 percent of its support units. The Army Guard consists of 10 combat divisions, 14 separate combat brigades, 4 divisional roundout brigades, 4 armored cavalry regiments, 3 medical brigades, 2 special forces groups, 1 infantry scout group (arctic reconnaissance) and 17 major command headquarters units.

The Army National Guard is crucial to the nation's first-line of defense. Over half of the Army's divisional capability is in the Army National Guard. Of the Army's 28 divisions, ten are solely Guard divisions with an additional 10 requiring Guard units of battalion or brigade size to bring them to their full combat potential.

The Army National Guard's force structure is broken down into: 10 divisions, 14 separate brigades, five divisional roundout brigades, three armored cavalry regiments, and two special forces groups. In addition, the Army Guard has the Army's only infantry scout group (arctic reconnaissance).

The Air National Guard has 91 flying units and 282 mission support units which, upon mobilization, would be gained by one of six major commands of the USAF. The gaining major commands are Tactical Air Command (TAC), Strategic Air Command (SAC), Military Airlift Command (MAC), Air Force Communications Command (AFCC), Pacific Air Forces (PACAF), and Alaskan Air Command (AAC).

The Air National Guard is a vital contributor to the Total Air Force mission. By the close of fiscal year '90, the Air Guard will be performing:

- 92 percent of the Total Air Force air defense mission,
- 55 percent of all Air Force tactical reconnaissance,
- 36 percent of tactical airlift,
- and will represent 24 percent of all U.S. Air Force fighters.

In the mission support areas, the Air National Guard comprises:

- 66 percent of the total Air Forces' combat communications units;
- 69 percent of its engineering and installation forces;
- and 30 percent of the U.S. Air Force civil engineering units.

The National Guard Bureau, a joint, Federal agency located in Washington D.C., formulates and administers National Guard programs to ensure the continued development and maintenance of Army and Air Guard units. Functioning as both an operating and staff agency, the National Guard Bureau serves as the channel of communications between the 54 states and U.S. territories where Guard units are located. The Chief, National Guard Bureau is nominated by the President and confirmed by the Senate. The current Chief, National Guard Bureau, is Lt. General John B. Conaway, (USAF) of Kentucky.

The National Guard offers its members a broad range of educational opportunities. These not only include skill training associated with their military occupational specialty, but in many instances cross over with skills utilized in their civilian occupations. The list of skills is not limited to those that are equipment oriented but includes management, medical, and other career fields. Some of these educational opportunities may even be pursued in civilian institutions, specifically that of the Clinical Specialist, which is compatible with a Licensed Practical Nurse or Licensed Vocational Nurse.

If openings exist, men and women between the ages of 17 and 35 may enlist for a period of four or six years followed by a 4 or 2 year inactive reserve period. The time required on inactive reserve duty status is contingent upon an enlistee's initial service obligation. (Initial service obligation plus inactive duty status must meet a time requirement of eight years.) While on inactive status, the service member is subject to recall should the need arise.

A woman between the ages of 17 and 35 who has no previous military experience may also enlist in the National Guard for a period of six years. Women in the Army National Guard will receive basic training at either Fort McClellan, Ala., Fort Dix, N.J., or Fort Jackson, S.C.; women in the Air National Guard train at Lackland Air Force Base, Tex. Advanced training takes place at appropriate training centers.

Guard members receive a full day's pay of their military rank for each unit training assembly attended. Additionally, they receive a day's pay of their military rank for each of their 15 days of annual training, plus any other days on active duty for training at military schools or special assignments. All such training counts toward retirement eligibility at age 60 with 20 or more years of qualifying service.

Veterans' Benefits

Although benefits of various kinds date back to Colonial days, veterans of World War I were the first to receive disability compensation, allotments for dependents, life insurance, and vocational rehabilitation. In the 1940's, these benefits were slowly broadened. On March 15, 1989, the Veterans Administration became the Department of Veterans Affairs.

The following benefits available to veterans require certain minimum periods of active duty during qualifying periods of service and generally are applicable only to those whose discharges are not dishonorable.

For information or assistance in applying for veterans benefits, write, call, or visit a VA Regional Office. Consult your local telephone directory under United States Government, Department of Veterans Affairs (VA) for the address and telephone number. Toll-free telephone service is available in all 50 States.

Unemployment allowances. Every effort is being made to secure employment for Vietnam veterans. Unemployment benefits are administered by the U.S. Department of Labor.

Loan Guaranty. VA will guarantee loans for a variety of purposes, such as: to buy or build a home; to purchase a manufactured home with or without a lot; and to refinance a home presently owned and occupied by the veteran. When the purpose of a refinancing loan is to lower the interest rate on an existing guaranteed loan then prior occupancy by the veteran or spouse will suffice. VA will guarantee the lender against loss up to 50% on loans of $45,000 or less, the lesser of $36,000 or 40% (never less than $22,500) on loans of more than $45,000, and the lesser of $46,000 or 25% on loans of more than $144,000. On mobile home loans, the amount of the guarantee is 40% of the loan to a maximum of $20,000. The interest rate may not exceed the maximum rate set by VA and in effect when the loan is made.

Compensation and rehabilitation benefits. These are available to those having some service-connected illness or disability.

Disability compensation. VA pays from $76 to $1,537 per month, and for specific conditions up to $4,392 per month, plus allowances for dependents, where the disability is rated 30% or more.

Vocational Rehabilitation. VA provides professional counseling, training and other assistance to help compensably service-disabled veterans who have an employment handicap to achieve maximum independence in daily living and, to the extent possible, to obtain and maintain suitable employment. Generally, a veteran may receive up to 48 months of this assistance during the 12 years from the date he or she is notified of entitlement to VA compensation. All the expenses of a veteran's rehabilitation program are paid by VA. In addition, the veteran receives a subsistence allowance which varies based on the rate of training and number of dependents. For example, a single veteran training full time would receive $333 monthly.

Vocational Training for VA Pension Recipients. Veterans who are awarded pension during the period from February 1, 1985, through January 31, 1992, may participate in a program of vocational training essentially identical to that provided in VA's vocational rehabilitation program. Certain veterans awarded pension before February 1, 1985 may also participate in this program. Participants do not receive any direct payments, such as subsistence allowance, while in training.

Medical and dental care. This includes care in VA and, in certain instances, in non-VA, or other federal hospitals. It also covers outpatient treatment at a VA field facility or, in some cases, by an approved private physician or dentist. Full domiciliary care is also provided where necessary. Nursing home care may be provided at certain VA medical facilities or in approved community nursing homes. Hospital and other medical care may also be provided for the spouse and child dependents of a veteran who is permanently and totally disabled due to a service-connected disability; or for survivors of a veteran who dies from a service-connected disability; or for survivors of a veteran who at the time of death had a total disability, permanent in nature, resulting from a service-connected disability. These latter benefits are usually provided in nonfederal facilities. Eligibility criteria for these benefits vary and certain veterans must agree to make a copayment for the care they receive from VA. Veterans and/or their dependents or survivors should always apply in advance. Contact the nearest VA medical facility.

Readjustment Counseling. VA provides readjustment counseling to veterans of the Vietnam Era in need of assistance in resolving post-war readjustment problems in the areas of employment, family, education, and personal readjustment including post-traumatic stress disorder. Services are provided at community-based Vet Centers and at VA Medical Centers in certain locations. Services include individual family and group counseling, employment and educational counseling, and assistance in obtaining referrals to various governmental and nongovernmental agencies with an interest in assisting Vietnam Era veterans. All Vietnam Era veterans are eligible for services except those with a type of discharge which may limit eligibility for VA services. Certain types of discharges are subject to special adjudication to determine eligibility. Contact the nearest Vet Center or VA facility to determine location of Vet Center.

Dependents' educational assistance. VA pays $404 a month for up to 45 months of schooling to spouses and children of veterans who died of service-connected causes or who were permanently and totally disabled from service-connected causes or died while permanently and totally disabled or who are missing in action, captured in the line of duty, or forcibly detained or interned in line of duty by a foreign power for more than 90 days. Students must usually be between 18 and 26.

Veterans readjustment education. Veterans and servicepersons who initially entered the military on or after Jan. 1, 1977, and before July 1, 1985, may receive educational assistance under a contributory plan. Individuals contribute $25 to $100 from military pay, up to a maximum of $2,700. This amount is matched by the Federal Government on a 2 for 1 basis. Participants, while on active duty, may make a lump sum contribution. Participants receive monthly payments for the number of months they contributed, or for 36 months, whichever is less. No initial enrollments are permitted after March 31, 1987.

Montgomery GI Bill. This Act provides education benefits for individuals entering the military after June 30, 1985. Servicepersons entering active duty after that date will have their basic pay reduced by $100 a month for the first 12 months of their service, unless they specifically elect not to participate in the program. Servicepersons eligible for post-Korean GI Bill benefits as of December 31, 1989, and who serve 3 years in active duty service after July 1, 1985, are also eligible for the new program, but will not have their basic pay reduced. Servicepersons who, after December 31, 1976, received commissions as officers from service academies or scholarship senior ROTC programs are not eligible for this program.

Active duty for three years (two years, if the initial obligated period of active duty is less than three years), or two years active duty plus four years in the Selected Reserve or National Guard will entitle an individual to $300 a month basic benefits. There is also a targeted, discretionary kicker of up to an additional $700 available. A supplemental benefit of up to an additional $300 with a targeted, discretionary kicker of up to $300 more is also available for certain additional active duty service.

An educational entitlement program is also available for members of the Selected Reserve. Eligibility applies to individuals who, after June 30, 1985 enlist, re-enlist, or extend an enlistment for a six-year period. Benefits may be paid to eligible members of the Selected Reserve who complete their initial period of active duty training. Full-time payments are $140 a month for 36 months.

Veterans' Benefits Improvement Act of 1989. Veterans awarded 100 percent disability compensation based upon unemployability during the period February 1, 1989, through January 31, 1992, for whom a vocational goal is feasible may participate in a rehabilitation program. Necessary training expenses, special equipment, etc., toward a definite job objective are paid for, plus a monthly allowance up to $333, with increased amounts for dependents, in addition to compensation. In addition, all veterans granted an unemployability rating before February 1, 1985, the start of the special program period, may receive special assistance in securing employment under the Vocational Rehabilitation Program. Any veteran with an unemployability rating who secures gainful employment during the special program period will be protected from reduction until such veteran has worked continuously for 12 months.

Pensions. Pension benefits are payable for wartime veterans permanently and totally disabled from non-service-connected causes. These benefits are based on need. Surviving spouses and children of wartime veterans have the same eligibility status, based on the veteran's honorable wartime service and their need.

Insurance. The VA life insurance programs have approximately 7.2 million policyholders with total coverage of about $216 billion. Detailed information on NSLI (National Service Life Insurance), USGLI (United States Government Life Insurance), and VMLI (Veterans Mortgage Life Insurance) may be obtained at any VA Office. Information regarding SGLI (Servicemen's Group Life Insurance) and VGLI (Veterans Group Life Insurance) may be obtained from the Office of Servicemen's Group Life Insurance, 213 Washington St., Newark, N.J. 07102

Burial benefits. Burial is provided in any VA national cemetery with available grave space to any deceased veteran of wartime or peacetime service, other than for training, who was discharged under conditions other than dishonorable. Also eligible for burial in a national cemetery are the veteran's spouse, widow, widower, minor children, and under certain conditions, unmarried adult children.

Headstone or marker. A government headstone or marker is furnished for any deceased veteran of wartime or peacetime service, other than for training, who was discharged under conditions other than dishonorable and is interred in a national, state veterans', or private cemetery. VA also will furnish markers to veterans' eligible dependents interred in a national or state veterans' cemetery.

America's Forgotten Korean Veterans

During a three-year duration, June 21, 1950, to July 27, 1953, the United States fought one of its toughest wars under the UN flag in Korea. During this period, 5,720,00 Americans served in the Armed Forces. Of those servicemen and women, 34,000 were killed in action, 8,000 of whom were missing in action, and later declared dead, and 20,000 others died of nonbattle causes, for a total of 54,000 deaths in service. In addition, 103,000 were wounded, and 7,000 were captured or interned. Only 4,000 of the latter were returned by the enemy. The rest are MIAs.

That the total deaths for three years fighting comes close to the ten-year total for Vietnam demonstrates the savageness of the fighting.

Just like our Vietnam veterans, they had experienced all the horrors of war and suffered from the same post-traumatic stress when the fighting was over. When the Korean veterans returned home, no special recognition was given them. There were no parades or praise. Unlike those returning from Vietnam, no one harassed them and there were no anti-war activists during the conflict. Theirs was considered a just cause and, as a result of their valor, South Korea has remained free for over the past forty years.

Unjustly, their great contribution to stopping Communist aggression in that part of the world was simply ignored by our nation. The Korean veterans had fought in what was later called the "Forgotten War."

Legislation was enacted in 1986 to authorize erection of a memorial in the Washington, D.C., area by the American Battle Monuments Commission primarily through private contributions. Over $5.4 million in private contributions have been received. Hyundai Motors America has contributed over $1 million.

Isn't it about time that we give the sacrifices of our Korean veterans the long-overdue recognition that they deserve? If you would like to help correct this injustice, write to the American Battle Monuments Commission, Massachusetts Ave., N.W., Washington, D.C. 20314. Attn: Korean War Veteran's Memorial.

The total cost for the monument will be $ 11 million. □

Casualties in World War I

Country	Total mobilized forces	Killed or died[1]	Wounded	Prisoners or missing	Total casualties
Austria-Hungary	7,800,000	1,200,000	3,620,000	2,200,000	7,020,000
Belgium	267,000	13,716	44,686	34,659	93,061
British Empire[2]	8,904,467	908,371	2,090,212	191,652	3,190,235
Bulgaria	1,200,000	87,500	152,390	27,029	266,919
France[2]	8,410,000	1,357,800	4,266,000	537,000	6,160,800
Germany	11,000,000	1,773,700	4,216,058	1,152,800	7,142,558
Greece	230,000	5,000	21,000	1,000	27,000
Italy	5,615,000	650,000	947,000	600,000	2,197,000
Japan	800,000	300	907	3	1,210
Montenegro	50,000	3,000	10,000	7,000	20,000
Portugal	100,000	7,222	13,751	12,318	33,291
Romania	750,000	335,706	120,000	80,000	535,706
Russia	12,000,000	1,700,000	4,950,000	2,500,000	9,150,000
Serbia	707,343	45,000	133,148	152,958	331,106
Turkey	2,850,000	325,000	400,000	250,000	975,000
United States	4,734,991	116,516	204,002	—	320,518

1. Includes deaths from all causes. 2. Official figures. NOTE: For additional U.S. figures, *see* the table on U.S. Casualties in Major Wars in this section.

Casualties in World War II

Country	Men in war	Battle deaths	Wounded
Australia	1,000,000	26,976	180,864
Austria	800,000	280,000	350,117
Belgium	625,000	8,460	55,513[1]
Brazil[2]	40,334	943	4,222
Bulgaria	339,760	6,671	21,878
Canada	1,086,343[7]	42,042[7]	53,145
China[3]	17,250,521	1,324,516	1,762,006
Czechoslovakia	—	6,683[4]	8,017
Denmark	—	4,339	—
Finland	500,000	79,047	50,000
France	—	201,568	400,000
Germany	20,000,000	3,250,000[4]	7,250,000
Greece	—	17,024	47,290
Hungary	—	147,435	89,313
India	2,393,891	32,121	64,354
Italy	3,100,000	149,496[4]	66,716
Japan	9,700,000	1,270,000	140,000
Netherlands	280,000	6,500	2,860
New Zealand	194,000	11,625[4]	17,000
Norway	75,000	2,000	—
Poland	—	664,000	530,000
Romania	650,000[5]	350,000[6]	—
South Africa	410,056	2,473	—
U.S.S.R.	—	6,115,000[4]	14,012,000
United Kingdom	5,896,000	357,116[4]	369,267
United States	16,112,566	291,557	670,846
Yugoslavia	3,741,000	305,000	425,000

1. Civilians only. 2. Army and Navy figures. 3. Figures cover period July 7, 1937–Sept. 2, 1945, and concern only Chinese regular troops. They do not include casualties suffered by guerrillas and local military corps. 4. Deaths from all causes. 5. Against Soviet Russia; 385,847 against Nazi Germany. 6. Against Soviet Russia; 169,822 against Nazi Germany. 7. National Defense Ctr., Canadian Forces Hq., Director of History. NOTE: The figures in this table are unofficial estimates obtained from various sources.

Military Pensions

The Military Reform Act of 1986 changed pensions for anyone entering the armed forces after August 1, 1986. Under the new law, those who retire after 20 years (and usually go on to a new career) will receive 40 percent of base pay for the three highest years. It rises to 75 percent after 30 years of service.

The bill also provided for annual cost-of-living increases.

Early retirement pensions are adjusted up to a base of 50 percent at age 62, with a 1 percent penalty added after the cost-of-living adjustment for each year of service less than 30 years.

U.S. Military Actions Other Than Declared Wars

Hawaii (1893): U.S. Marines, ordered to land by U.S. Minister John L. Stevens, aided the revolutionary Committee of Safety in overthrowing the native government. Stevens then proclaimed Hawaii a U.S. protectorate. Annexation, resisted by the Democratic administration in Washington, was not formally accomplished until 1898.

China (1900): Boxers (a group of Chinese revolutionists) occupied Peking and laid siege to foreign legations. U.S. troops joined an international expedition which relieved the city.

Panama (1903): After Colombia had rejected a proposed agreement for relinquishing sovereignty over the Panama Canal Zone, revolution broke out, aided by promoters of the Panama Canal Co. Two U.S. warships were standing by to protect American privileges. The U.S. recognized the Republic of Panama on November 6.

Dominican Republic (1904): When the Dominican Republic failed to meet debts owed to the U.S. and foreign creditors, President Theodore Roosevelt declared the U.S. intention of exercising "international police power" in the Western Hemisphere whenever necessary. The U.S. accordingly administered customs and managed debt payments of the Dominican Republic from 1905 to 1907.

Nicaragua (1911): The possibility of foreign control over Nicaragua's canal route led to U.S. intervention and agreement. The U.S. landed Marines in Nicaragua (Aug. 14, 1912) to protect American interests there. A small detachment remained until 1933.

Mexico (1914): Mexican dictator Victoriano Huerta, opposed by President Woodrow Wilson, had the support of European governments. An incident involving unarmed U.S. sailors in Tampico led to the landing of U.S. forces on Mexican soil. Veracruz was bombarded by the Navy to prevent the landing of munitions from a German vessel. At the point of war, both powers agreed to mediation by Argentina, Brazil, and Chile. Huerta abdicated, and Venustiano Carranza succeeded to the presidency.

Haiti (1915): U.S. Marines imposed a military occupation. Haiti signed a treaty making it a virtual protectorate of the U.S. until troops were withdrawn in 1934.

Mexico (1916): Raids by Pancho Villa cost American lives on both sides of the border. President Carranza consented to a punitive expedition led by Gen. John J. Pershing, but antagonism grew in Mexico. Wilson withdrew the U.S. force when war with Germany became imminent.

Dominican Republic (1916): Renewed intervention in the Dominican Republic with internal administration by U.S. naval officers lasted until 1924.

Korea (1950): In this undeclared war, which terminated with the July 27, 1953, truce at Panmunjom and the establishment of a neutral nations' supervisory commission, the U.S. and 15 member-nations of the U.N. came to the aid of the Republic of South Korea, whose 38th-parallel border was crossed by the invading Russian Communist-controlled North Koreans, who were later joined by the Chinese Communists.

Lebanon (1958 and 1983): Fearful of the newly formed U.A.R. abetting the rebels of his politically and economically torn country, President Camille Chamoun appealed to the U.S. for military assistance. U.S. troops landed in Beirut in mid-July and left before the end of the year, after internal and external quiet were restored. In September 1983, President Reagan ordered Marines to join an international peacekeeping force in Beirut. On October 23, 241 were killed in the terrorist bombing of the Marine compound. On February 7, 1984, Reagan ordered the Marine contingent withdrawn. He ended the U.S. role in Beirut on March 30 by releasing the Sixth Fleet from the international force.

Dominican Republic (1965): On April 28, when a political coup-turned-civil war endangered the lives of American nationals, President Lyndon B. Johnson rushed 400 marines into Santo Domingo, the beginning of an eventual U.S. peak-commitment of 30,000 troops, constituting the preponderant military strength of the OAS-created Inter-American Peace Force, and 6,500 troops, including 5,000 Americans, remained until after the peaceful inauguration of President Joaquín Balaguer on July 1, 1966, and the entire force left the country on September 20.

Vietnam: This longest war in U.S. history began with economic and technical assistance after 1954 Geneva accords ending the Indochinese War. By 1964 it had escalated into a major conflict.

This involvement spanning the administrations of five Presidents led to domestic discontent in the late 1960s. By April 1969, U.S. troop strength reached a peak of 543,400. Peace negotiations began in Paris in 1968 but proved fruitless. Finally, on Jan. 27, 1973, a peace accord was signed in Paris by the U.S., North and South Vietnam, and the Vietcong. Within 60 days, U.S. POWs were returned, and the U.S. withdrew all military forces from South Vietnam.

Grenada (1983): A left-wing military coup resulted in the intervention of a 1,900-man United States contingent, supported by token forces from Caribbean allies, which engaged an 800-man Cuban Force and secured the island within a few days. The American combat force was brought home two months later although a small non-combat unit was left behind to assist in peacekeeping functions.

Panama (1989): On Dec. 15, the Panamanian legislature proclaimed dictator Gen. Manuel Noriega the nation's "maximum leader," and declared a "state of war" with the United States. On Dec. 20th, following several attacks on Americans, Pres. George Bush ordered over 20,000 U.S. military forces into action in Panama to protect the lives of 35,000 American citizens he considered in "grave danger," to apprehend Gen. Noriega for trial in the U.S. on federal drug trafficking charges, to secure the safety of the Canal, and to defend democracy in Panama. Noriega surrendered to U.S. troops the first week in January 1990.

U.S. Nuclear Weapons Stockpile (June 1990)

Warhead/ Weapon	First produced	Yield (kilotons)	User	Number (warheads)	Status
Bombs					
B28*	8/58	70-1,450	AF	100	Being replaced by B61 and B83 bombs.
B43*	4/61	<1,000	AF, MC, N, NATO	350	Being replaced by new B61-3, B61-4, and B83 bombs.
B53*	8/62	9,000	AF	50	Being replaced by B83 bomb.
B57 strike bomb*	1/63	<1 to 20	AF, MC, N, NATO	775	To be replaced by B90 nuclear depth/strike bomb.
B57 depth bomb*	1/63	<1 to 20	N, NATO	825	Antisubmarine weapon, to be replaced by B90 nuclear depth/strike bomb.
B61-0, -1, -7	10/66	10 to 500	AF	900	Strategic bomb replacing B28.
B61-2, -5	3/75	10 to 345	N, MC	625	Tactical bomb replacing upgraded and redesignated B61-6, -8 for initial operation March 1991.
B61-3**, -4**	5/79	10 to 345	AF, NATO	1,500	Tactical bomb replacing B28, B43, and B57.
B83**	6/83	low to 1,200	AF	1,200	Replacing strategic B28, B43, and B53 bombs.
Artillery					
W33/8-inch*	1/57	<1 to 12	A, MC, NATO	700	A portion has been replaced by new 8-inch W79.
W48/155mm*	10/63	0.1	A, MC, NATO	900	To be replaced by non-enhanced-radiation W82 beginning 1991-92.
W79/8-inch	9/81	0.8	A	40	May have been converted to non-enhanced-radiation versions.
W79/8-inch	10/84	1.1	A, MC, NATO	300	Production completed August 1986.
Intermediate- and short-range missiles					
W50/Pershing 1a*	3/63	60, 200, 400	NATO	100	U.S. missiles were replaced by Pershing II/W85, 1983-85. Held in U.S. custody for 72 West German air force missiles, which will begin withdrawal in 1990.
W70-0, -1, -2/Lance	6/73	1 to 100	A, NATO	900	Follow-on Lance replacement cancelled.
W70-3/Lance (enhanced radiation)	5/81	<1 to 1	A	350	May have been converted to non-enhanced-radiation versions; in storage at army depots in U.S.
W85/Pershing II*	2/83	.3-80	A	100	Withdrawal under INF Treaty will be completed by May 31, 1991.
Submarine-launched ballistic missiles					
W68/Poseidon C3*	5/70	50	N	1,800	Final 11 submarines to be retired 1996-97.
W76/Trident I C4*	6/78	100	N	3,175	Approximately one half to be used on Trident II subs, 1993-2000.
W88/Trident II D5**	9/88	475	N	200	Plan to produce 200 per year throughout 1990s.
Intercontinental ballistic missiles					
W56/Minuteman II*	3/63	1,200	AF	455	To be retired.
W62/Minuteman III	3/70	170	AF	610	Partial replacement by Mk 12A/W78 and MX/W87.
W78/Minuteman III	8/79	335	AF	920	Retrofitted between Dec. 1979 and Feb. 1983.
W87-0/MX	4/86	300	AF	525	200-500 more for small ICBM if deployed in late 1990s.
Air-to-surface missiles and cruise missiles					
W69/SRAM*	10/71	170	AF	1,100	To be replaced by W89/SRAM II, 1994-96.
W80-0/Tomahawk**	12/83	5 to 150	N	325	SLCM, 758 planned; could cease at 400-450.
W80-1/ALCM	12/81	5 to 150	AF	1,660	Production ceased.
W80-1/ACM**	?/90	5 to 150	AF	10	First operational B-52H squadron planned for 1990, so some 1,300 could be produced.
W84/GLCM*	6/83	.2 to 150	AF	250	Being withdrawn under INF Treaty. Warheads could be dismantled or used in other systems.

*Weapons scheduled for partial or complete retirement in 1990s. **Weapons in production. A: Army; AF: Air Force; MC: Marine Corps; N: Navy; NATO: non-U.S. delivery systems. SRAM—short-range attack missile; SLCM—sea-launched cruise missile; ALCM—air-launched cruise missile; ACM—advanced air-launched cruise missile; GLCM—ground-launched cruise missile. In weapons nomenclature, B stands for "bomb" and W for "warhead." The number following the letter indicates the order in which it was introduced into the stockpile; for example, W69 followed W68. These are authors' estimates of stockpile breakdown of approximately 20,750 warheads. It is thought that large numbers of old warheads await dismantlement. It is estimated that the stockpile has decreased by some 1,750 warheads in the past year; this downward trend is likely to continue throughout the 1990s. The strategic percentage of the stockpile is likely to stabilize at 60-65 percent as tactical weapons are retired. Now, 61 percent are in strategic forces and 39 percent in tactical forces. By service, the stockpile is split 46 percent air force, 38 percent navy and marine corps, and 16 percent army. Five warheads are currently in production: W88/Trident II D5 SLBM, W80-1/ACM, B61-3, -4 tactical bomb, B83 bomb, and W80-0/SLCM. Five warhead types—W31/Nike-Hercules, W44/ASROC, W45/Terrier, B54/Special Atomic Demolition Munition, and W55/SUBROC—were removed from this year's table to reflect new information about retirements. Reprinted by permission of the *Bulletin of the Atomic Scientists*. Copyright © 1990 by the Educational Foundation for Nuclear Science, 6042 South Kimbark Avenue, Chicago, IL 60637, USA. A one year subscription is $30.

Estimated Soviet Nuclear Stockpile (July 1990)

Estimating the size and composition of the Soviet nuclear stockpile is extraordinarily difficult. The Soviet government's excessive secrecy and the lack of explicit public U.S. government estimates of Soviet nuclear warhead production and deployment mean that virtually no trustworthy official information is available. This table represents the most extensive public attempt to estimate the size of the Soviet stockpile. It is adapted from *Nuclear Weapons Databook Volume IV: Soviet Nuclear Forces* (New York: Ballinger, 1989), where each weapon category is treated in greater detail and the methodology is explained.

This estimate shows that the Soviet stockpile is almost 45 percent larger than the U.S. stockpile and is composed of a greater variety of nuclear weapons, including 17 ballistic missile types, 12 kinds of airplanes and helicopters, seven types of air-to-surface and seven types of surface-to-air missiles (including two kinds of ASW weapons (including two types of nuclear torpedoes), three calibers of artillery, atomic land mines, and possibly sea mines.

Among the five branches of the armed forces, the navy has the most types of nuclear weapons, followed by the strategic rocket forces and the air forces. The strategic rocket forces have the most warheads, with

about 8,000. Fifty-three percent of Soviet warheads are used for strategic forces (offense and defense) and 47 percent for nonstrategic forces. Unlike the U.S. stockpile, it is not known how many different warhead types or modifications exist for these systems. It is conceivable that several kinds of missiles all use the same warhead type. It is estimated that there are three different types of gravity bombs and two types of nuclear depth bombs. The Soviet nuclear arsenal seems to have peaked in 1988 at 33,000 and is undergoing a gradual decrease.

Developments and changes since last year include: continuing retirement of SS-11, SS-17, and SS-19 ICBMs coupled with deployments of SS-24 and SS-25 ICBMs, the modest growth of SLCMs, withdrawal from operation of all Bear A bombers, SA-1 SAMs, naval nuclear artillery, and nuclear capable MiG-21 Fishbed aircraft, withdrawal and destruction of many SS-20s and the last SS-4s. The table reflects a reassessment of the SA-N-6 SAM as a non-nuclear missile. As occurred in the U.S. military 10-20 years ago, certain military missions that currently have nuclear weapons will be phased out either unilaterally or by treaty. For example, SAM forces are being denuclearized.

Category/type	Weapon system	Launchers	Warheads
Strategic offense			
ICBMs	SS-11, SS-13, SS-17, SS-18, SS-19, SS-24, SS-25	1,353	7,300
SLBMs	SS-N-6, SS-N-8, SS-N-17, SS-N-18, SS-N-20, SS-N-23	914	4,000
Bombers	Blackjack, Bear B/C/G/H (AS-3 and AS-4 ASMs, AS-15 ALCMs, AS-16 SRAMs, bombs)	160	1,400
Subtotal			**12,700**
Strategic defense			
ABMs	Improved Galosh, Gazelle	100	110
SAMs	SA-2, SA-5, SA-10	6,050	3,000
Subtotal			**3,100**
Land-based nonstrategic			
Missiles	SS-20, Scud B, SS-21, FROG 3/5/7	1,470	3,600
Bombers and fighters	Backfire, Blinder, Badger, Fencer, Flogger, Fitter, (AS-2, AS-4, AS-5, AS-6, ASMs, bombs)	2,595	4,500
Artillery	152mm, 203mm, 240mm	7,000	2,000
Atomic demolitions		NA	NA
Subtotal			**10,000**
Naval nonstrategic			
Attack aircraft	Backfire, Blinder, Badger, Fencer, Flogger (AS-2, AS-4, AS-5, AS-6 ASMs, bombs)	395	1,000
SLCMs	SS-N-3, SS-N-7, SS-N-9, SS-N-12, SS-N-19, SS-N-21, SS-N-22	1,064	578
ASW aircraft	Mail, May, Bear F, Hormone A, Helix A	375	400
ASW weapons	SS-N-15, SS-N-16, FRAS-1, Type 65 and ET-80 torpedoes	534*	1,000
Anti-air weapons	SA-N-1, SA-N-3	51*	200
Coastal missiles	SSC-1b	100	100
Mines		NA	NA
Subtotal			**3,300**
Total			**30,000**

*Total number of ships and submarines, not launchers. ABM: anti-ballistic missile; ALCM: air-launched cruise missile; ASM: air-to-surface missile; ASW: Anti-submarine warfare; ICBM: intercontinental ballistic missile; SAM: surface-to-air missile; SLBM: submarine-launched ballistic missile; SLCM: sea-launched cruise missile; NA: not available. Reprinted by permission of the Bulletin of the Atomic Scientists. Copyright © 1990 by the Educational Foundation for Nuclear Science, 6042 South Kimbark Avenue, Chicago, IL 60637, USA. A one year subscription is $30.

The Battle of Tokyo

The change in the American bombing campaign against Tokyo to incendiary bombs instead of explosive bombs produced horrifyingly effective results. On March 9, 1945, 279 American B 29s—each carrying 6–8 tons of incendiaries—devastated Tokyo. A quarter of the total area of the city, nearly 16 square miles, was burnt out, and over 267,000 buildings were destroyed. Civilian casualties totaled approximately 185,000, while American attackers lost only 14 aircraft. In the next ten days

the United States dropped nearly 10,000 tons of incendiaries, devastating not only Tokyo but the cities of Osaka, Kobe, and Nagoya as well.

For three months early in 1945 the use of explosive bombs had had disappointing resu'ts, but civilian morale declined badly after the Tokyo fire-raid. Over 8 1/2 million people fled into the countryside, causing war production to practically cease. More than 600 major war factories were destroyed by bombing.

The Medal of Honor

Often called the Congressional Medal of Honor, it is the Nation's highest military award for "uncommon valor" by men and women in the armed forces. It is given for actions that are above and beyond the call of duty in combat against an armed enemy. The medal was first awarded by the Army on March 25, 1863, and then by the Navy on April 3, 1863. President Reagan awarded the last Medal of Honor to retired Master Sargeant Roy Benavidez, a Vietnam veteran, on February 24, 1981.

Recipients of the medal receive $200 per month for life, a right to burial at Arlington National Cemetary, admission for them or their children to a service academy if they qualify and quotas permit, and free travel on government aircraft to almost anywhere in the world, on a space-available basis.

In 1989, medals were restored to William F. Cody (Buffalo Bill) and four other scouts who had them revoked in 1917 due to a new ruling.

Medal of Honor Recipients[1]

	Total	Army	Navy	Marines	Air Force	Coast Guard
Civil War	1,520	1,196	307	17	—	—
Indian Wars (1861–98)	428	428				—
Korean Expedition (1871)	15	—	9	6	—	—
Spanish-American War	109	30	64	15	—	—
Philippines/Samoa (1899–1913)	91	70	12	9	—	—
Boxer Rebellion (1900)	59	4	22	33	—	—
Dominican Republic (1904)	3	—	—	3	—	—
Nicaragua (1911)	2	—	—	2	—	—
Mexico (Veracruz) (1914)	55	—	46	9	—	—
Haiti (1915)	6	—	—	6	—	—
Misc. (1865–1920)	166	1	161	4	—	—
World War I	123	95	21	7	—	—
Haitian Action (1919–20)	2	—	—	2	—	—
Misc. (1920–1940)	18	2	15	1	—	—
World War II	433	294	57	81	—	1
Korean War	131	78	7	42	4	—
Vietnam War	238	155	14	57	12	—
Total	3,399*	2,353	735	294	16	1

1. Total number of actual medals awarded is 3,417. This includes nine awarded to Unknown Soldiers, and some soldiers received more than one medal. *Source:* The Congressional Medal of Honor Society, New York, N.Y.

Average Military Strength[1]

Year	Army	Air Force	Navy	Marine Corps	Total
1942	1,992	[2]	416	89	2,498
1943	5,224	[2]	1,206	232	6,662
1944	7,507	[2]	2,386	398	10,290
1945	8,131	[2]	3,205	473	11,809
1950	632	415	412	80	1,539
1953	1,536	971	809	237	3,554
1954	1,477	939	767	242	3,425
1955	1,311	958	692	217	3,178
1960	871	828	617	173	2,489
1965	966	844	669	190	2,668
1970	1,432	834	732	295	3,293
1975	779	628	545	193	2,145
1980	762	561	525	185	2,033
1985	782	601	566	198	2,148
1988	769	591	581	197	2,139
1989	766	575	584	196	2,121

1. In thousands. Data represent averages of month-end strengths. 2. Air Force data prior to June 30, 1948 included with Army data. NOTE: Detail may not add to totals due to rounding. *Source:* Department of Defense.

The Birth of the Ballistic Missile

The forerunner of the modern ballistic missile was the World War II German liquid-fuel rocket bomb called the V-2 (V for "vengeance") first used in 1944. It carried a one-ton warhead of high explosives and could be fired from a mobile launcher. Its range was about 220 miles (354.04 km).

During the war, over 4,000 V-2s were launched against cities in Britain, France, and Belgium. At that time, there was no known defense against them. The United States and the Soviet Union used captured V-2s in post-war research and development of defense programs and space exploration.

SPACE

Why Mars Should Be Earth's Next Goal

By Oleg Borisov

The number one priority of the Soviet space program for the next two decades is sending a manned expedition to Mars, and the odds are improving that we could find evidence of past life upon our arrival. *Phobos 2* detected an unexpected diversity of surface materials—additional signs that Mars still has some surprises in store. We are calling for an international effort for this mission in the hope that the United States and other nations will join us. A joint mission would promote the idea of living in peace and would introduce humanism, respect, and mutual understanding into international relations. The new data from *Phobos 2* could be seen as an important boost toward a joint mission.

The Soviet Institute of Space Research of the Academy of Sciences gives four reasons why Mars is so attractive to scientists:

(1) Mars is similar to Earth. The Martian day, at 24 hours and 37 minutes, is only slightly longer than ours; the planet has an axis tilt that creates seasonal variations similar to those here; Mars, like Earth, has a wide range of terrains; and the temperatures on Mars, although very low at night, are comparable to Earth's during the day. By studying Mars and using methods of comparative planetology, we will gain insight into the history and structure of our own planet.

(2) There is evidence that Mars has experienced an interesting evolution of its climate and surface. Mars may once have had open bodies of water and a dense atmosphere. If so, we must learn why they disappeared.

(3) Mars is a prime candidate for extraterrestrial life, past, present, or future. Even if we find only the simplest form of life, it would revolutionize our world outlook and understanding of the origin of life on Earth.

(4) Mars, the only potentially habitable planet in our solar system besides Earth, is the first planet on which we can land and proclaim humankind a space civilization.

The Soviet program will include three phases. The first, planned for 1994-1996 and based on use of the Energia booster, will study the Martian surface and atmosphere using unmanned rovers, drilling units, balloons, and an orbiter that will survey the planet's surface from an altitude of 125 to 190 miles.

All the groundwork for the future manned mission will be done during this phase, including choosing sites of maximum interest to future crews. Scientists are interested in the history and geological structure of Mars. Craters, valleys, and volcanos will be examined closely for evidence that water was once plentiful on the Martian surface. Mariner 9 established that liquid water can exist on the Martian surface for only short periods—yet its cameras also revealed clear evidence of water erosion.

The unmanned rovers, powered by radioisotopes that will give them a lifespan of one to three years and a range of 300 miles or more, will be equipped with mini-labs that can analyze soil samples. The balloons, inspired by those successfully used in the Venusian atmosphere, will carry cameras that will be able to discern, from an altitude of 650 feet, details of the surface as small as a tennis ball. The balloon probes may last about two weeks in the thin Martian atmosphere and send back hundreds of millions of bits of information. For the first time man will have a bird's-eye view of the most remote parts of Mars.

The next phase, scheduled for 2000-2005, will be a rehearsal for the manned mission. The wide range of research tasks conducted during this phase will include more detailed studies by rovers. One lander will return to Earth with samples of Martian soil and polar ice for detailed physical, chemical, and biological analysis. Study of these samples may reveal whether water is still trapped in the subsurface permafrost. Soil taken from anywhere on the Martian surface could also answer questions about the conditions that have persisted on Mars for billions of years and left it barren while life here on Earth flourished.

If the first two phases of the program are successful, the first manned mission to Mars will take place in 2005-2010. It will require a very large spacecraft because, in addition to carrying a million or more pounds of fuel, the ship must accommodate humans for as long as three years. Just to exist in space for one day, each crew member will need several pounds of oxygen, four pounds of water, and three pounds of food. Because of these weight requirements, it may be necessary to use nuclear electric engines. Although these engines are low in thrust, they are more fuel-efficient than liquid rocket engines, and most important, they can operate for hundreds of days on end.

Once the explorers arrive on Mars, they will encounter the Martian atmosphere, which is unfit for breathing and by Earthly standards very thin. It is made up almost entirely of carbon dioxide, with traces of water vapor, and the atmospheric pressure near the surface is only 0.5 percent of Earth's. These conditions, as well as differences in temperature and gravity and the lack of water, will confine explorers of the Red Planet to spacesuits, special relaxation boxes, and well-sealed self-propelled vehicles.

The most exciting question for Mars explorers is whether the soil will reveal organic matter or traces of extinct life. Even though the U.S. *Viking* landers in 1976 turned up no positive signs of life, Lev Mukhin, a leading researcher from the Institute of Space Research, believes that these results were inconclusive, since the probes were of low

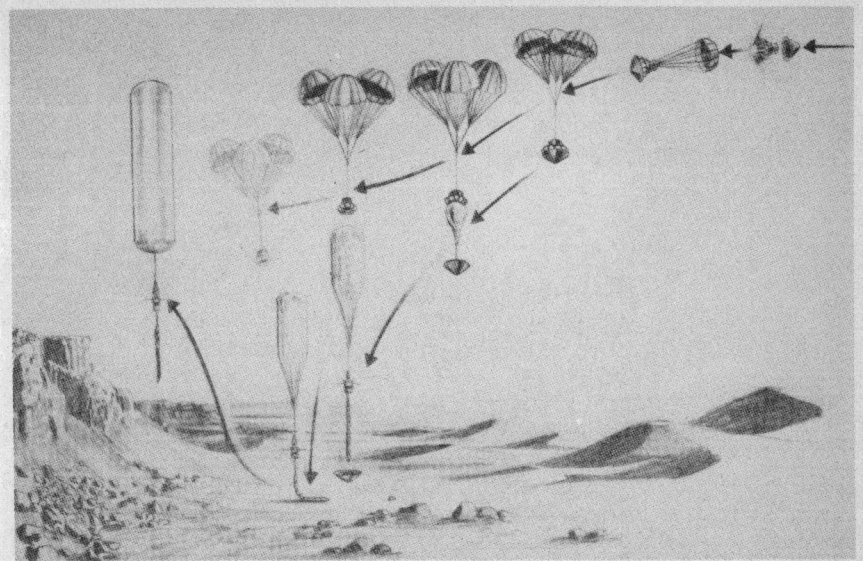

THE MARS BALLOON. The current Mars 94 program calls for two launches in October 1994 for arrival in September 1995. During the mission, the spacecraft will drop one or two balloons which will carry several scientific packages for analyzing Martian meteorological and surface conditions over a wide range of the planet.

The balloon segment of the mission is a joint U.S.S.R., France, and United States undertaking, which has greatly benefitted from the successful balloon deployed at Venus in 1985 under the Soviet VEGA program.

The American effort is being led by the Planetary Society and Titan Systems, Inc. Several balloon designs have been under evaluation in all three countries to maximize survivability of the balloon's expected ten-day lifetime without sacrificing scientific

opportunities in the face of uncertainities about the Martian atmosphere.

The selected balloon will carry both a suspended payload (gondola) and a distributed payload (SNAKE) which will come into contact with the planet's surface as the balloon descends during the Martian night. The sun's light will heat the gasses within the lightweight balloon during the daytime, causing the balloon to rise and drift with the winds above the planet's surface. At night, the gasses will cool, causing the balloon to descend and rest on the Martian soil.

The total mass of the balloon system is targeted for 60 to 65 kilograms (130 to 134 pounds). The gondola will weigh about 15 kilograms (33 pounds).

Illustration and major data: The Soviet Year in Space, 1989, Teledyne Brown Engineering.

sensitivity and examined only two small areas of the planet. New evidence collected by the Soviet spacecraft *Phobos 2* in 1989 shows that the composition of the Martian surface is varied. This contradicts the finding of the two *Viking* craft, which determined that the soil at two sites was very similar.

There is reason to be optimistic about the possibility of life on Mars, even if life had existed only in the remote past. If the early climates of Mars and Earth were similar shortly after the planets' formation, sedimentary rocks in ancient Martian riverbeds would be an ideal place to hunt for fossils of organisms. There is even a chance that a living plant cell or a bacterium could be found in a specimen. Scientists would have mixed feelings of delight and concern over such a discovery because it would raise the serious issue of pathogenicity. The immune system of Earthlings may prove powerless against attacks by microorganisms of extraterrestrial origin.

If a growing number of U.S. and Soviet scientists have their way, astronauts and cosmonauts will explore Mars together by the year 2010. Teams of engineers and scientists from both countries are plan-

ning unmanned missions for the 1990s, and there is a hope that politics will allow the two nations to cooperate in a joint mission that would help draw the Soviet Union and the United States closer. The consensus among many space scientists and leaders in both countries is that it is not only desirable to cooperate, it is necessary. The heavy financial burden of a manned expedition to Mars could be shared by the two countries instead of falling on one.

It would be easier to reach Mars than it was to reach the moon because no new technologies would have to be developed. We would only have to utilize those currently available. Traveling to Mars would be no more expensive than a major strategic weapons system. If shared by two or more countries the cost to each would be even less, and the possible benefits incalculable. ☐

Oleg Borisov is a Scientific Analyst with the Novosti Press Agency. This article was first published in *Air & Space*, March 1990, and is reprinted with the permission of the author.

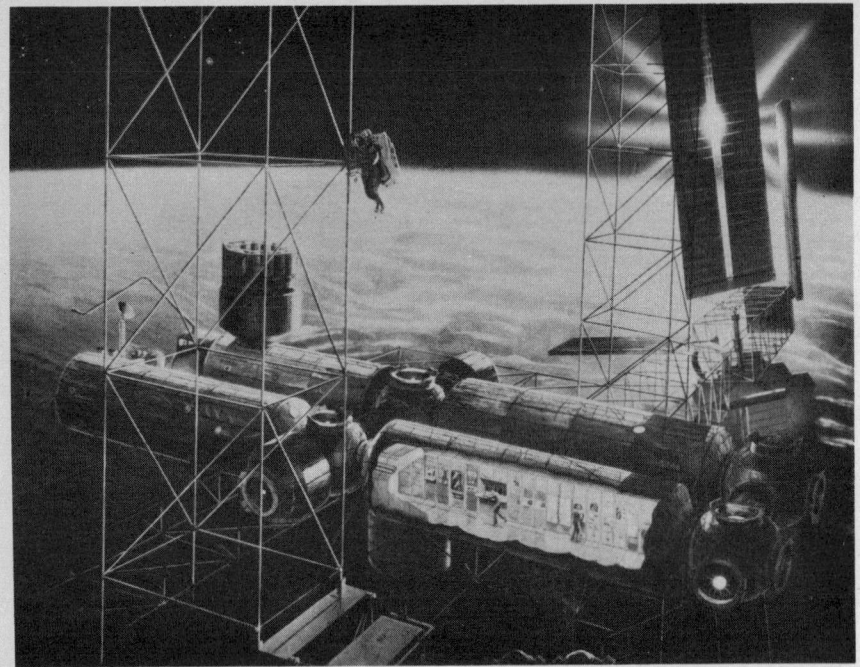

THE SPACE STATION *FREEDOM*. An artist's depiction of the United States' first permanently manned space station, *Freedom,* being assembled. It would be over 500 ft long (153 m) and would have four modules for living and working. Additional modules could be added when required and it eventually could be possible to house as many as 30 astronauts.

Freedom would be assembled in orbit almost 300 miles above the earth from materials brought aloft by space shuttles making 20 trips in two years' time. NASA would like funding to begin its construction in late 1995.

(*See* "Skylab/Space Station Differences," *Information Please Almanac,* 1989, for additional information.)

GALILEO
Long-Term Study of Jupiter

Galileo is a project to orbit Jupiter and send an instrumented probe into the giant planet's atmosphere. The Galileo mission will allow scientists to study—at close range and for almost two years—the largest planet in the solar system, its satellites and massive energy field. The project is named after the Italian astronomer Galileo Galilei, who on Jan. 7, 1610, discovered three of Jupiter's moons and later on January 13th discovered a fourth satellite. These four "Galilean" satellites—Io, Europa, Ganymede, and Callisto, are major targets for the mission. The spacecraft will study the chemical composition and physical state of Jupiter's atmosphere and the four moons, as well as the structure and dynamics of the Jovian magnetosphere.

During the 22-month life of the mission, the orbiter will complete 10 orbits of Jupiter while making a close flyby of at least one Galilean satellite on each orbit.

The spacecraft was carried aloft by the space shuttle *Atlantis* and launched toward Jupiter on Oct. 18, 1989. After a six-year journey, it will reach the planet in 1995. A comprehensive article about the Galileo mission was published in the 1988 edition of *Information Please Almanac.*

ULYSSES
International Solar Polar Mission

Ulysses is an international project to study the poles of the Sun and interstellar space above and below the poles. *Ulysses,* formerly called the International Solar Polar Mission, will launch a single 814-lb (370-kg) spacecraft into an orbit at right angles to the solar system's ecliptic plane. (The ecliptic is the plane in which the Earth and most of the planets orbit the Sun). This special orbit will allow the spacecraft to examine for the first time the regions of the Sun's north and south poles. Besides examining the Sun's energy fields, instruments on *Ulysses* will study other phenomena from the Milky Way and beyond.

While scientists have studied the Sun for centuries, they know very little about matter reaching the solar system from other nearby stars. This is because particles reaching the Sun's magnetic field from beyond the solar system are greatly changed by the Sun's magnetic field and by collision with particles flowing outward from the Sun. No spacecraft has ever left the solar system to make actual measurements of the interstellar medium.

It is hoped that the *Ulysses* spacecraft will be launched from the space shuttle *Discovery* in October 1990.

Mars Observer Scheduled For 1992

A long-awaited NASA mission to study the surface, atmosphere, interior, and magnetic field of Mars for a full Martian Year is being readied for a 1992 launch at the Jet Propulsion Laboratory, Pasadena, California. Called the *Mars Observer*, it will be the first in a planned series of Planetary Observer missions that will use a new class of spacecraft derived from Earth-orbiter designs. These missions will be of modest cost and are intended to explore objects of the inner solar system such as Venus, the Moon, Mars, and near-Earth asteroids and comets.

The *Mars Observer* will continue NASA's exploration of the red planet, which began with the *Mariner 4* mission in 1964-65, and continued with *Mariners 6* and *7* in 1969 and *Mariner 9* in 1971-72. This program reached its peak with the *Viking* orbiters and landers of 1975-82.

The new global studies of the planet's geology and atmosphere are expected to give scientists more information about the planet's evolution. One subject of particular interest is the role that water once played on Mars. While there is no liquid water on the surface of Mars now, the *Mariner* and *Viking* missions found ample evidence that liquid flowed there long ago.

In September 1992, an expendable commercial *Titan III* launch vehicle will carry *Mars Observer* and its booster into Earth orbit. From there, the Transfer Orbit Stage will boost the spacecraft into an interplanetary orbit leading to Mars.

After an 11-month cruise, *Mars Observer* will arrive at the red planet and be placed in a special orbit that will circle above Mars about every two hours. This mapping orbit will be sun-synchronized, so that sunlight will be at the same angle (early afternoon directly below the spacecraft) on the day side throughout the long observation period.

The mission will last for one Martian year (almost 687 Earth days) to allow the spacecraft to examine the planet through its four seasons.

The scientific objectives of the Mars mission are to: determine the global elemental and mineralogical character of the surface material; define the global topography and gravitational field; establish the nature of the magnetic field; determine the time and space distribution, abundance, sources and sinks of volatile material and dust over a seasonal cycle; and to explore the structure and aspects of the circulation of the atmosphere.

In addition, *Mars Observer* will participate in an ambitious international Mars investigation through an agreement with France and the Soviet Union. The participation is the Mars Balloon Relay Experiment.

The Soviet Mars '94 mission will deploy balloon-borne instrument packages in the atmosphere of Mars. (*See* The Mars Balloon, p. 317.)

THE CRAF/CASSINI MISSION

These projects combine two missions that will both use NASA's new *Mariner Mark II* spacecraft and greatly reduce the total cost. NASA plans to launch CRAF in 1995 and follow it with the Cassini mission in 1996.

Comet Rendezvous Asteroid Flyby (CRAF)

This mission will send a spacecraft to encounter an asteroid, and then to rendezvous with a comet and fly alongside it for nearly three years. CRAF will launch a heavily instrumented penetrator/lander into the comet's nucleus to measure temperatures and chemical composition. Other instruments will collect data on the comet's nucleus, its coma, and its dust and ion cloud and tail.

CRAF will be launched aboard a *Titan IV-Centaur* expendable launch vehicle in August 1995. The spacecraft would encounter an asteroid named 449 Hamburga in January 1998 en route to the comet. CRAF would take photographs and other scientific measurements during the encounter period. The asteroid is about 55 miles (88 kilometers) in diameter and is a carbonaceous type.

The spacecraft will subsequently arrive at a rendezvous point with Comet Kopff in August 2000. CRAF will fire its penetrator/lander at the comet in August 2001, and will continue to fly beside it for two and two-thirds years. The mission will end on March 31, 2003. It will mark the first time a spacecraft will have flown in formation with a comet.

Comet Kopff is named for August Adalbert Kopff, who discovered it on August 22, 1906. The comet travels between a region from just inside the orbit of Jupiter inward to perihelion near the orbit of Mars, 140 million miles (220 million kilometers) from the Sun. The CRAF spacecraft will fly within six miles (10 kilometers) of the comet's nucleus.

All of the phenomena associated with comets will be the target of CRAF's instruments. □

The Cassini Mission

The ringed planet Saturn, its major moon Titan, and complex system of at least 16 other satellites[1] will be the destination for NASA's and the European Space Agency's Cassini Mission. Cassini is named for the Italian-French astronomer, Gian Domenico Cassini, who discovered four of Saturn's major moons and a dark, narrow gap ("Cassini's Division") splitting the planet's rings.

Early during the spacecraft's four-year tour orbiting Saturn, it will launch a parachuted probe decending through Titan's dense atmosphere to the surface of the satellite which has unique organic-like chemistry that could provide clues to the origin of life on Earth.

Current plans call for Cassini to be launched in April 1996. NASA would provide the expendable Titan-Centaur launch vehicle and the Cassini orbiter spacecraft and the European Space Agency (ESA) would contribute the Titan probe. NASA and ESA member countries would provide science instruments for both the orbiter and probe.

In order to reach Saturn, Cassini will first execute flybys of the Earth and Jupiter to gain "gravity assist" boosts in velocity to send it on its way. The first flyby of Earth will take place 26 months after launch, followed by the Jupiter flyby some 19 months later. During the first leg of its trip, before its first Earth flyby, Cassini will navigate through part of the asteroid belt and could perform an encounter with the asteroid Maja in March 1997. Maja is a carbonaceous, or "C" type asteroid about 50 miles (78 kilometers) in diameter. Two small asteroids are being considered as possible additional targets, but only one of them could be visited.

The spacecraft's final encounter before proceeding to Saturn will be with Jupiter, which it will pass at a distance of about 2.2 million miles (3.6 million kilometers). Its flight path will take it for 130 days down through a region that no spacecraft has explored more than briefly—the giant planet's magnetotail. Cassini will fly down the magnetotail[2] of Jupiter, performing studies complementing NASA's CRAF mission and the Galileo mission to Jupiter.

Upon reaching Saturn in October 2002, the spacecraft will begin the first of some three dozen highly elliptical orbits during the remainder of its mission. Eighty-five days later, it will release its probe to Titan. Eleven days later, the probe will enter Titan's dense atmosphere and descend to the surface by parachute.

Because of the dense atmosphere shrouding the moon Titan, little is known of its surface. At Titan, scientists hope to gain a better understanding of abundances of elements and compounds in its atmosphere, winds, and temperatures, and its surface state and composition.

After relaying to Earth data from the Titan probe's experiments, Cassini will continue with orbits of Saturn and flybys of most of the planet's 16 or more moons. In addition to 36 close encounters with Titan, the spacecraft's orbits will allow it to study Saturn's polar regions after examining the planet's equatorial zone. □

---

1. The International Astronomical Union has officially recognized 17 Saturnian moons. Photographs from *Voyager* flybys suggest that others may exist. 2. A tube of Jupiter's energy field, which trails away from the sun for several million miles.

MAGELLAN
Venus Radar Mapper

On May 4, 1989, NASA'S unmanned spacecraft *Magellan* was launched from the shuttle *Discovery*. It was the first time a space probe was launched from a shuttle. *Magellan* is a spacecraft equipped with an imaging radar system designed to "see" through Venus' thick cloud-like cover and obtain detailed photographlike images of 90% of the planet's surface. Upon reaching the planet on August 10, 1990, the spacecraft will be placed in an elliptical orbit, circling Venus once every 3.1 hours and the radar will operate once each orbit for approximately 40 minutes, from an altitude of 190 to 1060 miles (300 to 1,700 kilometers). The mapping will continue for 243 days. □

Is There Ice on the Moon?

Unlike the rest of the Moon's surface, the temperature of its polar regions remains permanently about −390° to −315° F and some of its craters remain perpetually in the dark. Some scientists have speculated that ice may have accumulated in the dark craters over long eons of time.

NASA would like to launch a polar lunar orbiter known as the *Lunar Observer* in the mid-1990s to study the unknown regions of the Moon's poles and search for water, ice, and other useful volatiles that may exist on the Moon.

In December 1992, the U.S. *Galileo* spacecraft, during its first Earth flyby, will travel over the Moon's North Pole, presenting an opportunity to find signs of ice in the dark craters.

U.S. Unmanned Planetary and Lunar Programs

Lunar Orbiter. Series of spacecraft designed to orbit the Moon, taking pictures and obtaining data in support of the subsequent manned Apollo landings. The U.S. launched five *Lunar Orbiters* between Aug. 10, 1966 and Aug. 2, 1967.

Mariner. Designation for a series of spacecraft designed to fly past or orbit the planets, particularly Mercury, Venus, and Mars. *Mariners* provided the early information on Venus and Mars. *Mariner 9*, orbiting Mars in 1971, returned the most startling photographs of that planet to date, and helped pave the way for a *Viking* landing in 1976. *Mariner 10* explored Venus and Mercury in 1973 and was the first probe to use a planet's gravity to whip it toward another.

Pioneer. Designation for the United States' first series of sophisticated interplanetary spacecraft. *Pioneers 10* and *11* reached Jupiter in 1973 and 1974 and continued on to explore Saturn and the other outer planets. *Pioneer 11*, renamed *Pioneer Saturn*, examined the Saturn system in September 1979. Significant discoveries were the finding of a small new moon and a narrow new ring. In 1986, *Pioneer 10* was the first man-made object to escape the solar system. *Pioneer Venus 1* and *2* reached Venus in 1978 and provided detailed information about that planet's surface and atmosphere.

Ranger. NASA's earliest moon exploration program. Spacecraft were designed for a crash landing on the Moon, taking pictures and returning scientific data up to the moment of impact. Provided the first closeup views of the lunar surface. The *Rangers* provided more than 17,000 closeup pictures, giving us more information about the Moon in a few years than in all the time that had gone before.

Surveyor. Series of unmanned spacecraft designed to land gently on th : Moon and provide information on the surface in preparation for the manned lunar landings. Their legs were instrumented to return data on the surface hardness of the Moon. *Surveyor* dispelled the fear that Apollo spacecraft might sink several feet or more into the lunar dust.

Viking. Designation for two spacecraft designed to conduct detailed scientific examination of the planet Mars, including a search for life. *Viking 1* landed on July 20, 1976; *Viking 2*, Sept. 3, 1976. More was learned about the Red Planet in a few short months than in all the time that had gone before. But the question of life on Mars remains unresolved.

Voyager. Designation for two spacecraft designed to explore Jupiter and the other outer planets. *Voyager 1* and *Voyager 2* passed Jupiter in 1979 and sent back startling color TV images of that planet and its moons. They took a total of about 33,000 pictures. *Voyager 1* passed Saturn November 1980. *Voyager 2* passed Saturn August 1981 and Uranus in January 1986.

It encountered Neptune on August 29, 1989 and made many startling discoveries. Found four rings around the planet, six new moons, a Great Giant Spot, and evidence of volcanic-like activity on its largest moon, Triton. The spacecraft sent back over 9,000 pictures of the planet and its system.

On February 13, 1990, at a distance of 3.7 billion miles, *Voyager 1* took its final pictures—the sun and six of its planets as seen from deep space. NASA released the extraordinary images to the public on June 6, 1990. Only Mercury, Mars, and Pluto were not seen.

Notable Unmanned Lunar and Interplanetary Probes

Spacecraft	Launch date	Destination	Remarks
Pioneer 3 (U.S.)	Dec. 6, 1958	Moon	Max. alt.: 66,654 mi. Discovered outer Van Allen layer.
Luna 2 (U.S.S.R.)	Sept. 12, 1959	Moon	Impacted on Sept. 14. First space vehicle to reach moon.
Luna 3 (U.S.S.R.)	Oct. 4, 1959	Moon	Flew around Moon and transmitted first pictures of lunar far side, Oct. 7.
Mariner 2 (U.S.)	Aug. 27, 1962	Venus	Venus probe. Successful mid-course correction. Passed 21,648 mi. from Venus Dec. 14, 1962. Reported 800°F. surface temp. Contact lost Jan. 3, 1963 at 54 million mi.
Mariner 4 (U.S.)	Nov. 28, 1964	Mars	Transmitted first close-up pictures on June 14, 1965, from altitude of 6,000 mi.
Ranger 7 (U.S.)	July 28, 1964	Moon	Impacted near Crater Guericke 68.5 h after launch. Sent 4,316 pictures during last 15 min of flight as close as 1,000 ft above lunar surface.
Luna 9 (U.S.S.R.)	Jan. 31, 1966	Moon	3,428 lb. Instrument capsule of 220 lb soft-landed Feb. 3, 1966. Sent back about 30 pictures.
Surveyor 1 (U.S.)	May 30, 1966	Moon	Landed June 2, 1966. Sent almost 10,400 pictures, a number after surviving the 14-day lunar night.
Lunar Orbiter 1 (U.S.)	Aug. 10, 1966	Moon	Orbited Moon Aug. 14. 21 pictures made.
Surveyor 3 (U.S.)	April 17, 1967	Moon	Soft-landed 65 h after launch on Oceanus Procellarum. Scooped and tested lunar soil.
Venera 4 (U.S.S.R.)	June 12, 1967	Venus	Arrived Oct. 17. Instrument capsule sent temperature and chemical data.
Surveyor 5 (U.S.)	Sept. 8, 1967	Moon	Landed near lunar equator Sept. 10. Radiological analysis of lunar soil. Mechanical claw for digging soil.
Surveyor 7 (U.S.)	Jan. 6, 1968	Moon	Landed near Crater Tycho Jan. 10. Soil analysis. Sent 3,343 pictures.
Pioneer 9 (U.S.)	Nov. 8, 1968	Sun Orbit	Achieved orbit. Six experiments returned solar radiation data.
Venera 5 (U.S.S.R.)	Jan. 5, 1969	Venus	Landed May 16, 1969. Returned atmospheric data.
Mariner 6 (U.S.)	Feb. 24, 1969	Mars	Came within 2000 mi. of Mars July 31, 1969. Sent back data & TV pictures.
Luna 16 (U.S.S.R.)	Sept. 12, 1970	Moon	Soft-landed Sept. 20, scooped up rock, returned to Earth Sept. 24.
Luna 17 (U.S.S.R.)	Nov. 10, 1970	Moon	Soft-landed on Sea of Rains Nov. 17. Lunokhod 1, self-propelled vehicle, used for first time. Sent TV photos, made soil analysis, etc.
Mariner 9 (U.S.)	May 30, 1971	Mars	First craft to orbit Mars, Nov. 13. 7,300 pictures, 1st closeups of Mars' moon. Transmission ended Oct. 27, 1972.
Luna 20 (U.S.S.R.)	Feb. 14, 1972	Moon	Soft-landed Feb. 21 in Sea of Fertility. Returned Feb. 25 with rock samples.
Pioneer 10 (U.S.)	March 3, 1972	Jupiter	620-million-mile flight path through asteroid belt passed Jupiter Dec. 3, 1973, to give man first closeup of planet. In 1986, it became first man-made object to escape solar system.
Luna 21 (U.S.S.R.)	Jan. 8, 1973	Moon	Soft-landed Jan. 16. Lunokhod 2 (moon-car) scooped up soil samples, returned them to Earth Jan. 27.
Mariner 10 (U.S.)	Nov. 3, 1973	Venus, Mercury	Passed Venus Feb. 5, 1974. Arrived Mercury March 29, 1974, for man's first closeup look at planet. First time gravity of one planet (Venus) used to whip spacecraft toward another (Mercury).
Viking 1 (U.S.)	Aug. 20, 1975	Mars	Carrying life-detection labs. Landed July 20, 1976, for detailed scientific research, including pictures. Designed to work for only 90 days, it operated for almost 6 1/2 years before it went silent in November 1982.
Viking 2 (U.S.)	Sept. 9, 1975	Mars	Like Viking 1. Landed Sept. 3, 1976. Functioned 3 1/2 years.
Luna 24 (U.S.S.R.)	Aug. 9, 1976	Moon	Soft-landed Aug. 18, 1976. Returned soil samples Aug. 22, 1976.
Voyager 1 (U.S.)	Sept. 5, 1977	Jupiter, Saturn	Fly-by mission. Reached Jupiter in March 1979; passed Saturn Nov. 1980; passed Uranus 1986.
Voyager 2 (U.S.)	Aug. 20, 1977	Jupiter, Saturn, Uranus	Launched before *Voyager 1*. Encountered Jupiter in July 1979; flew by Saturn Aug. 1981; passed Uranus January 1986; scheduled to pass Neptune Aug. 24, 1989.
Pioneer Venus 1 (U.S.)	May 20, 1978	Venus	Arrived Dec. 4 and orbited Venus, photographing surface and atmosphere.
Pioneer Venus 2 (U.S.)	Aug. 8, 1978	Venus	Four-part multi-probe, landed Dec. 9.
Venera 13 (U.S.S.R.)	Oct. 30, 1981	Venus	Landed March 1, 1982. Took first X-ray fluorescence analysis of the planet's surface. Transmitted data 2 hours 7 minutes.
VEGA 1 (U.S.S.R.)	Deployed on Venus, June 10, 1985	Encounter with Halley's comet	In flyby over Venus while enroute to encounter with Halley's Comet, VEGA 1 and 2 dropped scientific capsules onto Venus to study atmosphere and surface material. Encountered Halley's Comet on March 6
VEGA 2 (U.S.S.R.)	Deployed on Venus, June 14, 1985		

Spacecraft	Launch date	Destination	Remarks
			and March 9, 1986. Took TV pictures, and studied comet's dust particles.
Suisei (Japan)	Encountered Hally's Comet March 8, 1986	Halley's Comet	Spacecraft made fly-by of comet and studied atmosphere with ultraviolet camera. Observed rotation nucleus.
Sakigake (Japan)	Encountered Halley's Comet March 10, 1986	Halley's Comet	Spacecraft made fly-by to study solar wind and magnetic fields. Detected plasma waves.
Giotto (ESA)	Encountered Halley's Comet March 13, 1986	Halley's Comet	European Space Agency spacecraft made closest approach to comet. Studied atmosphere and magnetic fields. Sent back best pictures of nucleus.
Phobos Mission (U.S.S.R.)	July 7 and July 12, 1988	Mars and Phobos	Two spacecraft to probe Martian moon Phobos starting April 1989. Were to study orbit, soil chemistry, send TV pictures and data of planet. Contact was lost with Phobos 1 in August 1988 and later with Phobos 2 in March 1989 after it reached the Martian moon.
Magellan (U.S.)	May 4, 1989	Venus	To arrive at Venus on Aug. 10, 1990 and make a geologic map of planet with a powerful radar.
Galileo (U.S.)	Oct. 18, 1989	Jupiter	To study Jupiter's atmosphere and its moons during 22-month mission.
Hiten (Japan)	Jan. 24, 1990	Moon	First Japanese unmanned spacecraft carried two small satellites without scientific instruments. One satellite placed in lunar orbit called *Hagoromo;* its transmitter later failed. The other in Earth orbit for future missions. Project was a practice test for later scientific missions in the 1990s.
Hubble Space Telescope (U.S., E.S.A.)[2]	April 25, 1990	Earth Orbit	Will study distant stars and galaxies and search for evidence of planets in other solar systems.
Mars Observer (U.S.)	Sept. 1992[1]	Mars	Spacecraft to arrive at Mars Aug. 1993 and orbit the planet for one full Martian year to study atmosphere and surface change during the planet's seasons.
Mars '94 (U.S.S.R.)	Oct. 1994[1]	Mars	Two spacecraft to study Mars over an 18-month period. Will investigate Martian surface and deploy a balloon-borne package to study the planet's atmosphere.

1. Tentative launch date. To be deployed by Space Shuttle. 2. European Space Agency (E.S.A.) responsible for furnishing the solar arrays, the Faint Object Camera, and participation in flight operations aspects of the mission.

U.S. Manned Space Flight Projects

Mercury. *Project Mercury,* America's first manned space program, was designed to further knowledge about man's capabilities in space. *Mercury 3* put the first American, Alan B. Shepard, into space. *Mercury 9,* with astronaut Gordon L. Cooper, was the longest flight.

Gemini. *Gemini* was an extension of *Project Mercury,* to determine the effects of prolonged space flight on man—two weeks or longer. "Walks in space" provided invaluable information for astronauts' later walks on the Moon. The *Gemini* spacecraft, twice as large as the *Mercury* capsule, accommodated two astronauts.

Apollo. *Apollo* was the designation for the United States' effort to land a man on the Moon and return him safely to Earth. The goal was successfully accomplished with *Apollo 11* on July 20, 1969, culminating eight years of rehearsal and centuries of dreaming. Astronauts Neil A. Armstrong and Col. Edwin E. Aldrin, Jr., scooped up and brought back the first lunar rocks ever seen on Earth—about 47 pounds. Six *Apollo* flights followed, ending with *Apollo 17* in December, 1972. The last three *Apollos* carried mechanized vehicles called lunar rovers for wide-ranging surface exploration of the Moon by astronauts. The rendezvous and docking of an *Apollo* spacecraft with a Russian *Soyuz* craft in Earth orbit on July 18, 1975, closed out the *Apollo* program.

Skylab. America's first Earth-orbiting space station. *Project Skylab* was designed to demonstrate that men can work and live in space for prolonged periods without ill effects. Originally the spent third stage of a Saturn 5 moon rocket, *Skylab* measured 118 feet from stem to stern, and carried the most varied assortment of experimental equipment ever assembled in a single spacecraft. Three three-man crews visited the space stations, spending more than 740 hours observing the Sun and bringing home more than 175,000 solar pictures. These were the first recordings of solar activity above Earth's obscuring atmosphere. *Skylab* also evaluated systems designed to gather information on Earth's resources and environmental conditions. *Skylab* biomedical findings indicated that man adapts well to space for at least a period of three months, provided he has a proper diet and adequately programmed exercise, sleep, work, and recreation periods. *Skylab* orbited Earth at a distance of about 300 miles. Five years after the last *Skylab* mission, the 77-ton space station's orbit began to deteriorate faster than expected, owing to unexpectedly high sunspot activity. On July 11, 1979, the parts of *Skylab* that did not burn up in the atmosphere came crashing down on parts of Australia and the Indian Ocean. No one was hurt.

Space Shuttle. The *Space Shuttle* (also known as the National Space Transportation System or STS) is a manned spacecraft design developed by NASA to reduce the cost of using space for commercial, scientific, and defense needs. The *Shuttle* is a manned rocket which, after depositing its payload in space, can be flown back to Earth like a conventional airplane and be available for re-use. Although most of its cargoes will be unmanned, the *Shuttle* can serve as an inhabited Earth-orbiting laboratory for up to 30 days. The NASA orbiter is 122.2 feet long and has a wingspan of 78.6 feet.

The *Space Shuttle Columbia* was successfully launched on April 12, 1981. It made five flights (the first four were test runs), the last completed on November 16, 1982. The second shuttle, *Challenger*, made its maiden flight on April 4, 1983. In April 1984, crew members of the *Challenger* captured, repaired, and returned the Solar Max satellite to orbit, making it the first time a disabled satellite had been repaired in space. The third shuttle, *Discovery*, made its first flight on August 30, 1984. The fourth space shuttle, *Atlantis*, made its maiden flight on Oct. 3, 1985.

A tragedy occurred on Jan. 28, 1986, when the shuttle *Challenger* exploded, killing the crew of seven 73 seconds after takeoff. It was the world's worst space flight disaster.

The first U.S. space mission since the *Challenger* disaster was launched 32 months later on Sept. 29, 1988, with the flight of *Discovery*. It had a crew of five and deployed a TDRS (Tracking Data Relay Satellite) communications satellite.

A new orbiter, the *Endeavour*, named after British explorer James Cook's first ship, is being built by Rockwell International, Inc. to replace the *Challenger*. It is scheduled for delivery to NASA's Kennedy Space Center, Cape Canaveral, Florida, in April 1991.

Soviet Manned
Space Flight Programs

Vostok. The Soviets' first manned capsule, roughly spherical, used to place the first six cosmonauts in Earth orbit (1961–65).

Voskhod. Adaptation of the *Vostok* capsule to accommodate two and three cosmonauts. *Voskhod 1* orbited three persons, and *Voskhod 2* orbited two persons performing the world's first manned extravehicular activity.

Soyuz. Late-model manned spacecraft with provisions for three cosmonauts and a "working compartment" accessible through a hatch. Soyuz is the Russian word for "union". Since 1973, all *Soyuz* spacecraft have carried two cosmonauts. *Soyuz 19,* launched July 15, 1975, docked with the American *Apollo* spacecraft.

Salyut. Earth-orbiting space station intended for prolonged occupancy and re-visitation by cosmonauts. They are usually launched by Soviet Proton rockets. *Salyut 1* was launched April 19, 1971. *Salyut 2,* launched April 3, 1973, malfunctioned in orbit and was never occupied. *Salyut 3* was launched June 25, 1974. *Salyut 4* was launched Dec. 26, 1974. *Salyut 5* was launched June 22, 1976. *Salyut 6* was launched on Sept. 29, 1977. *Salyut 7* was launched on April 19, 1982 and is still in orbit. It is slowly descending, and will re-enter the Earth's atmosphere in 1991. A record breaking Russian endurance flight was set (Feb. 8, 1984-Oct. 2, 1985) when Soviet astronauts spent 237 days in orbit aboard *Salyut-7.*

Mir. The latest Soviet space station was launched into orbit on Feb. 20, 1986. Since that time, two space endurance records have been set in the *Mir.* On Dec. 29, 1987, Col. Yuri Romanenko set a single-mission record of 326.5 days in space. On Dec. 21, 1989, Col. Vladimir Titov and Musa Manarov returned to Earth after spending 366 days aboard the orbiting space station.

Above: The Soviet space station *Mir (Peace)* was launched on Feb. 20, 1986. It is 43 ft long (13.10 m), has a diameter of 13.7 ft (4.14 m), and weighs 46,300 lb. Its two solar panels span about 100 ft (30 m). The Soviet Union has placed seven space stations in orbit since 1971. The *Mir* is equipped with six docking ports so it can be docked simultaneously with six spacecraft, including passenger, cargo, and research ships.

The Soviets launched the world's first space station, *Salyut 1,* on April 19, 1971. The *Salyuts* were 49.2 ft long (14.98 m) and 13.8 ft (4.16 m) maximum diameter. Photos by Tass and Novosti.

Notable Manned Space Flights

Designation and country	Date	Astronauts	Flight time (h/min)	Remarks
Vostok 1(U.S.S.R.)	April 12, 1961	Yuri A. Gagarin	1/48	First manned orbital flight
MR III (U.S.)	May 5, 1961	Alan B. Shepard, Jr.	0/15	Range 486 km (302 mi.), peak 187 km (116.5 mi.); capsule recovered. First American in space.
Vostok 2 (U.S.S.R.)	Aug. 6–7, 1961	Gherman S. Titov	25/18	First long-duration flight
MA VI (U.S.)	Feb. 20, 1962	John H. Glenn, Jr.	4/55	First American in orbit
MA IX (U.S.)	May 15–16, 1963	L. Gordon Cooper, Jr.	34/20	Longest Mercury flight
Vostok 6 (U.S.S.R.)	June 16–19, 1963	Valentina V. Tereshkova	70/50	First orbital flight by female cosmonaut
Voskhod 1 (U.S.S.R.)	Oct. 12, 1964	Vladimir M. Komarov; Konstantin P. Feoktistov; Boris G. Yegorov	24/17	First 3-man orbital flight; also first flight without space suits
Voskhod 2 (U.S.S.R.)	March 18, 1965	Alexei A. Leonov; Pavel I. Belyayev	26/2	First "space walk" (by Leonov), 10 min
GT III (U.S.)	March 23, 1965	Virgil I. Grissom; John W. Young	4/53	First manned test of Gemini spacecraft
GT IV (U.S.)	June 3–7, 1965	James A. McDivitt; Edward H. White, 2d	97/48	First American "space walk" (by White), lasting slightly over 20 min
GT VIII (U.S.)	March 16–17, 1966	Neil A. Armstrong; David R. Scott	10/42	First docking between manned spacecraft and an unmanned space vehicle (an orbiting Agena rocket)
Apollo 7 (U.S.)	Oct. 11–22, 1968	Walter M. Schirra, Jr.; Donn F. Eisele; R. Walter Cunningham	260/9	First manned test of Apollo command module; first live TV transmissions from orbit
Soyuz 3 (U.S.S.R.)	Oct. 26–30, 1968	Georgi T. Bergeovoi	94/51	First manned rendezvous and possible docking by Soviet cosmonaut
Apollo 8 (U.S.)	Dec. 21–27, 1968	Frank Borman; James A. Lovell, Jr.; William A. Anders	147/00	First spacecraft in circumlunar orbit; TV transmissions from this orbit
Apollo 9 (U.S.)	Mar. 3–13, 1969	James A. McDivitt; David R. Scott; Russell L. Schweikart	241/1	First manned flight of Lunar Module
Apollo 10 (U.S.)	May 18–26, 1969	Thomas P. Stafford; Eugene A. Cernan; John W. Young	192/3	First descent to within 9 miles of moon's surface by manned craft
Apollo 11 (U.S.)	July 16–24, 1969	Neil A. Armstrong; Edwin E. Aldrin, Jr.; Michael Collins	195/18	First manned landing and EVA on Moon; soil and rock samples collected; experiments left on lunar surface
Soyuz 6 (U.S.S.R.)	Oct. 11–16, 1969	Gorgiy Shonin; Valriy Kabasov	118/42	Three spacecraft and seven men put into earth orbit simultaneously for first time
Apollo 12 (U.S.)	Nov. 14–24, 1969	Charles Conrad, Jr.; Richard F. Gordon, Jr.; Alan Bean	244/36	Manned lunar landing mission; investigated Surveyor 3 spacecraft; collected lunar samples. EVA time: 15 h 30 min
Apollo 13 (U.S.)	April 11–17, 1970	James A. Lovell, Jr.; Fred W. Haise, Jr.; John L. Swigert, Jr.	142/54	Third manned lunar landing attempt; aborted due to pressure loss in liquid oxygen in service module and failure of fuel cells
Apollo 14 (U.S.)	Jan. 31–Feb. 9, 1971	Alan B. Shepard; Stuart A. Roosa; Edgar D. Mitchell	216/42	Third manned lunar landing; returned largest amount of lunar material
Soyuz 11 (U.S.S.R.)	June 6–30, 1971	Georgiy Tomofeyevich Dobrovolskiy; Vladislav Nikolayevich Volkov; Viktor Ivanovich Patsyev	569/40	Linked up with first space station, Salyut 1. Astronauts died just before re-entry due to loss of pressurization in spacecraft
Apollo 15 (U.S.)	July 26–Aug. 7, 1971	David R. Scott; James B. Irwin; Alfred M. Worden	295/12	Fourth manned lunar landing; first use of Lunar Rover propelled by Scott and Irwin; first live pictures of LM lift-off from Moon; exploration time: 18 hours
Apollo 16 (U.S.)	April 16–27, 1972	John W. Young; Thomas K. Mattingly; Charles M. Duke, Jr.	265/51	Fifth manned lunar landing; second use of Lunar Rover Vehicle, propelled by Young and Duke. Total exploration time on the Moon was 20 h 14 min, setting new record. Mattingly's in-flight "walk in space" was 1 h 23 min. Approximately 213 lb of lunar rock returned
Apollo 17 (U.S.)	Dec. 7–19, 1972	Eugene A. Cernan; Ronald E. Evans; Harrison H. Schmitt	301/51	Sixth and last manned lunar landing; third to carry lunar rover. Cernan and Schmitt, during three EVA's, completed total of 22 h 05 min 3 sec. USS Ticonderoga recovered crew and about 250 lbs of lunar samples
Skylab SL-2 (U.S.)	May 25–June 22, 1973	Charles Conrad, Jr.; Josep P. Kerwin; Paul J. Weitz	672/50	First manned Skylab launch. Established Skylab Orbital Assembly and conducted scientific and medical experiments
Skylab SL-3 (U.S.)	July 28–Sept. 25, 1973	Alan L. Bean, Jr.; Jack R. Lousma; Owen K. Garriott	1427/9	Second manned Skylab launch. New crew remained in space for 59 days, continuing scientific and medical experiments and earth observations from orbit

Designation and country	Date	Astronauts	Flight time (h/min)	Remarks
Skylab SL-4 (U.S.)	Nov. 16, 1973-Feb. 8, 1974	Gerald Carr; Edward Gibson; William Pogue	2017/16	Third manned Skylab launch; obtained medical data on crew for use in extending the duration of manned space flight; crews "walked in space" 4 times, totaling 44 h 40 min. Longest space mission yet—84 d 1 h 16 min. Splashdown in Pacific, Feb. 9, 1974
Apollo/Soyuz Test Project (U.S. and U.S.S.R.)	July 15-24, 1975 (U.S.)	U.S.: Brig. Gen. Thomas P. Stafford, Vance D. Brand, Donald K. Slayton	216/05	World's first international manned rendezvous and docking in space; aimed at developing a space rescue capability
	July 15-21, 1975 (U.S.S.R)	U.S.S.R.: Col. A. A. Leonov, V. N. Kubasov	223/35	Apollo and Soyuz docked and crewmen exchanged visits on July 17, 1975. Mission duration for Soyuz: 142 h 31 min. For Apollo: 217 h, 28 min.
Columbia (U.S.)	April 12-14, 1981	Capt. Robert L. Crippen; John W. Young	54/20	Maiden voyage of Space Shuttle, the first spacecraft designed specifically for re-use up to 100 times
Salyut 7 (U.S.S.R.)	Feb. 8, 1984— Oct. 2, 1985	Leonid Kizim; Vladimir Solovyov; Oleg Atkov	237 days	Record Soviet team endurance flight in orbiting space station.
Mir (U.S.S.R.)	Feb. 8, 1987— Dec. 29, 1987	Yuri V. Romanenko[2]	326.5 days	Record Soviet single endurance flight in orbiting space station.
Mir (U.S.S.R.)	Dec. 21, 1988— Dec. 21, 1989	Col. Vladimir Titov and Musa Manarov[3]	366 days	Record Soviet team endurance flight in orbiting space station.

1. Approximate time. NOTE: The letters MR stand for Mercury (capsule) and Redstone (rocket); MA, for Mercury and Atlas (rocket); GT, for Gemini (capsule) and Titan-II (rocket). The first astronaut listed in the Gemini and Apollo flights is the command pilot. The Mercury capsules had names: MR-III was *Freedom 7*, MR-IV was *Liberty Bell 7*, MA-VI was *Friendship 7*, MA-VII was *Aurora 7*, MA-VIII was *Sigma 7*, and MA-IX was *Faith 7*. The figure 7 referred to the fact that the first group of U.S. astronauts numbered seven men. Only one Gemini capsule had a name: GT-III was called *Molly Brown* (after the Broadway musical *The Unsinkable Molly Brown*); thereafter the practice of naming the capsules was discontinued. 2. Returned to earth with two fellow cosmonauts, Aleksandr P. Aleksandrov and Anatoly Levchenko, who had spent a shorter stay aboard the *Mir*. 3. Also returned to earth with French astronaut Jean-Loup Chrétien who spent 3-1/2 weeks aboard the *Mir*.

The Soviet Space Shuttle *Buran*

The successful test flight of the Soviet Union's first reusable space shuttle *Buran* (Russian for "snowstorm") (Shown at left on launch pad. Novosti photo) was made on Nov. 15, 1988. The unmanned flight circled the Earth for two orbits and lasted 3 hr 25 min.

The Soviet and American space shuttles closely resemble each other in size and appearance and have similar delta wings and vertical tail structures. Some major differences between the two shuttles are that the Soviet craft has no large rocket engines of its own. It uses the giant disposable *Energiya* rocket for most of its propulsion, and has only small rockets for maneuvering. The United States space shuttles have three reusable main engines to help lift it into orbit. The *Buran* also has larger payload capabilities than NASA's orbiters.

Unlike the American version, the *Buran* is designed for fully automatic flight, from takeoff to landing, a difficult engineering feat. By comparison, U.S. astronauts take control of their shuttles when making the final landing approach.

The crew cabin of *Buran* can accommodate two to four astronauts and has seats for six passengers or other crew members. The U.S. space shuttle can accommodate up to eight crew members. The Soviet shuttle will be adapted for docking with an advanced second-generation *Mir-2* space station.

The Soviet craft is 19 ft (5.6 m) in diameter compared with NASA's shuttle, 17 ft (5.2 m). The wingspan is 79.2 ft (24 m). NASA's orbiter is 78.6 ft (23.79 m). *Buran's* length is 119 ft (36 m), the U.S. shuttle is 122.2 ft long (37.24 m).

The Soviets had planned to make ten to twelve shuttle flights a year, but the *Buran* program was cut back to only one flight a year due to economic considerations. Manned *Buran* missions will start in 1992. Cosmonaut Igor Volk will be the pilot of the *Buran* when it makes its first manned flight in space. He took the Soviet space shuttle on its first 12-minute test flight, which remained in the Earth's atmosphere, and has continued to fly test missions in the *Buran*.

ASTRONOMY

Exploring Other Worlds and Protecting This One: The Connection

By Carl Sagan

The *Apollo* images of Earth from space revealed plainly the fragility and vulnerability of our lovely little world, and powerfully assisted the coming of age of a global ecological consciousness. Such pictures by themselves may be worth the whole cost of the space program, because their meaning has reached so many. But what is not so widely understood is how much vital and urgent information we have gained about our own world from robotic exploration of other worlds.

If we are stuck on one world, we are limited to a single case; we do not know what else is possible. Then like a linguist who knows only English, or a physicist who knows about gravity only from falling bodies on Earth, our insights are narrow and our predictive abilities severely circumscribed. But when we explore other worlds, our perspective widens. We gain a new understanding of worlds in general, including our own.

Robotic exploration of other worlds has already opened our eyes in many fields of Earth science, including the study of volcanoes, earthquakes and weather. It may turn out to have profound implications for biology, because all life on Earth is built on a common biochemical master plan. The discovery of a single extraterrestrial organism—even something as humble as a bacterium—would revolutionize biology. But the connection between exploring other worlds and protecting our own is most evident in the study of Earth's climate and the burgeoning threat to the climate that our technology now represents. Other planets provide important insights about what dumb things not to do to Earth.

Three environmental catastrophes, or potential catastrophes, have been uncovered accidentally, mainly in the last two decades: ozonosphere depletion, greenhouse warming and nuclear winter. I want briefly to sketch some of the ways in which planetary exploration aided and deepened these findings.

Thinning Ozone Shield

It was disquieting to discover that an inert material with all sorts of practical functions—it serves as the working fluid in refrigerators and air conditioners, as propellant for deodorants and other products in aerosol cans and as lightweight foamy packaging for fast foods, to name only a few—can pose a danger to life on Earth. Who would have figured it?

The molecules in question are called chlorofluorocarbons (CFCs). They are extremely chemically inert, which means they are invulnerable—

until they find themselves up in the ozone layer, where they are dissociated by sunlight. The chlorine atoms thus liberated deplete the ozone and let more ultraviolet light from the Sun reach the ground.

This increased ultraviolet intensity ushers in a ghastly procession of potential consequences involving not just skin cancer but the weakening of the human immune system and, most dangerous of all, the destruction of agriculture and of photosynthetic microorganisms at the base of the food chain on which most life on Earth depends.

The principal manufacturer of this material, the Dupont company (which gave it the brand name Freon)—after years of pooh-poohing the concern of environmentalists, after taking out full-page ads in newspapers and scientific magazines claiming that the uproar all came from wild extrapolations from inadequate data, that nobody had actually demonstrated any peril—that company has now announced that it will rapidly phase out all its CFC production. The precipitating event seems to have been the discovery in 1986 by British scientists of a hole in the Antarctic ozone layer. There is now good evidence of thinning of the ozone layer at other latitudes as well.

Who discovered that CFCs posed a threat to the ozone layer? Was it Dupont exercising corporate responsibility? Nope. Was it the Environmental Protection Agency protecting us? Nope. Was it the Department of Defense defending us? Nope. It was two ivory-tower, white-coated university scientists working in 1974 on something else—Sherwood Rowland and Mario Molina of the University of California, Irvine.

Their work used reaction rate constants of chemical reactions involving chlorine and other halogens, determined in part with NASA support. Why NASA? Because Venus has chlorine and fluorine molecules in its atmosphere—as discovered by US spacecraft and groundbased observations—and planetary aeronomers wanted to understand what's happening there.

Thank You, Venus

Confirming theoretical work on ozone depletion was done with a big computer model by a group led by Michael McElroy at Harvard. How is it they had all these branching networks of halogen chemical kinetics in their computer ready to go? Because they were working on the halogen chemistry of the atmosphere of Venus. Venus helped make the discovery that the Earth's ozone layer is in danger. (Such serendipity, by the way, is found in many discoveries in science.)

There is an absolutely unexpected connection between the atmospheric photochemistries of two planets, and suddenly a very practical result emerges from the most blue-sky, abstract kind of work, understanding the upper atmosphere of Venus.

There is also a Mars connection to ozone depletion on Earth. *Viking* found the surface of Mars to be lifeless and remarkably deficient even in simple organic molecules. This deficiency is widely understood as due to the lack of ozone in the martian atmosphere. Ultraviolet light from the Sun strikes the surface of Mars unimpeded; if any organic matter were there, it would be quickly destroyed by solar ultraviolet light or the oxidation products of solar ultraviolet light. Thus part of the reason that the topmost layers of Mars are antiseptic is that Mars has an ozone hole of planetary dimensions—a possibly useful cautionary tale for us, who are busily making holes in our ozone layer.

CO$_2$ and the Greenhouse Effect

Now let's look at global warming from the increasing greenhouse effect, which derives largely from carbon dioxide generated by the burning of fossil fuels—but also from the buildup of other infrared-absorbing gases (oxides of nitrogen, methane, those same CFCs and some other molecules). Some of the important recent work on global warming has been done by James Hansen and his colleagues at the Goddard Institute for Space Sciences, a NASA facility in New York City.

Hansen and his colleagues point out that over the last hundred years the five warmest years in terms of average global temperature have been in the 1980s. If their current projections prove correct, and world temperatures continue to be driven up by the increasing levels of carbon dioxide and other gases in Earth's atmosphere, then 1990 will be the warmest year in the last 120,000.

Some of the consequences projected by various climatologists to the middle and end of the next century include the conversion of the Soviet Ukraine and the American Midwest, the breadbasket of the world, to something approaching scrub deserts. The slow volume expansion of sea water, the melting of glacial and polar ice and later the collapse of the West Antarctic ice sheet would cause the inundation of every coastal city on the planet. Now that's serious. Mitigating this warming will be very expensive.

Hansen has played a major role before committees of the House and Senate, convincing them to take the threat of global warming seriously. How did Hansen get involved with the issue of Earth's climatic future in the first place? As a graduate student at the University of Iowa he wrote a doctoral thesis that attempted (mistakenly, we now know) to disprove the contention that Venus was hot because of a massive greenhouse effect there. Venus got Hansen thinking about the greenhouse effect.

Those who are skeptical about carbon dioxide greenhouse warming might profitably note the massive greenhouse on Venus, where the atmosphere is primarily carbon dioxide, the surface pressure is about 90 times that on Earth, and the surface temperature is about 900 degrees Fahrenheit (480 degrees Celsius). No one proposes that Venus' runaway greenhouse effect was caused by Venusians who burned too much coal, drove fuel-inefficient autos or cut down their forests. That's not the point. But the climatological history of our planetary neighbor, an otherwise Earthlike planet on which the surface became hot enough to melt tin or lead, is worth considering—especially by those who say that the increasing greenhouse effect on Earth will be self-correcting, that we don't really have to worry about it.

Nuclear Winter

Nuclear winter is the darkening and cooling of the Earth, mainly from fine smoke particles injected into the atmosphere from the burning of cities and petroleum facilities that would follow even a "small" nuclear war.

There has been a vigorous scientific debate on just how serious nuclear winter is likely to be. The debate has now largely converged. Most three-dimensional general circulation models now get nearly the same answer provided they use the same starting conditions. That answer is close to the results first announced in 1982/1983 by a team of five scientists, to which I'm proud to belong, called TTAPS (for Richard P. Turco, Owen B. Toon, Thomas Ackerman, James Pollack and myself). Of the five TTAPS scientists, three are full-time planetary scientists, and the other two have published many papers in planetary science.

The earliest intimation of nuclear winter came during the *Mariner 9* mission to Mars, when there was a global dust storm and we were unable to see the surface of the planet; the infrared spectrometer on *Mariner 9* found the high atmosphere to be warmer and the surface colder than it ought to have been. We sat down and tried to calculate how that could come about. Eventually this line of inquiry led us from dust storms on Mars to nuclear winter on Earth.

Planetary Perspective

Planetary science provides a global perspective, a big interdisciplinary picture that turns out to be very helpful in finding and attempting to define these looming climate catastrophes. When you cut your teeth studying other worlds, you develop a point of view—one very useful in understanding this world. There are probably other such catastrophes still to be uncovered. When they emerge, I think it likely that planetary science will play an important role in discovering and assessing them.

When I look at the evidence, I find that planetary exploration is of the most practical and urgent utility for us here on Earth. Even if we were not concerned about exploration, even if we did not have a nanogram of adventuresome spirit in us, even if we were only concerned for ourselves in the narrowest sense, planetary exploration would be a superb investment. NASA ought to make this case. □

Carl Sagan, President of The Planetary Society, is coauthor with Richard Turco of a forthcoming book on nuclear winter and its implications for strategic policy and doctrine, force structures and arms control treaties, "A Path Where No Man Thought: Nuclear Winter and the End of the Arms Race" (Random House, 1990). Dr. Sagan has just been awarded the Oersted Medal of the American Society of Physics Teachers. Copyright © 1990 by Carl Sagan. All Rights Reserved. First published in *The Planetary Report*. Reprinted by permission of the author.

Astronomical Terms

Planet is the term used for a body in orbit around the Sun. Its origin is Greek; even in antiquity it was known that a number of "stars" did not stay in the same relative positions to the others. There were five such restless "stars" known—Mercury, Venus, Mars, Jupiter, and Saturn—and the Greeks referred to them as *planetes,* a word which means "wanderers." That the earth is one of the planets was realized later. The additional planets were discovered after the invention of the telescope.

Satellite (or *moon*) is the term for a body in orbit around a planet. As long as our own Moon was the only moon known, there was no need for a general term for the moons of planets. But when Galileo Galilei discovered the four main moons of the planet Jupiter, Johannes Kepler (in a letter to Galileo) suggested "satellite" (from the Latin *satelles,* which means attendant) as a general term for such bodies. The word is used interchangeably with "moons": astronomers speak and write about the moons of Neptune, Saturn, etc. A satellite may be any size.

Orbit is the term for the path traveled by a body in space. It comes from the Latin *orbis,* which means circle, circuit, etc., and *orbita,* which means a rut or a wheel track. Theoretically, four mathematical figures are possible orbits: two are open (hyperbola and parabola) and two are closed (ellipse and circle), but in reality all closed orbits are ellipses. These ellipses can be nearly circular, as are the orbits of most planets, or very elongated, as are the orbits of most comets. In these orbits, the Sun is in one focal point of the ellipse, and the other focal point is empty. In the orbits of satellites, the planet stands in one focal point of the orbit. The *primary* of an orbit is the body in the focal point. For planets, the point of the orbit closest to the Sun is the *perihelion,* and the point farthest from the Sun is the *aphelion.* For orbits around the Earth, the corresponding terms are *perigee* and *apogee;* for orbits around other planets, corresponding terms are coined when necessary.

Two heavenly bodies are in *inferior* or *superior conjunction* when they have the same Right Ascension, or are in the same meridian; that is, when one is due north or south of the other. If the bodies appear near each other as seen from the Earth, they will rise and set at the same time. They are in *opposition* when they are opposite each other in the heavens: when one rises as the other is setting. *Greatest elongation* is the greatest apparent angular distance from the Sun, when a planet is most favorably suited for observation. Mercury can be seen with the naked eye only at about this time. An *occultation* of a planet or star is an eclipse of it by some other body, usually the Moon.

Stars are the basic units of population in the universe. Our Sun is the nearest star. Stars are very large (our Sun has a diameter of 865,400 miles—a comparatively small star). Stars are composed of intensely hot gasses, deriving their energy from nuclear reactions going on in their interiors.

Galaxies are immense systems containing billions of stars. All that you can see in the sky (with a very few exceptions) belongs to our galaxy—a system of roughly 200 billion stars. The few exceptions are other galaxies. Our own galaxy, the rim of which we see as the "Milky Way," is about 100,000 light-years in diameter and about 10,000 light-years in thickness. Its shape is roughly that of a thick lens; more precisely it is a "spiral nebula," a term first used for other galaxies when they were discovered and before it was realized that these were separate and distant galaxies. The spiral galaxy nearest to ours is in the constellation Andromeda. It is somewhat larger than our own galaxy and is visible to the naked eye.

Recent developments in radio astronomy have revealed additional celestial objects that are still incompletely understood.

Quasars ("quasi-stellar" objects), originally thought to be peculiar stars in our own galaxy, are now believed to be the most remote objects in the Universe. Spectral studies of quasars indicate that some are 9 billion light years away and moving away from us at the incredible rate of 150,000 miles per second. Quasars emit tremendous amounts of light and microwave radiation. Although they appear to be far smaller than ordinary galaxies, some quasars emit as much as 100 times more energy. Some astronomers believe that quasars are the cores of violently exploding galaxies.

Pulsars are believed to be rapidly spinning neutron stars, so crushed by their own gravity that a million tons of their matter would hardly fill a thimble. Pulsars are so named because they emit bursts of radio energy at regular intervals. Some have pulse rates as rapid as 10 per second.

A *black hole* is the theoretical end-product of the total gravitational collapse of a massive star or group of stars. Crushed even smaller than an incredibly dense neutron star, such a body may become so dense that not even light can escape its gravitational field. It has been suggested that black holes may be detectable in proximity to normal stars when they draw matter away from their visible neighbors. Strong sources of X-rays in our galaxy and beyond may also indicate the presence of black holes. One possible black hole now being studied is the invisible companion to a supergiant star in the constellation Cygnus.

Origin of the Universe

Evidence uncovered in recent years tends to confirm that the universe began its existence about 15 billion years ago as a dense, hot globule of gas expanding rapidly outward. At that time, the universe contained nothing but hydrogen and a small amount of helium. There were no stars and no planets. The first stars probably began to condense out of the primordial hydrogen when the universe was about 100 million years old and continued to form as the universe aged. The Sun arose in this way 4.6 billion years ago. Many stars came into being before the Sun was formed; many others formed after the Sun appeared. This process continues, and through telescopes we can now see stars forming out of compressed pockets of hydrogen in outer space.

Birth and Death of a Star

When a star begins to form as a dense cloud of gas, the individual hydrogen atoms fall toward the center of the cloud under the force of the star's gravity. As they fall, they pick up speed, and their energy increases. The increase in energy heats the gas. When this process has continued for some millions of years, the temperature reaches about 20 million degrees Fahrenheit. At this temperature, the hydrogen within the star ignites and burns in a continuing series of nuclear reactions in which all the elements in the universe are manufactured from hydrogen and helium. The onset of these re-

Astronomical Constants

Light-year (distance traveled by light in one year)	5,880,000,000,000 mi.
Parsec (parallax of one second, for stellar distances)	3.259 light-yrs.
Velocity of light	186,281.7 mi./sec.
Astronomical unit (A.U.), or mean distance earth-to-sun	ca. 93,000,000 mi.[1]
Mean distance, earth to moon	238,860 mi.
General precession	50″.26
Obliquity of the ecliptic	23° 27′8″.26−0″.4684(t−1900)[2]
Equatorial radius of the earth	3963.34 statute mi.
Polar radius of the earth	3949.99 statute mi.
Earth's mean radius	3958.89 statute mi.
Oblateness of the earth	1/297
Equatorial horizontal parallax of the moon	57′ 2″.70
Earth's mean velocity in orbit	18.5 mi./sec.
Sidereal year	365d.2564
Tropical year	365d.2422
Sidereal month	27d.3217
Synodic month	29d.5306
Mean sidereal day	23h56m4s.091 of mean solar time
Mean solar day	24h3m56s.555 of sidereal time

1. Actual mean distance derived from radar bounces: 92,935,700 mi. The value of 92,897,400 mi. (based on parallax of 8″.80) is used in calculations. 2. *t* refers to the year in question, for example, 1991.

actions marks the birth of a star. When a star begins to exhaust its hydrogen supply, its life nears an end. The first sign of old age is a swelling and reddening of its outer regions. Such an aging, swollen star is called a red giant. The Sun, a middle-aged star, will probably swell into a red giant in 5 billion years, vaporizing the earth and any creatures that may be left on its surface. When all its fuel has been exhausted, a star cannot generate sufficient pressure at its center to balance the crushing force of gravity. The star collapses under the force of its own weight; if it is a small star, it collapses gently and remains collapsed. Such a collapsed star, at its life's end, is called a white dwarf. The Sun will probably end its life in this way. A different fate awaits a large star. Its final collapse generates a violent explosion, blowing the innards of the star out into space. There, the materials of the exploded star mix with the primeval hydrogen of the universe. Later in the history of the galaxy, other stars are formed out of this mixture. The Sun is one of these stars. It contains the debris of countless other stars that exploded before the Sun was born.

Supernova 1987A

On Feb. 24, 1987, Canadian astronomer Ian Shelter at the Las Campas Observatory in Chile discovered a supernova—an exploding star—from a photograph taken on Feb. 23 of the Large Megallanic Cloud, a galaxy some 160,000 light years away from Earth. Astronomers believe that the dying star was Sanduleak −69°202, a 10-million-year-old blue supergiant.

Supernova 1987A was the closest and best studied supernova in almost 400 years. The last known one was observed by Johannes Kepler in 1604, four years before the telescope was invented.

On January 18 1989, astronomers reported evidence that they had sighted the birth of a pulsar, an extremely dense star spinning about 2,000 times per second in the debris left over from the explosion of supernova 1987A. If this discovery had been confirmed, it would have marked the first time the creation of a pulsar has been observed. However, in February 1990, it was discovered to have been

caused by a spurious signal from the TV cameras that are used to guide the telescope.

Formation of the Solar System

The sun's age was calculated in 1989 to be 4.49 billion years old, less than the 4.7 billion years previously believed. It was formed from a cloud of hydrogen mixed with small amounts of other substances that had been manufactured in the bodies of other stars before the Sun was born. This was the parent cloud of the solar system. The dense hot gas at the center of the cloud gave rise to the Sun; the outer regions of the cloud—cooler and less dense—gave birth to the planets.

Our solar system consists of one star (the Sun), nine planets and all their moons, several thousand minor planets called asteroids or planetoids, and an equally large number of comets.

The Sun

All the stars, including our Sun, are gigantic balls of superheated gas, kept hot by atomic reactions in their centers. In our Sun, this atomic reaction is hydrogen fusion: four hydrogen atoms are combined to form one helium atom. The temperature at the core of our Sun must be 20 million degrees centigrade, the surface temperature is around 6,000 degrees centigrade, or about 11,000 degrees Fahrenheit. The diameter of the sun is 865,400 miles, and its surface area is approximately 12,000 times that of the Earth. Compared with other stars, our Sun is just a bit below average in size and temperature. Its fuel supply (hydrogen) is estimated to last for another 5 billion years.

Our Sun is not motionless in space; in fact it has two proper motions. One is a seemingly straight-line motion in the direction of the constellation Hercules at the rate of about 12 miles per second. But since the Sun is a part of the Milky Way system and since the whole system rotates slowly around its own center, the Sun also moves at the rate of 175 miles per second as part of the rotating Milky Way system.

Quasars and Cosmology

Source: A Field Guide to the Stars and Planets, Donald H. Menzel and Jay M. Pasachoff.

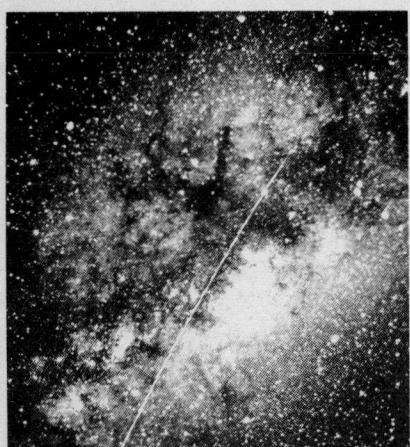

The Milky Way in Sagittarius. Astronomers believe that there may be a large black hole at the center of our own galaxy, the Milky Way, 30,000 light years away.

Quasars

It came as a surprise in 1960 when some of the sources of celestial radio waves appeared to be pointlike—"quasi-stellar"—instead of looking like galaxies. These "quasi-stellar radio sources"—*quasars,* for short—were discovered three years later to be extremely far away, when Maarten Schmidt discovered that the spectrum of one of them showed an extreme redshift. A class of radio-quiet quasars—quasi-stellar objects with huge redshifts—has since been discovered. We now know of over a thousand quasars.

The redshift can be expressed as the fraction or percentage by which the wavelengths of light are shifted. For speeds much slower than the speed of light, this fraction is the same as the fraction that the recession speed of the quasar is of the speed of light. For example, a redshift (called z) of 0.2 means that the wavelengths of light are shifted toward the red by 0.2 times (20% of) the original wavelength. It is also true that the galaxy or quasar emitting such light is receding from us at 0.2 times the speed of light, or 60,000 km/sec. A quasar with redshift of 1.0 has its wavelengths shifted by 1.0 times (100% of) the original wavelength; each wavelength is doubled. But Einstein's formulas from the special theory of relativity must be used to calculate how fast the quasars are receding; their velocities are always less than the speed of light.

The most distant quasar is redshifted by z = 3.78.[1] Few quasars with redshifts greater than 3 (300%) have been found, even though instruments exist that would be sensitive enough to do so. The farther out the quasar is, the farther back in time the light reaching us was emitted. That few quasars of the largest redshifts are found indicates that we

are seeing back to the instant at which the first quasars were formed—somewhat over 10 billion years ago.

Since quasars are so far away yet still send us some visible light and relatively strong radio radiation, the quasars must be astonishingly bright. Astronomers now agree that giant black holes are probably present in the centers of quasars. These black holes would contain millions of times the mass of the sun. As gas is sucked into the black holes, it heats up and gives off energy. Quasars may be a stage in the evolution of galaxies, for there is evidence that some quasars have structure around them not unlike that of galaxies. Since we see most quasars quite far away, we are seeing them far back in time, and we can conclude that the epoch at which quasars were brightest took place long ago.

Cosmology

Hubble's observations that the most distant galaxies are receding from us faster than closer galaxies can be explained if the universe were expanding in a way similar to the way a giant loaf of raisin bread rises. If you picture yourself as sitting on a raisin, all the other raisins will recede from you as the bread rises. Since there is more dough between you and the more distant raisins, the dough will expand more and the distant raisins will recede more rapidly than closer ones. Similarly, the universe is expanding. We have the same view no matter which raisin or galaxy we are on, so the fact that all raisins and galaxies seem to be receding doesn't say that we are at the center of the universe. Indeed, the universe has no center. (We would have to picture a loaf of raisin bread extending infinitely in all directions to get a more accurate analogy.)

Since the universe is uniformly expanding now, we can ask what happened in the past. As we go back in time, the universe must have been more compressed, until it was at quite a high density 15 billion or so years ago. Most models of the origin of the universe say that there then was a *big bang* that started the expansion. A new model—the *inflationary universe*—holds that the early universe grew larger rapidly for a short time before it settled down to its current rate of expansion. The big bang itself may not have occurred; the first matter could have formed as a chance fluctuation in the nothingness of space.

Astronomers ask what will happen to the universe in the future. The evidence is not all in. One possibility is that the universe is *open*—it will continue to expand forever. Another possibility is that the universe will eventually stop its expansion and begin to contract. We know that this cannot happen for at least 50 billion years more—at least three times longer than the current age of the universe—because we can observe the rate at which the universe is now expanding. Still, if the universe does contract in the long run, then we have a *closed universe* that will wind up in a *big crunch*. The inflationary model indicates that the universe will expand forever, but at a decreasing rate. □

1. In 1988, astronomers announced the discovery of a galaxy designated 4C41.17 which has a redshift of 3.8, making it the most distant galaxy observed.—Ed.

THE MILKY WAY GALAXY. Our sun is one of 200-billion stars banded together by gravity in an enormous spiral disk called the Milky Way Galaxy. The arrow indicates our position three-fifths of the way out from the center. It takes light 100,000 years to traverse our Galaxy, one of billions of galaxies in the universe. Copyright © 1984, Hansen Planetarium, Salt Lake City, Utah. Reproduced with Permission.

OUR PLACE IN THE GALAXY

In addition to this motion, the Sun rotates on its axis. Observing the motion of sun spots (darkish areas which look like enormous whirling storms) and solar flares, which are usually associated with sun spots, has shown that the rotational period of our Sun is just short of 25 days. But this figure is valid for the Sun's equator only; the sections near the Sun's poles seem to have a rotational period of 34 days. Naturally, since the Sun generates its own heat and light, there is no temperature difference between poles and equator.

What we call the Sun's "surface" is technically known as the photosphere. Since the whole Sun is a ball of very hot gas, there is really no such thing as a surface; it is a question of visual impression. The next layer outside the photosphere is known as the chromosphere, which extends several thousand miles beyond the photosphere. It is in steady motion, and often enormous prominences can be seen to burst from it, extending as much as 100,000 miles into space. Outside the chromosphere is the corona. The corona consists of very tenuous gases (essentially hydrogen) and makes a magnificent sight when the Sun is eclipsed.

The Moon

Mercury and Venus do not have any moons. Therefore, the Earth is the planet nearest the Sun to be orbited by a moon.

The next planet farther out, Mars, has two very small moons. Jupiter has four major moons and twelve minor ones. Saturn, the ringed planet, has seventeen known moons (and possibly more), of which one (Titan) is larger than the planet Mercury. Uranus has fifteen moons, (four of them large) as well as rings, while Neptune has one large and seven small moons. Pluto has one moon, discovered in 1978. Some astronomers still consider Pluto to be a "runaway moon" of Neptune.

Our own Moon, with a diameter of 2,160 miles, is one of the larger moons in our solar system and is especially large when compared with the planet that it orbits. In fact, the common center of gravity of the Earth-Moon system is only about 1,000 miles below the Earth's surface. The closest our Moon can come to us (its perigee) is 221,463 miles; the farthest it can go away (its apogee) is 252,710 miles. The period of rotation of our Moon is equal to its period of revolution around the Earth. Hence from Earth we can see only one hemisphere of the Moon. Both periods are 27 days, 7 hours, 43 minutes and 11.47 seconds. But while the rotation of the Moon is constant, its velocity in its orbit is not, since it moves more slowly in apogee than in perigee. Consequently, some portions near the rim which are not normally visible will appear briefly. This phenomenon is called "libration," and by taking advantage of the librations, astronomers have succeeded in mapping approximately 59% of the lunar surface. The other 41% can never be seen from the earth but has been mapped by American and Russian Moon-orbiting spacecraft.

Though the Moon goes around the Earth in the time mentioned, the interval from new Moon to new Moon is 29 days, 12 hours, 44 minutes and 2.78 seconds. This delay of nearly two days is due to the fact that the Earth is moving around the Sun, so that the Moon needs two extra days to reach a spot in its orbit where no part is illuminated by the Sun, as seen from Earth.

If the plane of the Earth's orbit around the Sun (the ecliptic) and the plane of the Moon's orbit around the Earth were the same, the Moon would be eclipsed by the Earth every time it is full, and the Sun would be eclipsed by the Moon every time

The Brightest Stars

Star	Constellation	Mag.	Dist. (l.-y.)	Star	Constellation	Mag.	Dist. (l.-y.)
Sirius	Canis Major	−1.6	8	Antares	Scorpius	1.2	170
Canopus	Carina	−0.9	650	Fomalhaut	Piscis Austrinus	1.3	27
Alpha Centauri	Centaurus	+0.1	4	Deneb	Cygnus	1.3	465
Vega[1]	Lyra	0.1	23	Regulus	Leo	1.3	70
Capella	Auriga	0.2	42	Beta Crucis	Crux	1.5	465
Arcturus	Boötes	0.2	32	Eta Carinae	Carina	1-7	—
Rigel	Orion	0.3	545	Alpha-one Crucis	Crux	1.6	150
Procyon	Canis Minor	0.5	10	Castor	Gemini	1.6	44
Achernar	Eridanus	0.6	70	Gamma Crucis	Crux	1.6	
Beta Centari	Centaurus	0.9	130	Epsilon Canis Majoris	Canis Major	1.6	325
Altair	Aquila	0.9	18	Epsilon Ursae Majoris	Ursa Major	1.7	50
Betelgeuse	Orion	0.9	600	Bellatrix	Orion	1.7	215
Aldebaran	Taurus	1.1	54	Lambda Scorpii	Scorpius	1.7	205
Spica	Virgo	1.2	190	Epsilon Carinae	Carina	1.7	325
Pollux	Gemini	1.2	31	Mira	Cetus	2-10	250

1. In 1984, the discovery of a possible planetary system around Vega was reported.

the Moon is "new" (it would be better to call it the "black Moon" when it is in this position). But because the two orbits do not coincide, the Moon's shadow normally misses the Earth and the Earth's shadow misses the Moon. The inclination of the two orbital planes to each other is 5 degrees. The tides are, of course, caused by the Moon with the help of the Sun, but in the open ocean they are surprisingly low, amounting to about one yard. The very high tides which can be observed near the shore in some places are due to funnelling effects of the shorelines. At new Moon and at full Moon the tides raised by the Moon are reinforced by the Sun; these are the "spring tides." If the Sun's tidal power acts at right angles to that of the Moon (quarter moons) we get the low "neap tides."

Our Planet Earth

The Earth, circling the Sun at an average distance of 93 million miles, is the fifth largest planet and the third from the Sun. It orbits the Sun at a speed of 67,000 miles per hour, making one revolution in 365 days, 5 hours, 48 minutes, and 45.51 seconds. The Earth completes one rotation on its axis every 23 hours, 56 minutes, and 4.09 seconds. Actually a bit pear-shaped rather than a true sphere, the Earth has a diameter of 7,927 miles at the Equator and a few miles less at the poles. It has an estimated mass of about 6.6 sextillion tons, with an average density of 5.52 grams per cubic centimeter. The Earth's surface area encompasses 196,949,970 square miles of which about three-fourths is water.

Origin of the Earth. The Earth, along with the other planets, is believed to have been born 4.5 billion years ago as a solidified cloud of dust and gases left over from the creation of the Sun. For perhaps 500 million years, the interior of the Earth stayed solid and relatively cool, perhaps 2000° F. The main ingredients, according to the best available evidence, were iron and silicates, with small amounts of other elements, some of them radioactive. As millions of years passed, energy released by radioactive decay—mostly of uranium, thorium, and potassium—gradually heated the Earth, melting some of its constituents. The iron melted before the silicates, and, being heavier, sank toward the center. This forced upward the silicates that it found

there. After many years, the iron reached the center, almost 4,000 miles deep, and began to accumulate. No eyes were around at that time to view the turmoil which must have taken place on the face of the Earth—gigantic heaves and bubbling of the surface, exploding volcanoes, and flowing lava covering everything in sight. Finally, the iron in the center accumulated as the core. Around it, a thin but fairly stable crust of solid rock formed as the Earth cooled. Depressions in the crust were natural basins in which water, rising from the interior of the planet through volcanoes and fissures, collected to form the oceans. Slowly the Earth acquired its present appearance.

The Earth Today. As a result of radioactive heating over millions of years, the Earth's molten *core* is probably fairly hot today, around 11,000° F. By comparison, lead melts at around 800° F. Most of the Earth's 2,100-mile-thick core is liquid, but there is evidence that the center of the core is solid. The liquid outer portion, about 95% of the core, is constantly in motion, causing the Earth to have a magnetic field that makes compass needles point north and south. The details are not known, but the latest evidence suggests that planets which have a magnetic field probably have a solid core or a partially liquid one.

Outside the core is the Earth's *mantle*, 1,800 miles thick, and extending nearly to the surface. The mantle is composed of heavy silicate rock, similar to that brought up by volcanic eruptions. It is somewhere between liquid and solid, slightly yielding, and therefore contributing to an active, moving Earth. Most of the Earth's radioactive material is in the thin *crust* which covers the mantle, but some is in the mantle and continues to give off heat. The crust's thickness ranges from 5 to 25 miles.

Scientists recently discovered that the Earth's core is not a perfect sphere. X-ray like images of inside the Earth show that there are vast mountains six to seven miles high and deep valleys on the core. These features are in an upside down relationship to the Earth's surface.

Continental Drift. A great deal of recent evidence confirms the theory that the continents of the Earth, made mostly of relatively light granite, float in the slightly yielding mantle, like logs in a pond. For many years it had been noticed that if North

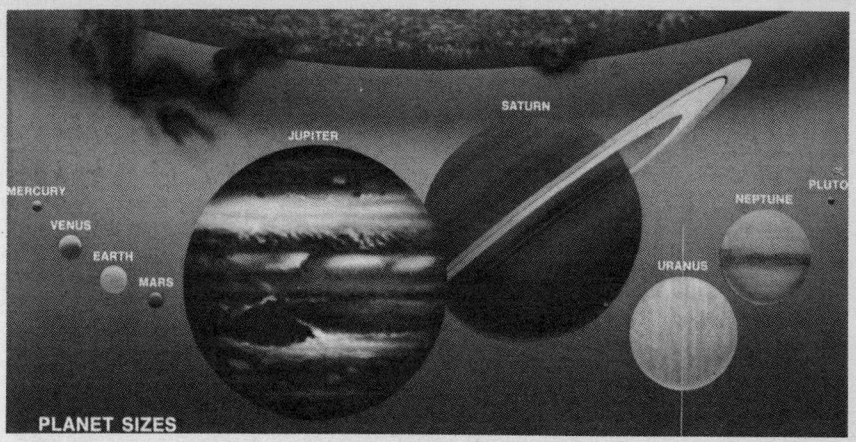

PLANET SIZES. Shown from left to right: Mercury, Venus, Earth, Mars, Jupiter, Saturn, Uranus, Neptune, and Pluto.

Copyright © 1984 Hansen Planetarium, Salt Lake City, Utah. Reproduced with Permission.

Basic Planetary Data

	Mercury	Venus	Earth	Mars	Jupiter
Mean distance from Sun (Millions of kilometers)	57.9	108.2	149.6	227.9	778.3
(Millions of miles)	36.0	67.24	92.9	141.71	483.88
Period of revolution	88 days	224.7 days	365.2 days	687 days	11.86 yrs
Rotation period	59 days	243 days retrograde	23 hr 56 min 4 sec	24 hr 37 min	9 hr 55 min 30 sec
Inclination of axis	Near 0°	3°	23°27'	25°12'	3°5'
Inclination of orbit to ecliptic	7°	3.4°	0°	1.9°	1.3°
Eccentricity of orbit	.206	.007	.017	.093	.048
Equatorial diameter (Kilometers)	4,880	12,100	12,756	6,794	142,800
(Miles)	3,032.4	7,519	7,926.2	4,194	88,736
Atmosphere (Main components)	Virtually none	Carbon dioxide	Nitrogen oxygen	Carbon dioxide	Hydrogen helium
Satellites	0	0	1	2	16
Rings	0	0	0	0	1

	Saturn	Uranus	Neptune	Pluto
Mean distance from Sun (Millions of kilometers)	1,427	2,870	4,497	5,900
(Millions of miles)	887.14	1,783.98	2,796.46	3,666
Period of revolution	29.46 yrs	84 yrs	165 yrs	248 yrs
Rotation period	10 hr 40 min 24 sec	16.8 hr(?) retrograde	16 hr 11 min(?)	6 days 9 hr 18 mins retrograde
Inclination of axis	26°44'	97°55'	28°48'	60° (?)
Inclination of orbit to ecliptic	2.5°	0.8°	1.8°	17.2°
Eccentricity of orbit	.056	.047	.009	.254
Equatorial diameter (Kilometers)	120,660	51,810	49,528	2,290 (?)
(Miles)	74,978	32,193	30,775	1,423 (?)
Atmosphere (Main components)	Hydrogen helium	Helium hydrogen methane	Hydrogen helium methane	None detected
Satellites	18+[1]	15	8	1
Rings	1,000 (?)	11	4	?

1. 1981 S13 discovered from *Voyager* photos in 1990. *Source:* Basic NASA data and other sources.

THE SOLAR SYSTEM

THE SOLAR SYSTEM. Orbiting around the Sun are Mercury, Venus, Earth, Mars, Jupiter, Saturn, Uranus, Neptune, and Pluto. Our Solar System was born nearly five billion years ago out of a cloud of interstellar gas and dust. Gravity caused this nebula to contract and flatten into a spinning disk. Near the center, where the density was greatest, a body formed which was so massive that its internal pressures ignited and sustained a nuclear reaction, creating a star we call the Sun. Elsewhere in the cloud, smaller bodies coalesced and cooled—nine planets, perhaps fifty moons, millions of asteroids, and billions of comets. Within our Milky Way Galaxy, there may be billions of other solar systems. Copyright © 1984 Hansen Planetarium, Salt Lake City, Utah. Reproduced with Permission.

and South America could be pushed toward western and southern Europe and western Africa, they would fit like pieces in a jigsaw puzzle. Today, there is little question—the continents have drifted widely and continue to do so.

In 10 million years, the world as we know it may be unrecognizable, with California drifting out to sea, Florida joining South America, and Africa moving farther away from Europe and Asia.

The Earth's Atmosphere. The thin blanket of atmosphere that envelops the Earth extends several hundred miles into space. From sea level—the very bottom of the ocean of air—to a height of about 60 miles, the air in the atmosphere is made up of the same gases in the same ratio: about 78% nitrogen, 21% oxygen, and the remaining 1% being a mixture of argon, carbon dioxide, and tiny amounts of neon, helium, krypton, xenon, and other gases. The atmosphere becomes less dense with increasing altitude: more than three-fourths of the Earth's huge envelope is concentrated in the first 5 to 10 miles above the surface. At sea level, a cubic foot of the atmosphere weighs about an ounce and a quarter. The entire atmosphere weighs 5,700,000,000,000,000 tons, and the force with which gravity holds it in place causes it to exert a pressure of nearly 15 pounds per square inch. Going out from the Earth's surface, the atmosphere is divided into five regions. The regions, and the heights to which they extend, are: *Troposphere*, 0 to 7 miles (at middle latitudes); *stratosphere*, 7 to 30 miles; *mesosphere*, 30 to 50 miles; *thermosphere*, 50 to 400 miles; and *exosphere*, above 400 miles. The boundaries between each of the regions are known respectively as the *tropopause, stratopause, mesopause,* and *thermopause.* Alternate terms often used for the layers above the troposphere are *ozonosphere* (for stratosphere) and *ionosphere* for the remaining upper layers.

The Seasons. Seasons are caused by the 23.4 degree tilt of the Earth's axis, which alternately turns the North and South Poles toward the Sun. Times when the Sun's apparent path crosses the Equator are known as *equinoxes.* Times when the Sun's apparent path is at the greatest distance from the Equator are known as *solstices.* The lengths of the days are most extreme at each solstice. If the Earth's axis were perpendicular to the plane of the Earth's orbit around the Sun, there would be no seasons, and the days always would be equal in length. Since the Earth's axis is at an angle, the Sun strikes the Earth directly at the Equator only twice a year: in March (vernal equinox) and September (autumnal equinox). In the Northern Hemisphere, spring begins at the vernal equinox, summer at the summer solstice, fall at the autumnal equinox, and winter at the winter solstice. The situation is reversed in the Southern Hemisphere.

Mercury

Mercury is the planet nearest the Sun. Appropriately named for the wing-footed Roman messenger of the gods, Mercury whizzes around the Sun at a speed of 30 miles per second completing one circuit in 88 days. The days and nights are long on Mercury. It takes 59 Earth days for Mercury to make a single rotation. It spins at a rate of about 10 kilometers (about 6 miles) per hour, measured at the equator, as compared to the Earth's spin of about 1,690 kilometers (about 1,000 miles) per hour at the equator.

The photographs *Mariner 10* (1974-75) radioed back to Earth revealed an ancient, heavily cratered surface on Mercury, closely resembling our own Moon. The pictures showed huge cliffs, or scarps, crisscrossing the planet. These apparently were created when Mercury's interior cooled and shrank, compressing the planet's crust. The cliffs are as high as two kilometers (1.2 miles) and as long as 1,500 kilometers (932 miles). Another unique feature is the Caloris Basin, a large impact crater about 1,300 kilometers (808 miles) in diameter.

Mercury, like the Earth, appears to have a crust of light silicate rock. Scientists believe it has a heavy iron-rich core that makes up about half of its volume.

Instruments onboard *Mariner 10* discovered that the planet has a weak magnetic field and a trace of atmosphere—a trillionth the density of the Earth's and composed chiefly of argon, neon, and helium. The spacecraft reported temperatures ranging from 510° C (950° F) on Mercury's sunlit side to −210° C (−346° F) on the dark side. Mercury literally bakes in daylight and freezes at night.

Until the *Mariner 10* probe, little was known about the planet. Even the best telescopic views from Earth showed Mercury as an indistinct object lacking any surface detail. The planet is so close to the Sun that it is usually lost in the Sun's glare.

● Mercury is a naked eye object at morning or evening twilight when it is at greatest elongation.

Venus

Although Venus is Earth's closest neighbor, very little is known about the planet because it is permanently covered by thick clouds. In 1962, Soviet and American space probes, coupled with Earth-based radar and infrared spectroscopy, began slowly unraveling some of the mystery surrounding Venus.

According to the latest results, Venus' atmosphere exerts a pressure at the surface 94.5 times greater than Earth's. Walking on Venus would be as difficult as walking a half-mile beneath the ocean. Because of a thick blanket of carbon dioxide, a "greenhouse effect" exists on Venus. Venus intercepts twice as much of the Sun's light as does the Earth. The light enters freely through the carbon dioxide gas and is changed to heat radiation in molecular collisions. But carbon dioxide prevents the heat from escaping. Consequently, the temperature of the surface of Venus is over 800° F, hot enough to melt lead.

The atmospheric composition of Venus is about 96% carbon dioxide, 4% nitrogen, and minor amounts of water, oxygen, and sulfur compounds. There are at least four distinct cloud and haze layers that exist at different altitudes above the planet's surface. The haze layers contain small aerosol particles, possibly droplets of sulfuric acid. A concentration of sulfur dioxide above the cloud tops has been observerd to be decreasing since 1978. The source of sulfur dioxide at this altitude is unknown; it may be injected by volcanic explosions or atmospheric overturning.

Measurements of the Venusian atmosphere and its cloud patterns reveal nearly constant high-speed zonal winds, about 100 meters per second (220 miles per hour) at the equator. The winds decrease toward the poles so that the atmosphere at cloud-top level rotates almost like a solid body. The wind speeds at the equator correspond to Venus' rotation period of four to five days at most latitudes. The circulation is always in the same direction—east to west—as Venus' slow retrograde motion.

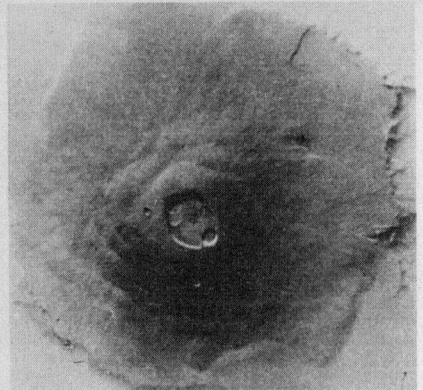

Giant Olympus Mons, the tallest volcano on Mars, is also the highest mountain in the solar system. It is 540 kilometers (336 miles) across and rises 10 miles higher than Mount Everest. NASA photo.

Earth's winds blow from west to east, the same direction as its rotation.

Venus is quite round, very different from the other planets and from the Moon. Venus has neither polar flattening nor an equatorial bulge. The diameter of Venus is 12,100 kilometers (7,519 miles). Venus has a retrograde axial rotation period of 243.1 Earth days. The surface atmospheric pressure is 1,396 pounds per square inch (95 Earth atmospheres). The planet's mean distance from the Sun is 108.2 million kilometers (67.2 million miles). The period of its revolution around the Sun is 224.7 days.

The highest point on Venus is the summit of Maxwell Montes, 10.8 kilometers (6.71 miles) above the mean level, more than a mile taller than Mount Everest. There is some evidence that this huge mountain is an active volcano. The lowest point is in the rift valley, Diana Chasma, 2.9 kilometers (1.8 miles) below the mean level. This point is about one-fifth the greatest depth on Earth in the Marianas Trench.

Venus has an extreme lowland basin, Atalanta Planitia, which is about the size of Earth's North Atlantic Ocean basin. The smooth surface of the Atalanta Planitia resembles the mare basins of the Moon.

There are only two highland or continental masses on Venus: Ishtar Terra and Aphrodite Terra. Ishtar Terra is 11 kilometers (6.8 miles) at its highest points (the highest peaks on Venus) and those of Aphrodite Terra rise to about 5 kilometers (3.10 miles) above the planet. Ishtar Terra is about the size of the continental United States and Aphrodite Terra is about the size of Africa.

Scientists are yet uncertain if Venus is geologically active. Lightning which was interpreted to result from active volcanism has been inferred from *Pioneer Venus Orbiter* electric measurements but the signals attributed to lightning may be the result of other causes.

The unmanned NASA spacecraft *Magellan* was launched on May 4, 1989, from the shuttle *Atlantis*. It was to arrive at Venus August 1990 and will map up to 90% of the planet. (*Also see* Space Section and Current Events.)

• Venus is the brightest of all the planets and is often visible in the morning or evening, when it is frequently referred to as the Morning Star or Evening Star. At its brightest, it can sometimes be seen with the naked eye in full daylight, if one knows where to look.

Mars

Mars, on the other side of the Earth from Venus, is Venus' direct opposite in terms of physical properties. Its atmosphere is cold, thin, and transparent, and readily permits observation of the planet's features. We know more about Mars than any other planet except Earth. Mars is a forbidding, rugged planet with huge volcanoes and deep chasms. The largest volcano, Olympus Mons rises 78,000 feet above the surface, higher than Mount Everest. The plains of Mars are pockmarked by the hits of thousands of meteors over the years.

Most of our information about Mars comes from the Mariner 9 spacecraft, which orbited the planet in 1971. Mariner 9, photographing 100% of the planet, uncovered spectacular geological formations, including a Martian Grand Canyon that dwarfs the one on Earth. The spacecraft's cameras also recorded what appeared to be dried riverbeds, suggesting the onetime presence of water on the planet. The latter idea gives encouragement to scientists looking for life on Mars, for where there is water, there may be life. However, by 1979, no evidence of life has been found. Temperatures near the equator range from −17 degrees F. in the daytime to −130 degrees F. at night.

Mars rotates upon its axis in nearly the same period as Earth—24 hours, 37 minutes—so that a Mars day is almost identical to an Earth day. Mars takes 687 days to make one trip around the Sun. Because of its eccentric orbit Mars' distance from the Sun can vary by about 36 million miles. Its distance from Earth can vary by as much as 200 million miles. The atmosphere of Mars is much thinner than Earth's; atmospheric pressure is about 1% that of our planet. Its gravity is one-third of Earth's. Major constituents are carbon dioxide and nitrogen. Water vapor and oxygen are minor constituents. Mars' polar caps, composed mostly of carbon dioxide, recede and advance according to the Martian seasons. Mars has four seasons like Earth, but they are much longer. For example, in the northern hemisphere, the Martian spring is 198 days, and the winter season lasts 158 days.

Mars was named for the Roman god of war, because when seen from Earth its distinct red color reminded the ancient people of blood. We know now that the reddish hue reflects the oxidized (rusted) iron in the surface material. The landing of two robot Viking spacecraft on the surface of Mars in 1976 provided more information about Mars in a few months than in all the time that has gone before.

The Martian Moons

Mars has two very small elliptical-shaped moons, Deimos and Phobos—the Greek names for the companions of the God Mars: Deimos (Terror) and Phobos (Fear). They were discovered in August 1877 by the American astronomer Asaph Hall of the U.S. Naval Observatory in Washington, D.C.

The inner satellite Phobos is 27 kilometers (16.78 miles) long and it revolves around the planet in 7.6 hours. The outer moon, Deimos, is 15 kilometers (9.32 miles) long and it circles the planet in 30.35

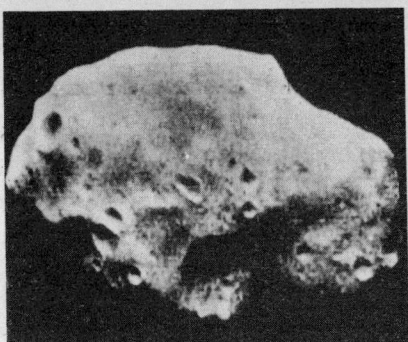

Phobos, Mars' tiny inner moon, is covered with a large number of craters.

hours. The short orbital period of Phobos means that the satellite travels around Mars twice in a Martian day. If an observer were suitably situated on the planet, he would see Phobos rise and set twice in a day.

Recent studies of Phobos indicate that its orbit is slowly decreasing downward and that in approximately 40 million years, it will crash into the planet's surface.

In 1988, the Soviet Union launched two spacecraft to study the geology, climate, and atmosphere of Mars, and explore its moon, Phobos. The attempt was unsuccessful as contact was lost with both spacecraft.

The Soviet Union plans to make unmanned studies of the Martian atmosphere and surface during 1994 to 1996. (*Also see* Space Section.)

Meteorites From Mars

Our knowledge of the origin and history of Mars has been greatly enhanced by recent research showing that a group of eight meteorites, labeled SNC[1] (named for towns where they were found: Shergotty, India, in 1865; Nakhla, Egypt, in 1911; and Chassigny, France, in 1815), are probably samples of Mars. This hypothesis is based largely on the composition of noble gases (particularly argon and xenon) trapped in the meteorites, and the Shergottites in particular, which resemble measurements of the Martian atmosphere made by the *Viking* spacecraft. Major element compositions of the SNCs are also similar to Martian soil analyses made by *Viking*.

These meteorites suggest that the Martian mantle is two to four times richer than Earth in moderately volatile elements such as potassium, rubidium, chlorine, bromine, sodium, zinc, and lead. In contrast, nitrogen, carbon dioxide, and the noble gases are more depleted than expected in the Martian atmosphere, suggesting an episode of severe atmospheric loss at some time in its history.

The relatively young isotopic ages of the SNC meteorites (1.3 billion years or less) suggest that Mars has been volcanically active during its recent past.

Scientists do not know how the meteorites were thrown off the Martian surface.

1. Pronounced "snick."

Jupiter

Jupiter is the largest planet in the solar system—a gaseous world as large as 1,300 Earths. Its equatorial diameter is 142,800 kilometers (88,736 miles), while from pole to pole, Jupiter measures only 133,500 kilometers (84,201 miles). For comparison, the diameter of the Earth is 12,756 kilometers (7,926.2 miles). The massive planet rotates at a dizzying speed—once every 9 hours and 55 minutes. It takes Jupiter almost 12 Earth years to complete a journey around the Sun.

The giant planet appears as a banded disk of turbulent clouds with all of its stripes running parallel to its bulging equator. Large dusky gray regions surround each pole. Darker Gray or brown stripes called belts intermingle with lighter, yellow-white stripes called zones. The belts are regions of descending air masses and the zones are rising cloudy air masses. The strongest winds—up to 400 kilometers (250 miles) per hour—are found at boundaries between the belts and zones.

This uniquely colorful atmosphere is mainly hydrogen and helium. It contains small amounts of methane, ammonia, ethane, acetylene, phosphene, germanium tetrahydride, and possibly hydrogen cyanide.

Cloud-type lightning bolts similar to those on Earth have been found in the Jovian atmosphere. At the polar regions, auroras have been observed. A very thin ring of material less than one kilometer (0.6 mile) in thickness and about 6,000 kilometers (4,000 miles) in radial extent has been observed circling the planet about 55,000 kilometers (35,000 miles) above the cloud tops.

The most prominent feature on Jupiter is its Great Red Spot, an oval larger than the planet Earth. It is a tremendous atmospheric storm that rotates counter-clockwise with one revolution every six days at the outer edge, while at the center almost no motion can be seen. The Spot is about 25,000 kilometers (16,000 miles) on its long axis, and would cover three Earths. The outer rim shows streamline shapes of 360-kilometer (225-mile) winds. Wind currents on the top flow east to west and currents on the top flow east to west and currents on the bottom flow west to east. The color of the Great Red Spot may indicate that it extends deep into the Jovian atmosphere.

The Spot was first seen more than three centuries ago. During the years, it has changed its color and size, and it escaped detection for nearly 50 years in the 1700s. *Voyager 1* and *2* found the

Jupiter's ring. A line has been drawn around a photograph of Jupiter to show the position of the extremely thin faint ring. NASA photo.

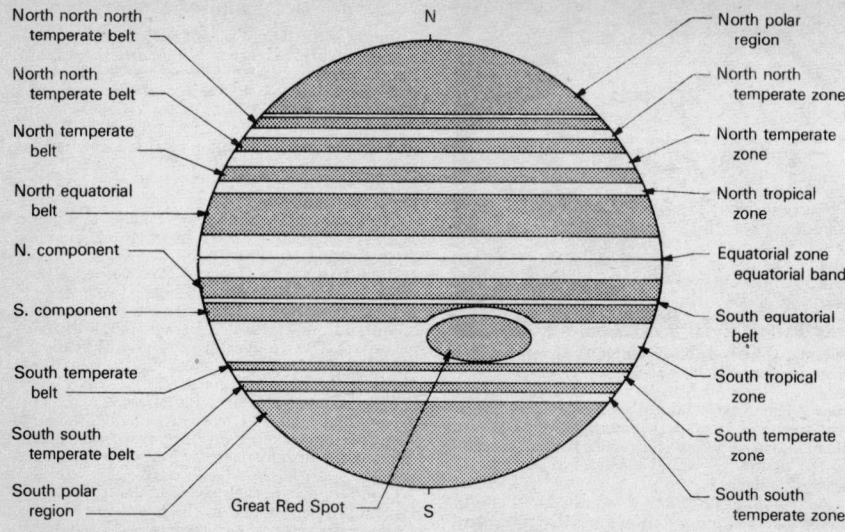

North north north temperate belt

North north temperate belt

North temperate belt

North equatorial belt

N. component

S. component

South temperate belt

South south temperate belt

South polar region

N

Great Red Spot

S

North polar region

North north temperate zone

North temperate zone

North tropical zone

Equatorial zone equatorial band

South equatorial belt

South tropical zone

South temperate zone

South south temperate zone

Schematic diagram of Jupiter's major features. NASA illustration.

Ganymede, Jupiter's largest satellite and also the largest known moon in the solar system. Its diverse surface indicates several periods of geologic activity.

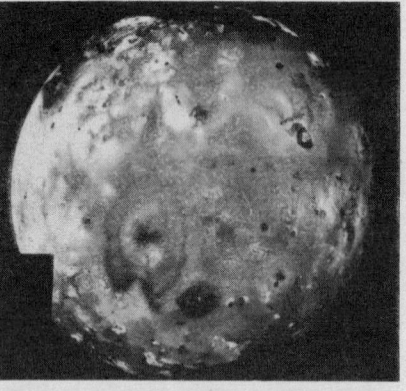

A computer-generated image of Io, the most volcanically active planetary body known in the solar system. Io's volcanoes and lava lakes cover the landscape and continually reface it, so that many impact craters have disappeared. NASA photo.

Great Red Spot to be cooler at the top than the surrounding clouds, indicating that the Spot may tower above them.

Jupiter emits 67% more heat than it absorbs from the Sun. This heat is thought to be accumulated during the planet's formation several billion years ago.

Jovian Moons

The four great moons of Jupiter were discovered by Galileo Galilei in January 1610, and are called the Galilean satellites after their discoverer. Their names are Io, Europa, Ganymede, and Callisto. Like our Moon, the satellites always keep the same face turned toward the Earth. Jupiter has 16 known satellites.

Ganymede

Ganymede, 5,270 kilometers (3,275 miles) in diameter, is Jupiter's largest moon, and also it is the largest satellite in the solar system. Ganymede is about one and one-half times the size of our Moon. It is heavily cratered and probably has the greatest variety of geologic process recorded on its surface.

Ganymede is half water and half rock, resulting in a density about two-thirds that of Europa, an ice-coated satellite. No atmosphere has been detected on it.

Europa

Europa, 3,130 kilometers (1,945 miles) in diameter, the brightest of Jupiter's Galilean satellites, may have a surface of thin ice crust overlying water or softer ice, with large-scale fracture and ridge systems appearing in the crust. Europa has a density about three times that of water, suggesting that it is a mixture of silicate rock and some water. Very few impact craters are visible on the surface, implying a continual resurfacing process, perhaps by the production of fresh ice or snow along cracks and cold glacier-like flows.

Callisto

Callisto, 4,840 kilometers (3,008 miles) in diameter, is the least active geologically of the Galilean satellites. Its icy, dirt-laden surface appears to be very ancient and heavily cratered. Callisto's density (less than twice that of water) is very close to that of Ganymede, yet there is little or no evidence of the crustal motion and internal activity that is visible on Ganymede.

Io

Io, 3,640 kilometers (2,262 miles) in diameter, is the most spectacular of the Galilean moons. Its brilliant colors of red, orange, and yellow set it apart from any other planet. Eight active volcanoes have been detected on Io, with some plumes extending up to 320 kilometers (200 miles) above the surface. The relative smoothness of Io's surface and its volcanic activity suggest that it has the youngest surface of Jupiter's moons. Its surface is composed of large amounts of sulfur and sulfur-dioxide frost, which account for the primarily yellow-orange surface color.

The volcanoes seem to eject a sufficient amount of sulfur dioxide to form a doughnut-shaped ring (torus) of ionized sulfur and oxygen atoms around Jupiter near Io's orbit. The Jovian magnetic field lines that go through the torus allow particles to precipitate into the polar regions of Jupiter, resulting in intense ultraviolet and visible auroras.

Amalthea

Amalthea, Jupiter's most innermost satellite, was discovered in 1892. It is so small—265 kilometers (165 miles) long and 150 kilometers (90 miles) wide—that it is extremely difficult to observe from Earth. Amalthea is an elongated, irregularly shaped satellite of reddish color. It orbits the planet every 12 hours and is in synchronous rotation, with its long axis always oriented toward Jupiter.

The Magnetosphere

Perhaps the largest structure in the solar system is the magnetosphere of Jupiter. This is the region of space which is filled with Jupiter's magnetic field and is bounded by the interaction of that magnetic field with the solar wind, which is the Sun's outward flow of charged particles. The plasma of electrically charged particles that exists in the magnetosphere is flattened into a large disk more than 4.8 million kilometers (3 million miles) in diameter, is coupled to the magnetic field, and rotates around Jupiter. The Galilean satellites are located in the inner regions of the magnetosphere and are subjected to intense radiation bombardment.

The intense radiation field that surrounds Jupiter is fatal to humans. If astronauts were one day able to approach the planet as close as the *Voyager 1* spacecraft did, they would receive a dose of 400,000 rads or roughly 1,000 times the lethal dose for humans.

In 1989, evidence from ground-based infrared spectra of Io indicated that the Jovian moon has hydrogen sulfide (H_2S) on its surface and in its atmosphere. It is the first time that the presence of H_2S has been detected outside the Earth.

● Even when nearest the Earth, Jupiter is still almost 400 million miles away. But because of its size, it may rival Venus in brilliance when near. Jupiter's four large moons may be seen through field glasses, moving rapidly around Jupiter and changing their position from night to night.

The United States launched its *Galileo* spacecraft toward Jupiter on Oct. 18, 1989. The unmanned spacecraft will reach Jupiter in 1995 and make a 22-month study of the planet.

Saturn

Saturn, the second largest planet in the solar system, is the least dense. Its mass is 95 times the mass of the Earth and its density is 0.70 gram per cubic centimeter, so that it would float in an ocean if there were one big enough to hold it.

Saturn radiates more energy than it receives from the Sun, about 80% more. However, the excess thermal energy cannot be primarily attributed to Saturn's primordial heat loss, as is speculated for Jupiter.

Saturn's diameter is 120,660 kilometers (74,978 miles) but 10% less at the poles, a consequence of its rapid rotation. Its axis of rotation is tilted by 27 degrees and the length of its day is 10 hours, 39 minutes, and 24 seconds.

Saturn is composed primarily of liquid metallic hydrogen (about 80%) and the second most common element is believed to be helium.

Saturn's atmospheric appearance is very similar to Jupiter's with dark and light cloud markings and swirls, eddies, and curling ribbons; the belts and zones are more numerous and a thick haze mutes the markings. The temperature ranges from 80° K to 90° K (176° F to −203° F).

Winds blow at extremely high speeds on Saturn. Near the equator, the *Voyagers* measured winds of about 500 meters per second (1,100 miles per hour). The winds blow primarily in an eastward direction.

Saturn's Rings

Saturn's spectacular ring system is unique in the solar system, with uncountable billions of tiny particles of water ice (with traces of other material) in orbit around the planet. The ring particles range in size from smaller than grains of sugar to as large as a house. The main rings stretch out from about 7,000 kilometers (4,350 miles) to above the atmosphere of the planet out to the F ring, a total span of 74,000 kilometers (45,984 miles). Saturn's rings can be likened to a phonograph, rings within rings numbering in the hundreds, and spokes in the B rings, and shepherding satellites controlling the F ring.

The main rings are called the A, B, and C rings moving from outside to inside. The gap between the A and B rings is called the Cassini Division and is named for the Italian-French astronomer, Gian Domenico Cassini, who discovered four of Saturn's major moons and the dark, narrow gap, "Cassini's Division," splitting the planet's rings.

Saturn's magnetic field has well-defined north and south magnetic poles, and is aligned with Saturn's axis of rotation to within one degree.

Saturn's Moons

Saturn has 18 recognized moons and there is evidence for several more. The five largest moons, Tethys, Dione, Rhea, Titan, and Iapetus, range from 1060 to 5150 kilometers (650 to 3,200 miles) in diameter. The planet's outstanding satellite is Titan, first discovered by the Dutch astronomer Christiaan Huygens in 1656.

Titan

Titan is remarkable because it is the only known moon in the solar system that has a substantial atmosphere—largely nitrogen with a minor amount of methane and a rich variety of other hydrocarbons. Its surface is completely hidden from view (except at infrared and radio wavelengths) by a dense, hazy atmosphere.

The diameter of Titan is 5,150 kilometers (3,200 miles) and it is the second largest satellite in the solar system after Jupiter's Ganymede. Titan is larger than the planet Mercury.

Titan's surface temperature is about −175° C (−280° F) and its surface pressure is about 50% greater than the surface pressure of the Earth. After the Voyager I flyby in 1980, scientists hypothesized that Titan may have an ocean of liquid hydrogen covering its surface. However, in 1990 it was shown that Titan's surface reflects and scatters radio waves, suggesting that the satellite has a solid surface with the possibility of small hydrocarbon lakes.

The new data was obtained by using NASA's 70-meter antenna in California to transmit powerful radio waves to Titan, and the Very Large Array in New Mexico as the receiver of the reflected waves.

NASA plans to send a scientific probe to the surface of Titan in August 2002 as part of its Cassini Mission. The probe will be provided by the European Space Agency (ESA). For further details, see the "Cassini Mission" in the special *Space* section of *Information Please Almanac*.

Other Notable Saturnian Moons

The other four largest moons of Saturn are: Tethys, Dione, Rhea, and Iapetus.

Tethys is 1,060 kilometers (650 miles) in diameter. Its surface is heavily cratered and it has a huge, globe-girdling canyon, Ithaca Chasma. Part of the canyon stretches over three-quarters of the satellite's surface. Ithaca Chasma is about 2,500 kilometers (1,550 miles) long. It has an average width of about 100 kilometers (62 miles) and a depth of 3 to 5 kilometers (1.8 to 3.1 miles).

Tethys also has a huge impact crater named Odysseus, 400 kilometers (244 miles) in diameter, or more than one-third its diameter.

Dione is slightly larger than Tethys, 1,120 kilometers (696 miles) and is more than half composed of water ice. It has bright, wispy markings resembling thin veils covering its features.

Rhea, the largest of the inner satellites, is 1,530 kilometers (951 miles) in diameter. It is composed mainly of water ice, causing its reflective surface to present an almost uniform white appearance.

Iapetus is the outermost of Saturn's icy satellites. Its appearance is unique because it has one dark and one bright hemisphere. The origin of the black coating of its dark face is unknown. Iapetus has a diameter of 1,460 kilometers (907 miles).

Other notable moons of Saturn are Mimas, Enceladus, Hyperion, and Phoebe.

Mimas is small, only 329 kilometers (244 miles) in diameter. It has a huge impact crater, Herschel, nearly one-third its diameter. The crater is about 130 kilometers (81 miles) wide and its icy peak rises almost 10 kilometers (6.2 miles) above the floor.

Mimas is believed to be composed mainly of water ice and to contain between 20 to 50% rock.

Enceladus is remarkable in that its surface shows signs of extensive and recent geological activity. There may be active water volcanism. The surface is extremely bright, reflecting more than 90% of incident sunlight. This suggests that its surface is composed of extremely pure ice without dust or rocks to contaminate it.

Enceladus has a diameter of 500 kilometers (310 miles).

Hyperion orbits between Iapetus and Titan. It is irregular in shape, measuring about 400 by 250 by 200 kilometers (248 by 155 by 124 miles). It may be a remnant of a much larger object which was shattered by impact with another space body. It appears that Hyperion is composed primarily of water ice.

Hyperion orbits Saturn in a randon-like motion ("chaotic tumbling").

Phoebe is Saturn's outermost satellite. It travels in a retrograde orbit at a distance of over 10 million kilometers (6.2 million miles) away from the planet. It is the darkest moon of Saturn and is the planet's only known satellite that does not keep the same face always turned to Saturn. It has been speculated that it is an asteroid that was captured by the planet.

Phoebe rotates in about nine hours and orbits Saturn in 406 days. It has a diameter of 200 kilometers (124 miles).

1981 S13 discovered in 1990 from *Voyager 2* photos taken in 1981. An official name is to be approved by the International Astronomical Union. The satellite is estimated to be about 20 kilometers (12.43 miles) in diameter, which makes it the planet's smallest known moon.

The remaining eight moons range from 25 to 190 kilometers (15 to 120 miles) in diameter. They are all non-spherical in shape.

NASA's planned Cassini Mission to Saturn in the later 1990s will shed more light on the planet's mysteries. (*See* Cassini Mission in the Space Section.)

● Saturn is the last of the planets visible to the naked eye. Saturn is never an object of overwhelming brilliance, but it looks like a bright star. The rings can be seen with a small telescope.

Uranus

Uranus, the first planet discovered in modern times by Sir William Herschel in 1781, is the seventh planet from the Sun, twice as far out as Saturn. Its mean distance from the Sun is 2,869 million kilometers (1,783 million miles). Uranus's equatorial diameter is 51,810 kilometers (32,200 miles). The

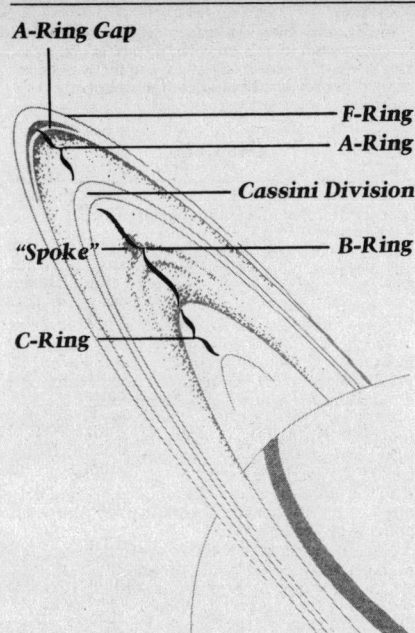

A-Ring Gap

F-Ring

A-Ring

Cassini Division

"Spoke"

B-Ring

C-Ring

NASA illustration of the divisions in Saturn's ring system.

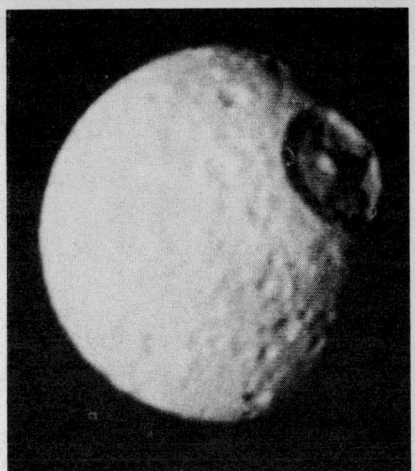

Photo of icy Mimias shows the largest meteorite crater which is about one-quarter the diameter of the entire moon. A huge mountain can be seen rising up almost 20,000 feet from the center of the crater. The crater's walls average 16,000 feet in height. NASA photo.

axis of Uranus is tilted at 97 degrees, so it goes around the Sun nearly lying on its side.

Due to Uranus' unusual inclination, the polar regions receive more sunlight during a Uranus year of 84 Earth years. Scientists had thought that the temperature of its poles would be warmer than that at its equator, but *Voyager 2* discovered that the equatorial temperatures were similar to the temperatures at the poles, −209° C (−344° F), implying that some redistribution of heat toward the equatorial region must occur within the atmosphere. The wind patterns are much like Saturn's, flowing parallel to the equator in the direction of the planet's rotation.

Ninety-eight percent of the upper atmosphere is composed of hydrogen and helium; the remaining two percent is methane. Scientists speculate that the bulk of the lower atmosphere is composed of water (perhaps as much as 50%), methane, and ammonia. Methane is responsible for Uranus' blue-green color because it selectively absorbs red sunlight and condenses to form clouds of ice crystals in the cooler, higher regions of Uranus' atmosphere.

It was also discovered that the planet's magnetic field was 60 degrees tilted from the planet's axis of rotation and offset from the planet's center by one-third of Uranus' radius. It may be generated at a depth where water is under sufficient pressure to be electrically conductive.

The Uranian Rings

Voyager 2 also expanded the body of information pertaining to the rings and moons of Uranus. *Voy-*

ager's cameras obtained the first images of nine previously known narrow rings and discovered at least two new rings, one narrow and one broadly diffused, bringing the total known rings to eleven. It was found that a highly structured distribution of fine dust exists throughout the ring system.

The outermost (epsilon) ring contains nothing smaller than fist-sized particles. It is flanked by two small moons discovered interior to the orbit of the Uranian moon Miranda. The moons exert a shepherding influence on the epsilon ring and on the outer edges of the gamma and delta rings.

All of the rings lie within one planetary radius[1] of Uranus' cloud tops. Most of Uranus' rings are narrow, ranging in width from 1 to 93 kilometers (0.6 to 58 miles) and are only a few kilometers thick. The Uranian rings are colorless and extremely dark. The dark material may be either irradiated methane ice or organic-rich minerals mixed with water-impregnated, silicon-based compounds. There is evidence that incomplete rings, or "ring arcs," exist at Uranus.

The Uranian Moons

There are 15 known moons of Uranus. In order of decreasing distance from the planet, the moons are Oberon, Titania, Umbriel, Ariel, Miranda, Puck, Belinda, Cressida, Portia, Rosalind, Desdemona, Juliet, Bianca, Ophelia, and Cordelia. Nine of the new moons range in size from 26 to 108 kilometers (16 to 67 miles) in diameter and, being closer to the planet, have faster periods of revolution (8 to 15 hours) than their more distant relatives.

1. The equatorial radius of Uranus is 25,560 kilometers (15,880 miles) at a pressure of 1 bar.

The Uranian moon Miranda is one of the strangest objects in the solar system. Photo shows some of its complex surface terrain. NASA photo.

Oberon and Titania

The two largest moons, Oberon, 1,516 kilometers (942 miles) in diameter, and Titania (1,580 kilometers (982 miles) in diameter, are less than half the diameter of Earth's moon. Titania, the reddest of Uranus' moons, may have endured global tectonics as evidenced by complex valleys and fault lines etched into its surface. Smooth sections indicate that volcanic resurfacing has taken place.

Umbriel and Ariel

Umbriel and Ariel are roughly three-fourths the size of Oberon and Titania. Umbriel is the darkest of the large moons with huge craters peppering its surface. Umbriel has a paucity of what are known as bright ray craters, which are formed on an older darker surface when bright submerged ice is excavated and sprayed by meteoroid impacts.

In contrast, the surface of Ariel, the brightest of the Uranian moons, is relatively free of pockmarks due to volcanism which periodically erases the damage done by foreign projectiles. However, there are several extremely deep cuts on Ariel's surface.

Miranda

The smallest of Uranus' large moons, Miranda, 472 kilometers (293 miles) in diameter, has been described as "the most bizarre body in the solar system," with the most geologically complex surface. Miranda's remarkable terrain consists of rolling, heavily cratered plains (the oldest known in the Uranian system) adjoined by three huge, 200 to 300 kilometer (120 to 180 mile) oval-to-trapezoidal regions known as coronae, which are characterized by networks of concentric canyons.

Puck

Puck was the first new moon discovered by *Voyager*, and is 154 kilometers (96 miles) in diameter and makes a trip around Uranus every 18 hours. Puck is shaped somewhat like a potato with a huge impact crater marring roughly one-fourth of its surface.

• Uranus can—on rare occasions—become bright enough to be seen with the naked eye, if one knows exactly where to look; normally, a good set of field glasses or a small portable telescope is required.

Neptune

Little was known about Neptune until August 1989, when NASA's *Voyager 2* became the first spacecraft to observe the planet. Passing about 4,950 kilometers (3,000 miles) above Neptune's north pole, *Voyager 2* made its closest approach to any planet since leaving Earth twelve years prior. The spacecraft passed about 40,000 kilometers (25,000 miles) from Neptune's largest moon, Triton, the last solid body that *Voyager 2* will have studied.

Nearly 4.5 billion kilometers (3 billion miles) from the Sun, Neptune orbits the Sun once in 165 years, and therefore has made not quite a full circle around the Sun since it was discovered.[1]

With an equatorial diameter of 49,528 kilometers (30,775 miles), Neptune is the smallest of our solar system's four gas giants.[2] Even so, its volume could hold nearly 60 Earths. Neptune is also denser than the other gas giants—Jupiter, Saturn, and Uranus, about 64% heavier than if it were composed entirely of water.

Neptune has a blue color as a result of methane in its atmosphere. Methane preferentially absorbs the longer wavelengths of sunlight (those near the red end of the spectrum). What are left to be reflected are colors at the blue end of the spectrum.

The atmosphere of Neptune is mainly composed of hydrogen, with helium and traces of methane and ammonia.

Neptune is a dynamic planet even though it receives only three percent as much sunlight as Jupiter does. Several large, dark spots are prominent features on the planet. The largest spot is about the size of the Earth and was designated the "Great Dark Spot" by its discoverers. It appears to be an anticyclone similar to Jupiter's Great Red Spot. While Neptune's Great Dark Spot is comparable in size, relative to the planet, and at the same latitude (22° south latitude) as Jupiter's Great Red Spot, it is far more variable in size and shape than its Jovian counterpart. Bright, wispy "cirrus-type" clouds overlay the Great Dark Spot at its southern and northeastern boundaries.

At about 42° south, a bright, irregularly shaped, eastward-moving cloud circles much faster than does the Great Dark Spot, "scooting" around Neptune in about 16 hours. This "scooter" may be a cloud plume rising between cloud decks.

Another spot, designated "D2," is located far to the south of the Great Dark Spot at 55° S latitude. It is almond-shaped, with a bright central core, and moves eastward around the planet in about 16 hours.

---

1. Astronomers have studied Neptune since Sept. 23, 1846, when Johann Gottfried Galle, of the Berlin Observatory, and Louis d'Arrest, an astronomy student, discovered the eighth planet on the basis of mathematical predictions by Urbain Jean Joseph Le Verrier. Similar predictions were made independently by John Couch Adams. Galileo Galilei had seen Neptune during several nights of observing Jupiter, in January 1613, but didn't realize he was seeing a new planet.
2. These four planets are about 4 to 12 times greater in diameter than Earth. They have no solid surfaces, but possess massive atmospheres that contain substantial amounts of hydrogen and helium with traces of other gases.

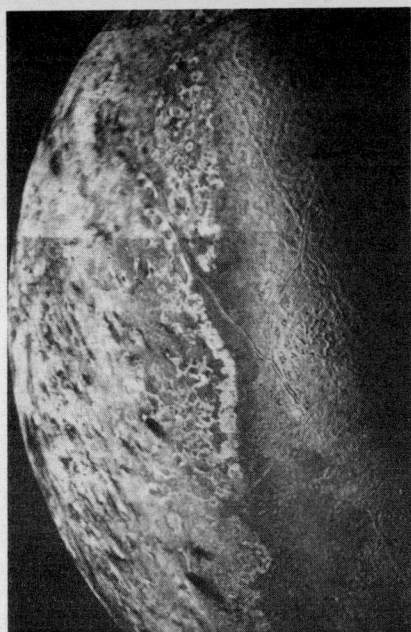

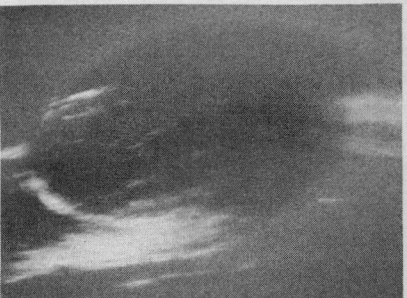

ABOVE LEFT: The rugged terrain of Triton, Neptune's largest moon. *Voyager 2* photographed geyser-like eruptions of nitrogen gas on Triton. ABOVE RIGHT: High-altitude clouds in Neptune's atmosphere. BELOW RIGHT: The Great Dark Spot is the most prominent feature in the planet's atmosphere. It is a counter-clockwise storm about the size of the Earth.

The atmosphere above Neptune's clouds is hotter near the equator, cooler in the mid-latitudes, and warm again at the south pole. Temperatures in the stratosphere were measured to be 750 kelvins (900° F), while at the 100 millibar pressure level, they were measured to be 55° K (−360° F).

Long, bright clouds, reminiscent of cirrus clouds on Earth, were seen high in Neptune's atmosphere. They appear to form above most of the methane, and consequently are not blue.

At northern low latitudes (27° N), *Voyager* captured images of cloud streaks casting their shadows on cloud decks estimated to be about 50 to 100 kilometers (30 to 60 miles) below. The widths of these cloud streaks range from 50 to 200 kilometers (30 to 125 miles). Cloud streaks were also seen in the southern polar regions (71° S) where the cloud heights were about 50 kilometers (30 miles).

Most of the winds on Neptune blow in a westward direction, which is retrograde, or opposite to the rotation of the planet. Near the Great Dark Spot, there are retrograde winds blowing up to 1,500 miles an hour—the strongest winds measured on any planet.

The Magnetic Field

Neptune's magnetic field is tilted 47 degrees from the planet's rotation axis, and is offset at least 0.55 radii (about 13,500 kilometers or 8,500 miles) from the physical center. The dynamo electric currents produced within the planet, therefore, must be relatively closer to the surface than for Earth, Jupiter, or Saturn. Because of its unusual orientation, and the tilt of the planet's rotation axis, Neptune's magnetic field goes through dramatic changes as the planet rotates in the solar wind.

Voyager's planetary radio astronomy instrument measured the periodic radio waves generated by the magnetic field and determined that the rotation rate of the interior of Neptune is 16 hours 7 minutes.

Voyager also detected auroras, similar to the northern and southern lights on Earth, in Neptune's atmosphere. Unlike those on Earth, due to Neptune's complex magnetic field, the auroras are extremely complicated processes that occur over wide regions of the planet, not just near the planet's magnetic poles.

Neptune's Moons

Triton

The largest of Neptune's eight known satellites, Triton is different from all other icy moons that *Voyager* has studied. Triton circles Neptune in a tilted, circular, retrograde orbit, completing an orbit in 5.875 days at an average distance of 330,000 kilometers (205,000 miles) above the planet's cloud tops.

Triton shows evidence of a remarkable geologic history, and *Voyager 2* images show active geyser-like eruptions spewing invisible nitrogen gas and dark dust particles 2 to eight kilometers (1 to 5 miles) into space.

Triton is about three-quarters the size of Earth's moon and has a diameter of about 2,705 kilometers (1,680 miles), and a mean density of about 2.066 grams per cubic centimeter. (The density of water is 1.0 gram per cubic centimeter.) This means that Triton contains more rock in its interior than the icy satellites of Saturn and Uranus do.

The relatively high density and the retrograde orbit offer strong evidence that Triton did not originate near Neptune, but is a captured object.

An extremely thin atmosphere extends as much as 800 kilometers (500 miles) above the satellite's surface. Tiny nitrogen ice particles may form thin clouds a few kilometers above the surface. Triton is very bright, reflecting 60 to 95% of the sunlight that strikes it. (By comparison, Earth's moon reflects only 11 percent.)

The atmospheric pressure at Triton's surface is about 14 microbars, a mere 1/70,000th the surface pressure on Earth. Temperature at the surface is about 38 kelvins (−391° F), making it the coldest surface of any body yet visited in the solar system.

The Smaller Satellites

In addition to the previously known moons Triton and Nereid, *Voyager 2* found six more satellites, making the total eight.

Nereid

Nereid was discovered in 1948 through Earth-based telescopes. Little is known about Nereid, which is slightly smaller than 1989N1[3], having a diameter of 340 kilometers (211 miles). The satellite's surface reflects about 14% of the sunlight that strikes it. Nereid's orbit is the most eccentric in the solar system, ranging from about 1,353,600 km (841,100 miles) to 9,623,700 (5,980,200 mi.).

1989N1 to 1989N6

1989N1. Like all six of Neptune's newly discovered small satellites, it is one of the darkest objects in the solar system—"as dark as soot" is a good description. It reflects only 6% of the sunlight that strikes it. 1989N1 is about 400 kilometers (250 miles) in diameter, larger than Nereid. It circles Neptune at a distance of about 92,800 kilometers (57,700 miles) above the cloud tops, and completes one orbit in 26 hours 54 minutes. Scientists say that it is about as large as a satellite can be without being pulled into a spherical shape by its own gravity.

1989N2. This object is only about 48,800 kilometers (30,300 miles) from Neptune and circles the planet in 13 hours 18 minutes. Its diameter is 190 kilometers (120 miles).

1989N3. The satellite is 27,700 kilometers (17,200 miles) from Neptune's clouds and makes one orbit every 8 hours. Its diameter is about 150 kilometers (90 miles).

1989N4. It lies 37,200 kilometers (23,100 miles) from Neptune. Its diameter is 180 kilometers (110 miles) and it completes an orbit in 10 hours 18 minutes.

1989N5. The satellite appears to be about 80 kilometers (50 miles) in diameter. It orbits Neptune in 7 hours 30 minutes some 25,200 kilometers (15,700 miles) above the cloud tops.

1989N6. The last satellite discovered, it is about 54 kilometers (33 miles) in diameter and orbits Neptune about 23,200 kilometers (14,400 miles) above the clouds in 7 hours 6 minutes.

1989N1 and its tiny companions are cratered and irregularly shaped—they are not round—and show no signs of any geologic modifications. All circle the planet in the same direction as Neptune rotates, and remain close to Neptune's equatorial plane.

Neptune's Rings

Voyager found four rings and evidence of ring *arcs* or incomplete rings. The "Main Ring" orbits Neptune at about 38,100 kilometers (23,700 miles) above the cloud tops. The "Inner Ring" is about 28,400 kilometers (17,700 miles) from Neptune's cloud tops. An "Inside Diffuse Ring"—a complete ring—is located about 17,100 kilometers (10,600 miles) from the planet's cloud tops. Some scientists suspect that this ring may extend all the way down to Neptune's cloud tops. An area called "the Plateau" is a broad, diffuse sheet of fine material just outside the so-called "Inner Ring." The fine material is approximately the size of smoke particles. All other rings contain a greater proportion of larger material.

Pluto

Pluto, the outermost and smallest planet in the solar system, looks more like a terrestrial planet than a gaseous planet. But so little is known about it, that it is difficult to classify. Appropriately named for the Roman god of the underworld, it must be frozen, dark, and dead. Pluto's mean distance from the Sun is 5,900 million kilometers (3,666 million miles).

In 1978, light curve studies gave evidence of a moon revolving around Pluto with the same period as Pluto's rotation. Therefore, it stays over the same point on Pluto's surface. In addition, it keeps the same face toward the planet. The satellite was later named Charon and is estimated to be about 1,284 kilometers (798 miles) in diameter. Recent estimates indicate Pluto's diameter is about about 2,290 kilometers (1,423 miles), making the pair more like a double planet than any other in the solar system. Previously, the Earth-Moon system held this distinction. The density of Pluto is slightly greater than that of water.

There is evidence that Pluto has an atmosphere containing methane and polar ice caps that increase and decrease in size with the planet's seasons.

Pluto was predicted by calculation when Percival Lowell noticed irregularities in the orbits of Uranus and Neptune. Clyde Tombaugh discovered the planet in 1930, precisely where Lowell predicted it would be. The name Pluto was chosen because the first two letters represent the initials of Percival Lowell.

● Pluto has the most eccentric orbit in the solar system, bringing it at times closer to the Sun than Neptune. Pluto is now approaching the perihelion of its orbit, and for the rest of this century will be closer to the Sun than Neptune. Even then, it can be seen only with a large telescope.

3. The new satellites have not yet been named. The temporary designations give the year of discovery, the planet that they are associated with, and the order of discovery. For example, 1989N1 was the first satellite of Neptune found that year.

The First Ten Minor Planets (Asteroids)

Name	Year of discovery	Mean distance from sun (millions of miles)	Orbital period (years)	Diameter (miles)	Magnitude
1. Ceres	1801	257.0	4.60	485	7.4
2. Pallas	1802	257.4	4.61	304	8.0
3. Juno	1804	247.8	4.36	118	8.7
4. Vesta	1807	219.3	3.63	243	6.5
5. Astraea	1845	239.3	4.14	50	9.9
6. Hebe	1847	225.2	3.78	121	8.5
7. Iris	1847	221.4	3.68	121	8.4
8. Flora	1847	204.4	3.27	56	8.9
9. Metis	1848	221.7	3.69	78	8.9
10. Hygeia	1849	222.6	5.59	40 (?)	9.5

The Asteroids

Between the orbits of Mars and Jupiter are an estimated 30,000 pieces of rocky debris, known collectively as the asteroids, or planetoids. The first and, incidentally, the largest was discovered during the New Year's night of 1801 by the Italian astronomer Father Piazzi, and its orbit was calculated by the German mathematician Karl Friedrich Gauss. (Gauss invented a new method of calculating orbits on that occasion.) A German amateur astronomer, the physician Olbers, discovered the second asteroid. The number now known, catalogued, and named is over 2,000; the estimated total is about 20 times that figure. A few asteroids do not move in orbits beyond the orbit of Mars, but in orbits which cross the orbit of Mars. The first of them was named Eros because of this peculiar orbit. It had become the rule to bestow female names on the asteroids, but when it was found that Eros crossed the orbit of a major planet, it received a male name. Since then around two dozen orbit-crossers have been discovered, and they are often referred to as the "male asteroids." A few of them—Albert, Adonis, Apollo, Amor, and Icarus—cross the orbit of the Earth, and two of them may come closer than our Moon; but the crossing is like a bridge crossing a highway, not like two highways intersecting. Hence there is very little danger of collision from these bodies. They are all small, three to five miles in diameter, and therefore very difficult objects to identify, even when quite close. Some scientists believe the asteroids represent the remains of an exploded planet.

Comets

Comets, according to the noted astronomer, Fred L. Whipple, are enormous "snowballs" of frozen gases (mostly carbon dioxide, methane, and water vapor) and contain very little solid material. The whole behavior of comets can then be explained as the behavior of frozen gas being heated by the Sun. When the comet Kohoutek made its first appearance to man in 1973, its behavior seemed to confirm this theory and later, the international study by five spacecraft that encountered Comet Halley in March 1986 confirmed Whipple's idea of the make-up of comets.

Since comets appear in the sky without any warning, people in classical times and especially during the Middle Ages believed that they had a special meaning, which, of course, was bad. Since a natural catastrophe of some sort of a military conflict occurs every year, it was quite simple to blame the comet that happened to be visible. But even in the past, there were some people who used logical reasoning. When, in Roman times, a comet was blamed for the loss of a battle and hence was called a "bad omen," a Roman writer observed that the victors in the battle probably did not think so.

Up until the middle of the sixteenth century, comets were believed to be phenomena of the upper atmosphere; they were usually "explained" as "burning vapors" which had risen from "distant swamps." That nobody had ever actually seen burning vapors rise from a swamp did not matter.

But a large comet which appeared in 1577 was carefully observed by Tycho Brahe, a Danish astronomer who is often, and with the best of reasons, called "eccentric" but who insisted on precise measurements for everything. It was Tycho Brahe's accumulation of literally thousands of precise measurements which later enable his younger collaborator, Johannes Kepler, to discover the laws of planetary motion. Measuring the motion of the comet of 1577, Tycho Brahe could show that it had been far beyond the atmosphere, even though he could not give figures for the distance. Tycho Brahe's work proved that comets were astronomical and not meteorological phenomena.

In 1682, the second Astronomer Royal of Great Britain, Dr. Edmond Halley, checked the orbit of a bright comet that was in the sky then and compared it with earlier comet orbits which were known in part. Halley found that the comet of 1682 was the third to move through what appeared to be the same orbit. And the three appearances were roughly 76 years apart. Halley concluded that this was the same comet, moving around the Sun in a closed orbit, like the planets. He predicted that it would reappear in 1758 or 1759. Halley himself died in 1742, but a large comet appeared sixteen years after his death as predicted and was immediately referred to as "Halley's comet."

In the Spring of 1973, the discovery of comet Kohoutek, apparently headed for a close-Christmastime rendezvous with the Sun, created worldwide excitement. The comet was a visual disappointment, but turned out to be a treasure trove of information on these little-understood celestial objects. Given an unprecedented advance notice of nine months on the advent of the fiery object, scientists were able to study the comet in visible, ultraviolet and infrared light; with optical telescopes, radio telescopes, and radar. They observed it from the ground, from high-flying aircraft, with instruments aboard unmanned satellites, with sounding rockets, and telescopes and cameras on the Earth-orbiting Skylab space station.

Halley's Comet appeared again in 1986, sparking a worldwide effort to study it up close. Five satellites in all took readings from the comet at various distances. Two Soviet craft, *Vega 1* and *Vega 2*, went in close to provide detailed pictures of the comet, including the first of the comet's core. The European Space Agency's craft, *Giotto*, entered the comet itself, coming to within 450 miles of the comet's center and successfully passing through its tail. In addition, two Japanese craft, the *Suisei* and the *Sakigake*, passed at a longer distance in order to analyze the cloud and tail of the comet and the effect of solar radiation upon it. The United States declined to launch a similar mission, citing budgetary constraints imposed by the shuttle program. A space telescope was to study Halley's Comet but was destroyed in the *Challenger* disaster.

The information gained included measurements of the size of the nucleus, an idea of its configuration and the rate of its rotation. The gas and dust of the comet were analyzed as was the material of the tail. This information is considered important because comets are believed to be debris from the formation of the solar system and to have changed little since then.

Astronomers refer to comets as "periodic" or as "non-periodic" comets, but the latter term does not mean that these comets have no period; it merely means that their period is not known. The actual periods of comets run from 3.3 years (the shortest known) to many thousands of years. Their orbits are elliptical, like those of the planets, but they are very eccentric, long and narrow ellipses. Only comet Schwassmann-Wachmann has an orbit which has such a low eccentricity (for a cometary orbit) that it could be the orbit of a minor planet.

When a comet, coming from deep space, approaches the Sun, it is at first indistinguishable from a minor planet. Somewhere between the orbits of Mars and Jupiter its outline becomes fuzzy; it is said to develop a "coma" (the word used here is the Latin word *coma*, which means "hair," not the phonetically identical Greek word which means "deep sleep"). Then, near the orbit of Mars, the comet develops its tail, which at first trails behind. This grows steadily as the comet comes closer and closer to the Sun. As it rounds the Sun (as first noticed by Girolamo Fracastoro) the tail always points away from the Sun so that the comet, when moving away from the Sun, points its tail ahead like the landing lights of an airplane.

The reason for this behavior is that the tail is pushed in these directions by the radiation pressure of the Sun. It sometimes happens that a comet loses its tail at perihelion; it then grows another one. Although the tail is clearly visible against the black of the sky, it is very tenuous. It has been said that if the tail of Halley's comet could be compressed to the density of iron, it would fit into a small suitcase.

Although very low in mass, comets are among the largest members of the solar system. The nucleus of a comet may be up to 10,000 miles in diameter; its coma between 10,000 and 50,000 miles in diameter; and its tail as long as 28 million miles.

Meteors and Meteorites

The term "meteor" for what is usually called a "shooting star" bears an unfortunate resemblance to the term "meteorology," the science of weather and weather forecasting. This resemblance is due to an ancient misunderstanding which wrongly considered meteors an atmospheric phenomenon. Actually, the streak of light in the sky that scientists call a meteor is essentially an astronomical phenomenon: the entry of a small piece of cosmic matter into our atmosphere.

The distinction between "meteors" and "fireballs" (formerly also called "bolides") is merely one of convenience; a fireball is an unusually bright meteor. Incidentally, it also means that a fireball is larger than a faint meteor.

Bodies which enter our atmosphere become visible when they are about 60 miles above the ground. The fact that they grow hot enough to emit light is not due to the "friction" of the atmosphere, as one can often read. The phenomenon responsible for the heating is one of compression. Unconfined air cannot move faster than the speed of sound. Since the entering meteorite moves with 30 to 60 times the speed of sound, the air simply cannot get out of the way. Therefore, it is compressed like the air in the cylinder of a Diesel engine and is heated by compression. This heat—or part of it—is transferred to the moving body. The details of this process are now fairly well understood as a result of re-entry tests with ballistic-missile nose cones.

The average weight of a body producing a faint "shooting star" is only a small fraction of an ounce. Even a bright fireball may not weigh more than 2 or 3 pounds. Naturally, the smaller bodies are worn to dust by the passage through the atmosphere; only rather large ones reach the ground. Those that are found are called meteorites. (The "meteor," to repeat, is the term for the light streak in the sky.)

The largest meteorite known is still imbedded in the ground near Grootfontein in SW Africa and is estimated to weight 70 tons. The second largest known is the 34-ton Anighito (on exhibit in the Hayden Planetarium, New York), which was found by Admiral Peary at Cape York in Greenland. The largest meteorite found in the United States is the Willamette meteorite (found in Oregon, weight ca. 15 tons), but large portions of this meteorite weathered away before it was found. Its weight as it struck the ground may have been 20 tons.

All these are iron meteorites (an iron meteorite normally contains about 7% nickel), which form one class of meteorites. The other class consists of the stony meteorites, and between them there are the so-called "stony irons." The so-called "tektites" consist of glass similar to our volcanic glass obsidian, and because of the similarity, there is doubt in a number of cases whether the glass is of terrestrial or of extra-terrestrial origin.

Though no meteorite larger than the Grootfontein is actually known, we do know that the Earth has, on occasion, been struck by much larger bodies. Evidence for such hits are the meteorite craters, of which an especially good example is located near the Cañon Diablo in Arizona. Another meteor crater in the United States is a rather old crater near Odessa, Texas. A large number of others are known, especially in eastern Canada; and for many "probables," meteoric origin has now been proved.

The meteor showers are caused by multitudes of very small bodies travelling in swarms. The Earth travels in its orbit through these swarms like a car driving through falling snow. The point from which the meteors seem to emanate is called the *radiant* and is named for the constellation in that

The 88 Recognized Constellations

In astronomical works, the Latin names of the constellations are used. The letter N or S following the Latin name indicates whether the constellation is located to the north or south of the Zodiac. The letter Z indicates that the constellation is within the Zodiac.

Latin name	Letter	English version	Latin name	Letter	English version	Latin name	Letter	English version
Andromeda	N	Andromeda	Delphinus	N	Dolphin	Pavo	S	Peacock
Antlia	S	Airpump	Dorado	S	Swordfish	Pegasus	N	Pegasus
Apus	S	Bird of Paradise			(Goldfish)	Perseus	N	Perseus
Aquarius	Z	Water Bearer	Draco	N	Dragon	Phoenix	S	Phoenix
Aquila	N	Eagle	Equuleus	N	Filly	Pictor	S	Painter (or his
Ara	S	Altar	Eridanus	S	Eridanus (river)			Easel)
Aries	Z	Ram	Fornax	S	Furnace	Pisces	Z	Fishes
Auriga	N	Charioteer	Gemini	Z	Twins	Piscis		
Boötes	N	Herdsmen	Grus	S	Crane	Austrinus	S	Southern Fish
Caelum	S	Sculptor's Tool	Hercules	N	Hercules	Puppis	S	Poop (of Argo)[1]
Camelopardalis	N	Giraffe	Horologium	S	Clock	Pyxis	S	Mariner's
Cancer	Z	Crab	Hydra	N	Sea Serpent			Compass
Canes Venatici	N	Hunting Dogs	Hydrus	S	Water Snake	Reticulum	S	Net
Canis Major	S	Great Dog	Indus	S	Indian	Sagitta	N	Arrow
Canis Minor	S	Little Dog	Lacerta	N	Lizard	Sagittarius	Z	Archer
Capricornus	Z	Goat (or Sea-	Leo	Z	Lion	Scorpius	Z	Scorpion
		Goat)	Leo Minor	N	Little Lion	Sculptor	S	Sculptor
Carina	S	Keel (of Argo)[1]	Lepus	S	Hare	Scutum	N	Shield
Cassiopeia	N	Cassiopeia	Libra	Z	Scales	Serpens	N	Serpent
Centaurus	S	Centaur	Lupus	S	Wolf	Sextans	S	Sextant
Cepheus	N	Cepheus	Lynx	N	Lynx	Taurus	Z	Bull
Cetus	S	Whale	Lyra	N	Lyre (Harp)	Telescopium	S	Telescope
Chameleon	S	Chameleon	Mensa	S	Table	Triangulum	N	Triangle
Circinus	S	Compasses			(mountain)	Triangulum	S	Southern
Columba	S	Dove	Microscopium	S	Microscope	Australe		Triangle
Coma Berenices	N	Berenice's Hair	Monoceros	S	Unicorn	Tucana	S	Toucan
Corona Australis	S	Southern Crown	Musca	S	Southern Fly	Ursa Major	N	Big Dipper
Corona Borealis	N	Northern Crown	Norma	S	Rule	Ursa Minor	N	Little Dipper
Corvus	S	Crow (Raven)			(straightedge)	Vela	S	Sail (of Argo)[1]
Crater	S	Cup	Octans	S	Octant	Virgo	Z	Virgin
Crux	S	Southern Cross	Ophiuchus	N	Serpent-Bearer	Volans	S	Flying Fish
Cygnus	N	Swan	Orion	S	Orion	Vulpecula	N	Fox

1. The original constellation Argo Navis (the Ship Argo) has been divided into Carina, Puppis, and Vela. Normally the brightest star in each constellation is designated by alpha, the first letter of the Greek alphabet, the second brightest by beta, the second letter of the Greek alphabet, and so forth. But the Greek letters run through Carina, Puppis, and Vela as if it were still one constellation.

area. The Perseid meteor shower in August is the most spectacular of the year, boasting at peak roughly 60 meteors per hour under good atmospheric conditions. The presence of a bright moon diminishes the number of visible meteors.

The Constellations

Constellations are groupings of stars which form patterns that can be easily recognized and remembered, for example, Orion and the Big Dipper. Actually, the stars of the majority of all constellations do not "belong together." Usually they are at greatly varying distances from the Earth and just happen to lie more or less in the same line of sight as seen from our solar system. But in a few cases the stars of a constellation are actually associated; most of the bright stars of the Big Dipper travel together and form what astronomers call an open cluster.

If you observe a planet, say Mars, for one complete revolution, you will see that it passes successively through twelve constellations. All planets (except Pluto at certain times) can be observed only in these twelve constellations, which form the so-called Zodiac, and the Sun also moves through the Zodiacal signs, though the Sun's apparent movement is actually caused by the movement of the Earth.

Although the constellations are due mainly to the optical accident of line of sight and have no real significance, astronomers have retained them as reference areas. It is much easier to speak of a star in Orion than to give its geometrical position in the sky. During the Astronomical Congress of 1928, it was decided to recognize 88 constellations. A description of their agreed-upon boundaries was published at Cambridge, England, in 1930, under the title *Atlas Céleste*.

The Auroras

The "northern lights" *(Aurora borealis)* as well as the "southern lights" *(Aurora australis)* are upper-atmosphere phenomena of astronomical origin. The auroras center around the magnetic (not the geographical) poles of the Earth, which explains why, in the Western Hemisphere, they have been seen as far to the south as New Orleans and Florida while the equivalent latitude in the Eastern Hemisphere never sees an aurora. The northern magnetic pole happens to be in the Western Hemisphere.

The lower limit of an aurora is at about 50 miles. Upper limits have been estimated to be as high as 400 miles. Since about 1880, a connection between the auroras on Earth and the sun spots has been suspected and has gradually come to be accepted. It was said that the sun spots probably eject "particles" (later the word *electrons* was substituted) which on striking the Earth's atmosphere, cause the auroras. But this explanation suffered from certain difficulties. Sometimes a very large sun spot group on the Sun, with individual spots bigger than the Earth itself, would not cause an aurora. Moreover, even if a sun spot caused an aurora, the time that passed between the appearance of the one and the occurrence of the other was highly unpredictable.

This problem of the time lag is, in all probability, solved by the discovery of the Van Allen layer by artificial satellite *Explorer I*. The Van Allen layer is a double layer of charged sub-atomic particles around the Earth. The inner layer, with its center some 1,500 miles from the ground, reaches from about 40° N. to about 40° S. and does not touch the atmosphere. The outer layer, much larger and with its center several thousand miles from the ground, does touch the atmosphere in the vicinity of the magnetic poles.

It seems probable that the "leakage" of electrons from the outer Van Allen layer causes the auroras. A new burst of electrons from the Sun seems to be caught in the outer layer first. Under the assumption that all electrons are first caught in the outer layer, the time lag can be understood. There has to be an "overflow" from the outer layer to produce an aurora.

The Atmosphere

Astronomically speaking, the presence of our atmosphere is deplorable. Though reasonably transparent to visible light, the atmosphere may absorb as much as 60% of the visible and near-visible light. It is opaque to most other wave-lengths, except certain fairly short radio waves. In addition to absorbing much light, our atmosphere bends light rays entering at a slant (for a given observer) so that the true position of a star close to the horizon is not what it seems to be. One effect is that we see the Sun above the horizon before it actually is. And the unsteady movement of the atmosphere causes the "twinkling" of the stars, which may be romantic but is a nuisance when it comes to observing.

The composition of our atmosphere near the ground is 78% nitrogen and 21% oxygen, the remaining 1% consisting of other gases, most of it argon. The composition stays the same to an altitude of at least 70 miles (except that higher up two impurities, carbon dioxide and water vapor, are missing), but the pressure drops very fast. At 18,000 feet, half of the total mass of the atmosphere is below, and at 100,000 feet, 99% of the mass of the atmosphere is below. The upper limit of the atmosphere is usually given as 120 miles; no definitive figure is possible, since there is no boundary line between the incredibly attenuated gases 120 miles up and space.

Astronomical Telescopes

Optical telescopes used in astronomy are of two basic kinds: refracting and reflecting. In the *refractor telescope*, a lens is used to collect light from a distant object and bring it to a focus. A second lens, the eyepiece, then magnifies the image which may be examined visually or photographed directly. The *reflector telescope* uses a concave mirror instead of a lens, which reflects the light rays back toward the upper end of the telescope where they are magnified and observed or photographed. Most large optical telescopes now being built are reflectors.

Radio telescopes are used to study radio waves coming from outside the Earth's atmosphere. The waves are gathered by an antenna or "dish," which is a parabolic reflecting surface made of metal or finely meshed wire. Radio signals have been received from the Sun, Moon, and planets, and from the center of our galaxy and other galaxies. Radio signals are the means by which the distant and mysterious quasars and pulsars were recently discovered.

Very Large Telescope

In December 1987, the European Southern Observatory (ESO) agreed to build a super telescope called the Very Large Telescope in the mountains of northern Chile. It will be the world's largest ground-based optical telescope and will consist of four 8-meter (26.24 ft) telescopes whose mirrors will combine their images to simulate a single mirror of 16-meter (52.49 ft) diameter.

It will take at least ten years to complete construction of the super telescope and will cost about $235 million.

The Hubble Space Telescope

The Edwin P. Hubble Space Telescope was released by the space shuttle *Discovery* on April 25, 1990. It is able to peer far out in space and back in time, producing imagery of unprecedented clarity, of galaxies, star systems, and some of the universe's more intriguing objects: quasars, pulsars, and exploding galaxies. It can distinguish fine details—in planetary atmospheres or nearby star fields—with ten times the clarity of the best ground observatories. When pointed at Jupiter, for example, the telescope will provide images comparable to those from Voyager flybys.

The $1.6-billion Hubble Space Telescope has a primary mirror 2.4 m (94 inches) in diameter. The mirror is almost half the diameter of the 5-m (200 inch) telescope at Mt. Palomar, the most powerful ground-based telescope in the western world.

After it was placed in orbit at 380 miles (611.5 km) altitude, the Hubble Telescope became the principal tool for exploring the universe through this decade and the next.

The Space telescope can view galaxies and quasars over distances up to 14 billion light years. Seeing that far will show us the universe as it was early in its lifetime and will reveal how matter has evolved over the eons. It will also teach us more about the large structure of the universe, providing clues as to whether the universe will continue to expand.

The first two test images taken by the orbiting telescope of an open star cluster, NGC 3535, in the southern-sky constellation Carina (the Ship's Keel) revealed a double star previously suspected but not seen before.

It was discovered in June that there was a spherical aberration in one of the telescope's mirrors and this defect may not be repaired until a June 1993 shuttle mission. In the meantime, observations are continuing with the equipment that is working correctly.

Conversion of Universal Time (U. T.) to Civil Time

U.T.	E.D.T.[1]	E.S.T.[2]	C.S.T.[3]	M.S.T.[4]	P.S.T.[5]	U.T.	E.D.T.[1]	E.S.T.[2]	C.S.T.[3]	M.S.T.[4]	P.S.T.[5]
00	*8P	*7P	*6P	*5P	*4P	12	8A	7A	6A	5A	4A
01	*9P	*8P	*7P	*6P	*5P	13	9A	8A	7A	6A	5A
02	*10P	*9P	*8P	*7P	*6P	14	10A	9A	8A	7A	6A
03	*11P	*10P	*9P	*8P	*7P	15	11A	10A	9A	8A	7A
04	M	*11P	*10P	*9P	*8P	16	N	11A	10A	9A	8A
05	1A	M	*11P	*10P	*9P	17	1P	N	11A	10A	9A
06	2A	1A	M	*11P	*10P	18	2P	1P	N	11A	10A
07	3A	2A	1A	M	*11P	19	3P	2P	1P	N	11A
08	4A	3A	2A	1A	M	20	4P	3P	2P	1P	N
09	5A	4A	3A	2A	1A	21	5P	4P	3P	2P	1P
10	6A	5A	4A	3A	2A	22	6P	5P	4P	3P	2P
11	7A	6A	5A	4A	3A	23	7P	6P	5P	4P	3P

1. Eastern Daylight Time. 2. Eastern Standard Time, same as Central Daylight Time. 3. Central Standard Time, same as Mountain Daylight Time. 4. Mountain Standard Time, same as Pacific Daylight Time. 5. Pacific Standard Time. NOTES: *denotes previous day. N = noon. M = midnight.

Phenomena, 1991

Configurations of Sun, Moon, and Planets

NOTE: The hour listings are in Universal Time. For conversion to United States time zones, see conversion table above.

JANUARY

d	h	
1	15	Venus 1°.2 S of Saturn
1	16	Mars stationary
2	23	Jupiter 2° N of Moon
3	03	Earth at perihelion
3	19	Mercury stationary
5	03	Neptune in conjunction with Sun
5	08	Vesta stationary
7	19	LAST QUARTER
12	03	Antares 0°.6 S of Moon(Occn.)
12	11	Moon at apogee
13	20	Mercury 4° N of Moon
14	09	Mercury greatest elong. W (24°)
16	00	NEW MOON (Eclipse)
17	18	Venus 3° S of Moon
18	08	Saturn in conjunction with Sun
23	14	FIRST QUARTER
23	17	Mercury 0°.4 N of Uranus
23	21	Pallas stationary
25	15	Mars 2° S of Moon
26	14	Mercury 1°.1 S of Neptune
28	09	Moon at perigee
29	00	Jupiter at opposition
30	05	Jupiter 1°.8 N of Moon
30	06	FULL MOON (Penumbral Eclipse)

FEBRUARY

5	16	Mercury 1°.2 S of Saturn
6	14	LAST QUARTER
8	11	Antares 0°.7 S of Moon(Occn.)
9	04	Moon at apogee
11	04	Uranus 1°.1 N of Moon(Occn.)
11	11	Neptune 1°.9 N of Moon
12	18	Saturn 0°.5 S of Moon(Occn.)
14	18	NEW MOON
17	02	Venus 6° S of Moon
21	23	FIRST QUARTER
22	08	Mars 8° N of Aldebaran
22	13	Mars 1°.6 S of Moon
25	01	Moon at perigee
25	14	Pluto stationary
26	09	Jupiter 1°.6 N of Moon
28	18	FULL MOON

MARCH

2	03	Mercury in superior conjunction
3	23	Ceres stationary
6	08	Pallas at opposition
7	19	Antares 0°.8 S of Moon(Occn.)
8	11	LAST QUARTER
9	01	Moon at apogee
10	15	Uranus 0°.9 N of Moon(Occn.)
10	21	Neptune 1°.8 N of Moon
12	08	Saturn 0°.9 S of Moon(Occn.)
16	08	NEW MOON
17	15	Mercury 5° S of Moon
19	00	Venus 5° S of Moon
21	03	Equinox
22	05	Moon at perigee
22	17	Mars 0°.7 S of Moon(Occn.)
23	06	FIRST QUARTER
25	13	Jupiter 1°.6 N of Moon
27	15	Mercury greatest elong. E(19°)
28	02	Pallas 0°.9 N of Moon(Occn.)
30	07	FULL MOON
30	14	Jupiter stationary

APRIL

4	03	Antares 1°.1 S of Moon(Occn.)
4	17	Mercury stationary
5	21	Moon at apogee
7	00	Uranus 0°.6 N of Moon(Occn.)
7	06	Neptune 1°.5 N of Moon
7	07	LAST QUARTER
8	21	Saturn 1°.4 S of Moon
10	00	Pallas stationary
14	20	NEW MOON
14	21	Mercury in inferior conjunction
17	16	Ceres at opposition
17	16	Venus 2° S of Moon
17	17	Moon at perigee
18	12	Uranus stationary
18	23	Neptune stationary
20	00	Mars 0°.6 N of Moon(Occn.)
21	13	FIRST QUARTER
21	19	Jupiter 1°.9 N of Moon
22	04	Venus 7° N of Aldebaran
27	06	Mercury stationary
28	21	FULL MOON

MAY

3	15	Moon at apogee
4	08	Uranus 0°.3 N of Moon(Occn.)
4	14	Neptune 1°.2 N of Moon
6	07	Saturn 1°.8 S of Moon
7	01	LAST QUARTER
10	03	Pluto at opposition
12	13	Mercury 9° S of Moon
12	18	Mercury greatest elong. W (26°)
14	05	NEW MOON
15	17	Moon at perigee
16	05	Mars 5° S of Pollux
17	00	Venus 1°.6 N of Moon
17	11	Saturn stationary
18	10	Mars 2° N of Moon
19	07	Jupiter 2° N of Moon
20	20	FIRST QUARTER
23	19	Juno stationary
28	12	FULL MOON
31	01	Venus 4° S of Pollux
31	03	Moon at apogee
31	13	Uranus 0°.2 N of Moon(Occn.)
31	20	Neptune 1°.1 N of Moon(Occn.)

JUNE

2	14	Saturn 2° S of Moon
5	15	LAST QUARTER
10	10	Ceres stationary
12	12	NEW MOON
13	00	Moon at perigee
13	22	Venus greatest elong. E(45°)
14	05	Mars 0°.6 N of Jupiter
15	20	Venus 4° N of Moon
15	22	Jupiter 3° N of Moon
16	00	Mars 4° N of Moon
17	05	Mercury in superior conjunction
17	23	Venus 1°.2 N of Jupiter
19	04	FIRST QUARTER
21	21	Solstice
23	12	Venus 0°.3 N of Mars
27	03	FULL MOON(Penumbral Eclipse)
27	07	Moon at apogee
27	17	Uranus 0°.3 N of Moon(Occn.)

28	00	Neptune 1°.1 N of Moon(Occn.)
29	18	Saturn 2° S of Moon
30	22	Mercury 5° S of Pollux

JULY

4	07	Uranus at opposition
5	03	LAST QUARTER
6	15	Earth at aphelion
8	00	Neptune at opposition
9	19	Vesta in conjunction with Sun
11	08	Venus 1°.0 S of Regulus
11	10	Moon at perigee
11	19	NEW MOON(Eclipse)
13	14	Mercury 3° N of Moon
13	17	Jupiter 3° N of Moon
14	15	Mars 5° N of Moon
14	16	Mars 0°.7 N of Regulus
14	18	Venus 3° N of Moon
15	08	Mercury 0°.08 S of Jupiter
16	23	Juno at opposition
17	05	Venus greatest brilliancy
18	15	FIRST QUARTER
22	06	Venus 4° S of Mars
24	11	Moon at apogee
24	21	Uranus 0°.4 N of Moon(Occn.)
25	02	Mercury greatest elong. E(27°)
25	05	Neptune 1°.2 N of Moon
26	18	FULL MOON(Penumbral Eclipse)
26	20	Saturn 1°.9 S of Moon
27	00	Saturn at opposition
27	01	Mercury 2° S of Regulus
30	04	Venus stationary

AUGUST

2	19	Pluto stationary
3	11	LAST QUARTER
7	04	Mercury stationary
7	06	Mercury 2° N of Venus
8	18	Moon at perigee
10	02	NEW MOON
11	07	Venus 3° S of Moon
11	08	Mercury 0°.6 S of Moon(Occn.)
12	08	Mars 6° N of Moon
17	00	Venus 9° S of Regulus
17	05	FIRST QUARTER
17	22	Jupiter in conjunction with Sun
20	02	Moon at apogee
21	02	Uranus 0°.4 N of Moon(Occn.)
21	10	Neptune 1°.2 N of Moon

21	21	Mercury in inferior conjunction
22	20	Venus in inferior conjunction
22	23	Saturn 1°.8 S of Moon
25	09	FULL MOON
29	05	Mercury 6° N of Venus
30	20	Mercury stationary

SEPTEMBER

1	18	LAST QUARTER
5	19	Moon at perigee
6	17	Venus 5° S of Moon
6	18	Juno stationary
7	05	Mercury 3° N of Moon
7	11	Jupiter 5° N of Moon
7	18	Mercury greatest elong. W(18°)
8	11	NEW MOON
10	02	Mars 6° N of Moon
10	08	Jupiter 0°.4 N of Regulus
10	10	Mercury 0°.07 S of Jupiter
10	10	Mercury 0°.3 N of Regulus
12	02	Venus stationary
15	22	FIRST QUARTER
17	09	Uranus 0°.2 N of Moon(Occn.)
17	15	Moon at apogee
17	17	Neptune 1°.0 N of Moon(Occn.)
19	04	Saturn 1°.8 S of Moon
19	09	Uranus stationary
23	13	Equinox
23	23	FULL MOON
26	05	Neptune stationary
28	23	Venus greatest brilliancy

OCTOBER

1	00	LAST QUARTER
2	18	Moon at perigee
3	17	Mercury in superior conjunction
4	15	Venus 0°.2 N of Moon(Occn.)
5	02	Saturn stationary
5	05	Jupiter 5° N of Moon
6	00	Mars 3° N of Spica
7	22	NEW MOON
8	04	Venus 3° S of Regulus
14	18	Uranus 0°.06 S of Moon(Occn.)
15	02	Neptune 0°.7 N of Moon (Occn.)
15	11	Moon at apogee
15	18	FIRST QUARTER
16	12	Saturn 2° S of Moon
17	03	Venus 2° S of Jupiter

23	11	FULL MOON
27	16	Moon at perigee
30	07	LAST QUARTER

NOVEMBER

1	20	Jupiter 6° N of Moon
2	09	Venus greatest elong. W(47°)
2	21	Venus 6° N of Moon
4	15	Pallas in conjunction with Sun
6	11	NEW MOON
8	05	Mercury 0°.7 N of Moon(Occn.)
8	09	Mars in conjunction with Sun
11	03	Uranus 0°.4 S of Moon(Occn.)
11	07	Mercury 2° N of Antares
11	11	Neptune 0°.4 N of Moon(Occn.)
12	08	Moon at apogee
12	22	Saturn 2°S of Moon
13	04	Pluto in conjunction with Sun
14	14	FIRST QUARTER
19	02	Mercury greatest elong. E(22°)
21	23	FULL MOON
24	02	Moon at perigee
28	15	LAST QUARTER
28	18	Mercury stationary
29	08	Jupiter 6° N of Moon
29	09	Venus 4° N of Spica

DECEMBER

2	14	Venus 8° N of Moon
6	04	NEW MOON
8	14	Uranus 0°.6 S of Moon(Occn.)
8	15	Mercury in inferior conjunction
8	20	Neptune 0°.2 N of Moon(Occn.)
10	02	Moon at apogee
10	10	Saturn 3° S of Moon
11	15	Mars 4° N of Antares
11	19	Ceres in conjunction with Sun
13	16	Mercury 3° N of Mars
14	10	FIRST QUARTER
15	22	Mercury 8° N of Antares
18	12	Mercury stationary
21	06	Mercury 7° N of Antares
21	10	FULL MOON(Eclipse)
22	09	Moon at perigee
22	09	Solstice
26	17	Jupiter 7° N of Moon
27	21	Mercury greatest elong. W(22°)
28	02	LAST QUARTER
31	12	Jupiter stationary

Eclipses of the Sun and the Moon, 1991

Jan. 15. Annular eclipse of the Sun. Visible east of Indonesia, south of New Guinea, Australia, New Zealand, part of Antarctica, and Polynesia.

Jan. 30. Penumbral eclipse of the Moon. The beginning of the penumbral phase visible in extreme eastern Asia, North America, Central America, South America, Greenland, Europe, most of Africa, the Palmer Peninsula of Antarctica, the Arctic regions, the eastern Pacific Ocean, and the Atlantic Ocean; the end visible in extreme eastern Asia, most of New Zealand, North America, Central America, South America, Greenland, the Arctic regions, the Pacific Ocean, and the northern Atlantic Ocean.

June 27. Penumbral eclipse of the Moon. The beginning of the penumbral phase visible in eastern North America, Central America, South America, Antarctica, Africa, Europe south of Scandinavia, the western Indian Ocean, the Atlantic Ocean, and the southeastern Pacific Ocean; the end visible in North America except for Alaska and northwestern Canada, Central America, South America, Antarctica, the western half of Africa, the western Iberian Peninsula of Europe, the Atlantic Ocean, and the southeastern Pacific Ocean.

July 11. Total eclipse of the Sun. Visible in the Hawaiian Islands, Southwestern United States except in the extreme northeast, Mexico, Central and South America except the extreme south.

July 26. Penumbral eclipse of the Moon. The beginning of the penumbral phase visible in southern and eastern Africa, most of Asia, Australia, New Zealand, most of Antarctica, the western Pacific Ocean, and the Indian Ocean; the end visible in most of Europe, most of Africa, most of Asia, Australia, southern New Zealand, Antarctica, the eastern South Atlantic Ocean, and the Indian Ocean.

Dec. 21. Partial eclipse of the Moon. The beginning of the umbral phase is visible in eastern Australia, New Zealand, northern and eastern Asia, North America, Central America, northwestern South America, Greenland, northern Scandinavia, the Arctic regions, the Pacific Ocean, and the northwestern Atlantic Ocean; the end visible in northern and eastern Asia, Australia, New Zealand, North America, Central America, Greenland, northern Scandinavia, the Arctic regions, and the Pacific Ocean.

DECLINATIONS OF SUN AND PLANETS, 1991

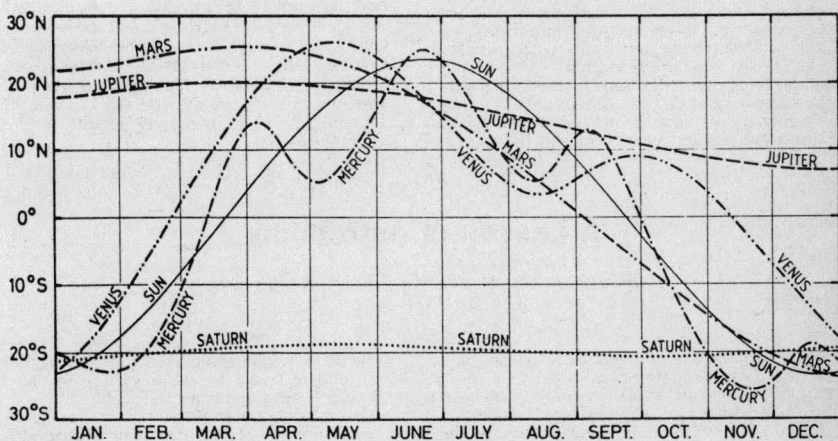

Visibility of Planets, 1991

Mercury can only be seen low in the east before sunrise, or low in the west after sunset (about the time of the beginning or end of civil twilight). It is visible in the mornings between the following approximate dates: January 1 to February 18, April 23 to June 10, August 30 to September 23, and December 14 to December 31. The planet is brighter at the end of each period (the best conditions in northern latitudes occur around the second week in September and, only in low northern latitudes, during the second and third weeks of January and the last 10 days of December, and in southern latitudes most of January and early February and from the end of April until the end of May). It is visible in the evenings between the following approximate dates: March 12 to April 6, June 25 to August 15, and October 18 to December 3. The planet is brighter at the end of each period (the best conditions in northern latitudes occur during the last two weeks of March and in southern latitudes from early July until just before mid-August and late October to late November).

Venus is a brilliant object in the evening sky from the beginning of the year until mid-August when it becomes too close to the Sun for observation. Towards the end of August it reappears in the morning sky where it stays until the end of the year. Venus is in conjunction with Saturn on January 1, with Jupiter on June 17 and October 17, with Mars on June 23 and July 22, and with Mercury on August 7 and 29.

Mars can be seen in January for more than half the night in Taurus, its eastward elongation gradu-

ally decreases (passing 8° N of *Aldebaran* on February 22) until it can only be seen in the evening sky passing from Taurus through Gemini (passing 5° S of *Pollux* on May 16), Cancer, Leo (passing 0.7° N of *Regulus* on July 14), and into Virgo where towards the end of September it becomes too close to the Sun for observation. It reappears in the morning sky in Ophiuchus in late December. Mars is in conjunction with Jupiter on June 14, with Venus on June 23 and July 22.

Jupiter can be seen for most of the night in Cancer, its westward elongation gradually increases until it is at opposition on January 29 when it can be seen throughout the night. Its eastward elongation then gradually decreases as it passes into Leo in mid-July where it can be seen only in the evening sky. In early August it becomes too close to the Sun for observation until the beginning of September when it reappears in the morning sky in Leo in which constellation it remains for the rest of the year (passing 0.4° N of *Regulus* on September 10). Its westward elongation gradually increases until by mid-December it can be seen for more than half the night. Jupiter is in conjunction with Mars on June 14, with Venus on June 17 and October 17 and with Mercury on July 15 and September 10.

Saturn can be seen on January 1 in the evening sky in Sagittarius then it becomes too close to the Sun for observation. It reappears in the morning sky in early February in Capricornus in which constellation it remains for the rest of the year. Its westward elongation gradually increases until it is at opposition on July 27 when it is visible throughout the night. Its eastward elongation then gradually decreases until from late October it can only be seen in the evening sky. Saturn is in conjunction with Venus on January 1 and with Mercury on February 5.

Uranus is too close to the Sun for observation until towards the end of January when it appears in the morning sky in Sagittarius, in which constellation it remains throughout the year. It is at opposition on July 4 when it can be seen throughout the night, after which its eastward elongation gradually decreases. From early October it can only be seen in the evening sky until the second half of December when it again becomes too close to the Sun for observation.

Neptune is too close to the Sun for observation until late January when it can be seen in the morning sky shortly before sunrise in Sagittarius, in which constellation it remains throughout the year. It

is at opposition on July 8 when it can be seen throughout the night. From mid-October it can only be seen in the evening sky until mid-December when it again becomes too close to the Sun for observation.

Do not confuse (1) Venus with Saturn on January 1, with Mars from the second week in June until near the end of July, with Jupiter for the third and fourth weeks of June and again the second and third weeks of October and with Mercury from the end of July until mid-August; on all occasions Venus is the brighter object. (2) Mercury with Saturn around the end of the first week of February when Mercury is the brighter object. (3) Jupiter with Mars for most of June and with Mercury around mid-July and the first half of September; on all occasions Jupiter is the brighter object. □

A Lesson in Astronomy

Reprinted by courtesy of the U.S. Naval Observatory

To understand where things are in the sky, and how the locations of the planets relate to each other, you have to understand one of the most basic things about astronomy—the *celestial sphere.*

Imagine, if you will, all the things in the sky—the Sun, Moon, planets, stars, etc.—no matter how far away they actually are, being on a gigantic transparent sphere, with the Earth at its center. The early Greeks believed this celestial sphere to be made out of some crystalline material, at a very great distance from the Earth.

From here things get easy. As the Earth rotates on its axis, we perceive the celestial sphere to be moving, and not the Earth. The sphere has two points around which it rotates, and we call them the celestial poles. The celestial poles are where the Earth's axis penetrates the celestial sphere. The north celestial pole is marked by Polaris, the North Star, which is relatively close to the pole. The south celestial pole has no bright star nearby to mark its place in the sky. Now, if we extend the Earth's equator on to the celestial sphere, we get the celestial equator. The celestial equator is 90° from the celestial poles. Straight up from where you happen to be is called the zenith, and straight down is called the nadir. The zenith forms the apex of the hemisphere of the celestial sphere that is above your horizon at any given time.

Now for something not so easy. As we watch the Sun rise and set on any given day it marks a path in the sky called a diurnal circle. In fact, any object on the celestial sphere will make a diurnal circle—the apparent path of an object made through the course of a day. If you marked the position of the Sun (in Right Ascension and Declination, see below) against the background of stars through the course of a year you would see another path on the celestial sphere—we call it the ecliptic. The ecliptic is the apparent path the Sun makes on the celestial sphere due to the Earth's revolution around the Sun. The ecliptic also represents the plane of the solar system. The inclination of the orbits of all other objects in the solar system are measured against it.

How do astronomers measure things on the celestial sphere? There are two ways. The first way is probably most familiar, called the altitude-azimuth, or horizon system. Altitude is the object's position in degrees above the horizon, and azimuth is the object's direction, measured in degrees from north (0°), moving east (just like a compass, east is 90°, south is 180°, etc.). Altitude-azimuth is always measured from the observer's position, and does not give you a universal position for an object. The best way to mark an object's position in the heavens is to use a fixed set of coordinates, much like the Earth's latitude and longitude. The celestial coordinate system most used is the Right Ascension and Declination system.

Right Ascension is measured in hours, not degrees, starting at the vernal equinox, a zero point equivalent to 0° longitude on the Earth, and is marked in one hour increments, measured east. Each one hour increment equals 15°, and there are 24 hours of Right Ascension. Declination is a measurement of degrees north or south of the celestial equator. Positive is above the celestial equator, and negative is below. For example, the bright star Sirius in the winter sky has a position of 6 hours, 44 minutes Right Ascension, and −16 degrees, 42 minutes Declination (abbreviated 6h 44m and −16° 42′).

The orientation of the observer to the celestial sphere is an important factor you cannot overlook. The first thing you should do is find the North Star. Once you have that in your sights, everything else will fall into place. If you know your latitude, you're in good shape, because your latitude marks your position north of the equator (if you are in the northern hemisphere). Your latitude is equal to the altitude of the North Star above the northern horizon. Subtract your latitude from 90° and you will have the altitude of the celestial equator above your southern horizon. It is best to have a star chart handy during an evening observing session, as most will have the ecliptic charted among the evening constellations.

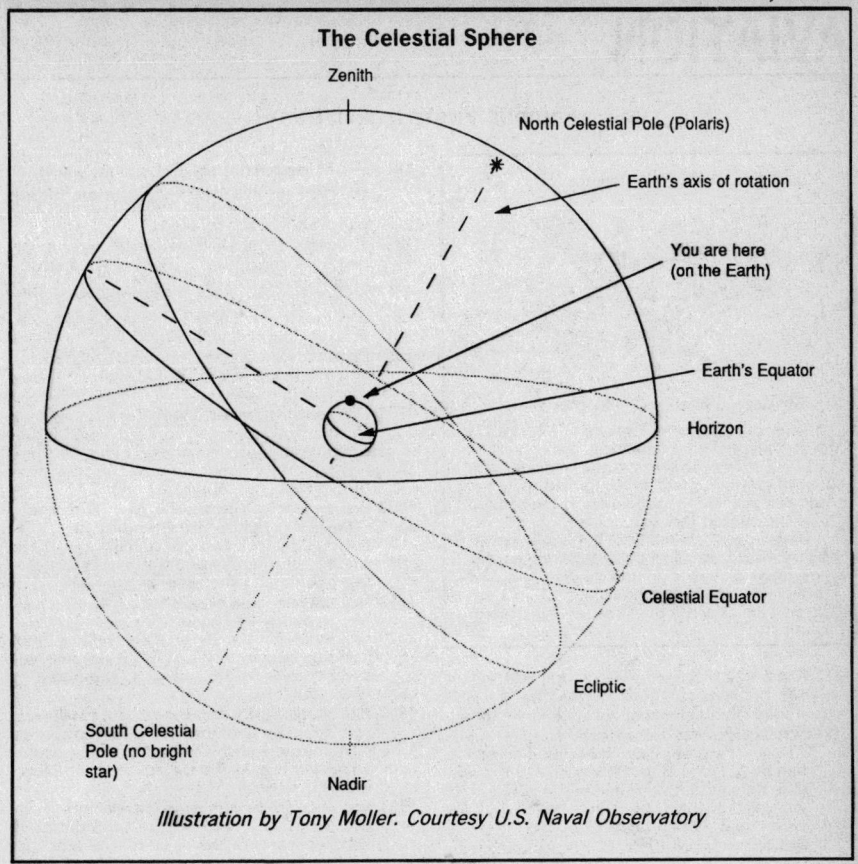

The Celestial Sphere

Zenith

North Celestial Pole (Polaris)

Earth's axis of rotation

You are here
(on the Earth)

Earth's Equator

Horizon

Celestial Equator

Ecliptic

South Celestial
Pole (no bright
star)

Nadir

Illustration by Tony Moller. Courtesy U.S. Naval Observatory.

Are We Alone?

Source: U.S. Naval Observatory.

Seventeen years ago, on November 16, 1974, the people of the planet Earth sent a purposeful message to interstellar space. Using a giant radio telescope in Puerto Rico, we beamed up a 3-minute message about ourselves to anyone listening in a cluster of stars in the constellation **Hercules.** We told them all about the solar system we live in, about the population of the world at the time, and about the atomic elements we're made of. We haven't heard back from anyone.

Moving outward, our message has traveled 17 light years so far, nearly four times the distance to the nearest star, *Alpha Centauri*, but needs at least another 24,983 years to get to the 300,000 closely packed stars in the Hercules cluster. Then it will be another 25,000 before we should expect to hear anything back.

Today, several programs around the world are tuned into the great beyond. Perhaps best known as SETI (for Search for Extra Terrestrial Intelligence), NASA is most heavily involved. Harvard runs the META (for Megachannel Extra Terrestrial Assay) receiver, which covers 64 times as many channels as its predecessor *Project Sentinel*. In 1992, a group of NASA scientists will begin a 10-year search for extraterrestrial intelligence using a radio spectrum analyzer that will tune into 10 million radio channels simultaneously. The radio telescopes used by the Naval Observatory are trained on 73 distant quasars, performing the essential mission-related work needed for precise navigation. They measure Earth rotation, and do astrometric research. In this program of observation, the same quasars are being monitored year after year.

Finding a signal from the great beyond would be momentous, a turning point. Definitively finding that there existed intelligent life elsewhere in our Universe would perhaps be the greatest event in all of human history. Mankind's view of itself would change irrevocably, and forever. □

AVIATION

Famous Firsts in Aviation

Cayley's Helicopter

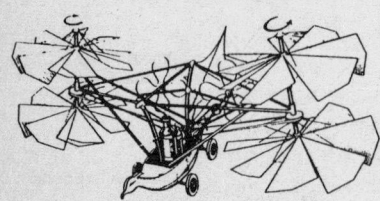

Sir George Cayley's Helicopter design

Sir George Cayley of England (1773-1857) designed the first practical helicopter in 1842-43. His remarkable machine had twin contra-rotating rotors which served as wings and two pusher-type propellers at the back to give the aircraft forward motion.

Cayley designed and built the first successful man-carrying glider in 1853 and sent his coachman aloft in it on its first flight. He also formulated the basic principles of modern aerodynamics and is the father of British aeronautics.

1782 **First balloon flight.** Jacques and Joseph Montgolfier of Annonay, France, sent up a small smoke-filled balloon about mid-November.

1783 **First hydrogen-filled balloon flight.** Jacques A. C. Charles, Paris physicist, supervised construction by A. J. and M. N. Robert of a 13-ft diameter balloon that was filled with hydrogen. It got up to about 3,000 ft and traveled about 16 mi. in a 45-min flight (Aug. 27).
First human balloon flights. A Frenchman, Jean Pilâtre de Rozier made the first captive-balloon ascension (Oct. 15). With the Marquis d'Arlandes, Pilâtre de Rozier made the first free flight, reaching a peak altitude of about 500 ft, and traveling about 5 1/2 mi. in 20 min (Nov. 21).

1784 **First powered balloon.** Gen. Jean Baptiste Marie Meusnier developed the first propeller-driven and elliptically-shaped balloon—the crew cranking three propellers on a common shaft to give the craft a speed of about 3 mph.
First woman to fly. Mme. Thible, a French opera singer (June 4).

1793 **First balloon flight in America.** Jean Pierre Blanchard, a French pilot, made it from Philadelphia to near Woodbury, Gloucester County, N.J., in a little over 45 min (Jan. 9).

1794 **First military use of the balloon.** Jean Marie Coutelle, using a balloon built for the French Army, made two 4-hr observation ascents. The military purpose of the ascents seems to have been to damage the enemy's morale.

1797 **First parachute jump.** André-Jacques Garnerin dropped from about 6,500 ft over Monceau Park in Paris in a 23-ft diameter parachute made of white canvas with a basket attached (Oct. 22).

1843 **First air transport company.** In London, William S. Henson and John Stringfellow filed articles of incorporation for the Aerial Transit Company (March 24). It failed.

1852 **First dirigible.** Henri Giffard, a French engineer, flew in a controllable (more or less) steam-engine powered balloon, 144 ft long and 39 ft in diameter, inflated with 88,000 cu ft of coal gas. It reached 6.7 mph on a flight from Paris to Trappe (Sept. 24).

1860 **First aerial photographers.** Samuel Archer King and William Black made two photos of Boston, still in existence.

1872 **First gas-engine powered dirigible.** Paul Haenlein, a German engineer, flew in a semi-rigid-frame dirigible, powered by a 4-cylinder internal-combustion engine running on coal gas drawn from the supporting bag.

1873 **First transatlantic attempt.** *The New York Daily Graphic* sponsored the attempt with a 400,000 cu ft balloon carrying a lifeboat. A rip in the bag during inflation brought collapse of the balloon and the project.

1897 **First successful metal dirigible.** An all-metal dirigible, designed by David Schwarz, a Hungarian, took off from Berlin's Tempelhof Field and, powered by a 16-hp Daimler engine, got several miles before leaking gas caused it to crash (Nov. 13).

1900 **First Zeppelin flight.** Germany's Count Ferdinand von Zeppelin flew the first of his long series of rigid-frame airships. It attained a speed of 18 mi. per h and got 3 1/2 mi. before its steering gear failed (July 2).

1903 **First successful heavier-than-air machine flight.** Aviation was really born on the sand dunes at Kitty Hawk, N.C., when Orville Wright

Moy's Aerial Steamer

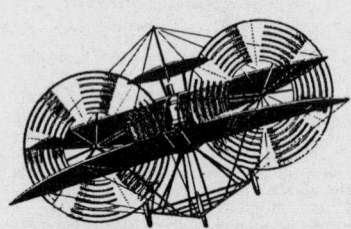

Thomas Moy's Aerial Steamer, 1875

Thomas Moy, a British Engineer, invented a steam-powered monoplane with 15-foot tandem wings and two large fan-shaped propellers. He named his flying machine "The Aerial Steamer." Moy demonstrated his airplane at London's Crystal Palace in 1875. While his pilotless aircraft never actually flew, it was able to rise about six inches off the ground under its own power while attached to a tether on a circular track.

Dec. 17, 1903. Orville Wright at the controls, Wilbur runs alongside him. (National Air and Space Museum, Smithsonian Institution)

crawled to his prone position between the wings of the biplane he and his brother Wilbur had built, opened the throttle of their homemade 12-hp engine and took to the air. He covered 120 ft in 12 sec. Later that day, in one of four flights, Wilbur stayed up 59 sec and covered 852 ft (Dec. 17).

1904 First airplane maneuvers. Orville Wright made the first turn with an airplane (Sept. 15); 5 days later his brother Wilbur made the first complete circle.

1905 First airplane flight over half an hour. Orville Wright kept his craft up 33 min 17 sec (Oct. 4).

1906 First European airplane flight. Alberto Santos-Dumont, a Brazilian, flew a heavier-than-air machine at Bagatelle Field, Paris (Sept. 13).

1908 First airplane fatality. Lt. Thomas E. Selfridge, U.S. Army Signal Corps, was in a group of officers evaluating the Wright plane at Fort Myer, Va. He was up about 75 ft with Orville Wright when the propeller hit a bracing wire and was broken, throwing the plane out of control, killing Selfridge and seriously injuring Wright (Sept. 17).

1909 First cross-Channel flight. Louis Blériot flew in a 25-hp Blériot VI monoplane from Les Baraques near Calais, France, and landed near Dover Castle, England, in a 26.61-mi. (38-km) 37-min flight across the English Channel (July 25).

1910 First licensed woman pilot. Baroness Raymonde de la Roche of France, who learned to fly in 1909, received ticket No. 36 on March 8.

First flight from shipboard. Lt. Eugene Ely, USN, took a Curtiss plane off from the deck of cruiser *Birmingham* at Hampton Roads, Va., and flew to Norfolk (Nov. 14). The following January, he reversed the process, flying from Camp Selfridge to the deck of the armored cruiser *Pennsylvania* in San Francisco Bay (Jan. 18).

1911 First U.S. woman pilot. Harriet Quimby, a magazine writer, who got ticket No. 37.

1912 First woman's cross-Channel flight. Harriet Quimby flew from Dover, England, across the English Channel, and landed at Hardelot, France (25 mi. south of Calais) in a Blériot monoplane

Harriet Quimby was the leading woman aviator of her day. (Leslie's Weekly Illustrated Newspaper)

loaned to her by Louis Blériot (April 16). She was later killed in a flying accident over Dorchester Bay during a Harvard-Boston aviation meet on July 1, 1912.

1913 First multi-engined aircraft. Built and flown by Igor Ivan Sikorsky while still in his native Russia.

1914 First aerial combat. In August, Allied and German pilots and observers started shooting at each other with pistols and rifles—with negligible results.

1915 First air raids on England. German Zeppelins started dropping bombs on four English communities (Jan. 19).

1918 First U.S. air squadron. The U.S. Army Air Corps made its first independent raids over enemy lines, in DH-4 planes (British-designed) powered with 400-hp American-designed Liberty engines (April 8).

First regular airmail service. Operated for the Post Office Department by the Army, the first regular service was inaugurated with one round trip a day (except Sunday) between Washington, D.C., and New York City (May 15).

1919 First transatlantic flight. The NC-4, one of four Curtiss flying boats commanded by Lt. Comdr. Albert C. Read, reached Lisbon, Por tugal, (May 27) after hops from Trepassy Bay, Newfoundland, to Horta, Azores (May 16–17), to Ponta Delgada (May 20). The Liberty-powered craft was piloted by Walter Hinton.

First nonstop transatlantic flight. Capt. John Alcock and Lt. Arthur Whitten Brown, British World War I flyers, made the 1,900 mi. from St. John's, Newfoundland, to Clifden, Ireland, in 16 h 12 min in a Vickers-Vimy bomber with two 350-hp Rolls-Royce engines (June 15–16).

First lighter-than-air transatlantic flight. The British dirigible R-34, commanded by Maj. George H. Scott, left Firth of Forth, Scotland, (July 2) and touched down at Mineola, L.I., 108 h later. The eastbound trip was made in 75 h (completed July 13).

First scheduled London-Paris passenger service (using airplanes). Aircraft Travel and Transport inaugurated London-Paris service (Aug. 25). Later the company started the first trans-channel mail service on the same route (Nov. 10).

1921 **First naval vessel sunk by aircraft.** Two battleships being scrapped by treaty were sunk by bombs dropped from Army planes in demonstration put on by Brig. Gen. William S. Mitchell (July 21).

First helium balloon. The C-7, non-rigid Navy dirigible was first to use non-inflammable helium as lifting gas, making a flight from Hampton Roads, Va., to Washington, D.C. (Dec. 1).

1922 **First member of Caterpillar Club.** Lt. (later Maj. Gen.) Harold Harris bailed out of a crippled plane he was testing at McCook Field, Dayton, Ohio (Oct. 20), and became the first man to join the Caterpillar Club—those whose lives have been saved by parachute.

1923 **First nonstop transcontinental flight.** Lts. John A. Macready and Oakley Kelly flew a single-engine Fokker T-2 nonstop from New York to San Diego, a distance of just over 2,500 mi. in 26 h 50 min (May 2–3).

First autogyro flight. Juan de la Cierva, a brilliant Spanish mathematician, made the first successful flight in a rotary wing aircraft in Madrid (June 9).

1924 **First round-the-world flight.** Four Douglas Cruiser biplanes of the U.S. Army Air Corps took off from Seattle under command of Maj. Frederick Martin (April 6). 175 days later, two of the planes (Lt. Lowell Smith's and Lt. Erik Nelson's) landed in Seattle after a circuitous route—one source saying 26,345 mi., another saying 27,553 mi.

1926 **First polar flight.** Then-Lt. Cmdr. Richard E. Byrd, acting as navigator, and Floyd Bennett as pilot, flew a trimotor Fokker from Kings Bay, Spitsbergen, over the North Pole and back in 15 1/2 h (May 8–9).

1927 **First solo, nonstop transatlantic flight.** Charles Augustus Lindbergh lifted his Wright-powered Ryan monoplane, *Spirit of St. Louis,* from Roosevelt Field, L.I., to stay aloft 33 h 39 min and travel 3,600 mi. to Le Bourget Field outside Paris (May 20–21).

First transatlantic passenger. Charles A. Levine was piloted by Clarence D. Chamberlin from Roosevelt Field, L.I., to Eisleben, Germany, in a Wright-powered Bellanca (June 4–5).

1928 **First east-west transatlantic crossing.** Baron Guenther von Huenefeld, piloted by German

Charles A. Lindbergh and *The Spirit of St. Louis.* (National Air and Space Museum, Smithsonian Institution)

Capt. Hermann Koehl and Irish Capt. James Fitzmaurice, left Dublin for New York City (April 12) in a single-engine all-metal Junkers monoplane. Some 37 h later, they crashed on Greely Island, Labrador. Rescued.

First U.S.-Australia flight. Sir Charles Kingsford-Smith and Capt. Charles T. P. Ulm, Australians, and two American navigators, Harry W. Lyon and James Warner, crossed the Pacific from Oakland to Brisbane. They went via Hawaii and the Fiji Islands in a trimotor Fokker (May 31–June 8).

First transarctic flight. Sir Hubert Wilkins, an Australian explorer and Carl Ben Eielson, who served as pilot, flew from Point Barrow, Alaska, to Spitsbergen (mid-April).

1929 **First of the endurance records.** With Air Corps Maj. Carl Spaatz in command and Capt. Ira Eaker as chief pilot, an Army Fokker, aided by refueling in the air, remained aloft 150 h 40 min at Los Angeles (Jan. 1–7).

First round-the-world airship flight. The LZ-127, known as the *Graf Zeppelin,* flew 21,300 miles in 20 days and 4 hours. Also set distance record (August).

First blind flight. James H. Doolittle proved the feasibility of instrument-guided flying when he took off and landed entirely on instruments (Sept. 24).

First rocket-engine flight. Fritz von Opel, a German auto maker, stayed aloft in his small rocket-powered craft for 75 sec, covering nearly 2 mi. (Sept. 30).

First South Pole flight. Comdr. Richard E. Byrd, with Bernt Balchen as pilot, Harold I. June, radio operator, and Capt. A. C. McKinley, photographer, flew a trimotor Fokker from the Bay of Whales, Little America, over the South Pole and back (Nov. 28–29).

1930 **First Paris–New York nonstop flight.** Dieudonné Coste and Maurice Bellonte, French pilots, flew a Hispano-powered Breguet biplane from Le Bourget Field to Valley Stream, L.I., in 37 h 18 min. (Sept. 2–3).

1931 **First flight into the stratosphere.** Auguste Piccard, a Swiss physicist, and Charles Knipfer ascended in a balloon from Augsburg, Germany, and reached a height of 51,793 ft in a 17-h flight that terminated on a glacier near Innsbruck, Austria (May 27).

First nonstop transpacific flight. Hugh Herndon and Clyde Pangborn took off from Sabishiro Beach, Japan, dropped their landing gear, and flew 4,860 mi. to near Wenatchee, Wash., in 41 h 13 min. (Oct. 4–5).

1932 **First woman's transatlantic solo.** Amelia Earhart, flying a Pratt & Whitney Wasp-powered Lockheed Vega, flew alone from Harbor Grace, Newfoundland, to Ireland in approximately 15 h (May 20–21).

First westbound transatlantic solo. James A. Mollison, a British pilot, took a de Havilland Puss Moth from Portmarnock, Ireland, to Pennfield, N.B. (Aug. 18).

First woman airline pilot. Ruth Rowland Nichols, first woman to hold three international records at the same time—speed, distance, altitude—was employed by N.Y.-New England Airways.

1933 **First round-the-world solo.** Wiley Post took a Lockheed Vega, *Winnie Mae*, 15,596 mi. around the world in 7 d 18 h 49 1/2 min (July 15–22).

1937 **First successful helicopter.** Hanna Reitsch, a German pilot, flew Dr. Heinrich Focke's FW-61 in free, fully controlled flight at Bremen (July 4).

1939 **First turbojet flight.** Just before their invasion of Poland, the Germans flew a Heinkel He-178 plane powered by a Heinkel S3B turbojet (Aug. 27).

1942 **First American jet plane flight.** Robert Stanley, chief pilot for Bell Aircraft Corp., flew the Bell XP-59 *Airacomet* at Muroc Army Base, Calif. (Oct. 1).

1947 **First piloted supersonic flight in an airplane.** Capt. Charles E. Yeager, U.S. Air Force, flew the X-1 rocket-powered research plane built by Bell Aircraft Corp., faster than the speed of sound at Muroc Air Force Base, California (Oct. 14).

1949 **First round-the-world nonstop flight.** Capt. James Gallagher and USAF crew of 13 flew a Boeing B-50A Superfortress around the world nonstop from Ft. Worth, returning to same point: 23,452 mi. in 94 h 1 min, with 4 aerial refuelings enroute (Feb. 27–March 2).

1950 **First nonstop transatlantic jet flight.** Col. David C. Schilling (USAF) flew 3,300 mi. from England to Limestone, Maine, in 10 h 1 min (Sept. 22).

1951 **First solo across North Pole.** Charles F. Blair, Jr., flew a converted P-51 (May 29).

1952 **First jetliner service.** De Havilland Comet flight inaugurated by BOAC between London and Johannesburg, South Africa (May 2). Flight, including stops, took 23 h 38 min.

First transatlantic helicopter flight. Capt. Vincent H. McGovern and 1st Lt. Harold W. Moore piloted 2 Sikorsky H-19s from Westover, Mass., to Prestwick, Scotland (3,410 mi.). Trip was made in 5 steps, with flying time of 42 h 25 min (July 15–31).

First transatlantic round trip in same day. British Canberra twin-jet bomber flew from Aldergrove, Northern Ireland, to Gander, Newfoundland, and back in 7 h 59 min flying time (Aug. 26).

1955 **First transcontinental round trip in same day.** Lt. John M. Conroy piloted F-86 Sabrejet across U.S. (Los Angeles–New York) and back—5,085 mi.—in 11 h 33 min 27 sec (May 21).

1957 **First round-the-world, nonstop jet plane flight.** Maj. Gen. Archie J. Old, Jr., USAF, led a flight of

Chuck Yeager alongside the Bell X-1 named *Glamorous Glennis* after his wife. (National Air and Space Museum, Smithsonian Institution)

3 Boeing B-52 bombers, powered with 8 10,000-lb. thrust Pratt & Whitney Aircraft J57 engines around the world in 45 h 19 min; distance 24,325 mi.; average speed 525 mph. (Completed Jan. 18.)

1958 **First transatlantic jet passenger service.** BOAC, New York to London (Oct. 4). Pan American started daily service, N.Y. to Paris (Oct. 26).

First domestic jet passenger service. National Airlines inaugurated service between New York and Miami (Dec. 10).

1968 **Prototype of world's first supersonic** airliner, the Soviet-designed Tupolev Tu-144 made first flight, Dec. 31. It first achieved supersonic speed on June 5, 1969.

1973 **First female pilot of a U.S. major scheduled airline.** Emily H. Warner became employed by Frontier Airlines on January 29 as second officer on a Boeing 737.

1976 **First regularly-scheduled commercial supersonic transport (SST) flights begin.** Air France and British Airways inaugurate service (January 21). Air France flies the Paris-Rio de Janeiro route; B.A., the London-Bahrain. Both airlines begin SST service to Washington, D.C. (May 24).

1977 **First successful man-powered aircraft.** Paul MacCready, an aeronautical engineer from Pasadena, Calif., was awarded the Kremer Prize for creating the world's first successful man-powered aircraft. The *Gossamer Condor* was flown by Bryan Allen over the required 3-mile course on Aug. 23.

1978 **First successful transatlantic balloon flight.** Three Albuquerque, N.M., men, Ben Abruzzo, Larry Newman, and Maxie Anderson, completed the crossing (Aug. 16. Landed, Aug. 17) in their helium-filled balloon, *Double Eagle II.*

1979 **First man-powered aircraft to fly across the English Channel.** The Kremer Prize for the Channel crossing was won by Bryan Allen who flew the *Gossamer Albatross* from Folkestone, England to Cap Gris-Nez, France, in 2 h 55 min (June 12).

1980 **First successful balloon flight over the North Pole.** Sidney Conn and his wife Eleanor, in hot-air balloon *Joy of Sound* (April 11).

First nonstop transcontinental balloon flight, and also record for longest overland voyage in a balloon. Maxie Anderson and his son, Kris, completed four-day flight from Fort Baker, Calif., to successful landing outside Matane, Quebec, on May 12 in their helium-filled balloon, *Kitty Hawk.*

World's 25 Busiest Airports in 1989

Airport	Passengers[1]	Cargo		Operations	
1. Chicago, Ill. (O'Hare)	59,130,007	958,430	(5)	780,658	(1)
2. Dallas/Ft. Worth, Texas	47,579,046	502,212	(17)	698,870	(2)
3. Los Angeles (International)	44,967,221	1,130,050	(4)	637,117	(4)
4. Atlanta, Georgia	43,312,285	540,749	(15)	665,930	(3)
5. London (Heathrow)	39,905,200	765,600	(7)	368,600	(22)
6. Tokyo, Japan (Haneda)	36,567,738	581,940	(13)	178,992	(79)
7. New York (Kennedy)	30,323,077	1,372,243	(1)	305,058	(34)
8. San Francisco	29,939,835	558,078	(14)	427,475	(12)
9. Denver, Colorado	27,568,033	273,388	(29)	463,797	(8)
10. Frankfurt, Fed. Rep. of Germany	26,006,900	1,223,207	(3)	325,472	(30)
11. Paris (Orly)	24,288,440	280,177	(27)	196,066	(70)
12. Miami, Fla. (International)	23,385,010	796,690	(6)	385,135	(17)
13. New York (LaGuardia)	23,158,317	107,237	(59)	349,116	(26)
14. Honolulu, Oahu, Hawaii	22,617,340	363,790	(21)	403,635	(14)
15. Boston, Massachusetts	22,272,690	340,903	(24)	388,792	(16)
16. Osaka, Japan	21,873,831	454,201	(18)	64,675	(217)
17. Detroit (Metro Wayne Co.)	21,495,159	179,279	(40)	374,520	(20)
18. London (Gatwick)	21,293,200	225,000	(34)	206,200	(64)
19. Newark, N.J. (International)	20,927,946	448,776	(19)	365,106	(23)
20. Phoenix, Arizona	20,710,790	94,506	(65)	484,940	(6)
21. Paris (Charles De Gaulle)	20,669,542	609,995	(10)	206,394	(62)
22. Toronto, Ont. (Pearson)	20,418,094	291,311	(26)	354,996	(25)
23. St. Louis, Missouri	20,015,015	91,998	(68)	428,875	(11)
24. Minneapolis/St. Paul, Minn.	19,400,815	242,483	(33)	364,030	(24)
25. Hong Kong, Hong Kong	17,431,124	751,060	(8)	94,300	(161)

1. Enplaned, deplaned, and transfer, in millions. NOTE: Figures in ( ) next to cargo and operations totals represent rank for those categories. *Source:* Airport Operators Council International.

First long-distance solar-powered flight. Janice Brown, 98-lb former teacher, flew tiny experimental solar-powered aircraft, *Solar Challenger* six miles in 22-min near Marana, Ariz. (Dec. 3). The craft was powered by a 2.75-hp engine.

First solar-powered aircraft to fly across the English Channel. Stephen R. Ptacek flew the 210-lb *Solar Challenger* at the average speed of 30 mph from Cormeilles-en-Vexin near Paris to the Royal Manston Air Force Base on England's southeastern coast in 5 h 30 min (July 7).

1984 First solo transatlantic balloon flight. Joe W. Kittinger landed Sept. 18 near Savona, Italy, in his helium-filled balloon *Rosie O'Grady's Balloon of Peace* after a flight of 3,535 miles from Caribou, Me.

1986 First nonstop flight around the world without refueling. From Edwards AFB, Calif., Dick Rutan and Jeana Yeager flew in *Voyager* around the world (24,986.727 mi.), returning to Edwards in 216 h 3 min 44 s (Dec. 14–23).

1987 First Transatlantic Hot-Air Balloon Flight. Richard Branson and Per Lindstrand flew 2,789.6 miles from Sugarloaf Mt., Maine, to Ireland in the hot-air balloon *Virgin Atlantic Flyer* (July 2-4).

World Class Helicopter Records

Selected records. *Source:* National Aeronautic Association.

Great Circle Distance Without Landing
International: 2,213.04 mi.; 3,561.55 km.
Robert G. Ferry (U.S.) in Hughes YOH-6A helicopter powered by Allison T-63-A-5 engine; from Culver City, Calif., to Ormond Beach, Fla., April 6–7, 1966.

Distance, Closed Circuit
International: 1,739.96 mi.; 2,800.20 km.

Jack Schweibold (U.S.) in Hughes YOH-6A helicopter powered by Allison T-62-A-5 engine; Edwards Air Force Base, Calif., March 26, 1966.

Altitude
International: 40,820 ft; 12,442 m.
Jean Boulet (France) in Alouette SA 315-001 "Lama" powered by Artouste IIIB 735 KW engine; Istres, France, June 21, 1972.

Altitude in Horizontal Flight
International: 36,122 ft; 11,010 m.
CWO James K. Church, (U.S.) in Sikorsky CH-54B helicopter powered by 2 P&W JFTD-12 engines; Stratford, CT., Nov. 4, 1971.

Speed Around the World
35.40 mph; 56.97 kph.
H. Ross Perot, Jr., pilot; J.W. Coburn, co-pilot (U.S.) in Bell 206 L-II Long Ranger, powered by one Allison 250-C28B of 435 hp. Elapsed time: 29 days 3 h 8 min 13 sec, Sept. 1–30, 1982.

Active Pilot Certificates Held[1]

(as of January 1)

Year	Total	Airline transport	Commercial	Private
1970	720,028	31,442	176,585	299,491
1975	733,728	41,002	192,425	305,848
~1980	814,667	63,652	182,097	343,276
1985	722,376	79,192	155,929	320,086
1987	699,653	91,287	143,635	300,949
1988	694,016	96,968	143,030	299,786
1989	700,010	102,087	144,540	293,179

1. Includes other pilot categories—helicopter, glider and lighter-than-air (17,660), and students (142,544). *Source:* Department of Transportation, Federal Aviation Administration.

THE WORLD'S FASTEST AIRCRAFT. The Lockheed SR-71 A/B "Blackbird" first produced in January 1966 was moth-balled in 1989. It is the world's fastest and highest flying production aircraft built. The Blackbird was unarmed and had a crew of two seated in tandem. The dimensions are: span 55 ft 7 in.; length 107 ft 5 in.; and height 18 ft 6 in. Its estimated maximum speed at 78,750 feet is over Mach 3, and its operational ceiling is above 80,000 feet. In a reconnaissance mission, the SR-71 could cover up to a 100,000 sq.-mi. area in one hour.

Before it was donated to the Smithsonian Institution, one of the SR-71's set a transcontinental speed record on March 6, 1990, distance: 2,404 miles, time: 1 hr 7 min 53.69 seconds, speed: 2,124.51 miles per hour. ☐

THE LAST U-2 SPYPLANE. Prior to its retirement in April 1989, the last flying U2-C, NASA 709, broke eight high-altitude records on April 17, including one that had never been set before—Time-to-Climb to 20,000 meters (65,617 feet) in 12 minutes and 13 seconds. The record breaking aircraft was flown to Robins AFB, Georgia, for display in the base's museum. NASA had used the plane for environmental missions, including taking the famous high-altitude photos of Mt. St. Helens shortly after the volcano erupted. ☐

Absolute World Records

(Maximum Performance in Any Class)
Source: National Aeronautic Association.

These official Absolute World Records are the supreme achievements of all the hundreds of records open to flying machines. They are the most outstanding of all the major types, and thus warrant the highest respect.

All types of airplanes are eligible for these few very special records. Airplanes may be powered by piston, turboprop, turbojet, rocket engines or a combination. They may be landplanes, seaplanes or amphibians; they may be lightplanes, business planes, military or commercial airplanes.

Over the years, many different categories of aircraft have held these records. In the past, the cost of developing high-performance aircraft has been so great that only airplanes created for military purposes have held these records. There have been two exceptions to this situation.

Most recently and most dramatically, the Rutan designed "Voyager" shattered the theory that only a complicated military behemoth could hold an Absolute World Record. The Voyager team and its nonstop, non-refueled flight around the world proved that the dreams of dedicated individuals, combined with creative engineering, new technology, and hard work, could conquer the world.

The other exception was the X-15 rocket-powered research airplane. Holder of one record, it was used for both civilian and military research during its highly productive lifetime.

Within the seven basic categories of Absolute Records for airplanes, again the Voyager stands out as a special achievement. This amateur, hand-built, experimental aircraft deserves special recognition because the others were are all military/civilian aircraft designed and built by major government facilities. They are: the little-known Soviet E-266M a rocket-boosted version of the MiG-25 "Foxbat" interceptor, which holds the absolute altitude record, the aforementioned North American X-15 which holds the record for carrier-launched altitude, and the Lockheed SR-71 "Blackbird" photoreconnaisance airplane which holds three records for speed and altitude.

As evidence of the exceptional status of these records, note that several are more than 10 years old. Since the performance of many new government-backed airplanes which might be superior to these is wrapped in a blanket of national security, the breaking of some of these records will depend as much on political considerations as on technical ones.

Speed Around The World, Nonstop, Nonrefueled

Speed (mph)	Date	Type plane	Pilots	Place
115.65	Dec. 14-23, 1986	*Voyager*	Dick Rutan & Jeana Yeager (U.S.)	Edwards AFB, Calif.—Edwards AFB, Calif.

Distance, Great Circle Without Landing, also Distance, Closed Circuit Without Landing

Distance (mi.)	Date	Pilots	Place
24,986.727	Dec. 14-23, 1986	Dick Rutan & Jeana Yeager (U.S.)	Edwards AFB, Calif.—Edwards AFB, Calif.

Speed Over a Straight Course

Speed (mph)	Date	Type plane	Pilot	Place
2,193.16	July 28, 1976	Lockheed SR-71A	Capt. Eldon W. Joersz (USAF)	Beale AFB, Calif.

Speed Over A Closed Circuit

Speed (mph)	Date	Type plane	Pilot	Place
2,092.294	July 27,1976	Lockheed SR-71A	Maj. Adolphus H. Bledsoe, Jr. (USAF)	Beale, AFB, Calif.

Altitude

Height (ft)	Date	Type plane	Pilot	Place
123,523.58	Aug. 31, 1977	MIG-25, E-266M	Alexander Fedotov (U.S.S.R.)	U.S.S.R.

Altitude in Horizontal Flight

Height (ft)	Date	Pilot	Place
85,068.997	July 28, 1976	Capt. Robert C. Helt (USAF)	Beale AFB, Calif.

Altitude, Aircraft Launched From A Carrier Airplane

Height (ft)	Date	Type plane	Pilot	Place
314,750.00	July 17, 1962	N. American X-15-1	Maj. Robert H. White (USAF)	Edwards AFB, Calif.

The Fuels of the Future

Every motor fuel available today pollutes the air, but gasoline is one of the dirtiest. Automobiles that run on gasoline emit unburned hydrocarbons and oxides of nitrogen, which react with sunlight to create smog. Automobiles account for about 30 percent of the nation's total carbon-dioxide emissions and for virtually all carbon-monoxide emissions in urban areas. Carbon dioxide is the main contributor to the greenhouse effect—the slow warming of the earth's atmosphere. Carbon monoxide is a toxic gas.

People who inhale gasoline exhaust may suffer from eye and respiratory-system irritation. Worse than that, the fumes contain a number of other airborne toxics, including benzene, a known carcinogen. The EPA estimates that toxic fumes from automobiles cause as many as 1,800 cases of cancer every year.

Gasoline doesn't have to contaminate the air as much as it does. But until recently most oil companies didn't pay much attention to formulating a less-polluting fuel. Now, however, Government interest in alternative fuels has threatened the oil industry's unchallenged domination of the motor-fuels market. So oil companies are hustling to concoct a cleaner gasoline.

Cleaning up Gasoline

The gasoline used today is a complex combination of as many as 100 different hydrocarbons, plus additives. In the past 10 or 15 years, as lead has been phased out of gasoline, refiners have altered the composition of gasoline to maintain the octane levels that lead used to provide. Unfortunately, these changes also increased emissions of airborne toxics.

To make a gasoline that results in less pollution overall, refiners will probably add oxygenated compounds, which allow more complete combustion. That would reduce the emission of both airborne toxics and carbon monoxide. The most common oxygenates are methanol (wood alcohol), ethanol (grain alcohol made from corn or sugar cane), and ethers made from methanol or ethanol.

But there's a catch. Although oxygenates decrease the release of carbon monoxide, they can increase smog formation. So oxygenated fuels make most sense in areas with carbon-monoxide problems but little smog. Some cities in Arizona, Colorado, and Nevada already require the use of oxygenated fuels during the winter, when carbon-monoxide levels peak, and of regular gasoline in the summer to lessen smog.

The American Petroleum Institute, 14 major oil companies, and all three domestic automakers recently joined forces in a clean-gasoline research project. The group predicts that an early version of the resulting product could be test-marketed as soon as this summer [1990]. (Last year, Atlantic Richfield Co. introduced in some California stations a lead-free fuel for older cars that would otherwise need leaded gasoline. The company says it will take more work to produce a cleaner unleaded gasoline.)

If refiners come up with a viable "clean" gasoline, the fuel would offer one obvious advantage over gasoline substitutes: It could be used in all existing and future cars without costly conversions. Further, any environmental benefits of clean gasoline would be felt immediately, which is not the case with other alternative-fuel programs. However, clean gasoline would do nothing to reduce carbon-dioxide emissions that cause global warming.

Vehicles that run on clean gasoline won't require design changes, but clean gasoline is expected to cost at least two or three cents more per gallon than today's gasoline.

Methanol: Hype and Reality

As the nation moves into the post-petroleum age, the chief rival to gasoline is methanol, an alcohol fuel made from coal, wood, natural gas, or garbage.

Methanol-powered vehicles will pollute less and have more pep, say the fuel's advocates, including the Bush Administration and the U.S. Environmental Protection Agency. Methanol exhaust contains at least 35 percent less smog-producing hydrocarbons and 30 to 40 percent less airborne toxics than gasoline. And the fuel's superior combustion gives cars designed to run on methanol up to 20 percent more horsepower and faster acceleration than gasoline-powered cars.

Critics of the fuel argue that methanol would be a nightmare for consumers. A gallon of methanol goes only half as far as a gallon of gasoline, so drivers would have to fill up more often. They would also have to take special care when refueling, since methanol can damage both metal and rubber. Slopped on the side of a car, the fuel can remove paint or change its color.

Methanol is far from an ideal fuel from an environmental perspective. Methanol exhaust contains four to eight times more formaldehyde than gasoline exhaust. Formaldehyde, the same stuff used to preserve dead frogs in high-school biology classes, contributes to ozone formation in the lower atmosphere. It's also an eye and respiratory-system irritant and a probable carcinogen. Automakers will have to design a catalyst to control formaldehyde emissions. (Methanol advocates counter that gasoline can produce almost as much atmospheric formaldehyde as methanol, although its formaldehyde forms in the air *after* the fumes leave the tailpipe.)

Methanol presents other problems as well. Cars that run on straight methanol can be hard to start at temperatures below 50° F. When the fuel burns, its flame is an almost-invisible blue; if you had an auto accident on a bright day, you might not immediately notice a fire. Methanol is also poisonous; swallowing as little as one ounce can blind or kill you.

Two of these drawbacks are overcome by a fuel blend known as M85—85 percent methanol and 15 percent gasoline. It can start cars at −20°, and it burns with gasoline's typical bright yellow flame. But M85 compromises some of methanol's clean-air benefits. For example, hydrocarbon emissions per mile from straight methanol are 90 percent lower than from gasoline, but M85 cuts hydrocarbon emissions by only 35 percent.

Automakers plan to make it difficult for people to swallow methanol accidentally by installing devices in fuel tanks that prevent the siphoning of fuel. The National Capital Poison Center at Georgetown University Hospital estimates that without such gadgets, nearly 200 people could die each year after accidentally swallowing methanol.

Methanol, the EPA predicts, will cost the same as regular gasoline, mile-for-mile. But oil-industry spokespeople and other researchers contend that methanol may cost as much as 50 percent more per mile than gasoline. Cars that use it may cost $300 to $2000 more to buy.

Some methanol advocates argue that a switch to methanol would help ease U.S. dependence on Middle East oil. But that's a debatable proposition. Most methanol would be produced from natural gas. Although the U.S., Canada, and Mexico have enough natural gas to provide methanol for about 10 percent of America's market, most of the fuel would likely be produced overseas, including the Middle East, near extensive natural-gas reserves. Methanol can also be made from coal, which is abundant in the U.S. But that method is expensive and dirty using current technology.

Methanol's impact on global warming depends on how the methanol is made. All methanol produces the same amount of carbon dioxide when burned. But when both production and combustion are considered, methanol made from natural gas generates about 10 percent less carbon dioxide than gasoline, while methanol made from coal produces up to 100 percent more.

Other Alternatives

Cars could run on fuels other than gasoline or methanol. Here are the most likely candidates:

Ethanol, the alcohol fuel made from corn and sugar cane, offers many of methanol's clean air benefits. It's also less corrosive than methanol and contains one-third more energy per gallon. Ethanol can help lower carbon-dioxide emissions because the plants it's made from use carbon dioxide from the air as they grow. Much of that benefit is, however, offset by the carbon-dioxide emissions from the tractors used to care for the crops and from the fermentation processes.

Ethanol is too expensive to compete as a straight motor fuel. It costs nearly twice as much as gasoline. Supplies are also limited. If 40 percent of the total U.S. grain harvest were turned into ethanol, it would provide just 10 percent of the fuel consumed in the U.S. each year.

Ethanol has been used as a gasoline extender and octane enhancer since the energy shortages of the 1970s, and it will undoubtedly continue to be important as an ingredient in clean gasoline. Today it's found in about 8 percent of the gasoline sold in the U.S.

Compressed natural gas, already used for cooking and heating, makes sense for fleet vehicles that service a limited geographic area and can return to a central point at night for refueling. It now powers more than 30,000 vehicles in the U.S.—from school buses in Oklahoma to United Parcel Service delivery trucks in Brooklyn, N.Y.

Compressed natural gas emits at least 40 percent less hydrocarbons and 30 percent less carbon dioxide per mile than gasoline. Carbon monoxide, formaldehyde, and airborne toxics are nearly eliminated. It's also cheap—about 70 cents for the energy equivalent of a gallon of gasoline at current prices.

But this gas isn't a practical alternative fuel for passenger cars; you'd either have to load down your car with extra fuel tanks or refuel every 100 miles or so. If compressed natural-gas cars reach the consumer market, they will cost about $800 more than conventional cars, in part to cover the cost of the heavy cylinders needed to keep the fuel under pressure.

Electricity remains the cleanest alternative to gasoline. Like battery-operated golf carts, electric cars would emit no exhaust, although the power plants that produced the electricity would probably burn the fuel *they* use in a less than pristine way. At this point, it is impractical to manufacture an electric-powered passenger car. The lead-acid batteries used in today's models weigh as much as 1000 pounds and require six to eight hours of recharging for every 60 to 100 miles. Significant technological breakthroughs will be needed before these vehicles can satisfy consumer needs.

Solar-hydrogen fuel may be the most promising of long-term alternatives. Large solar cells set up in sunny parts of the U.S. would convert the sun's energy into electricity, which would then be used to split water molecules and form hydrogen. Vehicles that run on hydrogen release only water vapor and oxides of nitrogen; they do not emit carbon dioxide or other gases that contribute to global warming. Research on this technology is under way, but hydrogen-powered passenger cars are unlikely to be available for decades. Even farther down the road are cars powered by solar-generated electricity. □

Reprinted with permission from "The Fuels of the Future," *Consumer Reports,* January, 1990.

The Stages of Invention

Alexander von Humbolt (1769-1859), the German naturalist, said that an invention goes through three stages: doubt of its existence, denial of its importance, and, finally, credit for its discovery going to someone else.

One example of the truth in this perception is the invention of the "Pullman," the railroad sleeping car. The first sleeper was built by Richard Imlay of Philadelphia. It ran between Chambersburg and Harrisburg, Pa., in 1838. At least eight railroads advertised some kind of sleeping car before 1850. Pullman's first car was not built until 1859. George M. Pullman and his friend Ben Field patented the folding upper berth in 1864. Pullman seems to have been a better businessman and a better promoter.

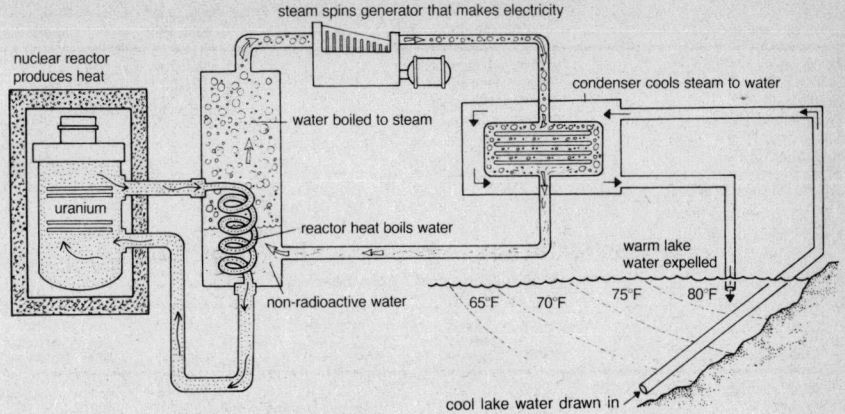

steam spins generator that makes electricity

nuclear reactor
produces heat

water boiled to steam

condenser cools steam to water

uranium

reactor heat boils water

warm lake
water expelled

non-radioactive water 65°F 70°F 75°F 80°F

cool lake water drawn in

Simplified diagram of a nuclear reactor. Laurel Cook, Boston, Ma.

Largest Nuclear Power Plants in the United States

(over a million kilowatts)

Plant	Operating utility	Capacity (kilowatts)	Year operative
South Texas 1, TX	Houston Lighting & Power	1,250,000	1988
South Texas 2	Houston Lighting	1,250,000	1989
Palo Verde 1, AZ	Arizona Public Service	1,221,000	1986
Palo Verde 2, AZ	Arizona Public Service	1,221,000	1986
Palo Verde 3, AZ	Arizona Public Service	1,221,000	1988
Perry 1, OH	Cleveland Electric Illumination	1,205,000	1987
Sequoyah 1, TN	Tennessee Valley Authority	1,148,000	1981
Sequoyah 2, TN	Tennessee Valley Authority	1,148,000	1982
Callaway, MO	Union Electric	1,145,000	1984
Grand Gulf 1, MS	System Energy Resources	1,142,000	1985
Millstone 3, CT	Northeast Nuclear Energy	1,142,000	1986
Catawba 1, SC	Duke Power Co.	1,129,000	1985
Catawba 2, SC	Duke Power Co.	1,129,000	1986
McGuire 1, NC	Duke Power Co.	1,129,000	1981
McGuire 2, NC	Duke Power Co.	1,129,000	1984
Wolf Creek 1, KS	Wolf Creek Nuclear Operating	1,128,000	1985
Braidwood 1, IL	Commonwealth Edison	1,120,000	1988
Braidwood 2, IL	Commonwealth Edison	1,120,000	1988
Salem 1, DE	Public Service Electric & Gas	1,106,000	1977
Salem 2, DE	Public Service Electric & Gas	1,106,000	1981
Byron 1, IL	Commonwealth Edison	1,105,000	1985
Byron 2, IL	Commonwealth Edison	1,105,000	1987
Vogtle 2	Georgia Power	1,083,000	1989
Trojan, OR	Portland General Electric	1,095,000	1976
Fermi 2, OH	Detroit Edison	1,093,000	1988
Diablo Canyon 2	Pacific Gas & Electric	1,087,000	1986
Nine Mile Point 2, NY	Niagara Mohawk Power	1,080,000	1988
San Onofre 3, CA	Southern California Edison	1,080,000	1984
Vogtle 1, GA	Georgia Power	1,079,000	1987
Waterford 3, LA	Louisiana Power & Light	1,075,000	1985
Diablo Canyon 1, CA	Pacific Gas & Electric	1,073,000	1985
San Onofre 2, CA	Southern California Edison	1,070,000	1983
Hope Creek 1, DE	Public Service Electric & Gas	1,067,000	1986
Browns Ferry 1, AL	Tennessee Valley Authority	1,065,000	1974
Browns Ferry 2, AL	Tennessee Valley Authority	1,065,000	1975
Browns Ferry 3, AL	Tennessee Valley Authority	1,065,000	1977
Limerick 2	Philadelphia Elec	1,065,000	1990
Cook 2, MI	Indiana & Michigan Power	1,060,000	1978
Limerick 1, PA	Philadelphia Electric	1,055,000	1986
Peach Bottom 2, PA	Philadelphia Electric	1,051,000	1974
Zion 1, IL	Commonwealth Edison	1,040,000	1973

Plant	Operating utility	Capacity (kilowatts)	Year operative
Zion 2, IL	Commonwealth Edison	1,040,000	1974
La Salle 1, IL	Commonwealth Edison	1,036,000	1984
La Salle 2, IL	Commonwealth Edison	1,036,000	1984
Peach Bottom 3, PA	Philadelphia Gas & Electric	1,035,000	1974
Susquehanna 1, PA	Pennsylvania Power & Light	1,032,000	1983
Susquehanna 2, PA	Pennsylvania Power & Light	1,032,000	1985

Source: Nuclear Regulatory Commission.

Production of Crude Petroleum by Countries

(in thousands of 42-gallon barrels)

Area and country	Est. 1990[1]	1989[1]	Est. percent change	Area and country	Est. 1990[1]	1989[1]	Est. percent change
Western Hemisphere	5,720,280	5,733,420	−0.2	Syria	136,510	102,930	32.6
Argentina	171,550	164,615	4.2	United Arab Emirates	753,360	590,935	27.5
Bolivia	6,935	6,570	5.6	Yemen, North[4]	65,700	71,175	−7.7
Brazil	228,490	202,575	12.8	Yemen, South[4]	3,650	3,650	—
Canada	524,870	575,605	−8.8	Asia Pacific	1,231,875	1,182,965	4.1
Chile	7,300	8,760	−16.7	Australia	200,020	178,120	12.3
Columbia	160,600	153,665	4.5	Brunei	54,750	53,290	2.7
Ecuador	101,470	105,485	−3.5	Burma	3,650	4,380	−16.7
Mexico	954,840	953,015	0.2	India	254,040	239,440	6.1
Peru	46,355	52,195	−11.2	Indonesia	446,760	447,125	−0.1
Trinidad	54,750	56,575	−3.2	Japan	4,015	4,380	−8.3
United States	2,724,360	2,854,300	−4.6	Malaysia	219,000	212,430	3.1
Venezuela	735,110	597,140	23.1	New Zealand	10,220	10,220	—
Western Europe	1,446,495	1,331,520	8.6	Pakistan	21,170	16,790	26.1
Austria	7,665	8,760	−12.5	Thailand	14,965	13,505	10.8
Denmark	41,975	38,690	8.5	Africa	2,129,045	1,825,730	16.6
France	23,725	23,725	—	Algeria	283,240	233,965	21.1
West Germany	26,280	28,105	−6.5	Angola/Cabinda[3]	167,900	166,075	1.1
Greece	6,570	6,935	−5.3	Cameroon	60,225	61,685	−2.4
Italy	32,850	25,550	28.6	Congo	58,765	55,845	5.2
Netherlands	23,360	25,915	−9.9	Egypt	313,170	313,170	—
Norway	570,860	493,115	15.8	Gabon	94,900	68,255	39.0
Spain	5,840	6,570	−11.1	Ivory Coast	730	1,095	−33.3
Turkey	21,535	18,615	15.7	Libya	474,500	373,760	27.0
United Kingdom	685,835	655,540	4.6	Nigeria	629,260	501,510	25.5
Middle East	6,327,275	5,472,810	15.6	Tunisia	36,135	37,960	−4.8
Bahrain	16,060	15,695	2.3	Zaire	9,125	10,585	−13.8
Iran	1,072,005	1,070,180	0.2	Communist Bloc	5,499,455	5,651,660	−2.7
Iraq	1,113,615	974,915	14.2	China	1,004,845	983,675	2.2
Kuwait	647,510	418,655	54.7	Romania	65,700	65,700	—
Neutral Zone[2]	146,000	146,730	−0.5	U.S.S.R.	4,352,625	4,526,000	−3.8
Oman	233,600	222,650	4.9	Other communist	76,285	76,285	—
Qatar	131,765	155,125	−15.1				
Saudi Arabia	2,007,500	1,700,170	18.1	**World Total**	**22,354,425**	**21,198,105**	**5.5**

1. Based on Jan.–Feb. average. 2. Shared by Kuwait and Saudi Arabia. 3. An enclave in West Africa on Atlantic coast between the Congo and Angola. 4. Based on data prior to union into Republic of Yemen. Totals may not add up due to rounding.

Energy Equivalents

(*Source:* Energy Information Administration.)

1 Btu of energy: one match tip, 250 calories (International Steam Table), or 0.25 kilocalories (food calories).

1,000 Btu of energy: two five-ounce glasses of table wine; 250 kilocalories (food calories), or 0.80 peanut butter and jelly sandwiches.

1 million Btu of energy: 90 pounds of coal, 120 pounds of oven dried hardwood, 8 gallons of motor gasoline, 10 therms of natural dry gas, 11 gallons of propane, 1.2 days of U.S. energy consumption per capita (1984), or two months dietary intake of a laborer.

1 barrel of crude oil: 14 days U.S. petroleum consumption per capita, 5.6 thousand cubic feet of dry natural gas, 0.26 short tons (520 pounds) of coal, or 1,700 kilowatts of electricity.

1 short ton of coal: 102 days of U.S. petroleum consumption per capita, 3.8 barrels of crude oil, 21 thousand cubic feet of dry natural gas, or 6,500 kilowatthours of electricity. ☐

Petroleum Imports by Country of Origin, 1980–1989

(Thousand barrels per day)

Year	Nigeria	Saudi Arabia	Venezuela	Other OPEC[1]	Total OPEC[2]	Total Arab OPEC[3]	Canada	Mexico	United Kingdom	Virgin Is. and Puerto Rico
1980	857	1,261	481	865	4,300	2,551	455	533	176	476
1981	620	1,129	406	491	3,323	1,848	447	522	375	389
1982	514	552	412	250	2,146	854	482	685	456	366
1983	302	337	422	223	1,862	632	547	826	382	322
1984	216	325	548	294	2,049	819	630	748	402	336
1985	293	168	605	264	1,830	472	770	816	310	275
1986	440	685	793	329	2,837	1,162	807	699	350	265
1987	535	751	804	390	3,060	1,274	848	655	352	294
1988	618	1,064	794	538	3,520	1,839	999	747	315	264
1989[4]	809	1,224	867	772	4,116	2,122	910	763	217	352

Source: 1. "Other OPEC" consists of Ecuador, Gabon, Iran, Iraq, Kuwait, Libya, Qatar, and United Arab Emirates. Prior to 1988, imports from the Neutral Zone between Kuwait and Saudi Arabia included in imports from Saudi Arabia. From 1988 forward, those imports are included in imports from "Other OPEC." 2. "Total OPEC" consists of Ecuador, Gabon, Indonesia, Iran, Nigeria, and Venezuela, as well as the Arab members. "Total OPEC" imports exclude petroleum imported into the United States indirectly from OPEC countries, primarily from Caribbean and West European refining areas, as petroleum products that were refined from crude oil produced in OPEC countries. 3. "Total Arab OPEC" consists of Algeria, Iraq, Kuwait, Libya, Qatar, Saudi Arabia, and United Arab Emirates. Imports from the Neutral Zone are included in imports from "Total Arab OPEC." 4. Preliminary. Note: Sum of components may not equal total due to independent rounding. Sources: ● 1960 through 1975—Bureau of Mines, *Minerals Yearbook,* "Crude Petroleum and Petroleum Products" Chapter. ● 1976 through 1980—Energy Information Administratio Data Reports, *P.A.D. Districts Supply/Demand, Annual.* ● 1981 through 1988—Energy Information Administration, *Petroleum Supply Annual.* ● 1989—Energy Information Administration, *Petroleum Supply Monthly,* Dec. 1989 (Feb. 1990).

Petroleum Exports by Country of Destination, 1980–1989

(Thousand Barrels per Day)

Year	Canada	Japan	Mexico	Netherlands	Belgium[1]	Italy	United Kingdom	France	Brazil	Virgin Is./ Puerto Rico
1980	108	32	28	23	20	14	7	11	4	220
1981	89	38	26	42	12	22	5	15	1	221
1982	85	68	53	85	17	32	14	24	8	211
1983	76	104	24	49	22	35	8	23	2	144
1984	83	92	35	37	21	39	14	18	1	152
1985	74	108	61	44	26	30	14	11	3	161
1986	85	110	56	58	30	39	8	11	3	112
1987	83	120	70	39	17	42	6	12	2	126
1988[2]	84	124	70	26	25	29	9	12	3	150
1989[2]	92	122	89	36	23	37	9	11	5	141

1. Including Luxembourg. 2. Preliminary. NOTE: Sum of components may not equal total due to independent rounding. *Source:* 1980—Energy Information Administration, Energy Data Reports, *Petroleum Statement, Annual.* ˙ 1981 through 1986—Energy Information Administration, *Petroleum Supply Annual.* ˙ 1987–88—Energy Information Administration, *Petroleum Supply Monthly.* 1989—Energy Information Administration, *Petroleum Supply Monthly,* Dec. 1989 (Feb.1990).

U.S. Motor Vehicle Fuel Consumption and Related Data

(1988 estimate)

Type of vehicle	Total travel (million vehicle miles)	Number of registered vehicles	Average miles traveled per vehicle	Fuel consumed (thousand gallons)	Average fuel consumption per vehicle (gallons)
All passenger vehicles	1,444,784	146,451,648	9,865	72,774,695	497
Total personal passenger vehicles	1,439,319	145,835,979	9,869	71,854,639	493
Cars	1,429,297	141,251,695	10,119	71,654,199	507
Motorcycles	10,022	4,584,284	2,186	200,440	44
All buses	5,465	615,669	8,877	920,056	1,494
All cargo vehicles	580,802	42,529,368	13,656	57,111,185	1,343
Single unit trucks	490,654	41,053,127	11,952	40,010,219	975
Combination	90,149	1,476,241	61,066	17,100,966	11,584
All motor vehicles	2,025,586	188,981,016	10,718	129,885,880	687

Source: Department of Transportation, Federal Highway Administration.

WEIGHTS & MEASURES

Measures and Weights

Source: Department of Commerce, National Bureau of Standards.

The International System (Metric)

The International System of Units is a modernized version of the metric system, established by international agreement, that i.e. provides a logical and interconnected framework for all measurements in science, industry, and commerce. The system is built on a foundation of seven basic units, and all other units are derived from them. (Use of metric weights and measures was legalized in the United States in 1866, and our customary units of weights and measures are defined in terms of the meter and kilogram.)

Length. Meter. Up until 1983, the meter was defined as 1,650,764.73 wavelengths in vacuum of the orange-red line of the spectrum of krypton-86. Since then, it is equal to the distance traveled by light in a vacuum in 1/299,792,458 of a second.

Time. Second. The second is defined as the duration of 9,192,631,770 cycles of the radiation associated with a specified transition of the cesium 133 atom.

Mass. Kilogram. The standard for the kilogram is a cylinder of platinum-iridium alloy kept by the International Bureau of Weights and Measures at Paris. A duplicate at the National Bureau of Standards serves as the mass standard for the United States. The kilogram is the only base unit still defined by a physical object.

Temperature. Kelvin. The kelvin is defined as the fraction 1/273.16 of the thermodynamic temperature of the triple point of water; that is, the point at which water forms an interface of solid, liquid and vapor. This is defined as 0.01° C on the Centigrade or Celsius scale and 32.02° F on the Fahrenheit scale. The temperature 0° K is called "absolute zero."

Electric Current. Ampere. The ampere is defined as that current that, if maintained in each of two long parallel wires separated by one meter in free space, would produce a force between the two wires (due to their magnetic fields) of 2×10^{-7} newton for each meter of length. (A newton is the unit of force which when applied to one kilogram mass would experience an acceleration of one meter per second per second.)

Luminous Inentsity. Candela. The candela is defined as the luminous intensity of 1/600,000 of a square meter of a cavity at the temperature of freezing platinum (2,042K).

Amount of Substance. Mole. The mole is the amount of substance of a system that contains as many elementary entities as there are atoms in 0.012 kilogram of carbon-12.

Tables of Metric Weights and Measures

LINEAR MEASURE

10 millimeters (mm) = 1 centimeter (cm)
10 centimeters = 1 decimeter (dm) = 100 millimeters
10 decimeters = 1 meter (m) = 1,000 millimeters
10 meters = 1 dekameter (dam)
10 dekameters = 1 hectometer (hm) = 100 meters
10 hectometers = 1 kilometer (km) = 1,000 meters

AREA MEASURE

100 square millimeters (mm²) = 1 sq centimeter (cm²)
10,000 square centimeters = 1 sq meter (m²) = 1,000,000 sq millimeters
100 square meters = 1 are (a)
100 ares = 1 hectare (ha) = 10,000 sq meters
100 hectares = 1 sq kilometer (km²) = 1,000,000 sq meters

VOLUME MEASURE

10 milliliters (ml) = 1 centiliter (cl)
10 centiliters = 1 deciliter (dl) = 100 milliliters
10 deciliters = 1 liter (1) = 1,000 milliliters
10 liters = 1 dekaliter (dal)
10 dekaliters = 1 hectoliter (hl) = 100 liters
10 hectoliters = 1 kiloliter (kl) = 1,000 liters

CUBIC MEASURE

1,000 cubic millimeters (mm³) = 1 cu centimeter (cm³)
1,000 cubic centimeters = 1 cu decimeter (dm³) = 1,000,000 cu millimeters
1,000 cubic decimeters = 1 cu meter (m³) = 1 stere = 1,000,000 cu centimeters = 1,000,000,000 cu millimeters

WEIGHT

10 milligrams (mg) = 1 centigram (cg)
10 centigrams = 1 decigram (dg) = 100 milligrams
10 decigrams = 1 gram (g) = 1,000 milligrams
10 grams = 1 dekagram (dag)
10 dekagrams = 1 hectogram (hg) = 100 grams
10 hectograms = 1 kilogram (kg) = 1,000 grams
1,000 kilograms = 1 metric ton (t)

Tables of Customary U.S. Weights and Measures

LINEAR MEASURE

12 inches (in.) = 1 foot (ft)
3 feet = 1 yard (yd)
5 1/2 yards = 1 rod (rd), pole, or perch (16 1/2 ft)
40 rods = 1 furlong (fur) = 220 yds = 660 ft
8 furlongs = 1 statute mile (mi.) = 1,760 yds = 5,280 ft
3 land miles = 1 league
5,280 feet = 1 statute or land mile
6,076.11549 feet = 1 international nautical mile

AREA MEASURE

144 square inches = 1 sq ft
9 square feet = 1 sq yd = 1,296 sq in.
30 1/4 square yards = 1 sq rd = 272 1/4 sq ft
160 square rods = 1 acre = 4,840 sq yds = 43,560 sq ft
640 acres = 1 sq mi.
1 mile square = 1 section (of land)
6 miles square = 1 township = 36 sections = 36 sq mi.

CUBIC MEASURE

1,728 cubic inches = 1 cu ft
27 cubic feet = 1 cu yd

LIQUID MEASURE

When necessary to distinguish the liquid pint or quart from the dry pint or quart, the word "liquid" or the abbreviation "liq" should be used in combination with the name or abbreviation of the liquid unit.

4 gills (gi) = 1 pint (pt) (= 28.875 cu in.)
2 pints = 1 quart (qt) (= 57.75 cu in.)
4 quarts = 1 gallon (gal) (= 231 cu in.) = 8 pts = 32 gills

APOTHECARIES' FLUID MEASURE

60 minims (min.) = 1 fluid dram (fl dr) (= 0.2256 cu in.)
8 fluid drams = 1 fluid ounce (fl oz) (= 1.8047 cu in.)
16 fluid ounces = 1 pt (= 28.875 cu in.) = 128 fl drs
2 pints = 1 qt (= 57.75 cu in.) = 32 fl oz = 256 fl drs
4 quarts = 1 gal (= 231 cu in.) = 128 fl oz = 1,024 fl drs

DRY MEASURE

When necessary to distinguish the dry pint or quart from the liquid pint or quart; the word "dry" should be used in combination with the name or abbreviation of the dry unit.

2 pints = 1 qt (=67.2006 cu in.)
8 quarts = 1 peck (pk) (=537.605 cu in.) = 16 pts
4 pecks = 1 bushel (bu) (= 2,150.42 cu in.) = 32 qts

AVOIRDUPOIS WEIGHT

When necessary to distinguish the avoirdupois dram from the apothecaries dram, or to distinguish the avoirdupois dram or ounce from the fluid dram or ounce, or to distinguish the avoirdupois ounce or pound from the troy or apothecaries, ounce or pound, the word "avoirdupois" or the abbreviation "avdp" should be used in combination with the name or abbreviation of the avoirdupois unit.
(The "grain" is the same in avoirdupois, troy, and apothecaries weights.)

27 11/32 grains = 1 dram (dr)
16 drams = 1 oz = 437 1/2 grains
16 ounces = 1 lb = 256 drams = 7,000 grains
100 pounds = 1 hundredweight (cwt)[1]
20 hundredweights = 1 ton (tn) = 2,000 lbs[1]

In "gross" or "long" measure, the following values are recognized:

112 pounds = 1 gross or long cwt[1]
20 gross or long hundredweights = 1 gross or long ton = 2,240 lbs[1]

1. When the terms "hundredweight" and "ton" are used unmodified, they are commonly understood to mean the 100-pound hundredweight and the 2,000-pound ton, respectively; these units may be designated "net" or "short" when necessary to distinguish them from the corresponding units in gross or long measure.

UNITS OF CIRCULAR MEASURE

Second (") = —
Minute (') = 60 seconds
Degree (°) = 60 minutes
Right angle = 90 degrees
Straight angle = 180 degrees
Circle = 360 degrees

TROY WEIGHT

24 grains = 1 pennyweight (dwt)
20 pennyweights = 1 ounce troy (oz t) = 480 grains
12 ounces troy = 1 pound troy (lb t) = 240 pennyweights = 5,760 grains

APOTHECARIES' WEIGHT

20 grains = 1 scruple (s ap)
3 scruples = 1 dram apothecaries' (dr ap) = 60 grains
8 drams apothecaries = 1 ounce apothecaries' (oz ap) = 24 scruples = 480 grains
12 ounces apothecaries = 1 pound apothecaries' (lb ap) = 96 drams apothecaries' = 288 scruples = 5,760 grains

GUNTER'S OR SURVEYOR'S CHAIN MEASURE

7.92 inches = 1 link (li)
100 links = 1 chain (ch) = 4 rods = 66 ft
80 chains = 1 statute mile = 320 rods = 5,280 ft

Metric and U.S. Equivalents

1 angstrom[1] (light wave measurement)	0.1 millimicron 0.000 1 micron 0.000 000 1 millimeter 0.000 000 004 inch	1 decimeter	3.937 inches
		1 dekameter	32.808 feet
1 cable's length	120 fathoms 720 feet 219.456 meters	1 fathom	6 feet 1.8288 meters
1 centimeter	0.3937 inch	1 foot	0.3048 meter
1 chain (Gunter's or surveyor's)	66 feet 20.1168 meters	1 furlong	10 chains (surveyor's) 660 feet 220 yards 1/8 statute mile 201.168 meters

1 inch	2.54 centimeters
1 kilometer	0.621 mile
1 league (land)	3 statute miles 4.828 kilometers
1 link (Gunter's or surveyor's)	7.92 inches 0.201 168 meter
1 meter	39.37 inches 1.094 yards
1 micron	0.001 millimeter 0.000 039 37 inch
1 mil	0.001 inch 0.025 4 millimeter
1 mile (statute or land)	5,280 feet 1.609 kilometers
1 mile (nautical international)	1.852 kilometers 1.151 statute miles 0.999 U.S. nautical miles
1 millimeter	0.03937 inch
1 millimicron (mμ)	0.001 micron 0.000 000 039 37 inch
1 nanometer	0.001 micrometer or 0.000 000 039 37 inch
1 point (typography)	0.013 837 inch 1/72 inch (approximately) 0.351 millimeter
1 rod, pole, or perch	16 1/2 feet 5.0292 meters
1 yard	0.9144 meter

AREAS OR SURFACES

1 acre	43,560 square feet 4,840 square yards 0.405 hectare
1 are	119.599 square yards 0.025 acre
1 hectare	2.471 acres
1 square centimeter	0.155 square inch
1 square decimeter	15.5 square inches
1 square foot	929.030 square centimeters
1 square inch	6.4516 square centimeters
1 square kilometer	0.386 square mile 247.105 acres
1 square meter	1.196 square yards 10.764 square feet
1 square mile	258.999 hectares
1 square millimeter	0.002 square inch
1 square rod, square pole or square perch	25.293 square meters
1 square yard	0.836 square meters

CAPACITIES OR VOLUMES

1 barrel, liquid	31 to 42 gallons[2]
1 barrel, standard for fruits, vegetables, and other dry commodities except cranberries	7,056 cubic inches 105 dry quarts 3.281 bushels, struck measure
1 barrel, standard, cranberry	5.286 cubic inches 86 45/64 dry quarts 2.709 bushels, struck measure
1 bushel (U.S.) struck measure	2,150.42 cubic inches 35.238 liters
1 bushel, heaped (U.S.)	2,747.715 cubic inches 1.278 bushels, struck measure[3]
1 cord (firewood)	128 cubic feet
1 cubic centimeter	0.061 cubic inch
1 cubic decimeter	61.024 cubic inches
1 cubic foot	7.481 gallons 28.316 cubic decimeters
1 cubic inch	0.554 fluid ounce 4.433 fluid drams 16.387 cubic centimeters
1 cubic meter	1.308 cubic yards
1 cubic yard	0.765 cubic meter
1 cup, measuring	8 fluid ounces 1/2 liquid pint
1 dram, fluid or liquid (U.S.)	1/8 fluid ounces 0.226 cubic inch 3.697 milliliters 1.041 British fluid drachms
1 dekaliter	2.642 gallons 1.135 pecks
1 gallon (U.S.)	231 cubic inches 3.785 liters 0.833 British gallon 128 U.S. fluid ounces
1 gallon (British Imperial)	277.42 cubic inches 1.201 U.S. gallons 4.546 liters 160 British fluid ounces
1 gill	7.219 cubic inches 4 fluid ounces 0.118 liter
1 hectoliter	26.418 gallons 2.838 bushels
1 liter	1.057 liquid quarts 0.908 dry quart 61.024 cubic inches
1 milliliter	0.271 fluid dram 16.231 minims 0.061 cubic inch
1 ounce, fluid or liquid (U.S.)	1.805 cubic inch 29.574 milliliters 1.041 British fluid ounces

1 peck	8.810 liters	1 hundredweight, net or short	100 pounds 45.359 kilograms
1 pint, dry	33.600 cubic inches 0.551 liter	1 kilogram	2.205 pounds
1 pint, liquid	28.875 cubic inches 0.473 liter	1 microgram [μg (the Greek letter mu in combination with the letter g)]	0.000 001 gram
1 quart, dry (U.S.)	67.201 cubic inches 1.101 liters 0.969 British quart	1 milligram	0.015 grain
1 quart, liquid (U.S.)	57.75 cubic inches 0.946 liter 0.833 British quart	1 ounce, avoirdupois	437.5 grains 0.911 troy or apothecaries, ounce 28.350 grams
1 quart (British)	69.354 cubic inches 1.032 U.S. dry quarts 1.201 U.S. liquid quarts	1 ounce, troy or apothecaries	480 grains 1.097 avoirdupois ounces 31.103 grams
1 tablespoon, measuring	3 teaspoons 4 fluid drams 1/2 fluid ounce	1 pennyweight	1.555 grams
1 teaspoon, measuring	1/3 tablespoon 1 1/3 fluid drams	1 point	0.01 carat 2 milligrams
1 assay ton[4]	29.167 grams	1 pound, avoirdupois	7,000 grains 1.215 troy or apothecaries pounds 453.592 37 grams
1 carat	200 milligrams 3.086 grains		
1 dram, apothecaries'	60 grains 3.888 grams	1 pound, troy or apothecaries	5,760 grains 0.823 avoirdupois pound 373.242 grams
1 dram, avoirdupois	27 11/32 (=27.344) grains 1.772 grams	1 ton, gross or long[5]	2,240 pounds 1.12 net tons 1.016 metric tons
1 grain	64.798 91 milligrams		
1 gram	15.432 grains 0.035 ounce, avoirdupois	1 ton, metric	2,204.623 pounds 0.984 gross ton 1.102 net tons
1 hundredweight, gross or long[5]	112 pounds 50.802 kilograms	1 ton, net or short	2,000 pounds 0.893 gross ton 0.907 metric ton

1. The angstrom is basically defined as 10^{-10} meter. 2. There is a variety of "barrels" established by law or usage. For example, federal taxes on fermented liquors are based on a barrel of 31 gallons; many state laws fix the "barrel for liquids" at 31 1/2 gallons; one state fixes a 36-gallon barrel for cistern measurement; federal law recognizes a 40-gallon barrel for "proof spirits"; by custom, 42 gallons comprise a barrel of crude oil or petroleum products for statistical purposes, and this equivalent is recognized "for liquids" by four states. 3. Frequently recognized as 1 1/4 bushels, struck measure. 4. Used in assaying. The assay ton bears the same relation to the milligram that a ton of 2,000 pounds avoirdupois bears to the ounce troy; hence the weight in milligrams of precious metal obtained from one assay ton of ore gives directly the number of troy ounces to the net ton. 5. The gross or long ton and hundredweight are used commercially in the United States to only a limited extent, usually in restricted industrial fields. These units are the same as the British "ton" and "hundredweight."

Miscellaneous Units of Measure

Acre: An area of 43,560 square feet. Originally, the area a yoke of oxen could plow in one day.

Agate: Originally a measurement of type size (5 1/2 points). Now equal to 1/14 inch. Used in printing for measuring column length.

Ampere: Unit of electric current. A potential difference of one volt across a resistance of one ohm produces a current of one ampere.

Astronomical Unit (A.U.): 93,000,000 miles, the average distance of the earth from the sun. Used in astronomy.

Bale: A large bundle of goods. In the U.S., the approximate weight of a bale of cotton is 500 pounds. The weight varies in other countries.

Board Foot (fbm): 144 cubic inches (12 in. × 12 in. × 1 in.). Used for lumber.

Bolt: 40 yards. Used for measuring cloth.

Btu: British thermal unit. Amount of heat needed to increase the temperature of one pound of water by one degree Fahrenheit (252 calories).

Carat (c): 200 milligrams or 3.086 grains troy.

Originally the weight of a seed of the carob tree in the Mediterranean region. Used for weighing precious stones. *See also* Karat.

Chain (ch): a chain 66 feet or one-tenth of a furlong in length, divided into 100 parts called links. One mile is equal to 80 chains. Used in surveying and sometimes called Gunter's or surveyor's chain.

Cubit: 18 inches or 45.72 cm. Derived from distance between elbow and tip of middle finger.

Decibel: Unit of relative loudness. One decibel is the smallest amount of change detectable by the human ear.

Ell, English: 1 1/4 yards or 1/32 bolt. Used for measuring cloth.

Freight Ton (also called Measurement Ton): 40 cubic feet of merchandise. Used for cargo freight.

Great Gross: 12 gross or 1728.

Gross: 12 dozen or 144.

Hand: 4 inches or 10.16 cm. Derived from the width of the hand. Used for measuring the height of horses at withers.

Hertz: Modern unit for measurement of electromagnetic wave frequencies (equivalent to "cycles per second").

Hogshead (hhd): 2 liquid barrels or 14,653 cubic inches.

Horsepower: The power needed to lift 33,000 pounds a distance of one foot in one minute (about 1 1/2 times the power an average horse can exert). Used for measuring power of steam engines, etc.

Karat (kt): A measure of the purity of gold, indicating how many parts out of 24 are pure. For example, 18 karat gold is 3/4 pure. Sometimes spelled *carat.*

Knot: Not a distance, but the rate of speed of one nautical mile per hour. Used for measuring speed of ships.

League: Rather indefinite and varying measure, but usually estimated at 3 miles in English-speaking countries.

Light-Year: 5,880,000,000,000 miles, the distance light travels in a vacuum in a year at the rate of 186,281.7 miles (299,792 kilometers) per second. (If an astronomical unit were represented by one inch, a light-year would be represented by about one mile.) Used for measurements in interstellar space.

Magnum: Two-quart bottle. Used for measuring wine, etc.

Ohm: Unit of electrical resistance. A circuit in which a potential difference of one volt produces a current of one ampere has a resistance of one ohm.

Parsec: Approximately 3.26 light-years or 19.2 trillion miles. Term is combination of first syllables of *pa*rallax and *sec*ond, and distance is that of imaginary star when lines drawn from it to both earth and sun form a maximum angle or parallax of one second (1/3600 degree). Used for measuring interstellar distances.

Pi (π): 3.14159265+. The ratio of the circumference of a circle to its diameter. For practical purposes, the value is used to four decimal places: 3.1416.

Pica: 1/6 inch or 12 points. Used in printing for measuring column width, etc.

Pipe: 2 hogsheads. Used for measuring wine and other liquids.

Point: .013837 (approximately 1/72) inch or 1/12 pica. Used in printing for measuring type size.

Quintal: 100,000 grams or 220.46 pounds avoirdupois.

Quire: Used for measuring paper. Sometimes 24 sheets but more often 25. There are 20 quires in a ream.

Ream: Used for measuring paper. Sometimes 480 sheets, but more often 500 sheets.

Roentgen: Dosage unit of radiation exposure produced by X-rays.

Score: 20 units.

Sound, Speed of: Usually placed at 1,088 ft per second at 32° F at sea level. It varies at other temperatures and in different media.

Span: 9 inches or 22.86 cm. Derived from the distance between the end of the thumb and the end of the little finger when both are outstretched.

Square: 100 square feet. Used in building.

Stone: Legally 14 pounds avoirdupois in Great Britain.

Therm: 100,000 Btu's.

Township: U. S. land measurement of almost 36 square miles. The south border is 6 miles long. The east and west borders, also 6 miles long, follow the meridians, making the north border slightly less than 6 miles long. Used in surveying.

Tun: 252 gallons, but often larger. Used for measuring wine and other liquids.

Watt: Unit of power. The power used by a current of one ampere across a potential difference of one volt equals one watt.

Kelvin Scale

Absolute zero, −273.16° on the Celsius (Centigrade) scale, is 0° Kelvin. Thus, degrees Kelvin are equivalent to degrees Celsius plus 273.16. The freezing point of water, 0° C. and 32° F., is 273.16° K. The conversion formula is K° = C° + 273.16.

Conversion of Miles to Kilometers and Kilometers to Miles

Miles	Kilometers	Miles	Kilometers	Miles	Kilometers	Kilometers	Miles	Kilometers	Miles	Kilometers	Miles
1	1.6	8	12.8	60	96.5	1	0.6	8	4.9	60	37.2
2	3.2	9	14.4	70	112.6	2	1.2	9	5.5	70	43.4
3	4.8	10	16.0	80	128.7	3	1.8	10	6.2	80	49.7
4	6.4	20	32.1	90	144.8	4	2.4	20	12.4	90	55.9
5	8.0	30	48.2	100	160.9	5	3.1	30	18.6	100	62.1
6	9.6	40	64.3	1,000	1609	6	3.7	40	24.8	1,000	621
7	11.2	50	80.4			7	4.3	50	31.0		

Bolts and Screws: Conversion from Fractions of an Inch to Millimeters

Inch	mm	Inch	mm	Inch	mm	Inch	mm
1/64	0.40	17/64	6.75	33/64	13.10	49/64	19.45
1/32	0/79	9/32	7.14	17/32	13.50	25/32	19.84
3/64	1.19	19/64	7.54	35/64	13.90	51/64	20.24
1/16	1.59	5/16	7.94	9/16	14.29	13/16	20.64
5/64	1.98	21/64	8.33	37/64	14.69	53/64	21.03
3/32	2.38	11/32	8.73	19/32	15.08	27/32	21.43
7/64	2.78	23/64	9.13	39/64	15.48	55/64	21.83
1/8	3.18	3/8	9.53	5/8	15.88	7/8	22.23
9/64	3.57	25/64	9.92	41/64	16.27	57/64	22.62
5/32	3.97	13/32	10.32	21/32	16.67	29/32	23.02
11/64	4.37	27/64	10.72	43/64	17.06	59/64	23.42
3/16	4.76	7/16	11.11	11/64	17.46	15/16	23.81
13/64	5.16	29/64	11.51	45/64	17.86	61/64	24.21
7/32	5.56	15/32	11.91	23/32	18.26	31/32	24.61
15/64	5.95	31/64	12.30	47/64	18.65	63/64	25.00
1/4	6.35	1/2	12.70	3/4	19.05	1	25.40

U.S.—Metric Cooking Conversions

U.S. customary system				Metric			
Capacity		Weight		Capacity		Weight	
1/5 teaspoon	1 milliliter	1 fluid oz	30 milliliters	1 milliliter	1/5 teaspoon	1 gram	.035 ounce
1 teaspoon	5 ml		28 grams	5 ml	1 teaspoon	100 grams	3.5 ounces
1 tablespoon	15 ml	1 pound	454 grams	15 ml	1 tablespoon	500 grams	1.10 pounds
1/5 cup	50 ml			34 ml	1 fluid oz	1 kilogram	2.205 pounds
1 cup	240 ml						35 oz
2 cups (1 pint)	470 ml			100 ml	3.4 fluid oz		
4 cups (1 quart)	.95 liter			240 ml	1 cup		
4 quarts (1 gal.)	3.8 liters			1 liter	34 fluid oz		
					4.2 cups		
					2.1 pints		
					1.06 quarts		
					0.26 gallon		

Cooking Measurement Equivalents

16 tablespoons = 1 cup
12 tablespoons = 3/4 cup
10 tablespoons + 2 teaspoons = 2/3 cup
8 tablespoons = 1/2 cup
6 tablespoons = 3/8 cup
5 tablespoons + 1 teaspoon = 1/3 cup
4 tablespoons = 1/4 cup

2 tablespoons = 1/8 cup
2 tablespoons + 2 teaspoons = 1/6 cup
1 tablespoon = 1/16 cup
2 cups = 1 pint
2 pints = 1 quart
3 teaspoons = 1 tablespoon
48 teaspoons = 1 cup

Prefixes and Multiples

Prefix	Symbol	Equivalent	Multiple/submultiple	Prefix	Symbol	Equivalent	Multiple/submultiple
atto	a	quintillionth part	10^{-18}	deci	d	tenth part	10^{-1}
femto	f	quadrillionth part	10^{-15}	deka	da	tenfold	10
pico	p	trillionth part	10^{-12}	hecto	h	hundredfold	10^2
nano	n	billionth part	10^{-9}	kilo	k	thousandfold	10^3
micro	μ	millionth part	10^{-6}	mega	M	millionfold	10^6
milli	m	thousandth part	10^{-3}	giga	G	billionfold	10^9
centi	c	hundredth part	10^{-2}	tera	T	trillionfold	10^{12}

Common Formulas

Circumference

Circle: $C = \pi d$, in which π is 3.1416 and d the diameter.

Area

Triangle: $A = \dfrac{ab}{2}$, in which a is the base and b the height.

Square: $A = a^2$, in which a is one of the sides.

Rectangle: $A = ab$, in which a is the base and b the height.

Trapezoid: $A = \dfrac{h(a+b)}{2}$, in which h is the height, a the longer parallel side, and b the shorter.

Regular pentagon: $A = 1.720a^2$, in which a is one of the sides.

Regular hexagon: $A = 2.598a^2$, in which a is one of the sides.

Regular octagon: $A = 4.828a^2$, in which a is one of the sides.

Circle: $A = \pi r^2$, in which π is 3.1416 and r the radius.

Volume

Cube: $V = a^3$, in which a is one of the edges.

Rectangular prism: $V = abc$, in which a is the length, b the width, and c the depth.

Pyramid: $V = \dfrac{Ah}{3}$, in which A is the area of the base and h the height.

Cylinder: $V = \pi r^2 h$, in which π is 3.1416, r the radius of the base, and h the height.

Cone: $V = \dfrac{\pi r^2 h}{3}$, in which π is 3.1416, r the radius of the base, and h the height.

Sphere: $V = \dfrac{4\pi r^3}{3}$, in which π is 3.1416 and r the radius.

Miscellaneous

Distance in feet traveled by falling body: $d = 16t^2$, in which t is the time in seconds.

Speed of sound in feet per second through any given temperature of air: $V = \dfrac{1087 \sqrt{273+t}}{16.52}$, in which t is the temperature Centigrade.

Cost in cents of operation of electrical device: $C = \dfrac{Wtc}{1000}$, in which W is the number of watts, t the time in hours, and c the cost in cents per kilowatt-hour.

Conversion of matter into energy (Einstein's Theorem): $E = mc^2$, in which E is the energy in ergs, m the mass of the matter in grams, and c the speed of light in centimeters per second. ($c^2 = 9.10^{20}$).

Decimal Equivalents of Common Fractions

1/2	.5000	1/10	.1000	2/7	.2857	3/11	.2727	5/9	.5556	7/11	.6364
1/3	.3333	1/11	.0909	2/9	.2222	4/5	.8000	5/11	.4545	7/12	.5833
1/4	.2500	1/12	.0833	2/11	.1818	4/7	.5714	5/12	.4167	8/9	.8889
1/5	.2000	1/16	.0625	3/4	.7500	4/9	.4444	6/7	.8571	8/11	.7273
1/6	.1667	1/32	.0313	3/5	.6000	4/11	.3636	6/11	.5455	9/10	.9000
1/7	.1429	1/64	.0156	3/7	.4286	5/6	.8333	7/8	.8750	9/11	.8182
1/8	.1250	2/3	.6667	3/8	.3750	5/7	.7143	7/9	.7778	10/11	.9091
1/9	.1111	2/5	.4000	3/10	.3000	5/8	.6250	7/10	.7000	11/12	.9167

Conversion Factors

To change	To	Multiply by	To change	To	Multiply by
acres	hectares	.4047	liters	pints (dry)	1.8162
acres	square feet	43,560	liters	pints (liquid)	2.1134
acres	square miles	.001562	liters	quarts (dry)	.9081
atmospheres	cms. of mercury	76	liters	quarts (liquid)	1.0567
BTU	horsepower-hour	.0003931	meters	feet	3.2808
BTU	kilowatt-hour	.0002928	meters	miles	.0006214
BTU/hour	watts	.2931	meters	yards	1.0936
bushels	cubic inches	2150.4	metric tons	tons (long)	.9842
bushels (U.S.)	hectoliters	.3524	metric tons	tons (short)	1.1023
centimeters	inches	.3937	miles	kilometers	1.6093
centimeters	feet	.03281	miles	feet	5280
circumference	radians	6.283	miles (nautical)	miles (statute)	1.1516
cubic feet	cubic meters	.0283	miles (statute)	miles (nautical)	.8684
cubic meters	cubic feet	35.3145	miles/hour	feet/minute	88
cubic meters	cubic yards	1.3079	millimeters	inches	.0394
cubic yards	cubic meters	.7646	ounces avdp.	grams	28.3495
degrees	radians	.01745	ounces	pounds	.0625
dynes	grams	.00102	ounces (troy)	ounces (avdp)	1.09714
fathoms	feet	6.0	pecks	liters	8.8096
feet	meters	.3048	pints (dry)	liters	.5506
feet	miles (nautical)	.0001645	pints (liquid)	liters	.4732
feet	miles (statute)	.0001894	pounds ap or t	kilograms	.3782
feet/second	miles/hour	.6818	pounds avdp	kilograms	.4536
furlongs	feet	660.0	pounds	ounces	16
furlongs	miles	.125	quarts (dry)	liters	1.1012
gallons (U.S.)	liters	3.7853	quarts (liquid)	liters	.9463
grains	grams	.0648	radians	degrees	57.30
grams	grains	15.4324	rods	meters	5.029
grams	ounces avdp	.0353	rods	feet	16.5
grams	pounds	.002205	square feet	square meters	.0929
hectares	acres	2.4710	square kilometers	square miles	.3861
hectoliters	bushels (U.S.)	2.8378	square meters	square feet	10.7639
horsepower	watts	745.7	square meters	square yards	1.1960
hours	days	.04167	square miles	square kilometers	2.5900
inches	millimeters	25.4000	square yards	square meters	.8361
inches	centimeters	2.5400	tons (long)	metric tons	1.016
kilograms	pounds avdp or t	2.2046	tons (short)	metric tons	.9072
kilometers	miles	.6214	tons (long)	pounds	2240
kilowatts	horsepower	1.341	tons (short)	pounds	2000
knots	nautical miles/hour	1.0	watts	Btu/hour	3.4129
knots	statute miles/hour	1.151	watts	horsepower	.001341
liters	gallons (U.S.)	.2642	yards	meters	.9144
liters	pecks	.1135	yards	miles	.0005682

Fahrenheit and Celsius (Centigrade) Scales

Zero on the Fahrenheit scale represents the temperature produced by the mixing of equal weights of snow and common salt.

	F	C
Boiling point of water	212°	100°
Freezing point of water	32°	0°
Absolute zero	−459.6°	−273.1°

Absolute zero is theoretically the lowest possible temperature, the point at which all molecular motion would cease.

To convert Fahrenheit to Celsius (Centigrade), subtract 32 and multiply by 5/9.

To convert Celsius (Centigrade) to Fahrenheit, multiply by 9/5 and add 32.

° Centigrade	° Fahrenheit	° Centigrade	° Fahrenheit
−273.1	−459.6	30	86
−250	−418	35	95
−200	−328	40	104
−150	−238	45	113
−100	−148	50	122
−50	−58	55	131
−40	−40	60	140
−30	−22	65	149
−20	−4	70	158
−10	14	75	167
0	32	80	176
5	41	85	185
10	50	90	194
15	59	95	203
20	68	**100**	**212**
25	77		

Roman Numerals

Roman numerals are expressed by letters of the alphabet and are rarely used today except for formality or variety.

There are three basic principles for reading Roman numerals:

1. A letter repeated once or twice repeats its value that many times. (XXX=30, CC=200, etc.).

2. One or more letters placed after another letter of greater value increases the greater value by the amount of the smaller. (VI=6, LXX=70, MCC=1200, etc.).

3. A letter placed before another letter of greater value decreases the greater value by the amount of the smaller. (IV=4, XC=90, CM=900, etc.).

Letter	Value	Letter	Value	Letter	Value	Letter	Value	Letter	Value
I	1	VII	7	XXX	30	LXXX	80	$\overline{V}$	5,000
II	2	VIII	8	XL	40	XC	90	$\overline{X}$	10,000
III	3	IX	9	L	50	C	100	$\overline{L}$	50,000
IV	4	X	10	LX	60	D	500	$\overline{C}$	100,000
V	5	XX	20	LXX	70	M	1,000	$\overline{D}$	500,000
VI	6							$\overline{M}$	1,000,000

Mean and Median

The mean, also called the average, of a series of quantities is obtained by finding the sum of the quantities and dividing it by the number of quantities. In the series 1,3,5,18,19,20,25, the mean or average is 13—i.e., 91 divided by 7.

The median of a series is that point which so divides it that half the quantities are on one side, half on the other. In the above series, the median is 18.

The median often better expresses the common-run, since it is not, as is the mean, affected by an excessively high or low figure. In the series 1,3,4, 7,55, the median of 4 is a truer expression of the common-run than is the mean of 14.

Prime Numbers Between 1 and 1,000

	2	3	5	7	11	13	17	19	23
29	31	37	41	43	47	53	59	61	67
71	73	79	83	89	97	101	103	107	109
113	127	131	137	139	149	151	157	163	167
173	179	181	191	193	197	199	211	223	227
229	233	239	241	251	257	263	269	271	277
281	283	293	307	311	313	317	331	337	347
349	353	359	367	373	379	383	389	397	401
409	419	421	431	433	439	443	449	457	461
463	467	479	487	491	499	503	509	521	523
541	547	557	563	569	571	577	587	593	599
601	607	613	617	619	631	641	643	647	653
659	661	673	677	683	691	701	709	719	727
733	739	743	751	757	761	769	773	787	797
809	811	821	823	827	829	839	853	857	859
863	877	881	883	887	907	911	919	929	937
941	947	953	967	971	977	983	991	997	(1009)

Definitions of Gold Terminology

The term "fineness" defines a gold content in parts per thousand. For example, a gold nugget containing 885 parts of pure gold, 100 parts of silver, and 15 parts of copper would be considered 885-fine.

The word "karat" indicates the proportion of solid gold in an alloy based on a total of 24 parts. Thus, 14-karat (14K) gold indicates a composition of 14 parts of gold and 10 parts of other metals.

The term "gold-filled" is used to describe articles of jewelry made of base metal which are covered on one or more surfaces with a layer of gold alloy. No article having a gold alloy portion of less than one twentieth by weight may be marked "gold-filled." Articles may be marked "rolled gold plate" provided the proportional fraction and fineness designations are also shown.

Electroplated jewelry items carrying at least 7 millionths of an inch of gold on significant surfaces may be labeled "electroplate." Plate thicknesses less than this may be marked "gold flashed" or "gold washed."

Portraits and Designs of U.S. Paper Currency[1]

Currency	Portrait	Design on back	Currency	Portrait	Design on back
$1	Washington	ONE between obverse and reverse of Great Seal of U.S.	$50	Grant	U.S. Capitol
			$100	Franklin	Independence Hall
$2[2]	Jefferson	Monticello	$500	McKinley	Ornate FIVE HUNDRED
$2[3]	Jefferson	"The Signing of the Declaration of Independence"	$1,000	Cleveland	Ornate ONE THOUSAND
			$5,000	Madison	Ornate FIVE THOUSAND
$5	Lincoln	Lincoln Memorial	$10,000	Chase	Ornate TEN THOUSAND
$10	Hamilton	U.S. Treasury Building	$100,000[4]	Wilson	Ornate ONE HUNDRED THOUSAND
$20	Jackson	White House			

1. Denominations of $500 and higher were discontinued in 1969. 2. Discontinued in 1966. 3. New issue, April 13, 1976.
4. For use only in transactions between Federal Reserve System and Treasury Department.

Major Religions of the World

Judaism

The determining factors of Judaism are: descendance from Israel, the *Torah*, and Tradition.

The name Israel (Jacob, a patriarch) also signifies his descendants as a people. During the 15th–13th centuries B.C., Israelite tribes, coming from South and East, gradually settled in Palestine, then inhabited by Canaanites. They were held together by Moses, who gave them religious unity in the worship of *Jahweh*, the God who had chosen Israel to be his people.

Under Judges, the 12 tribes at first formed an amphictyonic covenant. Saul established kingship (circa 1050 B.C.), and under David, his successor (1000–960 B.C.), the State of Israel comprised all of Palestine with Jerusalem as religio-political center. A golden era followed under Solomon (965–926 B.C.), who built *Jahweh* a temple.

After Solomon's death, the kingdom separated into Israel in the North and Judah in the South. A period of conflicts ensued, which ended with the conquest of Israel by Assyria in 722 B.C. The Babylonians defeated Judah in 586 B.C., destroying Jerusalem and its temple, and deporting many to Babylon.

The era of the kings is significant also in that the great prophets worked in that time, emphasizing faith in *Jahweh* as both God of Israel and God of the universe, and stressing social justice.

When the Persians permitted the Jews to return from exile (539 B.C.), temple and cult were restored in Jerusalem. The Persian rulers were succeeded by the Seleucides. The Maccabaean revolt against these Hellenistic kings gave independence to the Jews in 128 B.C., which lasted till the Romans occupied the country.

Important groups that exerted influence during these times were the Sadducees, priests in the temple in Jerusalem; the Pharisees, teachers of the Law in the synagogues; Essenes, a religious order (from whom Dead Sea Scrolls, discovered in 1947, came); Apocalyptists, who were expecting the heavenly Messiah; and Zealots, who were prepared to fight for national independence.

When the latter turned against Rome in A.D. 66, Roman armies under Titus suppressed the revolt,

Estimated Membership of the Principal Religions of the World

Statistics of the world's religions are only very rough approximations. Aside from Christianity, few religions, if any, attempt to keep statistical records; and even Protestants and Catholics employ different methods of counting members. All persons of whatever age who have received baptism in the Catholic Church are counted as members, while in most Protestant Churches only those who "join" the church are numbered. The compiling of statistics is further complicated by the fact that in China one may be at the same time a Confucian, a Taoist, and a Buddhist. In Japan, one may be both a Buddhist and a Shintoist.

Religion	Africa	Asia	Europe[1]	South America	North America	Oceania	World
Christians	293,547,000	236,700,000	515,110,000	10,240,000	234,600,000	21,700,000	1,711,897,000
Roman Catholics	110,264,000	111,028,000	265,750,000	81,800,000	95,200,000	7,660,000	971,702,000
Protestants	77,327,000	73,563,000	82,630,000	15,500,000	94,600,000	7,600,000	351,220,000
Orthodox	26,262,000	3,300,000	125,960,700	1,660,000	5,900,000	540,000	163,622,700
Anglicans	24,108,000	645,000	32,690,300	1,230,000	7,200,000	5,336,000	71,209,300
Other Christians	55,586,000	48,164,000	8,079,000	10,050,000	31,700,000	564,000	154,143,000
Muslims	263,132,000	608,500,000	46,460,000	1,200,000	5,220,000	99,500	924,611,500
Nonreligious	1,700,000	690,000,000	137,013,500	16,000,000	21,700,000	3,100,000	869,513,500
Hindus	1,450,000	685,000,000	595,100	750,000	1,100,000	310,000	689,205,100
Buddhists	14,000	310,000,000	512,000	495,000	400,000	17,000	311,438,000
Atheists	250,000	150,000,000	76,960,000	2,900,000	1,200,000	530,000	231,840,000
Chinese folk religionists	10,000	170,000,000	50,200	60,000	101,000	15,000	170,236,200
New-Religionists	15,000	125,000,000	35,500	460,000	1,300,000	9,000	126,819,500
Tribal religionists	66,240,000	23,500,000	200	950,000	50,000	70,000	90,810,200
Sikhs	23,000	17,350,000	217,100	7,000	230,000	8,000	17,735,100
Jews	300,000	4,310,000	4,547,000	1,010,000	7,100,000	90,000	17,357,000
Shamanists	900	10,500,000	200,400	200	500	200	10,702,200
Confucians	800	5,800,000	1,500	800	18,000	300	5,821,400
Baha'is	1,310,000	2,510,000	91,000	750,000	340,000	71,000	5,072,000
Jains	45,000	3,520,000	10,000	3,000	2,500	1,000	3,581,500
Shintoists	300	3,200,000	500	1,000	3,000	500	3,205,300
Other religionists	279,000	5,719,000	743,000	4,237,000	405,000	87,500	11,570,500
Total Population	628,317,000	3,051,609,000	782,547,000	439,064,000	273,770,000	26,109,000	5,201,416,000

1. Includes the U.S.S.R. *Source: Britannica Book of the Year, 1990.*

destroying Jerusalem and its temple in A.D. 70. The Jews were scattered in the *diaspora* (Dispersion), subject to oppressions until the Age of the Enlightenment (18th century) brought their emancipation, although persecutions did not end entirely.

The fall of the Jerusalem temple was an important event in the religious life of the Jews, which now developed around *Torah* (Law) and synagogue. Around A.D. 100 the Sacred Scriptures were codified. Synagogue worship became central, with readings from *Torah* and prophets. Most important prayers are the *Shema* (Hear) and the Prayer of the 18 Benedictions.

Religious life is guided by the commandments contained in the *Torah*: circumcision and *Sabbath*, as well as other ethical and ceremonial commandments.

The *Talmud*, based on the *Mishnah* and its interpretations, took place over many centuries in the Babylonian and Palestinian Schools. It was a strong binding force of Judaism in the Dispersion.

In the 12th century, Maimonides formulated his "13 Articles of Faith," which carried great authority. Fundamental in this creed are: belief in God and his oneness *(Sherma)*, belief in the changeless *Torah*, in the words of Moses and the prophets, belief in reward and punishment, the coming of the Messiah, and the resurrection of the dead.

Judaism is divided into theological schools, the main divisions of which are Orthodox, Conservative, and Reform.

Christianity

Christianity is founded upon Jesus Christ, to whose life the New Testament writings testify. Jesus, a Jew, was born in about 7 B.C. and assumed his public life, after his 30th year, in Galilee. The Gospels tell of many extraordinary deeds that accompanied his ministry. He proclaimed the Kingdom of God, a future reality that is at the same time already present. Nationalistic-Jewish expectations of the Messiah he rejected. Rather, he referred to himself as the "Son of Man," the Christ, who has power to forgive sins now and who shall also come as Judge at the end of time. Jesus set forth the religio-ethical demands for participation in the Kingdom of God as change of heart and love of God and neighbor.

At the Last Supper he signified his death as a sacrifice, which would inaugurate the New Covenant, by which many would be saved. Circa A.D. 30 he died on a cross in Jerusalem. The early Church carried on Jesus' proclamation, the apostle Paul emphasizing his death and resurrection.

The person of Jesus is fundamental to the Christian faith since it is believed that in his life, death, and resurrection, God's revelation became historically tangible. He is seen as the turning point in history, and man's relationship to God as determined by his attitude to Jesus.

Historically Christianity thus arose out of Judaism, claiming fulfillment of the promises of the Old Testament in Jesus. The early Church designated itself as "the true Israel," which expected the speedy return of Jesus. The mother church was at Jerusalem, but churches were soon founded in many other places. The apostle Paul was instrumental in founding and extending a Gentile Christianity that was free from Jewish legalism.

The new religion spread rapidly throughout the eastern and western parts of the Roman Empire. In coming to terms with other religious movements within the Empire, Christianity began to take definite shape as an organization in its doctrine, liturgy, and ministry circa A.D. 200. In the 4th century the Catholic Church had taken root in countries stretching from Spain in the West to Persia and India in the East. Christians had been repeatedly subject to persecution by the Roman state, but finally gained tolerance under Constantine the Great (A.D. 313). Since that time, the Church became favored under his successors and in 380 the Emperor Theodosius proclaimed Christianity the State religion. Paganism was suppressed and public life was gradually molded in accordance with Christian ethical demands.

It was in these years also that the Church was able to achieve a certain unity of doctrine. Due to differences of interpretation of basic doctrines concerning Christ, which threatened to divide the Catholic Church, a standard Christian Creed was formulated by bishops at successive Ecumenical Councils, the first of which was held in A.D. 325 (Nicaea). The chief doctrines formulated concerned the doctrine of the Trinity, i.e., that there is one God in three persons: Father, Son, and Holy Spirit (Constantinople, A.D. 381); and the nature of Christ as both divine and human (Chalcedon, A.D. 541).

Through differences and rivalry between East and West the unity of the Church was broken by schism in 1054. In 1517 a separation occurred in the Western Church with the Reformation. From the major Protestant denominations [Lutheran, Presbyterian, Anglican (Episcopalian)], many Free Churches separated themselves in an age of individualism.

In the 20th century, however, the direction is toward unity. The Ecumenical Movement led to the formation of the World Council of Churches in 1948 (Amsterdam), which has since been joined by many Protestant and Orthodox Churches.

Through its missionary activity Christianity has spread to most parts of the globe.

Eastern Orthodoxy

Eastern Orthodoxy comprises the faith and practice of Churches stemming from ancient Churches in the Eastern part of the Roman Empire. The term covers Orthodox Churches in communion with the See of Constantinople, Uniate Churches in communion with Rome, and Nestorian and Monophysite Churches.

The Orthodox, Catholic, Apostolic Church is the direct descendant of the Byzantine State Church and consists of a series of independent national

U. S. Church Membership

Religious group	Members
Protestant bodies and others	79,328,686
Roman Catholics	54,918,949
Jewish congregations[1]	5,935,000
Eastern churches	4,077,011
Old Catholic, Polish National Catholic, Armenian churches	826,889
Buddhists	100,000
Miscellaneous	197,203
Total[2]	145,383,738

1. Includes Orthodox, Conservative, and Reform. 2. As reported in the *1990 Yearbook of American & Canadian Churches* from statistics furnished by 219 religious bodies in the United States.

churches that are united by Doctrine, Liturgy, and Hierarchical organization (deacons and priests, who may either be married or be monks before ordination, and bishops, who must be celibates). The heads of these Churches are patriarchs or metropolitans; the Patriarch of Constantinople is only "first among equals." Rivalry between the Pope of Rome and the Patriarch of Constantinople, aided by differences and misunderstandings that existed for centuries between the Eastern and Western parts of the Empire, led to a schism in 1054. Repeated attempts at reunion have failed in past centuries. The mutual excommunication pronounced in that year was lifted in 1965, however, and because of greater interaction in theology between Orthodox Churches and those in the West, a climate of better understanding has been created in the 20th century. First contacts were with Anglicans and Old Catholics. Orthodox Churches belong to the World Council of Churches.

The Eastern Orthodox Churches recognize only the canons of the seven Ecumenical Councils (325–787) as binding for faith and they reject doctrines that have been added in the West.

The central worship service is called the Liturgy, which is understood as representation of God's acts of salvation. Its center is the celebration of the Eucharist, or Lord's Supper.

In their worship *icons* (sacred pictures) are used that have a sacramental meaning as representation. The Mother of Christ, angels, and saints are highly venerated.

The number of sacraments in the Orthodox Church is the same as in the Western Catholic Church.

Orthodox Churches are found in the Balkans and the Soviet Union also, since the 20th century, in Western Europe and other parts of the world, particularly in America.

Eastern Orthodoxy also includes the Uniate Churches that recognize the authority of the Pope but keep their own traditional liturgies and those Churches dating back to the 5th century that emancipated themselves from the Byzantine State Church: the Nestorian Church in the Near East and India with approximately half a million members and the Monophysite Churches with some 17 million members (Coptic, Ethiopian, Syrian, Armenian, and the Mar Thoma Church in India).

Roman Catholicism

Roman Catholicism comprises the belief and practice of the Roman Catholic Church. The Church stands under the authority of the Bishop of Rome, the Pope, and is ruled by him and bishops who are held to be, through ordination, successors of Peter and the Apostles, respectively. Fundamental to the structure of the Church is the juridical aspect: doctrine and sacraments are bound to the power of jurisdiction and consecration of the hierarchy. The Pope, as the head of the hierarchy of archbishops, bishops, priests, and deacons, has full ecclesiastical power, granted him by Christ, through Peter. As successor to Peter, he is the Vicar of Christ. The powers that others in the hierarchy possess are delegated.

Roman Catholics believe their Church to be the one, holy, catholic, and apostolic Church, possessing all the properties of the one, true Church of Christ.

The faith of the Church is understood to be identical with that taught by Christ and his Apostles and contained in Bible and Tradition, i.e. the original deposit of faith, to which nothing new may be added. New definitions of doctrines, such as the Immaculate Conception of Mary (1854) and the bodily Assumption of Mary (1950), have been declared by Popes, however, in accordance with the principle of development (implicit-explicit doctrine).

At Vatican Council I (1870) the Pope was proclaimed "endowed with infallibility, *ex cathedra*, i.e., when exercising the office of Pastor and Teacher of all Christians."

The center of Roman Catholic worship is the celebration of the Mass, the Eucharist, which is the commemoration of Christ's sacrificial death and of his resurrection. Other sacraments are Baptism, Confirmation, Confession, Matrimony, Ordination, and Extreme Unction, seven in all. The Virgin Mary and saints, and their relics, are highly venerated and prayers are made to them to intercede with God, in whose presence they are believed to dwell.

The Roman Catholic Church is the largest Christian organization in the world, found in most countries. Some 8 million belong to the Uniate rites, the vast majority to the Latin rite.

Since Vatican Council II (1962–65) and the effort to "update" the Church, many interesting changes and developments have been taking place.

Protestantism

Protestantism comprises the Christian churches that separated from Rome during the Reformation in the 16th century, initiated by an Augustinian monk, Martin Luther. "Protestant" was originally applied to followers of Luther, who protested at the Diet of Spires (1529) against the decree which prohibited all further ecclesiastical reforms. Subsequently, Protestantism came to mean rejection of attempts to tie God's revelation to earthly institutions, and a return to the Gospel and the Word of God as sole authority in matters of faith and practice. Central in the biblical message is the justification of the sinner by faith alone. The Church is understood as a fellowship and the priesthood of all believers stressed.

The Augsburg Confession (1530) was the principal statement of Lutheran faith and practice. It became a model for other Confessions of Faith, which in their turn had decisive influence on Church polity. Major Protestant denominations are the Lutheran, Reformed (Calvinist), Presbyterian, and Anglican (Episcopal). Smaller ones are the Mennonite, Schwenkfeldians, and Unitarians. In Great Britain and America there are the Congregationalists, Baptists, Quakers, Methodists, and other free church types of communities. (In regarding themselves as being faithful to original biblical Christianity, these Churches differ from such religious bodies as Unitarians, Mormons, Jehovah's Witnesses, and Christian Scientists, who either teach new doctrines or reject old ones.)

Since the latter part of the 19th century, national councils of churches have been established in many countries, e.g. the Federal Council of Churches of Christ in America in 1908. Denominations across countries joined in federations and world alliances, beginning with the Anglican Lambeth Conference in 1867.

Protestant missionary activity, particularly strong in the last century, resulted in the founding of many younger churches in Asia and Africa. The Ecumenical Movement, which originated with Protestant missions, aims at unity among Christians and churches.

Islam

Islam is the religion founded in Arabia by Mohammed between 610 and 632. Its more than 600 million adherents are found in countries stretching from Morocco in the West to Indonesia in the East.

Mohammed was born in A.D. 570 at Mecca and belonged to the Quraysh tribe, which was active in caravan trade. At the age of 25 he joined the caravan trade from Mecca to Syria in the employment of a rich widow, Khadiji, whom he married. Critical of the idolatry of the inhabitants of Mecca, he began to lead a contemplative life in the deserts. There he received a series of revelations. Encouraged by Khadiji, he gradually became convinced that he was given a God-appointed task to devote himself to the reform of religion and society. Idolatry was to be abandoned.

The *Hegira (Hijra)* (migration) of Mohammed from Mecca, where he was not honored, to Medina, where he was well received, occurred in 622 and marks the beginning of the Muslim era. In 630 he marched on Mecca and conquered it. He died at Medina in 632. His grave there has since been a place of pilgrimage.

Mohammed's followers, called Moslems, revered him as the prophet of *Allah* (God), beside whom there is no other God. Although he had no close knowledge of Judaism and Christianity, he considered himself succeeding and completing them as the seal of the Prophets. Sources of the Islamic faith are the *Qur'an*, regarded as the uncreated, eternal Word of God, and Tradition *(hadith)* regarding sayings and deeds of the prophet.

Islam means surrender to the will of *Allah*. He is the all-powerful, whose will is supreme and determines man's fate. Good deeds will be rewarded at the Last Judgment in paradise and evil deeds will be punished in hell.

The Five Pillars, primary duties, of Islam are: witness; confessing the oneness of God and of Mohammed, his prophet; prayer, to be performed five times a day; almsgiving to the poor and the mosque (house of worship); fasting during daylight hours in the month of Ramadan; and pilgrimage to Mecca at least once in the Moslem's lifetime.

Islam, upholding the law of brotherhood, succeeded in uniting an Arab world that had disintegrated into tribes and castes. Disagreements concerning the succession of the prophet caused a great division in Islam between *Sunnis* and *Shias.* Among these, other sects arose *(Wahhabi).* Doctrinal issues also led to the rise of different schools of thought in theology. Nevertheless, since Arab armies turned against Syria and Palestine in 635, Islam has expanded successfully under Mohammed's successors. Its rapid conquests in Asia and Africa are unsurpassed in history. Turning against Europe, Moslems conquered Spain in 713. In 1453 Constantinople fell into their hands and in 1529 Moslem armies besieged Vienna. Since then, Islam has lost its foothold in Europe.

In modern times it has made great gains in Africa.

Hinduism

In India alone there are more than 300 million adherents of Hinduism. In contrast to other religions, it has no founder. Considered the oldest religion in the world, it dates back, perhaps, to prehistoric times.

Hinduism is hard to define, there being no common creed, no one doctrine to bind Hindus together. Intellectually there is complete freedom of belief, and one can be monotheist, polytheist, or atheist. What matters is the social system: a Hindu is one born into a caste.

As a religion, Hinduism is founded on the sacred scriptures, written in Sanskrit and called the *Vedas* (*Veda*-knowledge). There are four Vedic books, among which the *Rig Veda* is the most important. It speaks of many gods and also deals with questions concerning the universe and creation. The dates of these works are unknown (1000 B.C.?).

The *Upanishads* (dated 1000–300 B.C.), commentaries on the Vedic texts, have philosophical speculations on the origin of the universe, the nature of deity, of *atman* (the human soul), and its relationship to *Brahman* (the universal soul).

Brahman is the principle and source of the universe who can be indicated only by negatives. As the divine intelligence, he is the ground of the visible world, a presence that pervades all beings. Thus the many Hindu deities came to be understood as manifestations of the one *Brahman* from whom everything proceeds and to whom everything ultimately returns. The religio-social system of Hinduism is based on the concept of reincarnation and transmigration in which all living beings, from plants below to gods above, are caught in a cosmic system that is an everlasting cycle of becoming and perishing.

Life is determined by the law of *karma,* according to which rebirth is dependent on moral behavior in a previous phase of existence. The doctrine of transmigration thus provides a rationale for the caste system. In this view, life on earth is regarded as transient *(maya)* and a burden. The goal of existence is liberation from the cycle of rebirth and redeath and entrance into the indescribable state of what in Buddhism is called *nirvana* (extinction of passion).

Further important sacred writings are the Epics *(puranas),* which contain legendary stories about gods and men. They are the *Mahabharata* (composed between 200 B.C. and A.D. 200) and the *Ramayana.* The former includes the *Bhagavad-Gita* (Song of the Lord), its most famous part, that tells of devotion to *Krishna* (Lord), who appears as an *avatar* (incarnation) of the god *Vishnu,* and of the duty of obeying caste rules. The work begins with a praise of the *yoga* (discipline) system.

The practice of Hinduism consists of rites and ceremonies, performed within the framework of the caste system and centering on the main socioreligious occasions of birth, marriage, and death. There are many Hindu temples, which are dwelling places of the deities and to which people bring offerings. There are also places of pilgrimage, the chief one being Benares on the Ganges, most sacred among the rivers in India.

In modern times work has been done to reform and revive Hinduism. One of the outstanding reformers was Ramakrishna (1836–86), who inspired many followers, one of whom founded the Ramakrishna mission, which seeks to convert others to its religion. The mission is active both in India and in other countries.

Buddhism

Founded in the 6th century B.C. in northern India by Gautama Buddha, who was born in southern Nepal as son to a king. His birth is surrounded by many legends, but Western scholars agree that he lived from 563 to 483 B.C. Warned by a sage that his son would become an ascetic or a universal monarch, the king confined him to his home. He was able to escape and began the life of a homeless wanderer in search of peace, passing through many disappointments until he finally came to the Tree of Enlightenment, under which he lived in meditation till enlightenment came to him and he became a Buddha (enlightened one).

Now he understood the origin of suffering, summarized in the *Four Noble Truths*, which constitutes the foundation of Buddhism. The Four are the truth of suffering, which all living beings must endure; of the origin of suffering, which is craving and which leads to rebirth; that it can be destroyed; and of the way that leads to cessation of pain, i.e., the *Noble Eightfold Way*, which is the rule of practical Buddhism: right views, right intention, right speech, right action, right livelihood, right effort, right concentration, and right ecstasy.

Nirvana is the goal of all existence, the state of complete redemption, into which the redeemed enters. Buddha's insight can free every man from the law of reincarnation through complete emptying of the self.

The nucleus of Buddha's church or association was originally formed by monks and lay-brothers, whose houses gradually became monasteries used as places for religious instruction. The worship service consisted of a sermon, expounding of Scripture, meditation, and confession. At a later stage pilgrimages to the holy places associated with the Buddha came into being, as well as veneration of relics.

In the 3rd century B.C., King Ashoka made Buddhism the State religion of India but, as centuries passed, it gradually fell into decay through splits, persecutions, and the hostile Brahmans. Buddhism spread to countries outside India, however.

At the beginning of the Christian era, there occurred a split that gave rise to two main types: *Hinayana* (Little Vehicle), or southern Buddhism, and *Mahayana* (Great Vehicle), or northern Buddhism. The former type, more individualistic, survived in Ceylon and southern Asia. *Hinayana* retained more closely the original teachings of the Buddha, which did not know of a personal god or soul. *Mahayana*, more social, polytheistic, and developing a pluralistic pompous cult, was strong in the Himalayas, Tibet, Mongolia, China, Korea, and Japan.

In the present century, Buddhism has found believers also in the West and Buddhist associations have been established in Europe and the U.S.

Confucianism

Confucius (K'ung Fu-tzu), born in the state of Lu (northern China), lived from 551 to 479 B.C. Tradition, exaggerating the importance of Confucius in life, has depicted him as a great statesman but, in fact, he seems to have been a private teacher. Anthologies of ancient Chinese classics, along with his own Analects *(Lun Yu)*, became the basis of Confucianism. These Analects were transmitted as a collection of his sayings as recorded by his students, with whom he discussed ethical and social problems. They developed into men of high moral standing, who served the State as administrators.

In his teachings, Confucius emphasized the importance of an old Chinese concept *(li)*, which has the connotation of proper conduct. There is some disagreement as to the religious ideas of Confucius, but he held high the concepts handed down from centuries before him. Thus he believed in Heaven *(T'ien)* and sacrificed to his ancestors. Ancestor worship he indeed encouraged as an expression of filial piety, which he considered the loftiest of virtues.

Piety to Confucius was the foundation of the family as well as the State. The family is the nucleus of the State, and the "five relations," between king and subject, father and son, man and wife, older and younger brother, and friend and friend, are determined by the virtues of love of fellow men, righteousness, and respect.

An extension of ancestor worship may be seen in the worship of Confucius, which became official in the 2nd century B.C. when the emperor, in recognition of Confucius' teachings as supporting the imperial rule, offered sacrifices at his tomb.

Mencius (Meng Tse), who lived around 400 B.C., did much to propagate and elaborate Confucianism in its concern with ordering society. Thus, for two millennia, Confucius' doctrine of State, with its emphasis on ethics and social morality, rooted in ancient Chinese tradition and developed and continued by his disciples, has been standard in China and the Far East.

With the revolution of 1911 in China, however, students, burning Confucius in effigy, called for the removal of "the old curiosity shop."

Shintoism

Shinto, the Chinese term for the Japanese *Kami no Michi*, i.e., the Way of the Gods, comprises the religious ideas and cult indigenous to Japan. *Kami*, or gods, considered divine forces of nature that are worshipped, may reside in rivers, trees, rocks, mountains, certain animals, or, particularly, in the sun and moon. The worship of ancestors, heroes, and deceased emperors was incorporated later.

After Buddhism had come from Korea, Japan's native religion at first resisted it. Then there followed a period of compromise and amalgamation with Buddhist beliefs and ceremonies, resulting, since the 9th century A.D., in a syncretistic religion, a Twofold Shinto. Buddhist deities came to be regarded as manifestations of Japanese deities and Buddhist priests took over most of the Shinto shrines.

In modern times Shinto regained independence from Buddhism. Under the reign of the Emperor Meiji (1868–1912) it became the official State religion, in which loyalty to the emperor was emphasized. The line of succession of emperors is traced back to the first Emperor Jimmu (660 B.C.) and beyond him to the Sun-goddess *Amaterasuomikami*.

The centers of worship are the shrines and temples in which the deities are believed to dwell and believers approach them through *torii* (gateways). Most important among the shrines is the imperial shrine of the Sun-goddess at Ise, where state ceremonies were once held in June and December. The *Yasukuni* shrine of the war dead in Tokyo is also well known.

Acts of worship consist of prayers, clapping of hands, acts of purification, and offerings. On feast days processions and performances of music and dancing take place and priests read prayers before the gods in the shrines, asking for good harvest, the well-being of people and emperor, etc. In Japanese homes there is a god-shelf, a small wooden shrine that contains the tablets bearing the names of ancestors. Offerings are made and candles lit before it.

After World War II the Allied Command ordered the disestablishment of State Shinto. To be distinguished from State Shinto is Sect Shinto, consisting of 13 recognized sects. These have arisen in modern times. Most important among them is *Tenrikyo* in Tenri City (Nara), in which healing by faith plays a central role.

Taoism

Taoism, a religion of China, was, according to tradition, founded by Lao Tse, a Chinese philosopher, long considered one of the prominent religious leaders from the 6th century B.C.

Data about him are for the most part legendary, however, and the *Tao Te Ching* (the classic of the Way and of its Power), traditionally ascribed to him, is now believed by many scholars to have originated in the 3rd century B.C. The book is composed in short chapters, written in aphoristic rhymes. Central are the word *Tao*, which means way or path and, in a deeper sense, signifies the principle that underlies the reality of this world and manifests itself in nature and in the lives of men, and the word *Te* (power).

The virtuous man draws power from being absorbed in *Tao*, the ultimate reality within an ever-changing world. By non-action and keeping away from human striving it is possible for man to live in harmony with the principles that underlie and govern the universe. *Tao* cannot be comprehended by reason and knowledge, but only by inward quiet.

Besides the *Tao Te Ching*, dating from approximately the same period, there are two Taoist works, written by Chuang Tse and Lieh Tse.

Theoretical Taoism of this classical philosophical movement of the 4th and 3rd centuries B.C. in China differed from popular Taoism, into which it gradually degenerated. The standard of theoretical Taoism was maintained in the classics, of course, and among the upper classes it continued to be alive until modern times.

Religious Taoism is a form of religion dealing with deities and spirits, magic and soothsaying. In the 2nd century A.D. it was organized with temples, cult, priests, and monasteries and was able to hold its own in the competition with Buddhism that came up at the same time.

After the 7th century A.D., however, Taoist religion further declined. Split into numerous sects, which often operate like secret societies, it has become a syncretistic folk religion in which some of the old deities and saints live on.

Roman Catholic Pontiffs

St. Peter, of Bethsaida in Galilee, Prince of the Apostles, was the first Pope. He lived first in Antioch and then in Rome for 25 years. In AD 64 or 67, he was martyred. St. Linus became the second Pope.

Name	Birthplace	Reigned From	Reigned To	Name	Birthplace	Reigned From	Reigned To
St. Linus	Tuscia	67	76	St. Innocent I	Albano	401	417
St. Anacletus (Cletus)	Rome	76	88	St. Zozimus	Greece	417	418
St. Clement	Rome	88	97	St. Boniface I	Rome	418	422
St. Evaristus	Greece	97	105	St. Celestine I	Campania	422	432
St. Alexander I	Rome	105	115	St. Sixtus III	Rome	432	440
St. Sixtus I	Rome	115	125	St. Leo I (the Great)	Tuscany	440	461
St. Telesphorus	Greece	125	136	St. Hilary	Sardinia	461	468
St. Hyginus	Greece	136	140	St. Simplicius	Tivoli	468	483
St. Pius I	Aquileia	140	155	St. Felix III (II)[2]	Rome	483	492
St. Anicetus	Syria	155	166	St. Gelasius I	Africa	492	496
St. Soter	Campania	166	175	Anastasius II	Rome	496	498
St. Eleutherius	Epirus	175	189	St. Symmachus	Sardinia	498	514
St. Victor I	Africa	189	199	St. Hormisdas	Frosinone	514	523
St. Zephyrinus	Rome	199	217	St. John I	Tuscany	523	526
St. Callistus I	Rome	217	222	St. Felix IV (III)	Samnium	526	530
St. Urban I	Rome	222	230	Boniface II	Rome	530	532
St. Pontian	Rome	230	235	John II	Rome	533	535
St. Anterus	Greece	235	236	St. Agapitus I	Rome	535	536
St. Fabian	Rome	236	250	St. Silverius	Campania	536	537
St. Cornelius	Rome	251	253	Vigilius	Rome	537	555
St. Lucius I	Rome	253	254	Pelagius I	Rome	556	561
St. Stephen I	Rome	254	257	John III	Rome	561	574
St. Sixtus II	Greece	257	258	Benedict I	Rome	575	579
St. Dionysius	Unknown	259	268	Pelagius II	Rome	579	590
St. Felix I	Rome	269	274	St. Gregory I (the Great)	Rome	590	604
St. Eutychian	Luni	275	283				
St. Caius	Dalmatia	283	296	Sabinianus	Tuscany	604	606
St. Marcellinus	Rome	296	304	Boniface III	Rome	607	607
St. Marcellus I	Rome	308	309	St. Boniface IV	Marsi	608	615
St. Eusebius	Greece	309[1]	309[1]	St. Deusdedit (Adeodatus I)	Rome	615	618
St. Meltiades	Africa	311	314				
St. Sylvester I	Rome	314	335	Boniface V	Naples	619	625
St. Marcus	Rome	336	336	Honorius I	Campania	625	638
St. Julius I	Rome	337	352	Severinus	Rome	640	640
Liberius	Rome	352	366	John IV	Dalmatia	640	642
St. Damasus I	Spain	366	384	Theodore I	Greece	642	649
St. Siricius	Rome	384	399	St. Martin I	Todi	649	655
St. Anastasius I	Rome	399	401	St. Eugene I[3]	Rome	654	657

Name	Birthplace	Reigned From	Reigned To	Name	Birthplace	Reigned From	Reigned To
St. Vitalian	Segni	657	672	Benedict IX	—	1045	1045
Adeodatus II	Rome	672	676	(2nd time)			
Donus	Rome	676	678	Gregory VI	Rome	1045	1046
St. Agatho	Sicily	678	681	Clement II	Saxony	1046	1047
St. Leo II	Sicily	682	683	Benedict IX	—	1047	1048
St. Benedict II	Rome	684	685	(3rd time)			
John V	Syria	685	686	Damasus II	Bavaria	1048	1048
Conon	Unknown	686	687	St. Leo IX	Alsace	1049	1054
St. Sergius I	Syria	687	701	Victor II	Germany	1055	1057
John VI	Greece	701	705	Stephen IX (X)	Lorraine	1057	1058
John VII	Greece	705	707	Nicholas II	Burgundy	1059	1061
Sisinnius	Syria	708	708	Alexander II	Milan	1061	1073
Constantine	Syria	708	715	St. Gregory VII	Tuscany	1073	1085
St. Gregory II	Rome	715	731	Bl. Victor III	Benevento	1086	1087
St. Gregory III	Syria	731	741	Bl. Urban II	France	1088	1099
St. Zachary	Greece	741	752	Paschal II	Ravenna	1099	1118
Stephen II (III)[4]	Rome	752	757	Gelasius II	Gaeta	1118	1119
St. Paul I	Rome	757	767	Callistus II	Burgundy	1119	1124
Stephen III (IV)	Sicily	768	772	Honorius II	Flagnano	1124	1130
Adrian I	Rome	772	795	Innocent II	Rome	1130	1143
St. Leo III	Rome	795	816	Celestine II	Città di	1143	1144
Stephen IV (V)	Rome	816	817		Castello		
St. Paschal I	Rome	817	824	Lucius II	Bologna	1144	1145
Eugene II	Rome	824	827	Bl. Eugene III	Pisa	1145	1153
Valentine	Rome	827	827	Anastasius IV	Rome	1153	1154
Gregory IV	Rome	827	844	Adrian IV	England	1154	1159
Sergius II	Rome	844	847	Alexander III	Siena	1159	1181
St. Leo IV	Rome	847	855	Lucius III	Lucca	1181	1185
Benedict III	Rome	855	858	Urban III	Milan	1185	1187
St. Nicholas I	Rome	858	867	Gregory VIII	Benevento	1187	1187
(the Great)				Clement III	Rome	1187	1191
Adrian II	Rome	867	872	Celestine III	Rome	1191	1198
John VIII	Rome	872	882	Innocent III	Anagni	1198	1216
Marinus I	Gallese	882	884	Honorius III	Rome	1216	1227
St. Adrian III	Rome	884	885	Gregory IX	Anagni	1227	1241
Stephen V (VI)	Rome	885	891	Celestine IV	Milan	1241	1241
Formosus	Portus	891	896	Innocent IV	Genoa	1243	1254
Boniface VI	Rome	896	896	Alexander IV	Anagni	1254	1261
Stephen VI (VII)	Rome	896	897	Urban IV	Troyes	1261	1264
Romanus	Gallese	897	897	Clement IV	France	1265	1268
Theodore II	Rome	897	897	Bl. Gregory X	Piacenza	1271	1276
John IX	Tivoli	898	900	Bl. Innocent V	Savoy	1276	1276
Benedict IV	Rome	900	903	Adrian V	Genoa	1276	1276
Leo V	Ardea	903	903	John XXI[7]	Portugal	1276	1277
Sergius III	Rome	904	911	Nicholas III	Rome	1277	1280
Anastasius III	Rome	911	913	Martin IV[8]	France	1281	1285
Landus	Sabina	913	914	Honorius IV	Rome	1285	1287
John X	Tossignano	914	928	Nicholas IV	Ascoli	1288	1292
Leo VI	Rome	928	928	St. Celestine V	Isernia	1294	1294
Stephen VII (VIII)	Rome	928	931	Boniface VIII	Anagni	1294	1303
John XI	Rome	931	935	Bl. Benedict XI	Treviso	1303	1304
Leo VII	Rome	936	939	Clement V	France	1305	1314
Stephen VIII (IX)	Rome	939	942	John XXII	Cahors	1316	1334
Marinus II	Rome	942	946	Benedict XII	France	1334	1342
Agapitus II	Rome	946	955	Clement VI	France	1342	1352
John XII	Tusculum	955	964	Innocent VI	France	1352	1362
Leo VIII[5]	Rome	963	965	Bl. Urban V	France	1362	1370
Benedict V[5]	Rome	964	966	Gregory XI	France	1370	1378
John XIII	Rome	965	972	Urban VI	Naples	1378	1389
Benedict VI	Rome	973	974	Boniface IX	Naples	1389	1404
Benedict VII	Rome	974	983	Innocent VII	Sulmona	1404	1406
John XIV	Pavia	983	984	Gregory XII	Venice	1406	1415
John XV	Rome	985	996	Martin V	Rome	1417	1431
Gregory V	Saxony	996	999	Eugene IV	Venice	1431	1447
Sylvester II	Auvergne	999	1003	Nicholas V	Sarzana	1447	1455
John XVII	Rome	1003	1003	Callistus III	Jativa	1455	1458
John XVIII	Rome	1004	1009	Pius II	Siena	1458	1464
Sergius IV	Rome	1009	1012	Paul II	Venice	1464	1471
Benedict VIII	Tusculum	1012	1024	Sixtus IV	Savona	1471	1484
John XIX	Tusculum	1024	1032	Innocent VIII	Genoa	1484	1492
Benedict IX[6]	Tusculum	1032	1044	Alexander VI	Jativa	1492	1503
Sylvester III	Rome	1045	1045				

Name	Birthplace	Reigned From	To	Name	Birthplace	Reigned From	To
Pius III	Siena	1503	1503	Bl. Innocent XI	Como	1676	1689
Julius II	Savona	1503	1513	Alexander VIII	Venice	1689	1691
Leo X	Florence	1513	1521	Innocent XII	Spinazzola	1691	1700
Adrian VI	Utrecht	1522	1523	Clement XI	Urbino	1700	1721
Clement VII	Florence	1523	1534	Innocent XIII	Rome	1721	1724
Paul III	Rome	1534	1549	Benedict XIII	Gravina	1724	1730
Julius III	Rome	1550	1555	Clement XII	Florence	1730	1740
Marcellus II	Montepulciano	1555	1555	Benedict XIV	Bologna	1740	1758
Paul IV	Naples	1555	1559	Clement XIII	Venice	1758	1769
Pius IV	Milan	1559	1565	Clement XIV	Rimini	1769	1774
St. Pius V	Bosco	1566	1572	Pius VI	Cesena	1775	1799
Gregory XIII	Bologna	1572	1585	Pius VII	Cesena	1800	1823
Sixtus V	Grottammare	1585	1590	Leo XII	Genga	1823	1829
Urban VII	Rome	1590	1590	Pius VIII	Cingoli	1829	1830
Gregory XIV	Cremona	1590	1591	Gregory XVI	Belluno	1831	1846
Innocent IX	Bologna	1591	1591	Pius IX	Senegallia	1846	1878
Clement VIII	Florence	1592	1605	Leo XIII	Carpineto	1878	1903
Leo XI	Florence	1605	1605	St. Pius X	Riese	1903	1914
Paul V	Rome	1605	1621	Benedict XV	Genoa	1914	1922
Gregory XV	Bologna	1621	1623	Pius XI	Desio	1922	1939
Urban VIII	Florence	1623	1644	Pius XII	Rome	1939	1958
Innocent X	Rome	1644	1655	John XXIII	Sotto il Monte	1958	1963
Alexander VII	Siena	1655	1667	Paul VI	Concesio	1963	1978
Clement IX	Pistoia	1667	1669	John Paul I	Forno di Canale	1978	1978
Clement X	Rome	1670	1676	John Paul II	Wadowice, Poland	1978	

1. Or 310. 2. He should be called Felix II, and his successors of the same name should be numbered accordingly. The discrepancy was caused by the erroneous insertion in some lists of the name of St. Felix of Rome, Martyr. 3. He was elected during the exile of St. Martin I, who endorsed him as Pope. 4. After St. Zachary died, a Roman priest named Stephen was elected but died before his consecration as Bishop of Rome. His name is not included in all lists for this reason. In view of this historical confusion, the *National Catholic Almanac* lists the true Stephen II as Stephen II (III), the true Stephen III as Stephen III (IV), etc. 5. Confusion exists concerning the legitimacy of claims. If the deposition of John was invalid, Leo was an antipope until after the end of Benedict's reign. If the deposition of John was valid, Leo was the legitimate Pope and Benedict an antipope. 6. If the triple removal of Benedict IX was not valid, Sylvester III, Gregory VI, and Clement II were antipopes. 7. Elimination was made of the name of John XX in an effort to rectify the numerical designation of Popes named John. The error dates back to the time of John XV. 8. The names of Marinus I and Marinus II were construed as Martin. In view of these two pontificates and the earlier reign of St. Martin I, this pontiff was called Martin IV. *Source: National Catholic Almanac, from Annuarto Pontificio.*

Books of the Bible

OLD TESTAMENT

Genesis	[1]Tobit	[1]Baruch
Exodus	[1]Judith	Ezekiel
Leviticus	Esther	Daniel
Numbers	[1]1 Maccabees	Hosea
Deuteronomy	[1]2 Maccabees	Joel
Joshua	Job	Amos
Judges	Psalms	Obadiah
Ruth	Proverbs	Jonah
I Samuel	Ecclesiastes	Micah
2 Samuel	Song of Songs/Solomon	Nahum
I Kings	[1]Wisdom	Habakkuk
2 Kings	[1]Sirach/Ecclesiasticus	Zephaniah
I Chronicles	Isaiah	Haggai
2 Chronicles	Jeremiah	Zechariah
Ezra	Lamentations	Malachi
Nehemiah		

NEW TESTAMENT

Matthew	Ephesians	Hebrews
Mark	Phillipians	James
Luke	Colossians	1 Peter
John	1 Thessalonians	2 Peter
Acts	2 Thessalonians	1 John
Romans	1 Timothy	2 John
1 Corinthians	2 Timothy	3 John
2 Corinthians	Titus	Jude
Galatians	Philemon	Revelation

1. These books are generally not accepted in the Protestant canon of Scripture, and Protestants refer to them as "Apocrypha." Catholic bibles include these books and refer to them as "Deuterocanonical." These disputed books were included in pre-Reformation Bibles.

GREAT DISASTERS

The following lists are not all-inclusive due to space limitations. Only disasters involving great loss of life and/or property, historical interest, or unusual circumstances are listed. Data as of July 1, 1990. For later disasters see *Current Events.*

Earthquakes and Volcanic Eruptions

A.D. 79 Aug. 24, Italy: eruption of Mt. Vesuvius buried cities of Pompeii and Herculaneum, killing thousands.

1556 Jan. 24, Shaanxi (Shensi) Province, China: most deadly earthquake in history; 830,000 killed.

1755 Nov. 1, Portugal: one of the most severe of recorded earthquakes leveled Lisbon and was felt as far away as southern France and North Africa; 10,000–20,000 killed in Lisbon.

1883 Aug. 26–28, Netherlands Indies: eruption of Krakatau; violent explosions destroyed two thirds of island. Sea waves occurred as far away as Cape Horn, and possibly England. Estimated 36,000 dead.

1902 May 8, Martinique, West Indies: Mt. Pelée erupted and wiped out city of St. Pierre; 40,000 dead.

1908 Dec. 28, Messina, Sicily: about 85,000 killed and city totally destroyed.

1915 Jan. 13, Avezzano, Italy: earthquake left 29,980 dead.

1920 Dec. 16, Gansu (Kansu) Province, China: earthquake killed 200,000.

1923 Sept. 1, Japan: earthquake destroyed third of Tokyo and most of Yokohama; more than 140,000 killed.

1933 March 10, Long Beach, Calif.: 117 left dead by earthquake.

1935 May 31, India: earthquake at Quetta killed an estimated 50,000.

1939 Jan. 24, Chile: earthquake razed 50,000 sq mi.; about 30,000 killed.

Dec. 27, Northern Turkey: severe quakes destroyed city of Erzingan; about 100,000 casualties.

1950 Aug. 15, India: earthquake affected 30,000 sq mi. in Assam; 20,000–30,000 believed killed.

1963 July 26, Skoplje, Yugoslavia: four fifths of city destroyed; 1,011 dead, 3,350 injured.

1964 March 27, Alaska: strongest earthquake ever to strike North America hit 80 miles east of Anchorage; followed by seismic wave 50 feet high that traveled 8,445 miles at 450 miles per hour; 117 killed.

1970 May 31, Peru: earthquake left 50,000 dead, 17,000 missing.

1972 April 10, Iran: 5,000 killed in earthquake 600 miles south of Teheran.

Dec. 22, Managua, Nicaragua: earthquake devastated city, leaving up to 6,000 dead.

1976 Feb. 4, Guatemala: earthquake left over 23,000 dead.

July 28, Tangshan, China: earthquake devastated 20-sq-mi. area of city leaving estimated 242,000 dead.

Aug. 17, Mindanao, Philippines: earthquake and tidal wave left up to 8,000 dead or missing.

1977 March 4, Bucharest: earthquake razed most of downtown Bucharest; 1,541 reported dead, over 11,000 injured.

1978 Sept. 16, Tabas, Iran: earthquake destroyed city in eastern Iran, leaving 25,000 dead.

1980 Nov. 23, Naples, Italy: 2,735 killed when earthquake struck southern Italy.

1982 Dec. 13, Yemen: 2,800 reported dead in earthquake.

1985 Sept. 19–20, Mexico: earthquake registering 8.1 on Richter scale struck central and southwestern regions, devastating part of Mexico City and three coastal states. An estimated 25,000 killed.

Nov. 14–16, Colombia: eruption of Nevada del Ruiz, 85 miles northwest of Bogotá, caused mud slides which buried most of the town of Armero and devastated Chinchiná. An estimated 25,000 were killed.

1988 Dec. 7, Armenia: An earthquake measuring 6.9 on the Richter scale killed nearly 25,000, injured 15,000, and left at least 400,000 homeless.

1989 Oct. 17, San Francisco Bay Area: An earthquake measuring 7.1 on the Richter Scale killed 67 and injured over 3,000. The quake damaged or destroyed over 100,000 buildings and caused billions of dollars of damage.

1990 June 21, Northwestern Iran. An earthquake measuring 7.7 on the Richter Scale destroyed cities, towns, and villages in Caspian Sea area. At least 50,000 dead, over 100,000 injured, and 500,000 homeless.

Floods, Avalanches, and Tidal Waves

1228 Holland: 100,000 persons reputedly drowned by sea flood in Friesland.

1642 China: rebels destroyed Kaifeng seawall; 300,000 drowned.

1896 June 15, Sanriku, Japan: earthquake and tidal wave killed 27,000.

1953 Northwest Europe: storm followed by floods devastated North Sea coastal areas. Netherlands was hardest hit with 1,794 dead.

1959 Dec. 2, Frejus, France: flood caused by collapse of Malpasset Dam left 412 dead.

1960 Agadir, Morocco: 10,000–12,000 dead as earthquake set off tidal wave and fire, destroying most of city.

1962 Jan. 10, Peru: avalanche down Huascaran, extinct Andean volcano, killed more than 3,000 persons.

1963 Oct. 9, Italy: landslide into the Vaiont Dam; flood killed about 2,000.

1966 Oct. 21, Aberfan, Wales: avalanche of coal, waste, mud, and rocks killed 144 persons, including 116 children in school.

1969 Jan. 18–26, Southern California: floods and mudslides from heavy rains caused widespread property damage; at least 100 dead. Another downpour (Feb. 23–26) caused further floods and mudslides; at least 18 dead.

1970 Nov. 13, East Pakistan: 200,000 killed by cyclone-driven tidal wave from Bay of Bengal. Over 100,000 missing.

1971 Sept. 29, Orissa State, India: cyclone and tidal wave off Bay of Bengal killed as many as 10,000.

1972 Feb. 26, Man, W. Va.: more than 118 died when slag-pile dam collapsed under pressure of torrential rains and flooded 17-mile valley.

June 9–10, Rapid City, S.D.: flash flood caused 237

Worst United States Disasters

Aircraft

1979 May 25, Chicago: American Airlines DC-10 lost left engine upon take-off and crashed seconds later, killing all 272 persons aboard and three on the ground in worst U.S. air disaster.

Dam

1928 March 12, Santa Paula, Calif.: collapse of St. Francis Dam left 450 dead.

Earthquake

1906 April 18, San Francisco: earthquake accompanied by fire razed more than 4 sq mi.; more than 500 dead or missing.

Explosion

1947 April 16-18, Texas City, Texas: Most of the city destroyed by a fire and subsequent explosion on the French freighter *Grandcamp* carrying a cargo of ammonium nitrate. At least 516 were killed and over 3,000 injured.

Fire

1871 Oct. 8, Peshtigo, Wis.: over 1,200 lives lost and 2 billion trees burned in forest fire.

Flood

1889 May 31, Johnstown, Pa.: more than 2,200 died in flood.

Hurricane

1900 Aug. 27-Sept. 15, Galveston, Tex.: over 6,000 died from devastation due to both winds and tidal wave.

Marine

1865 April 27, *Sultana*: boiler explosion on Mississippi River steamboat near Memphis, 1,547 killed.

Mine

1907 Dec. 6, Monongha, W. Va.: coal mine explosion killed 361.

Oil Spill

1989 Mar. 24, Prince William Sound, Alaska: Tanker, *Exxon Valdez*, hit an undersea reef and released 10 million plus gallons of oil into the waters, causing the worst oil spill in U.S. history.

Railroad

1918 July 9, Nashville, Tenn.: 101 killed in a two-train collision near Nashville.

Submarine

1963 April 10, *Thresher*: atomic-powered submarine sank in North Atlantic: 129 dead.

Tornado

1925 March 18, Great Tri-State Tornado: Missouri, Illinois, and Indiana; 695 deaths. Eight additional tornadoes in Kentucky, Tennessee, and Alabama raised day's toll to 792 dead.

deaths and $160 million in damage.
June 20, Eastern Seaboard: tropical storm Agnes, in 10-day rampage, caused widespread flash floods. Death toll was 129, 115,000 were left homeless, and damage estimated at $3.5 billion.
1976 Aug. 1, Loveland, Colo.: Flash flood along Route 34 in Big Thompson Canyon left 139 dead.
1977 Nov. 19, Andhra Pradesh State, India: cyclone and flood from Bay of Bengal left 7,000–10,000 dead.
1988 August-September, Bangladesh: Heaviest monsoon in 70 years inundates three-fourths of country, killing more than 1,300 people and leaving 30 million homeless. Damage is estimated at over $1 billion.

Storms and Weather

(For U.S. tornadoes and hurricanes, see Index)

1864 Oct. 5, India: most of Calcutta denuded by cyclone; 70,000 killed.
1930 Sept. 3, Santo Domingo: hurricane killed about 2,000 and injured 6,000.
1934 Sept. 21, Japan: hurricane killed more than 4,000 on Honshu.
1942 Oct. 16, India: cyclone devastated Bengal; about 40,000 lives lost.
1963 May 28–29, East Pakistan: cyclone killed about 22,000 along coast.
Oct. 2-7, Caribbean: Hurricane Flora killed up to 7,000 in Haiti and Cuba.

1965 May 11–12 and June 1–2, East Pakistan: cyclones killed about 47,000.
Dec. 15, Karachi, Pakistan: cyclone killed about 10,000.
1974 Sept. 20, Honduras: Hurricane Fifi struck northern section of country, leaving 8,000 dead, 100,000 homeless.
Dec. 25, Darwin, Australia: cyclone destroyed nearly the entire city, causing mass evacuation.
1977 Nov. 19, India: cyclone struck state of Andhra Pradesh, killing 10,000.

Fires and Explosions

1666 Sept. 2, England: "Great Fire of London" destroyed St. Paul's Church, etc. Damage £10 million.
1835 Dec. 16, New York City: 530 buildings destroyed by fire.
1871 Oct. 8, Chicago: the "Chicago Fire" burned 17,450 buildings, killed 250 persons; $196 million damage.
1872 Nov. 9, Boston: fire destroyed 800 buildings; $75-million damage.
1876 Dec. 5, New York City: fire in Brooklyn Theater killed more than 300.
1881 Dec. 8, Vienna: at least 620 died in fire at Ring Theatre.
1894 Sept. 1, Minnesota: forest fire over 480-square-mile area destroyed six towns and killed 480 people.
1900 May 1, Scofield, Utah: explosion of blasting powder in coal mine killed 200.

Nuclear Power Plant Accidents

1952 **Dec. 12, Chalk River, near Ottawa, Canada:** A partial meltdown of the reactor's uranium fuel core resulted after the accidental removal of four control rods. Although millions of gallons of radioactive water accumulated inside the reactor, there were no injuries.

1957 **Oct. 7, Windscale Pile No. 1, north of Liverpool, England:** Fire in a graphite-cooled reactor spewed radiation over the countryside, contaminating a 200 sq mi area.

South Ural Mountains: Explosion of radioactive wastes at Soviet nuclear weapons factory 12 miles from city of Kyshtym forces the evacuation of over 10,000 people from a contaminated area. No casualties were reported by Soviet officials.

1976 **near Greifswald, East Germany.** Radioactive core of reactor in the Lubmin nuclear power plant nearly melted down due to the failure of safety systems during a fire.

1979 **March 28, Three Mile Island, near Harrisburg, Pa.:** One of two reactors lost its coolant, which caused the radioactive fuel to overheat and caused a partial meltdown. Some radioactive material was released.

1986 **April 16, Chernobyl, near Kiev, U.S.S.R.:** Explosion and fire in the graphite core of one of four reactors released radioactive material which spread over part of the Soviet Union, Eastern Europe, Scandinavia, and later Western Europe, in the worst such accident to date.

June 30, Hoboken, N.J.: piers of North German Lloyd Steamship line burned; 326 dead.

1903 **Dec. 30, Chicago:** Iroquois Theatre fire killed 602.

1906 **March 10, France:** explosion in coal mine in Courrières killed 1,060.

1907 **Dec. 19, Jacobs Creek, Pa.:** explosion in coal mine left 239 dead.

1909 **Nov. 13, Cherry, Ill.:** explosion in coal mine killed 259.

1911 **March 25, New York City:** fire in Triangle Shirtwaist Factory fatal to 145.

1913 **Oct. 22, Dawson, N.M.:** coal mine explosion left 263 dead.

1917 **April 10, Eddystone, Pa.:** explosion in munitions plant killed 133.

Dec. 6, Canada: 1,600 people died when French ammunition ship *Mont Blanc* collided with Belgium steamer in Halifax Harbor.

1930 **April 21, Columbus, Ohio:** fire in Ohio State Penitentiary killed 320 convicts.

1937 **March 18, New London, Tex.:** explosion destroyed schoolhouse; 294 killed.

1942 **April 26, Manchuria:** explosion in Honkeiko Colliery killed 1,549.

Nov. 28, Boston: Cocoanut Grove nightclub fire killed 491.

1944 **July 6, Hartford, Conn.:** fire and ensuing stampede in main tent of Ringling Brothers Circus killed 168, injured 487.

July 17, Port Chicago, Calif.: 322 killed as ammunition ships explode.

Oct. 20, Cleveland: liquid-gas tanks exploded, killing 130.

1946 **Dec. 7, Atlanta:** fire in Winecoff Hotel killed 119.

1948 **Dec. 3, Shanghai:** Chinese passenger ship *Kiangya*, carrying refugees fleeing Communist troops during civil war, struck an old mine, exploded, and sank off Shanghai. Over 3,000 people are believed killed.

1949 **Sept. 2, China:** fire on Chongqing (Chungking) waterfront killed 1,700.

1954 **May 26, off Quonset Point, R.I.:** explosion and fire aboard aircraft carrier *Bennington* killed 103 crewmen.

1956 **Aug. 7, Colombia:** about 1,100 reported killed when seven army ammunition trucks exploded at Cali.

Aug. 8, Belgium: 262 died in coal mine fire at Marcinelle.

1960 **Jan. 21, Coalbrook, South Africa:** coal mine explosion killed 437.

Nov. 13, Syria: 152 children killed in moviehouse fire.

1961 **Dec. 17, Niteroi, Brazil:** circus fire fatal to 323.

1962 **Feb. 7, Saarland, West Germany:** coal mine gas explosion killed 298.

1963 **Nov. 9, Japan:** explosion in coal mine at Omuta killed 447.

1965 **May 28, India:** coal mine fire in state of Bihar killed 375.

June 1, near Fukuoka, Japan: coal mine explosion killed 236.

1967 **May 22, Brussels:** fire in L'Innovation, major department store, left 322 dead.

July 29, off North Vietnam: fire on U.S. carrier *Forrestal* killed 134.

1969 **Jan. 14, Pearl Harbor, Hawaii:** nuclear aircraft carrier *Enterprise* ripped by explosions; 27 dead, 82 injured.

1970 **Nov. 1, Saint-Laurent-du-Pont, France:** fire in dance hall killed 146 young people.

1972 **May 13, Osaka, Japan:** 118 people died in fire in nightclub on top floor of Sennichi department store.

June 6, Wankie, Rhodesia: explosion in coal mine killed 427.

1973 **Nov. 29, Kumamoto, Japan:** fire in Taiyo department store killed 101.

1974 **Feb. 1, Sao Paulo, Brazil:** fire in upper stories of bank building killed 189 persons, many of whom leaped to death.

1975 **Dec. 27, Dhanbad, India:** explosion in coal mine followed by flooding from nearby reservoir left 372 dead.

1977 **May 28, Southgate, Ky.:** fire in Beverly Hills Supper Club; 167 dead.

1978 **July 11, Tarragona, Spain:** 140 killed at coastal campsite when tank truck carrying liquid gas overturned and exploded.

Aug. 20, Abadan, Iran: nearly 400 killed when arsonists set fire to crowded theater.

1982 **Dec. 18–21, Caracas, Venezuela:** power-plant fire leaves 128 dead.

1986 **Dec. 31, San Juan, P. R.:** arson fire in Dupont Plaza Hotel set by three hotel employees kills 96.

1989 **April 19, off Puerto Rico:** A gun turret on the battleship *Iowa* exploded during a test-firing

THE WORST MARINE DISASTER IN U.S. HISTORY.

The Mississippi sidewheeler *Sultana* had a total capacity of 376 passengers and crew. On this occasion, the ship was jammed with some 2,400 Union soldiers who had recently been released from Confederate prison camps. The Civil War had ended several weeks before and the troops were cheerfully looking forward to returning home. There were about 100 civilian passengers aboard, men, women, and children, who occupied first-class cabins. The boat also had a cargo of horses, mules, hogs, and, surprisingly, a live ten-foot alligator that was kept in a wooden crate. On April 27, 1865, eight miles out of Memphis, Tennessee, the boiler exploded and the ship burst into flames. During the night, the *Sultana* burned down to the water line, while its survivors clung to floating debris. Some passengers were trapped aboard the flaming ship and died in the inferno. During the shipboard fire, one desperate individual managed to kill the alligator with a knife and used the crate to float to safety. Exactly how many people died in the disaster is not known. At least 1,547 lives were lost, exceeding the total of 1,513 for the 1912 sinking of the *Titanic*. Illustration: Courtesy of Mariners Museum.

while participating in training excercises in the Atlantic about 330 miles northeast of Puerto Rico; 47 crew members were killed. *Also see* Wartime Disasters, *U.S.S. Mississippi.*

June 3, Ural Mountains: Liquified petroleum gas leaking from a pipeline running alongside the Trans-Siberian railway near Uta, 720 miles east of Moscow, exploded and destroyed two passing passenger trains. About 500 travelers were killed and 723 injured of an estimated 1,200 passengers on both trains.

Oct. 23, Pasadena, Texas. A huge explosion followed by a series of others and a raging fire at a plastics manufacturing plant owned by Phillips Petroleum Co. killed 22 and injured more than 80 persons. A large leak of ethylene was presumed to be the cause.

1990 Jan. 14, Zaragoza, Spain. A fire at a discotheque killed 43 with poisonous smoke fumes.

March 25, New York City. Arson fire in illegal *Happy Land Social Club*, Bronx, killed 87.

Shipwrecks

1833 May 11, *Lady of the Lake:* bound from England to Quebec, struck iceberg; 215 perished.

1853 Sept. 29 *Annie Jane:* emigrant vessel off coast of Scotland; 348 died.

1898 Nov. 26, *City of Portland:* Loss of 157 off Cape Cod.

1904 June 15, *General Slocum:* excursion steamer burned in East River, New York; 1,021 perished.

1912 March 5, *Principe de Asturias:* Spanish steamer struck rock off Sebastien Point; 500 drowned.

April 15, *Titanic:* sank after colliding with iceberg; 1,513 died.

1914 May 29, *Empress of Ireland:* sank after collision in St. Lawrence River; 1,024 perished.

1915 July 24, *Eastland:* Great Lakes excursion steamer overturned in Chicago River; 812 died.

1928 Nov. 12, *Vestris:* British steamer sank in gale off Virginia; 110 died.

1931 June 14: French excursion steamer overturned in gale off St. Nazaire; approximately 450 died.

1934 Sept. 8, *Morro Castle:* 134 killed in fire off Asbury Park, N.J.

Space Accidents

1967 Jan. 27, Apollo 1: A fire aboard the space capsule on the ground at Cape Kennedy, Fla. killed astronauts Virgil L. Grissom, Edward H. White, and Roger Chaffee.
April 23-24, Soyuz 1: Vladimir M. Komarov was killed when his craft crashed after its parachute lines, released at 23,000 feet for re-entry, became snarled.

1971 June 6-30, Soyuz 11: Three cosmonauts, Georgi T. Dolrovolsky, Vladislav N. Volkov, and Viktor I. Patsayev, found dead in the craft after its automatic landing. Apparently the cause of death was loss of pressurization in the space craft during re-entry into the earth's atmosphere.

1980 March 18, U.S.S.R. A Vostok rocket exploded on its launch pad while being refueled, killing 50 at the Plesetsk Space Center.

1986 Jan 28, Challenger Space Shuttle: Exploded 73 seconds after lift off, killing all seven crew members. They were: Christa McAuliffe, Francis R. Scobee, Michael J. Smith, Judith A. Resnick, Ronald E. McNair, Ellison S. Onizuka, and Gregory B. Jarvis. A booster leak ignited the fuel, causing the explosion.

1939 May 23, *Squalus:* submarine with 59 men sank off Hampton Beach, N.H.; 33 saved.
June 1, Submarine *Thetis:* sank in Liverpool Bay, England; 99 perished.

1942 Oct. 2, *Queen Mary:* rammed and sank a British cruiser; 338 aboard the cruiser died.

1945 April 9: U.S. ship, loaded with aerial bombs, exploded at Bari, Italy; at least 360 killed.

1947 November, Yingkow: Unidentified Chinese troopship evacuating Nationalist troops from Manchuria sank, killing an estimated 6,000 persons.

1949 Sept. 17, *Noronic:* Canadian Great Lakes cruise ship burned at Toronto dock; about 130 died.

1952 April 26, *Hobson:* minesweeper collided with aircraft carrier *Wasp* and sank during night maneuvers in mid-Atlantic; 176 persons lost.

1953 Jan. 9, *Chang Tyong-Ho:* South Korean ferry foundered off Pusan; 249 reported dead.
Jan. 31, *Princess Victoria:* British ferry sank in Irish Sea; 133 lost.

1956 July 25, *Andrea Doria:* Italian liner collided with Swedish liner *Stockholm* off Nantucket Island, Mass., sinking next day; 52, mostly passengers on Italian ship, dead or unaccounted for; over 1,600 rescued.

1962 April 8, *Dara,* British liner, exploded and sank in Persian Gulf; 236 persons dead. Caused by time bomb.

1963 May 4: U.A.R. ferry capsized and sank in upper Nile; over 200 died.

1968 Late May, *Scorpion:* nuclear submarine sank in Atlantic 400 miles S.W. of Azores; 99 dead. (Located Oct. 31.)

1970 Dec. 15: ferry in Korean Strait capsized; 261 lost.

1976 Oct. 20, Luling, La.: *George Prince,* Mississippi River ferry, rammed by Norwegian tanker *Frosta;* 77 dead.

1983 May 25, *10th of Ramadan,* Nile steamer, caught fire and sank in Lake Nasser, near Aswan, Egypt; 272 dead and 75 missing.

1987 March 9, Belgium: British ferry capsizes after leaving Belgian port of Zeebrugge with 500 abroad; 134 drowned. Water rushing through open bow is believed to be probable cause.

1987 Dec. 20. Manila: Over 1,500 people killed when passenger ferry *Dona Paz* collided with oil tanker *Victor* off Mindoro Is., 110 miles south of Manila.

1989 April 7, Norwegian Sea: Fourty-two seamen died when Soviet Mike-class nuclear-powered submarine sank more than 300 miles off coast of Norway after an undersea accident and fire. Twenty-seven crew members were rescued.

1990 April 7, Skagerrak Strait off Norway. Suspected arson fire aboard Danish-owned North Sea ferry, *Scandinavian Star,* kills at least 110 passengers.
April 7, Myanmar (Burma). Double-decker ferry sinks in Gyaing River during a storm and 215 persons are believed drowned.

Aircraft Accidents

1921 Aug. 24, England: *AR-2* British dirigible, broke in two on trial trip near Hull; 62 died.

1925 Sept. 3, Caldwell, Ohio: U.S. dirigible *Shenandoah* broke apart; 14 dead.

1930 Oct. 5, Beauvais, France: British dirigible R 101 crashed, killing 47.

1933 April 4, New Jersey Coast: U.S. dirigible *Akron* crashed; 73 dead.

1937 May 6, Lakehurst, N.J.: German zeppelin *Hindenburg* destroyed by fire at tower mooring; 36 killed.

1945 July 28, New York City: U.S. Army bomber crashed into Empire State Building; 13 dead.

1952 Jan. 22, Elizabeth, N.J.: 29 killed, including former Secretary of War Robert P. Patterson, when airliner hit apartments; seven of dead were on ground.

1953 June 18, near Tokyo: crash of U.S. Air Force "Globemaster" killed 129 servicemen.

1960 Dec. 16, New York City: United and Trans World planes collided in fog, crashed in two boroughs, killing 134 in air and on ground.

1961 Feb. 15, near Brussels: 72 on board and farmer on ground killed in crash of Sabena plane; U.S. figure skating team wiped out.

1966 March 5, Japan: British airliner caught fire and crashed into Mt. Fuji; 124 dead.
Dec. 24, Binh Thai, South Vietnam: crash of military-chartered plane into village killed 129.

1970 Nov. 14, Huntington, W. Va.: chartered plane carrying 43 players and coaches of Marshall University football team crashed; 75 dead.

1971 July 30, Morioka, Japan: Japanese Boeing 727 and F-86 fighter collided in mid-air; toll was 162.
Sept. 4, near Juneau, Alaska: Alaska Airlines Boeing 727 crashed into Chilkoot Mountains; 111 killed.

1972 **Aug. 14, East Berlin, East Germany:** Soviet-built East German Ilyushin plane crashed, killing 156.
Dec. 3, Santa Cruz de Tenerife, Canary Islands: Spanish charter jet carrying West German tourists crashed on take-off; all 155 aboard killed.
Dec. 30, Miami, Fla.: Eastern Airlines Lockheed 1011 TriStar Jumbo jet crashed into Everglades; 101 killed, 75 survived.
1973 **Jan. 22, Kano, Nigeria:** 171 Nigerian Moslems returning from Mecca and five crewmen died in crash.
1973 **Feb. 21:** Civilian Libyan Arab Airlines Boeing 727 shot down by Israeli fighters over Sinai after it had strayed off course; 108 died, five survived. Officials claimed that the pilot had ignored fighters' warnings to land.
April 10, Hochwald, Switzerland: British airliner carrying tourists to Swiss fair crashed in blizzard; 106 dead.
July 11, Paris: Boeing 707 of Varig Airlines, en route to Rio de Janeiro, crashed near airport, killing 122 of 134 passengers.
1974 **March 3, Paris:** Turkish DC-10 jumbo jet crashed in forest shortly after take-off; all 346 passengers and crew killed.
Dec. 4, Colombo, Sri Lanka: Dutch DC-8 carrying Moslems to Mecca crashed on landing approach, killing all 191 persons aboard.
1975 **April 4, near Saigon, Vietnam:** Air Force Galaxy C-5A crashed after take-off, killing 172, mostly Vietnamese children.
Aug. 3, Agadir, Morocco: Chartered Boeing 707, returning Moroccan workers home after vacation in France, plunged into mountainside; all 188 aboard killed.
1976 **Sept. 10, Zagreb, Yugoslavia:** midair collision between British Airways Trident and Yugoslav charter DC-9 fatal to all 176 persons aboard; worst mid-air collision on record.
1977 **March 27, Santa Cruz de Tenerife, Canary Islands:** Pan American and KLM Boeing 747s collided on runway. All 249 on KLM plane and 333 of 394 aboard Pan Am jet killed. Total of 582 is highest for any type of aviation disaster.
1978 **Jan. 1, Bombay:** Air India 747 with 213 aboard exploded and plunged into sea minutes after takeoff.
Sept. 25, San Diego, Calif.: Pacific Southwest plane collided in midair with Cessna. All 135 on airliner, 2 in Cessna, and 7 on ground killed for total of 144.
Nov. 15, Colombo, Sri Lanka: Chartered Icelandic Airlines DC-8, carrying 249 Moslem pilgrims from Mecca, crashed in thunderstorm during landing approach; 183 killed.
1979 **Nov. 26, Jidda, Saudi Arabia:** Pakistan International Airlines 707 carrying pilgrims returning from Mecca crashed on take-off; all 156 aboard killed.
Nov. 28, Mt. Erebus, Antarctica: Air New Zealand DC-10 crashed on sightseeing flight; 257 killed.
1980 **March 14, Warsaw:** LOT Polish Airlines Ilyushin 62 crashed while attempting landing; 22 boxers and officials of a U.S. amateur boxing team killed along with 65 others.
April 25, Santa Cruz de Tenerife, Canary Islands: Chartered Boeing 727 carrying 138 British vacationers and crew of 8 crashed into mountain while approaching for landing; all killed.
Aug. 19, Riyadh, Saudi Arabia: all 301 aboard Saudi Arabian jet killed when burning plane made

safe landing but passengers were unable to escape.
1981 **Dec. 1, Ajaccio, Corsica:** Yugoslav DC-9 Super 80 carrying tourists crashed into mountain on landing approach, killing all 178 aboard.
1983 **June 28, near Cuenca, Ecuador, Ecuadorean** jetliner crashed in mountains, killing 119.
Aug. 30, near island of Sakhalin off Siberia, South Korean civilian jetliner shot down by Soviet fighter after it strayed off course into Soviet airspace. All 269 people aboard killed.
Nov. 26, Madrid: A Columbian Avianca Boeing 747 crashed near Mejorada del Campó Airport killing 183 persons aboard. Eleven people survived the accident.
1985 **June 23:** Air-India Boeing 747 exploded over the Atlantic off the coast of Ireland, all 329 aboard killed.
Aug. 12, Japan Air Lines Boeing 747 crashed into a mountain, killing 520 of the 524 aboard.
Dec. 12, A chartered Arrow Air DC-8, bringing American soldiers home for Christmas, crashed on takeoff from Gander, Newfoundland. All 256 aboard died.
1987 **May 9, Poland:** Polish airliner, Ilyushin 62M on charter flight to New York, crashes after take-off from Warsaw killing 183.
Aug. 16, Detroit: Northwest Airlines McDonnell Douglas MD-30 plunges to heavily traveled boulevard, killing 156. Girl 4, only survivor.
Nov. 26: South African Airways Boeing 747 goes down south of Mauritius in rough seas; 160 die.
Nov. 29: Korean Air Boeing 747 jetliner explodes from bomb planted by North Korean agents and crashes into sea off Burma, killing all 115 aboard.
1988 **July 3, Persian Gulf:** U.S. Navy cruiser *Vincennes* shot down Iran Air A300 Airbus, killing 290 persons, after mistaking it for an attacking jet fighter.
Aug. 28, Ramstein Air Force Base, West Germany: Three jets from Italian Air Force acrobatic team collided in mid-air during air show and crashed, killing 70 persons, including the pilots and spectators on the ground. It is worst air-show disaster in history.
Dec. 21, Lockerbie, Scotland: A New-York-bound Pan-Am Boeing 747 exploded in flight from a terrorist bomb and crashed into Scottish village, killing all 259 aboard and 11 persons on the ground. Passengers included 38 Syracuse University students and many U.S. military personnel.
1989 **Feb. 24, UAL 811:** About 100 miles southwest of Hawaii, a 10- × 40-ft hole blew open in the fuselage of a United Airlines Boeing 747. Nine passengers were sucked out of the jet liner to their deaths 20,000 ft over the Pacific; 27 other passengers were injured.
June 7, Paramaribo, Suriname: A Surinam Airways DC-8 carrying 174 passengers and nine crew members crashed into the jungle while making a third attempt to land in a thick fog, killing 168 aboard.

Railroad Accidents
1904 **Aug. 7, Eden, Colo.:** Train derailed on bridge during flash flood; 96 killed.

1910 **March 1, Wellington, Wash.:** two trains swept into canyon by avalanche; 96 dead.

1915 **May 22, Gretna, Scotland:** two passenger trains and troop train collided; 227 killed.

1917 **Dec. 12, Modane, France:** nearly 550 killed in derailment of troop train near mouth of Mt. Cenis tunnel.

1918 **Nov. 1, New York City:** derailment of subway train in Malbone St. tunnel in Brooklyn left 92 dead.

1939 **Dec. 22, near Magdeburg, Germany:** more than 125 killed in collision; 99 killed in another wreck near Friedrichshafen.

1943 **Dec. 16, near Rennert, N.C.:** 72 killed in derailment and collision of two Atlantic Coast Line trains.

1944 **March 2, near Salerno, Italy:** 521 suffocated when Italian train stalled in tunnel.

1949 **Oct. 22, near Nowy Dwor, Poland:** more than 200 reported killed in derailment of Danzig-Warsaw express.

1950 **Nov. 22, Richmond Hill, N.Y.:** 79 died when one Long Island Rail Road commuter train crashed into rear of another.

1951 **Feb. 6, Woodbridge, N.J.:** 85 died when Pennsylvania Railroad commuter train plunged through temporary overpass.

1952 **Oct. 8, Harrow-Wealdstone, England:** two express trains crashed into commuter train; 112 dead.

1953 **Dec. 24, near Sakvice, Czechoslovakia:** two trains crashed; over 100 dead.

1957 **Sept. 1, near Kendal, Jamaica:** about 175 killed when train plunged into ravine.

Sept. 29, near Montgomery, West Pakistan: express train crashed into standing oil train; nearly 300 killed.

Dec. 4, St. John's, England: 92 killed, 187 injured as one commuter train crashed into another in fog.

1960 **Nov. 14, Pardubice, Czechoslovakia:** two trains collided; 110 dead, 106 injured.

1962 **May 3, near Tokyo:** 163 killed and 400 injured when train crashed into wreckage of collision between inbound freight train and outbound commuter train.

1963 **Nov. 9, near Yokohama, Japan:** two passenger trains crashed into derailed freight, killing 162.

1964 **July 26, Custoias, Portugal:** passenger train derailed; 94 dead.

1970 **Feb. 4, near Buenos Aires:** 236 killed when express train crashed into standing commuter train.

1972 **July 21, Seville, Spain:** head-on crash of two passenger trains killed 76.

Oct. 6, near Saltillo, Mexico: train carrying religious pilgrims derailed and caught fire, killing 204 and injuring over 1,000.

Oct. 30, Chicago: two Illinois Central commuter trains collided during morning rush hour; 45 dead and over 200 injured.

1974 **Aug. 30, Zagreb, Yugoslavia:** train entering station derailed, killing 153 and injuring over 60.

1977 **Feb. 4, Chicago:** 11 killed and over 180 injured when elevated train hit rear of another, sending two cars to street.

1981 **June 6, Near Mansi, India:** Driver of train carrying over 500 passengers, braked to avoid hitting cow, causing train to plunge off a bridge into Baghmati River; 268 passengers were reported killed, but at least 300 more were missing.

1982 **Jan. 26, Algeria:** Derailment on Algiers—Oran line leaves up to 120 dead.

July 11, Tepic, Mexico: Nogales-Guadalajara train plunges down mountain gorge killing 120.

1988 **Dec. 12, South London:** A commuter train crashed into the rear of a stopped train killing 33 and injuring more than 110 passengers.

1989 **Jan. 15, Maizdi Khan, Bangladesh:** A train carrying Muslim pilgrims crashed head-on with a mail train killing at least 110 persons and injuring as many as 1,000. Many people were riding on the roof of the trains and between the cars.

1989 **Aug. 10, near Los Mochis, Mexico:** A second-class passenger train traveling from Mazatlán to Mexicali, plunged off a bridge at Puente del Rio Bamoa into the river and killed an estimated 85 people and injured 107.

1990 **Jan. 4, Sangi village, Sindh province, Pakistan:** An overcrowded sixteen-car passenger train was switched to the wrong track and rammed into a standing freight train. At least 210 persons were killed and 700 believed injured in what is said to be Pakistan's worst train disaster.

March 7, Philadelphia. Three passengers were killed and 162 injured when a six-car subway train derailed and crashed into a tunnel support beam.

April 15, near Kumrahar, Bihar State, India. An explosion aboard a moving commuter train caused a fire when a match was lit near a leaking gas cylinder, killing at least 80 people and injuring 65 others.

Oil Spills

1978 **March 16, off Portsall, France:** Wrecked supertanker *Amoco Cadiz* spilled 68 million gallons causing widespread environmental damage over 100 miles of coast of Brittany. Is world's largest tanker disaster.

1979 **June 8, Gulf of Mexico:** Exploratory oil well, Ixtoc 1, blew out, spilling an estimated 140 million gallons of crude into the open sea. Although it is the largest known oil spill, it had a low environmental impact.

1989 **Dec. 19. Off Las Palmas, the Canary Islands.** An explosion in Iranian supertanker, the *Kharg-5*, tore through its hull and caused 19 million gallons of crude oil to spill out into the Atlantic Ocean about 400 miles north of Las Palmas, forming a 100-square-mile oil slick.

Sports

1955 **June 11, Le Mans, France:** Racing car in Grand Prix hurtled into grandstand, killing 82 spectators.

1964 **May 24, Lima, Peru:** More than 300 soccer fans killed and over 500 injured during riot and panic following unpopular ruling by referee in Peru vs. Argentina soccer game. It is worst soccer disaster on record.

1971 **Jan. 2, Glasgow, Scotland:** Sixty-six persons killed in a crush at the Glasgow Rangers home stadium when fans trying to leave encountered fans trying to return to the stadium after hearing that a late goal had been scored.

1982 **Oct. 20, Moscow:** According to *Sovietsky Sport*, as many as 340 persons were killed at Lenin Stadium when exiting soccer fans collided with returning fans after final goal was scored. All the fans had been crowded into one section of stadium by police.

1985 May 11, Bradford, England: 56 persons burned to death and over 200 injured when fire engulfed the main grandstand at Bradford's soccer stadium.

May 29, Brussels, Belgium: Drunken group of British soccer fans supporting Liverpool club stormed stand filled with Italian supporters of Juventus team before European Champion's Cup final. While British fans attacked rival spectators at the Heysel Stadium, concrete retaining wall collapsed and 39 persons were crushed or trampled to death, 32 of them Italians. More than 400 persons were injured.

1988 March 12, Katmandu, Nepal: Some 80 soccer fans seeking cover during a violent hail storm at the national stadium were trampled to death in a stampede because the stadium doors were locked.

1989 April 15, Sheffield, England: Ninety-four people were killed and 170 injured at Hillsborough stadium when throngs of Liverpool soccer fans, many without tickets, collapsed a stadium barrier in a mad rush to see the game between Liverpool and Nottingham Forest. It was Britain's worst soccer disaster.

Miscellaneous

1980 Jan. 20, Sincelejo, Colombia: Bleachers at a bullring collapsed, leaving 222 dead.

March 30, Stavanger, Norway: Floating hotel in North Sea collapsed, killing 123 oil workers.

1981 July 18, Kansas City, Mo.: suspended walkway in Hyatt Regency Hotel collapses; 113 dead, 186 injured.

1984 Dec. 3, Bhopal, India: Toxic gas, methyl isocyanate, seeped from Union Carbide insecticide plant, killing more than 2,000; injuring about 150,000.

1987 Sept. 18. Goiânia, Brazil: 244 people contaminated with cesium-137 removed from steel cylinder taken from cancer-therapy machine in abandoned clinic and sold as scrap. Four people died in worst radiation disaster in Western Hemisphere.

1988 July 6, North Sea off Scotland: 166 workers killed in explosion and fire on Occidental Petroleum's Piper Alpha rig in North Sea off Scottish coast; 64 survivors rescued. It is the world's worst offshore oil disaster.

Wartime Disasters

1915 May 6: Despite German warnings, the Cunard Liner *Lusitania* sailed from New York for Liverpool, England, on May 1st and was sunk off the coast of Ireland by a German submarine. 1,198 passengers and crew, 128 of them Americans, died. Unknown to the passengers, the ship was carrying a cargo of small arms. The disaster contributed to the entry of the United States into World War I.

1916 Feb. 26: 3,100 people died when the French cruiser *Provence* was sunk by a German submarine in the Mediterranean.

1940 Sept. 13. The luxury liner *S.S. City of Benares* sailed from Liverpool with over 90 British children who were being evacuated to Canada to escape harm during World War II. About 600 miles out to sea, the ship was torpedoed by a German submarine during the night and only 13 of the children survived the disaster.[1]

1943 November, Gilbert Islands: While battleship *U.S.S. Mississippi* was bombarding Makin Atoll in Pacific during WW II, an accidental gun turret explosion killed 43 of her crew.

1944 Sept. 12, South China Sea: U.S. submarines torpedoed and sank two Japanese troop ships[2], the *Kachidoki Maru* and the *Rakuyo Maru*. Unknown to the submarines, the Japanese, in disregard for the rules of treatment of prisoners of war, had forced 2,000 British, Australian, and American POWs into the holds of the ships which were designed to hold only 300 troops. Later, when the subs discovered the tragedy, they sought to rescue as many survivors as possible. Japanese vessels picked up most of *Kachidoki Maru*'s prisoners but abandoned those from the *Rakuyo Maru*, taking only the Japanese survivors. Of the 1,300 POWs aboard the *Rakuyo Maru*, 159 were rescued, but only seven lived.

Oct. 24, South China Sea: The *Arisan Maru*[2] carrying 1,800 American prisoners was torpedoed by a U.S. submarine and sunk. The Japanese destroyer escort rescued Japanese military and civilian personnel and left the POWs to their fate. It is estimated that only ten prisoners survived the disaster.

Dec. 17-18, Philippine Sea: A typhoon struck U.S. Third Fleet's Task Force 38, sank three destroyers, damaged seven other ships, destroyed 186 aircraft, and killed 800 officers and men.

1945 Jan. 30: 7,700 persons died in world's largest marine disaster when the Nazi passenger ship *Wilhelm Gustoff* carrying Germans fleeing Poland was torpedoed in the Baltic by a Soviet submarine.

May 3, *Cap Arcona*: Several days before World War II ended in Europe, the German passenger ship carrying about 6,000, of which an estimated 5,000 were concentration camp prisoners, was sunk by British aircraft. An estimated 5,000 persons were killed, most of them prisoners who were about to gain their freedom.

July 29, near Leyte Gulf: The heavy cruiser *Indianapolis* was torpedoed and sunk by a Japanese submarine. Of the crew of 1,199 men, only 316 survived. Several days earlier, the *Indianapolis* had delivered a lead cylinder containing uranium (U-235) and the firing mechanism for the first atomic bomb to Tinian Island. Had the ship been sunk earlier while delivering its special cargo, WW II would have ended differently.

---

1. During the war (1939-40), some 10,000 children were evacuated to stay with foster parents in the United States and Canada. The sinking of the *City of Benares* ended the British government's evacuation program.
2. The ships had no identification that they were transporting prisoners of war.

When You Need Help,
Call the Citizens Emergency Center

Source: Bureau of Consular Affairs, U.S. Department of State.

A very important service of the U.S. Government that all travelers and their families should be aware of is the Citizens Emergency Center which deals with emergencies involving Americans abroad—Americans who die, become destitute, get sick, disappear, have accidents, or get arrested. In addition to these individual emergencies, the Center is also the U.S. State Department's focal point for *major* disasters involving Americans abroad, such as plane crashes, hijackings, natural disasters, and terrorist incidents.

Emergency assistance generally pertains to four categories: death, arrests, financial-medical problems, and welfare-whereabouts queries. The Center, working through the U.S. embassies and consulates abroad, serves as a link between the citizen in distress and his or her family in the United States.

Deaths

Persons traveling abroad on business, pleasure, or a study program rarely think about death. Nevertheless, approximately 6,000 Americans do die outside of the United States each year. The Citizens Emergency Center assists with the return of approximately 2,000 remains annually.

When an American dies abroad, a consular officer will notify the deceased's family and inform them of the options and costs for disposition of the remains. The costs for preparing and returning a body to the U.S. are high and are the responsibility of the family. Often local laws and procedures make returning a body to the United States for burial a lengthy process.

Arrests

Nearly 3,000 Americans are arrested abroad each year. Over 30% of these arrests are drug related and over 70% of the drug related arrests involve marijuana or cocaine.

The rights an American enjoys in this country do not apply abroad. Each country is sovereign and its laws apply to everyone who enters regardless of nationality. The U.S. Government cannot "spring" Americans from foreign jails. However, a consul will insist on prompt access to the arrested American, provide a list of reputable attorneys, provide information on the host country's legal system, offer to contact the arrested person's family or friends, visit on a regular basis, protest mistreatment, monitor jail conditions, provide dietary supplements if needed, and keep the State Department informed. The Center is the point of contact for family members and others who are concerned about an American arrested abroad.

Welfare/Whereabouts

The Center receives about 12,000 inquiries a year concerning the welfare or whereabouts of an American abroad. Many of the inquiries are from worried relatives who have not heard from the traveler. Others are attempts to notify a traveler about a family crisis at home.

Most of these inquiries are successfully resolved. However, occasionally, a person truly is missing. In that case, it is the responsibility of local authorities to investigate the matter. The State Department and U.S. consuls abroad do not conduct investigations. As happens in the United States, some missing persons are never found.

Financial Assistance

If an American finds him or herself destitute he/she can turn to a U.S. consular officer abroad for help. The Citizen's Emergency Center will assist by contacting the destitute person's family, friends, or business associates to raise private funds. The Center will transmit these funds to the destitute American.

The Center transfers approximately three million dollars a year in private emergency funds. It can also approve small government loans to destitute parties to tide them over until private funds arrive. Each year, over $500,000 are loaned to destitute Americans.

Medical Assistance

The Center works with U.S. consuls abroad to assist Americans who become physically or mentally ill while traveling. It will locate family members, guardians, and friends in the U.S., assist in transmitting private funds, and, when necessary, assist in the return of ill or injured Americans by commercial carrier.

The Privacy Act

The provisions of the Privacy Act are designed to protect the privacy and rights of Americans but occasionally they complicate the Center's efforts to assist citizens abroad. As a general rule, consular officers may not reveal information regarding an individual American's location, welfare, intentions, or problems to anyone, including family members, without the expressed consent of that individual. Although sympathetic to the distress that this can cause concerned families, consular officers must comply with the provisions of the Privacy Act.

Where to Call

The Citizens Emergency Center's telephone number is (202) 647-5225. It is staffed by 25 officers and clerical personnel and is open 8:15 A.M. to 10:00 P.M. EST, Monday through Friday, and 9:00 A.M. to 3:00 P.M. Saturday. At other times, including holidays, a duty officer can be reached through the State Department's main number: (202) 634-3600. □

U.S. Passport and Customs Information

Source: Department of State, Bureau of Consular Affairs and Department of the Treasury, Customs Service.

Passports

With a few exceptions, a passport is required for all U.S. citizens to depart and enter the United States and to enter most foreign countries. A valid U.S. passport is the best documentation of U.S. citizenship available. Persons who travel to a country where a U.S. passport is not required should be in possession of documentary evidence of their U.S. citizenship and identity to facilitate reentry into the United States. Travelers should check passport and visa requirements with consular officials of the countries to be visited well in advance of their departure date.

Application for a passport may be made at a passport agency; to a clerk of any Federal court or State court of record; or a judge or clerk of any probate court accepting applications; or at a post office selected to accept passport applications. Passport agencies are located in Boston, Chicago, Honolulu, Houston, Los Angeles, Miami, New Orleans, New York, Philadelphia, San Francisco, Seattle, Stamford, Conn., and Washington, D.C.

All persons are required to obtain individual passports in their own names. Neither spouses nor children may be included in each others' passports. Applicants between the ages of 13 and 18 must appear in person before the clerk or agent executing the application. For children under the age of 13, a parent or legal guardian may execute an application for them.

First time passport applicants must apply in person. Applicants must present evidence of citizenship (e.g., a certified copy of birth certificate), personal identification (e.g., a valid driver's license), two identical black and white or color photographs taken within six months (2×2 inches, with the image size measured from the bottom of the chin to the top of the head [including hair] not less than 1 inch nor more than 1 3/8 inches on a plain white or off-white background, vending machine photographs not acceptable), plus a completed passport application (DSP-11). If you were born abroad, you may also use as proof of citizenship: a Certificate of Naturalization, a Certificate of Citizenship, a Report of Birth abroad of a Citizen of the United States of America or a Certification of Birth. A fee of $35 plus a $7 execution fee is charged for adults 18 years and older for a passport valid for ten years from the date of issue. The fee for minor children under 18 years of age is $20 for a five-year passport plus $7 for the execution of the application.

You may apply for a passport by mail if you have been the bearer of a passport issued within 12 years prior to the date of a new application, are able to submit your most recent U.S. passport with your new application, and your previous passport was not issued before your 16th birthday. If you are eligible to apply by mail, include your previous passport, a completed, signed, and dated DSP-82 "Application for Passport by Mail," new photographs, and the passport fee of $35. The $7 execution fee is not required when applying by mail. Mail the application and attachments to one of the 13 passport agencies.

Passports may be presented for amendment to show a married name or legal change of name or to correct descriptive data. Any alterations to the passport by the bearer *other than* in the spaces provided for change of address and next of kin data are forbidden.

Loss, theft or destruction of a passport should be reported to Passport Services, 1425 K Street, N.W., Washington, D.C. 20524 immediately, or to the nearest passport agency. If you are overseas, report to the nearest U.S. Embassy or consulate and to local police authorities. Your passport is a valuable citizenship and identity document. It should be carefully safeguarded. Its loss could cause you unnecessary travel complications as well as significant expense. It is advisable to photocopy the data page of your passport and keep it in a place separate from your passport to facilitate the issuance of a replacement passport should one be necessary.

Customs

United States residents must declare all articles acquired abroad and in their possession at the time of their return. In addition, articles acquired in the U.S. Virgin Islands, American Samoa, or Guam and not accompanying you must be declared at the time of your return. The wearing or use of an article acquired abroad does *not* exempt it from duty. Customs declaration forms are distributed on vessels and planes, and should be prepared in advance of arrival for presentation to the customs inspectors.

If you have not exceeded the duty-free exemption allowed, you may make an oral declaration to the customs inspector. A written declaration is necessary when (1) total fair retail value of articles exceeds $1,400 ($400 tax-free exemption plus $1,000 dutiable at a flat 10% rate) (keep your sales slips); (2) over 1 liter of liquor, 200 cigarettes, or 100 cigars are included; (3) items are not intended for your personal or household use, or articles brought home for another person; and (4) when a customs duty or internal revenue tax is collectible on any article in your possession.

An exception to the above are regulations applicable to articles purchased in the U.S. Virgin Islands, American Samoa, or Guam where you may receive a customs exemption of $800. Not more than $400 of this exemption may be applied to merchandise obtained elsewhere than in these islands. Five liters of alcoholic beverages and 1000 cigarettes may be included provided not more than one liter and 200 cigarettes were acquired elsewhere than in these islands. Articles acquired in and sent from these islands to the United States may be claimed under your duty-free personal exemption if properly declared at the time of your return.

Articles accompanying you, in excess of your personal exemption, up to $1000 will be assessed at a flat rate of duty of 10% based on fair retail value in country of acquisition. (If articles were acquired in the insular possessions, the flat rate of duty is 5% and these goods may accompany you or be shipped home.) These articles must be for your personal use or for use as gifts and not for sale. This provision may be used every 30 days, excluding the day of your last arrival. Any items which have a "free" duty rate will be excluded before duty is calculated.

Other exemptions include in part: automobiles, boats, planes, or other vehicles taken abroad for noncommercial use. Foreign-made personal articles (e.g., watches, cameras, etc.) taken abroad should be registered with Customs before departure. Customs will register *only* serially numbered foreign-made items. Gifts of not more than $50 can be shipped back to the United States tax and duty free ($100 if mailed from the Virgin Islands, American Samoa, or Guam). Household effects and tools of trade which you take out of the United States are duty free at time of return.

Prohibited and restricted articles include in part: absinthe, narcotics and dangerous drugs, obscene articles and publications, seditious and treasonable materials, hazardous articles (e.g., fireworks, dangerous toys, toxic and poisonous substances, and switchblade knives), biological materials of public health or veterinary importance, fruit, vegetables and plants, meats, poultry and products thereof, birds, monkeys, and turtles.

If you understate the value of an article you declare, or if you otherwise misrepresent an article in your declaration, you may have to pay a penalty in addition to payment of duty. Under certain circumstances, the article could be seized and forfeited if the penalty is not paid.

If you fail to declare an article acquired abroad, not only is the article subject to seizure and forfeiture, but you will be liable for a personal penalty in an amount equal to the value of the article in the United States. In addition, you may also be liable to criminal prosecution.

If you carry more than $10,000 into or out of the United States in currency (either United States or foreign money), negotiable instruments in bearer form, or travelers checks, a report must be filed with United States Customs at the time you arrive or depart with such amounts.

As U.S. restrictions on travel to Cuba, North Korea, Vietnam, and Cambodia have been eased, the Office of Foreign Assets Control (FAC) issued a general license, effective March 21, 1977, which allows visitors to those countries to purchase a maximum of $100 worth of goods. This amount is based on retail value in the country where acquired. These articles must be for personal use—not for resale—and must accompany the traveler on his entry into the U.S. This allowance may be used only once every 6 months.

Foreign Embassies in the United States

Source: U.S. Department of State

Embassy of the Democratic Republic of Afghanistan, 2341 Wyoming Ave., N.W., Washington, D.C. 20008. Phone: (202) 234-3770, 3771.

Embassy of the Democratic & Popular Republic of Algeria, 2118 Kalorama Rd., N.W., Washington, D.C. 20008. Phone: (202) 265-2800.

Embassy of Antigua & Barbuda, 3400 International Dr., N.W., Suite 4M, Washington, D.C. 20008. Phone: (202) 362-5211, 5166, 5122.

Embassy of the Argentine Republic, 1600 New Hampshire Ave., N.W., Washington, D.C. 20009. Phone: (202) 939-6400 to 6403, inclusive.

Embassy of Australia, 1601 Massachusetts Ave., N.W., Washington, D.C. 20036. Phone: (202) 797-3000.

Embassy of Austria, 2343 Massachusetts Ave., N.W., Washington, D.C. 20008. Phone: (202) 483-4474.

Embassy of the Commonwealth of the Bahamas, 600 New Hampshire Ave., N.W., Suite 865, Washington, D.C. 20037. Phone: (202) 944-3390.

Embassy of the State of Bahrain, 3502 International Dr., N.W., Washington, D.C. 20008. Phone: (202) 342-0741, 0742.

Embassy of the People's Republic of Bangladesh, 2201 Wisconsin Ave., N.W., Washington, D.C. 20007. Phone: (202) 342-8372 to 8376.

Embassy of Barbados, 2144 Wyoming Ave., N.W., Washington, D.C. 20008. Phone: (202) 939-9218/9.

Embassy of Belgium, 3330 Garfield St., N.W., Washington, D.C. 20008. Phone: (202) 333-6900.

Embassy of Belize, 3400 International Dr., N.W., Suite 2J, Washington, D.C. 20008. Phone: (202) 363-4505.

Embassy of the People's Republic of Benin, 2737 Cathedral Ave., N.W., Washington, D.C. 20008. Phone: (202) 232-6656.

Embassy of Bolivia, 3014 Massachusetts Ave., N.W., Washington, D.C. 20008. Phone: (202) 483-4410, 4411 and 4412.

Embassy of the Republic of Botswana, 4301 Connecticut Ave., N.W., Suite 404, Washington, D.C. 20008. Phone: (202) 244-4990, 4991.

Brazilian Embassy, 3006 Massachusetts Ave.,

N.W., Washington, D.C. 20008. Phone: (202) 745-2700.

Embassy of the State of Brunei Darussalam, 2600 Virginia Ave., N.W., Suite 300, Washington, D.C. 20037. Phone: (202) 342-0159.

Embassy of the People's Republic of Bulgaria, 1621 22nd St., N.W., Washington, D.C. 20008. Phone: (202) 387-7969.

Embassy of Burkina Faso, 2340 Massachusetts Ave., N.W., Washington, D.C. 20008. Phone: (202) 332-5577, 6895.

Embassy of the Republic of Burundi, 2233 Wisconsin Ave., N.W., Suite 212, Washington, D.C. 20007. Phone: (202) 342-2574.

Embassy of the Republic of Cameroon, 2349 Massachusetts Ave., N.W., Washington, D.C. 20008. Phone: (202) 265-8790 to 8794.

Embassy of Canada, 501 Pennsylvania Ave., N.W., Washington, D.C. 20001. Phone: (202) 682-1740.

Embassy of the Republic of Cape Verde, 3415 Massachusetts Ave., N.W., Washington, D.C. 20007. Phone: (202) 965-6820.

Embassy of Central African Republic, 1618 22nd St. N.W., Washington, D.C. 20008. Phone: (202) 483-7800, 7801.

Embassy of the Republic of Chad, 2002 R St., N.W., Washington, D.C. 20009. Phone: (202) 462-4009.

Embassy of Chile, 1732 Massachusetts Ave., N.W., Washington, D.C. 20036. Phone: (202) 785-1746.

Embassy of the People's Republic of China, 2300 Connecticut Ave., N.W., Washington, D.C. 20008. Phone: (202) 328-2500, 2501 and 2502.

Embassy of Colombia, 2118 Leroy Pl., N.W., Washington, D.C. 20008. Phone: (202) 387-8338.

Embassy of the Federal and Islamic Republic of Comoros, c/o Permanent Mission of the Federal and Islamic Republic of Comoros to the United Nations, 336 E. 45th St., 2nd floor, New York, N.Y. 10017. Phone: (212) 972-8010.

Embassy of the People's Republic of the Congo, 4891 Colorado Ave., N.W., Washington, D.C. 20011. Phone: (202) 726-5500, 5501.

Embassy of Costa Rica, 1825 Connecticut Ave.,

N.W., Suite 211, Washington, D.C. 20009. Phone: (202) 234-2945 to 2947.

Embassy of the Republic of Cote d'Ivoire, 2424 Massachusetts Ave., N.W., Washington, D.C. 20008. Phone: (202) 797-0300.

Embassy of the Republic of Cyprus, 2211 R St. N.W., Washington, D.C. 20008. Phone: (202) 462-5772.

Embassy of the Czechoslovak Socialist Republic, 3900 Linnean Ave., N.W., Washington, D.C. 20008. Phone: (202) 363-6315, 6316.

Cuban Interests Section, 2630 and 2639 16th St., N.W., Washington, D.C. 20009. Phone: (202) 797-8518 to 8520, 8609 and 8610.

Royal Danish Embassy, 3200 Whitehaven St., N.W., Washington, D.C. 20008. Phone: (202) 234-4300.

Embassy of the Republic of Djibouti, 1430 K St. N.W., Suite 600, Washington, D.C. 20005. Phone: (202) 347-0254.

Embassy of the Dominican Republic, 1715 22nd St., N.W., Washington, D.C. 20008. Phone: (202) 332-6280.

Embassy of Ecuador, 2535 15th St., N.W., Washington, D.C. 20009. Phone: (202) 234-7200.

Embassy of the Arab Republic of Egypt, 2310 Decatur Pl., N.W., Washington, D.C. 20008. Phone: (202) 232-5400.

Embassy of El Salvador, 2308 California St., N.W., Washington, D.C. 20008. Phone: (202) 265-3480 to 3482.

Embassy of Equatorial Guinea, 801 Second Ave., Suite 1403, New York, N.Y. 10017. Phone: (212) 599-1523.

Legation of Estonia, 9 Rockefeller Plaza, New York, N.Y. 10020. Phone: (212) 247-1450.

Embassy of Ethiopia, 2134 Kalorama Rd., N.W., Washington, D.C. 20008. Phone: (202) 234-2281, 2282.

Embassy of Fiji, 2233 Wisconsin Ave., N.W., Suite 240, Washington, D.C. 20007. Phone: (202) 337-8320.

Embassy of Finland, 3216 New Mexico Ave., N.W., Washington, D.C. 20016. Phone: (202) 363-2430.

Embassy of France, 4101 Reservoir Rd., N.W., Washington, D.C. 20007. Phone: (202) 944-6000.

Embassy of the Gabonese Republic, 2034 20th St., N.W., Washington, D.C. 20009. Phone: (202) 797-1000.

Embassy of The Gambia, 1030 15th St., N.W., Suite 720, Washington, D.C. 20005. Phone: (202) 842-1356, 1359.

Embassy of the German Democratic Republic, 1717 Massachusetts Ave., N.W., Washington, D.C., 20036. Phone: (202) 232-3134.

Embassy of the Federal Republic of Germany, 4645 Reservoir Rd., N.W., Washington, D.C. 20007. Phone: (202) 298-4000.

Embassy of Ghana, 3512 International Dr., N.W., Washington, D.C. 20008 (202) 686-4520.

Embassy of Greece, 2221 Massachusetts Ave., N.W., Washington, D.C. 20008. Phone (202) 939-5800.

Embassy of Grenada, 1701 New Hampshire Ave., N.W., Washington, D.C. 20009. Phone: (202) 265-2561.

Embassy of Guatemala, 2220 R St., N.W., Washington, D.C. 20008. Phone: (202) 745-4952 to 4954.

Embassy of the Republic of Guinea, 2112 Leroy Pl., N.W., Washington, D.C. 20008. Phone: (202) 483-9420.

Embassy of the Republic of Guinea-Bissau, c/o of the Permanent Mission of the Republic of Guinea-Bissau, 211 E. 43rd St., Suite 604, New York, N.Y. 10017. Phone: (212) 661-3977.

Embassy of Guyana, 2490 Tracy Pl., N.W. Washington, D.C. 20008. Phone: (202) 265-6900/6903.

Embassy of Haiti, 2311 Massachusetts Ave., N.W., Washington, D.C. 20008. Phone: (202) 332-4090 to 4092.

Apostolic Nunciature of the Holy See, 3339 Massachusetts Ave., N.W., Washington, D.C. 20008. Phone: (202) 333-7121.

Embassy of Honduras, 3007 Tilden St., N.W., Washington, D.C. 20008. Phone: (202) 966-7702, 2604, 5008, 4596.

Embassy of the Republic of Hungary, 3910 Shoemaker St., N.W., Washington, D.C. 20008. Phone: (202) 362-6730.

Embassy of Iceland, 2022 Connecticut Ave., N.W., Washington, D.C. 20008. Phone: (202) 265-6653 to 6655.

Embassy of India, 2107 Massachusetts Ave., N.W., Washington, D.C. 20008. Phone: (202) 939-7000.

Embassy of the Republic of Indonesia, 2020 Massachusetts Ave., N.W., Washington, D.C. 20036. Phone: (202) 775-5200.

Embassy of the Republic of Iraq, 1801 P St., N.W., Washington, D.C. 20036. Phone: (202) 483-7500.

Embassy of Ireland, 2234 Massachusetts Ave., N.W., Washington, D.C. 20008. Phone: (202) 462-3939.

Embassy of Israel, 3514 International Dr., N.W., Washington, D.C. 20008. Phone: (202) 364-5500.

Embassy of Italy, 1601 Fuller St., N.W., Washington, D.C. 20009. Phone: (202) 328-5500.

Embassy of Jamaica, 1850 K St., N.W., Suite 355, Washington, D.C. 20006. Phone: (202) 452-0660.

Embassy of Japan, 2520 Massachusetts Ave., N.W., Washington, D.C. 20008. Phone: (202) 939-6700.

Embassy of the Hashemite Kingdom of Jordan, 3504 International Dr., N.W., Washington, D.C. 20008. Phone: (202) 966-2664.

Embassy of Kenya, 2249 R St., N.W., Washington, D.C. 20008. Phone: (202) 387-6101.

Embassy of Korea, 2370 Massachusetts Ave., N.W., Washington, D.C. 20008. Phone: (202) 939-5600.

Embassy of the State of Kuwait, 2940 Tilden St., N.W., Washington, D.C. 20008. Phone: (202) 966-0702.

Embassy of the Lao People's Democratic Republic, 2222 S St., N.W., Washington, D.C. 20008. Phone: (202) 332-6416, 6417.

Legation of Latvia, 4325 17th St., N.W., Washington, D.C. 20011. Phone: (202) 726-8213/8214.

Embassy of Lebanon, 2560 28th St., N.W., Washington, D.C. 20008. Phone: (202) 939-6300.

Embassy of the Kingdom of Lesotho, 2511 Massachusetts Ave., N.W., Washington, D.C. 20008. Phone: (202) 797-5534 to 5536.

Embassy of Liberia, 5201 16th St., N.W., Washington, D.C. 20011. Phone: (202) 291-0761.

Legation of Lithuania, 2622 16th St., N.W., Washington, D.C. Phone: (202) 234-5860/2639.

Embassy of Luxembourg, 2200 Massachusetts Ave., N.W., Washington, D.C. 20008. Phone: (202) 265-4171.

Embassy of the Democratic Republic of Madagascar, 2374 Massachusetts Ave., N.W., Washington, D.C. 20008. Phone: (202) 265-5525/5526.

Malawi Embassy, 2408 Massachusetts Ave., N.W., Washington, D.C. 20008. Phone: (202) 797-1007.

Embassy of Malaysia, 2401 Massachusetts Ave., N.W., Washington, D.C. 20008. Phone: (202) 328-2700.

Embassy of the Republic of Mali, 2130 R St., N.W., Washington, D.C. 20008. Phone: (202) 332-2249; (202) 939-8950.

Embassy of Malta, 2017 Connecticut Ave., N.W., Washington, D.C. 20008. Phone: (202) 462-3611/3612.

Embassy of the Republic of the Marshall Islands, 1901 Pennsylvania Ave., N.W., Washington, D.C. 20006. Phone: (202) 233-4952.

Embassy of the Islamic Republic of Mauritania, 2129 Leroy Pl., N.W., Washington, D.C. 20008. Phone: (202) 232-5700.

Embassy of Mauritius, 4301 Connecticut Ave., N.W., Suite 134, Washington, D.C. 20008. Phone: (202) 244-1491/1492.

Embassy of Mexico, 1911 Pennsylvania Ave., N.W., 20006, Washington, D.C. Phone: (202) 728-1600.

Embassy of the Federated States of Micronesia, 706 G St. S.E. 20003, Washington, D.C. Phone: (202) 544-2460.

Embassy of the Mongolian People's Republic, Washington, D.C. Phone: (202) 483-3176.

Embassy of Morocco, 1601 21st St., N.W., Washington, D.C. 20009. Phone: (202) 462-7979 to 7982.

Embassy of the People's Republic of Mozambique, 1990 M St., N.W., Suite 570, Washington, D.C. 20036. Phone: (202) 293-7146.

Embassy of the Union of Myanmar, 2300 S St., N.W., Washington, D.C. 20008. Phone: (202) 332-9044/9045.

Royal Nepalese Embassy, 2131 Leroy Pl., N.W., Washington, D.C. 20008. Phone: (202) 667-4550.

Embassy of the Netherlands, 4200 Linnean Ave., N.W., Washington, D.C. 20008. Phone: (202) 244-5300; after 6 p.m. (202) 244-5304.

Embassy of New Zealand, 37 Observatory Circle, N.W., Washington, D.C. 20008. Phone: (202) 328-4800.

Embassy of Nicaragua, 1627 New Hampshire Ave., N.W., Washington, D.C. 20009. Phone: (202) 939-6570.

Embassy of the Republic of Niger, 2204 R St., N.W., Washington, D.C. 20008. Phone: (202) 483-4224 to 4227.

Embassy of the Federal Republic of Nigeria, 2201 M St., N.W., Washington, D.C. 20037. Phone: (202) 822-1500.

Royal Norwegian Embassy, 2720 34th St., N.W., Washington, D.C. 20008. Phone: (202) 333-6000.

Embassy of the Sultanate of Oman, 2342 Massachusetts Ave., N.W., Washington, D.C. 20008. Phone: (202) 387-1980 to 1982.

Embassy of Pakistan, 2315 Massachusetts Ave., N.W., Washington, D.C. 20008. Phone: (202) 939-6200.

Embassy of Panama, 2862 McGill Terrace, N.W., Washington, D.C. 20008. Phone: (202) 483-1407.

Embassy of Papua New Guinea, 1330 Connecticut Ave., N.W., Suite 350, Washington, D.C. 20036. Phone: (202) 659-0856.

Embassy of Paraguay, 2400 Massachusetts Ave., N.W., Washington, D.C. 20008. Phone: (202) 483-6960 to 6962.

Embassy of Peru, 1700 Massachusetts Ave., N.W., Washington, D.C. 20036. Phone: (202) 833-9860 to 9869.

Embassy of the Philippines, 1617 Massachusetts Ave., N.W., Washington, D.C. 20036. Phone: (202) 483-1414.

Embassy of the Polish People's Republic, 2640 16th St., N.W., Washington, D.C. 20009. Phone: (202) 234-3800 to 3802.

Embassy of Portugal, 2125 Kalorama Rd., N.W., Washington, D.C. 20008. Phone: (202) 328-8610.

Embassy of the State of Qatar, 600 New Hampshire Ave., N.W., Suite 1180, Washington, D.C. 20037. Phone: (202) 338-0111.

Embassy of Romania, 1607 23rd St., N.W., Washington, D.C. 20008. Phone: (202) 232-4747.

Embassy of the Republic of Rwanda, 1714 New Hampshire Ave., N.W., Washington, D.C. 20009. Phone: (202) 232-2882.

Embassy of Saint Kitts and Nevis, 2501 M St., N.W., Suite 540, Washington, D.C. 20037. Phone: (202) 833-3550.

Embassy of Saint Lucia, 2100 M St., N.W., Suite 309, Washington, D.C. 20037. Phone: (202) 463-7378/7379.

Embassy of São Tomé and Príncipe, 801 Second Ave., Suite 1504, New York, N.Y. 10017 (temporary address). Phone: (212) 697-4211.

Embassy of Saudi Arabia, 601 New Hampshire Ave., N.W., Washington, D.C. 20037. Phone: (202) 342-3800.

Embassy of the Republic of Senegal, 2112 Wyoming Ave., N.W., Washington, D.C. 20008. Phone: (202) 234-0540/0541.

Embassy of the Republic of Seychelles, c/o Permanent Mission of the Republic of Seychelles to the United Nations, 820 Second Ave., Suite 900F, New York, N.Y. 10017. Phone: (212) 687-9766/9767.

Embassy of Sierra Leone, 1701 19th St., N.W., Washington, D.C. 20009. Phone: (202) 939-9261.

Embassy of the Republic of Singapore, 1824 R St., N.W., Washington, D.C. 20009. Phone: (202) 667-7555.

Embassy of the Somali Democratic Republic, 600 New Hampshire Ave., N.W., Suite 710, Washington, D.C. 20037. Phone: (202) 342-1575.

Embassy of South Africa, 3051 Massachusetts Ave., N.W., Washington, D.C. 20008. Phone: (202) 232-4400, 3451 to 3453.

Embassy of Spain, 2700 15th St., N.W., Washington, D.C. 20009. Phone: (202) 265-0190/0191.

Embassy of the Democratic Socialist Republic of Sri Lanka, 2148 Wyoming Ave., N.W., Washington, D.C. 20008. Phone: (202) 483-4025 to 4028.

Embassy of the Republic of the Sudan, 2210 Massachusetts Ave., N.W., Washington, D.C. 20008. Phone: (202) 338-8565 to 8570.

Embassy of the Republic of Suriname, 4301 Connecticut Ave., N.W., Suite 108, Washington, D.C. 20008. Phone: (202) 244-7488, 7490 to 7492.

Embassy of the Kingdom of Swaziland, 3400 International Drive N.W. 20008, Washington, D.C. Phone: (202) 362-6683/6685.

Embassy of Sweden, 600 New Hampshire Ave., N.W., Suite 1200, Washington, D.C. 20037. Phone: (202) 944-5600.

Embassy of Switzerland, 2900 Cathedral Ave., N.W., Washington, D.C. 20008. Phone: (202) 745-7900.

Embassy of the Syrian Arab Republic, 2215 Wyoming Ave., N.W., Washington, D.C. 20008. Phone: (202) 232-6313.

Embassy of the United Republic of Tanzania, 2139 R St., N.W., Washington, D.C. 20008. Phone: (202) 939-6125.

Embassy of Thailand, 2300 Kalorama Rd., N.W., N.W., Washington, D.C. 20008. Phone: (202) 483-7200.

Embassy of the Republic of Togo, 2208 Massachusetts Ave., N.W., Washington, D.C. 20008. Phone: (202) 234-4212/4213.

Embassy of Trinidad and Tobago, 1708 Massachusetts Ave., N.W., Washington, D.C. 20036. Phone: (202) 467-6490.

Embassy of Tunisia, 1515 Massachusetts Ave., N.W., Washington, D.C. 20005. Phone: (202) 862-1850.

Embassy of the Republic of Turkey, 1714 Massachusetts Ave. N.W., Washington, D.C. 20036. Phone: (202) 659-8200.

Embassy of the Republic of Uganda, 5909 16th St., N.W., Washington, D.C. 20011. Phone: (202) 726-7100 to 7102.

Embassy of the Union of Soviet Socialist Republics, 1125 16th St., N.W., Washington, D.C. 20036. Phone: (202) 628-7551/8548.

Embassy of the United Arab Emirates, 600 New Hampshire Ave., N.W., Suite 740, Washington, D.C. 20037. Phone: (202) 338-6500.

United Kingdom of Great Britain & Northern Ireland British Embassy, 3100 Massachusetts Ave., N.W., Washington, D.C. 20008. Phone: (202) 462-1340.

Embassy of Uruguay, 1918 F St., N.W., Washington D.C. 20006. Phone: (202) 331-1313 to 1316.

Embassy of Venezuela, 2445 Massachusetts Ave., N.W., Washington, D.C. 20008. Phone: (202) 797-3800.

Embassy of Western Samoa, 1155 15th St. N.W., # 510, Washington, D.C. 20005. Phone: (202) 833-1743.

Embassy of the Yemen Arab Republic, 600 New Hampshire Ave., N.W., Suite 840, Washington, D.C. 20037. Phone: (202) 965-4760/4761.

Embassy of the Socialist Federal Republic of Yugoslavia, 2410 California St., N.W., Washington, D.C. 20008. Phone: (202) 462-6566.

Embassy of the Republic of Zaire, 1800 New Hampshire Ave., N.W., Washington, D.C. 20009. Phone: (202) 234-7690/7691.

Embassy of the Republic of Zambia, 2419 Massachusetts Ave., N.W., Washington, D.C. 20008. Phone: (202) 265-9717 to 9721.

Embassy of Zimbabwe, 2852 McGill Terrace, N.W., Washington, D.C. 20008. Phone: (202) 332-7100.

Diplomatic Personnel To and From the U.S.

Country	U.S. Representative to[1]	Rank	Representative from[2]	Rank
Afghanistan	—	—	Mr. Miagol	Min.
Algeria	Christopher W. S. Ross	Amb.	Abderrahmane Bensid	Amb.
Antigua and Barbuda	(Vacancy)	Amb.	Edmund Hawkins Lake	Amb.
Argentina	Terance A. Todman	Amb.	Guido Jose Maria Di Tella	Amb.
Australia	Melvin F. Sembler	Amb.	Michael John Cook	Amb.
Austria	(Vacancy)	Amb.	Friedrich Hoess	Amb.
Bahamas	Chic Hecht	Amb.	Margaret E. McDonald	Amb.
Bahrain	Charles W. Hostler	Amb.	Ghazi Mohamed Algosaibi	Amb.
Bangladesh	Willard A. DePree	Amb.	A.H.S. Ataul Karim	Amb.
Barbados	(Vacancy)	Amb.	Sir William Douglas	Amb.
Belgium	Maynard W. Gitman	Amb.	Herman Dehennin	Amb.
Belize	Robert G. Rich, Jr.	Amb.	Edward A. Laing	Amb.
Benin	Harriet W. Isom	Amb.	Theophile Nata	Amb.
Bolivia	Robert S. Gelbard	Amb.	Jorge Crespo-Velasco	Amb.
Botswana	(Vacancy)	Amb.	Botsweletse Kingsley Sebele	Amb.
Brazil	Richard H. Melton	Amb.	Marcilio Marques Moreira	Amb.
Brunei	Christopher H. Phillips	Amb.	Dato Paduka Haji Mohd Suni	Amb.
Bulgaria	Sol Polansky	Amb.	Velichko F. Velichkov	Amb.
Burkina Faso	David H. Shinn	Amb.	Paul-Désiré Kabore	Amb.
Burundi	Cynthia S. Perry	Amb.	Julien Kavakure	Amb.
Cameroon	Frances D. Cook	Amb.	Paul Pondi	Amb.
Canada	Edward N. Ney	Amb.	Derek H. Burney	Amb.
Cape Verde	Francis T. McNamara	Amb.	Jose Luis Fernandes Lopes	Amb.
Central African Republic	Daniel H. Simpson	Amb.	Jean-Pierre Sohahong-Kombet	Amb.
Chad	(Vacancy)	Amb.	Mahamat Ali Adoum	Amb.
Chile	Charles A. Gillespie Jr.	Amb.	Patricio Silva	Amb.
China	James R. Lilley	Amb.	Qizhen Zhu	Amb.
Colombia	Thomas E. McNamara	Amb.	Victor Mosquera	Amb.
Comoros	Howard K. Walker	Amb.	Amini Ali Moumin	Amb.
Congo, People's Republic of	Leonard G. Shurtleff	Amb.	Ikourou-Yoka	Cd'A.
Costa Rica	(Vacancy)	Amb.	Danilo Jimenez	Amb.
Cyprus	(Vacancy)	Amb.	Michael E. Sherifis	Amb.
Czechoslovakia	Shirley Temple Black	Amb.	Rita Klimova	Amb.
Denmark	Keith L. Brown	Amb.	Peter P. Dyvig	Amb.
Djibouti	Robert S. Barrett IV		Roble Olhaye	Amb.
Dominica	—	—	—	—

Country	U.S. Representatives to[1]	Rank	Representative from[2]	Rank
Dominican Republic	Paul D. Taylor	Amb.	Carlos A. Morales	Amb.
Ecuador	(Vacancy)	Amb.	Jaime Moncayo	Amb.
Egypt	Frank G. Wisner	Amb.	El Sayed Abdel Raouf El Reedy	Amb.
El Salvador	William G. Walker	Amb.	Miguel Angel Salaverria	Amb.
Equatorial Guinea	Chester E. Norris, Jr.	Amb.	Damaso Obiang Ndong	Amb.
Ethiopia	Robert G. Houdek	Cd'A.	Girma Amare	Consul.
Fiji	Evelyn I. H. Teegen	Amb.	Abdul H. Yusuf	Consul.
Finland	John G. Weinmann	Amb.	Jukka Valtasaari	Amb.
France	Walter J. P. Curley	Amb.	Jacques Andreani	Amb.
Gabon	Keith L. Wauchope	Amb.	Jean Robert Odzaga	Amb.
Gambia	(Vacancy)	Amb.	Ousman A, Sallah	Amb.
Germany (East)	Richard C. Barkley	Amb.	Dr. Gerhard Herder	Amb.
Germany (West)	Vernon A. Walters	Amb.	Juergen Ruhfus	Amb.
Ghana	Raymond C. Ewing	Amb.	Eric K. Otoo	Amb.
Greece	Michael G. Sotirhos	Amb.	Christo Zacharakis	Amb.
Grenada	Ford Cooper	Cd'A.	Albert O. Xavier	Amb.
Guatemala	Thomas F. Stroock	Amb.	John Schwank	Amb.
Guinea	(Vacancy)	Amb.	Moussa Sangare	Amb.
Guinea-Bissau	William H. Jacobsen, Jr.	Amb.	Alfredo Lopes Cabral	Amb.
Guyana	Theresa A. Tull	Amb.	Dr. Cedric Hilburn Grant	Amb.
Haiti	Alvin P. Adams, Jr.	Amb.	Louis Harold Joseph	Min.-Consl.
Holy See	Thomas P. Melady	Amb.	Most Rev. Pio Laghi	Pro-Nuncio
Honduras	Cresencio S. Arcos	Amb.	Jorge Ramon Hernandez-Alcerro	Amb.
Hungary	Mark Palmer	Amb.	Peter Varkonyi	Amb.
Iceland	Charles E. Cobb, Jr.	Amb.	Ingvi S. Ingvarsson	Amb.
India	William Clark, Jr.	Amb.	Lalit Mansingh	Min.
Indonesia	John C. Monjo	Amb.	Abdul Rachman Ramly	Amb.
Iraq	April C. Glaspie	Amb.	Dr. Mohamed Sadiq Al-Mashat	Amb.
Ireland	Richard A. Moore	Amb.	Padraic N. MacKernan	Amb.
Israel	William A. Brown	Amb.	Moshe Arad	Amb.
Italy	Peter F. Secchia	Amb.	Rinaldo Petrignani	Amb.
Ivory Coast	Kenneth L. Brown	Amb.	Charles Gomis	Amb.
Jamaica	Glen A. Holden	Amb.	Keith Johnson	Amb.
Japan	Michael H. Armacost	Amb.	Ryohei Murata	Amb.
Jordan	Roscoe S. Suddarth	Amb.	Hussein A. Hammami	Amb.
Kenya	Smith Hempstone, Jr.	Amb.	Denis D. Afande	Amb.
Korea, South	Donald P. Gregg	Amb.	Tong-Jin Park	Amb.
Kuwait	W. Nathaniel Howell	Amb.	Shaikh Saud Nasir Al-Sabah	Amb.
Laos	Charles B. Salmon, Jr.	Cd'A.	Phonsavanh Sipaseuth	3rd Secy.
Lebanon	John T. McCarthy	Amb.	Nassib S. Lahoud	Amb.
Lesotho	(Vacancy)	Amb.	W. T. Van Tonder	Amb.
Liberia	James K. Bishop	Amb.	Eugenia A. Wordsworth-Stevenson	Amb.
Luxembourg	Edward M. Rowell	Amb.	Andre Philippe	Amb.
Madagascar	Howard K. Walker	Amb.	Pierrot J. Rajaonarivelo	Amb.
Malawi	George A. Trail, III	Amb.	Robert Mbaya	Amb.
Malaysia	Paul M. Cleveland	Amb.	Albert S. Talalla	Amb.
Mali	Robert M. Pringle	Amb.	Mohamed Alhousseyni Toure	Amb.
Malta	Sally J. Novetzke	Amb.	Salv. J. Stellini	Amb.
Marshall Islands	Samuel B. Thomsen	Cd'A.	Wilfred I. Kendall	Amb.
Mauritania	William H. Twaddell	Amb.	Abdellah Ould Daddah	Amb.
Mauritius	Penne Percy Korth	Amb.	Chitmansing Jesseramsing	Amb.
Mexico	John D. Negroponte	Amb.	Gustavo Petricioli	Amb.
Morocco	E. Michael Ussery	Amb.	Ali Bengelloun	Amb.
Mozambique	Melissa F. Wells	Amb.	Valeriano Ferrao	Amb.
Myanmar (Burma)	Burton Levin	Amb.	U. Myo Aung	Amb.
Nepal	Julia Chang Bloch	Amb.	Mohan Man Sainju	Amb.
Netherlands	C. Howard Wilkins, Jr.	Amb.	Johan H. Meesman	Amb.
New Zealand	Della M. Newman	Amb.	Harold Huyton Francis	Amb.
Nicaragua	(Vacancy)	Amb.	Leonor de Huper	Min.-Consl.
Niger	Carl C. Cundiff	Amb.	Moumouni Adamou Djermakoye	Amb.
Nigeria	Lannon Walker	Amb.	Hamzat Ahmadu	Amb.
Norway	Loret Miller Ruppe	Amb.	Kjeld Vibe	Amb.
Oman	Richard W. Boehm	Amb.	Awadh Bader Al-Shanfari	Amb.
Pakistan	Robert B. Oakley	Amb.	Zulfigar Ali Khan	Amb.
Panama	Arthur H. Davis	Amb.	Eduardo Vallarino	Amb.
Papua New Guinea	Robert W. Farrand	Amb.	Margaret Taylor	Amb.
Paraguay	Timothy L. Towell	Amb.	Marcos Martinez Mendieta	Amb.
Peru	Anthony C.E. Quainton	Amb.	Cesar G. Atala	Amb.
Philippines	Nicholas Platt	Amb.	Emmanuel Pelaez	Amb.
Poland	John R. Davis, Jr.	Amb.	Jan Kinast	Amb.

Country	U.S. Representatives to[1]	Rank	Representative from[2]	Rank
Portugal	Everett Ellis Briggs	Amb.	Joao Eduardo M. Pereira Bastos	Amb.
Qatar	Mark G. Hambley	Amb.	Dr. Hamad Abdelaziz Al-Kawari	Amb.
Romania	Alan Green, Jr.	Amb.	Virgil Constantinescu	Amb.
Rwanda	Leonard H. O. Spearman, Sr.	Amb.	Aloys Uwimana	Amb.
Saint Kitts and Nevis	—		Erstein M. Edwards	Amb.
Saint Lucia	—		Dr. Joseph Edsel Edmunds	Amb.
Saudi Arabia	Charles W. Freeman, Jr.	Amb.	Prince Bandar Bin Sultan	Amb.
Senegal	George E. Moose	Amb.	Ibra Deguene Ka	Amb.
Seychelles	James Moran	Amb.	Marc R. Marengo	2nd Secy.
Sierra Leone	Johnny Young	Amb.	Dr. George Carew	Amb.
Singapore	Robert D. Orr	Amb.	Tommy T.B. Koh	Amb.
Solomon Islands	Robert W. Farrand	Amb.	—	—
Somalia	T. Frank Crigler	Amb.	Abdikarim Ali Omar	Amb.
South Africa	William L. Swing	Amb.	Piet G.J. Koornhof	Amb.
Spain	Joseph Zappala	Amb.	Jaime de Ojeda y Eiseley	Amb.
Sri Lanka	Marion V. Creekmore	Amb.	W. Susanta DeAlwis	Amb.
Sudan	James R. Cheek	Amb.	Abdalla Ahmed Abdalla	Amb.
Suriname	Richard C. Howland	Amb.	Willem A. Udenhout	Amb.
Swaziland	(Vacancy)	Amb.	Absalom Vusani Mamba	Amb.
Sweden	Charles E. Rednam	Amb.	Anders Ingmar Thunborg	Amb.
Switzerland	Joseph B. Gildenhorn	Amb.	Edouard Brunner	Amb.
Syria	Edward P. Djerejian	Amb.	Bushra Kanafani	Min.
Tanzania	Edward DeJarnette, Jr.	Amb.	Ali A. Karume	Min.
Thailand	Daniel A. O'Donohue	Amb.	Vitthya Vejjajiva	Amb.
Togo	Rush W. Taylor Jr.	Amb.	Ellom-Kodjo Schuppius	Amb.
Trinidad and Tobago	Charles A. Gargano	Amb.	Angus Albert Khan	Amb.
Tunisia	Robert H. Pelletreau, Jr.	Amb.	Dr. Abdelaziz Hamzaoui	Amb.
Turkey	Morton I. Abramowitz	Amb.	Nuzhet Kandemir	Amb.
Uganda	John A. Burroughs, Jr.	Amb.	Stephen Kapimpina Katenta-Apuli	Amb.
U.S.S.R.	Jack F. Matlock, Jr.	Amb.	Yuriy V. Dubinin	Amb.
United Arab Emirates	Edward S. Walker, Jr.	Amb.	Abdulla bin Zayed Al-Nahayyan	Amb.
United Kingdom	Henry E. Catto	Amb.	Sir Antony Acland	Amb.
Uruguay	Malcolm R. Wilkey	Amb.	Juan Podesta Pinon	Amb.
Venezuela	(Vacancy)	Amb.	Simon Alberto Consalvi	Amb.
Western Samoa	Della M. Newman	Amb.	Tuaopepe Fili Wendt	Amb.
Yemen Arab Republic	Charles F. Dunbar	Amb.	Mohsin A. Alaini	Amb.
Yugoslavia	Warren Zimmerman	Amb.	Dzevad Mujezinovic	Amb.
Zaire	William C. Harrop	Amb.	Kalimba Wa Katana, Mushobekwa	Amb.
Zambia	Jeffrey Davidow	Amb.	Dr. Paul J.F. Lusaka	Amb.
Zimbabwe	J. Steven Rhodes	Amb.	Stanislaus Garikai Chigwedere	Amb.

1. As of May 1990. 2. As of May 1990. NOTE: Amb.=Ambassador; Cd'A.=Charge d'Affaires; Secy.=Secretary; Consl.=Counselor; Min.=Minister; P.O.=Principal Officer. *Source:* U.S. Department of State.

Health Hints for the International Traveler

*Source: U.S. Department of Health and Human Services, Public Health Service,
Centers for Disease Control*

Introduction

This article includes practical information on how to avoid potential health problems. Some of these recommendations are common-sense precautions; others have been scientifically documented.

Personal and specific preventive measures against certain diseases may require advance planning and advice from a physician concerning immunization and prophylaxis. If more specific information is needed, travelers should contact their local health department or physician.

Travelers who take prescription medications should carry an adequate supply accompanied by a signed and dated statement from a physician; the statement should indicate the major health problems and dosage of such medications, to provide information for medical authorities in case of emergency. The traveler should take an extra pair of glasses or lens prescription, and a card, tag, or bracelet that identifies any physical condition that may require emergency care.

Medical Care

If medical care is needed abroad, travel agents or the American Embassy or Consulate can usually provide names of hospitals, physicians, or emergency medical service agencies. Prior to departure, travelers should contact their own insurance companies concerning their coverage.

WHO Blood Transfusion Guidelines

There is a growing public awareness of the AIDS epidemic, and a resulting concern about acquiring the AIDS virus through blood transfusion. Systematic screening of blood donations is not yet feasible in all developing countries. Requests have been made by persons planning international travels, to have their own blood, or blood from their home country, available to them in case of urgent need. These requests raise logistic, technical and ethical issues which are not easy to resolve. Ultimately, the safety of blood for such persons will depend upon the quality of blood transfusion services in the host country. The strengthening of these services is of the highest priority. While efforts are being made to achieve this end, other approaches are also needed.

Basic Principles:

1. Unexpected, emergency, blood transfusion is rarely required. It is needed only in situations of massive hemorrhage like severe trauma, gynecological and obstetric emergency, or gastrointestinal bleeding.

2. In many cases, resuscitation can be achieved by use of colloid or crystalloid plasma expanders[1] instead of blood.

3. Blood transfusion is not free of risk, even in the best of conditions. In most developing countries, the risk is increased by limited technical resources for screening blood donors for HIV infection and other diseases transmissible by blood.

4. The international shipment of blood for transfusion is practical only when handled by agreement between two responsible organizations, such as national blood transfusion services. This mechanism is not useful for emergency needs of individual patients and should not be attempted by private individuals or organizations not operating recognized blood programs.

Therefore:

1. There are no medical indications for travelers to take blood with them from their home country.

2. The limited storage period of blood and the need for special equipment negate the feasibility of independent blood banking for individual travelers or small groups.

3. Blood should be transfused only when absolutely indicated. This applies even more forcefully in those countries where screening of blood for transmissible diseases is not yet widely performed.

Proposed Options:

1. When urgent resuscitation is necessary, the use of plasma expanders rather than blood should always be considered.

2. In case of emergency need of blood, use of plasma expanders and urgent evacuation home may be the actions of choice.

3. When blood transfusion cannot be avoided, the attending physician should make every effort to ensure that the blood has been screened for transmissible diseases, including HIV.

4. International travelers should: (a) take active steps to minimize the risk of injury; (b) establish a plan for dealing with medical emergencies; (c) support the development within countries of safe and adequate blood supplies.

This information is taken from the WHO publication "World Health Organization Global Programme on AIDS: Blood transfusion guidelines for international travelers."

Motion Sickness

Travelers with a history of motion sickness or sea sickness can attempt to avoid symptoms by taking anti-motion-sickness pills or antihistaminics before departure.

Pregnant Women

The problems that a pregnant woman might encounter during international travel are basically the same problems that other international travelers have. These have to do with exposure to infectious diseases and availability of good medical care. There is the additional potential problem that air travel late in pregnancy might precipitate labor.

Potential health problems vary from country to country; therefore, if the traveler has specific questions, she should be advised to check with the embassy or local consulate general office of the country in question before traveling.

Disabled Travelers

The Airport Operators Council International, Incorporated, publishes "Access Travel: A Guide to Accessibility of Terminals." The 40-page guide lists design features, facilities, and services for handicapped persons in 472 airport terminals in over 50 countries. Single copies are available at no cost from the Architectural and Transportation Barriers Compliance Board. For a copy, you may write or call, ATBCB, 1111 18th Street, N.W., Suite 50, Washington, D.C. 20036-3894, (202) 653-7834.

Risks From Food and Drink

Contaminated food and drink are common sources for the introduction of infection into the body. Among the more common infections that travelers may acquire from contaminated food and drink are *Escherichia coli* infections, shigellosis or bacillary dysentery, giardiasis, cryptosporidiosis, and hepatitis A. Other less common infectious disease risks for travelers include typhoid fever and other salmonelloses, cholera, infections caused by rotaviruses and Norwalk-like viruses, and a variety of protozoan and helminth parasites (other than those that cause giardiasis and cryptosporidiosis). Many of the infectious diseases transmitted in food and water can also be acquired directly through the fecal-oral route.

Water

Water that has been adequately chlorinated, using minimum recommended water-works standards as practiced in the United States, will afford significant protection against viral and bacterial waterborne diseases. However, chlorine treatment alone, as used in the routine disinfection of water, may not kill some enteric viruses and the parasitic organisms that cause giardiasis and amebiasis. In areas where chlorinated tap water is not available, or where hygiene and sanitation are poor, travelers should be advised that only the following may be safe to drink:

1. Beverages, such as tea and coffee, made with boiled water.

2. Canned or bottled *carbonated* beverages, in-

Treatment of Water With Tincture of Iodine

Tincture of iodine (from medicine chest or first aid kit)	Drops* to be added per quart or liter	
	Clear water	Cold or cloudy water†
2%	5	10

*1 drop = 0.05 ml.
Let stand for 30 minutes.
Water is safe to use.
†Very turbid or very cold water may require prolonged contact time; let stand up to several hours prior to use, if possible.

cluding *carbonated* bottled water and soft drinks.
3. Beer and wine.

Where water may be contaminated, ice (or containers for drinking) also should be considered contaminated. Thus, in these areas ice should not be used in beverages. If ice has been in contact with containers used for drinking, the containers should be thoroughly cleaned, preferably with soap and hot water, after the ice has been discarded.

It is safer to drink directly from a can or bottle of a beverage than from a questionable container. However, water on the outside of cans or bottles of beverages might be contaminated. Therefore, wet cans or bottles should be dried before being opened, and surfaces which are contacted directly by the mouth in drinking should first be wiped clean. Where water may be contaminated, travelers should avoid brushing their teeth with tap water.

Treatment of Water

Boiling is by far the most reliable method to make water of uncertain purity safe for drinking. Water should be brought to a vigorous boil and allowed to cool to room temperature—do not add ice. At very high altitudes, for an extra margin of safety, boil for several minutes or use chemical disinfection. Adding a pinch of salt to each quart, or pouring the water several times from one container to another will improve the taste.

Chemical disinfection with iodine is an alternative method of water treatment when it is not feasible to boil water. Two well-tested methods for disinfection with iodine are the use of tincture of iodine (*See* table), and the use of tetraglycine hydroperiodide tablets (Globaline, Potable-Aqua, Coghlan's,[2] etc.). The tablets are available from pharmacies and sporting goods stores. The manufacturer's instructions should be followed. If water is cloudy, the number of tablets should be doubled; if water is extremely cold, an attempt should be made to warm the water, and the recommended contact time should be increased to achieve reliable disinfection. Cloudy water should be strained through a clean cloth into a container to remove any sediment or floating matter, and then the water should be treated with heat or iodine. Chlorine, in various forms, has also been used for chemical disinfection. However, its germicidal activity varies greatly with pH, temperature, and organic content of the water to be purified, and is less reliable than iodine.

There are a variety of portable filters currently on the market which according to the manufacturers' data will provide safe drinking water. Although the iodide-impregnated resins and the microstrainer type filters will kill and/or remove many micoorganisms, there are very few published reports in the scientific literature dealing both with the methods used and the results of the tests employed to evaluate the efficacy of these filters against water-borne pathogens. Until there is sufficient independent verification of the efficacy of these filters, The Centers for Disease Control makes no recommendation regarding their use.

As a last resort, if no source of safe drinking water is available or can be obtained, tap water that is uncomfortably hot to touch is usually safe. After allowing such hot water to cool to room temperature in a thoroughly cleaned container, it may be used for brushing teeth, as well as for drinking.

Food

To avoid illness, food should be selected with care. All raw food is subject to contamination. Particularly in areas where hygiene and sanitation are inadequate, the traveler should be advised to avoid salads, uncooked vegetables, unpasteurized milk and milk products such as cheese, and to eat only food that has been cooked and is still hot, or fruit that has been peeled by the traveler. Undercooked and raw meat, fish, and shellfish may carry various intestinal pathogens.

The easiest way to guarantee a safe food source for an infant less than 6 months of age is to have the child breast-feed. If the infant has already been weaned from the breast, formula prepared from commercial powder and boiled water is the safest and most practical food.

Some species of fish and shellfish can contain poisonous biotoxins, even when well cooked. The most common type of fish poisoning in travelers is ciguatera fish poisoning. Red snapper, grouper, barracuda, amberjack, sea bass, and a wide range of tropical reef fish contain the toxin at unpredictable times. The potential for ciguatera poisoning exists in all subtropical and tropical insular areas of the West Indies, Pacific and Indian Oceans where the implicated fish species are consumed. ☐

1. See World Health Organization documents LAB/81,5: "Use of plasma volume substitutes and plasma in developing countries," for further details, and WHO/GPA/INF/88.5 "Guidelines for Treatment of Acute Blood Loss."

2. Use of trade names is for identification only and does not imply endorsement by the Public Health Service or the U.S. Department of Health and Human Services.

Travel Tips

The booklet, *Your Trip Abroad,* contains some valuable information on loss and theft of a passport as well as other travel tips. To obtain a copy, write to the Superintendent of Documents, U.S. Government Printing Office, Washington, D.C. 20402 and ask for publication #8969. The single copy price is $1.

Countries Requiring AIDS Testing for Entry

Source: United States Department of State, Bureau of Consular Affairs

Country	Required For	U.S. Test Accepted
Antigua and Barbuda	University students and those suspected of having the HIV virus	Yes
Australia	All applicants for permanent residence over age 16. Students or temporary residents staying over 12 months may be tested	Yes
Bahrain	Foreign workers in certain job categories, i.e. hotel staff, hairdressers, etc. are screened after entry	N/A
Belize	Certain foreign workers	Yes, if within past 3 months
British Virgin Islands	Intending immigrants and those wishing to work must certify they are free of HIV virus	Yes
Bulgaria	Certain groups of foreigners, such as university students who stay for prolonged periods of time. Holders of tourist passports staying over 30 days may be tested.	No
China, People's Republic of	Those staying more than 6 months	Yes, under certain conditions[1]
Costa Rica	All applicants for temporary residence permits or permanent resident status and students or tourists staying over 90 days	No
Cuba	All foreigners, excluding tourists	No, testing required to be performed on arrival
Cyprus	All foreigners working as entertainers	Yes
Czechoslovakia	Students and workers from countries with high number of AIDS cases	No, testing required to be performed on arrival
Egypt	All foreigners working or studying in Egypt for more than 60 days	No
German Democratic Republic	Those staying over 3 months	Yes, under certain conditions[1]
Germany, Federal Republic of (Bavaria only)	Applicants for residence permits staying over 180 days	No
Greece	Students receiving Greek Government scholarships and performing artists working in Greece	No
India	All students and anyone over 18 staying over 1 year, excluding accredited journalists, and those working in foreign missions	Yes, under certain conditions[1]
Iraq	Anyone staying over 5 days (Failure to have the test done will result in a fine of $1600)	Yes, under certain conditions[1] (To avoid $330 fee have test done in the U.S. before departing)
Kuwait	Those planning to obtain a residence permit for longer than 6 months	Yes
Libya	Those seeking residence permits, excluding official visitors	Yes
Marshall Islands, Republic of the	Although not yet implemented, legislation will require those planning to reside over 6 months to be tested	Yes under certain conditions[1]
Mongolia	Students and anyone planning to stay longer than 3 months must be tested before arrival	Yes
Pakistan	Those staying for over 1 year must certify they are free of HIV	Yes
Papua New Guinea	Those planning to work	Yes
Philippines	Applicants for permanent resident visas	Yes
Qatar	Those going to work or study	Yes, if within six months
Saudi Arabia	Applicants for work permits only	Yes
South Africa	Mine workers	Yes
St. Kitts and Nevis	Applicants for work permits or residency	Yes
Syria	Students and others staying over 1 year	Yes, under certain conditions[1]
Taiwan	Proposed legislation would require those planning to reside over 3 months to be tested	Uncertain
Thailand	Those suspected or confirmed of carrying AIDS are refused entry	Not Applicable
Union of Soviet Socialist Republics	Those staying more than 3 months	Yes
United Arab Emirates	Applicants for work or residence permits	No, testing required to be performed on arrival

1. Check with embassy in Washington, D.C. for detailed requirements. Data as of March 6, 1990.

State and City Tourism Offices

The following is a selected list of state, tourism offices. Where a toll-free 800 number is available, it is given.
However, the numbers are subject to change.

ALABAMA
Bureau of Tourism & Travel
532 S. Perry St.
Montgomery, AL 36104
205-242-4169 or
1-800-ALABAMA

ALASKA
Alaska Division of Tourism
P.O. Box E
Juneau, AK 99811
907-465-2010

ARIZONA
Arizona Office of Tourism
1100 West Washington
Phoenix, AZ 85007
602 542-TOUR

ARKANSAS
Arkansas Department of Parks
and Tourism
1 Capitol Mall
Little Rock, AR 72201
501-682-7777 or
1-800-NATURAL
(both in and out of state)

CALIFORNIA
California Office of Tourism
Department of Commerce
1121 L Street
Suite 103
Sacramento, CA 95814
Write or phone for free 200-
page Guide Information
Packet: (Outside Calif.) 800-
862-2543

COLORADO
Colorado Tourism Board
1625 Broadway, Suite 1700
Denver, CO 80202
303-592-5410
For a vacation planning kit,
call Toll-free 1-800-433-2656

CONNECTICUT
Tourism Promotion Service
CT Dept. of Economic Develop-
ment
865 Brook Street
Rocky Hill, CT 06067-3405
203-258-4290 or 800-CT
BOUND (nationwide, except
CT)

DELAWARE
Delaware Tourism Office
Delaware Development Office
99 Kings Highway
P.O. Box 1401
Dover, DE 19903
302-736-4271 or
1-800-441-8846
(out of state)

DISTRICT OF COLUMBIA
Washington Convention and
Visitors Association
1212 New York Ave., NW
Washington, D.C. 20005
202-789-7000

FLORIDA
Department of Commerce Visitors Inquiry
126 Van Buren St.
Tallahassee, FL 32399-2000
904-487-1462

GEORGIA
Tourist Division
P.O. Box 1776
Atlanta, GA 30301
404-656-3590

HAWAII
Hawaii Visitors Bureau
2270 Kalakaua Ave., Suite 801
Honolulu, HI 96815
808-923-1811

IDAHO
Department of Commerce
700 W. State St.
Second Floor
Boise, ID 83720
208-334-2470 or
1-800-635-7820

ILLINOIS
Illinois Department of Commerce and Community Af-
fairs, Bureau of Tourism
620 East Adams Street
Springfield, IL 62701
217-782-7139

INDIANA
Indiana Dept. of Commerce
Tourism & Film Development
Division
One North Capitol
Suite 700
Indianapolis, IN 46204-2288
317-232-8860 or
1-800-289-ONIN

IOWA
Iowa Department of Economic
Development
Division of Tourism
200 East Grand Avenue
Des Moines, IA 50309
515-281-3100

KANSAS
Travel & Tourism Development
Division
Department of Commerce
400 W. 8th St., 5th Floor
Topeka, KS 66603
913-296-2009

KENTUCKY
Department of Travel Develop-
ment
Capital Plaza Tower
Frankfort, KY 40601
502-564-4930 or
1-800-225-TRIP
(Continental United States and
provinces of Ontario and
Quebec, Canada)

LOUISIANA
Office of Tourism
P.O. Box 94291
Baton Rouge, LA 70804-9291
504-342-8119 or
1-800-33GUMBO

MAINE
Maine Publicity Bureau
97 Winthrop St., P.O. Box
2300
Hallowell, ME 04347-2300
207-289-2423

MARYLAND
Office of Tourism Development
217 E. Redwood St.
Baltimore, MD 21202
301-333-6611

MASSACHUSETTS
Office of Travel and Tourism
100 Cambridge St., 13th Floor
Boston, MA 02202
617-727-3201

MICHIGAN
Travel Bureau
Department of Commerce
P.O. Box 30226
Lansing, MI 48909
1-800-5432-YES

MINNESOTA
Minnesota Office of Tourism
375 Jackson St.
250 Skyway Level
Farm Credit Services Bldg.
St. Paul, MN 55101
612-296-5029 or
1-800-657-3700

MISSISSIPPI
Department of Economic and
Community Development
Tourism Development
P.O. Box 22825
Jackson, MS 39205
601-359-3297 or
1-800-647-2290

MISSOURI
Missouri Division of Tourism
Truman State Office Bldg.
301 W. High St.

Average Daily Temperatures (°F) in Tourist Cities

	January		April		July		October	
Location	High	Low	High	Low	High	Low	High	Low
U.S. CITIES (See Weather and Climate Section)								
CANADA								
Ottawa	21	3	51	31	81	58	54	37
Quebec	18	2	45	29	76	57	51	37
Toronto	30	16	50	34	79	59	56	40
Vancouver	41	32	58	40	74	54	57	44
MEXICO								
Acapulco	85	70	87	71	89	75	88	74
Mexico City	66	42	78	52	74	54	70	50
OVERSEAS								
Australia (Sydney)	78	65	71	58	60	46	71	56
Austria (Vienna)	34	26	57	41	75	59	55	44
Bahamas (Nassau)	77	65	81	69	88	75	85	73
Bermuda (Hamilton)	68	58	71	59	85	73	79	69
Brazil (Rio de Janeiro)	84	73	80	69	75	63	77	66
Denmark (Copenhagen)	36	29	50	37	72	55	53	42
Egypt (Cairo)	65	47	83	57	96	70	86	65
France (Paris)	42	32	60	41	76	55	59	44
Germany (Berlin)	35	26	55	38	74	55	55	41
Greece (Athens)	54	42	67	52	90	72	74	60
Hong Kong	64	56	75	67	87	78	81	73
India (Calcutta)	80	55	97	76	90	79	89	74
Italy (Rome)	54	39	68	46	88	64	73	53
Israel (Jerusalem)	55	41	73	50	87	63	81	59
Japan (Tokyo)	47	29	63	46	83	70	69	55
Nigeria (Lagos)	88	74	89	77	83	74	85	74
Netherlands (Amsterdam)	40	34	52	43	69	59	56	48
Puerto Rico (San Juan)	81	67	84	69	87	74	87	73
South Africa (Cape Town)	78	60	72	53	63	45	70	52
Spain (Madrid)	47	33	64	44	87	62	66	48
United Kingdom (London)	44	35	56	40	73	55	58	44
United Kingdom (Edinburgh)	43	35	50	39	65	52	53	44
U.S.S.R. (Moscow)	21	9	47	31	76	55	46	34
Venezuela (Caracas)	75	56	81	60	78	61	79	61
Yugoslavia (Belgrade)	37	27	64	45	84	61	65	47

P.O. Box 1055
Jefferson City, MO 65102
314-751-4133

MONTANA
Travel Montana
Deer Lodge, MT 59722
406-444-2654 or
    1-800-541-1447

NEBRASKA
Dept. of Economic Development
Division of Travel and Tourism
301 Centennial Mall South
P.O. Box 94666
Lincoln, NE 68509
402-471-3796 or
    1-800-742-7595 (in state)
    or 1-800-228-4307 (out of
    state)

NEVADA
Commission on Tourism
Capitol Complex
Carson City, NV 89710
1-800-Nevada-8

NEW HAMPSHIRE
Office of Vacation Travel
P.O. Box 856
Concord, NH 03301
603-271-2666
or for recorded weekly events,
    ski conditions, foliage reports
    1-800-258-3608
Toll free number is for north-
    east only

NEW JERSEY
Division of Travel and Tourism
CN-826
Trenton, NJ 08625
609-292-2470 or
    1-800-JERSEY-7

NEW MEXICO
New Mexico Tourism
& Travel Division ED & TD
Room 119, Joseph M. Montoya
    Bldg.
1100 St. Francis Dr.
Santa Fe, NM 87503
505-827-0291 or
    1-800-545-2040

NEW YORK
Division of Tourism
1 Commerce Plaza
Albany, NY 12245
Toll free from anywhere in the
    U.S. and its territorial posses-
    sions 1-800-225-5697.
From Canada, call (518)
    474-4116

NORTH CAROLINA
Travel and Tourism Division
Department of Commerce
430 North Salisbury St.
Raleigh, NC 27611
919-733-4171 or 1-800-VISIT
    NC

NORTH DAKOTA
North Dakota Tourism
    Promotion
Liberty Memorial Building
Capitol Grounds
Bismarck, ND 58505
701-224-2525 or
    1-800-437-2077 (out
    of state)
1-800-537-8879 (Canada)

OHIO
Ohio Division of Travel and
Tourism
P.O. Box 1001
Columbus, OH 43266-0101
614-466-8844 (Business Of-
fice)
1-800-BUCKEYE (National
Toll-Free Travel Hotline)

OKLAHOMA
Oklahoma Tourism and Recre-
ation Dept.
Literature Distribution Center
P.O. Box 60000
Oklahoma City, OK 73146
405-521-2409 (In Oklahoma
City area) or nationwide at
1-800-652-6552

OREGON
Tourism Division
Oregon Economic Development
775 Summer St. NE
Salem, OR 97310
503-373-1270 or
1-800-547-7842 (Out of
state); 1-800-543-8838 (in-
state)

PENNSYLVANIA
Bureau of Travel Marketing
453 Forum Building
Harrisburg, PA 17120
717-787-5453 (Business Office)
1-800-VISIT PA, ext. 257
(To order single free copy of
PA Travel Guide)

RHODE ISLAND
Rhode Island Tourism Division
7 Jackson Walkway
Providence, RI 02903
401-277-2601 or
1-800-556-2484

SOUTH CAROLINA
South Carolina Division of
Tourism
Box 71
Columbia, SC 29202
803-734-0235

SOUTH DAKOTA
Department of Tourism
Capitol Lake Plaza
Pierre, South Dakota 57501
605-773-3301 or
1-800-843-1930 out of SD;
1-800-952-2217 in SD

TENNESSEE
Department of Tourist Develop-
ment
P.O. Box 23170
Nashville, TN 37202
615-741-2158

TEXAS
Travel Information Services
State Highway Department
P.O. Box 5064
Austin, TX 78763-5064
512-483-3705

UTAH
Utah Travel Council
Council Hall, Capitol Hill
Salt Lake City, UT 84114
801-538-1030

VERMONT
Agency of Development and
Community Affairs
Travel Division
134 State St.
Montpelier, VT 05602
802-828-3236

VIRGINIA
Virginia Division of Tourism
1021 East Cary St.
Richmond, VA 23219
804-786-4484

WASHINGTON
Washington State Dept. of
Trade and Economic Develop-
ment
101 General Administration
Bldg.
AX-13
Olympia, WA 98504-0613
206-753-5630

WASHINGTON, D.C.
See District of Columbia

WEST VIRGINIA
Dept. of Commerce
State Capitol Complex
Charleston, WV 25305
304-348-2286 or
1-800-CALL-WVA

WISCONSIN
Department of Development
Division of Tourism Develop-
ment
Box 7606
Madison, WI 53707
Toll free in WI and neighbor
states 1-800-372-2737
others: 608-266-2161
Nationally 1-800-432-TRIP

WYOMING
Wyoming Travel Commission
I-25 at College Drive
Cheyenne, WY 82002-0660
307-777-7777 or
1-800-225-5996

Travel Advisories

Source: U.S. Department of State.

The Department of State tries to alert American travelers to adverse conditions abroad—including violence—through the travel advisory program. In consultation with our embassies and consulates overseas, and various bureaus of the Department of State, the Office of Overseas Citizens Services in the Bureau of Consular Affairs issues travel advisories about conditions in specific countries. Advisories generally do not pertain to isolated international terrorist incidents since these can occur anywhere and at any time. Some mention conditions of political or civil unrest which could pose a threat to personal safety.

There are only a few advisories in effect which advise avoiding all travel to a particular country because of a high incidence of terrorism within the region or because a long-term problem exists. Most of the security-related advisories do not recommend against travel to an entire country but suggest avoiding specific areas within a country where unrest is endemic.

Ask about current travel advisories for specific countries at any of the 13 regional U.S. passport agencies and at U.S. Embassies and consulates abroad. Travel advisories are also widely disseminated to interested organizations, travel associations, and airlines.

Travel advisories may be heard by calling (24 hours a day) the State Department's Citizens Emergency Center at 202-647-5225. □

Passport Travel Tips

The American Society of Travel Agents (ASTA) advises those traveling abroad to photocopy important pages in their passports, especially the pages featuring their photos and passport numbers, and dates and places of issue. Also copy those pages containing visas of countries you plan to visit.

In the case of a lost passport, U.S. embassies will usually accept photocopies as proof that you actually possess a passport. Losing a passport abroad can be a time-consuming and expensive process to replace.

Keep a list of your credit cards and other important numbers (driver's license, traveler's cheques) in a separate location from your cards in case they are lost. □

Road Mileages Between U.S. Cities[1]

Cities	Birmingham	Boston	Buffalo	Chicago	Cleveland	Dallas	Denver
Birmingham, Ala.	—	1,194	947	657	734	653	1,318
Boston, Mass.	1,194	—	457	983	639	1,815	1,991
Buffalo, N.Y.	947	457	—	536	192	1,387	1,561
Chicago, Ill.	657	983	536	—	344	931	1,050
Cleveland, Ohio	734	639	192	344	—	1,205	1,369
Dallas, Tex.	653	1,815	1,387	931	1,205	—	801
Denver, Colo	1,318	1,991	1,561	1,050	1,369	801	—
Detroit, Mich.	754	702	252	279	175	1,167	1,301
El Paso, Tex.	1,278	2,358	1,928	1,439	1,746	625	652
Houston, Tex.	692	1,886	1,532	1,092	1,358	242	1,032
Indianapolis, Ind.	492	940	510	189	318	877	1,051
Kansas City, Mo.	703	1,427	997	503	815	508	616
Los Angeles, Calif.	2,078	3,036	2,606	2,112	2,424	1,425	1,174
Louisville, Ky.	378	996	571	305	379	865	1,135
Memphis, Tenn.	249	1,345	965	546	773	470	1,069
Miami, Fla.	777	1,539	1,445	1,390	1,325	1,332	2,094
Minneapolis, Minn.	1,067	1,402	955	411	763	969	867
New Orleans, La.	347	1,541	1,294	947	1,102	504	1,305
New York, N.Y.	983	213	436	840	514	1,604	1,780
Omaha, Neb.	907	1,458	1,011	493	819	661	559
Philadelphia, Pa.	894	304	383	758	432	1,515	1,698
Phoenix, Ariz.	1,680	2,664	2,234	1,729	2,052	1,027	836
Pittsburgh, Pa.	792	597	219	457	131	1,237	1,411
St. Louis, Mo.	508	1,179	749	293	567	638	871
Salt Lake City, Utah	1,805	2,425	1,978	1,458	1,786	1,239	512
San Francisco, Calif.	2,385	3,179	2,732	2,212	2,540	1,765	1,266
Seattle, Wash.	2,612	3,043	2,596	2,052	2,404	2,122	1,373
Washington, D.C.	751	440	386	695	369	1,372	1,635

Cities	Detroit	El Paso	Houston	Indianapolis	Kansas City	Los Angeles	Louisville
Birmingham, Ala.	754	1,278	692	492	703	2,078	378
Boston, Mass.	702	2,358	1,886	940	1,427	3,036	996
Buffalo, N.Y.	252	1,928	1,532	510	997	2,606	571
Chicago, Ill.	279	1,439	1,092	189	503	2,112	305
Cleveland, Ohio	175	1,746	1,358	318	815	2,424	379
Dallas, Tex.	1,167	625	242	877	508	1,425	865
Denver, Colo.	1,310	652	1,032	1,051	616	1,174	1,135
Detroit, Mich.	—	1,696	1,312	290	760	2,369	378
El Paso, Tex.	1,696	—	756	1,418	936	800	1,443
Houston, Tex.	1,312	756	—	1,022	750	1,556	981
Indianapolis, Ind.	290	1,418	1,022	—	487	2,096	114
Kansas City, Mo.	760	936	750	487	—	1,609	519
Los Angeles, Calif.	2,369	800	1,556	2,096	1,609	—	2,128
Louisville, Ky.	378	1,443	981	114	519	2,128	—
Memphis, Tenn.	756	1,095	586	466	454	1,847	396
Miami, Fla.	1,409	1,957	1,237	1,225	1,479	2,757	1,111
Minneapolis, Minn.	698	1,353	1,211	600	466	2,041	716
New Orleans, La.	1,101	1,121	365	839	839	1,921	725
New York, N.Y.	671	2,147	1,675	729	1,216	2,825	785
Omaha, Neb.	754	1,015	903	590	204	1,733	704
Philadelphia, Pa.	589	2,065	1,586	647	1,134	2,743	703
Phoenix, Ariz.	1,986	402	1,158	1,713	1,226	398	1,749
Pittsburgh, Pa.	288	1,778	1,395	360	847	2,456	416
St. Louis, Mo.	529	1,179	799	239	255	1,864	264
Salt Lake City, Utah	1,721	877	1,465	1,545	1,128	728	1,647
San Francisco, Calif.	2,475	1,202	1,958	2,299	1,882	403	2,401
Seattle, Wash.	2,339	1,760	2,348	2,241	1,909	1,150	2,355
Washington, D.C.	526	1,997	1,443	565	1,071	2,680	601

1. These figures represent estimates and are subject to change.

Road Mileages Between U.S. Cities

Cities	Memphis	Miami	Minneapolis	New Orleans	New York	Omaha	Philadelphia
Birmingham, Ala.	249	777	1,067	347	983	907	894
Boston, Mass.	1,345	1,539	1,402	1,541	213	1,458	304
Buffalo, N.Y.	965	1,445	955	1,294	436	1,011	383
Chicago, Ill.	546	1,390	411	947	840	493	758
Cleveland, Ohio	773	1,325	763	1,102	514	819	432
Dallas, Tex.	470	1,332	969	504	1,604	661	1,515
Denver, Colo.	1,069	2,094	867	1,305	1,780	559	1,698
Detroit, Mich.	756	1,409	698	1,101	671	754	589
El Paso, Tex.	1,095	1,957	1,353	1,121	2,147	1,015	2,065
Houston, Tex.	586	1,237	1,211	365	1,675	903	1,586
Indianapolis, Ind.	466	1,225	600	839	729	590	647
Kansas City, Mo.	454	1,479	466	839	1,216	204	1,134
Los Angeles, Calif.	1,847	2,757	2,041	1,921	2,825	1,733	2,743
Louisville, Ky.	396	1,111	716	725	785	704	703
Memphis, Tenn.	—	1,025	854	401	1,134	658	1,045
Miami, Fla.	1,025	—	1,801	892	1,328	1,683	1,239
Minneapolis, Minn.	854	1,801	—	1,255	1,259	373	1,177
New Orleans, La.	401	892	1,255	—	1,330	1,043	1,241
New York, N.Y.	1,134	1,328	1,259	1,330	—	1,315	93
Omaha, Neb.	658	1,683	373	1,043	1,315	—	1,233
Philadelphia, Pa.	1,045	1,239	1,177	1,241	93	1,233	
Phoenix, Ariz.	1,464	2,359	1,644	1,523	2,442	1,305	2,360
Pittsburgh, Pa.	810	1,250	876	1,118	386	932	304
St. Louis, Mo.	295	1,241	559	696	968	459	886
Salt Lake City, Utah	1,556	2,571	1,243	1,743	2,282	967	2,200
San Francisco, Calif.	2,151	3,097	1,997	2,269	3,036	1,721	2,954
Seattle, Wash.	2,363	3,389	1,641	2,606	2,900	1,705	2,818
Washington, D.C.	902	1,101	1,114	1,098	229	1,170	140

Cities	Phoenix	Pittsburgh	St. Louis	Salt Lake City	San Francisco	Seattle	Washington
Birmingham, Ala.	1,680	792	508	1,805	2,385	2,612	751
Boston, Mass.	2,664	597	1,179	2,425	3,179	3,043	440
Buffalo, N.Y.	2,234	219	749	1,978	2,732	2,596	386
Chicago, Ill.	1,729	457	293	1,458	2,212	2,052	695
Cleveland, Ohio	2,052	131	567	1,786	2,540	2,404	369
Dallas, Tex.	1,027	1,237	638	1,239	1,765	2,122	1,372
Denver, Colo.	836	1,411	871	512	1,266	1,373	1,635
Detroit, Mich.	1,986	288	529	1,721	2,475	2,339	526
El Paso, Tex.	402	1,778	1,179	877	1,202	1,760	1,997
Houston, Tex.	1,158	1,395	799	1,465	1,958	2,348	1,443
Indianapolis, Ind.	1,713	360	239	1,545	2,299	2,241	565
Kansas City, Mo.	1,226	847	255	1,128	1,882	1,909	1,071
Los Angeles, Calif.	398	2,456	1,864	728	403	1,150	2,680
Louisville, Ky.	1,749	416	264	1,647	2,401	2,355	601
Memphis, Tenn.	1,464	810	295	1,556	2,151	2,363	902
Miami, Fla.	2,359	1,250	1,241	2,571	3,097	3,389	1,101
Minneapolis, Minn.	1,644	876	559	1,243	1,997	1,641	1,114
New Orleans, La.	1,523	1,118	696	1,743	2,269	2,626	1,098
New York, N.Y.	2,442	386	968	2,282	3,036	2,900	229
Omaha, Neb.	1,305	932	459	967	1,721	1,705	1,178
Philadelphia, Pa.	2,360	304	886	2,200	2,954	2,818	140
Phoenix, Ariz.		2,073	1,485	651	800	1,482	2,278
Pittsburgh, Pa.	2,073	—	599	1,899	2,653	2,517	241
St. Louis, Mo.	1,485	599	—	1,383	2,137	2,164	836
Salt Lake City, Utah	651	1,899	1,383	—	754	883	2,110
San Francisco, Calif.	800	2,653	2,137	754	—	817	2,864
Seattle, Wash.	1,482	2,517	2,164	883	817	—	2,755
Washington, D.C.	2,278	241	836	2,110	2,864	2,755	—

Air Distances Between U.S. Cities in Statute Miles

Cities	Birmingham	Boston	Buffalo	Chicago	Cleveland	Dallas	Denver
Birmingham, Ala.	—	1,052	776	578	618	581	1,095
Boston, Mass.	1,052	—	400	851	551	1,551	1,769
Buffalo, N. Y.	776	400	—	454	173	1,198	1,370
Chicago, Ill.	578	851	454	—	308	803	920
Cleveland, Ohio	618	551	173	308	—	1,025	1,227
Dallas, Tex.	581	1,551	1,198	803	1,025	—	663
Denver, Colo.	1,095	1,769	1,370	920	1,227	663	—
Detroit, Mich.	641	613	216	238	90	999	1,156
El Paso, Tex.	1,152	2,072	1,692	1,252	1,525	572	557
Houston, Tex.	567	1,605	1,286	940	1,114	225	879
Indianapolis, Ind.	433	807	435	165	263	763	1,000
Kansas City, Mo.	579	1,251	861	414	700	451	558
Los Angeles, Calif.	1,802	2,596	2,198	1,745	2,049	1,240	831
Louisville, Ky.	331	826	483	269	311	726	1,038
Memphis, Tenn.	217	1,137	803	482	630	420	879
Miami, Fla.	665	1,255	1,181	1,188	1,087	1,111	1,726
Minneapolis, Minn.	862	1,123	731	355	630	862	700
New Orleans, La.	312	1,359	1,086	833	924	443	1,082
New York, N. Y.	864	188	292	713	405	1,374	1,631
Omaha, Neb.	732	1,282	883	432	739	586	488
Philadelphia, Pa.	783	271	279	666	360	1,299	1,579
Phoenix, Ariz.	1,456	2,300	1,906	1,453	1,749	887	586
Pittsburgh, Pa.	608	483	178	410	115	1,070	1,320
St. Louis, Mo.	400	1,038	662	262	492	547	796
Salt Lake City, Utah	1,466	2,099	1,699	1,260	1,568	999	371
San Francisco, Calif.	2,013	2,699	2,300	1,858	2,166	1,483	949
Seattle, Wash.	2,082	2,493	2,117	1,737	2,026	1,681	1,021
Washington, D.C.	661	393	292	597	306	1,185	1,494

Cities	Detroit	El Paso	Houston	Indianapolis	Kansas City	Los Angeles	Louisville
Birmingham, Ala.	641	1,152	567	433	579	1,802	331
Boston, Mass.	613	2,072	1,605	807	1,251	2,596	826
Buffalo, N. Y.	216	1,692	1,286	435	861	2,198	483
Chicago, Ill.	238	1,252	940	165	414	1,745	269
Cleveland, Ohio	90	1,525	1,114	263	700	2,049	311
Dallas, Tex.	999	572	225	763	451	1,240	726
Denver, Colo.	1,156	557	879	1,000	558	831	1,038
Detroit, Mich.	—	1,479	1,105	240	645	1,983	316
El Paso, Tex.	1,479	—	676	1,264	839	701	1,254
Houston, Tex.	1,105	676	—	865	644	1,374	803
Indianapolis, Ind.	240	1,264	865	—	453	1,809	107
Kansas City, Mo.	645	839	644	453	—	1,356	480
Los Angeles, Calif.	1,983	701	1,374	1,809	1,356	—	1,829
Louisville, Ky.	316	1,254	803	107	480	1,829	—
Memphis, Tenn.	623	976	484	384	369	1,603	320
Miami, Fla.	1,152	1,643	968	1,024	1,241	2,339	919
Minneapolis, Minn.	543	1,157	1,056	511	413	1,524	605
New Orleans, La.	939	983	318	712	680	1,673	623
New York, N. Y.	482	1,905	1,420	646	1,097	2,451	652
Omaha, Neb.	669	878	794	525	166	1,315	580
Philadelphia, Pa.	443	1,836	1,341	585	1,038	2,394	582
Phoenix, Ariz.	1,690	346	1,017	1,499	1,049	357	1,508
Pittsburgh, Pa.	205	1,590	1,137	330	781	2,136	344
St. Louis, Mo.	455	1,034	679	231	238	1,589	242
Salt Lake City, Utah	1,492	689	1,200	1,356	925	579	1,402
San Francisco, Calif.	2,091	995	1,645	1,949	1,506	347	1,986
Seattle, Wash.	1,938	1,376	1,891	1,872	1,506	959	1,943
Washington, D.C.	396	1,728	1,220	494	945	2,300	476

Source: National Geodetic Survey.

Air Distances Between U.S. Cities in Statute Miles

Cities	Memphis	Miami	Minne-apolis	New Orleans	New York	Omaha	Phila-delphia
Birmingham, Ala.	217	665	862	312	864	732	783
Boston, Mass.	1,137	1,255	1,123	1,359	188	1,282	271
Buffalo, N. Y.	803	1,181	731	1,086	292	883	279
Chicago, Ill.	482	1,188	355	833	713	432	666
Cleveland, Ohio	630	1,087	630	924	405	739	360
Dallas, Tex.	420	1,111	862	443	1,374	586	1,299
Denver, Colo.	879	1,726	700	1,082	1,631	488	1,579
Detroit, Mich.	623	1,152	543	939	482	669	443
El Paso, Tex.	976	1,643	1,157	983	1,905	878	1,836
Houston, Tex.	484	968	1,056	318	1,420	794	1,341
Indianapolis, Ind.	384	1,024	511	712	646	525	585
Kansas City, Mo.	369	1,241	413	680	1,097	166	1,038
Los Angeles, Calif.	1,603	2,339	1,524	1,673	2,451	1,315	2,394
Louisville, Ky.	320	919	605	623	652	580	582
Memphis, Tenn.	—	872	699	358	957	529	881
Miami, Fla.	872	—	1,511	669	1,092	1,397	1,019
Minneapolis, Minn.	699	1,511	—	1,051	1,018	290	985
New Orleans, La.	358	669	1,051	—	1,171	847	1,089
New York, N. Y.	957	1,092	1,018	1,171	—	1,144	83
Omaha, Neb.	529	1,397	290	847	1,144	—	1,094
Philadelphia, Pa.	881	1,019	985	1,089	83	1,094	—
Phoenix, Ariz.	1,263	1,982	1,280	1,316	2,145	1,036	2,083
Pittsburgh, Pa.	660	1,010	743	919	317	836	259
St. Louis, Mo.	240	1,061	466	598	875	354	811
Salt Lake City, Utah	1,250	2,089	987	1,434	1,972	833	1,925
San Francisco, Calif.	1,802	2,594	1,584	1,926	2,571	1,429	2,523
Seattle, Wash.	1,867	2,734	1,395	2,101	2,408	1,369	2,380
Washington, D.C.	765	923	934	966	205	1,014	123

Cities	Phoenix	Pitts-burgh	St. Louis	Salt Lake City	San Francisco	Seattle	Wash-ington
Birmingham, Ala.	1,456	608	400	1,466	2,013	2,082	661
Boston, Mass.	2,300	483	1,038	2,099	2,699	2,493	393
Buffalo, N. Y.	1,906	178	662	1,699	2,300	2,117	292
Chicago, Ill.	1,453	410	262	1,260	1,858	1,737	597
Cleveland, Ohio	1,749	115	492	1,568	2,166	2,026	306
Dallas, Tex.	887	1,070	547	999	1,483	1,681	1,185
Denver, Colo.	586	1,320	796	371	949	1,021	1,494
Detroit, Mich.	1,690	205	455	1,492	2,091	1,938	396
El Paso, Tex.	346	1,590	1,034	689	995	1,376	1,728
Houston, Tex.	1,017	1,137	679	1,200	1,645	1,891	1,220
Indianapolis, Ind.	1,499	330	231	1,356	1,949	1,872	494
Kansas City, Mo.	1,049	781	238	925	1,506	1,506	945
Los Angeles, Calif.	357	2,136	1,589	579	347	959	2,300
Louisville, Ky.	1,508	344	242	1,402	1,986	1,943	476
Memphis, Tenn.	1,263	660	240	1,250	1,802	1,867	765
Miami, Fla.	1,982	1,010	1,061	2,089	2,594	2,734	923
Minneapolis, Minn.	1,280	743	466	987	1,584	1,395	934
New Orleans, La.	1,316	919	598	1,434	1,926	2,101	966
New York, N. Y.	2,145	317	875	1,972	2,571	2,408	205
Omaha, Neb.	1,036	836	354	833	1,429	1,369	1,014
Philadelphia, Pa.	2,083	259	811	1,925	2,523	2,380	123
Phoenix, Ariz.	—	1,828	1,272	504	653	1,114	1,983
Pittsburgh, Pa.	1,828	—	559	1,668	2,264	2,138	192
St. Louis, Mo.	1,272	559	—	1,162	1,744	1,724	712
Salt Lake City, Utah	504	1,668	1,162	—	600	701	1,848
San Francisco, Calif.	653	2,264	1,744	600	—	678	2,442
Seattle, Wash.	1,114	2,138	1,724	701	678	—	2,329
Washington, D.C.	1,983	192	712	1,848	2,442	2,329	—

Source: National Geodetic Survey.

Air Distances Between World Cities in Statute Miles

Cities	Berlin	Buenos Aires	Cairo	Calcutta	Cape Town	Caracas	Chicago
Berlin	—	7,402	1,795	4,368	5,981	5,247	4,405
Buenos Aires	7,402	—	7,345	10,265	4,269	3,168	5,598
Cairo	1,795	7,345	—	3,539	4,500	6,338	6,129
Calcutta	4,368	10,265	3,539	—	6,024	9,605	7,980
Cape Town, South Africa	5,981	4,269	4,500	6,024	—	6,365	8,494
Caracas, Venezuela	5,247	3,168	6,338	9,605	6,365	—	2,501
Chicago	4,405	5,598	6,129	7,980	8,494	2,501	—
Hong Kong	5,440	11,472	5,061	1,648	7,375	10,167	7,793
Honolulu, Hawaii	7,309	7,561	8,838	7,047	11,534	6,013	4,250
Istanbul	1,078	7,611	768	3,638	5,154	6,048	5,477
Lisbon	1,436	5,956	2,363	5,638	5,325	4,041	3,990
London	579	6,916	2,181	4,947	6,012	4,660	3,950
Los Angeles	5,724	6,170	7,520	8,090	9,992	3,632	1,745
Manila	6,132	11,051	5,704	2,203	7,486	10,620	8,143
Mexico City	6,047	4,592	7,688	9,492	8,517	2,232	1,691
Montreal	3,729	5,615	5,414	7,607	7,931	2,449	744
Moscow	1,004	8,376	1,803	3,321	6,300	6,173	4,974
New York	3,965	5,297	5,602	7,918	7,764	2,132	713
Paris	545	6,870	1,995	4,883	5,807	4,736	4,134
Rio de Janeiro	6,220	1,200	6,146	9,377	3,773	2,810	5,296
Rome	734	6,929	1,320	4,482	5,249	5,196	4,808
San Francisco	5,661	6,467	7,364	7,814	10,247	3,904	1,858
Shanghai, China	5,218	12,201	5,183	2,117	8,061	9,501	7,061
Stockholm	504	7,808	2,111	4,195	6,444	5,420	4,278
Sydney, Australia	10,006	7,330	8,952	5,685	6,843	9,513	9,272
Tokyo	5,540	11,408	5,935	3,194	9,156	8,799	6,299
Warsaw	320	7,662	1,630	4,048	5,958	5,517	4,667
Washington, D.C.	4,169	5,218	5,800	8,084	7,901	2,059	597

Cities	Hong Kong	Honolulu	Istanbul	Lisbon	London	Los Angeles	Manila
Berlin	5,440	7,309	1,078	1,436	579	5,724	6,132
Buenos Aires	11,472	7,561	7,611	5,956	6,916	6,170	11,051
Cairo	5,061	8,838	768	2,363	2,181	7,520	5,704
Calcutta	1,648	7,047	3,638	5,638	4,947	8,090	2,203
Cape Town, South Africa	7,375	11,534	5,154	5,325	6,012	9,992	7,486
Caracas, Venezuela	10,167	6,013	6,048	4,041	4,660	3,632	10,620
Chicago	7,793	4,250	5,477	3,990	3,950	1,745	8,143
Hong Kong	—	5,549	4,984	6,853	5,982	7,195	693
Honolulu, Hawaii	5,549	—	8,109	7,820	7,228	2,574	5,299
Istanbul	4,984	8,109	—	2,012	1,552	6,783	5,664
Lisbon	6,853	7,820	2,012	—	985	5,621	7,546
London	5,982	7,228	1,552	985	—	5,382	6,672
Los Angeles, Calif.	7,195	2,574	6,783	5,621	5,382	—	7,261
Manila	693	5,299	5,664	7,546	6,672	7,261	—
Mexico City	8,782	3,779	7,110	5,390	5,550	1,589	8,835
Montreal	7,729	4,910	4,789	3,246	3,282	2,427	8,186
Moscow	4,439	7,037	1,091	2,427	1,555	6,003	5,131
New York	8,054	4,964	4,975	3,364	3,458	2,451	8,498
Paris	5,985	7,438	1,400	904	213	5,588	6,677
Rio de Janeiro	11,021	8,285	6,389	4,796	5,766	6,331	11,259
Rome	5,768	8,022	843	1,161	887	6,732	6,457
San Francisco	6,897	2,393	6,703	5,666	5,357	347	6,967
Shanghai, China	764	4,941	4,962	6,654	5,715	6,438	1,150
Stockholm	5,113	6,862	1,348	1,856	890	5,454	5,797
Sydney, Australia	4,584	4,943	9,294	11,302	10,564	7,530	3,944
Tokyo	1,794	3,853	5,560	6,915	5,940	5,433	1,866
Warsaw	5,144	7,355	863	1,715	899	5,922	5,837
Washington, D.C.	8,147	4,519	5,215	3,562	3,663	2,300	8,562

Source: Encyclopaedia Britannica.

Air Distances Between World Cities in Statute Miles

Cities	Mexico City	Montreal	Moscow	New York	Paris	Rio de Janeiro	Rome
Berlin	6,047	3,729	1,004	3,965	545	6,220	734
Buenos Aires	4,592	5,615	8,376	5,297	6,870	1,200	6,929
Cairo	7,688	5,414	1,803	5,602	1,995	6,146	1,320
Calcutta	9,492	7,607	3,321	7,918	4,883	9,377	4,482
Cape Town, South Africa	8,517	7,931	6,300	7,764	5,807	3,773	5,249
Caracas, Venezuela	2,232	2,449	6,173	2,132	4,736	2,810	5,196
Chicago	1,691	744	4,974	713	4,134	5,296	4,808
Hong Kong	8,782	7,729	4,439	8,054	5,985	11,021	5,768
Honolulu	3,779	4,910	7,037	4,964	7,438	8,285	8,022
Istanbul	7,110	4,789	1,091	4,975	1,400	6,389	843
Lisbon	5,390	3,246	2,427	3,364	904	4,796	1,161
London	5,550	3,282	1,555	3,458	213	5,766	887
Los Angeles	1,589	2,427	6,003	2,451	5,588	6,331	6,732
Manila	8,835	8,186	5,131	8,498	6,677	11,259	6,457
Mexico City	—	2,318	6,663	2,094	5,716	4,771	6,366
Montreal	2,318	—	4,386	320	3,422	5,097	4,080
Moscow	6,663	4,386	—	4,665	1,544	7,175	1,474
New York	2,094	320	4,665	—	3,624	4,817	4,281
Paris	5,716	3,422	1,544	3,624	—	5,699	697
Rio de Janeiro	4,771	5,097	7,175	4,817	5,699	—	5,684
Rome	6,366	4,080	1,474	4,281	697	5,684	—
San Francisco	1,887	2,539	5,871	2,571	5,558	6,621	6,240
Shanghai, China	8,022	7,053	4,235	7,371	5,754	11,336	5,677
Stockholm	5,959	3,667	762	3,924	958	6,651	1,234
Sydney, Australia	8,052	9,954	9,012	9,933	10,544	8,306	10,136
Tokyo	7,021	6,383	4,647	6,740	6,034	11,533	6,135
Warsaw	6,365	4,009	715	4,344	849	6,467	817
Washington, D.C.	1,887	488	4,858	205	3,829	4,796	4,434

Cities	San Francisco	Shanghai	Stockholm	Sydney	Tokyo	Warsaw	Washington
Berlin	5,661	5,218	504	10,006	5,540	320	4,169
Buenos Aires	6,467	12,201	7,808	7,330	11,408	7,662	5,218
Cairo	7,364	5,183	2,111	8,952	5,935	1,630	5,800
Calcutta	7,814	2,117	4,195	5,685	3,194	4,048	8,084
Cape Town, South Africa	10,247	8,061	6,444	6,843	9,156	5,958	7,901
Caracas, Venezuela	3,904	9,501	5,420	9,513	8,799	5,517	2,059
Chicago	1,858	7,061	4,278	9,272	6,299	4,667	597
Hong Kong	6,897	764	5,113	4,584	1,794	5,144	8,147
Honolulu	2,393	4,941	6,862	4,943	3,853	7,355	4,519
Istanbul	6,703	4,962	1,348	9,294	5,560	863	5,215
Lisbon	5,666	6,654	1,856	11,302	6,915	1,715	3,562
London	5,357	5,715	890	10,564	5,940	899	3,663
Los Angeles	347	6,438	5,454	7,530	5,433	5,922	2,300
Manila	6,967	1,150	5,797	3,944	1,866	5,837	8,562
Mexico City	1,887	8,022	5,959	8,052	7,021	6,365	1,887
Montreal	2,539	7,053	3,667	9,954	6,383	4,009	488
Moscow	5,871	4,235	762	9,012	4,647	715	4,858
New York	2,571	7,371	3,924	9,933	6,740	4,344	205
Paris	5,558	5,754	958	10,544	6,034	849	3,829
Rio de Janeiro	6,621	11,336	6,651	8,306	11,533	6,467	4,796
Rome	6,240	5,677	1,234	10,136	6,135	817	4,434
San Francisco	—	6,140	5,361	7,416	5,135	5,841	2,442
Shanghai, China	6,140	—	4,825	4,899	1,097	4,951	7,448
Stockholm	5,361	4,825	—	9,696	5,051	501	4,123
Sydney, Australia	7,416	4,899	9,696	—	4,866	9,696	9,758
Tokyo	5,135	1,097	5,051	4,866	—	5,249	6,772
Warsaw	5,841	4,951	501	9,696	5,249	—	4,457
Washington, D.C.	2,442	7,448	4,123	9,758	6,772	4,457	—

Source: Encyclopaedia Britannica.

PERSONAL FINANCE

The ABCs of the New CDs

By Carole Gould

Certificates of deposit have been a favorite with security-minded investors for years, guaranteeing safety of principal while paying higher rates of interest than passbook savings accounts. True, they tied up your money for a certain period, but that meant you didn't have to think about it. CDs were simple, safe and predictable.

They're still safe, but everything else has changed. Since deregulation removed restrictions on the types of CDs that can be offered, the more creative financial institutions have flooded the market with new varieties. Finding the highest rate for the length of time you want to tie up your money isn't easy.

Oh, the plain-vanilla fixed-rate CD is still around. But now you can also find CDs with odd terms, variable rates, no penalties—even CDs linked to the stock market or sporting events. And banks, savings and loans and credit unions are no longer the sole sources; you can buy CDs from your stockbroker as well.

What's an investor to do?

For the understandably bewildered CD buyer, here are some of the more exotic CDs and how to find the best deal.

No-Penalty CDs. Federal law no longer requires financial institutions to charge for early withdrawals of principal. But many still deduct one to three months' interest on CDs of one year or less, three to six months' interest on longer terms.

Some no-penalty CDs let investors make withdrawals at any time. Others allow withdrawals at set intervals—every six months, say, or once a year. Caution: A no-penalty CD may pay a lower interest rate than the standard version.

Odd-Term CDs. Standard CDs come in six-month or one-year terms or longer. Today you can also find seven-, eight-, nine- and 15-month terms. In some cases the odd term allows a bank or S&L to advertise a higher rate. For example, a seven-month CD can be priced as much as a quarter-point higher than a standard six-month CD, even though the difference is just 30 days. Six- and seven-month CDs are commonly advertised in close proximity; read the fine print so you know what you're getting.

Some institutions use odd terms to market a tax angle. If a CD pays interest only at maturity, you can defer taxes on the interest until the following year. If you buy a seven-month CD in July 1991, for example, you'll pay no taxes on the interest until you file your 1992 tax return in April 1993. In other cases odd terms are just a gimmick; one bank sold an eight-month CD on 8/8/88.

The bottom line: Ask the representative how much money you will have in your pocket when the CD matures, then decide whether it pays to tie

up your funds for the extra time. So says Robert K. Heady, publisher of *100 Highest Yields*, a Florida newsletter that ranks the top-paying CD yields nationwide.

Variable-rate CDs. Sometimes known as adjustable-rate CDs, these are pegged to indexes like the prime rate or short-term Treasury bills. The buyer bets that rates will go up—but what goes up can also come down. When you choose a variable-rate CD, you give up the main virtue of the fixed-rate CD: a predictable return.

A case in point: At this writing the First New York Bank for Business is paying 1.5 points below the prime rate (10.5 percent) on its "floating rate CD." But because there is no minimum rate, or "floor," your return can plummet.

If you select a variable-rate CD, make sure the institution uses an independent index, and find out how often rates change.

Rising rate CDs. These pay a continually higher rate each time they are rolled over during a specified term. You would get a higher rate, for example, every six months over a period of three years.

Read the fine print: Banks and S&Ls may advertise only the highest rate paid during the final months. Don't be dazzled by the artificially inflated numbers; your real return will be lower because the CD earns less during the early months. Compute the average yield over the full term. Find out when the higher rates kick in—the earlier the better.

Stock-indexed CDs. This popular hybrid combines stock market performance with bank safety. Yields are tied to the market and there is no risk of principal. Like all CDs, the stock-indexed version is government-insured up to $100,000. The "bull" version lets you profit when the market rises; with the "bear" version, you bet on a market decline. As with any stock market investment, though, you gamble on your return.

Brokered CDs. Will you get a better deal on a CD from a bank or S&L or from a stockbroker? Buy from the broker, advises William E. Donoghue, publisher of *Donoghue's Moneyletter*, a consumer investment newsletter based in Holliston, Massachusetts. For one thing, brokers have access to CDs issued nationwide so you have more of a selection. For another, brokered CDs are traded on a secondary market, giving you the option to sell without penalty before the CD matures (some firms charge a small fee, however).

Carole Gould is the mutual funds columnist for the New York Times and writes on personal finance and investing for many national publications.

Sports/Election-linked CDs. Sports CDs were introduced by Skokie (Illinois) Federal Savings, which once issued a Super Bowl CD tied to the Chicago Bears. Since then, sports CDs have been indexed to baseball, basketball, football and hockey, to professional, college and even high school teams.

Some experts take a dim view of these types of innovations. "They're marketing gimmicks, not serious investment products because there's no way you can make a professional judgment," says Norberto Mehl, chairman of Banxquote Money Markets, a New York-based information service. Others, however, point out that the innovations help small and mid-sized institutions compete with the emerging super-regionals.

Here are some strategies from Robert Heady to help investors cope:

Ignore the promotional hype and ask the representative: "If I give you my money today, how much will I have—in dollars, not as a percentage, and after subtracting fees and charges—at the end of the term?"

Read the fine print to find the minimum deposit required to earn the advertised rate; some ads flaunt big numbers for deposits of $10,000 or $25,000; smaller accounts earn less.

Beware of high-rate promotional come-ons: Look at the average rate of the full term of the CD, not the rate for the last few months.

One final note: Compare each financial institution's real rate with rates offered by the competition. The old-fashioned, plain-vanilla CD just might pay more. □

Investing in U.S., Municipal, and Corporate Bonds

By Neal Ochsner

The typical investment you can make in a corporation, such as IBM or Exxon, is in either their stocks or bonds. Having stock is owning a small piece of the company; it is an equity investment. Stocks generally pay investors an annual share of whatever profit the company makes; this is called a dividend.

A bond is different. When you buy a bond, you are lending money to the bond issuer. In exchange, the issuer promises to pay a specific amount of interest on a regular basis (usually twice a year) for a specific period of time. At the end of that time, the bond matures and the issuer repays you the amount of money borrowed. That amount is the face amount of the bond.

As creditors of a company, bondholders must be paid any money due them before stockholders can be paid anything. As a result of this priority obligation, bonds issued by a company will always be a safer investment than stocks issued by the same company. While not all bonds are safer than all stocks, bonds generally offer a higher degree of safety than stocks.

The other major investment benefit of bonds is current income. Most bonds require regular payments of interest.

Although all bonds incorporate the basic features described above, there are a great many specific types of bonds with special features. The most important categories of bonds are bonds backed by the U.S. government, municipal bonds, and corporate bonds.

Excerpts from HOW TO MAKE BASIC INVESTMENT DECISIONS by Neal Oschsner part of the REAL LIFE, REAL ANSWERS series. Copyright © 1990 by Lee Simmons Associates. Reprinted by permission of Houghton Mifflin Co. REAL LIFE, REAL ANSWERS is a Registered Trademark of the John Hancock Mutual Life Insurance Company.

Bonds Backed by the U.S. Government

The only investments any government—federal, state, or local—offers to investors are various types of bonds. That makes sense, since you can't own a piece of a government, at least not any more than you do as a citizen. All securities you buy from a government are different ways of lending the government money. As with any bonds, the government pays interest on the loan and eventually repays the debt.

The money that the federal government takes in through taxes is not enough to pay for the expenses incurred each year by the government and all of its agencies and programs. The shortfall is well known to us as the budget deficit; it is financed by selling bonds.

The credit rating (the ability to repay bond debt) of an issuer is a major factor when you are considering investing in corporate bonds. This is not a problem with federal government bonds because the government has almost unlimited powers of taxation and the ability to print money. As a result, there is no way that the federal government can fail to repay its debt! Government bonds, therefore, have extremely high safety of principal and income.

There is a tax benefit associated with an investment in federal securities; you do not pay state taxes on the interest payments you receive. However, interest on U.S. bonds is subject to federal taxes.

The high level of safety and the tax benefits provided by federal securities mean that the government pays investors a lower current income and yield than do corporate bond issuers. Less risk in a security usually coincides with less return.

Different types of federal investments have distinct investment features. Some of these securities are purchased only by large pension funds, banks, and other financial institutions, but there are several that are purchased by individuals.

Treasury Bills

Treasury bills, or "T bills," as they are often known, are short-term securities. The smallest T bill has a denomination, or face value, of $10,000. There are weekly auctions for T bills with three-month and six-month maturities, and monthly auctions for one-year maturities. Instead of paying regular interest distributions to investors, T bills are sold on a "discount" basis. For example, suppose you buy a $10,000 one-year T bill paying 10 percent interest. The interest—$1,000—is deducted from the face amount when you purchase it. At maturity, you get the $10,000 face value.

The yield is thus higher than the stated interest on a T bill. In this case, you have invested $9,000 to get a $1,000 return, a yield of 11.1 percent on your investment. You can buy T bills through your broker or bank and pay a commission, or you can buy them by setting up a Treasury Direct account of your own. Call any Federal Reserve Bank for an application form.

If you buy direct, it is more difficult to sell a T bill before maturity. T bills bought through a broker or bank are traded on the over-the-counter (OTC) market and are highly liquid.

Treasury Notes and Bonds

T notes have maturities of one to ten years. T bonds are issued with maturities of at least ten years. The minimum face value for T notes with terms of less than four years is $5,000. Longer term T notes and T bonds may be bought in $1,000 denominations. Unlike T bills, which do not pay regular interest, both T notes and T bonds pay semiannual interest. However, the yield on these securities may be different from the stated interest rate. That is because, like T bills, T notes and T bonds are auctioned and priced on the basis of a discount off their face value.

For example, a T bond could pay 7.5 percent interest on a face value of $1,000, but have both a higher current return and yield to maturity if bought at a discount. Once again, the typical investor doesn't have to calculate exact yields. That information is in the newspaper or is available from your broker. What is important is that you have some idea of how these securities function so that you can ask your broker or financial adviser the right questions.

Series EE and HH Savings Bonds

Series EE Savings Bonds are bought at a 50 percent discount off their face value, and do not make regular interest distributions. They can be bought from the post office or commercial banks for as little as $25.

It costs $50 to buy a $100 Series EE Bond. This bond has an eight-year term, so an investor getting back $100 after eight years would get a 9 percent yield. However, if an investor has held the bond for at least five years, the return is set at 85 percent of the average yield of five-year Treasury notes and bonds, and not less than 6 percent. In recent years, the return has been greater than 9 percent.

The government has made Series EE Bonds especially attractive for families expecting future college expenses. Interest on bonds bought after January 1, 1990, will not be taxed if the bonds are used for tuition or other educational expenses.

Series HH Savings Bonds are for investors who require income. They are bought at their full face value (the minimum investment is $500), and they pay semiannual interest. Unlike T bills, notes and bonds, savings bonds are not transferable.

Ginnie Mae

The Government National Mortgage Association, known as GNMA or "Ginnie Mae," issues several different securities. All are backed by the government, but they are not exempt from state or local income tax. The purpose of Ginnie Mae is to provide money for Federal Housing Administration and Veterans Administration home mortgages. It raises the money to make these loans by issuing bonds. Each bond is backed by a large pool of individual home loans. If a few mortgages out of this pool were to default, there would still be enough money coming in from the other loans to make the necessary bond payments. The mortgage payments of individual home owners are therefore providing the money to pay interest to the holder of a Ginnie Mae security.

The government guarantees that the investor will get interest payments on time, and protects the investor in the event that too many mortgages go into default. Ginnie Mae investments are expensive; it costs $25,000 to get in the game unless you buy a mutual fund with this investment specialty. The problem with Ginnie Maes is that since home owners often repay their mortgages early, you cannot be sure how long a Ginnie Mae will last. Although the mortgages have 30-year terms, the average maturity of Ginnie Maes is 12 to 14 years. To make up for the uncertainty, yields are better than Treasuries.

Fannie Mae and Freddie Mac

The Federal National Mortgage Association (Fannie Mae) and Federal Home Loan Mortgage Corporation (Freddie Mac) are also government agencies involved in buying pools of home mortgages. However, these are "conventional" loans. The expense and uncertain maturities make them similar to Ginnie Maes, but there is a difference. The government guarantees interest payments for most Fannie Mae and Freddie Mac programs, but it does not always guarantee the principal. Each investment is in a well-diversified pool of mortgages, so the risk that you won't get all of your original investment back is not great, but it is higher than in the other securities we have discussed. To compensate for this risk, a higher interest rate is paid. With many different federal loan programs being sponsored by these agencies, it is important to understand the terms and features of the specific bonds you are considering.

Municipal Bonds

The federal government is not the only government that issues bonds in order to raise money for its needs. Municipal bonds, generally referred to as muni bonds or munis, are issued by states, territories, counties, cities, school districts, and other public agencies.

General obligation bonds are backed by the full credit of the issuer, while *revenue bonds* are paid for by a specific tax or revenues from a specific project, such as an airport or sewer system.

Just as the interest on U.S. securities is exempt from state and local taxes, the interest on muni bonds is exempt from federal income tax. In addition, most states do not charge state income tax to their own residents for the interest income on bonds issued by entities in that state. These tax benefits can significantly boost the effective yield to an investor. For example, a muni bond paying 8.5 percent interest to an investor in the 28 percent federal tax bracket is yielding the equivalent of an 11.8 percent pretax return. If the bond is from a municipal issuer in the investor's own state, and the combined state and federal tax liability is 35 percent, then the equivalent taxable yield rises to almost 13.1 percent.

There has been one exception to this interest exemption on muni bonds since the Tax Reform Act of 1986. Certain municipal bonds are considered "private activity bonds." Bonds in this category—intended to provide mortgage money for the development of new rental housing, commercial redevelopment, arenas and convention centers, and community parking—are fully taxable. Make it a point to ask about the tax status and treatment of a particular bond before you purchase it.

How Safe Is a Municipal Bond?

Most of the time municipal bonds are very safe investments. However, since no state or local authority has either the ability to print money or unlimited powers of taxation, municipal bonds are never quite as safe as federal obligations. And it isn't fair to assume that all municipal bonds are safer than corporate bonds; there are large corporations that have far greater assets than many municipalities. New York City stopped paying interest on its many bond issues for a while in the 1970s, and there was a serious, though unrealized, fear that the city would completely default.

Since it is not feasible for the individual investor to go around checking out the financial statements of various states and municipalities, a system has developed wherein bonds are given credit ratings.

The two largest credit-rating firms are Moody's and Standard & Poor's (often called "S&P"). Their principal business is to judge the ability of a bond issuer to pay its obligations. Most major municipal and corporate bond offerings are rated for their safety as investments by these firms as follows:

	Moody's	S&P
Highest	Aaa	AAA
Excellent	Aa	AA
Very Good	A	A
Good	Baa	BBB
	Ba	BB
	B	B
Speculative	Caa	CCC
	Ca	CC
	C	C
		D

If a bond issue receives one of the top four ratings by either firm, it is considered to be *investment grade*. Lower-rated bonds are more likely to default and involve a higher degree of investment risk; they are often called *junk bonds*. It is rare that a municipal bond will be "junk." This is more common in corporate bonds, and will be discussed in a later section.

The credit rating a bond issue receives has a direct effect on the interest rate it will pay to investors when it is issued. The higher the investment risk, the higher the yield. This is true of all bonds, not just municipal offerings.

Most municipal bond issues are tradable in the over-the-counter market, and are, therefore, highly liquid.

Equivalent Yield Table (%)

Yield of Tax-Exempt Munis	6.00	7.00	8.00	9.00	10.00
Equivalent Yield of Tax-able Investments					
15 percent federal bracket	7.06	8.24	9.41	10.59	11.76
28 percent federal bracket	8.33	9.72	11.11	12.50	13.89
35 percent combined federal and state bracket	9.23	10.77	12.31	13.85	15.38

Corporate Bonds

While there are many short-term federal and municipal securities, most corporate bonds have 10- to 30-year terms. If a corporation needs to borrow money for a shorter period of time, it will usually go to a bank.

The market for corporate bonds uses the same system of credit ratings as municipal bonds. Since corporations vary widely in their stability and financial strength, there is a broad spectrum of credit ratings in the corporate bond market. As bond ratings and safety move up, yield moves down. In order to raise money successfully, companies with "junk" credit ratings will often pay 3 to 8 percent more annual interest on their bonds than companies that have the coveted triple A rating. Still, since lower ratings do reflect a genuine risk that a company will not be able to meet its obligations when the time comes, the appeal of these high interest rates may be a mirage. Most conservative investors will want to limit their corporate bond investments to companies with one of the top three or four ratings.

The existence of credit ratings means you don't need to understand all the differences among various types of bonds. However, there are a few features and terms common to corporate bonds with which you should be familiar:

Call Features

Many bonds (both corporate and municipal) are callable. This means that the issuer may repay principal sooner than the maturity date in order to stop paying interest on the bonds. A company would do this when interest rates decline and the company can reduce its debt payments by issuing new bonds at a lower rate. If you are getting an attractive interest rate, you obviously do not want your bond investment to be called. For this reason, most bonds have some type of call protection, such as a period during which the bonds are not callable or a provision that requires a premium to be paid to investors who have their bonds called early. If you think you are locking away your money for a specific period of time, be sure to check the call provisions of bonds that you are considering.

Convertible Bonds

A few corporate bonds are convertible, meaning that they can be exchanged for a specified number of shares of stock in the same company. If the price of the stock rises above the conversion level while the bond is being held, then it is profitable to exercise your conversion rights. If the price of the stock does not go up, then you have the improved safety and current income of a bond. Because of this flexibility, the interest rate on convertible bonds is usually 3 to 4 percent lower than a conventional bond of the same company. The investment decision on a convertible bond should involve more research than just knowing the credit rating and yield of the issue. You should also make a judgment about the appreciation potential of the company's stock.

Zero-Coupon Bonds

Zeros, as they are known, are bonds that do not distribute interest payments on a current basis. Instead, the interest accrues and compounds, increasing the amount that will be repaid when the bond matures. At 7 percent interest, it would take a zero just 11 years to double in value. This can make a zero-coupon bond an effective way to provide for your children's college or any other future financial need that is time specific.

The catch is that the credit rating should be very good or you may never see anything. Also, even though you don't get a dividend distributed to you each year, you are still benefiting from the accrual (growth) of interest and must pay taxes on the annual "earnings." Zeros don't pay any cash, so that money has to come from someplace else. You won't

have this problem, of course, with zero-coupon, tax-exempt munis.

Junk Bonds

Junk bonds are bonds with credit ratings below investment grade. These bonds pay higher interest rates than other bond investments. There are some very fine, stable companies whose bonds are technically "junk." They may not qualify for the stringent requirements of the higher ratings because the companies have not been in business long enough or are too small. But it may be hard for the typical investor to differentiate between these companies and those that are just plain risky. The best advice is to tread cautiously in this area and seek professional financial advice. When assessing how your portfolio is diversified among various areas and levels of risk, count your junk bond investment in the high-risk column.

Corporate bonds are traded on the New York Stock Exchange and the over-the-counter market. The current prices of many major bond issues are shown in the daily financial pages of newspapers. As a result, it is easy to follow the value of corporate bond holdings and there is a high degree of liquidity. □

A Guide to Life Insurance

By Virginia Applegarth

Individual Policies

In addition to Social Security[1] and group coverage, the third main type of insurance is individual coverage. This coverage is purchased by you as an individual, either through an agent or directly from an insurance company. Individual life insurance policies generally have many more options and many more variations than group insurance.

Term Insurance

There are two basic types of life insurance policies—term and permanent. They both provide protection against death.

Term insurance offers pure insurance protection; all of the premium goes toward purchasing the risk coverage. The premium typically increases periodically (either every year, every five years, 10 years, etc.) and becomes very expensive by age 65 or so as the risk of death increases. There are several different types of term insurance to choose from.

Nonrenewable versus renewable. With nonrenewable term insurance, the policy is good for only a limited period of time (typically 5 to 20 years). This is usually the cheapest form of term insurance you can buy, but you cannot renew it. Even if you need insurance after the policy expires, you must apply for a new policy, take a new medical exam, and hope that you are healthy enough to qualify.

Renewable insurance is just that: it is renewable at the option of the policyholder regardless of his or her health, usually at least until age 70. Even if you are on your deathbed, the company must renew your policy. Renewable term contracts are generally more expensive than nonrenewable. However, because it is hard to predict your future health or insurance needs, you should select a renewable policy.

Convertible versus nonconvertible. With a convertible policy, you can trade in your term insurance policy for a permanent insurance policy (offering protection plus an investment element) without having to prove you are healthy. This feature is especially useful if you know that you need permanent protection but you cannot afford the premiums right now. Nonconvertible policies offer no such option.

Death benefits. In a level term policy, the death benefit stays the same as long as the policy stays in force. With decreasing term, on the other hand, the amount payable upon death will decrease to zero at the end of the term period. One of the most common decreasing term policies is a mortgage insurance policy.

Revertible versus nonrevertible. With a revertible policy, you can get a break on premiums if you can continue to prove your good health (which means additional paperwork every few years). If you cannot, premiums generally will be higher than if you had chosen a policy without this feature (a nonre-

Excerpts from HOW TO MAKE BASIC INVESTMENT DECISIONS by Neal Oschsner part of the REAL LIFE, REAL ANSWERS series. Copyright © 1990 by Lee Simmons Associates. Reprinted by permission of Houghton Mifflin Co. REAL LIFE, REAL ANSWERS is a Registered Trademark of the John Hancock Mutual Life Insurance Company.

Although this article is designed to provide accurate and authoritative information in regard to the subject matter covered, neither the author and general editors nor the publisher are engaged in rendering legal, accounting, or other professional service. If legal advice or expert assistance is required, the services of a competent professional should be sought.

1. Social Security information is provided in-depth in the special section on "Social Security & Aging," prepared by the editors of *Information Please Almanac*.

vertible policy). With a revertible policy, you are gambling that you will stay healthy; with a nonrevertible policy, you are not.

With all of these options to choose from, a good general recommendation is level death benefit, annual renewable and convertible term, nonrevertible and renewable to at least age 70.

Permanent Insurance

In contrast to term insurance, permanent insurance offers protection for your whole life. One major benefit of permanent insurance is that no matter how long you live, premiums will never increase. The insurance company accomplishes this by charging higher premiums than for term insurance in the early years and building up a reserve to help pay premiums in future years, when term premiums start to go up dramatically.

A permanent insurance policy offers protection against death coupled with a savings or investment account. In other words, you get something back whether you live or die. Permanent insurance is also attractive because under current tax laws the investment portion within the policy grows at a tax-deferred rate, so income taxes on the gains do not have to be paid unless and until the policy is cashed in.

Different types of permanent policies have different savings vehicles. However, they are all based on the concept that extra premiums paid in the early years go toward a savings or cash value account. This is why, if both policies were issued at the same age, the premium for a $100,000 permanent policy is more than for a $100,000 term policy in the early years and usually much less in later years.

Whole life. The best known type of permanent insurance (because it has been around for more than 100 years) is whole life, ordinary life, or straight life—all different names for the same product. It is called whole life because the death benefits continue for your entire life, although there are ways to stop payments earlier. Whole life offers a guaranteed premium and death benefit as well as a guaranteed minimum cash value, which you can borrow against if necessary.

Having cash value is like having a savings account within the policy that grows each year. If you die, the policy pays the death benefit amount. However, you can cancel the policy at any time during your life and get back the current cash value. This option can be helpful to supplement retirement income. In addition, many policies pay dividends that can increase your cash values and/or death benefits substantially.

Insurance companies are either stock companies (the stockholders own the company) or mutual companies (the policyholders technically own the company). If your whole life policy is with a mutual company, you will probably qualify for dividends. Dividends are technically a partial return of premium, so they are not taxable.

Interest-sensitive policies. A decade ago, thanks to competition and a changing investment environment, interest-sensitive permanent life insurance products were introduced. With interest-sensitive policies, the cash value part can fluctuate more widely than in whole life policies because it is more directly tied to interest rates. The distinguishing feature of interest-sensitive insurance contracts is that they separate out the insurance portion (the protection part) and the investment portion (the savings part). The policyholder receives periodic statements that list all charges taken out of his or her premiums, such as expenses, the cost of insurance, etc. The remaining premium goes into the investment portion.

Interest-sensitive products are more directly linked to the investment environment, which can sometimes make their value vary a great deal over short periods of time. With interest-sensitive products as a whole, you are assuming more risk than with a standard whole life policy. In return, however, you may enjoy greater investment returns than with a traditional product.

Universal life. The most popular type of interest-sensitive product today is universal life. You can have flexible premium payments, and there is a minimum guaranteed death benefit and interest rate. When a premium is paid, expense, insurance, and maintenance charges are deducted; the balance is put into your investment account. The insurance company decides which types of investments to make, and investment earnings are credited to the savings part after a variety of charges are taken out. Because you can sometimes skip payments on a universal life policy, you could easily find yourself suddenly faced with a large premium due to save the policy. It is crucial to have the self-discipline to pay the premium as originally planned.

Variable life. Another type of interest-sensitive insurance policy that allows the individual more investment flexibility is variable life. This product allows you to pick the type of investment you want. For the investment account, you typically can choose among money market, stock, bond, and real estate funds. You can also periodically change your investments in the account. However, although there is a guaranteed death benefit, there is very little premium flexibility and no minimum guaranteed cash value. Variable life is best suited to you if you are willing to take a fair amount of investment risk.

Variable universal life. A new contender in the interest-sensitive market is variable universal life, which combines features of both variable and universal products. Variable universal life contracts offer flexible premiums (like universal policies), as well as the ability to direct how your investment account is invested (like variables).

Special "Mostly Investment" Policies

Single Premium Life

With a single premium life policy, which can be single premium whole life or variable life, you pay one premium and immediately get a paid-up contract. In other words, you never have to pay another premium for the insurance coverage. The advantages are that the investment grows on a tax-deferred basis and, like traditional insurance products, the death benefit is income tax-free. The disadvantage is that new tax regulations (on policies issued after June 21, 1988) penalize many types of withdrawals from single premium policies, so you do not have ready access to your investment until age 59 1/2. Consult your tax adviser before purchasing such a policy.

Annuities

The other type of special policy is an annuity. With an annuity, you pay premiums and, in return, receive regular income for your life and sometimes even beyond, to your beneficiary. In buying an annuity, usually for retirement income, there are three basic decisions to make.

Single premium versus annual premium. Like a single premium life insurance contract, a single premium annuity requires only one premium and the policy is paid up. With an annual premium contract, however, annual premiums are paid for a defined period of time before the policy becomes paid up.

When benefits begin. With an immediate annuity, almost as soon as the insurance company receives the premium it begins to pay benefits. A deferred annuity means that benefit payments will be deferred for a specified period of time.

Fixed versus variable payments. With a fixed annuity, the insurance company agrees to pay a fixed monthly amount regardless of changes in inflation and investments. Variable annuity payments will fluctuate up and down, depending on the company's investment results and other factors. Each monthly payment may be different, or payments may vary on a yearly basis. With variable annuities, however, you still receive a minimum guaranteed monthly payment. Like single premium life contracts, annuities have the same disadvantages on many kinds of withdrawals before age 59 1/2. However, they also provide an income throughout your retirement, no matter how long you live, and sometimes even to your beneficiary. ☐

Additional Considerations

Source: A Consumer's Guide to Life Insurance, published by the American Council of Life Insurance.

Before the Purchase

When buying life insurance, you should read the contract carefully and, if necessary, ask your agent for a point-by-point explanation of the language. To help the consumer, many insurance companies have rewritten their contracts to make them more understandable. Keep in mind that these are legal documents and you should be familiar with what they promise, even though some technical terms are used.

In addition, the National Association of Insurance Commissioners and many state insurance departments have prepared buyer's guides to help you further understand life insurance terms, benefits and relative costs. Buyer's guides are distributed through your agent and insurance company, so be sure to ask for one. If you have more questions about companies or policies, you can check with your state insurance commissioner's office.

No matter how they are put together, however, life insurance policies can be divided into three parts. There's The First Page, which outlines the basic features of the contract; The Details, which spell out the basic agreement; and The Application, which is the information you give the company about yourself and which becomes part of the policy.

After the Purchase

After purchasing new life insurance, keep in mind that you have a 10-day "free look," which entitles you to change your mind. If you do so, the company will return your premium, without penalty.

It's a good idea to provide your beneficiaries with a photocopy of your policy, and your agent's name. If you have a lawyer, he or she should likewise have this information and know who your beneficiaries are.

Your beneficiaries should know where your policy is kept, because it may have to be sent to the company upon your death, along with a copy of the death certificate, in order to obtain the life insurance proceeds. You should keep your policy in a safe place at home and the name of the company and policy number in a safe deposit box in case your policy is misplaced or lost.

Your beneficiaries need not take your insurance proceeds in one lump sum. Many people select other options, such as a monthly income and a specific sum set aside for other purposes, perhaps retirement or college costs. Ask your agent about the settlement options available to you.

Switching Policies

If you already own life insurance, think twice if someone suggests that you replace it. Before you give up this protection make sure you are still insurable (check medical and any other qualification requirements). Also remember that you are now older than when you first purchased your policy, and a new one will cost more because of your age. Moreover, an older policy may have provisions that are not duplicated in some new ones. This does not mean that you should reject the idea of replacing a policy you already have, but rather that you should proceed with caution. It is recommended that you ask your agent or company for an opinion about the new proposal, so you hear both sides of the matter. ☐

Making Bank Deposits

When Will Your Money Be Available?

Source: Board of Governors of the Federal Reserve System.

In 1987, Congress passed a law that limits how long financial institutions may delay a customer's ability to use deposited funds. The law, called the Expedited Funds Availability Act, balances the risk to financial institutions with the needs of customers. As of September 1, 1988, all banks, savings and loan associations, savings banks, and credit unions

must let you use funds deposited in checking, share draft, or NOW accounts within a fixed number of days. They also must tell you, in writing, how soon you may use the money after making a deposit.

The law does not require an institution to delay your ability to use deposited funds; it only limits how long the delay may last. Many institutions have always let their long-term customers use deposited funds right away, and they may continue to do so under the new law. Even those institutions that do delay their customers' use of funds may make funds available sooner than the limits set in the new law. Some institutions, of course, may now take as much time as the established schedule allows. So, if availability of funds is a consideration for you, you may want to compare the policies of different institutions before deciding where you will deposit your funds.

How Soon Are Your Deposited Funds Available?

How quickly the funds must be available depends on the type of check you deposit and on the likelihood that it will be paid. For example, you may be able to use the money sooner when you deposit a U.S. Treasury check than when you deposit a check from an individual or a business. The time you have to wait may also depend on where the individual or business that gave you the check has their checking account. Your institution can expect to find out more quickly from a hometown institution than from a distant, out-of-state institution whether a check is backed by sufficient funds.

The following are usually the longest times that institutions can delay your use of deposited funds under the new law.

These times, based on business days, include all days except Saturdays, Sundays, and federal holidays.

Now let's look at how these rules affect the availability of your funds. Let's say that your institution decides to hold deposited funds for the longest time allowed by law. If you deposit a local check* on a Monday, you can use the deposited funds on Thursday—the third business day after the day of deposit. If you deposit the check on a Wednesday, however, you will have to wait until Monday to use your funds, because Saturday and Sunday are not business days and are not counted in figuring the time. If you deposit the check on a day when your institution is closed, on a Saturday, or on any business day after the cut-off time (usually 2 p.m.), the institution may treat the deposit as though you actually made it on the following business day.

At the end of the waiting period, your institution will pay checks that you have written, but it may not allow you to withdraw all the money in cash right away. Contact your institution to see whether it has special rules for cash withdrawals.

Deposits at an automated teller machine not belonging to your institution must be available on the same schedule as other deposits.

Are There Special Rules for New Accounts?

When you open an account, be sure to ask whether the institution has special rules regarding availability of funds for new customers. An institution may delay a new customer's use of deposited funds longer because it is not familiar with that person's history in using a checking account. These longer delays are allowed only during the first 30 days the account is open.

---

*Under the law, a check is a local check if it is deposited in an institution located in the same Federal Reserve check processing region as the paying bank. There are 48 Federal Reserve check processing regions in the nation.

Type of deposit	When the funds must be available to you
• cash • the first $100 of any deposit of checks • government, cashier's, certified, or teller's checks • checks written on another account at the same institution • direct deposit and other electronic credits	the next business day after the day of deposit (certain conditions may apply—check with your institution)
• checks written on local institutions	the second business day after the day of deposit
• checks written on nonlocal institutions • deposits made at an automated teller machine not belonging to your institution	the fifth business day after the day of deposit

May an Institution Delay Your Use of Deposited Funds Beyond the Usual Limits?

In certain instances, the law allows an institution to delay a customer's use of deposited funds longer than the usual limits, generally for four more business days. This longer limit gives an institution extra time to make sure a deposit is backed by sufficient funds. An institution may use this longer limit in the following circumstances:

• you redeposit a check that was returned unpaid.

• you have overdrawn your account repeatedly in the previous six months. (That is, you have not had enough money in the account to cover checks you wrote.)

• you deposit checks totalling more than $5,000 on any one day.

• your institution has reason to believe that the check you are depositing will not be paid.

If your institution uses the longer limit, it must tell you why it has done so and when you will be able to use the deposited funds. ☐

Additional Information

All institutions must send a notice explaining to their customers when they must use deposited funds. When you receive the notice, take the time to review it carefully. If you do not understand it, ask someone at your institution for help. If you write checks against funds not yet available for your use, you could end up owing charges on returned checks to your institution, as well as to the merchants or others who receive these checks from you.

Keep in mind that you are responsible should a check you deposit be returned unpaid. If you have already used some or all of the funds, you will have to reimburse your institution promptly.

The way you endorse a check for deposit could help hasten its clearing. When you endorse a check, make sure that your signature is near the edge of the left side on the back of the check. This will leave room for all the financial institutions handling the check to make their endorsements and move the check more quickly. ☐

Reducing Your Tax Bill: For Two-Income Couples

By Candace E. Trunzo

We may be in the twenty-first century by the time tax professionals are able to decipher all the provisions of the Tax Reform Act of 1986. What is clear is that tax planning for two-income couples is more important than ever. Perhaps you won't be able to go it alone and will need the help of a financial planner, or at least a savvy accountant to guide you.

For two-career couples, tax reform gave a little, but it took away even more. While it is true that rates are lower (a cap of 28 percent on taxable income replaced the 50 percent top rate), and personal exemptions are higher (from $1,080 in 1986 to $2,000 in 1989), the marriage penalty deduction—in which dual-income married couples were allowed to write off up to $3,000 a year—was abolished. In fact, two-career couples living together unmarried are more likely to get a break than their married counterparts. Two singles filing separate returns pay more of their income tax at the lower 15 percent rate than if they had to combine their incomes—or file separately—as a married couple.

Restricted Write-Offs

Rather than focus on what you can't do to keep more of your income, focus on the investment and tax-cutting strategies that are available.

Owning a home. A true tax shelter. You can fully deduct mortgage interest and property taxes as well as the interest on a home-equity loan (up to the price you paid plus improvements). Also, if you sell your home, you are allowed to defer the profit on the sale as long as you buy another house within two years that costs as much or more than the one you sold.

Filing separately. If either you or your spouse has high business or medical expenses, you may be able to reduce your bill by filing separate returns. Under the new law, you cannot qualify for a deduction unless your medical expenses, for example, exceed 7.5 percent of your adjusted gross income. If one of you had $5,000 in medical expenses, and together you earned $70,000, you could not take the deduction if you filed jointly. But if you earned $35,000 individually, you would qualify for a $2,375 write-off, the portion of the $5,000 that exceeds 7.5 percent of $35,000.

Individual Retirement Accounts (IRAs). If you and your spouse are not covered by a corporate pension or profit-sharing plan, you can still deduct up to $2,000 each and put the money into IRAs. Even if you are covered by a company plan, you can claim the entire deduction if your joint adjusted gross income does not exceed $40,000. The amount you can deduct decreases until you earn $50,000, when your contributions are no longer deductible. Even if you cannot deduct the contribution, an IRA is an easy way to get tax-free compounding on the earnings from your investments. You pay taxes only when you withdraw money from your account. If you take cash out before you reach 59 1/2, you will

---

Tax Advantages of Buying a Home

Particularly in the first few years of home ownership, you can get a hefty tax deduction thanks to a tax code that allows you to deduct all the interest you pay on your mortgage up to a $1 million mortgage limit. The sample case is that of a two-income couple who are buying a $93,000 home, the median-priced home, with a 10.5 percent 30-year mortgage. This sample is based on the 1988 tax rates for married couples filing jointly.

Adjusted gross income	$42,000
House price	93,000
Down payment (20 percent)	−18,600
Mortgage (@ 10.5 percent)	$74,400

Costs	
Annual mortgage payment	8,167
Annual real estate taxes	+1,860
Annual cost before taxes	$10,027

Itemized	Deductions
Annual interest on mortgage (average of first five years)	7,706
Real estate taxes	+1,860
Tax deductions (mortgage interest and real estate taxes)	$9,566
Tax liability using standard deduction of $5,000	6,500
Tax liability using itemized deductions above	−5,212
Savings for homeowners	$1,288

Source: "Home Guide 1990," National Association of Realtors.

---

also owe a tax penalty of 10 percent of the money withdrawn.

Keogh Plans. Those who are self-employed, even in a part-time business, can use a Keogh to shelter up to 25 percent of self-employment income or $30,000, whichever is less. Even if you have an IRA, you are allowed to have a Keogh. As with IRAs, your earnings from your investments are tax-

Excerpted from FINANCIAL PLANNING FOR THE TWO-CAREER FAMILY by Candace E. Trunzo, part of the REAL LIFE, REAL ANSWERS series. Copyright © 1990 by Lee Simmons Associates. Reprinted by permission of Houghton Mifflin Company. REAL LIFE, REAL ANSWERS is a Registered Trademark of the John Hancock Mutual Life Insurance Company.

free until you take the money out (at 59 1/2 or after). But there is a 10 percent penalty for early withdrawals.

There are several ways to set up a Keogh. The least complicated Keogh is a defined-contribution plan in which you have a fixed, maximum yearly payment. If you choose this type of plan, you have two options. The first is a money-purchase Keogh, in which you must contribute the same percentage every year (up to the smaller of 25 percent or $30,000) unless your business is losing money. The second option is more flexible because you can change your contributions each year. But if you use this option, you can only contribute up to 15 percent of your self-employment income.

Defined-benefit Keoghs are more complicated but make sense for older couples who need to play retirement catch-up. Let's say you are 50 and haven't saved a penny. With a defined-benefit plan, you can save—and deduct—whatever is necessary to let you retire on the average of your highest earnings in three consecutive years; you are not subject to the $30,000/25 percent maximum. You can deduct up to $94,023 if you intend to start making withdrawals at 65. Each year you are required to have an actuary audit your calculations for the IRS.

Simplified Employee Pensions (SEPs). Simplified employee pensions, known as SEPs, are similar to Keoghs. If you have a company with up to 25 employees, you can contribute up to 15 percent a year of each employee's gross income into his or her SEP; your company can take the contribution as a tax deduction. Like an IRA or a Keogh, SEPs can be opened with a bank, brokerage house, or mutual fund. If you pull your money out before you are 59 1/2, you also pay a 10 percent penalty for early withdrawal.

401(k) Plans. These company savings plans, if available to you and your spouse, are a painless way to save. Your contribution is automatically invested so you never have your hands on the money. You do not pay any tax on the earnings until you with-

draw the money. Since many companies match all or part of your contribution, that amounts to added tax-deferred earnings. The tax law has restricted once easy withdrawal privileges, however. Now, unless you use the money to pay medical bills, you pay a 10 percent penalty on early withdrawals of your own contributions. The rest is totally off-limits until you retire. Since you are investing pretax dollars, you have, in effect, a tax deduction. If you were in the 28 percent bracket and contributed the maximum allowed to your 401(k) last year ($7,637[1]), you would have reduced your tax bill by $2,135.

1. For 1990, this amount is $7,979—Ed.

Municipal bonds. Municipal bonds (or munis) are issued by state and local governments. The interest, usually paid twice a year, is free from federal taxes and sometimes state and local taxes too if you buy a bond that is issued in your state. Zero coupon municipal bonds are munis that are purchased at a large discount and then are redeemed at a much higher face value later on. You get the tax-free income all at once when you redeem the bond. The most affordable way to have a well-diversified portfolio of munis is through a municipal bond mutual fund or unit trust.

Whole life insurance, universal life insurance, variable life insurance, and variable annuities. With all these policies your earnings grow tax-deferred. The tax law has placed no limit on what you can contribute when you buy an annuity or insurance policy. Also, with life insurance you get a death benefit in the bargain.

Limited partnerships. While the tax law eliminated partnerships in which you could deduct more than was invested, low write-off deals are still available. Sold by stockbrokers and financial planners, these programs tend to be real estate partnerships that are not highly leveraged (do not rely on borrowing money). Instead they rely on property depreciation, mortgage interest, and property taxes for tax breaks. □

Qualifying for a Mortgage—How Much Can You Afford?

By Kenneth R. Harney

Qualifying Ratios

Virtually all lenders tie the amount of the mortgage they'll offer you to two key credit evaluation ratios. The first is the monthly housing cost-to-income ratio. As a general rule, conventional lenders will require that your monthly mortgage payment, consisting of principal, interest, taxes, and insurance (PITI), and any other related fees, such as condominium assessments, not exceed 25-28 percent of your gross monthly income. Expressed as a formula, the rule looks like this:

$$\frac{\text{Principal, interest, taxes, insurance, and fees}}{\text{Gross monthly income}} = \text{25-28 percent}$$

For example, let's say your monthly household income is $5,000. Using a typical 28 percent hous-

ing cost ratio, you should be able to afford a monthly mortgage expense of $1,400.

$$\frac{\$1,400 \text{ housing cost}}{\$5,000 \text{ gross income}} = 28 \text{ percent}$$

On certain types of loans, such as fixed-rate mortgages that require a large down payment, lenders will stretch this to 33 percent. But the 25-28 percent housing cost standard is used for most conventional (non-FHA or non-VA) loans. FHA and VA lenders use different qualifying criteria. The FHA, for instance, allows your "housing costs" (including PITI *and utilities and maintenance*) to equal 38 percent of your net monthly income. (Your net in-

---

Excerpted from "Choose a Mortgage to Suit Your Taste," by Kenneth R. Harney, HOME GUIDE 1990, with permission of the National Association of Realtors.

come is your gross income minus federal income tax withholding.)

The second credit evaluation ratio you'll encounter with every lender focuses on your total monthly debts—your housing costs and all other installment-type debts, such as car loans, revolving charge accounts, and personal debts.

Generally, most conventional lenders will require that your total regular installment debt should not exceed 33-38 percent of your gross monthly income. Expressed graphically, it would look like this:

$$\frac{\text{Mortgage debt, condo fees,}}{\text{and other monthly debt}} = 33\text{-}38 \text{ percent}$$

With the hypothetical $5,000 per month income, your total monthly debt—mortgage costs and other debts—shouldn't exceed $1,650 (if your lender uses the 33 percent ceiling) or $1,900 (if the lender uses the more liberal 38 percent maximum).

$$\frac{\$1,650 \text{ total monthly debt}}{\$5,000 \text{ gross monthly income}} = 33 \text{ percent}$$

or

$$\frac{\$1,900 \text{ total monthly debt}}{\$5,000 \text{ gross monthly income}} = 38 \text{ percent}$$

Again, you'll find variations among lenders and loan types. You'll also find that the FHA and the VA measure the ratios somewhat differently than do conventional lenders.

The bottom line on these ratios, however, is that they essentially put a limit on the size of the loan any lender will grant you. That, in turn, puts a lid on how much house you can afford.

Also Keep in Mind . . .

Other key determinants in virtually any lender's decision on how much to offer you include the following:

● **Credit history**—Your record on all types of debt repayments in the past is considered. The better your credit, the more comfortable the lender will be with a larger loan.

● **Assets**—These may run from bank accounts to autos and stocks. As you might expect, the more you have, the bigger the loan you're likely to get. That's true despite the fact that your mortgage will be secured solely by your real estate; in other words, if you default, your lender will foreclose on your house but won't go after your other assets.

● **Employment history and prospects**—Lenders may base their assessment of your creditworthiness in part on such factors as length of employment, steady growth in rank and earnings, and potential for additional earnings, such as salary increases, commissions, or bonuses.

● **Closing costs**—In calculating how large a mortgage you can handle, prudent lenders also consider the expected closing or settlement charges on the loan. They typically range from 2 to 5 percent of the home price. If you don't have the cash resources to pay the transfer taxes and recording, attorney's, title, and other fees, the maximum loan for which you qualify may be reduced. □

Reading the Fine Print

Source: The Mortgage Money Guide, Federal Trade Commission.

Before going ahead with a creative home loan, you may want to have a lawyer or other expert help you interpret the fine print. You may also want to consider some of the situations you could face when paying off your loan or selling your property. Also, make sure you understand the terms in your agreement—such as *acceleration, due on sale* clauses, and *waivers.*

An *acceleration clause* allows the lender to speed up the rate at which your loan comes due. Suppose you've missed a payment, and your contract gives the lender the right to "accelerate" the loan when a payment is missed. This means that the lender now has the power to force you to repay the entire loan immediately.

Here, taken from a mortgage contract, is a sample acceleration clause: *"In the event any installment of this note is not paid when due, time being of the essence, and such installment remains unpaid for thirty (30) days, the Holder of this Note may, at its option, without notice or demand, declare the entire principal sum then unpaid, together with secured interest and late charges thereon, immediately due and payable. The lender may without further notice or demand invoke the power of sale and any other remedies permitted by applicable law."*

Note the use of the term "without notice" above. If this contract provision is legal in your state, you have *waived* your right to notice. In other words, you've given up the right to be notified of some

occurrence—for example, a missed payment. If you've waived your right to notice of delinquency or default, and you've made a late payment, action may be initiated against you before you've been told; the lender may even start to foreclose.

Know whether your contract waives your right to notice. If so, obtain a clear understanding in advance of what you're giving up. And consider having your attorney check state law to determine if the waiver is legal.

A *due on sale* clause gives the lender the right to require immediate repayment of the balance you owe if the property changes hands. Here's an example of a due on sale clause: *"If all or any part of the Property or an interest therein is sold or transferred by Borrower without Lender's prior written consent . . . Lender may, at Lender's option, declare all the sums secured by this Mortgage to be immediately due and payable."*

Due on sale clauses have been included in many mortgage contracts for years. They are being enforced by lenders increasingly when buyers try to assume sellers' existing low rate mortgages. In these cases, the courts have frequently upheld the lender's right to raise the interest rate to the prevailing market level. So be especially careful when considering an "assumable mortgage." If your agreement has a due on sale provision, the assumption may not be legal, and you could be liable for thousands of additional dollars. □

Mortgage Highlights

Type	Description	Considerations
Fixed rate mortgage	Fixed interest rate, usually long-term; equal monthly payments of principal and interest until debt is paid in full.	Offers stability and long-term tax advantages. Interest rates may be higher than other types of financing. New fixed rates are rarely assumable.
Fifteen-year mortgage	Fixed interest rate. Requires down payment or monthly payments higher than 30-year loan. Loan is fully repaid over 15-year term.	Frequently offered at slightly reduced interest rate. Offers faster accumulation of equity than traditional fixed rate mortgage but has higher monthly payments. Involves paying less interest but this may result in fewer tax deductions.
Adjustable rate mortgage	Interest rate changes over the life of the loan, resulting in possible changes in your monthly payments, loan term, and/or principal. Some plans have rate or payment caps.	Starting interest rate is slightly below market, but payments can increase sharply and frequently if index increases. Payment caps prevent wide fluctuations in payments but may cause negative amortization. Rate caps limit amount total debt can expand.
Renegotiable rate mortgage (roll-over)	Interest rate and monthly payments are constant for several years; changes possible thereafter. Long-term mortgage.	Less frequent changes in interest rate offer some stability.
Balloon mortgage	Monthly payments based on fixed interest rate; usually short-term; payments may cover interest only with principal due in full at term end.	Offers low monthly payments but possibly no equity until loan is fully paid. When due, loan must be paid off or refinanced. Refinancing poses high risk if rates climb.
Graduated payment mortgage	Lower monthly payments rise gradually (usually over 5-10 years), then level off for duration of term. With adjustable interest rate, additional payment changes possible if index changes.	Easier to qualify for. Buyer's income must be able to keep pace with scheduled payment increases. With an adjustable rate, payment increases beyond the graduated payments can result in additional negative amortization.
Shared appreciation mortgage	Below-market interest rate and lower monthly payments, in exchange for a share of profits when property is sold or on a specified date. Many variations.	If home appreciates greatly, total cost of loan jumps. If home fails to appreciate, projected increase in value may still be due, requiring refinancing at possibly higher rates.
Assumable mortgage	Buyer takes over seller's original, below-market rate mortgage.	Lowers monthly payments. May be prohibited if "due on sale" clause is in original mortgage. Not permitted on most new fixed rate mortgages.
Seller take-back	Seller provides all or part of financing with a first or second mortgage.	May offer a below-market interest rate; may have a balloon payment requiring full payment in a few years or refinancing at market rates, which could sharply increase debt.
Wraparound	Seller keeps original low rate mortgage. Buyer makes payments to seller who forwards a portion to the lender holding original mortgage. Offers lower effective interest rate on total transaction.	Lender may call in old mortgage and require higher rate. If buyer defaults, seller must take legal action to collect debt.
Growing equity mortgage (rapid payoff mortgage)	Fixed interest rate but monthly payments may vary according to agreed-upon schedule or index.	Permits rapid payoff of debt because payment increases reduce principal. Buyer's income must be able to keep up with payment increases.
Land contract	Seller retains original mortgage. No transfer of title until loan is fully paid. Equal monthly payments based on below-market interest rate with unpaid principal due at loan end.	May offer no equity until loan is fully paid. Buyer has few protections if conflict arises during loan.
Buy-down	Developer (or other party) provides an interest subsidy which lowers monthly payments during the first few years of the loan. Can have fixed or adjustable interest rate.	Offers a break from higher payments during early years. Enables buyer with lower income to qualify. With adjustable rate mortgage, payments may jump substantially at end of subsidy. Developer may increase selling price.
Rent with option	Renter pays "option fee" for right to purchase property at specified time and agreed-upon price. Rent may or may not be applied to sales price.	Enables renter to buy time to obtain down payment and decide whether to purchase. Locks in price during inflationary times. Failure to take option means loss of option fee and rental payments.
Reverse annuity mortgage (equity conversion)	Borrower owns mortgage-free property and needs income. Lender makes monthly payments to borrower, using property as collateral.	Can provide homeowners with needed cash. At end of term, borrower must have money available to avoid selling property or refinancing.

Source: The Mortgage Money Guide, Federal Trade Commission.

Mortgage Payment Tables

Source: The Mortgage Money Guide, Federal Trade Commission.

8% Annual Percentage Rate

Amount financed	Monthly payments (principal and interest)*					
	5 Years	10 Years	15 Years	20 Years	25 Years	30 Years
$ 25,000	506.91	303.32	238.91	209.11	192.95	183.44
30,000	608.29	363.98	286.70	250.93	231.54	220.13
35,000	709.67	424.65	334.48	292.75	270.14	256.82
40,000	811.06	485.31	382.26	334.58	308.73	293.51
45,000	912.44	545.97	430.04	376.40	347.32	330.19
50,000	1013.82	606.64	477.83	418.22	385.91	366.88
60,000	1216.58	727.97	573.39	501.86	463.09	440.26
70,000	1419.35	849.29	668.96	585.51	540.27	513.64
80,000	1622.11	970.62	764.52	669.15	617.45	587.01
90,000	1824.88	1091.95	860.09	752.80	694.63	660.39
100,000	2027.64	1213.28	955.65	836.44	771.82	733.76

9% Annual Percentage Rate

Amount financed	Monthly payments (principal and interest)*					
	5 Years	10 Years	15 Years	20 Years	25 Years	30 Years
$ 25,000	518.96	316.69	253.57	224.93	209.80	201.16
30,000	622.75	380.03	304.28	269.92	251.76	241.39
35,000	726.54	443.36	354.99	314.90	293.72	281.62
40,000	830.33	506.70	405.71	359.89	335.68	321.85
45,000	934.13	570.04	456.42	404.88	377.64	362.08
50,000	1037.92	633.38	507.13	449.86	419.60	402.31
60,000	1245.50	760.05	608.56	539.84	503.52	482.77
70,000	1453.08	886.73	709.99	629.81	587.44	563.24
80,000	1660.67	1013.41	811.41	719.78	671.36	643.70
90,000	1868.25	1140.08	912.84	809.75	755.28	724.16
100,000	2075.84	1266.76	1014.27	899.73	839.20	804.62

10% Annual Percentage Rate

Amount financed	Monthly payments (principal and interest)*					
	5 Years	10 Years	15 Years	20 Years	25 Years	30 Years
$ 25,000	531.18	330.38	268.65	241.26	227.18	219.39
30,000	637.41	396.45	322.38	289.51	272.61	263.27
35,000	743.65	462.53	376.11	337.76	318.05	307.15
40,000	849.88	528.60	429.84	386.01	363.48	351.03
45,000	956.12	594.68	483.57	434.26	408.92	394.91
50,000	1062.35	660.75	537.30	482.51	454.35	438.79
60,000	1274.82	792.90	644.76	579.01	545.22	526.54
70,000	1487.29	925.06	752.22	675.52	636.09	614.30
80,000	1699.76	1057.20	859.68	772.02	726.96	702.06
90,000	1912.23	1189.36	967.14	868.52	817.83	789.81
100,000	2124.70	1321.51	1074.61	965.02	908.70	877.57

Losing Ground

Source: The Mortgage Money Guide, Federal Trade Commission.

Repaying debt gradually through payments of principal and interest is called amortization. Today's economic climate has given rise to a reverse process called negative amortization.

Negative amortization means that you are losing—not gaining—value, or equity. This is because your monthly payments may be too low to cover the interest rate agreed upon in the mortgage contract. Instead of paying the full interest costs now, you'll pay them later—either in larger payments or in more payments. You will also be paying interest on that interest.

In other words, the lender postpones collection of the money you owe by increasing the size of your debt. In extreme cases, you may even lose the equity you purchased with your down payment, leaving you in worse financial shape a few years

11% Annual Percentage Rate

Amount financed	Monthly payments (principal and interest)*					
	5 Years	10 Years	15 Years	20 Years	25 Years	30 Years
$ 25,000	543.56	344.38	284.15	258.05	245.03	238.08
30,000	652.27	413.25	340.98	309.66	294.03	285.70
35,000	760.98	482.13	397.81	361.27	343.04	333.31
40,000	869.70	551.00	454.64	412.88	392.05	380.93
45,000	978.41	619.88	511.47	464.48	441.05	428.55
50,000	1087.12	688.75	568.30	516.09	490.06	476.16
60,000	1304.54	826.50	681.96	619.31	588.07	571.39
70,000	1521.97	964.25	795.62	722.53	686.08	666.63
80,000	1739.39	1102.00	909.28	825.75	784.09	761.86
90,000	1956.81	1239.75	1022.94	928.97	882.10	857.09
100,000	2174.24	1377.50	1136.60	1032.19	980.11	952.32

12% Annual Percentage Rate

Amount financed	Monthly payments (principal and interest)*					
	5 Years	10 Years	15 Years	20 Years	25 Years	30 Years
$ 25,000	556.11	358.68	300.05	275.28	263.31	257.16
30,000	667.33	430.42	360.06	330.33	315.97	308.59
35,000	778.56	502.15	420.06	385.39	368.63	360.02
40,000	889.78	573.89	480.07	440.44	421.29	411.45
45,000	1001.00	645.62	540.08	495.49	473.96	462.88
50,000	1112.22	717.36	600.09	550.55	526.62	514.31
60,000	1334.67	860.83	720.11	660.66	631.93	617.17
70,000	1557.11	1004.30	840.12	770.77	737.26	720.03
80,000	1779.56	1147.77	960.14	880.87	842.58	822.90
90,000	2002.00	1291.24	1080.15	990.98	947.90	925.75
100,000	2224.44	1434.71	1200.17	1101.09	1053.23	1028.62

13% Annual Percentage Rate

Amount financed	Monthly payments (principal and interest)*					
	5 Years	10 Years	15 Years	20 Years	25 Years	30 Years
$ 25,000	568.83	373.28	316.32	292.90	281.96	276.55
30,000	682.60	447.94	379.58	351.48	338.36	331.86
35,000	796.36	522.59	442.84	410.06	394.75	387.17
40,000	910.13	597.25	506.10	468.64	451.14	442.48
45,000	1023.89	671.90	569.36	527.21	507.53	497.79
50,000	1137.66	746.56	632.63	585.79	563.92	553.10
60,000	1365.19	895.87	759.15	702.95	676.71	663.72
70,000	1592.72	1045.18	885.67	820.11	789.49	774.34
80,000	1820.25	1194.49	1012.20	937.27	902.27	884.96
90,000	2047.78	1343.80	1138.72	1054.42	1015.05	995.58
100,000	2275.31	1493.11	1265.25	1171.58	1127.84	1106.20

after you purchase your home than when you bought it.

Suppose you signed an adjustable rate mortgage for $50,000 in 1978. The index established your initial rate at 9.15%. It nearly doubled to 17.39% by 1981. If your monthly payments had kept pace with the index, they would have risen from $408 to $722. But because of a payment cap they stayed at $408. By 1981 your mortgage had swelled from $50,000 to $58,350, even though you had dutifully paid $408 every month for 48 months. In other words, you paid out $20,000 but you were $8,000 more in debt than you were three years earlier. During the next few years, despite the fact that the index fell gradually, you were still paying off the increases made to your principal from earlier years.

Certain loans, such as graduated payment mortgages, are structured so that you regain the lost ground with payments that eventually rise high enough to fully pay off your debt. And you may also be able to pay off the extra costs if your home is gaining rapidly in value or if your income is rising fast enough to meet the increased obligation. But if it isn't, you may realize a loss if, for example, you sign a below-market adjustable rate mortgage in January and try to sell the home in August when interest rates are higher. You could end up owing more than you'd make on the sale. ☐

14% Annual Percentage Rate

Amount financed	Monthly payments (principal and interest)*					
	5 Years	10 Years	15 Years	20 Years	25 Years	30 Years
$ 25,000	581.71	388.17	332.94	310.89	300.95	296.22
30,000	698.05	465.80	399.53	373.06	361.13	355.47
35,000	814.39	543.44	466.11	435.24	421.32	414.71
40,000	930.74	621.07	532.70	497.41	481.51	473.95
45,000	1047.08	698.70	599.29	559.59	541.70	533.20
50,000	1163.42	776.34	665.88	621.77	601.89	592.44
60,000	1396.10	931.60	799.05	746.12	722.26	710.93
70,000	1628.78	1086.87	932.22	870.47	842.64	829.42
80,000	1861.47	1242.14	1065.40	994.82	963.01	947.90
90,000	2094.14	1397.40	1198.57	1119.17	1083.38	1066.38
100,000	2326.83	1552.67	1331.75	1243.53	1203.77	1184.88

15% Annual Percentage Rate

Amount financed	Monthly payments (principal and interest)*					
	5 Years	10 Years	15 Years	20 Years	25 Years	30 Years
$ 25,000	594.75	403.34	349.90	329.20	320.21	316.12
30,000	713.70	484.01	419.88	395.04	384.25	379.34
35,000	832.65	564.68	489.86	460.88	448.30	442.56
40,000	951.60	645.34	559.84	526.72	512.34	505.78
45,000	1070.55	726.01	629.82	592.56	576.38	569.00
50,000	1189.50	806.68	699.80	658.40	640.42	632.23
60,000	1427.40	968.01	839.76	790.08	768.50	758.67
70,000	1665.30	1129.35	979.72	921.76	896.59	885.12
80,000	1903.20	1290.68	1119.67	1053.44	1024.67	1011.56
90,000	2141.09	1452.01	1259.63	1185.11	1152.75	1138.00
100,000	2379.00	1613.35	1399.59	1316.79	1280.84	1264.45

*For loans that fully pay off the debt over the loan term.

Know Homebuying Lingo

Source: National Association of Realtors

Amortization. The gradual repayment of a mortgage by periodic installments.

Annual percentage rate (APR). The total finance charge (interest, loan fees, points) expressed as a percentage of the loan amount.

Assessed value. The valuation placed on property by a public tax assessor as the basis of property taxes.

Binder. An agreement, accompanied by a deposit, whereby the buyer evidences good faith.

Cap. The maximum amount an interest or monthly payment can change, either at adjustment time or over the life of the mortgage.

Closing. The final step in transferring ownership of a property from the seller to the buyer.

Closing costs. Fees and expenses, not including the price of the home, payable by the seller and the buyer at the closing (e.g. brokerage commissions, title insurance premiums, and inspection, appraisal, recording, and attorney's fees).

Deed. A legal document conveying title to a property.

Escrow. The placement of money or documents with a third party for safekeeping pending the fulfillment or performance of a specified act or condition.

Lien. A legal claim against a property that must be paid when the property is sold.

Loan-to-value-ratio. The relationship between the amount of a home loan and the total value of the property. Lenders may limit their maximum loan to 80-95 percent of value.

Lock-in rate. A commitment made by lenders on a mortgage loan to "lock in" a certain rate pending loan approval. Lock-in periods vary.

Points. A dollar amount paid to the lender as a consideration for making the loan. A point is one percent of the loan amount; also called discount points.

Principal, interest, taxes, and insurance (PITI) payment. A periodic (typically monthly) payment that includes the principal and interest payment plus a contribution to the escrow account established by the lender to pay insurance premiums and property taxes on the mortgaged property.

Private mortgage insurance (PMI). Insurance issued to a lender by a private company to protect the lender against loss on a defaulted mortgage loan. Its use is usually limited to loans with high loan-to-value ratios. The borrower pays the premiums.

Shared equity mortgage. A home loan in which an investor is granted a share of the equity, thereby allowing the investor to participate in the proceeds from resale.

Title. A document that's evidence of ownership.

Title insurance. Protection for lenders and homeowners against financial loss resulting from legal debts in the title.

SOCIAL SECURITY & AGING

Can America Learn for Tomorrow From the Aging of Japan Today?

By Barry Robinson

Japan is changing. The "land of the new" is growing older—more rapidly than most. Its aging population will soon be one of the oldest in the world, and its people are trying to decide now how to deal with the dramatic demographic shifts which have already begun altering their futures forever.

In search of insights and inspiration, many of Japan's citizens have spent the last decade or so looking at the experiences of the United States and other industrialized nations in dealing with local manifestations of global aging trends. During the late 1970s, throughout the 80s, and continuing into the 90s, a steadily growing stream of Japanese government officials, business executives, academic researchers, journalists, gerontologists and older persons themselves have been visiting America to observe firsthand how we are responding to the impact and implications of aging.

Now, as the Japanese begin to adapt some of what they have been learning from other nations' experiences, we may be able to learn from studying them as they modify and apply what they have learned from studying our experiences. It's a process that's applicable to all nations, and one that, if we're all lucky, could go on indefinitely as we continue learning from each other's experiences for the ultimate benefit of all concerned.

For the present, however, the situation in Japan is not as critical as it is expected to be after the turn of the century. While aging faster than most other nations, Japan still has a proportionately smaller age 65 and over population than the United States and most western industrialized nations. In the U.S., the 30.4 million age 65+ people presently comprise 12.4% of the population, compared to 13 million and 10.3% in Japan today.

Japan will not really feel the full impact of its aging until well into the first quarter of the 21st century when, in 2025, 31.5 million people or 23.4% of its population will be 65 or over, and there are those who expect that percentage to continue rising. By 2030, however, the U.S. older population will have peaked at 66 million or 21.8%.

It is over the long run that the drastic differences in degree between the changes taking place in Japan and the United States become more readily apparent. In 1950, only 7.7% of Japan's population was over age 60, compared to 12.1% in the U.S. By

2020, those percentages are expected to rise to 26.2 and 22, respectively. According to consulting actuary David Healy of Towers, Perrin, Forster & Crosby, this adds up to an increase of 340% for Japan, but only 182% for the U.S.

Thus, while the U.S. will continue for the foreseeable future to have more older people than Japan, both the percentage of the population in this age group and the rate of its growth will be larger in Japan than in the U.S. When the needs and aspirations of "minority" groups within a nation's population are being taken into consideration in planning, percentages such as these can often count for far more than absolute numbers.

With the Japanese growing increasingly aware of the changes taking place in their midst, the situation has become the focus in recent years of a developing national dialogue which is being promoted to a great extent by the government itself in an effort to lay the groundwork now for building a consensus for the future when circumstances require it. And, the changes that are coming—and the changes that they will necessitate—will indeed require broad-based agreement.

Shifting Assets and Burdens

As in other Asian countries, the Japanese have a long tradition of reverence for elders and ancestors. While that tradition is still very much alive today, it is relatively easy to respect and treat one's elders well when there are comparatively few of them, as was the case in the not too distant past. Now, however, there are more elderly Japanese than ever before, and they are living longer than ever before—81.39 years for women and 75.61 years for men, the highest life expectancy in the world today. Thus, while it wants to "do right" by all of its older citizens, there is also the realization that the old rules and ways may no longer apply in a Japan that has changed in so many ways during the past century and especially in the years since World War II.

"The living conditions of the growing numbers of older people show a deepening division between two classes—those who enjoy a rich, relaxed 'silver' life with sufficient financial assets, and those who live in a tight financial situation, supporting themselves with a meager pension and ever-diminishing savings," points out Kimi Itakura in *Look Japan* magazine. "The first class provides a booming market for 'silver' leisure services and enterprises targetted at the over-60s."

It is among this second class that cause for justifiable concern arises, and this is particularly true in some of the almost universal aging-associated problem areas—such as housing, long-term care, changing work-retirement options, and intergenera-

Barry Robinson, associate editor of *Ageing International,* the journal of the International Federation on Ageing (IFA), has been maintaining liaison with Japan for the American Association of Retired Persons (AARP) since 1979, and has traveled there on several occasions to speak at symposia and confer with government officials and business leaders. He is the author of *Options for Older Americans, On The Beat: Policemen at Work,* and "The Vision of Aging: Sight and Insight" in *Aging and Human Visual Function* plus numerous articles in American and Japanese periodicals.

tional dependency—issues with which Japan, the U.S., and other industrialized nations have long been wrestling. In some cases, Japan has for better or for worse been following our lead in dealing with these issues while, in other instances, it is breaking its own trail and exploring paths the U.S. might wish to at least consider in formulating its plans.

For years, Japanese parents, grandparents, and children have frequently lived under the same roof, and caring for the elderly has almost always been a family responsibility, with the burden usually falling, fairly or unfairly, on the wife of the eldest son. Today, with multi-generational households no longer as common as they once were, many wives work, thus making them less available for caregiving chores. Nonetheless, Japan is the one remaining industrialized nation in which a large share of elderly parents still live with their adult children.

Still, Japan is searching for new ways to continue its tradition of caring for its elders within the context of changing circumstances. Out of this dilemma has come an increased emphasis on the idea of "productive aging" which encourages older people to remain active and self-sufficient, thereby reducing the government's and/or society's role in providing for them.

Work and Retirement

Japan's low birthrate in the years following the postwar "baby boom" is now beginning to result in a shrinking supply of young workers, a trend which is expected to peak early next century. Not only will this result in labor shortages, especially for entry level and less desirable jobs, but it will also increase the financial burden borne by active workers in supporting retired workers. In response, large Japanese corporations have recently begun raising the age at which workers retire from so-called lifetime (actually long-term) employment careers, while the government is in the process of doing the same to the age at which they become eligible to collect public pension benefits from the Japanese equivalent of Social Security.

Most Japanese employees receive their pension benefits in a lump sum when they retire (which can precede by several years their eligibility to collect the public pension at age 60 for men and 56 for women). If a worker receives a large lump sum and manages it well, he and his wife may be able to continue living comfortably without having to dip into their accumulated savings (with an average saving rate of about 17% of earned income, Japanese workers truly live up to their reputation as super savers).

Keep in mind, however, that a large percentage of Japanese work for relatively small firms offering neither the security of lifetime employment nor the benefit of high occupational pensions. As a result, these people rarely retire willingly, usually working right up to—and sometimes beyond—their eligibility for the government's public pension. In many ways, their situations are similar to those of older American workers without private pension coverage who are totally dependent upon personal savings and Social Security.

Thus, most Japanese older workers spend the period between the end of long-term employment and the beginning of their public pension eligibility in some sort of second career—often with a smaller firm in a related field, and sometimes with their original employers but at a lower level. Many

still seek some kind of employment even after their public pension payments begin. In recent years, a number of "silver manpower" programs have been established to find work for older persons, but most of the available jobs have been menial (such as cutting grass in parks) and therefore not particularly desirable. With Japan just now beginning to experience the first symptoms of its young worker shortfall, increased efforts are being made to pair older persons with appropriate job assignments, but it remains to be seen whether these approaches will prove any more successful than their predecessors—or than similar efforts in the U.S.

Health and Housing

Housing shortages are nothing new to Japan which, for all of its recent economic gains, remains a basically land-poor nation with roughly half the population of the U.S. but only 4% as much land (slightly less than the state of California). This is one of the reasons that land prices are so high throughout Japan, and particularly in its major cities, especially Tokyo, where the surging economy has given rise to an incredibly rapid escalation of real estate values in recent years. Seeking to benefit from this, many affluent older Japanese who own their homes in the Tokyo metropolitan area have begun selling their houses to major real estate companies, and then moving into new luxury retirement residences being developed in some cases by the same firms buying their former homes.

As in the United States, there has been a rapid expansion of expensive retirement housing amidst growing concern for the vast majority of middle class Japanese elders who are unable to afford such accommodations or to qualify for publicly supported low-income housing. The inadequate supply of suitable housing for Japan's aging middle class population (or, for that matter, land upon which to build it) led to talk some five years ago about the possibility of establishing "retirement colonies" of Japanese seniors in Europe, Australia, and the Americas. Originally proposed by the Ministry of International Trade and Industry, the concept was quickly abandoned after meeting with intense criticism from both the potential host countries and within Japan itself.

Closely related to housing and the whole idea of developing greater self-sufficiency among aged Japanese is the question of long-term care which is rapidly becoming as big an issue in Japan as it presently is in America. One reason that long-term care is such a troublesome issue in both countries is that it is extremely expensive and beyond the means of most families. Since Japan, unlike the U.S., has national health insurance, the cost would most likely be borne by the government and ultimately by taxpayers.

Another is that no one really wants to spend his or her final days or years in a custodial nursing home. Unlike an acute-care nursing facility from which people eventually return home after recuperating from a hospitalization for surgery or a major illness, institutionalization in a custodial facility tends to be permanent and usually stems from people no longer being able to care for themselves in their own homes.

In recent years, long-term care has begun to encompass the kind of medical and home care services that can help people continue living independently in their own homes, and thus avoid—or at least postpone—having to go into custodial nursing homes. Compared to the United States, Japan has relatively few custodial nursing homes and, while efforts are being made to increase the nation's supply of such facilities, greater emphasis is being placed on developing workable alternatives. This is the main thrust of the Ministry of Health and Welfare's recently announced "Ten-Year Gold Plan for the Welfare of the Aged," which calls for spending $43 billion during the decade to create and put in place a home care and support network for Japan's elders. In contrast, the United States is still vacillating on the question of what to do about long-term care as the need to do something grows greater and greater.

Reverence and Pragmatism

On virtually all levels of Japanese society today, there is at least a commitment to finding ways for dealing with the aging of its population and its anticipated ramifications. The best of intentions, however, do not always translate into actions that work.

"Twenty years or so from now, the Japanese babyboomers, who are supporting the present Japanese economy, will be in their 60s," notes Kimie Itakura. "Whether Japanese society can be called truly rich will depend on how they find their lives at that time. While the administration should initiate concrete plans to bring about an affluent aged society in the coming century, each person needs to prepare her or himself individually for old age."

Itakura's final thought is consistent with—and may even reflect some impact of—the government's desire to stimulate private initiatives in the aging arena, and thus limit its role as a provider. Where American aging policy has been moving ever so slowly over the years toward increased government involvement in at least funding programs and services, Japan's approach seems to be one of trying to move rapidly toward getting its government "out of the aging business."

Toward this end, the Ministry of Health and Welfare helped established the Elderly Service Providers Association in 1987 to encourage the corporate sector to become involved in creating services and products for Japan's aging population. In a way, this is good since most businesses generally tend to have more respect for people they regard as potential customers than for those whom they see as potential recipients of their corporate charitable contributions. Although ESPA is supposed to be independent of the government, many of its staff are on leave from the Ministry, and there is the general impression that, while the government is seeking to remove itself from the service provision process, it sees itself serving as a powerful chuka-isha or trusted intermediary which might intervene quickly and forcefully if corporations were to treat older consumers unfairly.

At the same time, the Ministry is also organizing Japan's senior citizenry to advocate and negotiate on its own behalf with both the corporate and political sectors by encouraging the further development of a diverse range of aging organizations. Serving as the Ministry's vehicle for this is the Foundation of Social Development for Senior Citizens which was originally established in 1974 as the Japan Institute for Gerontological Research and Development, and reorganized as the Foundation in 1989.

How well this approach to empowering Japan's aging population will work over the long run is still questionable. At the moment, most of the newer aging groups, which came into being during the 1980s, are still relatively small, having fewer than 10,000 members each. Many of them claim to have been inspired by—and, to some extent, patterned after—the 33-million-member American Association of Retired Persons. From the still growing numbers of Japanese visiting AARP's offices who say they intend to establish aging organizations, this tendency will probably continue for a while, but it is possible that no single Japanese aging group will achieve the same kind of dominance or size that enables AARP to tower over its peers in the U.S. Instead, we may see a number of smaller and medium-sized groups springing up among Japan's aged as an appropriate reflection of their socio-cultural structure, and this may work just as well—or even better—in Japan as the so-called AARP model does in America.

For all of its reverence and respect for its elders, Japan is still a country in which pragmatism prevails, enabling it to survive and overcome the various vicissitudes of war, weather, and wealth, and it is quite likely that both of these attitudes will come into play in confronting the aging of its population. While the United States has traditionally placed great value on practicality, its citizens are often motivated more by emotion, sentimentality, and a desire to "do the right thing" than by totally realistic considerations. Somewhere between these two poles of East/West values may lie the appropriate combination of how best to deal with the aging of the world. Whether Japan and the United States can learn these lessons from each other's experience in time to make a difference remains to be seen. ☐

Barriers to Employment of Older Workers

Source: U.S. Department of Agriculture

Early retirement (labor force withdrawal prior to age 65) has become the norm. By age 62, almost half of all men are out of the labor force, that is, neither working nor looking for a job. Anticipating a dramatic decline in the ratio of workers to retirees as the baby-boom generation becomes eligible for retirement early in the next century, Federal policy has been directed toward encouraging workers to extend their work lives. However, older workers who might want to work still face various institutional barriers through (1) the impact of Social Security regulations and pension policies on work activity, (2) the market for part-time jobs, and (3) age discrimination.

The Social Security amendments of 1983 contained several long-term provisions, designed to remove work disincentives. These include:

- Beginning in the year 2000, the retirement age at which beneficiaries are eligible to receive full benefits will increase gradually from 65 to 67.
- Reduced benefits will continue to be available at age 62, but reduction factors will be revised to a maximum of 30 percent (for workers entitled at 62 when the normal retirement age is 67) compared to the prior 20 percent reduction.
- The delayed retirement credit will increase by half a percentage point for every other year, from 3 percent for workers age 62 prior to 1987 to 8 percent per year for workers age 62 after 2004.
- Beginning in 1990, the withholding rate decreased from $1 of every $2 above the exempt amount for persons who attain full retirement age to $1 of every three dollars. ☐

Social Security

The original Social Security Act was passed in 1935 and amended in 1939, 1946, 1950, 1952, 1954, 1956, 1958, 1960, 1961, 1965, 1967, 1969, 1972, 1974, 1977, 1980-1984, 1986, and 1988-1989.

The act is administered by the Social Security Administration and the Health Care Financing Administration, and other agencies within the Department of Health and Human Services.

For purposes of clarity, the explanations given below will describe the provisions of the act as amended.

Old Age, Disability, and Survivors Insurance

Practically everyone who works fairly regularly is covered by social security. Most state and local government employees are covered under voluntary agreements between states and the Secretary of Health and Human Services. Workers not covered include most federal civilian employees hired prior to January 1984, career railroad workers, and a few other exceptions.

Cash tips count for Social Security if they amount to $20 or more in a month from employment with a single employer.

To qualify for benefits or make payments possible for your survivors, you must be in work covered by the law for a certain number of "quarters of coverage." Before 1978, a quarter of coverage was earned if a worker was paid $50 or more wages in a 3-month calendar quarter. A self-employed person got 4 "quarters of coverage" for a year in which his net earnings were $400 or more.

In 1978, a worker, whether employed or self-employed, received one quarter of coverage for each $250 of covered annual earnings up to a maximum of four for a year. The quarter of coverage measure was increased to $260 in 1979 and $290 in 1980, $310 in 1981, $340 in 1982, $370 in 1983, $390 in 1984, $410 in 1985, $440 in 1986, $460 in 1987, $470 in 1988, $500 in 1989, $520 in 1990, and will increase automatically in future years to keep pace with increases in average wages. The number of quarters needed differs for different persons and depends on the date of your birth; in general, it is related to the number of years after 1950, or after the year you reach 21, if later, and up to the year you reach 62, become disabled, or die. One "quarter of coverage" is required for each such year in order for you or your family to get benefits. No one will need more than 40 quarters. Your local Social Security office can tell you how long you need to work.

Who Pays for the Insurance?

Both workers and their employers pay for the workers' insurance. Self-employed persons pay their own social security contributions annually along with their income tax. The rates include the cost of Medicare hospital insurance. The contribution and benefit base is $51,300 for 1990, and will increase automatically in future years as earnings levels rise. The contribution rate schedules under present law are shown in a table in this section.

The separate payroll contribution to finance hospital insurance is placed in a separate trust fund in the U.S. Treasury. In addition, the medical insurance premiums, currently $29 for 1990 a month,

Social Security Contribution and Rate Schedule
(percent of covered earnings)

Year	Retirement, survivors, and disability insurance	Hospital insurance	Total
EMPLOYERS AND EMPLOYEES			
1978	4.95 %	1.10 %	6.05 %
1979-80	5.08	1.05	6.13
1981	5.35	1.30	6.65
1982-83	5.40	1.30	6.70
1984	5.70	1.30	7.00
1985	5.70	1.35	7.05
1986-87	5.70	1.45	7.15
1988-89	6.06	1.45	7.51
1990 & later	6.20	1.45	7.65
SELF-EMPLOYED			
1978	7.00 %	1.10 %	8.10 %
1979-80	7.05	1.05	8.10
1981	8.00	1.30	9.30
1982	8.05	1.30	9.35
1983	8.05	1.30	9.35
1984	11.40	2.60	*14.00
1985	11.40	2.70	*14.10
1986-87	11.40	2.90	*14.30
1988-89	12.12	2.90	*15.02
1990 & later	12.40	2.90	*15.30

*The law provides credit against self-employment tax liability in the following manner: 2.7% in 1984; 2.3% in 1985; 2.09% 1986-1989 and, beginning with the 1990 taxable year, the credit is replaced.

and the government's shares go into another separate trust fund.

How to Apply for Benefits

You apply for benefits by filing a claim either in person, by mail, or by telephone at any social security office. You can get the address either from the post office or from the phone book under the listing, United States Government—Department of Health and Human Services—Social Security Administration. You will need certain kinds of proof, depending upon the type of benefit you are claiming. If it is a retirement benefit, you should provide a birth or baptismal certificate. If you are unable to get these documents, other old documents showing your age or date of birth—such as census records, school records, early naturalization certificate, etc.—may be acceptable. A widow, or widower, 60 or older who is claiming widow's benefits based on his or her spouse's earnings should have both proof of age and a copy of the marriage certificate. A child claiming child's benefits should provide a birth certificate. If formal proof is not available, the Social Security office will tell you what kinds of information will be acceptable.

What Does Social Security Offer?

The Social Security contribution you pay gives you four different kinds of protection: (1) retire-

Delayed Retirement Credit Rates

Age 62	Monthly percentage	Yearly percentage
Prior to 1979	1/12 of 1%	1%
1979-1986	1/4 of 1%	3%
1987-1988	7/24 of 1%	3.5%
1989-1990	1/3 of 1%	4%
1991-1992	3/8 of 1%	4.5%
1993-1994	5/12 of 1%	5%
1995-1996	11/24 of 1%	5.5%
1997-1998	1/2 of 1%	6%
1999-2000	13/24 of 1%	6.5%
2001-2002	7/12 of 1%	7%
2003-2004	5/8 of 1%	7.5%
2005 or later	2/3 of 1%	8%

ment benefits, (2) survivors' benefits, (3) disability benefits, and (4) Medicare hospital insurance benefits.

Retirement benefits. Currently, a worker becomes eligible for the full amount of his retirement benefits at age 65, if he has retired under the definition in the law. A worker may retire at 62 and get 80% of his full benefit. The closer he is to age 65 when he starts collecting his benefit, the larger is the fraction of his full benefit that he will get.

The amount of the retirement benefit you are entitled to at 65 is the key to all other benefits under the program. The retirement benefit is based on covered earnings, generally those after 1950. Your covered earnings will be updated (indexed) to the second year before you reach age 62, become disabled, or die, and will reflect the increases in average wages that have occurred since the earnings were paid.

A worker who delays his retirement past age 65, or who does not receive a benefit for some months after age 65 because of high earnings will get a special credit that can mean a larger benefit. The credit adds to a worker's benefits 1% (3% for workers age 62 after 1978) for each year (1/12 of 1% for each month) from age 65 to age 70 for which he did not get benefits. (*See* table.)

The law provides a special minimum benefit at retirement for people who worked under Social Security for many years. The provision will help people who had low incomes, but above a specific level, in their working years. The amount of the special minimum depends on the number of years of coverage. For a worker retiring at 65 in Jan. 1990 with 30 or more years of coverage, the special minimum benefit would be $437.60 (effective December 1984). These benefits are reduced if a worker is under 65 and are increased automatically for increases in the cost of living.

If you retired at age 65 in Jan. 1990 with average earnings, you would get a benefit of $719.80.

If your spouse is also 65, then he or she will get a spouse's benefit that is equal to half your benefit. So if your benefit is $719.80, your spouse gets $354.90.

If your spouse is between ages 62 and 65, he or she can draw a reduced benefit; the amount depends on the number of months before 65 that he or she starts getting checks. If he or she draws his or her benefit when he or she is 62, he or she will get about 3/8 of your basic benefit, or $269.90. (He or she will get this amount for the rest of his or her life, unless you should die first; then he or she can

start getting widow's or widower's benefits, described below.)

If the spouse is entitled to a worker's retirement benefit on his or her own earnings, he or she can draw whichever amount is larger. If the spouse is entitled to a retirement benefit which is less than the spouse's benefit, he or she will receive his or her own retirement benefit plus the difference between the retirement benefit and the spouse's benefit.

If you have children under 18 or a child under age 19 in full-time attendance at an elementary or secondary school or a son or daughter who became totally disabled prior to reaching age 22, when you retire they will get a benefit equal to half your full retirement benefits (subject to maximum payments that can be made to a family). If your spouse is caring for a child who is under 16 or who became disabled before 22 (and getting benefits too), he or she is eligible for benefits, even if he or she is under 62.

In general, the highest retirement check that can be paid to a worker who retired at 65 in Jan. 1990 is about $975 a month. Maximum payment to the family of this retired worker is about $1,705.70 in Jan. 1990. When your children reach age 18, their benefits will stop except for children under age 19 attending an elementary or secondary school and except for a benefit that is going to a son or daughter who became totally disabled before attaining age 22. Such a person can continue to get his benefits as long as his disability meets the definition in the law.

If you are divorced, you can get Social Security benefits (the same as a spouse or widow, or widower), based on your ex-spouse's earnings record if you were married at least 10 years and if your ex-spouse has retired, become disabled, or died. If a divorced spouse has been divorced for at least 2 years, the spouse may be eligible for benefits even if the worker is not receiving benefits. However, both the worker and spouse must be age 62 or over and the worker must be fully insured.

Survivor benefits. This feature of the social security program gives your family valuable life insurance protection—in some cases benefits to a family could amount to $100,000 or more over a period of years. The amount of protection is again geared to what the worker would be entitled to if he had been age 65 when he died. Your survivors could get:

1. A one-time cash payment. [NOTE: There is no restriction on the use of the lump-sum death payment.] This "lump-sum death payment" is $255.

2. A benefit for each child until he reaches 18, or 19 if the child is in full-time attendance at an elementary or secondary school or at any age if disabled before 22. Each eligible child receives 75% of the basic benefit (subject to reduction for the family maximum). (A disabled child can continue to collect benefits after age 22.) If certain conditions are met, dependent grandchildren of insured workers can receive survivor or dependent benefits.

3. A benefit for your widow(er) at any age, if she/he has children under 16 or disabled in care. Her/his benefit is also 75% of the basic benefit. She/he can collect this as long as she/he has a child under 16 or disabled now "in care." Payments stop then (they will start again upon application when she/he is 60 at a slightly lower amount).

Total family survivor benefits are estimated to be

as high as $2,084.50 a month if the worker dies in 1990.

4. If there are no children either under 16 or disabled, your spouse can get a widow's, or widower's benefit starting at age 60. This would come to 71 1/2% of the basic amount at age 60. A widow, or widower, who first becomes entitled at 65 or later may get 100% of his or her deceased spouse's basic amount (provided neither he nor she ever drew reduced benefits).

5. Dependent parents can sometimes collect survivors' benefits. They are usually eligible if: (a) they were getting at least half their support from the deceased worker at (1) the time of the worker's death if the worker did not qualify for disability benefits before death, or (2) if the worker had been entitled to disability benefits which had not been terminated before death either at the beginning of the period of disability or at the time of death; (b) they have reached 62; and (c) they are not eligible for a greater retirement benefit based on their own earnings. A single surviving parent can then get 82 1/2% of the basic benefit. If two parents are eligible, each would get 75%.

Here is an example of survivors' benefits in one family situation: John Jones died at age 29 in June 1990 leaving a wife and two children aged one and three. He had average covered earnings under Social Security. Family survivors' benefits would include: (1) a cash lump-sum death payment of $255, and (2) a total monthly benefit of $1,317 for the family. When the children reach 18, their benefits stop unless they are attending an elementary or secondary school full time, in which case payments continue up to age 19. When the older child no longer collects benefits, the widow and younger child continue to get benefits until that child is 16. He will still get a benefit until age 18 (or age 19, if he continues in school), but Mrs. Jones' checks will stop. When Mrs. Jones becomes 60 (assuming she has not remarried), she will be able to get a reduced widow's benefit if she so chooses, or she can wait until age 65 to get a full benefit.

If in addition to your Social Security benefit as a wife, husband, widow, or widower you receive a pension based on your work in [public] employment not covered by Social Security, your benefit as a dependent or survivor will be reduced by 2/3rds of the amount of that pension. Under an exception in the law, your government pension will not affect your dependent's or survivor's benefit if you became eligible for that pension before December 1982 and if, at the time you apply or become entitled to your social security benefit as a dependent or survivor, you could have qualified for that benefit if the law in effect in January 1977 had remained in effect (i.e., at that time, men had to prove they were dependent upon their wives for support to be eligible for benefits as a dependent or survivor.) There are also several other exceptions in the law. Your government pension, however, currently will not affect any Social Security benefit based on your own work covered by social security.

Disability Benefits. Disability benefits can be paid to several groups of people:

Disabled workers under 65 and their families.

Persons disabled before 22 who continue to be disabled. These benefits are payable as early as 18 when a parent (or grandparent under certain circumstances) receives social security retirement or disability benefits or when an insured parent dies.

Disabled widows and widowers and (under cer-

Work Credit for Disability Benefits

Born after 1929, become disabled at age	Born before 1930, become disabled before 62 in	Years of work credit you need
42 or younger	1971	5
44	1973	5 1/2
46	1975	6
48	1977	6 1/2
50	1979	7
51	1980	7 1/4
52	1981	7 1/2
54	1983	8
56	1985	8 1/2
58	1987	9
60	1989	9 1/2
62 or older	1991 or later	10

NOTE: Five years of this credit must have been earned in the 10 years ending when you became disabled; years need not be continuous or in units of full years.

tain conditions) disabled surviving divorced spouses of workers who were insured at death. These benefits are payable as early as 50.

A disabled person is eligible for Medicare after being entitled to disability payments for 24 months.

If you are a worker and become severely disabled, you will be eligible for monthly benefits if you have worked under Social Security long enough and recently enough. The amount of work you will need depends on your age when you become disabled:

Before 24: You need credit for 1 1/2 years of work in the 3-year period ending when your disability begins.

24 through 30: You need credit for having worked half the time between 21 and the time you become disabled.

31 or older: All workers disabled at 31 or older—except the blind—need the amount of credit shown in the chart.

To be considered disabled under the social security law you must have a physical or mental condition which: (1) prevents you from doing any substantial gainful work; and (2) is expected to last (or has lasted) for at least 12 months, or is expected to result in death.

If you meet these conditions, you may be able to get payments even if your recovery from the disability is expected.

The medical evidence from your physician or other sources will show the severity of your condition and the extent to which it prevents you from doing substantial gainful work. Your age, education, training, and work experience also may be considered in deciding whether you are able to work.

If you can't do your regular work but can do other substantial gainful work, you will not be considered disabled. A person whose vision is no better than 20/200 even with glasses, or who has a limited visual field of 20 degrees or less, is considered "blind" under the social security law.

While you are receiving benefits as a disabled worker, payments can also be made to certain members of your family. These family members include:

Your unmarried children under 18.

Your children under 19 if they are unmarried

and attending an elementary or secondary school full time.

Your unmarried children 18 or older who were disabled before reaching 22 and continue to be disabled.

Your spouse at any age if she/he has in-care a child who is under 16 or disabled and who is getting benefits based on your social security record.

Your spouse 62 or older even if there are no children entitled to benefits.

A child may be eligible on a grandparent's social security record only if the child's parents are disabled or deceased and the child was living with and receiving 1/2 support from the grandparent at the time the grandparent qualified for benefits.

Benefits begin after a waiting period of 5 full calendar months. No benefits can be paid for these first 5 months of disability; therefore, the first payment is for the 6th full month. If you are disabled more than 6 full months before you apply, back benefits may be payable, but not before the 6th full month of disability. It is important to apply soon after the disability starts because back payments are limited to the 12 months preceding the month you apply.

Certain disabled people under 65 are eligible for Medicare. They include disabled workers at any age, persons who became disabled before age 22, and disabled widows and widowers age 50 or over who have been entitled to disability checks for 2 years or more.

Medicare protection generally ends when monthly disability benefits end, and can continue an additional 3 years after benefits stop because an individual returns to gainful work. (Under certain circumstances, former disability beneficiaries may purchase continued Medicare coverage. *See* "Do You Qualify for Hospital Insurance?" in this section.)

If a person becomes entitled to disability benefits again, Medicare coverage starts at the same time if a worker becomes disabled again within 5 years after benefits end (or within 7 years for a disabled widow, widower, or person disabled before age 22).

Benefits to workers disabled after 1978 and their dependents are based, in part, on earnings that have been adjusted to take account of increases in average wages since they were earned. The adjusted earnings are averaged together and a formula is applied to the adjusted average to figure the benefit rate.

Monthly benefits in Jan. 1990 or later can be as high as $1,152 for a worker and as high as $1,728 for a worker with a family. Once a person starts receiving benefits, the amount will increase automatically in future years to keep pace with the rising cost of living.

If you receive benefits as a disabled worker, an adult disabled since childhood, or a disabled widow or widower, you are not subject to the general rule under which some benefits are withheld if you have substantial earnings. There are special rules, which include medical considerations, for determining how any work you do might affect your disability payments.

If one of your dependents who is under 65 and who is not disabled works and earns more than $6,840 in 1990, some of the dependent's benefits may be withheld. In general, $1 in benefits is withheld for each $2 over $6,840. Different rules apply to your dependents who are 65 or over. A person 65 or over can earn $9,360 in 1990 without having benefits withheld. For persons 65 or over, $1 in benefits is withheld for $3 in earnings over $9,360.

The amount a person can earn without having any benefits withheld will increase in future years as the level of average wages rises.

If you are receiving disability benefits, you are required by law to let the Social Security Administration know if your condition improves or if you return to work no matter how little you earn.

If at any time medical evidence shows that you no longer meet the requirements for entitlement to disability benefits, you will still receive benefits for a 3-month period of adjustment. Benefits will then be stopped.

Whether or not you report a return to work or that your condition has improved, Social Security will review your claim periodically to see if you continue to meet the requirements for benefits.

If you are a disabled worker or a person disabled in childhood and you return to work in spite of a severe condition, your benefits may continue to be paid during a trial work period of up to 9 months—not necessarily consecutive months. This will give you a chance to test your ability to work. If after 9 months it is decided that you are able to do substantial gainful work, your benefits will be paid for an adjustment period of 3 additional months.

Thus, if you go to work in spite of your disability, you may continue to receive disability benefits for up to 12 months, even though the work is substantial gainful work. If it is decided that the work you are able to do is not substantial and gainful, you may continue to receive benefits. Of course, should you no longer meet the requirements for entitlement your benefits would be stopped after a 3-month adjustment period even though your trial work period might not be over.

Disabled widows and widowers also can have a trial work period. If your benefits are stopped because you return to work and you become unable to continue working within the next 33 months, your benefits can be restarted automatically. You do not have to file a new disability application.

You Can Earn Income Without Losing Benefits

If you are 70 or over you can earn any amount and still get all your benefits. If you are under 70, you can receive all benefits if your earnings do not exceed the annual exempt amount. The annual amount for 1990 is $9,360 for people 65 or over and $6,840 for people under 65.

If your earnings go over the annual amount, $1 in benefits is withheld for each $2 ($3 if age 65-69) of earnings above the limit.

The monthly measure used for 1977 and earlier years to determine whether benefits could be paid for any month during which they earned 1/12 or less of the annual exempt amount and did not do substantial work in their business has been eliminated. A person can now use the monthly test only in the first year that he or she has a month in which earnings do not exceed 1/12 of the annual exempt amount or does not perform substantial services in self-employment. If such a month occurs in 1990, a benefit can be paid for any month in which you earn $780 or less (if 65 or older) or $570 (if under 65) and don't perform substantial services in self-employment even though your total yearly earnings exceed the annual amount.

The annual exempt amount will increase automatically as the level of average wages rises.

If a worker's earnings exceed the exempt

amount, social security benefits to his dependents may be reduced. However, a dependent's benefits will not be reduced if another dependent has excess earnings.

Anyone earning over the annual exempt amount a year while receiving benefits (and under age 70) must report these earnings to the Social Security Administration. If you continue to work after you have applied for social security, your additional earnings may increase the amount of your monthly payment. This will be done automatically by the Social Security Administration. You need not ask for it.

Medicare

The Medicare program is administered by the Health Care Financing Administration.

Most people 65 and over and many under 65 who have been entitled to disability checks for at least 2 years have Medicare protection. So do insured people and their dependents who need a kidney transplant or dialysis treatment because of permanent kidney failure.

The hospital insurance part of Medicare helps pay the cost of inpatient hospital care and certain kinds of follow-up care. The medical insurance part helps pay for the cost of doctors' services, outpatient hospital services, and for certain other medical items and services.

A person who is eligible for monthly benefits at 65 gets hospital insurance automatically and does not have to pay a premium. He does pay a monthly premium for medical insurance.

Supplemental Security Income

The supplemental security income (SSI) program is a federally funded program administered by the Social Security Administration. Its basic purpose is to assure a minimum level of income to people who are elderly (65 or over), blind or disabled, and who have limited income and resources.

In 1990, the maximum Federal SSI payment was $386 a month for an individual and $579 a month for a couple. But in many States, SSI payments are much higher because the State adds to the Federal payment.

Countable resources must be valued at $2,000 or less for an individual or $3,000 or less for a couple. But not all the things people own count for SSI. For instance, the house a person lives in and the land around it, and usually, one car does not count.

Generally, depending on the State, people who get SSI can also get Medicaid to pay for their health care costs as well as food stamps and other social services. And in many States an application for SSI is an application for Medicaid, so people do not have to make separate applications. Certain people can also apply for food stamps at the same Social Security office where they apply for SSI.

Social Security representatives will need information about the income and resources and the citizenship or alien status of people applying for benefits. If the person is living with a spouse, or the application is for a disabled child living with parents, the same information is needed about the spouse/parents.

People who are age 65 or over will need proof of their age such as a birth or baptismal certificate. And if a person who is filing is disabled or blind, Social Security will need information about the impairment and its treatment history.

It helps if people have this information and evidence with them when they talk to their Social Security representative. But they do not need to have any of these things to **start** their application. All they need to do is to call Social Security to find out if they are eligible for SSI payments and the other benefits that come with it. Benefits are not retroactive, so delay can cost money.

The Social Security representative will explain just what information/evidence is needed for the SSI claim, and will provide help in getting it if help is needed. Most Social Security offices will make an appointment for an office visit or for a telephone interview if that is more convenient. Or people can just walk in, and wait until someone is free to help them.

Over 4.5 million people receive SSI benefits now. Many receive both SSI and Social Security. Do not wait. Call 1-800-234-5SSA, and find out more about SSI. Even the call is free!

How to Protect Your Social Security Record

Always show your Social Security card when you start a new job. In that way you will be sure that your earnings will be credited to *your* Social Security record and not someone else's. If you lose your Social Security card, apply for a new one at any Social Security office. When a woman marries, she should apply for a new card showing her married name (and the same number).

Public Assistance

The Federal government makes grants to the states to help them provide financial assistance, medical care, and social services to certain persons in need, including children dependent because of the death, absence from home, incapacity, or (in some states) unemployment of a parent. In addition, some help is provided from only state and/or local funds to some other needy persons.

Federal sharing in state cash assistance expenditures made in accordance with the Social Security Act is based on formulas which are set forth in the Act. The Social Security Act gives the states the option of using one of two formulas, whichever is to its benefit. One formula limits the amount of assistance payment in which there is federal sharing. The other formula permits federal sharing without a limit on the amount of assistance payment. Administrative costs in all the programs are shared equally by the federal and state governments.

Within these and other general patterns set by the requirements of the Social Security Act and their administrative interpretations, each state initiates and administers its own public assistance programs, including the determination of who is eligible to receive assistance, and how much can be granted and under what conditions. Assistance is in the form of cash payments made to recipients, except that direct payments are used for medical care, and restricted payments may be used in cases of mismanagement. Other social services are provided, in some instances, to help assistance recipients increase their capacity for self-care and self-support or to strengthen family life.

In the medical assistance Medicaid program, federal funds pay 50% to 83% of the costs for medical care. If it is to a state's benefit, it may use the Medicaid formula for federal sharing for its money payment programs, ignoring the maximum on dollar amounts per recipient.

Medicare Program

The Medicare program is a federal health-insurance program for persons 65 and over, disabled people under 65 who have been entitled to social security disability benefits at least 24 months, or have worked long enough in Federal employment to be insured for Medicare, and insured workers and their dependents at any age who need dialysis treatment or a kidney transplant because of permanent kidney failure.

Enacted under the Social Security Amendments of 1965, Medicare's official name is Title XVIII of the Social Security Act. These amendments also carried Title XIX, providing federal assistance to state medical-aid programs, which has come to be known as Medicaid.

Medicare

It will be helpful to your understanding of the Medicare program if you keep the following points in mind:

- The federal health-insurance program does not of itself offer medical services. It helps pay hospital, doctor, and other medical bills. You choose your own doctor, who prescribes your treatment and place of treatment. But, you should always make sure that health care facilities or persons who provide you with treatment or services are participating in Medicare. Usually, Medicare cannot pay for care from non-participating health care organizations.
- There are two parts of the program: (1) The hospital insurance part for the payment of most of the cost of covered care provided by participating hospitals, skilled nursing facilities, and home health agencies. (2) The medical insurance part which helps pay doctors' bills and certain other expenses.
- Another important point to remember: While Medicare pays the major share of the costs of many illnesses requiring hospitalization, it does not offer adequate protection for long-term illness or mental illness.
- Therefore, it may be advisable not to cancel any private health insurance you now carry. You may wish to cancel a policy whose benefits are duplicated by the federal program, and consider a new policy that will provide for the payment of costs not covered by the federal program. Private insurance companies offer policies supplementing the protection offered by the federal program.

If you want help in deciding whether to buy private supplemental insurance, ask at any social security office for the pamphlet, *Guide to health insurance for people with Medicare.* This free pamphlet describes the various types of supplemental insurance available.

Do You Qualify for Hospital Insurance?

If you're entitled to monthly social security or railroad retirement checks (as a worker, dependent, or survivor), you have hospital insurance protection automatically when you're 65. Disabled people under 65 will have hospital insurance automatically after they have been entitled to social security disability benefits for 24 months. Effective July 1, 1990, former disability beneficiaries will be able to purchase hospital insurance after their premium-free coverage stops due to work activity. Federal employees who are disabled before 65 may be eligible on the basis of Federal employment. (Disabled people who get railroad annuities must meet special requirements.) People 65 or older who are not entitled to monthly benefits must have worked long enough under Social Security or the railroad retirement system or in covered Federal employment to get hospital insurance without paying a monthly premium. If they do not have enough work, they can buy hospital insurance. The premium is $175 a month in 1990. People are eligible at any age if they need maintenance dialysis or a kidney transplant for permanent kidney failure and are getting monthly Social Security or railroad retirement benefits or have worked long enough.

To be sure your protection will start the month you reach 65, apply for Medicare insurance 3 months before reaching 65, even if you don't plan to retire.

Do You Qualify for Voluntary Medical Insurance?

The voluntary medical insurance plan is a vital supplement to the hospital plan. It helps pay for doctors' and other medical services. Many people have not been able to obtain such insurance from private companies because they could not afford it or because of their medical histories.

One difference between the hospital insurance plan and the medical insurance plan is that you do not have to be under the social security or railroad retirement systems to enroll in the medical plan. Almost anyone who is 65 or older or who is eligible for hospital insurance can enroll in medical insurance.

People who get social security benefits or retirement benefits under the railroad retirement system will be enrolled automatically for medical insurance—unless they say they don't want it—when they become entitled to hospital insurance. Automatic enrollment does not apply to people who plan to continue working past 65, who are disabled widows or widowers between 50 and 65 who aren't getting disability checks, who are 65 but have not worked long enough to be eligible for hospital insurance, who have permanent kidney failure, who are eligible for Medicare on the basis of Federal employment, or who live in Puerto Rico or foreign countries. These people have to apply for medical insurance if they want it. People who have medical insurance pay a monthly premium covering part of the cost of this protection. The other part is paid from general federal revenues. The basic premium for enrollees is $28.60 a month in 1990.

Is Other Insurance Necessary?

As already indicated, Medicare provides only partial reimbursement. Therefore, you should know how much medical cost you can bear and perhaps arrange for other insurance.

In 1990, for the first 60 days of inpatient hospital care in each benefit period, hospital insurance pays for all covered services except for the first $592.

For the 61st through 90th day of a covered inpatient hospital stay, hospital insurance pays for all covered services except for $148 a day. People who need to be in a hospital for more than 90 days in a benefit period can use some or all of their 60 lifetime reserve days. Hospital insurance pays for all covered services except for $296 a day for each reserve day used. Hospital insurance also does not pay the full cost of an inpatient stay in a skilled nursing facility.

Under medical insurance, the patient must meet an annual deductible. In 1990, the annual deductible is $75. After the patient has met the deductible, each year, medical insurance generally pays 80% of the approved amounts for any additional covered services the patient receives during the rest of the year.

How You Obtain Coverage

If you are receiving Social Security or railroad retirement monthly benefits, you will receive from the government information concerning Medicare about 3 months before you become entitled to hospital insurance.

All other eligible people have to file an application for Medicare. They should contact a social security office to apply for Medicare.

The Social Security System: Safe and Sound

By Gwendolyn S. King

As Commissioner of Social Security, I am heartened by the current debate on the future financing and continued long-term health of the Social Security program. Such discussions give the American people the chance to learn more about a program that is so important to so many.

Today, Social Security is financially sound. In fact, 1990 marks the 50th anniversary of Social Security's paying benefits, on time and in the right amount, to those who depend on them. And over the next four decades, the Social Security trust fund reserves are projected to grow substantially, ensuring that the program can make good on its commitment to pay monthly benefits to future generations of retirees.

The Bush Administration has a solemn commitment to protect and preserve Social Security. We need to assure its continued solvency and build even greater public confidence in the program. However, I have a unique responsibility as Commissioner to ensure that the current discussion on Social Security edifies, and does not confuse or mislead, the public on America's most important and successful social program. Based on much inaccurate information that has been disseminated to the public recently on this issue, I believe it is necessary to set the record straight on what is fact, and what is fiction.

Fiction: Social Security reserves are being used to finance general government operating expenses and, thus, are nothing more than worthless IOUs. They are not being invested for the public's benefit.

Fact: Section 201 of the Social Security Act stipulates that Social Security reserves are to be invested exclusively in interest-bearing U.S. government obligations. The law's creators intended that the public's money should be placed in the safest possible investment, backed by the full faith and credit of the U.S. government.

Because Social Security trust funds are invested in Treasury obligations, the money, after investment, has always been available to the government for its general operating needs.

Social Security dollars do draw interest. The Treasury pays the Social Security Trust Fund substantial interest payments—9.7 percent in the year ending June 30, 1989.

Fiction: Social Security reserves are sufficiently high, allowing a payroll tax cut and a return to the pay-as-you-go system.

Fact: The 1983 Social Security Rescue Amendments were adopted because of a realization that the pay-as-you-go philosophy left the system vulnerable to the effects of economic downturns. Back-to-back recessions in the late '70s and early '80s moved Social Security dangerously close to fiscal catastrophe. At one point, the contingency reserve contained only 14 percent of the next year's benefit expenditures, necessitating interfund borrowing from the Hospital Insurance Trust Fund.

At the begining of 1990, the Social Security Trust Fund had accumulated $188 billion. That money represents only nine months' worth of benefit payments. There is general agreement that a contingency of 100-150 percent of the funds needed to pay one year's worth of benefits should accumulate before changes in system financing are even discussed.

Fiction: The Social Security pay-roll tax is a regressive tax.

Fact: Social Security provides significant protection to surviving spouses and children, as well as to insured workers and their families in the event of disability. In fact, about 40 percent of Social Security benefit payments are in these non-retirement categories.

The Social Security benefit structure is highly progressive. It provides considerably higher benefits for low earners, in relation to their pre-retirement earnings, than for high-income workers. For workers retiring at age 65, Social Security benefits replace approximately 58 percent of earnings, 42 percent for mid-income Americans, and 24 percent for high-income earners.

Today, a low-income worker retiring at age 65 will gain back his or her lifetime Social Security tax contributions, plus interest, in about four years. High-income workers will gain their contribution back with interest in about seven years. □

Gwendolyn S. King is Commissioner of the Social Security Administration.

Source: Tax Federation. These opinions are not necessarily those of the Tax Federation or the *Information Please Almanac.*

WRITER'S GUIDE

A Concise Guide to Style

From *Webster's II New Riverside University Dictionary*. © 1984 by Houghton Mifflin Company.

This section discusses and illustrates the basic conventions of American capitalization, punctuation, and italicization.

Capitalization

Capitalize the following: 1. the first word of a sentence: Some spiders are poisonous; others are not. Are you my new neighbor?

2. the first word of a direct quotation, except when the quotation is split: Joyce asked, "Do you think that the lecture was interesting?" "No," I responded, "it was very boring." Tom Paine said, "The sublime and the ridiculous are often so nearly related that it is difficult to class them separately."

3. the first word of each line in a poem in traditional verse: Half a league, half a league,/Half a league onward,/All in the valley of Death/Rode the six hundred.—Alfred, Lord Tennyson

4. the names of people, of organizations and their members, of councils and congresses, and of historical periods and events: Marie Curie, Benevolent and Protective Order of Elks, an Elk, Protestant Episcopal Church, an Episcopalian, the Democratic Party, a Democrat, the Nuclear Regulatory Commission, the U.S. Senate, the Middle Ages, World War I, the Battle of Britain.

5. the names of places and geographic divisions, districts, regions, and locales: Richmond, Vermont, Argentina, Seventh Avenue, London Bridge, Arctic Circle, Eastern Hemisphere, Continental Divide, Middle East, Far North, Gulf States, East Coast, the North, the South Shore.

Do not capitalize words indicating compass points unless a specific region is referred to: Turn north onto Interstate 91.

6. the names of rivers, lakes, mountains, and oceans: Ohio River, Lake Como, Rocky Mountains, Atlantic Ocean.

7. the names of ships, aircraft, satellites, and space vehicles: U.S.S. *Arizona, Spirit of St. Louis,* the spy satellite Ferret-D, Voyager II, the space shuttle Challenger.

8. the names of nationalities, races, tribes, and languages: Spanish, Maori, Bantu, Russian.

9. words derived from proper names, except in their extended senses: the Byzantine Empire. *But:* byzantine office politics.

10. words indicating family relationships when used with a person's name as a title: Aunt Toni and Uncle Jack. *But:* my aunt and uncle, Toni and Jack Walker.

11. a title (i.e., civil, judicial, military, royal and noble, religious, and honorary) when preceding a name: Justice Marshall, General Jackson, Mayor Daley, Queen Victoria, Lord Mountbatten, Pope John Paul II, Professor Jacobson, Senator Byrd.

12. all references to the President and Vice President of the United States: The President has entered the hall. The Vice President presides over the Senate.

13. all key words in titles of literary, dramatic, artistic, and musical works: the novel *The Old Man and the Sea,* the short story "Notes from Underground," an article entitled "On Passive Verbs," James Dickey's poem "In the Tree House at Night," the play *Cat on a Hot Tin Roof,* Van Gogh's *Wheat Field and Cypress Trees,* Beethoven's *Emperor Concerto.*

14. *the* in the title of a newspaper if it is a part of the title: *The Wall Street Journal. But:* the New York *Daily News.*

15. the first word in the salutation and in the complimentary close of a letter: My dear Carol, Yours sincerely,

16. epithets and substitutes for the names of people and places: Old Hickory, Old Blood and Guts, The Oval Office, the Windy City.

17. words used in personifications: When is not Death at watch/Within those secret waters?/What wants he but to catch/Earth's heedless sons and daughters?—Edmund Blunden

18. the pronoun *I:* I told them that I had heard the news.

19. names for the Deity and sacred works: God, the Almighty, Jesus, Allah, the Supreme Being, the Bible, the Koran, the Talmud.

20. days of the week, months of the year, holidays, and holy days: Tuesday, May, Independence Day, Passover, Ramadan, Christmas.

21. the names of specific courts: The Supreme Court of the United States, the Massachusetts Appeals Court, the United States Court of Appeals for the First Circuit.

22. the names of treaties, accords, pacts, laws, and specific amendments: Panama Canal Treaty, Treaty of Paris, Geneva Accords, Warsaw Pact countries, Sherman Antitrust Law, Labor Management Relations Act, took the Fifth Amendment.

23. registered trademarks and service marks: Day-Glo, Comsat.

24. the names of geologic eras, periods, epochs, and strata and the names of prehistoric divisions: Paleozoic Era, Precambrian, Pleistocene, Age of Reptiles, Bronze Age, Stone Age.

25. the names of constellations, planets, and stars: Milky Way, Southern Crown, Saturn, Jupiter, Uranus, Polaris.

26. genus but not species names in binomial nomenclature: *Rana pipiens.*

27. New Latin names of classes, families, and all groups higher than genera in botanical and zoological nomenclature: Nematoda.

But do not capitalize derivatives from such names: nematodes.

28. many abbreviations and acronyms: Dec., Tues., Lt. Gen., M.F.A., UNESCO, MIRV.

Italicization

Use italics to:
1. indicate titles of books, plays, and epic poems:

436

War and Peace, The Importance of Being Earnest, Paradise Lost.

2. indicate titles of magazines and newspapers: *New York* magazine, *The Wall Street Journal*, the New York *Daily News.*

3. set off the titles of motion pictures and radio and television programs: *Star Wars, All Things Considered, Masterpiece Theater.*

4. indicate titles of major musical compositions: Handel's *Messiah*, Adam's *Giselle.*

5. set off the names of paintings and sculpture: *Mona Lisa, Pietà.*

6. indicate words, letters, or numbers that are referred to: The word *hiss* is onomatopoeic. *Can't* means *won't* in your lexicon. You form your *n*'s like *u*'s. A *6* looks like an inverted *9.*

7. indicate foreign words and phrases not yet assimilated into English: *C'est la vie* was the response to my complaint.

8. indicate the names of plaintiff and defendant in legal citations: *Roe* v. *Doe.*

9. emphasize a word or phrase: When you appear on the national news, you are *somebody.*

Use this device sparingly.

10. distinguish New Latin names of genera, species, subspecies, and varieties in botanical and zoological nomenclature: *Homo sapiens.*

11. set off the names of ships and aircraft but not space vehicles: U.S.S. *Arizona, Spirit of St. Louis,* Voyager II, the space shuttle Challenger, the spy satellite Ferret-D.

Punctuation

Apostrophe. 1. indicates the possessive case of singular and plural nouns, indefinite pronouns, and surnames combined with designations such as *Jr., Sr.,* and *II:* my sister's husband, my three sisters' husbands, anyone's guess, They answer each other's phones, John Smith, Jr.'s car.

2. indicates joint possession when used with the last of two or more nouns in a series: Doe and Roe's report.

3. indicates individual possession or authorship when used with each of two or more nouns in a series: Smith's, Roe's, and Doe's reports.

4. indicates the plurals of words, letters, and figures used as such: 60's and 70's; *x*'s, *y*'s, and *z*'s.

5. indicates omission of letters in contractions: aren't, that's, o'clock.

6. indicates omission of figures in dates: the class of '63.

Brackets. 1. enclose words or passages in quoted matter to indicate insertion of material written by someone other than the author: A tough but nervous, tenacious but restless race [the Yankees]; materially ambitious, yet prone to introspection. . . .—Samuel Eliot Morison

2. enclose material inserted within matter already in parentheses: (Vancouver [B.C.] January 1, 19—).

Colon. 1. introduces words, phrases, or clauses that explain, amplify, or summarize what has gone before: Suddenly I realized where we were: Rome.

There are two cardinal sins from which all the others spring: impatience and laziness.—Franz Kafka

2. introduces a long quotation: In his original draft of the *Declaration of Independence,* Jefferson wrote: "We hold these truths to be sacred and undeniable; that all men are created equal and independent, that from that equal creation they derive

rights inherent and inalienable. . . ."

3. introduces a list: We need the following items: pens, paper, pencils, blotters, and erasers.

4. separates chapter and verse numbers in Biblical references: James 1:4.

5. separates city from publisher in footnotes and bibliographies: Chicago: Riverside Press, 1983.

6. separates hour and minute(s) in time designations: 9:30 a.m., a 9:30 meeting.

7. follows the salutation in a business letter: Gentlemen:

Comma. 1. separates the clauses of a compound sentence connected by a coordinating conjunction: A difference exists between the musical works of Handel and Haydn, and it is a difference worth noting.

The comma may be omitted in short compound sentences: I heard what you said and I am furious. I got out of the car and I walked and walked.

2. separates *and* or *or* from the final item in a series of three or more: Red, yellow, and blue may be mixed to produce all colors.

3. separates two or more adjectives modifying the same noun if *and* could be used between them without altering the meaning: a solid, heavy gait. *But:* a polished mahogany dresser.

4. sets off nonrestrictive clauses or phrases (i.e., those that if eliminated would not affect the meaning of the sentences): The burglar, who had entered through the patio, went straight to the silver chest.

The comma should not be used when a clause is restrictive (i.e., essential to the meaning of the sentence): The burglar who had entered through the patio went straight to the silver chest; the other burglar searched for the wall safe.

5. sets off words or phrases in apposition to a noun or noun phrase: Plato, the famous Greek philosopher, was a student of Socrates.

The comma should not be used if such words or phrases precede the noun: The Greek philosopher Plato was a student of Socrates.

6. sets off transitional words and short expressions that require a pause in reading or speaking: Unfortunately, my friend was not well traveled. Did you, after all, find what you were looking for? I live with my family, of course.

7. sets off words used to introduce a sentence: No, I haven't been to Paris. Well, what do you think we should do now?

8. sets off a subordinate clause or a long phrase that precedes a principal clause: By the time we found the restaurant, we were starved. Of all the illustrations in the book, the most striking are those of the tapestries.

9. sets off short quotations and sayings: The candidate said, "Actions speak louder than words." "Talking of axes," said the Duchess, "chop off her head!"—Lewis Carroll

10. indicates omission of a word or words: To err is human; to forgive, divine.

11. sets off the year from the month in full dates: Nicholas II of Russia was shot on July 16, 1918.

But note that when only the month and the year are used, no comma appears: Nicholas II of Russia was shot in July 1918.

12. sets off city and state in geographic names: Atlanta, Georgia, is the transportation center of the South. 34 Beach Drive, Bedford, VA 24523.

13. separates series of four or more figures into thousands, millions, etc.: 67,000; 200,000.

14. sets off words used in direct address: I tell you, folks, all politics is applesauce.—Will Rogers Thank you for your expert assistance, Dolores.

15. Separates a tag question from the rest of a sentence: You forgot your keys again, didn't you?

16. sets off sentence elements that could be misunderstood if the comma were not used: Some time after, the actual date for the project was set.

17. follows the salutation in a personal letter and the complimentary close in a business or personal letter: Dear Jessica, Sincerely yours.

18. sets off titles and degrees from surnames and from the rest of a sentence: Walter T. Prescott, Jr.; Gregory A. Rossi, S.J.; Susan P. Green, M.D., presented the case.

Dash. 1. indicates a sudden break or abrupt change in continuity: "If—if you'll just let me explain—" the student stammered. And the problem—if there really is one—can then be solved.

2. sets apart an explanatory, a defining, or an emphatic phrase: Foods rich in protein—meat, fish, and eggs—should be eaten on a daily basis.

More important than winning the election, is governing the nation. That is the test of a political party—the acid, final test.—Adlai E. Stevenson

3. sets apart parenthetical matter: Wolsey, for all his faults—and he had many—was a great statesman, a man of natural dignity with a generous temperament. . . .—Jasper Ridley

4. marks an unfinished sentence: "But if my bus is late—" he began.

5. sets off a summarizing phrase or clause: The vital measure of a newspaper is not its size but its spirit—that is its responsibility to report the news fully, accurately, and fairly.—Arthur H. Sulzberger

6. sets off the name of an author or source, as at the end of a quotation: A poet can survive everything but a misprint.—Oscar Wilde

Ellipses. 1. indicate, by three spaced points, omission of words or sentences within quoted matter: Equipped by education to rule in the nineteenth century, . . . he lived and reigned in Russia in the twentieth century.—Robert K. Massie

2. indicate, by four spaced points, omission of words at the end of a sentence: The timidity of bureaucrats when it comes to dealing with . . . abuses is easy to explain. . . .—*New York*

3. indicate, when extended the length of a line, omission of one or more lines of poetry:
Roll   on,   thou   deep   and   dark   blue
    ocean—roll!
. . . .
Man marks the earth with ruin—his
    control
Stops with the shore.—Lord Byron

4. are sometimes used as a device, as for example, in advertising copy:
To help you Move and Grow
    with the Rigors of
Business in the 1980's . . .
    and Beyond.—*Journal of Business Strategy*

Exclamation Point. 1. terminates an emphatic or exclamatory sentence: Go home at once! You've got to be kidding!

2. terminates an emphatic interjection: Encore!

Hyphen. 1. indicates that part of a word of more than one syllable has been carried over from one line to the next:
During the revolution, the nation was beset with problems—looting, fight-
ing, and famine.

2. joins the elements of some compounds: great-grandparent, attorney-at-law, ne'er-do-well.

3. joins the elements of compound modifiers preceding nouns: high-school students, a fire-and-brimstone lecture, a two-hour meeting.

4. indicates that two or more compounds share a single base: four- and six-volume sets, eight- and nine-year olds.

5. separates the prefix and root in some combinations; check the Dictionary when in doubt about the spelling: anti-Nazi, re-elect, co-author, re-form/reform, re-cover/recover, re-creation/-recreation.

6. substitutes for the word *to* between typewritten inclusive words or figures: pp. 145-155, the Boston-New York air shuttle.

7. punctuates written-out compound numbers from 21 through 99: forty-six years of age, a person who is forty-six, two hundred fifty-nine dollars.

Parentheses. 1. enclose material that is not essential to a sentence and that if not included would not alter its meaning: After a few minutes (some say less) the blaze was extinguished.

2. often enclose letters or figures to indicate subdivisions of a series: A movement in sonata form consists of the following elements: (1) the exposition, (2) the development, and (3) the recapitulation.

3. enclose figures following and confirming written-out numbers, especially in legal and business documents: The fee for my services will be two thousand dollars ($2,000.00).

4. enclose an abbreviation for a term following the written-out term, when used for the first time in a text: The patient is suffering from acquired immune deficiency syndrome (AIDS).

Period. 1. terminates a complete declarative or mild imperative sentence: There could be no turning back as war's dark shadow settled irrevocably across the continent of Europe.—W. Bruce Lincoln. Return all the books when you can. Would you kindly affix your signature here.

2. terminates sentence fragments: Gray clouds—and what looks like a veil of rain falling behind the East German headland. A pair of ducks. A tired or dying swan, head buried in its back feathers, sits on the sand a few feet from the water's edge.—Anthony Bailey

3. follows some abbreviations: Dec., Rev., St., Blvd., pp., Co.

Question Mark. 1. punctuates a direct question: Have you seen the new play yet? Who goes there? *But:* I wonder who said "Nothing is easy in war." I asked if they planned to leave.

2. indicates uncertainty: Ferdinand Magellan (1480?-1521), Plato (427?-347 B.C.).

Quotation Marks. 1. Double quotation marks enclose direct quotations: "What was Paris like in the Twenties?" our daughter asked. "Ladies and Gentlemen," the Chief Usher said, "the President of the United States." Robert Louis Stevenson said that "it is better to be a fool than to be dead." When advised not to become a lawyer because the profession was already overcrowded, Daniel Webster replied, "There is always room at the top."

2. Double quotation marks enclose words or phrases to clarify their meaning or use or to indicate that they are being used in a special way: This was the border of what we often call "the West" or "the Free World." "The Windy City" is a name for Chicago.

3. Double quotation marks set off the translation of a foreign word or phrase: *die Grenze*, "the border."

4. Double quotation marks set off the titles of series of books, of articles or chapters in publications, of essays, of short stories and poems, of individual radio and television programs, and of songs and short musical pieces: "The Horizon Concise History" series; an article entitled "On Reflexive

Verbs in English"; Chapter Nine, "The Prince and the Peasant"; Pushkin's "The Queen of Spades"; Tennyson's "Ode on the Death of the Duke of Wellington"; "The Bob Hope Special"; Schubert's "Death and the Maiden."

5. Single quotation marks enclose quotations within quotations: The blurb for the piece proclaimed, "Two years ago at Geneva, South Vietnam was virtually sold down the river to the Communists. Today the spunky little . . . country is back on its own feet, thanks to 'a mandarin in a sharkskin suit who's upsetting the Red timetable.' "—Frances FitzGerald

Put commas and periods inside quotation marks; put semicolons and colons outside. Other punctuation, such as exclamation points and question marks, should be put inside the closing quotation marks only if part of the matter quoted.

Semicolon. 1. separates the clauses of a compound sentence having no coordinating conjunction: Do not let us speak of darker days; let us rather speak of sterner days.—Winston Churchill

2. separates the clauses of a compound sentence in which the clauses contain internal punctuation, even when the clauses are joined by conjunctions: Skis in hand, we trudged to the lodge, stowed our lunches, and donned our boots; and the rest of our party waited for us at the lifts.

3. separates elements of a series in which items already contain commas: Among those at the diplomatic reception were the Secretary of State; the daughter of the Ambassador to the Court of St. James's, formerly of London; and two United Nations delegates.

4. separates clauses of a compound sentence joined by a conjunctive adverb, such as *however, nonetheless,* or *hence:* We insisted upon a hearing; however, the Grievance Committee refused.

5. may be used instead of a comma to signal longer pauses for dramatic effect: But I want you to know that when I cross the river my last conscious thought will be of the Corps; and the Corps; and the Corps.—General Douglas MacArthur

Virgule. 1. separates successive divisions in an extended date: fiscal year 1983/84.

2. represents *per:* 35 km/hr, 1,800 ft/sec.

3. means *or* between the words *and* and *or:* Take water skis and/or fishing equipment when you visit the beach this summer.

4. separates two or more lines of poetry that are quoted and run in on successive lines of a text: The student actress had a memory lapse when she came to the lines "Double, double, toil and trouble/Fire burn and cauldron bubble/Eye of newt and toe of frog/Wool of bat and tongue of dog" and had to leave the stage in embarrassment.

Forms of Address[1]

Source: Webster's II New Riverside University Dictionary. Copyright © 1984 by Houghton Mifflin Company.

Academics

Dean, college or university. *Address:* Dean _____ _____. *Salutation:* Dear Dean _____.

President. *Address:* President _____ _____. *Salutation:* Dear President _____.

Professor, college or university. *Address:* Professor _____ _____. *Salutation:* Dear Professor _____.

Clerical and Religious Orders

Abbot. *Address:* The Right Reverend _____ _____ O.S.B. Abbot of _____. *Salutation:* Right Reverend Abbot or Dear Father Abbot.

Archbishop, Eastern Orthodox. *Address:* The Most Reverend Joseph, Archbishop of _____. *Salutation:* Your Eminence.

Archbishop, Roman Catholic. The Most Reverend _____ _____, Archbishop of _____. *Salutation:* Your Excellency.

Archdeacon, Episcopal. *Address:* The Venerable _____ _____, Archdeacon of _____. *Salutation:* Venerable Sir or Dear Archdeacon _____.

Bishop, Episcopal. *Address:* The Right Reverend _____ _____, Bishop of _____. *Salutation:* Right Reverend Sir or Dear Bishop _____.

Bishop, other Protestant. *Address:* The Reverend _____ _____. *Salutation:* Dear Bishop _____.

Bishop, Roman Catholic. *Address:* The Most Reverend _____ _____, Bishop of _____. *Salutation:* Your Excellency or Dear Bishop _____.

Brotherhood, Roman Catholic. *Address:* Brother _____ _____, C.F.C. *Salutation:* Dear Brother or Dear Brother Joseph.

Brotherhood, superior of. *Address:* Brother Joseph C.F.C. Superior. *Salutation:* Dear Brother Joseph.

Cardinal. *Address:* His Eminence Joseph Cardinal Stone. *Salutation:* Your Eminence.

Clergyman/woman, Protestant. *Address:* The Reverend _____ _____ or The Reverend _____ _____, D.D. *Salutation:* Dear Mr./Ms. _____ or Dear Dr. _____.

Dean of a cathedral, Episcopal. *Address:* The Very Reverend _____ _____, Dean of _____. *Salutation:* Dear Dean _____.

Monsignor. *Address:* The Right Reverend Monsignor _____ _____. *Salutation:* Dear Monsignor.

Patriarch, Greek Orthodox. *Address:* His All Holiness Patriarch Joseph. *Salutation:* Your All Holiness.

Patriarch, Russian Orthodox. *Address:* His Holiness the Patriarch of _____. *Salutation:* Your Holiness.

Pope. *Address:* His Holiness The Pope. *Salutation:* Your Holiness or Most Holy Father.

Priest, Roman Catholic. *Address:* The Reverend _____ _____, S.J. *Salutation:* Dear Reverend Father or Dear Father.

Rabbi, man or woman. *Address:* Rabbi _____ _____ or _____ _____ D.D.. *Salutation:* Dear Rabbi _____ or Dear Dr. _____.

Sisterhood, Roman Catholic. *Address:* Sister _____ _____, C.S.J. *Salutation:* Dear Sister or Dear Sister _____.

Sisterhood, superior of. *Address:* The Reverend Mother Superior, S.C. *Salutation:* Reverend Mother.

Diplomats

Ambassador, U.S. *Address:* The Honorable _____ _____ The Ambassador of the United States. *Salutation:* Sir/Madam or Dear Mr./Madam Ambassador.

Ambassador to the U.S. *Address:* His/Her Excellency _____ _____, The Ambassador of _____. *Salutation:* Excellency or Dear Mr./Madam Ambassador.

Chargé d'Affaires, U.S. *Address:* The Honorable _____ _____, United States Chargé d'Affaires. *Salutation:* Dear Mr./Ms. _____.

Consul, U.S. *Address:* _____ _____, Esq., United States Consul. *Salutation:* Dear Mr./Ms. _____.

Minister, U.S. or to U.S. *Address:* The Honorable _____ _____, The Minister of _____. *Salutation:* Sir/Madam or Dear Mr./Madame Minister.

Secretary General, United Nations. *Address:* His/Her Excellency _____ _____, Secretary General of the United Nations. *Salutation:* Dear Mr./Madam/Madame Secretary General.

United Nations Representative (Foreign). *Address:* His/Her Excellency _____ Representative of _____ to the United Nations. *Salutation:* Excellency or My dear Mr./Madame _____.

United Nations Representative (U.S.) *Address:* The Honorable _____ _____, United States Representative to the United Nations. *Salutation:* Sir/Madam or Dear Mr./Ms. _____.

Government Officials

Assemblyman. *Address:* The Honorable _____ _____. *Salutation:* Dear Mr./Ms. _____.

Associate Justice, U.S. Supreme Court. *Address:* Mr./Madam Justice _____. *Salutation:* Dear Mr./Madam Justice or Sir/Madam.

Attorney General, U.S. *Address:* The Honorable _____ _____, Attorney General of the United States. *Salutation:* Dear Mr./Madam or Attorney General.

Cabinet member: *Address:* The Honorable _____ _____, Secretary of _____. *Salutation:* Sir/Madam or Dear Mr./Madam Secretary.

Chief Justice, U.S. Supreme Court. *Address:* The Chief Justice of the United States. *Salutation:* Dear Mr. Chief Justice.

Commissioner (federal, state, local). *Address:* The Honorable _____ _____. *Salutation:* Dear Mr./Ms. _____.

Governor. *Address:* The Honorable _____ _____, Governor of _____. *Salutation:* Dear Governor _____.

Judge, Federal: *Address:* The Honorable _____ _____, Judge of the United States District Court for the _____, District of _____. *Salutation:*

Sir/Madam or Dear Judge _____.

Judge, state or local. *Address:* The Honorable _____ _____, Judge of the Court of _____. *Salutation:* Dear Judge _____.

Lieutenant Governor. *Address:* The Honorable _____ _____, Lieutenant Governor of _____. *Salutation:* Dear Mr./Ms. _____.

Mayor. *Address:* The Honorable _____ _____, Mayor of _____. *Salutation:* Dear Mayor _____.

President, U.S. *Address:* The President. *Salutation:* Dear Mr. President.

President, U.S., former. *Address:* The Honorable _____ _____. *Salutation:* Dear Mr. _____.

Representative, state. *Address:* The Honorable _____ _____. *Salutation:* Dear Mr./Ms. _____.

Representative, U.S. *Address:* The Honorable _____ _____, United States House of Representatives. *Salutation:* Dear Mr./Ms. _____.

Senator, state. *Address:* The Honorable _____ _____, The State Senate, State Capitol. *Salutation:* Dear Senator _____.

Senator, U.S. *Address:* The Honorable _____ _____, United States Senate. *Salutation:* Dear Senator _____.

Speaker, U.S. House of Representatives. *Address:* The Honorable _____ _____, Speaker of the House of Representatives. *Salutation:* Dear Mr./Madam Speaker.

Vice President, U.S. *Address:* The Vice President of the United States. *Salutation:* Sir or Dear Mr. Vice President.

Military and Naval Officers

Rank. *Address:* Full rank, USN (or USCG, USAF, USA, USMC). *Salutation:* Dear (full rank) _____.

Professions

Attorney. *Address:* Mr./Ms. _____ _____, Attorney at law or _____ _____, Esq. *Salutation:* Dear Mr./Ms. _____.

Dentist. *Address:* _____ _____, D.D.S. *Salutation:* Dear Dr. _____.

Physician. *Address:* _____ _____, M.D. *Salutation:* Dear Dr. _____.

Veterinarian. *Address:* _____ _____, D.V.M. *Salutation:* Dear Dr. _____.

1. Forms of address do not always follow set guidelines; the type of salutation is often determined by the relationship between correspondents or by the purpose and content of the letter. However, a general style applies to most occasions. In highly formal salutations, when the addressee is a woman, "Madam" should be substituted for "Sir." When the salutation is informal, "Ms.," "Miss," or "Mrs." should be substituted for "Mr." If a woman addressee has previously indicated a preference for a particular form of address, that form should be used.

Foreign Words and Phrases

(The English meanings given are not necessarily literal translations.)

Source: Webster's II New Riverside University Dictionary. Copyright © 1984 Houghton Mifflin Company.

à bientôt [Fr.]: goodbye; I'll see you later

à bon marché [Fr.]: at a bargain price

ab ovo [Lat.]: from the very beginning

à compte [Fr.]: on account

à deux [Fr.]: of or involving two individuals

ad infinitum [Lat.]: to infinity

ad valorem [Lat.]: according to the value

advocatus diaboli [Lat.]: devil's advocate

aide-toi, le ciel t'aidera [Fr.]: heaven helps those who help

themselves—La Fontaine

à la bonne heure [Fr.]: at a good time; splendid; all right

aloha oe [Hawaiian]: love to you; greetings; farewell

amende honorable [Fr.]: public apology; just restitution

amicus curiae [Lat.]: friend of the court

amor vincit omnia [Lat.]: love conquers all—Virgil

ancien regime [Fr.]: the old order

à peu près [Fr.]: almost; approximately

a priori [Lat.]: from the former

arrivederci [Ital.]: goodbye

ars est celare artem [Lat.]: (true) art is to conceal art

ars gratia artis [Lat.]: art for art's sake

ars longa, vita brevis [Lat.]: art is long, life short

au contraire [Fr.]: on the contrary

au courant [Fr.]: up-to-date

au fait [Fr.]: well-informed

auf Wiedersehen [G.]: goodbye

autres temps, autres moeurs [Fr.]: other times, other customs

à votre santé [Fr.]: to your health

ben trovato [Ital.]: ingenious

bête noire [Fr.]: one particularly disliked

bona fide [Lat.]: in good faith; genuine
bon appétit [Fr.]: good appetite
bon mot [Fr.]: a clever saying
bon vivant [Fr.]: an epicure
carpe diem [Lat.]: enjoy today
carte blanche [Fr.]: unrestricted power to act on one's own
causa sine qua non [Lat.]: indispensable condition or cause
cause célèbre [Fr.]: a highly controversial issue
caveat emptor [Lat.]: let the buyer beware
chacun à son goût [Fr.]: everyone to his own taste
circa [Lat.]: in approximately
comme ci comme ça [Fr.]: so-so
corpus delicti [Lat.]: the material evidence of the fact that a crime has been committed
coup de grâce [Fr.]: finishing blow
cri de coeur [Fr.]: heartfelt appeal
cum grano salis [Lat.]: with a grain of salt
d'accord [Fr.]: agreed
danke (schön) [G.]: thank you (very much)
de bonne grâce [Fr.]: with good grace
de facto [Lat.]: in reality or fact
de gustibus non est disputandum [Lat.]: there is no arguing in matters of taste
Deo gratias [Lat.]: thanks be to God
Deo volente [Lat.]: God willing
de profundis [Lat.]: from the depths
dernier cri [Fr.]: the newest fashion
deus ex machina [Lat.]: a contrived device to resolve a situation
dolce far niente [Ital.]: pleasant idleness
dramatis personae [Lat.]: characters in a play
ecce homo [Lat.]: behold the man
éminence grise [Fr.]: gray eminence; power behind the throne
en bloc [Fr.]: wholesale; as one
enfin [Fr.]: in conclusion
en masse [Fr.]: all together
en passant [Fr.]: in passing
en rapport [Fr.]: in sympathy or accord; in touch
entre nous [Fr.]: between ourselves; confidentially
ex animo [Lat.]: from the heart
ex gratia [Lat.]: as a favor
ex more [Lat.]: according to custom
experto credite [Lat.]: believe one who knows from experience
fait accompli [Fr.]: an accomplished fact, presumably irreversible
faute de mieux [Fr.]: for lack of anything better
faux pas [Fr.]: a social blunder
feux d'artifice [Fr.]: fireworks; dazzling display, as of wit

fiat justitia, ruat caelum [Lat.]: let justice be done even if the heavens fall
flagrante delicto [Lat.]: in the very act
folie de grandeur [Fr.]: delusion of grandeur
force de frappe [Fr.]: strike force—used esp. of nuclear forces
frisson [Fr.]: thrill; shudder
Gesundheit [G]: good health
gnōthi seauton [Gr.]: know thyself
gracias [Sp.]: thank you
grande dame [Fr.]: great lady
guten Tag [G]: good day; hello
habeas corpus [Lat.]: writ to bring a person before a court or judge
hasta la vista [Sp.]: see you later
haut monde [Fr.]: high society; the fashionable world
hoi polloi [Gk.]: the common people
honi soit qui mal y pense [Fr.]: shame to him who thinks evil of it—motto of the Order of the Garter
hors concours [Fr.]: out of the running
ich dien [G.]: I serve—motto of the Prince of Wales
inshallah [Ar.]: if Allah wills it; God willing
in vino veritas [Lat.]: in wine there is truth
ipso facto [Lat.]: by the fact itself
je ne sais quoi [Fr.]: I know not what; an elusive quality
jeu de mots [Fr.]: play on words
jeu d'esprit [Fr.]: play of wit
jeunesse dorée [Fr.]: gilded youth
Kinder, Kirche, Küche [G.]: children, church, kitchen
laissez faire [Fr.]: noninterference
l'art pour l'art [Fr.]: art for art's sake
le coeur a ses raisons que la raison ne connaît point [Fr.]: the heart has its reasons that reason knows nothing of—Pascal
l'état c'est moi [Fr.]: I am the state—Attributed to Louis XIV
mano a mano [Sp.]: hand to hand; together
mauvais goût [Fr.]: bad taste
mea culpa [Lat.]: I am to blame
meden agan [Gk.]: nothing in excess
mens sana in corpore sano [Lat.]: a healthy mind in a healthy body—Juvenal
mirabile dictu [Lat.]: wonderful to relate
modus operandi [Lat.]: a method of operating
n'est-ce pas? [Fr.]: isn't that so?
nicht wahr? [G.]: isn't that so?
n'importe [Fr.]: no matter
nom de plume [Fr.]: pen name
non compos mentis [Lat.]: not of sound mind
non sequitur [Lat.]: it does not fol-

low
omnia vincit amor [Lat.]: love conquers all—Virgil
O tempora! O mores! [Lat.]: O times! O morals!; what corrupt times we live in!—Cicero
per annum [Lat.]: by the year
per capita [Lat.]: per unit of population
per diem [Lat.]: by the day
persona non grata [Lat.]: unacceptable or unwelcome person
peu à peu [Fr.]: little by little
pièce d'occasion [Fr.]: musical or literary work composed for a special occasion
plus ça change, plus c'est la même chose [Fr.]: the more things change, the more they remain the same
post mortem [Lat.]: after death
prêt-à-porter [Fr.]: ready to wear
pro bono publico [Lat.]: for the public good
pro patria [Lat.]: for one's country
que será será [Sp.]: what will be will be
quid pro quo [Lat.]: something for something; an equal exchange
repondez s'il vous plaît [Fr.]: please reply— Used on invitation cards (abbr. R.S.V.P.)
requiescat in pace [Lat.]: rest in peace
salto mortale [Ital.]: deadly leap
salud [Sp.]: health; to your health
sans peur et sans reproche [Fr.]: without fear and above reproach; chivalrous
sans-souci [Fr.]: carefree pleasure
savoir-faire [Fr.]: the ability to say and do the correct thing
se non è vero, è ben trovato [Ital.]: even if it isn't true, it's a wonderful invention
shalom [Heb.]: peace, used as a greeting
sic transit gloria mundi [Lat.]: thus passes away the glory of the world
s'il vous plaît [Fr.]: if you please
sine die [Lat.]: with no day set for a future meeting; indefinitely
sine qua non [Lat.]: indispensable
status (in) quo [Lat.]: the existing condition
sui generis [Lat.]: unique; individual
tant pis [Fr.]: so much the worse
tempus fugit [Lat.]: time flies
terra incognita [Lat.]: unknown territory
ton [Fr.]: fashionable society
tout de suite [Fr.]: immediately; all at once
tout le monde [Fr.]: everybody; everyone of importance
uomo universale [Ital.]: universal man; one of broad education and ability
utile dulci [Lat.]: the useful with the pleasurable—Horace
veni, vidi, vici [Lat.]: I came, I saw,

I conquered—attributed to Julius
Caesar
vis-à-vis [Fr.]: face to face

vive la différence [Fr.]: long live
the difference (between the sexes)
wie geht's? [G.]: how are things?

wunderbar [G.]: wonderful
Wunderkind [G.]: child prodigy

Redundant Expressions

Redundancy— the needless repetition of ideas— is one of the principal obstacles to writing clear, precise prose. The elements repeated in the phrases and in the brief definitions are italicized. To eliminate redundancy, delete the italic elements in the phrases.

old antique: (= an object having special value because of its *age*, esp. a work of art or handicraft more than 100 years *old*)

ascend *upward*: (= to go or move *upward*)

assemble *together*: (= to bring or gather *together*)

pointed barb: (= a sharp *point* projecting in reverse direction to the main point of a weapon or tool)

first beginning: (= the *first* part)

big *in size*: (= of considerable *size*)

bisect *in two*: (= to cut *into two* equal parts)

blend *together*: (= to combine, mix, or go well *together*)

capitol *building*: (= a *building* in which a legislative body meets)

coalesce *together*: (= to grow or come *together* so as to form a whole)

collaborate *together* or *jointly*: (= to work *together*, esp. in a joint effort)

fellow colleague: (= a *fellow* member of a profession, staff, or academic faculty)

congregate *together*: (= to bring or come *together* in a crowd)

connect *together*: (= to join or fasten *together*)

consensus *of opinion*: (= collective *opinion*)

courthouse *building*: (= a *building* in which judicial courts or county government offices are housed)

habitual custom: (= a *habitual* practice)

descend *downward*: (= to move,

slope, extend, or incline *downward*)

endorse (a check) *on the back*: (= to write one's signature *on the back of*, e.g., a check)

erupt *violently*: (= to emerge *violently* or to become *violently* active)

explode *violently*: (= to burst *violently* from internal pressure)

real fact: (= something with *real*, demonstrable existence)

passing fad: (= a *passing* fashion)

few *in number*: (= amounting to or made up of a *small number*)

founder *and sink*: (= to *sink* beneath the water)

basic fundamental: (= a *basic* or essential part)

fuse *together*: (= to mix *together* by or as if by melting)

gather *together*: (= to come *together* or cause to come *together*)

free gift: (= something bestowed voluntarily and *without compensation*)

past history: (= a narrative of *past* events; something that took place *in the past*)

hoist *up*: (= to raise or to haul *up* with or as if with a mechanical device)

current or *present* incumbent: (= one *currently* holding an office)

new innovation: (= something *new* or unusual)

join *together*: (= to bring or put *together* so as to make continuous or form a unit)

knots *per hour*: (= a unit of speed, one nautical mile *per hour*, approx. 1.15 statute miles *per hour*)

large *in size*: (= greater than av-

erage *in size*)

merge *together*: (= to blend or cause to blend *together* gradually)

necessary need: (= something *necessary* or wanted)

universal panacea: (= a remedy for *all* diseases, evils, or difficulties)

continue *to* persist: (= to *continue* in existence)

individual person: (= an *individual* human being)

chief or *leading* or *main* protagonist: (= the *leading* character in a Greek drama or other literary form; a *leading* or *principal* figure)

original prototype: (= an *original* type, form, or instance that is a model on which later stages are based or judged)

protrude *out*: (= to push or thrust *outward*)

recall *back*: (= to summon *back* to awareness; to bring *back*)

recoil *back*: (= to kick or spring *back;* to shrink *back* in fear or loathing; to fall *back*)

recur *again* or *repeatedly*: (= to occur *again* or *repeatedly*)

temporary reprieve: (= *temporary* relief, as from danger or pain)

short *in length* or *height*: (= having very little *length* or *height*)

small *in size*: (= characterized by relatively little *size* or slight *dimensions*)

completely unanimous: (= being in *complete* harmony, accord, or agreement)

Telephone Solicitations

For your protection, don't buy anything over the telephone unless you initiate the call, you know who you have reached, and you believe the seller is reputable. To check on a company's reputation, call the Better Business Bureau or consumer protection office where the company is located. Be wary of any caller who insists on an immediate purchase decision. Ask for the name, address, and phone number where you can reach the caller after considering the solicitation. Don't be lured into buying otherwise unwanted merchandise by offers of promotional gifts or prizes.

Get the offer in writing before you buy. Look to see if there are conditions or restrictions that you were not told about on the phone.

Never give your credit card or social security number over the telephone as a verification of your identity. Don't use your credit card number to purchase anything unless you initiated the call or you know exactly with whom you are talking. □

DRUGS & DRUG ABUSE

A Primer on Drugs of Abuse

Main Sources: U.S. Department of Justice, Drug Enforcement Administration, U.S. Department of Education, National Institute on Drug Abuse.

NARCOTICS

The term narcotic in its medical meaning refers to opium and opium derivatives or synthetic substitutes.[1]

Narcotics are essential in the practice of medicine: they are the most effective agents known for the relief of intense pain. They are also used as cough suppressants as well as a centuries-old remedy for diarrhea.

Under medical supervision, narcotics are administered orally or by intramuscular injection. As drugs of abuse, however, they also are sniffed, smoked, or self-administered by the more direct routes of subcutaneous ("skin-popping") and intravenous ("mainlining") injection.

The relief of suffering, whether of physical or psychological origin, may result in a short-lived state of euphoria. The initial effects, however, are often unpleasant, leading many to conclude that those who persist in their illicit use may have latent personality disturbances. Narcotics tend to induce pinpoint pupils and reduced vision, together with drowsiness, apathy, decreased physical activity, and constipation. A larger dose may induce sleep, but there is an increasing possibility of nausea, vomiting, and respiratory depression—the major toxic effect of the opiates. Except in cases of acute intoxication, there is no loss of motor coordination or slurred speech as in the case of the depressants.

To the extent that the response may be felt to be pleasurable, its intensity may be expected to increase with the amount of the dose administered. Repeated use, however, will result in increasing tolerance: the user must administer progressively larger doses to attain the desired effect, thereby reinforcing the compulsive behavior known as drug dependence.

Physical dependence refers to an alteration of the normal functions of the body that necessitates the continued presence of a drug in order to prevent the withdrawal or abstinence syndrome, which is characteristic of each class of addictive drugs. The intensity of physical symptoms experienced during the withdrawal period is related directly to the amount of narcotic used each day.

Deprivation of an addictive drug causes increased excitability of those same bodily functions that have been depressed by its habitual use.

With the deprivation of narcotics, the first withdrawal signs are usually experienced shortly before the time of the next scheduled dose. Complaints, pleas, and demands by the addict are prominent, increasing in intensity and peaking from 36 to 72 hours after the last dose, then gradually subsiding. Symptoms, such as watery eyes, runny nose, yawning, and perspiration, appear about 8 to 12 hours after the last dose. Thereafter, the addict may fall

1. Cocaine, ecgonine, and coca leaves, classified as narcotics under the Controlled Substances Act (CSA), are discussed in the text on stimulants.

into a restless sleep. As the abstinence syndrome progresses, restlessness, irritability, loss of appetite, insomnia, goose flesh, tremors, and finally yawning and severe sneezing occur. These symptoms reach their peak at 48 to 72 hours. The patient is weak and depressed, with nausea and vomiting. Stomach cramps and diarrhea are common. Heart rate and blood pressure are elevated. Chills alternating with flushing and excessive sweating are also characteristic symptoms. Pains in the bones and muscles of the back and extremities occur as do muscle spasms and kicking movements, which may be the source of the expression "kicking the habit." At this time an individual may become suicidal. Without treatment the syndrome eventually runs its course and most of the symptoms will disappear in 7 to 10 days. How long it takes to restore physiological and psychological equilibrium, however, is unpredictable. For a few weeks following withdrawal the addict will continue to think and talk about his use of drugs and be particularly susceptible to an urge to use them again.

The withdrawal syndrome may be avoided by reducing the dose of narcotic over a one-to-three-week period. Detoxification of an addict can be accomplished by substituting oral methadone for the illicit narcotic and gradually reducing the dose. However, since the addict's entire pattern of life usually is built around drug taking, narcotic dependence is never entirely resolved by withdrawal alone.

Since addicts tend to become preoccupied with the daily ritual of obtaining and taking drugs, they often neglect themselves and may suffer from malnutrition, infections, and unattended diseases or injuries. Among the hazards of narcotic addiction are toxic reactions to contaminants, such as quindine, sugars, and talcum power, as well as unsterile needles and injection techniques, resulting in abscesses, blood poisoning, hepatitis, and AIDS.

Since there is no simple way to determine the purity of a drug that is sold on the street, the potency is unpredictable, posing the ever present danger of an unintentional overdose. A person with a mild overdose may be stuporous or asleep. Larger doses may induce a coma with slow, shallow respiration. The skin becomes clammy cold, the body limp, and the jaw relaxed; there is a danger that the tongue may fall back, blocking the air passageway. If the condition is sufficiently severe, convulsions may occur, followed by respiratory arrest and death. Specific antidotes for narcotic poisoning are available at hospitals.

NARCOTICS OF NATURAL ORIGIN

The poppy *Papaver somniferum* is the main source of the nonsynthetic narcotics. It was grown in the Mediterranean region as early as 300 B.C. and has since been cultivated in countries around the world, such as Hungary, Turkey, India, Burma,

China, Lebanon, Pakistan, Afghanistan, Laos, and Mexico.

The milky fluid that oozes from incisions in the unripe seedpod has, since ancient times, been scraped by hand and air dried to produce opium gum. A more modern method of harvesting is by the industrial poppy straw process of extracting alkaloids from the mature dried plant. The extract may be in either liquid, solid, or powder form. Most poppy straw concentrate made available commercially is a fine brownish powder with a distinct odor. More than 400 tons of opium or its equivalent in poppy straw concentrate are legally imported annually into the United States

Opium

There were no legal restrictions on the importation or use of opium until the early 1900s. In those days, patent medicines often contained opium without any warning label. Today, there are state, federal, and international laws governing the production and distribution of narcotics substances, and there is little abuse of opium in the United States.

At least 25 alkaloids can be extracted from opium. These fall into two general categories, each producing markedly different effects. The first, known as the phenanthrene alkaloids, represented by morphine and codeine, are used as analgesics and cough suppressants; the second, the isoquinoline alkaloids, represented by papaverine (an intestinal relaxant) and noscapine (a cough suppressant),

have no significant influence on the central nervous system and are not regulated under the Controlled Substances Act (CSA).

Although a small amount of opium is used to make antidiarrheal preparations, such as paregoric, virtually all the opium imported into this country is broken down into its alkaloid constituents, principally morphine and codeine.

Morphine

The principal constituent of opium, ranging in concentration from 4 to 21 percent, morphine is one of the most effective drugs known for the relief of pain. It is marketed in the form of white crystals, hypodermic tablets, and injectable preparations. Its licit use is restricted primarily to hospitals. Morphine is odorless, tastes bitter, and darkens with age. It may be administered subcutaneously, intramuscularly, or intravenously, the latter method being the one most frequently resorted to by addicts. Tolerance and dependence develop rapidly in the user. Only a small part of the morphine obtained from opium is used medically. Most of it is converted to codeine and, secondarily, to hydromorphone.

Codeine

This alkaloid is found in raw opium in concentrations ranging from 0.7 to 2.5 percent. It was first isolated in 1832 as an impurity in a batch of morphine. Although it occurs naturally, most codeine

The Controlled Substances Act

The Controlled Substances Act (CSA), Title II of the Comprehensive Drug Abuse Prevention and Control Act of 1970, is the legal foundation of the Government's fight against abuse of drugs and other substances. This law is a consolidation of numerous laws regulating the manufacture and distribution of narcotics, stimulants, depressants, and hallucinogens.

The CSA places all substances which were in some manner regulated under existing federal law into one of five schedules. This placement is based upon the substance's medical use, potential for abuse, and safety or dependence liability. The Act also provides a mechanism for substances to be controlled, or added to a schedule; decontrolled, or removed from control; and rescheduled or transferred from one schedule to another.

The five schedules are as follows:

Schedule I

√ The drug or other substance has a high potential for abuse.

√ The drug or other substance has no currently accepted medical use in treatment in the United States.

√ There is a lack of accepted safety for use of the drug or other substance under medical supervision.

Schedule II

√ The drug or other substance has a high potential for abuse.

√ The drug or other substance has a currently accepted medical use in treatment in the United States or a currently accepted medical use with severe restrictions.

√ Abuse of the drug or other substance may lead to severe psychological or physical dependence.

Schedule III

√ The drug or other substance has a potential for abuse less than the drugs or other substances in Schedules I and II.

√ The drug or other substance has a currently accepted medical use in treatment in the United States.

√ Abuse of the drug or other substance may lead to moderate or low physical dependence or high psychological dependence.

Schedule IV

√ The drug or other substance has a low potential for abuse relative to the drugs or other substances in Schedule III.

√ The drug or other substance has a currently accepted medical use in treatment in the United States.

√ Abuse of the drug or other substance may lead to limited physical dependence or psychological dependence relative to the drugs or other substances in Schedule III.

Schedule V

√ The drug or other substance has a low potential for abuse relative to the drugs or other substances in Schedule IV.

√ The drug or other substance has a currently accepted medical use in treatment in the United States.

√ Abuse of the drug or other substances may lead to limited physical dependence or psychological dependence relative to the drugs or other substances in Schedule IV.

is produced from morphine. As compared with morphine, codeine produces less analgesia, sedation, and respiratory depression. It is widely distributed in products of two general types. Codeine for the relief of moderate pain may consist of codeine tablets or be combined with other products, such as aspirin or acetaminophen (Tylenol). Some examples of liquid codeine preparations for the relief of coughs (antitussives) are Robitussin AC, Cheracol, and elixir of terpin hydrate with codeine. Codeine is also manufactured to a lesser extent in injectable form for the relief of pain. It is by far the most widely used naturally occurring narcotic in medical treatment.

Thebaine

A minor constituent of opium, thebaine is the principal alkaloid present in another species of poppy, *Papaver bracteatum*, which has been grown experimentally in the United States as well as in other parts of the world. Although chemically similar to both codeine and morphine, it produces stimulant rather than depressant effects. Thebaine is not used in this country for medical purposes, but it is converted into a variety of medically important compounds, including codeine, hydrocodone, oxycodone, oxymorphone, nalbuphine, naloxone, and the Bentley compounds. It is controlled in Schedule II of the CSA as well as under international law.

SEMI-SYNTHETIC NARCOTICS

The following narcotics are among the more significant synthetic substances that have been derived by modification of the chemicals contained in opium.

Heroin

First synthesized from morphine in 1874, heroin was not extensively used in medicine until the beginning of this century. The Bayer Company in Germany first started commercial production of the new pain remedy in 1898. While it received widespread acceptance, the medical profession for years remained unaware of its potential for addiction. The first comprehensive control of heroin in the United States was established with the Harrison Narcotic Act of 1914.

Pure heroin is a white powder with a bitter taste. Illicit heroin may vary in both form and color. Most illicit heroin is a powder which may vary in color from white to dark brown because of impurities left from the manufacturing process or the presence of additives, such as food coloring, cocoa, or brown sugar.

Pure heroin is rarely sold on the street. A "bag"—slang for a single dosage unit of heroin—may weigh about 100 mg, usually containing about five percent heroin. To increase the bulk of the material sold to the addict, diluents are mixed with the heroin in ratios ranging from 9 to 1 to as much as 99 to 1. Sugars, starch, powdered milk, and quinine are among the diluents used.

Another form of heroin known as "black tar" heroin has also become increasingly available in recent years, especially in the western United States. Black tar heroin is a crudely processed form of heroin illicitly manufactured in Mexico. It may be sticky like roofing tar or hard like coal, and it is dark brown to black in color. Black tar heroin is often sold on the street in its tar-like state, sometimes at purities ranging as high as 40-80 percent. Black tar heroin is sometimes diluted, however, by adding materials of similar consistency (such as burnt cornstarch), or by converting the tar heroin into a powder and adding conventional diluents, such as mannitol or quinine. It is most commonly used through injection.

Hydromorphone

Most commonly sold as Dilaudid, hydromorphone is the second oldest semi-synthetic narcotic analgesic. Marketed both in tablet and injectable form, it is shorter acting and more sedating than morphine, but its potency is from two to eight times as great. It is, therefore, a highly abusable drug, much sought after by narcotic addicts, who usually obtain it through fraudulent prescription or theft. The tablets, stronger than available liquid forms, may be dissolved and injected.

Oxycodone

Oxycodone is synthesized from thebaine. It is similar to codeine, but more potent and with a higher dependence potential. It is effective orally and is marketed in combination with aspirin as Percodan for the relief of pain. Addicts take Percodan orally or dissolve tablets in water, filter out the insoluble material, and "mainline" the active drug.

Etorphine and Diprenorphine

Two of the Bentley compounds, these substances are both made from thebaine. Etorphine is more than one thousand times as potent as morphine in its analgesic, sedative, and respiratory depressant effects. For human use, its potency is a distinct disadvantage because of the danger of overdose. Etorphine hydrochloride (M99) is used by veterinarians to immobilize large wild animals. Diprenorphine hydrochloride (M50-50), acting as an antagonist, counteracts the effects of etorphine. The manufacture and distribution of both substances are strictly regulated under the CSA.

SYNTHETIC NARCOTICS

In contrast to pharmaceutical products derived directly or indirectly from narcotics of natural origin, synthetic narcotics are produced entirely within the laboratory. A continuing search for a product that will retain the analgesic properties of morphine without the consequent dangers of tolerance and dependence has yet to yield a drug that is not susceptible to abuse. The two that are most widely available are meperidine and methadone.

Meperidine (Pethidine)

The first synthetic narcotic, meperidine, is chemically dissimilar to morphine but resembles it in its analgesic effect. It is probably the most widely used drug for the relief of moderate to severe pain. Available in pure form as well as in products containing other medicinal ingredients, it is administered either orally or by injection, the latter method being the most widely abused. Tolerance and dependence develop with chronic use, and large doses can result in convulsions or death.

Methadone and Related Drugs

German scientists synthesized methadone during World War II because of a shortage of morphine. Although chemically unlike morphine or heroin, it produces many of the same effects. Introduced into the United States in 1947 as an analgesic and distributed under such names as Amidone, Dolophine, and Methadone, it became widely used in the 1960s in the treatment of narcotic addicts. The effects of methadone differ from morphine-based drugs in that they have a longer duration of action, lasting up to 24 hours, thereby permitting administration only once a day in heroin detoxification and maintenance programs. Moreover, methadone is almost as effective when administered orally as it is by injection. But tolerance and dependence may develop, and withdrawal symptoms, though they develop more slowly and are less severe, are more prolonged. Ironically, methadone, designed to control narcotic addiction, has

Controlled Substances—Uses and Effects

Drugs/CSA schedules		Trade or other names	Medical uses	Physical dependency
NARCOTICS				
Opium	II III V	Dover's Powder, Paregoric Parepectolin	Analgesic, antidiarrheal	High
Morphine	II III	Morphine, MS-Contin, Roxanol, Roxanol-SR	Analgesic, antitussive	High
Codeine	II III V	Tylenol w/Codeine, Empirin w/Codeine, Robitussan A-C, Fiorinal w/Codeine	Analgesic, antitussive	Moderate
Heroin	I	Diacetylmorphine, Horse, Smack	None	High
Hydromorphone	II	Dilaudid	Analgesic	High
Meperidine (Pethidine)	II	Demerol, Mepergan	Analgesic	High
Methadone	II	Dolophine, Methadone, Methadose	Analgesic	High
Other Narcotics	I II III IV V	Numorphan, Percodan, Percocet, Tylox, Tussionex, Fentanyl, Darvon, Lomotil, Talwin[2]	Analgesic, antidiarrheal, antitussive	High-Low
DEPRESSANTS				
Chloral Hydrate	IV	Noctec	Hypnotic	Moderate
Barbiturates	II III IV	Amytal, Butisol, Fiorinal, Lotusate, Nembutal, Seconal, Tuinal, Phenobarbital	Anesthetic, anticonvulsant, sedative, hypnotic, veterinary euthanasia agent	High-Mod.
Benzodiazepines	IV	Ativan, Dalmane, Diazepam, Librium, Xanax, Serax, Valium, Tranxexe, Verstran, Versed, Halcion, Paxipam, Restoril	Antianxiety, anticonvulsant, sedative, hypnotic	Low
Methaqualone	I	Quaalude	Sedative, hypnotic	High
Glutethimide	III	Doriden	Sedative, hypnotic	High
Other Depressants	III IV	Equanil, Miltown, Noludar, Placidyl, Valmid	Antianxiety, sedative, hypnotic	Moderate
STIMULANTS				
Cocaine[1]	II	Coke, Flake, Snow, Crack	Local anesthetic	Possible
Amphetamines	II	Biphetamine, Delcobese, Desoxyn, Dexedrine, Obetrol	Attention deficit disorders, narcolepsy, weight control	Possible
Phenmetrazine	II	Preludin	Weight control	Possible
Methylphenidate	II	Ritalin	Attention deficit disorders, narcolepsy	Possible
Other Stimulants	III IV	Adipex, Cylert, Didrex, Ionamin, Melfiat, Plegine, Sanorex, Tenuate, Tepanil, Prelu-2	Weight control	Possible
HALLUCINOGENS				
LSD	I	Acid, Microdot	None	None
Mescaline and Peyote	I	Mexc, Buttons, Cactus	None	None
Amphetamine Variants	I	2,5-DMA, PMA, STP, MDA, MDMA, TMA, DOM, DOB	None	Unknown
Phencyclidine	II	PCP, Angel Dust, Hog	None	Unknown
Phencyclidine Analogues	I	PCE, PCPy, TCP	None	Unknown
Other Hallucinogens	I	Bufotenine, Ibogaine, DMT, DET, Psilocybin, Psilocyn	None	None
CANNABIS				
Marijuana	I	Pot, Acapulco Gold, Grass, Reefer, Sinsemilla, Thai Sticks	None	Unknown
Tetrahydrocannabinol	I II	THC, Marinol	Cancer chemotherapy antinauseant	Unknown
Hashish	I	Hash	None	Unknown
Hashish Oil	I	Hash Oil	None	Unknown

1. Designated a narcotic under the CSA. 2. Not designated a narcotic under the CSA.

emerged in some metropolitan areas as a major cause of overdose deaths.

Closely related chemically to methadone is the synthetic compound levo-alpha-acetylmethadol (LAAM), which has an even longer duration of action (from 48 to 72 hours), permitting a further reduction in clinic visits and the elimination of take-home medication. Its potential in the treatment of narcotic addicts is under investigation.

Another close relative of methadone is propoxyphene, first marketed in 1957 under the trade name Darvon for the relief of mild to moderate pain. Less dependence-producing than the other opiates, it is less effective as an analgesic. Propoxyphene is in Schedule II and preparations containing it are in Schedule IV.

Narcotic Antagonists

The deliberate effort to find an effective analgesic that is not dependence-producing led to the development of compounds known as narcotic antag-

Psychological dependence	Tolerance	Duration (hours)	Usual methods of administration	Possible effects	Effects of overdose	Withdrawal syndrome
High	Yes	3-6	Oral, smoked	Euphoria, drowsiness, respiratory depression, constricted pupils, nausea	Slow and shallow breathing, clammy skin, convulsions, coma, possible death	Watery eyes, runny nose, yawning, loss of appetite, irritability, tremors, panic, cramps, nausea, chills and sweating
High	Yes	3-6	Oral, smoked, injected			
Moderate	Yes	3-6	Oral, injected			
High	Yes	3-6	Injected, sniffed, smoked			
High	Yes	3-6	Oral, injected			
High	Yes	3-6	Oral, injected			
High-Low	Yes	12-24	Oral, injected			
High-Low	Yes	Variable	Oral, injected			
Moderate	Yes	5-8	Oral	Slurred speech, disorientation, drunken behavior without odor of alcohol	Shallow respiration, clammy skin, dilated pupils, weak and rapid pulse, coma, possible death	Anxiety, insomnia, tremors, delirium, convulsions, possible death
High-Mod.	Yes	1-16	Oral			
Low	Yes	4-8	Oral			
High	Yes	4-8	Oral			
Moderate	Yes	4-8	Oral			
Moderate	Yes	4-8	Oral			
High	Yes	1-2	Sniffed, smoked, injected	Increased alertness, excitation, euphoria, increased pulse rate & blood pressure, insomnia, loss of appetite	Agitation, increase in body temperature, hallucinations, convulsions, possible death	Apathy, long periods of sleep, irritability, depression, disorientation
High	Yes	2-4	Oral, injected			
High	Yes	2-4	Oral, injected			
Moderate	Yes	2-4	Oral, injected			
High	Yes	2-4	Oral, injected			
Unknown	Yes	8-12	Oral	Illusions and hallucinations, poor perception of time and distance	Longer, more intense "trip" episodes, psychosis, possible death	Withdrawal syndrome not reported
Unknown	Yes	8-12	Oral			
Unknown	Yes	Variable	Oral, injected			
High	Yes	Days	Smoked, oral, injected			
High	Yes	Days	Smoked, oral, injected			
Unknown	Possible	Variable	Smoked, oral, injected, sniffed			
Moderate	Yes	2-4	Smoked, oral	Euphoria, relaxed inhibitions, increased appetite, disoriented behavior	Fatigue, paranoia, possible psychosis	Insomnia, hyperactivity, and decreased appetite occasionally reported
Moderate	Yes	2-4	Smoked, oral			
Moderate	Yes	2-4	Smoked, oral			
Moderate	Yes	2-4	Smoked, oral			

Source: U.S. Department of Justice, Drug Enforcement Administration.

onists. These drugs, as the name implies, block or reverse the effects of narcotics. Naloxone (Narcan), having no morphine-like effects, was removed from the CSA when introduced as a specific antidote for narcotic poisoning in 1971. Nalorphine (Nalline), introduced into clinical medicine in 1951 and now in Schedule III, is called a narcotic agonist-antagonist. In a drug-free individual, it produces morphine-like effects; it counteracts these effects in an individual under the influence of narcotics.

Another agonist-antagonist is pentazocine (Talwin). Introduced as an analgesic in 1967, it was determined to be an abusable drug and placed under Schedule IV in 1979. On the street, pentazocine is frequently used in combination with another drug: tripelennamine. This combination is commonly referred to as "T's and B's" or "T's and Blues" with "T" referring to Talwin and "B" indicating the blue PBZ (tripelennamine) tablet.

A further attempt at reducing the abuse of this drug was made in 1983 with the addition of naloxone to the pentazocine tablets. The new product, Talwin Nx, contains a quantity of antagonist sufficient to counteract the morphine-like effects of pentazocine if the tablets are dissolved and injected.

DEPRESSANTS

Substances regulated under the CSA as depressants have a potential for abuse associated with both physical and psychological dependence. Taken as prescribed as a physician, depressants may be beneficial for the relief of anxiety, irritability, and tension, and for the symptomatic treatment of insomnia. In excessive amounts, however, they produce a state of intoxication that is remarkably similar to that of alcohol.

As in the case of alcohol, these effects may vary not only from person to person but from time to time in the same individual. Low doses produce mild sedation. Higher doses, insofar as they relieve anxiety or stress, may produce a temporary sense of well-being; they may also produce mood depression and apathy. In marked contrast to the effects of narcotics, however, intoxicating doses invariably result in impaired judgment, slurred speech, and loss of motor coordination. In addition to the dangers of disorientation, resulting in a high incidence of highway accidents, recurrent users incur risks of long-term involvement with depressants.

Tolerance to the intoxicating effects develops rapidly, leading to a progressive narrowing of the margin of safety between an intoxicating and lethal dose. The person who is unaware of the dangers of increasing dependence will often increase the daily dose up to 10 or 20 times the recommended therapeutic level. The source of supply may be no farther than the family medicine cabinet. Depressants are also frequently obtained by theft, illegal prescription, or purchase on the illicit market.

In the world of illicit drug use, depressants often are used as self-medication to soothe jangled nerves brought on by the use of stimulants, to quell the anxiety of "flashbacks" resulting from prior use of hallucinogens, or to ease withdrawal from heroin. The dangers, it should be stressed, are compounded when depressants are used in combination with alcohol or other drugs. Chronic intoxication, though it affects every age group, is not common in middle age. The problem often remains unrecognized until the user exhibits recur-

Trends in Annual Prevalence of Fourteen Types of Drugs
Among College Students 1-4 Years Beyond High School

	Percent who used in last twelve months							
	1980	1983	1985	1986	1987	1988	1989	'88-'89 change
Any illicit druge	56.2	49.8	46.3	45.0	40.1	37.4	36.7	−0.7
Any illicit druge other than marijuana	32.3	29.9	26.7	25.0	21.3	19.2	16.4	−2.8
Marijuana	51.2	45.2	41.7	40.9	37.0	34.6	33.6	−1.0
Inhalantsb	3.0	2.8	3.1	3.9	3.7	4.1	3.7	−0.4
Hallucinogens	8.5	6.5	5.0	6.0	5.9	5.3	5.1	−0.2
LSD	6.0	4.3	2.2	3.9	4.0	3.6	3.4	−0.2
Cocaine	16.8	17.3	17.3	17.1	13.7	10.0	8.2	−1.8
Crackc	n.a.	n.a.	n.a.	1.3	2.0	1.4	1.5	+0.1
Heroin	0.4	0.0	0.2	0.1	0.2	0.2	0.1	−0.1
Other opiatesa	5.1	3.8	2.4	4.0	3.1	3.1	3.2	+0.1
Stimulantsa	22.4	n.a.	n.a.	n.a.	n.a.	n.a.	n.a.	n.a.
Stimulants, adjusteda,d	n.a.	17.3	11.9	10.3	7.2	6.2	4.6	−1.6
Sedativesa	8.3	4.5	2.5	2.6	1.7	1.5	1.0	−0.5
Barbituratesa	2.9	2.2	1.3	2.0	1.2	1.1	1.0	−0.1
Methaqualonea	7.2	3.1	1.4	1.2	0.8	0.5	0.2	−0.3
Tranquilizersa	6.9	4.6	3.6	4.4	3.8	3.1	2.6	−0.5
Alcohol	90.5	91.6	92.0	91.5	90.9	89.6	89.6	0.0
Cigarettes	36.2	36.1	35.0	35.3	38.0	36.6	34.2	−2.4

a. Only drug use which was not under a doctor's orders is included here. b. This drug was asked about in four of the five questionnaire forms. c. This drug was asked about in one of the five questionnaire forms in 1986, and in two of the five questionnaire forms thereafter. d. Based on the data from the revised question, which attempts to exclude the inappropriate reporting of non-prescription stimulants. e. Use of "any illicit drug" includes any use of marijuana, hallucinogens, cocaine, and heroin, or any use of other opiates, stimulants, sedatives; or tranquilizers not under a doctor's orders. NOTE: n.a. = data not available.

Source: The University of Michigan 1989 annual study titled "Monitoring the Future," conducted under a series of research grants from the National Institute on Drug Abuse to the U-M Institute for Social Research.

rent confusion or an obvious inability to function. Depressants also serve as a means of suicide, a pattern particularly common among women.

The depressants vary with respect to their potential for overdose. Moderate depressant poisoning closely resembles alcoholic inebriation. The symptoms of severe depressant poisoning are coma, a cold clammy skin, a weak and rapid pulse, and a slow to rapid but shallow respiration. Death will follow if the reduced respiration and low blood pressure are not counteracted by proper medical treatment.

The abrupt cessation or reduction of high-dose depressant intake may result in a characteristic withdrawal syndrome, which should be recognized as a medical emergency more serious than that of any other drugs of abuse. An apparent improvement in the patient's condition may be the initial result of detoxification. Within 24 hours, however, minor withdrawal symptoms manifest themselves, among them anxiety and agitation, loss of appetite, nausea and vomiting, increased heart rate and excessive sweating, tremulousness and abdominal cramps. The symptoms usually peak during the second or third day of abstinence from the short-acting barbiturates or meprobamate; they may not be reached until the seventh or eighth day of abstinence from the long-acting barbiturates or benzodiazepines. It is during the peak period that the major withdrawal symptoms usually occur. The patient may experience convulsions indistinguishable from those occurring in grand mal epilepsy. More than half of those who experience convulsions will go on to develop delirium, often resulting in a psychotic state identical to the delirium tremens associated with the alcohol withdrawal syndrome. Detoxification and treatment must therefore be carried out under close medical supervision. While treatment techniques vary to some extent, they share common objectives: stabilization of the drug-dependent state to allay withdrawal symptoms followed by gradual withdrawal to prevent their recurrence.

Among the depressants that give rise to the general conditions described are chloral hydrate, a broad array of barbiturates, glutethimide, methaqualone, meprobamate, and the benzodiazepines.

Chloral Hydrate

The oldest of the hypnotic (sleep-inducing) drugs, chloral hydrate was first synthesized in 1862 and soon supplanted alcohol, opium, and cannabis preparations for inducing sedation and sleep. Its popularity declined after the introduction of the barbiturates. It has a penetrating, slightly acrid odor, and a bitter caustic taste. Its depressant effects, as well as resulting tolerance and dependence, are comparable to those of alcohol, and withdrawal symptoms resemble delirium tremens. Chloral hydrate is a liquid, marketed in the form of syrups and soft gelatin capsules. Cases of poisoning have occurred from mixing chloral hydrate with alcoholic drinks. Chloral hydrate is not a street drug of choice. Its main misuse is by older adults.

Barbiturates

Among the drugs most frequently prescribed to induce sedation and sleep by both physicians and veterinarians are the barbiturates. About 2,500 derivatives of barbituric acid have been synthesized,

How Long Drugs Stay in Urine	
Nicotine	24 to 48 hours
Marijuana	10 to 35 days
Cocaine	24 to 36 hours
Amphetamines	48 to 72 hours
PCP	48 to 78 hours
Valium, et al.	48 to 76 hours
Heroin	48 to 72 hours
Phenylpropanolamine*	24 to 48 hours

*The most commonly abused over the counter drug. *Source:* The National Parents' Resource Institute for Drug Education, Inc. (PRIDE).

but of these only about 15 remain in medical use. Small therapeutic doses tend to calm nervous conditions, and larger dozes cause sleep 20 to 60 minutes after oral administration. As in the case of alcohol, some individuals may experience a sense of excitement before sedation takes effect. If dosage is increased, however, the effects of the barbiturates may progress through successive stages of sedation, sleep, and coma to death from respiratory arrest and cardiovascular complications.

Barbiturates are classified as ultrashort, short, intermediate, and long-acting. The ultrashort-acting barbiturates produce anesthesia within one minute after intravenous administration. The rapid onset and brief duration of action make them undesirable for purposes of abuse. Those in current medical use are hexobarbital (Sombulex), methohexital (Brevital), thiamylal (Surital), and thiopental (Pentothal).

Among the short-acting and intermediate-acting barbiturates are pentobarbital (Nembutal), secobarbital (Seconal), and amobarbital (Amytal)—three of the drugs in the depressant category most sought after by abusers. The group also includes butabarbital (Butisol), talbutal (Lotusate), and aprobarbital (Alurate). After oral administration, the onset time of action is from 15 to 40 minutes and duration of action is up to 6 hours. Physicians prescribe short-acting barbiturates to induce sedation or sleep. Veterinarians use pentobarbital for anesthesia and euthanasia.

Long-acting barbiturates, which include phenobarbital (Luminal), mephobarbital or methylphenobarbital (Mebaral), and metharbital (Gemonil), have onset times of up to one hour and durations of action up to 16 hours. They are used medicinally as sedatives, hypnotics, and anticonvulsants. Their slow onset of action discourages their use for episodic intoxication, and they are not ordinarily distributed on the illicit market except when sold as something else. It should be emphasized, however, that all barbiturates result in a buildup of tolerance, and dependence on them is widespread.

Glutethimide

When glutethimide (Doriden) was introduced in 1954, it was said to be a safe barbiturate substitute without an addiction potential. Experience has shown, however, that glutethimide is yet another depressant having no particular advantage over the barbiturates and several important disadvantages. The sedative effects of glutethimide begin about 30 minutes after oral administration and last for 4 to 8 hours. Glutethimide is marketed as Doriden in 250 and 500 mg tablets. Because the effects

Reported Drug Use by High School Seniors, 1988

Drug	Used within the last:	
	12 months[1]	30 days
Marijuana	33.1%	18.0%
Inhalants	7.1	3.0
Hallucinogens	5.8	2.3
Cocaine	7.9	3.4
Heroin	.5	.2
Other opiates	4.6	1.6
Sedatives	3.7	1.4
Tranquilizers	4.8	1.5
Stimulants	10.9	4.6

1. Including the last 30 days. *Source: Drugs and Crime Facts, 1989,* Bureau of Justice Statistics.

Cocaine use among high school seniors during the late 1970s and early 1980s may have peaked in 1985.

Reported marijuana use by high school seniors within a twelve-month period fell to 33% in 1988, the lowest level since this survey began; similarly, the 18% reporting such use within the last 30 days was also the lowest in the period. However, self-reports of drug use among high school seniors underrepresent drug use among youth of that age group because high school dropouts and truants are not included, and these groups are expected to have more involvement with drugs than those who stay in school.

of this drug are of long duration, it is exceptionally difficult to reverse overdoses, which often result in death.

Methaqualone

Methaqualone is a synthetic sedative chemically unrelated to the barbiturates, glutethimide, or chloral hydrate. It has been widely abused and has caused many cases of serious poisoning. It was placed in Schedule II in 1973 and rescheduled to Schedule I in 1984. It is administered orally and is rapidly absorbed from the digestive tract. Large doses can cause coma, which may be accompanied by thrashing movements or convulsions. Continued heavy use of large doses leads to tolerance and dependence.

Methaqualone was marketed in the United States under various brand names, such as Quaalude, Parest, Mequin, Optimil, Somnafac, and Sopor. Mandrax is a European name for methaqualone in combination with an antihistamine.

Mecloqualone, a chemical similar to methaqualone in all significant respects, is not legally sold in the United States and is in Schedule I.

Meprobamate

Meprobamate, first synthesized in 1950, introduced the era of mild or "minor" tranquilizers. In the United States today more than 70 tons of meprobamate are distributed annually under its generic name, as well as under brand names such as Miltown, Equanil, and SK-Bamate. Meprobamate is prescribed primarily for the relief of anxiety, tension, and associated muscle spasms. Its onset and duration of action are like those of the intermediate-acting barbiturates; it differs from them in that it is a muscle relaxant, does not produce sleep at

therapeutic doses, and is relatively less toxic. Excessive use, however, can result in psychological and physical dependence.

Benzodiazepines

The benzodiazepine family of depressants relieve anxiety, tension, and muscle spasms, produce sedation, and prevent convulsions. These substances are marketed as anxiolytics (mild or minor tranquilizers), sedatives, hypnotics or anticonvulsants based to some extent on differences in their duration of action. Twelve members of this group currently are marketed in the United States. They are alprazolam (Xanax), chlordiazepoxide (Librium), clonazepam (Clonopin), clorazepate (Tranxene), diazepam (Valium), flurazepam (Dalmane), halazepam (Paxipam), lorazepam (Ativan), midazolam (Versed), oxazepam (Serax), prazepam (Centrax), quazepam (Dormalin), temazepam (Restoril), and triazolam (Halcion). While the margin of safety associated with these drugs is considerable, overdose can occur, and continuous use for several months can result in psychic or physical dependence.

Librium and Valium are among the most widely prescribed drugs in this country. These drugs have a relatively slow onset but long duration of action. Prolonged use of excessive doses may result in physical and psychological dependence. Withdrawal symptoms develop approximately one week to 10 days after continual high doses are abruptly discontinued. The delay in appearance of the abstinence syndrome is due to the slow elimination of the drug from the body. When these drugs are used to obtain a "high," they are usually taken in conjunction with another drug, such as alcohol.

STIMULANTS

The two most prevalent stimulants are nicotine in tobacco products and caffeine, the active ingredient of coffee, tea, and some bottled beverages that are sold in every supermarket. When used in moderation, these stimulants tend to relieve fatigue and increase alertness. They are an accepted part of our culture.

There are, however, more potent stimulants that because of their dependence-producing potential are under the regulatory control of the CSA. These controlled stimulants are available by prescription for medical purposes; they are also clandestinely manufactured for distribution on the illicit market.

Users tend to rely on stimulants to feel stronger, more decisive, and self-possessed. Because of the cumulative effects of the drugs, chronic users often follow a pattern of taking "uppers" in the morning and "downers," such as alcohol or sleeping pills, at night. Such chemical manipulation interferes with normal body processes and can lead to mental and physical illness.

Individuals who resort to stimulants for their euphoric effects consume large doses sporadically, over weekends or at night, often going on to experiment with other drugs of abuse. The consumption of stimulants may result in a temporary sense of exhilaration, superabundant energy, hyperactivity, extended wakefulness, and a loss of appetite. It may also induce irritability, anxiety, and apprehension. These effects are greatly intensified with administration by intravenous injection, which may produce a sudden sensation known as a "flash" or "rush." The protracted use of stimulants is fol-

Past and Present Cocaine Epidemics

By Constance Holden

In the late 1950s, when Yale University psychiatrist and drug historian David Musto was in medical school, there were only about 50,000 cocaine users in the United States. Musto says his professors would cite cocaine "as an example of a problem we used to have and has now been almost completely eliminated."

The old chestnut by George Santayana—about those who forget history being condemned to repeat it—seems particularly apt with regard to today's cocaine epidemic. Even in the mid-1970s, when cocaine use had begun a sharp climb, the Carter White House took a tolerant view. Jimmy Carter's drug adviser, psychiatrist Peter Bourne, went so far as to write that cocaine "is probably the most benign of illicit drugs currently in widespread use."*

Musto says Bourne and others had forgotten what happened around the country's first cocaine epidemic in the early years of this century. Cocaine (like opiates) used to be completely legal and widely available in a variety of products. But over the years prices fell and the sniffing, swallowing, and injecting of cocaine became widespread.

The year 1910 signalled the peak of the epidemic. In 20 years, says Musto, cocaine had been transformed from "a miracle drug to the most dangerous drug in America." In his annual message to Congress, President William Howard Taft said, "Cocaine is more appalling in its effects than any other habit-forming drug used in the United States."

Public fears eventually found expression in the passage of the first federal antinarcotics law, the Harrison Act of 1915. Although physicians were still allowed to dispense dangerous drugs, this loophole was tightened in Supreme Court rulings.

"Nothing is a better example of forgetting history," says Musto. And the forgetting was "intentional." During the 1930s and '40s, everyone thought the policy was working and mandatory drug education in the schools faded away, so "all the information from the first epidemic was not transmitted."

Despite the heroin epidemic of the late 1960s, the national mood was still one of relative toleration toward illicit drugs, marked by calls for legalization or decriminalization of marijuana, until the advent of the Reagan years.

Since then the tide has turned with a vengeance. Once again calls are being sounded for legalization—but this time against a background of increasing public intolerance of drugs. Musto, who calls legalization "a fad born of frustration," thinks its advocates are also guilty of forgetting history when they try to make analogies with Prohibition. For one thing, a great many Americans have always believed that alcohol is harmless in moderation. A more apt comparison would be to the laws against cocaine, but "you never read an article about how cocaine prohibition didn't work, because it was completely successful."

The reason for its success was the strong public consensus, which is far more crucial than any legal measures, says Musto. He sees a similar consensus building now, catalyzed by crack. But public fervor is a two-edged sword, says Musto, who fears that it could lead people to writing off the problems of inner cities as beyond redemption.

---

* *The American Disease: Origins of Narcotic Control* by David F. Musto (Oxford Univ. Press, New York, 1987).

Reprinted with permission from *Science*, Vol 246, Page 1377, Dec. 15, 1989. Copyright 1989 by the American Association for the Advancement of Science.

---

lowed, however, by a period of depression known as "crashing" that is invariably described as unpleasant. Since the depression can be easily counteracted by a further injection of stimulant, this abuse pattern becomes increasingly difficult to break. Heavy users may inject themselves every few hours, a process sometimes continued to the point of delirium, psychosis, or physical exhaustion.

Tolerance to both the euphoric and appetite suppressant effects develops rapidly. Doses large enough to overcome the insensitivity that develops may cause various mental aberrations, the early signs of which include repetitive grinding of the teeth, touching and picking the face and extremities, performing the same task over and over, a preoccupation with one's own processes, suspiciousness, and a sense of being watched. Paranoia with auditory and visual hallucinations characterizes the toxic syndrome resulting from continued high doses. Dizziness, tremor, agitation, hostility, panic, headache, flushed skin, chest pain with palpitations, excessive sweating, vomiting, and abdominal cramps are among the symptoms of a sublethal overdose. In the absence of medical intervention, high fever, convulsions, and cardiovascular collapse may precede the onset of death. It should be added that physical exertion increases the hazards

of stimulant use since accidental death is due in part to their effects on the cardiovascular and temperature regulating systems. Fatalities under conditions of extreme exertion have been reported among athletes who have taken stimulants in moderate amounts.

If withdrawn from stimulants, chronic high-dose users exhibit profound depression, apathy, fatigue, and disturbed sleep for up to 20 hours a day. The immediate withdrawal syndrome may last for several days. There may also be a lingering impairment of perception and thought processes. Anxiety, an incapacitating tenseness, and suicidal tendencies may persist for weeks or months. Many experts now interpret these symptoms as indicating that stimulant drugs are capable of producing physical dependence. Whether the withdrawal syndrome is physical or psychological in origin is, in this instance, academic since the stimulants are recognized as among the most potent agents of reward and reinforcement that underlie the problem of dependence.

Cocaine

The most potent stimulant of natural origin, cocaine is extracted from the leaves of the coca plant (Erythroxylon coca), which has been grown in the

Andean highlands of South America since prehistoric times. The leaves of the plant are chewed in the region for refreshment and relief from fatigue.

Pure cocaine, the principal psychoactive ingredient, was first isolated in the 1880s. It was used as an anesthetic in eye surgery for which no previously known drug had been suitable. It became particularly useful in surgery of the nose and throat because of its ability to anesthetize tissue while simultaneously constricting blood vessels and limiting bleeding. Many of its therapeutic applications are now obsolete because of the development of safer drugs as local anesthetics.

Illicit cocaine is usually distributed as a white crystalline powder, often diluted by a variety of other ingredients, the most common of which are sugars such as lactose, inositol, mannitol, and local anesthetics such as lidocaine. The frequent adulteration is to increase volume and thus to multiply profits.

The drug is most commonly administered by being "snorted" through the nasal passages. Symptoms of repeated use in this manner may resemble the congested nose of a common cold.

The intensity of the psychological effects of cocaine, as with many psychoactive drugs, depends on the rate of entry into the blood. Intravenous injection or smoking produces an almost immediate intense experience. Cocaine hydrochloride, the usual form in which cocaine is sold, while soluble in water and sometimes injected, is fairly insensitive to heat. Conversion of cocaine hydrochloride to cocaine base yields a substance that will become volatile when heated. "Crack," or cocaine base in the form of chips, chunks or "rocks," is usually vaporized in a pipe or smoked with plant material in a cigarette or a "joint." Inhalation of the cocaine fumes produces effects that are very fast in onset, very intense, and are quickly over. These intense effects are often followed within minutes by a dysphoric "crash," leading to frequently repeated doses and rapid addiction.

Because of the intensity of its pleasurable effects, cocaine has the potential for extraordinary psychic dependency. Recurrent users may resort to larger doses at shorter intervals until their lives are largely committed to their drug addiction. Anxiety, restlessness, and extreme irritability may indicate the onset of a toxic psychosis similar to paranoid schizophrenia. Tactile hallucinations so afflict some chronic users that they injure themselves in attempting to remove imaginary insects from under the skin. Others feel persecuted and fear that they are being watched and followed.

Excessive doses of cocaine may cause seizures and death from, for example, respiratory failure, stroke, cerebral hemorrhage, or heart failure. There is no specific treatment for cocaine overdose. Nor does tolerance develop to the toxic effects of cocaine. In fact, there are studies which indicate that repeated use lowers the dose at which toxicity occurs. There is no "safe" dose of cocaine.

Amphetamines

Amphetamine, dextroamphetamine, and methamphetamine are so similar in the effects they induce that they can be differentiated from one another only by laboratory analysis. Amphetamine was first used clinically in the mid-1930s to treat narcolepsy, a rare disorder resulting in an uncontrollable tendency to sleep. After the introduction of the amphetamines into medical practice, the number of conditions for which they were pre-

Reported Cocaine Use by High School Seniors

| Year | Used cocaine within the last: | |
	12 months[1]	30 days
1975	5.6%	1.9%
1976	6.0	2.0
1977	7.2	2.9
1978	9.0	3.9
1979	12.0	5.7
1980	12.3	5.2
1981	12.4	5.8
1982	11.5	5.0
1983	11.4	4.9
1984	11.6	5.8
1985	13.1	6.7
1986	12.7	6.2
1987	10.3	4.3
1988	7.9	3.4

1. Including the last 30 days. *Source: Drugs and Crime Facts, 1989,* Bureau of Justice Statistics.

scribed multiplied, as did the quantities made available.

For a time, they were sold without prescription in inhalers and other over-the-counter preparations. Abuse became popular. Many segments of the population, especially those concerned with extensive or irregular hours, were among those who used amphetamines orally in excessive amounts. "Speed freaks," who injected amphetamines, became known for their bizarre and often violent behavior. Over-the-counter availability (except inhalers) was terminated and amphetamines now are available only by prescription. Inhalers still are available over-the-counter.

Whereas a prescribed dose is between 2.5 and 15 mg per day, those on a "speed" binge have been known to inject as much as 1,000 mg every 2 or 3 hours. Recognition of the deleterious effects of these drugs and their limited therapeutic value led to a marked reduction in their use by the medical profession. The medical use of amphetamines is now limited to narcolepsy, attention deficit disorders in children, and certain cases of obesity—as a short-term adjunct to a restricted diet for patients resistant to other forms of therapy.

Their illicit use closely parallels that of cocaine in the range of its short-term and long-term effects. Despite broad recognition of the risks, clandestine laboratories produce vast quantities of amphetamines, particularly methamphetamine, for distribution on the illicit market.

Methamphetamine Abusers

According to a recent study by the National Institute on Drug Abuse, abusing populations are predominantly white, lower middle income, high school educated, young adults ranging in age from 20 to 35 years. Although clients in drug treatment programs for methamphetamine abuse report that the drug is commonly used by adolescent males, that group is not observed in morbidity and mortality data. Abuse patterns suggest an estimated two to four year latency period from first use to full addiction. Most treatment clients interviewed initiated use by intranasal snorting, but then turned to intravenous (IV) administration. Compulsive abuse accelerates with IV use because of the drug's rapid onset of action in a pattern similar to crack cocaine abuse. Although crack is not injected, inhalation of its vapors provides a rapid pulmonary delivery of the drug in concentrated dose to the brain promoting an intensified onset of action. This method, like IV methamphetamine use, triggers an initial, short term jolt which compels the user to repeat drug use again and again in a futile attempt to re-experience the drug's exhilarating effects. Additionally, needle sharing with methamphetamine appears common despite users' knowledge of HIV transmission risk. Thus, methamphetamine has been characterized as "white man's version of crack" and a "gateway to needle use and sharing."

Dosage levels reported by those interviewed varied according to how long methamphetamine had been used, the purity of the drug, and its route of administration. Doses tended to increase significantly with continued use, particularly with IV administration. The smallest unit of purchase was usually 1/4 gram which would provide approximately 4 doses to the first time, intranasal user. Quantities used by study participants ranged from less than 1/4 gram to 4 grams per day. A common unit of sale is called an *eightball*, reported to be 1/8 of an ounce or 3.5 grams which usually sold for $150. Prices for an eightball were mentioned as low as $90 and as high as $200.

Phenmetrazine (Preludin) and Methylphenidate (Ritalin)

The medical indications, patterns of abuse, and adverse effects of phenmetrazine (Preludin) and methylphenidate (Ritalin) compare closely with those of the other stimulants. Phenmetrazine is medically used only as an appetite suppressant and methylphenidate mainly for treatment of attention deficit disorders in children. They have been subject to abuse in countries where freely available, as they are here in localities where medical practitioners write prescriptions on demand. While the abuse of these drugs involves both oral and intravenous use, most of the abuse involves the injection of tablets dissolved in water. Complications arising from such use are common since the tablets contain insoluble materials which, when injected, block small blood vessels and cause serious damage, especially in the lungs and retina of the eye.

Anorectic Drugs

In recent years, a number of drugs have been manufactured and marketed to replace amphetamines as appetite suppressants. These so-called anorectic drugs include benzphetamine (Didrex), chlorphentermine (Pre-Sate, etc.), clortermine (Voranil), diethylpropion (Tenuate, Tepanil, etc.), fenfluramine (Pondimin), mazindol (Sanorex, Mazanor), phendimetrazine (Plegine, Bacarate, Melfiat, Statobex, Tanorex, etc.), phentermine (Ionamin, Adipex-P, etc.). They produce many of the effects of the amphetamines, but are generally less potent. All are controlled because of the similarity of their effects to those of the amphetamines. Fenfluramine differs somewhat from the others in that at low doses it produces sedation.

CANNABIS

Cannabis sativa L., the hemp plant, grows wild throughout most of the tropic and temperate regions of the world. It is a single species. This plant has long been cultivated for the tough fiber of the stem, the seed used in feed mixtures, and the oil as an ingredient of paint, as well as for its biologically active substances, most highly concentrated in the leaves and resinous flowering tops.

The plant material has been used as a drug for centuries. In 1839, it entered the annals of western medicine with the publication of an article surveying its therapeutic potential, including possible uses as an analgesic and anticonvulsant agent. It was alleged to be effective in treating a wide range of physical and mental ailments during the remainder of the 19th century. With the introduction of many new synthetic drugs in the 20th century, interest in it as a medication waned.

The controls imposed with the passage of the Marihuana Tax Act of 1937 further curtailed its use in treatment, and by 1941 it had been deleted from the *U.S. Pharmacopoeia* and the *National* Formulary, the official compendia of drugs. But advances continued to be made in the chemistry of cannabis. Among the many cannabinoids synthesized by the plant are cannabinol, cannabidiol, cannabinolidic acids, cannabigerol, cannabichromene, and several isomers of tetrahydrocannabinol, one of which is believed responsible for most of its characteristic psychoactive effects. This is delta-9-tetrahydrocannabinol (THC), one of 61 cannabinoids which are unique chemicals found only in cannabis.

Cannabis products are usually smoked in the form of loosely rolled cigarettes ("joints"). They may be used alone or in combination with other substances. They may also be administered orally, but are reported to be about three times more potent when smoked. The effects are felt within minutes, reach their peak in 10 to 30 minutes, and may linger for 2 or 3 hours.

A condensed description of these effects is apt to be inadequate or even misleading. So much depends upon the experience and expectations of the individual as well as the activity of the drug itself. Low doses tend to induce restlessness and an increasing sense of well-being, followed by a dreamy state of relaxation, and frequently hunger, especially a craving for sweets. Changes of sensory perception—a more vivid sense of sight, smell, touch, taste, and hearing—may be accompanied by subtle alterations in thought formation and expression. Stronger doses intensify reactions. The individual may experience shifting sensory imagery, rapidly fluctuating emotions, a flight of fragmentary thoughts with disturbed associations, an altered sense of self-identity, impaired memory, and a dulling of attention despite an illusion of heightened insight. This state of intoxication may not be noticeable to an observer. High doses may result in image distortion, a loss of personal identity, and fantasies and hallucination. Very high doses may result in a toxic psychosis.

During the past 20-25 years, there has been a resurgence in the scientific study of cannabis, one goal of which has been to develop therapeutic agents which, if used as directed in medical treatment, will not produce harmful side effects. THC can be synthesized in the laboratory. Because it is a liquid insoluble in water and it decomposes on exposure to air and light, it is administered in soft gelatin capsules. Research has resulted in development and marketing of a product containing THC for the control of nausea and vomiting caused by chemotherapeutic agents used in the treatment of cancer. None of the synthetic cannabinoids have so far been detected in the drug traffic.

Three drugs that come from cannabis are currently distributed on the U.S. illicit market. Having no currently accepted medical use in treatment in the United States, they remain under Schedule I of the CSA.

Marijuana

The term marijuana is used in this country to refer to the cannabis plant and to any part or extract of it that produces somatic or psychic changes in humans. A tobacco-like substance produced by drying the leaves and flowering tops of the plant, marijuana varies significantly in its potency, depending on the source and selectivity of plant materials used. Most wild U.S. cannabis is considered inferior because of a low concentration of THC, usually less than 0.5 percent. Jamaican, Colombian, and Mexican varieties range between 0.5 and 7 percent. The most selective produce is reputed to be sinsemilla (Spanish, *sin semilla:* without seed), prepared from the unpollinated female cannabis plant, samples of which have been found to contain up to 20 percent THC. Southeast Asian "Thai sticks," consisting of marijuana buds bound on short sections of bamboo, are encountered infrequently on the U.S. illicit market.

Hashish

The Middle East is the main source of hashish. It consists of the drug-rich resinous secretions of the cannabis plant, which are collected, dried, and then compressed into a variety of forms, such as balls, cakes, or cookie-like sheets. The THC content of hashish in the United States averages 3 percent.

Hashish Oil

The name is used by illicit drug users and dealers but is a misnomer in suggesting any resemblance to hashish other than its objective of further concentration. Hashish oil is produced by a process of repeated extraction of cannabis plant materials to yield a dark viscious liquid, current samples of which average about 20 percent THC. In terms of its psychoactive effect, a drop or two of this liquid on a cigarette is equal to a single "joint" of marijuana.

HALLUCINOGENS

Hallucinogenic drugs, both natural and synthetic, are substances that distort the perception of objective reality. They induce a state of excitation of the central nervous system, manifested by alterations of mood, usually euphoric, but sometimes severely depressive. Under the influence of hallucinogens, the senses of direction, distance, and time becomes disoriented. A user may speak of "seeing" sounds and "hearing" colors. If taken in a large enough dose, the drug produces delusions and visual hallucinations. Occasionally, depersonalization and depression are so severe that suicide is possible, but the most common danger is impaired judgment, leading to rash decisions and accidents. Persons in hallucinogenic states should, therefore, be closely supervised and upset as little as possible to keep them from harming themselves and others. Acute anxiety, restlessness, and sleeplessness are common until the drug wears off.

Long after hallucinogens are eliminated from the body, users may experience flashbacks—fragmentary recurrences of psychedelic effects—such as the intensification of a perceived color, the apparent motion of a fixed object, or the mistaking of one object for another. Recurrent use produces tolerance, which tends to encourage resorting to greater amounts. Although no evidence of physical dependence is detectable when the drugs are withdrawn, recurrent use tends to produce psychic dependence, varying according to the drug, the dose, and the individual user. It should be stressed that the hallucinogens are unpredictable in their effects each time they are used.

The abuse of hallucinogens in the United States reached a peak of popularity in the late 1960s, and a subsequent decline was attributed to broader awareness of their hazardous effects. Their abuse, however, reemerged in the late 1970s and has continued in this decade.

Peyote and Mescaline

The primary active ingredient of the peyote cactus is the hallucinogen *mescaline.* It is derived from the fleshy parts or buttons of this plant, which has been employed by Indians in northern Mexico from the earliest recorded time as a part of traditional religious rites. The Native American Church, which uses peyote in religious ceremonies, has been exempted from certain provisions of the CSA. Peyote, or mescal buttons, and mescaline should not be confused with mescal, the colorless Mexican liquor distilled from the leaves of maguey plants. Usually ground into a powder, peyote is taken orally. Mescaline can also be produced synthetically. A dose of 350 to 500 mg of mescaline produces illusions and hallucinations lasting from 5 to 12 hours.

DOM, DOB, MDA, and MDMA

Many chemical variations of mescaline and amphetamine have been synthesized in the laboratory, certain of which at various times have won acceptance among illicit drug users and traffickers. DOM (4-methyl-2,5-dimethoxyamphetamine), synthesized in 1963, was introduced in 1967 into the Haight-Asbury drug scene in San Francisco. At first named STP after a motor oil additive, the acronym was quickly reinterpreted to stand for "Serenity, Tranquility, and Peace." A host of related chemicals are illicitly manufactured, including DOB (4-bromo-2,5-dimethoxyamphetamine), MDA (3, 4-methylenedioxyamphetamine), and MDMA (3, 4-methylenedioxymethamphetamine) (XTC). These drugs differ from one another in their speed of onset, duration of action, potency, and capacity to modify mood with or without producing hallucinations. They are usually taken orally, sometimes "snorted," and rarely injected intravenously. Because they are produced in clandestine laboratories, they are seldom pure, and the dose in a tablet, in a capsule, or on a square of impregnated paper may be expected to vary considerably. The names of these drugs are sometimes used to misrepresent other chemicals.

Psilocybin and Psilocyn

Like the peyote cactus, Psilocybe mushrooms have been used for centuries in traditional Indian rites. When they are eaten, these "sacred" or "magic" mushrooms affect mood and perception in a manner similar to mescaline and LSD. Their active ingredients, psilocybin and psilocyn, are chemically related to LSD. They can now be made synthetically, but much of what is sold under these names on the illicit market consists of other chemical compounds.

LSD (LSD-25, lysergide)

LSD is an abbreviation of the German expression for lysergic acid diethylamide. It is produced from lysergic acid, a substance derived from the ergot fungus which grows on rye or from lysergic acid amide, a chemical found in morning glory seeds. Both of these precursor chemicals are in Schedule III of the CSA.

LSD was first synthesized in 1938. Its psychotomimetic effects were discovered in 1943 when a chemist accidentally took some LSD. As he began to experience the effects now known as a "trip," he was aware of vertigo and an intensification of light. Closing his eyes, he saw a stream of fantastic images of extraordinary vividness accompanied by a kaleidoscopic play of colors. This condition lasted for about two hours.

Because of the extremely high potency of LSD, its structural relationship to a chemical which is present in the brain, and its similarity in effects to certain aspects of psychosis, LSD was used as a tool of research to study the mechanism of mental illness. Although there was a marked decline from its initial popularity in illicit channels during the 1960s, there are indications that its illicit use once again may be increasing to some extent.

LSD is usually sold in the form of tablets, thin squares of gelatin ("window panes"), or impregnated paper ("blotter acid"). The average effective oral dose is from 30 to 50 micrograms, but the amount per dosage unit varies greatly. The effects of higher doses persist for 10 to 12 hours. Tolerance develops rapidly.

Phencyclidine (PCP) and Related Drugs

Phencyclidine was investigated in the 1950s as a human anesthetic, but, because of side effects of confusion and delirium, its development for human use was discontinued. It became commercially available for use in veterinary medicine in the 1960s under the trade name Sernylan. In 1978, however, the manufacturer stopped production. That same year phencyclidine was transferred from Schedule III to Schedule II of the CSA, together with two previously unscheduled precursor chemicals.[1] Most, if not all, phencyclidine on the U.S. illicit market is produced in clandestine laboratories.

More commonly known as PCP, it is sold under at least 50 other names, including Angel Dust, Crystal, Supergrass, Killer Weed, Embalming Fluid, and Rocket Fuel, that reflect the range of its bizarre and volatile effects. It is also frequently misrepresented as mescaline, LSD, or THC. In its pure form, it is a white crystalline powder that readily dissolves in water. Most PCP now contains contaminants resulting from its makeshift manufacture, causing the color to range from tan to brown and the consistency from a powder to a gummy mass. Although sold in tablets and capsules, as well as in powder and liquid form, it is commonly applied to a leafy material, such as parsley, mint, oregano, or marijuana, and smoked.

The drug is as variable in its effects as it is in its appearance. A moderate amount often produces in the user a sense of detachment, distance, and estrangement from the surroundings. Numbness, slurred or blocked speech, and a loss of coordination may be accompanied by a sense of strength and invulnerability. A blank stare, rapid and involuntary eye movements, and an exaggerated gait are among the more common observable effects. Auditory hallucinations, image distortion as in a fun-house mirror, and severe mood disorders may also occur, producing in some acute anxiety and a feeling of impending doom, in others paranoia and violent hostility. PCP is unique among popular drugs of abuse in its power to produce psychoses indistinguishable from schizophrenia. Although such extreme psychic reactions are usually associated with repeated use of the drug, they have been known to occur in some cases after only one dose and to last, or recur intermittently, long after the drug has left the body. Phencyclidine now poses greater risks to the user than any other drug of abuse, with the possible exception of crack—the smokable form of cocaine—whose street distribution and use by inhalation parallels that of PCP.

Modification of the manufacturing process may further yield chemically related analogues capable of producing, so far as is known, similar psychic effects. Three of these analogues have so far been encountered on the U.S. illicit market, where they have been sold as PCP.[2] In view of the severe behavioral toxicity of phencyclidine and its analogues, in November 1978 the Congress passed legislation increasing the penalties for manufacture, distribution, and possession with intent to distribute these chemicals. The penalties for manufacture, distribution, and possession with intent to distribute PCP were further increased by the Controlled Substances Penalties Amendments Act of 1984 and the Narcotics Penalties and Enforcement Act of 1986. There are enhanced penalties for violations involving specified quantities of PCP or substances containing PCP.

---

1. The chemicals are 1-phenylcyclohexylamine and 1-piperidinocyclohexanecarbonitrile (PCC).
2. The analogues are N-ethyl-1-phenylcyclohexylamine (PCE), 1-(1-phenylcyclohexyl)-pyrrolidine (PCP; PHP), and 1-[1-(2-thienyl-cyclohexyl)]-piperdine (TPCP; TCP).

ALCOHOL

Source: U.S. Department of Education.

Effects.—Alcohol consumption causes a number of marked changes in behavior. Even low doses significantly impair the judgment and coordination required to drive a car safely, increasing the likelihood that the driver will be involved in an accident. Low to moderate doses of alcohol also increase the incidence of a variety of aggressive acts, including spouse and child abuse. Moderate to high doses of alcohol cause marked impairments in higher mental functions, severely altering a person's ability to learn and remember information. Very high doses cause respiratory depression and death. If combined with other depressants of the central nervous system, much lower doses of alcohol will produce the effects just described.

Repeated use of alcohol can lead to dependence. Sudden cessation of alcohol intake is likely to produce withdrawal symptoms, including severe anxiety, tremors, hallucinations, and convulsions. Alcohol withdrawal can be life-threatening. Long-term consumption of large quantities of alcohol, particularly when combined with poor nutrition, can also lead to permanent damage to vital organs such as the brain and the liver.

Mothers who drink alcohol during pregnancy may give birth to infants with fetal alcohol syndrome. These infants have irreversible physical abnormalities and mental retardation. In addition, research indicates that children of alcoholic parents are at greater risk than other youngsters of becoming alcoholics.

Youth and Alcohol

Alcohol is the number one drug problem among youth. The easy availability, widespread acceptability, and extensive promotion of alcoholic beverages within our society make alcohol the most widely used and abused drug.

● Alcohol use is widespread. By their senior year of high school almost all students will have tried alcoholic beverages; 2 out of 3 will be current users; 1 in 20 will be daily users; and almost 4 out of 10 will consume 5 or more drinks in a row at least once every 2 weeks.

● Early alcohol use is associated with subsequent alcohol dependence and related health problems. Youth who use alcohol at a younger age are more likely to use alcohol heavily and to experience alcohol-related problems affecting their relationships with family and friends by late adolescence. Their school performance is likely to suffer, and they are more likely to be truant. They are also more likely to abuse other drugs and to get in trouble with the law, or, if they are girls, to become pregnant. ☐

TOBACCO

Source: U.S. Department of Education.

Effects.—The smoking of tobacco products is the chief avoidable cause of death in our society. Smokers are more likely than nonsmokers to contract heart disease—some 170,000 die each year from smoking-related coronary heart disease. Lung, larynx, esophageal, bladder, pancreatic, and kidney cancers also strike smokers at increased rates. Some 30 percent of cancer deaths (130,000 per year) are linked to smoking. Chronic obstructive lung diseases such as emphysema and chronic bronchitis are 10 times more likely to occur among smokers than among nonsmokers.

Smoking during pregnancy also poses serious risks. Spontaneous abortion, preterm birth, low birth weights, and fetal and infant deaths are all more likely to occur when the pregnant woman/mother is a smoker.

Cigarette smoke contains some 4,000 chemicals, several of which are known carcinogens. Other toxins and irritants found in smoke can produce eye, nose, and throat irritations. Carbon monoxide, another component of cigarette smoke, combines with hemoglobin in the blood stream to form carboxyhemoglobin, a substance that interferes with the body's ability to obtain and use oxygen.

Perhaps the most dangerous substance in tobacco smoke is nicotine. Although it is implicated in the onset of heart attacks and cancer, its most dangerous role is reinforcing and strengthening the desire to smoke. Because nicotine is highly addictive, addicts find it very difficult to stop smoking. Of 1,000 typical smokers, fewer than 20 percent succeed in stopping on the first try.

Although the harmful effects of smoking cannot be questioned, people who quit can make significant strides in repairing damage done by smoking. For pack-a-day smokers, the increased risk of heart attack dissipates after 10 years. The likelihood of contracting lung cancer as a result of smoking can also be greatly reduced by quitting. ☐

Sources of Information

A few of the sources of assistance or information to which you might turn are given below. Also see *Information Please* listing of Toll-Free Numbers for additional sources.

Parents' Resource Institute for Drug Education, Inc. (PRIDE).—This national resource and information center offers consultant services to parent groups, school personnel, and youth groups, and provides a drug-use survey service. It conducts an annual conference; publishes a newsletter, a youth group handbook, and other publications; and sells and rents books, films, videos, and slide programs. Membership is $20. The Hurt Building, 50 Hurt Plaza, Suite 210, Atlanta, Ga. 30303. Telephone (404) 577-4500; 1-800-241-9746.

U.S. Clearinghouse.—(A publication list is available on request, along with placement on a mailing list for new publications. Single copies are free.) National Clearinghouse for Alcohol and Drug Information (NCADI), P.O. Box 2345, Rockville, Md. 20852. Telephone (301) 468-2600

NCADI combines the clearinghouse activities previously administered by the National Institute on Alcoholism and Alcohol Abuse and the National Institute on Drug Abuse.

National Council on Alcoholism, Inc.—This national voluntary health agency provides information about alcoholism and alcohol problems through more than 300 local affiliates. 12 West 21st St., New York, N.Y. 10010. Telephone (212) 206-6770.

Institute on Black Chemical Abuse.—This institute provides training and technical assistance to programs that want to serve African-American/black clients and others of color more effectively. 2614 Nicollet Ave., Minneapolis, Minn. 55408. Telephone (612) 871-7878

Al-Anon Family Group Headquarters.—Al-Anon was established as a resource for family members and friends of alcoholics. It is a free, nonprofessional, worldwide organization with more than 30,000 groups. (See your telephone White Pages.)

Nar-Anon Family Group Headquarters.—This organization operates in a manner similar to Al-Anon and supports people who have friends or family members with drug problems. World Service Office, P.O. Box 2562, Palos Verdes Peninsula, Calif. 90274. Telephone (213) 547-5800.

American Council for Drug Education.—This organization provides information on drug use, develops media campaigns, reviews scientific findings, publishes books and a newsletter, and offers films and curriculum materials for preteens. 204 Monroe St., Rockville, Md. 20850. Telephone (301) 294-0600.

Narcotics Anonymous.—Similar to Alcoholics Anonymous, this program is a fellowship of men and women who meet to help one another with their drug dependency problems. World Service Office, P.O. Box 9999, Van Nuys, Calif. 91409. Telephone (818) 780-3951.

Families Anonymous.—This worldwide organization offers a 12-step, self-help program for families and friends of people with behavioral problems usually associated with drug abuse. The organization is similar in structure to Alcoholics Anonymous. P.O. Box 528, Van Nuys, Calif. 91408. Telephone (818) 989-7841.

GEOGRAPHY

World Geography
Explorations and Discoveries
(All years are A.D. unless B.C. is specified.)

Country or place	Event	Explorer or discoverer	Date
AFRICA			
Sierra Leone	Visited	Hanno, Carthaginian seaman	c. 520 B.C.
Congo River	Mouth discovered	Diogo Cão, Portuguese	c. 1484
Cape of Good Hope	Rounded	Bartolomeu Diaz, Portuguese	1488
Gambia River	Explored	Mungo Park, Scottish explorer	1795
Sahara	Crossed	Dixon Denham and Hugh Clapperton, English explorers	1822–23
Zambezi River	Discovered	David Livingstone, Scottish explorer	1851
Sudan	Explored	Heinrich Barth, German explorer	1852–55
Victoria Falls	Discovered	Livingstone	1855
Lake Tanganyika	Discovered	Richard Burton and John Speke, British explorers	1858
Congo River	Traced	Sir Henry M. Stanley, British explorer	1877
ASIA			
Punjab (India)	Visited	Alexander the Great	327 B.C.
China	Visited	Marco Polo, Italian traveler	c. 1272
Tibet	Visited	Odoric of Pordenone, Italian monk	c. 1325
Southern China	Explored	Niccolò dei Conti, Venetian traveler	c. 1440
India	Visited (Cape route)	Vasco da Gama, Portuguese navigator	1498
Japan	Visited	St. Francis Xavier of Spain	1549
Arabia	Explored	Carsten Niebuhr, German explorer	1762
China	Explored	Ferdinand Richthofen, German scientist	1868
Mongolia	Explored	Nikolai M. Przhevalsky, Russian explorer	1870–73
Central Asia	Explored	Sven Hedin, Swedish scientist	1890–1908
EUROPE			
Shetland Islands	Visited	Pytheas of Massilia (Marseille)	c. 325 B.C.
North Cape	Rounded	Ottar, Norwegian explorer	c. 870
Iceland	Colonized	Norwegian noblemen	c. 890–900
NORTH AMERICA			
Greenland	Colonized	Eric the Red, Norwegian	c. 985
Labrador; Nova Scotia (?)	Discovered	Leif Ericson, Norse explorer	1000
West Indies	Discovered	Christopher Columbus, Italian	1492
North America	Coast discovered	Giovanni Caboto (John Cabot), for British	1497
Pacific Ocean	Discovered	Vasco Núñez de Balboa, Spanish explorer	1513
Florida	Explored	Ponce de León, Spanish explorer	1513
Mexico	Conquered	Hernando Cortés, Spanish adventurer	1519–21
St. Lawrence River	Discovered	Jacques Cartier, French navigator	1534
Southwest U. S.	Explored	Francisco Coronado, Spanish explorer	1540–42
Colorado River	Discovered	Hernando de Alarcón, Spanish explorer	1540
Mississippi River	Discovered	Hernando de Soto, Spanish explorer	1541
Frobisher Bay	Discovered	Martin Frobisher, English seaman	1576
Maine Coast	Explored	Samuel de Champlain, French explorer	1604

Country or place	Event	Explorer or discover	Date
Jamestown, Va.	Settled	John Smith, English colonist	1607
Hudson River	Explored	Henry Hudson, English navigator	1609
Hudson Bay (Canada)	Discovered	Henry Hudson	1610
Baffin Bay	Discovered	William Baffin, English navigator	1616
Lake Michigan	Navigated	Jean Nicolet, French explorer	1634
Arkansas River	Discovered	Jacques Marquette and Louis Jolliet, French explorers	1673
Mississippi River	Explored	Sieur de La Salle, French explorer	1682
Bering Strait	Discovered	Vitus Bering, Danish explorer	1728
Alaska	Discovered	Vitus Bering	1741
Mackenzie River (Canada)	Discovered	Sir Alexander Mackenzie, Scottish-Canadian explorer	1789
Northwest U. S.	Explored	Meriwether Lewis and William Clark	1804–06
Northeast Passage (Arctic Ocean)	Navigated	Nils Nordenskjöld, Swedish explorer	1879
Greenland	Explored	Robert Peary, American explorer	1892
Northwest Passage	Navigated	Roald Amundsen, Norwegian explorer	1906
SOUTH AMERICA			
Continent	Visited	Columbus, Italian	1498
Brazil	Discovered	Pedro Alvarez Cabral, Portuguese	1500
Peru	Conquered	Francisco Pizarro, Spanish explorer	1532–33
Amazon River	Explored	Francisco Orellana, Spanish explorer	1541
Cape Horn	Discovered	Willem C. Schouten, Dutch navigator	1615
OCEANIA			
Papua New Guinea	Visited	Jorge de Menezes, Portuguese explorer	1526
Australia	Visited	Abel Janszoon Tasman, Dutch navigator	1642
Tasmania	Discovered		
Australia	Explored	John McDouall Stuart, English explorer	1828
Australia	Explored	Robert Burke and William Wills, Australian explorers	1861
New Zealand	Sighted (and named)	Abel Janszoon Tasman	1642
New Zealand	Visited	James Cook, English navigator	1769
ARCTIC, ANTARCTIC, AND MISCELLANEOUS			
Ocean exploration	Expedition	Magellan's ships circled globe	1519–22
Galápagos Islands	Visited	Diego de Rivadeneira, Spanish captain	1535
Spitsbergen	Visited	Willem Barents, Dutch navigator	1596
Antarctic Circle	Crossed	James Cook, English navigator	1773
Antarctica	Discovered	Nathaniel Palmer, U. S. whaler (archipelago) and Fabian Gottlieb von Bellingshausen, Russian admiral (mainland)	1820–21
Antarctica	Explored	Charles Wilkes, American explorer	1840
North Pole	Reached	Robert E. Peary, American explorer	1909
South Pole	Reached	Roald Amundsen, Norwegian explorer	1911

The Continents

A continent is defined as a large unbroken land mass completely surrounded by water, although in some cases continents are (or were in part) connected by land bridges.

The hypothesis first suggested late in the 19th century was that the continents consist of lighter rocks that rest on heavier crustal material in about the same manner that icebergs float on water. That the rocks forming the continents are lighter than the material below them and under the ocean bottoms is now established. As a consequence of this fact, Alfred Wegener (for the first time in 1912) suggested that the continents are slowly moving, at a rate of about one yard per century, so that their relative positions are not rigidly fixed. Many geologists that were originally skeptical have come to accept this theory of Continental Drift.

When describing a continent, it is important to remember that there is a fundamental difference between a deep ocean, like the Atlantic, and shallow seas, like the Baltic and most of the North Sea, which are merely flooded portions of a continent. Another and entirely different point to remember is that political considerations have often overridden geographical facts when it came to naming continents.

Geographically speaking, Europe, including the British Isles, is a large western peninsula of the continent of Asia; and many geographers, when referring to Europe and Asia, speak of the Eurasian Continent. But traditionally, Europe is counted as a separate continent, with the Ural and the Caucasus mountains forming the line of demarcation between Europe and Asia.

To the south of Europe, Asia has an odd-shaped peninsula jutting westward, which has a large number of political subdivisions. The northern section is taken up by Turkey; to the south of Turkey there are Syria, Iraq, Israel, Jordan, Saudi Arabia, and a number of smaller Arab countries. All this is part of Asia. Traditionally, the island of Cyprus in the Mediterranean is also considered to be part of Asia, while the island of Crete is counted as European.

The large islands of Java, Borneo, and Sumatra and the smaller islands near them are counted as part of "tropical Asia," while New Guinea is counted as related to Australia. In the case of the Americas, the problem arises as to whether they should be considered one or two continents. There are good arguments on both sides, but since there is now a land bridge between North and South America (in the past it was often flooded) and since no part of the sea east of the land bridge is deep ocean, it is more logical to consider the Americas as one continent.

Politically, based mainly on history, the Americas are divided into North America (from the Arctic to the Mexican border), Central America (from Mexico to Panama, with the Caribbean islands), and South America. Greenland is considered a section of North America, while Iceland is traditionally counted as a European island because of its political ties with the Scandinavian countries.

The island groups in the Pacific are often called "Oceania," but this name does *not* imply that scientists consider them the remains of a continent.

The seven continents are North America, South America, Europe, Asia, Africa, Australia, and Antarctica.

Volcanoes of the World

About 500 volcanoes have had recorded eruptions within historical times. Almost two thirds of these are in the Northern Hemisphere. Most volcanoes occur at the boundaries of the earth's crustal plates, such as the famous "Ring of Fire" that surrounds the Pacific Ocean plate. Of the world's active volcanoes, about 60% are along the perimeter of the Pacific, about 17% on mid-oceanic islands, about 14% in an arc along the south of the Indonesian islands, and about 9% in the Mediterranean area, Africa, and Asia Minor. Many of the world's volcanoes are submarine and have unrecorded eruptions.

Pacific "Ring of Fire"

NORTHWEST

Japan: At least 33 active vents.

Aso (5,223 ft; 1,592 m), on Kyushu, has one of the largest craters in the world.

Asama (over 8,300 ft; 2,530 m), on Honshu, is continuously active; violent eruption in 1783.

Azuma (nearly 7,700 ft; 2,347 m), on Honshu, erupted in 1900.

Chokai (7,300 ft; 2,225 m), on Honshu, erupted in 1974 after having been quiescent since 1861.

Fujiyama (Fujisan) (12,385 ft; 3,775 m), on Honshu, southwest of Tokyo. Symmetrical in outline, snow-covered. Regarded as a sacred mountain.

On-take (3,668 ft; 1,118 m), on peninsula of Kyushu. Strong smoke emissions and explosions began November 1973 and continued through 1974.

U.S.S.R.: Kamchatka peninsula, 14–18 active volcanoes. Klyuchevskaya (Kluchev) (15,500 ft; 4,724 m) reported active in 1974.

Kurile Islands: At least 13 active volcanoes and several submarine outbreaks.

SOUTHWEST

New Zealand: Mount Tarawera (3,645 ft; 1,112 m), on North Island, had a severe eruption in 1886 that destroyed the famous Pink and White sinter terraces of Rotomahana, a hot lake.

Ngauruhoe (7,515 ft; 2,291 m), on North Island, emits steam and vapor constantly. Erupted 1974.

Papua New Guinea: Karkar Island (4,920 ft; 1,500 m). Mild eruptions 1974.

Philippine Islands: About 100 eruptive centers; Hibok Hibok, on Camiguin, erupted September 1950 and again in December 1951, when about 750 were reported killed or missing; eruptions continued during 1952–53.

Taal (4,752 ft; 1,448 m), on Luzon. Major eruption in 1965 killed 190; erupted again, 1968.

Volcano Islands: Mount Suribachi (546 ft; 166 m), on Iwo Jima. A sulfurous steaming volcano. Raising of U.S. flag over Mount Suribachi was one of the dramatic episodes of World War II.

NORTHEAST

Alaska: Mount Wrangell (14,163 ft; 4,317 m) and Mount Katmai (about 6,700 ft; 2,042 m). On June 6, 1912, a violent eruption (Nova Rupta) of Mount Katmai occurred, during which the "Valley of Ten Thousand Smokes" was formed.

Aleutian Islands: There are 32 active vents known and numerous inactive cones. Akutan Island (over 4,000 ft; 1,220 m) erupted in 1974, with ash and debris rising over 300 ft.

Great Sitkin (5,741 ft; 1,750 m). Explosive activity February–September 1974, accompanied by earthquake originating at volcano that registered 2.3 on Richter scale.

Augustine Island: Augustine volcano (4,000 ft; 1,220 m) erupted March 27, 1986. It last erupted in 1976.

California, Oregon, Washington: Lassen Peak (10,453 ft; 3,186 m) in California is one of two observed active volcanoes in the U.S. outside Alaska and Hawaii. The last period of activity was 1914–17. Mt. St. Helens (9,677 ft; 2,950 m) in the Cascade Range of southwest Washington became active on March 27, 1980, and erupted on May 18 after being inactive since 1857. From April 15 through May 1, 1986, weak activity began for the first time in two years. Other mountains of volcanic origin include Mount Shasta (California), Mount Hood (Oregon), Mount Mazama (Oregon)—the mountain containing Crater Lake, Mount Rainier (Washington), and Mount Baker (Washington), which has

Continued on page 462

The Pacific Ocean "Ring of Fire"

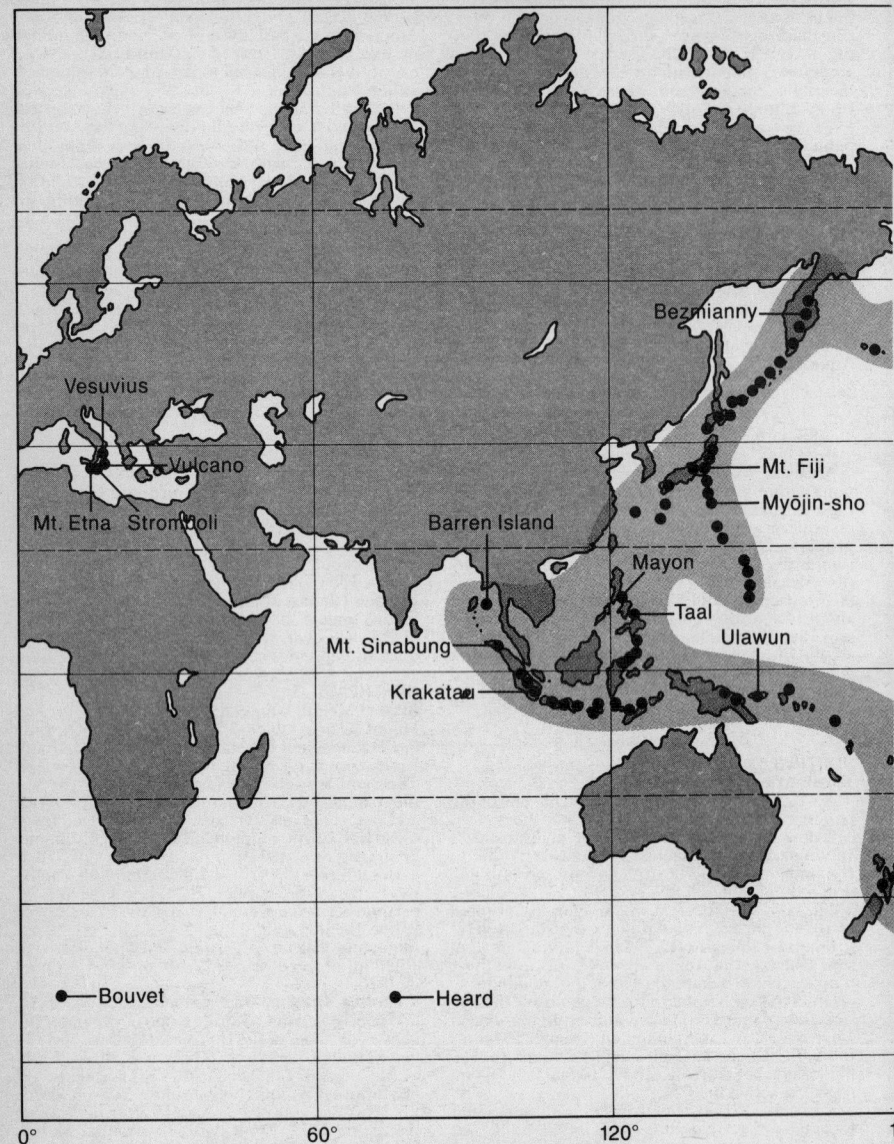

Bezmianny

Vesuvius

Vulcano

Mt. Etna Stromboli

Mt. Fiji

Myōjin-sho

Barren Island

Mayon

Taal

Ulawun

Mt. Sinabung

Krakatau

Bouvet

Heard

Volcanic Activity in the Solar System

(*Source:* U.S. Dept. of Interior, Geological Survey.)

From the 1976-1979 *Viking* mission, scientists have been able to study the volcanoes on Mars, and their studies are very revealing when compared with those of volcanoes on Earth. For example, Martian and Hawaiian volcanoes have gently sloping flanks, large multiple-collapse pits at their centers, and appear to be built of fluid lavas that have left their numerous flow features on their flanks. The most obvious difference between the two is size. The Martian shields are enormous. They can grow to over 17 miles in height and more than 350 miles across, in contrast to a maximum height of about 6 miles and width of 74 miles for the Hawaiian shields.

Source: U.S. Department of the Interior, U.S. Geological Survey.

Earth's Volcanic Origin

In July 1979, *Voyager-2* spacecraft images taken of Io, a moon of Jupiter, captured volcanoes in the actual process of eruption. The volcanic plumes photographed rose to some 60 to 100 miles above the surface of the moon. Thus active volcanism is taking place, at present, on at least one planetary body in addition to our Earth.

More than 80 percent of the Earth's surface—above and below sea level—is of volcanic origin. Gaseous emissions from volcanic vents over hundreds of millions of years formed the Earth's earliest oceans and atmosphere. Over geologic eons, countless volcanic eruptions have produced mountains, plateaus, and plains which erosion and weathering have transformed into fertile soils.

been steaming since October 1975, but gives no sign of an impending eruption.

SOUTHEAST

Chile and Argentina: About 25 active or potentially active.

Colombia: Huila (nearly 18,900 ft; 5,760 m), a vapor-emitting volcano, and Tolima (nearly 18,500 ft; 5,640 m). Eruption of Puracé (15,600 ft; 4,755 m) in 1949 killed 17 people. Nevado del Ruiz (16,200 ft; 4,938 m.), erupted Nov. 13, 1985, sending torrential floods of mud and water engulfing the town of Armero and killing more than 22,000 people.

Ecuador: Cayambe (nearly 19,000 ft; 5,791 m). Almost on the equator.

Cotopaxi (19,344 ft; 5,896 m). Perhaps highest active volcano in the world. Possesses a beautifully formed cone.

Reventador (11,434 ft; 3,485 m). Observed in active state in late 1973.

El Salvador: Izalco ("beacon of Central America") (7,830 ft; 2,387 m) first appeared in 1770 and is still growing (erupted in 1950, 1956; last erupted in October–November 1966). San Salvador (6,187 ft; 1,886 m) had a violent eruption in 1923. Conchagua (about 4100 ft; 1,250 m) erupted with considerable damage early in 1947.

Guatemala: Santa Maria Quezaltenango (12,361 ft; 3,768 m). Frequent activity between 1902–08 and 1922–28 after centuries of quiescence. Most dangerously active vent of Central America. Other volcanoes include Tajumulco (13,814 ft; 4,211 m) and Atitlán (11,633 ft; 3,546 m).

Mexico: Boquerón ("Big Mouth"), on San Benedicto, about 250 mi. south of Lower California. Newest volcano in Western Hemisphere, discovered September 1952.

Colima (about 14,000 ft; 4,270 m), in group that has had frequent eruptions.

Orizaba (Citlaltépetl) (18,701 ft; 5,700 m).

Parícutin (7,450 ft; 2,270 m). First appeared in February 1943. In less than a week, a cone over 140 ft high developed with a crater one quarter mile in circumference. Cone grew more than 1,500 ft (457 m) in 1943. Erupted 1952.

Popocatépetl (17,887 ft; 5,452 m). Large, deep, bell-shaped crater. Not entirely extinct; steam still escapes.

El Chinchonal (7,300 ft; 1,005.6 m) about 15 miles from Pichucalco. Long inactive, it erupted in March 1982.

Nicaragua: Volcanoes include Telica, Coseguina, and Momotombo. Between Momotombo on the west shore of Lake Managua and Coseguina overlooking the Gulf of Fonseca, there is a string of more than 20 cones, many still active. One of these, Cerro Negro, erupted in July 1947, with considerable damage and loss of life, and again in 1971.

Concepción (5,100 ft; 1,555 m). Ash eruptions 1973–74.

Mid-oceanic Islands

Canary Islands: Pico de Teide (12,192 ft; 3,716 m), on Tenerife.

Cape Verde Islands: Fogo (nearly 9,300 ft; 2,835 m). Severe eruption in 1857; quiescent until 1951.

Caribbean: La Soufrière (4,813 ft; 1,467 m), on Basse-Terre, Guadeloupe. Also called La Grande Soufrière. Violent activity in July–August 1976 caused evacuation of 73,000 people; renewed activity in April 1977 again caused thousands to flee their homes.

La Soufrière (4,048 ft; 1,234 m), on St. Vincent. Major eruption in 1902 killed over 1,000 people. Eruptions over 10-day period in April 1979 caused evacuation of northern two thirds of island.

Comoros: One volcano, Karthala (nearly 8,000 ft; 2,440 m), is visible for over 100 miles. Last erupted in 1904.

Hawaii: Mauna Loa ("Long Mountain") (13,680 ft; 4,170 m), on Hawaii, discharges from its high side vents more lava than any other volcano. Largest volcanic mountain in the world in cubic content. Area of crater is 3.7 sq mi. Violent eruption in June 1950, with lava pouring 25 miles into the ocean. Last major eruption in March 1984.

Mauna Kea (13,796 ft; 4,205 m), on Hawaii. Highest mountain in state.

Kilauea (4,090 ft; 1,247 m) is a vent in the side of Mauna Loa, but its eruptions are apparently independent. One of the most spectacular and active craters. Crater has an area of 4.14 sq mi. Earthquake in July 1975 caused major eruption. Eruptions began in September 1977 and reached a height of 980 ft (300 m). Activity ended Oct. 1. Became active again in January 1983, exploding in earnest in March 1983 forming the volcanic cone Pu'u O which has erupted periodically ever since. By May 1990, the lava flow had traveled 20 miles, obliterating the community of Kalapana on the southeast coast. By summer it had reached the Pacific Ocean.

Iceland: At least 25 volcanoes active in historical times. Very similar to Hawaiian volcanoes. Askja (over 4,700 ft; 1,433 m) is the largest.

Lesser Antilles (West Indian Islands): Mount Pelée (over 4,500 ft; 1,370 m), northwestern Martinique. Eruption in 1902 destroyed town of St. Pierre and killed approximately 40,000 people.

Réunion Island (east of Madagascar): Piton de la Fournaise (Le Volcan) (8,610 ft; 2,624 m). Large lava flows. Last erupted in 1972.

Samoan archipelago: Savai'i Island had an eruption in 1905 that caused considerable damage. Niuafoo (Tin Can), in the Tonga Islands, has a crater that extends 6,000 feet below and 600 feet above water.

Indonesia

Sumatra: Ninety volcanoes have been discovered; 12 are now active. The most famous, Krakatau, is a small volcanic island in the Sunda Strait. Numerous volcanic discharges occurred in 1883. One extremely violent explosion caused the disappearance of the highest peak and the northern part of the island. Fine dust was carried around the world in the upper atmosphere. Over 36,000 persons lost their lives in resultant tidal waves that were felt as far away as Cape Horn. Active in 1972.

Mediterranean Area

Italy: Mount Etna (10,902 ft; 3,323 m), eastern Sicily. Two new craters formed in eruptions of February–March 1947. Worst eruption in 50 years occurred November 1950–January 1951. Erupted again in 1974, 1975, 1977, 1978, 1979, and 1983.

Stromboli (about 3,000 ft; 914 m), Lipari Islands (north of Sicily). Called "Lighthouse of the Mediterranean." Reported active in 1971.

Mount Vesuvius (4,200 ft; 1,280 m), southeast of Naples. Only active volcano on European mainland. Pompeii buried by an eruption, A.D. 79.

Antarctica

The discovery of two small active volcanoes in 1982 brings to five the total number known on Antarctica. The new ones, 30 miles apart, are on the Weddell Sea side of the Antarctic Peninsula. The largest, Mount Erebus (13,000 ft; 3,962 m), rises from McMurdo Sound. Mount Melbourne (9,000 ft; 2,743 m) is in Victoria Land. The fifth, off the northern tip of the Antarctic Peninsula, is a crater known as Deception Island.

Principal Types of Volcanoes

(*Source:* U.S. Dept. of Interior, Geological Survey.)

The word "volcano" comes from the little island of Vulcano in the Mediterranean Sea off Sicily. Centuries ago, the people living in this area believed that Vulcano was the chimney of the forge of Vulcan—the blacksmith of the Roman gods. They thought that the hot lava fragments and clouds of dust erupting from Vulcano came from Vulcan's forge. Today, we know that volcanic eruptions are not supernatural but can be studied and interpreted by scientists.

Geologists generally group volcanoes into four main kinds—cinder cones, composite volcanoes, shield volcanoes, and lava domes.

Cinder Cones

Cinder cones are the simplest type of volcano. They are built from particles and blobs of congealed lava ejected from a single vent. As the gas-charged lava is blown violently into the air, it breaks into small fragments that solidify and fall as cinders around the vent to form a circular or oval cone. Most cinder cones have a bowl-shaped crater at the summit and rarely rise more than a thousand feet or so above their surroundings. Cinder cones are numerous in western North America as well as throughout other volcanic terrains of the world.

Composite Volcanoes

Some of the Earth's grandest mountains are composite volcanoes—sometimes called *stratovolcanoes*. They are typically steep-sided, symmetrical cones of large dimension built of alternating layers of lava flows, volcanic ash, cinders, blocks, and bombs and may rise as much as 8,000 feet above their bases. Some of the most conspicuous and beautiful mountains in the world are composite volcanoes, including Mount Fuji in Japan, Mount Cotopaxi in Ecuador, Mount Shasta in California, Mount Hood in Oregon, and Mount St. Helens and Mount Rainier in Washington.

Most composite volcanoes have a crater at the summit which contains a central vent or a clustered group of vents. Lavas either flow through breaks in the crater wall or issue from fissures on the flanks of the cone. Lava, solidified within the fissures, forms *dikes* that act as ribs which greatly strengthen the cone.

The essential feature of a composite volcano is a conduit system through which magma from a reservoir deep in the Earth's crust rises to the surface. The volcano is built up by the accumulation of material erupted through the conduit and increases in size as lava, cinders, ash, etc., are added to its slopes.

Shield Volcanoes

Shield volcanoes, the third type of volcano, are built almost entirely of fluid lava flows. Flow after flow pours out in all directions from a central summit vent, or group of vents, building a broad, gently sloping cone of flat, domical shape, with a profile much like that of a warrior's shield. They are built up slowly by the accretion of thousands of flows of highly fluid basaltic (from *basalt*, a hard, dense dark volcanic rock) lava that spread widely over great distances, and then cool as thin, gently dipping sheets. Lavas also commonly erupt from vents along fractures (rift zones) that develop on the flanks of the cone. Some of the largest volcanoes in the world are shield volcanoes. In northern California and Oregon, many shield volcanoes have diameters of 3 or 4 miles and heights of 1,500 to 2,000 feet. The Hawaiian Islands are composed of linear chains of these volcanoes, including Kilauea and Mauna Loa on the island of Hawaii.

In some shield-volcano eruptions, basaltic lava pours out quietly from long fissures instead of central vents and floods the surrounding countryside with lava flow upon lava flow, forming broad plateaus. Lava plateaus of this type can be seen in Iceland, southeastern Washington, eastern Oregon, and southern Idaho.

Lava Domes

Volcanic or lava domes are formed by relatively small, bulbous masses of lava too viscous to flow any great distance; consequently, on extrusion, the lava piles over and around its vent. A dome grows largely by expansion from within. As it grows its outer surface cools and hardens, then shatters, spilling loose fragments down its sides. Some domes form craggy knobs or spines over the volcanic vent, whereas others form short, steep-sided lava flows known as "coulees." Volcanic domes commonly occur within the craters or on the flanks of large composite volcanoes. The nearly circular Novarupta Dome that formed during the 1912 eruption of Katmai Volcano, Alaska, measures 800 feet across and 200 feet high. The internal structure of this dome—defined by layering of lava fanning upward and outward from the center—indicates that it grew largely by expansion from within. Mount Pelée in Martinique, West Indies, and Lassen Peak and Mono domes in California, are examples of lava domes.

Submarine Volcanoes

Submarine volcanoes and volcanic vents are common features on certain zones of the ocean floor. Some are active at the present time and, in shallow water, disclose their presence by blasting steam and rock-debris high above the surface of the sea. Many others lie at such great depths that the tremendous weight of the water above them results in high, confining pressure and prevents the formation and release of steam and gases. Even very large, deepwater eruptions may not disturb the ocean floor.

The famous black sand beaches of Hawaii were created virtually instantaneously by the violent interaction between hot lava and sea water.

Plate-Tectonics Theory—The Lithosphere Plates of the Earth

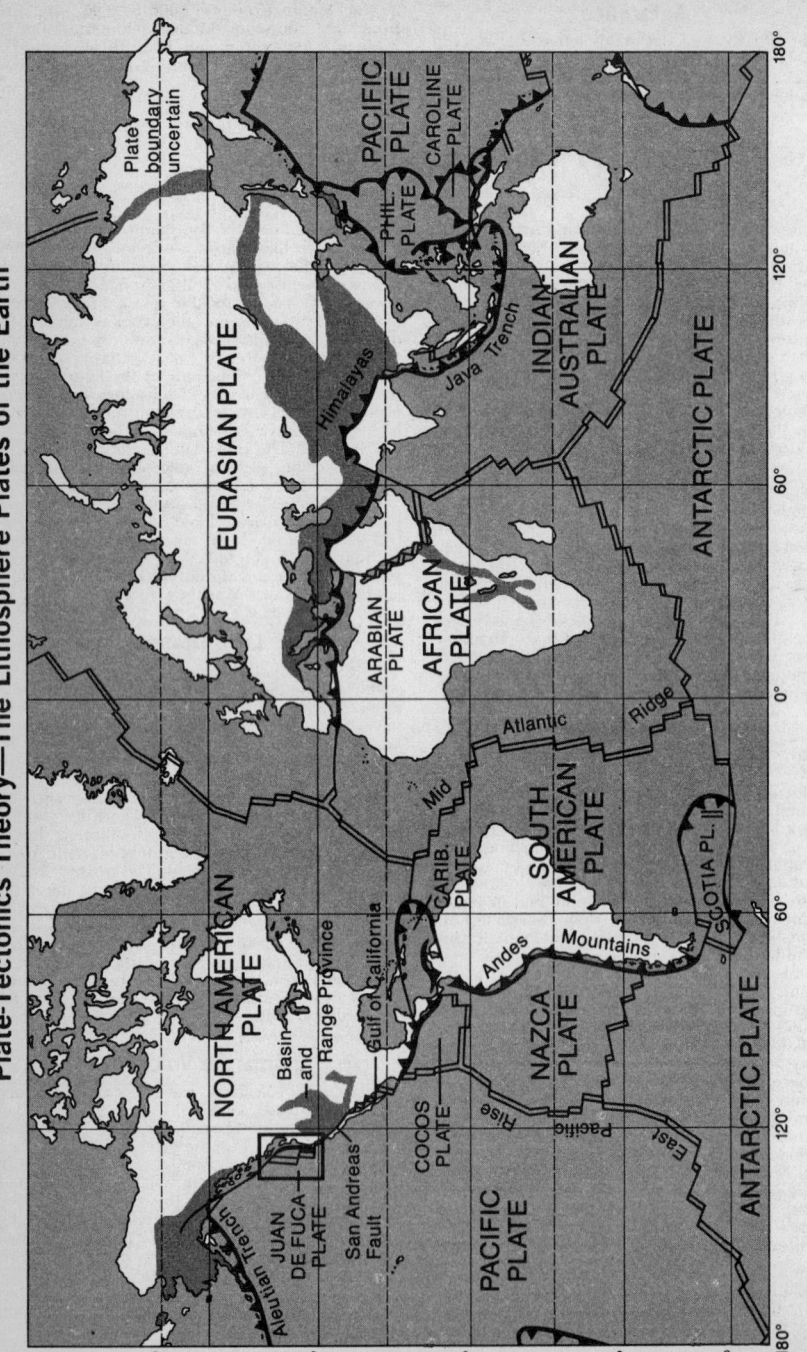

Source: U.S. Department of the Interior, U.S. Geological Survey.

World Population, Land Areas, and Elevations

Area	Estimated population, mid-1990	Approximate Land area sq mi.	Percent of total land area	Population density per sq mi.	Elevation, feet	
					Highest	Lowest
WORLD	5,321,000,000	58,433,000	100.0	91.0	Mt. Everest, Asia, 29,108	Dead Sea, Asia, 1,290 below sea level
ASIA, incl. Philippines, Indonesia, and European and Asiatic Turkey; excl. Asiatic U.S.S.R.	3,116,000,000	10,644,000	18.2	292.7	Mt. Everest, Tibet-Nepal, 29,108	Dead Sea, Israel-Jordan, 1,290 below sea level
AFRICA	661,000,000	11,707,000	20.0	56.5	Mt. Kilimanjaro, Tanzania, 19,340	Lake Assal, Djibouti, 571 below sea level
NORTH AMERICA, including Hawaii, Central America, and Caribbean region	430,000,000	9,360,000	16.0	45.9	Mt. McKinley, Alaska, 20,320	Death Valley, Calif., 282 below sea level
SOUTH AMERICA	296,000,000	6,883,000	11.8	43.0	Mt. Aconcagua, Arg.-Chile, 23,034	Valdes Peninsula, 131 below sea level
ANTARCTICA	—	6,000,000	10.3	—	Vinson Massif, Sentinel Range, 16,863	Sea level
EUROPE, incl. Iceland; excl. European U.S.S.R. and European Turkey	501,000,000	1,905,000	3.3	263.0	Mont Blanc, France, 15,781	Sea level
OCEANIA, incl. Australia, New Zealand, Melanesia, Micronesia, and Polynesia[2]	27,000,000	3,284,000	5.6	8.2	Mauna Kea, Hawaii, 13,796	Lake Eyre, Australia, 38 below sea level
U.S.S.R., both European and Asiatic	291,000,000	8,647,000	14.8	33.6	Communism Peak, Pamir, 24,590	Caspian Sea, 96 below sea level

1. In computing density per square mile, the area of Antarctica is omitted. 2. Although Hawaii is geographically part of Oceania, its population is included in the population figure for North America. *Source:* Population Reference Bureau, Inc.

Plate-Tectonics Theory

(*Source:* U.S. Dept. of the Interior, Geological Survey.)

According to the generally accepted "plate-tectonics" theory, scientists believe that the Earth's surface is broken into a number of shifting slabs or plates, which average about 50 miles in thickness. These plates move relative to one another above a hotter, deeper, more mobile zone at average rates as great as a few inches per year. Most of the world's active volcanoes are located along or near the boundaries between shifting plates and are called "plate-boundary" volcanoes. However, some active volcanoes are not associated with plate boundaries, and many of these so-called "intra-plate" volcanoes form roughly linear chains in the interior of some oceanic plates. The Hawaiian Islands provide perhaps the best example of an "intra-plate" volcanic chain, developed by the northwest-moving Pacific plate passing over an inferred "hot spot" that initiates the magma-generation and volcano-formation process. The peripheral areas of the Pacific Ocean Basin, containing the boundaries of several plates, are dotted by many active volcanoes that form the so-called "Ring of Fire." The "Ring" provides excellent examples of "plate-boundary" volcanoes, including Mount St. Helens.

The accompanying figure on page 464 shows the boundaries of lithosphere plates that are active at present. The double lines indicate zones of spreading from which plates are moving apart. The lines with barbs show zones of underthrusting (subduction), where one plate is sliding beneath another. The barbs on the lines indicate the overriding plate. The single line defines a strike-slip fault along which plates are sliding horizontally past one another. The stippled areas indicate a part of a continent, exclusive of that along a plate boundary, which is undergoing active extensional, compressional, or strike-slip faulting.

The Severity of an Earthquake

(Source: U.S. Dept. of the Interior, Geological Survey.)

The Richter Magnitude Scale

The Richter magnitude scale was developed in 1935 by Charles F. Richter of the California Institute of Technology as a mathematical device to compare the size of earthquakes. The magnitude of an earthquake is determined from the logarithm of the amplitude of waves recorded by seismographs. Adjustments are included in the magnitude formula to compensate for the variation in the distance between the various seismographs and the epicenter of the earthquakes. On the Richter Scale, magnitude is expressed in whole numbers and decimal fractions. For example, a magnitude of 5.3 might be computed for a moderate earthquake, and a strong earthquake might be rated as magnitude 6.3.

Because of the logarithmic basis of the scale, each whole-number increase in magnitude represents a tenfold increase in measured amplitude; as an estimate of energy, each whole number step in the magnitude scale corresponds to the release of about 31 times more energy than the amount associated with the preceding whole number value.

Earthquakes with magnitudes of about 2.0 or less are usually called microearthquakes; they are not commonly felt by people and are generally recorded only on local seismographs. Events with magnitudes of about 4.5 or greater—there are several thousand such shocks annually—are strong enough to be recorded by sensitive seismographs all over the world.

Great earthquakes, such as the 1906 Good Friday earthquake in San Francisco, have magnitudes of 8.0 or higher. On the average, one earthquake of such size occurs somewhere in the world each year. Although the Richter Scale has no upper limit, the largest known shocks have had magnitudes in the 8.8 to 8.9 range.

The Richter Scale is not used to express damage. An earthquake in a densely populated area which results in many deaths and considerable damage may have the same magnitude as a shock in a remote area that does nothing more than frighten the wildlife. Large-magnitude earthquakes that occur beneath the oceans may not even be felt by humans.

The Modified Mercalli Intensity Scale

The effect of an earthquake on the Earth's surface is called the intensity. The intensity scale consists of a series of certain key responses such as people awakening, movement of furniture, damage to chimneys, and finally—total destruction. Although numerous *intensity scales* have been developed over the last several hundred years to evaluate the effects of earthquakes, the one currently used in the United States is the Modified Mercalli (MM) Intensity Scale. It was developed in 1931 by the American seismologists Harry Wood and Frank Neumann. This scale, composed of 12 increasing levels of intensity that range from imperceptible shaking to catastrophic destruction, is designated by Roman numerals. It does not have a mathematical basis; instead it is an arbitrary ranking based on observed effects.

The Modified Mercalli Intensity value assigned to a specific site after an earthquake has a more meaningful measure of severity to the nonscientist than the magnitude because intensity refers to the effects actually experienced at that place. After the occurrence of widely-felt earthquakes, the Geological Survey mails questionnaires to postmasters in the disturbed area requesting the information so that intensity values can be assigned. The results of this postal canvass and information furnished by other sources are used to assign an intensity value, and to compile isoseismal maps that show the extent of various levels of intensity within the felt area. The maximum observed intensity generally occurs near the epicenter.

The *lower* numbers of the intensity scale generally deal with the manner in which the earthquake is felt by people. The *higher* numbers of the scale are based on observed structural damage. Structural engineers usually contribute information for assigning intensity values of VIII or above.

The Mexico City earthquake on September 19, 1985, was assigned an intensity of IX on the Mercalli Scale.

The following is an abbreviated description of the 12 levels of Modified Mercalli intensity.

I. Not felt except by a very few under especially favorable conditions.

II. Felt only by a few persons at rest, especially on upper floors of buildings. Delicately suspended objects may swing.

III. Felt quite noticeably by persons indoors, especially on upper floors of buildings. Many people do not recognize it as an earthquake. Standing motor cars may rock slightly. Vibration similar to the passing of a truck. Duration estimated.

IV. Felt indoors by many, outdoors by few during the day. At night, some awakened. Dishes, windows, doors disturbed; walls make cracking sound. Sensation like heavy truck striking building. Standing motor cars rocked noticeably.

V. Felt by nearly everyone; many awakened. Some dishes, windows broken. Unstable objects overturned. Pendulum clocks may stop.

VI. Felt by all, many frightened. Some heavy furniture moved; a few instances of fallen plaster. Damage slight.

VII. Damage negligible in buildings of good design and construction; slight to moderate in well-built ordinary structures; considerable damage in poorly built or badly designed structures; some chimneys broken.

VIII. Damage slight in specially designed structures; considerable damage in ordinary substantial buildings with partial collapse. Damage great in poorly built structures. Fall of chimneys, factory stacks, columns, monuments, walls. Heavy furniture overturned.

IX. Damage considerable in specially designed structures; well-designed frame structures thrown out of plumb. Damage great in substantial buildings, with partial collapse. Buildings shifted off foundations.

X. Some well-built wooden structures destroyed; most masonry and frame structures destroyed with foundations. Rails bent.

XI. Few, if any (masonry) structures remain standing. Bridges destroyed. Rails bent greatly.

XII. Damage total. Lines of sight and level are distorted. Objects thrown into the air.

Latitude and Longitude of World Cities
(and time corresponding to 12:00 noon, eastern standard time)

City	Lat. ° ′	Long. ° ′	Time	City	Lat. ° ′	Long. ° ′	Time
Aberdeen, Scotland	57 9 n	2 9 w	5:00 p.m.	La Paz, Bolivia	16 27 s	68 22 w	1:00 p.m.
Adelaide, Australia	34 55 s	138 36 e	2:30 a.m.[1]	Leeds, England	53 45 n	1 30 w	5:00 p.m.
Algiers	36 50 n	3 0 e	6:00 p.m.	Leningrad	59 56 n	30 18 e	8:00 p.m.
Amsterdam	52 22 n	4 53 e	6:00 p.m.	Lima, Peru	12 0 s	77 2 w	2:00 noon
Ankara, Turkey	39 55 n	32 55 e	7:00 p.m.	Lisbon	38 44 n	9 9 w	5:00 p.m.
Asunción, Paraguay	25 15 s	57 40 w	1:00 p.m.	Liverpool, England	53 25 n	3 0 w	5:00 p.m.
Athens	37 58 n	23 43 e	7:00 p.m.	London	51 32 n	0 5 w	5:00 p.m.
Auckland, New Zealand	36 52 s	174 45 e	5:00 a.m.[1]	Lyons, France	45 45 n	4 50 e	6:00 p.m.
Bangkok, Thailand	13 45 n	100 30 e	midnight[1]	Madrid	40 26 n	3 42 w	6:00 p.m.
Barcelona	41 23 n	2 9 e	6:00 p.m.	Manchester, England	53 30 n	2 15 w	5:00 p.m.
Belém, Brazil	1 28 s	48 29 w	2:00 p.m.	Manila	14 35 n	120 57 e	1:00 a.m.[1]
Belfast, Northern Ireland	54 37 n	5 56 w	5:00 p.m.	Marseilles, France	43 20 n	5 20 e	6:00 p.m.
				Mazatlán, Mexico	23 12 n	106 25 w	10:00 a.m.
Belgrade, Yugoslavia	44 52 n	20 32 e	6:00 p.m.	Mecca, Saudi Arabia	21 29 n	39 45 e	8:00 p.m.
Berlin	52 30 n	13 25 e	6:00 p.m.	Melbourne	37 47 s	144 58 e	3:00 a.m.[1]
Birmingham, England	52 25 n	1 55 w	5:00 p.m.	Mexico City	19 26 n	99 7 w	11:00 a.m.
Bogotá, Colombia	4 32 n	74 15 w	12:00 noon	Milan, Italy	45 27 n	9 10 e	6:00 p.m.
Bombay	19 0 n	72 48 e	10:30 p.m.	Montevideo, Uruguay	34 53 s	56 10 w	2:00 p.m.
Bordeaux, France	44 50 n	0 31 w	6:00 p.m.	Moscow	55 45 n	37 36 e	8:00 p.m.
Bremen, W. Germany	53 5 n	8 49 e	6:00 p.m.	Munich, Germany	48 8 n	11 35 e	6:00 p.m.
Brisbane, Australia	27 29 s	153 8 e	3:00 a.m.[1]	Nagasaki, Japan	32 48 n	129 57 e	2:00 a.m.[1]
Bristol, England	51 28 n	2 35 w	5:00 p.m.	Nagoya, Japan	35 7 n	136 56 e	2:00 a.m.[1]
Brussels	50 52 n	4 22 e	6:00 p.m.	Nairobi, Kenya	1 25 s	36 55 e	8:00 p.m.
Bucharest	44 25 n	26 7 e	7:00 p.m.	Nanjing (Nanking), China	32 3 n	118 53 e	1:00 a.m.[1]
Budapest	47 30 n	19 5 e	6:00 p.m.	Naples, Italy	40 50 n	14 15 e	6:00 p.m.
Buenos Aires	34 35 s	58 22 w	2:00 p.m.	Newcastle-on-Tyne, Eng.	54 58 n	1 37 w	5:00 p.m.
Cairo	30 2 n	31 21 e	7:00 p.m.	Odessa, U.S.S.R.	46 27 n	30 48 e	8:00 p.m.
Calcutta	22 34 n	88 24 e	10:30 p.m.	Osaka, Japan	34 32 n	135 30 e	2:00 a.m.[1]
Canton, China	23 7 n	113 15 e	1:00 a.m.[1]	Oslo	59 57 n	10 42 e	6:00 p.m.
Cape Town, South Africa	33 55 s	18 22 e	7:00 p.m.	Panama City, Panama	8 58 n	79 32 w	12:00 noon
				Paramaribo, Surinam	5 45 n	55 15 w	1:30 p.m.
Caracas, Venezuela	10 28 n	67 2 w	1:00 p.m.	Paris	48 48 n	2 20 e	6:00 p.m.
Cayenne, French Guiana	4 49 n	52 18 w	1:00 p.m.	Peking	39 55 n	116 25 e	1:00 a.m.[1]
Chihuahua, Mexico	28 37 n	106 5 w	11:00 a.m.	Perth, Australia	31 57 s	115 52 e	1:00 a.m.[1]
Chongqing, China	29 46 n	106 34 e	1:00 a.m.[1]	Plymouth, England	50 25 n	4 5 w	5:00 p.m.
Copenhagen	55 40 n	12 34 e	6:00 p.m.	Port Moresby, Papua New Guinea	9 25 s	147 8 e	3:00 a.m.[1]
Córdoba, Argentina	31 28 s	64 10 w	2:00 p.m.	Prague	50 5 n	14 26 e	6:00 p.m.
Dakar, Senegal	14 40 n	17 28 w	5:00 p.m.	Reykjavik, Iceland	64 4 n	21 58 w	4:00 p.m.
Darwin, Australia	12 28 s	130 51 e	2:30 a.m.[1]	Rio de Janeiro	22 57 s	43 12 w	2:00 p.m.
Djibouti	11 30 n	43 3 e	8:00 p.m.	Rome	41 54 n	12 27 e	6:00 p.m.
Dublin	53 20 n	6 15 w	5:00 p.m.	Salvador, Brazil	12 56 s	38 27 w	2:00 p.m.
Durban, South Africa	29 53 s	30 53 e	7:00 p.m.	Santiago, Chile	33 28 s	70 45 w	1:00 p.m.
Edinburgh, Scotland	55 55 n	3 10 w	5:00 p.m.	Sao Paulo, Brazil	23 31 s	46 31 w	2:00 p.m.
Frankfurt	50 7 n	8 41 e	6:00 p.m.	Shanghai, China	31 10 n	121 28 e	1:00 a.m.[1]
Georgetown, Guyana	6 45 n	58 15 w	1:15 p.m.	Singapore	1 14 n	103 55 e	0:30 a.m.[1]
Glasgow, Scotland	55 50 n	4 15 w	5:00 p.m.	Sofia, Bulgaria	42 40 n	23 20 e	7:00 p.m.
Guatemala City, Guatemala	14 37 n	90 31 w	11:00 a.m.	Stockholm	59 17 n	18 3 e	6:00 p.m.
Guayaquil, Ecuador	2 10 s	79 56 w	12:00 noon	Sydney, Australia	34 0 s	151 0 e	3:00 a.m.[1]
Hamburg	53 33 n	10 2 e	6:00 p.m.	Tananarive, Madagascar	18 50 s	47 33 e	8:00 p.m.
Hammerfest, Norway	70 38 n	23 38 e	6:00 p.m.	Teheran, Iran	35 45 n	51 45 e	8:30 p.m.
Havana	23 8 n	82 23 w	12:00 noon	Tokyo	35 40 n	139 45 e	2:00 a.m.[1]
Helsinki, Finland	60 10 n	25 0 e	7:00 p.m.	Tripoli, Libya	32 57 n	13 12 e	7:00 p.m.
Hobart, Tasmania	42 52 s	147 19 e	3:00 a.m.[1]	Venice	45 26 n	12 20 e	6:00 p.m.
Iquique, Chile	20 10 s	70 7 w	1:00 p.m.	Veracruz, Mexico	19 10 n	96 10 w	11:00 a.m.
Irkutsk, U.S.S.R.	52 30 n	104 20 e	1:00 a.m.	Vienna	48 14 n	16 20 e	6:00 p.m.
Jakarta, Indonesia	6 16 s	106 48 e	0:30 a.m.[1]	Vladivostok, U.S.S.R.	43 10 n	132 0 e	3:00 a.m.[1]
Johannesburg, South Africa	26 12 s	28 4 e	7:00 p.m.	Warsaw	52 14 n	21 0 e	6:00 p.m.
				Wellington, New Zealand	41 17 s	174 47 e	5:00 a.m.[1]
Kingston, Jamaica	17 59 n	76 49 w	12:00 noon	Yangon, Myanmar	16 50 n	96 0 e	11:30 p.m.
Kinshasa, Zaire	4 18 s	15 17 e	6:00 p.m.	Zürich	47 21 n	8 31 e	6:00 p.m.

1. On the following day.

Highest Mountain Peaks of the World
(For U.S. peaks, see Index)

Mountain peak	Range	Location	Height feet	Height meters
Everest	Himalayas	Nepal-Tibet	29,108	8,872
Godwin Austen (K-2)	Karakoram	Kashmir	29,064	8,858
Kanchenjunga	Himalayas	Nepal-Sikkim	28,208	8,598
Lhotse	Himalayas	Nepal-Tibet	27,890	8,501
Makalu	Himalayas	Tibet-Nepal	27,790	8,470
Dhaulagiri I	Himalayas	Nepal	26,810	8,172
Manaslu	Himalayas	Nepal	26,760	8,156
Cho Oyu	Himalayas	Nepal	26,750	8,153
Nanga Parbat	Himalayas	Kashmir	26,660	8,126
Annapurna I	Himalayas	Nepal	26,504	8,078
Gasherbrum I	Karakoram	Kashmir	26,470	8,068
Broad Peak	Karakoram	Kashmir	26,400	8,047
Gasherbrum II	Karakoram	Kashmir	26,360	8,033
Gosainthan	Himalayas	Tibet	26,291	8,013
Gasherbrum III	Karakoram	Kashmir	26,090	7,952
Annapurna II	Himalayas	Nepal	26,041	7,937
Gasherbrum IV	Karakoram	India	26,000	7,925
Kangbachen	Himalayas	Nepal	25,925	7,902
Gyachung Kang	Himalayas	Nepal	25,910	7,897
Himal Chuli	Himalayas	Nepal	25,895	7,893
Disteghil Sar	Karakoram	Kashmir	25,868	7,885
Nuptse	Himalayas	Nepal	25,850	7,829
Kunyang Kish	Karakoram	Kashmir	25,760	7,852
Dakum (Peak 29)	Himalayas	Nepal	25,760	7,852
Masherbrum	Karakoram	Kashmir	25,660	7,821
Nanda Devi	Himalayas	India	25,645	7,817
Chomolonzo	Himalayas	Nepal-Tibet	25,640	7,815
Rakaposhi	Karakoram	Kashmir	25,550	7,788
Batura	Karakoram	Kashmir	25,540	7,785
Kanjut Sar	Karakoram	Kashmir	25,460	7,760
Kamet	Himalayas	India-Tibet	25,447	7,756
Namche Barwa	Himalayas	Tibet	25,445	7,756
Dhaulagiri II	Himalayas	Nepal	25,427	7,750
Saltoro Kangri	Karakoram	India	25,400	7,742
Gurla Mandhata	Himalayas	Tibet	25,355	7,728
Ulugh Muztagh	Kunlun	Tibet	25,341	7,724
Trivor	Karakoram	Kashmir	25,330	7,721
Jannu	Himalayas	Nepal	25,294	7,710
Tirich Mir	Hindu Kush	Pakistan	25,230	7,690
Saser Kangri	Karakoram	India	25,170	7,672
Makalu II	Himalayas	Nepal	25,130	7,660
Chogolisa	Karakoram	India	25,110	7,654
Dhaulagiri IV	Himalayas	Nepal	25,064	7,639
Fang	Himalayas	Nepal	25,013	7,624
Kula Kangri	Himalayas	Bhutan	24,783	7,554
Changtse	Himalayas	Tibet	24,780	7,553
Muztagh Ata	Muztagh Ata	China	24,757	7,546
Skyang Kangri	Himalayas	Kashmir	24,750	7,544
Communism Peak	Pamir	U.S.S.R.	24,590	7,495
Victory Peak	Pamir	U.S.S.R.	24,406	7,439
Sia Kangri	Himalayas	Kashmir	24,340	7,419
Chamlang	Himalayas	Nepal	24,012	7,319
Alung Gangri	Himalayas	Tibet	23,999	7,315
Chomo Lhari	Himalayas	Tibet-Bhutan	23,996	7,314
Muztagh (K-5)	Kunlun	China	23,891	7,282
Amne Machin	Kunlun	China	23,490	7,160
Gaurisankar	Himalayas	Népal-Tibet	23,440	7,145
Lenin Peak	Pamir	U.S.S.R.	23,405	7,134
Korzhenevski Peak	Pamir	U.S.S.R.	23,310	7,105
Kangto	Himalayas	Tibet	23,260	7,090
Dunagiri	Himalayas	India	23,184	7,066
Pauhunri	Himalayas	India-Tibet	23,180	7,065
Aconcagua	Andes	Argentina-Chile	23,034	7,021
Revolution Peak	Pamir	U.S.S.R.	22,880	6,974
Kangchenjhan	Himalayas	India	22,700	6,919
Siniolchu	Himalayas	India	22,620	6,895

Mountain peak	Range	Location	Height feet	Height meters
Ojos des Salado	Andes	Argentina-Chile	22,588	6,885
Bonete	Andes	Argentina-Chile	22,546	6,872
Simvuo	Himalayas	India	22,346	6,811
Tup	Andes	Argentina	22,309	6,800
Kungpu	Himalayas	Bhutan	22,300	6,797
Falso-Azufre	Andes	Argentina-Chile	22,277	6,790
Moscow Peak	Pamir	U.S.S.R.	22,260	6,785
Veladero	Andes	Argentina	22,244	6,780
Pissis	Andes	Argentina	22,241	6,779
Mercedario	Andes	Argentina-Chile	22,211	6,770
Huascarán	Andes	Peru	22,198	6,766
Tocorpuri	Andes	Bolivia-Chile	22,162	6,755
Karl Marx Peak	Pamir	U.S.S.R.	22,067	6,726
Llullaillaco	Andes	Argentina-Chile	22,057	6,723
Libertador	Andes	Argentina	22,047	6,720
Kailas	Himalayas	Tibet	22,027	6,714
Lingtren	Himalayas	Nepal-Tibet	21,972	6,697
Incahuasi	Andes	Argentina-Chile	21,719	6,620
Carnicero	Andes	Peru	21,689	6,611
Kurumda	Pamir	U.S.S.R.	21,686	6,610
Garmo Peak	Pamir	U.S.S.R.	21,637	6,595
Sajama	Andes	Bolivia	21,555	6,570
Ancohuma	Andes	Bolivia	21,490	6,550
El Muerto	Andes	Argentina-Chile	21,456	6,540
Nacimiento	Andes	Argentina	21,302	6,493
Illimani	Andes	Bolivia	21,184	6,457
Antofalla	Andes	Argentina-Chile	21,129	6,440
Coropuña	Andes	Peru	21,079	6,425
Cuzco (Ausangate)	Andes	Peru	20,995	6,399
Toro	Andes	Argentina-Chile	20,932	6,380
Parinacota	Andes	Bolivia-Chile	20,768	6,330
Chimboraso	Andes	Ecuador	20,702	6,310
Salcantay	Andes	Peru	20,575	6,271
General Manuel Belgrano	Andes	Argentina	20,505	6,250
Chañi	Andes	Argentina	20,341	6,200
Caca Aca	Andes	Bolivia	20,328	6,196
McKinley	Alaska	Alaska	20,320	6,194
Vudor Peak	Pamir	U.S.S.R.	20,118	6,132
Condoriri	Andes	Bolivia	20,095	6,125
Solimana	Andes	Peru	20,069	6,117
Nevada	Andes	Argentina	20,023	6,103

Oceans and Seas

Name	Area sq mi.	Area sq km	Average depth feet	Average depth meters	Greatest known depth feet	Greatest known depth meters	Place greatest known depth
Pacific Ocean	64,000,000	165,760,000	13,215	4,028	35,820	10,918	Mindanao Deep
Atlantic Ocean	31,815,000	82,400,000	12,880	3,926	30,246	9,219	Puerto Rico Trough
Indian Ocean	25,300,000	65,526,700	13,002	3,963	24,460	7,455	Sunda Trench
Arctic Ocean	5,440,200	14,090,000	3,953	1,205	18,456	5,625	77° 45′ N; 175° W
Mediterranean Sea[1]	1,145,100	2,965,800	4,688	1,429	15,197	4,632	Off Cape Matapan, Greece
Caribbean Sea	1,049,500	2,718,200	8,685	2,647	22,788	6,946	Off Cayman Islands
South China Sea	895,400	2,319,000	5,419	1,652	16,456	5,016	West of Luzon
Bering Sea	884,900	2,291,900	5,075	1,547	15,659	4,773	Off Buldir Island
Gulf of Mexico	615,000	1,592,800	4,874	1,486	12,425	3,787	Sigsbee Deep
Okhotsk Sea	613,800	1,589,700	2,749	838	12,001	3,658	146° 10′ E; 46° 50′ N
East China Sea	482,300	1,249,200	617	188	9,126	2,782	25° 16′ N; 125° E
Hudson Bay	475,800	1,232,300	420	128	600	183	Near entrance
Japan Sea	389,100	1,007,800	4,429	1,350	12,276	3,742	Central Basin
Andaman Sea	308,100	797,700	2,854	870	12,392	3,777	Off Car Nicobar Island
North Sea	222,100	575,200	308	94	2,165	660	Skagerrak
Red Sea	169,100	438,000	1,611	491	7,254	2,211	Off Port Sudan
Baltic Sea	163,000	422,200	180	55	1,380	421	Off Gotland

1. Includes Black Sea and Sea of Azov. NOTE: For Caspian Sea, *see* Large Lakes of World elsewhere in this section.

World's Greatest Man-Made Lakes[1]

Name of dam	Location	Millions of cubic meters	Thousands of acre-feet	Year completed
Owen Falls	Uganda	204,800	166,000	1954
Kariba	Zimbabwe	181,592	147,218	1959
Bratsk	U.S.S.R.	169,270	137,220	1964
High Aswan (Sadd-el-Aali)	Egypt	168,000	136,200	1970
Akosombo	Ghana	148,000	120,000	1965
Daniel Johnson	Canada	141,852	115,000	1968
Guri (Raul Leoni)	Venezuela	136,000	110,256	1986
Krasnoyarsk	U.S.S.R.	73,300	59,425	1967
Bennett W.A.C.	Canada	70,309	57,006	1967
Zeya	U.S.S.R.	68,400	55,452	1978
Cabora Bassa	Mozambique	63,000	51,075	1974
LaGrande 2	Canada	61,720	50,037	1982
LaGrande 3	Canada	60,020	48,659	1982
Ust'—Ilimsk	U.S.S.R.	59,300	48,075	1980
Volga—V.I. Lenin	U.S.S.R.	58,000	47,020	1955
Caniapiscau	Canada	53,790	43,608	1981
Pati (Chapetón)	Argentina	53,700	43,535	UC
Upper Wainganga	India	50,700	41,103	1987
São Felix	Brazil	50,600	41,022	1986
Bukhtarma	U.S.S.R.	49,740	40,325	1960
Atatürk (Karababa)	Turkey	48,700	39,482	UC
Cerros Colorados	Argentina	48,000	38,914	1973
Irkutsk	U.S.S.R.	46,000	37,290	1956
Tucuruí	Brazil	36,375	29,489	1984
Vilyuy	U.S.S.R.	35,900	29,104	1967
Sanmenxia	China	35,400	28,700	1960
Hoover	Nevada/Arizona	35,154	28,500	1936
Sobridinho	Brazil	34,200	27,726	1981
Glen Canyon	Arizona	33,304	27,000	1964
Jenpeg	Canada	31,790	25,772	1975

1. Formed by construction of dams. NOTE: UC = under construction. *Source:* Department of the Interior, Bureau of Reclamation and *International Water Power and Dam Construction.*

Large Lakes of the World

Name and location	Area		Length		Maximum depth	
	sq mi.	sq km	mi.	km	feet	meters
Caspian Sea, U.S.S.R.-Iran[1]	152,239	394,299	745	1,199	3,104	946
Superior, U.S.-Canada	31,820	82,414	383	616	1,333	406
Victoria, Tanzania—Uganda	26,828	69,485	200	322	270	82
Aral, U.S.S.R.	25,659	66,457	266	428	223	68
Huron, U.S.-Canada	23,010	59,596	247	397	750	229
Michigan, U.S.	22,400	58,016	321	517	923	281
Tanganyika, Tanzania-Zaire	12,700	32,893	420	676	4,708	1,435
Baikal, U.S.S.R.	12,162	31,500	395	636	5,712	1,741
Great Bear, Canada	12,000	31,080	232	373	270	82
Nyasa, Malawi-Mozambique-Tanzania	11,600	30,044	360	579	2,316	706
Great Slave, Canada	11,170	28,930	298	480	2,015	614
Chad,[2] Chad-Niger-Nigeria	9,946	25,760	—	—	23	7
Erie, U.S.-Canada	9,930	25,719	241	388	210	64
Winnipeg, Canada	9,094	23,553	264	425	204	62
Ontario, U.S.-Canada	7,520	19,477	193	311	778	237
Balkash, U.S.S.R.	7,115	18,428	376	605	87	27
Ladoga, U.S.S.R.	7,000	18,130	124	200	738	225
Onega, U.S.S.R.	3,819	9,891	154	248	361	110
Titicaca, Bolivia-Peru	3,141	8,135	110	177	1,214	370
Nicaragua, Nicaragua	3,089	8,001	110	177	230	70
Athabaska, Canada	3,058	7,920	208	335	407	124
Rudolf, Kenya	2,473	6,405	154	248	—	—
Reindeer, Canada	2,444	6,330	152	245	—	—
Eyre, South Australia	2,400[3]	6,216	130	209	varies	varies
Issyk-Kul, U.S.S.R.	2,394	6,200	113	182	2,297	700
Urmia,[2] Iran	2,317	6,001	81	130	49	15
Torrens, South Australia	2,200	5,698	130	209	—	—
Vänern, Sweden	2,141	5,545	87	140	322	98

Name and location	Area		Length		Maximum depth	
	sq mi.	sq km	mi.	km	feet	meters
Winnipegosis, Canada	2,086	5,403	152	245	59	18
Mobutu Sese Seko, Uganda	2,046	5,299	100	161	180	55
Nettilling, Baffin Island, Canada	1,950	5,051	70	113	—	—
Nipigon, Canada	1,870	4,843	72	116	—	—
Manitoba, Canada	1,817	4,706	140	225	22	7
Great Salt, U.S.	1,800	4,662	75	121	15/25	5/8
Kioga, Uganda	1,700	4,403	50	80	about 30	9
Koko-Nor, China	1,630	4,222	66	106	—	—

1. The Caspian Sea is called "sea" because the Romans, finding it salty, named it *Mare Caspium*. Many geographers, however, consider it a lake because it is land-locked. 2. Figures represent high-water data. 3. Varies with the rainfall of the wet season. It has been reported to dry up almost completely on occasion.

Principal Rivers of the World

(For other U.S. rivers, see Index)

River	Source	Outflow	Approx. length	
			miles	km
Nile	Tributaries of Lake Victoria, Africa	Mediterranean Sea	4,180	6,690
Amazon	Glacier-fed lakes, Peru	Atlantic Ocean	3,912	6,296
Mississippi-Missouri-Red Rock	Source of Red Rock, Montana	Gulf of Mexico	3,880	6,240
Yangtze Kiang	Tibetan plateau, China	China Sea	3,602	5,797
Ob	Altai Mts., U.S.S.R.	Gulf of Ob	3,459	5,567
Yellow (Huang Ho)	Eastern part of Kunlan Mts., west China	Gulf of Chihli	2,900	4,667
Yenisei	Tannu-Ola Mts., western Tuva, U.S.S.R.	Arctic Ocean	2,800	4,506
Paraná	Confluence of Paranaiba and Grande rivers	Río de la Plata	2,795	4,498
Irtish	Altai Mts., U.S.S.R.	Ob River	2,758	4,438
Congo	Confluence of Lualaba and Luapula rivers, Zaire	Atlantic Ocean	2,716	4,371
Heilong (Amur)	Confluence of Shilka (U.S.S.R.) and Argun (Manchuria) rivers	Tatar Strait	2,704	4,352
Lena	Baikal Mts., U.S.S.R.	Arctic Ocean	2,652	4,268
Mackenzie	Head of Finlay River, British Columbia, Canada	Beaufort Sea (Arctic Ocean)	2,635	4,241
Niger	Guinea	Gulf of Guinea	2,600	4,184
Mekong	Tibetan highlands	South China Sea	2,500	4,023
Mississippi	Lake Itasca, Minnesota	Gulf of Mexico	2,348	3,779
Missouri	Confluence of Jefferson, Gallatin, and Madison rivers, Montana	Mississippi River	2,315	3,726
Volga	Valdai plateau, U.S.S.R.	Caspian Sea	2,291	3,687
Madeira	Confluence of Beni and Maumoré rivers, Bolivia-Brazil boundary	Amazon River	2,012	3,238
Purus	Peruvian Andes	Amazon River	1,993	3,207
São Francisco	Southwest Minas Gerais, Brazil	Atlantic Ocean	1,987	3,198
Yukon	Junction of Lewes and Pelly rivers, Yukon Territory, Canada	Bering Sea	1,979	3,185
St. Lawrence	Lake Ontario	Gulf of St. Lawrence	1,900	3,058
Rio Grande	San Juan Mts., Colorado	Gulf of Mexico	1,885	3,034
Brahmaputra	Himalayas	Ganges River	1,800	2,897
Indus	Himalayas	Arabian Sea	1,800	2,897
Danube	Black Forest, W. Germany	Black Sea	1,766	2,842

River	Source	Outflow	Approx. length	
			miles	km
Euphrates	Confluence of Murat Nehri and Kara Su rivers, Turkey	Shatt-al-Arab	1,739	2,799
Darling	Central part of Eastern Highlands, Australia	Murray River	1,702	2,739
Zambezi	11°21'S, 24°22'E, Zambia	Mozambique Channel	1,700	2,736
Tocantins	Goiás, Brazil	Pará River	1,677	2,699
Murray	Australian Alps, New South Wales	Indian Ocean	1,609	2,589
Nelson	Head of Bow River, western Alberta, Canada	Hudson Bay	1,600	2,575
Paraguay	Mato Grosso, Brazil	Paraná River	1,584	2,549
Ural	Southern Ural Mts., U.S.S.R.	Caspian Sea	1,574	2,533
Ganges	Himalayas	Bay of Bengal	1,557	2,506
Amu Darya (Oxus)	Nicholas Range, Pamir Mts., U.S.S.R.	Aral Sea	1,500	2,414
Japurá	Andes, Colombia	Amazon River	1,500	2,414
Salween	Tibet, south of Kunlun Mts.	Gulf of Martaban	1,500	2,414
Arkansas	Central Colorado	Mississippi River	1,459	2,348
Colorado	Grand County, Colorado	Gulf of California	1,450	2,333
Dnieper	Valdai Hills, U.S.S.R.	Black Sea	1,419	2,284
Ohio-Allegheny	Potter County, Pennsylvania	Mississippi River	1,306	2,102
Irrawaddy	Confluence of Nmai and Mali rivers, northeast Burma	Bay of Bengal	1,300	2,092
Orange	Lesotho	Atlantic Ocean	1,300	2,092
Orinoco	Serra Parima Mts., Venezuela	Atlantic Ocean	1,281	2,062
Pilcomayo	Andes Mts., Bolivia	Paraguay River	1,242	1,999
Xi Jiang (Si Kiang)	Eastern Yunnan Province, China	China Sea	1,236	1,989
Columbia	Columbia Lake, British Columbia, Canada	Pacific Ocean	1,232	1,983
Don	Tula, R.S.F.S.R., U.S.S.R.	Sea of Azov	1,223	1,968
Sungari	China-North Korea boundary	Amur River	1,215	1,955
Saskatchewan	Canadian Rocky Mts.	Lake Winnipeg	1,205	1,939
Peace	Stikine Mts., British Columbia, Canada	Great Slave River	1,195	1,923
Tigris	Taurus Mts., Turkey	Shatt-al-Arab	1,180	1,899

Highest Waterfalls of the World

Waterfall	Location	River	Height	
			feet	meters
Angel	Venezuela	Tributary of Caroni	3,281	1,000
Tugela	Natal, South Africa	Tugela	3,000	914
Cuquenán	Venezuela	Cuquenán	2,000	610
Sutherland	South Island, N.Z.	Arthur	1,904	580
Takkakaw	British Columbia	Tributary of Yoho	1,650	503
Ribbon (Yosemite)	California	Creek flowing into Yosemite	1,612	491
Upper Yosemite	California	Yosemite Creek, tributary of Merced	1,430	436
Gavarnie	Southwest France	Gave de Pau	1,384	422
Vettisfoss	Norway	Mörkedola	1,200	366
Widows' Tears (Yosemite)	California	Tributary of Merced	1,170	357
Staubbach	Switzerland	Staubbach (Lauterbrunnen Valley)	984	300

Waterfall	Location	River	Height feet	Height meters
Middle Cascade (Yosemite)	California	Yosemite Creek, tributary of Merced	909	277
King Edward VIII	Guyana	Courantyne	850	259
Gersoppa	India	Sharavati	829	253
Kaieteur	Guyana	Potaro	822	251
Skykje	Norway	In Skykjedal (valley of Inner Hardinger Fjord)	820	250
Kalambo	Tanzania-Zambia	—	720	219
Fairy (Mount Rainier Park)	Washington	Stevens Creek	700	213
Trummelbach	Switzerland	Trummelbach (Lauterbrunnen Valley)	700	213
Aniene (Teverone)	Italy	Tiber	680	207
Cascata delle Marmore	Italy	Velino, tributary of Nera	650	198
Maradalsfos	Norway	Stream flowing into Ejkisdalsvand (lake)	643	196
Feather	California	Fall River	640	195
Maletsunyane	Lesotho	Maletsunyane	630	192
Bridalveil (Yosemite)	California	Yosemite Creek	620	189
Multnomah	Oregon	Multnomah Creek, tributary of Columbia	620	189
Vøringsfos	Norway	Bjoreia	597	182
Nevada (Yosemite)	California	Merced	594	181
Skjeggedal	Norway	Tysso	525	160
Marina	Guyana	Tributary of Kuribrong, tributary of Potaro	500	152
Tequendama	Colombia	Funza, tributary of Magdalena	425	130
King George's	Cape of Good Hope, South Africa	Orange	400	122
Illilouette (Yosemite)	California	Illilouette Creek, tributary of Merced	370	113
Victoria	Rhodesia-Zambia boundary	Zambezi	355	108
Handöl	Sweden	Handöl Creek	345	105
Lower Yosemite	California	Yosemite	320	98
Comet (Mount Rainier Park)	Washington	Van Trump Creek	320	98
Vernal (Yosemite)	California	Merced	317	97
Virginia	Northwest Territories, Canada	South Nahanni, tributary of Mackenzie	315	96
Lower Yellowstone	Wyoming	Yellowstone	310	94

NOTE: Niagara Falls (New York-Ontario), though of great volume, has parallel drops of only 158 and 167 feet.

Large Islands of the World

Island	Location and status	Area sq mi.	Area sq km
Greenland	North Atlantic (Danish)	839,999	2,175,597
New Guinea	Southwest Pacific (Irian Jaya, Indonesian, west part; Papua New Guinea, east part)	316,615	820,033
Borneo	West mid-Pacific (Indonesian, south part; British protectorate, and Malaysian, north part)	286,914	743,107
Madagascar	Indian Ocean (Malagasy Republic)	226,657	587,042
Baffin	North Atlantic (Canadian)	183,810	476,068
Sumatra	Northeast Indian Ocean (Indonesian)	182,859	473,605
Honshu	Sea of Japan-Pacific (Japanese)	88,925	230,316
Great Britain	Off coast of NW Europe (England, Scotland, and Wales)	88,758	229,883
Ellesmere	Arctic Ocean (Canadian)	82,119	212,688
Victoria	Arctic Ocean (Canadian)	81,930	212,199
Celebes	West mid-Pacific (Indonesian)	72,986	189,034
South Island	South Pacific (New Zealand)	58,093	150,461
Java	Indian Ocean (Indonesian)	48,990	126,884
North Island	South Pacific (New Zealand)	44,281	114,688

Island	Location and status	Area sq mi.	Area sq km
Cuba	Caribbean Sea (republic)	44,218	114,525
Newfoundland	North Atlantic (Canadian)	42,734	110,681
Luzon	West mid-Pacific (Philippines)	40,420	104,688
Iceland	North Atlantic (republic)	39,768	102,999
Mindanao	West mid-Pacific (Philippines)	36,537	94,631
Ireland	West of Great Britain (republic, south part; United Kingdom, north part)	32,597	84,426
Hokkaido	Sea of Japan—Pacific (Japanese)	30,372	78,663
Hispaniola	Caribbean Sea (Dominican Republic, east part; Haiti, west part)	29,355	76,029
Tasmania	South of Australia (Australian)	26,215	67,897
Sri Lanka (Ceylon)	Indian Ocean (republic)	25,332	65,610
Sakhalin (Karafuto)	North of Japan (U.S.S.R.)	24,560	63,610
Banks	Arctic Ocean (Canadian)	23,230	60,166
Devon	Arctic Ocean (Canadian)	20,861	54,030
Tierra del Fuego	Southern tip of South America (Argentinian, east part; Chilean, west part)	18,605	48,187
Kyushu	Sea of Japan—Pacific (Japanese)	16,223	42,018
Melville	Arctic Ocean (Canadian)	16,141	41,805
Axel Heiberg	Arctic Ocean (Canadian)	15,779	40,868
Southampton	Hudson Bay (Canadian)	15,700	40,663

Principal Deserts of the World

Desert	Location	Approximate size	Approx. elevation, ft
Atacama	North Chile	400 mi. long	7,000–13,500
Black Rock	Northwest Nevada	About 1,000 sq mi.	2,000–8,500
Colorado	Southeast California from San Gorgonio Pass to Gulf of California	200 mi. long and a maximum width of 50 mi.	Few feet above to 250 below sea level
Dasht-e-Kavir	Southeast of Caspian Sea, Iran	—	2,000
Dasht-e-Lut	Northeast of Kerman, Iran	—	1,000
Gobi (Shamo)	Covers most of Mongolia	500,000 sq mi.	3,000–5,000
Great Arabian	Most of Arabia	1,500 mi. long	—
An Nafud (Red Desert)	South of Jauf	400 mi. by avg of 140 mi.	3,000
Dahna	Northeast of Nejd	400 mi. by 30 mi.	—
Rub' al-Khali	South portion of Nejd	Over 200,000 sq. mi.	—
Syrian (Al-Hamad)	North of lat. 30° N	—	1,850
Great Australian	Western portion of Australia	About one half the continent	600–1,000
Great Salt Lake	West of Great Salt Lake to Nevada—Utah boundary	About 110 mi. by 50 mi.	4,500
Kalahari	South Africa—South-West Africa	About 120,000 sq mi.	Over 3,000
Kara Kum (Desert of Kiva)	Southwest Turkmen, U.S.S.R.	115,000 sq mi.	—
Kyzyl Kum	Uzbek and Kazakh, U.S.S.R.	Over 100,000 sq. mi.	160 near Lake Aral to 2,000 in southeast
Libyan	Libya, Egypt, Sudan	Over 500,000 sq mi.	—
Mojave	North of Colorado Desert and south of Death Valley, southeast California	15,000 sq mi.	2,000
Nubian	From Red Sea to great west bend of the Nile, Sudan	—	2,500
Painted Desert	Northeast Arizona	Over 7,000 sq mi.	High plateau, 5,000
Sahara	North Africa to about lat. 15° N and from Red Sea to Atlantic Ocean	3,200 mi. greatest length along lat. 20° N; area over 3,500,000 sq mi.	440 below sea level to 11,000 above; avg elevation, 1,400–1,600
Takla Makan	South central Sinkiang, China	Over 100,000 sq mi.	—
Thar (Indian)	Pakistan-India	Nearly 100,000 sq mi.	Over 1,000

Interesting Caves and Caverns of the World

Aggtelek. In village of same name, northern Hungary. Large stalactitic cavern about 5 miles long.

Altamira Cave. Near Santander, Spain. Contains animal paintings (Old Stone Age art) on roof and walls.

Antiparos. On island of same name in the Grecian Archipelago. Some stalactites are 20 ft long. Brilliant colors and fantastic shapes.

Blue Grotto. On island of Capri, Italy. Cavern hollowed out in limestone by constant wave action. Now half filled with water because of sinking coast. Name derived from unusual blue light permeating the cave. Source of light is a submerged opening, light passing through the water.

Carlsbad Caverns. Southeast New Mexico. Largest underground labyrinth yet discovered. Three levels: 754, 900, and 1,320 ft below the surface.

Fingal's Cave. On island of Staffa off coast of western Scotland. Penetrates about 200 ft inland. Contains basaltic columns almost 40 ft high.

Ice Cave. Near Dobsina, Czechoslovakia. Noted for its beautiful crystal effects.

Jenolan Caves. In Blue Mountain plateau, New South Wales, Australia. Beautiful stalactitic formations.

Kent's Cavern. Near Torquay, England. Source of much information on Paleolithic man.

Luray Cavern. Near Luray, Va. Has large stalactitic and stalagmitic columns of many colors.

Mammoth Cave. Limestone cavern in central Kentucky. Cave area is about 10 miles in diameter but has at least 150 miles of irregular subterranean passageways at various levels. Temperature remains fairly constant at 54° F.

Peak Cavern or Devil's Hole. Derbyshire, England. About 2,250 ft into a mountain. Lowest part is about 600 ft below the surface.

Postojna (Postumia) Grotto. Near Postumia in Julian Alps, about 25 miles northeast of Trieste. Stalactitic cavern, largest in Europe. Piuca (Pivka) River flows through part of it. Caves have numerous beautiful stalactites.

Singing Cave. Iceland. A lava cave; name derived from echoes of people singing in it.

Wind Cave. In Black Hills of South Dakota. Limestone caverns with stalactites and stalagmites almost entirely missing. Variety of crystal formations called "boxwork."

Wyandotte Cave. In Crawford County, southern Indiana. A limestone cavern with five levels of passages; one of the largest in North America. "Monumental Mountain," approximately 135 ft high, is believed to be one of the world's largest underground "mountains."

U.S. Geography

Miscellaneous Data for the United States

Source: Department of the Interior, U.S. Geological Survey.

Highest point: Mount McKinley, Alaska	20,320 ft (6,198 m)
Lowest point: Death Valley, Calif.	282 ft (86 m) below sea level
Approximate mean altitude	2,500 ft (763 m)
Points farthest apart (50 states):	
Log Point, Elliot Key, Fla., and Kure Island, Hawaii	5,859 mi. (9,429 km)
Geographic center (50 states):	
In Butte County, S.D. (west of Castle Rock)	44° 58′ N. lat. 103° 46′ W. long.
Geographic center (48 conterminous states):	
In Smith County, Kan. (near Lebanon)	39° 50′ N. lat. 98° 35′ W. long.
Boundaries:	
Between Alaska and Canada	1,538 mi. (2,475 km)
Between the 48 conterminous states and Canada (incl. Great Lakes)	3,987 mi. (6,416 km)
Between the United States and Mexico	1,933 mi. (3,111 km)

Extreme Points of the United States (50 States)

Extreme point	Latitude	Longitude	Distance[1] mi.	km
Northernmost point: Point Barrow, Alaska	71°23′ N	156°29′ W	2,507	4,034
Easternmost point: West Quoddy Head, Me.	44°49′ N	66°57′ W	1,788	2,997
Southernmost point: Ka Lae (South Cape), Hawaii	18°55′ N	155°41′ W	3,463	5,573
Westernmost point: Pochnoi Point, Alaska (Semisopochnoi Island)	51°17′ N	172°09′ E	3,372	5,426

1. From geographic center of United States (incl. Alaska and Hawaii), west of Castle Rock, S.D., 44°58′ N. lat., 103°46′ W. long.

Highest, Lowest, and Mean Altitudes in the United States

State	Altitude, ft[1]	Highest point	Altitude, ft[1]	Lowest point	Altitude, ft[1]
Alabama	500	Cheaha Mountain	2,405	Gulf of Mexico	Sea level
Alaska	1,900	Mount McKinley	20,320	Pacific Ocean	Sea level
Arizona	4,100	Humphreys Peak	12,633	Colorado River	70
Arkansas	650	Magazine Mountain	2,753	Ouachita River	55
California	2,900	Mount Whitney	14,491[2]	Death Valley	282[3]
Colorado	6,800	Mount Elbert	14,433	Arkansas River	3,350
Connecticut	500	Mount Frissell, on south slope	2,380	Long Island Sound	Sea level
Delaware	60	On Ebright Road	442	Atlantic Ocean	Sea level
D.C.	150	Tenleytown, at Reno Reservoir	410	Potomac River	1
Florida	100	Sec. 30, T6N, R20W[4]	345	Atlantic Ocean	Sea level
Georgia	600	Brasstown Bald	4,784	Atlantic Ocean	Sea level
Hawaii	3,030	Puu Wekiu, Mauna Kea	13,796	Pacific Ocean	Sea level
Idaho	5,000	Borah Peak	12,662	Snake River	710
Illinois	600	Charles Mound	1,235	Mississippi River	279[5]
Indiana	700	Franklin Township, Wayne County	1,257	Ohio River	320[5]
Iowa	1,100	Sec. 29, T100N, R41W[6]	1,670	Mississippi River	480
Kansas	2,000	Mount Sunflower	4,039[7]	Verdigris River	679
Kentucky	750	Black Mountain	4,139	Mississippi River	257[5]
Louisiana	100	Driskill Mountain	535	New Orleans	8[3]
Maine	600	Mount Katahdin	5,267	Atlantic Ocean	Sea level
Maryland	350	Backbone Mountain	3,360	Atlantic Ocean	Sea level
Massachusetts	500	Mount Greylock	3,487	Atlantic Ocean	Sea level
Michigan	900	Mount Curwood	1,979	Lake Erie	572[5]
Minnesota	1,200	Eagle Mountain	2,301	Lake Superior	602
Mississippi	300	Woodall Mountain	806	Gulf of Mexico	Sea level
Missouri	800	Taum Sauk Mountain	1,772	St. Francis River	230[5]
Montana	3,400	Granite Peak	12,799	Kootenai River	1,800
Nebraska	2,600	Johnson Township, Kimball County	5,426	Missouri River	840
Nevada	5,500	Boundary Peak	13,140	Colorado River	479
New Hampshire	1,000	Mount Washington	6,288	Atlantic Ocean	Sea level
New Jersey	250	High Point	1,803[7]	Atlantic Ocean	Sea level
New Mexico	5,700	Wheeler Peak	13,161	Red Bluff Reservoir	2,842
New York	1,000	Mount Marcy	5,344	Atlantic Ocean	Sea level
North Carolina	700	Mount Mitchell	6,684	Atlantic Ocean	Sea level
North Dakota	1,900	White Butte	3,506	Red River	750
Ohio	850	Campbell Hill	1,549	Ohio River	455[5]
Oklahoma	1,300	Black Mesa	4,973	Little River	289
Oregon	3,300	Mount Hood	11,239	Pacific Ocean	Sea level
Pennsylvania	1,100	Mount Davis	3,213	Delaware River	Sea level
Rhode Island	200	Jerimoth Hill	812	Atlantic Ocean	Sea level
South Carolina	350	Sassafras Mountain	3,560	Atlantic Ocean	Sea level
South Dakota	2,200	Harney Peak	7,242	Big Stone Lake	966
Tennessee	900	Clingmans Dome	6,643	Mississippi River	178[5]
Texas	1,700	Guadalupe Peak	8,749	Gulf of Mexico	Sea level
Utah	6,100	Kings Peak	13,528	Beaverdam Wash	2,000
Vermont	1,000	Mount Mansfield	4,393	Lake Champlain	95
Virginia	950	Mount Rogers	5,729	Atlantic Ocean	Sea level
Washington	1,700	Mount Rainier	14,410	Pacific Ocean	Sea level
West Virginia	1,500	Spruce Knob	4,861	Potomac River	240
Wisconsin	1,050	Timms Hill	1,951	Lake Michigan	581[5]
Wyoming	6,700	Gannett Peak	13,804	Belle Fourche River	3,099
United States	2,500	Mount McKinley (Alaska)	20,320	Death Valley (California)	282[3]

1. Approximate mean altitude. 2. National Geodetic Survey. 3. Below sea level. 4. Walton County. 5. Corps of Engineers 6. Osceola County. 7. State Surveys *Source:* Department of the Interior, U.S. Geological Survey.

The Continental Divide

The Continental Divide is a ridge of high ground which runs irregularly north and south through the Rocky Mountains and separates eastward-flowing from westward-flowing streams. The waters which flow eastward empty into the Atlantic Ocean, chiefly by way of the Gulf of Mexico; those which flow westward empty into the Pacific.

Mason and Dixon's Line

Mason and Dixon's Line (often called the Mason-Dixon Line) is the boundary between Pennsylvania and Maryland, running at a north latitude of 39°43'19.11". The greater part of it was surveyed from 1763–67 by Charles Mason and Jeremiah Dixon, English astronomers who had been appointed to settle a dispute between the colonies. As the line was partly the boundary between the free and the slave states, it has come to signify the division between the North and the South.

Latitude and Longitude of U.S. and Canadian Cities
(and time corresponding to 12:00 noon, eastern standard time)

City	Lat. n ° '	Long. w ° '	Time	City	Lat. n ° '	Long. w ° '	Time
Albany, N.Y.	42 40	73 45	12:00 noon	Memphis, Tenn	35 9	90 3	11:00 a.m.
Albuquerque, N.M.	35 05	106 39	10:00 a.m.	Miami, Fla.	25 46	80 12	12:00 noon
Amarillo, Tex.	35 11	101 50	11:00 a.m.	Milwaukee	43 2	87 55	11:00 a.m.
Anchorage, Alaska	61 13	149 54	7:00 a.m.	Minneapolis	44 59	93 14	11:00 a.m.
Atlanta	33 45	84 23	12:00 noon	Mobile, Ala.	30 42	88 3	11:00 a.m.
Austin, Tex.	30 16	97 44	11:00 a.m.	Montgomery, Ala.	32 21	86 18	11:00 a.m.
Baker, Ore.	44 47	117 50	9:00 a.m.	Montpelier, Vt.	44 15	72 32	12:00 noon
Baltimore	39 18	76 38	12:00 noon	Montreal, Que.	45 30	73 35	12:00 noon
Bangor, Me.	44 48	68 47	12:00 noon	Moose Jaw, Sask.	50 37	105 31	10:00 a.m.
Birmingham, Ala.	33 30	86 50	11:00 a.m.	Nashville, Tenn.	36 10	86 47	11:00 a.m.
Bismarck, N.D.	46 48	100 47	11:00 a.m.	Nelson, B.C.	49 30	117 17	9:00 a.m.
Boise, Idaho	43 36	116 13	10:00 a.m.	Newark, N.J.	40 44	74 10	12:00 noon
Boston	42 21	71 5	12:00 noon	New Haven, Conn.	41 19	72 55	12:00 noon
Buffalo, N.Y.	42 55	78 50	12:00 noon	New Orleans	29 57	90 4	11:00 a.m.
Calgary, Alberta	51 1	114 1	10:00 a.m.	New York	40 47	73 58	12:00 noon
Carlsbad, N.M.	32 26	104 15	10:00 a.m.	Nome, Alaska	64 25	165 30	6:00 a.m.
Charleston, S.C.	32 47	79 56	12:00 noon	Oakland, Calif.	37 48	122 16	9:00 a.m.
Charleston, W. Va.	38 21	81 38	12:00 noon	Oklahoma City	35 26	97 28	11:00 a.m.
Charlotte, N.C.	35 14	80 50	12:00 noon	Omaha, Neb.	41 15	95 56	11:00 a.m.
Cheyenne, Wyo.	41 9	104 52	10:00 a.m.	Ottawa, Ont.	45 24	75 43	12:00 noon
Chicago	41 50	87 37	11:00 a.m.	Philadelphia	39 57	75 10	12:00 noon
Cincinnati	39 8	84 30	12:00 noon	Phoenix, Ariz.	33 29	112 4	10:00 a.m.
Cleveland	41 28	81 37	12:00 noon	Pierre, S.D.	44 22	100 21	11:00 a.m.
Columbia, S.C.	34 0	81 2	12:00 noon	Pittsburgh	40 27	79 57	12:00 noon
Columbus, Ohio	40 0	83 1	12:00 noon	Port Arthur, Ont.	48 30	89 17	11:00 a.m.
Dallas	32 46	96 46	11:00 a.m.	Portland, Me.	43 40	70 15	12:00 noon
Denver	39 45	105 0	10:00 a.m.	Portland, Ore.	45 31	122 41	9:00 a.m.
Des Moines, Iowa	41 35	93 37	11:00 a.m.	Providence, R.I.	41 50	71 24	12:00 noon
Detroit	42 20	83 3	12:00 noon	Quebec, Que.	46 49	71 11	12:00 noon
Dubuque, Iowa	42 31	90 40	11:00 a.m.	Raleigh, N.C.	35 46	78 39	12:00 noon
Duluth, Minn.	46 49	92 5	11:00 a.m.	Reno, Nev.	39 30	119 49	9:00 a.m.
Eastport, Me.	44 54	67 0	12:00 noon	Richfield, Utah	38 46	112 5	10:00 a.m.
El Centro, Calif.	32 38	115 33	9:00 a.m.	Richmond, Va.	37 33	77 29	12:00 noon
El Paso	31 46	106 29	10:00 a.m.	Roanoke, Va.	37 17	79 57	12:00 noon
Eugene, Ore.	44 3	123 5	9:00 a.m.	Sacramento, Calif.	38 35	121 30	9:00 a.m.
Fargo, N.D.	46 52	96 48	11:00 a.m.	St. John, N.B.	45 18	66 10	1:00 p.m.
Flagstaff, Ariz.	35 13	111 41	10:00 a.m.	St. Louis	38 35	90 12	11:00 a.m.
Fort Worth, Tex.	32 43	97 19	11:00 a.m.	Salt Lake City, Utah	40 46	111 54	10:00 a.m.
Fresno, Calif.	36 44	119 48	9:00 a.m.	San Antonio	29 23	98 33	11:00 a.m.
Grand Junction, Colo.	39 5	108 33	10:00 a.m.	San Diego, Calif.	32 42	117 10	9:00 a.m.
Grand Rapids, Mich.	42 58	85 40	12:00 noon	San Francisco	37 47	122 26	9:00 a.m.
Havre, Mont.	48 33	109 43	10:00 a.m.	San Jose, Calif.	37 20	121 53	9:00 a.m.
Helena, Mont.	46 35	112 2	10:00 a.m.	San Juan, P.R.	18 30	66 10	1:00 p.m.
Honolulu	21 18	157 50	7:00 a.m.	Santa Fe, N.M.	35 41	105 57	10:00 a.m.
Hot Springs, Ark.	34 31	93 3	11:00 a.m.	Savannah, Ga.	32 5	81 5	12:00 noon
Houston, Tex.	29 45	95 21	11:00 a.m.	Seattle	47 37	122 20	9:00 a.m.
Idaho Falls, Idaho	43 30	112 1	10:00 a.m.	Shreveport, La.	32 28	93 42	11:00 a.m.
Indianapolis	39 46	86 10	12:00 noon	Sioux Falls, S.D.	43 33	96 44	11:00 a.m.
Jackson, Miss.	32 20	90 12	11:00 a.m.	Sitka, Alaska	57 10	135 15	9:00 a.m.
Jacksonville, Fla.	30 22	81 40	12:00 noon	Spokane, Wash.	47 40	117 26	9:00 a.m.
Juneau, Alaska	58 18	134 24	9:00 a.m.	Springfield, Ill.	39 48	89 38	11:00 a.m.
Kansas City, Mo.	39 6	94 35	11:00 a.m.	Springfield, Mass.	42 6	72 34	12:00 noon
Key West, Fla.	24 33	81 48	12:00 noon	Springfield, Mo.	37 13	93 17	11:00 a.m.
Kingston, Ont.	44 15	76 30	12:00 noon	Syracuse, N.Y.	43 2	76 8	12:00 noon
Klamath Falls, Ore.	42 10	121 44	9:00 a.m.	Tampa, Fla.	27 57	82 27	12:00 noon
Knoxville, Tenn.	35 57	83 56	12:00 noon	Toledo, Ohio	41 39	83 33	12:00 noon
Las Vegas, Nev.	36 10	115 12	9:00 a.m.	Toronto, Ont.	43 40	79 24	12:00 noon
Lewiston, Idaho	46 24	117 2	9:00 a.m.	Tulsa, Okla.	36 09	95 59	11:00 a.m.
Lincoln, Neb.	40 50	96 40	11:00 a.m.	Victoria, B.C.	48 25	123 21	9:00 a.m.
London, Ont.	43 2	81 34	12:00 noon	Virginia Beach, Va.	36 51	75 58	12:00 noon
Long Beach, Calif.	33 46	118 11	9:00 a.m.	Washington, D.C.	38 53	77 02	12:00 noon
Los Angeles	34 3	118 15	9:00 a.m.	Wichita, Kan.	37 43	97 17	11:00 a.m.
Louisville, Ky.	38 15	85 46	12:00 noon	Wilmington, N.C.	34 14	77 57	12:00 noon
Manchester, N.H.	43 0	71 30	12:00 noon	Winnipeg, Man.	49 54	97 7	11:00 a.m.

Named Summits in the U.S. Over 14,000 Feet Above Sea Level

Name	State	Height	Name	State	Height	Name	State	Height
Mt. McKinley	Alaska	20,320	Castle Peak	Colo.	14,265	Mt. Eolus	Colo.	14,083
Mt. St. Elias	Alaska	18,008	Quandary Peak	Colo.	14,265	Windom Peak	Colo.	14,082
Mt. Foraker	Alaska	17,400	Mt. Evans	Colo.	14,264	Mt. Columbia	Colo.	14,073
Mt. Bona	Alaska	16,500	Longs Peak	Colo.	14,255	Mt. Augusta	Alaska	14,070
Mt. Blackburn	Alaska	16,390	Mt. Wilson	Colo.	14,246	Missouri Mtn.	Colo.	14,067
Mt. Sanford	Alaska	16,237	White Mtn.	Calif.	14,246	Humboldt Peak	Colo.	14,064
Mt. Vancouver	Alaska	15,979	North Palisade	Calif.	14,242	Mt. Bierstadt	Colo.	14,060
South Buttress	Alaska	15,885	Mt. Cameron	Colo.	14,238	Sunlight Peak	Colo.	14,059
Mt. Churchill	Alaska	15,638	Shavano Peak	Colo.	14,229	Split Mtn.	Calif.	14,058
Mt. Fairweather	Alaska	15,300	Crestone Needle	Colo.	14,197	Handies Peak	Colo.	14,048
Mt. Hubbard	Alaska	14,950	Mt. Belford	Colo.	14,197	Culebra Peak	Colo.	14,047
Mt. Bear	Alaska	14,831	Mt. Princeton	Colo.	14,197	Mt. Lindsey	Colo.	14,042
East Buttress	Alaska	14,730	Mt. Yale	Colo.	14,196	Ellingwood Point	Colo.	14,042
Mt. Hunter	Alaska	14,573	Mt. Bross	Colo.	14,172	Little Bear Peak	Colo.	14,037
Browne Tower	Alaska	14,530	Kit Carson Mtn.	Colo.	14,165	Mt. Sherman	Colo.	14,036
Mt. Alverstone	Alaska	14,500	Mt. Wrangell	Alaska	14,163	Redcloud Peak	Colo.	14,034
Mt. Whitney	Calif.	14,494[1]	Mt. Shasta	Calif.	14,162	Mt. Langley	Calif.	14,026
University Peak	Alaska	14,470	El Diente Peak	Colo.	14,159	Conundrum Peak	Colo.	14,022
Mt. Elbert	Colo.	14,433	Point Success	Wash.	14,158	Mt. Tyndall	Calif.	14,019
Mt. Massive	Colo.	14,421	Maroon Peak	Colo.	14,156	Pyramid Peak	Colo.	14,018
Mt. Harvard	Colo.	14,420	Tabeguache Mtn.	Colo.	14,155	Wilson Peak	Colo.	14,017
Mt. Rainier	Wash.	14,410	Mt. Oxford	Colo.	14,153	Wetterhorn Peak	Colo.	14,015
Mt. Williamson	Calif.	14,370	Mt. Sill	Calif.	14,153	North Maroon Peak	Colo.	14,014
La Plata Peak	Colo.	14,361	Mt. Sneffels	Colo.	14,150	San Luis Peak	Colo.	14,014
Blanca Peak	Colo.	14,345	Mt. Democrat	Colo.	14,148	Middle Palisade	Calif.	14,012
Uncompahgre Peak	Colo.	14,309	Capitol Peak	Colo.	14,130	Mt. Muir	Calif.	14,012
Crestone Peak	Colo.	14,294	Liberty Cap	Wash.	14,112	Mt. of the Holy Cross	Colo.	14,005
Mt. Lincoln	Colo.	14,286	Pikes Peak	Colo.	14,110	Huron Peak	Colo.	14,003
Grays Peak	Colo.	14,270	Snowmass Mtn.	Colo.	14,092	Thunderbolt Peak	Calif.	14,003
Mt. Antero	Colo.	14,269	Mt. Russell	Calif.	14,088	Sunshine Peak	Colo.	14,001
Torreys Peak	Colo.	14,267						

1. National Geodetic Survey. *Source:* Department of the Interior, U.S. Geological Survey.

Rivers of the United States
(350 or more miles long)

Alabama-Coosa (600 mi.; 966 km): From junction of Oostanula and Etowah R. in Georgia to Mobile R.

Altamaha-Ocmulgee (392 mi.; 631 km): From junction of Yellow R. and South R., Newton Co. in Georgia to Atlantic Ocean.

Apalachicola-Chattahoochee (524 mi.; 843 km): From Towns Co. in Georgia to Gulf of Mexico in Florida.

Arkansas (1,459 mi.; 2,348 km): From Lake Co. in Colorado to Mississippi R. in Arkansas.

Brazos (923 mi.; 1,490 km): From junction of Salt Fork and Double Mountain Fork in Texas to Gulf of Mexico.

Canadian (906 mi.; 1,458 km): From Las Animas Co. in Colorado to Arkansas R. in Oklahoma.

Cimarron (600 mi.; 966 km): From Colfax Co. in New Mexico to Arkansas R. in Oklahoma.

Colorado (1,450 mi.; 2,333 km): From Rocky Mountain National Park in Colorado to Gulf of California in Mexico.

Colorado (862 mi.; 1,387 km): From Dawson Co. in Texas to Matagorda Bay.

Columbia (1,243 mi.; 2,000 km): From Columbia Lake in British Columbia to Pacific Ocean (entering between Oregon and Washington).

Colville (350 mi.; 563 km): From Brooks Range in Alaska to Beaufort Sea.

Connecticut (407 mi.; 655 km): From Third Connecticut Lake in New Hampshire to Long Island Sound in Connecticut.

Cumberland (720 mi.; 1,159 km): From junction of Poor and Clover Forks in Harlan Co. in Kentucky to Ohio R.

Delaware (390 mi.; 628 km): From Schoharie Co. in New York to Liston Point, Delaware Bay.

Gila (649 mi.; 1,044 km): From Catron Co. in New Mexico to Colorado R. in Arizona.

Green (360 mi.; 579 km): From Lincoln Co. in Kentucky to Ohio R. in Kentucky.

Green (730 mi.; 1,175 km): From Sublette Co. in Wyoming to Colorado R. in Utah.

Illinois (420 mi.; 676 km): From St. Joseph Co. in Indiana to Mississippi R. at Grafton in Illinois.

James (sometimes called *Dakota*) (710 mi.; 1,143 km): From Wells Co. in North Dakota to Missouri R. in South Dakota.

Kanawha-New (352 mi.; 566 km): From junction of North and South Forks of New R. in North Carolina, through Virginia and West Virginia (New River becoming Kanawha River), to Ohio River.

Koyukuk (470 mi.; 756 km): From Brooks Range in Alaska to Yukon R.

Kuskokwim (724 mi.; 1,165 km): From Alaska Range in Alaska to Kuskokwim Bay.

Licking (350 mi.; 563 km): From Magoffin Co. in Kentucky to Ohio R. at Cincinnati in Ohio.

Little Missouri (560 mi.; 901 km): From Crook Co. in Wyoming to Missouri R. in North Dakota.

Milk (625 mi.; 1,006 km): From junction of forks in Alberta Province to Missouri R.

Coastline of the United States

State	General coastline[1]	Tidal shoreline[2]	State	General coastline[1]	Tidal shoreline[2]
	Lengths, statute miles			**Lengths, statute miles**	
Atlantic Coast:			Gulf Coast:		
Maine	228	3,478	Florida (Gulf)	770	5,095
New Hampshire	13	131	Alabama	53	607
Massachusetts	192	1,519	Mississippi	44	359
Rhode Island	40	384	Louisiana	397	7,721
Connecticut	—	618	Texas	367	3,359
New York	127	1,850	Total Gulf coast	1,631	17,141
New Jersey	130	1,792	Pacific Coast:		
Pennsylvania	—	89	California	840	3,427
Delaware	28	381	Oregon	296	1,410
Maryland	31	3,190	Washington	157	3,026
Virginia	112	3,315	Hawaii	750	1,052
North Carolina	301	3,375	Alaska (Pacific)	5,580	31,383
South Carolina	187	2,876	Total Pacific coast	7,623	40,298
Georgia	100	2,344	Arctic Coast:		
Florida (Atlantic)	580	3,331	Alaska (Arctic)	1,060	2,521
Total Atlantic coast	2,069	28,673	Total Arctic coast	1,060	2,521
			States Total	**12,383**	**88,633**

1. Figures are lengths of general outline of seacoast. Measurements made with unit measure of 30 minutes of latitude on charts as near scale of 1:1,200,000 as possible. Coastline of bays and sounds is included to point where they narrow to width of unit measure, and distance across at such point is included. 2. Figures obtained in 1939–40 with recording instrument on largest-scale maps and charts then available. Shoreline of outer coast, offshore islands, sounds, bays, rivers, and creeks is included to head of tidewater, or to point where tidal waters narrow to width of 100 feet. *Source:* Department of Commerce, National Oceanic and Atmospheric Administration, National Ocean Service.

Mississippi (2,340 mi.; 3,766 km): From Lake Itasca in Minnesota to mouth of Southwest Pass in La.

Mississippi-Missouri-Red Rock (3,710 mi.; 5,970 km): From source of Red Rock R. in Montana to mouth of Southwest Pass in Louisiana.

Missouri (2,315 mi.; 3,726 km): From junction of Jefferson R., Gallatin R., and Madison R. in Montana to Mississippi R. near St. Louis.

Missouri-Red Rock (2,540 mi.; 4,090 km): From source of Red Rock R. in Montana to Mississippi R. near St. Louis.

Mobile-Alabama-Coosa (645 mi.; 1,040 km): From junction of Etowah R. and Oostanula R. in Georgia to Mobile Bay.

Neosho (460 mi.; 740 km): From Morris Co. in Kansas to Arkansas R. in Oklahoma.

Niobrara (431 mi.; 694 km): From Niobrara Co. in Wyoming to Missouri R. in Nebraska.

Noatak (350 mi.; 563 km): From Brooks Range in Alaska to Kotzebue Sound.

North Canadian (800 mi.; 1,290 km): From Union Co. in New Mexico to Canadian R. in Oklahoma.

North Platte (618 mi.; 995 km): From Jackson Co. in Colorado to junction with So. Platte R. in Nebraska to form Platte R.

Ohio (981 mi.; 1,579 km): From junction of Allegheny R. and Monongahela R. at Pittsburgh to Mississippi R. between Illinois and Kentucky.

Ohio-Allegheny (1,306 mi.; 2,102 km): From Potter Co. in Pennsylvania to Mississippi R. at Cairo in Illinois.

Osage (500 mi.; 805 km): From east-central Kansas to Missouri R. near Jefferson City in Missouri.

Ouachita (605 mi.; 974 km): From Polk Co. in Arkansas to Red R. in Louisiana.

Pearl (411 mi.; 661 km): From Neshoba County in Mississippi to Gulf of Mexico (Mississippi-Louisiana).

Pecos (926 mi.; 1,490 km): From Mora Co. in New Mexico to Rio Grande in Texas.

Pee Dee-Yadkin (435 mi.; 700 km): From Watauga Co. in North Carolina to Winyah Bay in South Carolina.

Pend Oreille-Clark Fork (531 mi.; 855 km): Near Butte in Montana to Columbia R. on Washington-Canada border.

Porcupine (569 mi.; 916 km): From Yukon Territory, Canada, to Yukon R. in Alaska.

Potomac (383 mi.; 616 km): From Garrett Co. in Md. to Chesapeake Bay at Point Lookout in Md.

Powder (375 mi.; 603 km): From junction of forks in Johnson Co. in Wyoming to Yellowstone R. in Montana.

Red (1,290 mi.; 2,080 km): From source of Tierra Blanca Creek in Curry County, New Mexico to Mississippi R. in Louisiana.

Red (also called *Red River of the North*) (545 mi.; 877 km): From junction of Otter Tail R. and Bois de Sioux R. in Minnesota to Lake Winnipeg in Manitoba.

Republican (445 mi.; 716 km): From junction of North Fork and Arikaree R. in Nebraska to junction with Smoky Hill R. in Kansas to form the Kansas R.

Rio Grande (1,900 mi.; 3,060 km): From San Juan Co. in Colorado to Gulf of Mexico.

Roanoke (380 mi.; 612 km): From junction of forks in Montgomery Co. in Virginia to Albemarle Sound in North Carolina.

Sabine (380 mi.; 612 km): From junction of forks in Hunt Co. in Texas to Sabine Lake between Texas and Louisiana.

Sacramento (377 mi.; 607 km): From Siskiyou Co. in California to Suisun Bay.

Saint Francis (425 mi.; 684 km): From Iron Co. in Missouri to Mississippi R. in Arkansas.

Salmon (420 mi.; 676 km): From Custer Co. in Idaho to Snake R.

San Joaquin (350 mi.; 563 km): From junction of forks in Madera Co. in California to Suisun Bay.

San Juan (360 mi.; 579 km): From Archuleta Co. in Colorado to Colorado R. in Utah.

Santee-Wateree-Catawba (538 mi.; 866 km): From McDowell Co. in North Carolina to Atlantic Ocean in South Carolina.
Smoky Hill (540 mi.; 869 km): From Cheyenne Co. in Colorado to junction with Republican R. in Kansas to form Kansas R.
Snake (1,038 mi.; 1,670 km): From Ocean Plateau in Wyoming to Columbia R. in Washington.
South Platte (424 mi.; 682 km): From Park Co. in Colorado to junction with North Platte R. in Nebraska to form Platte R.
Susquehanna (444 mi.; 715 km): From Otsego Lake in New York to Chesapeake Bay in Maryland.
Tanana (659 mi.; 1,060 km): From Wrangell Mts. in Yukon Territory, Canada, to Yukon R. in Alaska.
Tennessee (652 mi.; 1,049 km): From junction of Holston R. and French Broad R. in Tennessee to Ohio R. in Kentucky.
Tennessee-French Broad (870 mi.; 1,400 km): From Bland Co. in Virginia to Ohio R. at Paducah

in Kentucky.
Tombigbee (525 mi.; 845 km): From junction of forks in Itawamba Co. in Mississippi to Mobile R. in Alabama.
Trinity (360 mi.; 579 km): From junction of forks in Dallas Co. in Texas to Galveston Bay.
Wabash (512 mi.; 824 km): From Darke Co. in Ohio to Ohio R. between Illinois and Indiana.
Washita (500 mi.; 805 km): From Hemphill Co. in Texas to Red R. in Oklahoma.
White (722 mi.; 1,160 km): From Madison Co. in Arkansas to Mississippi R.
Wisconsin (430 mi.; 692 km): From Vilas Co. in Wisconsin to Mississippi R.
Yellowstone (692 mi.; 1,110 km): From Park Co. in Wyoming to Missouri R. in North Dakota.
Yukon (1,979 mi.; 3,185 km): From junction of Lewes R. and Pelly R. in Yukon Territory, Canada, to Bering Sea in Alaska.

Soviet and U.S. Citizens Score Low in Geographic Literacy

In 1988 the National Geographic Society commissioned an international survey of geographic literacy of the adult population in six industrialized nations, in addition to the United States, (Japan, France, West Germany, the United Kingdom, Sweden, and Italy) and our two neighboring countries, Canada and Mexico. It was conducted by the Gallup Organization.

In the spring of 1989 the survey was expanded to include the Soviet Union where 1,500 adults living in Moscow and the industrial city of Kursk, 300 miles south of the capital, were tested. The results were surprising. While young Soviet adults scored significantly higher than their American counterparts, overall the Soviets did not do well. In correctly identifying places on a world map, adults of all age groups scored an average of 7.4 out of a possible 16. That put them at the bottom of the group of nations tested, along with Mexico. American adults ranked only slightly higher with 8.6 correct.

Among the 18-to-24-year olds, with a score of 9.3, the Soviets ranked in fourth place along with Canadians and Italians. Young American adults came in last, with an average of only 6.9 correct. Americans were the only nationality whose 18-to-24-year olds did worse than those over the age of 55. Soviet youth scored considerably better than their elders. Neil A. Upmeyer, a Gallup vice president, attributed the poor overall rankings of the Soviets to the low scores of those over 55, who grew up in war time without adequate educational opportunities.

The overall Soviet results fell short of Soviet researchers' expectations. "It was a shock," said Vladimir G. Andreyenkov, of the Soviet Academy of Sciences, which conducted the survey with Gallup. "I didn't believe Soviet citizens knew so little about geography." Even the better showing by young Soviet adults was not satisfactory, Andreyenkov said. "It's terrible in our society, where everybody believes that, in general, we teach our children well."

All those surveyed in the 10 nations were asked to locate the same 13 countries, Central America, the Pacific Ocean, and the Persian Gulf on an unmarked map of the world. For the Soviet survey Afghanistan, which borders it on the south, was added. In spite of a decade-long military involvement there, only four persons in 10 could find it on the world map.

However, only a third of Americans could locate Vietnam, and despite heavy involvement in the Persian Gulf and Central America on our part, 75 percent of the adults surveyed could not find the Persian Gulf and 45 percent could not locate Central America.

Generally, Soviets and Americans did best at recognizing their own countries and neighbors, but even here the results were surprising. What surprised Andreyenkov most about the Soviet results was that "not everybody; could identify the Soviet Union." Thirteen percent could not. Americans were equally inept at finding the United States. Fourteen percent—one in seven—could not.

Next to their own country, the United States was the country most recognized by the Soviet participants in the survey. Sixty-six percent correctly located the United States. Among Americans, 75 percent recognized the Soviet Union.

As was the case in the U.S. survey, the level of education played a major role in identification scores. The higher a respondent's education level, the higher the identification score.

In the case of the Soviets, those with less than a high school education had an overall score of 3.2, those with a high school degree scored an average of 7.3, those with some college scored a 10.2, and those with a college degree scored 10.8.

Gilbert M. Grosvenor, president of the National Geographic Society, found the results of the survey disturbing not only for the Soviet Union but also for the United States. "The superiority of Soviet young adults—indeed of all other young adults—reinforces the need to strengthen the teaching of geography in American classrooms." Nearly 90 percent of the Soviets surveyed—compared with 47 percent of the Americans—said they had taken a course devoted entirely to geography.

In response to questions on attitudes toward geography, a majority of Soviets felt that knowing where countries in the news are located is absolutely necessary to be considered a well-rounded person, putting them with France and Mexico, the only other countries where the majority of respondents expressed this view.

As if to underline this belief, Mr. Grosvenor said, "We share the same world, not only environmentally but economically. If we are to resolve problems of global pollution, deforestation, hunger, nuclear arms control, and population balance, we must be geographically literate."

NORTH AMERICA

LAMBERT AZIMUTHAL EQUAL-AREA
PROJECTION

SCALE OF MILES

0   200   400   600   800   1000

SCALE OF KILOMETERS

0   200 400 600 800 1000

Capitals .... ⊛
International Boundaries ____
Canals ____

© Copyright HAMMOND INCORPORATED, Maplewood, N.J.

MIDDLE AMERICA

BONNE PROJECTION

Copyright by C. S. HAMMOND & Co., N. Y.

SCALE OF MILES

| 0 | 200 | 400 | 600 |

KILOMETERS

| 0 | 200 | 400 | 600 |

Capitals of Countries ⊛
Other Capitals ⊛
International Boundaries ....

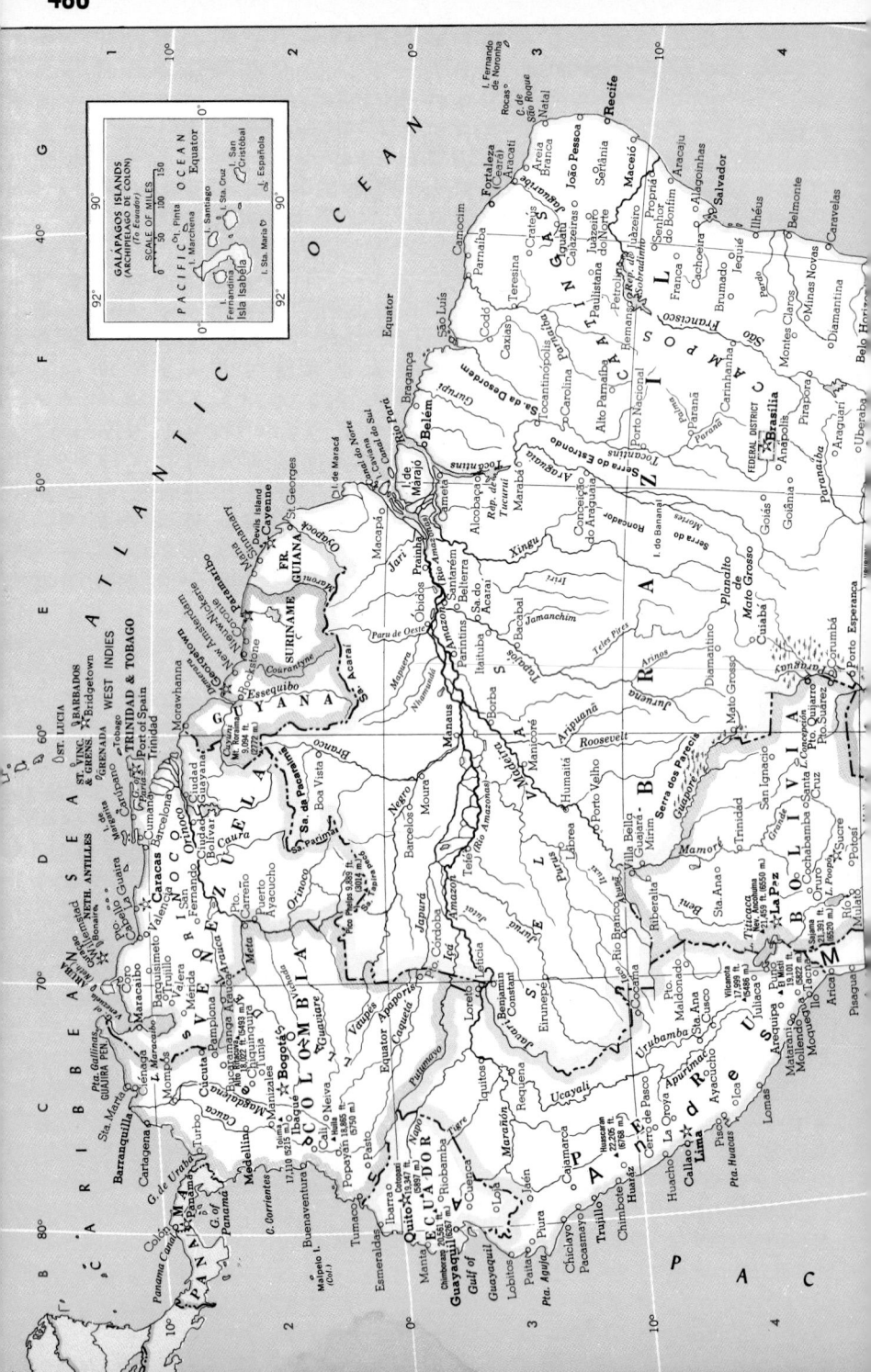

GALAPAGOS ISLANDS
(ARCHIPIÉLAGO DE COLÓN)
(To Ecuador)
SCALE OF MILES
0   50   100   150

PACIFIC OCEAN
Equator
Pinta
I. Marchena
San
Cristóbal
Santiago
I. Sta. Cruz
I. Española
Fernandina
Isla Isabela
I. Sta. María ⌀

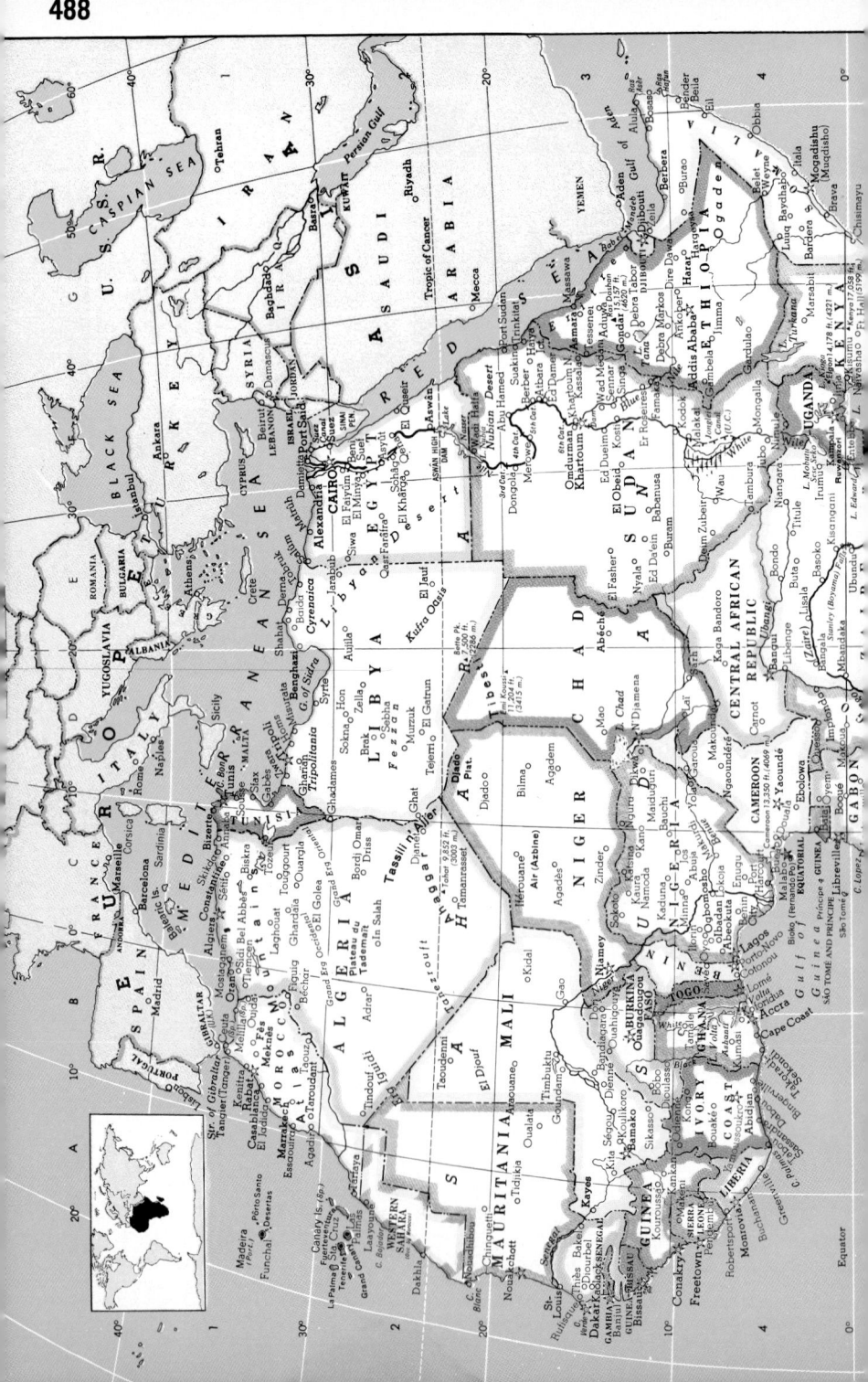

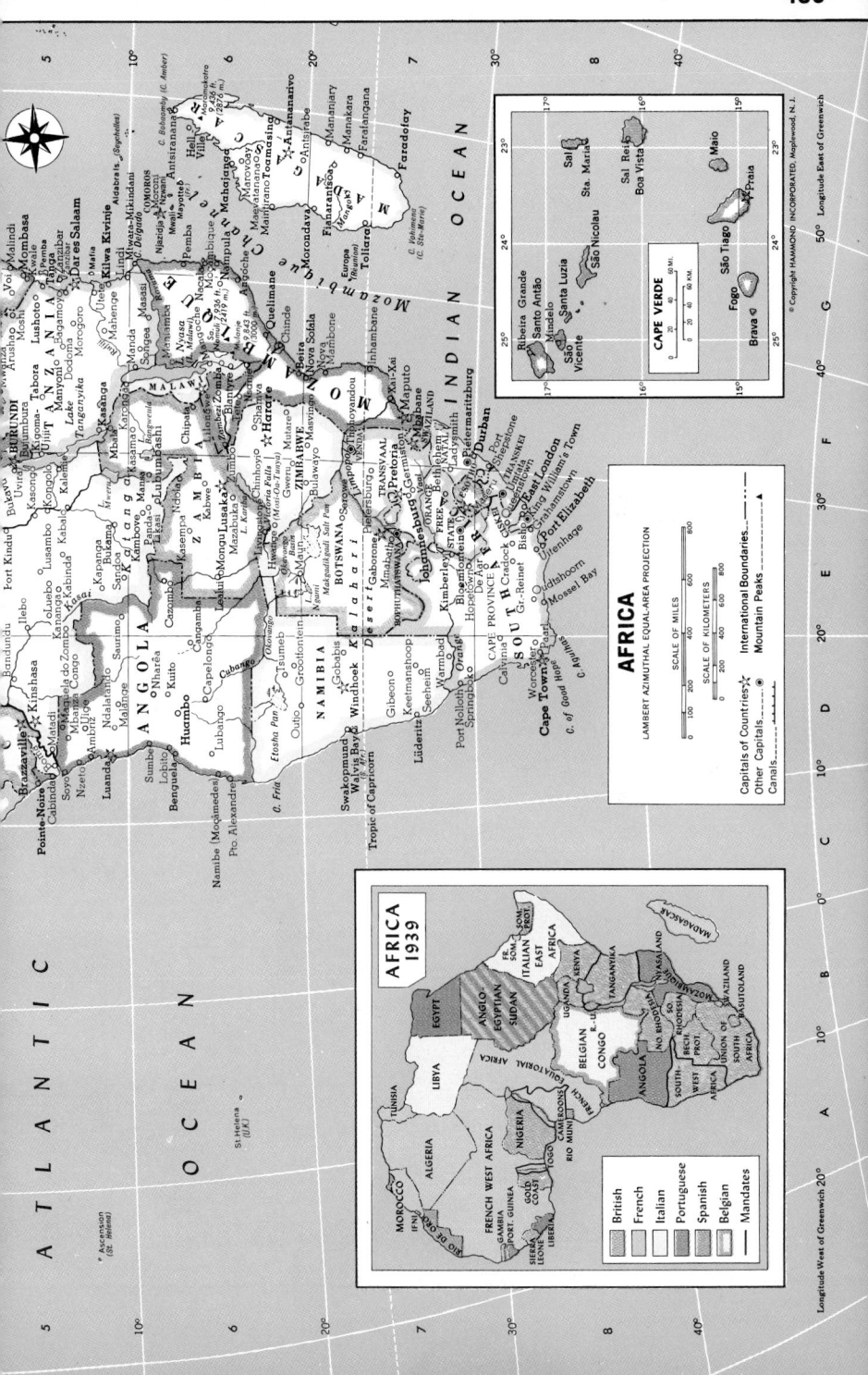

EUROPE

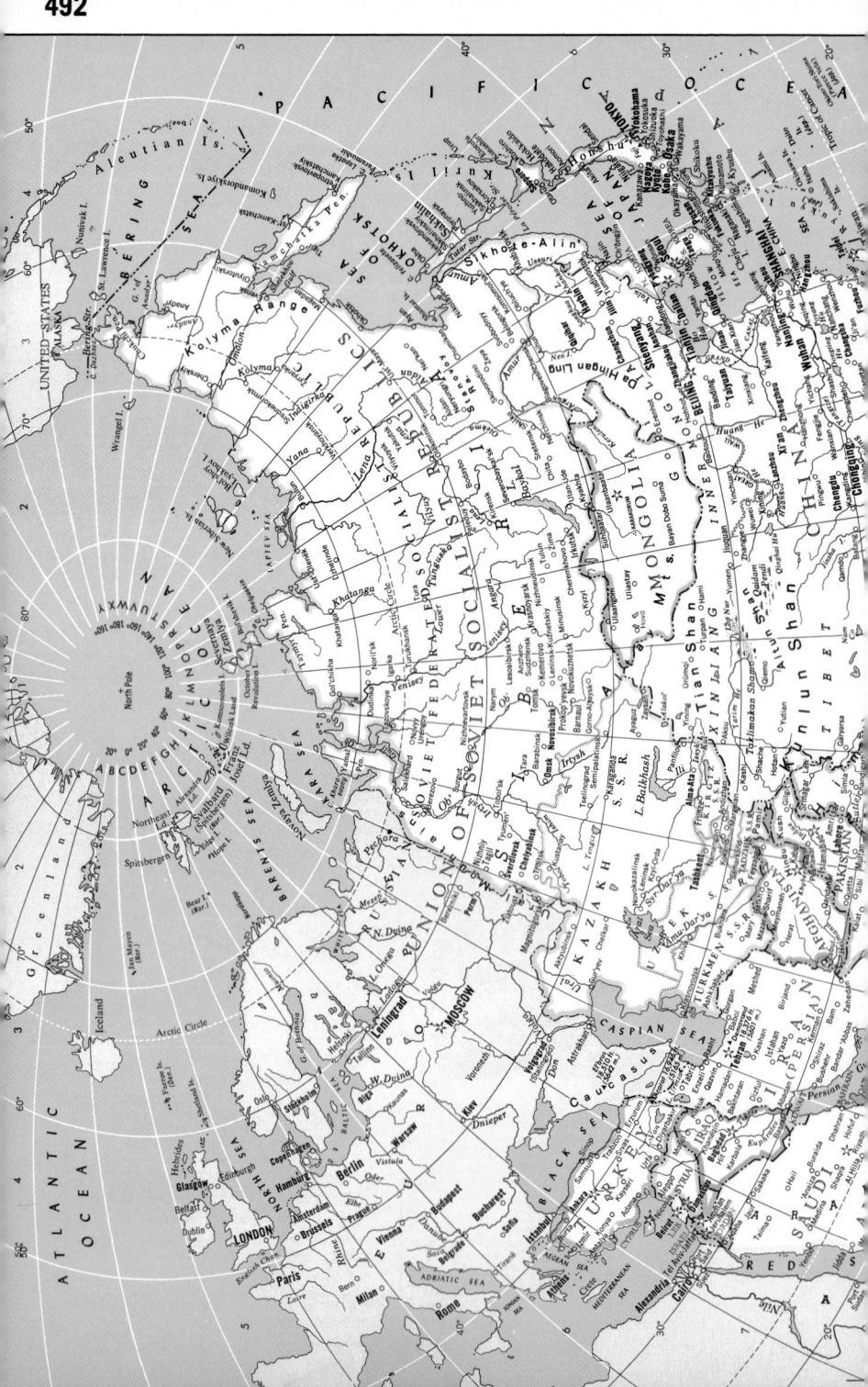

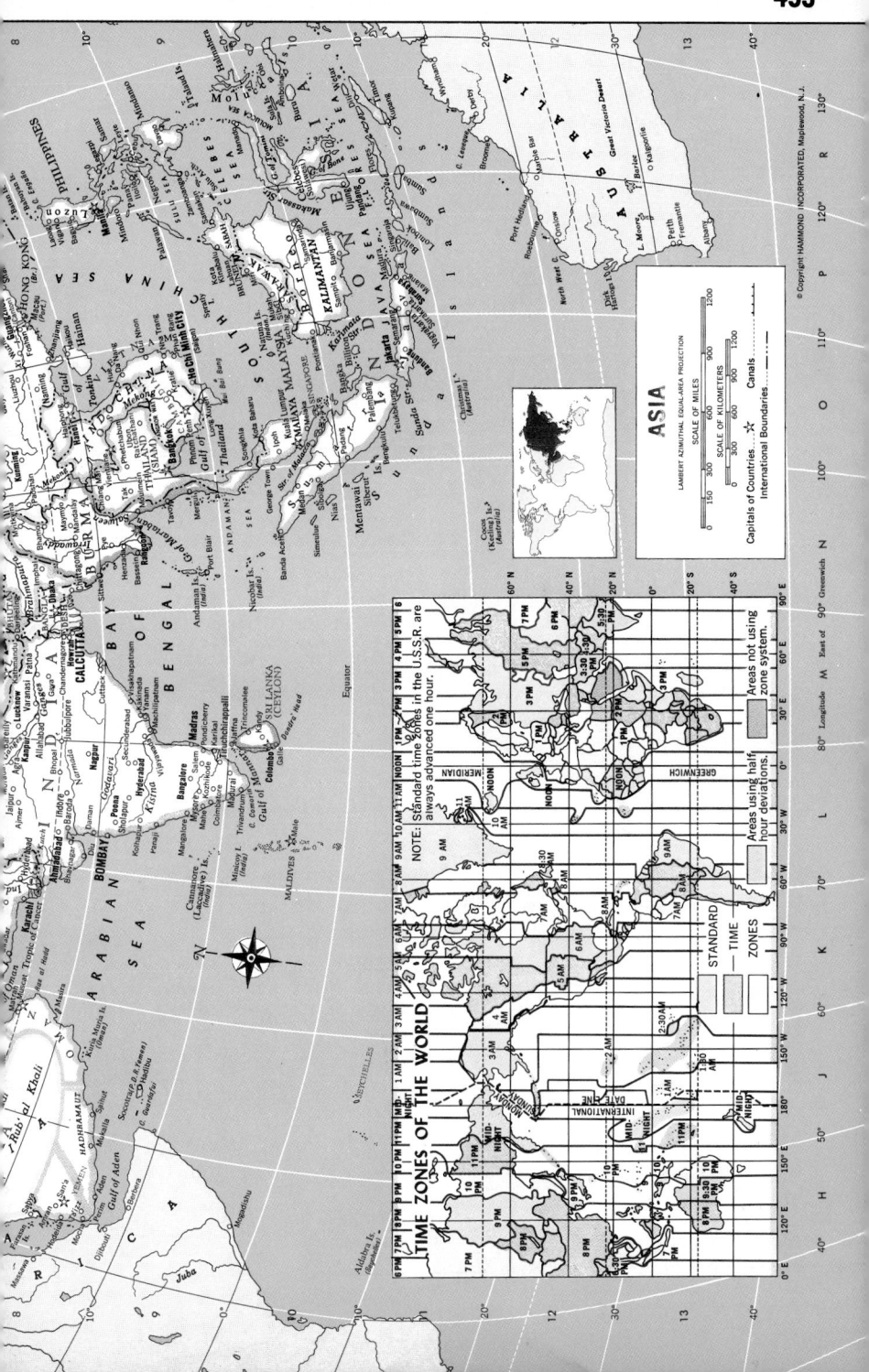

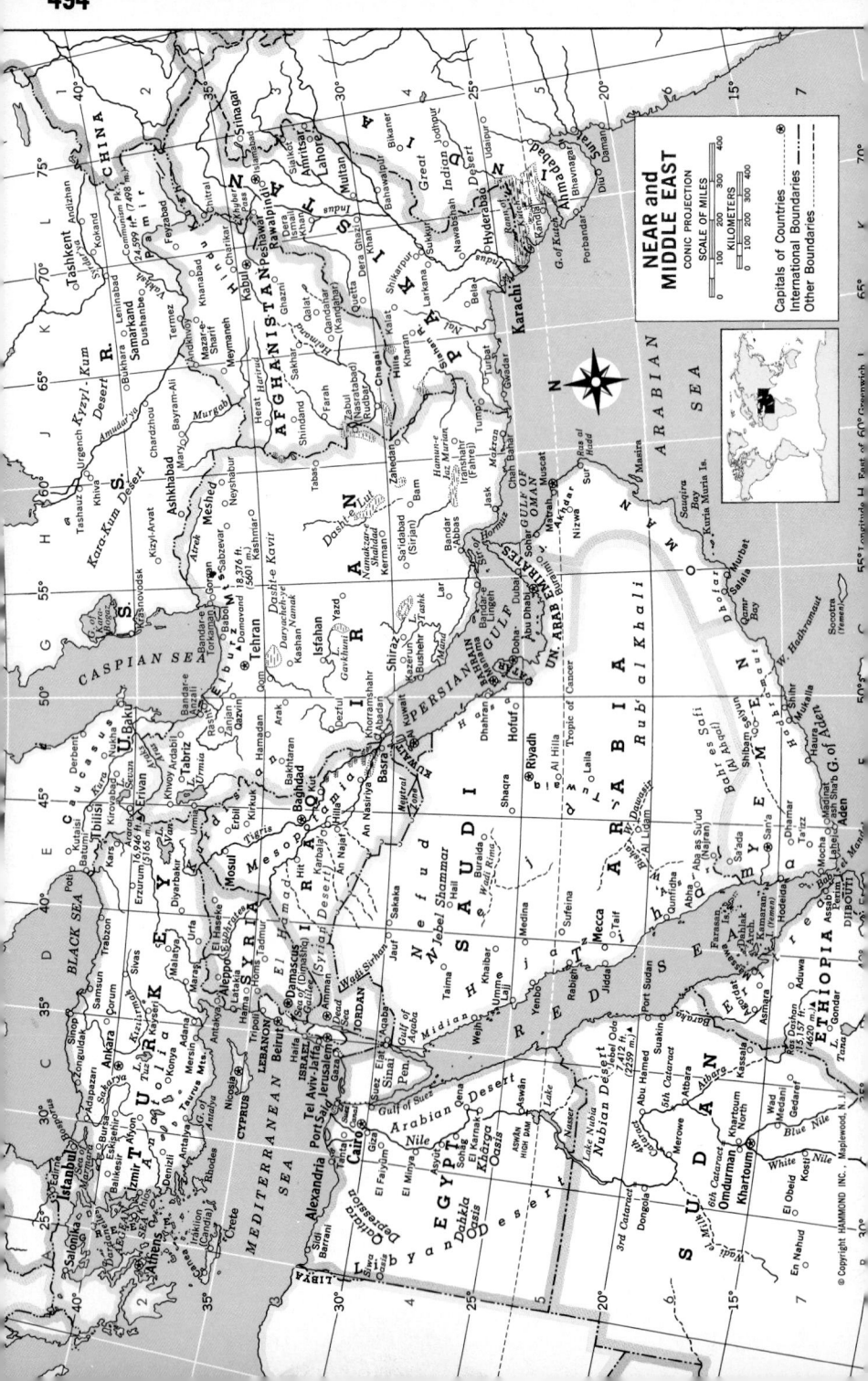

NEAR and MIDDLE EAST

CONIC PROJECTION

SCALE OF MILES

KILOMETERS

Capitals of Countries ⊛
International Boundaries
Other Boundaries

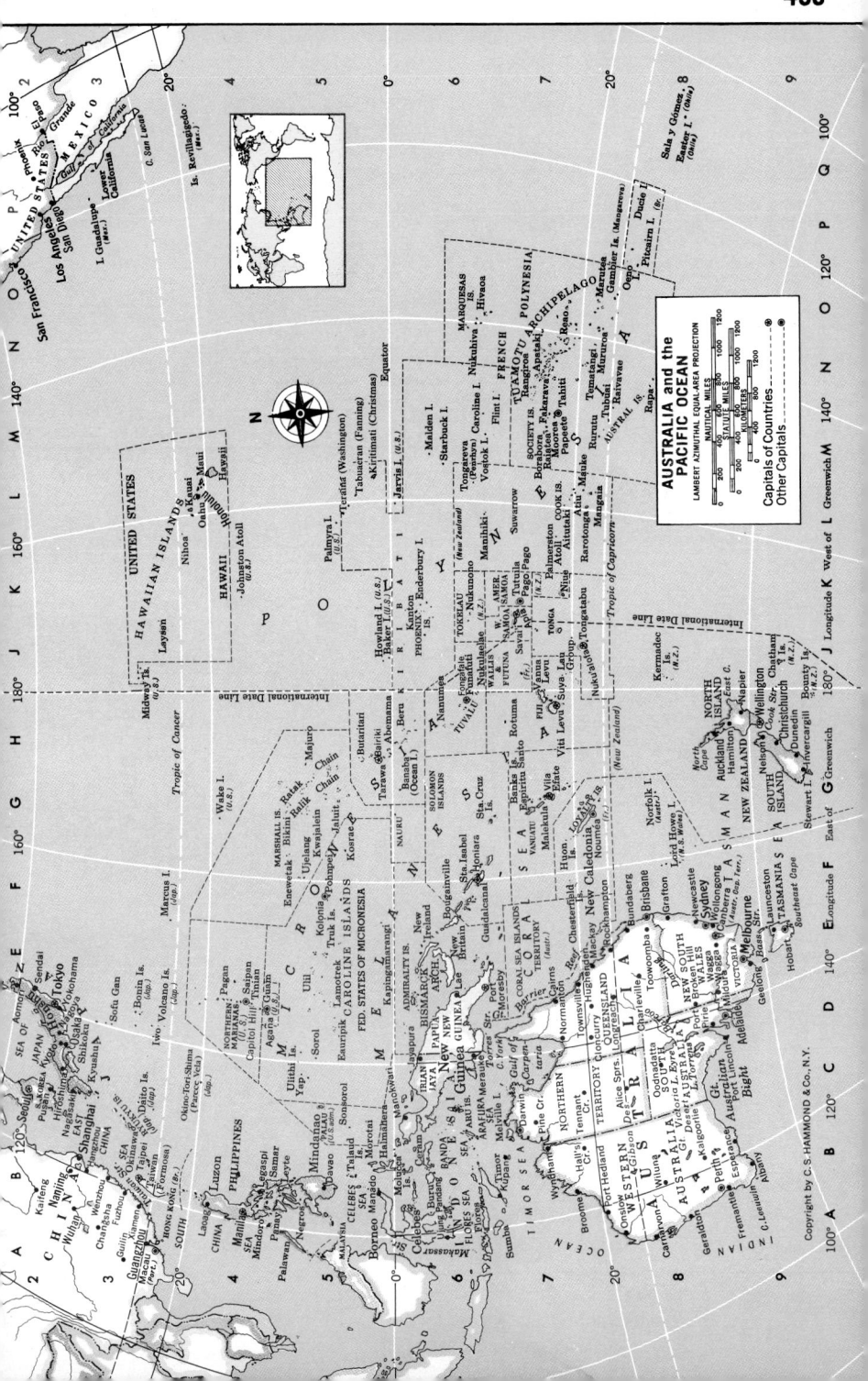

AUSTRALIA and the PACIFIC OCEAN

LAMBERT AZIMUTHAL EQUAL-AREA PROJECTION

NAUTICAL MILES
0   200   400   600   800   1000 1200

STATUTE MILES
0   200   400   600   800   1000 1200

KILOMETERS
0   200 400 600 800 1000 1200

Capitals of Countries .... ◉
Other Capitals .... ●

Copyright by C.S. HAMMOND & Co., N.Y.

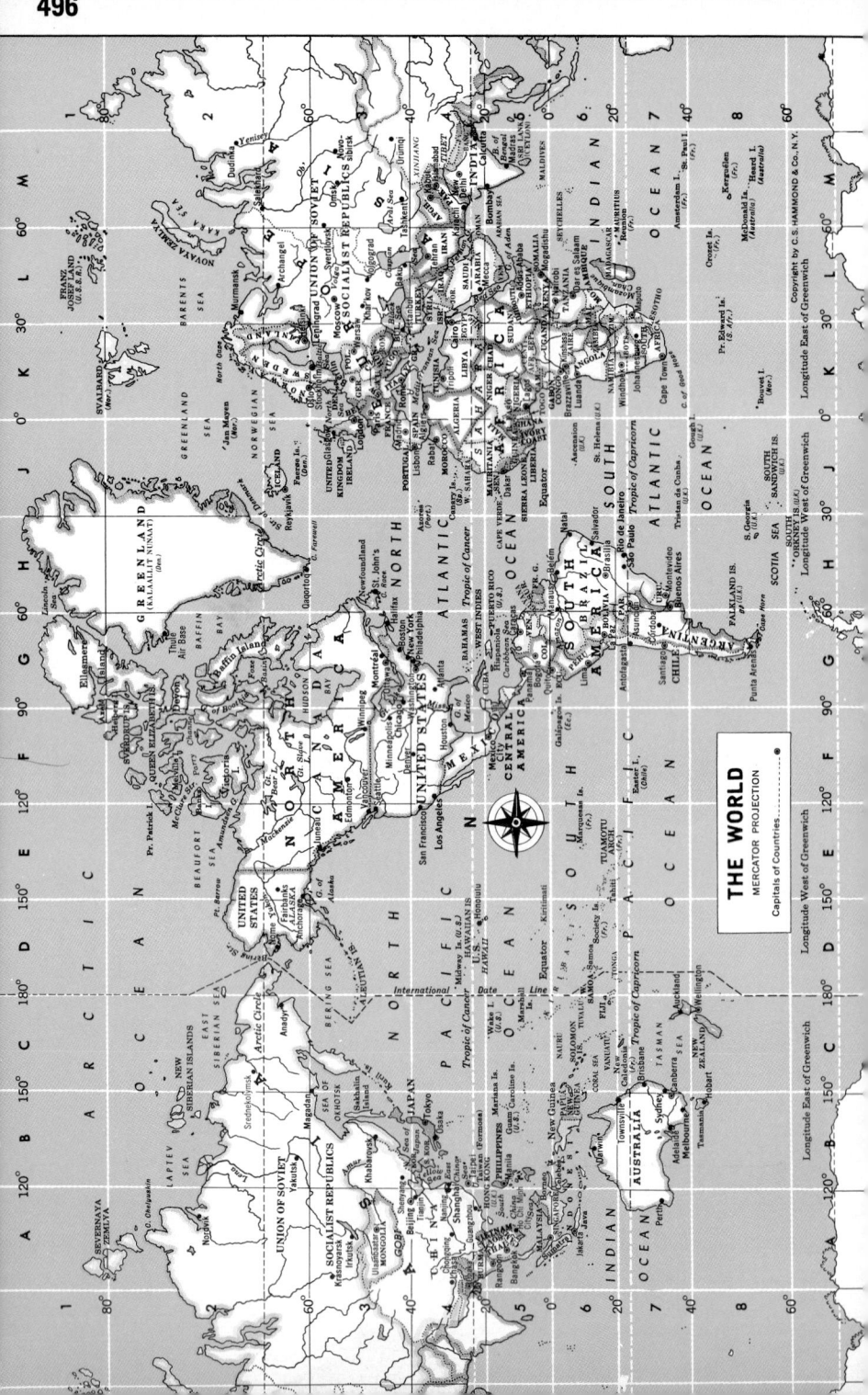

THE WORLD

MERCATOR PROJECTION

Capitals of Countries............

THE YEAR IN PICTURES

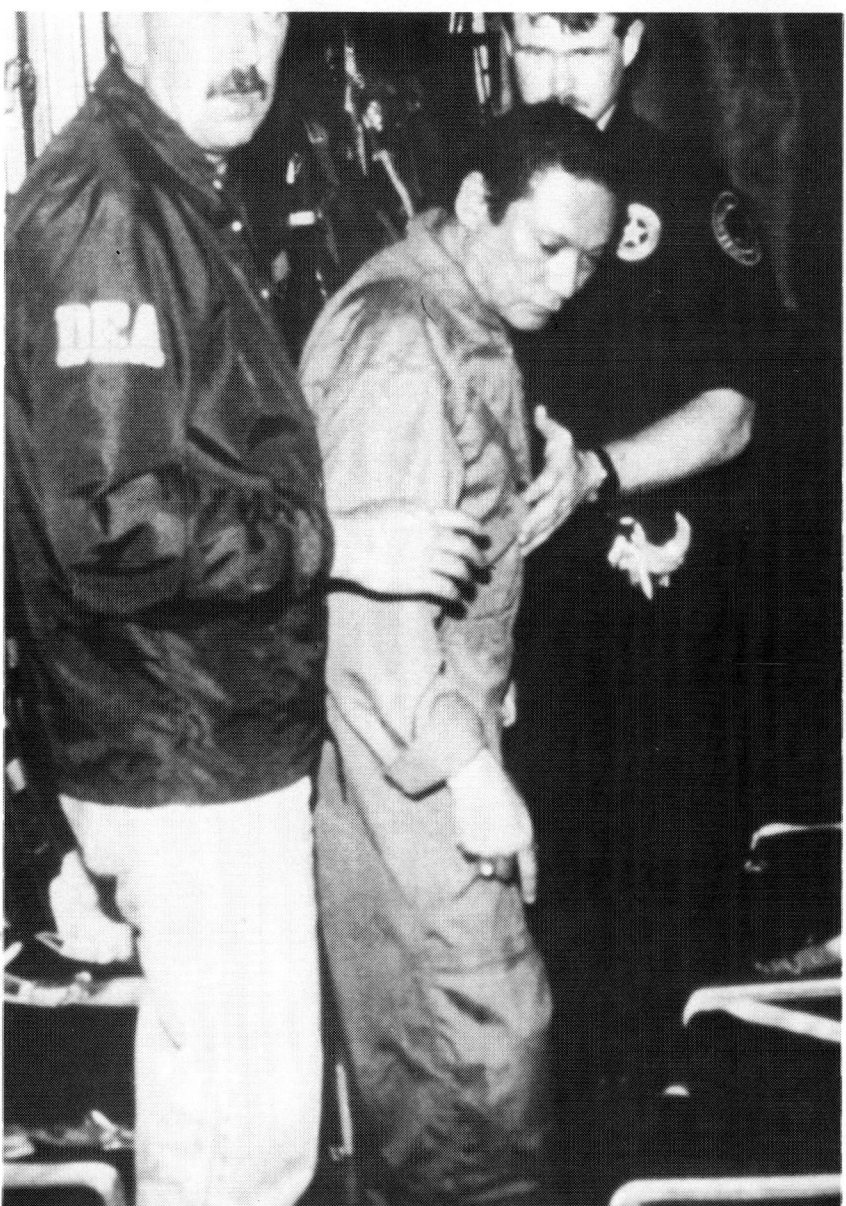

IN CUSTODY—After surrendering, Manuel Antonio Noriega is helped into a C-130 transport plane by U.S. Drug Enforcement Agents accompanying him to Miami to face trial on drug charges.

SWORN IN—L. Douglas Wilder (left), the first elected black governor in the United States, is sworn in as governor of Virginia by retired U.S. Supreme Court Justice Lewis F. Powell, Jr.; his daughter and son look on.

VICTORS—Violetta Barrios De Chamorro embraces her running mate, Virgilio Godoy, after winning in Nicaragua's national election.

ADDRESSES CONGRESS—Vaclav Havel, Czechoslovakian president, addresses a joint session of Congress with Vice President Dan Quayle and House Speaker Thomas Foley in attendance.

THROUGH THE WALL—A West Berlin couple enter East Berlin through a hole in the wall before it is dismantled by East Germany to allow free crossing.

INAUGURATED—Haiti's first woman president, Ertha Pascal Trouillot, receives a pledge of loyalty from General Herard Abraham during inauguration ceremonies in Port-au-Prince.

INDEPENDENT—Namibian President Sam Nujomo reads his inaugural speech at his country's independence ceremony.

AWASH—Flood waters from the Trinity River surround the homes of residents of Kenefick, Texas.

VIOLENCE—An anti-poll tax rally turns violent as protesters charge across demolished crowd barriers in London's Trafalgar Square.

WELCOME—President Bush greets former hostage Robert Polhill and his wife Ferial upon their arrival at the White House. Polhill had been held hostage for three years and three months.

HOMECOMING—Former hostage Frank Reed, with his wife Fifi and son Tarek, waves to hometowners during a parade in his honor in Malden, Mass. Reed had been held hostage for three and a half years.

SIGN ACCORDS—Soviet President Mikhail Gorbachev and President George Bush sign treaties during ceremonies ending their summit meeting. Joseph Reed, U.S. Chief of Protocol, looks on.

PRESIDENT—Soviet maverick Boris N. Yeltsin leaves the Kremlin following his election as president of the Russian Republic.

CROWD PLEASER—Soviet President Mikhail Gorbachev waves to the crowd at airport on his arrival in Minneapolis.

CONGRESSIONAL ACCLAIM—Nelson Mandela, surrounded by congressmen, waves to the audience after addressing a joint meeting of Congress.

TICKER TAPE WELCOME—Office workers shower ticker tape on Nelson Mandela's vehicle during his parade through the Wall Street area in Manhattan.

GRIM SEARCH—A team of divers search the mouth of Pipe Creek in southern Ohio for flood victims.

CRACKDOWN—Pro-government miners wielding clubs attack an anti-government demonstrator in University Square in Bucharest, Romania.

FIREFIGHTING—Fireboats spray water on the supertanker *Mega Borg* off the coast of Galveston, Texas, in an effort to cool the steel so flame-smothering foam can be sprayed on the ship. As a result of the accident millions of gallons of crude oil were spilled.

ON THEIR WAY—World leaders attending the 1990 Economic Summit in Houston walk to lunch on the Rice University campus. From left: Economic Community President Delors, Italian Prime Minister Andreotti, Japanese Prime Minister Kaifu, British Prime Minister Thatcher, West German Chancellor Kohl, French President Mitterrand, President Bush, and Canadian Prime Minister Mulroney.

ROYAL VISITOR—President Bush escorts Jordan's King Hussein upon his arrival for a meeting at Bush's Kennebunkport home.

REFUGEES—Albanians disembark at Brindisi, Italy, after fleeing from their homeland.

AN ILL WIND—A Plainfield, Ill., resident stands amid the ruins of his apartment—one of many destroyed when tornadoes swept through the area.

AT LAST—Signing of the 2 plus 4 agreement clears the way for the reunification of Germany. Left to right are: U.S., James Baker; Britain, Douglas Hurd; U.S.S.R., Eduard Shevardnaze; France, Roland Dumas; East Germany, Lothar de Maiziére; and West Germany, Hans-Dietrich Gensher.

DEPLOYED—Troops and armour from the U.S. Army 82nd Airborne take up a defensive position at a military facility in Saudi Arabia.

REFUGEES—Crowds of Egyptians wait to board a ferry at Jordanian Red Sea port of Aqaba for their return to Egypt.

HUSSEIN'S "GUESTS"—Scene on Iraqi television of President Hussein with Western hostages which outraged viewers around the world.

First Aid to Crossword Puzzlers

We cannot begin to list all the odd words you will meet with in your daily and Sunday crossword puzzles, for such words run into many thousands. But we have tried to include those that turn up most frequently, as well as many others that should be of help to you when you are unable to go any further.

Also, we do not guarantee that the definitions in your puzzle will be exactly the same as ours, although we have checked every word with a standard dictionary and have followed its definition.

In nearly every case, we have used as the key word the principal noun of the definition, rather than any adjective, adjective phrase, or noun used as an adjective. And, to simplify your searching, we have grouped the words according to the number of spaces you have to fill.

For a list of Foreign Phrases, *see* Index. For Rulers of England and Great Britain, France, Germany and Prussia, and Russia, *see* Countries of the World.

Words of Two Letters

Ambary, DA
And (French, Latin), ET
Article (Arabic), AL
  (French), LA, LE, UN
  (Spanish), EL, LA, UN
At the (French), AU
  (Spanish), AL
Behold, LO
Bird: Hawaiian, OO
Birthplace: Abraham's, UR
Bone, OS
Buddha, FO
Butterfly: Peacock, IO
Champagne, AY
Chaos, NU
Chief: Burmese, BO
Coin: Roman, AS
  Siamese, AT
Concerning, RE
Dialect: Chinese, WU
Double (Egy. relig.), KA
Drama: Japanese, NO
Egg (comb. form), OO
Esker, OS
Eye (Scotch), EE
Factor: Amplification, MU
Fifty (Greek), NU
Fish: Carplike, ID
Force, OD
Forty (Greek), MU
From (French, Latin, Spanish), DE

(Latin prefix), AB
From the (French), DU
God: Babylonian, EA, ZU
  Egyptian sun, RA
  Hindu unknown, KA
  Semitic, EL
Goddess: Babylonian, AI
  Greek earth, GE
Gold (heraldry), OR
Gulf: Arctic, OB
Heart (Egy. relig.), AB
Indian: South American, GE
King: Of Bashan, OG
Language: Artificial, RO
  Assamese, AO
Lava: Hawaiian, AA
Letter: Greek, MU, NU, PI, XI
  Hebrew, HE, PE
Lily: Palm, TI
Measure: Annamese, LY
  Chinese, HO, HU, KO, LI, MU, PU, TO, TU
  Japanese, GO, JO, MO, RI, SE, TO
  Metric land, AR
  Netherlands, EL
  Portuguese, PE
  Siamese, WA
  Swedish, AM
  Type, EM, EN
Monk: Buddhist, BO
Month: Jewish, AB

Mouth, OS
Mulberry: Indian, AL
Native: Burmese, WA
Note: Of Scale, DO, FA, MI, LA, RE, TI
Of (French, Latin, Spanish), DE
Of the (French), DU
One (Scotch), AE
Pagoda: Chinese, TA
Plant: East Indian fiber, DA
Ridge: Sandy, AS, OS
River: Russian, OB
Sloth: Three-toed, AI
Soul (Egy. relig.), BA
Sound: Hindu mystic, OM
Suffix: Comparative, ER
The. *See* Article
To the: French, AU
  Spanish, AL
Tree: Buddhist sacred, BO
Tribe: Assamese, AO
Type: Jumbled, PI
Weight: Annamese, TA
  Chinese, LI
  Danish, ES
  Japanese, MO
  Roman, AS
Whirlwind: Faeroe Is., OE
Yes (German), JA
  (Italian, Spanish), SI
  (Russian), DA

Words of Three Letters

Adherent: IST
Again, BIS
Age, ERA
Antelope: African, GNU, KOB
Apricot: Japanese, UME
Article (German), DAS, DEM, DEN, DER, DES, DIE, EIN
  (French), LES, UNE
  (Spanish), LAS, LOS, UNA
Banana: Polynesian, FEI
Barge, HOY
Bass: African, IYO
Beak, NEB, NIB
Beard: Grain, AWN
Beetle: June, DOR
Being, ENS
Berry: Hawthorn, HAW
Beverage: Hawaiian, AVA
Bird: Australian, EMU
  Crowlike, JAY
  Extinct, MOA

Fabulous, ROC
Frigate, IWA
Parson, POE, TUE, TUI
Sea, AUK
Blackbird, ANI, ANO
Born, NEE
Bronze: Roman, AES
Bugle: Yellow, IVA
By way of, VIA
Canton: Swiss, URI
Cap: Turkish, FEZ
Catnip, NEP
Character: In "Faerie Queene," UNA
Coin: Afghan, PUL
  Albanian, LEK
  British Guiana, BIT
  Bulgarian, LEV, LEW
  French, ECU, SOU
  Indian, PIE
  Japanese, SEN, YEN
  Korean, WON

Lithuanian, LIT
Macao, Timor, AVO
Palestinian, MIL
Persian, PUL
Peruvian, SOL
Rumanian, BAN, LEU, LEY
Scandinavian, ORE
Siamese, ATT
See also Money of account
Collection: Facts, ANA
Commune: Belgian, ANS, ATH
  Netherlands, EDE, EPE
Community: Russian, MIR
Constellation: Southern, ARA
Contraction: Poetic, EEN, EER, OER
Covering: Apex of roof, EPI
Crab: Fiddler, UCA
Crag: Rocky, TOR
Cry: Crow, rook, raven, CAW
Cup: Wine, AMA
Cymbal, Oriental, TAL, ZEL

Disease: Silkworm, UJI
Division: Danish territorial, AMT
  Geologic, EON
Doctrine, ISM
Dowry, DOT
Dry (French), SEC
Dynasty: Chinese, CHI, HAN, SUI, WEI, YIN
Eagle: Sea, ERN
Earth (comb. form), GEO
Egg: Louse, NIT
Eggs: Fish, ROE
Emmet, ANT
Enzyme, ASE
Equal (comb. form), ISO
Extension: building, ELL
Far (comb. form), TEL
Farewell, AVE
Fiber: Palm, TAL
Finial, EPI
Fish: Carplike, IDE
  Pikelike, GAR
Flatfish, DAB
Fleur-de-lis, LIS, LYS
Food: Hawaiian, POI
Formerly, NEE
Friend (French), AMI
Game: Card, LOO
Garment: Camel-hair, ABA
Gateway, DAR
Gazelle: Tibetan, GOA
Genus: Ducks, AIX
  Grasses, POA
  Grasses (maize), ZEA
  Herbs or shrubs, IVA
  Lizards, UTA
  Rodents (incl. house mice), MUS
  Ruminants (incl. cattle), BOS
  Swine, SUS
Gibbon: Malay, LAR
God: Assyrian, SIN
  Babylonian, ABU, ANU, BEL, HEA, SIN, UTU
  Irish sea, LER
  Phrygian, MEN
  Polynesian, ORO
Goddess: Babylonian, AYA
  Etruscan, UNI
  Hindu, SRI, UMA, VAC
  Teutonic, RAN
Governor: Algerian, DEY
  Turkish, BEY
Grampus, ORC
Grape, UVA
Grass: Meadow, POA
Gypsy, ROM
Hail, AVE
Hare: Female, DOE
Hawthorn, HAW
Hay: Spread for drying, TED
Herb: Japanese, UDO
  Perennial, PIA
  Used for blue dye, WAD
Herd: Whales, GAM, POD
Hero: Spanish, CID
High (music), ALT
Honey (pharm.), MEL
Humorist: American, ADE
I (Latin), EGO
I love (Latin), AMO
Indian: Algonquian, FOX, SAC, WEA
  Chimakuan, HOH
  Keresan, SIA
  Mayan, MAM
  Shoshonean, UTE
  Siouan, KAW, OTO
  South American, ITE, ONA, URO, URU, YAO
  Tierra del Fuego, ONA
  Wakashan, AHT
Ingot, PIG
Inlet: Narrow, RIA
Island: Cyclades, IOS
  Dodecanese, COS, KOS
  (French), ILE
  River, AIT

Jackdaw, DAW
John (Gaelic), IAN
Keelbill, ANI, ANO
Kiln, OST
King: British legendary LUD
Kobold, NIS
Lace: To make, TAT
Lamprey, EEL
Language: Artificial, IDO
  Bantu, ILA
  Siamese, LAO, TAI
Leaf: Palm, OLA, OLE
Leaving, ORT
Left: Cause to turn, HAW
Letter: Greek, CHI, ETA, PHI, PSI, RHO, TAU
  Hebrew, MEM, NUN, SIN, TAV, VAU
Lettuce, COS
Life (comb. form), BIO
Lily: Palm, TOI
Lizard, EFT
Louse: Young, NIT
Love (Anglo-Irish), GRA
Lute: Oriental, TAR
Macaw: Bralizian, ARA
Marble, TAW
Match: Shooting (French), TIR
Meadow, LEA
Measure: Abyssinian, TAT
  Algerian, PIK
  Annamese, GON, MAU, NGU, VUO, SAO, TAO, TAT
  Arabian, DEN, SAA
  Belgian, VAT
  Bulgarian, OKA, OKE
  Chinese, FEN, TOU, YIN
  Cloth, ELL
  Cyprus, OKA, OKE, PIK
  Czech, LAN, SAH
  Danish, FOD, MIL, POT
  Dominican Republic, ONA
  Dutch, old, AAM
  East Indian, KIT
  Egyptian, APT, HEN, PIK, ROB
  Electric, MHO, OHM
  Energy, ERG
  English, PIN
  Estonian, TUN
  French, POT
  German, AAM
  Greek, PIK
  Hebrew, CAB, HIN, KOR, LOG
  Hungarian, AKO
  Icelandic, FET
  Indian, GAZ, GUZ, JOW, KOS
  Japanese, BOO, CHO, KEN, RIN, SHO, SUN, TAN
  Malabar, ADY
  Metric land, ARE
  Netherlands, KAN, KOP, MUD, VAT, ZAK
  Norwegian, FOT, POT
  Persian, GAZ, GUZ, MOU, ZAR, ZER
  Polish, CAL
  Rangoon, DHA, LAN
  Roman, PES, URN
  Russian, FUT, LOF
  Scotch, COP
  Siamese, KEN, NIU, RAI, SAT, SEN, SOK, WAH, YOT
  Somaliland, TOP
  Spanish, PIE
  Straits Settlements, PAU, TUN
  Swedish, ALN, FOT, MIL, REF, TUM
  Swiss, POT
  Tunisian, SAA
  Turkish, OKA, OKE, PIK
  Wire, MIL
  Württemberg, IMI
  Yarn, LEA
  Yugoslavian, OKA, RIF
Milk, LAC
Milkfish, AWA
Moccasin, PAC
Money: Yap stone, FEI
Money of Account: Anglo-Saxon, ORA,

ORE
  French, SOU
  Indian, LAC
  Japanese, RIN
  Oman, GAJ
  Virgin Islands, BIT
  See also Coin
Monkey: Capuchin, SAI
Morsel, ORT
Mother: Peer Gynt's, ASE
Mountain: Asia Minor, IDA
Mulberry: Indian, AAL, ACH, AWL
Muttonbird: New Zealand, OII
Nahoor, SNA
Native: Mindanao, ATA
Neckpiece, BOA
Newt, EFT
No (Scotch), NAE
Note: Guido's highest, ELA
  Of scale, SOL
Nursemaid: Oriental, AMA, IYA
Ocher: Yellow, SIL
One (Scotch), YIN
Ornament: Pagoda, TEE
Oven: Polynesian, UMU
Ox: Tibetan, YAK
Pagoda: Chinese, TAA
Parrot: Hawk, HIA
  New Zealand, KEA
Part: Footlike, PES
Particle: Electrified, ION
Pasha, DEY
Pass: Mountain, COL
Paste: Rice, AME
Pea: Indian split, DAL
Peasant: Philippine, TAO
Penpoint, NEB, NIB
Piece out, EKE
Pigeon, NUN
Pine: Textile screw, ARA
Pistol (slang), GAT
Pit: Baking, IMU
Plant: Pepper, AVA
Play: By Capek, RUR
Poem: Old French, DIT
Porgy: Japanese, TAI
Priest: Biblical high, ELI
  Prince Ethiopian, RAS
Pseudonym: Dickens', BOZ
Queen: Fairy, MAB
Quince: Bengal, BEL
Record: Ship's, LOG
Refuse: Flax (Scotch), PAB, POB
Resin, LAC
Resort, SPA
Revolver (slang), GAT
Right: Cause to turn, GEE
River: Scotch or English, DEE
  (Spanish), RIO
  Swiss, AAR
Room: Harem, ODA
Rootstock: Fern, ROI
Rose (Persian), GUL
Ruff: Female, REE
Rule: Indian, RAJ
Sailor, GOB, TAR
Saint: Female (abbr.), STE
  Mohammedan, PIR
Salt, SAL
Sash: Japanese, OBI
Scrap, ORT
Seed: Poppy, MAW
  Small, PIP
Self, EGO
Serpent: Vedic sky, AHI
Sesame, TIL
Sheep: Female, EWE
  Indian, SHA
  Male, RAM
Sheepfold (Scotch), REE
Shelter, LEE
Shield, ECU
Shooting match (French), TIR
Shrew: European, ERD
Shrub: Evergreen, YEW
Silkworm, ERI

Snake, ASP, BOA
Soak, RET
Son-in-law: Mohammed's, ALI
Sorrel: Wood, OCA
Spade: Long, narrow, LOY
Spirit: Malignant, KER
Spot: Playing-card, PIP
Spread for drying, TED
Spring: Mineral, SPA
Sprite: Water, NIX
Statesman: Japanese, ITO
Stern: Toward, AFT
Stomach: Bird's, MAW
Street (French), RUE
Summer (French), ETE
Sun, SOL
Swamp, BOG, FEN
Swan: Male, COB
Tea: Chinese, CHA
Temple: Shinto, SHA
The. *See* Article
Thing (law), RES
Title: Etruscan, LAR
  Monk's, FRA
  Portuguese, DOM
  Spanish, DON
  Turkish, AGA, BEY
Tool: Cutting, ADZ, AXE
  Mining, GAD
  Piercing, AWL
Tree: Candlenut, AMA
  Central American, EBO
  East Indian, SAJ, SAL

Evergreen, YEW
Hawaiian, KOA, KOU
Indian, BEL, DAR
Linden, LIN
New Zealand, AKE
Philippine, DAO, TUA, TUI
Rubber, ULE
  South American, APA
Tribe: New Zealand, ATI
Turmeric, REA
Twice, BIS
Twin: Siamese, ENG
Uncle (dialect), EAM, EME
Veil: Chalice, AER, AIR
Vessel: Wine, AMA
Vestment: Ecclesiastical, ALB
Vetch: Bitter, ERS
Victorfish, AKU
Vine: New Zealand, AKA
  Philippine, IYO
Wallaba, APA
Wapiti, ELK
Water (French), EAU
Waterfall, LIN
Watering place: Prussian, EMS
Weave: Designating plain, UNI
Weight: Annamese, CAN
  Bulgarian, OKA, OKE
  Burmese, MOO, VIS
  Chinese, FEN, HAO, KIN, SSU, TAN,
    YIN
  Cyprus, OKA, OKE
  Danish, LOD, ORT, VOG

East Indian, TJI
Egyptian, KAT, OKA, OKE
English, for wool, TOD
German, LOT
Greek, MNA, OKA, OKE
Indian, SER
Japanese, FUN, KIN, RIN, SHI
Korean, KON
Malacca, KIP
Mongolian, LAN
Netherlands, ONS
Norwegian, LOD
Polish, LUT
Rangoon, PAI
Roman, BES
Russian, LOT
Siamese, BAT, HAP, PAI
Swedish, ASS, ORT
Turkish, OKA, OKE
Yugoslavian, OKA, OKE
Whales: Herd, GAM, POD
Wildebeest, GNU
Wing, ALA
Witticism, MOT
Wolframite, CAL
Worm: African, LOA
Wreath: Hawaiian, LEI
Yale, ELI
Yam: Hawaiian, HOI
Yes (French), OUI
Young: Bring forth, EAN
Z (letter), ZED

Words of Four Letters

Aborigine: Borneo, DYAK
Agave, ALOE
Animal: Footless, APOD
Ant: White, ANAI, ANAY
Antelope: African, ASSE, BISA, GUIB,
  KOBA, KUDU, ORYX, POKU, PUKU,
  TOPI, TORA
Apoplexy: Plant, ESCA
Apple, POME
Apricot, ANSU
Ardor, ELAN
Armadillo, APAR, PEBA, PEVA, TATU
Ascetic: Mohammedan, SUFI
Association: Chinese, TONG
Astronomer: Persian, OMAR
Avatar: Of Vishnu, RAMA
Axillary, ALAR
Band: Horizontal (heraldry), FESS
Barracuda, SPET
Bark: Mulberry, TAPA
Base: Column, DADO
Bearing (heraldry), ORLE
Beer: Russian, KVAS
Beige, ECRU
Being, ESSE
Beverage: Japanese rice, SAKE
Bird: Asian, MINA, MYNA
  Egyptian sacred, IBIS
  Extinct, DODO, MAMO
  Flightless, KIWI
  Gull-like, TERN
  Hawaiian, IIWI, MAMO
  Parson, KOKO
  Unfledged, EYAS
Birds: As class, AVES
Black, EBON
  (French), NOIR
Blackbird: European, MERL
Boat: Flat-bottomed, DORY
Bone: Forearm, ULNA
Bones, OSSA
Box, Japanese, INRO
Bravo (rare), EUGE
Buffalo: Indian wild, ARNA
Bull (Spanish), TORO
Burden, ONUS
Cabbage: Sliced, SLAW

Caliph: Mohammedan, OMAR
Canoe: Malay, PRAU, PROA
Cap: Military, KEPI
Cape, NESS
Capital: Ancient Irish, TARA
Case: Article, ETUI
Cat: Wild, BALU, EYRA
Chalcedony, SARD
Chamber: Indian ceremonial, KIVA
Channel: Brain, ITER
Cheese: Dutch, EDAM
Chest: Sepulchral stone, CIST
Chieftain: Arab, EMIR
Church: Part of, APSE, NAVE
  (Scotch), KIRK
Claim (law), LIEN
Cluster: Flower, CYME
Coin: Chinese, TAEL, YUAN
  German, MARK
  Indian, ANNA
  Iranian, RIAL
  Italian, LIRA
  Moroccan, OKIA
  Siamese, BAHT
  South American, PESO
  Spanish, DURO, PESO
  Turkish, PARA
Commune: Belgian, AATH
Composition: Musical, OPUS
Compound: Chemical, DIOL
Constellation: Southern, PAVO
Council: Russian, DUMA
Counsel, REDE
Covering: Seed, ARIL
Cross: Egyptian, ANKH
Cry: Bacchanalian, EVOE
Cup (Scotch), TASS
Cupbearer, SAKI
Dagger, DIRK
  Malay, KRIS
Dam: River, WEIR
Dash, ELAN
Date: Roman, IDES
Dawn: Pertaining to, EOAN
Dean: English, INGE
Decay: In fruit, BLET
Deer: Sambar, MAHA

Disease: Skin, ACNE
Disk: Solar, ATEN
Dog: Hunting, ALAN
Drink: Hindu intoxicating, SOMA
Duck, SMEE, SMEW, TEAL
Dynasty: Chinese, CHEN, CHIN, CHOU,
  CHOW, HSIA, MING, SUNG, TANG,
  TSIN
  Mongol, YUAN
Eagle: Biblical, GIER
  Sea, ERNE
Egyptian: Christian, COPT
Ear: Pertaining to, OTIC
Entrance: Mine, ADIT
Esau, EDOM
Escutcheon: Voided, ORLE
Eskers, OSAR
Evergreen: New Zealand, TAWA
Fairy: Persian, PERI
Family: Italian, ESTE
Far (comb. form), TELE
Farewell, VALE
Father (French), PERE
Fennel: Philippine, ANIS
Fever: Malarial, AGUE
Fiber: East Indian, JUTE
Firn, NEVE
Fish: Carplike, DACE
  Hawaiian, ULUA
  Herringlike, SHAD
  Mackerellike, CERO
  Marine, HAKE
  Sea, LING, MERO, OPAH
  Spiny-finned, GOBY
Food: Tropical, TARO
Foot: Metric, IAMB
Formerly, ERST
Founder: Of Carthage, DIDO
France: Southern, MIDI
Furze, ULEX
Gaelic, ERSE
Gaiter, SPAT
Game: Card, FARO, SKAT
Garlic: European wild, MOLY
Garment: Hindu, SARI
  Roman, TOGA
Gazelle, CORA

Gem, JADE, ONYX, OPAL, RUBY
Genus: Amphibians (incl. frogs), RANA
Amphibians (incl. tree toads), HYLA
Antelopes, ORYX
Auks, ALCA, URIA
Bees, APIS
Birds (American ostriches), RHEA
Birds (cranes), CRUS
Birds (magpies), PICA
Birds (peacocks), PAVO
Cetaceans, INIA
Ducks (incl. mallards), ANAS
Fishes (burbots), LOTA
Fishes (incl. bowfins), AMIA
Geese (snow geese), CHEN
Gulls, XEMA
Herbs, ARUM, GEUM
Insects (water scorpions), NEPA
Lilies, ALOE
Mammals (mankind), HOMO
Orchids, DISA
Owls, ASIO, BUBO, OTUS
Palms, NIPA
Sea birds, SULA
Sheep, OVIS
Shrubs, Eurasian, ULEX
Shrubs (hollies), ILEX
Shrubs (incl. Virginia Willow), ITEA
Shrubs, tropical, EVEA
Snakes (sand snakes), ERYX
Swans, OLOR
Trees, chocolate, COLA
Trees (ebony family), MABA
Trees (incl. maples), ACER
Trees (olives), OLEA
Trees, tropical, EVEA
Turtles, EMYS
Goat: Wild, IBEX, KRAS, TAHR, TAIR, THAR
God: Assyrian, ASUR
Babylonian, ADAD, ADUU, ENKI, ENZU, IRRA, NABU, NEBO, UTUG
Celtic, LLEU, LLEW
Hindu, AGNI, CIVA, DEVA, DEWA, KAMA, RAMA, SIVA, VAYU
Phrygian, ATYS
Semitic, BAAL
Teutonic, HLER
Goddess: Babylonian, ERUA, GULA
Hawaiian, PELE
Hindu, DEVI, KALI, SHRI, VACH
Gooseberry: Hawaiian, POHA
Gourd, PEPO
Grafted (heraldry), ENTE
Grandfather (obsolete), AIEL
Grandparents: Pertaining to, AVAL
Grass: Hawaiian, HILO
Gray (French), GRIS
Green (heraldry), VERT
Groom: Indian, SYCE
Half (prefix), DEMI, HEMI, SEMI
Hamlet, DORP
Hammer-head: Part of, PEEN
Handle, ANSA
Harp: Japanese, KOTO
Hartebeest, ASSE, TORA
Hautboy, OBOE
Hawk: Taken from nest (falconry), EYAS
Hearing (law), OYER
Heater: For liquids, ETNA
Herb: Aromatic, ANET, DILL
Fabulous, MOLY
Perennial, GEUM, SEGO
Pot, WORT
Used for blue dye, WADE, WOAD
Hill: Flat-topped, MESA
Sand, DENE, DUNE
Hoarfrost, RIME
Hog: Immature female, GILT
Holly, ILEX
House: Cow, BYRE
(Spanish), CASA
Ice: Floating, FLOE
Image, ICON, IKON

Incarnation: Of Vishnu, RAMA
Indian: Algonquian, CREE, SAUK
Central American, MAYA
Iroquoian, ERIE
Mexican, CORA
Peruvian, CANA, INCA, MORO
Shoshonean, HOPI
Siouan, OTOE
Southwestern, HOPI, PIMA, YUMA, ZUNI
Insect: Immature, PUPA
Instrument: Stringed, LUTE, LYRE
Ireland, EIRE, ERIN
Jacket: English, ETON
Jail (British), GAOL
Jar, OLLA
Judge: Mohammedan, CADI
Juniper: European, CADE
Kiln, OAST, OVEN
King: British legendary, LUDD, NUDD
Kiss, BUSS
Knife: Philippine, BOLO
Koran: Section of, SURA
Laborer: Spanish American, PEON
Lake: Mountain, TARN
(Scotch), LOCH
Lamp: Miner's, DAVY
Landing place: Indian, GHAT
Language: Buddhist, PALI
Japanese, AINU
Latvian, LETT
Layer: Of iris, UVEA
Leaf: Palm, OLAY, OLLA
Legislature: Ukrainian, RADA
Lemur, LORI
Leopard, PARD
Let it stand, STET
Letter: Greek, BETA, IOTA, ZETA
Hebrew, AYIN, BETH, CAPH, KOPH, RESH, SHIN, TETH, YODH
Papal, BULL
Lily, ALOE
Literature: Hindu sacred, VEDA
Lizard, GILA
Monitor, URAN
Loquat, BIWA
Magistrate: Genoese or Venetian, DOGE
Man (Latin), HOMO
Mark: Omission, DELE
armoset: South American, MICO
Meadow: Fertile, VEGA
Measure: Electric, VOLT, WATT
Force, DYNE
Hebrew, OMER
Printing, PICA
Spanish or Portuguese, VARA
Swiss land, IMMI
Medley, OLIO
Merganser, SMEW
Milk (French), LAIT
Molding, GULA
Curved, OGEE
Mongoose: Crab-eating, URVA
Monk: Tibetan, LAMA
Monkey: African, MONA, WAAG
Ceylonese, MAHA
Cochin-China, DOUC
South American, SAKI, TITI
Monkshood, ATIS
Month: Jewish, ADAR, ELUL, IYAR
Mother (French), MERE
Mountain: Thessaly, OSSA
Mouse: Meadow, VOLE
Mythology: Norse, EDDA
Nail (French), CLOU
Native: Philippine, MORO
Nest: Of pheasants, NIDE
Network, RETE
No (German), NEIN
Noble: Mohammedan, AMIR
Notice: Death, OBIT
Novel: By Zola, NANA
Nursemaid: Oriental AMAH, AYAH, EYAH
Nut: Philippine, PILI

Oak: Holm, ILEX
Oil (comb. form), OLEO
Ostrich: American, RHEA
Oven, KILN, OAST
Owl: Barn, LULU
Ox: Celebes wild, ANOE
Extinct wild, URUS
Palm, ATAP, NIPA, SAGO
Parliament, DIET
Parrot: New Zealand, KAKA
Pass: Indian mountain, GHAT
Passage: Closing (music), CODA
Peach: Clingstone, PAVY
Peasant: Indian, RYOT
Old English, CARL
Pepper: Australasian, KAVA
Perfume, ATAR
Persia, IRAN
Person: Extraordinary, ONER
Pickerel or pike, ESOX
Pitcher, EWER
Plant: Aromatic, NARD
Century, ALOE
Indigo, ANIL
Pepper, KAVA
Platform: Raised, DAIS
Plum: Wild, SLOE
Pods: Vegetable, OKRA, OKRO
Poem: Epic, EPOS
Poet: Persian, OMAR
Roman, OVID
Poison, BANE
Arrow, INEE
Porkfish, SISI
Portico: Greek, STOA
Premium, AGIO
Priest: Mohammedan, IMAM
Prima donna, DIVA
Prong: Fork, TINE
Pseudonym: Lamb's, ELIA
Queen: Carthaginian, DIDO
Hindu, RANI
Rabbit, CONY
Race: Of Japan, AINU
Rail: Ducklike, COOT
North American, SORA
Redshank, CLEE
Refuse: After pressing, MARC
Regiment: Turkish, ALAI
Reliquary, ARCA
Resort: Italian, LIDO
Ridges: Sandy, ASAR, OSAR
River: German, ELBE, ODER
Italian, ADDA
Siberian, LENA
Road: Roman, ITER
Rockfish: California, RENA
Rodent: Mouselike, VOLE
South American, PACA
Rootstock, TARO
Salamander, NEWT
Salmon: Silver, COHO
Young, PARR
Same (Greek), HOMO
(Latin), IDEM
Sauce: Fish, ALEC
School: English, ETON
Seaweed, AGAR, ALGA, KELP
Secular, LAIC
Sediment, SILT
Seed: Dill, ANET
Of vetch, TARE
Serf, ILOT
Sesame, TEEL
Settlement: Eskimo, ETAH
Shark: Atlantic, GATA
European, TOPE
Sheep: Wild, UDAD
Sheltered, ALEE
Shield, EGIS
Ship: Jason's, ARGO
Left side of, PORT
Two-masted, BRIG
Shrine: Buddhist, TOPE
Shrub: New Zealand, TUTU

Sign: Magic, RUNE
Silkworm, ERIA
Skin: Beaver, PLEW
Skink: Egyptian, ADDA
Slave, ESNE
Sloth: Two-toed, UNAU
Smooth, LENE
Snow: Glacial, NEVE
Soapstone, TALC
Society: African secret, EGBO, PORO
Son: Of Seth, ENOS
Song (German), LIED
  Unaccompanied, GLEE
Sound: Lung, RALE
Sour, ACID
Sow: Young, GILT
Spike: Brad-shaped, BROB
Spirit: Buddhist evil, MARA
Stake: Poker, ANTE
Star: Temporary, NOVA
Starch: East Indian, SAGO
Stone: Precious, OPAL
Strap: Bridle, REIN
Strewn (heraldry), SEME
Sweetsop, ATES, ATTA
Sword: Fencing, EPEE, FOIL
Tambourine: African, TAAR
Tapir: Brazilian, ANTA
Tax, CESS
Tea: South American, MATE
Therefore (Latin), ERGO
Thing: Extraordinary, ONER
Three (dice, cards, etc.), TREY
Thrush: Hawaiian, OMAO

Tide, NEAP
Tipster: Racing, TOUT
Tissue, TELA
Title: Etruscan, LARS
  Hindu, BABU
  Indian, RAJA
  Mohammedan, EMIR, IMAM
  Persian, BABA
  Spanish, DONA
  Turkish, AGHA, BABA
Toad: Largest-known, AGUA
  Tree, HYLA
Tool: Cutting, ADZE
Track: Deer, SLOT
Tract: Sandy, DENE
Tree: Apple, SORB
  Central American, EBOE
  East Indian, TEAK
  Eucalyptus, YATE
  Guiana and Trinidad, MORA
  Javanese, UPAS
  Linden, LIME, LINN, TEIL, TILL
  Sandarac, ARAR
  Sassafras, AGUE
  Tamarisk salt, ATLE
Tribe: Moro, SULU
Trout, CHAR
Urchin: Street, ARAB
Vessel: Arab, DHOW
Vestment: Ecclesiastical, COPE
Vetch, TARE
Vine: East Indian, SOMA
Violinist: Famous, AUER
Vortex, EDDY

Wampum, PEAG
Wapiti, STAG
Waste: Allowance for, TRET
Watchman: Indian, MINA
Water (Spanish), AGUA
Waterfall, LINN
Wavy (heraldry), ONDE, UNDE
Wax, CERE
  Chinese, PELA
Weed: Biblical, TARE
Weight: Ancient, MINA
  Danish (pl.), ESER
  East Asian, TAEL
  Greek, MINA
  Siamese, BAHT
Well done (rare), EUGE
Whale, CETE
  Killer, ORCA
  White, HUSE, HUSO
Whirlpool, EDDY
Wife: Of Geraint, ENID
Willow: Virginia, ITEA
Wine, PORT
Winged, ALAR
  (Heraldry), AILE
Wings, ALAE
Withered, SERE
Without (French), SANS
Wool: To comb, CARD
Work, OPUS
Wrong: Civil, TORT
Young: Bring forth, YEAN

Words of Five Letters

Abode of dead: Babylonian, ARALU
Aborigine: Borneo DAYAK
Aftersong, EPODE
Aloe, AGAVE
Animal: Footless, APODE
Ant, EMMET
Antelope: African, ADDAX, BEISA, CAAMA, ELAND, GUIBA,
  ORIBI, TIANG
  Goat, GORAL, SEROW
  Indian, SASIN
  Siberian, SAIGA
Arch: Pointed, OGIVE
Armadillo, APARA, POYOU, TATOU
Arrowroot, ARARU
Artery: Trunk, AORTA
Association: Russian, ARTEL
  Secret, CABAL
Author: English, READE
Automaton, GOLEM, ROBOT
Award: Motion-picture, OSCAR
Basket: Fishing, CREEL
Beer: Russian, KVASS
Bible: Mohammedan, KORAN
Bird: Asian, MINAH, MYNAH
  Indian, SHAMA
  Larklike, PIPIT
  Loonlike, GREBE
  Oscine, VIREO
  South American, AGAMI
  Swimming, GREBE
Black: (French), NOIRE
  (Heraldry), SABLE
Blackbird: European, MERLE, OUSEL, OUZEL
Block: Glacial, SERAC
Blue (heraldry), AZURE
Boat: Eskimo, BIDAR, UMIAK
Bobwhite, COLIN, QUAIL
Bone (comb. form), OSTEO
  Leg, TIBIA
  Thigh, FEMUR
Broom: Twig, BESOM
Brother (French), FRERE
  Moses, AARON
Canoe: Eskimo, BIDAR, KAYAK
Cape: Papal, FANON, ORALE
Caravansary, SERAI

Card: Old playing, TAROT
Caterpillar: New Zealand, AWETO
Catkin, AMENT
Cavity: Stone, GEODE
Cephalopod, SQUID
Cetacean, WHALE
Chariot, ESSED
Cheek: Pertaining to, MALAR
Chieftain: Arab, EMEER
Child (Scotch), BAIRN
Cigar, CLARO
Coating: Seed, TESTA
Cockatoo: Palm, ARARA
Coin: Costa Rican, COLON
  Danish, KRONE
  Ecuadorian, SUCRE
  English, GROAT, PENCE
  French, FRANC
  German, KRONE, TALER
  Hungarian, PENGO
  Icelandic, KRONA
  Indian, RUPEE
  Iraqi, DINAR
  Norwegian, KRONE
  Polish, ZLOTY
  Russian, COPEC, KOPEK, RUBLE
  Swedish, KRONA
  Turkish, ASPER
  Yugoslav, DINAR
Collar: Papal, FANON, ORALE
  Roman, RABAT
Commune: Italian, TREIA
Composition: Choral, MOTET
Compound: Chemical, ESTER
Conceal (law), ELOIN
Council: Ecclesiastical, SYNOD
Court: Anglo-Saxon, GEMOT
  Inner, PATIO
Crest: Mountain, ARETE
Crown: Papal, TIARA
Cuttlefish, SEPIA
Date: Roman, NONES
Decree: Mohammedan, IRADE
  Russian, UKASE
Deposit: Loam, LOESS
Desert: Gobi, SHAMO

Devilfish, MANTA
Disease: Cereals, ERGOT
Disk, PATEN
Dog: Wild, DHOLE, DINGO
Dormouse, LEROT
Drum, TABOR
Duck: Sea, EIDER
Dynasty: Chinese, CHING, LIANG, SHANG
Earthquake, SEISM
Eel, ELVER, MORAY
Ermine: European, STOAT
Ether: Crystalline, APIOL
Fabric: Velvetlike, PANNE
Fabulist, AESOP
Family: Italian, CENCI
Fiber: West Indian, SISAL
Fig: Smyrna, ELEME, ELEMI
Figure: Of speech, TROPE
Finch: European, SERIN
Fish: American small, KILLY
Flower: Garden, ASTER
Friend (Spanish), AMIGO
Fruit: Tropical, MANGO
Fungus: Rye, ERGOT
Furze, GORSE
Gateway, TORAN, TORII
Gem, AGATE, BERYL, PEARL, TOPAZ
Genus: Barnacles, LEPAS
   Bears, URSUS
   Birds (loons), GAVIA
   Birds (nuthatches), SITTA
   Cats, FELIS
   Dogs, CANIS
   Fishes (chiros), ELOPS
   Fishes (perch), PERCA
   Geese, ANSER
   Grasses, STIPA
   Grasses (incl. oats), AVENA
   Gulls, LARUS
   Hares, rabbits, LEPUS
   Hawks, BUTEO
   Herbs, old world, INULA
   Herbs, trailing or climbing, APIOS
   Herbs, tropical, TACCA, URENA
   Horses, EQUUS
   Insects (olive flies), DACUS
   Lice, plant, APHIS
   Lichens, USNEA
   Lizards, AGAMA
   Moles, TALPA
   Mollusks, OLIVA
   Monkeys, CEBUS
   Palms, ARECA
   Pigeons, GOURA
   Plants (amaryllis family), AGAVE
   Ruminants (goats), CAPRA
   Shrubs, Asiatic, SABIA
   Shrubs (heath), ERICA
   Shrubs (incl. raspberry), RUBUS
   Shrubs, tropical, IXORA, TREMA, URENA
   Ticks, ARGAS
   Trees (of elm family), TREMA, ULMUS
   Trees, tropical, IXORA, TREMA
Goat: Bezoar, PASAN
God: Assyrian, ASHIR, ASHUR, ASSUR
   Babylonian, DAGAN, SIRIS
   Gaelic, DAGDA
   Hindu, BHAGA, INDRA, SHIVA
   Japanese, EBISU
   Philistine, DAGON
   Phrygian, ATTIS
   Teutonic, AEGIR, GYMIR
   Welsh, DYLAN
Goddess: Babylonian, ISTAR, NANAI
   Hindu, DURGA, GAURI, SHREE
Group: Of six, HEXAD
Grove: Sacred to Diana, NEMUS
Growing out, ENATE
Guitar: Hindu, SITAR
Gull: PEWEE, PEWIT
Hartebeest, CAAMA
Headdress: Jewish or Persian, TIARA
   Liturgical, MITER, MITRE
Heath, ERICA
Herb: Grasslike marsh, SEDGE
Heron, EGRET

Hog: Young, SHOAT, SHOTE
Image, EIKON
Indian: Cariban, ARARA
   Iroquoian, HURON
   Mexican, AZTEC, OPATA, OTOMI
   Muskhogean, CREEK
   Siouan, OSAGE, TETON
   Spanish American, ARARA, CARIB
Inflorescence: Racemose, AMENT
Insect: Immature, LARVA
Intrigue, CABAL
Iris: Yellow, SEDGE
Juniper, GORSE, RETEM
Kidneys: Pertaining to, RENAL
King: British legendary, LLUDD
Kite: European, GLEDE
Kobold, NISSE
Land: Cultivated, ARADA, ARADO
   Landholder (Scotch), LAIRD, THANE
Language: Dravidian, TAMIL
Lariat, LASSO, REATA
Laughing, RIANT
Lawgiver: Athenian, DRACO, SOLON
Leaf: Calyx, SEPAL
   Fern, FROND
Lemur, LORIS
Letter: English, AITCH
   Greek, ALPHA, DELTA, GAMMA, KAPPA, OMEGA,
      SIGMA, THETA
   Hebrew, ALEPH, CHETH, GIMEL, SADHE, ZAYIN
Lichen, USNEA
Lighthouse, PHARE
Lizard: Old World, AGAMA
Loincloth, DHOTI
Louse: Plant, APHID
Macaw: Brazilian, ARARA
Mahogany: Philippine, ALMON
Mammal: Badgerlike, RATEL
   Civetlike, GENET
   Giraffelike, OKAPI
   Raccoonlike, COATI
Man (French), HOMME
Marble, AGATE
Mark: Insertion, CARET
Market place: Greek, AGORA
Marsupial: Australian, KOALA
Measure: Electric, FARAD, HENRY
   Energy, JOULE
   Metric, LITER, STERE
   Printing, AGATE
   Russian, VERST
Mixture: Smelting, MATTE
Mohicans: Last of, UNCAS
Molding: Convex, OVOLO, TORUS
Mole, TALPA
Monkey: African, PATAS
   Capuchin, SAJOU
   Howling, ARABA
Monkshood, ATEES
Month: Jewish, NISAN, SIVAN, TEBET
Museum (French), MUSEE
Musketeer, ATHOS
Native: Aleutian, ALEUT
   New Zealand, MAORI
Neckpiece: Ecclesiastical, AMICE
Nerve (comb. form), NEURO
Nest: Eagle's or hawk's, AERIE
   Insect's, NIDUS
Net: Fishing, SEINE
Newsstand, KIOSK
Nitrogen, AZOTE
Noble: Mohammedan, AMEER
Nodule: Stone, GEODE
Nostrils, NARES
Notched irregularly, EROSE
Nymph: Mohammedan, HOURI
Official: Roman, EDILE
Oleoresin, ELEMI
Opening: Mouthlike, STOMA
Oration: Funeral, ELOGE
Ostiole, STOMA
Page: Left-hand, VERSO
   Right-hand, RECTO
Palm, ARECA, BETEL
Park: Colorado, ESTES
Perfume, ATTAR

Philosopher: Greek, PLATO
Pillar: Stone, STELA, STELE
Pinnacle: Glacial, SERAC
Plain, LLANO
Plant: Century, AGAVE
   Climbing, LIANA
   Dwarf, CUMIN
   East Asian perennial, RAMIE
   Medicinal, SENNA
   Mustard family, CRESS
Plate: Communion, PATEN
Poem: Lyric, EPODE
Point: Lowest, NADIR
Poplar, ABELE, ALAMO, ASPEN
Porridge: Spanish American, ATOLE
Post: Stair, NEWEL
Priest: Mohammedan, IMAUM
Protozoan, AMEBA
Queen: (French), REINE
   Hindu, RANEE
Rabbit, CONEY
Rail, CRAKE
Red (heraldry), GULES
Religion: Moslem, ISLAM
Resin, ELEMI
Revoke (law), ADEEM
Rich man, MIDAS, NABOB
Ridge: Sandy, ESKAR, ESKER
River: French, LOIRE, SEINE
Rockfish: California, REINA
Rootstock: Fragrant, ORRIS
Ruff: Female, REEVE
Sack: Pack, KYACK
Salt: Ethereal, ESTER
Saltpeter, NITER, NITRE
Salutation: Eastern, SALAM
Sandpiper: Old World, TEREK
Scented, OLENT
School: Fish, SHOAL
   French public, LYCEE
Scriptures: Mohammedan, KORAN
Seaweeds, ALGAE
Seed: Aromatic, ANISE
Seraglio, HAREM, SERAI
Serf, HELOT
Sheep: Wild, AUDAD
Sheeplike, OVINE
Shield, AEGIS
Shoe: Wooden, SABOT
Shoots: Pickled bamboo, ACHAR
Shot: Billiard, CAROM, MASSE
Shrine: Buddhist, STUPA
Shrub: Burning bush, WAHOO
   Ornamental evergreen, TOYON
   Used in tanning, SUMAC
Silk: Watered, MOIRE
Sister (French), SOEUR
   (Latin), SOROR
Six: Group of, HEXAD
Skeleton: Marine, CORAL

Slave, HELOT
Snake, ABOMA, ADDER, COBRA, RACER
Soldier: French, POILU
   Indian, SEPOY
Sour, ACERB
Spirit: Air, ARIEL
Staff: Shepherd's, CROOK
Starwort, ASTER
Steel (German), STAHL
Stockade: Russian, ETAPE
Stop (nautical), AVAST
Storehouse, ETAPE
Subway: Parisian, METRO
Tapestry, ARRAS
Tea: Paraguayan, YERBA
Temple: Hawaiian, HEIAU
Terminal: Positive, ANODE
Theater: Greek, ODEON, ODEUM
Then (French), ALORS
Thread: Surgical, SETON
Thrush: Wilson's, VEERY
Title: Hindu, BABOO
   Indian, RAJAH, SAHEB, SAHIB
   Mohammedan, EMEER, IMAUM
Tree: Buddhist sacred, PIPAL
   East Indian cotton, SIMAL
   Hickory, PECAN
   Light-wooded, BALSA
   Malayan, TERAP
   Mediterranean, CAROB
   Mexican, ABETO
   Mexican pine, OCOTE
   New Zealand, MAIRE
   Philippine, ALMON
   Rain, SAMAN
   South American, UMBRA
   Tamarack, LARCH
   Tamarisk salt, ATLEE
   West Indian, ACANA
Trout, CHARR
Troy, ILION, ILIUM
Twin: Siamese, CHANG
Vestment: Ecclesiastical, STOLE
Violin: Famous, AMATI, STRAD
Volcano: Mud, SALSE
Wampum, PEAGE
War cry: Greek, ALALA
Wavy (heraldry), UNDEE
Weight: Jewish, GERAH
Wen, TALPA
Wheat, SPELT
Wheel: Persian water, NORIA
Whitefish, CISCO
Willow, OSIER
Window: Bay, ORIEL
Wine, MEDOC, RHINE, TINTA, TOKAY
Winged, ALATE
Woman (French), FEMME
Year: Excess of solar over lunar, EPACT
Zoroastrian, PARSI

Words of Six or More Letters

Agave, MAGUEY
Alkaloid: Crystalline, ESERIN, ESERINE
Alligator, CAYMAN
Amphibole, EDENITE, URALITE
Ant: White, TERMITE
Antelope: African, DIKDIK, DUIKER, GEMSBOK, IMPALA,
   KOODOO
   European, CHAMOIS
   Indian, NILGAI, NILGAU, NILGHAI, NILGHAU
Ape: Asian or East Indian, GIBBON
Appendage: Leaf, STIPEL, STIPULE
Armadillo, PELUDO, TATOUAY
Arrowroot, ARARAO
Ascetic: Jewish, ESSENE
Ass: Asian wild, ONAGER
Avatar: Of Vishnu, KRISHNA
Babylonian, ELAMITE
Badge: Shoulder, EPAULET
Baldness, ALOPECIA

Barracuda, SENNET
Bark: Aromatic, SINTOC
Bearlike, URSINE
Beetle, ELATER
Bible: Zoroastrian, AVESTA
Bird: Sea, PETREL
   South American, SERIEMA
   Wading, AVOCET, AVOSET
Bone: Leg, FIBULA
Branched, RAMATE
Brother (Latin), FRATER
Bunting: European, ORTOLAN
Call: Trumpet, SENNET
Canoe: Eskimo, BAIDAR, OOMIAK
Caravansary, IMARET
Cat: Asian or African, CHEETAH
   Leopardlike, OCELOT
Cenobite: Jewish, ESSENE
Centerpiece: Table, EPERGNE

Cetacean, DOLPHIN, PORPOISE
Chariot, ESSEDA, ESSEDE
Chief: Seminole, OSCEOLA
Claim: Release as (law), REMISE
Clock: Water, CLEPSYDRA
Cloud, CUMULUS, NIMBUS
Coach: French hackney, FIACRE
Coin: Czech, KORUNA
  Ethiopian, TALARI
  Finnish, MARKKA
  German, THALER
  Greek, DRACHMA
  Haitian, GOURDE
  Honduran, LEMPIRA
  Hungarian, FORINT
  Indo-Chinese, PIASTER
  Netherlands, GUILDER
  Panamanian, BALBOA
  Paraguayan, GUARANI
  Portuguese, ESCUDO
  Russian, COPECK, KOPECK, ROUBLE
  Spanish, PESETA
  Venezuelan, BOLIVAR
Communion: Last holy, VIATICUM
Conceal (law), ELOIGN
Confection, PRALINE
Construction: Sentence, SYNTAX
Convexity: Shaft of column, ENTASIS
Court: Anglo-Saxon, GEMOTE
Cow: Sea, DUGONG, MANATEE
Cylindrical, TERETE
Dagger, STILETTO
  Malay, CREESE, KREESE
Date: Roman, CALENDS, KALENDS
Deer, CARIBOU, WAPITI
Disease: Plant, ERINOSE
Doorkeeper, OSTIARY
Dragonflies: Order of, ODANATA
Drink: Of gods, NECTAR
Drum: TABOUR
  Moorish, ATABAL, ATTABAL
Duck: Fish-eating, MERGANSER
  Sea, SCOTER
Dynasty: Chinese, MANCHU
Eel, CONGER
Edit, REDACT
Envelope: Flower, PERIANTH
Eskimo, AMERIND
Ether: Crystalline, APIOLE
Excuse (law), ESSOIN
Eyespots, OCELLI
Fabric, ESTAMENE, ESTAMIN, ETAMINE
Falcon: European, KESTREL
Figure: Used as column, CARYATID, TELAMON
Fine: For punishment, AMERCE
Fish: Asian fresh-water, GOURAMI
  Pikelike, BARRACUDA
Five: Group of, PENTAD
Fly: African, TSETSE
Foot: Metric, ANAPEST, IAMBUS
Foxlike, VULPINE
Frying pan, SPIDER
Fur, KARAKUL
Galley: Greek or Roman, BIREME, TRIREME
Game: Card, ECARTE
Garment: Greek, CHLAMYS
Gateway, GOPURA, TORANA
Genus: Birds (ravens, crows), CORVUS
  Eels, CONGER
  Fishes, ANABAS
  Foxes, VULPES
  Herbs, ANEMONE
  Insects, CICADA
  Lemurs, GALAGO
  Mints (incl. catnip), NEPETA
  Mollusks, ANOMIA, ASTARTE, TEREDO
  Mollusks (incl. oysters), OSTREA
  Monkeys (spider monkeys), ATELES
  Thrushes (incl. robins), TURDUS
  Trees (of elm family), CELTIS
  Trees (inc. dogwood), CORNUS
  Trees, tropical American, SAPOTA
  Wrens, NANNUS
Gibbon, SIAMANG, WOUWOU
Gland: Salivary, RACEMOSE
Goat: Bezoar, PASANG

Goatlike, CAPRINE
God: Assyrian, ASHSHUR, ASSHUR
  Babylonian, BABBAR, MARDUK, MERODACH, NANNAR,
    NERGAL, SHAMASH
  Hindu, BRAHMA, KRISHNA, VISHNU
  Tahitian, TAAROA
Goddess: Babylonian, ISHTAR
  Hindu, CHANDI, HAIMAVATI, LAKSHMI, PARVATI,
    SARASVATI, SARASWATI
Government, POLITY
Governor: Persian, SATRAP
Grandson (Scotch), NEPOTE
Group: Of five, PENTAD
  Of nine, ENNEAD
  Of seven, HEPTAD
Hare: in first year, LEVERET
Harpsichord, SPINET
Herb: Alpine, EDELWEISS
  Chinese, GINSENG
  South African, FREESIA
Hermit, EREMITE
Hero: Legendary, PALADIN
Heron, BITTERN
Horselike, EQUINE
Hound: Short-legged, BEAGLE
House (French), MAISON
Idiot, CRETIN
Implement: Stone, NEOLITH
Incarnation: Hindu, AVATAR ▪
Indian, APACHE, COMANCHE, PAIUTE, SENECA
Inn: Turkish, IMARET
Insects: Order of, DIPTERA
Instrument: Japanese banjolike, SAMISEN
  Musical, CLAVIER, SPINET
Interstice, AREOLA
Ironwood, COLIMA
Juniper: Old Testament, RAETAM
Kettledrum, ATABAL
King: Fairy, OBERON
Kneecap, PATELLA
Knife, MACHETE
Langur: Sumatran, SIMPAI
Legislature: Spanish, CORTES
Lemur: African, GALAGO
  Madagascar, AYEAYE
Letter: Greek, EPSILON, LAMBDA, OMICRON, UPSILON
  Hebrew, DALETH, LAMEDH , SAMEKH
Lighthouse, PHAROS
Lizard, IGUANA
Llama, ALPACA
Lockjaw, TETANUS
Locust, CICADA, CICALA
Macaw: Brazilian, MARACAN
Maid: Of Astolat, ELAINE
Mammal: Madagascar, TENDRAC, TENREC
Man (Spanish), HOMBRE
Marmoset: South American, TAMARIN
Marsupial, BANDICOOT, WOMBAT
Massacre, POGROM
Mayor: Spanish, ALCALDE
Measure: Electric, AMPERE, COULOMB, KILOWATT
Medicine: Quack, NOSTRUM
Member: Religious order, CENOBITE
Molasses, TREACLE
Monkey: African, GRIVET, NISNAS
  Asian, LANGUR
  Philippine, MACHIN
  South American, PINCHE, SAIMIRI, SAMIRI, SAPAJOU
Monster, CHIMERA, GORGON
  (Comb. form), TERATO
  Cretan, MINOTAUR
Month: Jewish, HESHVAN, KISLEV, SHEBAT, TAMMUZ,
    TISHRI, VEADAR
Mountain: Asia Minor, ARARAT
Mulct, AMERCE
Musketeer, ARAMIS, PORTHOS
Nearsighted, MYOPIC
Net, TRAMMEL
New York City, GOTHAM
Nine: Group of, ENNEAD
Nobleman: Spanish, GRANDEE
Official: Roman, AEDILE
Onyx: Mexican, TECALI
Order: Dragonflies, ODANATA
  Insects, DIPTERA
Organ: Plant, PISTIL

Ornament: Shoulder, EPAULET
Overcoat: Military, CAPOTE
Ox: Wild, BANTENG
Oxidation: Bronze or copper, PATINA
Paralysis: Incomplete, PARESIS
Pear: Alligator, AVOCADO
Persimmon: Mexican, CHAPOTE
Pipe: Peace, CALUMET
Plaid (Scotch), TARTAN
Plain, PAMPAS, STEPPE, TUNDRA
Plant: Buttercup family, ANEMONE
  Century, MAGUEY
  On rocks, LICHEN
Plowing: Fit for, ARABLE
Poem: Heroic, EPOPEE
  Six-lined, SESTET
Point: Highest, ZENITH
Potion: Love, PHILTER, PHILTRE
Protozoan, AMOEBA
Punish, AMERCE
Purple (heraldry), PURPURE
Queen: Fairy, TITANIA
Race: Skiing, SLALOM
Rat, BANDICOOT, LEMMING
Retort, RIPOST, RIPOSTE
Ring: Harness, TERRET
  Little, ANNULET
Rodent: Jumping, JERBOA
  Spanish American, AGOUTI, AGOUTY
Sailor: East Indian, LASCAR
Salmon: Young, GRILSE
Salutation: Eastern, SALAAM
Sandpiper, PLOVER
Sandy, ARENOSE
Sapodilla, SAPOTA, SAPOTE
Saw: Surgical, TREPAN
Seven: Group of, HEPTAD
Sexes: Common to both, EPICENE
Shawl: Mexican, SERAPE
Sheathing: Flower, SPATHE
Sheep: Wild, AOUDAD, ARGALI
Shipworm, TEREDO
Shoes: Mercury's winged, TALARIA
Shortening: Syllable, SYSTOLE
Shrub, SPIRAEA
Sickle-shaped, FALCATE

Silver (heraldry), ARGENT
Snake, ANACONDA
Speech: Loss of, APHASIA
Spiral, HELICAL
Staff: Bishop's, CROSIER, CROZIER
Stalk: Plant, PETIOLE
State: Swiss, CANTON
Studio, ATELIER
Swan: Young, CYGNET
Swimming, NATANT
Sword-shaped, ENSATE
Terminal: Negative, CATHODE
Third (music), TIERCE
Thrust: Fencing, RIPOST, RIPOSTE
Tile: Pertaining to, TEGULAR
Tomb: Empty, CENOTAPH
Tooth (comb. form), ODONTO
Tower: Mohammedan, MINARET
Tree: African timber, BAOBAB
  Black gum, TUPELO
  East Indian, MARGOSA
  Locust, ACACIA
  Malayan, SINTOC
  Marmalade, SAPOTE
Urn: Tea, SAMOVAR
Vehicle, LANDAU, TROIKA
Verbose, PROLIX
Viceroy: Egyptian, KHEDIVE
Vulture: American, CONDOR
Warehouse (French), ENTREPOT
Whale: White, BELUGA
Whirlpool, VORTEX
Will: Addition to, CODICIL
  Having left, TESTATE
Wind, CHINOOK, MONSOON, SIMOOM, SIMOON, SI-
ROCCO
Window: In roof, DORMER

Wine, BARBERA, BURGUNDY, CABERNET, CHABLIS, CHI-
ANTI, CLARET, MUSCATEL, RIESLING, SAUTERNE,
SHERRY, ZINFANDEL

Wolfish, LUPINE
Woman: Boisterous, TERMAGANT
Woolly, LANATE
Workshop, ATELIER
Zoroastrian, PARSEE

Old-Testament Names

(We do not pretend that this list is all-inclusive. We include only those names which in our opinion one meets most often in crossword puzzles.)

Aaron: First high priest of Jews; son of Amram; brother of Miriam and Moses; father of Abihu, Eleazer, Ithamar, and Nadab.
Abel: Son of Adam; slain by Cain.
Abigail: Wife of Nabal; later, wife of David.
Abihu: Son of Aaron.
Abimelech: King of Gerar.
Abner: Commander of army of Saul and Ishbosheth; slain by Joab.
Abraham (or Abram): Patriarch; forefather of the Jews; son of Terah; husband of Sarah; father of Isaac and Ishmael.
Absalom: Son of David and Maacah; revolted against David; slain by Joab.
Achish: King of Gath; gave refuge to David.
Achsa (or Achsah): Daughter of Caleb; wife of Othniel.
Adah: Wife of Lamech.
Adam: First man; husband of Eve; father of Cain, Abel, and Seth.
Adonijah: Son of David and Haggith.
Agag: King of Amalek; spared by Saul; slain by Samuel.
Ahasuerus: King of Persia; husband of Vashti and, later, Esther; sometimes identified with Xerxes the Great.
Ahijah: Prophet; foretold accession of Jeroboam.
Ahinoam: Wife of David.
Amasa: Commander of army of David; slain by Joab.
Amnon: Son of David and Ahinoam; ravished Tamar; slain by Absalom.
Amram: Husband of Jochebed; father of Aaron, Miriam and Moses.

Asenath: Wife of Joseph.
Asher: Son of Jacob and Zilpah.
Balaam: Prophet; rebuked by his donkey for cursing God.
Barak: Jewish captain; associated with Deborah.
Baruch: Secretary to Jeremiah.
Bathsheba: Wife of Uriah; later, wife of David.
Belshazzar: Crown prince of Babylon.
Benaiah: Warrior of David; proclaimed Solomon King.
Ben-Hadad: Name of several kings of Damascus.
Benjamin: Son of Jacob and Rachel.
Bezaleel: Chief architect of tabernacle.
Bilhah: Servant of Rachel; mistress of Jacob.
Bildad: Comforter of Job.
Boaz: Husband of Ruth; father of Obed.
Cain: Son of Adam and Eve; slayer of Abel; father of Enoch.
Cainan: Son of Enos.
Caleb: Spy sent out by Moses to visit Canaan; father of Achsa.
Canaan: Son of Ham.
Chilion: Son of Elimelech; husband of Orpah.
Cush: Son of Ham; father of Nimrod.
Dan: Son of Jacob and Bilhah.
Daniel: Prophet; saved from lions by God.
Deborah: Hebrew prophetess; helped Israelites conquer Canaanites.
Delilah: Mistress and betrayer of Samson.
Elam: Son of Shem.
Eleazar: Son of Aaron; succeeded him as high priest.

Eli: High priest and judge; teacher of Samuel; father of Hophni and Phinehas.

Eliakim: Chief minister of Hezekiah.

Eliezer: Servant of Abraham.

Elihu: Comforter of Job.

Elijah (or Elias): Prophet; went to heaven in chariot of fire.

Elimelech: Husband of Naomi; father of Chilion and Mahlon.

Eliphaz: Comforter of Job.

Elisha (or Eliseus): Prophet; successor of Elijah.

Elkanah: Husband of Hannah; father of Samuel.

Enoch: Son of Cain.

Enoch: Father of Methuselah.

Enos: Son of Seth; father of Cainan.

Ephraim: Son of Joseph.

Esau: Son of Isaac and Rebecca; sold his birthright to his brother Jacob.

Esther: Jewish wife of Ahasuerus; saved Jews from Haman's plotting.

Eve: First woman; created from rib of Adam.

Ezra (or Esdras): Hebrew scribe and priest.

Gad: Son of Jacob and Zilpah.

Gehazi: Servant of Elisha.

Gideon: Israelite hero; defeated Midianites.

Goliath: Philistine giant; slain by David.

Hagar: Handmaid of Sarah; concubine of Abraham; mother of Ishmael.

Haggith: Mother of Adonijah.

Ham: Son of Noah; father of Cush, Mizraim, Phut, and Canaan.

Haman: Chief minister of Ahasuerus; hanged on gallows prepared for Mordecai.

Hannah: Wife of Elkanah; mother of Samuel.

Hanun: King of Ammonites.

Haran: Brother of Abraham; father of Lot.

Hazael: King of Damascus.

Hephzi-Bah: Wife of Hezekiah; mother of Mannaseh.

Hiram: King of Tyre.

Holofernes: General of Nebuchadnezzar; slain by Judith.

Hophni: Son of Eli.

Isaac: Hebrew patriarch; son of Abraham and Sarah; half brother of Ishmael; husband of Rebecca; father of Esau and Jacob.

Ishmael: Son of Abraham and Hagar; half brother of Isaac.

Issachar: Son of Jacob and Leah.

Ithamar: Son of Aaron.

Jabal: Son of Lamech and Adah.

Jabin: King of Hazor.

Jacob: Hebrew patriarch, founder of Israel; son of Isaac and Rebecca; husband of Leah and Rachel; father of Asher, Benjamin, Dan, Gad, Issachar, Joseph, Judah, Levi, Naphtali, Reuben, Simeon, and Zebulun.

Jael: Slayer of Sisera.

Japheth: Son of Noah.

Jehoiada: High priest; husband of Jehoshabeath; revolted against Athaliah and made Joash King of Judah.

Jehoshabeath (or Jehosheba): Daughter of Jehoram of Judah; wife of Jehoiada.

Jephthah: Judge in Israel; sacrificed his only daughter because of vow.

Jesse: Son of Obed; father of David.

Jethro: Midianite priest; father of Zipporah.

Jezebel: Phoenician princess; wife of Ahab; mother of Ahaziah, Athaliah, and Jehoram.

Joab: Commander in chief under David; slayer of Abner, Absalom, and Amasa.

Job: Patriarch; underwent many afflictions; comforted by Bildad, Elihu, Eliphaz and Zophar.

Jochebed: Wife of Amram.

Jonah: Prophet; cast into sea and swallowed by great fish.

Jonathan: Son of Saul; friend of David.

Joseph: Son of Jacob and Rachel; sold into slavery by his brothers; husband of Asenath; father of Ephraim and Manassah.

Joshua: Successor of Moses; son of Nun.

Jubal: Son of Lamech and Adah.

Judah: Son of Jacob and Leah.

Judith: Slayer of Holofernes.

Kish: Father of Saul.

Laban: Father of Leah and Rachel.

Lamech: Son of Methuselah; father of Noah.

Lamech: Husband of Adah and Zillah; father of Jabal, Jubal, and Tubal-Cain.

Leah: Daughter of Laban; wife of Jacob.

Levi: Son of Jacob and Leah.

Lot: Son of Haran; escaped destruction of Sodom.

Maacah: Mother of Absalom and Tamar.

Mahlon: Son of Elimelech; first husband of Ruth.

Manasseh: Son of Joseph.

Melchizedek: King of Salem.

Methuselah: Patriarch; son of Enoch; father of Lamech.

Michal: Daughter of Saul; wife of David.

Miriam: Prophetess; daughter of Amram; sister of Aaron and Moses.

Mizraim: Son of Ham.

Mordecai: Uncle of Esther; with her aid, saved Jews from Haman's plotting.

Moses: Prophet and lawgiver; son of Amram; brother of Aaron and Miriam; husband of Zipporah.

Naaman: Syrian captain; cured of leprosy by Elisha.

Nabal: Husband of Abigail.

Naboth: Owner of vineyard; stoned to death because he would not sell it to Ahab.

Nadab: Son of Aaron.

Nahor: Father of Terah.

Naomi: Wife of Elimelech; mother-in-law of Ruth.

Naphtali: Son of Jacob and Bilhah.

Nathan: Prophet; reproved David for causing Uriah's death.

Nebuchadnezzar (or Nebuchadrezzar): King of Babylon; destroyer of Jerusalem.

Nehemiah: Jewish leader; empowered by Artaxerxes to rebuild Jerusalem.

Nimrod: Mighty hunter; son of Cush.

Noah: Patriarch; Son of Lamech; escaped Deluge by building Ark; father of Ham, Japheth and Shem.

Nun (or Non): Father of Joshua.

Obed: Son of Boaz; father of Jesse.

Og: King of Bashan.

Orpah: Wife of Chilion.

Othniel: Kenezite; judge of Israel; husband of Achsa.

Phinehas: Son of Eleazer.

Phinehas: Son of Eli.

Phut (or Put): Son of Ham.

Potiphar: Egyptian official; bought Joseph.

Rachel: Wife of Jacob.

Rebecca (or Rebekah): Wife of Isaac.

Reuben: Son of Jacob and Leah.

Ruth: Wife of Mahlon, later of Boaz; daughter-in-law of Naomi.

Samson: Judge of Israel; famed for strength; betrayed by Delilah.

Samuel: Hebrew judge and prophet; son of Elkanah.

Sarah (or Sara, Sarai): Wife of Abraham.

Sennacherib: King of Assyria.

Seth: Son of Adam; father of Enos.

Shem: Son of Noah; father of Elam.

Simeon: Son of Jacob and Leah.

Sisera: Canaanite captain; slain by Jael.

Tamar: Daughter of David and Maachah; ravished by Amnon.

Terah: Son of Nahor; father of Abraham.

Tubal-Cain: Son of Lamech and Zillah.

Uriah: Husband of Bathsheba; sent to death in battle by David.

Vashti: Wife of Ahasuerus; set aside by him.

Zadok: High priest during David's reign.

Zebulun (or Zabulon): Son of Jacob and Leah.

Zillah: Wife of Lamech.

Zilpah: Servant of Leah; mistress of Jacob.

Zipporah: Daughter of Jethro; wife of Moses.

Zophar: Comforter of Job.

Kings of Judah and Israel

Kings Before Division of Kingdom

Saul: First King of Israel; son of Kish; father of Ish-Bosheth, Jonathan and Michal.

Ish-Bosheth (or Eshbaal): King of Israel; son of Saul.

David: King of Judah; later of Israel; son of Jesse; husband of Abigail, Ahinoam, Bathsheba, Michal, etc.; father of Absalom, Adonijah, Amnon, Solomon, Tamar, etc.

Solomon: King of Israel and Judah; son of David; father of Rehoboam.

Rehoboam: Son of Solomon; during his reign the kingdom was divided into Judah and Israel.

Kings of Judah (Southern Kingdom)

Rehoboam: First King.

Abijah (or Abijam or Abia): Son of Rehoboam.

Asa: Probably son of Abijah.

Jehoshaphat: Son of Asa.

Jehoram (or Joram): Son of Jehoshaphat; husband of Athaliah.

Ahaziah: Son of Jehoram and Athaliah.

Athaliah: Daughter of King Ahab of Israel and Jezebel; wife of Jehoram.

Joash (or Jehoash): Son of Ahaziah.

Amaziah: Son of Joash.

Uzziah (or Azariah): Son of Amaziah.

Jotham: Regent, later King; son of Uzziah.

Ahaz: Son of Jotham.

Hezekiah: Son of Ahaz; husband of Hephzi-Bah.

Manasseh: Son of Hezekiah and Hephzi-Bah.

Amon: Son of Manasseh.

Josiah (or Josias): Son of Amon.

Jehoahaz (or Joahaz): Son of Josiah.

Jehoiachin: Son of Jehoiakim.

Jehoiakim: Son of Josiah.

Zedekiah: Son of Josiah; kingdom overthrown by Babylonians under Nebuchadnezzar.

Kings of Israel (Northern Kingdom)

Jeroboam I: Led secession of Israel.

Nadab: Son of Jeroboam I.

Baasha: Overthrew Nadab.

Elah: Son of Baasha.

Zimri: Overthrew Elah.

Omri: Overthrew Zimri.

Ahab: Son of Omri; husband of Jezebel.

Ahaziah: Son of Ahab.

Jehoram (or Joram): Son of Ahab.

Jehu: Overthrew Jehoram.

Jehoahaz (or Joahaz): Son of Jehu.

Jehoash (or Joash): Son of Jehoahaz.

Jeroboam II: Son of Jehoash.

Zechariah: Son of Jeroboam II.

Shallum: Overthrew Zechariah.

Menahem: Overthrew Shallum.

Pekahiah: Son of Menahem.

Pekah: Overthrew Pekahiah.

Hoshea: Overthrew Pekah; kingdom overthrown by Assyrians under Sargon II.

Prophets

Major.—Isaiah, Jeremiah, Ezekiel, Daniel.

Minor.—Hosea, Obadiah, Nahum, Haggai, Joel, Jonah, Habakkuk, Zechariah, Amos, Micah, Zephaniah, Malachi.

Greek and Roman Mythology

(Most of the Greek deities were adopted by the Romans, although in many cases there was a change of name. In the list below, information is given under the Greek name; the name in parentheses is the Latin equivalent. However, all Latin names are listed with cross references to the Greek ones. In addition, there are several deities which were exclusively Roman.)

Acheron: *See* Rivers.

Achilles: Greek warrior; slew Hector at Troy; slain by Paris, who wounded him in his vulnerable heel.

Actaeon: Hunter; surprised Artemis bathing; changed by her to stag and killed by his dogs.

Admetus: King of Thessaly; his wife, Alcestis, offered to die in his place.

Adonis: Beautiful youth loved by Aphrodite.

Aeacus: One of three judges of dead in Hades; son of Zeus.

Aeëtes: King of Colchis; father of Medea; keeper of Golden Fleece.

Aegeus: Father of Theseus; believing Theseus killed in Crete, he drowned himself, Aegean Sea named for him.

Aegisthus: Son of Thyestes; slew Atreus; with Clytemnestra, his paramour, slew Agamemnon; slain by Orestes.

Aegyptus: Brother of Danaus; his sons, except Lynceus, slain by Danaides.

Aeneas: Trojan; son of Anchises and Aphrodite; after fall of Troy, led his followers eventually to Italy; loved and deserted Dido.

Aeolus: *See* Winds.

Aesculapius: *See* Asclepius.

Aeson: King of Ioclus; father of Jason; overthrown by his brother Pelias; restored to youth by Medea.

Aether: Personification of sky.

Aethra: Mother of Theseus.

Agamemnon: King of Mycenae; son of Atreus; brother of Menelaus; leader of Greeks against Troy; slain on his return home by Clytemnestra and Aegisthus.

Agiaia: *See* Graces.

Ajax: Greek warrior; killed himself at Troy because Achilles'

armor was awarded to Odysseus.

Alcestis: Wife of Admetus; offered to die in his place but saved from death by Hercules.

Alcmene: Wife of Amphitryon; mother by Zeus of Hercules.

Alcyone: *See* Pleiades.

Alecto: *See* Furies.

Alectryon: Youth changed by Ares into cock.

Althaea: Wife of Oeneus; mother of Meleager.

Amazons: Female warriors in Asia Minor; supported Troy against Greeks.

Amor: *See* Eros.

Amphion: Musician; husband of Niobe; charmed stones to build fortifications for Thebes.

Amphitrite: Sea goddess; wife of Poseidon.

Amphitryon: Husband of Alcmene.

Anchises: Father of Aeneas.

Ancile: Sacred shield that fell from heavens; palladium of Rome.

Andraemon: Husband of Dryope.

Andromache: Wife of Hector.

Andromeda: Daughter of Cepheus; chained to cliff for monster to devour; rescued by Perseus.

Anteia: Wife of Proetus; tried to induce Bellerophon to elope with her.

Anteros: God who avenged unrequited love.

Antigone: Daughter of Oedipus; accompanied him to Colonus; performed burial rite for Polynices and hanged herself.

Antinoüs: Leader of suitors of Penelope; slain by Odysseus.

Aphrodite (Venus): Goddess of love and beauty; daughter

of Zeus; mother of Eros.

Apollo: God of beauty, poetry, music; later identified with Helios as Phoebus Apollo; son of Zeus and Leto.

Aquilo: *See* Winds.

Arachne: Maiden who challenged Athena to weaving contest; changed to spider.

Ares (Mars): God of war; son of Zeus and Hera.

Argo: Ship in which Jason and followers sailed to Colchis for Golden Fleece.

Argus: Monster with hundred eyes; slain by Hermes; his eyes placed by Hera into peacock's tail.

Ariadne: Daughter of Minos; aided Theseus in slaying Minotaur; deserted by him on island of Naxos and married to Dionysus.

Arion: Musician; thrown overboard by pirates but saved by dolphin.

Artemis (Diana): Goddess of moon; huntress; twin sister of Apollo.

Asclepius (Aesculapius): Mortal son of Apollo; slain by Zeus for raising dead; later deified as god of medicine. Also known as Asklepios.

Astarte: Phoenician goddess of love; variously identified with Aphrodite, Selene, and Artemis.

Astraea: Goddess of Justice; daughter of Zeus and Themis.

Atalanta: Princess who challenged her suitors to a foot race; Hippomenes won race and married her.

Athena (Minerva): Goddess of wisdom; known poetically as Pallas Athene; sprang fully armed from head of Zeus.

Atlas: Titan; held world on his shoulders as punishment for warring against Zeus; son of Iapetus.

Atreus: King of Mycenae; father of Menelaus and Agamemnon; brother of Thyestes, three of whose sons he slew and served to him at banquet; slain by Aegisthus.

Atropos: *See* Fates.

Aurora: *See* Eos.

Auster: *See* Winds.

Avernus: Infernal regions; name derived from small vaporous lake near Vesuvius which was fabled to kill birds and vegetation.

Bacchus: *See* Dionysus.

Bellerophon: Corinthian hero; killed Chimera with aid of Pegasus; tried to reach Olympus on Pegasus and was thrown to his death.

Bellona: Roman goddess of war.

Boreas: *See* Winds.

Briareus: Monster of hundred hands; son of Uranus and Gaea.

Briseis: Captive maiden given to Achilles; taken by Agamemnon in exchange for loss of Chryseis, which caused Achilles to cease fighting, until death of Patroclus.

Cadmus: Brother of Europa; planter of dragon seeds from which first Thebans sprang.

Calliope: *See* Muses.

Calypso: Sea nymph; kept Odysseus on her island Ogygia for seven years.

Cassandra: Daughter of Priam; prophetess who was never believed; slain with Agamemnon.

Castor: *See* Dioscuri.

Celaeno: *See* Pleiades.

Centaurs: Beings half man and half horse; lived in mountains of Thessaly.

Cephalus: Hunter; accidentally killed his wife Procris with his spear.

Cepheus: King of Ethiopia; father of Andromeda.

Cerberus: Three-headed dog guarding entrance to Hades.

Ceres: *See* Demeter.

Chaos: Formless void; personified as first of gods.

Charon: Boatman on Styx who carried souls of dead to Hades; son of Erebus.

Charybdis: Female monster; personification of whirlpool.

Chimera: Female monster with head of lion, body of goat, tail of serpent; killed by Bellerophon.

Chiron: Most famous of centaurs.

Chronos: Personification of time.

Chryseis: Captive maiden given to Agamemnon; his refusal to accept ransom from her father Chryses caused Apollo to send plague on Greeks besieging Troy.

Circe: Sorceress; daughter of Helios; changed Odysseus' men into swine.

Clio: *See* Muses.

Clotho: *See* Fates.

Clytemnestra: Wife of Agamemnon, whom she slew with aid of her paramour, Aegisthus; slain by her son Orestes.

Cocytus: *See* Rivers.

Creon: Father of Jocasta; forbade burial of Polynices; ordered burial alive of Antigone.

Creüsa: Princess of Corinth, for whom Jason deserted Medea; slain by Medea, who sent her poisoned robe; also known as Glaüke.

Creusa: Wife of Aeneas; died fleeing Troy.

Cronus (Saturn): Titan; god of harvests; son of Uranus and Gaea; dethroned by his son Zeus.

Cupid: *See* Eros.

Cybele: Anatolian nature goddess; adopted by Greeks and identified with Rhea.

Cyclopes: Race of one-eyed giants (singular: Cyclops).

Daedalus: Athenian artificer; father of Icarus; builder of Labyrinth in Crete; devised wings attached with wax for him and Icarus to escape Crete.

Danae: Princess of Argos; mother of Perseus by Zeus, who appeared to her in form of golden shower.

Danaïdes: Daughters of Danaüs; at his command, all except Hypermnestra slew their husbands, the sons of Aegyptus.

Danaüs: Brother of Aegyptus; father of Danaïdes; slain by Lynceus.

Daphne: Nymph; pursued by Apollo; changed to laurel tree.

Decuma: *See* Fates.

Deino: *See* Graeae.

Demeter (Ceres): Goddess of agriculture; mother of Persephone.

Diana: *See* Artemis.

Dido: Founder and queen of Carthage; stabbed herself when deserted by Aeneas.

Diomedes: Greek hero; with Odysseus, entered Troy and carried off Palladium, sacred statue of Athena.

Diomedes: Owner of man-eating horses, which Hercules, as ninth labor, carried off.

Dione: Titan goddess; mother by Zeus of Aphrodite.

Dionysus (Bacchus): God of wine; son of Zeus and Semele.

Dioscuri: Twins Castor and Pollux; sons of Leda by Zeus.

Dis: *See* Hades.

Dryads: Wood nymphs.

Dryope: Maiden changed to Hamadryad.

Echo: Nymph who fell hopelessly in love with Narcissus; faded away except for her voice.

Electra: Daughter of Agamemnon and Clytemnestra; sister of Orestes; urged Orestes to slay Clytemnestra and Aegisthus.

Electra: *See* Pleiades.

Elysium: Abode of blessed dead.

Endymion: Mortal loved by Selene.

Enyo: *See* Graeae.

Eos (Aurora): Goddess of dawn.

Epimetheus: Brother of Prometheus; husband of Pandora.

Erato: *See* Muses.

Erebus: Spirit of darkness; son of Chaos.

Erinyes: *See* Furies.

Eris: Goddess of discord.

Eros (Amor or Cupid): God of love; son of Aphrodite.

Eteocles: Son of Oedipus, whom he succeeded to rule alternately with Polynices; refused to give up throne at end of year; he and Polynices slew each other.

Eumenides: *See* Furies.

Euphrosyne: *See* Graces.

Europa: Mortal loved by Zeus, who, in form of white bull, carried her off to Crete.

Eurus: *See* Winds.

Euryale: *See* Gorgons.

Eurydice: Nymph; wife of Orpheus.

Eurystheus: King of Argos; imposed twelve labors on Hercules.

Euterpe: *See* Muses.

Fates: Goddesses of destiny; Clotho (Spinner of thread of life), Lachesis (Determiner of length), and Atropos (Cutter of thread); also called Moirae. Identified by Romans with their goddesses of fate; Nona, Decuma, and Morta; called Parcae.

Fauns: Roman deities of woods and groves.

Faunus: *See* Pan.

Favonius: *See* Winds.

Flora: Roman goddess of flowers.

Fortuna: Roman goddess of fortune.

Furies: Avenging spirits; Alecto, Megaera, and Tisiphone; known also as Erinyes or Eumenides.

Gaea: Goddess of earth; daughter of Chaos; mother of Titans; known also as Ge, Gea, Gaia, etc.

Galatea: Statue of maiden carved from ivory by Pygmalion; given life by Aphrodite.

Galatea: Sea nymph; loved by Polyphemus.

Ganymede: Beautiful boy; successor to Hebe as cupbearer of gods.

Glaucus: Mortal who became sea divinity by eating magic grass.

Glauke: *See* Creüsa.

Golden Fleece: Fleece from ram that flew Phrixos to Colchis; Aeëtes placed it under guard of dragon; carried off by Jason.

Gorgons: Female monsters; Euryale, Medusa, and Stheno; had snakes for hair; their glances turned mortals to stone. *See* Medusa.

Graces: Beautiful goddesses: Aglaia (Brilliance), Euphrosyne (Joy), and Thalia (Bloom); daughters of Zeus.

Graeae: Sentinels for Gorgons; Deino, Enyo, and Pephredo; had one eye among them, which passed from one to another.

Hades (Dis): Name sometimes given Pluto; also, abode of dead, ruled by Pluto.

Haemon: Son of Creon; promised husband of Antigone; killed himself in her tomb.

Hamadryads: Tree nymphs.

Harpies: Monsters with heads of women and bodies of birds.

Hebe (Juventas): Goddess of youth; cupbearer of gods before Ganymede; daughter of Zeus and Hera.

Hecate: Goddess of sorcery and witchcraft.

Hector: Son of Priam; slayer of Patroclus; slain by Achilles.

Hecuba: Wife of Priam.

Helen: Fairest woman in world; daughter of Zeus and Leda; wife of Menelaus; carried to Troy by Paris, causing Trojan War.

Heliades: Daughters of Helios; mourned for Phaëthon and were changed to poplar trees.

Helios (Sol): God of sun; later identified with Apollo.

Helle: Sister of Phrixos; fell from ram of Golden Fleece; water where she fell named Hellespont.

Hephaestus (Vulcan): God of fire; celestial blacksmith; son of Zeus and Hera; husband of Aphrodite.

Hera (Juno): Queen of heaven; wife of Zeus.

Hercules: Hero and strong man; son of Zeus and Alcmene; performed twelve labors or deeds to be free from bondage under Eurystheus; after death, his mortal share was destroyed, and he became immortal. Also known as Herakles or Heracles. Labors: (1) killing Nemean lion; (2) killing Lernaean Hydra; (3) capturing Erymanthian boar; (4) capturing Cerynean hind; (5) killing man-eating Stymphalian birds; (6) procuring girdle of Hippolyte; (7) cleaning Augean stables; (8) capturing Cretan bull; (9) capturing man-eating horses of Diomedes; (10) capturing cattle of Geryon; (11) procuring golden apples of Hesperides; (12) bringing Cerberus up from Hades.

Hermes (Mercury): God of physicians and thieves; messenger of gods; son of Zeus and Maia.

Hero: Priestess of Aphrodite; Leander swam Hellespont nightly to see her; drowned herself at his death.

Hesperus: Evening star.

Hestia (Vesta): Goddess of hearth; sister of Zeus.

Hippolyte: Queen of Amazons; wife of Theseus.

Hippolytus: Son of Theseus and Hippolyte; falsely accused by Phaedra of trying to kidnap her; slain by Poseidon at request of Theseus.

Hippomenes: Husband of Atalanta, whom he beat in race by dropping golden apples, which she stopped to pick up.

Hyacinthus: Beautiful youth accidentally killed by Apollo, who caused flower to spring up from his blood.

Hydra: Nine-headed monster in marsh of Lerna; slain by Hercules.

Hygeia: Personification of health.

Hyman: God of marriage.

Hyperion: Titan; early sun god; father of Helios.

Hypermnestra: Daughter of Danaüs; refused to kill her husband Lynceus.

Hypnos (Somnus): God of sleep.

Iapetus: Titan; father of Atlas, Epimetheus, and Prometheus.

Icarus: Son of Daedalus; flew too near sun with wax-attached wings and fell into sea and was drowned.

Io: Mortal maiden loved by Zeus; changed by Hera into heifer.

Iobates: King of Lycia; sent Bellerophon to slay Chimera.

Iphigenia: Daughter of Agamemnon; offered as sacrifice to Artemis at Aulis; carried by Artemis to Tauris where she became priestess; escaped from there with Orestes.

Iris: Goddess of rainbow; messenger of Zeus and Hera.

Ismene: Daughter of Oedipus; sister of Antigone.

Iulus: Son of Aeneas.

Ixion: King of Lapithae; for making love to Hera he was bound to endlessly revolving wheel in Tartarus.

Janus: Roman god of gates and doors; represented with two opposite faces.

Jason: Son of Aeson; to gain throne of Ioclus from Pelias, went to Colchis and brought back Golden Fleece; married Medea; deserted her for Creüsa.

Jocasta: Wife of Laius; mother of Oedipus; unwittingly became wife of Oedipus; hanged herself when relationship was discovered.

Juno: *See* Hera.

Jupiter: *See* Zeus.

Juventas: *See* Hebe.

Lachesis: *See* Fates.

Laius: Father of Oedipus, by whom he was slain.

Laocoön: Priest of Apollo at Troy; warned against bringing wooden horse into Troy; destroyed with his two sons by serpents sent by Athena.

Lares: Roman ancestral spirits protecting descendants and homes.

Lavinia: Wife of Aeneas after defeat of Turnus.

Leander: Swam Hellespont nightly to see Hero; drowned in storm.

Leda: Mortal loved by Zeus in form of Swan; mother of Helen, Clytemnestra, Dioscuri.

Lethe: *See* Rivers.

Leto (Latona): Mother by Zeus of Artemis and Apollo.

Lucina: Roman goddess of childbirth; identified with Juno.

Lynceus: Son of Aegyptus; husband of Hypermnestra; slew Danaüs.

Maia: Daughter of Atlas; mother of Hermes.

Maia: *See* Pleiades.

Manes: Souls of dead Romans, particularly of ancestors.

Mars: *See* Ares.

Marsyas: Shepherd; challenged Apollo to music contest and lost; flayed alive by Apollo.

Medea: Sorceress; daughter of Aeëtes; helped Jason obtain Golden Fleece; when deserted by him for Creüsa, killed her children and Creüsa.

Medusa: Gorgon; slain by Perseus, who cut off her head.

Megaera: *See* Furies.

Meleager: Son of Althaea; his life would last as long as brand burning at his birth; Althaea quenched and saved it but destroyed it when Meleager slew his uncles.

Melpomene: *See* Muses.

Memnon: Ethiopian king; made immortal by Zeus; son of Tithonus and Eos.

Menelaus: King of Sparta; son of Atreus; brother of Agamemnon; husband of Helen.

Mercury: *See* Hermes.

Merope: *See* Pleiades.

Mezentius: Cruel Etruscan king; ally of Turnus against Aeneas; slain by Aeneas.

Midas: King of Phrygia; given gift of turning to gold all he touched.

Minerva: *See* Athena.

Minos: King of Crete; after death, one of three judges of dead in Hades; son of Zeus and Europa.

Minotaur: Monster, half man and half beast, kept in Labyrinth in Crete; slain by Theseus.

Mnemosyne: Goddess of memory; mother by Zeus of Muses.

Moirae: *See* Fates.

Momus: God of ridicule.

Morpheus: God of dreams.

Mors: *See* Thanatos.

Morta: *See* Fates.

Muses: Goddesses presiding over arts and sciences: Calliope (epic poetry), Clio (history), Erato (lyric and love poetry), Euterpe (music), Melpomene (tragedy), Polymnia or Polyhymnia (sacred poetry), Terpsichore (choral dance and song), Thalia (comedy and bucolic poetry), Urania (astronomy); daughters of Zeus and Mnemosyne.

Naiads: Nymphs of waters, streams, and fountains.

Napaeae: Wood nymphs.

Narcissus: Beautiful youth loved by Echo; in punishment for not returning her love, he was made to fall in love with his image reflected in pool; pined away and became flower.

Nemesis: Goddess of retribution.

Neoptolemus: Son of Achilles; slew Priam; also known as Pyrrhus.

Neptune: *See* Poseidon.

Nereids: Sea nymphs; attendants on Poseidon.

Nestor: King of Pylos; noted for wise counsel in expedition against Troy.

Nike: Goddess of victory.

Niobe: Daughter of Tantalus; wife of Amphion; her children slain by Apollo and Artemis; changed to stone but continued to weep her loss.

Nona: *See* Fates.

Notus: *See* Winds.

Nox: *See* Nyx.

Nymphs: Beautiful maidens; inferior deities of nature.

Nyx (Nox): Goddess of night.

Oceanids: Ocean nymphs; daughters of Oceanus.

Oceanus: Eldest of Titans; god of waters.

Odysseus (Ulysses): King of Ithaca; husband of Penelope; wandered ten years after fall of Troy before arriving home.

Oedipus: King of Thebes; son of Laius and Jocasta; unwittingly murdered Laius and married Jocasta; tore his eyes out when relationship was discovered.

Oenone: Nymph of Mount Ida; wife of Paris, who abandoned her; refused to cure him when he was poisoned by arrow of Philoctetes at Troy.

Ops: *See* Rhea.

Oreads: Mountain nymphs.

Orestes: Son of Agamemnon and Clytemnestra; brother of Electra; slew Clytemnestra and Aegisthus; pursued by Furies until his purification by Apollo.

Orion: Hunter; slain by Artemis and made heavenly constellation.

Orpheus: Famed musician; son of Apollo and Muse Calliope; husband of Eurydice.

Pales: Roman goddess of shepherds and herdsmen.

Palinurus: Aeneas' pilot; fell overboard in his sleep and was drowned.

Pan (Faunus): God of woods and fields; part goat; son of Hermes.

Pandora: Opener of box containing human ills; mortal wife of Epimetheus.

Parcae: *See* Fates.

Paris: Son of Priam; gave apple of discord to Aphrodite, for which she enabled him to carry off Helen; slew Achilles at Troy; slain by Philoctetes.

Patroclus: Great friend of Achilles; wore Achilles' armor and was slain by Hector.

Pegasus: Winged horse that sprang from Medusa's body at her death; ridden by Bellerophon when he slew Chimera.

Pelias: King of Iolcus; seized throne from his brother Aeson; sent Jason for Golden Fleece; slain unwittingly by his daughters at instigation of Medea.

Pelops: Son of Tantalus; his father cooked and served him to gods; restored to life; Peloponnesus named for him.

Penates: Roman household gods.

Penelope: Wife of Odysseus; waited faithfully for him for ten years while putting off numerous suitors.

Pephredo: *See* Graeae.

Periphetes: Giant; son of Hephaestus; slain by Theseus.

Persephone (Proserpine): Queen of infernal regions; daughter of Zeus and Demeter; wife of Pluto.

Perseus: Son of Zeus and Danaë; slew Medusa; rescued Andromeda from monster and married her.

Phaedra: Daughter of Minos; wife of Theseus; caused the death of her stepson, Hippolytus.

Phaethon: Son of Helios; drove his father's sun chariot and was struck down by Zeus before he set world on fire.

Philoctetes: Greek warrior who possessed Hercules' bow and arrows; slew Paris at Troy with poisoned arrow.

Phineus: Betrothed of Andromeda; tried to slay Perseus but turned to stone by Medusa's head.

Phlegethon: *See* Rivers.

Phosphor: Morning star.

Phrixos: Brother of Helle; carried by ram of Golden Fleece to Colchis.

Pirithous: Son of Ixion; friend of Theseus; tried to carry off Persephone from Hades; bound to enchanted rock by Pluto.

Pleiades: Alcyone, Celaeno, Electra, Maia, Merope, Sterope or Asterope, Taygeta; seven daughters of Atlas; transformed into heavenly constellation, of which six stars are visible (Merope is said to have hidden in shame for loving a mortal).

Pluto (Dis): God of Hades; brother of Zeus.

Plutus: God of wealth.

Pollux: *See* Dioscuri.

Polymnia: *See* Muses.

Polynices: Son of Oedipus; he and his brother Eteocles killed each other; burial rite, forbidden by Creon, performed by his sister Antigone.

Polyphemus: Cyclops; devoured six of Odysseus' men; blinded by Odysseus.

Polyxena: Daughter of Priam; betrothed to Achilles, whom Paris slew at their betrothal; sacrificed to shade of Achilles.

Pomona: Roman goddess of fruits.

Pontus: Sea god; son of Gaea.

Poseidon (Neptune): God of sea; brother of Zeus.

Priam: King of Troy; husband of Hecuba; ransomed Hector's body from Achilles; slain by Neoptolemus.

Priapus: God of regeneration.

Procris: Wife of Cephalus, who accidentally slew her.

Procrustes: Giant; stretched or cut off legs of victims to make them fit iron bed; slain by Theseus.

Proetus: Husband of Anteia; sent Bellerophon to Iobates to be put to death.

Prometheus: Titan; stole fire from heaven for man. Zeus punished him by chaining him to rock in Caucasus where vultures devoured his liver daily.

Proteus: Sea god; assumed various shapes when called on to prophesy.

Psyche: Beloved of Eros; punished by jealous Aphrodite; made immortal and united with Eros.

Pygmalion: King of Cyprus; carved ivory statue of maiden which Aphrodite gave life as Galatea.

Pyramus: Babylonian youth; made love to Thisbe through hole in wall; thinking Thisbe slain by lion, killed himself.

Pyrrhus: *See* Neoptolemus.

Python: Serpent born from slime left by Deluge; slain by Apollo.

Quirinus: Roman war god.

Remus: Brother of Romulus; slain by him.

Rhadamanthus: One of three judges of dead in Hades; son of Zeus and Europa.

Rhea (Ops): Daughter of Uranus and Gaea; wife of Cronus; mother of Zeus; identified with Cybele.

Rivers of Underworld: Acheron (woe), Cocytus (wailing), Lethe (forgetfulness), Phlegethon (fire), Styx (across which souls of dead were ferried by Charon).

Romulus: Founder of Rome; he and Remus suckled in infancy by she-wolf; slew Remus; deified by Romans.

Sarpedon: King of Lycia; son of Zeus and Europa; slain by Patroclus at Troy.

Saturn: *See* Cronus.

Satyrs: Hoofed demigods of woods and fields; companions of Dionysus.

Sciron: Robber; forced strangers to wash his feet, then hurled them into sea where tortoise devoured them; slain by Theseus.

Scylla: Female monster inhabiting rock opposite Charybdis; menaced passing sailors.

Selene: Goddess of moon.

Semele: Daughter of Cadmus; mother by Zeus of Dionysus; demanded Zeus appear before her in all his splendor and was destroyed by his lightnings.

Sibyls: Various prophetesses; most famous, Cumaean sibyl, accompanied Aeneas into Hades.

Sileni: Minor woodland deities similar to satyrs (singular: silenus). Sometimes Silenus refers to eldest of satyrs, son of Hermes or of Pan.

Silvanus: Roman god of woods and fields.

Sinis: Giant; bent pines, by which he hurled victims against side of mountain; slain by Theseus.

Sirens: Minor deities who lured sailors to destruction with their singing.

Sisyphus: King of Corinth; condemned in Tartarus to roll huge stone to top of hill; it always rolled back down again.

Sol: *See* Helios.

Somnus: *See* Hypnos.

Sphinx: Monster of Thebes; killed those who could not answer her riddle; slain by Oedipus. Name also refers to other monsters having body of lion, wings, and head and bust of woman.

Sterope: *See* Pleiades.

Stheno: *See* Gorgons.

Styx: *See* Rivers.

Symplegades: Clashing rocks at entrance to Black Sea; Argo passed through, causing them to become forever fixed.

Syrinx: Nymph pursued by Pan; changed to reeds, from which he made his pipes.

Tantalus: Cruel king; father of Pelops and Niobe; condemned in Tartarus to stand chin-deep in lake surrounded by fruit branches; as he tried to eat or drink, water or fruit always receded.

Tartarus: Underworld below Hades; often refers to Hades.

Taygeta: *See* Pleiades.

Telemachus: Son of Odysseus; made unsuccessful journey to find his father.

Tellus: Roman goddess of earth.

Terminus: Roman god of boundaries and landmarks.

Terpsichore: *See* Muses.

Terra: Roman earth goddess.

Thalia: *See* Graces; Muses.

Thanatos (Mors): God of death.

Themis: Titan goddess of laws of physical phenomena; daughter of Uranus; mother of Prometheus.

Theseus: Son of Aegeus; slew Minotaur; married and deserted Ariadne; later married Phaedra.

Thisbe: Beloved of Pyramus; killed herself at his death.

Thyestes: Brother of Atreus; Atreus killed three of his sons and served them to him at banquet.

Tiresias: Blind soothsayer of Thebes.

Tisiphone: *See* Furies.

Titans: Early gods from which Olympian gods were derived; children of Uranus and Gaea.

Tithonus: Mortal loved by Eos; changed into grasshopper.

Triton: Demigod of sea; son of Poseidon.

Turnus: King of Rutuli in Italy; betrothed to Lavinia; slain by Aeneas.

Ulysses: *See* Odysseus.

Urania: *See* Muses.

Uranus: Personification of Heaven; husband of Gaea; father of Titans; dethroned by his son Cronus.

Venus: *See* Aphrodite.

Vertumnus: Roman god of fruits and vegetables; husband of Pomona.

Vesta: *See* Hestia.

Vulcan: *See* Hephaestus.

Winds: Aeolus (keeper of winds), Boreas (Aquilo) (north wind), Eurus (east wind), Notus (Auster) (south wind), Zephyrus (Favonius) (west wind).

Zephyrus: *See* Winds.

Zeus (Jupiter): Chief of Olympian gods; son of Cronus and Rhea; husband of Hera.

Norse Mythology

Aesir: Chief gods of Asgard.

Andvari: Dwarf; robbed of gold and magic ring by Loki.

Angerbotha (Angrbotha): Giantess; mother by Loki of Fenrir, Hel, and Midgard serpent.

Asgard (Asgarth): Abode of gods.

Ask (Aske, Askr): First man; created by Odin, Hoenir, and Lothur.

Asynjur: Goddesses of Asgard.

Atli: Second husband of Gudrun; invited Gunnar and Hogni to his court, where they were slain; slain by Gudrun.

Audhumla (Audhumbla): Cow that nourished Ymir, created Buri by licking ice cliff.

Balder (Baldr, Baldur): God of light, spring, peace, joy; son of Odin; slain by Hoth at instigation of Loki.

Bifrost: Rainbow bridge connecting Midgard and Asgard.

Bragi (Brage): God of poetry; husband of Ithunn.

Branstock: Great oak in hall of Volsungs; into it, Odin thrust Gram, which only Sigmund could draw forth.

Brynhild: Valkyrie; wakened from magic sleep by Sigurd; married Gunnar; instigated death of Sigurd; killed herself and was burned on pyre beside Sigurd.

Bur (Bor): Son of Buri; father of Odin, Hoenir, and Lothur.

Buri (Bori): Progenitor of gods; father of Bur; created by Audhumla.

Embla: First woman; created by Odin, Hoenir, and Lothur.

Fafnir: Son of Rodmar, whom he slew for gold in Otter's skin; in form of dragon, guarded gold; slain by Sigurd.

Fenrir: Wolf; offspring of Loki; swallows Odin at Ragnarok and is slain by Vitharr.

Forseti: Son of Balder.

Frey (Freyr): God of fertility and crops; son of Njorth; originally one of Vanir.

Freya (Freyja): Goddess of love and beauty; sister of Frey; originally one of Vanir.

Frigg (Frigga): Goddess of sky; wife of Odin.

Garm: Watchdog of Hel; slays, and is slain by, Tyr at Ragnarok.

Gimle: Home of blessed after Ragnarok.

Giuki: King of Nibelungs; father of Gunnar, Hogni, Guttorm, and Gudrun.

Glathsheim (Gladsheim): Hall of gods in Asgard.

Gram (meaning "Angry"): Sigmund's sword; rewelded by Regin; used by Sigurd to slay Fafnir.

Greyfell: Sigmund's horse; descended from Sleipnir.

Grimhild: Mother of Gudrun; administered magic potion to Sigurd which made him forget Brynhild.

Gudrun: Daughter of Giuki; wife of Sigurd; later wife of Atli and Jonakr.

Gunnar: Son of Giuki; in his semblance Sigurd won Brynhild for him; slain at hall of Atli.

Guttorm: Son of Giuki; slew Sigurd at Brynhild's request.

Heimdall (Heimdallr): Guardian of Asgard.

Hel: Goddess of dead and queen of underworld; daughter of Loki.

Hiordis: Wife of Sigmund; mother of Sigurd.

Hoenir: One of creators of Ask and Embla; son of Bur.

Hogni: Son of Giuki; slain at hall of Atli.

Hoth (Hoder, Hodur): Blind god of night and darkness; slayer of Balder at instigation of Loki.

Ithunn (Ithun, Iduna): Keeper of golden apples of youth; wife of Bragi.

Jonakr: Third husband of Gudrun.

Jormunrek: Slayer of Swanhild; slain by sons of Gudrun.

Jotunnheim (Jotunheim): Abode of giants.

Lif and Lifthrasir: First man and woman after Ragnarok.

Loki: God of evil and mischief; instigator of Balder's death.

Lothur (Lodur): One of creators of Ask and Embla.

Midgard (Midgarth): Abode of mankind; the earth.

Midgard Serpent: Sea monster; offspring of Loki; slays, and is slain by, Thor at Ragnarok.

Mimir: Giant; guardian of well in Jotunnheim at root of Yggdrasill; knower of past and future.

Mjollnir: Magic hammer of Thor.

Nagifar: Ship to be used by giants in attacking Asgard at

Ragnarok; built from nails of dead men.

Nanna: Wife of Balder.

Nibelungs: Dwellers in northern kingdom ruled by Giuki.

Niflheim (Nifelheim): Outer region of cold and darkness; abode of Hel.

Njorth: Father of Frey and Freya; originally one of Vanir.

Norns: Demigoddesses of fate: Urth (Urdur) (Past), Verthandi (Verdandi) (Present), Skuld (Future).

Odin (Othin): Head of Aesir; creator of world with Vili and Ve; equivalent to Woden (Wodan, Wotan) in Teutonic mythology.

Otter: Son of Rodmar; slain by Loki; his skin filled with gold hoard of Andvari to appease Rodmar.

Ragnarok: Final destruction of present world in battle between gods and giants; some minor gods will survive, and Lif and Lifthrasir will repeople world.

Regin: Blacksmith; son of Rodmar; foster-father of Sigurd.

Rerir: King of Huns; son of Sigi.

Rodmar: Father of Regin, Otter, and Fafnir; demanded Otter's skin be filled with gold; slain by Fafnir, who stole gold.

Sif: Wife of Thor.

Siggeir: King of Goths; husband of Signy; he and his sons slew Volsung and his sons, except Sigmund; slain by Sigmund and Sinflotli.

Sigi: King of Huns; son of Odin.

Sigmund: Son of Volsung; brother of Signy, who bore him Sinflotli; husband of Hiordis, who bore him Sigurd.

Signy: Daughter of Volsung; sister of Sigmund; wife of Siggeir; mother by Sigmund of Sinflotli.

Sigurd: Son of Sigmund and Hiordis; wakened Brynhild from magic sleep; married Gudrun; slain by Guttorm at instigation of Brynhild.

Sigyn: Wife of Loki.

Sinflotli: Son of Sigmund and Signy.

Skuld: *See* Norns.

Sleipnir (Sleipner): Eight-legged horse of Odin.

Surt (Surtr): Fire demon; slays Frey at Ragnarok.

Svartalfaheim: Abode of dwarfs.

Swanhild: Daughter of Sigurd and Gudrun; slain by Jormunrek.

Thor: God of thunder; oldest son of Odin; equivalent to Germanic deity Donar.

Tyr: God of war; son of Odin; equivalent to Tiu in Teutonic mythology.

Ull (Ullr): Son of Sif; stepson of Thor.

Urth: *See* Norns.

Valhalla (Valhall): Great hall in Asgard where Odin received souls of heroes killed in battle.

Vali: Odin's son: Ragnarok survivor.

Valkyries: Virgins, messengers of Odin, who selected heroes to die in battle and took them to Valhalla; generally considered as nine in number.

Vanir: Early race of gods; three survivors, Njorth, Frey, and Freya, are associated with Aesir.

Ve: Brother of Odin; one of creators of world.

Verthandi: *See* Norns.

Vili: Brother of Odin; one of creators of world.

Vingolf: Abode of goddesses in Asgard.

Vitharr (Vithar): Son of Odin; survivor of Ragnarok.

Volsung: Descendant of Odin, and father of Signy, Sigmund; his descendants were called Volsungs.

Yggdrasill: Giant ash tree springing from body of Ymir and supporting universe; its roots extended to Asgard, Jotunnheim, and Niffheim.

Ymir (Ymer): Primeval frost giant killed by Odin, Vili, and Ve; world created from his body; also, from his body sprang Yggdrasill.

Egyptian Mythology

Aaru: Abode of the blessed dead.

Amen (Amon, Ammdn): One of chief Theban deities; united with sun god under form of Amen-Ra.

Amenti: Region of dead where souls were judged by Osiris.

Anubis: Guide of souls to Amenti; son of Osiris; jackal-headed.

Apis: Sacred bull, an embodiment of Ptah; identified with Osiris as Osiris-Apis or Serapis.

Geb (Keb, Seb): Earth god; father of Osiris; represented with goose on head.

Hathor (Athor): Goddess of love and mirth; cow-headed.

Horus: God of day; son of Osiris and Isis; hawk-headed.

Isis: Goddess of motherhood and fertility; sister and wife of Osiris.

Khepera: God of morning sun.

Khnemu (Khnum, Chnuphis, Chnemu, Chnum): Ram-headed god.

Khonsu (Khensu, Khuns): Son of Amen and Mut.

Mentu (Ment): Solar deity, sometimes considered god of

war; falcon-headed.

Min (Khem, Chem): Principle of physical life.

Mut (Maut): Wife of Amen.

Nephthys: Goddess of the dead; sister and wife of Set.

Nu: Chaos from which world was created, personified as a god.

Nut: Goddess of heavens; consort of Geb.

Osiris: God of underworld and judge of dead; son of Geb and Nut.

Ptah (Phtha): Chief deity of Memphis.

Ra: God of the Sun, the supreme god; son of Nut; Pharaohs claimed descent from him; represented as lion, cat, or falcon.

Serapis: God uniting attributes of Osiris and Apis.

Set (Seth): God of darkness or evil; brother and enemy of Osiris.

Shu: Solar deity; son of Ra and Hathor.

Tem (Atmu, Atum, Tum): Solar deity.

Thoth (Dhouti): God of wisdom and magic; scribe of gods; ibis-headed.

Modern Wedding Anniversary Gift List

Anniversary	Gift	Anniversary	Gift	Anniversary	Gift
1st	Gold jewelry	10th	Diamond jewelry	19th	Aquamarine
2nd	Garnet	11th	Turquoise	20th	Emerald
3rd	Pearls	12th	Jade	25th	Silver jubilee
4th	Blue topaz	13th	Citrine	30th	Pearl jubilee
5th	Sapphire	14th	Opal	35th	Emerald
6th	Amethyst	15th	Ruby	40th	Ruby
7th	Onyx	16th	Peridot	45th	Sapphire
8th	Tourmaline	17th	Watches	50th	Golden jubilee
9th	Lapis	18th	Cat's-eye	60th	Diamond jubilee

Source: Jewelry Industry Council.

SCIENCE

The Human Genome Project

By James D. Watson

When the United States declared its independence from England in 1776, most maps of North America did not include California, now one of the most populous, diverse, and wealthy states in the nation. Only after the Civil War were California and the American West carefully and systematically mapped out. Expeditions and surveys laid the foundation for renewed exploration of the vast resources available to Americans in the great West.

As the Nineties begin, we are poised to mount a similar effort of even greater importance—to construct the genetic map of humans; to chart the mysteries encoded in the 50,000 to 100,000 genes that make up our bodies.

The human genome represents all genetic material that composes a living person. The chemical composition of this material consists entirely of DNA (deoxyribonucleic acid), the hereditary molecule arranged into working units called genes. Mapping the genome consists of locating every gene on the 23 pairs of our chromosomes squeezed into the nucleus of every cell and sequencing the 3 billion DNA subunits that make up each gene.

The Human Genome Project hatched out of passionate debates during the past several years. The success of the project is a shared commitment among Congress, the National Institutes of Health, the U.S. Department of Energy, and many foreign governments. To mediate the logistics of this large international cooperation, the Human Genome Organization was founded. The expected cost of this extensive biological operation is $3 billion ($1 for every subunit in the DNA chain) over the next 15 years. Unlike other federally funded megaprojects, such as the *Apollo* moon program, the benefits will begin as soon as data start coming in. We won't have to wait for the completion of the genome to reap the benefits.

This is indeed an expensive endeavor, but the rewards from mapping the genome will be widespread. By defining the structure of DNA, researchers will be able to identify inherited patterns or specific markers on the DNA strand that indicate the source of hereditary diseases. Many of the disorders that dominate our world, such as heart disease, cancer, arthritis, alcoholism, and mental illness, may be caused by genetic abnormalities.

As we analyze the information hidden within the chemical composition of every gene in the human body, the role of medicine will shift from treatment to prevention. For instance, genetic analysis of a newborn may be used to screen for a wide range of genetic disorders. Whenever a defect is found, the child may be protected from illness by the proper diet or by avoiding environmental hazards. Mapping the human genome will also give doctors the tools to test adults for vulnerability to certain diseases before symptoms appear. And eventually drugs may be developed to correct deficiencies within genes that cause genetic errors, and perhaps defective genes may someday be replaced by healthy ones.

In order to fish a single gene out of the sea of genetic material in the body's cells, however, the pioneers exploring the genetic frontier must first push the limits of existing technology. New methods of automation must be cultivated before we can fulfill the goals of the genome project. These technological improvements (primarily advances in engineering) are already being created. A new technology that promises to help interpret data gathered from sequencing will scan the chemical composition of sequenced DNA and pick up patterns that will indicate common genetic functions.

The venture to map the human genome, however, is not without its dangers. We have already witnessed the violent abuse of genetics in the name of eugenics and racial hygiene (the hideous genocide of Jews in Nazi Germany) earlier in this century. The eugenics movement was initiated in the Twenties in Britain and the United States, where its supporters attempted to alter the human stock by controlled breeding through sterilization and laws to prevent racial intermarriages.

The shadows of past abuses loom in the background of genetic research. We can prevent such atrocities from recurring if scientists, doctors, and society at large refuse to cede control of genetic discoveries to those who would misuse them. And one day laws must be passed to protect individuals from harm that might occur from violation of medical confidentiality (between patients and their physicians), resulting from genetic profiles.

We are far more than our genes, but understanding our genes is extraordinarily important. How else can we understand what transforms a normal cell into one that indulges in unregulated growth to become a cancer? How else can we combat Alzheimer's disease, arthritis, or disorders of immunity that result more from "the enemies within" than from infections arising from external sources? The fruits of our labors will be masses of information about the most important set of instructions we can ever study—the human genome. The resulting mountain of knowledge will be mined for centuries, as we strive to conquer disease. □

James D. Watson, a pioneer in genetics, received the Nobel prize in medicine in 1962 for codiscovering the structure of DNA. Today he has a new challenge as director of the Human Genome Project. This article was first published in *OMNI*, June 1990.

Landmark Gene Therapy Approved

In July 1990, the Recombinant DNA Advisory Committee (RAC) and the National Institutes of Health (NIH) approved research proposals to treat volunteers with genetically altered cells.

One proposal calls for injecting gene-altered white cells into a group of men and women with advanced melanoma. Another proposal is to alter cells from a small group of children with an inherited immune disorder. □

Table of Geological Periods

It is now generally assumed that planets are formed by the accretion of gas and dust in a cosmic cloud, but there is no way of estimating the length of this process. Our earth acquired its present size, more or less, between 4,000 and 5,000 million years ago. Life on earth originated about 2,000 million years ago, but there are no good fossil remains from periods earlier than the Cambrian, which began about 550 million years ago. The largely unknown past before the Cambrian Period is referred to as the Pre-Cambrian and is subdivided into the Lower (or older) and Upper (or younger) Pre-Cambrian—also called the Archaeozoic and Proterozoic Eras.

The known geological history of the earth since the beginning of the Cambrian Period is subdivided into three "eras," each of which comprises a number of "periods." They, in turn, are subdivided into "subperiods." In a subperiod, a certain section may be especially well known because of rich fossil finds. Such a section is called a "formation," and it is usually identified by a place name.

Paleozoic Era

This era began 550 million years ago and lasted for 355 million years. The name was compounded from Greek *palaios* (old) and *zoön* (animal).

Period	Duration¹	Subperiods	Events
Cambrian (from *Cambria*, Latin name for Wales)	70	Lower Cambrian Middle Cambrian Upper Cambrian	Invertebrate sea life of many types, proliferating during this and the following period
Ordovician (from Latin *Ordovices*, people of early Britain)	85	Lower Ordovician Upper Odovician	
Silurian (from Latin *Silures*, people of early Wales)	40	Lower Silurian Upper Silurian	First known fishes; gigantic sea scorpions
Devonian (from Devonshire in England)	50	Lower Devonian Upper Devonian	Proliferation of fishes and other forms of sea life, land still largely lifeless
Carboniferous (from Latin *carbo* = coal + *fero* = to bear)	85	Lower or Mississippian Upper of Pennsylvanian	Period of maximum coal formation in swampy forests; early insects and first known amphibians
Permian (from district of Perm in Russia)	25	Lower Permian Upper Permian	Early reptiles and mammals; earliest form of turtles

Mesozoic Era

This era began 195 million years ago and lasted for 135 million years. The name was compounded from Greek *mesos* (middle) and *zoön* (animal). Popular name: Age of Reptiles.

Period	Duration¹	Subperiods	Events
Triassic (from *trias* = triad)	35	Lower or Buntsandstein (from German *bunt* = colorful + *Sandstein* = sandstone) Middle or Muschelkalk (from German *Muschel* = clam + *Kalk* = limestone) Upper or Keuper (old miners' term)	Early saurians
Jurassic (from Jura Mountains)	35	Lower or Black Jurassic, or Lias (from French *liais* = hard stone) Middle or Brown Jurassic, or Dogger (old provincial English for ironstone) Upper or White Jurassic, or Malm (Middle English for sand)	Many sea-going reptiles; early large dinosaurs; somewhat later, flying reptiles (pterosaurs), earliest known birds
Cretaceous (from Latin *creta* = chalk)	65	Lower Cretaceous Upper Cretaceous	Maximum development of dinosaurs; birds proliferating; oppossum-like mammals

Cenozoic Era

This era began 60 million years ago and includes the geological present. The name was compounded from Greek *kainos* (new) and *zoön* (animal). Popular name: Age of Mammals.

Period	Duration[1]	Subperiods	Events
Tertiary (originally thought to be the third of only three periods)	c. 60	Paleocene (from Greek *palaios* = old + *kainos* = new)	First mammals other than marsupials
		Eocene (from Greek *eos* = dawn + *kainos* = new)	Formation of amber; rich insect fauna; early bats
		Oligocene (from Greek *oligos* = few + *kainos* = new)	Steady increase of large mammals
		Miocene (from Greek *meios* = less + *kainos* = new)	
		Pliocene (from Greek *pleios* = more + *kainos* = new)	Mammals closely resembling present types; protohumans
Pleistocene (from Greek *pleistos* = most + *kainos* = new) (popular name: Ice Age)	1	Four major glaciations, named Günz, Mindel, Riss, and Würm, originally the names of rivers. Last glaciation ended 10,000 to 15,000 years ago	Various forms of early man
Holocene (from Greek *holos* = entire + *kainos* = new)		The present	The last 3,000 years are called "history"

1. In millions of years.

Chemical Elements

Element	Symbol	Atomic no.	Atomic weight	Specific gravity	Melting point °C	Boiling point °C	Number of isotopes[1]	Discoverer	Year
Actinium	Ac	89	227 [2]	10.07[2]	1050	3200 ±300	11	Debierne	1899
Aluminum	Al	13	26.9815	2.6989	660.37	2467	8	Wöhler	1827
Americium	Am	95	243 [6]	13.67	994 ±4	2607	13[3]	Seaborg et al.	1944
Antimony	Sb	51	121.75	6.691	630.74	1750	29	Early historic times	—
Argon	Ar	18	39.948	1.7837[4]	−189.2	−185.7	8	Rayleigh and Ramsay	1894
Arsenic (gray)	As	33	74.9216	5.73	817 (28 atm.)	613 [5]	14	Albertus Magnus	1250?
Astatine	At	85	−210	—	302	337	21	Corson et al.	1940
Barium	Ba	56	137.34	3.5	725	1640	25	Davy	1808
Berkelium	Bk	97	247[6]	14.00[7]	—	—	8[3]	Seaborg et al.	1949
Beryllium	Be	4	9.01218	1.848	1278 ±5	2970 (5 mm.)	6	Vauquelin	1798
Bismuth	Bi	83	208.9806	9.747	271.3	1560 ±5	19	Geoffroy	1753
Boron	B	5	10.81	2.37[8]	2300	2550 [5]	6	Gay-Lussac and Thénard; Davy	1808
Bromine	Br	35	79.904	3.12[4]	−7.2	58.78	19	Balard	1826
Cadmium	Cd	48	112.40	8.65	320.9	765	22	Stromeyer	1817
Calcium	Ca	20	40.08	1.55	839 ±2	1484	14	Davy	1808
Californium	Cf	98	251[6]	—	—	—	12[3]	Seaborg et al.	1950
Carbon	C	6	12.011	1.8–3.5[9]	−3550	4827	7	Prehistoric	—
Cerium	Ce	58	140.12	6.771	798 ±3	3257	19	Berzelius and Hisinger; Klaproth	1803
Cesium	Cs	55	132.9055	1.873	28.40	678.4	22	Bunsen and Kirchhoff	1860
Chlorine	Cl	17	35.453	1.56[4]	−100.98	−34.6	11	Scheele	1774
Chromium	Cr	24	51.996	7.18–7.20	1857 ±20	2672	9	Vauquelin	1797
Cobalt	Co	27	58.9332	8.9	1495	2870	14	Brandt	c.1735
Copper	Cu	29	63.546	8.96	1083.4±0.2	2567	11	Prehistoric	—
Curium	Cm	96	247[6]	13.51[2]	1340 ±40	—	13[3]	Seaborg et al.	1944
Dysprosium	Dy	66	162.50	8.540	1409	2335	21	Boisbaudran	1886
Einsteinium	Es	99	254[6]	—	—	—	12[3]	Ghiorso et al	1952
Erbium	Er	68	167.26	9.045	1522	2510	16	Mosander	1843
Europium	Eu	63	151.96	5.283	822 ±5	1597	21	Demarcay	1896
Fermium	Fm	100	257[6]	—	—	—	10[3]	Ghiorso et al	1953
Fluorine	F	9	18.9984	1.108[4]	−219.62	−188.14	6	Moissan	1886
Francium	Fr	87	223[6]	—	27[2]	677 [2]	21	Perey	1939
Gadolinium	Gd	64	157.25	7.898	1311 ±1	3233	17	Marignac	1880
Gallium	Ga	31	69.72	5.904	29.78	2403	14	Boisbaudran	1875
Germanium	Ge	32	72.59	5.323	937.4	2830	17	Winkler	1886
Gold	Au	79	196.9665	19.32	1064.43	2807	21	Prehistoric	—
Hafnium	Hf	72	178.49	13.31	2227 ±20	4602	17	Coster and von Hevesy	1923
Helium	He	2	4.00260	0.1785[4]	−272.2 (26 atm.)	−268.934	5	Janssen	1868
Holmium	Ho	67	164.9303	8.781	1470	2720	29	Delafontaine and Soret	1878
Hydrogen	H	1	1.0080	0.070[4]	−259.14	−252.87	3	Cavendish	1766

Element	Symbol	Atomic no.	Atomic weight	Specific gravity	Melting point °C	Boiling point °C	Number of isotopes[1]	Discoverer	Year
Indium	In	49	114.82	7.31	156.61	2080	34	Reich and Richter	1863
Iodine	I	53	126.9045	4.93	113.5	184.35	24	Courtois	1811
Iridium	Ir	77	192.22	22.42	2410	4130	25	Tennant	1803
Iron	Fe	26	55.847	7.894	1535	2750	10	Prehistoric	—
Krypton	Kr	36	83.80	3.733[4]	−156.6	−152.30±0.10	23	Ramsay and Travers	1898
Lanthanum	La	57	138.9055	6.166	920 ±5	3454	19	Mosander	1839
Lawrencium	Lr	103	257[6]	—	—	—	20[3]	Ghiorso et al.	1961
Lead	Pb	82	207.2	11.35	327.502	1740	29	Prehistoric	—
Lithium	Li	3	6.941	0.534	180.54	1347	5	Arfvedson	1817
Lutetium	Lu	71	174.97	9.835	1656 ±5	3315	22	Urbain	1907
Magnesium	Mg	12	24.305	1.738	648.8±0.5	1090	8	Black	1755
Manganese	Mn	25	54.9380	7.21−7.44[10]	1244 ±3	1962	11	Gahn, Scheele, and Bergman	1774
Mendelevium	Md	101	256[6]	—	—	—	3[3]	Ghiorso et al.	1955
Mercury	Hg	80	200.59	13.546	−38.87	356.58	26	Prehistoric	—
Molybdenum	Mo	42	95.94	10.22	2617	4612	20	Scheele	1778
Neodymium	Nd	60	144.24	6.80 & 7.004[10]	1010	3127	16	von Welsbach	1885
Neon	Ne	10	20.179	0.89990 (g/l 0°C/1 atm)	−248.67	−246.048	8	Ramsay and Travers	1898
Neptunium	Np	93	237.0482	20.25	640 ±1	3902	15[3]	McMillan and Abelson	1940
Nickel	Ni	28	58.71	8.902	1453	2732	11	Cronstedt	1751
Niobium (Columbium)	Nb	41	92.9064	8.57	2468 ±10	4742	24	Hatchett	1801
Nitrogen	N	7	14.0067	0.808[4]	−209.86	−195.8	8	Rutherford	1772
Nobelium	No	102	254[6]	—	—	—	7[3]	Ghiorso et al.	1957
Osmium	Os	76	190.2	22.57	3045 ±30	5027 ±100	19	Tennant	1803
Oxygen	O	8	15.9994	1.14[4]	−218.4	−182.962	8	Priestley	1774
Palladium	Pd	46	106.4	12.02	1552	3140	21	Wollaston	1803
Phosphorus	P	15	30.9738	1.82 (white)	44.1	280	7	Brand	1669
Platinum	Pt	78	195.09	21.45	1772	3827 ±100	32	Ulloa	1735
Plutonium	Pu	94	244[6]	19.84	641	3232	16[3]	Seaborg et al.	1940
Polonium	Po	84	210[6]	9.32	254	962	34	Curie	1898
Potassium	K	19	39.102	0.862	63.65	774	10	Davy	1807
Praseodymium	Pr	59	140.9077	6.772	931 ±4	3212	15	von Weisbach	1885
Promethium	Pm	61	145[6]	—	≈1080	2460?	14	Marinsky et al.	1945
Protactinium	Pa	91	231.0359	15.37[2]	<1600	—	14	Hahn and Meitner	1917
Radium	Ra	88	226.0254	5.0?	700	1140	15	P. and M. Curie	1898
Radon	Rn	86	222[6]	4.4[4]	−71	−61.8	20	Dorn	1900
Rhenium	Re	75	186.2	21.02	3180	5627[7]	21	Noddack, Berg, and Tacke	1925
Rhodium	Rh	45	102.9055	12.41	1966 ±3	3727 ±100	20	Wollaston	1803
Rubidium	Rb	37	85.4678	1.532	38.89	688	20	Bunsen and Kirchoff	1861
Ruthenium	Ru	44	101.07	12.44	2310	3900	16	Klaus	1844
Samarium	Sm	62	150.4	7.536	1072 ±5	1778	17	Boisbaudran	1879
Scandium	Sc	21	44.9559	2.989	1539	2832	15	Nilson	1879
Selenium	Se	34	78.96	4.79 (gray)	217	684.9±1	20	Berzelius	1817
Silicon	Si	14	28.086	2.33	1410	2355	8	Berzelius	1824
Silver	Ag	47	107.868	10.50	961.93	2212	27	Prehistoric	—
Sodium	Na	11	22.9898	0.971	97.81±0.03	882.9	7	Davy	1807
Strontium	Sr	38	87.62	2.54	769	1384	18	Davy	1808
Sulfur	S	16	32.06	2.07[11]	112.8	444.674	10	Prehistoric	—
Tantalum	Ta	73	180.9479	16.654	2996	5425 ± 100	19	Ekeberg	1801
Technetium	Tc	43	98.9062	11.50[2]	2172	4877	23	Perrier and Segrè	1937
Tellurium	Te	52	127.60	6.24	449.5±0.3	989.8±3.8	29	von Reichenstein	1782
Terbium	Tb	65	158.9254	8.234	1360 ±4	3041	24	Mosander	1843
Thallium	Tl	81	204.37	11.85	303.5	1457 ±10	28	Crookes	1861
Thorium	Th	90	232.0381	11.72	1750	4790	12	Berzelius	1828
Thulium	Tm	69	168.9342	9.314	1545 ±15	1727	18	Cleve	1879
Tin	Sn	50	118.69	7.31 (white)	231.9681	2270	28	Prehistoric	—
Titanium	Ti	22	47.90	4.55	1660 ±10	3287	9	Gregor	1791
Tungsten (Wolfram)	W	74	183.85	19.3	3410 ±20	5660	22	J. and F. d'Elhuyar	1783
Uranium	U	92	238.029	−18.95	1132.3±0.8	3818	15	Peligot	1841
Vanadium	V	23	50.9414	6.11	1890 ±10	3380	9	del Rio	1801
Xenon	Xe	54	131.30	3.52[4]	−111.9	−107.1±3	31	Ramsay and Travers	1898
Ytterbium	Yb	70	173.04	6.972	824 ±5	1193	16	Marignac	1878
Yttrium	Y	39	88.9059	4.457	1523 ±8	3337	21	Gadolin	1794
Zinc	Zn	30	65.38	7.133	419.58	907	15	Prehistoric	—
Zirconium	Zr	40	91.22	6.506[2]	1852 ±2	4377	20	Klaproth	1789

Elements No. 104, 105, and 106—See NOTE at end of footnotes.

1. Isotopes are different forms of the same element having the same atomic number but different atomic weights. 2. Calculated figure. 3. Artificially produced. 4. Liquid. 5. Sublimation point. 6. Mass number of the isotope of longest known life. 7. Estimated. 8. Amorphous. 9. Depending on whether amorphous, graphite or diamond. 10. Depending on allotropic form. 11. Rhombic. —Is approximately. < Is less than. NOTE: There is a dispute between groups at the Lawrence Berkeley Laboratory of the University of California and at the Dubna Laboratory in the Soviet Union concerning the discovery of elements 104, 105, and 106. The Lawrence Berkeley Laboratory claims that 104 and 105 were discovered in 1969 and 1970, respectively, by Ghiorso et al. and has suggested the names Rutherfordium and Hahnium. The U.S. laboratory claims also that Ghiorso et al. discovered element 106 in 1974. No name has yet been suggested for this element. Names will not be official until the controversy is resolved and they have been approved by the International Union of Pure and Applied Chemistry.

Federal Funding for R&D, by Budget Function, 1980-1990

(In millions of dollars)

Function	1990, est.	1989	1988	1987	1986	1985	1980
National defense	44,295	40,574	40,099	39,152	36,926	33,698	14,946
Health	8,229	7,724	7,076	6,556	5,565	5,418	3,694
Space research and technology	6,146	4,589	3,683	3,398	2,894	2,725	2,738
General science	2,652	2,379	2,160	2,042	1,873	1,862	1,233
Energy	2,333	2,427	2,126	2,053	2,286	2,389	3,603
Transportation	1,129	1,019	896	908	917	1,030	887
Natural resources and environment	1,140	1,208	1,160	1,133	1,062	1,059	999
Agriculture	901	910	882	822	815	836	585
Education, training, employment[2]	347	343	285	267	248	220	468
International affairs	169	141	224	223	211	210	125
Veterans benefits and services	199	212	195	215	183	193	126
Commerce and housing credit	132	134	122	110	111	114	101
Administration of justice	40	45	51	49	41	47	45
Community and regional develop	79	77	108	99	88	50	119
Total[1]	67,833	61,823	59,106	57,069	53,249	49,887	29,739

1. Includes functions not shown separately. 2. Includes social services. *Source:* U.S. National Science Foundation, *Federal R&D Funding by Budget Function,* annual. *Statistical Abstract of the United States, 1990.*

Biotechnology

Biotechnology is an ancient practice that includes such familiar applications as the use of yeast in baking bread and cultures in making cheese. Recent breakthroughs in biotechnology, such as recombinant DNA techniques, cell fusion, and gene therapy, offer unprecedented opportunities for improving the nation's productivity, health, and well being. Uncertainties in the returns on biotechnology investment, however, stemming from market barriers and regulation, have retarded the process.

The U.S. government proposes to spend $3.6 billion, an increase of $213 million over 1990, for biotechnology research and development.

Advances in biotechnology hold much promise. They can help improve the availability and quality of the food supply; prevent, identify, and cure disease; and reduce the hazards of industrial waste.

Cell fusion, the merging of the genetic material of two cells of different species, can accelerate the selective breeding process for producing hardier and more fruitful crops and livestock. Gene therapy, replacing defective genetic material with normal DNA, may enable doctors to attack directly the source of major diseases, including cancer.

In 1960, biotechnology as an industry was nearly non-existent. In 1989, U.S. businesses and government agencies invested about $5 billion in biotechnology research, development, and manufacturing.

High Energy Physics

As scientists probe further and further into the interior of atoms, they discover new "building blocks" or elementary particles. Today it is known that protons, neutrons, and various other particles are made up of even smaller particles known as quarks. Currently, investigations are underway at laboratories around the world to try to understand the forces between these quarks and to construct theories to explain the numbers and kinds of quarks, as well as their physical properties.

This research is accomplished using accelerators, machines that speed protons or electrons close to the speed of light and then allow controlled collisions between particles in order to probe the interactions that take place. The higher the energy of the colliding particles, the finer the probe into these particles.

Experiments in the United States are carried out mostly by university groups working at the nation's four large accelerator centers: the Stanford Linear Accelerator in California, the Brookhaven National Laboratory on Long Island, the Cornell Electron Storage Ring accelerator in New York State, and the Fermilab National Laboratory near Chicago.

The machine at Fermilab is the world's most energetic proton accelerator, pushing particles to energies as great as one trillion electron volts (1 TEV). It is expected to hold that distinction until the Superconducting Super Collider becomes operational in the late 1990s.

The Superconducting Super Collider

The Superconducting Super Collider (SSC) will accelerate counter-rotating beams of protons to an energy 20 times greater than that of the machine at Fermilab and then cause these beams to collide head-on. At such energies, scientists believe that they can explore aspects of matter that are unreachable using any existing facility.

The dominant feature of the Super Collider will be two rings of superconducting magnets in a tunnel 53 miles in circumference. By comparison, the largest existing U.S. circular accelerator (Fermilab) is 4 miles in circumference. Around this tunnel there will be six areas for researchers to conduct experiments on the colliding beams. The SSC will employ 2,500 scientists, engineers, and technicians and host an additional 500 visiting scientists from all over the world.

The 1991 Federal budget provides $318 million for the Super Collider, an increase of $100 million over the 1990 level.

The proposed site for the SSC is in Ellis County, Texas, for which an Environmental Impact Statement will be completed before construction begins. A proposed schedule calls for design and construction within 10 years (by 1998) at an estimated cost of $5.9 billion. □

SCIENCE & LEARNING

A Chronology of Major Developments from 1450 to the Present

Text from AN ENCYCLOPEDIA OF WORLD HISTORY by William L. Langer, The Fifth Edition, Copyright 1940, 1948, 1952, and © 1967, 1972 by Houghton Mifflin Company. Reprinted by permission of Houghton Mifflin Company.

Science

1469. Publication of Pliny's *Historia naturalis*, the first scientific book to be printed.

1527-1541. Philippus Paracelsus [Theophrastus von Hohenheim] (1493-1541) crusaded for the use of chemicals in the treatment of disease. He introduced the system of salt, sulfur, and mercury as the three prime "elements," from which all things are made.

1540. Posthumous publication of *De la pirotechnica*, a handbook of metallurgy containing information about smelting and ore reduction compiled by **Vannoccio Biringuccio** (1480-1539).

1543. Nicolaus Copernicus [Niklas Kopernik] (1473-1543) published *De revolutionibus orbium coelestium*, which asserted that the planets, including the earth, circle around a stationary sun. He believed this theory represented the true structure of the world.

1543. Andreas Vesalius (1514-1564) produced *De fabrica corporis humani*, an illustrated, systematic study of the human body. This work is a union of Renaissance artistic endeavor and of a revived interest in the empirical study of **human anatomy**.

1545. Jerome Cardan (1501-1576) published the solution of the **cubic equation** in *Ars Magna*. This solution, the first major advance in mathematics in the European Renaissance, was due to **Niccolò Tartaglia** (?1500-1557), and was used without his permission.

1546. Georgius Agricola [Georg Bauer] (1494-1555) applied observation rather than mere speculation to the study of rocks, publishing *De natura fossilium*, an early handbook of mineralogy, and *De re metallica* (1556), which dealt with mining and metallurgy.

1546. Girolamo Fracastoro (?1483-1553) developed the theory that **contagion** (infectious disease) is caused by a living agent transmitted from person to person.

1551-1587. Conrad Gesner (1516-1565) amassed in the first great Renaissance encyclopedia, *Historia animalium*, ancient and contemporary knowledge of the animal kingdom.

1554. Jean Fernel (1497-1558) codified the practical and theoretical medicine of the Renaissance, rejecting magic and astrology but emphasizing the functions of organs.

1572. Tycho Brahe (1546-1601) observed a bright new star, a *super nova*, and determined that it was beyond the moon, thereby destroying the prevailing Aristotelian notion that no change occurred in celestial regions. Through systematic

Johannes Kepler

Johannes Kepler, German astronomer and mathematician, was the founder of modern astronomy. He was born on Dec. 27, 1571, in the village of Weil-der-Stadt in the Duchy of Württenberg, Swabia. He studied mathematics, philosophy, theology, and astronomy at the University of Tüblingen, earning his M.A. in 1591.

Kepler became a teacher of mathematics and astronomy at Gratz, the Austrian province of Styria from 1594 to 1600. His writings on celestial orbits impressed the famous Danish astronomer Tycho Brahe who invited Kepler to join him at Prague. Kepler accepted and assisted Tycho in preparing new planetary tables. When Brahe died in 1601, Kepler succeeded him as Imperial Mathematician. He had access to all of Tycho Brahe's papers and 20 years of precise observations which he used to form the foundation of his three laws of planetary motion *(Kepler's Laws)* published between 1609 and 1618.

They are: (1) the path of a planet is an ellipse with the sun at one focus; (2) a line from the sun to a planet sweeps out equal areas in equal time periods; and (3) the square of the orbital period of a planet is proportional to the cube of its average distance from the sun.

Kepler spent the latter part of his life as a professor of mathematics at Linz, Austria. He died at Regensburg, Bavaria, on Nov. 15, 1630. □

observation, using instruments designed by himself, Tycho accumulated very accurate data on planetary and lunar positions and produced the **first modern star catalog.**

1583. Andrea Cesalpino (1519-1603) compiled the first modern **classification of plants** based on a comparative study of forms.

1585. Simon Stevin (1548-1620) published *La disme,* introducing decimal fractions into arithmetic. A year later he published treatises on **statics and hydrostatics.** The work on statics gave a mathematical proof of the law of the lever, elegantly proved the law of the inclined plane, and showed that two unequal weights fell through the same distance in the same time.

1591. François Viète [Vieta] (1540-1603) introduced **literal notation** in algebra, i.e., the systematic use of letters to represent both coefficients and unknown quantities in algebraic equations.

c. 1600. Dutch lens-grinders in Middleburg are thought to have constructed the **first refracting telescope** and the **compound microscope.**

1600. William Gilbert (1540-1603) provided in *De magnete* a methodical experimental study of the **electric and magnetic properties of bodies,** and established that the earth itself is a magnet.

1603. Johann Bayer (1572-1625) produced a **celestial atlas** which introduced the use of Greek letters to indicate the brightest stars in every constellation.

1609. Johannes Kepler (1571-1630) announced in *Astronomia nova* his first two **laws of planetary motion:** planets move in ellipses with the sun in one focus; the radius vector from the sun to a planet sweeps out equal areas in equal times. In *Harmonices mundi* (1619) he added his third law: the squares of the periods of revolution of all planets are proportional to the cubes of their mean distances from the sun.

1610. Galileo Galilei (1564-1642), in *Sidereus nuncius,* revealed the results of the first telescopic observations of celestial phenomena. He used these observations to destroy the Aristotelian-Ptolemaic cosmology and to argue for the plausibility of the Copernican system.

1614. John Napier (1550-1617) introduced **logarithms** as a computational tool.

1627. Kepler, on the basis of Tycho Brahe's observations and his own theories, compiled the *Rudolphine Tables (Tabulae Rudolfinae)* which made possible the calculation of future planetary positions and other astronomical events; they were standard for over a century.

1628. William Harvey (1578-1657) in his classic *Exercitatio anatomica de motu cordis et sanguinis in animalibus* blended reason, comparative observation, and experimentation to demonstrate the **circulation of the blood.**

1632. Galileo fashioned in *Dialogo sopra i due massimi sistemi del mondo Tolemaico e Copernicano* a brilliant polemical masterpiece, which clearly showed the superiority of the Copernican system over the Ptolemaic system of the world. This work led to **Galileo's trial and recantation** before the Roman Inquisition of the Catholic Church.

1637. René Descartes (1596-1650) published *Discours de la méthode,* an introduction to his philosophy, which served as a preface to his works on dioptrics, meteorology, and geometry. In the same year he published *La géometrie,* setting forth an **analytic geometry,** i.e., representation of geometric figures by algebraic equations and algebraic equations by geometric figures. **Pierre de Fermat** (?1608-1665) simultaneously and independently developed an analytic geometry. Both Descartes and Fermat applied analytic geometry to the finding of tangents to curves; Fermat also devised a general method for finding maxima and minima.

1638. Galileo in *Discorsi e demonstrazione matematiche intorno a due nuove scienze* established the basic principles of a mathematical description of falling bodies and projectile motion.

1642-1671. Blaise Pascal (1623-1662) constructed the first **adding machine** that could perform the operation of carrying. Some thirty years later, **Gottfried Wilhelm Leibniz** (1646-1716) invented a more complex calculating machine which would multiply rapidly by repeated additions.

1648. Jan Baptista van Helmont (1577-1644), in his

Galileo Galilei

The great Italian scientist, Galileo Galilei, was born in Pisa on Feb. 15, 1564. He taught mathematics at the University of Pisa from 1589 to 1592. He discovered that all falling bodies, large or small, descend with an equal velocity, but the famous story that he demonstrated this by experimenting with weights dropped from the Leaning Tower of Pisa is believed not to be true. From 1592 to 1610, he was a professor of mathematics at the University of Padua. After hearing about a simple magnifying device that was constructed in Holland, he was able to make the first complete astronomical telescope in 1609. Within a year, Galileo made some spectacular discoveries from his celestial observations. They included the four largest moons of Jupiter, the phases of Venus, the mountains and craters of the Moon, and the finding that the Milky Way is made up of myriads of single stars. Galileo's discovery that Venus goes through a complete cycle of phases was a major proof of Copernicus's idea that the sun rather than the Earth is the center of the solar system. His support of Copernicus's views conflicted with church dogma and, in 1616, he was ordered to refrain from teaching Copernicus's heliocentric view of the heavens. Despite the warning, he continued to support Copernican ideas, and in 1633, was summoned to Rome and tried by the Holy Inquisition. Galileo was convicted and made to recant his "false" belief that the Earth moves round the Sun. He was placed in house arrest at his retreat at Arcetri near Florence, where he remained until his death on Jan. 8, 1642.

Sir Isaac Newton

Sir Isaac Newton, the English mathematician and philosopher was born in Woolsthorpe, Lincolnshire, on Christmas day 1642. He earned his B.A. degree at Trinity College, Cambridge University in 1665. During this time he made his first discovery on fluxions but did not publish it. However, it has been established that he devised calculus independently of the German philosopher and mathematician Gottfried W. Leibnitz.

In 1666, according to the popular story, he was working in his garden at Woolsthorpe, when he supposedly reflected on the fall of an apple and it suggested to him the law of universal gravitation.

Newton's subsequent investigations include the nature of light. He experimented with sunlight refracted through a prism in a darkened room and discovered that ordinary white light contains the colors of the rainbow. His study of the laws of refraction and reflection led him to construct the first reflecting telescope in 1668.

Newton's other achievements were ·in the field of mechanics with his discovery of the second and third laws of motion. He became a member of the Royal Society in 1672.

He published his greatest work, "The Mathematical Principle of Natural Philosophy" in 1687 which presented his law of gravitation and laws of motion. He was knighted by Queen Anne in 1705.

Newton was elected president of the Royal Society in 1703 and remained in that office until his death in London on Mar. 20, 1727. He was given a national funeral and was the first scientist to be buried in Westminster Abbey.   □

posthumously published collected works, *Ortus medicinae,* assigned the name "gas" to the "wild spirits" which were produced in various chemical processes and argued that acid fermentation, not "innate heat," was the operative agent of digestion.

1654. Correspondence between Pascal and Fermat on mathematical treatment of games of chance resulted in the beginning of **probability theory.**

1655. John Wallis (1616-1703) published *Arithmetica infinitorum,* which studied infinite series, infinite products, solved problems of quadratures, and found tangents by use of infinitesimals.

1657. The foundation of the **Accademia del Cimento** of Florence, the first organized scientific academy and a center for the new experimental science which stemmed from the work of Galileo.

1659. Christiaan Huygens (1629-1695) revealed, in *Systema Saturnium,* that Saturn is surrounded by a thin, flat ring.

1660-1674. Robert Boyle (1627-1691) described his first **pneumatic pump,** an improvement on that invented by **Otto von Guericke** (1602-1686), in *New Experiments Physicomechanical, Touching the Spring of the Air.* In the second edition (1662) Boyle noted the relation between pressure and volume now called **Boyle's Law.** With this pump Boyle showed that animals die from a lack of air, not from the accumulation of noxious vapors. So began an era in respiration studies that included the elucidation of lung structure (1661) by **Marcello Malpighi** (1628-1694), the proof that fresh air is necessary for respiration (1667) by **Robert Hooke** (1635-1703), the observation that blood changes color when in contact with air (1667-1669) by **Richard Lower** (1631-1691), and the demonstration that the volume of air is reduced in respiration (1674) by **John Mayow** (1640-1679).

1662. Charles II of England chartered **The Royal Society of London,** an independent organization that became the major center of English scientific activity during the 17th and 18th centuries.

1662. Jeremiah Horrocks (1619-1641) predicted and was the first man to observe (1639) a **transit of Venus** across the disk of the sun. His work was posthumously published in *Venus in sole visa* (1662).

1665. Robert Hooke published *Micrographia,* containing descriptions of his microscopic observations. He first used the word *cells* to describe the lacework of rigid walls seen in cork. The observations of Hooke and other classical microscopists —**Marcello Malpighi, Nehemiah Grew** (1641-1712), **Jan Swammerdam** (1637-1680), **Antony van Leeuwenhoek** (1632-1723)—revealed the complex minute structure of living matter and the existence of micro-organisms.

1666. Louis XIV of France founded the **Académie Royale des Sciences,** a government-controlled and financed organization dedicated to experimental science. The activity of the Académie was regularly recorded in the *Journal des Savants,* one of the earliest scientific periodicals. In 1667 the king founded the **Observatoire de Paris** and named the Italian astronomer **Giovanni Domenico Cassini** (1625-1712) as its first director (1669).

1669. Isaac Newton (1642-1727) announced his calculus, in *De analysi per aequationes numero terminorum infinitas,* which circulated in manuscript but was first published in 1711. He further developed the calculus in *Methodus fluxionum et serierum infinitarum* (1671, published 1736), using as fundamental notions "fluxions" (time derivatives) and "fluents" (inverse of fluxions), fluents being interpreted as areas.

1671-1684. Cassini discovered four new **satellites of Saturn** and observed a dark marking in Saturn's ring.

1672. Newton presented to the Royal Society a reflecting telescope which he constructed on principles learned in his optical studies. Newton also published his "New Theory about Light and Colors" showing notably that white light is composed of the various spectral colors, each of which has a different index of refraction.

1673. Christiaan Huygens announced in *Horologium oscillatorium* the invention and theory of the **pendulum clock**. This work included theorems on centrifugal force in circular motion.

1675. Olaus Roemer (1644-1710), by studying the eclipses of Jupiter's moons, determined that light is transmitted with a finite, though very great, speed.

1675. Charles II of England established the **Royal Observatory, Greenwich** and designated **John Flamsteed** (1646-1719) as the first Astronomer Royal.

1678. Robert Hooke provided an account of the law of elastic force, *ut tensio, sic vis* (stress is proportional to strain), which is now known by his name.

1679. Edmé Mariotte (?1620-1684) announced his discovery of the constant **relation between the pressure and volume** of an enclosed quantity of air (discovered independently of Robert Boyle).

1684. Leibniz first published his **differential calculus,** based on work done independently of Newton during the period 1673-1676. Leibniz based his calculus on the finding of differentials, which he understood as infinitesimal differences, and defined the integral as an infinite sum of infinitesimals; the operations of summing and of finding the differences were mutually inverse. His vision of a universal symbolic language led him to devise notation of great heuristic power, such as d for differential and $\int$ for integral.

1686-1704. John Ray (1627-1705) in the three volumes of *Historia generalis plantarum* provided an able account of the structure, physiology, and distribution of plants and laid the foundations of modern **systematic classification.**

1687. Newton in his *Philosophiae naturalis principia mathematica* founded mechanics, both celestial and terrestrial, on his three axioms or **laws of motion.** He demonstrated that the sun attracts the planets and the earth attracts the moon with a force inversely proportional to the square of the distance between them. In his **principle of universal gravitation** he states that any two bodies attract each other with a force proportional to the product of their masses and inversely proportional to the square of the distance between them.

1688. Francesco Redi (1621-1697) challenged the ancient belief in spontaneous generation and began a two-century-long debate on the subject by his controlled experimentation on the production of maggots.

1696. Guillaume de L'Hôpital (1661-1704) published the first textbook of the **infinitesimal calculus,** *Analyse des infiniment petits,* based on the lectures of his teacher, **Johann Bernoulli** (1667-1748).

1697. Bernoulli showed that the curve of quickest descent was the cycloid, thereby solving the first problem of the **calculus of variations.**

1700. Gottfried Wilhelm Leibniz (1646-1716) was instrumental in the foundation of the **Berlin Academy,** Germany's first stable scientific organization.

1701-1713. Jakob (Jacques) Bernoulli (1654-1705) worked on problems (1701) which later became the calculus of variations. His *Ars conjectandi,* posthumously published in 1713, on probability theory, permutations and combinations, and binomial distribution.

Scientific Thought

1704. Isaac Newton (1642-1727), reporting on the optical researches he had undertaken since the 1660s, published his *Opticks.* He treated experimentally of the reflection, refraction, diffraction, and spectra of light.

He investigated the dispersion and composition of white light, showing that it is not homogeneous, as was traditionally thought, but decomposable into simple colors. The *Opticks* concluded with a group of "Queries," which in later editions developed Newton's speculations and conjectures concerning heat, chemical affinity, pneumatics, physiology, atomism, the nature of gravitation and the aether, the relation of the world of nature to God, and the proper manner of scientific inquiry. These speculations determined much of the experimental science of the 18th century.

1705. Edmund Halley (1656-1742) noted the resemblance in the paths of the comets of 1531, 1607, and 1682, and conjectured that these were different appearances of the same comet, now called *Halley's Comet.* He correctly predicted the return of this comet in 1758.

1708. Hermann Boerhaave (1668-1738) systematized physiology in the mechanistic terms of chemistry. As teacher of theoretical medicine at Leyden he influenced a whole generation of physicians.

1715. Brook Taylor (1685-1731) published *Methodus incrementorum directa et inversa,* the first treatise on finite differences and the source of *Taylor's series.* The series took on great importance in the work of **Leonhard Euler** (1707-1783) and **Joseph-Louis Lagrange** (1736-1813).

1717. Gabriel D. Fahrenheit (1686-1736) proposed the *Fahrenheit System* and a mode of calibrating thermometers.

1718. Etienne F. Geoffroy (1672-1731) published the first table of *chemical affinities,* a chart designed to indicate the reactivity of individual chemicals toward each other.

1725. Peter the Great founded the **Academy of Sciences** at St. Petersburg. The original resident membership of sixteen included thirteen Germans, two Swiss, and one Frenchman.

1725. John Flamsteed's (1646-1719) *Historia coelestis britannica,* a catalog of the positions of nearly 3,000 stars published posthumously. This replaced the catalog of **Tycho Brahe** as the standard reference source.

1727-1733. Stephen Hales (1677-1761) in *Vegetable Staticks* (1727) and *Haemastaticks* (1733) recorded a series of experiments in plant and animal physiology and demonstrated that biological phenomena, such as blood pressure, could be investigated on a quantitative basis. He also invented a pneumatic trough, an indispensible apparatus for collecting gases.

1728. James Bradley (1693-1762) explained an anomalous motion of the fixed stars by his discovery of the aberration of light.

1732. Boerhaave published *Elementa chemiae,* a standard chemistry textbook influential until the end of the 18th century.

1736. Leonhard Euler published *Mechanica sive motus analytice exposita,* generally considered to be the first systematic textbook of mechanics. During his life, Euler made fundamental contributions in many areas of analytical mechanics, e.g., the theory of the motion of rigid bodies, hydrodynamics, the application of variational principles in mechanics, and celestial mechanics.

1738. Pierre de Maupertuis (1698-1759) published *Sur la figure de la terre,* a report of a scientific expedition to Lapland which confirmed Newton's view that the earth is a spheroid flattened near the poles with a bulge near the equator.

1738. Daniel Bernoulli (1700-1782), in *Hydrodynamica,* presented investigations of the forces exerted by fluids, and presented an early version of the **kinetic theory of gases.**

1743. Alexis Clairaut (1713-1765) presented his *Théorie de la figure de la terre,* a mathematical investigation on hydrostatic principles of the shape of the earth.

1743-1744. Benjamin Franklin (1706-1790) was instrumental in the establishment of the **American Philosophical Society** at Philadelphia, America's first scientific society, devoted to "the promotion of useful knowledge."

1748. James Bradley reported his discovery, made earlier, of the **mutation of the earth's axis.**

1748. Euler published *Introductio in analysin infinitorum,* systematizing the calculus and emphasizing the study of functions, classifying differential equations, and treating trigonometric functions and equations of curves without reference to diagrams. He gave an elegant and highly influential exposition of the Leibnizian calculus, together with many new results of his own, in his *Institutiones calculi differentialis* (1755) and *Institutiones calculi integralis* (1768-1770).

1748. John Tuberville Needham (1713-1781), in *Observations upon the Generation, Composition, and Decomposition of Animal and Vegetable Substances,* reported that boiled, sealed flasks of broth teemed with "little animals" when opened. His rival **Lazzaro Spallanzani** (1729-1799) devised controlled experiments to test such factors as the amount of heating necessary to kill micro-organisms.

1750. Thomas Wright (1711-1786) suggested that the appearance of the Milky Way from the earth is due to the distribution of the visible stars in a disc.

1751. Robert Whytt (1714-1764) explicitly distinguished voluntary from involuntary motions, recognized that only a segment of the spinal cord is necessary for reflex action, and established the **study of reflexes** as a distinct branch of physiology.

1751-1754. Franklin published *Experiments and Observations on Electricity,* in which he explained his theory that electricity is a single fluid and used it to account for the properties of the Leyden jar and other known electrical phenomena. He deduced the principle of the **conservation of electric charge** from his theory, and established that lightning is identical with electricity produced by friction.

1755. Mikhail Lomonosov (1711-1765) played a leading role in the founding of **Moscow University.** Known for his work in chemistry, electricity, mechanics, and history, his major contribution was the establishment of the scientific tradition in Russia.

1756-1762. Joseph Black (1728-1799), in *Experiments upon Magnesia Alba* (1756), announced the isolation of a new gas, "fixed air" (carbon dioxide). In researches conducted between 1759 and 1762, but published posthumously (1803) in his *Lectures on the Elements of Chemistry,* he distinguished between temperature and quantity of heat, and introduced the terms and concepts *latent heat, heat of fusion, thermal capacity,* and *caloric.*

1756. Johann Lehmann (d. 1767) contributed to knowledge of geological succession by classifying orders of strata. Similar work was carried on by **Giovanni Arduino** (1713-1795), who gave the names *primary, secondary,* and *tertiary* to lithologically distinct sequences of strata; and earlier by **John Strachey** (1671-1743), whose "Observations on the Strata in the Somersetshire Coal Fields" (1719) established stratigraphical divisions and offered an early attempt at a structure section.

1758. Carl Linnaeus (1707-1778) in the tenth edition of his *Systema naturae* catalogued all known flora and fauna, (including man), and laid the basis for modern taxonomy by his consistent use of a **binomial nomenclature.**

1760-1761. Joseph-Louis Lagrange presented a complete *calculus of variations,* incorporating both old and new results in an elegant and systematic treatment.

1761. Giovanni Morgagni (1682-1771) presented in *De sedibus et causis morborum* a correlation of clinical symptoms and anatomic lesions challenging the notion of disease as an imbalance of humors.

1768-1779. Captain James Cook (1728-1779), an English naval officer, led three expeditions opening the Pacific to scientific explorers and collectors.

1771. Charles Messier (1730-1817) published the first installment of a star catalog which eventually recorded 103 nebulae and clusters.

1771-1794. John Hunter (1728-1793) raised surgery from a technical trade to the ranks of a science by connecting morphology with physiology and emphasizing the natural healing powers of the body.

1773-1784. Pierre Laplace (1749-1827) and **Lagrange** in a long series of papers finally solved the "long-term inequality" of Jupiter and Saturn, thus giving important evidence for the stability of the solar system.

1774-1817. Abraham Werner (1749/50-1817) propagated his view that features of the earth's crust are of aqueous origin (neptunism). Werner's methodical systematization of rocks and their formations helped found mineralogy as a science.

1774. Nicholas Desmarest (1725-1815) established the igneous origin of basalt in a study of the Auvergne volcanoes, thereby challenging neptunism.

1774-1786. Joseph Priestley (1733-1804) in his *Experiments and Observations on Different Kinds of Air* reported his studies on gases and announced the discovery of a number of water soluble gases, including ammonia, sulfur dioxide, and hydrogen chloride. In 1774 Priestley isolated **oxygen,** which he called "dephlogisticated air," in experiments with red calx of mercury.

1777. Carl Scheele (1742-1786) published his *Chemische Abhandlung von der Luft und dem Feuer.* He reported on his production of hydrogen in 1770 ("inflammable air"), his isolation of oxygen in 1773 ("fire air"), and his discoveries of many new and important substances, both organic and inorganic.

1779. Jan Ingenhousz (1730-1799) showed that plants make the atmosphere fit for breathing by producing oxygen during the day, that green leaves and stalks are the functional parts in this process, and that plants carry out respiration concomitantly with photosynthesis.

1780-1781. Claude Berthollet (1748-1822) and **Antoine Lavoisier** (1743-1794), using the new chemical techniques of pneumatic and combustion analysis, isolated carbon, oxygen, and hydrogen as the elements of organic substances. Their work opened a new era in elementary organic analysis and physiological chemistry.

1781. William Herschel (1738-1822) discovered by telescopic observation the planet *Uranus*, the first planet to be discovered in recorded history.

1783. John Goodricke (1764-1786) observed regular variations in the brightness of the star Algol and demonstrated that Algol was an eclipsing binary.

1784. René-Just Haüy (1743-1821/22) gave an exposition of the laws of crystal form in *Essai d'une théorie sur la structure des crystaux.*

1784. Henry Cavendish (1731-1810) published *Experiments on Air,* in which he showed from experimental results obtained in 1781 that the explosion of a mixture of two volumes of "inflammable air" (hydrogen) with one volume of "dephlogisticated air" (oxygen) produced water.

1784. Lavoisier and **Laplace** measured the amount of oxygen consumed and of carbon dioxide and heat produced in respiration and combustion.

1785-1789. Charles Augustin de Coulomb (1736-1806) published *Mémoires sur l'électricité et le magnétisme,* in which, by using a torsion balance, he measured the force of electric and magnetic attraction and repulsion and found it inversely proportional to the square of the distance between point charges or magnetic poles.

1788. Lagrange published *Méchanique analitique,* a strictly analytical treatment of mechanics. Here statics is founded on the principle of virtual velocities and dynamics on d'Alembert's principle.

1789. Lavoisier published his *Traité élémentaire de chimie* rejecting the phlogiston theory. He championed his new **theory of combustion** which maintained that oxygen supports combustion and respiration, and combines with metals to form a calx. He also presented a new and empirically determined list of chemical elements. Two years earlier, in collaboration with **Guyton de Morveau** (1737-1816), **Claude-Louis Berthollet** (1748-1822), and **Antoine Fourcroy** (1757-1809), he published a treatise outlining a new method of chemical nomenclature, essentially the one used today.

1790-1801. The revolutionary government of France decreed the adoption of a decimal system of weights, measures, and coinage (the **metric system**).

1791. Luigi Galvani (1737-1798) in a series of experiments reported in *De viribus electricitatis in motu musculari animalium,* postulated the existence of "animal electricity."

1793. The Académie Royale des Sciences was first suppressed by the revolutionary government and then reopened as a section of the **Institut de France.** Motivated by a new concern for applied science, the government established the **École Polytechnique** (1794), providing training and posts for eminent French scientists.

1795. James Hutton (1726-1797) published his *Theory of the Earth,* setting forth the uniformitarian principle that geological change is produced by continuous natural forces.

1798. Edward Jenner (1749-1823) described his success at using the scrapings from cowpox as a "vaccination" against smallpox.

1799. Carl Friedrich Gauss (1777-1855) gave the first rigorous proof of the fundamental theorem of algebra, that an nth degree algebraic equation with real coefficients has n roots.

1799. Joseph Louis Proust (1754-1826) announced the **law of definite proportions,** according to which the same chemical compound, however it is prepared, always contains the same elements combined in the same proportions by weight.

1800. Alessandro Volta (1745-1827), in his essay "On the Electricity Excited by the mere Contact of Conducting Substances of Different Kinds," disagreeing with **Luigi Galvani** (1791), showed that the electrically produced effects in muscular contraction arise not from an innate animal electricity, but from the moist contact of different metals. This observation led him to construct the voltaic pile, the forerunner of the modern battery and the first source of a continuous electric current.

Mathematics, Physics, and Astronomy

1799-1825. Pierre Laplace (1749-1827) published his *Traité de mécanique céleste,* in which he aimed at presenting analytically all of the developments in gravitational astronomy since the time of Newton.

1800. The Royal Institution of Great Britain, center for the diffusion of technical and scientific knowledge, was founded by the American **Benjamin Thompson (Count Rumford)** (1753-1814).

1801. Giuseppi Piazzi (1746-1826) discovered the first asteroid *Ceres;* its orbit was computed by Gauss.

1801. Carl Friedrich Gauss (1777-1855) published *Disquisitiones arithmeticae,* developing the theory of congruences, quadratic forms, and quadratic residues, using methods and concepts basic to the subsequent progress of number theory and algebra.

1802. Thomas Young (1773-1829) demonstrated in his paper "On the Theory of Light and Colours" that the properties of light, including interference phenomena, are satisfactorily explained by considering it as a periodic wave motion in an aether.

1803-1804. William Herschel (1738-1822) reported observations on six cases of double stars, and concluded that each was a binary or connected pair of stars in which each member influenced the motion of the other. This was the first observation of changes taking place under gravity beyond the solar system.

1815-1821. Augustin Fresnel (1788-1827), through a series of mathematical and experimental researches on interference, diffraction, polarization, and double refraction, was able to establish the **transverse wave theory of light.**

1820. Hans Oersted (1777-1851) showed that a magnetic needle placed near a current-carrying wire deviated from its position, and that the direction of deviation depended on the direction of current flow.

1820. André-Marie Ampère (1775-1836) repeated Oersted's experiments (1820), and reported his discovery that two current-carrying wires exercise a reciprocal action upon one another. He later established a mathematical theory of known electrical phenomena, and experimentally demonstrated the principles of the electrodynamics of adjacent current-carrying conductors.

1821-1859. Michael Faraday (1791-1867) demon-

Michael Faraday

Michael Faraday, the distinguished English physicist and chemist, was born of poor parents in Newington Butts on Sept. 22, 1791. Due to his family's poverty, his formal education was only in reading, writing, and the rudiments of mathematics.

At the age of 13, Faraday was apprenticed to a bookbinder and, because of the opportunities given him while learning the trade, he was able to read extensively about science during his free time.

In 1812, he obtained employment as laboratory assistant to Sir Humphrey Davy, the celebrated chemist and inventor, and was launched on his scientific career that led to many important discoveries.

Faraday discovered electromagnetic induction and developed the first dynamo. It was a simple device consisting of a copper disk that rotated between the poles of a permanent magnet. He also formulated the laws of electrolysis. Faraday gave us the familiar terms: *electrode, cathode, anode, anion, cation, ion, ionization, electrolyte,* and *electrolysis.*

He became a member of the Royal Institution in 1823 and was made a Fellow of the Royal Society in 1824. He was offered knighthood, and the presidency of the Royal Society but declined both honors. Michael Faraday died at Hampton Court, near London, on Aug. 25, 1867. ☐

---

strated electromagnetic rotation (1821) and discovered electromagnetic induction (1831). He independently discovered self-induced currents (1834), found two years earlier by **Joseph Henry** (1797-1878). He found the laws of electrochemical decomposition and conduction, and established a general theory of electrolysis. He also introduced the concept of *field* into physics. These and other investigations were collected in his *Experimental Researches in Electricity* (1839-1855) and in his *Experimental Researches in Chemistry and Physics* (1859).

1821-1823. Augustin-Louis Cauchy (1789-1857), who successfully sought rigor in analysis, gave the first essentially correct definition of limit in *Cours d'analyse* (1821). This work also contained the first systematic study of convergence of series and general tests for it, and the first theory of functions of a complex variable. He defined the derivative and integral in terms of limit, and obtained the fundamental theorem of calculus (1823).

1822. Joseph Fourier (1768-1830) published *Théorie analytique de la chaleur,* giving a mathematical theory of heat conduction. He introduced trigonometric series, *Fourier series* of arbitrary, piecewise, continuous functions, thus extending the notion of function.

1824. Nicolas Sadi Carnot (1796-1832) published *Réflexions sur la puissance motrice du feu.* Here he showed that the transformation of heat into motive power depends on the quantity of heat ("caloric"), and the temperature difference between the source and sink of heat. He also introduced the reversible cycle of a heat engine—now called the *Carnot cycle.*

1827. Georg S. Ohm (1789-1854) found that the ratio of electromotive force to the current, in an electric circuit, is a constant *(Ohm's Law)* and called this constant the resistance of the circuit.

1829-1832. Nikolai Lobacheyskii (1793-1856) and **János Bólyai** (1802-1860) independently developed the first **non-Euclidean geometries.**

1831. The foundation of the **British Association for the Advancement of Science,** dedicated to the promotion and professionalization of British science. The B.A.A.S. was based on a German model, **Gesellschaft deutscher Naturforscher,** and served as an example for the **American Association for the Advancement of Science** (1848).

1833. Charles Babbage (1792-1871) conceived an "analytical engine" (a large-scale digital calculator). In 1822, he had made a working model of a smaller, "difference engine" to calculate tables of functions by finite difference methods.

1833. Gauss, in his *Intensitas vis magnetica terrestris,* presented a rigorous mathematical analysis of the earth's magnetic field, and proposed a system of absolute units for the measurement of terrestrial magnetism.

1834. Adolphe Quetelet (1796-1874) initiated the **London Statistical Society,** and later helped found several other such groups. He applied the theory of probability to the statistics of society, especially in *Sur l'homme* (1835).

1835. Cauchy published the first existence proof for the solution of a differential equation.

1838-1839. Friedrich Bessel (1784-1846), **Friedrich Struve** (1793-1864), and **Thomas Henderson** (1798-1844) measured *stellar parallax* for the first time.

1842. Julius von Mayer (1814-1878) stated that the total amount of energy in the universe is constant (a form of the **first law of thermodynamics**), and that in natural processes energy is never lost, but only transformed from one kind to another.

1843-1846. John Adams (1819-1892) and **Urbain LeVerrier** (1811-1877) independently predicted the existence of a new planet and constructed its orbit from a consideration of irregularities in the motion of Uranus. This planet, later named *Neptune,* was sighted in 1846 by **Johann Galle** (1812-1910)—a great triumph for gravitational astronomy.

1843. James Joule (1818-1889) sought the connection between electricity, heat, and mechanical energy in "The Calorific Effects of Magneto-Electricity, and the Mechanical Value of Heat," and determined by four different procedures the mechanical equivalent of heat. In 1847 he enunciated the principle of the **conservation of energy.**

1846. The **Smithsonian Institution** for the increase and diffusion of knowledge was established by the United States Congress, utilizing the funds bequeathed by England's **James Smithson** (1765-1829).

1847. Hermann Helmholtz (1821-1894) announced the principle of the conservation of energy in *Über die Erhaltung der Kraft.* He discussed the principle in great theoretical detail and elucidated its meaning.

1848. William Thomson (Lord Kelvin) (1824-1907) established the absolute thermodynamic scale of temperature, which is named after him.

1849. Armand Fizeau (1819-1896) for the first time successfully measured the **speed of light** by observations which do not involve astronomical constants.

1849. Jean Bernard Foucault (1819-1868) measured the speed of light accurately in media other than air, and thereby determined that the speed of light in air is greater than in water. Later, in a famous pendulum experiment, he demonstrated that the earth rotates (1851).

1850. William Cranch Bond (1789-1859), using the Harvard College Observatory's 15-inch refractor, took the first photograph of a star.

1850. Rudolph Clausius (1822-1888) announced the **second law of thermodynamics:** heat cannot of itself pass from a colder to a warmer body. In *Über die bewegende Kraft der Wärme* (1865) he introduced the term *entropy,* stating that the entropy of the universe tends to increase.

1854. Bernhard Riemann (1826-1866) established the mathematical importance of non-Euclidean geometries, discussing them in his general theory of manifolds. In the same year he gave the most comprehensive and general definition of the classical definite integral, since called the *Riemann integral.*

1854. George Boole (1815-1864) published *The Laws of Thought,* an expansion of his 1847 work, *The Mathematical Analysis of Logic,* which marks the beginning of **symbolic logic,** i.e., the attempt to express the laws of thought in algebraic symbols.

Hermann von Helmholtz

Hermann Ludwig Ferdinand von Helmholtz, one of the 19th century's greatest scientists, was born in Potsdam, Germany, on Aug. 31, 1821. He studied medicine at the Royal Institute for Medicine and Surgery, Berlin, from 1838 to 1842. He later taught physics at the University of Berlin (1871-1894) and became the first director of the Physio-Technical Institute at Charlottenburg (1888-1894).

Helmholtz's studies led him to reject the doctrine of vitalism (*see* Vitalism, p. 454) and he concluded that all forces could be reduced ultimately to matter and motion. His famous paper, "On the Conservation of Force," published in 1847, included his mathematical formulation on the principle of conservation of energy, making him one of the originators of this idea.

Helmholtz also made many important contributions to physiology, optics, electrodynamics, and mathematics. He invented the opthalmoscope and opthalmometer.

He died in Charlottenburg on Sept. 8, 1894. □

James Clerk Maxwell

James Clerk Maxwell, the British physicist and creator of the electromagnetic theory of light, was born in Edinburgh, Scotland, on June 13, 1831. He studied at the University of Edinburgh and Trinity College, Cambridge, graduating in 1854. In 1855, he became a Fellow of Trinity, and was appointed Professor of Natural Philosophy and Astronomy at King's College London in 1860. He left King's College in 1865 to retire to private life and devote himself to research and writing on electricity and magnetism.

In 1871, Maxwell became the first Cavendish professor of experimental physics at Cambridge and directed the organization of the Cavendish laboratory which opened in 1874.

Basing his own study and research on that of Michael Faraday, he developed the mathematical interpretation of Faraday's electromagnetic field concepts. He published his famous *Treatise on Electricity and Magnetism* in 1873 which expounded a set of four equations that were applicable to electricity, magnetism, and light.

Maxwell also made important contributions to theoretical physics in the kinetic theory of gases. He is also known for his studies of color and color blindness. He invented the "Maxwell" disk and color box. Maxwell showed that you could produce any given color from a combination of three selected colors taken from the spectrum.

James Clerk Maxwell's work on electromagnetic theory ranks next to Newton's work on mechanics. He died on Nov. 5, 1879, at Cambridge. □

Max Planck

Max Carl Ernst Ludwig Planck was born on April 23, 1858, in Kiel, Germany. He studied at the University of Munich from 1874 to 1877. In 1877 he went to the University of Berlin where he received his Ph.D. for his dissertation on the second law of thermodynamics when he was 21 years old. He subsequently taught at the University of Munich and Kiel University.

In 1889, he became a professor at the University of Berlin, where he remained until 1928 when he retired.

While investigating the problem of black body[1] radiation, Planck discovered the algebraic equation that described it. Since his findings did not conform to the classical laws of physics, he continued to study the problem and, in 1900, announced his revolutionary theory that energy was not a continuous entity but came in discontinuous small bundles that he called quanta. His discovery had provided an understanding of the nature of light and of radiation in general.

Later research by scientists such as Albert Einstein and Niels Bohr confirmed his basic hypothesis and established the Quantum Theory of modern physics.

Planck was awarded the Nobel prize in physics in 1918 for his work on black body radiation. He died at the age of 89 on Oct. 3, 1947, in Göttingen.

1. Black body: a theoretically perfect absorber of all radiation falling on it, reflecting or transmitting none.

1860-1877. James Clerk Maxwell (1831-1879) and **Ludwig Boltzmann** (1844-1906) developed statistical mechanics, a theory of the behavior of a gas considered as a collection of large numbers of molecules obeying the laws of classical mechanics.

1863. The United States Congress approved creation of the **National Academy of Sciences** as a scientific adviser to the federal government and promoter of scientific research.

1868. William Huggins (1824-1910), noting a slight shift toward the red in the spectrum of Sirius, calculated the radial velocity of a star for the first time.

1870-1883. Georg Cantor (1845-1918) published his major works, founding the **theory of sets** (1870) and the **theory of transfinite numbers** (1883).

1872-1882. Richard Dedekind (1831-1916) gave arithmetic definitions of irrational numbers (the *Dedekind cut*), constituting the first rigorous theory of irrationals.

1873. Maxwell published his *Treatise on Electricity and Magnetism* where he described the properties of the electromagnetic field in a series of equations *(Maxwell equations)* which entailed the electromagnetic theory of light.

1877. Giovanni Schiaparelli (1835-1910) observed long, narrow, straight, intersecting, dark lines on Mars, which he called *canali.*

1877-1893. Francis Galton (1822-1911) and **Karl Pearson** (1857-1936) developed the major statistical tools of present-day social science, e.g. regression (Galton, 1877), correlation coefficients (Galton, 1888), moments and standard deviation (Pearson, 1893).

1878. William Crookes (1832-1919) showed that cathode rays proceed in straight lines are capable of turning a small wheel, can be deflected by a magnet, excite fluorescence in certain substances, and heat and sometimes even melt some metals.

1887. Heinrich Hertz (1857-1894) demonstrated the existence of electromagnetic waves in the space about a discharging Leyden jar, and found that electromagnetic waves were propagated with the velocity of light as Maxwell had predicted (1873). Hertz's work led to modern radio communications.

1895. Wilhelm K. Röntgen (1845-1923) announced the discovery of x-rays in *Eine neue Art von Strahlen.*

1895. John W. Strutt (Lord Rayleigh) (1842-1919) and **William Ramsay** (1852-1916) discovered the "inert" or "noble" gas *argon.* Ramsay later discovered the other noble gases: helium, krypton, neon, xenon, and radon.

1896. Alfred B. Nobel (1833-1896) endowed prizes for outstanding achievements in physics, chemistry, medicine, and physiology. The first prizes were awarded in 1901.

1896. Antoine H. Becquerel (1852-1908) discovered radioactivity in uranium compounds.

1897. Joseph John Thomson (1856-1940) announced the discovery of the **electron**, the first sub-atomic particle, and determined experimentally the ratio of its mass to its charge.

1900. Max Planck (1858-1947) stated that energy is not emitted continuously from radiating bodies, but in discrete parcels, or **quanta.**

1904. Marie Sklodowska Curie (1867-1934) showed that pitchblende (uranium ore) contained two new radioactive elements: **radium** and **polonium.**

Second from left: Albert Einstein, third from left: Max Planck

Albert Einstein

Albert Einstein, one of the greatest intellects in the history of mankind, was born of Jewish parents in Ulm, Wurttemberg, Germany, on March 14, 1879. Contrary to a popular legend that he failed math in his youth, Einstein was a gifted student in mathematics and physics. He earned his doctorate at the University of Zurich, Switzerland, in 1905. During the same year, he published four papers of major importance in physics, which included his special and general theory of relativity.

He became a Swiss citizen and taught at the University of Zurich in 1909, the German University of Prague in 1911, and returned to Zurich in 1912. In 1913, Einstein accepted the posts of titular professor of physics and director of theoretical physics at the Kaiser Wilhelm Institute in Berlin and renewed his German citizenship.

One of his predictions on the general theory of relativity, which concerned the bending of light rays from stars by the sun as they passed on their way to the earth, was verified in 1919 by British scientists studying a solar eclipse and brought him international fame.

Einstein was awarded the 1921 Nobel Prize in Physics for his work on the photoelectric effect.

After Hitler's rise to power in 1933, he was persecuted by the Nazi government and he gave up his German citizenship. Fortunately, he had accepted the post as head of the school of mathematics at the Institute for Advanced Study at Princeton in 1933 and remained there until his death. He eventually became a U.S. citizen.

Although Einstein was an ardent pacifist, he wrote to President Roosevelt in 1939 to investigate the use of atomic energy in bombs. He did this at the request of other scientists including Niels Bohr who suspected that the Nazis were developing a nuclear-fission device. After the war, Einstein was a leader in seeking international govermental control of nuclear energy.

A Zionist, Einstein was offered the presidency of Israel by David Ben-Gurion in 1952, but declined. He died in Princeton, N.J., on April 18, 1955. □

1905. Albert Einstein (1879-1955) announced his **special theory of relativity,** which required a fundamental revision in the traditionally held Newtonian views of space and time, and introduced the celebrated equation $E = mc^2$.

1905. Einstein attributed to radiation itself a particle structure, and by supposing each particle of light **(photon)** to carry a quantum of energy, explained the photoelectric effect.

1910-1913. Bertrand Russell (1872-1970) and **Alfred North Whitehead** (1861-1947) published *Principia Mathematica,* carrying out the reduction of arithmetic to symbolic logic. This work is the foundation of the calculus of propositions and modern symbolic logic.

1911. Robert A. Millikan (1868-1953) established that electric charge always consists of an integral multiple of a unit charge, which he determined with great accuracy, in his oil-drop experiment.

1911. Ernest Rutherford (1871-1937) introduced the nuclear **model of the atom,** i.e., a small positively charged nucleus, containing most of the mass of the atom, surrounded by electrons.

1911-1913. Ejnar Hertzsprung (1873-1967) studied double stars and their colors, especially in the Pléiades, and with **Henry Norris Russell** (1877-1957) devised the Hertzsprung-Russell Diagram, a graphic way of grouping stars by the relation between their absolute magnitudes and spectral types.

1912. Max von Laue (1879-1960) discovered **X-ray diffraction,** a powerful technique for directly observing the atomic structure of crystals.

1913. Niels Bohr (1885-1962) devised a new model of the atom by applying quantum theory to Rutherford's nuclear atom. Although this model violated classical electromagnetic theory it successfully accounted for the spectrum of hydrogen.

Niels Henrik David Bohr

Niels Bohr, the founder of the modern theory of atomic structure was born in Copenhagen on Oct. 7, 1885. He received his Ph.D in physics from the University of Copenhagen in 1911. His thesis on the electron theory of metals remains a classic today.

From 1912 to 1916, Bohr worked at Manchester University with Ernest Rutherford (1871-1937) who in 1911 had introduced the nuclear model of the atom, i.e., a small positively charged nucleus surrounded by negatively charged electrons. Bohr applied Planck's quantum theory to Rutherford's atomic structure, and in 1913, proposed a radical new concept of atomic structure (known as the Bohr atom) in which electrons travel around the nucleus in orbits that are determined by quantum conditions and not by classical laws alone. He left Manchester in 1916 to take a professorship at the University of Copenhagen, and in 1920 he assumed the directorship of the Institute of Theoretical Physics created for him at the University and remained in that position for the rest of his academic career.

His brilliant work on atomic structure won him the Nobel Prize for physics in 1922.

During World War II, Bohr escaped from the Nazi occupation of Denmark to Sweden in 1943, and from there to England. The same year, he visited the United States and made some technical contributions to atomic bomb research. However, he was greatly concerned for the future of the world and the control of these terrible weapons.

After the war, he returned to Denmark. He continued his efforts to further world peace and mutual understanding. He received the first Atoms for Peace award in 1957.

Bohr died in Copenhagen on Nov. 18, 1962. □

1915. Einstein announced his **general theory of relativity**, which explained the advance of Mercury's perihelion, and predicted the subsequently observed bending of light rays near the sun.

1918. Harlow Shapley (1885-1972), from an extensive study of the distribution of globular clusters and cepheid variable stars, increased the estimated size of our galaxy about ten times. He envisioned the galaxy as a flattened lens-shaped system of stars in which the solar system occupied a position far from the center.

1919. Rutherford found that the collision of alpha particles with nitrogen atoms resulted in the disintegration of the nitrogen and the production of hydrogen nuclei (protons) and an isotope of oxygen. He was the first person to achieve artificial transmutation of an element.

1919. Arthur S. Eddington (1882-1944) and others, by studying data obtained during a total solar eclipse, verified Einstein's prediction of the bending of light rays by the gravitational field of large masses.

1919-1929. Edwin P. Hubble (1889-1953) detected cepheid variable stars in the Andromeda Nebula, a discovery that allowed him to determine the distances between galaxies.

1924. Louis-Victor de Broglie (1892-1987) determined from theoretical considerations that the electron, which had been considered a particle, should behave as a wave under certain circumstances. Experimental confirmation was obtained in 1927 by Clinton Davisson (1881-1958) and Lester H. Germer.

1925. Wolfgang Pauli (1900-1958) announced the **exclusion principle** (in any atom no two electrons have identical sets of quantum numbers). This principle was an important aid in determining the electron structure of the heavier elements.

1925-1926. Werner Karl Heisenberg and Erwin Schrödinger (1887-1960) independently, and in different ways, laid the theoretical foundations of the new **quantum mechanics** which, though violating classical notions of causality, successfully predicts the behavior of atomic particles.

1927. George Lemaître in order to explain the red shift in the spectra from distant galaxies, introduced the concept of the **expanding universe**. Eddington pursued research in this subject from 1930.

1928. Paul A. Dirac by combining quantum mechanics and relativity theory, devised a relativistic **theory of the electron**.

1930. Vannevar Bush (1890-1974) and his associates placed into operation a "differential analyzer," the first modern analog computer.

1931. Ernest O. Lawrence (1901-1958) invented the **cyclotron**, a device for accelerating atomic particles, which has become the fundamental research tool in high-energy physics and has made possible the creation of trans-uranium elements.

1932. Karl Jansky reported the reception of radio waves from cosmic sources, making **radio astronomy** possible.

1938-1939. Otto Hahn (1879-1968) and Otto Strassmann bombarded uranium with neutrons and found an isotope of barium in the product (1938). Lise Meitner (1878-1968) and Otto Frisch explained this result by assuming the fission of the uranium nucleus (**nuclear fission**).

1942. Enrico Fermi (1901-1954) and associates built the first controlled self-sustaining **nuclear reactor**. Fermi was one of the chief architects of the theory of the atomic nucleus.

1944. Mark I, the **Harvard-IBM Automatic Sequence Controlled Calculator**, was put into operation at Harvard University. This was the first large-scale digital calculating machine.

1945. Vannevar Bush issued the report *Science: The Endless Frontier*, recommending the creation of a United States foundation for the support and encouragement of basic research and education in science. In 1950 the United States Congress established the **National Science Foun-**

dation to implement this recommendation.

1946. The foundation of the **United States Atomic Energy Commission** assured civilian control of United States developments in atomic energy.

1946. ENIAC (Electronic Numerical Integrator and Calculator) was put into operation at the University of Pennsylvania, the first electronic high speed digital calculating machine.

1951. Harold I. Ewen and **Edward M. Purcell** detected the 21-centimeter hydrogen spectral line in galactic radiation, which had been predicted in 1944 by **Hendrik van de Hulst.** This discovery has enabled astronomers to map the structure of the Milky Way.

Chemistry, Biology, and Geology

1799-1805. Georges Cuvier (1769-1832) founded **comparative anatomy** on functional grounds maintaining that the parts of the organism are correlated to the functioning whole.

1800-1802. Marie-François Bichat (1771-1802) stimulated the separate and systematic study of each anatomical structure and physiological function by his classification of the body into textures or *tissus* each with its particular vital property.

1801. Claude Berthollet (1748-1822) opposed the prevailing doctrine of elective affinities with his **law of mass action.**

1802. John Playfair (1748-1819), friend and disciple of **James Hutton** (1726-1797), produced *Illustrations of the Huttonian Theory of the Earth,* bringing a clear exposition of uniformitarianism to a wide audience and establishing this philosophy as the basis of modern geology.

1804. Nicholas de Saussure (1767-1845) explained the process of photosynthesis in terms of the new chemistry of **Antoine Lavoisier** (1743-1794).

1807. Humphry Davy (1778-1829), using the new voltaic battery, isolated the metals potassium and sodium.

1807. Establishment of **United States Coast Survey,** the first United States scientific agency.

1807. Foundation of the **Geological Society of London,** which served as a center for research and discussion and as a model for similar societies in other countries.

1808. John Dalton (1766-1844) published his *New System of Chemical Philosophy,* which established the quantitative atomic theory in chemistry.

1808. Joseph Gay-Lussac (1778-1850) announced his discovery of the law of combining volumes for gases, i.e., the ratios of the volumes of reacting gases are small whole numbers.

1809. Jean-Baptiste Lamarck (1744-1829), in *Philosophie zoologique,* gave the most complete explanation of his **theory of evolution.** He argued that through a combination of unconscious striving, the physiological effects of use and disuse, and the influence of the environment, anatomical parts became modified. Furthermore, he believed that by the "inheritance of acquired characteristics" living forms evolved in an everascending scale of perfection.

1811. Amedeo Avogadro (1776-1856) concluded that equal volumes of all gases at the same temperature and pressure contain equal numbers of molecules; in effect he distinguished between atoms and molecules, but his ideas were neglected until 1858.

1815. William Smith (1769-1839) published his famous **geological map of England and Wales,** and

Edwin Powell Hubble

Edwin Powell Hubble, the American astronomer who revolutionized our understanding of the universe was born in Marshfield, Mo., on Nov. 20, 1889. He studied physics at the University of Chicago and law at Oxford. After a brief practice at law, he returned to Chicago to work for a doctorate in astronomy.

Hubble did research at Yerkes Observatory, Williams Bay, Wis., from 1914 to 1917, and joined the Army following America's entrance in the war. He accepted a position on the staff of Mt. Wilson Observatory, Pasadena, Calif., in 1919 where at that time and up until 1948 the observatory's 100-inch Hooker reflector telescope was the most powerful in the world.

Hubble spend the rest of his life at Mt. Wilson and eventually became its director. He took time out from his work during World War II when he did research on ballistics (1942-1946).

During 1923-1924, Hubble studied the Andromeda nebula from photographs taken through the 100-inch telescope and discovered that it contained short-period variable stars. This observation led him to conclude that Andromeda was not part of our own Milky Way galaxy, but was an independent star system at a very great distance from our own. He went on to study many remote galaxies along with other astronomers, and in 1929 found the first observational evidence to support the theories that the universe is expanding. Hubble also classified galaxies according to their shapes and investigated many of their properties. He died at San Marino, Calif., on Sept. 28, 1953. □

established that specific strata can be identified by their fossil content, the principle upon which historical geology is founded. He also worked out the main divisions of the **Secondary** or **Mesozoic** strata.

Charles Darwin

Charles Robert Darwin, the English naturalist, was born in Shrewsbury, England, on Feb. 12, 1809. When he was sixteen, he attended Edinburgh University to study medicine and, in 1827, attended Christ's College, Cambridge, to prepare for the ministry. Although he received a B.A. degree in 1831, he was disinterested in both professions. However, while at Cambridge, he became keenly interested in natural history.

An important change took place in his life when, in 1831, he was able to obtain a position as official naturalist aboard the H.M.S. *Beagle* bound on an around-the-world scientific expedition. During the five-year voyage (1831-1836), Darwin saw many natural wonders and made many important observations which he recorded in voluminous notes. This great scientific adventure was the beginning of his career as one of England's leading biologists and provided him with the basis for his evolutionary theory of natural selection.

In 1859, he published his controversial book on the "Origin of Species." It soon received wide and stormy attention. His book on the "Descent of Man," published in 1871, proposed the idea that man descended from ape-like ancestors and added to the furor as it contradicted divine scripture.

When Charles Darwin died on April 19, 1882, many scientists had accepted his basic theories. He was buried at Westminster Abbey. ☐

1819. Pierre Dulong (1785-1838) and **Alexis Petit** (1791-1820) formulated the rule that the product of the relative atomic weight and the specific heat of an element is a constant. This made possible the experimental determination of relative atomic weights.

1819. René Laënnec (1781-1826) invented the stethoscope.

1822. François Magendie (1783-1855) showed that the sensory and motor functions arise from different spinal roots. He was anticipated in 1811 by the more discursive work of **Charles Bell** (1774-1842).

1828. Karl von Baer (1792-1876) founded modern comparative embryology with the publication of *Über Entwickelungsgeschichte der Thiere*. Here

he proclaimed that embryonic development is the history of increasing specificity.

1831-1836. Charles Darwin (1809-1882), as naturalist aboard *H. M. S. Beagle*, studied South American flora and fauna, and gathered information he was later to use in his theory of evolution.

c. 1831-1852. Roderick Murchison (1792-1871) and **Adam Sedgwick** (1785-1873) described the succession of Paleozoic strata in Wales, Murchison defining the *Silurian* system (1839) and Sedgwick defining the *Cambrian* system.

1838-1842. The United States Exploring Expedition, under the command of Lieut. **Charles Wilkes** (1798-1877), explored the Pacific Ocean, the first example of a United States government-sponsored scientific maritime venture.

1839. Theodor Schwann (1810-1882) extended the 1838 observations on plants cells of **Matthias Schleiden** (1804-1881) into the generalization that cells are the common structural and functional unit of all living organisms.

1840. Louis Agassiz (1807-1873) elucidated the role of glaciers in geological change and enunciated his ice age theory.

1846. William T. G. Morton (1819-1868) gave the first public demonstration of the use of **ether as an anaesthetic** in surgery.

1847. Carl Ludwig (1816-1895) perfected the kymograph, which became an invaluable measuring instrument for physiology.

1848. Louis Pasteur (1822-1895), in a series of brilliantly conceived and executed experiments, demonstrated the connection between the optical activity of organic molecules and crystalline structure, thus founding **stereochemistry.**

1848. Claude Bernard (1813-1878) demonstrated the ability of the liver to store sugar in the form of glycogen. His widely read *Introduction à l'étude de la médecine expérimentale* (1865) influenced literary men as well as scientists.

1852. Edward Frankland (1825-1899) announced his theory of **valency,** i.e., each atom has a certain "valency," or capacity for combining with a definite number of other atoms.

1856-1864. Bernard evolved the concept of the *milieu interieur,* envisioning that cells were autonomous physiological units, yet were dependent upon and protected by the internal environment of the whole organism.

1856-1866. Hermann Helmholtz (1821-1894) extended the doctrine of specific nerve energies developed by **Johannes Müller** to vision and hearing, indicating the penetration of physics and physiology into psychology.

1857-1860. Louis Pasteur demonstrated that fermentation was a product of yeast cell activity. This challenged the view of Liebig that the ferment was merely an unstable chemical substance.

1858. Rudolph Virchow (1821-1902) in *Die Cellularpathologie* declared that disease reflects an impairment of cellular organization. Here, too, he stated his famous generalization *"omnis cellula e cellula"* (all cells arise from cells) and described the cell as the basic element of the life process.

1858. Friedrich A. Kekulé (1829-1896) published *Über die Konstitution und die Metamorphosen der chemischen Verbindungen und über die chemische Natur des Kohlenstoffs*, in which he recognized that carbon is quadrivalent, and that carbon atoms link together to form long chains that serve as skeletons for organic molecules.

1859. Gustav R. Kirchhoff (1824-1887) and **Robert**

W. Bunsen (1811-1899) began researches that made **spectrum analysis** a powerful method for the investigation of matter. They showed that a chemical element was clearly characterized by its spectrum, and by spectrum analysis they were able to discover previously unknown elements.

1859. Darwin amassed twenty-five years of careful research in *The Origin of Species*. Inspired by the evidence in geology, paleontology, zoogeography, and domestic animal breeding, he declared that species evolved through variation and the natural selection of those individuals best suited to survive in given environmental conditions. A similar theory was developed independently by **Alfred R. Wallace** (1823-1913).

1860. Marcelin Berthelot (1827-1907) published *Chimie organique fondée sur la synthèse*, which showed that total synthesis of all classes of organic compounds from the elements carbon, hydrogen, oxygen, and nitrogen was possible.

1861. Alexander M. Butlerov (1828-1886) introduced the term "chemical structure" at a chemical meeting in Germany. Butlerov shares credit with **Kekulé** for the development of the theory of the structure of organic compounds.

1861. Pasteur, in a classic paper "Mémoire sur les corpuscles organisés qui existent dans l'atmosphère," described a series of experiments which confuted the doctrine of the spontaneous generation of micro-organisms.

1862-1877. Pasteur investigated several types of micro-organisms to advance the **germ theory of disease**. His evidence encouraged **Joseph Lister** (1827-1912) to initiate the practice of **antiseptic surgery** (1865).

1865. Gregor Mendel (1822-1884), an Augustinian monk, described cross-breeding experiments with peas which demonstrated the particulate nature of inheritance. He concluded that many traits segregated into dominant and recessive alternatives and that combined traits assorted independently. Little attention was paid to his results until 1900 when cytological work suggested such unit characters existed.

1869. Dmitri I. Mendeleev (1834-1907), in *Principles of Chemistry*, devised his periodic table of the chemical elements, which arranged the elements in the order of increasing atomic weight, noted the periodic recurrence of similar properties in groups of elements, and successfully predicted the properties of elements yet to be discovered.

1872-1876. *H. M. S. Challenger* made an extended voyage of scientific investigation, led by **Wyville Thomson** (1830-1882). The information gathered and reported largely by **John Murray** (1841-1914) gave much impetus to the science of **oceanography**.

1879. Ivan P. Pavlov (1849-1936) showed the production of gastric juices could be achieved without the introduction of food into the stomach. His work in the physiology of digestion led him to develop the concept of the acquired or *conditioned reflex*.

1879. The **United States Geological Survey** was founded, consolidating under one office the several surveys which had been gaining valuable information in western North America for over a decade. Under the directorship of **John W. Powell** (1834-1902) after 1881, the survey grew into a powerful agency for the progress of science in the United States.

1880. John Milne (1850-1913) developed the first accurate **seismograph**, permitting the careful

Louis Pasteur

Louis Pasteur, the French chemist and microbiologist for whom the pasteurization process was named, was born in Dole, France on December 27, 1822. He received his doctorate of sciences at the École Normale Supérieure in 1847 and at the age of 26 launched his career as a scientific innovator—showing the Paris Academy that certain chemical compounds split into mirror-image components. This finding formed the basis for his theory of molecular asymmetry showing that atomical arrangement affects the biological properties of chemicals.

By 1857 Pasteur was director of scientific studies at his alma mater; in 1863 he became dean of the science faculty at the University of Lille, where he began to study fermentation. Once proving that germs in air putrefy food, he devised a way to destroy germs with heat—a process now known as pasteurization.

In the following years Pasteur found ways to protect France's valued silkworms against disease, beer against decomposition, farm animals against various illnesses. On April 27, 1882 he was elected to the Académie Française, where he began his most significant study—into the prevention of rabies—and three years later saved the life of a nine-year-old boy. In 1888 the Pasteur Institute for the research, treatment and prevention of rabies was inaugurated in Paris. Pasteur headed the institute until his death on September 28, 1895. □

study of earthquakes and opening the way to new knowledge of the earth's interior.

1882. Robert Koch (1843-1910) described the etiology of the **tubercle bacillus**. This discovery led him (1884) to state *Koch's postulates*, a method for isolating micro-organisms and proving that they are specific causes, not merely concomitants, of disease.

1883. Ilia I. Mechnikov (1845-1916) described the action of phagocytic cells in transparent starfish larvae. His discovery led to a general explanation of local inflammation.

1883. Edouard van Beneden (1845-1901) described how the chromosomes are derived in equal num-

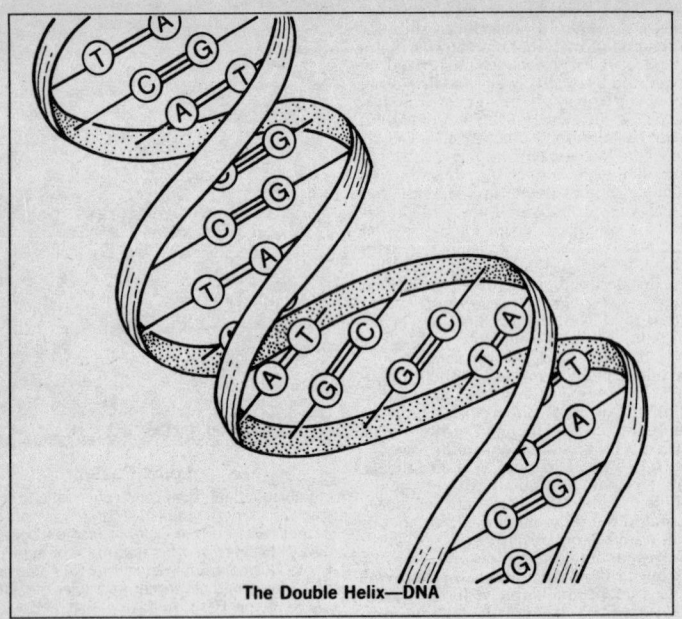

The Double Helix—DNA

bers from the conjugating germ cells. This led to the discovery of reduction division in the formation of the gametes.

1887. Svante A. Arrhenius (1859-1927) announced his theory of electrolytic dissociation, according to which most of the molecules of an electrolyte are immediately dissociated into two ions when dissolved.

1890. Emil von Behring (1854-1917) and **Shibasaburo Kitasato** (1856-1931) demonstrated that the serum of immunized rabbits neutralized the toxin of tetanus. This discovery opened the possibility that disease could be prevented through the stimulation of specific antibody production.

1892. August Weismann (1834-1914) described in *Das Keimplasma* his theory of the continuity of the germ plasm and a scheme for the unfolding of a particulate hereditary pattern in embryogenesis.

1893. Theobald Smith (1859-1934), in "Investigations into the Nature, Causation and Prevention of Southern Cattle Fever," demonstrated that parasites could act as vectors of disease.

1895. Wilhelm K. Röntgen (1845-1923) discovered x-rays and immediately realized that his discovery had a practical application in medicine.

1897. Eduard Buchner (1860-1917) discovered that *zymase*, a cell-free yeast extract, caused fermentation, thus resolving a long-standing controversy over "vital" and "inorganic" ferments.

1909. Paul Ehrlich (1854-1915) showed that the synthetic compound, *Salvarsan,* was an effective treatment for syphilis. This discovery was a tremendous stimulus to the field of chemotherapy. In 1935 **Gerhard Domagk** (1895-1964) made the fundamental discovery which led to the introduction and widespread use of **sulfa drugs.**

1911. Thomas H. Morgan (1866-1945) claimed that certain traits were genetically linked on the chromosome, thus visualizing a linear arrangement of genes and stimulating the construction of genetic maps.

1915. Alfred Wegener (1880-1930) gave the classic expression of the controversial theory of continental drift in *Die Entstehung der Kontinente und Ozeane.*

1927. Hermann J. Muller (1890-1967) announced that he had successfully induced mutations in fruit flies with x-rays. This provided a useful experimental tool, yet in retrospect gave warning to the generations of the 1940s and 1950s of a danger in the release of atomic energy.

1929. Alexander Fleming (1881-1955) announced that the common mold *Penicillium* had an inhibitory effect on certain pathogenic bacteria. It was not until 1943 under the pressures of World War II, however, that the first antibiotic, penicillin, was successfully developed.

1930. Ronald A. Fisher (1890-1962) established in *The Genetical Theory of Natural Selection* that superior genes have a significant selective advantage, thus testifying that Darwinian evolution was compatible with genetics.

1944. Ostwald T. Avery (1877-1955) and collaborators announced they had transmuted one type of pneumococcus bacteria into a second type by the transfer of DNA molecules.

1946. Willard F. Libby (1908-1980), and associates, developed *radiocarbon dating,* a method for ascertaining the absolute age of materials containing carbon.

1953. Francis H. C. Crick (1916-   ) and **James D. Watson** (1928-   ) offered a model for the structure of DNA which accounted for gene replication and conceived a biochemical code that could transmit a great variety of genetic information.

INVENTIONS & TECHNOLOGY

A Chronology of Major Developments from 1450 to the Present

Text from AN ENCYCLOPEDIA OF WORLD HISTORY by William L. Langer, The Fifth Edition, Copyright 1940, 1948, 1952, and © 1967, 1972 by Houghton Mifflin Company. Reprinted by permission of Houghton Mifflin Company.

c. 1450. Printing with moveable type introduced into Europe by **Johannes Gutenberg** (?1400-1468). **Laurens Coster** (1440), cheapened and widened the diffusion of knowledge. This development accompanied an increased use of woodblock illustrations.

1485. Publication of **Leon Battista Alberti's** (1404-1472) *De re aedificora* exemplifies the extended interests of Renaissance architects and artists in the realm of applied science. A more famous example is **Leonardo da Vinci** (1452-1519), who was a military engineer and speculated on various types of machines. Structural theory did not advance until the work of **Galileo Galilei** (*Dialogues concerning Two New Sciences*, 1638), **Christopher Wren**, and **Robert Hooke**. The revival of interest in classical architecture, sparked by the rediscovery of the works of Vitruvius, led architects to develop new techniques, flat ceiling, and the dome. Some architects of the period were **Filippo Brunelleschi** (?1377-1446), **François Mansard** (1598-1666), **Claude Perrault** (1613-1688), **François Blondel** (1617-1686), **Inigo Jones** (1573-1652), and **Christopher Wren** (1632-1723).

1500. The expansion of trade brought a **development in ship construction.** Galleys were in use until the 17th century but the fully rigged ship with stern-post rudder developed during the 15th century, and by 1700 the four-masted galleon had evolved.

c. 1510. First of the handbooks on metallurgy appeared, *Probierbergbüchlein* on assaying, *Bergbüchlein* on mining. In 1540 Vannocio Biringuccio's (1480-1539) *Pyrotechnica* published, the first practical, comprehensive metallurgy text by a professional metallurgist. Included were descriptions of alloying and cannon-molding processes. In 1556 *De re metallica* of Agricola (Georg Bauer), a physician in the mining area of Saxony, appeared. It covered all aspects of mining from the survey of the site through the equipment and methods of mining to assaying, blast and glass furnace descriptions as well as the treatment of iron, copper, and glass. Agricola was concerned with miners' health, and described the diseases to which they are prone.

1520. **Wheel lock** invented, probably in Italy, one of the steps to a single-handed pistol. **Rifling** of the gun barrel was a known technique, 1525, and by 1697 **iron cannon** were cast directly from the blast furnace.

1533. The principle of **triangulation** in surveying discovered by **Gemma Frisius**, a German. More technical maps began to appear to replace the earlier Portalan maps (first **road map of Europe** appeared in Germany, 1511). **Maritime charts** were improved; in 1536 **Pedro Nuñez** (1492-1577) wrote on the errors in the plain charts used at sea. In 1569 **Gerhard Mercator** [Kremer] (1512-1594) devised the mercator chart; in 1600

The true Effigies of Iohn Guttemberg Delineated from the Original Painting at Mentz in Germanie.

Johannes Gutenberg.

the first seaman's calendar appeared. The **telescope,** invented c. 1590, and the back-staff (1595) of **John Davis** (?1550-1605), superseded the older navigational instruments, the astrolabe and cross-staff.

c. 1589. William Lee (d. 1610) invented the first frame **knitting machine,** slowly accepted during the 17th century.

1560-1660. Increased **use of coal,** especially in England, as a power source. The output of coal in Newcastle rose from 32,951 tons in 1563-1564 to 529,032 tons in 1658-1659. The use of coal was dictated by serious deforestation both in England and on the Continent. By 1615 wood-fired glass furnaces were illegal in England; thus technology was stimulated by the necessity of using coal.

1575-1680. The evolution of the **glass-maker's** "chair." Many new techniques were introduced into glass-making, including those of producing ruby glass (before 1620), lead and white glass (1679).

1603. Cannon were bored in Spain. By 1650 lead shot was molded by means of a split mold.

1698. Thomas Savery's (?1650-1715) steam engine.

The steam mill of **Giovanni Branca**, 1629, was ill conceived, and the engine of **Denis Papin**, 1688, was not developed and had no effect on the Industrial Revolution.

1700. By this date many **foods and crops** were exchanged between Europe, Asia, and the Americas. From the New World came the **potato** (in Spain c. 1570), maize, tea, chocolate, **tobacco**. **Coffee** grew wild in Ethiopia (known c. 1450) and was introduced into Europe (in England by 1650). By this date **sugar** was a common, cheap commodity in England; cane was shipped to America to form the basis of the industry in the Caribbean in the 18th century. **Cotton** was exported to America where it became an important crop.

Technical achievements of this century in agriculture, mining, metallurgy, and machinery (prime movers, textiles, and machine tools) laid the groundwork for the Industrial Revolution, commencing about the mid-century, which markedly to change the nature of society and civilization. Industrialization, commencing first in England and first in the textile industry, was to urbanize society, transform the international power structure, and put its mark upon every aspect of modern life.

c. 1700. **Christopher Polhem** (1661-1751), the "Father of Swedish Technology," developed an improved **rolling mill** and utilized water power for primitive mass production.

1709-1717. Abraham Darby (1677-1717) produced iron from a **coke-fired blast furnace** at Coalbrookdale; despite shortage of charcoal, it took 50 years and improvements made in the method by his son Abraham Darby II before coke was regularly used for this purpose.

1712. Low pressure **steam pump** ("atmospheric engine") of **Thomas Newcomen** (1663-1729) used to pump water from mines. Newcomen utilized some features of **Denis Papin's** (1647-1714) atmospheric engine of 1695, but his invention was quite independent of **Thomas Savery's** (?1650-1715) first useful "fire-engine" of 1698. **John Smeaton** (1724-1792) made many empirical improvements of the Newcomen engine; he also designed bridges, harbors, canals, and the Eddystone Lighthouse (1759), and lowered the price of iron by his water-powered bellows (1761).

1716. Corps des Ponts et Chaussées established in France for civil engineering works; clear distinction made between civil engineer and architect. First improvements in **road-making** since Roman times with work of **P. M. J. Trésaguet** (1716-

1794) in France, and **John L. McAdam** (1756-1836) ("metalled" or "macadamized" roads) and **Thomas Telford** (1757-1834) in England. Trésaguet and Telford emphasized a road foundation of large stones, with smaller stones for top layer; McAdam stressed a roadtop impervious to water.

1722. First technical treatise on iron, *L'Art de convertir le fer forgé en acier et l'art d'adoucir le fer fondu*, by **René A. F. de Réaumur** (1683-1757). **Metallurgical techniques** developed during this century included **Benjamin Huntsman's** (1704-1776) crucible process for casting steel (1751), utilized for cutlery and instruments but not commercially successful until 1770; **Henry Cort's** (1740-1800) puddling process to produce wrought (bar) iron from cast iron in a reverberatory furnace (1784); and Cort's perfected rolling mill with grooved rollers (1784).

1732. Publication of **Jethro Tull's** (1674-1741) *New Horse Hoeing Husbandry* in which he described his innovations in **scientific cultivation**: seed drill (1701) to plant seed in rows rather than the older, casual method of tossing seeds; the horsehoe (introduced by Tull from France in 1714); and the technique of soil pulverization. **Robert Bakewell** (1725-1795) introduced selective breeding of livestock, and **Charles Townshend** (1674-1738) introduced useful new crops, turnips and clover, for winter fodder. The work of these pioneers in scientific cultivation, publicized by **Arthur Young** (1741-1820), helped to produce the **Agricultural Revolution,** which effected radical transformations in agricultural crops and techniques and a large increase in the production of foodstuffs and animal materials (wool, hides).

1733. John Kay (d. 1764?) patented the **flying shuttle,** the first of a series of inventions which were to transform the manufacture of textiles, substitute the factory system for the older method of domestic production, introduce power-driven machinery into manufacturing processes, and mark the first steps in the Industrial Revolution. Other landmarks in the industrialization of textile production were the **spinning jenny** invented (1764) by **James Hargreaves** (d. 1778); the spinning machine (**waterframe**) developed (1769) by **Richard Arkwright** (1732-1792), perhaps based on earlier machines for roller spinning (especially that devised by Lewis Paul in 1733 with some assistance from John Wyatt), and which made Arkwright Lancashire's largest cotton-manufacturer and one of England's richest

Major Developments 1450-1789

Development	See year	Development	See year	Development	See year
Architecture	1485	Flush toilet	1707	Roadmaps	1533
Agricultural		Glassmaking	1575-1680	Rolling mill	1700
developments	1732	Knitting machines	1589	Ship construction	1500
Blast furnace	1709-17	Lithography	1798	Semephore	1793
Bleaching	1785	Mapmaking	1533	Steam engines	1698,1776
Boring mill	1774	Marine chronometer	1797	Soda	1789
Cannon	1520,1603	Metallurgy	c.1510,1722	Telescope	1533
Canal building	1770	Optical glass	1798	Textile production	1733
Crops, New World	1700	Pumps	1712	Toolmaking	1797
Ceramics	1753	Road construction	1716	Wheel lock	1520

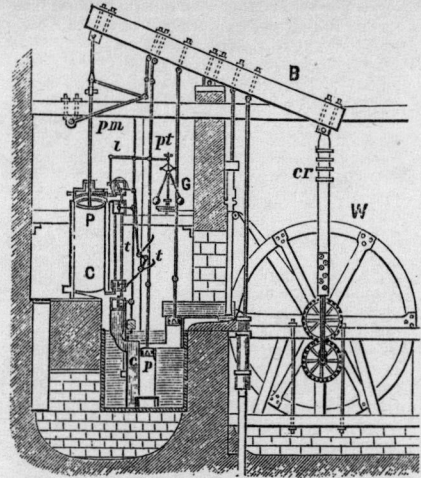

Watt's steam engine, 1784. His improved engines helped usher in the Industrial Revolution.

men; the spinning "mule" (1784) of **Samuel Crompton** (1753-1827); the power-loom (1785) of **Edmund Cartwright** (1743-1823), and the cotton gin (1793) of **Eli Whitney** (1765-1825).

1753. Publication by **Johann Heinrich Pott** of the *Lithogeoginoise pyrotechnique* on the **ceramic arts,** which developed during this period as Europeans sought to reproduce the much admired Chinese porcelain introduced to Europe in the later 17th century. First to produce quality china were the **Meissen** works in Saxony (Dresden China), followed by the French state manufactory at **Sèvres** (1768). The English developed bone-china (utilizing bone-ash as an ingredient). **Josiah Wedgwood** (1730-1795) was appointed royal potter (1762) and established his **Etruria** works in 1769. By the 1750's The Potteries, a series of towns in Staffordshire, had become the center of world production of inexpensive earthenware.

1754. Society for the Encouragement of Arts, Manufactures and Commerce (later, **The Royal Society of Arts**) established, inspiring the organization of similar societies in France, Netherlands, and Russia. The first exhibition of the industrial arts was held in Paris (1763). The French *Encyclopédie* (1751-1772) provided a comprehensive treatise, with illustrations, of contemporary technology.

1770. Completion of the English **Grand Trunk Canal** linking the Trent and the Mersey Rivers, giving the industrial towns of the Midlands a direct water route for exports and initiating a **canal-building** fever in England, which reached America and France in the early 19th century. Principal English canal engineers were **James Brindley** (1716-1772), **John Rennie** (1761-1821), and **Thomas Telford** (1757-1834).

1774. **John Wilkinson** (1728-1808) invented the **boring-mill.** Originally designed to bore cannon, this machine was to find its most important use in the boring of cylinders for

1776. The **steam engine** of **James Watt** (1736-1819). Based upon the older Newcomen engine, the first working model (1768, patented 1769) contained the separate steam condenser. Put into practical use in 1776, Watt's engine was not a commercial success until 1785, when Watt went into partnership with the entrepreneur **Matthew Boulton** (1728-1809) and only after further improvements had been made: the epicyclic (sun-and-planet) gear (1781) producing rotary motion by the reciprocal piston action, and the double-acting expansive engine (1782). (The "steam engine," actually a two-cylinder atmospheric pressure engine, of the Russian **Polzunov** [1729-1766] operated only for a short time [1767] and had no influence on subsequent engine development.)

1785. Introduction of **chemical bleaching** with chlorine *(eau de Javel)* by the French chemist **C. L. Berthollet** (1748-1822).

1789. The **Leblanc process** for obtaining soda from common salt invented by **Nicolas Leblanc** (1742-1806) in France, but first exploited in England.

1793. Claude Chappe (1763-1805) developed the **semaphore** (visual telegraph); rapid spread after success of first line from Paris-Lille.

1794. Establishment of **École Polytechnique,** premier institution of higher technological education in France; emphasis upon mathematics and applied science.

1797. Henry Maudslay (1771-1831) designed a **screw-cutting lathe,** made entirely of metal and utilizing a slide-rest. This tool was the culmination of much previous precision tool development, including the drill and lathe (1768-1780) of **Jacques de Vaucanson** (1709-1782), the screw-cutting lathe (1770) of **Jesse Ramsden** (1735-1800); the marine chronometer (1759) of **John Harrison** (1693-1776); the spring-winding machine of **Joseph Bramah** (1748-1814), who also invented the modern water closet (1778) and a hydraulic press (1796).

1798. P. L. Guinand (1748-1824), a Swiss, patented a stirring process for making optical glass which became the foundation of the great German **optical industry** of the 19th century.

1798. Aloys Senefelder (1771-1834) of Prague invented **lithography.**

The Industrial Revolution

The Industrial Revolution, begun in the latter half of the 18th century, expanded into new geographical areas, revolutionized older technologies, created new ones, and continued to transform society and human life during the 19th and 20th centuries. Although historians might debate as to whether several industrial revolutions occurred during this two-century span, whether there were different phases of the same revolution, or whether industrialization had reached the point of a "continuing revolution," there was no doubt that technological advances from the mid-18th century to the present had given man greatly increased mastery over his environment, while at the same time posing problems and even threats to man's continued existence.

The culmination of Britain's leadership in the Industrial Revolution was reached at the **Great Exhibition of 1851** in London; after that Britain's position declined relatively while new industrial giants, America and Germany near the close of the 19th century, and Russia in the 20th century, gained in technological strength.

Drake's oil well. He struck oil on August 27, 1859, at a depth of 69 feet.

Energy and Power

1800. The galvanic cell, or Voltaic pile, of **Alessandro Volta** (1745-1827) was the first electric battery (converting chemical energy into electrical energy).

1802. Richard Trevithick (1771-1833) built the first high-pressure steam engine, although the American **Oliver Evans** (1755-1819) had patented one in the United States in 1797. Other advances in steam-engine technology included the compound-engine (adding a high pressure cylinder to the original Watt engine) by **William McNaught** (1813-1881) in 1845.

1806. First gas-lighting of cotton mills. Improvements made in production and distribution of gas as heat source (**Bunsen burner,** 1855) and for illumination (**Welsbach gas-mantle,** 1885).

1827. Benoit Fourneyron (1802-1867) developed the **water-turbine.**

1832. The first mechanical generation of electricity by **Hippolyte Pixii.** Major improvements in **electric generators** followed: the improved armature (1856) designed by **Werner von Siemens** (1816-1892); and the ring-armature (1870) of **Zénobe T. Gramme** (1826-1901), which represented the first practical dynamo.

1854. Abraham Gesner (1797-1864) manufactured kerosene.

1859. William M. J. Rankine (1820-1872) published the first comprehensive manual of the steam engine. The steam engine stimulated theoretical studies in thermodynamics by Clapeyron, Clausius, Joule, Lord Kelvin, and Gibbs.

1859. Edwin L. Drake (1819-1880) drilled the first oil well in Titusville, Pennsylvania, opening up the Pennsylvania oil field and starting the large-scale commercial exploitation of petroleum. **First oil pipeline** (two-inch diameter, six miles long) constructed 1865 in Pennsylvania.

1876. Nicholas August Otto (1832-1891) built the first practical gas engine, working upon the so-called **Otto cycle,** which is now almost universally employed for all internal combustion engines. Otto's work was based upon previous engines of **Étienne Lenoir** (1822-1900) and **Alphonse Beau de Rochas** (1815-1891). The Otto cycle was employed in the gasoline engine patented (1885) by **Gottlieb Daimler** (1834-1900).

1882. The Pearl Street (New York City) electric generating station, a pioneer central power station designed by **Thomas A. Edison** (1847-1931), commenced operations a few months after Edison dynamos had been installed at Holborn Viaduct Station in England.

1884. Charles A. Parsons (1854-1931) patented the **steam turbine.** The steam turbine (1887) of the Swede **Gustav de Laval** (1845-1913) proved successful for engines of smaller power.

1886. Beginning of the first great **hydroelectric installation** at Niagara Falls.

1888. Nikola Tesla (1856-1943) invented the **alternating current electric motor;** he also made possible the polyphase transmission of power over long distances and pioneered the invention of radio.

1892. Rudolf Diesel (1858-1913) patented his heavy oil engine, first manufactured successfully in 1897.

1921. Tetraethyl lead, gasoline anti-knock additive, produced by **Thomas Midgley** (1889-1944).

1930-1937. Development of gas turbine unit for jet propulsion in aircraft by **Frank Whittle.**

1930-1935. Development of first commercially practicable **catalytic cracking system** for petroleum by **Eugene J. Houdry** (1892-1962).

1942. Dawn of the Nuclear Age. The first self-sustaining **nuclear chain reaction** achieved at Stagg Field, Chicago, by **Enrico Fermi** (1901-1954). The first full-scale use of nuclear fuel to produce electricity occurred at Calder Hall (England) in 1956.

1954. The **solar battery** developed by Bell Telephone Laboratories, making it possible to convert sunlight directly to electric power.

Major Developments in Energy and Power Sources

Development	See year	Development	See year	Development	See year
Catalytic Cracking	1930-35	Hydroelectric installation	1886	Tetracthyl lead	1921
Electric battery	1800	Kerosine	1854	Turbine, steam	1884
A.C. motor	1888	Diesel engine	1892	Turbine, jet-propulsion	1930-37
Electric generators	1832	Nuclear chain reaction	1942	Turbine, water	1827
Electric generating station	1882	Oil well	1859	Solar battery	1954
Gasoline engines	1876	Oil pipeline	1865		
Gas lightning	1806	Steam engine	1802, 1859		

Low-cost Bessemer steelmaking established the foundation of the modern steel industry.

Materials and Construction

1800. Pioneer suspension bridge, hung by iron chains, built by **James Finley** (c. 1762-1828) in Pennsylvania; wire suspension employed by **Marc Seguin** (1786-1875) in bridge near Lyons (1825). The American, **Ithiel Town** (1784-1844), patented his truss bridge (1820).

1817-1825. Building of the **Erie Canal,** the first great American civil engineering work.

1818. The **Institute of Civil Engineers** (London), the first professional engineering society, founded.

    Marc Isambard Brunel (1769-1849) patented the cast-iron **tunnel shield; Thomas Cochrane** (1830) used this shield to construct foundations on marshy ground.

1824. Joseph Aspdin (1779-1855) patented **Portland cement,** a hydraulic cement (impervious to water) as durable as that employed by the Romans.

1827. Gay-Lussac tower introduced in manufacture of sulfuric-acid, largely replacing John Roebuck's lead-chamber process (1746). **Herman Frasch** (1851-1914) developed process (1891) for mining sulfur (by superheated water and pumping to the surface).

1836. Galvanized iron introduced by Sorel in France. Galvanized fencing and barbed wire (c. 1880) helped to fence off large tracts of cattle land in American west during latter part of 19th century.

1839. Charles Goodyear (1800-1860) **vulcanized rubber.** Although introduced into Europe in 1615, rubber had not been commercially successful until a solvent for the latex was found (1765); bonding of rubber to cloth to produce raincoats (macintoshes) had been developed (1824) by **Charles Macintosh** (1766-1843).

1855. John A. Roebling (1806-1869) completed **wire cable bridge** at Niagara; Roebling utilized this same method for the **Brooklyn Bridge** (completed by his son, W.A. Roebling, in 1883), and it became standard construction technique for all great suspension bridges.

1856. Henry Bessemer (1813-1898) perfected the technique *(Bessemer process)* for converting pig iron into steel by directing an air blast upon the molten metal.

1856. *Mauve,* first of the **aniline** (coal-tar) **dyes,** discovered by **William H. Perkin** (1838-1907). Beginning of the synthetic dye industry, which was to develop greatly in Germany.

1861. Ernest Solvay (1838-1922) patented the Solvay ammonia process for the manufacture of soda.

1863. The **open-hearth process** for the manufacture of steel developed by the Martin brothers in France using the regenerative furnace devised (1856) by **Frederick Siemens** (1826-1904) (also known as the Siemens-Martin process).

1867. Alfred Nobel (1833-1896) manufactured **dynamite.** Guncotton and nitroglycerine both discovered in 1846, had previously been used for blasting purposes. In 1875 Nobel discovered blasting gelatine, from which arose the gelignite industry. Cordite, another explosive, patented 1889 by Frederick Abel and James Dewar.

1863. Henry Clifton Sorby (1826-1908) of Sheffield discovered the microstructure of steel, marking the beginning of **modern metallurgical science.**

1868. Robert F. Mushet (1811-1891) began the manufacture of **tungsten steel.** Other steel alloys also developed: chromium steel (France, 1877); manganese steel (Robert Hadfield, England, 1882); nickel steel (France, 1888); stainless steel (many inventors, 1911-1920).

Major Developments in Materials and Construction

Development	See year	Development	See year	Development	See year
Aluminum	1886	Dynamite	1867	Solvay ammonia process	1861
Aniline dyes	1856	Eiffel Tower	1889	Steelmaking, basic oxygen	1950
Bridge, wire cable	1855	Erie Canal	1817-25	Steelmaking, Bessemer	1856
Bridge, suspension	1800	Galvanized iron	1836	Steel-frame building	1928
Bridge, truss	1800	Institue of Civil Engineers	1818	Sulfuric acid	1827
Celluloid	1872	Modern metallurgy	1863	Tungsten steel	1868
Casting, shell molding	1941	Polymer	1909	Vulcanized rubber	1839
Cantilever technique,		Reinforced concrete	1947		
buildings	1947	Silicones	1945		

1872. John W. Hyatt (1837-1920) began commercial production of celluloid, discovered by Alexander Parkes (1855).

1877. Joseph Monier (1823-1906) patented a **reinforced concrete** beam. In the 1890s two other Frenchmen, Edmond Coignet and Francois Hennibique, utilized reinforced concrete for pipes, aqueducts, bridges, tunnels; E. L. Ransome employed it extensively in building construction.

1879. Percy Gilchrist (1851-1935) and **Sidney G. Thomas** (1850-1885) developed a method for making steel from phosphoric iron ores, thereby doubling in effect the world's potential steel production.

1886. Charles M. Hall (1863-1914) developed the electrolytic method of obtaining aluminum from its oxide (bauxite).

1889. Completion of the **Eiffel Tower;** wrought-iron superstructure on reinforced concrete base. Cast iron used for building construction earlier in the century by James Bogardus (1800-1874) for office buildings in New York and by Joseph Paxton (1801-1865) for Crystal Palace at Great Exhibition of 1851 (also employing wrought iron and glass, and prefabricated units). The first complete steel-frame structure was built in Chicago in 1890; steel made possible skyscrapers, as did the earlier invention (1854) of the elevator by **Elisha G. Otis** (1811-1861).

1902. Arthur D. Little (1863-1935) patented rayon, the **first cellulose fiber,** and also artificial silk. Earlier (1884) Louis, Count of Chardonet (1839-1924), had produced an artificial thread which was woven into a silk-like material. Cellophane developed by J. E. Brandenberger (1912); further developed by W.H. Church and K. E. Prindle (1926).

1909. The first polymer, **Bakelite,** discovered by **Leo H. Baekeland** (1863-1944). Subsequent development of polymers include neoprene, arising from work of Father Julius A. Nieuwland beginning in 1906; nylon, developed by Wallace H. Carothers and first manufactured in 1938; acrilan; orlon; dynel; and dacron (called terylene by its British inventors, J. R. Whinfield and J. T. Dickson, 1941). Synthetic polymers include elastomers, fibers, plastics. Silicon polymers developed c. 1945.

1928. The first steel-frame, glass-curtain-wall building completed. By 1960 this technique was practically universal for high buildings; developed

particularly by **L. Mies van der Rohe** (1886-1969).

1941. Shell molding, a revolutionary process producing more accurate castings cheaply, invented by **Johannes Croning.** Powder metallurgy, although known since Wollaston's work at the beginning of the 19th century, achieved extensive application in mid-20th century.

1945. Industrial development of silicones proceeded apace for a wide variety of applications, including lubricants for exceedingly high and low temperatures; binding of fiberglass; water-repellent agents; etc.

1947. Frank Lloyd Wright (1869-1959) extended pure cantilever technique (earlier employed with iron and steel construction in bridges) by using concrete slab cantilevers for S. C. Johnson Research Building (Racine, Wisconsin).

1950. Basic-oxygen process for manufacture of steel developed in Austria.

Machines and Industrial Techniques

1800. Eli Whitney (1765-1825) credited with introduction of **interchangeable parts** for manufacturing muskets. Although it had European precedents, the system of interchangeable parts became known as "the American system" because it was most fully exploited in the United States and became the foundation of the mass production characteristic of American industry at a later date.

1801. Joseph M. Jacquard (1752-1834) invented a loom for figured silk fabrics, later introduced into the making of worsteds. **William Horrocks** (1776-1849) developed the power loom (1813), improved (1822) by **Richard Roberts** (1789-1864). Machine combing of wool developed (1845); ring spinning frame (1830); the Brussels power loom invented by Erastus B. Bigelow (1814-1879) of Massachusetts for the weaving of carpets (1845); and the loom of J. H. Northrop of Massachusetts (1892), which was almost completely automatic.

1810. Friedrich Koenig's (1774-1833) **power-driven press** in use, followed by the flat bed press (1811). Other developments leading to mass production of printed matter, especially newspapers, were the rotary press of Robert Hoe (1846) and the web printing press, allowing for printing on a continuous roll (web) of paper by a rotary press, invented (1865) by William A. Bullock. In 1885 the linotype of **Ottmar Mergenthaler** (1854-1899) replaced monotype.

Major Developments in Machines and Industrial Techniques

Development	See year	Development	See year	Development	See year
Adding machines	1884	Electric driven machinery	1873	Printing presses and automatic typsetting	1810
Armament	1837	Interchangable manufacturing parts	1849-54	Refrigeration	1895
Automation	1947	Interchangeable firearm parts	1800	Resistance welder	1877
Ballpoint pen	1938	Laser	1920	Razors	1895
Bottlemaking	1898	Liquid air plant	1895	Screw gauge	1830
Calculators	1823-43	Looms	1801	Sewing machines	1846
Computers	1944, 1953	Managerial techniques	1920	Steam hammer	1839
Continuous rolling, steel sheet	1923	Milling machine	1855	Tanks	1915
Electric appliances	1882	Mass production	1914	Turret lathe	1855
Electric precipitation	1905-10			Zipper	1913

1823-1843. Charles Babbage (1792-1871) attempted to build calculating machines (following the lead of Thomas de Colmar, who built the first practical calculating machine in 1820; Babbage's machines were never completed, being too advanced for the technology of the time, but his theories formed a basis for later work in this field.

1830. Joseph Whitworth (1803-1887) developed the **standard screw gauge** and a machine to measure one-millionth of an inch, for standards. Made possible more precise machine tools for planing, gear-cutting, and milling.

1837. Rapid **development of armament,** keeping pace with improvements in metallurgy, machines, and explosives: **Henri J. Paixhans'** (1783-1854) shell-gun, adopted by France, 1837; rifled, breech-loading artillery used by Piedmont, 1845; the French '75, the first quick-firing artillery piece, firing both shrapnel and high explosive, 1898; the cast steel breech-loading Prussian artillery manufactured by the Krupps from 1849 on. In small arms, there was the Colt revolver (1835), the Dreyse needle-gun (1841), the Minié bullet (1849), Winchester repeating rifle (1860), Gatling machine gun (1861), French Chassepot (1866), and the Maxim gun (1884). The self-propelled torpedo was invented by Robert Whitehead (1823-1905) in 1864; smokeless powder appeared in 1884.

1839. Steam hammer invented by **James Nasmyth** (1808-1890). Also developments in drop-forging and die-stamping at this time.

1846. Elias Howe (1819-1867) invented the lockstitch sewing machine; in 1851 **Isaac M. Singer** (1811-1875) invented the first practical domestic **sewing machine.** This became the first major consumer appliance, soon followed by the **carpet sweeper** of M. R. Bissell (1876), and the **vacuum cleaner** (I. W. McGaffey, 1869; J. Thurman, 1899).

1849-1854. Exploiting the increasing accuracy of machine tools, **Samuel Colt** (1814-1862) and **Elisha Root** (1808-1865) developed a practical system for manufacturing interchangeable parts, especially in connection with Colt's revolver.

1855. Development of **turret lathe** by American machine-tool makers. First true **universal milling machine** designed (1862) by **Joseph R. Brown** (1810-1876). Other machine-tool improvements included Mushet's tool steel, increasing the cutting speed (high speed tool steel, 1898, by Taylor and White), gear-box mechanisms for better control, multiple-spindle lathes (1890), and tungsten carbide tools (1926).

1873. First **use of electricity to drive machinery,** Vienna. Quickly adopted, usually with the motor incorporated into the machine rather than separate.

1877. Elihu Thomson invented a **resistance welder.** N. W. Bernardos of Russia patented carbon-arc welding, although arc welding (most popularly employed process today) did not come into its own until invention of the coated electrode in the 1920s. Oxyacetylene torch (invented in 1900 by Edmund Fouche) and gas welding was the dominant process until recently. Development of inert-gas-shielded arc welding after 1942.

1882. Invention and use of electric appliances for consumer market: electric fan (S.S. Wheeler); flatiron (H. W. Seely, 1882); stove (W. S. Hadaway, 1896); separate attachable plug (H. Hubbell, 1904); sewing machine (Singer Co., 1889); washing machine (Hurling Co., 1907).

1884. Dorr E. Felt (1862-1930) made first accurate **comptometer. William S. Burroughs** (1857-1898) developed first successful recording **adding machine** (1888); Brunsviga calculating machine (1892).

1895. Carl Linde established **liquid air** plant. He had previously (1876) introduced the ammonia compressor machine (the first vapor compression machine invented by Jacob Perkins, 1834). Other refrigerating machines were: ammonia absorption machine (Carré, 1860), air refrigerator (Gorrie, 1845; improved by Kirk, 1862), open-cycle air machine (Giffard, 1873), and later by Bell and Coleman).

1895. King C. Gillette (1855-1932) invented **safety razor** with throwaway blades. **J. Schick** invented **electric razor** (1928). Stainless steel throwaway blades invented in Sweden (1962).

1898. M. J. Owens (1859-1923) invented automatic **bottle-making machine.**

1905-1910. Electric precipitation equipment for prevention of atmospheric pollution by industry, developed by Frederick G. Cottrell (1877-1948).

1913. G. Sundback invented a slide fastener (**zipper**); earlier version patented by W. L. Judson (1891).

1914. Conveyer-belt mass production employed in the United States most dramatically in Henry Ford's assembly line for Model T Ford automobile, which became the symbol for American industrial technique.

1915. Development of **tank in warfare** by British (Sir Ernest Swinton).

1920. Managerial techniques improved through development of "Scientific Management," whose principles were first enunciated by **Frederick W. Taylor** (1856-1915) in the first decade of the century. Taylor concentrated on time-motion studies. Other proponents of "rationalized" production were Frank Gilbreth and Charles Bedaux. Quality control developed 1926.

1920. J. C. Shaw developed a **sensing device,** controlled by a servomechanism, for a milling machine. Hydraulic trace of J. W. Anderson (1927) allowed the reproduction of complex shapes. Machine tools further supplemented by electrolytic and ultrasonic machines, and cutting machines guided by an electron beam. **Development of laser** (light amplification by simulated emission of radiation) by Theodore N. Maiman (1960), also used for precision cutting.

1923. First mill for hot continuous wide strip rolling of steel, based on work of John B. Tytus.

1938. Ladislao J. and George Biro patented the **ball-point pen.**

1944. Harvard IBM Automatic Sequence Controlled Calculator, the first automatic general-purpose **digital computer,** completed. ENIAC (electronic numerical integrator and calculator), the first electronic digital computer, built in 1946. Development of special purpose computers and data processor (1950), including programmed **teaching machines.**

1947. Word *Automation* coined by John Diebold and D. S. Harder, to define "self-powered, self-guiding and correcting mechanism," and later extended to include all elements of "automated factory" and extension to office and clerical procedures.

1953. Electronic computers with feedback mechanism (servomechanisms), made possible new field of **Cybernetics,** defined by **Norbert Wiener** (1953) as "the study of control and communication in the animal and the machine."

Major Developments in Agriculture and Food Technology

Development	See year	Development	See year	Development	See year
Artificial		DDT	1939	Plows	1837
insemination	1940	Evaporated milk	1860	Poultry farming	1950
Cream separator	1877	Farm implements	1850-80	Reapers	1834
Canning	1810	Frozen foods	1917	Refrigeration	1865
Chemical fertilizers	1880	Hydrogenation	1902	Sugarbeet industry	1801
Cotton picker	1889	Pasterurization	1861	Tractors	1892

Agricultural Production and Food Technology

1801. Franz K. Achard (1753-1821) built the first **sugar-beet factory** (Silesia). Sugar-beet cultivation and beet-sugar industry developed primarily in France and Germany.

1810. Nicolas Appert (c. 1750-1840) described system for food preservation by canning, using glass jars. Tin cans introduced 1811.

1834. Cyrus H. McCormick (1809-1884) patented his **reaper**, and began commercial manufacture c. 1840. Obed Hussey (1792-1860) invented a similar reaper simultaneously and independently.

1837. John Deere (1804-1886) introduced the **steel plow**. In 1819 Jethro Wood (1774-1834) had developed a cast-iron plow; and John Lane had introduced a steel-blade plowshare in 1833. James Oliver's (1823-1908) chilled plow of 1855 was improved by the Marsh brothers (1857). Mechanical power applied to plowing with the introduction of **cable plowing** (1859); by 1858 John Fowler had introduced the **steam plow**.

1850-1880. Improvements in farm implements included the revolving disc harrow (1847), binder (1850), corn planter (1853), two-horsestraddle-row cultivator (1856), combine harvester (1860), combine seed drill (1867), and sheaf-biding harvester (1878).

1860. Gail Borden (1801-1874) opened the first factory for the production of **evaporated milk.**

1861. After Louis Pasteur's work on microorganisms, **pasteurization** was introduced as a preservative for beer, wine, and milk.

1865. Development of **mechanical refrigeration** for preservation of food products, especially Thaddeus Lowe's (1832-1913) compression ice machine (1865) and Linde's ammonia compression refrigerator (1873).

1869. Transcontinental railway aided development of **meat-packing industry** in Chicago.

1877. Gustav de Laval (1845-1913) invented the centrifugal **cream separator.**

1880. Application of **chemical fertilizers** increased food production. J. B. Lawes manufactured superphosphates (1842); Chilean sodium nitrate beds exploited from c. 1870 until methods of fixing atmospheric nitrogen were developed after 1900 by Fritz Haber (1868-1934); use of potash as an inorganic fertilizer from Strassfurt deposits.

1889. Angus Campbell tested the first spindle type **cotton picker**; this type of machine was not fully developed and marketed successfully until the 1940s, competing with the machine devised by John and Mack Rust in 1924 and also commercially produced in the 1940s.

1892. Gasoline tractor came into use for farming. Caterpillar tractor developed 1931.

1902. W. Normann patented a process for hardening liquid fats by hydrogenation, making available an ample supply of solid fats for soap and food.

1917. Clarence Birdseye (1886-1956) began development of method for quick **freezing of foods** in small containers; placed on market in 1929.

1939. Paul Muller synthesized DDT for use as an insecticide. Othmar Zeidler had prepared DDT in 1874, but its insecticidal qualities had not been suspected.

1940. Development of **artificial insemination** to improve livestock breeding.

1945. Unit **packaging of foodstuffs** improved by development of plastic packaging films. Trend toward prepared "convenience" foods for household use.

1950. Mass-production, battery-raising of poultry increased production, lowered prices, and converted chicken and turkey from a holiday and Sunday luxury to an everyday food item.

Transportation and Communication

1802. Richard Trevithick (1771-1833) patented a steam carriage; earlier attempts to use steam power for transport purposes had been made by Nicolas Cugnot in France (1769); William Murdock in England (1785), and Oliver Evans in the United States. In 1804 Trevithick designed and built a locomotive to run on rails.

1807. Robert Fulton (1765-1815) sailed the *Clermont* from New York to Albany. This was by no means the first steamboat: the Marquis Claude de Jouffroy d'Abbans (1751-1832) had built a paddle-wheel steamer in France (1783); John Fitch (1743-1798) had launched a steamboat on the Delaware (1787); James Rumsey (1743-1792) on the Potomac (1787); and John Stevens (1749-1838) had designed a successful screw-propeller steamboat (1802). However, Fulton's boat was the first steamboat to represent a commercial success. By 1819 steam augmented sail on the first transatlantic steamship crossing of the *Savannah*.

Cugnot's steam carriage, 1770.

Stephenson's *Rocket* averaged 16 m.p.h. with a maximum speed of 29 m.p.h.

1814. George Stephenson (1781-1848) built his **first locomotive,** and in 1829 his *Rocket,* designed with the aid of his son Robert (1803-1859), won out in a competition with locomotives of other design and thereby set the pattern for future locomotive developments.

1825. Opening of the **Stockton-Darlington Railway,** the first successful railroad system, using a steam engine built by Stephenson. In 1829 the first railroads were opened in the United States (Pennsylvania) and France (Lyon-St. Étienne), both employing English-built locomotives. The first American locomotive was built (1830) by Peter Cooper (1791-1883).

1837. Charles Wheatstone (1802-1875) and **William F. Cooke** (1806-1879) patented the telegraph, which was also independently invented by the American **Samuel F. B. Morse** (1791-1872), whose **telegraphic code** was universally adopted. By 1866, **Cyrus W. Field** (1819-1892) succeeded in laying a **transatlantic cable,** after two previous failures and after overcoming tremendous financial and technical difficulties.

1839. Louis J. M. Daguerre (1787-1851) evolved the **daguerreotype photographic process,** based on the work of Joseph Nicéphore Niepce (1765-1833). Although **William H. F. Talbot** (1800-1877) produced paper positives (1841), the first fully practical medium for photography was the wet collodion plate process (1851) of Frederick S. Archer (1813-1857).

1860. Construction began on the **London underground railway** system, which was electrified in 1905. Construction began on the Paris *metro* in 1898, on New York City subway in 1900.

1864. George M. Pullman (1831-1897) built the first **sleeping car** specially constructed for that purpose.

1867. Ernest Michaux invented the **velocipede,** the first bicycle to put cranks and pedals directly on the front wheel; the "safety" bicycle with the geared chain-drive to rear wheel was introduced in 1885.

1869. Union Pacific and Central Pacific Railroads met to complete the **first transcontinental line** in America. The **Trans-Siberian Railway** was begun in 1891.

1869. Opening of the Suez Canal, the work of the French engineer **Ferdinand de Lesseps** (1805-1894).

1873. The Remington Company began manufacture of the **typewriter** patented by **Christopher L. Sholes** (1819-1890); shift-key system, with capital and small letters on same type bar, introduced in 1878.

1874. Stephen D. Field's (1846-1913) electrically powered **streetcar** began operation in New York City, replacing the horsecars introduced in 1832. The cable streetcar, invented by Andrew S. Hallidie (1836-1900), was put into use in San Francisco (1873). The first streetcars with overhead trolley lines were in use in Germany by 1884 and first installed in the United States at Richmond, Virginia, in 1888.

1876. Alexander Graham Bell (1847-1922) patented the **telephone.** The first telephone exchange installed in New Haven (1877) and an automatic switching system introduced in 1879. Much previous experimentation had been done on telephones, including that of Philip Reis of Germany (1861), Antonio Meucci of Italy (1857),

Bell demonstrating the long-distance capability of his invention at Salem, Mass., on March 15, 1877. A hook-up was made with Boston, 18 miles away, and an extended conversation took place between the two cities.

and Elisha Gray (simultaneously with Bell). The periodic insertion of loading coils (inductors), originated by M. I. Pupin (1899), made possible long distance transmission of telephone calls.

1878-1879. Joseph W. Swan (1828-1914) of England made the first successful carbon filament **electric lamp** in 1878; working independently **Thomas A. Edison** patented his **incandescent bulb** in 1879. Improved vacuum in the lamp bulb made possible by the high vacuum mercury pump developed by Hermann Springel (1865). At the same time successful experiments in public lighting were carried on with the use of arc lamps, the most successful systems being those of P. Jablochkoff (Paris, 1876) and Charles F. Brush (Cleveland, 1879). Tungsten filament lamp introduced in 1913.

1885. Karl Benz (1844-1929) produced the prototype of the **automobile** using an internal combustion motor operating on the Otto four-stroke cycle principle; the same year **Gottlieb Daimler** (1834-1900) also patented his **gasoline engine,** trying it first on a motorcycle, then on a four-wheeled vehicle. These may be said to have been the first automobiles, although there had been experiments with battery-powered electric automobiles from 1851 on and some previous internal combustion vehicles had been attempted by the Frenchman Étienne Lenoir (1859) and the Austrian Siegfried Marcus (1864). Other automobile pioneers included the Frenchmen Peugeot and Panhard. The first automobile patent in the United States was taken out by George B. Selden

(1879), but the Duryea (1895) was the first auto made for sale in the United States. **Henry Ford** (1863-1947) made his first car in 1896 and founded the Ford Motor Co. in 1903. Important in the development of the automobile was the invention (1888) of the **pneumatic tire** by **John B. Dunlop** (1840-1921).

1889-1890. Thomas Edison improved on his first **phonograph** (patented 1878) by substituting wax for the tinfoil-coated cylinders and by adding a loudspeaker to amplify the sounds produced by the diaphragm. Emile Berliner (1851-1929) improved the quality of sound reproduction (1890) by utilizing disk-records and better cutting technique.

1888. George Eastman (1854-1932) perfected the **hand camera** *(Kodak);* he had previously invented the first successful roll film (1880). Leo Backeland perfected (1893) a photographic paper *(Velox)* sufficiently sensitive to be printed by artificial light. Work of Rudolph Fischer and Siegrist in dye-coupler color processes (1910-1914) provided the basis for the development of a commercially practicable color film *(Kodachrome)* by Leopold Godowsky, Jr., and Leopold Mannes (1935).

1895. The first public **motion picture** showing in Paris, by **Louis** (1864-1948) and **Auguste** (1862-1954) **Lumière,** inventors of the **cinématographe.** This followed by a year the openeing of Edison's Kinetoscope Parlor (New York City) where the motion picture (peepshow) could be viewed by but one person at a time. Both these successful attempts at motion pictures had been preceded by earlier devices: the "thaumatrope" of J. A. Paris (1826); the magic lantern, devised by A. Kircher (1645) and improved by Pieter van Musschenbroek (1736); the multi-camera apparatus of Edward Muybridge (1872); the "photographic gun" of E. J. Marey (1882); the celluloid motion-picture film of William Friese-Green (1889). Prototype of the modern **film projector** was the Vitascope (1896), devised by **Charles Francis Jenkins** (1867-1934) and Thomas Armat on the basis of Edison's kinetoscope.

1895. Guglielmo Marconi (1874-1937) invented the **wireless telegraph,** based on the discovery (1887) of radio waves by Heinrich Hertz (1857-1894) (existence of these waves had been deduced by James Clerk Maxwell in 1873). Other contributors to wireless development were E. Branly, Thomas Edison, Alexander Popov (who contributed the aerial), Reginald E. Fessenden (improved transmitter, 1901). In 1901 Marconi succeeded in sending a wireless signal across the Atlantic.

1898. Valdemar Poulsen of Denmark invented the **magnetic recording of sound** (1898). F. Pfleumer of Germany replaced steel wire by plastic tape coated with magnetic material (1930's), and Marvin Camras of the United States made further developments in magnetic recording (1940s).

1904. John Ambrose Fleming (1849-1945) devised the diode thermionic valve (**radio tube**); **Lee de Forest** (1873-1961) invented the Audion (1906), a three-electrode vacuum tube (triode amplifier), thereby providing the basis for the development of **electronics.**

1911. Charles F. Kettering (1876-1958), who had previously invented lighting and ignition systems for the automobile, perfected the **electric self-starter.** The first fully **automatic transmission,** perfected by Earl A. Thompson, was introduced commercially in 1939. Harry Vickers and Francis W. Davis began work on hydraulic **power-assisted steering** systems in 1925 and 1926 respectively, and in 1951 power steering was introduced for passenger cars.

1913. Diesel-electric railway engines first used in Sweden. Coming into use in the United States during the later 1930's, they have largely replaced steam-locomotives.

1920. Frank Conrad (1874-1941) of the Westinghouse Co. began broadcasting radio programs in Pittsburgh, marking the **beginning of radio** as a mass communication medium.

1922. Herbert T. Kalmus developed **Technicolor,** first commercially successful color process for motion pictures.

1926. Sound Motion Pictures. Although Edison had attempted to put together his phonograph and motion picture inventions for sound movies as early as 1904, it was 1923 before de Forest successfully demonstrated his phono-film system for recording sound on the motion picture film. The first motion picture with sound accompaniment was publicly shown in 1926, the first talking picture in 1927.

1926. John L. Baird (1888-1946) successfully demonstrated **television** in England. His mechanical system of television, similar to that of C. F. Jenkins in the United States, was based on Paul von Nipkov's rotating disk (1886), but had technical limitations; modern electronic television developed from the cathode-ray tube (1897) of Ferdinand Braun and A. A. Campbell-Swinton's proposals (1911) for use of a cathode ray to scan an image. The crucial invention was the Iconoscope of the Russian-American **Vladimir Zworykin** (1889-1982), the device which transmits television images quickly and effectively. Philo Farnsworth of the United States contributed the image disector tube (1927). General broadcasting of television began in England in 1936, in the United States in 1941, but languished until after World War II. Peter C. Goldmark of Columbia Broadcasting System demonstrated (1940) sequential method of color television which gave way to compatible electronic system developed by R. C. A. in the 1950s.

1932. Edwin H. Land (1909-   ) invented the first practical synthetic light-polarizing material (**polaroid glass**), found useful in sunglasses, cameras, and scientific optical instruments. In 1947 he invented the **Polaroid Land camera,** which developed the film inside the camera and produced a photograph print within one minute; in 1962 he introduced color film for his camera.

1933. Fluorescent lamps introduced for floodlighting and advertising. Developments leading up to

Major Developments in Transportation and Communication

Development	See year	Development	See year	Development	See year
Aviation (see Aviation section)		Hand-held camera	1888	Sound recording	1898
Automobiles	1885	Polaroid glass, camera	1932	Steam power	1802
Self-starter	1911	Radar	1940-45	Steamboat	1807
Bicycles	1867	Radio tube	1904	Streetcar	1874
Electric lamp	1878-79	Radio broadcasts	1920	Submarine, nuclear	1950
Fluorescent lamp	1933	FM (frequency modulation)	1933	Suez Canal	1869
Maser	1954	Railroad system, first	1825	Telegraph	1837
Motion pictures	1895	Diesel-electric engines	1913	Wireless	1895
Technicolor	1922	Sleeping car	1864	Telephone	1876
3-D films	1953	Locomotive	1814	Television	1926
Cinerama	1953	London railway system	1860	Transistor	1948
Phonograph	1888-90	Transcontinental, first	1869	Typewriter	1873
Long-playing records	1948	Space (see Space section)		Xerography	1937
Photography, Daguerrotype	1839	Satellite	1957		

The world's first liquid-fuel rocket, 1926 (Smithsonian Institution photo)

this included experiments by George Stokes (1852) and Alexandre Becquerel (1859) to excite fluorescent materials by ultraviolet rays or in a discharge tube; Peter Cooper-Hewitt's invention of the mercury vapor lamp (1901); the introduction of the **Neon lamp** by Georges Claude and the work on cathodes by D. M. Moore and Wehnelt in the 1900's; and J. Risler's application of powder to the outside of tubular discharge lamps (1923). Subsequent developments have included increased cathode life and improved fluorescent powders.

1933. Edwin H. Armstrong (1890-1954), pioneer radio inventor (regenerative, i.e., feedback, circuit, 1912, and superheterodyne circuit, 1918), perfected **frequency modulation (FM)** providing static-free radio reception.

1937. Chester Carlson patented a new dry photographic process *(Xerography)* based upon principles of photoconductivity and electrostatics.

1939. Igor Sikorsky (1889-1972) flew the first **helicopter** of his design. The first helicopter capable of flight was the work of Ellehammer of Denmark (1912), based on C. Rendard's articulated rotor blade (1904) and G. A: Croco's cyclic pitch control (1906). Juan de la Cierva invented the autogiro (1922), differing from the helicopter in that its rotor auto-rotated and the engine drove a normal propeller. Further development work was done (1934-1936) by Louis Breguet and Heinrich Focke.

1939. First test flight of a **turbo-jet airplane** (Heinkel) with an engine designed by Hans von Ohain.

Simultaneous and parallel work on jet airplanes in Britain, based on turbo-jet engine designed by Frank Whittle (1930). (Also see special section on Aviation for additional information.)

1940-1945. Development of radar ("radio-detection-and-ranging") stimulated by World War II, for detection of aircraft, blind-bombing techniques, and naval search equipment. Based on Heinrich Hertz's demonstration (1887) that radio waves are reflected similarly to light rays, the technique was first applied by Edward Appleton in Britain (1924) and G. Breit and M. A. Tuve in the United States (1925) for investigating ionization in the upper atmosphere. Robert A. Watson-Watt showed the possibilities of employing radio waves to detect aircraft (1935); J. T. Randall and H. A. H. Boot developed the cavity magnetron for high-power microwave transmission. Simultaneously, radar development had been going on in Germany and the United States, including the development of equipment by Robert H. Page of the Naval Laboratory. After 1940 Britain and the United States co-operated in radar development, much of the work being done at the Radiation Laboratory in Cambridge, Mass.

1941-1945. Construction of 2,500 miles of large diameter (20-inch-24-inch) **pipelines** to deliver petroleum from oil-producing regions in Southwest United States to East Coast depots. Development of welding of steelpipe sections (1913-1914) cut leakage and made possible large-scale pipeline construction.

1948. Long-playing phonograph record introduced, based on Peter Goldmark's development of the narrow-groove vinyl plastic record, a lightweight pickup, and a slow-speed (33-1/3 r.p.m.), silent turntable.

1948. Basic research in semi-conductors at the Bell Telephone Laboratories resulted in the invention of the **transistor** by a group which included William Shockley, John Bardeen, and Walter H. Brattain. This tiny, rugged, amplifying device was increasingly used to replace vacuum tubes in electronic instruments. In 1954 the silicon transistor was developed.

1950. Development of **nuclear propulsion** for submarines and surface ships. The United States submarine *Nautilus* (1955), built under the stimulus exerted by Admiral Hyman Rickover, was the first submarine to pass under the North Polar ice cap. The Soviet icebreaker *Lenin* was the first nuclear-powered surface vessel.

1953. "Cinerama" system (invented and developed by Fred Waller) to produce three-dimensional films, released for commercial exhibition. At about the same time Cinemascope, employing a single large concave screen, and stereophonic sound were introduced for motion picture exhibition.

1954. Charles H. Townes (1915-   ) invented the **maser** (microwave amplification by the simulated emission of radiation), making it possible to transmit signals over great distances.

1957. Launching of first **man-made satellite**, *Sputnik I*, by Russia (Oct. 4) marked the beginning of the **Space Age**. This was the product of millennia of human dreams but, more materially, of the rocket researches of **Robert H. Goddard** (1882-1945) of the United States (first liquid-fuel rocket launched, 1926), the theoretical studies of the Russian **Konstantin Tsiolkovsky** (1903), and the German **Herman Oberth** (1923). (Also see special section on Space for additional information.)

Selected Scientific Inventions, Discoveries, and Theories

Abacus: *See* Calculating machine

Adding machine: *See* Calculating machine; Computer

Adrenaline: (isolation of) John Jacob Abel, U.S., 1897

Anesthetic: (first use of anesthetic—ether—on man) Crawford W. Long, U.S., 1842

Antibiotics: (first demonstration of antibiotic effect) Louis Pasteur, Jules-François Joubert, France, 1887; (penicillin, first modern antibiotic) Alexander Fleming, England, 1928

Antiseptic: (surgery) Joseph Lister, England, 1867

Antitoxin, diphtheria: Emil von Behring, Germany, 1890

Atomic theory: (ancient) Leucippus, Democritus, Greece, c.500 B.C.; Lucretius, Rome, c.100 B.C.; (modern) John Dalton, England, 1808

Bacteria: Anton van Leeuwenhoek, The Netherlands, 1683

Barometer: Evangelista Torricelli, Italy, 1643

Bicycle: Karl D. von Sauerbronn, Germany, 1816; (first modern model) James Starley, England, 1884

Bifocal lens: *See* Lens, bifocal

Blood, circulation of: William Harvey, England, 1628

Braille: Louis Braille, France, 1829

Bullet: (conical) Claude Minié, France, 1849

Calculating machine: (Abacus) China, c.190; (logarithms: made multiplying easier and thus calculators practical) John Napier, Scotland, 1614; (slide rule) William Oughtred, England, 1632; (digital calculator) Blaise Pascal, 1642; (multiplication machine) Gottfried Leibnitz, Germany, 1671; (important 19th-century contributors to modern machine) Frank S. Baldwin, Jay R. Monroe, Dorr E. Felt, W. T. Ohdner, William Burroughs, all U.S.; ("analytical engine" design, included concepts of programming, taping) Charles Babbage, England, 1835. *See also* Computer

Classification of plants and animals: (by genera and species) Carolus Linnaeus, Sweden, 1737-53

Clock, pendulum: Christian Huygens, The Netherlands, 1656

Combustion: (nature of) Antoine Lavoisier, France, 1777

Computer: (differential analyzer, mechanically operated) Vannevar Bush, U.S., 1928; (Mark I, first information-processing digital computer) Howard Aiken, U.S., 1944; (ENIAC, Electronic Numerical Integrator and Calculator, first all-electronic) J. Presper Eckert, John W. Mauchly, U.S., 1946; (stored-program concept) John von Neumann, U.S., 1947

Conditioned reflex: Ivan Pavlov, Russia, c.1910

Cosmetics: Egypt, c.4000 B.C.

Crossbow: China, c.300 B.C.

Cyclotron: Ernest O. Lawrence, U.S., 1931

Deuterium: (heavy hydrogen) Harold Urey, U.S., 1931

DNA: (deoxyribonucleic acid) Friedrich Meischer, Germany, 1869; (determination of double-helical structure) F. H. Crick, England, James D. Watson, U.S., 1953

Electromagnet: William Sturgeon, England, 1823

Electron: Sir Joseph J. Thompson, England, 1897

E = mc²: (equivalence of mass and energy) Albert

Section of Charles Babbage's Difference Engine, an ingenious calculating machine.

Einstein, Switzerland, 1907

Evolution: (by natural selection) Charles Darwin, England, 1859

Falling bodies, law of: Galileo Galilei, Italy, 1590

Fermentation: (micro-organisms as cause of) Louis Pasteur, France, c.1860

Geometry, elements of: Euclid, Alexandria, Egypt, c.300 B.C.

Gravitation, law of: Sir Isaac Newton, England, c. 1665 (published 1687)

Gunpowder: China, c.700

Gyrocompass: Elmer A. Sperry, U.S., 1905

Gyroscope: Léon Foucault, France, 1852

Helium first observed on sun: Sir Joseph Lockyer, England, 1868

Heredity, laws of: Gregor Mendel, Austria, 1865

Induction, electric: Joseph Henry, U.S., 1828

Insulin: Sir Frederick G. Banting, J. J. R. MacLeod, Canada, 1922

Intelligence testing: Alfred Binet, Theodore Simon, France, 1905

Isotopes: (concept of) Frederick Soddy, England, 1912; (stable isotopes) J. J. Thompson, England, 1913; (existence demonstrated by mass spectrography) Francis W. Ashton, 1919

Laser: (theoretical work on) Charles H. Townes, Arthur L. Schawlow, U.S., N. Basov, A. Prokhorov, U.S.S.R., 1958; (first working model) T. H. Maiman, U.S., 1960

Lens, bifocal: Benjamin Franklin, U.S., c.1760

Light, nature of: (wave theory) Christian Huygens, The Netherlands, 1678; (electromagnetic theory) James Clerk Maxwell, England, 1873
Light, speed of: (theory that light has finite velocity) Olaus Roemer, Denmark, 1675
Lightning rod: Benjamin Franklin, U.S., 1752
Logarithms: *See* Calculating machine
Loom: (horizontal, two-beamed) Egypt, c.4400 B.C.; (Jacquard drawloom, pattern controlled by punch cards) Jacques de Vaucanson, France, 1745, Joseph-Marie Jacquard, 1801; (flying shuttle) John Kay, England, 1733; (power-driven loom) Edmund Cartwright, England, 1785
Machine gun: James Puckle, England, 1718; Richard J. Gatling, U.S., 1861
Match: (phosphorus) François Derosne, France, 1816; (friction) Charles Sauria, France, 1831; (safety) J. E. Lundstrom, Sweden, 1855
Mendelian law: *See* Heredity
Microscope: (compound) Zacharias Janssen, The Netherlands, 1590; (electron) Vladimir Zworykin et al., U.S., Canada, Germany, 1932-1939
Neptunium: (first transuranic element, synthesis of) Edward M. McMillan, Philip H. Abelson, U.S., 1940
Neutron: James Chadwick, England, 1932
Neutron-induced radiation: Enrico Fermi et al., Italy, 1934
Nuclear fission: Otto Hahn, Fritz Strassmann, Germany, 1938
Ohm's law: (relationship between strength of electric current, electromotive force, and circuit resistance) Georg S. Ohm, Germany, 1827
Ozone: Christian Schönbein, Germany, 1839
Paper: China, c.100 B.C.
Parachute: Louis S. Lenormand, France, 1783
Pen: (fountain) Lewis E. Waterman, U.S., 1884; (ball-point, for marking on rough surfaces) John H. Loud, U.S., 1888; (ball-point, for handwriting) Lazlo Biro, Argentina, 1944
Penicillin: *See* Antibiotics
Periodic law: (that properties of elements are functions of their atomic weights) Dmitri Mendeleev, Russia, 1869
Periodic table: (arrangement of chemical elements based on periodic law) Dmitri Mendeleev, Russia, 1869
Plow, forked: Mesopotamia, before 3000 B.C.
Plutonium, synthesis of: Glenn T. Seaborg, Edwin M. McMillan, Arthur C. Wahl, Joseph W. Kennedy, U.S., 1941
Polio, vaccine against: (vaccine made from dead virus strains) Jonas E. Salk, U.S., 1954; (vaccine made from live virus strains) Albert Sabin, U.S., 1960
Positron: Carl D. Anderson, U.S., 1932
Pressure cooker: (early version) Denis Papin, France, 1679
Printing: (block) Japan, c.700; (movable type) Korea, c.1400; Johann Gutenberg, Germany, c. 1450 (lithography, offset) Aloys Senefelder, Germany, 1796; (rotary press) Richard Hoe, U.S., 1844; (linotype) Ottmar Mergenthaler, U.S., 1884
Programming, information: *See* Calculating machine
Propeller, screw: Sir Francis P. Smith, England, 1836; John Ericsson, England, worked independently of and simultaneously with Smith, 1837
Proton: Ernest Rutherford, England, 1919
Psychoanalysis: Sigmund Freud, Austria, c.1904
Quantum theory: Max Planck, Germany, 1901
Rabies immunization: Louis Pasteur, France, 1885
Radioactivity: (X-rays) Wilhelm K. Roentgen, Germany, 1895; (radioactivity of uranium) Henri Bec-

querel, France, 1896; (radioactive elements, radium and polonium in uranium ore) Marie Sklodowska-Curie, Pierre Curie, France, 1898; (classification of alpha and beta particle radiation) Pierre Curie, France, 1900; (gamma radiation) Paul-Ulrich Villard, France, 1900; (carbon dating) Willard F. Libby et al., U.S., 1955
Relativity: (special and general theories of) Albert Einstein, Switzerland, Germany, U.S., 1905-53
Roller bearing: (wooden for cartwheel) Germany or France, c.100 B.C.
Safety match: *See* Match
Solar system, universe: (sun-centered universe) Nicolaus Copernicus, Warsaw, 1543; (establishment of planetary orbits as elliptical) Johannes Kepler, Germany, 1609; (infinity of universe) Giordano Bruno, Italian monk, 1584
Spectrum: (heterogeneity of light) Sir Isaac Newton, England, 1665-66
Spermatozoa: Anton van Leeuwenhoek, The Netherlands, 1683
Spinning: (spinning wheel) India, introduced to Europe in Middle Ages; (Saxony wheel, continuous spinning of wool or cotton yarn) England, c.1500-1600; (spinning jenny) James Hargreaves, England, 1764; (spinning frame) Sir Richard Arkwright, England, 1769; (spinning mule, completed mechanization of spinning, permitting production of yarn to keep up with demands of modern looms) Samuel Crompton, England, 1779
Sulfa drugs: (parent compound, para-aminobenzenesulfanomide) Paul Gelmo, Austria, 1908; (antibacterial activity) Gerhard Domagk, Germany, 1935
Syphilis, test for: *See* Wassermann test
Thermometer: (open-column) Galileo Galilei, c. 1593; (clinical) Santorio Santorio, Padua, c. 1615; (mercury, also Fahrenheit scale) Gabriel D. Fahrenheit, Germany, 1714; (centigrade scale) Anders Celsius, Sweden, 1742; (absolute-temperature, or Kelvin, scale) William Thompson, Lord Kelvin, England, 1848
Toilet, flush: Product of Minoan civilization, Crete, c.2000 B.C. Alleged invention by "Thomas Crapper" is untrue.
Tractor: Benjamin Holt, U.S., 1900
Transformer, electric: William Stanley, U.S., 1885
Uncertainty principle: (that position and velocity of an object cannot both be measured exactly, at the same time) Werner Heisenberg, Germany, 1927
Vaccination: Edward Jenner, England, 1796
Van Allen (radiation) Belt: (around the earth) James Van Allen, U.S., 1958
Vitamins: (hypothesis of disease deficiency) Sir F. G. Hopkins, Casimir Funk, England, 1912; (vitamin A) Elmer V. McCollum, M. Davis, U.S., 1912-14; (vitamin B) Elmer V. McCollum, U.S., 1915-16; (thiamin, B_1) Casimir Funk, England, 1912; (riboflavin, B_2) D. T. Smith, E. G. Hendrick, U.S., 1926; (niacin) Conrad Elvehjem, U.S., 1937; (B_6) Paul Gyorgy, U.S., 1934; (vitamin C) C. A. Hoist, T. Froelich, Norway, 1912; (vitamin D) Elmer V. McCollum, U.S., 1922; (folic acid) Lucy Wills, England, 1933
Wassermann test: (for syphilis) August von Wassermann, Germany, 1906
Weaving, cloth: *See* Loom
Wheel: (cart, solid wood) Mesopotamia, c.3800-3600 B.C.
Windmill: Persia, c.600
X-ray: *See* Radioactivity
Zero: India, c.600; (absolute zero, cessation of all molecular energy) William Thompson, Lord Kelvin, England, 1848

ENVIRONMENT

Pollution Knows No Boundaries

By Sharon Begley

AS FAR AS LEE LIEBENSTEIN knows, Wisconsin farmers don't apply the pesticide toxaphene. It is, after all, a carcinogen banned in the United States. But the chemical, used in Latin America to kill grubs that feast on corn roots, has been showing up in the cold blue waters of Lake Superior and in the fish that live there.

Liebenstein, toxic substances specialist at Wisconsin's Department of Natural Resources, suspects toxaphene of hitchhiking on the winds, riding storm systems that sweep up from the Gulf of Mexico and swing over Oklahoma into the Great Lakes states. If he's right, the pesticide is one of the latest international terrorists, pollutants that cross political boundaries with impunity and prove that no place, no matter how remote, is immune to their threat. "Long-range transport of pesticides and industrial compounds," says Liebenstein, "is the new challenge."

Every austral springtime, chemicals used in air conditioners and other products rip a great hole in the ozone layer above Antarctica. The chief culprits, chlorofluorocarbons (CFCs), come from all over the globe, particularly developed countries in the northern hemisphere. Almost none is produced on the frozen land directly below. When British scientists discovered the hole in 1985, its size was bad enough: as big as the continental United States. But its location sent shivers into the environmental community. If CFCs can meander down to the South Pole from computer-chip assembly lines in Silicon Valley, from leaky air conditioners in Bangkok, from hairspray cans in Paris, no spot on Earth is safe from pollutants.

In a major foreign policy address last spring [1989], President Bush sounded the conservation mantra for the 1990s: "Environmental destruction respects no borders." It wasn't long ago that the rivers and oceans of the globe divided the world's states. Nature's gift to the mapmakers, they stopped foreign armies and impeded would-be emigrants. But now they have assumed an opposite role—offering free rides to pollutants. The more scientists discover about pollutants' effects and ability to travel great distances, the clearer it becomes how inadequate the world's response has been.

Pollution that crosses national boundaries creates global problems, most notably erosion of the ozone layer by chlorine atoms in CFCs and climate change threatened by greenhouse gases. But itinerant pollutants also leave their mark on more circumscribed areas:

• In 1986, 1,000 metric tons of dyes, insecticides and mercury spilled into the Rhine River after a fire at a Sandoz company warehouse in Basel, Switzerland. The spill carried noxious waste through West Germany all the way to the river's mouth at the North Sea in the Netherlands.

• That same year, the accident at the Chernobyl nuclear power plant in the Ukraine rained radioactive particles throughout the Northern Hemisphere.

• Every day, even without disasters, pesticides and toxic heavy metals such as mercury, cadmium and lead run off the land into rivers and seas, from the Chesapeake Bay to Puget Sound.

• Coal-fired utilities in the Midwest emit sulfur dioxide that floats on the westerly winds until it reaches the Adirondack Mountains and falls as acid rain.

Acid Rain

The atmosphere transports pollutants where water cannot: mercury from coal-fired power plants and from latex paints rides the air currents into lakes in the Upper Midwest. Eleven lakes studied in north-central Wisconsin have toxic mercury in their bottom sediments. Since almost all their water comes from precipitation, the mercury must be coming from the air. Lake Siskiwit on Isle Royale in Lake Superior contains dioxins and PCBs. Since about the only activities there are camping and wolf research, "the atmosphere must be the source," says Wisconsin's Liebenstein.

To pinpoint sources of pollution that might be as close as the next town or as far away as the next hemisphere, scientists are "fingerprinting" pollutants. Each geological source of lead, for instance, is chemically unique. In studies of lakes Erie and Ontario published last year, geochemist A. Russell Flegal of the University of California, Santa Cruz, found industrial leads from Canada in western Lake Ontario and U.S. leads in the southern half of Lake Erie.

When researchers fingerprinted acid rain, they also found evidence of border crossing. They traced the rain and snow that blight lakes and forests in the eastern United States and Canada to sources in the Midwest (see *National Wildlife*, February-March 1987). Rain, snow and fog are made acidic by sulfur dioxide and nitrogen oxides from vehicles, coal-fired power plants and nonferrous smelters. The pollutants can ride long distances on prevailing winds, and have corroded buildings and monuments, blighted forests and damaged thousands of streams and lakes in North America and Europe.

Using chemical fingerprints, investigators led by chemist Kenneth Rahn of the University of Rhode Island have found that up to 80 percent of the sulfate from sulfur dioxide falling in the northeastern United States originates in the Midwest. Nearly half the acid rain falling on eastern Canada comes from the United States; 10 percent of the acid rain in the northeastern United States comes from Canada. Swedish scientists have determined that as much as one-third the sulfur compounds that are added to their atmosphere come from as far away as East Germany, Poland and Czechoslovakia.

Because any country that is a source of acid rain is usually also a victim, there has been some progress in controlling it. In 1979, 32 European nations, plus Canada and the United States, signed the Convention on Long Range Transboundary Air Pollution, pledging in principle to reduce their 1980 sulfur emissions 30 percent by 1993. Canadà, West Germany, France, Norway, Sweden and Denmark went further, pledging reductions of 40 or 50 percent. But countries that contribute the most to acid rain—Britain, the United States and Poland—haven't taken the necessary steps to fulfill their pledge. Only last spring [1989], President Bush suggested new clean-air measures, reversing the years-long do-nothing stance of his predecessor, and proposed that America's sulfur dioxide emissions be slashed by 40 percent.

Ozone Depletion

Some pollutants mix so thoroughly with the atmosphere that they affect the globe no matter where they originate. Jerry Mahlmann of the Geophysical Fluid Dynamics Lab at Princeton notes that CFCs, for instance, disperse throughout the lower atmosphere within a year of being emitted. These odorless, colorless gases—used primarily as refrigerants, solvents, cleaning agents and plastic-foam blowers—stay in the atmosphere for decades; the two most common CFCs have lifetimes of 76 and 139 years.

Once in the stratosphere, 6 to 30 miles above the Earth's surface, their chlorine atoms act like chemical PacMen, gobbling the thin band of ozone that absorbs ultraviolet rays. Ozone is also depleted by halons, bromine-based compounds used in fire extinguishers. And scientists tell us that ozone is just as appetizing to chlorine from other sources, such as the solvents methyl chloroform, found in typing correction fluid, and carbon tetrachloride, used in dry cleaning.

The history of the ozone crisis offers one of the more cheering cases of world cooperation against a common threat. In 1974, chemists F. Sherwood Rowland and Mario Molina of the University of California hypothesized that CFCs could destroy stratospheric ozone. (Each chlorine atom can destroy more than 10,000 ozone molecules.) But government and academic estimates of how much ozone might be lost went up and down like a yo-yo: 7 percent, 16.5 percent, 2 percent.

It was just the kind of scientific uncertainty that policymakers blame when they want to avoid making policy. But this time was different. Even before the scientific case was settled, the United States, Canada, Norway and Sweden banned nonessential uses of CFCs in aerosol sprays in the late 1970s. The rest of the world did not. But the precedent was set.

In the fall of 1987, 34 nations meeting in Montreal pledged to freeze production at 1986 levels in 1990 and cut CFC production 50 percent by 1998. They also agreed to freeze consumption of halons by 1992. Halons, though relatively rare, are three to ten times more destructive of ozone than CFCs. Unfortunately, the ink on the treaty was hardly dry before it became apparent that it was totally inadequate. British scientists had already discovered the hole over the South Pole. But only after the Montreal pact did scientists agree that the hole was due to CFCs.

Says chemist Rowland, "The questions now are will it spread and how rapidly will it spread." Last austral spring (our fall) the hole covered about 10 million square miles, about the size of the record 1987 hole, exceeding scientists' predictions.

In 1988, NASA researchers reported that the land of the penguins wasn't the only region subject to CFC's destructive power: ozone concentrations in the Northern Hemisphere have fallen between 1.7 and 3 percent since 1979. Each 1 percent drop allows another 2 percent more UV rays to reach the planet's surface, calculates the Environmental Protection Agency (EPA), and triggers about 5 percent more human skin cancers. And in 1989, an Arctic expedition found chemicals and reactions similar to those in Antarctica at the North Pole, too.

If unchanged, the Montreal agreement would allow CFC concentrations to triple by 2075 and rise to 12.4 parts per billion in the atmosphere by 2100. (The "natural" level of chlorine in the atmosphere is .7 ppb.) accelerating the phaseout will make little difference. Even if CFCs are banned immediately, atmospheric levels of chlorine will continue to increase.

The gases last so long that those released years ago are still rising to the stratosphere and may destroy another 2 to 10 percent of the ozone cover by about 2050. Even phasing out CFCs completely by 2000 allows a rise from the current 2.7 ppb to about 7 ppb. Freezing emissions of carbon tetrachloride and methyl chloroform would help significantly, says NASA ozone specialist Robert Watson. Currently, carbon tetrachloride emissions are rising 1 percent a year. If both substances in addition to CFCs are phased out completely by the year 2000, chlorine levels will rise to only 5.2 ppb.

Spurred by such discoveries, 60 nations met in Helsinki last spring to review the Montreal accord. The European Economic Community, later joined by the United States and Canada, agreed in principle to push up the timetable so that CFCs would be phased out in 11 years.

But as in all cases of global pollution, attempts to save the ozone layer will fail without the cooperation of developing countries. Under the Montreal protocol, developing nations can increase CFC use. (China, India and Brazil, with 40 percent of world population, now account for little more than 2 percent of CFC use.) The Third World insists that it can't implement expensive CFC substitutes without help from its richer neighbors. The Chinese delegate to the Helsinki meeting said his country would adopt substitutes "only if this does not jeopardize our economic development."

Although the ozone layer will continue to diminish, at least the world has taken steps to mitigate the loss. The same cannot be said for greenhouse warming. In large part, that's because there is no scientific consensus that pollutants are already turning up the world's thermostat. They do agree that certain gases trap heat, and that warming is inevitable.

Greenhouse Warming

The chief greenhouse gas is carbon dioxide, emitted from the burning of fossil fuels and from deforestation: the burning of trees releases their carbon and leaves behind fewer trees to absorb carbon dioxide from the air. Forest burning accounts for 20 to 25 percent of the world's annual carbon dioxide emissions (6 billion tons), estimates the United Nations Environment Program (UNEP). Besides carbon dioxide, there are 39 other known gases responsible for half the global warming, says UNEP. The three most significant are methane, produced by such biological sources as cattle's digestive tracts and anerobic bacteria in rice paddies; nitrous oxide, primarily from bacteria; and CFCs. Over the last century, atmospheric carbon dioxide levels increased 25 percent, to 350 parts per million. At the rate things are going, levels should double in 60 years, reaching twice the pre-industrial level by 2030, predicts Ralph Cicerone of the National Center for Atmospheric Research. By then, his computerized simulations predict, mean global temperatures will rise 1.5 to 4.5 degrees C (2.7 to 8° F).

What will a greenhouse world be like? At high latitudes, winters will be shorter, wetter and warmer; summers longer, hotter and drier. Dry areas of the tropics and subtropics will be drier; humid areas will suffer more frequent and more violent storms. "Severe shocks to agriculture from major floods, persistent droughts, forest fires and crop pests will also change in frequency and magnitude," says Martin Parry of Birmingham University in Britain, who is leading a greenhouse study for the United Nations. The El Niño current off South America may become warmer more often, causing droughts in Brazil, Australia, India and parts of Africa. Agriculture belts will shift, moving several hundred kilometers northward for every 1-degree rise in average temperature.

Sea levels could rise 0.5 to 3.5 meters (19.5 in. to 11.5 ft) by 2100. Coasts and islands, home to half the world's people, would be inundated. Malibu and East Hampton aside, the overwhelming majority of coastal dwellers are poor and would have no easy escape from rising waters. "Those hardest hit are likely to be the developing nations," says UNEP director Mostafa Tolba.

Unlike their agreement that chlorine destroys ozone, scientists do not agree on whether the greenhouse effect has arrived yet. Many point to the evidence that the abnormally warm 1980s saw five of the hottest years on record. "The greenhouse is already beginning to affect the probability of summer heat waves and drought," argues James Hansen, directo. of the Goddard Institute for Space Studies, from 30 percent in the period from 1950 to 1980, to 60 to 70 percent now. "The greenhouse effect is already strong enough to load the climatic dice."

Since weather is driven by so many chaotic forces, a more reliable indicator of the greenhouse effect may be sea levels. They have risen 10 to 20 centimeters (4 to 8 inches) during the past century, reported researchers W.R. Peltier and A.M. Tushingham of the University of Toronto last year, due to thermal expansion of the water and the melting of ice sheets and glaciers. This could, they say,

"constitute an indication of global climate warming."

In 1988, NASA researchers reported that the land of the penguins wasn't the only region subject to CFC's destructive power: ozone concentrations in the Northern Hemisphere have fallen between 1.7 and 3 percent since 1979. Each 1 percent drop allows another 2 percent more UV rays to reach the planet's surface, calculates the Environmental Protection Agency (EPA), and triggers about 5 percent more human skin cancers. And in 1989, an Arctic expedition found chemicals and reactions similar to those in Antarctica at the North Pole, too.

In 1947, the International Court of Justice, an arm of the United Nations, declared, "Every state is under an obligation not to allow its territory to be used for acts contrary to the rights of other states." But laws cannot, and have not, stopped sovereign nations from doing as they please.

Appeals to the commonweal are seldom effective, particularly if the problem lies in the future, like a greenhouse world. The difficulty is even greater when pollution control competes with economic self-interest, or even survival. It's hard to get an Amazonian campesino alarmed about shifting agricultural belts in Iowa in the year 2050 when he has to feed his hungry family from slashed-and-burned fields tonight. Policy makers, too, faced with problems that seem to have no boundaries, feel "a sense of helplessness and inevitability, weighed down by depression," said Vermont governor Madeleine Kunin at a greenhouse conference last year in New York.

Still, now that pollution travels on an international passport, the days of dealing with it by pushing it into someone else's backyard are over. Skin cancer cases in Rome may increase because of Brazil's desire for modern refrigeration; agricultural belts in Canada may shift into regions of disastrously poor rainfall because of coal-burning in China.

A global threat requires global solutions. As Canadian Environment Minister Lucien Bouchard told the New York greenhouse conference last year, "It is clear that no one country alone can protect the planet." And no country, however well intentioned, can rest easy until the last recalcitrant nation cleans up its act. □

Sharon Begley is a science and environment writer for *Newsweek.* Copyright 1990 by the National Wildlife Federation. Reprinted with permission from the February/March 1990 issue of *National Wildlife.*

1990 Environmental Quality Index

Source: Copyright 1990 by the National Wildlife Federation.

Reprinted from the February-March issue of *National Wildlife Magazine.*

National Wildlife's annual Environmental Quality Index is a subjective analysis of the state of the nation's natural resources. The information included in each section is based on personal interviews, news reports, and the most current scientific studies. The judgments on resource trends represent the collective thinking of the editors and the National Wildlife Federation staff, based on consultation with government experts, private specialists, and academic researchers.

Wildlife: Worse. Wildlife in many areas of the United States continued to suffer from the lingering effects of the drought of 1988, and from the unusually harsh winter that followed in some regions. However, largely due to human intrusion, the numbers of several New England fish species, such as cod and haddock, are at record low levels because of overharvesting. Human intrusion also was affecting North America's waterfowl population, estimated to be near an all-time low. Wetland destruction by farming and other interests continued in the country at a rate of some 300,000 acres a year. Despite the vaunted Swampbuster provision of the 1985 U.S. Farm Act, which can deny federal subsidies to farmers who destroy wetlands, a study released last year said wetland drainage in 1987 was the highest in 20 years. Meanwhile waterfowl got a boost last summer [1989] when the Lake Thompson Watershed Restoration Project in South Dakota was dedicated.

Air: Worse. The problems that were so visible during 1988 did not go away. Once again, the worst of it involved not a continually degrading problem, but the discovery that an imperfectly understood dilemma had for some time been getting worse. In the case of toxic chemicals that are released into the air by American industry it was *far worse*. A 1985 estimate—that as much as 80 million pounds of poisons were being released into the nation's air every year—had been derided by U.S. industry as a wild overstatement of the case. The reality, as reported for 1987, turned out to be 30 times worse—a total of some 2.6 *billion* pounds. Another EPA report contained some good news. All five pervasive pollutants originally listed in the Clean Air Act of 1970—sulfur dioxide, nitrogen oxides, carbon monoxide, ozone, and particulates—were substantially reduced in the decade ending in 1987. But during the last two years of the period, levels of ozone (the most hazardous smog component) and particulates increased; those of nitrogen oxides stopped decreasing. In 1989, 81 U.S. cities remained unable to meet long-mandated standards for air quality and unpunished for their failure. Meanwhile, evidence continued to mount in 1989 on the need for tougher standards.

Water: Worse. As the year began, A Congressional subcommittee report detailed what one Congressman called "an absolutely horrendous problem" with coastal waters, involving far more than oil spills. "From the contaminated sediment of New Bedford Harbor to the closed beaches of Long Island, from declining shellfish harvests of Chesapeake Bay, to the rapidly disappearing wetlands of Louisiana, from the heavily polluted waters of San Francisco Bay to the Superfund sites in Puget Sound, the signs of damage and loss are pervasive."

Despite the problems besieging their coastal waters, Americans were showing signs in 1989 of far deeper worries about their supplies of drinking water. A National Wildlife Federation study of municipal water systems found more than 100,000 violations of federal drinking water regulations during 1988, affecting 38 million people.

Energy: Borderline Same/Worse. Americans continued their plunge toward the dark side of the fossil fuel era in 1989, still largely ignoring signs of trouble ahead. The nation continued to guzzle oil, importing more than it produced in the first half of 1989, for only the second time in history. The effect of the Alaska oil spill led to tabling plans for oil exploration and drilling in the Arctic National Wildlife Refuge, and a one-year ban on oil and gas leases off the California coast, much of the mid-Atlantic coast and Georges Bank, and off the Florida Keys and Alaska's Bristol Bay.

None of the trends holds out hope that energy will continue to be plentiful, reliable and cheap much longer. Those looking at natural gas as an alternative to oil in 1989 found sharply reduced estimates of reserves and predictions of substantial price increases. An attempt to foster renewed public acceptance of nuclear power gained little ground. Coal burning continued to face opposition due to its contribution to acid rain and the greenhouse effect.

Forests: Borderline Same/Worse. "Save a logger, kill a spotted owl." The bitter slogan summarizes how some people in the Pacific Northwest view the continuing agony of the lumber industry there. Last year [1989] at least 13 mills in Oregon and Washington shut down with a loss of 2,000 jobs. Many in the industry blamed the shutdowns on the controversy over the spotted owl; on the birds' behalf, conservationists successfully brought suit to deny the loggers access to some publicly owned old growth—among the last U.S. stands of virgin timber. The pressures of insatiable demand made themselves felt elsewhere in the country. In six Appalachian national forests, Forest Service plans envisioned boosting a cut that harvested 100 million board feet to more than 200 million by 1996. One objection—timber sales would bring less than roads and services would cost. Such economic arguments were thought most persuasive when Congress voted last year to stop all subsidized timber sales in Alaska's 17-million-acre Tongass National Forest.

Soil: Borderline Same/Worse. The drought of 1988 eased its grip on some parts of the American Midwest last year [1989], but not before it made a final sweeping blow. Last March, wind erosion damaged some 4.7 million acres of cropland in the Great Plains states. Plantings of mainstay crops such as corn and soybeans posted the best gains in five years. Meanwhile conservationists remained concerned about the health of land in the public domain: 600 million acres. Western ranchers use such publicly owned range for less than half the cost of grazing cattle on private rangelands. The effect of such bargain grazing on the land is all too obvious.

Quality of Life: Worse. It was a rare home in the United States that did not find itself shaken more than once in 1989 with worries about the quality of its environment, or the safety of its food and water supplies. Concern about ocean pollution played a part in the first slump in the nation's seafood industry in a decade. While the safety of urban drinking water supplies continued to come under scrutiny, rural areas in 38 states found toxic contamination in their wells. Fear of a different sort could be detected in the country's municipal council chambers. While county and city landfills are running out of room, the public shows few signs of either permitting the siting of new landfills or reducing the stream of waste emanating from the nation's households. ☐

Endangered Species

The number of threatened animal taxa identified by International Union for Conservation of Nature and Natural Resources (IUCN) is 4,589, comprised of 555 mammals, 1,073 birds, 186 reptiles, 54 amphibians, 596 fishes, and 2,125 invertebrates. However, except for birds, for which International Council for Bird Preservation (ICBP)/IUCN have now attempted a global review, these numbers represent only those taxa whose threatened status is known to IUCN; many, many more taxa, particularly invertebrates, are threatened, and becoming extinct every year undescribed and unknown to the scientific and conservation communities. Thus the number of threatened taxa identified by IUCN represents only the visible fraction of a much greater problem.

The following list comprises some of the more familiar species that are endangered. Due to space limitations, it does not include all mammals, birds, reptiles, amphibians, and fish on the 1988 IUCN Red List nor does it include any clams, crustaceans, snails, insects, or plants.

Some Endangered and Threatened Species of the World[1]

Common Name	Scientific name	Listed range
MAMMALS		
Bear, Baluchistan	Selenarctos thibetanus gedrosianus	Iran, Pakistan
Bear, Polar[2]	Ursus maritimus	Arctic
Cat, Pardel lynx	Felis pardina	Portugal, Spain
Cat, little spotted	Felis tigrina	Central & South America
Cheetah[2]	Acinonyx jubatus	Africa, Middle East Iran, U.S.S.R.
Cougar, Florida	Felis concolor coryi	U.S.
Deer, marsh[2]	Blastocerus dichotomus	Central South America
Deer, musk, Himalayan subspecies[2]	Moschus chrysogaster (subspecies)	Himalayas
Elephant, Asian	Elephas maximus	Asia
Gazelle, Clark's (Dibatag)[2]	Ammodorcas clarkei	Ethiopia, Somalia
Gazelle, slender-horned (Rhim)[2]	Gazella leptoceros	Sahara/Sahel
Gorilla, mountain	Gorilla gorilla beringei	Rwanda, Uganda, Zaire
Ibex, Walia	Capra walie	Ethiopia
Jaguar[2]	Panthera onca	U.S., Central & South America
Leopard[3]	Panthera pardus	Africa, Middle East, Asia
Leopard, snow	Panthera uncia	Asia
Lion, Asiatic	Panthera leo persica	India
Mandrill[2]	Mandrillus sphinx	Cameroon, Congo, Eq. Guinea, Gabon
Monkey, long-haired spider[2]	Ateles belzebuth	South America
Ocelot[2]	Felis pardalis	U.S., Central & South America
Orangutan	Pongo pygmaeus	Borneo, Sumatra
Prairie dog, Utah[2]	Cynomys parvidens	U.S.
Pronghorn, Sonoran	Antilocapra americana sonoriensis	Mexico, U.S.
Rat, Morro Bay kangaroo	Dipodomys heermanni morroensis	California
Rhinoceros, great Indian	Rhinoceros unicornis	India, Nepal
Sloth, maned	Bradypus torquatus	Brazil
Tiger	Panthera tigris	Asia
Wallaby, bridled nailtail	Onychogalea fraenata	Australia
Whale, humpback	Megaptera novaeangliae	All oceans
Wolf, gray[2]	Canis lupus	North America, Middle East, Eurasia
Wolf, red	Canis rufus	U.S.
Zebra, Cape Mountain	Equus zebra zebra	South Africa
BIRDS		
Albatross, short-tailed	Diomedea albatrus	Japan
Condor, California	Gymnogyps californianus	U.S.
Crane, whooping	Grus americana	Canada, U.S.
Crow, Hawaiian	Corvus tropicus	Hawaiian Islands
Kestrel, Mauritius	Falco punctatus	Mauritius
Parrot, paradise	Psephotus pulcherrimus	Australia
Stork, oriental white	Ciconia boyciana	China, Japan, South Korea, U.S.S.R.
Woodpecker, ivory-billed	Campephilus principalis	Cuba, U.S.
REPTILES		
Crocodile, American	Crocodylus acutus	Caribbean, Central America, U.S.
Iguana, Anegada ground	Cyclura pinguis	British Virgin Is.

Common Name	Scientific name	Listed range
Python, Indian[2]	Python molurus	South & Southeast Asia
Snake, Atlantic saltmarsh[4]	Nerodia fasciata taeniata	U.S.
AMPHIBIANS		
Frog, Israel painted[5]	Discoglossus nigriventer	Israel
Toad, Mount Nimba viviparous[2]	Nectophrynoides occidentalis	Guinea, Ivory Coast
FISH		
Catfish, giant[2]	Pangasianodon gigas	Mekong Basin
Trout, cutthroat[3]	Salmo clarki (subspecies)	U.S.

1. Unless otherwise indicated the species is rated endangered. 2. Vulnerable. 3. Threatened. 4. Rare. 5. Extinct? *Source: 1988 IUCN Red List of Threatened Animals,* published by the International Union for Conservation of Nature and Natural Resources/ United Nations Environment Programme, Avenue du Mont-Blanc, CH-1196 Gland, Switzerland.

Zoological Gardens

North America abounds in zoos from Canada to Mexico. The Metro Toronto Zoo, opened in 1974, is one of the largest in the world. Its six pavilions simulate the animals' natural habitats. So does the Calgary Zoo which also has a children's zoo. Mexico City's Chapultepec Park includes a large zoo featuring one of the few pairs of pandas outside of Red China, and a children's zoo.

The first zoological garden in the United States was established in Philadelphia in 1874. Since that time nearly every large city in the country has acquired a zoo. Among the largest are San Diego's on the West Coast; Chicago's Brookfield Zoo and those of St. Louis and Kansas City in the Middle West; New Orleans' Audubon Park and Zoological Garden in the South; and in the East the New York Zoological Society's park in the Bronx. The National Zoological Park in Washington, D.C., in a beautiful setting of hills, woods, and streams, was established in 1890 by an act of Congress. The major U.S. zoos now have created large natural-habitat areas for their collections.

In Europe, zoological gardens have long been popular public institutions. The modern concept of zoo keeping may be dated from 1752 with the founding of the Imperial Menagerie at the Schönbrunn Palace in Vienna. It was opened to the public in 1765 and is still in operation. In 1793 the zoological collection of the Jardin des Plantes was established in Paris in the Bois de Boulogne. At Antwerp the Royal Zoological Society founded a large menagerie in 1843. Now its aviary is noted for the principle of lighted and darkened spaces for confining the birds. Germany's famous Tiergarten zoo, in West Berlin, was founded in 1841 and officially opened in 1844. East Berlin has founded its own zoo.

In the British Isles, the Zoological Society of London established its collection in Regent's Park in 1828. It was also responsible for the establishment of the prototype of the open-range zoo, Whipsnade Park, in 1932. Edinburgh's zoo is famous for its collection of penguins, the largest colony in captivity.

U.S. Zoos and Aquariums

Source: The facilities listed are members of, and accredited by, the American Association of Zoological Parks and Aquariums to ensure that they are maintaining professional standards. It also accredits facilities outside of the United States.

Abilene Zoological Gardens, Texas
Akron Zoological Park, Ohio
Alexandria Zoological Park, La.
Arizona-Sonora Desert Museum, Tucson
Audubon Park and Zoological Garden, New Orleans
John Ball Zoological Gardens, Grand Rapids, Mich.
Baltimore Zoo, Md.
Beardsley Zoological Gardens, Bridgeport, Conn.
Belle Isle Zoo and Aquarium, Detroit
Bergen County Zoological Park, Paramus, N.J.
Binder Park Zoo, Battle Creek, Mich.
Birmingham Zoo, Ala.
Blank Park Zoo of Des Moines, Iowa
Brandywine Zoo, Wilmington, Del.
Brookgreen Gardens, Murrells Inlet, S.C.
Buffalo Zoological Gardens, N.Y.
Burnet Park Zoo, Syracuse, N.Y.
Busch Gardens, Tampa, Fla.
Caldwell Zoo, Texas
Cape May County Park Zoo, Cape May Court House, N.J.

Central Florida Zoological Park, Lake Monroe, Fla.
Central Park Zoo, New York, N.Y.
Central Texas Zoo, Waco, Texas
Cheyenne Mountain Zoological Park, Colorado Springs
Chicago Zoological Park, Brookfield, Ill.
Cincinnati Zoo and Botanical Garden, Ohio
Cleveland Metroparks Zoo, Ohio
Columbus Zoological Gardens, Ohio
Dallas Aquarium, Texas
Dallas Zoo, Texas
Denver Zoological Gardens, Colo.
Detroit Zoological Park, Mich.
Dickerson Park Zoo, Springfield, Mo.
Discovery Island, Buena Vista, Fla.
Dreher Park Zoo, West Palm Beach, Fla.
El Paso Zoological Park, Texas
Emporia Zoo, Kan.
Erie Zoo, Pa.
Florida Cypress Gardens, Inc., Fla.
Fort Wayne Children's Zoo, Ind.

Fort Worth Zoological Park, Texas
Fossil Rim Wildlife Ranch, Fort Worth, Texas
Fresno Zoo, Calif.
Glen Oak Zoo, Ill.
Greater Baton Rouge Zoo, La.
Greenville Zoo, S.C.
Hogle Zoological Gardens, Salt Lake City, Utah
Honolulu Zoo, Hawaii
Houston Zoological Gardens, Texas
Indianapolis Zoo, Ind.
International Crane Foundation, Baraboo, Wis.
Jackson Zoological Park, Miss.
Jacksonville Zoological Park, Fla.
Kansas City Zoological Gardens, Mo.
Knoxville Zoological Park, Tenn.
Lake Superior Zoological Gardens, Duluth, Minn.
Lincoln Park Zoological Gardens, Chicago
Little Rock Zoological Gardens, Ark.
Living Desert, The, Palm Desert, Calif.
Los Angeles Zoo, Calif.
Louisville Zoological Garden, Ky.
Lowry Park Zoological Garden, Tampa, Fla.
Marine World Africa USA, Redwood City, Calif.
Memphis Zoological Gardens and Aquarium, Tenn.
Mesker Park Zoo, Evansville, Ind.
Metro Washington Park Zoo, Portland, Ore.
Miami Metrozoo, Fla.
Micke Grove Zoo, Lodi, Calif.
Miller Park Zoo, Bloomington, Ill.
Milwaukee County Zoological Gardens, Wis.
Minnesota Zoological Garden, Apple Valley, Minn.
Monkey Jungle, Inc., Miami, Fla.
Monterey Bay Aquarium, Calif.
Montgomery Zoo, Ala.
Mystic Marinelife Aquarium, Mystic, Conn.
National Aquarium in Baltimore, Md.
National Zoological Park, Washington, D.C.
New England Aquarium, Boston
New York Aquarium, Brooklyn, N.Y.
New York Zoological Park, Bronx, N.Y.
North Carolina Zoological Park, Asheboro, N.C.
Northwest Trek Wildlife Park, Eatonville, Wash.
Oakland Zoo, Calif.
Oglebay's Good Children's Zoo, Wheeling, W.Va.
Oklahoma City Zoological Park, Okla.
Omaha's Henry Doorly Zoo, Neb.
Parrot Jungle and Gardens, Inc., Miami, Fla.
Clyde Peeling's Reptiland Ltd., Williamsport, Pa.
Philadelphia Zoological Garden, Pa.
Phoenix Zoo, Ariz.
Pittsburgh Aviary, Pa.
Pittsburgh Zoo, Pa.
Point Defiance Zoo and Aquarium, Tacoma, Wash.
Gladys Porter Zoo, Brownsville, Texas
Potawatomi Zoo, South Bend, Ind.

Potter Park Zoo, Lansing, Mich.
Racine Zoological Gardens, Wis.
Reid Park Zoo, Tucson, Ariz.
Lee Richardson Zoo, Garden City, Kan.
Rio Grande Zoological Park, Albuquerque, N.M.
Riverbanks Zoological Park, Columbia, S.C.
Riverside Zoo, Scottsbluff, Neb.
Henson Robinson Zoo, Springfield, Ill.
Roosevelt Zoo, Minot, N.D.
Ross Park Zoo, Binghamton, N.Y.
Sacramento Zoo, Calif.
St. Augustine Alligator Farm, Fla.
St. Louis Zoological Park, Mo.
St. Paul's Como Zoo, Minn.
Salisbury Zoological Park, Md.
San Antonio Zoological Gardens and Aquarium, Texas
San Diego Wild Animal Park, Calif.
San Diego Zoo, Calif.
San Francisco Zoological Gardens, Calif.
Santa Ana Zoo, Calif.
Santa Barbara Zoological Gardens, Calif.
Sante Fe Teaching Zoo, Fla.
Sea Life Park, Waimanalo, Hawaii
Sea World of California, San Diego
Sea World of Florida, Orlando
Sea World of Ohio, Aurora
Sea World of Texas, San Antonio
The Seattle Aquarium, Wash.
Sedgwick County Zoo and Botanical Garden, Wichita, Kan.
Seneca Park Zoo, Rochester, N.Y.
John G. Shedd Aquarium, Chicago
Staten Island Zoo, N.Y.
Sunset Zoological Park, Manhattan, Kan.
The Texas Zoo, Victoria, Texas
Toledo Zoological Gardens, Ohio
Topeka Zoological Park, Kan.
Trevor Zoo, Millbrook, N.Y.
Ellen Trout Zoo, Lufkin, Texas
Tulsa Zoological Park, Okla.
Utica Zoo, N.Y.
Van Saun Park Zoo, Paramus, N.J.
Henry Vilas Zoo, Madison, Wis.
Virginia Zoological Park, Norfolk, Va.
Waikiki Aquarium, Hawaii
Wild Animal Habitat, Kings Island, Ohio
Wildlife Safari, Inc. Winston, Ore.
Wildlife World Zoo, Litchfield Park, Ariz.
Roger Williams Park Zoo, Providence, R.I.
Woodland Park Zoological Gardens, Seattle
The ZOO, Gulf Breeze, Fla.
Zoo Atlanta, Ga.
ZOOAMERICA North American Wildlife Park, Hershey, Pa.

Animal Names: Male, Female, and Young

Animal	Male	Female	Young	Animal	Male	Female	Young	Animal	Male	Female	Young
Ass	Jack	Jenny	Foal	Duck	Drake	Duck	Duckling	Sheep	Ram	Ewe	Lamb
Bear	Boar	Sow	Cub	Elephant	Bull	Cow	Calf	Swan	Cob	Pen	Cygnet
Cat	Tom	Queen	Kitten	Fox	Dog	Vixen	Cub	Swine	Boar	Sow	Piglet
Cattle	Bull	Cow	Calf	Goose	Gander	Goose	Gosling	Tiger	Tiger	Tigress	Cub
Chicken	Rooster	Hen	Chick	Horse	Stallion	Mare	Foal	Whale	Bull	Cow	Calf
Deer	Buck	Doe	Fawn	Lion	Lion	Lioness	Cub	Wolf	Dog	Bitch	Pup
Dog	Dog	Bitch	Pup	Rabbit	Buck	Doe	Bunny				

Source: James Doherty, Curator of Mammals, N.Y. Zoological Society.

Gestation, Incubation, and Longevity of Certain Animals

Animal	Gestation or incubation, in days & (average)	Longevity, in years & (record exceptions)	Animal	Gestation or incubation, in days & (average)	Longevity, in years & (record exceptions)
Ass	365	18–20 (63)	Horse	329–345 (336)	20–25 (50+)
Bear	180–240 [1]	15–30 (47)	Kangaroo	32–39 [1]	4–6 (23)
Cat	52–69 (63)	10–12 (26+)	Lion	105–113 (108)	10 (29)
Chicken	22	7–8 (14)	Man	253–303	([2])
Cow	c. 280	9–12 (39)	Monkey	139–270 [1]	12–15[1](29)
Deer	197–300 [1]	10–15 (26)	Mouse	19–31 [1]	1–3 (4)
Dog	53–71 (63)	10–12 (24)	Parakeet (Budgerigar)	17–20 (18)	8 (12+)
Duck	21–35[1](28)	10 (15)	Pig	101–130 (115)	10 (22)
Elephant	510–730 (624) [1]	30–40 (71)	Pigeon	11–19	10–12 (39)
Fox	51–63 [1]	8–10 (14)	Rabbit	30–35 (31)	6–8 (15)
Goat	136–160 (151)	12 (17)	Rat	21	3 (5)
Groundhog	31–32	4–9	Sheep	144–152 (151) [1]	12 (16)
Guinea pig	58–75 (68)	3 (6)	Squirrel	44	8–9 (15)
Hamster, golden	15–17	2 (8)	Whale	365–547 [1]	—
Hippopotamus	220–255 (240)	30 (49+)	Wolf	60–63	10–12 (16)

1. Depending on kind. 2. For life expectancy charts, *see* Index. *Source:* James Doherty, Curator of Mammals, N.Y. Zoological Society.

Speed of Animals

Most of the following measurements are for maximum speeds over approximate quarter-mile distances. Exceptions—which are included to give a wide range of animals—are the lion and elephant, whose speeds were clocked in the act of charging; the whippet, which was timed over a 200-yard course; the cheetah over a 100-yard distance; man for a 15-yard segment of a 100-yard run; and the black mamba, six-lined race runner, spider, giant tortoise, three-toed sloth, and garden snail, which were measured over various small distances.

Animal	Speed mph	Animal	Speed mph	Animal	Speed mph
Cheetah	70	Mongolian wild ass	40	Man	27.89
Pronghorn antelope	61	Greyhound	39.35	Elephant	25
Wildebeest	50	Whippet	35.5	Black mamba snake	20
Lion	50	Rabbit (domestic)	35	Six-lined race runner	18
Thomson's gazelle	50	Mule deer	35	Squirrel	12
Quarter horse	47.5	Jackal	35	Pig (domestic)	11
Elk	45	Reindeer	32	Chicken	9
Cape hunting dog	45	Giraffe	32	Spider (Tegenearia atrica)	1.17
Coyote	43	White-tailed deer	30	Giant Tortoise	0.17
Gray fox	42	Wart hog	30	Three-toed sloth	0.15
Hyena	40	Grizzly bear	30	Garden snail	0.03
Zebra	40	Cat (domestic)	30		

Source: Natural History Magazine, March 1974, copyright 1974. The American Museum of Natural History; and James Doherty, Curator of Mammals, N.Y. Zoological Society.

Animal Group Terminology

Source: James Doherty, Curator of Mammals, N.Y. Zoological Society, and *Information Please* data.

ants: colony
bears: sleuth, sloth
bees: grist, hive, swarm
birds: flight, volery
cattle: drove
cats: clutter, clowder
chicks: brood, clutch
clams: bed
cranes: sedge, seige
crows: murder
doves: dule
ducks: brace, team
elephants: herd
elks: gang
finches: charm
fish: school, shoal, draught
foxes: leash, skulk
geese: flock, gaggle, skein
gnats: cloud, horde
goats: trip

gorillas: band
hares: down, husk
hawks: cast
hens: brood
hogs: drift
horses: pair, team
hounds: cry, mute, pack
kangaroos: troop
kittens: kindle, litter
larks: exaltation
lions: pride
locusts: plague
magpies: tidings
mules: span
nightingales: watch
oxen: yoke
oysters: bed
parrots: company
partridges: covey

peacocks: muster, ostentation
pheasants: nest, bouquet
pigs: litter
ponies: string
quail: bevy, covey
rabbits: nest
seals: pod
sheep: drove, flock
sparrows: host
storks: mustering
swans: bevy, wedge
swine: sounder
toads: knot
turkeys: rafter
turtles: bale
vipers: nest
whales: gam, pod
wolves: pack, route
woodcocks: fall

The National Park System

Source: Department of the Interior, National Park Service.

The National Park System of the United States is administered by the National Park Service, a bureau of the Department of the Interior. Started with the establishment of Yellowstone National Park in 1872, the system includes not only the most extraordinary and spectacular scenic exhibits in the United States but also a large number of sites distinguished either for their historic or prehistoric importance or scientific interest, or for their superior recreational assets. The number and extent of the various types of areas that make up the system follow.

Type of area	Number	Total acreage[1]	Type of area	Number	Total acreage[1]
International Historic Site	1	35.39	National Monument	79	4,844,417.44
National Battlefield	11	12,843.35	National Park	50	47,429,839.90
National Battlefield Park	3	8,725.30	National Parkway	4	168,600.30
National Battlefield Site	1	1.00	National Preserve	14	22,155,586.82
National Capital Park	1	6,468.88	National Recreation Area	18	3,697,199.88
National Historic Site	69	18,545.20	National Rivers[2]	14	552,703.54
National Historical Park	29	151,633.84	National Scenic Trail	3	172,540.92
National Lakeshore	4	227,262.71	National Seashore	10	596,663.08
National Mall	1	146.35	Park (other)	10	32,120.70
National Memorial	23	7,949.16	White House	1	18.07
National Military Park	9	34,046.71	Total	355	80,117,313.15

1. Acreages as of December 31, 1989. 2. National Park System units and components of the Wild & Scenic Rivers System.

National Parks

Name, location, and year authorized	Acreage	Outstanding characteristics
Acadia (Maine), 1919	41,408.63	Rugged seashore on Mt. Desert Island and adjacent mainland
Arches (Utah), 1971	73,378.98	Unusual stone arches, windows, pedestals caused by erosion
Badlands (S.D.), 1978	243,244.48	Arid land of fossils, prairie, bison, deer, bighorn, antelope
Big Bend (Tex.), 1935	802,541.30	Mountains and desert bordering the Rio Grande
Biscayne (Fla.), 1980	173,039.39	Aquatic, coral reef park south of Miami was a national monument, 1968–80
Bryce Canyon (Utah), 1924	35,835.08	Area of grotesque eroded rocks brilliantly colored
Canyonlands (Utah), 1964	337,570.43	Colorful wilderness with impressive red-rock canyons, spires, arches
Capitol Reef (Utah), 1971	241,904.26	Highly colored sedimentary rock formations in high, narrow gorges
Carlsbad Caverns (N.M.), 1930	46,755.33	The world's largest known caves
Channel Islands (Calif.) 1980	249,353.77	Area is rich in marine mammals, sea birds, endangered species and archeology
Crater Lake (Ore.), 1902	183,224.05	Deep blue lake in heart of inactive volcano
Denali (Alaska), 1917	4,716,726.00	Mt. McKinley National Park was renamed and enlarged by Act of Dec. 2, 1980. Contains Mt. McKinley, N. America's highest mountain (20,320 ft)
Everglades (Fla.), 1934	1,508,938.00	Subtropical area with abundant bird and animal life
Gates of the Arctic (Alaska), 1980	7,523,888.00	Diverse north central wilderness contains part of Brooks Range
Glacier (Mont.), 1910	1,013,572.42	Rocky Mountain scenery with many glaciers and lakes
Glacier Bay (Alaska), 1980	3,225,284.00	Park was a national monument (1925–1980) popular for wildlife, whale-watching, glacier-calving, and scenery
Grand Canyon (Ariz.), 1919	1,218,375.24	Mile-deep gorge, 4 to 18 miles wide, 217 miles long
Grand Teton (Wyo.), 1929	309,993.93	Picturesque range of high mountain peaks
Great Basin (Nev.), 1986	77,109.15	Exceptional scenic, biologic, and geologic attractions
Great Smoky Mts. (N.C.-Tenn.), 1926	520,269.44	Highest mountain range east of Black Hills; luxuriant plant life
Guadalupe Mountains (Tex.), 1966	86,416.01	Contains highest point in Texas: Guadalupe Peak (8,751 ft)
Haleakala (Hawaii), 1960	28,655.25	World-famous 10,023-ft. Haleakala volcano (dormant)
Hawaii Volcanoes (Hawaii), 1916	229,177.03	Spectacular volcanic area; luxuriant vegetation at lower levels
Hot Springs (Ark.), 1921	5,839.24	47 mineral hot springs said to have therapeutic value
Isle Royale (Mich.), 1931	571,790.11	Largest wilderness island in Lake Superior; moose, wolves, lakes
Katmai (Alaska), 1980	3,716,000.00	Expansion may assure brown bear's preservation. Park was national monument 1918–80; is known for fishing, 1912 eruption, bears

Name, location, and year authorized	Acreage	Outstanding characteristics
Kenai Fjords (Alaska), 1980	669,541.00	Mountain goats, marine mammals, birdlife are features at this seacoast park near Seward
Kings Canyon (Calif.), 1940	461,901.20	Huge canyons; high mountains; giant sequoias
Kobuk Valley (Alaska), 1980	1,750,421.00	Native culture and anthropology center around the broad Kobuk River in northwest Alaska
Lake Clark (Alaska), 1980	2,636,839.00	Park provides scenic and wilderness recreation across Cook Inlet from Anchorage
Lassen Volcanic (Calif.), 1916	106,372.36	Exhibits of impressive volcanic phenomena
Mammoth Cave (Ky.), 1926	52,419.00	Vast limestone labyrinth with underground river
Mesa Verde (Colo.), 1906	52,085.14	Best-preserved prehistoric cliff dwellings in United States
Mount Rainier (Wash.), 1899	235,404.00	Single-peak glacial system; dense forests, flowered meadows
North Cascades (Wash.), 1968	504,780.94	Roadless Alpine landscape; jagged peaks; mountain lakes; glaciers
Olympic (Wash.), 1938	921,942.14	Finest Pacific Northwest rain forest; scenic mountain park
Petrified Forest (Ariz.), 1962	93,532.57	Extensive natural exhibit of petrified wood
Redwood (Calif.), 1968	110,132.40	Coastal redwood forests; contains world's tallest known tree (369.2 ft)
Rocky Mountain (Colo.), 1915	265,200.07	Section of the Rocky Mountains; 107 named peaks over 10,000 ft
Samoa (American Samoa)	9,000.00	Samoa National Park, American Samoa: two rain forest preserves and a coral reef on the island of Ofu are home to unique tropical animals. The park also includes several thousand acres on the islands of Tutuila and Ta'u.
Sequoia (Calif.), 1890	402,482.38	Giant sequoias; magnificent High Sierra scenery, including Mt. Whitney
Shenandoah (Va.), 1926	195,382.13	Tree-covered mountains; scenic Skyline Drive
Theodore Roosevelt (N.D.), 1978	70,416.39	Scenic valley of Little Missouri River; T.R. Ranch; Wildlife
Virgin Islands (U.S. V.I.), 1956	14,688.87	Beaches; lush hills; prehistoric Carib Indian relics
Voyageurs (Minn.), 1971	218,035.93	Wildlife, canoeing, fishing, and hiking
Wind Cave (S.D.), 1903	28,292.08	Limestone caverns in Black Hills; buffalo herd
Wrangell-St. Elias (Alaska), 1980	8,331,604.00	Largest Park System area has abundant wildlife, second highest peak in U.S. (Mt. St. Elias); adjoins Canadian land
Yellowstone (Wyo.-Mont.-Idaho), 1872	2,219,790.71	World's greatest geyser area; abundant falls, wildlife, and canyons
Yosemite (Calif.), 1890	761,170.20	Mountains; inspiring gorges and waterfalls; giant sequoias
Zion (Utah), 1919	146,597.64	Multicolored gorge in heart of southern Utah desert

NATIONAL HISTORICAL PARKS

Name and location	Total acreage
Appomattox Court House (Va.)	1,325.08
Boston (Mass.)	41.03
Chaco Culture (N.M.)	33,974.29
Chesapeake and Ohio Canal (Md.-W.Va.-D.C.)	20,781.00
Colonial (Va.)	9,327.37
Cumberland Gap (Ky.-Tenn.-Va.)	20,274.42
George Rogers Clark (Ind.)	26.17
Harpers Ferry (W.Va.-Md.)	2,238.60
Independence (Pa.)	44.85
Jean Lafitte (La.)	20,020.00
Kalaupapa (Hawaii)	10,778.88
Klondike Goldrush (Alaska, Wash.)	13,191.35
Kaloko-Honokohau (Hawaii)	1,160.91
Lowell (Mass.)	136.04
Lyndon B. Johnson (Tex.)	1,570.61
Minute Man (Mass.)	750.00
Morristown (N.J.)	1,670.61
Natchez (Miss.)	80.00
Nez Perce (Idaho)	2,108.89
Púuchonua o Honaunau (Hawaii)	181.80
San Antonio Missions (Tex.)	492.66
San Franisco Maritime (Calif.)	50.00
San Juan Island (Wash.)	1,751.99
Saratoga (N.Y.)	3,392.82
Sitka (Alaska)	106.83
Valley Forge (Pa.)	3,468.06
War in the Pacific (Guam)	1,960.15

Name and location	Total acreage
Women's Rights (N.Y.)	5.54
Zuni-Cibola (N.M.)	800.00

NATIONAL MONUMENTS

Agate Fossil Beds (Neb.)	3,055.22
Alibates Flint Quarries (Tex.)	1,370.97
Aniakchak (Alaska)	137,176.00
Aztec Ruins (N.M.)	319.03
Bandelier (N.M.)	32,737.20
Black Canyon (Colo.)	20,766.14
Booker T. Washington (Va.)	223.92
Buck Island Reef (U.S. V.I.)	880.00
Cabrillo (Calif.)	137.06
Canyon de Chelly (Ariz.)	83,840.00
Cape Krusenstern (Alaska)	659,807.00
Capulin Volcano (N.M.)	792.84
Casa Grande (Ariz.)	472.50
Castillo de San Marcos (Fla.)	20.48
Castle Clinton (N.Y.)	1.00
Cedar Breaks (Utah)	6,154.60
Chiricahua (Ariz.)	11,984.80
Colorado (Colo.)	20,453.93
Congaree Swamp (S.C.)	22,200.00
Craters of the Moon (Idaho)	53,545.05
Custer Battlefield (Mont.)	765.34
Death Valley (Calif.-Nev.)	2,067,627.68
Devils Postpile (Calif.)	798.46
Devils Tower (Wyo.)	1,346.91
Dinosaur (Utah-Colo.)	210,844.02

Name and location	Total acreage
Effigy Mounds (Iowa)	1,481.39
El Malpais (N.M.)	114,942.15
El Morro (N.M.)	1,278.72
Florissant Fossil Beds (Colo.)	5,998.09
Fort Frederica (Ga.)	216.35
Fort Jefferson (Fla.)	64,700.00
Fort Matanzas (Fla.)	227.76
Fort McHenry (Md.)	43.26
Fort Pulaski (Ga.)	5,623.10
Fort Stanwix (N.Y.)	15.52
Fort Sumter (S.C.)	196.75
Fort Union (N.M.)	720.60
Fossil Butte (Wyo.)	8,198.00
George Washington Birthplace (Va.)	538.23
George Washington Carver (Mo.)	210.00
Gila Cliff Dwellings (N.M.)	533.13
Grand Portage (Minn.)	709.97
Great Sand Dunes (Colo.)	38,662.18
Hagerman Fossil Beds (Idaho)	4,280.00
Hohokam Pima (Ariz.)	1,690.00
Homestead (Neb.)	194.57
Hovenweep (Utah-Colo.)	784.93
Jewel Cave (S.D.)	1,273.51
John Day Fossil Beds (Ore.)	14,014.10
Joshua Tree (Calif.)	559,954.50
Lava Beds (Calif.)	46,559.87
Montezuma Castle (Ariz.)	857.69
Mound City Group (Ohio)	270.20
Muir Woods (Calif.)	553.55
Natural Bridges (Utah)	7,636.49
Navajo (Ariz.)	360.00
Ocmulgee (Ga.)	683.48
Oregon Caves (Ore.)	487.98
Organ Pipe Cactus (Ariz.)	330,688.86
Pecos (N.M.)	364.80
Pinnacles (Calif.)	16,265.44
Pipe Spring (Ariz.)	40.00
Pipestone (Minn.)	281.78
Poverty Point	910.85
Rainbow Bridge (Utah)	160.00
Russell Cave (Ala.)	310.45
Saguaro (Ariz.)	83,573.88
Salinas (N.M.)	1,076.94
Scotts Bluff (Neb.)	2,997.08
Statue of Liberty (N.Y.-N.J.)	58.38
Sunset Crater (Ariz.)	3,040.00
Timpanogos Cave (Utah)	250.00
Tonto (Ariz.)	1,120.00
Tumacacori (Ariz.)	16.52
Tuzigoot (Ariz.)	800.62
Walnut Canyon (Ariz.)	2,249.46
White Sands (N.M.)	143,732.92
Wupatki (Ariz.)	35,253.24
Yucca House (Colo.)	10.00

NATIONAL PRESERVES

Aniakchak (Alaska)	465,603.00
Bering Land Bridge (Alaska)	2,784,960.00
Big Cypress (Fla.)	716,000.00
Big Thicket (Tex.)	85,732.85
City of Rock, (Idaho)	14,407.19
Denali (Alaska)	1,311,365.00
Gates of the Arctic (Alaska)	948,629.00
Glacier Bay (Alaska)	57,884.00
Katmai (Alaska)	374,000.00
Lake Clark (Alaska)	1,407,293.00
Noatak (Alaska)	6,574,481.00
Timucuan Ecological and Historic Preserve (Fla.)	35,000.00
Wrangell-St. Elias (Alaska)	4,856,720.99
Yukon-Charley (Alaska)	2,523,509.00

Name and location	Total acreage

NATIONAL MILITARY PARKS

Chickamauga and Chattanooga (Ga.-Tenn.)	8,106.04
Fredericksburg and Spotsylvania (Va.)	5,907.45
Gettysburg (Pa.)	3,895.70
Guilford Courthouse (N.C.)	220.25
Horseshoe Bend (Ala.)	2,040.00
Kings Mountain (S.C.)	3,945.29
Pea Ridge (Ark.)	4,300.35
Shiloh (Tenn.)	3,837.50
Vicksburg (Miss.)	1,619.89

NATIONAL BATTLEFIELDS

Antietam (Md.)	3,244.42
Big Hole (Mont.)	655.61
Cowpens (S.C.)	841.56
Fort Donelson (Tenn.)	536.66
Fort Necessity (Pa.)	902.80
Monocacy (Md.)	1,647.01
Moores Creek (N.C.)	86.52
Petersburg (Va.)	2,735.38
Stones River (Tenn.)	402.91
Tupelo (Miss.)	1.00
Wilson's Creek (Mo.)	1,749.91

NATIONAL BATTLEFIELD PARKS

Kennesaw Mountain (Ga.)	2,884.52
Manassas (Va.)	5,071.61
Richmond (Va.)	769.16

NATIONAL BATTLEFIELD SITE

Brices Cross Roads (Miss.)	1.00

NATIONAL HISTORIC SITES

Abraham Lincoln Birthplace (Ky.)	116.50
Adams (Mass.)	9.82
Allegheny Portage Railroad (Pa.)	1,246.97
Andersonville (Ga.)	475.72
Andrew Johnson (Tenn.)	16.68
Bent's Old Fort (Colo.)	799.80
Boston African American (Mass.)	0.00
Carl Sandburg Home (N.C.)	263.52
Charles Pinckney (S.C.)	25.00
Christiansted (V.I.)	27.15
Clara Barton (Md.)	8.59
Edgar Allan Poe (Pa.)	0.52
Edison (N.J.)	21.25
Eisenhower (Pa.)	690.46
Eleanor Roosevelt (N.Y.)	180.50
Eugene O'Neill (Calif.)	13.19
Ford's Theatre (Lincoln Museum) (D.C.)	0.29
Fort Bowie (Ariz.)	1,000.00
Fort Davis (Tex.)	460.00
Fort Laramie (Wyo.)	832.85
Fort Larned (Kan.)	718.39
Fort Point (Calif.)	29.00
Fort Raleigh (N.C.)	157.27
Fort Scott (Kan.)	16.69
Fort Smith (Ark.-Okla.)	75.00
Fort Union Trading Post (N.D.-Mont.)	442.45
Fort Vancouver (Wash.)	208.89
Frederick Douglass Home (D.C.)	8.53
Frederick Law Olmsted (Mass.)	1.75
Friendship Hill (Pa.)	674.56
Golden Spike (Utah)	2,735.28
Grant-Kohrs Ranch (Mont.)	1,498.65
Hampton (Md.)	62.04
Harry S Truman (Mo.)	0.78
Herbert Hoover (Iowa)	186.80
Home of F. D. Roosevelt (N.Y.)	290.34
Hopewell Furnace (Pa.)	848.06
Hubbell Trading Post (Ariz.)	160.09

Name and location	Total acreage
James A. Garfield (Ohio)	7.82
Jefferson National Expansion Memorial (Mo.)	190.58
Jimmy Carter (Ga.)	69.55
John F. Kennedy (Mass.)	0.09
John Muir (Calif.)	338.90
Knife River Indian Villages (N.D.)	1,293.35
Lincoln Home (Ill.)	12.24
Longfellow (Mass.)	1.98
Maggie L. Walker (Va.)	1.29
Martin Luther King, Jr. (Ga.)	23.18
Martin Van Buren (N.Y.)	39.58
Ninety Six (S.C.)	989.14
Palo Alto Battlefield (Tex.)	50.00
Pennsylvania Avenue (D.C.)	0.00
Puukohola Heiau (Hawaii)	80.47
Sagamore Hill (N.Y.)	83.02
Saint-Gaudens (N.H.)	148.23
Saint Paul's Church (N.Y.)	6.13
Salem Maritime (Mass.)	8.95
San Juan (P.R.)	75.13
Saugus Iron Works (Mass.)	8.51
Springfield Armory (Mass.)	54.93
Steamtown (Pa.)	42.30
Theodore Roosevelt Birthplace (N.Y.)	0.11
Theodore Roosevelt Inaugural (N.Y.)	1.03
Thomas Stone (Md.)	328.25
Tuskegee Institute (Ala.)	74.39
Ulysses S. Grant (Mo.)	9.65
Vanderbilt Mansion (N.Y.)	211.65
Whitman Mission (Wash.)	98.15
William Howard Taft (Ohio)	3.07

NATIONAL MEMORIALS

Name and location	Total acreage
Arkansas Post (Ark.)	389.18
Arlington House, the Robert E. Lee Memorial (Va.)	27.91
Chamizal (Tex.)	54.90
Coronado (Ariz.)	4,750.22
De Sota (Fla.)	26.84
Federal Hall (N.Y.)	0.45
Fort Caroline (Fla.)	138.39
Fort Clatsop (Ore.)	125.20
General Grant (N.Y.)	0.76
Hamilton Grange (N.Y.)	0.11
John F. Kennedy Center for Performing Arts (D.C.)	17.50
Johnstown Flood (Pa.)	164.12
Lincoln Boyhood (Ind.)	199.65
Lincoln Memorial (D.C.)	109.63
Lyndon Baines Johnson Memorial Grove on the Potomac (D.C.)	17.00
Mount Rushmore (S.D.)	1,278.45
Roger Williams (R.I.)	4.56
Thaddeus Kosciuszko (Pa.)	0.02
Theodore Roosevelt Island (D.C.)	88.50
Thomas Jefferson Memorial (D.C.)	18.36
USS Arizona Memorial (Hawaii)	0.00
Washington Monument (D.C.)	106.01
Wright Brothers (N.C.)	431.40

NATIONAL CEMETERIES[1]

Name and location	Total acreage
Antietam (Md.)	11.36
Battleground (D.C.)	1.03
Fort Donelson (Tenn.)	15.34
Fredericksburg (Va.)	12.00
Gettysburg (Pa.)	20.58
Poplar Grove (Va.)	8.72
Shiloh (Tenn.)	10.05
Stones River (Tenn.)	20.09
Vicksburg (Miss.)	116.28
Yorktown (Va.)	2.91

NATIONAL SEASHORES

Name and location	Total acreage
Assateague Island (Md.-Va.)	39,630.93
Canaveral (Fla.)	57,661.69
Cape Cod (Mass.)	43,557.24
Cape Hatteras (N.C.)	30,319.43
Cape Lookout (N.C.)	28,243.36
Cumberland Island (Ga.)	36,415.09
Fire Island (N.Y.)	19,578.55
Gulf Islands (Fla.-Miss.)	139,775.46
Padre Island (Tex.)	130,434.27
Point Reyes (Calif.)	71,046.51

NATIONAL PARKWAYS

Name and location	Total acreage
Blue Ridge (Va.-N.C.)	85,950.36
George Washington Memorial (Va.-Md.)	7,130.63
John D. Rockefeller, Jr., Memorial (Wyo.)	23,777.22
Natchez Trace (Miss.-Tenn.-Ala.)	51,755.64

NATIONAL LAKESHORES

Name and location	Total acreage
Apostle Islands (Wis.)	69,371.89
Indiana Dunes (Ind.)	13,841.16
Pictured Rocks (Mich)	72,915.96
Sleeping Bear Dunes (Mich.)	71,133.70

NATIONAL SCENIC RIVERS AND RIVERWAYS

Name and location	Total acreage
Alagnak Wild River (Alaska)	24,038.00
Big South Fork National River & Recreation Area (Ky.-Tenn.)	122,960.00
Bluestone National Scenic River (W. Va.)	0.00
Buffalo (Ark.)	94,218.57
Delaware (N.Y.-N.J.-Pa.)	1,973.33
Lower St. Croix (Minn.-Wis.)	9,474.93
Mississippi National River & Recreation Area (Minn.)	0.00
Missouri National Recreational River (Neb., S.D.)	0.00
New River Gorge (W. Va.)	62,663.00
Obed Wild & Scenic River (Tenn.)	5,074.85
Ozark (Mo.)	80,788.34
Rio Grande Wild & Scenic (Tex.)	9,600.00
St. Croix (Minn.-Wis.)	67,431.86
Upper Delaware (N.Y., N.J.-Pa.)	75,000.00

NATIONAL CAPITAL PARKS

Name and location	Total acreage
National Capital Parks (D.C.-Va.-Md.)	6,467.85

WHITE HOUSE

Name and location	Total acreage
White House (D.C.)	18.07

1. The National Cemeteries are not independent areas of the National Park System; each is part of a military park, battlefield, etc., except Battleground. Their acreage is kept separately. Arlington National Cemetery is under the Department of the Army. *See* Index.

OTHER PARKS

Name and location	Total acreage
Catoctin Mountain (Md.)	5,770.22
Constitution Gardens, (D.C.)	52.00
Fort Washington Park (Md.)	341.00
Greenbelt Park (Md.)	1,175.99
Perry's Victory and International Peace Memorial (Ohio)	25.38
Piscataway (Md.)	4,262.52
Prince William Forest (Va.)	18,571.55
Rock Creek Park (D.C.)	1,754.37
Vietnam Veterans Memorial (D.C.)	2.00
Wolf Trap Farm Park for the Performing Arts (Va.)	130.28

NATIONAL RECREATION AREAS

Name and location	Total acreage
Amistad (Tex.)	57,292.44
Bighorn Canyon (Wyo.-Mont.)	120,296.22
Chattahoochee River (Ga.)	9,263.64
Chickasaw (Okla.)	9,521.91

Name and location	Total acreage
Coulee Dam (Wash.)	100,390.31
Curecanti (Colo.)	42,114.47
Cuyahoga Valley (Ohio)	42,437.76
Delaware Water Gap (Pa.-N.J.)	66,651.86
Gateway (N.Y.-N.J.)	26,310.93
Gauley River (W. Va.)	0.00
Glen Canyon (Ariz.-Utah)	1,236,880.00
Golden Gate (Calif.)	73,082.37
Lake Chelan (Wash.)	61,882.76
Lake Mead (Ariz.-Nev.)	1,495,665.52
Lake Meredith (Tex.)	44,977.63
Ross Lake (Wash.)	117,574.09
Santa Monica Mountains (Calif.)	150,050.00
Whiskeytown-Shasta-Trinity (Calif.)	42,503.46

NATIONAL SCENIC TRAIL

Appalachian (Maine, N.H., Vt., Mass., Conn., N.Y., N.J., Pa., Md., W.Va., Va., N.C., Tenn., Ga.)	161,545.92
Natchez Trace (Ga.-Ala.-Tenn.)	10,995.00
Potomac Heritage (D.C.-Md.-Va.-Pa.)	0.00

NATIONAL MALL

National Mall (D.C.)	146.35

INTERNATIONAL HISTORIC SITE

Saint Croix Island (Maine)	35.39

AFFILIATED AREAS

(National Historic Sites unless otherwise noted.)

American Memorial Park (N. Mariana Is.)	0.00
Benjamin Franklin (Pa.)[1]	0.00
Blackstone River Valley National Heritage Corridor (Mass., R.I.)	0.00
Chicago Portage (Ill.)	91.20

Name and location	Total acreage
Chimney Rock (Neb.)	83.36
David Berger (Ohio)[1]	0.00
Delaware and Lehigh Navigation Canal National Heritage Corridor (Pa.)	0.00
Ebey's Landing (Wash.)	8,000.00
Father Marquette (Mich.)[1]	52.00
Gloria Dei Church (Pa.)	3.71
Green Springs Historic District (Va.)	5,490.59
Historic Camden (S.C.)	0.00
Ice Age Scenic Trail (Wisc.)	0.00
Ice Age (Wis.)[2]	32,500.00
Iditarod National Historic Trail (Alaska)	0.00
Illinois and Michigan Canal National Heritage Corridor	0.00
International Peace Garden (N.D.)	2,330.30
Jamestown (Va.)	20.63
Lewis & Clark Natl. Historic Trail (Ill., Mo., Kan., Neb., Iowa, Idaho, S.D., N.D., Mont., Ore., Wash.)	0.00
M. McLeod Bethune Council House (D.C.)	0.00
McLoughlin House (Ore.)	0.63
Mormon Pioneer Natl. Historic Trail (Ill., Iowa, Neb., Wyo., Utah)	0.00
North Country Nat'l Scenic Trail (N.Y., Pa., Ohio, Mich., Wis., Minn., N.D.)	0.00
Oregon Natl. Historic Trail (Mo., Kan., Neb., Wyo., Idaho, Ore., Wash.)	0.00
Overmountain Victory Trail (Mo. to Ore.)	0.00
Pinelands Natl. Reserve (N.J.)	0.00
Red Hill Patrick Henry (Va.)[1]	0.00
Roosevelt-Campobello International Park (Canada)	2,721.50
Sewell-Belmont House National Historic Site (D.C.)	0.35
Touro Synagogue (R.I.)	0.23

1. National Memorial. 2. National Scientific Reserve.

Don't Eat the Flowers

There are more than 700 species of plants that grow in the United States that have been identified as dangerous if eaten. Among them are some that are commonly favored by gardeners—buttercups, daffodils, lily of the valley, sweet peas, oleander, azalea, bleeding heart, delphinium, and rhododendron. According to a survey of the nation's poison control centers, next to medicines, plants are the leading cause of poisoning in children under five years of age. A threefold increase in plant poisoning, from 1971 levels, is attributed to the house plant explosion and back-to-nature dining.

Water Supply of the World[1]

The Antarctic Icecap is the largest supply of fresh water, nearly 2 percent of the world's total of fresh and salt water. As can be seen from the table below, the amount of water in our atmosphere is over ten times as large as the water in all the rivers taken together. The fresh water actually available for human use in lakes and rivers and the accessible ground water amounts to only about one third of one percent of the world's total water supply.

	Surface area (square miles)	Volume (cubic miles)	Percentage of total
Salt Water			
The oceans	139,500,000	317,000,000	97.2
Inland seas and saline lakes	270,000	25,000	0.008
Fresh Water			
Freshwater lakes	330,000	30,000	0.009
All rivers (average level)	—	300	0.0001
Antarctic Icecap	6,000,000	6,300,000	1.9
Arctic Icecap and glaciers	900,000	680,000	0.21
Water in the atmosphere	197,000,000	3,100	0.001
Ground water within half a mile from surface	—	1,000,000	0.31
Deep-lying ground water	—	1,000,000	0.31
Total (rounded)	—	326,000,000	100.00

1. All figures are estimated. *Source:* Department of the Interior, Geological Survey.

CALENDAR & HOLIDAYS

1991

JANUARY

S	M	T	W	T	F	S
—	—	1	2	3	4	5
6	7	8	9	10	11	12
13	14	15	16	17	18	19
20	21	22	23	24	25	26
27	28	29	30	31		

1—New Year's Day
6—Epiphany
21—Martin Luther
King, Jr. Day

FEBRUARY

S	M	T	W	T	F	S
—	—	—	—	—	1	2
3	4	5	6	7	8	9
10	11	12	13	14	15	16
17	18	19	20	21	22	23
24	25	26	27	28		

2—Ground-hog Day
12—Lincoln's Birthday
13—Ash Wednesday
14—Valentine's Day
18—Washington's Birthday
Observed
28—Purim

MARCH

S	M	T	W	T	F	S
—	—	—	—	—	1	2
3	4	5	6	7	8	9
10	11	12	13	14	15	16
17	18	19	20	21	22	23
24	25	26	27	28	29	30
31						

17—St. Patrick's Day
18—1st Day of Rama-
dan
24—Palm Sunday
29—Good Friday
30—1st Day of Passover
31—Easter

APRIL

S	M	T	W	T	F	S
—	1	2	3	4	5	6
7	8	9	10	11	12	13
14	15	16	17	18	19	20
21	22	23	24	25	26	27
28	29	30				

7—Daylight Savings
Time begins

MAY

S	M	T	W	T	F	S
—	—	—	1	2	3	4
5	6	7	8	9	10	11
12	13	14	15	16	17	18
19	20	21	22	23	24	25
26	27	28	29	30	31	

9—Ascension Day
12—Mother's Day
19—1st Day of Shavuot
and Pentecost
30—Memorial Day

JUNE

S	M	T	W	T	F	S
—	—	—	—	—	—	1
2	3	4	5	6	7	8
9	10	11	12	13	14	15
16	17	18	19	20	21	22
23	24	25	26	27	28	29
30						

14—Flag Day
16—Father's Day

JULY

S	M	T	W	T	F	S
—	1	2	3	4	5	6
7	8	9	10	11	12	13
14	15	16	17	18	19	20
21	22	23	24	25	26	27
28	29	30	31			

1—Canada Day
4—Independence Day

AUGUST

S	M	T	W	T	F	S
—	—	—	—	1	2	3
4	5	6	7	8	9	10
11	12	13	14	15	16	17
18	19	20	21	22	23	24
25	26	27	28	29	30	31

SEPTEMBER

S	M	T	W	T	F	S
1	2	3	4	5	6	7
8	9	10	11	12	13	14
15	16	17	18	19	20	21
22	23	24	25	26	27	28
29	30					

2—Labor Day
9—1st Day of Rosh
Hashana
18—Yom Kippur

OCTOBER

S	M	T	W	T	F	S
—	—	1	2	3	4	5
6	7	8	9	10	11	12
13	14	15	16	17	18	19
20	21	22	23	24	25	26
27	28	29	30	31		

12—Columbus Day
14—Thanksgiving Day
(Canada)
27—Daylight Savings
Time ends
31—Halloween

NOVEMBER

S	M	T	W	T	F	S
—	—	—	—	—	1	2
3	4	5	6	7	8	9
10	11	12	13	14	15	16
17	18	19	20	21	22	23
24	25	26	27	28	29	30

1—All Saints Day
5—Election Day
11—Veterans Day
28—Thanksgiving

DECEMBER

S	M	T	W	T	F	S
1	2	3	4	5	6	7
8	9	10	11	12	13	14
15	16	17	18	19	20	21
22	23	24	25	26	27	28
29	30	31				

1—1st Sunday of
Advent
2—1st Day of
Hanukkah
25—Christmas

Seasons for the Northern Hemisphere, 1991

Eastern Standard Time

March 20, 10:02 p.m., sun enters sign of Aries; spring begins

June 21, 4:19 p.m., sun enters sign of Cancer; summer begins

Sept. 23, 7:48 a.m., sun enters sign of Libra; fall begins

Dec. 22, 3:54 a.m., sun enters sign of Capricorn; winter begins

1990

	JANUARY					
S	M	T	W	T	F	S
—	1	2	3	4	5	6
7	8	9	10	11	12	13
14	15	16	17	18	19	20
21	22	23	24	25	26	27
28	29	30	31			

	FEBRUARY					
S	M	T	W	T	F	S
—	—	—	—	1	2	3
4	5	6	7	8	9	10
11	12	13	14	15	16	17
18	19	20	21	22	23	24
25	26	27	28			

	MARCH					
S	M	T	W	T	F	S
—	—	—	—	1	2	3
4	5	6	7	8	9	10
11	12	13	14	15	16	17
18	19	20	21	22	23	24
25	26	27	28	29	30	31

	APRIL					
S	M	T	W	T	F	S
1	2	3	4	5	6	7
8	9	10	11	12	13	14
15	16	17	18	19	20	21
22	23	24	25	26	27	28
29	30					

	MAY					
S	M	T	W	T	F	S
—	—	1	2	3	4	5
6	7	8	9	10	11	12
13	14	15	16	17	18	19
20	21	22	23	24	25	26
27	28	29	30	31		

	JUNE					
S	M	T	W	T	F	S
—	—	—	—	—	1	2
3	4	5	6	7	8	9
10	11	12	13	14	15	16
17	18	19	20	21	22	23
24	25	26	27	28	29	30

	JULY					
S	M	T	W	T	F	S
1	2	3	4	5	6	7
8	9	10	11	12	13	14
15	16	17	18	19	20	21
22	23	24	25	26	27	28
29	30	31				

	AUGUST					
S	M	T	W	T	F	S
—	—	—	1	2	3	4
5	6	7	8	9	10	11
12	13	14	15	16	17	18
19	20	21	22	23	24	25
26	27	28	29	30	31	

	SEPTEMBER					
S	M	T	W	T	F	S
—	—	—	—	—	—	1
2	3	4	5	6	7	8
9	10	11	12	13	14	15
16	17	18	19	20	21	22
23	24	25	26	27	28	29
30						

	OCTOBER					
S	M	T	W	T	F	S
—	1	2	3	4	5	6
7	8	9	10	11	12	13
14	15	16	17	18	19	20
21	22	23	24	25	26	27
28	29	30	31			

	NOVEMBER					
S	M	T	W	T	F	S
—	—	—	—	1	2	3
4	5	6	7	8	9	10
11	12	13	14	15	16	17
18	19	20	21	22	23	24
25	26	27	28	29	30	

	DECEMBER					
S	M	T	W	T	F	S
—	—	—	—	—	—	1
2	3	4	5	6	7	8
9	10	11	12	13	14	15
16	17	18	19	20	21	22
23	24	25	26	27	28	29
30	31					

1992

	JANUARY					
S	M	T	W	T	F	S
—	—	—	1	2	3	4
5	6	7	8	9	10	11
12	13	14	15	16	17	18
19	20	21	22	23	24	25
26	27	28	29	30	31	

	FEBRUARY					
S	M	T	W	T	F	S
—	—	—	—	—	—	1
2	3	4	5	6	7	8
9	10	11	12	13	14	15
16	17	18	19	20	21	22
23	24	25	26	27	28	29

	MARCH					
S	M	T	W	T	F	S
1	2	3	4	5	6	7
8	9	10	11	12	13	14
15	16	17	18	19	20	21
22	23	24	25	26	27	28
29	30	31				

	APRIL					
S	M	T	W	T	F	S
—	—	—	1	2	3	4
5	6	7	8	9	10	11
12	13	14	15	16	17	18
19	20	21	22	23	24	25
26	27	28	29	30		

	MAY					
S	M	T	W	T	F	S
—	—	—	—	—	1	2
3	4	5	6	7	8	9
10	11	12	13	14	15	16
17	18	19	20	21	22	23
24	25	26	27	28	29	30
31						

	JUNE					
S	M	T	W	T	F	S
—	1	2	3	4	5	6
7	8	9	10	11	12	13
14	15	16	17	18	19	20
21	22	23	24	25	26	27
28	29	30				

	JULY					
S	M	T	W	T	F	S
—	—	—	1	2	3	4
5	6	7	8	9	10	11
12	13	14	15	16	17	18
19	20	21	22	23	24	25
26	27	28	29	30	31	

	AUGUST					
S	M	T	W	T	F	S
—	—	—	—	—	—	1
2	3	4	5	6	7	8
9	10	11	12	13	14	15
16	17	18	19	20	21	22
23	24	25	26	27	28	29
30	31					

	SEPTEMBER					
S	M	T	W	T	F	S
—	—	1	2	3	4	5
6	7	8	9	10	11	12
13	14	15	16	17	18	19
20	21	22	23	24	25	26
27	28	29	30			

	OCTOBER					
S	M	T	W	T	F	S
—	—	—	—	1	2	3
4	5	6	7	8	9	10
11	12	13	14	15	16	17
18	19	20	21	22	23	24
25	26	27	28	29	30	31

	NOVEMBER					
S	M	T	W	T	F	S
1	2	3	4	5	6	7
8	9	10	11	12	13	14
15	16	17	18	19	20	21
22	23	24	25	26	27	28
29	30					

	DECEMBER					
S	M	T	W	T	F	S
—	—	1	2	3	4	5
6	7	8	9	10	11	12
13	14	15	16	17	18	19
20	21	22	23	24	25	26
27	28	29	30	31		

Pre-Columbian Calendar Systems

The Mayans and the Aztecs both used two calendars—a sacred or ceremonial calendar of 260 days and a 365-day secular calendar that was divided into 18 months of 20 days each. An additional five days were added to complete the 365-day year.

The Mayans were able to approximate the true length of the tropical year with a greater accuracy than does the Gregorian calendar year we now use.

The tropical year is 365.2422 days. The Mayans determined it to be 365.2420 days, whereas the Gregorian calendar year is 365.2425.

Very little is known about the Inca calendar. Because the Incas did not have a written language, early reports about their calendar cannot be verified.

PERPETUAL CALENDAR

Year	No	Year	No	Year	No	Year	No	Year	No	Year	No
1800	4	1844	9	1888	8	1932	13	1976	12	2020	11
1801	5	1845	4	1889	3	1933	1	1977	7	2021	6
1802	6	1846	5	1890	4	1934	2	1978	1	2022	7
1803	7	1847	6	1891	5	1935	3	1979	2	2023	1
1804	8	1848	14	1892	13	1936	11	1980	10	2024	9
1805	3	1849	2	1893	1	1937	6	1981	5	2025	4
1806	4	1850	3	1894	2	1938	7	1982	6	2026	5
1807	5	1851	4	1895	3	1939	1	1983	7	2027	6
1808	13	1852	12	1896	11	1940	9	1984	8	2028	14
1809	1	1853	7	1897	6	1941	4	1985	3	2029	2
1810	2	1854	1	1898	7	1942	5	1986	4	2030	3
1811	3	1855	2	1899	1	1943	6	1987	5	2031	4
1812	11	1856	10	1900	2	1944	14	1988	13	2032	12
1813	6	1857	5	1901	3	1945	2	1989	1	2033	7
1814	7	1858	6	1902	4	1946	3	1990	2	2034	1
1815	1	1859	7	1903	5	1947	4	1991	3	2035	2
1816	9	1860	8	1904	13	1948	12	1992	11	2036	10
1817	4	1861	3	1905	1	1949	7	1993	6	2037	5
1818	5	1862	4	1906	2	1950	1	1994	7	2038	6
1819	6	1863	5	1907	3	1951	2	1995	1	2039	7
1820	14	1864	13	1908	11	1952	10	1996	9	2040	8
1821	2	1865	1	1909	6	1953	5	1997	4	2041	3
1822	3	1866	2	1910	7	1954	6	1998	5	2042	4
1823	4	1867	3	1911	1	1955	7	1999	6	2043	5
1824	12	1868	11	1912	9	1956	8	2000	14	2044	13
1825	7	1869	6	1913	4	1957	3	2001	2	2045	1
1826	1	1870	7	1914	5	1958	4	2002	3	2046	2
1827	2	1871	1	1915	6	1959	5	2003	4	2047	3
1828	10	1872	9	1916	14	1960	13	2004	12	2048	11
1829	5	1873	4	1917	2	1961	1	2005	7	2049	6
1830	6	1874	5	1918	3	1962	2	2006	1	2050	7
1831	7	1875	6	1919	4	1963	3	2007	2	2051	1
1832	8	1876	14	1920	12	1964	11	2008	10	2052	9
1833	3	1877	2	1921	7	1965	6	2009	5	2053	4
1834	4	1878	3	1922	1	1966	7	2010	6	2054	5
1835	5	1879	4	1923	2	1967	1	2011	7	2055	6
1836	13	1880	12	1924	10	1968	9	2012	8	2056	14
1837	1	1881	7	1925	5	1969	4	2013	3	2057	2
1838	2	1882	1	1926	6	1970	5	2014	4	2058	3
1839	3	1883	2	1927	7	1971	6	2015	5	2059	4
1840	11	1884	10	1928	8	1972	14	2016	13	2060	12
1841	6	1885	5	1929	3	1973	2	2017	1	2061	7
1842	7	1886	6	1930	4	1974	3	2018	2	2062	1
1843	1	1887	7	1931	5	1975	4	2019	3	2063	2

DIRECTIONS: The number given with each year in the key above is number of calendar to use for that year

Calendar 1

```
JANUARY              FEBRUARY             MARCH                APRIL
S  M  T  W  T  F  S  S  M  T  W  T  F  S  S  M  T  W  T  F  S  S  M  T  W  T  F  S
1  2  3  4  5  6  7              1  2  3  4              1  2  3  4                    1
8  9 10 11 12 13 14  5  6  7  8  9 10 11  5  6  7  8  9 10 11  2  3  4  5  6  7  8
15 16 17 18 19 20 21 12 13 14 15 16 17 18 12 13 14 15 16 17 18  9 10 11 12 13 14 15
22 23 24 25 26 27 28 19 20 21 22 23 24 25 19 20 21 22 23 24 25 16 17 18 19 20 21 22
29 30 31             26 27 28             26 27 28 29 30 31    23 24 25 26 27 28 29
                                                               30

MAY                  JUNE                 JULY                 AUGUST
S  M  T  W  T  F  S  S  M  T  W  T  F  S  S  M  T  W  T  F  S  S  M  T  W  T  F  S
      1  2  3  4  5              1  2  3                    1        1  2  3  4  5
6  7  8  9 10 11 12   4  5  6  7  8  9 10  2  3  4  5  6  7  8  6  7  8  9 10 11 12
13 14 15 16 17 18 19 11 12 13 14 15 16 17  9 10 11 12 13 14 15 13 14 15 16 17 18 19
20 21 22 23 24 25 26 18 19 20 21 22 23 24 16 17 18 19 20 21 22 20 21 22 23 24 25 26
27 28 29 30 31       25 26 27 28 29 30    23 24 25 26 27 28 29 27 28 29 30 31
                                          30 31

SEPTEMBER            OCTOBER              NOVEMBER             DECEMBER
S  M  T  W  T  F  S  S  M  T  W  T  F  S  S  M  T  W  T  F  S  S  M  T  W  T  F  S
               1  2  1  2  3  4  5  6  7              1  2  3                 1  2
3  4  5  6  7  8  9  8  9 10 11 12 13 14  4  5  6  7  8  9 10  3  4  5  6  7  8  9
10 11 12 13 14 15 16 15 16 17 18 19 20 21 11 12 13 14 15 16 17 10 11 12 13 14 15 16
17 18 19 20 21 22 23 22 23 24 25 26 27 28 18 19 20 21 22 23 24 17 18 19 20 21 22 23
24 25 26 27 28 29 30 29 30 31             25 26 27 28 29 30    24 25 26 27 28 29 30
                                                               31
```

Calendar 2

```
JANUARY              FEBRUARY             MARCH                APRIL
S  M  T  W  T  F  S  S  M  T  W  T  F  S  S  M  T  W  T  F  S  S  M  T  W  T  F  S
   1  2  3  4  5  6           1  2  3              1  2  3  4  1  2  3  4  5  6  7
7  8  9 10 11 12 13  4  5  6  7  8  9 10  5  6  7  8  9 10 11  8  9 10 11 12 13 14
14 15 16 17 18 19 20 11 12 13 14 15 16 17 12 13 14 15 16 17 18 15 16 17 18 19 20 21
21 22 23 24 25 26 27 18 19 20 21 22 23 24 19 20 21 22 23 24 25 22 23 24 25 26 27 28
28 29 30 31          25 26 27 28          26 27 28 29 30 31    29 30

MAY                  JUNE                 JULY                 AUGUST
S  M  T  W  T  F  S  S  M  T  W  T  F  S  S  M  T  W  T  F  S  S  M  T  W  T  F  S
      1  2  3  4  5                 1  2  1  2  3  4  5  6  7              1  2  3
6  7  8  9 10 11 12  3  4  5  6  7  8  9  8  9 10 11 12 13 14  4  5  6  7  8  9 10
13 14 15 16 17 18 19 10 11 12 13 14 15 16 15 16 17 18 19 20 21 11 12 13 14 15 16 17
20 21 22 23 24 25 26 17 18 19 20 21 22 23 22 23 24 25 26 27 28 18 19 20 21 22 23 24
27 28 29 30 31       24 25 26 27 28 29 30 29 30 31             25 26 27 28 29 30 31

SEPTEMBER            OCTOBER              NOVEMBER             DECEMBER
S  M  T  W  T  F  S  S  M  T  W  T  F  S  S  M  T  W  T  F  S  S  M  T  W  T  F  S
                  1     1  2  3  4  5  6           1  2  3                    1
2  3  4  5  6  7  8  7  8  9 10 11 12 13  4  5  6  7  8  9 10  2  3  4  5  6  7  8
9 10 11 12 13 14 15 14 15 16 17 18 19 20 11 12 13 14 15 16 17  9 10 11 12 13 14 15
16 17 18 19 20 21 22 21 22 23 24 25 26 27 18 19 20 21 22 23 24 16 17 18 19 20 21 22
23 24 25 26 27 28 29 28 29 30 31          25 26 27 28 29 30    23 24 25 26 27 28 29
30                                                             30 31
```

Calendar 3

```
JANUARY              FEBRUARY             MARCH                APRIL
S  M  T  W  T  F  S  S  M  T  W  T  F  S  S  M  T  W  T  F  S  S  M  T  W  T  F  S
      1  2  3  4  5                 1  2              1  2        1  2  3  4  5  6
6  7  8  9 10 11 12  3  4  5  6  7  8  9  3  4  5  6  7  8  9  7  8  9 10 11 12 13
13 14 15 16 17 18 19 10 11 12 13 14 15 16 10 11 12 13 14 15 16 14 15 16 17 18 19 20
20 21 22 23 24 25 26 17 18 19 20 21 22 23 17 18 19 20 21 22 23 21 22 23 24 25 26 27
27 28 29 30 31       24 25 26 27 28       24 25 26 27 28 29 30 28 29 30
                                          31

MAY                  JUNE                 JULY                 AUGUST
S  M  T  W  T  F  S  S  M  T  W  T  F  S  S  M  T  W  T  F  S  S  M  T  W  T  F  S
         1  2  3                    1     1  2  3  4  5  6           1  2  3
4  5  6  7  8  9 10  2  3  4  5  6  7  8  7  8  9 10 11 12 13  4  5  6  7  8  9 10
11 12 13 14 15 16 17  9 10 11 12 13 14 15 14 15 16 17 18 19 20 11 12 13 14 15 16 17
18 19 20 21 22 23 24 16 17 18 19 20 21 22 21 22 23 24 25 26 27 18 19 20 21 22 23 24
25 26 27 28 29 30 31 23 24 25 26 27 28 29 28 29 30 31          25 26 27 28 29 30 31
                     30

SEPTEMBER            OCTOBER              NOVEMBER             DECEMBER
S  M  T  W  T  F  S  S  M  T  W  T  F  S  S  M  T  W  T  F  S  S  M  T  W  T  F  S
1  2  3  4  5  6  7        1  2  3  4  5                 1  2  1  2  3  4  5  6  7
8  9 10 11 12 13 14  6  7  8  9 10 11 12  3  4  5  6  7  8  9  8  9 10 11 12 13 14
15 16 17 18 19 20 21 13 14 15 16 17 18 19 10 11 12 13 14 15 16 15 16 17 18 19 20 21
22 23 24 25 26 27 28 20 21 22 23 24 25 26 17 18 19 20 21 22 23 22 23 24 25 26 27 28
29 30                27 28 29 30 31       24 25 26 27 28 29 30 29 30 31
```

Calendar 4

```
JANUARY              FEBRUARY             MARCH                APRIL
S  M  T  W  T  F  S  S  M  T  W  T  F  S  S  M  T  W  T  F  S  S  M  T  W  T  F  S
         1  2  3  4                    1                    1        1  2  3  4  5
5  6  7  8  9 10 11  2  3  4  5  6  7  8  2  3  4  5  6  7  8  6  7  8  9 10 11 12
12 13 14 15 16 17 18  9 10 11 12 13 14 15  9 10 11 12 13 14 15 13 14 15 16 17 18 19
19 20 21 22 23 24 25 16 17 18 19 20 21 22 16 17 18 19 20 21 22 20 21 22 23 24 25 26
26 27 28 29 30 31    23 24 25 26 27 28    23 24 25 26 27 28 29 27 28 29 30
                                          30 31

MAY                  JUNE                 JULY                 AUGUST
S  M  T  W  T  F  S  S  M  T  W  T  F  S  S  M  T  W  T  F  S  S  M  T  W  T  F  S
         1  2  3     1  2  3  4  5  6  7        1  2  3  4  5                 1  2
4  5  6  7  8  9 10  8  9 10 11 12 13 14  6  7  8  9 10 11 12  3  4  5  6  7  8  9
11 12 13 14 15 16 17 15 16 17 18 19 20 21 13 14 15 16 17 18 19 10 11 12 13 14 15 16
18 19 20 21 22 23 24 22 23 24 25 26 27 28 20 21 22 23 24 25 26 17 18 19 20 21 22 23
25 26 27 28 29 30 31 29 30                27 28 29 30 31       24 25 26 27 28 29 30
                                                               31

SEPTEMBER            OCTOBER              NOVEMBER             DECEMBER
S  M  T  W  T  F  S  S  M  T  W  T  F  S  S  M  T  W  T  F  S  S  M  T  W  T  F  S
   1  2  3  4  5  6           1  2  3  4                    1     1  2  3  4  5  6
7  8  9 10 11 12 13  5  6  7  8  9 10 11  2  3  4  5  6  7  8  7  8  9 10 11 12 13
14 15 16 17 18 19 20 12 13 14 15 16 17 18  9 10 11 12 13 14 15 14 15 16 17 18 19 20
21 22 23 24 25 26 27 19 20 21 22 23 24 25 16 17 18 19 20 21 22 21 22 23 24 25 26 27
28 29 30             26 27 28 29 30 31    23 24 25 26 27 28 29 28 29 30 31
                                          30
```

Calendar 5

```
JANUARY              FEBRUARY             MARCH                APRIL
S  M  T  W  T  F  S  S  M  T  W  T  F  S  S  M  T  W  T  F  S  S  M  T  W  T  F  S
         1  2  3     1  2  3  4  5  6  7  1  2  3  4  5  6  7              1  2  3  4
4  5  6  7  8  9 10  8  9 10 11 12 13 14  8  9 10 11 12 13 14  5  6  7  8  9 10 11
11 12 13 14 15 16 17 15 16 17 18 19 20 21 15 16 17 18 19 20 21 12 13 14 15 16 17 18
18 19 20 21 22 23 24 22 23 24 25 26 27 28 22 23 24 25 26 27 28 19 20 21 22 23 24 25
25 26 27 28 29 30 31                      29 30 31             26 27 28 29 30

MAY                  JUNE                 JULY                 AUGUST
S  M  T  W  T  F  S  S  M  T  W  T  F  S  S  M  T  W  T  F  S  S  M  T  W  T  F  S
               1  2     1  2  3  4  5  6           1  2  3  4                    1
3  4  5  6  7  8  9  7  8  9 10 11 12 13  5  6  7  8  9 10 11  2  3  4  5  6  7  8
10 11 12 13 14 15 16 14 15 16 17 18 19 20 12 13 14 15 16 17 18  9 10 11 12 13 14 15
17 18 19 20 21 22 23 21 22 23 24 25 26 27 19 20 21 22 23 24 25 16 17 18 19 20 21 22
24 25 26 27 28 29 30 28 29 30             26 27 28 29 30 31    23 24 25 26 27 28 29
31                                                             30 31

SEPTEMBER            OCTOBER              NOVEMBER             DECEMBER
S  M  T  W  T  F  S  S  M  T  W  T  F  S  S  M  T  W  T  F  S  S  M  T  W  T  F  S
      1  2  3  4  5           1  2  3  4  1  2  3  4  5  6  7        1  2  3  4  5
6  7  8  9 10 11 12  4  5  6  7  8  9 10  8  9 10 11 12 13 14  6  7  8  9 10 11 12
13 14 15 16 17 18 19 11 12 13 14 15 16 17 15 16 17 18 19 20 21 13 14 15 16 17 18 19
20 21 22 23 24 25 26 18 19 20 21 22 23 24 22 23 24 25 26 27 28 20 21 22 23 24 25 26
27 28 29 30          25 26 27 28 29 30 31 29 30                27 28 29 30 31
```

Calendar 6

```
JANUARY              FEBRUARY             MARCH                APRIL
S  M  T  W  T  F  S  S  M  T  W  T  F  S  S  M  T  W  T  F  S  S  M  T  W  T  F  S
               1  2     1  2  3  4  5  6     1  2  3  4  5  6           1  2  3
3  4  5  6  7  8  9  7  8  9 10 11 12 13  7  8  9 10 11 12 13  4  5  6  7  8  9 10
10 11 12 13 14 15 16 14 15 16 17 18 19 20 14 15 16 17 18 19 20 11 12 13 14 15 16 17
17 18 19 20 21 22 23 21 22 23 24 25 26 27 21 22 23 24 25 26 27 18 19 20 21 22 23 24
24 25 26 27 28 29 30 28                   28 29 30 31          25 26 27 28 29 30
31

MAY                  JUNE                 JULY                 AUGUST
S  M  T  W  T  F  S  S  M  T  W  T  F  S  S  M  T  W  T  F  S  S  M  T  W  T  F  S
                  1        1  2  3  4  5           1  2  3     1  2  3  4  5  6  7
2  3  4  5  6  7  8  6  7  8  9 10 11 12  4  5  6  7  8  9 10  8  9 10 11 12 13 14
9 10 11 12 13 14 15 13 14 15 16 17 18 19 11 12 13 14 15 16 17 15 16 17 18 19 20 21
16 17 18 19 20 21 22 20 21 22 23 24 25 26 18 19 20 21 22 23 24 22 23 24 25 26 27 28
23 24 25 26 27 28 29 27 28 29 30          25 26 27 28 29 30 31 29 30 31
30 31

SEPTEMBER            OCTOBER              NOVEMBER             DECEMBER
S  M  T  W  T  F  S  S  M  T  W  T  F  S  S  M  T  W  T  F  S  S  M  T  W  T  F  S
         1  2  3  4                  1  2     1  2  3  4  5  6           1  2  3  4
5  6  7  8  9 10 11  3  4  5  6  7  8  9  7  8  9 10 11 12 13  5  6  7  8  9 10 11
12 13 14 15 16 17 18 10 11 12 13 14 15 16 14 15 16 17 18 19 20 12 13 14 15 16 17 18
19 20 21 22 23 24 25 17 18 19 20 21 22 23 21 22 23 24 25 26 27 19 20 21 22 23 24 25
26 27 28 29 30       24 25 26 27 28 29 30 28 29 30             26 27 28 29 30 31
                     31
```

7

JANUARY	FEBRUARY	MARCH	APRIL
S M T W T F S	S M T W T F S	S M T W T F S	S M T W T F S

8

JANUARY	FEBRUARY	MARCH	APRIL

9

JANUARY	FEBRUARY	MARCH	APRIL

10

JANUARY	FEBRUARY	MARCH	APRIL

11

JANUARY	FEBRUARY	MARCH	APRIL

12

JANUARY	FEBRUARY	MARCH	APRIL

13

JANUARY	FEBRUARY	MARCH	APRIL

14

JANUARY	FEBRUARY	MARCH	APRIL

Each calendar (numbered 7 through 14) contains twelve monthly grids arranged in three rows: JANUARY, FEBRUARY, MARCH, APRIL; MAY, JUNE, JULY, AUGUST; SEPTEMBER, OCTOBER, NOVEMBER, DECEMBER. Each month grid is headed by S M T W T F S with the numbered days below.

The Calendar

History of the Calendar

The purpose of a calendar is to reckon time in advance, to show how many days have to elapse until a certain event takes place—the harvest, a religious festival, or whatever. The earliest calendars, naturally, were crude, and they must have been strongly influenced by the geographical location of the people who made them. In the Scandinavian countries, for example, where the seasons are pronounced, the concept of the year was determined by the seasons, specifically by the end of winter. The Norsemen, before becoming Christians, are said to have had a calendar consisting of ten months of 30 days each.

But in warmer countries, where the seasons are less pronounced, the Moon became the basic unit for time reckoning; an old Jewish book actually makes the statement that "the Moon was created for the counting of the days." All the oldest calendars of which we have reliable information were lunar calendars, based on the time interval from one new moon to the next—a so-called "lunation." But even in a warm climate there are annual events that pay no attention to the phases of the Moon. In some areas it was a rainy season; in Egypt it was the annual flooding of the Nile. It was, therefore, necessary to regulate daily life and religious festivals by lunations, but to take care of the annual event in some other manner.

The calendar of the Assyrians was based on the phases of the Moon. The month began with the first appearance of the lunar crescent, and since this can best be observed in the evening, the day began with sunset. They knew that a lunation was 29 1/2 days long, so their lunar year had a duration of 354 days, falling eleven days short of the solar year.[1] After three years such a lunar calendar would be off by 33 days, or more than one lunation. We know that the Assyrians added an extra month from time to time, but we do not know whether they had developed a special rule for doing so or whether the priests proclaimed the necessity for an extra month from observation. If they made every third year a year of 13 lunations, their three-year period would cover 1,091 1/2 days (using their value of 29 1/2 days for one lunation), or just about four days too short. In one century this mistake would add up to 133 days by their reckoning (in reality closer to 134 days), requiring four extra lunations per century.

We now know that an eight-year period, consisting of five years with 12 months and three years with 13 months would lead to a difference of only 20 days per century, but we do not know whether such a calendar was actually used.

The best approximation that was possible in antiquity was a 19-year period, with seven of these 19 years having 13 months. This means that the period contained 235 months. This, still using the old value for a lunation, made a total of 6,932 1/2 days, while 19 solar years added up to 6,939.7 days, a difference of just one week per period and about five weeks per century. Even the 19-year period required constant adjustment, but it was the period that became the basis of the religious calendar of

the Jews. The Arabs used the same calendar at first, but Mohammed forbade shifting from 12 months to 13 months, so that the Islamic religious calendar, even today, has a lunar year of 354 days. As a result the Islamic religious festivals run through all the seasons of the year three times per century.

The Egyptians had a traditional calendar with 12 months of 30 days each. At one time they added five extra days at the end of every year. These turned into a five-day festival because it was thought to be unlucky to work during that time.

When Rome emerged as a world power, the difficulties of making a calendar were well known, but the Romans complicated their lives because of their superstition that even numbers were unlucky. Hence their months were 29 or 31 days long, with the exception of February, which had 28 days. However, four months of 31 days, seven months of 29 days, and one month of 28 days added up to only 355 days. Therefore, the Romans invented an extra month called Mercedonius of 22 or 23 days. It was added every second year.

Even with Mercedonius, the Roman calendar was so far off that Caesar, advised by the astronomer Sosigenes, ordered a sweeping reform in 45 B.C. One year, made 445 days long by imperial decree, brought the calendar back in step with the seasons. Then the solar year (with the value of 365 days and 6 hours) was made the basis of the calendar. The months were 30 or 31 days in length, and to take care of the six hours, every fourth year was made a 366-day year. Moreover, Caesar decreed, the year began with the first of January, not with the vernal equinox in late March.

This was the Julian calendar, named after Julius Caesar. It is still the calendar of the Eastern Orthodox churches.

However, the year is 11 1/2 minutes shorter than the figure written into Caesar's calendar by Sosigenes, and after a number of centuries, even 11 1/2 minutes add up. *See* table.

While Caesar could decree that the vernal equinox should not be used as the first day of the new year, the vernal equinox is still a fact of Nature that could not be disregarded. One of the first (as far as we know) to become alarmed about this was Roger Bacon. He sent a memorandum to Pope Clement IV, who apparently was not impressed. But Pope Sixtus IV (reigned 1471 to 1484) decided that another reform was needed and called the German astronomer Regiomontanus to Rome to advise him. Regiomontanus arrived in 1475, but one year later he died in an epidemic, one of the recurrent outbreaks of the plague. The Pope himself survived, but his reform plans died with Regiomontanus.

Less than a hundred years later, in 1545, the Council of Trent authorized the then Pope, Paul III, to reform the calendar once more. Most of the mathematical and astronomical work was done by Father Christopher Clavius, S.J. The immediate correction, advised by Father Clavius and ordered by Pope Gregory XIII, was that Thursday, Oct. 4, 1582, was to be the last day of the Julian calendar. The next day was Friday, with the date of October 15. For long-range accuracy, a formula suggested by the Vatican librarian Aloysius Giglio (latinized into Lilius) was adopted: every fourth year is a leap year *unless* it is a century year like 1700 or 1800. Century years can be leap years *only* when they are divisible by 400 (e.g., 1600). This rule elim-

---

1. The correct figures are: lunation: 29 d, 12 h, 44 min, 2.8 sec (29.530585 d); solar year: 365 d, 5 h, 48 min, 46 sec (365.242216 d); 12 lunations: 354 d, 8 h, 48 min, 34 sec (354.3671 d).

Drift of the Vernal Equinox in the Julian Calendar

Date	Julian year	Date	Julian year	Date	Julian year
March 21	325 A.D.	March 17	837 A.D.	March 13	1349 A.D.
March 20	453 A.D.	March 16	965 A.D.	March 12	1477 A.D.
March 19	581 A.D.	March 15	1093 A.D.	March 11	1605 A.D.
March 18	709 A.D.	March 14	1221 A.D.		

inates three leap years in four centuries, making the calendar sufficiently correct for all ordinary purposes.

Unfortunately, all the Protestant princes in 1582 chose to ignore the papal bull; they continued with the Julian calendar. It was not until 1698 that the German professor Erhard Weigel persuaded the Protestant rulers of Germany and of the Netherlands to change to the new calendar. In England the shift took place in 1752, and in Russia it needed the revolution to introduce the Gregorian calendar in 1918.

The average year of the Gregorian calendar, in spite of the leap year rule, is about 26 seconds longer than the earth's orbital period. But this discrepancy will need 3,323 years to build up to a single day.

Modern proposals for calendar reform do not aim at a "better" calendar, but at one that is more convenient to use, especially for commercial purposes. A 365-day year cannot be divided into equal halves or quarters; the number of days per month is haphazard; the months begin or end in the middle of a week; a holiday fixed by date (e.g., the Fourth of July) will wander through a week; a holiday fixed in another manner (e.g., Easter) can fall on thirty-five possible dates. The Gregorian calendar, admittedly, keeps the calendar dates in reasonable unison with astronomical events, but it still is full of minor annoyances. Moreover, you need a calendar every year to look up dates; an ideal calendar should be one that you can memorize for one year and that is valid for all other years, too.

In 1834 an Italian priest, Marco Mastrofini, suggested taking one day out of every year. It would be made a holiday and *not* be given the name of a weekday. That would make every year begin with January 1 as a Sunday. The leap-year day would be treated the same way, so that in leap years there would be two unnamed holidays at the end of the year.

About a decade later the philosopher Auguste Comte also suggested a 364-day calendar with an extra day, which he called Year Day.

Since then there have been other unsuccessful attempts at calendar reform.

Time and Calendar

The two natural cycles on which time measurements are based are the year and the day. The year is defined as the time required for the Earth to complete one revolution around the Sun, while the day is the time required for the Earth to complete one turn upon its axis. Unfortunately the Earth needs 365 days plus about six hours to go around the Sun once, so that the year does not consist of so and so many days; the fractional day has to be taken care of by an extra day every fourth year.

But because the Earth, while turning upon its axis, also moves around the Sun there are two kinds of days. A day may be defined as the interval between the highest point of the Sun in the sky on two successive days. This, averaged out over the year, produces the customary 24-hour day. But one might also define a day as the time interval between the moments when a certain point in the sky, say a conveniently located star, is directly overhead. This is called:

Sidereal time. Astronomers use a point which they call the "vernal equinox" for the actual determination. Such a sidereal day is somewhat shorter than the "solar day," namely by about 3 minutes and 56 seconds of so-called "mean solar time."

Apparent solar time is the time based directly on the Sun's position in the sky. In ordinary life the day runs from midnight to midnight. It begins when the Sun is invisible by being 12 hours from its zenith. Astronomers use the so-called "Julian Day," which runs from noon to noon; the concept was invented by the astronomer Joseph Scaliger, who named it after his father Julius. To avoid the problems caused by leap-year days and so forth, Scaliger picked a conveniently remote date in the past and suggested just counting days without regard to weeks, months, and years. The Julian Day for 0ʰ Jan. 31, 1990 is 244 7922.5. The reason for having the Julian Day run from noon to noon is the practical one that astronomical observations usually extend across the midnight hour, which would require a change in date (or in the Julian Day number) if the astronomical day, like the civil day, ran from midnight to midnight.

Mean solar time, rather than apparent solar time, is what is actually used most of the time. The mean solar time is based on the position of a fictitious "mean sun." The reason why this fictitious sun has to be introduced is the following: the Earth turns on its axis regularly; it needs the same number of seconds regardless of the season. But the movement of the Earth around the Sun is not regular because the Earth's orbit is an ellipse. This has the result (as explained in the section The Seasons) that the Earth moves faster in January and slower in July. Though it is the Earth that changes velocity, it looks to us as if the Sun did. In January, when the Earth moves faster, the *apparent* movement of the Sun looks faster. The "mean sun" of time measurements, then, is a sun that moves regularly all year round; the real Sun will be either ahead of or behind the "mean sun." The difference between the real Sun and the fictitious mean sun is called the *equation of time.*

When the real Sun is west of the mean sun we have the "sun fast" condition, with the real Sun crossing the meridian ahead of the mean sun. The opposite is the "sun slow" situation when the real Sun crosses the meridian after the mean sun. Of course, what is observed is the real Sun. The equation of time is needed to establish mean solar time, kept by the reference clocks.

But if all clocks were actually set by mean solar time we would be plagued by a welter of time differences that would be "correct" but a major nuisance. A clock on Long Island, correctly showing mean solar time for its location (this would be *local*

The Names of the Days

Latin	Saxon	English	French	Italian	Spanish	German
Dies Solis	Sun's Day	Sunday	Dimanche	domenica	domingo	Sonntag
Dies Lunae	Moon's Day	Monday	Lundi	lunedi	lunes	Montag
Dies Martis	Tiw's Day	Tuesday	Mardi	martedi	martes	Dienstag
Dies Mercurii	Woden's Day	Wednesday	Mercredi	mercoledi	miércoles	Mittwoch
Dies Jovis	Thor's Day	Thursday	Jeudi	giovedi	jueves	Donnerstag
Dies Veneris	Frigg's Day	Friday	Vendredi	venerdi	viernes	Freitag
Dies Saturni	Seterne's Day	Saturday	Samedi	sabato	sábado	Sonnabend

NOTE: The Romans gave one day of the week to each planet known, the Sun and Moon being considered planets in this connection. The Saxon names are a kind of translation of the Roman names: Tiw was substituted for Mars, Woden (Wotan) for Mercury, Thor for Jupiter (Jove), Frigg for Venus, and Seterne for Saturn. The English names are adapted Saxon. The Spanish and Italian names, which are normally not capitalized, and the French are derived from the Latin. The German names follow the Saxon pattern with two exceptions: Wednesday is Mittwoch (Middle of the Week), and Saturday is Sonnabend (Sunday's Eve).

civil time), would be slightly ahead of a clock in Newark, N.J. The Newark clock would be slightly ahead of a clock in Trenton, N.J., which, in turn, would be ahead of a clock in Philadelphia. This condition actually prevailed in the past until 1883, when *standard time* was introduced. Standard time is the correct mean solar time for a designated meridian, and this time is used for a certain area to the east and west of this meridian. In the U.S. four meridians have been designated to supply standard times; they are 75°, 90°, 105°, and 120° west of Greenwich. The 75° meridian determines Eastern Standard Time. It happens to run through Camden, N.J., where standard time, therefore, is also mean solar time and local civil time. The 90° meridian (which happens to pass through the western part of Memphis, Tenn.) determines Central Standard Time, the 105° meridian (passing through Denver) determines Mountain Standard Time, and the 120° meridian (which runs through Lake Tahoe) determines Pacific Standard Time.

Canada, extending over more territory from west to east, adds one time zone on either side: Atlantic Standard Time (based on 60° west of Greenwich) for New Brunswick, Nova Scotia, and Quebec, and Yukon Standard Time (determined by the 135° meridian) for its extreme West. Alaska, extending still farther to the west, adds two more time zones, Alaska Standard Time (determined by the 150° meridian that passes through Anchorage) and Nome Standard Time, based on the 165° meridian just east of Nome.

In general the Earth is divided into 24 such time zones, which run one hour apart. For practical purposes the time zones sometimes show indentations, and there are a few "subzones" that differ from the neighboring zone by only half an hour, e.g., Newfoundland.

The date line. While the time zones are based on the natural event of the Sun crossing the meridian, the date must be an arbitrary decision. The meridians are traditionally counted from the meridian of the observatory of Greenwich in England, which is called the zero meridian. The logical place for changing the date is 12 hours, or 180° from Greenwich. Fortunately, the 180th meridian runs mostly through the open Pacific. The date line makes a zigzag in the north to incorporate the eastern tip of Siberia into the Siberian time system and then another one to incorporate a number of islands into the Alaska time system. In the south there is a similar zigzag for the purpose of tying a number of British-owned islands to the New Zealand time system. Otherwise the date line is the same as 180° from Greenwich. At points to the east of the date line the calendar is one day earlier than at points to the west of it. A traveller going eastward across the date line from one island to another would not have to re-set his watch because he would stay inside the time zone (provided he does so where the date line does *not* coincide with the 180° meridian), but it would be the same time of the previous day.

The Seasons

The seasons are caused by the tilt of the Earth's axis (23.4°) and not by the fact that the Earth's orbit around the Sun is an ellipse. The average distance of the Earth from the Sun is 93 million miles; the difference between aphelion (farthest away) and perihelion (closest to the Sun) is 3 million miles, so that perihelion is about 91.4 million miles from the Sun. The Earth goes through the perihelion point a few days after New Year, just when the northern hemisphere has winter. Aphelion is passed during the first days in July. This by itself shows that the

The Names of the Months

January: named after Janus, protector of the gateway to heaven

February: named after Februalia, a time period when sacrifices were made to atone for sins

March: named after Mars, the god of war, presumably signifying that the campaigns interrupted by the winter could be resumed

April: from *aperire*, Latin for "to open" (buds)

May: named after Maia, the goddess of growth of plants

June: from *juvenis*, Latin for "youth"

July: named after Julius Caesar

August: named after Augustus, the first Roman Emperor

September: from *septem*, Latin for "seven"

October: from *octo*, Latin for "eight"

November: from *novem*, Latin for "nine"

December: from *decem*, Latin for "ten"

NOTE: The earliest Latin calendar was a 10-month one; thus September was the seventh month, October, the eighth, etc. July was originally called Quintilis, as the fifth month; August was originally called Sextilis, as the sixth month.

distance from the Sun is not important within these limits. What is important is that when the Earth passes through perihelion, the northern end of the Earth's axis happens to tilt away from the Sun, so that the areas beyond the Tropic of Cancer receive only slanting rays from a Sun low in the sky.

The tilt of the Earth's axis is responsible for four lines you find on every globe. When, say, the North Pole is tilted away from the Sun as much as possible, the farthest points in the North which can still be reached by the Sun's rays are 23 1/2° from the pole. This is the Arctic Circle. The Antarctic Circle is the corresponding limit 23.4° from the South Pole; the Sun's rays cannot reach beyond this point when we have mid-summer in the North.

When the Sun is vertically above the equator, the day is of equal length all over the Earth. This happens twice a year, and these are the "equinoxes" in March and in September. After having been over the equator in March, the Sun will seem to move northward. The northernmost point where the Sun can be straight overhead is 23.4° north of the equator. This is the Tropic of Cancer; the Sun can never be vertically overhead to the north of this line. Similarly the Sun cannot be vertically overhead to the south of a line 23.4° south of the equator—the Tropic of Capricorn.

This explains the climatic zones. In the belt (the Greek word *zone* means "belt") between the Tropic of Cancer and the Tropic of Capricorn, the Sun can be straight overhead; this is the tropical zone. The two zones where the Sun cannot be overhead but will be above the horizon every day of the year are the two temperate zones; the two areas where the Sun will not rise at all for varying lengths of time are the two polar areas, Arctic and Antarctic.

Holidays

Religious and Secular, 1991

Since 1971, by federal law, Washington's Birthday, Memorial Day, Columbus Day, and Veterans' Day have been celebrated on Mondays to create three-day weekends for federal employees. Many states now observe these holidays on the same Mondays. The dates given for the holidays listed below are the traditional ones.

New Year's Day, Tuesday, Jan. 1. A legal holiday in all states and the District of Columbia, New Year's Day has its origin in Roman Times, when sacrifices were offered to Janus, the two-faced Roman deity who looked back on the past and forward to the future.

Epiphany, Sunday, Jan. 6. Falls the twelfth day after Christmas and commemorates the manifestation of Jesus as the Son of God, as represented by the adoration of the Magi, the baptism of Jesus, and the miracle of the wine at the marriage feast at Cana. Epiphany originally marked the beginning of the carnival season preceding Lent, and the evening (sometimes the eve) is known as Twelfth Night.

Martin Luther King, Jr.'s Birthday, Tuesday, Jan. 15. Honors the late civil rights leader. Became a legal public holiday in 1986.

Ground-hog Day, Saturday, Feb. 2. Legend has it that if the ground-hog sees his shadow, he'll return to his hole, and winter will last another six weeks.

Lincoln's Birthday, Tuesday, Feb. 12. A legal holiday in many states, this day was first formally observed in Washington, D.C., in 1866, when both houses of Congress gathered for a memorial address in tribute to the assassinated President.

St. Valentine's Day, Thursday, Feb. 14. This day is the festival of two third-century martyrs, both named St. Valentine. It is not known why this day is associated with lovers. It may derive from an old pagan festival about this time of year, or it may have been inspired by the belief that birds mate on this day.

Washington's Birthday, Friday, Feb. 22. The birthday of George Washington is celebrated as a legal holiday in every state of the Union, the District of Columbia, and all territories. The observance began in 1796.

Shrove Tuesday, Feb. 12. Falls the day before Ash Wednesday and marks the end of the carnival season, which once began on Epiphany but is now usually celebrated the last three days before Lent. In France, the day is known as Mardi Gras (Fat Tuesday), and Mardi Gras celebrations are also held in several American cities, particularly in New Orleans. The day is sometimes called Pancake Tuesday by the English because fats, which were prohibited during Lent, had to be used up.

Ash Wednesday, Feb. 13. The first day of the Lenten season, which lasts 40 days. Having its origin sometime before A.D. 1000, it is a day of public penance and is marked in the Roman Catholic Church by the burning of the palms blessed on the previous year's Palm Sunday. With his thumb, the priest then marks a cross upon the forehead of each worshipper. The Anglican Church and a few Protestant groups in the United States also observe the day, but generally without the use of ashes.

Purim (Feast of Lots), Thursday, Feb. 28. A day of joy and feasting celebrating deliverance of the Jews from a massacre planned by the Persian Minister Haman. The Jewish Queen Esther interceded with her husband, King Ahasuerus, to spare the life of her uncle, Mordecai, and Haman was hanged on the same gallows he had built for Mordecai. The holiday is marked by the reading of the Book of Esther (megillah), and by the exchange of gifts, donations to the poor, and the presentation of Purim plays.

St. Patrick's Day, Sunday, March 17. St. Patrick, patron saint of Ireland, has been honored in America since the first days of the nation. There are many dinners and meetings but perhaps the most-notable part of the observance is the annual St. Patrick's Day parade on Fifth Avenue in New York City.

Palm Sunday, March 24. Is observed the Sunday

before Easter to commemorate the entry of Jesus into Jerusalem. The procession and the ceremonies introducing the benediction of palms probably had their origin in Jerusalem.

Good Friday, March 29. This day commemorates the Crucifixion, which is retold during services from the Gospel according to St. John. A feature in Roman Catholic churches is the Liturgy of the Passion; there is no Consecration, the Host having been consecrated the previous day. The eating of hot cross buns on this day is said to have started in England.

First Day of Passover (Pesach), Saturday, March 30. The Feast of the Passover, also called the Feast of Unleavened Bread, commemorates the escape of the Jews from Egypt. As the Jews fled they ate unleavened bread, and from that time the Jews have allowed no leavening in the houses during Passover, bread being replaced by matzoh.

Easter Sunday, March 31. Observed in all Christian churches, Easter commemorates the Resurrection of Jesus. It is celebrated on the first Sunday after the full moon which occurs on or next after March 21 and is therefore celebrated between March 22 and April 25 inclusive. This date was fixed by the Council of Nicaea in A.D. 325. The Orthodox Church celebrates Easter on April 15, 1990.

Ascension Day, Thursday, May 9. Took place in the presence of His apostles 40 days after the Resurrection of Jesus. It is traditionally held to have occurred on Mount Olivet in Bethany.

Mother's Day, Sunday, May 12. Observed the second Sunday in May, as proposed by Anna Jarvis of Philadelphia in 1907.

First Day of Shavuot (Hebrew Pentecost), Sunday, May 19. This festival, sometimes called the Feast of Weeks, or of Harvest, or of the First Fruits, falls 50 days after Passover and originally celebrated the end of the seven-week grain harvesting season. In later tradition, it also celebrated the giving of the Law to Moses on Mount Sinai.

Pentecost (Whitsunday), Sunday, May 19. This day commemorates the descent of the Holy Ghost upon the apostles 50 days after the Resurrection. The sermon by the Apostle Peter, which led to the baptism of 3,000 who professed belief, originated the ceremonies that have since been followed. "Whitsunday" is believed to have come from "white Sunday" when, among the English, white robes were worn by those baptized on the day.

Memorial Day, Thursday, May 30. Also known as Decoration Day, Memorial Day is a legal holiday in most of the states and in the territories, and is also observed by the armed forces. In 1868, Gen. John A. Logan, Commander in Chief of the Grand Army of the Republic, issued an order designating the day as one in which the graves of soldiers would be decorated. The holiday was originally devoted to honoring the memory of those who fell in the Civil War, but is now also dedicated to the memory of all war dead.

Flag Day, Friday, June 14. This day commemorates the adoption by the Continental Congress on June 14, 1777, of the Stars and Stripes as the U.S. flag. Although it is a legal holiday only in Pennsylvania,

President Truman, on Aug. 3, 1949, signed a bill requesting the President to call for its observance each year by proclamation.

Father's Day, Sunday, June 16. Observed the third Sunday in June. First celebrated June 19, 1910.

Independence Day, Thursday, July 4. The day of the adoption of the Declaration of Independence in 1776, celebrated in all states and territories. The observance began the next year in Philadelphia.

Labor Day, Monday, Sept. 2. Observed the first Monday in September in all states and territories, Labor Day was first celebrated in New York in 1882 under the sponsorship of the Central Labor Union, following the suggestion of Peter J. McGuire, of the Knights of Labor, that the day be set aside in honor of labor.

First Day of Rosh Hashana (Jewish New Year), Monday, Sept. 9. This day marks the beginning of the Jewish year 5752 and opens the Ten Days of Penitence closing with Yom Kippur.

Yom Kippur (Day of Atonement), Wednesday, Sept. 18. This day marks the end of the Ten Days of Penitence that began with Rosh Hashana. It is described in *Leviticus* as a "Sabbath of rest," and synagogue services begin the preceding sundown, resume the following morning, and continue to sundown.

First Day of Sukkot (Feast of Tabernacles) Monday, Sept. 23. This festival, also known as the Feast of the Ingathering, originally celebrated the fruit harvest, and the name comes from the booths or tabernacles in which the Jews lived during the harvest, although one tradition traces it to the shelters used by the Jews in their wandering through the wilderness. During the festival many Jews build small huts in their back yards or on the roofs of their houses.

Simhat Torah (Rejoicing of the Law), Tuesday, Oct. 1. This joyous holiday falls on the eighth day of Sukkot. It marks the end of the year's reading of the Torah (Five Books of Moses) in the synagogue every Saturday and the beginning of the new cycle of reading.

Columbus Day, Saturday, Oct. 12. A legal holiday in many states, commemorating the discovery of America by Columbus in 1492. Quite likely the first celebration of Columbus Day was that organized in 1792 by the Society of St. Tammany, or Columbian Order, widely known as Tammany Hall.

United Nations Day, Thursday, Oct. 24. Marking the founding of the United Nations.

Halloween, Thursday, Oct. 31. Eve of All Saints' Day, formerly called All Hallows and Hallowmass. Halloween is traditionally associated in some countries with old customs such as bonfires, masquerading, and the telling of ghost stories. These are old Celtic practices marking the beginning of winter.

All Saints' Day, Friday, Nov. 1. A Roman Catholic and Anglican holiday celebrating all saints, known and unknown.

Election Day, (legal holiday in certain states), Tuesday, Nov. 5. Since 1845, by Act of Congress, the first Tuesday after the first Monday in November is the date for choosing Presidential electors. State elections are also generally held on this day.

Veterans Day, Monday, Nov. 11. Armistice Day was established in 1926 to commemorate the signing in 1918 of the Armistice ending World War I. On June 1, 1954, the name was changed to Veterans Day to honor all men and women who have served America in its armed forces.

Thanksgiving, Thursday, Nov. 28. Observed nationally on the fourth Thursday in November by Act of Congress (1941), the first such national proclamation having been issued by President Lincoln in 1863, on the urging of Mrs. Sarah J. Hale, editor of *Godey's Lady's Book.* Most Americans believe that the holiday dates back to the day of thanks ordered by Governor Bradford of Plymouth Colony in New England in 1621, but scholars point out that days of thanks stem from ancient times.

First Sunday of Advent, Dec. 1. Advent is the season in which the faithful must prepare themselves for the advent of the Saviour on Christmas. The four Sundays before Christmas are marked by special church services.

First Day of Hanukkah (Festival of Lights), Monday, Dec. 2. This festival was instituted by Judas Maccabaeus in 165 B.C. to celebrate the purification of the Temple of Jerusalem, which had been desecrated three years earlier by Antiochus Epiphanes, who set up a pagan altar and offered sacrifices to Zeus Olympius. In Jewish homes, a light is lighted on each night of the eight-day festival.

Christmas (Feast of the Nativity), Wednesday, Dec. 25. The most widely celebrated holiday of the Christian year, Christmas is observed as the anniversary of the birth of Jesus. Christmas customs are centuries old. The mistletoe, for example, comes from the Druids, who, in hanging the mistletoe, hoped for peace and good fortune. Use of such plants as holly comes from the ancient belief that such plants blossomed at Christmas. Comparatively recent is the Christmas tree, first set up in Germany in the 17th century, and the use of candles on trees developed from the belief that candles appeared by miracle on the trees at Christmas. Colonial Manhattan Islanders introduced the name Santa Claus, a corruption of the Dutch name for the 4th-century Asia Minor St. Nicholas.

State Observances

January 6, Three Kings' Day: Puerto Rico.
January 8, Battle of New Orleans Day: Louisiana.
January 11, De Hostos' Birthday: Puerto Rico.
January 19, Robert E. Lee's Birthday: Arkansas, Florida, Kentucky, Louisiana, South Carolina, **(third Monday)** Alabama, Mississippi.
January 19, Confederate Heroes Day: Texas.
January (third Monday): Lee-Jackson-King Day: Virginia.
January 30, F.D.Roosevelt's Birthday: Kentucky.
February 15, Susan B. Anthony's Birthday: Florida, Minnesota.
March (first Tuesday), Town Meeting Day: Vermont.
March 2, Texas Independence Day: Texas.
March (first Monday), Casimir Pulaski's Birthday: Illinois.
March 17, Evacuation Day: Massachusetts (in Suffolk County).
March 20 (First Day of Spring), Youth Day: Oklahoma.
March 22, Abolition Day: Puerto Rico.
March 25, Maryland Day: Maryland.
March 26, Prince Jonah Kuhio Kalanianaole Day: Hawaii.
March (last Monday), Seward's Day: Alaska.
April 2, Pascua Florida Day: Florida
April 13, Thomas Jefferson's Birthday: Alabama, Oklahoma.
April 16, De Diego's Birthday: Puerto Rico.
April (third Monday), Patriots' Day: Maine, Massachusetts.
April 21, San Jacinto Day: Texas.
April 22, Arbor Day: Nebraska.
April 22, Oklahoma Day: Oklahoma.
April 26, Confederate Memorial Day: Florida, Georgia.
April (fourth Monday), Fast Day: New Hampshire.
April (last Monday), Confederate Memorial Day: Alabama, Mississippi.
May 1, Bird Day: Oklahoma.
May 8, Truman Day: Missouri.
May 11, Minnesota Day: Minnesota.

May 20, Mecklenburg Independence Day: North Carolina.
June (first Monday), Jefferson Davis's Birthday: Alabama, Mississippi.
June 3, Jefferson Davis's Birthday: Florida, South Carolina.
June 3, Confederate Memorial Day: Kentucky, Louisiana.
June 9, Senior Citizens Day: Oklahoma.
June 11, King Kamehameha I Day: Hawaii.
June 15, Separation Day: Delaware.
June 17, Bunker Hill Day: Massachusetts (in Suffolk County).
June 19, Emancipation Day: Texas.
June 20, West Virginia Day: West Virginia.
July 17, Muñoz Rivera's Birthday: Puerto Rico.
July 24, Pioneer Day: Utah.
July 25, Constitution Day: Puerto Rico.
July 27, Barbosa's Birthday: Puerto Rico.
August (first Sunday), American Family Day: Arizona.
August (first Monday), Colorado Day: Colorado.
August (second Monday), Victory Day: Rhode Island.
August 16, Bennington Battle Day: Vermont.
August (third Friday), Admission Day: Hawaii.
August 27, Lyndon B. Johnson's Birthday: Texas.
August 30, Huey P. Long Day: Louisiana.
September 9, Admission Day: California.
September 12, Defenders' Day: Maryland.
September 16, Cherokee Strip Day: Oklahoma.
September (first Saturday after full moon), Indian Day: Oklahoma.
October 10, Leif Erickson Day: Minnesota.
October 10, Oklahoma Historical Day: Oklahoma.
October 18, Alaska Day: Alaska.
October 31, Nevada Day: Nevada.
November 4, Will Rogers Day: Oklahoma.
November (week of the 16th), Oklahoma Heritage Week: Oklahoma.
November 19, Discovery Day: Puerto Rico.
December 7, Delaware Day: Delaware.

Movable Holidays, 1991–1994

CHRISTIAN AND SECULAR

Year	Ash Wednesday	Easter	Pentecost	Labor Day	Election Day	Thanksgiving	1st Sun. Advent
1991	Feb. 13	March 31	May 19	Sept. 2	Nov. 5	Nov. 28	Dec. 1
1992	March 4	April 19	June 7	Sept. 7	Nov. 3	Nov. 26	Nov. 29
1993	Feb. 24	April 11	May 30	Sept. 6	Nov. 2	Nov. 25	Nov. 28
1994	Feb. 16	April 3	May 22	Sept. 5	Nov. 8	Nov. 24	Nov. 27

Shrove Tuesday: 1 day before Ash Wednesday
Palm Sunday: 7 days before Easter
Maundy Thursday: 3 days before Easter
Good Friday: 2 days before Easter

Holy Saturday: 1 day before Easter
Ascension Day: 10 days before Pentecost
Trinity Sunday: 7 days after Pentecost
Corpus Christi: 11 days after Pentecost

NOTE: Easter is celebrated on April 7, 1991, by the Orthodox Church.

JEWISH

Year	Purim[1]	1st day Passover[2]	1st day Shavuot[3]	1st day Rosh Hashana[4]	Yom Kippur[5]	1st day Sukkot[6]	Simhat Torah[7]	1st day Hanukkah[8]
1991	Feb. 28	March 30	May 19	Sept. 9	Sept. 18	Sept. 23	Oct. 1	Dec. 2
1992	March 19	April 18	June 7	Sept. 28	Oct. 7	Oct. 12	Oct. 20	Dec. 20
1993	March 7	April 6	May 26	Sept. 16	Sept. 25	Sept. 30	Oct. 8	Dec. 9
1994	Feb. 25	March 27	May 16	Sept. 6	Sept. 15	Sept. 20	Sept. 28	Nov. 28

1. Feast of Lots. 2. Feast of Unleavened Bread. 3. Hebrew Pentecost; or Feast of Weeks, or of Harvest, or of First Fruits. 4. Jewish New Year. 5. Day of Atonement. 6. Feast of Tabernacles, or of the Ingathering. 7. Rejoicing of the Law. 8. Festival of Lights.

Length of Jewish holidays (O=Orthodox, C=Conservative, R=Reform):

Passover: O & C, 8 days (holy days: first 2 and last 2); R, 7 days (holy days: first and last)
Shavuot: O & C, 2 days; R, 1 day
Rosh Hashana: O & C, 2 days; R, 1 day.
Yom Kippur: All groups, 1 day

Sukkot: All groups, 7 days (holy days: O & C, first 2; R, first only)
O & C observe two additional days: Shemini Atseret (Eighth Day of the Feast) and Simhat Torah. R observes Shemini Atseret but not Simhat Torah
Hanukkah: All groups, 8 days

NOTE: All holidays begin at sundown on the evening before the date given.

Islamic 1991

March 18	First day of the month of Ramadan	
April 17	'Id al Fitr (Festival of end of Ramadan)	
July 5	'Id al-Adha (Festival of Sacrifice at time of annual pilgrimage to Mecca)	

July 13 First day of month of Muharram (beginning of liturgical year)
Sept. 22 Mawlid al-Nabi (Anniversary of Prophet Mohammed's birthday)

NOTE: All holidays begin at sundown on the evening before the date given.

Chinese Calendar

The Chinese lunar year is divided into 12 months of 29 or 30 days. The calendar is adjusted to the length of the solar year by the addition of extra months at regular intervals.

The years are arranged in major cycles of 60 years. Each successive year is named after one of 12 animals. These 12-year cycles are continuously repeated. The Chinese New Year is celebrated at the first new moon after the sun enters Aquarius—sometime between Jan. 21 and Feb. 19.

Rat	Ox	Tiger	Cat (Rabbit)	Dragon	Snake	Horse	Sheep (Goat)	Monkey	Rooster	Dog	Pig
1864	1865	1866	1867	1868	1869	1870	1871	1872	1873	1874	1875
1876	1877	1878	1879	1880	1881	1882	1883	1884	1885	1886	1887
1888	1889	1890	1891	1892	1893	1894	1895	1896	1897	1898	1899
1900	1901	1902	1903	1904	1905	1906	1907	1908	1909	1910	1911
1912	1913	1914	1915	1916	1917	1918	1919	1920	1921	1922	1923
1924	1925	1926	1927	1928	1929	1930	1931	1932	1933	1934	1935
1936	1937	1938	1939	1940	1941	1942	1943	1944	1945	1946	1947
1948	1949	1950	1951	1952	1953	1954	1955	1956	1957	1958	1959
1960	1961	1962	1963	1964	1965	1966	1967	1968	1969	1970	1971
1972	1973	1974	1975	1976	1977	1978	1979	1980	1981	1982	1983
1984	1985	1986	1987	1988	1989	1990	1991	1992	1993	1994	1995

National Holidays Around the World, 1991

Country	Date	Country	Date	Country	Date
Afghanistan	April 27	Ghana	March 6	Papua New Guinea	Sept. 16
Albania	Nov. 29	Greece	March 25	Paraguay	May 14
Algeria	Nov. 1	Grenada	Feb. 7	Peru	July 28
Angola	Nov. 11	Guatemala	Sept. 15	Philippines	June 12
Antigua and Barbuda	Nov. 1	Guinea	Oct. 2	Poland	July 22
Argentina	May 25	Guinea-Bissau	Sept. 24	Portugal	June 10
Australia	Jan. 26	Guyana	Feb. 23	Qatar	Sept. 3
Austria	Oct. 26	Haiti	Jan. 1	Romania	Aug. 23
Bahamas	July 10	Honduras	Sept. 15	Rwanda	July 1
Bahrain	Dec. 16	Hungary	April 4	St. Kitts and Nevis	Sept. 19
Bangladesh	March 26	Iceland	June 17	St. Lucia	Feb. 22
Barbados	Nov. 30	India	Jan. 26	St. Vincent and	
Belgium	July 21	Indonesia	Aug. 17	the Grenadines	Oct. 27
Belize	Sept. 21	Iran	Feb. 11	São Tomé and Príncipe	July 12
Benin	Nov. 30	Iraq	July 17	Saudi Arabia	Sept. 23
Bhutan	Dec. 17	Ireland	March 17	Senegal	April 4
Bolivia	Aug. 6	Israel	April 18[1]	Seychelles	June 5
Botswana	Sept. 30	Italy	June 2	Sierra Leone	April 27
Brazil	Sept. 7	Ivory Coast	Dec. 7	Singapore	Aug. 9
Brunei	Feb. 23	Jamaica	Aug. 5[2]	Solomon Islands	July 7
Bulgaria	Sept. 9	Japan	April 29	Somalia	Oct. 21
Burkina Faso	Aug. 4	Jordan	May 25	South Africa	May 31
Burundi	July 1	Kenya	Dec. 12	Spain	Oct. 12
Cambodia	April 17	Kuwait	Feb. 25	Sri Lanka	Feb. 4
Cameroon	May 20	Laos	Dec. 2	Sudan	Jan. 1
Canada	July 1	Lebanon	Nov. 22	Suriname	Nov. 25
Cape Verde	Sept. 12	Lesotho	Oct. 4	Swaziland	Sept. 6
Central African Republic	Dec. 1	Liberia	July 26	Sweden	June 6
Chad	June 7	Libya	Sept. 1	Switzerland	Aug. 1
Chile	Sept. 18	Luxembourg	June 23	Syria	April 17
China	Oct. 1	Madagascar	June 26	Tanzania	April 26
Colombia	July 20	Malawi	July 6	Thailand	Dec. 5
Comoros	July 6	Malaysia	Aug. 31	Togo	April 27
Congo	Aug. 15	Maldives	July 26	Trinidad and Tobago	Aug. 31
Costa Rica	Sept. 15	Mali	Sept. 22	Tunisia	June 1
Cuba	Jan. 1	Malta	March 31	Turkey	Oct. 29
Cyprus	Oct. 1	Mauritania	Nov. 28	Uganda	Oct. 9
Czechoslovakia	May 9	Mauritius	March 12	U.S.S.R.	Nov. 7
Denmark	April 16	Mexico	Sept. 16	United Arab Emirates	Dec. 2
Djibouti	June 27	Mongolia	July 11	United Kingdom	June 8[3]
Dominica	Nov. 3	Morocco	March 3	United States	July 4
Dominican Republic	Feb. 27	Mozambique	June 25	Uruguay	Aug. 25
Ecuador	Aug. 10	Myanmar	Jan. 4	Vanuatu	July 30
Egypt	July 23	Nepal	Dec. 28	Venezuela	July 5
El Salvador	Sept. 15	Netherlands	April 30	Viet Nam	Sept. 2
Equatorial Guinea	Oct. 12	New Zealand	Feb. 6	Western Samoa	June 1
Ethiopia	Sept. 12	Nicaragua	Sept. 15	Yemen, People's Dem.	
Fiji	Oct. 10	Niger	Dec. 18	Republic of	Oct. 14[4]
Finland	Dec. 6	Nigeria	Oct. 1	Yemen Arab Republic	Sept. 26[4]
France	July 14	Norway	May 17	Yugoslavia	Nov. 29
Gabon	Aug. 17	Oman	Nov. 18	Zaire	June 30
Gambia	Feb. 18	Pakistan	March 23	Zambia	Oct. 24
Germany, East	Oct. 7	Panama	Nov. 3	Zimbabwe	April 18

1. Changes yearly according to Hebrew calendar. 2. Celebrated on first Monday in August. 3. Celebrated the second Saturday in June. 4. Celebrated prior to unification in May 1990. *Source:* United Nations.

The Basic Unit of the World Calendar

Days	First month					Second month					Third month				
Sunday	1	8	15	22	29	—	5	12	19	26	—	3	10	17	24
Monday	2	9	16	23	30	—	6	13	20	27	—	4	11	18	25
Tuesday	3	10	17	24	31	—	7	14	21	28	—	5	12	19	26
Wednesday	4	11	18	25	—	1	8	15	22	29	—	6	13	20	27
Thursday	5	12	19	26	—	2	9	16	23	30	—	7	14	21	28
Friday	6	13	20	27	—	3	10	17	24	—	1	8	15	22	29
Saturday	7	14	21	28	—	4	11	18	25	—	2	9	16	23	30

CONSUMER'S RESOURCE GUIDE

Telemarketing Travel Fraud

Source: the Federal Trade Commission

Have you ever been tempted to buy one of those bargain-priced travel packages sold over the telephone? Be careful. Your dream adventure may be a misadventure if you fall victim to one of the travel scams sold over the phone. While some of these travel opportunities are legitimate, many of them are scam operations that are defrauding consumers out of millions of dollars each month.

How the Scams Work

These schemes take many forms. Increasingly common is one that involves travel clubs. A consumer pays a membership fee from $50 to $400 to receive a travel package that includes round-trip air transportation for one person and lodging for two people for a week in Hawaii, London, or another vacation place. The catch? You must purchase a high-priced, round-trip ticket for the second person from the fraudulent travel operation. You may wind up paying two to three times what it would cost if you purchased your own tickets in advance or through an airline or reputable travel agency. Another scam starts by sending you a postcard stating: "You have been specially selected to receive a free trip." The postcard instructs you to call a phone number, usually toll-free, for details about your trip. Once you call, you are told you must join their travel club to be eligible for the free trip. Sometimes, a credit card number is requested so that your account can be billed for the membership fee. Only after you join are you sent the vacation package with instructions on requesting reservations for your "prepaid trip." Usually, your reservation request must be accompanied by yet another fee. The catch here? New charges are being added at every step along the way. And, you never get your "free" trip because your reservations are not confirmed or you must comply with hard-to-meet hidden or expensive "conditions."

Telemarketing travel scams usually originate out of "boiler rooms." Skilled salespeople, often with years of experience selling dubious products and services over the phone, pitch travel packages that may sound legitimate, but often are not. These sales pitches usually have the following in common:

● **Oral Misrepresentations.** Whatever the particular scheme may be, telephone salespeople are likely to promise you a "deal" they cannot deliver. Unfortunately, you often do not realize this until after you have paid your money.

● **High Pressure/Time Pressure Tactics.** These scam operators are likely to tell you that they need your commitment to buy right away or that this special offer will not be available tomorrow. Often, they will brush aside your questions with vague answers.

● **"Affordable" Offers.** Unlike telephone fraud operators who try to persuade people to spend thousands of dollars on a particular investment scheme, travel scam operators usually pitch their offers in the $50 to $400 range. Because this amount is often in the price range of those planning vacations, the fraudulent scheme may appear to be a reasonably-priced package.

● **Contradictory Follow-up Material.** Some firms may agree to send you written confirmation of the deal. You usually will find, however, that the literature bears little resemblance to the offer you accepted. Often, the written materials will disclose additional terms, conditions, and costs.

How to Protect Yourself

No one wants unpleasant surprises on a vacation. Therefore, it pays to thoroughly investigate a travel package *before* you commit to a purchase. While it is sometimes difficult to tell a legitimate sales pitch from a fraudulent one, there are some things you can do to protect yourself.

● **Be wary of "great deals."** One tip-off to a scam is that the offer is very low-priced. Few legitimate businesses can afford to give away things of real value or to undercut substantially everyone else's price.

● **Do not be pressured into buying—NOW.** Generally, a good offer today will remain a good offer tomorrow. Legitimate businesses do not expect you to make an instant decision.

● **Ask detailed questions.** Find out exactly what the price covers—and does not cover. Ask if there are any additional charges later. Find out the names of the specific hotels, airports, airlines, and restaurants that your package includes. You may wish to contact these places yourself to double-check arrangements. Find out exact dates and times. Ask about cancellation policies and refunds. If the salesperson cannot give you detailed answers to these questions, this is not the deal for you.

● **Get all information in writing before you agree to buy.** Before purchasing a travel package, ask for detailed written information. Once you receive the information, make sure the written material confirms everything you were told by phone.

● **Do not give your credit card number over the phone.** One easy way for a scam operator to close a deal is to get your credit card number and then charge your account. Sometimes scam operators say they need the number for verification purposes only. Never give your credit or charge card numbers—or any other personal information (such as bank account numbers)—to unsolicited telephone salespeople.

● **Do not send money by messenger or overnight mail.** Instead of asking for your credit card number, some scam operators may ask you to send a check or money order right away—or offer to send a messenger to pick these up. If you use money rather than a credit card in the transaction, you lose your right to dispute fraudulent charges under the Fair Credit Billing Act. (*See* section entitled "What To Do If You Have Problems.")

● **Check out the company.** Before purchasing any travel package, check first with various government and private organizations to see if any complaints have been lodged against the travel firm calling you. A list of some of these organizations is included at the end of this brochure. Be aware, however, that fraudulent firms change their names frequently to avoid detection.

● **If in doubt, say "no."** Sometimes an offer appears legitimate, but you still have doubts. In that case, it is usually better to turn down the offer and hang up the phone. Remember, if something goes wrong, the likelihood of your receiving all your money back is very slim.

What To Do If You Have Problems

If you have problems with a travel package, try resolving your disputes first with the company that sold you the package. If you are not satisfied, try contacting your local consumer protection agency, Better Business Bureau, or state Attorney General.

In addition, you may want to write to the American Society of Travel Agents (ASTA) at P.O. Box 23992, Washington, D.C. 20026-3992, which may be able to mediate your dispute. Or, write to the Federal Trade Commission at 6th and Pennsylvania Avenue, N.W., Washington, D.C. 20580. Although the FTC does not generally intervene in individual disputes, the information you provide may indicate a pattern of possible law violations requiring action by the Commission.

If you charged your trip to a credit card, you may dispute the charges by writing to your credit card issuer at the address provided for billing disputes. Try to do this as soon as you receive your statement, but no later than 60 days after the bill's statement date. Under some circumstances under the Fair Credit Billing Act, your credit card issuer may have to absorb the charges if the seller does not resolve your dispute. If you did not authorize the charge, you are not responsible for its payment. ☐

Copyrights

Source: Library of Congress, Copyright Office.

U.S. is Now a Member of the Berne Union

On March 1, 1989, the United States joined the Berne Union by entering into an international treaty called the Berne Convention, whose full title is the Berne Convention for the Protection of Literary and Artistic Works. Also on that date, amendments to the U.S. copyright law that satisfy U.S. treaty obligations under the Convention took effect and some of them are listed herein. Contact the U.S. copyright office for details of Berne Convention obligations.

The U.S. Law continues to govern the protection and registration of works in the United States.

Beginning March 1, 1989, copyright in the works of U.S. authors is protected automatically in all member nations of the Berne Union and the works of foreign authors who are nationals of a Berne Union country, and works first published in a Berne Union country are automatically protected in the United States.

In order to fulfill its Berne Convention obligations, the United States made certain changes in its copyright law by passing the Berne Convention Implementation Act of 1988. These changes are not retroactive and are effective only on and after March 1, 1989.

The copyright law (Title 17 of the United States Code) was amended by the enactment of a statute for its general revision, Public Law 94–553 (90 Stat. 2541), which was signed by the President on October 19, 1976. The new law superseded the copyright act of 1909, as amended, which remained effective until the new enactment took effect on January 1, 1978.

Under the new law, all copyrightable works, whether published or unpublished, are subject to a single system of statutory protection which gives a copyright owner the exclusive right to reproduce the copyrighted work in copies or phonorecords and distribute them to the public by sale, rental, lease, or lending. Among the other rights given to

the owner of a copyright are the exclusive rights to prepare derivative works based upon the copyrighted work, to perform the work publicly if it be literary, musical, dramatic, choreographic, a pantomime, motion picture, or other audiovisual work, and in the case of literary, musical, dramatic, and choreographic works, pantomimes, and pictorial, graphic, or sculptural works, including the individual images of a motion picture or other audiovisual work, to display the copyrighted work publicly. All of these rights are subject to certain exceptions, including the principle of "fair use" which the new statute specifically recognizes.

Special provisions are included which permit compulsory licensing for the recording of musical compositions, noncommercial transmissions by public broadcasters of published musical and graphic works, performances of copyrighted music by jukeboxes, and the secondary transmission of copyrighted works on cable television systems.

Copyright protection under the new law extends to original works of authorship fixed in any tangible medium of expression, now known or later developed, from which they can be perceived, reproduced, or otherwise communicated, either directly or with the aid of a machine or device. Works of authorship include books, periodicals and other literary works, musical compositions with accompanying lyrics, dramas and dramatico-musical compositions, pantomimes and choreographic works, motion pictures and other audiovisual works, and sound recordings.

As a mandatory condition of copyright protection under the law in effect before 1978, all published copies of a work were required to bear a copyright notice. The 1976 Act provides for a notice on published copies, but omission or errors will not immediately result in forfeiture of the copyright, and can be corrected within certain time limits. Innocent infringers misled by the omission or error will be shielded from liability.

In accordance with the Berne agreement, mandatory notice of copyright has been abolished for works published for the first time on or after March

1, 1989. Failure to place a notice of copyright on copies or phonorecords of such works can no longer result in the loss of copyright.

Voluntary use of notice is encouraged. Placing a notice of copyright on published works is still strongly recommended. One of the benefits is that an infringer will not be able to claim that he or she "innocently infringed" a work. (A successful innocent infringement claim may result in a reduction in damages for infringement that the copyright owner would otherwise receive.)

A sample notice of copyright is: © 1991 John Brown.

The notice requirement for works incorporating a predominant portion of U.S. government work has been eliminated as of March 1, 1989. For these works to receive the evidentiary benefit of voluntary notice, in addition to the notice, a statement is required on the copies identifying what is copyrighted.

A sample is: © 1991 Jane Brown. Copyright claimed in Chapters 7-10, exclusive of U.S. government maps.

Notice Unchanged for Works Published Before March 1, 1989

The Berne Convention Implementation Act is not retroactive. Thus, the notice requirements that were in place before March 1, 1989, govern all works first published during that period (regardless of national origin).

● Works first published between January 1, 1978, and February 28, 1989: If a work was first published without notice during this period, it is still necessary to register the work before or within five years after publication and add the notice to copies distributed in the United States after discovery of the omission.

● Works first published before January 1, 1978: If a work was first published without the required notice before 1978, copyright was lost immediately (except for works seeking "ad interim" protection). Once copyright is lost, it can never be restored in the United States, except by special legislation.

Registration in the Copyright Office is not a condition of copyright protection but will be a prerequisite to bringing an action in a court of law for infringement. With certain exceptions, the remedies of statutory damages and attorney's fees will not be available for infringements occurring before registration. Copies or phonorecords published in the United States with notice of copyright are required to be deposited for the collections of the Library of Congress, not as a condition of copyright protection, but under provisions of the law subjecting the copyright owner to certain penalties for failure to deposit after a demand by the Register of Copyrights. Registration is permissive, but may be made either at the time the depository requirements are satisfied or at any other time during the subsistence of the copyright.

For works already under statutory protection, the new law retains the present term of copyright of 28 years from first publication (or from registration in some cases), renewable by certain persons for a second period of protection, but it increases the length of the second period to 47 years. Copyrights in their first term on January 1, 1978, must still be renewed during the last (28th) year of the original copyright term to receive the maximum statutory term of 75 years (a first term of 28 years plus a renewal term of 47 years).

Copyrights in their second term on January 1, 1978, are automatically extended up to a maximum of 75 years, without the need for further renewal. Unpublished works that are already in existence on January 1, 1978, but are not protected by statutory copyright and have not yet gone into the public domain, will generally obtain automatic Federal copyright protection for the author's life, plus an additional 50 years after the author's death, but in any event, for a minimal term of 25 years (that is, until December 31, 2002), and if the work is published before that date, then for an additional term of 25 years, through the end of 2027.

For works created on or after January 1, 1978, the new law provides a term lasting for the author's life, plus an additional 50 years after the author's death. For works made for hire, and for anonymous and pseudonymous works (unless the author's identity is revealed in Copyright Office records), the new term will be 75 years from publication or 100 years from creation, whichever is shorter. The new law provides that all terms of copyright will run through the end of the calendar year in which they would otherwise expire. This will not only affect the duration of copyrights, but also the time-limits for renewal registrations.

Works already in the public domain cannot be protected under the new law. The 1976 Act provides no procedure for restoring protection to works in which copyright has been lost for any reason. In general, works published before January 1, 1914, are not under copyright protection in the United States, at least insofar as any version published before that date is concerned.

The new law requires that all visually perceptible copies published in the United States or elsewhere bear a notice of copyright affixed in such manner and location as to give reasonable notice of the claim of copyright. (Abolished in or after March 1, 1989, according to the Berne agreement) The notice consists of the symbol © (the letter C in a circle), the word "Copyright," or the abbreviation "Copr.," and the year of first publication of the work, and the name of the owner of copyright in the work. EXAMPLE: © *1991 John Doe.*

The notice of copyright prescribed for sound recordings consists of the symbol ℗ (the letter P in a circle), the year of first publication of the sound recording, and the name of the owner of copyright in the sound recording, placed on the surface of the phonorecord, or on the phonorecord label or container, in such manner and location as to give reasonable notice of the claim of copyright. EXAMPLE: ℗ *1991 Doe Records, Inc.*

According to the Berne Agreement, copyright owners must deposit in the Copyright Office two complete copies or phonorecords of the best edition of all works subject to copyright that are publicly distributed in the United States, whether or not the work contains a notice of copyright. In general, this deposit requirement may be satisfied by registration. For more information about mandatory deposit, request Circular 7d.

Renewal Is Still Required

Works first federally copyrighted before 1978 must still be renewed in the 28th year in order to receive the second term of 47 years. If such a work is not timely renewed, it will fall into the public domain in the United States at the end of the 28th year.

Recordation

Recordation as a Prerequisite to an Infringement Suit. The copyright owner no longer has to record a transfer before bringing a copyright lawsuit in that owner's name.

Benefits of recordation. The benefits of recordation in the Copyright Office are unchanged:

● Under certain conditions, recordation establishes priorities between conflicting transfers and nonexclusive licenses;

● Under certain conditions, recordation establishes priority between conflicting transfers; and,

● Recordation establishes a public record of the contents of the transfer or document.

Jukebox Licenses

Section 116 of the 1976 Copyright Act provides for a compulsory license to publicly perform non-dramatic musical works by means of coin-operated phonorecord players (jukeboxes). The Berne Convention Implementation Act amends the law to provide for negotiated licenses between the user (the jukebox operator) and the copyright owner. If necessary, the parties are encouraged to submit to arbitration to facilitate negotiated licenses. Such licenses take precedence over the compulsory license.

For detailed information about the admendments to U.S. copyright law under the Berne Convention agreement, request circulars 93, "Highlights of U.S. Adherence to the Berne Convention," and 93a, "The United States Joins The Berne Union" from the Copyright Office.

For publications, call the Forms and Publications Hotline, 202-707-9100, or write:
Copyright Office
Publications Section, LM-455
Library of Congress
Washington, D.C. 20559

To speak with an information specialist or to request further information, call 202-479-0700, or write:
Copyright Office
Information Section, LM-401
Library of Congress
Washington, D.C. 20559

Counterfeit Products

Source: U.S. Office of Consumer Affairs.

Counterfeit products include any product bearing an unauthorized representation of a manufacturer's trademark or trade name. Examples of products which have been counterfeited include prescription and over-the-counter drugs, clothing, credit cards, watches, pacemakers, and machine and automobile replacement parts. Because counterfeit products are often of sub-standard quality, there are potential safety risks which may cause personal injury as well as economic loss.

Avoiding counterfeit products takes practice. The following are usually associated with counterfeit products:

● incorrect, smeared or blurred product packaging
● incorrect spelling of brand name
● no warranty or guarantee available
● "unbelievably" low prices

Unemployment Insurance

Unemployment insurance is managed jointly by the states and the federal government. Most states began paying benefits in 1938 and 1939.

Under What Conditions Can the Worker Collect?

The laws vary from state to state. In general, a waiting period of one week is required after a claim is filed before collecting unemployment insurance; the worker must be able to work, must not have quit without good cause or have been discharged for misconduct; he must not be involved in a labor dispute; above all, he must be ready and willing to work. He may be disqualified if he refuses, without good cause, to accept a job which is suitable for him in terms of his qualifications and experience, unless the wages, hours and working conditions offered are substantially less favorable than those prevailing for similar jobs in the community.

The unemployed worker must go to the local state employment security office and register for work. If that office has a suitable opening available, he must accept it or lose his unemployment payments, unless he has good cause for the refusal. If a worker moves out of his own state, he can still collect at his new residence; the state in which he is now located will act as agent for the other state, which will pay his benefits.

Benefits are paid only to unemployed workers who have had at least a certain amount of recent

past employment or earnings in a job covered by the state law. The amount of employment or earnings, and the period used to measure them, vary from state to state, but the intent of the various laws is to limit benefits to workers whose recent records indicate that they are members of the labor force. The amount of benefits an unemployed worker may receive for any week is also determined by application to his past wages of a formula specified in the law. The general objective is to provide a weekly benefit which is about half the worker's customary weekly wages, up to a maximum set by the law (see table). In a majority of states, the total benefits a worker may receive in a 12-month period is limited to a fraction of his total wages in a prior 12-month period, as well as to a stated number of weeks. Thus, not all workers in a state are entitled to benefits for the number of weeks shown in the table.

Who Pays for the Insurance?

The total cost is borne by the employer in all but a few states. Each state has a sliding scale of rates. The standard rate is set at 6.2% of taxable payroll in most states. But employers with records of less unemployment (that is, with fewer unemployment benefits paid to their former workers) are rewarded with rates lower than the standard state rate.

During periods of high unemployment in a state,

federal-state extended benefits are available to workers who have exhausted their regular benefits. An unemployed worker may receive benefits equal to the weekly benefit he received under the state program for one half the weeks of his basic entitlement to benefits up to a maximum (including regular benefits) of 39 weeks.

Federal Programs

Amendments to the Social Security Act provided unemployment insurance for Federal civilian employees (1954) and for ex-servicemen (1958). Benefits under these programs are paid by state employment security agencies as agents of the federal government under agreements with the Secretary of Labor. For federal civilian employees, eligibility for benefits and the amount of benefits paid are determined according to the terms and conditions of the applicable state unemployment insurance law. Ex-servicemen are subject to specific eligibility and benefit payment provisions: benefits are not payable before the fifth week subsequent to the week of release or discharge from service and such benefits are limited to 13 weeks of duration.

State Unemployment Compensation Maximums, 1990

State	Weekly benefit[1]	Maximum duration, weeks	State	Weekly benefit[1]	Maximum duration, weeks
Alabama	150	26	Nebraska	134	26
Alaska	188–260	26	Nevada	194	26
Arizona	155	26	New Hampshire	162	26
Arkansas	215	26	New Jersey	279	26
California	190	26	New Mexico	170	26
Colorado	224	26	New York	245	26
Connecticut	252–302	26	North Carolina	236	26
Delaware	225	26	North Dakota	187	26
D.C.	293	26	Ohio	184–291	26
Florida	200	26	Oklahoma	197	26
Georgia	175	26	Oregon	238	26
Hawaii	256	26	Pennsylvania	280–288	26
Idaho	200	26	Puerto Rico	110	20
Illinois	199–260	26	Rhode Island	258–323	26
Indiana	96–161	26	South Carolina	165	26
Iowa	181–222	26	South Dakota	140	26
Kansas	216	26	Tennessee	160	26
Kentucky	186	26	Texas	217	26
Louisiana	181	26	Utah	214	26
Maine	180–270	26	Vermont	178	26
Maryland	205	26	Virgin Islands	163	26
Massachusetts	272–408	30	Virginia	176	26
Michigan	275	26	Washington	237	30
Minnesota	255	26	West Virginia	245	26
Mississippi	145	26	Wisconsin	225	26
Missouri	160	26	Wyoming	200	26
Montana	190	26			

1. Maximum amounts. When two amounts are shown, higher includes dependents' allowances. *Source:* Department of Labor, Employment and Training Administration.

Trademarks

Source: Department of Commerce, Patent and Trademark Office.

A trademark may be defined as a word, letter, device, or symbol, as well as some combination of these, which is used in connection with merchandise and which points distinctly to the origin of the goods.

Certificates of registration of trademarks are issued under the seal of the Patent and Trademark Office and may be registered by the owner if he is engaged in interstate or foreign commerce which may lawfully be regulated by Congress since any Federal jurisdiction over trademarks arises under the commerce clause of the Constitution. Effective November 16, 1989, applications to register may also be based on a "bona fide intention to use the mark in commerce." Trademarks may be registered by foreign owners who comply with our law, as well as by citizens of foreign countries with which the U.S. has treaties relating to trademarks. American citizens may register trademarks in for-

eign countries by complying with the laws of those countries. The right to registration and protection of trademarks in many foreign countries is guaranteed by treaties.

General jurisdiction in trademark cases involving Federal Registrations is given to Federal courts. Adverse decisions of examiners on applications for registration are appealable to the Trademark Trial and Appeal Board, whose affirmances, and decisions in *inter partes* proceedings, are subject to court review. Before adopting a trademark, a person should make a search of prior marks to avoid infringing unwittingly upon them.

The duration of a trademark registration is 10 years, but it may be renewed indefinitely for 10-year periods, provided the trademark is still in use at the time of expiration.

The application fee is $175.

Patents

Source: Department of Commerce, Patent and Trademark Office.

A patent, in the most general sense, is a document issued by a government, conferring some special right or privilege. The term is now restricted mainly to patents for inventions; occasionally, land patents.

The grant of a patent for an invention gives the inventor the privilege, for a limited period of time, of excluding others from making, using, or selling a certain article. However, it does not give him the right to make, use, or sell his own invention if it is an improvement on some unexpired patent whose claims are infringed thereby.

In the U.S., the law provides that a patent may be granted, for a term of 17 years, to any person who has invented or discovered any new and useful art, machine, manufacture, or composition of matter, as well as any new and useful improvements thereof. A patent may also be granted to a person who has invented or discovered and asexually reproduced a new and distinct variety of plant (other than a tuber-propagated one) or has invented a new, original and ornamental design for an article of manufacture.

A patent is granted only upon a regularly filed application, complete in all respects; upon payment of the fees; and upon determination that the disclosure is complete and that the invention is new, useful, and, in view of the prior art, unobvious to one skilled in the art. The disclosure must be of such nature as to enable others to reproduce the invention.

A complete application, which must be addressed to the Commissioner of Patents and Trademarks, Washington, D.C. 20231, consists of a specification with one or more claims; oath or declaration; drawing (whenever the nature of the case admits of it); and a basic filing fee of $185.00.[1] The filing fee is not returned to the applicant if the patent is refused. If the patent is allowed, another fee of $310.00[1] is required before the patent is issued. The fee for design patent application is $75.00; the issue fee is $110.00[1]. Maintenance fees are required on utility patents at stipulated intervals.

Applications are ordinarily considered in the order in which they are received. Patents are not granted for printed matter, for methods of doing business, or for devices for which claims contrary to natural laws are made. Applications for a perpetual-motion machine have been made from time to time, but until a working model is presented that actually fulfills the claim, no patent will be issued.

1. Fees quoted are for small entities. Fees are double for corporations.

Beware of Illegal Patent Services

It is illegal under patent law (35 USC 33) for anyone to hold himself out as qualified to prepare and prosecute patent applications unless he is registered with the Patent Office. Also, Patent Office regulations forbid registered practitioners advertising for patent business. Some inventors, unaware of this, enter into binding contracts with persons and firms which advertise their assistance in making patent searches, preparing drawings, specifications, and patent applications, only to discover much later that their applications require the services of fully qualified agents or attorneys.

Birthstones

Month	Stone	Month	Stone
January	Garnet	July	Ruby or Star Ruby
February	Amethyst	August	Peridot or Sardonyx
March	Aquamarine or Bloodstone	September	Sapphire or Star Sapphire
April	Diamond	October	Opal or Tourmaline
May	Emerald	November	Topaz or Citrine
June	Pearl, Alexandrite or Moonstone	December	Turquoise, Lapis Lazuli, Blue Zircon or Blue Topaz

Source: Jewelry Industry Council.

Additional Consumer Information

Consult the following special sections of *Information Please Almanac* for specific consumer information

837	Accredited Senior Colleges	529	Science
42	Business & Economy	426	Social Security & Aging
576	Calendar & Holidays	391	Travel
433	Drugs & Drug Abuse	70	Taxes
361	Energy	596	Toll-Free Numbers
78	First Aid	599	U.S. Societies & Associations
80	Nutrition & Health	302	Where to Find out More
411	Personal Finance	436	Writer's Guide
989	Postage	366	Weights & Measures

State Consumer Protection Offices

Source: U.S. Office of Consumer Affairs.

State consumer protection offices resolve individual consumer complaints, conduct informational and educational programs, and enforce consumer protection and fraud laws. Most of these offices require complaints in writing. Call to find out the correct procedure for filing a complaint and what sales documents are needed. Phone numbers are subject to change.

Alabama
Montgomery (205) 261-7334
1 (800) 392-5658 (Alabama only)

Alaska
Anchorage (907) 279-0428
Fairbanks (907) 456-8588

Arizona
Phoenix (602) 542-3702 (fraud only)
1 (800) 352-8431 (Arizona only)

Arkansas
Little Rock (501) 682-2007
1 (800) 482-8982 (Arkansas only)

California
Sacramento-Consumer Affairs (916) 445-0660 (complaint assistance)
(916) 445-1254 (consumer information)
(916) 322-3360 (Attorney General)
1 (800) 952-5225 (California only)
(916) 366-5100 (auto repairs)
1 (800) 952-5210 (California only-auto repairs)
Los Angeles (213) 974-1452

Colorado
Denver (303) 866-5167
(303) 866-3561 (agriculture)

Connecticut
Hartford (203) 566-4999
1 (800) 842-2649 (Connecticut only)

Delaware
Wilmington (302) 571-3250
(302) 571-3849 (economic crime)

District of Columbia
Washington, DC (202) 727-7000

Florida
Tallahassee (904) 488-2226
1 (800) 327-3382 (education)
Miami (305) 377-5619

Georgia
Atlanta (404) 656-7000
1 (800) 282-5808 (Georgia only)

Hawaii
Honolulu (808) 548-2560 (legal-Hawaii only)
(808) 548-2540 (complaints-Hawaii only)
Hilo (808) 961-7433
Lihue (808) 245-4365
Wailuku (808) 244-4387

Illinois
Springfield (217) 782-0244
1 (800) 642-3112 (Illinois only)
Chicago (312) 917-3580
(312) 917-3289 (citizens' rights)

Indiana
Indianapolis (317) 232-6330
1 (800) 382-5516 (Indiana only)

Iowa
Des Moines (515) 281-3592
1 (800) 358-5510 (Iowa only)
(515) 281-5926 (consumer protection)

Kansas
Topeka (913) 296-3751
1 (800) 432-2310 (Kansas only)

Kentucky
Frankfort (502) 564-2200
1 (800) 432-9257 (Kentucky only)

Louisiana
Baton Rouge (504) 342-7013
New Orleans (504) 568-5472

Maine
Augusta (207) 582-8718
(207) 289-3716 (9 a.m.-1 p.m.)
Portland (207) 797-8978 (1 p.m.-4 p.m.)

Maryland
Baltimore (301) 528-8662 (9 a.m.-2 p.m.)
Hagerstown (301) 791-4780
Glen Burnie (301) 768-7420
Salisbury (301) 543-6620

Massachusetts
Boston (617) 727-8400 (information & referral only)
(617) 727-7780 (information & referral only)
Springfield (413) 784-1240

Michigan
Lansing (517) 373-1140
(517) 373-0947 (Consumers Council)
(517) 373-7858 (automotive regulation)
1 (800) 292-4204 (Michigan only)

Minnesota
Duluth (218) 723-4891
St. Paul (612) 296-2331

Mississippi
Jackson (601) 354-6018
(601) 354-7063 (agriculture and commerce)
Biloxi (601) 436-6000

Missouri
Jefferson City (314) 751-4962
(314) 751-2616 (trade offenses)
1 (800) 392-8222 (Missouri only)

Montana
Helena (406) 444-4312

Nebraska
Lincoln (402) 471-4723

Nevada
Carson City (702) 885-4340
Las Vegas (702) 486-4150

New Hampshire
Concord (603) 271-3641

New Jersey
Newark (201) 648-4010 (consumer affairs)

(201) 648-4730 (Attorney General)
Trenton (609) 292-7087
1 (800) 792-8600 (New Jersey only)

New Mexico
Santa Fe (505) 872-6910
1 (800) 432-2070 (New Mexico only)

New York
Albany (518) 474-8583
(518) 474-5481
New York (212) 587-4908
(212) 341-2300

North Carolina
Raleigh
(919) 733-7741

North Dakota
Bismarck (701) 224-2210
(701) 224-3404 (Consumer Fraud)
1 (800) 472-2600 (North Dakota only)

Ohio
Columbus (614) 466-4986
1 (800) 282-0515 (Ohio only)
(614) 466-9605 (Consumers' Counsel)
1 (800) 282-9448 (Ohio only)

Oklahoma
Oklahoma City (405) 521-3921
(405) 521-3653

Oregon
Salem (503) 378-4320

Pennsylvania
Allentown (215) 821-6690
Erie (814) 871-4371
Harrisburg (717) 787-9707
1 (800) 441-2555 (Pennsylvania only)
(717) 783-5048 (utilities only)
(717) 787-7109 (consumer protection)
Scranton (717) 963-4913
Philadelphia (215) 560-2414
Pittsburgh (412) 565-5135

Puerto Rico
Old San Juan (809) 721-2900
Santurce (809) 722-7555

Rhode Island
Providence (401) 277-2104
(401) 277-2764

South Carolina
Columbia (803) 734-3970 (fraud)
(803) 734-9452 (Consumer affairs)
1 (800) 922-1594 (South Carolina only)
(803) 734-0457 (State Ombudsman)

South Dakota
Pierre (605) 773-4400

Tennessee
Nashville (615) 741-2672 (consumer protection)

(615) 741-4737 (consumer affairs)
1 (800) 342-8385 (Tennessee only)
Texas
Austin (512) 463-2070
Dallas (214) 742-8944
El Paso (915) 772-9476
Houston (713) 223-5886
Lubbock (806) 747-5238
McAllen (512) 682-4547
San Antonio (512) 225-4191
Utah
Salt Lake City (801) 530-6601
(801) 538-1331 (consumer affairs)
Vermont
Montpelier (802) 828-3171
(802) 828-2436 (agriculture)

Virgin Islands
St. Thomas (809) 774-3130
Virginia
Richmond (804) 786-2116
(804) 786-2042 (agriculture)
1 (800) 552-9963 (Virginia only)
Washington
Olympia (206) 753-6210
Seattle (206) 464-7744
1 (800) 551-4636 (Washington only)
Spokane (509) 456-3123
Tacoma (206) 593-2904
West Virginia
Charleston (304) 348-8986
1 (800) 368-8808 (West Virginia only)

(304) 348-7890
Wisconsin
Altoona (715) 839-3848
Green Bay (414) 436-4087 (agriculture)
Milwaukee (414) 257-8956 (agriculture)
(414) 227-4948
Madison (608) 266-1852 (Consumer protection)
1 (800) 362-8189 (Wisconsin only)
(608) 266-9836 (agriculture)
1 (800) 362-3020 (Wisconsin only)
Wyoming
Cheyenne (307) 777-7841, 6286

How to Write a Complaint Letter

Source: United States Office of Consumer Affairs.

●Include your name, address, and home and work phone numbers.

●Type your letter if possible. If it is handwritten, make sure it is neat and easy to read.

●Make your letter brief and to the point. Include all important facts about your purchase, including the date and place where you made the purchase and any information you can give about the product or service such as serial or model numbers or specific type of service.

●State exactly what you want done about the problem and how long you are willing to wait to get it resolved. Be reasonable.

●Include all documents regarding your problem. Be sure to send COPIES, not originals.

●Avoid writing an angry, sarcastic, or threatening letter. The person reading your letter probably was not responsible for your problem, but may be very helpful in resolving it.

●Keep a copy of the letter for your records.

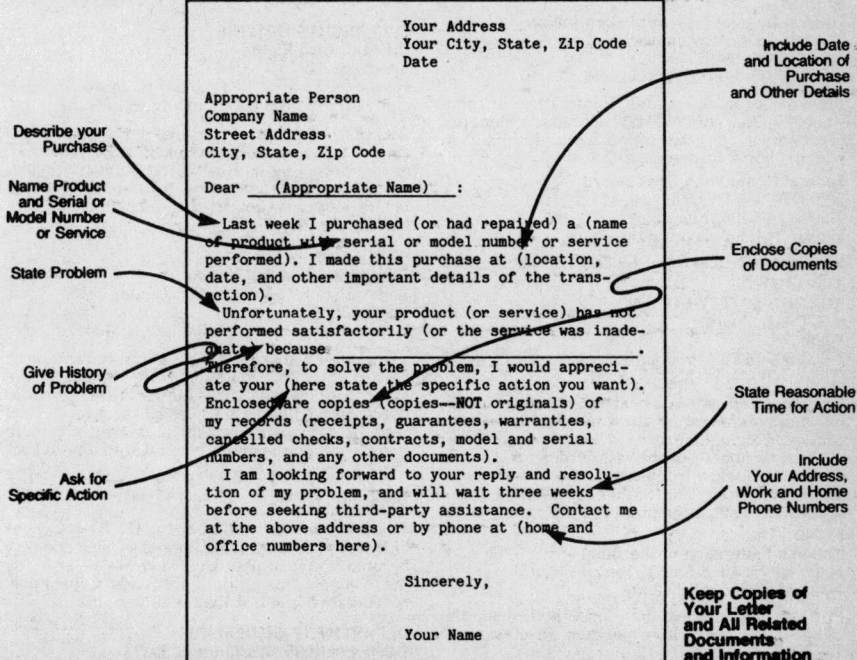

TOLL-FREE NUMBERS

AIDS
National AIDS Hotline
U.S. Public Health Service
1-800-342-2437
SIDA (Spanish line) 1-800-344-7432
TTY (hearing impaired) 1-800-243-7889
Hours: 24 hours, 7 days

Provides the latest information to the public about
Acquired Immune Deficiency Syndrome (AIDS).

AIDS Drugs Hotline
National Institute of Allergies and Infectious Diseases
1-800-874-2572
Hours: 9 a.m.–7 p.m., Mon.-Fri.

Callers learn the status of research and how to get
into an FDA clinical trial.

AUTOMOBILE
Auto Safety Hotline
National Highway Traffic Safety Administration
202-366-0123 (Washington, D.C.)
1-800-424-9393 (Elsewhere)
Hours: 8:00–4:00, EST Mon.–Fri.
Answering service after hours

Handles complaints on safety-related defects, and
receives reports of vehicle safety problems. Provides information and in some cases literature on:
●motor vehicle safety recalls ●car seats
●automobile equipment ●tires ●motor homes
●drunk driving ●gas mileage

BANKING
Federal Deposit Insurance Corporation
202-898-3536 (Washington, D.C.)
1-800-424-5488 (Elsewhere)
Hours: 9:00–4:00, EST Mon.–Fri.

Provides general banking information on consumer banking laws. Will refer consumer to proper
regulatory agency that supervises institution complaint is being filed against.

Federal Home Loan Bank Board
202-377-6988 (Washington, D.C.)
1-800-424-5405 (Elsewhere)
Hours: 24-hour recording

Provides information on federal adjustable mortgage rates.

BOATING SAFETY HOTLINE
U.S. Coast Guard
1-800-368-5647
1-202-267-0972 (Washington, D.C.)
Hours: 8:00–4:00 EST Mon.-Fri.

Provides information on boats, safe boating, and associated equipment involved in safety defect (recall) campaigns for past five model years. Takes
complaints about possible safety defects. Cannot
resolve non-safety problems between consumer
and manufacturer and cannot recommend or endorse specific boats or products.

BLIND
National Federation of the Blind
1-800-638-7518, 8-5 EST, Mon.-Fri.
1-301-659-9314 (Maryland)

Provides job information. Concerned about the
rights of the blind. Free package of information
about blindness.

CHEMICALS
Chemical Referral Center
1-800-262-8200
1-202-887-1315 (Washington, D.C.)
Hours: 9:00-6:00, EST, Mon.-Fri.

Refers callers to health and safety contacts at
chemical manufacturers.

CHILD ABUSE
Parents Anonymous
1-800-352-0386 (California)
1-800-421-0353 (Elsewhere)
Hours: 8:30–5:00 Mon.–Fri., PST
Has a 24-hour hotline.

American Child Protective Association, Inc.
1-800-KID-WATCH
Hours: 24 hours, 7 days.

"Kid Watch Radio Alert Program" presents information through the radio stations to the public that
a missing child situation exists. The Kid Watch Public Awareness Program has helped fingerprint over
40,000 children.

CIVICS
National Civic League
1-800-223-6004
303-832-6515 in Colorado
Hours: 8 A.M.—5 P.M. MST, Mon.-Fri.

Nonprofit organization that seeks to improve state
and local governments.

CIVIL RIGHTS HOTLINE
Office of Civil Rights
1-800-368-1019
Hours: 9:00—5:30, EST Mon.-Fri. Answering machine after 5:30 p.m., including weekends.

Accepts complaints regarding discrimination on
the basis of race, color, national origin, handicap,
or age occurring in Health and Human Services
programs, i.e. in admission to hospitals, nursing
homes, day care centers, or federally funded state
health care assistance.

EDUCATION
Federal Student Aid Hotline
Federal Student Information Center
1-800-333-INFO
Hours: 9:00 A.M.—5:30 P.M., EST, Mon.-Fri.

The Center will help students file an application or
correct a Student Aid Report (SAR), explain the Request for Information Transfer (RIT) process,
check on whether a school takes part in Federal
Student Aid programs, explain student eligibility
requirements, and mail a Federal Student Aid Fact
sheet to callers if desired.

1-800-MIS-USED

This number is the hotline to the U.S. Department
of Education's Inspector General's Office and is to
be used if you suspect any fraud, waste, or abuse
involving Federal student aid funds. Callers may
remain anonymous if they wish.

DEPARTMENT OF DEFENSE
1-800-424-9098 (Washington, D.C.)

223-5080 (Autovon Line)
693-5080 (FTS)
Hours: 8:00–4:30, EST

Operated for citizens to report suspected cases of fraud and waste involving the Department of Defense. The anonymity of callers will be respected.

DRUG ABUSE
National Institute on Drug Abuse
1-800-662-HELP
Hours: 9:00–3:00 Monday to Friday), 12:00–3:00 (Saturday & Sunday).

Provides information on drug abuse, and treatment referrals.

National Cocaine Hotline
1-800-COCAINE
Hours: 24 hours—7days

Provides information on cocaine and drug-related problems for cocaine abusers.

PRIDE Drug Information Hotline
Parents' Resource Institute for Drug Education (PRIDE)
1-800-677-7433
Hours: 8:30 A.M.—5:00 P.M., EST Mon.-Fri.

A national resource and information center, PRIDE refers concerned parents to parent groups in their state or local area; gives information on how parents can form a group in their community; provides telephone consultation and referrals to emergency health centers; and maintains a series of drug information tapes that callers can listen to, free of charge, by calling after 5 P.M.

ALCOHOLISM
National Council on Alcoholism Information Line
1-800-622-2255
Hours: 24 hours—7 days

The National Council on Alcoholism, Inc. (NCA), is a national nonprofit organization that combats alcoholism, other drug addictions, and related problems. The council also provides referral services to families and individuals seeking help with alcoholism or other drug problems.

Mothers Against Drunk Driving (MADD)
1-800-438-6233
Hours: 24-hours (Business hours: 9 A.M.—5 P.M. Central Time, Mon.-Fri.)
In New York state, call 1-800-245-6233

Provides counseling, victim hotline, and nearest chapter referrals. Sends free literature.

"Just Say No Clubs" Hotline (Drug Abuse)
"Just Say No" International
1-800-258-2766
Hours: 8:00 A.M.—5:00 P.M., PCT, Mon.-Fri.

These nationwide clubs provide support and positive peer reinforcement to youngsters through workshops, seminars, newsletters, walk-a-thons, and a variety of other activities. Clubs are organized by schools, communities, and parent groups.

ELECTIONS
Federal Election Commission
Clearinghouse on Election Administration
1-800-424-9530
202-376-3120 (Wash. D.C., Alaska, and Hawaii)
Hours: 8:30—5:30, EST Mon.-Fri.

Provides information on campaign financing.

ENERGY
Conservation and Renewable Energy Inquiry and Referral Service
1-800-523-2929
Hours: 9:00–5:00, EST Mon.-Fri.

Provides non-technical information on solar, wind, and other energy heating and cooling technologies, energy conservation, and alcohol fuels.

ENVIRONMENT
Hazardous Waste
RCRA Superfund Hotline
Environmental Protection Agency
202-382-3000 (Washington, D.C.)
1-800-424-9346 (Elsewhere)
Hours: 8:30-7:30, EST Mon.-Fri.

Provides information and interpretation of federal hazardous waste regulations. Will provide referrals regarding other hazardous waste matters.

Pesticide Hotline
National Pesticide Telecommunications Network
1-800-858-7378
Hours: 24 hours—7 days

Provides information on health hazards, cleanup and disposal of pesticides. Will refer callers to human and animal poison control centers in their states if necessary.

Radon Hotline
1-800-SOS-RADON
Hours: 24-hour recording.

Provides information about radon and how to test for the gas in your home.

FOOD
The Meat and Poultry Hotline
U.S. Department of Agriculture
1-800-535-4555
202-477-3333 in Washington, D.C.
Hours: 10 A.M.—4 P.M. EST, Mon.-Fri.

Provides information on proper handling, preparation, storing, and cooking of meat, poultry, and eggs. Answers questions about the safe cooking of poultry and meat in microwave ovens.

GAY-LESBIAN HOTLINE
National Gay/Lesbian Crisisline/AIDS 800 (NGLC)
1-800-SOS-GAYS
Hours: 5:00–10:00 p.m., EST, M–F; (Sept.–May, Sat., 1–5)

Provides information on gay/lesbian life styles, AIDS; referrals to resources and gay/lesbian events in the caller's community.

HEALTH CARE
ALZHEIMER'S DISEASE
Alzheimer's Disease and Related Disorders Association, Inc.
1-800-621-0379
1-800-572-6037 (Illinois)
Hours: 24 hours, 7 days

Information and referral service. Provides support for patients and their families, aids research efforts, etc.

Cancer Information Service
National Cancer Institute
National Institutes of Health
Department of Health & Human Services

1-800-638-6694 (National)
1-800-4-Cancer (State)
Hours: 9:00 A.M.–10:00 P.M., EST Mon.–Fri.

Provides information on cancer, prevention, treatment and ongoing research; fills requests for pamphlets and other literature on cancer.

National Health Information Center
Department of Health & Human Services
301-565-4167 (Maryland)
1-800-336-4797 (Elsewhere)
Hours: 9:00–5:00 EST Mon.–Fri.

Provides referrals to sources of information on health-related issues.

Sexually Transmitted Diseases (STDs)
National STD Hotline
Operated by The American Social Health Association
1-800-227-8922
Hours: 8 A.M.—11 P.M. EST Mon.-Fri.

Provides latest information about STDs (sometimes called VD) and where to get confidential, free treatment in your area.

HOUSING
Fair Housing Discrimination Hotline
Fair Housing and Equal Opportunity
Department of Housing and Urban Development
202-708-3500 (Washington, D.C.)
1-800-424-8590 (Elsewhere)
Hours: 8:45—5:15, EST Mon.—Fri.

Receives housing discrimination complaints due to race, color, religion, sex, familial status, handicap, or national origin.

INSURANCE
Federal Crime Insurance
Federal Emergency Management Administration
301-251-1660 (Maryland)
1-800-638-8780 (Elsewhere)
Hours: 8:30–5:00, EST Mon.–Fri.
Answering service after hours.

Provides information on federal crime insurance for both homes and businesses which have been robbed or burglarized.

National Flood Insurance
1-800-492-6605 (Maryland)
1-800-638-6831 (Alaska, Hawaii, Puerto Rico, Virgin Islands, Guam)
1-800-638-6620 (Elsewhere)
Hours: 8:00–8:00, EST Mon.–Fri.

Provides information on community participation in the flood program (emergency or regular). If the community does not have a program, it is not eligible for government-subsidized insurance relief. Complaints are referred to the proper office within the agency.

PREGNANCY
Pro-Choice
Abortion Hotline
National Abortion Federation
1-800-772-9100
Hours: 9:30 A.M.—5:30 P.M. EST, Mon.-Fri.

Provides facts about abortion, counseling, and referrals to member clinics.

Right-To-Life
Birthright, Inc. (U.S.A.)
1-800-848-LOVE
1-800-328-LOVE in Canada
Hours: 8 A.M.—12 midnight, EST 7-days

Birthright, Inc. provides alternative advice to abortion. Operates crisis centers, and provides help such as pregnancy testing, housing, medical care, and adoption referral.

Birth Control
Birth Control Information Line
Sponsored by The American College of Obstetricians and Gynecologists and The American Academy of Family Physicians
1-800-468-3637
Hours: 24 hours, 7-days

Will send booklet with the facts you need to know about contraceptives.

PRODUCT SAFETY
Consumer Product Safety Commission
1-800-638-2772
Hours: 10:30–4:00, EST Mon.–Fri.

Provides recorded information on the safety of consumer products. Receives reports of product-related deaths, illnesses, and injuries. Products are not rated or recommended.

RUNAWAYS
Runaway Hotline
1-800-231-6946 (U.S.A. except Texas)
1-800-392-3352 (Texas)
Hours: 24 hours, 7 days

Helps runaways by referring them to shelters, clinics, local hotlines. Will relay messages from the runaway to the parent.

SOCIAL SECURITY AND MEDICARE FRAUD
Inspector General Hotline
Department of Health and Human Services
1-800-368-5779
Hours: 10:00–4:00, EST Mon.-Fri.

Takes calls on fraud in Social Security payments or abuse, Medicaid and Medicare fraud and other HHS programs. Recording machine after hours.

VIETNAM VETERANS
Vietnam Veterans of America
1-800-424-7275 (answering machine)
202-332-2700 (Washington, D.C.)
Hours: 9:00–5:30, EST Mon.-Fri.

Answering machine takes messages for information and help. Provides information on Agent Orange, post-traumatic stress disorder, and other matters. Will answer questions on direct line.

Veterans of the Vietnam War, Inc.
1-800-VIETNAM
1-800-NAM-9090 (Pennsylvania)
Hours: 8 a.m.–6 p.m., Mon.-Fri., service after hours

Provides information on filing claims against the Agent Orange Settlement, filing claims for veterans benefits with the VA, how to take the VA to court, and information on MIAs and POWs. Veterans newsletter is available, also provides Veterans location services.

U.S. SOCIETIES & ASSOCIATIONS

Source: Information Please questionnaires to organizations. Names are listed alphabetically according to key word in title; figure in parentheses is year of founding; other figure is membership. An asterisk (*) before a name indicates that up-to-date information has not been provided.

The following is a partial list selected for general readership interest. A comprehensive listing of approximately 20,000 national and international organizations can be found in the "Encyclopedia of Associations," 20th Ed., 1986, Vol. I, Parts 1-3 (Katherine Gruber, Editor; Iris Cloyd, Research Editor), published by Gale Research Company, Book Tower, Detroit, Mich. 48226, available in most public libraries.

Abortion Federation, National (1977): 1436 U St. N.W., Suite 103, Washington, D.C., 20009. 285. Phone: (202) 667-5881.

Abortion Rights Action League, National (1969): 1101 14th St. N.W., Washington, D.C. 20005. 400,000. Phone: (202) 408-4600.

Accountants, American Institute of Certified Public (1887): 1211 Avenue of the Americas, New York, N.Y. 10036. 284,000. Phone: (212) 575-6200.

Accountants, National Association of (1919): 10 Paragon Dr., Montvale, N.J., 07645-1760. 85,000. Phone: (201) 573-9000.

Acoustical Society of America (1929): 500 Sunnyside Blvd., Woodbury, N.Y. 11797. 6,200. Phone: (516) 349-7800.

ACSM: American Congress on Surveying and Mapping (1941): 5410 Grosvenor Lane, Bethesda, Md. 20814. 23,000. Phone: (301) 493-0200.

Actors' Equity Association (1913): 165 W. 46th St., New York, N.Y. 10036. Phone: (212) 869-8530.

Actuaries, Society of (1949): 475 N. Martingale Rd., Suite 800, Schaumburg, Ill. 60173-2226. 12,200. Phone: (708) 706-3500.

Adirondack Mountain Club (1922): RD 3, Box 3055, Luzerne Rd., Lake George, N.Y. 12845. 17,000. Phone: (518) 668-4447.

Aeronautic Association, National (1905): 1815 N. Fort Myer Dr., Arlington, Va. 22209. 250,000. Phone: (703) 527-0226.

Aeronautics and Astronautics, American Institute of (1932): 370 L'Enfant Promenade S.W., Washington, D.C. 20024. 42,000. Phone: (202) 646-7400.

Aerospace Industries Association of America (1919): 1250 Eye St. N.W., Washington, D.C. 20005. 53 companies. Phone: (202) 371-8400.

Aerospace Medical Association (1929): 320 S. Henry St., Alexandria, Va. 22314-3524. 4,350. Phone: (703) 739-2240.

African-American Institute, The (1953): 833 United Nations Plaza, New York, N.Y. 10017. Phone: (212) 949-5666.

AFS Intercultural Programs (1947): 313 E. 43rd St., New York, N.Y. 10017. 100,000. Phone: (212) 949-4242 or (800) AFS-INFO.

Aging Association, American (1970): 600 S. 42nd St., Omaha, Neb. 68198-4635. 500. Phone: (402) 559-4416.

Agricultural Engineers, American Society of (1907): 2950 Niles Rd., St. Joseph, Mich. 49085. 12,000. Phone: (616) 429-0300.

Agricultural History Society (1919): 1301 New York Ave. N.W., Washington, D.C. 20005-4788. 1,400. Phone: (202) 786-3307.

Agronomy, American Society of (1907): 677 S. Segoe Rd., Madison, Wis. 53711-1086. 13,000. Phone: (608) 273-8080.

Air & Waste Management Association (1907): P.O. Box 2861, Pittsburgh, Pa. 15230. 10,000. Phone: (412) 232-3444.

Aircraft Association, Experimental (1953): 3000 Poberezny Rd., Oshkosh, Wis. 54903-3086. 125,000. Phone: (414) 426-4800.

Aircraft Owners and Pilots Association (1939): 421 Aviation Way, Frederick, Md. 21701-4798. 300,000. Phone: (301) 695-2000.

Air Force Association (1946): 1501 Lee Highway, Arlington, Va., 22209-1198. 196,000. Phone: (703) 247-5800.

Air Line Pilots Association (1931): 1625 Massachusetts Ave. N.W., Washington, D.C. 20036 and 535 Herndon Pkwy., Herndon, Va. 22070. 41,000. Phone: (703) 689-2270.

Air Transport Association of America (1936): 1709 New York Ave. N.W., Washington, D.C. 20006. 21 airlines. Phone: (202) 626-4000.

Al-Anon Family Group Headquarters, Inc. (1951): P.O. Box 862, Midtown Station, New York, N.Y. 10018-0862. 31,000 groups worldwide. Phone: (800) 356-9996.

Alcoholics Anonymous (1935): P.O. Box 459, Grand Central Station, New York, N.Y. 10163. 1,800,000. Address communications to General Service Office. Phone: (212) 686-1100.

Alcoholism, and Drug Dependence, National Council on (1944): 12 W. 21st St., New York, N.Y. 10010. 200 affiliates. Phone: (212) 206-6770.

Alcohol Problems, American Council on (1895): 3426 Bridgeland Dr., Bridgeton, Mo. 63044. 3,500. Phone: (314) 739-5944.

Alexander Graham Bell Association for the Deaf (1890): 3417 Volta Place N.W., Washington, D.C. 20007. 6,000. Phone: (202) 337-5220.

Allergy and Immunology, American Academy of (1943): 611 E. Wells St., Milwaukee, Wis. 53202. 4,045. Phone: (414) 272-6071.

Alzheimer's Disease and Related Disorders Association, Inc., (1980): 70 E. Lake St., Suite 600, Chicago, Ill. 60601-5997. 210 Chapters and Affiliates, over 1,600 Family Support Groups. Toll-free information: 1-800-621-0379; in Illinois: 1 (800) 572-6037.

***American Federation of Labor and Congress of Industrial Organizations (AFL-CIO)** (1955): 815 16th St. N.W., Washington, D.C. 20006. 14,100,000. Phone: (202) 637-5010.

American Film and Video Association (formerly Educational Film Library Assn.) (1943): 920 Barnsdale Rd., Suite 152, La Grange Park, Ill. 60525. 1,400. Phone: (708) 482-4000.

American Foundrymen's Society, Inc. (1896): 505 State St., Des Plaines, Ill. 60016-8399. 14,000. Phone: (708) 824-0181.

American Friends Service Committee (1917): 1501 Cherry St., Philadelphia, Pa. 19102. Phone: (215) 241-7000.

American Historical Association (1884): 400 A St. S.E., Washington, D.C. 20003. 15,000. Phone: (202) 544-2422.

American Indian Affairs, Association on (1923): 95 Madison Ave., New York, N.Y. 10016. 35,000. Phone: (212) 689-8720.

*****American Legion, The** (1919): P.O. Box 1055, Indianapolis, Ind. 46206. 2,900,000. Phone: (317) 635-8411.

American Legion Auxiliary (1919): 777 N. Meridian St., Indianapolis, Ind. 46204. 955,000. Phone: (317) 635-6291.

American Mensa, Ltd. (1960): 2626 E. 14th St., Brooklyn, N.Y. 11235-3992. Phone: (718) 934-3700.

American Montessori Society (1960): 150 Fifth Ave., New York, N.Y. 10011. 12,000. Phone: (212) 924-3209.

American Philosophical Society (1743): 104 S. 5th St., Philadelphia, Pa. 19106-3387. 600. Phone: (215) 440-3400.

American Planning Association (1909): 1776 Massachusetts Ave. N.W., Washington, D.C. 20036 (headquarters). 26,000. Phone: (202) 872-0611. Membership office: 1313 E. 60th St., Chicago, Ill. 60637. (312) 955-9100.

Americans for Democratic Action, Inc. (1947): 1511 "K" St. N.W., Suite 941, Washington, D.C. 20005. 40,000. Phone: (202) 638-6447.

American Society for Public Administration (ASPA) (1939): 1120 G St. N.W., Suite 500, Washington, D.C. 20005. 16,000. Phone: (202) 393-7878.

American Society of CLU & ChFC (1928): 270 Bryn Mawr Ave., Bryn Mawr, Pa. 19010. Phone: (215) 526-2500.

American Universities, Association of (1900): One Dupont Circle N.W., Suite 730, Washington, D.C. 20036. Phone: (202) 466-5030.

AMIDEAST (America-Mideast Educational and Training Services) (1951): 1100 17th St. N.W., Washington, D.C. 20036-4601. 200. Phone: (202) 785-0022.

Amnesty International/USA (1961): 322 Eighth Ave., New York, N.Y. 10001. 385,000. Phone: (212) 807-8400.

AMVETS (American Veterans of World War II, Korea, and Vietnam) (1944): 4647 Forbes Blvd., Lanham, Md. 20706. 200,000. Phone: (301) 459-9600.

Animal Protection Institute of America (1968): 2831 Fruitridge Rd., P.O. Box 22505, Sacramento, Calif. 95822. Phone: (916) 731-5521.

*****Animals, Fund For** (1967): 200 W. 57th St., New York, N.Y. 10019. 175,000. Phone: (212) 246-2096.

Animals, The American Society for the Prevention of Cruelty to (ASPCA) (1866): 441 E. 92nd St., New York, N.Y. 10128. 300,000. Phone: (212) 876-7700..

Animal Welfare Institute (1951): P.O. Box 3650, Washington, D.C. 20007. 8,600. Phone: (202) 337-2332.

Anthropological Association, American (1902): 1703 New Hampshire Ave. N.W., Washington, D.C. 20009. 11,500. Phone: (202) 232-8800.

Anti-Defamation League of B'nai B'rith (1913): 823 United Nations Plaza, New York, N.Y. 10017. Phone: (212) 490-2525.

Antiquarian Society, American (1812): 185 Salisbury St., Worcester, Mass. 01609. 530. Phone: (508) 755-5221.

Anti-Vivisection Society, The American (1883): Suite 204, Noble Plaza, 801 Old York Rd., Jenkintown, Pa. 19046. 15,000. Phone: (215) 887-0816.

Appraisers, American Society of (1936): P.O. Box 17265, Washington, D.C. 20041. 5,600. Phone: (703) 478-2228.

Arbitration Association, American (1926): 140 W. 51st St., New York, N.Y. 10020. 5,500. Phone: (212) 484-4000.

*****Arboriculture, International Society of** (1924): 303 W. University, Urbana, Ill. 61801-1746. 5,200. Phone: (217) 328-2032.

Archaeological Institute of America (1879): 675 Commonwealth Ave., Boston, Mass. 02215. 8,000. Phone: (617) 353-9361.

Architects, American Institute of (1857): 1735 New York Ave. N.W., Washington, D.C. 20006. 56,000. Phone: (202) 626-7300.

Architectural Historians, Society of (1940): 1232 Pine St., Philadelphia, Pa. 19107. 4,000. Phone: (215) 735-0224.

Army, Association of the United States (1950): 2425 Wilson Blvd., Arlington, Va. 22210-0860. 150,000. Phone: (703) 841-4300.

*****Arthritis Foundation** (1948): 1314 Spring St., N.W., Atlanta, Ga. 30309. 72 local chapters. Phone: (404) 872-7100.

Arts, National Endowment for the (1965): 1100 Pennsylvania Ave. N.W., Washington, D.C. 20506. Phone: (202) 682-5400.

Arts, The American Federation of (1909): 41 E. 65th St., New York, N.Y. 10021. 1,400. Phone: (212) 988-7700. Museum Services Division: 74 New Montgomery St., Suite 206, San Francisco, Calif. 94105. Phone: (415) 974-1230.

Arts and Letters, American Academy and Institute of (1898): 633 W. 155th St., New York, N.Y. 10032. 250. Phone: (212) 368-5900.

ASM INTERNATIONAL (1913): Materials Park, Ohio 44073. 54,000. Phone: (216) 338-5151.

Astronomical Society, American (1899): Astronomy Program, University of Maryland, College Park, Md. 20742. 5,048. Phone: (301) 454-0818.

Atheists, American (1963): P.O. Box 140195, Austin, Tex. 78714-0195. 40,000 Families. Phone: (512) 458-1244.

Auctioneers Association, National (1949): 8880 Ballentine, Overland Park, Kan. 66214. 6,000. Phone: (913) 541-8084.

Audubon Society, National (1905): 950 Third Ave., New York, N.Y. 10022. 546,000. Phone: (212) 832-3200.

Authors League of America (1912): 234 W. 44th St., New York, N.Y. 10036. 14,000. Phone: (212) 391-9198.

Autism Society of America (1965): 1234 Massachusetts Ave. N.W., Washington, D.C. 20005. 10,000. Phone: (202) 783-0125.

Automobile Association, American (1902): 1000 AAA Dr., Heathrow, Fla., 32746-5063. Phone: (407) 444-7000.

Automobile Club, National (1924): Bayside Plaza, 188 The Embarcadero, #300, San Francisco, Calif. 94105. 300,000. Phone: (415) 777-4000.

Automobile Dealers Association, National (1917): 8400 Westpark Dr., McLean, Va. 22102. 20,000. Phone: (703) 821-7100.

Automotive Engineers, Inc., Society of (1905): 400 Commonwealth Dr., Warrendale, Pa. 15096. 55,000. Phone: (412) 776-4841.

Automotive Hall of Fame (1939): P.O. Box 1727, Midland, Mich. 48641-1727. Phone: (517) 631-5760.

Bar Association, American (1878): 750 N. Lake Shore Dr., Chicago, Ill. 60611. 371,000. Phone: (312) 988-5000.

Bar Association, Federal (1920): 1815 H St. N.W., Suite 408, Washington, D.C. 20006-3697. 15,000. Phone: (202) 638-0252.

Barber Shop Quartet Singing in America, Society for the Preservation and Encouragement of (1938): 6315 Third Ave., Kenosha, Wis., 53140-5199. 38,000. Phone: (414) 656-8440.

Better Business Bureaus, Council of (1970): 4200 Wilson Blvd., Suite 800, Arlington, Va. 22203. Phone: (703) 276-0100.

Bible Society, American (1816): 1865 Broadway, New York, N.Y. 10023. 320,000. Phone: (212) 581-7400.

Biblical Literature, Society of (1880): 1549 Clairmont Rd., Suite 204, Decatur, Ga. 30033-4635. 7,000. Phone: (404) 636-4744.

Bibliographical Society of America (1904): P.O. Box 397, Grand Central Station, New York, N.Y. 10163. 1,300. Phone: (212) 995-9151.

Bide-A-Wee Home Association, Inc. (1903): 410 E. 38th St., New York, N.Y. 10016. 26,000. Phone: Adoptions (pets) (212) 532-4455; Clinic and Hospital (212) 532-5884.

Big Brothers/Big Sisters of America (1977): 230 N. 13th St., Philadelphia, Pa. 19107. Phone: (215) 567-7000.

Biochemistry and Molecular Biology, American Society for (1906): 9650 Rockville Pike, Bethesda, Md. 20814. 8,000. Phone: (301) 530-7145.

Biological Sciences, American Institute of (1947): 730 11th St. N.W., Washington, D.C. 20001-4521. 12,500. Phone: (202) 628-1500.

Blind, American Council of the (1961): 1010 Vermont Ave. N.W., Suite 1100, Washington, D.C. 20005. 20,000. Phone: (202) 393-3666.

Blind, National Federation of the (1940): 1800 Johnson St., Baltimore, Md. 21230. 50,000. Phone: (301) 659-9314.

Blindness, National Society to Prevent (1908): 500 E. Remington Rd., Schaumburg, Ill. 60173-4557. 26 affiliates. Phone: (708) 843-2020.

Blindness, Research to Prevent (1960): 598 Madison Ave., New York, N.Y. 10022. 3,300. Phone: (212) 752-4333.

Blue Cross and Blue Shield Association (1948 and 1946): 676 N. St. Clair St., Chicago, Ill. 60611. 74 Plans. Phone: (312) 440-6000.

B'nai B'rith International (1843): 1640 Rhode Island Ave. N.W., Washington, D.C. 20036. 500,000. Phone: (202) 857-6500.

Booksellers Association, American (1900): 137 W. 25th St., New York, N.Y. 10001. 8,000. Phone: (212) 463-8450.

Botanical Gardens & Arboreta, American Association of (1971): 786 Church Rd., Wayne, Pa. 19087. 1,800. Phone: (215) 688-1120.

Boys and Girls Clubs of America (1906): 771 First Ave., New York, N.Y. 10017. 1,410,995. Phone: (212) 351-5900.

Boy Scouts of America (1910): 1325 Walnut Hill Lane, P.O. Box 152079, Irving, Tex. 75015-2079. 5,339,184. Phone: (214) 580-2000.

Bridge, Tunnel, and Turnpike Association, International (1932): 2120 L St. N.W., Suite 305, Washington, D.C. 20037. 215 agencies. Phone: (202) 659-4620.

Broadcasters, National Association of (1922): 1771 N St. N.W., Washington, D.C. 20036. 6,000. Phone: (202) 429-5300.

Brookings Institution, The (1916): 1775 Massachusetts Ave. N.W., Washington, D.C. 20036. Phone: (202) 797-6000.

Brooks Bird Club, Inc., The (1932): 707 Warwood Ave., Wheeling, W. Va. 26003. 1,000. Phone: (304) 547-5253.

Business Clubs, National Association of American (1922): 3315 No. Main St., High Point, N.C. 27265. 6,800. Phone: (919) 869-2166.

Business Education Association, National (1946): 1914 Association Dr., Reston, Va. 22091. 16,000. Phone: (703) 860-8300.

Business Women's Association, American (1949): 9100 Ward Parkway, P.O. Box 8728, Kansas City, Mo. 64114. More than 100,000. Phone: (816) 361-6621.

Campers & Hikers Association, National (1949): 4804 Transit Rd., Bldg. 2, Depew, N.Y. 14043-4704. 24,000 families. Phone: (716) 668-6242.

Camp Fire Boys and Girls (1910): 4601 Madison Ave., Kansas City, Mo. 64112. 600,000. Phone: (816) 756-1950.

Camping Association, The American (1910): 5000 State Rd. 67 N., Martinsville, Ind. 46151. 5,500. Phone: (317) 342-8456.

Cancer Society, American (1913): 1599 Clifton Rd., N.E., Atlanta Ga. 30329. 2,646,070 volunteers. Phone: (404) 320-3333. Cancer information: (800) ACS-2345.

CARE, Inc. (1945): 660 First Ave., New York, N.Y. 10016. 20 agencies plus 23 public members. Phone: (212) 686-3110.

Carnegie Endowment for International Peace (1910): 2400 N St. N.W., Washington, D.C. 20037. Phone: (202) 862-7900.

Cartoonists Society, National (1946): 157 W. 57th St., Suite 904, New York, N.Y. 10019. Phone: (212) 333-7606.

Catholic Charities USA (1910): 1319 F St. N.W., Washington, D.C. 20004. 4,000 individuals, 800 agencies and institutions. Phone: (202) 639-8400.

Catholic Daughters of the Americas (1903): 10 W. 71st St., New York, N.Y. 10023. 150,000. Phone: (212) 877-3041.

Catholic Historical Society, American (1884): 263 S. Fourth St., Philadelphia, Pa. 19106. 950. Phone: (215) 925-5752.

Catholic War Veterans of the U.S.A. Inc. (1935): 419 N. Lee St., Alexandria, Va. 22314. 30,000. Phone: (703) 549-3622.

Ceramic Society, Inc., The American (1899): 757 Brooksedge Plaza Dr., Westerville, Ohio 43081-6136. Phone: (614) 890-4700; FAX (614) 899-6109; TWA: 7101109409.

Cerebral Palsy Associations, Inc., United (1949): 7 Penn Plaza, Suite 804, New York, N.Y. 10001. 180 affiliates. Phone: 1 (800) USA IUCP.

Chamber of Commerce of the U.S. (1912): 1615 H St. N.W., Washington, D.C. 20062. 180,000. Phone: (202) 659-6000.

Chemical Engineers, American Institute of (1908): 345 E. 47th St., New York, N.Y. 10017. 50,000. Phone: (212) 705-7338.

Chemical Manufacturers Association, Inc. (1872): 2501 M St. N.W., Washington, D.C. 20037. 175 companies. Phone: (202) 887-1100.

Chemical Society, American (1876): 1155 16th St. N.W., Washington, D.C. 20036. 140,089. Phone: (202) 872-4600.

Chemists, American Institute of (1923): 7315 Wisconsin Ave., Bethesda, Md. 20814. 7,000. Phone: (301) 652-2447.

Chess Federation, United States (1939): 186 Rt. 9W, New Windsor, N.Y. 12553. 60,000. Phone: (914) 562-8350.

Child Labor Committee, National (1904): 1501 Broadway, Rm. 1111, New York, N.Y. 10036. Phone: (212) 840-1801.

Children, American Association for Protecting (a Div. of the American Humane Association) (1877): 9725 E. Hampden, Denver, Colo. 80231. Phone: (303) 695-0811.

Children's Aid Society, The (1853): 105 E. 22nd St., New York, N.Y. 10010. Child welfare services, community centers, camps and health services. Phone: (212) 949-4800.

Children's Book Council (1945): 568 Broadway, New York, N.Y. 10012. 61 publishing houses. Phone: (212) 966-1990.

Child Welfare League of America (1920): 440 First St. N.W., Suite 310, Washington, D.C. 20001. Phone: (202) 638-2952.

*Chiropractic Association, American (1963): 1701 Clarendon Blvd., Arlington, Va. 22209. 21, 300. Phone: (703) 276-8800.

Christians and Jews, National Conference of (1928): 71 Fifth Ave., New York, N.Y. 10003. 200,000. Phone: (212) 206-0006.

Churches of Christ in the USA, National Council of the (1950): 475 Riverside Drive, New York, N.Y. 10115. 32 Protestant and Orthodox communions. Phone: (212) 870-2511.

Cities, National League of (1924): 1301 Pennsylvania Ave. N.W., Washington, D.C. 20004. 16,000 cities and towns. Phone: (202) 626-3000.

Civil Air Patrol (1941): Maxwell AFB, Ala. 36112-5572. 70,000. Phone: (205) 293-5463.

Civil Engineers, American Society of (1852): 345 E. 47th St., New York, N.Y. 10017. 160,000. Phone: (212) 705-7496.

Civil Liberties Union, American (1920): 132 W. 43rd St., New York, N.Y. 10036. 290,000. Phone: (212) 944-9800.

Clinical Chemistry, Inc., American Association for (1948): 2029 K St., N.W., 7th Floor, Washington, D.C. 20006. 9,000. Phone (202) 857-0717.

Clinical Pathologists, American Society of (1922): 2100 W. Harrison St., Chicago, Ill. 60612. 34, 000. Phone: (312) 738-1336.

Collectors Association, American (1939): Box 39106, Minneapolis, Minn. 55439-0106. Over 3,400 debt collection agencies. Phone: (612) 926-6547.

College Board, The (1900): 45 Columbus Ave., New York, N.Y. 10023-6992. 2,700 institutions. Phone: (212) 713-8000.

College Placement Council (1956): 62 E. Highland Ave., Bethlehem, Pa. 18017. 3,100. Phone: (215) 868-1421.

Colored Women's Clubs, National Association of (1896): 5808 16th St. N.W., Washington, D.C. 20011. 40,000. Phone: (202) 726-2044.

Common Cause (1970): 2030 M St. N.W., Washington, D.C. 20036. 280,000. Phone: (202) 833-1200.

Community and Junior Colleges, American Association of (1920): One Dupont Circle N.W., Suite 410, Washington, D.C. 20036-1176. 1,113 institutions. Phone: (202) 728-0200.

Community Cultural Center Association, American (1978): 19 Foothills Dr., Pompton Plains, N.J. 07444. Phone: (201) 835-2661.

Composers, Authors, and Publishers, American Society of (ASCAP) (1914): One Lincoln Plaza, New York, N.Y. 10023. 40,000. Phone: (212) 595-3050.

Composers/USA, National Association of (1932): P.O. Box 49652, Barrington Station, Los Angeles, Calif. 90049. 550. Phone: (213) 541-8213.

Congress of Racial Equality (CORE) (1942): 1457 Flatbush Ave., Brooklyn, N.Y. 11210. Nationwide network of chapters. Phone: (718) 434-3580.

Conscientious Objectors, Central Committee for (1948): 2208 South St., Philadelphia, Pa. 19146. Phone: (215) 545-4626.

Conservation Engineers, Association of (1961): Alabama Dept. of Cons. & Natural Resources, Engineering Section, 64 N. Union St., Montgomery, Ala 36130. Phone: (205) 242-3476.

Consulting Chemists & Chemical Engineers, Inc., Association of (1928): 310 Madison Ave., Rm. 1423, New York, N.Y. 10017. 130. Phone: (212) 983-3160.

Consulting Organizations, Council of (1989): 230 Park Ave., Suite 544, New York, N.Y. 10169. 2,100. Phone: (212) 697-8262.

Consumer Federation of America (1968): 1424 16th St. N.W., Washington, D.C. 20036. 240 member organizations. Phone: (202) 387-6121.

Consumer Interests, American Council on (1953): 240 Stanley Hall, Univ. of Missouri, Columbia, Mo. 65211. 1,800. Phone: (314) 882-3817.

Consumers League, National (1899): 815 15th St. N.W., Suite 516, Washington, D.C. 20005. Phone: (202) 639-8140.

Consumers Union (1936): 256 Washington St., Mt. Vernon, N.Y. 10553. 4,600,000 subscribers to *Consumer Reports*. Phone: (914) 667-9400.

Contract Bridge League, American (1927): 2990 Airways Blvd., Memphis, Tenn. 38116-3847. Phone: (901) 332-5586.

Cooperative Business Association, National (formerly Cooperative League of the U.S.A) (1916): 1401 New York Ave. N.W., Suite 1100, Washington, D.C. 20005. Phone: (202) 638-6222.

Counselors and Family Therapists, National Academy of (1972): 55 Morris Ave., Springfield, N.J. 07081-1422. Phone: (201) 379-7496.

Country Music Association (1958): Box 22299, Nashville, Tenn. 37202. 6,000. Phone: (615) 244-2840.

Credit Association, International (1912): P.O. Box 27357, St. Louis, Mo. 63141-1757. 11,500 members, 125 local associations. Phone: (314) 991-3030.

Credit Management, National Association of (1896): 8815 Centre Park Dr., Suite 200, Columbia, Md. 21045. Phone: (301) 740-5560.

Credit Union National Association (1934): P.O. Box 431, Madison, Wis. 53701. 52 state leagues representing 15,000 credit unions. Phone: (608) 231-4000.

Crime and Delinquency, National Council on (1907): 685 Market St., #620, San Francisco, Calif. 94105. Nationwide membership. Phone: (415) 896-6223.

*Criminal Investigators Association, International (ICIA) (1982): P.O. Box 15350, Chevy Chase, Md. 20815. 1,000. Phone: (202) 293-9088.

*CSA/USA, Celiac Sprue Association/United States of America: P.O. Box 31700, Omaha, Neb. 68131-0700. 6 regions in U.S., 36 chapters, 60 active resource units. Phone: (402) 558-0600.

Dairy Council, National (1915): 6300 N. River Rd., Rosement, Ill. 60018. Phone: (708) 696-1020.

Daughters of the American Revolution, National Society (1890): 1776 D St. N.W., Washington, D.C. 20006. 200,000. Phone: (202) 628-1776.

Daughters of the Confederacy, United (1894): 328 N. Boulevard, Richmond, Va. 23220-4057. 27,000. Phone: (804) 355-1636.

Deaf, National Association of the (1880): 814 Thayer Ave., Silver Spring, Md. 20910. Phone: (301) 587-1788.

Defenders of Wildlife (1947): 1244 19th St. N.W., Washington, D.C. 20036. 80,000. Phone: (202) 659-9510.

Defense Preparedness Association, American (1919): Two Colonial Place, Suite 400, 2101 Wilson Blvd., Arlington, Va. 22201-3061. 45,000 individual, 1,000 corporate. Phone: (703) 522-1820.

Dental Association, American (1859): 211 E. Chicago Ave., Chicago, Ill. 60611. 150,000. Phone: (312) 440-2500.

Diabetes Association, American (1940): 1660 Duke St., Alexandria, Va. 22314. Phone: (703) 549-1500.

Dignity (1969): 1500 Massachusetts Ave. N.W., Suite 11, Washington, D.C. 20005. 5,000. Phone: (202) 861-0017.

Disabled American Veterans (1920): 807 Maine Ave. S.W., Washington, D.C. 20024. Phone: (202) 554-3501.

Dowsers, Inc., The American Society of (1961): Danville, Vt. 05828. 3,500. Phone: (802) 684-3417.

Drug, Chemical, & Allied Trades Association, Inc., The (1890): 2 Roosevelt Ave., Syosset, N.Y. 11791. 575. Phone (516) 496-3317.

Ducks Unlimited, Inc. (1937): One Waterfowl Way, Long Grove, Ill. 60047. 550,000. Phone: (708) 438-4300.

Earthwatch (1970): 680 Mt. Auburn St., Box 403, Watertown, Mass. 02272. 40,000. Phone: (617) 926-8200.

Eastern Star, Order of, General Grand Chapter (1876): 1618 New Hampshire Ave. N.W., Washington, D.C. 20009. 2,087,063. Phone: (202) 667-4737.

Easter Seal Society, The National (1921): 70 E. Lake St., Chicago, Ill. 60601. 58 affiliated state societies and Puerto Rico. Phone: (312) 726-6200 and (312) 726-4258.

Economic Association, American (1885): 1313 21st Ave. So., Nashville, Tenn. 37212. 20,000 members, 5,500 inst. subscribers. Phone: (615) 322-2595.

Economic Development, Committee for (1942): 477 Madison Ave., New York, N.Y. 10022. 250 trustees. Phone: (212) 688-2063.

Edison Electric Institute (1933): 701 Pennsylvania Ave. N.W., Washington, D.C. 20004.

Education, American Council on (1918): One Dupont Circle N.W., Washington, D.C. 20036. 1,750 institutional members. Phone: (202) 939-9300.

Education, Council for Advancement and Support of (1974): 11 Dupont Circle N.W., Suite 400, Washington, D.C. 20036-1207. 13,500. Phone: (202) 328-5900.

Educational Exchange, International, Council on (1947): 205 E. 42nd St., New York, N.Y. 10017. 203. Phone: (212) 661-1414.

Educational Research Association, American (1906): 1230 17th St. N.W., Washington, D.C. 20036. 16,000. Phone: (202) 223-9485.

Education Association, National (1857): 1201 16th St. N.W., Washington, D.C. 20036-3290. 2 million. Phone: (202) 833-4000.

Electrochemical Society, The (1902): 10 S. Main St., Pennington, N.J. 08534. 6,274. Phone: (609) 737-1902.

Electronic Industries Association (1924): 2001 Pennsylvania Ave. N.W. Washington, D.C. 20006-1813. 1,000 member companies. Phone: (202) 457-4900.

Electroplaters and Surface Finishers Society, American (1909): 12644 Research Pkwy., Orlando, Fla. 32826. 10,000. Phone: (407) 281-6441.

Elks of the U.S.A., Benevolent and Protective Order of the (1868): 2750 Lake View Ave., Chicago, Ill. 60614. 1,500,000. Phone: (312) 477-2750.

Energy Engineers, Association of (1977): 4025 Pleasantdale Rd., Suite 420, Atlanta, Ga. 30340. 7,500. Phone: (404) 447-5083.

English-Speaking Union of the United States (1920): 16 E. 69th St., New York, N.Y. 10021. 25,000. Phone: (212) 879-6800.

Entomological Society of America (1889): 9301 Annapolis Rd., Lanham, Md. 20706. 9,000. Phone: (301) 731-4535.

Esperanto League for North America, The (1952): P.O. Box 1129, El Cerrito, Calif. 94530. Over 1,000. Phone: (415) 653-0998.

Exceptional Children, The Council for (1922): 1920 Association Dr., Reston, Va. 22091. 53,000. Phone: (703) 620-3660.

Experimental Test Pilots, The Society of (1956): 44814 Elm St., Lancaster, Calif. 93534. 1,800. Phone: (805) 942-9574.

Exploration Geophysicists, Society of (1930): P.O. Box 702740, Tulsa, Okla. 74170. 15,000. Phone: (918) 493-3516.

Family Physicians, American Academy of (1947): 8880 Ward Pkwy., Kansas City, Mo. 64114. 68,000. Phone: (816) 333-9700.

Family Relations, National Council on (1938): 3989 Central Ave. N.E., #550, Minneapolis, Minn. 55421. 4,000. Phone: (612) 781-9331.

Family Service America (1911): 11700 W. Lake Park Dr., Park Place, Milwaukee, Wis. 53224. Approx. 300 member agencies. Phone: (414) 359-1040.

Farm Bureau Federation, American (1919): 225 Touhy Ave., Park Ridge, Ill. 60068. 3.7 million member families. Phone: (312) 399-5700.

Farmer Cooperatives, National Council of (1929): 50 F St. N.W., Washington, D.C. 20001. 135. Phone: (202) 626-8700.

Federal Employees, National Federation of (1917): 1016 16th St. N.W., Washington, D.C. 20036. Rep. 150,000. Phone: (202) 862-4400.

Feline and Canine Friends, Inc. (1973): 505 N. Bush St., Anaheim, Calif. 92805. 1,000. Phone: (714) 635-7975.

Fellowship of Reconciliation (1915): Box 271, Nyack, N.Y. 10960. 35,000. Phone: (914) 358-4601.

Female Executives, •National Association for (1972): 127 W. 24th St., New York, N.Y. 10011. 220,000. Phone: (212) 645-0770.

FFA Organization, National (1928): 5632 Mt. Vernon Memorial Hwy., P.O. Box 15160, Alexandria, Va. 22309-0160. 397,107. Phone: (703) 360-3600.

Fire Protection Association, National (1896): One Batterymarch Park, P.O. Box 9101, Quincy, Mass. 02269-9101. 54,000. Phone: (617) 770-3999.

Flag Foundation, National (1968): Flag Plaza, Pittsburgh, Pa. 15219. 3,000+. Phone: (412) 261-1776.

Fleet Reserve Association (1924): 1303 New Hampshire Ave. N.W., Washington, D.C. 20036. 160,000. Phone: (202) 785-2768.

Flight Test Engineers, Society of (1968): P.O. Box 4047, Lancaster, Calif. 93539. 1,100. Phone: (805) 948-3067.

Foreign Policy Association (1918): 729 Seventh Ave., New York, N.Y. 10019. Phone: (212) 764-4050.

Foreign Relations, Council on (1921): 58 E. 68th St., New York, N.Y. 10021. 2,400. Phone: (212) 734-0400.

*Foreign Study, American Institute for** (1965): 102 Greenwich Ave., Greenwich, Conn. 06830. 325,000. Phone: (203) 869-9090.

Foreign Trade Council, Inc., National (1914): 100 E. 42nd St., New York, N.Y. 10017. Over 550 companies. Phone: (212) 867-5630. Also, 1625 K St. N.W., Washington, D.C. 20006. Phone: (202) 887-0278.

Forensic Sciences, American Academy of (1948): 218 E. Cache La Poudre/80903, P.O. Box 669, Colorado Springs, Colo. 80901-0669. 3,500. Phone: (719) 636-1100.

*Forest Council, American** (1932): 1250 Connecticut Ave. N.W., Suite 320, Washington, D.C. 20036. 100. Phone: (202) 463-2455.

Foresters, Society of American (1900): 5400 Grosvenor Lane, Bethesda, Md. 20814-2198. 19,000. Phone: (301) 897-8720.

Forestry Association, American (1875): 1516 P St. N.W., Washington, D.C. 20005. 35,000. Phone: (202) 667-3300.

Fortean Organization, International (1965): P.O. Box 367, Arlington, Va. 22210-0367. 900. Phone: (703) 522-9232.

Foster Parents Plan International (1937). Box 804, East Greenwich, R.I. 02818. Phone: (401) 826-2500.

4-H Program (early 1900s): Room 3860-S, U.S. Department of Agriculture, Washington, D.C. 20250. 5,492,120. Phone: (202) 447-5853.

Freedom of Information Center (1958): 20 Walter Williams Hall, Univ. of Missouri, Columbia, Mo. 65211. Phone: (314) 882-4856.

French-American Chamber of Commerce in the U.S. Inc. (1896): 509 Madison Ave., Suite 1900, New York, N.Y. 10022. 605. Trade Association. Phone: (212) 371-4466.

French Institute/Alliance Française (1911): 22 E. 60th St., New York, N.Y. 10022. 9,000. Phone: (212) 355-6100.

Friendship and Good Will, International Society of (Esperanto) (1978): 211 W. Fourth Ave., P.O. Box 2637, Gastonia, N.C. 28053-2637. 3,850 in 162 countries. Phone: (704) 864-7906.

Friends of Animals Inc. (1957): P.O. Box 1244, Norwalk, Conn. 06856. 104,000. Phone: (203) 866-5223. For low-cost spay/neuter info. call: 1 (800) 631-2212.

Friends of the Earth (1969): 218 D St. S.E., Washington, D.C. 20003. Phone: (202) 544-2600.

Future Homemakers of America, Inc. (1945): 1910 Association Dr., Reston, Va. 22091. 285,000. Phone: (703) 476-4900.

Gamblers Anonymous: Box 17173, Los Angeles, Calif. 90017. Phone: (213) 386-8789.

*Genealogical Society, National** (1903): 4527 17th St. N., Arlington, Va. 22207. 10,000. Phone: (703) 525-0050.

Genetic Association, American (1903): P.O. Box 39, Buckeystown, Md. 21717. 1,600. Phone: (301) 695-9292.

Geographers, Association of American (1904): Dept. 199, 1718 M St. N. W. Washington, D.C. 20036. 6,300. Phone: (202) 234-1450.

Geographical Society, The American (1851): 156 Fifth Ave., Suite 600, New York, N.Y. 10010. 7,002. Phone: (212) 242-0214.

Geographic Education, National Council for (1915): Indiana University of Pennsylvania, Indiana, Pa. 15705. 3,500. Phone: (412) 357-6290.

Geographic Society, National (1888): 17th and M Sts. N.W., Washington, D.C. 20036. 10,500,000. Phone: (202) 857-7000.

Geological Institute, American (1948): 4220 King St., Alexandria, Va. 22302. 21 member societies representing 70,000 geoscientists. Phone: (703) 379-2480.

Geological Society of America, Inc. (1888): 3300 Penrose Pl., P.O. Box 9140, Boulder, Colo. 80301. 17,000. Phone: (303) 447-2020.

Geriatrics Society, American (1942): 770 Lexington Ave., Suite 400, New York, N.Y. 10021. 6,200. Phone: (212) 308-1414.

German American National Congress, The (Deutsch-Amerikanischer National Kongress—DANK) (1958): 4740 N. Western Ave., Chicago, Ill. 60625. 30,000, plus Associates. Phone: (312) 275-1100.

Gideons International, The (1889): 2900 Lebanon Rd., Nashville, Tenn. 37214. 100,000. Phone: (615) 883-8533.

Gifted, The Association for the (1958): The Council for Exceptional Children, 1920 Association Dr., Reston, Va. 22091. 2,200. Phone: (703) 620-3660.

Girls Clubs of America (1945): 30 E. 33rd St., New York, N.Y. 10016. 250,000. Phone: (212) 689-3700.

Girl Scouts of the U.S.A. (1912): 830 Third Ave., New York, N.Y. 10022. 3,166,000. Phone: (212) 940-7500.

Graphic Artists, Society of American (1916): 32 Union Square, Rm. 1214, New York, N.Y. 10003. Phone: (212) 260-5706.

Graphoanalysis Society, International (1929): 111 N. Canal St., Chicago, Ill. 60606. 10,000. Phone: (312) 930-9446.

Gray Panthers Project Fund (1970): 1424 16th St. N.W., Suite 602, Washington, D.C. 20036. Over 80 chapters. Phone: (202) 387-3111.

*Greenpeace U.S.A.** (1979): 1436 U St. N.W., Washington, D.C. 20009. 800,000. Phone: (202) 462-1177.

Group Psychotherapy Association, American (1942): 25 E. 21st St., 6th Floor, New York, N.Y. 10010. 3,500 Phone: (212) 477-2677.

Guide Dog Foundation for the Blind, Inc. (1946): 371 E. Jericho Turnpike, Smithtown, N.Y. 11787. 1,326. Phone: (516) 265-2121; outside N.Y. state call 1 (800) 548-4337.

Hadassah, The Women's Zionist Organization of America (1912): 50 W. 58th St., New York, N.Y. 10019. 385,000. Phone: (212) 355-7900.

Handgun Control, Inc. (1974): 1225 Eye St. N.W., Washington, D.C. 20005. 250,000. Phone: (202) 898-0792.

Health, Physical Education, Recreation, and Dance, American Alliance for (1885): 1900 Association Dr., Reston, Va. 22091. 35,000. Phone: (703) 476-3400.

*Heart Association, American (1924): 7320 Greenville Ave., Dallas, Tex. 75231-4599. 2,000,000 volunteers. Phone: (214) 373-6300.

Heating, Refrigerating, and Air-Conditioning Engineers, Inc., American Society of (1894): 1791 Tullie Circle N.E., Atlanta, Ga. 30329. 50,000. Phone: (404) 636-8400.

Helicopter Association International (1948): 1619 Duke St., Alexandria, Va. 22314-3439. Phone: (703) 683-4646.

Hemispheric Affairs, Council on (1975): 724 9th St. N.W., Rm. 401, Washington, D.C. 20001. Phone: (202) 393-3322.

Historians, The Organization of American (1907): Indiana Univ., 112 N. Bryan St., Bloomington, Ind 47408. 8,500. Phone: (812) 855-7311.

Historic Preservation, National Trust for (1949): 1785 Massachusetts Ave. N.W., Washington, D.C. 20036. 250,000. Phone: (202) 673-4000.

Home Economics Association, American (1909): 1555 King St., Alexandria, Va. 22314. 26,000. Phone: 1 (800) 424-8080.

Horse Council, Inc., American (1969): 1700 K St. N.W., Washington, D.C. 20006. More than 170 organizations and 2,200 individuals. Phone: (202) 296-4031.

Horse Shows Association, Inc., American (1917): 220 E. 42nd St., New York, N.Y. 10017-5806. 55,000. Phone: (212) 972-2472.

Horticultural Association, National Junior (1935): 441 E. Pine, Freemont, Mich. 49412. 12,500. Phone: (616) 924-5237.

Horticultural Society, American (1922): Box 0105, Mt. Vernon, Va. 22121. 20,000. Phone: (703) 768-5700.

Hospital Association, American (1898): 840 N. Lake Shore Dr., Chicago, Ill. 60611. 5,500 institutions. Phone: (312) 280-6000.

Housing Science, International Association for (1972): P.O. Box 340254, Coral Gables/Miami, Fla. 33114. 500 professionals. Phone: (305) 448-3532.

Humane Association, American (1877): P.O. Box 1266, Denver, Colo. 80201-1266. Phone: (303) 792-9900.

Humane Society of the United States (1954): 2100 L St. N.W., Washington, D.C. 20037. 1,000,000. Phone: (202) 452-1100.

Humanities, National Endowment for the (1965): 1100 Pennsylvania Ave. N.W., Washington, D.C. 20506. Phone: (202) 786-0438.

Hydrogen Energy, International Association for (1975): P.O. Box 248266, Coral Gables, Fla. 33124. 2,500. Phone: (305) 284-4666.

Illustrators, Society of (1901): 128 E. 63rd St., New York, N.Y. 10021. 975. Phone: (212) 838-2560.

Industrial Engineers, Institute of (1948): 25 Technology Park/Atlanta, Norcross, Ga. 30092. 40,000. Phone: (404) 449-0460.

Interfraternity Conference, National (1909): 3901 W. 86th St., Suite 390, Indianapolis, Ind. 46268. 59. Phone: (317) 872-1112.

Investment Management and Research, Association for (1947): 1633 Broadway, 16th floor, New York, N.Y. 10019. 17,500. Phone: (212) 957-2860.

Iron and Steel Institute, American (1908): 1133 15th St. N.W., Washington, D.C. 20005-2701. 1,200. Phone: (202) 452-7100.

Izaak Walton League of America (1922): 1401 Wilson Blvd., Level B, Arlington, Va. 22209. 50,000. Phone: (703) 528-1818.

Jaycees, The United States (1920): P.O. Box 7,

Tulsa, Okla. 74121. 240,000. Phone: (918) 584-2481.

Jewish Community Centers, World Confederation of (1946): 12 Hess St., Jerusalem, Israel 94185. Phone: (02) 231 371.

Jewish Congress, American (1918): 15 E. 84th St., New York, N.Y. 10028. 50,000. Phone: (212) 879-4500.

Jewish Historical Society, American (1892): 2 Thornton Rd., Waltham, Mass. 02154. 3,500. Phone: (617) 891-8110.

Jewish War Veterans of the U.S.A. (1896): 1811 R St. N.W., Washington, D.C. 20009-1659. Phone: (202) 265-6280.

Jewish Women, National Council of (1893): 53 W. 23rd St., New York, N.Y. 10010. 100,000. Phone: (212) 645-4048.

John Birch Society (1958): P.O. Box 8040, Appleton, Wis. 54913. Under 100,000. Phone: (414) 749-3780.

Journalists, Society of Professional, (1909): 53 W. Jackson Blvd., Suite 731, Chicago, Ill. 60604-3610. 20,000. Phone: (312) 922-7424.

Journalists and Authors, American Society of (1948): 1501 Broadway, Suite 1907, New York, N.Y. 10036. 750. Phone: (212) 997-0947.

Judaism, American Council for (1943): P.O. Box 9009, Alexandria, Va. 22304. 10,000. Phone: (703) 836-2546.

Junior Achievement Inc. (1919): 45 Clubhouse Dr., Colorado Springs, Colo. 80906. 9,201,108. Phone: (719) 540-8000.

Junior Leagues International, Inc., Association of (1921): 660 First Ave., New York, N.Y. 10016. 277 Leagues, 182,000 members. Phone: (212) 683-1515.

Junior Statesmen of America (1934): 650 Bair Island Rd., Suite 201, Redwood City, Calif. 94063. 10,000. Phone: (415) 366-2700.

JWB (1917): 15 E. 26th St., New York, N.Y. 10010-1579. 275 affiliated Jewish Community Centers, YM-YWHAs, and camps. Phone: (212) 532-4949.

Kennel Club, American (1884): 51 Madison Ave., New York, N.Y. 10010. 463 member clubs. Phone: (212) 696-8200.

Kiwanis International (1915): 3636 Woodview Trace, Indianapolis, Ind. 46268-3196. 323,000. Phone: (317) 875-8755.

Knights of Columbus (1882): One Columbus Plaza, New Haven, Conn. 06507. 1,484,860. Phone: (203) 772-2130.

Knights of Pythias, Supreme Lodge (1864): 2785 E. Desert Inn Rd. #116, Las Vegas, Nev. 89121. 100,000. Phone: (702) 735-3302.

Knights Templar, Grand Encampment of (1816): 14 E. Jackson Blvd., Suite 1700, Chicago, Ill. 60604. 340,000. Phone: (312) 427-5670.

La Leche League International (1956): 9616 Minneapolis Ave., Franklin Park, Ill. 60131-8209. 40,000. Phone: (708) 455-7730.

Law, American Society of International (1906): 2223 Massachusetts Ave. N.W., Washington, D.C. 20008. 4,500. Phone: (202) 265-4313.

League of Women Voters of the U.S. (1920): 1730 M St. N.W., Washington, D.C. 20036. 114,000. Phone: (202) 429-1965.

Legal Aid and Defender Association, National (1911): 1625 K St. N.W., Suite 800, Washington, D.C. 20006. 5,000. Phone: (202) 452-0620.

Legal Secretaries, National Association of (1950): 2250 E. 73rd St., Suite 550, Tulsa, Okla. 74136-6864. 18,000. Phone: (918) 493-3540.

Leukemia Society of America (1949): 733 Third Ave., New York, N.Y. 10017. Phone: (212) 573-8484.

Library Association, American (1876): 50 E. Huron St., Chicago, Ill. 60611. 50,000. Phone: (312) 944-6780.

Life Insurance, American Council of (1976): 1001 Pennsylvania Ave. N.W., Washington, D.C. 20004-2599. 617. Phone: (202) 624-2000.

Life Underwriters, National Association of (1890): 1922 F St. N.W., Washington, D.C. 20006. Phone: (202) 331-6000.

Lions Clubs International (1917): 300 22nd St., Oak Brook, Ill. 60521-8842. 1,363,323. Phone: (708) 571-5466.

Longwave Club of America (1974): 45 Wildflower Rd., Levittown, Pa. 19057. 530. Phone: (215) 945-0543.

Lung Association, American (1904): 1740 Broadway, New York, N.Y. 10019-4374. 132 constituent and affiliate associations. Phone: (212) 315-8700.

Magazine Editors, American Society of (1963): 575 Lexington Ave., New York, N.Y. 10022. 650. Phone: (212) 752-0055.

Magazine Publishers of America (1919): 575 Lexington Ave., New York, N.Y. 10022. 292 member companies; 1,250 publications. Phone: (212) 752-0055.

Management Association, American (1923): 135 W. 50th St., New York, N.Y. 10020. 75,000. Phone: (212) 586-8100.

Manufacturers, National Association of (1895): 1331 Pennsylvania Ave. N.W., Suite 1500–North Lobby, Washington, D.C. 20004-1703. 13,500. Phone: (202) 637-3065.

*Manufacturers' Agents National Association (MANA) (1947): 23016 Mill Creek Rd., P.O. Box 3467, Laguna Hills, Calif. 92654. 9,000. Phone: (714) 859-4040.

March of Dimes Birth Defects Foundation (1938): 1275 Mamaroneck Ave., White Plains, N.Y. 10605. 133 chapters. Phone: (914) 428-7100.

Marine Conservation, Center for (formerly Center for Environmental Education, est. 1972): 1725 De Sales St. N.W., Suite 500, Washington, D.C. 20036. 110,000. Phone: (202) 429-5609.

Marine Corps Association (1913): Bldg. #715, Marine Corps Base, Quantico, Va. 22134. 104, 419. Phone: 1 (800) 336-0291.

Marine Corps League (1923): 8626 Lee Hwy., Fairfax, Va. Correspondence address: P.O. Box 3070, Merrifield, Va. 22116. 30,000. Phone: (703) 207-9588 or (703) 207-9589.

Marine Technology Society (1963): 1825 K St. N.W., Suite 218, Washington, D.C. 20006. 2,500. Phone: (202) 775-5966.

Masons, Ancient and Accepted Scottish Rite, Northern Masonic Jurisdiction, Supreme Council 33 (1867): 33 Marrett Rd., Lexington, Mass. 02173. 424,602. Phone: (617) 862-4410.

Masons, Ancient and Accepted Scottish Rite, Southern Jurisdiction, Supreme Council (1801): 1733 16th St. N.W., Washington, D.C. 20009. 575,746. Phone: (202) 232-3579.

Masons, Royal Arch, General Grand Chapter International (1797): 1084 New Circle Rd. N.E., Lexington, Ky. 40505. 277,340. Phone: (606) 252-4618.

Massachusetts Audubon Society (1896): South Great Rd., Lincoln, Mass. 01773. 45,000 member households. Phone: (508) 259-9500.

Mathematical Association of America (1915): 1529 18th St. N.W., Washington, D.C. 20036.

33,000. Phone: (202) 387-5200.

Mathematical Society, American (1888): P.O. Box 6248, Providence, R.I. 02940. 22,611. Phone: (401) 455-4000.

Mathematical Statistics, Institute of (1935): 3401 Investment Blvd. #7, Hayward, Calif. 94545. 3,800. Phone: (415) 783-8141.

Mayflower Descendants, General Society of (1897): 4 Winslow St., P.O. Box 3297, Plymouth, Mass. 02361. 25,000. Phone: (508) 746-3188.

Mayors, U.S. Conference of (1932): 1620 Eye St. N.W., Washington, D.C. 20006. 8 standing committees. Phone: (202) 293-7330.

Mechanical Engineers, American Society of (1880): 345 E. 47th St., New York, N.Y. 10017. 119,000. Phone: (212) 705-7722.

Mechanics, American Academy of (1969): Dept. of Ames, R-011, University of Calif., San Diego, La Jolla, Calif. 92093. 1,200. Phone: (619) 534-4772.

Medical Association, American (1847): 535 N. Dearborn St., Chicago, Ill. 60610-4377. Phone: (312) 645-5000.

Medical Library Association (1898): Six N. Michigan Ave., Suite 300, Chicago, Ill. 60602. 5,000. Phone: (312) 419-9094.

Mental Health Association, National (1909): 1021 Prince St., Alexandria, Va., 22314-2971. 1,000, 000. Phone: (703) 684-7722.

Meteorological Society, American (1919): 45 Beacon St., Boston, Mass. 02108. 10,000. Phone: (617) 227-2425.

Military Chaplains Association of the U.S.A. (1925): P.O. Box 645, Riverdale, Md. 20737. 1, 550. Phone: (302) 674-3306.

Mining, Metallurgy and Exploration, Society for; The Minerals, Metals & Materials Society (1871): 345 E. 47th St., New York, N.Y. 10017. 4 Member Societies: Society of Mining Engineers, The Minerals, Metals and Materials Society, Iron & Steel Society, Society of Petroleum Engineers. Phone: (212) 705-7695.

Mining and Metallurgical Society of America (1910): 210 Post St., Suite 1102, San Francisco, Calif. 94108. Phone: (415) 398-6925.

Model Aeronautics, Academy of (1936): 1810 Samuel Morse Dr., Reston, Va. 22090. 150,000. Phone: (703) 435-0750.

Modern Language Association of America (1883): 10 Astor Place, New York, N.Y. 10003. 31,547. Phone: (212) 475-9500.

Modern Woodmen of America (1883): 1701 1st Ave., Rock Island, Ill. 61201. 630,000. Phone: (309) 786-6481.

Moose, Loyal Order of (1888): Mooseheart, Ill. 60539. 1,804,198. Phone: (708) 859-2000.

Mothers Against Drunk Driving (MADD) (1980): 669 Airport Fwy., Suite 310, Hurst, Tex. 76053. 1.8 million. Phone: (817) 268-6233.

Motion Picture & Television Engineers, Society of (1916): 595 W. Hartsdale Ave., White Plains, N.Y. 10607. 9,500. Phone: (914) 761-1100.

Motion Picture Arts & Sciences, Academy of (1927): 8949 Wilshire Blvd., Beverly Hills, Calif. 90211. Phone: (213) 278-8990.

Multiple Sclerosis Society, National (1946): 205 E. 42nd St., New York, N.Y. 10017-5706. 370, 000. Phone: (212) 986-3240.

Muscular Dystrophy Association (1950): 810 Seventh Ave., New York, N.Y. 10019. 2,300,000 volunteers. Phone: (212) 586-0808.

Museum of Natural History, American (1869): Central Park West at 79th St., New York, N.Y. 10024-5192. 505,000. Phone: (212) 769-5100.

*Museums, American Association of (1906): 1225 Eye St. N.W., Suite 200, Washington, D.C. 20005. 10,000. Phone: (202) 289-1818.

Music Council, National (1940): 40 W. 37th St., Fifth floor, New York, N.Y. 10018. 50 National Music Organizations. Phone: (212) 563-3734.

Musicians, American Federation of (1896): 1501 Broadway, Suite 600 Paramount Bldg., New York, N.Y. 10036. 230,000. Phone: (212) 869-1330.

*Music Publishers Association, Inc., National (1917): 205 E. 42nd St., New York, N.Y. 10017. Trade Organization/Harry Fox Agency-Licensing Organization. Phone: (212) 370-5330.

Muzzle Loading Rifle Association, National (1933): P.O. Box 67, Friendship, Ind. 47021. 30,000. Phone: (812) 667-5131.

NAFSA: Association of International Educators (1948): k860 19th St. N.W., Washington, D.C. 20009. 6,200. Phone: (202) 462-4811.

*Narcolepsy and Cataplexy Foundation of America (1975): 1410 York Ave., Suite 2D, Mail Box 22, New York, N.Y. 10021. 3,991. Phone: (212) 628-6315.

National Association for the Advancement of Colored People (1909): 4805 Mt. Hope Dr., Baltimore, Md. 21215. 450,000. Phone: (301) 358-8900.

National Grange, The (1867): 1616 H St. N.W., Washington, D.C. 20006. 330,000. Phone: (202) 628-3507.

National PTA (National Congress of Parents and Teachers) (1897): 700 N. Rush St., Chicago, Ill. 60611. 6.6 million. Phone: (312) 787-0977.

Natural Science for Youth Foundation (1961): 130 Azalea Dr., Roswell, Ga. 30075. 350. Phone: (404) 594-9367.

Nature Conservancy, The (1951): 1815 N. Lynn St., Arlington, Va. 22209. 530,000. Phone: (703) 841-5300.

Naval Architects and Marine Engineers, The Society of (1893): 601 Pavonia Ave., Jersey City, N.J. 07306. 12,200. Phone: (201) 798-4800.

Naval Engineers, American Society of (1888): 1452 Duke St., Alexandria, Va. 22314. 9,000. Phone: (703) 836-6727.

Naval Institute, United States (1873): Annapolis, Md. 21402. 110,000. Phone: (301) 268-6110.

Navigation, The Institute of (1945): 1026 16th St. N.W., #104, Washington, D.C. 20036. 3,200. Phone: (202) 783-4121.

Navy League of the United States (1902): 2300 Wilson Blvd., Arlington, Va. 22201. 70,500; Dudley L. Carlson, Executive Director.

Neurofibromatosis Foundation, The National (1978): 141 Fifth Ave., Suite 7-S, New York, N.Y. 10010. 27,000. Phone: (212) 460-8980; toll-free outside N.Y. state 1 (800) 323-7938.

Newspaper Editors, American Society of (1922): P.O. Box 17004, Washington, D.C. 20041. 1,000. Phone: (703) 648-1144.

Newspaper Publishers Association, American (1887): The Newspaper Center, P.O. Box 17407, Dulles International Airport, Washington, D.C. 20041. 1,430. Phone: (703) 648-1000.

Ninety-Second Street Young Men's and Young Women's Hebrew Association (1874): 1395 Lexington Ave., New York, N.Y. 10128. Phone: (212) 427-6000.

Nondestructive Testing, Inc., The American Society for (1941): 1711 Arlingate Lane, P.O. Box 28518, Columbus, Ohio 43228-0518. 10,000. Phone: Natl. 1-800-222-ASNT; Ohio 1-800-NDT-OHIO.

NOT SAFE (National Organization Taunting Safety and Fairness Everywhere) (1980): P.O. Box 5743, Montecito, Calif. 93108. 975. Phone: (805) 969-6217.

Nuclear Society, American (1954): 555 N. Kensington Ave., La Grange Park, Ill. 60525. 16,000. Phone: (708) 352-6611.

Numismatic Association, American (1891): 818 N. Cascade Ave., Colorado Springs, Colo. 80903-3279. 34,000. Phone: (719) 632-2646; (800) 367-9723.

Nurses' Association, American (1896): 2420 Pershing Rd., Kansas City, Mo. 64108. 196,000. Phone: (816) 474-5720.

Nutrition, American Institute of (1928): 9650 Rockville Pike, Bethesda, Md. 20814. 2,700. Phone: (301) 530-7050.

Odd Fellows, Sovereign Grand Lodge, Independent Order of (1819): 422 N. Trade St., Winston-Salem, N.C. 27101. 700,000. Phone: (919) 725-5955.

Olympic Committee, United States (1921): 1750 East Boulder St., Colorado Springs, Colo. 80909. Phone: (719) 632-5551.

Optical Society of America (1916): 2010 Massachusetts Ave. N.W., Washington, D.C. 20036. 10,000. Phone: (202) 223-8130.

Optimist International (1919): 4494 Lindell Blvd., St. Louis, Mo. 63108. 170,000. Phone: (314) 371-6000.

Optometric Association, American (1898): 243 N. Lindbergh Blvd., St. Louis, Mo. 63141. 27,000. Phone: (314) 991-4100.

Organization of American States, General Secretariat (1890): 1889 F St. N.W., Washington, D.C. 20006. 32 member nations. Phone: (202) 458-3000.

Ornithologists' Union, American (1883): c/o National Museum of Natural History, Smithsonian Institution, Washington, D.C. 20560. 5,000. Phone: (202) 357-1970.

ORT Federation, American (1922): 817 Broadway, New York, N.Y. 10003. 160,000. Phone: (212) 677-4400.

Osteopathic Association, American: 142 E. Ontario St., Chicago, Ill. 60611-3269. Phone: (312) 280-5800.

Overeaters Anonymous (1960): P.O. Box 92870, Los Angeles, Calif. 90009. 150,000. Phone: (213) 542-8363.

Parents Without Partners (1957): 8807 Colesville Rd., Silver Spring, Md. 20910. 130,000. Phone: (301) 588-9354 or 1 (800) 637-7974.

Parks & Conservation Association, National (1919): 1015 31st St. N.W., Washington, D.C. 20007. 150,000. Phone: (202) 944-8530.

Pathologists, American Association of (1976): 9650 Rockville Pike, Bethesda, Md. 20814. 2,300. Phone: (301) 530-7130.

People for the American Way (1980): 2000 M St. N.W., Suite 400, Washington, D.C. 20036. 280,000. Phone: (202) 467-4999.

Petroleum Geologists, American Association of (1917): P.O. Box 979, Tulsa, Okla. 74101-0979. 36,000. Phone: (918) 584-2555.

Pharmaceutical Association, American (1852): 2215 Constitution Ave. N.W., Washington, D.C. 20037. 38,200. Phone: (202) 628-4410.

Philatelic Society, American (1886): P.O. Box 8000, State College, Pa. 16803. 57,000. Phone: (814) 237-3803.

Photogrammetry and Remote Sensing, American Society for (1934): 5410 Grosvenor Lane, Suite 210, Bethesda, Md. 20814-2160. Phone: (301) 493-0290.

Photographic Society of America (1934): 3000 United Founders Blvd., Suite 103, Oklahoma City, Okla. 73112. Phone: (405) 843-1437.

Photography, International Center of (1974): 1130 Fifth Ave., New York, N.Y. 10128. Phone: (212) 860-1777.

Physical Society, American (1899): 335 E. 45th St., New York, N.Y. 10017. 39,000. Phone: (212) 682-7341.

Physical Therapy Association, American (APTA) (1921): 1111 N. Fairfax St., Alexandria, Va. 22314. 50,000. Phone: (703) 684-2782.

Physics, American Institute of (1931): 335 E. 45th St., New York, N.Y. 10017. 102,500. Phone: (212) 661-9404.

Pilot Club International (1921): Pilot International World Headquarters, 244 College St., P.O. Box 4844, Macon, Ga. 31213. 21,000. Phone: (912) 743-7403.

Planetary Society, The (1979): 65 N. Catalina Ave., Pasadena, Calif. 91106. 120,000. Phone: (818) 793-5100.

Planned Parenthood® Federation of America, Inc., (1916): 810 Seventh Ave., New York, N.Y. 10019. 175 affiliates. Phone: (212) 541-7800.

Plastics Engineers, Society of (1942): 14 Fairfield Dr., Brookfield, Conn. 06804-0403. 35,000. Phone: (203) 775-0471.

Police, American Federation of (1966): Records Center, 1100 N.E. 125th St., North Miami, Fla. 33161. 55,000. Phone: (305) 891-1700.

Police, International Association of Chiefs of (1893): 1110 N. Glebe Rd., Suite 200, Arlington, Va. 22201. 14,500. Phone (703) 243-6500.

Police Hall of Fame, American (1960): 3801 Biscayne Blvd., Miami, Fla. 33137. 55,000. Phone: (305) 891-1700.

Political and Social Science, American Academy of (1889): 3937 Chestnut St., Philadelphia, Pa. 19104. Phone: (215) 386-4594.

Political Science, Academy of (1880): 475 Riverside Dr., Suite 1274, New York, N.Y. 10115-0012. 9,000. Phone: (212) 870-2500.

Powder Metallurgy Institute, American (1958): 105 College Rd. East, Princeton, N.J. 08540. 2, 400. Phone: (609) 452-7700.

Practical Nurse Education and Service, National Association for (1951): 1400 Spring St., Suite 310, Silver Spring, Md. 20910. Phone: (301) 588-2491.

Press Club, National (1908): National Press Bldg., 529 14th St. N.W., Washington, D.C. 20045. 4,800. Phone: (202) 662-7500.

Professional Engineers, National Society of (1934): 1420 King St., Alexandria, Va. 22314. 75,000. Phone: (703) 684-2800.

Professional Photographers of America, Inc. (1880): 1090 Executive Way, Des Plaines, Ill. 60018. 17,000. Phone: (708) 299-8161.

Psychiatric Association, American (1844): 1400 K St. N.W., Washington, D.C. 20005. 36,335. Phone: (202) 682-6000.

Psychoanalytic Association, The American (1911): 309 E. 49th St., New York, N.Y. 10017. 3,000 psychoanalysts. Phone: (212) 752-0450.

Psychological Association, American (1892): 1200 17th St. N.W., Washington, D.C. 20036. 96,000. Phone: (202) 955-7600.

Public Health Association, American (1872): 1015 15th St. N.W., Washington, D.C. 20005. 50,000+. Phone: (202) 789-5600.

Puppeteers of America (1937): 5 Cricklewood Path, Pasadena, Calif. 91107. Phone: (818) 797-5748.

Quality Control, The American Society for (1946): 310 W. Wisconsin Ave., Milwaukee, Wis. 53203. 70,000. Phone: (414) 272-8575.

Railroads, Association of American (1934): 50 F St. N.W., Washington, D.C. 20001. Phone: (202) 639-2100.

Realtors, National Association of (1908): 430 N. Michigan Ave., Chicago, Ill. 60611. 766,317. Phone: (312) 329-8200.

Recording Arts and Sciences, Inc., National Academy of (1958): 303 N. Glenoaks Blvd., Suite 140, Burbank, Calif. 91502. 7,300. Phone: (213) 849-1313.

Red Cross, American (1881): 17th and D Sts. N.W., Washington, D.C. 20006. Over 2,800 chapters. Phone: (202) 737-8300.

Rehabilitation Association, National (1925): 633 S. Washington St., Alexandria, Va. 22314-4193. 18,000. Phone: (703) 836-0850.

Research and Enlightenment, Association for (1931): 67th St. & Atlantic Ave. (P.O. Box 595), Virginia Beach, Va. 23451. 90,000. Phone: (804) 428-3588.

Reserve Officers Association of the United States (1922): 1 Constitution Ave. N.E., Washington, D.C. 20002. 125,000. Phone: (202) 479-2200.

***Retarded Citizens, Association for** (1950): 2501 Avenue J, Arlington, Tex. 76006. 1,300 chapters. Phone: (817) 640-0204.

Retired Federal Employees, National Association of (1921): 1533 New Hampshire Ave. N.W., Washington, D.C. 20036-1279. 500,000. Phone: (202) 234-0832.

***Retired Persons, American Association of** (1958): 1909 K St. N.W., Washington, D.C. 20049. 29,000,000. Phone: (202) 872-4700.

Reye's Syndrome Foundation, National (1974): 426 N. Lewis St., Bryan, Ohio 43506. Phone: (800) 233-7393. In Ohio: 1 (800) 231-7393.

RID-USA (Remove Intoxicated Drivers) (1978): Box 520, Schenectady, N.Y. 12301. Over 155/40 state chapters. Phone: (518) 372-0034.

Rifle Association of America, National (1871): 1600 Rhode Island Ave. N.W., Washington, D.C. 20036. 3,000,000. Phone: (202) 828-6000.

Right to Life, National Committee (1973): 419 7th St. N.W., Washington, D.C. 20004. Phone: (202) 626-8800.

Rotary International (1905): One Rotary Center, 1560 Sherman Ave., Evanston, Ill. 60201. 1,090, 000 in 167 countries. Phone: (708) 866-3000.

Safety Council, National (1913): 444 N. Michigan Ave., Chicago, Ill. 60611. Phone: (312) 527-4800.

Salvation Army, The (1865): 799 Bloomfield Ave., Verona, N.J. 07044. 433,443. Phone: (201) 239-0606.

SANE/FREEZE: Campaign for Global Security (a merger of SANE and the Nuclear Weapons Freeze Campaign) (1957): 1819 H St. N.W., Suite 1000, Washington, D.C. 20006. 170,000. Phone: (202) 862-9740.

Save-the-Redwoods League (1918): 114 Sansome St., Suite 605, San Francisco, Calif. 94104. 45, 000. Phone: (415) 362-2352.

Savings Institutions, National Council of (1920): 1101 15th St. N.W., Suite 400, Washington, D.C. 20005. Phone: (202) 857-3100.

Science, American Association for the Advancement of (1848): 1333 H St. N.W., Washington, D.C. 20005. 133,000. Phone: (202) 326-6400.

Science and Health, American Council on (1978): 1995 Broadway, 16th Floor, New York, N.Y. 10023. Phone: (212) 362-7044.

Science Fiction Society, World (1939): c/o Southern California Institute for Fan Interests, P.O. Box 8442, Van Nuys, Calif. 91409. 6,000. Phone: (818) 366-3827.

Science Writers, Inc., National Association of (1934): P.O. Box 294, Greenlawn, N.Y. 11740. 1,600. Phone: (516) 757-5664.

Scientists, Federation of American (FAS) (1945): 307 Massachusetts Ave. N.E., Washington, D.C. 20002. 4,000. Phone: (202) 546-3300.

SCRABBLE® Association, National (1972): P.O. Box 700, Front Street Garden, Greenport, N.Y. 11944. 15,000. Phone: (516) 477-0033.

Screen Actors Guild (1933): 7065 Hollywood Blvd., Hollywood, Calif. 90028. 73,000. Phone: (213) 465-4600.

Sculpture Society, National (1893): 15 E. 26th St., New York, N.Y. 10010. 350. Phone: (212) 889-6960.

Seeing Eye Inc., The (1929): P.O. Box 375. Morristown, N.J. 07963-0375. Phone: (201) 539-4425.

***Senior Citizens, National Alliance of** (1974): 2525 Wilson Blvd., Arlington, Va. 22201. 2.2 million. Phone: (703) 528-4380.

Separationists, Society of (1963): P.O. Box 140195, Austin, Tex. 78714-0195. 37,216 families. Phone: (512) 458-1244.

Shrine of North America (Shriners Hospitals) (1872): Box 31356, Tampa, Fla. 33631-3356. 774,184. Phone: (813) 281-0300.

Sierra Club (1892): 730 Polk St., San Francisco, Calif. 94109. 500,000. Phone: (415) 776-2211.

SIETAR INTERNATIONAL (1974) 733 15th St. N.W., Suite 900, Washington, D.C. 20005. 1, 500. Phone: (202) 737-5000.

Simon Wiesenthal Center (1978): 9760 W. Pico Blvd., Los Angeles, Calif. 90035. 370,000. Phone: (213) 553-9036.

Small Business United, National (1937): 1155 15th St. N.W., #710, Washington, D.C. 20005. 50,000. Phone: (202) 293-8830.

Social Work Education, Council on (1919): 1600 Duke St., Alexandria, Va. 22314. Phone: (703) 683-8080.

Social Workers, National Association of (1955): 7981 Eastern Ave., Silver Spring, Md. 20910. Phone: (301) 565-0333.

Sociological Association, American (1905): 1722 N St. N.W., Washington, D.C. 20036. 12,600. Phone: (202) 833-3410.

Soil and Water Conservation Society (1945): 7515 N.E. Ankeny Rd., Ankeny, Iowa 50021. 13,000. Phone: (515) 289-2331.

Songwriters Guild of America, The (1931): 276 Fifth Ave., New York, N.Y. 10001. 4,200. Phone: (212) 686-6820.

Sons of Italy in America, Order (1905): 219 E St. N.E., Washington, D.C. 20002. 175,000. Phone: (202) 547-2900.

Sons of the American Revolution, National Society of the (1889): 1000 S. 4th St., Louisville, Ky. 40203. 26,000. Phone: (502) 589-1776.

Soroptimist International of the Americas (1921): 1616 Walnut St., Philadelphia, Pa. 19103. 50, 000. Phone: (215) 732-0512.

Southern Association on Children Under Six (1948): Box 5403, Brady Station, Little Rock, Ark. 72215. 16,000. Phone: (501) 663-0353.

Space Education Association, U.S. (1973): 746 Turnpike Rd., Elizabethtown, Pa. 17022-1161. 1,000. Phone: (717) 367-3265.

Space Society, National (1974): 922 Pennsylvania Ave. S.E., Washington, D.C. 20003. 28,000. Phone: (202) 543-1900.

Special Olympics International (1968): 1350 New York Ave. N.W., Suite 500, Washington, D.C., 20005. 1,000,000. Phone: (202) 628-3630.

***Speech-Language-Hearing Association, American** (1925): 10801 Rockville Pike, Rockville, Md. 20852. 46,000. Phone: (301) 897-5700.

Sports Car Club of America Inc. (1944): 9033 E. Easter Place, Englewood, Colo. 80112. 54,000. Phone: (303) 694-7222.

State Garden Clubs, Inc., National Council of (1929): 4401 Magnolia Ave., St. Louis, Mo. 63110. 308,623. Phone: (314) 776-7574.

***State Governments, The Council of** (1933): P.O. Box 11910, Iron Works Pike, Lexington, Ky. 40578. All state officials, all 50 states. Phone: (606) 252-2291.

Statistical Association, American (1839): 1429 Duke St., Alexandria, Va. 22314. 15,103.

Student Association, United States (1947): 1012 14th St. N.W., #207, Washington, D.C. 20005. Phone: (202) 347-8772.

Surgeons, American College of (1913): 55 E. Erie, St., Chicago, Ill. 60611. 50,000+. Phone: (312) 664-4050.

Symphony Orchestra League, American (1942): 777 Fourteenth St. N.W., Suite 500, Washington, D.C. 20005. 4,713. Phone: (202) 628-0099.

TASH: The Association for Persons with Severe Handicaps (1973): 7010 Roosevelt Way N.E., Seattle, Wash. 98115. 8,500. Phone: (206) 523-8446.

Tax Foundation, Inc. (1937): 470 L'Enfant Plaza S.W., Suite 7112, Washington, D.C. 20024. Phone: (202) 863-5454.

***Teachers, American Federation of** (1916): 555 New Jersey Ave. N.W., Washington, D.C., 20001. 660,000. Phone: (202) 879-4400.

***Television Arts and Sciences, National Academy of** (1948): 111 W. 57th St., New York, N.Y., 10019. 15,000. Phone: (212) 586-8424.

***Testing & Materials, American Society for** (1898): 1916 Race St., Philadelphia, Pa. 19103. 32,000. Phone: (215) 299-5400.

Theatre Guild (1919): 226 W. 47th St., New York, N.Y. 10036. 105,000. Phone: (212) 869-5470.

Theosophical Society in America, The (1875): P.O. Box 270, Wheaton, Ill. 60189-0270. 5, 600. Phone: (708) 668-1571.

Tin Can Sailors, Inc. (1976): Battleship Cove, Fall River, Mass. 02721. 12,087. Phone: (617) 678-1905.

Toastmasters International (1924): P.O. Box 9052, Mission Viejo, Calif. 92690-7052, and 23182 Arroyo Vista, Rancho Santa Margarita, Calif. 92688. Phone: (714) 858-8255. 92711. 142,500. Phone: (714) 542-6793.

TOUGHLOVE International (1977): P.O. Box 1069, Doylestown, Pa. 18901. 750 registered groups. Phone: (215) 348-7090.

TransAfrica Forum (1982): 545 Eighth St. S.E., Suite 200, Washington, D.C. 20003. Phone: (202) 547-2550.

Travel Agents, American Society of (ASTA) (1931): P.O. Box 23992, Washington, D.C. 20026-3992. 23,000. Phone: (703) 739-2782.

Travelers Aid Services (1905/1982); 2 Lafayette St., New York, N.Y. 10007. Lucy N. Friedman, Executive Director. (Result of merger of Travelers Aid Society of New York and Victim Services Agency in 1982). Phone: (212) 577-7700.

Tuberous Sclerosis Association, Inc., National (1975): 4351 Garden City Dr., Suite 660, Landover, Md. 20785. 5,000. Phone: 1 (800) 225-NTSA and (301) 459-9888.

UFOs, National Investigations Committee on (1967): 14617 Victory Blvd., Suite 4, Van Nuys, Calif. 91411. Phone: (818) 989-5942.

UNICEF, U.S. Committee for (1947): 333 E. 38th St., New York, N.Y. 10016. 20,000 volunteers. Phone: (212) 686-5522.

Union of Concerned Scientists(1969): 26 Church St., Cambridge, Mass. 02238. Phone: (617) 547-5552.

United Jewish Appeal (1939): 99 Park Ave., New York, N.Y. 10016. Phone: (212) 818-9100.

United Negro College Fund Inc. (1944): 500 E. 62nd St., New York, N.Y. 10021. Phone: (212) 326-1100.

United Way of America (1918): 701 N. Fairfax St., Alexandria, Va. 22314. 2,300 local United Ways. Phone: (703) 836-7100.

University Foundation, International (1973): 1301 S. Noland Rd., Independence, Mo. 64055. 35,000. Phone: (816) 461-3633.

University Women, American Association of (1881): 1111 16th St. N.W., Washington, D.C. 20036. 140,000. Phone: (202) 785-7700.

Urban League, National (1910): 500 E. 62nd St., New York, N.Y. 10021. 116. Phone: (212) 310-9000.

USO (United Service Organizations) (1941): 601 Indiana Ave. N.W., Washington, D.C. 20004. Phone: (202) 783-8121.

Variety Clubs International (1927): 1560 Broadway, Suite 1209, New York, N.Y. 10036. 15,000. Phone: (212) 704-9872.

Veterans Committee, American (AVC) (1944): 1717 Massachusetts Ave. N.W., Suite 203, Washington, D.C. 20036. 25,000. Phone: (202) 667-0090.

Veterans of Foreign Wars of the U.S. (1899): V. F.W. Bldg., 34th and Broadway, Kansas City, Mo. 64111. V.F.W. and Auxiliary, 2,850,000. Phone: (816) 756-3390.

Veterinary Medical Association, American (1863): 930 N. Meacham Rd., Schaumburg, Ill. 60196-1074. 49,000. Phone: (708) 605-8070.

Visually Handicapped, Division for the (1948): The Council for Exceptional Children, 1920 Association Dr., Reston, Va. 22091. 1,000. Phone: (703) 620-3660.

Volunteers of America (1896): 3813 N. Causeway Blvd., Metairie, La. 70002. Provides human services in over 200 communities. Phone: (504) 837-2652.

War Resisters League (1923): 339 Lafayette St., New York, N.Y. 10012. 18,000. Phone: (212) 228-0450.

Washington Legal Foundation (1976): 1705 N St. N.W., Washington, D.C. 20036. 200,000. Phone: (202) 857-0240.

Water Quality Association (1974): 4151 Naperville Rd., Lisle, Ill. 60532. Phone: (708) 505-0160.

Water Resources Association, American (1964): 5410 Grosvenor Lane, Suite 220, Bethesda, Md. 20814. 4,000. Phone: (301) 493-8600.

Welding Society, American (1919): 550 N.W. Le-

Jeune Rd., Miami, Fla. 33126. 36,631. Phone: (305) 443-9353; toll free (800) 443-9353.

Wildlife Federation, National (1936): 1400 16th St. N.W., Washington, D.C. 20036. 5,800,000. Phone: (202) 797-6800.

Wildlife Fund, World (1961): 1250 24th St. N.W., Washington, D.C. 20037. 800,000. Phone: (202) 293-4800.

Woman's Christian Temperance Union, National (1874): 1730 Chicago Ave., Evanston, Ill. 60201. Under 50,000. Phone: (312) 864-1396.

Women, National Organization for (NOW) (1966): 1000 16th St. N.W., Suite 700, Washington, D.C. 20036-5705. 270,000. Phone: (202) 331-0066.

Women's American ORT (1927): 315 Park Ave. South, New York, N.Y. 10010. Over 1,250 Chapters. Phone: (212) 505-7700.

Women's Clubs, General Federation of (1890): 1734 N St., N.W., Washington, D.C. 20036. 400,000. Phone: (202) 347-3168.

Women's Educational and Industrial Union (1877): 356 Boylston St., Boston, Mass. 02116. 2,200. Phone: (617) 536-5651.

Women's International League for Peace and Freedom (1915): 1213 Race St., Philadelphia, Pa. 19107-1691. 50,000. Phone: (215) 563-7110.

World Future Society (1966): 4916 Saint Elmo Ave., Bethesda, Md. 20814. 30,000. Phone: (301) 656-8274.

World Health, American Association for (1951): 2001 S St. N.W., Suite 530, Washington, D.C. 20009. 1,100. Phone: (202) 265-0286.

World Peace, International Association of Educators for (1969): P.O. Box 3282, Mastin Lake Station, Huntsville, Ala. 35810. 20,000. Phone: (205) 534-5501.

World Peace Foundation (1910): 22 Batterymarch St., Boston, Mass. 02109. Phone: (617) 482-3875.

Worldwatch Institute (1974): 1776 Massachusetts Ave. N.W., Washington, D.C. 20036. Research organization. Phone: (202) 452-1999.

Writers Union, National (1983): 13 Astor Pl., 7th Fl., New York, NY 10003. 2,900. Phone: (212) 254-0279.

YMCA of the USA (1844): 101 N. Wacker Dr., Chicago, Ill. 60606. 12,800,000. Phone: (312) 977-0031.

Young Women's Christian Association of the U.S.A. (1858 in U.S.A., 1855 in England): 726 Broadway, New York, N.Y. 10003. 2,030,922. Phone: (212) 614-2846.

Youth Hostels, Inc., American (1934): P.O. Box 37613, Washington, D.C. 20013-7613. 100,000. Phone: (202) 783-6161.

Zero Population Growth (1968): 1400 Sixteenth St. N.W., Suite 320, Washington, D.C. 20036. 28,000. Phone: (202) 332-2200.

Zionist Organization of America (1897): ZOA House, 4 E. 34th St., New York, N.Y. 10016. 135,000. Phone: (212) 481-1500.

Zoological Parks and Aquariums, American Association of (1924): Oglebay Park, Wheeling, W. Va. 26003. 5,600. Phone: (304) 242-2160.

Zoologists, American Society of (1890): 104 Sirius Circle, Thousand Oaks, Calif. 91360. 4,000. Phone: (805) 492-3585.

Conservation Hall of Fame

The new headquarters office of the National Wildlife Federation features a Conservation Hall of Fame which is open to the public Monday through Friday, 8:00 a.m. to 4:30 p.m.

The first person to be so honored was Theodore Roosevelt, the nation's 25th president.

THE DECLARATION OF INDEPENDENCE

In Congress, July 4, 1776

The unanimous Declaration of the thirteen united States of America.

When in the Course of human events it becomes necessary for one people to dissolve the political bands which have connected them with another, and to assume among the powers of the earth, the separate and equal station to which the Laws of Nature and of Nature's God entitle them, a decent respect to the opinions of mankind requires that they should declare the causes which impel them to the separation.

We hold these truths to be self-evident, that all men are created equal, that they are endowed by their Creator with certain unalienable Rights, that among these are Life, Liberty and the pursuit of Happiness.—That to secure these rights, Governments are instituted among Men, deriving their just powers from the consent of the governed,—That whenever any Form of Government becomes destructive of these ends, it is the Right of the People to alter or to abolish it, and to institute new Government, laying its foundation on such principles and organizing its powers in such form, as to them shall seem most likely to effect their Safety and Happiness. Prudence, indeed, will dictate that Governments long established should not be changed for light and transient causes; and accordingly all experience hath shewn that mankind are more disposed to suffer, while evils are sufferable, than to right themselves by abolishing the forms to which they are accustomed. But when a long train of abuses and usurpations, pursuing invariably the same Object evinces a design to reduce them under absolute Despotism, it is their right, it is their duty, to throw off such Government, and to provide new Guards for their future security.—Such has been the patient sufferance of these Colonies; and such is now the necessity which constrains them to alter their former Systems of Government. The history of the present King of Great Britain is a history of repeated injuries and usurpations, all having in direct object the establishment of an absolute Tyranny over these States. To prove this, let Facts be submitted to a candid world.

He has refused his Assent to Laws, the most wholesome and necessary for the public good.

He has forbidden his Governors to pass Laws of immediate and pressing importance, unless suspended in their operation till his Assent should be obtained; and when so suspended, he has utterly neglected to attend to them.

He has refused to pass other Laws for the accommodation of large districts of people, unless those people would relinquish the right of Representation in the Legislature, a right inestimable to them and formidable to tyrants only.

He has called together legislative bodies at places unusual, uncomfortable, and distant from the depository of their Public Records, for the sole purpose of fatiguing them into compliance with his measures.

He has dissolved Representative Houses repeatedly, for opposing with manly firmness his invasions on the rights of the people.

He has refused for a long time, after such dissolutions, to cause others to be elected; whereby the Legislative Powers, incapable of Annihilation, have returned to the People at large for their exercise; the State remaining in the mean time exposed to all the dangers of invasion from without, and convulsions within.

He has endeavoured to prevent the population of these States; for that purpose obstructing the Laws for Naturalization of Foreigners; refusing to pass others to encourage their migrations hither, and raising the conditions of new Appropriations of Lands.

He has obstructed the Administration of Justice, by refusing his Assent to Laws for establishing Judiciary Powers.

He has made Judges dependent on his Will alone, for the tenure of their offices, and the amount and payment of their salaries.

He has erected a multitude of New Offices, and sent hither swarms of Officers to harass our people, and eat out their substance.

He has kept among us, in times of peace, Standing Armies without the Consent of our legislatures.

He has affected to render the Military independent of and superior to the Civil Power.

He has combined with others to subject us to a jurisdiction foreign to our constitution, and unacknowledged by our laws; giving his Assent to their Acts of pretended Legislation:

For quartering large bodies of armed troops among us:

For protecting them, by a mock Trial, from punishment for any Murders which they should commit on the Inhabitants of these States:

For cutting off our Trade with all parts of the

NOTE: On April 12, 1776, the legislature of North Carolina authorized its delegates to the Continental Congress to join with others in a declaration of separation from Great Britain; the first colony to instruct its delegates to take the actual initiative was Virginia on May 15. On June 7, 1776, Richard Henry Lee of Virginia offered a resolution to the Congress to the effect "that these United Colonies are, and of right ought to be, free and independent States. . . ." A committee, consisting of Thomas Jefferson, John Adams, Benjamin Franklin, Robert R. Livingston, and Roger Sherman was organized to "prepare a declaration to the effect of the said first resolution." The Declaration of Independence was adopted on July 4, 1776.

Most delegates signed the Declaration August 2, but George Wythe (Va.) signed August 27; Richard Henry Lee (Va.), Elbridge Gerry (Mass.), and Oliver Wolcott (Conn.) in September; Matthew Thornton (N.H.), not a delegate until September, in November; and Thomas McKean (Del.), although present on July 4, not until 1781 by special permission, having served in the army in the interim.

world:

For imposing Taxes on us without our Consent:

For depriving us in many cases, of the benefits of Trial by Jury:

For transporting us beyond Seas to be tried for pretended offences:

For abolishing the free System of English Laws in a neighbouring Province, establishing therein an Arbitrary government, and enlarging its Boundaries so as to render it at once an example and fit instrument for introducing the same absolute rule into these Colonies:

For taking away our Charters, abolishing our most valuable Laws and altering fundamentally the Forms of our Governments:

For suspending our own Legislatures, and declaring themselves invested with power to legislate for us in all cases whatsoever.

He has abdicated Government here, by declaring us out of his Protection and waging War against us.

He has plundered our seas, ravaged our Coasts, burnt our towns, and destroyed the lives of our people.

He is at this time transporting large Armies of foreign Mercenaries to compleat the works of death, desolation, and tyranny, already begun with circumstances of Cruelty & Perfidy scarcely paralleled in the most barbarous ages, and totally unworthy the Head of a civilized nation.

He has constrained our fellow Citizens taken Captive on the high Seas to bear Arms against their Country, to become the executioners of their friends and Brethren, or to fall themselves by their Hands.

He has excited domestic insurrections amongst us, and has endeavoured to bring on the inhabitants of our frontiers, the merciless Indian Savages, whose known rule of warfare, is an undistinguished destruction of all ages, sexes and conditions.

In every stage of these Oppressions We have Petitioned for Redress in the most humble terms: Our repeated Petitions have been answered only by repeated injury. A Prince, whose character is thus marked by every act which may define a Tyrant, is unfit to be the ruler of a free people.

Nor have We been wanting in attentions to our Brittish brethren. We have warned them from time to time of attempts by their legislature to extend an unwarrantable jurisdiction over us. We have reminded them of the circumstances of our emigration and settlement here. We have appealed to their native justice and magnanimity, and we have conjured them by the ties of our common kindred to disavow these usurpations, which would inevitably interrupt our connections and correspondence. They too have been deaf to the voice of justice and consanguinity. We must, therefore, acquiesce in the necessity, which denounces our Separation, and hold them, as we hold the rest of mankind, Enemies in War, in Peace Friends.

We, therefore, the Representatives of the United States of America, in General Congress, Assembled, appealing to the Supreme Judge of the world for the rectitude of our intentions, do, in the Name, and by Authority of the good People of these Colonies, solemnly publish and declare, That these United Colonies are, and of Right ought to be Free and Independent States; that they are Absolved from all Allegiance to the British Crown, and that all political connection between them and the State of Great Britain, is and ought to be totally dissolved; and that as Free and Independent States, they have full Power to levy War, conclude Peace, contract Alliances, establish Commerce, and to do all other Acts and Things which Independent States may of right do.—And for the support of this Declaration, with a firm reliance on the protection of Divine Providence, we mutually pledge to each other our Lives, our Fortunes and our sacred Honor. —John Hancock

New Hampshire
Josiah Bartlett
Wm. Whipple
Matthew Thornton

Rhode Island
Step. Hopkins
William Ellery

Connecticut
Roger Sherman
Sam'el Huntington
Wm. Williams
Oliver Wolcott

New York
Wm. Floyd
Phil. Livingston
Frans. Lewis
Lewis Morris

New Jersey
Richd. Stockton
Jno. Witherspoon
Fras. Hopkinson
John Hart
Abra. Clark

Pennsylvania
Robt. Morris
Benjamin Rush
Benj. Franklin
John Morton
Geo. Clymer
Jas. Smith
Geo. Taylor
James Wilson
Geo. Ross

Massachusetts-Bay
Saml. Adams
John Adams
Robt. Treat Paine
Elbridge Gerry

Delaware
Caesar Rodney
Geo. Read
Tho. M'Kean

Maryland
Samuel Chase
Wm. Paca
Thos. Stone
Charles Carroll of Carrollton

Virginia
George Wythe
Richard Henry Lee
Th. Jefferson
Benj. Harrison
Ths. Nelson, Jr.
Francis Lightfoot Lee
Carter Braxton

North Carolina
Wm. Hooper
Joseph Hewes
John Penn

South Carolina
Edward Rutledge
Thos. Heyward, Junr.
Thomas Lynch, Junr.
Arthur Middleton

Georgia
Button Gwinnett
Lyman Hall
Geo. Walton

Constitution of the United States of America

(Historical text has been edited to conform to contemporary American usage.
The bracketed words are designations for your convenience; they are not part of the Constitution.)

The oldest federal constitution in existence was framed by a convention of delegates from twelve of the thirteen original states in Philadelphia in May, 1787, Rhode Island failing to send a delegate. George Washington presided over the session, which lasted until September 17, 1787. The draft (originally a preamble and seven Articles) was submitted to all thirteen states and was to become effective when ratified by nine states. It went into effect on the first Wednesday in March, 1789, having been ratified by New Hampshire, the ninth state to approve, on June 21, 1788. The states ratified the Constitution in the following order:

Delaware	December 7, 1787	South Carolina	May 23, 1788
Pennsylvania	December 12, 1787	New Hampshire	June 21, 1788
New Jersey	December 18, 1787	Virginia	June 25, 1788
Georgia	January 2, 1788	New York	July 26, 1788
Connecticut	January 9, 1788	North Carolina	November 21, 1789
Massachusetts	February 6, 1788	Rhode Island	May 29, 1790
Maryland	April 28, 1788		

[Preamble]

We the people of the United States, in order to form a more perfect Union, establish justice, insure domestic tranquility, provide for the common defence, promote the general welfare, and secure the blessings of liberty to ourselves and our posterity, do ordain and establish this Constitution for the United States of America.

Article I

Section 1

[Legislative powers vested in Congress.] All legislative powers herein granted shall be vested in a Congress of the United States, which shall consist of a Senate and House of Representatives.

Section 2

[Composition of the House of Representatives.—1.] The House of Representatives shall be composed of members chosen every second year by the people of the several States, and the electors in each State shall have the qualifications requisite for electors of the most numerous branch of the State Legislature.

[Qualifications of Representatives.—2.] No Person shall be a Representative who shall not have attained to the age of twenty-five years, and been seven years a citizen of the United States, and who shall not, when elected, be an inhabitant of that State in which he shall be chosen.

[Apportionment of Representatives and direct taxes—census.[1]—3.] (Representatives and direct taxes shall be apportioned among the several States which may be included within this Union, according to their respective numbers, which shall be determined by adding to the whole number of free persons, including those bound to service for a term of years, and excluding Indians not taxed, three fifths of all other persons.) The actual enumeration shall be made within three years after the first meeting of the Congress of the United States, and within every subsequent term of ten years, in such manner as they shall by law direct. The number of Representatives shall not exceed one for every thirty thousand, but each State shall have at least one Representative; and until such enumeration shall be made, the State of New Hampshire shall be entitled to choose three, Massachusetts eight, Rhode-Island and Providence Plantations one, Connecticut five, New York six, New Jersey four, Pennsylvania eight, Delaware one, Maryland six, Virginia ten, North Carolina five, South Carolina five, and Georgia three.

[Filling of vacancies in representation.—4.] When vacancies happen in the representation from any State, the Executive Authority thereof shall issue writs of election to fill such vacancies.

[Selection of officers; power of impeachment.—5.] The House of Representatives shall choose their Speaker and other officers; and shall have the sole power of impeachment.

Section 3[2]

[The Senate.—1.] The Senate of the United States shall be composed of two Senators from each State, chosen by the Legislature thereof, for six years; and each Senator shall have one vote.

[Classification of Senators; filling of vacancies.—2.] Immediately after they shall be assembled in consequence of the first election, they shall be divided as equally as may be into three classes. The seats of the Senators of the first class shall be vacated at the expiration of the second year, of the second class at the expiration of the fourth year, and of the third class at the expiration of the sixth year, so that one-third may be chosen every second year; and if vacancies happen by resignation, or otherwise, during the recess of the Legislature of any State, the Executive thereof may make temporary appointments (until the next meeting of the Legislature, which shall then fill such vacancies).

[Qualification of Senators.—3.] No person shall be a Senator who shall not have attained to the age of thirty years, and been nine years a citizen of the United States, and who shall not, when elected, be an inhabitant of that State for which he shall be chosen.

[Vice President to be President of Senate.—4.] The Vice President of the United States shall be President of the Senate, but shall have no vote, unless they be equally divided.

[Selection of Senate officers; President pro tempore.—5.] The Senate shall choose their other officers, and also a President pro tempore, in the absence of the Vice President, or when he shall exercise the office of President of the United States.

[Senate to try impeachments.—6.] The Senate

shall have the sole power to try all impeachments. When sitting for that purpose, they shall be on oath or affirmation. When the President of the United States is tried, the Chief Justice shall preside: and no person shall be convicted without the concurrence of two thirds of the members present.

[**Judgment in cases of Impeachment.—7.**] Judgment in cases of impeachment shall not extend further than to removal from office, and disqualification to hold and enjoy any office of honor, trust, or profit under the United States: but the party convicted shall nevertheless be liable and subject to indictment, trial, judgment and punishment, according to Law.

Section 4

[**Control of congressional elections.—1.**] The times, places, and manner of holding elections for Senators and Representatives, shall be prescribed in each State by the Legislature thereof; but the Congress may at any time by law make or alter such regulations, except as to the places of choosing Senators.

[**Time for assembling of Congress.³—2.**] The Congress shall assemble at least once in every year, and such meeting shall be on the first Monday in December, unless they shall by law appoint a different day.

Section 5

[**Each house to be the judge of the election and qualifications of its members; regulations as to quorum.—1.**] Each House shall be the judge of the elections, returns, and qualifications of its own members, and a majority of each shall constitute a quorum to do business; but a smaller number may adjourn from day to day, and may be authorized to compel the attendance of absent members, in such manner, and under such penalties as each House may provide.

[**Each house to determine its own rules.—2.**] Each House may determine the rules of its proceedings, punish its members for disorderly behavior, and, with the concurrence of two thirds, expel a member.

[**Journals and yeas and nays.—3.**] Each House shall keep a journal of its proceedings, and from time to time publish the same, excepting such parts as may in their judgment require secrecy; and the yeas and nays of the members of either House on any question shall, at the desire of one fifth of those present, be entered on the journal.

[**Adjournment.—4.**] Neither House, during the session of Congress, shall, without the consent of the other, adjourn for more than three days, nor to any other place than that in which the two Houses shall be sitting.

Section 6

[**Compensation and privileges of members of Congress.—1.**] The Senators and Representatives shall receive a compensation for their services, to be ascertained by law, and paid out of the Treasury of the United States. They shall in all cases, except treason, felony, and breach of the peace, be privileged from arrest during their attendance at the session of their respective Houses, and in going to and returning from the same; and for any speech or debate in either House, they shall not be questioned in any other place.

[**Incompatible offices; exclusions.—2.**] No Senator or Representative shall, during the time for which he was elected, be appointed to any civil office under the authority of the United States, which

shall have been created, or the emoluments whereof shall have been increased during such time; and no person holding any office under the United States shall be a member of either House during his continuance in office.

Section 7

[**Revenue bills to originate in House.—1.**] All bills for raising revenue shall originate in the House of Representatives; but the Senate may propose or concur with amendments as on other bills.

[**Manner of passing bills; veto power of President.—2.**] Every bill which shall have passed the House of Representatives and the Senate, shall, before it becomes a law, be presented to the President of the United States; if he approve he shall sign it, but if not he shall return it, with his objections to that House in which it shall have originated, who shall enter the objections at large on their journal, and proceed to reconsider it. If after such reconsideration two thirds of that House shall agree to pass the bill, it shall be sent, together with the objections, to the other House, by which it shall likewise be reconsidered, and if approved by two thirds of that House, it shall become a law. But in all such cases the votes of both Houses shall be determined by yeas and nays, and the names of the persons voting for and against the bill shall be entered on the journal of each house, respectively. If any bill shall not be returned by the President within ten days (Sundays excepted) after it shall have been presented to him, the same shall be a law, in like manner as if he had signed it, unless the Congress by their adjournment prevent its return, in which case it shall not be a law.

[**Concurrent orders or resolutions, to be passed by President.—3.**] Every order, resolution, or vote to which the concurrence of the Senate and House of Representatives may be necessary (except on a question of adjournment) shall be presented to the President of the United States; and before the same shall take effect, shall be approved by him, or being disapproved by him, shall be repassed by two thirds of the Senate and House of Representatives, according to the rules and limitations prescribed in the case of a bill.

Section 8

[**General powers of Congress.⁴**]

[**Taxes, duties, imposts, and excises.—1.**] The Congress shall have power to lay and collect taxes, duties, imposts and excises, to pay the debts and provide for the common defense and general welfare of the United States; but all duties, imposts and excises shall be uniform throughout the United States;

[**Borrowing of money.—2.**] To borrow money on the credit of the United States;

[**Regulation of commerce.—3.**] To regulate commerce with foreign nations, and among the several States, and with the Indian tribes;

[**Naturalization and bankruptcy.—4.**] To establish a uniform rule of naturalization, and uniform laws on the subject of bankruptcies throughout the United States;

[**Money, weights and measures.—5.**] To coin money, regulate the value thereof, and of foreign coin, and fix the standard of weights and measures;

[**Counterfeiting.—6.**] To provide for the punishment of counterfeiting the securities and current coin of the United States;

[**Post offices.—7.**] To establish post offices and post roads;

[**Patents and copyrights.—8.**] To promote the

progress of science and useful arts, by securing for limited times to authors and inventors the exclusive right to their respective writings and discoveries;

[Inferior courts.—9.] To constitute tribunals inferior to the Supreme Court;

[Piracies and felonies.—10.] To define and punish piracies and felonies committed on the high seas, and offences against the law of nations;

[War; marque and reprisal.—11.] To declare war, grant letters of marque and reprisal, and make rules concerning captures on land and water;

[Armies.—12.] To raise and support armies, but no appropriation of money to that use shall be for a longer term than two years;

[Navy.—13.] To provide and maintain a navy;

[Land and naval forces.—14.] To make rules for the government and regulation of the land and naval forces;

[Calling out militia.—15.] To provide for calling forth the militia to execute the laws of the Union, suppress insurrections, and repel invasions.

[Organizing, arming, and disciplining militia.—16.] To provide for organizing, arming, and disciplining, the militia, and for governing such part of them as may be employed in the service of the United States, reserving to the States, respectively, the appointment of the officers, and the authority of training the militia according to the discipline prescribed by Congress;

[Exclusive legislation over District of Columbia.—17.] To exercise exclusive legislation in all cases whatsoever, over such district (not exceeding ten miles square) as may, by cession of particular States, and the acceptance of Congress, become the seat of the Government of the United States, and to exercise like authority over all places purchased by the consent of the Legislature of the State in which the same shall be, for the erection of forts, magazines, arsenals, dock-yards, and other needful buildings;—And

[To enact laws necessary to enforce Constitution.—18.] To make all laws which shall be necessary and proper for carrying into execution the foregoing powers, and all other powers vested by this Constitution in the Government of the United States, or in any department or officer thereof.

Section 9

[Migration or importation of certain persons not to be prohibited before 1808.—1.] The migration or importation of such persons as any of the States now existing shall think proper to admit, shall not be prohibited by the Congress prior to the year one thousand eight hundred and eight, but a tax or duty may be imposed on such importation, not exceeding ten dollars for each person.

[Writ of habeas corpus not to be suspended; exception.—2.] The privilege of the writ of habeas corpus shall not be suspended, unless when in cases of rebellion or invasion the public safety may require it.

[Bills of attainder and ex post facto laws prohibited.—3.] No bill of attainder or ex post facto law shall be passed.

[Capitation and other direct taxes.—4.] No capitation, or other direct, tax shall be laid, unless in proportion to the census or enumeration herein before directed to be taken.[5]

[Exports not to be taxed.—5.] No tax or duty shall be laid on articles exported from any State.

[No preference to be given to ports of any States; interstate shipping.—6.] No preference shall be given by any regulation of commerce or revenue to the ports of one State over those of another: nor shall vessels bound to, or from, one State, be obliged to enter, clear, or pay duties in another.

[Money, how drawn from treasury; financial statements to be published.—7.] No money shall be drawn from the Treasury, but in consequence of appropriations made by law; and a regular statement and account of the receipts and expenditures of all public money shall be published from time to time.

[Titles of nobility not to be granted; acceptance by government officers of favors from foreign powers.—8.] No title of nobility shall be granted by the United States: and no person holding any office of profit or trust under them, shall, without the consent of the Congress, accept of any present, emolument, office, or title, of any kind whatever, from any king, prince, or foreign state.

Section 10

[Limitations of the powers of the several States.—1.] No State shall enter into any treaty, alliance, or confederation; grant letters of marque and reprisal; coin money; emit bills of credit; make any thing but gold and silver coin a tender in payment of debts; pass any bill of attainder, ex post facto law, or law impairing the obligation of contracts, or grant any title of nobility.

[State imposts and duties.—2.] No State shall, without the consent of the Congress, lay any imposts or duties on imports or exports, except what may be absolutely necessary for executing its inspection laws; and the net produce of all duties and imposts, laid by any State on imports or exports, shall be for the use of the Treasury of the United States; and all such laws shall be subject to the revision and control of the Congress.

[Further restrictions on powers of States.—3.] No State shall, without the consent of Congress, lay any duty of tonnage, keep troops, or ships of war in time of peace, enter into any agreement or compact with another state, or with a foreign power, or engage in war, unless actually invaded, or in such imminent danger as will not admit of delay.

Article II

Section 1

[The President; the executive power.—1.] The executive power shall be vested in a President of the United States of America. He shall hold his office during the term of four years, and, together with the Vice President, chosen for the same term, be elected, as follows

[Appointment and qualifications of presidential electors.—2.] Each State shall appoint, in such manner as the Legislature thereof may direct, a number of electors, equal to the whole number of Senators and Representatives to which the State may be entitled in the Congress: but no Senator or Representative, or person holding an office of trust or profit under the United States, shall be appointed an elector.

[Original method of electing the President and Vice President.[6]] (The electors shall meet in their respective States, and vote by ballot for two persons, of whom at least shall not be an inhabitant of the same State with themselves. And they shall make a list of all the persons voted for, and of the number of votes for each; which list they shall sign and certify, and transmit sealed to the seat of the Government of the United States, directed to the

President of the Senate. The President of the Senate shall, in the presence of the Senate and House of Representatives, open all the certificates, and the votes shall then be counted. The person having the greatest number of votes shall be the President, if such number be a majority of the whole number of electors appointed; and if there be more than one who have such majority, and have an equal number of votes, then the House of Representatives shall immediately choose by ballot one of them for President; and if no person have a majority, then from the five highest on the list the said House shall in like manner choose the President. But in choosing the President, the votes shall be taken by States, the representation from each State having one vote; A quorum for this purpose shall consist of a member or members from two thirds of the States, and a majority of all the states shall be necessary to a choice. In every case, after the choice of the President, the person having the greatest number of votes of the electors shall be the Vice President. But if there should remain two or more who have equal votes, the Senate should choose from them by ballot the Vice President.)

[**Congress may determine time of choosing electors and day for casting their votes.—3.**] The Congress may determine the time of choosing the electors, and the day on which they shall give their votes; which day shall be the same throughout the United States.

[**Qualifications for the office of President.[7]—4.**] No person except a natural born citizen, or a citizen of the United States, at the time of the adoption of this Constitution, shall be eligible to the office of President; neither shall any person be eligible to that office who shall not have attained to the age of thirty-five years, and been fourteen years a resident within the United States.

[**Filling vacancy in the office of President.[8]—5.**] In case of the removal of the President from office, or of his death, resignation, or inability to discharge the powers and duties of the said office, the same shall devolve on the Vice President, and the Congress may by law provide for the case of removal, death, resignation or inability, both of the President and Vice President, declaring what officer shall then act as President, and such officer shall act accordingly, until the disability be removed, or a President shall be elected.

[**Compensation of the President.—6.**] The President shall, at stated times, receive for his services, a compensation, which shall neither be increased nor diminished during the period for which he shall have been elected, and he shall not receive within that period any other emolument from the United States, or any of them.

[**Oath to be taken by the President.—7.**] Before he enter on the execution of his office, he shall take the following oath or affirmation:—"I do solemnly swear (or affirm) that I will faithfully execute the office of President of the United States, and will to the best of my ability, preserve, protect, and defend the Constitution of the United States."

Section 2

[**The President to be commander in chief of army and navy and head of executive departments; may grant reprieves and pardons.—1.**] The President shall be Commander in Chief of the Army and Navy of the United States, and of the militia of the several States, when called into the actual service of the United States; he may require the opinion, in writing, of the principal officer in each of the executive departments, upon any subject relating to the duties of their respective offices, and he shall have power to grant reprieves and pardons for offences against the United States, except in cases of impeachment.

[**President may, with concurrence of Senate, make treaties, appoint ambassadors, etc.; appointment of inferior officers, authority of Congress over.—2.**] He shall have power, by and with the advice and consent of the Senate, to make treaties, provided two thirds of the Senators present concur; and he shall nominate, and by and with the advice and consent of the Senate, shall appoint ambassadors, other public ministers and consuls, judges of the Supreme Court, and all other officers of the United States, whose appointments are not herein otherwise provided for, and which shall be established by law: but the Congress may by law vest the appointment of such inferior officers, as they think proper, in the President alone, in the courts of law, or in the heads of departments.

[**President may fill vacancies in office during recess of Senate.—3.**] The President shall have power to fill up all vacancies that may happen during the recess of the Senate, by granting commissions which shall expire at the end of their session.

Section 3

[**President to give advice to Congress; may convene or adjourn it on certain occasions; to receive ambassadors, etc.; have laws executed and commission all officers.**] He shall from time to time give to the Congress information of the state of the Union, and recommend to their consideration such measures as he shall judge necessary and expedient; he may, on extraordinary occasions, convene both Houses, or either of them, and in case of disagreement between them, with respect to the time of adjournment, he may adjourn them to such time as he shall think proper; he shall receive ambassadors and other public ministers: he shall take care that the laws be faithfully executed, and shall commission all the officers of the United States.

Section 4

[**All civil officers removable by impeachment.**] The President, Vice President, and all civil officers of the United States shall be removed from office on impeachment for, and conviction of, treason, bribery, or other high crimes and misdemeanors.

Article III

Section 1

[**Judicial powers; how vested; term of office and compensation of judges.**] The judicial Power of the United States, shall be vested in one Supreme Court, and in such inferior courts as the Congress may from time to time ordain and establish. The judges, both of the supreme and inferior courts, shall hold their offices during good behavior, and shall, at stated times, receive for their services, a compensation, which shall not be diminished during their continuance in office.

Section 2

[**Jurisdiction of Federal courts.[9]—1.**] The judicial power shall extend to all cases, in law and equity, arising under this Constitution, the laws of the United States, and treaties made, or which shall be made, under their authority; to all cases affecting ambassadors, other public ministers and consuls; to all cases of admiralty and maritime jurisdiction; to controversies to which the United States, shall be a party; to controversies between two or more States; between a State and citizens of another State; between citizens of different States; between citizens of the same State claiming lands under grants of different states, and between a State, or the citizens thereof, and foreign states, citizens, or subjects.

[**Original and appellate jurisdiction of Supreme Court.—2.**] In all cases affecting ambassadors, other public ministers and consuls, and those in which a State shall be party, the Supreme Court shall have original jurisdiction. In all the other cases before mentioned, the Supreme Court shall have appellate jurisdiction, both as to law and fact, with such exceptions, and under such regulations, as the Congress shall make.

[**Trial of all crimes, except impeachment, to be by jury.—3.**] The trial of all crimes, except in cases of impeachment, shall be by jury; and such trial shall be held in the State where the said crimes shall have been committed; but when not committed within any State, the trial shall be at such place or places as the Congress may by law have directed.

Section 3

[**Treason defined; conviction of.—1.**] Treason against the United States, shall consist only in levying war against them, or, in adhering to their enemies, giving them aid and comfort. No person shall be convicted of treason unless on the testimony of two witnesses to the same overt act, or on confession in open court.

[**Congress to declare punishment for treason; proviso.—2.**] The Congress shall have power to declare the punishment of treason, but no attainder of treason shall work corruption of blood, or forfeiture except during the life of the person attained.

Article IV

Section 1

[**Each State to give full faith and credit to the public acts and records of other States.**] Full faith and credit shall be given in each State to the public acts, records, and judicial proceedings of every other State. And the Congress may by general laws prescribe the manner in which such acts, records, and proceedings shall be proved, and the effect thereof.

Section 2

[**Privileges of citizens.—1.**] The citizens of each State shall be entitled to all privileges and immunities of citizens in the several States.

[**Extradition between the several States.—2.**] A person charged in any State with treason, felony, or other crime, who shall flee from justice, and be found in another State, shall on demand of the Executive authority of the State from which he fled, be delivered up, to be removed to the State having jurisdiction of the crime.

[**Persons held to labor or service in one State, fleeing to another, to be returned.—3.**] No person held to service or labor in one State, under the laws thereof, escaping into another, shall, in conse-

quence of any law or regulation therein, be discharged from such service or labor, but shall be delivered up on claim of the party to whom such service or labor may be due.

Section 3

[**New States.—1.**] New States may be admitted by the Congress into this Union; but no new State shall be formed or erected within the jurisdiction of any other State; nor any State be formed by the junction of two or more States, or parts of States, without the consent of the Legislatures of the States concerned as well as of the Congress.

[**Regulations concerning territory.—2.**] The Congress shall have power to dispose of and make all needful rules and regulations respecting the territory or other property belonging to the United States; and nothing in this Constitution shall be so construed as to prejudice any claims of the United States, or of any particular State.

Section 4

[**Republican form of government and protection guaranteed the several States.**] The United States shall guarantee to every State in this Union a Republican form of government, and shall protect each of them against invasion; and on application of the Legislature, or of the Executive (when the Legislature cannot be convened) against domestic violence.

Article V

[**Ways in which the Constitution can be amended.**] The Congress, whenever two thirds of both Houses shall deem it necessary, shall propose amendments to this Constitution, or, on the application of the Legislatures of two thirds of the several States shall call a convention for proposing amendments, which, in either case, shall be valid to all intents and purposes, as part of this Constitution, when ratified by the Legislatures of three fourths of the several States, or by conventions in three fourths thereof, as the one or the other mode of ratification may be proposed by the Congress; provided that no amendment which may be made prior to the year one thousand eight hundred and eight shall in any manner affect the first and fourth clauses in the ninth Section of the first Article; and that no State, without its consent, shall be deprived of its equal suffrage in the Senate.

Article VI

[**Debts contracted under the confederation secured.—1.**] All debts contracted and engagements entered into, before the adoption of this Constitution, shall be as valid against the United States under this Constitution, as under the Confederation.

[**Constitution, laws, and treaties of the United States to be supreme.—2.**] This Constitution, and the laws of the United States which shall be made in pursuance thereof; and all treaties made, or which shall be made, under the authority of the United States, shall be the supreme law of the land; and the judges in every State shall be bound thereby, any thing in the Constitution or laws of

1. The clause included in parentheses is amended by the 14th Amendment, Section 2. 2. The first paragraph of this section and the part of the second paragraph included in parentheses are amended by the 17th Amendment. 3. Amended by the 20th Amendment, Section 2. 4. By the 16th Amendment, Congress is given the power to lay and collect taxes on income. 5. See the 16th Amendment. 6. This clause has been superseded by the 12th Amendment. 7. For qualifications of the Vice President, see 12th Amendment. 8. Amended by the 20th Amendment, Sections 3 and 4. 9. This section is abridged by the 11th Amendment. 10. See the 13th Amendment.

any State to the contrary notwithstanding.

[Who shall take constitutional oath; no religious test as to official qualification.—3.] The Senators and Representatives before mentioned, and the members of the several State Legislatures, and all executive and judicial officers, both of the United States and of the several States, shall be bound by oath or affirmation, to support this Constitution; but no religious test shall ever be required as a qualification to any office or public trust under the United States.

Article VII

[Constitution to be considered adopted when ratified by nine States.] The ratification of the conventions of nine States shall be sufficient for the establishment of this Constitution between the States so ratifying the same.

Done in convention by the unanimous consent of the States present the seventeenth day of September in the year of our Lord one thousand seven hundred and eighty seven and of the independence of the United States of America the Twelfth. In witness whereof we have hereunto subscribed our names.

GEORGE WASHINGTON
President and Deputy from Virginia

NEW HAMPSHIRE
John Langdon   Nicholas Gilman

MASSACHUSETTS
Nathaniel Gorham   Rufus King

CONNECTICUT
Wm. Saml. Johnson   Roger Sherman

NEW YORK
Alexander Hamilton

NEW JERSEY
Wil. Livingston   Wm. Paterson
David Brearley   Jona. Dayton

PENNSYLVANIA
B. Franklin   Thomas Mifflin
Robt. Morris   Geo. Clymer·
Thos. FitzSimons   Jared Ingersoll
James Wilson   Gouv. Morris

DELAWARE
Geo. Read   Gunning Bedford Jun.
John Dickinson   Richard Bassett
Jaco. Broom

MARYLAND
James McHenry   Dan. of St. Thos. Jenifer
Danl. Carroll

VIRGINIA
John Blair   James Madison, Jr.

NORTH CAROLINA
Wm. Blount   Richd Dobbs Spaight
Hu. Williamson

SOUTH CAROLINA
J. Rutledge   Charles Cotesworth
Charles Pinckney   Pinckney
                            Pierce Butler

GEORGIA
William Few   Abr. Baldwin
Attest: William Jackson, Secretary

Amendments to the Constitution of the United States

(Amendments I to X inclusive, popularly known as the Bill of Rights, were proposed and sent to the states by the first session of the First Congress. They were ratified Dec. 15, 1791.)

Article I

[Freedom of religion, speech, of the press, and right of petition.] Congress shall make no law respecting an establishment of religion, or prohibiting the free exercise thereof; or abridging the freedom of speech, or of the press; or the right of the people peaceably to assemble, and to petition the Government for a redress of grievances.

Article II

[Right of people to bear arms not to be infringed.] A well regulated militia, being necessary to the security of a free State, the right of the people to keep and bear arms, shall not be infringed.

Article III

[Quartering of troops.] No soldier shall, in time of peace be quartered in any house, without the consent of the owner, nor in time of war, but in a manner to be prescribed by law.

Article IV

[Persons and houses to be secure from unreasonable searches and seizures.] The right of the people to be secure in their persons, houses, papers, and effects, against unreasonable searches and seizures, shall not be violated, and no warrants shall issue, but upon probable cause, supported by oath or affirmation, and particularly describing the place to be searched, and the persons or things to be seized.

Article V

[Trials for crimes; just compensation for private property taken for public use.] No person shall be held to answer for a capital, or otherwise infamous crime, unless on a presentment or indictment of a Grand Jury, except in cases arising in the land or naval forces, or in the militia, when in actual service in time of war or public danger; nor shall any person be subject for the same offence to be twice put in jeopardy of life or limb; nor shall be compelled in any criminal case to be a witness, against himself, nor be deprived of life, liberty, or property, without due process of law; nor shall private property be taken for public use, without just compensation.

Article VI

[Civil rights in trials for crimes enumerated.] In all criminal prosecutions, the accused shall enjoy the right to a speedy and public trial, by an impartial jury of the State and district wherein the crime shall have been committed, which district shall have been previously ascertained by law, and to be informed of the nature and cause of the accusation; to be confronted with the witnesses against him; to have compulsory process for obtaining witnesses in his favor, and to have the assistance of counsel for his defense.

Article VII

[Civil rights in civil suits.] In suits at common law, where the value in controversy shall exceed twenty dollars, the right of trial by jury shall be preserved, and no fact tried by a jury, shall be otherwise re-examined in any court of the United States, than according to the rules of the common law.

Article VIII

[Excessive bail, fines, and punishments prohibited.] Excessive bail shall not be required, nor excessive fines imposed, nor cruel and unusual punishments inflicted.

Article IX

[Reserved rights of people.] The enumeration in the Constitution, of certain rights, shall not be construed to deny or disparage others retained by the people.

Article X

[Powers not delegated, reserved to states and people respectively.] The powers not delegated to the United States by the Constitution, nor prohibited by it to the States, are reserved to the States, respectively, or to the people.

Article XI

(The proposed amendment was sent to the states Mar. 5, 1794, by the Third Congress. It was ratified Feb. 7, 1795.)

[Judicial power of United States not to extend to suits against a State.] The judicial power of the United States shall not be construed to extend to any suit in law or equity, commenced or prosecuted against one of the United States by citizens of another State, or by citizens or subjects of any foreign state.

Article XII

(The proposed amendment was sent to the states Dec. 12, 1803, by the Eighth Congress. It was ratified July 27, 1804.)

[Present mode of electing President and Vice-President by electors.[1]] The electors shall meet in their respective states, and vote by ballot for President and Vice President, one of whom, at least, shall not be an inhabitant of the same state with themselves; they shall name in their ballots the person voted for as President, and in distinct ballots the person voted for as Vice President, and they shall make distinct lists of all persons voted for as President, and of all persons voted for as Vice President, and of the number of votes for each, which lists they shall sign and certify, and transmit sealed to the seat of the government of the United States, directed to the President of the Senate; the President of the Senate shall, in the presence of the Senate and House of Representatives, open all the certificates and the votes shall then be counted; the person having the greatest number of votes for President, shall be the President, if such number be a majority of the whole number of electors appointed; and if no person have such majority, then from the persons having the highest numbers not exceeding three on the list of those voted for as President, the House of Representatives shall choose immediately, by ballot, the President. But in choosing the President, the votes shall be taken by states, the representation from each State having one vote; a quorum for this purpose shall consist of a member or members from two thirds of the states, and a majority of all the states shall be necessary to a choice. And if the House of Representatives shall not choose a President whenever the right of choice shall devolve upon them, before the fourth day of March next following, then the Vice President shall act as President, as in the case of the death or other constitutional disability of the President. The person having the greatest number of votes as Vice President, shall be the Vice President, if such number be a majority of the whole number of electors appointed, and if no person have a majority, then from the two highest numbers on the list, the Senate shall choose the Vice President; a quorum for the purpose shall consist of two thirds of the whole number of Senators, and a majority of the whole number shall be necessary to a choice. But no person constitutionally ineligible to the office of President shall be eligible to that of Vice President of the United States.

Article XIII

(The proposed amendment was sent to the states Feb. 1, 1865, by the Thirty-eighth Congress. It was ratified Dec. 6, 1865.)

Section 1

[Slavery prohibited.] Neither slavery nor involuntary servitude, except as a punishment for crime whereof the party shall have been duly convicted, shall exist within the United States, or any place subject to their jurisdiction.

Section 2

[Congress given power to enforce this article.] Congress shall have power to enforce this article by appropriate legislation.

Article XIV

(The proposed amendment was sent to the states June 16, 1866, by the Thirty-ninth Congress. It was ratified July 9, 1868.)

Section 1

[Citizenship defined; privileges of citizens.] All persons born or naturalized in the United States, and subject to the jurisdiction thereof, are citizens of the United States and of the State wherein they reside. No State shall make or enforce any law which shall abridge the privileges or immunities of citizens of the United States; nor shall any State deprive any person of life, liberty, or property, without due process of law; nor deny to any person within its jurisdiction the equal protection of the laws.

Section 2

[**Apportionment of Representatives.**] Representatives shall be apportioned among the several States according to their respective numbers, counting the whole number of persons in each State, excluding Indians not taxed. But when the right to vote at any election for the choice of electors for President and Vice President of the United States, Representatives in Congress, the executive and judicial officers of a State, or the members of the Legislature thereof, is denied to any of the male inhabitants of such State, being twenty-one years of age, and citizens of the United States, or in any way abridged, except for participation in rebellion, or other crime, the basis of representation therein shall be reduced in the proportion which the number of such male citizens shall bear to the whole number of male citizens twenty-one years of age in such State.

Section 3

[**Disqualification for office; removal of disability.**] No person shall be a Senator or Representative in Congress, or elector of President and Vice President, or hold any office, civil or military, under the United States, or under any State, who, having previously taken an oath, as a member of Congress, or as an officer of the United States, or as a member of any State Legislature, or as an executive or judicial officer of any State, to support the Constitution of the United States, shall have engaged in insurrection or rebellion against the same, or given aid or comfort to the enemies thereof. But Congress may be a vote of two thirds of each House, remove such disability.

Section 4

[**Public debt not to be questioned; payment of debts and claims incurred in aid of rebellion forbidden.**] The validity of the public debt of the United States, authorized by law, including debts incurred for payment of pensions and bounties for services in suppressing insurrection or rebellion, shall not be questioned. But neither the United States nor any State shall assume or pay any debt or obligation incurred in aid of insurrection or rebellion against the United States, or any claim for the loss or emancipation of any slave; but all such debts, obligations, and claims shall be held illegal and void.

Section 5

[**Congress given power to enforce this article.**] The Congress shall have power to enforce, by appropriate legislation, the provisions of this article.

Article XV

(The proposed amendment was sent to the states Feb. 27, 1869, by the Fortieth Congress. It was ratified Feb. 3, 1870.)

Section 1

[**Right of certain citizens to vote established.**] The right of citizens of the United States to vote shall not be denied or abridged by the United States or by any State on account of race, color, or previous condition of servitude.

Section 2

[**Congress given power to enforce this article.**] The Congress shall have power to enforce this article by appropriate legislation.

Article XVI

(The proposed amendment was sent to the states July 12, 1909, by the Sixty-first Congress. It was ratified Feb. 3, 1913.)

[**Taxes on income; Congress given power to lay and collect.**] The Congress shall have power to lay and collect taxes on incomes, from whatever source derived, without apportionment among the several States, and without regard to any census or enumeration.

Article XVII

(The proposed amendment was sent to the states May 16, 1912, by the Sixty-second Congress. It was ratified April 8, 1913.)

[**Election of United States Senators; filling of vacancies; qualifications of electors.**] The Senate of the United States shall be composed of two Senators from each State, elected by the people thereof, for six years; and each Senator shall have one vote. The electors in each State shall have the qualifications requisite for electors of the most numerous branch of the State Legislatures.

When vacancies happen in the representation of any State in the Senate, the executive authority of such State shall issue writs of election to fill such vacancies: Provided, that the legislature of any State may empower the executive thereof to make temporary appointment until the people fill the vacancies by election as the legislature may direct.

This amendment shall not be so construed as to affect the election or term of any Senator chosen before it becomes valid as part of the Constitution.

Article XVIII[2]

(The proposed amendment was sent to the states Dec. 18, 1917, by the Sixty-fifth Congress. It was ratified by three quarters of the states by Jan. 16, 1919, and became effective Jan. 16, 1920.)

Section 1

[**Manufacture, sale, or transportation of intoxicating liquors, for beverage purposes, prohibited.**] After one year from the ratification of this article the manufacture, sale, or transportation of intoxicating liquors within, the importation thereof into, or the exportation thereof from the United States and all territory subject to the jurisdiction thereof for beverage purposes is hereby prohibited.

Section 2

[**Congress and the several States given concurrent power to pass appropriate legislation to enforce this article.**] The Congress and the several States shall have concurrent power to enforce this article by appropriate legislation.

Section 3

[**Provisions of article to become operative, when adopted by three fourths of the States.**] This article shall be inoperative unless it shall have been ratified as an amendment to the Constitution by the legislatures of the several States, as provided in the Constitution, within seven years from the date of the submission hereof to the States by Congress.

Article XIX

(The proposed amendment was sent to the states June 4, 1919, by the Sixty-sixth Congress. It was ratified Aug. 18, 1920.)

[The right of citizens to vote shall not be denied because of sex.] The right of citizens of the United States to vote shall not be denied or abridged by the United States or by any State on account of sex.

[Congress given power to enforce this article.] Congress shall have power to enforce this article by appropriate legislation.

Article XX

(The proposed amendment, sometimes called the "Lame Duck Amendment," was sent to the states Mar. 3, 1932, by the Seventy-second Congress. It was ratified Jan. 23, 1933; but, in accordance with Section 5, Sections 1 and 2 did not go into effect until Oct. 15, 1933.)

Section 1

[Terms of President, Vice President, Senators, and Representatives.] The terms of the President and Vice President shall end at noon on the twentieth day of January, and the terms of Senators and Representatives at noon on the third day of January, of the years in which such terms would have ended if this article had not been ratified; and the terms of their successors shall then begin.

Section 2

[Time of assembling Congress.] The Congress shall assemble at least once in every year, and such meeting shall begin at noon on the third day of January, unless they shall by law appoint a different day.

Section 3

[Filling vacancy in office of President.] If, at the time fixed for the beginning of the term of the President, the President-elect shall have died, the Vice President-elect shall become President. If a President shall not have been chosen before the time fixed for the beginning of his term, or if the President-elect shall have failed to qualify, then the Vice President shall have qualified; and the Congress may by law provide for the case wherein neither a President-elect nor a Vice President-elect shall have qualified, declaring who shall then act as President, or the manner in which one who is to act shall be selected, and such person shall act accordingly until a President or Vice President shall have qualified.

Section 4

[Power of Congress in Presidential succession.] The Congress may by law provide for the case of the death of any of the persons from whom the House of Representatives may choose a President whenever the right of choice shall have devolved upon them, and for the case of the death of any of the persons from whom the Senate may choose a Vice President whenever the right of choice shall have devolved upon them.

Section 5

[Time of taking effect.] Sections 1 and 2 shall take effect on the 15th day of October following the ratification of this article.

Section 6

[Ratification.] This article shall be inoperative unless it shall have been ratified as an amendment to the Constitution by the legislatures of three-fourths of the several States within seven years from the date of its submission.

Article XXI

(The proposed amendment was sent to the states Feb. 20, 1933, by the Seventy-second Congress. It was ratified Dec. 5, 1933.)

Section 1

[Repeal of Prohibition Amendment.] The eighteenth article of amendment to the Constitution of the United States is hereby repealed.

Section 2

[Transportation of intoxicating liquors.] The transportation or importation into any State, territory, or possession of the United States for delivery or use therein of intoxicating liquors, in violation of the laws thereof, is hereby prohibited.

Section 3

[Ratification.] This article shall be inoperative unless it shall have been ratified as an amendment to the Constitution by convention in the several States, as provided in the Constitution, within seven years from the date of the submission thereof to the States by the Congress.

Article XXII

(The proposed amendment was sent to the states Mar. 21, 1947, by the Eightieth Congress. It was ratified Feb. 27, 1951.)

Section 1

[Limit to number of terms a President may serve.] No person shall be elected to the office of the President more than twice, and no person who has held the office of President, or acted as President, for more than two years of a term to which some other person was elected President shall be elected to the office of the President more than once. But this article shall not apply to any person holding the office of President when this article was proposed by the Congress, and shall not prevent any person who may be holding the office of President, or acting as President, during the term within which this article becomes operative from holding the office of President or acting as President during the remainder of such term.

Section 2

[Ratification.] This article shall be inoperative unless it shall have been ratified as an amendment to the Constitution by the legislatures of three fourths of the several States within seven years from the date of its submission to the States by the Congress.

Article XXIII

(The proposed amendment was sent to the states June 16, 1960, by the Eighty-sixth Congress. It was ratified March 29, 1961.)

Section 1

[Electors for the District of Columbia.] The District constituting the seat of Government of the United States shall appoint in such manner as the Congress may direct:

A number of electors of President and Vice President equal to the whole number of Senators and Representatives in Congress to which the District would be entitled if it were a State, but in no event more than the least populous State; they shall be in addition to those appointed by the States, but they shall be considered, for the purposes of the election of President and Vice President, to be electors appointed by a State; and they shall meet in the District and perform such duties as provided by the twelfth article of amendment.

Section 2

[Congress given power to enforce this article.] The Congress shall have the power to enforce this article by appropriate legislation.

Article XXIV

(The proposed amendment was sent to the states Aug. 27, 1962, by the Eighty-seventh Congress. It was ratified Jan. 23, 1964.)

Section 1

[Payment of poll tax or other taxes not to be prerequisite for voting in federal elections.] The right of citizens of the United States to vote in any primary or other election for President or Vice President, for electors for President or Vice President, or for Senator or Representative in Congress, shall not be denied or abridged by the United States or any State by reasons of failure to pay any poll tax or other tax.

Section 2

[Congress given power to enforce this article.] The Congress shall have the power to enforce this article by appropriate legislation.

Article XXV

(The proposed amendment was sent to the states July 6, 1965, by the Eighty-ninth Congress. It was ratified Feb. 10, 1967.)

Section 1

[Succession of Vice President to Presidency.] In case of the removal of the President from office or of his death or resignation, the Vice President shall become President.

Section 2

[Vacancy in office of Vice President.] Whenever there is a vacancy in the office of the Vice President, the President shall nominate a Vice President who shall take office upon confirmation by a majority vote of both Houses of Congress.

Section 3

[Vice President as Acting President.] Whenever the President transmits to the President pro tempore of the Senate and the Speaker of the House of Representatives his written declaration that he is unable to discharge the powers and duties of his

office, and until he transmits to them a written declaration to the contrary, such powers and duties shall be discharged by the Vice President as Acting President.

Section 4

[Vice President as Acting President.] Whenever the Vice President and a majority of either the principal officers of the executive departments or of such other body as Congress may by law provide, transmit to the President pro tempore of the Senate and the Speaker of the House of Representatives their written declaration that the President is unable to discharge the powers and duties of his office, the Vice President shall immediately assume the powers and duties of the office as Acting President.

Thereafter, when the President transmits to the President pro tempore of the Senate and the Speaker of the House of Representatives his written declaration that no inability exists, he shall resume the powers and duties of his office unless the Vice President and a majority of either the principal officers of the executive department or of such other body as Congress may by law provide, transmit within four days to the President pro tempore of the Senate and the Speaker of the House of Representatives their written declaration that the President is unable to discharge the powers and duties of his office. Thereupon Congress shall decide the issue, assembling within forty-eight hours for that purpose if not in session. If the Congress, within twenty-one days after receipt of the latter written declaration, or, if Congress is not in session, within twenty-one days after Congress is required to assemble, determines by two thirds vote of both Houses that the President is unable to discharge the powers and duties of his office, the Vice President shall continue to discharge the same as Acting President; otherwise, the President shall resume the powers and duties of his office.

Article XXVI

(The proposed amendment was sent to the states Mar. 23, 1971, by the Ninety-second Congress. It was ratified July 1, 1971.)

Section 1

[Voting for 18-year-olds.] The right of citizens of the United States, who are 18 years of age or older, to vote shall not be denied or abridged by the United States or by any state on account of age.

Section 2

[Congress given power to enforce this article.] The Congress shall have power to enforce this article by appropriate legislation.

1. Amended by the 20th Amendment, Sections 3 and 4. 2. Repealed by the 21st Amendment.

The White House

Source: Department of the Interior, U.S. National Park Service.

The White House, the official residence of the President, is at 1600 Pennsylvania Avenue in Washington, D.C. 20500 The site, covering about 18 acres, was selected by President Washington and Pierre Charles L'Enfant, and the architect was James Hoban. The design appears to have been influenced by Leinster House, Dublin, and James Gibb's *Book of Architecture.* The cornerstone was laid Oct. 13, 1792, and the first residents were President and Mrs. John Adams in November 1800. The building was fired by the British in 1814.

From December 1948 to March 1952, the interior of the White House was rebuilt, and the outer walls were strengthened.

The rooms for public functions are on the first floor; the second and third floors are used as the residence of the President and First Family. The most celebrated public room is the East Room, where formal receptions take place. Other public rooms are the Red Room, the Green Room, and the Blue Room. The State Dining Room is used for formal dinners. There are 132 rooms.

The Mayflower Compact

On Sept. 6, 1620, the *Mayflower*, a sailing vessel of about 180 tons, started her memorable voyage from Plymouth, England, with about 100[1] pilgrims aboard, bound for Virginia to establish a private permanent colony in North America. Arriving at what is now Provincetown, Mass., on Nov. 11 (Nov. 21, new style calendar), 41 of the passengers signed the famous "Mayflower Compact" as the boat lay at anchor in that Cape Cod harbor. A small detail of the pilgrims, led by William Bradford, assigned to select a place for permanent settlement landed at what is now Plymouth, Mass., on Dec. 21 (n.s.).

The text of the compact follows:

In the name of God, Amen. We, whose names are underwritten, the Loyal Subjects of our dread Sovereign Lord, King *James*, by the Grace of God, of *Great Britain, France and Ireland*, King, *Defender of the Faith, &*

Having undertaken for the Glory of God, and Advancement of the Christian Faith, and the Honour of our King and Country, a voyage to plant the first colony in the northern Parts of Virginia; do by these Presents, solemnly and mutually in the Presence of God and one of another, covenant and combine ourselves together into a civil Body Politick, for our better Ordering and Preservation, and Furtherance of the Ends aforesaid; And by Virtue hereof to enact, constitute, and frame, such just and equal Laws, Ordinances, Acts, Constitutions and Offices, from time to time, as shall be thought most meet and convenient for the General good of the Colony; unto which we promise all due Submission and Obedience.

In Witness whereof we have hereunto subscribed our names at *Cape Cod* the eleventh of *November*, in the Reign of our Sovereign Lord, King *James* of *England, France* and *Ireland*, the eighteenth, and of *Scotland* the fifty-fourth. *Anno Domini*, 1620

John Carver	William Mullins	John Billington	Peter Brown
Digery Priest	Thomas English	Thomas Tinker	John Turner
William Brewster	John Howland	Samuel Fuller	Edward Tilly
Edmund Margesson	Stephen Hopkins	Richard Clark	John Craxton
John Alden	Edward Winslow	John Allerton	Thomas Rogers
George Soule	Gilbert Winslow	Richard Warren	John Goodman
James Chilton	Miles Standish	Edward Liester	Edward Fuller
Francis Cooke	Richard Bitteridge	William Bradford	Richard Gardiner
Moses Fletcher	Francis Eaton	Thomas Williams	William White
John Ridgate	John Tilly	Isaac Allerton	Edward Doten
Christopher Martin			

1. Historians differ as to whether 100, 101, or 102 passengers were aboard.

The Monroe Doctrine

The Monroe Doctrine was announced in President James Monroe's message to Congress, during his second term on Dec. 2, 1823, in part as follows:

"In the discussions to which this interest has given rise, and in the arrangements by which they may terminate, the occasion has been deemed proper for asserting as a principle in which rights and interests of the United States are involved, that the American continents, by the free and independent condition which they have assumed and maintain, are henceforth not to be considered as subjects for future colonization by any European power. . . . We owe it, therefore, to candor and to the amicable relations existing between the United States and those powers to declare that we should consider any attempt on their part to extend their system to any portion of this hemisphere as dangerous to our peace and safety. With the existing colonies or dependencies of any European power we have not interfered and shall not interfere. But with the governments who have declared their independence and maintain it, and whose independence we have, on great consideration and on just principles, acknowledged, we could not view any interposition for the purpose of oppressing them or controlling in any other manner their destiny by any European power in any other light than as the manifestation of an unfriendly disposition toward the United States."

Order of Presidential Succession

1. The Vice President
2. Speaker of the House
3. President pro tempore of the Senate
4. Secretary of State
5. Secretary of the Treasury
6. Secretary of Defense
7. Attorney General
8. Secretary of the Interior
9. Secretary of Agriculture
10. Secretary of Commerce
11. Secretary of Labor
12. Secretary of Health and Human Services
13. Secretary of Housing and Urban Development
14. Secretary of Transportation
15. Secretary of Energy
16. Secretary of Education

NOTE: An official cannot succeed to the Presidency unless that person meets the Constitutional requirements.

The Star-Spangled Banner

Francis Scott Key, 1814

O say, can you see, by the dawn's early light,
What so proudly we hail'd at the twilight's last gleaming?
Whose broad stripes and bright stars, thro' the perilous fight,
O'er the ramparts we watch'd, were so gallantly streaming?
And the rockets' red glare, the bombs bursting in air,
Gave proof thro' the night that our flag was still there.
O say, does that star-spangled banner yet wave
O'er the land of the free and the home of the brave?

On the shore dimly seen thro' the mists of the deep,
Where the foe's haughty host in dread silence reposes,
What is that which the breeze, o'er the towering steep,
As it fitfully blows, half conceals, half discloses?
Now it catches the gleam of the morning's first beam,
In full glory reflected, now shines on the stream:
'T is the star-spangled banner: O, long may it wave
O'er the land of the free and the home of the brave!

And where is that band who so vauntingly swore
That the havoc of war and the battle's confusion,
A home and a country should leave us no more?
Their blood has wash'd out their foul footsteps' pollution.
No refuge could save the hireling and slave
From the terror of flight or the gloom of the grave:
And the star-spangled banner in triumph doth wave
O'er the land of the free and the home of the brave.

O thus be it ever when free-men shall stand
Between their lov'd home and the war's desolation;
Blest with vict'ry and peace, may the heav'n-rescued land
Praise the Pow'r that hath made and preserv'd us a nation!
Then conquer we must, when our cause it is just,
And this be our motto: "In God is our trust!"
And the star-spangled banner in triumph shall wave
O'er the land of the free and the home of the brave!

On Sept. 13, 1814, Francis Scott Key visited the British fleet in Chesapeake Bay to secure the release of Dr. William Beanes, who had been captured after the burning of Washington, D.C. The release was secured, but Key was detained on ship overnight during the shelling of Fort McHenry, one of the forts defending Baltimore. In the morning, he was so delighted to see the American flag still flying over the fort that he began a poem to commemorate the occasion. First published under the title "Defense of Fort M'Henry," and later as "The Star-Spangled Banner," the poem soon attained wide popularity as sung to the tune "To Anacreon in Heaven." The origin of this tune is obscure, but it may have been written by John Stafford Smith, a British composer born in 1750. "The Star-Spangled Banner" was officially made the National Anthem by Congress in 1931, although it had been already adopted as such by the Army and the Navy.

The Emancipation Proclamation

January 1, 1863

By the President of the United
States of America:

A Proclamation.
Whereas on the 22d day of September, A.D. 1862, a proclamation was issued by the President of the United States, containing, among other things, the following, to wit:
"That on the 1st day of January, A.D. 1863, all persons held as slaves within any State or designated part of a State the people whereof shall then be in rebellion against the United States shall be then, thenceforward, and forever free; and the executive government of the United States, including the military and naval authority thereof, will recognize and maintain the freedom of such persons, and will do not act or acts to repress such persons, or any of them, in any efforts they may make for their actual freedom.
"That the executive will on the 1st day of January aforesaid, by proclamation, designate the States and parts of States, if any, in which the people thereof, respectively, shall then be in rebellion against the United States; and the fact that any State or the people thereof shall on that day be in good faith represented in the Congress of the United States by members chosen thereto at elections wherein a majority of the qualified voters of such States shall have participated shall, in the absence of strong countervailing testimony, be deemed conclusive evidence that such State and the people thereof are not then in rebellion against the United States."
Now, therefore, I, Abraham Lincoln, President

of the United States, by virtue of the power in me vested as Commander-in-Chief of the Army and Navy of the United States in time of actual armed rebellion against the authority and government of the United States, and as a fit and necessary war measure for suppressing said rebellion, do, on this 1st day of January, A.D. 1863, and in accordance with my purpose so to do, publicly proclaimed for the full period of one hundred days from the first day above mentioned, order and designate as the States and parts of States wherein the people thereof, respectively, are this day in rebellion against the United States the following, to wit:

Arkansas, Texas, Louisiana (except the parishes of St. Bernard, Plaquemines, Jefferson, St. John, St. Charles, St. James, Ascension, Assumption, Terrebonne, Lafourche, St. Mary, St. Martin, and Orleans, including the city of New Orleans), Mississippi, Alabama, Florida, Georgia, South Carolina, North Carolina, and Virginia (except the forty-eight counties designated as West Virginia, and also the counties of Berkeley, Accomac, Northhampton, Elizabeth City, York, Princess Anne, and Norfolk, including the cities of Norfolk and Portsmouth), and which excepted parts are for the present left precisely as if this proclamation were not issued.

And by virtue of the power and for the purpose aforesaid, I do order and declare that all persons held as slaves within said designated States and parts of States are, and henceforward shall be, free; and that the Executive Government of the United States, including the military and naval authorities thereof, will recognize and maintain the freedom of said persons.

And I hereby enjoin upon the people so declared to be free to abstain from all violence, unless in necessary self-defense; and I recommend to them that, in all cases when allowed, they labor faithfully for reasonable wages.

And I further declare and make known that such persons of suitable condition will be received into the armed service of the United States to garrison forts, positions, stations, and other places, and to man vessels of all sorts in said service.

And upon this act, sincerely believed to be an act of justice, warranted by the Constitution upon military necessity, I invoke the considerate judgment of mankind and the gracious favor of Almighty God.

The Confederate States of America

State	Seceded from Union	Readmitted to Union[1]	State	Seceded from Union	Readmitted to Union[1]
1. South Carolina	Dec. 20, 1860	July 9, 1868	7. Texas	March 2, 1861	March 30, 1870
2. Mississippi	Jan. 9, 1861	Feb. 23, 1870	8. Virginia	April 17, 1861	Jan. 26, 1870
3. Florida	Jan. 10, 1861	June 25, 1868	9. Arkansas	May 6, 1861	June 22, 1868
4. Alabama	Jan. 11, 1861	July 13, 1868	10. North Carolina	May 20, 1861	July 4, 1868
5. Georgia	Jan. 19, 1861	July 15, 1870[2]	11. Tennessee	June 8, 1861	July 24, 1866
6. Louisiana	Jan. 26, 1861	July 9, 1868			

1. Date of readmission to representation in U.S. House of Representatives. 2. Second readmission date. First date was July 21, 1868, but the representatives were unseated March 5, 1869. NOTE: Four other slave states—Delaware, Kentucky, Maryland, and Missouri—remained in the Union.

Lincoln's Gettysburg Address

The Battle of Gettysburg, one of the most noted battles of the Civil War, was fought on July 1, 2, and 3, 1863. On Nov. 19, 1863, the field was dedicated as a national cemetery by President Lincoln in a two-minute speech that was to become immortal. At the time of its delivery the speech was relegated to the inside pages of the papers, while a two-hour address by Edward Everett, the leading orator of the time, caught the headlines.

The following is the text of the address revised by President Lincoln from his own notes:

Fourscore and seven years ago our fathers brought forth on this continent a new nation conceived in liberty and dedicated to the proposition that all men are created equal. Now we are engaged in a great civil war testing whether that nation, or any nation so conceived and so dedicated, can long endure. We are met on a great battlefield of that war. We have come to dedicate a portion of that field as a final resting-place for those who here gave their lives that that nation might live. It is altogether fitting and proper that we should do this. But, in a larger sense, we cannot dedicate, we cannot consecrate, we cannot hallow this ground. The brave men, living and dead, who struggled here have consecrated it far above our poor power to add or detract. The world will little note nor long remember what we say here, but it can never forget what they did here. It is for us the living rather to be dedicated here to the unfinished work which they who fought here have thus far so nobly advanced. It is rather for us to be here dedicated to the great task remaining before us—that from these honored dead we take increased devotion to that cause for which they gave the last full measure of devotion—that we here highly resolve that these dead shall not have died in vain, that this nation under God shall have a new birth of freedom, and that government of the people, by the people, for the people shall not perish from the earth.

The Early Congresses

At the urging of Massachusetts and Virginia, the First Continental Congress met in Philadelphia on Sept. 5, 1774, and was attended by representatives of all the colonies except Georgia. Patrick Henry of Virginia declared: "The distinctions between Pennsylvanians, New Yorkers and New Englanders are no more. I am not a Virginian but an American." This Congress, which adjourned Oct. 26, 1774, passed intercolonial resolutions calling for extensive boycott by the colonies against British trade.

The following year, most of the delegates from the colonies were chosen by popular election to attend the Second Continental Congress, which assembled in Philadelphia on May 10. As war had already begun between the colonies and England, the chief problems before the Congress were the procuring of military supplies, the establishment of an army and proper defenses, the issuing of continental bills of credit, etc. On June 15, 1775, George Washington was elected to command the Conti-

nental army. Congress adjourned Dec. 12, 1776.

Other Continental Congresses were held in Baltimore (1776–77), Philadelphia (1777), Lancaster, Pa. (1777), York, Pa. (1777–78), and Philadelphia (1778–81).

In 1781, the Articles of Confederation, although establishing a league of the thirteen states rather than a strong central government, provided for the continuance of Congress. Known thereafter as the Congress of the Confederation, it held sessions in Philadelphia (1781–83), Princeton, N.J. (1783), Annapolis, Md. (1783–84), and Trenton, N.J. (1784). Five sessions were held in New York City between the years 1785 and 1789.

The Congress of the United States, established by the ratification of the Constitution, held its first meeting on March 4, 1789, in New York City. Several sessions of Congress were held in Philadelphia, and the first meeting in Washington, D.C., was on Nov. 17, 1800.

Presidents of the Continental Congresses

Name	Elected	Birth and Death Dates	Name	Elected	Birth and Death Dates
Peyton Randolph, Va.	9/5/1774	c.1721-1775	John Hanson, Md.	11/5/1781	1715-1783
Henry Middleton, S.C.	10/22/1774	1717-1784	Elias Boudinot, N.J.	11/4/1782	1740-1821
Peyton Randolph, Va.	5/10/1775	c.1721-1775	Thomas Mifflin, Pa.	11/3/1783	1744-1800
John Hancock, Mass.	5/24/1775	1737-1793	Richard Henry Lee, Va.	11/30/1784	1732-1794
Henry Laurens, S.C.	11/1/1777	1724-1792	John Hancock, Mass.[1]	11/23/1785	1737-1793
John Jay, N.Y.	12/10/1778	1745-1829	Nathaniel Gorham, Mass.	6/6/1786	1738-1796
Samuel Huntington, Conn.	9/28/1779	1731-1796	Arthur St. Clair, Pa.	2/2/1787	1734-1818
Thomas McKean, Del.	7/10/1781	1734-1817	Cyrus Griffin, Va.	1/22/1788	1748-1810

1. Resigned May 29, 1786, never having served, because of continued illness.

The Great Seal of the U.S.

On July 4, 1776, the Continental Congress appointed a committee consisting of Benjamin Franklin, John Adams, and Thomas Jefferson "to bring in a device for a seal of the United States of America." After many delays, a verbal description of a design by William Barton was finally approved by Congress on June 20, 1782. The seal shows an American bald eagle with a ribbon in its mouth bearing the device *E pluribus unum* (One out of many). In its talons are the arrows of war and an olive branch of peace. On the reverse side it shows an unfinished pyramid with an eye (the eye of Providence) above it. Although this description was adopted in 1782, the first drawing was not made until four years later, and no die has ever been cut.

The American's Creed

William Tyler Page

"I believe in the United States of America as a government of the people, by the people, for the people; whose just powers are derived from the consent of the governed; a democracy in a republic; a sovereign Nation of many sovereign States; a perfect union, one and inseparable; established upon those principles of freedom, equality, justice, and humanity for which American patriots sacrificed their lives and fortunes.

"I therefore believe it is my duty to my country to love it, to support its Constitution, to obey its laws, to respect its flag, and to defend it against all enemies."

NOTE: William Tyler Page, Clerk of the U.S. House of Representatives, wrote "The American's Creed" in 1917. It was accepted by the House on behalf of the American people on April 3, 1918.

U.S. Capitol

When the French architect and engineer Maj. Pierre L'Enfant first began to lay out the plans for a new Federal city (now Washington, D.C.), he noted that Jenkins' Hill, overlooking the area, seemed to be "a pedestal waiting for a monument." It was here that the U.S. Capitol would be built. The basic structure as we know it today evolved over a period of more than 150 years. In 1792 a competition was held for the design of a capitol building. Dr. William Thornton, a physician and amateur architect, submitted the winning plan, a simple, low-lying structure of classical proportions with a shallow dome. Later, internal modifications were made by Benjamin Henry Latrobe. After the building was burned by the British in 1814, Latrobe and architect Charles Bulfinch were responsible for its reconstruction. Finally, under Thomas Walter, who was Architect of the Capitol from 1851 to 1865, the House and Senate wings and the imposing cast iron dome topped with the Statue of Freedom were added, and the Capitol assumed the form we see today. It was in the old Senate chamber that Daniel Webster cried out, "Liberty and Union, now and forever, one and inseparable!" In Statuary Hall, which used to be the old House chamber, a small disk on the floor marks the spot where John Quincy Adams was fatally stricken after more than 50 years of service to his country. A whisper from one side of this room can be heard across the vast space of the hall. Visitors can see the original Supreme Court chamber a floor below the Rotunda.

In addition to its historical association, the Capitol Building is also a vast artistic treasure house. The works of such famous artists as Gilbert Stuart, Rembrandt Peale, and John Trumbull are displayed on the walls. The Great Rotunda, with its 180-foot- (54.9-m-) high dome, is decorated with a massive fresco by Constantino Brumidi, which extends some 300 feet (90 m) in circumference. Throughout the building are many paintings of events in U.S. history and sculptures of outstanding Americans. The Capitol itself is situated on a 68-acre (27.5-ha) park designed by the 19th-century landscape architect Frederick Law Olmsted. There are free guided tours of the Capitol, which include admission to the House and Senate galleries. Those who wish to visit the visitors' gallery in either wing without taking the tour may obtain passes from their Senators or Congressmen. Visitors may ride on the monorail subway that joins the House and Senate wings of the Capitol with the Congressional office buildings.

Washington Monument

Construction of this magnificent Washington, D.C., monument, which draws some two million visitors a year, took nearly a century of planning, building, and controversy. Provision for a large equestrian statue of George Washington was made in the original city plan, but the project was soon dropped. After Washington's death it was taken up again, and a number of false starts and changes of design were made. Finally, in 1848, work was begun on the monument that stands today. The design, by architect Robert Mills, then featured an ornate base. In 1854, however, political squabbling and a lack of money brought construction to a halt. Work was resumed in 1880, and the monument was completed in 1884 and opened to the public in 1888. The tapered shaft, faced with white marble and rising from walls 15 feet thick (4.6 m) at the base was modeled after the obelisks of ancient Egypt. The monument, one of the tallest masonry constructions in the world, stands just over 555 feet (169 m). Memorial stones from the 50 States, foreign countries, and organizations line the interior walls. The top, reached only by elevator, commands a panoramic view of the city.

The Liberty Bell

The Liberty Bell was cast in England in 1752 for the Pennsylvania Statehouse (now named Independence Hall) in Philadelphia. It was recast in Philadelphia in 1753. It is inscribed with the words, "Proclaim liberty throughout all the land unto all the inhabitants thereof" (Lev. 25:10). The bell was rung on July 8, 1776, for the first public reading of the Declaration of Independence. Hidden in Allentown during the British occupation of Philadelphia, it was replaced in Independence Hall in 1778. The bell cracked on July 8, 1835, while tolling the death of Chief Justice John Marshall. In 1976 the Liberty Bell was moved to a special exhibition building near Independence Hall.

Arlington National Cemetery

Arlington National Cemetery occupies 612 acres in Virginia on the Potomac River, directly opposite Washington. This land was part of the estate of John Parke Custis, Martha Washington's son. His son, George Washington Parke Custis, built the mansion which later became the home of Robert E. Lee. In 1864, Arlington became a military cemetery. More than 200,000 servicemembers and their dependents are buried there. Expansion of the cemetery began in 1966, using a 180-acre tract of land directly east of the present site.

In 1921, an Unknown American Soldier of World War I was buried in the cemetery; the monument at the Tomb was opened to the public without ceremony in 1932. Two additional Unknowns, one from World War II and one from the Korean War, were buried May 30, 1958. The Unknown Serviceman of Vietnam was buried on May 28, 1984. The inscription carved on the Tomb of the Unknowns reads:

HERE RESTS IN
HONORED GLORY
AN AMERICAN
SOLDIER
KNOWN BUT TO GOD

History of the Flag

Source: Encyclopaedia Britannica.

The first official American flag, the Continental or Grand Union flag, was displayed on Prospect Hill, Jan. 1, 1776, in the American lines besieging Boston. It had 13 alternate red and white stripes, with the British Union Jack in the upper left corner.

On June 14, 1777, the Continental Congress adopted the design for a new flag, which actually was the Continental flag with the red cross of St. George and the white cross of St. Andrew replaced on the blue field by 13 stars, one for each state. No rule was made as to the arrangement of the stars, and while they were usually shown in a circle, there were various other designs. It is uncertain when the new flag was first flown, but its first official announcement is believed to have been on Sept. 3, 1777.

The first public assertion that Betsy Ross made the first Stars and Stripes appeared in a paper read before the Historical Society of Pennsylvania on March 14, 1870, by William J. Canby, a grandson. However, Mr. Canby on later investigation found no official documents of any action by Congress on the flag before June 14, 1777. Betsy Ross's own story, according to her daughter, was that Washington, Robert Morris, and George Ross, as representatives of Congress, visited her in Philadelphia in June 1776, showing her a rough draft of the flag and asking her if she could make one. However, the only actual record of the manufacture of flags by Betsy Ross is a voucher in Harrisburg, Pa., for 14 pounds and some shillings for flags for the Pennsylvania navy.

On Jan. 13, 1794, Congress voted to add two stars and two stripes to the flag in recognition of the admission of Vermont and Kentucky to the Union. By 1818, there were 20 states in the Union, and as it was obvious that the flag would soon become unwieldy, Congress voted April 18 to return to the original 13 stripes and to indicate the admission of a new state simply by the addition of a star the following July 4. The 49th star, for Alaska, was added July 4, 1959; and the 50th star, for Hawaii, was added July 4, 1960.

The first Confederate flag, adopted in 1861 by the Confederate convention in Montgomery, Ala., was called the Stars and Bars; but because of its similarity in colors to the American flag, there was much confusion in the Battle of Bull Run. To remedy this situation, Gen. G. T. Beauregard suggested a battle flag, which was used by the Southern armies throughout the war. The flag consisted of a red field on which was placed a blue cross of St. Andrew separated from the field by a white fillet and adorned with 13[1] white stars for the Confederate states. In May 1863, at Richmond, an official flag was adopted by the Confederate Congress. This flag was white and twice as long as wide; the union, two-thirds the width of the flag, contained the battle flag designed for Gen. Beauregard. A broad transverse stripe of red was added Feb. 4, 1865, so that the flag might not be mistaken for a signal of truce.

1. 11 states formally seceded, and unofficial groups in Kentucky and Missouri adopted ordinances of secession. On this basis, these two states were admitted to the Confederacy, although the official state governments remained in the Union.

The Pledge of Allegiance[1] to the Flag

"I pledge allegiance to the Flag of the United States of America, and to the Republic for which it stands, one Nation under God,[2] indivisible, with liberty and justice for all."

1. The original pledge was published in the Sept. 8, 1892, issue of *The Youth's Companion* in Boston. For years, the authorship was in dispute between James B. Upham and Francis Bellamy of the magazine's staff. In 1939, after a study of the controversy, the United States Flag Association decided that authorship be credited to Bellamy. 2. The phrase "under God" was added to the pledge on June 14, 1954.

The Statue of Liberty

The Statue of Liberty ("Liberty Enlightening the World") is a 225-ton, steel-reinforced copper female figure, 152 ft in height, facing the ocean from Liberty[1] Island in New York Harbor. The right hand holds aloft a torch, and the left hand carries a tablet upon which is inscribed: "July IV MDCCLXXVI."

The statue was designed by Frédéric Auguste Bartholdi of Alsace as a gift to the United States from the people of France to memorialize the alliance of the two countries in the American Revolution and their abiding friendship. The French people contributed the $250,000 cost.

The 150-foot pedestal was designed by Richard M. Hunt and built by Gen. Charles P. Stone, both Americans. It contains steel underpinnings designed by Alexander Eiffel of France to support the statue. The $270,000 cost was borne by popular subscription in this country. President Grover Cleveland accepted the statue for the United States on Oct. 28, 1886.

On Sept. 26, 1972, President Richard M. Nixon

1. Called Bedloe's Island prior to 1956.

dedicated the American Museum of Immigration, housed in structural additions to the base of the statue. In 1984 scaffolding went up for a major restoration and the torch was extinguished on July 4. It was relit with much ceremony July 4, 1986 to mark its centennial.

On a tablet inside the pedestal is engraved the following sonnet, written by Emma Lazarus (1849–1887):

The New Colossus

Not like the brazen giant of Greek fame.
With conquering limbs astride from land to land;
Here at our sea-washed, sunset gates shall stand
A mighty woman with a torch, whose flame
Is the imprisoned lightning, and her name
Mother of Exiles. From her beacon-hand
Glows world-wide welcome; her mild eyes command
The air-bridged harbor that twin cities frame.
"Keep, ancient lands, your storied pomp!" cries she
With silent lips. "Give me your tired, your poor,
Your huddled masses yearning to breathe free,
The wretched refuse of your teeming shore.
Send these, the homeless, tempest-tost to me,
I lift my lamp beside the golden door!"

Presidents

Name and (party)[1]	Term	State of birth	Born	Died	Religion	Age at inaug.	Age at death
1. Washington (F)[2]	1789–1797	Va.	2/22/1732	12/14/1799	Episcopalian	57	67
2. J. Adams (F)	1797–1801	Mass.	10/30/1735	7/4/1826	Unitarian	61	90
3. Jefferson (DR)	1801–1809	Va.	4/13/1743	7/4/1826	Deist	57	83
4. Madison (DR)	1809–1817	Va.	3/16/1751	6/28/1836	Episcopalian	57	85
5. Monroe (DR)	1817–1825	Va.	4/28/1758	7/4/1831	Episcopalian	58	73
6. J. Q. Adams (DR)	1825–1829	Mass.	7/11/1767	2/23/1848	Unitarian	57	80
7. Jackson (D)	1829–1837	S.C.	3/15/1767	6/8/1845	Presbyterian	61	78
8. Van Buren (D)	1837–1841	N.Y.	12/5/1782	7/24/1862	Reformed Dutch	54	79
9. W. H. Harrison (W)[3]	1841	Va.	2/9/1773	4/4/1841	Episcopalian	68	68
10. Tyler (W)	1841–1845	Va.	3/29/1790	1/18/1862	Episcopalian	51	71
11. Polk (D)	1845–1849	N.C.	11/2/1795	6/15/1849	Methodist	49	53
12. Taylor (W)[3]	1849–1850	Va.	11/24/1784	7/9/1850	Episcopalian	64	65
13. Fillmore (W)	1850–1853	N.Y.	1/7/1800	3/8/1874	Unitarian	50	74
14. Pierce (D)	1853–1857	N.H.	11/23/1804	10/8/1869	Episcopalian	48	64
15. Buchanan (D)	1857–1861	Pa.	4/23/1791	6/1/1868	Presbyterian	65	77
16. Lincoln (R)[4]	1861–1865	Ky.	2/12/1809	4/15/1865	Liberal	52	56
17. A. Johnson (U)[5]	1865–1869	N.C.	12/29/1808	7/31/1875	([6])	56	66
18. Grant (R)	1869–1877	Ohio	4/27/1822	7/23/1885	Methodist	46	63
19. Hayes (R)	1877–1881	Ohio	10/4/1822	1/17/1893	Methodist	54	70
20. Garfield (R)[4]	1881	Ohio	11/19/1831	9/19/1881	Disciples of Christ	49	49
21. Arthur (R)	1881–1885	Vt.	10/5/1830	11/18/1886	Episcopalian	50	56
22. Cleveland (D)	1885–1889	N.J.	3/18/1837	6/24/1908	Presbyterian	47	71
23. B. Harrison (R)	1889–1893	Ohio	8/20/1833	3/13/1901	Presbyterian	55	67
24. Cleveland (D)[7]	1893–1897	—	—	—	—	55	—
25. McKinley (R)[4]	1897–1901	Ohio	1/29/1843	9/14/1901	Methodist	54	58
26. T. Roosevelt (R)	1901–1909	N.Y.	10/27/1858	1/6/1919	Reformed Dutch	42	60
27. Taft (R)	1909–1913	Ohio	9/15/1857	3/8/1930	Unitarian	51	72
28. Wilson (D)	1913–1921	Va.	12/28/1856	2/3/1924	Presbyterian	56	67
29. Harding (R)[3]	1921–1923	Ohio	11/2/1865	8/2/1923	Baptist	55	57
30. Coolidge (R)	1923–1929	Vt.	7/4/1872	1/5/1933	Congregationalist	51	60
31. Hoover (R)	1929–1933	Iowa	8/10/1874	10/20/1964	Quaker	54	90
32. F. D. Roosevelt (D)[3]	1933–1945	N.Y.	1/30/1882	4/12/1945	Episcopalian	51	63
33. Truman (D)	1945–1953	Mo.	5/8/1884	12/26/1972	Baptist	60	88
34. Eisenhower (R)	1953–1961	Tex.	10/14/1890	3/28/1969	Presbyterian	62	78
35. Kennedy (D)[4]	1961–1963	Mass.	5/29/1917	11/22/1963	Roman Catholic	43	46
36. L. B. Johnson (D)	1963–1969	Tex.	8/27/1908	1/22/1973	Disciples of Christ	55	64
37. Nixon (R)[8]	1969–1974	Calif.	1/9/1913	—	Quaker	56	—
38. Ford (R)	1974–1977	Neb.	7/14/1913	—	Episcopalian	61	—
39. Carter (D)	1977–1981	Ga.	10/1/1924	—	Southern Baptist	52	—
40. Reagan (R)	1981–1989	Ill.	2/6/1911	—	Disciples of Christ	69	—
41. Bush (R)	1989–	Mass.	6/12/24	—	Episcopalian	64	—

1. F—Federalist; DR—Democratic-Republican; D—Democratic; W—Whig; R—Republican; U—Union. 2. No party for first election. The party system in the U.S. made its appearance during Washington's first term. 3. Died in office. 4. Assassinated in office. 5. The Republican National Convention of 1864 adopted the name Union Party. It renominated Lincoln for President; for Vice President it nominated Johnson, a War Democrat. Although frequently listed as a Republican Vice President and President, Johnson undoubtedly considered himself strictly a member of the Union Party. When that party broke apart after 1868, he returned to the Democratic Party. 6. Johnson was not a professed church member; however, he admired the Baptist principles of church government. 7. Second nonconsecutive term. 8. Resigned Aug. 9, 1974.

Vice Presidents

Name and (party)[1]	Term	State of birth	Birth and death dates	President served under
1. John Adams (F)[2]	1789–1797	Massachusetts	1735–1826	Washington
2. Thomas Jefferson (DR)	1797–1801	Virginia	1743–1826	J. Adams
3. Aaron Burr (DR)	1801–1805	New Jersey	1756–1836	Jefferson
4. George Clinton (DR)[3]	1805–1812	New York	1739–1812	Jefferson and Madison
5. Elbridge Gerry (DR)[3]	1813–1814	Massachusetts	1744–1814	Madison
6. Daniel D. Tompkins (DR)	1817–1825	New York	1774–1825	Monroe
7. John C. Calhoun[4]	1825–1832	South Carolina	1782–1850	J. Q. Adams and Jackson
8. Martin Van Buren (D)	1833–1837	New York	1782–1862	Jackson
9. Richard M. Johnson (D)	1837–1841	Kentucky	1780–1850	Van Buren
10. John Tyler (W)[5]	1841	Virginia	1790–1862	W. H. Harrison
11. George M. Dallas (D)	1845–1849	Pennsylvania	1792–1864	Polk
12. Millard Fillmore (W)[5]	1849–1850	New York	1800–1874	Taylor
13. William R. King (D)[3]	1853	North Carolina	1786–1853	Pierce
14. John C. Breckinridge (D)	1857–1861	Kentucky	1821–1875	Buchanan

Name and (party)[1]	Term	State of birth	Birth and death dates	President served under
15. Hannibal Hamlin (R)	1861–1865	Maine	1809–1891	Lincoln
16. Andrew Johnson (U)[5]	1865	North Carolina	1808–1875	Lincoln
17. Schuyler Colfax (R)	1869–1873	New York	1823–1885	Grant
18. Henry Wilson (R)[3]	1873–1875	New Hampshire	1812–1875	Grant
19. William A. Wheeler (R)	1877–1881	New York	1819–1887	Hayes
20. Chester A. Arthur (R)[5]	1881	Vermont	1830–1886	Garfield
21. Thomas A. Hendricks (D)[3]	1885	Ohio	1819–1885	Cleveland
22. Levi P. Morton (R)	1889–1893	Vermont	1824–1920	B. Harrison
23. Adlai E. Stevenson (D)	1893–1897	Kentucky	1835–1914	Cleveland
24. Garret A. Hobart (R)[3]	1897–1899	New Jersey	1844–1899	McKinley
25. Theodore Roosevelt (R)[5]	1901	New York	1858–1919	McKinley
26. Charles W. Fairbanks (R)	1905–1909	Ohio	1852–1918	T. Roosevelt
27. James S. Sherman (R)[3]	1909–1912	New York	1855–1912	Taft
28. Thomas R. Marshall (D)	1913–1921	Indiana	1854–1925	Wilson
29. Calvin Coolidge (R)[5]	1921–1923	Vermont	1872–1933	Harding
30. Charles G. Dawes (R)	1925–1929	Ohio	1865–1951	Coolidge
31. Charles Curtis (R)	1929–1933	Kansas	1860–1936	Hoover
32. John N. Garner (D)	1933–1941	Texas	1868–1967	F. D. Roosevelt
33. Henry A. Wallace (D)	1941–1945	Iowa	1888–1965	F. D. Roosevelt
34. Harry S. Truman (D)[5]	1945	Missouri	1884–1972	F. D. Roosevelt
35. Alben W. Barkley (D)	1949–1953	Kentucky	1877–1956	Truman
36. Richard M. Nixon (R)	1953–1961	California	1913–	Eisenhower
37. Lyndon B. Johnson (D)[5]	1961–1963	Texas	1908–1973	Kennedy
38. Hubert H. Humphrey (D)	1965–1969	South Dakota	1911–1978	Johnson
39. Spiro T. Agnew (R)[6]	1969–1973	Maryland	1918–	Nixon
40. Gerald R. Ford (R)[7]	1973–1974	Nebraska	1913–	Nixon
41. Nelson A. Rockefeller (R)[8]	1974–1977	Maine	1908–1979	Ford
42. Walter F. Mondale (D)	1977–1981	Minnesota	1928–	Carter
43. George Bush (R)	1981–1989	Massachusetts	1924–	Reagan
44. J. Danforth Quayle (R)	1989–	Indiana	1947–	Bush

1. F—Federalist; DR—Democratic-Republican; D—Democratic; W—Whig; R—Republican; U—Union. 2. No party for first election. The party system in the U.S. made its appearance during Washington's first term as President. 3. Died in office. 4. Democratic-Republican with J. Q. Adams; Democratic with Jackson. Calhoun resigned in 1832 to become a U.S. Senator. 5. Succeeded to presidency on death of President. 6. Resigned Oct. 10, 1973, after pleading no contest to Federal income tax evasion charges. 7. Nominated by Nixon on Oct. 12, 1973, under provisions of 25th Amendment. Confirmed by Congress on Dec. 6, 1973, and was sworn in same day. He became President Aug. 9, 1974, upon Nixon's resignation. 8. Nominated by Ford Aug. 20, 1974; confirmed by Congress on Dec. 19, 1974, and was sworn in same day.

Burial Places of the Presidents

President	Burial place	President	Burial place
Washington	Mt. Vernon, Va.	Grant	New York City
J. Adams	Quincy, Mass.	Hayes	Fremont, Ohio
Jefferson	Charlottesville, Va.	Garfield	Cleveland, Ohio
Madison	Montpelier Station, Va.	Arthur	Albany, N.Y.
Monroe	Richmond, Va.	Cleveland	Princeton, N.J.
J. Q. Adams	Quincy, Mass.	B. Harrison	Indianapolis
Jackson	The Hermitage, nr. Nashville, Tenn.	McKinley	Canton, Ohio
		T. Roosevelt	Oyster Bay, N.Y.
Van Buren	Kinderhook, N.Y.	Taft	Arlington National Cemetery
W. H. Harrison	North Bend, Ohio	Wilson	Washington National Cathedral
Tyler	Richmond, Va.	Harding	Marion, Ohio
Polk	Nashville, Tenn.	Coolidge	Plymouth, Vt.
Taylor	Louisville, Ky.	Hoover	West Branch, Iowa
Fillmore	Buffalo, N.Y.	F. D. Roosevelt	Hyde Park, N.Y.
Pierce	Concord, N.H.	Truman	Independence, Mo.
Buchanan	Lancaster, Pa.	Eisenhower	Abilene, Kan.
Lincoln	Springfield, Ill.	Kennedy	Arlington National Cemetery
A. Johnson	Greeneville, Tenn.	L. B. Johnson	Stonewall, Tex.

"In God We Trust"

"In God We Trust" first appeared on U.S. coins after April 22, 1864, when Congress passed an act authorizing the coinage of a 2-cent piece bearing this motto. Thereafter, Congress extended its use to other coins. On July 30, 1956, it became the national motto.

Wives and Children of the Presidents

President	Wife's name	Year and place of wife's birth	Married	Wife died	Children of President[1] Sons	Children of President[1] Daughters
Washington	Martha Dandridge Custis	1732, Va.	1759	1802	—	—
John Adams	Abigail Smith	1744, Mass.	1764	1818	3	2
Jefferson	Martha Wayles Skelton	1748, Va.	1772	1782	1	5
Madison	Dorothy "Dolley" Payne Todd	1768, N.C.	1794	1849	—	—
Monroe	Elizabeth "Eliza" Kortright	1768, N.Y.	1786	1830	—	2
J. Q. Adams	Louisa Catherine Johnson	1775, England	1797	1852	3	1
Jackson	Mrs. Rachel Donelson Robards	1767, Va.	1791	1828	—	—
Van Buren	Hannah Hoes	1788, N.Y.	1807	1819	4	—
W. H. Harrison	Anna Symmes	1775, N.J.	1795	1864	6	4
Tyler	Letitia Christian	1790, Va.	1813	1842	3	4
	Julia Gardiner	1820, N.Y.	1844	1889	5	2
Polk	Sarah Childress	1803, Tenn.	1824	1891	—	—
Taylor	Margaret Smith	1788, Md.	1810	1852	1	5
Fillmore	Abigail Powers	1798, N.Y.	1826	1853	1	1
	Caroline Carmichael McIntosh	1813, N.J.	1858	1881	—	—
Pierce	Jane Means Appleton	1806, N.H.	1834	1863	3	—
Buchanan	(Unmarried)	—	—	—	—	—
Lincoln	Mary Todd	1818, Ky.	1842	1882	4	—
A. Johnson	Eliza McCardle	1810, Tenn.	1827	1876	3	2
Grant	Julia Dent	1826, Mo.	1848	1902	3	1
Hayes	Lucy Ware Webb	1831, Ohio	1852	1889	7	1
Garfield	Lucretia Rudolph	1832, Ohio	1858	1918	5	2
Arthur	Ellen Lewis Herndon	1837, Va.	1859	1880	2	1
Cleveland	Frances Folsom	1864, N.Y.	1886	1947	2	3
B. Harrison	Caroline Lavinia Scott	1832, Ohio	1853	1892	1	1
	Mary Scott Lord Dimmick	1858, Pa.	1896	1948	—	1
McKinley	Ida Saxton	1847, Ohio	1871	1907	—	2
T. Roosevelt	Alice Hathaway Lee	1861, Mass.	1880	1884	—	1
	Edith Kermit Carow	1861, Conn.	1886	1948	4	1
Taft	Helen Herron	1861, Ohio	1886	1943	2	1
Wilson	Ellen Louise Axson	1860, Ga.	1885	1914	—	3
	Edith Bolling Galt	1872, Va.	1915	1961	—	—
Harding	Florence Kling DeWolfe	1860, Ohio	1891	1924	—	—
Coolidge	Grace Anna Goodhue	1879, Vt.	1905	1957	2	—
Hoover	Lou Henry	1875, Iowa	1899	1944	2	—
F. D. Roosevelt	Anna Eleanor Roosevelt	1884, N.Y.	1905	1962	5	1
Truman	Bess Wallace	1885, Mo.	1919	1982	—	1
Eisenhower	Mamie Geneva Doud	1896, Iowa	1916	1979	2	—
Kennedy	Jacqueline Lee Bouvier	1929, N.Y.	1953	—	2	1
L. B. Johnson	Claudia Alta "Lady Bird" Taylor	1912, Tex.	1934	—	—	2
Nixon	Thelma Catherine "Pat" Ryan	1912, Nev.	1940	—	—	2
Ford	Elizabeth "Betty" Bloomer Warren	1918, Ill.	1948	—	3	1
Carter	Rosalynn Smith	1928, Ga.	1946	—	3	1
Reagan	Jane Wyman	1914, Mo.	1940[2]	—	1[3]	1
	Nancy Davis	1921 (?)[4], N.Y.	1952	—	1	1
Bush	Barbara Pierce	1925, N.Y.	1945	—	4	2

1. Includes children who died in infancy. 2. Divorced in 1948. 3. Adopted. 4. Birthday officially given as 1923 but her high school and college records show 1921 for year of birth.

Elections

How a President Is Nominated and Elected

The National Conventions of both major parties are held during the summer of a presidential-election year. Earlier, each party selects delegates by primaries, conventions, committees, etc.

For their 1988 National Convention, the Republicans allow each state a base of 6 delegates at large; the District of Columbia, 14; Puerto Rico, 14; Guam and the Virgin Islands, 4 each. In addition, each state receives 3 district delegates for each representative it has in the House of Representatives, regardless of political affiliation. This did not apply to the District of Columbia, Puerto Rico, Guam and the Virgin Islands.

Each state is awarded additional delegates at large on the basis of having supported the Republican candidate for President in 1984 and electing Republican candidates for Senator, Governor, and U.S. Representative between 1984 and 1987 inclusive.

The number of delegates at the 1988 convention, held in New Orleans starting August 15, was 2,277.

Following was the apportionment of delegates:

Alabama	38	Florida	82	Kentucky	38	Montana	20	Ohio	88	Texas	111
Alaska	19	Georgia	48	Louisiana	41	Nebraska	25	Oklahoma	36	Utah	26
Arizona	33	Guam	4	Maine	22	Nevada	20	Oregon	32	Vermont	17
Arkansas	27	Hawaii	20	Maryland	41	N.H.	23	Pa.	96	V.I.	4
California	175	Idaho	22	Mass.	52	N. Jersey	64	P.R.	14	Virginia	50
Colorado	36	Illinois	92	Michigan	77	New Mexico	26	R.I.	21	Washington	41
Connecticut	35	Indiana	51	Minnesota	31	New York	136	S.C.	37	W. Va.	28
Delaware	17	Iowa	37	Mississippi	31	N.C.	54	S.D.	18	Wisconsin	47
D.C.	14	Kansas	34	Missouri	47	N.D.	16	Tennessee	45	Wyoming	18

The Democrats base the number of delegates on a state's showing in the 1984 and 1986 elections. At the 1988 convention, held in Atlanta starting July 18, there were 4,203[1,2] delegates casting 4,161 votes. Following is the apportionment by states:

Alabama	65	Florida	154	Kentucky	65	Montana	28	Ohio	183	Texas	212
Alaska	17	Georgia	94	Louisiana	76	Nebraska	30	Oklahoma	56	Utah	28
Arizona	43	Guam	10[1]	Maine	29	Nevada	23	Oregon	54	Vermont	20
Arkansas	48	Hawaii	28	Maryland	84	N. H.	22	Pa.	202	V.I.	11
California	368[1]	Idaho	24	Mass.	119	New Jersey	125	P.R.	61[1]	Virginia	86
Colorado	55	Illinois	200	Michigan	162	New Mexico	30	R.I.	28	Washington	77
Connecticut	63	Indiana	91[1]	Minnesota	91	New York	292	S.C.	53	W. Va.	47
Delaware	19	Iowa	61	Mississippi	47	N.C.	95	S.D.	20	Wisconsin	91
D. C.	24	Kansas	45	Missouri	88	N.D.	22	Tennessee	84	Wyoming	18

1. Fractional votes. 2. Includes 22[1] delegates for Democrats Abroad and 12[1] for American Samoa.

The Conventions

At each convention, a temporary chairman is chosen. After a credentials committee seats the delegates, a permanent chairman is elected. The convention then votes on a platform, drawn up by the platform committee.

By the third or fourth day, presidential nominations begin. The chairman calls the roll of states alphabetically. A state may place a candidate in nomination or yield to another state.

Voting, again alphabetically by roll call of states, begins after all nominations have been made and seconded. A simple majority is required in each party, although this may require many ballots.

Finally, the vice-presidential candidate is selected. Although there is no law saying that the candidates *must* come from different states, it is, practically, necessary for this to be the case. Otherwise, according to the Constitution (*see* Amendment XII), electors from that state could vote for only one of the candidates and would have to cast their other vote for some person of another state. This could result in a presidential candidate's receiving a majority electoral vote and his running mate's failing to.

The Electoral College

The next step in the process is the nomination of electors in each state, according to its laws. These electors must not be Federal office holders. In the November election, the voters cast their votes for electors, not for President. In some states, the ballots include only the names of the presidential and vice-presidential candidates; in others, they include only names of the electors. Nowadays, it is rare for electors to be split between parties. The last such occurrence was in North Carolina in 1968[1]; the last before that, in Tennessee in 1948.

On three occasions (1824, 1876, and 1888), the presidential candidate with the largest popular vote failed to obtain an electoral-vote majority.

Each state has as many electors as it has Senators and Representatives. For the 1984 election, the total electors were 538, based on 100 Senators, 435 Representatives, plus 3 electoral votes from the District of Columbia as a result of the 23rd Amendment to the Constitution.

On the first Monday after the second Wednesday in December, the electors cast their votes in their respective state capitols. Constitutionally they may vote for someone other than the party candidate but usually they do not since they are pledged to one party and its candidate on the ballot. Should the presidential or vice-presidential candidate die between the November election and the December meetings, the electors pledged to vote for him could vote for whomever they pleased. However, it seems certain that the national committee would attempt to get an agreement among the state party leaders for a replacement candidate.

The votes of the electors, certified by the states, are sent to Congress, where the president of the Senate opens the certificates and has them counted in the presence of both Houses on January 6. The new President is inaugurated at noon on January 20.

Should no candidate receive a majority of the electoral vote for President, the House of Representatives chooses a President from among the three highest candidates, voting, not as individuals, but as states, with a majority (now 26) needed to elect. Should no vice-presidential candidate obtain the majority, the Senate, voting as individuals, chooses from the highest two.

1. In 1956, 1 of Alabama's 11 electoral votes was cast for Walter B. Jones. In 1960, 6 of Alabama's 11 electoral votes and 1 of Oklahoma's 8 electoral votes were cast for Harry Flood Byrd. (Byrd also received all 8 of Mississippi's electoral votes.)

National Political Conventions Since 1856

Opening date	Party	Where held	Opening date	Party	Where held
June 17, 1856	Republican	Philadelphia	June 10, 1924	Republican	Cleveland
June 2, 1856	Democratic	Cincinnati	June 24, 1924[2]	Democratic	New York City
May 16, 1860	Republican	Chicago	June 12, 1928	Republican	Kansas City
April 23, 1860	Democratic	Charleston and Baltimore	June 26, 1928	Democratic	Houston
			June 14, 1932	Republican	Chicago
June 7, 1864	Republican[1]	Baltimore	June 27, 1932	Democratic	Chicago
Aug. 29, 1864	Democratic	Chicago	June 9, 1936	Republican	Cleveland
May 20, 1868	Republican	Chicago	June 23, 1936	Democratic	Philadelphia
July 4, 1868	Democratic	New York City	June 24, 1940	Republican	Philadelphia
June 5, 1872	Republican	Philadelphia	July 15, 1940	Democratic	Chicago
June 9, 1872	Democratic	Baltimore	June 26, 1944	Republican	Chicago
June 14, 1876	Republican	Cincinnati	July 19, 1944	Democratic	Chicago
June 28, 1876	Democratic	St. Louis	June 21, 1948	Republican	Philadelphia
June 2, 1880	Republican	Chicago	July 12, 1948	Democratic	Philadelphia
June 23, 1880	Democratic	Cincinnati	July 17, 1948	(3)	Birmingham
June 3, 1884	Republican	Chicago	July 22, 1948	Progressive	Philadelphia
July 11, 1884	Democratic	Chicago	July 7, 1952	Republican	Chicago
June 19, 1888	Republican	Chicago	July 21, 1952	Democratic	Chicago
June 6, 1888	Democratic	St. Louis	Aug. 20, 1956	Republican	San Francisco
June 7, 1892	Republican	Minneapolis	Aug. 13, 1956	Democratic	Chicago
June 21, 1892	Democratic	Chicago	July 25, 1960	Republican	Chicago
June 16, 1896	Republican	St. Louis	July 11, 1960	Democratic	Los Angeles
July 7, 1896	Democratic	Chicago	July 13, 1964	Republican	San Francisco
June 19, 1900	Republican	Philadelphia	Aug. 24, 1964	Democratic	Atlantic City
July 4, 1900	Democratic	Kansas City	Aug. 5, 1968	Republican	Miami Beach
June 21, 1904	Republican	Chicago	Aug. 26, 1968	Democratic	Chicago
July 6, 1904	Democratic	St. Louis	July 10, 1972	Democratic	Miami Beach
June 16, 1908	Republican	Chicago	Aug. 21, 1972	Republican	Miami Beach
July 7, 1908	Democratic	Denver	July 12, 1976	Democratic	New York City
June 18, 1912	Republican	Chicago	Aug. 16, 1976	Republican	Kansas City, Mo.
June 25, 1912	Democratic	Baltimore	Aug. 11, 1980	Democratic	New York City
June 7, 1916	Republican	Chicago	July 14, 1980	Republican	Detroit
June 14, 1916	Democratic	St. Louis	Aug. 20, 1984	Republican	Dallas
June 8, 1920	Republican	Chicago	July 16, 1984	Democratic	San Francisco
June 28, 1920	Democratic	San Francisco	July 18, 1988	Democratic	Atlanta
			Aug. 15, 1988	Republican	New Orleans

1. The Convention adopted name Union party to attract War Democrats and others favoring prosecution of war. 2. In session until July 10, 1924. 3. States' Rights delegates from 13 Southern states.

National Committee Chairmen Since 1944

Chairman and (state)	Term	Chairman and (state)	Term
REPUBLICAN		**DEMOCRATIC**	
Herbert Brownell, Jr. (N.Y.)	1944–46	Robert E. Hannegan (Mo.)	1944–47
Carroll Reece (Tenn.)	1946–48	J. Howard McGrath (R.I.)	1947–49
Hugh D. Scott, Jr. (Pa.)	1948–49	William M. Boyle, Jr. (Mo.)	1949–51
Guy G. Gabrielson (N.J.)	1949–52	Frank E. McKinney (Ind.)	1951–52
Arthur E. Summerfield (Mich.)	1952–53	Stephen A. Mitchell (Ill.)	1952–54
Wesley Roberts (Kan.)	1953–	Paul M. Butler (Ind.)	1955–60
Leonard W. Hall (N.Y.)	1953–57	Henry M. Jackson (Wash.)	1960–61
Meade Alcorn (Conn.)	1957–59	John M. Bailey (Conn.)	1961–68
Thruston B. Morton (Ky.)	1959–61	Lawrence F. O'Brien (Mass.)	1968–69
William E. Miller (N.Y.)	1961–64	Fred R. Harris (Okla.)	1969–70
Dean Burch (Ariz.)	1964–65	Lawrence F. O'Brien (Mass.)	1970–72
Ray C. Bliss (Ohio)	1965–69	Jean Westwood (Utah)	1972
Rogers C. B. Morton (Md.)	1969–71	Robert S. Strauss (Tex.)	1972–77
Robert Dole (Kan.)	1971–73	Kenneth M. Curtis (Me.)	1977
George H. Bush (Tex.)	1973–74	John C. White (Tex.)	1977–81
Mary Louise Smith (Iowa)	1974–77	Charles T. Manatt (Calif.)	1981–85
William E. Brock III (Tenn.)	1977–81	Paul G. Kirk, Jr. (Mass.)	1985–89
Richard Richards (Utah)	1981–83	Ronald H. Brown (D.C.)	1989
Frank J. Fahrenkopf, Jr. (Nevada)	1983–89		
Lee Atwater (S.C.)	1989–		

Republican National Committee: 310 First St., S.E., Washington, D. C. 20003.
Democratic National Committee: 430 South Capitol St., S.E., Washington, D.C. 20003.

Presidential Elections, 1789 to 1988

For the original method of electing the President and the Vice President (elections of 1789, 1792, 1796, and 1800), see Article II, Section 1, of the Constitution. The election of 1804 was the first one in which the electors voted for President and Vice President on separate ballots. (See Amendment XII to the Constitution.)

Year	Presidential candidates	Party	Electoral vote	Year	Presidential candidates	Party	Electoral vote
1789[1]	George Washington	(no party)	69	1796	John Adams	Federalist	71
	John Adams	(no party)	34		Thomas Jefferson	Dem.-Rep.	68
	Scattering	(no party)	35		Thomas Pinckney	Federalist	59
	Votes not cast		8		Aaron Burr	Dem.-Rep.	30
					Scattering		48
1792	George Washington	Federalist	132				
	John Adams	Federalist	77	1800[2]	Thomas Jefferson	Dem.-Rep.	73
	George Clinton	Anti-Federalist	50		Aaron Burr	Dem.-Rep.	73
	Thomas Jefferson	Anti-Federalist	4		John Adams	Federalist	65
	Aaron Burr	Anti-Federalist	1		Charles C. Pinckney	Federalist	64
	Votes not cast		6		John Jay	Federalist	1

Year	Presidential candidates	Party	Electoral vote	Vice-presidential candidates	Party	Electoral vote
1804	Thomas Jefferson	Dem.-Rep.	162	George Clinton	Dem.-Rep.	162
	Charles C. Pinckney	Federalist	14	Rufus King	Federalist	14
1808	James Madison	Dem.-Rep.	122	George Clinton	Dem.-Rep.	113
	Charles C. Pinckney	Federalist	47	Rufus King	Federalist	47
	George Clinton	Dem.-Rep.	6	John Langdon	Ind. (no party)	9
	Votes not cast		1	James Madison	Dem.-Rep.	3
				James Monroe	Dem.-Rep.	3
				Votes not cast		1
1812	James Madison	Dem.-Rep.	128	Elbridge Gerry	Dem.-Rep.	131
	De Witt Clinton	Federalist	89	Jared Ingersoll	Federalist	86
	Votes not cast		1	Votes not cast		1
1816	James Monroe	Dem.-Rep.	183	Daniel D. Tompkins	Dem.-Rep.	183
	Rufus King	Federalist	34	John E. Howard	Federalist	22
	Votes not cast		4	James Ross	Ind. (no party)	5
				John Marshall	Federalist	4
				Robert G. Harper	Ind. (no party)	3
				Votes not cast		4
1820	James Monroe	Dem-Rep	231	Daniel D. Tompkins	Dem.-Rep.	218
	John Quincy Adams	Ind. (no party)	1	Richard Stockton	Ind. (no party)	8
	Votes not cast		3	Daniel Rodney	Ind. (no party)	4
				Richard Rush	Ind. (no party)	1
				Robert G. Harper	Ind. (no party)	1
				Votes not cast		3
1824[3]	John Quincy Adams	(no party)	84	John C. Calhoun	(no party)	182
	Andrew Jackson	(no party)	99	Nathan Sanford	(no party)	30
	William H. Crawford	(no party)	41	Nathaniel Macon	(no party)	24
	Henry Clay	(no party)	37	Andrew Jackson	(no party)	13
				Martin Van Buren	(no party)	9
				Henry Clay	(no party)	2
				Votes not cast		1
1828	Andrew Jackson	Democratic	178	John C. Calhoun	Democratic	171
	John Quincy Adams	Natl. Rep.	83	Richard Rush	Natl. Rep.	83
				William Smith	Democratic	7
1832	Andrew Jackson	Democratic	219	Martin Van Buren	Democratic	189
	Henry Clay	Natl. Rep.	49	John Sergeant	Natl. Rep.	49
	John Floyd	Ind. (no party)	11	Henry Lee	Ind. (no party)	11
	William Wirt	Antimasonic[4]	7	Amos Ellmaker	Antimasonic	7
	Votes not cast		2	William Wilkins	Ind. (no party)	30
				Votes not cast		2

Year	Presidential candidates	Party	Electoral vote	Vice-presidential candidates	Party	Electoral vote
1836	Martin Van Buren	Democratic	170	Richard M. Johnson[5]	Democratic	147
	William H. Harrison	Whig	73	Francis Granger	Whig	77
	Hugh L. White	Whig	26	John Tyler	Whig	47
	Daniel Webster	Whig	14	William Smith	Ind. (no party)	23
	W. P. Mangum	Ind. (no party)	11			
1840	William H. Harrison[6]	Whig	234	John Tyler	Whig	234
	Martin Van Buren	Democratic	60	Richard M. Johnson	Democratic	48
				L. W. Tazewell	Ind. (no party)	11
				James K. Polk	Democratic	1
1844	James K. Polk	Democratic	170	George M. Dallas	Democratic	170
	Henry Clay	Whig	105	Theo. Frelinghuysen	Whig	105
1848	Zachary Taylor[7]	Whig	163	Millard Fillmore	Whig	163
	Lewis Cass	Democratic	127	William O. Butler	Democratic	127
1852	Franklin Pierce	Democratic	254	William R. King	Democratic	254
	Winfield Scott	Whig	42	William A. Graham	Whig	42
1856	James Buchanan	Democratic	174	John C. Breckinridge	Democratic	174
	John C. Fremont	Republican	114	William L. Dayton	Republican	114
	Millard Fillmore	American[8]	8	A. J. Donelson	American[8]	8
1860	Abraham Lincoln	Republican	180	Hannibal Hamlin	Republican	180
	John C. Breckinridge	Democratic	72	Joseph Lane	Democratic	72
	John Bell	Const. Union	39	Edward Everett	Const. Union	39
	Stephen A. Douglas	Democratic	12	H. V. Johnson	Democratic	12
1864	Abraham Lincoln[9]	Union[10]	212	Andrew Johnson	Union[15]	212
	George B. McClellan	Democratic	21	G. H. Pendleton	Democratic	21
1868	Ulysses S. Grant	Republican	214	Schuyler Colfax	Republican	214
	Horatio Seymour	Democratic	80	Francis P. Blair, Jr.	Democratic	80
	Votes not counted[11]		23	Votes not counted[11]		23

Year	Presidential candidates	Party	Electoral vote	Popular vote	Vice-presidential candidates and party
1872	Ulysses S. Grant	Republican	286	3,597,132	Henry Wilson—R
	Horace Greeley	Dem., Liberal Rep.	([12])	2,834,125	B. Gratz Brown—D, LR—(47)
	Thomas A. Hendricks	Democratic	42		Scattering—(19)
	B. Gratz Brown	Dem., Liberal Rep.	18		Votes not counted—(14)
	Charles J. Jenkins	Democratic	2		
	David Davis	Democratic	1		
	Votes not counted		17		
1876[13]	Rutherford B. Hayes	Republican	185	4,033,768	William A. Wheeler—R
	Samuel J. Tilden	Democratic	184	4,285,992	Thomas A. Hendricks—D
	Peter Cooper	Greenback	0	81,737	Samuel F. Cary—G
1880	James A. Garfield[14]	Republican	214	4,449,053	Chester A. Arthur—R
	Winfield S. Hancock	Democratic	155	4,442,035	William H. English—D
	James B. Weaver	Greenback	0	308,578	B. J. Chambers—G
1884	Grover Cleveland	Democratic	219	4,911,017	Thomas A. Hendricks—D
	James G. Blaine	Republican	182	4,848,334	John A. Logan—R
	Benjamin F. Butler	Greenback	0	175,370	A. M. West—G
	John P. St. John	Prohibition	0	150,369	William Daniel—P
1888	Benjamin Harrison	Republican	233	5,440,216	Levi P. Morton—R
	Grover Cleveland	Democratic	168	5,538,233	A. G. Thurman—D
	Clinton B. Fisk	Prohibition	0	249,506	John A. Brooks—P
	Alson J. Streeter	Union Labor	0	146,935	Charles E. Cunningham—UL
1892	Grover Cleveland	Democratic	277	5,556,918	Adlai E. Stevenson—D
	Benjamin Harrison	Republican	145	5,176,108	Whitelaw Reid—R
	James B. Weaver	People's[15]	22	1,041,028	James G. Field—Peo
	John Bidwell	Prohibition	0	264,133	James B. Cranfill—P

Year	Presidential candidates	Party	Electoral vote	Popular vote	Vice-presidential candidates and party
1896	William McKinley	Republican	271	7,035,638	Garret A. Hobart—R
	William J. Bryan	Dem., People's[15]	176	6,467,946	Arthur Sewall—D—(149)
					Thomas E. Watson—Peo—(27)
	John M. Palmer	Natl. Dem.	0	133,148	Simon B. Buckner—ND
	Joshua Levering	Prohibition	0	132,007	Hale Johnson—P
1900	William McKinley[16]	Republican	292	7,219,530	Theodore Roosevelt—R
	William J. Bryan	Dem., People's[15]	155	6,358,071	Adlai E. Stevenson—D, Peo
	Eugene V. Debs	Social Democratic	0	94,768	Job Harriman—SD
1904	Theodore Roosevelt	Republican	336	7,628,834	Charles W. Fairbanks—R
	Alton B. Parker	Democratic	140	5,084,491	Henry G. Davis—D
	Eugene V. Debs	Socialist	0	402,400	Benjamin Hanford—S
1908	William H. Taft	Republican	321	7,679,006	James S. Sherman—R
	William J. Bryan	Democratic	162	6,409,106	John W. Kern—D
	Eugene V. Debs	Socialist	0	402,820	Benjamin Hanford—S
1912	Woodrow Wilson	Democratic	435	6,286,214	Thomas R. Marshall—D
	Theodore Roosevelt	Progressive	88	4,126,020	Hiram Johnson—Prog
	William H. Taft	Republican	8	3,483,922	Nicholas M. Butler—R[17]
	Eugene V. Debs	Socialist	0	897,011	Emil Seidel—S
1916	Woodrow Wilson	Democratic	277	9,129,606	Thomas R. Marshall—D
	Charles E. Hughes	Republican	254	8,538,221	Charles W. Fairbanks—R
	A. L. Benson	Socialist	0	585,113	G. R. Kirkpatrick—S
1920	Warren G. Harding[18]	Republican	404	16,152,200	Calvin Coolidge—R
	James M. Cox	Democratic	127	9,147,353	Franklin D. Roosevelt—D
	Eugene V. Debs	Socialist	0	917,799	Seymour Stedman—S
1924	Calvin Coolidge	Republican	382	15,725,016	Charles G. Dawes—R
	John W. Davis	Democratic	136	8,385,586	Charles W. Bryan—D
	Robert M LaFollette	Progressive, Socialist	13	4,822,856	Burton K. Wheeler—Prog S
1928	Herbert Hoover	Republican	444	21,392,190	Charles Curtis—R
	Alfred E. Smith	Democratic	87	15,016,443	Joseph T. Robinson—D
	Norman Thomas	Socialist	0	267,420	James H. Maurer—S
1932	Franklin D. Roosevelt	Democratic	472	22,821,857	John N. Garner—D
	Herbert Hoover	Republican	59	15,761,841	Charles Curtis—R
	Norman Thomas	Socialist	0	884,781	James H. Maurer—S
1936	Franklin D. Roosevelt	Democratic	523	27,751,597	John N. Garner—D
	Alfred M. Landon	Republican	8	16,679,583	Frank Knox—R
	Norman Thomas	Socialist	0	187,720	George Nelson—S
1940	Franklin D. Roosevelt	Democratic	449	27,244,160	Henry A. Wallace—D
	Wendell L. Willkie	Republican	82	22,305,198	Charles L. McNary—R
	Norman Thomas	Socialist	0	99,557	Maynard C. Krueger—S
1944	Franklin D. Roosevelt[19]	Democratic	432	25,602,504	Harry S. Truman—D
	Thomas E. Dewey	Republican	99	22,006,285	John W. Bricker—R
	Norman Thomas	Socialist	0	80,518	Darlington Hoopes—S
1948	Harry S. Truman	Democratic	303	24,179,345	Alben W. Barkley—D
	Thomas E. Dewey	Republican	189	21,991,291	Earl Warren—R
	J. Strom Thurmond	States' Rights Dem.	39	1,176,125	Fielding L. Wright—SR
	Henry A. Wallace	Progressive	0	1,157,326	Glen Taylor—Prog
	Norman Thomas	Socialist	0	139,572	Tucker P. Smith—S
1952	Dwight D. Eisenhower	Republican	442	33,936,234	Richard M. Nixon—R
	Adlai E. Stevenson	Democratic	89	27,314,992	John J. Sparkman—D
1956	Dwight D. Eisenhower	Republican	457	35,590,472	Richard M. Nixon—R
	Adlai E. Stevenson	Democratic	73[20]	26,022,752	Estes Kefauver—D
1960	John F. Kennedy[22]	Democratic	303	34,226,731	Lyndon B. Johnson—D
	Richard M. Nixon	Republican	219[21]	34,108,157	Henry Cabot Lodge—R

Year	Presidential candidates	Party	Electoral vote	Popular vote	Vice-presidential candidates and party
1964	Lyndon B. Johnson	Democratic	486	43,129,484	Hubert H. Humphrey—D
	Barry M. Goldwater	Republican	52	27,178,188	William E. Miller—R
1968	Richard M. Nixon	Republican	301	31,785,480	Spiro T. Agnew—R
	Hubert H. Humphrey	Democratic	191	31,275,166	Edmund S. Muskie—D
	George C. Wallace	American Independent	46	9,906,473	Curtis F. LeMay—AI
1972	Richard M. Nixon[23]	Republican	520[24]	47,169,911	Spiro T. Agnew—R
	George McGovern	Democratic	17	29,170,383	Sargent Shriver—D
	John G. Schmitz	American	0	1,099,482	Thomas J. Anderson—A
1976	Jimmy Carter	Democratic	297	40,830,763	Walter F. Mondale—D
	Gerald R. Ford	Republican	240[25]	39,147,973	Robert J. Dole—R
	Eugene J. McCarthy	Independent	0	756,631	None
1980	Ronald Reagan	Republican	489	43,899,248	George Bush—R
	Jimmy Carter	Democratic	49	36,481,435	Walter F. Mondale—D
	John B. Anderson	Independent	0	5,719,437	Patrick J. Lucey—I
1984	Ronald Reagan	Republican	525	54,455,075	George Bush—R
	Walter F. Mondale	Democratic	13	37,577,185	Geraldine A. Ferraro—D
1988	George H. Bush	Republican	426	48,886,097	J. Danforth Quayle—R
	Michael S. Dukakis	Democratic	111[26]	41,809,074	Lloyd Bentsen—D

1. Only 10 states participated in the election. The New York legislature chose no electors, and North Carolina and Rhode Island had not yet ratified the Constitution. 2. As Jefferson and Burr were tied, the House of Representatives chose the President. In a vote by states, 10 votes were cast for Jefferson, 4 for Burr; 2 votes were not cast. 3. As no candidate had an electoral-vote majority, the House of Representatives chose the President from the first three. In a vote by states, 13 votes were cast for Adams, 7 for Jackson, and 4 for Crawford. 4. The Antimasonic Party on Sept. 26, 1831, was the first party to hold a nominating convention to choose candidates for President and Vice-President. 5. As Johnson did not have an electoral-vote majority, the Senate chose him 33–14 over Granger, the others being legally out of the race. 6. Harrison died April 4, 1841, and Tyler succeeded him April 6. 7. Taylor died July 9, 1850, and Fillmore succeeded him July 10. 8. Also known as the Know-Nothing Party. 9. Lincoln died April 15, 1865, and Johnson succeeded him the same day. 10. Name adopted by the Republican National Convention of 1864. Johnson was a War Democrat. 11. 23 Southern electoral votes were excluded. 12. See Election of 1872 in *Unusual Voting Results* under Elections, Presidential, in Index. 13. See Election of 1876 in *Unusual Voting Results* under Elections, Presidential, in Index. 14. Garfield died Sept. 19, 1881, and Arthur succeeded him Sept. 20. 15. Members of People's Party were called Populists. 16. McKinley died Sept. 14, 1901, and Roosevelt succeeded him the same day. 17. James S. Sherman, Republican candidate for Vice President, died Oct. 30, 1912, and the Republican electoral votes were cast for Butler. 18. Harding died Aug. 2, 1923, and Coolidge succeeded him Aug. 3. 19. Roosevelt died April 12, 1945, and Truman succeeded him the same day. 20. One electoral vote from Alabama was cast for Walter B. Jones. 21. Sen. Harry F. Byrd received 15 electoral votes. 22. Kennedy died Nov. 22, 1963, and Johnson succeeded him the same day. 23. Nixon resigned Aug. 9, 1974, and Gerald R. Ford succeeded him the same day. 24. One electoral vote from Virginia was cast for John Hospers, Libertarian Party. 25. One electoral vote from Washington was cast for Ronald Reagan. 26. One electoral vote from West Virginia was cast for Lloyd Bentsen.

Qualifications for Voting

The Supreme Court decision of March 21, 1972, declared lengthy requirements for voting in state and local elections unconstitutional and suggested that 30 days was an ample period. Most of the states have changed or eliminated their durational residency requirements to comply with the ruling, as shown.

NO DURATIONAL RESIDENCY REQUIREMENT

Alabama,[6] Arkansas, Connecticut,[13] Delaware,[12] District of Columbia,[16] Florida,[5] Georgia,[2] Hawaii,[2] Iowa,[6] Maine, Maryland, Massachusetts,[3] Missouri,[4] Nebraska,[9] New Hampshire,[17] New Mexico,[7] North Carolina, Oklahoma, South Carolina,[2] South Dakota,[10] Tennessee,[20] Texas, Virginia, West Virginia,[2] Wyoming[2]

30-DAY RESIDENCY REQUIREMENT

Alaska,[18] Arizona,[11] Idaho,[17] Illinois, Indiana, Kentucky,[2] Louisiana,[8] Michigan, Mississippi,[2] Montana, Nevada, New Jersey, New York, North Dakota,[3] Ohio, Pennsylvania, Rhode Island, Utah, Washington

OTHER

California,[19] Colorado,[1] Kansas, Minnesota[15] and Oregon, 20 days; Vermont, 17 days;[14] Wisconsin, 10 days

1. 32 days. 2. 30-day registration requirement. 3. No residency required to register to vote. 4. Must be registered by the fourth Wednesday prior to election. 5. 30-day registration requirement for national elections; 30-day for state elections. 6. 10-day registration requirement. In-person registration by 5 PM, eleven days before election date. 7. Must register 28 days before election. 8. 24 days prior to any election. 9. Registration requirement, 2nd Friday prior to elections 10. 15-day registration requirement. 11. Residency in the state 50 days next preceding the election except 30 days for presidential election. 12. Must reside in Delaware and register by the last day that the books are open for registration. 13. Registration deadline 21st day before election; registration and party enrollment deadline the day before primary; unaffiliated voters may vote in Republican primaries for *some* offices. 14. Administrative cut-off date for processing applications. 15. Permits registration and voting on election day with approved ID. 16. Registration stops 30 days before any election and until 15 days after. Voters must inform Board of Elections of change of address within 30 days of moving. 17. Registration requirement, 10 days prior

to elections. 18. If otherwise qualified but has not been a resident of the election district for at least 30 days preceding the date of a presidential election, is entitled to register and vote for presidential and vice–presidential candidates. 19. 29 days before an election. 20. Must be resident of state for a period of at least 20 days prior to registration. *Source: Information Please* questionnaires to the states. 20. Must be resident of state for a period of at least 20 days prior to registration.

Unusual Voting Results

Election of 1872

The presidential and vice-presidential candidates of the Liberal Republicans and the northern Democrats in 1872 were Horace Greeley and B. Gratz Brown. Greeley died Nov. 29, 1872, before his 66 electors voted. In the electoral balloting for President, 63 of Greeley's votes were scattered among four other men, including Brown.

Election of 1876

In the election of 1876 Samuel J. Tilden, the Democratic candidate, received a popular majority but lacked one undisputed electoral vote to carry a clear majority of the electoral college. The crux of the problem was in the 22 electoral votes which were in dispute because Florida, Louisiana, South Carolina, and Oregon each sent in two sets of election returns. In the three southern states, Republican election boards threw out enough Democratic votes to certify the Republican candidate, Hayes. In Oregon, the Democratic governor disqualified a Republican elector, replacing him with a Democrat. Since the Senate was Republican and the House of Representatives Democratic, it seemed useless to refer the disputed returns to the two houses for solution. Instead Congress appointed an Electoral Commission with five representatives each from the Senate, the House, and the Supreme Court. All but one Justice was named, giving the Commission seven Republican and seven Democratic members. The naming of the fifth Justice was left to the other four. He was a Republican who first favored Tilden but, under pressure from his party, switched to Hayes, ensuring his election by the Commission voting 8 to 7 on party lines.

Minority Presidents

Fifteen candidates have become President of the United States with a popular vote less than 50% of the total cast. It should be noted, however, that in elections before 1872, presidential electors were not chosen by popular vote in all states. Adams' election in 1824 was by the House of Representatives, which chose him over Jackson, who had a plurality of both electoral and popular votes, but not a majority in the electoral college.

Besides Jackson in 1824, only two other candidates receiving the largest popular vote have failed to gain a majority in the electoral college—Samuel J. Tilden (D) in 1876 and Grover Cleveland (D) in 1888.

The "minority" Presidents follow:

Vote Received by Minority Presidents

Year	President	Electoral	Popular vote
		Percent	Percent
1824	John Q. Adams	31.8	29.8
1844	James K. Polk (D)	61.8	49.3
1848	Zachary Taylor (W)	56.2	47.3
1856	James Buchanan (D)	58.7	45.3
1860	Abraham Lincoln (R)	59.4	39.9
1876	Rutherford B. Hayes (R)	50.1	47.9
1880	James A. Garfield (R)	57.9	48.3
1884	Grover Cleveland (D)	54.6	48.8
1888	Benjamin Harrison (R)	58.1	47.8
1892	Grover Cleveland (D)	62.4	46.0
1912	Woodrow Wilson (D)	81.9	41.8
1916	Woodrow Wilson (D)	52.1	49.3
1948	Harry S. Truman (D)	57.1	49.5
1960	John F. Kennedy (D)	56.4	49.7
1968	Richard M. Nixon (R)	56.1	43.4

How a Bill Becomes a Law

When a Senator or a Representative introduces a bill, he sends it to the clerk of his house, who gives it a number and title. This is the *first reading*, and the bill is referred to the proper committee.

The committee may decide the bill is unwise or unnecessary and *table* it, thus killing it at once. Or it may decide the bill is worthwhile and hold hearings to listen to facts and opinions presented by experts and other interested persons. After members of the committee have debated the bill and perhaps offered amendments, a vote is taken; and if the vote is favorable, the bill is sent back to the floor of the house.

The clerk reads the bill sentence by sentence to the house, and this is known as the *second reading*. Members may then debate the bill and offer amendments. In the House of Representatives, the time for debate is limited by a *cloture rule*, but there is no such restriction in the Senate for cloture, where 60 votes are required. This makes possible a *filibuster*, in which one or more opponents hold the floor to defeat the bill.

The *third reading* is by title only, and the bill is put to a vote, which may be by voice or roll call, depending on the circumstances and parliamentary rules. Members who must be absent at the time but who wish to record their vote may be paired if each negative vote has a balancing affirmative one.

The bill then goes to the other house of Congress, where it may be defeated, or passed with or without amendments. If the bill is defeated, it dies. If it is passed with amendments, a joint Congressional committee must be appointed by both houses to iron out the differences.

After its final passage by both houses, the bill is sent to the President. If he approves, he signs it, and the bill becomes a law. However, if he disapproves, he *vetoes* the bill by refusing to sign it and sending it back to the house of origin with his reasons for the veto. The objections are read and debated, and a roll-call vote is taken. If the bill receives less than a two-thirds vote, it is defeated and goes no farther. But if it receives a two-thirds vote or greater, it is sent to the other house for a vote. If that house also passes it by a two-thirds vote, the President's veto is *overridden*, and the bill becomes a law.

Should the President desire neither to sign nor to veto the bill, he may retain it for ten days, Sundays excepted, after which time it automatically becomes a law without signature. However, if Congress has adjourned within those ten days, the bill is automatically killed, that process of indirect rejection being known as a *pocket veto*.

Government Officials
Cabinet Members With Dates of Appointment

Although the Constitution made no provision for a President's advisory group, the heads of the three executive departments (State, Treasury, and War) and the Attorney General were organized by Washington into such a group; and by about 1793, the name "Cabinet" was applied to it. With the exception of the Attorney General up to 1870 and the Postmaster General from 1829 to 1872, Cabinet members have been heads of executive departments.

A Cabinet member is appointed by the President, subject to the confirmation of the Senate; and as his term is not fixed, he may be replaced at any time by the President. At a change in Administration, it is customary for him to tender his resignation, but he remains in office until a successor is appointed.

The table of Cabinet members lists only those members who actually served after being duly commissioned.

The dates shown are those of appointment. "Cont." indicates that the term continued from the previous Administration for a substantial amount of time.

With the creation of the Department of Transportation in 1966, the Cabinet consisted of 12 members. This figure was reduced to 11 when the Post Office Department became an independent agency in 1970 but, with the establishment in 1977 of a Department of Energy, became 12 again. Creation of the Department of Education in 1980 raised the number to 13. Creation of the Department of Veterans' Affairs in 1989 raised the number to 14.

WASHINGTON

Secretary of State	Thomas Jefferson 1789
	Edmund Randolph 1794
	Timothy Pickering 1795
Secretary of the Treasury	Alexander Hamilton 1789
	Oliver Wolcott, Jr. 1795
Secretary of War	Henry Knox 1789
	Timothy Pickering 1795
	James McHenry 1796
Attorney General	Edmund Randolph 1789
	William Bradford 1794
	Charles Lee 1795

J. ADAMS

Secretary of State	Timothy Pickering (Cont.)
	John Marshall 1800
Secretary of the Treasury	Oliver Wolcott, Jr. (Cont.)
	Samuel Dexter 1801
Secretary of War	James McHenry (Cont.)
	Samuel Dexter 1800
Attorney General	Charles Lee (Cont.)
Secretary of the Navy	Benjamin Stoddert 1798

JEFFERSON

Secretary of State	James Madison 1801
Secretary of the Treasury	Samuel Dexter (Cont.)
	Albert Gallatin 1801
Secretary of War	Henry Dearborn 1801
Attorney General	Levi Lincoln 1801
	Robert Smith 1805
	John Breckinridge 1805
	Caesar A. Rodney 1807
Secretary of the Navy	Benjamin Stoddert (Cont.)
	Robert Smith 1801

MADISON

Secretary of State	Robert Smith 1809
	James Monroe 1811
Secretary of the Treasury	Albert Gallatin (Cont.)
	George W. Campbell 1814
	Alexander J. Dallas 1814
	William H. Crawford 1816
Secretary of War	William Eustis 1809
	John Armstrong 1813

	James Monroe 1814
	William H. Crawford 1815
Attorney General	Caesar A. Rodney (Cont.)
	William Pinckney 1811
	Richard Rush 1814
Secretary of the Navy	Paul Hamilton 1809
	William Jones 1813
	B. W. Crowninshield 1814

MONROE

Secretary of State	John Quincy Adams 1817
Secretary of the Treasury	William H. Crawford (Cont.)
Secretary of War	John C. Calhoun 1817
Attorney General	Richard Rush (Cont.)
	William Wirt 1817
Secretary of the Navy	B. W. Crowninshield (Cont.)
	Smith Thompson 1818
	Samuel L. Southard 1823

J. Q. ADAMS

Secretary of State	Henry Clay 1825
Secretary of the Treasury	Richard Rush 1825
Secretary of War	James Barbour 1825
	Peter B. Porter 1828
Attorney General	William Wirt (Cont.)
Secretary of the Navy	Samuel L. Southard (Cont.)

JACKSON

Secretary of State	Martin Van Buren 1829
	Edward Livingston 1831
	Louis McLane 1833
	John Forsyth 1834
Secretary of the Treasury	Samuel D. Ingham 1829
	Louis McLane 1831
	William J. Duane 1833
	Roger B. Taney[3] 1833
	Levi Woodbury 1834
Secretary of War	John H. Eaton 1829
	Lewis Cass 1831
Attorney General	John M. Berrien 1829
	Roger B. Taney 1831
	Benjamin F. Butler 1833
Postmaster General[ ]	William T. Barry 1829
	Amos Kendall 1835
Secretary of the Navy	John Branch 1829
	Levi Woodbury 1831
	Mahlon Dickerson 1834

VAN BUREN

Secretary of State	John Forsyth (Cont.)
Secretary of the Treasury	Levi Woodbury (Cont.)
Secretary of War	Joel R. Poinsett 1837
Attorney General	Benjamin F. Butler (Cont.)
	Felix Grundy 1838
	Henry D. Gilpin 1840
Postmaster General	Amos Kendall (Cont.)
	John M. Niles 1840
Secretary of the Navy	Mahlon Dickerson (Cont.)
	James K. Paulding 1838

W. H. HARRISON

Secretary of State	Daniel Webster 1841
Secretary of the Treasury	Thomas Ewing 1841
Secretary of War	John Bell 1841
Attorney General	John J. Crittenden 1841
Postmaster General	Francis Granger 1841
Secretary of the Navy	George E. Badger 1841

TYLER

Secretary of State	Daniel Webster (Cont.)
	Abel P. Upshur 1843
	John C. Calhoun 1844
Secretary of the Treasury	Thomas Ewing (Cont.)
	Walter Forward 1841
	John C. Spencer[3] 1843
	George M. Bibb 1844
Secretary of War	John Bell (Cont.)
	John C. Spencer 1841
	James M. Porter[3] 1843
	William Wilkins 1844
Attorney General	John J. Crittenden (Cont.)
	Hugh S. Legaré 1841
	John Nelson 1843
Postmaster General	Francis Granger (Cont.)
	Charles A. Wickliffe 1841
Secretary of the Navy	George E. Badger (Cont.)
	Abel P. Upshur 1841
	David Henshaw[3] 1843
	Thomas W. Gilmer 1844
	John Y. Mason 1844

POLK

Secretary of State	James Buchanan 1845
Secretary of the Treasury	Robert J. Walker 1845
Secretary of War	William L. Marcy 1845
Attorney General	John Y. Mason 1845
	Nathan Clifford 1846
	Isaac Toucey 1848
Postmaster General	Cave Johnson 1845
Secretary of the Navy	George Bancroft 1845
	John Y. Mason 1846

TAYLOR

Secretary of State	John M. Clayton 1849
Secretary of the Treasury	William M. Meredith 1849
Secretary of War	George W. Crawford 1849
Attorney General	Reverdy Johnson 1849
Postmaster General	Jacob Collamer 1849
Secretary of the Navy	William B. Preston 1849
Secretary of the Interior	Thomas Ewing 1849

FILLMORE

Secretary of State	Daniel Webster 1850
	Edward Everett 1852
Secretary of the Treasury	Thomas Corwin 1850
Secretary of War	Charles M. Conrad 1850
Attorney General	John J. Crittenden 1850
Postmaster General	Nathan K. Hall 1850
	Samuel D. Hubbard 1852
Secretary of the Navy	William A. Graham 1850
	John P. Kennedy 1852
Secretary of the Interior	Thos. M. T. McKennan 1850
	Alex. H. H. Stuart 1850

PIERCE

Secretary of State	William L. Marcy 1853
Secretary of the Treasury	James Guthrie 1853
Secretary of War	Jefferson Davis 1853
Attorney General	Caleb Cushing 1853
Postmaster General	James Campbell 1853
Secretary of the Navy	James C. Dobbin 1853
Secretary of the Interior	Robert McClelland 1853

BUCHANAN

Secretary of State	Lewis Cass 1857
	Jeremiah S. Black 1860
Secretary of the Treasury	Howell Cobb 1857
	Philip F. Thomas 1860
	John A. Dix 1861
Secretary of War	John B. Floyd 1857
	Joseph Holt 1861
Attorney General	Jeremiah S. Black 1857
	Edwin M. Stanton 1860
Postmaster General	Aaron V. Brown 1857
	Joseph Holt 1859
	Horatio King 1861
Secretary of the Navy	Isaac Toucey 1857
Secretary of the Interior	Jacob Thompson 1857

LINCOLN

Secretary of State	William H. Seward 1861
Secretary of the Treasury	Salmon P. Chase 1861
	William P. Fessenden 1864
	Hugh McCulloch 1865
Secretary of War	Simon Cameron 1861
	Edwin M. Stanton 1862
Attorney General	Edward Bates 1861
	James Speed 1864
Postmaster General	Montgomery Blair 1861
	William Dennison 1864
Secretary of the Navy	Gideon Welles 1861
Secretary of the Interior	Caleb B. Smith 1861
	John P. Usher 1863

A. JOHNSON

Secretary of State	William H. Seward (Cont.)
Secretary of the Treasury	Hugh McCulloch (Cont.)
Secretary of War	Edwin M. Stanton (Cont.)
	John M. Schofield 1868
Attorney General	James Speed (Cont.)
	Henry Stanbery 1866
	William M. Evarts 1868
Postmaster General	William Dennison (Cont.)
	Alexander W. Randall 1866
Secretary of the Navy	Gideon Welles (Cont.)
Secretary of the Interior	John P. Usher (Cont.)
	James Harlan 1865
	Orville H. Browning 1866

GRANT

Secretary of State	Elihu B. Washburne 1869
	Hamilton Fish 1869
Secretary of the Treasury	George S. Boutwell 1869
	William A. Richardson 1873
	Benjamin H. Bristow 1874
	Lot M. Morrill 1876
Secretary of War	John A. Rawlins 1869
	William W. Belknap 1869
	Alphonso Taft 1876
	James D. Cameron 1876
Attorney General	Ebenezer R. Hoar 1869
	Amos T. Akerman 1870
	George H. Williams 1871
	Edwards Pierrepont 1875
	Alphonso Taft 1876
Postmaster General	John A. J. Creswell 1869
	Marshall Jewell 1874
	James N. Tyner 1876
Secretary of the Navy	Adolph E. Borie 1869
	George M. Robeson 1869
Secretary of the Interior	Jacob D. Cox 1869
	Columbus Delano 1870
	Zachariah Chandler 1875

HAYES

Secretary of State	William M. Evarts 1877
Secretary of the Treasury	John Sherman 1877
Secretary of War	George W. McCrary 1877
	Alexander Ramsey 1879
Attorney General	Charles Devens 1877
Postmaster General	David M. Key 1877
	Horace Maynard 1880

Secretary of the Navy	Richard W. Thompson 1877
	Nathan Goff, Jr. 1881
Secretary of the Interior	Carl Schurz 1877

GARFIELD

Secretary of State	James G. Blaine 1881
Secretary of the Treasury	William Windom 1881
Secretary of War	Robert T. Lincoln 1881
Attorney General	Wayne MacVeagh 1881
Postmaster General	Thomas L. James 1881
Secretary of the Navy	William H. Hunt 1881
Secretary of the Interior	Samuel J. Kirkwood 1881

ARTHUR

Secretary of State	James G. Blaine (Cont.)
	F. T. Frelinghuysen 1881
Secretary of the Treasury	William Windom (Cont.)
	Charles J. Folger 1881
	Walter Q. Gresham 1884
	Hugh McCulloch 1884
Secretary of War	Robert T. Lincoln (Cont.)
Attorney General	Wayne MacVeagh (Cont.)
	Benjamin H. Brewster 1881
Postmaster General	Thomas L. James (Cont.)
	Timothy O. Howe 1881
	Walter Q. Gresham 1883
	Frank Hatton 1884
Secretary of the Navy	William H. Hunt (Cont.)
	William E. Chandler 1882
Secretary of the Interior	Samuel J. Kirkwood (Cont.)
	Henry M. Teller 1882

CLEVELAND

Secretary of State	Thomas F. Bayard 1885
Secretary of the Treasury	Daniel Manning 1885
	Charles S. Fairchild 1887
Secretary of War	William C. Endicott 1885
Attorney General	Augustus H. Garland 1885
Postmaster General	William F. Vilas 1885
	Don M. Dickinson 1888
Secretary of the Navy	William C. Whitney 1885
Secretary of the Interior	Lucius Q. C. Lamar 1885
	William F. Vilas 1888
Secretary of Agriculture	Norman J. Colman 1889

B. HARRISON

Secretary of State	James G. Blaine 1889
	John W. Foster 1892
Secretary of the Treasury	William Windom 1889
	Charles Foster 1891
Secretary of War	Redfield Proctor 1889
	Stephen B. Elkins 1891
Attorney General	William H. H. Miller 1889
Postmaster General	John Wanamaker 1889
Secretary of the Navy	Benjamin F. Tracy 1889
Secretary of the Interior	John W. Noble 1889
Secretary of Agriculture	Jeremiah M. Rusk 1889

CLEVELAND

Secretary of State	Walter Q. Gresham 1893
	Richard Olney 1895
Secretary of the Treasury	John G. Carlisle 1893
Secretary of War	Daniel S. Lamont 1893
Attorney General	Richard Olney 1893
	Judson Harmon 1895
Postmaster General	Wilson S. Bissell 1893
	William L. Wilson 1895
Secretary of the Navy	Hilary A. Herbert 1893
Secretary of the Interior	Hoke Smith 1893
	David R. Francis 1896
Secretary of Agriculture	Julius Sterling Morton 1893

McKINLEY

Secretary of State	John Sherman 1897
	William R. Day 1898
	John Hay 1898
Secretary of the Treasury	Lyman J. Gage 1897
Secretary of War	Russell A. Alger 1897
	Elihu Root 1899
Attorney General	Joseph McKenna 1897
	John W. Griggs 1898

	Philander C. Knox 1901
Postmaster General	James A. Gary 1897
	Charles E. Smith 1898
Secretary of the Navy	John D. Long 1897
Secretary of the Interior	Cornelius N. Bliss 1897
	Ethan A. Hitchcock 1898
Secretary of Agriculture	James Wilson 1897

T. ROOSEVELT

Secretary of State	John Hay (Cont.)
	Elihu Root 1905
	Robert Bacon 1909
Secretary of the Treasury	Lyman J. Gage (Cont.)
	Leslie M. Shaw 1902
	George B. Cortelyou 1907
Secretary of War	Elihu Root (Cont.)
	William H. Taft 1904
	Luke E. Wright 1908
Attorney General	Philander C. Knox (Cont.)
	William H. Moody 1904
	Charles J. Bonaparte 1906
Postmaster General	Charles E. Smith (Cont.)
	Henry C. Payne 1902
	Robert J. Wynne 1904
	George B. Cortelyou 1905
	George von L. Meyer 1907
Secretary of the Navy	John D. Long (Cont.)
	William H. Moody 1902
	Paul Morton 1904
	Charles E. Bonaparte 1905
	Victor H. Metcalf 1906
	Truman H. Newberry 1908
Secretary of the Interior	Ethan A. Hitchcock (Cont.)
	James R. Garfield 1907
Secretary of Agriculture	James Wilson (Cont.)
Secretary of Commerce and Labor	
	George B. Cortelyou 1903
	Victor H. Metcalf 1904
	Oscar S. Straus 1906

TAFT

Secretary of State	Philander C. Knox 1909
Secretary of the Treasury	Franklin MacVeagh 1909
Secretary of War	Jacob M. Dickinson 1909
	Henry L. Stimson 1911
Attorney General	George W. Wickersham 1909
Postmaster General	Frank H. Hitchcock 1909
Secretary of the Navy	George von L. Meyer 1909
Secretary of the Interior	Richard A. Ballinger 1909
	Walter L. Fisher 1911
Secretary of Agriculture	James Wilson (Cont.)
Secretary of Commerce and Labor	
	Charles Nagel 1909

WILSON

Secretary of State	William J. Bryan 1913
	Robert Lansing 1915
	Bainbridge Colby 1920
Secretary of the Treasury	William G. McAdoo 1913
	Carter Glass 1918
	David F. Houston 1920
Secretary of War	Lindley M. Garrison 1913
	Newton D. Baker 1916
Attorney General	James C. McReynolds 1913
	Thomas W. Gregory 1914
	A. Mitchell Palmer 1919
Postmaster General	Albert S. Burleson 1913
Secretary of the Navy	Josephus Daniels 1913
Secretary of the Interior	Franklin K. Lane 1913
	John B. Payne 1920
Secretary of Agriculture	David F. Houston 1913
	Edwin T. Meredith 1920
Secretary of Commerce	William C. Redfield 1913
	Joshua W. Alexander 1919
Secretary of Labor	William B. Wilson 1913

HARDING

Secretary of State	Charles E. Hughes 1921
Secretary of the Treasury	Andrew W. Mellon 1921
Secretary of War	John W. Weeks 1921
Attorney General	Harry M. Daugherty 1921
Postmaster General	Will H. Hays 1921

	Hubert Work 1922
	Harry S. New 1923
Secretary of the Navy	Edwin Denby 1921
Secretary of the Interior	Albert B. Fall 1921
	Hubert Work 1923
Secretary of Agriculture	Henry C. Wallace 1921
Secretary of Commerce	Herbert Hoover 1921
Secretary of Labor	James J. Davis 1921

COOLIDGE

Secretary of State	Charles E. Hughes (Cont.)
	Frank B. Kellogg 1925
Secretary of the Treasury	Andrew W. Mellon (Cont.)
Secretary of War	John W. Weeks (Cont.)
	Dwight F. Davis 1925
Attorney General	Harry M. Daughtery (Cont.)
	Harlan F. Stone 1924
	John G. Sargent 1925
Postmaster General	Harry S. New (Cont.)
Secretary of the Navy	Edwin Denby (Cont.)
	Curtis D. Wilbur 1924
Secretary of the Interior	Hubert Work (Cont.)
	Roy O. West 1928
Secretary of Agriculture	Henry C. Wallace (Cont.)
	Howard M. Gore 1924
	William M. Jardine 1925
Secretary of Commerce	Herbert Hoover (Cont.)
	William F. Whiting 1928
Secretary of Labor	James J. Davis (Cont.)

HOOVER

Secretary of State	Frank B. Kellogg (Cont.)
	Henry L. Stimson 1929
Secretary of the Treasury	Andrew W. Mellon (Cont.)
	Ogden L. Mills 1932
Secretary of War	James W. Good 1929
	Patrick J. Hurley 1929
Attorney General	William D. Mitchell 1929
Postmaster General	Walter F. Brown 1929
Secretary of the Navy	Charles F. Adams 1929
Secretary of the Interior	Ray Lyman Wilbur 1929
Secretary of Agriculture	Arthur M. Hyde 1929
Secretary of Commerce	Robert P. Lamont 1929
	Roy D. Chapin 1932
Secretary of Labor	James J. Davis (Cont.)
	William N. Doak 1930

F. D. ROOSEVELT

Secretary of State	Cordell Hull 1933
	E. R. Stettinius, Jr. 1944
Secretary of the Treasury	William H. Woodin 1933
	Henry Morgenthau, Jr. 1934
Secretary of War	George H. Dern 1933
	Harry H. Woodring 1936
	Henry L. Stimson 1940
Attorney General	Homer S. Cummings 1933
	Frank Murphy 1939
	Robert H. Jackson 1940
	Francis Biddle 1941
Postmaster General	James A. Farley 1933
	Frank C. Walker 1940
Secretary of the Navy	Claude A. Swanson 1933
	Charles Edison 1940
	Frank Knox 1940
	James Forrestal 1944
Secretary of the Interior	Harold L. Ickes 1933
Secretary of Agriculture	Henry A. Wallace 1933
	Claude R. Wickard 1940
Secretary of Commerce	Daniel C. Roper 1933
	Harry L. Hopkins 1938
	Jesse H. Jones 1940
	Henry A. Wallace 1945
Secretary of Labor	Frances Perkins 1933

TRUMAN

Secretary of State	E. R. Stettinius, Jr. (Cont.)
	James F. Byrnes 1945
	George C. Marshall 1947
	Dean Acheson 1949
Secretary of the Treasury	Henry Morgenthau, Jr. (Cont.)
	Frederick M. Vinson 1945
	John W. Snyder 1946

Secretary of Defense	James Forrestal 1947
	Louis A. Johnson 1949
	George C. Marshall 1950
	Robert A. Lovett 1951
Attorney General	Francis Biddle (Cont.)
	Tom C. Clark 1945
	J. Howard McGrath 1949
	James P. McGranery 1952
Postmaster General	Frank C. Walker (Cont.)
	Robert E. Hannegan 1945
	Jesse M. Donaldson 1947
Secretary of the Interior	Harold L. Ickes (Cont.)
	Julius A. Krug 1946
	Oscar L. Chapman 1949
Secretary of Agriculture	Claude R. Wickard (Cont.)
	Clinton P. Anderson 1945
	Charles F. Brannan 1948
Secretary of Commerce	Henry A. Wallace (Cont.)
	W. Averell Harriman 1946
	Charles Sawyer 1948
Secretary of Labor	Frances Perkins (Cont.)
	Lewis B. Schwellenbach 1945
	Maurice J. Tobin 1948
Secretary of War[2]	Henry L. Stimson (Cont.)
	Robert P. Patterson 1945
	Kenneth C. Royall 1947
Secretary of the Navy[2]	James Forrestal (Cont.)

EISENHOWER

Secretary of State	John Foster Dulles 1953
	Christian A. Herter 1959
Secretary of the Treasury	George M. Humphrey 1953
	Robert B. Anderson 1957
Secretary of Defense	Charles E. Wilson 1953
	Neil H. McElroy 1957
	Thomas S. Gates, Jr. 1959
Attorney General	Herbert Brownell, Jr. 1953
	William P. Rogers 1958
Postmaster General	Arthur E. Summerfield 1953
Secretary of the Interior	Douglas McKay 1953
	Frederick A. Seaton 1956
Secretary of Agriculture	Ezra Taft Benson 1953
Secretary of Commerce	Sinclair Weeks 1953
	Lewis L. Strauss[3] 1958
	Frederick H. Mueller 1959
Secretary of Labor	Martin P. Durkin 1953
	James P. Mitchell 1953
Secretary of Health, Education,	
and Welfare	Oveta Culp Hobby 1953
	Marion B. Folsom 1955
	Arthur S. Flemming 1958

KENNEDY

Secretary of State	Dean Rusk 1961
Secretary of the Treasury	C. Douglas Dillon 1961
Secretary of Defense	Robert S. McNamara 1961
Attorney General	Robert F. Kennedy 1961
Postmaster General	J. Edward Day 1961
	John A. Gronouski 1963
Secretary of the Interior	Stewart L. Udall 1961
Secretary of Agriculture	Orville L. Freeman 1961
Secretary of Commerce	Luther H. Hodges 1961
Secretary of Labor	Arthur J. Goldberg 1961
	W. Willard Wirtz 1962
Secretary of Health, Education,	
and Welfare	Abraham A. Ribicoff 1961
	Anthony J. Celebrezze 1962

L. B. JOHNSON

Secretary of State	Dean Rusk (Cont.)
Secretary of the Treasury	C. Douglas Dillon (Cont.)
	Henry H. Fowler 1965
	Joseph W. Barr[4] 1968
Secretary of Defense	Robert S. McNamara (Cont.)
	Clark M. Clifford 1968
Attorney General	Robert F. Kennedy (Cont.)
	N. de B. Katzenbach 1965
	Ramsey Clark 1967
Postmaster General	John A. Gronouski (Cont.)
	Lawrence F. O'Brien 1965
	W. Marvin Watson 1968
Secretary of the Interior	Stewart L. Udall (Cont.)
Secretary of Agriculture	Orville L. Freeman (Cont.)

Secretary of Commerce	Luther H. Hodges (Cont.)
	John T. Connor 1964
	A. B. Trowbridge 1967
	C. R. Smith 1968
Secretary of Labor	W. Willard Wirtz (Cont.)
Secretary of Health, Education, and Welfare	Anthony J. Celebrezze (Cont.)
	John W. Gardner 1965
	Wilbur J. Cohen 1968
Secretary of Housing and Urban Development	Robert C. Weaver 1966
	Robert C. Wood[4] 1969
Secretary of Transportation	Alan S. Boyd 1966

NIXON

Secretary of State	William P. Rogers 1969
	Henry A. Kissinger 1973
Secretary of the Treasury	David M. Kennedy 1969
	John B. Connally 1971
	George P. Shultz 1972
	William E. Simon 1974
Secretary of Defense	Melvin R. Laird 1969
	Eliot L. Richardson 1973
	James R. Schlesinger 1973
Attorney General	John N. Mitchell 1969
	Richard G. Kleindienst 1972
	Eliot L. Richardson 1973
	William B. Saxbe 1974
Postmaster General[5]	William M. Blount 1969
Secretary of the Interior	Walter J. Hickel 1969
	Rogers C. B. Morton 1971
Secretary of Agriculture	Clifford M. Hardin 1969
	Earl L. Butz 1971
Secretary of Commerce	Maurice H. Stans 1969
	Peter G. Peterson 1972
	Frederick B. Dent 1973
Secretary of Labor	George P. Shultz 1969
	James D. Hodgson 1970
	Peter J. Brennan 1973
Secretary of Health, Education, and Welfare	Robert H. Finch 1969
	Eliot L. Richardson 1970
	Caspar W. Weinberger 1973
Secretary of Housing and Urban Development	George Romney 1969
	James T. Lynn 1973
Secretary of Transportation	John A. Volpe 1969
	Claude S. Brinegar 1973

FORD

Secretary of State	Henry A. Kissinger (Cont.)
Secretary of the Treasury	William E. Simon (Cont.)
Secretary of Defense	James R. Schlesinger (Cont.)
	Donald H. Rumsfeld 1975
Attorney General	William B. Saxbe (Cont.)
	Edward H. Levi 1975
Secretary of the Interior	Rogers C. B. Morton (Cont.)
	Stanley K. Hathaway 1975
	Thomas S. Kleppe 1975
Secretary of Agriculture	Earl L. Butz (Cont.)
	John Knebel 1976
Secretary of Commerce	Frederick B. Dent (Cont.)
	Rogers C. B. Morton 1975
	Elliot L. Richardson 1976
Secretary of Labor	Peter J. Brennan (Cont.)
	John T. Dunlop 1975
	William J. Usery, Jr. 1976
Secretary of Health, Education, and Welfare	Caspar W. Weinberger (Cont.)
	F. David Mathews 1975
Secretary of Housing and Urban Development	James T. Lynn (Cont.)
	Carla A. Hills 1975
Secretary of Transportation	Claude S. Brinegar (Cont.)
	William T. Coleman, Jr. 1975

CARTER

Secretary of State	Cyrus R. Vance 1977
	Edmund S. Muskie 1980

Secretary of the Treasury	W. Michael Blumenthal 1977
	G. William Miller 1979
Secretary of Defense	Harold Brown 1977
Attorney General	Griffin B. Bell 1977
	Benjamin R. Civiletti 1979
Secretary of the Interior	Cecil D. Andrus 1977
Secretary of Agriculture	Bob S. Bergland 1977
Secretary of Commerce	Juanita M. Kreps 1977
	Philip M. Klutznick 1979
Secretary of Labor	F. Ray Marshall 1977
Secretary of Health and Human Services[6]	Joseph A. Califano, Jr. 1977
	Patricia Roberts Harris 1979
Secretary of Housing and Urban Development	Patricia Roberts Harris 1977
	Moon Landrieu 1979
Secretary of Transportation	Brock Adams 1977
	Neil E. Goldschmidt 1979
Secretary of Energy	James R. Schlesinger 1977
	Charles W. Duncan, Jr. 1979
Secretary of Education	Shirley Mount Hufstedler 1979

REAGAN

Secretary of State	Alexander M. Haig, Jr. 1981
	George P. Shultz 1982
Secretary of the Treasury	Donald T. Regan 1981
	James A. Baker 3rd 1985
	Nicholas F. Brady 1988
Secretary of Defense	Caspar W. Weinberger 1981
	Frank C. Carlucci 1987
Attorney General	William French Smith 1981
	Edwin Meese 3rd 1985
	Richard L. Thornburgh 1988
Secretary of the Interior	James G. Watt 1981
	William P. Clark 1983
	Donald P. Hodel 1985
Secretary of Agriculture	John R. Block 1981
	Richard E. Lyng 1986
Secretary of Commerce	Malcolm Baldrige 1981
	C. William Verity, Jr. 1987
Secretary of Labor	Raymond J. Donovan 1981
	William E. Brock 1985
	Ann Dore McLaughlin 1987
Secretary of Health and Human Services	Richard S. Schweiker 1981
	Margaret M. Heckler 1983
	Otis R. Bowen 1985
Secretary of Housing and Urban Development	Samuel R. Pierce, Jr. 1981
Secretary of Transportation	Andrew L. Lewis, Jr. 1981
	Elizabeth H. Dole 1983
	James H. Burnley 4th 1987
Secretary of Energy	James B. Edwards 1981
	Donald P. Hodel 1983
	John S. Herrington 1985
Secretary of Education	T. H. Bell 1981
	William J. Bennett 1985
	Lauro F. Cavazos 1988

BUSH

Secretary of State	James A. Baker 3d 1989
Secretary of the Treasury	Nicholas F. Brady (Cont.)
Secretary of Defense	Richard Cheney 1989
Attorney General	Richard L. Thornburgh (Cont.)
Secretary of the Interior	Manuel Lujan Jr. 1989
Secretary of Agriculture	Clayton K. Yeutter 1989
Secretary of Commerce	Robert A. Mosbacher Sr. 1989
Secretary of Labor	Elizabeth H. Dole 1989
Secretary of Health and Human Services	Louis W. Sullivan 1989
Secretary of Housing and Urban Development	Jack F. Kemp 1989
Secretary of Transportation	Samuel K. Skinner 1989
Secretary of Energy	James D. Watkins 1989
Secretary of Education	Lauro F. Cavazos (Cont.)
Secretary of Veterans Affairs	Edward J. Derwinski 1989

1. The Postmaster General did not become a Cabinet member until 1829. Earlier Postmasters General were: Samuel Osgood (1789), Timothy Pickering (1791), Joseph Habersham (1795), Gideon Granger (1801), Return J. Meigs, Jr. (1814), and John McLean (1823). 2. On July 26, 1947, the Departments of War and of the Navy were incorporated into the Department of Defense. 3. Not confirmed by the Senate. 4. Recess appointment. 5. The Postmaster General is no longer a Cabinet member. 6. Known as Department of Health, Education, and Welfare until May 1980.

Figures and Legends in American Folklore

Appleseed, Johnny (John Chapman, 1774–1847): Massachusetts-born nurseryman; reputed to have spread seeds and seedlings from which rose orchards of the Midwest.

Billy the Kid (William H. Bonney, 1859–1881): New York-born desperado; killed his first man before he reached his teens; after short life of crime in Wild West, was gunned down by Sheriff Pat Garrett; symbol of lawless West.

Boone, Daniel (1734–1820): Frontiersman and Indian fighter, about whom legends of early America have been built; figured in Byron's *Don Juan*.

Brodie, Steve (1863–1901): Reputed to have dived off Brooklyn Bridge on July 23, 1886. (Whether he actually did so has never been proved.)

Buffalo Bill (William F. Cody, 1846–1917): Buffalo hunter and Indian scout; much of legend about him and Wild West stems from his own Wild West show, which he operated in late 19th century.

Bunyan, Paul: Mythical lumberjack; subject of tall tales throughout timber country (that he dug Grand Canyon, for example).

Crockett, David (1786–1836): Frontiersman and member of U.S. Congress, about whom legends have been built of heroic feats; died in defense of Alamo.

Fritchie (or Frietchie), Barbara: Symbol of patriotism; in ballad by John Greenleaf Whittier, 90-year-old Barbara Fritchie defiantly waves Stars and Stripes as "Stonewall" Jackson's Confederate troops march through Frederick, Md.

James, Jesse (1847–1882): Bank and train robber; folklore has given him quality of American Robin Hood.

Jones, Casey (John Luther Jones, 1863–1900): Example of heroic locomotive engineer given to feats of prowess; died in wreck with his hand on brake lever when his Illinois Central "Cannonball" express hit freight train at Vaughan, Miss.

Ross, Betsy (1752–1836): Member of Philadelphia flag-making family; reported to have designed and sewn first American flag. (Report is without confirmation.)

Uncle Sam: Personification of United States and its people; origin uncertain; may be based on inspector of government supplies in Revolutionary War and War of 1812.

Assassinations and Attempts in U. S. Since 1865

Cermak, Anton J. (Mayor of Chicago): Shot Feb. 15, 1933, in Miami by Giuseppe Zangara, who attempted to assassinate Franklin D. Roosevelt; Cermak died March 6.

Ford, Gerald R. (President of U.S.): Escaped assassination attempt Sept. 5, 1975, in Sacramento, Calif., by Lynette Alice (Squeaky) Fromm, who pointed but did not fire .45-caliber pistol. Escaped assassination attempt in San Francisco, Calif., Sept. 22, 1975, by Sara Jane Moore, who fired one shot from a .38-caliber pistol that was deflected.

Garfield, James A. (President of U.S.): Shot July 2, 1881, in Washington, D.C., by Charles J. Guiteau; died Sept. 19.

Jordan, Vernon E., Jr. (civil rights leader): Shot and critically wounded in assassination attempt May 29, 1980, in Fort Wayne, Ind.

Kennedy, John F. (President of U.S.): Shot Nov. 22, 1963, in Dallas, Tex., allegedly by Lee Harvey Oswald; died same day. Injured was Gov. John B. Connally of Texas. Oswald was shot and killed two days later by Jack Ruby.

Kennedy, Robert F. (U.S. Senator from New York): Shot June 5, 1968, in Los Angeles by Sirhan Bishara Sirhan; died June 6.

King, Martin Luther, Jr. (civil rights leader): Shot April 4, 1968, in Memphis by James Earl Ray; died same day.

Lincoln, Abraham (President of U.S.): Shot April 14, 1865, in Washington, D.C., by John Wilkes Booth; died April 15.

Long, Huey P. (U.S. Senator from Louisiana): Shot Sept. 8, 1935, in Baton Rouge by Dr. Carl A. Weiss; died Sept. 10.

McKinley, William (President of U.S.): Shot Sept. 6, 1901, in Buffalo by Leon Czolgosz; died Sept. 14.

Reagan, Ronald (President of U.S.): Shot in left lung in Washington by John W. Hinckley, Jr., on March 30, 1981; three others also wounded.

Roosevelt, Franklin D. (President-elect of U.S.): Escaped assassination unhurt Feb. 15, 1933, in Miami. *See* Cermak.

Roosevelt, Theodore (ex-President of U.S.): Escaped assassination (though shot) Oct. 14, 1912, in Milwaukee while campaigning for President.

Seward, William H. (Secretary of State): Escaped assassination (though injured) April 14, 1865, in Washington, D.C., by Lewis Powell (or Paine), accomplice of John Wilkes Booth.

Truman, Harry S. (President of U.S.): Escaped assassination unhurt Nov. 1, 1950, in Washington, D.C., as 2 Puerto Rican nationalists attempted to shoot their way into Blair House.

Wallace, George C. (Governor of Alabama): Shot and critically wounded in assassination attempt May 15, 1972, at Laurel, Md., by Arthur Herman Bremer. Wallace paralyzed from waist down.

Impeachments of Federal Officials

Source: Congressional Directory

The procedure for the impeachment of Federal officials is detailed in Article I, Section 3, of the Constitution. See Index.

The Senate has sat as a court of impeachment in

the following cases:

William Blount, Senator from Tennessee; charges dismissed for want of jurisdiction, January 14, 1799.

John Pickering, Judge of the U.S. District Court for New Hampshire; removed from office March 12, 1804.

Samuel Chase, Associate Justice of the Supreme Court; acquitted March 1, 1805.

James H. Peck, Judge of the U.S. District Court for Missouri; acquitted Jan. 31, 1831.

West H. Humphreys, Judge of the U.S. District Court for the middle, eastern, and western districts of Tennessee; removed from office June 26, 1862.

Andrew Johnson, President of the United States; acquitted May 26, 1868.

William W. Belknap, Secretary of War; acquitted Aug. 1, 1876.

Charles Swayne, Judge of the U.S. District Court for the northern district of Florida; acquitted Feb. 27, 1905.

Robert W. Archbald, Associate Judge, U.S. Commerce Court; removed Jan. 13, 1913.

George W. English, Judge of the U.S. District Court for eastern district of Illinois; resigned Nov. 4, 1926; proceedings dismissed.

Harold Louderback, Judge of the U.S. District Court for the northern district of California; acquitted May 24, 1933.

Halsted L. Ritter, Judge of the U.S. District Court for the southern district of Florida; removed from office April 17, 1936.

Harry E. Claiborne, Judge of the U.S. District Court for the district of Nevada; removed from office October 9, 1986.

Alcee L. Hastings, Judge of the U.S. District Court for the southern district of Florida; removed from office October 20, 1989.

Walter L. Nixon, Jr., Judge of the U.S. District Court for Mississippi; removed from office November 3, 1989.

Members of the Supreme Court of the United States

Name; apptd. from	Service Term	Yrs	Birth Place	Date	Died	Religion
CHIEF JUSTICES						
John Jay, N.Y.	1789-1795	5	N.Y.	1745	1829	Episcopal
John Rutledge, S.C.	1795	0	S.C.	1739	1800	Church of England
Oliver Ellsworth, Conn.	1796-1800	4	Conn.	1745	1807	Congregational
John Marshall, Va.	1801-1835	34	Va.	1755	1835	Episcopal
Roger B. Taney, Md.	1836-1864	28	Md.	1777	1864	Roman Catholic
Salmon P. Chase, Ohio	1864-1873	8	N.H.	1808	1873	Episcopal
Morrison R. Waite, Ohio	1874-1888	14	Conn.	1816	1888	Episcopal
Melville W. Fuller, Ill.	1888-1910	21	Me.	1833	1910	Episcopal
Edward D. White, La.	1910-1921	10	La.	1845	1921	Roman Catholic
William H. Taft, Conn.	1921-1930	8	Ohio	1857	1930	Unitarian
Charles E. Hughes, N.Y.	1930-1941	11	N.Y.	1862	1948	Baptist
Harlan F. Stone, N.Y.	1941-1946	4	N.H.	1872	1946	Episcopal
Frederick M. Vinson, Ky.	1946-1953	7	Ky.	1890	1953	Methodist
Earl Warren, Calif.	1953-1969	15	Calif.	1891	1974	Protestant
Warren E. Burger, Va.	1969-1986	17	Minn.	1907	—	Presbyterian
William H. Rehnquist, Ariz.	1986-		Wis.	1924	—	Lutheran
ASSOCIATE JUSTICES						
James Wilson, Pa.	1789-1798	8	Scotland	1742	1798	Episcopal
John Rutledge, S.C.	1790-1791	1	S.C.	1739	1800	Church of England
William Cushing, Mass.	1790-1810	20	Mass.	1732	1810	Unitarian
John Blair, Va.	1790-1796	5	Va.	1732	1800	Presbyterian
James Iredell, N.C.	1790-1799	9	England	1751	1799	Episcopal
Thomas Johnson, Md.	1792-1793	0	Md.	1732	1819	Episcopal
William Paterson, N.J.	1793-1806	13	Ireland	1745	1806	Protestant
Samuel Chase, Md.	1796-1811	15	Md.	1741	1811	Episcopal
Bushrod Washington, Va.	1799-1829	30	Va.	1762	1829	Episcopal
Alfred Moore, N.C.	1800-1804	3	N.C.	1755	1810	Episcopal
William Johnson, S.C.	1804-1834	30	S.C.	1771	1834	Presbyterian
Brockholst Livingston, N.Y.	1807-1823	16	N.Y.	1757	1823	Presbyterian
Thomas Todd, Ky.	1807-1826	18	Va.	1765	1826	Presbyterian
Gabriel Duval, Md.	1811-1835	23	Md.	1752	1844	French Protestant
Joseph Story, Mass.	1812-1845	33	Mass.	1779	1845	Unitarian
Smith Thompson, N.Y.	1823-1843	20	N.Y.	1768	1843	Presbyterian
Robert Trimble, Ky.	1826-1828	2	Va.	1777	1828	Protestant
John McLean, Ohio	1830-1861	31	N.J.	1785	1861	Methodist-Epis.
Henry Baldwin, Pa.	1830-1844	14	Conn.	1780	1844	Trinity Church
James M. Wayne, Ga.	1835-1867	32	Ga.	1790	1867	Protestant
Philip P. Barbour, Va.	1836-1841	4	Va.	1783	1841	Episcopal
John Catron, Tenn.	1837-1865	28	Pa.	1786	1865	Presbyterian
John McKinley, Ala.	1837-1852	14	Va.	1780	1852	Protestant
Peter V. Daniel, Va.	1841-1860	18	Va.	1784	1860	Episcopal
Samuel Nelson, N.Y.	1845-1872	27	N.Y.	1792	1873	Protestant

Name; apptd. from	Service Term	Yrs	Birth Place	Date	Died	Religion
Levi Woodbury, N.H.	1845-1851	5	N.H.	1789	1851	Protestant
Robert C. Grier, Pa.	1846-1870	23	Pa.	1794	1870	Presbyterian
Benjamin R. Curtis, Mass.	1851-1857	5	Mass.	1809	1874	(²)
John A. Campbell, Ala.	1853-1861	8	Ga.	1811	1889	Episcopal
Nathan Clifford, Maine	1858-1881	23	N.H.	1803	1881	(¹)
Noah H. Swayne, Ohio	1862-1881	18	Va.	1804	1884	Quaker
Samuel F. Miller, Iowa	1862-1890	28	Ky.	1816	1890	Unitarian
David Davis, Ill.	1862-1877	14	Md.	1815	1886	(⁴)
Stephen J. Field, Calif.	1863-1897	34	Conn.	1816	1899	Episcopal
William Strong, Pa.	1870-1880	10	Conn.	1808	1895	Presbyterian
Joseph P. Bradley, N.J.	1870-1892	21	N.Y.	1813	1892	Presbyterian
Ward Hunt, N.Y.	1872-1882	9	N.Y.	1810	1886	Episcopal
John M. Harlan, Ky.	1877-1911	33	Ky.	1833	1911	Presbyterian
William B. Woods, Ga.	1880-1887	6	Ohio	1824	1887	Protestant
Stanley Matthews, Ohio	1881-1889	7	Ohio	1824	1889	Presbyterian
Horace Gray, Mass.	1882-1902	20	Mass.	1828	1902	(³)
Samuel Blatchford, N.Y.	1882-1893	11	N.Y.	1820	1893	Presbyterian
Lucius Q. C. Lamar, Miss.	1888-1893	5	Ga.	1825	1893	Methodist
David J. Brewer, Kan.	1889-1910	20	Asia Minor	1837	1910	Protestant
Henry B. Brown, Mich.	1890-1906	15	Mass.	1836	1913	Protestant
George Shiras, Jr., Pa.	1892-1903	10	Pa.	1832	1924	Presbyterian
Howell E. Jackson, Tenn.	1893-1895	2	Tenn.	1832	1895	Baptist
Edward D. White, La.	1894-1910	16	La.	1845	1921	Roman Catholic
Rufus W. Peckham, N.Y.	1895-1909	13	N.Y.	1838	1909	Episcopal
Joseph McKenna, Calif.	1898-1925	26	Pa.	1843	1926	Roman Catholic
Oliver W. Holmes, Mass.	1902-1932	29	Mass.	1841	1935	Unitarian
William R. Day, Ohio	1903-1922	19	Ohio	1849	1923	Protestant
William H. Moody, Mass.	1906-1910	3	Mass.	1853	1917	Episcopal
Horace H. Lurton, Tenn.	1909-1914	4	Ky.	1844	1914	Episcopal
Charles E. Hughes, N.Y.	1910-1916	5	N.Y.	1862	1948	Baptist
Willis Van Devanter, Wyo.	1910-1937	26	Ind.	1859	1941	Episcopal
Joseph R. Lamar, Ga.	1910-1916	4	Ga.	1857	1916	Ch. of Disciples
Mahlon Pitney, N.J.	1912-1922	10	N.J.	1858	1924	Presbyterian
James C. McReynolds, Tenn.	1914-1941	26	Ky.	1862	1946	Disciples of Christ
Louis D. Brandeis, Mass.	1916-1939	22	Ky.	1856	1941	Jewish
John H. Clarke, Ohio	1916-1922	5	Ohio	1857	1945	Protestant
George Sutherland, Utah	1922-1938	15	England	1862	1942	Episcopal
Pierce Butler, Minn.	1923-1939	16	Minn.	1866	1939	Roman Catholic
Edward T. Sanford, Tenn.	1923-1930	7	Tenn.	1865	1930	Episcopal
Harlan F. Stone, N.Y.	1925-1941	16	N.H.	1872	1946	Episcopal
Owen J. Roberts, Pa.	1930-1945	15	Pa.	1875	1955	Episcopal
Benjamin N. Cardozo, N.Y.	1932-1938	6	N.Y.	1870	1938	Jewish
Hugo L. Black, Ala.	1937-1971	34	Ala.	1886	1971	Baptist
Stanley F. Reed, Ky.	1938-1957	19	Ky.	1884	1980	Protestant
Felix Frankfurter, Mass.	1939-1962	23	Austria	1882	1965	Jewish
William O. Douglas, Conn.	1939-1975	36	Minn.	1898	1980	Presbyterian
Frank Murphy, Mich.	1940-1949	9	Mich.	1890	1949	Roman Catholic
James F. Byrnes, S.C.	1941-1942	1	S.C.	1879	1972	Episcopal
Robert H. Jackson, Pa.	1941-1954	13	N.Y.	1892	1954	Episcopal
Wiley B. Rutledge, Iowa	1943-1949	6	Ky.	1894	1949	Unitarian
Harold H. Burton, Ohio	1945-1958	13	Mass.	1888	1964	Unitarian
Tom C. Clark, Tex.	1949-1967	17	Tex.	1899	1977	Presbyterian
Sherman Minton, Ind.	1949-1956	7	Ind.	1890	1965	Roman Catholic
John M. Harlan, N.Y.	1955-1971	16	Ill.	1899	1971	Presbyterian
William J. Brennan, Jr., N.J.⁵	1956-1990	33	N.J.	1906	—	Roman Catholic
Charles E. Whittaker, Mo.	1957-1962	5	Kan.	1901	1973	Methodist
Potter Stewart, Ohio	1958-1981	23	Mich.	1915	1985	Episcopal
Byron R. White, Colo.	1962-	—	Colo.	1917	—	Episcopal
Arthur J. Goldberg, Ill.	1962-1965	2	Ill.	1908	—	Jewish
Abe Fortas, Tenn.	1965-1969	3	Tenn.	1910	1982	Jewish
Thurgood Marshall, N.Y.	1967-	—	Md.	1908	—	Episcopalian
Harry A. Blackmun, Minn.	1970-	—	Ill.	1908	—	Methodist
Lewis F. Powell, Jr., Va.	1972-1987	15	Va.	1907	—	Presbyterian
William H. Rehnquist, Ariz.	1972-1986	14	Wis.	1924	—	Lutheran
John Paul Stevens, Ill.	1975-	—	Ill.	1920	—	Protestant
Sandra Day O'Connor, Ariz.	1981-	—	Tex.	1930	—	Episcopal
Antonin Scalia, D.C.	1986-	—	N.J.	1936	—	Roman Catholic
Anthony M. Kennedy, Calif.	1988-	—	Calif.	1936	—	n.a.

1. Congregational; later Unitarian. 2. Unitarian; then Episcopal. 3. Unitarian or Congregational. 4. Not a member of any church. 5. David H. Souter nominated to fill vacancy. *See* Current Events for confirmation or another nomination. NOTE: n.a.=not available.

Executive Departments and Agencies
Source: Congressional Directory, 1989–1990
Unless otherwise indicated, addresses shown are in Washington, D.C.

CENTRAL INTELLIGENCE AGENCY (CIA)
Washington, D.C. (20505).
　Established: 1947.
　Director: William H. Webster.
COUNCIL OF ECONOMIC ADVISERS (CEA)
Executive Office Bldg. (20500).
　Members: 3.
　Established: Feb. 20, 1946.
　Chairman: Michael J. Boskin
COUNCIL ON ENVIRONMENTAL QUALITY
722 Jackson Pl., N.W. (20006).
　Members: 3.
　Established: 1969.
　Chairman: A. Alan Hill.
NATIONAL SECURITY COUNCIL (NSC)
Old Executive Office Bldg. (20506).
　Members: 4.
　Established: July 26, 1947.
　Chairman: The President.
　Other members: Vice President; Secretary of State; Secretary of Defense.
OFFICE OF ADMINISTRATION
Old Executive Office Bldg. (20500).
　Established: Dec. 12, 1977.
　Director: Paul Bateman
OFFICE OF MANAGEMENT AND BUDGET
Executive Office Bldg. (20503).
　Established: July 1, 1970.
　Director: Richard Darman
OFFICE OF SCIENCE AND TECHNOLOGY POLICY
Old Executive Office Building (20506).
　Established: May 11, 1976
　Director: William R. Graham
OFFICE OF THE UNITED STATES TRADE REPRESENTATIVE
600 17th St., N.W. (20506).
　Established: Jan. 15, 1963.
　Trade Representative: Carla A. Hills
OFFICE OF POLICY DEVELOPMENT
1600 Pennsylvania Ave., N.W. (20500).
　Established: Jan. 21, 1981.
　Director: William L. Roper
OFFICE OF NATIONAL DRUG CONTROL POLICY
Suite 1011, 1825 Connecticut Ave., N.W. (20009)
　Established: March 13, 1989
　Director: William J. Bennett

Executive Departments

DEPARTMENT OF STATE
2201 C St., N.W. (20520).
　Established: 1781 as Department of Foreign Affairs; reconstituted, 1789, following adoption of Constitution; name changed to Department of State Sept. 15, 1789.
　Secretary: James A. Baker III
　Deputy Secretary: Lawrence S. Eagleburger
　Chief Delegate to U.N.: Vernon A. Walters.
DEPARTMENT OF THE TREASURY
15th St. & Pennsylvania Ave., N.W. (20220).
　Established: Sept. 2, 1789.
　Secretary: Nicholas F. Brady
　Deputy Secretary: M. Peter McPherson
　Treasurer of the U.S.: Catalina Vasquez Villalpando
　Comptroller of the Currency: Robert L. Clarke.
DEPARTMENT OF DEFENSE
The Pentagon (20301).
　Established: July 26, 1947, as National Department Establishment; name changed to Department of Defense on Aug. 10, 1949. Subordinate to Secretary of Defense are Secretaries of Army, Navy, Air Force.
　Secretary: Richard Cheney
　Deputy Secretary: Donald J. Atwood
　Secretary of Army: Richard L. Armitage
　Secretary of Navy: H. Lawrence Garrett III
　Secretary of Air Force: Donald B. Rice
　Commandant of Marine Corps: Gen. Alfred M. Gray.
　Joint Chiefs of Staff: Gen. Colin L. Powell, Chairman; Adm. Frank B. Kelso II, Navy; Gen. John M. Loh (acting), Air Force; Gen. Carl E. Vuono, Army; Gen. Alfred M. Gray, Marine Corps.
DEPARTMENT OF JUSTICE
Constitution Ave. between 9th & 10th Sts., N.W. (20530).
　Established: Office of Attorney General was created Sept. 24, 1789. Although he was one of original Cabinet members, he was not executive department head until June 22, 1870, when Department of Justice was established.
　Attorney General: Richard L. Thornburgh
　Deputy Attorney General: William P. Barr
　Solicitor General: Kenneth W. Starr
　Director of FBI: William Steele Sessions.
DEPARTMENT OF THE INTERIOR
C St. between 18th & 19th Sts., N.W. (20240).
　Established: March 3, 1849.
　Secretary: Manuel Lujan, Jr.
　Under Secretary: Frank A. Bracken
DEPARTMENT OF AGRICULTURE
Independence Ave. between 12th & 14th Sts., S.W. (20250).
　Established: May 15, 1862. Administered by Commissioner of Agriculture until 1889, when it was made executive department.
　Secretary: Clayton Yeutter
　Deputy Secretary: Jack C. Parnell
DEPARTMENT OF COMMERCE
14th St. between Constitution Ave. & E St., N.W. (20230).
　Established: Department of Commerce and Labor was created Feb. 14, 1903. On March 4, 1913, all labor activities were transferred out of Department of Commerce and Labor and it was renamed Department of Commerce.
　Secretary: Robert A. Mosbacher
　Deputy Secretary: Thomas J. Murrin
DEPARTMENT OF LABOR
200 Constitution Ave., N.W. (20210).
　Established: Bureau of Labor was created in 1884 under Department of the Interior; later became independent department without executive rank. Returned to bureau status in Department of Commerce and Labor, but on March 4, 1913, became independent executive department under its present name.
　Secretary: Elizabeth H. Dole
　Deputy Secretary: Roderick DeArment
DEPARTMENT OF HEALTH AND HUMAN SERVICES[1]
200 Independence Ave., S.W. (20201).
　Established: April 11, 1953, replacing Federal Security Agency created in 1939.
　Secretary: Louis W. Sullivan

Surgeon General: Dr. Antonia Novello
1. Originally Department of Health, Education and Welfare. Name changed in May 1980 when Department of Education was activated.

DEPARTMENT OF HOUSING AND URBAN DEVELOPMENT
451 7th St., S.W. (20410).
Established: 1965, replacing Housing and Home Finance Agency created in 1947.
Secretary: Jack Kemp
Under Secretary: Alfred A. DelliBovi

DEPARTMENT OF TRANSPORTATION
400 7th St., S.W. (20590).
Established: Oct. 15, 1966, as result of Department of Transportation Act, which became effective April 1, 1967.
Secretary: Samuel K. Skinner
Deputy Secretary: Elaine L. Chao

DEPARTMENT OF ENERGY
1000 Independence Ave., S.W. (20585).
Established: Aug. 1977.
Secretary: James D. Watkins
Deputy Secretary: W. Henson Moore

DEPARTMENT OF EDUCATION
400 Maryland Avenue, S.W. (20202).
Established: Oct. 17, 1979.
Secretary: Lauro F. Cavazos
Under Secretary: Ted Sanders

DEPARTMENT OF VETERANS' AFFAIRS
810 Vermont Avenue, N.W. (20420)
Established: March 15, 1989, replacing Veterans Administration created in 1930.
Secretary: Edward J. Derwinski
Deputy Secretary: Anthony J. Principi

Major Independent Agencies

ACTION
806 Connecticut Ave., N.W. (20525).
Established: July 1, 1971.
Director: Jane Kenny

CONSUMER PRODUCT SAFETY COMMISSION
5401 Westbard Ave., Bethesda, Md. (20207).
Members: 5.
Established: Oct. 27, 1972.
Chairman: Jacqueline Jones-Smith

ENVIRONMENTAL PROTECTION AGENCY (EPA)
401 M St., S.W. (20460).
Established: Dec. 2, 1970.
Administrator: William K. Reilly

EQUAL EMPLOYMENT OPPORTUNITY COMMISSION (EEOC)
1801 L St., N.W. (20507).
Members: 5.
Established: July 2, 1965.
Chairman: Evan J. Kemp, Jr.

FARM CREDIT ADMINISTRATION (FCA)
1501 Farm Credit Dr., McLean, Va. (22102).
Members: 13.
Established: July 17, 1916.
Chairman of Federal Farm Credit Board: Harold B. Steele

FEDERAL COMMUNICATIONS COMMISSION (FCC)
1919 M St., N.W. (20554).
Members: 7.
Established: 1934.
Chairman: Alfred C. Silkes

FEDERAL DEPOSIT INSURANCE CORPORATION (FDIC)
550 17th St., N.W. (20429).
Members: 3.

Established: June 16, 1933.
Chairman: L. William Seidman.

FEDERAL ELECTION COMMISSION (FEC)
999 E St., N.W. (20463).
Members: 6.
Established: 1974.
Chairman: Lee Ann Elliott

FEDERAL MARITIME COMMISSION
1100 L St., N.W. (20573).
Members: 5.
Established: Aug. 12, 1961.
Chairman: James J. Carey (acting)

FEDERAL MEDIATION AND CONCILIATION SERVICE (FMCS)
2100 K St., N.W. (20427).
Established: 1947.
Director: Bernard E. DeLury

FEDERAL RESERVE SYSTEM (FRS), BOARD OF GOVERNORS OF
20th St. & Constitution Ave., N.W. (20551).
Members: 7.
Established: Dec. 23, 1913.
Chairman: Alan Greenspan.

FEDERAL TRADE COMMISSION (FTC)
Pennsylvania Ave. at 6th St., N.W. (20580).
Members: 5.
Established: Sept. 26, 1914.
Chairman: Daniel Oliver

GENERAL SERVICES ADMINISTRATION (GSA)
18th and F Sts., N.W. (20405).
Established: July 1, 1949.
Administrator: Richard G. Austin

INTERSTATE COMMERCE COMMISSION (ICC)
12th St. & Constitution Ave., N.W. (20423).
Members: 7.
Established: Feb. 4, 1887.
Chairman: Edward Philbin

NATIONAL AERONAUTICS AND SPACE ADMINISTRATION (NASA)
600 Independence Ave. (20546).
Established: 1958.
Administrator: Rear Adm. Richard H. Truly

NATIONAL FOUNDATION ON THE ARTS AND THE HUMANITIES
1100 Pennsylvania Ave., N.W., (20506).
Established: 1965.
Chairmen: National Endowment for the Arts, John E. Frohnmayer; National Endowment for the Humanities, Lynne V. Cheney

NATIONAL LABOR RELATIONS BOARD (NLRB)
1717 Pennsylvania Ave., N.W. (20570).
Members: 5.
Established: July 5, 1935.
Chairman: James M. Stephens

NATIONAL MEDIATION BOARD
1425 K St., N.W. (20572).
Members: 3
Established: June 21, 1934.
Chairman: Joshua M. Javits

NATIONAL SCIENCE FOUNDATION (NSF)
1800 G St., N.W. (20550).
Established: 1950.
Director: Mary L. Good

NATIONAL TRANSPORTATION SAFETY BOARD
800 Independence Ave., S.W. (20594).
Members: 5
Established: April 1, 1975.
Chairman: James L. Kolstad (acting)

NUCLEAR REGULATORY COMMISSION (NRC)
Washington, DC (20555).
Members: 5.
Established: Jan. 19, 1975.
Chairman: Kenneth Carr

OFFICE OF PERSONNEL MANAGEMENT (OPM)
1900 E St., N.W. (20415).
Members: 3
Established: Jan. 1, 1979.
Director: Constance B. Newman

SECURITIES AND EXCHANGE COMMISSION (SEC)
450 5th St., N.W. (20549).
Members: 5.
Established: July 2, 1934
Chairman: Richard C. Breeden

SELECTIVE SERVICE SYSTEM (SSS)
National Headquarters (20435).
Established: Sept. 16, 1940.
Director: Gen. Samuel K. Lessey, Jr.

SMALL BUSINESS ADMINISTRATION (SBA)
1441 L St., N.W. (20416).
Established: July 30, 1953.
Administrator: Susan S. Engeleiter

TENNESSEE VALLEY AUTHORITY (TVA)
400 West Summit Hill Drive, Knoxville, Tenn. (37902).
Washington office: Capitol Hill Office Bldg., 412 First St., S.E. (20444).
Members of Board of Directors: 3.
Established: May 18, 1933.
Chairman: Marvin Runyon

U.S. AGENCY FOR INTERNATIONAL DEVELOPMENT
320 21st St., N.W. (20523).
Established: Oct. 1, 1979.
Administrator: Ronald Roskins

U.S. ARMS CONTROL AND DISARMAMENT AGENCY
320 21st St., N.W., (20451).
Established: Sept. 26, 1961.
Director: Ronald F. Lehman II

U.S. COMMISSION ON CIVIL RIGHTS
1121 Vermont Avenue, N.W. (20425).
Members: 8.
Established: 1957.
Chairman: Arthur A. Fletcher

U.S. INFORMATION AGENCY
301 Fourth St., S.W. (20547).
Established: April 1, 1978.
Director: Bruce Gelb

U.S. INTERNATIONAL TRADE COMMISSION
701 E St., N.W. (20436).
Members: 6.
Established: Sept. 8, 1916.
Chairman: Anne E. Brunsdale

U.S. POSTAL SERVICE
475 L'Enfant Plaza West, S.W. (20260).
Postmaster General: Anthony M. Frank
Deputy Postmaster General: Michael S. Coughlin.
Established: Office of Postmaster General and temporary post office system created in 1789. Act of Feb. 20, 1792, made detailed provisions for Post Office Department. In 1970 became independent agency headed by 11-member board of governors.

Other Independent Agencies

Administrative Conference of the United States—2120 L St., N.W. (20037).

American Battle Monuments Commission—5127 Pulaski Bldg. 20 Massachusetts Ave. (20314).

Appalachian Regional Commission—1666 Connecticut Ave., N.W. (20235).

Board for International Broadcasting—Suite 400, 1201 Connecticut Ave., N.W. (20036).

Commission of Fine Arts—708 Jackson Place, N.W. (20006).

Commodity Futures Trading Commission—2033 K St., N.W. (20581).

Export-Import Bank of the United States—811 Vermont Ave., N.W. (20571).

Federal Emergency Management Agency—500 C St., S.W. (20472).

Federal Home Loan Bank Board—1700 G St., N.W. (20552).

Federal Labor Relations Authority—500 C St., S.W. (20424).

Inter-American Foundation—1515 Wilson Blvd., Arlington, Va. (22209).

Merit Systems Protection Board—1120 Vermont Ave., N.W. (20419).

National Commission on Libraries and Information Science—7th & D Sts., S.W. (20024).

National Credit Union Administration—1776 G St., N.W. (20456).

Occupational Safety and Health Review Commission—1825 K St., N.W. (20006).

Panama Canal Commission—2000 L St., N.W. (20036).

Peace Corps—806 Connecticut Ave., N.W. (20526).

Pension Benefit Guaranty Corporation—2020 K St., N.W. (20006).

Postal Rate Commission—1333 H St., N.W. (20268).

President's Committee on Employment of the Handicapped—1111 20th St., N.W. (20036).

President's Council on Physical Fitness and Sports—450 5th St., S.W. (20001).

Railroad Retirement Board (RRB)—844 Rush St., Chicago, Ill. (60611); Washington Liaison Office: Suite 558, 2000 L St. (20036).

U.S. Parole Commission—5550 Friendship Blvd., Chevy Chase, Md. (20815).

Legislative Department

Architect of the Capitol—U.S. Capitol Building (20515)

General Accounting Office (GAO)—441 G St., N.W. (20548)

Government Printing Office (GPO)—North Capitol & H Sts., N.W. (20401)

Library of Congress—10 First St. S.E. (20540)

Office of Technology Assessment—600 Pennsylvania Ave., S.E. (20510)

United States Botanic Garden—Office of Director, 245 First St., S.W. (20024)

Quasi-Official Agencies

American National Red Cross—430 17th St., N.W. (20006).

Legal Services Corporation—400 Virginia Ave. S.W. (20024).

National Academy of Sciences, National Academy of Engineering, National Research Council, Institute of Medicine—2101 Constitution Ave., N.W. (20418).

National Railroad Passenger Corporation (Amtrak)—400 N. Capitol St., N.W. (20001).

Smithsonian Institution—1000 Jefferson Dr., S.W. (20560).

U.S. Railway Association—955 L'Enfant Plaza North, S.W. (20595).

Biographies of the Presidents

GEORGE WASHINGTON was born on Feb. 22, 1732 (Feb. 11, 1731/2, old style) in Westmoreland County, Va. While in his teens, he trained as a surveyor, and at the age of 20 he was appointed adjutant in the Virginia militia. For the next three years, he fought in the wars against the French and Indians, serving as Gen. Edward Braddock's aide in the disastrous campaign against Fort Duquesne. In 1759, he resigned from the militia, married Martha Dandridge Custis, a widow, and settled down as a gentleman farmer at Mount Vernon, Va.

As a militiaman, Washington had been exposed to the arrogance of the British officers, and his experience as a planter with British commercial restrictions increased his anti-British sentiment. He opposed the Stamp Act of 1765 and after 1770 became increasingly prominent in organizing resistance. A delegate to the Continental Congress, Washington was selected as commander in chief of the Continental Army and took command at Cambridge, Mass., on July 3, 1775.

Inadequately supported and sometimes covertly sabotaged by the Congress, in charge of troops who were inexperienced, badly equipped, and impatient of discipline, Washington conducted the war on the policy of avoiding major engagements with the British and wearing them down by harrassing tactics. His able generalship, along with the French alliance and the growing weariness within Britain, brought the war to a conclusion with the surrender of Cornwallis at Yorktown, Va., on Oct. 19, 1781.

The chaotic years under the Articles of Confederation led Washington to return to public life in the hope of promoting the formation of a strong central government. He presided over the Constitutional Convention and yielded to the universal demand that he serve as first President. He was inaugurated on April 30, 1789, in New York, the first national capital. In office, he sought to unite the nation and establish the authority of the new government at home and abroad. Greatly distressed by the emergence of the Hamilton-Jefferson rivalry, Washington worked to maintain neutrality but actually sympathized more with Hamilton. Following his unanimous re-election in 1792, his second term was dominated by the Federalists. His Farewell Address on Sept. 17, 1796 (published but never delivered) rebuked party spirit and warned against "permanent alliances" with foreign powers.

He died at Mount Vernon on Dec. 14, 1799.

JOHN ADAMS was born on Oct. 30 (Oct. 19, old style), 1735, at Braintree (now Quincy), Mass. A Harvard graduate, he considered teaching and the ministry but finally turned to law and was admitted to the bar in 1758. Six years later, he married Abigail Smith. He opposed the Stamp Act, served as lawyer for patriots indicted by the British, and by the time of the Continental Congresses, was in the vanguard of the movement for independence. In 1778, he went to France as commissioner. Subsequently he helped negotiate the peace treaty with Britain, and in 1785 became envoy to London. Resigning in 1788, he was elected Vice President under Washington and was re-elected in 1792.

Though a Federalist, Adams did not get along with Hamilton, who sought to prevent his election to the presidency in 1796 and thereafter intrigued against his administration. In 1798, Adam's independent policy averted a war with France but completed the break with Hamilton and the right-wing Federalists; at the same time, the enactment of the Alien and Sedition Acts, directed against foreigners and against critics of the government, exasperated the Jeffersonian opposition. The split between Adams and Hamilton resulted in Jefferson's becoming the next President. Adams retired to his home in Quincy. He and Jefferson died on the same day, July 4, 1826, the 50th anniversary of the signing of the Declaration of Independence.

His *Defence of the Constitutions of Government of the United States* (1787) contains original and striking, if conservative, political ideas.

THOMAS JEFFERSON was born on April 13 (April 2, old style), 1743, at Shadwell in Goochland (now Albemarle) County, Va. A William and Mary graduate, he studied law, but from the start showed an interest in science and philosophy. His literary skill and political clarity brought him to the forefront of the revolutionary movement in Virginia. As delegate to the Continental Congress, he drafted the Declaration of Independence. In 1776, he entered the Virginia House of Delegates and initiated a comprehensive reform program for the abolition of feudal survivals in land tenure and the separation of church and state.

In 1779, he became governor, but constitutional limitations on his power, combined with his own lack of executive energy, caused an unsatisfactory administration, culminating in Jefferson's virtual abdication when the British invaded Virginia in 1781. He retired to his beautiful home at Monticello, Va., to his family. His wife, Martha Wayles Skelton, whom he married in 1772, died in 1782.

Jefferson's *Notes on Virginia* (1784–85) illustrate his many-faceted interests, his limitless intellectual curiosity, his deep faith in agrarian democracy. Sent to Congress in 1783, he helped lay down the decimal system and drafted basic reports on the organization of the western lands. In 1785 he was appointed minister to France, where the Anglo-Saxon liberalism he had drawn from John Locke, the British philosopher, was stimulated by contact with the thought that would soon ferment in the French Revolution. In 1789, Washington appointed him Secretary of State. While favoring the Constitution and a strengthened central government, Jefferson came to believe that Hamilton contemplated the establishment of a monarchy. Growing differences resulted in Jefferson's resignation on Dec. 31, 1793.

Elected vice president in 1796, Jefferson continued to serve as spiritual leader of the opposition to Federalism, particularly to the repressive Alien and Sedition Acts. He was elected President in 1801 by the House of Representatives as a result of Hamilton's decision to throw the Federalist votes to him rather than to Aaron Burr, who had tied him in electoral votes. He was the first President to be inaugurated in Washington, which he had helped to design.

The purchase of Louisiana from France in 1803, though in violation of Jefferson's earlier constitutional scruples, was the most notable act of his administration. Re-elected in 1804, with the Federalist Charles C. Pinckney opposing him, Jefferson tried desperately to keep the United States out of the Napoleonic Wars in Europe, employing to this end the unpopular embargo policy.

After his retirement to Monticello in 1809, he developed his interest in education, founding the University of Virginia and watching its development with never-flagging interest. He died at Monticello on July 4, 1826. Jefferson had an enormous variety of interests and skills, ranging from education and science to architecture and music.

JAMES MADISON was born in Port Conway, Va., on March 16, 1751 (March 5, 1750/1, old style). A Princeton graduate, he joined the struggle for independence on his return to Virginia in 1771. In the 1770s and 1780s he was active in state politics, where he championed the Jefferson reform program, and in the Continental Congress. Madison was influential in the Constitutional Convention as leader of the group favoring a strong central government and as recorder of the debates; and he subsequently wrote, in collaboration with Alexander Hamilton and John Jay, the *Federalist* papers to aid the campaign for the adoption of the Constitution.

Serving in the new Congress, Madison soon emerged as the leader in the House of the men who opposed Hamilton's financial program and his pro-British leanings in foreign policy. Retiring from Congress in 1797, he continued to be active in Virginia and drafted the Virginia Resolution protesting the Alien and Sedition Acts. His intimacy with Jefferson made him the natural choice for Secretary of State in 1801.

In 1809, Madison succeeded Jefferson as President, defeating Charles C. Pinckney. His attractive wife, Dolley Payne Todd, whom he married in 1794, brought a new social sparkle to the executive mansion. In the meantime, increasing tension with Britain culminated in the War of 1812—a war for which the United States was unprepared and for which Madison lacked the executive talent to clear out incompetence and mobilize the nation's energies. Madison was re-elected in 1812, running against the Federalist De Witt Clinton. In 1814, the British actually captured Washington and forced Madison to flee to Virginia.

Madison's domestic program capitulated to the Hamiltonian policies that he had resisted 20 years before and he now signed bills to establish a United States Bank and a higher tariff.

After his presidency, he remained in retirement in Virginia until his death on June 28, 1836.

JAMES MONROE was born on April 28, 1758, in Westmoreland County, Va. A William and Mary graduate, he served in the army during the first years of the Revolution and was wounded at Trenton. He then entered Virginia politics and later national politics under the sponsorship of Jefferson. In 1786, he married Elizabeth (Eliza) Kortright.

Fearing centralization, Monroe opposed the adoption of the Constitution and, as senator from Virginia, was highly critical of the Hamiltonian program. In 1794, he was appointed minister to France, where his ardent sympathies with the Revolution exceeded the wishes of the State Department. His troubled diplomatic career ended with his recall in 1796. From 1799 to 1802, he was governor of Virginia. In 1803, Jefferson sent him to France to help negotiate the Louisiana Purchase and for the next few years he was active in various negotiations on the Continent.

In 1808, Monroe flirted with the radical wing of the Republican Party, which opposed Madison's candidacy; but the presidential boom came to naught and, after a brief term as governor of Virginia in 1811, Monroe accepted Madison's offer to become Secretary of State. During the War of 1812, he vainly sought a field command and instead served as Secretary of War from September 1814 to March 1815.

Elected President in 1816 over the Federalist Rufus King, and re-elected without opposition in 1820, Monroe, the last of the Virginia dynasty, pursued the course of systematic tranquilization that won for his administrations the name "the era of good feeling." He continued Madison's surrender to the Hamiltonian domestic program, signed the Missouri Compromise, acquired Florida, and with the able assistance of his Secretary of State, John Quincy Adams, promulgated the Monroe Doctrine in 1823, declaring against foreign colonization or intervention in the Americas. He died in New York City on July 4, 1831, the third president to die on the anniversary of Independence.

JOHN QUINCY ADAMS was born on July 11, 1767, at Braintree (now Quincy), Mass., the son of John Adams, the second President. He spent his early years in Europe with his father, graduated from Harvard, and entered law practice. His anti-Jeffersonian newspaper articles won him political attention. In 1794, he became minister to the Netherlands, the first of several diplomatic posts that occupied him until his return to Boston in 1801. In 1797, he married Louisa Catherine Johnson.

In 1803, Adams was elected to the Senate, nominally as a Federalist, but his repeated displays of independence on such issues as the Louisiana Purchase and the embargo caused his party to demand his resignation and ostracize him socially. In 1809, Madison rewarded him for his support of Jefferson by appointing him minister to St. Petersburg. He helped negotiate the Treaty of Ghent in 1814, and in 1815 became minister to London. In 1817 Monroe appointed him Secretary of State where he served with great distinction, gaining Florida from Spain without hostilities and playing an equal part with Monroe in formulating the Monroe Doctrine.

When no presidential candidate received a majority of electoral votes in 1824, Adams, with the support of Henry Clay, was elected by the House in 1825 over Andrew Jackson, who had the original plurality. Adams had ambitious plans of government activity to foster internal improvements and promote the arts and sciences, but congressional obstructionism, combined with his own unwillingness or inability to play the role of a politician, resulted in little being accomplished. After being defeated for re-elected by Jackson in 1828, he successfully ran for the House of Representatives in 1830. There though nominally a Whig, he pursued as ever an independent course. He led the fight to force Congress to receive antislavery petitions and fathered the Smithsonian Institution.

Stricken on the floor of the House, he died on Feb. 23, 1848. His long and detailed *Diary* gives a unique picture of the personalities and politics of the times.

ANDREW JACKSON was born on March 15, 1767, in what is now generally agreed to be Waxhaw, S.C. After a turbulent boyhood as an orphan and a British prisoner, he moved west to Tennessee, where he soon qualified for law practice but found time for such frontier pleasures as horse racing, cockfighting, and dueling. His marriage to Rachel Donelson Robards in 1791 was complicated by subsequent legal uncertainties about the status of her divorce. During the 1790s, Jackson served in the Tennessee Constitutional Convention, the United States House of Representatives and Senate, and on the Tennessee Supreme Court.

After some years as a country gentleman, living at the Hermitage near Nashville, Jackson in 1812 was given command of Tennessee troops sent against the Creeks. He defeated the Indians at Horseshoe Bend in 1814; subsequently he became a major general and won the Battle of New Orleans over veteran British troops, though after the treaty of peace had been signed at Ghent. In 1818, Jackson invaded Florida, captured Pensacola, and hanged two Englishmen named Arbuthnot and Ambrister, creating an international incident. A presidential boom began for him in 1821, and to foster it, he returned to the Senate (1823–25). Though he won a plurality of electoral votes in 1824, he lost in the House when Clay threw his strength to Adams. Four years later, he easily defeated Adams.

As President, Jackson greatly expanded the power and prestige of the presidential office and carried through an unprecedented program of domestic reform, vetoing the bill to extend the United States Bank, moving toward a hard-money currency policy, and checking the program of federal internal improvements. He also vindicated federal authority against South Carolina with its doctrine of nullification and against France on the question of debts. The support given his policies by the workingmen of the East as well as by the farmers of the East, West, and South resulted in his triumphant re-election in 1832 over Clay.

After watching the inauguration of his handpicked successor, Martin Van Buren, Jackson retired to the Hermitage, where he maintained a lively interest in national affairs until his death on June 8, 1845.

MARTIN VAN BUREN was born on Dec. 5, 1782, at Kinderhook, N.Y. After graduating from the village school, he became a law clerk, entered practice in 1803, and soon became active in state politics as state senator and attorney general. In 1820, he was elected to the United States Senate. He threw the support of his efficient political organization, known as the Albany Regency, to William H. Crawford in 1824 and to Jackson in 1828. After leading the opposition to Adams's administration in the Senate, he served briefly as governor of New York (1828–29) and resigned to become Jackson's Secretary of State. He was soon on close personal terms with Jackson and played an important part in the Jacksonian program.

In 1832, Van Buren became vice president; in 1836, President. The Panic of 1837 overshadowed his term. He attributed it to the overexpansion of the credit and favored the establishment of an independent treasury as repository for the federal funds. In 1840, he established a 10-hour day on public works. Defeated by Harrison in 1840, he was the leading contender for the Democratic nomination in 1844 until he publicly opposed immediate annexation of Texas, and was subsequently beaten by the Southern delegations at the Baltimore convention. This incident increased his growing misgivings about the slave power.

After working behind the scenes among the antislavery Democrats, Van Buren joined in the movement that led to the Free-Soil Party and became its candidate for President in 1848. He subsequently returned to the Democratic Party while

continuing to object to its pro-Southern policy. He died in Kinderhook on July 24, 1862. His *Autobiography* throws valuable sidelights on the political history of the times.

His wife, Hannah Hoes, whom he married in 1807, died in 1819.

WILLIAM HENRY HARRISON was born in Charles City County, Va., on Feb. 9, 1773. Joining the army in 1791, he was active in Indian fighting in the Northwest, became secretary of the Northwest Territory in 1798 and governor of Indiana in 1800. He married Anna Symmes in 1795. Growing discontent over white encroachments on Indian lands led to the formation of an Indian alliance under Tecumseh to resist further aggressions. In 1811, Harrison won a nominal victory over the Indians at Tippecanoe and in 1813 a more decisive one at the Battle of the Thames, where Tecumseh was killed.

After resigning from the army in 1814, Harrison had an obscure career in politics and diplomacy, ending up 20 years later as a county recorder in Ohio. Nominated for President in 1835 as a military hero whom the conservative politicians hoped to be able to control, he ran surprisingly well against Van Buren in 1836. Four years later, he defeated Van Buren but caught penumonia and died in Washington on April 4, 1841, a month after his inauguration. Harrison was the first president to die in office.

JOHN TYLER was born in Charles City County, Va., on March 29, 1790. A William and Mary graduate, he entered law practice and politics, serving in the House of Representatives (1817–21), as governor of Virginia (1825–27), and as senator (1827–36). A strict constructionist, he supported Crawford in 1824 and Jackson in 1828, but broke with Jackson over his United States Bank policy and became a member of the Southern state-rights group that cooperated with the Whigs. In 1836, he resigned from the Senate rather than follow instructions from the Virginia legislature to vote for a resolution expunging censure of Jackson from the Senate record.

Elected vice president on the Whig ticket in 1840, Tyler succeeded to the presidency on Harrison's death. His strict-constructionist views soon caused a split with the Henry Clay wing of the Whig party and a stalemate on domestic questions. Tyler's more considerable achievements were his support of the Webster-Ashbûrton Treaty with Britain and his success in bringing about the annexation of Texas.

After his presidency he lived in retirement in Virginia until the outbreak of the Civil War, when he emerged briefly as chairman of a peace convention and then as delegate to the provisional Congress of the Confederacy. He died on Jan. 18, 1862. He married Letitia Christian in 1813 and, two years after her death in 1842, Julia Gardiner.

JAMES KNOX POLK was born in Mecklenburg County, N.C., on Nov. 2, 1795. A graduate of the University of North Carolina, he moved west to Tennessee, was admitted to the bar, and soon became prominent in state politics. In 1825, he was elected to the House of Representatives, where he opposed Adams and, after 1829, became Jackson's floor leader in the fight against the Bank. In 1835, he became Speaker of the House. Four years later, he was elected governor of Tennessee, but was beaten in tries for re-election in 1841 and 1843.

The supporters of Van Buren for the Democratic

nomination in 1844 counted on Polk as his running mate; but, when Van Buren's stand on Texas alienated Southern support, the convention swung to Polk on the ninth ballot. He was elected over Henry Clay, the Whig candidate. Rapidly disillusioning those who thought that he would not run his own administration, Polk proceeded steadily and precisely to achieve four major objectives—the acquisition of California, the settlement of the Oregon question, the reduction of the tariff, and the establishment of the independent treasury. He also enlarged the Monroe Doctrine to exclude all non-American intervention in American affairs, whether forcible or not, and he forced Mexico into a war that he waged to a successful conclusion.

His wife, Sarah Childress, whom he married in 1824, was a woman of charm and ability. Polk died in Nashville, Tenn., on June 15, 1849.

ZACHARY TAYLOR was born at Montebello, Orange County, Va., on Nov. 24, 1784. Embarking on a military career in 1808, Taylor fought in the War of 1812, the Black Hawk War, and the Seminole War, meanwhile holding garrison jobs on the frontier or desk jobs in Washington. A brigadier general as a result of his victory over the Seminoles at Lake Okeechobee (1837), Taylor held a succession of Southwestern commands and in 1846 established a base on the Rio Grande, where his forces engaged in hostilities that precipitated the war with Mexico. He captured Monterrey in September 1846 and, disregarding Polk's orders to stay on the defensive, defeated Santa Anna at Buena Vista in February 1847, ending the war in the northern provinces.

Though Taylor had never cast a vote for president, his party affiliations were Whiggish and his availability was increased by his difficulties with Polk. He was elected president over the Democrat Lewis Cass. During the revival of the slavery controversy, which was to result in the Compromise of 1850, Taylor began to take an increasingly firm stand against appeasing the South; but he died in Washington on July 9, 1850, during the fight over the Compromise. He married Margaret Mackall Smith in 1810. His bluff and simple soldierly qualities won him the name Old Rough and Ready.

MILLARD FILLMORE was born at Locke, Cayuga County, N.Y., on Jan. 7, 1800. A lawyer, he entered politics with the Anti-Masonic Party under the sponsorship of Thurlow Weed, editor and party boss, and subsequently followed Weed into the Whig Party. He served in the House of Representatives (1833–35 and 1837–43) and played a leading role in writing the tariff of 1842. Defeated for governor of New York in 1844, he became State comptroller in 1848, was put on the Whig ticket with Taylor as a concession to the Clay wing of the party, and became president upon Taylor's death in 1850.

As president, Fillmore broke with Weed and William H. Seward and associated himself with the pro-Southern Whigs, supporting the Compromise of 1850. Defeated for the Whig nomination in 1852, he ran for president in 1856 as candidate of the American, or Know-Nothing Party, which sought to unite the country against foreigners in the alleged hope of diverting it from the explosive slavery issue. Fillmore opposed Lincoln during the Civil War. He died in Buffalo on March 8, 1874.

He was married in 1826 to Abigail Powers, who died in 1853, and in 1858 to Caroline Carmichael McIntosh.

FRANKLIN PIERCE was born at Hillsboro, N.H., on Nov. 23, 1804. A Bowdoin graduate, lawyer, and Jacksonian Democrat, he won rapid political advancement in the party, in part because of the prestige of his father, Gov. Benjamin Pierce. By 1831 he was Speaker of the New Hampshire House of Representatives; from 1833 to 1837, he served in the federal House and from 1837 to 1842 in the Senate. His wife, Jane Means Appleton, whom he married in 1834, disliked Washington and the somewhat dissipated life led by Pierce; in 1842 Pierce resigned from the Senate and began a successful law practice in Concord, N.H. During the Mexican War, he was a brigadier general.

Thereafter Pierce continued to oppose antislavery tendencies within the Democratic Party. As a result, he was the Southern choice to break the deadlock at the Democratic convention of 1852 and was nominated on the 49th ballot. In the election, Pierce overwhelmed Gen. Winfield Scott, the Whig candidate.

As president, Pierce followed a course of appeasing the South at home and of playing with schemes of territorial expansion abroad. The failure of his foreign and domestic policies prevented his renomination; and he died in Concord on Oct. 8, 1869, in relative obscurity.

JAMES BUCHANAN was born near Mercersburg, Pa., on April 23, 1791. A Dickinson graduate and a lawyer, he entered Pennsylvania politics as a Federalist. With the disappearance of the Federalist Party, he became a Jacksonian Democrat. He served with ability in the House (1821–31), as minister to St. Petersburg (1832–33), and in the Senate (1834–45), and in 1845 became Polk's Secretary of State. In 1853, Pierce appointed Buchanan minister to Britain, where he participated with other American diplomats in Europe in drafting the expansionist Ostend Manifesto.

He was elected president in 1856, defeating John C. Frémont, the Republican candidate, and former President Millard Fillmore of the American Party. The growing crisis over slavery presented Buchanan with problems he lacked the will to tackle. His appeasement of the South alienated the Stephen Douglas wing of the Democratic Party without reducing Southern militancy on slavery issues. While denying the right of secession, Buchanan also denied that the federal government could do anything about it. He supported the administration during the Civil War and died in Lancaster, Pa., on June 1, 1868.

The only president to remain a bachelor throughout his term, Buchanan used his charming niece, Harriet Lane, as White House hostess.

ABRAHAM LINCOLN was born in Hardin (now Larue) County, Ky., on Feb. 12, 1809. His family moved to Indiana and then to Illinois, and Lincoln gained what education he could along the way. While reading law, he worked in a store, managed a mill, surveyed, and split rails. In 1834, he went to the Illinois legislature as a Whig and became the party's floor leader. For the next 20 years he practiced law in Springfield, except for a single term (1847–49) in Congress, where he denounced the Mexican War. In 1855, he was a candidate for senator and the next year he joined the new Republican Party.

A leading but unsuccessful candidate for the vice-presidential nomination with Frémont, Lincoln gained national attention in 1858 when, as

Republican candidate for senator from Illinois, he engaged in a series of debates with Stephen A. Douglas, the Democratic candidate. He lost the election, but continued to prepare the way for the 1860 Republican convention and was rewarded with the presidential nomination on the third ballot. He won the election over three opponents.

From the start, Lincoln made clear that, unlike Buchanan, he believed the national government had the power to crush the rebellion. Not an abolitionist, he held the slavery issue subordinate to that of preserving the Union, but soon perceived that the war could not be brought to a successful conclusion without freeing the slaves. His administration was hampered by the incompetence of many Union generals, the inexperience of the troops, and the harassing political tactics both of the Republican Radicals, who favored a hard policy toward the South, and the Democratic Copperheads, who desired a negotiated peace. The Gettysburg Address of Nov. 19, 1863, marks the high point in the record of American eloquence. Lincoln's long search for a winning combination finally brought Generals Ulysses S. Grant and William T. Sherman on the top; and their series of victories in 1864 dispelled the mutterings from both Radicals and Peace Democrats that at one time seemed to threaten Lincoln's re-election. He was re-elected in 1864, defeating Gen. George B. McClellan, the Democratic candidate. His inaugural address urged leniency toward the South: "With malice toward none, with charity for all . . . let us strive on to finish the work we are in; to bind up the nation's wounds . . ." This policy aroused growing opposition on the part of the Republican Radicals, but before the matter could be put to the test, Lincoln was shot by the actor John Wilkes Booth at Ford's Theater, Washington, on April 14, 1865. He died the next morning.

Lincoln's marriage to Mary Todd in 1842 was often unhappy and turbulent, in part because of his wife's pronounced instability.

ANDREW JOHNSON was born at Raleigh, N.C., on Dec. 29, 1808. Self-educated, he became a tailor in Greeneville, Tenn., but soon went into politics, where he rose steadily. He served in the House of Representatives (1843–54), as governor of Tennessee (1853–57), and as a senator (1857–62). Politically he was a Jacksonian Democrat and his specialty was the fight for a more equitable land policy. Alone among the Southern Senators, he stood by the Union during the Civil War. In 1862, he became war governor of Tennessee and carried out a thankless and difficult job with great courage. Johnson became Lincoln's running mate in 1864 as a result of an attempt to give the ticket a nonpartisan and nonsectional character. Succeeding to the presidency on Lincoln's death, Johnson sought to carry out Lincoln's policy, but without his political skill. The result was a hopeless conflict with the Radical Republicans who dominated Congress, passed measures over Johnson's vetoes, and attempted to limit the power of the executive concerning appointments and removals. The conflict culminated with Johnson's impeachment for attempting to remove his disloyal Secretary of War in defiance of the Tenure of Office Act which required senatorial concurrence for such dismissals. The opposition failed by one vote to get the two thirds necessary for conviction.

After his presidency, Johnson maintained an interest in politics and in 1875 was again elected to the Senate. He died near Carter Station, Tenn., on July 31, 1875. He married Eliza McCardle in 1827.

ULYSSES SIMPSON GRANT was born (as Hiram Ulysses Grant) at Point Pleasant, Ohio, on April 27, 1822. He graduated from West Point in 1843 and served without particular distinction in the Mexican War. In 1848 he married Julia Dent. He resigned from the army in 1854, after warnings from his commanding officer about his drinking habits, and for the next six years held a wide variety of jobs in the Middle West. With the outbreak of the Civil War, he sought a command and soon, to his surprise, was made a brigadier general. His continuing successes in the western theaters, culminating in the capture of Vicksburg, Miss., in 1863, brought him national fame and soon the command of all the Union armies. Grant's dogged, implacable policy of concentrating on dividing and destroying the Confederate armies brought the war to an end in 1865. The next year, he was made full general.

In 1868, as Republican candidate for president, Grant was elected over the Democrat, Horatio Seymour. From the start, Grant showed his unfitness for the office. His Cabinet was weak, his domestic policy was confused, many of his intimate associates were corrupt. The notable achievement in foreign affairs was the settlement of controversies with Great Britain in the Treaty of London (1871), negotiated by his able Secretary of State, Hamilton Fish.

Running for re-election in 1872, he defeated Horace Greeley, the Democratic and Liberal Republican candidate. The Panic of 1873 graft scandals close to the presidency created difficulties for his second term.

After retiring from office, Grant toured Europe for two years and returned in time to accede to a third-term boom, but was beaten in the convention of 1880. Illness and bad business judgment darkened his last years, but he worked steadily at the *Personal Memoirs*, which were to be so successful when published after his death at Mount McGregor, near Saratoga, N.Y., on July 23, 1885.

RUTHERFORD BIRCHARD HAYES was born in Delaware, Ohio, on Oct. 4, 1822. A graduate of Kenyon College and the Harvard Law School, he practiced law in Lower Sandusky (now Fremont) and then in Cincinnati. In 1852 he married Lucy Webb. A Whig, he joined the Republican party in 1855. During the Civil War he rose to major general. He served in the House of Representatives from 1865 to 1867 and then confirmed a reputation for honesty and efficiency in two terms as Governor of Ohio (1868–72). His election to a third term in 1875 made him the logical candidate for those Republicans who wished to stop James G. Blaine in 1876, and he was nominated.

The result of the election was in doubt for some time and hinged upon disputed returns from South Carolina, Louisiana, Florida, and Oregon. Samuel J. Tilden, the Democrat, had the larger popular vote but was adjudged by the strictly partisan decisions of the Electoral Commission to have one fewer electoral vote, 185 to 184. The national acceptance of this result was due in part to the general understanding that Hayes would pursue a conciliatory policy toward the South. He withdrew the troops from the South, took a conservative position on financial and labor issues, and urged civil service reform.

Hayes served only one term by his own wish and

spent the rest of his life in various humanitarian endeavors. He died in Fremont on Jan. 17, 1893.

JAMES ABRAM GARFIELD, the last president to be born in a log cabin, was born in Cuyahoga County, Ohio, on Nov. 19, 1831. A Williams graduate, he taught school for a time and entered Republican politics in Ohio. In 1858, he married Lucretia Rudolph. During the Civil War, he had a promising career, rising to major general of volunteers; but he resigned in 1863, having been elected to the House of Representatives, where he served until 1880. His oratorical and parliamentary abilities soon made him the leading Republican in the House, though his record was marred by his unorthodox acceptance of a fee in the DeGolyer paving contract case and by suspicions of his complicity in the Crédit Mobilier scandal.

In 1880, Garfield was elected to the Senate, but instead became the presidential candidate on the 36th ballot as a result of a deadlock in the Republican convention. In the election, he defeated Gen. Winfield Scott Hancock, the Democratic candidate. Garfield's administration was barely under way when he was shot by Charles J. Guiteau, a disappointed office seeker, in Washington on July 2, 1881. He died in Elberton, N.J., on Sept. 19.

CHESTER ALAN ARTHUR was born at Fairfield, Vt., on Oct. 5, 1830. A graduate of Union College, he became a successful New York lawyer. In 1859, he married Ellen Herndon. During the Civil War, he held administrative jobs in the Republican state administration and in 1871 was appointed collector of the Port of New York by Grant. This post gave him control over considerable patronage. Though not personally corrupt, Arthur managed his power in the interests of the New York machine so openly that President Hayes in 1877 called for an investigation and the next year Arthur was suspended.

In 1880 Arthur was nominated for vice president in the hope of conciliating the followers of Grant and the powerful New York machine. As president upon Garfield's death, Arthur, stepping out of his familiar role as spoilsman, backed civil service reform, reorganized the Cabinet, and prosecuted political associates accused of post office graft. Losing machine support and failing to gain the reformers, he was not nominated for a full term in 1884. He died in New York City on Nov. 18, 1886.

STEPHEN GROVER CLEVELAND was born at Caldwell, N.J., on March 18, 1837. He was admitted to the bar in Buffalo, N.Y., in 1859 and lived there as a lawyer, with occasional incursions into Democratic politics, for more than 20 years. He did not participate in the Civil War. As mayor of Buffalo in 1881, he carried through a reform program so ably that the Democrats ran him successfully for governor in 1882. In 1884 he won the Democratic nomination for President. The campaign contrasted Cleveland's spotless public career with the uncertain record of James G. Blaine, the Republican candidate, and Cleveland received enough Mugwump (independent Republican) support to win.

As president, Cleveland pushed civil service reform, opposed the pension grab and attacked the high tariff rates. While in the White House, he married Frances Folsom in 1886. Renominated in 1888, Cleveland was defeated by Benjamin Harrison, polling more popular but fewer electoral votes. In 1892, he was elected over Harrison. When the Panic of 1893 burst upon the country, Cleveland's attempts to solve it by sound-money measures alienated the free-silver wing of the party, while his tariff policy alienated the protectionists. In 1894, he sent troops to break the Pullman strike. In foreign affairs, his firmness caused Great Britain to back down in the Venezuela border dispute.

In his last years Cleveland was an active and much-respected public figure. He died in Princeton, N.J., on June 24, 1908.

BENJAMIN HARRISON was born in North Bend, Ohio, on Aug. 20, 1833, the grandson of William Henry Harrison, the ninth president. A graduate of Miami University in Ohio, he took up the law in Indiana and became active in Republican politics. In 1853, he married Caroline Lavinia Scott. During the Civil War, he rose to brigadier general. A sound-money Republican, he was elected senator from Indiana in 1880. In 1888, he received the Republican nomination for President on the eighth ballot. Though behind on the popular vote, he won over Grover Cleveland in the electoral college by 233 to 168.

As President, Harrison failed to please either the bosses or the reform element in the party. In foreign affairs he backed Secretary of State Blaine, whose policy foreshadowed later American imperialism. Harrison was renominated in 1892 but lost to Cleveland. His wife died in the White House in 1892 and Harrison married her niece, Mary Scott (Lord) Dimmick, in 1896. After his presidency, he resumed law practice. He died in Indianapolis on March 13, 1901.

WILLIAM McKINLEY was born in Niles, Ohio, on Jan. 29, 1843. He taught school, then served in the Civil War, rising from the ranks to become a major. Subsequently he opened a law office in Canton, Ohio, and in 1871 married Ida Saxton. Elected to Congress in 1876, he served there until 1891, except for 1883–85. His faithful advocacy of business interests culminated in the passage of the highly protective McKinley Tariff of 1890. With the support of Mark Hanna, a shrewd Cleveland businessman interested in safeguarding tariff protection, McKinley became governor of Ohio in 1892 and Republican presidential candidate in 1896. The business community, alarmed by the progressivism of William Jennings Bryan, the Democratic candidate, spent considerable money to assure McKinley's victory.

The chief event of McKinley's administration was the war with Spain, which resulted in our acquisition of the Philippines and other islands. With imperialism an issue, McKinley defeated Bryan again in 1900. On Sept. 6, 1901, he was shot at Buffalo, N.Y., by Leon F. Czolgosz, an anarchist, and he died there eight days later.

THEODORE ROOSEVELT was born in New York City on Oct. 27, 1858. A Harvard graduate, he was early interested in ranching, in politics, and in writing picturesque historical narratives. He was a Republican member of the New York Assembly in 1882–84, an unsuccessful candidate for mayor of New York in 1886, a U.S. Civil Service Commissioner under Benjamin Harrison, Police Commissioner of New York City in 1895, and Assistant Secretary of the Navy under McKinley in 1897. He resigned in 1898 to help organize a volunteer regiment, the Rough Riders, and take a more direct part in the war with Spain. He was elected governor of New York in 1898 and vice president in 1900, in spite of lack of enthusiasm on the part of the bosses.

Assuming the presidency of the assassinated McKinley in 1901, Roosevelt embarked on a wide-ranging program of government reform and conservation of natural resources. He ordered antitrust suits against several large corporations, threatened to intervene in the anthracite coal strike of 1902, which prompted the operators to accept arbitration, and, in general, championed the rights of the "little man" and fought the "malefactors of great wealth." He was also responsible for such progressive legislation as the Elkins Act of 1901, which outlawed freight rebates by railroads; the bill establishing the Department of Commerce and Labor; the Hepburn Act, which gave the I.C.C. greater control over the railroads; the Meat Inspection Act; and the Pure Food and Drug Act.

In foreign affairs, Roosevelt pursued a strong policy, permitting the instigation of a revolt in Panama to dispose of Colombian objections to the Panama Canal and helping to maintain the balance of power in the East by bringing the Russo-Japanese War to an end, for which he won the Nobel Peace Prize, the first American to achieve a Nobel prize in any category. In 1904, he decisively defeated Alton B. Parker, his conservative Democratic opponent.

Roosevelt's increasing coldness toward his successor, William Howard Taft, led him to overlook his earlier disclaimer of third-term ambitions and to re-enter politics. Defeated by the machine in the Republican convention of 1912, he organized the Progressive Party (Bull Moose) and polled more votes than Taft, though the split brought about the election of Woodrow Wilson. From 1915 on, Roosevelt strongly favored intervention in the European war. He became deeply embittered at Wilson's refusal to allow him to raise a volunteer division. He died in Oyster Bay, N.Y., on Jan. 6, 1919. He was married twice: in 1880 to Alice Hathaway Lee, who died in 1884, and in 1886 to Edith Kermit Carow.

WILLIAM HOWARD TAFT was born in Cincinnati on Sept. 15, 1857. A Yale graduate, he entered Ohio Republican politics in the 1880s. In 1886 he married Helen Herron. From 1887 to 1890, he served on the Ohio Superior Court; 1890–92, as solicitor general of the United States; 1892–1900, on the federal circuit court. In 1900 McKinley appointed him president of the Philippine Commission and in 1901 governor general. Taft had great success in pacifying the Filipinos, solving the problem of the church lands, improving economic conditions, and establishing limited self-government. His period as Secretary of War (1904–08) further demonstrated his capacity as administrator and conciliator, and he was Roosevelt's hand-picked successor in 1908. In the election, he polled 321 electoral votes to 162 for William Jennings Bryan, who was running for the presidency for the third time.

Though he carried on many of Roosevelt's policies, Taft got into increasing trouble with the progressive wing of the party and displayed mounting irritability and indecision. After his defeat in 1912, he became professor of constitutional law at Yale. In 1921 he was appointed Chief Justice of the

United States. He died in Washington on March 8, 1930.

THOMAS WOODROW WILSON was born in Staunton, Va., on Dec. 28, 1856. A Princeton graduate, he turned from law practice to post-graduate work in political science at Johns Hopkins University, receiving his Ph.D. in 1886. He taught at Bryn Mawr, Wesleyan, and Princeton, and in 1902 was made president of Princeton. After an unsuccessful attempt to democratize the social life of the university, he welcomed an invitation in 1910 to be the Democratic gubernatorial candidate in New Jersey, and was elected. His success in fighting the machine and putting through a reform program attracted national attention.

In 1912, at the Democratic convention in Baltimore, Wilson won the nomination on the 46th ballot and went on to defeat Roosevelt and Taft in the election. Wilson proceeded under the standard of the New Freedom to enact a program of domestic reform, including the Federal Reserve Act, the Clayton Antitrust Act, the establishment of the Federal Trade Commission, and other measures designed to restore competition in the face of the great monopolies. In foreign affairs, while privately sympathetic with the Allies, he strove to maintain neutrality in the European war and warned both sides against encroachments on American interests.

Re-elected in 1916 as a peace candidate, he tried to mediate between the warring nations; but when the Germans resumed unrestricted submarine warfare in 1917, Wilson brought the United States into what he now believed was a war to make the world safe for democracy. He supplied the classic formulations of Allied war aims and the armistice of Nov. 11, 1918 was negotiated on the basis of Wilson's Fourteen Points. In 1919 he strove at Versailles to lay the foundations for enduring peace. He accepted the imperfections of the Versailles Treaty in the expectation that they could be remedied by action within the League of Nations. He probably could have secured ratification of the treaty by the Senate if he had adopted a more conciliatory attitude toward the mild reservationists; but his insistence on all or nothing eventually caused the diehard isolationists and diehard Wilsonites to unite in rejecting a compromise.

In September 1919 Wilson suffered a paralytic stroke that limited his activity. After leaving the presidency he lived on in retirement in Washington, dying on Feb. 3, 1924. He was married twice—in 1885 to Ellen Louise Axson, who died in 1914, and in 1915 to Edith Bolling Galt.

WARREN GAMALIEL HARDING was born in Morrow County, Ohio, on Nov. 2, 1865. After attending Ohio Central College, Harding became interested in journalism and in 1884 bought the *Marion* (Ohio) *Star*. In 1891 he married a wealthy widow, Florence Kling De Wolfe. As his paper prospered, he entered Republican politics, serving as state senator (1899–1903) and as lieutenant governor (1904–06). In 1910, he was defeated for governor, but in 1914 was elected to the Senate. His reputation as an orator made him the keynoter at the 1916 Republican convention.

When the 1920 convention was deadlocked between Leonard Wood and Frank O. Lowden, Harding became the dark-horse nominee on his solemn affirmation that there was no reason in his past that he should not be. Straddling the League question, Harding was easily elected over James M. Cox, his Democratic opponent. His Cabinet contained some able men, but also some manifestly unfit for public office. Harding's own intimates were mediocre when they were not corrupt. The impending disclosure of the Teapot Dome scandal in the Interior Department and illegal practices in the Justice Department and Veterans' Bureau, as well as political setbacks, profoundly worried him. On his return from Alaska in 1923, he died unexpectedly in San Francisco on Aug. 2.

JOHN CALVIN COOLIDGE was born in Plymouth, Vt., on July 4, 1872. An Amherst graduate, he went into law practice at Northampton, Mass., in 1897. He married Grace Anna Goodhue in 1905. He entered Republican state politics, becoming successively mayor of Northampton, state senator, lieutenant governor and, in 1919, governor. His use of the state militia to end the Boston police strike in 1919 won him a somewhat undeserved reputation for decisive action and brought him the Republican vice-presidential nomination in 1920. After Harding's death Coolidge handled the Washington scandals with care and finally managed to save the Republican Party from public blame for the widespread corruption.

In 1924, Coolidge was elected without difficulty, defeating the Democrat, John W. Davis, and Robert M. La Follette running on the Progressive ticket. His second term, like his first, was characterized by a general satisfaction with the existing economic order. He stated that he did not choose to run in 1928.

After his presidency, Coolidge lived quietly in Northampton, writing an unilluminating *Autobiography* and conducting a syndicated column. He died there on Jan. 5, 1933.

HERBERT CLARK HOOVER was born at West Branch, Iowa, on Aug. 10, 1874, the first president to be born west of the Mississippi. A Stanford graduate, he worked from 1895 to 1913 as a mining engineer and consultant throughout the world. In 1899, he married Lou Henry. During World War I, he served with distinction as chairman of the American Relief Committee in London, as chairman of the Commission for Relief in Belgium, and as U.S. Food Administrator. His political affiliations were still too indeterminate for him to be mentioned as a possibility for either the Republican or Democratic nomination in 1920, but after the election he served Harding and Coolidge as Secretary of Commerce.

In the election of 1928, Hoover overwhelmed Gov. Alfred E. Smith of New York, the Democratic candidate and the first Roman Catholic to run for the presidency. He soon faced the worst depression in the nation's history, but his attacks upon it were hampered by his devotion to the theory that the forces that brought the crisis would soon bring the revival and then by his belief that there were too many areas in which the federal government had no power to act. In a succession of vetoes, he struck down measures proposing a national employment system or national relief, he reduced income tax rates, and only at the end of his term did he yield to popular pressure and set up agencies such as the Reconstruction Finance Corporation to make emergency loans to assist business.

After his 1932 defeat, Hoover returned to private business. In 1946, President Truman charged him with various world food missions; and from 1947 to 1949 and 1953 to 1955, he was head of the Commission on Organization of the Executive Branch of the Government. He died in New York City on Oct. 20, 1964.

FRANKLIN DELANO ROOSEVELT was born in Hyde Park, N.Y., on Jan. 30, 1882. A Harvard graduate, he attended Columbia Law School and was admitted to the New York bar. In 1910, he was elected to the New York State Senate as a Democrat. Re-elected in 1912, he was appointed Assistant Secretary of the Navy by Woodrow Wilson the next year. In 1920, his radiant personality and his war service resulted in his nomination for vice president as James M. Cox's running mate. After his defeat, he returned to law practice in New York. In August 1921, Roosevelt was stricken with infantile paralysis while on vacation at Campobello, New Brunswick. After a long and gallant fight, he recovered partial use of his legs. In 1924 and 1928, he led the fight at the Democratic national conventions for the nomination of Gov. Alfred E. Smith of New York, and in 1928 Roosevelt was himself induced to run for governor of New York. He was elected, and was re-elected in 1930.

In 1932, Roosevelt received the Democratic nomination for president and immediately launched a campaign that brought new spirit to a weary and discouraged nation. He defeated Hoover by a wide margin. His first term was characterized by an unfolding of the New Deal program, with greater benefits for labor, the farmers, and the unemployed, and the progressive estrangement of most of the business community.

At an early stage, Roosevelt became aware of the menace to world peace posed by totalitarian fascism, and from 1937 on he tried to focus public attention on the trend of events in Europe and Asia. As a result, he was widely denounced as a warmonger. He was re-elected in 1936 over Gov. Alfred M. Landon of Kansas by the overwhelming electoral margin of 523 to 8, and the gathering international crisis prompted him to run for an unprecedented third term in 1940. He defeated Wendell L. Willkie.

Roosevelt's program to bring maximum aid to Britain and, after June 1941, to Russia was opposed, until the Japanese attack on Pearl Harbor restored national unity. During the war, Roosevelt shelved the New Deal in the interests of conciliating the business community, both in order to get full production during the war and to prepare the way for a united acceptance of the peace settlements after the war. A series of conferences with Winston Churchill and Joseph Stalin laid down the bases for the postwar world. In 1944 he was elected to a fourth term, running against Gov. Thomas E. Dewey of New York.

On April 12, 1945, Roosevelt died of a cerebral hemorrhage at Warm Springs, Ga., shortly after his return from the Yalta Conference. His wife, Anna Eleanor Roosevelt, whom he married in 1905, was a woman of great ability who made significant contributions to her husband's policies.

HARRY S. TRUMAN was born on a farm near Lamar, Mo., on May 8, 1884. During World War I, he served in France as a captain with the 129th Field Artillery. He married Bess Wallace in 1919. After engaging briefly and unsuccessfully in the haberdashery business in Kansas City, Mo., Truman entered local politics. Under the sponsorship of Thomas Pendergast, Democratic boss of Missouri, he held a number of local offices, preserving his personal honesty in the midst of a notoriously corrupt political machine. In 1934, he was elected to the Senate and was re-elected in 1940. During his first term he was a loyal but quiet supporter of the New Deal, but in his second term, an appointment as head of a Senate committee to investigate war production brought out his special qualities of honesty, common sense, and hard work, and he won widespread respect.

Elected vice president in 1944, Truman became president upon Roosevelt's sudden death in April 1945 and was immediately faced with the problems of winding down the war against the Axis and preparing the nation for postwar adjustment.

The years 1947–48 were distinguished by civil-rights proposals, the Truman Doctrine to contain the spread of Communism, and the Marshall Plan to aid in the economic reconstruction of war-ravaged nations. Truman's general record, highlighted by a vigorous Fair Deal campaign, brought about his unexpected election in 1948 over the heavily favored Thomas E. Dewey.

Truman's second term was primarily concerned with the Cold War with the Soviet Union, the implementing of the North Atlantic Pact, the United Nations police action in Korea, and the vast rearmament program with its accompanying problems of economic stabilization.

On March 29, 1952, Truman announced that he would not run again for the presidency. After leaving the White House, he returned to his home in Independence, Mo., to write his memoirs. He further busied himself with the Harry S. Truman Library there. He died in Kansas City, Mo., on Dec. 26, 1972.

DWIGHT DAVID EISENHOWER was born in Denison, Tex., on Oct. 14, 1890. His ancestors lived in Germany and emigrated to America, settling in Pennsylvania, early in the 18th century. His father, David, had a general store in Hope, Kan., which failed. After a brief time in Texas, the family moved to Abilene, Kan.

After graduating from Abilene High School in 1909, Eisenhower did odd jobs for almost two years. He won an appointment to the Naval Academy at Annapolis, but was too old for admittance. Then he received an appointment in 1910 to West Point, from which he graduated as a second lieutenant in 1915.

He did not see service in World War I, having been stationed at Fort Sam Houston, Tex. There he met Mamie Geneva Doud, whom he married in Denver on July 1, 1916, and by whom he had two sons: Doud Dwight (died in infancy) and John Sheldon Doud.

Eisenhower served in the Philippines from 1935 to 1939 with Gen. Douglas MacArthur. Afterward, Gen. George C. Marshall, the Army Chief of Staff, brought him into the War Department's General Staff and in 1942 placed him in command of the invasion of North Africa. In 1944, he was made Supreme Allied Commander for the invasion of Europe.

After the war, Eisenhower served as Army Chief of Staff from November 1945 until February 1948, when he was appointed president of Columbia University.

In December 1950, President Truman recalled Eisenhower to active duty to command the North Atlantic Treaty Organization forces in Europe. He held his post until the end of May 1952.

At the Republican convention of 1952 in Chicago, Eisenhower won the presidential nomination on the first ballot in a close race with Senator Robert A. Taft of Ohio. In the election, he defeated Gov. Adlai E. Stevenson of Illinois.

Through two terms, Eisenhower hewed to moderate domestic policies. He sought peace through Free World strength in an era of new nationalisms, nuclear missiles, and space exploration. He fostered alliances pledging the United States to resist Red aggression in Europe, Asia, and Latin America. The Eisenhower Doctrine of 1957 extended commitments to the Middle East.

At home, the popular president lacked Republican Congressional majorities after 1954, but he was re-elected in 1956 by 457 electoral votes to 73 for Stevenson.

While retaining most Fair Deal programs, he stressed "fiscal responsibility" in domestic affairs. A moderate in civil rights, he sent troops to Little Rock, Ark., to enforce court-ordered school integration.

With his wartime rank restored by Congress, Eisenhower returned to private life and the role of elder statesman, with his vigor hardly impaired by a heart attack, an ileitis operation, and a mild stroke suffered while in office. He died in Washington on March 28, 1969.

JOHN FITZGERALD KENNEDY was born in Brookline, Mass., on May 29, 1917. His father, Joseph P. Kennedy, was Ambassador to Great Britain from 1937 to 1940.

Kennedy was graduated from Harvard University in 1940 and joined the Navy the next year. He became skipper of a PT boat that was sunk in the Pacific by a Japanese destroyer. Although given up for lost, he swam to a safe island, towing an injured enlisted man.

After recovering from a war-aggravated spinal injury, Kennedy entered politics in 1946 and was elected to Congress. In 1952, he ran against Senator Henry Cabot Lodge, Jr., of Massachusetts, and won.

Kennedy was married on Sept. 12, 1953, to Jacqueline Lee Bouvier, by whom he had three children: Caroline, John Fitzgerald, Jr., and Patrick Bouvier (died in infancy).

In 1957 Kennedy won the Pulitzer Prize for a book he had written earlier, *Profiles in Courage.*

After strenuous primary battles, Kennedy won the Democratic presidential nomination on the first ballot at the 1960 Los Angeles convention. With a plurality of only 118,574 votes, he carried the election over Vice President Richard M. Nixon and became the first Roman Catholic president.

Kennedy brought to the White House the dynamic idea of a "New Frontier" approach in dealing with problems at home, abroad, and in the dimensions of space. Out of his leadership in his first few months in office came the 10-year Alliance for Progress to aid Latin America, the Peace Corps, and accelerated programs that brought the first Americans into orbit in the race into space.

Failure of the U.S.-supported Cuban invasion in April 1961 led to the entrenchment of the Communist-backed Castro regime, only 90 miles from United States soil. When it became known that Soviet offensive missiles were being installed in Cuba in 1962, Kennedy ordered a naval "quarantine" of the island and moved troops into position to eliminate this threat to U.S. security. The world seemed on the brink of a nuclear war until Soviet Premier Khrushchev ordered the removal of the missiles.

A sudden "thaw," or the appearance of one, in the cold war came with the agreement with the Soviet Union on a limited test-ban treaty signed in Moscow on Aug. 6, 1963.

In his domestic policies, Kennedy's proposals for medical care for the aged, expanded area redevelopment, and aid to education were defeated, but on minimum wage, trade legislation, and other measures he won important victories.

Widespread racial disorders and demonstrations led to Kennedy's proposing sweeping civil rights legislation. As his third year in office drew to a close, he also recommended an $11-billion tax cut to bolster the economy. Both measures were pending in Congress when Kennedy, looking forward to a second term, journeyed to Texas for a series of speeches.

While riding in a procession in Dallas on Nov. 22, 1963, he was shot to death by an assassin firing from an upper floor of a building. The alleged assassin, Lee Harvey Oswald, was killed two days later in the Dallas city jail by Jack Ruby, owner of a striptease place.

At 46 years of age, Kennedy became the fourth president to be assassinated and the eighth to die in office.

LYNDON BAINES JOHNSON was born in Stonewall, Tex., on Aug. 27, 1908. On both sides of his family he had a political heritage mingled with a Baptist background of preachers and teachers. Both his father and his paternal grandfather served in the Texas House of Representatives.

After his graduation from Southwest Texas State Teachers College, Johnson taught school for two years. He went to Washington in 1932 as secretary to Rep. Richard M. Kleberg. During this time, he married Claudia Alta Taylor, known as "Lady Bird." They had two children: Lynda Bird and Luci Baines.

In 1935, Johnson became Texas administrator for the National Youth Administration. Two years later, he was elected to Congress as an all-out supporter of Franklin D. Roosevelt, and served until 1949. He was the first member of Congress to enlist in the armed forces after the attack on Pearl Harbor. He served in the Navy in the Pacific and won a Silver Star.

Johnson was elected to the Senate in 1948 after he had captured the Democratic nomination by only 87 votes. He was 40 years old. He became the Senate Democratic leader in 1953. A heart attack in 1955 threatened to end his political career, but he recovered fully and resumed his duties.

At the height of his power as Senate leader, Johnson sought the Democratic nomination for president in 1960. When he lost to John F. Kennedy, he surprised even some of his closest associates by accepting second place on the ticket.

Johnson was riding in another car in the motorcade when Kennedy was assassinated in Dallas on Nov. 22, 1963. He took the oath of office in the presidential jet on the Dallas airfield.

With Johnson's insistent backing, Congress finally adopted a far-reaching civil-rights bill, a voting-rights bill, a Medicare program for the aged, and measures to improve education and conservation. Congress also began what Johnson described as "an all-out war" on poverty.

Amassing a record-breaking majority of nearly 16 million votes, Johnson was elected president in his own right in 1964, defeating Senator Barry Goldwater of Arizona.

The double tragedy of a war in Southeast Asia and urban riots at home marked Johnson's last two years in office. Faced with disunity in the nation and challenges within his own party, Johnson surprised the country on March 31, 1968, with the announcement that he would not be a candidate for re-election. He died of a heart attack suffered at his LBJ Ranch on Jan. 22, 1973.

RICHARD MILHOUS NIXON was born in Yorba Linda, Calif., on Jan. 9, 1913, to Midwestern-bred parents, Francis A. and Hannah Milhous Nixon, who raised their five sons as Quakers.

Nixon was a high school debater and was undergraduate president at Whittier College in California, where he was graduated in 1934. As a scholarship student at Duke University Law School in North Carolina, he graduated third in his class in 1937.

After five years as a lawyer, Nixon joined the Navy in August 1942. He was an air transport officer in the South Pacific and a legal officer stateside before his discharge in 1946 as a lieutenant commander.

Running for Congress in California as a Republican in 1946, Nixon defeated Rep. Jerry Voorhis. As a member of the House Un-American Activities Committee, he made a name as an investigator of Alger Hiss, a former high State Department official, who was later jailed for perjury. In 1950, Nixon defeated Rep. Helen Gahagan Douglas, a Democrat, for the Senate. He was criticized for portraying her as a Communist dupe.

Nixon's anti-Communism, his Western base, and his youth figured in his selection in 1952 to run for vice president on the ticket headed by Dwight D. Eisenhower. Demands for Nixon's withdrawal followed disclosure that California businessmen had paid some of his Senate office expenses. He televised rebuttal, known as "the Checkers speech" (named for a cocker spaniel given to the Nixons), brought him support from the public and from Eisenhower. The ticket won easily in 1952 and again in 1956.

Eisenhower gave Nixon substantive assignments, including missions to 56 countries. In Moscow in 1959, Nixon won acclaim for his defense of U.S. interests in an impromptu "kitchen debate" with Soviet Premier Nikita S. Khrushchev.

Nixon lost the 1960 race for the presidency to John F. Kennedy.

In 1962, Nixon failed in a bid for California's governorship and seemed to be finished as a national candidate. He became a Wall Street lawyer, but kept his old party ties and developed new ones through constant travels to speak for Republicans.

Nixon won the 1968 Republican presidential nomination after a shrewd primary campaign, then made Gov. Spiro T. Agnew of Maryland his surprise choice for vice president. In the election, they edged out the Democratic ticket headed by Vice President Hubert H. Humphrey by 510,314 votes out of 73,212,065 cast.

Committed to wind down the U.S. role in the Vietnamese War, Nixon pursued "Vietnamization"—training and equipping South Vietnamese to do their own fighting. American ground combat forces in Vietnam fell steadily from 540,000 when Nixon took office to none in 1973 when the military draft was ended. But there was heavy continuing use of U.S. air power.

Nixon improved relations with Moscow and reopened the long-closed door to mainland China with a good-will trip there in February 1972. In May of that year, he visited Moscow and signed agreements on arms limitation and trade expansion and approved plans for a joint U.S.-Soviet space mission in 1975.

Inflation was a campaign issue for Nixon, but he failed to master it as president. On Aug. 15, 1971, with unemployment edging up, Nixon abruptly announced a new economic policy: a 90-day wage-price freeze, stimulative tax cuts, a temporary 10% tariff, and spending cuts. A second phase, imposing guidelines on wage, price and rent boosts, was announced October 7.

The economy responded in time for the 1972 campaign, in which Nixon played up his foreign-policy achievements. Played down was the burglary on June 17, 1972, of Democratic national headquarters in the Watergate apartment complex in Washington. The Nixon-Agnew re-election campaign cost a record $60 million and swamped the Democratic ticket headed by Senator George McGovern of South Dakota with a plurality of 17,999,528 out of 77,718,554 votes. Only Massachusetts, with 14 electoral votes, and the District of Columbia, with 3, went for McGovern.

In January 1973, hints of a cover-up emerged at the trial of six men found guilty of the Watergate burglary. With a Senate investigation under way, Nixon announced on April 30 the resignations of his top aides, H. R. Haldeman and John D. Ehrlichman, and the dismissal of White House counsel John Dean III. Dean was the star witness at televised Senate hearings that exposed both a White House cover-up of Watergate and massive illegalities in Republican fund-raising in 1972.

The hearings also disclosed that Nixon had routinely tape-recorded his office meetings and telephone conversations.

On Oct. 10, 1973, Agnew resigned as vice president, then pleaded no-contest to a negotiated federal charge of evading income taxes on alleged bribes. Two days later, Nixon nominated the House minority leader, Rep. Gerald R. Ford of Michigan, as the new vice president. Congress confirmed Ford on Dec. 6, 1973.

In June 1974, Nixon visited Israel and four Arab nations. Then he met in Moscow with Soviet leader Leonid I. Brezhnev and reached preliminary nuclear arms limitation agreements.

But, in the month after his return, Watergate ended the Nixon regime. On July 24 the Supreme Court ordered Nixon to surrender subpoenaed tapes. On July 30, the Judiciary Committee referred three impeachment articles to the full membership. On August 5, Nixon bowed to the Supreme Court and released tapes showing he halted an FBI probe of the Watergate burglary six days after it occurred. It was in effect an admission of obstruction of justice, and impeachment appeared inevitable.

Nixon resigned on Aug. 9, 1974, the first president ever to do so. A month later, President Ford issued an unconditional pardon for any offenses Nixon might have committed as president, thus forestalling possible prosecution.

In 1940, Nixon married Thelma Catherine (Pat) Ryan. They had two daughters, Patricia (Tricia) Cox and Julie, who married Dwight David Eisenhower II, grandson of the former president.

GERALD RUDOLPH FORD was born in Omaha, Neb., on July 14, 1913, the only child of Leslie and Dorothy Gardner King. His parents were divorced in 1915. His mother moved to Grand Rapids, Mich., and married Gerald R. Ford. The boy was renamed for his stepfather.

Ford captained his high school football team in Grand Rapids, and a football scholarship took him to the University of Michigan, where he starred as varsity center before his graduation in 1935. A job as 'assistant football coach at Yale gave him an opportunity to attend Yale Law School, from which he graduated in the top third of his class in 1941.

He returned to Grand Rapids to practice law, but entered the Navy in April 1942. He saw wartime service in the Pacific on the light aircraft carrier *Monterey* and was a lieutenant commander when he returned to Grand Rapids early in 1946 to resume law practice and dabble in politics.

Ford was elected to Congress in 1948 for the first of his 13 terms in the House. He was soon assigned to the influential Appropriations Committee and rose to become the ranking Republican on the subcommittee on Defense Department appropriations and an expert in the field.

As a legislator, Ford described himself as "a moderate on domestic issues, a conservative in fiscal affairs, and a dyed-in-the-wool internationalist." He carried the ball for Pentagon appropriations, was a hawk on the war in Vietnam, and kept a low profile on civil-rights issues.

He was also dependable and hard-working and popular with his colleagues. In 1963, he was elected chairman of the House Republican Conference. He served in 1963–64 as a member of the Warren Commission that investigated the assassination of John F. Kennedy. A revolt by dissatisfied younger Republicans in 1965 made him minority leader.

Ford shelved his hopes for the Speakership on Oct. 12, 1973, when Nixon nominated him to fill the vice presidency left vacant by Agnew's resignation under fire. It was the first use of the procedures for filling vacancies in the vice presidency laid down in the 25th Amendment to the Constitution, which Ford had helped enact.

Congress confirmed Ford as vice president on Dec. 6, 1973. Once in office, he said he did not believe Nixon had been involved in the Watergate scandals, but criticized his stubborn court battle against releasing tape recordings of Watergate-related conversations for use as evidence.

The scandals led to Nixon's unprecedented resignation on Aug. 9, 1974, and Ford was sworn in immediately as the 38th president, the first to enter the White House without winning a national election.

Ford assured the nation when he took office that "our long national nightmare is over" and pledged "openness and candor" in all his actions. He won a warm response from the Democratic 93rd Congress when he said he wanted "a good marriage" rather than a honeymoon with his former colleagues. In December 1974 Congressional majorities backed his choice of former New York Gov. Nelson A. Rockefeller as his successor in the again-vacant vice presidency.

The cordiality was chilled by Ford's announcement on Sept. 8, 1974, that he had granted an unconditional pardon to Nixon for any crimes he might have committed as president. Although no formal charges were pending, Ford said he feared "ugly passions" would be aroused if Nixon were brought to trial. The pardon was widely criticized.

To fight inflation, the new president first proposed fiscal restraints and spending curbs and a 5% tax surcharge that got nowhere in the Senate and House. Congress again rebuffed Ford in the spring of 1975 when he appealed for emergency military aid to help the governments of South Vietnam and Cambodia resist massive Communist offensives.

In November 1974, Ford visited Japan, South Korea, and the Soviet Union, where he and Soviet leader Leonid I. Brezhnev conferred in Vladivostok and reached a tentative agreement to limit the number of strategic offensive nuclear weapons. It was Ford's first meeting as president with Brezhnev, who planned a return visit to Washington in the fall of 1975.

Politically, Ford's fortunes improved steadily in the first half of 1975. Badly divided Democrats in Congress were unable to muster votes to override his vetoes of spending bills that exceeded his budget. He faced some right-wing opposition in his own party, but moved to pre-empt it with an early announcement—on July 8, 1975—of his intention to be a candidate in 1976.

Early state primaries in 1976 suggested an easy victory for Ford despite Ronald Reagan's bitter attacks on administration foreign policy and defense programs. But later Reagan primary successes threatened the President's lead. At the Kansas City convention, Ford was nominated by the narrow margin of 1,187 to 1,070. But Reagan had moved the party to the right, and Ford himself was regarded as a caretaker president lacking in strength and vision. He was defeated in November by Jimmy Carter.

In 1948, Ford married Elizabeth Anne (Betty) Bloomer. They had four children, Michael Gerald, John Gardner, Steven Meigs, and Susan Elizabeth.

JAMES EARL CARTER, JR., was born in the tiny village of Plains, Ga., Oct. 1, 1924, and grew up on the family farm at nearby Archery. Both parents were fifth-generation Georgians. His father, James Earl Carter, was known as a segregationist, but treated his black and white workers equally. Carter's mother, Lillian Gordy, was a matriarchal presence in home and community and opposed the then-prevailing code of racial inequality. The future President was baptized in 1935 in the conservative Southern Baptist Church and spoke often of being a "born again" Christian, although committed to the separation of church and state.

Carter married Rosalynn Smith, a neighbor, in 1946. Their first child, John William, was born a year later in Portsmouth, Va. Their other children are James Earl III, born in Honolulu in 1950; Donnel Jeffrey, born in New London, Conn., in 1952, and Amy Lynn, born in Plains in 1967.

In 1946 Carter was graduated from the U.S. Naval Academy at Annapolis and served in the nuclear-submarine program under Adm. Hyman G. Rickover. In 1954, after his father's death, he resigned from the Navy to take over the family's flourishing warehouse and cotton gin, with several thousand acres for growing seed peanuts.

Carter was elected to the Georgia Senate in 1962. In 1966 he lost the race for Governor, but was elected in 1970. His term brought a state government reorganization, sharply reduced agencies, increased economy and efficiency, and new social programs, all with no general tax increase. In 1972 the peanut farmer-politician set his sights on the Presidency and in 1974 built a base for himself as he criss-crossed the country as chairman of the Democratic Campaign Committee, appealing for revival and reform. In 1975 his image as a typical Southern white was erased when he won support of most of the old Southern civil-rights coalition after endorsement by Rep. Andrew Young, black Democrat from Atlanta, who had been the closest aide to the Rev. Martin Luther King, Jr. At Carter's 1971 inauguration as Governor he had called for an end to all forms of racial discrimination.

In the 1976 spring primaries, he won 19 out of 31 with a broad appeal to conservatives and liberals, black and white, poor and well-to-do. Throughout his campaigning Carter set forth his policies in his soft Southern voice, and with his electric-blue stare faced down skeptics who joked about "Jimmy Who?" His toothy smile became his trademark. He was nominated on the first roll-call vote of the 1976 Bicentennial Democratic National Convention in New York, and defeated Gerald R. Ford in November. Likewise, in 1980 he was renominated on the first ballot after vanquishing Senator Edward M. Kennedy of Massachusetts in the primaries. At the convention he defeated the Kennedy forces in their attempt to block a party rule that bound a large majority of pledged delegates to vote for Carter. In the election campaign, Carter attacked his rivals, Ronald Reagan and John B. Anderson, independent, with the warning that a Reagan Republican victory would heighten the risk of war and impede civil rights and economic opportunity. In November Carter lost to Reagan, who won 489 Electoral College votes and 51% of the popular tally, to 49 electoral votes and 41% for Carter.

In his one term, Carter fought hard for his programs against resistance from an independent-minded Democratic Congress that frustrated many pet projects although it overrode only two vetoes. Many of his difficulties were traced to his aides' brusqueness in dealing with Capitol Hill and insensitivity to Congressional feelings and tradition. Observers generally viewed public dissatisfaction with the "stagflation" economy as a principal factor in his defeat. Others included his jittery performance in the debate Oct. 28 with Reagan and the final uncertainties in the negotiations for freeing the Iranians' hostages, along with earlier staff problems, friction with Congress, long gasoline lines, and the months-long Iranian crisis, including the abortive sally in April 1980 to free the hostages. The President, however, did deflect criticism resulting from the activities of his brother, Billy. Yet, assessments of his record noted many positive elements. There was, for one thing, peace throughout his term, with no American combat deaths and with a brake on the advocates of force. Regarded as perhaps his greatest personal achievements were the Camp David accords between Israel and Egypt and the resulting treaty—the first between Israel and an Arab neighbor. The treaty with China and the Panama Canal treaties were also major achievements. Carter worked for nuclear-arms control. His concern for international human rights was credited with saving lives and reducing torture, and he supported the British policy that ended internecine warfare in Rhodesia, now Zimbabwe. Domestically, his environmental record was a major accomplishment. His judicial appointments won acclaim; the Southerner who had forsworn racism made 265 choices for the Federal bench that included minority members and women. On energy, he ended by price decontrols the practice of holding U.S. petroleum prices far below world levels. —*Arthur P. Reed, Jr.*

RONALD WILSON REAGAN rode to the Presidency in 1980 on a tide of resurgent right-wing sentiment among an electorate battered by winds of unwanted change, longing for a distant, simpler era.

He left office in January 1989 with two-thirds of the American people approving his performance during his two terms. It was the highest rating for any retiring President since World War II. In his farewell speech, Reagan exhorted the nation to cling to the revival of patriotism that he had fostered. And he spoke proudly of the economic recovery during his Administrations, although regretting the huge budget deficit, for which, in part, many blamed his policies.

Reagan had retained the public's affection as he applied his political magic to policy goals. His place in history will rest, perhaps, on the short- and intermediate-range missile treaty consummated on a cordial visit to the Soviet Union that he had once reviled as an "evil empire." Its provisions, including a ground-breaking agreement on verification inspection, were formulated in four days of summit talks in Moscow in May 1988 with the Soviet leader, Mikhail S. Gorbachev.

And Reagan can point to numerous domestic achievements: sharp cuts in income tax rates, sweeping tax reform; creating economic growth without inflation, reducing the unemployment rate, among others. He failed, however, to win the "Reagan Revolution" on such issues as abortion and school prayer, and he seemed aloof from "sleazy" conduct by some top officials.

In his final months Reagan campaigned aggressively to win election as President for his two-term Vice President, George Bush.

Reagan's popularity with the public dipped sharply in 1986 when the Iran-Contra scandal broke, shortly after the Democrats gained control of the Senate. Observers agreed that Reagan's presidency had been weakened, if temporarily, by the two unrelated events. Then the weeks-long Congressional hearings in the summer of 1987 heard an array of Administration officials, present and former, tell their tales of a White House riven by deceit and undercover maneuvering. Yet no breath of illegality touched the President's personal reputation; on Aug. 12, 1987, he told the nation that he had not known of questionable activities but agreed that he was "ultimately accountable."

Ronald Reagan, actor turned politician, New Dealer turned conservative, came to the films and politics from a thoroughly Middle-American background—middle class, Middle West and small town. He was born in Tampico, Ill., Feb. 6, 1911, the second son of John Edward Reagan and Nelle Wilson Reagan, and the family later moved to Dixon, Ill. The father, of Irish descent, was a shop clerk and merchant with Democratic sympathies. It was an impoverished family; young Ronald sold homemade popcorn at high school games and worked as a lifeguard to earn money for his college tuition. When the father got a New Deal WPA job, the future President became an ardent Roosevelt Democrat.

Reagan won a B.A. degree in 1932 from Eureka (Ill.) College, where a photographic memory aided in his studies and in debating and college theatricals. In a Depression year, he was making $100 a week as a sports announcer for radio station WHO in Des Moines, Iowa, from 1932 to 1937. His career as a film and TV actor stretched from 1937 to 1966, and his salary climbed to $3,500 a week. As a World War II captain in Army film studios, Reagan recoiled from what he saw as the laziness of Civil Service workers, and moved to the Right. As president of the Screen Actors Guild, he resisted what he considered a Communist plot to subvert the film industry. With advancing age, Reagan left leading-man roles and became a television spokesman for the General Electric Company at $150,000.

With oratorical skill his trademark, Reagan became an active Republican. At the behest of a small group of conservative Southern California businessmen, he ran for governor with a pledge to cut spending, and was elected by almost a million votes over the political veteran, Democratic Gov. Edmund G. Brown, father of the later governor.

In the 1980 election battle against Jimmy Carter, Reagan broadened his appeal by espousing moderate policies, gaining much of his support from disaffected Democrats and blue-collar workers. The incoming Administration immediately set out to "turn the government around" with a new economic program. Over strenuous Congressional opposition, Reagan triumphed on his "supply side" theory to stimulate production and control inflation through tax cuts and sharp reductions in government spending.

The President won high acclaim for his nomination of Sandra Day O'Connor as the first woman on the Supreme Court. His later nominations met increasing opposition but did much to tilt the Court's orientation to the Right.

In 1982, the President's popularity had slipped as the economy declined into the worst recession in 40 years, with persistent high unemployment and interest rates. Initial support for "supply side" economics faded but the President won crucial battles in Congress.

Internationally, Reagan confronted numerous critical problems in his first term. The successful invasion of Grenada accomplished much diplomatically. But the intervention in Lebanon and the withdrawal of Marines after a disastrous terrorist attack were regarded as military failures.

The popular President won reelection in the 1984 landslide, with the economy improving and inflation under control. Domestically, a tax reform bill that Reagan backed became law. But the constantly growing budget deficit remained a constant irritant, with the President and Congress persistently at odds over priorities in spending for defense and domestic programs. His foreign policy met stiffening opposition, with Congress increasingly reluctant to increase spending for the Nicarguan "Contras" and the Pentagon to expand the development of the MX missile. But even severe critics praised Reagan's restrained but decisive handling of the crisis following the hijacking of an American plane in Beirut by Moslem extremists. The attack on Libya in April 1986 galvanized the nation, although it drew scathing disapproval from the NATO alliance.

Barely three months into his first term, Reagan was the target of an assassin's bullet; his courageous comeback won public admiration.

Reagan is devoted to his wife, Nancy, whom he married after his divorce from the screen actress Jane Wyman. The children of the first marriage are Maureen, his daughter by Miss Wyman, and Michael, an adopted son. In the present marriage the children are Patricia and Ron.

—Arthur P. Reed, Jr.

GEORGE H. BUSH entered the Presidency on January 20, 1989, with his theme harmony and conciliation after the often turbulent Reagan years. With his calm and unassuming manner, he emerged from his subordinate Vice-Presidential role with an air of quiet authority. His Inaugural address emphasized, "A new breeze is blowing, and the old bipartisanship must be made new again."

In his first months, the 65-year-old President, the nation's 41st, established himself as his own man and all but erased memories of what many had regarded as his fiercely abrasive Presidential election campaign of 1988 and questionable tactics against his Democratic opponent. People liked his easy style and readiness to compromise even as he remained a staunch conservative, although that readiness had made some conservatives uneasy.

Bush's Cabinet choices reflected a pragmatic desire for an efficient nonideological Government.

But in his second year, 1990, the President confronted a mounting array of problems, his most critical being on the domestic side. Chief among them were the staggering and mushrooming budget deficit and the savings and loan crisis, which threatened to cost the taxpayers billions of dollars. Other vexing issues were the question of cutting defense expenditures with consequent economic dislocation, the war on drugs, education, and the environment.

With his usual cautious instinct, the President nominated the scholarly David Souter, with broadly conservative views, for the Supreme Court. Thus he hoped to avoid another bruising fight that would further rend the nation over the tinderbox issues of abortion, civil rights, and affirmative action. And the President was careful to say he had avoided "the litmus test approach."

In foreign affairs, mid-1990 saw the President coping with the kaleidoscopic changes in Central and Eastern Europe, which at times seemed to be slipping beyond U.S. influence. But Bush dealt easily with the Soviet leader, Mikhail Gorbachev, at their second annual summit conference, in Washington in May and June. The two signed a broad understanding including cuts in nuclear arms and chemical weapons, and Bush signed the trade treaty sought by Gorbachev.

Bush also took a leading role in the London NATO conference that declared four decades of Cold War at an end. At the ensuing Houston economic summit meeting Bush won a concession by which the leaders acceded to his wish for no timetables limiting emission of gases that might cause global warming. But at home the President's popularity slipped sharply from its near record 76 percent public approval following the invasion of Panama in late 1989. This plunge followed his recantation of his "no new taxes" pledge as he sat down with Congressional leaders to devise a strategy to tame the budget deficit and cope with a faltering economy.

In his first year Bush, a World War II hero, had won plaudits at home and abroad for his confident, competent conduct at the NATO 40th anniversary summit meeting at Brussels, the Paris economic conference, on his tour of Eastern Europe, and at the Malta conference with Gorbachev. Grave challenges in that year were the Lebanon hostage crisis and the ongoing war on the drug traffic.

Domestically, Bush had to cope with such issues as the Exxon Valdez oil spill in Alaska and the dispute over flag-burning restrictions, which was resolved, if only for a time, in mid-1990.

Bush, scion of an aristocratic New England fam-

ily, came to the White House after a long career in public service, in which he held top positions in national and international organizations. As Vice President, he avoided the appearance of direct involvement in the Iran-Contra affair while not seeming to shy away from the President.

Earlier, in the 1960s, Bush won two contests for a Texas Republican seat in the House of Representatives, but lost two bids for a Senate seat and one for the Presidency. After his second race for the Senate, President Nixon appointed him U.S. delegate to the United Nations with the rank of Ambassador and he later became Republican National Chairman. He headed the United States liaison office in Beijing before becoming Director of Central Intelligence.

In 1980 Bush became Reagan's running mate despite earlier criticism of Reagan "voodoo economics" and by the 1984 election had won acclaim for devotion to Reagan's conservative agenda despite his own reputation as somewhat more liberally inclined. Nevertheless, die-hard right-wingers could find satisfaction in Bush's war record and his Government service, particularly with the C.I.A. Throughout he remained influential in White House decisions, particularly in foreign affairs.

In the 1988 campaign, Bush's choice of Senator Dan Quayle of Indiana for Vice President surprised his friends and provoked criticism and ridicule that continued even after the Administration was established in office. Nonetheless Bush strongly defended his choice.

The future President joined the Navy after war broke out and at 18 became the Navy's youngest commissioned pilot, serving from 1942 to 1945. The man later derided by some as a "wimp" fought the Japanese on 58 missions and was shot down once. He won the Distinguished Flying Cross.

Throughout his whole career, Bush had the backing of an established family, headed by his father, the autocratic and wealthy Prescott Bush, who was elected to the Senate from Connecticut in 1952. And his family helped the young patrician became established in his early business ventures, a rich uncle raising most of the capital required for founding a new oil company in Texas.

George Herbert Walker Bush was born June 12, 1924, in Milton, Mass., to Prescott and Dorothy Bush. The family later moved to Connecticut. The youth studied at the elite Phillips Academy in Andover, Mass., before entering the Navy.

After the war, Bush earned an economics degree and a Phi Beta Kappa key in two and a half years at Yale University. While there he captained the baseball team and was initiated into "Skull and Bones," the prestigious Yale secret society.

In 1945 Bush married Barbara Pierce of Rye, N.Y., daughter of a magazine publisher. With his bride, Bush moved to Texas instead of entering his father's investment banking business. There he founded his oil company and in 1980 reported an estimated wealth of $1.4 million.

The Bushes have lived in 17 cities and more than a score of homes and have traveled in as many countries. In her husband's frequent absences during the early years, Mrs. Bush was often matriarch of a family of four boys and a girl. Bush is close to his immediate family and to 10 grandchildren, a sister, and three brothers.

Bush sold his Houston home several years ago and moved from the Vice President's dwelling to the White House, and lives there and at the family estate at Kennebunkport, Maine.

—Arthur P. Reed, Jr.

WEATHER & CLIMATE

Climate of 100 Selected U.S. Cities

City	Average Monthly Temperature (°F)[1]				Precipitation		Snowfall	
	Jan.	April	July	Oct.	Average (in.)[1]	annual (days)[2]	Average annual (in.)[2]	Years[2]
Albany, N.Y.	21.1	46.6	71.4	50.5	35.74	134	65.5	38
Albuquerque, N.M.	34.8	55.1	78.8	57.4	8.12	59	10.6	45
Anchorage, Alaska	13.0	35.4	58.1	34.6	15.20	115	69.2	41 [3]
Asheville, N.C.	36.8	55.7	73.2	56.0	47.71	124	17.5	20
Atlanta, Ga.	41.9	61.8	78.6	62.2	48.61	115	1.9	50
Atlantic City, N.J.	31.8	51.0	74.4	55.5	41.93	112	16.4	40 [3]
Austin, Texas	49.1	68.7	84.7	69.8	31.50	83	0.9	43
Baltimore, Md.	32.7	54.0	76.8	56.9	41.84	113	21.8	34
Baton Rouge, La.	50.8	68.4	82.1	68.2	55.77	108	0.1	34 [3]
Billings, Mont.	20.9	44.6	72.3	49.3	15.09	96	57.2	50
Birmingham, Ala.	42.9	62.8	80.1	62.6	54.52	117	1.3	41
Bismark, N.D.	6.7	42.5	70.4	46.1	15.36	96	40.3	45
Boise, Idaho	29.9	48.6	74.6	51.9	11.71	92	21.4	45
Boston, Mass.	29.6	48.7	73.5	54.8	43.81	127	41.8	49 [3]
Bridgeport, Conn.	29.5	48.6	74.0	56.0	41.56	117	26.0	36
Buffalo, N.Y.	23.5	45.4	70.7	51.5	37.52	169	92.2	41
Burlington, Vt.	16.6	42.7	69.6	47.9	33.69	153	78.2	41
Caribou, Maine	10.7	37.3	65.1	43.1	36.59	160	113.3	45
Casper, Wyom.	22.2	42.1	70.9	47.1	11.43	95	80.5	34
Charleston, S.C.	47.9	64.3	80.5	65.8	51.59	113	0.6	42
Charleston, W.Va.	32.9	55.3	74.5	55.9	42.43	151	31.5	37
Charlotte, N.C.	40.5	60.3	78.5	60.7	43.16	111	6.1	45
Cheyenne, Wyom.	26.1	41.8	68.9	47.5	13.31	98	54.1	49
Chicago, Ill.	21.4	48.8	73.0	53.5	33.34	127	40.3	26
Cleveland, Ohio	25.5	48.1	71.6	53.2	35.40	156	53.6	43
Columbia, S.C.	44.7	63.8	81.0	63.4	49.12	109	1.9	37
Columbus, Ohio	27.1	51.4	73.8	53.9	36.97	137	28.3	37 [3]
Concord, N.H.	19.9	44.1	69.5	48.3	36.53	125	64.5	43
Dallas–Ft. Worth, Texas	44.0	65.9	86.3	67.9	29.46	78	3.1	31
Denver, Colo.	29.5	47.4	73.4	51.9	15.31	88	59.8	50
Des Moines, Iowa	18.6	50.5	76.3	54.2	30.83	107	34.7	45
Detroit, Mich.	23.4	47.3	71.9	51.9	30.97	133	40.4	26
Dodge City, Kan.	29.5	54.3	80.0	57.7	20.66	78	19.5	42
Duluth, Minn.	6.3	38.3	65.4	44.2	29.68	135	77.4	41 [3]
El Paso, Texas	44.2	63.6	82.5	63.6	7.82	47	5.2	45
Fairbanks, Alaska	-12.7	30.2	61.5	25.1	10.37	106	67.5	33
Fargo, N.D.	4.3	42.1	70.6	46.3	19.59	100	35.9	42
Grand Junction, Colo.	25.5	51.7	78.9	54.9	8.00	72	26.1	38
Grand Rapids, Mich.	22.0	46.3	71.4	50.9	34.35	143	72.4	21
Hartford, Conn.	25.2	48.8	73.4	52.4	44.39	127	50.0	30
Helena, Mont.	18.1	42.3	67.9	45.1	11.37	96	47.9	44
Honolulu, Hawaii	72.6	75.7	80.1	79.5	23.47	100	0.0	38 [3]
Houston, Texas	51.4	68.7	83.1	69.7	44.76	105	0.4	50
Indianapolis, Ind.	26.0	52.4	75.1	54.8	39.12	125	23.1	53 [3]
Jackson, Miss.	45.7	65.1	81.9	65.0	52.82	109	1.2	21
Jacksonville, Fla.	53.2	67.7	81.3	69.5	52.76	116	T	43
Juneau, Alaska	21.8	39.1	55.7	41.8	53.15	220	102.8	41
Kansas City, Mo.	28.4	56.9	80.9	59.6	29.27	98	20.0	43
Knoxville, Tenn.	38.2	59.6	77.6	59.5	47.29	127	12.3	42
Las Vegas, Nev.	44.5	63.5	90.2	67.5	4.19	26	1.4	36
Lexington, Ky.	31.5	55.1	75.9	56.8	45.68	131	16.3	40
Little Rock, Ark.	39.9	62.4	82.1	63.1	49.20	104	5.4	42
Long Beach, Calif.	55.2	60.9	72.8	67.5	11.54	32	T	41 [3]
Los Angeles, Calif.	56.0	59.5	69.0	66.3	12.08	36	T	49
Louisville, Ky.	32.5	56.6	77.6	57.7	43.56	125	17.5	37
Madison, Wisc.	15.6	45.8	70.6	49.5	30.84	118	40.8	36
Memphis, Tenn.	39.6	62.6	82.1	62.9	51.57	107	5.5	34
Miami, Fla.	67.1	75.3	82.5	77.9	57.55	129	0.0	42
Milwaukee, Wisc.	18.7	44.6	70.5	50.9	30.94	125	47.0	44

City	Average Monthly Temperature (°F)[1]				Precipitation		Snowfall	
	Jan.	April	July	Oct.	Average (in.)[1]	annual (days)[2]	Average annual (in.)[2]	Years[2]
Minneapolis-St. Paul, Minn.	11.2	46.0	73.1	49.6	26.36	115	48.9	46
Mobile, Ala.	50.8	68.0	82.2	68.5	64.64	123	0.3	43
Montgomery, Ala.	46.7	65.2	81.7	65.3	49.16	108	0.3	40
Mt. Washington, N.H.	5.1	22.4	48.7	30.5	89.92	209	246.8	52
Nashville, Tenn.	37.1	59.7	79.4	60.2	48.49	119	11.1	43
Newark, N.J.	31.2	52.1	76.8	57.2	42.34	122	28.2	43
New Orleans, La.	52.4	68.7	82.1	69.2	59.74	114	0.2	38[3]
New York, N.Y.	31.8	51.9	76.4	57.5	42.82	119	26.1	40[3]
Norfolk, Va.	39.9	58.2	78.4	61.3	45.22	115	7.9	36
Oklahoma City, Okla.	35.9	60.2	82.1	62.3	30.89	82	9.0	45
Olympia, Wash.	37.2	47.3	63.0	50.1	50.96	164	18.0	43
Omaha, Neb.	20.2	52.2	77.7	54.5	30.34	98	31.1	49[3]
Philadelphia, Pa.	31.2	52.9	76.5	56.5	41.42	117	21.9	42[3]
Phoenix, Ariz.	52.3	68.1	92.3	73.4	7.11	36	T	47[3]
Pittsburgh, Pa.	26.7	50.1	72.0	52.5	36.30	154	44.6	32
Portland, Maine	21.5	42.8	68.1	48.5	43.52	128	72.4	44
Portland, Ore.	38.9	50.4	67.7	54.3	37.39	154	6.8	44
Providence, R.I.	28.2	47.9	72.5	53.2	45.32	124	37.1	31
Raleigh, N.C.	39.6	59.4	77.7	59.7	41.76	112	7.7	40
Reno, Nev.	32.2	46.4	69.5	50.3	7.49	51	25.3	42
Richmond, Va.	36.6	57.9	77.8	58.6	44.07	113	14.6	47
Roswell, N.M.	41.4	61.9	81.4	61.7	9.70	52	11.4	37[3]
Sacramento, Calif.	45.3	58.2	75.6	63.9	17.10	58	0.1	36[3]
Salt Lake City, Utah	28.6	49.2	77.5	53.0	15.31	90	59.1	56
San Antonio, Texas	50.4	69.6	84.6	70.2	29.13	81	0.4	42
San Diego, Calif.	56.8	61.2	70.3	67.5	9.32	43	T	44
San Francisco, Calif.	48.5	54.8	62.2	60.6	19.71	63	T	57
Savannah, Ga.	49.1	66.0	81.2	66.9	49.70	111	0.3	34
Seattle-Tacoma, Wash.	39.1	48.7	64.8	52.4	38.60	158	12.8	40
Sioux Falls, S.D.	12.4	46.4	74.0	49.4	24.12	96	39.9	39
Spokane, Wash.	25.7	45.8	69.7	47.5	16.71	114	51.5	37
Springfield, Ill.	24.6	53.3	76.5	56.0	33.78	114	24.5	37
St. Louis, Mo.	28.8	56.1	78.9	57.9	33.91	111	19.8	48[3]
Tampa, Fla.	59.8	71.5	82.1	74.4	46.73	107	T	38
Toledo, Ohio	23.1	47.8	71.8	51.7	31.78	137	38.3	29
Tucson, Ariz.	51.1	64.9	86.2	70.4	11.14	52	1.2	44
Tulsa, Okla.	35.2	61.0	83.2	62.6	38.77	89	9.0	46
Vero Beach, Fla.	61.9	71.7	81.1	75.2	51.41	n.a.	n.a.	0
Washington, D.C.	35.2	56.7	78.9	59.3	39.00	112	17.0	41[3]
Wilmington, Del.	31.2	52.4	76.0	56.3	41.38	117	20.9	37
Wichita, Kan.	29.6	56.3	81.4	59.1	28.61	85	16.4	31

1. Based on 30 year period 1951–80. Data latest available. 2. Data through 1984 based on number of years as indicated in Years column. 3. For snowfall data where number of years differ from that for precipitation data. T = trace. n.a. = not available. *Source:* National Oceanic and Atmospheric Administration.

Wind Chill Factors

Wind speed (mph)	Thermometer reading (degrees Fahrenheit)																
	35	30	25	20	15	10	5	0	−5	−10	−15	−20	−25	−30	−35	−40	−45
5	33	27	21	19	12	7	0	−5	−10	−15	−21	−26	−31	−36	−42	−47	−52
10	22	16	10	3	−3	−9	−15	−22	−27	−34	−40	−46	−52	−58	−64	−71	−77
15	16	9	2	−5	−11	−18	−25	−31	−38	−45	−51	−58	−65	−72	−78	−85	−92
20	12	4	−3	−10	−17	−24	−31	−39	−46	−53	−60	−67	−74	−81	−88	−95	−103
25	8	1	−7	−15	−22	−29	−36	−44	−51	−59	−66	−74	−81	−88	−96	−103	−110
30	6	−2	−10	−18	−25	−33	−41	−49	−56	−64	−71	−79	−86	−93	−101	−109	−116
35	4	−4	−12	−20	−27	−35	−43	−52	−58	−67	−74	−82	−89	−97	−105	−113	−120
40	3	−5	−13	−21	−29	−37	−45	−53	−60	−69	−76	−84	−92	−100	−107	−115	−123
45	2	−6	−14	−22	−30	−38	−46	−54	−62	−70	−78	−85	−93	−102	−109	−117	−125

NOTES: This chart gives equivalent temperatures for combinations of wind speed and temperatures. For example, the combination of a temperature of 10° Fahrenheit and a wind blowing at 10 mph has a cooling power equal to −9° F. Wind speeds of higher than 45 mph have little additional cooling effect.

World and U.S. Extremes of Climate

Highest recorded temperature

	Place	Date	Degree Fahrenheit	Degree Centigrade
World (Africa)	El Azizia, Libya	Sept. 13, 1922	136	58
North America (U.S.)	Death Valley, Calif.	July 10, 1913	134	57
Asia	Tirat Tsvi, Israel	June 21, 1942	129	54
Australia	Cloncurry, Queensland	Jan. 16, 1889	128	53
Europe	Seville, Spain	Aug. 4, 1881	122	50
South America	Rivadavia, Argentina	Dec. 11, 1905	120	49
Canada	Midale and Yellow Grass, Saskatchewan	July 5, 1937	113	45
Persian Gulf (sea-surface)		August 5, 1924	96	36
South Pole		Dec. 27, 1978	7.5	−14
Antarctica	Vanda Station	Jan. 5, 1974	59	15

Lowest recorded temperature

	Place	Date	Degree Fahrenheit	Degree Centigrade
World (Antarctica)	Vostok	July 21, 1983	−129	−89
Asia	Verkhoyansk/Oimekon	Feb. 6, 1933	−90	−68
Greenland	Northice	Jan. 9, 1954	−87	−66
North America (excl. Greenland)	Snag, Yukon, Canada	Feb. 3, 1947	−81	−63
Alaska	Prospect Creek, Endicott Mts.	Jan. 23, 1971	−80	−62
U.S., excluding Alaska	Rogers Pass, Mont.	Jan. 20, 1954	−70	−56.5
Europe	Ust 'Shchugor, U.S.S.R.	n.a.	−67	−55
South America	Sarmiento, Argentina	Jan. 1, 1907	−27	−33
Africa	Ifrane, Morocco	Feb. 11, 1935	−11	−24
Australia	Charlotte Pass, N.S.W.	July 22, 1947	−8	−22
United States	Prospect Creek, Alaska	Jan. 23, 1971	−80	−62

Greatest rainfalls

	Place	Date	Inches	Centimeters
1 minute (World)	Unionville, Md.	July 4, 1956	1.23	3.1
20 minutes (World)	Curtea-de-Arges, Romania	July 7, 1889	8.1	20.5
42 minutes (World)	Holt, Mo.	June 22, 1947	12	30.5
12 hours (World)	Foc-Foc, La Réunion	Jan. 7-8, 1966	45	114
24 hours (World)	Foc-Foc, La Réunion	Jan. 7-8, 1966	72	182.5
24 hours (N. Hemisphere)	Paishih, Taiwan	Sept. 10-11, 1963	49	125
24 hours (Australia)	Bellenden Ker, Queensland	Jan. 4, 1979	44	114
24 hours (U.S.)	Alvin, Texas	July 25-26, 1979	43	109
24 hours (Canada)	Ucluelet Brynnor Mines, British Columbia	Oct. 6, 1967	19	49
5 days (World)	Commerson, La Réunion	Jan. 23-28, 1980	156	395
1 month (World)	Cherrapunji, India	July 1861	366	930
12 months (World)	Cherrapunji, India	Aug. 1860-Aug. 1861	1,042	2,647
12 months (U.S.)	Kukui, Maui, Hawaii	Dec. 1981-Dec. 1982	739	1878

Greatest snowfalls

	Place	Date	Inches	Centimeters
1 month (U.S.)	Tamarack, Calif.	Jan. 1911	390	991
24 hours (N. America)	Silver Lake, Colo.	April 14-15, 1921	76	192.5
24 hours (Alaska)	Thompson Pass	Dec. 29, 1955	62	157.5
19 hours (France)	Bessans	April 5-6, 1969	68	173
1 storm (N. America)	Mt. Shasta Ski Bowl, Calif.	Feb. 13-19, 1959	189	480
1 storm (Alaska)	Thompson Pass	Dec. 26-31, 1955	175	445.5
1 season (N. America)	Paradise Ranger Sta., Wash.	1971-1972	1,122	2,850
1 season (Alaska)	Thompson Pass	1952-1953	974.5	2,475
1 season (Canada)	Revelstoke Mt. Copeland, British Columbia	1971-1972	964	2,446.5

Source: U.S. Army Corps of Engineers, Engineer Topographic Laboratories.

Devastating North Atlantic Hurricanes of the 20th Century

The following is a selected list of North Atlantic hurricanes based on casualties, damage, and general public interest. Facts about each storm are taken from Weather records, although in some cases only estimates of wind speed are available. Data given in this list pertain only to U.S. land areas except where indicated otherwise.

Date	Areas hardest hit	Land stations with highest wind speed	Deaths (U.S. only)	Est. damage (millions)	Remarks
1900, Aug. 27–Sept. 15	Galveston, Tex.	Galveston, Tex. (120[1] mph)	6,000	$30	Damage due to both winds and storm wave. Galveston Is. inundated.
1909, Sept. 10–21	Louisiana and Mississippi	New Orleans, La. (53 mph)	350	5	Winds 50–75 mi. W of New Orleans, where deaths occurred, were stronger than 68 mph.
1915, Aug. 5–23	East Texas and Louisiana	Galveston, Tex. (120 mph)	275	50	Water 5–6 ft deep in Galveston business district. 90% of homes demolished. Warnings issued well ahead of time.
1915, Sept. 22–Oct. 1	Mid-Gulf Coast	Burrwood, La. (140 mph)	275	13	Many casualties due to persons insisting on staying in low-lying areas despite warnings.
1919, Sept. 2–15	Florida, Louisiana, and Texas	Sand Key, Fla. (84[1] mph)	287	22	488 persons drowned at sea.
1926, Sept. 11–22	Florida and Alabama	Miami, Fla. (138 mph)	243	112	Most deaths were in Miami area. Said to have been one of most destructive storms of century.
1928, Sept. 6–20	Southern Florida	Lake Okeechobee, Fla. (75[1] mph)	1,836	25	1,870 injured. Nearly all deaths were in Lake Okeechobee area. Winds estimated as high as 160 mph caused Lake to overflow into populated areas.
1935, Aug. 29–Sept. 10	Southern Florida	Tampa, Fla. (86 mph)	408	6	Sustained winds over Florida Keys est. 150–200 mph. Remembered as "Labor Day Storm."
1938, Sept. 10–22	Long Island and Southern New England	Blue Hills Obs., Mass. (183 mph)	600	306	Unusually destructive. Storm center moved as fast as 56 mph at times. 1,754 injured.
1944, Sept. 9–16	North Carolina to New England	Cape Henry, Va. (150[1] mph)	46	100	344 deaths at sea. Shipping lanes were crowded with war-time activity.
1944, Oct. 12–23	Florida	Dry Tortugas Is. (120 mph)	18	100	About 300 were killed in Cuba area before storm reached U.S. Evacuation of thousands from threatened areas in Fla. prevented higher toll.
1947, Sept. 4–21	Florida and Mid-Gulf Coast	Hillsboro Light, Fla. (155 mph)	51	110	Wind damage especially heavy along Gulf Coast and Florida east coast.
1954, Aug. 25–31	North Carolina to New England	Block Island, R.I. (135 mph)	60	461	"CAROL"—more damage than any other single storm to this date. Water and high waves flooded low-lying areas; 1,000 injuries in Long Island—New England area.
1954, Sept. 2–14	New Jersey to New England	Block Island, R.I. (87 mph)	21	40	"EDNA"—New England again heavily hit. Gusts of 120 mph at Martha's Vineyard, Mass.
1954, Oct. 5–18	South Carolina to New York	New York, N.Y. (113 mph) (See Remarks)	95	252	"HAZEL"—several N.C. localities had winds of 130–150 mph with unusually heavy wave damage resulting. Est. 400–1,000 casualties in Haiti. In Canada there were 78 deaths, mostly due to flooding.
1955, Aug. 7–21	North Carolina to New England	Wilmington, N.C. (83 mph)	184	832	"DIANE"—worst floods in history in Southern New England. 16 in. of rain in Hartford area.
1957, June 25–28	Texas to Alabama	Sabine/Pass, Tex. (100 mph)	390	150	"AUDREY"—gave an early start to the hurricane season and wiped out Cameron, La. Two weeks later "BERTHA" struck same area.

Date	Areas hardest hit	Land stations with highest wind speed	Deaths (U.S. only)	Est. damage (millions)	Remarks
1960, Aug. 29–Sept. 13	Florida to New England	Ft. Myers, Fla. (92 mph) Block Island, R.I. (130 mph) (See Remarks)	50	500	"DONNA"—hurricane winds from a single storm swept the entire Atlantic seaboard from Florida to New England for the first time in a 75-year record. Winds estimated near 140 mph with gusts 175–180 mph on Central Keys and lower southwest Florida coast. 115 deaths in Antilles, most from flash floods in Puerto Rico.
1961, Sept. 3–15	Texas coast	Port Lavaca, Tex. (145 mph)	46	408	"CARLA"—devastated Texas Gulf Coast Cities with 15-foot tides and 15-inch rains. Gusts to 175 mph at Port Lavaca.
1964, Aug. 20–Sept. 5	Southern Florida, Eastern Virginia	Miami, Fla. (110 mph)	3	129	"CLEO"—first hurricane in Miami area since 1950. Killed 214 in Caribbean area.
1964, Aug. 28–Sept. 16	Northeastern Florida, Southern Georgia	St. Augustine, Fla. (125 mph)	5	250	"DORA"—first storm of full hurricane force on record to move inland from east over northeastern Florida.
1965, Aug. 27–Sept. 12	Southern Florida and Louisiana	Port Sulphur, La. (136 mph)	75	1,420	"BETSY"—Damage in Louisiana, $1.2 billion. 27,000 homes destroyed, 17,500 injured or ill, 300,000 evacuated. Gusts of 165 mph at Pine Key, Fla.
1967, Sept. 5–22	Southern Texas	Brownsville, Texas (109 mph gust)	15	200	"BEULAH"—main damage was caused by torrential rains.
1969, Aug. 14–22	Mississippi, Louisiana, Alabama, Virginia, W. Virginia	Oil drilling rig east of Boothville, La. (172 mph)	256	1,420	"CAMILLE"—68 additional persons missing. One of most destructive killer storms ever to hit U.S.
1970, July 23–Aug. 5	Texas coast	Corpus Christi, Tex. (130 mph)	11	453.8	"CELIA"—Gusts of 161 mph recorded.
1972, June 14–23	Florida to New York	Key West, Fla. (43 mph)	117	2,100	"AGNES"—Devastating floods with many record-breaking river crests. Pa. hardest hit, with 50 deaths.
1975, Sept. 13–24	Florida and Southern Alabama	Ozark, Ala. (104 mph)	21	490	"ELOISE"—Structures destroyed from Panama City Beach, Fla., to Ft. Walton Beach, Fla. Major flooding from rainfall.
1976, Aug. 6–10	New York, New Jersey, and Southern New England	Bridgeport, Conn. (77 mph gust)	5	100	"BELLE"—Crop damage in the Northeast. Considerable Inland stream and road flooding.
1979, Aug. 25–Sept. 7	Florida to New England	Fort Pierce, Fla. (95 mph gust)	5	320	"DAVID"—1200 deaths in the Dominican Republic. Homes 80 percent destroyed in Dominica.
1979, Aug. 29–Sept. 14	Alabama and Mississippi	Dauphin Island, Alabama (145 mph gust)	5	2300	"FREDERIC"—highest dollar damage ever in the United States.
1980, Aug. 3–10	Caribbean Islands to Texas Gulf Coast	Port Mansfield, Texas (120 mph gust)	28	300	"ALLEN"—Highest tides in 61 years. Over 200 killed in Caribbean Islands. Extensive crop damage in Caribbean.
1983, Aug. 15–21	Texas Coast	Hobby Airport (94 mph)	21	2000	"ALICIA"—Extensive damage in Galveston/Houston area.
1985, Aug. 28–Sept. 4	Florida to Mississippi	Dauphin Island, Ala. (96 mph)	4	1,000	"ELENA"—one million persons evacuated.
1985, Sept. 16—27	North Carolina Outer Banks and Long Island, N.Y.	Chesapeake Bay Bridge (92 mph)	8	1,000	"GLORIA"—downed trees and power outages across southern New England.
1985, Oct. 26–Nov. 1	Louisiana	Pensacola, Fla. (63 mph gust)	12	1,500	"JUAN"—Serious damage to offshore oil rigs. Sustained flooding over SE Louisiana.

Date	Areas hardest hit	Land stations with highest wind speed	Deaths (U.S. only)	Est. damage (millions)	Remarks
1989, Sept. 10–22	Caribbean Islands from Guadeloupe to Puerto Rico; South Carolina and North Carolina	Roosevelt Roads, P.R. (104 mph) Charleston, S.C. (87 mph)	49	7,000	"HUGO"–Storm surge flood waters reached 20 feet above normal along portions of S.C. Coast. New record high dollar damage.

1. Wind-measuring equipment disabled at speed indicated. NOTE: Additional hurricanes may be listed in *Current Events*.
Source: Department of Commerce, National Oceanic and Atmospheric Administration.

Tornadoes That Caused Outstanding Damage

Date	Number of tornadoes	Deaths	Property losses	States in which storms occurred
1884, Feb. 19	60	800	(1)	Mississippi, Alabama, North and South Carolina, Tennessee, Kentucky, Indiana
1917, May 26–27	(1)	249	$5,555,000	Illinois, Indiana, Arkansas, Kentucky, Tennessee, Alabama, Mississippi
1920, April 20	6	220	3,525,000	Mississippi, Alabama, Tennessee
1924, April 29–30	22	115	4,372,300	Oklahoma, Arkansas, Alabama, Georgia, Louisiana, North and South Carolina, Virginia
1924, June 28	4	96	13,050,000	Ohio and Pennsylvania
1925, March 18	8	792	17,872,000	Missouri, Illinois, Indiana, Kentucky, Tennessee, Alabama
1927, May 8–9	36	227	7,877,000	Texas, Louisiana, Missouri, Nebraska, Indiana, Michigan
1932, March 21	27	321	5,514,000	Alabama, Mississippi, Georgia, Tennessee
1936, April 5–6	22	498	21,800,000	Arkansas, Alabama, Tennessee, Georgia, South Carolina
1944, June 23	4	153	5,160,000	Pennsylvania, West Virginia, Maryland
1947, April 9–10	8	167	10,030,750	Texas, Oklahoma, Kansas
1952, March 21–22	31	343	15,327,100	Arkansas, Tennessee, Missouri, Mississippi, Alabama, Kentucky
1953, June 7–9	12	234	93,230,840	Michigan, Ohio, and New England states
1953, May 11	1	114	39,500,000	Texas
1955, May 25	13	102	11,747,500	Oklahoma and Kansas
1965, April 11–12	47	257	200,000,000	Iowa, Illinois, Wisconsin, Michigan, Indiana, Ohio
1968, May 15	7	63	65,000,000	Arkansas, Iowa, Illinois
1970, May 11	1	26	135,000,000	Texas
1971, Feb. 21	(1)	117	17,000,000	Louisiana, Mississippi
1973, March 31	2	9	115,000,000	Georgia, South Carolina
1973, May 26–28	96	22	(1)	Hawaii and 18 states in South, Southwest, Midwest, and East
1974, April 3–4	144	307	500,000,000 +	13 states in East, South, and Midwest
1975, May 6	3	3	400,000,000 +	Nebraska
1977, April 4	7	22	15,000,000	Alabama
1978, Dec. 3	13	4	100,000,000 +	Louisiana and Arkansas
1979, April 10	10	54	(1)	Texas and Oklahoma
1979, Oct. 3	1	3	200,000,000	Connecticut
1980, May 13	1	5	40,000,000	Michigan
1980, Aug. 9–11	29	0	50,000,000 +	Texas
1981, April 4	1	3	12,900,000	Wisconsin
1983, July 3	22	0	11,000,000 +	Wisconsin
1984, April 26–27	47	16	n.a.	Iowa, Illinois, Kansas, Louisiana, Michigan, Minnesota, Missouri, Oklahoma, South Dakota, Wisconsin
1985, May 31	30	76	102,500,000 +	Ohio, Pennsylvania, New York
1986, Feb. 5	1	2	50,000,000	Texas
1987, Feb. 27	1	6	28,000,000	Laurel, Miss.
1987, May 22	1	30	1,300,000	Saragosa, Texas
1987, Nov. 15-16	49	11	70,000,000 +	Louisiana, Mississippi, Oklahoma, Texas
1988, Nov. 15-16	44	7	35,000,000 +	Arkansas, Illinois, Iowa, Kansas, Missouri, Oklahoma, Texas
1988, Nov. 28	1	2	77,500,000	Raleigh, N.C.
1989, May 5	17	7	64,000,000 +	Georgia, South Carolina, North Carolina
1989, Nov. 15	1	21	100,000,000	Huntsville, Alabama
1989, Nov. 15-16	39	30	100,000,000 +	Alabama, Arkansas, Georgia, Tennesse, New Jersey, Pennsylvania, New York

1. Not definitely known; believed to be large. NOTE: Additional storms may be listed in the *Current Events* section. n.a. = not available. *Source:* Department of Commerce, National Oceanic and Atmospheric Administration.

November 15-16, A Good Time to Head for the Cellar

1987	49 tornadoes	11 killed	$70 + million damage
1988	44 tornadoes	7 killed	$35 + million damage
1989	39 tornadoes	30 killed	$100 + million damage

Tropical Storms and Hurricanes, 1886–1989

	Jan.–April	May	June	July	Aug.	Sept.	Oct.	Nov.	Dec.	Total
Number of tropical storms (incl. hurricanes)	3	14	56	66	209	298	181	42	6	875
Number of tropical storms that reached hurricane intensity	1	3	23	35	147	187	91	21	3	511

Other Recorded Extremes

Highest average annual mean temperature (World): Dallol, Ethiopia (Oct. 1960-Dec. 1966), 94° F (35° C). **(U.S.):** Key West, Fla. (30-year normal), 78.2° F (25.7° C).

Lowest average annual mean temperature (Antarctica): Plateau Station −70° F (−57° C). **(U.S.):** Barrow, Alaska (30-year normal), 9.3° F (−13° C).

Greatest average yearly rainfall (U.S.): Mt. Waialeale, Kauai, Hawaii (32-year avg), 460 in. (1,168 cm). **(India):** Cherrapunji (74-year avg), 450 in. (1,143 cm).

Minimum average yearly rainfall (Chile): Arica (59-year avg), 0.03 in. (0.08 cm) (no rainfall for 14 consecutive years). **(U.S.):** Death Valley, Calif. (42-year avg), 1.63 in. (4.14 cm). Bagdad, Calif., holds the U.S. record for the longest period with no measurable rain, 767 days, from Oct. 3, 1912 to Nov. 8, 1914).

Hottest summer avg in Western Hemisphere (U.S.): Death Valley, Calif., 98° F (36.7° C).

Longest hot spell (W. Australia): Marble Bar, 100° F (38° C) (or above) for 162 consecutive days, Oct. 30, 1923-Apr. 7, 1924.

Largest hailstone (U.S.): Coffeyville, KS, 17.5 in. (44.5 cm), Sept. 3, 1979.

Weather Glossary

blizzard: storm characterized by strong winds, low temperatures, and large amounts of snow.

blowing snow: snow lifted from ground surface by wind; restricts visibility.

cold wave warning: indicates that a change to abnormally cold weather is expected; greater than normal protective measures will be required.

cyclone: circulation of winds rotating counterclockwise in the northern hemisphere and clockwise in the southern hemisphere. Hurricanes and tornadoes are both examples of cyclones.

drifting snow: strong winds will blow loose or falling snow into significant drifts.

drizzle: uniform close precipitation of tiny drops with diameter less than .02 inch.

flash flood: dangerous rapid rise of water levels in streams, rivers, or over land area.

freezing rain or drizzle: rain or drizzle that freezes on contact with the ground or other objects forming a coating of ice on exposed surfaces.

gale warning: winds in the 33–48 knot (38–55 mph) range forecast.

hail: small balls of ice falling separately or in lumps; usually associated with thunderstorms and temperatures that may be well above freezing.

hazardous driving warnings: indicates that drizzle, freezing rain, snow, sleet, or strong winds make driving conditions difficult.

heavy snow warnings: issued when 4 inches or more of snow are expected to fall in a 12-hour period or when 6 inches or more are anticipated in a 24-hour period.

hurricane: devastating cyclonic storm; winds over 74 mph near storm center; usually tropical in origin; called cyclone in Indian Ocean, typhoon in the Pacific.

hurricane warning: winds in excess of 64 knots (74 mph) in connection with hurricane.

rain: precipitation of liquid particles with diameters larger than .02 inch.

sleet: translucent or transparent ice pellets; frozen rain; generally a winter phenomenon.

small craft warning: indicates winds as high as 33 knots (38 mph) and sea conditions dangerous to small boats.

snow flurries: snow falling for a short time at intermittent periods; accumulations are usually small.

snow squall: brief, intense falls of snow, usually accompanied by gusty winds.

storm warnings: winds greater than 48 knots (55 mph) are forecast.

temperature-humidity index (THI): measure of personal discomfort based on the combined effects of temperature and humidity. Most people are uncomfortable when the THI is 75. A THI of 80 produces acute discomfort for almost everyone.

tidal waves: series of ocean waves caused by earthquakes; can reach speeds of 600 mph; they grow in height as they reach shore and can crest as high as 100 feet.

thunder: the sound produced by the rapid expansion of air heated by lightning.

tornado: dangerous whirlwind associated with the cumulonimbus clouds of severe thunderstorms; winds up to 300 mph.

tornado warning: tornado has actually been detected by radar or sighted in designated area.

tornado watch: potential exists in the watch area for storms that could contain tornadoes.

travelers' warning: *see* hazardous driving warning.

tsunami: *see* tidal waves.

wind-chill factor: combined effect of temperature and wind speed as compared to equivalent temperature in calm air.

Record Highest Temperatures by State

State	Temp, °F	Date	Station	Elevation, feet
Alabama	112	Sept. 5, 1925	Centerville	345
Alaska	100	June 27, 1915	Fort Yukon	est. 420
Arizona	127	July 7, 1905*	Parker	345
Arkansas	120	Aug. 10, 1936	Ozark	396
California	134	July 10, 1913	Greenland Ranch	−178
Colorado	118	July 11, 1888	Bennett	5,484
Connecticut	105	July 22, 1926	Waterbury	400
Delaware	110	July 21, 1930	Millsboro	20
Florida	109	June 29, 1931	Monticello	207
Georgia	113	May 27, 1978	Greenville	860
Hawaii	100	Apr. 27, 1931	Pahala	850
Idaho	118	July 28, 1934	Orofino	1,027
Illinois	117	July 14, 1954	E. St. Louis	410
Indiana	116	July 14, 1936	Collegeville	672
Iowa	118	July 20, 1934	Keokuk	614
Kansas	121	July 24, 1936*	Alton (near)	1,651
Kentucky	114	July 28, 1930	Greensburg	581
Louisiana	114	Aug. 10, 1936	Plain Dealing	268
Maine	105	July 10, 1911*	North Bridgton	450
Maryland	109	July 10, 1936*	Cumberland & Frederick	623;325
Massachusetts	107	Aug. 2, 1975	New Bedford & Chester	120;640
Michigan	112	July 13, 1936	Mio	963
Minnesota	114	July 6, 1936*	Moorhead	904
Mississippi	115	July 29, 1930	Holly Springs	600
Missouri	118	July 14, 1954*	Warsaw & Union	687;560
Montana	117	July 5, 1937	Medicine Lake	1,950
Nebraska	118	July 24, 1936*	Minden	2,169
Nevada	122	June 23, 1954*	Overton	1,240
New Hampshire	106	July 4, 1911	Nashua	125
New Jersey	110	July 10, 1936	Runyon	18
New Mexico	116	July 14, 1934*	Orogrande	4,171
New York	108	July 22, 1926	Troy	35
North Carolina	109	Sept. 7, 1954*	Weldon	81
North Dakota	121	July 6, 1936	Steele	1,857
Ohio	113	July 21, 1934*	Gallipolis (near)	673
Oklahoma	120	July 26, 1943*	Tishomingo	670
Oregon	119	Aug. 10, 1898	Pendleton	1,074
Pennsylvania	111	July 10, 1936*	Phoenixville	100
Rhode Island	104	Aug. 2, 1975	Providence	51
South Carolina	111	June 28, 1954*	Camden	170
South Dakota	120	July 5, 1936	Gannvalley	1,750
Tennessee	113	Aug. 9, 1930*	Perryville	377
Texas	120	Aug. 12, 1936	Seymour	1,291
Utah	116	June 28, 1892	Saint George	2,880
Vermont	105	July 4, 1911	Vernon	310
Virginia	110	July 15, 1954	Balcony Falls	725
Washington	118	Aug. 5, 1961*	Ice Harbor Dam	475
West Virginia	112	July 10, 1936*	Martinsburg	435
Wisconsin	114	July 13, 1936	Wisconsin Dells	900
Wyoming	114	July 12, 1900	Basin	3,500

*Also on earlier dates at the same or other places. *Source:* National Oceanic and Atmospheric Administration, Environmental Data and Information Service, National Climatic Center, Asheville, N.C.

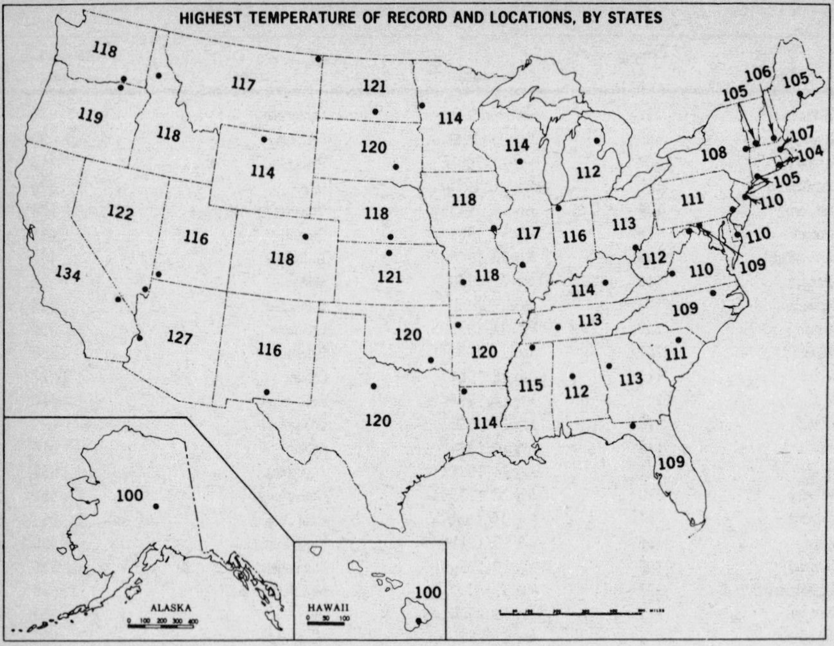

HIGHEST TEMPERATURE OF RECORD AND LOCATIONS, BY STATES

118 117 121 114 114 112 106 105 105 107 104 105 108 111 110 110 109 119 118 114 120 120 118 118 113 111 112 110 122 116 118 117 116 114 134 127 116 121 118 114 109 120 113 109 111 120 115 112 113 120 114 109

ALASKA 100

HAWAII 100

Source: National Oceanic and Atmospheric Administration.

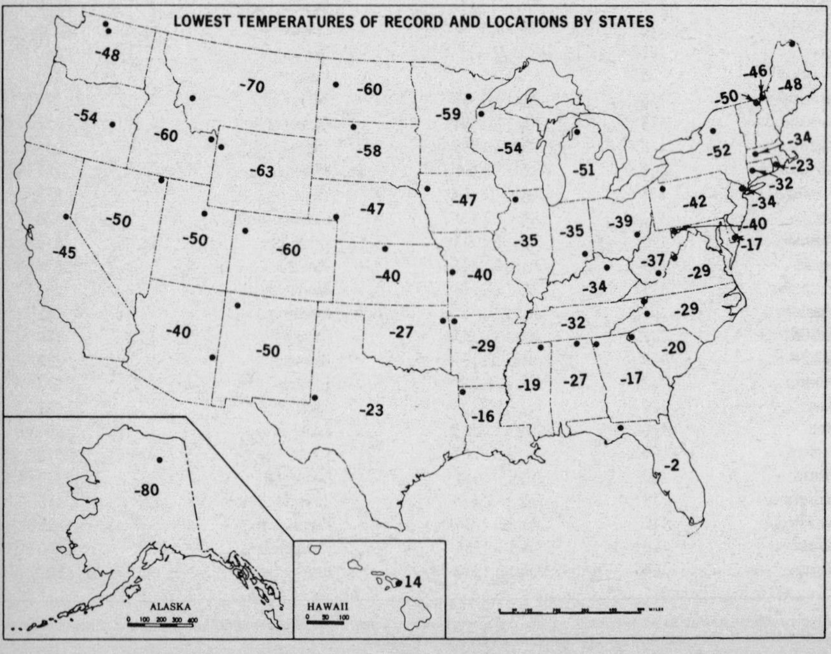

LOWEST TEMPERATURES OF RECORD AND LOCATIONS BY STATES

-48 -70 -60 -59 -46 -50 -48 -54 -60 -58 -54 -52 -34 -63 -51 -42 -23 -50 -50 -47 -47 -34 -45 -60 -40 -40 -35 -35 -39 -40 -17 -40 -50 -27 -29 -37 -29 -34 -32 -29 -19 -27 -17 -20 -23 -16 -2

ALASKA -80

HAWAII 14

Record Lowest Temperatures by State

State	Temp, °F	Date	Station	Elevation, feet
Alabama	−27	Jan. 30, 1966	New Market	760
Alaska	−80	Jan. 23, 1971	Prospect Creek	1,100
Arizona	−40	Jan. 7, 1971	Hawley Lake	8,180
Arkansas	−29	Feb. 13, 1905	Pond	1,250
California	−45	Jan. 20, 1937	Boca	5,532
Colorado	−60	Jan. 1, 1979*	Maybell	5,920
Connecticut	−32	Feb. 16, 1943	Falls Village	585
Delaware	−17	Jan. 17, 1893	Millsboro	20
Florida	−2	Feb. 13, 1899	Tallahassee	193
Georgia	−17	Jan. 27, 1940	CCC Camp F-16	est. 1,000
Hawaii	14	Jan. 2, 1961	Haleakala, Maui Is	9,750
Idaho	−60	Jan. 18, 1943	Island Park Dam	6,285
Illinois	−35	Jan. 22, 1930	Mount Carroll	817
Indiana	−35	Feb. 2, 1951	Greensburg	954
Iowa	−47	Jan. 12, 1912	Washta	1,157
Kansas	−40	Feb. 13, 1905	Lebanon	1,812
Kentucky	−34	Jan. 28, 1963	Cynthiana	684
Louisiana	−16	Feb. 13, 1899	Minden	194
Maine	−48	Jan. 19, 1925	Van Buren	510
Maryland	−40	Jan. 13, 1912	Oakland	2,461
Massachusetts	−34	Jan. 18, 1957	Birch Hill Dam	840
Michigan	−51	Feb. 9, 1934	Vanderbilt	785
Minnesota	−59	Feb. 16, 1903*	Pokegama Dam	1,280
Mississippi	−19	Jan. 30, 1966	Corinth	420
Missouri	−40	Feb. 13, 1905	Warsaw	700
Montana	−70	Jan. 20, 1954	Rogers Pass	5,470
Nebraska	−47	Feb. 12, 1899	Camp Clarke	3,700
Nevada	−50	Jan. 8, 1937	San Jacinto	5,200
New Hampshire	−46	Jan. 28, 1925	Pittsburg	1,575
New Jersey	−34	Jan. 5, 1904	River Vale	70
New Mexico	−50	Feb. 1, 1951	Gavilan	7,350
New York	−52	Feb. 18, 1979*	Old Forge	1,720
North Carolina	−29	Jan. 30, 1966	Mt. Mitchell	6,525
North Dakota	−60	Feb. 15, 1936	Parshall	1,929
Ohio	−39	Feb. 10, 1899	Milligan	800
Oklahoma	−27	Jan. 18, 1930	Watts	958
Oregon	−54	Feb. 10, 1933*	Seneca	4,700
Pennsylvania	−42	Jan. 5, 1904	Smethport	est. 1,500
Rhode Island	−23	Jan. 11, 1942	Kingston	100
South Carolina	−20	Jan. 18, 1977	Caesars Head	3,100
South Dakota	−58	Feb. 17, 1936	McIntosh	2,277
Tennessee	−32	Dec. 30, 1917	Mountain City	2,471
Texas	−23	Feb. 8, 1933*	Seminole	3,275
Utah	−50	Jan. 5, 1913*	Strawberry Tunnel	7,650
Vermont	−50	Dec. 30, 1933	Bloomfield	915
Virginia	−29	Feb. 10, 1899	Monterey	—
Washington	−48	Dec. 30, 1968	Mazama & Winthrop	2,120;1,765
West Virginia	−37	Dec. 30, 1917	Lewisburg	2,200
Wisconsin	−54	Jan. 24, 1922	Danbury	908
Wyoming	−63	Feb. 9, 1933	Moran	6,770

*Also on earlier dates at the same or other places. Source: National Oceanic and Atmospheric Administration, Environmental Data and Information Service, National Climatic Center, Asheville, N.C.

Temperature Extremes in The United States

Source: National Oceanic and Atmospheric Administration, Environmental Data and Information Service, and National Center Climatic Center

The Highest Temperature Extremes

Greenland Ranch, California, with 134° F (56.67° C) on July 10, 1913, holds the record for the highest temperature ever officially observed in the United States. This station was located in barren Death Valley, 178 feet below sea level. Death Valley is about 140 miles long, four to six miles wide, and oriented north to south in southwestern California. Much of the valley is below sea level and is flanked by towering mountain ranges with Mt. Whitney, the highest landmark in the 48 conterminous states, rising to 14,495 feet above sea level, less than 100 miles to the west. Death Valley has the hottest summers in the Western Hemisphere, and is the only known place in the United States where nightime temperatures sometimes remain above 100° F (37.78° C).

The highest annual normal (1941-70 mean) temperature in the United States, 78.2° F (25.67° C), and the highest summer (June-August) normal temperature, 92.8° F (33.78° C), are for Death Valley, California. The highest winter (December-February) normal temperature is 72.8° F (22.67° C) for Honolulu, Hawaii.

Amazing temperature rises of 40° to 50° F (4.44 to 10° C) in a few minutes occasionally may be brought about by chinook winds.[1]

Some Outstanding Temperature Rises

In 12 hours: 83° F (46.11° C), Granville, N.D., Feb. 21, 1918, from −33° F to 50° F (−36.11 to 10° C) from early morning to late afternoon.

In 15 minutes: 42° F (23.34° C), Fort Assiniboine, Mont., Jan. 19, 1892, from −5° F to 37° F (−20.56 to 2.78° C).

In seven minutes: 34° F (1.11° C), Kipp, Mont., Dec. 1, 1896. The observer also reported that a total rise of 80° F (26.67° C) occurred in a few hours and that 30 inches of snow disappeared in one-half day.

In two minutes: 49° F (27.22° C), Spearfish, S.D., Jan. 22, 1943 from −4° F (20° C) at 7:30 a.m. to 45° F (7.22° C) at 7:32 a.m.

The Lowest Temperature Extremes

The lowest temperature on record in the United States, −79.8° F (−62.1° C), was observed at Pros-pect Creek Camp in the Endicott Mountains of northern Alaska (latitude 66° 48′N, longitude 150° 40′W) on Jan. 23, 1971. The lowest ever recorded in the conterminous 48 states, −69.7° F (−56.5° C), occurred at Rogers Pass, in Lewis and Clark County, Mont., on Jan. 20, 1954. Rogers Pass is in mountainous and heavily forested terrain about one-half mile east of and 140 feet below the summit of the Continental Divide.

The lowest annual normal (1941-70 mean) temperature in the United States is 9.3° F (−12.68° C) for Barrow, Alaska, which lies on the Arctic coast. Barrow also has the coolest summers (June-August) with a normal temperature of 36.4° F (2.44° C). The lowest winter (December-February) normal temperature, is −15.7° F (−26.5° C) for Barter Island on the arctic coast of northeast Alaska.

In the 48 conterminous states, Mt. Washington, N.H. (elevation 6,262 feet) has the lowest annual normal temperature 26.9° F (−2.72° C) and the lowest normal summer temperature, 46.8° F (8.22° C). A few stations in the northeastern United States and in the upper Rocky Mountains have normal annual temperatures in the 30s; summer normal temperatures at these stations are in the low 50s. Winter normal temperatures are lowest in northeastern North Dakota, 5.6° F (−14.23° C) for Langdon Experiment Farm, and in northwestern Minnesota, 5.3° F (−14.83° C) for Hallock.

Some Outstanding Temperature Falls

In 24 hours: 100° F (55.57° C), Browing, Mont., Jan. 23-24, 1916, from 44° to −56° F (6.67° to −48.9° C).

In 12 hours: 84° F (46.67° C), Fairfield, Mont., Dec. 24, 1924, from 63° (17.22° C) at noon to −21° F (−29.45° C) at midnight.

In 2 hours: 62° F (34.45° C), Rapid City, S.D., Jan. 12, 1911, from 49° F (9.45° C) at 6:00 a.m. to −13° F (−25° C) at 8:00 a.m.

In 27 minutes: 58° F (32.22° C), Spearfish, S.D., Jan. 22, 1943, from 54° F (12.22° C) at 9:00 a.m. to −4° F (−20° C) at 9:27 a.m.

In 15 minutes: 63° F (26.11° C), Rapid City, S.D., Jan. 10, 1911, from 55° F (12.78° C) at 7:00 a.m. to 8° F (−13.33° C). at 7:15 a.m.

1. A warm, dry wind that descends from the eastern slopes of the Rocky Mountains, causing a rapid rise in temperature.

Winter Indoor Comfort and Relative Humidity

Compared to summer when the moisture content of the air (relative humidity) is an important factor of body discomfort, air moisture has a lesser effect on the human body during outdoor winter activities. But it is a big factor for winter indoor comfort because it has a direct bearing on health and energy consumption.

The colder the outdoor temperature, the more heat must be added indoors for body comfort. However, the heat that is added will cause a drying effect and lower the indoor relative humidity, unless an indoor moisture source is present.

While a room temperature between 71° and 77° F may be comfortable for short periods of time under very dry conditions, prolonged exposure to dry air has varying effects on the human body and usually causes discomfort. The moisture content of the air is important, and by increasing the rela-

Average Indoor Relative Humidity, %, for January

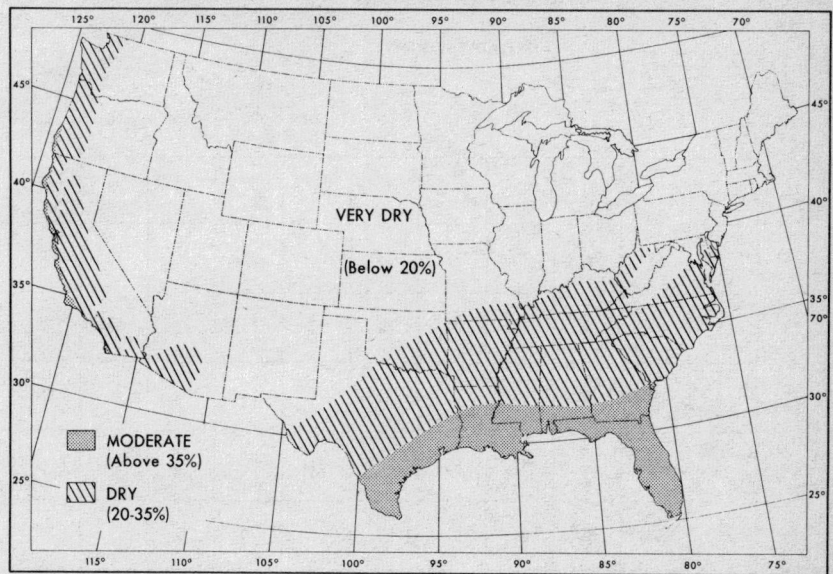

Source: National Oceanic and Atmospheric Administration, Environmental Data and Information Service, National Climatic Center.

tive humidity to above 50% within the above temperature range, 80% or more of all average dressed persons would feel comfortable.

Effects of Dry Air on the Body

Studies have shown that dry air has four main effects on the human body:

1. Breathing dry air is a potential health hazard which can cause such respiratory ailments as asthma, bronchitis, sinusitis, and nosebleeds, or general dehydration since body fluids are depleted during respiration.

2. Skin moisture evaporation can cause skin irritations and eye itching.

3. Irritative effects, such as static electricity which causes mild shocks when metal is touched, are common when the air moisture is low.

4. The "apparent temperature" of the air is lower than what the thermometer indicates, and the body "feels" colder.

These problems can be reduced by simply increasing the indoor relative humidity. This can be done through use of humidifiers, vaporizers, steam generators, sources such as large pans, or water containers made of porous ceramics. Even wet towels or water in a bathtub will be of some help. The lower the room temperature the easier the relative humidity can be brought to its desired level. A relative humidity indicator (hygrometer) may be of assistance in determining the humidity in the house.

Referring to item 4, a more detailed discussion is necessary. While the indoor temperature as read

from a thermometer may be 75° F, the apparent temperature (what it feels like) may be warmer or colder depending on the moisture content of the air. Apparent temperature can vary as much as 8° F within a relative humidity range of 10 to 80 percent (these limits are generally possible in a closed room). Because of evaporation the human body cools when exposed to dry air, and the sense of coldness increases as the humidity decreases. With a room temperature of 70° F, for example, a person will feel colder in a dry room than in a moist room; this is especially noticeable when entering a dry room after bathing.

The table on the following page gives apparent temperatures for various combinations of room temperature and relative humidity. As an example of how to read the table, a room temperature of 70° F combined with a relative humidity of 10% feels like 64° F, but at 80% it feels like 71° F.

Although degrees of comfort vary with age, health, activity, clothing, and body characteristics, the table can be used as a general guideline when raising the apparent temperature and the level of comfort through an increase in room moisture, rather than by an addition of heat to the room. This method of changing the apparent temperature can give the direct benefit of reducing heating costs because comfort can be maintained with a lower thermostat setting if moisture is added. For example, an apparent comfortable temperature can be maintained with a thermostat setting of 75° F with 20% relative humidity or with a 70° F setting with 80 percent humidity. A relative humidity of 20 percent is common for homes without a humidifier during winter in the northern United States.

Apparent Temperature for Values of Room Temperature and Relative Humidity

RELATIVE HUMIDITY (%)

ROOM TEMPERATURE (°F)	0	10	20	30	40	50	60	70	80	90	100
75	68	69	71	72	74	75	76	76	77	78	79
74	66	68	69	71	72	73	74	75	76	77	78
73	65	67	68	70	71	72	73	74	75	76	77
72	64	65	67	68	70	71	72	73	74	75	76
71	63	64	66	67	68	70	71	72	73	74	75
70	63	64	65	66	67	68	69	70	71	72	73
69	62	63	64	65	66	67	68	69	70	71	72
68	61	62	63	64	65	66	67	68	69	70	71
67	60	61	62	63	64	65	66	67	68	68	69
66	59	60	61	62	63	64	65	66	67	67	68
65	59	60	61	61	62	63	64	65	65	66	67
64	58	59	60	60	61	62	63	64	64	65	66
63	57	58	59	59	60	61	62	62	63	64	64
62	56	57	58	58	59	60	61	61	62	63	63
61	56	57	57	58	59	59	60	60	61	61	62
60	55	56	56	57	58	58	59	59	60	60	61

Source: National Oceanic and Atmospheric Administration, Environmental Data and Information Service and National Climatic Center.

Many public figures not listed here may be found elsewhere in the *Information Please Almanac*.

  41 Governors
  629 Presidents
  631 Presidents' Wives
  34 Senators
  899 Sports Personalities
  645 Supreme Court Justices
  629 Vice Presidents

A name in parentheses is the original name or form of name. Localities are places of birth. Country name in parenthesis is the present-day name. Dates of birth appear as month/day/year. **Boldface** years in parentheses are dates of **(birth-death).**

Information has been gathered from many sources, including the individuals themselves. However, the *Information Please Almanac* cannot guarantee the accuracy of every individual item.

A

Aalto, Alvar (architect); Kuortane, Finland **(1898-1976)**
Abbado, Claudio (orchestra conductor); Milan, Italy, 1933
Abbott, Bud (William) (comedian); Asbury Park, N.J. **(1898-1974)**
Abbott, George (stage producer); Forestville, N.Y., 6/25/1887
Abel, Walter (actor); St. Paul **(1898-1987)**
Abelard, Peter (theologian); nr. Nantes, France **(1079-1142)**
Abernathy, Ralph (civil rights leader); Linden, Ala., **(1926-1990)**
Acheson, Dean (statesman); Middletown, Conn. **(1893-1971)**
Acuff, Roy Claxton (musician); nr. Maynardsville, Tenn. 9/15/1903
Adams, Charles Francis (diplomat); Boston **(1807-1886)**
Adams, Don (actor); New York City, 4/19/1926
Adams, Edie (Edie Enke) (actress); Kingston, Pa., 4/16/1929
Adams, Franklin Pierce (columnist and author); Chicago **(1881-1960)**
Adams, Henry Brooks (historian); Boston **(1838-1918)**
Adams, Joey (comedian); New York City, 1/6/1911
Adams, Mason (actor); New York City, 2/26/19
Adams, Maude (Maude Kiskadden) (actress); Salt Lake City, **(1872-1953)**
Adams, Samuel (American Revolutionary patriot); Boston **(1722-1803)**
Adamson, Joy (naturalist); Troppau, Silesia **(1910-1980)**
Addams, Charles (cartoonist); Westfield, N.J., **(1912-1988)**
Addams, Jane (social worker); Cedarville, Ill. **(1860-1935)**
Adderley, Julian "Cannonball" (jazz saxophonist); Tampa, Fla. **(1928-1975)**
Ade, George (humorist); Kentland, Ind. **(1866-1944)**
Adenauer, Konrad (statesman); Cologne, Germany **(1876-1967)**
Adler, Alfred (psychoanalyst); Vienna **(1870-1937)**
Adler, Larry (musician); Baltimore, 2/10/1914
Adler, Richard (songwriter); New York City, 8/3/1921
Adoree, Renée (Renée La Fonte) (actress); Lille, France **(1898-1933)**
Aeschylus (dramatist); Eleusis (Greece) **(525-456 B.C.)**
Aesop (fabulist); birthplace unknown **(lived c. 600 B.C.)**
Aherne, Brian (actor); King's Norton, England **(1902-1986)**
Aiello, Danny (actor); New York City, 6/20/33
Aiken, Conrad (poet); Savannah, Ga. **(1889-1973)**
Ailey, Alvin (choreographer); Rogers, Tex., **(1931-1989)**
Albanese, Licia (operatic soprano); Bari, Italy, 7/22/1913
Albee, Edward (playwright); Washington, D.C., 3/12/1928
Albers, Josef (painter); Bottrop, Germany **(1888-1976)**
Albert, Eddie (Edward Albert Heimberger) (actor); Rock Island, Ill., 4/22/1908
Albert, Edward (actor); Los Angeles, 2/20/51
Albertson, Jack (actor); Malden, Mass. **(1910?-1981)**
Albright, Lola (actress); Akron, Ohio, 7/20/1925
Alcott, Louisa May (novelist); Germantown, Pa. **(1832-1888)**
Alda, Alan (actor); New York City, 1/28/1936
Alda, Robert (Alphonso d'Abruzzo) (actor); New York City **(1914-1986)**
Alden, John (American Pilgrim); England **(1599?-1687)**
Alexander, Jane (Quigley) (actress); Boston, 10/28/39
Alexander the Great (monarch and conqueror); Pella, Macedonia (Greece) **(356-323 B.C.)**
Alger, Horatio (author); Revere, Mass. **(1834-1899)**
Algren, Nelson (novelist); Detroit **(1909-1981)**
Allen, Debbie (dancer-choreographer, actress); Houston, Tex., 1/16/50
Allen, Ethan (American Revolutionary soldier); Litchfield, Conn. **(1738-1789)**
Allen, Fred (John Florence Sullivan) (comedian); Cambridge, Mass. **(1894-1956)**
Allen, Gracie (Grace Ethel Cecile Rosalie Allen) (comedienne); San Francisco **(1906-1964)**
Allen, Mel (Melvin Israel) (sportscaster); Birmingham, Ala.,

2/14/1913
Allen, Peter (actor); Tenterfield, Australia, 2/10/1944
Allen, Steve (TV entertainer); New York City, 12/26/1921
Allen, Woody (Allen Stewart Konigsberg) (actor, writer, and director); Brooklyn, N.Y., 12/1/1935
Alley, Kirstie (actress); Wichita, Kan., 1/12/55
Allison, Fran (actress); LaPorte City, Iowa, **(1908?-1989)**
Allman, Gregg (singer); Nashville, Tenn., 12/8/1947
Allyson, June (Jan Allyson) (actress); New York City, 10/7/1923
Alonso, Alicia (ballerina); Havana, 12/21/1921(?)
Alpert, Herb (band leader); Los Angeles, 3/31/1935(?)
Alsop, Joseph W., Jr. (journalist); Avon, Conn., **(1910-1989)**
Alsop, Stewart (journalist); Avon, Conn. **(1914-1974)**
Altman, Robert (film director); Kansas City, Mo., 2/20/1925
Amati, Nicola (violin maker); Cremona, Italy **(1596-1684)**
Ambler, Eric (suspense writer); London, 6/28/1909
Ameche, Don (Dominic Amici) (actor); Kenosha, Wis., 5/31/1908
Ames, Leon (actor); Portland, Ind., 1/20/03
Amis, Kingsley (novelist); London, 4/16/1922
Amory, Cleveland (writer and conservationist); Nahant, Mass., 9/2/1917
Amos (Freeman F. Gosden) (radio comedian); Richmond, Va., **(1899-1982)**
Amos, John (actor); Newark, N.J., 12/27/41
Amsterdam, Morey (actor); Chicago, 12/14/1914
Andersen, Hans Christian (author of fairy-tales); Odense, Denmark **(1805-1875)**
Anderson, Eddie. *See* Rochester
Anderson, Harry (actor); Newport, R.I., 10/14/52
Anderson, Ib (ballet dancer); Copenhagen, 12/14/1954
Anderson, Jack (journalist); Long Beach, Calif., 10/19/1922
Anderson, Dame Judith (actress); Adelaide, Australia, 2/10/1898
Anderson, Lindsay (Gordon) (director); Bangalore, India, 4/17/1923
Anderson, Loni (actress); St. Paul, Minn. 8/5/45
Anderson, Lynn (singer); Grand Forks, N.D., 9/26/1947
Anderson, Marian (contralto); Philadelphia, 2/17/1902
Anderson, Maxwell (dramatist); Atlantic, Pa. **(1888-1959)**
Anderson, Richard Dean (actor); Minneapolis, Minn., 1/23/50
Anderson, Robert (playwright); New York City, 4/28/1917
Andersson, Bibi (actress); Stockholm, 11/11/1935
Andress, Ursula (actress); Switzerland, 3/19/1938
Andrews, Dana (actor); Collins, Miss., 1/1/1909
Andrews, Julie (Julia Wells) (actress and singer); Walton-on-Thames, England, 10/1/1935
Andrews, La Verne (singer); Minneapolis **(1916-1967)**
Andrews, Maxene (singer); Minneapolis, 1/3/1918
Andrews, Patti (singer); Minneapolis, 2/16/1920
Andy (Charles J. Correll) (radio comedian); Peoria, Ill. **(1890-1972)**
Angeles, Victoria de los (Victoria Gamez Cima) (operatic soprano); Barcelona, 11/1/1924
Anka, Paul (singer and composer); Ottawa, 7/30/1941
Ann-Margret (Ann-Margret Olsson) (actress); Valsjobyn, Sweden, 4/28/1941
Annabella (actress); Paris, 1912
Anouilh, Jean (playwright); Bordeaux, France **(1910-1987)**
Anthony, Susan Brownell (woman suffragist); Adams, Mass. **(1820-1906)**
Antonioni, Michelangelo (director); Ferrara, Italy, 9/29/1912
Antony, Mark (Marcus Antonius) (statesman); Rome **(83?-30 B.C.)**
Anuszkiewicz, Richard (painter); Erie, Pa., 5/23/1930
Aquinas, St. Thomas (philosopher); nr. Aquino (Italy) **(1225?-1274)**
Arbuckle, Roscoe "Fatty" (actor and director); San Jose, Calif. **(1887-1933)**
Archimedes (physicist and mathematician); Syracuse, Sicily **(287?-212 B.C.)**
Archipenko, Alexandre (sculptor); Kiev, Russia **(1887-1964)**
Arden, Elizabeth (Florence Nightingale Graham) (cosmetics executive);

Woodbridge, Canada **(1891-1966)**
Arden, Eve (Eunice Quedens) (actress); Mill Valley, Calif., 4/30/1912
Arendt, Hannah (historian); Hannover, Germany **(1906-1975)**
Aristophanes (dramatist); Athens 448?-380 B.C.)
Aristotle (philosopher); Stagirus, Macedonia (384-322 B.C.)
Arkin, Alan (actor and director); New York City, 3/26/1934
Arledge, Roone (TV executive); Forest Hills, N.Y., 7/8/1931
Arlen, Harold (Hyman Arluck) (composer); Buffalo, N.Y. **(1905-1986)**
Arlen, Richard (actor); Charlottesville, Va. **(1900-1976)**
Arliss, George (actor); London **(1868-1946)**
Armstrong, Louis ("Satchmo") (musician); New Orleans **(1900-1971)**
Armstrong-Jones, Anthony. *See* Snowdon, Earl of
Arnaz, Desi (Desiderio) (actor and producer); Santiago, Cuba **(1917-1986)**
Arness, James (James Aurness) (TV actor); Minneapolis, 5/26/1923
Arno, Peter (cartoonist); New York City **(1904-1968)**
Arnold, Benedict (American Revolutionary War general, charged with treason); Norwich, Conn. **(1741-1801)**
Arnold, Eddy (singer); Henderson, Tenn., 5/15/1918
Arnold, Edward (actor); New York City **(1890-1956)**
Arnold, Matthew (poet and critic); Laleham, England **(1822-1888)**
Arp, Jean (sculptor and painter); Strasbourg (France) **(1887-1966)**
Arpino, Gerald (choreographer); Staten Island, N.Y., 1/14/28
Arquette, Cliff ("Charley Weaver") (actor); Toledo, Ohio **(1905-1974)**
Arquette, Rosanna (actress); New York City, 8/10/59
Arrau, Claudio (pianist); Chillán, Chile, 2/6/1903
Arroyo, Martina (soprano); New York City, 2/2/1940
Arthur, Bea (Bernice Frankel) (actress); New York City, 5/13/1926(?)
Arthur, Jean (Gladys Greene) (actress); New York City, 10/17/1905
Asch, Sholem (novelist); Kutno, Poland **(1880-1957)**
Ashcroft, Dame Peggy (actress); Croydon, England, 12/22/07
Ashkenazy, Vladimir (concert pianist); Gorki, U.S.S.R., 7/6/1937
Ashley, Elizabeth (actress); Ocala, Fla., 8/30/1939
Ashton, Sir Frederick William Mallandaine (choreographer); Guayaquil, Ecuador **(1904-1988)**
Asimov, Isaac (author); Petrovichi, Russia, 1/2/1920
Asner, Edward (actor); Kansas City, Mo., 11/15/1929
Astaire, Fred (Frederick Austerlitz) (dancer and actor); Omaha, Neb. **(1899-1987)**
Astin, John (actor; director); Baltimore, Md., 3/30/30
Astor, John Jacob (financier); Waldorf (Germany) **(1763-1848)**
Astor, Mary (Lucile Langhanke) (actress); Quincy, Ill. **(1906-1987)**
Atkins, Chet (guitarist); nr. Luttrell, Tenn., 6/20/1924
Atkinson, Brooks (drama critic); Melrose, Mass. **(1894-1984)**
Attenborough, Richard (actor-director) Cambridge, England, 8/29/1923
Attila (King of Huns, called "Scourge of God") **(406?-453)**
Attlee, Clement R ichard (statesman); London **(1883-1967)**
Atwill, Lionel (actor); Croydon, England, **(1885-1946)**
Auberjonois, Rene (actor); New York City, 6/1/40
Auchincloss, Louis (author); Lawrence, N.Y., 9/27/1917
Auden, W(ystan) H(ugh) (poet); York, England **(1907-1973)**
Audubon, John James (naturalist and painter); Haiti **(1785-1851)**
Auer, Leopold (violinist and teacher); Veszprém, Hungary **(1845-1930)**
Auer, Mischa (actor); St. Petersburg, Russia **(1905-1967)**
Augustine, Saint (Aurelius Augustinus) (theologian); Tagaste, Numidia (Algeria) **(354-430)**
Augustus (Gaius Octavius) (Roman emperor); Rome (63 B.C.-A.D. 14)
Aumont, Jean-Pierre (actor); Paris, 1/5/1913
Austen, Jane (novelist); Steventon, England **(1775-1817)**
Autry, Gene (singer and actor); Tioga, Tex., 9/29/1907
Avalon, Frankie (singer); Philadelphia, 9/18/1940
Avedon, Richard (photographer); New York City, 5/15/1923
Avery, Milton (painter); Altmar, N.Y. **(1893-1965)**
Ax, Emanuel (pianist); Lvov, U.S.S.R., 6/8/1949
Axelrod, George (playwright); New York City, 6/9/1922
Ayckbourn, Alan (playwright); London, 4/12/1939
Ayckroyd, Dan (actor); Ottawa, Ont., Canada, 7/1/1952
Ayres, Agnes (actress); Carbondale, Ill., **(1896-1940)**
Ayres, Lew (actor); Minneapolis, 12/28/1908
Aznavour, Charles (singer, composer); Paris, France 5/22/24

B

Bacall, Lauren (Betty Joan Perske) (actress); New York City, 9/16/1924
Bach, Johann Sebastian (composer); Eisenach (East Germany) **(1685-1750)**
Bach, Karl Phillipp Emanuel (composer); Weimar (East Germany) **(1714-1788)**
Bacharach, Burt (songwriter); Kansas City, Mo., 5/12/1929
Backus, Jim (actor); Cleveland, **(1913-1989)**
Bacon, Francis (painter); Dublin, 1910

Bacon, Francis (philosopher and essayist); London **(1561-1626)**
Bacon, Roger (philosopher and scientist); Ilchester, England **(1214?-1294)**
Baedeker, Karl (travel-guidebook publisher); Essen (Germany) **(1801-1859)**
Baez, Joan (folk singer); Staten Island, N.Y., 1/9/1941
Bagnold, Enid (novelist); Rochester, England **(1889-1981)**
Bailey, F. Lee (lawyer); Waltham, Mass., 6/10/1933
Bailey, Pearl (singer); Newport News, Va. **(1918-1990)**
Bain, Conrad (actor); Lethbridge, Alberta, Canada, 2/4/23
Bainter, Fay (actress); Los Angeles **(1891-1968)**
Baio, Scott (actor); Brooklyn, N.Y., 9/22/61
Baird, Bil (William B.) (puppeteer); Grand Island, Neb **(1904-1987)**
Baker, Anita (singer); Toledo, Ohio, 1958
Baker, Carroll (actress); Johnstown, Pa., 5/28/1931
Baker, Josephine (singer and dancer); St. Louis **(1906-1975)**
Baker, Russell (columnist); Loudoun County, Va., 8/14/1925
Balanchine, George (choreographer); St. Petersburg, Russia **(1904-1983)**
Balboa, Vasco Nuñez de (explorer); Jerez de los Caballeros (Spain) **(1475-1517)**
Baldwin, Faith (novelist); New Rochelle, N.Y. **(1893-1978)**
Baldwin, James (novelist); New York City **(1924-1987)**
Balenciaga, Cristóbal (fashion designer); Guetaria, Spain **(1895-1972)**
Ball, Lucille (Désirée) (actress and producer); Celoron (nr. Jamestown), N.Y. **(1911-1989)**
Ballard, Kaye (Catherine Gloria Balotta) (actress); Cleveland, 11/20/1926
Balmain, Pierre (fashion designer); St.-Jean-de-Maurienne, France **(1914-1982)**
Balsam, Martin (actor); New York City, 11/4/1919
Balzac, Honoré de (novelist); Tours, France **(1799-1850)**
Bancroft, Anne (Annemarie Italiano) (actress); New York City, 9/17/1931
Bancroft, George (actor); Philadelphia **(1882-1956)**
Bankhead, Tallulah (actress); Huntsville, Ala. **(1903-1963)**
Banneker, Benjamin (almanacker and mathematician-astronomer on District of Columbia site survey); Ellicott, Md. **(1731-1806)**
Banting, Fredrick Grant (physiologist); Alliston, Ont., Canada **(1891-1941)**
Bara, Theda (Theodosia Goodman) (actress); Cincinnati **(1890-1955)**
Barber, Red (Walter Lanier) (sportscaster); Columbus, Miss., 2/17/1908
Barber, Samuel (composer); West Chester, Pa. **(1910-1981)**
Bardot, Brigitte (actress); Paris, 1935
Barenboim, Daniel (concert pianist and conductor); Buenos Aires, 11/15/1942
Bari, Lynn (actress); Roanoke, Va., 12/18/13 (?)
Barker, Bob (host); Darrington, Wash., 12/12/23
Barnard, Christiaan N. (heart surgeon); Beauford West, South Africa, 1923
Barnes, Priscilla (actress); Fort Dix, N.J., 12/7/55
Barnum, Phineas Taylor (showman); Bethel, Conn. **(1810-1891)**
Barr, Roseanne (actress); Salt Lake City, 11/3/1952
Barrie, Sir James Matthew (author); Kirriemuir, Scotland **(1860-1937)**
Barrie, Wendy (actress); Hong Kong **(1913-1978)**
Barry, Gene (Eugene Klass) (actor); New York City, 6/4/1922
Barry, John (naval officer); County Wexford, Ireland **(1745-1803)**
Barrymore, Diana (actress); New York City **(1921-1960)**
Barrymore, Ethel (Ethel Blythe) (actress); Philadelphia **(1879-1959)**
Barrymore, Georgiana Drew (actress); Philadelphia **(1856-1893)**
Barrymore, John (John Blythe) (actor); Philadelphia **(1882-1942)**
Barrymore, Lionel (Lionel Blythe) (actor); Philadelphia **(1878-1954)**
Barrymore, Maurice (Herbert Blythe) (actor and playwright); Agra, India **(1847-1905)**
Barthelme, Donald (novelist); Philadelphia **(1931-1989)**
Barthelmess, Richard (actor); New York City **(1897-1963)**
Bartholomew, Freddie (actor); London, 3/28/1924
Bartók, Béla (composer); Nagyszentmiklos (Romania) **(1881-1945)**
Barton, Clara (founder of American Red Cross); Oxford, Mass. **(1821-1912)**
Baruch, Bernard Mannes (statesman), Camden, S.C. **(1870-1965)**
Baryshnikov, Mikhail Nikolayevich (ballet dancer and artistic director); Riga, Latvia, 1/27/1948
Basehart, Richard (actor); Zanesville, Ohio **(1914-1984)**
Basie, Count (William) (band leader); Red Bank, N.J. **(1904-1984)**
Basinger, Kim (actress); Athens, Ga., 8/8/53
Bassey, Shirley (singer); Cardiff, Wales, 1/8/1937
Batchelor, Clarence Daniel (political cartoonist); Osage City, Kan. **(1888-1977)**
Bateman, Jason (actor); Rye, N.Y. 1/14/69
Bateman, Justine (actress); Rye, N.Y., 2/19/66
Bates, Alan (actor); Allestree, England, 2/17/1934
Battle, Kathleen (soprano); Portsmouth, Ohio, 8/13/48
Baudelaire, Charles Pierre (poet); Paris **(1821-1867)**

Baudouin (King); Palace of Laeken, Belgium, 9/7/1930
Baxter, Anne (actress); Michigan City, Ind. (1923-1985)
Baxter, Warner (actor); Columbus, Ohio (1891-1951)
Baxter-Birney, Meredith (actress); Los Angeles, 6/21/47
Bean, Orson (Dallas Frederick Burrows) (actor); Burlington, Vt., 7/22/1928
Beardsley, Aubrey Vincent (illustrator); Brighton, England (1872-1898)
Beaton, Cecil (photographer and designer); London (1904-1980)
Beatty, Clyde (animal trainer); Chillicothe, Ohio (1903-1965)
Beatty, Warren (actor and producer); Richmond, Va., 3/30/1937
Beaumont, Francis (dramatist); Grace-Dieu, England (1584-1616)
Beavers, Louise (actress); Cincinnati, Ohio (1902-1962)
Becket, Thomas à (Archbishop of Canterbury); London (1118?-1170)
Beckett, Samuel (playwright); Dublin (1906-1989)
Beckmann, Max (painter); Leipzig, Germany (1884-1950)
Bede, Saint ("The Venerable Bede") (scholar); Monkwearmouth, England (673-735)
Beecham, Sir Thomas (conductor); St. Helens, England (1879-1961)
Beecher, Henry Ward (clergyman); Litchfield, Conn. (1813-1887)
Beerbohm, Sir Max (author); London (1872-1956)
Beery, Noah (actor); Kansas City, Mo. (1884-1946)
Beery, Noah, Jr. (actor); New York City, 8/10/1916
Beery, Wallace (actor); Kansas City, Mo. (1886-1949)
Beethoven, Ludwig von (composer); Bonn (Germany) (1770-1827)
Begley, Ed (actor); Hartford, Conn. (1901-1970)
Belafonte, Harry (singer and actor); New York City, 3/1/1927
Belafonte-Harper, Shari (actress); New York City, 9/22/54
Belasco, David (dramatist and producer); San Francisco (1854-1931)
Bel Geddes, Barbara (actress); New York City, 10/31/22
Bell, Alexander Graham (inventor); Edinburgh, Scotland (1847-1922)
Bellamy, Edward (author); Chicopee Falls, Mass. (1850-1898)
Bellamy, Ralph (actor); Chicago, 6/17/1904
Bellini, Giovanni (painter); Venice (c.1430-1516)
Bellow, Saul (novelist); Lachine, Quebec, Canada, 6/10/1915
Bellows, George Wesley (painter and lithographer); Columbus, Ohio (1882-1925)
Belmondo, Jean-Paul (actor); Neuilly-sur-Seine, France, 4/9/1933
Belushi, Jim (actor); Chicago, 6/15/54
Belushi, John (comedian, actor); Chicago (1949-1982)
Benchley, Peter Bradford (novelist); New York City, 5/8/1940
Benchley, Robert Charles (humorist); Worcester, Mass. (1889-1945)
Bendix, William (actor); New York City (1906-1964)
Benedict, Dirk (actor); Helena, Mont., 3/1/44
Benes, Eduard (statesman); Kozlany (Czechoslovakia) (1884-1948)
Benét, Stephen Vincent (poet and story writer); Bethlehem, Pa. (1898-1943)
Benét, William Rose (poet and novelist); Ft. Hamilton, Brooklyn, N.Y. (1886-1950)
Ben-Gurion, David (David Green) (statesman); Plónsk (Poland) (1886-1973)
Benjamin, Richard (actor); New York City, 5/22/1938
Bennett, Constance (actress); New York City (1905-1965)
Bennett, Enoch Arnold (novelist and dramatist); Hanley, England (1867-1931)
Bennett, James Gordon (editor); Keith, Scotland (1795-1872)
Bennett, Joan (actress); Palisades, N.J., 2/27/1910
Bennett, Robert Russell (composer); Kansas City, Mo., (1894-1981)
Bennett, Tony (Anthony Benedetto) (singer); Astoria, Queens, N.Y., 8/3/1926
Benny, Jack (Benjamin Kubelsky) (comedian); Chicago (1894-1974)
Benson, Robby (actor); Dallas, Tex., 1/21/56
Bentham, Jeremy Heinrich (economist); London (1748-1832)
Benton, Thomas Hart (painter); Neosho, Mo. (1889-1975)
Berg, Alban (composer); Vienna (1885-1935)
Berg, Gertrude (writer and actress); New York City (1899-1966)
Bergen, Candice (actress); Beverly Hills, Calif., 5/9/1946
Bergen, Edgar (ventriloquist); Chicago, (1903-1978)
Bergen, Polly (actress and singer); Knoxville, Tenn., 7/14/1930
Bergerac, Cyrano de (poet); Paris (1619-1655)
Bergman, Ingmar (film director); Uppsala, Sweden, 7/14/1918
Bergman, Ingrid (actress); Stockholm (1918-1982)
Bergson, Henri (philosopher); Paris (1859-1941)
Berkeley, Busby (choreographer, director); Los Angeles (1885-1976)
Berle, Milton (Milton Berlinger) (comedian); New York City, 7/12/1908
Berlin, Irving (Israel Baline) (songwriter); Temum, Russia (1888-1989)
Berlioz, Louis Hector (composer); La Côte-Saint-André, France (1803-1869)
Berman, Lazar (concert pianist); Leningrad, 1930.
Berman, Shelley (Sheldon) (comedian); Chicago, 2/3/1926
Bernardi, Herschel (actor); New York City (1922-1986)
Bernhardt, Sarah (Rosine Bernard) (actress); Paris (1844-1923)

Bernini, Gian Lorenzo (sculptor and painter); Naples (Italy) (1598-1680)
Bernoulli, Jacques (scientist); Basel, Switzerland (1654-1705)
Bernsen, Corbin (actor); North Hollywood, Calif., 7/7/?
Bertinelli, Valerie (actress); Wilmington, Del., 4/23/60
Bernstein, Leonard (conductor); Lawrence, Mass., 8/25/1918
Berry, Chuck (Charles Edward Berry) (singer); San Jose, Calif., 1/15/1926
Berry, Ken (actor); Moline, Ill., 11/3/30
Betjeman, Sir John (Poet Laureate); London (1906-1984)
Bettelheim, Bruno (psychoanalyst); Vienna (1903-1990)
Bickford, Charles (actor); Cambridge, Mass. (1889-1967)
Bierce, Ambrose Gwinnett (journalist); Meigs County, Ohio (1842-1914?)
Bikel, Theodore (actor and folk singer); Vienna, 5/2/1924
Bing, Sir Rudolf (opera manager); Vienna, 1/9/1902
Bingham, George Caleb (painter); Augusta Co., Va. (1811-1879)
Bishop, Joey (Joseph Gottlieb) (comedian); New York City, 2/3/1919
Bismarck-Schönhausen, Prince Otto Eduard Leopold von (statesman); Schönhausen (East Germany) (1815-1898)
Bisset, Jacqueline (actress); Weybridge, England, 9/13/1944
Bixby, Bill (actor); San Francisco, 1/22/1934
Bizet, Georges (Alexandre César Léopold Bizet) (composer); Paris (1838-1875)
Bjoerling, Jussi (tenor); Stora Tuna, Sweden (1911-1960)
Black, Cilla (singer and actress); Liverpool, England, 5/27/1943
Black, Karen (actress); Park Ridge, Ill., 7/1/1942
Black, Shirley Temple (former actress); Santa Monica, Calif., 4/23/1928
Blackmer, Sidney (actor); Salisbury, N.C. (1898-1973)
Blackstone, Sir William (jurist); London (1723-1780)
Blaine, Vivian (actress and singer); Newark, N.J., 11/21/1924
Blair, Janet (actress); Altoona, Pa., 4/23/1921
Blake, Amanda (Beverly Louise Neill) (actress); Buffalo, N.Y. (1929-1989)
Blake, Eubie (James Hubert) (pianist); Baltimore, (1883-1983)
Blake, Robert (Michael Gubitosi) (actor); Nutley, N.J., 9/18/1933
Blake, William (poet and artist); London (1757-1827)
Blanc, Mel(vin Jerome) (actor and voice specialist); San Francisco (1908-1989)
Blass, Bill (fashion designer); Fort Wayne, Ind., 6/22/1922
Bloch, Ernest (composer); Geneva (1880-1959)
Blondell, Joan (actress); New York City (1909-1979)
Bloom, Claire (actress); London, 2/15/1931
Bloomgarden, Kermit (producer); Brooklyn, N.Y. (1904-1976)
Blore, Eric (actor); London (1887-1959)
Blue, Monte (actor); Indianapolis (1890-1963)
Blyth, Ann (actress); New York City, 8/16/1928
Boccaccio, Giovanni (author); Paris (1313-1375)
Boccherini, Luigi (Rodolfo) (composer); Lucca, Italy (1743-1805)
Boccioni, Umberto (painter and sculptor); Reggio di Calabria, Italy (1882-1916)
Bock, Jerry (composer); New Haven, Conn., 11/23/1928
Bogarde, Dirk (Derek Van den Bogaerde) (film actor and director); London, 3/28/1921
Bogart, Humphrey DeForest (actor); New York City (1899-1957)
Bogdanovich, Peter (producer and director); Kingston, N.Y., 7/30/1939
Bohlen, Charles E. (diplomat); Clayton, N.Y. (1904-1974)
Bohr, Niels (atomic physicist); Copenhagen (1885-1962)
Boland, Mary (actress); Philadelphia, Pa. (1880-1965)
Boles, John (actor); Greenville, Tex. (1895-1969)
Bolger, Ray (dancer and actor); Dorchester, Mass (1904-1987)
Bolivar, Simón (South American liberator); Caracas, Venezuela (1783-1830)
Bologna, Giovanni da (sculptor); Douai (France) (1529-1608)
Bombeck, Erma (author, columnist); Dayton, Ohio 2/21/1927
Bonaparte, Napoleon (Emperor of the French); Ajaccio, Corsica (France) (1769-1821)
Bond, Julian (Georgia legislator); Nashville, Tenn., 1/14/1940
Bondi, Beulah (actress); Chicago (1883-1981)
Bonet, Lisa (actress); San Francisco, 11/16/67
Bonnard, Pierre (painter); Fontenayaux-Roses, France (1867-1947)
Bon Jovi, Jon (musician, songwriter); Sayreville, N.J., 3/2/62
Bono, Sonny (Salvatore) (singer); Detroit, 2/16/1935
Boone, Daniel (frontiersman); nr. Reading, Pa. (1734-1820)
Boone, Pat (Charles) (singer); Jacksonville, Fla., 6/1/1934
Boone, Richard (actor); Los Angeles (1917-1981)
Booth, Edwin Thomas (actor); Bel Air, Md. (1833-1893)
Booth, Evangeline Cory (religious leader); London (1865-1950)
Booth, John Wilkes (actor; assassin of Lincoln); Harford County, Md. (1838-1865)
Booth, Shirley (Thelma Booth Ford) (actress); New York City, 8/30/1907
Bordoni, Irene (actress); Ajaccio (France) (1895-1953)
Borge, Victor (pianist and comedian); Copenhagen, 1/3/1909

Borgia, Cesare (nobleman and soldier); Rome **(1475?-1507)**
Borgia, Lucrezia (Duchess of Ferrara); Rome **(1480-1519)**
Borgnine, Ernest (actor); Hamden, Conn., 1/24/1917
Borromini, Francesco (architect); Bissone (Italy) **(1599-1667)**
Bosch, Hieronymus (Hieronymus van Aeken) (painter); Hertogenbosch (Netherlands) **(c.1450-1516)**
Bosley, Tom (actor); Chicago, 10/1/1927
Bostwick, Barry (actor); San Mateo, Calif., 2/24/45
Boswell, Connee (singer); New Orleans **(1907-1976)**
Boswell, James (diarist and biographer); Edinburgh, Scotland **(1740-1795)**
Botticelli, Sandro (Alessandro di Mariano dei Filipepi) (painter); Florence (Italy) **(1444?-1510)**
Bottoms, Joseph (actor); Santa Barbara, Calif., 4/16/33
Bottoms, Timothy (actor); Santa Barbara, Calif., 8/30/50
Boulez, Pierre (conductor); Montbrison, France, 3/26/1925
Bourke-White, Margaret (photographer); New York City **(1906-1971)**
Bow, Clara (actress); Brooklyn, N.Y. **(1905-1965)**
Bowen, Catherine Drinker (biographer); Haverford, Pa. **(1897-1973)**
Bowes, Edward (radio show director); San Francisco **(1874-1946)**
Bowie, David (David Robert Jones) (actor and musician); London, 1/8/1947(?)
Bowie, James (soldier); Burke County, Ga. **(1799-1836)**
Bowles, Chester (diplomat); Springfield, Mass. **(1901-1986)**
Boxleitner, Bruce (actor); Elgin, Ill., 5/12/50
Boyce, William (composer); London? **(1710-1779)**
Boyd, Bill (William) ("Hopalong Cassidy") (actor); Cambridge, Ohio **(1898-1972)**
Boyd, Stephen (Stephen Millar) (actor); Belfast, Northern Ireland **(1928-1977)**
Boyer, Charles (actor); Figeac, France **(1899-1978)**
Boy George (George Alan O'Dowd) (singer); London, 1961
Boyle, Peter (actor); Philadelphia, 10/18/33
Boyle, Robert (scientist); Lismore Castle, Munster, Ireland **(1627-1691)**
Bracken, Eddie (actor); Astoria, Queens, N.Y., 2/7/1920
Bradbury, Ray Douglas (science-fiction writer); Waukegan, Ill., 8/22/1920
Bradlee, Benjamin C. (editor); Boston, 8/26/1921
Bradley, Ed (broadcast journalist); Philadelphia, Pa., 6/22/1941
Bradley, Omar N. (5-star general); Clark, Mo. **(1893-1981)**
Brady, Alice (actress); New York City **(1892-1939)**
Brady, Scott (actor); Brooklyn, N.Y., **(1924-1985)**
Brahe, Tycho (astronomer); Knudstrup, Denmark **(1546-1601)**
Brahms, Johannes (composer); Hamburg **(1833-1897)**
Braille, Louis (teacher of blind); Coupvray, France **(1809-1862)**
Brailowsky, Alexander (pianist); Kiev, Russia **(1896-1976)**
Bramante, Donato D'Agnolo (architect); Monte Asdrualdo (now Fermignano, Italy) **(1444-1514)**
Brancusi, Constantin (sculptor); Pestisani, Romania **(1876-1957)**
Brando, Marlon (actor); Omaha, Neb., 4/3/1924
Brandt, Willy (Herbert Frahm) (ex-Chancellor); Lübeck, Germany, 12/18/1913
Braque, Georges (painter); Argenteuil, France **(1882-1963)**
Brazzi, Rossano (actor); Bologna, Italy, 9/18/1916
Brecht, Bertolt (dramatist and poet); Augsburg, Bavaria **(1898-1956)**
Brel, Jacques (singer and composer); Brussels, **(1929-1978)**
Brennan, Walter (actor); Lynn, Mass. **(1894-1974)**
Brent, George (actor); Dublin **(1904-1979)**
Breslin, Jimmy (journalist); Jamaica, Queens, N.Y., 10/17/1930
Breuer, Marcel (architect and designer); Pécs, Hungary **(1902-1981)**
Brewer, Teresa (singer); Toledo, Ohio, 5/7/1931
Brewster, Kingman, Jr. (ex-president of Yale); Longmeadow, Mass. **(1919-1988)**
Brezhnev, Leonid I. (Communist Party Secretary); Dneprodzerzhinsk, Ukraine **(1906-1982)**
Brice, Fanny (Fannie Borach) (comedienne); New York City **(1892-1951)**
Bridges, Beau (actor); Los Angeles, 12/9/1941
Bridges, Jeff (actor); Los Angeles, 12/4/49
Bridges, Lloyd (actor); San Leandro, Calif. 1/15/1913
Brinkley, David (TV newscaster); Wilmington, N.C., 7/10/1920
Britt, May (Maybritt Wilkins) (actress); Sweden, 3/22/1936
Britten, Benjamin (composer); Lowestoft, England **(1913-1976)**
Britton, Barbara (actress); Long Beach, Calif. **(1920-1980)**
Broderick, Helen (actress); Philadelphia, Pa. **(1891-1959)**
Brolin, James (actor); Los Angeles, 7/18/40
Bromfield, Louis (novelist); Mansfield, Ohio **(1896-1956)**
Bronson, Charles (Charles Buchinsky) (actor); Ehrenfeld, Pa., 11/3/1922(?)
Brontë, Charlotte (novelist); Thornton, England **(1816-1855)**
Brontë, Emily Jane (novelist); Thornton, England **(1818-1848)**
Bronzino, Agnolo (painter); Monticelli (Italy) **(1503-1572)**
Brook, Peter (director); London, 3/21/1925
Brooke, Rupert (poet); Rugby, England **(1887-1915)**
Brooks, Geraldine (Geraldine Stroock) (actress); New York City **(1925-1977)**
Brooks, Gwendolyn (poet); Topeka, Kan., 6/7/1917
Brooks, Mel (Melvin Kaminsky) (writer and film director); Brooklyn, N.Y., 1926(?)
Brosnan, Pierce (actor); County Meath, Ireland, 5/16/52
Brothers, Joyce (Bauer) (psychologist, author, radio-TV personality); New York City, 1927(?)
Broun, Matthew Heywood Campbell (journalist); Brooklyn, N.Y. **(1888-1939)**
Brown, Helen Gurley (author); Green Forest, Ark., 2/18/1922
Brown, James (singer); Augusta, Ga., 5/3/1934
Brown, Joe E. (comedian); Holgate, Ohio **(1892-1973)**
Brown, John (abolitionist); Torrington, Conn. **(1800-1859)**
Brown, John Mason (critic); Louisville, Ky. **(1900-1969)**
Brown, Les (band leader); Reinerton, Pa., 1912
Brown, Pamela (actress); London **(1918-1975)**
Brown, Vanessa (Smylla Brind) (actress); Vienna, 3/24/1928
Browne, Jackson (singer and guitarist); Heidelberg, Germany, 10/9/late 1940s
Browning, Elizabeth Barrett (poet); Durham, England **(1806-1861)**
Browning, Robert (poet); London **(1812-1889)**
Brubeck, Dave (musician); Concord, Calif., 12/6/1920
Bruce, Lenny (comedian); Long Island, N.Y. **(1926-1966)**
Bruce, Nigel (actor); Ensenada, Mexico **(1895-1953)**
Bruce, Virginia (actress); Minneapolis, Minn. **(1910-1982)**
Brueghel, Pieter (painter); nr. Breda, Flanders (Netherlands) **(1520?-1569)**
Bruhn, Erik (Belton Evers) (ballet dancer); Copenhagen **(1928-1986)**
Brunelleschi, Filippo (architect); Florence (Italy) **(1377-1446)**
Bruno, Giordano (philosopher); Nola, Italy **(1548-1600)**
Brutus, Marcus Junius (Roman politician); **(85?-42 b.c.)**
Bryan, William Jennings (orator and politician); Salem, Ill. **(1860-1925)**
Bryant, Anita (singer); Barnsdall, Okla., 3/25/1940
Bryant, William Cullen (poet and editor); Cummington, Mass. **(1794-1878)**
Brynner, Yul (Taidje Khan) (actor); Sakhalin Island, Russia **(1920-1985)**
Brzezinski, Zbigniew (ex-presidential adviser); Warsaw, 3/28/1928
Buber, Martin (philosopher and theologian); Vienna **(1878-1965)**
Bucchanan, Jack (actor); Glasgow, Scotland **(1891-1957)**
Buchanan, Edgar (actor); Humansville, Mo., **(1903-1979)**
Buchholz, Horst (actor); Berlin, 12/4/1933
Buchwald, Art (Arthur) (columnist); Mount Vernon, N.Y., 10/20/1925
Buck, Pearl S(ydenstricker) (author); Hillsboro, W. Va. **(1892-1973)**
Buckley, William F., Jr. (journalist); New York City, 11/24/1925
Buddha. *See* Gautama Buddha
Buffalo Bill (William Frederick Cody) (scout); Scott County, Iowa **(1846-1917)**
Bujold, Genevieve (actress); Montreal, 7/1/1942
Bujones, Fernando (ballet dancer); Miami, Fla., 3/9/1955
Bullins, Ed (playwright); Philadelphia, 7/2/1935
Bullock, Jm J. (actor); Casper Wyom., 2/9/?
Bumbry, Grace (mezzo-soprano); St. Louis, 1/4/1937
Bunche, Ralph J. (statesman); Detroit **(1904-1971)**
Bundy, McGeorge (educator); Boston, 3/30/1919
Bundy, William Putnam (editor); Washington, D.C., 9/24/1917
Buñuel, Luis (film director); Calanda, Spain, **(1900-1983)**
Bunyan, John (preacher and author); Elstow, England **(1628-1688)**
Burbank, Luther (horticulturist); Lancaster, Mass. **(1849-1926)**
Burke, Adm. Arleigh A. (ex-Chief of Naval Operations); Boulder, Colo., 10/19/1901
Burke, Billie (comedienne); Washington, D.C. **(1885-1970)**
Burke, Delta (actress); Orlando, Fla., 7/30/56
Burke, Edmund (statesman); Dublin **(1729-1797)**
Burne-Jones, Edward Coley (painter); Birmingham, England **(1833-1898)**
Burnett, Carol (comedienne); San Antonio, 4/26/1936
Burnette, Smiley (Lester Alvin) (actor); Summum, Ill. **(1911-1967)**
Burney, Fanny (Frances) (writer); King's Lynn, England **(1752-1840)**
Burns, George (Nathan Birnbaum) (comedian); New York City, 1/20/1896
Burns, Robert (poet); Alloway, Scotland **(1759-1796)**
Burr, Aaron (political leader); Newark, N.J. **(1756-1836)**
Burr, Raymond (William Stacey Burr) (actor); New Westminster, British Columbia, Canada, 5/21/1917
Burroughs, Edgar Rice (novelist); Chicago **(1875-1950)**
Burrows, Abe (playwright and director); New York City, **(1910-1985)**
Burstyn, Ellen (Edna Rae Gillooly) (actress); Detroit, 12/7/1932
Burton, LaVar (actor); Landsthul, Germany, 2/16/57
Burton, Richard (Richard Jenkins) (actor); Pontrhydfen, Wales **(1925-1984)**
Bush, Vannevar (scientist); Everett, Mass. **(1890-1974)**
Bushman, Francis X. (actor); Baltimore **(1883-1966)**
Butkus, Dick (actor); Chicago, 12/9/42

Butler, Samuel (author); Langar, England **(1835-1902)**
Butterworth, Charles (actor); South Bend, Ind. **(1896-1946)**
Buttons, Red (Aaron Chwatt) (actor); New York City, 2/5/1919
Buzzi, Ruth (comedienne); Wequetequock, Conn., 7/24/1936
Byington, Spring (actress); Colorado Springs, Colo. **(1893-1971)**
Byrd, Richard Evelyn (polar explorer); Winchester, Va. **(1888-1957)**
Byron, George Gordon (6th Baron Byron) (poet); London **(1788-1824)**

C

Caan, James (actor); The Bronx, N.Y., 3/26/1939
Caballé, Montserrat (soprano); Barcelona, Spain, 4/12/33
Cabot, Bruce (actor); Carlsbad, N.M. **(1904-1972)**
Cabot, John (Giovanni Caboto) (navigator); Genoa (?) **(1450-1498)**
Cabot, Sebastian (navigator); Venice **(1476?-1557)**
Cadmus, Paul (painter and etcher); New York City, 12/17/1904
Caesar, Gaius Julius (statesman); Rome (100?-44 B.C.)
Caesar, Sid (comedian); Yonkers, N.Y., 9/8/1922
Cagney, James (actor); New York City **(1899-1986)**
Cahn, Sammy (songwriter); New York City, 6/18/1913
Caine, Michael (Maurice J. Micklewhite) (actor); London, 3/14/1933
Calder, Alexander (sculptor); Lawnton, Pa. **(1898-1976)**
Calderón del al Barca, Pedro (dramatist); Madrid **(1600-1681)**
Caldwell, Erskine (novelist); White Oak, Ga **(1903-1987)**
Caldwell, Sarah (opera director and conductor); Maryville, Mo., 1928
Caldwell, Taylor (novelist); Manchester, England **(1900-1985)**
Caldwell, Zoe (actress); Hawthorn, Australia, 9/14/1933
Calhern, Louis (Carl Henry Vogt) (actor); Brooklyn, N.Y. **(1895-1956)**
Calhoun, John Caldwell (statesman); nr. Calhoun Mills, S.C. **(1782-1850)**
Calisher, Hortense (novelist); New York City, 12/20/1911
Callas, Maria (Maria Calogeropoulos) (dramatic soprano); New York City **(1923-1977)**
Calloway, Cab (Cabell) (band leader); Rochester, N.Y., 12/25/1907
Calvet, Corinne (actress); Paris, 4/30/1926
Calvin, John (Jean Chauvin) (religious reformer); Noyon, Picardy **(1509-1564)**
Cambridge, Godfrey (comedian); New York City **(1933-1976)**
Cameron, Rod (Rod Cox) (actor); Calgary, Alberta, Canada, **(1912-1983)**
Campbell, Glen (singer); nr. Delight, Ark., 4/22/1938
Campbell, Mrs. Patrick (Beatrice Stella Tanner) (actress); London **(1865-1940)**
Camus, Albert (author); Mondovi, Algeria **(1913-1960)**
Canaletto, (Giovanni Antonio Canale); (painter) Venice **(1697-1768)**
Candy, John (actor, comedian); Toronto, Ont., Canada, 10/31/50
Caniff, Milton (cartoonist); Hillsboro, Ohio **(1907-1988)**
Cannon, Dyan (actress); Tacoma, Wash., 1/4/1937
Canova, Judy (comedienne); Jacksonville, Fla., **(1916-1983)**
Cantinflas (Mario Moreno) (comedian); Mexico City, 8/12/1911
Cantor, Eddie (Edward Iskowitz) (actor); New York City **(1892-1964)**
Cantrell, Lana (singer); Sydney, Australia, 1944
Capote, Truman (novelist); New Orleans **(1924-1984)**
Capp, Al (Alfred Gerald Caplin) (cartoonist); New Haven, Conn. **(1909-1979)**
Capra, Frank (film producer, director); Palermo, Italy, 5/18/1897
Caravaggio, Michelangelo Merisi da (painter); Caravaggio (Italy) **(1573-1610)**
Cardin, Pierre (fashion designer); nr. Venice, 7/7/1922
Cardinale, Claudia (actress); Tunis, Tunisia, 1939
Carey, Harry (actor); New York City **(1878-1947)**
Carey, Macdonald (actor); Sioux City, Iowa, 3/15/1913
Carlin, George (comedian); Bronx, N.Y., 5/12/37
Carlisle, Kitty (singer and actress); New Orleans, 9/3/1915
Carlson, Richard (actor); Albert Lea, Minn., **(1912-1977)**
Carlyle, Thomas (essayist and historian); Ecclefechan, Scotland **(1795-1881)**
Carmichael, Hoagy (Hoagland Howard) (songwriter); Bloomington, Ind. **(1899-1981)**
Carne, Judy (Joyce Botterill) (singer); Northampton, England, 1939
Carnegie, Andrew (industrialist); Dunfermline, Scotland **(1835-1919)**
Carney, Art (actor); Mt. Vernon, N.Y., 11/4/1918
Carnovsky, Morris (actor); St. Louis, 9/5/1897
Caron, Leslie (actress); Paris, 7/1/1931
Carr, Vikki (singer); El Paso, 7/19/1942
Carracci, Annibale (painter); Bologna (Italy) **(1560-1609)**
Carracci, Lodovico (painter); Bologna (Italy) **(1555-1619)**
Carradine, David (actor); Hollywood, Calif., 12/8/1936
Carradine, John (actor); New York City **(1906-1988)**
Carradine, Keith (actor); San Mateo, Calif., 8/8/49
Carreras, José (tenor); Barcelona, Spain, 12/5/1946
Carrillo, Leo (actor); Los Angeles **(1881-1961)**
Carroll, Diahann (Carol Diahann Johnson) (singer and actress); Bronx, N.Y., 7/17/1935

Carroll, Leo G. (actor); Weedon, England **(1892-1972)**
Carroll, Lewis (Charles Lutwidge Dodgson) (author and mathematician); Daresbury, England **(1832-1898)**
Carroll, Madeleine (actress); West Bromwich, England **(1906-1987)**
Carroll, Nancy (actress); New York City **(1904-1965)**
Carroll, Pat (comedienne); Shreveport, La., 5/5/1927
Carson, Jack (actor); Carmen, Man., Canada **(1910-1963)**
Carson, Johnny (TV entertainer); Corning, Iowa, 10/23/1925
Carson, Kit (Christopher) (scout); Madison County, Ky. **(1809-1868)**
Carson, Rachel (biologist and author); Springdale, Pa. **(1907-1964)**
Carter, Dixie (actress); McLemoresville, Tenn., 5/25/39
Carter, Jack (comedian); New York City, 1923
Carter, Lynda (actress); Phoenix, Ariz., 7/24/51
Cartier, Jacques (explorer); Saint-Malo, Brittany (France) **(1491-1557)**
Cartier-Brisson, Henri (photographer); Chanteloup, France, 8/22/1908
Cartland, Barbara (author); England, 7/9/1901
Caruso, Enrico (Errico) (tenor); Naples, Italy **(1873-1921)**
Carver, George Washington (botanist); Missouri **(1864-1943)**
Cary, Arthur Joyce Lunel (novelist); Londonderry, Ireland **(1888-1957)**
Casals, Pablo (cellist); Vendrell, Spain **(1876-1973)**
Casanova de Seingalt, Giovanni Jacopo (adventurer); Venice **(1725-1798)**
Cash, Johnny (singer); nr. Kingsland, Ark., 2/26/1932
Cass, Peggy (comedienne); Boston, 5/21/1924
Cassatt, Mary (painter); Allegheny, Pa. **(1844-1926)**
Cassavetes, John (actor and director); New York City **(1929-1989)**
Cassidy, David (singer); New York City, 4/12/1950
Cassidy, Jack (actor); Richmond Hill, Queens, N.Y. **(1927-1976)**
Cassidy, Shaun (actor); Los Angeles, 9/27/58
Cassini, Oleg (Oleg Lolewski-Cassini) (fashion designer); Paris, 4/11/1913
Castagno, Andrea del (painter); San Martino a Corella (Italy) **(c.1421-1457)**
Castellano, Richard (actor); New York City **(1934-1988)**
Castle, Irene (Irene Foote) (actress and dancer); New Rochelle, N.Y. **(1893-1969)**
Castle, Vernon Blythe (dancer and aviator); Norwich, England **(1887-1918)**
Castro Ruz, Fidel (Premier); Mayari, Oriente, Cuba, 8/13/1926
Cather, Willa Sibert (novelist); Winchester, Va. **(1876-1947)**
Cato, Marcus Porcius (called Cato the Elder) (statesman); Tusculum (Italy) (234-149 B.C.)
Catt, Carrie Chapman Lane (woman suffragist); Ripon, Wis. **(1859-1947)**
Catton, Bruce (historian); Petoskey, Mich. **(1899-1978)**
Cauldfield, Joan (actress); East Orange, N.J., 6/1/22
Cavallaro, Carmen (band leader); New York City, 1913
Cavett, Dick (Richard) (TV entertainer); Gibbon, Neb., 11/19/1936
Cellini, Benvenuto (goldsmith and sculptor); Florence (Italy) **(1500-1571)**
Cervantes Saavedra, Miguel de (novelist); Alcalá de Henares, Spain **(1547-1616)**
Cézanne, Paul (painter); Aix-en-Provence, France **(1839-1906)**
Chagall, Marc (painter); Vitebsk, Russia, **(1887-1985)**
Chaliapin, Feodor Ivanovitch (operatic basso); Kazan, Russia **(1873-1938)**
Chamberlain, Arthur Neville (statesman); Edgbaston, England **(1869-1940)**
Chamberlain, Richard (actor); Los Angeles, 3/31/1935(?)
Champion, Gower (choreographer); Geneva, Ill. **(1921-1980)**
Champion, Marge (actress and dancer); Los Angeles, 9/2/1923
Champlain, Samuel de (explorer); nr. Rochefort, France **(1567?-1635)**
Chancellor, John (TV commentator); Chicago, 7/14/1927
Chandler, Jeff (actor); Brooklyn, N.Y. **(1918-1961)**
Chandler, Raymond (writer); Chicago **(1883-1959)**
Chanel, "Coco" (Gabriel Bonheur) (fashion designer); Issoire, France **(1883-1971)**
Chaney, Lon (actor); Colorado Springs, Colo. **(1883-1930)**
Channing, Carol (actress); Seattle, 1/31/1923
Channing, Stockard (actress); New York City, 2/13/44
Chaplin, Geraldine (actress); Santa Monica, Calif., 7/31/1944
Chaplin, Sir Charles (actor); London **(1889-1977)**
Charisse, Cyd (Tula Finklea) (dancer and actress); Amarillo, Tex., 3/8/1923
Charlemagne (Holy Roman Emperor); birthplace unknown **(742-814)**
Charles, Ray (Ray Charles Robinson) (pianist, singer, and songwriter); Albany Ga., 9/23/1930
Charo (Maria Rosario Pilar Martinez) (actress); Murcia, Spain 1/15/51
Chase, Chaz (actor, director); Baltimore, Md. **(1893-1940)**
Chase, Chevy (Cornelius Crane Chase) (comedian); New York City, 10/8/1943

Chase, Ilka (author and actress); New York City (1905-1978)
Chase, Lucia (founder Ballet Theatre [now American Ballet Theatre]); Waterbury, Conn. (1907-1986)
Chatterton, Ruth (actress); New York City (1893-1961)
Chaucer, Geoffrey (poet); London (1340?-1400)
Chávez, Carlos (composer); nr. Mexico City (1899-1978)
Chavez, Cesar (labor leader); nr. Yuma, Ariz., 3/31/1927
Chayefsky, Paddy (Sidney) (playwright); New York City, (1923-1981)
Checker, Chubby (Ernest Evans) (performer); Philadelphia, 10/3/1941
Cheever, John (novelist); Quincy, Mass. (1912-1982)
Chekhov, Anton Pavlovich (dramatist and short-story writer); Taganrog, Russia (1860-1904)
Cher (Cherilyn LaPiere) (singer); El Centro, Calif., 5/20/1946
Cherubini, Luigi (composer); Florence (1760-1842)
Chesterton, Gilbert Keith (author); Kensington, England (1874-1936)
Chevalier, Maurice (entertainer); Paris (1888-1972)
Chiang Kai-shek (Chief of State); Feng-hwa, China (1887-1975)
Child, Julia (food expert); Pasadena, Calif., 8/15/1912
Chippendale, Thomas (cabinet-maker); Otley, England (1718?-1779)
Chirico, Giorgio de (painter); Vólos, Greece, (1888-1978)
Chopin, Frédéric François (composer); nr. Warsaw (1810-1849)
Chou En-lai. See Zhou Enlai
Christian, Linda (Blanca Rosa Welter) (actress); Tampico, Mexico, 11/13/1924
Christie, Agatha (mystery writer); Torquay, England, (1890-1976)
Christie, Julie (actress); Chukua, India, 4/14/1941
Christopher, Jordon (actor and musician); Youngstown, Ohio, 1941
Christy, June (singer); Springfield, Ill., 1925
Churchill, Sir Winston Leonard Spencer (statesman); Blenheim Palace, Oxfordshire, England (1874-1965)
Cicero, Marcus Tullius (orator and statesman); Arpinum (Italy) (106-43 B.C.)
Cid, El (Rodrigo (or Ruy) Díez de Bivar) (Spanish national hero); nr. Burgos, Spain (1040?-1099)
Cilento, Diane (actress); Queensland, Australia, 10/5/1933
Cimabue, Giovanni (painter); Florence (Italy) (c.1240-c.1302)
Cimino, Michael (film director); New York City, 1943(?)
Clair, René (René Chomette) (film director); Paris (1898-1981)
Claire, Ina (Ina Fagan) (actress); Washington, D.C., (1895-1985)
Clapton, Eric (singer and guitarist); Ripley, England, 3/30/1945
Clark, Bobby (comedian, actor); Springfield, Ohio (1888-1960)
Clark, Dane (Barney Zanville) (actor); New York City, 2/18/1915
Clark, Dick (TV personality); Mt. Vernon, N.Y., 11/30/1929
Clark, Mark W. (general); Madison Barracks, N.Y. (1896-1984)
Clark, Petula (singer); Epsom, England, 11/15/1934
Clark, Roy (country music artist); Meherrin, Va., 4/15/1933
Clark, William (explorer); Caroline County, Va. (1770-1838)
Clarke, Arthur C. (science fiction writer); Minehead, England, 12/16/1917
Clary, Robert (actor); Paris, France, 3/1/26
Claude Lorrain (Claude Gellée) (painter); Champagne, France (1600-1682)
Clausewitz, Karl von (military strategist); Burg (East Germany) (1780-1831)
Clay, Henry (statesman); Hanover County, Va. (1777-1852)
Clay, Lucius D. (banker, ex-general); Marietta, Ga. (1897-1978)
Clayburgh, Jill (actress); New York City, 4/30/1944
Cleese, John (writer, actor); Weston-super-Mare, England, 10/27/39
Clemenceau, Georges (statesman); Mouilleron-en-Pareds, Vondée, France (1841-1929)
Clemens, Samuel L. See Mark Twain
Cleopatra (Queen of Egypt); Alexandria, Egypt (69-30 B.C.)
Cliburn, Van (Harvey Lavan Cliburn, Jr.) (concert pianist); Shreveport, La., 7/12/1934
Clifford, Clark M. (ex-Secretary of Defense); Ft. Scott, Kan., 12/25/1906
Clift, Montgomery (actor); Omaha, Neb. (1920-1966)
Clooney, Rosemary (singer); Maysville, Ky., 5/23/1928
Close, Glenn (actress); Greenwich, Conn., 3/19/1947
Clurman, Harold (stage producer); New York City (1901-1980)
Cobb, Irvin Shrewsbury (humorist); Paducah, Ky. (1876-1944)
Cobb, Lee J. (Leo Jacob) (actor); New York City (1911-1976)
Coburn, Charles Douville (actor); Savannah, Ga. (1877-1961)
Coburn, James (actor); Laurel, Neb., 8/31/1928
Coca, Imogene (comedienne); Philadelphia, 11/18/1908
Cocker, Joe (John Robert Cocker) (singer); Sheffield, England, 5/20/1944
Coco, James (actor); New York City (1929-1987)
Cocteau, Jean (author); Maison-Lafitte, France (1891-1963)
Cody, W. F. See Buffalo Bill
Cohan, George Michael (actor and dramatist); Providence, R.I. (1878-1942)
Cohn, Mindy (actress); Los Angeles, 5/20/66
Colbert, Claudette (Lily Chauchoin) (actress); Paris, 9/13/1903
Colby, William E. (ex-Director of CIA); St. Paul, 1/4/1920

Cole, Nat "King" (singer); Montgomery, Ala. (1919-1965)
Cole, Natalie (singer); Los Angeles, 2/6/1950
Cole, Thomas (painter); Lancashire, England (1801-1848)
Coleman, Dabney (actor); Corpus Christi, Tex., 1/2/32
Coleman, Gary (actor); Zion, Ill., 2/8/68
Coleridge, Samuel Taylor (poet); Ottery St. Mary, England (1772-1834)
Colette (Sidonie-Gabrielle Colette) (novelist); St.-Sauveur, France (c. 1873-1954)
Collier, Constance (actress); Windsor, England (1878-1955)
Collingwood, Charles (TV commentator); Three Rivers, Mich. (1917-1985)
Collins, Dorothy (Marjorie Chandler) (singer); Windsor, Ontario, Canada, 11/18/1926
Collins, Joan (actress); London 5/23/1933
Collins, Judy (singer); Seattle, 5/1/1939
Colman, Ronald (actor); Richmond, England (1891-1958)
Colonna, Jerry (comedian); Boston (1905-1986)
Columbo, Russ (singer, bandleader); San Francisco (1908-1934)
Columbus, Christopher (Cristoforo Colombo) (discoverer of America); Genoa (Italy) (1451-1506)
Comden, Betty (writer); New York City, 5/3/1919
Comenius, Johann Amos (educational reformer) Nivnice, Moravia (Czechoslovakia) (1592-1670)
Commager, Henry Steele (historian); Pittsburgh, 10/25/1902
Como, Perry (Pierino) (singer); Canonsburg, Pa., 5/18/1912
Compton, Karl Taylor (physicist); Wooster, Ohio (1887-1954)
Comte, Auguste (philosopher); Montpellier, France (1798-1857)
Conant, James B. (educator and statesman); Dorchester, Mass. (1893-1978)
Condon, Eddie (jazz musician); Goodland, Ind. (1905-1973)
Confucius (K'ung Fu-tzu) (philosopher); Shantung province, China (c. 551-479 B.C.)
Congreve, William (dramatist); nr. Leeds, England (1670-1729)
Connelly, Marc (playwright); McKeesport, Pa. (1890-1980)
Connery, Sean (actor); Edinburgh, Scotland, 8/25/1930
Conniff, Ray (band leader); Attleboro, Mass., 11/6/1916
Connolly, Walter (actor); Cincinnati, Ohio (1887-1940)
Connors, Chuck (actor); Brooklyn, N.Y., 4/10/1921
Connors, Mike (Krekor Ohanian) (actor); Fresno, Calif., 8/15/1925
Conrad, Joseph (Teodor Jozef Konrad Korzeniowski) (novelist); Berdichev, Ukraine (1857-1924)
Conrad, Robert (Conrad Robert Falk) (actor); Chicago, 3/1/1935
Conrad, William (actor); Louisville, Ky., 9/27/1920
Conried, Hans (Frank Foster) (actor); Baltimore (1915-1982)
Constable, John (painter); East Bergholt, Suffolk, England (1776-1837)
Constantine II (ex-king); Athens, 6/2/1940
Constantine, Michael (actor); Reading, Pa., 5/22/27
Conte, Richard (actor); New York City (1916-1975)
Conti, Tom (actor); Paisley, Scotland, 11/22/1941
Converse, Frank (actor); St. Louis, 1938
Convy, Bert (actor, host); St. Louis, Mo., 5/23/33
Conway, Tim (comedian); Chagrin Falls, Ohio, 12/15/1933
Coogan, Jackie (actor); Los Angeles (1914-1984)
Cook, Peter (actor, writer); Torquay, England, 11/17/37
Cooke, Alistair (Alfred Alistair); (TV narrator and journalist); Manchester, England, 11/20/1908
Cooley, Denton A(rthur) (heart surgeon); Houston, Tex., 8/22/1920
Coolidge, Rita (singer); Nashville, Tenn., 1944
Cooper, Alice (Vincent Furnier) (rock musician); Detroit, 2/4/1948
Cooper, Gary (Frank James Cooper) (actor); Helena, Mont. (1901-1961)
Cooper, Dame Gladys (actress); Lewisham, England (1898-1971)
Cooper, Jackie (actor and director); Los Angeles, 9/15/1922
Cooper, James Fenimore (novelist); Burlington, N.J. (1789-1851)
Cooper, Peter (industrialist and philanthropist); New York City (1791-1883)
Copernicus, Nicolaus (Mikolaj Kopernik) (astronomer); Thorn, Poland (1473-1543)
Copland, Aaron (composer); Brooklyn, N.Y., 11/14/1900
Copley, John Singleton (painter); Boston, Mass. (1738-1815)
Copperfield, David (illusionist); Matuchen, N.J., 9/16/1956
Coppola, Francis Ford (film director); Detroit, 4/7/1939
Corelli, Arcangelo (composer); Fusignano, Italy (1653-1713)
Corelli, Franco (operatic tenor); Ancona, Italy, 4/8/1923
Corneille, Pierre (dramatist); Rouen, France (1606-1684)
Cornell, Katharine (actress); Berlin (1893-1974)
Coret, Jean Baptiste Camille (painter); Paris (1796-1875)
Correggio, Antonio Allegri da (painter); Correggio (Italy) (1494-1534)
Corsaro, Frank (opera director); New York harbor, 12/22/1924
Cortés (or Cortez), Hernando (explorer); Medellin, Spain (1485-1547)
Cosby, Bill (actor); Philadelphia, 7/12/1937
Cosell, Howard (Howard Cohen) (sportscaster); Winston-Salem, N.C.,

3/25/1920
Costa-Gavras, Henri (Kostantinos Gavras) (film director); Athens, 1933
Costello, Dolores (actress); Pittsburgh, Pa. **(1905-1979)**
Costello, Elvis (Declan Patrick McManus) (singer-musician-song-writer); London, 1954
Costello, Lou (comedian); Paterson, N.J. **(1908-1959)**
Costello, Maurice (actor); Pittsburgh **(1877-1950)**
Cotten, Joseph (actor); Petersburg, Va., 5/15/1905
Couperin, François (composer); Paris **(1668-1733)**
Courbet, Gustave (painter); Ornans, France **(1819-1877)**
Courrèges, André (fashion designer); Pau, France, 3/9/1923
Courtenay, Tom (actor); Hull, England, 2/25/1937
Cousins, Norman (publisher); Union Hill, N.J., 6/24/1915
Cousteau, Jacques-Yves (marine explorer); St. André-de-Cubzac, France, 6/11/1910
Coward, Sir Noel (playwright and actor); Teddington, England **(1899-1973)**
Cowl, Jane (actress); Boston **(1887-1950)**
Cowles, Gardner, Jr. (newspaper publisher); Algona, Iowa, **(1903-1985)**
Cowper, William (poet); Great Berkhamstead, England **(1731-1800)**
Cox, Wally (actor); Detroit, Mich. **(1924-1973)**
Cozzens, James Gould (novelist); Chicago **(1903-1978)**
Crabbe, Buster (Clarence) (actor); Oakland, Calif. **(1908-1983)**
Crain, Jeanne (actress); Barstow, Calif., 5/25/1925
Cranach, Lucas, the elder (painter); Kronach (Germany) **(1472-1553)**
Crane, Hart (poet); Garrettsville, Ohio **(1899-1932)**
Crane, Stephen (novelist and poet); Newark, N.J. **(1871-1900)**
Cranmer, Thomas (churchman); Aslacton, England **(1489-1556)**
Crawford, Broderick (actor); Philadelphia **(1911-1986)**
Crawford, Cheryl (stage producer); Akron, Ohio **(1902-1986)**
Crawford, Joan (Lucille LeSueur) (actress and business executive); San Antonio **(1908-1977)**
Cregar, Laird (actor); Philadelphia, Pa. **(1916-1944)**
Crenna, Richard (actor); Los Angeles, 11/30/1927
Crespin, Régine (operatic soprano); Marseilles, France, 2/23/1929
Crichton, (John) Michael (novelist); Chicago, 10/23/1942
Crisp, Donald (actor); London **(1880-1974)**
Croce, Benedetto (philosopher); Peseasseroli, Aquila, Italy **(1866-1952)**
Croce, Jim (singer); Philadelphia **(1942-1973)**
Crockett, Davy (David) (frontiersman); Greene County, Tenn. **(1786-1836)**
Cromwell, Oliver (statesman); Huntingdon, England **(1599-1658)**
Cronin, A. J. (Archibald J. Cronin) (novelist); Cardross, Scotland **(1896-1981)**
Cronkite, Walter (TV newscaster); St. Joseph, Mo., 11/4/1916
Cronyn, Hume (actor); London, Ontario, Canada, 7/18/1911
Crosby, Bing (Harry Lillis) (singer, actor); Tacoma, Wash. **(1904-1977)**
Crosby, Bob (musician); Spokane, Wash., 8/23/1913
Crosby, Cathy Lee (actress); Los Angeles, 12/2/48
Crosby, Norm (comedian); Boston, 9/15/27
Cross, Ben (Bernard) (actor); Paddington, England, 12/16/1947
Cross, Milton (opera commentator); New York City **(1897-1975)**
Crouse, Russel (playwright); Findlay, Ohio **(1893-1966)**
Cruise, Tom (actor); Syracuse, N.Y., 7/3/1962
Crystal, Billy (comedian, actor); Long Beach, L.I., N.Y., 3/14/47
Cugat, Xavier (band leader); Barcelona, Spain, 1/1/1900
Cukor, George (film director); New York City **(1899-1983)**
Cullen, Bill (William Lawrence Cullen) (radio and TV entertainer); Pittsburgh **(1920-1990)**
Culp, Robert (actor); Berkeley, Calif., 8/16/1930
Cummings, E. E. (Edward Estlin Cummings) (poet); Cambridge, Mass. **(1894-1962)**
Cummings, Robert (actor); Joplin, Mo., 6/9/1910
Curie, Marie (Marja Sklodowska) (physical chemist); Warsaw **(1867-1934)**
Curie, Pierre (physicist); Paris **(1859-1906)**
Curtin, Jane (actress); Cambridge, Mass., 9/6/47
Curtin, Phyllis (soprano); Clarksburg, W.Va., 12/3/1927
Curtis, Jamie Lee (actress); Los Angeles, 11/22/58
Curtis, Tony (Bernard Schwartz) (actor); Bronx, N.Y., 6/3/1925
Curzon, Clifford (concert pianist); London **(1907-1982)**
Custer, George Armstrong (army officer); New Rumley, Ohio **(1839-1876)**

D

da Gama, Vasco (explorer); Sines, Portugal **(1460-1524)**
Daguerre, Louis (photographic pioneer); nr. Paris **(1787-1851)**
Dahl, Arlene (actress); Minneapolis, 8/11/1928
Dailey, Dan (actor and dancer); New York City, **(1917-1978)**

Dale, Jim (actor,singer, songwriter); Rothwell, England, 8/15/35
Daley, Richard J. (Mayor of Chicago); Chicago **(1902-1976)**
Dali, Salvador (painter); Figueras, Spain **(1904-1989)**
Dalton, Abby (actress); Las Vegas, Nev., 8/15/32
Dalton, John (chemist); nr. Cockermouth, England **(1766-1844)**
Daly, James (actor); Wisconsin Rapids, Wis. **(1918-1978)**
Daly, John (radio and TV news analyst); Johannesburg, South Africa, 2/20/1914
Daly, Tyne (actress); Madison, Wis. 2/21/47
d'Amboise, Jacques (ballet dancer); Dedham, Mass., 7/28/1934
Damone, Vic (Vito Farinola) (singer); Brooklyn, N.Y., 6/12/1928
Damrosch, Walter Johannes (orchestra conductor); Breslau (Poland) **(1862-1950)**
Dana, Charles Anderson (editor); Hinsdale, N.H. **(1819-1897)**
Dandridge, Dorothy (actress); Cleveland **(1923-1965)**
Dangerfield, Rodney (comedian); Babylon, L.I., N.Y., 1921
Daniels, Bebe (Virginia Daniels) (actress); Dallas **(1901-1971)**
Daniels, William (actor); Brooklyn, N.Y., 3/31/27
Danilova, Alexandra (ballerina); Peterhof, Russia, 1/20/1904
Dannay, Frederic (novelist, pseudonym Ellery Queen); Brooklyn, N.Y. **(1905-1982)**
Danner, Blythe (actress); Philadelphia, 1944(?)
D'Annunzio, Gabriele (soldier and author); Francaville at Mare, Pescara, Italy **(1863-1938)**
Danson, Ted (actor); San Diego, Calif., 12/29/47
Dante (or Durante) Alighieri (poet); Florence (Italy) **(1265-1321)**
Danton, Georges Jacques (French Revolutionary leader); Arcis-sur-Aube, France **(1759-1794)**
Danza, Tony (actor); Brooklyn, N.Y., 4/21/51
Darnell, Linda (actress); Dallas **(1921-1965)**
Darren, James (actor); Philadelphia, 6/8/1936
Darrieux, Danielle (actress); Bordeaux, France, 5/1/1917
Darrow, Clarence Seward (lawyer); Kinsman, Ohio **(1857-1938)**
Darwell, Jane (actress); Palmyra, Mo. **(1879-1967)**
Darwin, Charles Robert (naturalist); Shrewsbury, England **(1809-1882)**
daSilva, Howard (actor); Cleveland **(1909-1986)**
Dassin, Jules (film director); Middletown, Conn., 12/18/1911
Daumier, Honoré (caricaturist); Marseilles, France **(1808-1879)**
Dauphin, Claude (actor); Corbeil, France **(1903-1978)**
Davenport, Harry (actor); New York City **(1866-1949)**
David, Jacques-Louis (painter); Paris **(1748-1825)**
David (King of Israel and Judah) **(died c. 973** B.C.)
Davidson, John (singer and actor); Pittsburgh, 12/13/1941
Davies, Marion (Marion Douras) (actress); New York City **(1898?-1961)**
da Vinci, Leonardo (painter and scientist); Vinci, Tuscany (Italy) **(1452-1519)**
Davis, Ann B. (actress); Schenectady, N.Y., 5/5/26
Davis, Bette (actress); Lowell, Mass. **(1908-1989)**
Davis, Elmer Holmes (radio commentator); Aurora, Ind. **(1890-1958)**
Davis, Jefferson (President of the Confederacy); Christian (now Todd) County, Ky. **(1808-1889)**
Davis, Joan (actress); St. Paul, Minn., **(1907-1961)**
Davis, Mac (singer); Lubbock, Tex., 1/21/1942
Davis, Miles (jazz trumpeter); Alton, Ill., 5/25/1926
Davis, Ossie (actor and writer); Cogdell, Ga., 12/18/1917
Davis, Sammy, Jr. (actor and singer); New York City **(1925-1990)**
Davis, Skeeter (Mary Francis Penick) (singer); Dry Ridge, Ky., 12/30/1931
Davis, Stuart (painter); Philadelphia **(1894-1964)**
Dawber, Pam (actress); Farmington Hills, Mich., 10/18/51
Dawson, Richard (actor, host); Gosport, Hampshire, England, 11/20/32
Day, Dennis (singer); New York City **(1917-1988)**
Day, Doris (Doris von Kappelhoff) (singer and actress); Cincinnati, 4/3/1924
Day, Laraine (La Raine Johnson) (actress); Roosevelt, Utah, 10/13/1920
Dayan, Moshe (ex-Defense Minister of Israel); Dagania, Palestine **(1915-1981)**
Dean, James (actor); Marion, Ind. **(1931-1955)**
Dean, Jimmy (singer); Seth Ward, nr. Plainview, Tex., 8/10/1928
De Bakey, Michael E. (heart surgeon); Lake Charles, La., 9/7/1908
de Beauvoir, Simone (novelist and philosopher); Paris **(1908-1986)**
Debs, Eugene Victor (Socialist leader); Terre Haute, Ind. **(1855-1926)**
Debussy, Claude Achille (composer); St. Germain-en-Laye, France **(1862-1918)**
DeCamp, Rosemary (actress); Prescott, Ariz., 11/14/14(?)
De Carlo, Yvonne (Peggy Yvonne Middleton) (actress); Vancouver, B.C., Canada, 9/1/1924
de Chirico, Giorgio (painter); Volos, Greece, **(1888-1978)**
Dee, Francis (actress); Los Angeles, 11/26/07
Dee, Ruby (actress); Cleveland, Ohio, 10/27/23(?)
Dee, Sandra (Alexandra Zuck) (actress); Bayonne, N.J., 4/23/1942
Defoe, Daniel (novelist); London **(1659?-1731)**

Defore, Don (actor); Cedar Rapids, Iowa, 8/25/17
Degas, Hilaire Germain Edgar (painter); Paris **(1834-1917)**
de Gaulle, Charles André Joseph Marie (soldier and statesman); Lille, France **(1890-1970)**
DeHaven, Gloria (actress); Los Angeles, 7/23/1925
de Havilland, Olivia (actress); Tokyo, 7/1/1916
Dekker, Albert (actor); Brooklyn, N.Y. **(1904-1968)**
de Kooning, Willem (painter); Rotterdam, 4/24/1904
Delacroix, Eugène (painter); Charenton-St. Maurice, France **(1798-1863)**
de la Renta, Oscar (fashion designer); Santo Domingo, Dominican Republic, 7/22/1932
Delaunay, Robert (painter); Paris **(1885-1941)**
De Laurentiis, Dino (film producer); Torre Annunziata, Bay of Naples, Italy, 8/8/1919
della Robbia, Andrea (sculptor) Florence **(1435-1525)**
della Robbia, Luca (sculptor); Florence **(1400-1482)**
Delon, Alain (actor); Sceaux, France, 11/8/1935
Del Rio, Dolores (Dolores Ansunsolo) (actress); Durango, Mexico **(1905-1983)**
DeLuise, Dom (comedian); Brooklyn, N.Y., 8/1/1933
Demarest, William (actor); St. Paul **(1892-1983)**
de Mille, Agnes (choreographer); New York City 9/18/1905
De Mille, Cecil Blount (film director); Ashfield, Mass. **(1881-1959)**
Demosthenes (orator); Athens **(385?-322** B.C.)
Deneuve, Catherine (actress); Paris, 10/22/1943
De Niro, Robert (actor); New York City, 8/17/1943
Dennehy, Brian (actor); Brigeport, Conn., 7/9/40
Denning, Richard (actor); Poughkeepsie, N.Y., 3/27/14
Dennis, Sandy (actress); Hastings, Neb., 4/27/1937
Denny, Reginald (actor); Richmond, England **(1891-1967)**
Denver, John (Henry John Deutschendorf, Jr.) (singer); Roswell, N.M., 12/31/1943
De Palma, Brian (film director); Newark, N.J., 9/11/1940
Derain, André (painter); Chatou, Seine-et-Oise, France **(1880-1954)**
Derek, John (actor, director); Los Angeles, 8/12/26
Dern, Bruce (actor); Chicago, 6/4/1936
Descartes, René (philosopher and mathematician); La Haye, France **(1596-1650)**
De Seversky, Alexander P. (aviator); Tiflis, Russia **(1894-1974)**
De Sica, Vittorio (film direct r); Sora, Italy **(1901-1974)**
Desmond, Johnny (composer); Detroit **(1921-1985)**
Desmond, William (actor); Dublin **(1878-1949)**
De Soto, Hernando (explorer); Barcarrota, Spain **(1500?-1542)**
De Valera, Eamon (ex-President of Ireland); New York City **(1882-1975)**
Devane, William (actor); Albany, N.Y., 9/5/39
Devine, Andy (actor); Flagstaff, Ariz. **(1905-1977)**
DeVito, Danny (Daniel Michael); (actor, director); Neptune, N.J., 11/17/1944
De Vries, Peter (novelist); Chicago, 2/27/1910
de Waart, Edo (conductor); Amsterdam, the Netherlands, 6/1/41
Dewey, George (admiral); Montpelier, Vt. **(1837-1917)**
Dewey, John (philosopher and educator); Burlington, Vt. **(1859-1952)**
Dewey, Thomas E. (politician); Owosso, Mich. **(1902-1971)**
Dewhurst, Colleen (actress); Montreal, 1926(?)
De Wilde, Brandon (actor); Brookly, N.Y. **(1942-1972)**
DeWitt, Joyce (actress); Wheeling W.Va., 4/23/49
De Wolfe, Billy (actor); Wollaston, Mass. **(1907-1974)**
Dey, Susan (actress); Pekin, Ill., 12/10/52
Diamond, Neil (singer); Brooklyn, N.Y., 1/24/1941
Diana (Diana Frances Spencer) (Princess of Wales); Sandringham, England, 7/1/61
Dichter, Misha (pianist); Shanghai, 9/27/1945
Dickens, Charles John Huffam (novelist); Portsea, England **(1812-1870)**
Dickey, James (poet); Atlanta, 2/2/1923
Dickinson, Angie (Angeline Brown) (actress); Kulm, N.D., 9/30/1932
Dickinson, Emily Elizabeth (poet); Amherst, Mass. **(1830-1886)**
Diddley, Bo (Elias McDaniel) (guitarist); McComb, Miss., 12/30/1928
Diderot, Denis (encyclopedist); Langres, France **(1713-1784)**
Diefenbaker, John G. (ex-Prime Minister); Grey County, Ontario, Canada **(1895-1979)**
Dietrich, Marlene (Maria Magdalena von Losch) (actress); Berlin, 12/27/1901
Diggs, Dudley (actor); Dublin **(1879-1947)**
Diller, Phyllis (Phyllis Driver) (comedienne); Lima, Ohio, 7/17/1917
Dillman, Bradford (actor); San Francisco, 4/14/1930
Dine, Jim (painter); Cincinnati, 6/16/1935
Diogenes (philosopher); Sinope (Turkey) **(412?-323** B.C.**)**
Dion (Dion DiMucci) (singer); Bronx, N.Y., 7/18/1939
Dior, Christian (fashion designer); Granville, France **(1905-1957)**
Disney, Walt(er) Elias (film animator and producer); Chicago **(1901-1966)**
Disraeli, Benjamin (Earl of Beaconsfield) (statesman); London **(1804-1881)**
Dix, Dorothea (civil rights reformer); Hampden, Me. **(1802-1887)**
Dix, Richard (Ernest Carlton Brimmer) (actor); St. Paul **(1894-1949)**
Dixon, Jeane (Jeane Pinckert) (seer); Medford, Wis., 1918
Dobbs, Mattiwilda (soprano); Atlanta, Ga., 7/11/1925
Doctorow, E(dgar) L(aurence) (novelist); New York City, 1/6/1931
Dodgson, C. L. *See* Carroll, Lewis.
Dolin, Anton (dancer); Slinfold, England **(1904-1983)**
Domingo, Placido (tenor); Madrid, 1/21/1941
Domino, Fats (Antoine) (musician); New Orleans, 2/26/1928
Donahue, Phil (television personality); Cleveland, 12/21/1935
Donahue, Troy (actor); New York City, 1/27/36(?)
Donat, Robert (actor); Withington, England **(1905-1958)**
Donatello (Donato Niccolò di Betto Bardi) (sculptor); Florence **(c. 1386-1466)**
Donley, Brian (actor); Portadown, Ireland **(1849-1972)**
Donovan (Donovan Leitch) (singer and songwriter); Glasgow, Scotland, 2/10/1946
Donne, John (poet); London **(1573-1631)**
Doolittle, James H. (ex-Air Force general); Alameda, Calif., 12/14/1896
Dorati, Antal (orchestra conductor); Budapest **(1906-1988)**
Dorsey, Jimmy (band leader); Shenandoah, Pa. **(1904-1957)**
Dorsey, Tommy (band leader); Mahonoy Plains, Pa. **(1905-1956)**
Dos Passos, John (author); Chicago **(1896-1970)**
Dostoevski, Fyodor Mikhailovich (novelist); Moscow **(1821-1881)**
Dotrice, Roy (actor); Guernsey, Channel Islands, England, 5/26/23
Douglas, Helen Gahagan (ex-Representative); Boonton, N.J. **(1900-1980)**
Douglas, Kirk (Issur Danielovitch) (actor); Amsterdam, N.Y., 12/9/1916
Douglas, Melvyn (Melvyn Hesselberg) (actor); Macon, Ga., **(1901-1981)**
Douglas, Michael (actor; movie producer); New Brunswick, N.J., 9/25/1944
Douglas, Mike (Michael D. Dowd, Jr.) (TV personality); Chicago, 8/11/1925
Douglas, Paul (actor); Philadelphia **(1907-1959)**
Douglas, Stephen Arnold (politician); Brandon, Vt. **(1813-1861)**
Dowling, Eddie (Edward Goucher) (actor and stage producer); Woonsocket, R.I., **(1894-1976)**
Down, Lesley-Anne (actress); London, England, 3/17/54
Downs, Hugh (TV entertainer); Akron, Ohio, 2/14/1921
Doyle, Sir Arthur Conan (novelist and spiritualist); Edinburgh, Scotland **(1859-1930)**
Doyle, David (actor); Omaha, Neb., 12/1/25
Drake, Alfred (singer and actor); New York City, 10/7/1914
Drake, Sir Francis (navigator); Tavistock, England **(1545-1596)**
Dreiser, Theodore (writer); Terre Haute, Ind. **(1871-1945)**
Dressler, Marie (Leila Koeber) (actress); Cobourg, Ontario, Canada **(1869-1934)**
Dreyfus, Alfred (French army officer); Mulhouse (France) **(1859-1935)**
Dreyfuss, Richard (actor); Brooklyn, N.Y., 10/29/1947
Drury, Allen (novelist); Houston, 9/2/1918
Dryden, John (poet); Northamptonshire, England **(1631-1700)**
Dryer, Fred (actor); Hawthorne, Calif., 7/6/46
Dru, Joan (actress); Logan, W. Va., 1/31/23
Dubček, Alexander (ex-President of Czechoslovakia); Uhroved (Czechoslovakia), 11/27/1921
Dubinsky, David (David Dobnievski) (labor leader); Brest-Litovsk (U.S.S.R.) **(1892-1982)**
Duchamp, Marcel (painter); Blainville, France **(1887-1968)**
Duchin, Eddy (pianist, bandleader); Cambridge, Mass. **(1909-1951)**
Duchin, Peter (pianist and band leader); New York City, 7/28/1937
Dufay, Guillaume (composer); Cambrai, France **(c. 1400-1474)**
Duff, Howard (actor); Bremerton, Wash. **(1917-1990)**
Duffy, Julia (actress); Minneapolis, Minn., 6/27/50
Dufy, Raoul (painter); Le Havre, France **(1877-1953)**
Duke, James B. (industrialist); nr. Durham, N.C. **(1856-1925)**
Duke, Patty (Anna Marie Duke) (actress); New York City, 12/14/1946
Dullea, Keir (actor); Cleveland, 5/30/1936(?)
Dulles, Allen Welsh (ex-Director of CIA); Watertown, N.Y. **(1893-1969)**
Dulles, John Foster (statesman); Washington, D.C. **(1888-1959)**
Dumas, Alexandre (called Dumas fils) (novelist); Paris **(1824-1895)**
Dumas, Alexandre (called Dumas père) (novelist); Villers-Cotterets, France **(1802-1870)**
du Maurier, Daphne (novelist); London **(1907-1989)**
du Maurier, George Louis Palmella Busson (novelist); Paris **(1834-1896)**
Dumont, Margaret (actress); **(1889-1965)**
Dunaway, Faye (actress); Bascom, Fla., 1/14/1941
Duncan, Isadora (dancer); San Francisco **(1878-1927)**
Duncan, Sandy (actress); Henderson, Tex., 2/20/1946
Dunham, Katherine (dancer, choreographer); Chicago, 1914

Dunn, James (actor); Santa Monica, Calif. (1905-1967)
Dunne, Irene (actress); Louisville, Ky. (1901?-1990)
Dunnock, Mildred (actress); Baltimore, 1/25/1906
Duns Scotus, John (theologian); Duns, Scotland (1265-1303)
Du Pont, Pierre S. (economist); Paris (1739-1817)
Durante, Jimmy (comedian); New York City (1893-1980)
Durbin, Deanna (Edna Mae) (actress); Winnipeg, Canada, 12/4/1922
Dürer, Albrecht (painter and engraver); Nürnberg (Germany) (1471-1528)
Durning, Charles (actor); Highland Falls, N.Y., 2/28/23
Durrell, Lawrence George (novelist); Julundur, India, 2/27/1912
Duryea, Dan (actor); White Plains, N.Y. (1907-1968)
Duse, Eleonora (actress); Chioggia, Italy (1859-1924)
Dussault, Nancy (actress); Pensacola, Fla., 6/30/36
Duvalier, Jean-Claude (ex-President; son of "Papa Doc"); Port-au-Prince, Haiti, 7/3/1951
Duvall, Robert (actor); San Diego, Calif., 1931
Duvall, Shelley (actress); Houston, Tex., 1950
Dvořák, Antonin (composer); Nelahozeves (Czechoslovakia) (1841-1904)
Dylan, Bob (Robert Zimmerman) (folk singer and composer); Duluth, Minn., 5/24/1941
Dysart, Richard (actor); Brighton, Mass., 3/30/?

E

Eagels, Joanne (actress); Kansas City, Mo. (1894-1929)
Eakins, Thomas (painter and sculptor); Philadelphia, (1844-1916)
Earhart, Amelia (aviator); Atchison, Kan. (1898-1937)
Eastman, George (inventor); Waterville, N.Y. (1854-1932)
Eastwood, Clint (actor); San Francisco, 5/31/1930
Ebert, Roger (film critic); Urbana, Ill., 6/18/42
Ebsen, Buddy (Christian Ebsen, Jr.) (actor); Belleville, Ill., 4/2/1908
Eckstine, Billy (singer); Pittsburgh, 7/8/1914
Eddy, Mary Baker (founder of Christian Science Church); Bow, N.H. (1821-1910)
Eddy, Nelson (baritone and actor); Providence, R.I. (1901-1967)
Eden, Sir Anthony (Earl of Avon) (ex-Prime Minister); Durham, England (1897-1977)
Eden, Barbara (actress); Tucson, Ariz., 8/23/34
Edison, Thomas Alva (inventor); Milan, Ohio (1847-1931)
Edwards, Anthony (actor); Santa Barbara, Calif., 7/19/?
Edwards, Blake (film writer-producer); Tulsa, Okla. 7/26/1922
Edwards, Jonathan (theologian); East Windsor, Conn. (1703-1758)
Edwards, Ralph (TV and radio producer); Merino, Colo., 1913
Edwards, Vincent (actor); Brooklyn, N.Y., 7/7/1928
Egan, Richard (actor); San Francisco (1923-1987)
Eggar, Samantha (actress); London, 5/3/1939
Eglevsky, André (ballet dancer); Moscow (1917-1977)
Ehrlich, Paul (bacteriologist); Strzelin (Poland) (1854-1915)
Eikenberry, Jill (actress); New Haven, Conn., 1/21/47
Einstein, Albert (physicist); Ulm, Germany (1879-1955)
Eisenhower, Milton S. (educator); Abilene, Kan., (1899-1985)
Eisenstaedt, Alfred (photographer and photojournalist); Dirschau (Poland), 12/6/1898
Ekberg, Anita (actress); Malmö, Sweden, 9/29/1931
Ekland, Britt (Britt-Marie) (actress); Stockholm, Sweden, 1942
Eldridge, Florence (Florence McKechnie) (actress); Brooklyn, N.Y., (1901-1988)
Elgar, Sir Edward (composer); Worcester, England (1857-1934)
Elgart, Larry (band leader); New London, Conn., 3/20/1922
El Greco (Domenicos Theotocopoulos) (painter); Candia, Crete (Greece) (c.1541-1614)
Eliot, George (Mary Ann Evans) (novelist); Chilvers Coton, England (1819-1880)
Eliot, Thomas Stearns (poet); St. Louis (1888-1965)
Ellington, Duke (Edward Kennedy) (jazz musician); Washington, D.C. (1899-1974)
Elliot, "Mama" Cass (Ellen Naomi Cohen) (singer); Baltimore (1941-1974)
Elliott, Denholm (actor); London, 5/31/22
Elliott, Sam (actor); California, 8/9/44
Elman, Mischa (violinist); Stalnoye, Ukraine (1891-1967)
Emerson, Ralph Waldo (philosopher and poet); Boston (1803-1882)
Enesco, Georges (composer); Dorohoi, Romania (1881-1955)
Engels, Friedrich (Socialist writer); Barmen (Germany) (1820-1895)
Englund, Robert (actor); Glendale, Calif., 6/6/49
Entremont, Philippe (concert pianist); Rheims, France, 6/7/1934
Epicurus (philosopher); Samos (Greece) (341-270 B.C.)
Epstein, Sir Jacob (sculptor); New York City (1880-1959)
Erasmus, Desiderius (Gerhard Gerhards) (scholar); Rotterdam (1466?-1536)
Erhard, Ludwig (ex-Chancellor); Furth, Germany (1897-1977)
Erickson, Leif (actor); Alameda, Calif. (1911-1986)
Ericson, Leif (navigator); (c. 10th century A.D.)

Erikson, Erik H. (psychoanalyst); Frankfurt, Germany, 6/15/1902
Ernst, Max (painter); Bruhl, Germany (1891-1976)
Erté (Romain de Tirtoff) (artist, designer); St. Petersburg, Russia (1892-1990)
Estrada, Erik (actor); New York City, 3/16/49
Euclid (mathematician); Megara (Greece) (c. 300 B.C.)
Euler, Leonhard (mathematician); Basel, Switzerland (1707-1783)
Euripides (dramatist); Salamis (Greece) (c.484-407 B.C.)
Evans, Dale (Frances Butts) (actress and singer); Uvalde, Tex., 10/31/1912
Evans, Dame Edith (actress); London (1888-1976)
Evans, Linda (actress); Hartford, Conn., 11/18/1942
Evans, Maurice (actor); Dorchester, England (1901-1989)
Everett, Chad (actor); (Raymon Lee Cramton) South Bend, Ind., 6/11/1936
Evers, Charles (civil rights leader); Decatur, Miss., 9/14/1923(?)
Evers, Medgar (civil rights leader); Decatur, Miss. (1925-1963)
Evigan, Greg (actor); South Amboy, N.J., 10/14/53
Ewell, Tom (Yewell Tompkins) (actor); Owensboro, Ky., 4/29/1909

F

Fabares, Shelley (actress); Santa Monica, Calif., 1/19/44
Fabian (Fabian Anthony Forte) (singer); Philadelphia, 2/6/1943
Fabray, Nanette (Nanette Fabarés) (actress); San Diego, Calif., 10/27/1922
Fadiman, Clifton (literary critic); Brooklyn, N.Y., 5/15/1904
Fahrenheit, Gabriel (German physicist); Danzig (Poland); (1686-1736)
Fairbanks, Douglas (Douglas Ulman) (actor); Denver (1883-1939)
Fairbanks, Douglas, Jr. (actor); New York City, 12/9/1909
Fairchild, Morgan (actress); Dallas, Tex., 2/3/50
Faith, Percy (conductor); Toronto (1908-1976)
Falk, Peter (actor); New York City, 9/16/1927
Falla, Manuel de (composer); Cadiz, Spain (1876-1946)
Faraday, Michael (physicist); Newington, England (1791-1867)
Farber, Barry (radio-TV broadcaster); Baltimore, Md., 1930
Farentino, James (actor); Brooklyn, N.Y., 2/24/1938
Farmer, Frances (actress); Seattle, Wash. (1913-1970)
Farmer, James (civil rights leader); Marshall, Tex., 1/12/1920
Farnum, William (actor); Boston (1876-1953)
Farr, Jamie (actor); Toledo, Ohio, 7/1/34
Farrar, Geraldine (soprano, actress); Melrose, Mass. (1882-1967)
Farrell, Charles (actor); Onset Bay, Mass. (1901-1990)
Farrell, Eileen (operatic soprano); Willimantic, Conn., 2/13/1920
Farrell, Glenda (actress); Enid, Okla. (1904-1971)
Farrell, James T. (novelist); Chicago (1904-1979)
Farrell, Mike (actor); St. Paul, Minn., 2/6/39
Farrell, Suzanne (Roberta Sue Ficker) (ballerina); Cincinnati, 8/16/1945
Farrow, Mia (actress); Los Angeles, 2/9/1946
Fasanella, Ralph (painter); New York City, 9/2/1914
Fassbinder, Rainer Werner (film and stage director); Bad Wörishofen, West Germany (1946-1982)
Fast, Howard (novelist); New York City, 11/11/1914
Faulkner, William (novelist); New Albany, Miss. (1897-1962)
Fauré, Gabriel Urbain (composer); Pamiers, France (1845-1924)
Fawcett, Farrah (actress); Corpus Christi, Tex., 2/2/1947?(?)
Faye, Alice (Ann Leppert) (actress); New York City, 5/5/1915
Feiffer, Jules (cartoonist); New York City, 1/26/1929
Feininger, Lyonel (painter); New York City (1871-1956)
Feldman, Marty (actor, screenwriter, director); London (1938-1982)
Feldon, Barbara (actress); Pittsburgh, 3/12/1941
Feliciano, José (singer); Larez, Puerto Rico, 9/10/1945
Felker, Clay S. (editor and publisher); St. Louis, 10/2/1925(?)
Fell, Norman (actor); Philadelphia, 3/24/23
Fellini, Federico (film director); Rimini, Italy, 1/20/1920
Fender, Freddie (Baldemar Huerta) (singer); San Benito, Tex., 1937
Ferber, Edna (novelist); Kalamazoo, Mich. (1885-1968)
Ferguson, Maynard (jazz trumpeter); Verdun, Quebec, Canada, 5/4/1928
Fermi, Enrico (atomic physicist); Rome (1901-1954)
Fernandel (Fernand Joseph Desire Contandin) (actor); Marseilles, France (1903-1971)
Ferrer, José (actor and director); Santurce, Puerto Rico, 1/8/1912
Ferrer, Mel (actor); Elberon, N.J., 8/25/1917
Ferrigno, Lou (actor); Brooklyn, N.Y., 11/9/52
Fetchit, Stepin (Lincoln Theodore Perry) (comedian); Key West, Fla. (1902-1985)
Fiedler, Arthur (conductor); Boston (1894-1979)
Field, Betty (actress); Boston (1918-1973)
Field, Eugene (poet); St. Louis (1850-1895)
Field, Marshall (merchant); nr. Conway, Mass. (1834-1906)
Field, Sally (actress); Pasadena, Calif., 11/6/1946
Fielding, Henry (novelist); nr. Glastonbury, England (1707-1754)

Fields, Gracie (comedienne); Rochdale, England **(1898-1979)**
Fields, Totie (comedienne); Hartford, Conn. **(1931-1978)**
Fields, W. C. (William Claude Dukenfield) (comedian); Philadelphia **(1880-1946)**
Fierstein, Harvey (Forbes) (playwright and actor); Brooklyn, 6/6/1954
Filene, Edward A. (merchant); **(1860-1937)**
Finch, Peter (actor); Kensington, England **(1916-1977)**
Finney, Albert (actor); Salford, England, 5/9/1936
Firkusny, Rudolf (pianist); Napajedia (Czechoslovakia), 2/11/1912
Fischer-Dieskau, Dietrich (baritone); Berlin, 5/28/1925
Fisher, Carrie (actress); Los Angeles, 10/21/56
Fisher, Eddie (Edwin) (singer); Philadelphia, 8/10/1928
Fitzgerald, Barry (William Joseph Shields) (actor); Dublin **(1888-1961)**
Fitzgerald, Edward (radio broadcaster); Troy, N.Y. **(1898(?)-1982)**
Fitzgerald, Ella (singer); Newport News, Va., 4/25/1918
Fitzgerald, F. Scott (Francis Scott Key) (novelist); St. Paul, Minn. **(1896-1940)**
Fitzgerald, Geraldine (actress); Dublin, 11/24/1914
Fitzgerald, Pegeen (radio broadcaster); Norcatur, Kan. **(1910-1989)**
Flack, Roberta (singer); Black Mountain, N.C., 2/10/1940
Flagstad, Kirsten (Wagnerian soprano); Hamar, Norway **(1895-1962)**
Flatt, Lester Raymond (bluegrass musician); Overton County, Tenn. **(1914-1979)**
Flaubert, Gustave (novelist); Rouen, France **(1821-1880)**
Fleming, Sir Alexander (bacteriologist); Lochfield, Scotland **(1881-1955)**
Fleming, Rhonda (Marilyn Louis) (actress); Los Angeles, 8/10/1923
Fletcher, John (dramatist); Rye? England **(1579-1625)**
Flynn, Errol (actor); Hobart, Tasmania **(1909-1959)**
Foch, Nina (actress); Leyden, Netherlands, 4/20/1924
Fodor, Eugene (violinist); Turkey Creek, Colo., 3/5/1950
Fokine, Michel (dancer, choreographer); St. Petersburg, Russia **(1880-1942)**
Fonda, Henry (actor); Grand Island, Neb. **(1905-1982)**
Fonda, Jane (actress); New York City, 12/21/1937
Fonda, Peter (actor); New York City, 2/23/1939
Fontaine, Frank (singer and comedian); Cambridge, Mass. **(1920-1979)**
Fontaine, Joan (Joan de Havilland) (actress); Tokyo, 10/22/1917
Fontanne, Lynn (actress); London, **(1887-1983)**
Fonteyn, Dame Margot (Margaret Hookham) (ballerina); Reigate, England, 5/18/1919
Forbes, Malcolm S(tevenson) (publisher and sportsman); Brooklyn, N.Y. **(1919-1990)**
Ford, Glenn (Gwyllyn Ford) (actor); Quebec, 5/1/1916
Ford, Harrison (actor); Chicago, 7/13/1942
Ford, Henry (industrialist); Greenfield, Mich. **(1863-1947)**
Ford, Henry, II (auto maker); Detroit **(1917-1987)**
Ford, John (film director); Cape Elizabeth, Me. **(1895-1973)**
Ford, Paul (actor); Baltimore **(1901-1976)**
Ford, Tennessee Ernie (Ernie Jennings Ford) (singer); Bristol, Tenn., 2/13/1919
Forrester, Maureen (contralto); Montreal, 7/25/1930
Forsythe, John (actor); Carney's Point, N.J., 1/29/1918
Fosdick, Harry Emerson (clergyman); Buffalo, N.Y. **(1878-1968)**
Fosse, Bob (Robert Louis) (choreographer and director); Chicago **(1927-1987)**
Foster, Jodie (actress); Bronx, N.Y., 1963
Foster, Preston (actor); Ocean City, N.J. **(1900-1970)**
Foster, Stephen Collins (composer); nr. Pittsburgh **(1826-1864)**
Fox, Michael J. (actor); Edmonton, Alta., Canada, 6/9/1961
Foxx, Redd (John Elroy Sanford) (actor and comedian); St. Louis, 12/9/1922
Foy, Eddie, Jr. (dancer and actor); New Rochelle, N.Y. **(1905-1983)**
Fra Angelico (Giovanni da Fiesole) (painter); Vicchio in the Mugello, Tuscany (Italy) **(c.1387-1455)**
Fracci, Carla (ballerina); Milan, Italy, 8/20/1936
Fragonard, Jean Honoré (painter); Grasse, France **(1732-1806)**
Frampton, Peter (rock musician); Beckenham, England, 4/20/1950
France, Anatole (Jacques Anatole François Thibault) (author); Paris **(1844-1924)**
Francescatti, Zino (violinist); Marseilles, France, 8/9/1905
Franciosa, Anthony (Anthony Papaleo) (actor); New York City, 10/25/1928
Francis, Anne (actress); Ossining, N.Y., 7/16/30
Francis, Arlene (Arlene Francis Kazanjian) (actress); Boston, 10/20/1908
Francis, Connie (Concetta Franconero) (singer); Newark, N.J., 12/12/1938
Francis, Genie (actress); Englewood, N.J., 5/26/62
Francis, Kay (Katherine Edwina Gibbs) (actress); Oklahoma City **(1903-1968)**
Francis of Assisi, Saint (Giovanni Francesco Barnardone) (founder of Franciscans); Assisi, Italy **(1182-1226)**

Franck, César Auguste (composer); Liège (Belgium) **(1822-1890)**
Franco Bahamonde, Francisco (Chief of State); El Ferrol, Spain **(1892-1975)**
Franklin, Aretha (singer); Memphis, Tenn., 3/25/1942
Franklin, Benjamin (statesman and scientist); Boston **(1706-1790)**
Franklin, Bonnie (actress); Santa Monica, Calif., 1/6/44
Frann, Mary (actress); St. Louis, Mo., 2/27/43
Frazer, Sir James George (anthropologist); Glasgow, Scotland **(1854-1941)**
Freud, Sigmund (psychoanalyst); Moravia (Czechoslovakia) **(1856-1939)**
Friedan, Betty (Betty Naomi Goldstein) (feminist); Peoria, Ill., 2/4/1921
Fromm, Erich (psychoanalyst); Frankfurt-am-Main, Germany **(1900-1980)**
Frost, David (TV entertainer); Tenterden, England, 4/7/1939
Frost, Robert Lee (poet); San Francisco **(1874-1963)**
Fry, Christopher (playwright); Bristol, England, 12/18/1907
Frye, David (impressionist); Brooklyn, N.Y., 1934
Fugard, Athol (playwright); Middleburg, South Africa, 6/11/1932
Fuller, R(ichard) Buckminster (Jr.) (architect and educator); Milton, Mass. **(1895-1983)**
Fulton, Robert (inventor); Lancaster County, Pa. **(1765-1815)**
Funicello, Annette (actress); Los Angeles, 10/22/42
Funt, Allen (TV producer); Brooklyn, N.Y., 9/16/1914
Furness, Betty (Elizabeth) (ex-actress and consumer advocate); New York City, 1/3/1916

G

Gabel, Martin (actor and producer); Philadelphia **(1912-1986)**
Gabin, Jean (actor); Paris **(1904-1976)**
Gable, (William) Clark (actor); Cadiz, Ohio **(1901-1960)**
Gabo, Naum (sculptor); Briansk, Russia **(1890-1977)**
Gabor, Eva (actress); Budapest, 2/11/1926(?)
Gabor, Zsa Zsa (Sari) (actress); Budapest, 2/6/1919(?)
Gabrieli, Giovanni (composer); Venice **(c.1557-1612)**
Gainsborough, Thomas (painter); Sudbury, Suffolk, England **(1727-1788)**
Galbraith, John Kenneth (economist); Iona Station, Ontario, Canada, 10/15/1908
Galilei, Galileo (astronomer and physicist); Pisa (Italy) **(1564-1642)**
Gallico, Paul (novelist); New York City **(1897-1976)**
Gallup, George H. (poll taker); Jefferson, Iowa **(1901-1984)**
Galsworthy, John (novelist and dramatist); Coombe, England **(1867-1933)**
Galway, James (flutist); Belfast, Northern Ireland, 12/8/1939
Gambling, John A. (radio broadcaster); New York City, 1930
Gandhi, Indira (Indira Nehru) (Prime Minister); Allahabad, India **(1917-1984)**
Gandhi, Mohandas Karamchand (called Mahatma Gandhi) (Hindu leader); Porbandar, India **(1869-1948)**
Gannett, Frank E. (editor and publisher); **(1876-1957)**
Garagiola, Joe (Joseph Henry) (sportscaster); St. Louis, 2/12/1926
Garbo, Greta (Greta Gustafsson) (actress); Stockholm **(1905-1990)**
Garcia Lorca, Frederico (author); Fuente Vaqueros, Spain **(1898-1936)**
Garden, Mary (soprano); Aberdeen, Scotland **(1874-1967)**
Gardenia, Vincent (actor); Naples, Italy, 1/7/22
Gardner, Ava (actress); Smithfield, N.C. **(1922-1990)**
Gardner, Erle Stanley (novelist); Malden, Mass. **(1889-1970)**
Garfield, John (Jules Garfinkle) (actor); New York City **(1913-1952)**
Garfunkel, Art (Arthur) (singer); Newark, N.J., 11/5/1941
Gargan, William (actor); Brooklyn, N.Y., **(1905-1979)**
Garibaldi, Giuseppe (Italian nationalist leader); Nice, France **(1807-1882)**
Garland, Judy (Frances Gumm) (actress and singer); Grand Rapids, Minn. **(1922-1969)**
Garner, Erroll (jazz pianist); Pittsburgh **(1921-1977)**
Garner, James (James Bumgarner) (actor); Norman, Okla., 4/7/1928
Garner, Peggy Ann (actress); Canton, Ohio **(1932-1984)**
Garr, Teri (actress); Lakewood, Ohio, 12/11/49
Garrett, Betty (actress); St. Joseph, Mo., 5/23/1919
Garrick, David (actor); Hereford, England **(1717-1779)**
Garrison, William Lloyd (abolitionist); Newburyport, Mass. **(1805-1879)**
Garroway, Dave (TV host); Schenectady, N.Y. **(1913-1982)**
Garson, Greer (actress); County Down, Northern Ireland, 9/29/1912(?)
Gary, John (singer); Watertown, N.Y., 11/29/1932
Gassman, Vittorio (film actor and director); Genoa, Italy, 9/1/1922
Gaudí, Antonio (architect); Reus, Spain **(1852-1926)**
Gauguin, Eugène Henri Paul (painter); Paris **(1848-1903)**
Gautama Buddha (Prince Siddhartha) (philosopher); Kapilavastu (India) **(563?-?483 B.C.)**

Gavin, John (actor, diplomat); Los Angeles, 4/8/1935

Gayle, Crystal (Brenda Gayle Webb) (singer); Paintsville, Ky., 1/9/51

Gaynor, Janet (actress); Philadelphia (1906-1984)

Gaynor, Mitzi (Francesca Mitzi Marlene de Czanyi von Gerber) (actress); Chicago, 9/4/1931

Gazzara, Ben (Biago Anthony Gazzara) (actor); New York City, 8/28/1930

Gebel-Williams, Gunther (animal trainer); Schweidnitz (Poland), 1934

Gedda, Nicolai (tenor); Stockholm, Sweden, 7/11/25

Geddes, Barbara Bel (actress); New York City, 10/31/1922

Genet, Jean (playwright); Paris (1910-1986)

Genghis Khan (Temujin) (conqueror); nr. Lake Baikal, Russia (1162-1227)

Genn, Leo (actor); London (1905-1978)

Gentry, Bobbie (Roberta Streeter) (singer); Chickasaw Co., Miss., 7/27/1944

George, David Lloyd (statesman); Manchester, England (1863-1945)

Gere, Richard (actor); Philadelphia, 1950

Gericault, Jean Louis (painter); Rouen, France (1791-1824)

Geronimo (Goyathlay) (Apache chieftain); Arizona (1829-1909)

Gershwin, George (composer); Brooklyn, N.Y. (1898-1937)

Gershwin, Ira (lyricist); New York City, (1896-1983)

Getty, J. Paul (oil executive); Minneapolis (1892-1976)

Getz, Stan (saxophonist); Philadelphia, 2/2/1927

Ghiberti, Lorenzo (goldsmith and sculptor); Florence (1378-1455)

Ghostley, Alice (actress); Eve, Mo., 8/14/26

Giacometti, Alberto (sculptor); Switzerland (1901-1966)

Giannini, Giancarlo (actor); La Spezia, Italy, 8/1/1942

Gibbon, Edward (historian); Putney, England (1737-1794)

Gibson, Charles Dana (illustrator); Roxbury, Mass. (1867-1944)

Gibson, Henry (actor, comedian); Germantown, Pa., 9/21/35

Gibson, Hoot (Edward) (actor); Tememah, Neb. (1892-1962)

Gibson, Mel (actor); Peekskill, N.Y., 1/3/56

Gide, André (author); Paris (1869-1951)

Gielgud, Sir John (actor); London, 4/14/1904

Gilbert, John (movie actor); Logan, Utah (1897-1936)

Gilbert, Melissa (actress); Los Angeles, 5/8/64

Gilbert, Sir William Schwenck (librettist); London (1836-1911)

Gilels, Emil (concert pianist); Odessa, Ukraine (1916-1985)

Gillespie, Dizzy (John Birks Gillespie) (jazz trumpeter); Cheraw, S.C., 10/21/1917

Gillette, William (actor); Hartford, Conn. (1855-1932)

Gimbel, Bernard F. (merchant); Vincennes, Ind. (1885-1966)

Gingold, Hermione (actress and comedienne); London (1897-1987)

Ginsberg, Allen (poet); Newark, N.J., 6/3/1926

Giordano, Luca (painter); Naples, Italy (1632-1705)

Giorgione (painter); Castelfranco, (Italy) (c.1477-1510)

Giotto di Bondone (painter); Vespignamo (Italy) (c.1266-1337)

Giovanni, Nikki (poet); Knoxville, Tenn., 6/7/1943

Giroud, Françoise (French government official); Geneva, 9/21/1916

Gish, Dorothy (actress); Massillon, Ohio (1898-1968)

Gish, Lillian (Lillian de Guiche) (actress); Springfield, Ohio, 10/14/1896(?)

Givenchy, Hubert (fashion designer); Beauvais, France, 2/21/1927

Gladstone, William Ewart (statesman); Liverpool, England (1809-1898)

Glaser, Paul Michael (actor, director); Cambridge, Mass., 3/25/43

Glass, Philip (composer); Baltimore, 1/31/1937

Gleason, Jackie (comedian); Brooklyn, N.Y. (1916-1987)

Gleason, James (actor); New York City (1886-1959)

Gless, Sharon (actress); Los Angeles, 5/31/43

Gluck, Christoph Willibald (composer); Erasbach (Germany) (1714-1787)

Gobel, George (comedian); Chicago, 5/20/1920

Godard, Jean Luc (film director); Paris, 12/3/1930

Goddard, Robert Hutchings (father of modern rocketry); Worcester, Mass. (1882-1945)

Goddard, Paulette (Marion Levy) (actress); Great Neck, N.Y. (1911?-1990)

Godfrey, Arthur (entertainer); New York City (1903-1983)

Godunov, Alexander (ballet dancer); Sakhalin, U.S.S.R. 11/28/1949

Goebbels, Joseph Paul (Nazi leader); Rheydt, Germany (1897-1945)

Goering, Hermann (Nazi leader); Rosenheim, Germany (1893-1946)

Goethals, George Washington (engineer); Brooklyn, N.Y. (1858-1928)

Goethe, Johann Wolfgang von (poet); Frankfurt-am-Main, Germany (1749-1832)

Gogol, Nikolai Vasilievich (novelist); nr. Mirgorod, Ukraine (1809-1852)

Goldberg, Rube (cartoonist); San Francisco (1883-1970)

Goldberg, Whoopi (actress); New York City, 1949 (?)

Goldblum, Jeff (actor); Pittsburgh, Pa., 10/22/52

Golden, Harry (Harry Goldhurst) (author); New York City (1902-1981)

Goldsmith, Oliver (dramatist and poet); County Longford, Ireland (1728-1774)

Goldwyn, Samuel (Samuel Goldfish) (film producer); Warsaw (1882-1974)

Golenpaul, Dan (creator of Information Please radio show and editor of almanac of same name); New York City (1900-1974)

Gompers, Samuel (labor leader); London (1850-1924)

Goodall, Jane (Baroness van Lawick-Goodall) (ethologist); London, 4/3/1934

Goodman, Benny (clarinetist); Chicago (1909-1986)

Goodyear, Charles (inventor); New Haven; Conn. (1800-1860)

Gorbachev, Mikhail Sergeyevich (Soviet leader); Privolnoye, U.S.S.R., 3/2/1931

Gordimer, Nadine (novelist and short-story writer); Springs, South Africa, 12/20/1923

Gordon, Max (stage producer); New York City; (1892-1978)

Gordon, Ruth (actress); Wollaston, Mass. (1896-1985)

Gordy, Berry, Jr. (record company executive); Detroit, 11/28/1929

Gore, Lesley (singer); Tenafly, N.J., 1946

Goren, Charles H. (bridge expert); Philadelphia, 3/4/1901

Gorki, Maxim (Alexei Maximovich Peshkov) (author); Nizhni Novgorod, Russia (1868-1936)

Gorky, Arshile (painter); Armenia (1904-1948)

Gormé, Eydie (singer); Bronx, N.Y., 8/16/1932

Gorshin, Frank (actor); Pittsburgh, 4/5/1934

Gosden, Freeman F. *See* Amos

Gossett, Louis, Jr. (actor); Brooklyn, N.Y., 5/27/36

Gottschalk, Louis Moreau (pianist, composer); New Orleans, La. (1829-1869)

Gould, Chester (cartoonist); Pawnee, Okla. (1900-1985)

Gould, Elliott (Elliott Goldstein) (actor); Brooklyn, N.Y., 8/29/1938

Gould, Glenn (concert pianist); Toronto, (1932-1982)

Gould, Morton (composer); Richmond Hill, Queens, N.Y., 12/10/1913

Goulet, Robert (singer); Lawrence, Mass., 11/26/1933

Gounod, Charles François (composer); Paris (1818-1893)

Goya y Lucientes, Francisco José de (painter); Fuendetodos, Spain (1746-1828)

Grable, Betty (actress); St. Louis (1916-1973)

Grace, Princess of Monaco (Grace Kelly) (ex-actress); Philadelphia (1929-1982)

Graham, Bill (Wolfgang Grajonca) (rock impresario); Berlin, 1931

Graham, Billy (William F.) (evangelist); Charlotte, N.C., 11/7/1918

Graham, Katharine Meyer (newspaper publisher); New York City, 6/16/1917

Graham, Martha (choreographer); Pittsburgh, 5/11/1894(?)

Graham, Virgina (actress,host); Chicago, 7/4/13

Grahame, Gloria (Gloria Hallwood) (actress); Los Angeles (1929-1981)

Grainger, Percy Aldridge (pianist and composer); Melbourne, Australia (1882-1961)

Gramm, Donald (Grambach) (bass-baritone); Milwaukee (1927-1983)

Granger, Farley (actor); San Jose, Calif., 7/1/1925

Granger, Stewart (James Stewart) (actor); London, 5/6/1913

Grant, Cary (Alexander Archibald Leach) (actor); Bristol, England (1904-1986)

Grant, Kathryn (actress); Houston, Tex. 1933

Grant, Lee (Lyova Haskell Rosenthal) (actress); New York City, 10/31/1930

Granville, Bonita (actress); New York City (1923-1988)

Grass, Günter (novelist); Danzig (Poland), 10/16/1927

Grauer, Ben (radio and TV announcer); New York City (1908-1977)

Graves, Peter (Peter Arness) (actor); Minneapolis, 3/18/1926

Graves, Robert (writer); London (1895-1985)

Gray, Barry (Bernard Yaroslaw) (radio interviewer); Atlantic City, N.J., 7/2/1916

Gray, Dolores (singer and actress); Chicago, 6/7/1930

Gray, Linda (actress); Santa Monica, Calif., 9/12/40

Gray, Thomas (poet); London (1716-1771)

Grayson, Kathryn (Zelma Hednick) (singer and actress); Winston-Salem, N.C., 2/9/1923

Greco, Buddy (singer); Philadelphia, 8/14/1926

Greco, José (dancer); Montorio nei Frentani, Itàly, 12/23/1918

Greeley, Horace (journalist and politician); Amherst, N.H. (1811-1872)

Green, Adolph (actor and lyricist); New York City, 12/2/1915

Green, Al (singer); Forrest City, Ark., 4/13/1946

Greene, Graham (novelist); Berkhamsted, England, 10/2/1904

Greene, Lorne (actor); Ottawa (1915-1987)

Greene, Martyn (actor); London (1899-1975)

Greene, Michele (actress); Las Vegas, Nev., 2/3/?

Greene, Shecky (comedian, actor); Chicago, 4/8/25

Greenstreet, Sydney (actor); Sandwich, England (1879-1954)

Greenwood, Charlotte (actress); Philadelphia, Pa. (1893-1978)

Greenwood, Joan (actress and director); London (1921-1987)

Greer, Germaine (feminist); Melbourne, 1/29/1939

Gregory, Cynthia (ballerina); Los Angeles, 7/8/1946

Gregory, Dick (comedian); St. Louis, 1932
Greuze, Jean-Baptiste (painter); Tournus, France **(1725-1805)**
Grey, Joel (Joel Katz) (actor); Cleveland, 4/11/1932
Grey, Zane (author); Zanesville, Ohio **(1875-1939)**
Grieg, Edvard Hagerup (composer); Bergen, Norway **(1843-1907)**
Grier, Roosevelt (entertainer and former athlete); Cuthbert, Ga., 7/14/1932
Griffin, Merv (TV entertainer); San Mateo, Calif., 7/6/1925
Griffith, Andy (actor); Mount Airy, N.C., 6/1/1926
Griffith, David Lewelyn Wark (film producer); La Grange, Ky. **(1875-1948)**
Griffith, Melanie (actress); New York City, 8/9/57
Grigorovich, Yuri (choreographer); Leningrad, 1/1/1927
Grimes, Tammy (actress); Lynn, Mass., 1/30/1934
Grimm, Jacob (author of fairy tales); Hanau (Germany) **(1785-1863)**
Grimm, Wilhelm (author of fairy tales); Hanau (Germany) **(1786-1859)**
Gris, Juan (José Victoriano González) (painter); Madrid **(1887-1927)**
Grizzard, George (actor); Roanoke Rapids, N.C., 4/1/1928
Grodin, Charles (actor); Pittsburgh, Pa., 4/21/35
Groh, David (actor); Brooklyn, N.Y., 5/21/39
Gromyko, Andrei A. (diplomat); Starye Gromyki, Russia **(1909-1989)**
Gropius, Walter (architect); Berlin **(1883-1969)**
Gropper, William (painter, illustrator); New York City **(1897-1977)**
Gross, Michael (actor); Chicago, 6/21/47
Grosz, George (painter); Germany **(1893-1959)**
Guardino, Harry (actor); New York City, 12/23/1925
Guggenheim, Meyer (capitalist); Langnau, Switzerland **(1828-1905)**
Guillaume, Robert (actor); St. Louis, Mo. 11/30/27
Guinness, Sir Alec (actor); London, 4/2/1914
Guitry, Sacha (Alexandre) (actor and film director); St. Petersburg, Russia **(1885-1957)**
Gumbel, Bryant Charles (TV newscaster); New Orleans, 9/29/1948
Gunther, John (author); Chicago **(1901-1970)**
Gutenberg, Johannes (printer); Mainz (Germany) **(1400?-?1468)**
Guthrie, Arlo (singer); New York City, 7/10/1947
Guthrie, Woody (folk singer and composer); Okemah, Okla. **(1912-1967)**
Gwenn, Edmund (actor); London **(1875-1959)**
Gwynne, Fred (actor); New York City, 7/10/26

H

Hackett, Bobby (trumpeter); Providence, R.I. **(1915-1976)**
Hackett, Buddy (Leonard Hacker) (comedian and actor); Brooklyn, N.Y., 8/31/1924
Hackman, Gene (actor); San Bernardino, Calif., 1/30/1931
Hagen, Uta (actress); Göttingen, Germany, 6/12/1919
Haggard, Merle (songwriter); Bakersfield, Calif., 4/6/1937
Hagman, Larry (actor); Weatherford, Tex., 1931
Haig, Alexander Meigs, Jr. (ex-Secretary of State and ex-general); Bala-Cynwyd, Pa., 12/2/1924
Haile Selassie (Ras Tafari Makonnen) (ex-Emperor); Ethiopia **(1892-1975)**
Hailey, Arthur (novelist); Luton, England, 4/5/1920
Halberstam, David (journalist); New York City, 4/10/1934
Hale, Alan (actor, director); Washington, D.C. **(1892-1950)**
Hale, Barbara (actress); DeKalb, Ill., 4/18/21
Hale, Edward Everett (clergyman and author); Boston **(1822-1909)**
Hale, Nathan (American Revolutionary officer); Coventry, Conn. **(1755-1776)**
Halevi, Judah (Jewish poet); Toledo, Spain **(1085-1140)**
Haley, Alex (writer); Ithaca, N.Y., 8/11/1921
Haley, Jack (actor); Boston **(1899-1979)**
Hall, Arsenio (comedian); Cleveland, Ohio, 2/12/?
Hall, Donald (Andrew, Jr.) (poet) New Haven, Conn., 9/20/1928
Hall, Huntz (actor); New York City, 1920
Hall, Monty (TV personality); Winnipeg, Canada, 1923
Halley, Edmund (astronomer); London **(1656-1742)**
Hals, Frans (painter); Antwerp (Netherlands) **(1580?-1666)**
Halsey, William Frederick, Jr. (naval officer); Elizabeth, N.J. **(1882-1959)**
Hamel, Veronica (actress); Philadelphia, Pa., 11/20/43
Hamill, Pete (journalist); Brooklyn, N.Y., 6/24/1935
Hamilton, Alexander (statesman); Nevis, British West Indies **(1757?-1804)**
Hamilton, George (actor); Memphis, Tenn., 8/12/1939
Hamilton, Margaret (actress); Cleveland **(1902-1985)**
Hamlin, Harry (actor); Pasadena, Calif., 10/30/51
Hamlisch, Marvin (composer and pianist); New York City, 6/2/1944
Hammarskjöld, Dag (U.N. Secretary-General); Jönköping, Sweden **(1905-1961)**
Hammerstein, Oscar, II (librettist and stage producer); New York City **(1895-1960)**
Hampden, Walter (Walter Hampden Dougherty) (actor); Brooklyn, N.Y.

(1879-1955)
Hampshire, Susan (actress); London, 5/12/38
Hampton, Lionel (vibraharpist and band leader); Birmingham, Ala., 4/12/1913
Hamsun, Knut (Knut Pedersen) (novelist); Lom, Norway **(1859-1952)**
Hancock, John (statesman); Braintree, Mass. **(1737-1793)**
Hand, Learned (jurist); Albany, N.Y. **(1872-1961)**
Handel, George Frederick (Georg Friedrich Händel) (composer); Halle (East Germany) **(1685-1759)**
Handy, William Christopher (blues composer); Florence, Ala. **(1873-1958)**
Hanks, Tom (actor); Concord, Calif., 7/9/1956
Hannibal (Carthaginian general); North Africa **(247-182** B.C.)
Hanson, Howard (conductor); Wahoo, Neb., **(1896-1981)**
Harburg, E. Y. "Yip" (songwriter); New York City **(1896-1981)**
Harding, Ann (actress); San Antonio, Tex. **(1902-1981)**
Hardwicke, Sir Cedric (actor); Stourbridge, England **(1893-1964)**
Hardy, Oliver (comedian); Atlanta **(1892-1957)**
Hardy, Thomas (novelist); Dorsetshire, England **(1840-1928)**
Harkness, Edward S. (capitalist); Cleveland **(1874-1940)**
Harlow, Jean (Harlean Carpentier) (actress); Kansas City, Mo. **(1911-1937)**
Harnick, Sheldon (lyricist); Chicago, 4/30/1924
Harper, Valerie (actress); Suffern, N.Y., 8/22/1940(?)
Harrell, Lynn (cellist); New York City, 1/30/1944
Harriman, W. (William) Averell (ex-Governor of New York); New York City **(1891-1986)**
Harrington, Pat., Jr. (actor, comedian); New York City, 8/13/29
Harris, Barbara (actress); Evanston, Ill., 1935
Harris, Emmylou (singer); Birmingham, Ala., 1949
Harris, Julie (actress); Grosse Pointe Park, Mich., 12/2/1925
Harris, Phil (actor and band leader); Linton, Ind., 6/24/1906
Harris, Richard (actor); Limerick, Ireland, 10/1/1933
Harris, Rosemary (actress); Ashby, England, 9/19/1930
Harris, Roy (composer); Lincoln County, Okla. **(1898-1979)**
Harrison, George (singer and songwriter); Liverpool, England, 2/25/1943
Harrison, Gregory (actor); Avalon, Catalina Island, Calif., 5/31/50
Harrison, Sir Rex (Reginald Carey) (actor); Huyton, England, **(1908-1990)**
Hart, Lorenz (lyricist); New York **(1895-1943)**
Hart, Mary (host); Sioux Falls, S.D., c.1950
Hart, Moss (playwright); New York City **(1904-1961)**
Hart, William S. (actor); Newburgh, N.Y. **(1862-1946)**
Harte, Bret (Francis Brett Harte) (author); Albany, N.Y. **(1836-1902)**
Hartford, Huntington (George Huntington Hartford II) (A.&P. heir); New York City, 4/18/1911
Hartford, John (singer and banjoist); New York City, 12/30/1937
Hartley, Mariette (actress); New York City, 6/21/40
Hartman, David Downs (TV newscaster); Pawtucket, R.I., 5/19/1935
Hartman, Elizabeth (actress); Youngstown, Ohio **(1941-1987)**
Hartman, Lisa (actress); Houston, Tex., 6/1/56
Harvey, Laurence (Larushka Skikne) (actor); Joniskis, Lithuania **(1928-1973)**
Harvey, William (physician); Folkestone, England **(1578-1657)**
Hasselhoff, David (actor); Baltimore, Md., 7/17/52
Hasso, Signe (actress); Stockholm, 8/15/1915
Havoc, June (June Hovick) (actress); Seattle, 1916
Haver, June (actress); Rock Island, Ill., 6/10/1926
Hawkins, Jack (actor); London **(1910-1973)**
Hawn, Goldie (actress); Washington, D.C., 11/21/1945
Haworth, Jill (actress); Sussex, England, 1945
Hawthorne, Nathaniel (novelist); Salem, Mass. **(1804-1864)**
Hay, John Milton (statesman); Salem, Ind. **(1838-1905)**
Hayakawa, Sessue (actor); Honshu, Japan **(1890-1973)**
Hayden, Melissa (ballerina); Toronto, 4/25/1923
Hayden, Sterling (Sterling Relyea Walter) (actor and writer); Montclair, N.J. **(1916-1986)**
Haydn, Franz Joseph (composer); Rohrau (Austria) **(1732-1809)**
Hayes, Helen (Helen Hayes Brown) (actress); Washington, D.C., 10/10/1900
Hayes, Isaac (composer); Covington, Tenn., 8/20/1942
Hayes, Peter Lind (comedian, singer); San Francisco, 6/25/15
Haymes, Dick (singer, actor); Buenos Aires **(1916-1980)**
Hayward, Leland (producer); Nebraska City, Neb. **(1902-1971)**
Hayward, Louis (actor); Johannesburg, South Africa **(1909-1985)**
Hayward, Susan (Edythe Marrener) (actress); Brooklyn, N.Y. **(1919?-1975)**
Hayworth, Rita (Margarita Cansino) (actress); New York City **(1918-1987)**
Head, Edith (costume designer); Los Angeles **(1907-1981)**
Hearst, William Randolph (publisher); San Francisco **(1863-1951)**
Hearst, William Randolph, Jr. (publisher); New York City, 1/27/1908
Heath, Edward (ex-Prime Minister); Broadstairs, England, 7/9/1916
Heatherton, Joey (actress); Rockville Centre, N.Y., 9/14/1944
Hecht, Ben (author); New York City **(1894-1964)**

Heckart, Eileen (actress); Columbus, Ohio, 3/29/1919

Heflin, Van (Emmet Evan Heflin) (actor); Walters, Okla. **(1910-1971)**

Hefner, Hugh (publisher); Chicago, 4/9/1926

Hegel, Georg Wilhelm Friedrich (philosopher); Stuttgart (Germany) **(1770-1831)**

Heifetz, Jascha (concert violinist); Vilna, Russia **(1901-1987)**

Heine, Heinrich (Harry) (poet); Düsseldorf (Germany) **(1797-1856)**

Heinemann, Gustav (ex-President of Germany); Schweim, Germany **(1899-1976)**

Heisenberg, Werner Karl (physicist); Würzburg, Germany **(1901-1976)**

Held, Anna (comedienne); Paris, France **(1873(?)-1918)**

Heller, Joseph (novelist); Brooklyn, N.Y., 5/1/1923

Hellman, Lillian (playwright); New Orleans **(1905-1984)**

Helmond, Katherine (actress); Galveston, Tex., 7/5/34(?)

Hemingway, Ernest Miller (novelist); Oak Park, Ill. **(1899-1961)**

Hemingway, Margaux (actress); Portland, Ore., Feb. 1955

Hemmings, David (actor); Guilford, England, 11/2/1941

Henderson, Florence (actress); Dale, Ind., 2/14/1934

Henderson, Skitch (Lyle Russell Cedric) (conductor and pianist); Birmingham, England(?), 1/27/1918

Hendrix, Jimi (James Marshall Hendrix) (guitarist); Seattle **(1942-1970)**

Henley, Beth (playwright-actress); Jackson, Miss., 5/8/1952

Henner, Marilu (actress); Chicago, 4/6/52

Henning, Doug (magician and actor); Winnipeg, Canada, 1947(?)

Henreid, Paul (actor); Trieste, 1/10/1908

Henri, Robert (painter); Cincinnati **(1865-1926)**

Henry, O. (William Sydney Porter) (story writer); Greensboro, N.C. **(1862-1910)**

Henry, Patrick (statesman); Hanover County, Va. **(1736-1799)**

Henson, Jim (puppeteer); Greenville, Miss. **(1936-1990)**

Hepburn, Audrey (actress); Brussels, Belgium, 5/4/1929

Hepburn, Katharine (actress); Hartford, Conn., 11/8/1909

Hepplewhite, George (furniture designer); England **(?-1786)**

Hepworth, Barbara (sculptor); Wakefield, England **(1903-1975)**

Herachel, William (Frederich Wilhelm) (astronomer); Hanover, Germany **(1738-1822)**

Herbert, George (poet); Montgomery Castle, Wales **(1593-1633)**

Herbert, Victor (composer); Dublin **(1859-1924)**

Herblock (Herbert L. Block) (political cartoonist); Chicago, 10/13/1909

Herman, Pee-wee (Paul Reubens) (comedian); Peekskill, N.Y., 1952

Herman, Woody (Woodrow Charles) (band leader); Milwaukee **(1913-1987)**

Herod (Herodes) (called Herod the Great) (King of Judea) **(73?-4 B.C.)**

Herodotus (historian); Halicarnassus, Asia Minor (Turkey) **(c. 484-425 B.C.)**

Herrick, Robert (poet); London? **(1591-1674)**

Hershey, Barbara (actress); Hollywood, Calif., 2/5/48(?)

Hershfield, Harry (humorist and raconteur); Cedar Rapids, Iowa **(1885-1974)**

Hersholt, Jean (actor); Copenhagen **(1886-1956)**

Hesburgh, Theodore M. (educator); Syracuse, N.Y., 5/2/1917

Hesseman, Howard (actor); Salem, Ore., 2/27/40

Heston, Charlton (actor); Evanston, Ill., 10/4/1924

Heyerdahl, Thor (ethnologist and explorer); Larvik, Norway, 10/6/1914

Hildegarde (Hildegarde Loretta Sell) (singer); Adell, Wis., 2/1/1906

Hill, Arthur (actor); Melfort, Canada, 8/1/1922

Hill, Benny (comedian); Southampton, England, 1/21/25

Hillary, Sir Edmund (mountain climber); New Zealand, 7/20/1919

Hiller, Wendy (actress); Bramhall, England, 8/15/1912

Hillerman, John (actor); Denison, Tex., 12/20(?)/32

Hilliard, Harriet. *See* Nelson, Harriet

Hindemith, Paul (composer); Hanau, Germany **(1895-1963)**

Hines, Earl "Fatha" (jazz pianist); Duquesne, Pa. **(1905-1983)**

Hines, Gregory (dancer, actor); New York City, 2/14/46

Hines, Jerome (Jerome Heinz) (basso); Los Angeles, 11/8/1921

Hingle, Pat (actor); Denver, 7/19/1924

Hippocrates (physician); Cos, Greece **(c. 460-c. 377 B.C.)**

Hirohito (Emperor); Tokyo, **(1901-1989)**

Hiroshige, Ando (painter); Edo? (Tokyo) **(1797-1858)**

Hirsch, Judd (actor); New York City, 3/15/1935

Hirschfeld, Al (Albert) (cartoonist); St. Louis, 6/21/1903

Hirschhorn, Joseph Herman (financier, speculator, and art collector); Mitau, Latvia **(1899-1981)**

Hirt, Al (trumpeter); New Orleans, 11/7/1922

Hitchcock, Alfred J. (film director); London **(1899-1980)**

Hitler, Adolf (German dictator); Braunau, Austria **(1889-1945)**

Hitzig, William Maxwell (physician); Austria, 12/15/1904

Hobbes, Thomas (philosopher); Westport, England **(1588-1679)**

Hobson, Laura Z. (Laura K. Zametkin) (novelist); New York City **(1900-1986)**

Hockney, David (artist); Bradford, England, 7/9/1937

Hodges, Eddie (actor); Hattiesburg, Miss., 3/5/1947

Hoffa, James R(iddle) (labor leader); Brazil, Ind. **(1913-75?)** presumed murdered.

Hoffman, Dustin (film actor and director); Los Angeles, 8/8/1937

Hofmann, Hans (painter); Germany **(1880-1966)**

Hogan, Paul (actor); Lightning Ridge, NSW, Australia, 1941 (?)

Hogarth, William (painter and engraver); London **(1697-1764)**

Hokusai, Katauhika (artist); Yedo, Japan **(1760-1849)**

Holbein, Hans (the Elder) (painter); Augsburg (Germany) **(1465?-1524)**

Holbein, Hans (the Younger) (painter); Augsburg (Germany) **(1497?-1543)**

Holbrook, Hal (actor); Cleveland, 2/17/1925

Holden, William (William Franklin Beedle, Jr.) (actor); O'Fallon, Ill. **(1918-1981)**

Holder, Geoffrey (dancer); Port-of-Spain, Trinidad, 8/1/1930

Holiday, Billie (Eleanora Fagan) (jazz-blues singer); Baltimore **(1915-1959)**

Holliday, Judy (Judith Tuvim) (comedienne); New York City **(1922-1965)**

Holliday, Polly (actress); Jasper, Ala., 7/2/37

Holliman, Earl (actor); Delhi, La., 9/11/28

Holloway, Stanley (actor); London **(1890-1982)**

Holloway, Sterling (actor); Cedartown, Ga., 1905

Holm, Celeste (actress); New York City, 4/29/1919

Holmes, Oliver Wendell (jurist); Boston **(1841-1935)**

Holt, Jack (actor); Winchester, Va. **(1888-1951)**

Holt, Tim (actor); Beverly Hills, Calif. **(1918-1973)**

Holtz, Lou (comedian); San Francisco **(1898-1980)**

Home, Lord (Alexander Frederick Douglas-Home) (diplomat); London, 7/2/1903

Homeier, Skip (George Vincent Homeier) (actor); Chicago, 10/5/1930

Homer, Winslow (painter); Boston, Mass. **(1836-1910)**

Homer (Greek poet) **(c.850 B.C.?)**

Homolka, Oscar (actor); Vienna **(1898-1978)**

Honegger, Arthur (composer); Le Havre, France **(1892-1955)**

Hook, Sidney (philosopher); New York City, **(1902-1989)**

Hoover, J. Edgar (FBI director); Washington, D.C. **(1895-1972)**

Hope, Bob (Leslie Townes Hope) (comedian); London, 5/29/1903

Hopkins, Anthony (actor); Port Talbot, Wales, 12/31/1937

Hopkins, Gerald Manley (poet); Stratford, England **(1844-1899)**

Hopkins, Johns (financier); Anne Arundel County, Md. **(1795-1873)**

Hopkins, Miriam (actress); Bainbridge, Ga. **(1902-1972)**

Hopper, Dennis (actor); Dodge City, Kan., 5/17/1936

Hopper, Edward (painter); Nyack, N.Y. **(1882-1967)**

Horace (Quintus Horatius Flaccus) (poet); Venosa (Italy) **(65-8 B.C.)**

Horne, Lena (singer); Brooklyn, N.Y., 6/30/1917

Horne, Marilyn (mezzo-soprano); Bradford, Pa., 1/16/1934

Horowitz, Vladimir (pianist); Kiev, Russia **(1903-1989)**

Horsley, Lee (actor); Muleshoe, Tex., 5/15/55

Horton, Edward Everett (comedian); Brooklyn, N.Y. **(1887-1970)**

Hoskins, Bob (actor); Bury St. Edminds, England, 10/26/42

Houdini, Harry (Ehrich Weiss) (magician); Appleton, Wis. **(1874-1926)**

Houseman, John (Jacques Haussmann) (producer, director, and actor); Bucharest **(1902-1988)**

Housman, A(lfred) E(dward) (poet); Fockburg, England **(1859-1936)**

Houston, Samuel (political leader); Rockbridge County, Va. **(1793-1863)**

Houston, Whitney (singer); Newark, N.J., 8/9/63

Howard, Ken (actor); El Centro, Calif., 3/28/44

Howard, Leslie (Leslie Stainer) (actor); London **(1893-1943)**

Howard, Ron (actor, producer, director); Duncan, Okla., 3/1/54

Howard, Trevor (actor); Kent, England **(1916-1988)**

Howe, Elias (inventor); Spencer, Mass. **(1819-1867)**

Howe, Irving (literary critic); New York City, 6/11/1920

Howe, Julia Ward (poet and reformer); New York City **(1819-1910)**

Howes, Sally Ann (actress); London, 7/20/1934

Hudson, Henry (English navigator) **(?-1611)**

Hudson, Rock (born Roy Scherer, Jr.; took Roy Fitzgerald as legal name) (actor); Winnetka, Ill., **(1925-1985)**

Hughes, Barnard (actor); Bedford Hills, N.Y., 7/16/15

Hughes, Charles Evans (jurist); Glens Falls, N.Y. **(1862-1948)**

Hughes, Howard (industrialist and film producer); Houston **(1905-1976)**

Hughes, Langston (poet); Joplin, Mo. **(1902-1967)**

Hugo, Victor Marie (author); Besançon, France **(1802-1885)**

Hulce, Tom (actor); Detroit, Mich., 12/6/53

Hull, Henry (actor); Louisville, Ky. **(1890-1977)**

Hume, David (philosopher); Edinburgh, Scotland **(1711-1776)**

Humperdinck, Engelbert (Arnold Dorsey) (singer); Madras, India, 5/2/1936

Humperdinck, Engelbert (composer); Siegburg (Germany) **(1854-1921)**

Hunt, H. L. (industrialist); nr. Vandalia, Ill. **(1889-1974)**

Hunt, Marsha (actress); Chicago, 10/17/1917
Hunter, Kim (Janet Cole) (actress); Detroit, 11/12/1922
Hunter, Tab (Arthur Andrew Gelien) (actor); New York City, 7/11/1931
Huntley, Chet (TV newscaster); Cardwell, Mont. **(1911-1974)**
Hurok, Sol (Solomon) (impresario); Pogar, Russia **(1884-1974)**
Hurst, Fannie (novelist); Hamilton, Ohio **(1889-1968)**
Hurt, John (actor); Shirebrook, England, 1/22/1940
Hurt, William (actor); Washington, D.C., 3/20/50
Hus, Jan (Bohemian religious reformer); Husinetz, nr. Budweis (Czechoslovakia) **(c.1369-1415)**
Husing, Ted (sportscaster); New York City **(1901-1962)**
Hussein I (King); Jordan, 11/14/1935
Hussey, Ruth (Ruth Carol O'Rourke) (actress); Providence, R.I., 10/30/14
Huston, John (film director and writer); Nevada, Mo. **(1906-1987)**
Huston, Walter (Walter Houghston) (actor); Toronto **(1884-1950)**
Hutchins, Robert M. (educator); Brooklyn, N.Y. **(1899-1977)**
Hutton, Barbara (Woolworth heiress); New York City **(1912-1979)**
Hutton, Betty (Betty Thornburg) (actress); Battle Creek, Mich., 2/26/1921
Hutton, Lauren (actress, model); Charleston, S.C., 11/17/43
Hutton, Timothy (actor); Los Angeles, 8/16/1960
Huxley, Aldous (author); Godalming, England **(1894-1963)**
Huxley, Sir Julian S. (biologist and author); London **(1887-1975)**
Huxley, Thomas Henry (biologist); Ealing, England **(1825-1895)**

I

Ian, Janis (singer); New York City, 5/7/1951
Ibsen, Henrik (dramatist); Skien, Norway **(1828-1906)**
Inge, William (playwright); Independence, Kan. **(1913-1973)**
Ingres, Jean Auguste Dominique (painter); Montauban, France **(1780-1867)**
Inness, George (painter); nr. Newburgh, N.Y. **(1825-1894)**
Ionesco, Eugene (playwright); Slatina, Romania, 11/26/1912
Ireland, Jill (actress); London, **(1936-1990)**
Ireland, John (actor); Vancouver, B.C., Canada, 1/30/1915
Irons, Jeremy (actor); Cowes, Isle of Wight, England, 9/19/1948
Irving, Amy (actress); Palo Alto, Calif., 9/10/1953
Irving, John (Winslow) (writer); Exeter, N.H., 3/2/1942
Irving, Washington (author); New York City **(1783-1859)**
Isherwood, Christopher (novelist and playwright); nr. Dilsey and High Lane, England **(1904-1986)**
Iturbi, José (concert pianist); Valencia, Spain **(1895-1980)**
Ives, Burl (Icle Ivanhoe) (singer); Hunt, Ill., 6/14/1909
Ives, Charles E(dward) (composer); Danbury, Conn. **(1874-1954)**

J

Jackson, Anne (actress); Millvale, Pa., 9/3/1926
Jackson, Glenda (actress); Hoylake, England, 1937(?)
Jackson, Gordon (actor); Glasgow, Scotland, **(1923-1990)**
Jackson, Rev. Jesse (civil rights leader); Greenville, S.C., 10/8/1941
Jackson, Kate (actress); Birmingham, Ala., 10/29/1949
Jackson, Mahalia (gospel singer); New Orleans **(1911-1972)**
Jackson, Michael (singer); Gary, Ind., 8/29/1958
Jackson, Thomas Jonathan ("Stonewall") (general); Clarksburg, Va. (now W. Va.) **(1824-1863)**
Jacobi, Derek (actor); Leytonstone, England, 10/22/38
Jacobi, Lou (actor); Toronto, 12/26/1913
Jacobs, Jane (urbanologist); Scranton, Pa., 5/1/1916
Jaffe, Sam (actor); New York City **(1891-1984)**
Jagger, Dean (actor); Lima, Ohio, 11/7/1903
Jagger, Mick (Michael Phillip) (singer); Dartford, England, 7/26/1944
James, Harry (trumpeter); Albany, Ga. **(1916-1983)**
James, Henry (novelist); New York City **(1843-1916)**
James, Jesse Woodson (outlaw); Clay County, Mo. **(1847-1882)**
James, William (psychologist); New York City **(1842-1910)**
Jameson, (Margaret) Storm (novelist); Whitby, England **(1897-1986)**
Janis, Byron (pianist); McKeesport, Pa., 3/24/1928
Janis, Conrad (actor, musician); New York City, 2/11/28
Jannings, Emil (actor); Brooklyn, N.Y. **(1886-1950)**
Janssen, David (David Meyer) (actor); Naponee, Neb. **(1930-1980)**
Jay, John (statesman and jurist); New York City **(1745-1829)**
Jeanmaire, Renée (dancer); Paris, 4/29/1924
Jenner, Edward (physician); Berkeley, England **(1749-1823)**
Jennings, Waylon (singer); Littlefield, Tex., 1937
Jessel, George (entertainer); New York City **(1898-1981)**
Jessup, Philip C. (diplomat); New York City, 1/5/1897
Jiang Qing (political leader); Chucheng, China, 1913 (?)
Jillian, Ann (actress); Cambridge, Mass., 1/29/51
Joan of Arc (Jeanne d'Arc) (saint and patriot); Domremy-la-Pucelle,

France **(1412-1431)**
Joel, Billy (singer); New York City, 5/9/1949
Joffrey, Robert (Abdullah Jaffa Bey Khan) (choreographer); Seattle **(1930-1988)**
John, Elton (Reginald Kenneth Dwight) (singer and pianist); Pinner, England, 3/25/1947
Johns, Glynis (actress); Pretoria, South Africa, 10/5/1923
Johns, Jasper (painter and sculptor); Augusta, Ga., 5/15/1930
Johnson, Don (actor); Flatt Creek, Mo., 12/15/49
Johnson, James Weldon (author and educator); Jacksonville, Fla. (1871-1938)
Johnson, Philip Cortalyou (architect); Cleveland, Ohio, 7/8/1906
Johnson, Samuel (lexicographer and author); Lichfield, England **(1709-1784)**
Johnson, Van (actor); Newport, R.I., 8/20/1916
Joliot-Curie, Frédéric (physicist); Paris **(1900-1958)**
Joliot-Curie, Irène (Irène Curie) (physicist); France **(1897-1956)**
Jolliet (or Joliet), Louis (explorer); Beaupré, Canada **(1645-1700)**
Jolson, Al (Asa Yoelson) (actor and singer); St. Petersburg, Russia **(1886-1950)**
Jones, Allan (singer, actor); Old Forge, Pa., 10/14/08
Jones, Buck (Charles Frederick Gebhart) (actor); Vincennes, Ind. **(1889-1942)**
Jones, Carolyn (singer and actress); Amarillo, Tex., **(1933-1983)**
Jones, Dean (actor); Morgan County, Ala., 1/25/1935
Jones, George (singer); Saratoga, Tex., 9/12/1931
Jones, Inigo (architect); London **(1573-1652)**
Jones, James (novelist); Robinson, Ill. **(1921-1977)**
Jones, James Earl (actor); Arkabutla, Miss., 1/17/1931
Jones, Jennifer (Phyllis Isley) (actress); Tulsa, Okla., 3/2/1919
Jones, John Paul (John Paul) (naval officer); Scotland **(1747-1792)**
Jones, Quincy (composer); Chicago, 3/14/1933
Jones, Shirley (singer and actress); Smithtown, Pa., 3/31/1934
Jones, Spike (host, orchestra leader); Long Beach, Calif. **(1911-1965)**
Jones, Tom (Thomas Jones Woodward) (singer); Pontypridd, Wales, 6/7/1940
Jong, Erica (writer); New York City, 3/26/1942
Jonson, Ben (Benjamin) (poet and dramatist); Westminster, England **(1572-1637)**
Joplin, Janis (singer); Port Arthur, Tex. **(1943-1970)**
Jordan, James Edward (radio actor-Fibber McGee); Peoria, Ill. **(1896-1988)**
Jordan, Marian (radio actress-Molly of Fibber McGee and Molly); Peoria, Ill. **(1898-1961)**
Jory, Victor (actor); Dawson City, Yukon, Canada **(1902-1982)**
Josquin des Prés (usually known as Josquin) (composer); Conde-sur-L'Escaut?, Hainaut (France or Belgium) **(c.1445-1521)**
Jourdan, Louis (Louis Gendre) (actor); Marseilles, France, 6/19/1920
Joyce, James (novelist); Dublin **(1882-1941)**
Juárez, Benito Pablo (statesman); Guelatao, Mexico **(1806-1872)**
Julia, Raul (Raúl Rafael Carlos Julia y Arcelay) (actor); San Juan, Puerto Rico, 3/9/1940
Juliana (Queen); The Hague, Netherlands, 4/30/1909
Jung, Carl Gustav (psychoanalyst); Basel, Switzerland **(1875-1961)**
Jurado, Katy (actress); Guadalajara, Mexico, 1927

K

Kabalevsky, Dmitri (composer); St. Petersburg, Russia **(1904-1987)**
Kafka, Franz (author); Prague **(1883-1924)**
Kádár, János (Communist Party leader); Hungary, 1912
Kahn, Gus (songwriter); Coblenz, Germany **(1886-1941)**
Kahn, Louis I. (architect); Oesel Island, Estonia **(1901-1974)**
Kahn, Madeline (actress); Boston, 9/29/1942
Kaminska, Ida (actress); Odessa, Russia **(1899-1980)**
Kandinsky, Wassily (painter); Moscow **(1866-1944)**
Kane, Helen (actress, singer); Bronx, N.Y. **(1903-1966)**
Kanin, Garson (playwright); Rochester, N.Y., 11/24/1912
Kant, Immanuel (philosopher); Königsberg (Kaliningrad, U.S.S.R.) **(1724-1804)**
Kantor, MacKinlay (novelist); Webster City, Iowa **(1904-1977)**
Kaplan, Gabe (Gabriel) (actor); Brooklyn, N.Y., 3/31/1945
Karloff, Boris (William Henry Pratt) (actor); London **(1887-1969)**
Kasem, Casey (disc jockey); Detroit, Mich., 4/27/1932
Katt, William (actor); Los Angeles, 2/16/50
Kaufman, George S. (playwright); Pittsburgh **(1889-1961)**
Kavner, Julie (actress); Los Angeles, 9/7/51
Kaye, Danny (David Daniel Kominski) (comedian); Brooklyn, N.Y. **(1913-1987)**
Kaye, Sammy (band leader); Cleveland **(1910-1987)**
Kazan, Elia (director); Constantinople, Turkey, 9/7/1909
Kazan, Lainie (Levine) (singer); New York City, 5/15/1940
Keach, Stacy (actor); Savannah, Ga., 6/2/1941
Kean, Edmund (actor); London **(1787-1833)**
Keaton, Buster (Joseph Frank Keaton) (comedian); Piqua, Kan. **(1896-**

1966)
Keaton, Diane (actress); Los Angeles, 1/5/1946
Keats, John (poet); London **(1795-1821)**
Keel, Howard (singer and actor); Gillespie, Ill., 4/13/1919
Keeler, Ruby (Lehy Keeler) (actress and dancer); Halifax, Nova Scotia, Canada, 8/25/1910
Kefauver, Estes (legislator); Madisonville, Tenn. **(1903-1963)**
Keith, Brian (actor); Bayonne, N.J., 11/14/1921
Keller, Helen Adams (author and educator); Tuscumbia, Ala. **(1880-1968)**
Kellerman, Sally (actress); Long Beach, Calif., 6/2/1938
Kelley, DeForest (actor); Atlanta, Ga., 1/20/20
Kelly, Emmett (clown); Sedan, Kan., **(1898-1979)**
Kelly, Gene (dancer and actor); Pittsburgh, 8/23/1912
Kelly, Grace. *See* Grace, Princess of Monaco.
Kelly, Nancy (actress); Lowell, Mass., 3/25/21
Kelly, Patsy (actress and comedienne); Brooklyn, N.Y. **(1910-1981)**
Kelly, Walt (cartoonist); Philadelphia **(1913-1973)**
Kemal Ataturk (Mustafa Kemal) (Turkish soldier and statesman); Salonika (Greece) **(1881-1938)**
Kemble, Fanny (Frances Anne) (actress); London **(1809-1893)**
Kempis, Thomas a (mystic); Kempis, Prussia (Germany) **(1380-1471)**
Kennan, George F. (diplomat); Milwaukee, 2/16/1904
Kennedy, Arthur (actor); Worcester, Mass. **(1914-1990)**
Kennedy, George (actor); New York City, 2/18/1925
Kennedy, Jacqueline. *See* Onassis, Jacqueline
Kennedy, Joseph P. (financier); Boston **(1888-1969)**
Kennedy, Robert Francis (legislator); Brookline, Mass. **(1925-1968)**
Kennedy, Rose Fitzgerald (President's mother); Boston, 7/22/1890
Kent, Allegra (ballerina); Santa Monica, Calif., 8/11/38
Kent, Rockwell (painter); Tarrytown Heights, N.Y. **(1882-1971)**
Kenton, Stan (Stanley Newcomb) (jazz musician); Wichita, Kan. **(1912-1979)**
Kepler, Johannes (astronomer); Weil (Germany) **(1571-1630)**
Kercheval, Ken (actor); Wolcottville, Ind., 7/15/35
Kerensky, Alexander Fedorovich (statesman); Simbirks, Russia **(1881-1970)**
Kern, Jerome David (composer); New York City **(1885-1945)**
Kerns, Joanna (actress); San Francisco, 2/12/53
Kerr, Deborah (actress); Helensburgh, Scotland, 9/30/1921
Kettering, Charles F. (engineer and inventor); nr. Loudonville, Ohio **(1876-1958)**
Key, Francis Scott (lawyer and author of national anthem); Frederick (now Carroll) County, Md. **(1779-1843)**
Keyes, Frances Parkinson (novelist); Charlottesville, Va. **(1885-1970)**
Keynes, (1st Baron of Tilton) (John Maynard Keynes) (economist); Cambridge, England **(1883-1946)**
Khachaturian, Aram (composer); Tiflis, Russia **(1903-1978)**
Khrushchev, Nikita S. (Soviet leader); Kalinovka, nr. Kursk, Ukraine **(1894-1971)**
Kibbee, Guy (actor); El Paso **(1886-1956)**
Kidd, Michael (choreographer); Brooklyn, N.Y., 1917
Kidd, William (called Captain Kidd) (pirate); Greenock, Scotland **(1645?-1701)**
Kidder, Margot (actress); Yellowknife, N.W.T., Canada, 10/17/48
Kiepura, Jan (tenor); Sosnowiec, Poland **(1904(?)-1966)**
Kieran, John (writer); New York City **(1892-1981)**
Kierkegaard, Sören Aalys (philosopher); Copenhagen **(1813-1855)**
Kiesinger, Kurt Georg (diplomat); Ebingen, Germany **(1904-1988)**
Kiley, Richard (actor and singer); Chicago, 3/31/1922
Kilmer, Alfred Joyce (poet); New Brunswick, N.J. **(1886-1918)**
King, Alan (Irwin Alan Kniberg) (entertainer); Brooklyn, N.Y., 12/26/1927
King, B.B. (Riley King) (guitarist); Itta Bena, Miss., 9/16/1925
King, Carole (singer and songwriter); Brooklyn, N.Y., 2/9/1941
King, Coretta Scott (civil rights leader); Marion, Ala., 4/27/1927
King, Dennis (actor, singer); Coventry, England **(1897-1971)**
King, Martin Luther, Jr. (civil rights leader); Atlanta **(1929-1968)**
King, Pee Wee (Frank) (singer); Abrams, Wis., 2/18/1914
King, Stephen (writer); Portland, Maine, 9/21/1947
Kingsley, Ben (Krishna Bhanji) (actor); Snainton, England, 12/31/1943
Kingsley, Sidney (Sidney Kirschner) (playwright); New York City, 10/18/1906
Kinski, Nastassja (Nastassja Nakszynski) (actress); West Berlin, 1/24/1961
Kipling, Rudyard (author); Bombay **(1865-1936)**
Kipnis, Alexander (basso); Ukraine, **(1891-1978)**
Kirby, George (comedian); Chicago, **1923(?)**
Kirk, Grayson (educator); Jeffersonville, Ohio, 10/12/1903
Kirk, Lisa (actress and singer); Charleroi, Pa., 1925
Kirk, Phyllis (actress); Plainfield, N.J., 9/18/1930
Kirkland, Gelsey (ballerina); Bethlehem, Pa., 12/29/1952
Kirkpatrick, Jeane Jordan (educator-public affairs); Duncan, Okla., 11/19/1926

Kirkpatrick, Ralph (harpsichordist); Leominster, Mass. **(1911-1984)**
Kirkwood, James (actor); Grand Rapids, Mich. **(1883-1963)**
Kirsten, Dorothy (soprano); Montclair, N.J., 7/6/1919
Kissinger, Henry (Heinz Alfred Kissinger) (ex-Secretary of State); Furth, Germany, 5/27/1923
Kitt, Eartha (singer); North, S.C., 1/26/1928
Klee, Paul (painter); Münchenbuchsee, nr. Bern, Switzerland **(1879-1940)**
Klein, Calvin (fashion designer); Bronx, N.Y., 11/19/1942
Klein, Robert (comedian); New York City, 2/8/1942
Kline, Kevin (actor); St. Louis, Mo., 10/24/47
Kleist, Henrich von (poet); Frankfurt an der Oder (East Germany) **(1777-1811)**
Klemperer, Otto (conductor); Breslau (Poland) **(1885-1973)**
Klemperer, Werner (actor); Cologne, Germany, 3/22/1920
Klugman, Jack (actor); Philadelphia, 4/27/1922
Knievel, Evel (Robert Craig) (daredevil motorcyclist); Butte, Mont., 10/17/1938
Knight, Gladys (singer); Atlanta, 5/28/1944
Knight, Ted (Tadeus Wladyslaw Konopka) (actor); Terryville, Conn., **(1923-1986)**
Knight, John S. (publisher); Bluefield, W. Va. **(1894-1981)**
Knopf, Alfred A. (publisher); New York City, **(1892-1984)**
Knotts, Don (actor); Morgantown, W.Va., 7/21/1924
Knox, John (religious reformer); Haddington, East Lothian, Scotland **(1505-1572)**
Koch, Robert (physician); Klausthal (Germany) **(1843-1910)**
Koestler, Arthur (novelist); Budapest **(1905-1983)**
Kokoschka, Oskar (painter); Pöchlarn Austria **(1886-1980)**
Koope:, Al (singer and pianist); Brooklyn, N.Y., 2/5/1944
Kopell, Bernie (actor); New York City, 6/21/33
Koppel, Ted (broadcast journalist); Lancashire, England, 2/8/1940
Korman, Harvey (actor); Chicago, 2/15/1927
Kosciusko, Thaddeus (Tadeusz Andrzej Bonawentura Kosciuszko) (military officer); Grand Duchy of Lithuania **(1746-1817)**
Kossuth, Lajos (patriot); Monok, Hungary **(1802-1894)**
Kostelanetz, André (orchestra conductor); St. Petersburg, Russia **(1901-1980)**
Kosygin, Aleksei N. (Premier); St. Petersburg, Russia **(1904-1980)**
Koussevitzky, Serge (Sergei) Alexandrovitch (orchestra conductor); Vishni Volochek, Tver, Russia **(1874-1951)**
Kovacs, Ernie (comedian); Trenton, N.J. **(1919-1962)**
Kramer, Stanley E. (film producer and director); New York City, 9/29/1913
Kràus, Lili (pianist); Budapest **(1905-1986)**
Kreisler, Fritz (violinist and composer); Vienna **(1875-1962)**
Kresge, S. S. (merchant); Bald Mount, Pa. **(1867-1966)**
Krips, Josef (orchestra conductor); Vienna **(1902-1974)**
Kristofferson, Kris (singer); Brownsville, Tex., 6/22/1936
Kruger, Otto (actor); Toledo, Ohio **(1885-1974)**
Krupa, Gene (drummer); Chicago **(1909-1973)**
Krupp, Alfred (munitions magnate); Essen, Germany **(1812-1887)**
Kubelik, Rafael (conductor); Bychory (Czechoslovakia), 6/29/1914
Kublai Khan (Mongol conqueror) **(1216-1294)**
Kubrick, Stanley (producer and director); New York City, 7/26/1928
Kuralt, Charles (TV journalist); Wilmington, N.C., 9/10/1934
Kurosawa, Akira (film director); Tokyo, 3/23/1910
Kurtz, Efrem (conductor); St. Petersburg, Russia, 11/7/1900
Kurtz, Swoosie (actress); Omaha, Neb., 9/6/44
Ky, Nguyen Cao (ex-Vice President of South Vietnam); Son Tay (Vietnam), 9/8/1930

L

LaBelle, Patti (singer, actress); Philadelphia, Pa., 10/4/44
Ladd, Alan (actor); Hot Springs, Ark. **(1913-1964)**
Ladd, Cheryl (Cheryl Stoppelmoor) (actress); Huron, S.D., 7/12/1951
Ladd, Diane (actress); Meridian, Miss., 11/29/32
Lafayette, Marquis de (Marie Joseph Paul Yves Roch Gilbert du Motier) (military officer); Auvergne, France **(1757-1834)**
Lafitte, Jean (pirate); Bayonne? France **(1780-1826)**
La Follette, Robert Marin (politician); Primrose, Wis. **(1855-1925)**
La Guardia, Fiorello Henry (Mayor of New York); New York City **(1882-1947)**
Lahr, Bert (Irving Lahrheim) (comedian); New York City **(1895-1967)**
Laine, Cleo (Clementina Dinah Campbell) (singer, actress); Southall, England, 10/28/27
Laine, Frankie (Frank Paul LoVecchio) (singer); Chicago, 3/30/1913
Laird, Melvin (ex-Secretary of Defense); Omaha, Neb., 9/1/1922
Lake, Veronica (actress); Brooklyn, N.Y. **(1919-1973)**
Lamarck, Chevalier de (Jean Baptiste Pierre Antoine de Monet) (naturalist); Bazantin, France **(1744-1829)**
Lamarr, Hedy (Hedwig Kiesler) (actress); Vienna, 1915
Lamas, Fernando (actor); Buenos Aires, **(1915-1982)**
Lamas, Lorenzo (actor); Los Angeles, 1/20/58

Lamb, Charles (Elia) (essayist); London (1775-1834)

L'Amour, Louis (author); Jamestown, N.D., (1908-1988)

Lamour, Dorothy (Dorothy Kaumeyer) (actress); New Orleans, 10/10/1914

Lancaster, Burt (actor); New York City, 11/2/1913

Lanchester, Elsa (Elsa Sullivan) (actress); London (1902-1986)

Landau, Martin (actor); Brooklyn, N.Y. 1934

Landers, Ann (columnist); Sioux City, Iowa, 7/4/1918

Landon, Michael (Eugene Maurice Orowitz) (actor); Forest Hills, Queens, N.Y., 10/31/1936(?)

Lane, Abbe (singer); New York City, 1933

Lang, Fritz (film director); Vienna (1890-1976)

Lang, Paul Henry (music critic); Budapest, 8/28/1901

Lange, Hope (actress); Redding Ridge, Conn., 11/28/1933

Lange, Jessica (actress); Cloquet, Minn., 4/20/49

Langella, Frank (actor); Bayonne, N.J., 1/1/1940

Langford, Frances (singer); Lakeland, Fla., 4/4/1913

Langmuir, Irving (chemist); Brooklyn, N.Y. (1881-1957)

Langtry, Lillie (Emily Le Breton) (actress); Island of Jersey (1852-1929)

Lansbury, Angela (actress); London, 10/16/1925

Lansing, Robert (Robert Howell Brown) (actor); San Diego, Calif., 6/5/1928

Lanza, Mario (Alfred Arnold Cocozza) (singer and actor); Philadelphia (1925-1959)

Lao-Tzu (or Lao-Tse) (Li Erh) (philosopher); Honan Province, China (c. 604-531 B.C.)

Lardner, Ring (Ringgold Wilmar Lardner) (story writer); Niles, Mich. (1885-1933)

La Rouchefoucauld, Francois duc de (author); Paris (1613-1680)

Larroquette, John (actor); New Orleans, 11/25/47

La Salle, Sieur de (Robert Cavelier) (explorer); Rouen, France (1643-1687)

Lasser, Louise (actress); New York City, 1940(?)

Lauder, Sir Harry (Harry MacLennan) (singer); Portobello, Scotland (1870-1950)

Laughton, Charles (actor); Scarborough, England (1899-1962)

Lauper, Cyndi (singer); New York City, 6/20/53

Laurel, Stan (Arthur Jefferson) (comedian); Ulverston, England (1890-1965)

Laurents, Arthur (playwright); New York City, 7/14/1918

Laurie, Piper (Rosetta Jacobs) (actress); Detroit, 1/22/1932

Lavin, Linda (actress); Portland, Me., 10/15/37

Lavoisier, Antoine-Laurent (chemist); Paris (1743-1794)

Lawford, Peter (actor); London (1923-1984)

Lawrence, David Herbert (novelist); Nottingham, England (1885-1930)

Lawrence, Gertrude (Gertrud Klasen) (actress); London (1900-1952)

Lawrence, Marjorie (singer); Deans Marsh, Australia (1908-1979)

Lawrence, Steve (Sidney Leibowitz) (singer); Brooklyn, N.Y., 7/8/1935

Lawrence of Arabia (Thomas Edward Lawrence, later changed to Shaw) (author and soldier); Tremadoc, Wales (1888-1935)

Lawrence, Vicki (actress); Inglewood, Calif., 3/26/49

Leach, Robin (host, producer); London, c.1941

Leachman, Cloris (actress); Des Moines, Iowa, 4/30/1926(?)

Lean, David (film director); Croydon, England, 3/25/1908

Lear, Edward (nonsense poet); London (1812-1888)

Lear, Evelyn (Shulman) (soprano); Brooklyn, N.Y., 1/8/29(?)

Lear, Norman (TV producer); New Haven, Conn., 7/27/22

Learned, Michael (actress); Washington, D.C., 4/9/39

le Carré, John (David John Moore Cornwell) (novelist); Poole, England, 10/19/1931

Le Corbusier (Charles Edouard Jeanneret) (architect); La Chaux-de-Fonds, Switzerland (1887-1965)

Lederer, Francis (actor); Prague, 11/6/1906

Lee, Christopher (actor); London, 5/27/1922

Lee, Gypsy Rose (Rose Louise Hovick) (entertainer); Seattle (1914-1970)

Lee, Manfred B. (novelist, pseudonym Ellery Queen); Brooklyn, N.Y. (1905-1971)

Lee, Michele (actress, singer); Los Angeles, 6/24/42

Lee, Peggy (Norma Engstrom) (singer); Jamestown, N.D., 5/26/1920

Lee, Robert Edward (Confederate general); Stratford Estate, Va. (1807-1870)

Leeuwenhoek, Anton van (zoologist); Delft (Netherlands) (1632-1723)

Le Gallienne, Eva (actress); London, 1/11/1899

Lehár, Franz (composer); Komárom (Czechoslovakia) (1870-1948)

Lehman, Herbert H. (Governor and Senator); New York City (1878-1963)

Lehmann, Lotte (soprano); Perleberg (Germany) (1888-1976)

Leibniz, Gottfried W. von (scientist); Leipzig (East Germany) (1646-1716)

Leigh, Janet (Jeanetta Morrison) (actress); Merced, Calif., 7/6/1927

Leigh, Vivien (Vivien Mary Hartley) (actress); Darjeeling, India (1913-1967)

Leighton, Margaret (actress); nr. Birmingham, England (1922-1976)

Leinsdorf, Erich (conductor); Vienna, 2/4/1912

Lemmon, Jack (actor); Boston, 2/8/1925

Lenin, Vladimir (Vladimir Ilich Ulyanov) (Soviet leader); Simbirsk, Russia (1870-1924)

Lennon, Dianne (singer); Los Angeles, 12/1/39

Lennon, Janet (singer); Culver City, Calif., 11/15/46

Lennon, John (singer and songwriter); Liverpool, England (1940-1980)

Lennon, Kathy (singer); Santa Monica, Calif., 8/22/42

Lennon, Peggy (singer); Los Angeles, 4/8/41

Leno, Jay (comedian); New Rochelle, N.Y., 4/28/1950

Lenya, Lotte (Karoline Blamauer) (singer and actress); Vienna, Austria (1898-1981)

Leonard, Sheldon (actor and director); New York City, 2/22/1907

Lerner, Alan Jay (lyricist); New York City (1918-1986)

Lerner, Max (columnist); Minsk, Russia, 12/20/1902

Le Roy, Mervyn (film producer); San Francisco (1900-1987)

Leslie, Joan (actress); Detroit, 1/26/1925

Lessing, Doris (novelist); Kermanshah, Iran, 10/22/1919

Lester, Mark (actor); Richmond, England, 1958

Letterman, David (TV personality); Indianapolis, 1947

Levant, Oscar (pianist); Pittsburgh (1906-1972)

Levene, Sam (actor); New York City (1905-1980)

Levenson, Sam (humorist); New York City (1911-1980)

Levi, Carlo (novelist); Turin, Italy (1902-1975)

Levine, James (music director, Metropolitan Opera); Cincinnati, 6/23/1943

Levine, Joseph E. (film producer); Boston (1905-1987)

Lewis, Jerry (Joseph Levitch) (comedian and film director); Newark, N.J., 3/16/1926

Lewis, Jerry Lee (singer); Ferriday, La., 9/29/1935

Lewis, John Llewellyn (labor leader); Lucas, Iowa (1880-1969)

Lewis, Meriwether (explorer); Albemarle Co., Va. (1774-1809)

Lewis, Shari (Shari Hurwitz) (puppeteer); New York City, 1/17/1934

Lewis, Sinclair (novelist); Sauk Centre, Minn. (1885-1951)

Lewis, Ted (entertainer); Circleville, Ohio (1891-1971)

Ley, Willy (science writer); Berlin (1906-1969)

Liberace (Wladziu Liberace) (pianist); West Allis, Wis. (1919-1987)

Lichtenstein, Roy (painter); New York City, 10/27/1923

Lie, Trygve Halvdan (first U.N. Secretary-General); Oslo (1896-1968)

Light, Judith (actress); Trenton, N.J., 2/9/49

Lightfoot, Gordon (singer and songwriter); Orillia, Ontario, Canada, 11/17/1938

Lillie, Beatrice (Lady Peel) (actress and comedienne); Toronto (1898-1989)

Lin Yutang (author); Changchow, China (1895-1976)

Lind, Jenny (Johanna Maria Lind) (soprano); Stockholm (1820-1887)

Lindbergh, Anne Morrow (author); Englewood, N.J., 6/22/1906

Lindbergh, Charles A. (aviator); Detroit (1902-1974)

Linden, Hal (Harold Lipshitz) (actor); New York City, 3/20/1931

Lindfors, Viveca (actress); Uppsala, Sweden, 12/29/20

Lindsay, Howard (playwright); Waterford, N.Y. (1889-1968)

Lindsay, John Vliet (ex-Mayor of New York City); New York City, 11/24/1921

Lindstrom, Pia (TV newscaster); Stockholm, 11/?/1938

Linkletter, Art (radio-TV personality); Moose Jaw, Saskatchewan, Canada, 7/17/1912

Linnaeus, Carolus (Carl von Linné) (botanist); Råshult, Sweden (1707-1778)

Lipchitz, Jacques (sculptor); Druskieniki, Latvia (1891-1973)

Lippi, Fra Filippo (painter); Florence (1406-1469)

Lippmann, Walter (columnist, author, and political analyst); New York City (1889-1974)

Lister, (1st Baron of Lyme Regis) (Joseph Lister) (surgeon); Upton, England (1827-1912)

Liszt, Franz (composer and pianist); Raiding (Hungary) (1811-1886)

Lithgow, John (actor); Rochester, N.Y., 6/6/45

Little, Cleavon (actor and comedian); Chickasha, Okla., 6/1/1939

Little, Rich (impressionist); Ottawa, 11/26/1938

Livesey, Roger (actor); Barry, Wales (1906-1976)

Livingstone, David (missionary and explorer); Lanarkshire, Scotland (1813-1873)

Livingstone, Mary (Sadye Marks) (comedienne); Seattle (1909-1983)

Llewellyn, Richard (novelist); St. David's, Wales (1906-1983)

Lloyd, Harold (comedian); Burchard, Neb. (1894-1971)

Lloyd George, David (Earl of Dwyfor) (statesman); Manchester, England (1863-1945)

Lloyd Webber, Andrew (composer); London, England, 3/22/1948

Locke, John (philosopher); Somersetshire, England (1632-1704)

Lockhart, Gene (actor); London, Ontario, Canada (1891-1957)

Lockhart, June (actress); New York City, 6/25/1925

Lockwood, Margaret (actress); Karachi (Pakistan) (1916-1990)

Lodge, Henry Cabot (legislator); Boston (1850-1924)

Lodge, Henry Cabot, Jr. (diplomat); Nahant, Mass. (1902-1985)

Loesser, Frank (composer); New York City **(1910-1969)**
Loewe, Frederick (composer); Vienna **(1901-1988)**
Logan, Joshua (director and producer); Texarkana, Tex. **(1908-1988)**
Lollobrigida, Gina (actress); Subiaco, Italy, 1928
Lombard, Carole (Carol Jane Peters) (actress); Ft. Wayne, Ind. **(1908-1942)**
Lombardo, Guy (band leader); London, Ontario, Canada **(1902-1977)**
London, George (baritone); Montreal **(1920-1985)**
London, Jack (John Griffith London) (novelist); San Francisco **(1876-1916)**
London, Julie (Julie Peck) (singer and actress); Santa Rosa, Calif., 9/26/1926
Long, Huey Pierce (politician); Winnfield, La. **(1893-1935)**
Long, Shelly (actress); Fort Wayne, Ind., 8/23/49
Longfellow, Henry Wadsworth (poet); Portland, Me. **(1807-1882)**
Longworth, Alice Roosevelt (social figure); New York City **(1884-1980)**
Loos, Anita (novelist); Sissons, Calif., **(1888-1981)**
Lopez, Trini (singer); Dallas, Tex., 5/15/37
Lopez, Vincent (band leader); Brooklyn, N.Y. **(1895-1975)**
Lord, Jack (John Joseph Ryan) (actor); New York City, 12/30/1930
Loren, Sophia (Sofia Scicolone) (actress); Rome, 9/20/1934
Lorre, Peter (Laszlo Löewenstein) (actor); Rosenberg (Czechoslovakia) **(1904-1964)**
Loudon. Dorothy (actress, singer); Boston, 9/17/1933
Louise, Tina (actress); New York City, 2/11/1937
Lovecraft, Howard Phillips (author); Providence, R.I., **(1890-1937)**
Lowe, Edmund (actor); San Jose, Calif. **(1892-1971)**
Lowell, Amy (poet); Brookline, Mass. **(1874-1925)**
Lowell, James Russell (poet); Cambridge, Mass. **(1819-1891)**
Lowell, Robert (poet); Boston **(1917-1977)**
Loy, Myrna (Myrna Williams) (actress); nr. Helena, Mont., 8/2/1905
Loyola, St. Ignatius of (Iñigo de Oñez y Loyola) (founder of Jesuits); Gúipuzcoa Province, Spain **(1491-1556)**
Lubitsch, Ernst (film director); Berlin **(1892-1947)**
Lucas, George (film director); Modesto, Calif., 5/14/44
Lucci, Susan (actress); Scarsdale, N.Y., 12/23/1948
Luce, Clare Boothe (playwright and former Ambassador); New York City **(1903-1987)**
Luce, Henry Robinson (editor and publisher); Tengchow, China **(1898-1967)**
Ludlum, Robert (author); New York City, 5/25/1927
Lugosi, Bela (Bela Lugosi Blasko) (actor); Logos, Hungary **(1888-1956)**
Lukas, Paul (actor); Budapest **(1895-1971)**
Lully, Jean Baptiste (French composer); Florence **(1639-1687)**
Lumet, Sidney (film and TV director); Philadelphia, 6/25/1924
Lunden, Joan (TV host); Fair Oaks, Calif., 9/19/1950
Lunt, Alfred (actor); Milwaukee **(1892-1977)**
Lupino, Ida (actress and director); London, 2/4/1918
LuPone, Patti (actress; singer); Northport, N.Y., 4/21/1949
Luther, Martin (religious reformer); Eisleben (East Germany) **(1483-1546)**
Lynde, Paul (comedian); Mt. Vernon, Ohio **(1926-1982)**
Lynley, Carol (actress); New York City, 2/13/1942
Lynn, Jeffrey (actor); Auburn, Mass., 1909
Lynn, Loretta (singer); Butcher's Hollow, Ky., 4/14/1935

M

Ma, Yo-Yo (cellist); Paris, 10/7/1955
Maazel, Lorin (conductor); Neuilly, France, 3/5/1930
MacArthur, Charles (playwright); Scranton, Pa. **(1895-1956)**
MacArthur, Douglas (five-star general); Little Rock Barracks, Ark. **(1880-1964)**
MacArthur, James (actor); Los Angeles, 12/8/1937
Macaulay, Thomas Babington (author); Rothley Temple, England **(1800-1859)**
MacCorkindale, Simon (actor); Ely, England, 2/12/53
MacDermot, Galt (composer); Montreal, 12/19/1928
MacDonald, James Ramsay (statesman); Lossiemouth, Scotland **(1866-1937)**
MacDonald, Jeanette (actress and soprano); Philadelphia **(1907-1965)**
Macdonald, Ross (Kenneth Millar) (mystery writer); Los Gatos, Calif. **(1915-1983)**
MacDowell, Edward Alexander (composer); New York City **(1861-1908)**
Macfadden, Bernarr (physical culturist); nr. Mill Spring, Mo. **(1868-1955)**
MacGraw, Ali (actress); New York City, 4/1/1939
Machaut, Guillaume de (composer); Marchault, France **(1300-1377)**
Machiavelli, Niccolò (political philosopher); Florence (Italy) **(1469-1527)**
Mack, Ted (TV personality); Greeley, Colo. **(1904-1976)**

MacKenzie, Gisele (Marie Marguerite Louise Gisele LaFleche) (singer and actress); Winnipeg, Manitoba, Canada, 1/10/1927
Mackie, Bob (designer); Monterey Park, Calif., 3/24/1940
MacLaine, Shirley (Shirley MacLean Beatty) (actress); Richmond, Va., 4/24/1934
MacLeish, Archibald (poet); Glencoe, Ill. **(1892-1982)**
Macmillan, Harold (ex-Prime Minister); London **(1894-1986)**
MacMurray, Fred (actor); Kankakee, Ill., 8/30/1908
MacNeil, Cornell (baritone); Minneapolis, 1925
MacRae, Gordon (singer); East Orange, N.J. **(1921-1986)**
MacRae, Sheila (comedienne); London, 9/24/1924
Madison, Guy (Robert Moseley) (actor); Bakersfield, Calif., 1/19/1922
Madonna (Madonna Louise Ciccone) (singer); Bay City, Mich., 8/16/58
Maeterlinck, Count Maurice (author); Ghent, Belgium **(1862-1949)**
Magellan, Ferdinand (Fernando de Magalhaes) (navigator); Sabrosa, Portugal **(1480?-1521)**
Magnani, Anna (actress); Rome **(1908-1973)**
Magritte, René (painter); Belgium **(1898-1967)**
Magsaysay, Ramón (statesman); Iba, Luzon, Philippines **(1907-1957)**
Mahan, Alfred Thayer (naval historian); West Point, N.Y. **(1840-1914)**
Mahler, Gustav (composer and conductor); Kalischt (Czechoslovakia) **(1860-1911)**
Mailer, Norman (novelist); Long Branch, N.J., 1/31/1923
Maillol, Aristide (sculptor); Banyuls-sur-Mer, Rousillion, France **(1861-1944)**
Maimonides, Moses (Jewish philosopher); Cordoba, Spain **(1135-1204)**
Main, Marjorie (Mary Tomlinson Krebs) (actress); Acton, Ind. **(1890-1975)**
Mainbocher (Main Rousseau Bocher) (fashion designer); Chicago **(1891-1976)**
Majors, Lee (actor); Wyandotte, Mich., 4/23/1940
Makarova, Natalia (ballerina); Leningrad, 11/21/1940
Makeba, Miriam (singer); Johannesburg, South Africa, 3/4/1932
Malamud, Bernard (novelist); Brooklyn, N.Y., **(1914-1986)**
Malden, Karl (Miaden Sekulovich) (actor); Chicago, 3/22/1913
Malkovich, John (actor); Christopher, Ill., 12/9/53
Malle, Louis (director); Thumeries, France, 10/30/32
Malone, Dorothy (actress); Chicago, 1/30/1925
Malraux, André (author); Paris **(1901-1976)**
Malthus, Thomas Robert (economist); nr. Dorking, England **(1766-1834)**
Mamet, David (playwright); Chicago, 11/30/1947
Manchester, Melissa (singer); Bronx, N.Y., 2/15/1951
Manchester, William (writer); Attleboro, Mass., 4/1/1922
Mancini, Henry (composer and conductor); Cleveland, 4/16/1924
Mandela, Nelson (Rolihlahla) (South African political activist) Umtata, Transkei, 1918
Mandela, Winnie (Nomzamo) (South African political activist); Pondoland district of the Transkei, 1936(?)
Mandrell, Barbara (singer); Houston, 12/25/1948
Manet, Edouard (painter); Paris **(1832-1883)**
Mangano, Silvana (actress); Rome **(1930-1989)**
Mangione, Chuck (hornist, pianist, and composer); Rochester, N.Y., 11/29/1940
Manilow, Barry (singer); Brooklyn, N.Y., 6/17/1946
Mankiewicz, Frank F. (columnist); New York City, 5/16/1924
Mankiewicz, Joseph L. (film writer and director); Wilkes-Barre, Pa., 2/11/1909
Mann, Horace (educator); Franklin, Mass. **(1796-1859)**
Mann, Thomas (novelist); Lübeck, Germany **(1875-1955)**
Mannes, Marya (writer); New York City, 11/14/1904
Mansfield, Jayne (Jayne Palmer) (actress); Bryn Mawr, Pa. **(1932-1967)**
Mansfield, Katherine (story writer); Wellington, New Zealand **(1888-1923)**
Mantovani, Annunzio (conductor); Venice **(1905-1980)**
Mao Zedong (Tse-tung) (Chinese leader); Shao Shan, China **(1893-1976)**
Mapplethorpe, Robert (photographer); Floral Park, Queens, N.Y. **(1946-1989)**
Marat, Jean Paul (French revolutionist); Boudry, Neuchâtei, Switzerland **(1743-1793)**
Marceau, Marcel (mime); Strasbourg, France, 3/22/1923
March, Fredric (Frederick Bickel) (actor); Racine, Wis. **(1897-1975)**
Marchand, Nancy (actress); Buffalo, N.Y., 6/19/28
Marconi, Guglielmo (inventor); Bologna, Italy **(1874-1937)**
Marcus Aurelius (Marcus Annius Verus) (Roman emperor); Rome **(121-180)**
Marcuse, Herbert (philosopher); Berlin, **(1898-1979)**
Margaret Rose (Princess); Glamis Castle, Angus, Scotland, 8/21/1930
Margrethe II (Queen); Copenhagen, 4/16/1940

Marie Antoinette (Josephe Jeanne Marie Antoinette) (Queen of France); Vienna (1755-1793)

Marisol (sculptor); Venezuela, 1930

Markham, Edwin (poet); Oregon City, Ore. (1852-1940)

Markova, Dame Alicia (Lilian Alice Marks) (ballerina); London, 12/1/1910

Marley, Bob (reggae singer and songwriter); Kingston, Jamaica (1945-1981)

Marlowe, Christopher (dramatist); Canterbury, England (1564-1593)

Marlowe, Julia (Sarah Frances Frost) (actress); Cumberlandshire, England (1866-1950)

Marquand, J(ohn) P(hillips) (novelist); Wilmington, Del. (1893-1960)

Marquette, Jacques (missionary and explorer); Laon, France (1637-1675)

Marriner, Neville (conductor); Lincoln, England, 4/15/1924

Marsalis, Wynton (musician); New Orleans, La., 10/18/61

Marsh, Jean (actress); Stoke Newington, England, 7/1/1934

Marshall, E.G. (actor); Owatonna, Minn., 6/18/1910

Marshall, George Catlett (general); Uniontown, Pa. (1880-1959)

Marshall, Herbert (actor); London (1890-1968)

Marshall, John (jurist); nr. Germantown, Va. (1755-1835)

Marshall, Penny (actress); New York City, 10/15/1942

Martin, Dean (Dino Crocetti) (singer and actor); Steubenville, Ohio, 6/17/1917

Martin, Mary (singer and actress); Weatherford, Tex., 12/1/1913

Martin, Steve (comedian); Waco, Tex., 1945(?)

Martin, Tony (Alvin Morris) (singer); San Francisco, 12/25/1913

Martinelli, Giovanni (tenor); Montagnana, Italy (1885-1969)

Martins, Peter (dancer-choreographer); Copenhagen, 10/27/1945

Marvell, Andrew (poet); Winestead, England (1621-1678)

Marvin, Lee (actor); New York City (1924-1987)

Marx, Chico (Leonard) (comedian); New York City (1891-1961)

Marx, Groucho (Julius) (comedian); New York City (1890-1977)

Marx, Harpo (Arthur) (comedian); New York City (1893-1964)

Marx, Karl (Socialist writer); Treves (Germany) (1818-1883)

Marx, Zeppo (Herbert) (comedian); New York City (1901-1979)

Mary Stuart (Queen of Scotland); Linlithgow, Scotland (1542-1587)

Masaryk, Jan Garrigue (statesman); Prague (Czechoslovakia) (1886-1948)

Masaryk, Thomas Garrigue (statesman); Hodonin (Czechoslovakia) (1850-1937)

Masefield, John (poet); Ledbury, England (1878-1967)

Masekela, Hugh (trumpeter); Wilbank, South Africa, 4/4/1939

Mason, Jackie (comedian); Sheboygan, Wis., 6/9/30(?)

Mason, James (actor); Huddersfield, England (1909-1984)

Mason, Marsha (actress); St. Louis, Mo., 4/3/42

Massenet, Jules Emile Frédéric (composer); Montaud, France (1842-1912)

Massey, Raymond (actor); Toronto, (1896-1983)

Massine, Léonide (choreographer); Moscow, (1895-1979)

Masters, Edgar Lee (poet); Garnett, Kan. (1869-1950)

Mastroianni, Marcello (actor); Fontana Liri, Italy, 9/28/1924

Mather, Cotton (clergyman); Boston (1663-1728)

Mathis, Johnny (singer); San Francisco, 9/30/1935

Matisse, Henri (painter); Le Cateau, France (1869-1954)

Matthau, Walter (Walter Matuschanskayasky) (actor); New York City, 10/1/1920

Mature, Victor (actor); Louisville, Ky., 1/19/1916

Maugham, W(illiam) Somerset (author); Paris (1874-1965)

Mauldin, Bill (political cartoonist); Mountain Park, N.M., 10/29/1921

Maupassant, Henri René Albert Guy de (story writer); Normandy, France (1850-1893)

Maurois, André (Emile Herzog) (author); Elbauf, France (1885-1967)

Maximilian (Ferdinand Maximilian Joseph) (Emperor of Mexico); Vienna (1832-1867)

Maxwell, James Clerk (physicist); Edinburgh, Scotland (1831-1879)

May, Elaine (Elaine Berlin) (entertainer-writer); Philadelphia, 4/21/1932

May, Rollo (psychologist); Ada, Ohio, 4/21/1909

Mayall, John (singer and songwriter); Manchester, England, 11/29/1933

Mayer, Louis B. (motion picture executive); Minsk, Russia (1885-1957)

Mayo, Charles H. (surgeon); Rochester, Minn. (1865-1939)

Mayo, Charles W. (surgeon); Rochester, Minn. (1898-1968)

Mayo, Virginia (Jones) (actress); St. Louis, 1920

Mayo, William J. (surgeon); Le Sueur, Minn. (1861-1939)

Mayron, Melanie (actress); Philadelphia, 10/20/1952

Mazzini, Giuseppe (patriot); Genoa (1805-1872)

McBride, Mary Margaret (radio personality); Paris, Mo. (1899-1976)

McBride, Patricia (ballerina); Teaneck, N.J., 8/23/1942

McCallum, David (actor); Glasgow, Scotland, 9/19/1933

McCambridge, Mercedes (actress); Joliet, Ill., 3/17/1918

McCarthy, Eugene J. (ex-Senator); Watkins, Minn., 3/29/1916

McCarthy, Joseph Raymond (Senator); Grand Chute, Wis. (1908-1957)

McCarthy, Kevin (actor); Seattle, 2/15/1914

McCarthy, Mary (novelist); Seattle (1912-1989)

McCartney, Paul (singer and songwriter); Liverpool, England, 6/18/1942

McClanahan, Rue (actress); Healdton, Okla., 2/21/1935

McClellan, George Brinton (general); Philadelphia (1826-1885)

McClintock, Barbara (geneticist); Hartford, Conn., 6/16/1902

McCloy, John J. (lawyer and banker); Philadelphia, 3/31/1895

McClure, Doug (actor); Glendale, Calif., 5/11/1938

McCormack, John (tenor); Athlone, Ireland (1884-1945)

McCormack, John W. (ex-Speaker of House); Boston (1891-1980)

McCormack, Patty (actress); New York City, 8/21/1945

McCormick, Cyrus Hall (inventor); Rockbridge County, Va. (1809-1884)

McCormick, Myron (actor); Albany, Ind. (1907-1962)

McCoy, Col. Tim (actor); Saginaw, Mich. (1891-1978)

McCracken, James (dramatic tenor); Gary, Ind. (1926-1988)

McCrea, Joel (actor); Los Angeles, 11/5/1905

McCullers, Carson (novelist); Columbus, Ga. (1917-1967)

McDaniel, Hattie (actress); Wichita, Kan. (1895-1952)

McDowall, Roddy (actor); London, 9/17/1928

McDowell, Malcolm (actor); Leeds, England, 6/19/1943

McFarland, Spanky (George Emmett) (actor); Fort Worth, Tex., 10/2/28

McGavin, Darren (actor); San Joaquin, Calif., 5/7/1922

McGinley, Phyllis (poet and writer); Ontario, Ore. (1905-1978)

McGoohan, Patrick (actor); Astoria, Queens, N.Y., 1928

McGovern, Maureen (singer); Youngstown, Ohio, 7/27/1949

McGuire, Dorothy (actress); Omaha, Neb. 6/14/1919

McKellen, Ian (actor); Burnley, England, 5/25/1939

McKenna, Siobhan (actress); Belfast, Northern Ireland (1923-1986)

McKuen, Rod (singer and composer); Oakland, Calif., 4/29/1933

McLaglen, Victor (actor); Tunbridge Wells, Kent, England (1886-1959)

McLaughlin, John (guitarist); Yorkshire, England, 1942

McLean, Don (singer and songwriter); New Rochelle, N.Y., 10/2/1945

McLuhan, Marshall (Herbert Marshall) (communications writer); Edmonton, Canada (1911-1980)

McMahon, Ed (TV personality); Detroit, 3/6/1923

McNamara, Robert S. (former president of World Bank); San Francisco, 6/9/1916

McQueen, Butterfly (Thelma) (actress); Tampa, Fla., 1/8/11

McQueen, Steve (Terence Stephen McQueen) (actor); Indianapolis (1930-1980)

McRaney, Gerald (actor); Collins, Miss., 8/19/47

Mead, Margaret (anthropologist); Philadelphia, (1901-1978)

Meadows, Audrey (actress); Wu Chang, China, 1922(?)

Meadows, Jayne (actress); Wu Chang, China 9/27/1926

Meany, George (labor leader); New York City (1894-1980)

Meara, Anne (actress); New York City, 1929

Medici, Lorenzo de' (called Lorenzo the Magnificent) (Florentine ruler); Florence (Italy) (1449-1492)

Meek, Donald (actor); Glasgow, Scotland (1880-1946)

Meeker, Ralph (Ralph Rathgeber) (actor); Minneapolis, (1920-1988)

Mehta, Zubin (conductor); Bombay, 4/29/1936

Meir, Golda (Golda Myerson, nee Mabovitz) (ex-Premier of Israel); Kiev, Russia (1898-1978)

Melanie (Melanie Safka) (singer and songwriter); New York City, 2/3/1947

Melba, Dame Nellie (Helen Porter Mitchell) (soprano); nr. Melbourne (1861-1931)

Melchior, Lauritz (Lebrecht Hommel) (heroic tenor); Copenhagen (1890-1973)

Mellon, Andrew William (financier); Pittsburgh (1855-1937)

Melville, Herman (novelist); New York City (1819-1891)

Mencken, Henry Louis (writer); Baltimore (1880-1956)

Mendel, Gregor Johann (geneticist); Heinzendorf, Austrian Silesia (1822-1884)

Mendeleyev, Dmitri Ivanovich (chemist); Tobolsk, Russia (1834-1907)

Mendelssohn-Bartholdy, Jakob Ludwig Felix (composer); Hamburg (1809-1847)

Mendès-France, Pierre (ex-Premier); Paris (1905-1982)

Menjou, Adolphe (actor); Pittsburgh (1890-1963)

Mennin, Peter (Peter Mennini) (composer); Erie, Pa. (1923-1983)

Menninger, William C. (psychiatrist); Topeka, Kan. (1899-1966)

Menotti, Gian Carlo (composer); Cadegliano, Italy, 7/7/1911

Menuhin, Yehudi (violinist and conductor); New York City, 4/22/1916

Menzies, Robert Gordon (ex-Prime Minister); Jeparit, Australia (1894-1978)

Mercer, Johnny (songwriter); Savannah, Ga. (1909-1976)

Mercer, Mabel (singer); Burton-on-Trent, England (1900-1984)

Mercer, Marian (actress, singer); Akron, Ohio, 11/26/35

Mercouri, Melina (actress); Athens, 10/18/1925

Meredith, Burgess (actor); Cleveland, 11/16/1908

Merkel, Una (actress); Covington, Ky. (1903-1986)

Merman, Ethel (Ethel Zimmerman) (singer and actress); Astoria, Queens, N.Y. **(1909-1984)**

Merrick, David (David Margulois) (stage producer); St. Louis, 11/27/1912

Merrill, Dina (actress); New York City, 12/9/1925

Merrill, Gary (actor); Hartford, Conn. **(1915-1990)**

Merrill, Robert (baritone); Brooklyn, N.Y., 6/4/1919

Merton, Thomas (clergyman and writer); France **(1915-1968)**

Mesmer, Franz Anton (physician); Itzmang, nr. Constance (Germany) **(1733-1815)**

Mesta, Perle (social figure); Sturgis, Mich. **(1889-1975)**

Metternich, Prince Klemens Wenzel Nepomuk Lothar von (statesman); Coblenz (Germany) **(1773-1859)**

Michelangelo Buonarroti (painter, sculptor, and architect); Caprese (Italy) **(1475-1564)**

Michener, James A. (novelist); New York City, 2/3/1907

Mickiewicz, Adam (Polish poet); Zozie, Belorussia (U.S.S.R.) **(1798-1855)**

Midler, Bette (singer); Honolulu, 1945

Mielziner, Jo (stage designer); Paris **(1901-1976)**

Mies van der Rohe, Ludwig (architect and designer); Aachen, Germany **(1886-1969)**

Mikoyan, Anastas I. (diplomat); Sanain, Armenia, **(1895-1978)**

Miles, Sarah (actress); Essex, England, 12/31/1943

Miles, Sylvia (actress); New York City, 9/9/1932

Miles, Vera (Vera Ralston) (actress); nr. Boise City, Okla., 8/23/1930

Milhaud, Darius (composer); Aix-en-Provence, France **(1892-1974)**

Mill, John Stuart (philosopher); London, **(1806-1873)**

Milland, Ray (Reginald Truscott-Jones) (actor); Neath, Wales **(1907-1986)**

Millay, Edna St. Vincent (poet); Rockland, Me. **(1892-1950)**

Miller, Ann (Lucille Ann Collier) (dancer and actress); Cherino, Tex., 4/12/1923

Miller, Arthur (playwright); New York City, 10/17/1915

Miller, Glenn (band leader); Clarinda, Iowa **(1904-1944)**

Miller, Henry (novelist); New York City **(1891-1980)**

Miller, Jason (John Miller) (playwright); New York City, 1939(?)

Miller, Marilyn (dancer-singer, actress); Evansville, Ind. **(1898-1936)**

Miller, Mitch (Mitchell) (musician); Rochester, N.Y., 7/4/1911

Miller, Roger (singer); Fort Worth, 1/2/1936

Millet, Jean François (painter); Gruchy, France **(1814-1875)**

Millett, Kate (feminist); St. Paul, 9/14/1934

Millikan, Robert A. (physicist); Morrison, Ill. **(1869-1953)**

Mills, Donna (actress); Chicago, 12/11/41

Mills, Hayley (actress); London, 4/18/1946

Mills, John (actor); Felixstowe, England, 2/22/1908

Mills, Juliet (actress); London, 11/21/41

Milne, A(lan) A(lexander) (author); London **(1882-1956)**

Milner, Martin (actor); Detroit, Mich., 12/28/1931

Milnes, Sherrill (baritone); Downers Grove, Ill., 1/10/35

Milstein, Nathan (concert violinist); Odessa, Russia, 12/31/1904

Milton, John (poet); London **(1608-1674)**

Mimieux, Yvette (actress); Hollywood, Calif., 1/8/1941

Mineo, Sal (actor); New York City **(1939-1976)**

Minnelli, Liza (singer and actress); Hollywood, Calif., 3/12/1946

Minnelli, Vincente (film director); Chicago **(1913-1986)**

Minuit, Peter (Governor of New Amsterdam); Wesel (Germany) **(1580-1638)**

Miranda, Carmen (Maria do Carmo da Cunha) (singer and dancer); Lisbon **(1913-1955)**

Miró, Joan (painter); Barcelona **(1893-1983)**

Mitchell, Cameron (actor); Dallastown, Pa., 4/11/1918

Mitchell, Guy (actor); Detroit, 2/27/1927

Mitchell, John N. (former Attorney General); Detroit **(1913-1988)**

Mitchell, Joni (Roberta Joan Anderson) (singer and songwriter); Ft. Macleod, Canada, 11/7/1943

Mitchell, Margaret (novelist); Atlanta **(1900-1949)**

Mitchell, Thomas (actor); Elizabeth, N.J. **(1892-1962)**

Mitchum, Robert (actor); Bridgeport, Conn., 8/6/1917

Mitropoulos, Dimitri (orchestra conductor); Athens **(1896-1960)**

Mix, Tom (actor); Mix Run, Pa. **(1880-1940)**

Modigliani, Amedeo (painter); Leghorn, Italy **(1884-1920)**

Moffo, Anna (soprano); Wayne, Pa., 6/27/1934

Mohammed (prophet); Mecca (Saudi Arabia) **(570-632)**

Molière (Jean Baptiste Poquelin) (dramatist); Paris **(1622-1673)**

Moll, Richard (actor); Pasadena, Calif. 1/13/(?)

Molnar, Ferenc (dramatist); Budapest **(1878-1952)**

Molotov, Vyacheslav M. (V. M. Skryabin) (diplomat); Kukarka, Russia **(1890-1986)**

Mondrian, Piet (painter); Amersfoort, Netherlands **(1872-1944)**

Monet, Claude (painter); Paris **(1840-1926)**

Monk, Meredith (choreographer-composer-performing artist); Lima, Peru, 11/20/1942

Monk, Thelonious (pianist); Rocky Mount, N.C. **(1918-1982)**

Monroe, Marilyn (Norma Jean Mortenson or Baker) (actress); Los Angeles **(1926-1962)**

Monroe, Vaughn (Wilton) (band leader); Akron, Ohio **(1912-1973)**

Monsarrat, Nicholas (novelist); Liverpool, England, **(1910-1979)**

Montaigne, Michel Eyquem de (essayist); nr. Bordeaux, France **(1533-1592)**

Montalban, Ricardo (actor); Mexico City, 11/25/1920

Montand, Yves (Yvo Montand Livi) (actor and singer); Monsummano, Italy, 10/13/1921

Montesquieu, Charles-Louis de Secondat, baron de La Brède and de, (philosopher) nr. Borleaux, France **(1689-1755)**

Monteux, Pierre (conductor); Paris **(1875-1964)**

Monteverdi, Claudio (composer); Cremona? Italy **(1567-1643)**

Montez, Maria (actress); Dominican Republican **(1918-1951)**

Montezuma II (Aztec emperor); Mexico **(1480?-1520)**

Montgomery, Elizabeth (actress); Hollywood, Calif., 4/15/1933

Montgomery, George (George Montgomery Letz) (actor); Brady, Mont., 8/29/1916

Montgomery, Robert (Henry, Jr.) (actor); Beacon, N.Y. **(1904-1981)**

Montgomery of Alamein, 1st Viscount of Hindhead (Sir Bernard Law Montgomery) (military leader); London **(1887-1976)**

Montoya, Carlos (guitarist); Madrid, 12/13/1903

Moore, Clement Clarke (author); New York City **(1779-1863)**

Moore, Dudley (actor-writer-musician); Dagenham, England, 4/19/1935

Moore, Garry (Thomas Garrison Morfit) (TV personality); Baltimore, 1/31/1915

Moore, Grace (soprano); Jellico, Tenn. **(1901-1947)**

Moore, Henry (sculptor); Castleford, England **(1898-1986)**

Moore, Marianne (poet); Kirkwood, Mo. **(1887-1972)**

Moore, Mary Tyler (actress); Brooklyn, N.Y., 12/29/1937

Moore, Melba (Beatrice) (singer and actress); New York City, 10/27/1945

Moore, Roger (actor); London, 10/14/1927(?)

Moore, Thomas (poet); Dublin **(1779-1852)**

Moore, Victor (actor); Hammonton, N.J. **(1876-1962)**

Moorehead, Agnes (actress); Clinton, Mass. **(1906-1974)**

More, Henry (philosopher); Grantham, England **(1614-1687)**

More, Sir Thomas (statesman and author); London **(1478-1535)**

Moreau, Jeanne (actress); Paris, 1/23/1928

Moreno, Rita (Rosita Dolores Alverio) (actress); Humacao, Puerto Rico, 12/11/1931

Morgan, Dennis (actor); Prentice, Wis., 12/10/1920

Morgan, Frank (actor); New York City **(1890-1949)**

Morgan, Harry (actor); Detroit, 4/10/1915

Morgan, Helen (singer); Danville, Ohio **(1900?-1941)**

Morgan, Henry (comedian); New York City, 3/31/1915

Morgan, Jane (Florence Currier) (singer); Boston, 1920

Morgan, John Pierpont (financier); Hartford, Conn. **(1837-1913)**

Morgan, Ralph (actor); New York City **(1882-1956)**

Moriarty, Michael (actor); Detroit, 4/5/1941

Morini, Erica (concert violinist); Vienna, 1/5/1910

Morison, Samuel Eliot (historian); Boston **(1887-1976)**

Morley, Christopher Darlington (novelist); Haverford, Pa. **(1890-1957)**

Morley, Robert (actor); Semley, England, 5/26/1908

Morris, Chester (actor); New York City **(1901-1970)**

Morris, Wayne (actor); Los Angeles, Calif. **(1914-1959)**

Morrison, Jim (James Douglas Morrison) (singer and songwriter); Melbourne, Fla. **(1943-1971)**

Morse, Marston (mathematician); Waterville, Me. **(1892-1977)**

Morse, Robert (actor); Newton, Mass., 5/18/1931

Morse, Samuel Finley Breese (painter and inventor); Charlestown, Mass. **(1791-1872)**

Moses, Grandma (Mrs. Anna Mary Robertson Moses) (painter); Greenwich, N.Y. **(1860-1961)**

Moses, Robert (urban planner); New Haven, Conn., **(1888-1981)**

Mostel, Zero (Samuel Joel Mostel) (actor); Brooklyn, N.Y. **(1915-1977)**

Moussorgsky, Modest Petrovich (composer); Karev, Russia **(1839-1881)**

Mowbray, Alan (actor); London **(1896-1969)**

Moyers, Bill D. (Billy Don) (journalist); Hugo, Okla., 6/5/1934

Moynihan, Daniel Patrick (New York Senator); Tulsa, Okla., 3/16/1927

Mozart, Wolfgang Amadeus (Johannes Chrysostomus Wolfgangus Theophilus Mozart) (composer); Salzburg (Austria) **(1756-1791)**

Mudd, Roger (TV newscaster); Washington, D.C., 2/9/1928

Muggeridge, Malcolm (Thomas) (writer); Croydon, England, 3/24/1903

Muhammad, Elijah (Elijah Poole) (religious leader); Sandersville, Ga. **(1897-1975)**

Mulgrew, Kate (actress); Dubuque, Iowa, 4/?/1929

Mulhare, Edward (actor); Ireland, 1923

Mumford, Lewis (cultural historian and city planner); Flushing, Queens, N.Y. **(1895-1990)**

Munch, Edvard (painter); Löten, Norway **(1863-1944)**

Munchhausen, Karl Friedrick Hieronymus, baron von (anecdotist);

Hanover, Germany **(1720-1797)**
Muni, Paul (Muni Weisenfreund) (actor); Lemburg (Ukraine) **(1895-1967)**
Munsel, Patrice (soprano); Spokane, Wash., 5/14/1925
Murdoch, Iris (novelist); Dublin, 7/15/1919
Murdoch, Rupert (publisher); Melbourne, 3/11/1931
Murillo, Bartolomé Esteban (painter); Seville, Spain **(1617-1682)**
Murphy, Audie (actor and war hero); Kingston, Tex. **(1924-1971)**
Murphy, Eddie (actor-comedian); Brooklyn, N.Y. 4/3/61
Murphy, George (actor, dancer, and ex-Senator); New Haven, Conn., 7/4/1902
Murray, Arthur (dance teacher); New York City, 4/4/1895
Murray, Bill (actor-comedian); Wilmette, Ill. 9/21/1950
Murray, Kathryn (dance teacher); Jersey City, N.J., 1906
Murray, Ken (Don Court) (producer); Nyack, N.Y. **(1903-1988)**
Murray, Mae (Marie Adrienne Koenig) (actress); Portsmouth, Va. **(1890-1965)**
Murrow, Edward R. (commentator and government official); Greensboro, N.C. **(1908-1965)**
Mussolini, Benito (Italian dictator); Dovia, Forli, Italy **(1883-1945)**
Muti, Riccardo (orchestra conductor); Naples, Italy, 7/28/41
Mutter, Anne-Sophie (violinist); Rheinfelden, West Germany, 6/29/63
Myerson, Bess (consumer advocate); Bronx, N.Y., 1924
Myrdal, Gunnar (sociologist and economist); Gustaf Parish, Sweden **(1898-1987)**

N

Nabokov, Vladimir (novelist); St. Petersburg, Russia **(1899-1977)**
Nabors, Jim (actor and singer); Sylacauga, Ala., 6/12/1932
Nader, Ralph (consumer advocate); Winsted, Conn., 2/27/1934
Nagel, Conrad (actor); Keokuk, Iowa **(1897-1970)**
Naish, J. Carrol (actor); New York City **(1900-1973)**
Naldi, Nita (Anita Donna Dooley) (actress); New York City **(1899-1961)**
Napoleon Bonaparte. *See* Bonaparte, Napoleon
Nash, Graham (singer); Blackpool, England, 1942
Nash, Ogden (poet); Rye, N.Y. **(1902-1971)**
Nasser, Gamal Abdel (statesman); Beni Mor, Egypt **(1918-1970)**
Nast, Thomas (cartoonist); Landau (Germany) **(1840-1902)**
Nation, Carry Amelia (temperance leader); Garrard County, Ky. **(1846-1911)**
Natwick, Mildred (actress); Baltimore, 6/19/1908
Nazimova, Alla (actress); Yalta, Crimea, Russia **(1879-1945)**
Neagle, Anna (Marjorie Robertson) (actress); London **(1908-1986)**
Neal, Patricia (actress); Packard, Ky., 1/20/1926
Neff, Hildegarde (actress); Ulm, Germany, 12/28/1925
Negri, Pola (Apolina Mathias-Chalupec) (actress); Bromberg (Poland) **(1899-1987)**
Nehru, Jawaharlal (first Prime Minister of India); Allahabad, India **(1889-1964)**
Nelligan, Kate (actress); London, Ont., Canada, 3/16/51
Nelson, Barry (Neilsen) (actor); San Francisco, 1920
Nelson, David (actor); New York City, 10/24/1936
Nelson, Harriet Hilliard (Peggy Lou Snyder) (actress); Des Moines, Iowa, 1914
Nelson, Ozzie (Oswald) (actor); Jersey City, N.J. **(1907-1975)**
Nelson, Ricky (Eric) (singer and actor); Teaneck, N.J. **(1940-1985)**
Nelson, Viscount Horatio (naval officer); Burnham Thorpe, England **(1758-1805)**
Nelson, Willie (singer); Waco, Texas, 4/30/1933
Nenni, Pietro (Socialist leader); Faenza, Italy **(1891-1980)**
Nero (Nero Claudius Caesar Drusus Germanicus) (Roman emperor); Antium (Italy) **(37-68)**
Nero, Peter (pianist); New York City, 5/22/1934
Nesbitt, Cathleen (actress); Cheshire, England **(1889-1982)**
Nevelson, Louise (sculptor); Kiev, Russia **(1899-1988)**
Newhart, Bob (entertainer); Chicago, 9/5/1929
Newhouse, Samuel I. (publisher); New York City **(1895-1979)**
Newley, Anthony (actor and song writer); London, 9/24/1931
Newman, Edwin (news commentator); New York City, 1/25/1919
Newman, John Henry (prelate); London **(1801-1890)**
Newman, Paul (actor and director); Cleveland, 1/26/1925
Newman, Randy (singer); Los Angeles, 11/28/1943
Newton, Huey (black activist); New Orleans, 2/17/1942
Newton, Sir Isaac (mathematician and scientist); nr. Grantham, England **(1642-1727)**
Newton, Wayne (singer); Norfolk, Va., 4/3/1942
Newton-John, Olivia (singer); Cambridge, England, 9/26/1948
Nichols, Mike (Michael Peschkowsky) (stage and film director); Berlin, 11/6/1931
Nicholson, Jack (actor); Neptune, N.J., 4/22/1937
Nietzsche, Friedrich Wilhelm (philosopher); nr. Lützen Saxony (East Germany) **(1844-1900)**

Nightingale, Florence (nurse); Florence (Italy) **(1820-1910)**
Nijinsky, Vaslav (ballet dancer); Warsaw **(1890-1950)**
Nilsson, Birgit (soprano); West Karup, Sweden, 5/17/1923
Nilsson, Harry (singer and songwriter); Brooklyn, N.Y., 6/15/1941
Nimitz, Chester W. (naval officer); Fredericksburg, Tex. **(1885-1966)**
Nimoy, Leonard (actor); Boston, 3/26/1931
Nin, Anais (author and diarist); Neuilly, France **(1903-1977)**
Niven, David (actor); Kirriemuir, Scotland **(1910-1983)**
Nizer, Louis (lawyer and author); London, 2/6/1902
Nobel, Alfred Bernhard (industrialist); Stockholm **(1833-1896)**
Noguchi, Isamu (sculptor); Los Angeles **(1904-1988)**
Nolan, Lloyd (actor); San Francisco **(1902-1985)**
Nolte, Nick (actor); Omaha, Neb., 1942
Norell, Norman (Norman Levinson) (fashion designer); Noblesville, Ind. **(1900-1972)**
Norman, Jessye (soprano); Augusta, Ga., 9/15/45
Norman, Marsha (Marsha Williams) (playwright); Louisville, Ky., 9/21/1947
Normand, Mabel (actress); Boston **(1894-1930)**
Norstad, Gen. Lauris (ex-commander of NATO forces); Minneapolis **(1907-1988)**
North, John Ringling (circus director); Baraboo, Wis. **(1903-1985)**
North, Sheree (actress); Los Angeles, 1/17/1933
Norton, Eleanor Holmes (New York City government official, lawyer); Washington, D.C., 6/13/1937
Nostradamus (Michel de Notredame) (astrologer); St. Rémy, France **(1503-1566)**
Novaes, Guiomar (pianist); São João de Boa Vista, Brazil **(1895-1979)**
Novak, Kim (Marilyn Novak) (actress); Chicago, 2/13/1933
Novarro, Ramon (Ramon Samaniegoes) (actor); Durango, Mexico **(1899-1968)**
Novello, Ivor (actor, playwright, composer); Cardiff, Wales **(1893-1951)**
Nugent, Elliott (actor and director); Dover, Ohio, **(1899-1980)**
Nureyev, Rudolf (ballet dancer); U.S.S.R., 3/17/1938
Nuyen, France (actress); Marseilles, France, 7/31/1939
Nyro, Laura (singer and songwriter); Bronx, N.Y., 1947

O

Oakie, Jack (actor); Sedalia, Mo. **(1903-1978)**
Oakley, Annie (Phoebe Anne Oakley Mozee) (markswoman); Darke County, Ohio **(1860-1926)**
Oates, Joyce Carol (novelist); Lockport, N.Y., 6/16/1938
Oberon, Merle (Estelle Merle O'Brien Thompson) (actress); Calcutta, India **(1911-1979)**
Oberth, Hermann (rocketry and space flight pioneer); Hermannstadt, Romania **(1894-1989)**
O'Brian, Hugh (Hugh J. Krampe) (actor); Rochester, N.Y., 4/19/1930
O'Brien, Edmond (actor); New York City **(1915-1985)**
O'Brien, Margaret (Angela Maxine O'Brien) (actress); San Diego, Calif., 1/15/1937
O'Brien, Pat (William Joseph O'Brien, Jr.) (actor); Milwaukee, **(1899-1983)**
O'Casey, Sean (playwright); Dublin **(1881-1964)**
Ochs, Adolph Simon (publisher); Cincinnati **(1858-1935)**
O'Connor, Carroll (actor); New York City, 8/2/1924
O'Connor, Donald (actor); Chicago, 8/28/1925
Odets, Clifford (playwright); Philadelphia **(1906-1963)**
Odetta (Odetta Holmes) (folk singer and actress); Birmingham, Ala., 12/31/1930
Offenbach, Jacques (composer); Cologne, Germany **(1819-1880)**
O'Hara, John (novelist); Pottsville, Pa. **(1905-1970)**
O'Hara, Maureen (Maureen FitzSimons) (actress); Dublin, 8/17/1921
Ohlsson, Garrick (pianist); Bronxville, N.Y., 4/3/1948
Ohrbach, Jerry (actor-singer); Bronx, N.Y., 10/20/1935
Oistrakh, David (concert violinist); Odessa, Russia **(1908-1974)**
O'Keefe, Dennis (actor); Fort Madison, Iowa **(1908-1968)**
O'Keeffe, Georgia (painter); Sun Prairie, Wis. **(1887-1986)**
Oland, Warner (actor); Umea, Sweden **(1880-1938)**
Olav V (King of Norway); Sandringham, England, 7/2/1903
Oldenburg, Claes (painter); Stockholm, Sweden, 1/28/1929
Oliver, Edna May (actress); Malden, Mass. **(1883-1942)**
Olivier, Lord (Laurence) (actor); Dorking, England **(1907-1989)**
Olmsted, Frederick Law (landscape architect); Hartford, Conn. **(1822-1903)**
Olsen, Ole (John Sigvard Olsen) (comedian); Peru, Ind. **(1892-1963)**
Omar Khayyam (poet and astronomer); Nishapur (Iran) **(died c. 1123)**
Onassis, Aristotle (shipping executive); Smyrna, Turkey **(1906-1975)**
Onassis, Christina (shipping executive); New York City **(1950-1988)**
Onassis, Jacqueline Kennedy (Jacqueline Bouvier) (President's

widow); Southampton, N.Y., 7/28/1929
O'Neal, Ryan (Patrick) (actor); Los Angeles, 4/20/1941
O'Neal, Tatum (actress); Los Angeles, Calif., 11/5/1963
O'Neill, Eugene Gladstone (playwright); New York City (1888-1953)
O'Neill, Jennifer (actress); Rio de Janeiro, 2/20/1949
Oppenheimer, J. Robert (nuclear physicist); New York City (1904-1967)
Orff, Carl (composer); Munich, Germany (1895-1982)
Orlando, Tony (Michael Anthony Orlando Cassavitis) (singer); New York City, 4/3/1944
Ormandy, Eugene (conductor); Budapest (1899-1985)
Orozco, José Clemente (painter); Zapotlán, Jalisco, Mexico (1883-1949)
Orwell, George (Eric Arthur Blair) (British author); Motihari, India (1903-1950)
Osborn, Paul (playwright); Evansville, Ind. (1901-1988)
Osborne, John (playwright); London, 12/12/1929
Osler, Sir William (physician); Bondhead, Ontario, Canada (1849-1919)
Osmond, Donny (singer); Ogden, Utah, 12/9/1957
Osmond, Marie (singer); Ogden, Utah, 1959
O'Sullivan, Maureen (actress); County Roscommon, Ireland, 5/17/1911
Otis, Elisha (inventor); Halifax, Vt. (1811-1861)
O'Toole, Peter (actor); Connemara, Ireland, 8/2/1933
Ouspenskaya, Maria (actress); Tula, Russia (1876-1949)
Ovid (Publius Ovidius Naso) (poet); Sulmona (Italy) (43 B.C.-?A.D. 17)
Owen, Reginald (actor); Wheathampstead, England (1887-1972)
Owens, Buck (Alvis Edgar Owens) (singer); Sherman, Tex., 8/12/1929
Ozawa, Seiji (orchestra conductor); Hoten, Japan, 9/1/35

P

Paar, Jack (TV personality); Canton, Ohio, 5/1/1918
Pacino, Al (Alfred) (actor); New York City, 4/25/1940
Packard, Vance (author); Granville Summit, Pa., 5/22/1914
Paderewski, Ignace Jan (pianist and statesman); Kurylowka, Russian Podolia (1860-1941)
Paganini, Nicolò (violinist); Genoa (Italy) (1782-1840)
Page, Geraldine (actress); Kirksville, Mo. (1924-1987)
Page, Patti (Clara Ann Fowler) (singer and entertainer); Claremore, Okla., 11/8/1927
Paige, Janis (actress); Tacoma, Wash., 9/16/1922
Paine, Thomas (political philosopher); Thetford, England (1737-1809)
Palance, Jack (Walter Palanuik) (actor); Lattimer, Pa., 2/18/1920
Palestrina, Giovanni Pierluigi da (composer); Palestrina, Italy (1526-1594)
Paley, William S. (broadcasting executive); Chicago, 9/28/1901
Palladio, Andrea (architect); Padua or Vicenza (Italy) (1508-1580)
Pallette, Eugene (actor); Winfield, Kan. (1889-1954)
Palmer, Betsy (actress); East Chicago, Ind., 1929
Palmer, Lilli (Lilli Peiser) (actress); Posen (Germany) (1914-1986)
Palmerston, Henry John Templeton (3rd Viscount) (statesman); Broadlands, England (1784-1865)
Pangborn, Franklin (actor); Newark, N.J. (1893-1958)
Papanicolaou, George N. (physician); Coumi, Greece (1883-1962)
Papas, Irene (actress); Chiliomodion, Greece, 1929
Papp, Joseph (Joseph Papirofsky) (stage producer and director); Brooklyn, N.Y., 6/22/1921
Paracelaus, Philippus (Aureolus Theophrastus Bombastus von Hohenheim) (physican); Einsiedeln, Switzerland (1493-1541)
Park, Chung Hee (President of South Korea); Sangmo-ri, Korea (1917-1979)
Parker, Dorothy (Dorothy Rothschild) (author); West End, N.J. (1893-1967)
Parker, Eleanor (actress); Cedarville, Ohio, 6/26/1922
Parker, Fess (actor); Fort Worth, Tex., 1925
Parker, Jean (actress); Butte, Mont., 8/11/12
Parker, Suzy (model and actress); San Antonio, 10/28/1933
Parkinson, C(yril) Northcote (historian); Durham, England, 7/30/1909
Parks, Bert (Bert Jacobson) (entertainer); Atlanta, 12/30/1914
Parks, Gordon (film director); Ft. Scott, Kan., 11/30/1912
Parnell, Charles Stewart (statesman); Avondale, Ireland (1846-1891)
Parnis, Mollie (Mollie Parnis Livingston) (fashion designer); New York City, 3/18/1905
Parsons, Estelle (actress); Marblehead, Mass., 11/20/1927
Parton, Dolly (singer); Locust Ridge, Tenn. 1/19/1946
Pascal, Blaise (philosopher); Clermont, France (1623-1662)
Pasternak, Boris Leonidovich (author); Moscow (1890-1960)
Pasternak, Joseph (film producer); Silagy-Somlyo, Romania, 9/19/1901

Pasteur, Louis (chemist); Dôle, France (1822-1895)
Pastor, Tony (Antonio) (actor, theater manager); New York City (1837-1908)
Paton, Alan (author); Pietermaritzburg, South Africa (1903-1988)
Patti, Adelina (soprano); Madrid (1843-1919)
Patton, George Smith, Jr. (general); San Gabriel, Calif., (1885-1945)
Paul, Les (Lester William Polfus) (guitarist); Waukesha, Wis., 6/9/1915
Paul VI (Giovanni Battista Montini) (Pope); Concesio, nr. Brescia, Italy (1897-1978)
Pauley, Jane (TV newscaster); Indianapolis, 10/31/1950
Pauling, Linus Carl (chemist); Portland, Ore., 2/28/1901
Pavarotti, Luciano (tenor); Modena, Italy, 10/12/1935
Pavlov, Ivan Petrovich (physiologist); Ryazan district, Russia (1849-1936)
Pavlova, Anna (ballerina); St. Petersburg, Russia (1885-1931)
Paxinou, Katina (actress); Piraeus, Greece (1900-1973)
Payne, John (actor); Roanoke, Va. (1912-1989)
Peale, Norman Vincent (clergyman); Bowersville, Ohio, 5/31/1898
Pearl, Minnie (Sarah Ophelia Colley Cannon) (comedienne and singer); Centerville, Tenn., 10/25/1912
Pears, Peter (tenor); Farnham, England (1910-1986)
Pearson, Drew (Andrew Russel Pearson) (columnist); Evanston, Ill. (1897-1969)
Pearson, Lester B. (statesman); Toronto (1897-1972)
Peary, Robert Edwin (explorer); Cresson, Pa. (1856-1920)
Peck, Gregory (actor); La Jolla, Calif., 4/5/1916
Peckinpah, Sam (film director); Fresno, Calif. (1925-1984)
Peerce, Jan (tenor); New York City (1904-1984)
Pegler, (James) Westbrook (columnist); Minneapolis, (1894-1969)
Pei, I(eoh) M(ing) (architect); Canton, China, 4/26/1917
Penn, Arthur (stage and film director); Philadelphia, 9/27/1922
Penn, William (American colonist); London (1644-1718)
Penner, Joe (comedian); Hungary (1904-1941)
Penney, James C. (merchant); Hamilton, Mo. (1875-1971)
Peppard, George (actor); Detroit, 10/1/1928
Pepys, Samuel (diarist); Bampton, England (1633-1703)
Perelman, S(idney) J(oseph) (writer); Brooklyn, N.Y. (1904-1979)
Pergolesi, Giovanni Battista (composer); Jesi, Italy (1710-1736)
Pericles (statesman); Athens (died 429 B.C.)
Perkins, Osgood (actor); West Newton, Mass. (1892-1937)
Perkins, Tony (Anthony) (actor); New York City, 4/14/1932
Perlman, Itzhak (violinist); Tel Aviv, Israel, 8/31/1945
Perlman, Rhea (actress); Brooklyn, N.Y., 3/31/48
Perón, Isabel (María Estela Martínez Cartas) (former chief of state); La Rioja, Argentina, 2/4/1931
Perón, Juan D. (statesman); nr. Lobos, Argentina (1895-1974)
Perón, Maria Eva Duarte de (political leader); Los Toldos, Argentina (1919-1952)
Perrine, Valerie (actress and dancer); Galveston, Tex., 9/3/1943
Pershing, John Joseph (general); Linn County, Mo. (1860-1948)
Pestalozzi, Johann (educator); Zurich, Switzerland (1746-1827)
Peters, Bernadette (Bernadette Lazzara) (actress); New York City, 2/28/1944
Peters, Brock (actor-singer); New York City, 7/2/1927
Peters, Jean (actress); Canton, Ohio, 10/15/1926
Peters, Roberta (Roberta Peterman) (soprano); New York City, 5/4/1930
Petit, Roland (choreographer and dancer); Villemombe, France, 1924
Petrarch (Francesco Petrarca) (poet); Arezzo (Italy) (1304-1374)
Pfeiffer, Michelle (actress); Santa Ana, Calif., 4/29/58
Philip (Philip Mountbatten) (Duke of Edinburgh); Corfu, Greece, 6/10/1921
Piaf, Edith (Edith Gassion) (chanteuse); Paris (1916-1963)
Piatigorsky, Gregor (cellist); Ekaterinoslav, Russia (1903-1976)
Piazza, Ben (actor); Little Rock, Ark., 7/30/1934
Piazza, Marguerite (soprano); New Orleans, 5/6/1926
Picasso, Pablo (painter and sculptor); Málaga, Spain (1881-1973)
Pickford, Jack (Jack Smith) (actor); Toronto (1896-1933)
Pickford, Mary (Gladys Mary Smith) (actress); Toronto (1893-1979)
Picon, Molly (actress); New York City, 6/1/1898
Pidgeon, Walter (actor); East St. John, New Brunswick, Canada (1898-1984)
Pinter, Harold (playwright); London, 10/10/1930
Pinza, Ezio (basso); Rome (1892-1957)
Pirandello, Luigi (dramatist and novelist); nr. Girgenti, Italy (1867-1936)
Piranesi, Giambattista (artist); Mestre, Italy (1720-1778)
Pissaro, Camille Jacob (painter); St. Thomas (U.S. Virgin Islands) (1830-1903)
Piston, Walter (composer); Rockland, Me. (1894-1976)
Pitman, Sir (Isaac) James (educator and publisher); Bath, England, 8/14/1901
Pitt, William ("Younger Pitt") (statesman); nr. Bromley, England (1759-1806)
Pitts, ZaSu (actress); Parsons, Kan. (1898-1963)

Pius XII (Eugenio Pacelli) (Pope); Rome **(1876-1958)**
Pizarro, Francisco (explorer); Trujillo, Spain **(1470?-1541)**
Planck, Max (physicist); Kiel, Germany **(1858-1947)**
Plato (Aristocies) (philosopher); Athens (?) **(427?-347 B.C.)**
Pleasence, Donald (actor); Worksop, England, 10/5/1919
Pleshette, Suzanne (actress); New York City, 1/31/1937
Plimpton, George (author); New York City, 3/18/1927
Plisetskaya, Maya (ballerina); Moscow, 11/20/1925
Plowright, Joan (actress); Brigg, England, 10/28/1929
Plummer, Christopher (actor); Toronto, 12/13/1929
Plutarch (biographer); Chaeronea (Greece) **(46?-?120)**
Pocahontas (Matoaka) (American Indian princess); Virginia (?) **(1595?-1617)**
Podhoretz, Norman (author); Brooklyn, N.Y., 1/16/1930
Poe, Edgar Allan (poet and story writer); Boston, Mass. **(1809-1849)**
Poitier, Sidney (film actor and director); Miami, Fla., 2/20/1927
Polanski, Roman (film director); Paris, 8/18/1933
Pollard, Michael J. (actor); Passaic, N.J., 5/30/1939
Pollock, Jackson (painter); Cody, Wyo. **(1912-1956)**
Polo, Marco (traveler); Venice **(1254?-?1324)**
Pompadour, Mme. de (Jeanne Antoinette Poisson) (courtesan); Versailles **(1721-1764)**
Pompey (Gnaeus Pompeius Magnus) (general); Rome (?) **(106-48 B.C.)**
Ponce de León, Juan (explorer); Servas, Spain **(1460?-1521)**
Pons, Lily (coloratura soprano); Cannes, France **(1904-1976)**
Ponselle, Rosa (soprano); Meriden, Conn. **(1897-1981)**
Ponti, Carlo (director); Milan, Italy, 12/11/1913
Pope, Alexander (poet); London **(1688-1744)**
Porter, Cole (songwriter); Peru, Ind. **(1892?-1964)**
Porter, Katherine Anne (novelist); Indian Creek, Tex. **(1891-1980)**
Post, Wiley (aviator); Grand Plain, Tex. **(1900-1935)**
Poston, Tom (actor); Columbus, Ohio, 10/17/1927
Potëmkin, Grigori Aleksandrovich, Prince (statesman); Khizovo (Khizov, Belorussia, U.S.S.R.) **(1739-1791)**
Potok, Chaim (author); New York City, 2/17/1929
Poulenc, Francis (composer); Paris **(1899-1963)**
Pound, Ezra (poet); Hailey, Idaho **(1885-1972)**
Poussin, Nicolas (painter); Villers, France **(1594-1665)** ·
Powell, Adam Clayton, Jr. (Congressman); New Haven, Conn. **(1908-1972)**
Powell, Dick (actor); Mt. View, Ark. **(1904-1963)**
Powell, Eleanor (actress and tap dancer); Springfield, Mass. **(1912-1982)**
Powell, Jane (Suzanne Burce) (actress and singer); Portland, Ore., 4/1/1929
Powell, William (actor); Pittsburgh, **(1892-1984)**
Power, Tyrone (actor); Cincinnati, Ohio **(1914-1958)**
Powers, Stephanie (Taffy Paul) (actress); Hollywood, Calif., 11/12/1942
Praxiteles (sculptor); Athens **(c.370-c.330 B.C.)**
Preminger, Otto (film director and producer); Vienna **(1906-1986)**
Prentiss, Paula (Paula Ragusa) (actress); San Antonio, 1939
Presley, Elvis (singer and actor); Tupelo, Miss. **(1935-1977)**
Presley, Priscilla (actress); Brooklyn, N.Y., 5/24/45
Preston, Robert (Robert Preston Meservey) (actor); Newton Highlands, Mass **(1918-1987)**
Previn, André (conductor); Berlin, 4/6/1929
Previn, Dory (singer); Rahway, N.J., 10/22/1929(?)
Price, Leontyne (Mary) (soprano); Laurel, Miss., 2/10/1927
Price, Ray (country music artist); Perryville, Tex., 1/12/1926
Price, Vincent (actor); St. Louis, 5/27/1911
Pride, Charley (singer); Sledge, Miss., 3/18/1938(?)
Priestley, J. B. (John B.) (author); Bradford, England **(1894-1984)**
Priestley, Joseph (chemist); nr. Leeds, England **(1733-1804)**
Primrose, William (violist); Glasgow, Scotland **(1904-1982)**
Prince (Prince Roger Nelson) (singer); Minneapolis, 6/7/58
Prince, Harold (stage producer); New York City, 1/30/1928
Principal, Victoria (actress); Fukuoka, Japan, 1/3/45(?)
Prinze, Freddie (actor); New York City **(1954-1977)**
Pritchett, V(ictor) S(awdon) (literary critic); Ipswich, England, 12/16/1900
Procter, William (scientist); Cincinnati **(1872-1951)**
Prokofiev, Sergei Sergeevich (composer); St. Petersburg, Russia **(1891-1953)**
Proust, Marcel (novelist); Paris **(1871-1922)**
Provine, Dorothy (actress); Deadwood, S. Dak., 1/20/1937
Prowse, Juliet (actress); Bombay, 9/25/1936
Pryor, Richard (comedian); Peoria, Ill., 12/1/1940
Ptolemy (Claudius Ptolemaeus) (astronomer and geographer); Ptolemais Hermii (Egypt) **(2nd century A.D.)**
Pucci, Emilio (Marchese di Barsento) (fashion designer); Naples, Italy, 11/20/1914
Puccini, Giacomo (composer); Lucca, Italy **(1858-1924)**
Puente, Tito (band leader); New York City, 4/20/1923
Pulaski, Casimir (military officer); Podolia, Poland **(1748-1779)**

Pulitzer, Joseph (publisher); Makó (Hungary) **(1847-1911)**
Pullman, George (inventor); Brockton, N.Y. **(1831-1897)**
Purcell, Henry (composer); London **(1658-1695)**
Pusey, Nathan M. (educator); Council Bluffs, Iowa, 4/4/1907
Pushkin, Alexander Sergeevich (poet and dramatist); Moscow **(1799-1837)**
Puzo, Mario (novelist); New York City, 10/15/1921
Pyle, Ernest Taylor (journalist); Dana, Ind. **(1900-1945)**
Pythagoras (mathematician and philosopher); Samos (Greece) **(6th century B.C.)**

Q

Quaid, Randy, (actor); Houston, Texas, 10/1/1950
Quayle, Anthony (actor); Ainsdale, England **(1913-1989)**
Queen, Ellery: pen name of the late Frederic Dannay and the late Manfred B. Lee
Queler, Eve (conductor); New York City, 1/1/1936
Quennell, Peter Courtney (biographer); Bromley, England, 3/9/1905
Quinn, Anthony (actor); Chihuahua, Mexico, 4/21/1916

R

Rabe, David (playwright); Dubuque, Iowa, 3/10/1940
Rabelais, François (satirist); nr. Chinon, France **(1494?-1553)**
Rabi, I(sidor) I(saac) (physicist); Rymanow (Poland) **(1898-1988)**
Rachmaninoff, Sergei Wassilievitch (pianist and composer); Oneg Estate, Novgorod, Russia **(1873-1943)**
Racine, Jean Baptiste (dramatist); La Ferté-Milon, France **(1639-1699)**
Radner, Gilda (comedienne); Detroit **(1946-1989)**
Raft, George (actor); New York City **(1895-1980)**
Rainer, Luise (actress); Vienna, 1912
Raines, Ella (actress); Snoqualmie Falls, Wash. **(1921-1988)**
Rainier III (Prince); Monaco, 5/31/1923
Rains, Claude (actor); London **(1889-1967)**
Raitt, Bonnie (singer); Burbank, Calif., 11/8/1949
Raitt, John (actor/singer); Santa Ana, Calif., 1/29(?)/17
Raleigh, Sir Walter (courtier and navigator); London **(1552?-1618)**
Rambeau, Marjorie (actress); San Francisco **(1889-1970)**
Rameau, Jean-Philippe (composer); Dijon? France **(1683-1764)**
Rampal, Jean-Pierre (Louis) (flutist); Marseilles, France, 7/1/22
Randall, Tony (Leonard Rosenberg) (actor); Tulsa, Okla., 2/26/1920
Randolph, A(sa) Philip (labor leader); Crescent City, Fla. **(1889-1979)**
Raphael (Raffaello Santi) (painter and architect); Urbino (Italy) **(1483-1520)**
Rasputin, Grigori Efimovich (monk); Tobolsk Province, Russia **(1871?-1916)**
Rathbone, Basil (actor); Johannesburg, South Africa **(1892-1967)**
Rather, Dan (TV newscaster); Wharton, Tex., 10/31/1931
Ratoff, Gregory (film director); St. Petersburg, Russia **(1897-1960)**
Rattigan, Terence (playwright); London **(1911-1977)**
Rauschenberg, Robert (painter); Port Arthur, Tex., 10/22/1925
Ravel, Maurice Joseph (composer); Ciboure, France **(1875-1937)**
Rawls, Lou (singer); Chicago, 12/1/1935
Ray, Aldo (DaRe) (actor); Pen Argyl, Pa., 9/25/26
Ray, Gene Anthony (actor, dancer); Harlem, N.Y., 5/24/63
Ray, Man (painter); Philadelphia **(1890-1976)**
Ray, Satyajit (film director); Calcutta, 5/2/1922
Rayburn, Gene (TV personality); Christopher, Ill., 12/22/1917
Raye, Martha (Margie Yvonne Reed) (comedienne and actress); Butte, Mont., 8/27/1916
Raymond, Gene (actor); New York City, 8/13/1908
Reasoner, Harry (TV commentator); Dakota City, Iowa, 4/17/1923
Redding, Otis (singer); Dawson, Ga. **(1941-1967)**
Reddy, Helen (singer); Melbourne, 10/25/1941
Redford, Robert (Charles Robert Redford, Jr.) (actor); Santa Monica, Calif., 8/18/1937
Redgrave, Lynn (actress); London, 3/8/1943
Redgrave, Sir Michael (actor); Bristol, England **(1908-1985)**
Redgrave, Vanessa (actress); London, 1/30/1937
Reed, Donna (actress); Denison, Iowa **(1921-1986)**
Reed, Rex (critic); Ft. Worth, 10/2/1940
Reed, Walter (army surgeon); Belroi, Va. **(1851-1902)**
Reese, Della (Deloreese Patricia Early) (singer); Detroit, 7/6/1932
Reeve, Christopher (actor); New York City, 9/25/52
Reeves, Jim (singer); Panola County, Tex. **(1923-1964)**
Reich, Steve (composer); New York City, 10/3/1936
Reid, Wallace (actor); St. Louis **(1891-1923)**
Reiner, Carl (actor); New York City, 3/20/1922
Reiner, Fritz (conductor); Budapest **(1888-1963)**
Reiner, Robert (actor); Bronx, N.Y., 1945
Reinhardt, Max (Max Goldmann) (theater producer); nr. Vienna

(1873-1943)
Remarque, Erich Maria (novelist); Osnabrük, Germany (1898-1970)
Rembrandt (Rembrandt Harmensz van Rijn) (painter); Leyden (Netherlands) (1605-1669)
Remick, Lee (Ann) (actress); Boston, 12/14/1935
Rennert, Günther (opera director and producer); Essen, Germany, 4/1/1911
Rennie, Michael (actor); Bradford, England (1909-1971)
Renoir, Jean (film director and writer); Paris, (1894-1979)
Renoir, Pierre Auguste (painter); Limoges, France (1841-1919)
Resnais, Alain (film director); Vannes, France, 6/3/1922
Resnik, Regina (mezzo-soprano); New York City, 8/30/1922
Respighi, Ottorino (composer); Bologna, Italy (1879-1936)
Reston, James (journalist); Clydebank, Scotland, 11/3/1909
Reuther, Walter (labor leader); Wheeling, W. Va. (1907-1970)
Revere, Paul (silversmith and hero of famous ride); Boston (1735-1818)
Revson, Charles (business executive); Boston (1906-1975)
Reynolds, Burt (actor); Waycross, Ga., 2/11/1936
Renolds, Debbie (Marie Frances Reynolds) (actress); El Paso, 4/1/1932
Reynolds, Sir Joshua (painter); nr. Plymouth, England (1723-1792)
Reynolds, Marjorie (Goodspeed) (actress); Buhl, Idaho, 8/12/21
Rhodes, Cecil John (South African statesman); Bishop Stortford, England (1853-1902)
Rice, Elmer (playwright); New York City (1892-1967)
Rice, Grantland (sports writer); Murfreesboro, Tenn. (1880-1954)
Rich, Buddy (Bernard) (drummer); Brooklyn, N.Y. (1917-1987)
Rich, Charlie (singer); Colt, Ark., 12/14/1932
Richardson, Elliot L. (ex-Cabinet member); Boston, 7/20/1920
Richardson, Sir Ralph (actor); Cheltenham, England (1902-1983)
Richardson, Tony (director); Shipley, England, 6/5/1928
Richelieu, Duc de (Armand Jean du Plessis) (cardinal); Paris (1585-1642)
Richie, Lionel (singer-songwriter); Tuskegee, Ala., 1949 (?)
Richter, Charles Francis (seismologist); Hamilton, Canada (1900-1985)
Richter, Sviatosiav (pianist); Zhitomir, Ukraine, 3/20/1914
Rickenbacker, Edward V. (aviator); Columbus, Ohio (1890-1973)
Rickles, Don (comedian); New York City, 5/8/1926
Rickover, Vice Admiral Hyman G. (atomic energy expert); Russia (1900-1986)
Riddle, Nelson (composer); Hackensack, N.J. (1921-1985)
Ride, Sally K(risten) (astronaut, astrophysicist); Encino, Calif., 5/26/1951
Ridgway, General Matthew B. (ex-Army Chief of Staff); Ft. Monroe, Va., 3/3/1895
Rigg, Diana (actress); Doncaster, England, 7/20/1938
Riley, James Whitcomb (poet); Greenfield, Ind. (1849-1916)
Rimsky-Korsakov, Nikolai Andreevich (composer); Tikhvin, Russia (1844-1908)
Rinehart, Mary (née Roberts) (novelist); Pittsburgh (1876-1958)
Ritchard, Cyril (actor and director); Sydney, Australia (1898-1977)
Ritter, John (Jonathan) (actor); Burbank, Calif., 9/17/1948
Ritter, Tex (Woodward Maurice Ritter) (singer); Panola County, Tex., (1905-1973)
Ritter, Thelma (actress); Brooklyn, N.Y. (1905-1969)
Rivera, Chita (Dolores Conchita Figuero del Rivero) (dancer-actress-singer); Washington, D.C. 1/23/1933
Rivera, Diego (painter); Guanajuato, Mexico (1886-1957)
Rivera, Geraldo (Miguel) (TV newscaster); New York City, 7/3/1943
Rivers, Joan (comedienne); Brooklyn, N.Y., 6/8/1933
Rivers, Larry (Yitzroch Loiza Grossberg) (painter); New York City, 8/17/1923
Robards, Jason, Jr. (actor); Chicago, 7/26/1922
Robards, Jason, Sr. (actor); Hillsdale, Mich. (1892-1963)
Robbins, Harold (Harold Rubin) (novelist); New York City, 5/21/1916
Robbins, Jerome (Jerome Rabinowitz) (choreographer); New York City, 10/11/1918
Robbins, Marty (singer); Glendale, Ariz., (1925-1982)
Roberts, Eric (actor); Bilox, Miss., 4/18/1956
Roberts, (Granville) Oral (evangelist and publisher); nr. Ada, Okla., 1/24/1918
Robertson, Cliff (actor); La Jolla, Calif., 9/9/1925
Robertson, Dale (Dayle) (actor); Oklahoma City, 7/14/1923
Robeson, Paul (singer and actor); Princeton, N.J., (1898-1976)
Robespierre, Maximilien François Marie Isidore de (French Revolutionist); Arras, France (1758-1794)
Robinson, Bill "Bojangles" (Luther) (dancer); Richmond, Va. (1878-1949)
Robinson, Edward G. (Emanuel Goldenberg) (actor); Bucharest (1893-1973)
Robinson, Edwin Arlington (poet); Head Tide, Me. (1869-1935)
Robson, Dame Flora (actress); South Shields, England (1902-1984)
Robson, May (actress); Melbourne, Australia (1858-1942)
Rochester (Eddie Anderson) (actor); Oakland, Calif. (1905-1977)

Rockefeller, David (banker); New York City, 6/12/1915
Rockefeller, John Davison (capitalist); Richford, N.Y. (1839-1937)
Rockefeller, John Davison, Jr. (industrialist); Cleveland (1874-1960)
Rockefeller, John D., 3rd (philanthropist); New York City (1906-1978)
Rockefeller, Laurance S. (conservationist); New York City, 5/26/1910
Rockwell, Norman (painter and illustrator); New York City, (1894-1978)
Rodgers, Jimmie (singer); Meridian, Miss. (1897-1933)
Rodgers, Richard (composer); New York City (1902-1979)
Rodin, François Auguste René (sculptor); Paris (1840-1917)
Rodzinski, Artur (conductor); Spalato, Dalmatia (1894-1958)
Roentgen, Wilhelm Konrad (physicist); Lennep, Prussia (1845-1923)
Rogers, Buddy (Charles) (actor); Olathe, Kan., 8/13/1904
Rogers, Fred (Television producer, host); Latrobe, Pa., 3/20/28
Rogers, Ginger (Virginia McMath) (dancer and actress); Independence, Mo., 7/16/1911
Rogers, Kenny (singer); Houston, 1939(?)
Rogers, Roy (Leonard Slye) (actor); Cincinnati, 11/5/1912
Rogers, Wayne (actor); Birmingham, Ala. 4/7/33
Rogers, Will (William Penn Adair Rogers) (humorist); Oologah, Okla. (1879-1935)
Rogers, William P. (ex-Secretary of State); Norfolk, N.Y., 6/23/1913
Roland, Gilbert (actor); Juarez, Mexico, 12/11/1905
Rolland, Romain (author); Clamecy, France (1866-1944)
Rollins, Sonny (saxophonist); New York City, 9/7/1930
Romberg, Sigmund (composer); Szeged (Hungary) (1887-1951)
Rome, Harold (composer); Hartford, Conn., 5/27/1908
Romero, Cesar (actor); New York City, 2/15/1907
Romney, George W. (ex-Secretary of HUD); Chihuahua, Mexico, 7/8/1907
Romulo, Carlos P. (diplomat and educator); Manila (1899-1985)
Ronsard, Pierre de (poet); La Possonnière nr. Couture (Couture-sur-Loir, France) (1524-1585)
Ronstadt, Linda (singer); Tucson, Ariz., 7/30/1946
Rooney, Andy (TV personality); Albany, N.Y., 1/14/1919
Rooney, Mickey (Joe Yule, Jr.) (actor); Brooklyn, N.Y., 9/23/1920
Roosevelt, Anna Eleanor (reformer and humanitarian); New York City (1884-1962)
Rorem, Ned (composer); Richmond, Ind., 10/23/23
Rose, Billy (showman); New York City (1899-1966)
Rose, Leonard (concert cellist); Washington, D.C. (1918-1984)
Ross, Betsy (Betsey Griscom) (flagmaker); Philadelphia (1752-1836)
Ross, Diana (singer); Detroit, 3/26/1944
Ross, Katharine (actress); Hollywood, Calif., 1/29/1943
Rossellini, Isabella (model, actress); Rome, Italy, 6/18/1952
Rossellini, Roberto (film director); Rome (1906-1977)
Rossetti, Dante Gabriel (painter and poet); London (1828-1882)
Rossini, Gioacchino Antonio (composer); Pesaro (Italy) (1792-1868)
Rostand, Edmond (dramatist); Marseilles, France (1868-1918)
Rostow, Walt Whitman (economist); New York City, 10/7/1916
Rostropovich, Mstislav (cellist and conductor); Baku, U.S.S.R., 3/27/1927
Roth, Lillian (singer); Boston (1910-1980)
Roth, Philip (novelist); Newark, N.J., 3/19/1933
Rothko, Mark (Marcus Rothkovich) (painter); Russia (1903-1970)
Rouault, Georges (painter); Paris (1871-1958)
Roundtree, Richard (actor); New Rochelle, N.Y., 9/7/1942
Rousseau, Henri (painter); Laval, France (1844-1910)
Rousseau, Jean Jacques (philosopher); Geneva (1712-1778)
Rovere, Richard H. (journalist); Jersey City, N.J., 5/5/1915
Rowan, Dan (comedian); Beggs, Okla. (1922-1987)
Rowlands, Gena (actress); Cambria, Wis., 6/19/1936(?)
Rubens, Sir Peter Paul (painter); Siegen (Germany) (1577-1640)
Rubinstein, Arthur (concert pianist); Lódz (Poland) (1887-1982)
Rubinstein, Helena (cosmetics executive); Krakow (Poland) (1882?-1965)
Rubinstein, John (actor, composer); Los Angeles, 12/8/46
Rudel, Julius (conductor); Vienna, 3/6/1921
Ruffo, Titta (baritone); Italy (1878-1953)
Ruggles, Charles (actor); Los Angeles (1892-1970)
Rule, Janice (actress); Norwood, Ohio, 8/15/1931
Runcie, Robert (Alexander Kennedy) (Archbishop of Canterbury); Liverpool, England, 10/2/1921
Runyon, (Alfred) Damon (journalist); Manhattan, Kan. (1884-1945)
Rusk, Dean (ex-Sec. of State); Cherokee County, Ga., 2/9/1909
Ruskin, John (art critic); London (1819-1900)
Russell, Lord Bertrand (Arthur William) (mathematician and philosopher); Trelleck, Wales (1872-1970)
Russell, Jane (actress); Bemidji, Minn., 6/21/1921
Russell, Ken (film director); Southhampton, England, 4/3/27
Russell, Leon (pianist and singer); Lawton, Okla., 4/2/1941
Russell, Lillian (Helen Louise Leonard) (soprano); Clinton, Iowa (1861-1965)
Russell, Mark (satirist); Buffalo, N.Y., 8/23/32

Russell, Nipsy (comedian); Atlanta, 1924(?)
Russell, Rosalind (actress); Waterbury, Conn. **(1912-1976)**
Rustin, Bayard (civil rights leader); West Chester, Pa. **(1910-1987)**
Rutherford, Dame Margaret (actress); London **(1892-1972)**
Ryan, Robert (actor); Chicago **(1909-1973)**
Rydell, Bobby (singer); Philadelphia, 1942
Rysanek, Leonie (dramatic soprano); Vienna, 11/14/1928

S

Saarinen, Eero (architect); Finland **(1910-1961)**
Sabin, Albert B. (polio researcher); Bialystok (Poland), 8/26/1906
Sabu (Dastagir) (actor); Karapur, India **(1924-1963)**
Sadat, Anwar el- (President); Egypt **(1918-1981)**
Sade, Marquis de (Donatien Alphonse Francois, Comte de Sade) (libertine and writer); Paris **(1740-1814)**
Safer, Morley (TV newscaster); Toronto, 11/8/1931
Sagan, Carl (Edward) (astronomer, astrophysicist); New York City, 11/9/1934
Sagan, Françoise (novelist); Cajarc, France, 6/21/1935
Sahl, Mort (Morton Lyon Sahl) (comedian); Montreal, 5/11/1927
Saint, Eva Marie (actress); Newark, N.J., 7/4/1924
Saint-Gaudens, Augustus (sculptor); Dublin **(1848-1907)**
St. Denis, Ruth (dancer,choreographer); Newark, N.J. **(1878-1968)**
St. James, Susan (Susan Miller) (actress); Los Angeles, 8/14/1946
St. John, Jill (actress); Los Angeles, 8/19/1940
St. Johns, Adela Rogers (journalist and author); Los Angeles **(1894-1988)**
Saint-Laurent, Yves (Henri Donat Mathieu) (fashion designer); Oran, Algeria, 8/1/1936
Saint-Saens, Charles Camille (composer); Paris **(1835-1921)**
Sainte-Marie, Buffy (Beverly) (folk singer); Craven, Saskatchewan, Canada, 2/20/1942(?)
Sales, Soupy (Milton Hines); Franklinton, N.C., 1/6/26
Salinger, J(erome) D(avid) (novelist); New York City, 1/1/1919
Salisbury, Harrison E. (journalist); Minneapolis, 11/14/1908
Salk, Jonas (polio researcher); New York City, 10/28/1914
Salk, Leo (psychologist); New York City, 1926
Salomon, Haym (American Revolution financier); Leszno, Poland **(1740-1785)**
Sand, George (Amandine Lucille Aurore Dudevant, née Dupin) (novelist); Paris **(1804-1876)**
Sandburg, Carl (poet and biographer); Galesburg, Ill. **(1878-1967)**
Sanders, George (actor); St. Petersburg, Russia **(1906-1972)**
Sands, Tommy (singer); Chicago, 8/27/1937
Sanger, Margaret (birth control leader); Corning, N.Y. **(1883-1966)**
Santayana, George (philosopher); Madrid **(1863-1952)**
Sappho (poet); Lesbos (Greece) (lived c. 600 B.C.)
Sargent, John Singer (painter); Florence, Italy **(1856-1925)**
Sarnoff, David (radio executive); Minsk, Russia **(1891-1971)**
Saroyan, William (novelist); Fresno, Calif. **(1908-1981)**
Sarrazin, Michael (actor); Quebec, 5/22/1940
Sarto, Andrea del (Andrea Domenico d'Agnolo di Francesco) (painter); Florence (Italy) **(1486-1531)**
Sartre, Jean-Paul (existentialist writer); Paris **(1905-1980)**
Sassoon, Vidal (hair stylist); London, 1/(?)/1928
Saul (King of Israel) (11th century B.C.)
Savalas, Telly (actor); Garden City, N.Y., 1/21/1924(?)
Savonarola, Girolamo (religious reformer); Ferrara, Italy **(1452-1498)**
Sawyer, Diane (broadcast journalist); Glasgow, Ky., 12/22/1945
Sayão, Bidú (soprano); Rio de Janeiro, 5/11/1902
Scaasi, Arnold (Arnold Isaacs) (fashion designer); Montreal
Scarlatti, Alessandro (composer); Palermo, Italy **(1659-1725)**
Scarlatti, Domenico (composer); Naples, Italy **(1685-1757)**
Scavullo, Francesco (photographer); Staten Island, N.Y. 1/16/1929
Schary, Dore (producer and writer); Newark, N.J. **(1905-1980)**
Schell, Maria (actress); Vienna, 1/15/1926
Schell, Maximilian (actor); Vienna, 12/8/1930
Schiaparelli, Elsa (fashion designer); Rome **(1890?-1973)**
Schiff, Dorothy (newspaper publisher); New York City **(1903-1989)**
Schildkraut, Joseph (actor); Vienna **(1896-1964)**
Schiller, Johann Christoph Friedrich von (dramatist and poet); Marbach (Germany) **(1759-1805)**
Schipa, Tito (tenor); Lecce, Italy **(1890-1965)**
Schippers, Thomas (conductor); Kalamazoo, Mich. **(1930-1977)**
Schlegel, Friedrich von (philosopher); Hanover? Germany **(1772-1829)**
Schlesinger, Arthur M., Jr. (historian); Columbus, Ohio, 10/15/1917
Schnabel, Artur (pianist,composer); Lipnik, Austria **(1882-1951)**
Schneider, Romy (Rose-Marie Albach) (actress); Vienna **(1938-1982)**
Schoenberg, Arnold (composer); Vienna **(1874-1951)**
Schopenhauer, Arthur (philosopher); Danzig (Poland) **(1788-1860)**
Schubert, Franz Peter (composer); Vienna **(1797-1828)**

Schulberg, Budd (novelist); New York City, 3/27/1914
Schulz, Charles M. (cartoonist); Minneapolis, 11/26/1922
Schuman, Robert (statesman); Luxembourg **(1886-1963)**
Schuman, William (composer); New York City, 8/4/1910
Schumann, Robert Alexander (composer); Zwickau (East Germany) **(1810-1856)**
Schumann-Heink, Ernestine (contralto); near Prague **(1861-1936)**
Schwartz, Arthur (song writer); Brooklyn, N.Y. **(1900-1984)**
Schwarzenegger, Arnold (bodybuilder, actor); Graz, Austria, 7/30/47
Schwarzkopf, Elisabeth (soprano); Jarotschin, Poznán (Poland), 12/9/1915
Schweitzer, Albert (humanitarian); Kaysersburg, Upper Alsace **(1875-1965)**
Scofield, Paul (actor); Hurstpierpoint, England, 1/21/1922
Scorsese, Martin (film director); Flushing, N.Y., 11/17/1942
Scott, George C. (actor); Wise, Va., 10/18/1927
Scott, Hazel (singer, pianist); Port of Spain, Trinidad **(1920-1981)**
Scott, Lizabeth (Emma Matso) (actress); Scranton, Pa., 1923
Scott, Martha (actress); Jamesport, Mo., 9/22/1914
Scott, Randolph (Randolph Crane) (actor); Orange County, Va **(1898-1987)**
Scott, Robert Falcon (explorer); Devonport, England **(1868-1912)**
Scott, Sir Walter (novelist); Edinburgh, Scotland **(1771-1832)**
Scott, Zachary (actor); Austin, Tex. **(1914-1965)**
Scotto, Renata (operatic soprano); Savona, Italy, 2/?/1936?
Scruggs, Earl Eugene (bluegrass musician); Cleveland County, N.C., 1/6/1924
Sebastian, John (composer); New York City, 3/17/1944
Seberg, Jean (actress); Marshalltown, Iowa **(1938-1979)**
Sedaka, Neil (singer); Brooklyn, N.Y., 3/13/1939
Seeger, Pete (folk singer); New York City, 5/3/1919
Segal, Erich (novelist); Brooklyn, N.Y., 6/16/1937
Segal, George (actor); New York City, 2/13/1936
Segovia, Andrés (guitarist); Linares, Spain **(1893-1987)**
Selleck, Tom (actor); Detroit, 1/29/1945
Sellars, Peter (theater director); Pittsburgh, Pa., 1958 (?)
Sellers, Peter (actor); Southsea, England **(1925-1980)**
Selznick, David O. (film producer); Pittsburgh **(1902-1965)**
Sendak, Maurice (Bernard) (children's book author and illustrator); Brooklyn, N.Y., 6/10/1928
Sennett, Mack (Michael Sinnott) (film producer); Richmond, Quebec, Canada **(1880-1960)**
Serkin, Peter (pianist); New York City, 7/24/1947
Serkin, Rudolf (pianist); Eger (Hungary), 3/28/1903
Serling, Rod (story writer); Syracuse, N.Y. **(1924-1975)**
Sessions, Roger (composer); Brooklyn, N.Y. **(1896-1985)**
Seurat, Georges (painter); Paris **(1859-1891)**
Seuss, Dr. (Theodor Seuss Geisel) (author and illustrator); Springfield, Mass., 3/2/1904
Sevareid, Eric (TV commentator); Velva, N.D., 11/26/1912
Severinsen, Doc (Carl) (band leader); Arlington, Ore., 7/7/1927
Sexton, Anne (poet); Newton, Mass. **(1928-1974)**
Seymour, Jane (actress); Wimbledon, England, 2/15/51
Shaffer, Peter (playwright); Liverpool, England, 5/15/1926
Shahn, Ben(jamin) (painter); Kaunas, Lithuania **(1898-1969)**
Shakespeare, William (dramatist); Stratford on Avon, England **(1564-1616)**
Shandling, Garry (comedian); Chicago, Ill., 1950
Shankar, Ravi (sitar player); Benares, India, 4/7/1920
Shanker, Albert (labor leader); New York City, 9/14/1928
Sharif, Omar (Michael Shalhoub) (actor); Alexandria, Egypt, 4/10/1932
Shatner, William (actor); Montreal, 3/22/1931
Shaw, Artie (Arthur Arshawsky) (band leader); New York City, 5/23/1910
Shaw, George Bernard (dramatist); Dublin, **(1856-1950)**
Shaw, Irwin (novelist); Brooklyn, N.Y., **(1913-1984)**
Shaw, Robert (actor); Lancashire, England **(1927-1978)**
Shaw, Robert (chorale conductor); Red Bluff, Calif., 4/30/1916
Shawn, Ted (Edwin Myers Shawn) (dancer,choreographer); Kansas City, Mo. **(1891-1972)**
Shearer, Moira (ballerina); Dunfermline, Scotland, 1/17/1926
Shearer, Norma (actress); Montreal, **(1902?-1983)**
Shearing, George (pianist); London, 8/13/1920
Sheen, Fulton J. (Peter Sheen) (Roman Catholic bishop); El Paso, Ill. **(1895-1979)**
Sheen, Martin (Ramon Estevez) (actor); Dayton, Ohio, 8/3/1940
Shelley, Percy Bysshe (poet); nr. Horsham, England **(1792-1822)**
Shepard, Sam (playwright); Ft. Sheridan, Ill. 11/5/1943
Shepherd, Cybill (actress); Memphis, Tenn., 2/18/50
Sheraton, Thomas (furniture designer); Stockton-on-Tees, England **(1751-1806)**
Sheridan, Ann (actress); Denton, Tex. **(1915-1967)**
Sheridan, Philip (army officer); Albany, N.Y. **(1831-1888)**
Sheridan, Richard Brinsley (dramatist); Dublin, **(1751-1816)**
Sherman, William Tecumseh (army officer); Lancaster, Ohio **(1820-**

1891)

Sherwood, Robert Emmet (playwright); New Rochelle, N.Y. (1896-1955)

Shevardnadze, Eduard Amvrosiyevich (Minister of Foreign Affairs, U.S.S.R.); Mamati, Georgia, U.S.S.R. 1/25/1928

Shields, Brooke (actress); New York City, 5/31/1965

Shire, Talia (Coppola) (actress) Lake Success, N.Y. 4/25/46(?)

Shirer, William L. (journalist and historian); Chicago, 2/23/1904

Shirley, Anne (actress); New York City, 4/17/18

Sholokhov, Mikhail (novelist); Veshenskaya, Russia (1905-1984)

Shore, Dinah (Frances Rose Shore) (singer); Winchester, Tenn., 3/1/1917(?)

Short, Bobby (Robert Waltrip Short) (singer and pianist); Danville, Ill., 9/15/1924

Shostakovich, Dmitri (composer); St. Petersburg, Russia (1906-1975)

Shriner, Herb (humorist,host); Toledo, Ohio (1918-1970)

Shriver, Maria (TV co-host); Chicago, 11/6/1955

Shriver, Sargent (Robert Sargent Shriver, Jr.) (business executive); Westminster, Md., 11/9/1915

Shulman, Max (novelist); St. Paul (1919-1988)

Sibelius, Jean (Johann Julius Christian Sibelius) (composer); Tavastehus (Finland) (1865-1957)

Siddons, Sarah (Sarah Kemble) (actress); Wales (1755-1831)

Sidney, Sylvia (actress); New York City, 8/8/1910

Siepi, Cesare (basso); Milan, Italy, 2/10/1923

Signoret, Simone (Simone Kaminker) (actress); Wiesbaden, Germany (1921-1985)

Sikorsky, Igor I. (inventor); Kiev, Russia (1889-1972)

Sills, Beverly (Belle Silverman) (soprano, opera director); Brooklyn, N.Y., 5/25/1929

Sills, Milton (actor); Chicago (1882-1930)

Silone, Ignazio (Secondo Tranquilli) (novelist); Pescina del Marsi, Italy (1900-1978)

Silverman, Fred (broadcasting executive); New York City, 9/13/1937

Silvers, Phil (Philip Silversmith) (comedian); Brooklyn, N.Y. (1912-1985)

Sim, Alastair (actor); Edinburgh, Scotland (1900-1976)

Simenon, Georges (Georges Sim) (mystery writer); Liège, Belgium (1903-1989)

Simmons, Jean (actress); Crouch Hill, London, 1/31/1929

Simon, Carly (singer and songwriter); New York City, 6/25/1945

Simon, Neil (playwright); Bronx, N.Y., 7/4/1927

Simon, Norton (business executive); Portland, Ore., 2/5/1907

Simon, Paul (singer and songwriter); Newark, N.J., 11/5/1942

Simon, Simone (actress); Marseilles, France, 4/23/1914

Simone, Nina (Eunice Kathleen Waymoa) (singer and pianist); Tryon, N.C., 2/21/1933

Sinatra, Frank (Francis Albert) (singer and actor); Hoboken, N.J., 12/12/1915

Sinclair, Upton Beall (novelist); Baltimore (1878-1968)

Singer, Isaac Bashevis (novelist); Radzymin (Poland), 7/14/1904

Siqueiros, David (painter); Chihuahua, Mexico (1896-1974)

Sisley, Alfred (painter); Paris (1839-1899)

Sitting Bull (Prairie Sioux Indian Chief); on Grand River, S.D. (c. 1835-1890)

Skelton, Red (Richard) (comedian); Vincennes, Ind., 7/18/1913

Skinner, B(urrhus) F(rederic) (psychologist); Susquehanna, Pa. (1904-1990)

Skinner, Cornelia Otis (writer and actress); Chicago, (1901-1979)

Skinner, Otis (actor); Cambridge, Mass. (1858-1942)

Slatkin, Leonard (conductor); Los Angeles, 9/1/1944

Slezak, Walter (actor); Vienna (1902-1983)

Sloan, Alfred P., Jr. (industrialist); New Haven, Conn. (1875-1965)

Sloan, John (painter); Lock Haven, Pa. (1871-1951)

Smetana, Bedrich (composer); Litomysl (Czechoslovakia) (1824-1884)

Smith, Adam (economist); Kirkaldy, Scotland (1723-1790)

Smith, Alexis (actress); Penticon, Canada, 6/8/1921

Smith, Alfred Emanuel (politician); New York City (1873-1944)

Smith, Sir C. Aubrey (actor); London (1863-1948)

Smith, David (sculptor); Decatur, Ind. (1906-1965)

Smith, H. Allen (humorist); McLeansboro, Ill. (1907-1976)

Smith, Howard K. (TV commentator); Ferriday, La., 5/12/1914

Smith, Jaclyn (actress); Houston, 10/26/47

Smith, John (American colonist); Willoughby, Lincolnshire, England (1580-1631)

Smith, Joseph (religious leader); Sharon, Vt. (1805-1844)

Smith, Kate (Kathryn) (singer); Greenville, Va. (1909-1986)

Smith, Dame Maggie (actress); Ilford, England, 12/28/1934

Smith, Red (Walter) (sports columnist); Green Bay, Wis. (1905-1982)

Smits, Jimmy (actor); New York City, 7/9/58

Smollet, Tobias (novelist); Dalquhurn, Scotland (1721-1771)

Smothers, Dick (Richard) (comedian); Governors Island, New York City, 11/20/1939

Smothers, Tom (Thomas) (comedian); Governors Island, New York

City, 2/2/1937

Snow, Lord (Charles Percy) (author); Leicester, England (1905-1980)

Snowdon, Earl of (Anthony Armstrong-Jones) (photographer); London, 3/7/1930

Snyder, Tom (TV personality); Milwaukee, 5/12/1936

Socrates (philosopher); Athens (469-399 B.C.)

Solomon (King of Israel); Jerusalem (?) (died c. 933 B.C.)

Solon (lawgiver); Salamis (Greece) (638?-559 B.C.)

Solti, Sir Georg (conductor); Budapest, 10/21/1912

Solzhenitsyn, Aleksandr (novelist); Kislovodsk, Russia, 12/11/1918

Somers, Suzanne (Suzanne Mahoney) (actress); San Bruno, Calif., 10/16/1946

Somes, Michael (ballet dancer); Horsley, England, 1917

Sommer, Elke (Elke Schletz) (actress); Berlin, 11/5/1942

Sondheim, Stephen (composer); New York City, 3/22/1930

Sontag, Susan (author and film director); New York City, 1/28/1933

Sophocles (dramatist); nr. Athens (496?-406 B.C.)

Sothern, Ann (Harriette Lake) (actress); Valley City, N.D., 1/22/1909

Soul, David (David Solberg) (actor); Chicago, 8/28/(?)

Sousa, John Philip (composer); Washington, D.C. (1854-1932)

Soyer, Raphael (painter); Borisoglebsk, Russia (1899-1987)

Spaak, Paul-Henri (statesman); Brussels (1899-1972)

Spacek, Sissy (Mary Elizabeth) (actress); Quitman, Tex., 12/25/1949

Spark, Muriel (novelist); Edinburgh, Scotland, 2/1/1918

Sparks, Ned (actor); Ontario (1883-1957)

Spector, Phil (rock producer); Bronx, N.Y., 12/25/1940

Spencer, Herbert (philosopher); Derby, England (1820-1903)

Spender, Stephen (poet); nr. London, 2/28/1909

Spengler, Oswald (philosopher); Blankenburg, (East Germany) (1880-1936)

Spenser, Edmund (poet); London (1552?-1599)

Spewack, Bella (playwright); Hungary (1899-1990)

Spiegel, Sam (producer); Jaroslaw (Poland) (1901-1985)

Spielberg, Steven (film director); Cincinnati, 12/18/1947

Spillane, Mickey (Frank Spillane) (mystery writer); Brooklyn, N.Y., 3/9/1918

Spinoza, Baruch (philosopher); Amsterdam (Netherlands) (1632-1677)

Spitalny, Phil (orchestra leader); (1890-1970)

Spivak, Lawrence (TV producer); Brooklyn, N.Y., 1900

Spock, Benjamin (pediatrician); New Haven, Conn., 5/2/1903

Springsteen, Bruce (singer and songwriter); Freehold, N.J., 9/23/1949

Sproul, Robert G. (educator); San Francisco (1891-1975)

Stack, Robert (actor); Los Angeles, 1/13/1919

Stafford, Jo (singer); Coalinga, Calif., 1918

Stalin, Joseph Vissarionovich (Iosif V. Dzhugashvili) (Soviet leader); nr. Tiflis, Russia (1879-1953)

Stalina, Svetlana Alliluyeva (Stalin's daughter); Moscow, 2/28/1926

Stallone, Sylvester (actor and writer); New York City, 7/6/1946

Stamp, Terrence (actor); London, 1938

Stander, Lionel (actor); New York City, 1/11/08

Standing, Sir Guy (actor); London (1873-1937)

Stang, Arnold (comedian); Chelsea, Mass., 1925

Stanislavski (Konstantin Sergeevich Alekseev) (stage producer); Moscow (1863-1938)

Stanley, Sir Henry Morton (John Rowlands) (explorer); Denbigh, Wales (1841-1904)

Stanley, Kim (Patricia Reid) (actress); Tularosa, N.M., 2/11/1925

Stans, Maurice H. (ex-Secretary of Commerce); Shakope, Minn., 3/22/1908

Stanton, Frank (broadcasting executive); Muskegon, Mich., 3/20/1908

Stanwyck, Barbara (Ruby Stevens) (actress); Brooklyn, N.Y. (1907-1990)

Stapleton, Jean (Jeanne Murray) (actress); New York City, 1/19/1923

Stapleton, Maureen (actress); Troy, N.Y., 6/21/1925

Starker, Janós (cellist); Budapest 7/5/1926

Starr, Kay (Starks) (singer); Dougherty, Okla., 7/21/1922

Starr, Ringo (Richard Starkey) (singer and songwriter); Liverpool, England, 7/7/1940

Stassen, Harold E. (ex-government official); West St. Paul, Minn., 4/13/1907

Steber, Eleanor (soprano); Wheeling, W. Va., 7/17/16

Steegmuller, Francis (biographer); New Haven, Conn., 7/3/1906

Steele, Tommy (singer); London, 12/17/1936

Stegner, Wallace (Earle) (novelist and critic); Lake Mills, Iowa, 2/18/1909

Steichen, Edward Jean (photographer, artist); Luxembourg (1879-1973)

Steiger, Rod (Rodney) (actor); Westhampton, N.Y., 4/14/1925

Stein, Gertrude (author); Allegheny, Pa. (1874-1946)

Steinbeck, John Ernst (novelist); Salinas, Calif. (1902-1968)

Steinberg, David (comedian); Winnipeg, Manitoba, Canada, 8/19/1942

Steinberg, William (conductor); Cologne, Germany **(1899-1978)**
Steinem, Gloria (feminist); Toledo, Ohio, 3/25/1934
Steinmetz, Charles (electrical engineer); Breslau (Poland) **(1865-1923)**
Stendhal (Marie Henri Beyle) (novelist); Grenoble, France **(1783-1842)**
Sterling, Jan (actress); New York City, 4/3/1923
Stern, Isaac (concert violinist); Kreminlecz, Russia, 7/21/1920
Sterne, Laurence (novelist); Clonmel, Ireland **(1713-1768)**
Stevens, Cat (Steven Georgiou) (singer and songwriter); London, 7/?/1947
Stevens, Connie (Concetta Ingolia) (singer); Brooklyn, N.Y., 8/8/1938
Stevens, George (film director); Oakland, Calif. **(1905-1975)**
Stevens, Risë (mezzo-soprano); New York City, 6/11/1913
Stevens, Stella (actress); Yazoo City, Miss., 10/1/1936
Stevenson, Adlai Ewing (statesman); Los Angeles **(1900-1965)**
Stevenson, McLean (actor); Bloomington, Ill., 11/14/1929(?)
Stevenson, Parker (actor); Philadelphia, Pa., 6/4/52
Stevenson, Robert Louis Balfour (novelist and poet); Edinburgh, Scotland **(1850-1894)**
Stewart, James (actor); Indiana, Pa., 5/20/1908
Stewart, Rod (Roderick David) (singer); London, 1/10/1945
Stickney, Dorothy (actress); Dickinson, N.D. 6/21/1903
Stieglitz, Alfred (photographer); Hoboken, N.J. **(1864-1946)**
Stiers, David Ogden (actor); Peoria, Ill., 10/31/42
Stiller, Jerry (actor); Brooklyn, N.Y., 6/8/29
Stills, Stephen (singer and songwriter); Dallas, 1/3/1945
Sting (Gordon Matthew Sumner) (singer and composer); Wallsend, England, 10/2/1951
Stockwell, Dean (actor); North Hollywood, Calif., 3/5/36
Stokes, Carl (TV newscaster); Cleveland, 6/21/1927
Stokowski, Leopold (conductor); London **(1882-1977)**
Stone, Edward Durell (architect); Fayetteville, Ark. **(1902-1978)**
Stone, Ezra (actor and producer); New Bedford, Mass., 12/2/1917
Stone, I(sidor) F(einstein) (journalist); Philadelphia **(1907-1989)**
Stone, Irving (Irving Tennenbaum) (novelist); San Francisco **(1903-1989)**
Stone, Lewis (actor); Worcester, Mass. **(1879-1953)**
Stone, Lucy (woman suffragist); nr. West Brookfield, Mass. **(1818-1893)**
Stone, Sly (Sylvester) (rock musician); 1944
Stoppard, Tom (Thomas Straussler) (playwright); Zlin, Czechoslovakia, 7/3/1937
Storm, Gale (actress); Bloomington, Tex., 1922
Stout, Rex (mystery writer); Noblesville, Ind. **(1886-1975)**
Stowe, Harriet Elizabeth Beecher (novelist); Litchfield, Conn. **(1811-1896)**
Stradivari, Antonio (violinmaker); Cremona (Italy) **(1644-1737)**
Straight, Beatrice (actress); Old Westbury, N.Y., 8/2/16(?)
Strasberg, Lee (stage director); Budanov, Austria **(1901-1982)**
Strasberg, Susan (actress); New York City, 5/22/1938
Stratas, Teresa (soprano); Toronto, Ont., Canada, 5/26/38
Straus, Oskar (composer); Vienna **(1870-1954)**
Strauss, Johann (composer); Vienna **(1825-1899)**
Strauss, Lewis L. (naval officer and scientist); Charleston, W. Va. **(1896-1974)**
Strauss, Peter (actor); New York City, 2/20/1947
Strauss, Richard (composer); Munich, Germany **(1864-1949)**
Stravinsky, Igor (composer); Orlenbaum, Russia **(1882-1971)**
Streep, Meryl (Mary Louise) (actress); Summit, N.J., 6/22/1949
Streisand, Barbra (singer and actress); Brooklyn, N.Y., 4/24/1942
Stritch, Elaine (actress); Detroit, 2/2/1925(?)
Struthers, Sally Ann (actress); Portland, Ore., 7/28/1948
Stuart, Gilbert Charles (painter); Rhode Island **(1755-1828)**
Stuart, James Ewell Brown (known as Jeb) (Confederate army officer); Patrick County, Va. **(1833-1864)**
Sturges, Preston (director, screenwriter, playwright); Chicago **(1898-1959)**
Stuyvesant, Peter (Governor of New Amsterdam); West Friesland (Netherlands) **(1592-1672)**
Styne, Jule (Julius Kerwin Stein) (songwriter); London, 12/31/1905
Styron, William (William Clark Styron, Jr.) (novelist); Newport News, Va., 6/11/1925
Sullavan, Margaret Brooke (actress); Norfolk, Va. **(1911-1960)**
Sullivan, Sir Arthur Seymour (composer); London **(1842-1900)**
Sullivan, Barry (Patrick Barry) (actor); New York City, 8/29/1912
Sullivan, Ed (columnist and TV personality); New York City **(1901-1974)**
Sullivan, Frank (Francis John) (humorist); Saratoga Springs, N.Y. **(1892-1976)**
Sullivan, Louis Henry (architect); Boston, Mass. **(1856-1924)**
Sulzberger, Arthur Ochs (newspaper publisher); New York City, 2/5/1926
Sumac, Yma (singer); Ichocan, Peru, 9/10/1927
Summer, Donna (La Donna Andrea Gaines) (singer); Boston, 12/31/1948

Summerville, Slim (George) (actor); Albuquerque, N.M. **(1892-1946)**
Sun Yat-sen (statesman); nr. Macao **(1866-1925)**
Susann, Jacqueline (novelist); Philadelphia **(1926?-1974)**
Susskind, David (TV producer); New York City **(1920-1987)**
Sutherland, Donald (actor); St. John, N.B., Canada, 7/17/34
Sutherland, Joan (soprano); Sydney, Australia, 11/7/1926
Suzuki, Pat (actress); Cressey, Calif., 1931
Swados, Elizabeth (composer, playwright); Buffalo, N.Y., 2/5/1951
Swanson, Gloria (Gloria May Josephine Svensson) (actress); Chicago, **(1899-1983)**
Swarthout, Gladys (soprano); Deepwater, Mo. **(1904-1969)**
Swayze, John Cameron (news commentator); Wichita, Kan., 4/4/1906
Swayze, Patrick (actor, dancer); Houston, Tex., 8/18/54
Swendenborg, Emanuel (scientist, philosopher, mystic); Stockholm **(1688-1772)**
Swift, Jonathan (satirist); Dublin **(1667-1745)**
Swinburne, Algernon Charles (poet); London **(1837-1909)**
Swit, Loretta (actress); Passaic, N.J., 11/4/37
Swope, Herbert Bayard (journalist); St. Louis **(1882-1958)**
Sydow, von, Max (Carl Adolf von Sydow) (actor); Lund, Sweden, 4/10/1929
Synge, John Millington (dramatist); nr. Dublin **(1871-1909)**
Szilard, Leo (physicist); Budapest **(1898-1964)**

T

Taft, Robert Alphonso (legislator); Cincinnati **(1889-1953)**
Tagore, Sir Rabindranath (poet); Calcutta **(1861-1941)**
Tallchief, Maria (ballerina); Fairfax, Okla., 1/24/1925
Talleyrand-Périgord, Charles Maurice de (statesman); Paris **(1754-1838)**
Talmadge, Norma (actress); Niagara Falls, N.Y. **(1897-1957)**
Talvela, Martti (basso); Hiitola, Finalnd **(1935-1989)**
Tamerlane (Timur) (Mongol conqueror); nr. Samarkand (U.S.S.R.) **(1336?-1405)**
Tamiroff, Akim (actor) Baku, Russia **(1899-1972)**
Tandy, Jessica (actress); London, 6/7/1909
Tarkington, (Newton) Booth (novelist); Indianapolis **(1869-1946)**
Tate, Allen (John Orley) (poet and critic); Winchester, Ky., **(1899-1979)**
Tate, Sharon (actress); Dallas **(1943-1969)**
Tati, Jacques (Jacques Tatischeff) (actor); Pecq, France **(1908-1982)**
Taylor, Deems (composer); New York City **(1885-1966)**
Taylor, Elizabeth (actress); London, 2/27/1932
Taylor, Estelle (actress); Wilmington, Del. **(1899-1958)**
Taylor, Harold (educator); Toronto, 9/28/1914
Taylor, James (singer and songwriter); Boston, 3/12/1948
Taylor, (Joseph) Deems (composer); New York City **(1885-1966)**
Taylor, Laurette (Laurette Cooney) (actress); New York City **(1884-1946)**
Taylor, Gen. Maxwell D. (former Army Chief of Staff); Keytesville, Mo **(1901-1987)**
Taylor, Robert (Spangler Arlington Brugh) (actor); Filley, Neb. **(1911-1969)**
Taylor, Rod (actor); Sydney, Australia, 1/11/1930
Tchaikovsky, Peter (Pëtr) Ilich (composer); Votkinsk, Russia **(1840-1893)**
Teasdale, Sara (poet); St. Louis **(1884-1933)**
Tebaldi, Renata (lyric soprano); Pesaro, Italy, 1/2/1922
Tecumseh (Shawnee Indian chief); nr. Springfield, Ohio **(1768?-1813)**
Te Kanawa, Kiri (soprano); Gisborne, New Zealand, 1946(?)
Telemann, Georg Philipp (composer); Magdeburg (East Germany) **(1681-1767)**
Teller, Edward (atomic physicist); Budapest, 1/15/1908
Temple, Shirley. *See* Black, Shirley Temple
Templeton, Alec Andrew (pianist, composer); Cardiff, Wales **(1910-1963)**
Tennille, Toni (singer); Montgomery, Ala., 5/8/43
Tennyson, Alfred (1st Baron Tennyson) (poet); Somersby, England **(1809-1892)**
Terhune, Albert Payson (novelist and journalist); Newark, N.J. **(1872-1942)**
Terkel, Studs (writer-interviewer); New York City, 5/16/1912
Terry, Ellen Alicia (actress); Coventry, England **(1848-1928)**
Terry-Thomas (Thomas Terry Hoar Stevens) (actor); London, 7/14/1911
Tesla, Nikola (electrical engineer and inventor); Smiljan (Yugoslavia) **(1856-1943)**
Thackeray, William Makepeace (novelist); Calcutta **(1811-1863)**
Thalberg, Irving G. (producer); Brooklyn, N.Y. **(1899-1936)**
Thant, U (U.N. statesman); Pantanaw (Burma) **(1909-1974)**
Tharp, Twyla (dancer and choreographer); Portland, Ind.,

7/1/1941(?)

Thatcher, Margaret (Prime Minister); Grantham, England, 10/13/1925

Thaxter, Phyllis (actress); Portland, Me., 1921

Thebom, Blanche (mezzo-soprano); Monessen, Pa., 9/19/1919

Theodorakis, Mikis (composer); Chios, Greece, 7/29/1925

Thicke, Alan (actor); Kirland Lake, Ont., Canada, 3/1/47

Thieu, Nguyen Van (ex-President of South Vietnam); Trithuy (Vietnam) 4/5/1923

Thomas, Danny (Amos Jacobs) (entertainer and TV producer); Deerfield, Mich., 1/6/1914

Thomas, Dylan Marlais (poet); Carmarthenshire, Wales **(1914-1953)**

Thomas, Lowell (explorer, commentator); Woodington, Ohio **(1892-1981)**

Thomas, Marlo (actress); Detroit, 11/21/1943

Thomas, Michael Tilson (conductor); Hollywood, Calif., 12/21/1944

Thomas, Norman Mattoon (Socialist leader): Marion, Ohio **(1884-1968)**

Thomas, Philip Michael (actor); Columbus, Ohio, 5/26/49

Thomas, Richard (actor); New York City, 6/13/1951

Thompson, Dorothy (writer); Lancaster, N.Y. **(1894-1961)**

Thompson, Hunter (Stockton) (writer); Louisville, Ky. 7/18/1939

Thompson, Sada (actress); Des Moines, Iowa, 9/27/1929

Thomson, Virgil (Garnett) (composer); Kansas City, Mo. **(1896-1989)**

Thoreau, Henry David (naturalist and author); Concord, Mass. **(1817-1862)**

Thorndike, Dame Sybil (actress); Gainsborough, England **(1882-1976)**

Thurber, James Grover (author and cartoonist); Columbus, Ohio **(1894-1961)**

Tibbett, Lawrence (baritone); Bakersfield, Calif. **(1896-1960)**

Tiegs, Cheryl (model,actress); Minnesota, 9/25/47

Tierney, Gene (actress); Brooklyn, N.Y., 11/20/1920

Tiffin, Pamela (actress); Oklahoma City, 10/13/1942

Tillstrom, Burr (puppeteer); Chicago **(1917-1985)**

Tintoretto, Il (Jacopo Robusti) (painter); Venice **(1518-1594)**

Tiny Tim (Herbert Khaury) (entertainer); New York City, 1923(?)

Tiomkin, Dmitri (composer); St. Petersburg, Russia **(1894-1979)**

Titian (Tiziano Vecelli) (painter); Pieve di Cadore (Italy) **(1477-1576)**

Tito (Josip Broz or Brozovich) (President of Yugoslavia); Croatia (Yugoslavia) **(1892-1980)**

Tocqueville, Alexis de (writer); Verneuil, France **(1805-1859)**

Todd, Ann (actress); Hartford, England, 1/24/09

Todd, Michael (producer); Minneapolis, Minn. **(1907-1958)**

Todd, Richard (actor); Dublin, Ireland, 6/11/19

Todd, Thelma (actress); Lawrence, Mass. **(1905-1935)**

Tolstoi, Count Leo (Lev) Nikolaevich (novelist); Tula Province, Russia **(1828-1910)**

Tomlin, Lily (comedienne); Detroit, 1939(?)

Tone, Franchot (actor); Niagara Falls, N.Y. **(1905-1968)**

Toomey, Regis (actor); Pittsburg, Pa., 8/13/02

Tormé, Mel (Melvin) (singer); Chicago, 9/13/1925

Torn, Rip (Elmore Torn, Jr.) (actor and director); Temple, Tex., 2/6/1931

Torquamada, Tomás de (Spanish Inquisitor); Valladolid, Spain **(1420-1498)**

Toscanini, Arturo (orchestra conductor); Parma, Italy **(1867-1957)**

Toulouse-Lautrec (Henri Marie Raymond de Toulouse-Lautrec Monfa) (painter); Albi, France **(1864-1901)**

Toynbee, Arnold J. (historian); London **(1889-1975)**

Tracy, Lee (actor); Atlanta, Ga. **(1898-1968)**

Tracy, Spencer (actor); Milwaukee **(1900-1967)**

Traubel, Helen (Wagnerian soprano); St. Louis **(1903-1972)**

Travanti, Daniel J. (actor); Kenosha, Wis., 3/7/40

Travolta, John (actor); Englewood, N.J., 2/18/1954

Treacher, Arthur (actor); Brighton, England **(1894-1975)**

Tree, Sir Herbert Beerbolm (actor-manager); London **(1853-1917)**

Trevor, Claire (actress); New York City, 1911

Trigère, (Pauline (fashion designer); Paris, 11/4/1912

Trilling, Lionel (author and educator); New York City **(1905-1975)**

Trotsky, Leon (Lev Davidovich Bronstein) (statesman); Elisavetgrad, Russia **(1879-1940)**

Troyanos, Tatiana (mezzo-soprano); New York City, 9/12/38

Trudeau, Garry (cartoonist); New York City, 1948

Trudeau, Pierre Elliott (former Prime Minister); Montreal, 10/18/1919

Truffaut, François (film director); Paris **(1932-1984)**

Trujillo y Molina, Rafael Leonidas (Dominican Republic dictator); San Cristóbal, Dominican Republic **(1891-1961)**

Truman, Margaret (author); Independence, Mo., 2/17/1924

Tryon, Thomas (actor and novelist); Hartford, Conn., 1/14/1926

Tsiolkovsky, Konstantin E. (father of cosmonautics); Izhevskoye, Russia **(1857-1935)**

Tuchman, Barbara (Wertheim) (historian, author); New York City **(1912-1989)**

Tucker, Forrest (actor); Plainfield, Ind. **(1919-1986)**

Tucker, Richard (tenor); New York City **(1914-1975)**

Tucker, Sophie (Sophie Abuza) (singer); Europe **(1884?-1966)**

Tudor, Antony (choreographer); London **(1909-1987)**

Tune, Tommy (dancer-choreographer); Wichita Falls, Tex., 2/28/1939

Turgenev, Ivan Sergeevich (novelist); Orel, Russia **(1818-1883)**

Turner, Ike (singer); Clarksdale, Miss., 11/?/1931

Turner, Joseph M.W. (painter); London **(1775-1851)**

Turner, Kathleen (actress); Springfield, Mo., 1956 (?)

Turner, Lana (Julia Jean Mildred Frances Turner) (actress); Wallace, Idaho, 2/8/1920

Turner, Nat (civil rights leader); Southampton County, Va. **(1800-1831)**

Turner, Tina (Annie Mae Bullock) (singer); Brownsville, Tex., 1939

Turpin, Ben (comedian); New Orleans **(1874-1940)**

Tushingham, Rita (actress); Liverpool, England, 3/14/1942

Twain, Mark (Samuel Langhorne Clemens) (author); Florida, Mo. **(1835-1910)**

Tweed, William Marcy (politician); New York City **(1823-1878)**

Twiggy (Leslie Hornby) (model); London, 9/19/1949

Twining, Gen. Nathan F. (former Air Force Chief of Staff); Monroe, Wis. **(1897-1982)**

Twitty, Conway (Harold Lloyd Jenkins) (singer and guitarist); Friars Point, Miss., 9/1/1933

Tyson, Cicely (actress); New York City, 12/19/1939(?)

U

Udall, Stewart L. (ex-Secretary of the Interior); St. Johns, Ariz., 1/31/1920

Uggams, Leslie (singer and actress); New York City, 5/25/1943

Ulanova, Galina (ballerina); St. Petersburg, Russia, 1/10/1910

Ullman, Tracey (actress, singer); Slough, England, 12/30/59

Ullmann, Liv (actress); Tokyo, 12/16/1939

Ulric, Lenore (actress); New Ulm, Minn. **(1894-1970)**

Untermeyer, Louis (anthologist and poet); New York City **(1885-1977)**

Updike, John (novelist); Shillington, Pa., 3/18/1932

Urey, Harold C. (physicist); Walkerton, Ind. **(1893-1981)**

Uris, Leon (novelist); Baltimore, 8/3/1924

Ustinov, Peter (actor and producer); London, 4/16/1921

Utrillo, Maurice (painter); Paris **(1883-1955)**

V

Vaccaro, Brenda (actress); Brooklyn, N.Y., 11/18/1939

Vadim, Roger (Roger Vadim Plemiannikov) (film director); Paris, 1/26/1928

Valentine, Karen (actress); Santa Rosa, Calif., 1947

Valentino, Rudolph (Rodolpho d'Antonguolla) (actor); Castellaneta, Italy **(1895-1926)**

Valentino (Valentino Garavani) (fashion designer); nr. Milan, Italy, 5/11/1932

Vallee, Rudy (Hubert Prior Rudy Vallée) (band leader and singer); Island Pond, Vt. **(1901-1986)**

Valli, Frankie (Frank Castellaccio) (singer); Newark, N.J., 5/3/1937

Van Allen, James Alfred (space physicist); Mt. Pleasant, Iowa, 9/7/1914

Van Buren, Abigail (Mrs. Morton Phillips) (columnist); Sioux City, Iowa, 7/4/1918

Vance, Vivian (actress); Cherryvale, Kan. **(1912-1979)**

Vanderbilt, Alfred G. (sportsman); London, 9/22/1912

Vanderbilt, Cornelius (financier); Port Richmond, N.Y. **(1794-1877)**

Vanderbilt, Gloria (fashion designer) New York City, 2/20/1924

Van Doren, Carl (writer and educator); Hope, Ill. **(1885-1950)**

Van Doren, Mamie (actress); Rowena, S.D., 2/6/1933

Van Dyke, Dick (actor); West Plains, Mo., 12/13/1925

Vandyke (or Van Dyck), Sir Anthony (painter); Antwerp (Belgium) **(1599-1641)**

Van Eyck, Jan (painter); Maeseyck (Belgium) **(c.1390-1441)**

Van Fleet, Jo (actress); Oakland, Calif., 12/30/19

van Gogh, Vincent (painter); Groot Zundert, Brabant **(1853-1890)**

van Hamel, Martine (ballerina); Brussels, 11/16/1945

Van Heusen, Jimmy (Edward Chester Babcock) (songwriter); Syracuse, N.Y. **(1913-1990)**

Van Patten, Dick (actor); Richmond Hill, N.Y., 12/9/28

Van Peebles, Melvin (playwright); Chicago, 9/21/1932

Vaughan, Sarah (singer); Newark, N.J. **(1924-1990)**

Vaughan Williams, Ralph (composer); Down Ampney, England **(1872-1958)**

Vaughn, Robert (actor); New York City, 11/22/1932

Veidt, Conrad (actor); Potsdam, Germany **(1893-1943)**

Velázquez, Diego Rodriguez de Silva y (painter); Seville, Spain **(1599-**

1660)
Velez, Lupe (Guadelupe Velez de Villalobos) (actress); San Luis Potosi, Mexico **(1908-1944)**
Venturi, Robert (Charles) (architect); Philadelphia, 6/25/1925
Verdi, Giuseppe (composer); Roncole (Italy) **(1813-1901)**
Verdon, Gwen (actress); Culver City, Calif., 1/13/1925
Vereen, Ben (actor and singer); Miami, Fla., 10/10/1946
Vermeer, Jan (or Jan van der Meer van Delft) (painter); Delft (Netherlands) **(1632-1675)**
Verne, Jules (author); Nantes, France **(1828-1905)**
Veronese, Paolo (Paolo Cagliari) (painter); Verona **(1528-1588)**
Verrazano, Giovanni da (navigator); Florence (Italy) **(1485?-1528)**
Verrett, Shirley (mezzo-soprano); New Orleans, 5/31/1933
Vesalius, Andreas (anatomist); Brussels, Belgium **(1515-1564)**
Vespucci, Amerigo (navigator); Florence (Italy) **(1454-1512)**
Vickers, Jon (tenor); Prince Albert, Sask, Canada, 10/29/1926
Vico, Giovanni Battista (philosopher); Naples, Italy **(1668-1744)**
Vidal, Gore (novelist); West Point, N.Y., 10/3/1925
Vidor, King (film director and producer); Galveston, Tex. **(1895-1982)**
Vigoda, Abe (actor); New York City, 2/24/21
Villa, Pancho (Doroteo Arango) (bandit); Rio Grande, Mexico **(1877-1923)**
Villella, Edward (ballet dancer); Bayside, Queens, N.Y., 10/1/1936
Villon, François (François de Montcorbier) (poet); Paris **(1431-1463)**
Vincent, Helen (actress); Beaumont, Tex., 9/17/07
Vinton, Bobby (singer); Canonsburg, Pa., 4/16/1935(?)
Virgil (or Vergil) (Publius Vergilius Maro) (poet); nr. Mantua (Italy) **(70-19** B.C.)
Vishnevskaya, Galina (soprano); Leningrad, 10/25/1926
Vivaldi, Antonio (composer); Venice **(1678-1741)**
Vlaminck, Maurice de (painter); Paris **(1876-1958)**
Voight, Jon (actor); Yonkers, N.Y., 12/29/1938
Volta, Alessandro (scientist); Como, Italy **(1745-1827)**
Voltaire (François Marie Arouet) (author); Paris **(1694-1778)**
von Aroldingen, Karin (Karin Awny Hannelore Reinbold von Aroedingen and Eltzinger) (ballet dancer); Greiz (East Germany) 7/9/1941
von Braun, Wernher (rocket scientist); Wirsitz, Germany **(1912-1977)**
von Furstenberg, Betsy (Elizabeth Caroline Maria Agatha Felicitas Therese von Furstenberg-Hedringen) (actress); Nelheim-Heusen, Germany, 8/16/1935
von Fürstenberg, Diane (Diane Simone Michelle Halfin) (fashion designer); Brussels, 12/31/1946
von Hindenburg, Paul (statesman); Posen (Poland) **(1847-1934)**
von Karajan, Herbert (conductor); Salzburg (Austria) **(1908-1989)**
Vonnegut, Kurt, Jr. (novelist); Indianapolis, 11/11/1922
Von Stade, Frederica (mezzo-soprano); Somerville, N.J., 1945
Von Stroheim, Erich Oswald Hans Carl Maria von Nordenwall (film actor and director); Vienna **(1885-1957)**
Von Zell, Harry (announcer); Indianapolis, Ind. **(1906-1981)**
Vreeland, Diana (Diana Dalziel) (fashion journalist and museum consultant); Paris **(1903?-1989)**

W

Wagner, Lindsay (actress); Los Angeles, 6/22/1949
Wagner, Robert (actor); Detroit, 2/10/1930
Wagner, Robert F. (ex-Mayor of New York City); New York City, 4/20/1910
Wagner, Wilhelm Richard (composer); Leipzig (East Germany) **(1813-1883)**
Waldheim, Kurt (ex-U.N. Secretary-General); St. Andrae-Wörden, Austria, 12/21/1918
Walker, Clint (actor); Hartford, Ill., 5/30/1927
Walker, Nancy (Ann Myrtle Swoyer); (actress and comedienne); Philadelphia, 5/10/1922
Wallace, DeWitt (publisher); St. Paul **(1889-1981)**
Wallace, George C. (ex-governor); Clio, Ala. 8/25/19
Wallace, Irving (novelist); Chicago **(1916-1990)**
Wallace, Mike (Myron Wallace) (TV interviewer and commentator); Brookline, Mass., 5/9/1918
Wallach, Eli (actor); Brooklyn, N.Y., 12/7/1915
Wallenstein, Alfred (conductor); Chicago **(1898-1983)**
Waller, Thomas "Fats" (pianist); New York City **(1904-1943)**
Wallis, Hal (film producer); Chicago **(1899-1986)**
Walpole, Horace (statesman and novelist); London **(1717-1797)**
Waltari, Mika (novelist); Helsinki, Finland, **(1903-1979)**
Walter, Bruno (Bruno Walter Schlesinger) (orchestra conductor); Berlin **(1876-1962)**
Walters, Barbara (TV commentator); Boston, 9/25/1931
Walton, Izaak (author); Stafford, England **(1593-1683)**
Wambaugh, Joseph (author and screenwriter); East Pittsburgh, Pa., 1/22/1937

Wanamaker, John (merchant); Philadelphia **(1838-1922)**
Wanamaker, Sam (actor,director); Chicago, 6/14/19
Ward, Barbara (economist); York, England **(1914-1981)**
Warhol, Andy (artist and producer); Pennsylvania **(1928(?)-1987)**
Waring, Fred (band leader); Tyrone, Pa., **(1900-1984)**
Warner, H. B. (Henry Bryan Warner Lickford) (actor); London **(1876-1958)**
Warren, Lesley Ann (actress); New York City, 8/16/46
Warren, Robert Penn (novelist); Guthrie, Ky. **(1905-1989)**
Warrick, Ruth (actress); St. Joseph, Mo., 6/29/15
Warwick, Dionne (singer); East Orange, N.J., 1941
Washington, Booker Taliaferro (educator); Franklin County, Va. **(1856-1915)**
Waters, Ethel (actress and singer); Chester, Pa. **(1896-1977)**
Waters, Muddy (McKinley Morganfield) (singer and guitarist); Rolling Fork, Miss. **(1915-1983)**
Waterson, Sam (actor); Cambridge, Mass., 11/15/1940
Watson, Thomas John (industrialist); Campbell, N.Y. **(1874-1956)**
Watt, James (inventor); Greenock, Scotland **(1736-1819)**
Watteau, Jean-Antoine (painter); Valanciennes, France **(1684-1721)**
Wattleton, Faye (family planning advocate); St. Louis, Mo., 7/8/43
Watts, André (concert pianist); Nuremberg, Germany, 6/20/1946
Waugh, Alec (Alexander Raban Waugh) (novelist); London **(1898-1981)**
Waugh, Evelyn (satirist); London **(1903-1966)**
Wayne, Anthony (military officer); Waynesboro (family farm), nr. Paoli, Pa. **(1745-1796)**
Wayne, David (David McMeekan); (actor); Traverse City, Mich., 1/30/1914
Wayne, John (Marion Michael Morrison) (actor); Winterset, Iowa, **(1907-1979)**
Weaver, Dennis (actor); Joplin, Mo., 6/4/1925
Weaver, Fritz (actor); Pittsburgh, Pa., 1/19/26
Weaver, Sigourney (actress); New York City, 10/8/1949
Webb, Clifton (Webb Parmelee Hollenbeck) (actor); Indianapolis **(1893-1966)**
Webb, Jack (film actor and producer); Santa Monica, Calif. **(1920-1982)**
Weber, Karl Maria Friedrich Ernst von (composer); nr. Lübeck (Germany) **(1786-1826)**
Webster, Daniel (statesman); Salisbury, N.H. **(1782-1852)**
Webster, Margaret (producer, director, actress); New York City **(1905-1973)**
Webster, Noah (lexicographer); West Hartford, Conn. **(1758-1843)**
Weill, Kurt (composer); Dessau, (East Germany) **(1900-1950)**
Weir, Peter (film director); Sydney, Australia, 8/21/1944
Weizmann, Chaim (statesman); Grodno Province, Russia **(1874-1952)**
Welch, Raquel (Raquel Tejada) (actress); Chicago, 9/5/1942
Weld, Tuesday (Susan) (actress); New York City, 8/27/1943
Welk, Lawrence (band leader); Strasburg, N.D., 3/11/1903
Welles, Orson (actor and producer); Kenosha, Wis. **(1915-1985)**
Wellington, Duke of (Arthur Wellesley) (statesman); Ireland **(1769-1852)**
Wells, H(erbert) G(eorge) (author); Bromley, England **(1866-1946)**
Welty, Eudora (novelist); Jackson, Miss., 4/13/1909
Werfel, Franz (novelist); Prague **(1890-1945)**
Werner, Oskar (Josef Schliessmayer) (film actor and director); Vienna **(1922-1984)**
Wertmuller, Lina (film director); Rome, 1926(?)
Wesley, John (religious leader); Epworth Rectory, Lincolnshire, England **(1703-1791)**
West, Dame Rebecca (Cicily Fairfield); (novelist); County Kerry, Ireland **(1892-1983)**
West, Jessamyn (novelist); nr. North Vernon, Ind. **(1902-1984)**
West, Mae (actress); Brooklyn, N.Y. **(1893-1980)**
West, Nathanael (Nathan Weinstein) (novelist); New York City **(1902-1940)**
Westheimer, Ruth (Karola Ruth Siegel) (psychologist, author, broadcaster); Frankfurt, Germany, 1928
Westinghouse, George (inventor); Central Bridge, N.Y. **(1846-1914)**
Westmoreland, William Childs (ex-Army Chief of Staff); Saxon, S.C., 3/26/1914
Wharton, Edith Newbold (née Jones) (novelist); New York City **(1862-1937)**
Wheeler, Bert (Albert Jerome Wheeler) (comedian); Paterson, N.J. **(1895-1968)**
Whistler, James Abbott McNeill (painter and etcher); Lowell, Mass. **(1834-1903)**
White, Betty (actress); Oak Park, Ill., 1/17/24(?)
White, E(lwyn) B(rooks) (author); Mt. Vernon, N.Y. **(1899-1985)**
White, Pearl (actress); Green Ridge, Mo. **(1889-1938)**
White, Stanford (architect); New York City **(1853-1906)**
White, Theodore H. (historian); Boston **(1915-1986)**
White, Vanna (TV personality); Conway, S.C., 2/18/1957
White, William Allen (journalist); Emporia, Kan. **(1868-1944)**

Whitehead, Alfred North (mathematician and philosopher); Isle of Thanet, England (1861-1947)
Whiteman, Paul (band leader); Denver (1891-1967)
Whiting, Margaret (singer, actress); Detroit, Mich., 7/22/24
Whitman, Walt (Walter) (poet); West Hills, N.Y. (1819-1892)
Whitmore, James (actor); White Plains, N.Y., 10/1/1921
Whitney, Cornelius Vanderbilt (sportsman); New York City, 2/20/1899
Whitney, Eli (inventor); Westboro, Mass. (1765-1825)
Whitney, John Hay (publisher); Ellsworth, Me. (1904-1982)
Whittier, John Greenleaf (poet); Haverhill, Mass. (1807-1892)
Whitty, Dame May (actress); Liverpool, England (1865-1948)
Widmark, Richard (actor); Sunrise, Minn., 12/26/1914
Wiesel, Elie (Eliezer) (author); Signet, Romania, 9/30/1928
Wilde, Cornel (film actor and producer); New York City (1915-1989)
Wilde, Oscar Fingal O'Flahertie Wills (author); Dublin (1854-1900)
Wilder, Billy (film producer and director); Vienna, 6/22/1906
Wilder, Gene (Jerome Silberman) (actor); Milwaukee, 6/11/1935(?)
Wilder, Thornton (author); Madison, Wis. (1897-1975)
Wilding, Michael (actor); Westcliff, England (1912-1979)
Wilkins, Roy (civil rights leader); St. Louis (1901-1981)
Williams, Andy (singer); Wall Lake, Iowa, 12/3/1930
Williams, Billy Dee (actor); New York City, 4/6/1937
Williams, Cindy (actress); Van Nuys, Calif., 8/22/(?)
Williams, Edward Bennett (lawyer); Hartford, Conn. (1920-1988)
Williams, Emlyn (actor and playwright); Mostyn, Wales (1905-1987)
Williams, Esther (actress); Los Angeles, 8/8/1923
Williams, Gluyas (cartoonist); San Francisco (1888-1982)
Williams, Hank, Sr. (Hiram King Williams) (singer); Georgiana, Ala. (1923-1953)
Williams, Joe (singer); Cordele, Ga., 12/12/1918
Williams, Paul (singer, composer, actor); Omaha, Neb., 9/19/1940
Williams, Robin (comedian); Chicago, 7/?/1952
Williams, Roger (clergyman); London (1603?-1683)
Williams, Tennessee (Thomas L. Williams) (playwright); Columbus, Miss. (1911-1983)
Williams, William Carlos (physician and poet); Rutherford, N.J. (1883-1963)
Williamson, Nicol (actor); Hamilton, Scotland, 9/14/38
Willkie, Wendell Lewis (lawyer); Elwood, Ind. (1892-1944)
Willis, Bruce (actor); Germany, 3/19/1955
Willson, Meredith (composer); Mason City, Iowa (1902-1984)
Wilson, August (poet, writer, playwright); Pittsburgh, Pa., 1945
Wilson, Don (radio and TV announcer); Lincoln, Neb. (1900-1982)
Wilson, Dooley (actor, musician); Tyler, Tex. (1894-1953)
Wilson, Edmund (literary critic and author); Red Bank, N.J. (1895-1972)
Wilson, Flip (Clerow) (comedian); Jersey City, N.J., 12/8/1933
Wilson, Harold (ex-Prime Minister); Huddersfield, England, 3/11/1916
Wilson, Marie (actress); Anaheim, Calif. (1916-1972)
Wilson, Nancy (singer); Chillicothe, Ohio, 2/20/1937
Wilson, Sloan (novelist); Norwalk, Conn., 5/8/1920
Winchell, Walter (columnist); New York City (1897-1972)
Windsor, Duchess of (Bessie Wallis Warfield); Blue Ridge Summit, Pa. (1896-1986)
Windsor, Duke of (formerly King Edward VIII of England); Richmond Park, England (1894-1972)
Winfrey, Oprah (talk show hostess, actress); Kosciuska, Miss., 1/29/1954
Winger, Debra (actress); Cleveland, Ohio, 1955
Winkler, Henry (actor); New York City, 10/30/1945
Winninger, Charles (actor); Athen, Wis. (1884-1969)
Winningham, Mare (actress); Phoenix, Ariz., 5/16/1959
Winter, Johnny (guitarist); Leland, Miss., 2/23/1944
Winters, Jonathan (comedian); Dayton, Ohio, 11/11/1925
Winters, Shelley (Shirley Schrift) (actress); East St. Louis, Ill., 8/18/1922
Winthrop, John (first Governor, Massachusetts Bay Colony); Suffolk, England (1588-1649)
Wise, Stephen Samuel (rabbi); Budapest (1874-1949)
Withers, Jane (actress); Atlanta, 1927
Wittgenstein, Ludwig (Josef Johann) (philosopher); Vienna (1889-1951)
Wodehouse, P(elham) G(renville) (novelist); Guildford, England (1881-1975)
Wolfe, Thomas Clayton (novelist); Asheville, N.C. (1900-1938)
Wolfe, Tom (journalist); Richmond, Va., 3/2/1931
Wolsey, Thomas (prelate and statesman); Ipswich, England (1475?-1530)
Wonder, Stevie (Steveland Judkins, later Steveland Morris) (singer and songwriter); Saginaw, Mich., 5/13/1950
Wong, Anna May (Lu Tsong Wong) (actress); Los Angeles (1907-1961)
Wood, Grant (painter); Anamosa, Iowa (1892-1942)
Wood, Natalie (Natasha Gurdin) (film actress); San Francisco (1938-

1981)
Wood, Peggy (Margaret) (actress); Brooklyn, N.Y. (1892-1978)
Woodhouse, Barbara (Blackburn) (dog trainer, author, TV personality): Rathfarnham, Ireland (1910-1988)
Woodward, Edward (actor); Croydon, England, 6/1/30
Woodward, Joanne (film actress); Thomasville, Ga., 2/27/1930
Woolf, Adeline Virginia (née Stephens) (novelist); London (1882-1941)
Woollcott, Alexander (author-critic); Phalanx, N.J. (1887-1943)
Woolley, Monty (Edgar Montillion Woolley) (actor); New York City (1888-1963)
Woolworth, Frank (merchant); Rodman, N.Y. (1852-1919)
Wopat, Tom (actor); Lodi, Wis., 9/9/50
Wordsworth, William (poet); Cockermouth, England (1770-1850)
Wouk, Herman (novelist); New York City, 5/27/1915
Wray, Fay (actress); Alberta, Canada, 1907
Wren, Sir Christopher (architect); East Knoyle, England (1632-1723)
Wright, Frank Lloyd (architect); Richland Center, Wis. (1869-1959)
Wright, Martha (singer); Seattle, Wash., 3/23/26
Wright, Orville (inventor); Dayton, Ohio (1871-1948)
Wright, Richard (novelist); nr. Natchez, Miss. (1908-1960)
Wright, Teresa (actress); New York City, 10/27/1918
Wright, Wilbur (inventor); Millville, Ind. (1867-1912)
Wyatt, Jane (film actress); Campgaw, N.J., 8/12/1912
Wycliffe, John (church reformer); Hipswell, England (1320-1384)
Wyeth, Andrew (painter); Chadds Ford, Pa., 7/12/1917
Wyler, William (film director); Mulhouse (France), (1902-1981)
Wyman, Jane (Sarah Jane Fulks) (actress); St. Joseph, Mo., 1/4/1914
Wynette, Tammy (Wynette Pugh) (singer); Tupelo, Miss. 5/5/1942
Wynn, Ed (Isaiah Edwin Leopold) (comedian); Philadelphia (1886-1966)
Wynn, Keenan (actor); New York City (1916-1986)
Wynter, Dana (actress); London, 6/8/1930

X

Xavier, St. Francis (Jesuit missionary); Pamplona, Navarre (Spain) (1506-1552)
Xenophon (soldier, historian and essayist): Athens, Greece, (434(?)-355(?) B.C.)
Xerxes, the Great (king): Persian Empire, (519(?)-465 B.C.)

Y

Yeats, William Butler (poet); nr. Dublin (1865-1939)
Yevtushenko, Yevgeny (poet); Zima, U.S.S.R., 7/18/1933
York, Alvin Cullun (Sergeant York, World War I hero): Tennessee (1887-1964)
York, Michael (actor); Fulmer, England, 3/27/1942
York, Susannah (Fletcher) (actress); London, 1/9/1942
Yorty, Samuel W. (ex-Mayor of Los Angeles); Lincoln, Neb., 10/1/1909
Yothers, Tina (actress); Whittier, Calif., 5/5/73
Young, Alan (actor); North Shield, England, 11/19/1919
Young, Brigham (religious leader); Whitingham, Vt. (1801-1877)
Young, Gig (Byron Barr) (actor); St. Cloud, Minn. (1917-1978)
Young, Loretta (Gretchen Young) (actress); Salt Lake City, Utah, 1/6/1913
Young, Neil (singer and songwriter); Toronto, 11/12/1945
Young, Robert (actor); Chicago, 2/22/1907
Young, Roland (actor); London (1887-1953)
Youngman, Henny (comedian); Liverpool, England, 1/12/1906

Z

Zanuck, Darryl F. (film producer); Wahoo, Neb. (1902-1979)
Zappa, Frank (Francis Vincent Zappa, Jr.) (singer and songwriter); Baltimore, 12/21/1940
Zeffirelli, Franco (director); Florence, Italy, 2/12/1923
Zenger, John Peter (printer and journalist): Germany, (1697-1746)
Zhou Enlai (Premier); Hualyin, China (1898-1976)
Ziegfeld, Florenz (theatrical producer); Chicago (1869-1932)
Zimbalist, Efrem (concert violinist); Rostov-on-Don, Russia (1889-1985)
Zimbalist, Efrem, Jr. (actor); New York City, 11/30/1923
Zimbalist, Stephanie (actress); New York City, 10/8/56
Zola, Emile (novelist); Paris (1840-1902)
Zoroaster (religious leader); Persian Empire (c. 6th century B.C.)
Zukerman, Pinchas (violinist); Tel Aviv, Israel 7/16/1948
Zukor, Adolph (film executive); Risce, Hungary (1873-1976)
Zweig, Stefan (author); Vienna (1881-1942)
Zwingli, Huldrych (humanist); Wildaus, Switzerland (1484-1531)

AWARDS

Nobel Prizes

The Nobel prizes are awarded under the will of Alfred Bernhard Nobel, Swedish chemist and engineer, who died in 1896. The interest of the fund is divided annually among the persons who have made the most outstanding contributions in the fields of physics, chemistry, and physiology or medicine, who have produced the most distinguished literary work of an idealist tendency, and who have contributed most toward world peace.

In 1968, a Nobel Prize of economic sciences was established by Riksbank, the Swedish bank, in celebration of its 300th anniversary. The prize was awarded for the first time in 1969.

The prizes for physics and chemistry are awarded by the Swedish Academy of Science in Stockholm, the one for physiology or medicine by the Caroline Medical Institute in Stockholm, that for literature by the academy in Stockholm, and that for peace by a committee of five elected by the Norwegian Storting. The distribution of prizes was begun on December 10, 1901, the anniversary of Nobel's death. The amount of each prize varies with the income from the fund and currently is about $190,000. No Nobel prizes were awarded for 1940, 1941, and 1942; prizes for Literature were not awarded for 1914, 1918, and 1943.

PEACE

1901 Henri Dunant (Switzerland); Frederick Passy (France)
1902 Elie Ducommun and Albert Gobat (Switzerland)
1903 Sir William R. Cremer (England)
1904 Institut de Droit International (Belgium)
1905 Bertha von Suttner (Austria)
1906 Theodore Roosevelt (U.S.)
1907 Ernesto T. Moneta (Italy) and Louis Renault (France)
1908 Klas P. Arnoldson (Sweden) and Frederik Bajer (Denmark)
1909 Auguste M. F. Beernaert (Belgium) and Baron Paul H. B. B. d'Estournelles de Constant de Rebecque (France)
1910 Bureau International Permanent de la Paix (Switzerland)
1911 Tobias M. C. Asser (Holland) and Alfred H. Fried (Austria)
1912 Elihu Root (U.S.)
1913 Henri La Fontaine (Belgium)
1915 No award
1916 No award
1917 International Red Cross
1919 Woodrow Wilson (U.S.)
1920 Léon Bourgeois (France)
1921 Karl H. Branting (Sweden) and Christian L. Lange (Norway)
1922 Fridtjof Nansen (Norway)
1923 No award
1924 No award
1925 Sir Austen Chamberlain (England) and Charles G. Dawes (U.S.)
1926 Aristide Briand (France) and Gustav Stresemann (Germany)
1927 Ferdinand Buisson (France) and Ludwig Quidde (Germany)
1928 No award
1929 Frank B. Kellogg (U.S.)
1930 Lars O. J. Söderblom (Sweden)
1931 Jane Addams and Nicholas M. Butler (U.S.)
1932 No award
1933 Sir Norman Angell (England)
1934 Arthur Henderson (England)
1935 Karl von Ossietzky (Germany)
1936 Carlos de S. Lamas (Argentina)
1937 Lord Cecil of Chelwood (England)
1938 Office International Nansen pour les Réfugiés (Switzerland)
1939 No award
1944 International Red Cross
1945 Cordell Hull (U.S.)
1946 Emily G. Balch and John R. Mott (U.S.)
1947 American Friends Service Committee (U.S.) and British Society of Friends' Service Council (England)
1948 No award
1949 Lord John Boyd Orr (Scotland)
1950 Ralph J. Bunche (U.S.)
1951 Léon Jouhaux (France)
1952 Albert Schweitzer (French Equatorial Africa)
1953 George C. Marshall (U.S.)
1954 Office of U.N. High Commissioner for Refugees
1955 No award
1956 No award
1957 Lester B. Pearson (Canada)
1958 Rev. Dominique Georges Henri Pire (Belgium)
1959 Philip John Noel-Baker (England)
1960 Albert John Luthuli (South Africa)
1961 Dag Hammarskjöld (Sweden)
1962 Linus Pauling (U.S.)
1963 Intl. Comm. of Red Cross; League of Red Cross Societies (both Geneva)
1964 Rev. Dr. Martin Luther King, Jr. (U.S.)
1965 UNICEF (United Nations Children's Fund)
1966 No award
1967 No award
1968 René Cassin (France)
1969 International Labour Organization
1970 Norman E. Borlaug (U.S.)
1971 Willy Brandt (West Germany)
1972 No award
1973 Henry A. Kissinger (U.S.); Le Duc Tho (North Vietnam)[1]
1974 Eisaku Sato (Japan); Sean MacBride (Ireland)
1975 Andrei D. Sakharov (U.S.S.R.)
1976 Mairead Corrigan and Betty Williams (both Northern Ireland)
1977 Amnesty International
1978 Menachem Begin (Israel) and Anwar el-Sadat (Egypt)
1979 Mother Teresa of Calcutta (India)
1980 Adolfo Pérez Esquivel (Argentina)
1981 Office of the United Nations High Commissioner for Refugees
1982 Alva Myrdal (Sweden) and Alfonso García Robles (Mexico)
1983 Lech Walesa (Poland)
1984 Bishop Desmond Tutu (South Africa)
1985 International Physicians for the Prevention of Nuclear War
1986 Elie Wiesel (U.S.)
1987 Oscar Arias Sánchez (Costa Rica)

1. Le Duc Tho refused prize, charging that peace had not yet been really established in South Vietnam.

1988 U.N. Peacekeeping Forces
1989 Dalai Lama (Tibet)

LITERATURE

1901 René F. A. Sully Prudhomme (France)
1902 Theodor Mommsen (Germany)
1903 Björnstjerne Björnson (Norway)
1904 Frédéric Mistral (France) and José Echegaray (Spain)
1905 Henryk Sienkiewicz (Poland)
1906 Giosuè Carducci (Italy)
1907 Rudyard Kipling (England)
1908 Rudolf Eucken (Germany)
1909 Selma Lagerlöf (Sweden)
1910 Paul von Heyse (Germany)
1911 Maurice Maeterlinck (Belgium)
1912 Gerhart Hauptmann (Germany)
1913 Rabindranath Tagore (India)
1915 Romain Rolland (France)
1916 Verner von Heidenstam (Sweden)
1917 Karl Gjellerup (Denmark) and Henrik Pontoppidan (Denmark)
1919 Carl Spitteler (Switzerland)
1920 Knut Hamsun (Norway)
1921 Anatole France (France)
1922 Jacinto Benavente (Spain)
1923 William B. Yeats (Ireland)
1924 Wladyslaw Reymont (Poland)
1925 George Bernard Shaw (Ireland)
1926 Grazia Deledda (Italy)
1927 Henri Bergson (France)
1928 Sigrid Undset (Norway)
1929 Thomas Mann (Germany)
1930 Sinclair Lewis (U.S.)
1931 Erik A. Karlfeldt (Sweden)
1932 John Galsworthy (England)
1933 Ivan G. Bunin (Russia)
1934 Luigi Pirandello (Italy)
1935 No award
1936 Eugene O'Neill (U.S.)
1937 Roger Martin du Gard (France)
1938 Pearl S. Buck (U.S.)
1939 Frans Eemil Sillanpää (Finland)
1944 Johannes V. Jensen (Denmark)
1945 Gabriela Mistral (Chile)
1946 Hermann Hesse (Switzerland)
1947 André Gide (France)
1948 Thomas Stearns Eliot (England)
1949 William Faulkner (U.S.)
1950 Bertrand Russell (England)
1951 Pär Lagerkvist (Sweden)
1952 François Mauriac (France)
1953 Sir Winston Churchill (England)
1954 Ernest Hemingway (U.S.)
1955 Halldór Kiljan Laxness (Iceland)
1956 Juan Ramón Jiménez (Spain)
1957 Albert Camus (France)
1958 Boris Pasternak (U.S.S.R.) (declined)
1959 Salvatore Quasimodo (Italy)
1960 St-John Perse (Alexis St.-Léger Léger) (France)
1961 Ivo Andric (Yugoslavia)
1962 John Steinbeck (U.S.)
1963 Giorgios Seferis (Seferiades) (Greece)
1964 Jean-Paul Sartre (France) (declined)
1965 Mikhail Sholokhov (U.S.S.R.)
1966 Shmuel Yosef Agnon (Israel) and Nelly Sachs (Sweden)
1967 Miguel Angel Asturias (Guatemala)
1968 Yasunari Kawabata (Japan)
1969 Samuel Beckett (Ireland)
1970 Aleksandr Solzhenitsyn (U.S.S.R.)
1971 Pablo Neruda (Chile)
1972 Heinrich Böll (Germany)

1973 Patrick White (Australia)
1974 Eyvind Johnson and Harry Martinson (both Sweden)
1975 Eugenio Montale (Italy)
1976 Saul Bellow (U.S.)
1977 Vicente Aleixandre (Spain)
1978 Isaac Bashevis Singer (U.S.)
1979 Odysseus Elytis (Greece)
1980 Czeslaw Milosz (U.S.)
1981 Elias Canetti (Bulgaria)
1982 Gabriel García Márquez (Colombia)
1983 William Golding (England)
1984 Jaroslav Seifert (Czechoslovakia)
1985 Claude Simon (France)
1986 Wole Soyinka (Nigeria)
1987 Joseph Brodsky (U.S.)
1988 Naguib Mahfouz (Egypt)
1989 Camilo José Cela (Spain)

PHYSICS

1901 Wilhelm K. Roentgen (Germany), for discovery of Roentgen rays
1902 Hendrik A. Lorentz and Pieter Zeeman (Netherlands), for work on influence of magnetism upon radiation
1903 A. Henri Becquerel (France), for work on spontaneous radioactivity; and Pierre and Marie Curie (France), for study of radiation
1904 John Strutt (Lord Rayleigh) (England), for discovery of argon in investigating gas density
1905 Philipp Lenard (Germany), for work with cathode rays
1906 Sir Joseph Thomson (England), for investigations on passage of electricity through gases
1907 Albert A. Michelson (U.S.), for spectroscopic and metrologic investigations
1908 Gabriel Lippmann (France), for method of reproducing colors by photography
1909 Guglielmo Marconi (Italy) and Ferdinand Braun (Germany), for development of wireless
1910 Johannes D. van der Waals (Netherlands), for work with the equation of state for gases and liquids
1911 Wilhelm Wien (Germany), for his laws governing the radiation of heat
1912 Gustaf Dalén (Sweden), for discovery of automatic regulators used in lighting lighthouses and light buoys
1913 Heike Kamerlingh-Onnes (Netherlands), for work leading to production of liquid helium
1914 Max von Laue (Germany), for discovery of diffraction of Roentgen rays passing through crystals
1915 Sir William Bragg and William L. Bragg (England), for analysis of crystal structure by X rays
1916 No award
1917 Charles G. Barkla (England), for discovery of Roentgen radiation of the elements
1918 Max Planck (Germany), discoveries in connection with quantum theory
1919 Johannes Stark (Germany), discovery of Doppler effect in Canal rays and decomposition of spectrum lines by electric fields
1920 Charles E. Guillaume (Switzerland), for discoveries of anomalies in nickel steel alloys
1921 Albert Einstein (Germany), for discovery of the law of the photoelectric effect
1922 Niels Bohr (Denmark), for investigation of structure of atoms and radiations emanating from them
1923 Robert A. Millikan (U.S.), for work on elementary charge of electricity and photoelectric phenomena
1924 Karl M. G. Siegbahn (Sweden), for investiga-

tions in X-ray spectroscopy

1925 James Franck and Gustav Hertz (Germany), for discovery of laws governing impact of electrons upon atoms

1926 Jean B. Perrin (France), for work on discontinuous nous structure of matter and discovery of the equilibrium of sedimentation

1927 Arthur H. Compton (U.S.), for discovery of Compton phenomenon; and Charles T. R. Wilson (England), for method of perceiving paths taken by electrically charged particles

1928 In 1929, the 1928 prize was awarded to Sir Owen Richardson (England), for work on the phenomenon of thermionics and discovery of the Richardson Law

1929 Prince Louis Victor de Broglie (France), for discovery of the wave character of electrons

1930 Sir Chandrasekhara Raman (India), for work on diffusion of light and discovery of the Raman effect

1931 No award

1932 In 1933, the prize for 1932 was awarded to Werner Heisenberg (Germany), for creation of the quantum mechanics

1933 Erwin Schrödinger (Austria) and Paul A. M. Dirac (England), for discovery of new fertile forms of the atomic theory

1934 No award

1935 James Chadwick (England), for discovery of the neutron

1936 Victor F. Hess (Austria), for discovery of cosmic radiation; and Carl D. Anderson (U.S.), for discovery of the positron

1937 Clinton J. Davisson (U.S.) and George P. Thomson (England), for discovery of diffraction of electrons by crystals

1938 Enrico Fermi (Italy), for identification of new radioactivity elements and discovery of nuclear reactions effected by slow neutrons

1939 Ernest Orlando Lawrence (U.S.), for development of the cyclotron

1943 Otto Stern (U.S.), for detection of magnetic momentum of protons

1944 Isidor Isaac Rabi (U.S.), for work on magnetic movements of atomic particles

1945 Wolfgang Pauli (Austria), for work on atomic fissions

1946 Percy Williams Bridgman (U.S.), for studies and inventions in high-pressure physics

1947 Sir Edward Appleton (England), for discovery of layer which reflects radio short waves in the ionosphere

1948 Patrick M. S. Blackett (England), for improvement on Wilson chamber and discoveries in cosmic radiation

1949 Hideki Yukawa (Japan), for mathematical prediction, in 1935, of the meson

1950 Cecil Frank Powell (England), for method of photographic study of atom nucleus, and for discoveries about mesons

1951 Sir John Douglas Cockcroft (England) and Ernest T. S. Walton (Ireland), for work in 1932 on transmutation of atomic nuclei

1952 Edward Mills Purcell and Felix Bloch (U.S.), for work in measurement of magnetic fields in atomic nuclei

1953 Fritz Zernike (Netherlands), for development of "phase contrast" microscope

1954 Max Born (England), for work in quantum mechanics; and Walther Bothe (Germany), for work in cosmic radiation

1955 Polykarp Kusch and Willis E. Lamb, Jr. (U.S.), for atomic measurements

1956 William Shockley, Walter H. Brattain, and John Bardeen (U.S.), for developing electronic transistor

1957 Tsung Dao Lee and Chen Ning Yang (China), for disproving principle of conservation of parity

1958 Pavel A. Cherenkov, Ilya M. Frank, and Igor E. Tamm (U.S.S.R.), for work resulting in development of cosmic-ray counter

1959 Emilio Segre and Owen Chamberlain (U.S.), for demonstrating the existence of the anti-proton

1960 Donald A. Glaser (U.S.), for invention of "bubble chamber" to study subatomic particles

1961 Robert Hofstadter (U.S.), for determination of shape and size of atomic nucleus; Rudolf Mössbauer (Germany), for method of producing and measuring recoil-free gamma rays

1962 Lev D. Landau (U.S.S.R.), for his theories about condensed matter

1963 Eugene Paul Wigner, Maria Goeppert Mayer (both U.S.), and J. Hans D. Jensen (Germany), for research on structure of atom and its nucleus

1964 Charles Hard Townes (U.S.), Nikolai G. Basov, and Aleksandr M. Prochorov (both U.S.S.R.), for developing maser and laser principle of producing high-intensity radiation

1965 Richard P. Feynman, Julian S. Schwinger (both U.S.), and Shinichiro Tomonaga (Japan), for research in quantum electrodynamics

1966 Alfred Kastler (France), for work on energy levels inside atom

1967 Hans A. Bethe (U.S.), for work on energy production of stars

1968 Luis Walter Alvarez (U.S.), for study of subatomic particles

1969 Murray Gell-Mann (U.S.), for study of subatomic particles

1970 Hannes Alfvén (Sweden), for theories in plasma physics; and Louis Néel (France), for discoveries in antiferromagnetism and ferrimagnetism

1971 Dennis Gabor (England), for invention of holographic method of three-dimensional imagery

1972 John Bardeen, Leon N. Cooper, and John Robert Schrieffer (all U.S.), for theory of superconductivity, where electrical resistance in certain metals vanishes above absolute zero temperature

1973 Ivar Giaever (U.S.), Leo Esaki (Japan), and Brian D. Josephson (U.K.), for theories that have advanced and expanded the field of miniature electronics

1974 Antony Hewish (England), for discovery of pulsars; Martin Ryle (England), for using radiotelescopes to probe outer space with high degree of precision

1975 James Rainwater (U.S.) and Ben Mottelson and Aage N. Bohr (both Denmark), for showing that the atomic nucleus is asymmetrical

1976 Burton Richter and Samuel C. C. Ting (both U.S.), for discovery of subatomic particles known as J and psi

1977 Philip W. Anderson and John H. Van Vleck (both U.S.), and Nevill F. Mott (U.K.), for work underlying computer memories and electronic devices

1978 Arno A. Penzias and Robert W. Wilson (both U.S.), for work in cosmic microwave radiation; Piotr L. Kapitsa (U.S.S.R.), for basic inventions and discoveries in low-temperature physics

1979 Steven Weinberg and Sheldon L. Glashow (both U.S.) and Abdus Salam (Pakistan), for developing theory that electromagnetism and the "weak" force, which causes radioactive decay in some atomic nuclei, are facets of the same phenomenon

1980 James W. Cronin and Val L. Fitch (both U.S.), for work concerning the assymetry of subatomic particles

1981 Nicolaas Bloembergen and Arthur L. Schawlow (both U.S.) and Kai M. Siegbahn (Sweden), for developing technologies with lasers and other devices to probe the secrets of complex forms of matter

1982 Kenneth G. Wilson (U.S.), for analysis of changes in matter under pressure and temperature

1983 Subrahmanyam Chandrasekhar and William A. Fowler (both U.S.) for complementary research on processes involved in the evolution of stars

1984 Carlo Rubbia (Italy) and Simon van der Meer (Netherlands), for their role in discovering three subatomic particles, a step toward developing a single theory to account for all natural forces

1985 Klaus von Klitzing (Germany), for developing an exact way of measuring electrical conductivity

1986 Ernst Ruska, Gerd Binnig (both Germany) and Heinrich Rohrer (Switzerland) for work on microscopes

1987 K. Alex Müller (Switzerland) and J. Georg Bednorz (Germany) for their discovery of high-temperature superconductors

1988 Leon M. Lederman, Melvin Schwartz, and Jack Steinberger (all U.S.) for research that improved the understanding of elementary particles and forces.

1989 Norman F. Ramsey (U.S.), for work leading to development of the atomic clock, and Hans G. Dehmelt (U.S.) and Wolfgang Paul (Germany) for developing methods to isolate atoms and subatomic particles.

CHEMISTRY

1901 Jacobus H. van't Hoff (Netherlands), for laws of chemical dynamics and osmotic pressure in solutions

1902 Emil Fischer (Germany), for experiments in sugar and purin groups of substances

1903 Svante A. Arrhenius (Sweden), for his electrolytic theory of dissociation

1904 Sir William Ramsay (England), for discovery and determination of place of inert gaseous elements in air

1905 Adolf von Baeyer (Germany), for work on organic dyes and hydroaromatic combinations

1906 Henri Moissan (France), for isolation of fluorine, and introduction of electric furnace

1907 Eduard Buchner (Germany), discovery of cell-less fermentation and investigations in biological chemistry

1908 Sir Ernest Rutherford (England), for investigations into disintegration of elements

1909 Wilhelm Ostwald (Germany), for work on catalysis and investigations into chemical equilibrium and reaction rates

1910 Otto Wallach (Germany), for work in the field of alicyclic compounds

1911 Marie Curie (France), for discovery of elements radium and polonium

1912 Victor Grignard (France), for reagent discovered by him; and Paul Sabatier (France), for methods of hydrogenating organic compounds

1913 Alfred Werner (Switzerland), for linking up atoms within the molecule

1914 Theodore W. Richards (U.S.), for determining atomic weight of many chemical elements

1915 Richard Willstätter (Germany), for research into coloring matter of plants, especially chlorophyll

1916 No award

1917 No award

1918 Fritz Haber (Germany), for synthetic production of ammonia

1919 No award

1920 Walther Nernst (Germany), for work in thermochemistry

1921 Frederick Soddy (England), for investigations into origin and nature of isotopes

1922 Francis W. Aston (England), for discovery of isotopes in nonradioactive elements and for discovery of the whole number rule

1923 Fritz Pregl (Austria), for method of microanalysis of organic substances discovered by him

1924 No award

1925 In 1926, the 1925 prize was awarded to Richard Zsigmondy (Germany), for work on the heterogeneous nature of colloid solutions

1926 Theodor Svedberg (Sweden), for work on disperse systems

1927 In 1928, the 1927 prize was awarded to Heinrich Wieland (Germany), for investigations of bile acids and kindred substances

1928 Adolf Windaus (Germany), for investigations on constitution of the sterols and their connection with vitamins

1929 Sir Arthur Harden (England) and Hans K. A. S. von Euler-Chelpin (Sweden), for research of fermentation of sugars

1930 Hans Fischer (Germany), for work on coloring matter of blood and leaves and for his synthesis of hemin

1931 Karl Bosch and Friedrich Bergius (Germany), for invention and development of chemical high-pressure methods

1932 Irving Langmuir (U.S.), for work in realm of surface chemistry

1933 No award

1934 Harold C. Urey (U.S.), for discovery of heavy hydrogen

1935 Frédéric and Irène Joliot-Curie (France), for synthesis of new radioactive elements

1936 Peter J. W. Debye (Netherlands), for investigations on dipole moments and diffraction of X rays and electrons in gases

1937 Walter N. Haworth (England), for research on carbohydrates and Vitamin C; and Paul Karrer (Switzerland), for work on carotenoids, flavins, and Vitamins A and B

1938 Richard Kuhn (Germany), for carotinoid study and vitamin research (declined)

1939 Adolf Butenandt (Germany), for work on sexual hormones (declined the prize); and Leopold Ruzicka (Switzerland), for work with polymethylenes

1943 Georg Hevesy De Heves (Hungary), for work on use of isotopes as indicators

1944 Otto Hahn (Germany), for work on atomic fission

1945 Artturi Illmari Virtanen (Finland), for research in the field of conservation of fodder

1946 James B. Sumner (U.S.), for crystallizing enzymes; John H. Northrop and Wendell M. Stanley (U.S.), for preparing enzymes and virus proteins in pure form

1947 Sir Robert Robinson (England), for research in plant substances

1948 Arne Tiselius (Sweden), for biochemical discoveries and isolation of mouse paralysis virus

1949 William Francis Giauque (U.S.), for research in thermodynamics, especially effects of low temperature

1950 Otto Diels and Kurt Alder (Germany), for discovery of diene synthesis enabling scientists to study structure of organic matter

1951 Glenn T. Seaborg and Edwin H. McMillan (U.S.), for discovery of plutonium

1952 Archer John Porter Martin and Richard Laurence Millington Synge (England), for development of partition chromatography

1953 Hermann Staudinger (Germany), for research in giant molecules

1954 Linus C. Pauling (U.S.), for study of forces holding together protein and other molecules

1955 Vincent du Vigneaud (U.S.), for work on pituitary hormones

1956 Sir Cyril Hinshelwood (England) and Nikolai N. Semenov (U.S.S.R.), for parallel research on chemical reaction kinetics

1957 Sir Alexander Todd (England), for research with chemical compounds that are factors in heredity

1958 Frederick Sanger (England), for determining molecular structure of insulin

1959 Jaroslav Heyrovsky (Czechoslovakia), for development of polarography, an electrochemical method of analysis

1960 Willard F. Libby (U.S.), for "atomic time clock" to measure age of objects by measuring their radioactivity

1961 Melvin Calvin (U.S.), for establishing chemical steps during photosynthesis

1962 Max F. Perutz and John C. Kendrew (England), for mapping protein molecules with X-rays

1963 Carl Ziegler (Germany) and Giulio Natta (Italy), for work in uniting simple hydrocarbons into large molecule substances

1964 Dorothy Mary Crowfoot Hodgkin (England), for determining structure of compounds needed in combating pernicious anemia

1965 Robert B. Woodward (U.S.), for work in synthesizing complicated organic compounds

1966 Robert Sanderson Mulliken (U.S.), for research on bond holding atoms together in molecule

1967 Manfred Eigen (Germany), Ronald G. W. Norrish, and George Porter (both England), for work in high-speed chemical reactions

1968 Lars Onsager (U.S.), for development of system of equations in thermodynamics

1969 Derek H. R. Barton (England) and Odd Hassel (Norway), for study of organic molecules

1970 Luis F. Leloir (Argentina), for discovery of sugar nucleotides and their role in biosynthesis of carbohydrates

1971 Gerhard Herzberg (Canada), for contributions to knowledge of electronic structure and geometry of molecules, particularly free radicals

1972 Christian Boehmer Anfinsen, Stanford Moore, and William Howard Stein (all U.S.), for pioneering studies in enzymes

1973 Ernst Otto Fischer (W. Germany) and Geoffrey Wilkinson (U.K.), for work that could solve problem of automobile exhaust pollution

1974 Paul J. Flory (U.S.), for developing analytic methods to study properties and molecular structure of long-chain molecules

1975 John W. Cornforth (Australia) and Vladimir Prelog (Switzerland), for research on structure of biological molecules such as antibiotics and cholesterol

1976 William N. Lipscomb, Jr. (U.S.), for work on the structure and bonding mechanisms of boranes

1977 Ilya Prigogine (Belgium), for contributions to nonequilibrium thermodynamics, particularly the theory of dissipative structures

1978 Peter Mitchell (U.K.), for contributions to the understanding of biological energy transfer

1979 Herbert C. Brown (U.S.) and Georg Wittig (West Germany), for developing a group of substances that facilitate very difficult chemical reactions

1980 Paul Berg and Walter Gilbert (both U.S.) and Frederick Sanger (England), for developing methods to map the structure and function of DNA, the substance that controls the activity of the cell

1981 Roald Hoffmann (U.S.) and Kenichi Fukui (Japan), for applying quantum-mechanics theories to predict the course of chemical reactions

1982 Aaron Klug (U.K.), for research in the detailed structures of viruses and components of life

1983 Henry Taube (U.S.), for research on how electrons transfer between molecules in chemical reactions

1984 R. Bruce Merrifield (U.S.) for research that revolutionized the study of proteins

1985 Herbert A. Hauptman and Jerome Karle (both U.S.) for their outstanding achievements in the development of direct methods for the determination of crystal structures

1986 Dudley R. Herschback, Yuan T. Lee (both U.S.), and John C. Polanyi (Canada) for their work on "reaction dynamics"

1987 Donald J. Cram and Charles J. Pedersen (both U.S.) and Jean-Marie Lehn (France), for wide-ranging research that has included the creation of artificial molecules that can mimic vital chemical reactions of the processes of life.

1988 Johann Deisenhofer, Robert Huber, and Hartmut Michel (all West Germany) for unraveling the structure of proteins that play a crucial role in photosynthesis.

1989 Thomas R. Cech and Sidney Altman (both U.S.) for their discovery, independently, that RNA could actively aid chemical reactions in the cells.

PHYSIOLOGY OR MEDICINE

1901 Emil A. von Behring (Germany), for work on serum therapy against diptheria

1902 Sir Ronald Ross (England), for work on malaria

1903 Niels R. Finsen (Denmark), for his treatment of lupus vulgaris with concentrated light rays

1904 Ivan P. Pavlov (U.S.S.R.), for work on the physiology of digestion

1905 Robert Koch (Germany), for work on tuberculosis

1906 Camillo Golgi (Italy) and Santiago Ramón y Cajal (Spain), for work on structure of the nervous system

1907 Charles L. A. Laveran (France), for work with protozoa in the generation of disease

1908 Paul Ehrlich (Germany), and Elie Metchnikoff (U.S.S.R.), for work on immunity

1909 Theodor Kocher (Switzerland), for work on the thyroid gland

1910 Albrecht Kossel (Germany), for achievements

in the chemistry of the cell

1911 Allvar Gullstrand (Sweden), for work on the dioptrics of the eye

1912 Alexis Carrel (France), for work on vascular ligature and grafting of blood vessels and organs

1913 Charles Richet (France), for work on anaphylaxy

1914 Robert Bárány (Austria), for work on physiology and pathology of the vestibular system

1915-1918 No award

1919 Jules Bordet (Belgium), for discoveries in connection with immunity

1920 August Krogh (Denmark), for discovery of regulation of capillaries' motor mechanism

1921 No award

1922 In 1923, the 1922 prize was shared by Archibald V. Hill (England), for discovery relating to heat-production in muscles; and Otto Meyerhof (Germany), for correlation between consumption of oxygen and production of lactic acid in muscles

1923 Sir Frederick Banting (Canada) and John J. R. Macleod (Scotland), for discovery of insulin

1924 Willem Einthoven (Netherlands), for discovery of the mechanism of the electrocardiogram

1925 No award

1926 Johannes Fibiger (Denmark), for discovery of the Spiroptera carcinoma

1927 Julius Wagner-Jauregg (Austria), for use of malaria inoculation in treatment of dementia paralytica

1928 Charles Nicolle (France), for work on typhus exanthematicus

1929 Christiaan Eijkman (Netherlands), for discovery of the antineuritic vitamins; and Sir Frederick Hopkins (England), for discovery of growth-promoting vitamins

1930 Karl Landsteiner (U.S.), for discovery of human blood groups

1931 Otto H. Warburg (Germany), for discovery of the character and mode of action of the respiratory ferment

1932 Sir Charles Sherrington (England) and Edgar D. Adrian (U.S.), for discoveries of the function of the neuron

1933 Thomas H. Morgan (U.S.), for discoveries on hereditary function of the chromosomes

1934 George H. Whipple, George R. Minot, and William P. Murphy (U.S.), for discovery of liver therapy against anemias

1935 Hans Spemann (Germany), for discovery of the organizer-effect in embryonic development

1936 Sir Henry Dale (England) and Otto Loewi (Germany), for discoveries on chemical transmission of nerve impulses

1937 Albert Szent-Györgyi von Nagyrapolt (Hungary), for discoveries on biological combustion

1938 Corneille Heymans (Belgium), for determining importance of sinus and aorta mechanisms in the regulation of respiration

1939 Gerhard Domagk (Germany), for antibacterial effect of prontocilate

1943 Henrik Dam (Denmark) and Edward A. Doisy (U.S.), for analysis of Vitamin K

1944 Joseph Erlanger and Herbert Spencer Gasser (U.S.), for work on functions of the nerve threads

1945 Sir Alexander Fleming, Ernst Boris Chain, and Sir Howard Florey (England), for discovery of penicillin

1946 Herman J. Muller (U.S.), for hereditary effects of X-rays on genes

1947 Carl F. and Gerty T. Cori (U.S.), for work on animal starch metabolism; Bernardo A. Houssay (Argentina), for study of pituitary

1948 Paul Mueller (Switzerland), for discovery of insect-killing properties of DDT

1949 Walter Rudolf Hess (Switzerland), for research on brain control of body; and Antonio Caetano de Abreu Freire Egas Moniz (Portugal), for development of brain operation

1950 Philip S. Hench, Edward C. Kendall (both U.S.), and Tadeus Reichstein (Switzerland), for discoveries about hormones of adrenal cortex

1951 Max Theiler (South Africa), for development of anti-yellow-fever vaccine

1952 Selman A. Waksman (U.S.), for co-discovery of streptomycin

1953 Fritz A. Lipmann (Germany-U.S.) and Hans Adolph Krebs (Germany-England), for studies of living cells

1954 John F. Enders, Thomas H. Weller, and Frederick C. Robbins (U.S.), for work with cultivation of polio virus

1955 Hugo Theorell (Sweden), for work on oxidation enzymes

1956 Dickinson W. Richards, Jr., André F. Cournand (both U.S.), and Werner Forssmann (Germany), for new techniques in treating heart disease

1957 Daniel Bovet (Italy), for development of drugs to relieve allergies and relax muscles during surgery

1958 Joshua Lederberg (U.S.), for work with genetic mechanisms; George W. Beadle and Edward L. Tatum (U.S.), for discovering how genes transmit hereditary characteristics

1959 Severo Ochoa and Arthur Kornberg (U.S.), for discoveries related to compounds within chromosomes, which play a vital role in heredity

1960 Sir Macfarlane Burnet (Australia) and Peter Brian Medawar (England), for discovery of acquired immunological tolerance

1961 Georg von Bekesy (U.S.), for discoveries about physical mechanisms of stimulation within cochlea

1962 James D. Watson (U.S.), Maurice H. F. Wilkins, and Francis H. C. Crick (England), for determining structure of deoxyribonucleic acid (DNA)

1963 Alan Lloyd Hodgkin, Andrew Fielding Huxley (both England), and Sir John Carew Eccles (Australia), for research on nerve cells

1964 Konrad E. Bloch (U.S.) and Feodor Lynen (Germany), for research on mechanism and regulation of cholesterol and fatty acid metabolism

1965 François Jacob, André Lwolff, and Jacques Monod (France), for study of regulatory activities in body cells

1966 Charles Brenton Huggins (U.S.), for studies in hormone treatment of cancer of prostate; Francis Peyton Rous (U.S.), for discovery of tumor-producing viruses

1967 Haldan K. Hartline, George Wald, and Ragnar Granit (U.S.), for work on human eye

1968 Robert W. Holley, Har Gobind Khorana, and Marshall W. Nirenberg (U.S.), for studies of genetic code

1969 Max Delbruck, Alfred D. Hershey, and Salvador E. Luria (U.S.), for study of mechanism of virus infection in living cells

1970 Julius Axelrod (U.S.), Ulf S. von Euler (Sweden), and Sir Bernard Katz (England), for studies of how nerve impulses are transmitted within the body

1971 Earl W. Sutherland, Jr. (U.S.), for research on how hormones work

1972 Gerald M. Edelman (U.S.), and Rodney R. Porter (U.K.), for research on the chemical structure and nature of antibodies

1973 Karl von Frisch and Konrad Lorenz (Austria), and Nikolaas Tinbergen (Netherlands), for their studies of individual and social behavior patterns

1974 George E. Palade and Christian de Duve (both U.S.) and Albert Claude (Belgium), for contributions to understanding inner workings of living cells

1975 David Baltimore, Howard M. Temin, and Renato Dulbecco (all U.S.), for work in interaction between tumor viruses and genetic material of the cell

1976 Baruch S. Blumberg and D. Carleton Gajdusek (U.S.), for discoveries concerning new mechanisms for the origin and dissemination of infectious diseases

1977 Rosalyn S. Yalow, Roger C. L. Guillemin, and Andrew V. Schally (all U.S.), for research in role of hormones in chemistry of the body

1978 Daniel Nathans and Hamilton Smith (both U.S.) and Werner Arber (Switzerland), for discovery of restriction enzymes and their application to problems of molecular genetics

1979 Allan McLeod Cormack (U.S.) and Godfrey Newbold Hounsfield (England), for developing computed axial tomography (CAT scan) X-ray technique

1980 Baruj Benacerraf and George D. Snell (both U.S.) and Jean Dausset (France), for discoveries that explain how the structure of cells relates to organ transplants and diseases

1981 Roger W. Sperry and David H. Hubel (both U.S.) and Torsten N. Wiesel (Sweden), for studies vital to understanding the organization and functioning of the brain

1982 Sune Bergstrom and Bengt Samuelsson (Sweden) and John R. Vane (U.K.), for research in prostaglandins, a hormonelike substance involved in a wide range of illnesses

1983 Barbara McClintock (U.S.), for her discovery of mobile genes in the chromosomes of a plant that change the future generations of plants they produce

1984 Cesar Milstein (U.K./Argentina) Georges J.F. Kohler (West Germany), and Niels K. Jerne (U.K./Denmark) for their work in immunology

1985 Michael S. Brown and Joseph L. Goldstein (both U.S.) for their work which has drastically widened our understanding of the cholesterol metabolism and increased our possibilities to prevent and treat atherosclerosis and heart attacks

1986 Rita Levi-Montalcini (dual U.S./Italy) and Stanley Cohen (U.S.) for their contributions to the understanding of substances that influence cell growth

1987 Susumu Tonegawa (Japan), for his discoveries of how the body can suddenly marshal its immunological defenses against millions of different disease agents that it has never encountered before.

1988 Gertrude B. Elion, George H. Hitchings (both U.S.) and Sir James Black (U.K.) for their discoveries of important principles for drug treatment.

1989 J. Michael Bishop and Harold E. Varmus (both U.S.) for their unifying theory of cancer development.

ECONOMIC SCIENCE

1969 Ragnar Frisch (Norway) and Jan Tinbergen (Netherlands), for work in econometrics (application of mathematics and statistical methods to economic theories and problems)

1970 Paul A. Samuelson (U.S.), for efforts to raise the level of scientific analysis in economic theory

1971 Simon Kuznets (U.S.), for developing concept of using a country's gross national product to determine its economic growth

1972 Kenneth J. Arrow (U.S.) and Sir John R. Hicks (U.K.), for theories that help to assess business risk and government economic and welfare policies

1973 Wassily Leontief (U.S.), for devising the input-output technique to determine how different sectors of an economy interact

1974 Gunnar Myrdal (Sweden) and Friedrich A. von Hayek (U.K.), for pioneering analysis of the interdependence of economic, social and institutional phenomena

1975 Leonid V. Kantorovich (U.S.S.R.) and Tjalling C. Koopmans (U.S.), for work on the theory of optimum allocation of resources

1976 Milton Friedman (U.S.), for work in consumption analysis and monetary history and theory, and for demonstration of complexity of stabilization policy

1977 Bertil Ohlin (Sweden) and James E. Meade (U.K.), for contributions to theory of international trade and international capital movements

1978 Herbert A. Simon (U.S.), for research into the decision-making process within economic organizations

1979 Sir Arthur Lewis (England) and Theodore Schultz (U.S.), for work on economic problems of developing nations

1980 Lawrence R. Klein (U.S.), for developing models for forecasting economic trends and shaping policies to deal with them

1981 James Tobin (U.S.), for analyses of financial markets and their influence on spending and saving by families and businesses

1982 George J. Stigler (U.S.), for work on government regulation in the economy and the functioning of industry

1983 Gerard Debreu (U.S.), in recognition of his work on the basic economic problem of how prices operate to balance what producers supply with what buyers want.

1984 Sir Richard Stone (U.K.), for his work to develop the systems widely used to measure the performance of national economics

1985 Franco Modigliani (U.S.) for his pioneering work in analyzing the behavior of household savers and the functioning of financial markets

1986 James M. Buchanan (U.S.) for his development of new methods for analyzing economic and political decision-making

1987 Robert M. Solow (U.S.), for seminal contributions to the theory of economic growth.

1988 Maurice Allais (France) for his pioneering development of theories to better understand market behavior and the efficient use of resources.

1989 Trygve Haavelmo (Norway) for his pioneering work in methods for testing economic theories.

Motion Picture Academy Awards (Oscars)

1928

Picture: *Wings,* Paramount
Director: Frank Borzage, *Seventh Heaven;* Lewis Milestone, *Two Arabian Nights*
Actress: Janet Gaynor, *Seventh Heaven, Street Angel, Sunrise*
Actor: Emil Jannings, *The Way of All Flesh, The Last Command*

1929

Picture: *The Broadway Melody,* M-G-M
Director: Frank Lloyd, *The Divine Lady*
Actress: Mary Pickford, *Coquette*
Actor: Warner Baxter, *In Old Arizona*

1930

Picture: *All Quiet on the Western Front,* Universal
Director: Lewis Milestone, *All Quiet on the Western Front*
Actress: Norma Shearer, *The Divorcee*
Actor: George Arliss, *Disraeli*

1931

Picture: *Cimarron:* RKO Radio
Director: Norman Taurog, *Skippy*
Actress: Marie Dressler, *Min and Bill*
Actor: Lionel Barrymore, *A Free Soul*

1932

Picture: *Grand Hotel,* M-G-M
Director: Frank Borzage, *Bad Girl*
Actress: Helen Hayes, *The Sin of Madelon Claudet*
Actor: Fredric March, *Dr. Jekyll and Mr. Hyde,* and Wallace Beery, *The Champ*

1933

Picture: *Cavalcade,* Fox
Director: Frank Lloyd, *Cavalcade*
Actress: Katharine Hepburn, *Morning Glory*
Actor: Charles Laughton, *The Private Life of Henry VIII*

1934

Picture: *It Happened One Night,* Columbia
Director: Frank Capra, *It Happened One Night*
Actress: Claudette Colbert, *It Happened One Night*
Actor: Clark Gable, *It Happened One Night*

1935

Picture: *Mutiny on the Bounty,* M-G-M
Director: John Ford, *The Informer*
Actress: Bette Davis, *Dangerous*
Actor: Victor McLaglen, *The Informer*

1936

Picture: *The Great Ziegfeld,* M-G-M
Director: Frank Capra, *Mr. Deeds Goes to Town*
Actress: Luise Rainer, *The Great Ziegfeld*
Actor: Paul Muni, *The Story of Louis Pasteur*
Supporting Actress: Gale Sondergaard, *Anthony Adverse*
Supporting Actor: Walter Brennan, *Come and Get It*

1937

Picture: *The Life of Emile Zola,* Warner Bros.
Director: Leo McCarey, *The Awful Truth*
Actress: Luise Rainer, *The Good Earth*
Actor: Spencer Tracy, *Captains Courageous*
Supporting Actress: Alice Brady, *In Old Chicago*
Supporting Actor: Joseph Schildkraut, *The Life of Emile Zola*

1938

Picture: *You Can't Take It with You,* Columbia
Director: Frank Capra, *You Can't Take It with You*
Actress: Bette Davis, *Jezebel*
Actor: Spencer Tracy, *Boys Town*
Supporting Actress: Fay Bainter, *Jezebel*
Supporting Actor: Walter Brennan, *Kentucky*

1939

Picture: *Gone with the Wind,* Selznick-M-G-M
Director: Victor Fleming, *Gone with the Wind*
Actress: Vivien Leigh, *Gone with the Wind*
Actor: Robert Donat, *Goodbye, Mr. Chips*
Supporting Actress: Hattie McDaniel, *Gone with the Wind*
Supporting Actor: Thomas Mitchell, *Stagecoach*

1940

Picture: *Rebecca,* Selznick-UA
Director: John Ford, *The Grapes of Wrath*
Actress: Ginger Rogers, *Kitty Foyle*
Actor: James Stewart, *The Philadelphia Story*
Supporting Actress: Jane Darwell, *The Grapes of Wrath*
Supporting Actor: Walter Brennan, *The Westerner*

1941

Picture: *How Green Was My Valley,* 20th Century-Fox
Director: John Ford, *How Green Was My Valley*
Actress: Joan Fontaine, *Suspicion*
Actor: Gary Cooper, *Sergeant York*
Supporting Actress: Mary Astor, *The Great Lie*
Supporting Actor: Donald Crisp, *How Green Was My Valley*

1942

Picture: *Mrs. Miniver,* M-G-M
Director: William Wyler, *Mrs. Miniver*
Actress: Greer Garson, *Mrs. Miniver*
Actor: James Cagney, *Yankee Doodle Dandy*
Supporting Actress: Teresa Wright, *Mrs. Miniver*
Supporting Actor: Van Heflin, *Johnny Eager*

1943

Picture: *Casablanca,* Warner Bros.
Director: Michael Curtiz, *Casablanca*
Actress: Jennifer Jones, *The Song of Bernadette*
Actor: Paul Lukas, *Watch on the Rhine*
Supporting Actress: Katina Paxinou, *For Whom the Bell Tolls*
Supporting Actor: Charles Coburn, *The More the Merrier*

1944

Picture: *Going My Way,* Paramount
Director: Leo McCarey, *Going My Way*
Actress: Ingrid Bergman, *Gaslight*
Actor: Bing Crosby, *Going My Way*
Supporting Actress: Ethel Barrymore, *None But the Lonely Heart*
Supporting Actor: Barry Fitzgerald, *Going My Way*

1945

Picture: *The Lost Weekend,* Paramount
Director: Billy Wilder, *The Lost Weekend*
Actress: Joan Crawford, *Mildred Pierce*
Actor: Ray Milland, *The Lost Weekend*
Supporting Actress: Anne Revere, *National Velvet*
Supporting Actor: James Dunn, *A Tree Grows in Brooklyn*

1946

Picture: *The Best Years of Our Lives*, Goldwyn-RKO Radio
Director: William Wyler, *The Best Years of Our Lives*
Actress: Olivia de Havilland, *To Each His Own*
Actor: Fredric March, *The Best Years of Our Lives*
Supporting Actress: Anne Baxter, *The Razor's Edge*
Supporting Actor: Harold Russell, *The Best Years of Our Lives*

1947

Picture: *Gentleman's Agreement*, 20th Century-Fox
Director: Elia Kazan, *Gentleman's Agreement*
Actress: Loretta Young, *The Farmer's Daughter*
Actor: Ronald Colman, *A Double Life*
Supporting Actress: Celeste Holm, *Gentleman's Agreement*
Supporting Actor: Edmund Gwenn, *Miracle on 34th Street*

1948

Picture: *Hamlet,* Rank-Two Cities-U-I
Director: John Huston, *Treasure of Sierra Madre*
Actress: Jane Wyman, *Johnny Belinda*
Actor: Laurence Olivier, *Hamlet*
Supporting Actress: Claire Trevor, *Key Largo*
Supporting Actor: Walter Huston, *Treasure of Sierra Madre*

1949

Picture: *All the King's Men,* Rossen-Columbia
Director: Joseph L. Mankiewicz, *A Letter to Three Wives*
Actress: Olivia de Havilland, *The Heiress*
Actor: Broderick Crawford, *All the King's Men*
Supporting Actress: Mercedes McCambridge, *All the King's Men*
Supporting Actor: Dean Jagger, *Twelve O'Clock High*

1950

Picture: *All About Eve,* 20th Century-Fox
Director: Joseph L. Mankiewicz, *All About Eve*
Actress: Judy Holliday, *Born Yesterday*
Actor: José Ferrer, *Cyrano de Bergerac*
Supporting Actress: Josephine Hull, *Harvey*
Supporting Actor: George Sanders, *All About Eve*

1951

Picture: *An American in Paris,* M-G-M
Director: George Stevens, *A Place in the Sun*
Actress: Vivien Leigh, *A Streetcar Named Desire*
Actor: Humphrey Bogart, *The African Queen*
Supporting Actress: Kim Hunter, *A Streetcar Named Desire*
Supporting Actor: Karl Malden, *A Streetcar Named Desire*

1952

Picture: *The Greatest Show on Earth,* DeMille-Paramount
Director: John Ford, *The Quiet Man*
Actress: Shirley Booth, *Come Back, Little Sheba*
Actor: Gary Cooper, *High Noon*
Supporting Actress: Gloria Grahame, *The Bad and the Beautiful*
Supporting Actor: Anthony Quinn, *Viva Zapata!*

1953

Picture: *From Here to Eternity,* Columbia
Director: Fred Zinnemann, *From Here to Eternity*
Actress: Audrey Hepburn, *Roman Holiday*
Actor: William Holden, *Stalag 17*
Supporting Actress: Donna Reed, *From Here to Eternity*
Supporting Actor: Frank Sinatra, *From Here to Eternity*

1954

Picture: *On the Waterfront,* Horizon-American Corp., Columbia
Director: Elia Kazan, *On the Waterfront*
Actress: Grace Kelly, *The Country Girl*
Actor: Marlon Brando, *On the Waterfront*
Supporting Actress: Eva Marie Saint, *On the Waterfront*
Supporting Actor: Edmond O'Brien, *The Barefoot Contessa*

1955

Picture: *Marty,* Hecht and Lancaster, United Artists
Director: Delbert Mann, *Marty*
Actress: Anna Magnani, *The Rose Tattoo*
Actor: Ernest Borgnine, *Marty*
Supporting Actress: Jo Van Fleet, *East of Eden*
Supporting Actor: Jack Lemmon, *Mister Roberts*

1956

Picture: *Around the World in 80 Days,* Michael Todd Co., Inc.-U.A.
Director: George Stevens, *Giant*
Actress: Ingrid Bergman, *Anastasia*
Actor: Yul Brynner, *The King and I*
Supporting Actress: Dorothy Malone, *Written on the Wind*
Supporting Actor: Anthony Quinn, *Lust for Life*

1957

Picture: *The Bridge on the River Kwai,* Horizon Picture, Columbia
Director: David Lean, *The Bridge on the River Kwai*
Actress: Joanne Woodward, *The Three Faces of Eve*
Actor: Alec Guinness, *The Bridge on the River Kwai*
Supporting Actress: Miyoshi Umeki, *Sayonara*
Supporting Actor: Red Buttons, *Sayonara*

1958

Picture: *Gigi,* Arthur Freed Productions, Inc., M-G-M
Director: Vincente Minnelli, *Gigi*
Actress: Susan Hayward, *I Want to Live!*
Actor: David Niven, *Separate Tables*
Supporting Actress: Wendy Hiller, *Separate Tables*
Supporting Actor: Burl Ives, *The Big Country*

1959

Picture: *Ben-Hur,* M-G-M
Director: William Wyler, *Ben-Hur*
Actress: Simone Signoret, *Room at the Top*
Actor: Charlton Heston, *Ben-Hur*
Supporting Actress: Shelley Winters, *The Diary of Anne Frank*
Supporting Actor: Hugh Griffith, *Ben-Hur*

1960

Picture: *The Apartment,* Mirisch Co., Inc., United Artists
Director: Billy Wilder, *The Apartment*
Actress: Elizabeth Taylor, *Butterfield 8*
Actor: Burt Lancaster, *Elmer Gantry*
Supporting Actress: Shirley Jones, *Elmer Gantry*
Supporting Actor: Peter Ustinov, *Spartacus*

1961

Picture: *West Side Story,* Mirisch Pictures, Inc., and B and P Enterprises, Inc., United Artists

Director: Robert Wise and Jerome Robbins, *West Side Story*
Actress: Sophia Loren, *Two Women*
Actor: Maximillian Schell, *Judgment at Nuremberg*
Supporting Actress: Rita Moreno, *West Side Story*
Supporting Actor: George Chakiris, *West Side Story*

1962

Picture: *Lawrence of Arabia,* Horizon Pictures, Ltd.-Columbia
Director: David Lean, *Lawrence of Arabia*
Actress: Anne Bancroft, *The Miracle Worker*
Actor: Gregory Peck, *To Kill a Mockingbird*
Supporting Actress: Patty Duke, *The Miracle Worker*
Supporting Actor: Ed Begley, *Sweet Bird of Youth*

1963

Picture: *Tom Jones,* A Woodfall Production, UA-Lopert Pictures
Director: Tony Richardson, *Tom Jones*
Actress: Patricia Neal, *Hud*
Actor: Sidney Poitier, *Lilies of the Field*
Supporting Actress: Margaret Rutherford, *The V.I.P.s*
Supporting Actor: Melvyn Douglas, *Hud*

1964

Picture: *My Fair Lady,* Warner Bros.
Director: George Cukor, *My Fair Lady*
Actress: Julie Andrews, *Mary Poppins*
Actor: Rex Harrison, *My Fair Lady*
Supporting Actress: Lila Kedrova, *Zorba the Greek*
Supporting Actor: Peter Ustinov, *Topkapi*

1965

Picture: *The Sound of Music,* Argyle Enterprises Production, 20th Century-Fox
Director: Robert Wise, *The Sound of Music*
Actress: Julie Christie, *Darling*
Actor: Lee Marvin, *Cat Ballou*
Supporting Actress: Shelley Winters, *A Patch of Blue*
Supporting Actor: Martin Balsam, *A Thousand Clowns*

1966

Picture: *A Man for All Seasons,* Highland Films, Ltd., Production, Columbia
Director: Fred Zinnemann, *A Man for All Seasons*
Actress: Elizabeth Taylor, *Who's Afraid of Virginia Woolf?*
Actor: Paul Scofield, *A Man for All Seasons*
Supporting Actress: Sandy Dennis, *Who's Afraid of Virginia Woolf?*
Supporting Actor: Walter Matthau, *The Fortune Cookie*

1967

Picture: *In the Heat of the Night,* Mirisch Corp. Productions, United Artists
Director: Mike Nichols, *The Graduate*
Actress: Katharine Hepburn, *Guess Who's Coming to Dinner*
Actor: Rod Steiger, *In the Heat of the Night*
Supporting Actress: Estelle Parsons, *Bonnie and Clyde*
Supporting Actor: George Kennedy, *Cool Hand Luke*

1968

Picture: *Oliver!,* Columbia Pictures
Director: Sir Carol Reed, *Oliver!*
Actress: Katharine Hepburn, *The Lion in Winter* and Barbara Streisand, *Funny Girl*
Actor: Cliff Robertson, *Charly*

Supporting Actress: Ruth Gordon, *Rosemary's Baby*
Supporting Actor: Jack Albertson, *The Subject Was Roses*

1969

Picture: *Midnight Cowboy,* Jerome Hellman-John Schlesinger Production, United Artists
Director: John Schlesinger, *Midnight Cowboy*
Actress: Maggie Smith, *The Prime of Miss Jean Brodie*
Actor: John Wayne, *True Grit*
Supporting Actress: Goldie Hawn, *Cactus Flower*
Supporting Actor: Gig Young, *They Shoot Horses Don't They?*

1970

Picture: *Patton,* Frank McCarthy-Franklin J. Schaffner Production, 20th Century Fox
Director: Franklin J. Schaffner, *Patton*
Actress: Glenda Jackson, *Women in Love*
Actor: George C. Scott, *Patton*
Supporting Actress: Helen Hayes, *Airport*
Supporting Actor: John Mills, *Ryan's Daughter*

1971

Picture: *The French Connection,* D'Antoni Productions, 20th Century-Fox
Director: William Friedkin, *The French Connection*
Actress: Jane Fonda, *Klute*
Actor: Gene Hackman, *The French Connection*
Supporting Actress: Cloris Leachman, *The Last Picture Show*
Supporting Actor: Ben Johnson, *The Last Picture Show*

1972

Picture: *The Godfather,* Albert S. Ruddy Production, Paramount
Director: Bob Fosse, *Cabaret*
Actress: Liza Minnelli, *Cabaret*
Actor: Marlon Brando, *The Godfather*
Supporting Actress: Eileen Heckart, *Butterflies Are Free*
Supporting Actor: Joel Gray, *Cabaret*

1973

Picture: *The Sting,* Universal-Bill-Phillips-George Roy Hill Production, Universal
Director: George Roy Hill, *The Sting*
Actress: Glenda Jackson, *A Touch of Class*
Actor: Jack Lemmon, *Save the Tiger*
Supporting Actress: Tatum O'Neal, *Paper Moon*
Supporting Actor: John Houseman, *The Paper Chase*

1974

Picture: *The Godfather, Part II,* Coppola Co. Production, Paramount
Director: Francis Ford Coppola, *The Godfather, Part II*
Actress: Ellen Burstyn, *Alice Doesn't Live Here Anymore*
Actor: Art Carney, *Harry and Tonto*
Supporting Actress: Ingrid Bergman, *Murder on the Orient Express*
Supporting Actor: Robert De Niro, *The Godfather, Part II*

1975

Picture: *One Flew Over the Cuckoo's Nest,* Fantasy Films Production, United Artists
Director: Milos Forman, *One Flew Over the Cuckoo's Nest*
Actress: Louise Fletcher, *One Flew Over the Cuckoo's Nest*

Actor: Jack Nicholson, *One Flew Over the Cuckoo's Nest*
Supporting Actress: Lee Grant, *Shampoo*
Supporting Actor: George Burns, *The Sunshine Boys*

1976

Picture: *Rocky,* Robert Chartoff-Irwin Winkler Production, United Artists
Director: John G. Avildsen, *Rocky*
Actress: Faye Dunaway, *Network*
Actor: Peter Finch, *Network*
Supporting Actress: Beatrice Straight, *Network*
Supporting Actor: Jason Robards, *All the President's Men*

1977

Picture: *Annie Hall,* Jack Rollins-Charles H. Joffe Production, United Artists
Director: Woody Allen, *Annie Hall*
Actress: Diane Keaton, *Annie Hall*
Actor: Richard Dreyfuss, *The Goodbye Girl*
Supporting Actress: Vanessa Redgrave, *Julia*
Supporting Actor: Jason Robards, *Julia*

1978

Picture: *The Deer Hunter,* Michael Cimino Film Production, Universal
Director: Michael Cimino, *The Deer Hunter*
Actress: Jane Fonda, *Coming Home*
Actor: Jon Voight, *Coming Home*
Supporting Actress: Maggie Smith, *California Suite*
Supporting Actor: Christopher Walken, *The Deer Hunter*

1979

Picture: *Kramer vs. Kramer,* Stanley Jaffe Production, Columbia Pictures
Director: Robert Benton, *Kramer vs. Kramer*
Actress: Sally Field, *Norma Rae*
Actor: Dustin Hoffman, *Kramer vs. Kramer*
Supporting Actress: Meryl Streep, *Kramer vs. Kramer*
Supporting Actor: Melvyn Douglas, *Being There*

1980

Picture: *Ordinary People,* Wildwood Enterprises Production, Paramount
Director: Robert Redford, *Ordinary People*
Actress: Sissy Spacek, *Coal Miner's Daughter*
Actor: Robert De Niro, *Raging Bull*
Supporting Actress: Mary Steenburgen, *Melvin and Howard*
Supporting Actor: Timothy Hutton, *Ordinary People*

1981

Picture: *Chariots of Fire,* Enigma Productions, Ladd Company/Warner Bros.
Director: Warren Beatty, *Reds*
Actress: Katharine Hepburn, *On Golden Pond*
Actor: Henry Fonda, *On Golden Pond*
Supporting Actress: Maureen Stapleton, *Reds*
Supporting Actor: John Gielgud, *Arthur*

1982

Picture: *Gandhi,* Indo-British Films Production/Columbia
Director: Richard Attenborough, *Gandhi*
Actress: Meryl Streep, *Sophie's Choice*
Actor: Ben Kingsley, *Gandhi*
Supporting Actress: Jessica Lange, *Tootsie*
Supporting Actor: Louis Gossett, Jr., *An Officer and a Gentleman*

1983

Picture: *Terms of Endearment,* Paramount
Director: James L. Brooks, *Terms of Endearment*
Actress: Shirley MacLaine, *Terms of Endearment*
Actor: Robert Duvall, *Tender Mercies*
Supporting Actress: Linda Hunt, *The Year of Living Dangerously*
Supporting Actor: Jack Nicholson, *Terms of Endearment*

1984

Picture: *Amadeus,* Orion Pictures
Director: Milos Forman, *Amadeus*
Actress: Sally Field, *Places in the Heart*
Actor: F. Murray Abraham, *Amadeus*
Supporting Actress: Dame Peggy Ashcroft, *A Passage to India*
Supporting Actor: Haing S. Ngor, *The Killing Fields*

1985

Picture: *Out of Africa,* Universal
Director: Sydney Pollack, *Out of Africa*
Actress: Geraldine Page, *The Trip to Bountiful*
Actor: William Hurt, *Kiss of the Spider Woman*
Supporting Actress: Anjelica Huston, *Prizzi's Honor*
Supporting Actor: Don Ameche, *Cocoon*

1986

Picture: *Platoon,* Orion Pictures
Director: Oliver Stone, *Platoon*
Actress: Marlee Matlin, *Children of a Lesser God*
Actor: Paul Newman, *The Color of Money*
Supporting Actress: Dianne Wiest, *Hannah and Her Sisters*
Supporting Actor: Michael Caine, *Hannah and Her Sisters*

1987

Picture: *The Last Emperor,* Columbia Pictures
Director: Bernardo Bertolucci, *The Last Emperor*
Actress: Cher, *Moonstruck*
Actor: Michael Douglas, *Wall Street*
Supporting Actress: Olympia Dukakis, *Moonstruck*
Supporting Actor: Sean Connery, *The Untouchables*

1988

Picture: *Rain Man,* United Artists
Director: Barry Levinson, *Rain Man*
Actress: Jodie Foster, *The Accused*
Actor: Dustin Hoffman, *Rain Man*
Supporting Actress: Geena Davis, *The Accidental Tourist*
Supporting Actor: Kevin Kline: *A Fish Named Wanda*

1989

Picture: *Driving Miss Daisy,* Warner Brothers
Director: Oliver Stone, *Born on the Fourth of July*
Actress: Jessica Tandy, *Driving Miss Daisy*
Actor: Daniel Day-Lewis, *My Left Foot*
Supporting Actress: Brenda Fricker, *My Left Foot*
Supporting Actor: Denzel Washington, *Glory*

Other Academy Awards for 1989

Art direction: Anton Furst and Peter Young, *Batman*
Cinematography: Freddie Francis, *Glory*
Costume design: Phyllis Dalton, *Henry V*
Documentary (feature): *Common Threads: Stories From the Quilt;* **(short subject):** *The Johnstown Flood*

Editing: David Brenner and Joe Hutshing, *Born on the Fourth of July*

Foreign-language film: *Cinema Paradiso,* Italy

Makeup: Manlio Rocchetti, *Driving Miss Daisy*

Music (original score): Alan Menken, *The Little Mermaid*

Screenplay (original): Tom Schulman, *Dead Poets Society;* **(adaption):** Alfred Uhry, *Driving Miss Daisy*

Short subject (live-action): *Work Experience;* **(animated):** *Balance*

Song: Alan Menken and Howard Ashman, *Under the Sea* from *The Little Mermaid*

Sound: Donald O. Mitchell, Gregg C. Rudloff, Elliot Tyson, and Russell Williams 2nd, *Glory*

Sound editing: Ben Burtt and Richard Hymns, *Indiana Jones and the Last Crusade*

Visual effects: John Bruno, Dennis Muren, Hoyt Yeatman, and Dennis Skotak, *The Abyss*

Honorary Award: Akira Kurosawa

Jean Hersholt Humanitarian Award: Howard W. Koch

Gordon E. Sawyer Technical Award: Pierre Angenieux

National Society of Film Critics Awards, 1989

Best Film: *Drugstore Cowboy,* Gus Van Sam Jr.

Best Actress: Michelle Pfeiffer, *The Fabulous Baker Boys*

Best Actor: Daniel Day-Lewis, *My Left Foot*

Best Supporting Actress: Anjelica Huston, *Enemies, a Love Story*

Best Supporting Actor: Beau Bridges, *The Fabulous Baker Boys*

Best Director: Gus Van Sam Jr., *Drugstore Cowboy*

Best Screenplay: *Drugstore Cowboy,* Gus Van Sam Jr. and Dan Yost

Best Cinematography: Michael Ballhaus, *The Fabulous Baker Boys*

Best Documentary: *Roger and Me,* Michael Moore

George Foster Peabody Awards for Broadcasting, 1989

Radio

KCBS-AM San Francisco: *Earthquake '89*

CBS, New York: *China in Crisis*

National Public Radio, Washington, D.C.: Scott Simon's Radio Essays on *Weekend Edition Saturday*

Canadian Broadcasting Corporation, Toronto: *Lost Innocence: The Children of World War II*

D. Roberts, independent producer, American Public Radio's *Soundprint* series, for *Mei Mei: A Daughter's Song*

Texaco Inc. and the Metropolitan Opera Association, honoring a half-century of continuous Saturday afternoon radio broadcasts, the longest continuing sponsorship of a national program in broadcasting history.

Television

WCSC, Charleston, S.C.: for providing a "lifeline for viewers deprived of water, communications and other essential services" after Hurricane Hugo.

KGO, San Francisco: for public service after the 1989 earthquake, when it served as an information clearinghouse.

KING, Seattle: *Project Home Team*

KRON, San Francisco: *I Want to Go Home*

Cable News Network, Atlanta: for coverage of the China crisis.

Central Independent Television, London: *Cambodia Year 10*

MTV New York: *Decade*

CBS and Motown-Pangaea Productions, in association with **Quintex Entertainment:** *Lonesome Dove*

ABC and the Black-Marlens Company, in association with **New World Television:** *The Wonder Years*

ABC and Sacret, in association with **Warner Brothers Television:** *China Beach: Vets*

ABC, Lou Rudolph Films, Motown Productions and Allarcom and Fries Entertainment: *Small Sacrifices*

Beyond International Group, Sydney, Australia: *The Great Wall of Iron*

HBO, New York: *Common Threads: Stories From the Quilt*

KCNC, Denver: *Yellowstone: Four Seasons After Fire*

Public Affairs Television, New York: *The Public Mind*

WLOX, Biloxi, Miss.: *Did They Die in Vain?*

Film News Now—the American Documentary, New York: *Who Killed Vincent Chin?*

Children's Television Workshop, New York: *Sesame Street*

NBC News, New York: NBC News Special: *To Be an American* and Tom Brokaw

Personal Awards

David Brinkley, ABC-TV, "attesting to the exceptional contributions he has made to broadcasting during his tenure as one of this country's richest treasures."

J. Leonard Reinsch, a pioneer in broadcasting, cable, and political communication, for a lifetime of outstanding service to his chosen profession.

Poets Laureate of England

Edmund Spenser	1591–1599	Laurence Eusden	1718-1730	Alfred Lord Tennyson	1850-1892
Samuel Daniel	1599–1619	Colley Cibber	1730-1757	Alfred Austin	1896-1913
Ben Jonson	1619–1637	William Whitehead	1757-1785	Robert Bridges	1913-1930
William Davenant	1638–1668	Thomas Warton	1785-1790	John Masefield	1930-1967
John Dryden[1]	1670–1689	Henry James Pye	1790-1813	C. Day Lewis	1967-1972
Thomas Shadwell	1689–1692	Robert Southey	1813-1843	Sir John Betjeman	1972-1984
Nahum Tate	1692–1715	William Wordsworth	1843-1850	Ted Hughes	1984-
Nicholas Rowe	1715-1718				

1. First to bear the title officially. *Source: Encyclopaedia Britannica.*

Pulitzer Prize Awards

(For years not listed, no award was made.)

Source: Columbia University.

Pulitzer Prizes in Journalism

MERITORIOUS PUBLIC SERVICE

1918 *New York Times;* also special award to Minna Lewinson and Henry Beetle Hough
1919 *Milwaukee Journal*
1921 *Boston Post*
1922 *New York World*
1923 *Memphis Commercial Appeal*
1924 *New York World*
1926 *Columbus* (Ga.) *Enquirer Sun*
1927 *Canton* (Ohio) *Daily News*
1928 *Indianapolis Times*
1929 *New York Evening World*
1931 *Atlanta Constitution*
1932 *Indianapolis News*
1933 *New York World-Telegram*
1934 *Medford* (Ore.) *Mail Tribune*
1935 *Sacramento Bee*
1936 *Cedar Rapids* (Iowa) *Gazette*
1937 *St. Louis Post-Dispatch*
1938 *Bismarck* (N.D.) *Tribune*
1939 *Miami Daily News*
1940 *Waterbury* (Conn.) *Republican* and *American*
1941 *St. Louis Post-Dispatch*
1942 *Los Angeles Times*
1943 *Omaha World-Herald*
1944 *New York Times*
1945 *Detroit Free Press*
1946 *Scranton* (Pa.) *Times*
1947 *Baltimore Sun*
1948 *St. Louis Post-Dispatch*
1949 (Lincoln) *Nebraska State Journal*
1950 *Chicago Daily News;* and *St. Louis Post-Dispatch*
1951 *Miami Herald;* and *Brooklyn Eagle*
1952 *St. Louis Post-Dispatch*
1953 *Whiteville* (N.C.) *News Reporter;* and *Tabor City* (N.C.) *Tribune*
1954 *Newsday* (Garden City, L.I.)
1955 *Columbus* (Ga.) *Ledger* and *Sunday Ledger-Enquirer*
1956 *Watsonville* (Calif.) *Register-Pajaronian*
1957 *Chicago Daily News*
1958 (Little Rock) *Arkansas Gazette*
1959 *Utica* (N.Y.) *Observer Dispatch* and *Utica Daily Press*
1960 *Los Angeles Times*
1961 *Amarillo* (Tex.) *Globe-Times*
1962 *Panama City* (Fla.) *News-Herald*
1963 *Chicago Daily News*
1964 *St. Petersburg* (Fla.) *Times*
1965 *Hutchinson* (Kan.) *News*
1966 *Boston Globe*
1967 *Louisville Courier-Journal* and *Milwaukee Journal*
1968 *Riverside* (Calif.) *Press-Enterprise*
1969 *Los Angeles Times*
1970 *Newsday* (Garden City, L.I.)
1971 *Winston-Salem* (N.C.) *Journal and Sentinel*
1972 *New York Times*
1973 *Washington Post*
1974 *Newsday* (Garden City, L.I.)
1975 *Boston Globe*
1976 *Anchorage* (Alaska) *Daily News*
1977 *Lufkin* (Tex.) *News*
1978 *Philadelphia Inquirer*

1979 *Point Reyes* (Calif.) *Light*
1980 Gannett News Service
1981 *Charlotte* (N.C.) *Observer*
1982 *Detroit News*
1983 *Jackson* (Miss.) *Clarion-Ledger*
1984 *Los Angeles Times*
1985 *The Fort Worth Star-Telegram*
1986 *Denver Post*
1987 Andrew Schneider and Matthew Brelis, *Pittsburgh Press*
1988 *Charlotte* (N.C.) *Observer*
1989 *Anchorage Daily News*
1990 *Philadelphia Inquirer* and *Washington* (N.C.) *Daily News*

EDITORIAL

1917 *New York Tribune*
1918 *Louisville Courier-Journal*
1920 Harvey E. Newbranch *(Omaha Evening World-Herald)*
1922 Frank M. O'Brien *(New York Herald)*
1923 William Allen White *(Emporia* [Kan.] *Gazette)*
1924 *Boston Herald* (Frank Buxton); special prize: Frank I. Cobb *(New York World)*
1925 *Charleston* (S.C.) *News and Courier*
1926 *New York Times* (Edward M. Kingsbury)
1927 *Boston Herald* (F. Lauriston Bullard)
1928 Grover Cleveland Hall *(Montgomery* [Ala.] *Advertiser)*
1929 Louis Isaac Jaffe *(Norfolk Virginian-Pilot)*
1931 Charles S. Ryckman *(Fremont* [Neb.] *Tribune)*
1933 *Kansas City* (Mo.) *Star*
1934 E. P. Chase *(Atlantic* [Iowa] *News Telegraph)*
1936 Felix Morley *(Washington Post);* George B. Parker (Scripps-Howard Newspapers)
1937 John W. Owens *(Baltimore Sun)*
1938 W. W. Waymack *(Des Moines Register and Tribune)*
1939 Ronald G. Callvert *(Portland Oregonian)*
1940 Bart Howard *(St. Louis Post-Dispatch)*
1941 Reuben Maury *(New York Daily News)*
1942 Geoffrey Parsons *(New York Herald Tribune)*
1943 Forrest W. Seymour *(Des Moines Register and Tribune)*
1944 *Kansas City* (Mo.) *Star* (Henry J. Haskell)
1945 George W. Potter *(Providence* [R.I.] *Journal-Bulletin)*
1946 Hodding Carter ([Greenville, Miss.] *Delta Democrat-Times)*
1947 William H. Grimes *(Wall Street Journal)*
1948 Virginius Dabney *(Richmond Times-Dispatch)*
1949 John H. Crider *(Boston Herald);* Herbert Elliston *(Washington Post)*
1950 Carl M. Saunders *(Jackson* [Mich.] *Citizen Patriot)*
1951 William H. Fitzpatrick *(New Orleans States)*
1952 Louis LaCoss *(St. Louis Globe-Democrat)*
1953 Vermont C. Royster *(Wall Street Journal)*
1954 *Boston Herald* (Don Murray)
1955 *Detroit Free Press* (Royce Howes)
1956 Lauren K. Soth *(Des Moines Register and Tribune)*
1957 Buford Boone *(Tuscaloosa* [Ala.] *News)*
1958 Harry S. Ashmore *(Arkansas Gazette)*
1959 Ralph McGill *(Atlanta Constitution)*

1960 Lenoir Chambers *(Virginian-Pilot)*
1961 William J. Dorvillier *(San Juan* [P.R.] *Star)*
1962 Thomas M. Storke *(Santa Barbara* [Calif.] *News-Press)*
1963 Ira B. Harkey, Jr. *(Pascagoula* [Miss.] *Chronicle)*
1964 Hazel Brannon Smith *(Lexington* [Miss.] *Advertiser)*
1965 John R. Harrison *(Gainesville* [Fla.] *Daily Sun)*
1966 Robert Lasch *(St. Louis Post-Dispatch)*
1967 Eugene Patterson *(Atlanta Constitution)*
1968 John S. Knight (Knight Newspapers)
1969 Paul Greenberg *(Pine Bluff* [Ark.] *Commercial)*
1970 Phillip L. Geyelin *(Washington Post)*
1971 Horance G. Davis, Jr. *(Gainesville* [Fla.] *Sun)*
1972 John Strohmeyer *(Bethlehem* [Pa.] *Globe Times)*
1973 Roger Bourne Linscott *(Berkshire Eagle* [Pittsfield, Mass.])
1974 F. Gilman Spencer *(Trenton* [N.J.] *Trentonian)*
1975 John Daniell Maurice *(Charleston* [W. Va.] *Daily Mail)*
1976 Philip P. Kerby *(Los Angeles Times)*
1977 Warren L. Lerude, Foster Church and Norman F. Cardoza *(Reno* [Nev.] *Gazette* and *Nevada State Journal)*
1978 Meg Greenfield *(Washington Post)*
1979 Edwin M. Yoder, Jr. *(Washington Star)*
1980 Robert L. Bartley *(Wall Street Journal)*
1981 Not awarded
1982 Jack Rosenthal *(New York Times)*
1983 *Miami Herald*
1984 Albert Scardino *(Georgia Gazette)*
1985 Richard Aregood *(Philadelphia Daily News)*
1986 Jack Fuller *(Chicago Tribune)*
1987 Jonathan Freedman *(San Diego Tribune)*
1988 Jane E. Healy *(Orlando* Fla. *Sentinel)*
1989 Lois Wille *(Chicago Tribune)*
1990 Thomas J. Hylton *(Pottstown* (Pa.) *Mercury)*

CORRESPONDENCE

1929 Paul Scott Mowrer *(Chicago Daily News)*
1930 Leland Stowe *(New York Herald Tribune)*
1931 H. R. Knickerbocker *(Philadelphia Public Ledger* and *New York Evening Post)*
1932 Walter Duranty *(New York Times);* Charles G. Ross *(St. Louis Post-Dispatch)*
1933 Edgar Ansel Mowrer *(Chicago Daily News)*
1934 Frederick T. Birchall *(New York Times)*
1935 Arthur Krock *(New York Times)*
1936 Wilfred C. Barber *(Chicago Tribune)*
1937 Anne O'Hare McCormick *(New York Times)*
1938 Arthur Krock *(New York Times)*
1939 Louis P. Lochner (Associated Press)
1940 Otto D. Tolischus *(New York Times)*
1941 Group award[1]
1942 Carlos P. Romulo *(Philippines Herald)*
1943 Hanson W. Baldwin *(New York Times)*
1944 Ernie Pyle (Scripps-Howard Newspaper Alliance)
1945 Harold V. (Hal) Boyle (Associated Press)
1946 Arnaldo Cortesi *(New York Times)*
1947 Brooks Atkinson *(New York Times)*
1948 Discontinued

EDITORIAL CARTOONING

1922 Rollin Kirby *(New York World)*
1924 Jay Norwood Darling *(New York Tribune)*
1925 Rollin Kirby *(New York World)*
1926 D. R. Fitzpatrick *(St. Louis Post-Dispatch)*

1. For the public services and the individual achievements of American news reporters in the war zones.

1927 Nelson Harding *(Brooklyn Eagle)*
1928 Nelson Harding *(Brooklyn Eagle)*
1929 Rollin Kirby *(New York World)*
1930 Charles R. Macauley *(Brooklyn Eagle)*
1931 Edmund Duffy *(Baltimore Sun)*
1932 John T. McCutcheon *(Chicago Tribune)*
1933 H. M. Talburt *(Washington Daily News)*
1934 Edmund Duffy *(Baltimore Sun)*
1935 Ross A. Lewis *(Milwaukee Journal)*
1937 C. D. Batchelor *(New York Daily News)*
1938 Vaughn Shoemaker *(Chicago Daily News)*
1939 Charles G. Werner *(Daily Oklahoman* [Oklahoma City])
1940 Edmund Duffy *(Baltimore Sun)*
1941 Jacob Burck *(Chicago Times)*
1942 Herbert L. Block (NEA Service)
1943 Jay Norwood Darling *(New York Herald Tribune)*
1944 Clifford K. Berryman *(Washington Evening Star)*
1945 Bill Mauldin (United Features Syndicate)
1946 Bruce Alexander Russell *(Los Angeles Times)*
1947 Vaughn Shoemaker *(Chicago Daily News)*
1948 Reuben L. Goldberg *(New York Sun)*
1949 Lute Pease *(Newark Evening News)*
1950 James T. Berryman *(Washington Evening Star)*
1951 Reg (Reginald W.) Manning *(Arizona Republic* [Phoenix])
1952 Fred L. Packer *(New York Mirror)*
1953 Edward D. Kuekes *(Cleveland Plain Dealer)*
1954 Herbert L. Block *(Washington Post* and *Times-Herald)*
1955 Daniel R. Fitzpatrick *(St. Louis Post-Dispatch)*
1956 Robert York *(Louisville Times)*
1957 Tom Little *(Nashville Tennessean)*
1958 Bruce M. Shanks *(Buffalo Evening News)*
1959 Bill Mauldin *(St. Louis Post-Dispatch)*
1961 Carey Orr *(Chicago Tribune)*
1962 Edmund S. Valtman *(Hartford Times)*
1963 Frank Miller *(Des Moines Register)*
1964 Paul Conrad (formerly of *Denver Post,* later on *Los Angeles Times)*
1966 Don Wright *(Miami News)*
1967 Patrick B. Oliphant *(Denver Post)*
1968 Eugene Gray Payne *(Charlotte* [N.C.] *Observer)*
1969 John Fischetti *(Chicago Daily News)*
1970 Thomas F. Darcy *(Newsday* [Garden City, L.I.])
1971 Paul Conrad *(Los Angeles Times)*
1972 Jeffrey K. MacNelly *(Richmond* [Va.] *News Leader)*
1974 Paul Szep *(Boston Globe)*
1975 Garry Trudeau (Universal Press Syndicate)
1976 Tony Auth *(Philadelphia Inquirer)*
1977 Paul Szep *(Boston Globe)*
1978 Jeffrey K. MacNelly *(Richmond* [Va.] *News Leader)*
1979 Herbert L. Block *(Washington Post)*
1980 Don Wright *(Miami News)*
1981 Mike Peters *(Dayton* [Ohio] *Daily News)*
1982 Ben Sargent *(Austin* [Tex.] *American-Statesman)*
1983 Richard Locher *(Chicago Tribune)*
1984 Paul Conrad *(Los Angeles Times)*
1985 Jeff MacNelly *(Chicago Tribune)*
1986 Jules Feiffer *(Village Voice)*
1987 Berke Breathed *(Washington Post* Writers Group)
1988 Doug Marlette *(Atlanta Constitution* and *Charlotte* [N.C.] *Observer)*
1989 Jack Higgins *(Chicago Sun-Times)*
1990 Tom Toles *(Buffalo News)*

NEWS PHOTOGRAPHY

1942 Milton Brooks *(Detroit News)*

1943 Frank Noel (Associated Press)
1944 Frank Filan (Associated Press); Earle L. Bunker *(Omaha World-Herald)*
1945 Joe Rosenthal (Associated Press)
1947 Arnold Hardy
1948 Frank Cushing *(Boston Traveler)*
1949 Nat Fein *(New York Herald Tribune)*
1950 Bill Crouch *(Oakland Tribune)*
1951 Max Desfor (Associated Press)
1952 John Robinson and Don Ultang *(Des Moines Register & Tribune)*
1953 William M. Gallagher *(Flint* [Mich.] *Journal)*
1954 Mrs. Walter M. Schau
1955 John L. Gaunt, Jr. *(Los Angeles Times)*
1956 *New York Daily News*
1957 Harry A. Trask *(Boston Traveler)*
1958 William C. Beall *(Washington Daily News)*
1959 William Seaman *(Minneapolis Star)*
1960 Andrew Lopez (United Press International)
1961 Yasushi Nagao (Mainichi Newspapers, Tokyo)
1962 Paul Vathis (Harrisburg [Pa.] bureau of Associated Press)
1963 Hector Rondon *(La Republica,* Caracas, Venezuela)
1964 Robert H. Jackson *(Dallas Times Herald)*
1965 Horst Faas (Associated Press)
1966 Kyoichi Sawada (United Press International)
1967 Jack R. Thornell (Associated Press)
1968 News: Rocco Morabito *(Jacksonville* [Fla.] *Journal);* features: Toshio Sakai (United Press International)
1969 Spot news: Edward T. Adams (Associated Press); features: Moneta Sleet, Jr.
1970 Spot news: Steve Starr (Associated Press); features: Dallas Kinney *(Palm Beach Post)*
1971 Spot news: John Paul Filo *(Valley Daily News and Daily Dispatch* [Tarentum and New Kensington, Pa.]); features: Jack Dykinga *(Chicago Sun-Times)*
1972 Spot news: Horst Faas and Michel Laurent (Associated Press); features: Dave Kennerly (United Press International)
1973 Spot news: Huynh Cong Ut *(Associated Press);* features: Brian Lanker *(Topeka Capital-Journal)*
1974 Spot news: Anthony K. Roberts (Associated Press); features: Slava Veder (Associated Press)
1975 Spot news: Gerald H. Gay *(Seattle Times);* features: Matthew Lewis *(Washington Post)*
1976 Spot news: Stanley J. Forman *(Boston Herald-American);* features: photographic staff of *Louisville Courier-Journal* and *Times*
1977 Spot news: Neal Ulevich (Associated Press) and Stanley J. Forman *(Boston Herald-American);* features: Robin Hood *(Chattanooga News-Free Press)*
1978 Spot news: John Blair, freelance, Evansville, Ind.; features: J. Ross Baughman (Associated Press)
1979 Spot news: Thomas J. Kelly, 3rd *(Pottstown* [Pa.] *Mercury);* features: photographic staff of *Boston Herald-American*
1980 Features: Erwin H. Hagler *(Dallas Times Herald)*
1981 Spot news: Larry C. Price *(Fort Worth Star-Telegram);* features: Taro M. Yamasaki *(Detroit Free Press)*
1982 Spot news: Ron Edmonds (Associated Press); features: John H. White *(Chicago Sun-Times)*
1983 Spot news: Bill Foley (Associated Press); features: James B. Dickman *(Dallas Times Herald)*
1984 Spot news: Stan Grossfeld *(Boston Globe);* features: Anthony Suau *(Denver Post)*
1985 Spot news: photographic staff of *Register,* Santa Ana, Calif.; features: Stan Grossfeld *(Boston Globe)*
1986 Spot news: Michel duCille and Carol Guzy *(Miami Herald);* features: Tom Gralish *(Philadelphia Inquirer)*
1987 Spot news: Kim Komenich *(San Francisco Examiner);* features: David Peterson *(Des Moines Register)*
1988 Spot news: Scott Shaw *(Odessa* [Texas] *American);* features: Michel duCille *(Miami Herald)*
1989 Spot news: Ron Olshwanger *(St. Louis Post-Dispatch);* features: Manny Crisostomo *(Detroit Free Press)*
1990 Spot news: *Oakland Tribune;* features: David C. Turnley *(Detroit Free Press)*

NATIONAL TELEGRAPHIC REPORTING

1942 Louis Stark *(New York Times)*
1944 Dewey L. Fleming *(Baltimore Sun)*
1945 James Reston *(New York Times)*
1946 Edward A. Harris *(St. Louis Post-Dispatch)*
1947 Edward T. Folliard *(Washington Post)*

NATIONAL REPORTING

1948 Bert Andrews *(New York Herald Tribune);* Nat S. Finney *(Minneapolis Tribune)*
1949 C. P. Trussel *(New York Times)*
1950 Edwin O. Guthman *(Seattle Times)*
1952 Anthony Leviero *(New York Times)*
1953 Don Whitehead (Associated Press)
1954 Richard Wilson (Cowles Newspapers)
1955 Anthony Lewis *(Washington Daily News)*
1956 Charles L. Bartlett *(Chattanooga Times)*
1957 James Reston *(New York Times)*
1958 Relman Morin (Associated Press) and Clark Mollenhoff *(Des Moines Register & Tribune)*
1959 Howard Van Smith *(Miami News)*
1960 Vance Trimble (Scripps-Howard Newspaper Alliance)
1961 Edward R. Cony *(Wall Street Journal)*
1962 Nathan G. Caldwell and Gene S. Graham *(Nashville Tennessean)*
1963 Anthony Lewis *(New York Times)*
1964 Merriman Smith (United Press International)
1965 Louis M. Kohlmeier *(Wall Street Journal)*
1966 Haynes Johnson *(Washington Evening Star)*
1967 Stanley Penn and Monroe Karmin *(Wall Street Journal)*
1968 Howard James *(Christian Science Monitor);* Nathan K. (Nick) Kotz *(Des Moines Register* and *Minneapolis Tribune)*
1969 Robert Cahn *(Christian Science Monitor)*
1970 William J. Eaton *(Chicago Daily News)*
1971 Lucinda Franks and Thomas Powers (United Press International)
1972 Jack Anderson *(United Feature Syndicate)*
1973 Robert Boyd and Clark Hoyt *(Knight Newspapers)*
1974 Jack White *(Providence* [R.I.] *Journal-Bulletin);* and James R. Polk *(Washington Star-News)*
1975 Donald L. Barlett and James B. Steele *(Philadelphia Inquirer)*
1976 James Risser *(Des Moines Register)*
1977 Walter Mears (Associated Press)
1978 Gaylord D. Shaw *(Los Angeles Times)*
1979 James Risser *(Des Moines Register)*
1980 Bette Swenson Orsini and Charles Stafford *(St. Petersburg Times)*
1981 John M. Crewdson *(New York Times)*
1982 Rick Atkinson *(Kansas City* [Mo.] *Times)*
1983 *Boston Globe*
1984 John N. Wilford *(New York Times)*

1985 Thomas J. Knudson (*Des Moines Register*)
1986 Craig Flournoy and George Rodrigue *(Dallas Morning News)* and Arthur Howe *(Philadelphia Inquirer)*
1987 *Miami Herald,* staff; *New York Times,* staff
1988 Tim Weiner *(Philadelphia Inquirer)*
1989 Donald L. Barlett and James B. Steele *(Philadelphia Inquirer)*
1990 Ross Anderson, Bill Dietrich, Mary Ann Gwinn, and Eric Nalder *(Seattle Times)*

INTERNATIONAL TELEGRAPHIC REPORTING

1942 Laurence Edmund Allen (Associated Press)
1943 Ira Wolfert (North American Newspaper Alliance, Inc.)
1944 Daniel De Luce (Associated Press)
1945 Mark S. Watson *(Baltimore Sun)*
1946 Homer W. Bigart *(New York Herald Tribune)*
1947 Eddy Gilmore (Associated Press)

INTERNATIONAL REPORTING

1948 Paul W. Ward *(Baltimore Sun)*
1949 Price Day *(Baltimore Sun)*
1950 Edmund Stevens *(Christian Science Monitor)*
1951 Keyes Beech and Fred Sparks *(Chicago Daily News);* Homer Bigart and Marguerite Higgins *(New York Herald Tribune);* Relman Morin and Don Whitehead (Associated Press)
1952 John M. Hightower (Associated Press)
1953 Austin C. Wehrwein *(Milwaukee Journal)*
1954 Jim G. Lucas (Scripps-Howard Newspapers)
1955 Harrison E. Salisbury *(New York Times)*
1956 William Randolph Hearst, Jr. and Frank Conniff (Hearst Newspapers) and Kingsbury Smith (INS)
1957 Russell Jones (United Press)
1958 *New York Times*
1959 Joseph Martin and Philip Santora *(New York Daily News)*
1960 A. M. Rosenthal *(New York Times)*
1961 Lynn Heinzerling (Associated Press)
1962 Walter Lippmann (New York Herald Tribune Syndicate)
1963 Hal Hendrix *(Miami News)*
1964 Malcolm W. Browne (Associated Press) and David Halberstam *(New York Times)*
1965 J. A. Livingston *(Philadelphia Bulletin)*
1966 Peter Arnett (Associated Press)
1967 R. John Hughes *(Christian Science Monitor)*
1968 Alfred Friendly *(Washington Post)*
1969 William Tuohy *(Los Angeles Times)*
1970 Seymour M. Hersh (Dispatch News Service)
1971 Jimmie Lee Hoagland *(Washington Post)*
1972 Peter R. Kann *(Wall Street Journal)*
1973 Max Frankel *(New York Times)*
1974 Hedrick Smith *(New York Times)*
1975 William Mullen and Ovie Carter *(Chicago Tribune)*
1976 Sydney H. Schanberg *(New York Times)*
1978 Henry Kamm *(New York Times)*
1979 Richard Ben Cramer *(Philadelphia Inquirer)*
1980 Joel Brinkley and Jay Mather *(Louisville Courier-Journal)*
1981 Shirley Christian *(Miami Herald)*
1982 John Darnton *(New York Times)*
1983 Thomas L. Friedman *(New York Times)*
1984 Karen E. House *(Wall Street Journal)*
1985 Josh Friedman, Dennis Bell, and Ozier Muhammad *(Newsday)*
1986 Lewis M. Simons, Pete Carey, and Katherine Ellison *(San Jose Mercury News)*
1987 Michael Parks *(Los Angeles Times)*
1988 Thomas L. Friedman *(New York Times)*

1989 Bill Keller *(New York Times);* Glenn Frankel *(Washington Post)*
1990 Nicholas D. Kristof and Sheryl WuDunn *(New York Times)*

REPORTING

1917 Herbert B. Swope *(New York World)*
1918 Harold A. Littledale *(New York Evening Post)*
1920 John J. Leary, Jr. *(New York World)*
1921 Louis Seibold *(New York World)*
1922 Kirke L. Simpson (Associated Press)
1923 Alva Johnston *(New York Times)*
1924 Magner White *(San Diego Sun)*
1925 James W. Mulroy and Alvin H. Goldstein *(Chicago Daily News)*
1926 William Burke Miller *(Louisville Courier-Journal)*
1927 John T. Rogers *(St. Louis Post-Dispatch)*
1929 Paul Y. Anderson *(St. Louis Post-Dispatch)*
1930 Russell D. Owen *(New York Times);* special award: W. O. Dapping *(Auburn* [N.Y.] *Citizen)*
1931 A. B. MacDonald *(Kansas City* [Mo.] *Star)*
1932 W. C. Richards, D. D. Martin, J. S. Pooler, F. D. Webb, J. N. W. Sloan (all of *Detroit Free Press)*
1933 Francis A. Jamieson (Associated Press)
1934 Royce Brier *(San Francisco Chronicle)*
1935 William H. Taylor *(New York Herald Tribune)*
1936 Lauren D. Lyman *(New York Times)*
1937 John J. O'Neill *(New York Herald Tribune);* William Leonard Laurence *(New York Times);* Howard W. Blakeslee (Associated Press); Gobind Behari Lal (Universal Service); David Dietz (Scripps-Howard Newspapers)
1938 Raymond Sprigle *(Pittsburg Post-Gazette)*
1939 Thomas L. Stokes *(New York World-Telegram)*
1940 S. Burton Heath *(New York World-Telegram)*
1941 Westbrook Pegler *(New York World-Telegram)*
1942 Stanton Delaplane *(San Francisco Chronicle)*
1943 George Weller *(Chicago Daily News)*
1944 Paul Schoenstein and associates *(New York Journal-American)*
1945 Jack S. McDowell *(San Francisco Call-Bulletin)*
1946 William Leonard Laurence *(New York Times)*
1947 Frederick Woltman *(New York World-Telegram)*
1948 George E. Goodwin *(Atlanta Journal)*
1949 Malcolm Johnson *(New York Sun)*
1950 Meyer Berger *(New York Times)*
1951 Edward S. Montgomery *(San Francisco Examiner)*
1952 George de Carvalho *(San Francisco Chronicle)*
1953 Editorial staff *(Providence Journal and Evening Bulletin);*[1] Edward J. Mowery *(New York World-Telegram and Sun)*[2]
1954 *Vicksburg* (Miss.) *Sunday Post-Herald;*[1] Alvin Scott McCoy *(Kansas City* [Mo.] *Star)*[2]
1955 Mrs. Caro Brown *(Alice* [Tex.] *Daily Echo);*[1] Roland Kenneth Towery *(Cuero* [Tex.] *Record)*[2]
1956 Lee Hills *(Detroit Free Press);*[1] Arthur Daley *(New York Times)*[2]
1957 *Salt Lake Tribune;*[1] Wallace Turner and William Lambert *(Portland Oregonian)*[2]
1958 *Fargo* [N.D.] *Forum;*[1] George Beveridge *(Washington* [D.C.] *Evening Star)*[2]
1959 Mary Lou Werner *(Washington* [D.C.] *Evening Star);*[1] John Harold Brislin *(Scranton* [Pa.] *Tribune & Scrantonian)*[2]
1960 Jack Nelson *(Atlanta Constitution);*[1] Miriam Ottenberg *(Washington Evening Star)*[2]
1961 Sanche de Gramont *(New York Herald Tribune);*[1] Edgar May *(Buffalo Evening News)*[2]
1962 Robert D. Mullins *(Deseret News,* Salt Lake City);[1] George Bliss *(Chicago Tribune)*[2]
1963 Sylvan Fox, Anthony Shannon, and William

Longgood *(New York World-Telegram and Sun)*;[1] Oscar Griffin, Jr. (former editor of *Pecos* [Tex.] *Independent and Enterprise,* now on staff of *Houston Chronicle)*[2]

1. Reporting under pressure of edition deadlines. 2. Reporting not under pressure of edition deadlines.

GENERAL LOCAL REPORTING

1964 Norman C. Miller *(Wall Street Journal)*
1965 Melvin H. Ruder *(Hungry Horse News,* Columbia Falls, Mont.)
1966 Staff of *Los Angeles Times*
1967 Robert V. Cox *(Chambersburg* [Pa.] *Public Opinion)*
1968 Staff of *Detroit Free Press*
1969 John Fetterman *(Louisville Times* and *Courier-Journal)*
1970 Thomas Fitzpatrick *(Chicago Sun-Times)*
1971 Staff of *Akron* (Ohio) *Beacon*
1972 Richard Cooper and John Machacek *(Rochester* [N.Y.] *Times-Union)*
1973 *Chicago Tribune*
1974 Arthur M. Petacque and Hugh F. Hough *(Chicago Sun-Times)*
1975 *Xenia* (Ohio) *Daily Gazette*
1976 Gene Miller *(Miami Herald)*
1977 Margo Huston *(Milwaukee Journal)*
1978 Richard Whitt *(Louisville Courier-Journal)*
1979 Staff of *San Diego* (Calif.) *Evening Tribune*
1980 Staff of *Philadelphia Inquirer*
1981 *Longview* (Wash.) *Daily News*
1982 *Kansas City* (Mo.) *Star* and *Kansas City* (Mo.) *Times*
1983 *Fort Wayne* (Ind.) *News-Sentinel*
1984 *Newsday*

GENERAL NEWS REPORTING

1985 Thomas Turcol *(Virginian-Pilot and Ledger-Star)*
1986 Edna Buchanan *(Miami Herald)*
1987 *Akron Beacon Journal,* staff
1988 *Alabama Journal* (Montgomery), staff, *Lawrence* (Mass.) *Eagle-Tribune,* staff
1989 *Louisville Courier-Journal* staff
1990 *San Jose* (Calif.) *Mercury News*

SPECIAL LOCAL REPORTING

1964 James V. Magee, Albert V. Gaudiosi, and Frederick A. Meyer *(Philadelphia Bulletin)*
1965 Gene Goltz *(Houston Post)*
1966 John A. Frasca *(Tampa Tribune)*
1967 Gene Miller *(Miami Herald)*
1968 J. Anthony Lukas *(New York Times)*
1969 Albert L. Delugach and Denny Walsh *(St. Louis Globe-Democrat)*
1970 Harold Eugene Martin *(Montgomery Advertiser)*
1971 William Hugh Jones *(Chicago Tribune)*
1972 Timothy Leland, Gerard N. O'Neill, Stephen A. Kurkjian, and Ann DeSantis *(Boston Globe)*
1973 Sun Newspapers of Omaha, Neb.
1974 William Sherman *(New York Daily News)*
1975 *Indianapolis Star*
1976 *Chicago Tribune*
1977 Acel Moore and Wendell Rawls, Jr. *(Philadelphia Inquirer)*
1978 Anthony R. Dolan *(Stamford* [Conn.] *Advocate)*
1979 Gilbert M. Gaul and Elliot G. Jaspin *(Pottsville* [Pa.] *Republican)*
1980 Nils J. Bruzelius, Alexander B. Hawes, Jr., Stephen A. Kurkjian, Robert M. Porterfield, and Joan Vennochi *(Boston Globe)*
1981 Clark Hallas and Robert B. Lowe *(Arizona Daily Star,* Tucson)
1982 Paul Henderson *(Seattle Times)*
1983 Loretta Tofani *(Washington Post)*
1984 *Boston Globe*

INVESTIGATIVE REPORTING

1985 Lucy Morgan and Jack Reed *(St. Petersburg* [Fla.] *Times)* and William K. Marimow *(Philadelphia Inquirer)*
1986 Jeffrey A. Marx and Michael M. York *(Lexington* [Ky.] *Herald Leader)*
1987 Daniel R. Biddle, H.G. Bissinger, and Fredric N. Tulsky *(Philadelphia Inquirer)*
1988 Dean Baquet, William C. Gaines, and Ann Marie Lipinski *(Chicago Tribune)*
1989 Bill Dedman *(Atlanta Journal and Constitution)*
1990 Lou Kilzer and Chris Ison *(Minneapolis-St. Paul Star Tribune)*

FEATURE WRITING

1979 Jon D. Franklin *(Baltimore Evening Sun)*
1980 Madeleine Blais *(Miami Herald)*
1981 Teresa Carpenter *(Village Voice,* New York)
1982 Saul Pett (Associated Press)
1983 Nan Robertson *(New York Times)*
1984 Peter M. Rinearson *(Seattle Times)*
1985 Alice Steinbach *(Baltimore Sun)*
1986 John Camp *(St. Paul Pioneer Press and Dispatch)*
1987 Steve Twomey *(Philadelphia Inquirer)*
1988 Jacqui Banaszynski *(St. Paul Pioneer Press Dispatch)*
1989 David Zucchino *(Philadelphia Inquirer)*
1990 Dave Curtin *(Colorado Springs Gazette Telegraph)*

COMMENTARY

1970 Marquis W. Childs *(St. Louis Post-Dispatch)*
1971 William A. Caldwell *(Record* [Hackensack, N.J.])
1972 Mike Royko *(Chicago Daily News)*
1973 David S. Broder *(Washington Post)*
1974 Edwin A. Roberts, Jr. *(National Observer)*
1975 Mary McGrory *(Washington Star)*
1976 Walter W. (Red) Smith *(New York Times)*
1977 George F. Will *(Washington Post* Writers Group)
1978 William Safire *(New York Times)*
1979 Russell Baker *(New York Times)*
1980 Ellen H. Goodman *(Boston Globe)*
1981 Dave Anderson *(New York Times)*
1982 Art Buchwald *(Los Angeles Times* Syndicate)
1983 Claude Sitton *(Raleigh* [N.C.] *News & Observer)*
1984 Vermont Royster *(Wall Street Journal)*
1985 Murray Kempton *(Newsday)*
1986 Jimmy Breslin *(New York Daily News)*
1987 Charles Krauthammer *(Washington Post* Writers Group)
1988 Dave Barry *(Miami Herald)*
1989 Clarence Page *(Chicago Tribune)*
1990 Jim Murray *(Los Angeles Times)*

CRITICISM

1970 Ada Louise Huxtable *(New York Times)*
1971 Harold C. Schonberg *(New York Times)*
1972 Frank Peters, Jr. *(St. Louis Post-Dispatch)*
1973 Ronald Powers *(Chicago Sun-Times)*
1974 Emily Genauer *(Newsday* Syndicate)
1975 Roger Ebert *(Chicago Sun-Times)*
1976 Alan M. Kriegsman *(Washington Post)*
1977 William McPherson *(Washington Post)*
1978 Walter Kerr *(New York Times)*
1979 Paul Gapp *(Chicago Tribune)*
1980 William A. Henry, 3rd *(Boston Globe)*

1981 Jonathan Yardley *(Washington Star)*
1982 Martin Bernheimer *(Los Angeles Times)*
1983 Manuela Hoelterhoff *(Wall Street Journal)*
1984 Paul Goldberger *(New York Times)*
1985 Howard Rosenberg (*Los Angeles Times*)
1986 Donal Henahan *(New York Times)*
1987 Richard Eder *(Los Angeles Times)*
1988 Tom Shales *(Washington Post)*
1989 Michael Skube *(News and Observer,* Raleigh, N.C.)
1990 Allan Temko *(San Francisco Chronicle)*

EXPLANATORY JOURNALISM

1985 Jon Franklin *(Baltimore Evening Sun)*
1986 *New York Times*
1987 Jeff Lyon and Peter Gorner *(Chicago Tribune)*
1988 Daniel Hertzberg and James B. Stewart *(Wall Street Journal)*
1989 David Hanners, William Snyder, and Karen Blessen *(Dallas Morning News)*
1990 David A. Vise and Coll *(Washington Post)*

SPECIALIZED REPORTING

1985 Randall Savage and Jackie Crosby *(Macon* [Ga.] *Telegraph and News*)
1986 Andrew Schneider and Mary Pat Flaherty *(Pittsburgh Press)*
1987 Alex S. Jones *(New York Times)*
1988 Walt Bogdanich *(Wall Street Journal)*
1989 Edward Humes *(Orange County Register)*
1990 Tamar Stieber *(Albuquerque* (N.M.) *Journal)*

SPECIAL CITATIONS

1938 *Edmonton* (Alberta) *Journal,* special bronze plaque for editorial leadership in defense of freedom of press in Province of Alberta.
1941 *New York Times* for the public educational value of its foreign news report.
1944 Byron Price, Director of the Office of Censorship, for the creation and administration of the newspaper and radio codes. Mrs. William Allen White, for her husband's interest and services during the past seven years as a member of the Advisory Board of the Graduate School of Journalism, Columbia University. Richard Rodgers and Oscar Hammerstein II for their musical *Oklahoma!*
1945 The cartographers of the American press for their war maps.
1947 (Pulitzer centennial year.) Columbia University

and the Graduate School of Journalism for their efforts to maintain and advance the high standards governing the Pulitzer Prize awards. The *St. Louis Post-Dispatch* for its unswerving adherence to the public and professional ideals of its founder and its leadership in American journalism.
1948 Dr. Frank D. Fackenthal for his interest and service.
1951 Cyrus L. Sulzberger *(New York Times)* for his exclusive interview with Archbishop Stepinac in a Yugoslav prison.
1952 *Kansas City Star* for coverage of 1951 floods; Max Kase *(New York Journal-American)* for exposures of bribery in college basketball.
1953 *New York Times* for its 17-year publication of "News of the Week in Review"; and Lester Markel, its founder.
1957 Kenneth Roberts for his historical novels.
1958 Walter Lippmann *(New York Herald Tribune)* for his "wisdom, perception and high sense of responsibility" in his commentary on national and international affairs.
1960 Garrett Mattingly, for *The Armada.*
1961 *American Heritage Picture History of the Civil War,* as distinguished example of American book publishing.
1964 Gannett Newspapers, Rochester, N.Y.
1973 James Thomas Flexner for his biography *George Washington.*
1974 Roger Sessions for his "life's work in music."
1976 John Hohenberg for "services for 22 years as administrator of the Pulitzer Prizes"; Scott Joplin for his contributions to American music.
1977 Alex Haley for his novel, *Roots.*
1978 E.B. White of *New Yorker* magazine and Richard L. Strout of *Christian Science Monitor.*
1982 Milton Babbitt, "for his life's work as a distinguished and seminal American composer."
1984 Theodor Seuss Geisel (Dr. Seuss) for "books full of playful rhymes, nonsense words and strange illustrations."
1985 William H. Schuman for "more than a half century of contribution to American music as a composer and educational leader."
1987 Joseph Pulitzer Jr., "for extraordinary services to American journalism and letters during his 31 years as chairman of the Pulitzer Prize Board and for his accomplishments as an editor and publisher."

Pulitzer Prizes in Letters

FICTION[1]

1918 *His Family.* Ernest Poole
1919 *The Magnificent Ambersons.* Booth Tarkington
1921 *The Age of Innocence.* Edith Wharton
1922 *Alice Adams.* Booth Tarkington
1923 *One of Ours.* Willa Cather
1924 *The Able McLaughlins.* Margaret Wilson
1925 *So Big.* Edna Ferber
1926 *Arrowsmith.* Sinclair Lewis
1927 *Early Autumn.* Louis Bromfield
1928 *The Bridge of San Luis Rey.* Thornton Wilder
1929 *Scarlet Sister Mary.* Julia Peterkin
1930 *Laughing Boy.* Oliver La Farge
1931 *Years of Grace.* Margaret Ayer Barnes
1932 *The Good Earth.* Pearl S. Buck
1933 *The Store.* T. S. Stribling
1934 *Lamb in His Bosom.* Caroline Miller

1. Before 1948, award was for novels only.

1935 *Now in November.* Josephine Winslow Johnson
1936 *Honey in the Horn.* Harold L. Davis
1937 *Gone With the Wind.* Margaret Mitchell
1938 *The Late George Apley.* John Phillips Marquand
1939 *The Yearling.* Marjorie Kinnan Rawlings
1940 *The Grapes of Wrath.* John Steinbeck
1942 *In This Our Life.* Ellen Glasgow
1943 *Dragon's Teeth.* Upton Sinclair
1944 *Journey in the Dark.* Martin Flavin
1945 *A Bell for Adano.* John Hersey
1947 *All the King's Men.* Robert Penn Warren
1948 *Tales of the South Pacific.* James A. Michener
1949 *Guard of Honor.* James Gould Cozzens
1950 *The Way West.* A. B. Guthrie, Jr.
1951 *The Town.* Conrad Richter
1952 *The Caine Mutiny.* Herman Wouk
1953 *The Old Man and the Sea.* Ernest Hemingway
1955 *A Fable.* William Faulkner
1956 *Andersonville.* MacKinlay Kantor

1958 *A Death in the Family.* James Agee
1959 *The Travels of Jaimie McPheeters.* Robert Lewis Taylor
1960 *Advise and Consent.* Allen Drury
1961 *To Kill a Mockingbird.* Harper Lee
1962 *The Edge of Sadness.* Edwin O'Connor
1963 *The Reivers.* William Faulkner
1965 *The Keepers of the House.* Shirley Ann Grau
1966 *Collected Stories of Katherine Anne Porter.* Katherine Anne Porter
1967 *The Fixer.* Bernard Malamud
1968 *The Confessions of Nat Turner.* William Styron
1969 *House Made of Dawn.* N. Scott Momaday
1970 *Collected Stories.* Jean Stafford
1972 *Angle of Repose.* Wallace Stegner
1973 *The Optimist's Daughter.* Eudora Welty
1975 *The Killer Angels.* Michael Shaara
1976 *Humboldt's Gift.* Saul Bellow
1978 *Elbow Room.* James Alan McPherson
1979 *The Stories of John Cheever.* John Cheever
1980 *The Executioner's Song.* Norman Mailer
1981 *A Confederacy of Dunces.* John Kennedy Toole
1982 *Rabbit Is Rich.* John Updike
1983 *The Color Purple.* Alice Walker
1984 *Ironweed.* William Kennedy
1985 *Foreign Affairs,* Alison Lurie
1986 *Lonesome Dove,* Larry McMurtry
1987 *A Summons to Memphis,* Peter Taylor
1988 *Beloved,* Toni Morrison
1989 *Breathing Lessons,* Anne Tyler
1990 *The Mambo Kings Play Songs of Love,* Oscar Hijeulos

1957 *Long Day's Journey Into Night.* Eugene O'Neill
1958 *Look Homeward, Ángel.* Ketti Frings
1959 *J.B.* Archibald MacLeish
1960 *Fiorello!* George Abbott, Jerome Weidman, Jerry Bock, and Sheldon Harnick
1961 *All the Way Home.* Tad Mosel
1962 *How to Succeed in Business Without Really Trying.* Frank Loesser and Abe Burrows
1965 *The Subject Was Roses.* Frank D. Gilroy
1967 *A Delicate Balance.* Edward Albee
1969 *The Great White Hope.* Howard Sackler
1970 *No Place to Be Somebody.* Charles Gordone
1971 *The Effect of Gamma Rays on Man-in-the-Moon Marigolds.* Paul Zindel
1973 *That Championship Season.* Jason Miller
1975 *Seascape.* Edward Albee
1976 *A Chorus Line.* Conceived by Michael Bennett
1977 *The Shadow Box.* Michael Cristofer
1978 *The Gin Game.* Donald L. Coburn
1979 *Buried Child.* Sam Shepard
1980 *Talley's Folly.* Lanford Wilson
1981 *Crimes of the Heart.* Beth Henley
1982 *A Soldier's Play.* Charles Fuller
1983 *'Night, Mother.* Marsha Norman
1984 *Glengarry Glen Ross.* David Mamet
1985 *Sunday in the Park with George.* Stephen Sondheim and James Lapine
1987 *Fences.* August Wilson
1988 *Driving Miss Daisy.* Alfred Uhry
1989 *The Heidi Chronicles,* Wendy Wasserstein
1990 *The Piano Lesson,* August Wilson

HISTORY OF UNITED STATES

1917 *With Americans of Past and Present Days.* J. J. Jusserand, Ambassador of France to United States
1918 *A History of the Civil War, 1861–1865.* James Ford Rhodes
1920 *The War With Mexico.* Justin H. Smith
1921 *The Victory at Sea.* William Sowden Sims in collaboration with Burton J. Hendrick
1922 *The Founding of New England.* James Truslow Adams
1923 *The Supreme Court in United States History.* Charles Warren
1924 *The American Revolution—A Constitutional Interpretation.* Charles Howard McIlwain
1925 *A History of the American Frontier.* Frederic L. Paxson
1926 *The History of the United States.* Edward Channing
1927 *Pinckney's Treaty.* Samuel Flagg Bemis
1928 *Main Currents in American Thought.* Vernon Louis Parrington
1929 *The Organization and Administration of the Union Army, 1861–1865.* Fred Albert Shannon
1930 *The War of Independence.* Claude H. Van Tyne
1931 *The Coming of the War: 1914.* Bernadotte E. Schmitt
1932 *My Experiences in the World War.* John J. Pershing
1933 *The Significance of Sections in American History.* Frederick J. Turner
1934 *The People's Choice.* Herbert Agar
1935 *The Colonial Period of American History.* Charles McLean Andrews
1936 *The Constitutional History of the United States.* Andrew C. McLaughlin
1937 *The Flowering of New England.* Van Wyck Brooks
1938 *The Road to Reunion, 1865–1900.* Paul Herman Buck

DRAMA

1918 *Why Marry?* Jesse Lynch Williams
1920 *Beyond the Horizon.* Eugene O'Neill
1921 *Miss Lulu Bett.* Zona Gale
1922 *Anna Christie.* Eugene O'Neill
1923 *Icebound.* Owen Davis
1924 *Hell-Bent Fer Heaven.* Hatcher Hughes
1925 *They Knew What They Wanted.* Sidney Howard
1926 *Craig's Wife.* George Kelly
1927 *In Abraham's Bosom.* Paul Green
1928 *Strange Interlude.* Eugene O'Neill
1929 *Street Scene.* Elmer L. Rice
1930 *The Green Pastures.* Marc Connelly
1931 *Alison's House.* Susan Glaspell
1932 *Of Thee I Sing.* George S. Kaufman, Morrie Ryskind, and Ira Gershwin
1933 *Both Your Houses.* Maxwell Anderson
1934 *Men in White.* Sidney Kingsley
1935 *The Old Maid.* Zöe Akins
1936 *Idiot's Delight.* Robert E. Sherwood
1937 *You Can't Take It With You.* Moss Hart and George S. Kaufman
1938 *Our Town.* Thornton Wilder
1939 *Abe Lincoln in Illinois.* Robert E. Sherwood
1940 *The Time of Your Life.* William Saroyan
1941 *There Shall Be No Night.* Robert E. Sherwood
1943 *The Skin of Our Teeth.* Thornton Wilder
1945 *Harvey.* Mary Chase
1946 *State of the Union.* Russel Crouse and Howard Lindsay
1948 *A Streetcar Named Desire.* Tennessee Williams
1949 *Death of a Salesman.* Arthur Miller
1950 *South Pacific.* Richard Rodgers, Oscar Hammerstein II, and Joshua Logan
1952 *The Shrike.* Joseph Kramm
1953 *Picnic.* William Inge
1954 *The Teahouse of the August Moon.* John Patrick
1955 *Cat on a Hot Tin Roof.* Tennessee Williams
1956 *The Diary of Anne Frank.* Frances Goodrich and Albert Hackett

1939 *A History of American Magazines.* Frank Luther Mott
1940 *Abraham Lincoln: The War Years.* Carl Sandburg
1941 *The Atlantic Migration, 1607–1860.* Marcus Lee Hansen
1942 *Reveille in Washington.* Margaret Leech
1943 *Paul Revere and the World He Lived In.* Esther Forbes
1944 *The Growth of American Thought.* Merle Curti
1945 *Unfinished Business.* Stephen Bonsal
1946 *The Age of Jackson.* Arthur M. Schlesinger, Jr.
1947 *Scientists Against Time.* James Phinney Baxter, 3rd
1948 *Across the Wide Missouri.* Bernard DeVoto
1949 *The Disruption of American Democracy.* Roy Franklin Nichols
1950 *Art and Life in America.* Oliver W. Larkin
1951 *The Old Northwest, Pioneer Period 1815–1840.* R. Carlyle Buley
1952 *The Uprooted.* Oscar Handlin
1953 *The Era of Good Feelings.* George Dangerfield
1954 *A Stillness at Appomattox.* Bruce Catton
1955 *Great River: The Rio Grande in North American History.* Paul Horgan
1956 *The Age of Reform.* Richard Hofstadter
1957 *Russia Leaves the War: Soviet-American Relations, 1917–1920.* George F. Kennan
1958 *Banks and Politics in America: From the Revolution to the Civil War.* Bray Hammond
1959 *The Republican Era: 1869–1901.* Leonard D. White, assisted by Jean Schneider
1960 *In the Days of McKinley.* Margaret Leech
1961 *Between War and Peace: The Potsdam Conference.* Herbert Feis
1962 *The Triumphant Empire, Thunder-Clouds Gather in the West.* Lawrence H. Gipson
1963 *Washington, Village and Capital, 1800–1878.* Constance McLaughlin Green
1964 *Puritan Village: The Formation of a New England Town.* Sumner Chilton Powell
1965 *The Greenback Era.* Irwin Unger
1966 *Life of the Mind in America.* Perry Miller
1967 *Exploration and Empire: The Explorer and Scientist in the Winning of the American West.* William H. Goetzmann
1968 *The Ideological Origins of the American Revolution.* Bernard Bailyn
1969 *Origins of the Fifth Amendment.* Leonard W. Levy
1970 *Present at the Creation: My Years in the State Department.* Dean Acheson
1971 *Roosevelt: The Soldier of Freedom.* James McGregor Burns
1972 *Neither Black Nor White. Slavery and Race Relations in Brazil and the United States.* Carl N. Degler
1973 *People of Paradox: An Inquiry Concerning the Origin of American Civilization.* Michael Kammen
1974 *The Americans: The Democratic Experience, Vol. 3.* Daniel J. Boorstin
1975 *Jefferson and His Time.* Dumas Malone
1976 *Lamy of Santa Fe.* Paul Horgan
1977 *The Impending Crisis: 1841–1861.* David M. Potter (posth)
1978 *The Invisible Hand: The Managerial Revolution in American Business.* Alfred D. Chandler, Jr.
1979 *The Dred Scott Case: Its Significance in Law and Politics.* Don E. Fehrenbacher
1980 *Been in the Storm So Long.* Leon F. Litwack
1981 *American Education: The National Experience; 1783–1876.* Lawrence A. Cremin
1982 *Mary Chestnut's Civil War.* C. Vann Woodward, editor
1983 *The Transformation of Virginia, 1740–1790.* Rhys L. Isaac
1985 *The Prophets of Regulation.* Thomas K. McCraw
1986 *. . . the Heavens and the Earth: A Political History of the Space Age.* Walter A. McDougall
1987 *Voyagers to the West: A Passage in the Peopling of America on the Eve of the Revolution.* Bernard Bailyn
1988 *The Launching of Modern American Science 1846-1876.* Robert V. Bruce
1989 *Parting the Waters,* Taylor Branch; *Battle Cry of Freedom,* James M. McPherson
1990 *In Our Image: America's Empire in the Philippines,* Stanley Karnow

BIOGRAPHY OR AUTOBIOGRAPHY

1917 *Julia Ward Howe.* Laura E. Richards and Maude Howe Elliott, assisted by Florence Howe Hall
1918 *Benjamin Franklin, Self-Revealed.* William Cabell Bruce
1919 *The Education of Henry Adams.* Henry Adams
1920 *The Life of John Marshall.* Albert J. Beveridge
1921 *The Americanization of Edward Bok.* Edward Bok
1922 *A Daughter of the Middle Border.* Hamlin Garland
1923 *The Life and Letters of Walter H. Page,* Burton J. Hendrick
1924 *From Immigrant to Inventor.* Michael Idvorsky Pupin
1925 *Barrett Wendell and His Letters.* M. A. DeWolfe Howe
1926 *The Life of Sir William Osler.* Harvey Cushing
1927 *Whitman.* Emory Holloway
1928 *The American Orchestra and Theodore Thomas.* Charles Edward Russell
1929 *The Training of an American. The Earlier Life and Letters of Walter H. Page.* Burton J. Hendrick
1930 *The Raven.* Marquis James
1931 *Charles W. Eliot.* Henry James
1932 *Theodore Roosevelt.* Henry F. Pringle
1933 *Grover Cleveland.* Allan Nevins
1934 *John Hay.* Tyler Dennett
1935 *R. E. Lee.* Douglas S. Freeman
1936 *The Thought and Character of William James.* Ralph Barton Perry
1937 *Hamilton Fish.* Allan Nevins
1938 *Pedlar's Progress.* Odell Shepard; *Andrew Jackson.* Marquis James
1939 *Benjamin Franklin.* Carl Van Doren
1940 *Woodrow Wilson. Life and Letters,* Vols. VII and VIII. Ray Stannard Baker
1941 *Jonathan Edwards.* Ola E. Winslow
1942 *Crusader in Crinoline.* Forrest Wilson
1943 *Admiral of the Ocean Sea.* Samuel Eliot Morison
1944 *The American Leonardo: The Life of Samuel F. B. Morse.* Carleton Mabee
1945 *George Bancroft: Brahmin Rebel.* Russel Blaine Nye
1946 *Son of the Wilderness.* Linnie Marsh Wolfe
1947 *The Autobiography of William Allen White*
1948 *Forgotten First Citizen: John Bigelow.* Margaret Clapp
1949 *Roosevelt and Hopkins.* Robert E. Sherwood
1950 *John Quincy Adams and the Foundations of American Foreign Policy.* Samuel Flagg Bemis
1951 *John C. Calhoun: American Portrait.* Margaret Louise Coit
1952 *Charles Evans Hughes.* Merlo J. Pusey

1953 *Edmund Pendleton, 1721–1803.* David J. Mays
1954 *The Spirit of St. Louis.* Charles A. Lindbergh
1955 *The Taft Story.* William S. White
1956 *Benjamin Henry Latrobe.* Talbot F. Hamlin
1957 *Profiles in Courage.* John F. Kennedy
1958 *George Washington.* Douglas Southall Freeman (Vols. 1–6) and John Alexander Carroll and Mary Wells Ashworth (Vol. 7)
1959 *Woodrow Wilson, American Prophet.* Arthur Walworth
1960 *John Paul Jones.* Samuel Eliot Morison
1961 *Charles Sumner and the Coming of the Civil War.* David Donald
1963 *Henry James: Vol. II, The Conquest of London, 1870–1881; Vol. III, The Middle Years, 1881–1895.* Leon Edel
1964 *John Keats.* Walter Jackson Bate
1965 *Henry Adams* (3 Vols.). Ernest Samuels
1966 *A Thousand Days.* Arthur M. Schlesinger, Jr.
1967 *Mr. Clemens and Mark Twain.* Justin Kaplan
1968 *Memoirs, 1925–1950.* George F. Kennan
1969 *The Man From New York.* B. L. Reid
1970 *Huey Long.* T. Harry Williams
1971 *Robert Frost: The Years of Triumph, 1915–1938.* Lawrence Thompson
1972 *Eleanor and Franklin: The Story of Their Relationship Based on Eleanor Roosevelt's Private Papers.* Joseph P. Lash
1973 *Luce and His Empire.* W. A. Swanberg
1974 *O'Neill, Son and Artist.* Louis Sheaffer
1975 *The Power Broker: Robert Moses and the Fall of New York.* Robert A. Caro
1976 *Edith Wharton: A Biography.* Richard W. B. Lewis
1977 *A Prince of Our Disorder.* John E. Mack
1978 *Samuel Johnson.* Walter Jackson Bate
1979 *Days of Sorrow and Pain: Leo Baeck and the Berlin Jews.* Leonard Baker
1980 *The Rise of Theodore Roosevelt.* Edmund Morris
1981 *Peter the Great.* Robert K. Massie
1982 *Grant: A Biography.* William S. McFeely
1983 *Growing Up.* Russell Baker
1984 *Booker T. Washington.* Louis R. Harlan
1985 *The Life and Times of Cotton Mather,* Kenneth Silverman
1986 *Louise Bogan: A Portrait,* Elizabeth Frank
1987 *Bearing the Cross: Martin Luther King Jr. and the Southern Christian Leadership Conference,* David J. Garrow
1988 *Look Homeward: A Life of Thomas Wolfe.* David Herbert Donald
1989 *Oscar Wilde.* Richard Ellmann
1990 *Machiavelli in Hell,* Sebastian de Grazia

POETRY[1]

1918 *Love Songs.* Sara Teasdale
1919 *Old Road to Paradise.* Margaret Widdemer; *Corn Huskers.* Carl Sandburg
1922 *Collected Poems.* Edwin Arlington Robinson
1923 *The Ballad of the Harp-Weaver; A Few Figs from Thistles;* eight sonnets in *American Poetry, 1922, A Miscellany.* Edna St. Vincent Millay
1924 *New Hampshire: A Poem With Notes and Grace Notes.* Robert Frost
1925 *The Man Who Died Twice.* Edwin Arlington Robinson
1926 *What's O'Clock.* Amy Lowell
1927 *Fiddler's Farewell.* Leonora Speyer

1928 *Tristram.* Edwin Arlington Robinson
1929 *John Brown's Body.* Stephen Vincent Benét
1930 *Selected Poems.* Conrad Aiken
1931 *Collected Poems.* Robert Frost
1932 *The Flowering Stone.* George Dillon
1933 *Conquistador.* Archibald MacLeish
1934 *Collected Verse.* Robert Hillyer
1935 *Bright Ambush.* Audrey Wurdemann
1936 *Strange Holiness.* Robert P. T. Coffin
1937 *A Further Range.* Robert Frost
1938 *Cold Morning Sky.* Marya Zaturenska
1939 *Selected Poems.* John Gould Fletcher
1940 *Collected Poems.* Mark Van Doren
1941 *Sunderland Capture.* Leonard Bacon
1942 *The Dust Which Is God.* William Rose Benét
1943 *A Witness Tree.* Robert Frost
1944 *Western Star.* Stephen Vincent Benét
1945 *V-Letter and Other Poems.* Karl Shapiro
1947 *Lord Weary's Castle.* Robert Lowell
1948 *The Age of Anxiety.* W. H. Auden
1949 *Terror and Decorum.* Peter Viereck
1950 *Annie Allen.* Gwendolyn Brooks
1951 *Complete Poems.* Carl Sandburg
1952 *Collected Poems.* Marianne Moore
1953 *Collected Poems, 1917–1952.* Archibald MacLeish
1954 *The Waking.* Theodore Roethke
1955 *Collected Poems.* Wallace Stevens
1956 *Poems—North & South.* Elizabeth Bishop
1957 *Things of This World.* Richard Wilbur
1958 *Promises: Poems, 1954–1956.* Robert Penn Warren
1959 *Selected Poems, 1928–1958.* Stanley Kunitz
1960 *Heart's Needle.* William Snodgrass
1961 *Times Three: Selected Verse From Three Decades.* Phyllis McGinley
1962 *Poems.* Alan Dugan
1963 *Pictures From Breughel.* William Carlos Williams
1964 *At the End of the Open Road.* Louis Simpson
1965 *77 Dream Songs.* John Berryman
1966 *Selected Poems.* Richard Eberhart
1967 *Live or Die.* Anne Sexton
1968 *The Hard Hours.* Anthony Hecht
1969 *Of Being Numerous.* George Oppen
1970 *Untitled Subjects.* Richard Howard
1971 *The Carrier of Ladders.* William S. Merwin
1972 *Collected Poems.* James Wright
1973 *Up Country.* Maxine Winokur Kumin
1974 *The Dolphin.* Robert Lowell
1975 *Turtle Island.* Gary Snyder
1976 *Self-Portrait in a Convex Mirror.* John Ashbery
1977 *Divine Comedies.* James Merrill
1978 *Collected Poems.* Howard Nemerov
1979 *Now and Then: Poems, 1976–1978.* Robert Penn Warren.
1980 *Selected Poems.* Donald Rodney Justice
1981 *The Morning of the Poem.* James Schuyler
1982 *The Collected Poems.* Sylvia Plath
1983 *Selected Poems.* Galway Kinnell
1984 *American Primitive.* Mary Oliver
1985 *Yin,* Carolyn Kizer
1986 *The Flying Change,* Henry Taylor
1987 *Thomas and Beulah,* Rita Dove
1988 *Partial Accounts: New and Selected Poems.* William Meredith
1989 *New and Collected Poems.* Richard Wilbur
1990 *The World Doesn't End,* Charles Simic

GENERAL NONFICTION

1962 *The Making of the President, 1960.* Theodore H. White
1963 *The Guns of August.* Barbara W. Tuchman

1964 *Anti-Intellectualism in American Life*. Richard Hofstadter
1965 *O Strange New World*. Howard Mumford Jones
1966 *Wandering Through Winter*. Edwin Way Teale
1967 *The Problem of Slavery in Western Culture*. David Brion Davis
1968 *Rousseau and Revolution*. Will and Ariel Durant
1969 *So Human an Animal*. Rene Jules Dubos; *The Armies of the Night*. Norman Mailer
1970 *Gandhi's Truth*. Erik H. Erikson
1971 *The Rising Sun*. John Toland
1972 *Stilwell and the American Experience in China, 1911–1945*. Barbara W. Tuchman
1973 *Fire in the Lake: The Vietnamese and the Americans in Vietnam*. Frances FitzGerald; and *Children of Crisis* (Vols. 1 and 2). Robert M. Coles
1974 *The Denial of Death*. Ernest Becker
1975 *Pilgrim at Tinker Creek*. Annie Dillard
1976 *Why Survive? Being Old in America*. Robert N. Butler
1977 *Beautiful Swimmers: Watermen, Crabs and the Chesapeake Bay*. William W. Warner
1978 *The Dragons of Eden*. Carl Sagan
1979 *On Human Nature*. Edward O. Wilson
1980 *Gödel, Escher, Bach: An Eternal Golden Braid*. Douglas R. Hofstadter
1981 *Fin-de-Siecle Vienna: Politics and Culture*. Carl E. Schorske
1982 *The Soul of a New Machine*. Tracy Kidder
1983 *Is There No Place on Earth for Me?* Susan Sheehan
1984 *Social Transformation of American Medicine*. Paul Starr
1985 *The Good War: An Oral History of World War II*, Studs Terkel
1986 *Move Your Shadow: South Africa, Black and White*, Joseph Lelyveld; *Common Ground: A Turbulent Decade in the Lives of Three American Families*, J. Anthony Lukas
1987 *Arab and Jew: Wounded Spirits in a Promised Land*, David K. Shipler
1988 *The Making of the Atomic Bomb*. Richard Rhodes
1989 *A Bright Shining Lie*. Neil Sheehan
1990 *And Their Children After Them*, Dale Maharidge and Michael Williamson

PULITZER PRIZES IN MUSIC

1943 *Secular Cantata No. 2, A Free Song*. William Schuman
1944 *Symphony No. 4* (Op. 34). Howard Hanson
1945 *Appalachian Spring*. Aaron Copland
1946 *The Canticle of the Sun*. Leo Sowerby
1947 *Symphony No. 3*. Charles Ives
1948 *Symphony No. 3*. Walter Piston
1949 *Louisiana Story* music. Virgil Thomson
1950 *The Consul*. Gian Carlo Menotti
1951 Music for opera *Giants in the Earth*. Douglas Stuart Moore
1952 *Symphony Concertante*. Gail Kubik
1954 *Concerto for Two Pianos and Orchestra*. Quincy Porter
1955 *The Saint of Bleecker Street*. Gian Carlo Menotti
1956 *Symphony No. 3*. Ernst Toch
1957 *Meditations on Ecclesiastes*. Norman Dello Joio
1958 *Vanessa*. Samuel Barber
1959 *Concerto for Piano and Orchestra*. John La Montaine
1960 *Second String Quartet*. Elliott Carter
1961 *Symphony No. 7*. Walter Piston
1962 *The Crucible*. Robert Ward
1963 *Piano Concerto No. 1*. Samuel Barber
1966 *Variations for Orchestra*. Leslie Bassett
1967 *Quartet No. 3*. Leon Kirchner
1968 *Echoes of Time and the River*. George Crumb
1969 *String Quartet No. 3*. Karel Husa
1970 *Time's Encomium*. Charles Wuorinen
1971 *Synchronisms No. 6 for Piano and Electronic Sound*. Mario Davidowsky
1972 *Windows*. Jacob Druckman
1973 *String Quartet No. 3*. Elliott Carter
1974 *Notturno*. Donald Martino
1975 *From the Diary of Virginia Woolf*. Dominick Argento
1976 *Air Music*. Ned Rorem
1977 *Visions of Terror and Wonder*. Richard Wernick
1978 *Déjà Vu for Percussion Quartet and Orchestra*. Michael Colgrass
1979 *Aftertones of Infinity*. Joseph Schwantner
1980 *In Memory of a Summer Day*. David Del Tredici
1981 Not awarded
1982 *Concerto for Orchestra*. Roger Sessions
1983 *Three Movements for Orchestra*. Ellen T. Zwilich
1984 *Canti del Sole*. Bernard Rands
1985 *Symphony RiverRun*, Stephen Albert
1986 *Wind Quintet IV*, George Perle
1987 *The Flight Into Egypt*, John Harbison
1988 *12 New Etudes for Piano*. William Bolcom
1989 *Whispers Out of Time*, Roger Reynolds
1990 *Duplicates: A Concerto for Two Pianos and Orchestra*, Mel Powell

Enrico Fermi Award

Named in honor of Enrico Fermi, the atomic pioneer, the $100,000 award is given in recognition of "exceptional and altogether outstanding" scientific and technical achievement in atomic energy.

1954 Enrico Fermi
1956 John von Neumann
1957 Ernest O. Lawrence
1958 Eugene P. Wigner
1959 Glenn T. Seaborg
1961 Hans A. Bethe
1962 Edward Teller
1963 J. Robert Oppenheimer
1964 Hyman G. Rickover
1966 Otto Hahn, Lise Meitner, and Fritz Strassman
1968 John A. Wheeler
1969 Walter H. Zinn

1970 Norris E. Bradbury
1971 Shields Warren and Stafford L. Warren
1972 Manson Benedict
1976 William L. Russell
1978 Harold M. Agnew and Wolfgang K.H. Panofsky
1980 Alvin M. Weinberg and Rudolf E. Peirls
1981 W. Bennett Lewis
1982 Herbert Anderson and Seth Neddermeyer

1983 Alexander Hollaender and John Lawrence
1984 Robert R. Wilson and Georges Vendryès
1985 Norman C. Rasmussen and Marshall N. Rosenblath
1986 Ernest D. Courant and M. Stanley Livingston
1987 Luis W. Alvarez and Gerald F. Tape
1988 Richard B. Setlow and Victor F. Weisskopf
1989 Award not given

New York Drama Critics' Circle Awards

1935–36
Winterset, Maxwell Anderson
1936–37
High Tor, Maxwell Anderson
1937–38
Of Mice and Men, John Steinbeck
Shadow and Substance, Paul Vincent Carroll[1]
1938–39
(No award) *The White Steed,* Paul Vincent Carroll[1]
1939–40
The Time of Your Life, William Saroyan
1940–41
Watch on the Rhine, Lillian Hellman
The Corn Is Green, Emlyn Williams[1]
1941–42
(No award) *Blithe Spirit,* Noel Coward[1]
1942–43
The Patriots, Sidney Kingsley
1943–44
(No award) *Jacobowsky and the Colonel.* Franz Werfel and S. N. Behrman[1]
1944–45
The Glass Menagerie, Tennessee Williams
1945–46
(No award) *Carousel,* Richard Rodgers and Oscar Hammerstein II[2]
1946–47
All My Sons, Arthur Miller
No Exit, Jean-Paul Sartre[1]
Brigadoon, Alan Jay Lerner and Frederick Loewe[2]
1947–48
A Streetcar Named Desire, Tennessee Williams
The Winslow Boy, Terence Rattigan[1]
1948–49
Death of a Salesman, Arthur Miller
The Madwoman of Chaillot, Jean Giraudoux and Maurice Valency[1]
South Pacific, Richard Rodgers, Oscar Hammerstein II, and Joshua Logan[2]
1949–50
The Member of the Wedding, Carson McCullers
The Cocktail Party, T. S. Eliot[1]
The Consul, Gian Carlo Menotti[2]
1950–51
Darkness at Noon, Sidney Kingsley[3]
The Lady's Not for Burning, Christopher Fry[1]
Guys and Dolls, Abe Burrows, Jo Swerling, and Frank Loesser[2]
1951–52
I Am a Camera, John Van Druten[4]
Venus Observed, Christopher Fry[1]
Pal Joey, Richard Rodgers, Lorenz Hart, and John O'Hara[2]
Don Juan in Hell, George B. Shaw[5]
1952–53
Picnic, William Inge *The Love of Four Colonels,* by Peter Ustinov[1]
Wonderful Town, Joseph Fields, Jerome Chodorov, Betty Comden, Adolph Green, and Leonard Bernstein[2]
1953–54
The Teahouse of the August Moon, John Patrick
Ondine, Jean Giraudoux[1]
The Golden Apple, John Latouche and Jerome Moross[2]
1954–55
Cat on a Hot Tin Roof, Tennessee Williams
Witness for the Prosecution, Agatha Christie[1]
The Saint of Bleecker Street, Gian Carlo Menotti[2]
1955–56
The Diary of Anne Frank, Frances Goodrich and Albert Hackett

Tiger at the Gates, Jean Giraudoux and Christopher Fry[1]
My Fair Lady, Frederick Loewe and Alan Jay Lerner[2]
1956–57
Long Day's Journey Into Night, Eugene O'Neill
Waltz of the Toreadors, Jean Anouilh[1]
The Most Happy Fella, Frank Loesser[2] [6]
1957–58
Look Homeward, Angel, Ketti Frings[7]
Look Back in Anger, John Osborne[1]
The Music Man, Meredith Willson[2]
1958–59
A Raisin in the Sun, Lorraine Hansberry
The Visit, Friedrich Duerrenmatt-Maurice Valency[1]
La Plume de ma Tante, Robert Dhery and Gerard Calvi[2]
1959–60
Toys in the Attic, Lillian Hellman
Five Finger Exercise, Peter Shaffer[1]
Fiorello!, Jerome Weidman, George Abbott, Jerry Bock, and Sheldon Harnick[2]
1960–61
All the Way Home, Tad Mosel[3]
A Taste of Honey, Shelagh Delaney[1]
Carnival, Michael Stewart[2]
1961–62
The Night of the Iguana, Tennessee Williams
A Man for All Seasons, Robert Bolt[1]
How to Succeed in Business Without Really Trying, Abe Burrows, Jack Weinstock, Willie Gilbert, and Frank Loesser[2] [9]
1962–63
Who's Afraid of Virginia Woolf?, Edward Albee
Beyond the Fringe, Alan Bennett, Peter Cook, Jonathan Miller, and Dudley Moore[10]
1963–64
Luther, John Osborne
Hello, Dolly!, Michael Stewart and Jerry Herman[2] [11]
The Trojan Women, Euripides[10] [12]
1964–65
The Subject Was Roses, Frank D. Gilroy
Fiddler on the Roof, Joseph Stein, Jerry Bock, and Sheldon Harnick[2] [13]
1965–66
The Persecution and Assassination of Marat as Performed by the Inmates of the Asylum of Charenton Under the Direction of the Marquis de Sade, Peter Weiss
The Man of La Mancha, Dale Wasserman, Mitch Leigh, and Joe Darion
1966–67
The Homecoming, Harold Pinter
Cabaret, Joe Masteroff, John Kander, and Fred Ebb[2] [14]
1967–68
Rosencrantz and Guildenstern Are Dead, Tom Stoppard
Your Own Thing, Donald Driver, Hal Hester, and Danny Apolinar[2]
1968–69
The Great White Hope, Howard Sackler
1776, Sherman Edwards and Peter Stone[2]
1969–70
Borstal Boy, Frank McMahon[15]
The Effect of Gamma Rays on Man-in-the-Moon Marigolds, Paul Zindel[16]
Company, George Furth and Stephen Sondheim[2]
1970–71
Home, David Storey
The House of Blue Leaves, John Guare[16]

Follies, James Goldman and Stephen Sondheim[2]
1971–72
That Championship Season, Jason Miller
Two Gentlemen of Verona, adapted by John Guare and Mel Shapiro[2]
The Screens, Jean Genet[1]
1972–73
The Changing Room, David Storey
The Hot l Baltimore, by Lanford Wilson[16]
A Little Night Music, Hugh Wheeler and Stephen Sondheim[2]
1973–74
The Contractors, David Storey
Short Eyes, Miguel Piñero[16]
Candide, Leonard Bernstein, Hugh Wheeler, and Richard Wilbur[2]
1974–75
Equus, Peter Shaffer
The Taking of Miss Janie, Ed Bullins[16]
A Chorus Line, James Kirkwood and Nicholas Dante[2]
1975–76
Travesties, Tom Stoppard
Streamers, David Rabe[16]
Pacific Overtures, Stephen Sondheim, John Weidman, and Hugh Wheeler[2]
1976–77
Otherwise Engaged, Simon Gray
American Buffalo, David Mamet[16]
Annie, Thomas Meehan, Charles Strouse, and Martin Charnin[2]
1977–78
Da, Hugh Leonard
Ain't Misbehavin', conceived by Richard Maltby, Jr.[2]
1978–79
The Elephant Man, Bernard Pomerance
Sweeney Todd, Hugh Wheeler and Stephen Sondheim[2]
1979–80
Talley's Folly, Lanford Wilson
Evita,[2] Andrew Lloyd Webber and Tim Rice
Betrayal, Harold Pinter[1]
1980–81
A Lesson From Aloes, Athol Fugard
Crimes of the Heart, Beth Henley[16]
1981–82
The Life and Adventures of Nicholas Nickleby, adapted by David Edgar
A Soldier's Play, Charles Fuller[16]

1982–83
Brighton Beach Memoirs, Neil Simon
Plenty, David Hare[1]
Little Shop of Horrors, Alan Menken and Howard Ashman[2][17]
1983–84
The Real Thing, Tom Stoppard
Glengarry Glen Ross, David Mamet[16]
Sunday in the Park with George, Stephen W Sondheim and James Lapine[2]
1984–85
Ma Rainey's Black Bottom, August Wilson
(No award for best musical or foreign play)
1985–86
Lie of the Mind, Sam Shepard
Benefactors, Michael Frayn[1]
The Search for Signs of Intelligent Life in the Universe, Lily Tomlin and Jane Wagner[18]
(No award for best musical)
1986-87
Fences, August Wilson
Les Liaisons Dangereuses, Christopher Hampton[1]
Les Miserables, Claude-Michel Schonberg and Alain Boublil[2]
1987-88
Joe Turner's Come and Gone, August Wilson
The Road to Mecca, Athol Fugard[1]
Into the Woods, Stephen Sondheim and James Lapine[2]
1988-89
The Heidi Chronicles, Wendy Wasserstein
Aristocrats, Brian Friel[1]
Largely New York, Bill Irwin[18]
(No award for best musical)
1989–90
The Piano Lesson, August Wilson
Privates on Parade, Peter Nichols[1]
City of Angels, Larry Gelbart, Cy Coleman, and David Zippel[2]

1. Citation for best foreign play. 2. Citation for best musical. 3. Based on a novel by Arthur Koestler. 4. Based on Christopher Isherwood's *Berlin Stories*. 5. For "distinguished and original contribution to the theater." 6. Based on Sidney Howard's *They Knew What They Wanted*. 7. Based on a novel by Thomas Wolfe. 8. Based on James Agee's *A Death in the Family*. 9. Based on a book by Shepherd Mead. 10. Special citation. 11. Based on Thornton Wilder's *The Matchmaker*. 12. Translated by Edith Hamilton. 13. Based on Sholem Aleichem's Tevye stories, translated by Arnold Perl. 14. Based on John Van Druten's *I Am a Camera*, which won the award for the best play in 1951–52. 15. Based on Brendan Behan's autobiography. 16. Citation for best American play. 17. Based on a story by Roger Corman. 18. Special citation.

Antoinette Perry (Tony) Awards, 1990

Dramatic Play: *The Grapes of Wrath*, Frank Galati
Musical: *City of Angels*
Actor (play): Robert Morse, *Tru*
Actress (play): Maggie Smith, *Lettice and Lovage*
Actor, featured (play): Charles Durning, *Cat on a Hot Tin Roof*
Actress, featured (play): Margaret Tyzack, *Lettice and Lovage*
Actor (musical): James Naughton, *City of Angels*
Actress (musical): Tyne Daly, *Gypsy*
Actor, featured (musical): Michael Jeter, *Grand Hotel*
Actress, featured (musical): Randy Graff, *City of Angels*

Director (play): Frank Galati, *Grapes of Wrath*
Director (musical): Tommy Tune, *Grand Hotel*
Best book of a musical: Larry Gelbart, *City of Angels*
Best original musical score: Cy Coleman and David Zippel, *City of Angeles*
Scenic design: Robin Wagner, *City of Angels*
Costume design: Santo Loquasto, *Grand Hotel*
Choreography: Tommy Tune, *Grand Hotel*
Revival: *Gypsy*
Special award: Seattle Repertory Theater for best regional theater.
Tony Honor for Excellence in the Theater: Alfred Drake.

Poets Laureate of the United States

The post was established in 1985. Appointment is for a one-year term, but is renewable.

Robert Penn Warren	1986-1987	Howard Nemerov	1988-1990
Richard Wilbur	1987-1988	Mark Strand	1990

1990 Obie Award Winners

Best New American Play: Craig Lucas, *Prelude to a Kiss;* Suzan-Lori Parks, *Imperceptible Mutabilities in the Third Kingdom;* Mac Wellman, *Bad Penny; Crowbar; Terminal Hip*

Performance: Alec Baldwin, *Prelude to a Kiss;* Elzbieta Czyzewska, *Crowbar;* Karen Evans-Kandel, *Lear;* Marcia Jean Kurtz, *The Loman Family Picnic; When She Danced;* Ruth Maleczech, *Lear;* Greg Mehrten, *Lear;* Stephen Mellor, *Terminal Hip;* Isabell Monk, *Lear;* Jean Stapleton, *Mountain Language; The Birthday Party;* Pamala Tyson, *Imperceptible Mutabilities in the Third Kingdom;* Courtney B. Vance, *My Children! My Africa!;* Danitra Vance, *Spunk;* Lillias White, *Romance in Hard Times*

Sustained Excellence in Performance: Mary Shultz

Direction: Liz Diamond, *Imperceptible Mutabilities in the Third Kingdom;* Norman Rene, *Prelude to a Kiss;* Jim Simpson, *Bad Penny;* George C. Wolfe, *Spunk*

Sustained Excellence of Sound Design: Daniel Moses Schreier

Sustained Excellence of Set Design: George Tsypin

Special Citations: Eric Bogosian, *Sex, Drugs, Rock & Roll;* Dan Hurlin, *A Cool Million;* Joseph Papp, for his courageous stand against censorship

Theater Grants: Dixon Place, Pregones, Wow Cafe

Workshop Grants: BACA Downtown New Works Project and 52nd Street Project

Sustained Achievement: Act Up

Winners of Bollingen Prize in Poetry

($5,000[1] award is given biennially. It is administered by Yale University and the Bollingen Foundation.)

1949	Ezra Pound	1963	Robert Frost
1950	Wallace Stevens	1965	Horace Gregory
1951	John Crowe Ransom	1967	Robert Penn Warren
1952	Marianne Moore	1969	John Berryman and Karl Shapiro
1953	Archibald MacLeish and William Carlos Williams	1971	Richard Wilbur and Mona Van Duyn
1954	W. H. Auden	1973	James Merrill
1955	Léonie Adams and Louise Bogan	1975	Archie Randolph Ammons
1956	Conrad Aiken	1977	David Ignatow
1957	Allen Tate	1979	W. S. Merwin
1958	E.E. Cummings	1981	Howard Nemerov and May Swenson
1959	Theodore Roethke	1983	Anthony Hecht and John Hollander
1960	Delmore Schwartz	1985	John Ashbery and Fred Chappell
1961	Yvor Winters	1987	Stanley Kunitz
1962	John Hall Wheelock and Richard Eberhart	1989	Edgar Bowers

1. Beginning 1989 award increased to $10,000.

National Book Critics Circle Awards, 1990

Fiction: *Billy Bathgate* by E. L. Doctorow (Random House)

General nonfiction: *The Broken Cord* by Michael Dorris (Harper & Row)

Poetry: *Transparent Gestures* by Rodney Jones (Houghton Mifflin)

Criticism: *Not By Fact Alone: Essays on the Writing and Reading of History* by John Clive (Alfred A. Knopf)

Biography/Autobiography: *A First Class Temperament: The Emergence of Franklin Roosevelt* by Geoffrey C. Ward (Harper & Row)

American Library Association Awards for Children's Books, 1989

John Newbery Medal for best book: *Number the Stars,* Lois Lowry (Houghton Mifflin)

Newbery Honor Books: *Afternoon of the Elves,* Janet Taylor Lisle (Orchard Books/Franklin Watts Inc.); *Shabanu, Daughter of the Wind,* Suzanne Fisher Staples (Alfred A. Knopf, Inc.); *The Winter Room,* Gary Paulsen (A Richard Jackson Book/Orchard Books)

Randolph Caldecott Medal for best picture book: *Lon Po Po: A Red-Riding Hood Story from China,*

illustrated and translated by Ed Young (Philomel Books)

Caldecott Honor Books: *Hershel and the Hanukkah Goblins,* illustrated by Trina Schart Hyman, written by Eric Kimmel (Holiday House); *The Talking Eggs,* illustrated by Jerry Pickney, written by Robert D. San Souci (Dial Books for Young Readers); *Bill Peet: An Autobiography* illustrated and written by Bill Peet (Houghton Mifflin); *Color Zoo,* illustrated and written by Lois Ehlert (J.P. Lippincott)

National Book Awards, 1989

Established by Association of American Publishers

(American Book Awards 1980-86. Reverted to original name in 1987.)

Fiction: *Spartina* by John Casey (Alfred A. Knopf)

Nonfiction: *From Beirut to Jerusalem* by Thomas L. Friedman (Farrar, Straus & Giroux)

The National Book Award Medal for Distinguished Contribution to American Letters: Daniel J. Boorstin, author and Librarian of Congress Emeritus

Awards of the Society of Professional Journalists, 1989

(Sigma Delta Chi)

Deadline reporting: The staff, San Francisco *Examiner*

Non-deadline reporting: Tom Hallman Jr., Dave Hogan, Holley Gilbert, Julie Tripp, Fred Leeson, James Long, and Lauren Cowen, *The Oregonian* (Portland)

Investigative reporting: Bob Paynter, Keith McKnight, and Andrew Zajac, *Beacon Journal* (Akron, Ohio)

Feature writing: Tom Archdeacon, *Dayton Daily News*

Editorial writing: Lawrence Levy, *Newsday* (Long Island, N.Y.)

Washington correspondence: Bill Lambrecht, *St. Louis Post-Dispatch*

Foreign correspondence: Nora Boustany, *The Washington Post*

Public service in newspaper journalism: *The Lexington (Ky.) Herald-Leader* (circulation more than 100,000); *Washington (N.C.) Daily News* and *The Patriot Ledger* (Quincy, Mass.) (circulation less than 100,000)

News photography: Patrick Davison, *The Albuquerque Tribune*

Editorial cartooning: Don Wright, *The Palm Beach Post*

Magazine reporting: Daniel Golden, *The Boston Globe Magazine*

Public service in magazine journalism: *Common Cause* and *The New Yorker*

Radio spot news: KCBS, San Francisco

Editorializing on radio: Catherine Cahan, WBBM, Chicago

Radio investigative reporting: Phil Rogers, WBBM, Chicago

Public service in radio journalism: KGO, San Francisco

Television spot-news reporting: KGO staff, San Francisco

Public service in television journalism: WITI, Milwaukee (networks and top-40 markets); KSAT, San Antonio (all other markets)

Television editorials: Ed Quinn, Paul Sands, Don Lundy, Judy Vance, and John Beatty, KGTV, San Diego

Television investigative reporting: Mark Feldstein, reporter, and Diane Sperrazza, producer, WUSA, Washington, D.C.

Research about journalism: Gregory Gordon and Ronald E. Cohen, *Down to the Wire: UPI's Fight for Survival*

Alfred I. du Pont-Columbia University Broadcast News Awards

Gold Baton Award: *Frontline,* PBS

Silver Baton Awards: *CBS News,* for coverage of the Chinese student rebellion; *CNN* for its live Chinese coverage; *ABC News* and Koppel Communications, for a "Koppel Report" special "Tragedy at Tiananman: The Untold Story"; WETA of Washington, for "Arab and Jew: Wounded Spirits in a Promised Land"; WFAA of Dallas and its investigative reporter Byron Harris for coverage of failures of savings and loans institutions in Texas; KCET of Los Angeles, for reports on medical issues; Maryland Public Television for a documentary on the disproportionate incidence of AIDS in black and Hispanic

communities; WJXT of Jacsonville, Fla., for reports on the roots of the city's drug crisis; WBRZ of Batob Rouge, La., for an investigative report on corruption in the state insurance industry; Appalshop, a small company in Kentucky, won the award for independent television production, for tracing efforts by landowners to overturn a law allowing the sale of mining rights on personal property in Kentucky.

Silver Baton Award for Radio News: National Public Radio, for 16 reports on "AIDS and Black America: Breaking the Silence."

1990 Jefferson Awards

The Jefferson Awards, to honor the highest ideals and achievements in the field of public service, are sponsored by the American Institute for Public Service. The Institute was founded in 1972 and the first awards were presented in 1973.

Four categories of national winners receive a $5,000 grant; the five winners in the other category, Outstanding Public Service Benefiting Local Communities, share the grant equally. In addition all of the recipients receive a gold on silver medallion donated by the Franklin Mint.

Beginning in 1990, through an agreement with *Weekly Reader,* elementary school students became eligible for the awards.

The Greatest Public Service Performed by an Elected or Appointed Official: General Colin Powell, Chairman, Joint Chiefs of Staff, for helping restore democracy in Panama, and for strengthening America's image around the world.

The Greatest Public Service Performed by a Private Citizen: Jimmy Carter, former U.S. President, for his special dignity and character in fighting for world peace, free elections in Nicaragua, and the needs of the homeless.

The Greatest Public Service Benefiting the Disad-

vantaged: Jaime Escalante, teacher, Garfield High School, East Los Angeles, Calif., for his special ability to inspire students—especially minority students—to achieve national excellence.

The Greatest Public Service Performed by an Individual Thirty-five Years or Under: Anne Donahue, Executive Director, Covenant House, Calif., for her tireless efforts in behalf of the homeless.

Outstanding Public Service Benefiting Local Communities: Officer Wayne Barton, Boca Raton, Fla., for implementing an after-school and summer camp program for inner city youth, and providing them hope for the future. John H. Bell, Novato, Calif., for creating special camp for children with cancer and other life threatening illnesses. Queen Hyler, Milwaukee, Wis., for putting herself on the frontlines in the war on drugs. Dr. Viola S. Taylor, Richmond, Va., for providing emergency shelter and care to abused, battered, neglected, and runaway children. Jane Van Sant, Kansas City, Mo., for building a community support program for adults with severe and persistent mental illness.

The Weekly Reader/Jefferson Award: Kevin Lutes, Grade 6, Forest Park School, Brazil, Ind., and Brian Berlinski, Grade 4, P.S. No. 2, Clifton, N.J.

Major Grammy Awards for Recording in 1989

Source: National Academy of Recording Arts and Sciences.

Record: "Wind Beneath My Wings," Bette Midler (Atlantic)

Album: "Nick of Time," Bonnie Raitt (Capitol)

Song: "Wind Beneath My Wings," Larry Henley and Jeff Silbar (Atlantic)

New Artist: Milli Vanilli (Arista)

Pop Vocalists: (Female) Bonnie Raitt, "Nick of Time" (Capitol); (Male) Michael Bolton, "How Am I Supposed to Live Without You" (Columbia/CBS)

Pop Duo or Group: Linda Ronstadt and Aaron Neville, "Don't Know Much" (Elektra)

Pop Instrumental: Neville Brothers, "Healing Chant" (A&M)

Rock Vocalists: (Female) Bonnie Raitt, "Nick of Time" (Capitol); (Male) Don Henley, "The End of the Innocence" (Geffen)

Rock Duo or Group: Traveling Wilburys "Traveling Wilburys Volume One" (Wilbury/Warner Bros.)

Rock Instrumental: Jeff Beck, Terry Bozzio and Tony Hymas, "Jeff Beck's Guitar Shop with Terry Bozzio and Tony Hymas (Epic)

Hard Rock: Living Color, "Cult of Personality" (Epic)

Metal: Metallica, "One" (Elektra)

Rhythm and Blues Vocalists: (Female) Antia Baker, "Giving You the Best That I Got" (Elektra); (Male) Bobby Brown, "Every Little Step" (MCA)

Rhythm and Blues Duo or Group: Soul II Soul featuring Caron Wheeler, "Back to Life" (Virgin)

Rhythm and Blues Instrumental: Soul II Soul, "African Dance" (Virgin)

Rhythm and Blues Song: "If You Don't Know Me By Now," Kenny Gamble and Leon Huff. (Elektra)

Traditional Blues: John Lee Hooker and Bonnie Raitt, "I'm In the Mood" (Chameleon Music Group)

Contemporary Blues: Stevie Ray Vaughan and Double Trouble, "In Step" (Epic)

Rap: Young MC, "Busta Move" (Delicious Vinyl)

New Age: Peter Gabriel, "Passion—Music for the Last Temptation of Christ" (Geffen)

Jazz Fusion: Pat Metheny Group, "Letter from Home" (Geffen)

Jazz Vocalists: (Female) Ruth Brown, "Blues on Broadway" (Fantasy); (Male) Harry Connick, Jr., "When Harry Met Sally" (Columbia/CBS)

Jazz Duo or Group: Dr. John and Rickie Lee Jones, "Makin' Whoopee" (Warner Bros.)

Jazz Instrumentalists: (Soloist) Miles Davis, "Aura" (Columbia/CBS); (Group) Chick Corea Akoustic Band, "Chick Corea Akoustic Band" (GRP)

Jazz, Big Band: Miles Davis, "Aura" (Columbia/CBS)

Country Vocalists: (Female) k.d. lang, "Absolute Torch and Twang (Sire); (Males) Lyle Lovett, "Lyle Lovett and His Large Band" (MCA)

Country Duo or Group: The Nitty Gritty Dirt Band, "Will the Circle Be Unbroken Volume Two" (Universal)

Country Instrumental: Randy Scruggs, "Amazing Grace" (Universal)

Country Song: "After All This Time," Rodney Crowell (Columbia)

Gospel Vocalists: (Female) Cece Winans, "Don't Cry" (Capitol); (Male) Bebe Winans, "Meantime" (Capitol)

Gospel Duo or Group: Take 6, "The Savior Is Waiting" (World)

Soul Gospel Vocalists: (Female, Male) Al Green, "As Long As We're Together" (A&M)

Soul Gospel Duo, Group, Choir or Chorus: Daniel Winans & Choir, "Let Brotherly Love Continue" (Rejoice)

Latin Pop: Jose Feliciano, "Cielito Lindo" (EMI)

Tropical Latin: Celia Cruz & Ray Barretto, "Ritmo en el Corazon (Fania)

Best Mexican/American Performance: Los Lobos, "La Pistola y El Corazon" (Warner Bros./Slash)

Traditional Folk: Bulgarian State Female Vocal Choir, "Le Mystere des Voix Bulgares, Vol. II" (Elektra/Nonesuch)

Best Contemporary Folk: Indigo Girls, "Indigo Girls" (Epic)

Best Polka: Jimmy Sturr and His Orchestra, "All In My Love for You" (Starr)

Reggae: Ziggy Marley and the Melody Makers, "One Bright Day" (Virgin)

For Children: "The Rock-a-Bye Collection Vol. I", Tanya Goodman, David Lehman, and J. Aaron Brown, producers (Jaba Records)

Comedy: "P.D.Q. Bach: 1712 Overture & Other Musical Assaults," Professor Peter Schickele (Telarc)

Spoken Word: "It's Always Something," Gilda Radner (Simon and Schuster Audio)

Cast Show Album: "Jerome Robbins' Broadway," Jay David Saks, album producer; Jason Alexander, Debbie Shapiro, and Robert La Fasse lyricists and composers.

Instrumental Composition: Danny Elfman, "The Batman Theme" (Warner Bros.)

Instrumental Arrangement: Dave Grusin, "Suite from 'The Milagro Beanfield War' " (GRP)

Music Video—Short Form: "Leave Me Alone," Michael Jackson (Epic)

Music Video—Long Form: "Rhythm Nation 1814," Janet Jackson (A&M)

Historical Album: "Chuck Berry—The Chess Box," Andy McKaie, album producer (Chess-MCA)

Classical Album: "Bartok: 6 String Quartets," Emerson String Quartet, Wolf Erichson, album producer (Deutsche Grammophon)

Classical Orchestral Performance: "Mahler: Symphony No. 3 in D Minor," Leonard Berstein and The New York Philharmonic (Deutsche Grammophon)

Classical Soloist with Orchestra: Yo-Yo Ma (David Zinman conducting Baltimore Symphony Orchestra), "Barber: Cello Concerto, Opus 22/ Britten: Symphony for Cello & Orchestra, Opus 68" (CBS Masterworks); **Without Orchestra:** Andras Schiff, "Bach: English Suites, BWV 806-11" (London)

Chamber Music: Emerson String Quartet, "Bartok: 6 String Quartets" (Deutsche Grammophon)

Classical Vocal Soloist: Dawn Upshaw, "Knoxville—Summer of 1915 (Music of Barber, Menotti, Harbison, Stravinsky)" (Elektra/Nonesuch)

Classical Choral: "Britten: War Requiem," Robert Shaw, conductor, Atlanta Symphony Orchestra and Chorus and Atlanta Boy Choir (Telarc)

Opera: Wagner: "Die Walkuere," James Levine, conductor, Metropolitan Opera Orchestra (Deutsche Grammophon)

Contemporary Composition: "Reich: Different Trains," Steve Reich (Elektra/Nonesuch)

Producers: Non-Classical, Peter Asher; **Classical,** Robert Woods

Engineers: Non-Classical, George Massenburg, "Cry Like a Rainstorm—Howl Like the Wind"; (Elektra); **Classical,** Jack Renner, "Britten: War Requiem" (Telarc)

Presidential Medal of Freedom

The nation's highest civilian award, the Presidential Medal of Freedom, was established in 1963 by President John F. Kennedy to continue and expand Presidential recognition of meritorious service which, since 1945, had been granted as the Medal of Freedom. Kennedy selected the first recipients, but was assassinated before he could make the presentations. They were made by President Johnson. NOTE: An asterisk following a year denotes a posthumous award.

SELECTED BY PRESIDENT KENNEDY

Marian Anderson (contralto)	1963
Ralph J. Bunche (statesman)	1963
Ellsworth Bunker (diplomat)	1963
Pablo Casals (cellist)	1963
Genevieve Caulfield (educator)	1963
James B. Conant (educator)	1963
John F. Enders (bacteriologist)	1963
Felix Frankfurter (jurist)	1963
Karl Horton (youth authority)	1963
Robert J. Kiphuth (athletic director)	1963
Edwin H. Land (inventor)	1963
Herbert H. Lehman (statesman)	1963*
Robert A. Lovett (statesman)	1963
J. Clifford MacDonald (educator)	1963*
John J. McCloy (banker and statesman)	1963
George Meany (labor leader)	1963
Alexander Meiklejohn (philosopher)	1963
Ludwig Mies van der Rohe (architect)	1963
Jean Monnet (European statesman)	1963
Luis Muñoz-Marin (Governor of Puerto Rico)	1963
Clarence B. Randall (industrialist)	1963
Rudolf Serkin (pianist)	1963
Edward Steichen (photographer)	1963
George W. Taylor (educator)	1963
Alan T. Waterman (scientist)	1963
Mark S. Watson (journalist)	1963
Annie D. Wauneka (public health worker)	1963
E. B. White (author)	1963
Thornton N. Wilder (author)	1963
Edmund Wilson (author and critic)	1963
Andrew Wyeth (artist)	1963

AWARDED BY PRESIDENT JOHNSON

Dean G. Acheson (statesman)	1964
Eugene R. Black (banker)	1969
Detlev W. Bronk (neurophysiologist)	1964
McGeorge Bundy (government service)	1969
Ellsworth Bunker (diplomat)	1968
Clark Clifford (statesman)	1969
Aaron Copland (composer)	1964
Michael E. DeBakey (surgeon)	1969
Willem de Kooning (artist)	1964
Walt Disney (cartoon film producer)	1964
J. Frank Dobie (author)	1964
David Dubinsky (labor leader)	1969
Lena F. Edwards (physician and humanitarian)	1964
Thomas Stearns Eliot (poet)	1964
Ralph Ellison (author)	1969
Lynn Fontanne (actress)	1964
Henry Ford II (industrialist)	1969
John W. Gardner (educator)	1964
W. Averell Harriman (statesman)	1969
Rev. Theodore M. Hesburgh (educator)	1964
Bob Hope (comedian)	1969
John XXIII (Pope)	1963*
Clarence L. Johnson (aircraft engineer)	1964
Edgar F. Kaiser (industrialist)	1969
Frederick R. Kappel (telecommunications executive)	1964
Helen A. Keller (educator)	1964
John Fitzgerald Kennedy (U.S. President)	1963*
Robert W. Komer (government service)	1968
Mary Lasker (philanthropist)	1969
John L. Lewis (labor leader)	1964
Walter Lippmann (journalist)	1964
Eugene M. Locke (diplomat)	1968

Alfred Lunt (actor)	1964
John W. Macy, Jr. (government service)	1969
Ralph McGill (journalist)	1964
Robert S. McNamara (government service)	1968
Samuel Eliot Morison (historian)	1964
Lewis Mumford (urban planner and critic)	1964
Edward R. Murrow (radio-TV commentator)	1964
Reinhold Niebuhr (theologian)	1964
Gregory Peck (actor)	1969
Leontyne Price (soprano)	1964
A. Philip Randolph (labor leader)	1964
Laurance S. Rockefeller (conservationist)	1969
Walt Whitman Rostow (government service)	1969
Dean Rusk (statesman)	1969
Carl Sandburg (poet and biographer)	1964
Merriman Smith (journalist)	1969
John Steinbeck (author)	1964
Helen B. Taussig (pediatrician)	1964
Cyrus R. Vance (government service)	1969
Carl Vinson (legislator)	1964
Thomas J. Watson, Jr. (industrialist)	1964
James E. Webb (NASA administrator)	1968
Paul Dudley White (physician)	1964
William S. White (journalist)	1969
Roy Wilkins (social welfare executive)	1969
Whitney M. Young, Jr. (social welfare executive)	1969

AWARDED BY PRESIDENT NIXON

Edwin E. Aldrin (astronaut)	1969
Apollo 13 Mission Operations Team	1970
Neil A. Armstrong (astronaut)	1969
Earl Charles Behrens (journalist)	1970
Manlio Brosio (NATO secretary general)	1971
Michael Collins (astronaut)	1969
Edward K. (Duke) Ellington (musician)	1969
Edward T. Folliard (journalist)	1970
John Ford (film director)	1973
Samuel Goldwyn (film producer)	1971
Fred Wallace Haise, Jr. (astronaut)	1970
William M. Henry (journalist)	1970*
Paul G. Hoffman (statesman)	1974
William J. Hopkins (White House service)	1971
Arthur Krock (journalist)	1970
Melvin R. Laird (government service)	1974
David Lawrence (journalist)	1970
George Gould Lincoln (journalist)	1970
James A. Lovell, Jr. (astronaut)	1970
Dr. Charles L. Lowman (orthopedist)	1974
Raymond Moley (journalist)	1970
Eugene Ormandy (conductor)	1970
William P. Rogers (diplomat)	1973
Adela Rogers St. Johns (journalist)	1970
John Leonard Swigert, Jr. (astronaut)	1970
John Paul Vann (adviser, Vietnam war)	1972*
DeWitt and Lila Wallace (founders, *Reader's Digest*)	1972

AWARDED BY PRESIDENT FORD

I. W. Abel (labor leader)	1977
John Bardeen (physicist)	1977
Irving Berlin (composer)	1977
Norman Borlaug (agricultural scientist)	1977
Gen. Omar N. Bradley (soldier)	1977
David K. E. Bruce (diplomat)	1976
Arleigh Burke (national security)	1977
Alexander Calder (sculptor)	1977
Bruce Catton (historian)	1977

Joseph P. DiMaggio (baseball star)	1977
Ariel Durant (author)	1977
Will Durant (author)	1977
Arthur Fiedler (conductor)	1977
Henry J. Friendly (jurist)	1977
Martha Graham (dancer-choreographer)	1976
Claudia "Lady Bird" Johnson (service to U.S. scenic beauty)	1977
Henry A. Kissinger (statesman)	1977
Archibald MacLeish (poet)	1977
James A. Michener (author)	1977
Georgia O'Keeffe (artist)	1977
Jesse Owens (track champion)	1976
Nelson A. Rockefeller (government service)	1977
Norman Rockwell (illustrator)	1977
Arthur Rubinstein (pianist)	1976
Donald H. Rumsfeld (government service)	1977
Katherine Filene Shouse (service to the performing arts)	1977
Lowell Thomas (radio-TV commentator)	1977
James D. Watson (biochemist)	1977

AWARDED BY PRESIDENT CARTER

Ansel Adams (photographer)	1980
Horace M. Albright (government service)	1980
Roger Baldwin (civil libertarian)	1981
Harold Brown (government service)	1981
Zbigniew Brzezinski (government service)	1981
Rachel Carson (author)	1980*
Lucia Chase (ballet director)	1980
Warren M. Christopher (government service)	1981
Walter Cronkite (TV newscaster)	1981
Kirk Douglas (actor)	1981
Arthur J. Goldberg (government service)	1978
Hubert H. Humphrey (government service)	1980*
Archbishop Iakovos (churchman)	1980
Lyndon B. Johnson (U.S. President)	1980*
Rev. Dr. Martin Luther King, Jr. (civil rights leader)	1977*
Margaret Craig McNamara (educator)	1981
Margaret Mead (anthropologist)	1979*
Karl Menninger (psychiatrist)	1981
Clarence Mitchell, Jr. (civil rights leader)	1980
Edmund S. Muskie (government service)	1981
Esther Peterson (government service)	1981
Roger Tory Peterson (ornithologist)	1980
Adm. Hyman Rickover (national security)	1980
Jonas Salk (medical research)	1977
Beverly Sills (opera singer)	1980
Gerard C. Smith (government service)	1981
Robert S. Strauss (government service)	1981
Elbert Parr Tuttle (government service)	1981
Earl Warren (government service)	1981*
Robert Penn Warren (author and poet)	1980
John Wayne (actor)	1980*
Eudora Welty (author)	1980
Tennessee Williams (playwright)	1980
Andrew M. Young (government service)	1981

AWARDED BY PRESIDENT REAGAN

Walter H. Annenberg (publisher and diplomat)	1986
Anne L. Armstrong (diplomat)	1987
Howard H. Baker, Jr. (government service)	1984
George Balanchine (choreographer)	1983
Malcolm Baldrige (government service)	1988*
Count Basie (jazz pianist)	1985*
Pearl Bailey Bellson (entertainer and humanitarian)	1988
Earl (Red) Blaik (football coach)	1986
James H. (Eubie) Blake (composer-pianist)	1981
Irving Brown (labor leader)	1988
Paul W. (Bear) Bryant (football coach)	1983*
Warren Burger (former Chief Justice)	1987
James Burnham (editor-historian)	1983
James Francis Cagney (actor)	1984

The Right Honorable Lord Carrington (Secretary General of NATO)	1988
Whittaker Chambers (public servant)	1984*
James Cheek (educator)	1983
Leo Cherne (economist-humanitarian)	1984
Terence Cardinal Cooke, His Eminence (theologian)	1984*
Denton Arthur Cooley, M.D. (heart surgeon)	1984
Jacques-Yves Cousteau (marine explorer)	1985
Justin W. Dart Sr. (businessman)	1987*
Tennessee Ernie Ford (singer)	1984
Milton Friedman (economist)	1988
R. Buckminster Fuller (architect-geometrician)	1983
Hector P. Garcia, M.D. (humanitarian)	1984
Barry Goldwater (government service)	1986
Gen. Andrew J. Goodpaster (soldier-diplomat)	1984
Rev. Billy Graham (evangelist)	1983
Ella T. Grasso (Connecticut governor)	1981*
Philip C. Habib (diplomat)	1982
Bryce N. Harlow (government service)	1981
Helen Hayes (actress)	1986
Eric Hoffer (philosopher-longshoreman)	1983
Jerome Holland (educator and ambassador)	1985*
Sidney Hook (philosopher-educator)	1985
Vladimir Horowitz (pianist)	1985
Henry Martin Jackson (government service)	1984*
Jacob K. Javits (government service)	1983
Walter H. Judd (government service)	1981
Irving Kaufman (jurist)	1987
Danny Kaye (actor)	1987*
Jeane J. Kirkpatrick (government service)	1985
Lincoln Kirstein (ballet director)	1984
Louis L'Amour (author)	1984
Morris I. Leibman (lawyer)	1981
Gen. Lyman L. Lemnitzer (soldier)	1987
George M. Low (educator and administrator NASA)	1985*
Clare Boothe Luce (author-diplomat)	1983
Joseph M.A.H. Luns (diplomat-NATO)	1984
Jean Faircloth MacArthur (patriot)	1988
Dumas Malone (historian)	1983
Michael Mansfield (government service)	1989
J. Willard Marriott (businessman)	1988*
John A. McCone (government service)	1987
Mabel Mercer (jazz singer)	1983
Paul Nitze (government service)	1985
David Packard (public service, businessman)	1988
Frederick Patterson (educator)	1987
Norman Vincent Peale (theologian)	1984
Nathan Perlmutter (public service)	1987
Simon Ramo (industrialist)	1983
Frank Reynolds (TV anchor)	1985*
Gen. Matthew B. Ridgway (soldier)	1986
S. Dillon Ripley (cultural and public service)	1985
Jack Roosevelt Robinson (baseball player)	1984*
Gen. Carlos P. Romulo (Philippino statesman)	1984
Mstislav Rostropovich (cellist-conductor)	1987
Vermont Royster (journalist)	1986
Albert B. Sabin (medical research)	1986
Mohamed Anwar el-Sadat (statesman)	1984*
George P. Shultz (gov. service)	1989
Eunice Kennedy Shriver (humanitarian)	1984
Frank Sinatra (entertainer)	1985
Kate Smith (singer)	1982
Roger L. Stevens (theatrical producer)	1988
James Stewart (actor)	1985
Mother Teresa (humanitarian)	1985
Charles B. Thornton (industrialist)	1981
William B. Walsh (humanitarian)	1987
Gen. Albert Coady Wedemeyer (national security)	1985
Casper W. Weinberger (government service)	1987
Meredith Willson (composer)	1987*
Albert and Roberta Wohlstetter (government service)	1985
Charles E. Yeager (public service)	1985

AWARDED BY PRESIDENT BUSH

Lucille Ball (entertainer)	1989*
C. Douglas Dillon (public servant)	1989
James H. Doolittle (aviation pioneer)	1989

George F. Kennen (public servant and author)	1989
Claude D. Pepper (public servant)	1989
Margaret Chase Smith (public servant)	1989
Lech Walesa (human rights champion)	1989

Recipients of Kennedy Center Honors

The Kennedy Center for the Performing Arts in Washington, D.C., created its Honors awards in 1978 to recognize the achievements of five distinguished contributors to the performing arts. Following are the recipients:

1978: Marian Anderson (contralto), Fred Astaire (dancer-actor), Richard Rodgers (Broadway composer), Arthur Rubinstein (pianist), George Balanchine (choreographer).

1979: Ella Fitzgerald (jazz singer), Henry Fonda (actor), Martha Graham (dancer-choreographer), Tennessee Williams (playwright), Aaron Copland (composer).

1980: James Cagney (actor), Leonard Bernstein (composer-conductor), Agnes de Mille (choreographer), Lynn Fontanne (actress), Leontyne Price (soprano).

1981: Count Basie (jazz composer-pianist), Cary Grant (actor), Helen Hayes (actress), Jerome Robbins (choreographer), Rudolf Serkin (pianist).

1982: George Abbott (Broadway producer), Lillian Gish (actress), Benny Goodman (jazz clarinetist), Gene Kelly (dancer-actor), Eugene Ormandy (conductor).

1983: Katherine Dunham (dancer-choreographer), Elia Kazan (director-author), James Stew-

art (actor), Virgil Thomson (music critic-composer), Frank Sinatra (singer).

1984: Lena Horne (singer), Danny Kaye (comedian-actor), Gian Carlo Menotti (composer), Arthur Miller (playwright), Isaac Stern (violinist).

1985: Merce Cunningham (dancer-choreographer), Irene Dunne (actress), Bob Hope (comedian), Alan Jay Lerner (lyricist-playwright), Frederick Loewe (composer), Beverly Sills (soprano and opera administrator).

1986: Lucille Ball (comedienne), Ray Charles (musician), Yehudi Menuhin (violinist), Antony Tudor (choreographer), Hume Cronyn and Jessica Tandy (husband-and-wife acting team).

1987: Perry Como (singer), Bette Davis (actress), Sammy Davis Jr. (entertainer), Nathan Milstein (violinist), Alwin Nikolais (choreographer).

1988: Alvin Ailey (choreographer), George Burns (comedian-actor), Myrna Loy (actress), Alexander Schneider (violinist), Roger L. Stevens (theatrical producer and the Kennedy Center's founding chairman).

1989: Harry Belafonte (sinter-actor), Claudette Colbert (actress), Alexandra Danilova (ballerina-teacher), Mary Martin (actress), William Schuman (composer)

1990 Christopher Awards

Adult Books

Among Schoolchildren, by Tracy Kidder (Houghton Mifflin)

The Bishop's Boys: A Life of Wilbur and Orville Wright, by Tom D. Crouch (W.W. Norton)

The Broken Cord, by Michael Dorris (Harper & Row)

The Case Against Divorce, by Diane Medved, Ph.D. (Donald I. Fine)

The Crosswinds of Freedom, by James MacGregor Burns (Alfred A. Knopf)

An Exposure of the Heart, by Rebecca Busselle (W. W. Norton)

I Raise My Eyes To Say Yes, by Ruth Sienkiewicz-Mercer and Steven B. Kaplan (Houghton Mifflin)

The Steven McDonald Story, by Steven McDonald and Patti Ann McDonald with E. J. Kahn II (Donald I. Fine)

Young People's Books

Keeping a Christmas Secret, by Phyllis Reynolds Naylor, illustrated by Lena Shiffman (Atheneum)

William and Grandpa, by Alice Schertle, illustrated by Lydia Dabcovich (Lothrop, Lee & Shepard)

Can the Whales Be Saved?, by Dr. Philip Whitfield (Viking Kestrel)

So Much To Tell You . . . , by John Marsden (Young Adult, Little Brown and Company)

Television Specials

American Playhouse: The Silence at Bethany (PBS)

Everybody's Baby: The Rescue of Jessica McClure (ABC)

Fatal Addictions: An NBC News Special

A Mother's Courage: The Mary Thomas Story (NBC)

My Name Is Bill W. (ABC)

No Place Like Home (CBS)

The Struggle for Democracy (CBC/PBS/WQED)

Super Chief—The Life and Legacy of Earl Warren (PBS)

Films

Driving Miss Daisy (Warner Bros.)

Field of Dreams (Universal)

My Left Foot (Miramax)

Romero (Four Stars Entertainment/A Paulist Picture)

The James Keller Youth Award

Eunice Kennedy Shriver

Special Christopher Award

Bob Hope for a half-century of entertainment and dedication to our servicemen and women

1989 Bancroft Prizes in American History

Dark Journey: Black Mississippians in the Age of Jim Crow, by Neil R. McMillen (University of Illinois Press)

The Indian's New World: Catawbas and Their

Neighbors from European Contact Through the Era of Removal, by James H. Merrell (University of North Carolina Press)

ENTERTAINMENT & CULTURE

Notable Books, 1989

This list has been compiled by the Notable Books Council, Reference and Adult Services, a division of the American Library Association for use by the general reader and by librarians who work with adult readers. The titles were selected for their significant contribution to the expansion of knowledge or for the pleasure they can provide to adult readers. Criteria include wide general appeal and literary merit.

Fiction
Atwood, Margaret, **Cat's Eye,** Doubleday
Bausch, Richard, **Mr. Field's Daughter,** Simon & Schuster/Linden Press
Boyle, T. Coraghessan, **If the River Was Whiskey,** Viking
Burgess, Anthony, **Any Old Iron,** Random
Busch, Frederick, **Absent Friends,** Knopf
Casey, John, **Spartina,** Knopf
Desai, Anita, **Baumgartner's Bombay,** Knopf
Gordon, Mary, **The Other Side,** Viking
Hamill, Pete, **Loving Women: A Novel of the Fifties,** Random
Irving, John, **A Prayer for Owen Meany,** Morrow
Ishiguro, Kazuo, **The Remains of the Day,** Knopf
Kingsolver, Barbara, **Homeland,** Harper
Ozick, Cynthia, **The Shawl,** Knopf
Schaeffer, Susan Fromberg, **Buffalo Afternoon,** Knopf
Tan, Amy, **The Joy Luck Club,** Putnam
Wilson, Robley, **Terrible Kisses,** Simon & Schuster
Yehoshua, A.B., **Five Seasons,** translated by Hillel Halkin, Doubleday

Poetry
Carver, Raymond, **A New Path to the Waterfall,** Atlantic Monthly Press
An Ear to the Ground: An Anthology of Contemporary American Poetry, edited by Marie Harris and Kathleen Aguero, University of Georgia
Poets for Life: Seventy-six Poets Respond to AIDS, edited by Michael Klein, Crown

Nonfiction
Bentsen, Cheryl, **Maasai Days,** Summit
Branch, Taylor, **Parting the Waters: America in the King Years, 1954-63,** Simon & Schuster
Conway, Jill Ker, **The Road from Coorain,** Knopf
Dorris, Michael, **The Broken Cord,** Harper
Duberman, Martin Bauml, **Paul Robeson,** Knopf
Friedman, Thomas L., **From Beirut to Jerusalem,** Farrar
Hirsch, Kathleen, **Songs from the Alley,** Ticknor & Fields
Kidder, Tracy, **Among Schoolchildren,** Houghton Mifflin
Kluver, Billy, and Martin, Julie, **Ki Ki's Paris: Artists and Lovers, 1900-1930,** Abrams
Takaki, Ronald, **Strangers from a Different Shore: A History of Asian Americans,** Little, Brown

Source: Reprinted by permission of the American Library Association. Issued as a pamphlet by ALA, 50 E. Huron St., Chicago, Ill. 60611, annually in the spring for the preceding year. © American Library Association 1990.

Major U.S. Symphony Orchestras and Their Music Directors

Source: American Symphony Orchestra League.

Atlanta Symphony: Yoel Levi
Baltimore Symphony: David Zinman
Boston Symphony: Seiji Ozawa
Buffalo Philharmonic: Wilfred J. Larson
Chicago Symphony: Daniel Barenboim[1]
Cincinnati Symphony: Jesus Lopez-Cobos
Cleveland Orchestra: Christoph von Dohnanyi
Columbus Symphony: Christian Badea
Dallas Symphony: Eduardo Mata
Denver Symphony: Sixten Ehrling[2]
Detroit Symphony: Gunther Herbig
Houston Symphony: Christoph Eschenbach
Indianapolis Symphony: Raymond Leppard
Los Angeles Philharmonic: André Previn[7]
Milwaukee Symphony: Zdenek Macal
Minnesota Orchestra: Edo de Waart
National Symphony (D.C.): Mstislav Rostropovich

New Jersey Symphony: Hugh Wolff
New Orleans Symphony: Maxim Shostakovich
New York Philharmonic: Zubin Mehta[3]
Oregon Symphony: James DePreist
Philadelphia Orchestra: Riccardo Muti
Phoenix Symphony Orchestra: James Saderes
Pittsburgh Symphony: Lorin Maazel
Rochester Philharmonic: Mark Elder
Saint Louis Symphony: Leonard Slatkin
[5]**Saint Paul Chamber Orchestra:** Hugh Wolff[4]
San Antonio Symphony: Zdenek Macal[4,6]
San Diego Symphony: Yoav Talmi[8]
San Francisco Symphony: Herbert Blomstedt
Seattle Symphony: Gerard Schwarz
Syracuse Symphony: Kazuyoshi Akiyama
Utah Symphony: Joseph Silverstein

1. Starting 1990–91 season. 2. Music Advisor. 3. Through 1990–91. 4. Principal Conductor. 5. Artistic Commission also includes Christopher Hogwood, Director of Music and John Adams, Creative Chair. 6. Artistic Director. 7. Resigned as Music Director but continues as conductor. Esa-Pekka Salonen takes over as Music Director with the 1992–93 season. 8. Lynn Harrell remains as music advisor.

A Chorus Line Ends

The final curtain fell the night of April 28, 1990, on the longest-running show in Broadway's history. *A Chorus Line* ended its run of nearly 15 years and 6,137 performances with a gathering of former performers on stage with the final cast members.

Major Public Libraries

City (branches)	Volumes	Circulation	Budget (in millions)	City (branches)	Volumes	Circulation	Budget (in millions)
Akron-Summit County, Ohio (17)	1,205,000	2,770,609	$12.0	Louisville, Ky. (14)	1,011,033	2,842,406	$ 8.2
Albuquerque, N.M. (11)	697,869	2,649,554	4.4	Madison, Wis. (7)	699,100	2,210,278	5.4
Annapolis, Md. (13)	1,790,177	4,358,087	9.3	Memphis, Tenn. (22)	3,459,059	2,685,577	11.2
Atlanta-Fulton County (25)	1,790,965	2,300,684	17.6	Miami-Dade County, Fla. (30)	2,386,204	4,203,180	31.0
Austin, Tex. (16)	964,468	2,393,572	7.7	Milwaukee (12)	2,149,938	3,327,589	14.1
Baltimore (31)	2,148,625	1,505,323	16.3	Minneapolis (14)	1,888,934	3,012,111	13.4
Baton Rouge, La. (9)	640,385	1,733,200	7.9	Nashville-Davidson			
Birmingham, Ala. (19)	1,117,221	1,472,390	8.8	County, Tenn. (16)	638,514	1,876,397	7.0
Boston (25)	6,141,482	1,959,237	27.1	Newark, N.J. (11)	1,228,000	1,105,649	9.8
Buffalo-Erie County, N.Y. (58)	4,430,812[1]	6,740,110	17.2	New Orleans (15)	1,039,264	1,159,303	6.0
Charleston-Kanawha				*New York City:*			
County, W.Va. (8)	550,000	833,651	3.1	†The New York Public Library			
Charlotte, N.C. (19)	1,233,936	2,600,000	10.4	Branches (82)	3,386,287	10,407,829	72.0
Chicago (80)	5,458,215	7,657,392	63.0	Research	9,834,933		52.9
Cincinnati (41)	4,007,140	8,504,461	24.6	Brooklyn (60)	4,829,764	8,273,949	30.4
Cleveland (29)	2,690,194	4,550,994	31.8	Queens (62)	6,575,738	12,848,695	41.1
Columbus Metropolitan,				Norfolk, Va. (11)	880,564	823,908	4.1
Ohio (20)	1,610,558	5,869,434	25.2	Oklahoma City-County (10)	933,241	4,184,437	9.6
Dallas (19)	2,409,864	4,364,027	17.2	Omaha, Neb. (10)	619,425	2,196,824	6.6
Dayton-Montgomery				Philadelphia (52)	4,916,380	4,912,414	41.6
County, Ohio (19)	1,536,865	5,239,231	12.4	Phoenix, Ariz. (10)	1,618,390	5,398,827	12.0
Denver (21)	2,850,000	3,396,268	13.6	Pittsburgh (20)	1,880,241	2,841,120	12.6
Des Moines, Iowa (5)	527,800	1,246,350	3.4	Portland-Multnomah			
Detroit (25)	2,746,021	1,743,314	21.9	County, Ore. (14)	1,249,324	4,512,596	13.3
D.C. (26)	1,620,073	1,979,475	18.8	Providence, R.I. (9)	1,005,201	554,144	4.3
El Paso (9)	475,000	1,268,435	4.2	Richmond, Va. (10)	774,779	854,242	3.3
Erie, Pa. (6)	450,000	1,494,318	2.6	Rochester, N.Y. (11)	1,517,712	1,587,691	10.3
Evansville-Vanderburgh				Sacramento, Calif. (24)	1,663,893	3,977,515	18.0
County, Ind. (7)	833,465	1,417,804	4.1	St. Louis (14)	1,203,960	1,538,296	10.0
Fairfax County, Va. (22)	2,300,000	8,500,000	19.7	St. Paul (12)	740,171	2,414,263	6.3
Fort Wayne-Allen				St. Petersburg, Fla. (5)	445,000	1,300,000	2.8
County, Ind. (14)	2,015,967	2,929,244	7.9	Salt Lake City-County,			
Fort Worth (10)	2,186,563	3,356,148	5.9	Utah (15)	1,131,805	3,479,199	9.7
Grand Rapids, Mich. (5)	1,884,484	1,006,934	3.9	San Antonio (17)	1,858,522	3,578,687	8.9
Greenville City-County, S.C. (11)	547,526	1,268,144	3.8	San Diego, Calif. (31)	1,652,444	5,067,972	17.1[3]
Hawaii State Public Library				San Francisco (26)	1,937,954	3,163,931	18.2
System (49)[2]	2,388,106	6,187,214	21.1	San Jose, Calif. (18)	1,184,228	3,885,600	17.0
Houston (33)	3,583,445	6,304,000	14.9	Seattle (19)	1,752,156	4,922,013	16.5
Independence, Mo. (26)	1,700,000	3,950,000	13.7	Springfield, Mass. (8)	694,451	1,395,779	5.4
Indianapolis-Marion				Tampa, Fla. (17)	1,840,000	3,128,160	13.4
County (21)	1,644,727	5,885,226	16.1	Tucson, Ariz. (17)*	1,013,750	4,309,200	9.6
Jackson-Hinds County, Miss. (12)	602,989	884,297	2.4	Tulsa City-County, Okla. (20)	850,044	3,236,081	8.5
Jacksonville, Fla. (11)	1,923,843	2,775,145	9.4	Wichita, Kan. (11)	900,943	1,591,080	4.2
Kansas City, Mo. (9)	1,585,017	1,753,000	9.0	Winston-Salem-			
Knoxville, Tenn. (16)	640,608	1,638,964	3.7	Forsyth County, N.C. (8)	380,000	2,100,000	5.0
Lincoln, Neb. (7)	624,758	1,629,631	3.3	Worcester, Mass. (7)	542,444	848,163	3.3
Long Beach, Calif. (11)	1,004,205	2,824,651	10.8	Youngstown-			
Los Angeles (County) (63)	5,500,000	10,000,000	38.1	Mahoning County, Ohio (22)	709,484	1,477,664	7.8

1. Includes books, periodicals, musical scores, recordings, CDs, films, videos, maps, posters. 2. State-wide system. 3. Includes $3.3 million capital improvements and $1.2 million grant-funded services. †Includes Manhattan, Bronx, and Staten Island. *Did not reply to questionnaire.

Glossary of Art Movements

Abstract Expressionism. American art movement of the 1940s that emphasized form and color within a nonrepresentational framework. Jackson Pollock initiated the revolutionary technique of splattering the paint directly on canvas to achieve the subconscious interpretation of the artist's inner vision of reality.

Art Deco. A 1920s style characterized by setbacks, zigzag forms, and the use of chrome and plastic ornamentation. New York's Chrysler Building is an architectural example of the style.

Art Nouveau. An 1890s style in architecture, graphic arts, and interior decoration characterized by writhing forms, curving lines, and asymmetrical organization. Some critics regard the style as the first stage of modern architecture.

Ashcan School. A group of New York realist artists, formed in 1908, who abandoned decorous subject matter and portrayed the more common as well as the sordid aspects of city life.

Assemblage (Collage). Forms of modern sculpture and painting utilizing readymades, found objects, and pasted fragments to form an abstract composition. Louise Nevelson's boxlike enclosures, each with its own composition of assembled objects, illustrate the style in sculpture. Pablo Picasso developed the technique of cutting and pasting natural or manufactured materials to a painted or unpainted surface.

Barbizon School (Landscape Painting). A group of painters who, around the middle of the 19th century, reacted against classical landscape and advocated a direct study of nature. They were influenced by English and Dutch landscape masters. Theodore Rousseau, one of the principal figures of the group, led the fight for outdoor painting. In this respect, the school was a forerunner of Impressionism.

Baroque. European art and architecture of the 17th and 18th centuries. Giovanni Bernini, a major exponent of the style, believed in the union of the arts of architecture, painting, and sculpture to overwhelm the spectator with ornate and highly dramatized themes. Although the style originated in Rome as the instrument of the Church, it spread throughout Europe in such monumental creations as the Palace of Versailles.

Beaux Arts. Elaborate and formal architectural style characterized by symmetry and an abundance of sculptured ornamentation. New York's old Custom House at Bowling Green is an example of the style.

Black or Afro-American Art. The work of American artists of African descent produced in various styles characterized by a mood of protest and a search for identity and historical roots.

Classicism. A form of art derived from the study of Greek and Roman styles characterized by harmony, balance, and serenity. In contrast, the Romantic Movement gave free rein to the artist's imagination and to the love of the exotic.

Constructivism. A form of sculpture using wood, metal, glass, and modern industrial materials expressing the technological society. The mobiles of Alexander Calder are examples of the movement.

Cubism. Early 20th-century French movement marked by a revolutionary departure from representational art. Pablo Picasso and Georges Bracque penetrated the surface of objects, stressing basic abstract geometric forms that presented the object from many angles simultaneously.

Dada. A product of the turbulent and cynical post-World War I period, this anti-art movement extolled the irrational, the absurd, the nihilistic, and the nonsensical. The reproduction of Mona Lisa adorned with a mustache is a famous example. The movement is regarded as a precursor of Surrealism. Some critics regard HAPPENINGS as a recent development of Dada. This movement incorporates environment and spectators as active and important ingredients in the production of random events.

Expressionism. A 20th-century European art movement that stresses the expression of emotion and the inner vision of the artist rather than the exact representation of nature. Distorted lines and shapes and exaggerated colors are used for emotional impact. Vincent Van Gogh is regarded as the precursor of this movement.

Fauvism. The name "wild beasts" was given to the group of early 20th-century French painters because their work was characterized by distortion and violent colors. Henri Matisse and Georges Roualt were leaders of this group.

Futurism. This early 20th-century movement originating in Italy glorified the machine age and attempted to represent machines and figures in motion. The aesthetics of Futurism affirmed the beauty of technological society.

Genre. This French word meaning "type" now refers to paintings that depict scenes of everyday life without any attempt at idealization. Genre paintings can be found in all ages, but the Dutch productions of peasant and tavern scenes are typical.

Impressionism. Late 19th-century French school dedicated to defining transitory visual impressions painted directly from nature, with light and color of primary importance. If the atmosphere changed, a totally different picture would emerge. It was not the object or event that counted but the visual impression as caught at a certain time of day under a certain light. Claude Monet and Camille Pissarro were leaders of the movement.

Mannerism. A mid-16th century movement, Italian in origin, although El Greco was a major practitioner of the style. The human figure, distorted and elongated, was the most frequent subject.

Neoclassicism. An 18th-century reaction to the excesses of Baroque and Rococo, this European art movement tried to recreate the art of Greece and Rome by imitating the ancient classics both in style and subject matter.

Neoimpressionism. A school of painting associated with George Seurat and his followers in late 19th-century France that sought to make Impressionism more precise and formal. They employed a technique of juxtaposing dots of primary colors to achieve brighter secondary colors, with the mixture left to the eye to complete (pointillism).

Op Art. The 1960s movement known as Optical Painting is characterized by geometrical forms that create an optical illusion in which the eye is required to blend the colors at a certain distance.

Pop Art. In this return to representational art, the artist returns to the world of tangible objects in a reaction against abstraction. Materials are drawn from the everyday world of popular culture—comic strips, canned goods, and science fiction.

Realism. A development in mid-19th-century France lead by Gustave Courbet. Its aim was to depict the customs, ideas, and appearances of the time using scenes from everyday life.

Rococo. A French style of interior decoration developed during the reign of Louis XV consisting mainly of asymmetrical arrangements of curves in paneling, porcelain, and gold and silver objects. The characteristics of ornate curves, prettiness, and gaiety can also be found in the painting and sculpture of the period.

Surrealism. A further development of Collage, Cubism, and Dada, this 20th-century movement stresses the weird, the fantastic, and the dream-world of the subconscious.

Symbolism. As part of a general European movement in the latter part of the 19th century, it was closely allied with Symbolism in literature. It marked a turning away from painting by observation to transforming fact into a symbol of inner experience. Gauguin was an early practitioner.

Top Pop Albums 1980-1989

1980 **The Wall,** Pink Floyd (Columbia)
1981 **Hi Infidelity,** REO Speedwagon (Epic)
1982 **Asia,** Asia (Geffen)
1983 **Thriller,** Michael Jackson (Epic)
1984 **Thriller,** Michael Jackson (Epic)
1985 **Born in the USA,** Bruce Springsteen (Columbia)
1986 **Whitney Houston,** Whitney Houston (Arista)
1987 **Slippery When Wet,** Bon Jovi (Mercury)
1988 **Faith,** George Michael (Columbia)
1989 **Don't Be Cruel,** Bobby Brown (MCA)
Source: © 1990 BPI Communications, Inc. Used with permission from *Billboard.*

Top 10 Classical Crossover Albums, 1989

1. **Show Boat,** Von Stade, Hadley, Stratas (McGlinn) (Angel)
2. **James Galway's Greatest Hits,** James Galway (RCA)
3. **Ute Lemper Sings Kurt Weill,** Ute Lemper (London)
4. **Victory at Sea,** Cincinnati Pops (Kunzell) (Telarc)
5. **Big Band Hit Parade,** Cincinnati Pops (Kunzell) (Telarc)
6. **Digital Jukebox,** Boston Pops (Williams) (Philips)
7. **The Sound of Music,** Von Stade, Cincinnati Pops (Kunzell) (Telarc)
8. **A Disney Spectacular,** Cincinnati Pops (Kunzell) (Telarc)
9. **1712 Overture,** P.D.Q. Bach (Telarc)
10. **Mancini's Greatest Hits,** Cincinnati Pops (Kunzell) (Telarc)
Source: © 1990 BPI Communications, Inc. Used with permission from *Billboard.*

Top 10 Pop Compact Discs, 1989

1. **The Raw & the Cooked,** Fine Young Cannibals (I.R.S.)
2. **Traveling Wilburys,** Traveling Wilburys (Wilbury)
3. **Full Moon Fever,** Tom Petty (MCA)
4. **Forever Your Girl,** Paula Abdul (Virgin)
5. **Don't Be Cruel,** Bobby Brown (MCA)
6. **Girl You Know It's True,** Milli Vanilli (Arista)
7. **Like a Prayer,** Madonna (Sire)
8. **Shooting Rubberbands at the Stars,** Edie Brickell & New Bohemians (Geffen)
9. **Giving You the Best That I Got,** Anita Baker (Elektra)
10. **Repeat Offender,** Richard Marx (EMI)
Source: © 1990 BPI Communications, Inc. Used with permission from *Billboard.*

VCR & TV Sales to Retailers, 1989

Color TV[1]	21,706,124
Projection TV	265,300
Total TV	21,971,424
Home VCR	12,046,098
Camcorders[2]	2,286,326

1. Excludes projection television. 2. Included in home VCR.
Source: Electronic Industries Association Consumer Electronics Group.

Top Soundtracks 1980-1989

1980 **The Rose** (Atlantic)
1981 **The Jazz Singer** (Capitol)
1982 **Chariots of Fire** (Polydor)
1983 **Flashdance** (Casablanca)
1984 **Footloose** (Columbia)
1985 **Beverly Hills Cop** (MCA)
1986 **Top Gun** (Columbia)
1987 **Top Gun** (Columbia)
1988 **Dirty Dancing** (RCA)
1989 **Beaches** (Atlantic)
Source: © 1990 BPI Communications, Inc. Used with permission from *Billboard.*

Top Black Albums 1980-1989

1980 **Off the Wall,** Michael Jackson (Epic)
1981 **Street Songs,** Rick James (Gordy)
1982 **Raise,** Earth, Wind & Fire (ARC/Columbia)
1983 **Thriller,** Michael Jackson (Epic)
1984 **Can't Slow Down,** Lionel Richie (Motown)
1985 **Emergency,** Kool & The Gang (De-Lite)
1986 **Whitney Houston,** Whitney Houston (Arista)
1987 **Just Like the First Time,** Freddie Jackson (Capitol)
1988 **Make It Last Forever,** Keith Sweat (Vintertainment)
1989 **Guy,** Guy (Uptown)
Source: © 1990 BPI Communications, Inc. Used with permission from *Billboard.*

Top Country Albums 1980-1989

1980 **Kenny,** Kenny Rogers (United Artists)
1981 **9 to 5,** Dolly Parton (RCA)
1982 **Always on My Mind,** Willie Nelson (Columbia)
1983 **Mountain Music,** Alabama (RCA)
1984 **Don't Cheat in Our Hometown,** Ricky Skaggs (Sugar Hill/Epic)
1985 **40 Hour Week,** Alabama (RCA)
1986 **Rockin' With the Rhythm,** The Judds (RCA/Curb)
1987 **Storms of Life,** Randy Travis (Warner Bros.)
1988 **Always & Forever,** Randy Travis (Warner Bros.)
1989 **Loving Proof,** Ricky Van Shelton (Columbia)
Source: © 1990 BPI Communications, Inc. Used with permission from *Billboard.*

Top Classical Albums 1980-1989

1980 **O Sole Mio: Neopolitan Songs,** Luciano Pavarotti (London)
1981 **Pavarotti's Greatest Hits,** Luciano Pavarotti (London)
1982 **Pachelbel: Canon,** Paillard Chamber Orchestra (RCA)
1983 **Bach: Goldberg Variations,** Glenn Could (CBS)
1984 **Pachelbel: Kanon,** Paillard Chamber Orchestra (RCA)
1985 **Amadeus** (Neville Marriner) (Fantasy)
1986 **Horowitz: The Last Romantic,** Vladimir Horowitz (DG)
1987 **Horowitz in Moscow,** Vladimir Horowitz (DG)
1988 **Horowitz Plays Mozart,** Vladimir Horowitz (DG)
1989 **The Movies Go to the Opera,** Various artists (Angel)
Source: © 1990 BPI Communications, Inc. Used with permission from *Billboard.*

Top 10 Classical Albums, 1989

1. **The Movies Go To the Opera,** Various Artists (Angel)
2. **Verdi & Puccini: Arias,** Kiri Te Kanawa (CBS)
3. **Pavarotti at Carnegie Hall,** Luciano Pavarotti (London)
4. **Wagner: The 'Ring' Without Words,** Berlin Philharmonic (Maazel) (Telarc)
5. **Berlioz: Symphony Fantastique,** London Classical Players (Norrington) (Angel)
6. **Portrait of Wynton Marsalis,** Wynton Marsalis (CBS)
7. **Barber/Britten: Cello Concertos,** Yo-Yo Ma (CBS)
8. **Beethoven: Symphony No. 3,** London Classical Players (Norrington) (Angel)
9. **Horowitz at Home,** Vladimir Horowitz (DG)
10. **Beethoven: Symphonies No. 1 & 6,** London Classical Players (Norrington) (Angel)

Source: © 1990 BPI Communications, Inc. Used with permission from *Billboard.*

Artists of the Year, 1989

Based on combined singles and albums chart performance—through sales and radio play—during the year.

Single of the Year: Look Away, Chicago
Album of the Year: Don't Be Cruel, Bobby Brown
Female Artist of the Year: Paula Abdul
Male Artist of the Year: Bobby Brown
Group of the Year: Guns N' Roses
New Artist of the Year: New Kids on the Block
Country Artist of the Year: Randy Travis
Black Artist of the Year: Bobby Brown
Adult Contemporary Artist of the Year: Madonna
Jazz Artist of the Year: Charlie Parker
Classical Artist of the Year: Kiri Te Kanawa
Soundtrack of the Year: Beaches

Source: © 1990 BPI Communications, Inc. Used with permission from *Billboard.*

Top 10 Pop Single Recordings, 1989

1. **Look Away,** Chicago (Reprise)
2. **My Prerogative,** Bobby Brown (MCA)
3. **Every Rose Has Its Thorn,** Poison (Enigma)
4. **Straight Up,** Paula Abdul (Virgin)
5. **Miss You Much,** Janet Jackson (A&M)
6. **Cold Hearted,** Paula Abdul (Virgin)
7. **Wind Beneath My Wings (From 'Beaches'),** Bette Midler (Atlantic)
8. **Girl You Know It's True,** Milli Vanilli (Arista)
9. **Baby, I Love Your Way/Freebird Medley,** Will To Power (Epic)
10. **Giving You the Best That I Got,** Anita Baker (Elektra)

Source: © 1990 BPI Communications, Inc. Used with permission from *Billboard.*

Top 10 Country Single Recordings, 1989

1. **Better Man,** Clint Black (RCA)
2. **Killin' Time,** Clint Black (RCA)
3. **She's Got a Single Thing in Mind,** Conway Twitty (MCA)
4. **Lovin' Only Me,** Ricky Skaggs (Epic)
5. **I Got Dreams,** Steve Wariner (MCA)
6. **Above and Beyond,** Rodney Crowell (Columbia)
7. **I'm No Stranger to the Rain,** Keith Whitley (RCA)
8. **Let Me Tell You About Love,** The Judds (Curb/RCA)
9. **What's Going On in Your World,** George Strait (MCA)
10. **Nothing I Can Do About It Now,** Willie Nelson (Columbia)

Source: © 1990 BPI Communications, Inc. Used with permission from *Billboard.*

Top 10 Pop Albums, 1989

1. **Don't Be Cruel,** Bobby Brown (MCA)
2. **Hangin' Tough,** New Kids on the Block (Columbia)
3. **Forever Your Girl,** Paula Abdul (Virgin)
4. **New Jersey,** Bon Jovi (Mercury)
5. **Appetite for Destruction,** Guns N' Roses (Geffen)
6. **The Raw & the Cooked,** Fine Young Cannibals (I.R.S.)
7. **G N'R Lies,** Guns N' Roses (Geffen)
8. **Traveling Wilburys,** Traveling Wilburys (Wilbury)
9. **Hysteria,** Def Leppard (Mercury)
10. **Girl You Know It's True,** Milli Vanilli (Arista)

Source: © 1990 BPI Communications, Inc. Used with permission from *Billboard.*

Manufacturers' Dollar[1] Shipments of Recordings

(in millions)

	1986	1987	1988	1989
Singles	228	203	180.4	116.4
LP's/EP's	983	793	532.3	220.3
CD's	930	1,593	2,089.9	2,587.7
Cassettes	2,500	2,959	3,385.1	3,345.8
Cassette singles[2]	—	14	57.3	194.6

1. List price value. 2. New configuration. *Source:* Recording Industry Association of America, Inc.

Top 10 Black Single Recordings, 1989

1. **Superwoman,** Karyn White (Warner Bros.)
2. **Keep on Movin',** Soul II Soul (Featuring Caron Wheeler) (Virgin)
3. **So Good,** Al Jarreau (Reprise)
4. **Shower Me With Your Love,** Surface (Columbia)
5. **Don't Make Me Over,** Sybil (Next Plateau)
6. **Something In the Way (You Make Me Feel),** Stephanie Mills (MCA)
7. **Baby Come To Me,** Regina Belle (Columbia)
8. **Love Saw It,** Karyn White (Warner Bros.)
9. **Wild Thing,** Tone Loc (Delicious Vinyl)
10. **Start of a Romance,** Skyy (Atlantic)

Source: © 1990 BPI Communications, Inc. Used with permission from *Billboard.*

Top 15 Regularly Scheduled Network Programs, Nov. 1989

Rank	Program name (network)	Total percent of TV households
1.	Bill Cosby Show (NBC)	23.6
1.	Roseanne (ABC)	23.6
3.	Cheers (NBC)	22.3
4.	A Different World (NBC)	22.1
5.	Golden Girls (NBC)	21.2
6.	60 Minutes (CBS)	20.9
7.	Empty Nest (NBC)	20.2
8.	Murder She Wrote (CBS)	19.6
9.	Wonder Years (ABC)	19.4
10.	Dear John (NBC)	19.2
11.	L.A. Law (NBC)	18.9
12.	Who's The Boss? (ABC)	18.4
12.	NFL Monday Night Football (ABC)	18.4
14.	Unsolved Mysteries (NBC)	18.1
15.	Coach (ABC)	17.8
	Total U.S. TV households 92,100,000	

NOTE: Percentages are calculated from average audience viewings, 5 minutes or longer and 2 or more telecasts. *Source:* Nielsen Media Research, 1990 Nielsen Report on Television.

Top 15 Syndicated TV Programs 1989–90 Season

Rank	Program	Rating (% U.S.)[1]
1.	Wheel of Fortune, M-F	14.0
2.	Jeopardy	12.4
3.	Oprah Winfrey Show	9.7
3.	Star Trek	9.7[2]
5.	Cosby Show-Syndicated	9.6[2]
6.	Universal Pictures Debut Network	9.1[2]
7.	Current Affair	8.6[2]
8.	Wheel of Fortune, Weekend	8.4
9.	Entertainment Tonight	8.1[2]
10.	TriStar Showcase	7.1[2]
11.	Donahue	6.6
12.	National Geographic On Assignment	6.2[2]
13.	Geraldo	5.9[2]
13.	TV Net Movie	5.9[2]
15.	MGM Premiere Network III	5.6[2]

1. 9/18/89-12/31/89. 2. Includes multiple exposures. *Source:* Nielsen Syndication Service National TV Ratings.

Top Sports Shows 1989–90[1]*

Rank	Program name (network)	Rating (% of TV households)
1.	Super Bowl XXIV (CBS)	39.0
2.	NFC Championship Game (CBS)	26.4
3.	AFC Championship Game (NBC)	26.2
4.	AFC Playoff Steelers vs. Broncos (NBC)	24.5
5.	NFC Playoff Rams vs. Giants (CBS)	22.3

1. Sept. 18, 1989, through June 10, 1990.

Top Evening News Shows 1989–90[1]*

Rank	Program name (network)	Rating (% of TV households)
1.	World News Tonight (ABC)	11.0
2.	CBS Evening News	10.1
3.	NBC Nightly News	9.9

1. Sept. 18, 1989, through April 15, 1990.

Top Miniseries 1989–90[1][2]*

Rank	Program name (network)	Rating (% of TV households)
1.	The Kennedys of Massachusetts (ABC)	16.6
2.	Drug Wars: The Camarena Story (NBC)	15.3
3.	Jesus of Nazareth (NBC)	11.3

1. Sept. 18, 1989, through June 10, 1990. 2. Three or more parts.

Top Specials 1989–90[1]*

Rank	Program name (network)	Rating (% of TV households)
1.	Academy Awards (ABC)	27.9
2.	I Love Lucy: The Very First Episode (CBS)	21.2
3.	Barbara Walters Special with Beatty, Schwarzenegger, and Chase (ABC)	20.4
4.	Saturday Night Live 15th Anniversary Special (NBC)	20.3
5.	American Music Awards (ABC)	20.0

1. Sept. 18, 1989, through June 10, 1990.

Top Morning News Shows 1989–90[1]*

Rank	Program name (network)	Rating (% of TV households)
1.	Good Morning America (ABC)	4.4
2.	Today (NBC)	4.0
3.	CBS This Morning	2.6

1. Sept. 18, 1989, through April 15, 1990.

Top Soap Operas 1989–90[1]*

Rank	Program name (network)	Rating (% of TV households)
1.	The Young and the Restless (CBS)	8.0
2.	General Hospital (ABC)	7.4
3.	All My Children (ABC)	6.5
4.	One Life to Live (CBS)	6.3
5.	As the World Turns (CBS)	5.8

1. Sept. 18, 1989, through April 15, 1990.

Weekly TV Viewing by Age
(in hours and minutes)

	Time per week	
	Nov. 1989	Nov. 1988
Women 18–34 years old	29 h 16 min	28 h 53 min
Women 35–54	31 h 28 min	32 h 28 min
Women 55 and over	41 h 19 min	41 h 01 min
Men 18–34	24 h 51 min	25 h 44 min
Men 35–54	27 h 52 min	27 h 01 min
Men 55 and over	38 h 22 min	37 h 32 min
Female Teens	21 h 16 min	21 h 18 min
Male Teens	22 h 18 min	22 h 36 min
Children 6–11	23 h 39 min	23 h 17 min
Children 2–5	27 h 49 min	25 h 43 min
Total Persons (2+)	**29 h 52 min**	**29 h 40 min**

NOTE: All figures are estimates based on Nielsen Television Index NAD Report. *Source:* Nielsen Media Research, Nielsen Report on Television.

Television Network Addresses

American Broadcasting Companies (ABC)
77 W. 66th Street
New York, N.Y. 10023
Canadian Broadcasting Corporation (CBC)
1500 Bronson Avenue
Ottawa, Ontario, Canada K1G 3J5
Columbia Broadcasting System (CBS)
51 W. 52nd Street
New York, N.Y. 10019
Fox Television (WNYW)
205 E. 67th Street
New York, N.Y. 10021
National Broadcasting Company (NBC)
30 Rockefeller Plaza
New York, N.Y. 10020
Public Broadcasting Service (PBS)
1320 Braddock Place
Alexandria, Va. 22314
Westinghouse Broadcasting (Group W)
90 Park Avenue
New York, N.Y. 10016

Persons Viewing Prime Time[1]
(in millions)

	Total persons
Monday	99.3
Tuesday	99.6
Wednesday	92.8
Thursday	96.3
Friday	90.2
Saturday	91.0
Sunday	107.3
Total average	**96.6**

1. Average minute audiences Nov. 1989. NOTE: Prime time is 8–11 p.m. (EST) except Sun. 7–11 pm. Excludes unusual days. *Source:* Nielsen Media Research, Nielsen Report on Television.

Average Hours of Household TV Usage
(in hours and minutes per day)

	Yearly average	February	July
1981–82	6 h 48 min	7 h 22 min	6 h 09 min
1982–83	6 h 55 min	7 h 33 min	6 h 23 min
1983–84	7 h 08 min	7 h 38 min	6 h 26 min
1984–85	7 h 07 min	7 h 49 min	6 h 34 min
1985–86	7 h 10 min	7 h 48 min	6 h 37 min
1986–87	7 h 05 min	7 h 35 min	6 h 32 min
1987–88	6 h 55 min	7 h 38 min	6 h 31 min
1988–89	7 h 02 min	7 h 32 min	6 h 27 min

NOTE: Estimates are based on total U.S. TV households Sept.-Aug. 48 week average, excluding unusual days. *Source:* Nielsen Media Research, Nielsen Report on Television.

Audience Composition by Selected Program Type[1]
(Average Minute Audience)

	General drama	Suspense and mystery drama	Situation comedy	Informational[2] 6-7 p.m.	Feature films	All regular network programs 7–11 p.m.
Women (18 and over)	9,020,000	10,370,000	10,560,000	7,270,000	10,730,000	9,620,000
Men (18 and over)	5,890,000	7,320,000	6,530,000	5,470,000	7,230,000	7,010,000
Teens (12-17)	820,000	740,000	2,070,000	380,000	1,130,000	1,240,000
Children (2-11)	1,400,000	1,450,000	3,400,000	790,000	1,570,000	2,030,000
Total persons (2+)	**17,130,000**	**19,880,000**	**22,560,000**	**13,910,000**	**20,660,000**	**19,900,000**

1. All figures are estimated for the period Nov. 1989. 2. Multiweekly viewing. *Source:* Nielsen Media Research, 1990 Nielsen Report on Television.

Hours of TV Usage Per Week by Household Income

	Under $30,000	$30,000+	$40,000+	$50,000+	$60,000+
Nov. 1987	n.a.	49 h 38 min	48 h 29 min	n.a.	n.a.
Nov. 1988	52 h 43 min	49 h 22 min	48 h 44 min	48 h 26 min	47 h 49 min
Nov. 1989	52 h 59 min	48 h 47 min	48 h 19 min	46 h 54 min	46 h 20 min

Source: Nielsen Media Research, Nielsen Report on Television. NOTE: n.a. = not available.

Source of Household Viewing—Prime Time
Pay Cable, Basic Cable, and Non-Cable Households
(Mon.-Sun. 8–11 pm)

	Nov. 1989			Nov. 1988			Nov. 1987		
	Pay cable	Basic cable	Non-cable	Pay cable	Basic cable	Non-cable	Pay cable	Basic cable	Non-cable
% TV Usage	65.6	60.3	56.5	67.7	63.1	57.7	68.7	59.3	56.8
Pay Cable	9.7	—	—	11.8	—	—	10.4	—	—
Cable-originated programming	14.8	14.1	—	13.5	13.1	—	10.8	10.1	—
Other-on-air stations	14.2	14.0	15.8	14.2	14.7	16.1	14.9	13.6	14.7
Network affiliated stations	37.5	37.5	44.9	38.1	40.9	46.0	42.6	39.6	46.7
Network share	(57)	(62)	(79)	(56)	(65)	(80)	(62)	(67)	(82)

Source: Nielsen Media Research, Nielsen Report on Television.

Major U.S. Fairs and Expositions

1853 Crystal Palace Exposition, New York City: modeled on similar fair held in London.

1876 Centennial Exposition, Philadelphia: celebrating 100th year of independence.

1893 World's Columbian Exposition, Chicago: commemorating 400th anniversary of Columbus' voyage to America.

1894 Midwinter International Exposition, San Francisco: promoting business revival after Depression of 1893.

1898 Trans-Mississippi and International Exposition, Omaha, Neb.: exhibiting products, resources, industries, and civilization of states and territories west of the Mississippi River.

1901 Pan-American Exposition, Buffalo, N.Y.: promoting social and commercial interest of Western Hemisphere nations.

1904 Louisiana Purchase Exposition, St. Louis: marking 100th anniversary of major land acquisition from France and opening up of the West.

1905 Lewis and Clark Centennial Exposition, Portland, Ore.: commemorating 100th anniversary of exploration of a land route to the Pacific.

1907 Jamestown Ter Centennial Exposition, Hampton Roads, Va.: marking 300th anniversary of first permanent English settlement in America.

1909 Alaska-Yukon-Pacific Exposition, Seattle: celebrating growth of the Puget Sound area.

1915–16 Panama-Pacific International Exposition, San Francisco: celebrating opening of the Panama Canal.

1915–16 Panama-California Exposition, San Diego: promoting resources and opportunities for development and commerce of the Western states.

1926 Sesquicentennial Exposition, Philadelphia: marking 150th year of independence.

1933–34 Century of Progress International Exposition, Chicago: celebrating 100th anniversary of incorporation of Chicago as a city.

1935 California Pacific International Exposition, San Diego: marking 400 years of progress since the first Spaniard landed on the West Coast.

1939–40 New York World's Fair, New York City: "The World of Tomorrow," symbolized by Trylon and Perisphere. Officially commemorating 150th anniversary of inauguration of George Washington as President in New York.

1939–40 Golden Gate International Exposition, Treasure Island, San Francisco: celebrating new Golden Gate Bridge and Oakland Bay Bridge.

1962 The Century 21 Exposition, Seattle: "Man in the Space Age," symbolized by 600-foot steel space needle.

1964–65 New York World's Fair, New York City: "Peace Through Understanding."

1974 Expo '74, Spokane: "Tomorrow's Fresh, New Environment."

1982 World's Fair, Knoxville, Tenn.: "Energy Turns the World," symbolized by the bronze-globed Sunsphere.

1984 Louisiana World Exposition, New Orleans: "The World of Rivers."

Longest Broadway Runs[1]

1. A Chorus Line (M) (1975-90)	6,137
2. Oh, Calcutta (M) (1976-89)	5,959
3. 42nd Street (M) (1980-89)	3,486
4. Grease (M) (1972-80)	3,388
5. Cats (M) (1982-)	3,269
6. Fiddler on the Roof (1964-72)	3,242
7. Life with Father (1939-47)	3,224
8. Tobacco Road (1933-41)	3,182
9. Hello, Dolly! (M) (1964-71)	2,844
10. My Fair Lady (M) (1956-62)	2,717
11. Annie (M) (1977-83)	2,377
11. Oklahoma (M) (1943-48)	2,377
13. Man of La Mancha (M) (1965-71)	2,328
14. Abie's Irish Rose (1922-27)	2,327
15. Pippin (M) (1971-77)	1,994
16. South Pacific (M) (1949-54)	1,925
17. Magic Show (M) (1974-78)	1,920
18. Deathtrap (1978-82)	1,792
19. Gemini (1977-81)	1,788
20. Harvey (1944-49)	1,775
21. Dancin' (M) (1978-82)	1,774
22. Cage aux Folies (M) (1983-87)	1,761
23. Hair (M) (1968-72)	1,750
24. The Wiz (M) (1975-79)	1,672
25. Born Yesterday (1946-49)	1,642

1. As of Aug. 8, 1990. M = musical. Years are those of opening and closing.

Motion Picture Revenues

All-Time Top Money Makers[1]		Top Rentals 1989[2]	
1. E.T. The Extra-Terrestrial (Universal, 1982)	$228,618,939	1. Batman (Warner Brothers)	$150,500,000
2. Star Wars (20th Century-Fox, 1977)	193,500,000	2. Indiana Jones and the Last Crusade (Paramount)	115,500,000
3. Return of the Jedi (20th Century-Fox, 1983)	168,002,414	3. Lethal Weapon 2 (Warner Brothers)	79,500,000
4. Batman (Warner Brothers, 1989)	150,500,000	4. Honey, I Shrunk the Kids (Buena Vista)	71,097,000
5. The Empire Strikes Back (20th Century-Fox, 1980)	141,600,000	5 Rain Man (continuing 1989 run)	65,000,000
6. Ghostbusters (Columbia, 1984)	130,211,324	6. Back to the Future, Part II (Columbia)	63,000,000
7. Jaws (Universal, 1975)	129,549,325	7. Ghostbusters II (Columbia)	61,649,019
8. Raiders of the Lost Ark (Paramount, 1981)	115,598,000	8. Look Who's Talking (Tri-Star)	55,000,000
9. Indiana Jones and the Last Crusade (Paramount, 1989)	115,500,000	9. Parenthood (Universal)	48,600,000
10. Indiana Jones and the Temple of Doom (Paramount, 1984)	109,000,000	10. Dead Poets Society (Buena Vista)	47,596,000
11. Beverly Hills Cop (Paramount, 1984)	108,000,000	11. National Lampoon's Christmas Vacation (Warner Brothers)	42,000,000
12. Back to the Future (Universal, 1985)	104,408,738	12. When Harry Met Sally (Columbia)	41,976,751
13. Grease (Paramount, 1978)	96,300,000	13. Harlem Nights (Paramount)	35,000,000
14. Tootsie (Columbia, 1982)	96,292,736	14. Turner & Hooch (Buena Vista)	34,263,000
15. The Exorcist (Warner Brothers, 1973)	89,000,000	15. The War of the Roses (20th Century-Fox)	33,000,000
16. The Godfather (Paramount, 1972)	86,275,000	16. Field of Dreams (Universal)	30,309,587
17. Rain Man (United Artists, 1989)	86,000,000	17. The Little Mermaid (Buena Vista)	30,000,000
18. Superman (Warner Brothers, 1978)	82,800,000	18. Uncle Buck (Universal)	29,190,348
19. Close Encounters of the Third Kind (Columbia, 1977/1980)	82,750,000	19. The Abyss (20th Century-Fox)	28,700,000
20. Three Men and a Baby (Buena Vista, 1987)	81,356,000	20. Sea of Love (Universal)	27,500,000
21. Who Framed Roger Rabbit (Buena Vista, 1988)	81,244,000	21. Star Trek V: The Final Frontier (Paramount)	27,100,000
22. Beverly Hills Cop II (Paramount, 1987)	80,857,776	22. Pet Sematary (Paramount)	26,400,000
23. The Sound of Music (20th Century-Fox, 1965)	79,748,000	23. Steel Magnolias (Tri-Star)	26,000,000
24. Grelims (Warner Brothers, 1984)	79,500,000	24. Twins (continuing 1989 run)	25,237,000
24. Lethal Weapon 2 (Warner Brothers, 1989)	79,500,000	25. Beaches (Buena Vista, December 1988)	24,882,000

NOTE: United States and Canada only. 1. Figures are not to be confused with gross box-office receipts from sale of tickets. 2. Figures are total rentals collected by film distributors as of Dec. 31, 1989. *Source:* Reprinted with permission from *Variety Inc.*

Miss America Winners

1921 Margaret Gorman, Washington, D.C.
1922-23 Mary Campbell, Columbus, Ohio
1924 Ruth Malcolmson, Philadelphia, Pa.
1925 Fay Lamphier, Oakland, Calif.
1926 Norma Smallwood, Tulsa, Okla.
1927 Lois Delaner, Joliet, Ill.
1933 Marion Bergeron, West Haven, Conn.
1935 Henrietta Leaver, Pittsburgh, Pa.
1936 Rose Coyle, Philadelphia, Pa.
1937 Bette Cooper, Bertrand Island, N.J.
1938 Marilyn Meseke, Marion, Ohio
1939 Patricia Donnelly, Detroit, Mich.
1940 Frances Marie Burke, Philadelphia, Pa.
1941 Rosemary LaPlanche, Los Angeles, Calif.
1942 Jo-Caroll Dennison, Tyler, Texas
1943 Jean Bartel, Los Angeles, Calif.
1944 Venus Ramey, Washington, D.C.
1945 Bess Myerson, New York, N.Y.
1946 Marilyn Buferd, Los Angeles, Calif.
1947 Barbara Walker, Memphis, Tenn.
1948 BeBe Shopp, Hopkins, Minn.
1949 Jacque Mercer, Litchfield, Ariz.
1951 Yolande Betbeze, Mobile, Ala.
1952 Coleen Kay Hutchins, Salt Lake City, Utah
1953 Neva Jane Langley, Macon, Ga.
1954 Evelyn Margaret Ay, Ephrata, Pa.
1955 Lee Meriwether, San Francisco, Calif.
1956 Sharon Ritchie, Denver, Colo.
1957 Marian McKnight, Manning, S.C.
1958 Marilyn Van Derbur, Denver, Colo.
1959 Mary Ann Mobley, Brandon, Miss.
1960 Lynda Lee Mead, Natchez, Miss.
1961 Nancy Fleming, Montague, Mich.

1962 Maria Fletcher, Asheville, N.C.
1963 Jacquelyn Mayer, Sandusky, Ohio
1964 Donna Axum, El Dorado, Ark.
1965 Vonda Kay Van Dyke, Phoenix, Ariz.
1966 Deborah Irene Bryant, Overland Park, Kan.
1967 Jane Anne Jayroe, Laverne, Okla.
1968 Debra Dene Barnes, Moran, Kan.
1969 Judith Anne Ford, Belvidere, Ill.
1970 Pamela Anne Eldred, Birmingham, Mich.
1971 Phyllis Ann George, Denton, Texas
1972 Laurie Lea Schaefer, Columbus, Ohio
1973 Terry Anne Meeuwsen, DePere, Wis.
1974 Rebecca Ann King, Denver, Colo.
1975 Shirley Cothran, Fort Worth, Texas
1976 Tawney Elaine Godin, Yonkers, N.Y.
1977 Dorothy Kathleen Benham, Edina, Minn.
1978 Susan Perkins, Columbus, Ohio
1979 Kylene Baker, Galax, Va.
1980 Cheryl Prewitt, Ackerman, Miss.
1981 Susan Powell, Elk City, Okla.
1982 Elizabeth Ward, Russellville, Ark.
1983 Debra Maffett, Anaheim, Calif.
1984 Vanessa Williams, Milwood, N.Y.[1]
    Suzette Charles, Mays Landing, N.J.
1985 Sharlene Wells, Salt Lake City, Utah
1986 Susan Akin, Meridian, Miss.
1987 Kellye Cash, Memphis, Tenn.
1988 Kaye Lani Rae Rafko, Toledo, Ohio
1989 Gretchen Elizabeth Carlson, Anoka, Minn.
1990 Debbye Turner, Mexico, Mo.
1991 (*See* Current Events)
1. Resigned July 23, 1984.

U.S. STATES & CITIES

States and Territories

Sources for state estimated populations, populations under 18, and over 65 are latest data provided by the U.S. Census Bureau. They include Armed Forces residing in each state. Sources for estimated Black, Hispanic populations, legal immigrants, and net migration are provided courtesy of the Population Reference Bureau, Inc. NOTE: Estimated *net* migration differs from "immigrants admitted" in that it implicitly includes the effects of illegal immigration and emigration. Largest cities include incorporated places only, as defined by the U.S. Census Bureau. They do not include adjacent or suburban areas as do the Metropolitan Statistical Areas found in the "U.S. Statistics" section of this Almanac. For secession and readmission dates of the former Confederate states, *see* Index. For lists of Governors, Senators, and Representatives, *see* Index. For additional state information, *see* the sections on "Business and the Economy," "Elections," "Taxes," and "U.S. Statistics."

ALABAMA

Capital: Montgomery
Governor: Guy Hunt, R (to Jan. 1991)
Lieut. Governor: Jim E. Folsom, Jr., D (to Jan. 1991)
Secy. of State: Perry Hand, R (to Jan. 1991)
Comptroller: Robert Childree
Atty. General: Don Siegelman, D (to Jan. 1991)
Organized as territory: March 3, 1817
Entered Union & (rank): Dec. 14, 1819 (22)
Present constitution adopted: 1901
Motto: *Audemus jura nostra defendere* (We dare defend our rights)
State flower: Camellia (1959)
State bird: Yellowhammer (1927)
State song: "Alabama" (1931)
State tree: Southern pine (longleaf) (1949)
State salt water fish: Tarpon (1955)
State fresh water fish: Largemouth Bass (1975)
State horse: Racking horse (1975)
Official mineral: Hematite (1967)
Official rock: Marble (1969)
State game bird: Wild Turkey (1980)
State dance: Square dance (1981)
State nut: Pecan (1982)
State fossil: Species *Basilosaurus Cetoides* (1984)
Nickname: Yellowhammer State
Origin of name: May come from Choctaw meaning "thicket-clearers" or "vegetation-gatherers"
1980 population (1980 census) & (rank): 3,893,888 (22)
1989 est. population (July 1) & (rank): 4,118,000 (22)
1991 proj. population: 4,210,000
1980 land area & (rank): 50,767 sq mi. (131,487 sq km) (28)
Geographic center: In Chilton Co., 12 mi. SW of Clanton
Number of counties: 67
Largest cities (1980 census): Birmingham, 284,413; Mobile, 200,452; Montgomery, 178,157; Huntsville, 142,513; Tuscaloosa, 75,143; Gadsden, 47,565
State forests: 21 (48,000 ac.)
State parks: 22 (45,614 ac.)
1989 percent pop. below age 18: 26.9
1989 percent pop. age 65 and over: 12.7
Est. Black population (1985): 1,055,000
Est. Hispanic population (1985): 18,000
1987-88 Est. total net migration & (rate): −3,698 (−0.9%)
1987-88 (fiscal year) legal immigrants: 1,597

Spanish explorers are believed to have arrived at Mobile Bay in 1519, and the territory was visited in 1540 by the explorer Hernando de Soto. The first permanent European settlement in Alabama was founded by the French at Fort Louis in 1702. The British gained control of the area in 1763 by the Treaty of Paris, but had to cede almost all the Alabama region to the U.S. after the American Revolution. The Confederacy was founded at Montgomery in February 1861 and, for a time, the city was the Confederate capital.

During the last part of the 19th century, the economy of the state slowly improved. At Tuskegee Institute, founded in 1881 by Booker T. Washington, Dr. George Washington Carver carried out his famous agricultural research.

In the 1950s and '60s, Alabama was the site of such landmark civil-rights actions as the bus boycott in Montgomery (1955–56) and the "Freedom March" from Selma to Montgomery (1965).

Today paper, chemicals, rubber and plastics, apparel and textiles, and primary metals comprise the leading industries of Alabama. Continuing as a major manufacturer of coal, iron, and steel, Birmingham is also noted for its world-renowned medical center, especially for heart surgery. The state ranks high in the production of poultry, soybeans, milk, vegetables, livestock, wheat, cattle, cotton, peanuts, fruits, hogs, and corn.

Points of interest include the Space and Rocket Center at Huntsville, the White House of the Confederacy, and Shakespeare Festival Theater Complex in Montgomery, and Russell Cave near Bridgeport, and the Gulf Coast area.

ALASKA

Capital: Juneau
Governor: Steve Cowper, D (to Dec. 1990)
Lieut. Governor: Stephen McAlpine, D (to Dec. 1990)
Commissioner of Administration: John Andrews, D (to Dec. 1990)
Atty. General: Douglas B. Baily (to Dec. 1990)
Organized as territory: 1912
Entered Union & (rank): Jan. 3, 1959 (49)
Constitution ratified: April 24, 1956
Motto: North to the Future
State flower: Forget-me-not (1949)
State tree: Sitka spruce (1962)
State bird: Willow ptarmigan (1955)
State fish: King salmon (1962)
State song: "Alaska's Flag" (1955)
State gem: Jade (1968)
State marine mammal: Bowhead Whale (1983)
State fossil: Woolly Mammoth (1986)
State mineral: Gold (1968)
State sport: Dog Mushing (1972)
Nickname: The state is commonly called "The Last Frontier" or "Land of the Midnight Sun"
Origin of name: Corruption of Aleut word meaning "great land" or "that which the sea breaks against"
1980 population (1980 census) & (rank): 401,851 (50)
1989 est. population (July 1) & (rank): 527,000 (49)
1991 proj. population: 588,000

1980 land area & (rank): 570,833 sq mi. (1,478,458 sq km) (1)
Geographic center: 60 mi. NW of Mt. McKinley
Number of boroughs: 12
Largest cities (1988 est.): Anchorage, 246,139; Fairbanks, 27,141; Juneau, 29,946; Ketchikan (Borough), 12,982; Ketchikan (City), 7,601; Sitka, 8,102; Kodiak, 6,774; Bethel, 4,462
State forests: None
State parks: 5; 59 waysides and areas (3.3 million ac.)
1989 percent pop. below age 18: 31.3
1989 percent pop. age 65 and over: 4.1
Est. Black population (1985): 18,000
Est. Hispanic population (1985): 12,000
1987-88 Est. total net migration & (rate): −9,693 (−18.5%)
1987-88 (fiscal year) legal immigrants: 992

Vitus Bering, a Dane working for the Russians, and Alexei Chirikov discovered the Alaskan mainland and the Aleutian Islands in 1741. The tremendous land mass of Alaska—equal to one fifth of the continental U.S.—was unexplored in 1867 when Secretary of State William Seward arranged for its purchase from the Russians for $7,200,000. The transfer of the territory took place on Oct. 18, 1867. Despite a price of about two cents an acre, the purchase was widely ridiculed as "Seward's Folly." The first official census (1880) reported a total of 33,426 Alaskans, all but 430 being of aboriginal stock. The Gold Rush of 1898 resulted in a mass influx of more than 30,000 people. Since then, Alaska has returned billions of dollars' worth of products to the U.S.

In 1968, a large oil and gas reservoir near Prudhoe Bay on the Arctic Coast was found. The Prudhoe Bay reservoir, with an estimated recoverable 10 billion barrels of oil and 27 trillion cubic feet of gas, is twice as large as any other oil field in North America. The Trans-Alaska pipeline was completed in 1977 at a cost of $7.7 billion. On June 20, oil started flowing through the 800-mile-long pipeline from Prudhoe Bay to the port of Valdez.

Other industries important to Alaska's economy are fisheries, wood and wood products, and furs, and tourism.

Denali National Park and Mendenhall Glacier in North Tongass National Forest are of interest, as is the large totem pole collection at Sitka National Historical Park. The Katmai National Park includes the "Valley of Ten Thousand Smokes," an area of active volcanoes.

ARIZONA

Capital: Phoenix
Governor: Rose Mofford, D (to Jan. 1991)
Secy. of State: Jim Shumway, D (to Jan. 1991)
Atty. General: Bob Corbin, R (to Jan. 1991)
State Treasurer: Ray Rottas, R (to Jan. 1991)
Organized as territory: Feb. 24, 1863
Entered Union & (rank): Feb. 14, 1912 (48)
Present constitution adopted: 1911
Motto: *Ditat Deus* (God enriches)
State flower: Flower of saguaro cactus (1931)
State bird: Cactus wren (1931)
State colors: Blue and old gold (1915)
State song: "Arizona March Song" (1919)
State tree: Paloverde (1957)
Nickname: Grand Canyon State
Origin of name: From the Indian "Arizonac," meaning "little spring"

1980 population (1980 census) & (rank): 2,718,215 (29)
1989 est. population (July 1) & (rank): 3,556,000 (24)
1991 proj. population: 3,852,000
1980 land area & (rank): 113,508 sq mi. (293,986 sq km) (6)
Geographic center: In Yavapai Co., 55 mi. ESE of Prescott
Number of counties: 15
Largest cities (1980 census): Phoenix, 789,704; Tucson, 330,537; Mesa, 152,453; Tempe, 106,743; Glendale, 97,172; Scottsdale, 86,622; Yuma, 42,481
State forests: None
State parks: 24
1989 percent pop. below age 18: 27.6
1989 percent pop. age 65 and over: 13.1
Est. Black population (1985): 92,000
Est. Hispanic population (1985): 533,000
1987-88 Est. total net migration & (rate): 52,136 (15.1%)
1987-88 (fiscal year) legal immigrants: 7,189

Marcos de Niza, a Spanish Franciscan friar, was the first European to explore Arizona. He entered the area in 1539 in search of the mythical Seven Cities of Gold. Although he was followed a year later by another gold seeker, Francisco Vásquez de Coronado, most of the early settlement was for missionary purposes. In 1776 the Spanish established Fort Tucson. In 1848, after the Mexican War, most of the Arizona territory became part of the U.S., and the southern portion of the territory was added by the Gadsden Purchase in 1853.

In 1973 the world's biggest dam, the New Cornelia Tailings, was completed near Ajo.

Arizona history is rich in legends of America's Old West. It was here that the great Indian chiefs Geronimo and Cochise led their people against the frontiersmen. Tombstone, Ariz., was the site of the West's most famous shoot-out—the gunfight at the O.K. Corral. Today, Arizona has the largest U.S. Indian population; more than 14 tribes are represented on 19 reservations.

Manufacturing has become Arizona's most important industry. Principal products include electrical, communications, and aeronautical items. The state produces over half the country's copper. Agriculture is also important to the state's economy.

State attractions include such famous scenery as the Grand Canyon, the Petrified Forest, and the Painted Desert. Hoover Dam, Lake Mead, Fort Apache, and the reconstructed London Bridge at Lake Havasu City are of particular interest.

ARKANSAS

Capital: Little Rock
Governor: Bill Clinton, D (to Jan. 1991)
Lieut. Governor: Winston Bryant, D (to Jan. 1991)
Secy. of State: W. J. McCuen, D (to Jan. 1991)
Atty. General: Steve Clark (to Jan. 1991)
Auditor of State: Julia Hughes Jones, D (to Jan. 1991)
Treasurer of State: Jimmie Lou Fisher, D (to Jan. 1991)
Land Commissioner: Charles Daniels, D (to Jan. 1991)
Organized as territory: March 2, 1819
Entered Union & (rank): June 15, 1836 (25)
Present constitution adopted: 1874
Motto: *Regnat populus* (The people rule)
State flower: Apple Blossom (1901)
State tree: Pine (1939)
State bird: Mockingbird (1929)
State insect: Honeybee (1973)
State song: "Arkansas" (1963)
Nickname: Land of Opportunity

Origin of name: From the Quapaw Indians
1980 population (1980 census) & (rank): 2,286,435 (33)
1989 est. population (July 1) & (rank): 2,406,000 (33)
1991 proj. population: 2,439,000
1980 land area & (rank): 52,078 sq mi. (134,883 sq km) (27)
Geographic center: In Pulaski Co., 12 mi. NW of Little Rock
Number of counties: 75
Largest cities (1980 census): Little Rock, 158,461; Fort Smith, 71,626; North Little Rock, 64,288; Pine Bluff, 56,636; Fayetteville, 36,608; Hot Springs, 35,781
State forests: None
State parks: 44
1989 percent pop. below age 18: 27.0
1989 percent pop. age 65 and over: 14.8
Est. Black population (1985): 392,000
Est. Hispanic population (1985): 14,000
1987-88 Est. total net migration & (rate): −2,980 (−1.2%)
1987-88 (fiscal year) legal immigrants: 861

Hernando de Soto, in 1541, was among the early European explorers to visit the territory. It was a Frenchman, Henri de Tonti, who in 1686 founded the first permanent white settlement—the Arkansas Post. In 1803 the area was acquired by the U.S. as part of the Louisiana Purchase.

Food products are the state's largest employing sector, with lumber and wood products a close second. Arkansas is also a leader in the production of cotton, rice, and soybeans. The state produces 97% of the nation's high-grade domestic bauxite ore—the source of aluminum. It also has the country's only active diamond mine; located near Murfreesboro, it is operated as a tourist attraction.

Hot Springs National Park, and Buffalo National River in the Ozarks are major state attractions.

Blanchard Springs Caverns, the Arkansas Territorial Restoration at Little Rock, and the Arkansas Folk Center in Mountain View are of interest.

CALIFORNIA

Capital: Sacramento
Governor: George Deukmejian, R (to Jan. 1991)
Lieut. Governor: Leo McCarthy, D (to Jan. 1991)
Secy. of State: March Fong Eu, D (to Jan. 1991)
Controller: Gray Davis, D (to Jan. 1991)
Atty. General: John Van de Kamp, D (to Jan. 1991)
Treasurer: Jesse M. Unruh, D (to Jan. 1991)
Entered Union & (rank): Sept. 9, 1850 (31)
Present constitution adopted: 1879
Motto: *Eureka* (I have found it)
State flower: Golden poppy (1903)
State tree: California redwoods *(Sequoia sempervirens & Sequoia gigantea)* (1937 & 1953)
State bird: California valley quail (1931)
State animal: California grizzly bear (1953)
State fish: California golden trout (1947)
State colors: Blue and gold (1951)
State song: "I Love You, California" (1951)
Nickname: Golden State
Origin of name: From a book, *Las Sergas de Esplandián,* by Garcia Ordóñez de Montalvo, c. 1500
1980 population (1980 census) & (rank): 23,667,902 (1)
1989 est. population (July 1) & (rank): 29,063,000 (1)
1991 proj. population: 29,627,000
1980 land area & (rank): 156,299 sq mi. (404,815 sq km) (3)
Geographic center: In Madera Co., 35 mi. NE of Madera
Number of counties: 58

Largest cities (1980 census): Los Angeles, 2,966,850; San Diego, 875,538; San Francisco, 678,974; San Jose, 629,442; Long Beach, 361,334; Oakland, 339,337
State forests: 8 (70,283 ac.)
State parks and beaches: 180 (723,000 ac.)
1989 percent pop. below age 18: 26.6
1989 percent pop. age 65 and over: 10.6
Est. Black population (1985): 2,074,000
Est. Hispanic population (1985): 5,873,000
1987-88 Est. total net migration & (rate): 364,243 (13.0%)
1987-88 (fiscal year) legal immigrants: 161,164

Although California was sighted by Spanish navigator Juan Rodríguez Cabrillo in 1542, its first Spanish mission (at San Diego) was not established until 1769. California became a U.S. Territory in 1847 when Mexico surrendered it to John C. Frémont. On Jan. 24, 1848, James W. Marshall discovered gold at Sutter's Mill, starting the California Gold Rush and bringing settlers to the state in large numbers.

In 1964, the U.S. Census Bureau estimated that California had become the most populous state, surpassing New York. California also leads the country in personal income and consumer expenditures.

Leading industries include manufacturing (transportation equipment, machinery, and electronic equipment), agriculture, biotechnology, and tourism. Principal natural resources include timber, petroleum, cement, and natural gas.

More immigrants settle in California than any other state—27% of the nation's total in 1986. The influx was led by new arrivals from Mexico and the Philippines.

Death Valley, in the southeast, is 282 feet below sea level, the lowest point in the nation; and Mt. Whitney (14,491 ft) is the highest point in the contiguous 48 states. Lassen Peak is one of two active U.S. volcanos outside of Alaska and Hawaii; its last eruptions were recorded in 1917. The General Sherman Tree in Sequoia National Park is estimated to be about 3,500 years old and a stand of bristlecone pine trees in the White Mountains may be over 4,000 years old.

Other points of interest include Yosemite National Park, Disneyland, Hollywood, the Golden Gate bridge, San Simeon State Park, and Point Reyes National Seashore.

COLORADO

Capital: Denver
Governor: Roy Romer, D (to Jan. 1991)
Lieut. Governor: Michael Callihan, D (to Jan. 1991)
Secy. of State: Natalie Meyer, R (to Jan 1991)
Treasurer: Gail Schoettler, D (to Jan. 1991)
Controller: James A. Stroup
Atty. General: Duane Woodard, D (to Jan. 1991)
Organized as territory: Feb. 28, 1861
Entered Union & (rank): Aug. 1, 1876 (38)
Present constitution adopted: 1876
Motto: *Nil sine Numine* (Nothing without Providence)
State flower: Rocky Mountain columbine (1899)
State tree: Colorado blue spruce (1939)
State bird: Lark bunting (1931)
State animal: Rocky Mountain bighorn sheep (1961)
State gemstone: Aquamarine (1971)
State colors: Blue and white (1911)
State song: "Where the Columbines Grow" (1915)
Nickname: Centennial State

Origin of name: From the Spanish, "ruddy" or "red"
1980 population (1980 census) & (rank): 2,889,964 (28)
1989 est. population (July 1) & rank: 3,317,000 (26)
1991 proj. population: 3,476,000
1980 land area & (rank): 103,595 sq mi. (268,311 sq km) (8)
Geographic center: In Park Co., 30 mi. NW of Pikes Peak
Number of counties: 63
Largest cities (1980 census): Denver, 492,365; Colorado Springs, 214,821; Aurora, 158,588; Lakewood, 113,808; Pueblo, 101,686; Arvada, 84,576; Boulder, 76,685
State forests: 1 (71,000 ac.)
1989 percent pop. below age 18: 26.1
1989 percent pop. age 65 and over: 9.8
Est. Black population (1985): 120,000
Est. Hispanic population (1985): 384,000
1987-88 Est. total net migration & (rate): −24,879 (−7.5%)
1987-88 (fiscal year) legal immigrants: 4,562

First visited by Spanish explorers in the 1500s, the territory was claimed for Spain by Juan de Ulibarri in 1706. The U.S. obtained eastern Colorado as part of the Louisiana Purchase in 1803, the central portion in 1845 with the admission of Texas as a state, and the western part in 1848 as a result of the Mexican War.

Colorado has the highest mean elevation of any state, with more than 1,000 Rocky Mountain peaks over 10,000 feet high and 54 towering above 14,000 feet. Pikes Peak, the most famous of these mountains, was discovered by U.S. Army Lieut. Zebulon M. Pike in 1806.

Once primarily a mining and agricultural state, Colorado's economy is now driven by the service-producing industries, which provide jobs for more than four-fifths of the state's non-farm work force. In addition, tourism is extremely important to the state's economy. The ski industry accounts for approximately one-third of the state's tourism market. The main tourist attractions in the state include Rocky Mountain National Park, Curecanti National Recreation Area, Mesa Verde National Park, and the Great Sand Dunes and Dinosaur National Monuments.

The two primary facets of Colorado's manufacturing industry are advanced technology and defense.

The mining industry, which includes oil and gas, coal, and metal mining, is still important to Colorado's economy, though it employs only 1.5 percent of the state's workforce. Gold production is growing in importance, and Denver is now home to companies that control half of the nation's gold production. The farm industry, which is primarily concentrated in livestock, is also an important element of the state's economy. The primary crops in Colorado are corn, hay, and wheat.

CONNECTICUT

Capital: Hartford
Governor: William A. O'Neill, D (to Jan. 1991)
Lieut. Governor: Joseph J. Fauliso, D (to Jan. 1991)
Secy. of State: Julia H. Tashjian, D (to Jan. 1991)
Comptroller: J. Edward Caldwell, D (to Jan. 1991)
Treasurer: Francisco L. Borges, D (to Jan. 1991)
Atty. General: Clarine Nardi Riddle, D (to Jan. 1991)
Entered Union & (rank): Jan. 9, 1788 (5)
Present constitution adopted: Dec. 30, 1965
Motto: *Qui transtulit sustinet* (He who transplanted still sustains)

State flower: Mountain laurel (1907)
State tree: White Oak (1947)
State animal: Sperm whale (1975)
State bird: American robin (1943)
State Hero: Nathan Hale (1985)
State insect: Praying mantis (1977)
State mineral: Garnet (1977)
State song: "Yankee Doodle" (1978)
State ship: USS Nautilus (SSN571) (1983)
Official designation: *Constitution State* (1959)
Nickname: Nutmeg State
Origin of name: From an Indian word (Quinnehtukqut) meaning "beside the long tidal river"
1980 population (1980 census) & (rank): 3,107,576 (25)
1989 est. population (July 1) & (rank): 3,239,000 (28)
1991 proj. population: 3,300,000
1980 land area & (rank): 4,872 sq mi. (12,618 km) (48)
Geographic center: In Hartford Co., at East Berlin
Number of counties: 8
Largest cities (1980 census): Bridgeport, 142,546; Hartford, 136,392; New Haven, 126,109; Waterbury, 103,266; Stamford, 102,453; Norwalk, 77,767
State forests: 30 (139,377 ac.)
State parks: 89 (30,647 ac.)
1989 percent pop. below age 18: 23.4
1989 percent pop. age 65 and over: 13.6
Est. Black population (1985): 244,000
Est. Hispanic population (1985): 139,000
1987-88 Est. total net migration & (rate): 1,759 (0.5%)
1987-88 (fiscal year) legal immigrants: 8,058

The Dutch navigator, Adriaen Block, was the first European of record to explore the area, sailing up the Connecticut River in 1614. In 1633, Dutch colonists built a fort and trading post near present-day Hartford, but soon lost control to English Puritans migrating south from the Massachusetts Bay Colony.

English settlements, established in the 1630s at Windsor, Wethersfield, and Hartford, united in 1639 to form the Connecticut Colony and adopted the *Fundamental Orders*, considered the world's first written constitution.

The colony's royal charter of 1662 was exceptionally liberal. When Gov. Edmund Andros tried to seize it in 1687, it was hidden in the Hartford Oak, commemorated in Charter Oak Place.

Connecticut played a prominent role in the Revolutionary War, serving as the Continental Army's major supplier. Sometimes called the "Arsenal of the Nation," the state became one of the most industrialized in the nation.

Today, Connecticut factories produce weapons, sewing machines, jet engines, helicopters, motors, hardware and tools, cutlery, clocks, locks, ball bearings, silverware, and submarines. Hartford, which has the oldest U.S. newspaper still being published—the *Courant,* established 1764—is the insurance capital of the nation.

Poultry, fruit, and dairy products account for the largest portion of farm income, and Connecticut shade-grown tobacco is acknowledged to be the nation's most valuable crop, per acre.

Connecticut is a popular resort area with its 250-mile Long Island Sound shoreline and many inland lakes. Among the major points of interest are Yale University's Gallery of Fine Arts and Peabody Museum. Other famous museums include the P.T. Barnum, Winchester Gun, and American Clock and Watch. The town of Mystic features a recreated 19th-century New England seaport and the Mystic Marinelife Aquarium.

DELAWARE

Capital: Dover
Governor: Michael N. Castle, R (to Jan. 1993)
Lieut. Governor: Dale E. Wolf, R (to Jan. 1993)
Secy. of State: Michael Harkins, R (Pleasure of Governor)
State Treasurer: Janet C. Rzewnicki, R (to Jan. 1991)
Atty. General: Charles M. Oberly III, D (to Jan. 1991)
Entered Union & (rank): Dec. 7, 1787 (1)
Present constitution adopted: 1897
Motto: Liberty and independence
State colors: Colonial blue and buff
State flower: Peach blossom (1895)
State tree: American holly (1939)
State bird: Blue Hen chicken (1939)
State insect: Ladybug (1974)
State fish: Weakfish, *Cynoscion regalis* (1981)
State song: "Our Delaware"
Nicknames: Diamond State; First State; Small Wonder
Origin of name: From Delaware River and Bay; named in turn for Sir Thomas West, Lord De La Warr
1980 population (1980 census) & (rank): 594,338 (47)
1989 est. population (July 1) & (rank): 673,000 (47)
1991 proj. population: 673,000
1980 land area & (rank): 1,932 sq mi. (5,005 sq km) (49)
Geographic center: In Kent Co., 11 mi. S of Dover
Number of counties: 3
Largest cities (1980 census): Wilmington, 70,195; Newark, 25,247; Dover, 23,512; Elsmere, 6,493; Milford, 5,356; Seaford, 5,256; New Castle, 4,709; Lewes, 2,197
State forests: 3 (6,149 ac.)
State parks: 10
1989 percent pop. below age 18: 25.0
1989 percent pop. age 65 and over: 11.8
Est. Black population (1985): 106,000
Est. Hispanic population (1985): 10,000
1987-88 Est. total net migration & (rate): 7,722 (11.8%)
1987-88 (fiscal year) legal immigrants: 621

Henry Hudson, sailing under the Dutch flag, is credited with Delaware's discovery in 1609. The following year, Capt. Samuel Argall of Virginia named Delaware for his colony's governor, Thomas West, Baron De La Warr. An attempted Dutch settlement failed in 1631. Swedish colonization began at Fort Christina (now Wilmington) in 1638, but New Sweden fell to Dutch forces led by New Netherlands' Gov. Peter Stuyvesant in 1655.

England took over the area in 1664 and it was transferred to William Penn as the southern Three Counties in 1682. Semiautonomous after 1704, Delaware fought as a separate state in the American Revolution and became the first state to ratify the constitution in 1787.

During the Civil War, although a slave state, Delaware did not secede from the Union.

In 1802, Éleuthère Irénée du Pont established a gunpowder mill near Wilmington that laid the foundation for Delaware's huge chemical industry. Delaware's manufactured products now also include vulcanized fiber, textiles, paper, medical supplies, metal products, machinery, machine tools, and automobiles.

Delaware also grows a great variety of fruits and vegetables and is a U.S. pioneer in the food-canning industry. Corn, soybeans, potatoes, and hay are important crops. Delaware's broiler chicken farms supply the big Eastern markets; fishing and dairy products are other important industries.

Points of interest include the Fort Christina Monument, Hagley Museum, Holy Trinity Church (erected in 1698, the oldest Protestant church in the United States still in use), and Winterthur Museum, in and near Wilmington; central New Castle, an almost unchanged late 18th-century capital; and the Delaware Museum of Natural History.

Popular recreation areas include Cape Henlopen, Delaware Seashore, Trapp Pond State Park, and Rehoboth Beach.

DISTRICT OF COLUMBIA

See listing at end of *50 Largest Cities of the United States.*

FLORIDA

Capital: Tallahassee
Governor: Bob Martinez, R (to Jan. 1991)
Lieut. Governor: Bobby Brantley, R (to Jan. 1991)
Secy. of State: George Firestone, D (to Jan. 1991)
Comptroller: Gerald Lewis, D (to Jan. 1991)
Commissioner of Agriculture: Doyle Connor, D (to Jan. 1991)
Atty. General: Bob Butterworth, D (to Jan. 1991)
Organized as territory: March 30, 1822
Entered Union & (rank): March 3, 1845 (27)
Present constitution adopted: 1969
Motto: In God we trust (1868)
State flower: Orange blossom (1909)
State bird: Mockingbird (1927)
State song: "Suwannee River" (1935)
Nickname: Sunshine State (1970)
Origin of name: From the Spanish, meaning "feast of flowers" (Easter)
1980 population (1980 census) & (rank): 9,746,324 (7)
1989 est. population (July 1) & (rank): 12,671,000 (4)
1991 proj. population: 13,098,000
1980 land area & (rank): 54,153 sq mi. (140,256 sq km) (26)
Geographic center: In Hernando Co., 12 mi. NNW of Brooksville
Number of counties: 67
Largest cities (1984 est.): Jacksonville, 571,421; Miami, 383,027; Tampa, 275,512; St. Petersburg, 242,115; Fort Lauderdale, 152,053; Hialeah, 157,137
State forests: 3 (306,881 ac.)
State parks: 105 (215,820 ac.)
1989 percent pop. below age 18: 22.7
1989 percent pop. age 65 and over: 18.0
Est. Black population (1985): 1,565,000
Est. Hispanic population (1985): 1,102,000
1987-88 Est. total net migration & (rate): 266,353 (21.9%)
1987-88 (fiscal year) legal immigrants: 54,654

In 1513, Ponce De Leon, seeking the mythical "Fountain of Youth," discovered and named Florida, claiming it for Spain. Later, Florida would be held at different times by Spain and England until Spain finally sold it to the United States in 1819. (Incidentally, France established a colony named Fort Caroline in 1564 in the state that was to become Florida.)

Florida's early 19th-century history as a U.S. territory was marked by wars with the Seminole Indians that did not end until 1842, although a treaty was actually never signed.

One of the nation's fastest-growing states, Florida's population has gone from 2.8 million in 1950 to more than 11.3 million in 1985.

Florida's economy rests on a solid base of tourism (in 1989 the state entertained more than 38.7 million visitors from all over the world), manufacturing, and agriculture.

In recent years, oranges and grapefruit lead Florida's crop list, followed by vegetables, potatoes, melons, strawberries, sugar cane, dairy products, cattle and calves, and forest products.

Major tourist attractions are Miami Beach, Palm Beach, St. Augustine (founded in 1565, thus the oldest permanent city in the U.S.), Daytona Beach, and Fort Lauderdale on the East Coast. West Coast resorts include Sarasota, Tampa, Key West and St. Petersburg. Disney World, located on a 27,000-acre site near Orlando, is a popular attraction.

Also drawing many visitors are the NASA Kennedy Space Center's Spaceport USA, located in the town of Kennedy Space Center, Everglades National Park, and the Epcot Center.

GEORGIA

Capital: Atlanta
Governor: Joe Frank Harris, D (to Jan. 1991)
Lieut. Governor: Zell Miller, D (to Jan. 1991)
Secy. of State: Max Cleland, D (to Jan. 1991)
Insurance Commissioner: Warren Evans, D (to Jan. 1991)
Atty. General: Michael J. Bowers, D (to Jan. 1991)
Entered Union & (rank): Jan. 2, 1788 (4)
Present constitution adopted: 1977
Motto: Wisdom, justice, and moderation
State flower: Cherokee rose (1916)
State tree: Live oak (1937)
State bird: Brown thrasher (1935)
State song: "Georgia on my Mind" (1922)
Nicknames: Peach State, Empire State of the South
Origin of name: In honor of George II of England
1980 population (1980 census) & (rank): 5,463,105 (13)
1989 est. population (July 1) & (rank): 6,436,000 (11)
1991 proj. population: 6,801,000
1980 land area & (rank): 58,910 sq mi. (152,577 sq km) (21)
Geographic center: In Twiggs Co., 18 mi. SE of Macon
Number of counties: 159
Largest cities (1980 census): Atlanta, 425,022; Columbus, 169,441; Savannah, 141,634; Macon, 116,860; Albany, 74,550; Augusta, 47,532; Athens, 42,549; Warner Robins, 39,893
State forests: 25,258,000 ac. (67% of total state area)
State parks: 53 (42,600 ac.)
1989 percent pop. below age 18: 27.9
1989 percent pop. age 65 and over: 10.1
Est. Black population (1985): 1,600,000
Est. Hispanic population (1985): 48,000
1987-88 Est. total net migration & (rate): 62,565 (10.0%)
1987-88 (fiscal year) legal immigrants: 6,118

Hernando de Soto, the Spanish explorer, first traveled parts of Georgia in 1540. British claims later conflicted with those of Spain. After obtaining a royal charter, Gen. James Oglethorpe established the first permanent settlement in Georgia in 1733 as a refuge for English debtors. In 1742, Oglethorpe defeated Spanish invaders in the Battle of Bloody Marsh.

A Confederate stronghold, Georgia was the scene of extensive military action during the Civil War. Union General William T. Sherman burned Atlanta and destroyed a 60-mile wide path to the coast where he captured Savannah in 1864.

The largest state east of the Mississippi, Georgia is typical of the changing South with an ever-increasing industrial development. Atlanta, largest city in the state, is the communications and transportation center for the Southeast and the area's chief distributor of goods.

Georgia leads the nation in the production of paper and board, tufted textile products, and processed chicken. Other major manufactured products are transportation equipment, food products, apparel, and chemicals.

Important agricultural products are corn, cotton, tobacco, soybeans, eggs, and peaches. Georgia produces twice as many peanuts as the next leading state. From its vast stands of pine come more than half the world's resins and turpentine and 74.4% of the U.S. supply. Georgia is also a leader in the production of marble, kaolin, barite, and bauxite.

Principal tourist attractions in Georgia include the Okefenokee National Wildlife Refuge, Andersonville Prison Park and National Cemetery, Chickamauga and Chattanooga National Military Park, the Little White House at Warm Springs where Pres. Franklin D. Roosevelt died in 1945, Sea Island, the enormous Confederate Memorial at Stone Mountain, Kennesaw Mountain National Battlefield Park, and Cumberland Island National Seashore.

HAWAII

Capital: Honolulu (on Oahu)
Governor: John Waihee, D (to Dec. 1990)
Lieut. Governor: Ben Cayetano, D (to Dec. 1990)
Comptroller: Russel S. Nagata, D (to Dec. 1990)
Atty. General: Warren Price, D (to Dec. 1990)
Organized as territory: 1900
Entered Union & (rank): Aug. 21, 1959 (50)
Motto: *Ua Mau Ke Ea O Ka Aina I Ka Pono* (The life of the land is perpetuated in righteousness)
State flower: Hibiscus (yellow) (1988)
State song: "Hawaii Ponoi" (1967)
State bird: Nene (Hawaiian goose) (1957)
State tree: Kukui (Candlenut) (1959)
Nickname: Aloha State (1959)
Origin of name: Uncertain. The islands may have been named by Hawaii Loa, their traditional discoverer. Or they may have been named after Hawaii or Hawaiki, the traditional home of the Polynesians.
1980 population (1980 census) & (rank): 964,691 (39)
1989 est. population (July 1) & (rank): 1,112,000 (39)
1991 proj. population: 1,161,000
1980 land area & (rank): 6,425 sq mi. (16,641 sq km) (47)
Geographic center: Between islands of Hawaii and Maui
Number of counties: 4 plus one non-functioning county (Kalawao)
Largest cities (1980 census): Honolulu, 365,048; Pearl City, 42,575; Kailua, 35,812; Hilo, 35,269[1]
State parks and historic sites: 76
1989 percent pop. below age 18: 25.9
1989 percent pop. age 65 and over: 10.7
Est. Black population (1985): 23,000
Est. Hispanic population (1985): 72,000
1987-88 Est. total net migration & (rate): 3,500 (3.2%)
1987-88 (fiscal year) legal immigrants: 6,796

1. There are no political boundaries to Honolulu or any other place, but statistical boundaries are assigned under state law.

First settled by Polynesians sailing from other Pacific islands between 300 and 600 A.D., Hawaii was visited in 1778 by British Captain James Cook who called the group the Sandwich Islands.

Hawaii was a native kingdom throughout most of the 19th century when the expansion of the vital sugar industry (pineapple came after 1898) meant increasing U.S. business and political involvement. In 1893, Queen Liliuokalani was deposed and a year later the Republic of Hawaii was established with Sanford B. Dole as president. Then, following its annexation in 1898, Hawaii became a U.S. Territory in 1900.

The Japanese attack on the naval base at Pearl Harbor on Dec. 7, 1941, was directly responsible for U.S. entry into World War II.

Hawaii, 2,397 miles west-southwest of San Francisco, is a 1,523-mile chain of islets and eight main islands—Hawaii, Kahoolawe, Maui, Lanai, Molokai, Oahu, Kauai, and Niihau. The Northwestern Hawaiian Islands, other than Midway, are administratively part of Hawaii.

The temperature is mild and Hawaii's soil is fertile for tropical fruits and vegetables. Cane sugar and pineapple are the chief products. Hawaii also grows coffee, bananas and nuts. The tourist business is Hawaii's largest source of outside income.

Hawaii's highest peak is Mauna Kea (13,796 ft.). Mauna Loa (13,679 ft.) is the largest volcanic mountain in the world in cubic content.

Among the major points of interest are Hawaii Volcanoes National Park (Hawaii), Haleakala National Park (Maui), Puuhonua o Honaunau National Historical Park (Hawaii), Polynesian Cultural Center (Oahu), the U.S.S. *Arizona* Memorial at Pearl Harbor, and Iolani Palace (the only royal palace in the U.S.), Bishop Museum, and Waikiki Beach (all in Honolulu).

IDAHO

Capital: Boise
Governor: Cecil D. Andrus, D (to Jan. 1991)
Lieut. Governor: C. L. "Butch" Otter, R (to Jan. 1991)
Secy. of State: Pete T. Cenarrusa, R (to Jan. 1991)
State Auditor: J.D. Williams, D (to Jan. 1991)
Atty. General: James Jones, R (to Jan. 1991)
Treasurer: Lydia Justice Edwards, R (to Jan. 1991)
Organized as territory: March 3, 1863
Entered Union & (rank): July 3, 1890 (43)
Present constitution adopted: 1890
Motto: *Esto perpetua* (It is forever)
State flower: Syringa (1931)
State tree: White pine (1935)
State bird: Mountain bluebird (1931)
State horse: Appaloosa (1975)
State gem: Star garnet (1967)
State song: "Here We Have Idaho"
State folk dance: Square Dance
Nicknames: Gem State; Spud State; Panhandle State
Origin of name: Unknown. It is an invented name and has no Indian translation meaning "Gem of the Mountains." Meaning of name, if any, is unknown.
1980 population (1980 census) & (rank): 943,935 (41)
1989 est. population (July 1) & (rank): 1,014,000 (42)
1991 proj. population: 1,021,000
1980 land area & (rank): 82,412 sq mi. (213,449 sq km) (11)
Geographic center: In Custer Co., at Custer, SW of Challis
Number of counties: 44, plus small part of Yellowstone National Park
Largest cities (1988 est.): Boise, 111,030; Pocatello, 43,520; Idaho Falls, 44,250; Nampa, 28,320; Twin Falls, 27,540; Lewiston, 27,990; Coeur d'Alene, 24,040
State forests: 881,000 ac.
State parks: 21 (42,161) ac.
1989 percent pop. below age 18: 30.0
1989 percent pop. age 65 and over: 11.9
Est. Black population (1985): 3,000
Est. Hispanic population (1985): 42,000

1987-88 Est. total net migration & (rate): −5,633 (−5.6%)
1987-88 (fiscal year) legal immigrants: 682

After its acquisition by the U.S. as part of the Louisiana Purchase in 1803, the region was explored by Meriwether Lewis and William Clark in 1805–06. Northwest boundary disputes with Great Britain were settled by the Oregon Treaty in 1846 and the first permanent U.S. settlement in Idaho was established by the Mormons at Franklin in 1860.

After gold was discovered on Orofino Creek in 1860, prospectors swarmed into the territory, but left little more than a number of ghost towns.

In the 1870s, growing white occupation of Indian lands led to a series of battles between U.S. forces and the Nez Percé, Bannock, and Sheepeater tribes.

Mining, lumbering, and irrigation farming have been important for years. Idaho produces more than one third of all the silver mined in the U.S. It also ranks high among the states in antimony, lead, cobalt, garnet, phosphate rock, vanadium, zinc, and mercury.

Idaho's most impressive growth began when World War II military needs made processing agricultural products a big industry, particularly the dehydrating and freezing of potatoes. The state produces about one fourth of the nation's potato crop, as well as wheat, apples, corn, barley, sugar beets, and hops.

With the growth of winter sports, tourism now outranks mining in dollar revenue. Idaho's many streams and lakes provide fishing, camping, and boating sites. The nation's largest elk herds draw hunters from all over the world and the famed Sun Valley resort attracts thousands of visitors to its swimming and skiing facilities.

Other points of interest are the Craters of the Moon National Monument; Nez Percé National Historic Park, which includes many sites visited by Lewis and Clark; and the State Historical Museum in Boise.

ILLINOIS

Capital: Springfield
Governor: James R. Thompson, R (to Jan. 1991)
Lieut. Governor: George H. Ryan, R (to Jan. 1991)
Secy. of State: Jim Edgar, R (to Jan. 1991)
Comptroller: Roland J. Burris, D (to Jan. 1991)
Atty. General: Neil F. Hartigan, D (to Jan. 1991)
Treasurer: Jerry Cosentino, D (to Jan. 1991)
Organized as territory: Feb. 3, 1809
Entered Union & (rank): Dec. 3, 1818 (21)
Present constitution adopted: 1970
Motto: State sovereignty, national union
State flower: Violet (1908)
State tree: White oak (1973)
State bird: Cardinal (1929)
State animal: White-tailed deer (1982)
State fish: Bluegill (1987)
State insect: Monarch butterfly (1975)
State song: "Illinois" (1925)
State mineral: Fluorite (1965)
Nickname: Prairie State
Origin of name: From an Indian word and French suffix meaning "tribe of superior men"
1980 population (1980 census) & (rank): 11,426,518 (5)
1989 est. population (July 1) & (rank): 11,658,000 (6)
1991 proj. population: 11,622,000
1980 land area & (rank): 55,645 sq mi. (144,120 sq km) (24)

Geographic center: In Logan County 28 mi. NE of Springfield

Number of counties: 102

Largest cities (1984 census): Chicago, 2,992,472; Rockford, 136,531; Peoria, 117,113; Springfield, 101,570; Decatur, 91,851; Aurora, 85,735

Public use areas: 187 (275,000 ac.), incl. state parks, memorials, forests and conservation areas

1989 percent pop. below age 18: 25.5

1989 percent pop. age 65 and over: 12.3

Est. Black population (1985): 1,775,000

Est. Hispanic population (1985): 755,000

1987-88 Est. total net migration & (rate): −48,024 (−4.1%)

1987-88 (fiscal year) legal immigrants: 25,995

French explorers Marquette and Joliet, in 1673, were the first Europeans of record to visit the region. In 1699 French settlers established the first permanent settlement at Cahokia, near present-day East St. Louis.

Great Britain obtained the region at the end of the French and Indian War in 1763. The area figured prominently in frontier struggles during the Revolutionary War and in Indian wars during the early 19th century.

Significant episodes in the state's early history include the growing migration of Eastern settlers following the opening of the Erie Canal in 1825; the Black Hawk War, which virtually ended the Indian troubles in the area; and the rise of Abraham Lincoln from farm laborer to President-elect.

Today, Illinois stands high in manufacturing, coal mining, agriculture, and oil production. The sprawling Chicago district (including a slice of Indiana) is a great iron and steel producer, meat packer, grain exchange, and railroad center. Chicago is also famous as a Great Lakes port.

Illinois ranks first in the nation in export of agricultural products and second in hog production. An important dairying state, Illinois is also a leader in corn, oats, wheat, barley, rye, truck vegetables, and the nursery products.

The state manufactures a great variety of industrial and consumer products: railroad cars, clothing, furniture, tractors, liquor, watches, and farm implements are just some of the items made in its factories and plants.

Central Illinois is noted for shrines and memorials associated with the life of Abraham Lincoln. In Springfield are the Lincoln Home, the Lincoln Tomb, and the restored Old State Capitol. Other points of interest are the home of Mormon leader Joseph Smith in Nauvoo and, in Chicago: the Art Institute, Field Museum, Museum of Science and Industry, Shedd Aquarium, Adler Planetarium, Merchandise Mart, and Chicago Portage National Historic Site.

INDIANA

Capital: Indianapolis

Governor: Birch Evans Bayh III, D (to Jan. 1993)

Lieut. Governor: Frank O'Bannon, D (to Jan. 1993)

Secy. of State: Joseph H. Hogsett, D (to Dec. 1990)

Treasurer: Majorie H. O'Laughlin, R (to Feb. 1991)

Atty. General: Linley E. Pearson, R (to Jan. 1993)

Auditor: Ann G. Devore, R (to Dec. 1990)

Organized as territory: May 7, 1800

Entered Union & (rank): Dec. 11, 1816 (19)

Present constitution adopted: 1851

Motto: The Crossroads of America

State flower: Peony (1957)

State tree: Tulip tree (1931)

State bird: Cardinal (1933)

State song: "On the Banks of the Wabash, Far Away" (1913)

Nickname: Hoosier State

Origin of name: Meaning "land of Indians"

1980 population (1980 census) & (rank): 5,490,224 (12)

1989 est. population (July 1) & (rank): 5,593,000 (14)

1991 proj. population: 5,555,000

1980 land area & (rank): 35,932 sq mi. (93,064 sq km) (38)

Geographic center: In Boone Co., 14 mi. NNW of Indianapolis

Number of Counties: 92

Largest cities (1980 census): Indianapolis, 700,807; Fort Wayne, 172,028; Gary, 151,953; Evansville, 130,496; South Bend, 109,727; Hammond, 93,714; Muncie, 77,216

State parks: 19 (54,126 ac.)

State memorials: 16 (941.977 ac.)

1989 percent pop. below age 18: 26.1

1989 percent pop. age 65 and over: 12.4

Est. Black population (1985): 436,000

Est. Hispanic population (1985): 83,000

1987-88 Est. total net migration & (rate): −3,367 (−0.6%)

1987-88 (fiscal year) legal immigrants: 2,279

First explored for France by La Salle in 1679–80, the region figured importantly in the Franco-British struggle for North America that culminated with British victory in 1763.

George Rogers Clark led American forces against the British in the area during the Revolutionary War and, prior to becoming a state, Indiana was the scene of frequent Indian uprisings until the victory of Gen. William Henry Harrison at Tippecanoe in 1811.

Indiana's 41-mile Lake Michigan waterfront—one of the world's great industrial centers—turns out iron, steel, and oil products. Products include automobile parts and accessories, mobile homes and recreational vehicles, truck and bus bodies, aircraft engines, farm machinery, and fabricated structural steel. Phonograph records, wood office furniture, and pharmaceuticals are also manufactured.

The state is a leader in agriculture with corn the principal crop. Hogs, soybeans, wheat, oats, rye, tomatoes, onions, and poultry also contribute heavily to Indiana's agricultural output. Much of the building limestone used in the U.S. is quarried in Indiana which is also a large producer of coal.

Wyandotte Cave, one of the largest in the U.S., is located in Crawford County in southern Indiana and West Baden and French Lick are well known for their mineral springs. Other attractions include Indiana Dunes National Lakeshore, Indianapolis Motor Speedway, Lincoln Boyhood National Memorial, and the George Rogers Clark National Historical Park.

IOWA

Capital: Des Moines

Governor: Terry E. Branstad, R (to Jan. 1991)

Lieut. Governor: Jo Ann Zimmerman, D (to Jan. 1991)

Secy. of State: Elaine Baxter, D (to Jan. 1991)

Treasurer: Michael L. Fitzgerald, D (to Jan. 1991)

Atty. General: Tom Miller, D (to Jan. 1991)

Organized as territory: June 12, 1838

Entered Union & (rank): Dec. 28, 1846 (29)
Present constitution adopted: 1857
Motto: Our liberties we prize and our rights we will maintain
State flower: Wild rose (1897)
State bird: Eastern goldfinch (1933)
State colors: Red, white, and blue (in state flag)
State song: "Song of Iowa"
Nickname: Hawkeye State
Origin of name: Probably from an Indian word meaning "I-o-w-a, this is the place," or "The Beautiful Land"
1980 population (1980 census) & (rank): 2,913,808 (27)
1989 est. population (July 1) & (rank): 2,840,000 (29)
1991 proj. population: 2,737,000
1980 land area & (rank): 55,965 sq mi. (144,950 sq km) (24)
Geographic center: In Story Co., 5 mi. NE of Ames
Number of counties: 99
Largest cities (1980 census): Des Moines, 191,003; Cedar Rapids, 110,243; Davenport, 103,264; Sioux City, 82,003; Waterloo, 75,985; Dubuque, 62,321; Council Bluffs, 56,449; Iowa City, 50,508; Ames, 45,775
State forests: 5 (28,000 ac.)
State parks: 84 (49,237)
1989 percent pop. below age 18: 24.9
1989 percent pop. age 65 and over: 15.1
Est. Black population (1985): 45,000
Est. Hispanic population (1985): 26,000
1987-88 Est. total net migration & (rate): 575 (0.2%)
1987-88 (fiscal year) legal immigrants: 1,579

The first Europeans to visit the area were the French explorers, Father Jacques Marquette and Louis Joliet in 1673. The U.S. obtained control of the area in 1803 as part of the Louisiana Purchase.

During the first half of the 19th century, there was heavy fighting between white settlers and Indians. Lands were taken from the Indians after the Black Hawk War in 1832 and again in 1836 and 1837.

When Iowa became a state in 1846, its capital was Iowa City; the more centrally located Des Moines became the new capital in 1857. At that time, the state's present boundaries were also drawn.

Although Iowa produces a tenth of the nation's food supply, the value of Iowa's manufactured products is three times that of its agriculture. Major industries are food and associated products, non-electrical machinery, electrical equipment, printing and publishing, and fabricated products.

Iowa stands in a class by itself as an agricultural state. Its farms sell over $9 billion worth of crops and livestock annually. Iowa is second in the nation in all livestock and hog marketings, with about 24% of the pork supply and 8% of the grain-fed cattle. Iowa's forests produce hardwood lumber, particularly walnut, and its mineral products include cement, limestone, sand, gravel, gypsum, and coal.

Tourist attractions include the Herbert Hoover birthplace and library near West Branch; the Amana Colonies; Fort Dodge Historical Museum, Fort, and Stockade; the Iowa State Fair at Des Moines in August; and the Effigy Mounds National Monument at Marquette, a prehistoric Indian burial site.

KANSAS

Capital: Topeka
Governor: Mike Hayden, R (to Jan. 1991)
Lieut. Governor: Jack D. Walker, R (to Jan. 1991)

Secy. of State: Bill Graves, R (to Jan. 1991)
Treasurer: Joan Finney, D (to Jan. 1991)
Atty. General: Robert T. Stephan, R (to Jan. 1991)
Organized as territory: May 30, 1854
Entered Union & (rank): Jan. 29, 1861 (34)
Present constitution adopted: 1859
Motto: *Ad astra per aspera* (To the stars through difficulties)
State flower: Sunflower (1903)
State tree: Cottonwood (1937)
State bird: Western meadow lark (1937)
State animal: Buffalo (1955)
State song: "Home on the Range" (1947)
Nicknames: Sunflower State; Jayhawk State
Origin of name: From a Siouan word meaning "people of the south wind"
1980 population (1980 census) & (rank): 2,363,679 (32)
1989 est. population (July 1) & (rank): 2,513,000 (32)
1991 proj. population: 2,498,000
1980 land area & (rank): 81,778 sq mi. (211,805 sq km) (13)
Geographic center: In Barton Co., 15 mi. NE of Great Bend
Number of counties: 105
Largest cities (1980 census): Wichita, 279,835; Kansas City, 161,148; Topeka, 115,266; Overland Park, 81,784; Lawrence, 52,738; Salina, 41,843; Hutchinson, 40,284
State parks: 22 (14,394 ac.)
1989 percent pop. below age 18: 26.2
1989 percent pop. age 65 and over: 13.7
Est. Black population (1985): 137,000
Est. Hispanic population (1985): 70,000
1987-88 Est. total net migration & (rate): 3,638 (1.5%)
1987-88 (fiscal year) legal immigrants: 1,804

Spanish explorer Francisco de Coronado, in 1541, is considered the first European to have traveled this region. La Salle's extensive land claims for France (1682) included present-day Kansas. Ceded to Spain by France in 1763, the territory reverted back to France in 1800 and was sold to the U.S. as part of the Louisiana Purchase in 1803.

Lewis and Clark, Zebulon Pike, and Stephen H. Long explored the region between 1803 and 1819. The first permanent settlements in Kansas were outposts—Fort Leavenworth (1827), Fort Scott (1842), and Fort Riley (1853)—established to protect travelers along the Santa Fe and Oregon Trails.

Just before the Civil War, the conflict between the pro- and anti-slavery forces earned the region the grim title "Bleeding Kansas."

Today, wheat fields, oil well derricks, herds of cattle, and grain storage elevators are chief features of the Kansas landscape. A leading wheat-growing state, Kansas also raises corn, sorghums, oats, barley, soy beans, and potatoes. Kansas stands high in petroleum production and mines zinc, coal, salt, and lead. It is also the nation's leading producer of helium.

Wichita is one of the nation's leading aircraft manufacturing centers, ranking first in production of private aircraft. Kansas City is an important transportation, milling, and meat-packing center.

Points of interest include the new Kansas Museum of History at Topeka, the Eisenhower boyhood home and the new Eisenhower Memorial Museum and Presidential Library at Abilene, John Brown's cabin at Osawatomie, recreated Front Street in Dodge City, Fort Larned (once the most important military post on the Santa Fe Trail), and Fort Leavenworth and Fort Riley.

KENTUCKY

Capital: Frankfort
Governor: Wallace G. Wilkinson, D (to Dec. 1991)
Lieut. Governor: Brereton C. Jones, D (to Dec. 1991)
Secy. of State: Bremer Ehrler, D (to Jan. 1992)
State Treasurer: Robert Meade, D (to Jan. 1992)
State Auditor: Bob Babbage, D (to Jan. 1992)
Atty. General: Fred Cowan, D (to Jan. 1992)
Entered Union & (rank): June 1, 1792 (15)
Present constitution adopted: 1891
Motto: United we stand, divided we fall
State tree: Coffeetree
State flower: Goldenrod
State bird: Kentucky cardinal
State song: "My Old Kentucky Home"
Nickname: Bluegrass State
Origin of name: From an Iroquoian word "Ken-tah-ten"
    meaning "land of tomorrow"
1980 population (1980 census) & (rank): 3,660,777 (23)
1989 est. population (July 1) & (rank): 3,727,000 (23)
1991 proj. population: 3,747,000
1980 land area & (rank): 39,669 sq mi. (102,743 sq km)
    (37)
Geographic center: In Marion Co., 3 mi. NNW of Lebanon
Number of counties: 120
Largest cities (1985 proj.): Louisville, 293,834; Lexington,
    214,072; Owensboro, 56,419; Covington, 47,725;
    Bowling Green, 45,549; Paducah, 29,699; Hopkinsville,
    30,406
State forests: 9 (44,173 ac.)
State parks: 43 (40,574 ac.)
1989 percent pop. below age 18: 25.9
1989 percent pop. age 65 and over: 12.7
Est. Black population (1985): 264,000
Est. Hispanic population (1985): 14,000
1987-88 Est. total net migration & (rate): −12,551
    (−3.4%)
1987-88 (fiscal year) legal immigrants: 1,381

Kentucky was the first region west of the Allegheny Mountains settled by American pioneers. James Harrod established the first permanent settlement at Harrodsburg in 1774; the following year Daniel Boone, who had explored the area in 1767, blazed the Wilderness Trail and founded Boonesboro.

Politically, the Kentucky region was originally part of Virginia, but early statehood was gained in 1792.

During the Civil War, as a slaveholding state with a considerable abolitionist population, Kentucky was caught in the middle of the conflict, supplying both Union and Confederate forces with thousands of troops.

In recent years, manufacturing has shown important gains, but agriculture and mining are still vital to Kentucky's economy. Kentucky prides itself on producing some of the nation's best tobacco, horses, and whiskey. Corn, soybeans, wheat, fruit, hogs, cattle, and dairy farming are also important.

Among the manufactured items produced in the state are furniture, aluminum ware, brooms, shoes, lumber products, machinery, textiles, and iron and steel products. Kentucky also produces significant amounts of petroleum, natural gas, fluorspar, clay, and stone. However, coal accounts for 90% of the total mineral income.

Louisville, the largest city, famed for the Kentucky Derby at Churchill Downs, is also the location of a large state university, whiskey distilleries, and cigarette factories. The Bluegrass country around Lexington is the home of some of the world's finest race horses. Other attractions are Mammoth Cave, the George S. Patton, Jr., Military Museum at Fort Knox, and Old Fort Harrod State Park.

LOUISIANA

Capital: Baton Rouge
Governor: Buddy Roemer, D (to Jan. 1992)
Lieut. Governor: Paul J. Hardy, D (to Jan. 1992)
Secy. of State: W. Fox McKeithen, R (to Jan. 1992)
Treasurer: Mary Landrieu, D (to Jan. 1992)
Atty. General: Gen. Wm. J. Guste, Jr., D (to Jan. 1992)
Organized as territory: March 26, 1804
Entered Union & (rank): April 30, 1812 (18)
Present constitution adopted: 1974
Motto: Union, justice, and confidence
State flower: Magnolia (1900)
State tree: Bald cypress (1963)
State bird: Pelican (1958)
State song: "Give Me Louisiana," and "You Are My
    Sunshine"
Nicknames: Pelican State; Sportsman's Paradise; Creole
    State; Sugar State
Origin of name: In honor of Louis XIV of France
1980 population (1980 census) & (rank): 4,205,900 (19)
1989 est. population (July 1) & (rank): 4,382,000 (20)
1991 proj. population: 4,515,000
1980 land area & (rank): 44,521 sq mi. (115,309 sq km)
    (33)
Geographic center: In Avoyelles Parish, 3 mi. SE of
    Marksville
Number of parishes (counties): 64
Largest cities (1980 census): New Orleans, 557,927;
    Baton Rouge, 219,419; Shreveport, 205,820; Lafayette,
    81,961; Lake Charles, 75,226; Monroe, 57,597;
    Alexandria, 51,565
State forests: 1 (8,000 ac.)
State parks: 30 (13,932 ac.)
1989 percent pop. below age 18: 29.1
1989 percent pop. age 65 and over: 11.1
Est. Black population (1985): 1,348,000
Est. Hispanic population (1985): 98,000
1987-88 Est. total net migration & (rate): −37,466
    (−8.5%)
1987-88 (fiscal year) legal immigrants: 3,824

Louisiana has a rich, colorful historical background. Early Spanish explorers were Piñeda, 1519; Cabeza de Vaca, 1528; and de Soto in 1541. La Salle reached the mouth of the Mississippi and claimed all the land drained by it and its tributaries for Louis XIV of France in 1682.

Louisiana became a French crown colony in 1731, was ceded to Spain in 1763, returned to France in 1800, and sold by Napoleon to the U.S. as part of the Louisiana Purchase (with large territories to the north and northwest) in 1803.

In 1815, Gen. Andrew Jackson's troops defeated a larger British army in the Battle of New Orleans, neither side aware that the treaty ending the War of 1812 had been signed.

As to total value of its mineral output, Louisiana is a leader in natural gas, salt, petroleum, and sulfur production. Much of the oil and sulfur comes from offshore deposits. The state also produces large crops of sweet potatoes, rice, sugarcane, pecans, soybeans, corn, and cotton.

Leading manufactures include chemicals, processed food, petroleum and coal products, paper, lumber and wood products, transportation equipment, and apparel.

Louisiana marshes supply most of the nation's muskrat fur as well as that of opossum, raccoon, mink, and otter, and large numbers of game birds.

Major points of interest include New Orleans with its French Quarter and Superdome, plantation homes near Natchitoches and New Iberia, Cajun country in the Mississippi delta region, Chalmette National Historical Park, and the state capital at Baton Rouge.

MAINE

Capital: Augusta
Governor: John R. McKernan, Jr., R (to Jan. 1991)
Secy. of State: Rodney F. Quinn, D (to Jan. 1989)
Controller: David A. Bourne, R (term indefinite)
Atty. General: James Tierney, D (to Jan. 1991)
Entered Union & (rank): March 15, 1820 (23)
Present constitution adopted: 1820
Motto: *Dirigo* (I direct)
State flower: White pine cone and tassel (1895)
State tree: White pine tree (1945)
State bird: Chickadee (1927)
State fish: Landlocked salmon (1969)
State mineral: Tourmaline (1971)
State song: "State of Maine Song" (1937)
Nickname: Pine Tree State
Origin of name: First used to distinguish the mainland from the offshore islands. It has been considered a compliment to Henrietta Maria, Queen of Charles I of England. She was said to have owned the province of Mayne in France.
1980 population (1980 census) & (rank): 1,124,660 (38)
1989 est. population (July 1) & (rank): 1,222,000 (38)
1991 proj. population: 1,220,000
1980 land area & (rank): 30,995 sq mi. (80,277 sq km) (39)
Geographic center: In Piscataquis Co., 18 mi. N of Dover-Foxcroft
Number of counties: 16
Largest cities (1980 census): Portland, 61,572; Lewiston, 40,481; Bangor, 31,643; Auburn, 23,128; South Portland, 22,712; Augusta, 21,819; Biddeford, 19,638
State forests: 1 (21,000 ac.)
State parks: 26 (247,627 ac.)
State historic sites: 18 (403 ac.)
1989 percent pop. below age 18: 24.9
1989 percent pop. age 65 and over: 13.4
Est. Black population (1985): 4,000
Est. Hispanic population (1985): 4,000
1987-88 Est. total net migration & (rate): 13,577 (11.4%)
1987-88 (fiscal year) legal immigrants: 855

John Cabot and his son, Sebastian, are believed to have visited the Maine coast in 1498. However, the first permanent English settlements were not established until more than a century later, in 1623.

The first naval action of the Revolutionary War occurred in 1775 when colonials captured the British sloop *Margaretta* off Machias on the Maine coast. In that same year, the British burned Falmouth (now Portland).

Long governed by Massachusetts, Maine became the 23rd state as part of the Missouri Compromise in 1820.

Maine produces 98% of the nation's low-bush blueberries. Farm income is also derived from apples, potatoes, dairy products, and vegetables, with poultry and eggs the largest items.

The state is one of the world's largest pulp-paper producers. It ranks fifth in boot-and-shoe manufacturing. With more than 90% of its area forested,

Maine turns out wood products from boats to toothpicks.

Maine leads the world in the production of the familiar flat tins of sardines, producing more than 100 million of them annually. Lobstermen normally catch 80–90% of the nation's true total of lobsters.

A scenic seacoast, beaches, lakes, mountains, and resorts make Maine a popular vacationland. There are more than 2,500 lakes and 5,000 streams, plus 26 state parks, to attract hunters, fishermen, skiers, and campers.

Major points of interest are: Bar Harbor, Allagash National Wilderness Waterway, the Wadsworth-Longfellow House in Portland, Roosevelt Campobello International Park, and the St. Croix Island National Monument.

MARYLAND

Capital: Annapolis
Governor: William Donald Schaefer, D (to Jan. 1991)
Lieut. Gov.: Melvin A. Steinberg, D (to Jan. 1991)
Secy. of State: Winfield M. Kelly, Jr., D (appointed by governor)
Comptroller of the Treasury: Louis L. Goldstein, D (to Jan. 1991)
Treasurer: Lucille Maurer, D (to Jan. 1991)
Atty. General: J. Joseph Curran, Jr., D (to Jan. 1991)
Entered Union & (rank): April 28, 1788 (7)
Present constitution adopted: 1867
Motto: *Fatti maschii, parole femine* (Manly deeds, womanly words)
State flower: Black-eyed susan (1918)
State tree: White oak (1941)
State bird: Baltimore oriole (1947)
State dog: Chesapeake Bay retriever (1964)
State fish: Rockfish (1965)
State crustacean: Maryland Blue Crab (1989)
State insect: Baltimore checkerspot butterfly (1973)
State boat: Skipjack (1985)
State sport: Jousting (1962)
State song: "Maryland! My Maryland!" (1939)
Nicknames: Free State; Old Line State
Origin of name: In honor of Henrietta Maria (Queen of Charles I of England)
1980 population (1980 census) & (rank): 4,216,975 (18)
1989 est. population (July 1) & (rank): 4,694,000 (19)
1991 proj. population: 4,792,000
1980 land area & (rank): 9,837 sq mi. (25,477 sq km) (42)
Geographic center: In Prince Georges Co., 4 1/2 mi. NW of Davidsonville
Number of counties: 23, and 1 independent city
Largest cities (1980 census): Baltimore, 786,775; Rockville, 43,811; Hagerstown, 34,132; Bowie, 33,695; Annapolis, 31,740; Frederick, 28,086; Gaithersburg, 26,424
State forests: 13 (132,944 ac.)
State parks: 47 (87,670 ac.)
1989 percent pop. below age 18: 24.7
1989 percent pop. age 65 and over: 10.8
Est. Black population (1985): 1,076,000
Est. Hispanic population (1985): 71,000
1987-88 Est. total net migration & (rate): 51,599 (11.3%)
1987-88 (fiscal year) legal immigrants: 11,846

In 1608, Chesapeake Bay was explored by Capt. John Smith. Charles I granted a royal charter to Cecil Calvert, Lord Baltimore, in 1632 and English Roman Catholics landed on St. Clement's (now Blakistone Island) in 1634. Religious freedom, granted all Christians in the Toleration act passed by the Maryland assembly in 1649, was ended by a Puritan revolt, 1654–58.

From 1763 to 1767, Charles Mason and Jeremiah Dixon surveyed Maryland's northern boundary line with Pennsylvania. In 1791, Maryland ceded land to form the District of Columbia.

In 1814, when the British unsuccessfully tried to capture Baltimore, the bombardment of Fort McHenry inspired Francis Scott Key to write *The Star Spangled Banner.*

The Baltimore clipper ship trade developed during the 19th Century. The battles of South Mountain and Antietam (1862) and Monocacy (1864) were fought in this state.

In 1904, the Great Fire of Baltimore occurred. In 1937, the City of Greenbelt, a New Deal model community, was chartered.

Maryland is almost cut in two by the Chesapeake Bay, and the many estuaries and rivers create one of the longest waterfronts of any state. The Bay produces more seafood—oysters, crabs, clams, fin fish—than any comparable body of water. Important agricultural products, in order of cash value, are chickens, dairy products, corn, cattle, tobacco, and vegetables. Maryland is a leader in vegetable canning. Sand, gravel, lime and cement, stone, coal, and clay are the chief mineral products.

Manufacturing industries produce missiles, airplanes, steel, clothing, and chemicals. Baltimore, home of The Johns Hopkins University and Hospital, ranks as the nation's second port in foreign tonnage. Annapolis, site of the U.S. Naval Academy, has one of the earliest state houses (1772–79) still in regular use by a State government.

Among the popular attractions in Maryland are the Fort McHenry National Monument, Harpers Ferry and Chesapeake and Ohio Canal, National Aquarium, and Maryland Science Center at Baltimore's Inner Harbor, National Historical Parks, Historic St. Mary's City restoration near Leonardtown, USS *Constellation* at Baltimore, U.S. Naval Academy in Annapolis, Goddard Space Flight Center at Greenbelt, Assateague Island National Seashore, Ocean City beach resort, and Catoctin Mountain, Ft. Frederick, and Piscataway parks.

MASSACHUSETTS

Capital: Boston
Governor: Michael S. Dukakis, D (to Jan. 1991)
Lieut. Governor: Evelyn F. Murphy, D (to Jan. 1991)
Secy. of the Commonwealth: Michael Joseph Connolly, D (to Jan. 1991)
Treasurer & Receiver-General: Robert Q. Crane, D (to Jan. 1991)
Auditor of the Commonwealth: A. Joseph DeNucci, D (to Jan. 1991)
Atty. General: James M. Shannon, D (to Jan. 1991)
Entered Union & (rank): Feb. 6, 1788 (6)
Motto: *Ense petit placidam sub libertate quietem* (By the sword we seek peace, but peace only under liberty)
State flower: Mayflower (1918)
State tree: American elm (1941)
State bird: Chickadee (1941)
State colors: Blue and gold
State song: "All Hail to Massachusetts" (1966)
State beverage: Cranberry juice (1970)
State insect: Ladybug (1974)
Nicknames: Bay State; Old Colony State
Origin of name: From two Indian words meaning "Great mountain place"

1980 population (1980 census) & (rank): 5,737,037 (11)
1989 est. population (July 1) & (rank): 5,913,000 (13)
1991 proj. population: 5,898,000
1980 land area & (rank): 7,824 sq mi. (20,265 sq km) (45)
Geographic center: In Worcester Co., in S part of city of Worcester
Number of counties: 14
Largest cities (1980 census): Boston, 562,994; Worcester, 161,799; Springfield, 152,319; New Bedford, 98,478; Cambridge, 95,322; Brockton, 95,172; Fall River, 94,574
State forests and parks: 129 (242,000 ac.)[1]
1989 percent pop. below age 18: 22.6
1989 percent pop. age 65 and over: 13.8
Est. Black population (1985): 258,000
Est. Hispanic population (1985): 154,000
1987-88 Est. total net migration & (rate): 3,633 (0.6%)
1987-88 (fiscal year) legal immigrants: 16,630

1. The Metropolitan District Commission, an agency of the Commonwealth serving municipalities in the Boston area, has about 14,000 acres of parkways and reservations under its jurisdiction.

Massachusetts has played a significant role in American history since the Pilgrims, seeking religious freedom, founded Plymouth Colony in 1620.

As one of the most important of the 13 colonies, Massachusetts became a leader in resisting British oppression. In 1773, the Boston Tea Party protested unjust taxation. The Minutemen started the American Revolution by battling British troops at Lexington and Concord on April 19, 1775.

During the 19th century, Massachusetts was famous for the vigorous intellectual activity of famous writers and educators and for its expanding commercial fishing, shipping, and manufacturing interests.

Massachusetts pioneered in the manufacture of textiles and shoes. Today, these industries have been replaced in importance by activity in the electronics and communications equipment fields.

The state's cranberry crop is the nation's largest. Also important are dairy and poultry products, nursery and greenhouse produce, vegetables, and fruit.

Tourism has become an important factor in the economy of the state because of its numerous recreational areas and historical landmarks.

Cape Cod has summer theaters, water sports, and an artists' colony at Provincetown. Tanglewood, in the Berkshires, features the summer concerts of the Boston Symphony.

Among the many other points of interest are Old Sturbridge Village, Minute Man National Historical Park between Lexington and Concord, and, in Boston: Old North Church, Old State House, Faneuil Hall, the USS *Constitution* and the John F. Kennedy Library.

MICHIGAN

Capital: Lansing
Governor: James J. Blanchard, D (to Jan. 1991)
Lieut. Governor: Martha W. Griffiths, D (to Jan. 1991)
Secy. of State: Richard H. Austin, D (to Jan. 1991)
Atty. General: Frank J. Kelley, D (to Jan. 1991)
Organized as territory: Jan. 11, 1805
Entered Union & (rank): Jan. 26, 1837 (26)
Present constitution adopted: April 1, 1963, (effective Jan. 1, 1964)

Motto: *Si quaeris peninsulam amoenam circumspice* (If you seek a pleasant peninsula, look around you)
State flower: Apple blossom (1897)
State bird: Robin (1931)
State Fishes: Trout (1965), Brook trout (1988)
State gem: Isle Royal Greenstone (Chlorastrolite) (1972)
State stone: Petoskey stone (1965)
Nickname: Wolverine State
Origin of name: From two Indian words meaning "great lake"
1980 population (1980 census) & (rank): 9,262,078 (8)
1989 est. population (July 1) & (rank): 9,273,000 (8)
1991 proj. population: 9,314,000
1980 land area & (rank): 56,954 sq mi. (147,511 sq km) (22)
Geographic center: In Wexford Co., 5 mi. NNW of Cadillac
Number of counties: 83
Largest cities (1980 census): Detroit, 1,203,339; Grand Rapids, 181,843; Warren, 161,134; Flint, 159,611; Lansing, 130,414; Sterling Heights, 108,999; Ann Arbor, 107,966
State forests: 6 (3,762,184 ac.)
State parks and recreation areas: 92 (250,000)
1989 percent pop. below age 18: 26.4
1989 percent pop. age 65 and over: 11.9
Est. Black population (1985): 1,243,000
Est. Hispanic population (1985): 155,000
1987-88 Est. total net migration & (rate): −24,827 (−2.7%)
1987-88 (fiscal year) legal immigrants: 8,929

Indian tribes were living in the Michigan region when the first European, Etienne Brulé of France, arrived in 1618. Other French explorers, including Marquette, Joliet, and La Salle, followed, and the first permanent settlement was established in 1668 at Sault Ste. Marie. France was ousted from the territory by Great Britain in 1763, following the French and Indian War.

After the Revolutionary War, the U.S. acquired most of the region, which remained the scene of constant conflict between the British and U.S. forces and their respective Indian allies through the War of 1812.

Bordering on four of the five Great Lakes, Michigan is divided into Upper and Lower Peninsulas by the Straits of Mackinac, which link Lakes Michigan and Huron. The two parts of the state are connected by the Mackinac Bridge, one of the world's longest suspension bridges. To the north, connecting Lakes Superior and Huron are the busy Sault Ste. Marie Canals.

While Michigan ranks first among the states in production of motor vehicles and parts, it is also a leader in many other manufacturing and processing lines including prepared cereals, machine tools, airplane parts, refrigerators, hardware, steel springs, and furniture.

The state produces important amounts of iron, copper, iodine, gypsum, bromine, salt, lime, gravel, and cement. Michigan's farms grow apples, cherries, pears, grapes, potatoes, and sugar beets and the annual value of its forest products is estimated at $2 billion. With over 36,000 miles of streams, some 11,000 lakes, and a 2,000 mile shoreline, Michigan is a prime area for both commercial and sport fishing.

Points of interest are the automobile plants in Dearborn, Detroit, Flint, Lansing, and Pontiac; Mackinac Island; Pictured Rocks and Sleeping Bear Dunes National Lakeshores, Greenfield Village near Dearborn; and the many summer resorts along both the inland and Great Lakes.

MINNESOTA

Capital: St. Paul
Governor: Rudy Perpich, D (to Jan. 1991)
Lieut. Governor: Marlene Johnson, D (to Jan. 1991)
Secy. of State: Joan Growe, D (to Jan. 1991)
State Auditor: Arne Carlson, R (to Jan. 1991)
Atty. General: Hubert H. Humphrey III, D (to Jan. 1991)
State Treasurer: Michael McGrath, D (to Jan. 1991)
Organized as territory: March 3, 1849
Entered Union & (rank): May 11, 1858 (32)
Present constitution adopted: 1858
Motto: L'Etoile du Nord (The North Star)
State flower: Showy lady slipper (1902)
State tree: Red (or Norway) pine (1953)
State bird: Common loon (also called Great Northern Diver) (1961)
State song: "Hail Minnesota" (1945)
Nicknames: North Star State; Gopher State; Land of 10,000 Lakes
Origin of name: From a Dakota Indian word meaning "sky-tinted water"
1980 population (1980 census) & (rank): 4,075,970 (21)
1989 est. population (July 1) & (rank): 4,353,000 (21)
1991 proj. population: 4,348,000
1980 land area & (rank): 79,548 sq mi. (206,030 sq km) (14)
Geographic center: In Crow Wing Co., 10 mi. SW of Brainerd
Number of counties: 87
Largest cities (1980 census): Minneapolis, 370,951; St. Paul, 270,230; Duluth, 92,811; Bloomington, 81,831; Rochester, 57,890; Edina, 46,073
State forests: 55 (2,984,000 ac.)
State parks: 92 (202,205 ac.)
1989 percent pop. below age 18: 25.9
1989 percent pop. age 65 and over: 12.6
Est. Black population (1985): 64,000
Est. Hispanic population (1985): 34,000
1987-88 Est. total net migration & (rate): 32,393 (7.6%)
1987-88 (fiscal year) legal immigrants: 5,621

Following the visits of several French explorers, fur traders, and missionaries, including Marquette and Joliet and La Salle, the region was claimed for Louis XIV by Daniel Greysolon, Sieur Duluth, in 1679.

The U.S. acquired eastern Minnesota from Great Britain after the Revolutionary War and 20 years later bought the western part from France in the Louisiana Purchase of 1803. Much of the region was explored by U.S. Army Lt. Zebulon M. Pike before cession of the northern strip of Minnesota bordering Canada by Britain in 1818.

The state is rich in natural resources. A few square miles of land in the north in the Mesabi, Cuyuna, and Vermillion ranges, produce more than 60% of the nation's iron ore. The state's farms rank high in yields of corn, wheat, rye, alfalfa, and sugar beets. Other leading farm products include butter, eggs, milk, potatoes, green peas, barley, and livestock.

Minnesota's factory production includes nonelectrical machinery, fabricated metals, flour-mill products, plastics, electronic computers, scientific instruments, and processed foods.

Minneapolis is the trade center of the Northwest; St. Paul is the nation's biggest publisher of calendars and law books. These "twin cities" are the nation's third largest trucking center. Duluth has the nation's largest inland harbor and now handles a significant amount of foreign trade. Rochester is the home of the Mayo Clinic, an internationally famous medical center.

Today, tourism is a major revenue producer in Minnesota, with fishing, hunting, water sports, and winter sports bringing in millions of visitors each year.

Among the most popular attractions are the St. Paul Winter Carnival; the Tyrone Guthrie Theatre, the Institute of Arts, Walker Art Center, and Minnehaha Park, in Minneapolis; Voyageurs National Park; North Shore Drive; and the Minnesota Zoological Gardens.

MISSISSIPPI

Capital: Jackson
Governor: Ray Mabus, D (to Jan. 1992)
Lieut. Governor: Brad Dye, D (to Jan. 1992)
Secy. of State: Dick Molpus, D (to Jan. 1992)
Treasurer: Marshall Bennett, D (to Jan. 1992)
Atty. General: Mike Moore, D (to Jan. 1992)
Organized as Territory: April 7, 1798
Entered Union & (rank): Dec. 10, 1817 (20)
Present constitution adopted: 1890
Motto: *Virtute et armis* (By valor and arms)
State flower: Flower or bloom of the magnolia or evergreen magnolia (1952)
State tree: Magnolia (1938)
State bird: Mockingbird (1944)
State song: "Go, Mississippi" (1962)
Nickname: Magnolia State
Origin of name: From an Indian word meaning "Father of Waters"
1980 population (1980 census) & (rank): 2,520,638 (31)
1989 est. population (July 1) & (rank): 2,621,000 (31)
1991 proj. population: 2,718,000
1980 land area & (rank): 47,233 sq mi. (122,333 sq km) (31)
Geographic center: In Leake Co., 9 mi. WNW of Carthage
Number of counties: 82
Largest cities (1980 census): Jackson, 202,895; Biloxi, 49,311; Hattiesburg, 40,829; Greenville, 40,613; Gulfport, 39,676; Pascagoula, 29,318
State forests: 1 (1,760 ac.)
State parks: 27 (16,763 ac.)
1989 percent pop. below age 18: 29.4
1989 percent pop. age 65 and over: 12.4
Est. Black population (1985): 949,000
Est. Hispanic population (1985): 12,000
1987-88 Est. total net migration & (rate): −16,655 (−6.4%)
1987-88 (fiscal year) legal immigrants: 862

First explored for Spain by Hernando de Soto who discovered the Mississippi River in 1540, the region was later claimed by France. In 1699, a French group under Sieur d'Iberville established the first permanent settlement near present-day Biloxi.

Great Britain took over the area in 1763 after the French and Indian War, ceding it to the U.S. in 1783 after the Revolution. Spain did not relinquish its claims until 1798, and in 1810 the U.S. annexed West Florida from Spain, including what is now southern Mississippi.

For a little more than one hundred years, from shortly after the state's founding through the Great Depression, cotton was the undisputed king of Mississippi's largely agrarian economy. Over the last half-century, however, Mississippi has progressively deepened its commitment to diversification by balancing agricultural output with increased industrial activity.

Today, agriculture continues as a major segment of the state's economy. Soybeans have supplanted cotton as the largest crop—Mississippi is now third in cotton production—and the state's farmlands yield important harvests of corn, peanuts, pecans, rice, sugarcane, sweet potatoes, and hay, as well as poultry and eggs. Mississippi is also the world's leading producer of pond-raised catfish.

The state abounds in historical landmarks and is the home of the Vicksburg National Military Park. Other National Park Service areas are Brices Cross Roads National Battlefield Site, Tupelo National Battlefield, and part of Natchez Trace National Parkway. Pre-Civil War mansions are the special pride of Natchez, Oxford, Hattiesburg, and Jackson.

MISSOURI

Capital: Jefferson City
Governor: John D. Ashcroft, R (to Jan. 1993)
Lieut. Governor: Mel Carnahan, D (to Jan. 1993)
Secy. of State: Roy D. Blunt, R (to Jan. 1993)
Auditor: Margaret Kelly, R (to Jan. 1991)
Treasurer: Wendell Bailey, R (to Jan. 1993)
Atty. General: William L. Webster, R (to Jan. 1993)
Organized as territory: June 4, 1812
Entered Union & (rank): Aug. 10, 1821 (24)
Present constitution adopted: 1945
Motto: *Salus populi suprema lex esto* (The welfare of the people shall be the supreme law)
State flower: Hawthorn (1923)
State bird: Bluebird (1927)
State colors: Red, white, and blue (1913)
State song: "Missouri Waltz" (1949)
State fossil: Crinoidea (1989)
State musical instrument: Fiddle (1987)
State rock: Mozarkite (1967)
State mineral: Galena (1967)
State insect: Honeybee (1985)
Nickname: Show-me State
Origin of name: Named after a tribe called Missouri Indians. "Missouri" means "town of the large canoes."
1980 population (1980 census) & (rank): 4,916,686 (15)
1989 est. population (July 1) & (rank): 5,159,000 (15)
1991 proj. population: 5,219,000
1980 land area & (rank): 68,945 sq mi. (178,568 sq km) (18)
Geographic center: In Miller Co., 20 mi. SW of Jefferson City
Number of counties: 114, plus 1 independent city
Largest cities (1980 census): St. Louis, 453,085; Kansas City, 448,159; Springfield, 133,116; Independence, 111,806; St. Joseph, 76,961; Columbia, 62,061; Florissant, 55,372
State forests and Tower sites: 134 (308,978 ac.)
State parks: 73 (105,325 ac.)[1]
1989 percent pop. below age 18: 25.3
1989 percent pop. age 65 and over: 13.9
Est. Black population (1985): 545,000
Est. Hispanic population (1985): 48,000
1987-88 Est. total net migration & (rate): 9,849 (1.9%)
1987-88 (fiscal year) legal immigrants: 2,715

1. Includes 45 historic sites.

De Soto visited the Missouri area in 1541. France's claim to the entire region was based on La Salle's travels in 1682. French fur traders established Ste. Genevieve in 1735 and St. Louis was first settled in 1764.

The U.S. gained Missouri from France as part of the Louisiana Purchase in 1803, and the territory was admitted as a state following the Missouri Compromise of 1820. Throughout the pre-Civil War period and during the war, Missourians were sharply divided in their opinions about slavery and in their allegiances, supplying both Union and Confederate forces with troops. However, the state itself remained in the Union.

Historically, Missouri played a leading role as a gateway to the West, St. Joseph being the eastern starting point of the Pony Express, while the much-traveled Santa Fe and Oregon Trails began in Independence. Now a popular vacationland, Missouri has 11 major lakes and numerous fishing streams, springs, and caves. Bagnell Dam, across the Osage River in the Ozarks, completed in 1931, created one of the largest man-made lakes in the world, covering 65,000 acres of surface area.

Manufacturing, paced by the aerospace industry, provides more income and jobs than any other segment of the economy. Missouri is also a leading producer of transportation equipment, shoes, lead, and beer. Among the major crops are corn, soybeans, wheat, oats, barley, potatoes, tobacco, and cotton.

Points of interest include Mark Twain's boyhood home and Mark Twain Cave (Hannibal), the Harry S. Truman Library and Museum (Independence), the house where Jesse James was killed in St. Joseph, Jefferson National Expansion Memorial (St. Louis), and the Ozark National Scenic Riverway.

MONTANA

Capital: Helena
Governor: Stan Stephens, R (to Jan. 1993)
Lieut. Governor: Allen Kolstad, R (to Jan. 1993)
Secy. of State: Mike Cooney, D (to Jan. 1993)
Auditor: Andrea Bennett, R (to Jan. 1993)
Atty. General: Marc Racicot, R (to Jan. 1993)
Organized as territory: May 26, 1864
Entered Union & (rank): Nov. 8, 1889 (41)
Present constitution adopted: 1972
Motto: *Oro y plata* (Gold and silver)
State flower: Bitterroot (1895)
State tree: Ponderosa pine (1949)
State stones: Sapphire and agate (1969)
State bird: Western meadow lark (1931)
State song: "Montana" (1945)
Nickname: Treasure State
Origin of name: Chosen from Latin dictionary by J. M. Ashley. It is a Latinized Spanish word.
1980 population (1980 census) & (rank): 786,690 (44)
1989 est. population (July 1) & (rank): 806,000 (44)
1991 proj. population: 803,000
1980 land area & (rank): 145,388 sq mi. (376,564 sq km) (4)
Geographic center: In Fergus Co., 12 mi. W of Lewistown
Number of counties: 56, plus small part of Yellowstone National Park
Largest cities (1980 census): Billings, 66,824; Great Falls, 56,725; Butte-Silver Bow, 37,205; Missoula, 33,388; Helena, 23,938; Bozeman, 21,645; Havre, 10,891
State forests: 7 (214,000 ac.)
State parks and recreation areas: 110 (18,273 ac.)
1989 percent pop. below age 18: 27.0
1989 percent pop. age 65 and over: 13.2
Est. Black population (1985): 2,000
Est. Hispanic population (1985): 11,000
1987-88 Est. total net migration & (rate): −5,622 (−7.0%)
1987-88 (fiscal year) legal immigrants: 341

First explored for France by François and Louis-Joseph Verendrye in the early 1740s, much of the region was acquired by the U.S. from France as part of the Louisiana Purchase in 1803. Before western Montana was obtained from Great Britain

in the Oregon Treaty of 1846, American trading posts and forts had been established in the territory.

The major Indian wars (1867–1877) included the famous 1876 Battle of the Little Big Horn, better known as "Custer's Last Stand," in which Cheyennes and Sioux killed George A. Custer and more than 200 of his men in southeastern Montana.

Much of Montana's early history was concerned with mining with copper, lead, zinc, silver, coal, and oil as principal products.

Butte is the center of the area that once supplied half of the U.S. copper.

Fields of grain cover much of Montana's plains; it ranks high among the states in wheat and barley, with rye, oats, flaxseed, sugar beets, and potatoes other important crops. Sheep and cattle raising make significant contributions to the economy.

Tourist attractions include hunting, fishing, skiing, and dude ranching. Glacier National Park, on the Continental Divide, is a scenic and vacation wonderland with 60 glaciers, 200 lakes, and many streams with good trout fishing.

Other major points of interest include the Custer Battlefield National Monument, Virginia City, Yellowstone National Park, Museum of the Plains Indians at Browning, and the Fort Union Trading Post and Grant-Kohr's Ranch National Historic Sites.

NEBRASKA

Capital: Lincoln
Governor: Kay A. Orr, R (to Jan. 1991)
Lieut. Governor: Wm. Nichol, R (to Jan. 1991)
Secy. of State: Allen J. Beermann, R (to Jan. 1991)
Atty. General: Robert Spire, R (to Jan. 1991)
Auditor: Ray A. C. Johnson, R (to Jan. 1991)
Treasurer: Frank Marsh, R (to Jan. 1991)
Organized as territory: May 30, 1854
Entered Union & (rank): March 1, 1867 (37)
Present constitution adopted: Nov. 1, 1875 (extensively amended 1919-20)
Motto: Equality before the law
State flower: Goldenrod (1895)
State tree: Cottonwood (1972)
State bird: Western meadow lark (1929)
State insect: Honey Bee (1975)
State gem stone: Blue agate (1967)
State rock: Prairie agate (1967)
State fossil: Mammoth (1967)
State song: "Beautiful Nebraska" (1967)
Nicknames: Cornhusker State; Beef State; The Tree Planter State
Origin of name: From an Oto Indian word meaning "flat water"
1980 population (1980 census) & (rank): 1,569,825 (35)
1989 est. population (July 1) & (rank): 1,611,000 (36)
1991 proj. population: 1,585,000
1980 land area & (rank): 76,644 sq mi. (198,508 sq km) (15)
Geographic center: In Custer Co., 10 mi. NW of Broken Bow
Number of counties: 93
Largest cities (1980 census): Omaha, 313,911; Lincoln, 171,932; Grand Island, 33,180; North Platte, 24,479; Fremont, 23,979; Hastings, 23,045; Bellevue, 21,813
State forests: None
State parks: 93 areas, 4 categories, 5 major areas
1989 percent pop. below age 18: 26.3
1989 percent pop. age 65 and over: 13.9
Est. Black population (1985): 53,000
Est. Hispanic population (1985): 30,000
1987-88 Est. total net migration & (rate): −914 (−0.6%)
1987-88 (fiscal year) legal immigrants: 760

French fur traders first visited Nebraska in the early 1700s. Part of the Louisiana Purchase in 1803, Nebraska was explored by Lewis and Clark in 1804–06.

Robert Stuart pioneered the Oregon Trail across Nebraska in 1812–13 and the first permanent settlement was established at Bellevue in 1823. Western Nebraska was acquired by treaty following the Mexican War in 1848. The Union Pacific began its transcontinental railroad at Omaha in 1865. In 1937, Nebraska became the only state in the Union to have a unicameral (one-house) legislature. Members are elected to it without party designation.

Nebraska is a leading grain-producer with bumper crops of rye, corn, and wheat. More varieties of grass, valuable for forage, grow in this state than in any other in the nation.

The state's sizable cattle and hog industries make Dakota City and Lexington the nation's largest meat-packing center and the largest cattle markets in the world.

Manufacturing has become diversified in Nebraska, strengthening the state's economic base. Firms making electronic components, auto accessories, pharmaceuticals, and mobile homes have joined such older industries as clothing, farm machinery, chemicals, and transportation equipment. Oil was discovered in 1939 and natural gas in 1949.

Among the principal attractions are Agate Fossil Beds, Homestead, and Scotts Bluff National Monuments; Chimney Rock National Historic Site; a recreated pioneer village at Minden; SAC Museum at Bellevue; the Stuhr Museum of the Prairie Pioneer with 57 original 19th-century buildings near Grand Island; the Sheldon Memorial Art Gallery at the University of Nebraska in Lincoln; and the Lied Center for the Performing Arts located on the University of Nebraska campus in Lincoln.

NEVADA

Capital: Carson City
Governor (acting) and Lieut. Governor: Robert J. Miller, D (to Jan. 1991)
Secy. of State: Frankie Sue Del Papa, D (to Jan. 1991)
State Treasurer: Ken Santor, R (to Jan. 1991)
Controller: Darrel R. Daines, R (to Jan. 1991)
Atty. General: Brian McKay, R (to Jan. 1991)
Organized as territory: March 2, 1861
Entered Union & (rank): Oct. 31, 1864 (36)
Present constitution adopted: 1864
Motto: All for Our Country
State flower: Sagebrush (1967)
State trees: Single-leaf pinon (1953) and Bristlecone Pine (1987)
State bird: Mountain bluebird (1967)
State animal: Desert bighorn sheep (1973)
State colors: Silver and blue (1983)
State song: "Home Means Nevada" (1933)
Nicknames: Sagebrush State; Silver State; Battle-born State
Origin of name: Spanish: "snowcapped"
1980 population (1980 census) & (rank): 800,493 (43)
1989 est. population (July 1) & (rank): 1,111,000 (41)
1991 proj. population: 1,102,000
1980 land area & (rank): 109,894 sq mi. (284,624 sq km) (7)
Geographic center: In Lander Co., 26 mi. SE of Austin
Number of counties: 16, plus 1 independent city
Largest cities (est. as of July 1, 1985): Las Vegas, 193,052; Reno, 115,464; North Las Vegas, 45,920; Sparks, 49,612; Carson City, 35,400; Henderson, 37,046; Boulder City, 11,425
State forests: None

State parks: 20 (150,000 ac., including leased lands)
1989 percent pop. below age 18: 25.0
1989 percent pop. age 65 and over: 10.9
Est. Black population (1985): 61,000
Est. Hispanic population (1985): 70,000
1987-88 Est. total net migration & (rate): 39,879 (38.7%)
1987-88 (fiscal year) legal immigrants: 2,562

Trappers and traders, including Jedediah Smith, and Peter Skene Ogden, entered the Nevada area in the 1820s. In 1843–45, John C. Fremont and Kit Carson explored the Great Basin and Sierra Nevada.

In 1848 following the Mexican War, the U.S. obtained the region and the first permanent settlement was a Mormon trading post near present-day Genoa.

The driest state in the nation with an average annual rainfall of only about 7 inches,[1] much of Nevada is uninhabited, sagebrush-covered desert.

Nevada was made famous by the discovery of the fabulous Comstock Lode in 1859 and its mines have produced large quantities of gold, silver, copper, lead, zinc, mercury, barite, and tungsten. Oil was discovered in 1954. Gold now far exceeds all other minerals in value of production.

In 1931, the state created two industries, divorce and gambling. For many years, Reno and Las Vegas were the "divorce capitals of the nation." More liberal divorce laws in many states have ended this distinction, but Nevada is the gambling and entertainment capital of the U.S. State gambling taxes account for 42% of general fund tax revenues. Although Nevada leads the nation in per capita gambling revenue, it ranks only fourth in total gambling revenue.

Near Las Vegas, on the Colorado River, stands Hoover Dam, which impounds the waters of Lake Mead, one of the world's largest artificial lakes.

The state's agricultural crop consists mainly of hay, alfalfa seed, barley, wheat, and potatoes.

Nevada manufactures gaming equipment; lawn and garden irrigation devices; titanium products; seismic and machinery monitoring devices; and specialty printing.

Major resort areas flourish in Lake Tahoe, Reno, and Las Vegas. Recreation areas include those at Pyramid Lake, Lake Tahoe, and Lake Mead and Lake Mohave, both in Lake Mead National Recreation Area. Among the other attractions are Hoover Dam, Virginia City, and Great Basin National Park (includes Lehman Caves).

1. Wettest part of state receives about 40 inches of precipitation per year, while driest spot has less than four inches per year.

NEW HAMPSHIRE

Capital: Concord
Governor: Judd A. Gregg, R (to Jan. 1991)
Treasurer: Georgie A. Thomas, R (to Dec. 1990)
Secy. of State: William M. Gardner, D (to Dec. 1990)
Commissioner: George C. Jones, R
Atty. General: John R. Arnold, R (to March 1993)
Entered Union & (rank): June 21, 1788 (9)
Present constitution adopted: 1784
Motto: Live free or die
State flower: Purple lilac (1919)
State tree: White birch (1947)
State bird: Purple finch (1957)
State songs: "Old New Hampshire" (1949) and "New Hampshire, My New Hampshire" (1963)

Nickname: Granite State
Origin of name: From the English county of Hampshire
1980 population (1980 census) & (rank): 920,610 (42)
1989 est. population (July 1) & (rank): 1,107,000 (40)
1991 proj. population: 1,167,000
1980 land area & (rank): 8,993 sq mi. (23,292 sq km) (44)
Geographic center: In Belknap Co., 3 mi. E of Ashland
Number of counties: 10
Largest cities (1987 est.): Manchester, 100,600; Nashua, 80,694; Concord, 37,024; Portsmouth, 26,887; Dover, 25,716; Rochester, 25,381; Keene, 22,403; Derry, 26, 388; Salem, 25,303; Merrimack, 24,215.
State forests & parks: 175 (96,975 ac.)
1989 percent pop. below age 18: 25.2
1989 percent pop. age 65 and over: 11.4
Est. Black population (1985): 5,000
Est. Hispanic population (1985): 6,000
1987-88 Est. total net migration & (rate): 20,387 (19%)
1987-88 (fiscal year) legal immigrants: 1,070

Under an English land grant, Capt. John Smith sent settlers to establish a fishing colony at the mouth of the Piscataqua River, near present-day Rye and Dover, in 1623. Capt. John Mason, who participated in the founding of Portsmouth in 1630, gave New Hampshire its name.

After a 38-year period of union with Massachusetts, New Hampshire was made a separate royal colony in 1679. As leaders in the revolutionary cause, New Hampshire delegates received the honor of being the first to vote for the Declaration of Independence on July 4, 1776. New Hampshire is the only state that ever played host at the formal conclusion of a foreign war when, in 1905, Portsmouth was the scene of the treaty ending the Russo-Japanese War.

Abundant water power early turned New Hampshire into an industrial state and manufacturing is the principal source of income in the state. The most important industrial products are electrical and other machinery, textiles, pulp and paper products, and stone and clay products.

Dairy and poultry farming and growing fruit, truck vegetables, corn, potatoes, and hay are the major agricultural pursuits.

Tourism, because of New Hampshire's scenic and recreational resources, now brings over $2.2 billion into the state annually.

Vacation attractions include Lake Winnipesaukee, largest of 1,300 lakes and ponds; the 724,000-acre White Mountain National Forest; Daniel Webster's birthplace near Franklin; Strawbery Banke, restored building of the original settlement at Portsmouth; and the famous "Old Man of the Mountain" granite head profile, the state's official emblem, at Franconia.

NEW JERSEY

Capital: Trenton
Governor: James J. Florio, D (to Jan. 1994)
Secy. of State: Joan Haberle, D (to Jan. 1994)
Treasurer: Douglas Berman, D (to Jan. 1994)
Atty. General: Robert Del Tufo, D (to Jan. 1994)
Entered Union & (rank): Dec. 18, 1787 (3)
Present constitution adopted: 1947
Motto: Liberty and prosperity
State flower: Purple violet (1913)
State bird: Eastern goldfinch (1935)
State insect: Honeybee (1974)
State tree: Red oak (1950)
State animal: Horse (1977)

State colors: Buff and blue (1965)
Nickname: Garden State
Origin of name: From the Channel Isle of Jersey
1980 population (1980 census) & (rank): 7,364,823 (9)
1989 est. population (July 1) & (rank): 7,736,000 (9)
1991 proj. population: 7,971,000
1980 land area & (rank): 7,468 sq mi. (19,342 sq km) (46)
Geographic center: In Mercer Co., 5 mi. SE of Trenton
Number of counties: 21
Largest cities (1980 census): Newark, 329,248; Jersey City, 223,532; Paterson, 137,970; Elizabeth, 106,201; Trenton, 92,124; Camden, 84,910; Clifton, 77,690
State forests: 11
State parks: 35 (67,111 ac.)
1989 percent pop. below age 18: 23.7
1989 percent pop. age 65 and over: 13.2
Est. Black population (1985): 1,025,000
Est. Hispanic population (1985): 573,000
1987-88 Est. total net migration & (rate): 5,801 (0.8%)
1987-88 (fiscal year) legal immigrants: 30,849

New Jersey's early colonial history was involved with that of New York (New Netherlands), of which it was a part. One year after the Dutch surrender to England in 1664, New Jersey was organized as an English colony under Gov. Philip Carteret.

In the late 1600s the colony was divided between Carteret and William Penn; later it would be administered by the royal governor of New York. Finally, in 1738, New Jersey was separated from New York under its own royal governor, Lewis Morris.

Because of its key location between New York City and Philadelphia, New Jersey saw much fighting during the American Revolution.

Today, New Jersey, an area of wide industrial diversification, is known as the Crossroads of the East. Products from over 15,000 factories can be delivered overnight to almost 60 million people, representing 12 states and the District of Columbia. The greatest single industry is chemicals and New Jersey is one of the foremost research centers in the world. Many large oil refineries are located in northern New Jersey and other important manufactures are pharmaceuticals, instruments, machinery, electrical goods, and apparel.

Of the total land area, 37% is forested. Farmland is declining. In 1987 there were about 7,600 farms, with over 500,000 acres under harvest. The state ranks high in production of almost all garden vegetables. Tomatoes, asparagus, corn, and blueberries are important crops, and poultry farming and dairying make significant contributions to the state's economy.

Tourism is the second largest industry in New Jersey. The state has numerous resort areas on 127 miles of Atlantic coastline. In 1977, New Jersey voters approved legislation allowing legalized casino gambling in Atlantic City. Points of interest include the Walt Whitman House in Camden, the Delaware Water Gap, the Edison National Historic Site in West Orange, and Princeton University.

NEW MEXICO

Capital: Santa Fe
Governor: Garrey E. Carruthers, R (to Jan. 1991)
Lieut. Governor: Jack Stahl, R (to Jan. 1991)
Secy. of State: Rebecca Vigil-Giron, D (to Jan. 1991)
Atty. General: Hal Stratton, R (to Jan. 1991)
State Auditor: Harroll H. Adams, D (to Jan. 1991)

State Treasurer: James B. Lewis, D (to Jan. 1991)
Commissioner of Public Lands: William R. Humphries, R (to Jan. 1991)
Organized as territory: Sept. 9, 1850
Entered Union & (rank): Jan. 6, 1912 (47)
Present constitution adopted: 1911
Motto: *Crescit eundo* (It grows as it goes)
State flower: Yucca (1927)
State tree: Pinon (1949)
State animal: Black bear (1963)
State bird: Roadrunner (1949)
State fish: Cutthroat trout (1955)
State vegetables: Chile and frijol (1965)
State gem: Turquoise (1967)
State colors: Red and yellow of old Spain (1925)
State song: "O Fair New Mexico" (1917)
Spanish language state song: "Asi Es Nuevo Mejico" (1971)
Nicknames: Land of Enchantment; Sunshine State
Origin of name: From the country of Mexico
1980 population (1980 census) & (rank): 1,302,894 (37)
1989 est. population (July 1) & (rank): 1,528,000 (37)
1991 proj. population: 1,669,000
1980 land area & (rank): 121,335 sq mi. (314,258 sq km) (5)
Geographic center: In Torrance Co., 12 mi. SSW of Willard
Number of counties: 33
Largest cities (July 1, 1984 est.): Albuquerque, 350,575; Santa Fe, 52,274; Las Cruces, 50,275; Roswell, 45,702; Farmington, 37,332; Hobbs, 35,029
State-owned forested land: 933,000 ac.
State parks: 29 (105,012 ac.)
1989 percent pop. below age 18: 29.7
1989 percent pop. age 65 and over: 10.5
Est. Black population (1985): 29,000
Est. Hispanic population (1985): 551,000
1987-88 Est. total net migration & (rate): −6,023 (−4.0%)
1987-88 (fiscal year) legal immigrants: 2,302

Francisco Vásquez de Coronado, Spanish explorer searching for gold, traveled the region that became New Mexico in 1540–42. In 1598 the first Spanish settlement was established on the Rio Grande River by Juan de Onate and in 1610 Santa Fe was founded and made the capital of New Mexico.

The U.S. acquired most of New Mexico in 1848, as a result of the Mexican War, and the remainder in the 1853 Gadsden Purchase. Union troops captured the territory from the Confederates during the Civil War. With the surrender of Geronimo in 1886, the Apache Wars and most of the Indian troubles in the area were ended.

Since 1945, New Mexico has been a leader in energy research and development with extensive experiments conducted at Los Alamos Scientific Laboratory and Sandia Laboratories in the nuclear, solar, and geothermal areas.

Minerals are the state's richest natural resource and New Mexico is one of the U.S. leaders in output of uranium and potassium salts. Petroleum, natural gas, copper, gold, silver, zinc, lead, and molybdenum also contribute heavily to the state's income.

The principal manufacturing industries include food products, chemicals, transportation equipment, lumber, electrical machinery, and stone-clay-glass products. More than two thirds of New Mexico's farm income comes from livestock products, especially sheep. Cotton, pecans, and sorghum are the most important field crops. Corn, peanuts, beans, onions, chile, and lettuce are also grown.

Tourist attractions in New Mexico include the Carlsbad Caverns National Park, Inscription Rock at El Morro National Monument, the ruins at Fort Union, Billy the Kid mementos at Lincoln, the White Sands and Gila Cliff Dwellings National Monuments, and the Chaco Culture National Historical Park.

NEW YORK

Capital: Albany
Governor: Mario M. Cuomo, D (to Jan. 1991)
Lieut. Governor: Stan Lundine, D (to Jan. 1991)
Secy. of State: Gail S. Shaffer, D (to Jan. 1991)
Comptroller: Edward V. Regan, R (to Jan. 1991)
Atty. General: Robert Abrams, D (to Jan. 1991)
Entered Union & (rank): July 26, 1788 (11)
Present constitution adopted: 1777 (last revised 1938)
Motto: *Excelsior* (Ever upward)
State animal: Beaver (1975)
State fish: Brook trout (1975)
State gem: Garnet (1969)
State flower: Rose (1955)
State tree: Sugar maple (1956)
State bird: Bluebird (1970)
State insect: Ladybug (1989)
State song: "I Love New York" (1980)
Nickname: Empire State
Origin of name: In honor of the English Duke of York
1980 population (1980 census) & (rank): 17,558,072 (2)
1989 est. population (July 1) & (rank): 17,950,000 (2)
1991 proj. population: 17,789,000
1980 land area & (rank): 47,377 sq mi. (122,707 sq km) (30)
Geographic center: In Madison Co., 12 mi. S of Oneida and 26 mi. SW of Utica
Number of counties: 62
Largest cities (1986 est.): New York, 7,352,700; Buffalo, 313,570; Rochester, 229,780; Yonkers, 183,000; Syracuse, 153,610; Albany, 94,540; Utica, 66,180
State forest preserves: Adirondacks, 2,500,000 ac., Catskills, 250,000 ac.
State parks: 150 (250,000 ac.)
1989 percent pop. below age 18: 24.3
1989 percent pop. age 65 and over: 13.0
Est. Black population (1985): 2,733,000
Est. Hispanic population (1985): 1,879,000
1987-88 Est. total net migration & (rate): −25,111 (−1.4%)
1987-88 (fiscal year) legal immigrants: 114,194

Giovanni da Verrazano, Italian-born navigator sailing for France, discovered New York Bay in 1524. Henry Hudson, an Englishman employed by the Dutch, reached the bay and sailed up the river now bearing his name in 1609, the same year that northern New York was explored and claimed for France by Samuel de Champlain.

In 1624 the first permanent Dutch settlement was established at Fort Orange (now Albany); one year later Peter Minuit is said to have purchased Manhattan Island from the Indians for trinkets worth about $24 and founded the Dutch colony of New Amsterdam (now New York City), which was surrendered to the English in 1664.

For a short time, New York City was the U.S. capital and George Washington was inaugurated there as first President on April 30, 1789.

New York's extremely rapid commercial growth may be partly attributed to Governor De Witt Clinton, who pushed through the construction of the Erie Canal (Buffalo to Albany), which was opened in 1825. Today, the 559-mile Governor Thomas E. Dewey Thruway connects New York

City with Buffalo and with Connecticut, Massachusetts, and Pennsylvania express highways. Two toll-free superhighways, the Adirondack Northway (linking Albany with the Canadian border) and the North-South-Expressway (crossing central New York from the Pennsylvania border to the Thousand Islands) have been opened.

New York, with the great metropolis of New York City, is the spectacular nerve center of the nation. It is a leader in manufacturing, foreign trade, commercial and financial transactions, book and magazine publishing, and theatrical production.

New York City is not only a national but an international leader. A leading seaport, its John F. Kennedy International Airport is one of the busiest airports in the world. It is the largest manufacturing center in the country and its apparel industry is the city's largest manufacturing employer, with printing and publishing second.

Nearly all the rest of the state's manufacturing is done on Long Island, along the Hudson River north to Albany and through the Mohawk Valley, Central New York, and Southern Tier regions to Buffalo. The St. Lawrence seaway and power projects have opened the North Country to industrial expansion and have given the state a second seacoast.

The state ranks second in the nation in manufacturing with 1,208,400 employees in 1988. The principal industries are apparel, printing and publishing, leather products, instruments and electronic equipment.

The convention and tourist business is one of the state's most important sources of income.

New York farms are famous for raising cattle and calves, producing corn for grain, poultry, and the raising of vegetables and fruits. The state is a leading wine producer.

Among the major points of interest are Castle Clinton, Fort Stanwix, and Statue of Liberty National Monuments; Niagara Falls; U.S. Military Academy at West Point; National Historic Sites that include homes of Franklin D. Roosevelt at Hyde Park and Theodore Roosevelt in Oyster Bay and New York City; National Memorials, including Grant's Tomb and Federal Hall in New York City; Fort Ticonderoga; the Baseball Hall of Fame in Cooperstown; and the United Nations, skyscrapers, museums, theaters, and parks in New York City.

NORTH CAROLINA

Capital: Raleigh
Governor: James G. Martin, R (to Jan. 1993)
Lieut. Governor: James C. Gardner, R (to Jan. 1993)
Secy. of State: Rufus L. Edmisten, D (to Jan. 1993)
Treasurer: Harlan E. Boyles (to Jan. 1993)
Auditor: Edward Renfrow, D (to Jan. 1993)
Atty. General: Lacey H. Thornburg, D (to Jan. 1993)
Entered Union & (rank): Nov. 21, 1789 (12)
Present constitution adopted: 1971
Motto: *Esse quam videri* (To be rather than to seem)
State flower: Dogwood (1941)
State tree: Pine (1963)
State bird: Cardinal (1943)
State mammal: Gray Squirrel (1969)
State insect: Honeybee (1973)
State Reptile: Turtle (1979)
State gem stone: Emerald (1973)
State shell: Scotch bonnet (1965)
State historic boat: Shad Boat (1987)
State beverage: Mike (1987)
State rock: Granite (1979)

State dog: Plott Hound (1989)
State song: "The Old North State" (1927)
State colors: Red and blue (1945)
Nickname: Tar Heel State
Origin of name: In honor of Charles I of England
1980 population (1980 census) & (rank): 5,881,766 (10)
1989 est. population (July 1) & (rank): 6,571,000 (10)
1991 proj. population: 6,777,000
1980 land area & (rank): 48,843 sq mi. (126,504 sq km) (29)
Geographic center: In Chatham Co., 10 mi. NW of Sanford
Number of counties: 100
Largest cities (est. as of July 1, 1984): Charlotte, 367,860; Raleigh, 186,720; Greensboro, 181,970; Winston-Salem, 148,690; Durham, 115,430; Fayetteville, 78,805
State forests: 1
State parks: 30 (125,000 ac.)
1989 percent pop. below age 18: 25.0
1989 percent pop. age 65 and over: 12.1
Est. Black population (1985): 1,392,000
Est. Hispanic population (1985): 39,000
1987-88 Est. total net migration & (rate): 41,965 (6.5%)
1987-88 (fiscal year) legal immigrants: 3,181

English colonists, sent by Sir Walter Raleigh, unsuccessfully attempted to settle Roanoke Island in 1585 and 1587. Virginia Dare, born there in 1587, was the first child of English parentage born in America.

In 1653 the first permanent settlements were established by English colonists from Virginia near the Roanoke and Chowan Rivers.

The region was established as an English proprietary colony in 1663–65 and its early history was the scene of Culpepper's Rebellion (1677), the Quaker-led Cary Rebellion of 1708, the Tuscarora Indian War in 1711–13, and many pirate raids.

During the American Revolution, there was relatively little fighting within the state, but many North Carolinians saw action elsewhere. Despite considerable pro-Union, anti-slavery sentiment, North Carolina joined the Confederacy.

North Carolina is the nation's largest furniture, tobacco, brick, and textile producer. It holds second place in the Southeast in population and first place in the value of its industrial and agricultural production. This production is highly diversified, with metalworking, chemicals, and paper constituting enormous industries. Tobacco, corn, cotton, hay, peanuts, and truck and vegetable crops are of major importance. It is the country's leading producer of mica and lithium.

Tourism is also important, with travelers and vacationers spending more than $1 billion annually in North Carolina. Sports include year-round golfing, skiing at mountain resorts, both fresh and salt water fishing, and hunting.

Among the major attractions are the Great Smoky Mountains, the Blue Ridge National Parkway, the Cape Hatteras and Cape Lookout National Seashores, the Wright Brothers National Memorial at Kitty Hawk, Guilford Courthouse and Moores Creek National Military Parks, Carl Sandburg's home near Hendersonville, and the Old Salem Restoration in Winston-Salem.

NORTH DAKOTA

Capital: Bismarck
Governor: George A. Sinner, D (to Dec. 1992)
Lieut. Governor: Lloyd Omdahl, D (to Jan. 1993)
Secy. of State: Jim Kusler, D (to Jan. 1993)
Auditor: Robert W. Peterson, R (to Jan. 1993)

State Treasurer: Robert Hanson, D (to Jan. 1993)
Atty. General: Nicholas Spaeth, D (to Jan. 1993)
Organized as territory: March 2, 1861
Entered Union & (rank): Nov. 2, 1889 (39)
Present constitution adopted: 1889
Motto: Liberty and union, now and forever: one and inseparable
State tree: American Elm (1947)
State bird: Western meadow lark (1947)
State song: "North Dakota Hymn" (1947)
Nickname: Sioux State; Flickertail State, Peace Garden State
Origin of name: From the Dakotah tribe, meaning "allies"
1980 population (1980 census) & (rank): 652,717 (46)
1989 est. population (July 1) & (rank): 660,000 (46)
1991 proj. population: 656,000
1980 land area & (rank): 70,665 sq mi. (183,022 sq km) (17)
Geographic center: In Sheridan Co., 5 mi. SW of McClusky
Number of counties: 53
Largest cities (1980 census): Fargo, 61,383; Bismarck, 44,485; Grand Forks, 43,765; Minot, 32,843; Jamestown, 16,280; Dickinson, 15,924; Mandan, 15,513
State forests: None
State parks: 14 (14,922.6 ac.)
1989 percent pop. below age 18: 27.2
1989 percent pop. age 65 and over: 13.9
Est. Black population (1985): 3,000
Est. Hispanic population (1985): 3,000
1987-88 Est. total net migration & (rate): −4,812 (−7.2%)
1987-88 (fiscal year) legal immigrants: 305

North Dakota was explored in 1738–40 by French Canadians led by Vérendrye. In 1803, the U.S. acquired most of North Dakota from France in the Louisiana Purchase. Lewis and Clark explored the region in 1804–06 and the first settlements were made at Pembina in 1812 by Scottish and Irish families while this area was still in dispute between the U.S. and Great Britain.

In 1818, the U.S. obtained the northeastern part of North Dakota by treaty with Great Britain and took possession of Pembina in 1823.

North Dakota is the most rural of all the states, with farms covering more than 90% of the land. Only Kansas produces more wheat, and the state's coal and oil reserves are plentiful.

Other agricultural products include barley, rye, oats, and flaxseed, sugar beets, and hay; beef cattle, sheep, and hogs.

Recently, manufacturing industries have grown, especially food processing and farm equipment. The state also produces natural gas, lignite, salt, clay, sand, and gravel.

The Garrison Dam on the Missouri River provides extensive irrigation and produces 400,000 kilowatts of electricity for the Missouri Basin areas.

Known for its waterfowl, grouse, and deer hunting and bass, trout, and northern pike fishing, North Dakota has 20 state parks and recreation areas. Points of interest include the International Peace Garden near Dunseith, Fort Union Trading Post National Historic Site, the State Capitol at Bismarck, the Badlands, and Fort Lincoln, now a state park, from which Gen. George Custer set out on his last campaign in 1876.

OHIO

Capital: Columbus
Governor: Richard F. Celeste, D (to Jan. 1991)
Lieut. Governor: Paul Leonard, D (to Jan. 1991)
Secy. of State: Sherrod Brown, D (to Jan. 1991)

Auditor: Thomas E. Ferguson, D (to Jan. 1991)
Treasurer: Mary Ellen Withrow, D (to Jan. 1991)
Atty. General: Anthony J. Celebrezze, Jr., D (to Jan. 1991)
Entered Union & (rank): March 1, 1803 (17)
Present constitution adopted: 1851
Motto: With God, all things are possible
State flower: Scarlet carnation (1904)
State tree: Buckeye (1953)
State bird: Cardinal (1933)
State insect: Ladybug (1975)
State gem stone: Flint (1965)
State song: "Beautiful Ohio" (1969)
State drink: Tomato juice (1965)
Nickname: Buckeye State
Origin of name: From an Iroquoian word meaning "great river"
1980 population (1980 census) & (rank): 10,797,630 (6)
1989 est. population (July 1) & (rank): 10,907,000 (7)
1991 proj. population: 10,792,000
1980 land area & (rank): 41,004 sq mi. (106,201 sq km) (35)
Geographic center: In Delaware Co., 25 mi. NNE of Columbus
Number of counties: 88
Largest cities (1980 census): Cleveland, 573,822; Columbus, 565,032; Cincinnati, 385,457; Toledo, 354,635; Akron, 237,177; Dayton, 203,371; Youngstown, 115,436
State forests: 19 (172,744 ac.)
State parks: 71 (198,027 ac.)
1989 percent pop. below age 18: 25.9
1989 percent pop. age 65 and over: 12.8
Est. Black population (1985): 1,136
Est. Hispanic population (1985): 108,000
1987-88 Est. total net migration & (rate): −19,138 (−1.8%)
1987-88 (fiscal year) legal immigrants: 5,930

First explored for France by La Salle in 1669, the Ohio region became British property after the French and Indian War. Ohio was acquired by the U.S. after the Revolutionary War in 1783 and, in 1788, the first permanent settlement was established at Marietta, capital of the Northwest Territory.

The 1790s saw severe fighting with the Indians in Ohio; a major battle was won by Maj. Gen. Anthony Wayne at Fallen Timbers in 1794. In the War of 1812, Commodore Oliver H. Perry defeated the British in the Battle of Lake Erie on Sept. 10, 1813.

Ohio is one of the nation's industrial leaders, ranking third in the value of manufactured products. Important manufacturing centers are located in or near Ohio's major cities. Akron is known for rubber; Canton for roller bearings; Cincinnati for jet engines and machine tools; Cleveland for auto assembly and parts, refining, and steel; Dayton for office machines, refrigeration, and heating and auto equipment; Youngstown and Steubenville for steel; and Toledo for glass and auto parts.

The state's thousands of factories almost overshadow its importance in agriculture and mining. Its fertile soil produces soybeans, corn, oats, grapes, and clover. More than half of Ohio's farm receipts come from dairying and sheep and hog raising. Ohio is the top state in lime production and among the leaders in coal, clay, salt, sand, and gravel. Petroleum, gypsum, cement, and natural gas are also important.

Tourism is a valuable revenue producer, bringing in over $3 billion annually. Attractions include the Indian burial grounds at Mound City Group

National Monument, Perry's Victory International Peace Memorial, the Pro Football Hall of Fame at Canton, and the homes of Presidents Grant, Taft, Hayes, Harding, and Garfield.

OKLAHOMA

Capital: Oklahoma City
Governor: Henry Bellmon, R (to Jan. 1991)
Lieut. Governor: Robert S. Kerr, III, D (to Jan. 1991)
Secy. of State: Hannah Diggs Atkins, D (to Jan. 1991)
Treasurer: Ellis Edwards, D (to Jan. 1991)
Atty. General: Robert Henry, D (to Jan. 1991)
Organized as territory: May 2, 1890
Entered Union & (rank): Nov. 16, 1907 (46)
Present constitution adopted: 1907
Motto: *Labor omnia vincit* (Labor conquers all things)
State flower: Mistletoe (1893)
State tree: Redbud (1937)
State bird: Scissor-tailed flycatcher (1951)
State animal: Bison (1972)
State reptile: Mountain boomer lizard (1969)
State stone: Rose Rock (barite rose) (1968)
State colors: Green and white (1915)
State song: "Oklahoma" (1953)
Nickname: Sooner State
Origin of name: From two Choctaw Indian words meaning "red people"
1980 population (1980 census) & (rank): 3,025,290 (26)
1989 est. population (July 1) & (rank): 3,224,000 (27)
1991 proj. population: 3,287,000
1980 land area & (rank): 68,655 sq mi. (177,817 sq km) (19)
Geographic center: In Oklahoma Co., 8 mi. N of Oklahoma City
Number of counties: 77
Largest cities (1980 census): Oklahoma City, 403,213; Tulsa, 360,919; Lawton, 80,054; Norman, 68,020; Enid, 50,363; Midwest City, 49,559; Muskogee, 40,011
State forests: None
State parks: 36 (57,487 ac.)
1989 percent pop. below age 18: 26.4
1989 percent pop. age 65 and over: 13.3
Est. Black population (1985): 228,000
Est. Hispanic population (1985): 70,000
1987-88 Est. total net migration & (rate): −18,349 (−5.6%)
1987-88 (fiscal year) legal immigrants: 2,131

Francisco Vásquez de Coronado first explored the region for Spain in 1541. The U.S. acquired most of Oklahoma in 1803 in the Louisiana Purchase from France; the Western Panhandle region became U.S. territory with the annexation of Texas in 1845.

Set aside as Indian Territory in 1834, the region was divided into Indian Territory and Oklahoma Territory on May 2, 1890. The two were combined to make a new state, Oklahoma, on Nov. 16, 1907.

On April 22, 1889, the first day homesteading was permitted, 50,000 people swarmed into the area. Those who tried to beat the noon starting gun were called "Sooners." Hence the state's nickname.

Oil made Oklahoma a rich state, but natural gas production was never surpassed it. Oil refining, meat packing, food processing, and machinery manufacturing (especially construction and oil equipment) are important industries.

Other minerals produced in Oklahoma include helium, gypsum, zinc, cement, coal, copper, and silver.

Oklahoma's rich plains produce bumper yields of wheat, as well as large crops of sorghum, hay, cotton, and peanuts. More than half of Oklahoma's annual farm receipts are contributed by livestock products, including cattle, dairy products, and broilers.

Tourist attractions include the National Cowboy Hall of Fame in Oklahoma City, the Will Rogers Memorial in Claremore, the Cherokee Cultural Center with a restored Cherokee village, the restored Fort Gibson Stockade near Muskogee, and the Lake Texoma recreation area, Pari-Mutuel horse racing at Remington Park in Oklahoma City, and Blue Ribbon Downs in Sallisaw.

OREGON

Capital: Salem
Governor: Neil Goldschmidt, D (to Jan. 1991)
Secy. of State: Barbara Roberts, R (to Jan. 1993)
Treasurer: Tony Meeker, R (to Jan. 1993)
Atty. General: David B. Frohnmayer, R (to Jan. 1993)
Organized as territory: Aug. 14, 1848
Entered Union & (rank): Feb. 14, 1859 (33)
Present constitution adopted: 1859
Motto: "Alis volat Propriis" ("She flies with her own wings") (1987)
State flower: Oregon grape (1899)
State tree: Douglas fir (1939)
State animal: Beaver (1969)
State bird: Western meadow lark (1927)
State fish: Chinook salmon (1961)
State rock: Thunderegg (1965)
State colors: Navy blue and gold (1959)
State song: "Oregon, My Oregon" (1927)
Nickname: Beaver State
Poet Laureate: William E. Stafford (1974)
Origin of name: Unknown. However, it is generally accepted that the name, first used by Jonathan Carver in 1778, was taken from the writings of Maj. Robert Rogers, an English army officer.
1980 population (1980 census) & (rank): 2,633,105 (30)
1989 est. population (July 1) & (rank): 2,820,000 (30)
1991 proj. population: 2,781,000
1980 land area & (rank): 96,184 sq mi. (249,117 sq km) (10)
Geographic center: In Crook Co., 25 mi. SSE of Prineville
Number of counties: 36
Largest cities (est. as of July 1, 1985): Portland, 379,000; Eugene, 106,100; Salem, 94,600; Medford, 41,975; Springfield, 40,690
State forests: 820,000 ac.
State parks: 240 (93,330 ac.)
1989 percent pop. below age 18: 24.7
1989 percent pop. age 65 and over: 13.9
Est. Black population (1985): 41,000
Est. Hispanic population (1985): 76,000
1987-88 Est. total net migration & (rate): 29,609 (10.8%)
1987-88 (fiscal year) legal immigrants: 3,687

Spanish and English sailors are believed to have sighted the Oregon coast in the 1500s and 1600s. Capt. James Cook, seeking the Northwest Passage, charted some of the coastline in 1778. In 1792, Capt. Robert Gray, in the *Columbia*, discovered the river named after his ship and claimed the area for the U.S.

In 1805 the Lewis and Clark expedition explored the area and John Jacob Astor's fur depot, Astoria, was founded in 1811. Disputes for control of Oregon between American settlers and the Hudson Bay Company were finally resolved in the 1846 Oregon Treaty in which Great Britain gave up claims to the region.

Oregon has a five-billion-dollar wood processing industry. Its salmon-fishing industry is one of the world's largest.

In agriculture, the state leads in growing peppermint, winter pears, fresh plums, prunes, blackberries, boysenberries, filberts, Blue Lake beans, and cover seed crops, and also raises strawberries, hops, wheat and other grains, sugar beets, potatoes, green peas, fiber flax, dairy products, livestock and poultry, apples, pears, and cherries. Oregon is the source of all the nickel produced in the U.S.

With the low-cost electric power provided by Bonneville Dam, McNary Dam, and other dams in the Pacific Northwest, Oregon has developed steadily as a manufacturing state. Leading manufactures are lumber and plywood, metalwork, machinery, aluminum, chemicals, paper, food packing, and electronic equipment.

Crater Lake National Park, Mount Hood, and Bonneville Dam on the Columbia are major tourist attractions. Oregon Dunes National Recreation Area has been established near Florence. Other points of interest include the Oregon Caves National Monument, Cape Perpetua in Siuslaw National Forest, Columbia River Gorge between The Dalles and Troutdale, and Hells Canyon.

PENNSYLVANIA

Capital: Harrisburg
Governor: Robert P. Casey, D (to Jan. 1991)
Lieut. Governor: Mark S. Singel, D (to Jan. 1991)
Secy. of the Commonwealth: Christopher A. Lewis, D (at the pleasure of the Governor)
Auditor General: Barbara Hafer, R (to Jan. 1993)
Atty. General: Ernest D. Preate, Jr., R (to Jan. 1993)
Entered Union & (rank): Dec. 12, 1787 (2)
Present constitution adopted: 1874
Motto: Virtue, liberty, and independence
State flower: Mountain laurel (1933)
State tree: Hemlock (1931)
State bird: Ruffed grouse (1931)
State dog: Great Dane (1965)
State colors: Blue and gold (1907)
State song: None
Nickname: Keystone State
Origin of name: In honor of Adm. Sir. William Penn, father of William Penn. It means "Penn's Woodland."
1980 population (1980 census) & (rank): 11,863,895 (4)
1989 est. population (July 1) & (rank): 12,040,000 (5)
1991 proj. population: 11,806,000
1980 land area & (rank): 44,888 sq mi. (116,260 sq km) (32)
Geographic center: In Centre Co., 2 1/2 mi. SW of Bellefonte
Number of counties: 67
Largest cities (1980 census): Philadelphia, 1,688,210; Pittsburgh, 423,959; Erie, 119,123; Allentown, 103, 758; Scranton, 88,117; Reading, 78,686; Bethlehem, 70,419
State forests: 1,930,108 ac.
State parks: 120 (297,438 ac.)
1989 percent pop. below age 18: 23.6
1989 percent pop. age 65 and over: 15.1
Est. Black population (1985): 1,102,000
Est. Hispanic population (1985): 159,000
1987-88 Est. total net migration & (rate): 22,688 (1.9%)
1987-88 (fiscal year) legal immigrants: 10,599

Rich in historic lore, Pennsylvania territory was disputed in the early 1600s among the Dutch, the Swedes, and the English. England acquired the region in 1664 with the capture of New York and in 1681 Pennsylvania was granted to William Penn, a Quaker, by King Charles II.

Philadelphia was the seat of the federal government almost continuously from 1776 to 1800; there the Declaration of Independence was signed in 1776 and the U.S. Constitution drawn up in 1787. Valley Forge, of Revolutionary War fame, and Gettysburg, the turning-point of the Civil War, are both in Pennsylvania. The Liberty Bell is located in a glass pavilion across from Independence Hall in Philadelphia.

With the decline of the coal, steel and railroad industries, Pennsylvania's industry has diversified, though the state still leads the country in the production of specialty steel. Pennsylvania is a leader in the production of chemicals, food, and electrical machinery and produces 10% of the nations's cement. Also important are brick and tiles, glass, limestone, and slate. Data processing is also increasingly important.

Pennsylvania's nine million agricultural acres produce a wide variety of crops and its farms are the backbone of the state's economy. Leading products are milk, poultry and eggs, a variety of fruits, sweet corn, potatoes, mushrooms, cheese, beans, hay, maple syrup, and even Christmas trees.

Pennsylvania has the largest rural population in the nation. The state's farmers sell more than $3 billion in crops and livestock annually and agribusiness and food-related industries account for another $35 billion in economic activity annually.

Tourists now spend approximately $6 billion in Pennsylvania annually. Among the chief attractions: the Gettysburg National Military Park, Valley Forge National Historical Park, Independence National Historical Park in Philadelphia, the Pennsylvania Dutch region, the Eisenhower farm near Gettysburg, and the Delaware Water Gap National Recreation Area.

RHODE ISLAND

Capital: Providence
Governor: Edward D. DiPrete, R (to Jan. 1991)
Lieut. Governor: Roger N. Begin (to Jan. 1991)
Secy. of State: Kathleen S. Connell, D (to Jan. 1991)
Controller: Lawrence Franklin, Jr. (civil service)
Atty. General: James E. O'Neil, D (to Jan. 1991)
Entered Union & (rank): May 29, 1790 (13)
Present constitution adopted: 1843
Motto: Hope
State flower: Violet (unofficial) (1968)
State tree: Red maple (official) (1964)
State bird: Rhode Island Red (official) (1954)
State shell: Quahog (official)
State mineral: Bowenite
State stone: Cumberlandite
State colors: Blue, white, and gold (in state flag)
State song: "Rhode Island" (1946)
Nickname: The Ocean State
Origin of name: From the Greek Island of Rhodes
1980 population (1980 census) & (rank): 947,154 (40)
1989 est. population (July 1) & (rank): 998,000 (43)
1991 proj. population: 1,008,000
1980 land area & (rank): 1,055 sq mi. (2,732 sq km) (50)
Geographic center: In Kent Co., 1 mi. SSW of Crompton
Number of counties: 5
Largest cities (1980 census): Providence, 156,804; Warwick, 87,123; Cranston, 71,992; Pawtucket, 71,204; East Providence, 50,980; Woonsocket, 45,914

State forests: 11 (20,900 ac.)
State parks: 17 (8,200 ac.)
1989 percent pop. below age 18: 23.1
1989 percent pop. age 65 and over: 14.8
Est. Black population (1985): 34,000
Est. Hispanic population (1985): 20,000
1987-88 Est. total net migration & (rate): 2,865 (2.9%)
1987-88 (fiscal year) legal immigrants: 2,425

From its beginnings, Rhode Island has been distinguished by its support for freedom of conscience and action, started by Roger Williams, who was exiled by the Massachusetts Bay Colony Puritans in 1636, and was the founder of the present state capital, Providence. Williams was followed by other religious exiles who founded Pocasset, now Portsmouth, in 1638 and Newport in 1639.

The first Baptist church in the U.S. was established in Providence in 1638 and Rhode Island provided a haven for Quakers in 1657 and for Jews from Holland in 1659.

Rhode Island's rebellious, authority-defying nature was further demonstrated by the burnings of the British revenue cutters *Liberty* and *Gaspee* prior to the Revolution, by its early declaration of independence from Great Britain in May 1776, its refusal to participate actively in the War of 1812, and by Dorr's Rebellion of 1842, which protested property requirements for voting.

Rhode Island, smallest of the fifty states, is densely populated and highly industrialized. It is a primary center for jewelry manufacturing in the United States. Electronics, metal, plastic products, and boat and ship construction are other important industries. Non-manufacturing employment includes research in health and medical areas, and the ocean environment. Providence is a wholesale distribution center for New England.

Two of New England's fishing ports are at Galilee and Newport. Rural areas of the state support small-scale farming including grapes for local wineries, dairy, and poultry products.

Tourism is one of Rhode Island's largest industries, generating over a billion dollars a year in revenue.

Newport became famous as the summer capital of society in the mid-19th century. Touro Synagogue (1763) is the oldest in the U.S. Other points of interest include the Roger Williams National Memorial in Providence, Samuel Slater's Mill in Pawtucket, the General Nathanael Greene Homestead in Coventry and Block Island.

SOUTH CAROLINA

Capital: Columbia
Governor: Carroll Campbell, R (to Jan. 1991)
Lieut. Governor: Nick Theodore, D (to Jan. 1991)
Secy. of State: John T. Campbell, D (to Jan. 1991)
Comptroller General: Earl E. Morris, Jr. (to Jan. 1991)
Atty. General: T. Travis Medlock, D (to Jan. 1991)
Entered Union & (rank): May 23, 1788 (8).
Present constitution adopted: 1895
Mottoes: *Animis opibusque parati* (Prepared in mind and resources) and *Dum spiro spero* (While I breathe, I hope)
State flower: Carolina yellow jessamine (1924)
State tree: Palmetto tree (1939)
State bird: Carolina wren (1948)
State song: "Carolina" (1911)
Nickname: Palmetto State
Origin of name: In honor of Charles I of England

1980 population (1980 census) & (rank): 3,121,820 (24)
1989 est. population (July 1) & (rank): 3,512,000 (25)
1991 proj. population: 3,589,000
1980 land area & (rank): 30,203 sq mi. (78,227 sq km) (40)
Geographic center: In Richland Co., 13 mi. SE of Columbia
Number of counties: 46
Largest cities (1980 census): Columbia, 100,385; Charleston, 69,510; North Charleston, 62,534; Greenville, 58,242; Spartanburg, 43,826; Rock Hill, 35,344
State forests: 4 (124,052 ac.)
State parks: 50 (61,726 ac.)
1989 percent pop. below age 18: 27.1
1989 percent pop. age 65 and over: 11.1
Est. Black population (1985): 1,012,000
Est. Hispanic population (1985): 20,000
1987-88 Est. total net migration & (rate): 19,708 (5.7%)
1987-88 (fiscal year) legal immigrants: 1,480

Following exploration of the coast in 1521 by De Gordillo, the Spanish tried unsuccessfully to establish a colony near present-day Georgetown in 1526 and the French also failed to colonize Parris Island near Fort Royal in 1562.

The first English settlement was made in 1670 at Albemarle Point on the Ashley River, but poor conditions drove the settlers to the site of Charleston (originally called Charles Town). South Carolina, officially separated from North Carolina in 1729, was the scene of extensive military action during the Revolution and again during the Civil War. The Civil War began in 1861 as South Carolina troops fired on federal Fort Sumter in Charleston Harbor and the state was the first to secede from the Union.

Once primarily agricultural, South Carolina has built so many large textile and other mills that today its factories produce eight times the output of its farms in cash value. Charleston makes asbestos, wood, pulp, and steel products; chemicals, machinery, and apparel are also important.

Farms have become fewer but larger in recent years. South Carolina grows more peaches than any other state except California; it ranks fourth in tobacco. Other farm products include cotton, peanuts, sweet potatoes, soybeans, corn, and oats. Poultry and dairy products are also important revenue producers.

Points of interest include Fort Sumter National Monument, Fort Moultrie, Fort Johnson, and aircraft carrier USS *Yorktown* in Charleston Harbor; the Middleton, Magnolia, and Cypress Gardens in Charleston; Cowpens National Battlefield; and the Hilton Head resorts.

SOUTH DAKOTA

Capital: Pierre
Governor: George S. Mickelson, R (to Jan. 1991)
Lieut. Governor: Walter Dale Miller, R (to Jan. 1991)
Atty. General: Roger Tellinghuisen, R (to Jan. 1991)
Secy. of State: Joyce Hazeltine, R (to Jan. 1991)
State Auditor: Vern Larson, R (to Jan. 1991)
State Treasurer: David L. Volk, R (to Jan. 1991)
Organized as territory: March 2, 1861
Entered Union & (rank): Nov. 2, 1889 (40)
Present constitution adopted: 1889
Motto: Under God the people rule
State flower: American pasqueflower (1903)
State grass: Western wheat grass (1970)

State tree: Black Hills spruce (1947)
State bird: Ring-necked pheasant (1943)
State insect: Honeybee (1978)
State animal: Coyote (1949)
State mineral stone: Rose quartz (1966)
State gem stone: Fairburn agate (1966)
State colors: Blue and gold (in state flag)
State song: "Hail! South Dakota" (1943)
State fish: Walleye (1982)
State musical instrument: Fiddle (1989)
Nicknames: Sunshine State; Coyote State
Origin of name: Same as for North Dakota
1980 population (1980 census) & (rank): 690,768 (45)
1989 est. population (July 1) & (rank): 715,000 (45)
1991 proj. population: 709,000
1980 land area & (rank): 75,952 sq mi. (196,715 sq km) (16)
Geographic center: In Hughes Co., 8 mi. NE of Pierre
Number of counties: 67 (64 county governments)
Largest cities (1980 census): Sioux Falls, 81,343; Rapid City, 46,492; Aberdeen, 25,851; Watertown, 15,649; Brookings, 14,951; Mitchell, 13,916; Huron, 13,000
State forests: None[1]
State parks: 13 plus 39 recreational areas (87,269 ac.)[2]
1989 percent pop. below age 18: 27.4
1989 percent pop. age 65 and over: 14.4
Est. Black population (1985): 3,000
Est. Hispanic population (1985): 4,000
1987-88 Est. total net migration & (rate): −799 (−1.1%)
1987-88 (fiscal year) legal immigrants: 304

1. No designated state forests; about 13,000 ac. of state land is forestland. 2. Acreage includes 39 recreation areas and 80 roadside parks, in addition to 12 state parks.

Exploration of this area began in 1743 when Louis-Joseph and François Verendrye came from France in search of a route to the Pacific.

The U.S. acquired the region as part of the Louisiana Purchase in 1803 and it was explored by Lewis and Clark in 1804–06. Fort Pierre, the first permanent settlement, was established in 1817 and, in 1831, the first Missouri River steamboat reached the fort.

Settlement of South Dakota did not begin in earnest until the arrival of the railroad in 1873 and the discovery of gold in the Black Hills the following year.

Agriculture is the state's leading industry. South Dakota is a leading state in the production of rye, wheat, alfalfa, sunflower seed, flaxseed, and livestock.

South Dakota is the nation's second leading producer of gold and the Homestake Mine is the richest in the U.S. Other minerals produced include berylium, bentonite, granite, silver, petroleum, and uranium.

Processing of foods produced by farms and ranches is the largest South Dakota manufacturing industry, followed by lumber, wood products, and machinery, including farm equipment.

The Black Hills are the highest mountains east of the Rockies. Mt. Rushmore, in this group, is famous for the likenesses of Washington, Jefferson, Lincoln, and Theodore Roosevelt, which were carved in granite by Gutzon Borglum. A memorial to Crazy Horse is also being carved in granite near Custer.

Other tourist attractions include the Badlands; the World's Only Corn Palace in Mitchell; and the city of Deadwood where Wild Bill Hickok was killed in 1876 and where gambling was recently legalized to truly recapture city's Old West flavor.

TENNESSEE

Capital: Nashville
Governor: Ned Ray McWherther, D (to Jan. 1991)
Lieut. Governor: John S. Wilder, D (to Jan. 1991)
Secy. of State: Bryant Millsops, D (to Jan. 1991)
Atty. General: Charles W. Burson, D (Jan. 1991)
State Treasurer: Steve Adams, D (to Jan. 1991)
Entered Union & (rank): June 1, 1796 (16)
Present constitution adopted: 1870; amended 1953, 1960, 1966, 1972, 1978
Motto: "Tennessee—America at its best!" (1965)
State flower: Iris (1933)
State tree: Tulip poplar (1947)
State bird: Mockingbird (1933)
State horse: Tennessee walking horse
State animal: Raccoon (1971)
State wild flower: Passion flower (1973)
State song: "Tennessee Waltz" (1965)
Nickname: Volunteer State
Origin of name: Of Cherokee origin; the exact meaning is unknown
1980 population (1980 census) & (rank): 4,591,120 (17)
1989 est. population (July 1) & (rank): 4,940,000 (16)
1991 proj. population: 5,010,000
1980 land area & (rank): 41,155 sq mi. (106,591 sq km) (34)
Geographic center: In Rutherford Co., 5 mi. NE of Murfreesboro
Number of counties: 95
Largest cities (1980 census): Memphis, 646,174; Nashville, 455,651; Knoxville, 175,045; Chattanooga, 169,558; Clarksville, 54,777; Jackson, 49,131
State forests: 14 (155,752 ac.)
State parks: 21 (130,000 ac.)
1989 percent pop. below age 18: 25.4
1989 percent pop. age 65 and over: 12.6
Est. Black population (1985): 766,000
Est. Hispanic population (1985): 18,000
1987-88 Est. total net migration & (rate): 17,188 (3.5%)
1987-88 (fiscal year) legal immigrants: 2,276

First visited by the Spanish explorer de Soto in 1541, the Tennessee area would later be claimed by both France and England as a result of the 1670s and 1680s explorations of Marquette and Joliet, La Salle, and the Englishmen James Needham and Gabriel Arthur.

Great Britain obtained the region following the French and Indian War in 1763 and it was rapidly occupied by settlers moving in from Virginia and the Carolinas.

During 1784–87, the settlers formed the "state" of Franklin, which was disbanded when the region was allowed to send representatives to the North Carolina legislature. In 1790 Congress organized the territory south of the Ohio River and Tennessee joined the Union in 1796.

Although Tennessee joined the Confederacy during the Civil War, there was much pro-Union sentiment in the state, which was the scene of extensive military action.

The state is now predominantly industrial; in 1980, 60.4% of its population lived in urban areas. Among the most important products are chemicals, textiles, apparel, electrical machinery, furniture, and leather goods. Other lines include food processing, lumber, primary metals, and metal products. The state is known as the U.S. hardwood-flooring center and ranks first in the production of marble, zinc, pyrite, and ball clay.

Tennessee is one of the leading tobacco-producing states in the nation and its farming income is also derived from livestock and dairy products as well as corn, cotton, and soybeans.

With six other states, Tennessee shares the extensive federal reservoir developments on the Tennessee and Cumberland River systems. The Tennessee Valley Authority operates a number of dams and reservoirs in the state.

Among the major points of interest: the Andrew Johnson National Historic Site at Greenville, American Museum of Atomic Energy at Oak Ridge, Great Smoky Mountains National Park, The Hermitage (home of Andrew Jackson near Nashville), Rock City Gardens near Chattanooga, and three National Military Parks.

TEXAS

Capital: Austin
Governor: William P. Clements, R (to Jan. 1991)
Lieut. Governor: William P. Hobby, D (to Jan. 1991)
Secy. of State: George Bayoud, R (Apptd. by Govr.)
Treasurer: Ann W. Richards, D (to Jan. 1991)
Comptroller: Bob Bullock, D (to Jan. 1991)
Atty. General: Jim Mattox, D (to Jan. 1991)
Entered Union & (rank): Dec. 29, 1845 (28)
Present constitution adopted: 1876
Motto: Friendship
State flower: Bluebonnet (1901)
State tree: Pecan (1919)
State bird: Mockingbird (1927)
State song: "Texas, Our Texas" (1930)
State fish: Guadalupe bass (1989)
State seashell: Lightning whelk (1987)
Nickname: Lone Star State
Origin of name: From an Indian word meaning "friends"
1980 population (1980 census) & (rank): 14,229,191 (3)
1989 est. population (July 1) & (rank): 16,991,000 (3)
1991 proj. population: 17,973,000
1980 land area & (rank): 262,017 sq mi. (678,623 sq km) (2)
Geographic center: In McCulloch Co., 15 mi. NE of Brady
Number of counties: 254
Largest cities (1980 census): Houston, 1,595,138; Dallas, 904,078; San Antonio, 785,023; El Paso, 425,259; Fort Worth, 385,164; Austin, 345,496
State forests: 4 (6,306 ac.)
State parks: 83 (64 developed)
1989 percent pop. below age 18: 29.1
1989 percent pop. age 65 and over: 10.1
Est. Black population (1985): 1,910,000
Est. Hispanic population (1985): 3,690,000
1987-88 Est. total net migration & (rate): −122,979 (−7.3%)
1987-88 (fiscal year) legal immigrants: 42,349

Spanish explorers, including Cabeza de Vaca and Coronado, were the first to visit the region in the 16th and 17th centuries, settling at Ysleta near El Paso in 1682. In 1685, La Salle established a short-lived French colony at Matagorda Bay.

Americans, led by Stephen F. Austin, began to settle along the Brazos River in 1821 when Texas was controlled by Mexico, recently independent from Spain. In 1836, following a brief war between the American settlers in Texas and the Mexican government, and famous for the battles of the Alamo and San Jacinto, the Independent Republic of Texas was proclaimed with Sam Houston as president.

After Texas became the 28th U.S. state in 1845, border disputes led to the Mexican War of 1846–48.

Today, Texas, second only to Alaska in land area,

leads all other states in such categories as oil, cattle, sheep, and cotton. Possessing enormous natural resources, Texas is a major agricultural state and an industrial giant.

Sulfur, salt, helium, asphalt, graphite, bromine, natural gas, cement, and clays give Texas first place in mineral production. Chemicals, oil refining, food processing, machinery, and transportation equipment are among the major Texas manufacturing industries.

Texas ranches and farms produce beef cattle, poultry, rice, pecans, peanuts, sorghum, and an extensive variety of fruits and vegetables.

Millions of tourists spend well over $2 billion annually visiting more than 70 state parks, recreation areas, and points of interest such as the Gulf Coast resort area, the Lyndon B. Johnson Space Center in Houston, the Alamo in San Antonio, the state capital in Austin, and the Big Bend and Guadalupe Mountains National Parks.

UTAH

Capital: Salt Lake City
Governor: Norman H. Bangerter, R (to Jan. 1993)
Lieut. Governor: W. Val Oveson, R (to Jan. 1993)
Atty. General: David Wilkinson, R (to Jan. 1993)
Organized as territory: Sept. 9, 1850
Entered Union & (rank): Jan. 4, 1896 (45)
Present constitution adopted: 1896
Motto: Industry
State flower: Sego lily (1911)
State tree: Blue spruce (1933)
State bird: Seagull (1955)
State emblem: Beehive (1959)
State song: "Utah, We Love Thee" (1953)
Nickname: Beehive State
Origin of name: From the Ute tribe, meaning "people of the mountains"
1970 population & (rank): 1,059,273 (36)
1980 population (1980 census) & (rank): 1,461,037 (36)
1989 est. population (July 1) & (rank): 1,707,000 (35)
1991 proj. population: 1,802,000
1980 land area & (rank): 82,073 sq mi. (212,569 sq km) (12)
Geographic center: In Sanpete Co., 3 mi. N. of Manti
Number of counties: 29
Largest cities (1980 census): Salt Lake City, 163,697; Provo, 52,210; Ogden, 64,407; Orem, 52,399; Sandy City, 52,210; Bountiful, 32,877; West Jordan, 27,192; Logan, 26,844; Murray, 25,750
State forests: None
State parks: 44 (64,097 ac.)
1989 percent pop. below age 18: 36.9
1989 percent pop. age 65 and over: 8.6
Est. Black population (1985): 12,000
Est. Hispanic population (1985): 71,000
1987-88 Est. total net migration & (rate): −16,440 (−9.8%)
1987-88 (fiscal year) legal immigrants: 1,995

The region was first explored for Spain by Franciscan friars, Escalante and Dominguez in 1776. In 1824 the famous American frontiersman Jim Bridger discovered the Great Salt Lake.

Fleeing the religious persecution encountered in eastern and middle-western states, the Mormons reached the Great Salt Lake in 1847 and began to build Salt Lake City. The U.S. acquired the Utah region in the treaty ending the Mexican War in 1848 and the first transcontinental railroad was completed with the driving of a golden spike at Promontory Summit in 1869.

Mormon difficulties with the federal government about polygamy did not end until the Mormon Church renounced the practice in 1890, six years before Utah became a state.

In recent years, manufacturing, trade, and service have become Utah's most important industries, ahead of mining, agriculture, and tourism. The state's factories produce transportation equipment, food products, machinery, metal products, and electrical equipment. Utah has also become an important aerospace research and production center and is a leading warehousing and distribution point for much of the western U.S.

Rich in natural resources, Utah has long been a leading producer of copper, gold, silver, lead, zinc, and molybdenum. Oil has also become a major product; with Colorado and Wyoming, Utah shares what have been called the world's richest oil shale deposits.

Ranked eighth among the states in number of sheep in 1989, Utah also produces large crops of apricots and cherries as well as sugar beets, potatoes, onions, alfalfa, winter wheat, and beans. Utah's farmlands and crops require extensive irrigation.

Utah is a great vacationland with 11,000 miles of fishing streams and 147,000 acres of lakes and reservoirs. Among the many tourist attractions are Arches, Bryce Canyon, Canyonlands, Capitol Reef, and Zion National Parks; Dinosaur, Natural Bridges, and Rainbow Bridge National Monuments; the Mormon Tabernacle in Salt Lake City; and Monument Valley.

VERMONT

Capital: Montpelier
Governor: Madeleine M. Kunin, D (to Jan. 1991)
Lieut. Governor: Howard B. Dean, D (to Jan. 1991)
Secy. of State: James H. Douglas, R (to Jan. 1991)
Treasurer: Paul W. Ruse, Jr., D (to Jan. 1991)
Auditor of Accounts: Alexander V. Acebo, R (to Jan. 1991)
Atty. General: Jeffrey L. Amestoy, R (to Jan. 1991)
Entered Union & (rank): March 4, 1791 (14)
Present constitution adopted: 1793
Motto: Vermont, Freedom, and Unity
State flower: Red clover (1894)
State tree: Sugar maple (1949)
State bird: Hermit thrush (1941)
State animal: Morgan horse (1961)
State insect: Honeybee (1978)
State song: "Hail, Vermont!" (1938)
Nickname: Green Mountain State
Origin of name: From the French "vert mont," meaning "green mountain"
1980 population (1980 census) & (rank): 511,456 (48)
1989 est. population (July 1) & (rank): 567,000 (48)
1991 proj. population: 566,000
1980 land area & (rank): 9,273 sq mi. (24,017 sq km) (43)
Geographic center: In Washington Co., 3 mi. E of Roxbury
Number of counties: 14
Largest cities (1980 census): Burlington, 37,712; Rutland, 18,436; South Burlington, 10,679; Barre, 9,824; Montpelier, 8,241; St. Albans, 7,308; Winooski, 6,318
State forests: 34 (113,953 ac.)
State parks: 45 (31,325 ac.)
1989 percent pop. below age 18: 25.0
1989 percent pop. age 65 and over: 11.9
Est. Black population (1985): 2,000
Est. Hispanic population (1985): 4,000
1987-88 Est. total net migration & (rate): 6,673 (12.1%)
1987-88 (fiscal year) legal immigrants: 517

The Vermont region was explored and claimed for France by Samuel de Champlain in 1609 and the first French settlement was established at Fort Ste. Anne in 1666. The first English settlers moved into the area in 1724 and built Fort Drummer on the site of present-day Brattleboro. England gained control of the area in 1763 after the French and Indian War.

First organized to drive settlers from New York out of Vermont, the Green Mountain Boys, led by Ethan Allen, won fame by capturing Fort Ticonderoga from the British on May 10, 1775, in the early days of the Revolution.

In 1777 Vermont adopted its first constitution abolishing slavery and providing for universal male suffrage without property qualifications. In 1791 Vermont became the first state after the original 13 to join the Union.

Vermont leads the nation in the production of monument granite, marble, and maple syrup. It is also a leader in the production of asbestos and talc.

In ratio to population, Vermont keeps more dairy cows than any other state. Vermont's soil is devoted to dairying, truck farming, and fruit growing because the rugged, rocky terrain discourages extensive farming.

Principal industrial products include electrical equipment, fabricated metal products, printing and publishing, and paper and allied products.

Tourism is a major industry in Vermont. Vermont's many famous ski areas include Stowe, Killington, Mt. Snow, Bromley, Jay Peak, and Sugarbush. Hunting and fishing also attract many visitors to Vermont each year. Among the many points of interest are the Green Mountain National Forest, Bennington Battle Monument, the Calvin Coolidge Homestead at Plymouth, and the Marble Exhibit in Proctor.

VIRGINIA

Capital: Richmond
Governor: L. Douglas Wilder, D (to Jan. 1994)
Lieut. Governor: Donald S. Beyer, Jr., D (to Jan. 1994)
Secy. of the Commonwealth: Pamela M. Wornack (apptd. by governor)
Comptroller: Edward J. Mazur (apptd. by governor)
Atty. General: Mary Sue Terry, D (to Jan. 1994)
Entered Union & (rank): June 25, 1788 (10)
Present constitution adopted: 1970
Motto: *Sic semper tyrannis* (Thus always to tyrants)
State flower: American dogwood (1918)
State bird: Cardinal (1950)
State dog: American foxhound (1966)
State shell: Oyster shell (1974)
State song: "Carry Me Back to Old Virginia" (1940)
Nicknames: The Old Dominion; Mother of Presidents
Origin of name: In honor of Elizabeth "Virgin Queen" of England
1980 population (1980 census) & (rank): 5,346,818 (14)
1989 est. population (July 1) & (rank): 6,098,000 (12)
1991 proj. population: 6,242,000
1980 land area & (rank): 39,704 sq mi. (102,832 sq km) (36)
Geographic center: In Buckingham Co., 5 mi. SW of Buckingham
Number of counties: 95, plus 41 independent cities
Largest cities (1980 census): Norfolk, 266,979; Virginia Beach, 262,199; Richmond, 219,214; Newport News, 144,903; Hampton, 122,617; Chesapeake, 114,486
State forests: 8 (49,566 ac.)
State parks and recreational parks: 27, plus 3 in process of acquisition and/or development (42,722 ac.)[1]

1989 percent pop. below age 18: 24.3
1989 percent pop. age 65 and over: 10.8
Est. Black population (1985): 1,091,000
Est. Hispanic population (1985): 87,000
1987-88 Est. total net migration & (rate): 58,483 (9.8%)
1987-88 (fiscal year) legal immigrants: 11,235

1. Does not include portion of Breaks Interstate Park (Va.-Ky., 1,200 ac.) which lies in Virginia.

The history of America is closely tied to that of Virginia, particularly in the Colonial period. Jamestown, founded in 1607, was the first permanent English settlement in North America and slavery was introduced there in 1619. The surrenders ending both the American Revolution (Yorktown) and the Civil War (Appomattox) occurred in Virginia. The state is called the "Mother of Presidents" because eight chief executives of the United States were born there.

Today, Virginia has a large number of diversified manufacturing industries including transportation equipment, textiles, food processing and electric and electronic equipment. Other important lines are printing, chemicals, apparel, and lumber and wood products.

Agriculture remains an important sector in the Virginia economy and the state ranks among the leaders in the U.S. in tobacco, peanuts, apples, and peaches. Other crops include corn, vegetables, and barley. Famous for its turkeys and Smithfield hams, Virginia also has a large dairy industry.

Coal mining accounts for roughly 75% of Virginia's mineral output, and lime, kyanite, and stone are also mined.

Points of interest include Mt. Vernon and other places associated with George Washington; Monticello, home of Thomas Jefferson; Stratford, home of the Lees; Richmond, capital of the Confederacy and of Virginia; and Williamsburg, the restored Colonial capital.

The Chesapeake Bay Bridge-Tunnel spans the mouth of Chesapeake Bay, connecting Cape Charles with Norfolk. Consisting of a series of low trestles, two bridges and two mile-long tunnels, the complex is 18 miles (29 km) long. It was opened in 1964.

Other attractions are the Shenandoah National Park, Fredericksburg and Spotsylvania National Military Park, the Booker T. Washington birthplace near Roanoke, Arlington House (the Robert E. Lee Memorial), the Skyline Drive, and the Blue Ridge National Parkway.

WASHINGTON

Capital: Olympia
Governor: Booth Gardner, D (to 1989)
Lieut. Governor: Joel Pritchard, D (to 1991)
Secy. of State: Ralph Munro (to 1991)
State Treasurer: Daniel K. Grimm (to 1991)
Atty. General: Kenneth O. Eikenberry (to 1991)
Organized as territory: March 2, 1853
Entered Union & (rank): Nov. 11, 1889 (42)
Present constitution adopted: 1889
Motto: *Al-Ki* (Indian word meaning "by and by")
State flower: Rhododendron (1949)
State tree: Western hemlock (1947)
State bird: Willow goldfinch (1951)
State fish: Steelhead trout (1969)
State gem: Petrified wood (1975)
State colors: Green and gold (1925)
State song: "Washington, My Home" (1959)
State dance: Square dance (1979)

Nicknames: Evergreen State; Chinook State
Origin of name: In honor of George Washington
1980 population (1980 census) & (rank): 4,132,156 (18)
1989 est. population (July 1) & (rank): 4,761,000 (18)
1991 proj. population: 4,699,000
1980 land area & (rank): 66,511 sq mi (172,264 sq km) (20)
Geographic center: In Chelan Co., 10 mi. WSW of Wenatchee
Number of counties: 39
Largest cities (1980 census): Seattle, 493,846; Spokane, 171,300; Tacoma, 158,501; Bellevue, 73,903; Everett, 54,413; Yakima, 49,826; Bellingham, 45,794
State forest lands: 1,922,880 ac.
State parks: 202 (171,700 ac.)[1]
1989 percent pop. below age 18: 25.6
1989 percent pop. age 65 and over: 11.9
Est. Black population (1985): 122,000
Est. Hispanic population (1985): 142,000
1987-88 Est. total net migration & (rate): 70,600 (15.4%)
1987-88 (fiscal year) legal immigrants: 9,684

1. Parks and undeveloped areas administered by Parks and Recreation Dept. Game Dept. administers wildlife and recreation areas totaling 762,895 acres.

As part of the vast Oregon Country, Washington territory was visited by Spanish, American, and British explorers—Bruno Heceta for Spain in 1775, the American Capt. Robert Gray in 1792, and Capt. George Vancouver for Britain in 1792–94. Lewis and Clark explored the Columbia River region and coastal areas for the U.S. in 1805–06.

Rival American and British settlers and conflicting territorial claims threatened war in the early 1840s. However, in 1846 the Oregon Treaty set the boundary at the 49th parallel and war was averted.

Washington is a leading lumber producer. Its rugged surface is rich in stands of Douglas fir, hemlock, ponderosa and white pine, spruce, larch, and cedar. The state holds first place in apples, blueberries, hops, and red raspberries and it ranks high in potatoes, winter wheat, pears, grapes, apricots, and strawberries. Livestock and livestock products make important contributions to total farm revenue and the commercial fishing catch of salmon, halibut, and bottomfish makes a significant contribution to the state's economy.

Manufacturing industries in Washington include aircraft and missiles, shipbuilding and other transportation equipment, lumber, food processing, metals and metal products, chemicals, and machinery.

The Columbia River contains one third of the potential water power in the U.S., harnessed by such dams as the Grand Coulee, one of the greatest power producers in the world. Washington has 90 dams throughout the state built for irrigation, power, flood control, and water storage. Its abundance of electrical power makes Washington the nation's largest producer of refined aluminum.

Among the major points of interest: Mt. Rainier, Olympic, and North Cascades. In 1980, Mount St. Helens, a peak in the Cascade Range in Southwestern Washington erupted on May 18th. Also of interest are National Parks; Whitman Mission and Fort Vancouver National Historic Sites; and the Pacific Science Center and Space Needle in Seattle.

WEST VIRGINIA

Capital: Charleston
Governor: Gaston Caperton, D (to Jan. 1993)

Secy. of State: Ken Heckler, D (to Jan. 1993)
State Auditor: Glen Gainer (to Jan. 1993)
Atty. General: Charlie Brown, D (to Jan. 1993)
Entered Union & (rank): June 20, 1863 (35)
Present constitution adopted: 1872
Motto: *Montani semper liberi* (Mountaineers are always free)
State flower: Rhododendron (1903)
State tree: Sugar maple (1949)
State bird: Cardinal (1949)
State animal: Black bear (1973)
State colors: Blue and gold (official) (1863)
State songs: "West Virginia, My Home Sweet Home," "The West Virginia Hills," and "This Is My West Virginia" (adopted by Legislature in 1947, 1961 and 1963 as official state songs)
Nickname: Mountain State
Origin of name: Same as for Virginia
1980 population (1980 census) & (rank): 1,949,644 (34)
1989 est. population (July 1) & (rank): 1,857,000 (34)
1991 proj. population: 1,842,000
1980 land area & (rank): 24,282 sq mi. (62,468 sq km) (41)
Geographic center: In Braxton Co., 4 mi. E of Sutton
Number of counties: 55
Largest cities (1980 census): Charleston, 63,968; Huntington, 63,684; Wheeling, 43,070; Parkersburg, 39,967; Morgantown, 27,605; Weirton, 25,371
State forests: 9 (79,081 ac.)
State parks: 34 (72,599 ac.)
1989 percent pop. below age 18: 24.9
1989 percent pop. age 65 and over: 14.6
Est. Black population (1985): 64,000
Est. Hispanic population (1985): 8,000
1987-88 Est. total net migration & (rate): −2,933 (−1.6%)
1987-88 (fiscal year) legal immigrants: 530

West Virginia's early history from 1609 until 1863 is largely shared with Virginia, of which it was a part until Virginia seceded from the Union in 1861. Then the delegates of 40 western counties formed their own government, which was granted statehood in 1863.

First permanent settlement dates from 1731 when Morgan Morgan founded Mill Creek. In 1742 coal was discovered on the Coal River, an event that would be of great significance in determining West Virginia's future.

The state usually ranks 3rd in bituminous coal production with about 15% of the U.S. total. It also is a leader in steel, glass, aluminum, and chemical manufactures; natural gas, oil, quarry products, and hardwood lumber.

Major cash farm products are poultry and eggs, dairy products, apples, and feed crops. More than 75% of West Virginia is covered with forests.

Tourism is increasingly popular in mountainous West Virginia and visitors spend over $2.3 billion (1989) annually. More than a million acres have been set aside in 34 state parks and recreation areas and in 9 state forests, and national forests.

Major points of interest include Harpers Ferry and New River Gorge National River, The Greenbrier and Berkeley Springs resorts, the scenic railroad at Cass, and the historic homes in the Eastern Panhandle.

WISCONSIN

Capital: Madison
Governor: Tommy G. Thompson, R (to Jan. 1991)
Lieut. Governor: Scott McCallum, R (to Jan. 1991)
Secy. of State: Douglas J. La Follette, D (to Jan. 1991)

State Treasurer: Charles P. Smith, D (to Jan. 1991)
Atty. General: Donald J. Hanaway, R (to Jan. 1991)
Superintendent of Public Instruction: Herbert J. Grover, Nonpartisan (to July 1993)
Organized as territory: July 4, 1836
Entered Union & (rank): May 29, 1848 (30)
Present constitution adopted: 1848
Motto: Forward
State flower: Wood violet (1949)
State tree: Sugar maple (1949)
State bird: Robin (1949)
State animal: Badger; "wild life" animal: white-tailed deer (1957); "domestic" animal: dairy cow (1971)
State insect: Honeybee (1977)
State fish: Musky (Muskellunge) (1955)
State song: "On Wisconsin"
State mineral: Galena (1971)
State rock: Red Granite (1971)
State symbol of peace: Mourning Dove (1971)
State soil: Antigo Silt Loam (1983)
State fossil: Trilobite (1985)
State dog: American Water Spaniel (1986)
State beverage: Milk (1988)
Nickname: Badger State
Origin of name: French corruption of an Indian word whose meaning is disputed
1980 population (1980 census) & (rank): 4,705,767 (16)
1989 est. population (July 1) & (rank): 4,867,000 (17)
1991 proj. population: 4,812,000
1980 land area & (rank): 54,426 sq mi. (140,964 sq km) (25)
Geographic center: In Wood Co., 9 mi. SE of Marshfield
Number of counties: 72
Largest cities (1980 census): Milwaukee, 636,236; Madison, 170,616; Green Bay, 87,899; Racine, 85,725; Kenosha, 77,685; West Allis, 63,982; Appleton, 58,913
State forests: 9 (476,000 ac.)
State parks & scenic trails: 49 parks, 13 trails (66,185 ac.)
1989 percent pop. below age 18: 25.8
1989 percent pop. age 65 and over: 13.4
Est. Black population (1985): 204,000
Est. Hispanic population (1985): 66,000
1987-88 Est. total net migration & (rate): 19,330 (4.0%)
1987-88 (fiscal year) legal immigrants: 2,912

The Wisconsin region was first explored for France by Jean Nicolet, who landed at Green Bay in 1634. In 1660 a French trading post and Roman Catholic mission were established near present-day Ashland.

Great Britain obtained the region in settlement of the French and Indian War in 1763; the U.S. acquired it in 1783 after the Revolutionary War. However, Great Britain retained actual control until after the War of 1812. The region was successively governed as part of the territories of Indiana, Illinois, and Michigan between 1800 and 1836, when it became a separate territory.

Wisconsin leads the nation in milk and cheese production. In 1988 the state ranked first in the number of milk cows (1,740,000) and produced 17.5% of the nation's total output of milk. Other important farm products are peas, beans, corn, potatoes, oats, hay, and cranberries.

The chief industrial products of the state are automobiles, machinery, furniture, paper, beer, and processed foods. Wisconsin ranks second among the 47 paper-producing states.

Wisconsin pioneered in social legislation, providing pensions for the blind (1907), aid to dependent children (1913), and old-age assistance (1925). In labor legislation, the state was the first to enact an unemployment compensation law (1932) and the first in which a workman's compensation law actually took effect. Wisconsin had the first state-wide primary-election law and the first successful income-tax law. In April 1984, Wisconsin became the first state to adopt the Uniform Marital Property Act. The act took effect on January 1, 1986.

The state has over 8,500 lakes, of which Winnebago is the largest. Water sports, ice-boating, and fishing are popular, as are skiing and hunting. Public parks and forests take up one seventh of the land, with 49 state parks, 9 state forests, 13 state trails, 3 recreational areas, and 2 national forests.

Among the many points of interest are the Apostle Islands National Lakeshore; Ice Age National Scientific Reserve; the Circus World Museum at Baraboo; the Wolf, St. Croix, and Lower St. Croix national scenic riverways; and the Wisconsin Dells.

WYOMING

Capital: Cheyenne
Governor: Michael J. Sullivan, D (to Jan. 1991)
Secy. of State: Kathy Karpan, D (to Jan. 1991)
Auditor: Jack Sidi, R (to Jan. 1991)
Treasurer: Stanford S. Smith, R (to Jan. 1991)
Atty. General: Joseph B. Meyer, D (apptd. by Governor)
Organized as territory: May 19, 1869
Entered Union & (rank): July 10, 1890 (44)
Present constitution adopted: 1890
Motto: Equal rights (1955)
State flower: Indian paintbrush (1917)
State tree: Cottonwood (1947)
State bird: Meadow lark (1927)
State gemstone: Jade (1967)
State insignia: Bucking horse (unofficial)
State song: "Wyoming" (1955)
Nickname: Equality State
Origin of name: From the Delaware Indian word, meaning "mountains and valleys alternating"; the same as the Wyoming Valley in Pennsylvania
1980 population (1980 census) & (rank): 469,557 (49)
1989 est. population (July 1) & (rank): 475,000 (50)
1991 proj. population: 501,000
1980 land area & (rank): 96,989 sq mi. (251,201 sq km) (9)
Geographic center: In Fremont Co., 58 mi. ENE of Lander
Number of counties: 23, plus Yellowstone National Park
Largest cities (1980 census): Casper, 51,016; Cheyenne, 47,283; Laramie, 24,410; Rock Springs, 19,458;

Sheridan, 15,146; Green River, 12,807; Gillette, 12,134
State forests: None
State parks: 9 (44,732 ac.)
1989 percent pop. below age 18: 28.6
1989 percent pop. age 65 and over: 9.8
Est. Black population (1985): 4,000
Est. Hispanic population (1985): 27,000
1987-88 Est. total net migration & (rate): −4,494 (−9.3%)
1987-88 (fiscal year) legal immigrants: 261

The U.S. acquired the territory from France as part of the Louisiana Purchase in 1803. John Colter, a fur-trapper, is the first white man known to have entered present Wyoming. In 1807 he explored the Yellowstone area and brought back news of its geysers and hot springs.

Robert Stuart pioneered the Oregon Trail across Wyoming in 1812–13 and, in 1834, Fort Laramie, the first permanent trading post in Wyoming, was built. Western Wyoming was obtained by the U.S. in the 1846 Oregon Treaty with Great Britain and as a result of the treaty ending the Mexican War in 1848.

When the Wyoming Territory was organized in 1869 Wyoming women became the first in the nation to obtain the right to vote. In 1925 Mrs. Nellie Tayloe Ross was elected first woman governor in the United States.

Wyoming's towering mountains and vast plains provide spectacular scenery, grazing lands for sheep and cattle, and rich mineral deposits.

Mining, particularly oil and natural gas, is the most important industry. In 1990, Wyoming led the nation in sodium carbonate (natrona) and bentonite production, and was second in uranium.

Wyoming ranks second among the states in wool production. In January 1989, its sheep numbered 837,000, exceeded only by Texas and California; it also had 1,330,000 cattle. Principal crops include wheat, oats, sugar beets, corn, potatoes, barley, and alfalfa.

Second in mean elevation to Colorado, Wyoming has many attractions for the tourist trade, notably Yellowstone National Park. Cheyenne is famous for its annual "Frontier Days" celebration. Flaming Gorge, the Fort Laramie National Historic Site, and Devils Tower and Fossil Butte National Monuments are other National points of interest.

Self-Governing Areas

PUERTO RICO

Capital: San Juan
Governor: Rafael Hernández-Colón, Popular Democratic Party
Song: "La Borinqueña"
1980 population: 3,196,520
1989 population (July): 3,300,707 (growth rate 0.2%)
1989 net migration rate: −10 migrants per 1,000 population
Language: Spanish (official), English is understood.
Literacy rate: 89%
Labor force (1988): 1,062,000; 23% government, 20% trade, 18% manufacturing, 4% agriculture, 35% other.
Ethnic divisions: Almost entirely Hispanic.
Largest cities (1980 census): San Juan, 424,600; Bayamón, 185,087; Ponce, 161,739; Carolina, 147,835, Caguas, 87,214; Mayagüez, 82,968

Puerto Rico is an island about 100 miles long and 35 miles wide at the northeastern end of the Caribbean Sea. It is a self-governing Commonwealth freely and voluntarily associated with the U.S. Under its Constitution, a Governor and a Legislative Assembly are elected by direct vote for a four-year period. The judiciary is vested in a Supreme Court and lower courts established by law. The people elect a Resident Commissioner to the U.S. House of Representatives, where he has a voice but no vote. The island was formerly an unincorporated territory of the U.S. after being ceded by Spain as a result of the Spanish-American War.

The Commonwealth, established in 1952, has one of the highest standards of living in Latin America. Featuring Puerto Rican economic development is Operation Bootstrap. There are now over 1,600 manufacturing plants which have been created by this program. It has also greatly increased transportation and communications facilities, electric power, housing, and other industries.

The island's chief exports are chemicals, apparel, fish products and electronic products.

Columbus discovered the island on his second voyage to America in 1493.

The U.S. Congress is considering two bills, S.712 and HR 4765, that would allow Puerto Ricans to choose either statehood, independence, or continued commonwealth status. A plebiscite will be held June 4, 1991.

GUAM

Capital: Agaña
Governor: Joseph F. Ada
1980 population: 105,979
1980 land area: 209 sq mi. (541 sq km)
1989 population (July): 138,093 (growth rate 2.8%)
1989 net migration: 7 migrants per 1,000 population
Ethnic divisions: Chamorro, 50%; Filipino, 25%; Caucasian, 10%; Chinese, Japanese, Korean, and other, 15%
Language: English and Chamorro, most residents bilingual;

Japanese also widely spoken
Literacy rate: 90%
Labor force (1986): 42,000; 45% government, 55% other

Guam, the largest of the Mariana Islands, is independent of the trusteeship assigned to the U.S. in 1947. It was acquired by the U.S. from Spain in 1898 (occupied 1899) and was placed under the Navy Department.

In World War II, Guam was seized by the Japanese on Dec. 11, 1941; but on July 21, 1944, it was once more in U.S. hands.

On Aug. 1, 1950, President Truman signed a bill which granted U.S. citizenship to the people of Guam and established self-government. However, the people do not vote in national elections. In 1972 Guam elected its first delegate to the U.S. Congress. The Executive Branch of the Guam government is under the general supervision of the U.S. Secretary of the Interior. In November 1970, Guam elected its first Governor.

Military installations and tourism are important factors in Guam's economy.

Non-Self-Governing Territories

AMERICAN SAMOA

Capital: Pago Pago
Governor: Peter T. Coleman
Lieut. Governor: Galeai Poumele
1986 population: 36,260
1989 population (July): 40,625 (growth rate 2.7%)
1989 net migration rate: −11 migrants per 1,000 population
Ethnic divisions: Samoan (Polynesian) 90%; Caucasian, 2%; Tongan 2%; other 6%
Language: Samoan (closely related to Hawaiian and other Polynesian languages) and English; most people are bilingual
Literacy rate: 99%
Labor force (1986): 10,000; 48% government, 33% tuna canneries, 19% other
1980 land area: 77 sq mi (199 sq km)

American Samoa, a group of five volcanic islands and two coral atolls located some 2,600 miles south of Hawaii in the South Pacific Ocean, is an unincorporated, unorganized territory of the U.S., administered by the Department of the Interior.

By the Treaty of Berlin, signed Dec. 2, 1899, and ratified Feb. 16, 1900, the U.S. was internationally acknowledged to have rights extending over all the islands of the Samoa group east of longitude 171° west of Greenwich. On April 17, 1900, the chiefs of Tutuila and Aunu'u ceded those islands to the U.S. In 1904, the King and chiefs of Manu'a ceded the islands of Ofu, Olosega and Tau (composing the Manu'a group) to the U.S. Swains Island, some 214 miles north of Samoa, was included as part of the territory by Act of Congress March 4, 1925; and on Feb. 20, 1929, Congress formally accepted sovereignty over the entire group and placed the responsibility for administration in the hands of the President. From 1900 to 1951, by Presidential direction, the Department of the Navy governed the territory. On July 1, 1951, administration was transferred to the Department of the Interior. The first Constitution for the territory was signed on

April 27, 1960, and became effective on Oct. 17, 1960. It was revised in 1967.

Congress has provided for a non-voting delegate to sit in the House of Representatives in 1981.

The principal products are canned tuna, pet food, fish meal, mats, and handicrafts.

BAKER, HOWLAND, AND JARVIS ISLANDS

These Pacific islands were not to play a role in the extraterritorial plans of the U.S. until May 13, 1936. President F. D. Roosevelt, at that time, placed them under the control and jurisdiction of the Secretary of the Interior for administration purposes.

The three islands have a tropical climate with scant rainfall, constant wind, and a burning sun.

Baker Island is a saucer-shaped atoll with an area of approximately one square mile. It is about 1,650 miles from Hawaii.

Howland Island, 36 miles to the northwest, is approximately one and a half miles long and half a mile wide. It is a low-lying, nearly level, sandy, coral island surrounded by a narrow fringing reef.

Jarvis Island is several hundred miles to the east and is approximately one and three quarter miles long by one mile wide. It is a sandy coral island surrounded by a a narrow fringing reef.

Baker, Howland, and Jarvis have been uninhabited since 1942. In 1974, these islands became part of the National Wildlife Refuge System, administered by the U.S. Fish & Wildlife Service, Department of the Interior.

CANTON AND ENDERBURY ISLANDS

Canton and Enderbury islands, the largest of the Phoenix group, are jointly administered by the U.S. and Great Britain after an agreement signed April 6, 1939. The status of Canton and Enderbury was the subject of negotiations between the U.S., U.K., and Gilbert Islands Governments in 1979. The negotiations resulted in the signing on September 20, 1979, of a Treaty of Friendship between the U.S. and the Republic of Kiribati. The Republic of Kiribati declared its independence on July 12, 1979.

Canton is triangular in shape and the largest of the eight islands of this group. It lies about 1,600 miles southwest of Hawaii and was discovered at the turn of the 18th century by U.S. whalers. After World War II it served as an aviation support facility, and later as a missile tracking station.

Enderbury is rectangular in shape and is 2.75 miles long by 1 mile wide. It is unpopulated and lies about 35 miles southeast of Canton.

JOHNSTON ATOLL

Johnston is a coral atoll about 700 miles southwest of Hawaii. It consists of four small islands—Johnston Island, Sand Island, Hikina Island, and Akau Island—which lie on a reef about 9 miles long in a northeast-southwest direction.

The atoll was discovered by Capt. Charles James Johnston of *H.M.S. Cornwallis* in 1807. In 1858 it was claimed by Hawaii, and later became a U.S. possession.

Johnston Atoll is a Naval Defense Sea Area and Airspace Reservation and is closed to the public. The administration of Johnston Atoll is under the jurisdiction of the Defense Nuclear Agency, Commander, Johnston Atoll (FCDNA), APO San Francisco, CA 96305.

KINGMAN REEF

Kingman Reef, located about 1,000 miles south of Hawaii, was discovered by Capt. E. Fanning in 1798, but named for Capt. W. E. Kingman, who rediscovered it in 1853. The reef, drying only on its northeast, east and southeast edges, is of atoll character. The reef is triangular in shape, with its apex northward; it is about 9.5 miles long, east and west, and 5 miles wide, north and south, within the 100-fathom curve.

A United States possession, Kingman Reef is a Naval Defense Sea Area and Airspace Reservation, and is closed to the public. The Airspace Entry Control has been suspended, but is subject to immediate reinstatement without notice. No vessel, except those authorized by the Secretary of the Navy, shall be navigated in the area within the 3-mile limit.

MIDWAY ISLANDS

Midway Islands, lying about 1,150 miles west-northwest of Hawaii, were discovered by Captain N. C. Brooks of the Hawaiian bark *Gambia* on July 5, 1859, in the name of the United States. The atoll was formally declared a U.S. possession in 1867, and in 1903 Theodore Roosevelt made it a naval reservation.

Midway Islands consist of a circular atoll, 6 miles in diameter, and enclosing two islands. Eastern Island, on its southeast side, is triangular in shape, and about 1.2 miles long. Sand Island on its south side, is about 2.25 miles long in a northeast-southwest direction.

The Midway Islands are within a Naval Defense Sea Area. The Navy Department maintains an installation and has jurisdiction over the atoll. Permission to enter the Naval Defense Sea Area must be obtained in advance from the Commander Third Fleet (N31), Pearl Harbor, HI 96860.

U.S. VIRGIN ISLANDS

Capital: Charlotte Amalie (on St. Thomas)
Governor: Alexander A. Farrelly
1980 population: 96,569
1986 population: 109,800 (St. Croix, 52,260; St. Thomas, 52,260; St. John, 2,940)
1980 land area: 132 sq mi (342 sq km): St. Croix, 84 sq. mi. (207 sq km), St. Thomas, 32 sq mi (83 sq km), St. John, 20 sq mi. (52 sq km)
1989 population (July): 109,105 (growth rate 1.4%)
1989 net migration rate: −1 migrants per 1,000 population
Ethnic divisions: West Indian, 74% (45% born in the Virgin Islands and 29% born elsewhere in the West Indies), U.S. mainland, 13%; Puerto Rican, 5%; other 8%; black, 80%, white 15%, other 5%; 14% of Hispanic origin.
Language: English (official), but Spanish and Creole are widely spoken.
Literacy rate: 90%
Labor force (1987): 45,000

The Virgin Islands, consisting of nine main islands and some 75 islets, were discovered by Columbus in 1493. Since 1666, England has held six of the main islands; the other three (St. Croix, St. Thomas, and St. John), as well as about 50 of the islets, were eventually acquired by Denmark, which named them the Danish West Indies. In 1917, these islands were purchased by the U.S. from Denmark for $25 million.

Congress granted U.S. citizenship to Virgin Islanders in 1927; and, in 1931, administration was transferred from the Navy to the Department of the Interior. Universal suffrage was given in 1936 to all persons who could read and write the English language. The Governor was elected by popular vote for the first time in 1970; previously he had been appointed by the President of the U.S. A unicameral 15-man legislature serves the Virgin Islands, and Congressional legislation gave the islands a non-voting Representative in Congress.

The "Constitution" of the Virgin Islands is the Revised Organic Act of 1954 in which the U.S. Congress defines the three branches of the territorial government, i.e., the Executive Branch, the Legislative Branch, and the Judicial Branch. Residents of the islands substantially enjoy the same rights as those enjoyed by mainlanders with one important exception: citizens of the U.S. who are residents may not vote in presidential elections.

There is limited farming, fishing, and cattle raising. Industrial products include rum, watches, costume jewelry, pharmaceuticals, and petroleum products. Tourism is the principal industry.

WAKE ISLAND

Wake Island, about halfway between Midway and Guam, is an atoll comprising the three islets of Wilkes, Peale, and Wake. They were discovered by the British in 1796 and annexed by the U.S. in 1899. The entire area comprises 3 square miles and has no native population. In 1938, Pan American Airways established a seaplane base and Wake Island has been used as a commercial base since then. On Dec. 8, 1941, it was attacked by the Japanese, who finally took possession on Dec. 23. It was surrendered by the Japanese on Sept. 4, 1945.

The President, acting pursuant to the Hawaii Omnibus Act, assigned responsibility for Wake to the Secretary of the Interior in 1962. The Department of Transportation exercised civil administration of Wake through an agreement with the Department of the Interior until June 1972, at which time the Department of the Air Force assumed responsibility for the Territory.

Trust Territory of the Pacific Islands (Micronesia)

In 1885, Germany assumed a protectorate over the Marshall Islands; and, in 1899, she purchased the Northern Mariana and Caroline Islands from Spain. These islands were occupied by the Japanese in 1914 and were mandated to Japan by the League of Nations in 1919. On April 2, 1947, the U. N. Security Council approved a trusteeship agreement proposed by the U.S. under which the Northern Mariana, Caroline, and Marshall Islands became a Strategic Trust Territory under the administration of the U.S. The measure was approved by the President, with the agreement of Congress, on July 18, 1947. Administration was transferred from the Navy to the Department of the Interior on July 1, 1951. However, during 1953, administration of the islands of the Northern Marianas, except Rota, was transferred back to the Navy. The Department of the Interior again took over administration of these islands in July, 1962. The 1980 population of the Northern Marianas was 16,780.

In February 1975 a covenant was signed by the U.S. and the Marianas Political Status Commission that would make the 14 islands in the Northern Marianas a commonwealth under American sovereignty. The covenant was overwhelmingly ratified by the people of the islands and was approved by President Ford on March 24, 1976.

On April 9, 1978, in Hilo, Hawaii, the heads of the three Micronesian political status commissions and the U.S. negotiator signed a statement of agreed principles which is intended to form the basis of a free association relationship between the U.S. and Micronesia. Compact of Free Association was signed by the U.S. and the Micronesian commissions in 1982. The terms of the Compact of Free Association between the United States and the Federated States of Micronesia became effective as of November 3, 1986.

The entire group with a 1980 population of 116,149 comprises more than 2,000 islands, but the total land area is only 533 sq mi. (1,381 sq km), many of the islands being only tiny coral reefs.

The Micronesians are the main ethnic group; however, the inhabitants of two outlying islands, Kapingamarangi and Nukuoro, are Polynesian. The population of the Trust Territory in 1980 was estimated to be 116,974.

CAROLINE ISLANDS

The Caroline Islands, east of the Philippines and south of the Marianas, include the Yap, Truk, and the Palau groups and the islands of Ponape and Kusqie, as well as many coral atolls.

The islands are composed chiefly of volcanic rock, and their peaks rise 2,000 to 3,000 feet above sea level. Chief exports of the islands are copra, fish products, and handicrafts.

MARIANA ISLANDS

The Mariana Islands, east of the Philippines and south of Japan, include the islands of Guam, Rota, Saipan, Tinian, Pagan, Guguan, Agrihan, and Aguijan. Guam, the largest, is independent of the trusteeship, having been acquired by the U.S. from Spain in 1898. (For more information, *see* the entry on Guam in this section.) The remaining islands, referred to as the Commonwealth of the Northern Mariana Islands became part of the Unites States pursuant to P.L. 94-241 as of November 3, 1986.

Chief crops are copra and fresh fruits and vegetables.

REPUBLIC OF THE MARSHALL ISLANDS

The Government of the United States and the Republic of the Marshall Islands signed a Compact of Free Association on October 15, 1986, which became effective as of October 21, 1986. The termination of the Trusteeship Agreement became effective on November 3, 1986.

The Marshall Islands, east of the Carolines, are divided into two chains: the western or Ralik group, including the atolls Jaluit, Kwajalein, Wotho, Bikini, and Eniwetok; and the eastern or Ratak group, including the atolls Mili, Majuro, Maloelap, Wotje, and Likiep.

The islands are of the coral-reef type and rise only a few feet above sea level. The chief crop is coconuts; exports include copra, tortoise shell, mother-of-pearl, etc.

Bikini and Eniwetok were the scene of several atom-bomb tests after World War II. In April 1977, some 55 original inhabitants, the forerunner of 450 returnees, were resettled after an absence of 30 years.

Tabulated Data on State Governments

State	Governor		Legislature[1]						Highest Court[2]		
	Term, years	Annual salary	Member-ship		Term, yrs.		Salaries of members[5]		Mem-bers	Term, years	Annual salary[6]
			U[3]	L[4]	U[3]	L[4]					
Alabama	4[10]	70,222[16]	35	105	4	4	45.00	per diem[22]	9	6	83,880[6]
Alaska	4	81,648	20	40	4	2	22,140	per annum	5	([8])	85,278
Arizona	4	75,000	30	60	2	2	15,000	per annum	5	6	75,000
Arkansas	4	35,000	35	100	4	2	7,500	per annum[25]	7	8	67,660[6]

State	Governor Term, years	Governor Annual salary	Legislature[1] Membership U[3]	L[4]	Term, yrs U[3]	L[4]	Salaries of members[5]	Highest Court[2] Members	Term, years	Annual salary[6]
California	4	85,000	40	80	4	2	40,816[32] per annum	7	([30])	115,161[6]
Colorado	4	70,000	35	65	4	2	17,500 per annum	7	10	72,000[6]
Connecticut	4	78,000	36	151	2	2	16,760 per biennium	7	8	100,621[6]
Delaware	4[9]	80,000	21	41	4	2	22,173 per annum	5	12	98,700
Florida	4[10]	100,883.40	40	120	4	2	21,684 per annum	7	6	97,518
Georgia	4[9]	88,872	56	180	2	2	10,379.76 per annum	7	6	90,514
Hawaii	4	94,780	25	51	4	2	27,000[33] per year	5	10	78,500[6]
Idaho	4	55,000	42	84	2	2	30 per diem[34]	5	6	65,874
Illinois	4	93,266	59	118	4-2	2	35,661 per annum	7	10	93,266
Indiana	4[10]	77,200	50	100	4	2	11,600 per annum	5	([24])	66,000[6]
Iowa	4	72,500	50	100	4	2	16,000 per annum	9	8	78,900[6]
Kansas*	4	65,000	40	125	4	2	120 per diem[22]	7	6	59,143[31]
Kentucky	4[7]	74,649	38	100	4	2	100 per diem[22]	7	8	75,313[6]
Louisiana	4	73,440	39	105	4	4	16,800 per annum	7	10	66,566
Maine	4	70,000[16]	35	151	2	2	10,500 per annum[16]	7	7	77,300
Maryland	4[10]	120,000	47	141	4	4	27,000[5] per annum	7	10	99,000[6]
Massachusetts	4	75,000	40	160	6	2	45,000 per annum	7*	([13])*	90,450[6]
Michigan	4	106,690[16]	38	110	4	2	45,450[16] per annum[16]	7	8	106,610
Minnesota	4	91,460	67	134	4	2	26,395 per annum[16]	9	6	73,981[6]
Mississippi	4	63,000	52	122	4	4	10,000 per session[5]	9	8	59,000
Missouri	4[10]	88,541	34	163	4	2	22,414 per annum[5]	7	12	85,602
Montana	4	53,006	50	100	4	2	52.13 per diem[16]	6	8	50,452[6]
Nebraska	4[10]	65,000	49[11]	—	4[11]	—	12,000 per annum	7	6	77,000
Nevada	4	90,000	21	42	4	2	7,800 per biennium	5	6	85,000
New Hampshire	2	75,753	24	([12])	2	2	200 per biennium	5	([13])	86,625[6]
New Jersey	4[10]	85,000	40	80	4[14]	2	35,000[36] per annum	7	7[15]	93,000[6]
New Mexico	4[7]	63,000	42	70	4	2	75 per diem	5	8	75,000
New York	4	130,000	61	150	2	2	57,500 per annum	7	14	115,000[6]
North Carolina	4[9]	116,316[16]	50	120	2	2	11,124 per annum[16]	7	8	84,456[6]
North Dakota	4	65,200[16]	53	106	4	2	90 per diem[16][23]	5	10	62,306[6]
Ohio	4	100,000	33	99	4	2	40,407 per annum	7	6	96,350
Oklahoma	4	70,000	48	101	4	2	32,000[16] per annum	([19])	6	71,406[6]
Oregon	4[10]	75,000	30	60	4	2	937[31] per annum	7	6	74,172[6]
Pennsylvania	4[10]	105,000	50	203	4	2	47,000 per annum	7	10	91,500
Rhode Island	2	69,900	50	100	2	2	5 per diem[17]	5	([18])	99,560
South Carolina	4	84,897	46	124	4	2	10,000 per annum	5	10	83,883[6]
South Dakota	4[10]	60,816	35	70	2	2	8,000 per biennium	5	3[27]	64,700
Tennessee	4	85,000	33	99	4	2	16,500 per annum	5	8	85,500[26]
Texas	4	93,432	31	150	4	2	7,200[5] per annum	([20])	9	82,000
Utah	4	72,800	29	75	4	2	65 per diem[16]	5	10	75,000[6]
Vermont	2	75,800	30	150	2	2	480 per week[21]	5	6	68,055[6]
Virginia	4[7]	108,000	40	100	4	2	18,000 per annum	7	12	94,907[6]
Washington*	4	93,900	49	98	4	2	15,000 per annum	9	6	82,700
West Virginia	4[10]	72,000	34	100	4	2	6,500[16] per annum	5	12	55,000
Wisconsin	4	86,149	33	99	4	2	31,236 per annum	7	10	82,706
Wyoming	4	70,000	30	64	4	2	75[16] per diem[16]	5	8	66,500

1. General Assembly in Ark., Colo., Conn., Del., Ga., Ind., Ky., Md., Mo., N.C., Ohio, Pa., R.I., S.C., Tenn., Vt., Va., Legislative Assembly in N.D., Ore.; General Court in Mass., N.H.; Legislature in other states. Meets biennially in Calif., Ky., Me., Mont., Nev., N.J., N.C., N.D., Ore., Pa., Texas, Wash. Wyo Legislature meets annually. Regular general session on odd numbered years and a budget session on even numbered years. Ark. G.A. meets every other year for 60 days in odd numbered years.; meets annually in other states. 2. Court of Appeals in Md., N.Y., Supreme Court of Virginia in Va., Supreme Judicial Court in Me., Mass.; Supreme Court in other states. 3. Upper house: Senate in all states. 4. Lower house: Assembly in Calif., Nev., N.Y., Wis.; House of Delegates in Md., Va., W.Va.; General Assembly in N.J.; House of Representatives in other states. 5. Does not include additional payments for expenses, mileage, special sessions, etc., or additional per diem payments beyond salary shown. 6. In some states, Chief Justice receives a higher salary. 7. Cannot succeed himself. 8. Appointed for 3 years; thereafter subject to approval or rejection on a nonpartisan ballot for 10-year term. 9. May serve only 2 terms, consecutive or otherwise. 10. May not serve 3rd consecutive term. 11. Unicameral legislature. 12. Constitutional number: 375–400. 13. Until 70 years old. 14. When term begins in Jan. of 2nd year following U.S. census, term shall be 2 years. 15. 2nd term receive tenure, mandatory retirement at 70. 16. Plus additional expenses. 17. For 60 days only. 18. Term of good behavior. 19. 9 members in Supreme Court, highest in civil cases; 5 in Court of Criminal Appeals. 20. 9 members in Supreme Court, highest in civil cases; 9 in Court of Criminal Appeals. 21. To limit of $11,000 per biennium; $2,000 for special session. 22. When in session. 23. Plus $180 per month when not in session. 24. Appointed for 2 years; thereafter elected popularly for 10-year term. 25. To receive cost of living increase not to exceed 10% in the two year period. 26. Adjusted annually according to increase in Consumer Price Index. 27. Subsequent terms, 8 years. 28. Plus $600 per month whether legislature is in session or not. 29. As of July 1, 1986. 30. Terms vary. 31. Plus $400 monthly when not in session and per diem allowance when in session. 32. As of Dec. 5, 1988. 33. As of Jan. 1, 1989. 34. $30 per day while in session and $15 per day otherwise, plus per diem and mileage. 35. Plus $75,000 allowance for entertaining and other expenses. 36. Each legislator receives $60,000 annually for appointment of personal staff aides. 37. Salary not to exceed one thousand dollars per month. NOTE: An asterisk (*) indicates that up-to-date information has not been provided. *Source: Information Please* questionnaires to the states.

50 Largest Cities of the United States

(According to population estimates, July 1988)

Data supplied by Bureau of the Census and by the cities in response to *Information Please* questionnaires. Ranking of 50 largest cities latest available census data published as of August 1990. Civilian labor force (SMA, Jan. 1990); Percent employed and unemployed (SMA Jan. 1990); Per capita personal income (SMA Sept. 1989).

ALBUQUERQUE, N.M.

Incorporated as city: 1891
Mayor: Louis E. Saavedra (to Dec. 1993)
1988 est. population & rank: 378,480 (36)
1980 population (1980 census) & (rank): 332,336 (44)
Land area: 134.4 sq mi. (347 sq km)
Altitude: 4,958 ft.
Location: Central part of state on Rio Grande River
County: Bernalillo
Churches: 211
City-owned parks: 135
Radio stations: 30
Television stations: 7
1980 CENSUS: Population 65 and over, 8.4%; **under 18,** 27.8%; **Black,** 2.5%; **Spanish, origin,** 33.8%
CIVILIAN LABOR FORCE: 259,900
Unemployed: 11,000, **Percent:** 4.3
Per capita personal income: $15,019
Chamber of Commerce: Greater Albuquerque Chamber of Commerce, 401 2nd St., N.W., Albuquerque, N.M. 87102. Albuquerque Hispano Chamber of Commerce, 1520 Central Ave., S.E., Albuquerque, N.M. 87106

ATLANTA, GA.

Incorporated as city: 1847
Mayor: Maynard Jackson (to Jan. 1994)
1988 est. population & (rank): 420,220 (31)
1980 population (1980 census) & (rank): 425,022 (29)
City land area: 136 sq mi. (352.2 sq km)
Altitude: Highest, 1,050 ft; lowest, 940
Location: In northwest central part of state, near Chattahoochee River
Counties: Fulton and DeKalb
Churches (18-county area): 1,500+
City-owned parks: 277 (3,178 ac.)
Radio stations (18-county area): AM, 7; FM, 20
Television stations (18-county area): 7 commercial; 2 PBS
1980 CENSUS: Population 65 and over, 11.5%; **under 18,** 26.8%; **Black,** 66.6%; **Spanish, origin** 1.4%
CIVILIAN LABOR FORCE: 1,530,400
Unemployed: 76,300, **Percent:** 5
Per capita personal income: $18,400
Chamber of Commerce: Atlanta Chamber of Commerce, 235 International Blvd., Atlanta, Ga. 30301; Information is gathered on the **18-county MSA**

AUSTIN, TEX.

Incorporated as city: 1839
Mayor: Lee Cooke (to May 1991)
1988 est. population & (rank): 464,690 (27)
1980 population (1980 census) & (rank): 345,890 (42)
Land area: 116.0 sq mi. (300 sq km)
Altitude: From 425 ft. to over 1000 ft. elevation
Location: In south central part of state, on the Colorado River
County: Seat of Travis Co.
Churches: 353 churches, representing 45 denominations

City-owned parks and playgrounds: 160 (10,000 ac.)
Radio stations: AM, 6; FM, 12
Television stations: 3 commercial; 1 PBS; 1 independent
1980 CENSUS: Population 65 and over, 7.5%; **under 18,** 24.5%; **Black,** 12.2%; **Spanish, origin** 18.7%
CIVILIAN LABOR FORCE: 428,400
Unemployed: 18,100, **Percent:** 4.2
Per capita personal income: $15,342
Chamber of Commerce: Greater Austin Chamber of Commerce, P.O. Box 1967, Austin, Tex. 78767

BALTIMORE, MD.

Incorporated as city: 1797
Mayor: Kurt L. Schmoke (to Dec. 1991)
1988 est. population & (rank): 751,400 (11)
1980 population (1980 census) & (rank): 786,741 (10)
Land area: 80.3 sq mi. (208 sq km)
Altitude: Highest, 490 ft; lowest, sea level
Location: On Patapsco River, about 12 mi. from Chesapeake Bay
County: Independent city
Churches: Roman Catholic, 72; Jewish, 50; Protestant and others, 344
City-owned parks: 347 park areas and tracts (6,314 ac.)
Radio stations: AM, 11; FM, 9
Television stations: 7
1980 CENSUS: Population 65 and over, 12.8%; **under 18,** 26.9%; **Black,** 54.8%; **Spanish, origin,** 1.0%
CIVILIAN LABOR FORCE: 1,196,100
Unemployed: 54,000, **Percent:** 5.4
Per capita personal income: $19,010
Chamber of Commerce: Greater Baltimore Committee, 111 S. Calvert St., Ste. 1500, Baltimore, MD 21202

BOSTON, MASS.

Incorporated as city: 1822
Mayor: Raymond L. Flynn (to Jan. 1992)
1988 est. population & (rank): 577,830 (19)
1980 population (1980 census) & (rank): 562,994 (20)
Land area: 47.2 sq mi. (122 sq km)
Altitude: Highest, 330 ft; lowest, sea level
Location: On Massachusetts Bay, at mouths of Charles and Mystic Rivers
County: Seat of Suffolk Co.
Churches: Protestant, 187; Roman Catholic, 72; Jewish, 28; others, 100
City-owned parks, playgrounds, etc.: 2,276.36 ac.
Radio stations: AM, 9; FM, 12
Television stations: 10
1980 CENSUS: Population 65 and over, 12.7%; **under 18,** 21.6%; **Black,** 22.4%; **Spanish, origin,** 6.4%
CIVILIAN LABOR FORCE: 1,538,800[1]
Unemployed: 62,700[1], **Percent:** 4.1[1]
Per capita personal income: $20,355

Chamber of Commerce: Boston Chamber of Commerce, 600 Atlantic Ave., Boston, Mass. 02210
1. Boston-Lawrence-Salem-Lowell-Brockton NECMA.

BUFFALO, N.Y.

Incorporated as city: 1832
Mayor: James Griffin (to Dec. 1993)
1988 est. population & (rank): 313,570 (50)
1980 population (1980 census) & (rank): 357,870 (39)
Land area: 42.67 sq. mi. (109 sq. km)
Altitude: Highest 705 ft; lowest 571.84 ft;
Location: At east end of Lake Erie, on Niagara River
County: Seat of Erie Co.
Churches: 60 denominations, with over 1,100 churches
County-owned parks: 9 public parks (3,000 ac.)
Radio stations: AM 10; FM 13
Television stations: 8 (plus reception from 3 Canadian Stations)
1980 CENSUS: Population 65 and over, 15.0%; under 18, 25.2%; **Black,** 26.6%; **Spanish, origin,** 2.7%
CIVILIAN LABOR FORCE: 458,700
Unemployed: 24,700, **Percent:** 5.4
Per capita personal income: $16,342
Chamber of Commerce: Greater Buffalo Chamber of Commerce, 107 Delaware Avenue, Buffalo, NY 14202

CHARLOTTE, N.C.

Incorporated as city: 1768
Mayor: Sue Myrick (to Nov. 1991)
1988 est. population & (rank): 367,860 (42)
1980 population (1980 census) & (rank): 315,474 (47)
1990 est. population: 390,000
Land area: 172.1 sq mi. (446 sq km)
Altitude: 765 ft
Location: In the southern part of state near the border of South Carolina
County: Seat of Mecklenburg Co.
Churches: Protestant, over 400; Roman Catholic, 8; Jewish, 3; Greek Orthodox, 1
City-owned parks and parkways: 113
Radio stations: AM, 8; FM, 12
Television stations: 4 commercial; 2 PBS
1980 CENSUS: Population 65 and over, 8.6%; under 18, 27.8%; **Black,** 31.0%; **Spanish, origin,** 1.1%
CIVILIAN LABOR FORCE: 639,500[1]
Unemployed: 23,800,[1] **Percent:** 3.7[1]
Per capita personal income: $16,348[1]
Chamber of Commerce: Charlotte Chamber, P.O. Box 32785, Charlotte, N.C., 28232
1. Charlotte-Gastonia Rock Hill, NC-SC.

CHICAGO, ILL.

Incorporated as city: 1837
Mayor: Richard M. Daley (to April 1991)
1988 est. population & (rank): 2,977,520 (3)
1980 population (1980 census) & (rank): 3,005,072 (2)
Land area: 228.475 sq mi. (591.1 sq km)
Altitude: Highest, 672 ft; lowest, 578.5
Location: On lower west shore of Lake Michigan
County: Seat of Cook Co.
Churches: Protestant, 850; Roman Catholic, 252; Jewish, 51
City-owned parks: 563
Radio stations: AM, 17; FM, 23
Television stations: 12
1980 CENSUS: Population 65 and over, 11.4%; under 18,

28.4%; **Black,** 39.8%; **Spanish, origin,** 14.0%
CIVILIAN LABOR FORCE: 3,305,500[1]
Unemployed: 203,200[1], **Percent:** 6.1[1]
Per capita personal income: $19,060
Chamber of Commerce: Chicago Association of Commerce & Industry, 200 N. LaSalle, Chicago, Ill. 60601
1. PMSA.

CINCINNATI, OHIO

Incorporated as city: 1819
Mayor: Charles Luken (to Nov. 1991)
City Manager: Scott Johnson
1988 est. population & (rank): 370,480 (40)
1980 population (1980 census) & (rank): 385,410 (32)
Land area: 78.1 sq mi. (202 sq km)
Altitude: Highest, 960 ft; lowest, 441
Location: In southwestern corner of state on Ohio River
County: Seat of Hamilton Co.
Churches: 850
City-owned parks: 96 (4,345 ac.)
Radio stations: AM, 9; FM, 15 (Greater Cincinnati)
Television stations: 6
1980 CENSUS: Population 65 and over, 14.5%; under 18, 25.2%; **Black,** 33.8%; **Spanish, origin,** 0.8%
CIVILIAN LABOR FORCE: 779,700[1]
Unemployed: 39,400[1], **Percent:** 5.1[1]
Per capita personal income: $16,633[1]
Chamber of Commerce: Cincinnati Chamber of Commerce, 120 W Fifth St., Cincinnati, Ohio 45202
1. PMSA.

CLEVELAND, OHIO

Incorporated as city: 1836
Mayor: Michael R. White (to Dec. 1993)
1988 est. population & (rank): 521,370 (22)
1980 population (1980 census) & (rank): 573,822 (18)
Land area: 79.0 sq mi. (205 sq km)
Altitude: Highest, 1048 ft; lowest, 573
Location: On Lake Erie at mouth of Cuyahoga River
County: Seat of Cuyahoga Co.
Churches: [1] Protestant, 980; Roman Catholic, 187; Jewish, 31; Eastern Orthodox, 22
City-owned parks: 41 (1,930 ac.)
Radio stations: AM, 15; FM, 17
Television stations: 7
1980 CENSUS: Population 65 and over, 13.0%; under 18, 27.8%; **Black,** 43.8%; **Spanish, origin,** 3.1%
CIVILIAN LABOR FORCE: 945,100[1]
Unemployed: 57,100[1], **Percent:** 6.0[1]
Per capita personal income: $18,168[1]
Chamber of Commerce: Greater Cleveland Growth Association, 690 Huntington Building, Cleveland, Ohio 44115
1. PMSA.

COLUMBUS, OHIO

Incorporated as city: 1834
Mayor: Dana G. Rinehart (to Jan. 1992)
1988 est. population & (rank): 569,570 (20)
1980 population (1980 census) & (rank): 565,032 (19)
Land area: 193.5 sq mi. (500 sq km)
Altitude: Highest, 902 ft; lowest, 702
Location: In central part of state, on Scioto River
County: Seat of Franklin Co.
Churches: Protestant, 436; Roman Catholic, 62; Jewish, 5;

Other, 8
City-owned parks: 407 (12,070 ac.)
Radio stations: AM, 10; FM, 16
Television stations: 8 commercial, 3 PBS
1980 CENSUS: Population 65 and over, 8.9%; **under 18,** 25.8%; **Black,** 22.1%; **Spanish, origin,** 0.8%
CIVILIAN LABOR FORCE: 727,200
Unemployed: 42,900, **Percent:** 5.9
Per capita personal income: $16,251
Chamber of Commerce: Columbus Area Chamber of Commerce, P.O. Box 1527, Columbus, Ohio 43216

DALLAS, TEX.

Incorporated as city: 1856
Mayor: Annette Strauss (to April 1991)
City Manager: Jan Hart (apptd. April 1990)
1988 est. population & (rank): 987,360 (8)
1980 population (1980 census) & (rank): 904,599 (7)
Land area: 378 sq mi. (979 sq km)
Altitude: Highest, 750 ft; lowest, 375
Location: In northeastern part of state, on Trinity River
County: Seat of Dallas Co.
Churches: 1,974 (in Dallas Co.)
City-owned parks: 296 (47,025 ac.)
Radio stations: AM, 19; FM, 30
Television stations: 10 commercial, 1 PBS
1980 CENSUS: Population 65 and over, 9.5%; **under 18,** 27.0%; **Black,** 29.4%; **Spanish, origin,** 12.3%
CIVILIAN LABOR FORCE: 1,431,400
Unemployed: 64,600, **Percent:** 4.5
Per capita personal income: $18,580
Chamber of Commerce: Dallas Chamber of Commerce, 1201 Elm, Dallas, Tex. 75270

DENVER, COLO.

Incorporated as city: 1861
Mayor: Federico Pena (to July 1991)
1988 est. population & (rank): 494,200 (25)
1980 population (1980 census) & (rank): 492,694 (24)
Land area: 110.6 sq mi. (287 sq km)
Altitude: Highest, 5,470 ft; lowest, 5,130
Location: In northeast central part of state, on South Platte River
County: Coextensive with Denver Co.
Churches:[1] Protestant, 815; Roman Catholic, 63; Jewish, 13
City-owned parks: 155 (3,600 ac.)
City-owned mountain parks: 40 (13,448 ac.)
Radio stations: AM, 18; FM, 13[1]
Television stations: 5
1980 CENSUS: Population 65 and over, 12.6%; **under 18,** 22.5%; **Black,** 12.0%; **Spanish, origin,** 18.8%
CIVILIAN LABOR FORCE: 874,100
Unemployed: 43,400, **Percent:** 5.0
Per capita personal income: $18,155
Chamber of Commerce: Denver Chamber of Commerce, 1301 Welton, Denver, Colo. 80204
1. Metropolitan area.

DETROIT, MICH.

Incorporated as city: 1815
Mayor: Coleman A. Young (to Jan. 1994)
1988 est. population & (rank): 1,035,920 (7)

1980 population (1980 census) & (rank): 1,203,369 (6)
Land area: 143 sq mi. (370 sq km)
Altitude: Highest, 685 ft; lowest, 574
Location: In southeastern part of state, on Detroit River
County: Seat of Wayne Co.
Churches:[1] Protestant, 1,165; Roman Catholic, 89; Jewish, 2
City-owned parks: 56 parks (3,843 ac.); 393 sites (5,838 ac.)
Radio stations: AM, 27; FM, 30 (includes 3 in Windsor, Ont.)
Television stations: 8[2] (includes 1 in Windsor, Ont.)
1980 CENSUS: Population 65 and over, 11.7%; **under 18,** 30.3%; **Black,** 63.1%; **Spanish, origin,** 2.4%
CIVILIAN LABOR FORCE: 2,172,600
Unemployed: 189,200, **Percent:** 8.7
Per capita personal income: $18,554
Chamber of Commerce: Greater Detroit Chamber of Commerce, 622 W. Lafayette, Detroit, Mich. 48226
1. Six-county metropolitan area. 2. Within four counties of Metro Detroit.

EL PASO, TEX.

Incorporated as city: 1873
Mayor: Suzanne F. Azar (to June 1991)
1988 est. population & (rank): 510,970 (23)
1980 population (1980 census) & (rank): 425,259 (28)
Land area: 247.4 sq mi. (641 sq km)
Altitude: 4,000 ft
Location: In far western part of state, on Rio Grande
County: Seat of El Paso Co.
Churches: Protestant, 320; Roman Catholic, 39; Jewish, 3; others, 20
City-owned parks: 116[1] (1,180 ac.)
Radio stations: AM, 18; FM, 17
Television stations: 6
1980 CENSUS: Population 65 and over, 6.9%; **under 18,** 35.0%; **Black,** 3.2%; **Spanish, origin,** 62.5%
CIVILIAN LABOR FORCE: 249,700
Unemployed: 24,100, **Percent:** 9.7
Per capita personal income: $10,008
Chamber of Commerce: El Paso Chamber of Commerce, 10 Civic Center Plaza, El Paso, Tex. 79944
1. Includes 109 developed and 7 undeveloped parks.

FORT WORTH, TEX.

Incorporated as city: 1873
Mayor: Bob Bolen (to May 1991)
City Manager: David Ivory
1988 est. population & (rank): 426,610 (30)
1980 population (1980 census) & (rank): 385,164 (33)
Land area: 293.03 sq mi. (758.96 sq km)
Altitude: Highest, 780 ft; lowest, 520
Location: In north central part of state, on Trinity River
County: Seat of Tarrant Co.
Churches: Protestant, 392; Roman Catholic, 16; Jewish, 2
City-owned parks: 136 (8,189 ac.; 3,500 ac. in Nature Center)
Radio stations: AM, 6; FM, 8
Television stations: 6 (2 local)
1980 CENSUS: Population 65 and over, 11.8%; **under 18,** 27.1%; **Black,** 22.8%; **Spanish, origin,** 12.6%
CIVILIAN LABOR FORCE: 716,100
Unemployed: 33,400, **Percent:** 4.7
Per capita personal income: $16,551

Chamber of Commerce: Fort Worth Chamber of Commerce, 700 Throckmorton, Fort Worth, Tex. 76102

HONOLULU, HAWAII

Incorporated as city and county: 1907
Mayor: Frank F. Fasi (to Jan. 1993)
1988 est. population & (rank): 376,110 (37)
1980 population (1980 census) & (rank): 367,878 (36)
Land area: 600 sq mi. (1,554 sq km)[1]
Altitude: Highest, 4,025 ft; lowest, sea level
Location: The city and county government's jurisdiction includes the entire island of Oahu
Churches: Roman Catholic, 34; Buddhist, 34; Jewish, 2; Protestant and others, 329
City-owned parks: 5,386 ac.
Radio stations: AM, 15; FM, 13
Television stations: 10
1980 CENSUS: Population 65 and over, 10.4%; **under 18,** 23.1%; **Black,** 1.2%; **Spanish, origin,** 5.2%
CIVILIAN LABOR FORCE: 385,800
Unemployed: 10,400, **Percent:** 2.7
Per capita personal income: $17,540
Chamber of Commerce: Chamber of Commerce of Hawaii, 735 Bishop St., Honolulu, Hawaii 96813
1. City and county area. The census bureau does not include the entire city and county in its census of Honolulu. If it did, the 1980 census and rank would be 762,565 (12).

HOUSTON, TEX.

Incorporated as city: 1837
Mayor: Kathryn J. Whitmire (to Dec. 1991)
1988 est. population & (rank): 1,698,090 (4)
1980 population (1980 census) & (rank): 1,595,138 (5)
Land area: 578.68 sq mi. (1,490 sq km)
Altitude: Highest, 120 ft; lowest, sea level
Location: In southeastern part of state, near Gulf of Mexico
County: Seat of Harris Co.
Churches: 1,750[2]
City-owned parks: 324 (32,500 ac.)
Radio stations: AM, 23; FM, 28[1]
Television stations: 10 commercial, 1 PBS
Poet Laureate: HUY-LUC Khoi Tien Bui
1980 CENSUS: Population 65 and over, 6.9%; **under 18,** 28.4%; **Black,** 27.6%; **Spanish, origin,** 17.6%
CIVILIAN LABOR FORCE: 1,666,900
Unemployed: 79,000, **Percent:** 4.7
Per capita personal income: $16,192
Chamber of Commerce: Greater Houston Partnership, 1100 Milam Building, 25th Fl., Houston, Tex. 77002
1. Includes annexations since 1970. 2. Harris County.

INDIANAPOLIS, IND.

Incorporated as city: 1832 (reincorporated 1838)
Mayor: William H. Hudnut III (to Jan. 1992)
1988 est. population & (rank): 727,130 (14)
1980 population (1980 census) & (rank): 700,807 (12)
Land area: 352.0 sq mi. (912 sq km)
Altitude: Highest, 840 ft; lowest, 700
Location: In central part of the state, on West Fork of White River
County: Seat of Marion Co.
Churches: 1,200[1]
City-owned parks: 134 (10,753 ac.)
Radio stations: AM, 9; FM, 18

Television stations: 7[1]
1980 CENSUS: Population 65 and over, 10.3%; **under 18,** 28.6%; **Black,** 21.8%; **Spanish, origin,** 0.9%
CIVILIAN LABOR FORCE: 682,400
Unemployed: 29,400, **Percent:** 4.3
Per capita personal income: $16,987
Chamber of Commerce: Indianapolis Chamber of Commerce, 320 N Meridian St., Indianapolis, Ind. 46202
1. Marion County.

JACKSONVILLE, FLA.

Incorporated as city: 1822
Mayor: Tommy Hazouri (to July 1, 1991)
1988 est. population & (rank): 635,430 (16)
1980 population (1980 census) & (rank): 540,920 (22)
Land area: 759.6 sq mi. (1,967 sq km)
Altitude: Highest, 71 ft; lowest, sea level
Location: On St. Johns River, 20 miles from Atlantic Ocean
County: Duval
Churches: Protestant, 762; Roman Catholic, 27; Jewish, 5; others, 23
City-owned parks and playgrounds: 138 (1,522 ac.)
Radio stations: AM, 16; FM, 12
Television stations: 6 commercial, 1 PBS
1980 CENSUS: Population 65 and over, 9.6%; **under 18,** 28.8%; **Black,** 25.4%; **Spanish, origin,** 1.8%
CIVILIAN LABOR FORCE: 446,600
Unemployed: 27,300, **Percent:** 6.1
Per capita personal income: $15,452
Chamber of Commerce: Jacksonville Area Chamber of Commerce, Jacksonville, Fla. 32202

KANSAS CITY, MO.

Incorporated as city: 1850
Mayor: Richard L. Berkley (to April 10, 1991)
City Manager: David H. Olson (apptd. Nov. 1984)
1988 est. population & (rank): 438,950 (28)
1980 population (1980 census) & (rank): 448,028 (27)
Land area: 317.00 sq mi. (819 sq km)
Altitude: Highest, 1,014 ft; lowest, 722
Location: In western part of state, at juncture of Missouri and Kansas Rivers
County: Located in Jackson, Clay, and Platte & Cass Co.
Churches: 1,100 churches of all denominations
City-owned parks and playgrounds: 177 (7,646 ac.)
Radio stations: AM, 14; FM, 13[1]
Television stations: 6[1]
1980 CENSUS: Population 65 and over, 12.3%; **under 18,** 26.5%; **Black,** 27.4%; **Spanish, origin,** 3.3%
CIVILIAN LABOR FORCE: 847,800
Unemployed: 50,400, **Percent:** 5.9
Per capita personal income: $17,078
Chamber of Commerce: Chamber of Commerce of Greater Kansas City, 920 Main St., Kansas City, Mo. 64105
1. Metropolitan area.

LONG BEACH, CALIF.

Incorporated as city: 1888
Mayor: Ernie Kell (to third Tuesday of 1994)
City Manager: James C. Hankla
1988 est. population & (rank): 415,040 (33)
1980 population (1980 census) & (rank): 361,496 (37)

Land area: 49.8 sq mi. (129 sq km)
Altitude: Highest, 170 ft; lowest, sea level
Location: On San Pedro Bay, south of Los Angeles
County: Los Angeles
Churches: 236
City-owned parks: 42 (1,182 ac.)
Radio stations: AM, 2; FM, 2
Television stations: 1 (cable)
1980 CENSUS: Population 65 and over, 14.0%; **under 18,** 22.9%; **Black,** 11.3%; **Spanish, origin,** 14.0%
CIVILIAN LABOR FORCE: 4,373,000[1]
Unemployed: 257,000,[1] **Percent:** 5.9
Per capita personal income: $18,790[1]
Chamber of Commerce: Long Beach Area Chamber of Commerce, P.O. Box 690, Long Beach, CA 90801, (213) 436-1251
1. Los Angeles-Long Beach MSA.

LOS ANGELES, CALIF.

Incorporated as city: 1850
Mayor: Tom Bradley (to June 1993)
1988 est. population & (rank): 3,352,710 (2)
1980 population (1980 census) & (rank): 2,968,528 (3)
Land area: 470 sq mi. (1,217 sq km)
Altitude: Highest, 5,081 ft; lowest, sea level
Location: In southwestern part of state, on Pacific Ocean
County: Seat of Los Angeles Co.
Churches: 2,000 of all denominations
City-owned parks: 355 (15,357 ac.)
Radio stations: AM, 35; FM, 53
Television stations: 18
1980 CENSUS: Population 65 and over, 10.6%; **under 18,** 25.1%; **Black,** 17.0%; **Spanish, origin,** 27.5%
CIVILIAN LABOR FORCE: 4,373,000[1]
Unemployed: 257,000,[1] **Percent:** 5.9[1]
Per capita personal income: $18,790[1]
Chamber of Commerce: Los Angeles Chamber of Commerce, 404 S Bixel St., Los Angeles, Calif. 90017
1. Los Angeles-Long Beach MSA.

MEMPHIS, TENN.

Incorporated as city: 1826
Mayor: Richard C. Hackett (to Dec. 1991)
1988 est. population & (rank): 645,190 (15)
1980 population (1980 census) & (rank): 646,170 (14)
Land area: 281 sq mi. (751.30 sq km)
Altitude: Highest, 331 ft
Location: In southwestern corner of state, on Mississippi River
County: Seat of Shelby Co.
Churches: 800
Parks and playgrounds: 172 (5,363 ac.)
Radio stations: AM, 12; FM, 8
Television stations: 6
1980 CENSUS: Population 65 and over, 10.4%; **under 18,** 29.1%; **Black,** 47.6%; **Spanish, origin,** 0.8%
CIVILIAN LABOR FORCE: 460,500
Unemployed: 20,500, **Percent:** 4.4
Per capita personal income: $15,456
Chamber of Commerce: Memphis Area Chamber of Commerce, P.O. Box 224, Memphis, Tenn. 38103

MIAMI, FLA.

Incorporated as city: 1896
Mayor: Xavier L. Suarez (to Nov. 1993)
City manager: Cesar Odio (apptd. Dec. 1985)

1988 est. population & (rank): 371,100 (39)
1980 population (1980 census) & (rank): 346,681 (41)
Land area: 34.3 sq mi. (89 sq km)
Altitude: Average, 12 ft
Location: In southeastern part of state, on Biscayne Bay
County: Seat of Dade Co.
Churches: Protestant, 258; Roman Catholic, 12; Jewish, 4
City-owned parks: 103
Radio stations: AM, 9; FM, 9
Television stations: 8 commercial, 2 PBS
1980 CENSUS: Population 65 and over, 17.0%; **under 18,** 21.4%; **Black,** 25.1%; **Spanish, origin,** 55.9%
CIVILIAN LABOR FORCE: 934,200[1]
Unemployed: 59,400, **Percent:** 6.4
Per capita personal income: $16,874[1]
Chamber of Commerce: Greater Miami Chamber of Commerce, 1601 Biscayne Blvd., Miami, Fla. 33132
1. Miami-Hialeah PMSA.

MILWAUKEE, WIS.

Incorporated as city: 1846
Mayor: John O. Norquist (to April 1992)
1988 est. population & (rank): 599,380 (18)
1980 population (1980 census) & (rank): 636,298 (16)
Land area: 95.8 sq mi. (248 sq km)
Altitude: 580.60 ft
Location: In southeastern part of state, on Lake Michigan
County: Seat of Milwaukee Co.
Churches: 411
County-owned parks: 14,758 ac.
Radio stations: AM, 15; FM, 8
Television stations: 10
1985 SPECIAL CENSUS: Population 65 and over: 12.8%; **under 18,** 26.6%; **Black,** 25.3%; **Spanish, origin,** 4.6%
CIVILIAN LABOR FORCE: 764,400
Unemployed: 33,500, **Percent:** 4.4
Per capita personal income: $17,880[1]
Chamber of Commerce: Metropolitan Milwaukee Association of Commerce, 828 N. Broadway, Milwaukee, Wis. 53202; Milwaukee Minority Chamber of Commerce, 2821 N. 4th St., Milwaukee, Wis. 53212; Hispanic Chamber of Commerce, 1125 W. National Ave., Milwaukee, Wis. 53204
1. PMSA.

MINNEAPOLIS, MINN.

Incorporated as city: 1867
Mayor: Donald M. Fraser (to Jan. 1994)
1988 est. population & (rank): 344,670 (46)
1980 population (1980 census) & (rank): 370,951 (34)
Land area: 55.1 sq mi. (143 sq km)
Altitude: Highest, 945 ft; lowest, 695
Location: In southeast central part of state, on Mississippi River
County: Seat of Hennepin Co.
Churches: 419
City-owned parks: 153
Radio stations: AM, 17; FM, 15 (metro area)
Television stations: 6 (metro area)
1980 CENSUS: Population 65 and over, 15.4%; **under 18,** 20.0%; **Black,** 7.7%; **Spanish, origin,** 1.3%
CIVILIAN LABOR FORCE: 1,400,800[1]
Unemployed: 48,800, **Percent:** 3.5
Per capita personal income: $19,371
Chamber of Commerce: Greater Minneapolis Chamber of Commerce, 15 S Fifth Street, Minneapolis, Minn. 55402
1. Minneapolis-St. Paul MSA.

NASHVILLE-DAVIDSON, TENN.

Incorporated as city: 1806
Mayor: Bill Boner (to August, 1991)
1988 est. population & (rank): 481,400 (26)
1980 population (1980 census) & (rank): 455,651 (25)
Land area: 533 sq mi. (1,380 sq km)
Altitude: Highest, 1,100 ft; lowest, approx. 400 ft
Location: In north central part of state, on Cumberland River
County: Davidson
Churches: Protestant, 739; Roman Catholic, 15; Jewish, 3
City-owned parks: 72 (6,650 ac.)
Radio stations: AM, 11; FM, 8
Television stations: 7
1980 CENSUS: Population 65 and over, 11.0%; **under 18,** 25.0%; **Black,** 23.3%; **Spanish, origin,** 0.8%
CIVILIAN LABOR FORCE: 524,900
Unemployed: 20,100, **Percent:** 3.8
Per capita personal income: $16,258
Chamber of Commerce: Nashville Area Chamber of Commerce, 161 Fourth Ave. North, Nashville, Tenn. 37219

NEWARK, N.J.

Incorporated as city: 1836
Mayor: Sharpe James (to June 1994)
1988 est. population & (rank): 313,800 (49)
1980 population (1980 census) & (rank): 329,248 (46)
Land area: 24.1 sq mi. (62 sq km)
Altitude: Highest, 273.4 ft; lowest, sea level
Location: In northeastern part of state, on Passaic River and Newark Bay
County: Seat of Essex Co.
Churches: Roman Catholic, 37; Jewish, 2; Protestant and others, 250
City-owned parks: 40 (and 20 mini parks); (39.3 ac.)
County-governed parks in city: 7 (743.97 ac.)
Radio stations: AM, 2; FM, 4
Television stations: 3
1980 CENSUS: Population 65 and over, 8.8%; **under 18,** 34.1%; **Black,** 58.2%; **Spanish, origin,** 18.6%
CIVILIAN LABOR FORCE: 964,900
Unemployed: 50,000, **Percent:** 5.2
Per capita personal income: $22,963[1]
Chamber of Commerce: Greater Newark Chamber of Commerce, 40 Clinton St., Newark, N.J. 07102
1. PMSA.

NEW ORLEANS, LA.

Incorporated as city: 1805
Mayor: Sidney J. Barthelemy (to May 1994)
1988 est. population & (rank): 531,700 (21)
1980 population (1980 census) & (rank): 557,927 (21)
Land area: 199.4 sq mi. (516 sq km)
Altitude: Highest, 15 ft; lowest, −4
Location: In southeastern part of state, between Mississippi River and Lake Ponchartrain
Parish: Seat of Orleans Parish
Churches: 644
City-owned parks: 266 (4,460 ac.)
Radio stations: AM, 12; FM, 13
Television stations: 8
1980 CENSUS: Population 65 and over, 11.7%; **under 18,** 28.8%; **Black,** 55.3%; **Spanish, origin,** 3.4%
CIVILIAN LABOR FORCE: 574,800
Unemployed: 35,300, **Percent:** 6.1
Per capita personal income: $14,034

Chamber of Commerce: The Chamber/New Orleans and the River Region, 301 Camp Street, New Orleans, La. 70130

NEW YORK, N.Y.

Chartered as "Greater New York": 1898
Mayor: David N. Dinkins (to Dec. 31, 1993)
Borough Presidents: Bronx, Fernando Ferrer; Brooklyn, Howard Golden; Manhattan, Ruth W. Messinger; Queens, Claire Shulman; Staten Island, Guy V. Molinari
1988 est. population & (rank): 7,352,700 (1)[1]
1980 population (1980 census) & (rank): 7.071,639 (1)[1]
Land area: 314.7 sq mi. (815 sq km) (Queens, 112.83; Brooklyn, 74.45; Staten Island, 60.06; Bronx, 43.63; Manhattan, 23.73)
Altitude: Highest, 410 ft; lowest, sea level
Location: In south of state, at mouth of Hudson River (also known as the North River as it passes Manhattan)
Counties: Consists of 5 counties: Bronx, Kings (Brooklyn), New York (Manhattan), Queens, Richmond (Staten Island)
Churches: Protestant, 1,766; Jewish, 1,256; Roman Catholic, 437; Orthodox, 66
City-owned parks: 1,701 (26,138 ac.)
Radio stations: AM, 13; FM, 18
Television stations: 6 commercial, 1 public
1980 CENSUS: Population 65 and over, 13.5%; **under 18,** 25.0%; **Black,** 25.2%; **Spanish, origin,** 19.9%
CIVILIAN LABOR FORCE: 3,414,000
Unemployed: 240,000, **Percent:** 7.0
Per capita personal income: $20,396[2]
Chamber of Commerce: New York Chamber of Commerce and Industry, 65 Liberty St., New York, N.Y. 10005
1. For population of boroughs, *see* Index. 2. PMSA.

OAKLAND, CALIF.

Incorporated as city: 1854
Mayor: Lionel J. Wilson (to Jan., 1991)
City Manager: Henry L. Gardner (apptd. June 1981)
1988 est. population & (rank): 356,860 (44)
1980 population (1980 census) & (rank): 339,337 (43)
Land area: 53.9 sq mi.
Altitude: Highest, 1,700 ft; lowest, sea level
Location: In west central part of state, on east side of San Francisco Bay
County: Seat of Alameda Co.
Churches: 374, representing over 78 denominations in the City; over 500 churches in Alameda County
City-owned parks: 2,196 ac.
Radio stations: AM, 3; FM, 2
Television stations: 9 commercial; 3 PBS
1980 CENSUS: Population 65 and over, 13.2%; **under 18,** 24.3%; **Black,** 46.9%; **Spanish, origin,** 9.6%
CIVILIAN LABOR FORCE: 1,003,600
Unemployed: 43,800, **Percent:** 4.0
Per capita personal income: $21,096[1]
Chamber of Commerce: Oakland Chamber of Commerce, 475 Fourteenth St., Oakland, Calif. 94612-1903
1. PMSA.

OKLAHOMA CITY, OKLA.

Incorporated as city: 1890
Mayor: Ron Norick
City Manager: Paula Hearn
1988 est. population & (rank): 434,380 (29)
1980 population (1980 census) & (rank): 404,014 (31)

Land area: 623 sq mi. (1,679.1 sq km)
Altitude: Highest, 1,320 ft; lowest, 1,140
Location: In central part of state, on North Canadian River
County: Seat of Oklahoma Co.
Churches: Roman Catholic, 15; Jewish, 2; Protestant and others, 741
City-owned parks: 138 (3,944 ac.)
Television stations: 8
Radio stations: AM, 10; FM, 14
1980 CENSUS: Population 65 and over, 11.3%; **under 18,** 27.0%; **Black,** 14.6%; **Spanish, origin,** 2.8%
CIVILIAN LABOR FORCE: 496,100
Unemployed: 35,700, **Percent:** 7.2
Per capita personal income: $14,612
Chamber of Commerce: Oklahoma City Chamber of Commerce, 1 Santa Fe Plaza, Oklahoma City, Okla. 73102

OMAHA, NEB.

Incorporated as city: 1857
Mayor: P.J. Morgan (to June 1993)
1988 est. population & (rank): 353,170 (45)
1980 population (1980 census) & (rank): 314,255 (48)
Land area: 102.98 sq mi.
Altitude: Highest, 1,270 ft
Location: In eastern part of state, on Missouri River
County: Seat of Douglas Co.
Churches: Protestant, 246; Roman Catholic, 44; Jewish, 4
City-owned parks: 159 (over 7,000 ac.)
Radio stations: AM, 7; FM, 13
Television stations: 4
1980 CENSUS: Population 65 and over, 12.2%; **under 18,** 27.5%; **Black,** 12.0%; **Spanish, origin,** 2.3%
CIVILIAN LABOR FORCE: 339,500
Unemployed: 11,100, **Percent:** 3.3
Per capita personal income: $15,873
Chamber of Commerce: Omaha Chamber of Commerce, 1301 Harway St., Omaha, Neb. 68102

PHILADELPHIA, PA.

First charter as city: 1701
Mayor: W. Wilson Goode (to Nov. 1991)
1988 est. population & (rank): 1,647,000 (5)
1980 population (1980 census) & (rank): 1,688,210 (4)
Land area: 136.0 sq mi. (352 sq km)
Altitude: Highest, 440 ft; lowest, sea level
Location: In southeastern part of state, at junction of Schuylkill and Delaware Rivers
County: Seat of Philadelphia Co. (coterminous)
Churches: Roman Catholic, 133; Jewish, 55; Protestant and others, 830
City-owned parks: 630 (10,252 ac.)
Television stations: 8
1980 CENSUS: Population 65 and over, 14.1%; **under 18,** 25.9%; **Black,** 37.8%; **Spanish, origin,** 3.8%
CIVILIAN LABOR FORCE: 2,409,600
Unemployed: 114,100, **Percent:** 4.7
Per capita personal income: $18,504[1]
Chamber of Commerce: Philadelphia Chamber of Commerce, 1346 Chestnut St., Suite 800, Philadelphia, Pa. 19107
1. PMSA.

PHOENIX, ARIZ.

Incorporated as city: 1881
Mayor: Paul Johnson (to Jan. 1992)
City Manager: Marvin A. Andrews (appt. Oct. 1976)
1988 est. population & (rank): 923,750 (10)
1980 population (1980 census) & (rank): 789,704 (9)
Land area: 403.4 sq mi. (1,044 sq km)
Altitude: Highest, 2,740 ft.; lowest, 1,017
Location: In center of state, on Salt River
County: Seat of Maricopa Co.
City-owned parks: 135 (29,925 ac.)
Radio stations: AM, 18; FM, 17
Television stations: 9 commercial; 1 PBS
1980 CENSUS: Population 65 and over, 9.3%; **under 18,** 29.0%; **Black,** 4.8%; **Spanish, origin,** 14.8%
CIVILIAN LABOR FORCE: 1,046,100
Unemployed: 38,700, **Percent:** 3.7
Per capita personal income: $16,815
Chamber of Commerce: Phoenix Chamber of Commerce, 34 W. Monroe St., Phoenix, Ariz. 85003

PITTSBURGH, PA.

Incorporated as city: 1816
Mayor: Sophie Masloff (to Jan. 1994)
1988 est. population & (rank): 375,230 (38)
1980 population (1980 census) & (rank): 423,960 (30)
Land area: 55.5 sq mi. (144 sq km)
Altitude: Highest, 1,240 ft; lowest, 715
Location: In southwestern part of state, at beginning of Ohio River
County: Seat of Allegheny Co.
Churches: Protestant, 348; Roman Catholic, 86; Jewish, 28; Orthodox, 26
City-owned parks and playgrounds: 270 (2,572 ac.)
Radio stations: AM, 12; FM, 20
Television stations: 8
1980 CENSUS[1]: Population 65 and over, 16.0%; **under 18,** 21.4%; **Black,** 24.0%; **Spanish, origin,** 0.8%
CIVILIAN LABOR FORCE[2]: 984,400
Unemployed: 57,200, **Percent:** 5.8
Per capita personal income: $16,484[3]
Chamber of Commerce: The Chamber of Commerce of Greater Pittsburgh, 3 Gateway Center, Pittsburgh, Pa. 15222
1. For city only. 2. For whole metro area (4 counties). 3. PMSA.

PORTLAND, ORE.

Incorporated as city: 1851
Mayor: John (Bud) Clark (till Jan. 1993)
1988 est. population & (rank): 418,470 (32)
1980 est. population (1980 census) & rank: 368,146 (35)
Land area: 134.08 sq mi. (350 sq. km.)
Altitude: Highest, 1073 ft; lowest, sea level
Location: In northwestern part of the state on Willamette River
County: Seat of Multnomah Co.
Churches: Protestant, 450; Roman Catholic, 48; Jewish, 9; Buddhist, 6; other, 190
City-owned parks: 200 (over 9,400 ac.)
Radio stations: AM: 14, FM: 14
Television stations: 5 commercial, 1 public
1980 CENSUS: Population 65 and over, 15.3%; **under 18,** 21.8%; **Black,** 7.6%; **Spanish, origin,** 2.1%
CIVILIAN LABOR FORCE: 671,000

Unemployed: 27,200, **Percent:** 4.1
Per capita personal income: $16,837[1]
Chamber of Commerce: Portland Chamber of Commerce, 221 NW 2nd Ave., Portland, Ore. 97209
1. PMSA.

SACRAMENTO, CALIF.

Incorporated as city: 1849
Mayor: Anne Rudin (to Sept. 1991)
1988 est. population & (rank): 338,220 (48)
1980 population (1980 census) & (rank): 275,741 (52)
Land area: 98 sq mi. (249 sq km)
County: Seat of Sacramento Co.
City park & recreational facilities: 120+ (2,000+ ac.)
Television stations: 7
1980 CENSUS: Population 65 and over, 13.6%; **under 18,** 24.6%; **Black,** 13.4%; **Spanish, origin,** 14.2%
CIVILIAN LABOR FORCE: 726,200
Unemployed: 35,500, **Percent:** 4.9
Per capita personal income: $17,050
Chamber of Commerce: Sacramento Chamber of Commerce, 917 7th St., Sacramento, Calif. 95814; West Sacramento Chamber of Commerce, 834-C Jefferson Blvd., Sacramento, Calif. 95691

ST. LOUIS, MO.

Incorporated as city: 1822
Mayor: Vincent Schoemehl, Jr. (to April 1993)
1988 est. population & (rank): 403,700 (34)
1980 population (1980 census) & (rank): 452,804 (26)
Land area: 61.4 sq mi. (159 sq km)
Altitude: Highest, 616 ft; lowest, 413
Location: In east central part of state, on Mississippi River
County: Independent city
Churches: 900[1]
City-owned parks: 89 (2,639 ac.)
Radio stations: AM, 21; FM 27[1]
Television stations: 6 commercial; 1 PBS
1980 CENSUS: Population 65 and over, 17.6%; **under 18,** 26.1%; **Black,** 45.6%; **Spanish, origin,** 1.2%
CIVILIAN LABOR FORCE: 1,250,600
Unemployed: 83,400, **Percent:** 6.7
Per capita personal income: $14,080
Chamber of Commerce: St. Louis Regional Commerce and Growth Association, 100 S. Fourth St., Ste. 500, St. Louis, Mo. 63102
1. Metropolitan area.

SAN ANTONIO, TEX.

Incorporated as city: 1837
Mayor: Lila Cockrell (to May 1991)
City Manager: Alexander J. Briseno (apptd. April 27, 1990)
1988 est. population & (rank): 941,150 (9)
1980 population (1980 census) & (rank): 785,940 (11)
Land area: 328.53 sq mi. (841.89 sq km)
Altitude: 700 ft
Location: In south central part of state, on San Antonio River
County: Seat of Bexar Co.
City-owned parks: Approximately 6,235.9 ac.
Radio stations: AM, 15; FM, 12
Television stations: 8
1980 CENSUS: Population 65 and over, 9.5%; **under 18,** 32.2%; **Black,** 7.3%; **Spanish, origin,** 53.7%
CIVILIAN LABOR FORCE: 602,300
Unemployed: 36,300, **Percent:** 6.0

Per capita personal income: $13,436
Chamber of Commerce: Greater San Antonio Chamber of Commerce, P.O. Box 1628, 602 E Commerce, San Antonio, Tex. 78296

SAN DIEGO, CALIF.

Incorporated as city: 1850
Mayor: Maureen O'Connor (to Dec. 11, 1992)
City Manager: John Lockwood (apptd. Sept. 1986)
1988 est. population & (rank): 1,070,310 (6)
1980 population (1980 census) & (rank): 875,538 (8)
Land area: 330.7 sq miles (857 sq km)
Altitude: Highest, 1,591 ft; lowest, sea level
Location: In southwesternmost part of state, on San Diego Bay
County: Seat of San Diego Co.
Churches: Roman Catholic, 39; Jewish, 9; Protestant, 334; Eastern Orthodox, 8; other, 18
City park and recreation facilities: 164 (17,207 ac.)
Radio stations: AM, 8; FM, 18
Television stations: 9
1980 CENSUS: Population 65 and over, 9.7%; **under 18,** 24.1%; **Black,** 8.9%; **Spanish, origin,** 14.9%
CIVILIAN LABOR FORCE: 1,167,700
Unemployed: 44,400, **Percent:** 3.8
Per capita personal income: $17,576
Chamber of Commerce: San Diego Chamber of Commerce, 110 West C St., Ste. 1600, San Diego, Calif. 92101

SAN FRANCISCO, CALIF.

Incorporated as city: 1850
Mayor: Art Agnos (to Jan. 1992)
1988 est. population & (rank): 731,600 (13)
1980 population (1980 census) & (rank): 678,974 (13)
Land area: 46.1 sq mi. (120 sq km)
Altitude: Highest, 925 ft; lowest, sea level
Location: In northern part of state between Pacific Ocean and San Francisco Bay
County: Coextensive with San Francisco Co.
Churches: 540 of all denominations
City-owned parks and squares: 225
Radio stations: 29
Television stations: 10
1980 CENSUS: Population 65 and over, 15.4%; **under 18,** 17.2%; **Black,** 12.7%; **Spanish, origin,** 12.3%
CIVILIAN LABOR FORCE: 874,200
Unemployed: 28,800, **Percent:** 3.3
Per capita personal income: $26,309[1]
Chamber of Commerce: Greater San Francisco Chamber of Commerce, 465 California St., San Francisco, Calif. 94104
1. PMSA.

SAN JOSE, CALIF.

Incorporated as city: 1850
Mayor: Thomas McEnery (to Dec. 31, 1990)
City Manager: Leslie R. White (apptd. May 1989)
1988 est. population & (rank): 738,420 (12)
1980 population (1980 census) & (rank): 629,402 (17)
Land area: 172.9 sq mi. (447 sq km)
Altitude: Highest, 4,372 ft.; lowest, sea level
Location: In northern part of state, on south San Francisco Bay, 50 miles south of San Francisco
County: Seat of Santa Clara County

Churches: 403
City-owned parks and playgrounds: 152 (3,136 ac.)
Radio stations: 14
Television stations: 4
1980 CENSUS: Population 65 and over, 6.2%; **under 18,** 31.0%; **Black,** 4.6%; **Spanish, origin,** 22.3%
CIVILIAN LABOR FORCE: 816,800
Unemployed: 30,100, **Percent:** 3.7
Per capita personal income: $23,181
Chamber of Commerce: San Jose Chamber of Commerce, One Paseo de San Antonio, San Jose, Calif. 95113

SEATTLE, WASH.

Incorporated as city: 1869
Mayor: Norman B. Rice (to Dec. 31, 1993)
1988 est. population & (rank): 502,200 (24)
1980 population (1980 census) & (rank): 493,846 (23)
Land area: 144.6 sq mi. (375 sq km)
Altitude: Highest, 540 ft; lowest, sea level
Location: In west central part of state, on Puget Sound
County: Seat of King Co.
Churches: Roman Catholic, 36; Jewish, 13; Protestant and others, 535
City-owned parks, playgrounds, etc.: 278 (4,773.4 ac.)
Radio stations: AM, 22; FM, 26
Television stations: 3 commercial; 1 educational
1980 CENSUS: Population 65 and over, 15.4%; **under 18,** 17.6%; **Black,** 9.5%; **Spanish, origin,** 2.6%
CIVILIAN LABOR FORCE: 1,133,000
Unemployed: 47,800, **Percent:** 4.2
Per capita personal income: $19,703[1]
Chamber of Commerce: Seattle Chamber of Commerce, 1200 One Union Square, Seattle, Wash. 98101
1. PMSA.

TOLEDO, OHIO

Incorporated as city: 1837
Mayor: John McHugh (to Dec. 1991)
City Manager: Phillip Hawkey
1988 est. population & (rank): 340,760 (47)
1980 population (1980 census) & (rank): 354,635 (40)
Land area: 84.2 sq mi. (218 sq km)
Altitude: 630 ft
Location: In northwestern part of state, on Maumee River at Lake Erie
County: Seat of Lucas Co.
Churches: Protestant, 301; Roman Catholic, 55; Jewish, 4; others, 98
City-owned parks and playgrounds: 134 (2,650.90 ac.)
Radio stations: AM, 8; FM, 8
Television stations: 6
1980 CENSUS: Population 65 and over, 12.5%; **under 18,** 28.1%; **Black,** 17.4%; **Spanish, origin,** 3.0%
CIVILIAN LABOR FORCE: 315,800
Unemployed: 32,800, **Percent:** 10.4
Per capita personal income: $16,083
Chamber of Commerce: Toledo Area Chamber of Commerce, 218 Huron St., Toledo, Ohio 43604

TUCSON, ARIZ.

Incorporated as city: 1877
Mayor: Thomas J. Volgy (to Dec. 1991)
1988 est. population & (rank): 385,720 (35)
1980 population (1980 census) & (rank): 330,537 (45)
Land area: 130 sq mi. (336.7 sq km)
Altitude: 2,500 ft
Location: In southeastern part of state, on the Santa Cruz River
County: Seat of Pima Co.
Churches: Protestant, 325; Roman Catholic, 40; other, 74
City-owned parks and parkways: (25,349 ac.)
Radio stations: AM, 16; FM, 11
Television stations: 3 commercial; 1 educational; 4 other
1980 CENSUS: Population 65 and over, 11.7%; **under 18,** 25.5%; **Black,** 3.7%; **Spanish, origin,** 24.9%
CIVILIAN LABOR FORCE: 306,200
Unemployed: 11,300, **Percent:** 3.7
Per capita personal income: $14,362
Chamber of Commerce: Tucson Metropolitan Chamber of Commerce, P.O. Box 991, Tucson, Ariz. 85702

TULSA, OKLA.

Incorporated as city: 1898
Mayor: Rodger Randle (to May 1994)
1988 est. population & (rank): 368,330 (41)
1980 population (1980 census) & (rank): 360,919 (38)
Land area: 192.459 sq mi. (499 sq km)
Altitude: 674 ft
Location: In northeastern part of state, on Arkansas River
County: Seat of Tulsa Co.
Churches: Protestant, 593; Roman Catholic, 32; Jewish, 2; others, 4
City parks and playgrounds: 113 (5,338 ac.)
Radio stations: AM, 7; FM, 8
Television stations: 5 commercial; 1 PBS; 1 cable
1980 CENSUS: Population 65 and over, 10.8%; **under 18,** 25.8%; **Black,** 11.8%; **Spanish, origin,** 1.7%
CIVILIAN LABOR FORCE: 334,500
Unemployed: 19,800, **Percent:** 5.9
Per capita personal income: $15,075
Chamber of Commerce: Metropolitan Tulsa Chamber of Commerce, 616 S Boston, Tulsa, Okla. 74119

VIRGINIA BEACH, VA.

Incorporated as city: 1963
Mayor: Meyera E. Obendorf (to June 30, 1992)
1988 est. population & (rank): 365,300 (43)
1980 population (1980 census) & (rank): 262,199 (56)
Land area: 258.7 sq mi. (670 sq km)
Altitude: 12 ft
Location: Southeastern most portion of state, on Atlantic coastline
County: None
Churches: Protestant, 159; Catholic, 8; Jewish, 4
City-owned parks: 151 (1,748 ac.)
Radio stations: AM 18, FM 22
Television stations: 4 commercial, 1 PBS, 1 cable
1980 CENSUS: Population 65 and over, 4.5%; **under 18,** 30.7%; **Black,** 10.0%; **Spanish, origin,** 2.0%
CIVILIAN LABOR FORCE: 612,500[1]
Unemployed: 34,800[1], **Percent:** 4.4[1]
Per capita personal income: $15,051[1]
Chamber of Commerce: Hampton Roads Chamber of Commerce, 4512 Virginia Beach Blvd., Virginia Beach, Va., 23456
1. Norfolk-Virginia Beach-Newport News MSA.

WASHINGTON, D.C.

Land ceded to Congress: 1788 by Maryland; 1789 by Virginia (retroceded to Virginia Sept. 7, 1846)
Seat of government transferred to D. C.: Dec. 1, 1800
Created municipal corporation: Feb. 21, 1871
Mayor: Marion Barry, Jr. (to Jan. 1991)
Motto: *Justitia omnibus* (Justice to all)
Flower: American beauty rose
Tree: Scarlet oak
Origin of name: In honor of Columbus
1988 est. population & (rank): 617,000 (17)
1980 population (1980 census) & (rank): 638,432 (15)
Land area: 68.25 sq mi. (176.12 sq km)
Geographic center: Near corner of Fourth and L Sts., NW
Altitude: Highest, 420 ft; lowest, sea level
Location: Between Virginia and Maryland, on Potomac River
Churches: Protestant, 610; Roman Catholic, 45; Jewish, 15
City parks: 753 (7,725 ac.)
Radio stations: AM, 29; FM, 26
Television stations: 6 (including 2 UHF stations)
1980 CENSUS: Population 65 and over, 11.6%; **under 18,** 22.5%; **Black,** 70.3%; **Spanish, origin,** 2.8%
CIVILIAN LABOR FORCE: 2,206,900
Unemployed: 60,800, **Percent:** 2.8
Per capita personal income: $23,175
Board of Trade: Greater Washington Board of Trade, 1129 20th Street, N.W., Washington, D.C. 20036
Chamber of Commerce: D.C. Chamber of Commerce, 1319 F St., NW, Washington, D.C. 20004

The District of Columbia—identical with the City of Washington—is the capital of the United States and the first carefully planned capital in the world.

D.C. history began in 1790 when Congress directed selection of a new capital site, 10 miles square, along the Potomac. When the site was determined, it included 30.75 square miles on the Virginia side of the river. In 1846, however, Congress returned that area to Virginia, leaving the 68.25 square miles ceded by Maryland.

The city was planned and partly laid out by Major Pierre Charles L. 'Enfant, a French engineer. This work was perfected and completed by Major Andrew Ellicott and Benjamin Banneker, a freeborn black man, who was an astronomer and mathematician. In 1814, during the War of 1812, a British force fired the capital, and it was from the white paint applied to cover fire damage that the President's home was called the White House.

Until Nov. 3, 1967, the District of Columbia was administered by three commissioners appointed by the President. On that day, a government consisting of a mayor-commissioner and a 9-member Council, all appointed by the President with the approval of the Senate, took office. On May 7, 1974, the citizens of the District of Columbia approved a Home Rule Charter, giving them an elected mayor and 13-member council—their first elected municipal government in more than a century. The District also has one non-voting member in the House of Representatives and an elected Board of Education.

On Aug. 22, 1978, Congress passed a proposed constitutional amendment to give Washington, D.C., voting representation in the Congress. The amendment had to be ratified by at least 28 state legislatures within seven years to become effective. As of 1985 it died.

A petition asking for the District's admission to the Union as the 51st State was filed in Congress on September 9, 1983. The District is continuing this drive for statehood.

Largest Cities in the United States

(Over 100,000 population, estimate)

City and State	Population July 1988	Rank 1988	Rank 1980	City and State	Population July 1988	Rank 1988	Rank 1980
New York, N.Y.	7,352,700	1	1	Kansas City, Mo.	438,950	28	27
Los Angeles, Calif.	3,352,710	2	3	Oklahoma City, Okla.	434,380	29	31
Chicago, Ill.	2,977,520	3	2	Fort Worth, Tex.	426,610	30	33
Houston, Tex.	1,698,090	4	5	Atlanta, Ga.	420,220	31	29
Philadelphia, Pa.	1,647,000	5	4	Portland, Ore.	418,470	32	35
San Diego, Calif.	1,070,310	6	8	Long Beach, Calif.	415,040	33	37
Detroit, Mich.	1,035,920	7	6	St. Louis, Mo.	403,700	34	26
Dallas, Tex.	987,360	8	7	Tucson, Ariz.	385,720	35	45
San Antonio, Tex.	941,150	9	11	Albuquerque, N.M.	378,480	36	44
Phoenix, Ariz.	923,750	10	9	Honolulu, Hawaii[1]	376,110	37	36
Baltimore, Md.	751,400	11	10	Pittsburgh, Pa.	375,230	38	30
San Jose, Calif.	738,420	12	17	Miami, Fla.	371,100	39	41
San Francisco, Calif.	731,600	13	13	Cincinnati, Ohio	370,480	40	32
Indianapolis, Ind.	727,130	14	12	Tulsa, Okla.	368,330	41	38
Memphis, Tenn.	645,190	15	14	Charlotte, N.C.	367,860	42	47
Jacksonville, Fla.	635,430	16	22	Virginia Beach, Va.	365,300	43	56
Washington, D.C.	617,000	17	15	Oakland, Calif.	356,860	44	43
Milwaukee, Wis.	599,380	18	16	Omaha, Neb.	353,170	45	48
Boston, Mass.	577,830	19	20	Minneapolis, Minn.	344,670	46	34
Columbus, Ohio	569,570	20	19	Toledo, Ohio	340,760	47	40
New Orleans, La.	531,700	21	21	Sacramento, Calif.	338,220	48	52
Cleveland, Ohio	521,370	22	18	Newark, N.J.	313,800	49	46
El Paso, Tex.	510,970	23	28	Buffalo, N.Y.	313,570	50	39
Seattle, Wash.	502,200	24	23	Fresno, Calif.	307,090	51	65
Denver, Colo.	492,200	25	24	Wichita, Kan.	295,320	52	51
Nashville–Davidson, Tenn	481,400	26	25	Norfolk, Va.	286,500	53	55
Austin, Tex.	464,690	27	42	Colorado Springs, Colo.	283,110	54	66

City and State	Population July 1988	Rank 1988	Rank 1980
Louisville, Ky.	281,880	55	49
Tampa, Fla.	281,790	56	53
Mesa, Ariz.	280,360	57	102
Birmingham, Ala.	277,280	58	50
Corpus Christi, Tex.	260,930	59	60
St. Paul, Minn.	259,110	60	54
Arlington, Tex.	257,460	61	94
Anaheim, Calif.	244,670	62	63
Santa Ana, Calif.	239,540	63	69
St. Petersburg, Fla.	235,450	64	58
Baton Rouge, La.[2]	235,270	65	62
Rochester, N.Y.	229,780	66	57
Lexington–Fayette, Ky.	225,700	67	68
Akron, Ohio	221,510	68	59
Aurora, Colo.	218,720	69	97
Anchorage, Alaska	218,500	70	78
Shreveport, La.	218,010	71	67
Jersey City, N.J.	217,630	72	61
Richmond, Va.	213,300	73	64
Riverside, Calif.	210,630	74	84
Las Vegas, Nev.	210,620	75	89
Mobile, Ala.	208,820	76	71
Jackson, Miss.	201,250	77	70
Montgomery, Ala.	193,510	78	76
Des Moines, Iowa	192,910	79	74
Stockton, Calif.	190,680	80	107
Lubbock, Tex.	188,090	81	79
Lincoln, Nebr.	187,890	82	81
Huntington Beach, Calif.	186,880	83	85
Raleigh, N.C.	186,720	84	105
Grand Rapids, Mich.	185,370	85	75
Yonkers, N.Y.	183,000	86	72
Greensboro, N.C.	181,970	87	100
Garland, Tex.	180,450	88	115
Little Rock, Ark.	180,090	89	96
Fort Wayne, Ind.	179,810	90	80
Madison, Wis.	178,180	91	83
Dayton, Ohio	178,000	92	73
Columbus, Ga.	177,680	93	88
Knoxville, Tenn.	172,080	94	77
Spokane, Wash.	170,900	95	82
Fremont, Calif.	166,590	96	119
Amarillo, Tex.	166,010	97	106
Tacoma, Wash.	163,960	98	98
Chattanooga, Tenn.	162,670	99	87
Hialeah, Fla.	162,080	100	108
Glendale, Calif.	161,210	101	114
Kansas City, Kan.	160,630	102	92
Newport News, Va.	160,100	103	109
Huntsville, Ala.	159,450	104	111
Bakersfield, Calif.	157,650	105	152
Worcester, Mass.	156,190	106	91
Providence, R.I.	156,160	107	99
Orlando, Fla.	155,950	108	124
Syracuse, N.Y.	153,610	109	86
Salt Lake City, Utah	152,740	110	90
Springfield, Mass.	150,320	111	103
Winston-Salem, N.C.	148,690	112	120
Modesto, Calif.	148,670	113	147
San Bernardino, Calif.	148,420	114	131
Chesapeake, Va.	147,800	115	137
Savannah, Ga.	145,980	116	112
Fort Lauderdale, Fla.	145,610	117	101
Warren, Mich.	145,410	118	93
Springfield, Mo.	142,690	119	118
Flint, Mich.	141,620	120	95
Tempe, Ariz.	140,440	121	148
Glendale, Ariz.	140,170	122	-
Bridgeport, Conn.	139,770	123	110
Paterson, N.J.	138,620	124	116
Torrance, Calif.	137,940	125	123
Garden Grove, Calif.	135,310	126	127
Rockford, Ill.	134,500	127	113
Irving, Tex.	133,000	128	142
Gary, Ind.	132,460	129	104
Pasadena, Calif.	132,010	130	134
Hartford, Conn.	131,300	131	117
Hampton, Va.	130,800	132	128
Oxnard, Calif.	130,080	133	145
Evansville, Ind.	128,210	134	121
Chula Vista, Calif.	126,240	135	155
Tallahassee, Fla.	125,640	136	153
Lansing, Mich.	124,960	137	122
Laredo, Tex.	124,730	138	-
New Haven, Conn.	123,840	139	125
Ontario, Calif.	123,380	140	-
Topeka, Kan.	122,360	141	132
Scottsdale, Ariz.	121,740	142	-
Pomona, Calif.	120,470	143	-
Hollywood, Fla.	120,140	144	129
Lakewood, Colo.	119,340	145	138
Plano, Tex.	118,790	146	-
Macon, Ga.	117,940	147	135
Pasadena, Tex.	116,880	148	139
Sunnyvale, Calif.	116,180	149	149
Durham, N.C.	115,430	150	168
Reno, Nev.	115,130	151	169
Independence, Mo.	115,090	152	140
Sterling Heights, Mich.	114,720	153	144
Beaumont, Tex.	114,210	154	133
Erie, Pa.	112,800	155	130
Oceanside, Calif.	112,630	156	-
Boise City, Idaho	111,030	157	162
Cedar Rapids, Iowa	110,300	158	141
Fullerton, Calif.	109,740	159	163
Peoria, Ill.	109,560	160	128
Abilene, Tex.	109,110	161	-
Ann Arbor, Mich.	108,440	162	146
Alexandria, Va.	108,400	163	160
Santa Rosa, Calif.	108,220	164	-
Concord, Calif.	108,040	165	155
Eugene, Ore.	108,030	166	151
Portsmouth, Va.	107,500	167	154
Overland Park, Kan.	106,860	168	-
South Bend, Ind.	106,190	169	143
Orange, Calif.	105,710	170	-
Allentown, Pa.	105,200	171	156
Elizabeth, N.J.	105,150	172	150
Waterbury, Conn.	104,520	173	158
Brownsville, Tex.	104,510	174	-
Inglewood, Calif.	103,920	175	-
Berkeley, Calif.	103,660	176	157
Hayward, Calif.	103,600	177	-
Waco, Tex.	103,420	178	166
Thousand Oaks, Calif.	101,530	179	-
Youngstown, Ohio	101,150	180	136
Livonia, Mich.	101,100	181	153
Salinas, Calif.	101,090	182	-
Pueblo, Colo.	101,070	183	165
Vallejo, Calif.	100,730	184	-
Stamford, Conn.	100,260	185	161
Irvine, Calif.	100,130	186	-

1. The estimates shown here are for Honolulu census designated place, which is treated as the city by the Census Bureau, rather than the Honolulu city/county governmental unit. 2. The estimates shown here are for Baton Rouge city, not the Baton Rouge/East Baton Rouge Parish government. Data are latest Census Bureau report. *Source:* U.S. Department of Commerce, Bureau of the Census, November 1989.

Tabulated Data on City Governments

City	Mayor		City manager's salary[2]	Council or Commission			
	Term, years	Salary[1]		Name	Members	Term, years	Salary[3]
Albuquerque, N.M.	4	$59,509	$52,500[4]	Council	9	4	$5,951
Atlanta	4	100,000	—	Council	19	4	22,000[27]
Austin, Tex.	3	35,006	113,880	Council	6	3	30,014
Baltimore	4	60,000	—	Council	19	4	29,000
Boston	4	100,000	—	Council	13	2	45,000
Buffalo, N.Y.	4	64,100	—	Council	13	2[5]	38,000
Charlotte, N.C.	2	14,800	106,780	Council	11	2	8,000
Chicago	4	80,000	—	Council	50	4	40,000
Cincinnati	2	40,738	93,695	Council	9	2	37,238
Cleveland	4	80,000	—	Council	21	4	33,663
Columbus, Ohio	4	81,990	—	Council	7	4	25,000
Dallas	2	50[6]	—	Council	11	2	50[6]
Denver*	4	77,400	—	Council	13	4	28,680[21, 28]
Detroit	4	130,000	—	Council	9	4	60,000[29]
El Paso	2	25,000	—	Council	7[7]	2	15,000
Fort Worth	2	75[8]	96,000	Council	8	2	75[8]
Honolulu	4	84,725	89,488[2]	Council	9	4	35,000[3]
Houston	2	115,192	—	Council	14	2	30,718
Indianapolis	4	82,260	—	Council	29	4	8,971[10]
Jacksonville, Fla.	4	92,448	76,230[11]	Council	19	4	21,174[3]
Kansas City, Mo.	4	48,000	101,220	Council	13	4	20,000
Long Beach, Calif.	4	13,892[25]	105,000	Council	9	4	17,004
Los Angeles	4	102,537	137,056[4]	Council	15	4	61,522
Memphis, Tenn.	4	82,500	72,800	Council	13	4	6,000
Miami, Fla.	2	4,992[13]	96,595.20	Commission	5	4	4,992
Milwaukee	4	81,770	—	Council	16	4	37,700
Minneapolis	4	65,000	82,711	Council	13	4	48,000
Nashville, Tenn.	4	75,000	—	Council	41	4	5,400
Newark, N.J.	4	80,689.69	83,749.44[15]	Council	9	4	37,655.19[23]
New Orleans	4	81,742	71,028	Council	7	4	42,500
New York	4	130,000	112,000	Council	51	4	55,000
Oakland, Calif.	4	80,000	120,997.56	Council	9[7]	4	([16])
Oklahoma City	4	2,000	75,000	Council	8	4	20[17]
Omaha, Neb.	4	65,480	—	Council	7	4	16,700[3]
Philadelphia	4	84,550	95,000[18]	Council	17	4	40,000
Phoenix, Ariz.	2	37,500	115,280	Council	9[7]	2	18,000
Pittsburgh	4	67,324	—	Council	9	4	38,387
Portland, Ore.	4	69,638	—	Council	4	4	58,635
Sacramento	4	8,100[30]	112,000	Council	9[12]	4	8,100[31]
St. Louis	4	71,266	—	Board of Aldermen	29	4	18,500[32]
San Antonio	2	3,000[19]	102,000	Council	11[7]	2	20[20]
San Diego, Calif.	4	60,000	121,000	Council	8	4	45,000
San Francisco	4	122,356	121,212[33]	Board of Supervisors	11	4	23,924
San Jose, Calif.	4	72,000[34]	117,387[34]	Council	10	4	48,000[34]
Seattle	4	91,440	—	Council	9	4	61,146
Toledo, Ohio	2	36,000	85,000	Council	9[12]	2	7,800
Tucson, Ariz.	4	24,000	100,000	Council	7	4	12,000
Tulsa, Okla.	4	70,000	—	Council	9	2	12,000
Virginia Beach, Va.	2	17,000	90,000	Council	11	4	15,000
Washington, D.C.	4	90,705	83,600[35]	Council	13	4	69,500[22]

1. Annual salary unless otherwise indicated. 2. Annual salary. City Manager's term is indefinite and at will of Council (or Mayor). 3. Annual salary unless otherwise indicated. In some cities, President of Council receives a higher salary. 4. City Administrative Officer appointed by Mayor, approved by Council. 5. For 9 District Councilmen; 4 years for 3 Councilmen-at-Large. 6. Per Council meeting; not over $2,600 per year. 7. Including Mayor. 8. Per week and per Council meeting. 9. Managing Director appointed by Mayor; no Council approval required. 10. 102 per council meeting at a maxium of 21 meetings. $56 per committee meeting at a maximum of 40 meetings. 11. Chief Administrative Officer appointed by Mayor; not subject to Council confirmation. 12. Including Mayor and Vice-Mayor. 13. Plus $2,500 expense account. 14. No City Manager; salary is for Deputy Mayor. 15. Business Administrator, appointed by Mayor and confirmed by Council. 16. $1,180 per month as council member; additional $1,212.75 per month as member of Redevelopment Agency. 17. Per Council meeting; not to exceed 5 meetings a month. 18. Appointed by Mayor, with title of Managing Director. 19. Plus Council pay. 20. Per Council meeting; not over $1,040 per year. 21. Council President receives $28,992. 22. Council Chairman receives $79,500. 23. Annual allowance in lieu of expenses: Council members $13,000; Council President $15,000. 24. Plus $4,000 in travel expenses. 25. Plus $1,200 per month expense account. 26. Council President receives $105,000. 27. Council President earns $53,000; Vice President earns $30,500. 28. Council President receives $33,680. 29. Council President receives $63,000. 30. Plus $4,800 annual expense account, $4,800 annual secretary expense allowance and $4,800 annual vehicle expense allowance. 31. Plus $3,600 annual expense account and $4,800 annual vehicle expense allowance. 32. For 12 Aldermen $18,500, 16 Aldermen $21,460. 33. Chief Administrative Officer, $121,212. 34. Plus $4,200 automatic allowance. 35. City Administrator/Deputy Mayor for operations. NOTE: An asterisk (*) indicates up-to-date information not provided. *Source: Information Please* questionnaires to the cities.

U.S. STATISTICS

How We're Changing—An Overview

Source: U.S. Bureau of The Census, *Current Population Reports,* Series P-23, January 1990.

Our Population Is Growing by About 1 Percent Per Year

On January 1, 1990, the Census Bureau estimated that the resident population of the United States was 249.6 million, about 2.5 million higher than the 1989 New Year's Day figure. Since the 1980 census, our population has increased by 23.1 million, or 10.2 percent.

In 1989, the Nation had about 3.9 million births, 2.1 million deaths, and a net immigration of 700,000. Births since 1985 have been at their highest level since the mid-1960s.

March 1989 estimates, which were restricted to the civilian noninstitutional population, show 29.7 million Blacks, 12.3 percent of the total population. At the same date, there were 20.1 million Hispanics (who may be of any race), 8.3 percent of the total population. (Data on the White and Black populations are based on a race question; data on the Hispanic population are based on an ethnic origin question.)

Our Growth Will Slow and Possibly Stop Within 50 Years

Using the middle series projection, the Census Bureau sees the population peaking at about 302 million in 2038, and then declining slowly. Long term, we assume 1.8 births per woman, an average life span of 81 years, and an annual net immigration of 500,000.

The lowest series projects that the population will peak at 265 million in 2016, and the highest series sees an increase to 278 million in 2000 and to 388 million in 2040. The long-term assumptions for the lowest series are 1.5 births, a 78-year life span, and 300,000 net immigration; for the highest series, they are 2.2 births, an 88-year life span, and 800,000 immigration.

The elderly population will increase at a moderate rate until about 2010. Then, the 1946-64 Baby Boom generation will begin to enter the 65-and-over age group and accelerate the elderly rate of growth. It is projected that the elderly population will increase from 31.6% in 1990 to 68.5% in 2050. (Middle series projections.)

The South and West Are Our Most Rapidly Growing Regions

These two regions experienced 87 percent of our Nation's growth between 1980 and 1989; 90 percent of our growth in the 1970s was concentrated in these areas, compared with 61 percent in the 1960s. The proportion of the population living in the South and West rose from 48 percent in 1970 to 52 percent in 1980 to 55 percent in 1989.

Fifty-one percent of the decade's growth has occurred in California, Texas, and Florida (up from 42 percent in the 1970s and 32 percent in the 1960s). In 1989, 11.7 percent of U.S. residents lived in California—the highest concentration in one State since 1860, when 12.3 percent lived in New York. California alone had more residents in 1989 (29.1 million) than did the 21 least populous States combined.

Nevada, Alaska, and Arizona grew the fastest between 1980 and 1989; only West Virginia, Iowa, and the District of Columbia lost population during that time.

Population Growth Is Concentrated in Metropolitan Areas

In 1988, 77 percent of all Americans lived in the 283 designated metropolitan areas. These areas grew by 9.7 percent between 1980 and 1988, while the nonmetropolitan population increased by just 4.5 percent.

Forty-nine percent of the Nation's population lived in the 37 metropolitan areas with 1 million or more people. The most rapid growth between 1980 and 1988 in these areas occurred in Phoenix (34.5 percent), Dallas-Ft. Worth (28.5 percent), and Atlanta (28 percent). The largest numerical growth was in Los Angeles (2.3 million), followed by Dallas-Ft. Worth (835,000).

The Long Decline of the Farm Population Has Stopped

Our farm population was 5 million in 1988, unchanged from the 1987 figure. Between 1940 and 1980, the number of Americans living on farms dropped from 31 million to 6 million.

In 1988, 51 percent of the farm population lived in the Midwest, and 30 percent lived in the South. In 1950, the situation was reversed: 32 percent lived in the Midwest, and 52 percent lived in the South.

Average Household Size Reached a Record Low

The average number of people per household in 1989 was 2.62, compared with 2.76 in 1980 and 3.14 in 1970.

There were 92.8 million households in 1989, up by 15 percent since 1980. Seventy-one percent of these households contained families, down from 74 percent in 1980 and 81 percent in 1970. (Families have at least two members, including at least one relative of the householder.)

Nonfamily households increased rapidly from 11.9 million in 1970 to 21.2 million in 1980 and more slowly to 27 million in 1989. Currently, people living alone account for 84 percent of these nonfamily situations.

Women With Newborns Have Increased Their Labor Force Participation

In 1988, 51 percent of women 18 to 44 years old with infants under 1 year old were in the labor force, compared with 38 percent in 1980 and 31 percent in 1976. Women with less than a high school education increased their rate from 26 percent in 1976 to 34 percent in 1988. Women who were college graduates saw their rate jump from 39 percent to 60 percent during the same period.

In 1988, 33 percent of all births were to women in their thirties, compared with only 19 percent in 1976. This change reflects not only the increased birth rates to women in this age group, but also the large numbers of Baby Boomers now of childbearing age. The overall fertility rate has not changed significantly since 1976, however, and the average number of lifetime births expected by women 18 to 34 years old has remained between 2.0 and 2.1 during the past decade.

Voter Turnout Hit a New Low in the Presidential Election

Only 57 percent of the voting-age population reported that they went to the polls in November 1988. This reported rate was down from 60 percent in 1984, and well below the 69 percent reported in 1964, the first year that the Census Bureau collected data on voting. (Reported voting rates tend to be high; the actual figure in 1988 was about 50 percent.)

Voting rates vary widely by people's characteristics. In 1988, the reported rates were 59 percent for Whites and 52 percent for Blacks. The rate was 29 percent for Hispanics (37 percent of Hispanics surveyed were not U.S. citizens, so they were ineligible to register). People 45 and over voted at a rate of 68 percent, compared with 36 percent for 18- to 24-year-olds. College graduates reported a rate of 78 percent, while people with 8 or fewer years of school had a rate of 37 percent.

Poverty and Median Family Income Were Unchanged in 1988

There were 31.7 million people below the official government poverty level in 1988—13.0 percent of the population. These figures, revisions of estimates published earlier, are not significantly different from those for 1987. Median family income in 1988 ($32,190) also was not significantly different from the 1987 figure after adjusting for the 4.1 percent increase in consumer prices. The 1988 poverty rate for Whites was 10.1%, for Blacks 31.3%, for Hispanics 26.7%, and all races 13.0%. The 1988 median family income for Whites was $33,920, for Blacks $19,330, for Hispanics $21,770, and all races $32,190. They are not significantly different from the rates in 1987.

Real per capita income increased by 1.7 percent between 1987 and 1988—it reached a record high of $13,120. At the same time, real median earnings of men working year-round, full-time dropped by 1.3 percent in 1988 to $26,660; their female counterparts' earnings ($17,610) did not change significantly. The ratio of female to male earnings was .66 in 1988, up from .60 in 1980.

(Income and poverty figures are based on pre-tax money income before deductions and without non-cash benefits.)

Homeownership Rate Held Steady in 1989

In the third quarter of 1989, owners lived in 64 percent of occupied housing units, unchanged from the rate a year earlier, but lower than the third quarter 1980 rate of 66 percent. The rental vacancy rate was 7.3 percent in the third quarter of 1989, down from 7.8 percent a year earlier. The homeowner vacancy rate has remained in the 1-2 percent range during the 1980s.

There were 105.5 million housing units in the Nation in the third quarter of 1989: 93.6 million (88.7 percent) were occupied and 11.9 million (11.3 percent) were vacant. ☐

Population Shifts: 1790 to 1990

Source: U.S. Bureau of the Census, *Census and You,*
Bicentennial issue.

The population of the United States increased from 3.9 million at the first census in 1790 to an estimated 250 million in 1990. This tremendous growth has been accompanied by a striking change in population distribution as the nation developed from its primarily rural and agricultural beginnings on the Atlantic Coast to a highly urbanized and industrialized transcontinental nation.

During this period, the center of population (defined generally as the point at which an imaginary U.S. map would balance if each person weighed the same) has shifted west about 800 miles from a point east of Baltimore to a point southwest of St. Louis.

In 1790, the population was nearly equally divided between the North and the South. During the following century, growth was more rapid in the North, which increased its share to 63 percent in 1890.

Within the North, growth was more rapid in the Midwest, which had 36 percent of the nation's population in 1890, than in the Northeast, which had 28 percent.

The South's share dropped to 32 percent, while the West, which was first enumerated as part of the United States in 1850, had the remaining 5 percent of the total population in 1890.

The past century has brought additional changes in the distribution of population. The North's share dropped to a record low 45 percent in 1989 (20 percent in the Northeast and 24 percent in the Midwest), while the West's proportion increased rapidly, reaching a record high 21 percent in 1989.

The South's share was 32 percent in 1940, as in 1890, and then increased to 34 percent in 1989, its highest proportion in more than a century.

Population

Colonial Population Estimates (in round numbers)

Year	Population	Year	Population	Year	Population	Year	Population
1610	350	1660	75,100	1710	331,700	1760	1,593,600
1620	2,300	1670	111,900	1720	466,200	1770	2,148,100
1630	4,600	1680	151,500	1730	629,400	1780	2,780,400
1640	26,600	1690	210,400	1740	905,600		
1650	50,400	1700	250,900	1750	1,170,800		

National Censuses[1]

Year	Resident population[2]	Land area, sq mi.	Pop. per sq mi.	Year	Resident population[2]	Land area, sq mi.	Pop. per sq mi.
1790	3,929,214	864,746	4.5	1890	62,947,714	2,969,640	21.2
1800	5,308,483	864,746	6.1	1900	75,994,575	2,969,834	25.6
1810	7,239,881	1,681,828	4.3	1910	91,972,266	2,969,565	31.0
1820	9,638,453	1,749,462	5.5	1920	105,710,620	2,969,451	35.6
1830	12,866,020	1,749,462	7.4	1930	122,775,046	2,977,128	41.2
1840	17,069,453	1,749,462	9.8	1940	131,669,275	2,977,128	44.2
1850	23,191,876	2,940,042	7.9	1950	150,697,361	2,974,726	50.7
1860	31,443,321	2,969,640	10.6	1960	179,323,175	3,540,911	50.6
1870	39,818,449	2,969,640	13.4	1970	203,302,031	3,540,023	57.4
1880	50,155,783	2,969,640	16.9	1980	226,545,805	3,618,770	62.6

1. Beginning with 1960, figures include Alaska and Hawaii. 2. Excludes armed forces overseas. *Source:* Department of Commerce, Bureau of the Census.

Population Distribution by Age, Race, Nativity, and Sex

Year	Total	Under 5	5–19	20–44	45–64	65 and over	White Total[1]	Native born	Foreign born	Black	Other races[1]
PERCENT DISTRIBUTION											
1860[2]	100.0	15.4	35.8	35.7	10.4	2.7	85.6	72.6	13.0	14.1	0.3
1870[2]	100.0	14.3	35.4	35.4	11.9	3.0	87.1	72.9	14.2	12.7	0.2
1880[2]	100.0	13.8	34.3	35.9	12.6	3.4	86.5	73.4	13.1	13.1	0.3
1890[3]	100.0	12.2	33.9	36.9	13.1	3.9	87.5	73.0	14.5	11.9	0.3
1900	100.0	12.1	32.3	37.7	13.7	4.1	87.9	74.5	13.4	11.6	0.5
1910	100.0	11.6	30.4	39.0	14.6	4.3	88.9	74.4	14.5	10.7	0.4
1920	100.0	10.9	29.8	38.4	16.1	4.7	89.7	76.7	13.0	9.9	0.4
1930	100.0	9.3	29.5	38.3	17.4	5.4	89.8	78.4	11.4	9.7	0.5
1940	100.0	8.0	26.4	38.9	19.8	6.8	89.8	81.1	8.7	9.8	0.4
1950	100.0	10.7	23.2	37.6	20.3	8.1	89.5	82.8	6.7	10.0	0.5
1960	100.0	11.3	27.1	32.2	20.1	9.2	88.6	83.4	5.2	10.5	0.9
1970[2]	100.0	8.4	29.5	31.7	20.6	9.8	87.6	83.4	4.3	11.1	1.4
1980	100.0	7.2	24.8	37.1	19.6	11.3	83.1	n.a.	n.a.	11.7	5.2
MALES PER 100 FEMALES											
1860[2]	104.7	102.4	101.2	107.9	111.5	98.3	105.3	103.7	115.1	99.6	260.8
1870[2]	102.2	102.9	101.2	99.2	114.5	100.5	102.8	100.6	115.3	96.2	400.7
1880[2]	103.6	103.0	101.3	104.0	110.2	101.4	104.0	102.1	115.9	97.8	362.2
1890[3]	105.0	103.6	101.4	107.3	108.3	104.2	105.4	102.9	118.7	99.5	165.2
1900	104.4	102.1	100.9	105.8	110.7	102.0	104.9	102.8	117.4	98.6	185.2
1910	106.0	102.5	101.3	108.1	114.4	101.1	106.6	102.7	129.2	98.9	185.6
1920	104.0	102.5	100.8	102.8	115.2	101.3	104.4	101.7	121.7	99.2	156.6
1930	102.5	103.0	101.4	100.5	109.1	100.5	102.9	101.1	115.8	97.0	150.6
1940	100.7	103.2	102.0	98.1	105.2	95.5	101.2	100.1	111.1	95.0	140.5

		Age				Race and nativity				
							White[1]			
Year	Total	Under 5	5–19	20–44	45–62	65 and over	Total	Native born	Foreign born	Black	Other races[1]
1950	98.6	103.9	102.5	96.2	100.1	89.6	99.0	98.8	102.0	93.7	129.7
1960	97.1	103.4	102.7	95.6	95.7	82.8	97.4	97.6	94.2	93.3	109.7
1970[2]	94.8	104.0	103.3	95.1	91.6	72.1	95.3	95.9	83.8	90.8	100.2
1980	94.5	104.7	104.0	98.1	90.7	67.6	94.8	n.a.	n.a.	89.6	100.3

1. The 1980 census data for white and other races categories are not directly comparable to those shown for the preceding years because of the changes in the way some persons reported their race, as well as changes in 1980 procedures relating to racial classification. 2. Excludes persons for whom age is not available. 3. Excludes persons enumerated in the Indian Territory and on Indian reservations. NOTES: Data exclude Armed Forces overseas. Beginning in 1960, includes Alaska and Hawaii. n.a. = not available. *Source:* Department of Commerce, Bureau of the Census.

Population and Rank of Large Metropolitan Areas, 1980–1988

(over 150,000)

Standard metropolitan statistical area	1988 Est. Number	1988 Est. Rank	1980 Census Number	1980 Census Rank	Change 1980–88 Number	Change 1980–88 %
Akron, Ohio	653,500	—	660,328	—	−6,900	−1.0
Albany-Schenectady-Troy, N.Y.	850,800	48	835,880	46	15,000	1.8
Albuquerque, N.M.	493,100	75	420,262	79	72,800	17.3
Allentown-Bethlehem, Pa.-N.J.	677,100	56	635,481	54	41,600	6.6
Amarillo, Texas	196,300	156	173,699	157	22,600	13.0
Anaheim-Santa Ana, Calif.	2,257,000	—	1,932,921	—	324,079	16.8
Anchorage, Alaska	218,500	147	174,431	156	44,100	25.3
Ann Arbor, Mich.	267,800	—	264,740	—	3,100	1.2
Appleton-Oshkosh-Neenah, Wis.	312,900	112	291,369	107	21,500	7.4
Asheville, N.C.	173,100	169	160,934	171	12,100	7.5
Atlanta	2,736,600	13	2,138,143	16	598,400	28.0
Atlantic City, N.J.	309,200	114	276,385	113	32,800	11.9
Augusta, Ga.-S.C.	396,400	89	345,923	95	50,500	14.6
Aurora-Elgin, Ill.	355,400	—	315,607	—	39,700	12.6
Austin, Texas	748,500	52	536,688	63	211,800	39.5
Bakersfield, Calif.	520,000	71	403,089	84	116,900	29.0
Baltimore	2,342,500	18	2,199,497	15	143,000	6.5
Baton Rouge, La.	536,500	68	494,151	69	42,400	8.6
Beaumont-Port Arthur, Texas	363,900	98	375,497	88	−9,300	−2.5
Beaver County, Pa.	189,800	—	204,441	—	−14,600	−7.2
Benton Harbor, Mich.	166,600	177	171,276	161	−4,700	−2.8
Bergen-Passaic, N.J.	1,292,300	—	1,292,970	—	−700	−0.1
Biloxi-Gulfport, Miss.	205,000	154	182,161	153	22,800	12.5
Binghamton, N.Y.	260,200	128	263,460	123	−3,200	−1.2
Birmingham, Ala.	923,400	46	884,014	42	39,400	4.5
Boise City, Idaho	200,700	155	173,125	158	27,600	15.9
Boston	2,845,000	—	2,805,911	—	39,000	1.4
Bradenton, Fla.	186,900	161	148,445	181	38,500	25.9
Brazoria, Texas	184,600	—	169,587	—	15,000	8.8
Bremerton, Wash.	180,900	166	147,152	182	33,700	22.9
Bridgeport-Milford, Conn.	444,000	—	438,557	—	5,400	1.2
Brockton, Mass.	186,800	—	182,891	—	3,900	2.1
Brownsville-Harlingen, Texas	264,000	124	209,727	138	54,300	25.9
Buffalo, N.Y.	958,700	—	1,015,472	—	−56,800	−5.6
Canton, Ohio	401,400	88	404,421	83	−3,000	−0.8
Cedar Rapids, Iowa	171,500	173	169,775	163	1,700	1.0
Champaign-Urbana-Rantoul, Ill.	172,100	171	168,392	164	3,700	2.2
Charleston, S.C.	510,800	73	430,346	76	80,400	18.7
Charleston, W. Va.	260,800	126	269,595	118	−8,800	−3.3
Charlotte-Gastonia-Rock Hill, N.C.-S.C.	1,112,000	35	971,447	36	140,600	14.5
Chattanooga, Tenn.-Ga.	438,100	81	426,540	77	11,700	2.7
Chicago	6,216,300	3	6,060,401	3	155,900	2.6
Chico, Calif.	174,500	168	143,851	184	30,600	21.3
Cincinnati, Ohio-Ky.-Ind.	1,448,800	—	1,401,471	—	47,300	3.4
Clarksville-Hopkinsville, Tenn.-Ky.	158,900	180	150,220	179	8,600	5.7
Cleveland	1,845,000	—	1,898,825	—	−53,800	−2.8
Colorado Springs, Colo.	393,900	92	309,424	105	84,500	27.3
Columbia, S.C.	456,500	78	409,955	82	46,500	11.3
Columbus, Ga.-Ala.	246,900	132	239,196	131	7,700	3.2
Columbus, Ohio	1,344,300	29	1,243,827	28	100,500	8.1

Standard metropolitan statistical area	1988 Est.		1980 Census		Change, 1980–88	
	Number	Rank	Number	Rank	Number	%
Corpus Christi, Texas	358,000	100	326,228	99	31,800	9.7
Dallas-Fort Worth	3,766,100	8	2,930,539	10	835,500	28.5
Danbury, Conn.	190,800	—	170,369	—	20,500	12.6
Davenport-Rock Island-Moline, Iowa-Ill.	364,200	97	384,749	86	−20,500	−5.3
Dayton-Springfield, Ohio	948,000	44	942,083	39	5,900	0.6
Daytona Beach, Fla.	348,400	105	258,762	124	89,600	34.6
Denver-Boulder, Colo.	1,858,000	22	1,618,461	21	239,500	14.8
Des Moines, Iowa	391,800	93	367,561	89	24,200	6.6
Detroit, Mich.	4,352,400	—	4,488,024	—	−135,600	−3.0
Duluth, Minn.-Wis.	241,400	136	266,650	119	−25,300	−9.5
El Paso, Texas	585,900	67	479,899	70	106,000	22.1
Erie, Pa.	277,000	121	279,780	111	−2,800	−1.0
Eugene-Springfield, Ore.	270,100	122	275,226	115	−5,100	−1.9
Evansville, Ind.-Ky.	281,200	120	276,252	114	5,000	1.8
Fall River, Mass.-R.I.	153,800	—	157,222	—	−3,500	−2.2
Fayetteville, N.C.	255,700	130	247,160	127	8,500	3.5
Flint, Mich.	430,700	82	450,449	73	−19,700	−4.4
Fort Collins-Loveland, Colo.	182,000	164	149,184	180	32,800	22.0
Fort Lauderdale-Hollywood-Pompano Beach, Fla.	1,187,000	—	1,018,257	—	168,700	16.6
Fort Myers-Cape Coral, Fla.	309,100	115	205,266	140	103,900	50.6
Fort Pierce, Fla.	231,800	141	151,196	178	80,600	53.3
Fort Smith, Ark.-Okla.	180,700	167	162,813	169	17,900	11.0
Fort Wayne, Ind.	367,400	96	354,156	93	13,200	3.7
Fresno, Calif.	614,800	64	514,621	67	100,200	19.5
Gainesville, Fla.	207,600	153	171,392	160	36,200	21.1
Galveston-Texas City, Texas	210,000	—	195,738	—	14,200	7.3
Gary-Hammond, Ind.	612,200	—	642,733	—	−30,500	−4.8
Grand Rapids, Mich.	665,200	57	601,680	56	63,500	10.6
Green Bay, Wis.	191,200	158	175,280	155	16,000	9.1
Greensboro-Winston-Salem-High Point, N.C.	924,700	45	851,444	44	73,300	8.6
Greenville-Spartanburg, S.C.	621,400	62	570,211	59	51,200	9.0
Hamilton-Middletown, Ohio	279,700	—	258,787	—	20,900	8.1
Harrisburg-Lebanon-Carlisle, Pa.	591,100	66	556,242	62	34,900	6.3
Hartford, Conn.	755,400	—	715,923	—	39,500	5.5
Hickory, N.C.	222,100	144	202,711	142	19,400	9.6
Honolulu	838,500	50	762,565	47	75,900	10.0
Houma-Thibodaux, La.	183,100	163	176,876	154	6,300	3.5
Houston, Texas	3,247,000	—	2,734,617	—	512,300	18.7
Huntington-Ashland, W.Va.-Ky.-Ohio	322,300	111	336,410	97	−14,100	−4.2
Huntsville, Ala.	236,700	139	196,966	144	39,800	20.2
Indianapolis	1,236,600	32	1,166,575	30	70,000	6.0
Jackson, Miss.	396,200	90	362,038	92	34,200	9.4
Jacksonville, Fla.	898,100	47	722,252	50	175,800	24.3
Jersey City, N.J.	542,200	—	556,972	—	−14,800	−2.7
Johnson City-Kingsport-Bristol, Tenn.-Va.	442,300	80	433,638	75	8,700	2.0
Johnstown, Pa.	250,600	131	264,506	121	−13,900	−5.3
Joliet, Ill.	379,200	—	355,042	—	24,100	6.8
Kalamazoo, Mich.	217,900	148	212,378	136	5,500	2.6
Kansas City, Mo.-Kan.	1,575,400	24	1,433,464	25	141,900	9.9
Killeen-Temple, Texas	239,600	138	214,587	135	25,000	11.6
Knoxville, Tenn.	599,600	65	565,970	60	33,600	5.9
Lafayette, La.	209,600	152	190,231	150	19,400	10.2
Lake Charles, La.	172,400	170	167,223	165	5,100	3.1
Lake County, Ill.	495,300	—	440,387	—	55,000	12.5
Lakeland-Winter Haven, Fla.	395,800	91	321,652	101	74,100	23.0
Lancaster, Pa.	414,100	85	362,346	91	51,800	14.3
Lansing-East Lansing, Mich.	428,400	83	419,750	80	8,600	2.1
Las Vegas, Nev.	631,300	60	463,087	72	168,200	36.3
Lawrence-Haverhill, Mass.-N.H.	380,600	—	339,090	—	41,600	12.3
Lexington-Fayette, Ky.	347,900	106	317,548	103	30,400	9.6
Lima, Ohio	156,700	181	154,795	175	1,900	1.3
Lincoln, Neb.	211,600	151	192,884	147	18,700	9.7
Little Rock-North Little Rock, Ark.	513,100	72	474,464	71	38,600	8.1
Longview-Marshall, Texas	166,600	176	151,760	176	14,900	9.8
Lorain-Elyria, Ohio	207,500	—	274,909	—	−4,500	−1.6
Los Angeles-Long Beach, Calif.	8,587,800	2	7,477,422	2	1,110,600	14.9
Louisville, Ky.-Ind.	967,000	42	956,486	38	10,500	1.1
Lowell, Mass.-N.H.	261,600	—	243,142	—	18,400	7.6
Lubbock, Texas	226,800	143	211,651	137	15,100	7.2
Macon-Warner Robins, Ga.	288,500	118	263,591	122	23,100	8.8
Madison, Wis.	352,800	102	323,545	100	29,300	9.1
McAllen-Edinburg-Mission, Texas	387,900	95	283,323	110	104,600	36.9

Standard metropolitan statistical area	1988 Est.		1980 Census		Change, 1980-88	
	Number	Rank	Number	Rank	Number	%
Melbourne-Titusville-Palm Bay, Fla.	388,300	94	272,959	116	115,300	42.3
Memphis, Tenn.-Ark.-Miss.	979,300	39	913,472	40	65,800	7.2
Merced, Calif.	170,000	174	134,557	197	35,500	26.3
Miami-Hialeah, Fla.	1,813,500	—	1,625,611	—	188,000	11.6
Middlesex-Somerset-Hunterdon, N.J.	978,300	—	886,383	—	91,900	10.4
Milwaukee, Wis.	1,398,000	—	1,397,020	—	900	0.1
Minneapolis-St. Paul, Minn.-Wis.	2,387,500	16	2,137,133	17	250,400	11.7
Mobile, Ala.	485,600	76	443,536	74	42,100	9.5
Modesto, Calif.	341,000	108	265,900	120	75,100	28.3
Monmouth-Ocean, N.J.	969,500	—	849,211	—	120,300	14.2
Montgomery, Ala.	300,800	116	272,687	117	28,100	10.3
Muskegon, Mich.	161,300	179	157,589	173	3,700	2.4
Nashua, N.H.	177,300	—	142,527	—	34,700	24.4
Nashville, Tenn.	971,800	40	850,505	45	121,300	14.3
Nassau-Suffolk, N.Y.	2,639,000	—	2,605,813	—	33,100	1.3
Newark, N.J.	1,886,200	—	1,879,147	—	7,100	0.4
New Bedford, Mass.	167,900	175	166,699	166	1,200	0.7
New Haven-Meriden, Conn.	523,700	69	500,462	68	23,300	4.7
New London-Norwich, Conn.-R.I.	259,300	129	250,839	125	8,500	3.4
New Orleans	1,306,900	31	1,256,668	27	50,300	4.0
New York, N.Y.	8,567,000	1	8,274,961	1	292,000	3.5
Niagara Falls, N.Y.	216,900	—	227,354	—	−10,400	−4.6
Norfolk-Virginia Beach-Newport News, Va.	1,380,200	28	1,160,311	31	219,900	19.0
Oakland, Calif.	2,006,300	—	1,761,710	—	244,500	13.9
Ocala, Fla.	189,800	159	122,488	212	67,400	55.0
Oklahoma City, Okla.	963,800	43	860,969	43	102,800	11.9
Olympia, Wash.	156,600	182	124,264	211	32,400	26.1
Omaha, Neb.-Iowa	621,600	61	585,122	57	36,500	6.2
Orange County, N.Y.	293,500	—	259,603	—	33,900	13.1
Orlando, Fla.	971,200	41	699,906	51	271,300	38.8
Oxnard-Ventura, Calif.	647,300	—	529,174	—	118,100	22.3
Parkersburg-Marietta, W.Va.-Ohio	154,400	183	157,889	172	−3,500	−2.2
Pawtucket-Woonsocket-Attleboro, R.I.-Mass.	324,800	—	307,403	—	17,400	5.7
Pensacola, Fla.	349,900	103	289,782	109	60,200	20.8
Peoria, Ill.	340,400	109	365,864	90	−25,500	−7.0
Philadelphia, Pa.-N.J.	4,920,400	—	4,716,559	—	203,900	4.3
Phoenix, Ariz.	2,029,500	20	1,509,262	24	520,400	34.5
Pittsburgh	2,094,300	—	2,218,870	—	−124,600	−5.6
Portland, Maine	212,200	150	193,831	145	18,400	9.5
Portland, Ore.	1,188,000	—	1,105,750	—	82,300	7.4
Portsmouth-Dover-Rochester, N.H.-Maine	220,400	146	190,938	148	29,500	15.4
Poughkeepsie, N.Y.	262,200	125	245,055	129	17,200	7.0
Providence, R.I.	646,800	—	618,514	—	28,300	4.6
Provo-Orem, Utah	242,700	135	218,106	134	24,600	11.3
Racine, Wis.	173,800	—	173,132	—	600	0.4
Raleigh-Durham, N.C.	683,500	55	560,774	61	122,700	21.9
Reading, Pa.	329,100	110	312,509	104	16,600	5.3
Reno, Nev.	239,700	137	193,623	146	46,100	23.8
Richmond-Petersburg, Va.	844,300	49	761,311	48	83,000	10.9
Riverside-San Bernardino, Calif.	2,277,600	—	1,558,215	—	719,400	46.2
Roanoke, Va.	221,600	145	220,393	133	1,200	0.5
Rochester, N.Y.	980,100	38	971,230	37	8,900	0.9
Rockford, Ill.	282,200	119	279,514	112	2,700	1.0
Sacramento, Calif.	1,385,200	27	1,099,814	32	285,400	25.9
Saginaw-Bay City-Midland, Mich.	406,200	87	421,518	78	−15,400	−3.6
St. Cloud, Minn.	181,200	165	163,256	168	18,000	11.0
St. Louis, Mo.-Ill.	2,466,700	14	2,376,971	14	89,700	3.8
Salem-Gloucester, Mass.	258,700	—	258,231	—	500	0.2
Salem, Ore.	269,800	123	249,895	126	19,900	8.0
Salinas-Seaside-Monterey, Calif.	348,800	104	290,444	108	58,300	20.1
Salt Lake City-Ogden, Utah	1,065,000	37	910,222	41	154,800	17.0
San Antonio, Texas	1,323,200	30	1,072,125	34	251,000	23.4
San Diego, Calif.	2,370,400	17	1,861,846	19	508,600	27.3
San Francisco-Oakland, Calif.	3,596,400	—	3,250,605	—	345,700	10.6
San Jose, Calif.	1,432,000	—	1,295,071	—	137,000	10.6
Santa Barbara-Santa Maria-Lompoc, Calif.	343,100	107	298,694	106	44,500	14.9
Santa Cruz, Calif.	226,700	—	188,141	—	38,000	20.5
Santa Rosa-Petaluma, Calif.	366,000	—	299,681	—	66,300	22.1
Sarasota, Fla.	260,600	127	202,251	143	58,400	28.9
Savannah, Ga.	244,400	133	220,553	132	23,800	10.8
Scranton-Wilkes-Barre, Pa.	736,600	53	728,796	49	7,800	1.1
Seattle, Wash.	1,861,700	—	1,607,618	—	254,000	15.8

Standard metropolitan statistical area	1988 Est.		1980 Census		Change, 1980–88	
	Number	Rank	Number	Rank	Number	%
Shreveport, La.	359,100	99	333,158	98	26,000	7.8
South Bend-Mishawaka, Ind.	244,200	134	241,617	130	2,600	1.1
Spokane, Wash.	356,400	101	341,835	96	14,600	4.3
Springfield, Ill.	191,700	157	187,770	151	4,000	2.1
Springfield, Mass.	522,500	70	515,259	66	7,300	1.4
Springfield, Mo.	234,300	140	207,704	139	26,600	12.8
Stamford, Conn.	191,800	—	198,854	—	−7,100	−3.6
Stockton, Calif.	455,700	79	347,342	94	108,400	31.2
Syracuse, N.Y.	650,300	53	642,971	53	7,300	1.1
Tacoma, Wash.	559,100	—	485,667	—	73,500	15.1
Tallahassee, Fla.	228,600	142	190,329	149	38,300	20.1
Tampa-St. Petersburg-Clearwater, Fla.	1,995,100	21	1,613,621	22	381,500	23.6
Toledo, Ohio	616,500	63	616,864	55	−400	−0.1
Topeka, Kan.	164,800	178	154,916	174	9,900	6.4
Trenton, N.J.	331,000	—	307,863	—	23,100	7.5
Tucson, Ariz.	636,000	59	531,443	64	104,600	19.7
Tulsa, Okla.	727,600	54	657,173	52	70,400	10.7
Tyler, Texas	152,600	184	128,366	206	24,200	18.9
Utica-Rome, N.Y.	312,600	113	320,180	102	−7,600	−2.4
Vallejo-Fairfield-Napa, Calif.	420,700	—	334,402	—	86,300	25.8
Vancouver, Wash.	226,200	—	192,227	—	34,000	17.7
Visalia-Tulare-Porterville, Calif.	297,900	117	245,738	128	52,200	21.2
Waco, Texas	188,000	160	170,755	162	17,300	10.1
Washington, D.C.-Md.-Va.	3,734,200	9	3,250,921	8	483,200	14.9
Waterbury, Conn.	215,800	149	204,968	141	10,900	6.3
West Palm Beach-Boca Raton-Delray Beach, Fla.	818,500	51	576,754	58	241,700	41.9
Wheeling, W.Va.-Ohio	171,500	172	185,566	152	−14,000	−7.6
Wichita, Kan.	483,100	77	442,401	75	40,700	9.2
Wilmington, Del.-N.J.-Md.	573,500	—	523,221	—	50,300	9.6
Worcester, Mass.	415,700	84	402,918	85	12,800	3.2
Yakima, Wash.	185,500	162	172,508	159	13,000	7.6
York, Pa.	410,400	86	381,255	87	29,100	7.6
Youngstown-Warren, Ohio	501,700	74	531,350	65	−29,600	−5.6

NOTE: A standard metropolitan statistical area (SMSA) is one of a large population nucleus together with adjacent communities that have a high degree of economic and social integration with that nucleus. — Source does not list rank separately. It is given for the Consolidated Metropolitan Statistical Area of which this area is a part. *Source:* Bureau of the Census.

Resident Population by Age, Sex, Race, and Hispanic Origin, 1989[1]

(in thousands)

Age	White		Black		Other races		Hispanic origin[2]		All persons	
	Male	Female	Male	Female	Male	Female	Male	Female	Male	Female
Under 5	7,716	7,335	1,469	1,421	414	399	1,131	1,091	9,598	9,155
5-9	7,504	7,124	1,423	1,378	394	389	1,019	977	9,321	8,891
10-14	6,973	6,601	1,362	1,318	355	342	957	920	8,689	8,260
15-19	7,327	7,015	1,394	1,365	371	341	905	868	9,091	8,721
20-24	7,731	7,628	1,279	1,372	357	335	996	928	9,368	9,334
25-29	9,142	8,960	1,342	1,485	381	389	1,159	1,029	10,865	10,834
30-34	9,385	9,182	1,289	1,455	404	420	1,026	933	11,078	11,058
35-39	8,342	8,283	1,035	1,225	354	382	779	757	9,731	9,890
40-44	7,229	7,321	782	945	283	322	582	603	8,294	8,588
45-49	5,758	5,915	626	769	217	237	427	457	6,601	6,920
50-54	4,791	4,998	544	679	174	189	346	380	5,509	5,866
55-59	4,480	4,830	508	608	133	167	293	329	5,121	5,605
60-64	4,498	5,071	467	567	113	150	249	291	5,079	5,788
65-69	4,130	4,899	402	515	100	125	181	220	4,631	5,538
70-74	3,120	4,074	274	386	69	89	110	153	3,464	4,549
75-79	2,147	3,282	187	299	51	66	77	120	2,385	3,648
80-84	1,189	2,220	91	165	26	37	46	74	1,306	2,422
85 and over	761	2,000	72	164	17	27	32	59	849	2,192
All ages	102,223	106,738	14,545	16,115	4,213	4,404	10,317	10,188	120,982	127,258
16 and over	78,686	84,404	10,027	11,743	2,979	3,208	7,027	7,024	91,693	99,354
18 and over	75,862	81,725	9,466	11,200	2,832	3,072	6,666	6,678	88,160	95,997
65 and over	11,347	16,475	1,025	1,529	264	344	447	626	12,636	18,348
Median age	32.5	34.7	26.3	29.1	27.9	30.1	25.7	26.5	31.6	33.8
Mean age	34.6	37.4	29.3	32.0	29.7	31.7	27.4	29.0	33.8	36.5

1. July 1, 1989. 2. Persons of Hispanic origin may be of any race. *Source:* U.S. Bureau of the Census.

Population by State

State	1980	Percent change, 1970–80	Pop. per sq. mi., 1980	Pop. rank, 1980	1970	1950	1900	1790
Alabama	3,893,888	+13.1	76.7	22	3,444,354	3,061,743	1,828,697	—
Alaska	401,851	+32.8	0.7	50	302,583	128,643	63,592	—
Arizona	2,718,215	+53.1	23.9	29	1,775,399	749,587	122,931	—
Arkansas	2,286,435	+18.9	43.9	33	1,923,322	1,909,511	1,311,564	—
California	23,667,902	+18.5	151.4	1	19,971,069	10,586,223	1,485,053	—
Colorado	2,889,964	+30.8	27.9	28	2,209,596	1,325,089	539,700	—
Connecticut	3,107,576	+ 2.5	637.8	25	3,032,217	2,007,280	908,420	237,946
Delaware	594,338	+ 8.4	307.6	47	548,104	318,085	184,735	59,096
D.C.	638,333	−15.6	—	—	756,668	802,178	278,718	—
Florida	9,746,324	+43.5	180.0	7	6,791,418	2,771,305	528,542	—
Georgia	5,463,105	+19.1	94.1	13	4,587,930	3,444,578	2,216,331	82,548
Hawaii	964,691	+25.3	150.1	39	769,913	499,794	154,001	—
Idaho	943,935	+32.4	11.5	41	713,015	588,637	161,772	—
Illinois	11,426,518	+ 2.8	205.3	5	11,110,285	8,712,176	4,821,550	—
Indiana	5,490,224	+ 5.7	152.8	12	5,195,392	3,934,224	2,516,462	—
Iowa	2,913,808	+ 3.1	52.1	27	2,825,368	2,621,073	2,231,853	—
Kansas	2,363,679	+ 5.1	28.9	32	2,249,071	1,905,299	1,470,495	—
Kentucky	3,660,777	+13.7	92.3	23	3,220,711	2,944,806	2,147,174	73,677
Louisiana	4,205,900	+15.4	94.5	19	3,644,637	2,683,516	1,381,625	—
Maine	1,124,660	+13.2	36.3	38	993,722	913,774	694,466	96,540
Maryland	4,216,975	+ 7.5	428.7	18	3,923,897	2,343,001	1,188,044	319,728
Massachusetts	5,737,037	+ 0.8	733.3	11	5,689,170	4,690,514	2,805,346	378,787
Michigan	9,262,078	+ 4.3	162.6	8	8,881,826	6,371,766	2,420,982	—
Minnesota	4,075,970	+ 7.1	51.2	21	3,806,103	2,982,483	1,751,394	—
Mississippi	2,520,638	+13.7	53.4	31	2,216,994	2,178,914	1,551,270	—
Missouri	4,916,686	+ 5.1	71.3	15	4,677,623	3,954,653	3,106,665	—
Montana	786,690	+13.3	5.4	44	694,409	591,024	243,329	—
Nebraska	1,569,825	+ 5.7	20.5	35	1,485,333	1,325,510	1,066,300	—
Nevada	800,493	+63.8	7.3	43	488,738	160,083	42,335	—
New Hampshire	920,610	+24.8	102.4	42	737,681	533,242	411,588	141,885
New Jersey	7,364,823	+ 2.7	986.2	9	7,171,112	4,835,329	1,883,669	184,139
New Mexico	1,302,894	+28.1	10.7	37	1,017,055	681,187	195,310	—
New York	17,558,072	− 3.7	370.6	2	18,241,391	14,830,192	7,268,894	340,120
North Carolina	5,881,766	+15.7	120.4	10	5,084,411	4,061,929	1,893,810	393,751
North Dakota	652,717	+ 5.7	9.4	46	617,792	619,636	319,146	—
Ohio	10,797,630	+ 1.3	263.3	6	10,657,423	7,946,627	4,157,545	—
Oklahoma	3,025,290	+18.2	44.1	26	2,559,463	2,233,351	790,391[1]	—
Oregon	2,633,105	+25.9	27.4	30	2,091,533	1,521,341	413,536	—
Pennsylvania	11,863,895	+ 0.5	264.3	4	11,800,766	10,498,012	6,302,115	434,373
Rhode Island	947,154	− 0.3	897.8	40	949,723	791,896	428,556	68,825
South Carolina	3,121,820	+20.5	103.4	24	2,590,713	2,117,027	1,340,316	249,073
South Dakota	690,768	+ 3.7	9.1	45	666,257	652,740	401,570	—
Tennessee	4,591,120	+16.9	111.6	17	3,926,018	3,291,718	2,020,616	35,691
Texas	14,229,191	+27.1	54.3	3	11,198,655	7,711,194	3,048,710	—
Utah	1,461,037	+37.9	17.8	36	1,059,273	688,862	276,749	—
Vermont	511,456	+15.0	55.2	48	444,732	377,747	343,641	85,425
Virginia	5,346,818	+14.9	134.7	14	4,651,448	3,318,680	1,854,184	747,610[2]
Washington	4,132,156	+21.1	62.1	20	3,413,244	2,378,963	518,103	—
West Virginia	1,949,644	+11.8	80.8	34	1,744,237	2,005,552	958,800	—
Wisconsin	4,705,767	+ 6.5	86.5	16	4,417,821	3,434,575	2,069,042	—
Wyoming	469,557	+41.3	4.8	49	332,416	290,529	92,531	—
Total U.S.	226,545,805	+11.4	62.6	—	203,302,031	151,325,798	76,212,168	3,929,214

1. Includes population of Indian Territory: 1900, 392,960. 2. Until 1863, Virginia included what is now West Virginia. *Source:* Department of Commerce, Bureau of the Census.

The Rise in Singleness

Over the past two decades, substantial changes have occurred in the marital status and living arrangements of Americans. One of the most notable changes has been an increasing single population.

Adults are more likely to be single today than they were in 1970. Young adults are postponing marriage beyond the age at which most persons have married in the past, and young and middle-aged adults are becoming single for the second, third, or fourth time because of divorce. Elderly persons are finding themselves single once more because of the death of their spouses. The single population aged 18 and over rose from 38 million in 1970 (28 percent of all adults) to 66 million in 1988 (37 percent of all adults).

Incorporated Places Over 25,000 Population

Asterisk denotes more than one ZIP code for a city and refers to Postmaster. To find the ZIP code for a particular address, consult the ZIP code directory available in every post office. For latest population figures of many cities, see listing for individual states in the United States section.

City and major ZIP code	1980 census	1970 census	City and major ZIP code	1980 census	1970 census
Aberdeen, SD (57401)	25,851	26,476	Bellflower, CA (90706)	53,441	52,334
Abilene, TX (79604*)	98,315	89,653	Bell Gardens, CA (90201)	34,117	29,308
Addison, IL (60101)	29,759	24,482	Bellingham, WA (98225*)	45,794	39,375
Akron, OH (44309*)	237,177	275,425	Beloit, WI (53511)	35,207	35,729
Alameda, CA (94501)	63,852	70,968	Bergenfield, NJ (07621)	25,568	29,000
Albany, GA (31706*)	74,550	72,623	Berkeley, CA (94704*)	103,328	114,091
Albany, NY (12212*)	101,727	115,781	Berwyn, IL (60402)	46,840	52,502
Albany, OR (97321)	26,678	18,181	Bessemer, AL (35020*)	31,729	33,428
Albuquerque, NM (87101*)	331,767	244,501	Bethel Park, PA (15102)	34,755	34,758
Alexandria, LA (71301*)	51,565	41,811	Bethlehem, PA (18016*)	70,419	72,686
Alexandria, VA (22313*)	103,217	110,927	Bettendorf, IA (52722)	27,381	22,126
Alhambra, CA (91802*)	64,615	62,125	Beverly, MA (01915)	37,655	38,348
Allen Park, MI (48101)	34,196	40,747	Beverly Hills, CA (90213*)	32,367	33,416
Allentown, PA (18101*)	103,758	109,871	Billings, MT (59101*)	66,842	61,581
Alton, IL (62002)	34,171	39,700	Biloxi, MS (39530*)	49,311	48,486
Altoona, PA (16603*)	57,078	63,115	Binghamton, NY (13902*)	55,860	64,123
Amarillo, TX (79120*)	149,230	127,010	Birmingham, AL (35203*)	284,413	300,910
Ames, IA (50010)	45,775	39,505	Bismarck, ND (58501)	44,485	34,703
Amherst, MA (01002)	33,229	26,331	Blacksburg, VA (24060)	30,638	9,384
Anaheim, CA (92803*)	219,311	166,408	Blaine, MN (55433)	28,558	20,573
Anchorage, AK (99502*)	174,431	48,081	Bloomfield, NJ (07003)	47,792	52,029
Anderson, IN (46018*)	64,695	70,787	Bloomington, IL (61701)	44,189	39,992
Anderson, SC (29621*)	27,965	27,556	Bloomington, IN (47401)	52,044	43,262
Annapolis, MD (21401*)	31,740	30,095	Bloomington, MN (55420*)	81,831	81,970
Ann Arbor, MI (48106*)	107,966	100,035	Blue Springs, MO (64015)	25,927	6,779
Anniston, AL (36201*)	29,523	31,533	Boca Raton, FL (33432*)	49,505	28,506
Antioch, CA (94509)	42,683	28,060	Boise, ID (83708*)	102,160	74,990
Appleton, WI (54911*)	58,913	56,377	Bolingbrook, IL (60439)	37,261	7,651
Arcadia, CA (91006)	45,994	45,138	Bossier City, LA (71111*)	50,817	43,769
Arlington, TX (76010*)	160,113	90,229	Boston, MA (02205*)	562,994	641,071
Arlington Heights, IL (60004*)	66,116	65,058	Boulder, CO (80302*)	76,685	66,870
Arvada, CO (80001*)	84,576	49,844	Bountiful, UT (84010)	32,877	27,751
Asheville, NC (28810*)	53,583	57,820	Bowie, MD (20715*)	33,695	35,028
Ashland, KY (41101)	27,064	29,245	Bowling Green, KY (42101)	40,450	36,705
Athens, GA (30601*)	42,549	44,342	Bowling Green, OH (43402)	25,728	14,656
Atlanta, GA (30304*)	425,022	495,039	Boynton Beach, FL (33435*)	35,624	18,115
Atlantic City, NJ (08401*)	40,199	47,859	Bradenton, FL (33506*)	30,170	21,040
Attleboro, MA (02703)	34,196	32,907	Brea, CA (92621)	27,913	18,447
Auburn, AL (36830)	28,471	22,767	Bremerton, WA (98310*)	36,208	35,307
Auburn, NY (13021)	32,548	34,599	Bridgeport, CT (06602*)	142,546	156,542
Auburn, WA (98002*)	26,417	21,653	Bristol, CT (06010)	57,370	55,487
Augusta, GA (30901*)	47,532	59,864	Brockton, MA (02403*)	95,172	89,040
Aurora, CO (80010*)	158,588	74,974	Broken Arrow, OK (74012*)	35,761	11,018
Aurora, IL (60507*)	81,293	74,389	Brookfield, WI (53005)	34,035	31,761
Austin, TX (78710*)	345,496	253,539	Brooklyn Center, MN (55429*)	31,230	35,173
Azusa, CA (91702)	29,380	25,217	Brooklyn Park, MN (55007)	43,332	26,230
Bakersfield, CA (93302*)	105,735	69,515	Brook Park, OH (44142)	26,195	30,774
Baldwin Park, CA (91706)	50,554	47,285	Brownsville, TX (78520*)	84,997	52,522
Baltimore, MD (21233*)	786,775	905,787	Brunswick, OH (44212)	28,104	15,852
Bangor, ME (04401)	31,643	33,168	Bryan, TX (77801*)	44,337	33,719
Barberton, OH (44203)	29,751	33,052	Buena Park, CA (90622*)	64,165	63,646
Bartlesville, OK (74003*)	34,568	29,683	Buffalo, NY (14240*)	357,870	462,768
Baton Rouge, LA (70821*)	219,419	165,921	Burbank, CA (91505*)	84,625	88,871
Battle Creek, MI (49016*)	35,724	38,931	Burbank, IL (60459)	28,462	—
Bay City, MI (48706)	41,593	49,449	Burlingame, CA (94010)	26,173	27,320
Bayonne, NJ (07002)	65,047	72,743	Burlington, IA (52601)	29,529	32,366
Baytown, TX (77520*)	56,923	43,980	Burlington, NC (27215)	37,266	35,930
Beaumont, TX (77704*)	118,102	117,548	Burlington, VT (05401)	37,712	38,633
Beavercreek, OH (45401)	31,589	—	Burnsville, MN (55337)	35,674	19,940
Beaverton, OR (97005*)	30,582	18,577	Burton, MI (48502)	29,976	—
Bell, CA (90201)	25,450	21,836	Butte, MT (59701)	37,205	23,368
Belleville, IL (62220*)	41,580	41,223	Calumet City, IL (60409)	39,697	33,107
Belleville, NJ (07109)	35,367	37,629	Camarillo, CA (93010)	37,797	19,219
Bellevue, WA (98009*)	73,903	61,196	Cambridge, MA (02140)	95,322	100,361

City and major ZIP code	1980 census	1970 census	City and major ZIP code	1980 census	1970 census
Camden, NJ (08101*)	84,910	102,551	Cupertino, CA (95014)	34,015	17,895
Campbell, CA (95008)	27,067	23,797	Cuyahoga Falls, OH (44222*)	43,890	49,815
Canton, OH (44711*)	93,077	110,053	Cypress, CA (90630)	40,391	31,569
Cape Coral, FL (33910)	32,103	—	Dallas, TX (75260*)	904,078	844,401
Cape Girardeau, MO (63701)	34,361	31,282	Daly City, CA (94015*)	78,519	66,922
Carbondale, IL (62901)	26,414	22,816	Danbury, CT (06810*)	60,470	50,781
Carlsbad, CA (92008)	35,490	14,944	Danville, IL (61832)	38,985	42,570
Carlsbad, NM (88220)	25,496	21,297	Danville, VA (24541*)	45,642	46,391
Carrollton, TX (75006*)	40,595	13,855	Davenport, IA (52802*)	103,264	98,469
Carson, CA (90749)	81,221	71,150	Davis, CA (95616)	36,640	23,488
Carson City, NV (89701)	32,022	15,468	Dayton, OH (45401*)	193,444	243,023
Casper, WY (82601*)	51,016	39,361	Daytona Beach, FL (32015*)	54,176	45,327
Cedar Falls, IA (50613)	36,322	29,597	Dearborn, MI (48120*)	90,660	104,199
Cedar Rapids, IA (52401*)	110,243	110,642	Dearborn Heights, MI (48127)	67,706	80,069
Cerritos, CA (90701)	53,020	15,856	Decatur, AL (35602*)	42,002	38,044
Champaign, IL (61820*)	58,133	56,837	Decatur, IL (62521*)	94,081	90,397
Chandler, AZ (85224)	29,673	13,763	Deerfield Beach, FL (33441)	39,193	16,662
Chapel Hill, NC (27514)	32,421	26,199	De Kalb, IL (60115)	33,099	32,949
Charleston, SC (29423*)	69,510	66,945	Del City, OK (73155*)	28,424	27,133
Charleston, WV (25301*)	63,968	71,505	Delray Beach, FL (33444*)	34,325	19,915
Charlotte, NC (28228*)	314,447	241,420	Del Rio, TX (78840)	30,034	21,330
Charlottesville, VA (22906*)	39,916	38,880	Denton, TX (76201*)	48,063	39,874
Chattanooga, TN (37401*)	169,558	119,923	Denver, CO (80202*)	492,365	514,678
Chelsea, MA (02150)	25,431	30,625	Des Moines, IA (50318*)	191,003	201,404
Chesapeake, VA (23320*)	114,486	89,580	Des Plaines, IL (60018*)	53,568	57,239
Chester, PA (19013*)	45,794	56,331	Detroit, MI (48233*)	1,203,339	1,514,063
Cheyenne, WY (82001*)	47,283	41,254	Dothan, AL (36303*)	48,750	36,733
Chicago, IL (60607*)	3,005,072	3,369,357	Downers Grove, IL (60515*)	42,572	32,544
Chicago Heights, IL (60411)	37,026	40,900	Downey, CA (90241*)	82,602	88,573
Chico, CA (95926)	26,603	19,580	Dubuque, IA (52001)	62,321	62,309
Chicopee, MA (01021*)	55,112	66,676	Duluth, MN (55806*)	92,811	100,578
Chino, CA (91710)	40,165	20,411	Duncanville, TX (75138*)	27,781	14,105
Chula Vista, CA (92010*)	83,927	67,901	Dunedin, FL (33528)	30,203	17,639
Cicero, IL (60650)	61,232	67,058	Durham, NC (27701*)	100,538	95,438
Cincinnati, OH (45234*)	385,457	453,514	East Chicago, IN (46312)	39,786	49,982
Claremont, CA (91711)	30,950	24,776	East Cleveland, OH (44112)	36,957	39,660
Clarksville, TN (37041*)	54,777	31,719	East Detroit, MI (48021)	38,280	45,920
Clearwater, FL (33575*)	85,528	52,074	East Lansing, MI (48823)	51,392	47,540
Cleveland, OH (44101*)	573,822	750,879	Easton, PA (18042)	26,027	29,450
Cleveland, TN (37311)	26,415	21,446	East Orange, NJ (07019*)	77,690	75,471
Cleveland Heights, OH (44118)	56,438	60,767	East Point, GA (30364)	37,486	39,315
Clifton, NJ (07015*)	74,388	82,437	East Providence, RI (02914)	50,980	48,207
Clinton, IA (52732)	32,828	34,719	East St. Louis, IL (62201*)	55,200	70,169
Clovis, CA (93612)	33,021	13,856	Eau Claire, WI (54701*)	51,509	44,619
Clovis, NM (88101)	31,194	28,495	Edina, MN (55424*)	46,073	44,046
College Station, TX (77840)	37,272	17,676	Edmond, OK (73034)	34,637	16,633
Colorado Springs, CO (80901*)	214,821	135,517	Edmonds, WA (98020)	27,679	23,684
Columbia, MO (65201*)	62,061	58,812	El Cajon, CA (92020*)	73,892	52,273
Columbia, SC (29201*)	100,385	113,542	El Dorado, AR (71730)	25,270	25,283
Columbia, TN (38401)	26,571	21,471	Elgin, IL (60120)	63,798	55,691
Columbus, GA (31908*)	169,441	155,028	Elizabeth, NJ (07207*)	106,201	112,654
Columbus, IN (47201*)	30,614	26,457	Elk Grove, CA (60007)	28,907	20,346
Columbus, MS (39701*)	27,383	25,795	Elkhart, IN (46515*)	41,305	43,152
Columbus, OH (43216*)	565,032	540,025	Elmhurst, IL (60126)	44,276	46,392
Compton, CA (90220*)	81,286	78,547	Elmira, NY (14901*)	35,327	39,945
Concord, CA (94520*)	103,255	85,164	El Monte, CA (91734*)	79,494	69,892
Concord, NH (03301*)	30,400	30,022	El Paso, TX (79910*)	425,259	322,261
Coon Rapids, MN (55433)	35,826	30,505	Elyria, OH (44035*)	57,538	53,427
Coral Gables, FL (33114)	43,241	42,494	Emporia, KS (66801)	25,287	23,327
Coral Springs, FL (33065)	37,349	1,489	Englewood, CO (80110*)	30,021	33,695
Corona, CA (91720)	37,791	27,519	Enid, OK (73701)	50,363	44,986
Corpus Christi, TX (78408*)	231,999	204,525	Erie, PA (16515*)	119,123	129,265
Corvallis, OR (97333*)	40,960	35,056	Escondido, CA (92025*)	64,355	36,792
Costa Mesa, CA (92626*)	82,562	72,660	Euclid, OH (44117)	59,999	71,552
Council Bluffs, IA (51501)	56,449	60,348	Eugene, OR (97401*)	105,624	79,028
Covina, CA (91722*)	33,751	30,395	Evanston, IL (60204*)	73,706	80,113
Covington, KY (41011*)	49,563	52,535	Evansville, IN (47708*)	130,496	138,764
Cranston, RI (02910*)	71,992	74,287	Everett, MA (02149)	37,195	42,485
Crystal, MN (55428*)	25,543	30,925	Everett, WA (98201*)	54,413	53,622
Culver City, CA (90230)	38,139	34,451	Fairborn, OH (45324)	29,702	32,267
Cumberland, MD (21502*)	25,933	29,724	Fairfield, CA (94533)	58,099	44,146

City and major ZIP code	1980 census	1970 census	City and major ZIP code	1980 census	1970 census
Fairfield, OH (45014)	30,777	14,680	Gulfport, MS (39503*)	39,676	40,791
Fair Lawn, NJ (07410)	32,229	38,040	Hackensack, NJ (07602*)	36,039	36,008
Fall River, MA (02722*)	92,574	96,898	Hagerstown, MD (21740)	34,132	35,862
Fargo, ND (58102*)	61,383	53,365	Hallandale, FL (33009)	36,517	23,849
Farmington, NM (87401)	31,222	21,979	Haltom City, TX (76117)	29,014	28,127
Farmington Hills, MI (48024)	58,056	—	Hamilton, OH (45012*)	63,189	67,865
Fayetteville, AR (72701)	36,608	30,729	Hammond, IN (46320*)	93,714	107,983
Fayetteville, NC (28302*)	59,507	53,510	Hampton, VA (23670*)	122,617	120,779
Ferndale, MI (48220)	26,227	30,850	Hanover Park, IL (60103)	28,850	11,735
Findlay, OH (45840)	35,594	35,800	Harlingen, TX (78551*)	43,543	33,503
Fitchburg, MA (01420)	39,580	43,343	Harrisburg, PA (17105*)	53,264	68,061
Flagstaff, AZ (86001)	34,743	26,117	Hartford, CT (06101*)	136,392	158,017
Flint, MI (48502*)	159,611	193,317	Harvey, IL (60426)	35,810	34,636
Florence, AL (35631*)	37,029	34,031	Hattiesburg, MS (39401)	40,829	38,277
Florence, SC (29501)	29,176	25,997	Haverhill, MA (01830)	46,865	46,120
Florissant, MO (63033*)	55,372	65,908	Hawthorne, CA (90250)	56,447	53,304
Fond du Lac, WI (54935)	35,863	35,515	Hayward, CA (94544*)	94,342	93,058
Fontana, CA (92335)	37,107	20,673	Hazleton, PA (18201)	27,318	30,426
Fort Collins, CO (80521*)	65,092	43,337	Hempstead, NY (11551*)	40,404	39,411
Fort Dodge, IA (50501)	29,423	31,263	Hendersonville, TN (37075)	26,561	412
Fort Lauderdale, FL (33310*)	153,279	139,590	Hialeah, FL (33010*)	145,254	102,452
Fort Lee, NJ (07024)	32,449	30,631	Highland, IN (46322)	25,935	24,947
Fort Myers, FL (33906*)	36,638	27,351	Highland Park, IL (60035)	30,611	32,263
Fort Pierce, FL (33450*)	33,802	29,721	Highland Park, MI (48203)	27,909	35,444
Fort Smith, AR (72901*)	71,626	62,802	High Point, NC (27260*)	63,808	63,229
Fort Wayne, IN (46802*)	172,028	178,269	Hillsboro, OR (97123*)	27,664	14,675
Fort Worth, TX (76101*)	385,164	393,455	Hilo, HI (96720)	35,269	26,353
Fountain Valley, CA (92728)	55,080	31,886	Hobbs, NM (88240)	29,153	26,025
Frankfort, KY (40601)	25,973	21,902	Hoboken, NJ (07030)	42,460	45,380
Frederick, MD (21701)	28,086	23,641	Hoffman Estates, IL (60195)	37,272	22,238
Freeport, IL (61032)	26,266	27,736	Holland, MI (49423)	26,281	26,479
Freeport, NY (11520)	38,272	40,374	Hollywood, FL (33022*)	121,323	106,873
Fremont, CA (94538*)	131,945	100,869	Holyoke, MA (01040)	44,678	50,112
Fresno, CA (93706*)	218,202	165,655	Honolulu, HI (96820*)	365,048	324,871
Fridley, MN (55432)	30,228	29,233	Hopkinsville, KY (42240)	27,318	21,395
Fullerton, CA (92631*)	102,034	85,987	Hot Springs, AR (71901*)	35,781	35,631
Gadsden, AL (35901*)	47,565	53,928	Houma, LA (70360)	32,602	30,922
Gainesville, FL (32602*)	81,371	64,510	Houston, TX (77201*)	1,595,138	1,233,535
Gaithersburg, MD (20877*)	26,424	8,344	Huber Heights, OH (45424)	35,480	—
Galesburg, IL (61401)	35,305	36,290	Huntington, WV (25704*)	63,684	74,315
Galveston, TX (77553*)	61,902	61,809	Huntington Beach, CA (92647*)	170,505	115,960
Gardena, CA (90247*)	45,165	41,021	Huntington Park, CA (90255)	46,223	33,744
Garden City, MI (48135)	35,640	41,864	Huntsville, AL (35813*)	142,513	139,282
Garden Grove, CA (92640*)	123,307	121,155	Hurst, TX (76053)	31,420	27,215
Garfield, NJ (07026)	26,803	30,797	Hutchinson, KS (67501)	40,284	36,885
Garfield Heights, OH (44125)	34,938	41,417	Idaho Falls, ID (83401*)	39,590	35,776
Garland, TX (75040*)	138,857	81,437	Independence, MO (64051*)	111,806	111,630
Gary, IN (46401*)	151,953	175,415	Indianapolis, IN (46206*)	700,807	736,856
Gastonia, NC (28052)	47,333	47,322	Inglewood, CA (90311*)	94,245	89,985
Glendale, AZ (85301*)	97,172	36,228	Inkster, MI (48141)	35,190	38,595
Glendale, CA (91209*)	139,060	132,664	Iowa City, IA (52240*)	50,508	46,850
Glendora, CA (91740)	38,500	32,143	Irvine, CA (92713)	62,134	—
Glenview, IL (60025)	32,060	24,880	Irving, TX (75061*)	109,943	97,260
Gloucester, MA (01930)	27,768	27,941	Irvington, NJ (07111)	61,493	59,743
Goldsboro, NC (27530)	31,871	26,960	Ithaca, NY (14850)	28,732	26,226
Grand Forks, ND (58201)	43,765	39,008	Jackson, MI (49201*)	39,739	45,484
Grand Island, NE (68801)	33,180	32,358	Jackson, MS (39205*)	202,895	153,968
Grand Junction, CO (81501*)	27,956	20,170	Jackson, TN (38301*)	49,131	39,996
Grand Prairie, TX (75051*)	71,462	50,904	Jacksonville, AR (72076)	27,589	19,832
Grand Rapids, MI (49501*)	181,843	197,649	Jacksonville, FL (32203*)	540,920	504,265
Granite City, IL (62040)	36,815	40,685	Jamestown, NY (14701)	35,775	39,795
Great Falls, MT (59403*)	56,725	60,091	Janesville, WI (53545*)	51,071	46,426
Greeley, CO (80631*)	53,006	38,902	Jefferson City, MO (65101)	33,619	32,407
Green Bay, WI (54301*)	87,899	87,809	Jersey City, NJ (07303*)	223,532	260,350
Greenfield, WI (53220)	31,467	24,424	Johnson City, TN (37601)	39,753	33,770
Greensboro, NC (27420*)	155,642	144,076	Johnstown, PA (15901*)	35,496	42,476
Greenville, MS (38701*)	40,613	39,648	Joliet, IL (60436*)	77,956	78,827
Greenville, NC (27834)	35,740	29,063	Jonesboro, AR (72401)	31,530	27,050
Greenville, SC (29602*)	58,242	61,436	Joplin, MO (64801)	39,023	39,256
Gresham, OR (97030)	33,005	10,030	Kalamazoo, MI (49001*)	79,722	85,555

City and major ZIP code	1980 census	1970 census	City and major ZIP code	1980 census	1970 census
Kankakee, IL (60901)	30,141	30,944	Lorain, OH (44052*)	75,416	78,185
Kansas City, KS (66110*)	161,148	168,213	Los Altos, CA (94022)	25,769	25,062
Kansas City, MO (64108*)	448,159	507,330	Los Angeles, CA (90052*)	2,966,850	2,811,801
Kearny, NJ (07032)	35,735	37,585	Los Gatos, CA (95030)	26,906	22,613
Kenner, LA (70062*)	66,382	29,858	Louisville, KY (40231*)	298,840	361,706
Kennewick, WA (99336)	34,397	15,212	Loveland, CO (80537)	30,244	16,220
Kenosha, WI (53141*)	77,685	78,805	Lowell, MA (01853*)	92,418	94,239
Kent, OH (44240)	26,164	28,183	Lubbock, TX (79408*)	173,979	149,101
Kentwood, MI (49508)	30,438	20,310	Lufkin, TX (75901)	28,562	23,049
Kettering, OH (45429)	61,186	71,864	Lynchburg, VA (24506*)	66,743	54,083
Killeen, TX (76541*)	46,296	35,507	Lynn, MA (01901*)	78,471	90,294
Kingsport, TN (37662*)	32,027	31,938	Lynwood, CA (90262)	48,548	43,354
Kingsville, TX (78363)	28,808	28,915	Macon, GA (31213*)	116,896	122,423
Kinston, NC (28501)	25,234	23,020	Madison, WI (53707*)	170,616	171,809
Kirkwood, MO (63122)	27,987	31,679	Madison Heights, MI (48071)	35,375	38,599
Knoxville, TN (37901*)	175,045	174,587	Malden, MA (02148)	53,386	56,127
Kokomo, IN (46902*)	47,808	44,042	Manchester, NH (03103*)	90,936	87,754
La Crosse, WI (54601*)	48,347	50,286	Manhattan, KS (66502)	32,644	27,575
Lafayette, IN (47901*)	43,011	44,955	Manhattan Beach, CA (90266)	31,542	35,352
Lafayette, LA (70501*)	81,961	68,908	Manitowoc, WI (54220)	32,547	33,430
La Habra, CA (90631)	45,232	41,350	Mankato, MN (56001)	28,651	30,895
Lake Charles, LA (70601*)	75,226	77,998	Mansfield, OH (44901*)	53,927	55,047
Lakeland, FL (33802*)	47,406	42,803	Maple Heights, OH (44137)	29,735	34,093
Lakewood, CA (90714*)	74,654	83,025	Maplewood, MN (55109)	26,990	25,186
Lakewood, CO (80215)	113,808	92,743	Margate, FL (33063*)	35,900	8,867
Lakewood, OH (44107)	61,963	70,173	Marietta, GA (30060*)	30,829	27,216
Lake Worth, FL (33461*)	27,048	23,714	Marion, IN (46952*)	35,874	39,607
La Mesa, CA (92041)	50,308	39,178	Marion, OH (43302)	37,040	38,646
La Mirada, CA (90638)	40,986	30,808	Marlborough, MA (01752)	30,617	27,936
Lancaster, CA (93534*)	48,027	—	Marshalltown, IA (50158)	26,938	26,219
Lancaster, OH (43130)	34,953	32,911	Mason City, IA (50401)	30,144	30,279
Lancaster, PA (17604*)	54,725	57,690	Massillon, OH (44646)	30,557	32,539
Lansing, IL (60438)	29,039	25,805	Maywood, IL (60153)	27,998	29,019
Lansing, MI (48924*)	130,414	131,403	McAllen, TX (78501)	66,281	37,636
La Puente, CA (91747*)	30,882	31,092	McKeesport, PA (15134*)	31,012	37,977
Laredo, TX (78041*)	91,449	69,024	Medford, MA (02155)	58,076	64,397
Largo, FL (33540*)	58,977	24,230	Medford, OR (97501)	39,603	28,973
Las Cruces, NM (88001*)	45,086	37,857	Melbourne, FL (32901*)	46,536	40,236
Las Vegas, NV (89114*)	164,674	125,787	Melrose, MA (02176)	30,055	33,180
Lauderdale Lakes, FL (33313)	25,426	10,577	Memphis, TN (38101*)	646,174	623,988
Lauderhill, FL (33313)	37,271	8,465	Menlo Park, CA (94025)	26,369	26,826
Lawrence, IN (46226)	25,591	16,353	Menomonee Falls, WI (53051)	27,845	31,697
Lawrence, KS (66044)	52,738	45,698	Mentor, OH (44060)	42,065	36,912
Lawrence, MA (01842*)	63,175	66,915	Merced, CA (95340)	36,499	22,670
Lawton, OK (73501*)	80,054	74,470	Meriden, CT (06450)	57,118	55,959
Leavenworth, KS (66048)	33,656	25,147	Meridian, MS (39301)	46,577	45,083
Lebanon, PA (17042)	25,711	28,572	Merrillville, IN (46410)	27,677	—
Lee's Summit, MO (64063)	28,741	16,230	Mesa, AZ (85201*)	152,453	63,049
Leominster, MA (01453)	34,508	32,939	Mesquite, TX (75149*)	67,053	55,131
Lewiston, ID (83501)	27,986	26,068	Miami, FL (33152*)	346,865	334,859
Lewiston, ME (04240)	40,481	41,779	Miami Beach, FL (33139)	96,298	87,072
Lexington, KY (40511*)	204,165	108,137	Michigan City, IN (46360)	36,850	39,369
Lima, OH (45802*)	47,381	53,734	Middletown, CT (06457)	39,040	36,924
Lincoln, NE (68501*)	171,932	149,518	Middletown, OH (45042)	43,719	48,767
Lincoln Park, MI (48146)	45,105	52,984	Midland, MI (48640)	37,250	35,176
Linden, NJ (07036)	37,836	41,409	Midland, TX (79702*)	70,525	59,463
Lindenhurst, NY (11757)	26,919	28,359	Midwest City, OK (73140*)	49,559	48,212
Little Rock, AR (72231*)	158,461	132,483	Milford, CT (06460)	49,101	50,858
Littleton, CO (80120*)	28,631	26,466	Milpitas, CA (95035)	37,820	26,561
Livermore, CA (94550)	48,349	37,703	Milwaukee, WI (53201*)	636,236	717,372
Livonia, MI (48150*)	104,814	110,109	Minneapolis, MN (55401*)	370,951	434,400
Lodi, CA (95240)	35,221	28,691	Minnetonka, MN (55343)	38,683	35,776
Logan, UT (84321)	26,844	22,333	Minot, ND (58701)	32,843	32,290
Lombard, IL (60148)	37,295	34,043	Miramar, FL (33023)	32,813	23,997
Lompoc, CA (93436)	26,267	25,284	Mishawaka, IN (46544*)	40,201	36,060
Long Beach, CA (90809*)	361,334	358,879	Missoula, MT (59806*)	33,388	29,497
Long Beach, NY (11561)	34,073	33,127	Mobile, AL (36601*)	200,452	190,026
Long Branch, NJ (07740)	29,819	31,774	Modesto, CA (95350*)	106,602	61,712
Longmont, CO (80501)	42,942	23,209	Moline, IL (61265)	45,709	46,237
Longview, TX (75602*)	62,762	45,547	Monroe, LA (71203*)	57,597	56,374
Longview, WA (98632)	31,052	28,373	Monroeville, PA (15146)	30,977	29,011

City and major ZIP code	1980 census	1970 census
Monrovia, CA (91016)	30,531	30,562
Montclair, NJ (07042*)	38,321	44,043
Montebello, CA (90640)	52,929	42,807
Monterey, CA (93940)	27,558	26,302
Monterey Park, CA (91754)	54,338	49,166
Montgomery, AL (36119*)	177,857	133,386
Moore, OK (73153*)	35,063	18,761
Moorhead, MN (56560)	29,998	29,687
Morgantown, WV (26505)	27,605	29,431
Mountain View, CA (94042*)	58,655	54,132
Mount Prospect, IL (60056)	52,634	34,995
Mount Vernon, NY (10551*)	66,713	72,778
Muncie, IN (47302*)	77,216	69,082
Murfreesboro, TN (37130)	32,845	26,360
Murray, UT (84107)	25,750	21,206
Muskegon, MI (49440*)	40,823	44,631
Muskogee, OK (74401)	40,011	37,331
Nacogdoches, TX (75961)	27,149	22,544
Nampa, ID (83651)	25,112	20,768
Napa, CA (94558*)	50,879	36,103
Naperville, IL (60566*)	42,330	22,794
Nashua, NH (03061*)	67,865	55,820
Nashville, TN (37202*)	455,651	426,029
National City, CA (92050)	48,772	43,184
Naugatuck, CT (06770)	26,456	23,034
New Albany, IN (47150)	37,103	38,402
Newark, CA (94560)	32,126	27,153
Newark, DE (19711*)	25,247	21,298
Newark, NJ (07102*)	329,248	381,930
Newark, OH (43055)	41,200	41,836
New Bedford, MA (02741*)	98,478	101,777
New Berlin, WI (53151)	30,529	26,910
New Britain, CT (06050*)	73,840	83,441
New Brunswick, NJ (08901*)	41,442	41,885
New Castle, PA (16101*)	33,621	38,559
New Haven, CT (06511*)	126,109	137,707
New Iberia, LA (70560)	32,766	30,147
New London, CT (06320)	28,842	31,630
New Orleans, LA (70113*)	557,927	593,471
Newport, RI (02840)	29,259	34,562
Newport Beach, CA (92660*)	62,556	49,582
Newport News, VA (23607*)	144,903	138,177
New Rochelle, NY (10802*)	70,794	75,385
Newton, MA (02158)	83,622	91,263
New York, NY (10001*)	7,071,639	7,895,563
Bronx borough (10451*)	1,168,972	1,471,701
Brooklyn borough (11201*)	2,230,936	2,602,012
Manhattan borough (10001*)	1,428,285	1,539,233
Queens borough[1]	1,891,325	1,987,174
Staten Island borough (10314*)	352,121	295,443
Niagara Falls, NY (14302*)	71,384	85,615
Niles, IL (60648)	30,363	31,432
Norfolk, VA (23501*)	266,979	307,951
Normal, IL (61761)	35,672	26,396
Norman, OK (73070*)	68,020	52,117
Norristown, PA (19401*)	34,684	38,169
Northampton, MA (01060)	29,286	29,664
Northbrook, IL (60062)	30,778	25,422
North Charleston, SC (29406)	62,534	—
North Chicago, IL (60064)	38,774	47,275
Northglenn, CO (80233)	29,847	27,785
North Las Vegas, NV (89030)	42,739	46,067
North Little Rock, AR (72114*)	64,288	60,040
North Miami, FL (33161)	42,566	34,767
North Miami Beach, FL (33160)	36,553	30,544
North Olmsted, OH (44070)	36,486	34,861
North Richland Hills, TX (76118)	30,592	16,514
North Tonawanda, NY (14120)	35,760	36,012
Norwalk, CA (90650)	85,286	90,164
Norwalk, CT (06856*)	77,767	79,288

City and major ZIP code	1980 census	1970 census
Norwich, CT (06360)	38,074	41,739
Norwood, OH (45212*)	26,342	30,420
Novato, CA (94947)	43,916	31,006
Nutley, NJ (07110)	28,998	31,913
Oak Forest, IL (60452)	26,096	19,271
Oakland, CA (94615*)	339,337	361,561
Oak Lawn, IL (60454*)	60,590	60,305
Oak Park, IL (60301*)	54,887	62,511
Oak Park, MI (48237)	31,537	36,762
Oak Ridge, TN (37830)	27,662	28,319
Ocala, FL (32678*)	37,170	22,583
Oceanside, CA (92054*)	76,698	40,494
Odessa, TX (79760*)	90,027	78,380
Ogden, UT (84401*)	64,407	69,478
Oklahoma City, OK (73125*)	403,136	368,164
Olathe, KS (66061*)	37,258	17,917
Olympia, WA (98501*)	27,447	23,296
Omaha, NE (68108*)	313,911	346,929
Ontario, CA (91761*)	88,820	64,118
Orange, CA (92667*)	91,788	77,365
Orange, NJ (07051*)	31,136	32,566
Orem, UT (84057*)	52,399	25,729
Orlando, FL (32802*)	128,291	99,006
Oshkosh, WI (54901)	49,620	53,082
Ottumwa, IA (52501)	27,381	29,610
Overland Park, KS (66204)	81,784	77,934
Owensboro, KY (43201)	54,450	50,329
Oxnard, CA (93030*)	108,195	71,225
Pacifica, CA (94044)	36,866	36,020
Paducah, KY (42001)	29,315	31,627
Palatine, IL (60067*)	32,166	26,050
Palm Springs, CA (92263*)	32,366	20,936
Palo Alto, CA (94303*)	55,225	56,040
Panama City, FL (32401*)	33,346	32,096
Paramount, CA (90723)	36,407	34,734
Paramus, NJ (07652)	26,474	28,381
Paris, TX (75460)	25,498	23,441
Parkersburg, WV (26101*)	39,967	44,208
Park Forest, IL (60466)	26,222	30,638
Park Ridge, IL (60068)	38,704	42,614
Parma, OH (44129)	92,548	100,216
Pasadena, CA (91109*)	118,550	112,951
Pasadena, TX (77501*)	112,560	89,957
Pascagoula, MS (39567)	29,318	27,264
Passaic, NJ (07055)	52,463	55,124
Paterson, NJ (07510*)	137,970	144,824
Pawtucket, RI (02860*)	71,204	76,984
Peabody, MA (01960)	45,976	48,080
Pembroke Pines, FL (33024)	35,776	15,496
Pensacola, FL (32501*)	57,619	59,507
Peoria, IL (61601*)	124,160	126,963
Perth Amboy, NJ (08861*)	38,951	38,798
Petaluma, CA (94952)	33,834	24,870
Petersburg, VA (23804*)	41,055	36,103
Phenix City, AL (36867)	26,928	25,281
Philadelphia, PA (19104*)	1,688,210	1,949,996
Phoenix, AZ (85026*)	789,704	584,303
Pico Rivera, CA (90660)	53,387	54,170
Pine Bluff, AR (71601*)	56,636	57,389
Pinellas Park, FL (33565)	32,811	22,287
Pittsburg, CA (94565)	33,034	21,423
Pittsburgh, PA (15219*)	423,959	520,089
Pittsfield, MA (01201)	51,974	57,020
Placentia, CA (92670)	35,041	21,948
Plainfield, NJ (07061*)	45,555	46,862
Plano, TX (75074*)	72,331	17,872
Plantation, FL (33318)	48,653	23,523
Pleasant Hill, CA (94523)	25,124	24,610
Pleasanton, CA (94566)	35,160	18,328

City and major ZIP code	1980 census	1970 census
Plum, PA (15239)	25,390	21,932
Plymouth, MN (55447*)	31,615	18,077
Pocatello, ID (83201)	46,340	40,036
Pomona, CA (91766*)	92,742	87,384
Pompano Beach, FL (33060*)	52,618	38,587
Ponca City, OK (74601*)	26,238	25,940
Pontiac, MI (48056*)	76,715	85,279
Portage, IN (46368)	27,409	19,127
Portage, MI (49081)	38,157	33,590
Port Arthur, TX (77640)	61,251	57,371
Port Huron, MI (48060)	33,981	35,794
Portland, ME (04101*)	61,572	65,116
Portland, OR (97208*)	366,383	379,967
Portsmouth, NH (03801)	26,254	25,717
Portsmouth, OH (45662)	25,943	27,633
Portsmouth, VA (23705*)	104,577	110,963
Poughkeepsie, NY (12601*)	29,757	32,029
Prichard, AL (36610*)	39,541	41,578
Providence, RI (02940*)	156,804	179,116
Provo, UT (84603*)	74,108	53,131
Pueblo, CO (81003*)	101,686	97,774
Quincy, IL (62301)	42,554	45,288
Quincy, MA (02269)	84,743	87,966
Racine, WI (53401*)	85,725	95,162
Rahway, NJ (07065*)	26,723	29,114
Raleigh, NC (27611*)	150,255	122,830
Rancho Cucamonga, CA (91730)	55,250	—
Rancho Palos Verdes, CA (90274)	36,577	—
Rapid City, SD (57701)	46,492	43,836
Raytown, MO (64133*)	31,759	33,306
Reading, PA (19603*)	78,686	87,643
Redding, CA (96001*)	41,995	16,659
Redlands, CA (92373)	43,619	36,355
Redondo Beach, CA (90277*)	57,102	57,451
Redwood City, CA (94064*)	54,951	55,686
Reno, NV (89510*)	100,756	72,863
Renton, WA (98057*)	30,612	25,878
Revere, MA (02151)	42,423	43,159
Rialto, CA (92376)	37,474	28,370
Richardson, TX (75080*)	72,496	48,405
Richfield, MN (55423)	37,851	47,231
Richland, WA (99352)	33,578	26,290
Richmond, CA (94802*)	74,676	79,043
Richmond, IN (47374)	41,349	43,999
Richmond, VA (23232*)	219,214	249,332
Ridgewood, NJ (07451*)	25,208	27,547
Riverside, CA (92507*)	170,591	140,089
Riviera Beach, FL (33404)	26,489	21,401
Roanoke, VA (24022*)	100,220	92,115
Rochester, MN (55901*)	57,890	53,766
Rochester, NY (14692*)	241,741	295,011
Rockford, IL (61125*)	139,712	147,370
Rock Hill, SC (29730)	35,344	33,846
Rock Island, IL (61201)	47,036	50,166
Rockville, MD (20850*)	43,811	42,739
Rockville Centre, NY (11570)	25,412	27,444
Rocky Mount, NC (27801)	41,283	34,284
Rome, GA (30161)	29,654	30,759
Rome, NY (13440)	43,826	50,148
Rosemead, CA (91770)	42,604	40,972
Roseville, MI (48066)	54,311	60,529
Roseville, MN (55113*)	35,820	34,438
Roswell, NM (88201)	39,676	33,908
Royal Oak, MI (48068*)	70,893	86,238
Sacramento, CA (95813*)	275,741	257,105
Saginaw, MI (48065*)	77,508	91,849
St. Charles, MO (63301)	36,087	31,834
St. Clair Shores, MI (48080*)	76,210	88,093
St. Cloud, MN (56301)	42,566	39,691
St. Joseph, MO (64501*)	76,691	72,748
St. Louis, MO (63155*)	453,085	622,236

City and major ZIP code	1980 census	1970 census
St. Louis Park, MN (55426*)	42,931	48,883
St. Paul, MN (55101*)	270,230	309,866
St. Petersburg, FL (33730*)	238,647	216,159
Salem, MA (01970)	38,220	40,556
Salem, OR (97301*)	89,233	68,725
Salina, KS (67401)	41,843	37,714
Salinas, CA (93907*)	80,479	58,896
Salt Lake City, UT (84119*)	163,697	175,885
San Angelo, TX (76902*)	73,240	63,884
San Antonio, TX (78284*)	786,023	654,153
San Bernardino, CA (92403*)	118,794	106,869
San Bruno, CA (94066)	35,417	36,254
San Buenaventura (Ventura), CA (93002*)	74,393	57,964
San Clemente, CA (92672)	27,325	17,063
San Diego, CA (92199*)	875,538	697,471
Sandusky, OH (44870)	31,360	32,674
Sandy City, UT (84070*)	52,210	6,438
San Francisco, CA (94188*)	678,974	715,674
San Gabriel, CA (91776*)	30,072	29,336
San Jose, CA (95101*)	629,546	459,913
San Leandro, CA (94577*)	63,952	68,698
San Luis Obispo, CA (93401)	34,252	28,036
San Mateo, CA (94402*)	77,561	78,991
San Rafael, CA (94901*)	44,700	38,977
Santa Ana, CA (92711*)	204,023	155,710
Santa Barbara, CA (93102*)	74,414	70,215
Santa Clara, CA (95050*)	87,746	86,118
Santa Cruz, CA (95060*)	41,483	32,076
Santa Fe, NM (87501*)	48,953	41,167
Santa Maria, CA (93456*)	39,685	32,749
Santa Monica, CA (90406*)	88,314	88,289
Santa Rosa, CA (95402*)	83,320	50,006
Sarasota, FL (33578*)	48,868	40,237
Saratoga, CA (95070)	29,261	26,810
Savannah, GA (31401*)	141,390	118,349
Sayreville, NJ (08872)	29,969	32,508
Schaumburg, IL (60194)	53,305	18,531
Schenectady, NY (12301*)	67,972	77,958
Scottsdale, AZ (85251*)	88,622	67,823
Scranton, PA (18505*)	88,117	102,696
Seal Beach, CA (90740)	25,975	24,441
Seaside, CA (93955)	36,567	36,883
Seattle, WA (98109*)	493,846	530,831
Selma, AL (36701)	26,684	27,379
Shaker Heights, OH (44120)	32,487	36,306
Shawnee, KS (66202*)	29,653	20,946
Shawnee, OK (74801)	26,506	25,075
Sheboygan, WI (53081)	48,085	48,484
Shelton, CT (06484)	31,314	27,165
Sherman, TX (75090)	30,413	29,061
Shreveport, LA (71102*)	205,820	182,064
Simi Valley, CA (93065*)	77,500	59,832
Sioux City, IA (51101*)	82,003	85,925
Sioux Falls, SD (57101*)	81,343	72,488
Skokie, IL (60076*)	60,278	68,322
Slidell, LA (70458)	26,718	16,101
Somerville, MA (02143)	77,372	88,779
Somerville, NJ (08876)	29,969	32,508
South Bend, IN (46624*)	109,727	125,580
South Euclid, OH (44121)	25,713	29,579
Southfield, MI (48037*)	75,568	69,285
South Gate, CA (90280)	66,784	56,909
Southgate, MI (48195)	32,058	33,909
South San Francisco, CA (94080)	49,393	46,646
Sparks, NV (89431)	40,780	24,187
Spartanburg, SC (29301*)	43,826	44,546
Spokane, WA (99210*)	171,300	170,516
Springfield, IL (62703*)	100,054	91,753
Springfield, MA (01101*)	152,319	163,905
Springfield, MO (65801*)	133,116	120,096

City and major ZIP code	1980 census	1970 census	City and major ZIP code	1980 census	1970 census
Springfield, OH (45501*)	72,563	81,941	Visalia, CA (93277*)	49,729	27,130
Springfield, OR (97477*)	41,621	26,874	Vista, CA (92083)	35,834	24,688
Stamford, CT (06904*)	102,453	108,798	Waco, TX (76701*)	101,261	95,326
State College, PA (16801*)	36,130	32,833	Walla Walla, WA (99362)	25,618	23,619
Sterling Heights, MI (48077)	108,999	61,365	Walnut Creek, CA (94596*)	53,643	39,844
Steubenville, OH (43952)	26,400	30,771	Waltham, MA (02154)	58,200	61,582
Stillwater, OK (74074*)	38,268	31,126	Warner Robins, GA (31093)	39,893	33,491
Stockton, CA (95208*)	149,779	109,963	Warren, MI (48089*)	161,134	179,260
Stow, OH (44224)	25,303	20,061	Warren, OH (44481*)	56,629	63,494
Strongsville, OH (44136)	28,577	15,182	Warwick, RI (02887*)	87,123	83,694
Suffolk, VA (23434*)	47,621	9,858	Washington, DC (20013*)	638,432	756,668
Sunnyvale, CA (94086*)	106,618	95,976	Waterbury, CT (06701*)	103,266	108,033
Sunrise, FL (33338)	39,681	7,403	Waterloo, IA (50701*)	75,985	75,533
Superior, WI (54880)	29,571	32,237	Watertown, NY (13601)	27,861	30,787
Syracuse, NY (13220*)	170,105	197,297	Waukegan, IL (60085*)	67,653	65,134
Tacoma, WA (98413*)	158,501	154,407	Waukesha, WI (53186)	50,365	39,695
Tallahassee, FL (32301*)	81,548	72,624	Wausau, WI (54401)	32,426	32,806
Tamarac, FL (33320)	29,376	5,193	Wauwatosa, WI (53213)	51,308	58,676
Tampa, FL (33630*)	271,523	277,714	Weirton, WV (26062)	25,371	27,131
Taunton, MA (02780)	45,001	43,756	West Allis, WI (53213)	63,982	71,649
Taylor, MI (48180)	77,568	70,020	West Covina, CA (91793*)	80,291	68,034
Tempe, AZ (85282*)	106,743	63,550	Westfield, MA (01085)	36,465	31,433
Temple, TX (76501*)	42,354	33,431	Westfield, NJ (07091*)	30,447	33,720
Temple City, CA (91780)	28,972	31,034	West Haven, CT (06516)	53,184	52,851
Terre Haute, IN (47808*)	61,125	70,335	West Jordan, UT (84084)	27,192	4,221
Texarkana, TX (75501*)	31,271	30,497	Westland, MI (48185)	84,603	86,749
Texas City, TX (77590*)	41,403	38,908	West Memphis, AR (72301)	28,138	26,070
Thornton, CO (80229)	40,343	13,326	West Mifflin, PA (15122)	26,279	28,070
Thousand Oaks, CA (91360*)	77,072	35,873	Westminster, CA (92683)	71,133	60,076
Tinley Park, IL (60477)	26,171	12,572	Westminster, CO (80030*)	50,211	19,512
Titusville, FL (32780)	31,910	30,515	West New York, NJ (07093)	39,194	40,627
Toledo, OH (43601*)	354,635	383,062	West Orange, NJ (07052)	39,510	43,715
Topeka, KS (66603*)	115,266	125,011	West Palm Beach, FL (33401*)	63,305	57,375
Torrance, CA (90510*)	129,881	134,968	Wheaton, IL (60187)	43,043	31,138
Torrington, CT (06790)	30,987	31,952	Wheat Ridge, CO (80033)	30,293	29,778
Trenton, NJ (08650*)	92,124	104,786	Wheeling, WV (26003)	43,070	48,188
Troy, MI (48099*)	67,102	39,419	White Plains, NY (10602*)	46,999	50,346
Troy, NY (12180*)	56,638	62,918	Whittier, CA (90605*)	69,717	72,863
Tucson, AZ (85726*)	330,537	262,933	Wichita, KS (67276*)	279,835	276,554
Tulsa, OK (74101*)	360,919	330,350	Wichita Falls, TX (76307*)	94,201	96,265
Turlock, CA (95380)	26,287	13,992	Wilkes-Barre, PA (18701*)	51,551	58,856
Tuscaloosa, AL (35403*)	75,211	65,773	Williamsport, PA (17701)	33,401	37,918
Tustin, CA (92680)	32,317	22,313	Wilmette, IL (60091)	28,229	32,134
Twin Falls, ID (83301)	26,209	21,914	Wilmington, DE (19850*)	70,195	80,386
Tyler, TX (75712*)	70,508	57,770	Wilmington, NC (28402*)	44,000	46,169
Union City, CA (94587)	39,406	14,724	Wilson, NC (27893)	34,424	29,347
Union City, NJ (07087)	55,593	57,305	Winona, MN (55987)	25,075	26,438
University City, MO (63130)	42,738	47,527	Winston-Salem, NC (27102*)	131,885	133,683
Upland, CA (91786)	47,647	32,551	Woburn, MA (01801)	36,626	37,406
Upper Arlington, OH (43221)	35,648	38,727	Woodland, CA (95695)	30,235	20,677
Urbana, IL (61801)	35,978	33,976	Woonsocket, RI (02895)	45,914	46,820
Utica, NY (13504*)	75,632	91,373	Worcester, MA (01613*)	161,799	176,572
Vacaville, CA (95688)	43,367	21,690	Wyandotte, MI (48192)	34,006	41,061
Valdosta, GA (31601)	37,596	32,303	Wyoming, MI (49509)	59,616	56,560
Vallejo, CA (94590*)	80,303	71,710	Yakima, WA (98903*)	49,826	45,588
Valley Stream, NY (11580*)	35,769	40,413	Yonkers, NY (10701*)	195,351	204,297
Vancouver, WA (98661*)	42,834	41,859	Yorba Linda, CA (92686)	28,254	11,856
Vicksburg, MS (39180)	25,434	25,478	York, PA (17405*)	44,619	50,335
Victoria, TX (77901*)	50,695	41,349	Youngstown, OH (44501*)	115,436	140,909
Vineland, NJ (08360)	53,753	47,399	Yuma, AZ (85364*)	42,481	29,007
Virginia Beach, VA (23450*)	262,199	172,106	Zanesville, OH (43701)	28,655	33,045

1. Queens has four major ZIP codes: 11690*—Far Rockaway; 11351*—Flushing; 11431*—Jamaica; 11101*—Long Island City. *Sources:* Department of Commerce, Bureau of the Census; *National ZIP Code & Post Office Directory.*

Single-Parent Families Are Increasing

The substantial increase in single-parent situations is one of the most important recent changes in family composition. Between 1970 and 1988, the number of single-parent family groups more than doubled, from 3.8 million to 9.4 million. Of the approximately 63.2 million children under the age of 18 in 1988, 15.3 million were living with only one parent.

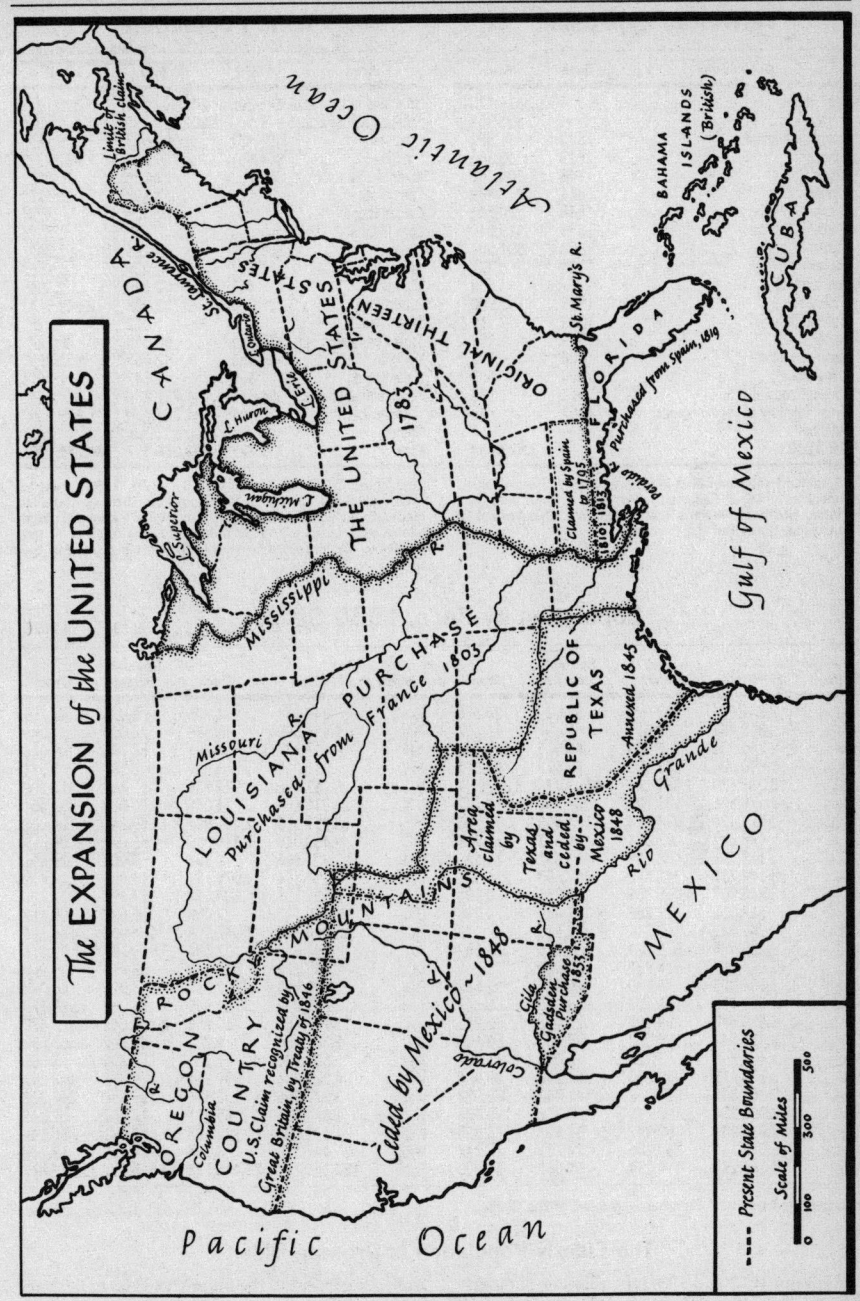

The EXPANSION of the UNITED STATES

CANADA

Limit of British claim

St. Lawrence R.

L. Ontario

L. Erie

L. Superior

L. Huron

L. Michigan

Atlantic Ocean

THE UNITED STATES 1783

ORIGINAL THIRTEEN STATES

St. Mary's R.

FLORIDA

Purchased from Spain, 1819

BAHAMA ISLANDS (British)

CUBA

Gulf of Mexico

Claimed by Spain to 1795

1810–1813

Perdido

Mississippi R.

Missouri R.

LOUISIANA PURCHASE
Purchased from France 1803

REPUBLIC OF TEXAS
Annexed 1845

Area claimed by Texas and ceded by Mexico 1848

Rio Grande

MEXICO

ROCK MOUNTAINS

OREGON COUNTRY
U.S. Claim recognized by Great Britain, by Treaty of 1846

Columbia R.

Ceded by Mexico ~ 1848

Colorado R.

Gila R.

Gadsden Purchase 1853

Pacific Ocean

- - - - Present State Boundaries

Scale of Miles
0 100 300 500

Map from AN ENCYCLOPEDIA OF WORLD HISTORY by William L. Langer, The Fifth Edition, Copyright 1940, 1948, 1952, and © 1967, 1972 by Houghton Mifflin Company. Reprinted by permission of Houghton Mifflin Company.

Territorial Expansion

Accession	Date	Area[1]
United States	—	3,618,770
Territory in 1790	—	891,364
Louisiana Purchase	1803	831,321
Florida	1819	69,866
Texas	1845	384,958
Oregon	1846	283,439
Mexican Cession	1848	530,706
Gadsden Purchase	1853	29,640
Alaska	1867	591,004
Hawaii	1898	6,471
Other territory	—	4,664
Philippines	1898	115,600[2]
Puerto Rico	1899	3,515
Guam	1899	209
American Samoa	1900	77
Canal Zone[3]	1904	553
Virgin Islands of U.S.	1917	132
Trust Territory of Pacific Islands	1947	717[4]
All other	—	14
Total, 1980	—	3,623,434

1. Total land and water area in square miles. 2. Became independent in 1946. 3. Reverted to Panama. 4. Land area only; includes Northern Mariana Islands. *Source:* Department of Commerce, Bureau of the Census.

Total Population

Area	1980	1970	1960
50 states of U.S.	226,545,805	203,302,031	179,323,175
48 coterminous	225,179,263	202,229,535	178,464,236
Alaska	401,851	302,583	226,167
Hawaii	964,691	769,913	632,772
American Samoa	32,297	27,159	20,051
Canal Zone	([1])	44,198	42,122
Canton Island	—	n.a.	320
Corn Islands	—	([2])	1,872
Guam	105,979	84,996	67,044
Johnston Atoll	327	1,007	156
Midway	453	2,220	2,356
Puerto Rico	3,196,520	2,712,033	2,349,544
Swan Islands	n.a.	22	28
Trust Ter. of Pac. Is.	132,929[3]	90,940	70,724
Virgin Is. of U.S.	96,569	62,468	32,099
Wake Island	302	1,647	1,097
Population abroad	995,546	1,737,836	1,374,421
Armed forces	515,408	1,057,776	609,720
Other[4]	n.a.	n.a.	n.a.
Total	231,106,727	208,066,557	183,285,009

1. Granted independence on Oct. 1, 1979. 2. Returned to Nicaragua April 25, 1971. 3. Includes Northern Mariana Islands. 4. Includes Baker Island, Enderbury Island, Howland Island, and Jarvis Island, all uninhabited. NOTE: n.a. = unavailable. *Source:* Department of Commerce, Bureau of the Census.

Population by Race, 1980 Census

State	White	Black	Spanish origin	Other	State	White	Black	Spanish origin	Other
Ala.	2,869,688	995,623	33,100	24,750	Mont.	740,148	1,786	9,974	44,756
Alaska	308,455	13,619	9,497	78,407	Neb.	1,490,569	48,389	28,020	31,048
Ariz.	2,240,033	75,034	440,915	402,799	Nev.	699,377	50,791	53,786	49,016
Ark.	1,890,002	373,192	17,873	22,319	N.H.	910,099	3,990	5,587	6,521
Calif.	18,031,689	1,819,282	4,543,770	3,817,591	N.J.	6,127,090	924,786	491,867	312,282
Colo.	2,570,596	101,702	339,300	216,517	N.M.	976,465	24,042	476,089	299,461
Conn.	2,799,420	217,433	124,499	90,723	N.Y.	13,961,106	2,401,842	1,659,245	1,194,340
Del.	488,543	95,971	9,671	10,711	N.C.	4,453,010	1,316,050	56,607	105,369
D.C.	171,796	488,229	17,652	17,626	N.D.	625,536	2,568	3,903	24,591
Fla.	8,178,387	1,342,478	857,898	219,127	Ohio	9,597,266	1,076,734	119,880	123,419
Ga.	3,948,007	1,465,457	61,261	50,801	Okla.	2,597,783	204,658	57,413	222,825
Hawaii	318,608	17,352	71,479	629,040	Ore.	2,490,192	37,059	65,833	105,412
Idaho	901,641	2,716	36,615	39,578	Pa.	10,654,325	1,047,609	154,004	164,794
Ill.	9,225,575	1,675,229	635,525	517,657	R.I.	896,692	27,584	19,707	22,878
Ind.	5,004,567	414,732	87,020	70,880	S.C.	2,145,122	948,146	33,414	25,940
Iowa	2,838,805	41,700	25,536	32,882	S.D.	638,955	2,144	4,028	49,079
Kan.	2,167,752	126,127	63,333	69,329	Tenn.	3,835,078	725,949	34,081	29,723
Ky.	3,379,648	259,490	27,403	22,295	Tex.	11,197,663	1,710,250	2,985,643	1,320,470
La.	2,911,243	1,237,263	99,105	55,466	Utah	1,382,550	9,225	60,302	69,262
Me.	1,109,850	3,128	5,005	11,682	Vt.	506,736	1,135	3,304	3,585
Md.	3,158,412	958,050	64,740	99,984	Va.	4,229,734	1,008,311	79,873	108,234
Mass.	5,362,836	221,279	141,043	152,922	Wash.	3,777,296	105,544	119,986	247,323
Mich.	7,868,956	1,198,710	162,388	190,678	W. Va.	1,874,751	65,051	12,707	9,842
Minn.	3,936,948	53,342	32,124	86,858	Wis.	4,442,598	182,593	62,981	80,144
Miss.	1,615,190	887,206	24,731	18,242	Wyo.	447,716	3,364	24,499	19,736
Mo.	4,346,267	514,274	51,667	56,903	Total	188,340,790	26,488,218	14,605,883	11,675,817

Source: Department of Commerce, Bureau of the Census.

The Elderly Population Is Growing Older

Between 1977 and 1987, the number of elderly (65 and over) increased from 23.9 million to 29.9 million, or from 10.8 to 12.2 percent of the population. The elderly population is itself growing older. The oldest old (persons aged 85 and over) increased from 5.6 percent of the elderly in 1960 to 9.6 percent in 1987.

Women dominate older age groups. In 1987, for example, 72 percent of people 85 years and over were women. Women tend to outlive men.

Immigration to U.S. by Country of Origin

(Figures are totals, not annual averages, and were tabulated as follows: 1820–67, alien passengers arrived; 1868–91 and 1895–97, immigrant aliens arrived; 1892–94 and 1898 to present, immigrant aliens admitted. Data before 1906 relate to country whence alien came; 1906–80, to country of last permanent residence; 1981 to present data based on country of birth.

Countries	1989	1820-1989	1981-89	1971-80	1961-70	1951-60	1941-50	1820-1940
Europe: Albania[1]	67	3,008	397	329	98	59	85	2,040
Austria[2]	476	2,660,618	3,936	9,478	20,621	67,106	24,860	2,534,617
Belgium	507	208,473	4,983	5,329	9,192	18,575	12,189	158,205
Bulgaria[3]	245	70,036	1,894	1,188	619	104	375	65,856
Czechoslovakia[1]	934	148,604	10,030	6,023	3,273	918	8,347	120,013
Denmark	564	369,727	4,685	4,439	9,201	10,984	5,393	335,025
Estonia[1]	14	1,274	117	91	163	185	212	506
Finland[1]	300	36,952	2,871	2,868	4,192	4,925	2,503	19,593
France	2,422	775,333	20,099	25,069	45,237	51,121	38,809	594,998
Germany[2]	6,641	7,053,918	62,414	74,414	190,796	477,765	226,578	6,021,951
Great Britain	12,892	5,084,974	124,997	137,374	213,822	202,824	139,306	4,266,561
Greece	2,157	691,581	26,054	92,369	85,969	47,608	8,973	430,608
Hungary[2]	1,051	1,669,182	7,967	6,550	5,401	36,637	3,469	1,609,158
Ireland	6,785	4,715,478	22,314	11,490	32,966	48,362	14,789	4,580,557
Italy[1]	2,636	5,335,187	29,333	129,368	214,111	185,491	57,661	4,719,223
Latvia[1]	55	2,934	312	207	510	352	361	1,192
Lithuania[1]	58	4,346	410	248	562	242	683	2,201
Luxembourg[1]	16	3,135	203	307	556	684	820	565
Netherlands	1,114	372,449	10,455	10,492	30,606	52,277	14,860	253,759
Norway[4]	462	752,912	3,357	3,941	15,484	22,935	10,100	697,095
Poland[5]	9,610	594,446	71,362	37,234	53,539	9,985	7,571	414,755
Portugal	3,588	496,645	35,815	101,710	76,065	19,588	7,423	256,044
Romania[6]	4,497	208,224	34,240	12,393	2,531	1,039	1,076	156,945
Spain	1,369	278,346	13,631	39,141	44,659	7,894	2,898	170,123
Sweden[4]	1,034	1,390,188	8,971	6,531	17,116	21,697	10,665	1,325,208
Switzerland	752	356,785	6,195	8,235	18,453	17,675	10,547	295,680
U.S.S.R.[7]	11,009	3,444,467	58,438	38,961	2,465	671	571	3,343,361
Yugoslavia[3]	2,158	133,525	16,016	30,540	20,381	8,225	1,576	56,787
Other Europe	208	60,722	2,463	4,049	4,904	9,799	3,447	36,060
Total Europe	73,621	36,923,469	583,959	800,368	1,123,492	1,325,727	621,147	32,468,776
Asia: China[8]	39,959	903,062	335,433	124,326	34,764	9,657	16,709	382,173
India	28,517	433,446	228,516	164,134	27,189	1,973	1,761	9,873
Israel	3,829	124,541	31,274	37,713	29,602	25,476	476	—
Japan[9]	4,446	452,270	37,111	49,775	39,988	46,250	1,555	277,591
Turkey	1,813	407,275	18,181	13,399	10,142	3,519	798	361,236
Other Asia	202,404	3,408,093	1,797,149	1,198,831	285,957	66,374	15,729	44,053
Total Asia[10]	280,968	5,728,687	2,447,664	1,588,178	427,642	153,249	37,028	1,074,926
America: Canada and Newfoundland[11]	10,618	4,239,506	100,859	169,939	413,310	377,952	171,718	3,005,728
Central America	33,904	596,961	245,421	134,640	101,330	44,751	21,665	49,154
Mexico[12]	66,445	2,868,341	635,455	640,294	453,937	299,811	60,589	778,255
South America	44,753	1,144,441	355,985	295,741	257,954	91,628	21,831	121,302
West Indies	79,348	2,598,894	767,768	741,126	470,213	123,091	49,725	446,971
Other America[12]	99	110,574	906	995	19,630	59,711	29,276	•56
Total America	235,167	11,558,717	2,106,394	1,982,735	1,716,374	996,944	354,804	4,401,466
Africa	18,450	306,855	149,603	80,779	28,954	14,092	7,367	26,060
Australia and New Zealand	2,229	140,938	17,480	23,788	19,562	11,506	13,805	54,437
Pacific Islands[13]	1,667	53,503	17,184	17,454	5,560	1,470	746	11,089
Countries not specified[14]	8	266,548	121	12	93	12,491	142	253,689
Total all countries	612,110	54,978,717	5,322,765	4,493,314	3,321,677	2,515,479	1,035,039	38,290,443

1. Countries established since beginning of World War I are included with countries to which they belonged. 2. Data for Austria-Hungary not reported until 1861. Austria and Hungary recorded separately after 1905, Austria included with Germany 1938–45. 3. Bulgaria, Serbia, Montenegro first reported in 1899. Bulgaria reported separately since 1920. In 1920, separate enumeration for Kingdom of Serbs, Croats, Slovenes; since 1922, recorded as Yugoslavia. 4. Norway included with Sweden 1820–68. 5. Included with Austria-Hungary, Germany, and Russia 1899–1919. 6. No record of immigration until 1880. 7. From 1931–63, the U.S.S.R. was broken down into European U.S.S.R. and Asian U.S.S.R. Since 1964, total U.S.S.R. has been reported in Europe. 8. Beginning in 1957, China includes Taiwan. 9. No record of immigration until 1861. 10. From 1934, Asia included Philippines; before 1934, recorded in separate tables as insular travel. 11. Includes all British North American possessions, 1820–98. 12. No record of immigration, 1886–93. 13. Included with "Countries not specified" prior to 1925. 14. Includes 32,897 persons returning in 1906 to their homes in U.S. *Source:* Department of Justice, Immigration and Naturalization Service. NOTE: Data are latest available.

Immigrant and Nonimmigrant Aliens Admitted to U.S.

Period[1]	Immigrants	Non-immigrants	Total	Period[1]	Immigrants	Non-immigrants	Total
1901–10	8,795,386	1,007,909	9,803,295	1982	594,131	11,779,359	12,373,490
1911–20	5,735,811	1,376,271	7,112,082	1983[2]	559,763	9,849,458	10,409,221
1921–30	4,107,209	1,774,896	5,882,090	1984	543,903	9,426,759	9,970,662
1931–40	528,431	1,574,071	2,102,502	1985	570,009	9,675,650	10,245,659
1941–50	1,035,039	2,461,359	3,496,398	1986	601,708	10,471,024	11,072,732
1951–60	2,515,479	7,113,023	9,628,502	1987	601,516	12,272,866	12,874,382
1961–70	3,321,677	24,107,224	27,428,901	1988	643,025	14,591,735	15,234,760
1971–77	2,797,209	45,236,597	48,033,806	1989	612,110	16,144,576	16,756,686

1. Fiscal year ending June 30 prior to 1977. After 1977 for fiscal year ending Sept. 30. 2. Nonimmigrant figures for calendar year 1983. Nonimmigrant aliens include visitors for business or pleasure, students, foreign government officials, and others temporarily in the U.S. *Source:* Department of Justice, Immigration and Naturalization Service.

Persons Naturalized Since 1907

Period[1]	Civilian	Military	Total	Period[1]	Civilian	Military	Total
1907–30	2,713,389	300,506	3,013,895	1985	238,394	3,266	244,717[2]
1931–40	1,498,573	19,891	1,518,464	1986	275,352	2,901	280,623[3]
1941–50	1,837,229	149,799	1,987,028	1987	224,100	2,402	227,008[4]
1951–60	1,148,241	41,705	1,189,946	1988	239,541	2,296	242,063[5]
1961–70	1,084,195	36,068	1,120,263	1989	231,198	1,954	233,777[6]
1971–80	1,397,846	66,926	1,464,772	1907–89	11,588,147	641,582	12,238,532[7]

1. Fiscal year ending June 30. Starting 1977, fiscal year ending Sept. 30. 2. Including 3,057 unidentified. 3. Including 2,370 unidentified. 4. Including 506 unidentified. 5. Including 226 unidentified. 6. Including 625 unidentified. 7. Including 8,803 unidentified. *Source:* Department of Justice, Immigration and Naturalization Service. NOTE: Data are latest available.

Population of Largest Indian Reservations, 1987

Navajo (Ariz., N.M., Utah)	173,018	Rosebud (S.D.)	11,685[1]	Zuni (N.M.)	8,135
Cherokee (Okla.)	58,232	Gila River (Ariz.)	10,688	Pawnee (Okla.)	7,657
Creek (Okla.)	54,606	Papago-Sells (Ariz.)	10,138	Northern Pueblos (N.M.)	7,651
Choctaw (Okla.)	21,858	Turtle Mountain (N.D.)	9,889	Shawnee (Okla., Texas)	7,263
Pine Ridge (S.D.)	19,246	Hopi (Ariz.)	9,040	Blackfeet (Mont.)	7,193
Southern Pueblos (N.M.)	17,079	Standing Rock (N.D., S.D.)	8,612	Yakima (Wash.)	6,846
Chicksaw (Okla.)	11,780	Fort Apache (Ariz.)	8,421	Wind River (Wyo.)	5,124

NOTE: The Bureau of Indian Affairs lists 861,500 Indians residing on or near Federal reservations as of January 1987. The total Indian population of the United States, according to the 1980 updated census, is 1,534,000, including Aleuts and Eskimos. *Source:* Department of the Interior, Bureau of Indian Affairs. 1. 1984 data. NOTE: Figures are most recent available.

Persons Below Poverty Level
by Age, Region, Race, and Hispanic Origin, 1988

	Number below poverty level (1,000)				Percent below poverty level			
Age and region	All races[2]	White	Black	Hispanic origin[1]	All races[2]	White	Black	Hispanic origin[1]
Under 16 years	11,550	6,931	3,978	2,468	20.4	15.2	45.4	38.9
16 to 21	3,328	2,043	1,046	559	15.7	11.8	34.0	27.4
22 to 44	9,470	6,379	2,573	1,627	10.5	8.4	23.6	20.6
45 to 64	4,047	2,816	1,045	500	8.8	7.0	22.4	17.9
65 and older	3,482	2,595	785	225	12.0	10.0	32.2	22.4
Northeast	5,117	3,704	1,145	917	10.2	8.4	22.9	28.4
Midwest	6,842	4,604	1,996	332	11.5	8.7	34.8	22.3
South	13,591	7,615	5,693	1,963	16.2	11.6	34.3	30.4
West	6,328	4,842	592	2,167	12.7	11.3	23.6	24.4
Total	31,878	20,765	9,426	5,379	13.1	10.1	31.6	26.8

1. Persons of Hispanic origin may be of any race. 2. Includes race not shown separately. *Source:* U.S. Bureau of the Census.

Revised Population Projections to 2080[1,2]
(in millions)

Sex, race, age group	2000	2050	2070	2080	Sex, race, age group	2000	2050	2070	2080
MALE, WHITE	108.8	110.3	105.6	103.6	**FEMALE, BLACK**	18.3	24.7	25.0	25.0
Up to 19 years	29.7	37.3	23.9	23.4	Up to 19 years	5.8	5.6	5.3	5.2
20 to 39 years	31.4	27.4	25.9	25.3	20 to 39 years	5.6	6.2	5.9	5.7
40 to 59 years	30.7	27.6	26.7	25.7	40 to 59 years	4.4	6.0	6.1	6.0
60 to 79 years	14.2	22.8	21.7	21.6	60 to 79 years	2.0	5.0	5.4	5.6
80 and over	2.8	7.4	7.5	7.6	80 and over	0.4	1.8	2.2	2.4
FEMALE, WHITE	112.7	116.2	110.9	108.7	**TOTALS**[3]	268.3	299.8	294.6	292.2
Up to 19 years	28.2	24.0	22.7	22.2	Up to 19 years	73.3	66.7	64.0	63.0
20 to 39 years	30.6	26.7	25.2	24.6	20 to 39 years	76.6	73.1	70.4	69.2
40 to 59 years	31.0	27.6	26.6	25.6	40 to 59 years	72.8	73.0	72.5	70.9
60 to 79 years	17.2	25.1	23.8	23.5	60 to 79 years	36.2	62.0	61.7	62.2
80 and over	5.7	12.9	12.5	12.7	80 and over	9.3	24.9	25.9	26.9
MALE, BLACK	16.7	22.4	22.7	22.6	Males	131.2	145.3	142.9	141.7
Up to 19 years	6.1	5.9	5.6	5.4	Females	137.1	154.5	151.7	150.5
20 to 39 years	5.2	5.8	5.5	5.4	White	221.5	226.6.	216.5	212.3
40 to 59 years	3.7	5.3	5.4	5.3	Black	35.1	47.1	47.7	47.6
60 to 79 years	1.6	4.3	4.8	5.0	Median age	36.4	42.7	43.6	43.9
80 and over	0.2	1.1	1.4	1.5					

1. Based on Population Report issued January 1989 revising prior Report issued May 1984. 2. Based on average of 1.8 lifetime births per woman. 3. Includes all races. NOTE: Zero population growth is expected to be reached by 2050. Details may not add because of rounding. *Source:* Department of Commerce, Bureau of the Census.

Marriage and Divorce

Marriages and Divorces

	Marriage		Divorce[1]			Marriage		Divorce[1]	
Year	Number	Rate[2]	Number	Rate[2]	Year	Number	Rate[2]	Number	Rate[2]
1900	709,000	9.3	55,751	.7	1966	1,857,000	9.5	499,000	2.5
1905	842,000	10.0	67,976	.8	1967	1,927,000	9.7	523,000	2.6
1910	948,166	10.3	83,045	.9	1968	2,069,258	10.4	584,000	2.9
1915	1,007,595	10.0	104,298	1.0	1969	2,145,438	10.6	639,000	3.2
1920	1,274,476	12.0	170,505	1.6	1970	2,158,802	10.6	708,000	3.5
1925	1,188,334	10.3	175,449	1.5	1971	2,190,481	10.6	773,000	3.7
1930	1,126,856	9.2	195,961	1.6	1972	2,282,154	11.0	845,000	4.1
1935	1,327,000	10.4	218,000	1.7	1973	2,284,108	10.9	915,000	4.4
1940	1,595,879	12.1	264,000	2.0	1974	2,229,667	10.5	977,000	4.6
1945	1,612,992	12.2	485,000	3.5	1975	2,152,662	10.1	1,036,000	4.9
1950	1,667,231	11.1	385,144	2.6	1976	2,154,807	10.0	1,083,000	5.0
1953	1,546,000	9.8	390,000	2.5	1977	2,178,367	10.1	1,091,000	5.0
1954	1,490,000	9.2	379,000	2.4	1978	2,282,272	10.5	1,130,000	5.2
1955	1,531,000	9.3	377,000	2.3	1979	2,341,799	10.6	1,181,000	5.4
1956	1,585,000	9.5	382,000	2.3	1980	2,406,708	10.6	1,182,000	5.2
1957	1,518,000	8.9	381,000	2.2	1981	2,438,000	10.6	1,219,000	5.3
1958	1,451,000	8.4	368,000	2.1	1982	2,495,000	10.8	1,180,000	5.1
1959	1,494,000	8.5	395,000	2.2	1983	2,444,000	10.5	1,179,000	5.0
1960	1,523,000	8.5	393,000	2.2	1984	2,487,000	10.5	1,155,000	4.9
1961	1,548,000	8.5	414,000	2.3	1985	2,425,000	10.2	1,187,000	5.0
1962	1,577,000	8.5	413,000	2.2	1986	2,400,000	10.0	1,159,000	4.8
1963	1,654,000	8.8	428,000	2.3	1987	2,421,000	9.9	1,157,000	4.8
1964	1,725,000	9.0	450,000	2.4	1988	2,389,000	9.7	1,183,000	4.8
1965	1,800,000	9.3	479,000	2.5	1989[3]	2,404,000	9.7	1,163,000	4.7

1. Includes annulments. 2. Per 1,000 population. Divorce rates for 1941–46 are based on population including armed forces overseas. Marriage rates are based on population excluding armed forces overseas. 3. Provisional. NOTE: Marriage and divorce figures for most years include some estimated data. Alaska is included beginning 1959, Hawaii beginning 1960. *Source:* Department of Health and Human Services, National Center for Health Statistics.

Percent of Population Ever Married

Age group, years[1]	1989	1980	1970	1960	1950	1940	1930	1920	1910	1900
Males: 15 to 19	1.2	2.7	2.6	3.3	2.9	1.5	1.5	1.8	1.0	0.9
20 to 24	22.6	31.2	45.3	46.9	41.0	27.8	29.0	29.1	24.7	22.2
25 to 29	54.1	67.0	80.9	79.2	76.2	64.0	63.2	60.5	57.1	54.1
30 to 34	74.2	84.1	90.6	88.1	86.8	79.3	78.8	75.8	73.9	72.3
35 to 44	87.9	92.5	93.3	91.9	90.4	86.0	85.7	83.8	83.3	83.0
45 to 54	93.3	93.9	92.5	92.6	91.5	88.9	88.6	88.0	88.8	89.7
Females: 15 to 19	4.8	8.8	9.7	13.5	14.4	10.0	11.0	10.8	9.8	9.4
20 to 24	37.5	49.8	64.2	71.6	67.7	52.8	53.9	54.4	51.5	48.4
25 to 29	70.6	79.1	89.5	89.5	86.7	77.2	78.3	76.9	75.0	72.4
30 to 34	83.1	90.5	93.8	93.1	90.7	85.3	86.8	85.1	83.8	83.4
35 to 44	91.8	94.5	94.8	93.9	91.7	89.6	90.0	88.6	88.6	88.9
45 to 54	94.6	95.3	95.1	93.0	92.2	91.3	90.9	90.4	91.4	92.2

1. Prior to 1980 data are for persons 14 years and older. *Source:* Department of Commerce, Bureau of the Census.

Persons Living Alone, by Sex and Age

(numbers in thousands)

Sex and age[1]	1989 Number	1989 Percent	1980 Number	1980 Percent	1975 Number	1975 Percent	1970 Number	1970 Percent	1960 Number	1960 Percent
BOTH SEXES										
15 to 24 years	1,315	5.8	1,726	9.4	1,111	8.0	556	5.1	234	3.3
25 to 44 years	7,067	31.1	4,729	25.8	2,744	19.7	1,604	14.8	1,212	17.2
45 to 64 years	5,476	24.1	4,514	24.7	4,076	29.2	3,622	33.4	2,720	38.5
65 years and over	8,851	39.0	7,328	40.1	6,008	43.1	5,071	46.7	2,898	41.0
Total, 15 years and over	**22,708**	**100.0**	**18,296**	**100.0**	**13,939**	**100.0**	**10,851**	**100.0**	**7,063**	**100.0**
MALE										
15 to 24 years	733	8.0	947	13.6	610	4.4	274	2.5	124	1.8
25 to 44 years	4,362	47.4	2,920	41.9	1,689	12.1	933	8.6	686	9.7
45 to 64 years	2,181	23.7	1,613	23.2	1,329	9.5	1,152	10.6	965	13.7
65 years and over	1,916	20.8	1,486	21.3	1,290	9.3	1,174	10.8	853	12.1
Total, 15 years and over	**9,193**	**100.0**	**6,966**	**100.0**	**4,918**	**35.3**	**3,532**	**32.5**	**2,628**	**37.2**
FEMALE										
15 to 24 years	581	4.3	779	6.9	501	3.6	282	2.6	110	1.6
25 to 44 years	2,705	20.0	1,809	16.0	1,055	7.6	671	6.2	526	7.4
45 to 64 years	3,295	24.4	2,901	25.6	2,747	19.7	2,470	22.8	1,755	24.8
65 years and over	6,935	51.3	5,842	51.6	4,718	33.8	3,897	35.9	2,045	29.0
Total, 15 years and over	**13,515**	**100.0**	**11,330**	**100.0**	**9,021**	**64.7**	**7,319**	**67.5**	**4,436**	**62.8**

1. Prior to 1980, data are for persons 14 years and older. NOTE: Details may not add because of rounding. *Source:* Department of Commerce, Bureau of the Census.

Characteristics of Unmarried-Couple Households, 1989

(number in thousands)

Characteristics	Number	Percent
Unmarried-couple households	2,764	100.0
Age of householders:		
Under 25 years	671	24.3
25–44 years	1,693	61.3
45–64 years	303	11.0
65 years and over	97	3.5

Characteristics	Number	Percent
Presence of children:		
No children under 15 years	1,906	69.0
Some children under 15 years	858	31.0
Sex of householders:		
Male	1,666	60.3
Female	1,098	39.7

Source: U.S. Bureau of the Census.

Households, Families, and Married Couples

Date	Households		Families		Married couples
	Number	Average population per household	Number	Average population per family	Number
June 1890	12,690,000	4.93	—	—	—
April 1930	29,905,000	4.11	—	—	25,174,000
April 1940	34,949,000	3.67	32,166,000	3.76	28,517,000
April 1950	43,554,000	3.37	39,303,000	3.54	36,091,000
April 1955	47,874,000	3.33	41,951,000	3.59	37,556,000
March 1960[1]	52,799,000	3.33	45,111,000	3.67	40,200,000
March 1965	57,436,000	3.29	47,956,000	3.70	42,478,000
March 1970	63,401,000	3.14	51,586,000	3.58	45,373,000
March 1975	71,120,000	2.94	55,712,000	3.42	47,547,000
March 1980	80,776,000	2.76	59,550,000	3.29	49,714,000
March 1985	86,789,000	2.69	62,706,000	3.23	51,114,000
March 1987	89,479,000	2.66	64,491,000	3.19	52,286,000
March 1988	91,066,000	2.64	65,133,000	3.17	52,613,000
March 1989	92,830,000	2.62	65,837,000	3.16	52,100,000

1. First year in which figures for Alaska and Hawaii are included. *Source:* Department of Commerce, Bureau of the Census.

Families Maintained by Women, With No Husband Present
(numbers in thousands)

	1989		1980		1975		1970		1960	
	Number	Percent	Number	Percent	Number	Percent	Number	Percent	Number	Percent
Age of women:										
Under 35 years	3,753	34.5	3,015	34.6	2,356	32.5	1,364	24.4	796	17.7
35 to 44 years	2,824	25.9	1,916	22.0	1,510	20.9	1,074	19.2	940	20.9
45 to 64 years	2,833	26.0	2,514	28.9	2,266	31.3	2,021	36.1	1,731	38.5
65 years and over	1,480	13.6	1,260	14.5	1,108	15.3	1,131	20.2	1,027	22.9
Median age	40.8	—	41.7	—	43.4	—	48.5	—	50.1	—
Presence of children:										
No own children under 18 years	4,371	40.1	3,260	37.4	2,838	39.2	2,665	47.7	2,397	53.3
With own children under 18 years	6,519	59.9	5,445	62.6	4,404	60.8	2,926	52.3	2,097	46.7
Total own children under 18 years	11,329	—	10,204	—	9,227	—	6,694	—	4,674	—
Average per family	1.04	—	1.17	—	1.27	—	1.20	—	1.04	—
Average per family with children	1.74	—	1.87	—	2.10	—	2.29	—	2.24	—
Race:										
White	7,342	67.4	6,052	69.5	5,212	72.0	4,165	74.5	3,547	78.9
Black[1]	3,223	29.6	2,495	28.7	1,940	26.8	1,382	24.7	947	21.1
Other	325	3.0	158	1.8	90	1.2	44	0.8	n.a.	n.a.
Marital status:										
Married, husband absent	1,864	17.1	1,769	20.3	1,647	22.7	1,326	23.7	1,099	24.5
Widowed	2,600	23.9	2,570	29.5	2,559	35.3	2,396	42.9	2,325	51.7
Divorced	3,966	36.4	3,008	34.6	2,110	29.1	1,259	22.5	694	15.4
Never married	2,460	22.6	1,359	15.6	926	12.8	610	10.9	376	8.4
Total families maintained by women	10,890	100.0	8,705	100.0	7,242	100.0	5,591	100.0	4,494	100.0

1. Includes other races in 1960. NOTE: n.a. = not available. (—) as shown in this table, means "not applicable." *Source:* Department of Commerce, Bureau of the Census.

Median Age at First Marriage

Year	Males	Females	Year	Males	Females	Year	Males	Females	Year	Males	Females
1900	25.9	21.9	1930	24.3	21.3	1960	22.8	20.3	1987	25.8	23.6
1910	25.1	21.6	1940	24.3	21.5	1970	23.2	20.8	1988	25.9	23.6
1920	24.6	21.2	1950	22.8	20.3	1980	24.7	22.0	1989	26.2	23.8

Source: Department of Commerce, Bureau of the Census.

Selected Family Characteristics

Characteristics[1]	1988 Number (thousands)	1988 Median income
ALL RACES		
All families	65,837	32,191
Type of residence		
Nonfarm	64,486	32,317
Farm	1,351	27,222
Location of residence		
Inside metropolitan areas	50,573	34,841
1,000,000 or more	31,817	36,917
Inside central cities	11,709	28,726
Outside central cities	20,108	41,320
Under 1,000,000	18,756	31,480
Inside central cities	7,596	29,088
Outside central cities	11,161	33,149
Outside metropolitan areas	15,263	25,894
Region		
Northeast	13,518	36,454
Midwest	16,096	32,887
South	23,200	28,951
West	13,022	33,082
Type of family		
Married-couple family	52,100	36,389
Wife in paid labor force	29,713	42,709
Wife not in paid labor force	22,387	27,220
Male householder, no wife present	2,847	26,827
Female householder, no husband present	10,890	15,346
Number of earners		
No earners	9,438	13,729
1 earner	18,189	23,872
2 earners	28,984	38,702
3 earners	6,680	48,977
4 earners or more	2,546	64,920
Size of family		
2 persons	27,377	27,075
3 persons	15,444	33,614
4 persons	14,068	39,051
5 persons	6,056	35,993
6 persons	1,901	36,307
7 persons or more	990	31,221
Occupation group of longest job of householder	(No longer available)	
Tenure status		
Owner occupied	n.a.	n.a.
Renter occupied	n.a.	n.a.
Occupier paid no cash rent	n.a.	n.a.
Educational attainment of householder		
Elementary	n.a.	n.a.
High school	n.a.	n.a.
College	n.a.	n.a.
1 to 3 years	n.a.	n.a.
4 years or more	n.a.	n.a.
4 years	n.a.	n.a.
5 years or more	n.a.	n.a.
Total, 25 years and over	n.a.	n.a.
WHITE		
All families	56,492	33,915
Type of residence		

Characteristics	1988 Number (thousands)	1988 Median income
Nonfarm	55,154	34,127
Farm	1,338	27,390
Location of residence		
Inside metropolitan areas	42,737	36,652
1,000,000 or more	26,284	39,321
Inside central cities	8,166	32,593
Outside central cities	18,119	42,009
Under 1,000,000	16,453	32,864
Inside central cities	6,126	31,359
Outside central cities	10,327	33,860
Outside metropolitan areas	13,755	27,029
Region		
Northeast	11,905	37,588
Midwest	14,406	34,246
South	18,777	31,475
West	11,405	33,478
Type of family		
Married-couple family	46,877	36,840
Wife in paid labor force	26,402	43,182
Wife not in paid labor force	20,475	27,958
Male householder, no wife present	2,274	28,935
Female householder, no husband present	7,342	17,672
Number of earners		
No earners	7,820	15,552
1 earner	15,107	25,993
2 earners	25,513	39,413
3 earners	5,798	49,927
4 earners or more	2,255	65,853
BLACK		
All families	7,409	19,329
Type of residence		
Nonfarm	7,400	19,360
Farm	10	(B)
Location of residence		
Inside metropolitan areas	6,180	20,509
1,000,000 or more	4,289	21,678
Inside central cities	2,945	18,821
Outside central cities	1,344	28,912
Under 1,000,000	1,891	17,935
Inside central cities	1,276	18,346
Outside central cities	615	17,175
Outside metropolitan areas	1,229	14,551
Region		
Northeast	1,225	24,495
Midwest	1,427	17,469
South	4,118	17,545
West	640	25,840
Type of family		
Married-couple family	3,722	30,385
Wife in paid labor force	2,414	36,709
Wife not in paid labor force	1,308	18,515
Male householder, no wife present	464	17,853
Female householder, no husband present	3,223	10,657

Characteristics[1]	1988 Number (thousands)	1988 Median income	Characteristics	1988 Number (thousands)	1988 Median income
Number of earners			Region		
No earners	1,364	6,108	Northeast	865	20,591
1 earner	2,573	14,006	Midwest	346	28,732
2 earners	2,654	31,875	South	1,560	19,851
3 earners	639	42,002	West	2,052	22,655
4 earners or more	179	53,635			
			Type of family		
SPANISH ORIGIN OF HOUSEHOLDER[2]			Married-couple family	3,398	25,667
All families	4,823	21,769	Wife in paid labor force	1,766	31,864
Type of residence			Wife not in paid labor force	1,632	19,117
Nonfarm	4,792	21,847	Male householder, no		
Farm	31	(B)	wife present	314	21,937
Location of residence			Female householder, no husband present	1,112	10,687
Inside metropolitan areas	4,454	22,181			
1,000,000 or more	3,398	23,163			
Inside central cities	1,968	20,076	Number of earners		
Outside central cities	1,430	27,908	No earners	622	6,545
Under 1,000,000	1,056	18,782	1 earner	1,568	15,841
Inside central cities	603	17,777	2 earners	1,891	28,406
Outside central cities	454	20,057	3 earners	530	36,897
Outside metropolitan areas	369	17,205	4 earners or more	213	49,138

1. Family data as of March 1989. 2. Persons of Spanish origin may be of any race. n.a. = not available. (B) Base less than 75,000. *Source:* Department of Commerce, Bureau of the Census. NOTE: Data are the latest available.

Births

Live Births and Birth Rates

Year	Births[1]	Rate[2]	Year	Births[1]	Rate[2]	Year	Births[1]	Rate[2]
1910	2,777,000	30.1	1955	4,104,000	25.0	1972	3,258,411	15.6
1915	2,965,000	29.5	1956[3]	4,218,000	25.2	1973	3,136,965	14.9
1920	2,950,000	27.7	1957[3]	4,308,000	25.3	1974	3,159,958	14.9
1925	2,909,000	25.1	1958[3]	4,255,000	24.5	1975	3,144,198	14.8
1930	2,618,000	21.3	1959[3]	4,295,000	24.3	1976	3,167,788	14.8
1935	2,377,000	18.7	1960[3]	4,257,850	23.7	1977	3,326,632	15.4
1940	2,559,000	19.4	1961[3]	4,268,326	23.3	1978	3,333,279	15.3
1945	2,858,000	20.4	1962[3]	4,167,362	22.4	1979	3,494,398	15.9
1946	3,411,000	24.1	1963[3]	4,098,020	21.7	1980	3,612,258	15.9
1947	3,817,000	26.6	1964[3]	4,027,490	21.0	1982	3,680,537	15.9
1948	3,637,000	24.9	1965[3]	3,760,358	19.4	1983	3,638,933	15.5
1949	3,649,000	24.5	1966[3]	3,606,274	18.4	1984	3,669,141	15.5
1950	3,632,000	24.1	1967[4]	3,520,959	17.8	1985	3,760,561	15.8
1951[3]	3,823,000	24.9	1968[3]	3,501,564	17.5	1986	3,731,000	15.5
1952[3]	3,913,000	25.1	1969[3]	3,600,206	17.8	1987	3,829,000	15.7
1953[3]	3,965,000	25.1	1970[3]	3,731,386	18.4	1988	3,913,000	15.9
1954[3]	4,078,000	25.3	1971[3]	3,555,970	17.2	1989[5]	4,021,000	16.2

1. Figures through 1959 include adjustment for underregistration; beginning 1960, figures represent number registered. For comparison, the 1959 registered count was 4,245,000. 2. Rates are per 1,000 population estimated as of July 1 for each year except 1940, 1950, 1960, 1970, and 1980, which are as of April 1, the census date; for 1942–46 based on population including armed forces overseas. 3. Based on 50% sample of births. 4. Based on a 20 to 50% sample of births. 5. Provisional. NOTE: Alaska is included beginning 1959; Hawaii beginning 1960. Since 1972, based on 100% of births in selected states and on 50% sample in all other states. *Sources:* Department of Health and Human Services, National Center for Health Statistics.

Live Births by Age of Mother

Year[1] and race	Total	Age of mother							
		Under 15 yr	15–19 yr	20–24 yr	25–29 yr	30–34 yr	35–39 yr	40–44 yr	45 yr and over
1940	2,558,647	3,865	332,667	799,537	693,268	431,468	222,015	68,269	7,558
1945	2,858,449	4,028	298,868	832,746	785,299	554,906	296,852	78,853	6,897
1950	3,631,512	5,413	432,911	1,155,167	1,041,360	610,816	302,780	77,743	5,322
1955	4,014,112	6,181	493,770	1,290,939	1,133,155	732,540	352,320	89,777	5,430
1960	4,257,850	6,780	586,966	1,426,912	1,092,816	687,722	359,908	91,564	5,182
1965	3,760,358	7,768	590,894	1,337,350	925,732	529,376	282,908	81,716	4,614
1970	3,731,386	11,752	644,708	1,418,874	994,904	427,806	180,244	49,952	3,146
1975	3,144,198	12,642	582,238	1,093,676	936,786	375,500	115,409	26,319	1,628
1980	3,612,258	10,169	552,161	1,226,200	1,108,291	550,354	140,793	23,090	1,200
1984	3,669,141	9,965	469,682	1,141,578	1,165,711	658,496	195,755	26,846	1,108
1985	3,760,561	10,220	467,485	1,141,320	1,201,350	696,354	214,336	28,334	1,162
1986	3,756,547	10,176	461,905	1,102,119	1,199,519	721,395	230,335	29,847	1,251
1987	3,809,394	10,311	462,312	1,075,454	1,216,080	760,695	247,984	34,781	1,375
White	2,992,488	4,009	308,099	821,749	999,153	630,048	200,947	27,497	986
Black	641,567	5,981	138,872	213,427	161,047	87,476	30,116	4,470	178
Other	175,339	321	15,341	40,680	55,880	43,171	16,921	2,814	211

1. Data for 1940–55 are adjusted for underregistration. Beginning 1960, registered births only are shown. Data for 1960–70 based on a 50% sample of births. For 1972–84, based on 100% of births in selected states and on 50% sample in all other states. Beginning 1960, including Alaska and Hawaii. NOTE: Data refer only to births occurring within the U.S. Figures are shown to the last digit as computed for convenience in summation. They are not assumed to be accurate to the last digit. Figures for age of mother not stated are distributed. *Source:* Department of Health and Human Services, National Center for Health Statistics.

Births to Unmarried Women
(in thousands, except as indicated)

Age and race	1987	1985	1980	1975	1970	1965	1960	1955	1950
By age of mother:									
Under 15 years	9.6	9.4	9.0	11.0	9.5	6.1	4.6	3.9	3.2
15–19 years	293.0	270.9	262.8	222.5	190.4	123.1	87.1	68.9	56.0
20–24 years	331.3	300.4	237.3	134.0	126.7	90.7	68.0	55.7	43.1
25–29 years	179.3	152.0	99.6	50.2	40.6	36.8	32.1	28.0	20.9
30–34 years	84.2	67.3	41.0	19.8	19.1	19.6	18.9	16.1	10.8
35–39 years	30.3	24.0	13.2	8.1	9.4	11.4	10.6	8.3	6.0
40 years and over	5.5	4.1	2.9	2.3	3.0	3.7	3.0	2.4	1.7
By race:									
White	498.6	433.0	320.1	186.4	175.1	123.7	82.5	64.2	53.5
Black and other	434.4	395.2	345.7	261.6	223.6	167.5	141.8	119.2	88.1
Total of above births	**933.0**	**828.2**	**665.8**	**447.9**	**398.7**	**291.2**	**224.3**	**183.4**	**141.6**
Percent of all births[1]	24.5	22.0	18.4	14.2	10.7	7.7	5.3	4.5	3.9
Rate[2]	36.1	32.8	29.4	24.8	26.4	23.4	21.8	19.3	14.1

1. Through 1955, based on data adjusted for underregistration; thereafter, registered births. 2. Rate per 1,000 unmarried (never married, widowed, and divorced) women, 15–44 years old. *Source:* Department of Health and Human Services, National Center for Health Statistics. NOTE: Data are latest available.

Women, Work, and Pregnancy

Between 1961 and 1985, the proportion of women having work experience before the birth of their first child increased. Among women who had their first births in 1961-65, 60 percent worked six or more months continuously before the birth of their first child; by 1981-85, 75 percent had reported a similar work experience.

Employment during pregnancy also became increasingly common; it rose from 44 percent in 1961-65 to 65 percent in 1981-85. The women most likely to work during first pregnancy are relatively older women, White women, and women who had at least a high school education.

Most women who work during pregnancy are full-time workers: since 1961, between 80 and 90 percent of pregnant workers reported that the last job they held before their child's birth was a full-time job (35 or more hours worked per week). Among women who worked during their first pregnancy in 1981-85, 78 percent worked during their last trimester (less then three months before their child's birth), and 47 percent were still at work less than one month before their child's birth.

Live Births and Birth Rates

State	1988[1] number	1988[1] rate	1987 number	1987 rate	State	1988[1] number	1988[1] rate	1987 number	1987 rate
Alabama	59,611	14.5	59,207	14.5	Montana	11,356	14.1	11,976	14.8
Alaska	11,037	21.1	11,441	21.8	Nebraska	24,363	15.2	23,657	14.8
Arizona	65,608	18.8	63,449	18.7	Nevada	18,589	17.6	16,279	16.2
Arkansas	34,554	14.4	33,375	14.0	New Hampshire	17,186	15.8	16,435	15.5
California	514,247	18.2	494,053	17.9	New Jersey	114,118	14.8	111,344	14.5
Colorado	53,014	16.1	54,314	16.5	New Mexico	27,438	18.2	30,169	20.1
Connecticut	46,868	14.5	46,547	14.5	New York	277,291	15.5	270,390	15.2
Delaware	10,915	16.5	10,032	15.6	North Carolina	98,183	15.1	93,405	14.6
D.C.	19,290	31.3	20,406	32.8	North Dakota	11,433	17.1	11,545	17.2
Florida	184,854	15.0	174,688	14.5	Ohio	165,258	15.2	156,900	14.5
Georgia	107,108	16.9	104,881	16.9	Oklahoma	46,874	14.5	45,535	13.9
Hawaii	19,055	17.4	18,602	17.2	Oregon	41,305	14.9	39,708	14.6
Idaho	15,564	15.5	15,956	16.0	Pennsylvania	167,144	13.9	166,287	13.9
Illinois	180,526	15.5	177,564	15.3	Rhode Island	14,481	14.6	14,519	14.7
Indiana	81,421	14.7	77,694	14.0	South Carolina	53,285	15.4	50,693	14.8
Iowa	38,506	13.6	38,736	13.7	South Dakota	11,297	15.8	11,514	16.2
Kansas	37,895	15.2	37,167	15.0	Tennessee	79,140	16.2	71,343	14.7
Kentucky	51,109	13.7	51,075	13.7	Texas	306,782	18.2	308,229	18.4
Louisiana	75,170	17.1	75,313	16.9	Utah	37,260	22.0	35,927	21.4
Maine	15,961	13.2	16,155	13.6	Vermont	8,538	15.3	7,226	13.2
Maryland	68,412	14.8	64,692	14.3	Virginia	90,498	15.0	87,002	14.7
Massachusetts	91,988	15.6	86,934	14.8	Washington	68,242	14.7	73,836	16.3
Michigan	140,229	15.2	136,374	14.8	West Virginia	22,585	12.0	23,572	12.4
Minnesota	66,579	15.5	64,068	15.1	Wisconsin	69,893	14.4	70,467	14.7
Mississippi	41,115	15.7	40,506	15.4	Wyoming	6,697	14.0	7,107	14.5
Missouri	75,844	14.8	75,950	14.9	**Total**	**3,913,000**	**15.9**	**3,829,000**	**15.7**

1. Provisional. NOTE: Provisional data by place of occurrence. Rates are per 1,000 population. *Source:* Department of Health and Human Services, National Center for Health Statistics.

Live Births by Race or National Origin

Race	1987	1986	Race	1987	1986
White	2,992,488	2,970,439	Chinese	19,293	18,284
Black	641,567	621,221	Filipino	23,636	22,490
American Indian[1]	43,707	42,645	Other[2]	75,880	68,844
Japanese	9,822	9,654	Total[3]	3,809,394	3,756,547

1. Includes Eskimos and Aleuts. 2. Hawaiian and other Asian or Pacific Islander. 3. Includes births of other races not shown separately. Data are latest available. *Source:* Department of Health and Human Services, National Center for Health Statistics.

Live Births by Sex and Sex Ratio[1]

Year	Total[2] Male	Female	Males per 1,000 females	White Male	Female	Males per 1,000 females	Black Male	Female	Males per 1,000 females
1978[3]	1,709,394	1,623,885	1,053	1,378,222	1,302,894	1,058	279,598	271,942	1,028
1979[3]	1,791,267	1,703,131	1,052	1,442,981	1,365,439	1,057	293,013	284,842	1,029
1980[3]	1,852,616	1,759,642	1,053	1,490,140	1,408,592	1,058	299,033	290,583	1,029
1981[3]	1,860,272	1,768,966	1,052	1,494,437	1,414,232	1,057	297,864	289,933	1,027
1982[3]	1,885,676	1,794,861	1,051	1,509,704	1,432,350	1,054	301,121	291,520	1,033
1983[3]	1,865,553	1,773,380	1,052	1,492,385	1,411,865	1,057	297,011	289,016	1,028
1984[3]	1,879,490	1,789,651	1,050	1,500,326	1,423,176	1,054	300,951	291,794	1,031
1985	1,927,983	1,832,578	1,052	1,536,646	1,454,727	1,056	308,575	299,618	1,030
1986	1,924,868	1,831,679	1,051	1,523,914	1,446,525	1,053	315,788	305,433	1,034
1987	1,951,153	1,858,241	1,050	1,535,517	1,456,971	1,054	325,259	316,308	1,028

1. Excludes births to nonresidents of U.S. 2. Includes races other than white and black. 3. Based on 100% of births for selected states and 50% sample in all others. *Source:* Department of Health and Human Services, National Center for Health Statistics. NOTE: Data are latest available.

Abortions and Abortion Rates

State	Numbers of abortions			Abortion occurence rate[1]			Change 1985-88
	1988	1987	1985	1988	1987	1985	
Alabama	18,220	19,630	19,380	18.7	20.2	20.2	−1.5
Alaska	2,390	2,560	3,450	18.2	19.7	27.7	−9.5
Arizona	23,070	22,130	22,330	28.8	28.2	29.9	−1.1
Arkansas	6,250	7,030	5,420	11.6	13.1	10.1	1.5
California	311,720	300,830	304,130	45.9	45.0	47.9	−2.1
Colorado	18,740	18,850	24,350	22.4	22.4	28.8	−6.4
Connecticut	23,650	22,380	21,850	31.2	29.4	29.3	1.8
Delaware	5,710	5,680	4,590	35.7	35.9	30.9	4.8
District of Columbia	26,120	25,840	23,910	163.3	158.5	145.9	17.4
Florida	82,850	80,560	76,650	31.5	31.2	31.8	−0.3
Georgia	36,720	36,030	38,340	23.5	23.3	26.1	−2.6
Hawaii	11,170	11,290	11,160	43.0	44.1	43.7	−0.7
Idaho	1,920	1,980	2,660	8.2	8.5	11.1	−2.8
Illinois	72,570	72,180	64,960	26.4	26.2	23.8	2.6
Indiana	15,760	14,750	16,090	11.9	11.2	12.2	−0.2
Iowa	9,420	8,900	9,930	14.6	13.8	15.0	−0.4
Kansas	11,440	11,430	10,150	20.1	20.2	18.2	2.0
Kentucky	11,520	11,550	9,820	13.0	13.1	11.0	2.0
Louisiana	17,340	16,550	19,240	16.3	15.4	17.4	−1.1
Maine	4,620	4,950	4,960	16.2	17.7	18.6	−2.4
Maryland	32,670	31,240	29,480	28.6	27.6	26.9	1.7
Massachusetts	43,720	41,490	40,310	30.2	28.7	29.3	0.9
Michigan	63,410	61,060	64,390	28.5	27.3	28.7	−0.3
Minnesota	18,580	17,810	16,850	18.2	17.5	16.6	1.6
Mississippi	5,120	5,430	5,890	8.4	8.9	9.7	−1.3
Missouri	19,490	20,190	20,100	16.4	17.0	17.3	−0.9
Montana	3,050	3,280	3,710	16.5	17.7	19.0	−2.5
Nebraska	6,490	6,580	6,680	17.7	18.0	18.2	−0.4
Nevada	10,190	10,710	9,910	40.3	43.9	40.5	−0.2
New Hampshire	4,710	4,680	7,030	17.5	17.8	29.0	−11.5
New Jersey	63,900	63,570	69,190	35.1	34.9	39.6	−4.5
New Mexico	6,810	6,650	6,110	19.1	18.6	17.4	1.8
New York	183,980	184,420	195,120	43.3	43.3	47.4	−4.0
North Carolina	39,720	37,630	34,180	25.4	24.2	22.6	2.8
North Dakota	2,230	2,560	2,850	14.9	17.0	18.5	−3.6
Ohio	53,400	51,490	57,360	21.0	20.2	22.4	−1.4
Oklahoma	12,120	11,000	13,100	16.2	14.5	17.1	−0.9
Oregon	15,960	14,370	15,230	23.9	21.8	22.3	1.7
Pennsylvania	51,830	51,800	57,370	18.9	18.9	21.3	−2.4
Rhode Island	7,190	7,390	7,770	30.6	31.3	35.5	−4.9
South Carolina	14,160	12,770	11,200	16.7	15.2	13.7	3.1
South Dakota	900	860	1,650	5.7	5.5	10.6	−4.9
Tennessee	22,090	22,050	22,350	18.9	18.9	19.1	−0.2
Texas	100,690	100,210	100,820	24.8	24.7	25.5	−0.7
Utah	5,030	4,830	4,440	12.8	12.4	11.1	1.7
Vermont	3,580	3,690	3,430	25.8	26.9	26.2	−0.5
Virginia	35,420	34,410	34,180	23.7	23.3	24.0	−0.3
Washington	31,220	29,840	30,990	27.6	26.9	28.0	−0.4
West Virginia	3,270	2,990	4,590	7.5	6.8	10.1	−2.6
Wisconsin	18,040	18,330	17,830	16.0	16.3	15.7	0.2
Wyoming	600	680	1,070	5.1	5.7	7.9	−2.8
Total	**1,590,750**	**1,559,110**	**1,588,550**	**27.3**	**26.9**	**28.0**	**−0.7**

1. Rate per 1,000 women aged 15–44. NOTES: Number of abortions are rounded to nearest 10. *Source:* Stanley K. Henshaw and Jennifer Van Vort, "Abortion Services in the United States, 1987 and 1988," *Family Planning Perspectives,* Volume 22, Number 3, May/June 1990, p. 104. © The Alan Guttmacher Institute.

The Elderly Are Homeowners

There were 58 million homeowners in the United States in 1987; about 15 million of them were 65 years or older. Of the 33 million householders who rented their homes, 5 million were elderly.

Seventy-five percent of elderly householders owned the home in which they lived. In contrast, among younger Americans only 61 percent were homeowners. The elderly most likely to own homes were in the South (8 out of 10) and those least likely to were in the Northeast (2 out of 3).

Elderly owners were somewhat less likely to live in metropolitan areas than younger owners. Still, most elderly owners lived in metropolitan areas; 27 percent did not.

The proportion of householders owning their own homes has grown more rapidly among the elderly. In 1960, 69 percent owned their own homes; by 1987, 75 percent did. Among younger householders ownership rose only one percent.

Mortality
Death Rates for Selected Causes

Cause of death	Death rates per 100,000							
	1989[1]	1988[1]	1985	1980	1950	1945–49	1920–24[4]	1900–04[4]
Typhoid fever	n.a.	n.a.	—	0.0	0.1	0.2	7.3	26.7
Communicable diseases of childhood	n.a.	n.a.	n.a.	0.0	1.3	2.3	33.8	65.2
Measles	0.0	—	—	0.0	0.3	0.6	7.3	10.0
Scarlet fever	n.a.	n.a.	1.0	0.0	0.2	0.1	4.0	11.8
Whooping cough	0.0	—	—	0.0	0.7	1.0	8.9	10.7
Diphtheria	n.a.	n.a.	—	0.0	0.3	0.7	13.7	32.7
Pneumonia and influenza	30.3	31.5	27.9	23.3	31.3	41.3	140.3	184.3
Influenza	0.5	0.8	0.8	1.1	4.4	5.0	34.8	22.8
Pneumonia	29.7	30.7	27.1	22.0	26.9	37.2	105.5	161.5
Tuberculosis	0.7	0.8	0.7	0.8	22.5	33.3	96.7	184.7
Cancer	199.9	198.2	191.7	182.5	139.8	134.0	86.9	67.7
Diabetes mellitus	18.7	16.1	16.2	15.0	16.2	24.1	17.1	12.2
Major cardiovascular diseases	375.3	394.5	410.7	434.5	510.8	493.1	369.9	359.5
Diseases of the heart	295.9	311.7	325.0	335.2	356.8	325.1	169.8	153.0
Cerebrovascular diseases	58.9	60.9	64.0	74.6	104.0	93.8	93.5	106.3
Nephritis and nephrosis	8.9	9.1	9.4	7.6	16.4	48.4	81.5	84.3
Syphilis	0.0	0.0	0.0	0.1	5.0	8.4	17.6	12.9
Appendicitis	0.2	0.2	0.2	0.3	2.0	3.5	14.0	9.4
Accidents, all forms	37.2	39.7	38.6	46.0	60.6	67.6	70.8	79.2
Motor vehicle accidents	18.9	20.4	18.8	23.0	23.1	22.3	12.9	n.a.
Infant mortality[2]	n.a.	9.9	10.6	12.5	29.2	33.3	76.7	n.a.
Neonatal mortality[2]	n.a.	6.4	7.0	8.4	20.5	22.9	39.7	n.a.
Fetal mortality[3]	n.a.	n.a.	7.9	9.2	19.2	21.6	n.a.	n.a.
Maternal mortality[2]	n.a.	n.a.	0.1	0.1	0.8	1.4	6.9	n.a.
All causes	868.1	883.9	890.8	883.4	960.1	1,000.6	1,157.4	1,621.6

1. Based on a 10% sample of deaths. 2. Rates per 1,000 live births. 3. Ratio per 1,000 births. 4. Includes only deaths occurring within the registration areas. Beginning with 1933, area includes the entire United States; Alaska included beginning in 1959 and Hawaii in 1960. Rates per 100,000 population residing in areas, enumerated as of April 1 for 1940, 1950, and 1980 and estimated as of July 1 for all other years. Due to changes in statistical methods, death rates are not strictly comparable. n.a. = not available. *Source:* Department of Health and Human Services, National Center for Health Statistics.

Accident Rates, 1988

Class of accident		One every	Class of accident		One every
All accidents	Deaths	5 minutes	Workers off-job	Deaths	14 minutes
	Injuries	3 seconds		Injuries	11 seconds
Motor-vehicle	Deaths	11 minutes	Home	Deaths	23 minutes
	Injuries	18 seconds		Injuries	9 seconds
Work	Deaths	50 minutes	Public non-motor-vehicle	Deaths	29 minutes
	Injuries	18 seconds		Injuries	14 seconds

NOTE: Data are latest available. *Source:* National Safety Council.

Improper Driving as Factor in Accidents, 1988

Kind of improper driving	Fatal accidents			Injury accidents			All accidents[1]		
	Total	Urban	Rural	Total	Urban	Rural	Total	Urban	Rural
Improper driving	61.4	59.6	62.2	69.5	70.4	67.8	67.2	68.0	65.5
Speed too fast[2]	30.3	28.2	31.2	25.1	22.0	30.4	20.4	17.9	26.0
Right of way	11.3	17.0	8.9	23.8	28.9	15.3	22.8	26.3	15.3
Failed to yield	7.3	10.0	6.2	16.7	19.5	12.1	17.1	19.3	12.6
Passed stop sign	2.2	2.6	1.9	2.3	2.5	2.0	1.8	1.8	1.6
Disregarded signal	1.8	4.4	0.8	4.8	6.9	1.2	3.9	5.2	1.1
Drove left of center	8.1	3.3	10.2	3.1	1.2	6.1	2.8	1.5	5.5
Improper overtaking	5.1	3.7	5.7	2.0	1.6	2.7	2.5	2.3	2.9
Made improper turn	0.5	0.5	0.5	1.5	1.8	1.0	2.6	3.0	1.6
Followed too closely	0.4	0.4	0.4	5.7	6.8	3.7	6.2	7.1	4.3
Other improper driving	5.7	6.5	5.3	8.3	8.1	8.6	9.9	9.9	9.9
No improper driving stated	38.6	40.4	37.8	30.5	29.6	32.2	32.8	32.0	34.5
Total	100.0%	100.0%	100.0%	100.0%	100.0%	100.0%	100.0%	100.0%	100.0%

1. Principally property-damage accidents, but also includes fatal and injury accidents. 2. Includes "speed too fast for conditions." *Source:* Urban and rural reports from six state traffic authorities to National Safety Council. NOTE: Figures are latest available.

Motor-Vehicle Deaths by Type of Accident

Year	Pedes-trians	Other motor vehicles	Railroad trains	Street cars	Pedalcycles	Animal-drawn vehicle or animal	Fixed objects	Deaths from non-collision accidents	Total deaths[1]
						Deaths from collisions with—			
1975	8,400	19,550	979	1	1,000	100	3,130	12,700	45,853
1980	9,700	23,000	739	1	1,200	100	3,700	14,700	53,172
1984	8,500	20,000	630	0	1,100	100	3,200	12,700	46,263
1985	8,300	19,900	500	(2)	1,100	100	2,800	12,900	45,600
1986	8,300	20,500	600	(2)	1,200	100	3,300	13,900	47,900
1987	8,500	20,500	600	(2)	1,400	100	3,400	14,200	48,700
1988	8,800	21,200	600	(2)	1,100	100	3,300	13,900	49,000

1. Totals do not equal sums of various types because totals are estimated. 2. Data not available for these years. NOTE: Figures are latest available. *Source:* National Safety Council.

Accidental Deaths by Principal Types

Year	Motor vehicle	Falls	Drown-ing	Fire burns	Ingestion of food or object	Fire-arms	Poison (solid, liquid)	Poison by gas
1981	51,385	12,628	6,277	5,697	3,331	1,871	3,243	1,280
1982	45,779	12,077	6,351	5,210	3,254	1,756	3,474	1,259
1983	44,452	12,024	6,353	5,028	3,387	1,695	3,382	1,251
1984	46,263	11,937	5,388	5,010	3,541	1,668	3,808	1,103
1985	45,600	11,700	5,300	4,900	3,600	1,800	3,600	1,000
1986	47,900	11,000	5,600	4,800	3,600	1,800	4,000	900
1987	48,700	11,300	5,300	4,800	3,200	1,400	4,400	1,000
1988	49,000	12,000	5,000	5,000	3,600	1,400	5,300	1,000

NOTE: Figures are latest available. *Source:* National Safety Council.

Deaths and Death Rates

State	Total deaths 1988 number	Total deaths 1988 rate[1]	Motor vehicle traffic deaths 1988 number	Motor vehicle traffic deaths 1988 rate[2]	State	Total deaths 1988 number	Total deaths 1988 rate[1]	Motor vehicle traffic deaths 1988 number	Motor vehicle traffic deaths 1988 rate[2]
Alabama	39,016	9.5	1,023	2.7	Montana	6,736	8.4	198	2.4
Alaska	2,059	3.9	97	2.3	Nebraska	15,123	9.4	291	1.9
Arizona	28,446	8.2	944	3.0	Nevada	9,166	8.7	286	3.2
Arkansas	25,278	10.6	610	3.2	New Hampshire	8,658	8.0	163	1.7
California	208,161	7.4	5,381	2.3	New Jersey	71,773	9.3	1,052	1.8
Colorado	21,712	6.6	496	1.8	New Mexico	10,476	7.0	487	3.1
Connecticut	28,757	8.9	486	1.7	New York	174,299	9.7	2,237	2.3
Delaware	5,866	8.9	164	2.6	North Carolina	58,164	9.0	1,587	2.7
D.C.	8,972	14.5	63	1.9	North Dakota	6,055	9.1	104	1.7
Florida	132,370	10.7	3,092	3.1	Ohio	100,625	9.3	1,748	2.2
Georgia	52,815	8.3	1,633	2.5	Oklahoma	29,174	9.0	642	2.1
Hawaii	6,324	5.8	149	2.0	Oregon	24,868	9.0	677	3.0
Idaho	7,391	7.4	257	3.0	Pennsylvania	127,156	10.6	1,932	2.4
Illinois	101,165	8.7	1,862	2.4	Rhode Island	9,930	10.0	125	2.1
Indiana	50,396	9.1	1,104	2.5	South Carolina	28,348	8.2	1,034	3.1
Iowa	27,753	9.8	556	2.6	South Dakota	6,564	9.2	147	2.3
Kansas	22,660	9.1	483	2.2	Tennessee	50,720	10.4	1,266	3.0
Kentucky	35,557	9.5	840	2.6	Texas	124,514	7.4	3,395	2.2
Louisiana	38,640	8.8	923	3.1	Utah	9,695	5.7	297	2.3
Maine	11,331	9.4	246	2.1	Vermont	5,267	9.5	128	2.4
Maryland	37,789	8.2	793	2.0	Virginia	46,984	7.8	1,069	1.9
Massachusetts	57,715	9.8	731	1.7	Washington	36,372	7.8	785	2.0
Michigan	78,882	8.5	1,699	2.2	West Virginia	19,649	10.5	460	3.2
Minnesota	35,246	8.2	615	1.6	Wisconsin	43,399	8.9	813	1.9
Mississippi	24,005	9.2	722	3.4	Wyoming	3,042	6.4	155	2.7
Missouri	54,495	10.6	1,104	2.5	Total	2,259,558	8.8	49,000	2.5

1. Provisional rates per 1,000 population, by place of occurrence. 2. Per 100 million vehicle-miles. *Sources:* Department of Health and Human Services, National Center for Health Statistics; National Safety Council.

Annual Death Rates

Year	Rate	Year	Rate	Year	Deaths	Rate
1900	17.2	1942	10.3	1966	1,863,149	9.5
1905	15.9	1943	10.9	1967	1,851,323	9.4
1910	14.7	1944	10.6	1968	1,930,082	9.7
1915	13.2	1945	10.6	1969	1,921,990	9.5
1920	13.0	1946	10.0	1970[1]	1,921,031	9.5
1924	11.6	1947	10.1	1971	1,927,542	9.3
1925	11.7	1948	9.9	1972	1,963,944	9.4
1926	12.1	1949	9.7	1973	1,973,003	9.3
1927	11.3	1950	9.6	1974	1,934,388	9.1
1928	12.0	1951	9.7	1975	1,892,879	8.8
1929	11.9	1952	9.6	1976	1,909,440	8.8
1930	11.3	1953	9.6	1977	1,899,597	8.6
1931	11.1	1954	9.2	1978	1,927,788	8.7
1932	10.9	1955	9.3	1979	1,913,841	8.5
1933	10.7	1956	9.4	1980	1,989,841	8.7
1934	11.1	1957	9.6	1982	1,974,797	8.5
1935	10.9	1958	9.5	1983	2,019,201	8.6
1936	11.6	1959	9.4	1984	2,039,369	8.6
1937	11.3	1960	9.5	1985	2,086,440	8.7
1938	10.6	1962	9.5	1986	2,099,000	8.7
1939	10.6	1963	9.6	1987	2,127,000	8.7
1940	10.8	1964	9.4	1988	2,171,000	8.8
1941	10.5	1965	9.4	1989[2]	2,155,000	8.7

1. First year for which deaths of nonresidents are excluded. 2. Provisional. NOTE: Includes only deaths occurring within the registration states. Beginning with 1933, area includes entire U.S.; with 1959 includes Alaska, and with 1960 includes Hawaii. Excludes fetal deaths. Rates per 1,000 population residing in area, as of April 1 for 1940, 1950, 1960, 1970, and 1980, and estimated as of July 1 for all other years. *Sources:* Department of Health and Human Services, National Center for Health Statistics.

Death Rates by Age, Race, and Sex

Age	1988[1]	1987	1986	1980	1970[2]	1960	1988[1]	1987	1986	1980	1970[2]	1960
	White males						White females					
Under 1 year	9.4	9.4	9.8	12.3	21.1	26.9	6.9	7.4	7.6	9.6	16.1	20.1
1–4	0.5	0.5	0.5	0.7	0.8	1.0	0.4	0.4	0.4	0.5	0.8	0.9
5–14	0.3	0.3	0.3	0.4	0.5	0.5	0.2	0.2	0.2	0.2	0.3	0.3
15–24	1.4	1.4	1.5	1.7	1.7	1.4	0.5	0.5	0.5	0.5	0.6	0.5
25–34	1.7	1.7	1.7	1.7	1.8	1.6	0.6	0.6	0.6	0.7	0.8	0.9
35–44	2.5	2.5	2.5	2.6	3.4	3.3	1.2	1.2	1.2	1.2	1.9	1.9
45–54	5.7	5.8	6.0	7.0	8.8	9.3	3.1	3.3	3.3	3.7	4.6	4.6
55–64	15.6	15.5	15.7	17.3	22.0	22.3	8.7	8.5	8.5	8.8	10.1	10.8
65–74	35.3	35.5	36.3	40.4	48.1	48.5	19.9	20.0	20.3	20.7	24.7	27.8
75–84	82.3	82.1	83.4	88.3	101.0	103.0	51.5	50.8	51.0	54.0	67.0	77.0
85 and over	189.3	184.3	185.7	191.0	185.5	217.5	147.3	144.9	145.0	149.8	159.8	194.8
	All other males						All other females					
Under 1 year	19.0	19.4	19.1	23.5	40.2	51.9	16.4	15.7	15.2	19.4	31.7	40.7
1–4	0.8	0.8	0.8	1.0	1.4	2.1	0.5	0.7	0.7	0.8	1.2	1.7
5–14	0.4	0.4	0.4	0.4	0.6	0.8	0.3	0.2	0.3	0.3	0.4	0.5
15–24	2.0	1.9	1.8	2.0	3.0	2.1	0.7	0.6	0.6	0.7	1.1	1.1
25–34	3.4	3.3	3.3	3.6	5.0	3.9	1.2	1.3	1.3	1.4	2.2	2.6
35–44	5.6	5.7	5.5	5.9	8.7	7.3	2.4	2.5	2.5	2.9	4.9	5.5
45–54	10.7	10.6	10.7	13.1	16.5	15.5	5.2	5.6	5.7	6.9	9.8	11.4
55–64	21.3	21.8	22.5	26.1	30.5	31.5	12.1	12.7	12.9	14.2	18.9	24.1
65–74	40.1	42.3	43.0	47.5	54.7	56.6	25.3	25.7	25.9	28.6	36.8	39.8
75–84	83.2	83.4	84.6	86.9	89.8	86.6	53.8	55.4	56.0	58.6	63.9	67.1
85 and over	145.3	145.1	147.6	157.7	114.1	152.4	115.2	118.1	120.2	119.2	102.9	128.7

1. Provisional. Based on a 10% sample of deaths. 2. Beginning 1970 excludes deaths of nonresidents of U.S. NOTE: Excludes fetal deaths. Rates are per 1,000 population in each group, enumerated as of April 1 for 1960, 1970, and 1980, and estimated as of July 1 for all other years. NOTE: Data are latest available. *Sources:* Department of Health and Human Services, National Center for Health Statistics.

Expectation of Life

Expectation of Life in the United States

Calendar period	Age								
	0	10	20	30	40	50	60	70	80
WHITE MALES									
1850[1]	38.3	48.0	40.1	34.0	27.9	21.6	15.6	10.2	5.9
1890[1]	42.50	48.45	40.66	34.05	27.37	20.72	14.73	9.35	5.40
1900–1902[2]	48.23	50.59	42.19	34.88	27.74	20.76	14.35	9.03	5.10
1909–1911[2]	50.23	51.32	42.71	34.87	27.43	20.39	13.98	8.83	5.09
1919–1921[3]	56.34	54.15	45.60	37.65	29.86	22.22	15.25	9.51	5.47
1929–1931	59.12	54.96	46.02	37.54	29.22	21.51	14.72	9.20	5.26
1939–1941	62.81	57.03	47.76	38.80	30.03	21.96	15.05	9.42	5.38
1949–1951	66.31	58.98	49.52	40.29	31.17	22.83	15.76	10.07	5.88
1959–1961[5]	67.55	59.78	50.25	40.98	31.73	23.22	16.01	10.29	5.89
1969–1971[6]	67.94	59.69	50.22	41.07	31.87	23.34	16.07	10.38	6.18
1979–1981	70.82	61.98	52.45	43.31	34.04	25.26	17.56	11.35	6.76
1985	71.9	62.9	53.3	44.0	34.7	25.8	18.0	11.6	6.8
1986	72.0	62.9	53.4	44.2	34.9	26.1	18.2	11.7	6.9
1987	72.2	63.1	53.6	44.3	35.1	26.2	18.3	11.8	6.9
WHITE FEMALES									
1850[1]	40.5	47.2	40.2	35.4	29.8	23.5	17.0	11.3	6.4
1890[1]	44.46	49.62	42.03	35.36	28.76	22.09	15.70	10.15	5.75
1900–1902[2]	51.08	52.15	43.77	36.42	29.17	21.89	15.23	9.59	5.50
1909–1911[2]	53.62	53.57	44.88	36.96	29.26	21.74	14.92	9.38	5.35
1919–1921[3]	58.53	55.17	46.46	38.72	30.94	23.12	15.93	9.94	5.70
1929–1931	62.67	57.65	48.52	39.99	31.52	23.41	16.05	9.98	5.63
1939–1941	67.29	60.85	51.38	42.21	33.25	24.72	17.00	10.50	5.88
1949–1951	72.03	64.26	54.56	45.00	35.64	26.76	18.64	11.68	6.59
1959–1961[5]	74.19	66.05	56.29	46.63	37.13	28.08	19.69	12.38	6.67
1969–1971[6]	75.49	66.97	57.24	47.60	38.12	29.11	20.79	13.37	7.59
1979–1981	78.22	69.21	59.44	49.76	40.16	30.96	22.45	14.89	8.65
1985	78.7	69.6	59.8	50.1	40.4	31.1	22.6	15.0	8.7
1986	78.8	69.6	59.9	50.1	40.5	31.2	22.6	15.1	8.8
1987	78.9	69.7	59.9	50.2	40.6	31.3	22.7	15.1	8.8
ALL OTHER MALES[4]									
1900–1902[2]	32.54	41.90	35.11	29.25	23.12	17.34	12.62	8.33	5.12
1909–1911[2]	34.05	40.65	33.46	27.33	21.57	16.21	11.67	8.00	5.53
1919–1921[3]	47.14	45.99	38.36	32.51	26.53	20.47	14.74	9.58	5.83
1929–1931	47.55	44.27	35.95	29.45	23.36	17.92	13.15	8.78	5.42
1939–1941	52.33	48.54	39.74	32.25	25.23	19.18	14.38	10.06	6.46
1949–1951	58.91	52.96	43.73	35.31	27.29	20.25	14.91	10.74	7.07
1959–1961[5]	61.48	55.19	45.78	37.05	28.72	21.28	15.29	10.81	6.87
1969–1971[6]	60.98	53.67	44.37	36.20	28.29	21.24	15.35	10.68	7.57
1979–1981	65.63	57.40	47.87	39.13	30.64	22.92	16.54	11.36	7.22
1985	67.2	58.7	49.1	40.2	31.6	23.7	16.9	11.4	7.2
1986	67.2	58.7	49.1	40.3	31.8	23.9	17.0	11.5	7.1
1987	67.3	58.8	49.2	40.4	32.0	24.1	17.2	11.6	7.2
ALL OTHER FEMALES[4]									
1900–1902[2]	35.04	43.02	36.89	30.70	24.37	18.67	13.60	9.62	6.48
1909–1911[2]	37.67	42.84	36.14	29.61	23.34	17.65	12.78	9.22	6.05
1919–1921[3]	46.92	44.54	37.15	31.48	25.60	19.76	14.69	10.25	6.58
1929–1931	49.51	45.33	37.22	30.67	24.30	18.60	14.22	10.38	6.90
1939–1941	55.51	50.83	42.14	34.52	27.31	21.04	16.14	11.81	8.00
1949–1951	62.70	56.17	46.77	38.02	29.82	22.67	16.95	12.29	8.15
1959–1961[5]	66.47	59.72	50.07	40.83	32.16	24.31	17.83	12.46	7.66
1969–1971[6]	69.05	61.49	51.85	42.61	33.87	25.97	19.02	13.30	9.01
1979–1981	74.00	65.64	55.88	46.39	37.16	28.59	20.49	14.44	9.17
1985	75.0	66.3	56.5	47.0	37.7	28.9	21.1	14.4	8.9
1986	75.1	66.4	56.6	47.1	37.8	29.1	21.2	14.5	8.9
1987	75.2	66.5	56.7	47.2	38.0	29.2	21.3	14.6	8.9

1. Massachusetts only; white and nonwhite combined, the latter being about 1% of the total. 2. Original Death Registration States. 3. Death Registration States of 1920. 4. Data for periods 1900–1902 to 1929–1931 relate to blacks only. 5. Alaska and Hawaii included beginning in 1959. 6. Deaths of nonresidents of the United States excluded starting in 1970. *Sources: Department of Health and Human Services, National Center for Health Statistics.*

Expectation of Life and Mortality Probabilities, 1987

	Expectation of life in years					Mortality probability per 1,000				
		White		All other			White		All other	
Age	Total persons	Male	Female	Male	Female	Total persons	Male	Female	Male	Female
0	75.0	72.2	78.9	67.3	75.2	10.1	9.6	7.6	17.0	14.0
1	74.7	71.9	78.5	67.4	75.3	0.7	0.7	0.6	1.1	0.8
2	73.8	71.0	77.6	66.5	74.3	0.5	0.5	0.4	0.8	0.7
3	72.8	70.0	76.6	65.6	73.4	0.4	0.4	0.3	0.7	0.6
4	71.9	69.0	75.6	64.6	72.4	0.4	0.4	0.3	0.6	0.4
5	70.9	68.1	74.7	63.6	71.4	0.3	0.3	0.2	0.5	0.4
6	69.9	67.1	73.7	62.7	70.5	0.3	0.3	0.2	0.4	0.3
7	68.9	66.1	72.7	61.7	69.5	0.2	0.3	0.2	0.4	0.2
8	67.9	65.1	71.7	60.7	68.5	0.2	0.3	0.2	0.3	0.2
9	66.9	64.1	70.7	59.7	67.5	0.2	0.2	0.1	0.3	0.2
10	66.0	63.1	69.7	58.8	66.5	0.2	0.2	0.1	0.3	0.2
11	65.0	62.2	68.7	57.8	65.5	0.2	0.2	0.1	0.3	0.2
12	64.0	61.2	67.7	56.8	64.6	0.2	0.3	0.2	0.4	0.2
13	63.0	60.2	66.8	55.8	63.6	0.3	0.4	0.2	0.5	0.2
14	62.0	59.2	65.8	54.8	62.6	0.5	0.6	0.3	0.7	0.3
15	61.0	58.2	64.8	53.9	61.6	0.6	0.8	0.4	0.9	0.3
16	60.1	57.3	63.8	52.9	60.6	0.8	1.0	0.5	1.1	0.4
17	59.1	56.4	62.8	52.0	59.6	0.9	1.2	0.5	1.3	0.5
18	58.2	55.4	61.9	51.0	58.7	1.0	1.3	0.5	1.6	0.5
19	57.2	54.5	60.9	50.1	57.7	1.0	1.4	0.5	1.8	0.6
20	56.3	53.6	59.9	49.2	56.7	1.1	1.5	0.5	2.1	0.7
21	55.3	52.6	59.0	48.3	55.8	1.1	1.6	0.5	2.3	0.8
22	54.4	51.7	58.0	47.4	54.8	1.2	1.6	0.5	2.5	0.8
23	53.5	50.8	57.0	46.5	53.9	1.2	1.6	0.5	2.6	0.9
24	52.5	49.9	56.1	45.7	52.9	1.2	1.6	0.5	2.7	0.9
25	51.6	49.0	55.1	44.8	52.0	1.2	1.6	0.5	2.7	0.9
26	50.7	48.0	54.1	43.9	51.0	1.2	1.5	0.6	2.7	1.0
27	49.7	47.1	53.1	43.0	50.0	1.2	1.5	0.6	2.8	1.0
28	48.8	46.2	52.2	42.1	49.1	1.2	1.6	0.6	3.0	1.1
29	47.8	45.3	51.2	41.3	48.2	1.3	1.6	0.6	3.2	1.2
30	46.9	44.3	50.2	40.4	47.2	1.3	1.7	0.6	3.4	1.3
31	46.0	43.4	49.3	39.5	46.3	1.4	1.7	0.7	3.6	1.5
32	45.0	42.5	48.3	38.7	45.3	1.5	1.8	0.7	3.8	1.6
33	44.1	41.6	47.3	37.8	44.4	1.5	1.9	0.7	4.0	1.7
34	43.1	40.6	46.4	37.0	43.5	1.6	1.9	0.8	4.3	1.8
35	42.2	39.7	45.4	36.1	42.6	1.7	2.0	0.8	4.6	1.9
36	41.3	38.8	44.4	35.3	41.6	1.8	2.1	0.9	4.9	2.0
37	40.4	37.9	43.5	34.5	40.7	1.9	2.2	1.0	5.2	2.1
38	39.4	37.0	42.5	33.6	39.8	2.0	2.3	1.0	5.5	2.2
39	38.5	36.0	41.6	32.8	38.9	2.1	2.4	1.1	5.7	2.4
40	37.6	35.1	40.6	32.0	38.0	2.2	2.5	1.2	5.9	2.6
41	36.7	34.2	39.7	31.2	37.1	2.3	2.7	1.3	6.2	2.8
42	35.8	33.3	38.7	30.4	36.2	2.4	2.8	1.4	6.4	3.0
43	34.8	32.4	37.8	29.6	35.3	2.6	3.1	1.6	6.8	3.2
44	33.9	31.5	36.8	28.8	34.4	2.9	3.3	1.8	7.1	3.5
45	33.0	30.6	35.9	28.0	33.5	3.2	3.6	2.0	7.5	3.7
46	32.1	29.7	35.0	27.2	32.6	3.5	4.0	2.2	7.9	4.0
47	31.2	28.8	34.0	26.4	31.8	3.8	4.4	2.5	8.5	4.3
48	30.4	27.9	33.1	25.6	30.9	4.2	4.8	2.7	9.2	4.8
49	29.5	27.1	32.2	24.9	30.1	4.6	5.4	3.0	10.0	5.3
50	28.6	26.2	31.3	24.1	29.2	5.1	6.0	3.4	11.0	5.8
51	27.8	25.4	30.4	23.4	28.4	5.7	6.6	3.7	11.9	6.4
52	26.9	24.5	29.5	22.6	27.6	6.2	7.3	4.1	12.9	7.0
53	26.1	23.7	28.6	21.9	26.7	6.8	8.1	4.5	13.7	7.5
54	25.3	22.9	27.8	21.2	25.9	7.4	8.9	4.9	14.5	8.0
55	24.4	22.1	26.9	20.5	25.2	8.0	9.8	5.3	15.3	8.5
56	23.6	21.3	26.0	19.8	24.4	8.7	10.7	5.8	16.2	9.0
57	22.8	20.5	25.2	19.2	23.6	9.5	11.8	6.4	17.4	9.8
58	22.1	19.8	24.3	18.5	22.8	10.5	13.1	7.1	18.8	10.7
59	21.3	19.0	23.5	17.8	22.1	11.6	14.4	7.8	20.5	11.9
60	20.5	18.3	22.7	17.2	21.3	12.7	16.0	8.6	22.4	13.2
61	19.8	17.6	21.9	16.6	20.6	14.0	17.6	9.5	24.4	14.5
62	19.1	16.9	21.1	16.0	19.9	15.2	19.2	10.4	26.3	15.7
63	18.3	16.2	20.3	15.4	19.2	16.4	20.7	11.3	28.0	16.7
64	17.6	15.6	19.5	14.8	18.5	17.6	22.2	12.3	29.7	17.6
65	16.9	14.9	18.8	14.3	17.8	18.8	23.8	13.3	31.3	18.6

Age	Total persons	White Male	White Female	All other Male	All other Female	Total persons	White Male	White Female	All other Male	All other Female
		Expectation of life in years					Mortality probability per 1,000			
66	16.3	14.3	18.0	13.7	17.2	20.2	25.5	14.4	33.2	19.6
67	15.6	13.6	17.3	13.2	16.5	21.8	27.7	15.7	35.3	20.9
68	14.9	13.0	16.5	12.6	15.8	23.8	30.3	17.1	37.8	22.6
69	14.3	12.4	15.8	12.1	15.2	26.0	33.5	18.8	40.6	24.6
70	13.6	11.8	15.1	11.6	14.6	28.5	36.9	20.6	43.7	26.8
71	13.0	11.2	14.4	11.1	13.9	31.1	40.6	22.6	47.0	29.1
72	12.4	10.7	13.7	10.6	13.3	33.8	44.4	24.7	50.3	31.4
73	11.9	10.2	13.1	10.2	12.8	36.6	48.3	27.0	53.6	33.4
74	11.3	9.6	12.4	9.7	12.2	39.6	52.4	29.5	56.8	35.4
75	10.7	9.1	11.8	9.3	11.6	42.8	56.7	32.3	60.1	37.6
76	10.2	8.7	11.2	8.8	11.1	46.3	61.5	35.4	63.9	40.1
77	9.7	8.2	10.6	8.4	10.5	50.2	66.7	38.9	68.3	43.3
78	9.1	7.8	10.0	8.0	10.0	54.7	72.6	42.9	73.5	47.2
79	8.6	7.3	9.4	7.6	9.4	59.6	79.1	47.4	79.6	52.0
80	8.2	6.9	8.8	7.2	8.9	65.3	86.2	52.5	86.8	57.7
81	7.7	6.5	8.3	6.9	8.4	71.6	94.1	58.4	95.1	64.6
82	7.2	6.1	7.8	6.5	8.0	78.9	102.6	65.3	104.9	72.7
83	6.8	5.8	7.3	6.2	7.6	87.1	111.8	73.3	116.3	82.3
84	6.4	5.5	6.8	6.0	7.2	96.5	121.4	83.0	129.8	93.8
85	6.1	5.2	6.4	5.8	6.9	—	—	—	—	—

Source: Department of Health and Human Services, National Center for Health Statistics.

Average Lifetime in Years by Sex, State, 1979-1981

State	Both sexes Number	Both sexes Rank	Male	Female	State	Both sexes Number	Both sexes Rank	Male	Female
Alabama	72.53	45	68.28	76.79	Montana	73.93	25	70.47	77.68
Alaska	72.24	46	68.71	76.87	Nebraska	75.49	6	71.73	79.29
Arizona	74.30	21	70.46	78.34	Nevada	72.64	44	69.26	76.48
Arkansas	73.72	29	69.73	77.83	New Hampshire	74.98	15	71.43	78.42
California	74.57	20	71.09	78.02	New Jersey	74.00	23[1]	70.48	77.39
Colorado	75.30	9	71.78	78.80	New Mexico	74.01	22	69.91	78.34
Connecticut	75.12	12	71.51	78.57	New York	73.70	30	70.02	77.18
Delaware	73.21	40	69.56	76.78	North Carolina	72.96	42	68.60	77.35
D.C.	69.20	—	64.55	73.70	North Dakota	75.71	5	72.09	79.68
Florida	74.00	23[1]	70.08	77.98	Ohio	73.49	35	69.85	77.06
Georgia	72.22	47	68.01	76.35	Oklahoma	73.67	31[1]	69.63	77.81
Hawaii	77.02	1	74.08	80.33	Oregon	74.99	14	71.35	78.77
Idaho	75.19	10	71.52	79.15	Pennsylvania	73.58	34	69.90	77.16
Illinois	73.37	37	69.55	77.13	Rhode Island	74.76	18	70.96	78.33
Indiana	73.84	27[1]	70.16	77.46	South Carolina	71.85	49	67.56	76.12
Iowa	75.81	3	72.00	79.60	South Dakota	74.97	16	71.03	79.21
Kansas	75.31	8	71.60	78.99	Tennessee	73.30	39	69.15	77.47
Kentucky	73.06	41	69.14	77.12	Texas	73.64	33	69.70	77.67
Louisiana	71.74	50	67.64	75.89	Utah	75.76	4	72.38	79.18
Maine	74.59	19	70.78	78.41	Vermont	74.79	17	71.06	78.49
Maryland	73.32	38	69.71	76.83	Virginia	73.43	36	69.60	77.27
Massachusetts	75.01	13	71.27	78.46	Washington	75.13	11	71.74	78.57
Michigan	73.67	31[1]	70.07	77.29	West Virginia	72.84	43	68.86	76.93
Minnesota	76.15	2	72.52	79.82	Wisconsin	75.35	7	71.86	78.87
Mississippi	71.98	48	67.64	76.39	Wyoming	73.85	26	69.95	78.20
Missouri	73.84	27[1]	69.92	77.72	United States	73.88	—	70.11	77.62

1. Florida and New Jersey share the same rank of 23; Indiana and Missouri share the same rank of 27; Michigan and Oklahoma share the same rank of 31. Therefore, the numbers 24, 28, and 32 are omitted in order for the states to total 50. *Source:* U.S. National Center for Health Statistics, *U.S. Decennial Life Tables for 1979-81, Vol II State Life Tables* (each state), August 1985, from *Statistical Abstract of the United States, 1990.*

Women Still Live Longer Than Men

Although the difference in life expectancy for males and females has narrowed since the late 1970s, women are still expected to outlive men by an average of 6.9 years. Throughout the 1972-1979 period there was a difference of 7.7 and 7.8 years. The difference had been widening from 1900 to 1972.

Recidivism of Prisoners

Source: U.S. Bureau of Justice Statistics

In April 1989, the Bureau of Justice Statistics released a special report on the recidivism of 108,580 persons in 11 states in 1983, representing more than half of all released state prisoners that year. These findings were based on a sample of more than 16,000 released prisoners, representing all those from the 11 states during 1983.

According to the study, an estimated 62.5% of the released prisoners had been rearrested for a felony or serious misdemeanor; 46.8% had been reconvicted; and 41.4% returned to prison or jail within three years after their release.

An estimated 67,898 of the prisoners were rearrested and charged with 326,746 new offenses by year-end 1986. More than 50,000 of the new charges were violent offenses, including 2,282 homicides, 1,451 kidnappings, 1,291 rapes, 2,262 other sexual assaults, 17,060 robberies, and 22,633 other assaults.

Approximately 40% of the released prisoners had previously escaped from custody, been absent without leave (AWOL), or had a prior revocation of parole or probation. An estimated 73% of these prisoners were rearrested within three years of their release.

Released prisoners were often rearrested for the same type of crime for which they had served time in prison. Within three years, 31.9% of released burglars were rearrested for burglary; 24.8% of drug offenders were rearrested for a drug offense; and 19.6% of robbers were rearrested for robbery.

Released rapists were 10.5 times more likely than nonrapists to be rearrested for rape, and released murderers were about five times more likely than other offenders to be rearrested for homicide.

The combination of a prisoner's age when released and the number of prior arrests was very strongly related to recidivism: an estimated 94.1% of prisoners age 18 to 24 with 11 or more prior arrests were rearrested within three years. □

Profile of Felons Convicted in State Courts

(*Source:* Bureau of Justice Statistics.)

The following overview is excerpted from the Nation Judicial Reporting Program (NJRP), *Profile of Felons Convicted in State Courts, 1986,* that summarizes the number of persons convicted on a felony in State courts and the sentences that they received. The data published January 1990 are the latest available.

● In 1986 State courts nationwide convicted about 583,000 persons of a felony—507,000 (87%) were men and 76,000 were women. Approximately 103,000 men and 7,000 women were convicted of a violent felony that year. Other findings include the following:

● Among all felons convicted in 1986, about 344,000 (59%) were white, 233,000 (40%) were black,

Recidivism of State Prisoners Released in 1983

Time after release	Percent of released prisoners who were:		
	Re-arrested	Recon-victed	Reincar-cerated
6 months	25.0 %	11.3 %	8.4 %
1 year	39.3	23.1	18.6
2 years	54.5	38.3	32.8
3 years	62.5	46.8	41.4

Source: U.S. Department of Justice, Bureau of Justice Statistics, 1989. Data are latest available.

and an estimated 6,000 (1%) were of other races (American Indian, Alaska Native, Asian, or Pacific Islander).

● The average age of convicted felons was 29 years. Half of all felons were in their twenties when sentenced.

● Nine percent of the convicted women and 20% of the convicted men had a violent conviction offense. Among whites, 17% of those convicted of a felony had a violent conviction offense; among blacks, 22%.

● Male felons were more likely than female felons (49% versus 30%) to have received a prison sentence. They were also more likely to have received a death sentence for murder or nonnegligent manslaughter (2% versus one-tenth of 1%), and were more likely to have received a sentence to life in prison (1% versus one-tenth of 1%).

● Men sentenced to State prison had an average sentence length of 7 years, while women had an

Prevalence of Violence Among State Prisoners Released in 1983

Among persons released from State prison in 1983, an estimated 77% had been arrested at least once in the past or rearrested after their release for a violent offense.

Nature of violent record	Percent arrested at some time for a violent offense
Prior arrest charge	52.1 %
Most serious charge when released	34.6
Arrest charge within 3 years after release	22.7
Ever charged	77.0

Source: U.S. Department of Justice, Bureau of Justice Statistics, 1989. Data are latest available.

average prison sentence of 5 years. Men were sentenced to local jail for an average of 9 months, and women, 6 months. Men's larger proportion of violent conviction offenses partly explains men's greater likelihood of a sentence to incarceration and longer average sentences.

• Equal percentages of whites and blacks (2%) received the death penalty for murder or nonnegligent manslaughter, and equal percentages of whites and blacks (1%) received a life sentence for a felony conviction. Comparisons of other types of sentences and other measures of sentence length did not reveal measurable differences between the races.

• The estimated 583,000 felons were convicted of about 900,000 felonies. About 74% of convicted felons had one felony conviction offense, 16% had two, and the remaining 10% had three or more. Felons with multiple conviction offenses were more likely to receive a prison sentence. Prison sentences accounted for 41% of felons with one conviction offense, 58% of felons with two offenses, and 66% of felons with three or more.

Comparing Sentences by Race

Sentences whites and blacks received in 1986 were not measurably different, meaning that a high chance existed that differences in data actually reflected particular conditions of the sampled counties and cases rather than real differences for all sentences in 1986. Assuming that recorded differences did accurately reflect real differences, an explanation for them was sought through an investigation of two legal factors that affect sentences: offense seriousness and State sentencing practices.

The survey recorded a 5-percentage-point difference between the races in the percentage receiving a prison sentence (50% of blacks versus 45% of whites). However, the offenses of blacks were, in the aggregate, more serious than those of whites (22% of blacks had a violent conviction offense versus 17% of whites). Also, blacks and whites were subject to different State sentencing practices insofar as blacks and whites were distributed differently geographically across the sampled States. Controlling for the two factors of offense seriousness and State sentencing practices narrowed the racial difference in percentages receiving a

prison sentence to 3 percentage points. Also, controlling for the two factors completely eliminated the 2-percentage-point difference in percentages receiving a jail sentence (21% of whites versus 19% of blacks).

The NJRP survey recorded several racial differences in average sentence lengths: prison terms of 88 months for whites versus 79 months for blacks, a difference of 9 months; jail terms of 8 months for whites versus 9 months for blacks, a difference of 1 month; and probation terms of 46 months for whites versus 60 months for blacks, a difference of 14 months. After controlling for differences in their offenses and in their geographical distributions, however, the racial difference in prison terms was reduced from 9 months to 6 months, and the racial difference in probation terms disappeared. Only the 1-month racial difference in jail terms remained unchanged.

The overall conclusion drawn from the investigation is that whites and blacks received generally similar sentences, once legally relevant differences between them were taken into account. □

Number of Arrest Charges for State Prisoners Released in 1983

Arrest charge	Number of arrest charges	
	Prior to release	After release, 1983-86
Total	**1,333,293**	**326,746**
Violent offenses	214,778	50,121
Homicide[a]	12,185	2,282
Kidnaping	5,622	1,451
Rape	8,922	1,291
Other sexual assault	10,335	2,626
Robbery	84,166	17,060
Assault	84,497	22,633
Other violent	9,051	2,778
Property offenses	628,320	141,416
Burglary	184,690	36,483
Larceny/theft	199,450	51,268
Motor vehicle theft	54,157	8,649
Arson	3,294	647
Fraud	82,522	20,233
Stolen property	60,873	13,738
Other property	43,334	10,398
Drug offenses	149,881	46,382
Possession	69,438	20,684
Trafficking	22,429	5,788
Other/unspecified	58,014	19,910
Public-order offenses	307,191	79,773
Weapons	55,539	12,791
Probation/parole violations	44,962	15,395
Traffic offenses	35,300	5,844
Other public-order	171,390	45,743
Other offenses	12,957	1,111
Unknown[b]	20,166	7,943

Source: U.S. Department of Justice, Bureau of Justice Statistics, 1989. Data latest available. Note: Data are based on an estimated 108,580 prisoners who were released from prison in 11 States in 1983 and who were still alive in 1987.
a. Homicide includes murder, nonnegligent manslaughter, and negligent manslaughter. b. Unknown charges include those that could not be converted to an NCRP offense code and those not coded because only 6 charges were recorded for each arrest.

Largest Prison Population and Incarceration Rates, 1988

10 States with largest prison populations	Number of inmates	10 States with highest incarceration rates*	Prisoners per 100,000 residents
Calif.	76,171	Nev.	452
N. Y.	44,560	S. C.	370
Tex.	40,437	La.	368
Fla.	34,732	Ala.	355
Mich.	27,714	Del.	354
Ohio	26,113	Ariz.	329
Ill.	21,081	Okla.	323
Ga.	18,787	Ala.	300
Penna.	17,879	Mich.	299
N. C.	17,069	Md.	291

Source: Bureau of Justice Statistics Bulletin, Latest Data.
NOTE: *The District of Columbia as a wholly urban jurisdiction is excluded.

Estimated Arrests, 1989[1]

Murder and non-negligent manslaughter	22,300	Weapons—carrying, possession, etc.	225,200
Forcible rape	39,110	Prostitution and commercial vice	107,400
Robbery	165,060	Sex offenses, except forcible rape	
Aggravated assault	459,000	and prostitution	104,800
Burglary	468,900	Drug abuse violations	1,361,700
Larceny—theft	1,604,400	Gambling	20,600
Motor vehicle theft	228,500	Offenses against family and children	74,200
Arson	18,600	Driving under the influence	1,736,200
Total violent crime	685,500	Liquor laws	657,300
Total property crime	2,320,400	Drunkenness	822,500
Other assaults	978,900	Disorderly conduct	776,600
Forgery and counterfeiting	105,400	Vagrancy	33,800
Fraud	376,600	All other offenses, except traffic	3,214,700
Embezzlement	18,200	Curfew and loitering law violations	77,400
Stolen property—buying, receiving, possessing	176,800	Runaways	159,200
Vandalism	307,800	**Total[2]**	**14,340,900**

1. Arrest totals based on all reporting agencies and estimates for unreported areas. 2. Because of rounding, items may not add to totals. *Source:* Department of Justice, Federal Bureau of Investigation, *Uniform Crime Reports for the United States,* 1990.

Number of Arrests by Sex and Age

	Male				Female			
	Total		Under 18		Total		Under 18	
Offense	1989	1988	1989	1988	1989	1988	1989	1988
Serious crimes	1,710,524	1,618,898	479,812	466,148	456,518	433,172	114,579	110,384
Murder[1]	14,852	14,088	1,955	1,653	1,989	1,946	131	117
Forcible rape	27,796	27,540	4,229	4,000	325	337	97	81
Robbery	113,833	103,381	26,762	22,873	10,682	9,516	2,472	1,845
Aggravated assault	281,196	256,648	36,948	31,979	43,215	39,865	6,360	5,781
Burglary—breaking or entering	301,083	292,797	97,063	98,655	29,332	26,951	8,450	7,970
Larceny—theft	807,350	774,266	245,167	246,330	351,647	337,566	89,319	87,865
Motor vehicle theft	152,777	138,044	62,373	55,276	17,502	15,153	7,169	6,175
Arson	11,637	12,134	5,315	5,382	1,826	1,838	581	550
All other								
Other assaults	601,494	555,328	81,513	72,408	111,903	99,462	24,154	21,434
Forgery and counterfeiting	47,584	45,800	3,829	3,975	24,458	23,451	1,755	1,901
Fraud	140,787	131,845	6,305	8,855	116,831	106,054	2,655	2,942
Embezzlement	7,029	6,503	574	502	4,658	4,011	485	367
Stolen property—buying, receiving, possessing	113,096	104,621	28,972	26,785	15,106	13,847	2,901	2,722
Vandalism	201,279	191,052	82,112	78,712	24,949	23,117	8,094	7,504
Weapons—carrying, possessing, etc.	154,504	145,659	27,698	24,602	12,925	12,205	1,929	1,788
Prostitution and commercialized vice	25,483	26,317	490	518	57,315	53,663	709	942
Sex offenses, except forcible rape and prostitution	70,737	69,780	11,632	11,421	5,810	5,563	896	847
Drug abuse violations	825,247	694,729	73,379	65,904	161,102	126,545	9,565	9,212
Gambling	13,455	15,062	796	719	2,437	2,747	33	41
Offenses against family and children	42,724	37,241	1,181	1,208	9,366	8,129	656	686
Driving under the influence	1,054,789	1,044,658	11,981	13,859	147,565	142,174	1,930	2,147
Liquor laws	377,973	367,758	77,985	84,386	87,729	82,551	29,958	30,954
Drunkenness	543,426	535,277	13,187	14,465	58,270	54,583	2,666	2,696
Disorderly conduct	477,016	446,788	73,141	68,652	108,625	101,888	17,863	16,282
Vagrancy	24,008	23,843	1,822	1,934	3,063	3,205	322	378
All other offenses, except traffic	1,911,497	1,788,764	185,607	185,955	372,711	341,880	48,525	47,957
Curfew and loitering law violations	46,040	48,880	46,040	48,880	15,888	16,628	15,888	16,628
Runaways	52,067	51,551	52,067	51,551	65,978	64,911	65,978	64,911
Total	**8,440,759**	**7,950,354**	**1,260,123**	**1,231,439**	**1,863,207**	**1,719,786**	**351,541**	**342,773**

1. Includes non-negligent manslaughter. NOTE: 8,978 agencies reporting; 1989 estimated population 180,712,000. *Source:* Department of Justice, Federal Bureau of Investigation, *Uniform Crime Reports for the United States, 1990.*

Arrests by Race, 1989

Offense	White	Black	Other[1]	Total	Offense	White	Black	Other[1]	Total
Serious crimes	1,426,123	869,261	45,876	2,341,260	Prostitution and				
Murder[2]	7,567	10,118	259	17,944	commercial vice	50,862	36,391	1,273	88,526
Forcible rape	15,768	14,209	493	30,470	Sex offenses, except				
Robbery	45,437	86,832	1,414	133,683	forcible rape and				
Aggravated assault	203,457	144,574	5,837	353,868	prostitution	63,643	18,270	1,429	83,342
Burglary	235,043	114,901	5,969	355,913	Drug abuse violation	613,800	452,574	7,971	1,074,345
Larceny-theft	806,752	417,442	27,923	1,252,117	Gambling	8,154	7,846	1,148	17,148
Motor vehicle theft	101,260	77,594	3,780	182,634	Offenses against				
Arson	10,839	3,591	201	14,631	family and children	37,671	18,435	2,060	58,166
All other					Driving under the				
Other assaults	475,488	281,237	13,962	770,687	influence	1,171,282	119,684	23,590	1,314,556
Forgery and					Liquor laws	439,416	47,883	14,433	501,732
counterfeiting	51,661	28,022	1,063	80,746	Drunkenness	530,926	118,312	17,328	666,566
Fraud	193,247	94,597	1,908	289,752	Disorderly conduct	405,800	229,286	9,906	644,992
Embezzlement	8,501	4,337	160	12,998	Vagrancy	16,876	12,070	611	29,557
Stolen property—					All other offenses				
buying, receiving,					except traffic	1,544,864	878,860	49,193	2,472,917
possessing	78,164	61,598	1,616	141,378	Suspicion	6,085	7,656	106	13,847
Vandalism	182,678	60,177	4,314	247,169	Curfew and loitering				
Weapons—carrying,					law violations	47,246	15,896	1,780	64,922
possession, etc.	101,522	76,264	2,551	180,337	Runaways	105,129	20,521	3,935	129,585
					Total	**7,559,138**	**3,459,177**	**206,213**	**11,224,528**

1. Includes American Indian, Alaskan Native, and Asian or Pacific Islander. 2. Includes non-negligent manslaughter. NOTE: Figures represent arrests reported by 10,479 agencies serving a total 1989 population of 199,394,000 as estimated by FBI. *Source:* Department of Justice, Federal Bureau of Investigation, *Uniform Crime Reports for the United States, 1990.*

Total Arrests, by Age Groups, 1989

Age	Arrests	Age	Arrests	Age	Arrests	Age	Arrests	Age	Arrests
Under 15	585,521	18	555,940	22	451,093	30–34	1,585,889	50–54	194,502
15	314,077	19	550,768	23	444,548	35–39	1,017,116	55 and	
16	385,198	20	503,402	24	452,783	40–44	591,426	over	287,976
17	460,022	21	472,525	25–29	2,073,706	45–49	334,803	**Total**	**11,261,295**

NOTE: Based on reports furnished to the FBI by 10,503 agencies covering a 1989 estimated population of 199,947,000. *Source:* Department of Justice, Federal Bureau of Investigation, *Uniform Crime Reports for the United States, 1990.*

Federal Prosecutions of Public Corruption: 1979 to 1988

(Prosecution of persons who have corrupted public office in violation of Federal Criminal Statutes. As of Dec. 31, 1988)

Prosecution status	1988	1987	1986	1985	1984	1983	1982	1981	1980	1979
Total:[1] Indicted	1,274	1,340	1,192	1,182	936	1,073	729	878	721	687
Convicted	1,067	1,075	1,027	997	934	972	671	730	552	555
Awaiting trial	288	368	246	256	269	222	186	231	213	187
Federal officials: Indicted	629	651	596	563	408	460[2]	158	198	123	128
Convicted	529	545	523	470	429	424[2]	147	159	131	115
Awaiting trial	86	118	83	90	77	58	38	23	16	21
State officials: Indicted	66	102	88	79	58	81	49	87	72	58
Convicted	69	76	71	66	52	65	43	66	51	32
Awaiting trial	14	26	24	20	21	26	18	36	28	30
Local officials: Indicted	276	246	232	248	203	270	257	244	247	212
Convicted	229	204	207	221	196	226	232	211	168	156
Awaiting trial	79	89	55	49	74	61	58	102	82	67

1. Includes individuals who are neither public officials nor employees, but who were involved with public officials or employees in violating the law, now shown separately. 2. Increases in the number indicted and convicted between 1982 and 1983 resulted from a greater focus on federal corruption nationwide and more consistent reporting of cases involving lower-level employees. NOTE: Figures are latest available. *Source:* U.S. Department of Justice, *Federal Prosecutions of Corrupt Public Officials, 1970–1980,* and *Report to Congress on the Activities and Operations of the Public Integrity Section,* annual.

Law Enforcement Officers Killed or Assaulted: 1979 to 1988

(Covers officers killed feloniously and accidentally in line of duty; includes federal officers.)

	1988	1987	1986	1985	1984	1983	1982	1981	1980	1979
Northeast	17	24	15	19	21	20	17	17	31	21
Midwest	18	31	19	23	22	26	41	29	23	28
South	77	51	62	64	69	64	75	80	72	77
West	39	40	29	29	32	34	27	27	32	32
Puerto Rico	1	1	6	10	3	6	3	3	6	4
Total killed	**155[7]**	**147**	**131**	**148[6]**	**147**	**152[5]**	**164[4]**	**157[3]**	**165[1]**	**164[2]**
Assaults:										
Population (1,000)[8]	186,418	190,025	196,030	198,935	195,794	198,341	176,563	177,836	182,288	182,027
Number of—										
Agencies	8,866	8,957	9,755	9,906	10,002	9,908	8,829	9,019	9,235	9,638
Police officers	369,743	378,977	380,249	389,808	372,268	377,620	319,101	332,856	345,554	340,764
Firearm	2,759	2,789	2,852	2,793	2,654	3,067	2,642	3,330	3,295	3,237
Knife or cutting instrument	1,367	1,561	1,614	1,715	1,662	1,829	1,452	1,733	1,653	1,720
Other dangerous weapon	5,573	5,685	5,721	5,263	5,148	5,527	4,879	4,800	5,415	5,543
Hands, fists, feet, etc.	49,053	53,807	54,072	51,953	50,689	51,901	46,802	47,253	47,484	48,531
Total assaulted	**58,752**	**63,842**	**64,259**	**61,724**	**60,153**	**62,324**	**55,775**	**57,116**	**57,847**	**59,031**

1. Includes one officer in Virgin Islands. 2. Includes 2 officers in Guam. 3. Includes one officer in American Samoa. 4. Includes one officer in Mariana Islands. 5. Includes one officer each in Guam and Mariana Islands. 6. Includes one officer in Guam and 2 in foreign locations. 7. Includes one officer in American Samoa and 2 in foreign locations. 8. Represents the number of persons covered by agencies shown. *Source: Statistical Abstract of the United States, 1990.*

Full-Time Law Enforcement Employees, 1989

City	Officers	Civilians	Total	1988 Total	City	Officers	Civilians	Total	1988 Total
Atlanta	1,518	331	1,849	1,704	Minneapolis	740	132	872	828
Baltimore	2,915	540	3,455	3,546	New Orleans	N.A.	N.A.	N.A.	1,636
Birmingham, Ala.	700	193	893	844	New York	25,858	9,747	35,605	36,027
Boston	N.A.	N.A.	N.A.	2,618	Newark, N.J.	1,064	192	1,256	1,291
Buffalo, N.Y.	1,039	141	1,180	1,154	Norfolk, Va.	638	72	710	696
Chicago	11,828	1,641	13,469	13,833	Oakland, Calif.	610	376	986	824
Cincinnati	933	219	1,152	1,135	Oklahoma City	810	219	1,029	983
Cleveland	1,743	373	2,116	2,074	Omaha, Neb.	631	148	779	750
Columbus, Ohio	1,335	335	1,670	1,670	Philadelphia	6,263	927	7,190	6,935
Dallas	2,472	844	3,316	3,161	Phoenix, Ariz.	1,917	697	2,614	2,479
Denver	1,334	233	1,567	1,566	Pittsburgh	1,076	38	1,114	1,125
Detroit	4,756	635	5,391	4,263	Portland, Ore.	746	186	932	1,063
El Paso	756	224	980	886	Rochester, N.Y.	641	121	762	752
Fort Worth	981	304	1,285	1,243	St. Louis	1,561	628	2,189	2,115
Honolulu	1,761	424	2,185	2,084	St. Paul	537	167	704	642
Houston	4,088	1,366	5,454	5,271	San Antonio	1,486	326	1,812	1,769
Indianapolis	997	355	1,352	1,370	San Diego, Calif.	1,857	697	2,554	2,408
Jacksonville, Fla.	1,174	849	2,023	1,811	San Francisco	1,769	713	2,482	2,512
Kansas City, Mo.	1,132	572	1,704	1,697	San Jose, Calif.	1,061	223	1,284	1,229
Long Beach, Calif.	654	367	1,021	962	Seattle	1,185	404	1,589	1,575
Los Angeles	7,893	2,585	10,478	10,023	Tampa, Fla.	743	237	980	945
Louisville, Ky.	663	186	849	832	Toledo, Ohio	706	55	761	806
Memphis, Tenn.	1,353	428	1,781	1,696	Tucson, Ariz.	N.A.	N.A.	N.A.	942
Miami, Fla.	1,113	437	1,550	1,358	Tulsa, Okla.	668	154	822	837
Milwaukee	1,950	393	2,343	2,334	Washington, D.C.	3,974	742	4,716	4,638

NOTE: As of Oct. 31, 1989. n.a. = not available. *Source:* Department of Justice, Federal Bureau of Investigation, *Uniform Crime Reports for the United States, 1990.*

Adolescent Drug Dealers

Most of them are not necessarily involved in other or more serious criminal activity. Most sell marijuana, amphetamines, and tranquilizers less than once a month to support their own use. Their buyers are almost always known to them and they typically distribute drugs in homes or cars, not in public places. They do not consider these activities "serious crimes." □

U.S. District Courts—Criminal Cases Commenced and Defendants Disposed of, by Nature of Offense: 1985 and 1988

[For years ending June 30]

Nature of offense	1988 cases com- menced[1]	Not convicted Total	Not convicted Ac- quitted	Convicted[2] Total	Convicted[2] Guilty plea[3]	Convicted[2] Court or jury	Sentenced Im- prison- ment	Sentenced Proba- tion	Sentenced Fine and other	1985 Cases com- menced[1]	1985 De- fend- ants dis- posed of
General offenses:											
Homicide	147	40	16	110	86	24	94	6	10	160	170
Robbery	1,283	131	27	1,064	927	137	990	72	2	1,236	1,387
Assault	617	163	37	436	338	98	267	138	31	552	555
Burglary	124	19	1	92	84	8	75	15	2	158	165
Larceny—theft	3,531	706	103	3,159	2,899	260	1,161	1,701	297	3,571	4,108
Embezzlement and fraud	9,433	1,571	240	9,609	8,736	873	4,004	5,334	271	7,912	9,044
Auto theft	293	59	14	323	291	32	224	92	7	300	461
Forgery, counterfeiting	1,674	293	39	1,777	1,666	111	853	910	14	2,118	2,372
Sex offenses	511	64	20	374	315	59	215	154	5	266	200
DAPCA[4]	10,291	2,588	420	13,162	11,044	2,118	9,983	3,042	137	6,690	11,177
Misc. general offenses	15,599	4,255	604	12,796	11,128	1,668	4,607	4,593	3,596	15,583	17,721
Total	**43,503**	**9,889**	**1,521**	**42,902**	**37,514**	**5,388**	**22,473**	**16,057**	**4,372**	**38,546**	**47,360**

1. Excludes transfers. 2. Convicted and sentenced. 3. Includes nolo contendere. 4. All marijuana, narcotics, and controlled substances under the Drug Abuse Prevention and Control Act. *Source: Statistical Abstract of the United States,* 1990.

Murder Victims by Weapons Used

Year	Murder victims, total	Guns Total	Guns Percent	Cutting or stabbing	Blunt object[1]	Strangu- lation, hands, fists, feet or pushing	Arson[3]	All other[2]
1965	8,773	5,015	57.2	2,021	505	894	226	112
1970	13,649	9,039	66.2	2,424	604	1,031	353	198
1971	16,183	10,712	66.2	3,017	645	1,295	314	200
1972	15,832	10,379	65.6	2,974	672	1,291	331	185
1973	17,123	11,249	65.7	2,985	848	1,445	173	423
1974	18,632	12,474	66.9	3,228	976	1,417	153	384
1975	18,642	12,061	64.7	3,245	1,001	1,646	193	496
1979	20,591	13,040	63.3	3,954	997	1,557	276	767
1980	21,860	13,650	62.0	4,212	1,094	1,666	291	947
1981	20,053	12,523	62.4	3,886	1,038	1,469	258	658
1982	19,485	11,721	60.2	4,065	957	1,657	279	630
1983	18,673	10,895	58.0	4,075	1,062	1,656	216	769
1984	16,689	9,819	58.8	3,540	973	1,407	192	758
1985	17,545	10,296	58.7	3,694	972	1,491	243	849
1986	19,257	11,381	59.1	3,957	1,099	1,651	230	939
1987	17,963	10,612	59.1	3,643	1,045	1,525	200	938
1988	17,971	10,895	60.6	3,457	1,126	1,426	255	812
1989	18,954	11,832	62.4	3,458	1,128	1,416	234	886

1. Refers to club, hammer, etc. 2. Includes poison, explosives, unknown, drowning, asphyxiation, narcotics, other means, and weapons not stated. 3. Before 1973, includes drowning. *Source:* Department of Justice, Federal Bureau of Investigation, *Uniform Crime Reports for the United States, 1990.*

Women Drug Offenders

Women offenders are not likely to be high-rate robbers or assaulters, but about one-third of addicted women offenders are prostitutes. Others commit many thefts. Few become top-level or even mid-level drug dealers. Over half, however, play an active role in the lowest levels of the drug trade and facilitate as many sales as men also involved at the lowest levels.

Many of the seriously drug-involved women have children. Those who continue to inject drugs during pregnancy may have infants born addicted. Additionally, because they frequently share needles with other addicts, they are at high risk of contracting AIDS and their children are also at high risk of contracting AIDS. □

Crime Rates for Population Groups and Selected Cities, 1988
(offenses known to the police per 100,000 population, as of July 1)

Group and city	Violent crime					Property crime				
	Mur-der	Forc-ible rape	Rob-bery	Aggra-vated assault	Total	Bur-glary—break-ing or enter-ing	Lar-ceny-theft	Motor vehicle theft	Total	Total all crimes
Total 7,434 cities	10.5	47	318	462	836	1,539	3,967	788	6,295	7,130
MSA's (Metropolitan Statistical Areas)	9	43	278	422	752	1,457	3,506	713	5,676	6,428
Other Cities	4	25	55	286	371	1,042	3,298	210	4,550	4,921
Rural Areas	5	18	15	141	180	672	973	114	1,759	1,938
Selected Cities:										
Baltimore	30.6	68	968	861	1,927	1,866	4,268	1,105	7,239	9,166
Chicago	22.0	(1)	968	1,202	(1)	1,739	4,295	1,503	7,537	(1)
Dallas	36.0	128	948	964	2,077	4,180	8,092	2,393	14,665	16,742
Detroit	57.9	133	1,194	989	2,375	2,958	3,981	2,772	9,711	12,085
Houston	25.5	70	582	471	1,149	2,908	4,491	1,763	9,163	10,311
Indianapolis	16.3	87	303	760	1,166	1,596	2,640	740	4,977	6,143
Los Angeles	21.6	59	770	1,111	1,961	1,499	3,531	1,685	6,714	8,676
Memphis	26.0	129	667	511	1,333	2,436	3,307	2,067	7,810	9,143
New York	25.8	46	1,179	967	2,218	1,731	4,199	1,633	7,562	9,780
Philadelphia	22.4	55	537	421	1,035	1,231	2,544	1,227	5,002	6,037
Phoenix	11.1	47	265	568	891	2,190	5,374	695	8,259	9,150
San Antonio	15.3	57	306	186	564	2,957	7,548	1,411	11,916	12,479
San Diego	13.4	36	298	506	854	1,634	4,278	2,247	8,159	9,013
San Francisco	12.2	60	646	560	1,278	1,346	4,863	1,270	7,479	8,757
Washington, D.C.	59.5	27	918	918	1,921	1,983	4,610	1,392	7,985	9,907

1. The rates for 1988 forcible rape, violent crime, and total crime are not shown because the forcible rape figures were not in accordance with national Uniform Crime Reporting guidelines. *Source: Statistical Abstract of the United States 1990.*

Percent of Firearms Usage in Selected Crimes, by Region: 1987–1989

Region	Murder[1]			Aggravated assault			Robbery		
	1989	1988	1987	1989	1988	1987	1989	1988	1987
Northeast	60.1	57.3	54.8	16.3	15.9	14.9	29.0	27.1	25.3
Midwest	58.8	59.0	57.7	23.6	23.1	24.4	33.0	33.4	32.6
South	65.8	64.4	62.9	25.3	26.3	25.6	39.2	40.8	39.7
West	61.6	59.2	56.4	19.5	18.4	17.7	32.4	33.1	33.8
U.S. Total	62.4	60.7	59.1	21.5	21.1	21.4	33.2	33.4	33.0

1. Murder includes non-negligent manslaughter. *Source:* U.S. Federal Bureau of Investigation, *Crime in the United States,* annual.

Reported Child Neglect and Abuse Cases: 1985 to 1987

Division	Percent change 1986-87	Total number of reports (1,000)			Reports per 1,000 population		
		1987	1986	1985	1987	1986	1985
New England	4.0	99.8	95.8	59.9	7.8	7.5	4.7
Middle Atlantic	6.3	242.5	228.1	152.2	6.5	6.1	4.1
North Central	-1.2	515.2	521.4	316.4	18.2	19.3	11.1
South Atlantic	-1.9	293.4	299.2	225.0	7.0	7.3	5.6
South Central	-3.0	302.4	311.7	249.9	14.8	15.1	12.9
Mountain	29.6	128.2	98.9	77.6	9.7	7.6	6.1
Pacific	6.1	443.7	418.3	218.4	12.1	11.7	6.2
U.S. Total	2.6	2,025.2	1,973.4	1,299.4	8.3	8.2	5.4

NOTE: Figures are latest available. *Source:* American Humane Association, *National Analysis of Official Child Neglect and Abuse Reporting,* annual.

Trends in Offender Drug Use

Between 1974 and 1986, the proportion of state prisoners under the influence of an illegal drug at the time of the offense for which they were incarcerated grew from 25% to 35%. Those found to be under the influence of cocaine at the time of their offense grew from 1% to 10.7% while those under the influence of heroin fell from 16.2% to 7%.

In 1979, 42.7% of the 288,086 state prisoners either had been convicted of a drug crime or were daily users of illegal drugs in the month preceding the offense for which they were imprisoned. In 1986, 46.8% of the 500,725 state prisoners were actively involved with illegal drugs either as users or by conviction for a drug crime.

More than half of the state prisoners who had ever used a major drug regularly said such use began after their first arrest—51% not until more than a year after.

For the typical state prisoner who used drugs:
- first use of any drug occurred at age 15
- first use of a major drug occurred at age 17
- first regular use of a major drug began at age 18

First use and first regular use of major drugs began an average of two years earlier among white than black inmates. □

Drug Use by Youthful Offenders, 1987

Type of drug	All races[a]		
	Ever used drugs	Used drugs regularly[b]	Committed current offense under influence of drugs
All ages[c,d]			
Any drug	82.7 %	63.1 %	39.4 %
Marijuana	81.2	59.0	30.0
Cocaine	46.1	21.5	12.8
Amphetamines	36.3	15.5	6.0
LSD	28.9	11.9	6.5
Barbiturates	27.3	8.9	2.7
PCP	22.6	8.9	4.9
Quaaludes	14.6	3.0	.7
Heroin	13.0	5.2	3.4
Under age 18[d,e]			
Any drug	80.6 %	59.7 %	39.1 %
Marijuana	79.4	56.6	31.7
Cocaine	42.6	19.6	12.9
Amphetamines	37.8	15.6	6.4
LSD	26.7	11.5	7.3
Barbiturates	28.4	9.3	2.8
PCP	18.7	6.4	3.4
Quaaludes	14.9	3.1	.9
Heroin	11.9	4.5	2.9
Age 18 or older[d,f]			
Any drug	88.2 %	72.3 %	40.3 %
Marijuana	85.9	65.4	25.4
Cocaine	55.3	26.7	12.6
Amphetamines	32.5	15.2	4.9
LSD	34.7	13.2	4.2
Barbiturates	24.4	7.9	2.4
PCP	33.0	15.5	9.0
Quaaludes	13.7	2.7	.3
Heroin	16.0	7.0	4.7

a. Include American Indians, Alaska Natives, Asians, and Pacific Islanders. b. Used drugs one or more times a week for at least a month. c. The numbers of youthful offenders of all ages were 25,024 all races, 13,272 white offenders, and 10,296 black offenders. d. The number of youth may differ slightly from that reported on other tables because of missing data for some characteristics. e. The numbers of youthful offenders under age 18 were 18,226 all races, 9,565 white offenders, and 7,541 black offenders. f. The numbers of youthful offenders age 18 or older were 6,798 all races, 3,707 white offenders, and 2,755 black offenders. NOTE: Survey respondents were residents of long-term, State-operated juvenile facilities. Percentages for specific drugs do not add to the percentage of youth using any drug because of multiple drug use. *Source:* Bureau of Justice Statistics, December 1989. Latest data.

Sentencing for Drug Violations

The average Federal sentence for drug offenses rose from almost four years in 1980 to more than 5.5 years in 1987.

A Bureau of Justice Statistics study of felony court sentencing in 1986 found that 64% of the persons convicted of drug trafficking were sentenced to some kind of incarceration—27% to jail and 37% to prison. In the 75 largest counties, 75% of those convicted of drug trafficking were sentenced to incarceration (40% to jail and 35% to prison). This may reflect the small amounts of illegal drugs (sometimes only ounces) needed to allow a defendant to be charged with "possession with intent to sell" rather than possession only.

Average Times Served By Federal Prisoners

Offense	Avg. time served, mos.	% Sentence served
All	43.3	59.1
Robbery	72.9	49.0
Drug	38.5	58.6
Weapons	31.5	69.4
Monetary Crime	26.5	63.8

State Prison Inmates Under the Influence of Drugs at Time of Current Offense

Type of drug	Percent of all inmates who were under the influence of a drug at the time of the offense		
	1974	1979	1986
Any drug	25.3%	32.3%	35.4%
Major drug			
Cocaine	1.0%	4.6%	10.7%
Heroin	16.2	8.7	7.0
PCP	—	2.3	2.2
LSD	—	2.0	1.6
Methadone	1.7	.7	.8
Other drug			
Marijuana or hashish	10.3%	17.6%	18.6%
Amphetamines	5.3	5.2	4.2
Barbiturates	5.5	5.7	3.3
Methaqualone	—	—	1.6
Other drugs	3.0	1.6	3.9

Source: Bureau of Justice Statistics, "Drug Use and Crime," July 1988. Latest data.

Prisoners Under Sentence of Death

Characteristic	1988	1987	1986	Characteristic	1988	1987	1986
White	1,238	1,128	1,006	Marital status:			
Black and other	886	839	775	Never married	898	856	772
Under 20 years	11	10	19	Married	594	571	525
20–24 years	195	222	217	Divorced or separated[2]	632	557	484
25–34 years	1,048	969	872	Time elapsed since sentencing:			
35–54 years	823	744	639	Less than 12 months	293	295	293
55 years and over	47	39	34	12–47 months	812	804	757
				48–71 months	409	412	376
Schooling completed:				72 months and over	610	473	355
7 years or less	180	181	164	Legal status at arrest:			
8 years	184	183	174	Not under sentence	1,207	1,123	992
9–11 years	692	650	577	On parole or probation	545[3]	480[3]	409[3]
12 years	657	591	515	In prison or escaped	93	91	82
More than 12 years	180	168	143	Unknown	279	290	298
Unknown	231	211	208	**Total**	**2,124**	**1,967**[1]	**1,781**

1. Revisions to the total number of prisoners were not carried to the characteristics except for race. 2. Includes widows, widowers, and unknown. 3. Includes 20 persons on mandatory conditional release, work release, leave, AWOL, or bail for 1986; 22 for 1987; 24 for 1988. NOTE: As of Dec. 31. Excludes prisoners under sentence of death confined in local correctional systems pending appeal or who had not been committed to prison. *Source:* U.S. Bureau of Justice Statistics, *Capital Punishment,* annual.

Methods of Execution[1]

State	Method	State	Method
Alabama[2]	Electrocution	Nevada[2]	Lethal injection
Alaska	No death penalty	New Hampshire[2]	Lethal injection
Arizona[2]	Lethal gas	New Jersey	Lethal injection[5]
Arkansas[2]	Lethal injection	New Mexico	Lethal injection
California*	Lethal gas	New York	No death penalty
Colorado[2]	Lethal injection[7]	North Carolina[2]	Lethal gas or injection
Connecticut[2]	Electrocution	North Dakota	No death penalty
Delaware	Lethal injection[3]	Ohio[2]	Electrocution
D.C.	No death penalty	Oklahoma	Lethal injection
Florida	Electrocution	Oregon	Lethal injection[5]
Georgia[2]	Electrocution	Pennsylvania[2]	Electrocution
Hawaii	No death penalty	Rhode Island	No death penalty
Idaho[2]	Lethal injection[9]	South Carolina[2]	Electrocution
Illinois	Lethal injection	South Dakota	Lethal injection
Indiana[2]	Electrocution	Tennessee[2]	Electrocution
Iowa	No death penalty	Texas[2]	Lethal injection
Kansas	No death penalty	Utah[2]	Firing squad or lethal injection
Kentucky[2]	Electrocution	Vermont	No death penalty
Louisiana[2]	Electrocution	Virginia	Electrocution
Maine*	No death penalty	Washington[2*]	Hanging or lethal injection
Maryland[2]	Lethal gas	West Virginia	No death penalty
Massachusetts*	No death penalty	Wisconsin	No death penalty
Michigan	No death penalty	Wyoming	Lethal injection
Minnesota	No death penalty	U.S. (Fed. Govt.)	[4]
Mississippi[2]	Lethal injection[8]	American Samoa	No death penalty
Missouri	Lethal injection	Guam	No death penalty
Montana[2]	Hanging, or lethal injection[6]	Puerto Rico	No death penalty
Nebraska[2]	Electrocution	Virgin Islands	No death penalty

1. On July 1, 1976, by a 7-2 decision, the U.S. Supreme Court upheld the death penalty as not being "cruel or unusual." However, in another ruling the same day, the Court, by a 5-4 vote, stated that states may not impose "mandatory" capital punishment on every person convicted of murder. These decisions left uncertain the fate of condemned persons throughout the U.S. On Oct. 4, the Court refused to reconsider its July ruling, which allows some states to proceed with executions of condemned prisoners. The first execution in this country since 1967 was in Utah on Jan. 17, 1977. Gary Mark Gilmore was executed by shooting. 2. Voted to restore death penalty after June 29, 1972, Supreme Court decision ruling capital punishment unconstitutional. 3. Prisoners originally sentenced to death prior to June 1986 may opt instead to hang. Those sentenced after June 1986 have no choice but lethal injection. 4. Is that of the state in which the execution takes place. 5. Death penalty has been passed, but not been used. 6. Defendant may choose between hanging and a lethal injection. 7. Applies to offenses committed on or after July, 1 1988. Prior to that date the method of execution is lethal gas. 8. Prisoners sentenced prior to July 1, 1984, shall be executed by lethal gas. 9. If the director of the Idaho Department of Corrections finds it impractical to carry out a lethal injection, he may instead use a firing squad. *Source: Information Please* questionnaires to the states. NOTE: An asterisk after the name of the state indicates non-reply.

Motor Vehicle Laws, 1990

State	Age for license		Age for driver's license[1]			Driver's license duration	Fee	Annual safety inspection required
	Motor-cycle	Moped	Regular	Learner's	Restrictive			
Alabama	14	14	16	15[5]	14[11]	4 yrs.	$15.00	no[17]
Alaska	14	14	16	14	14[6,11]	5	10.00	no[17]
Arizona	16	16	18	15 7 mo.[5,6]	16[6]	4	7	no[18]
Arkansas	16	10	16	(5)	14[6,9]	2 or 4	7/13.00	yes
California	18	15 1/2	18	15[4,7]	16[4]	4	10.00	no[17]
Colorado	16	16	21	15 1/2[5]	16[6]	4	15.00	no[19]
Connecticut	18	16	18		16[4]	2 or 4	24.75/38	yes[20]
Delaware	18	16	18	(5)	16[4,6]	5	12.50	yes
D. C.	16	16	18	(5)	16[6]	4	15.00	yes
Florida	15	15	16	(5)	15[6]	4 or 6	15.00	no
Georgia	16	15	21	15	16[6]	4	4.50	no[19]
Hawaii	15	15	18	(5)	15[6]	4[13]	3-12.00	yes
Idaho	16	16	16	(5)	14[4]	3	13.50	no
Illinois	18	16[25]	18	(5)	16[4,6]	4 or 5	10.00	no[23]
Indiana	16	15	18	15[8]	16 1 mo.[4,6]	4[14]	6.00	no
Iowa	16	14	18	14	16[4]	4[2]	8.00/16.00	([17])
Kansas	14	14	16	(5)	14	4	8/12.00	([17])
Kentucky	16	16	18	(5)	16[6]	4	8.00	no
Louisiana	15	15	17	(6)	15[15]	4	15.50	yes
Maine	17	16	17	(5)	16[4]	4	18.00	yes
Maryland	18	16	18	15 9 mo.	16[4,6]	4	20.00	no[24]
Massachusetts	17	16	18	(5)	16 1/2[4]	4	35.00	yes[21]
Michigan	18	15	18		16[4,6]	2 or 4	6/12.00	no[17]
Minnesota	18	15	19	15[8]	16[4]	4	15.00	no[17]
Mississippi	15	15	15	(5)		4	13.00	yes
Missouri	16	16	16		15[4]	3	7.50	yes
Montana	16	16	18	(5)	15[4,6]	4	16/24.00	no
Nebraska	16	14	16	15[9]	14	4	10.00	no
Nevada	16	16	16	15 1/2[5]	14[6,10]	4	9.00[15]	no
New Hampshire	18	16	16[4]		16[5]	4	30.00	yes[21]
New Jersey	17	15	17		16	4	16-17.50	yes
New Mexico	16	13	16	15	14[12]	4	10.00	no
New York	16	16	17[4]		16[6]	4	17.50	yes
North Carolina	18	16	18	15[6]	16[4]	4	15.00	yes
North Dakota	16	14	16	(5)	14[4,6]	4	10.00	no[17]
Ohio	18	14	16	16[5,6]	14[3]	2 or 4	7/14.00	no[19]
Oklahoma	14		16	(8)	15 1/2[4]	4	18.00	yes
Oregon	16	16	16	15[5]	14	4	25.00	no[17]
Pennsylvania	16	16	18	16[6,7]	16[6]	4	5.00	yes
Rhode Island	18	16	18	(5)	16[4]	5	20.00	yes
South Carolina	15	13	16	15[9]	15	4	10.00	yes
South Dakota	14	14	16	(5)	14[9]	4	6.00	no
Tennessee	16	14	16	15	15[4,7]	4	14.00	no
Texas	18	15	16[4]	15	15[4,7]	4	16.00	yes
Utah	16	16	16[4]			4	10.00	yes
Vermont	18	16	18	15[22]	16[7]	2 or 4	10/16.00	yes
Virginia	18	16	18	15 8 mo.[5,6,7]	16[4,6]	5	12.00	yes
Washington	18	16	18	15[5,8]	16[4]	4	14.00	no[25]
West Virginia	16	16	18	(5)	16[6]	4	10.00	yes
Wisconsin	18	16	16[4]	(5)	16[6]	4	9.00	no
Wyoming	16	15	16	15[6,7]	14[6,7]	4	10.00	no

1. Full driving privileges at age given in "Regular" column. A license restricted or qualified in some manner may be obtained at age given in "Restricted" column. 2. 2 years if under 18 or over 70. 3. Upon proof of hardship. 4. Must have completed approved driver education course. 5. Learner's permit required. 6. Guardian's or parental consent required. 7. Driver with learner's permit must be accompanied by locally licensed operator 18 years or older. 8. Must be enrolled in driver education course. 9. Driver with learner's permit must be accompanied by locally licensed operator 21 years or older. 10. To and from school or transporting handicapped. 11. Restricted to mopeds. 12. For use while enrolled in driver education course. Must be accompanied by instructor. 13. 2 years if 15-24 or over 65. 14. 3 years if over 75. 15. If 65 or over, a $4 fee. 17. State troopers are authorized to inspect at their discretion. 18. Arizona emission inspection fee $7.00. 19. Annual emissions test in some counties. 20. Used motor vehicles being registered in Connecticut from out-of-state are required to be inspected and approved and Connecticut cars 10 years old and older must be inspected upon being sold or transferred. 21. Annual emissions test. 22. Must be accompanied by licensed operator 25 years or older or a school driver training instructor. 23. Trucks and buses only. 24. All used vehicles upon resale or transfer. 25. Required on out-of-state or salvaged vehicles. Emissions tested in some counties. NOTES: A driver's license is required in every state. The national speed limit is 55 miles per hour. All states have an *implied consent* Chemical Test Law for alcohol. *Source:* American Automobile Association.

School Enrollment, October 1989
(in thousands)

Age	White		Black		Spanish origin[1]		All races	
	Enrolled	Percent	Enrolled	Percent	Enrolled	Percent	Enrolled	Percent
3 and 4 years	2,370	39.4	407	38.9	202	23.8	2,898	39.1
5 and 6 years	5,598	95.2	1,084	94.9	785	92.8	6,990	95.2
7 to 9 years	8,729	99.2	1,630	99.0	1,181	98.0	10,833	99.2
10 to 13 years	10,909	99.4	2,131	99.4	1,456	99.3	13,598	99.4
14 to 15 years	5,197	98.8	1,023	99.4	706	96.5	6,493	98.8
16 and 17 years	4,993	92.3	1,033	93.7	554	86.4	6,254	92.7
18 and 19 years	3,392	56.4	541	50.2	327	44.6	4,125	56.0
20 and 21 years	2,208	39.5	309	30.7	152	18.8	2,630	38.5
22 to 24 years	1,841	20.0	253	17.2	153	12.0	2,207	19.9
25 to 29 years	1,659	9.4	168	6.4	129	6.6	1,960	9.3
30 to 34 years	1,028	5.6	130	4.9	76	3.8	1,248	5.7
Total	47,923	48.4	8,707	51.3	5,722	45.8	59,235	49.1

1. Persons of Spanish origin may be of any race. NOTE: Figures include persons enrolled in nursery school, kindergarten, elementary school, high school, and college. *Source:* Department of Commerce, Bureau of the Census.

Persons Not Enrolled in School, October 1989
(in thousands)

Age	Popu-lation	Total not enrolled		High school graduate		Not high school graduate (dropouts)[1]	
		Number	Percent	Number	Percent	Number	Percent
14 and 15 years	6,571	79	1.2	8	0.1	70	1.1
16 and 17 years	6,746	492	7.3	97	1.4	395	5.9
18 and 19 years	7,361	3,236	44.0	2,204	29.9	1,033	14.0
20 and 21 years	6,828	4,198	61.5	3,103	45.4	1,095	16.0
22 to 24 years	11,072	8,865	80.1	7,350	66.4	1,516	13.7

1. Persons who are not enrolled in school and who are not high school graduates are considered dropouts. *Source:* Department of Commerce, Bureau of the Census.

School Enrollment by Grade, Control, and Race
(in thousands)

Grade level and type of control	White			Black			All races[1]		
	Oct. 1989[3]	Oct. 1980[4]	Oct. 1970	Oct. 1989[3]	Oct. 1980[4]	Oct. 1970	Oct. 1989[3]	Oct. 1980[4]	Oct. 1970
Nursery school: Public	712	432	198	216	180	129	971	633	333
Private	1,681	1,205	695	150	115	49	1,906	1,354	763
Kindergarten: Public	2,611	2,172	2,233	557	440	374	3,293	2,690	2,674
Private	506	423	473	44	50	53	575	486	536
Grades 1–8: Public	20,468	19,743	24,923	4,296	4,058	4,668	25,897	24,398	30,001
Private	2,399	2,768	3,715	232	202	200	2,740	3,051	3,949
Grades 9–12: Public	9,443	12,056[2]	11,599	2,027	2,200[2]	1,794	11,980	14,556[2]	13,545
Private	730	—	1,124	42	—	41	809	—	1,170
College: Public	7,219	8,875[2]	5,168	932	1,007[2]	422	8,576	10,180[2]	5,699
Private	2,158	—	1,591	208	—	100	2,490	—	1,714
Total: Public	40,453	—	44,121	8,028	—	7,387	50,717	—	52,225
Private	7,474	—	7,598	676	—	443	8,520	—	8,132
Grand Total	47,927	47,673	51,719	8,704	8,251	7,830	59,237	57,348	60,357

1. Includes persons of Spanish origin. 2. Total public and private. Breakdown not available. 3. Estimates controlled to 1980 census base. 4. Estimates controlled to 1970 census base. *Source:* Department of Commerce, Bureau of the Census.

State Compulsory School Attendance Laws

State	Enactment[1]	Age limits	State	Enactment[1]	Age limits
Alabama	1915	7–16	Montana[4]	1883	7–16
Alaska[2]	1929	7–16	Nebraska	1887	7–16
Arizona	1899	8–16	Nevada	1873	7–17
Arkansas	1909	7–17	New Hampshire	1871	6–16
California	1874	6–16	New Jersey	1875	6–16
Colorado	1889	7–16	New Mexico	1891	6–18
Connecticut	1872	7–16	New York[5]	1874	6–16
Delaware	1907	5–16	North Carolina	1907	7–16
D. C.	1864	7–17	North Dakota	1883	7–16
Florida	1915	6–16	Ohio	1877	6–18
Georgia	1916	7–16	Oklahoma	1907	7–18
Hawaii	1896	6–18	Oregon	1889	7–18
Idaho	1887	7–16	Pennsylvania	1895	8–17
Illinois	1883	7–16	Rhode Island	1883	6–16
Indiana	1897	7–16	South Carolina[6]	1915	5–17
Iowa	1902	7–16	South Dakota[4]	1883	7–16
Kansas	1874	7–16	Tennessee	1905	7–17
Kentucky[3]	1896	6–16	Texas[7]	1915	7–16
Louisiana	1910	7–17	Utah	1890	6–18
Maine	1875	7–17	Vermont	1867	7–16
Maryland	1902	6–16	Virginia	1908	5–17
Massachusetts	1852	6–16	Washington	1871	8–18
Michigan	1871	6–16	West Virginia	1897	6–16
Minnesota	1885	7–16	Wisconsin	1879	6–18
Mississippi	1918	6–14	Wyoming	1876	7–16
Missouri	1905	7–16			

1. Date of enactment of first compulsory attendance law. 2. Ages 7 to 16 or high school graduation. 3. Must have parental signature for leaving school between ages of 16 and 18. 4. May leave after completion of eighth grade. 5. The ages are 6 to 17 for New York City and Buffalo. 6. Permits parental waiver of kindergarten at age 5. 7. Must complete academic year in which 16th birthday occurs. *Source:* Department of Education, National Center for Educational Statistics.

High School and College Graduates

School Year	High School			College[1]		
	Men	Women	Total	Men	Women	Total
1900	38,075	56,808	94,883	22,173	5,237	27,410
1910	63,676	92,753	156,429	28,762	8,437	37,199
1920	123,684	187,582	311,266	31,980	16,642	48,622
1929–30	300,376	366,528	666,904	73,615	48,869	122,484
1939–40	578,718	642,757	1,221,475	109,546	76,954	186,500
1949–50	570,700	629,000	1,199,700	328,841	103,217	432,058
1959–60	898,000	966,000	1,864,000	254,063	138,377	392,440
1964–65	1,314,000	1,351,000	2,665,000	316,286	213,717	530,003
1968–69	1,402,000	1,427,000	2,829,000	444,380	319,805	764,185
1969–70	1,433,000	1,463,000	2,896,000	484,174	343,060	827,234
1970–71	1,456,000	1,487,000	2,943,000	511,138	366,538	877,676
1971–72	1,490,000	1,518,000	3,008,000	541,313	389,371	930,684
1972–73	1,501,000	1,536,000	3,037,000	564,680	407,700	972,380
1973–74	1,515,000	1,565,000	3,080,000	575,843	423,749	999,592
1974–75	1,541,000	1,599,000	3,140,000	553,797	425,052	978,849
1975–76	1,554,000	1,601,000	3,155,000	557,817	430,578	988,395
1976–77	1,548,000	1,606,000	3,154,000	547,919	435,989	983,908
1977–78	1,535,000	1,599,000	3,134,000	487,000	434,000	921,000
1978–79	1,531,800	1,602,400	3,134,200	529,996	460,242	990,238
1979–80	1,500,000	1,558,000	3,058,000	526,327	473,221	999,548
1980–81	1,483,000	1,537,000	3,020,000	470,000	465,000	935,000
1981–82	1,474,000	1,527,000	3,001,000	473,000	480,000	953,000
1982–83	1,437,000	1,451,000	2,888,000	479,140	490,370	969,510
1983–84	n.a.	n.a.	2,767,000	482,319	491,990	974,309
1984–85	n.a.	n.a.	2,677,000	482,528	496,949	979,477
1985–86	n.a.	n.a.	2,642,000	485,923	501,900	987,823
1986–87	n.a.	n.a.	2,698,000	480,854[2]	510,485[2]	991,339[2]
1987–88	n.a.	n.a.	2,793,000[3]	472,000[3]	517,000[3]	989,000[3]

1. Includes bachelor's and first-professional degrees for years 1900–1960. 2. Preliminary data. 3. Estimated. n.a. = not available. NOTE: Includes graduates from public and private schools. Beginning in 1959–60, figures include Alaska and Hawaii. Because of rounding, details may not add to totals. Most recent data available. *Source:* Department of Education, Center for Education Statistics.

Federal Funds for Some Major Programs for Education, Fiscal Year 1991[1]

Program	Amount in thousands	Program	Amount in thousands
Elementary–secondary		Higher education facilities	20,900
Educationally disadvantaged	$ 5,838,939	Aid for institutional development	209,890
Special programs	1,704,916	**Vocational education**	7,148
Bilingual education	205,537	**Adult basic and secondary education**	246,862
School assistance in federally		**Education for the handicapped**	
affected areas	660,854	State grant program	1,615,125
Higher education		Preschool grants	257,730
Program development	62,171	Special populations	n.a.
Student assistance		Training and information	n.a.
Pell grants	4,923,642	All other	82,701
Work study/grants	610,675	**Indian education**	75,762
Direct loans to students	473,650	**Education research and improvement**	174,726
Special programs for the disadvantaged	269,739	**Total**	**$17,432,057**

1. Estimated outlay for fiscal year 1991. n.a. = not available. *Source: Budget of the United States Government,* Fiscal Year 1991.

Funding for Public Elementary and Secondary Education, 1980–81 to 1986–87

(In thousands except percent)

School year	Total	Federal	State	Local[1]	% Federal	% State	% Local[1]
1980–81	105,949,087	9,768,262	50,182,659	45,998,166	9.2	47.4	43.4
1981–82	110,191,257	8,186,466	52,436,435	49,568,356	7.4	47.6	45.0
1982–83	117,497,502	8,339,990	56,282,157	52,875,354	7.1	47.9	45.0
1983–84	126,055,419	8,576,547	60,232,981	57,245,892	6.8	47.8	45.4
1984–85[2]	137,350,722	8,952,358	66,983,340	61,415,023	6.5	48.8	44.7
1984-85	137,294,678	9,105,569	67,168,684	61,020,425	6.6	48.9	44.4
1985-86	149,004,882	9,956,009	73,673,174	65,375,698	6.7	49.4	43.9
1986–87	158,827,473	10,145,899	79,022,572	69,659,003	6.4	49.8	43.9

1. Includes a relatively small amount from nongovernmental sources (gifts and tuition and transportation fees from patrons). *Source:* U.S. Department of Education, National Center for Education Statistics.

Major U.S. College and University Libraries

(Top 50 based on number of volumes in library)

Institution	Volumes	Microforms[1]	Institution	Volumes	Microforms[1]
Harvard	11,781,270	5,230,504	New York	3,031,621	2,529,260
Yale	8,718,619	3,137,720	Iowa	3,018,599	3,202,544
U of Illinois–Urbana	7,561,615	3,374,194	U of Kansas	2,973,134	2,109,557
U of California–Berkeley	7,366,672	4,255,519	U of Pittsburg	2,789,211	2,366,794
U of Michigan	6,237,521	3,710,700	U of Georgia	2,788,311	4,054,277
U of Texas	6,066,136	4,220,837	Johns Hopkins	2,784,642	1,480,444
U of California–Los Angeles	5,976,588	5,473,071	U of Florida	2,782,279	2,704,384
Columbia	5,894,135	3,913,294	Rochester	2,639,518	2,397,217
Stanford	5,753,147	3,343,162	U of Southern California	2,580,183	2,954,438
Cornell	5,144,830	4,759,356	SUNY-Buffalo	2,534,391	3,611,446
U of Chicago	5,063,051	1,473,403	Arizona State	2,466,274	3,117,172
U of Wisconsin	4,908,985	3,143,060	U of Missouri	2,446,491	4,708,404
U of Washington	4,815,209	5,170,917	Louisiana State	2,408,565	2,016,610
U of Minnesota	4,537,087	2,766,010	South Carolina	2,367,144	2,982,832
Ohio State	4,338,474	3,124,060	U of Massachusetts	2,345,974	1,715,655
Princeton	4,175,904	2,458,236	U of Hawaii	2,312,229	3,600,171
Indiana	4,045,828	1,624,710	Wayne State	2,309,698	2,044,008
Duke	3,757,814	1,385,578	U of California-Davis	2,306,831	2,705,395
North Carolina	3,635,509	3,013,887	Syracuse	2,285,707	3,408,965
U of Pennsylvania	3,576,227	2,368,423	U of Oklahoma	2,261,724	2,774,476
U of Arizona	3,424,698	3,880,539	U of Colorado	2,227,963	1,273,941
Michigan State	3,373,215	3,412,157	Washington U-St. Louis	2,221,176	1,750,903
Rutgers	3,129,861	3,536,150	U of Connecticut	2,210,528	2,534,835
U of Virginia	3,091,445	4,095,457	Brown	2,172,889	1,093,406
Pennsylvania State	3,043,837	3,057,959	MIT	2,141,174	1,687,035

1. Includes reels of microfilm and number of microcards, microprint sheets, and microfiches. Northwestern data are unavailable. *Source:* Association of Research Libraries.

College and University Endowments, 1988–89

(top 75 in millions of dollars)

Institution	Endowment (market value)	Voluntary support[1]	Expen- ditures[2]	Institution	Endowment (market value)	Voluntary support[1]	Expen- ditures[2]
Harvard U	$4,479.0	$185.4	$951.7	Swarthmore C	$304.9	$12.0	$41.4
Princeton U	2,351.1	80.3	253.5	U of Delaware	297.1	11.2	221.8
Yale U	2,342.1	122.8	569.3	Grinnell C	293.4	5.2	26.1
Stanford U	2,087.0	188.6	804.0	Ohio State U	293.4	68.6	754.8
Columbia U	1,443.3	110.4	738.8	Carnegie-Mellon U	291.3	31.2	231.3
Texas A&M U	1,406.8	50.2	215.6	Wake Forest U	284.7	25.5	181.6
Washington U	1,315.5	49.3	461.6	Wesleyan U	275.1	12.3	63.0
Massachusetts Inst. of Tech.	1,256.2	95.7	547.1	Pomona C	271.1	17.3	34.0
Northwestern U	1,065.8	68.5	460.2	Texas Christian U	269.4	11.3	62.7
Emory U	1,001.6	31.7	260.7	Indiana U	267.4	40.4	700.1
U of Chicago	973.8	66.6	412.4	Trinity U	266.7	6.3	36.2
Rice U	970.8	21.4	104.2	Amherst C	266.5	12.5	42.2
Cornell U	885.1	157.1	806.9	George Washington U	265.8	17.8	249.8
U of Pennsylvania	761.4	121.9	585.9	Loyola U-Chicago	257.2	30.5	139.7
Dartmouth C	632.0	47.5	180.7	U of Pittsburgh	257.2	28.4	473.4
Vanderbilt U	556.7	36.4	273.2	Berea C	252.1	11.8	17.5
New York U	542.8	61.8	675.4	Boston C	250.0	16.5	147.7
U of Notre Dame	541.6	44.9	114.2	U of Richmond	249.7	8.4	46.7
U of Rochester	538.1	39.0	270.1	U of Wisconsin-Madison	243.5	102.2	746.8
Mayo Medical School	537.0	31.9	127.3	Georgetown U	241.1	30.1	250.5
Johns Hopkins U	527.2	84.1	608.3	Oberlin C	235.7	15.0	57.1
Rockefeller U	523.3	20.6	88.6	Baylor U	235.5	25.7	91.6
California Inst. of Tech.	503.0	48.0	177.4	Lehigh U	225.7	26.7	139.7
U of Virginia	468.6	47.6	323.6	Vassar C	224.1	13.8	46.1
U of Michigan	467.8	70.7	861.6	Tulane U of Louisiana	221.7	24.0	192.8
U of Southern California	459.8	102.6	603.0	Middlebury C	217.2	10.5	44.7
Duke U	453.0	102.0	404.4	Rensselaer Poly. Inst.	206.5	22.3	126.6
U of Minnesota	433.9	100.2	912.3	Macalester C	203.8	5.6	27.3
U of California–Berkeley	415.3	68.3	682.8	U of Kansas	203.6	26.6	198.1
Brown U	410.0	38.2	178.7	Lafayette C	202.2	13.3	38.2
Case Western Reserve U	380.9	35.1	225.0	U of California-Los Angeles	196.0	72.8	948.0
Princeton Theol. Sem.	356.0	5.5	20.3	Boston U	194.7	27.7	456.2
Wellesley C	341.7	28.3	77.5	Thomas Jefferson U	190.3	15.4	150.6
Southern Methodist U	336.0	23.2	120.6	U of Tennessee	189.7	32.2	568.9
Smith C	329.5	31.5	82.0	U of North Carolina at Chapel Hill	189.2	49.2	464.4
U of Texas–Austin	323.8	35.5	520.1	Loyola U-New Orleans	184.1	4.5	42.9
Williams C	306.9	14.9	51.0	Pennsylvania State U	171.7	55.2	753.1
Purdue U	305.0	25.7	490.4				

1. Gifts from business, alumni, religious denominations, and others. 2. Figure represents about 80% of typical operating budget. Does not include auxiliary enterprises and capital outlays. NOTE: C = College; U = University. *Source:* Council for Aid to Education.

Institutions of Higher Education—Average Salaries and Fringe Benefits for Faculty Members, 1970-1989[1]

(in thousands of dollars)

Control and Academic Rank	1989	1988	1987	1986	1985	1984	1983	1982	1980	1975	1970
Average Salaries											
Public: All ranks	39.6	37.2	35.8	33.4	31.2	29.4	28.6	26.2	22.1	16.6	13.1
Professor	50.1	47.2	45.3	42.3	39.6	37.1	36.0	33.7	28.8	21.7	17.3
Associate professor	37.9	35.6	34.2	32.2	30.2	28.4	27.5	25.7	21.9	16.7	13.2
Assistant professor	31.7	29.6	28.5	26.7	25.0	23.5	22.6	21.2	18.0	13.7	10.9
Instructor	23.9	22.2	21.8	20.9	19.5	19.1	17.7	16.7	14.8	11.2	9.1
Private:[2] All ranks	42.4	39.7	37.8	35.4	33.0	31.1	29.2	26.8	22.1	16.6	13.1
Professor	55.9	52.2	50.3	47.0	44.1	41.5	38.8	35.8	30.1	22.4	17.8
Associate professor	38.8	36.6	34.9	32.9	30.9	29.4	27.5	25.4	21.0	16.0	12.6
Assistant professor	31.9	28.3	26.8	25.0	23.7	22.1	20.4	17.0	13.0	10.3	
Instructor	24.1	22.7	20.4	19.8	19.0	18.4	17.6	15.9	13.3	10.9	8.6
Average Fringe Benefits—All Ranks Combined											
Public	9.0	8.2	7.8	7.3	7.0	6.0	5.4	5.1	3.9	2.5	1.9
Private[2]	10.0	9.2	8.6	8.0	7.2	6.4	5.7	5.4	4.1	2.8	2.2

1. Figures are for 9 months teaching for full-time faculty members in four-year colleges and universities. 2. Excludes church-related colleges and universities. *Source:* U.S. Bureau of the Census, *Statistical Abstract of the United States: 1990.*

Accredited U.S. Senior Colleges and Universities

Source: The Guidance Information System™, a product of Houghton Mifflin Company, Software Division.

Schools listed are four-year institutions that offer at least a Bachelor's degree and are fully accredited by one of the institutional and professional accrediting associations. Included are accredited colleges outside the U.S.

Tuition, room, and board listed are average annual figures (including fees) subject to fluctuation, usually covering two semesters, two out of three trimesters, or three out of four quarters, depending on the school calendar.

For further information, write to the Registrar of the school concerned.

NOTE: n.a. = information not available. — = does not apply. Enrollment figures are approximate. (C) = Coeducational, (M) = primarily for men, (W) = primarily for women.

Abbreviations used for controls:

AB	American Baptist	ID	Interdenominational
AG	Assemblies of God	Ind	Independent
AL	American Lutheran	L	Lutheran
AME	African Methodist Episcopal	LCA	Lutheran Church of America
B	Baptist	LDS	Latter Day Saints
BC	Brethren in Christ	M	Methodist
Br	Brethren	MB	Mennonite Brethren
CB	Church of Brethren	MC	Missionary Church
CC	Church of Christ	Men	Mennonite
CE	Christian Evangelical	Mor	Moravian
CG	Church of God	Naz	Nazarene
ChC	Christian Church	ND	Non-denominational
CMA	Christian & Missionary Alliance	OBS	Open Bible Standard
CME	Christian Methodist Episcopal	P	Private
CP	Cumberland Presbyterian	PH	Pentecostal Holiness
CR	Christian Reformed	Pub	Public
DC	Disciples of Christ	PUS	Presbyterian, U.S.
E	Episcopal	RC	Roman Catholic
EC	Evangelical Covenant	RCA	Reformed Church in America
EFC	Evangelical Free Church	RP	Reformed Presbyterian
EL	Evangelical Lutheran	SB	Southern Baptist
F	Friends	SDA	Seventh Day Adventist
FG	Foursquare Gospel	UCC	United Church of Christ
FM	Free Methodist	UM	United Methodist
FWB	Free Will Baptist	UP	United Presbyterian
GGF	Grace Gospel Fellowship	W	Wesleyan
		WM	Wesleyan Methodist

Institution and location	Enrollment	Control	Tuition ($) Res.	Tuition ($) Nonres.	Rm/Bd ($)
Abilene Christian University; Abilene, Tex. 79699	3,687 (C)	P/CC	4,536	4,536	2,700
Academy of Art College; San Francisco, Calif. 94108	2,156 (C)	P	4,800	4,800	5,400
Academy of the New Church College; Bryn Athyn, Pa. 19009	139 (C)	P	2,928	2,928	2,709
Adams State College; Alamosa, Colo. 81102	2,098 (C)	Pub	1,350	3,510	2,580
Adelphi University; Garden City, N.Y. 11530	5,122 (C)	P	8,600	8,600	4,860
Adrian College; Adrian, Mich. 49221	1,207 (C)	P/UM	8,890	8,890	2,700
Aeronautics, College of; Flushing, N.Y. 11371	1,200 (C)	P	5,600	5,600	n.a.
Aero-Space Institute; Chicago, Ill. 60605-10717	50 (C)	P	4,800	4,800	n.a.
Agnes Scott College; Decatur, Ga. 30030	526 (W)	P	10,450	10,450	4,180
Akron, University of; Akron, Ohio 44325	24,857 (C)	Pub	2,277	5,593	2,950
Alabama, University of; Tuscaloosa, Ala. 35487-0132	15,296 (C)	Pub	1,724	4,260	2,980
Alabama, University of–Birmingham; Birmingham, Ala. 35294	10,057 (C)	Pub	1,823	3,473	3,870
Alabama, University of–Huntsville; Huntsville, Ala. 35899	6,113 (C)	Pub	1,905	3,810	2,685
Alabama A&M University; Normal, Ala. 35762	3,354 (C)	Pub	1,248	2,236	2,036
Alabama State University; Montgomery, Ala. 36101-0271	4,024 (C)	Pub	1,268	2,428	1,991
Alaska, University of–Anchorage; Anchorage, Alas. 99508	4,091 (C)	Pub	941	2,765	3,200
Alaska, University of–Fairbanks; Fairbanks, Alas. 99701	7,028 (C)	Pub	1,512	3,540	2,540
Alaska Southeast, University of–Juneau; Juneau, Alas. 99801	2,756 (C)	Pub	1,112	3,140	3,480
Alaska Bible College; Glennallen, Alas. 99588	90 (C)	P/ID	2,190	2,190	3,000
Alaska Pacific University; Anchorage, Alas. 99508	1,267 (C)	P/UM	6,200	6,200	3,900
Albany College of Pharmacy; Albany, N.Y. 12208	650 (C)	P	6,225	6,225	3,600
Albany State College; Albany, Ga. 31705	1,800 (C)	Pub	1,476	3,765	2,190
Albertus Magnus College; New Haven, Conn. 06511	507 (C)	P/RC	8,818	8,818	4,695
Albion College; Albion, Mich. 49224	1,700 (C)	P/UM	9,282	9,282	3,682
Albright College; Reading, Pa. 19603	1,306 (C)	P/UM	11,800	11,800	3,620
Alcorn State University; Lorman, Miss. 39096	2,757 (C)	Pub	1,700	4,582	1,750
Alderson–Broaddus College; Philippi, W. Va. 26416	760 (C)	P/AB	7,336	7,336	2,490
Alfred University; Alfred, N.Y. 14802	2,270 (C)	P	11,880	11,880	3,874

Institution and location	Enrollment	Control	Tuition ($) Res.	Tuition ($) Nonres.	Rm/Bd ($)
Alice Lloyd College; Pippa Passes, Ky. 41844	517 (C)	P	2,580	2,580	2,250
Allegheny College; Meadville, Pa. 16335	1,965 (C)	P	14,000	14,000	3,890
Allentown College of St. Francis de Sales; Center Valley, Pa. 18034	891 (C)	P/RC	7,180	7,180	3,790
Alma College; Alma, Mich. 48801	1,241 (C)	P	9,132	9,132	3,390
Alvernia College; Reading, Pa. 19607	1,113 (C)	P/RC	6,166	6,166	3,300
Alverno College; Milwaukee, Wis. 53215	2,310 (W)	P	5,966	5,966	3,460
Ambassador College; Pasadena, Calif. 91129	640 (C)	P	1,500	1,500	2,300
Amber University; Garland, Tex. 75041	600 (C)	P	3,780	3,780	n.a.
American Baptist College; Nashville, Tenn. 37207	163 (C)	P/B	1,650	1,650	1,486
American University of Paris; 75007 Paris, France	972 (C)	P	11,080	11,080	n.a.
American College of Switzerland; 1854 Leysin (HM), Switzerland	300 (C)	P	16,035	16,035	3,279
American Conservatory of Music; Chicago, Ill. 60602	124 (C)	P	6,000	6,000	n.a.
American International College; Springfield, Mass. 01109	1,391 (C)	P	7,731	7,731	3,600
American University; Washington, D.C. 20016	7,335 (C)	P	11,336	11,336	5,228
American University in Cairo; New York, N.Y. 10017	2,447 (C)	P	6,840	6,840	3,580
American University of Beirut; Beirut, Lebanon	4,500 (C)	P	3,200	3,200	2,925
American Universtity of Puerto Rico; Bayamon, PR 00619	4,255 (C)	P	1,900	1,900	n.a.
Amherst College; Amherst, Mass. 01002	1,570 (C)	P	13,780	13,780	4,200
Anderson University; Anderson, Ind. 46012	1,866 (C)	P/CG	7,330	7,330	2,610
Andrews University; Berrien Springs, Mich. 49104	2,009 (C)	P/SDA	7,761	7,761	3,078
Angelo State University; San Angelo, Tex. 76909	6,003 (C)	Pub	975	4,095	3,280
Anna Maria College for Men and Women; Paxton, Mass. 01612	604 (C)	P	7,700	7,700	4,020
Antillian College; Mayaguez, P.R. 00709	817 (C)	P/SDA	2,550	2,550	1,440
Antioch College; Yellow Springs, Ohio 45387	568 (C)	P	11,460	11,460	3,330
Antioch Los Angeles; Marina Del Rey, Calif. 90292	182 (C)	P	6,300	6,300	n.a.
Antioch Santa Barbara; Santa Barbara, Calif. 93101	48 (C)	P	6,000	6,000	n.a.
Antioch School for Adult & Experiential Learning; Yellow Springs, Ohio 45387	167 (C)	P	4,140	4,140	n.a.
Antioch Seattle; Seattle, Wash. 98121	91 (C)	P	6,300	6,300	n.a.
Appalachian Bible College; Bradley, W. Va. 25818	182 (C)	P/Ind	3,140	3,140	2,600
Appalachian State University; Boone, N.C. 28608	10,652 (C)	Pub	1,075	4,892	2,110
Aquinas College; Grand Rapids, Mich. 49506	2,159 (C)	P/RC	7,494	7,494	3,484
Arizona, University of; Tucson, Ariz. 85721	27,932 (C)	Pub	1,362	5,484	3,192
Arizona College of the Bible; Phoenix, Ariz. 85021	177 (C)	P/ID	3,790	3,790	2,770
Arizona State University; Tempe, Ariz. 85287-0112	32,606 (C)	Pub	1,362	5,484	3,520
Arkansas, Univ. of; Fayetteville, Ark. 72701	11,513 (C)	Pub	1,548	3,900	2,750
Arkansas, Univ. of–Little Rock; Little Rock, Ark. 72204	9,405 (C)	Pub	1,550	3,850	n.a.
Arkansas, Univ. of–Monticello; Monticello, Ark. 71655	1,854 (C)	Pub	1,410	3,230	1,880
Arkansas, Univ. of–Pine Bluff; Pine Bluff, Ark. 71601	3,333 (C)	Pub	1,300	3,038	1,940
Arkansas Baptist College; Little Rock, Ark. 72202	233 (C)	P	4,670	4,670	2,200
Arkansas College; Batesville, Ark. 72501	831 (C)	P/PUS	5,455	5,455	2,660
Arkansas State University; State University, Ark. 72467	9,026 (C)	Pub	1,200	2,450	2,010
Arkansas Tech. University; Russellville, Ark. 72801	3,453 (C)	Pub	1,100	2,150	1,940
Arlington Baptist College; Arlington, Tex. 76012	168 (C)	P	2,250	2,250	2,350
Armstrong College; Berkeley, Calif. 94704	150 (C)	P	4,057	4,057	n.a.
Armstrong State College; Savannah, Ga. 31419	2,750 (C)	Pub	1,365	3,747	2,790
Arnold & Marie Schwartz College of Pharmacy & Health Sciences. See Long Island University Center, Brooklyn Center					
Art Academy of Cincinnati; Cincinnati, Ohio 45202	250 (C)	P	5,825	5,825	n.a.
Art Center College of Design; Pasadena, Calif. 91103	1,268 (C)	P	10,309	10,309	n.a.
Art Institute of Chicago, School of the; Chicago, Ill. 60603	1,843 (C)	P	9,300	9,300	n.a.
Art Institute of Southern California; Laguna Beach, Calif. 92651	130 (C)	P	6,950	6,950	n.a.
Arts, The University of the; Philadelphia, Pa. 19102	1,228 (C)	P	8,400	8,400	4,300
Asbury College; Wilmore, Ky. 40390	993 (C)	P	6,308	6,308	2,127
Ashland University; Ashland, Ohio 44805	1,651 (C)	P/BR	8,632	8,632	3,568
Assumption College; Worcester, Mass. 01615-0005	1,810 (C)	P/RC	8,675	8,675	4,450
Athens State College; Athens, Ala. 35611	1,392 (C)	Pub	1,080	2,160	825
Atlanta Christian College; East Point, Ga. 30344	169 (C)	P	2,716	2,716	2,590
Atlanta College of Art; Atlanta, Ga. 30309	340 (C)	P	7,000	7,000	4,320
Atlantic, College of the; Bar Harbor, Maine 04609	217 (C)	P	10,405	10,405	3,700
Atlantic Christian College; Wilson, N.C. 27893	1,434 (C)	P/DC	5,500	5,500	2,600
Atlantic Union College; South Lancaster, Mass. 01561	795 (C)	P	8,185	8,185	2,800
Auburn University; Auburn University, Ala. 36849	19,349 (C)	Pub	1,476	4,428	2,750
Auburn University–Montgomery; Montgomery, Ala. 36193	4,450 (C)	Pub	1,215	3,645	2,890
Augsburg College; Minneapolis, Minn. 55454	2,554 (C)	P/AL	9,484	9,484	3,580
Augusta College; Augusta, Ga. 30910	3,934 (C)	Pub	1,296	3,585	3,195
Augustana College; Rock Island, Ill. 61201	2,013 (C)	P/LCA	8,751	8,751	2,994
Augustana College; Sioux Falls, S.D. 57197	1,952 (C)	P/AL	8,640	8,640	2,650
Aurora University; Aurora, Ill. 60506	1,523 (C)	P	8,100	8,100	3,480
Austin College; Sherman, Tex. 75090	1,210 (C)	P/PUS	8,735	8,735	3,497
Austin Peay State University; Clarksville, Tenn. 37040	4,784 (C)	Pub	1,210	4,166	2,160
Averett College; Danville, Va. 24541-3692	900 (C)	P/SB	6,900	6,900	3,920
Avila College; Kansas City, Mo. 64145	1,485 (C)	P/RC	6,580	6,580	2,900

Institution and location	Enrollment	Control	Tuition ($) Res.	Tuition ($) Nonres.	Rm/Bd ($)
Azusa Pacific University; Azusa, Calif. 91702	1,629 (C)	P	7,900	7,900	3,550
Babson College; Wellesley, Mass. 02157	1,546 (C)	P	12,570	12,570	5,858
Baker University; Baldwin City, Kan. 66006	848 (C)	P/UM	5,820	5,820	2,990
Baldwin–Wallace College; Berea, Ohio 44017	2,494 (C)	P/UM	8,625	8,625	3,501
Ball State University; Muncie, Ind. 47306	18,993 (C)	Pub	1,992	4,590	2,600
Baltimore, University of; Baltimore, Md. 21201	3,104 (C)	Pub	2,047	3,635	n.a.
Baltimore Hebrew University; Baltimore, Md. 21215	552 (C)	P	1,800	1,800	n.a.
Baptist Bible College; Springfield, Mo. 65803	742 (C)	P/B	1,600	1,600	2,190
Baptist Bible College of Pennsylvania; Clarks Summit, Pa. 18411	494 (C)	P	4,747	4,747	2,600
Baptist Christian College; Shreveport, La. 71108	350 (C)	P	2,100	2,100	n.a.
Baptist College at Charleston; Charleston, S.C. 29411	2,052 (C)	P/SB	5,832	5,832	2,902
Barat College; Lake Forest, Ill. 60045	674 (C)	P	7,020	7,020	3,000
Barber–Scotia College; Concord, N.C. 28025	370 (C)	P/UP	3,330	3,330	2,287
Bard College; Annandale-on-Hudson, N.Y. 12504	930 (C)	P	14,630	14,630	4,760
Barnard College of Columbia University; New York, N.Y. 10027	2,200 (W)	P	13,942	13,942	6,010
Barry University; Miami Shores, Fla. 33161	3,932 (C)	P	7,790	7,790	4,200
Bartlesville Wesleyan College; Bartlesville, Okla. 74003	489 (C)	P	5,170	5,170	2,700
Bassist College; Portland, Ore. 97201	157 (C)	P	7,500	7,500	4,000
Bates College; Lewiston, Maine 04240	1,500 (C)	P	19,905	19,905	—
Baylor University; Waco, Tex. 76798-7032	10,389 (C)	P/SB	5,110	5,110	3,330
Beaver College; Glenside, Pa. 19038	1,203 (C)	P	10,015	10,015	4,400
Behrend College. *See* Pennsylvania State University					
Beirut University College; Beirut, Lebanon	2,438 (C)	P	10,015	10,015	500
Belhaven College; Jackson, Miss. 39202	693 (C)	P/PUS	5,370	5,370	2,040
Bellarmine College; Louisville, Ky. 40205	2,102 (C)	P/RC	6,000	6,000	2,700
Bellevue College; Bellevue, Neb. 68005	1,956 (C)	P	2,370	2,370	n.a.
Bellin College of Nursing; Green Bay, Wis. 54305-5000	161 (C)	P	5,222	5,222	n.a.
Belmont Abbey College; Belmont, N.C. 28012	1,033 (C)	P/RC	4,260	5,360	2,886
Belmont College; Nashville, Tenn. 37203	2,508 (C)	P/SB	4,650	4,650	2,080
Beloit College; Beloit, Wis. 53511	1,090 (C)	P	11,994	11,994	3,204
Bemidji State University; Bemidji, Minn. 56601	4,642 (C)	Pub	1,944	2,976	2,259
Benedict College; Columbia, S.C. 29204	1,448 (C)	P	3,796	3,796	1,980
Benedictine College; Atchison, Kan. 66002	803 (C)	P/RC	6,560	6,560	2,805
Bennett College; Greensboro, N.C. 27401	602 (W)	P/UM	5,230	5,230	2,250
Bennington College; Bennington, Vt. 05201	593 (C)	P	17,790	17,790	3,760
Bentley College; Waltham, Mass. 02254	3,860 (C)	P	10,610	10,610	4,232
Berea College; Berea, Ky. 40404	1,550 (C)	P	170	170	2,205
Berklee College of Music; Boston, Mass. 02215	2,784 (C)	P	8,340	8,340	5,790
Bernard M. Baruch Coll. *See* New York, City Univ. of					
Berry College; Mount Berry, Ga. 30149	1,714 (C)	P	5,880	5,880	3,496
Bethany Bible College; Santa Cruz, Calif. 95066	533 (C)	P/AG	5,350	5,350	2,800
Bethany College; Bethany, W. Va. 36032	844 (C)	P/DC	9,768	9,768	3,402
Bethany College; Lindsborg, Kan. 67456	722 (C)	P	5,992	5,992	2,912
Bethel College; McKenzie, Tenn. 38201	469 (C)	P/CP	3,600	3,600	2,100
Bethel College; Mishawaka, Ind. 46545	570 (C)	P/MC	6,250	6,250	2,500
Bethel College; North Newton, Kan. 67117	614 (C)	P	6,990	6,990	2,800
Bethel College; St. Paul, Minn. 55112	1,800 (C)	P/B	9,250	9,250	3,380
Bethune–Cookman College; Daytona Beach, Fla. 32015	2,141 (C)	P	4,134	4,134	2,545
Biola University; La Mirada, Calif. 90639	1,838 (C)	P	9,172	9,172	3,820
Birmingham–Southern College; Birmingham, Ala. 35254	1,846 (C)	P/UM	8,380	8,380	3,280
Blackburn College; Carlinville, Ill. 62626	469 (C)	P	6,800	6,800	3,400
Black Hills State University; Spearfish, S.D. 57783	2,412 (C)	Pub	1,720	3,012	1,991
Bloomfield College; Bloomfield, N.J. 07003	1,484 (C)	P	6,750	6,750	3,320
Bloomsburg State Coll. *See* Bloomsburg Univ. of Pennsylvania					
Bloomsburg University of Pennsylvania; Bloomsburg, Pa. 17815	6,606 (C)	Pub	2,338	3,772	2,110
Bluefield College; Bluefield, Va. 24605	366 (C)	P/SB	4,920	4,920	3,320
Bluefield State College; Bluefield, W. Va. 24701	2,487 (C)	Pub	1,170	2,770	n.a.
Blue Mountain College; Blue Mountain, Miss. 38610	374 (W)	P/SB	3,180	3,180	1,940
Bluffton College; Bluffton, Ohio 45817	623 (C)	P	7,065	7,065	2,901
Bob Jones University; Greenville, S.C. 29614	4.096 (C)	P	3,340	3,340	3,060
Boca Raton, College of; Boca Raton, Fla. 33431	1,100 (C)	P	10,900	10,900	4,400
Boise State University; Boise, Idaho 83725	10,401 (C)	Pub	1,180	3,080	2,400
Boricua College; New York, N.Y. 10032	1,072 (C)	P	4,300	4,300	n.a.
Borromeo College of Ohio; Wickliffe, Ohio 44092	45 (M)	P/RC	4,500	4,500	2,300
Boston Architecture Center School of Architecture; Boston, Mass. 02115	653 (C)	P	2,280	2,280	n.a.
Boston College; Chestnut Hill, Mass. 02167	8,752 (C)	P/RC	13,077	13,077	5,830
Boston Conservatory; Boston, Mass. 02215	385 (C)	P	8,210	8,210	4,900
Boston University; Boston, Mass. 02215	14,714 (C)	P	15,165	15,165	5,960
Bowdoin College; Brunswick, Maine 04011	1,350 (C)	P	14,060	14,060	4,920
Bowie State College; Bowie, Md. 20715	2,265 (C)	Pub	1,991	3,533	3,238
Bowling Green State University; Bowling Green, Ohio 43403	15,707 (C)	Pub	2,644	6,504	2,344
Bradford College; Bradford, Mass. 01835	456 (C)	P	9,850	9,850	5,050

Institution and location	Enrollment	Control	Tuition ($) Res.	Tuition ($) Nonres.	Rm/Bd ($)
Bradley University; Peoria, Ill. 61625	4,910 (C)	P	8,500	8,500	3,750
Brandeis University; Waltham, Mass. 02254	2,881 (C)	P	13,890	13,890	5,820
Brenau: The Women's College; Gainesville, Ga. 30501	489 (W)	P	6,018	6,018	4,982
Brescia College; Owensboro, Ky. 42301	666 (C)	P/RC	4,600	4,600	2,300
Brewton–Parker College; Mount Vernon, Ga. 30445	1,350 (C)	P	2,900	2,900	2,100
Briar Cliff College; Sioux City, Iowa 51104	1,120 (C)	P/RC	7,980	7,980	2,973
Bridgeport, University of; Bridgeport, Conn. 06601	3,146 (C)	P	10,027	10,027	4,410
Bridgeport Engineering Institute; Bridgeport, Conn. 06606	830 (C)	P	5,850	5,850	n.a.
Bridgewater College; Bridgewater, Va. 22812	985 (C)	P	7,650	7,650	3,750
Bridgewater State College; Bridgewater, Mass. 02325	5,270 (C)	Pub	1,402	3,898	2,810
Brigham Young University; Provo, Utah 84602	26,600 (C)	P/LDS	1,800	1,800	2,750
Brigham Young University–Hawaii; Laie, Oahu, Hawaii 96762	2,040 (C)	P/LDS	2,160	2,160	2,355
Brooklyn Center. See Long Island University Center					
Brooklyn College. See New York, City University of					
Bristol University; Bristol, Tenn. 37621	700 (C)	P	3,600	3,600	n.a.
Brooks Institute of Photography; Santa Barbara, Calif. 93108	612 (C)	P	7,650	7,650	n.a.
Brown University; Providence, R.I. 02912	5,804 (C)	P	14,375	14,375	4,590
Bryan College; Dayton, Tenn. 37321	551 (C)	P	5,770	5,770	3,430
Bryant College; Smithfield, R.I. 02917	3,041 (C)	P	8,719	8,719	5,401
Bryn Mawr College; Bryn Mawr, Pa. 19010	1,177 (W)	P	13,200	13,200	5,100
Bucknell University; Lewisburg, Pa. 17837	3,344 (C)	P	14,800	14,800	3,825
Buena Vista College; Storm Lake, Iowa 50588	1,086 (C)	P	10,000	10,000	2,794
Burlington College; Burlington, Vt. 05401	213 (C)	P	6,030	6,030	n.a.
Butler University; Indianapolis, Ind. 46208	2,375 (C)	P	8,825	8,825	3,255
Cabrini College; Radnor, Pa. 19087	720 (C)	P	5,885	5,885	4,100
Caldwell College; Caldwell, N.J. 07006	1,069 (C)	P	7,200	7,200	3,800
California, University of; Berkeley, Calif. 94720:	22,262 (C)	Pub	1,670	7,470	4,134
UC–Berkeley; Berkeley, Calif. 94720	22,671 (C)	Pub	1,670	7,470	4,134
UC–Davis; Davis, Calif. 95616	17,202 (C)	Pub	1,676	7,592	4,741
UC–Irvine; Irvine, Calif. 92717	13,150 (C)	Pub	1,828	7,627	5,250
UC–Los Angeles; Los Angeles, Calif. 90024	23,883 (C)	Pub	1,634	7,433	3,700
UC–Riverside; Riverside, Calif. 92521	6,747 (C)	Pub	1,644	7,560	4,850
UC–San Diego; La Jolla, Calif. 92093	14,105 (C)	Pub	1,767	5,799	5,175
UC–Santa Barbara; Santa Barbara, Calif. 93106	16,853 (C)	Pub	1,578	5,799	4,736
UC–Santa Cruz; Santa Cruz, Calif. 95064	8,659 (C)	Pub	1,833	7,632	4,628
California Baptist College; Riverside, Calif. 92504	617 (C)	P	5,076	5,076	4,198
California College of Arts and Crafts; Oakland, Calif. 94618	1,044 (C)	P	8,580	8,580	3,700
California Institute of Technology; Pasadena, Calif. 91125	796 (C)	P	12,489	12,489	3,947
California Institute of the Arts; Valencia, Calif. 91355	640 (C)	P	11,200	11,200	4,000
California Lutheran University; Thousand Oaks, Calif. 91360	1,634 (C)	P/AL	8,750	8,750	4,000
California Maritime Academy; Vallejo, Calif. 94590	410 (C)	Pub	1,175	4,152	3,595
California Polytechnic State University; San Luis Obispo, Calif. 93407	16,568 (C)	Pub	948	5,604	3,960
California State Coll. (Pa.). See California Univ. of Pennsylvania					
California State Polytechnic University–Pomona; Pomona, Calif. 91768	17,933 (C)	Pub	820	5,670	4,116
California State University–Bakersfield; Bakersfield, Calif. 93311-1099	3,560 (C)	Pub	878	5,548	3,475
California State University–Chico; Chico, Calif. 95929	14,491 (C)	Pub	884	6,554	3,462
California St. Univ.–Dominguez Hills; Carson, Calif. 90747	6,158 (C)	Pub	832	4,663	4,480
California State Univ.–Fresno; Fresno, Calif. 93740	5,854 (C)	Pub	864	5,400	3,600
California State Univ.–Fullerton; Fullerton, Calif. 92634	20,862 (C)	Pub	916	6,586	4,056
California State Univ.–Hayward; Hayward, Calif. 94542	9,405 (C)	Pub	823	4,572	3,650
California State Univ.–Long Beach; Long Beach, Calif. 90840	28,729 (C)	Pub	862	5,670	4,200
California State Univ.–Los Angeles; Los Angeles, Calif. 90032	15,148 (C)	Pub	786	4,314	3,785
California State Univ.–Northridge; Northridge, Calif. 91330	25,420 (C)	Pub	942	5,478	4,900
California State Univ.–Sacramento; Sacramento, Calif. 95819	19,885 (C)	Pub	734	5,360	3,546
California State Univ.–San Bernardino; San Bernardino, Calif. 92407	7,914 (C)	Pub	845	5,670	4,043
California State Univ.–Stanislaus; Turlock, Calif. 95380	3,848 (C)	Pub	810	5,178	3,200
California Univ. of Pennsylvania; California, Pa. 15419	4,681 (C)	Pub	2,500	3,922	2,180
Calumet College of St. Joseph; Whiting, Ind. 46394	1,059 (C)	P/RC	3,600	3,600	n.a.
Calvary Bible College; Kansas City, Mo. 64147	328 (C)	P	3,220	3,220	2,320
Calvin College; Grand Rapids, Mich. 49506	4,190 (C)	P/CR	7,350	7,350	3,100
Cameron University; Lawton, Okla. 73505	5,206 (C)	Pub	1,209	2,965	1,862
Campbellsville College; Campbellsville, Ky. 42718	671 (C)	P/SB	4,500	4,500	2,760
Campbell University; Buies Creek, N.C. 27506	3,773 (C)	P/SB	6,386	6,386	2,504
Canisius College; Buffalo, N.Y. 14208	3,787 (C)	P	8,100	8,100	4,100
Capital University; Columbus, Ohio 43209	2,015 (C)	P/AL	9,530	9,530	3,330
Capitol College; Laurel, Md. 20708	777 (C)	P	5,580	5,580	4,076
Cardinal Stritch College; Milwaukee, Wis. 53217	1,836 (C)	P/RC	6,040	6,040	2,950
Carleton College; Northfield, Minn. 55057	1,850 (C)	P	14,070	14,070	2,880
Carlow College; Pittsburgh, Pa. 15213	962 (W)	P/RC	8,347	8,347	4,000

Institution and location	Enrollment	Control	Tuition ($) Res.	Tuition ($) Nonres.	Rm/Bd ($)
Carnegie-Mellon University; Pittsburgh, Pa. 15213	4,273 (C)	P	14,080	14,080	4,720
Carroll College; Helena, Mont. 59625	1,330 (C)	P/RC	6,174	6,174	3,118
Carroll College; Waukesha, Wis. 53186	1,478 (C)	P/UP	9,360	9,360	3,070
Carson–Newman College; Jefferson City, Tenn. 37760	1,922 (C)	P/SB	6,080	6,080	2,610
Carthage College; Kenosha, Wis. 53140	1,070 (C)	P/LCA	9,500	9,500	3,250
Case Western Reserve University; Cleveland, Ohio 44106	3,017 (C)	P	12,800	12,800	4,620
Castleton State College; Castleton, Vt. 05735	1,442 (C)	Pub	2,920	5,900	3,920
Catawba College; Salisbury, N.C. 28144	1,026 (C)	P/UCC	7,300	7,300	3,500
Catholic University of America; Washington, D.C. 20064	2,950 (C)	P	10,150	10,150	5,060
Catholic University of Puerto Rico; Ponce, P.R. 00732	11,474 (C)	P/RC	2,237	2,237	2,265
Cayey University College. *See* Puerto Rico, University of					
Cedar Crest College; Allentown, Pa. 18104-6196	497 (W)	P	11,130	11,130	4,556
Cedarville College; Cedarville, Ohio 45314	1,879 (C)	P/B	5,238	5,238	3,255
Centenary College; Hackettstown, N.J. 07840	736 (C)	P	8,650	8,650	4,200
Centenary College of Louisiana; Shreveport, La. 71104	849 (C)	P/UM	6,500	6,500	2,910
Center for Creative Studies, College of Art and Design; Detroit, Mich. 48202	953 (C)	P	7,870	7,870	3,700
Central Arkansas, University of; Conway, Ark. 72032	6,670 (C)	Pub	1,230	2,430	2,012
Central Baptist College; Conway, Ark. 72032	182 (C)	P/B	2,085	2,085	1,700
Central Bible College; Springfield, Mo. 65803	886 (C)	P/AG	2,680	2,680	2,600
Central Christian College of the Bible; Moberly, Mo. 65270	79 (C)	P/ChC	1,984	1,984	1,920
Central College; Pella, Iowa 50219	1,751 (C)	P/RCA	7,938	7,938	3,075
Central Connecticut State University; New Britain, Conn. 06050	11,250 (C)	Pub	1,992	4,784	3,514
Central Florida, University of; Orlando, Fla. 32816	13,608 (C)	Pub	1,255	4,013	3,620
Central Methodist College; Fayette, Mo. 65248	754 (C)	P/UM	6,100	6,100	2,950
Central Michigan University; Mt. Pleasant, Mich. 48859	15,628 (C)	Pub	1,945	4,795	3,160
Central Missouri State University; Warrensburg, Mo. 64093	9,456 (C)	Pub	1,484	2,744	2,480
Central State University; Edmond, Okla. 73034	10,940 (C)	Pub	1,065	2,811	1,992
Central State University; Wilberforce, Ohio 45384	2,550 (C)	Pub	2,124	4,332	3,753
Central Texas, University of; Killeen, Tex. 76540	336 (C)	P	3,660	3,660	2,484
Central Washington University; Ellensburg, Wash. 98926	6,398 (C)	Pub	1,674	5,712	2,993
Central Wesleyan College; Central, S.C. 29630	439 (C)	P/WM	5,880	5,880	2,600
Centre College; Danville, Ky. 40422	861 (C)	P	9,200	9,200	3,620
Chadron State College; Chadron, Neb. 69337	2,143 (C)	Pub	1,361	2,036	2,132
Chaminade University of Honolulu; Honolulu, Hawaii 96816	2,213 (C)	P/RC	5,540	6,290	3,570
Chapman College; Orange, Calif. 92666	1,586 (C)	P	11,450	11,450	4,050
Charleston, College of; Charleston, S.C. 29424	5,767 (C)	Pub	2,300	4,600	2,850
Charleston, University of; Charleston, W. Va. 25304	1,527 (C)	P	6,750	6,750	3,300
Charter Oak College; Farmington, Conn. 06032-1909	940 (C)	Pub	200	300	n.a.
Chatham College; Pittsburgh, Pa. 15232	686 (W)	P	9,100	9,100	4,100
Chestnut Hill College; Philadelphia, Pa. 19118-2695	620 (W)	P/RC	7,500	7,500	3,800
Cheyney University of Pennsylvania; Cheyney, Pa. 19319	1,160 (C)	Pub	2,388	4,244	2,556
Chicago, University of—The College; Chicago, Ill. 60637	3,349 (C)	P	14,985	14,985	5,390
Chicago State University; Chicago, Ill. 60628	4,644 (C)	Pub	1,772	4,916	n.a.
Christ College–Irvine; Irvine, Calif. 92715	577 (C)	P/L	6,735	6,735	3,570
Christian Brothers College; Memphis, Tenn. 38104	1,758 (C)	P/RC	6,860	6,860	3,070
Christian Heritage College; El Cajon, Calif. 92019	396 (C)	P	5,720	5,720	2,866
Christian Life College; Stockton, Calif. 95210	173 (C)	P	1,770	1,770	2,085
Christopher Newport College; Newport News, Va. 23606–2998	4,832 (C)	Pub	1,870	3,600	n.a.
Church College of Hawaii. *See* Brigham Young University—Hawaii Campus					
Cincinnati, University of; Cincinnati, Ohio 45221	29,207 (C)	Pub	2,840	6,777	3,950
Cincinnati Bible College; Cincinnati, Ohio 45204	633 (C)	P	3,366	3,366	2,826
Cincinnati College of Mortuary Science Cohen Center; Cincinnati, Ohio 45212	130 (C)	P	3,132	3,132	1,666
Circleville Bible College; Circleville, Ohio 43113	162 (C)	P/CC	3,514	3,514	2,580
Citadel–The Military College of South Carolina; Charleston, S.C. 29409	2,131 (M)	Pub	7,764	10,612	—
City College (NYC). *See* New York, City University of					
City University; Bellevue, Wash. 98008	2,222 (C)	P	5,355	5,355	n.a.
Claflin College; Orangeburg, S.C. 29115	756 (C)	P/UM	3,568	3,568	1,890
Claremont Colleges:					
Claremont McKenna College; Claremont, Calif. 91711	845 (C)	P	12,900	12,900	4,550
Claremont Men's College. *See* Claremont McKenna College					
Harvey Mudd College; Claremont, Calif. 91711–5990	556 (C)	P	13,360	13,360	5,580
Pitzer College; Claremont, Calif. 91711	750 (C)	P	14,995	14,995	5,690
Pomona College; Claremont, Calif. 91711	1,375 (C)	P	13,130	13,130	5,200
Scripps College; Claremont, Calif. 91711	607 (W)	P	12,890	12,890	5,550
Clarion State College. *See* Clarion University of Pennsylvania					
Clarion University of Pennsylvania; Clarion, Pa. 16214	5,833 (C)	Pub	2,160	4,034	2,360
Clark Atlanta University; Atlanta, Ga. 30314	1,883 (C)	P	4,900	4,900	2,684
Clarke College; Dubuque, Iowa 52001	777 (C)	P/RC	7,980	7,980	2,865
Clarkson University; Potsdam, N.Y. 13676	3,035 (C)	P	12,800	12,800	4,485
Clark University; Worcester, Mass. 01610	2,262 (C)	P	14,000	14,000	4,500

Institution and location	Enrollment	Control	Tuition ($) Res.	Nonres.	Rm/Bd ($)
Clarkson College of Technology. *See* Clarkson University					
Clearwater Christian College; Clearwater, Fla. 33519	295 (C)	P	3,770	3,770	3,000
Cleary College; Ypsilanti, Mich. 48197	940 (C)	P	3,825	3,825	n.a.
Clemson University; Clemson, S.C. 29634	11,774 (C)	Pub	2,478	6,618	2,908
Cleveland College of Jewish Studies; Beachwood, Ohio 44122	350 (C)	P	3,000	3,000	n.a.
Cleveland Institute of Art; Cleveland, Ohio 44106	517 (C)	P	9,000	9,000	4,380
Cleveland Institute of Music; Cleveland, Ohio 44106	167 (C)	P	9,375	9,375	4,380
Cleveland State University; Cleveland, Ohio 44115	13,000 (C)	Pub	2,277	4,554	2,907
Clinch Valley College. *See* Virginia, University of					
Coe College; Cedar Rapids, Iowa 52402	1,217 (C)	P/UP	9,530	9,530	3,720
Cogswell College; Cupertino, Calif. 95014	243 (C)	P	6,240	6,240	n.a.
Coker College; Hartsville, S.C. 29550	736 (C)	P	6,660	6,660	3,228
Colby College; Waterville, Me. 04901	1,695 (C)	P	14,120	14,120	4,860
Colby-Sawyer College; New London, N.H. 03257	500 (C)	P	10,350	10,350	4,170
Coleman College; La Mesa, Calif. 92041	962 (C)	P	7,565	7,565	n.a.
Colgate University; Hamilton, N.Y. 13346	2,687 (C)	P	13,710	13,710	4,540
College for Human Services; New York, N.Y. 10014. *See* Human Services, College for					
College Misericordia; Dallas, Pa. 18612	900 (C)	P/RC	6,880	6,880	3,700
College of Great Falls; Great Falls, Mont. 59405. *See* Great Falls, College of					
Colorado, University of; Boulder, Colo. 80309:					
U. of Colorado–Boulder; Boulder, Colo. 80309	18,927 (C)	Pub	2,000	4,000	3,500
U. of Colorado–Colorado Springs; Colorado Springs, Colo. 80933	4,216 (C)	Pub	1,792	5,366	n.a.
U. of Colorado–Denver; Denver, Colo. 80202	5,843 (C)	Pub	1,678	6,420	n.a.
Colorado Christian University; Lakewood, Colo. 80226	658 (C)	P	4,080	4,080	4,100
Colorado College; Colorado Springs, Colo. 80903	1,940 (C)	P	12,710	12,710	3,410
Colorado School of Mines; Golden, Colo. 80401	1,614 (C)	Pub	3,672	9,588	3,600
Colorado State University; Fort Collins, Colo. 80523	16,911 (C)	Pub	2,096	6,108	3,600
Colorado Technical College; Colorado Springs, Colo. 80907	1,150 (C)	P	5,670	5,670	n.a.
Colorado Women's College. *See* Denver, Univ. of					
Columbia Bible College and Seminary; Columbia, S.C. 29230	508 (C)	P	4,200	4,200	2,424
Columbia Christian College; Portland, Ore. 97216	268 (C)	P	4,560	4,560	2,474
Columbia College; Chicago, Ill. 60605	5,298 (C)	P	4,996	4,996	n.a.
Columbia College; Columbia, Mo. 65216	714 (C)	P	6,190	6,190	2,796
Columbia College; Columbia, S.C. 29203	1,133 (W)	P/UM	7,975	7,975	3,015
Columbia College–Hollywood; Los Angeles, Calif. 90038	225 (C)	P	5,600	5,600	n.a.
Columbia Union College; Takoma Park, Md. 20912	1,224 (C)	P/SDA	7,930	7,930	3,690
Columbia University–Columbia College; New York, N.Y. 10027	2,900 (C)	P	13,961	13,961	5,415
Columbus College; Columbus, Ga. 31993	3,482 (C)	Pub	1,365	3,747	n.a.
Columbus College of Art and Design; Columbus, Ohio 43215	1,461 (C)	P	6,900	6,900	4,000
Conception Seminary College; Conception, Mo. 64433	65 (M)	P/RC	4,160	4,160	2,820
Concord College; Athens, W. Va. 24712	2,450 (C)	Pub	1,224	3,014	2,620
Concordia College; Ann Arbor, Mich. 48105	416 (C)	P/L	7,296	7,296	3,456
Concordia College; Bronxville, N.Y. 10708	560 (C)	P/L	6,790	6,790	3,700
Concordia College; Moorhead, Minn. 56560	2,884 (C)	P/AL	8,125	8,125	2,525
Concordia College; Portland, Ore. 97211	555 (C)	P	7,050	7,050	2,800
Concordia College; River Forest, Ill. 60305	952 (C)	P/L	6,848	6,848	3,411
Concordia College; St. Paul, Minn. 55104	1,133 (C)	P/L	7,800	7,800	2,850
Concordia College; Seward, Neb. 68434	829 (C)	P	6,295	6,295	2,550
Concordia Lutheran College; Austin, Tex. 78705	603 (C)	P/L	5,250	5,250	3,000
Concordia University; Mequon, Wis. 53092	1,442 (C)	P	6,700	6,700	3,100
Connecticut, University of; Storrs, Conn. 06269	13,715 (C)	Pub	2,623	6,803	3,660
Connecticut College; New London, Conn. 06320	1,650 (C)	P	15,175	15,175	4,800
Conservatory of Music of Puerto Rico; Hato Rey, P.R. 00918	264 (C)	Pub	210	210	n.a.
Converse College; Spartanburg, S.C. 29301	892 (W)	P	9,875	9,875	3,000
Cooper Union; New York, N.Y. 10003	973 (C)	P	300	300	5,250
Coppin State College; Baltimore, Md. 21216	2,240 (C)	Pub	1,896	3,364	n.a.
Corcoran School of Art; Washington, D.C. 20006	306 (C)	P	7,680	7,680	4,400
Cornell College; Mt. Vernon, Iowa 52314	1,129 (C)	P	9,980	9,980	3,510
Cornell University; Ithaca, N.Y. 14853	7,603 (C)	P	15,164	15,164	4,990
Cornish College of the Arts; Seattle, Wash. 98102	549 (C)	P	6,890	6,890	n.a.
Corpus Christi State Univ.; Corpus Christi, Tex. 78412	4,141 (C)	Pub	990	4,110	1,900
Covenant College; Lookout Mountain, Ga. 30750	548 (C)	P/RP	6,750	6,750	2,960
Creighton University; Omaha, Neb. 68178	4,053 (C)	P	7,436	7,436	3,300
Crichton College; Memphis, Tenn. 38182	318 (C)	P	3,384	3,384	2,780
Culver-Stockton College; Canton, Mo. 63435	1,067 (C)	P	6,260	6,260	2,340
Cumberland College; Williamsburg, Ky. 40769	1,904 (C)	P/SB	4,930	4,930	2,726
Cumberland University of Tennessee; Lebanon, Tenn. 37087	707 (C)	P	4,075	4,075	2,640
Curry College; Milton, Mass. 02186	932 (C)	P	10,250	10,250	5,250
Curtis Institute of Music; Philadelphia, Pa. 19103	110 (C)	P	250	250	n.a.
C. W. Post Center. *See* Long Island Univ. Center					

Institution and location	Enrollment	Control	Tuition ($) Res.	Tuition ($) Nonres.	Rm/Bd ($)
Daemen College; Amherst, N.Y. 14226	1,532 (C)	P	6,850	6,850	3,550
Dakota State University; Madison, S.D. 57042	1,224 (C)	Pub	1,678	1,844	1,900
Dakota Wesleyan University; Mitchell, S.D. 57301	636 (C)	P/UM	5,700	5,700	2,497
Dallas, University of; Irving, Tex. 75062	1,016 (C)	P/RC	7,900	7,900	3,615
Dallas Baptist University; Dallas, Tex. 75211	1,627 (C)	P/SB	3,360	3,360	2,887
Dallas Christian College; Dallas, Tex. 75234	114 (C)	P/ChC	2,040	2,040	2,500
Dana College; Blair, Neb. 68008	493 (C)	P/AL	6,580	6,580	2,640
Daniel Webster College; Nashua, N.H. 03063	570 (C)	P	9,096	9,096	3,950
Dartmouth College; Hanover, N.H. 03755	3,795 (C)	P	15,372	15,372	5,124
David Lipscomb College; Nashville, Tenn. 37203	2,284 (C)	P/CC	4,080	4,080	2,970
Davidson College; Davidson, N.C. 28036	1,406 (C)	P/PUS	11,327	11,327	3,567
Davis and Elkins College; Elkins, W. Va. 26241	811 (C)	P/PUS	6,800	6,800	3,500
Dayton, University of; Dayton, Ohio 45469	7,366 (C)	P/RC	7,720	7,720	3,510
Defiance College; Defiance, Ohio 43512	1,006 (C)	P/UCC	7,184	7,184	2,800
Delaware, University of; Newark, Del. 19716	13,311 (C)	P	2,990	7,200	2,972
Delaware State College; Dover, Del. 19901	2,510 (C)	Pub	1,000	2,550	2,300
Delaware Valley College of Science and Agriculture; Doylestown, Pa. 18901	1,100 (C)	P	8,125	8,125	3,615
Delta State University; Cleveland, Miss. 38732	3,008 (C)	Pub	1,604	2,786	1,557
Denison University; Granville, Ohio 43023	2,024 (C)	P	13,510	13,510	3,740
Denver, University of; Denver, Colo. 80208	2,798 (C)	P	10,944	10,944	4,500
CWC Campus Weekend College–Women's Program; Denver, Colo. 80220	423 (W)	P	6,300	6,300	n.a.
DePaul University; Chicago, Ill. 60604	9,198 (C)	P	8,000	8,000	3,500
DePauw University; Greencastle, Ind. 46135	2,415 (C)	P/UM	11,500	11,500	4,150
Deree College–Division of the American College of Greece; Athens, Greece GR-153 42	2,477 (C)	P	2,288	2,288	n.a.
Design Institute of San Diego; San Diego, Calif. 92121	190 (C)	P	5,700	5,700	n.a.
Detroit, University of; Detroit, Mich. 48221	3,206 (C)	P/RC	8,460	8,460	3,050
Detroit Bible College. *See* William Tyndale College					
Detroit College of Business; Dearborn, Mich. 48126	4,061 (C)	P	4,248	4,248	n.a.
DeVry Institute of Technology; Chicago, Ill. 60618	3,531 (C)	P	4,525	4,525	n.a.
DeVry Institute of Technology; City of Industry, Calif. 91744	1,909 (C)	P	4,735	4,735	n.a.
DeVry Institute of Technology; Columbus, Ohio 43209	2,593 (C)	P	7,035	7,035	n.a.
DeVry Institute of Technology; Decatur, Ga. 30341	3,023 (C)	P	4,525	4,525	n.a.
DeVry Institute of Technology; Irving, Tex. 75038	2,327 (C)	P	4,525	4,525	n.a.
DeVry Institute of Technology; Kansas City, Mo. 64131	1,632 (C)	P	6,750	6,750	n.a.
DeVry Institute of Technology; Lombard, Ill. 60148	2,356 (C)	P	4,670	4,670	n.a.
DeVry Institute of Technology; Phoenix, Ariz. 85021	2,700 (C)	P	4,525	4,525	n.a.
DeVry Technical Institute; Woodbridge, N.J. 07095	2,861 (C)	P	4,525	4,525	n.a.
Dickinson College; Carlisle, Pa. 17013	1,977 (C)	P/UM	14,400	14,400	4,230
Dickinson State University; Dickinson, N.D. 58601	1,402 (C)	Pub	1,659	4,731	1,750
Dillard University; New Orleans, La. 70122	1,200 (C)	P	4,800	4,800	2,900
District of Columbia, Univ. of the; Washington, D.C. 20008	9,084 (C)	Pub	664	2,464	n.a.
Divine Word College; Epworth, Iowa 52045	64 (M)	P/RC	4,635	4,635	1,200
Doane College; Crete, Neb. 68333	651 (C)	P/UCC	7,250	7,250	2,325
Dr. Martin Luther College; New Ulm, Minn. 56073	443 (C)	P/EL	3,095	3,095	1,650
Dominican College of Blauvelt; Orangeburg, N.Y. 10962	1,4800 (C)	P	6,250	6,250	4,750
Dominican College of San Rafael; San Rafael, Calif. 94901	426 (C)	P/RC	9,300	9,300	4,800
Dominican School of Philosophy and Theology; Berkeley, Calif. 94709	8 (C)	P/RC	4,500	4,500	n.a.
Don Bosco College; Newton, N.J. 07860	42 (M)	P/RC	3,150	3,150	2,120
Dordt College; Sioux Center, Iowa 51250	1,038 (C)	P	7,100	7,100	2,200
Dowling College; Oakdale, N.Y. 11769	2,992 (C)	P	6,330	6,330	2,560
Drake University; Des Moines, Iowa 50311	3,979 (C)	P	10,290	10,290	4,055
Drew University–College of Liberal Arts; Madison, N.J. 07940	1,475 (C)	P/UM	14,926	14,926	4,475
Drexel University; Philadelphia, Pa. 19104	7,100 (C)	P	9,551	9,551	4,500
Drury College; Springfield, Mo. 65802	1,125 (C)	P/UCC	6,950	6,950	2,639
Dubuque, University of; Dubuque, Iowa 52001	835 (C)	P/UP	7,850	7,850	2,900
Duke University; Durham, N.C. 27706	5,950 (C)	P	14,063	14,063	4,686
Duquesne University; Pittsburgh, Pa. 15282	3,979 (C)	P/RC	8,040	8,040	3,917
Dyke College; Cleveland, Ohio 44115	1,380 (C)	P	4,590	4,590	n.a.
D'Youville College; Buffalo, N.Y. 14201	1,200 (C)	P	6,400	6,400	3,100
Earlham College; Richmond, Ind. 47374	1,200 (C)	P/F	11,610	11,610	3,393
East Carolina University; Greenville, N.C. 27834	12,982 (C)	Pub	978	5,350	2,425
East Central University; Ada, Okla. 74820-6899	3,606 (C)	Pub	1,200	4,140	1,988
Eastern College; St. Davids, Pa. 19087	958 (C)	P/AB	8,110	8,110	3,220
Eastern Connecticut State Univ.; Willimantic, Conn. 06226	4,104 (C)	Pub	1,884	4,676	3,264
Eastern Illinois University; Charleston, Ill. 61920	9,403 (C)	Pub	2,052	5,196	2,388
Eastern Kentucky University; Richmond, Ky. 40475	12,497 (C)	Pub	1,180	3,300	2,436
Eastern Mennonite College; Harrisonburg, Va. 22801	969 (C)	P/Men	6,910	6,910	3,080
Eastern Michigan University; Ypsilanti, Mich. 48197	17,643 (C)	Pub	1,852	4,774	3,192
Eastern Montana College; Billings, Mont. 59101	3,539 (C)	Pub	1,308	2,991	2,839
Eastern Nazarene College; Quincy, Mass. 02170	746 (C)	P/Naz	7,020	7,020	3,100

Institution and location	Enrollment	Control	Tuition ($) Res.	Tuition ($) Nonres.	Rm/Bd ($)
Eastern New Mexico University; Portales, N.M. 88130	3,095 (C)	Pub	1,140	4,014	2,026
Eastern Oregon State College; La Grande, Ore. 97850	1,767 (C)	Pub	1,755	1,755	2,840
Eastern Washington University; Cheney, Wash. 99004	7,543 (C)	Pub	1,611	5,649	2,971
Eastman School of Music; Rochester, N.Y. 14604	411 (C)	P	12,438	12,438	4,600
East Stroudsburg University of Pennsylvania; East Stroudsburg, Pa. 18301	4,311 (C)	Pub	2,392	4,248	2,632
East Tennessee State University; Johnson City, Tenn. 37614	11,195 (C)	Pub	1,278	4,232	2,322
East Texas Baptist University; Marshall, Tex. 75670	716 (C)	P/SB	4,050	4,050	2,750
East Texas State University; Commerce, Tex. 75428	4,881 (C)	Pub	930	4,050	3,200
East–West University; Chicago, Ill. 60605	226 (C)	P	4,830	4,830	n.a.
Eckerd College; St. Petersburg, Fla. 33711	1,350 (C)	P/PUS	12,280	12,280	3,030
Edgewood College; Madison, Wis. 53711	1,275 (C)	P/RC	5,990	5,990	2,900
Edinboro University of Pennsylvania; Edinboro, Pa. 16444	6,339 (C)	Pub	2,320	3,846	2,182
Edward Waters College; Jacksonville, Fla. 32209	686 (C)	P	3,116	3,116	3,540
Electronic Data Processing College of Puerto Rico; Hato Rey, P.R. 00918	1,176 (C)	P	2,334	2,334	n.a.
Elizabeth City State University; Elizabeth City, N.C. 27909	1,680 (C)	Pub	1,182	5,024	2,464
Elizabethtown College; Elizabethtown, Pa. 17022	1,451 (C)	P/CB	9,500	9,500	3,500
Elmhurst College; Elmhurst, Ill. 60126	1,733 (C)	P/UCC	7,166	7,166	3,064
Elmira College; Elmira, N.Y. 14901	841 (C)	P	10,100	10,100	3,700
Elms College; Chicopee, Mass. 01013-2839	600 (W)	P	8,100	8,100	3,900
Elon College; Elon College, N.C. 27244	3,197 (C)	P/UCC	6,170	6,170	3,150
Embry–Riddle Aeronautical Univ.–Daytona Beach Campus; Daytona Beach, Fla. 32014	5,197 (C)	P	5,200	5,200	3,780
Prescott Campus; Prescott, Ariz. 86301	1,770 (C)	P	5,200	5,200	3,780
Emerson College; Boston, Mass. 02116	2,065 (C)	P	12,096	12,096	6,832
Emmanuel College; Boston, Mass. 02115	877 (W)	P/RC	9,185	9,185	4,666
Emmanuel College School of Christian Ministries; Franklin Springs, Ga. 30639	38 (C)	P/PH	3,360	3,360	2,490
Emory and Henry College; Emory, Va. 24327	788 (C)	P/UM	6,800	6,800	3,700
Emory University; Atlanta, Ga. 30322	5,333 (C)	P	13,500	13,500	4,300
Emporia State University; Emporia, Kan. 66801	3,881 (C)	Pub	1,285	3,179	2,370
Endicott College; Beverly, Mass. 01915	775 (W)	P	8,340	8,340	4,730
Erskine College; Due West, S.C. 29639	497 (C)	P/RP	8,075	8,075	3,105
Esther Boyer College of Music, Temple University; Philadelphia, Pa. 19122	350 (C)	Pub	3,996	7,258	4,056
ETI Technical College; Cleveland, Ohio 44114	900 (C)	P	3,800	3,800	2,905
Eugene Bible College; Eugene, Ore. 97405	124 (C)	P/OBS	2,993	2,993	2,130
Eureka College; Eureka, Ill. 61530	430 (C)	P/DC	7,775	7,775	2,920
Evangel College; Springfield, Mo. 65802	1,564 (C)	P/AG	4,970	4,970	2,770
Evansville, University of; Evansville, Ind. 47722	3,006 (C)	P/UM	8,200	8,200	3,320
Evergreen State College; Olympia, Wash. 98505	3,250 (C)	Pub	1,611	5,649	3,384
Fairfield University; Fairfield, Conn. 06430	2,933 (C)	P/RC	10,570	10,570	4,750
Fairhaven College–Western Washington University; Bellingham, Wash. 98225	250 (C)	Pub	1,611	5,649	3,500
Fairleigh Dickinson Univ.–Madison; Madison, N.J. 07940	2,478 (C)	P	7,440	7,440	4,078
Fairleigh Dickinson Univ.–Rutherford; Rutherford, N.J. 07070	1,413 (C)	P	7,936	7,936	4,698
Fairleigh Dickinson Univ.–Teaneck; Teaneck, N.J. 07666	3,376 (C)	P	7,440	7,440	4,078
Fairmont State College; Fairmont, W. Va. 26554	6,136 (C)	Pub	1,200	3,000	2,660
Faith Baptist Bible College and Theological Seminary; Ankeny, Iowa 50021	·283 (C)	P/B	3,500	3,500	2,612
Faulkner University; Montgomery, Ala. 36193	1,690 (C)	P	3,750	3,750	2,600
Fayetteville State University; Fayetteville, N.C. 28301	2,307 (C)	Pub	1,054	5,426	7,576
Felician College; Lodi, N.J. 07644	700 (C)	P/RC	6,500	6,500	n.a.
Ferris State University; Big Rapids, Mich. 49307	11,561 (C)	Pub	2,133	4,434	2,781
Ferrum College; Ferrum, Va. 24088	1,238 (C)	P/UM	6,500	6,500	3,000
Findlay, University of; Findlay, Ohio 45840	2,215 (C)	P/CG	8,064	8,064	3,536
Finlay Engineering College; Kansas City, Mo. 64114	100 (C)	P	3,500	3,500	n.a.
Fisk University; Nashville, Tenn. 37203	520 (C)	P	4,600	4,600	2,285
Fitchburg State College; Fitchburg, Mass. 01420	5,671 (C)	Pub	1,630	4,468	2,844
Flagler College; St. Augustine, Fla. 32085	1,159 (C)	P	4,320	4,320	2,670
Flaming Rainbow University; Stilwell, Okla. 74960	227 (C)	P	3,400	3,400	n.a.
Florida, University of; Gainesville, Fla. 32611	26,491 (C)	Pub	1,229	3,988	3,210
Florida A&M University; Tallahassee, Fla. 32307	6,457 (C)	Pub	1,258	3,938	2,337
Florida Atlantic University; Boca Raton, Fla. 33431	8,346 (C)	Pub	1,300	4,040	3,345
Florida Baptist Theological College; Graceville, Fla. 32440	386 (C)	P	1,254	1,254	2,300
Florida Christian College; Kissimmee, Fla. 34744	123 (C)	P	2,777	2,777	2,999
Florida Institute of Technology; Melbourne, Fla. 32901	3,004 (C)	P	8,955	8,955	3,300
Florida International University; Miami, Fla. 33199	14,814 (C)	Pub	1,250	4,065	3,610
Florida Memorial College; Miami, Fla. 33054	1,750 (C)	P/AB	4,100	4,100	1,460
Florida Southern College; Lakeland, Fla. 33801	1,766 (C)	P/UM	6,080	6,080	3,870
Florida State University; Tallahassee, Fla. 32306	19,799 (C)	Pub	1,230	3,960	3,100

Institution and location	Enrollment	Control	Tuition ($) Res.	Nonres.	Rm/Bd ($)
Fontbonne College; St. Louis, Mo. 63105	797 (C)	P/RC	6,725	6,725	3,296
Fordham Univ.–Rose Hill Campus; New York, N.Y. 10458	6,481 (C)	P	9,365	9,365	4,900
Forsyth School for Dental Hygienists; Boston, Mass. 02115	117 (C)	P	10,130	10,130	6,249
Fort Hays State University; Hays, Kan. 67601	3,750 (C)	Pub	1,470	3,600	2,502
Fort Lauderdale College; Fort Lauderdale, Fla. 33301	500 (C)	P	4,400	4,400	4,200
Fort Lewis College; Durango, Colo. 81301	3,842 (C)	Pub	1,286	4,440	2,388
Fort Valley State College; Fort Valley, Ga. 31030	1,748 (C)	Pub	1,510	3,912	2,220
Framingham State College; Framingham, Mass. 01701	3,359 (C)	Pub	1,701	4,729	2,828
Franciscan University of Steubenville; Steubenville, Ohio 43952	1,375 (C)	P	6,070	6,070	3,400
Francis Marion College; Florence, S.C. 29501	3,662 (C)	Pub	1,550	3,100	2,830
Franklin and Marshall College; Lancaster, Pa. 17604-3003	1,876 (C)	P/UCC	19,420	19,420	–
Franklin College; Franklin, Ind. 46131	801 (C)	P/AB	8,170	8,170	3,110
Franklin College; Sorengo, Switzerland	200 (C)	P	10,400	10,400	6,000
Franklin Pierce College; Rindge, N.H. 03461	1,300 (C)	P	9,600	9,600	3,880
Franklin University; Columbus, Ohio 43215-5399	3,946 (C)	P	3,816	3,816	n.a.
Freed–Hardeman University; Henderson, Tenn. 38340	1,150 (C)	P/CC	4,640	4,640	2,810
Free Will Baptist Bible College; Nashville, Tenn. 37205	332 (C)	P/FWB	2,641	2,641	2,456
Fresno Pacific College; Fresno, Calif. 93702	464 (C)	P/MB	7,500	7,500	3,170
Friends Bible College; Haviland, Kan. 67059	92 (C)	P/F	4,350	4,350	2,200
Friends University; Wichita, Kan. 67213	1,001 (C)	P/F	6,835	6,835	2,520
Friends World College; Huntington, N.Y. 11743	300 (C)	P	9,000	9,000	4,750
Frostburg State University; Frostburg, Md. 21532	3,927 (C)	Pub	2,016	3,666	3,690
Furman University; Greenville, S.C. 29613	2,522 (C)	P/SB	9,156	9,156	3,504
Gallaudet University, Washington, D.C. 20002	1,558 (C)	P	3,304	3,304	3,735
Gannon University; Erie, Pa. 16541	3,975 (C)	P/RC	7,000	7,000	2,690
Gardner–Webb College; Boiling Springs, N.C. 28017	824 (C)	P/SB	5,770	5,770	3,086
General Motors Institute. See GMI Engineering and Management Institute					
Geneva College; Beaver Falls, Pa. 15010	1,264 (C)	P/RC	7,184	7,184	3,480
George Fox College; Newberg, Ore. 97132	802 (C)	P/F	7,585	7,585	3,120
George Mason University; Fairfax, Va. 22030	12,874 (C)	Pub	2,292	5,076	4,250
Georgetown College; Georgetown, Ky. 40324	1,028 (C)	P/SB	5,266	5,266	3,200
Georgetown University; Washington, D.C. 20057	5,835 (C)	P/RC	13,250	13,250	5,460
George Washington University; Washington, D.C. 20052	6,380 (C)	P	11,775	11,775	5,600
Georgia, University of; Athens, Ga. 30602	26,547 (C)	Pub	1,917	5,040	2,961
Georgia College; Milledgeville, Ga. 31061	3,539 (C)	Pub	1,413	2,601	2,073
Georgia Institute of Technology; Atlanta, Ga. 30332	9,324 (C)	Pub	1,962	5,811	3,723
Georgia Southern University; Statesboro, Ga. 30458	10,029 (C)	Pub	1,506	3,888	2,505
Georgia Southwestern College; Americus, Ga. 31709	1,778 (C)	Pub	1,446	3,828	2,085
Georgian Court College; Lakewood, N.J. 08701	1,584 (W)	P/RC	6,655	6,655	3,650
Georgia State University; Atlanta, Ga. 30303	16,232 (C)	Pub	1,749	5,844	n.a.
Gettysburg College; Gettysburg, Pa. 17325	1,900 (C)	P/L	13,625	13,625	3,160
Glassboro State College; Glassboro, N.J. 08208	5,400 (C)	Pub	2,120	3,020	4,325
Glenville State College; Glenville, W. Va. 26351	2,185 (C)	Pub	1,150	2,900	2,510
GMI Engineering & Management Institute; Flint, Mich. 48504	2,569 (C)	P	7,482	7,482	2,430
Goddard College; Plainfield, Vt. 05667	225 (C)	P	13,166	13,166	–
Golden Gate University; San Francisco, Calif. 94105	2,036 (C)	P	4,508	4,508	n.a.
Goldey Beacom College; Wilmington, Del. 19808	1,800 (C)	P	4,500	4,500	3,800
Gonzaga University; Spokane, Wash. 99258	2,592 (C)	P	8,750	8,750	3,350
Gordon College, Wenham, Mass 01984	1,216 (C)	P	9,299	9,299	3,696
Goshen College; Goshen, Ind. 46526	1,152 (C)	P/MEN	7,205	7,205	3,105
Goucher College; Baltimore, Md. 21204	942 (C)	P	10,800	10,800	5,040
Governors State University; University Park, Ill. 60466	2,691 (C)	Pub	1,646	4,838	n.a.
Grace Bible College; Grand Rapids, Mich. 49509	130 (C)	P/GGF	3,300	3,300	2,350
Grace College; Winona Lake, Ind. 46590	738 (C)	P	6,110	6,110	3,004
Grace College of the Bible; Omaha, Neb. 68108	239 (C)	P/Ind	3,060	3,060	2,130
Graceland College; Lamoni, Iowa 50140	898 (C)	P	6,770	6,770	2,420
Grambling State University; Grambling, La. 71245	5,518 (C)	Pub	1,600	2,950	2,612
Grand Canyon University; Phoenix, Ariz. 85017	1,835 (C)	P/SB	5,503	5,503	2,280
Grand Rapids Baptist College; Grand Rapids, Mich. 49505	752 (C)	P/B	4,846	4,846	3,330
Grand Valley State University; Allendale, Mich. 49401-9401	9,020 (C)	Pub	1,926	4,542	3,100
Grand View College; Des Moines, Iowa 50316	1,349 (C)	P/LCA	5,790	5,790	2,420
Gratz College; Philadelphia, Pa. 19141	92 (C)	P	2,100	2,100	n.a.
Great Falls, College of; Great Falls, Mont. 59405	1,127 (C)	P/RC	3,790	3,790	n.a.
Great Lakes Bible College; Lansing, Mich. 48901	127 (C)	P/CC	3,108	3,108	3,850
Green Mountain College; Poultney, Vt. 05764	600 (C)	P	6,775	6,775	3,900
Greensboro College; Greensboro, N.C. 27401	1,078 (C)	P/UM	5,646	5,646	2,906
Greenville College; Greenville, Ill. 62246	753 (C)	P/FM	7,164	7,164	3,211
Griffin College; Seattle, Wash. 98121	1,700 (C)	P	5,200	5,200	n.a.
Grinnell College; Grinnell, Iowa 50112	1,276 (C)	P	11,708	11,708	3,380
Grove City College; Grove City, Pa. 16127	2,163 (C)	P	4,050	4,050	2,220
Guam, University of; Mangilao, Guam 96913	1,788 (C)	Pub	1,408	2,136	2,905

Institution and location	Enrollment	Control	Tuition ($) Res.	Tuition ($) Nonres.	Rm/Bd ($)
Guilford College; Greensboro, N.C. 27410	1,233 (C)	P/F	9,540	9,540	3,922
Gustavus Adolphus College; St. Peter, Minn. 56082	2,349 (C)	P/LCA	10,900	10,900	2,850
Gwynedd–Mercy College; Gwynedd Valley, Pa. 19437	1,861 (C)	P/RC	6,650	6,650	3,500
Hahnemann University School of Health Sciences and Humanities; Philadelphia, Pa. 19102	793 (C)	P	6,585	6,585	4,000
Hamilton College; Clinton, N.Y. 13323	1,654 (C)	P	15,750	15,750	4,350
Hamline University; St. Paul, Minn. 55104	1,430 (C)	P/UM	10,875	10,875	3,460
Hampden–Sydney College; Hampden–Sydney, Va. 23943	944 (M)	P	10,155	10,155	3,280
Hampshire College; Amherst, Mass. 01002	1,282 (C)	P	14,730	14,730	3,905
Hampton University, Hampton, Va. 23668	4,490 (C)	P	4,800	4,800	3,450
Hannibal–LeGrange College; Hannibal, Mo. 63401	830 (C)	P/SB	4,300	4,300	1,900
Hanover College; Hanover, Ind. 47243	1,074 (C)	P/UP	6,000	6,000	2,670
Harding University; Searcy, Ark. 72143	3,284 (C)	P/CC	4,250	4,250	2,600
Hardin–Simmons University; Abilene, Tex. 79698	1,580 (C)	P	4,410	4,410	2,486
Harrington Institute of Interior Design; Chicago, Ill. 60605	411 (C)	P	6,975	6,975	n.a.
Harris–Stowe State College; St. Louis, Mo. 63103	1,400 (C)	Pub	1,230	2,400	n.a.
Hartford, University of; West Hartford, Conn. 06117	5,597 (C)	P	10,992	10,992	4,766
Hartwick College; Oneonta, N.Y. 13820	1,496 (C)	P	12,200	12,200	4,050
Harvard and Radcliffe Colleges; Cambridge, Mass. 02138	6,587 (C)	P	14,560	14,560	4,835
Harvey Mudd College. *See* Claremont Colleges					
Hastings College; Hastings, Neb. 68901	911 (C)	P/UP	6,990	6,990	2,610
Haverford College; Haverford, Pa. 19041	1,105 (C)	P	13,750	13,750	4,700
Hawaii, Univ. of–Hilo Colleges of Arts and Sciences and Agriculture; Hilo, Hawaii 96720-4091	1,249 (C)	Pub	450	2,510	3,254
Hawaii, University of–Manoa; Honolulu, Hawaii 96822	12,763 (C)	Pub	1,230	3,680	3,276
Hawaii, University of–West Oahu; Pearl City, Hawaii 96782	601 (C)	Pub	830	2,490	n.a.
Hawaii Loa College; Kaneohe, Hawaii 96744	490 (C)	P	7,800	7,800	4,200
Hawaii Pacific College; Honolulu, Hawaii 96813	4,488 (C)	P	4,800	4,800	n.a.
Health Sciences, University of–School of Related Health Sciences; North Chicago, Ill. 60064	58 (C)	P	6,031	6,031	n.a.
Hebrew Theological College; Skokie, Ill. 60077	93 (C)	P	4,795	4,795	3,790
Heidelberg College; Tiffin, Ohio 44883	1,129 (C)	P	10,001	10,001	3,220
Hellenic College; Brookline, Mass. 02146	49 (C)	P	4,842	4,842	2,900
Henderson State University; Arkadelphia, Ark. 71923	3,027 (C)	Pub	1,070	2,400	2,090
Hendrix College; Conway, Ark. 72032	1,029 (C)	P/UM	6,210	6,210	2,475
Herbert H. Lehman College. *See* New York; City University of					
Heritage College; Toppenish, Wash. 98948	383 (C)	P	3,088	3,088	n.a.
High Point College; High Point, N.C. 27261	2,023 (C)	P/UM	6,085	6,085	2,985
Hillsdale College; Hillsdale, Mich. 49242	1,075 (C)	P	8,850	8,850	3,780
Hillsdale Free Will Baptist College; Moore, Okla. 73153	116 (C)	P	1,950	1,950	2,470
Hiram College; Hiram, Ohio 44234	930 (C)	P	11,241	11,241	3,531
Hobart and William Smith Colleges; Geneva, N.Y. 14456	1,950 (C)	P	13,785	13,785	4,946
Hofstra University; Hempstead, N.Y. 11550	8,541 (C)	P	8,430	8,430	4,580
Hollins College; Roanoke, Va. 24020	919 (W)	P	9,900	9,900	4,100
Holy Apostles College and Seminary; Cromwell, Conn. 06416	85 (C)	P/RC	3,000	3,000	4,320
Holy Cross, College of the; Worcester, Mass. 01610	2,684 (C)	P/RC	14,200	14,200	5,400
Holy Family College; Philadelphia, Pa. 19914	886 (C)	P	6,500	6,500	n.a.
Holy Names College; Oakland, Calif. 94619	540 (C)	P/RC	8,500	8,500	4,122
Hong Kong Baptist College; Kowloon, Hong Kong	2,731 (C)	Pub	1,100	1,100	n.a.
Hood College; Frederick, Md 21701	1,176 (W)	P	11,525	11,525	5,600
Hope College, Holland, Mich. 49423	2,770 (C)	P/RCA	9,366	9,366	3,670
Houghton College, Houghton, N.Y. 14744	1,164 (C)	P/W	7,468	7,468	2,900
Houghton College–Buffalo Suburban Campus; West Seneca, N.Y. 14225	86 (C)	P	6,874	6,874	2,816
Houston, Univ. of; Houston, Tex. 77004	18,684 (C)	Pub	930	4,050	3,300
Houston, Univ. of–Clear Lake; Houston, Tex. 77058	3,782 (C)	Pub	914	4,154	n.a.
Houston, Univ. of–Downtown; Houston, Tex 77002	7,409 (C)	Pub	902	4,130	3,034
Houston, Univ. of–Victoria; Victoria, Tex. 77901	480 (C)	Pub	900	4,020	n.a.
Houston Baptist University; Houston, Tex 77074	1,868 (C)	P	4,695	4,695	2,590
Howard Payne University; Brownwood, Tex 76801	1,247 (C)	P/SB	3,725	3,725	2,310
Howard University; Washington, D.C. 20059	8,820 (C)	P	5,910	5,910	3,200
Human Services, College for; New York, N.Y. 10014	911 (C)	P	8,400	8,400	n.a.
Humboldt State University; Arcata, Calif. 95521	6,245 (C)	Pub	852	5,388	3,600
Hunter College. *See* New York; City University of					
Huntingdon College; Montgomery, Ala 36194	866 (C)	P/UM	5,160	5,160	2,900
Huntington College; Huntington, Ind. 46750	549 (C)	P/BC	7,250	7,250	3,010
Huron College; Huron, S.D. 57350	510 (C)	P	5,500	5,500	2,618
Husson College; Bangor, Me. 04401	1,650 (C)	P	7,135	7,135	3,638
Huston–Tillotson College; Austin, Tex. 78702	502 (C)	P	3,950	3,950	2,669
Idaho, College of; Caldwell, Idaho 83605	574 (C)	P	8,900	8,900	2,395
Idaho, University of; Moscow, Idaho 83843	6,955 (C)	Pub	1,098	3,298	2,364
Idaho State University; Pocatello, Idaho 83209	6,047 (C)	Pub	1,086	2,986	2,488

Institution and location	Enrollment	Control	Tuition ($) Res.	Tuition ($) Nonres.	Rm/Bd ($)
Illinois, Univ. of, at Chicago; Chicago, Ill. 60680	15,945 (C)	Pub	2,730	6,270	4,048
Illinois, Univ. of, at Urbana–Champaign; Urbana, Ill. 61801	25,750 (C)	Pub	2,788	6,328	3,442
Illinois Benedictine College; Lisle, Ill. 60532	1,651 (C)	P/RC	7,620	7,620	3,350
Illinois College; Jacksonville, Ill. 62650	813 (C)	P	5,500	5,500	3,100
Illinois Institute of Technology; Chicago, Ill. 60616	2,612 (C)	P	10,500	10,500	3,942
Illinois State University; Normal, Ill. 61761	19,358 (C)	Pub	2,187	5,615	2,479
Illinois Wesleyan University; Bloomington, Ill. 61702	1,731 (C)	P	10,085	10,085	3,475
Immaculata College; Immaculata, Pa. 19345	1,950 (W)	P/RC	7,250	7,250	4,120
Incarnate Word College; San Antonio, Tex. 78209	1,959 (C)	P/RC	6,700	6,700	3,230
Indiana Institute of Technology; Fort Wayne, Ind. 46803	904 (C)	P	5,850	5,850	3,030
Indianapolis, University of; Indianapolis, Ind. 46227	2,725 (C)	P	8,280	8,280	3,250
Indiana State University; Terre Haute, Ind. 47809	10,501 (C)	Pub	1,992	4,726	2,944
Indiana University of Pennsylvania; Indiana, Pa. 15705	12,611 (C)	Pub	2,524	4,380	2,350
Indiana University–Bloomington; Bloomington, Ind. 47405	25,386 (C)	Pub	2,077	6,288	2,920
Indiana University–East; Richmond, Ind. 47374	1,541 (C)	Pub	1,724	4,214	n.a.
Indiana University–Kokomo; Kokomo, Ind. 46902	2,857 (C)	Pub	1,350	3,342	n.a.
Indiana University–Northwest; Gary, Ind. 46408	4,100 (C)	Pub	1,724	4,214	n.a.
Indiana University–Purdue University at Fort Wayne; Fort Wayne, Ind. 46805	9,998 (C)	Pub	1,349	3,340	n.a.
Indiana University–Purdue University at Indianapolis; Indianapolis, Ind. 46202–5143	20,087 (C)	Pub	1,971	5,859	2,332
Indiana University–South Bend; South Bend, Ind. 46634	5,513 (C)	Pub	1,724	4,214	n.a.
Indiana University–Southeast; New Albany, Ind. 47150	4,931 (C)	Pub	1,350	3,342	n.a.
Indiana Wesleyan University; Marion, Ind. 46953	1,105 (C)	P	6,420	6,420	2,930
Industrial Engineering College of Chicago; Chicago, Ill. 60601	140 (C)	P	4,160	4,160	n.a.
Insurance, College of; New York, N.Y. 10007	650 (C)	P	7,440	7,440	6,600
Inter-American University–Arecibo Regional College; Arecibo, P.R. 00612	3,715 (C)	P	2,445	2,445	n.a.
International Bible College; Florence, Ala. 35630	153 (C)	P	1,964	1,964	2,400
International Institute of A.C.E.; Lewisville, Tex. 75067	75 (C)	P	2,000	2,000	2,800
International Institute of the Americas of World University; Carolina, P.R. 00628	4,600 (C)	P	2,280	2,280	n.a.
International Training, School for; Brattleboro, Vt. 05301	80 (C)	P	8,660	8,660	3,218
Iona College; New Rochelle, N.Y. 10801	3,420 (C)	P	7,390	7,390	5,050
Iowa, University of; Iowa City, Iowa 52242	20,160 (C)	Pub	1,826	5,982	2,580
Iowa State University; Ames, Iowa 50011	21,086 (C)	Pub	1,880	5,982	2,720
Iowa Wesleyan College; Mount Pleasant, Iowa 52641	652 (C)	P/UM	6,500	6,500	2,750
Ithaca College; Ithaca, N.Y. 14850	5,493 (C)	P	10,200	10,200	4,360
ITT Technical Institute; West Covina, Calif. 91790-2767	700 (C)	P	6,490	6,490	n.a.
Jackson College for Women. *See* Tufts University					
Jackson State University; Jackson, Miss. 39217	6,500 (C)	Pub	1,500	2,676	2,094
Jacksonville State University; Jacksonville, Ala. 36265	7,272 (C)	Pub	1,200	1,800	2,075
Jacksonville University; Jacksonville, Fla. 32211	1,927 (C)	P	6,900	6,900	3,340
James Madison University; Harrisonburg, Va. 22807	9,557 (C)	Pub	2,834	5,426	3,496
Jamestown College; Jamestown, N.D. 58401	772 (C)	P/UP	6,420	6,420	2,980
Jarvis Christian College; Hawkins, Tex. 75765	560 (C)	P	3,780	3,780	2,712
Jersey City State College; Jersey City, N.J. 07305	5,345 (C)	Pub	2,002	2,602	4,420
Jewish Theological Seminary of America; New York, N.Y. 10027	145 (C)	P	5,320	5,320	5,200
John Brown University; Siloam Springs, Ark. 72761	929 (C)	P	4,900	4,900	2,860
John Carroll University; University Heights, Ohio 44118	3,400 (C)	P/RC	7,424	7,424	4,230
John F. Kennedy University–Evenings; Orinda, Calif. 94563	395 (C)	P	4,920	4,920	n.a.
John Jay Coll. of Criminal Justice. *See* New York, City Univ. of					
Johns Hopkins Universtiy; Baltimore, Md. 21218	2,898 (C)	P	14,360	14,360	5,180
Johnson and Wales University; Providence, R.I. 02903	7,019 (C)	P	7,194	7,194	3,150
Johnson Bible College; Knoxville, Tenn. 37998	395 (C)	P/Chc	2,750	2,750	3,100
Johnson C. Smith University; Charlotte, N.C. 28216	1,197 (C)	P	4,448	4,448	2,186
Johnson State College; Johnson, Vt. 05656	1,200 (C)	Pub	2,605	5,389	3,666
Johnston College, Calif. *See* Redlands, University of					
John Wesley College; High Point, N.C. 27260	56 (C)	P	2,772	2,772	1,200
Jones College—Jacksonville; Jacksonville, Fla. 32211	1,700 (C)	P	3,240	3,240	n.a.
Jordan College; Cedar Springs, Mich. 49319	2,140 (C)	P	4,340	4,340	n.a.
Judson College; Elgin, Ill. 60120	498 (C)	P/B	6,690	6,690	3,590
Judson College; Marion, Ala. 36756	411 (W)	P/SB	3,500	3,500	2,490
Juilliard School; New York, N.Y. 10023	502 (C)	P	9,450	9,450	7,700
Juniata College; Huntingdon, Pa. 16652	1,134 (C)	P	11,520	11,520	3,470
Kalamazoo College; Kalamazoo, Mich. 49007	1,270 (C)	P/AB	10,736	10,736	3,516
Kansas, University of; Lawrence, Kan. 66045	19,185 (C)	Pub	1,448	4,246	2,336
Kansas, University of, Medical Center; Kansas City, Kan. 66103	597 (C)	Pub	1,212	4,010	n.a.
Kansas City Art Institute; Kansas City, Mo. 64111	533 (C)	P	9,150	9,150	3,150
Kansas City College and Bible School; Overland Park, Kan. 66204	100 (C)	P	2,040	2,040	2,250
Kansas Newman College; Wichita, Kan 67213	751 (C)	P	5,390	5,390	2,625
Kansas State University; Manhattan, Kan 66506	20,110 (C)	Pub	1,562	4,686	2,565

Institution and location	Enrollment	Control	Tuition ($) Res.	Nonres.	Rm/Bd ($)
Kansas Wesleyan University; Salina, Kan 67401	550 (C)	P/UM	5,720	5,720	2,800
Kean College of New Jersey; Union, N.J. 07083	10,907 (C)	Pub	1,950	2,640	2,920
Kearney State College; Kearney, Neb. 68849	7,263 (C)	Pub	1,360	2,080	2,010
Keene State College; Keene, N.H. 03431	3,098 (C)	Pub	2,213	5,873	3,162
Kendall College; Evanston, Ill. 60201	387 (C)	P	5,901	5,901	3,777
Kendall College of Art and Design; Grand Rapids, Mich. 49503	742 (C)	P	7,650	7,650	n.a.
Kennesaw College, Marietta, Ga. 30061	8,404 (C)	Pub	1,296	3,678	n.a.
Kent State University; Kent, Ohio 44242	18,995 (C)	Pub	2,826	5,426	2,872
Kentucky, University of; Lexington, Ky. 40506	17,260 (C)	Pub	1,559	4,320	2,600
Kentucky Christian College; Grayson, Ky. 41143	491 (C)	P/ChC	2,806	2,806	2,620
Kentucky State University; Frankfort, Ky. 40601	2,116 (C)	Pub	1,060	3,120	2,284
Kentucky Wesleyan College; Owensboro, Ky. 42301	830 (C)	P/UM	5,000	5,000	2,900
Kenyon College; Gambier, Ohio 43022	1,553 (C)	P	13,585	13,585	3,215
Keuka College; Keuka Park, N.Y. 14478	600 (C)	P	7,450	7,450	3,580
King College; Bristol, Tenn. 37620	600 (C)	P/PUS	5,900	5,900	3,050
Kings College; Briarcliff Manor, N.Y. 10510	508 (C)	P/ND	7,515	7,515	3,520
King's College; Wilkes-Barre, Pa 18711	2,324 (C)	P/RC	7,700	7,700	3,800
Knox College; Galesburg, Ill. 61401	1,050 (C)	P	11,559	11,559	3,411
Knoxville College; Knoxville, Tenn. 37921	1,225 (C)	P	4,800	4,800	3,400
Kutztown University; Kutztown, PA 19530	6,519 (C)	Pub	2,370	4,226	2,424
Laboratory Institute of Merchandising; New York, N.Y. 10022	258 (C)	P	7,200	7,200	n.a.
Lafayette College; Easton, Pa. 18042	2,303 (C)	P	14,000	14,000	4,575
LaGrange College; LaGrange, Ga. 30240	964 (C)	P/UM	4,725	4,725	2,715
Lake Erie College; Painesville, Ohio 44077	613 (C)	P	7,360	7,360	3,630
Lake Forest College; Lake Forest, Ill. 60045	1,121 (C)	P	12,780	12,780	2,870
Lakeland College; Sheboygan, Wis. 53082	1,766 (C)	P/UCC	7,445	7,445	3,100
Lake Superior State University; Sault Ste. Marie, Mich. 49783	2,959 (C)	Pub	1,920	3,819	3,166
Lamar University; Beaumont, Tex. 77710	10,347 (C)	Pub	782	3,278	2,500
Lambuth College; Jackson, Tenn. 38301	767 (C)	P/UM	4,196	4,196	2,858
Lancaster Bible College; Lancaster, Pa. 17601	387 (C)	P	5,720	5,720	2,690
Lander College; Greenwood S.C. 29649	2,301 (C)	Pub	2,090	2,990	2,390
Lane College; Jackson, Tenn. 38301	525 (C)	P/CME	4,000	4,000	2,242
Langston University; Langston, Okla. 73050	2,103 (C)	Pub	1,640	2,812	1,050
Laredo State University; Laredo, Tex. 78040-9960	541 (C)	Pub	1,338	4,398	n.a.
La Roche College; Pittsburgh, Pa. 15237	1,868 (C)	P	5,910	5,910	3,320
La Salle University; Philadelphia, Pa. 19141	3,565 (C)	P/RC	9,100	9,100	4,220
La Verne, University of; La Verne, Calif 91750	1,485 (C)	P	10,060	10,060	3,646
Lawrence Technological University; Southfield, Mich. 48075	5,400 (C)	P	4,578	4,578	3,500
Lawrence University; Appleton, Wis. 54912	1,242 (C)	P	13,710	13,710	3,237
Lebanon Valley College; Annville, Pa. 17003	840 (C)	P/UM	10,650	10,650	4,240
Lee College; Cleveland, Tenn. 37311	1,331 (C)	P	3,450	3,450	2,426
Lee College of the University of Judaism; Los Angeles, Calif. 90077	70 (C)	P	6,550	6,550	4,895
Lehigh University; Bethlehem, Pa. 18015	4,615 (C)	P	13,550	13,550	4,370
Le Moyne College; Syracuse, N.Y. 13214-1399	1,877 (C)	P	8,210	8,210	3,750
Le Moyne–Owen College; Memphis, Tenn. 38126	955 (C)	P	3,380	3,380	n.a.
Lenoir–Rhyne College; Hickory, N.C. 28603	1,465 (C)	P/LCA	7,250	7,250	2,890
Lesley College; Cambridge, Mass. 02138-2790	525 (W)	P	9,490	9,490	4,600
LeTourneau University; Longview, Tex. 75607	773 (C)	P	6,710	6,710	3,830
Lewis and Clark College; Portland, Ore. 97219	1,911 (C)	P	11,796	11,796	3,867
Lewis-Clark State College; Lewiston, Idaho 83501	2,275 (C)	Pub	1,040	2,940	2,720
Lewis University; Romeoville, Ill. 60441	2,920 (C)	P/RC	6,784	6,784	3,350
Liberty University; Lynchburg, Va. 24506	8,367 (C)	P/B	4,750	4,750	3,400
L.I.F.E. Bible College; Los Angeles, Calif. 90086-2529	370 (C)	P/FG	2,880	2,880	2,169
L.I.F.E. Bible College East; Christiansburg, V.A. 24073	96 (C)	P	1,685	1,685	1,785
Limestone College, Gaffney, S.C. 29340	295 (C)	P	5,860	5,860	2,830
Lincoln Christian College; Lincoln, Ill. 62656	327 (C)	P/CC	3,332	3,332	2,270
Lincoln Memorial University; Harrogate, Tenn. 37752	1,659 (C)	P	3,980	3,980	2,400
Lincoln University; San Francisco, Calif. 94118	159 (C)	P	600	600	n.a.
Lincoln University; Jefferson City, Mo. 65101	2,745 (C)	Pub	1,340	2,680	2,728
Lincoln University; Lincoln University, Pa. 19352	1,053 (C)	Pub	2,732	3,832	2,615
Lindenwood College; St. Charles, Mo. 63301	500 (C)	P	7,600	7,600	3,900
Lindsey Wilson College; Columbia, Ky. 42728	1,060 (C)	P	4,496	4,496	2,980
Linfield College; McMinnville, Ore. 97128	1,283 (C)	P	10,300	10,300	3,270
Livingstone College; Salisbury, N.C. 28144	580 (C)	P/AME	4,010	4,010	2,268
Livingstone University; Livingston, Ala. 35470	1,557 (C)	Pub	1,401	1,401	1,944
Lock Haven University of Pennsylvania; Lock Haven, Pa. 17745	2,985 (C)	Pub	2,318	4,214	2,274
Loma Linda University; Loma Linda, Calif. 92350	2,322 (C)	P/SDA	8,550	8,550	3,235
Loma Linda University–La Sierra; Riverside, Calif. 92515	1,800 (C)	P/SDA	8,550	8,550	3,066
Long Island University; Greenvale, N.Y. 11548:					
Brooklyn Campus; Brooklyn, N.Y. 11210	3,441 (C)	P	7,500	7,500	5,400
C.W. Post Campus; Greenvale, N.Y. 11548	5,126 (C)	P	8,400	8,400	4,600
Southampton Campus; Southampton, N.Y. 11968	1,145 (C)	P	8.450	8,450	4,922

Institution and location	Enrollment	Control	Tuition ($) Res.	Tuition ($) Nonres.	Rm/Bd ($)
Longwood College; Farmville, Va. 23901	2,956 (C)	Pub	2,700	4,950	3,074
Loras College; Dubuque, Iowa 52001	1,984 (C)	P	8,065	8,065	3,000
Louisiana College; Pineville, La. 71359	1,017 (C)	P/SB	3,247	3,247	3,062
Louisiana State Univ. and A&M Coll.; Baton Rouge, La. 70803	22,256 (C)	Pub	2,017	5,217	2,600
LSU–Shreveport; Shreveport, La. 71115	3,594 (C)	Pub	1,910	4,830	n.a.
Louisiana Tech University; Ruston, La. 71272	9,043 (C)	Pub	1,822	2,980	2,115
Louisville, University of; Louisville, Ky. 40292	17,835 (C)	Pub	1,488	4,248	1,680
Lourdes College; Sylvania, Ohio 43560	886 (C)	P/RC	4,660	4,660	n.a.
Lowell, University of; Lowell, Mass. 01854	11,555 (C)	Pub	2,249	5,377	3,854
Loyola College; Baltimore, Md. 21210	3,049 (C)	P/RC	9,640	9,640	5,080
Loyola Marymount University; Los Angeles, Calif. 90045	3,902 (C)	P/RC	9,431	9,431	4,680
Loyola University; New Orleans, La. 70118	3,594 (C)	P/RC	7,775	7,775	4,000
Loyola University of Chicago; Chicago, Ill. 60611	5,655 (C)	P	7,710	7,710	4,254
Lubbock Christian University; Lubbock, Tex. 79407	1,079 (C)	P/CC	5,630	5,630	2,330
Lutheran Bible Institute of Seattle; Issaquah, Wash. 98027	143 (C)	P/L	4,495	4,495	2,875
Luther College; Decorah, Iowa 52101	2,214 (C)	P/AL	9,750	9,750	3,100
Lycoming College; Williamsport, Pa. 17701	1,163 (C)	P	9,280	9,280	3,400
Lynchburg College; Lynchburg, Va. 24501	1,600 (C)	P	8,800	8,800	4,300
Lyndon State College; Lyndonville, Vt. 05851	948 (C)	Pub	2,700	5,484	3,666
Macalester College; St. Paul, Minn. 55105	1,847 (C)	P	12,370	12,370	3,714
MacMurray College; Jacksonville, Ill. 62650	620 (C)	P/UM	7,200	7,200	3,000
Madonna College; Livonia, Mich. 48150	3,742 (C)	P	3,720	3,720	2,950
Maharishi International University; Fairfield, Iowa 52556	298 (C)	P	7,080	7,080	2,532
Maine, Univ. of, at Augusta; Augusta, Me. 04330	4,342 (C)	Pub	1,605	3,825	n.a.
Maine, Univ. of, at Farmington; Farmington, Me. 04938	2,427 (C)	Pub	2,070	4,620	3,338
Maine, Univ. of, at Fort Kent; Fort Kent, Me. 04743-1292	594 (C)	Pub	1,710	4,140	3,075
Maine, Univ. of, at Machias; Machias, Me. 04654	876 (C)	Pub	1,795	2,215	3,045
Maine, Univ. of, at Orono; Orono, Me. 04469	10,682 (C)	Pub	1,970	5,030	3,390
Maine, Univ. of, at Presque Isle; Presque Isle, Me. 04769	1,410 (C)	Pub	1,780	4,210	3,088
Maine Maritime Academy—College of Engineering, Transportation, and Management; Castine, Me. 04420	530 (C)	Pub	3,215	5,345	3,550
Mallinckrodt College of the North Shore; Wilmette, Ill. 60091	272 (C)	P/RC	3,750	3,750	n.a.
Malone College; Canton, Ohio 44709	1,457 (C)	P/F	6,634	6,634	2,800
Manchester College; North Manchester, Ind. 46962	1,028 (C)	P/CB	7,260	7,260	2,810
Manhattan Christian College; Manhattan, Kan. 66502	206 (C)	P/CC	2,890	2,890	2,320
Manhattan College; Riverdale, N.Y. 10471	3,340 (C)	P	9,600	9,600	5,250
Manhattan School of Music; New York, N.Y. 10027	416 (C)	P	8,900	8,900	n.a.
Manhattanville College; Purchase, N.Y. 10577	1,050 (C)	P	9,846	4,676	4,676
Mankato State University; Mankato, Minn. 56001	14,206 (C)	Pub	1,884	2,966	2,275
Mannes College of Music; New York, N.Y. 10024	120 (C)	P	8,500	8,500	4,900
Mansfield University of Pennsylvania; Mansfield, Pa. 16933	2,661 (C)	Pub	2,453	4,309	2,316
Marian College; Indianapolis, Ind. 46222	1,233 (C)	P/RC	5,866	5,866	2,570
Marian College of Fond du Lac; Fond du Lac, Wis. 54935	875 (C)	P/RC	6,800	6,800	2,800
Marietta College; Marietta, Ohio 45750	1,285 (C)	P	10,250	10,250	3,000
Marist College; Poughkeepsie, N.Y. 12601	2,941 (C)	P	8,300	8,300	4,700
Marlboro College; Marlboro, Vt. 05344	268 (C)	P	14,000	14,000	4,820
Marquette University; Milwaukee, Wis. 53233	9,163 (C)	P	8,284	8,284	3,450
Mars Hill College; Mars Hill, N.C. 28754	1,097 (C)	P/SB	5,650	5,650	2,650
Marshall University; Huntington, W. Va. 25705	10,581 (C)	Pub	1,487	3,557	3,356
Martin Center College; Indianapolis, Ind. 46218	475 (C)	P	4,500	4,500	n.a.
Mary, University of; Bismarck, N.D. 58504	1,190 (C)	P	4,800	4,800	2,250
Mary Baldwin College; Staunton, Va. 24401	685 (W)	P/PUS	8,450	8,450	6,050
Marycrest College; Davenport, Iowa 52804	1,309 (C)	P/RC	7,200	7,200	2,700
Marygrove College; Detroit, Mich. 48221	1,022 (C)	P/RC	5,603	5,603	3,200
Mary Hardin–Baylor, University of; Belton, Tex. 76513	1,501 (C)	P/SB	4,185	4,185	2,625
Maryland, Univ. of–Baltimore County; Baltimore, Md. 21228	8,840 (C)	Pub	2,204	5,860	3,801
Maryland, Univ. of–College Park; College Park, Md. 20742	27,902 (C)	Pub	2,096	5,754	4,178
Maryland, Univ. of–Eastern Shore; Princess Anne, Md. 21853	1,484 (C)	Pub	2,683	5,573	3,364
Maryland, Univ. of, University College; College Park, Md. 20742	11,466 (C)	Pub	2,910	2,910	n.a.
Maryland Institute–College of Art; Baltimore, Md. 21217	850 (C)	P	9,650	9,650	3,825
Marylhurst College; Marylhurst, Ore. 97036	1,564 (W)	P	6,345	6,345	n.a.
Marymount College; Tarrytown, N.Y. 10591	1,122 (W)	P	8,750	8,750	4,996
Marymount Manhattan College; New York, N.Y. 10021	1,484 (W)	P	7,860	7,860	3,800
Marymount Univ.; Arlington, Va. 22207	1,878 (C)	P	9,072	9,072	4,550
Maryville College; Maryville, Tenn. 37801	787 (C)	P	6,995	6,995	3,395
Maryville College–St. Louis; St. Louis, Mo. 63141	2,377 (C)	P	6,800	6,800	3,500
Mary Washington College; Fredericksburg, Va. 22401	3,146 (C)	Pub	2,304	4,980	3,878
Marywood College; Scranton, Pa. 18509	2,085 (C)	P/RC	7,050	7,050	3,500
Massachusetts, Univ. of–Amherst; Amherst, Mass. 01003	19,778 (C)	Pub	2,400	5,900	2,900
Massachusetts, Univ. of–Boston; Boston, Mass. 02125	10,399 (C)	Pub	1,995	5,901	n.a.
Massachusetts College of Art; Boston, Mass. 02115	1,112 (C)	Pub	1,594	4,150	n.a.
Massachusetts College of Pharmacy and Allied Health Sciences; Boston, Mass. 02115	785 (C)	P	7,824	7,824	5,570

Institution and location	Enrollment	Control	Tuition ($) Res.	Tuition ($) Nonres.	Rm/Bd ($)
Massachusetts Institute of Technology; Cambridge, Mass. 02139	4,242 (C)	P	14,500	14,500	4,835
Massachusetts Maritime Academy; Buzzards Bay, Mass. 02532	600 (C)	Pub	1,544	4,100	3,150
Master's College, The; Newhall, Calif. 91322	845 (C)	P/B	6,450	6,450	3,690
Mayville State University; Mayville, N.D. 58257	764 (C)	Pub	1,356	3,156	1,980
McKendree College; Lebanon, Ill. 62258	1,100 (C)	P/UM	6,836	6,836	3,000
McMurry College; Abilene, Tex. 79697	1,703 (C)	P/UM	4,260	4,260	2,080
McNeese State University; Lake Charles, La. 70609	6,371 (C)	Pub	1,396	2,746	1,700
McPherson College; McPherson, Kan. 67460	485 (C)	P/CB	6,660	6,660	3,110
Medaille College; Buffalo, N.Y. 14214	1,021 (C)	P	5,550	5,550	n.a.
Medical College of Georgia; Augusta, Ga. 30912	780 (C)	Pub	1,802	4,970	3,222
Medical University of South Carolina; Charleston, S.C. 29425	915 (C)	Pub	1,750	3,500	3,300
Memphis College of Art; Memphis, Tenn. 38112	254 (C)	P	6,750	6,750	4,000
Memphis State University; Memphis, Tenn. 38152	16,179 (C)	Pub	1,354	4,088	2,730
Menlo College; Atherton, Calif. 94027-4185	537 (C)	P	10,552	10,552	5,738
Mercer University; Macon, Ga. 31207	2,596 (C)	P/SB	7,309	7,309	3,278
Mercer University–Atlanta; Atlanta, Ga. 30341	1,405 (C)	P/SB	5,468	5,468	n.a.
Mercy College; Dobbs Ferry, N.Y. 10522	5,283 (C)	P	6,000	6,000	n.a.
Mercy College of Detroit; Detroit, Mich. 48219	2,325 (C)	P/RC	6,258	6,258	1,800
Mercyhurst College; Erie, Pa. 16546	2,067 (C)	P/RC	8,125	8,125	3,075
Meredith College; Raleigh, N.C. 27607	1,935 (W)	P	4,910	4,910	2,470
Merrimack College; North Andover, Mass. 01845	2,357 (C)	P/RC	8,900	8,900	4,900
Mesa State College; Grand Junction, Colo. 81502	3,958 (C)	Pub	1,268	3,258	2,654
Messiah College; Grantham, Pa. 17027	2,280 (C)	P	8,000	8,000	3,990
Methodist College; Fayetteville, N.C. 28311-1499	1,447 (C)	P	7,200	7,200	3,000
Metropolitan State College; Denver, Colo. 80204	16,238 (C)	Pub	1,434	4,622	n.a.
Metropolitan State University; St. Paul, Minn. 55101	5,538 (C)	Pub	1,637	1,701	n.a.
Miami, University of; Coral Gables, Fla. 33124	8,714 (C)	P	13,050	13,050	5,162
Miami Christian College; Miami, Fla. 33167	155 (C)	P	4,930	4,930	2,760
Miami University; Oxford, Ohio 45056	14,528 (C)	Pub	3,400	6,600	2,890
Michigan, Univ. of–Ann Arbor; Ann Arbor, Mich. 48109	35,216 (C)	Pub	2,876	9,888	3,425
Michigan, Univ. of–Dearborn; Dearborn, Mich. 48128	6,680 (C)	Pub	2,670	7,180	n.a.
Michigan, Univ. of–Flint; Flint, Mich. 48502	6,100 (C)	Pub	2,104	6,860	n.a.
Michigan Christian College; Rochester Hills, Mich. 48063	281 (C)	P	3,840	3,840	3,030
Michigan State University; East Lansing, Mich. 48824	42,695 (C)	Pub	2,933	7,399	2,960
Michigan Technological University; Houghton, Mich. 49931	6,158 (C)	Pub	2,286	5,547	3,016
Mid-America Bible College; Oklahoma City, Okla. 73170	259 (C)	P/CG	3,924	3,924	2,100
Mid-America Nazarene College; Olathe, Kan. 66061	1,121 (C)	P	5,090	5,090	2,990
Middlebury College; Middlebury, Vt. 05753	1,950 (C)	P	19,160	19,160	–
Middle Tennessee State University; Murfreesboro, Tenn. 37132	11,850 (C)	Pub	1,254	4,208	1,862
Midland Lutheran College; Fremont, Neb. 68025	910 (C)	P/L	6,900	6,900	2,400
Midway College; Midway, Ky. 40347	335 (W)	P	4,130	4,130	3,080
Midwestern State University; Wichita Falls, Tex. 76308	4,711 (C)	Pub	1,110	4,230	2,340
Miles College; Birmingham, Ala. 35208	566 (C)	P/CME	3,760	3,760	2,300
Millersville University of Pennsylvania; Millersville, Pa. 17551	7,001 (C)	Pub	2,536	4,392	2,810
Milligan College; Milligan College, Tenn. 37682	600 (C)	P	5,416	5,416	2,458
Millikin University; Decatur, Ill. 62522	1,625 (C)	P	9,256	9,256	3,544
Millsaps College; Jackson, Miss. 39210	1,325 (C)	P/UM	8,060	8,060	3,080
Mills College; Oakland, Calif. 94613	789 (W)	P	13,005	13,005	5,400
Milwaukee Institute of Art and Design; Milwaukee, Wis. 53202	408 (C)	P	6,200	6,200	n.a.
Milwaukee School of Engineering; Milwaukee, Wis. 53201-0644	1,808 (C)	P	7,800	7,800	3,000
Minneapolis Coll. of Art and Design; Minneapolis, Minn. 55404	629 (C)	P	8,650	8,650	3,400
Minnesota, Univ. of–Duluth; Duluth, Minn. 55812	7,365 (C)	Pub	2,105	4,880	2,850
Minnesota, Univ. of–Morris; Morris, Minn. 56267	2,041 (C)	Pub	2,415	5,664	2,835
Minnesota, Univ. of–Twin Cities; Minneapolis, Minn. 55455	29,278 (C)	Pub	2,337	5,341	2,900
Minnesota Bible College; Rochester, Minn. 55902	90 (C)	P/CC	2,700	2,700	2,860
Minot State University; Minot, N.D. 58701	2,950 (C)	Pub	1,257	2,937	1,620
Mississippi, University of; University, Miss. 38677	7,589 (C)	Pub	1,790	2,972	2,204
Mississippi, Univ. of, Medical Center; Jackson, Miss. 39216	472 (C)	Pub	1,595	2,777	2,324
Mississippi College; Clinton, Miss. 39058	2,078 (C)	P	4,432	4,432	2,250
Mississippi State University; Mississippi State, Miss. 39762	11,123 (C)	Pub	1,794	2,976	2,500
Mississippi University for Women; Columbus, Miss. 39701	2,109 (C)	Pub	1,780	2,963	2,092
Mississippi Valley State University; Itta Bena, Miss. 38941	1,848 (C)	Pub	1,700	2,882	1,725
Missouri, Univ. of–Columbia; Columbia, Mo. 65211	18,196 (C)	Pub	1,807	5,158	2,851
Missouri, Univ. of–Kansas City; Kansas City, Mo. 64110	6,925 (C)	Pub	2,026	2,026	3,065
Missouri, Univ. of–Rolla; Rolla, Mo. 65401	4,138 (C)	Pub	2,152	5,743	3,080
Missouri, Univ. of–St. Louis; St. Louis, Mo. 63121	10,495 (C)	Pub	1,980	5,571	n.a.
Missouri Baptist College; St. Louis, Mo. 63141	951 (C)	P/SB	4,990	4,990	2,300
Missouri Southern State College; Joplin, Mo. 64801	5,901 (C)	Pub	1,116	2,182	2,220
Missouri Valley College; Marshall, Mo. 65340	1,130 (C)	P	7,479	7,479	4,356
Missouri Western State College; St. Joseph, Mo. 64507	4,135 (C)	Pub	1,236	2,322	1,972
Mobile College; Mobile, Ala. 36613	1,032 (C)	P/SB	4,260	4,260	2,872
Molloy College; Rockville Centre, N.Y. 11570	1,385 (C)	P/RC	7,300	7,300	n.a.

Institution and location	Enrollment	Control	Tuition ($) Res.	Tuition ($) Nonres.	Rm/Bd ($)
Monmouth College; Monmouth, Ill. 61462	671 (C)	P/UP	11,450	11,450	3,150
Monmouth College; West Long Branch, N.J. 07764	3,078 (C)	P	8,320	8,320	4,032
Montana, University of; Missoula, Mont. 59812	7,841 (C)	Pub	1,448	3,521	3,029
Montana College of Mineral Science and Technology; Butte, Mont. 59701	1,690 (C)	Pub	1,309	3,382	3,000
Montana State University; Bozeman, Mont. 59717	10,024 (C)	Pub	1,343	3,161	2,800
Montclair State College; Upper Montclair, N.J. 07043	10,224 (C)	Pub	2,055	2,865	3,904
Monterey Institute of Intl. Studies; Monterey, Calif. 93940	99 (C)	P	9,545	9,545	n.a.
Montevallo, University of; Montevallo, Ala. 35115	2,379 (C)	Pub	1,620	2,944	2,734
Montreat–Anderson College; Montreat, N.C. 28757	386 (C)	P	4,784	4,784	2,872
Moody Bible Institute; Chicago, Ill. 60610	1,410 (C)	P	650	650	3,600
Moore College of Art and Design; Philadelphia, Pa. 19103	654 (W)	P	9,700	9,700	4,600
Moorhead State University; Moorhead, Minn. 56560	9,100 (C)	Pub	1,751	2,765	2,256
Morávian College; Bethlehem, Pa. 18018	1,215 (C)	P/Mor	11,660	11,660	3,780
Morehead State University; Morehead, Ky. 40351	6,512 (C)	Pub	1,190	3,310	2,330
Morehouse College; Atlanta, Ga. 30314	2,606 (M)	P	5,550	5,550	3,600
Morgan State University; Baltimore, Md. 21239	3,604 (C)	Pub	1,922	3,832	4,156
Morningside College; Sioux City, Iowa 51106	1,126 (C)	P/UM	8,466	8,466	2,830
Morris Brown College; Atlanta, Ga. 30314	1,500 (C)	P/AME	4,900	4,900	2,600
Morris College; Sumter, S.C. 29150	700 (C)	P	3,127	3,127	2,158
Morrison College/Reno Business College; Reno, Nev. 89503	300 (C)	P	5,000	5,000	n.a.
Mount Angel Seminary; St. Benedict, Ore. 97373	25 (M)	P/RC	3,030	3,030	2,800
Mount Holyoke College; South Hadley, Mass. 01075	1,954 (W)	P	14,000	14,000	4,300
Mount Ida College; Newton Centre, Mass. 02159	1,340 (C)	P	7,685	7,685	5,535
Mount Marty College; Yankton, S.D. 57078	629 (C)	P/RC	5,775	5,775	2,460
Mount Mary College; Milwaukee, Wis. 53222	1,420 (W)	P/RC	6,150	6,150	2,550
Mount Mercy College; Cedar Rapids, Iowa 52402	1,591 (C)	P	7,050	7,050	2,835
Mount Olive College; Mount Olive, N.C. 28365	997 (C)	P	4,995	4,995	2,550
Mount St. Joseph, College of; Mount St. Joseph, Ohio 45051	2,343 (C)	P/RC	7,600	7,600	3,690
Mount Saint Mary College; Newburgh, N.Y. 12550	1,106 (C)	P	6,150	6,150	3,700
Mount Saint Mary's College; Emmitsburg, Md. 21727	1,452 (C)	P/RC	9,100	9,100	5,300
Mount St. Clare College; Clinton, Iowa 52732	335 (C)	P	6,080	6,080	2,800
Mount St. Mary's College; Los Angeles, Calif. 90049	981 (W)	P/RC	9,250	9,250	4,535
Mount Saint Vincent, College of; New York, N.Y. 10471	936 (C)	P	8,900	8,900	4,550
Mount Senario College; Ladysmith, Wis. 54848	489 (C)	P	5,600	5,600	2,300
Mount Union College; Alliance, Ohio 44601	1,249 (C)	P	10,070	10,070	2,930
Mount Vernon College; Washington, D.C. 20007	528 (W)	P	11,805	11,805	5,805
Mount Vernon Nazarene College; Mount Vernon, Ohio 43050	1,087 (C)	P	5,194	5,194	2,840
Muhlenberg College; Allentown, Pa. 18104	1,615 (C)	P/L	14,015	14,015	3,950
Multnomah School of the Bible; Portland, Ore. 97220	569 (C)	P	4,650	4,650	2,600
Mundelein College; Chicago, Ill. 60660	1,010 (W)	P/RC	7,500	7,500	3,000
Murray State University; Murray, Ky. 42071	6,717 (C)	Pub	1,290	3,650	2,280
Museum of Fine Arts, School of the–Tufts University; Boston, Mass. 02115	706 (C)	P	9,250	9,250	n.a.
Museum Art School, Portland. See Pacific Northwest College of Art					
Muskingum College; Concord, Ohio 43762	1,140 (C)	P/UP	10,980	10,980	3,300
NAES College; Chicago, Ill. 60659	119 (C)	P	3,395	3,395	n.a.
Naropa Institute; Boulder, Colo. 80302	130 (C)	P	7,580	7,580	n.a.
Nathaniel Hawthorne College. See Hawthorne College					
National College–Albuquerque; Albuquerque, N.M. 87108	134 (C)	P	4,290	4,290	n.a.
National College, Colorado Springs Branch; Colorado Springs, Colo. 80909	320 (C)	P	3,800	3,800	n.a.
National College; Rapid City, S.D. 57709	585 (C)	P	5,460	5,460	2,790
National–Louis University; Evanston, Ill. 60201	2,226 (C)	P	6,975	6,975	4,065
National University; San Diego, Calif. 92108	7,121 (C)	P	5,405	5,405	n.a.
Nazareth College in Kalamazoo; Nazareth, Mich. 49001-1282	564 (C)	P	7,156	7,156	3,082
Nazareth College of Rochester; Rochester, N.Y. 14610	1,394 (C)	P	8,020	8,020	4,070
Nebraska, University of–Lincoln; Lincoln, Neb. 68588-0415	19,775 (C)	Pub	1,790	4,415	2,450
Nebraska, University of–Omaha; Omaha, Neb. 68182	14,829 (C)	Pub	1,368	3,524	n.a.
Nebraska Christian College; Norfolk, Neb. 68701	129 (C)	P	2,440	2,440	2,200
Nebraska Wesleyan University; Lincoln, Neb. 68504	1,607 (C)	P/UM	7,188	7,188	2,570
Neumann College; Aston, Pa. 19014	1,073 (C)	P	6,760	6,760	n.a.
Nevada, University of–Las Vegas; Las Vegas, Nev. 89154	16,320 (C)	Pub	1,500	4,500	3,500
Nevada, University of–Reno; Reno, Nev. 89557	7,507 (C)	Pub	1,280	4,280	2,600
Newberry College; Newberry, S.C. 29108	701 (C)	P/LCA	7,000	7,000	2,800
New College of California; San Francisco, Calif. 94110	200 (C)	P	5,000	5,000	n.a.
New College of the University of South Florida; Sarasota, Fla. 34243-2197	525 (C)	Pub	1,419	4,730	3,300
New England, University of; Biddeford, Me. 04005	691 (C)	P	8,700	8,700	4,200
New England College; Henniker, N.H. 03242	1,073 (C)	P	9,790	9,790	4,200
New England College–Arundel Campus; Sussex BN18 0DA, England	220 (C)	P	9,790	9,790	4,200
New England Conservatory of Music; Boston, Mass. 02115	412 (C)	P	11,100	11,100	5,400
New England Institute of Technology; Warwick, R.I. 02886	1,950 (C)	P	6,225	6,225	n.a.
New Hampshire, University of; Durham, N.H. 03824	9,919 (C)	Pub	3,014	8,804	3,276
New Hampshire College; Manchester, N.H. 03104	1,500 (C)	P	8,840	8,840	4,380

Institution and location	Enrollment	Control	Tuition ($) Res.	Tuition ($) Nonres.	Rm/Bd ($)
New Haven, University of; West Haven, Conn. 06516	3,839 (C)	P	8,454	8,454	4,120
New Jersey Institute of Technology; Newark, N.J. 07102	4,704 (C)	Pub	3,560	6,620	4,300
New Mexico, University of; Albuquerque, N.M. 87131	20,028 (C)	Pub	1,222	4,572	2,850
New Mexico Highlands University; Las Vegas, N.M. 87701	1,563 (C)	Pub	1,104	4,062	2,094
New Mexico Inst. of Mining & Technology; Socorro, N.M. 87801	1,127 (C)	Pub	884	4,212	2,500
New Mexico State University; Las Cruces, N.M. 88003-0001	13,284 (C)	Pub	1,386	5,082	3,706
New Orleans, University of; New Orleans, La. 70148	16,109 (C)	Pub	1,666	4,138	2,368
New Rochelle, College of–School of Arts & Sciences and School of Nursing; New Rochelle, N.Y. 10801	636 (W)	P	8,550	8,550	3,920
New School for Social Research Eugene Lang College; New York, N.Y. 10011	350 (C)	P	9,140	9,140	5,900
New York, City University of; New York, N.Y. 10021:					
Bernard M. Baruch College; New York, N.Y. 10010	13,666 (C)	Pub	1,250	4,050	n.a.
Brooklyn College; Brooklyn, N.Y. 11210	11,825 (C)	Pub	1,355	4,155	n.a.
City College; New York, N.Y. 10031	10,179 (C)	Pub	1,345	4,145	n.a.
College of Staten Island; Staten Island, N.Y. 10301	9,679 (C)	Pub	1,344	4,144	n.a.
Herbert H. Lehman College; Bronx, N.Y. 10468	7,841 (C)	Pub	1,340	4,140	n.a.
Hunter College; New York, N.Y. 10021	16,091 (C)	Pub	1,342	4,142	3,200
John Jay College of Criminal Justice; New York, N.Y. 10019	6,769 (C)	Pub	1,350	4,200	n.a.
Medgar Evers College; Brooklyn, N.Y. 11225	2,823 (C)	Pub	1,225	2,025	n.a.
New York City Technical College; Brooklyn, N.Y. 11201	10,323 (C)	Pub	1,274	4,054	n.a.
Queens College; Flushing, N.Y. 11367	17,500 (C)	Pub	1,250	4,050	n.a.
York College; Jamaica, N.Y. 11451	4,826 (C)	Pub	1,347	4,122	n.a.
New York, State University of; Albany, N.Y. 12246:					
SUNY–Albany; Albany, N.Y. 12222	11,788 (C)	Pub	1,478	4,700	3,103
SUNY–Buffalo; Buffalo, N.Y. 14214	18,888 (C)	Pub	1,490	4,840	3,732
SUNY–College at Brockport; Brockport, N.Y. 14420	6,788 (C)	Pub	1,586	4,936	3,690
SUNY–College at Buffalo; Buffalo, N.Y. 14222	10,684 (C)	Pub	1,465	3,315	3,030
SUNY–College at Cortland; Cortland, N.Y. 13045	3,467 (C)	Pub	1,528	4,878	3,200
SUNY–College at Fredonia; Fredonia, N.Y. 14063	4,473 (C)	Pub	1,529	4,879	3,580
SUNY–College at Geneseo; Geneseo, N.Y. 14454–1471	4,939 (C)	Pub	1,500	4,900	3,050
SUNY–College at New Paltz; New Paltz, N.Y. 12561	4,696 (C)	Pub	1,495	4,095	3,360
SUNY–College at Old Westbury; Old Westbury, N.Y. 11568	3,999 (C)	Pub	1,350	3,292	3,984
SUNY–College at Oneonta; Oneonta, N.Y. 13820	5,501 (C)	Pub	1,686	5,036	3,588
SUNY–College at Oswego; Oswego, N.Y. 13126	6,622 (C)	Pub	1,350	3,950	3,102
SUNY–College at Plattsburgh; Plattsburgh, N.Y. 12901	5,754 (C)	Pub	1,350	3,950	3,166
SUNY–College at Potsdam; Potsdam, N.Y. 13676	4,000 (C)	Pub	1,490	3,355	3,200
SUNY–College of Agriculture and Life Sciences at Cornell University; Ithaca, N.Y. 14853	3,150 (C)	Pub	5,944	10,884	4,900
SUNY–College of Environmental Science and Forestry; Syracuse, N.Y. 13210	927 (C)	Pub	1,460	4,760	5,210
SUNY–College of Human Ecology at Cornell University; Ithaca, N.Y. 14853	1,220 (C)	Pub	5,994	10,884	4,900
SUNY–College of Technology–Farmingdale; Farmingdale, N.Y. 11735	10,802 (C)	Pub	1,542	3,950	3,850
SUNY–Empire State College; Saratoga Springs, N.Y. 12866	7,072 (C)	Pub	1,350	3,237	n.a.
SUNY–Fashion Institute of Technology; New York, N.Y. 10001-5992	4,296 (C)	Pub	1,560	3,460	4,355
SUNY–Health Science Center at Syracuse; Syracuse, N.Y. 13210	276 (C)	Pub	1,440	4,040	3,493
SUNY–Institute of Technology at Utica/Rome; Utica, N.Y. 13054	2,330 (C)	Pub ·	1,510	4,860	n.a.
SUNY–Maritime College; Throggs Neck, N.Y. 10465	760 (C)	Pub	1,495	4,945	3,632
SUNY–Purchase; Purchase, N.Y. 10577	3,864 (C)	Pub	1,350	4,095	3,286
SUNY–School of Industrial and Labor Relations at Cornell University; Ithaca, N.Y. 14853	660 (C)	Pub	5,944	10,884	4,900
SUNY–Stony Brook; Stony Brook, N.Y. 11794	11,210 (C)	Pub	1,500	4,700	5,000
SUNY–University Center at Binghamton; Binghamton, N.Y. 13901	9,310 (C)	Pub	1,350	4,103	3,784
New York City Technical Coll. *See* New York, City Univ. of					
New York Institute of Technology; Old Westbury, N.Y. 11568	6,428 (C)	P	6,232	6,232	n.a.
New York Institute of Technology, Metropolitan Center; New York N.Y. 10023	2,841 (C)	P	6,232	6,232	n.a.
New York Institute of Technology Central Islip Campus; Central Islip, N.Y. 11722	1,616 (C)	P	6,232	6,232	3,500
New York School of Interior Design; New York, N.Y. 10022	809 (C)	P	7,370	7,370	n.a.
New York University; New York, N.Y. 10011	14,608 (C)	P	13,286	13,286	6,348
New York, University of the State of, Regents College Degrees; Albany, N.Y. 12230	14,372 (C)	Pub	375	375	n.a.
Niagara University; Niagara University, N.Y. 14109	2,495 (C)	P	7,640	7,640	3,617
Nicholls State University; Thibodaux, La. 70310	6,511 (C)	Pub	1,510	3,310	1,980
Nichols College; Dudley, Mass. 01570	848 (C)	P	7,130	7,130	4,100
Norfolk State University; Norfolk, Va. 23504	7,047 (C)	Pub	1,606	3,156	2,730
North Adams State College; North Adams, Mass. 01247	2,204 (C)	Pub	1,750	4,575	3,300
North Alabama, University of; Florence, Ala. 35632	4,880 (C)	Pub	1,224	1,749	2,264
North Carolina, Univ. of–Asheville; Asheville, N.C. 28804	3,233 (C)	Pub	940	4,782	2,770
North Carolina, Univ. of–Chapel Hill; Chapel Hill, N.C. 27514	15,251 (C)	Pub	1,007	5,509	3,280
North Carolina, Univ. of–Charlotte; Charlotte, N.C. 28223	11,143 (C)	Pub	821	4,659	2,402
North Carolina, Univ. of–Greensboro; Greensboro, N.C. 27412	8,946 (C)	Pub	1,269	5,771	3,140
North Carolina, Univ. of–Wilmington; Wilmington, N.C. 28403	6,288 (C)	Pub	1,068	5,440	2,756

Institution and location	Enrollment	Control	Tuition ($) Res.	Tuition ($) Nonres.	Rm/Bd ($)
North Carolina Agricultural and Technical State University; Greensboro, N.C. 27411	5,396 (C)	Pub	899	4,737	2,188
North Carolina Central University; Durham,, N.C. 27707	3,532 (C)	Pub	983	4,821	2,536
North Carolina School of the Arts; Winston-Salem, N.C. 27127-2189	502 (C)	Pub	1,191	5,523	2,727
North Carolina State University–Raleigh; Raleigh, N.C. 27695	24,021 (C)	Pub	922	4,876	2,770
North Carolina Wesleyan College; Rocky Mount, N.C. 27801	1,504 (C)	P/UM	6,730	6,730	3,250
North Central Bible College; Minneapolis, Minn. 55404	1,167 (C)	P	4,420	4,420	2,750
North Central College; Naperville, Ill. 60566–7063	2,081 (C)	P	9,096	9,096	3,528
North Dakota, University of; Grand Forks, N.D. 58202	10,140 (C)	Pub	1,724	3,986	2,258
North Dakota State University; Fargo, N.D. 58105	8,518 (C)	Pub	1,656	3,918	2,118
Northeastern Bible College; Essex Fells, N.J. 07021	193 (C)	P	5,000	5,000	2,750
Northeastern Illinois University, Chicago, Ill. 60625	7,454 (C)	Pub	1,706	4,870	n.a.
Northeastern State Univ.; Tahlequah, Okla. 74464	6,009 (C)	Pub	1,255	3,268	1,880
Northeastern University; Boston, Mass. 02115	15,497 (C)	P	9,458	9,458	5,970
Northeast Louisiana University; Monroe, La. 71209	9,522 (C)	Pub	1,603	2,743	2,000
Northeast Missouri State University; Kirksville, Mo. 63501	5,432 (C)	Pub	1,608	3,072	2,304
Northern Arizona University; Flagstaff, Ariz. 86011	11,029 (C)	Pub	1,528	5,904	2,800
Northern Colorado, University of; Greeley, Colo. 80639	8,016 (C)	Pub	1,726	4,462	3,058
North Georgia College; Dahlonega, Ga. 30597	2,077 (C)	Pub	1,431	3,813	2,100
Northern Illinois University; DeKalb, Ill. 60115	18,029 (C)	Pub	2,227	5,655	3,440
Northern Iowa, University of; Cedar Falls, Iowa 50614	10,517 (C)	Pub	1,810	4,650	2,150
Northern Kentucky University; Highland Heights, Ky. 41076	9,265 (C)	Pub	1,140	3,260	3,836
Northern Michigan University; Marquette, Mich. 49855	7,607 (C)	Pub	1,987	3,907	3,157
Northern Montana College; Havre, Mont. 59501	1,686 (C)	Pub	1,051	2,370	2,400
Northern State College; Aberdeen, S.D. 57401	3,100 (C)	Pub	2,144	2,816	1,651
North Florida, University of; Jacksonville, Fla. 32216	6,085 (C)	Pub	1,100	3,600	2,800
Northland College; Ashland, Wis. 54806	547 (C)	P	6,850	6,850	3,240
North Park College; Chicago, Ill. 60625	1,083 (C)	P/EC	9,100	9,100	3,300
Northrop University; Los Angeles, Calif. 90045	1,181 (C)	P	9,120	9,120	8,402
North Texas, University of; Denton, Tex. 76203	19,970 (C)	Pub	1,024	4,144	3,154
Northwest Christian College; Eugene, Ore. 97401	279 (C)	P/DC	5,237	5,237	2,788
Northwest College; Kirkland, Wash. 98083-0579	695 (C)	P	5,145	5,145	2,300
Northwestern College; Orange City, Iowa 51041	1,049 (C)	P/RCA	7,400	7,400	2,700
Northwestern College; St. Paul, Minn. 55113	1,036 (C)	P/ID	8,310	8,310	2,595
Northwestern Oklahoma State University; Alva, Okla. 73717	1,537 (C)	Pub	1,263	3,137	1,648
Northwestern State Univ. of Louisiana; Natchitoches, La. 71497	5,757 (C)	Pub	1,752	3,192	2,000
Northwestern University; Evanston, Ill. 60201-3060	7,405 (C)	P	12,996	12,996	4,380
Northwest Missouri State University; Maryville, Mo. 64468	4,600 (C)	Pub	1,320	2,415	2,300
Northwest Nazarene College; Nampa, Idaho 83651	1,095 (C)	P/Naz	5,823	5,823	2,529
Northwood Institute of Florida; West Palm Beach, Fla. 33409	450 (C)	P	7,080	7,080	4,515
Northwood Institute of Michigan; Midland, Mich. 48640	1,850 (C)	P	6,780	6,780	3,345
Northwood Institute of Texas; Cedar Hill, Tex. 75104	215 (C)	P	6,780	6,780	3,645
Norwich University; Northfield, Vt. 05663	1,653 (C)	P	11,200	11,200	4,300
Notre Dame, College of; Belmont, Calif. 94002	591 (C)	P/RC	9,240	9,240	4,500
Notre Dame, University of; Notre Dame, Ind. 46556	7,500 (C)	P	11,500	11,500	3,200
Notre Dame College; Manchester, N.H. 03104	520 (C)	P/RC	7,125	7,125	3,900
Notre Dame of Maryland, College of; Baltimore, Md. 21210	690 (W)	P/RC	8,800	8,800	4,600
Notre Dame College of Ohio; Cleveland, Ohio 44121	827 (W)	P/RC	6,270	6,270	3,200
Nova University; Ft. Lauderdale, Fla. 33314	2,400 (C)	P	5,550	5,550	4,100
Nyack College; Nyack, N.Y. 10960	519 (C)	P/CMA	6,380	6,380	3,080
Oakland City College; Oakland City, Ind. 47660	625 (C)	P/B	5,990	5,990	2,430
Oakland University; Rochester, Mich. 48063	9,952 (C)	Pub	2,100	5,600	2,932
Oakwood College; Huntsville, Ala. 35896	1,000 (C)	P/SDA	5,331	5,331	3,051
Oberlin College; Oberlin, Ohio 44074	2,850 (C)	P	14,220	14,220	4,620
Oblate College; Washington, D.C. 20017	5[1] (C)	P/RC	3,550	3,550	n.a.
Occidental College; Los Angeles, Calif. 90041	1,677 (C)	P	13,044	13,044	4,860
Oglala Lakota College; Kyle, S.D. 57752	800 (C)	Pub	800	800	n.a.
Oglethorpe University; Atlanta, Ga. 30319	972 (C)	P	9,300	9,300	4,000
Ohio Dominican College; Columbus, Ohio 43219	1,257 (C)	P/RC	6,300	6,300	3,500
Ohio Institute of Technology; Columbus. See DeVry Institute of Technology, Columbus					
Ohio Northern University; Ada, Ohio 45810	2,222 (C)	P	10,845	10,845	3,195
Ohio State University; Columbus, Ohio 43210	40,122 (C)	Pub	2,190	6,279	3,507
Ohio State University–Lima; Lima, Ohio 45804	1,236 (C)	Pub	2,106	6,195	n.a.
Ohio State University–Mansfield; Mansfield, Ohio 44906	1,194 (C)	Pub	2,106	6,195	n.a.
Ohio State University–Marion; Marion, Ohio 43302	1,054 (C)	Pub	2,106	6,195	n.a.
Ohio State University–Newark; Newark, Ohio 43055	1,419 (C)	Pub	2,106	6,195	n.a.
Ohio University; Athens, Ohio 45701	14,500 (C)	Pub	2,730	5,992	3,549
Ohio University–Lancaster; Lancaster, Ohio 43130	1,500 (C)	Pub	2,070	4,929	n.a.
Ohio University–Zanesville; Zanesville, Ohio 43701	985 (C)	Pub	2,070	4,929	n.a.
Ohio Valley College; Parkersburg, W.Va. 26101	224 (C)	P	3,952	3,952	3,004
Ohio Wesleyan University; Delaware, Ohio 43015	1,775 (C)	P	11,128	11,128	4,230

Institution and location	Enrollment	Control	Tuition ($) Res.	Tuition ($) Nonres.	Rm/Bd ($)
Oklahoma, University of–Norman; Norman, Okla. 73019	16,375 (C)	Pub	1,000	3,004	2,772
Oklahoma, University of–Health Sciences Center; Oklahoma City, Okla. 73190	986 (C)	Pub	1,419	4,581	n.a.
Oklahoma Baptist University; Shawnee, Okla. 74801	2,173 (C)	P	3,700	3,700	2,450
Oklahoma Christian College; Oklahoma City, Okla. 73136-1100	1,611 (C)	P	3,830	3,830	2,390
Oklahoma City University; Oklahoma City, Okla. 73106	1,627 (C)	P	4,858	4,858	3,380
Oklahoma Panhandle State University; Goodwell, Okla. 73939	1,276 (C)	Pub	885	2,370	1,580
Oklahoma State University; Stillwater, Okla. 74078	15,695 (C)	Pub	1,522	4,478	2,620
Old Dominion University; Norfolk, Va. 23508	11,514 (C)	Pub	2,414	4,622	3,858
Olivet College; Olivet, Mich. 49076	784 (C)	P/UCC	7,360	7,360	2,740
Olivet Nazarene University; Kankakee, Ill. 60901	1,566 (C)	P/Naz	5,548	5,548	3,078
Oral Roberts University; Tulsa, Okla. 74171	3,250 (C)	P	5,395	5,395	3,660
Oregon, University of; Eugene, Ore. 97403	13,786 (C)	Pub	1,782	5,043	3,389
Oregon Art Institute–Pacific Northwest College of Art; Portland, Ore. 97205	201 (C)	P	5,730	5,730	n.a.
Oregon Coll. of Education. *See* Western Oregon State Coll.					
Oregon Health Sciences University; Portland, Ore. 97201	400 (C)	Pub	2,061	4,929	2,849
Oregon Institute of Technology; Klamath Falls, Ore. 97601	2,851 (C)	Pub	1,606	4,481	2,688
Oregon State University; Corvallis, Ore. 97331	12,890 (C)	Pub	1,604	4,472	2,772
Orlando College; Orlando, Fla. 32810	810 (C)	P	3,037	3,037	n.a.
Otis Art Institute of Parsons School of Design; Los Angeles, Calif. 90057	735 (C)	P	9,140	9,140	3,750
Ottawa University; Ottawa, Kan. 66067	525 (C)	P/AB	5,990	5,990	2,899
Ottawa University–Phoenix Center; Phoenix, Ariz. 85021	505 (C)	P	2,880	2,880	n.a.
Otterbein College; Westerville, Ohio 43081	2,315 (C)	P/UM	10,095	10,095	3,690
Ouachita Baptist University; Arkadelphia, Ark. 71923	1,428 (C)	P/B	4,410	4,410	2,000
Our Lady of Angels College. *See* Neumann College					
Our Lady of Holy Cross College; New Orleans, La. 70131-7399	1,033 (C)	P/RC	4,600	4,600	n.a.
Our Lady of the Lake–University of San Antonio; San Antonio, Tex. 78285	1,666 (C)	P/RC	5,650	5,650	3,030
Ozark Christian College; Joplin, Mo. 64801	535 (C)	P	2,360	2,360	1,990
Ozarks, School of the; Point Lookout, Mo. 65726	1,434 (C)	P	1,072	1,072	1,600
Ozarks, University of the; Clarksville, Ark. 72830	796 (C)	P/UP	3,010	3,010	2,160
Pace University; New York, N.Y. 10038	7,239 (C)	P	7,880	7,880	4,000
Pace University–College of White Plains; White Plains, N.Y. 10603	1,561 (C)	P	7,600	7,600	4,000
Pace University–Pleasantville-Briarcliff; Pleasantville, N.Y. 10570	4,104 (C)	P	7,600	7,600	4,000
Pacific, University of the; Stockton, Calif. 95211	3,600 (C)	P	13,622	13,622	4,598
Pacific Christian College; Fullerton, Calif. 92631	489 (C)	P/ChC	5,000	5,000	2,800
Pacific Lutheran University; Tacoma, Wash. 98447	3,255 (C)	P	10,449	10,449	3,780
Pacific Oaks College; Pasadena, Calif. 91103	50 (C)	P	8,200	8,200	n.a.
Pacific States University; Los Angeles, Calif. 94508	300 (C)	P	3,240	3,240	n.a.
Pacific Union College; Angwin, Calif. 94508	1,537 (C)	P/SDA	7,980	7,980	2,880
Pacific University; Forest Grove, Ore. 97116	832 (C)	P/UCC	10,200	10,200	3,175
Paier College of Art, Inc.; Hamden, Conn. 06511	312 (C)	P	8,610	8,610	n.a.
Paine College; Augusta, Ga. 30910	708 (C)	P/UM	4,500	4,500	2,400
Palm Beach Atlantic College; West Palm Beach, Fla. 33401	1,375 (C)	P/SB	5,400	5,400	2,600
Pan American University; Edinburg, Tex. 78539	9,000 (C)	Pub	972	4,716	2,080
Park College; Parkville, Mo. 64152	479 (C)	P/LDS	5,700	5,700	2,600
Parks College of St. Louis University; Cahokia, Ill. 62206	1,100 (C)	P/RC	5,280	5,280	3,100
Parsons School of Design; New York, N.Y. 10011	1,740 (C)	P	10,110	10,110	4,950
Patten College; Oakland, Calif. 94601	228 (C)	P/CE	3,150	3,150	3,790
Paul Quinn College; Waco, Tex. 76704	509 (C)	P	2,900	2,900	2,750
Peabody Conservatory of Music; Baltimore, Md. 21202	256 (C)	P	10,425	10,425	4,230
Pembroke State University; Pembroke, N.C. 28372	2,712 (C)	Pub	800	4,642	1,920
Pennsylvania, University of; Philadelphia, Pa. 19104	9,949 (C)	P	13,950	13,950	5,400
Pennsylvania State Erie–Behrend College; Erie, Pa. 16563	2,667 (C)	Pub	3,754	7,900	3,330
Pennsylvania State Harrisburg–The Capital College; Middletown, Pa. 17057	1,937 (C)	Pub	3,754	7,900	3,330
Pennsylvania State University–Park; University Park, Pa. 16802	31,251 (C)	Pub	3,754	7,900	3,330
Pepperdine University School of Business and Management; Culver City, Calif. 90230	600 (C)	P	13,500	13,500	n.a.
Pepperdine University–Seaver College; Malibu, Calif. 90265	2,562 (C)	P	14,250	14,250	5,740
Peru State College; Peru, Neb. 68421	1,700 (C)	Pub	1,375	1,955	2,150
Pfeiffer College; Misenheimer, N.C. 28109	811 (C)	P/UM	5,535	5,535	2,710
Pharmacy, School of (Ga.). *See* Mercer Univ.					
Philadelphia College of Bible; Langhorne, Pa. 19047	591 (C)	P	5,515	5,515	3,200
Philadelphia College of Pharmacy and Science; Philadelphia, Pa. 19104	1,558 (C)	P	7,750	7,750	3,450
Philadelphia College of Textiles and Science; Philadelphia, Pa. 19144	1,820 (C)	P	7,800	7,800	3,980
Philander Smith College; Little Rock, Ark. 72202	572 (C)	P/UM	2,236	2,236	2,300
Phillips University; Enid, Okla. 73702	808 (C)	P	4,918	4,918	2,318
Phoenix, University of; Phoenix, Ariz. 85040	3,023 (C)	P	5,478	5,478	n.a.
Piedmont Bible College; Winston-Salem, N.C. 27101	268 (C)	P	2,800	2,800	2,100
Piedmont College; Demorest, Ga. 30535	530 (C)	P	3,330	3,330	2,895

Institution and location	Enrollment	Control	Tuition ($) Res.	Tuition ($) Nonres.	Rm/Bd ($)
Pikeville College; Pikeville, Ky. 41501	753 (C)	P/UP	3,700	3,700	2,300
Pillsbury Baptist Bible College; Owatonna, Minn. 55060	394 (C)	P	3,600	3,600	2,450
Pine Manor College; Chestnut Hill, Mass. 02167	550 (W)	P	10,900	10,900	5,800
Pittsburgh, University of; Pittsburgh, Pa. 15260	18,861 (C)	Pub	4,086	8,106	3,314
Pittsburgh, University of–Bradford; Bradford, Pa. 16701-2898	954 (C)	Pub	4,060	8,080	3,320
Pittsburgh, University of–Greensburg; Greensburg, Pa. 15601	1,452 (C)	Pub	4,050	8,070	2,970
Pittsburgh, University of–Johnstown; Johnstown, Pa. 15904	3,270 (C)	Pub	4,030	8,050	3,034
Pittsburg State University; Pittsburg, Kan. 66762	4,165 (C)	Pub	1,236	3,310	2,470
Pitzer College. *See* Claremont Colleges.					
Plymouth State College; Plymouth, N.H. 03264	3,400 (C)	Pub	2,154	5,814	3,226
Point Loma Nazarene College; San Diego, Calif. 92106	1,837 (C)	P/Naz	7,221	7,221	3,390
Point Park College; Pittsburgh, Pa. 15222	2,713 (C)	P	6,860	6,860	3,390
Polytechnic University; Brooklyn, N.Y. 11201	1,879 (C)	P	11,900	11,900	4,000
Pomona College. *See* Claremont Colleges.					
Pontifical College Josephinum; Columbus, Ohio 43235-1498	97 (M)	P/RC	3,990	3,990	2,240
Portland, University of; Portland, Ore. 97203	2,084 (C)	P	7,665	7,665	3,130
Portland School of Art; Portland, Me. 04101	300 (C)	P	7,550	7,550	4,018
Portland State University; Portland, Ore. 97207	12,494 (C)	Pub	1,806	4,938	3,434
Post College; Waterbury, Conn. 06708	1,654 (C)	P	8,760	8,760	3,910
Potsdam Coll. of Arts & Science. *See* New York, State Univ. of					
Prairie View A&M University; Prairie View, Tex. 77446	4,834 (C)	Pub	931	4,051	2,938
Pratt Institute; Brooklyn, N.Y. 11205	2,784 (C)	P	9,460	9,460	4,805
Presbyterian College; Clinton, S.C. 29325	1,146 (C)	P	8,756	8,756	2,984
Prescott College; Prescott, Ariz. 86301	320 (C)	P	6,200	6,200	n.a.
Princeton University; Princeton, N.J. 08544	4,524 (C)	P	14,390	14,390	4,817
Principia College; Elsah, Ill. 62028	614 (C)	P	10,065	10,065	4,090
Providence College; Providence, R.I. 02918	3,805 (C)	P	9,450	9,450	4,300
Puerto Rico, University of–Cayey University College; Cayey, P.R. 00633	3,357 (C)	Pub	662	2,000	n.a.
Puerto Rico, University of–Humacao University College; Humacao, P.R. 00661	3,892 (C)	Pub	707	2,257	n.a.
Puerto Rico, University of–Mayaguez Campus; Mayaguez, P.R. 00708	9,123 (C)	Pub	590	2,890	n.a.
Puerto Rico, University of–Medical Science; San Juan, P.R. 00936	1,037 (C)	Pub	(²)	(³)	n.a.
Puget Sound, University of; Tacoma, Wash. 98416	3,214 (C)	P	11,400	11,400	3,800
Puget Sound Christian College; Edmonds, Wash. 98020	82 (C)	P	3,990	3,990	2,720
Purdue University; West Lafayette, Ind. 47907	29,674 (C)	Pub	2,020	6,118	3,056
Purdue University–Calumet; Hammond, Ind. 46323	7,437 (C)	Pub	1,789	4,504	n.a.
Purdue University–North Central; Westville, Ind. 46323	3,013 (C)	Pub	1,677	4,223	n.a.
Queens College; Charlotte, N.C. 28274	1,178 (C)	P/PUS	7,550	7,550	3,850
Queens College (NYC). *See* New York, City University of					
Quincy College; Quincy, Ill. 62301	1,425 (C)	P/RC	7,000	7,000	2,910
Quinnipiac College; Hamden, Conn. 06518	2,950 (C)	P	9,140	9,140	4,580
Rabbinical College of America; Morristown, N.J. 07960	230 (M)	P	4,100	4,100	3,400
Rabbinical Seminary of America; Forest Hills, N.Y. 11375	200 (M)	P	3,000	3,000	3,000
Radcliffe College. *See* Harvard and Radcliffe Colleges					
Radford University; Radford, Va. 24142	9,175 (C)	Pub	2,128	4,128	3,454
Ramapo College of New Jersey; Mahwah, N.J. 07403	4,058 (C)	Pub	2,145	2,745	3,900
Randolph–Macon College; Ashland, Va. 23005	1,120 (C)	P	9,130	9,130	3,945
Randolph–Macon Woman's College; Lynchburg, Va. 24503	765 (W)	P/UM	10,750	10,750	4,750
Redlands, University of; Redlands, Calif. 92373-0999	1,220 (C)	P	11,890	11,890	4,740
Reed College; Portland, Ore. 97202	1,261 (C)	P	14,520	14,520	4,300
Reformed Bible College; Grand Rapids, Mich. 49506	166 (C)	P	4,320	4,320	2,600
Regis College; Denver, Colo. 80221	1,041 (C)	P/RC	8,660	8,660	4,200
Regis College; Weston, Mass. 02193	1,025 (W)	P/RC	9,080	9,080	4,520
Rensselaer Polytechnic Institute; Troy, N.Y. 12180	4,195 (C)	P	15,375	15,375	4,815
Research College of Nursing; Kansas City, Mo. 64132	133 (C)	P	6,850	6,850	3,200
Rhode Island, University of; Kingston, R.I. 02881	12,646 (C)	Pub	2,437	6,819	4,230
Rhode Island, University of, College of Continuing Education; Providence, R.I. 02908-5090	4,400 (C)	Pub	(⁴)	(⁵)	n.a.
Rhode Island College; Providence, R.I. 02908	5,433 (C)	Pub	1,703	4,331	3,950
Rhode Island School of Design; Providence, R.I. 02903	1,800 (C)	P	12,210	12,210	5,200
Rhodes College Memphis; Memphis, Tenn. 38112	1,386 (C)	P/PUS	11,628	11,628	4,282
Rice University; Houston, Tex. 77251	2,741 (C)	P	6,900	6,900	4,600
Richmond, University of; Richmond, Va. 23173	2,749 (C)	P/B	10,850	10,850	2,715
Richmond College; Surrey, TW10 6JP England	995 (C)	P	8,565	8,565	4,500
Rider College; Lawrenceville, N.J. 08648	3,032 (C)	P	9,950	9,950	4,330
Ringling School of Art and Design; Sarasota, Fla. 34234	457 (C)	P	7,300	7,300	4,200
Ripon College; Ripon, Wis. 54971	859 (C)	P	11,104	11,104	2,635
Rivier College; Nashua, N.H. 03060	650 (W)	P/RC	7,350	7,350	3,780
Roanoke Bible College; Elizabeth City, N.C. 27909	130 (C)	P	2,000	2,000	2,000
Roanoke College; Salem, Va. 24153	1,696 (C)	P/LCA	9,400	9,400	3,600

Institution and location	Enrollment	Control	Tuition ($) Res.	Tuition ($) Nonres.	Rm/Bd ($)
Robert Morris College; Coraopolis, Pa. 15108	4,945 (C)	P	4,590	4,590	3,200
Roberts Wesleyan College; Rochester, N.Y. 14624	864 (C)	P/FM	7,890	7,890	2,826
Rio Grande, University of; Rio Grande, Ohio 45674	2,000 (C)	P	2,073	4,420	2,765
Rochester, University of; Rochester, N.Y. 14627	4,822 (C)	P	13,425	13,425	5,069
Rochester Institute of Technology; Rochester, N.Y. 14623	11,692 (C)	P	10,959	10,959	4,701
Rockford College; Rockford, Ill. 61108	1,108 (C)	P	8,030	8,030	3,000
Rockhurst College; Kansas City, Mo. 64110	3,085 (C)	P/RC	7,050	7,050	3,300
Rocky Mountain College; Billings, Mont. 59102	705 (C)	P	5,800	5,800	2,900
Roger Williams College; Bristol, R.I. 02809	2,060 (C)	P	9,108	9,108	4,770
Rollins College; Winter Park, Fla. 32789	1,477 (C)	P	12,500	12,500	4,085
Roosevelt University; Chicago, Ill. 60605	4,258 (C)	P	6,822	6,822	4,200
Rosary College; River Forest, Ill. 60305-1099	1,042 (C)	P/RC	7,740	7,740	3,460
Rose–Hulman Institute of Technology; Terre Haute, Ind. 47803	1,325 (M)	P	10,100	10,100	3,300
Rosemont College; Rosemont, Pa. 19010	613 (W)	P/RC	8,350	8,350	5,160
Rush University Colleges of Nursing and Health Sciences; Chicago, Ill. 60612	175 (C)	P	6,870	6,870	2,698
Russell Sage College; Troy, N.Y. 12180	1,227 (W)	P	8,970	8,970	3,700
Rust College; Holly Springs, Miss. 38635	936 (C)	P	4,152	4,152	1,848
Rutgers University–Camden College of Arts and Sciences; Camden, N.J. 08102	3,063 (C)	Pub	2,941	5,609	3,635
Rutgers University–College of Engineering; New Brunswick, N.J. 08903	2,567 (C)	Pub	3,402	6,360	3,661
Rutgers University–College of Nursing–Newark; Newark, N.J. 07102	412 (C)	Pub	2,939	5,607	3,916
Rutgers University–College of Pharmacy; New Brunswick, N.J. 08903	774 (C)	Pub	3,402	6,360	3,661
Rutgers University–Cook College; New Brunswick, N.J. 08903	3,009 (C)	Pub	3,402	6,360	3,661
Rutgers University–Douglass College; New Brunswick, N.J. 08903	3,341 (W)	Pub	3,090	5,758	3,661
Rutgers University–Livingston College; New Brunswick, N.J. 08903	3,576 (C)	Pub	3,111	5,779	3,661
Rutgers University–Mason Gross School of the Arts; New Brunswick, N.J. 08903	420 (C)	Pub	3,116	5,786	3,661
Rutgers University–Newark College of Arts and Sciences; Newark, N.J. 07102	3,621 (C)	Pub	2,946	5,614	n.a.
Rutgers University–Rutgers College; New Brunswick, N.J. 08903	8,563 (C)	Pub	3,102	5,770	3,661
Rutgers University–University College–Camden; Camden, N.J. 08102	973 (C)	Pub	(⁶)	(⁷)	n.a.
Rutgers University–University College–New Brunswick; New Brunswick, N.J. 08903	3,101 (C)	Pub	(⁶)	(⁷)	n.a.
Rutgers University–University College–Newark; Newark, N.J. 07102	1,978 (C)	Pub	(⁶)	(⁷)	n.a.
Sacred Heart, Univ. of the; Santurce, P.R. 00924	7,044 (C)	P/RC	3,130	3,130	3,340
Sacred Heart Seminary; Detroit, Mich. 48206	554 (C)	P/RC	2,850	2,850	2,350
Sacred Heart University; Fairfield, Conn. 06432	3,407 (C)	P	7,220	7,220	n.a.
Saginaw Valley State University; University Center, Mich. 48710	5,263 (C)	Pub	2,131	4,363	3,036
St. Alphonsus College; Suffield, Conn. 06078	43 (M)	P/RC	3,300	3,300	2,100
St. Ambrose University; Davenport, Iowa 52803	1,650 (C)	P/RC	7,320	7,320	3,010
St. Andrews Presbyterian College; Laurinburg, N.C. 28352	833 (C)	P/PUS	7,650	7,650	3,455
Saint Anselm College; Manchester, N.H. 03102	1,833 (C)	P	9,420	9,420	4,760
St. Augustine's College; Raleigh, N.C. 27611	1,716 (C)	P/E	4,250	4,250	2,800
St. Benedict, College of; St. Joseph, Minn. 56374-2099	1,852 (W)	P/RC	9,430	9,430	3,360
St. Bonaventure University; St. Bonaventure, N.Y. 14778	2,396 (C)	P	8,582	8,582	4,294
St. Catherine, College of; St. Paul, Minn. 55105	2,463 (W)	P/RC	9,248	9,248	3,356
St. Cloud State University; St. Cloud, Minn. 56301	14,429 (C)	Pub	1,872	2,803	2,267
St. Edward's University; Austin, Tex. 78704	2,524 (C)	P/RC	7,184	7,184	3,400
St. Elizabeth, College of; Convent Station, N.J. 07961	1,074 (W)	P	7,500	7,500	3,700
St. Francis, College of; Joliet, Ill. 60435	1,107 (C)	P/RC	7,100	7,100	3,500
St. Francis College; Brooklyn Heights, N.Y. 11201	1,248 (C)	P	5,200	5,200	n.a.
St. Francis College; Fort Wayne, Ind. 46808	897 (C)	P/RC	6,599	6,599	3,300
St. Francis College; Loretto, Pa. 15940	1,025 (C)	P/RC	8,758	8,758	4,120
St. Hyacinth College and Seminary; Granby, Mass. 01033	50 (M)	P/RC	3,600	3,600	4,000
St. John Fisher College; Rochester, N.Y. 14618	1,571 (C)	P	8,510	8,510	4,480
St. John's College; Annapolis, Md. 21404	410 (C)	P	12,990	12,990	4,410
St. John's College; Santa Fe, N.M. 87501	389 (C)	P	11,880	11,880	3,996
St. John's Seminary College; Camarillo, Calif. 93010	86 (M)	P/RC	4,012	4,012	—
St. John's Seminary College of Liberal Arts; Brighton, Mass. 02135	70 (M)	P/RC	3,600	3,600	2,600
St. John's University; Collegeville, Minn. 56321	1,939 (M)	P/RC	9,510	9,510	3,500
St. John's University–Queens—Staten Island; Jamaica, N.Y. 11439	14,380 (C)	P/RC	6,860	6,860	n.a.
St. John Vianney College Seminary; Miami, Fla. 33165	50 (M)	P	5,500	5,500	3,000
St. Joseph College; West Hartford, Conn. 06117	793 (W)	P/RC	9,800	9,800	4,145
St. Joseph in Vermont, College of; Rutland, Vt. 05701	391 (C)	P/RC	6,000	6,000	3,500
St. Joseph's College; Brooklyn, N.Y. 11205	794 (C)	P	5,200	5,200	n.a.
Saint Joseph's College; Rensselaer, Ind. 47978	933 (C)	P/RC	8,610	8,610	3,370

Institution and location	Enrollment	Control	Tuition ($) Res.	Tuition ($) Nonres.	Rm/Bd ($)
St. Joseph's College–Suffolk; Patchogue, N.Y. 11772	1,766 (C)	P	5,286	5,286	n.a.
Saint Joseph's College; Windham, Me. 04062-1198	663 (C)	P/RC	8,025	8,025	4,000
St. Joseph Seminary College; St. Benedict, La. 70457	59 (M)	P	3,800	3,800	3,000
Saint Joseph's University; Philadelphia, Pa. 19131	2,400 (C)	P/RC	9,750	9,750	4,700
St. Lawrence University; Canton, N.Y. 13617	2,077 (C)	P	13,505	13,505	4,345
Saint Leo College; Saint Leo, Fla. 33574	6,071 (C)	P/RC	6,932	6,932	3,260
St. Louis Christian College; Florissant, Mo. 63033	123 (C)	P	2,760	2,760	1,860
St. Louis College of Pharmacy; St. Louis, Mo. 63110	738 (C)	P	4,700	4,700	3,200
St. Louis Conservatory of Music; St. Louis, Mo. 63130	70 (C)	P	7,750	7,750	n.a.
St. Louis University; St. Louis, Mo. 63103	7,556 (C)	P	8,480	8,450	4,000
St. Martin's College; Lacey, Wash. 98503	577 (C)	P	9,600	9,600	3,360
St. Mary, College of; Omaha, Neb. 68124	1,133 (W)	P/RC	6,600	6,600	2,800
Saint Mary College; Leavenworth, Kan. 66048	448 (C)	P	5,820	5,820	3,080
St. Mary of the Plains College; Dodge City, Kan. 67801	911 (C)	P/RC	5,310	5,310	2,800
St. Mary-of-the-Woods Coll.; St. Mary-of-the-Woods, Ind. 47876	858 (W)	P/RC	7,635	7,635	3,135
St. Mary's College; Notre Dame, Ind. 46556	1,881 (W)	P/RC	9,322	9,322	3,947
St. Mary's College; Orchard Lake, Mich. 48033	307 (C)	P	3,325	3,325	2,700
St. Mary's College; Winona, Minn. 55987	1,275 (C)	P	8,665	8,665	2,820
St. Mary's College of California; Moraga, Calif. 94575	2,000 (C)	P/RC	10,294	10,294	5,058
St. Mary's College of Maryland; St. Mary's City, Md. 20686	1,595 (C)	Pub	2,620	4,220	3,900
St. Mary's University of San Antonio; San Antonio, Tex. 78284	2,404 (C)	P/RC	6,133	6,133	2,780
Saint Meinrad College; St. Meinrad, Ind. 47577	127 (M)	P/RC	4,013	4,013	3,924
Saint Michael's College; Colchester, Vt. 05439	1,751 (C)	P/RC	10,549	10,549	4,810
St. Norbert College; De Pere, Wis. 54115	1,950 (C)	P/RC	9,515	9,515	3,560
St. Olaf College; Northfield, Minn. 55057	3,132 (C)	P/AL	11,200	11,200	3,100
St. Paul Bible College; Bible College, Minn. 55375	528 (C)	P/CMA	5,560	5,560	3,010
Saint Paul's College; Lawrenceville, Va. 23868	736 (C)	P	3,950	3,950	2,855
Saint Peter's College; Jersey City, N.J. 07306	3,152 (C)	P/RC	6,683	6,683	4,120
Saint Rose, The College of; Albany, N.Y. 12203	2,209 (C)	P	7,184	7,184	4,250
St. Scholastica, College of; Duluth, Minn. 55811	1,741 (C)	P/RC	9,192	9,192	3,018
St. Thomas, College of; St. Paul, Minn. 55105	5,129 (C)	P	8,992	8,992	3,136
St. Thomas, University of; Houston, Tex. 77006	1,032 (C)	P/RC	4,464	4,464	3,040
St. Thomas Aquinas College; Sparkill, N.Y. 10968	1,886 (C)	P	6,100	6,100	4,400
Saint Thomas University; Miami, Fla. 33054	2,100 (C)	P/RC	6,900	6,900	3,600
Saint Vincent College; Latrobe, Pa. 15650	1,189 (C)	P/RC	8,339	8,339	3,280
St. Xavier College; Chicago, Ill. 60655	2,085 (C)	P/RC	6,540	6,540	2,765
Salem College; Winston–Salem, N.C. 27108	651 (W)	P	8,425	8,425	5,300
Salem State College; Salem, Mass. 01970	5,388 (C)	Pub	1,374	3,870	2,652
Salem–Teikyo University; Salem, W.Va. 26426	714 (C)	P	6,083	6,083	3,580
Salisbury State University, Salisbury, Md. 21801	4,840 (C)	Pub	2,330	3,996	3,890
Salve Regina University; Newport, R.I. 02840-4192	1,830 (C)	P	10,650	10,650	5,200
Samford University; Birmingham, Ala. 35229	3,203 (C)	P/SB	5,500	5,500	2,964
Sam Houston State University; Huntsville, Tex. 77341	12,359 (C)	Pub	1,060	4,180	2,467
San Diego, University of; San Diego, Calif. 92110	3,670 (C)	P/RC	10,370	10,370	5,000
San Diego State University; San Diego, Calif. 92182	28,712 (C)	Pub	888	5,424	3,968
Imperial Valley Campus; Calexico, Calif. 92231	253 (C)	Pub	838	5,500	n.a.
San Francisco, University of; San Francisco, Calif. 94117	2,664 (C)	P/RC	9,102	9,102	4,562
San Francisco Art Institute; San Francisco, Calif. 94133	514 (C)	P	11,550	11,550	n.a.
San Francisco Conservatory of Music; San Francisco, Calif. 94122	174 (C)	P	8,550	8,550	n.a.
San Francisco State Univ.; San Francisco, Calif. 94132	22,251 (C)	Pub	750	5,160	3,198
Sangamon State University; Springfield, Ill. 62708	2,342 (C)	Pub	1,824	4,944	5,530
San Jose Bible College; San Jose, Calif. 95108	348 (C)	P/ChC	4,611	4,611	2,460
San Jose State University; San Jose, Calif. 95192-0009	22,748 (C)	Pub	936	5,472	4,500
Santa Clara University; Santa Clara, Calif. 95053	3,777 (C)	P/RC	9,618	9,618	4,686
Santa Fe, College of; Santa Fe, N.M. 87501	1,482 (C)	P/RC	7,506	7,506	2,580
Sarah Lawrence College; Bronxville, N.Y. 10708	1,000 (C)	P	13,960	13,960	5,730
Savannah College of Art and Design; Savannah, Ga. 31401	1,293 (C)	P	6,150	6,150	4,150
Savannah State College; Savannah, Ga. 31404	1,754 (C)	Pub	1,461	3,603	2,025
Schiller International University; 6900 Heidelberg, W. Ger.	1,311 (C)	P	8,350	8,350	5,500
Schreiner College; Kerrville, Tex. 78028	658 (C)	P	6,975	6,975	4,800
Science and Arts, University of, of Oklahoma; Chickasha, Okla. 73018	1,451 (C)	Pub	1,317	3,616	1,820
Scranton, University of; Scranton, Pa. 18510	3,849 (C)	P/RC	8,800	8,800	4,000
Scripps College. *See* Claremont Colleges					
Seattle Pacific University; Seattle, Wash. 98119	2,444 (C)	P/FM	9,050	9,050	3,432
Seattle University; Seattle, Wash. 98122	3,361 (C)	P/RC	9,990	9,990	3,723
Seaver College. *See* Pepperdine University					
Selma University; Selma, Ala. 36701	217 (C)	P	2,100	2,100	1,740
Seton Hall University; South Orange, N.J. 07079	5,138 (C)	P/RC	9,790	9,790	5,222
Seton Hill College; Greensburg, Pa. 15601	976 (W)	P	7,500	7,500	3,280
Shawnee State University; Portsmouth, Ohio 45662	2,900 (C)	Pub	2,133	2,500	2,100
Shaw University; Raleigh, N.C. 27611	1,500 (C)	P	5,300	5,300	4,400
Sheldon Jackson College; Sitka, Alaska 99835	280 (C)	P/UP	5,390	5,390	4,100

Institution and location	Enrollment	Control	Tuition ($) Res.	Tuition ($) Nonres.	Rm/Bd ($)
Shenandoah College and Conservatory; Winchester, Va. 22601-9986	892 (C)	P	10,000	10,000	3,000
Shepherd College; Shepherdstown, W. Va. 25443	3,600 (C)	Pub	1,254	3,044	2,890
Shimer College; Waukegan, Ill. 60085	100 (C)	P	7,950	7,950	3,145
Shippensburg University of Pennsylvania; Shippensburg, Pa. 17257	5,324 (C)	Pub	2,396	3,818	2,282
Shorter College; Rome, Ga. 30161	832 (C)	P	4,930	4,930	3,770
Siena College; Loudonville, N.Y. 12211	3,596 (C)	P	7,350	7,350	4,055
Siena Heights College; Adrian, Mich. 49221	1,511 (C)	P	6,600	6,600	3,380
Sierra Nevada College; Incline Village, Nev. 89450	300 (C)	P	6,000	6,000	4,000
Silver Lake College; Manitowoc, Wis. 54220	694 (C)	P/RC	6,500	6,500	n.a.
Simmons Bible College; Louisville, Ky. 40210	103 (C)	P	520	520	n.a.
Simmons College; Boston, Mass. 02115	1,451 (W)	P	13,312	13,312	5,668
Simon's Rock of Bard College; Great Barrington, Mass. 01230	298 (C)	P	13,280	13,280	4,430
Simpson College; Indianola, Iowa 50125	1,737 (C)	P	8,900	8,900	3,075
Simpson College; Redding, Calif. 96003	242 (C)	P/CMA	5,804	5,804	3,300
Sinte Gleska College; Rosebud, S.D. 57570	485 (C)	P	1,298	1,298	n.a.
Sioux Falls College; Sioux Falls, S.D. 57105	900 (C)	P/B	6,900	6,900	2,485
Skidmore College; Saratoga Springs, N.Y. 12866	2,174 (C)	P	14,685	14,685	4,915
Slippery Rock State College. See Slippery Rock University of Pennsylvania					
Slippery Rock Univ. of Pennsylvania; Slippery Rock, Pa. 16057	6,866 (C)	Pub	2,504	4,034	2,656
Smith College; Northampton, Mass. 01063	2,660 (W)	P	13,380	13,380	5,170
Sojourner–Douglass College; Baltimore, Md. 21205	402 (C)	P	4,515	4,515	n.a.
Sonoma State University; Rohnert Park, Calif. 94928	4,983 (C)	Pub	852	4,959	4,113
South, University of the; Sewanee, Tenn. 37375	1,075 (C)	P/E	11,690	11,690	3,010
South Alabama, University of; Mobile, Ala. 36688	9,195 (C)	Pub	1,875	2,475	2,280
Southampton College. See Long Island Univ. Center					
South Carolina, University of; Columbia, S.C. 29208	15,962 (C)	Pub	2,448	5,548	2,603
South Carolina, Univ. of–Aiken; Aiken, S.C. 29801	2,528 (C)	Pub	1,700	3,540	2,340
South Carolina, Univ. of–Coastal Carolina; Conway, S.C. 29526	4,101 (C)	Pub	1,750	3,890	3,800
South Carolina, Univ. of–Spartanburg; Spartanburg, S.C. 29303	3,247 (C)	Pub	1,750	3,890	2,410
South Carolina State College; Orangeburg, S.C. 29117	3,531 (C)	Pub	1,450	2,980	2,286
South Dakota, University of; Vermillion, S.D. 57069	5,136 (C)	Pub	1,906	2,424	2,146
South Dakota School of Mines and Technology; Rapid City, S.D. 57701	1,881 (C)	Pub	2,145	3,769	1,920
South Dakota State University; Brookings, S.D. 57007	6,366 (C)	Pub	1,835	3,363	1,750
Southeast Missouri State Univ.; Cape Girardeau, Mo. 63701	7,810 (C)	Pub	1,580	3,200	2,550
Southeastern Baptist College; Laurel, Miss. 39440	79 (C)	P	2,080	2,080	1,600
Southeastern Bible College; Birmingham, Ala. 35243	296 (C)	P/ID	3,400	3,400	2,400
Southeastern College; Lakeland, Fla. 33801	1,155 (C)	P/AG	2,500	2,500	1,800
Southeastern Louisiana University; Hammond, La. 70402	8,637 (C)	Pub	1,703	3,503	2,280
Southeastern Massachusetts University; North Dartmouth, Mass. 02747	5,354 (C)	Pub	1,677	4,983	3,980
Southeastern Oklahoma State Univ.; Durant, Okla. 74701	3,616 (C)	Pub	804	1,992	1,704
Southeastern University; Washington, D.C. 20024	559 (C)	P	4,470	4,470	n.a.
Southern Arkansas University; Magnolia, Ark. 71753	2,165 (C)	Pub	1,050	1,680	2,100
Southern Baptist College; Walnut Ridge, Ark. 72476	475 (C)	P	2,706	2,706	2,258
Southern California, Univ. of; Los Angeles, Calif. 90089	15,585 (C)	P	14,375	14,375	5,650
Southern California College; Costa Mesa, Calif. 92626	828 (C)	P/AG	6,170	6,170	3,100
Southern California Institute of Architecture; Santa Monica, Calif. 90404	310 (C)	P	7,960	7,960	n.a.
Southern College of Seventh–Day Adventists; Collegedale, Tenn. 37315	1,526 (C)	P/SDA	6,650	6,650	2,864
Southern College of Technology; Marietta, Ga. 30060	3,843 (C)	Pub	1,380	3,765	3,065
Southern Colorado, University of; Pueblo, Colo. 81001	3,909 (C)	Pub	1,536	5,275	3,170
Southern Connecticut State Univ.; New Haven, Conn. 06515	6,222 (C)	Pub	1,420	3,830	3,324
Southern Illinois Univ.–Carbondale; Carbondale, Ill. 62901	20,126 (C)	Pub	2,166	5,286	2,636
Southern Illinois Univ.–Edwardsville; Edwardsville, Ill. 62026	8,552 (C)	Pub	1,798	4,720	4,520
Southern Indiana, University of; Evansville, Ind. 47714	5,713 (C)	Pub	1,664	4,036	2,750
Southern Maine, University of; Gorham, Me. 04038	9,424 (C)	Pub	1,913	5,243	3,570
Southern Methodist University; Dallas, Tex. 75275	5,749 (C)	P/UM	8,764	8,764	4,498
Southern Missionary College. See Southern College of Seventh-Day Adventists					
Southern Mississippi, Univ. of; Hattiesburg, Miss. 39406	9,379 (C)	Pub	1,834	3,016	2,280
Southern Nazarene Univ.; Bethany, Okla. 73008	1,254 (C)	P	4,200	4,200	2,688
Southern Oregon State College; Ashland, Ore. 97520	4,453 (C)	Pub	1,692	4,482	2,895
Southern University–Baton Rouge; Baton Rouge, La. 70813	9,448 (C)	Pub	1,354	2,876	2,370
Southern University–New Orleans; New Orleans, La. 70126	3,200 (C)	Pub	1,372	2,930	n.a.
Southern Utah State College; Cedar City, Utah 84720	3,600 (C)	Pub	1,345	3,596	2,070
Southern Vermont College; Bennington, Vt. 05201	635 (C)	P	6,330	6,330	3,360
South Florida, University of; Tampa, Fla. 33620	20,604 (C)	Pub	1,250	3,850	2,750
Southwest, College of the; Hobbs, N.M. 88240	215 (C)	P	2,230	2,230	2,750
Southwest Baptist University; Bolivar, Mo. 65613	2,909 (C)	P	6,917	6,917	2,210
Southwestern Adventist College; Keene, Tex. 76059	758 (C)	P	6,224	6,224	3,178
Southwestern Assemblies of God College; Waxahachie, Tex. 75165	622 (C)	P	2,600	2,600	2,500

Institution and location	Enrollment	Control	Tuition ($) Res.	Tuition ($) Nonres.	Rm/Bd ($)
Southwestern College; Winfield, Kan. 67156	663 (C)	P/UM	4,152	4,152	2,464
Southwestern Conservative Baptist Bible College; Phoenix, Ariz. 85032	163 (C)	P/B	4,090	4,090	1,850
Southwestern Louisiana, University of; Lafayette, La. 70504	14,103 (C)	Pub	1,490	3,140	1,945
Southwestern Oklahoma State Univ.; Weatherford, Okla. 73096	5,355 (C)	Pub	1,172	2,928	1,600
Southwestern University; Georgetown, Tex. 78626	1,219 (C)	P/UM	8,500	8,500	3,910
Southwest Missouri State Univ.; Springfield, Mo. 65804	17,681 (C)	Pub	1,322	2,618	2,280
Southwest State University; Marshall, Minn. 56258	2,814 (C)	Pub	1,800	3,000	2,400
Southwest Texas State Univ.; San Marcos, Tex. 78666	20,511 (C)	Pub	1,042	4,162	2,968
Spalding University; Louisville, Ky. 40203	799 (C)	P/RC	5,100	5,100	2,560
Spelman College; Atlanta, Ga. 30314	1,742 (W)	P	4,792	4,792	4,130
Spertus College of Judaica; Chicago, Ill. 60605	100 (C)	P	4,215	4,215	n.a.
Spring Arbor College; Spring Arbor, Mich. 49283	807 (C)	P	7,190	7,190	2,783
Springfield College; Springfield, Mass. 01109	2,350 (C)	P	7,854	7,854	3,600
Spring Garden College; Philadelphia, Pa. 19119	1,465 (C)	P	7,600	7,600	4,000
Spring Hill College; Mobile, Ala. 36608	932 (C)	P/RC	8,740	8,740	3,960
Stanford University; Stanford, Calif. 94305	6,457 (C)	P	14,280	14,280	5,930
Staten Island, Coll. of (NYC). See New York, City Univ. of					
Stephen F. Austin State Univ. Nacogcoches, Tex. 75962	11,471 (C)	Pub	900	3,262	2,950
Stephens College; Columbia, Mo. 65215	1,256 (W)	P	10,425	10,425	4,200
Sterling College; Sterling, Kan. 67579	503 (C)	P/PUS	6,150	6,150	2,800
Stetson University; Deland, Fla. 32720	2,113 (C)	P	8,440	8,440	3,600
Stevens Institute of Technology; Hoboken, N.J. 07030	1,600 (C)	P	14,400	14,400	4,440
Stillman College; Tuscaloosa, Ala. 35403	791 (C)	P/PUS	3,550	3,550	2,450
Stockton State College; Pomona, N.J. 08240	5,297 (C)	Pub	1,952	2,592	3,600
Stonehill College; North Easton, Mass. 02357	1,908 (C)	P/RC	9,650	9,650	5,020
Strayer College; Washington, D.C. 20036	1,185 (C)	P	3,645	3,645	n.a.
Suffolk University; Boston, Mass. 02108	2,887 (C)	P	7,328	7,328	n.a.
Susquehanna University; Selinsgrove, Pa. 17870	1,465 (C)	P/L	9,565	9,565	3,375
Swarthmore College; Swarthmore, Pa. 19081	1,302 (C)	P	14,530	14,530	4,920
Sweet Briar College; Sweet Briar, Va. 24595	579 (W)	P	10,890	10,890	4,000
Syracuse University; Syracuse, N.Y. 13210	12,577 (C)	P	11,034	11,034	5,125
Tabor College; Hillsboro, Kan. 67063	436 (C)	P/MB	5,650	5,650	2,550
Talladega College; Talladega, Ala. 35160	615 (C)	P	3,709	3,709	2,030
Tampa, University of; Tampa, Fla. 33606	2,136 (C)	P	9,260	9,260	3,600
Tampa College; Tampa, Fla. 33614	1,264 (C)	P	3,600	3,600	n.a.
Tarkio College; Tarkio, MO. 64491	553 (C)	P/UP	6,660	6,660	3,200
Tarleton State University; Stephensville, Tex. 76402	4,951 (C)	Pub	540	3,600	2,736
Taylor University; Upland, Ind. 46989	1,708 (C)	P/ID	8,648	8,648	3,357
Temple University, Philadelphia, Pa. 19122	22,336 (C)	Pub	3,514	6,172	3,596
Temple University–Ambler; Ambler, Pa. 19002	4,284 (C)	Pub	3,996	7,258	4,056
Tennessee, Univ. of–Chattanooga; Chattanooga, Tenn. 37402	6,595 (C)	Pub	1,376	4,328	4,376
Tennessee, Univ. of–Knoxville; Knoxville, Tenn. 37966	19,578 (C)	Pub	1,466	4,200	2,990
Tennessee, Univ. of–Martin; Martin, Tenn. 38238	4,700 (C)	Pub	1,430	4,364	2,360
Tennessee, Univ. of–Memphis, Health Science Center; Memphis, Tenn. 38163	326 (C)	Pub	1,644	4,650	2,892
Tennessee State University; Nashville, Tenn. 37203	7,012 (C)	Pub	1,202	3,938	2,246
Tennessee Technological Univ.; Cookeville, Tenn. 38505	7,044 (C)	Pub	1,358	4,312	1,250
Tennessee Temple University; Chattanooga, Tenn. 37404	1,400 (C)	P/B	3,560	3,560	2,800
Tennessee Wesleyan College; Athens, Tenn. 37303	601 (C)	P/UM	4,976	4,976	3,000
Texas, University of–Arlington; Arlington, Tex. 76019	19,796 (C)	Pub	850	3,346	3,700
Texas, University of–Austin; Austin, Tex. 78712	35,007 (C)	Pub	830	3,730	3,288
Texas, University of–Dallas; Richardson, Tex. 75083	4,311 (C)	Pub	886	3,990	n.a.
Texas, University of–El Paso; El Paso, Tex. 79968	13,232 (C)	Pub	925	4,045	2,600
Texas, University of–Health Science Center–San Antonio; San Antonio, Tex. 78284	691 (C)	Pub	504	3,000	n.a.
Texas, University of, Medical Branch–Galveston; Galveston, Tex. 77550	655 (C)	Pub	864	5,760	5,400
Texas, University of–Permian Basin; Odessa, Tex. 79762	1,258 (C)	Pub	855	3,975	2,900
Texas, University of–San Antonio; San Antonio, Tex. 78285	11,736 (C)	Pub	930	4,050	2,850
Texas, University of, Southwestern Medical Ctr. at Dallas; Dallas, Tex. 75235	332 (C)	Pub	990	5,400	n.a.
Texas, University of–Tyler; Tyler, Tex. 75701	2,335 (C)	Pub	861	3,695	n.a.
Texas A&I University–Kingsville; Kingsville, Tex. 78363	4,911 (C)	Pub	910	4,030	2,624
Texas A&M University; College Station, Tex. 77843	31,843 (C)	Pub	1,200	4,320	3,734
Texas A&M University at Galveston; Galveston, Tex. 77553	936 (C)	Pub	970	4,395	3,119
Texas Christian University; Fort Worth, Tex. 76129	5,684 (C)	P/DC	6,300	6,300	3,520
Texas College; Tyler, Tex. 75702	450 (C)	P/CME	1,130	1,130	2,300
Texas Lutheran College; Seguin, Tex. 78155	1,014 (C)	P	5,300	5,300	2,640
Texas Southern University; Houston, Tex. 77004	6,498 (C)	Pub	988	4,316	3,250
Texas Tech University; Lubbock, Tex. 79409	20,749 (C)	Pub	1,131	4,241	3,249
Texas Wesleyan University; Fort Worth, Tex. 76105	1,300 (C)	P/UM	4,800	4,800	3,080
Texas Woman's University; Denton, Tex. 76204	4,167 (W)	Pub	904	4,024	2,625
Thiel College; Greenville, Pa. 16125	918 (C)	P/LCA	8,310	8,310	3,990

Institution and location	Enrollment	Control	Tuition ($) Res.	Tuition ($) Nonres.	Rm/Bd ($)
Thomas A. Edison State College, Trenton, N.J. 08625	7,202 (C)	Pub	185	300	n.a.
Thomas Aquinas College; Santa Paula, Calif. 93060	176 (C)	P/RC	9,000	9,000	4,430
Thomas College; Waterville, Me. 04901	384 (C)	P	6,750	6,750	3,670
Thomas Jefferson University, College of Allied Health Sciences; Philadelphia, Pa. 19107	1,190 (C)	P	9,850	9,850	4,650
Thomas More College; Crestview Hills, Ky. 41017	1,126 (C)	P	6,950	6,950	3,210
Tiffin University; Tiffin, Ohio 44883	815 (C)	P	5,500	5,500	3,160
Toccoa Falls College; Toccoa Falls, Ga. 30598	795 (C)	P	3,910	3,910	2,530
Toledo, University of; Toledo, Ohio 43606	20,688 (C)	Pub	2,232	5,085	2,625
Tougaloo College; Tougaloo, Miss. 39174	788 (C)	P	3,879	3,879	1,550
Touro College; New York, N.Y. 10036	4,298 (C)	P	5,550	5,550	5,800
Towson State University; Towson, Md. 21204-7097	13,464 (C)	Pub	2,188	3,852	4,280
Transylvania University; Lexington, Ky. 40508	816 (C)	P/DC	8,302	8,302	3,498
Trenton State College; Trenton, N.J. 08650	6,760 (C)	Pub	2,342	2,342	4,620
Trevecca Nazarene College; Nashville, Tenn. 37210	781 (C)	P	3,990	3,990	2,368
Tri-State University; Angola, Ind. 46703	997 (C)	P	6,624	6,624	3,030
Trinity Bible College; Ellendale, N.D. 58436	456 (C)	P	3,950	3,950	2,988
Trinity Christian College; Palos Heights, Ill. 60463	534 (C)	P/CR	6,540	6,540	2,765
Trinity College; Burlington, Vt. 05401	999 (W)	P/RC	8,000	8,000	4,140
Trinity College; Deerfield, Ill. 60015	824 (C)	P/EFC	7,300	7,300	3,370
Trinity College; Hartford, Conn. 06106	1,886 (C)	P	14,300	14,300	4,200
Trinity College; Washington, D.C. 20017	906 (W)	P/RC	9,425	9,425	5,700
Trinity University; San Antonio, Tex. 78284	2,383 (C)	P	9,676	9,676	4,340
Troy State University; Troy, Ala. 36802	3,642 (C)	Pub	1,320	1,985	2,264
Troy State University-Dothan; Dothan, Ala. 36301	1,192 (C)	Pub	1,254	1,614	n.a.
Troy State University-Montgomery; Montgomery, Ala. 36195-4419	2,131 (C)	Pub	1,260	1,890	n.a.
Tufts University; Medford, Mass. 02155	4,683 (C)	P	13,975	13,975	5,120
Tulane University; New Orleans, La. 70118	7,320 (C)	P	14,230	14,230	5,150
Tulsa, University of; Tulsa, Okla. 74104	2,951 (C)	P	7,950	7,950	3,300
Tusculum College; Greeneville, Tenn. 37743	659 (C)	P/UP	5,240	5,240	2,860
Tuskegee University; Tuskegee, Ala. 36088	3,096 (C)	P	5,000	5,000	2,500
Union College; Barbourville, Ky. 40906	782 (C)	P	4,850	4,850	2,150
Union College; Lincoln, Neb. 68506	627 (C)	P/SDA	7,000	7,000	2,270
Union College; Schenectady, N.Y. 12308	2,031 (C)	P	13,355	13,355	4,695
Union Institute, The; Cincinnati, Ohio 45202-2407	300 (C)	P	6,900	6,900	n.a.
Union University; Jackson, Tenn. 38305	2,209 (C)	P/SB	4,250	4,250	2,110
U.S. Air Force Academy; Colorado Springs, Colo. 80840	4,405 (C)	Pub	1,000	1,000	—
U.S. Coast Guard Academy; New London, Conn. 06320	872 (C)	Pub	1,500	1,500	—
U.S. International University; San Diego, Calif. 92131	1,254 (C)	P	7,650	7,650	3,840
U.S. Merchant Marine Academy; Kings Point, N.Y. 11024	844 (C)	Pub	2,513	2,513	—
U.S. Military Academy; West Point, N.Y. 10996	4,322 (C)	Pub	1,000	1,000	—
U.S. Naval Academy; Annapolis, Md. 21402	4,500 (C)	Pub	1,500	1,500	—
Unity College; Unity, Me. 04988	370 (C)	P	6,050	7,350	4,100
Universidad de las Americas—Puebla; Puebla, Mexico 72820	4,488 (C)	P	4,000	4,000	1,000
Universidad Politecnica de Puerto Rico; Hato Rey, San Juan, P.R. 00918	3,116 (C)	P	(*)	(*)	n.a.
Upper Iowa University; Fayette, Iowa 52142	1,299 (C)	P	7,540	7,540	1,860
Upsala College; East Orange, N.J. 07019	1,228 (C)	P	8,500	8,500	3,500
Urbana Univ.; Urbana, Ohio 43078	315 (C)	P	6,507	6,507	3,160
Ursinus College; Collegeville, Pa. 19426	1,128 (C)	P	11,400	11,400	4,250
Ursuline College; Pepper Pike, Ohio 44124	427 (C)	P/RC	5,700	5,700	3,600
Utah, University of; Salt Lake City, Utah 84112	19,373 (C)	Pub	1,517	4,187	1,499
Utah State University; Logan, Utah 84322	10,230 (C)	Pub	1,482	4,113	2,445
Utica College of Syracuse University; Utica, N.Y. 13502	2,431 (C)	P	8,500	8,500	3,700
Valdosta State College; Valdosta, Ga. 31698	6,191 (C)	Pub	1,422	3,711	2,070
Valley City State University; Valley City, N.D. 58072	1,154 (C)	Pub	1,338	3,108	1,830
Valley Forge Christian College; Phoenixville, Pa. 19460	511 (C)	P/AG	3,135	3,135	2,494
Valparaiso University; Valparaiso, Ind. 46383	3,431 (C)	P/L	8,238	8,238	2,530
Vanderbilt University; Nashville, Tenn. 37212	5,268 (C)	P	12,625	12,625	4,695
VanderCook College of Music; Chicago, Ill. 60616	104 (C)	P	7,545	7,545	3,992
Vassar College; Poughkeepsie, N.Y. 12601	2,306 (C)	P	13,840	13,840	4,700
Vennard College; University Park, Iowa 52595	143 (C)	P	3,869	3,869	2,050
Vermont, University of; Burlington, Vt. 05401-3596	8,032 (C)	Pub	3,650	11,650	3,858
Villa Julie College; Stevenson, Md. 21153	1,459 (C)	P	4,990	4,990	n.a.
Villa Maria College; Erie, Pa. 16505	699 (W)	P	6,300	6,300	3,200
Villanova University; Villanova, Pa. 19085	6,400 (C)	P	9,800	9,800	4,800
Virginia, University of; Charlottesville, Va. 22906	11,199 (C)	Pub	2,708	7,088	3,000
Virginia, University of—Clinch Valley College; Wise, Va. 24293	1,594 (C)	Pub	1,574	2,534	2,680
Virginia Commonwealth University; Richmond, Va. 23284-2526	15,632 (C)	Pub	2,547	6,042	3,300
Virginia Intermont College; Bristol, Va. 24201	521 (C)	P/B	5,980	5,980	3,620
Virginia Military Institute; Lexington, Va. 24450	1,300 (M)	Pub	3,560	7,660	2,980

Institution and location	Enrollment	Control	Tuition ($) Res.	Tuition ($) Nonres.	Rm/Bd ($)
Virginia Polytechnic Institute and State University; Blacksburg, Va. 24061	18,149 (C)	Pub	2,730	5,706	2,464
Virginia State University; Petersburg, Va. 23803	3,308 (C)	Pub	3,071	5,135	3,602
Virginia Union University; Richmond, Va. 23220	1,112 (C)	P/B	5,311	5,311	2,634
Virginia Wesleyan College; Norfolk–Virginia Beach, Va. 23502	1,280 (C)	P/UM	8,100	8,100	4,100
Virgin Islands, University of the; St. Thomas, V.I. 00802	2,471 (C)	Pub	1,024	2,992	3,328
Visual Arts, School of; New York, N.Y. 10010	2,035 (C)	P	9,800	9,800	3,500
Viterbo College; La Crosse, Wis. 54601	1,022 (C)	P/RC	7,200	7,200	2,950
Voorhees College; Denmark, S.C. 29042	574 (C)	P/E	3,150	3,150	2,522
Wabash College; Crawfordsville, Ind. 47933	832 (M)	P	9,800	9,800	3,470
Wadhams Hall Seminary—College; Ogdensburg, N.Y. 13669	50 (M)	P	3,195	3,195	3,200
Wagner College; Staten Island, N.Y. 10301	1,380 (C)	P/L	9,250	9,250	4,700
Wake Forest University; Winston–Salem, N.C. 27109	3,541 (C)	P/B	9,700	9,700	3,550
Walla Walla College; College Place, Wash. 99324	1,528 (C)	P/SDA	8,430	8,430	3,950
Walsh College; Canton, Ohio 44720	1,444 (C)	P/RC	6,016	6,016	3,100
Walsh College of Accountancy and Business Administration; Troy, Mich. 48007	1,734 (C)	P	3,824	3,824	n.a.
Warner Pacific College; Portland, Ore. 97215	390 (C)	P/CG	7,044	7,044	3,188
Warner Southern College; Lake Wales, Fla. 33853	423 (C)	P/CG	4,610	4,610	2,580
Warren Wilson College; Swannanoa, N.C. 28778	470 (C)	P	7,500	7,500	812
Wartburg College; Waverly, Iowa 50677	1,459 (C)	P/AL	8,130	8,130	2,810
Washburn University; Topeka, Kan. 66621	5,492 (C)	Pub	2,190	3,240	2,734
Washington, University of; Seattle, Wash. 98195	24,272 (C)	Pub	1,827	5,082	3,660
Washington and Jefferson College; Washington, Pa. 15301	1,224 (C)	P	10,740	10,740	3,090
Washington and Lee University; Lexington, Va. 24450	1,592 (C)	P	10,970	10,970	3,900
Washington Bible College; Lanham, Md. 20706	321 (C)	P	4,800	4,800	2,950
Washington College; Chestertown, Md. 21620	899 (C)	P	11,400	11,400	4,600
Washington State University; Pullman, Wash. 99164	13,255 (C)	Pub	1,798	4,998	2,900
Washington University; St. Louis, Mo. 63130	4,925 (C)	P	13,600	13,600	4,610
Wayland Baptist University; Plainview, Tex. 79072	1,726 (C)	P	3,789	3,789	2,482
Waynesburg College; Waynesburg, Pa. 15370	1,155 (C)	P	6,630	6,630	2,780
Wayne State College; Wayne, Neb. 68787	2,618 (C)	Pub	1,337	2,057	2,190
Wayne State University; Detroit, Mich. 48202	20,592 (C)	Pub	2,100	4,600	2,700
Webber College; Babson Park, Fla. 33827	301 (C)	P	5,340	5,340	3,340
Webb Institute of Naval Architecture; Glen Cove, N.Y. 11542	80 (C)	P	—	—	3,750
Weber State College; Ogden, Utah 84408	12,783 (C)	Pub	1,308	3,513	2,205
Webster University; St. Louis, Mo. 63119	2,034 (C)	P	6,820	6,820	3,306
Wellesley College; Wellesley, Mass. 02181	2,200 (W)	P	14,840	14,840	5,310
Wells College; Aurora, N.Y. 13026	438 (W)	P	11,690	11,690	4,300
Wentworth Institute of Technology; Boston, Mass. 02115	3,800 (C)	P	7,079	7,079	5,334
Wesleyan College; Macon, Ga. 31297	524 (W)	P/M	8,700	8,700	3,850
Wesleyan University; Middletown, Conn. 06457	2,672 (C)	P	15,185	15,185	4,845
Wesley College; Dover, Del. 19901	1,295 (C)	P	7,255	7,255	3,725
Wesley College; Florence, Miss. 39073	65 (C)	P/M	1,700	1,700	2,000
Westbrook College; Portland, Maine 04103	458 (C)	P	8,400	8,400	4,120
West Chester Univ. of Pennsylvania; West Chester, Pa. 19383	9,770 (C)	Pub	2,398	4,254	2,956
West Coast Christian College; Fresno, Calif. 93710	274 (C)	P/CG	2,880	2,880	2,640
West Coast University; Los Angeles, Calif. 90020	850 (C)	P	7,500	7,500	n.a.
Western Baptist College; Salem, Ore. 97301	358 (C)	P/B	5,622	5,622	2,943
Western Carolina University; Cullowhee, N.C. 28723	4,992 (C)	Pub	1,028	5,400	2,180
Western Connecticut State University; Danbury, Conn. 06810	5,284 (C)	Pub	1,662	3,722	3,092
Western Illinois University; Macomb, Ill. 61455	9,724 (C)	Pub	1,791	4,455	2,445
Western International University; Phoenix, Ariz. 85021	500 (C)	P	3,960	3,960	n.a.
Western Kentucky University; Bowling Green, Ky. 42101	12,009 (C)	Pub	1,160	3,280	2,470
Western Maryland College; Westminster, Md. 21157	1,326 (C)	P	11,590	11,590	4,390
Western Michigan University; Kalamazoo, Mich. 49008	19,928 (C)	Pub	2,130	5,040	3,160
Western Montana College; Dillon, Mont. 59725	1,097 (C)	Pub	1,274	2,957	2,902
Western New England College; Springfield, Mass. 01119	2,872 (C)	P	7,468	7,468	4,456
Western New Mexico University; Silver City, N.M. 88061	1,546 (C)	Pub	966	4,100	2,230
Western Oregon State College; Monmouth, Ore. 97361	3,461 (C)	Pub	1,806	4,566	2,940
Western State College of Colorado; Gunnison, Colo. 81230	2,500 (C)	Pub	1,906	4,660	2,786
Western Washington University; Bellingham, Wash. 98225	9,322 (C)	Pub	1,611	5,649	3,200
Westfield State College; Westfield, Mass. 01085	3,043 (C)	Pub	1,413	3,909	2,822
West Florida, University of; Pensacola, Fla. 32514	5,924 (C)	Pub	1,200	3,900	3,700
West Georgia College; Carrollton, Ga. 30118	5,599 (C)	Pub	1,524	3,906	2,127
West Liberty State College; West Liberty, W. Va. 26074	2,435 (C)	Pub	1,160	2,890	2,640
West Los Angeles, University of, School of Paralegal Studies; Los Angeles, Calif. 90066	319 (C)	P	2,904	2,904	n.a.
Westmar College; Le Mars, Iowa 51031	566 (C)	P/UM	7,922	7,922	3,150
Westminster Choir College; Princeton, N.J. 08540	226 (C)	P	9,900	9,900	4,250
Westminster College; Fulton, Mo. 65251	734 (C)	P	7,700	7,700	3,300
Westminster College; New Wilmington, Pa. 16172	1,321 (C)	P/UP	9,620	9,620	2,730

Institution and location	Enrollment	Control	Tuition ($) Res.	Tuition ($) Nonres.	Rm/Bd ($)
Westminster Coll. of Salt Lake City; Salt Lake City, Utah 84105	1,551 (C)	P	6,060	6,060	4,040
Westmont College; Santa Barbara, Calif. 93108	1,251 (C)	P	10,900	10,900	4,650
West Oahu College. *See* Hawaii, University of.					
West Texas State University; Canyon, Tex. 79016	4,671 (C)	Pub	952	4,072	2,508
West Virginia Institute of Technology; Montgomery, W. Va. 25136	2,836 (C)	Pub	1,110	2,840	2,870
West Virginia State College; Institute, W. Va. 25112	4,509 (C)	Pub	1,092	2,672	2,450
West Virginia University; Morgantown, W. Va. 26506	13,769 (C)	Pub	1,692	4,222	3,389
West Virginia Wesleyan College; Buckhannon, W. Va. 26201	1,484 (C)	P/UM	10,930	10,930	3,000
Wheaton College; Norton, Mass. 02766	1,219 (C)	P	14,470	14,470	5,030
Wheaton College; Wheaton, Ill. 60187	2,229 (C)	P	8,836	8,836	3,640
Wheeling Jesuit College; Wheeling, W. Va. 26003	1,068 (C)	P	7,515	7,515	3,550
Wheelock College; Boston, Mass. 02215	691 (C)	P	9,696	9,696	4,680
White Plains, Coll. of, of Pace Univ. *See* Pace Univ.					
Whitman College; Walla Walla, Wash. 99362	1,239 (C)	P	11,920	11,920	4,130
Whittier College; Whittier, Calif. 90608	1,063 (C)	P	11,672	11,672	4,300
Whitworth College; Spokane, Wash. 99251	1,237 (C)	P/UP	9,500	9,500	3,600
Wichita State University; Wichita, Kan. 67208	13,720 (C)	Pub	1,450	3,200	2,600
Widener University; Chester, Pa. 19013	2,616 (C)	P	8,290	8,290	3,700
Wilberforce University; Wilberforce, Ohio 45384	737 (C)	P/AME	5,674	5,674	3,020
Wiley College; Marshall, Tex. 75670	557 (C)	P	3,946	3,946	2,544
Wilkes College; Wilkes-Barre, Pa. 18766	1,886 (C)	P	7,730	7,730	3,560
Willamette University; Salem, Ore. 97301	1,535 (C)	P	10,680	10,680	3,750
William and Mary, College of; Williamsburg, Va. 23185	5,300 (C)	Pub	3,156	8,382	3,578
William Carey College; Hattiesburg, Miss. 39401	1,546 (C)	P	2,885	2,885	2,000
William Jewell College; Liberty, Mo. 64068	1,426 (C)	P/B	7,450	7,450	2,530
William Paterson College; Wayne, N.J. 07470	7,441 (C)	Pub	1,776	2,376	3,316
William Penn College; Oskaloosa, Iowa 52577	671 (C)	P/F	7,500	7,500	2,550
Williams College; Williamstown, Mass. 01267	2,060 (C)	P	14,195	14,195	4,670
William Smith College. *See* Hobart and William Smith Colleges					
William Tyndale College; Farmington Hills, Mich. 48108	431 (C)	P	4,270	4,270	3,000
William Woods College; Fulton, Mo. 65251	730 (W)	P	7,400	7,400	3,200
Wilmington College; New Castle, Del. 19720	1,036 (C)	P	4,400	4,440	n.a.
Wilmington College of Ohio; Wilmington, Ohio 45177	890 (C)	P/F	7,980	7,980	3,000
Wilson College; Chambersburg, Pa. 17201-1285	713 (W)	P/UP	9,414	9,414	4,102
Wingate College; Wingate, N.C. 28174	1,534 (C)	P/SB	5,670	5,670	2,650
Winona State University; Winona, Minn. 55987	7,000 (C)	Pub	2,000	2,000	2,450
Winston-Salem State University; Winston-Salem, N.C. 27110	2,532 (C)	Pub	896	4,268	2,265
Winthrop College; Rock Hill, S.C. 29733	4,400 (C)	Pub	2,326	4,118	2,272
Wisconsin, University of—Eau Claire; Eau Claire, Wis. 54701	10,573 (C)	Pub	1,735	5,096	2,290
Wisconsin, University of—Green Bay; Green Bay, Wis. 54302	4,991 (C)	Pub	1,680	5,042	2,350
Wisconsin, University of—La Crosse; La Crosse, Wis. 54601	8,411 (C)	Pub	1,769	5,130	1,950
Wisconsin, University of—Madison; Madison, Wis. 53706	29,625 (C)	Pub	2,004	6,137	3,290
Wisconsin, University of—Milwaukee; Milwaukee, Wis. 53201	20,686 (C)	Pub	2,054	6,186	3,476
Wisconsin, University of—Oshkosh; Oshkosh, Wis. 54901	9,473 (C)	Pub	1,689	5,050	1,950
Wisconsin, University of—Parkside; Kenosha, Wis. 53141	4,896 (C)	Pub	1,698	4,059	2,756
Wisconsin, University of—Platteville; Platteville, Wis. 53818	5,080 (C)	Pub	1,658	4,740	2,030
Wisconsin, University of—River Falls; River Falls, Wis. 54022	4,583 (C)	Pub	1,755	5,116	2,292
Wisconsin, University of—Stevens Point; Stevens Point, Wis. 54481	7,872 (C)	Pub	1,777	5,138	2,488
Wisconsin, University of—Stout; Menomonie, Wis. 54751	6,779 (C)	Pub	1,776	5,136	2,158
Wisconsin, University of—Superior; Superior, Wis. 54880	2,112 (C)	Pub	1,678	5,039	2,102
Wisconsin, University of—Whitewater; Whitewater, Wis. 53190	9,147 (C)	Pub	1,760	5,120	2,096
Wisconsin Lutheran College; Milwaukee, Wis. 53226	261 (C)	P	6,860	6,860	3,100
Wittenberg University; Springfield, Ohio 45501	2,341 (C)	P	11,100	11,100	4,263
Wofford College; Spartanburg, S.C. 29301	1,121 (C)	P/UM	9,015	9,015	3,950
Woodbury University; Burbanks, Calif. 91510-7846	865 (C)	P	9,342	9,342	5,100
Wooster, College of; Wooster, Ohio 44691	1,891 (C)	P	16,420	16,420	—
Worcester Polytechnic Institute; Worcester, Mass. 01609	2,829 (C)	P	13,080	13,080	4,310
Worcester State College; Worcester, Mass. 01602	3,600 (C)	Pub	1,296	3,792	2,680
World College West; Petaluma, Calif. 94952	135 (C)	P	8,850	8,850	3,900
Wright State University; Dayton, Ohio 45435	13,940 (C)	Pub	2,244	4,488	3,432
Wyoming, University of; Laramie, Wyo. 82071	9,187 (C)	Pub	1,003	3,039	2,960
Xavier University; Cincinnati, Ohio 45207	3,779 (C)	P	9,000	9,000	3,910
Xavier University of Louisiana; New Orleans, La. 70125	2,226 (C)	P	5,500	5,500	2,900
Yale University; New Haven, Conn. 06520	5,183 (C)	P	14,000	14,000	5,310
Yeshiva University; New York, N.Y. 10033-3299	1,773 (C)	P	9,420	9,420	4,800
York College of Pennsylvania; York, Pa. 17405	2,680 (C)	P	3,760	3,760	2,598
Youngstown State Univ.; Youngstown, Ohio 44555	13,538 (C)	Pub	2,001	3,201	3,000

1. Graduate school only. 2. $15 per credit. 3. $50 per credit. 4. $79 per credit. 5. $250 per credit. 6. $74 per credit. 7. $148 per credit. 8. $65 per credit.

Selected Degree Abbreviations

A.B. Bachelor of Arts
AeEng. Aeronautical Engineer
A.M.T. Master of Arts in Teaching
B.A. Bachelor of Arts
B.A.E. Bachelor of Arts in Education, or Bachelor of Art Education, Aeronautical Engineering, Agricultural Engineering, or Architectural Engineering
B.Ag. Bachelor of Agriculture
B.A.M. Bachelor of Applied Mathematics
B.Arch. Bachelor of Architecture
B.B.A. Bachelor of Business Administration
B.C.E. Bachelor of Civil Engineering
B.Ch.E. Bachelor of Chemical Engineering
B.C.L. Bachelor of Canon Law
B.D. Bachelor of Divinity
B.E. Bachelor of Education or Bachelor of Engineering
B.E.E. Bachelor of Electrical Engineering
B.F. Bachelor of Forestry
B.F.A. Bachelor of Fine Arts
B.J. Bachelor of Journalism
B.L.S. Bachelor of Liberal Studies or Bachelor of Library Science
B.Lit. Bachelor of Literature
B.M. Bachelor of Medicine or Bachelor of Music
B.M.S. Bachelor of Marine Science
B.N. Bachelor of Nursing
B.Pharm. Bachelor of Pharmacy
B.R.E. Bachelor of Religious Education
B.S. Bachelor of Science
B.S.Ed. Bachelor of Science in Education
C.E. Civil Engineer
Ch.E. Chemical Engineer
D.B.A. Doctor of Business Administration
D.C. Doctor of Chiropractic
D.D. Doctor of Divinity[1]
D.D.S. Doctor of Dental Surgery or Doctor of Dental Science
D.L.S. Doctor of Library Science
D.M.D. Doctor of Dental Medicine
D.O. Doctor of Osteopathy
D.M.S. Doctor of Medical Science
D.P.A. Doctor of Public Administration[2]
D.P.H. Doctor of Public Health
D.R.E. Doctor of Religious Education
D.S.W. Doctor of Social Welfare or Doctor of Social Work
D.Sc. Doctor of Science[3]
D.V.M. Doctor of Veterinary Medicine
Ed.D. Doctor of Education[2]
Ed.S. Education Specialist
E.E. Electrical Engineer

E.M. Engineer of Mines
E.Met. Engineer of Metallurgy
I.E. Industrial Engineer or Industrial Engineering
J.D. Doctor of Laws[2]
J.S.D. Doctor of Juristic Science
L.H.D. Doctor of Humane Letters[3]
Litt.B. Bachelor of Letters
Litt.M. Master of Letters[4]
LL.B. Bachelor of Laws
LL.D. Doctor of Laws[3]
LL.M. Master of Laws
M.A. Master of Arts
M.Aero.E. Master of Aeronautical Engineering
M.B.A. Master of Business Administration
M.C.E. Master of Christian Education or Master of Civil Engineering
M.C.S. Master of Computer Science
M.D. Doctor of Medicine
M.Div. Master of Divinity
M.E. Master of Engineering
M.Ed. Master of Education
M.Eng. Master of Engineering
M.F.A. Master of Fine Arts
M.H.A. Master of Hospital Administration
M.L.S. Master of Library Science
M.M. Master of Music
M.M.E. Master of Mechanical Engineering or Master of Music Education
M.Mus. Master of Music
M.N. Master of Nursing
M.R.E. Master of Religious Education
M.S. Master of Science
M.S.W. Master of Social Work
M.Th. Master of Theology
Nuc.E. Nuclear Engineer
O.D. Doctor of Optometry
Pharm.D. Doctor of Pharmacy[2]
Ph.B. Bachelor of Philosophy
Ph.D. Doctor of Philosophy
S.B. Bachelor of Science
Sc.D. Doctor of Science[3]
S.J.D. Doctor of Juridical Science or Doctor of the Science of Law
S.Sc.D. Doctor of Social Science
S.T.B. Bachelor of Sacred Theology
S.T.D. Doctor of Sacred Theology
S.T.M. Master of Sacred Theology
Th.B. Bachelor of Theology
Th.D. Doctor of Theology
Th.M. Master of Theology

1. Honorary. 2. Earned and honorary. 3. Usually honorary. 4. Sometimes honorary.

Academic Costume: Colors Associated With Fields

Field	Color	Field	Color
Agriculture	Maize	Medicine	Green
Arts, Letters, Humanities	White	Music	Pink
Commerce, Accountancy, Business	Drab	Nursing	Apricot
		Oratory (Speech)	Silver gray
Dentistry	Lilac	Pharmacy	Olive green
Economics	Copper	Philosophy	Dark blue
Education	Light blue	Physical Education	Sage green
Engineering	Orange	Public Admin. including Foreign Service	Peacock blue
Fine Arts, Architecture	Brown	Public Health	Salmon pink
Forestry	Russet	Science	Golden yellow
Journalism	Crimson	Social Work	Citron
Law	Purple	Theology	Scarlet
Library Science	Lemon	Veterinary Science	Gray

1991 Special Sports Events

JANUARY

S	M	T	W	T	F	S
		1	2	3	4	5
6	7	**8**	9	10	11	12
13	14	15	16	17	18	**19**
20	**21**	22	23	24	25	26
27	28	29	30	31		

Days
1 New Year's Day
21 Martin Luther King Day
Events
1 Eight Bowl Games
8-11 NCAA Convention (Nashville)
13-26 Australian Open (Melbourne)
19 NHL All-Star Game (Chicago)
20 NFL Conference Championships
27 Super Bowl XXV (Tampa)

FEBRUARY

S	M	T	W	T	F	S
					1	**2**
3	4	5	6	7	8	9
10	11	12	**13**	**14**	15	16
17	**18**	19	20	21	22	23
24	25	26	27	28		

Days
2 Groundhog Day
13 Ash Wednesday
14 Valentine's Day
18 Presidents' Day
Events
3 NFL Pro Bowl (Honolulu)
10 NBA All-Star Game (Charlotte)
10-17 US Figure Skating
Championships
(Minneapolis)
17 Daytona 500 (Daytona Beach)

MARCH

S	M	T	W	T	F	S
					1	2
3	4	5	6	7	8	9
10	**11**	12	13	14	15	16
17	18	19	**20**	21	22	23
24	25	26	27	28	**29**	**30**
31						

Days
17 St. Patrick's Day
20 First Day of Spring
29 Good Friday
30 First Day of Passover
31 Easter Sunday
Events
11-17 World Figure Skating
Championships (Munich)
29-31 NCAA Women's Basketball
Final Four (New Orleans)
30-Apr 1 NCAA Men's Basketball
Final Four (Indianapolis)

APRIL

S	M	T	W	T	F	S
	1	2	**3**	4	5	6
7	**8**	9	10	11	12	13
14	**15**	16	17	18	19	20
21	22	23	24	**25**	26	27
28	29	30				

Days
7 Daylight Savings Begins
(Spring ahead)
Events
3 NHL Playoffs Begin
8 Baseball Opening Day
11-14 Masters Golf (Augusta)
15 Boston Marathon
21-22 NFL Draft (New York)
25 NBA Playoffs Begin

MAY

S	M	T	W	T	F	S
			1	2	3	**4**
5	6	7	8	9	10	11
12	13	14	15	16	17	**18**
19	20	21	22	23	24	25
26	**27**	28	29	30	**31**	

Days
12 Mother's Day
27 Memorial Day
Events
4 Kentucky Derby (Louisville)
18 Preakness Stakes (Baltimore)
26 Indianapolis 500
27-Jun 9 French Open Tennis (Paris)
31-Jun 8 College World Series
(Omaha)

JUNE

S	M	T	W	T	F	S
						1
2	3	4	5	6	7	**8**
9	10	11	12	**13**	**14**	15
16	17	18	19	20	**21**	22
23	**24**	25	26	27	28	29
30						

Days
14 Flag Day
16 Father's Day
21 First Day of Summer
Events
8 Belmont Stakes (Elmont, NY)
13-16 US Open Golf (Chaska, MN)
24-Jul 7 Wimbledon Tennis

JULY

S	M	T	W	T	F	S
	1	2	3	**4**	5	6
7	8	9	10	**11**	**12**	13
14	15	16	17	**18**	19	20
21	22	23	24	**25**	26	27
28	29	30	31			

Days
1 Canada Day
4 Independence Day
Events
9 Baseball All-Star Game (Toronto)
11-14 US Women's Open Golf
(Ft.Worth)
12-21 US Olympic Festival (Los Angeles)
18-21 British Open (Royal Birkdale)
25-28 US Senior Open Golf (Detroit)

AUGUST

S	M	T	W	T	F	S
				1	2	**3**
4	5	6	7	**8**	9	10
11	12	13	14	15	16	17
18	19	20	21	22	23	**24**
25	**26**	27	28	29	30	31

Events
3-18 Pan American Games
(Havana)
8-11 PGA Championship
(Carmel, IN)
24-Sep 1 World Track & Field Championships (Tokyo)
26-Sep 8 US Open Tennis
(Flushing, NY)

SEPTEMBER

S	M	T	W	T	F	S
1	**2**	3	4	5	6	7
8	**9**	10	11	12	13	14
15	16	17	**18**	19	20	21
22	**23**	24	25	26	27	28
29	30					

Days
2 Labor Day
9 First Day of Rosh Hashanah
18 Yom Kippur
23 First Day of Fall
Events
1 NFL Regular Season Opens

OCTOBER

S	M	T	W	T	F	S
		1	2	3	4	5
6	7	**8**	9	10	11	**12**
13	**14**	15	16	17	18	**19**
20	21	22	23	24	25	**26**
27	28	29	30	**31**		

Days
14 Columbus Day
27 Daylight Savings Time Ends
(Fall back)
31 Halloween
Events
6 Baseball Regular Season Ends
8 Baseball Playoffs Begin
12 Oklahoma vs Texas (Dallas)
19 World Series Begins
26 USC at Notre Dame

NOVEMBER

S	M	T	W	T	F	S
					1	**2**
3	4	**5**	6	7	8	9
10	**11**	12	13	14	15	**16**
17	18	19	20	21	**22**	**23**
24	25	26	27	**28**	29	**30**

Days
5 Election Day
11 Veteran's Day
28 Thanksgiving
Events
2 Breeders' Cup (Louisville)
3 New York City Marathon
16 Miami, FL at Florida St.
23 Harvard at Yale
Ohio St. at Michigan
Oklahoma at Nebraska
UCLA at USC
24 CFL Grey Cup (Winnipeg)
30 Alabama vs Auburn (Birmingham)

DECEMBER

S	M	T	W	T	F	S
1	**2**	3	4	5	**6**	**7**
8	9	10	11	12	13	14
15	16	17	18	19	20	21
22	**23**	24	**25**	**26**	27	**28**
29	30	31				

Days
2 First Day of Hanukkah
22 First Day of Winter
25 Christmas
26 Boxing Day (Canada)
Events
6-15 National Finals Rodeo (Las Vegas)
7 Army vs Navy (Philadelphia)
23 NFL Regular Season Ends
28 NFL Playoffs Begin

THE OLYMPIC GAMES

(W)—Site of Winter Games. (S)—Site of Summer Games

1896	Athens	1936	Berlin (S)	1972	Sapporo, Japan (W)
1900	Paris	1948	St. Moritz (W)	1972	Munich (S)
1904	St. Louis	1948	London (S)	1976	Innsbruck, Austria (W)
1906	Athens	1952	Oslo (W)	1976	Montreal (S)
1908	London	1952	Helsinki (S)	1980	Lake Placid (W)
1912	Stockholm	1956	Cortina d'Ampezzo, Italy (W)	1980	Moscow (S)
1920	Antwerp	1956	Melbourne (S)	1984	Sarajevo, Yugoslavia (W)
1924	Chamonix (W)	1960	Squaw Valley, Calif. (W)	1984	Los Angeles (S)
1924	Paris (S)	1960	Rome (S)	1988	Calgary, Alberta (W)
1928	St. Moritz (W)	1964	Innsbruck, Austria (W)	1988	Seoul, South Korea (S)
1928	Amsterdam (S)	1964	Tokyo (S)	1992	Albertville, France (W)
1932	Lake Placid (W)	1968	Grenoble, France (W)	1992	Barcelona, Spain (S)
1932	Los Angeles (S)	1968	Mexico City (S)	1994	Lillehammer, Norway (W)
1936	Garmisch-Partenkirchen (W)				

The first Olympic Games of which there is record were held in 776 B.C., and consisted of one event, a great foot race of about 200 yards held on a plain by the River Alpheus (now the Ruphia) just outside the little town of Olympia in Greece. It was from that date that the Greeks began to keep their calendar by "Olympiads," the four-year spans between the celebrations of the famous games.

The modern Olympic Games, which started in Athens in 1896, are the result of the devotion of a French educator, Baron Pierre de Coubertin, to the idea that, since young people and athletics have gone together through the ages, education and athletics might go hand-in-hand toward a better international understanding.

The principal organization responsible for the staging of the Games every four years is the International Olympic Committee (IOC). Other important roles are played by the National Olympic Committees in each participating country, international sports federations, and the organizing committee of the host city.

The headquarters of the 89-member International Olympic Committee are in Lausanne, Switzerland. The president of the IOC is Juan Antonio Samaranch of Spain.

The Olympic motto is "Citius, Altius, Fortius,"—"Faster, Higher, Stronger." The Olympic symbol is five interlocking circles colored blue, yellow, black, green, and red, on a white background, representing the five continents. At least one of those colors appears in the national flag of every country.

The ideal of peaceful international athletic competition has been severely tested in past Olympiads, dating back to the 1972 raid by Arab terrorists on the Olympic village in Munich, Germany. Eleven Israelis, five terrorists, and a German police officer were all killed in the seige.

In 1976, political problems kept one-quarter of the IOC-member nations from competing. The most pressing was the conflict over recognition of Taiwan or Mainland China as the correct representative of that country. An additional 31 nations withdrew over the failure to bar New Zealand, which had a soccer team touring apartheid South Africa.

A total of 66 nations, including the United States, did not participate in 1980, over the Soviet Union's invasion of Afghanistan. Those Summer Games were scheduled for Moscow.

Considering this action, it was almost inevitable that the Soviet Union would take some similar action for the 1984 games, held in Los Angeles. Officially, the Soviet Union, and nearly the entire Soviet-communist bloc, withdrew over dissatisfaction with security measures in Los Angeles.

The 1988 Summer Olympics were held in Seoul, South Korea. For the first time since 1976, all the Eastern bloc countries competed against the nations of the West.

Winter Games

FIGURE SKATING—MEN

1908	Ulrich Salchow, Sweden
1920	Gillis Grafstrom, Sweden
1924	Gillis Grafstrom, Sweden
1928	Gillis Grafstrom, Sweden
1932	Karl Schaefer, Austria
1936	Karl Schaefer, Austria
1948	Richard Button, United States
1952	Richard Button, United States
1956	Hayes Alan Jenkins, United States
1960	David Jenkins, United States
1964	Manfred Schnelldorfer, Germany
1968	Wolfgang Schwartz, Austria
1972	Ondrej Nepela, Czechoslovakia
1976	John Curry, Great Britain
1980	Robin Cousins, Great Britain
1984	Scott Hamilton, United States
1988	Brian Boitano, United States

FIGURE SKATING—WOMEN

1908	Madge Syers, Britain
1920	Magda Julin–Maurey, Sweden
1924	Herma Szabo-Planck, Austria
1928	Sonja Henie, Norway
1932	Sonja Henie, Norway
1936	Sonja Henie, Norway
1948	Barbara Ann Scott, Canada
1952	Jeannette Altwegg, Great Britain
1956	Tenley Albright, United States
1960	Carol Heiss, United States
1964	Sjoukje Dijkstra, Netherlands
1968	Peggy Fleming, United States

1972	Beatrix Schuba, Austria
1976	Dorothy Hamill, United States
1980	Anett Poetzsch, East Germany
1984	Katarina Witt, East Germany
1988	Katarina Witt, East Germany

SPEED SKATING—MEN

(U.S. winners only)

500 Meters

1924	Charles Jewtraw	44.0
1932	John A. Shea	43.4
1952	Kenneth Henry	43.2
1964	Terrence McDermott	40.1
1980	Eric Heiden	38.03

1,000 Meters

| 1976 | Peter Mueller | 1:19.32 |
| 1980 | Eric Heiden | 1:15.18 |

1,500 Meters

| 1932 | John A. Shea | 2:57.5 |
| 1980 | Eric Heiden | 1:55.44 |

5,000 Meters

| 1932 | Irving Jaffee | 9:40.8 |
| 1980 | Eric Heiden | 7:02.29 |

10,000 Meters

| 1932 | Irving Jaffee | 19:13.6 |
| 1980 | Eric Heiden | 14:28.13 |

SPEED SKATING—WOMEN

500 Meters

1972	Anne Henning	43.33
1976	Sheila Young	42.76
1988	Bonnie Blair,	39.10[1]

1,500 Meters

| 1972 | Dianne Holum | 2:20.85 |

1. World Record

SKIING, ALPINE—MEN

Downhill

1948	Henri Oreiller, France	2m55.0s
1952	Zeno Colo, Italy	2m30.8s
1956	Anton Sailer, Austria	2m52.2s
1960	Jean Vuarnet, France	2m06.2s
1964	Egon Zimmermann, Austria	2m18.16s
1968	Jean-Claude Killy, France	1m59.85s
1972	Bernhard Russi, Switzerland	1m51.43s
1976	Franz Klammer, Austria	1m45.72s
1980	Leonhard Stock, Austria	1m45.50s
1984	Bill Johnson, United States	1m45.59s
1988	Pirmin Zurbriggen, Switzerland	1m59.63s

Slalom

| 1948 | Edi Reinalter, Switzerland | 2m10.3s |
| 1952 | Othmar Schneider, Austria | 2m00.0s |

DISTRIBUTION OF MEDALS
1988 WINTER GAMES

(Calgary, Alberta)

	Gold	Silver	Bronze	Total
Soviet Union	11	9	9	29
East Germany	9	10	6	25
Switzerland	5	5	5	15
Austria	3	5	2	10
West Germany	2	4	2	8
Finland	4	1	2	7
Netherlands	3	2	2	7
Sweden	4	0	2	6
United States	2	1	3	6
Italy	2	1	2	5
Norway	0	3	2	5
Canada	0	2	3	5
Yugoslavia	0	2	1	3
Czechoslovakia	0	1	2	3
France	1	0	1	2
Japan	0	0	1	1
Liechtenstein	0	0	0	1

1956	Anton Sailer, Austria	194.7 pts.
1960	Ernst Hinterseer, Austria	2m08.9s
1964	Josef Stiegler, Austria	2m10.13
1968	Jean-Claude Killy, France	1m39.73s
1972	Francisco Fernandez Ochoa, Spain	1m49.27s
1976	Piero Gros, Italy	2m03.29s
1980	Ingemar Stenmark, Sweden	1m44.26s
1984	Phil Mahre, United States	1m39.41s
1988	Alberto Tomba, Italy	1m39.47s

Giant Slalom

1952	Stein Eriksen, Norway	2m25.0s
1956	Anton Sailer, Austria	3m00.1s
1960	Roger Staub, Switzerland	1m48.3s
1964	François Bonlieu, France	1m46.71s
1968	Jean-Claude Killy, France	3m29.28s
1972	Gustavo Thoeni, Italy	3m09.52s
1976	Heini Hemmi, Switzerland	3m26.97s
1980	Ingemar Stenmark, Sweden	2m40.74s
1984	Max Julen, Switzerland	1m20.54s
1988	Alberto Tomba, Italy	2m06.37s

SKIING, ALPINE—WOMEN

Downhill

1948	Hedi Schlunegger, Switzerland	2m28.3s
1952	Trude Jochum-Beiser, Austria	1m47.1s
1956	Madeleine Berthod, Switzerland	1m40.1s
1960	Heidi Biebl, Germany	1m37.6s
1964	Christl Haas, Austria	1m55.39s
1968	Olga Pall, Austria	1m40.87s
1972	Marie-Therese Nadig, Switzerland	1m36.68s
1976	Rosi Mittermeier, West Germany	1m46.16s
1980	Annemarie Proell Moser, Austria	1m37.52s
1984	Michela Figini, Switzerland	1m13.36s
1988	Marina Kiehl, West Germany	1m25.86s

Slalom

1948	Gretchen Fraser, United States	1m57.2s
1952	Andrea Mead Lawrence, United States	2m10.6s
1956	Renee Colliard, Switzerland	112.3 pts.
1960	Anne Heggtveigt, Canada	1m49.6s
1964	Christine Goitschel, France	1m29.86s
1968	Marielle Goitschel, France	1m25.86s
1972	Barbara Cochran, United States	1m31.24s

1976	Rosi Mittermeier, West Germany	1m30.54s
1980	Hanni Wenzel, Liechtenstein	1m25.09s
1984	Paoletta Magoni, Italy	1m36.47s
1988	Vreni Schneider, Switzerland	1m36.69s

Giant Slalom

1952	Andrea M. Lawrence, United States	2m06.8s
1956	Ossi Reichert, Germany	1m56.5s
1960	Yvonne Ruegg, Switzerland	1m39.9s
1964	Marielle Goitschel, France	1m52.24s
1968	Nancy Greene, Canada	1m51.97s
1972	Marie-Therese Nadig, Switzerland	1m29.90s
1976	Kathy Kreiner, Canada	1m29.13s
1980	Hanni Wenzel, Liechtenstein	2m41.66s
1984	Debbie Armstrong, United States	2m20.98s
1988	Vreni Schneider, Switzerland	2m06.49s

SKIING, NORDIC, JUMPING

90-Meter Hill

		Points
1924	Jacob T. Thams, Norway	227.5
1928	Alfred Andersen, Norway	230.5
1932	Birger Ruud, Norway	228.0
1936	Birger Ruud, Norway	232.0
1948	Peter Hugsted, Norway	228.1
1952	A. Bergmann, Norway	226.0
1956	Antti Hyvarinen, Finland	227.0
1960	Helmut Recknagel, Germany	227.2
1964	Toralf Engan, Norway	230.7
1968	Vladimir Beloussov, U.S.S.R.	231.3
1972	Wojciech Fortuna, Poland	219.9
1976	Karl Schnabl, Austria	234.8
1980	Jouko Tormanen, Finland	271.0
1984	Matti Nykanen, Finland	231.2
1988	Matti Nykanen, Finland	224.0

Small Hill (70 meters)

1964	Veikko Kankkonen, Finland	229.9
1968	Jiri Raska, Czechoslovakia	216.5
1972	Yukio Kasaya, Japan	244.2
1976	Hans-Georg Aschenbach, East Germany	252.0
1980	Anton Innauer, Austria	266.3
1984	Jens Weissflog, East Germany	215.2
1988	Matti Nykanen, Finland	229.1

ICE HOCKEY

1920	Canada	1960	United States
1924	Canada	1964	U.S.S.R.
1928	Canada	1968	U.S.S.R.
1932	Canada	1972	U.S.S.R.
1936	Great Britain	1976	U.S.S.R.
1948	Canada	1980	United States
1952	Canada	1984	U.S.S.R.
1956	U.S.S.R.	1988	U.S.S.R.

FINAL OVER-ALL 1988 OLYMPIC HOCKEY STANDINGS

	W	L	T	Pts	GF	GA
1. Soviet Union	4	1	0	8	25	7
2. Finland	3	1	1	7	18	10
3. Sweden	2	1	2	6	16	18
Canada	2	2	1	5	17	14
West Germany	1	4	0	2	8	26
Czechoslovakia	1	4	0	2	12	22

1. won gold medal 2. won silver medal 3. won bronze medal

Championship
Soviet Union 7, Sweden 1

Second Place
Finland 2, Soviet Union 1

Third Place
Sweden 3, West Germany 2

Fourth Place
Canada 6, Czechoslovakia 3

Seventh Place
United States 8, Switzerland 4

Ninth Place
Austria 3, Poland 2

Other 1988 Winter Olympic Games Champions

Biathlon
10-kilometer—Frank-Peter Roetsch, East Germany
20 kilometer—Frank-Peter Roetsch, East Germany
30-kilometer relay—Soviet Union

Bobsledding
2-man—U.S.S.R. I
4-man—Switzerland I

Figure Skating
Pairs—Ekaterina Gordeeva and Sergeir Grinkov, U.S.S.R.
Dance—Natalia Bestemianova and Andrei Boukine, U.S.S.R.

Speed Skating—Men
500m—Jens-Uew Mey, East Germany
1,000m—Nikolai Gouliaev, U.S.S.R.
1,500m—Andre Hoffmann, East Germany
5,000m—Tomas Gustafson, Sweden
10,000m—Tomas Gustafson, Sweden

Speed Skating—Women
500m—Bonnie Blair, United States
1,000m—Christa Rothenberger, East Germany

1,500m—Yvonne Van Gennip, The Netherlands
3,000m—Yvonne Van Gennip, The Netherlands
5,000m—Yvonne Van Gennip, The Netherlands

Luge
Men's singles—Jens Mueller, East Germany
Men's doubles—Joerg Hoffmann and Jochen Pietzsch, East Germany

Skiing, Nordic—Men
Combined team—West Germany
Combined—Hippolyt Kempf, Switzerland
Men's 15-kilometer—Mikhail Deviatiarov, U.S.S.R.
Men's 30-kilometer—Alexei Prokourorov, U.S.S.R.
Men's 50-kilometer—Gunde Svan, Sweden
40-kilometer relay—Sweden
70-m jump—Matti Nykaenen, Finland
90-m jump—Matti Nykaenen, Finland

Skiing, Nordic—Women
Women's 5-kilometer—Marjo Matikainen, Finland
Women's 10-kilometer—Vida Ventsene, U.S.S.R.
Women's 20-kilometer—Tamara Tikhonova, U.S.S.R.
20-kilometer relay—U.S.S.R.

Summer Games

TRACK AND FIELD—MEN

100-Meter Dash

1896	Thomas Burke, United States	12s
1900	Francis W. Jarvis, United States	10.8s
1904	Archie Hahn, United States	11s
1906	Archie Hahn, United States	11.2s
1908	Reginald Walker, South Africa	10.8s
1912	Ralph Craig, United States	10.8s
1920	Charles Paddock, United States	10.8s
1924	Harold Abrahams, Great Britain	10.6s
1928	Percy Williams, Canada	10.8s
1932	Eddie Tolan, United States	10.3s
1936	Jesse Owens, United States	10.3s[1]
1948	Harrison Dillard, United States	10.3s
1952	Lindy Remigino, United States	10.4s
1956	Bobby Morrow, United States	10.5s
1960	Armin Hary, Germany	10.2s
1964	Robert Hayes, United States	10s
1968	James Hines, United States	9.9s
1972	Valery Borzov, U.S.S.R.	10.14s
1976	Hasely Crawford, Trinidad and Tobago	10.06s
1980	Allan Wells, Britain	10.25s
1984	Carl Lewis, United States	9.99s
1988	Carl Lewis, United States	9.92s[2]

1. Wind assisted. 2. Lewis was awarded the gold medal when Ben Johnson of Canada, the original winner in 09.79s, was stripped of his medal after testing positive for steroid use.

200-Meter Dash

1900	John Tewksbury, United States	22.2s
1904	Archie Hahn, United States	21.6s
1908	Robert Kerr, Canada	22.6s
1912	Ralph Craig, United States	21.7s
1920	Allan Woodring, United States	22s
1924	Jackson Scholz, United States	21.6s
1928	Percy Williams, Canada	21.8s
1932	Eddie Tolan, United States	21.2s
1936	Jesse Owens, United States	20.7s
1948	Melvin E. Patton, United States	21.1s
1952	Andrew Stanfield, United States	20.7s
1956	Bobby Morrow, United States	20.6s
1960	Livio Berruti, Italy	20.5s
1964	Henry Carr, United States	20.3s
1968	Tommie Smith, United States	19.8s
1972	Valery Borzov, U.S.S.R.	20s
1976	Don Quarrie, Jamaica	20.23s
1980	Pietro Mennea, Italy	20.19s
1984	Carl Lewis, United States	19.80s
1988	Joe DeLoach, United States	19.75s

400-Meter Dash

1896	Thomas Burke, United States	54.2s
1900	Maxwell Long, United States	49.4s
1904	Harry Hillman, United States	49.2s
1906	Paul Pilgrim, United States	53.2s
1908	Wyndham Halswelle, Great Britain (walkover)	50s
1912	Charles Reidpath, United States	48.2s
1920	Bevil Rudd, South Africa	49.6s
1924	Eric Liddell, Great Britain	47.6s
1928	Ray Barbuti, United States	47.8s
1932	William Carr, United States	46.2s
1936	Archie Williams, United States	46.5s
1948	Arthur Wint, Jamaica, B.W.I.	46.2s
1952	George Rhoden, Jamaica, B.W.I.	45.9s
1956	Charles Jenkins, United States	46.7s
1960	Otis Davis, United States	44.9s
1964	Mike Larrabee, United States	45.1s
1968	Lee Evans, United States	43.8s
1972	Vincent Matthews, United States	44.66s

1976	Alberto Juantorena, Cuba	44.26s
1980	Viktor Markin, U.S.S.R.	44.60s
1984	Alonzo Babers, United States	44.27s
1988	Steve Lewis, United States	43.87s

800-Meter Run

1896	Edwin Flack, Australia	2m11s
1900	Alfred Tysoe, Great Britain	2m1.4s
1904	James Lightbody, United States	1m56s
1906	Paul Pilgrim, United States	2m1.2s
1908	Mel Sheppard, United States	1m52.8s
1912	Ted Meredith, United States	1m51.9s
1920	Albert Hill, Great Britain	1m53.4s
1924	Douglas Lowe, Great Britain	1m52.4s
1928	Douglas Lowe, Great Britain	1m51.8s
1932	Thomas Hampson, Great Britain	1m49.8s
1936	John Woodruff, United States	1m52.9s
1948	Malvin Whitfield, United States	1m49.2s
1952	Malvin Whitfield, United States	1m49.2s
1956	Tom Courtney, United States	1m47.7s
1960	Peter Snell, New Zealand	1m46.3s
1964	Peter Snell, New Zealand	1m45.1s
1968	Ralph Doubell, Australia	1m44.3s
1972	David Wottle, United States	1m45.9s
1976	Alberto Juantorena, Cuba	1m43.5s
1980	Steve Ovett, Britain	1m45.4s
1984	Joaquin Cruz, Brazil	1m43.0s
1988	Paul Ereng, Kenya	1m43.45s

1,500-Meter Run

1896	Edwin Flack, Australia	4m33.2s
1900	Charles Bennett, Great Britain	4m6s
1904	James Lightbody, United States	4m5.4s
1906	James Lightbody, United States	4m12s
1908	Mel Sheppard, United States	4m3.4s
1912	Arnold Jackson, Great Britain	3m56.8s
1920	Albert Hill, Great Britain	4m1.8s
1924	Paavo Nurmi, Finland	3m53.6s
1928	Harry Larva, Finland	3m53.2s
1932	Luigi Beccali, Italy	3m51.2s
1936	Jack Lovelock, New Zealand	3m47.8s
1948	Henri Eriksson, Sweden	3m49.8s
1952	Joseph Barthel, Luxembourg	3m45.2s
1956	Ron Delany, Ireland	3m41.2s
1960	Herb Elliott, Australia	3m35.6s
1964	Peter Snell, New Zealand	3m38.1s
1968	Kipchoge Keino, Kenya	3m34.9s
1972	Pekka Vasala, Finland	3m36.3s
1976	John Walker, New Zealand	3m39.17s
1980	Sebastian Coe, Britain	3m38.4s
1984	Sebastian Coe, Britain	3m32.53s
1988	Peter Rono, Kenya	3m35.96s

5,000-Meter Run

1912	Hannes Kolehmainen, Finland	14m36.6s
1920	Joseph Guillemot, France	14m55.6s
1924	Paavo Nurmi, Finland	14m31.2s
1928	Willie Ritola, Finland	14m38s
1932	Lauri Lehtinen, Finland	14m30s
1936	Gunnar Hockert, Finland	14m22.2s
1948	Gaston Reiff, Belgium	14m17.6s
1952	Emil Zatopek, Czechoslovakia	14m6.6s
1956	Vladimir Kuts, U.S.S.R.	13m39.6s
1960	Murray Halberg, New Zealand	13m43.4s
1964	Bob Schul, United States	13m48.8s
1968	Mohamed Gammoudi, Tunisia	14m.05s
1972	Lasse Viren, Finland	13m26.4s
1976	Lasse Viren, Finland	13m24.76s
1980	Miruts Yifter, Ethiopia	13m21s
1984	Saud Aouita, Morocco	13m5.59s

1988   John Ngugi, Kenya   13m11.70s

10,000-Meter Run

1912	Hannes Kolehmainen, Finland	31m20.8s
1920	Paavo Nurmi, Finland	31m45.8s
1924	Willie Ritola, Finland	30m23.2s
1928	Paavo Nurmi, Finland	30m18.8s
1932	Janusz Kusocinski, Poland	30m11.4s
1936	Ilmari Salminen, Finland	30m15.4s
1948	Emil Zatopek, Czechoslovakia	29m59.6s
1952	Emil Zatopek, Czechoslovakia	29m17s
1956	Vladimir Kuts, U.S.S.R.	28m45.6s
1960	Peter Bolotnikov, U.S.S.R.	28m32.2s
1964	Billy Mills, United States	28m24.4s
1968	Naftali Temu, Kenya	29m27.4s
1972	Lasse Viren, Finland	27m38.4s
1976	Lasse Viren, Finland	27m40.38s
1980	Miruts Yifter, Ethiopia	27m42.7s
1984	Alberto Cova, Italy	27m47.5s
1988	Mly Brahim Boutaib, Morocco	27m21.46s

Marathon

1896	Spiridon Loues, Greece	2h58m50s
1900	Michel Teato, France	2h59m45s
1904	Thomas Hicks, United States	3h28m53s
1906	William J. Sherring, Canada	2h51m23.65s
1908	John J. Hayes, United States	2h55m18.4s
1912	Kenneth McArthur, South Africa	2h36m54.8s
1920	Hannes Kolehmainen, Finland	2h32m35.8s
1924	Albin Stenroos, Finland	2h41m22.6s
1928	A. B. El Quafi, France	2h32m57s
1932	Juan Zabala, Argentina	2h31m36s
1936	Kitei Son, Japan	2h29m19.2s
1948	Delfo Cabrera, Argentina	2h34m51.6s
1952	Emil Zatopek, Czechoslovakia	2h23m3.2s
1956	Alain Mimoun, France	2h25m
1960	Abebe Bikila, Ethiopia	2h15m16.2s
1964	Abebe Bikila, Ethiopia	2h12m11.2s
1968	Mamo Wold, Ethiopia	2h20m26.4s
1972	Frank Shorter, United States	2h12m19.8s
1976	Walter Cierpinski, East Germany	2h09m55s
1980	Walter Cierpinski, East Germany	2h11m3s
1984	Carlos Lopes, Portugal	2hr9m.55s
1988	Gelindo Bordin, Italy	2hr10m47s

110-Meter Hurdles

1896	Thomas Curtis, United States	17.6s
1900	Alvin Kraenzlein, United States	15.4s
1904	Frederick Schule, United States	16s
1906	R. G. Leavitt, United States	16.2s
1908	Forrest Smithson, United States	15s
1912	Frederick Kelly, United States	15.1s
1920	Earl Thomson, Canada	14.8s
1924	Daniel Kinsey, United States	15s
1928	Sydney Atkinson, South Africa	14.8s
1932	George Saling, United States	14.6s
1936	Forrest Towns, United States	14.2s
1948	William Porter, United States	13.9s
1952	Harrison Dillard, United States	13.7s
1956	Lee Calhoun, United States	13.5s
1960	Lee Calhoun, United States	13.8s
1964	Hayes Jones, United States	13.6s
1968	Willie Davenport, United States	13.3s
1972	Rodney Milburn, United States	13.24s
1976	Guy Drut, France	13.30s
1980	Thomas Munkett, East Germany	13.39s
1984	Roger Kingdom, United States	13.20s
1988	Roger Kingdom, United States	12.98s

200-Meter Hurdles

| 1900 | Alvin Kraenzlein, United States | 25.4s |
| 1904 | Harry Hillman, United States | 24.6s |

400-Meter Hurdles

1900	John Tewksbury, United States	57.6s
1904	Harry Hillman, United States	53s
1908	Charles Bacon, United States	55s
1920	Frank Loomis, United States	54s
1924	F. Morgan Taylor, United States	52.6s
1928	Lord David Burghley, Great Britain	53.4s
1932	Robert Tisdall, Ireland	51.8s[1]
1936	Glenn Hardin, United States	52.4s
1948	Roy Cochran, United States	51.1s
1952	Charles Moore, United States	50.8s
1956	Glenn Davis, United States	50.1s
1960	Glenn Davis, United States	49.3s
1964	Rex Cawley, United States	49.6s
1968	David Hemery, Great Britain	48.1s
1972	John Akii-Bua, Uganda	47.8s
1976	Edwin Moses, United States	47.64s
1980	Volker Beck, East Germany	48.70s
1984	Edwin Moses, United States	47.75s
1988	Andre Phillips, United States	47.19s

1. Record not allowed.

2,500-Meter Steeplechase

| 1900 | George Orton, United States | 7m34s |
| 1904 | James Lightbody, United States | 7m39.6s |

3,000-Meter Steeplechase

1920	Percy Hodge, Great Britain	10m0.4s
1924	Willie Ritola, Finland	9m33.6s
1928	Toivo Loukola, Finland	9m21.8s
1932	Volmari Iso-Hollo, Finland	10m33.4s[1]
1936	Volmåri Iso-Hollo, Finland	9m3.8s
1948	Thure Sjoestrand, Sweden	9m4.6s
1952	Horace Ashenfelter, United States	8m45.4s
1956	Chris Brasher, Great Britain	8m41.2s
1960	Zdzislaw Krzyskowiak, Poland	8m34.2s
1964	Gaston Roelants, Belgium	8m30.8s
1968	Amos Biwott, Kenya	8m51s
1972	Kipchoge Keino, Kenya	8m23.6s
1976	Anders Gardervd, Sweden	8m08.02s
1980	Bronislaw Malinowski, Poland	8m9.7s
1984	Julius Korir, Kenya	8m11.80s
1988	Julius Karluki, Kenya	8m05.51s

1. About 3,450 meters—extra lap by error.

10,000-Meter Walk

1912	George Goulding, Canada	46m28.4s
1920	Ugo Frigerio, Italy	48m6.2s
1924	Ugo Frigerio, Italy	47m49s
1948	John Mikaelsson, Sweden	45m13.2s
1952	John Mikaelsson, Sweden	45m2.8s

20,000-Meter Walk

1956	Leonid Spirin, U.S.S.R.	1h31m27.4s
1960	Vladimir Golubnichy, U.S.S.R.	1h34m7.2s
1964	Ken Mathews, Great Britain	1h29m34s
1968	Vladimir Golubnichy, U.S.S.R.	1h33m58.4s
1972	Peter Frenkel, East Germany	1h26m42.4s
1976	Daniel Bautista, Mexico	1h24m40.6s
1980	Maurizio Damiliano, Italy	1h23m35.5s
1984	Ernesto Conto, Mexico	1m23.13s
1988	Jozef Pribilinec, Czechoslovakia	1h19m57s

50,000-Meter Walk

1932	Thomas W. Green, Great Britain	4h50m10s
1936	Harold Whitlock, Great Britain	4h30m41.1s
1948	John Ljunggren, Sweden	4h41m52s
1952	Giuseppe Dordoni, Italy	4h28m7.8s
1956	Norman Read, New Zealand	4h30m42.8s
1960	Donald Thompson, Great Britain	4h25m30s
1964	Abdon Pamich, Italy	4h11m12.4s
1968	Christoph Hohne, East Germany	4h20m13.6s
1972	Bern Kannernberg, West Germany	3h56m11.6s

1980	Hartwig Gauder, East Germany	3h49m24s
1984	Raul Gonzalez, Mexico	3hr47m26s
1988	Viacheslau Ivanenko, U.S.S.R.	3hr38m29s

400-Meter Relay (4 × 100)

1912	Great Britain	42.4s
1920	United States	42.2s
1924	United States	41s
1928	United States	41s
1932	United States	40s
1936	United States	39.8s
1948	United States	40.6s
1952	United States	40.1s
1956	United States	39.5s
1960	Germany	39.5s
1964	United States	39s
1968	United States	38.2s
1972	United States	38.19s
1976	United States	38.33s
1980	U.S.S.R.	38.26s
1984	United States	37.83s
1988	U.S.S.R.	38.19s

1,600-Meter Relay (4 × 400)

1912	United States	3m16.6s
1920	Great Britain	3m22.2s
1924	United States	3m16s
1928	United States	3m14.2s
1932	United States	3m8.2s
1936	Great Britain	3m9s
1948	United States	3m10.4s
1952	Jamaica, B.W.I.	3m3.9s
1956	United States	3m4.8s
1960	United States	3m2.2s
1964	United States	3m0.7s
1968	United States	2m56.1s
1972	Kenya	2m59.8s
1976	United States	2m58.65s
1980	U.S.S.R.	3m01.1s
1984	United States	2m57.91s
1988	United States	2m56.16s

Team Race

		Pts
1900	Great Britain (5,000 meters)	26
1904	United States (4 miles)	27
1908	Great Britain (3 miles)	6
1912	United States (3,000 meters)	9
1920	United States (3,000 meters)	10
1924	Finland (3,000 meters)	9

Standing High Jump

1900	Ray Ewry, United States	5 ft 5 in.
1904	Ray Ewry, United States	4 ft 11 in.
1906	Ray Ewry, United States	5 ft 1 5/8 in.
1908	Ray Ewry, United States	5 ft 2 in.
1912	Platt Adams, United States	5 ft 4 1/8 in.

Running High Jump

1896	Ellery Clark, United States	5 ft 11 1/4 in.
1900	Irving Baxter, United States	6 ft 2 3/4 in.
1904	Samuel Jones, United States	5 ft 11 in.
1906	Con Leahy, Ireland	5 ft 9 7/8 in.
1908	Harry Porter, United States	6 ft 3 in.
1912	Alma Richards, United States	6 ft 4 in.
1920	Richmond Landon, United States	6 ft 4 1/4 in.
1924	Harold Osborn, United States	6 ft 5 15/16 in.
1928	Robert W. King, United States	6 ft 4 3/8 in.
1932	Duncan McNaughton, Canada	6 ft 5 5/8 in.
1936	Cornelius Johnson, United States	6 ft 7 15/16 in.
1948	John Winter, Australia	6 ft 6 in.
1952	Walter Davis, United States	6 ft 8 5/16 in.
1956	Charles Dumas, United States	6 ft 11 1/4 in.
1960	Robert Shavlakadze, U.S.S.R.	7 ft 1 in.

1964	Valeri Brumel, U.S.S.R.	7 ft 1 3/4 in.
1968	Dick Fosbury, United States	7 ft 4 1/4 in.
1972	Yuri Tarmak, U.S.S.R.	7 ft 3 3/4 in.
1976	Jacek Wszola, Poland	(2.25m) 7 ft 4 1/2 in.
1980	Gerd Wessig, East Germany	7 ft 8 3/4 in.
1984	Dietmar Mogenburg, West Germany	7 ft 8 1/2 in.
1988	Guennadi Avdeenko, U.S.S.R.	7 ft 9 1/2 in.

Long Jump

1896	Ellery Clark, United States	20 ft 9 3/4 in.
1900	Alvin Kraenzlein, United States	23 ft 6 7/8 in.
1904	Myer Prinstein, United States	24 ft 1 in.
1906	Myer Prinstein, United States	23 ft 7 1/2 in.
1908	Frank Irons, United States	24 ft 6 1/2 in.
1912	Albert Gutterson, United States	24 ft 11 1/4 in.
1920	William Pettersson, Sweden	23 ft 5 1/2 in.
1924	DeHart Hubbard, United States	24 ft 5 1/8 in.
1928	Edward B. Hamm, United States	25 ft 4 3/4 in.
1932	Edward Gordon, United States	25 ft 3/4 in.
1936	Jesse Owens, United States	26 ft. 5 5/16 in.
1948	Willie Steele, United States	25 ft 8 in.
1952	Jerome Biffle, United States	24 ft 10 in.
1956	Gregory Bell, United States	25 ft 8 1/4 in.
1960	Ralph Boston, United States	26 ft 7 3/4 in.
1964	Lynn Davies, Great Britain	26 ft 5 3/4 in.
1968	Bob Beamon, United States	29 ft 2 1/2 in.
1972	Randy Williams, United States	27 ft 1/2 in.
1976	Arnie Robinson, United States	(8.35m) 24 ft 7 3/4 in.
1980	Lutz Dombrowski, E. Germany	28 ft 1/4 in.
1984	Carl Lewis, United States	28 ft 1/4 in.
1988	Carl Lewis, United States	28 ft 7 1/4 in.

Triple Jump

1896	James B. Connolly, United States	45 ft
1900	Myer Prinstein, United States	47 ft 4 1/4 in.
1904	Myer Prinstein, United States	47 ft
1906	P. G. O'Connor, Ireland	46 ft 2 in.
1908	Timothy Ahearne, Great Britain	48 ft 11 1/4 in.
1912	Gustaf Lindblom, Sweden	48 ft 5 1/8 in.
1920	Vilho Tuulos, Finland	47 ft 6 7/8 in.
1924	Archie Winter, Australia	50 ft 11 1/8 in.
1928	Mikio Oda, Japan	49 ft 10 13/16 in.
1932	Chuhei Nambu, Japan	51 ft 7 in.
1936	Naoto Tajima, Japan	52 ft 5 7/8 in.
1948	Arne Ahman, Sweden	50 ft 6 1/4 in.
1952	Adhemar da Silva, Brazil	53 ft 2 1/2 in.
1956	Adhemar da Silva, Brazil	53 ft 7 1/2 in.
1960	Jozef Schmidt, Poland	55 ft 1 3/4 in.
1964	Jozef Schmidt, Poland	55 ft 3 1/4 in.
1968	Viktor Saneyev, U.S.S.R.	57 ft 3/4 in.
1972	Viktor Saneyev, U.S.S.R.	56 ft 11 in.
1976	Viktor Saneyev, U.S.S.R.	(17.29m) 56 ft 8 3/4 in.
1980	Jaak Uudmae, U.S.S.R.	56 ft 11 1/8 in.
1984	Al Joyner, United States	56 ft 7 1/2 in.
1988	Hristo Markov, Bulgaria	57 ft 9 1/4 in.

Pole Vault

1896	William Hoyt, United States	10 ft 9 3/4 in.
1900	Irving Baxter, United States	10 ft 9 7/8 in.
1904	Charles Dvorak, United States	11 ft 6 in.
1906	Fernand Gouder, France	11 ft 6 in.
1908	Alfred Gilbert, United States, and Edward Cook, United States (tie)	12 ft 2 in.
1912	Harry Babcock, United States	12 ft 11 1/2 in.
1920	Frank Foss, United States	13 ft 5 9/16 in.
1924	Lee Barnes, United States	12 ft 11 1/2 in.
1928	Sabin W. Carr, United States	13 ft 9 3/8 in.
1932	William Miller, United States	14 ft 1 7/8 in.
1936	Earle Meadows, United States	14 ft 3 1/4 in.
1948	Guinn Smith, United States	14 ft 1 1/4 in.
1952	Robert Richards, United States	14 ft 11 1/8 in.
1956	Robert Richards, United States	14 ft 11 1/2 in.
1960	Don Bragg, United States	15 ft 5 1/8 in.

1964	Fred Hansen, United States	16 ft 8 3/4 in.
1968	Bob Seagren, United States	17 ft 8 1/2 in.
1972	Wolfgang Nordwig, East Germany	18 ft 1/2 in.
1976	Tadeusz Slusarski, Poland	(5.50m) 18 ft 1/2 in.
1980	Wladyslaw Kozakiewicz, Poland	18 ft 11 1/2 in.
1984	Pierre Quinon, France	18 ft 10 1/4 in.
1988	Sergei Bubka, U.S.S.R.	19 ft. 4 1/4 in.

16-lb Shot-Put

1896	Robert Garrett, United States	36 ft 9 3/4 in.
1900	Richard Sheldon, United States	46 ft 3 1/8 in.
1904	Ralph Rose, United States	48 ft 7 in.
1906	Martin Sheridan, United States	40 ft 4 4/5 in.
1908	Ralph Rose, United States	46 ft 7 1/2 in.
1912	Pat McDonald, United States	50 ft 4 in.
1920	Ville Porhola, Finland	48 ft 7 1/8 in.
1924	Clarence Houser, United States	49 ft 2 1/2 in.
1928	John Kuck, United States	52 ft 11 11/16 in.
1932	Leo Sexton, United States	52 ft 6 3/16 in.
1936	Hans Woellke, Germany	53 ft 1 3/4 in.
1948	Wilbur Thompson, United States	56 ft 2 in.
1952	Parry O'Brien, United States	57 ft 1 1/2 in.
1956	Parry O'Brien, United States	60 ft 11 in.
1960	Bill Nieder, United States	64 ft 6 3/4 in.
1964	Dallas Long, United States	66 ft 8 1/4 in.
1968	Randy Matson, United States	67 ft 4 3/4 in.
1972	Wladyslaw Komar, Poland	69 ft 6 in.
1976	Udo Beyer, East Germany	(21.05m) 69 ft 3/4 in.
1980	Vladimir Kiselyov, U.S.S.R.	70 ft 1/2 in.
1984	Alessandro Andrei, Italy	69 ft 9 in.
1988	Uhf Timmerman, East Germany	73 ft 8 3/4 in.

Discus Throw

1896	Robert Garrett, United States	95 ft 7 1/2 in.
1900	Rudolf Bauer, Hungary	118 ft 2 7/8 in.
1904	Martin Sheridan, United States	128 ft 10 1/2 in.
1906	Martin Sheridan, United States	136 ft 1/3 in.
1908	Martin Sheridan, United States	134 ft 2 in.
1912	Armas Taipale, Finland	145 ft 9/16 in.
1920	Elmer Niklander, Finland	146 ft 7 in.
1924	Clarence Houser, United States	151 ft 5 1/4 in.
1928	Clarence Houser, United States	155 ft 2 4/5 in.
1932	John Anderson, United States	162 ft 4 7/8 in.
1936	Ken Carpenter, United States	165 ft 7 3/8 in.
1948	Adolfo Consolini, Italy	173 ft 2 in.
1952	Simeon Iness, United States	180 ft 6 1/2 in.
1956	Al Oerter, United States	184 ft 10 1/2 in.
1960	Al Oerter, United States	194 ft 2 in.
1964	Al Oerter, United States	200 ft 1 1/2 in.
1968	Al Oerter, United States	212 ft 6 in.
1972	Ludvik Danek, Czechoslovakia	211 ft 3 in.
1976	Mac Wilkins, United States	(67.5m) 221 ft 5 in.
1980	Viktor Rashchupkin, U.S.S.R.	218 ft 8 in.
1984	Rolf Dannenberg, West Germany	218 ft 6 in.
1988	Jurgen Schult, East Germany	225 ft 9 1/4 in.

Javelin Throw

1906	Eric Lemming, Sweden	175 ft 6 in.
1908	Eric Lemming, Sweden	179 ft 10 1/2 in.
1912	Eric Lemming, Sweden	198 ft 11 1/4 in.
1920	Jonni Myyra, Finland	215 ft 9 3/4 in.
1924	Jonni Myyra, Finland	206 ft 6 3/4 in.
1928	Eric Lundquist, Sweden	218 ft 6 1/8 in.
1932	Matti Jarvinen, Finland	238 ft 7 in.
1936	Gerhard Stoeck, Germany	235 ft 8 5/16 in.
1948	Kaj Rautavaara, Finland	228 ft 10 1/2 in.
1952	Cy Young, United States	242 ft 3/4 in.
1956	Egil Danielsen, Norway	281 ft 2 1/4 in.
1960	Viktor Tsibulenko, U.S.S.R.	277 ft 8 3/8 in.
1964	Pauli Nevala, Finland	271 ft 2 1/4 in.
1968	Janis Lusis, U.S.S.R.	295 ft 7 in.
1972	Klaus Wolfermann, West Germany	296 ft 10 in.
1976	Miklos Nemeth, Hungary	(94.58m) 310 ft 4 in.

1980	Dainis Kula, U.S.S.R.	299 ft 2 3/8 in.
1984	Arto Haerkoenen, Finland	284 ft 8 in.
1988	Tapio Korjus, Finland	276 ft 6 in.

16-lb Hammer Throw

1900	John Flanagan, United States	167 ft 4 in.
1904	John Flanagan, United States	168 ft 1 in.
1908	John Flanagan, United States	170 ft 4 1/4 in.
1912	Matt McGrath, United States	179 ft 7 1/8 in.
1920	Pat Ryan, United States	173 ft 5 5/8 in.
1924	Fred Tootell, United States	174 ft 10 1/4 in.
1928	Patrick O'Callaghan, Ireland	168 ft 7 1/2 in.
1932	Patrick O'Callaghan, Ireland	176 ft 11 1/8 in.
1936	Karl Hein, Germany	185 ft 4 in.
1948	Imre Nemeth, Hungary	183 ft 11 1/2 in.
1952	Jozsef Csermak, Hungary	197 ft 11 9/16 in.
1956	Harold Connolly, United States	207 ft 2 3/4 in.
1960	Vasily Rudenkov, U.S.S.R.	220 ft 1 5/8 in.
1964	Romuald Klim, U.S.S.R.	228 ft 9 1/2 in.
1968	Gyula Zsivotzky, Hungary	240 ft 8 in.
1972	Anatoly Bondarchuk, U.S.S.R.	247 ft 8 1/2 in.
1976	Yuri Sedykh, U.S.S.R.	(77.52m) 254 ft 4 in.
1980	Yuri Sedykh, U.S.S.R.	(81.80m) 268 ft 4 1/2 in.
1984	Juha Tiainen, Finland	256 ft 2 in.
1988	Sergei Litvinov, U.S.S.R.	278 ft 2 1/2 in.

Decathlon

1912	Jim Thorpe, United States	—
	Hugo Wieslander, Sweden	—
1920	Helge Lovland, Norway	6,804.35 pts.
1924	Harold Osborn, United States	7,710.775 pts.
1928	Paavo Yrjola, Finland	8,053.29 pts.
1932	James Bausch, United States	8,462.23 pts.
1936	Glenn Morris, United States	7,900 pts.[1]
1948	Robert B. Mathias, United States	7,139 pts.
1952	Robert B. Mathias, United States	7,887 pts.
1956	Milton Campbell, United States	7,937 pts.
1960	Rafer Johnson, United States	8,392 pts.
1964	Willi Holdorf, Germany	7,887 pts.[1]
1968	Bill Toomey, United States	8,193 pts.
1972	Nikolai Avilov, U.S.S.R.	8,454 pts.
1976	Bruce Jenner, United States	8,618 pts.
1980	Daley Thompson, Britain	8,495 pts.
1984	Daley Thompson, Britain	8,797 pts.
1988	Christian Schenk, East Germany	8,488 pts.

1. Point system revised.

TRACK AND FIELD—WOMEN

100-Meter Dash

1928	Elizabeth Robinson, United States	12.2s
1932	Stella Walsh, Poland	11.9s
1936	Helen Stephens, United States	11.5s
1948	Fanny Blankers-Koen, Netherlands	11.9s
1952	Marjorie Jackson, Australia	11.5s
1956	Betty Cuthbert, Australia	11.5s
1960	Wilma Rudolph, United States	11s
1964	Wyomia Tyus, United States	11.4s
1968	Wyomia Tyus, United States	11s
1972	Renate Stecher, East Germany	11.07s
1976	Annegret Richter, West Germany	11.08s
1980	Lyudmila Kondratyeva, U.S.S.R.	11.06s
1984	Evelyn Ashford, United States	10.97s
1988	Florence Griffith-Joyner, United States	10.54s

200-Meter Dash

1948	Fanny Blankers-Koen, Netherlands	24.4s
1952	Marjorie Jackson, Australia	23.7s
1956	Betty Cuthbert, Australia	23.4s
1960	Wilma Rudolph, United States	24s
1964	Edith McGuire, United States	23s

1968	Irena Szewinska, Poland	22.5s
1972	Renate Stecher, East Germany	22.4s
1976	Baerbel Eckert, East Germany	22.37s
1980	Barbara Wockel, East Germany	22.03s
1984	Valerie Brisco-Hooks, United States	21.81s
1988	Florence Griffith-Joyner, United States	21.34s

400-Meter Dash

1964	Betty Cuthbert, Australia	52s
1968	Colette Besson, France	52s
1972	Monika Zehrt, East Germany	51.08s
1976	Irena Szewinska, Poland	49.29s
1980	Marita Koch, East Germany	48.88s
1984	Valerie Brisco-Hooks, United States	48.83s
1988	Olga Bryzguina, U.S.S.R.	48.65s

800-Meter Run

1928	Lina Radke, Germany	2m16.8s
1960	Ljudmila Shevcova, U.S.S.R.	2m4.3s
1964	Ann Packer, Great Britain	2m1.1s
1968	Madeline Manning, United States	2m0.9s
1972	Hildegard Falck, West Germany	1m58.6s
1976	Tatiana Kazankina, U.S.S.R.	1m54.94s
1980	Nadezhda Olizarenko, U.S.S.R.	1m53.5s
1984	Doina Melinte, Romania	1m57.60s
1988	Sigrun Wodars, East Germany	1m56.10s

1,500-Meter Run

1972	Ludmila Bragina, U.S.S.R.	4m01.4s
1976	Tatiana Kazankina, U.S.S.R.	4m05.48s
1980	Tatiana Kazankina, U.S.S.R.	3m56.6s
1984	Gabriella Dorio, Italy	4m03.25s
1988	Paula Ivan, Romania	3m53.96s

3,000-Meter Run

1984	Maricica Puica, Romania	8m35.96s
1988	Tatiana Samolenko, U.S.S.R.	8m26.53s

80-Meter Hurdles

1932	Mildred Didrikson, United States	11.7s
1936	Trebisonda Valla, Italy	11.7s
1948	Fanny Blankers-Koen, Netherlands	11.2s
1952	Shirley S. de la Hunty, Australia	10.9s
1956	Shirley S. de la Hunty, Australia	10.7s
1960	Irina Press, U.S.S.R.	10.8s
1964	Karin Balzer, Germany	10.5s[1]
1968	Maureen Caird, Australia	10.3s

1. Wind assisted.

100-Meter Hurdles

1972	Annelie Ehrhardt, East Germany	12.59s
1976	Johanna Schaller, East Germany	12.77s
1980	Vera Komisova, U.S.S.R.	12.56s
1984	Benita Fitzgerald-Brown, United States	12.84s
1988	Jordanka Donkova, Bulgaria	12.38s

400-Meter Hurdle

1984	Nawai El Moutawakel, Morocco	54.61s
1988	Debra Flintoff-King, Australia	53.17s

400-Meter Relay

1928	Canada	48.4s
1932	United States	47s
1936	United States	46.9s
1948	Netherlands	47.5s
1952	United States	45.9s
1956	Australia	44.5s
1960	United States	44.5s
1964	Poland	43.6s
1968	United States	42.8s
1972	West Germany	42.81s

1976	East Germany	42.55s
1980	East Germany	41.60s
1984	United States	41.65s
1988	United States	41.98s

1,600-Meter Relay

1972	East Germany	3m23s
1976	East Germany	3m19.23s
1980	U.S.S.R.	3m20.2s
1984	United States	3m18.29s
1988	U.S.S.R.	3m15.18s

Marathon

1984	Joan Benoit, United States	2 hr 24 m 52s
1988	Rosa Mota, Portugal	2 hr 25 m 40s

Running High Jump

1928	Ethel Catherwood, Canada	5 ft 3 in.
1932	Jean Shiley, United States	5 ft 5 1/4 in.
1936	Ibolya Csak, Hungary	5 ft 3 in.
1948	Alice Coachman, United States	5 ft 6 1/8 in.
1952	Ester Brand, South Africa	5 ft 5 3/4 in.
1956	Mildred McDaniel, United States	5 ft 9 1/4 in.
1960	Iolanda Balas, Romania	6 ft 3/4 in.
1964	Iolanda Balas, U.S.S.R.	6 ft 2 3/4 in.
1968	Miloslava Rezkova, Czechoslovakia	5 ft 11 3/4 in.
1972	Ulrike Meyfarth, West Germany	6 ft 3 5/8 in.
1976	Rosemarie Ackerman, E. Germany	(1.93m) 6 ft 4 in.
1980	Sara Simeoni, Italy	6 ft 5 1/2 in.
1984	Ulrike Meyfarth, West Germany	6 ft 7 1/2 in.
1988	Louise Ritter, United States	6 ft 8 in.

Long Jump

1948	Olga Gyarmati, Hungary	18 ft 8 1/4 in.
1952	Yvette Williams, New Zealand	20 ft 5 3/4 in.
1956	Elzbieta Krzesinska, Poland	20 ft 9 3/4 in.
1960	Vera Krepkina, U.S.S.R.	20 ft 10 3/4 in.
1964	Mary Rand, Great Britain	22 ft 2 in.
1968	Viorica Ciscopoleanu, Romania	22 ft 4 1/2 in.
1972	Heidemarie Rosendahl, West Germany	22 ft 3 in.
1976	Angela Voigt, East Germany	(6.72m) 22 ft 1/2 in.
1980	Tatiana Kolpakova, U.S.S.R.	23 ft 2 in.
1984	Anisoara Stanciu, Romania	22 ft 10 in.
1988	Jackie Joyner-Kersee, United States	24 ft 3 1/2 in.

Shot-Put

1948	Micheline Ostermeyer, France	45 ft 1 1/2 in.
1952	Galina Zybina, U.S.S.R.	50 ft 1 1/2 in.
1956	Tamara Tishkyevich, U.S.S.R.	54 ft 5 in.
1960	Tamara Press, U.S.S.R.	56 ft 9 7/8 in.
1964	Tamara Press, U.S.S.R.	59 ft 6 in.
1968	Margitta Gummel, East Germany	64 ft 4 in.
1972	Nadezhda Chizhova, U.S.S.R.	69 ft
1976	Ivanka Christova, Bulgaria	(21.16m) 69 ft 5 in.
1980	Ilona Sluplanek, East Germany	73 ft 6 in.
1984	Claudia Losch, West Germany	67 ft 2 1/4 in.
1988	Natalya Lisovskaya, U.S.S.R.	72 ft 11 1/2 in.

Discus Throw

1928	Helena Konopacka, Poland	129 ft 11 7/8 in.
1932	Lillian Copeland, United States	133 ft 2 in.
1936	Gisela Mauermayer, Germany	156 ft 3 3/16 in.
1948	Micheline Ostermeyer, France	137 ft 6 1/2 in.
1952	Nina Romaschkova, U.S.S.R.	168 ft 8 7/16 in.
1956	Olga Fikotova, Czechoslovakia	176 ft 1 1/2 in.
1960	Nina Ponomareva, U.S.S.R.	180 ft 8 1/4 in.
1964	Tamara Press, U.S.S.R.	187 ft 10 3/4 in.
1968	Lia Manoliu, Romania	191 ft 2 1/2 in.
1972	Faina Melnik, U.S.S.R.	218 ft 7 in.

1976	Evelin Schlaak, East Germany	(69.0m) 226 ft 4 in.
1980	Evelin Jahl, East Germany	229 ft 6 1/2 in.
1984	Ria Stalman, Netherlands	214 ft 5 in.
1988	Martina Hellmann, East Germany	237 ft 2 1/4 in.

Javelin Throw

1932	Mildred Didrikson, United States	143 ft 4 in.
1936	Tilly Fleischer, Germany	148 ft 2 3/4 in.
1948	Herma Bauma, Austria	149 ft 6 in.
1952	Dana Zatopek, Czechoslovakia	165 ft 7 in.
1956	Inessa Janzeme, U.S.S.R.	176 ft 8 in.
1960	Elvira Ozolina, U.S.S.R.	183 ft 8 in.
1964	Mihaela Penes, Romania	198 ft 7 1/2 in.
1968	Angela Nemeth, Hungary	198 ft 0 in.
1972	Ruth Fuchs, East Germany	209 ft 7 in.
1976	Ruth Fuchs, East Germany	(65.94m) 216 ft 4 in.
1980	Maria Colon, Cuba	224 ft 5 in.
1984	Tessa Sanderson, Britain	228 ft 2 in.
1988	Petra Felke, East Germany	245 ft

Pentathlon

1964	Irina Press, U.S.S.R.	5,246 pts.
1968	Ingrid Becker, West Germany	5,098 pts.
1972	Mary Peters, Britain	4,801 pts.
1976	Siegrun Siegl, East Germany	4,745 pts.
1980	Nadyezhda Tkachenko, U.S.S.R.	5,083 pts.
1984	Daniele Masala, Italy	5,469 pts.
1988	Jackie Joyner-Kersee, United States	7,291 pts.

SWIMMING—MEN

50 Meter Freestyle

| 1988 | Matt Biondi, United States | 22.14s |

100 Meter Freestyle

1896	Alfred Hajos, Hungary	1m22.2s
1904	Zoltan de Halmay, Hungary	1m2.8s[1]
1906	Charles Daniels, United States	1m13s
1908	Charles Daniels, United States	1m5.6s
1912	Duke P. Kahanamoku, United States	1m3.4s
1920	Duke P. Kahanamoku, United States	1m1.4s
1924	John Weissmuller, United States	59s
1928	John Weissmuller, United States	58.6s
1932	Yasuji Miyazaki, Japan	58.2s
1936	Ferenc Csik, Hungary	57.6s
1948	Walter Ris, United States	57.3s
1952	Clarke Scholes, United States	57.4s
1956	Jon Henricks, Australia	55.4s
1960	John Devitt, Australia	55.2s
1964	Don Schollander, United States	53.4s
1968	Michael Wenden, Australia	52.2s
1972	Mark Spitz, United States	51.22s
1976	Jim Montgomery, United States	49.99s
1980	Jorg Woithe, East Germany	50.40s
1984	Rowdy Gaines, United States	49.80s
1988	Matt Brondi, United States	48.63s

1. 100 yards.

200-Meter Freestyle

1900	Frederick Lane, Australia	2m25.2s
1904	Charles Daniels, United States	2m44.2s[1]
1968	Michael Wenden, Australia	1m55.2s
1972	Mark Spitz, United States	1m52.78s
1976	Bruce Furniss, United States	1m50.29s
1980	Sergei Kopliakov, U.S.S.R.	1m49.81s
1984	Michael Gross, West Germany	1m47.44s
1988	Duncan Armstrong, Australia	1m47.25s

1. 220 yards.

400-Meter Freestyle

1896	Paul Neumann, Austria	8m12.6s[1]
1904	Charles Daniels, United States	6m16.2s[2]
1906	Otto Sheff, Austria	6m23.8s
1908	Henry Taylor, Great Britain	5m36.8s
1912	George Hodgson, Canada	5m24.4s

1920	Norman Ross, United States	5m26.8s
1926	Jonn Weissmuller, United States	5m4.2s
1928	Albert Zorilla, Argentina	5m1.6s
1932	Clarence Crabbe, United States	4m48.4s
1936	Jack Medica, United States	4m44.5s
1948	William Smith, United States	4m41s
1952	Jean Boiteux, France	4m30.7s
1956	Murray Rose, Australia	4m27.3s
1960	Murray Rose, Australia	4m18.3s
1964	Don Schollander, United States	4m12.2s
1968	Mike Burton, United States	4m9s
1972	Bradford Cooper, Australia	4m00.27s[3]
1976	Brian Goodell, United States	3m51.93s
1980	Vladimir Salnikov, U.S.S.R.	3m51.31s
1984	George DiCarlo, United States	3m51.23s
1988	Uwe Dassier, East Germany	3m46.95s

1. 500 meters. 2. 440 yards. 3. Rick DeMont, United States, won but was disqualified following day for medical reasons.

1,500 Meter Freestyle

1904	Emil Rausch, Germany	27m18.2s[1]
1906	Henry Taylor, Great Britain	28m28s[2]
1908	Henry Taylor, Great Britain	22m48.4s
1912	George Hodgson, Canada	22m
1920	Norman Ross, United States	22m23.2s
1924	Andrew Charlton, Australia	20m6.6s
1928	Arne Borg, Sweden	19m51.8s
1932	Kusuo Kitamura, Japan	19m12.4s
1936	Noboru Terada, Japan	19m13.7s
1948	James McLane, United States	19m18.5s
1952	Ford Konno, United States	18m30s
1956	Murray Rose, Australia	17m58.9s
1960	Jon Konrads, Australia	17m19.6s
1964	Robert Windle, Australia	17m1.7s
1968	Michael Burton, United States	16m38.9s
1972	Michael Burton, United States	15m52.58s
1976	Brian Goodell, United States	15m02.4s
1980	Vladimir Salnikov, U.S.S.R.	14m58.27s
1984	Michael O'Brien, United States	15m05.2s
1988	Vladimir Salnikov, U.S.S.R.	15m00.4s

1. One mile. 2. 1,600 meters

100-Meter Backstroke

1904	Walter Brack, Germany	1m16.8s[1]
1908	Arno Bieberstein, Germany	1m24.6s
1912	Harry Hebner, United States	1m21.2s
1920	Warren Kealoha, United States	1m15.2s
1924	Warren Kealoha, United States	1m13.2s
1928	George Kojac, United States	1m8.2s
1932	Masaji Kiyokawa, Japan	1m8.6s
1936	Adolph Kiefer, United States	1m5.9s
1948	Allen Stack, United States	1m6.4s
1952	Yoshinobu Oyakawa, United States	1m5.4s
1956	David Thiele, Australia	1m2.2s
1960	David Thiele, Australia	1m1.9s
1968	Roland Matthes, East Germany	58.7s
1972	Roland Matthes, East Germany	56.58s
1976	John Naber, United States	55.49s
1980	Bengt Baron, Sweden	56.53s
1984	Rick Carey, United States	55.79s
1988	Daichi Suzuki, Japan	55.05s

1. 100 yards

200-Meter Backstroke

1900	Ernst Hoppenberg, Germany	2m47s
1964	Jed Graef, United States	2m10.3s
1968	Roland Matthes, East Germany	2m9.6s
1972	Roland Matthes, East Germany	2m2.82s
1976	John Naber, United States	1m59.19s
1980	Sandor Wladar, Hungary	2:01.93s
1984	Rick Carey, United States	2m00.23s
1988	Igor Polianski, U.S.S.R.	1m59.37s

100-Meter Breaststroke

1968	Donald McKenzie, United States	1m7.7s
1972	Nobutaka Taguchi, Japan	1m4.94s
1976	John Hencken, United States	1m03.11s
1980	Duncan Goodhew, Britain	1m03.34s
1984	Steve Lindquist, United States	1m01.65s
1988	Adrian Moorhouse, Great Britain	1m02.04s

200-Meter Breaststroke

1908	Frederick Holman, Great Britain	3m9.2s
1912	Walter Bathe, Germany	3m1.8s
1920	Haken Malmroth, Sweden	3m4.4s
1924	Robert Skelton, United States	2m56.6s
1928	Yoshiyuki Tsuruta, Japan	2m48.8s
1932	Yoshiyuki Tsuruta, Japan	2m45.4s
1936	Tetsuo Hamuro, Japan	2m41.5s
1948	Joseph Verdeur, United States	2m39.3s
1952	John Davies, Australia	2m34.4s
1956	Masura Furukawa, Japan	2m34.7s
1960	Bill Mulliken, United States	2m37.4s
1964	Ian O'Brien, Australia	2m27.8s
1968	Felipe Munoz, Mexico	2m28.7s
1972	John Hencken, United States	2m21.55s
1976	David Wilkie, Britain	2m15.11s
1980	Robertas Zulpa, U.S.S.R.	2m15.85s
1984	Victor Davis, Canada	2m13.34s
1988	Jozsef Szabo, Hungary	2m13.52s

100-Meter Butterfly

1968	Douglas Russell, United States	55.9s
1972	Mark Spitz, United States	54.27s
1976	Matt Vogel, United States	54.35s
1980	Par Arvidsson, Sweden	54.92s
1984	Michael Gross, West Germany	53.08s
1988	Anthony Nesty, Surinam	53.0s

200-Meter Butterfly

1956	Bill Yorzyk, United States	2m19.3s
1960	Mike Troy, United States	2m12.8s
1964	Kevin Berry, Australia	2m6.6s
1968	Carl Robie, United States	2m8.7s
1972	Mark Spitz, United States	2m00.7s
1976	Mike Bruner, United States	1m59.23s
1980	Sergei Fesenko, U.S.S.R.	1m59.76s
1984	Jon Sieben, Australia	1m57.0s
1988	Michael Gross, East Germany	1m56.94s

200-Meter Individual Medley

1968	Charles Hickcox, United States	2m12s
1972	Gunnar Larsson, Sweden	2m7.17s
1988	Tamas Darnyi, Hungary	2m0.17s

400-Meter Individual Medley

1964	Dick Roth, United States	4m45.4s
1968	Charles Hickcox, United States	4m48.4s
1972	Gunnar Larsson, Sweden	4m31.98s
1976	Rod Strachan, United States	4m23.68s
1980	Aleksandr Sidorenko, U.S.S.R.	4m22.8s
1984	Alex Baumann, Canada	4m17.41s
1988	Tamas Darnyi, Hungary	4m14.75s

400-Meter Freestyle Relay

1964	United States	3m32.2s
1968	United States	3m31.7s
1972	United States	3m26.42s
1988	United States	3m16.53s

800-Meter Freestyle Relay

1908	Great Britain	10m55.6s
1912	Australia	10m11.2s
1920	United States	10m4.4s
1924	United States	9m53.4s
1928	United States	9m36.2s
1932	Japan	8m58.4s
1936	Japan	8m51.5s
1948	United States	8m46s
1952	United States	8m31.1s
1956	Australia	8m23.6s
1960	United States	8m10.2s
1964	United States	7m52.1s
1968	United States	7m52.3s
1972	United States	7m35.78s
1976	United States	7m23.22s
1980	U.S.S.R.	7m23.50s
1984	United States	7m16.59s
1988	United States	7m12.51s

400-Meter Medley Relay

1960	United States	4m5.4s
1964	United States	3m58.4s
1968	United States	3m54.9s
1972	United States	3m48.16s
1976	United States	3m42.22s
1980	Australia	3m45.70s
1984	United States	3m39.30s
1988	United States	3m36.93s

Springboard Dive

		Points
1908	Albert Zuerner, Germany	85.5
1912	Paul Guenther, Germany	79.23
1920	Louis Kuehn, United States	675
1924	Albert White, United States	696.4
1928	Pete Desjardins, United States	185.04
1932	Michael Galitzen, United States	161.38
1936	Richard Degener, United States	163.57
1948	Bruce Harlan, United States	163.64
1952	David Browning, United States	205.59
1956	Robert Clotworthy, United States	159.56
1960	Gary Tobian, United States	170.00
1964	Ken Sitzberger, United States	159.90
1968	Bernard Wrightson, United States	170.15
1972	Vladimir Vasin, U.S.S.R.	594.00
1976	Phil Boggs, United States	619.05
1980	Alexsandr Portnov, U.S.S.R.	905.02
1984	Greg Louganis, United States	754.41
1988	Greg Louganis, United States	730.80

Platform Dive

		Points
1904	G. E. Sheldon, United States	12.75
1906	Gottlob Walz, Germany	156
1908	Hialmar Johansson, Sweden	83.75
1912	Erik Adlerz, Sweden	73.94
1920	Clarence Pinkston, United States	100.67
1924	Albert White, United States	487.3
1928	Pete Desjardins, United States	98.74
1932	Harold Smith, United States	124.80
1936	Marshall Wayne, United States	113.58
1948	Samuel Lee, United States	130.05
1952	Samuel Lee, United States	156.28
1956	Joaquin Capilla, Mexico	152.44
1960	Bob Webster, United States	165.56
1964	Bob Webster, United States	148.58
1968	Klaus Dibiasi, Italy	164.18
1972	Klaus Dibiasi, Italy	504.12
1976	Klaus Dibiasi, Italy	600.51
1980	Falk Hoffman, E. Germany	835.65
1984	Greg Louganis, United States	710.91
1988	Greg Louganis, United States	638.61

SWIMMING—WOMEN

50-Meter Freestyle

1988	Kristin Otto, East Germany	25.49s

100-Meter Freestyle

1912	Fanny Durack, Australia	1m22.2s

1920	Ethelda Bleibtrey, United States	1m13.6s
1924	Ethel Lackie, United States	1m12.4s
1928	Albina Osipowich, United States	1m11s
1932	Helene Madison, United States	1m6.8s
1936	Hendrika Mastenbroek, Netherlands	1m5.9s
1948	Greta Andersen, Denmark	1m6.3s
1952	Katalin Szoke, Hungary	1m6.8s
1956	Dawn Fraser, Australia	1m2s
1960	Dawn Fraser, Australia	1m1.2s
1964	Dawn Fraser, Australia	59.5s
1968	Marge Jan Henne, United States	1m
1972	Sandra Neilson, United States	58.59s
1976	Kornelia Ender, East Germany	55.65s
1980	Barbara Krause, East Germany	54.79s
1984	Carrie Steinseifer, United States	55.92s
1988	Kristin Otto, East Germany	54.93s

200-Meter Freestyle

1968	Debbie Meyer, United States	2m10.5s
1972	Shane Gould, Australia	2m3.56s
1976	Kornelia Ender, East Germany	1m59.26s
1980	Barbara Krause, East Germany	1m58.33s
1984	Mary Wayle, United States	1m59.23s
1988	Heike Friedrich, East Germany	1m57.65s

400-Meter Freestyle

1920	Ethelda Bleibtrey, United States	4m34s[1]
1924	Martha Norelius, United States	6m2.2s
1928	Martha Norelius, United States	5m42.8s
1932	Helene Madison, United States	5m28.5s
1936	Hendrika Mastenbroek, Netherlands	5m26.4s
1948	Ann Curtis, United States	5m17.8s
1952	Valerie Gyenge, Hungary	5m12.1s
1956	Lorraine Crapp, Australia	4m54.6s
1960	Chris von Saltza, United States	4m50.6s
1964	Ginny Duenkel, United States	4m43.3s
1968	Debbie Meyer, United States	4m31.8s
1972	Shane Gould, Australia	4m19.04s
1976	Petra Thumer, East Germany	4m09.89s
1980	Ines Diers, East Germany	4m08.76s
1984	Tiffany Cohen, United States	4m07.10s
1988	Janet Evans, United States	4m03.85s

1. 300 meters.

800-Meter Freestyle

1968	Debbie Meyer, United States	9m24s
1972	Keena Rothhammer, United States	8m53.68s
1976	Petra Thumer, East Germany	8m37.14s
1980	Michelle Ford, Australia	8m28.90s
1984	Tiffany Cohen, United States	8m24.95s
1988	Janet Evans, United States	8m20.20s

100-Meter Backstroke

1924	Sybil Bauer, United States	1m23.2s
1928	Marie Braun, Netherlands	1m22s
1932	Eleanor Holm, United States	1m19.4s
1936	Dina Senff, Netherlands	1m18.9s
1948	Karen Harup, Denmark	1m14.4s
1952	Joan Harrison, South Africa	1m14.3s
1956	Judy Grinham, Great Britain	1m12.9s
1960	Lynn Burke, United States	1m9.3s
1964	Cathy Ferguson, United States	1m7.7s
1968	Kaye Hall, United States	1m6.2s
1972	Melissa Belote, United States	1m5.78s
1976	Ulrike Richter, East Germany	1m01.83s
1980	Rica Reinisch, East Germany	1m00.86s
1984	Theresa Andrews, United States	1m02.55s
1988	Kristin Otto, East Germany	1m0.89s

200-Meter Backstroke

1968	Pokey Watson, United States	2m24.8s
1972	Melissa Belote, United States	2m19.19s

1976	Ulrike Richter, East Germany	2m13.43s
1980	Rica Reinisch, East Germany	2m11.77s
1984	Jolanda DeRover, Netherlands	2m12.38s
1988	Krisztina Egerszegi, Hungary	2m09.29s

100-Meter Breaststroke

1968	Djurdjica Bjedov, Yugoslavia	1m15.8s
1972	Catherine Carr, United States	1m13.58s
1976	Hannelore Anke, East Germany	1m11.16s
1980	Ute Geweniger, East Germany	1m10.22s
1984	Petra Van Staveren, Netherlands	1m09.88s
1988	Tania Dangalakova, Bulgaria	1m07.95s

200-Meter Breaststroke

1924	Lucy Morton, Great Britain	3m33.2s
1928	Hilde Schrader, Germany	3m12.6s
1932	Clare Dennis, Australia	3m6.3s
1936	Hideko Maehata, Japan	3m3.6s
1948	Nel van Vliet, Netherlands	2m57.2s
1952	Eva Szekely, Hungary	2m51.7s
1956	Ursula Happe, Germany	2m53.1s
1960	Anita Lonsbrough, Great Britain	2m49.5s
1964	Galina Prozumenschikova, U.S.S.R.	2m46.4s
1968	Sharon Wichman, United States	2m44.4s
1972	Beverly Whitfield, Australia	2m41.71s
1976	Marina Koshevaia, U.S.S.R.	2m33.35s
1980	Lina Kachushite, U.S.S.R.	2m29.54s
1984	Anne Ottenbrite, Canada	2m30.38s
1988	Silke Hoerner, East Germany	2m26.71s

100-Meter Butterfly

1956	Shelley Mann, United States	1m11s
1960	Carolyn Schuler, United States	1m9.5s
1964	Sharon Stouder, United States	1m4.7s
1968	Lynn McClements, Australia	1m5.5s
1972	Mayumi Aoki, Japan	1m3.34s
1976	Kornelia Ender, East Germany	1m00.13s
1980	Caren Metschuck, East Germany	1m00.42s
1984	Mary Meagher, United States	59.26s
1988	Kristin Otto, East Germany	59s

200-Meter Butterfly

1968	Ada Kok, Netherlands	2m24.7s
1972	Karen Moe, United States	2m15.57s
1976	Andrea Pollack, East Germany	2m11.41s
1980	Ines Geissler, East Germany	2m10.44s
1984	Mary Meagher, United States	2m06.90s
1988	Kathleen Nord, East Germany	2m9.51s

200-Meter Individual Medley

1968	Claudia Kolb, United States	2m24.7s
1972	Shane Gould, Australia	2m23.07s
1984	Tracy Caulkins, United States	2m12.64s
1988	Daniela Hunger, East Germany	2m12.59s

400-Meter Individual Medley

1964	Donna de Varona, United States	5m18.7s
1968	Claudia Kolb, United States	5m8.5s
1972	Gail Neall, Australia	5m2.97s
1976	Ulrike Tauber, East Germany	4m42.77s
1980	Petra Schneider, East Germany	4m36.29s
1984	Tracy Caulkins, United States	4m39.21s
1988	Janet Evans, United States	4m37.76s

400-Meter Freestyle Relay

1912	Great Britain	5m52.8s
1920	United States	5m11.6s
1924	United States	4m58.8s
1928	United States	4m47.6s
1932	United States	4m38s
1936	Netherlands	4m36s
1948	United States	4m29.2s

1952	Hungary	4m24.4s
1956	Australia	4m17.1s
1960	United States	4m8.9s
1964	United States	4m3.8s
1968	United States	4m2.5s
1972	United States	3m55.19s
1976	United States	3m44.82s
1980	East Germany	3m42.71s
1984	United States	3m44.43s
1988	East Germany	3m40.63s

400-Meter Medley Relay

1960	United States	4m41.1s
1964	United States	4m33.9s
1968	United States	4m28.3s
1972	United States	4m20.75s
1976	East Germany	4m07.95s
1980	East Germany	4m06.67s
1984	United States	4m08.34s
1988	East Germany	4m03.74s

Springboard Dive

		Points
1920	Aileen Riggin, United States	539.90
1924	Elizabeth Becker, United States	474.5
1928	Helen Meany, United States	78.62
1932	Georgia Coleman, United States	87.52
1936	Marjorie Gestring, United States	89.27
1948	Victoria M. Draves, United States	108.74
1952	Patricia McCormick, United States	147.30
1956	Patricia McCormick, United States	142.36
1960	Ingrid Kramer, Germany	155.81
1964	Ingrid Kramer Engel, Germany	145.00
1968	Sue Gossick, United States	150.77
1972	Micki King, United States	450.03
1976	Jennifer Chandler, United States	506.19
1980	Irina Kalinina, U.S.S.R.	725.91
1984	Sylvie Bernier, Canada	530.70
1988	Gao Min, China	580.23

Platform Dive

		Points
1912	Greta Johansson, Sweden	39.9
1920	Stefani Fryland, Denmark	34.60
1924	Caroline Smith, United States	166
1928	Elizabeth B. Pinkston, United States	31.60
1932	Dorothy Poynton, United States	40.26
1936	Dorothy Poynton Hill, United States	33.92
1948	Victoria M. Draves, United States	68.87
1952	Patricia McCormick, United States	79.37
1956	Patricia McCormick, United States	84.85
1960	Ingrid Kramer, Germany	91.28
1964	Lesley Bush, United States	99.80
1968	Milena Duchkova, Czechoslovakia	109.59
1972	Ulrika Knape, Sweden	390.00
1976	Elena Vaytsekhovskaia, U.S.S.R.	406.59
1980	Martina Jaschke, East Germany	596.25
1984	Zhou Jihong, China	435.51
1988	Xu Yanmei, China	445.20

BASKETBALL—MEN

1904	United States	1968	United States
1936	United States	1972	U.S.S.R.
1948	United States	1976	United States
1952	United States	1980	Yugoslavia
1956	United States	1984	United States
1960	United States	1988	U.S.S.R.
1964	United States		

BASKETBALL—WOMEN

1976	U.S.S.R.	1984	United States
1980	U.S.S.R.	1988	United States

DISTRIBUTION OF MEDALS
1988 SUMMER GAMES

Country	Gold	Silver	Bronze	Total
Soviet Union	55	31	46	132
East Germany	37	35	30	102
United States	36	31	27	94
West Germany	11	14	15	40
Bulgaria	10	12	13	35
South Korea	12	10	11	33
China	5	11	12	28
Romania	7	11	6	24
Britain	5	10	9	24
Hungary	11	6	6	23
France	6	4	6	16
Poland	2	5	9	16
Italy	6	4	4	14
Japan	4	3	7	14
Australia	3	6	5	14
New Zealand	3	2	8	13
Yugoslavia	3	4	5	12
Sweden	0	4	7	11
Canada	3	2	5	10
Kenya	5	2	2	9
The Netherlands	2	2	5	9
Czechoslovakia	3	3	2	8
Brazil	1	2	3	6
Norway	2	3	0	5
Denmark	2	1	1	4
Finland	1	1	2	4
Spain	1	1	2	4
Switzerland	0	2	2	4
Morocco	1	0	2	3
Turkey	1	1	0	2
Jamaica	0	2	0	2
Argentina	0	1	1	2
Belgium	0	0	2	2
Mexico	0	0	2	2
Austria	1	0	0	1
Portugal	1	0	0	1
Suriname	1	0	0	1
Chile	0	1	0	1
Costa Rica	0	1	0	1
Indonesia	0	1	0	1
Iran	0	1	0	1
Neth. Antilles	0	1	0	1
Peru	0	1	0	1
Senegal	0	1	0	1
Virgin Islands	0	1	0	1
Colombia	0	0	1	1
Djibouti	0	0	1	1
Greece	0	0	1	1
Mongolia	0	0	1	1
Pakistan	0	0	1	1
Philippines	0	0	1	1
Thailand	0	0	1	1

BOXING

(U.S. winners only)

(U.S. boycotted Olympics in 1980)

Flyweight—112 pounds (51 kilograms)

1904	George V. Finnegan	1952	Nate Brooks
1920	Frank De Genaro	1976	Leo Randolph
1924	Fidel La Barba	1984	Steve McCrory

Bantamweight—119 (54 kg)

1904	O.L. Kirk	1988	Kennedy McKinney

Featherweight—126 pounds (57 kg)

1904	O.L. Kirk	1984	Meldrick Taylor
1924	Jackie Fields		

Lightweight—132 pounds (60 kg)

1904	H.J. Spanger	1976	Howard Davis
1920	Samuel Mosberg	1984	Pernell Whitaker
1968	Ronnie Harris		

Light Welterweight—140 pounds (63.5 kg)

1952	Charles Adkins	1976	Ray Leonard
1972	Ray Seales	1984	Jerry Page

Welterweight—148 pounds (67 kg)

1904	Al Young	1984	Mark Breland
1932	Edward Flynn		

Light Middleweight—157 pounds (71 kg)

1960	Wilbert McClure	1984	Frank Tate

Middleweight—165 pounds (75 kg)

1904	Charles Mayer	1960	Eddie Cook
1932	Carmen Barth	1976	Michael Spinks
1952	Floyd Patterson		

Light Heavyweight—179 pounds (81 kg)

1920	Edward Eagan	1960	Cassius Clay
1952	Norvel Lee	1976	Leon Spinks
1956	James Boyd	1988	Andrew Maynard

Heavyweight—201 pounds

1904	Sam Berger	1968	George Foreman
1952	Edward Sanders	1984	Henry Tillman
1956	Pete Rademacher	1988	Ray Mercer
1964	Joe Frazier		

Super Heavyweight (unlimited)

1984	Tyrell Biggs

Sixty-one Nations Competed in Seoul Paralympics

The Games of the 8th Seoul Paralympics opened at the Seoul Olympic Stadium on Oct. 15, 1988, with the attendance of 4,278 disabled athletes from 61 nations, the largest turnout in the event's history.

The sports competition for the disabled took place at the games venues in Seoul Sports Complex, Olympic Park and Kyonggi-do area under the ideals of "challenge and overcoming," "peace and friendship," and "participation and equality."

They competed in 16 sports including archery, track and field, fencing, judo, cycling, shooting, soccer, swimming and pingpong.

Other competitions were basketball, weightlifting and powerlifting, lawn bowling, boccia, goal ball, and snooker.

Among the participating nations, the United States fielded the largest number of participants with 376 in 12 games, followed by Britain with 242 in 15 games and host Korea with 239 in 16 games.

The nations participating in the Seoul Paralympics included the Soviet Union, China, Yugoslavia, Hungary, Bulgaria, Poland, and Czechoslovakia.

Koh Kwi-Nam, president of the Seoul Paralympics Organizing Committee (SPOC), said 8,325 people including physically handicapped citizens and their family members as well as those suffering other plights were invited to the Opening Ceremony.

The Seoul Paralympics served as an occasion to enhance the recognition by the Korean people of the physically handicapped and cement friendly relationships among the disabled from around the world, he said.

The Athletes Village for the Seoul Paralympics, consisting of 1,316 apartments in 10 buildings, was built at a 57,666-square-meter site, about 4 kilometers away from the Olympic Stadium.

A total of 5,911 volunteers worked for the Games as interpreter-guides for foreign athletes and officials, and assistants in competition operation, administration, logistics, security, and medical services. □

Coubertin Founded Modern Olympics

In the late 1880s, Baron Pierre de Coubertin of France conceived the idea of holding a modern olympics every four years to diminish tensions between world nations through the ennoblement of amateur sports and the general spirit of competition. Accordingly, he organized a conference in Paris in 1884 for this purpose. Thirteen countries sent representatives and 21 other nations sent their messages of support.

Baron de Coubertin wanted the first modern olympics to be held in Paris, but a motion was passed to hold them in Athens, Greece in 1896. At that time, most of the games consisted of track and field events.

De Coubertin died in Geneva in 1937, but his heart was buried near the Temple of Hera at Olympia. In honor of this remarkable man who shaped the ideals of the modern games, each olympic torch bearer must visit de Courbertin's tomb with the lighted torch before beginning the run to the host city.

JIM THORPE'S OLYMPIC MEDALS

More than 70 years after he won the pentathlon and decathlon at Stockholm, Sweden, Jim Thorpe's Olympic gold medals were returned posthumously to him by the International Olympic Committee. Thorpe, an Oklahoma Sac and Fox Indian, became one of the greatest all-around athletes ever produced in America. He was an all-American football player at the Carlisle Institute, an Indian trade school in Pennsylvania, and starred in baseball and track and field. After winning the medals in the 1912 Olympics, he was forced to give them up when he admitted he had played two seasons for money as a semipro baseball player in 1909 and 1910. Under the rules, he had lost his amateur status by taking money and thus was theoretically ineligible for the Olympics. In October of 1982, after many years of vigorous efforts by his family and other officials in athletics, the I.O.C. reinstated Thorpe in its archives as a co-winner of the two events. At ceremonies in Los Angeles in January 1983, Antonio Samaranch, president of the I.O.C. presented Thorpe's children with gold medals to replace those he had turned back. Thorpe, who later in his career played major-league baseball and pro football, died at the age of 65 in 1953.

Other 1988 Summer Olympic Games Champions

Archery
Men—Jay Barrs, United States
Men's Team—South Korea
Women—Kim Soo-nyung, South Korea
Women's Team—South Korea

Baseball
Men—United States

Canoeing
500 m—Olaf Heukrodt, East Germany
1,000 m—Ivan Klementiev, U.S.S.R.
500-m pairs—U.S.S.R. (Victor Reneiski and Nikolai Jouravski)
1,000-m pairs—U.S.S.R. (Victor Reneiski and Nikolai Jouravski)

Kayak—Women
500 m—Vania Guecheva, Bulgaria
500-m pairs—East Germany (Birgit Schmidt and Anke Nothnagel)
500-m fours—East Germany

Kayak—Men
500 m—Zsolt Gyulay, Hungary
500-m pairs—New Zealand (Ian Ferguson and Paul MacDonald)
1,000 m—Greg Barton, United States
1,000-m pairs—United States (Greg Barton and Norman Bellingham)
1,000-m fours—Hungary

Cycling—Men
196.9-km Individual road race—Olaf Ludwig, East Germany
Individual time trial—Alexander Kirichenko, U.S.S.R.
100-km Team time trial—East Germany
4,000-m Individual pursuit—Gintaoutas Umaras, U.S.S.R.
Match sprint—Lutz Hesslich, East Germany
4,000-m Team, Pursuit—U.S.S.R.
Points race—Dan Frost, Denmark

Cycling—Women
Sprint—Erika Salumiae, U.S.S.R.
Individual road race—Monique Knol, Holland

Equestrian
Dressage—Nicole Uphoff, West Germany
Dressage team—West Germany
Jumping—Pierre Durand, France
Jumping team—West Germany
Three-day event—Mark Todd, New Zealand
Team three-day event—West Germany

Fencing
Foil—Stefano Cerioni, Italy
Team foil—U.S.S.R.
Epee—Arnd Schmitt, West Germany
Team epee—France
Sabre—Jeanfrancois Lamour, France
Team sabre—Hungary
Women's foil—Anja Fichtel, West Germany
Women's team foil—West Germany

Gymnastics—Men
All-around—Vladimir Artemov, U.S.S.R.
Floor exercise—Sergei Kharikov, U.S.S.R.
Horizontal bar—Vladimir Artemov, U.S.S.R.
Parallel bars—Vladimir Artemov, U.S.S.R.
Pommel horse—Zsolt Borkai, Hungary; Dmitri Bilozertchev, U.S.S.R.; Lyubomir Gueraskov, Bulgaria

Rings—Holger Berendt, East Germany; Dmitri Bilozertchev, U.S.S.R.
Vault—Lou Yun, China
Team—U.S.S.R.

Gymnastics—Women
All-around—Elena Shoushounova, U.S.S.R.
Balance beam—Daniela Silivas, Romania
Floor exercise—Daniela Silivas, Romania
Rhythmic Gymnastics—Marina Lobatch, U.S.S.R.
Uneven bars—Daniela Silivas, Romania
Vault—Svetlana Boguinskaia, U.S.S.R.
Team—U.S.S.R.

Judo
133 lb—Kim Jae-Yup, South Korea
143 lb—Lee Kyung-keun, South Korea
156 lb—Marc Alexandre, France
171 lb—Waldemar Legien, Poland
189 lb—Peter Seisenbacher, Austria
209 lb—Aurelio Miguel, Brazil
Over 209 lb—Hitoshi Saito, Japan

Modern Pentathlon
Individual—Janos Martinek, Hungary
Team—Hungary

Rowing—Men
Singles—Thomas Lange, East Germany
Doubles—Holland
Quadruples—Italy
Pairs—Great Britain
Pairs with coxswain—Italy
Fours—East Germany
Fours with coxswain—East Germany
Eights—West Germany

Rowing—Women
Singles—Jutta Behrendt, East Germany
Doubles—East Germany
Pairs—Romania
Fours with coxswain—East Germany
Quadruple sculls—East Germany
Eights—East Germany

Shooting—Men
Free pistol—Sorin Babii, Romania
Rapid-fire pistol—Afanasi Kouzming, U.S.S.R.
Small-bore rifle—Miroslav Varga, Czechoslovakia
Small-bore rifle, 3-position—Malcolm Cooper, Great Britain
Rifle running game target—Tor Heiestad, Norway
Trap—Dimitri Monakov, U.S.S.R.
Air rifle—Goran Maksimovic, Yugoslavia

Shooting—Women
Air rifle—Irina Chilova, U.S.S.R.
Small-bore rifle—Silvia Sperber, West Germany
Air pistol—Jasna Sekaric, Yugoslavia
Rapid-fire pistol—Nino Saloukvadze, U.S.S.R.

Synchronized Swimming
Solo—Carolyn Waldo, Canada
Duet—Canada (Carolyn Waldo and Michelle Cameron)

Table Tennis
Men's singles—Yoo Nam-kyu, South Korea
Men's doubles—China (Chen Longcan and Wei Qingguang)

Women's singles—Chen Jing, China
Women's doubles—South Korea (Hyun Jung-hwa and Yang Young-ja)

Tennis
Men's singles—Miloslav Mecir, Czechoslovakia
Men's doubles—United States (Ken Flach and Robert Seguso)
Women's singles—Steffi Graf, West Germany
Women's doubles—United States (Pam Shriver and Zina Garrison)

Weight Lifting
115 lb—Sevdalin Marinov, Bulgaria
126 lb—Oxen Mirzoian, U.S.S.R.
132 lb—Naim Suleymanoglu, Turkey
149 lb—Joachim Kunz, East Germany
165 lb—Borislav Guidikov, Bulgaria
182 lb—Israil Arsamakov, U.S.S.R.
198 lb—Anatoli Khrapatyi, U.S.S.R.
220 lb—Pavel Kousnetzov, U.S.S.R.
242 lb—Yuri Zacharevich, U.S.S.R.
Over 242—Alexandre Kurlovich, U.S.S.R.

Wrestling—Freestyle
105.5 lb—Takashi Kobayashi, Japan
114.5 lb—Mitsuru Sato, Japan
125.5 lb—Sergei Beloglazov, U.S.S.R.
136.5 lb—John Smith, United States
149.5 lb—Arsen Fadzaev, U.S.S.R.
162.5 lb—Kenneth Monday, United States
180 lb—Han Myung-woo, South Korea
198 lb—Makharbek Khadartsev, U.S.S.R.
220 lb—Vasile Puscasu, Romania
286 lb—David Gobedjichvili, U.S.S.R.

Wrestling—Greco-Roman
105.5 lb—Vincenzo Maenza, Italy
114.5 lb—Jon Ronningen, Norway
125.5 lb—Andras Sike, Hungary
135.25 lb—Kamandar Madjivov, U.S.S.R.
149.5 lb—Levon Djoulfalakian, U.S.S.R.
162.75 lb—Kim Young-nam, South Korea
180.25 lb—Mikhail Mamiachvili, U.S.S.R.
198 lb—Atanas Komchev, Bulgaria
220 lb—Andrzej Wronski, Poland
286 lb—Alexandre Kareline, U.S.S.R.

Yachting
Board sailing—Bruce Kendall, New Zealand
Finn—Jose Luis Doreste, Spain
Flying Dutchman—Denmark (Jorgen Bojsen-Moller and Christian Gronborg)
470 Class—France (Thierry Peponnet and Luc Pillot)
Soling—East Germany
Star—Great Britain (Michael McIntyre and Pmilip Bryn Vaile)
Tornado—France (Jean Yves Le Deroff and Nicolas Henard)
Women's 470—United States (Allison Jolly and Lynne Jewell)

Team Champions
Field hockey, men—Great Britain
Field hockey, women—Australia
Handball, men—U.S.S.R.
Handball, women—South Korea
Soccer—U.S.S.R.
Volleyball, men—United States
Volleyball—U.S.S.R.
Water polo—Yugoslavia

FOOTBALL

The pastime of kicking around a ball goes back beyond the limits of recorded history. Ancient savage tribes played football of a primitive kind. There was a ball-kicking game played by Athenians, Spartans, and Corinthians 2500 years ago, which the Greeks called *Episkuros*. The Romans had a somewhat similar game called *Harpastum* and are supposed to have carried the game with them when they invaded the British Isles in the First Century, B.C.

Undoubtedly the game known in the United States as Football traces directly to the English game of Rugby, though the modifications have been many. Informal football was played on college lawns well over a century ago, and an annual Freshman-Sophomore series of "scrimmages" began at Yale in 1840. The first formal intercollegiate football game was the Princeton-Rutgers contest at New Brunswick, N.J., on Nov. 6, 1869, with Rutgers winning by 6 goals to 4.

In those days, games were played with 25, 20, 15, or 11 men on a side. In 1880, there was a convention at which Walter Camp of Yale persuaded the delegates to agree to a rule calling for 11 players on a side. The game grew so rough that it was attacked as brutal, and some colleges abandoned the sport. Conditions were so bad in 1906 that President Theodore Roosevelt called a meeting of Yale, Harvard, and Princeton representatives at the White House in the hope of reforming and improving the game. The outcome was that the game, with the forward pass introduced and some other modifications of the rules inserted, became faster and cleaner.

The first professional game was played in 1895 at Latrobe, Pa. The National Football League was founded in 1921. The All-American Conference went into action in 1946. At the end of the 1949 season the two circuits merged, retaining the name of the older league. In 1960, the American Football League began operations. In 1970, the leagues merged. The United States Football League played its first season in 1983, from March to July. It suspended spring operation after the 1985 season, and planned a 1986 move to fall, but suspended operations again. It did not function as a league through 1987.

College Football

NATIONAL COLLEGE FOOTBALL CHAMPIONS

The "National Collegiate A. A. Football Guide" recognizes as unofficial national champion the team selected each year by press association polls. Where The Associated Press poll (of writers) does not agree with the United Press International poll (of coaches), the guide lists both teams selected.

1937	Pittsburgh	1950	Oklahoma	1961	Alabama	1972	So. California	1981	Clemson
1938	Texas Christian	1951	Tennessee	1962	So. California	1973	Notre Dame and	1982	Penn State
1939	Texas A & M	1952	Michigan State	1963	Texas		U. of Alabama	1983	Miami
1940	Minnesota	1953	Maryland	1964	Alabama	1974	Oklahoma and	1984	Brigham Young
1941	Minnesota	1954	Ohio State and	1965	Alabama and		So. California	1985	Oklahoma
1942	Ohio State		U.C.L.A.		Michigan State	1975	Oklahoma	1986	Penn State
1943	Notre Dame	1955	Oklahoma	1966	Notre Dame	1976	Pittsburgh	1987	Miami
1944	Army	1956	Oklahoma	1967	So. California	1977	Notre Dame	1988	Notre Dame
1945	Army	1957	Auburn and	1968	Ohio State	1978	Alabama and	1989	Miami
1946	Notre Dame		Ohio State	1969	Texas		So. California		
1947	Notre Dame	1958	Louisiana State	1970	Texas and Nebraska	1979	Alabama		
1948	Michigan	1959	Syracuse	1971	Nebraska	1980	Georgia		
1949	Notre Dame	1960	Minnesota						

RECORD OF ANNUAL MAJOR BOWL COLLEGE FOOTBALL GAMES

Rose Bowl
(At Pasadena, Calif.)

1902	Michigan 49, Stanford 0	1930	So. California 47, Pittsburgh 14	1948	Michigan 49, So. California 0
1916	Washington State 14, Brown 0	1931	Alabama 24, Washington State 0	1949	Northwestern 20, California 14
1917	Oregon 14, Pennsylvania 0	1932	So. California 21, Tulane 12	1950	Ohio State 17, California 14
1918	Mare Island Marines 19, Camp Lewis 7	1933	So. California 35, Pittsburgh 0	1951	Michigan 14, California 6
1919	Great Lakes 17, Mare Island Marines 0	1934	Columbia 7, Stanford 0	1952	Illinois 40, Stanford 7
		1935	Alabama 29, Stanford 13	1953	So. California 7, Wisconsin 0
1920	Harvard 7, Oregon 6	1936	Stanford 7, So. Methodist 0	1954	Michigan State 28, U.C.L.A. 20
1921	California 28, Ohio State 0	1937	Pittsburgh 21, Washington 0	1955	Ohio State 20, So. California 7
1922	Washington and Jefferson 0, California 0	1938	California 13, Alabama 0	1956	Michigan State 17, U.C.L.A. 14
		1939	So. California 7, Duke 3	1957	Iowa 35, Oregon State 19
		1940	So. California 14, Tennessee 0	1958	Ohio State 10, Oregon 7
1923	So. California 14, Penn State 3	1941	Stanford 21, Nebraska 13	1959	Iowa 38, California 12
1924	Navy 14, Washington 14	1942	Oregon State 20, Duke 16[1]	1960	Washington 44, Wisconsin 8
1925	Notre Dame 27, Stanford 10	1943	Georgia 9, U.C.L.A. 0	1961	Washington 17, Minnesota 7
1926	Alabama 20, Washington 19	1944	So. California 29, Washington 0	1962	Minnesota 21, U.C.L.A. 3
1927	Alabama 7, Stanford 7	1945	So. California 25, Tennessee 0	1963	So. California 42, Wisconsin 37
1928	Stanford 7, Pittsburgh 6	1946	Alabama 34, So. California 14	1964	Illinois 17, Washington 7
1929	Georgia Tech 8, California 7	1947	Illinois 45, U.C.L.A. 14	1965	Michigan 34, Oregon State 7

1966 U.C.L.A. 14, Michigan State 12
1967 Purdue 14, So. California 13
1968 So. California 14, Indiana 3
1969 Ohio State 27, So. California 16
1970 So. California 10, Michigan 3
1971 Stanford 27, Ohio State 17
1972 Stanford 13, Michigan 12
1973 So. California 42, Ohio State 17
1974 Ohio State 42, So. California 21
1975 So. California 18, Ohio State 17
1976 U.C.L.A. 23, Ohio State 10
1977 So. California 14, Michigan 6
1978 Washington 27, Michigan 20
1979 So. California 17, Michigan 10
1980 So. California 17, Ohio State 16
1981 Michigan 23, Washington 6
1982 Washington 28, Iowa 0
1983 U.C.L.A. 24, Michigan 14
1984 U.C.L.A. 45, Illinois 9
1985 USC 20, Ohio St. 17
1986 U.C.L.A. 45, Iowa 28
1987 Arizona State 22, Michigan 15
1988 Michigan State 20, USC 17
1989 Michigan 22, So. California 14
1990 USC 17, Michigan 10

1. Played at Durham, N.C.

Orange Bowl
(At Miami)

1933 Miami (Fla.) 7, Manhattan 0
1934 Duquesne 33, Miami (Fla.) 7
1935 Bucknell 26, Miami (Fla.) 0
1936 Catholic 20, Mississippi 19
1937 Duquesne 13, Mississippi State 12
1938 Auburn 6, Michigan State 0
1939 Tennessee 17, Oklahoma 0
1940 Georgia Tech 21, Missouri 7
1941 Mississippi State 14, Georgetown 7
1942 Georgia 40, Texas Christian 26
1943 Alabama 37, Boston College 21
1944 Louisiana State 19, Texas A&M 14
1945 Tulsa 26, Georgia Tech 12
1946 Miami (Fla.) 13, Holy Cross 6
1947 Rice 8, Tennessee 0
1948 Georgia Tech 20, Kansas 14
1949 Texas 41, Georgia 28
1950 Santa Clara 21, Kentucky 13
1951 Clemson 15, Miami (Fla.) 14
1952 Georgia Tech 17, Baylor 14
1953 Alabama 61, Syracuse 6
1954 Oklahoma 7, Maryland 0
1955 Duke 34, Nebraska 7
1956 Oklahoma 20, Maryland 6
1957 Colorado 27, Clemson 21
1958 Oklahoma 48, Duke 21
1959 Oklahoma 21, Syracuse 6
1960 Georgia 14, Missouri 0
1961 Missouri 21, Navy 14
1962 Louisiana State 25, Colorado 7
1963 Alabama 17, Oklahoma 0
1964 Nebraska 13, Auburn 7
1965 Texas 21, Alabama 17
1966 Alabama 39, Nebraska 28
1967 Florida 27, Georgia Tech 12
1968 Oklahoma 26, Tennessee 24
1969 Penn State 15, Kansas 14
1970 Penn State 10, Missouri 3
1971 Nebraska 17, Louisiana State 12
1972 Nebraska 38, Alabama 6
1973 Nebraska 40, Notre Dame 6
1974 Penn State 16, Louisiana State 9
1975 Notre Dame 13, Alabama 11
1976 Oklahoma 14, Michigan 6
1977 Ohio State 27, Colorado 10

1978 Arkansas 31, Oklahoma 6
1979 Oklahoma 31, Nebraska 24
1980 Oklahoma 24, Florida State 7
1981 Oklahoma 18, Florida State 17
1982 Clemson 22, Nebraska 15
1983 Nebraska 21, Louisiana State 20
1984 Miami 31, Nebraska 30
1985 Washington 28, Oklahoma 17
1986 Oklahoma 25, Penn St. 10
1987 Oklahoma 42, Arkansas 8
1988 Miami 20, Oklahoma 14
1989 Miami 23, Nebraska 3
1990 Notre Dame 21, Colorado 6

Sugar Bowl
(At New Orleans)

1935 Tulane 20, Temple 14
1936 Texas Christian 3, Louisiana State 2
1937 Santa Clara 21, Louisiana State 14
1938 Santa Clara 6, Louisiana State 0
1939 Texas Christian 15, Carnegie Tech 7
1940 Texas A & M 14, Tulane 13
1941 Boston College 19, Tennessee 13
1942 Fordham 2, Missouri 0
1943 Tennessee 14, Tulsa 7
1944 Georgia Tech 20, Tulsa 18
1945 Duke 29, Alabama 26
1946 Oklahoma A & M 33, St. Mary's (Calif.) 13
1947 Georgia 20, North Carolina 10
1948 Texas 27, Alabama 7
1949 Oklahoma 14, North Carolina 6
1950 Oklahoma 35, Louisiana State 0
1951 Kentucky 13, Oklahoma 7
1952 Maryland 28, Tennessee 13
1953 Georgia Tech 24, Mississippi 7
1954 Georgia Tech 42, West Virginia 19
1955 Navy 21, Mississippi 0
1956 Georgia Tech 7, Pittsburgh 0
1957 Baylor 13, Tennessee 7
1958 Mississippi 39, Texas 7
1959 Louisiana State 7, Clemson 0
1960 Mississippi 21, Louisiana State 0
1961 Mississippi 14, Rice 6
1962 Alabama 10, Arkansas 3
1963 Mississippi 17, Arkansas 13
1964 Alabama 12, Mississippi 7
1965 Louisiana State 13, Syracuse 10
1966 Missouri 20, Florida 18
1967 Alabama 34, Nebraska 7
1968 Louisiana State 20, Wyoming 13
1969 Arkansas 16, Georgia 2
1970 Mississippi 27, Arkansas 22
1971 Tennessee 34, Air Force Academy 13
1972 Oklahoma 40, Auburn 22
1973 Oklahoma 14, Penn State 0
1974 Notre Dame 24, Alabama 23
1975 Nebraska 13, Florida 10
1976 Alabama 13, Penn State 6
1977 Pittsburgh 27, Georgia 3
1978 Alabama 35, Ohio State 6
1979 Alabama 14, Penn State 7
1980 Alabama 24, Arkansas 9
1981 Georgia 17, Notre Dame 10
1982 Pittsburgh 24, Georgia 20
1983 Penn State 27, Georgia 23
1984 Auburn 9, Michigan 7
1985 Nebraska 28, LSU 10
1986 Tennessee 35, Miami, Fla. 7
1987 Nebraska 30, Louisiana State 15
1988 Syracuse 16, Auburn 16 (tie)
1989 Florida State 13, Auburn 7
1990 Miami 33, Alabama 25

Cotton Bowl
(At Dallas)

1937 Texas Christian 16, Marquette 6
1938 Rice 28, Colorado 14
1939 St. Mary's (Calif.) 20, Texas Tech. 13
1940 Clemson 6, Boston College 3
1941 Texas A & M 13, Fordham 12
1942 Alabama 29, Texas A & M 21
1943 Texas 14, Georgia Tech 7
1944 Randolph Field 7, Texas 7
1945 Oklahoma A & M 34, Texas Christian 0
1946 Texas 40, Missouri 27
1947 Louisiana State 0, Arkansas 0
1948 So. Methodist 13, Penn State 13
1949 So. Methodist 21, Oregon 13
1950 Rice 27, North Carolina 13
1951 Tennessee 20, Texas 14
1952 Kentucky 20, Texas Christian 7
1953 Texas 16, Tennessee 0
1954 Rice 28, Alabama 6
1955 Georgia Tech 14, Arkansas 6
1956 Mississippi 14, Texas Christian 13
1957 Texas Christian 28, Syracuse 27
1958 Navy 20, Rice 7
1959 Air Force 0, Texas Christian 0
1960 Syracuse 23, Texas 14
1961 Duke 7, Arkansas 6
1962 Texas 12, Mississippi 7
1963 Louisiana State 13, Texas 0
1964 Texas 28, Navy 6
1965 Arkansas 10, Nebraska 7
1966 Louisiana State 14, Arkansas 7
1967 Georgia 24, So. Methodist 9
1968 Texas A & M 20, Alabama 16
1969 Texas 36, Tennessee 13
1970 Texas 21, Notre Dame 17
1971 Notre Dame 24, Texas 11
1972 Penn State 30, Texas 6
1973 Texas 17, Alabama 13
1974 Nebraska 19, Texas 3
1975 Penn State 41, Baylor 20
1976 Arkansas 31, Georgia 10
1977 Houston 30, Maryland 21
1978 Notre Dame 38, Texas 10
1979 Notre Dame 35, Houston 34
1980 Houston 17, Nebraska 14
1981 Alabama 30, Baylor 2
1982 Texas 14, Alabama 12
1983 Southern Methodist 7, Pittsburgh 3
1984 Georgia 10, Texas 9
1985 Boston College 45, Houston 28
1986 Texas A & M 36, Auburn 16
1987 Ohio State 28, Texas A & M 12
1988 Texas A & M 35, Notre Dame 10
1989 UCLA 17, Arkansas 3
1990 Tennessee 31, Arkansas 27

Gator Bowl
(At Jacksonville, Fla. Played on Saturday nearest New Year's Day of year indicated)

1953 Florida 14, Tulsa 13
1954 Texas Tech 35, Auburn 13
1955 Auburn 33, Baylor 13
1956 Vanderbilt 25, Auburn 13
1957 Georgia Tech 21, Pittsburgh 14
1958 Tennessee 3, Texas A & M 0
1959 Mississippi 7, Florida 3
1960 Arkansas 14, Georgia Tech 7
1961 Florida 13, Baylor 12
1962 Penn State 30, Georgia Tech 15
1963 Florida 17, Penn State 7

1964 No. Carolina 35, Air Force 0	1973 Auburn 24, Colorado 3	1982 North Carolina 31, Arkansas 27
1965 Florida State 36, Oklahoma 19	1974 Texas Tech 28, Tennessee 19	1983 Florida State 31, West Virginia 12
1966 Georgia Tech 31, Texas Tech 21	1975 Auburn 27, Texas 3	1984 Florida 14, Iowa 6
1967 Tennessee 18, Syracuse 12	1976 Maryland 13, Florida 0	1985 Oklahoma St. 21, South Carolina 14
1968 Penn State 17, Florida State 17	1977 Notre Dame 20, Penn State 9	1986 Florida State 34, Oklahoma St. 23
1969 Missouri 35, Alabama 10	1978 Pittsburgh 34, Clemson 3	1987 Clemson 27, Stanford 21
1970 Florida 14, Tennessee 13	1979 Clemson 17, Ohio State 15	1988 LSU 30, South Carolina 13
1971 Auburn 35, Mississippi 28	1980 North Carolina 17, Michigan 15	1989 Georgia 34, Michigan St. 27
1972 Georgia 7, North Carolina 3	1981 Pittsburgh 37, South Carolina 9	1990 Clemson 27, West Virginia 7

RESULTS OF OTHER 1989 SEASON BOWL GAMES

All-American (Birmingham, Ala., Dec. 28)—Texas Tech 49, Duke 21
Aloha (Honolulu, Dec. 25)—Michigan State 33, Hawaii 13
California (Fresno, Dec. 9)—Fresno State 27, Ball State 6
Copper (Tucson, Ariz., Dec. 31)—Arizona 17, N.C. State 10
Fiesta (Tempe, Ariz., Jan 1)—Florida State 41, Nebraska 17
Florida Citrus (Orlando, Jan. 1)—Illinois 31, Virginia 21
Freedom (Anaheim, Calif., Dec. 30)—Washington 34, Florida 7

Hall of Fame (Tampa, Fla., Jan. 1)—Auburn 31, Ohio State 14
Holiday (San Diego, Dec. 29)—Penn State 50, Brigham Young 39
Independence (Shreveport, La., Dec. 16)—Oregon 27, Tulsa 24
Liberty (Memphis, Dec. 28)—Mississippi 42, Air Force 29
Peach (Atlanta, Dec. 30)—Syracuse 19, Georgia 18
Sun (El Paso, Tex., Dec. 30)—Pittsburgh 31, Texas A&M 28

HEISMAN MEMORIAL TROPHY WINNERS

The Heisman Memorial Trophy is presented annually by the Downtown Athletic Club of New York City to the nation's outstanding college football player, as determined by a poll of sportswriters and sportscasters.

1935 Jay Berwanger, Chicago	1953 Johnny Lattner, Notre Dame	1971 Pat Sullivan, Auburn
1936 Larry Kelley, Yale	1954 Alan Ameche, Wisconsin	1972 Johnny Rodgers, Nebraska
1937 Clinton Frank, Yale	1955 Howard Cassady, Ohio State	1973 John Cappelletti, Penn State
1938 Davey O'Brien, Texas Christian	1956 Paul Hornung, Notre Dame	1974-75 Archie Griffin, Ohio State
1939 Nile Kinnick, Iowa	1957 John Crow, Texas A & M	1976 Tony Dorsett, Pittsburgh
1940 Tom Harmon, Michigan	1958 Pete Dawkins, Army	1977 Earl Campbell, Texas
1941 Bruce Smith, Minnesota	1959 Billy Cannon, Louisiana State	1978 Billy Sims, Oklahoma
1942 Frank Sinkwich, Georgia	1960 Joe Bellino, Navy	1979 Charles White, Southern California
1943 Angelo Bertelli, Notre Dame	1961 Ernie Davis, Syracuse	1980 George Rogers, South Carolina
1944 Leslie Horvath, Ohio State	1962 Terry Baker, Oregon State	1981 Marcus Allen, Southern California
1945 Felix Blanchard, Army	1963 Roger Staubach, Navy	1982 Hershel Walker, Georgia
1946 Glenn Davis, Army	1964 John Huarte, Notre Dame	1983 Mike Rozier, Nebraska
1947 Johnny Lujack, Notre Dame	1965 Mike Garrett, Southern California	1984 Doug Flutie, Boston College
1948 Doak Walker, So. Methodist	1966 Steve Spurrier, Florida	1985 Bo Jackson, Auburn
1949 Leon Hart, Notre Dame	1967 Gary Beban, U.C.L.A.	1986 Vinnie Testeverde, Miami
1950 Vic Janowicz, Ohio State	1968 O. J. Simpson, Southern California	1987 Tim Brown, Notre Dame
1951 Dick Kazmaier, Princeton	1969 Steve Owens, Oklahoma	1988 Barry Sanders, Oklahoma State
1952 Billy Vessels, Oklahoma	1970 Jim Plunkett, Stanford	1989 Andre Ware, Houston

1989 N.C.A.A. CHAMPIONSHIP PLAYOFFS

DIVISION I-AA

Quarterfinals

Stephen F. Austin 55, Southwest Missouri St. 25
Georgia Southern 45, Middle Tennessee St. 3
Montana 25, Eastern Illinois 19
Furman 42, Youngstown State 23

Semifinals

Stephen F. Austin 21, Furman 19
Georgia Southern 45, Montana 15

Championship

Georgia Southern 37, Stephen F. Austin 34

DIVISION II

Quarterfinals

Jacksonville State 21, North Dakota State 17
Mississippi College 55, St. Cloud State (Minn.) 24
Angelo State (Tex.) 24, Pittsburg State (Kan.) 21
Indiana (Pa.) 17, Portland State (Ore.) 0

Semifinals

Jacksonville State 34, Angelo State (Tex.) 16
Mississippi College 26, Indiana (Pa.) 14

Championship

Mississippi College 3, Jacksonville State 0

DIVISION III

Quarterfinals

Dayton 28, Millikin (Ill.) 16
Union (N.Y.) 45, Montclair State (N.J.) 6
Ferrum (Va.) 49, Lycoming (Pa.) 24
St. John's (Minn.) 27, Central (Iowa) 34

Semifinals

Union (N.Y.) 37, Ferrum (Va.) 21
Dayton 28, St. John's (Minn.) 0

Championship

Dayton 17, Union 7

NATIONAL ASSOCIATION OF INTERCOLLEGIATE ATHLETICS 1989 CHAMPIONSHIPS

DIVISION I

Quarterfinals

Adams State (Col.) 30, Northwestern Oklahoma 22
Central State (Ohio) 56, Moorhead State (Minn.) 7
Carson–Newman (Tenn.) 51, West Virginia Tech 13
Emporia State (Kan.) 32, Harding (Ark.) 9

Semifinals

Carson–Newman 20, Central State 17
Emporia State 51, Adams State 44

Championship

Carson–Newman 34, Emporia State 20

DIVISION II

Quarterfinals

Central Washington 49, Dickinson State (N.D.) 7
Wisconsin–La Crosse 29, Nebraska–Wesleyan 0
Baker (Kan.) 35, Missouri Valley 28
Westminster (Pa.) 34, Tarleton State (Tex.) 0

Semifinals

Wisconsin–La Crosse 21, Baker 6
Westminster 21, Central Washington 10

Championship

Westminster 51, Wisconsin–La Crosse 30

COLLEGE FOOTBALL HALL OF FAME

(Kings Island, Interstate 71, Kings Mills, Ohio) (Date given is player's last year of competition)

Players

Abell, Earl—Colgate, 1915
Agase, Alex—Purdue/Illinois, 1946
Agganis, Harry—Boston Univ., 1952
Albert, Frank—Stanford, 1941
Aldrich, Chas. (Ki)—T.C.U., 1938
Aldrich, Malcolm—Yale, 1921
Alexander, John—Syracuse, 1920
Alworth, Lance—Arkansas, 1961
Ameche, Alan (Horse)—Wisconsin, 1954
Amling, Warren—Ohio State, 1946
Anderson, Donny—Texas Tech, 1965
Anderson, H. (Hunk)—Notre Dame, 1921
Atkins, Doug—Tennessee, 1952
Bacon, C. Everett—Wesleyan, 1912
Bagnell, Francis (Reds)—Penn, 1950
Baker, Hobart (Hobey)—Princeton, 1913
Baker, John—So. Calif., 1931
Baker, Terry—Oregon State, 1962
Ballin, Harold—Princeton, 1914
Banker, Bill—Tulane, 1929
Banonis, Vince—Detroit, 1941
Barnes, Stanley—S. California, 1921
Barrett, Charles—Cornell, 1915
Baston, Bert—Minnesota, 1916
Battles, Cliff—W. Va. Wesleyan, 1931
Baugh, Sammy—Texas Christian U., 1936
Baughan, Maxie—Georgia Tech, 1959
Bausch, James—Kansas, 1930
Beagle, Ron—Navy, 1955
Beban, Gary—UCLA, 1967
Beckett, John—Oregon, 1913
Bednarik, Chuck—Pennsylvania, 1948
Behm, Forrest—Nebraska, 1940
Bellino, Joe—Navy, 1960
Below, Marty—Wisconsin, 1923
Benbrook, A.—Michigan, 1911
Bertelli, A.—Notre Dame, 1943
Berry, Charlie—Lafayette, 1924
Berwanger, John (Jay)—Chicago, 1935
Bettencourt, Larry—St. Mary's, 1927
Blanchard, Felix (Doc)—Army, 1946
Bock, Ed—Iowa State, 1938
Bomar, Lynn—Vanderbilt, 1924
Bomeisler, Doug (Bo)—Yale, 1913
Booth, Albie—Yale, 1931
Borries, Fred—Navy, 1934
Bosely, Bruce—West Virginia, 1955
Bosseler, Don—Miami, Fla., 1956
Bottari, Vic—California, 1939
Boynton, Ben—Williams, 1920
Bozis, Al—Georgetown, 1941
Brewer, Charles—Harvard, 1895
Bright, John—Drake, 1951
Brodie, John—Stanford, 1956
Brooke, George—Pennsylvania, 1895
Brown, George—Navy, San Diego St., 1947
Brown, Gordon—Yale, 1900
Brown, John, Jr.—Navy, 1913
Brown, Johnny Mack—Alabama, 1925
Brown, Raymond (Tay)—So. California, 1932
Bunker, Paul—Army, 1902
Burton, Ron—Northwestern, 1956
Butkus, Dick—Illinois, 1964
Butler, Robert—Wisconsin, 1912
Cafego, George—Tennessee, 1939
Cagle, Chris—SW La./Army, 1929
Cain, John—Alabama, 1932
Cameron, Eddie—Wash. & Lee, 1924
Campbell, David C.—Harvard, 1901
Campbell, Earl—Texas, 1977

Cannon, Billy—L.S.U., 1959
Cannon, Jack—Notre Dame, 1929
Carideo, Frank—Notre Dame, 1930
Caroline, J.C.—Illinois, 1954
Carney, Charles—Illinois, 1921
Carpenter, Bill—Army, 1959
Carpenter, C. Hunter—VPI, 1905
Carroll, Charles—Washington, 1928
Casey, Edward L.—Harvard, 1919
Cassady, Howard—Ohio State, 1955
Chamberlain, Guy—Nebraska, 1915
Chapman, Sam—Cal.–Berkeley, 1938
Chappuis, Bob—Michigan, 1947
Christman, Paul—Missouri, 1940
Clark, Earl (Dutch)—Colo. College, 1929
Cleary, Paul—USC, 1947
Clevenger, Zora—Indiana, 1903
Cloud, Jack—William & Mary, 1948
Cochran, Gary—Princeton, 1895
Cody, Josh—Vanderbilt, 1920
Coleman, Don—Mich. State, 1951
Conerly, Chuck—Mississippi, 1947
Connor, George—Notre Dame, 1947
Corbin, W.—Yale, 1888
Corbus, William—Stanford, 1933
Cowan, Hector—Princeton, 1889
Coy, Edward H. (Tad)—Yale, 1909
Crawford, Fred—Duke, 1933
Crow, John D.—Texas A&M, 1957
Crowley, James—Notre Dame, 1924
Csonka, Larry—Syracuse, 1967
Cutter, Slade—Navy, 1934
Czarobski, Ziggie—Notre Dame, 1947
Dale, Carroll—Virginia Tech, 1959
Dalrymple, Gerald—Tulane, 1931
Daniell, James—Ohio State, 1941
Dalton, John—Navy, 1912
Daly, Charles—Harvard/Army, 1902
Daniell, Averell—Pittsburgh, 1936
Davies, Tom—Pittsburgh, 1921
Davis, Ernest—Syracuse, 1961
Davis, Glenn—Army, 1946
Davis, Robert T.—Georgia Tech, 1947
Dawkins, Pete—Army, 1958
De Rogatis, Al—Duke, 1940
DesJardien, Paul—Chicago, 1914
Devine, Aubrey—Iowa, 1921
DeWitt, John—Princeton, 1903
Ditka, Mike—Pittsburgh 1960
Dobbs, Glenn—Tulsa, 1942
Dodd, Bobby—Tennessee, 1930
Donan, Holland—Princeton, 1950
Donchess, Joseph—Pittsburgh, 1929
Dougherty, Nathan—Tennessee, 1909
Drahos, Nick—Cornell, 1940
Driscoll, Paddy—Northwestern, 1917
Drury, Morley—So. California, 1927
Dudley, William (Bill)—Virginia, 1941
Eckersall, Walter—Chicago, 1906
Edwards, Turk—Washington State, 1931
Edwards, William—Princeton, 1900
Eichenlaub, R.—Notre Dame, 1913
Elliott, Chalmers—Purdue, 1944 & Michigan, 1947
Evans, Ray—Kansas, 1947
Exendine, Albert—Carlisle, 1908
Falaschi, Nello—Santa Clara, 1937
Fears, Tom—Santa Clara/UCLA, 1947
Feathers, Beattie—Tennessee, 1933
Fenimore, Robert—Oklahoma State, 1947
Fenton, G.E. (Doc)—La. State U., 1910
Ferraro, John—So. California, 1944

Fesler, Wesley—Ohio State, 1930
Fincher, Bill—Georgia Tech, 1920
Fischer, Bill—Notre Dame, 1948
Fish, Hamilton—Harvard, 1909
Fisher, Robert—Harvard, 1911
Flowers, Abe—Georgia Tech, 1920
Fortmann, Daniel—Colgate, 1935
Francis, Sam—Nebraska, 1936
Franco, Edmund (Ed)—Fordham, 1937
Frank, Clint—Yale, 1937
Franz, Rodney—California, 1949
Friedman, Benny—Michigan, 1926
Gabriel, Roman—North Carolina St., 1961
Gain, Bob—Kentucky, 1950
Galiffa, Arnold—Army, 1949
Gallarneau, Hugh—Stanford, 1941
Garbisch, Edgar—Army, 1924
Garrett, Mike—USC, 1965
Gelbert, Charles—Pennsylvania, 1896
Geyer, Forest—Oklahoma, 1915
Giel, Paul—Minnesota, 1953
Gifford, Frank—So. California, 1951
Gilbert, Walter—Auburn, 1936
Gipp, George—Notre Dame, 1920
Gladchuk, Chet—Boston College, 1940
Glass, Bill—Baylor, 1956
Goldberg, Marshall—Pittsburgh, 1938
Goodreault, Gene—Boston College, 1940
Gordon, Walter—California, 1918
Governale, Paul—Columbia, 1942
Graham, Otto—Northwestern, 1943
Grange, Harold (Red)—Illinois, 1925
Grayson, Robert—Stanford, 1935
Green, Joe—North Texas State, 1968
Griese, Bob—Purdue, 1966
Griffin, Archie—Ohio State, 1975
Gulick, Merel—Hobart, 1929
Guyon, Joe—Georgia Tech, 1919
Hale, Edwin—Mississippi Col, 1921
Ham, Jack—Penn State, 1970
Hamilton, Robert (Bones)—Stanford, 1935
Hamilton, Tom—Navy, 1925
Hanson, Vic—Syracuse, 1926
Hardwick, H. (Tack)—Harvard, 1914
Hare, T. Truxton—Pennsylvania, 1900
Harley, Chick—Ohio State, 1919
Harmon, Tom—Michigan, 1940
Harpster, Howard—Carnegie Tech, 1928
Hart, Edward J.—Princeton, 1911
Hart, Leon—Notre Dame, 1949
Hartman, Bill—Georgia, 1937
Hazel, Homer—Rutgers, 1924
Healey, Ed—Dartmouth, 1916
Heffelfinger, W. (Pudge)—Yale, 1891
Hein, Mel—Washington State, 1930
Heinrich, Don—Washington, 1952
Hendricks, Ted—Miami, 1968
Henry, Wilber—Wash. & Jefferson, 1919
Herschberger, Clarence—Chicago, 1899
Herwig, Robert—California, 1937
Heston, Willie—Michigan, 1904
Hickman, Herman—Tennessee, 1931
Hickok, William—Yale, 1895
Hill, Dan—Duke, 1938
Hillebrand, A.R. (Doc)—Princeton, 1900
Hinkey, Frank—Yale, 1894
Hinkle, Carl—Vanderbilt, 1937
Hinkle, Clark—Bucknell, 1932
Hirsch, Elroy—Wis./Mich., 1943
Hitchcock, James—Auburn, 1932
Hoffman, Frank—Notre Dame, 1931

Hogan, James J.—Yale, 1904
Holland, Jerome (Brud)—Cornell, 1938
Holleder, Don—Army, 1955
Hollenbeck, William—Penn., 1908
Holovak, Michael—Boston College, 1942
Holub, E.J.—Texas Tech, 1960
Hornung, Paul—Notre Dame, 1956
Horrell, Edwin—California, 1924
Horvath, Les—Ohio State, 1944
Howe, Arthur—Yale, 1911
Howell, Millard (Dixie)—Alabama, 1934
Hubbard, Cal—Centenary, 1926
Hubbard, John—Amherst, 1906
Hubert, Allison—Alabama, 1925
Huff, Robert Lee (Sam)—W. Va., 1955
Humble, Weldon G.—Rice, 1946
Hunt, Joel—Texas A&M, 1927
Huntington, Ellery—Colgate, 1914
Hutson, Don—Alabama, 1934
Ingram, James—Navy, 1906
Isbell, Cecil—Purdue, 1937
Jablonsky, Harvey—Wash. U./Army, 1933
Janowicz, Vic—Ohio State, 1951
Jenkins, Darold—Missouri, 1941
Jensen, Jack—Cal-Berkeley, 1948
Joesting, Herbert—Minnesota, 1927
Johnson, James—Carlisle, 1903
Johnson, Robert—Tennessee, 1967
Jones, Calvin—Iowa, 1955
Jones, Gomer—Ohio State, 1935
Jordan, Lee Roy—Alabama, 1962
Juhan, Frank—Univ. of South, 1910
Justice, Charlie—North Carolina, 1949
Kaer, Mort—So. California, 1926
Kavanaugh, Kenneth—La. State U., 1939
Kaw, Edgar—Cornell, 1922
Kazmaier, Richard—Princeton, 1951
Keck, James—Princeton, 1921
Kelley, Larry—Yale, 1936
Kelly, William—Montana, 1926
Kenna, Ed—Syracuse, 1966
Kern, George—Boston College, 1941
Ketcham, Henry—Yale, 1913
Keyes, Leroy—Purdue, 1968
Killinger, William—Penn State, 1922
Kimbrough, John—Texas A&M, 1940
Kinard, Frank—Mississippi, 1937
King, Phillip—Princeton, 1893
Kinnick, Nile—Iowa, 1939
Kipke, Harry—Michigan, 1923
Kirkpatrick, John Reed—Yale, 1910
Kitzmiller, John—Oregon, 1929
Koch, Barton—Baylor, 1931
Kitner, Malcolm—Texas, 1942
Kramer, Ron—Michigan, 1956
Krueger, Charlie—Texas A&M, 1957
Kwalick, Ted—Penn State, 1968
Lach, Steve—Duke, 1941
Lane, Myles—Dartmouth, 1927
Lattner, Joseph J.—Notre Dame, 1953
Lauricella, Hank—Tennessee, 1952
Lautenschlaeger—Tulane, 1925
Layden, Elmer—Notre Dame, 1924
Layne, Bobby—Texas, 1947
Lea, Langdon—Princeton, 1895
LeBaron, Eddie—Univ. of Pacific, 1949
Leech, James—Va. Mil. Inst., 1920
Lester, Darrell—Texas Christian, 1935
Lilly, Bob—Texas Christian, 1960
Little, Floyd—Syracuse, 1966
Lio, Augie—Georgetown, 1940
Locke, Gordon—Iowa, 1922
Lourie, Don—Princeton, 1921
Lucas, Richard—Penn State, 1959
Luckman, Sid—Columbia, 1938
Lujack, John—Notre Dame, 1947
Lund, J.L. (Pug)—Minnesota, 1934
Macomber, Bart—Illinois, 1915
MacLeod, Robert—Dartmouth, 1938
Maegle, Dick—Rice, 1954
Mahan, Edward W.—Harvard, 1915
Majors, John—Tennessee, 1956
Mallory, William—Yale, 1893
Mancha, Vaughn—Alabama, 1947
Mann, Gerald—So. Methodist, 1927
Manning, Archie—Mississippi, 1970

Manske, Edgar—Northwestern, 1933
Markov, Vic—Washington, 1937
Marshall, Robert—Minnesota, 1907
Matson, Ollie—San Fran. U., 1952
Matthews, Ray—Texas Christ. U., 1928
Maulbetsch, John—Michigan, 1914
Mauthe, J.L. (Pete)—Penn State, 1912
Maxwell, Robert—Chi./Swarthmore, 1906
McAfee, George—Duke, 1939
McClung, Thomas L.—Yale, 1891
McColl, William F.—Stanford, 1951
McCormick, James B.—Princeton, 1907
McDonald, Tom—Oklahoma, 1956
McDowall, Jack—No. Car. State, 1927
McElhenny, Hugh—Washington, 1951
McEver, Gene—Tennessee, 1931
McEwan, John—Minn./Army, 1916
McFadden, J.B.—Clemson, 1939
McFadin, Bud—Texas, 1950
McGee, Mike—Duke, 1959
McGinley, Edward—Pennsylvania, 1924
McGovern, J.—Minnesota, 1910
McGraw, Thurman—Colorado State, 1949
McKeever, Mike—USC, 1960
McLaren, George—Pittsburgh, 1918
McMillan, Dan—U.S.C./Calif., 1922
McMillin, A.N. (Bo)—Centre, 1921
McWhorter, Robert—Georgia, 1913
Mercer, Leroy—Pennsylvania, 1912
Meredith, Don—Southern Methodist, 1959
Metzger, Bert—Notre Dame, 1930
Mickal, Abe—La. State U., 1935
Miller, Creighton—Notre Dame, 1943
Miller, Don—Notre Dame, 1925
Miller, Edgar (Rip)—Notre Dame, 1924
Miller, Eugene—Penn State, 1913
Miller, Fred—Notre Dame, 1928
Millner, Wayne—Notre Dame, 1935
Milstead, Century—Wabash, Yale, 1923
Minds, John—Pennsylvania, 1897
Minisi, Anthony—Navy, Pennsylvania, 1947
Moffatt, Alex—Princeton, 1884
Molinski, Ed—Tennessee, 1940
Montgomery, Cliff—Columbia, 1933
Moomaw, Donn—U.C.L.A., 1952
Morley, William—Columbia, 1903
Morris, George—Georgia Tech, 1952
Morton, William—Dartmouth, 1931
Moscrip, Monk—Stanford, 1935
Muller, Harold (Brick)—Calif., 1922
Nagurski, Bronko—Minnesota, 1929
Nevers, Ernie—Stanford, 1925
Newell, Marshall—Harvard, 1893
Newman, Harry—Michigan, 1932
Nobis, Tommy—Texas, 1965
Nomellini, Leo—Minnesota, 1949
Oberlander, Andrew—Dartmouth, 1925
O'Brien, Davey—Texas Christ. U., 1938
O'Dea, Pat—Wisconsin, 1899
O'Hearn, J.—Cornell, 1915
Olds, Robin—Army, 1942
Oliphant, Elmer—Purdue/Army, 1917
Olsen, Merlin—Utah State, 1961
Oosterbaan, Ben—Michigan, 1927
O'Rourke, Charles—Boston College, 1940
Orsi, John—Colgate, 1931
Osgood, W.D.—Cornell/Penn, 1895
Osmanski, William—Holy Cross, 1938
Owen, George—Harvard, 1922
Owens, Jim—Oklahoma, 1949
Pardee, Jack—Texas A & M, 1956
Parilli, Vito (Babe)—Kentucky, 1951
Parker, Clarence (Ace)—Duke, 1936
Parker, Jackie—Miss. State, 1953
Parker, James—Ohio State, 1956
Pazzetti, V.J.—Wes./Lehigh, 1912
Peabody, Endicott—Harvard, 1941
Peck, Robert—Pittsburgh, 1916
Pennock, Stanley B.—Harvard, 1914
Pfann, George—Cornell, 1923
Phillips, H.D.—U. of South, 1904
Pingel, John—Michigan State, 1938
Pihos, Pete—Indiana, 1945
Pinckert, Ernie—So. California, 1931
Plunkett, Jim—Stanford, 1970
Poe, Arthur—Princeton, 1899

Pollard, Fritz—Brown, 1916
Poole, Barney—Miss./Army, 1947
Pregulman, Merv—Michigan, 1943
Price, Eddie—Tulane, 1949
Pund, Henry—Georgia Tech, 1928
Ramsey, Gerrard—Wm. & Mary, 1942
Reeds, Claude—Oklahoma, 1913
Reid, Mike—Penn St. 1970
Reid, Steve—Northwestern, 1936
Reid, William—Harvard, 1900
Renfro, Mel—Oregon, 1963
Rentner, Ernest—Northwestern, 1932
Reynolds, Robert—Nebraska, 1952
Reynolds, Robert—Stanford, 1935
Richter, Les—California, 1951
Riley, John—Northwestern, 1931
Rinehart, Charles—Lafayette, 1897
Rodgers, Ira—West Virginia, 1919
Rogers, Edward L.—Minnesota, 1903
Romig, Joe—Colorado, 1961
Rosenberg, Aaron—So. California, 1934
Rote, Kyle—So. Methodist, 1950
Routt, Joe—Texas A&M, 1937
Salmon, Louis—Notre Dame, 1904
Sauer, George—Nebraska, 1933
Sayers, Gale—Kansas, 1964
Scarbath, Jack—Maryland, 1952
Scarlett, Hunter—Pennsylvania, 1909
Schloredt, Bob—Washington, 1960
Schoonover, Wear—Arkansas, 1929
Schreiner, Dave—Wisconsin, 1942
Schultz, Adolf (Germany)—Mich., 1908
Schwab, Frank—Lafayette, 1922
Schwartz, Marchmont—Notre Dame, 1931
Schwegler, Paul—Washington, 1931
Scott, Clyde—Arkansas, 1949
Scott, Richard—Navy 1947
Scott, Tom—Virginia, 1953
Seibels, Henry—Sewanee, 1899
Sellers, Ron—Florida State, 1968
Selmon, Lee Roy—Oklahoma, 1975
Shakespeare, Bill—Notre Dame, 1935
Shelton, Murray—Cornell, 1915
Shevlin, Tom—Yale, 1905
Shively, Bernie—Illinois, 1926
Simons, Claude—Tulane, 1934
Simpson, O.J.—So. Calif., 1968
Sington, Fred—Alabama, 1930
Sinkwich, Frank—Georgia, 1942
Sitko, Emil—Notre Dame, 1949
Skladany, Joe—Pittsburgh, 1933
Slater, F.F. (Duke)—Iowa, 1921
Smith, Bruce—Minnesota, 1941
Smith, Bubba—Michigan State, 1966
Smith, Ernie—So. California, 1932
Smith, Harry—So. California, 1939
Smith, Jim Ray—Baylor, 1954
Smith, John (Clipper)—Notre Dame, 1927
Smith, Riley—Alabama, 1935
Smith, Vernon—Georgia, 1931
Snow, Neil—Michigan, 1901
Sparlis, Al—U.C.L.A., 1945
Spears, Clarence W.—Dartmouth, 1915
Spears, W.D.—Vanderbilt, 1927
Sprackling, William—Brown, 1911
Sprague, M. (Bud)—Texas/Army, 1928
Spurrier, Steve—Florida, 1966
Stafford, Harrison—Texas, 1932
Stagg, Amos Alonzo—Yale, 1889
Starcevich, Max—Washington, 1936
Staubach, Roger—Navy, 1963
Steffen, Walter—Chicago, 1908
Steffy, Joe—Army, 1947
Stein, Herbert—Pittsburgh, 1921
Steuber, Robert—Missouri, 1943
Stevens, Mal—Yale, 1923
Stinchcomb, Gaylord—Ohio State, 1920
Stevenson, Vincent—Pennsylvania, 1905
Strom, Brock—Air Force, 1959
Strong, Ken—New York Univ., 1928
Strupper, George—Georgia Tech, 1917
Stuhldreher, Harry—Notre Dame, 1924
Stydahar, Joe—West Virginia, 1935
Suffridge, Robert—Tennessee, 1940
Suhey, Steve—Pennsylvania State, 1947
Sundstrom, Frank—Cornell, 1923

Swanson, Clarence—Nebraska, 1921
Swiacki, Bill—Holy Cross/Colombia, 1947
Swink, Jim—Texas Christian, 1956
Taliaferro, George—Indiana, 1948
Tarkenton, Fran—Georgia, 1960
Tavener, John—Indiana, 1944
Taylor, Charles—Stanford, 1942
Thomas, Aurelius—Ohio St., 1957
Thompson, Joe—Pittsburgh, 1907
Thorne, Samuel B.—Yale, 1906
Thorpe, Jim—Carlisle, 1912
Ticknor, Ben—Harvard, 1930
Tigert, John—Vanderbilt, 1904
Tinsley, Gaynell—La. State U., 1936
Tipton, Eric—Duke, 1938
Tonnemaker, Clayton—Minnesota, 1949
Torrey, Robert—Pennsylvania, 1906
Travis, Ed Tarkio—Missouri, 1920
Trippi, Charles—Georgia, 1946
Tryon, J. Edward—Colgate, 1925
Utay, Joe—Texas A&M, 1907
Van Brocklin, Norm—Oregon, 1948
Van Sickel, Dale—Florida, 1929
Van Surdam, Henderson—Wesleyan, 1905
Very, Dexter—Penn State, 1912
Vessels, Billy—Oklahoma, 1952
Vick, Ernie—Michigan, 1921
Wagner, Huber—Pittsburgh, 1913

Walker, Doak—So. Methodist, 1949
Wallace, Bill—Rice, 1935
Walsh, Adam—Notre Dame, 1924
Warburton, I. (Cotton)—So. Calif., 1934
Ward, Robert (Bob)—Maryland, 1951
Warner, William—Cornell, 1903
Washington, Ken—U.C.L.A., 1939
Webster, George—Michigan St. 1966
Wedemeyer, Herman J.—St. Mary's, 1947
Weekes, Harold—Columbia, 1902
Weir, Ed—Nebraska, 1925
Welch, Gus—Carlisle, 1914
Weller, John—Princeton, 1935
Wendell, Percy—Harvard, 1913
West, D. Belford—Colgate, 1919
Westfall, Bob—Michigan, 1941
Weyand, Alex—Army, 1915
Wharton, Charles—Pennsylvania, 1896
Wheeler, Arthur—Princeton, 1894
White, Byron (Whizzer)—Colorado, 1937
Whitmire, Don—Alabama/Navy, 1944
Wickhorst, Frank—Navy, 1926
Widseth, Ed—Minnesota, 1936
Wildung, Richard—Minnesota, 1942
Williams, Bob—Notre Dame, 1950
Williams, James—Rice, 1949
Willis, William—Ohio State, 1945
Wilson, George—Washington, 1925

Wilson, George—Lafayette, 1928
Wilson, Harry—Penn State/Army, 1923
Wistert, Albert A.—Michigan, 1942
Wistert, Al—Michigan, 1949
Wistert, Frank (Whitey)—Mich., 1933
Wood, Barry—Harvard, 1931
Wojciechowicz, Alex—Fordham, 1936
Wyant, Andrew—Bucknell/Chicago, 1894
Wyatt, Bowden—Tennessee, 1938
Wyckoff, Clint—Cornell, 1896
Yarr, Tom—Notre Dame, 1931
Yary, Ron—USC, 1968
Yoder, Lloyd—Carnegie Tech, 1926
Young, Claude (Buddy)—Illinois, 1946
Young, Harry—Wash. & Lee, 1916
Young, Walter—Oklahoma, 1938
Zarnas, Gus—Ohio State, 1937

Coaches

Bill Alexander
Dr. Ed Anderson
Ike Armstrong
Harry Baujan
Matty Bell
Hugo Bezdek
Dana X. Bible
Bernie Bierman
Bob Blackman
Earl (Red) Blaik
Frank Broyles
Paul "Bear" Bryant
Charles W. Caldwell
Walter Camp
Len Casanova
Frank Cavanaugh
Richard Colman
Fritz Crisler
Duffy Daugherty
Bob Devaney
Dan Devine
Gil Dobie
Michael Donohue

Gus Dorais
Bill Edwards
Charles (Rip) Engle
Don Faurot
Jake Gaither
Sid Gillman
Ernest Godfrey
Ray Graves
Andy Gustafson
Jack Harding
Edward K. Hall
Richard Harlow
Jesse Harper
Percy Haughton
Woody Hayes
John W. Heisman
R. A. (Bob) Higgins
Orin E. Hollingberry
Frank Howard
William Ingram
Morley Jennings
Howard Jones
L. (Biff) Jones

Thomas (Tad) Jones
Ralph (Shug) Jordan
Andy Kerr
Frank Leahy
George E. Little
Lou Little
El (Slip) Madigan
Charley McClendon
Herbert McCracken
Daniel McGugin
John McKay
DeOrmond (Tuss) Mc-
  Laughry
L. R. (Dutch) Meyer
Bernie Moore
Scrappy Moore
Jack Mollenkopf
Ray Morrison
George A. Munger
Clarence Munn
Frank Murray
William Murray
Ed (Hooks) Mylin

Earle (Greasy) Neale
Jess Neely
David Nelson
Robert Neyland
Homer Norton
Frank (Buck) O'Neill
Bennie Owen
Ara Parseghian
Doyt Perry
James Phalea
E. N. Robinson
Knute Rockne
E. L. (Dick) Romney
William W. Roper
Darrell Royal
George F. Sanford
Francis A. Schmidt
Floyd (Ben) Schwartz-
  walder
Clark Shaughnessy
Buck Shaw
Andrew L. Smith
Carl Snavely

Amos A. Stagg
Jock Sutherland
James Tatum
Frank W. Thomas
Thad Vann
John H. Vaught
Wallace Wade
Lynn Waldorf
Glenn (Pop) Warner
E. E. (Tad) Wieman
John W. Wilce
Bud Wilkinson
Henry L. Williams
George W. Woodruff
Warren Woodson
Fielding H. Yost
Robert Zuppke

NFL TEAM NICKNAMES AND HOME FIELD CAPACITIES

AMERICAN CONFERENCE
Eastern Division

Buffalo Bills	Rich Stadium (AT)	80,020
Indianapolis Colts[1]	Hoosier Dome (AT)	61,500
Miami Dolphins	Joe Robbie Stadium (G)	75,000
New England Patriots	Sullivan Stadium (ST)	61,297
New York Jets[2]	Giants Stadium (AT)	76,891

Central Division

Cincinnati Bengals	Riverfront Stadium (AT)	59,754
Cleveland Browns	Municipal Stadium (G)	80,322
Houston Oilers	Astrodome (AT)	50,496
Pittsburgh Steelers	Three Rivers Stadium (AT)	59,000

Western Division

Denver Broncos	Mile High Stadium (G)	75,103
Kansas City Chiefs	Arrowhead Stadium (TT)	78,067
Los Angeles Raiders[3]	Memorial Coliseum (G)	92,498
San Diego Chargers	Jack Murphy Stadium (G)	53,675
Seattle Seahawks	Kingdome (AT)	64,757

1. Moved franchise from Baltimore prior to 1984 season. 2.
Moved to Giants Stadium; East Rutherford, N.J. prior to
1984 season. 3. Moved franchise to Los Angeles for 1982
season. Shift is still being argued in courts, as city of Oakland
tries to regain franchise.

NATIONAL CONFERENCE
Eastern Division

Dallas Cowboys	Texas Stadium (TT)	65,101
New York Giants	Giants Stadium (AT)[1]	76,891
Philadelphia Eagles	Veterans Stadium (AT)	72,204
Phoenix Cardinals	Sun Devil Stadium (G)	70,491
Washington Redskins	R.F. Kennedy Stadium (G)	55,045

Central Division

Chicago Bears	Soldier Field (AT)	65,793
Detroit Lions	Pontiac Silverdome (AT)	80,638
Green Bay Packers	Lambeau Field (G)	56,189
	Milwaukee Stadium (G)	55,958
Minnesota Vikings	Hubert Humphrey	62,212
	Metrodome (ST)	
Tampa Bay Buccaneers	Tampa Stadium (G)	72,812

Western Division

Atlanta Falcons	Atlanta-Fulton Stadium (G)	60,748
Los Angeles Rams	Anaheim Stadium (G)	69,007
New Orleans Saints	Louisiana Superdome (AT)	71,330

San Francisco 49ers   Candlestick Park (G)   61,185

1. At East Rutherford, N.J. NOTE: Stadium playing surfaces in parentheses: (AT) Astro Turf; (G) Grass; (ST) Super Turf; (TT) Tartan Turf.

Professional Football

NATIONAL FOOTBALL LEAGUE FINAL STANDING 1989

AMERICAN FOOTBALL CONFERENCE
Eastern Division

	W	L	T	Pct	Pts	Op
Buffalo[1]	9	7	0	.563	409	317
Indianapolis	8	8	0	.500	298	301
Miami	8	8	0	.500	331	379
New England	5	11	0	.313	297	391
N.Y. Jets	4	12	0	.250	253	411

Central Division

	W	L	T	Pct	Pts	Op
Cleveland[1]	9	6	1	.594	334	254
Houston[2]	9	7	0	.563	365	412
Pittsburgh[2]	9	7	0	.563	265	326
Cincinnati	8	8	0	.500	404	285

Western Division

	W	L	T	Pct	Pts	Op
Denver[1]	11	5	0	.688	362	226
Kansas City	8	7	1	.531	318	286
L.A. Raiders	8	8	0	.500	315	297
Seattle	7	9	0	.438	241	327
San Diego	6	10	0	.375	266	290

1. Clinched division title; 2. Wild Card for playoffs.
Indianapolis finished ahead of Miami because of better conference rec-

NATIONAL FOOTBALL CONFERENCE
Eastern Division

	W	L	T	Pct	Pts	Op
N.Y. Giants[1]	12	4	0	.750	348	252
Philadelphia[2]	11	5	0	.688	342	274
Washington	10	6	0	.625	386	308
Phoenix	5	11	0	.313	258	377
Dallas	1	15	0	.063	204	393

Central Division

	W	L	T	Pct	Pts	Op
Minnesota[1]	10	6	0	.625	351	275
Green Bay	10	6	0	.625	362	356
Detroit	7	9	0	.438	312	364
Chicago	6	10	0	.375	358	377
Tampa Bay	5	11	0	.313	320	419

Western Division

	W	L	T	Pct	Pts	Op
San Francisco[1]	14	2	0	.875	442	253
L.A. Rams[2]	11	5	0	.688	426	344
New Orleans	9	7	0	.563	386	301
Atlanta	3	13	0	.188	279	437

ord (7-5 vs. 6-8). Houston finished ahead of Pittsburgh because of head-to-head sweep (2-0). Minnesota finished ahead of Green Bay because of better division record (6-2 vs. 5-3).

LEAGUE CHAMPIONSHIP—SUPER BOWL XXIV

(January 28, 1990, at The Superdome, New Orleans, La.; Attendance: 72,919)

Scoring

	1st Q	2nd Q	3rd Q	4th Q	Final
San Francisco (NFC)	13	14	14	14	- 55
Denver (AFC)	3	0	7	0	- 10

Scoring— San Francisco: Touchdowns: Rice, 20-yard pass from Montana (Cofer kick); Jones, 7-yard pass from Montana (kick failed); Rathman, 1-yard run (Cofer kick); Rice, 38-yard pass from Montana (Cofer kick); Rice, 28-yard pass from Montana (Cofer kick); Taylor, 35-yard pass from Montana (Cofer kick); Rathman, 4-yard run (Cofer kick); Craig, 1-yard run (Cofer kick). Denver: Touchdowns: Elway, 3-yard run (Treadwell kick). Field goals: Treadwell 42.

Statistics of the Game

	San Francisco	Denver
First downs	28	12
Third down eff	8-15	3-11
Fourth down eff	2-2	0-0
Total net yards	461	167
Net yards rushing	144	64
Net yards passing	317	103
Punts–avg.	4-40	6-39
Total return yardage	129	207
Penalties–yds	4-38	0-0
Fumbles–lost	0-0	3-2
Time of possession	39:31	20:29

SUPER BOWLS I–XXIV

Game	Date	Winner	Loser	Site	Attendance
XXIV	Jan. 28, 1990	San Francisco (NFC) 55	Denver (AFC) 10	Superdome, New Orleans	72,919
XXIII	Jan. 22, 1989	San Francisco (NFC) 20	Cincinnati (AFC) 16	Joe Robbie Stadium, Miami, Fla.	75,179
XXII	Jan. 31, 1988	Washington (NFC) 42	Denver (AFC) 10	Jack Murphy Stadium, San Diego, Calif.	73,302
XXI	Jan. 25, 1987	Giants (NFC) 39	Denver (AFC) 20	Rose Bowl, Pasadena, Calif.	101,063
XX	Jan. 26, 1986	Chicago (NFC) 46	New England (AFC) 10	Superdome, New Orleans	73,818
XIX	Jan. 20, 1985	San Francisco (NFC) 38	Miami (AFC) 16	Stanford Stadium, Palo Alto, Calif.	84,059
XVIII	Jan. 22, 1984	Los Angeles Raiders (AFC) 38	Washington (NFC) 9	Tampa Stadium, Tampa, Fla	72,920
XVII	Jan. 30, 1983	Washington (NFC) 27	Miami (AFC) 17	Rose Bowl, Pasadena, Calif.	103,667
XVI	Jan. 24, 1982	San Francisco (NFC) 26	Cincinnati (AFC) 21	Silverdome, Pontiac, Mich.	81,270
XV	Jan. 25, 1981	Oakland (AFC) 27	Philadelphia (NFC) 10	Superdome, New Orleans	75,500
XIV	Jan. 20, 1980	Pittsburgh (AFC) 31	Los Angeles (NFC) 19	Rose Bowl, Pasadena	103,985
XIII	Jan. 21, 1979	Pittsburgh (AFC) 35	Dallas (NFC) 31	Orange Bowl, Miami	79,484
XII	Jan. 15, 1978	Dallas (NFC) 27	Denver (AFC) 10	Superdome, New Orleans	75,583
XI	Jan. 9, 1977	Oakland (AFC) 32	Minnesota (NFC) 14	Rose Bowl, Pasadena	103,424

X	Jan. 18, 1976	Pittsburgh (AFC) 21	Dallas (NFC) 17	Orange Bowl, Miami	80,187
IX	Jan. 12, 1975	Pittsburgh (AFC) 16	Minnesota (NFC) 6	Tulane Stadium, New Orleans	80,997
VIII	Jan. 13, 1974	Miami (AFC) 24	Minnesota (NFC) 7	Rice Stadium, Houston	71,882
VII	Jan. 14, 1973	Miami (AFC) 14	Washington (NFC) 7	Memorial Coliseum, Los Angeles	90,182
VI	Jan. 16, 1972	Dallas (NFC) 24	Miami (AFC) 3	Tulane Stadium, New Orleans	81,591
V	Jan. 17, 1971	Baltimore (AFC) 16	Dallas (NFC) 13	Orange Bowl, Miami	79,204
IV	Jan. 11, 1970	Kansas City (AFL) 23	Minnesota (NFL) 7	Tulane Stadium, New Orleans	80,562
III	Jan. 12, 1969	New York (AFL) 16	Baltimore (NFL) 7	Orange Bowl, Miami	75,389
II	Jan. 14, 1968	Green Bay (NFL) 33	Oakland (AFL) 14	Orange Bowl, Miami	75,546
I	Jan. 15, 1967	Green Bay (NFL) 35	Kansas City (AFL) 10	Memorial Coliseum, Los Angeles	61,946

NOTE: Super Bowls I to IV were played before the American Football League and National Football League merged into the NFL, which was divided into two conferences, the NFC and AFC.

NATIONAL LEAGUE CHAMPIONS

Year	Champion (W-L-T)	Year	Champion (W-L-T)	Year	Champion (W-L-T)
1921	Chicago Bears (Staley's) (10–1–1)	1925	Chicago Cardinals (11–2–1)	1929	Green Bay Packers (12–0–1)
1922	Canton Bulldogs (10–0–2)	1926	Frankford Yellow Jackets (14–1–1)	1930	Green Bay Packers (10–3–1)
1923	Canton Bulldogs (11–0–1)	1927	New York Giants (11–1–1)	1931	Green Bay Packers (12–2–0)
1924	Cleveland Indians (7–1–1)	1928	Providence Steamrollers (8–1–2)	1932	Chicago Bears (7–1–6)

Year	Eastern Conference winners (W-L-T)	Western Conference winners (W-L-T)	League champion playoff results
1933	New York Giants (11–3–0)	Chicago Bears (10–2–1)	Chicago Bears 23, New York 21
1934	New York Giants (8–5–0)	Chicago Bears (13–0–0)	New York 30, Chicago Bears 13
1935	New York Giants (9–3–0)	Detroit Lions (7–3–2)	Detroit 26, New York 7
1936	Boston Redskins (7–5–0)	Green Bay Packers (10–1–1)	Green Bay 21, Boston 6
1937	Washington Redskins (8–3–0)	Chicago Bears (9–1–1)	Washington 28, Chicago Bears 21
1938	New York Giants (8–2–1)	Green Bay Packers (8–3–0)	New York 23, Green Bay 17
1939	New York Giants (9–1–1)	Green Bay Packers (9–2–0)	Green Bay 27, New York 0
1940	Washington Redskins (9–2–0)	Chicago Bears (8–3–0)	Chicago Bears 73, Washington 0
1941	New York Giants (8–3–0)	Chicago Bears (10–1–1)²	Chicago Bears 37, New York 9
1942	Washington Redskins (10–1–1)	Chicago Bears (11–0–0)	Washington 14, Chicago Bears 6
1943	Washington Redskins (6–3–1)²	Chicago Bears (8–1–1)	Chicago Bears 41, Washington 21
1944	New York Giants (8–1–1)	Green Bay Packers (8–2–0)	Green Bay 14, New York 7
1945	Washington Redskins (8–2–0)	Cleveland Rams (9–1–0)	Cleveland 15, Washington 14
1946	New York Giants (7–3–1)	Chicago Bears (8–2–1)	Chicago Bears 24, New York 14
1947	Philadelphia Eagles (8–4–0)²	Chicago Cardinals (9–3–0)	Chicago Cardinals 28, Philadelphia 21
1948	Philadelphia Eagles (9–2–1)	Chicago Cardinals (11–1–0)	Philadelphia 7, Chicago Cardinals 0
1949	Philadelphia Eagles (11–1–0)	Los Angeles Rams (8–2–2)	Philadelphia 14, Los Angeles 0
1950¹	Cleveland Browns (10–2–0)²	Los Angeles Rams (9–3–0)²	Cleveland 30, Los Angeles 28
1951¹	Cleveland Browns (11–1–0)	Los Angeles Rams (8–4–0)	Los Angeles 24, Cleveland 17
1952¹	Cleveland Browns (8–4–0)	Detroit Lions (9–3–0)²	Detroit 17, Cleveland 7
1953	Cleveland Browns (11–1–0)	Detroit Lions (10–2–0)	Detroit 17, Cleveland 16
1954	Cleveland Browns (9–3–0)	Detroit Lions (9–2–1)	Cleveland 56, Detroit 10
1955	Cleveland Browns (9–2–1)	Los Angeles Rams (8–3–1)	Cleveland 38, Los Angeles 14
1956	New York Giants (8–3–1)	Chicago Bears (9–2–1)	New York 47, Chicago Bears 7
1957	Cleveland Browns (9–2–1)	Detroit Lions (8–4–0)²	Detroit 59, Cleveland 14
1958	New York Giants (9–3–0)²	Baltimore Colts (9–3–0)	Baltimore 23, New York 17³
1959	New York Giants (10–2–0)	Baltimore Colts (9–3–0)	Baltimore 31, New York 16
1960	Philadelphia Eagles (10–2–0)	Green Bay Packers (8–4–0)	Philadelphia 17, Green Bay 13
1961	New York Giants (10–3–1)	Green Bay Packers (11–3–0)	Green Bay 37, New York 0
1962	New York Giants (12–2–0)	Green Bay Packers (13–1–0)	Green Bay 16, New York 7
1963	New York Giants (11–3–0)	Chicago Bears (11–1–2)	Chicago 14, New York 10
1964	Cleveland Browns (10–3–1)	Baltimore Colts (12–2–0)	Cleveland 27, Baltimore 0
1965	Cleveland Browns (11–3–0)	Green Bay Packers (11–3–1)²	Green Bay 23, Cleveland 12
1966	Dallas Cowboys (10–3–1)	Green Bay Packers (12–2–0)	Green Bay 34, Dallas 27
1967	Dallas Cowboys (9–5–0)²	Green Bay Packers (9–4–1)²	Green Bay 21, Dallas 17
1968	Cleveland Browns (10–4–0)²	Baltimore Colts (13–1–0)²	Baltimore 34, Cleveland 0
1969	Cleveland Browns (10–3–1)²	Minnesota Vikings (12–2–0)²	Minnesota 27, Cleveland 7

1. League was divided into American and National Conferences, 1950–52 and again in 1970, when leagues merged. 2. Won divisional playoff. 3. Won at 8:15 of sudden death overtime period.

NATIONAL CONFERENCE CHAMPIONS

Year	Eastern Division	Central Division	Western Division	Champion
1970	Dallas Cowboys (10–4–0)	Minnesota Vikings (12–2–0)	San Francisco 49ers (10–3–1)	Dallas
1971	Dallas Cowboys (11–3–0)	Minnesota Vikings (11–3–0)	San Francisco 49ers (9–5–0)	Dallas
1972	Washington Redskins (11–3–0)	Green Bay Packers (10–4–0)	San Francisco 49ers (8–5–1)	Washington
1973	Dallas Cowboys (10–4–0)	Minnesota Vikings (12–2–0)	Los Angeles Rams (12–2–0)	Minnesota
1974	St. Louis Cardinals (10–4–0)	Minnesota Vikings (10–4–0)	Los Angeles Rams (10–4–0)	Minnesota
1975	St. Louis Cardinals (11–3–0)	Minnesota Vikings (12–2–0)	Los Angeles Rams (10–4–0)	Dallas
1976	Dallas Cowboys (11–3–0)	Minnesota Vikings (11–2–1)	Los Angeles Rams (10–3–1)	Minnesota

1977	Dallas Cowboys (12–2–0)	Minnesota Vikings (9–5–0)	Los Angeles Rams (10–4–0)	Dallas
1978	Dallas Cowboys (12–4–0)	Minnesota Vikings (8–7–1)	Los Angeles Rams (12–4–0)	Dallas
1979	Dallas Cowboys (11–5–0)	Tampa Bay Buccaneers (10–6–0)	Los Angeles Rams (9–7–0)	Los Angeles
1980	Philadelphia Eagles (12–4–0)	Minnesota Vikings (9–7–0)	Atlanta Falcons (12–4–0)	Philadelphia
1981	Dallas Cowboys (12–4–0)	Tampa Bay Buccaneers (9–7–0)	San Francisco 49ers (13–3–0)	San Francisco
1982*	Washington Redskins won conference title and also had best regular-season record (8–1–0)			
1983	Washington Redskins (14–2–0)	Detroit Lions (8–8–0)	San Francisco 49ers (10–6–0)	Washington
1984	Washington Redskins (11–5–0)	Chicago Bears (10–6–0)	San Francisco 49ers (15–1–0)	San Francisco
1985	Dallas Cowboys (10-6-0)	Chicago Bears (15-1-0)	Los Angeles Rams (11-5-0)	Chicago
1986	New York Giants (14–2–0)	Chicago Bears (14–2–0)	San Francisco 49ers (10–5–1)	New York
1987	Washington Redskins (11–4–0)	Chicago Bears (11–4–0)	San Francisco 49ers (13–2–0)	Washington
1988	Philadelphia Eagles (10–6–0)	Chicago Bears (12–4–0)	San Francisco 49ers (10–6–0)	San Francisco
1989	New York Giants (12–4–0)	Minnesota Vikings (10–6–0)	San Francisco 49ers (14–2–0)	San Francisco

*Schedule reduced to 9 games from usual 16, with no standings kept in Eastern, Central, and Western Divisions, because of 57-day player strike.

AMERICAN CONFERENCE CHAMPIONS

Year	Eastern Division	Central Division	Western Division	Champion
1970	Baltimore Colts (11–2–1)	Cincinnati Bengals (8–6–0)	Oakland Raiders (8–4–2)	Baltimore
1971	Miami Dolphins (10–3–1)	Cleveland Browns (9–5–0)	Kansas City Chiefs (10–3–1)	Miami
1972	Miami Dolphins (14–0–0)	Pittsburgh Steelers (11–3–0)	Oakland Raiders (10–3–1)	Miami
1973	Miami Dolphins (12–2–0)	Cincinnati Bengals (10–4–0)	Oakland Raiders (9–4–1)	Miami
1974	Miami Dolphins (11–3–0)	Pittsburgh Steelers (10–3–1)	Oakland Raiders (12–2–0)	Pittsburgh
1975	Baltimore Colts (10–4–0)	Pittsburgh Steelers (12–2–0)	Oakland Raiders (11–3–0)	Pittsburgh
1976	Baltimore Colts (11–3–0)	Pittsburgh Steelers (10–4–0)	Oakland Raiders (13–1–0)	Oakland
1977	Baltimore Colts (10–4–0)	Pittsburgh Steelers (9–5–0)	Denver Broncos (12–2–0)	Denver
1978	New England Patriots (11–5–0)	Pittsburgh Steelers (14–2–0)	Denver Broncos (10–6–0)	Pittsburgh
1979	Miami Dolphins (10–6–0)	Pittsburgh Steelers (12–4–0)	San Diego Chargers (12–4–0)	Pittsburgh
1980	Buffalo Bills (11–5–0)	Cleveland Browns (11–5–0)	San Diego Chargers (11–5–0)	Oakland
1981	Miami Dolphins (11–4–1)	Cincinnati Bengals (12–4–0)	San Diego Chargers (10–6–0)	Cincinnati
1982*	Miami Dolphins won the conference title, but the Los Angeles Raiders had best regular-season record (8–1–0).			
1983	Miami (12–4–0)	Pittsburgh (10–6–0)	Los Angeles Raiders (12–4–0)	Los Angeles
1984	Miami (14–2–0)	Pittsburgh (9–7–0)	Denver (13–3–0)	Miami
1985	Miami (12-4-0)	Cleveland (8-8)	Los Angeles Raiders (12-4-0)	New England
1986	New England (11–5–0)	Cleveland (12–4–0)	Denver (11–5–0)	Denver
1987	Indianapolis Colts (9–6–0)	Cleveland Browns (10–5–0)	Denver Broncos (10–4–1)	Denver
1988	Buffalo Bills (12–4–0)	Cincinnati Bengals (12–4–0)	Seattle Seahawks (9–7–0)	Cincinnati
1989	Buffalo Bills (9–7–0)	Cleveland Browns (9–6–1)	Denver Broncos (11–5–0)	Denver

*Schedule reduced to 9 games from usual 16, with no standings kept in Eastern, Central, and Western Divisions, because of 57-day player strike.

AMERICAN LEAGUE CHAMPIONS

Year	Eastern Division (W-L-T)	Western Division (W-L-T)	League champion, playoff results
1960	Houston Oilers (10-4-0)	Los Angeles Chargers (10-4-0)	Houston 24, Los Angeles 16
1961	Houston Oilers (10-3-1)	San Diego Chargers (12-2-0)	Houston 10, San Diego 3
1962	Houston Oilers (11-3-0)	Dallas Texans (11-3-0)	Dallas 20, Houston 17[1]
1963	Boston Patriots (8-6-1)[2]	San Diego Chargers (11-3-0)	San Diego 51, Boston 10
1964	Buffalo Bills (12-2-0)	San Diego Chargers (8-5-1)	Buffalo 20, San Diego 7
1965	Buffalo Bills (10-3-1)	San Diego Chargers (9-2-3)	Buffalo 23, San Diego 0
1966	Buffalo Bills (9-4-1)	Kansas City Chiefs (11-2-1)	Kansas City 31, Buffalo 7
1967	Houston Oilers (9-4-1)	Oakland Raiders (13-1-0)	Oakland 40, Houston 7
1968	New York Jets (11-3-0)	Oakland Raiders (12-2-0)[2]	New York 27, Oakland 23
1969	New York Jets (10-4-0)	Oakland Raiders (12-1-1)	Kansas City 17, Oakland 7[3]

1. Won at 2:45 of second sudden death overtime period. 2. Won divisional playoff. 3. Kansas City defeated New York, 13–6, and Oakland defeated Houston, 56–7, in interdivisional playoffs.

PRO FOOTBALL HALL OF FAME

(National Football Museum, Canton, Ohio)

Teams named are those with which player is best identified; figures in parentheses indicate number of playing seasons.

Adderley, Herb, defensive back, Packers, Cowboys (12)	1961–72	Steelers, N.F.L. Commissioner	1946–59
		Bell, Bobby, linebacker, Chiefs (12)	1963–74
Alworth, Lance, wide receiver, Chargers, Cowboys (11)	1962–72	Berry, Raymond, end, Colts (13)	1955–67
		Bidwell, Charles W., owner Chicago Cardinals	1933–47
Atkins, Doug, defensive end, Browns, Bears, Saints (17)	1953–69	Biletnikoff, Fred, wide receiver, Raiders (14)	1965–1978
		Blanda, George, quarterback-kicker, Bears,	
Badgro, Morris, end, N.Y. Yankees, Giants, Bklyn. Dodgers (8)	1927, 1930–36	Oilers, Raiders (27)	1949–75
		Blount, Mel, cornerback, Pittsburgh Steelers (14)	1970–83
Battles, Cliff, back, Redskins (6)	1932–37	Bradshaw, Terry, quarterback, Pittsburgh Steelers (14)	1970–83
Baugh, Sammy, quarterback, Redskins (16)	1937–52	Brown, Jim, fullback, Browns (9)	1957–65
Bednarik, Chuck, center-linebacker, Eagles (14)	1949–62	Brown, Paul E., coach, Browns (1946–62),	
Bell, Bert, N.F.L. founder, owner Eagles and		Bengals (1968–75)	1946–75

Brown, Roosevelt, tackle, Giants (13) — 1953–65
Brown, Willie, cornerback, Broncos, Raiders (16) — 1963–78
Buchanan, Buck, tackle, Chiefs (11) — 1963–73
Butkus, Dick, linebacker, Bears (9) — 1965–73
Canadeo, Tony, back, Packers (11) — 1941–52
Carr, Joe, president N.F.L. (18) — 1921–39
Chamberlin, Guy, end 4 teams (9) — 1919–27
Christiansen, Jack, defensive back, Lions (8) — 1951–58
Clark, Earl (Dutch), Qback, Spartans, Lions (7) — 1931–38
Connor, George, tackle, linebacker, Bears (8) — 1948–55
Conzelman, Jimmy, Qback 5 teams (10), owner — 1921–48
Csonka, Larry, back, Dolphins, Giants (11) — 1968–79
Davis, Willie, defensive end, Packers (10) — 1960–69
Dawson, Len, quarterback, Steelers, Browns, Texans, Chiefs (19) — 1957–75
Ditka, Mike, tight end, Bears, Eagles, Cowboys (12) — 1961–72
Donovan, Art, defensive tackle, Colts (12) — 1950–61
Driscoll, John (Paddy), Qback, Cards, Bears (11) — 1919–29
Dudley, Bill, back, Steelers, Lions, Redskins (9) — 1942–53
Edwards, Albert Glen (Turk), tackle, Redskins (9) — 1932–40
Ewbank, Weeb, coach Colts, Jets (20) — 1954–73
Fears, Tom, end, Rams (9); coach, Saints — 1948–56
Flaherty, Ray, end, Yankees, Giants (9); coach, Redskins, Yankees (14) — 1928–49
Ford, Len, end, def. end, Browns, Packers (11) — 1948–58
Fortmann, Daniel J., guard, Bears (8) — 1936–43
Gatski, Frank, offensive lineman, Browns (12) — 1946–57
George, Bill, linebacker, Bears, Rams (15) — 1952–66
Gifford, Frank, back, Giants (12) — 1952–64
Gillman, Sid, coach, Rams, Chargers, Oilers (18) — 1955–70, 73–74
Graham, Otto, quarterback, Browns (10) — 1946–55
Grange, Harold (Red), back, Bears, Yankees (9) — 1925–34
Greene, Joe, defensive tackle, Steelers (13) — 1968–81
Gregg, Forrest, tackle, Packers (15) — 1956–71
Griese, Bob, quarterback, Dolphins (14) — 1967–80
Groza, Lou, place-kicker, tackle, Browns (21) — 1946–67
Guyon, Joe, back, 6 teams (8) — 1919–27
Halas, George, N.F.L. founder, owner and coach, Staleys and Bears, end (11) — 1919–67
Ham, Jack, linebacker, Steelers (13) — 1970–82
Harris, Franco, running back, Steelers, Seahawks (13) — 1972–84
Healey, Ed, tackle, Bears (8) — 1920–27
Hein, Mel, center, Giants (15) — 1931–45
Hendricks, Ted, linebacker, Colts, Packers, Raiders (15) — 1969–83
Henry, Wilbur (Pete), tackle, Bulldogs, Giants (8) — 1920–28
Herber, Arnie, Qback, Packers, Giants (13) — 1930–45
Hewitt, Bill, end, Bears, Eagles (9) — 1932–43
Hinkle, Clarke, fullback, Packers (10) — 1932–41
Hirsch, Elroy (Crazy Legs), back, end, Rams (12) — 1946–57
Hornung, Paul, running back, Packers (9) — 1957–62, 1964–66
Houston, Ken def. back, Oilers, Redskins (14) — 1967–80
Hubbard, R. (Cal), tackle, Giants, Packers (9) — 1927–36
Huff, Sam, linebacker, Giants, Redskins (13) — 1956–67, 1969
Hunt, Lamar, Founder A.F.L., owner Texans, Chiefs — 1959–
Hutson, Don, end, Packers (11) — 1935–45
Johnson, John Henry, back, 49ers, Lions, Steelers, Oilers (13) — 1954–66
Jones, David (Deacon), defensive end, Rams, Chargers, Redskins (14) — 1961–74
Jurgensen, Sonny, quarterback, Eagles, Redskins (18) — 1957–74
Kiesling, Walt, guard 6 teams (13) — 1926–38
Kinard, Frank (Bruiser), tackle, Dodgers (9) — 1938–47
Lambeau, Earl (Curly), N.F.L. founder, coach, end, back, Packers (11) — 1919–53
Lambert, Jack, linebacker, Steelers (11) — 1974–84
Landry, Tom, coach, Cowboys (29) — 1960–88
Lane, Richard (Night Train), defensive back, Rams, Cardinals, Lions (14) — 1952–65
Langer, Jim, center, Dolphins, Vikings (12) — 1970–81
Lanier, Willie, linebacker, Chiefs (11) — 1967–77
Lary, Yale, defensive back, punter, Lions (11) — 1952–64
Laveill, Dante, end, Browns (7) — 1946–56
Layne, Bobby, Qback, Bears, Lions, Steelers (15) — 1948–62
Leemans, Alphonse (Tuffy), back, Giants (8) — 1936–43
Lilly, Bob, defensive tackle, Cowboys (14) — 1961–74
Lombardi, Vince, coach, Packers, Redskins (11) — 1959–70
Luckman, Sid, quarterback, Bears (12) — 1939–50
Lyman, Roy (Link), tackle, Bulldogs, Bears (11) — 1922–34
Mara, Tim, N.F.L. founder, owner Giants — 1925–59
Marchetti, Gino, defensive end, Colts (14) — 1952–66

Marshall, George P., N.F.L. founder, owner Redskins — 1932–65
Matson, Ollie, back, Cardinals, Rams, Lions, Eagles (14) — 1952–66
Maynard, Don, receiver, Giants, Jets, Cardinals (15) — 1958–73
McAfee, George, back, Bears (8) — 1940–50
McCormack, Mike, tackle, N.Y. Yankees, Cleveland Browns (10) — 1951–62
McElhenny, Hugh, back, 49ers, Vikings, Giants (13) — 1952–64
McNally, John (Blood), back, 7 teams (15) — 1925–39
Michalske, August, guard, Yankees, Packers (11) — 1926–37
Millner, Wayne, end, Redskins (7) — 1936–45
Mitchell, Bobby, wide receiver, Browns, Redskins (11) — 1958–68
Mix, Ron, tackle, Chargers (11) — 1960–71
Moore, Lenny, back, Colts (12) — 1956–67
Motley, Marion, fullback, Browns, Steelers (9) — 1946–55
Musso, George, guard-tackle, Bears (12) — 1933–44
Nagurski, Bronko, fullback, Bears (9) — 1930–43
Namath, Joe, quarterback, Jets, Rams (13) — 1965–77
Neale, Earle (Greasy), coach, Eagles — 1941–50
Nevers, Ernie, fullback, Chicago Cardinals (5) — 1926–31
Nitschke, Ray, linebacker, Packers (15) — 1958–72
Nomellini, Leo, defensive tackle, 49ers (14) — 1950–63
Olsen, Merlin, defensive tackle, Rams (15) — 1962–76
Otto, Jim, center, Raiders (15) — 1960–74
Owen, Steve, tackle, Giants (9), coach, Giants (13) — 1924–53
Page, Alan, defensive tackle, Vikings, Bears (15) — 1967–81
Parker, Clarence (Ace), quarterback, Dodgers (7) — 1937–46
Parker, Jim, guard, tackle, Colts (11) — 1957–67
Perry, Joe, fullback, 49ers, Colts (16) — 1948–63
Pihos, Pete, end, Eagles (9) — 1947–55
Ray, Hugh, Shorty, N.F.L. advisor — 1938–52
Reeves, Dan, owner Rams — 1941–71
Ringo, Jim, center, Packers (15) — 1953–67
Robustelli, Andy, def. end, Rams, Giants (14) — 1951–64
Rooney, Art, N.F.L. founder, owner Steelers — 1933–
Rozelle, Pete, commissioner, NFL, — 1960–89
St. Claire, Bob, tackle, 49ers (11) — 1953–63
Sayers, Gale, back, Bears (7) — 1965–71
Schmidt, Joe, linebacker, Lions (13) — 1953–65
Shell, Art, tackle, Raiders (15) — 1968–82
Simpson, O.J., back, Bills, 49ers (11) — 1969–79
Starr, Bart, quarterback, coach, Packers (16) — 1956–71
Staubach, Roger, quarterback, Cowboys (11) — 1969–79
Stautner, Ernie, defensive tackle, Steelers (14) — 1950–63
Strong, Ken, back, Giants, Yankees (14) — 1929–47
Stydahar, Joe, tackle, Bears (9); coach, Rams, Cardinals (3) — 1936–54
Tarkenton, Fran, quarterback, Vikings, Giants (18) — 1961–78
Taylor, Charlie, wide receiver, Redskins (14) — 1964–77
Taylor, Jim, fullback, Packers, Saints (10) — 1958–67
Thorpe, Jim, back, 7 teams (12) — 1915–28
Tittle, Y. A., Qback, Colts, 49ers, Giants (17) — 1948–64
Trafton, George, center, Bears (13) — 1920–32
Trippi, Charley, back, Chicago Cardinals (9) — 1947–55
Tunnell, Emlen, def. back, Giants, Packers (14) — 1948–61
Turner, Clyde (Bulldog), center, Bears (13) — 1940–52
Unitas, John, quarterback, Colts (18) — 1956–73
Upshaw, Gene, guard, Raiders (15) — 1967–81
Van Brocklin, Norm, Qback, Rams, Eagles (12) — 1949–60
Van Buren, Steve, back, Eagles (8) — 1944–51
Walker, Doak, running back, def. back, kicker, Lions (6) — 1950–55
Warfield, Paul, wide receiver, Browns, Dolphins (13) — 1964–74, 76–77
Waterfield, Bob, quarterback, Rams (8) — 1945–52
Weinmeister, Arnie, tackle, N.Y. Yankees, Giants (6) — 1948–53
Willis, Bill, Guard, Browns (8) — 1946–53
Wilson, Larry, defensive back, Cardinals (13) — 1960–72
Wood, Willie, safety, Packers (12) — 1960–71
Wojciechowicz, Alex, center, Lions, Eagles (13) — 1938–50

N.F.L. INDIVIDUAL LIFETIME, SEASON, AND GAME RECORDS
(American Football League records were incorporated into N.F.L. records after merger of the leagues)

All-Time Leading Touchdown Scorers
(Through 1989 season)

Player	Yrs	Rush.	Rec.	Returns	TD
Jim Brown	9	106	20	0	126
Walter Payton	13	110	15	0	125
John Riggins	14	104	12	0	116
Lenny Moore	12	63	48	2	113
Don Huston	11	3	99	3	105
Steve Largent	14	1	100	0	101
Franco Harris	13	91	9	0	100
Jim Taylor	10	83	10	0	93
Tony Dorsett	12	77	13	1	91
Bobby Mitchell	11	18	65	8	91

All-Time Leading Receivers
(Through 1989)

Rank	Player	Yrs	Pass rec	Yds	Avg	TD
1.	Steve Largent	14	819	13,089	16.0	100
2.	Charlie Joiner	18	750	12,146	16.2	65
3.	Art Monk[1]	10	662	9,165	13.8	47
4.	Charley Taylor	13	649	9,110	14.0	79
5.	Ozzie Newsome	12	639	7,740	12.1	45
6.	Don Maynard	15	633	11,834	18.7	88
7.	Raymond Berry	13	631	9,275	14.7	68
8.	James Lofton[1]	12	607	11,251	18.5	57
9.	Harold Carmichael	14	590	8,985	15.2	79
10.	Fred Biletnikoff	14	589	8,974	15.2	76

1. Still active in 1990.

All-Time Leading Passers
(Minimum 1,500 attempts. Through 1989.)

Rank	Player	Yrs	Att	Comp	Yds	TD	Int	Rating
1.	Joe Montana[1]	11	4,059	2,593	31,054	216	107	94.0
2.	Dan Marino[1]	7	3,650	2,174	27,853	220	125	89.3
3.	Boomer Esiason[1]	6	2,285	1,296	18,350	126	76	87.3
4.	Dave Krieg[1]	10	2,842	1,644	20,858	169	116	83.7
5.	Roger Staubach	11	2,958	1,685	22,700	153	109	83.4
6.	Bernie Kosar[1]	5	1,940	1,134	13,888	75	47	83.4
7.	Ken O'Brien[1]	6	2,467	1,471	17,589	96	68	83.0
8.	Jim Kelly[1]	4	1,742	1,032	12,901	81	63	82.7
9.	Neil Lomax	8	3,153	1,817	22,771	136	90	82.7
10.	Sonny Jergensen	18	4,262	2,433	32,224	255	189	82.6
11.	Len Dawson	19	3,741	2,136	28,711	239	183	82.6
12.	Ken Anderson	16	4,475	2,654	32,838	197	160	81.9
13.	Danny White	13	2,950	1,761	21,959	155	132	81.7
14.	Bart Starr	16	3,149	1,808	24,718	152	138	80.5
15.	Fran Tarkenton	18	6,467	3,686	47,003	342	266	80.4
16.	Tony Eason[1]	7	1,536	898	10,987	61	50	80.3
17.	Dan Fouts	15	5,604	3,297	43,040	254	242	80.2
18.	Jim McMahon[1]	8	1,831	1,050	13,335	77	66	79.2
19.	Bert Jones	10	2,551	1,430	18,190	124	101	78.2
20.	Johnny Unitas	18	5,186	2,830	40,239	290	253	78.2

1. Active player in 1990 season.

All-Time Leading Scorers
(Through 1989)

Rank	Player	Yrs	TD	FG	PAT	Pts
1.	George Blanda	26	9	335	943	2,002
2.	Jan Stenrud	19	0	373	580	1,699
3.	Jim Turner	16	1	304	521	1,439
4.	Mark Mosley	16	0	300	482	1,382
5.	Jim Bakken	17	0	282	534	1,380
6.	Fred Cox[1]	15	0	282	519	1,865
7.	Lou Groza	17	1	234	641	1,349
8.	Pat Leahy[1]	16	0	255	496	1,261
9.	Chris Bahr[1]	14	0	241	490	1,213
10.	Gino Capalletti	11	42	176	350	1,130
11.	Ray Wersching	15	0	222	456	1,122
12.	Don Cockroft	13	0	216	432	1,080
13.	Garo Yepremian	14	0	210	444	1,074
14.	Bruce Gossett	11	0	219	374	1,031
15.	Nick Lowery[1]	11	0	225	338	1,013

1. Active in 1990 season.

All-Time Leading Rushers
(Through 1989)

Rank	Player	Yrs	Att	Yds	Avg	TD
1.	Walter Payton	13	3,838	16,726	4.4	110
2.	Tony Dorsett	12	2,936	12,739	4.3	77
3.	Jim Brown	9	2,359	12,312	5.2	106
4.	Franco Harris	13	2,949	12,120	4.1	91
5.	John Riggins	14	2,916	11,352	3.9	104
6.	O.J. Simpson	11	2,404	11,236	4.7	61
7.	Eric Dickerson[1]	7	2,450	11,226	4.6	82
8.	Earl Campbell	8	2,187	9,407	4.3	74
9.	Ottis Anderson[1]	11	2,274	9,317	4.1	69
10.	Jim Taylor	10	1,941	8,597	4.4	83
11.	Joe Perry	14	1,737	8,378	4.8	53
12.	Larry Csonka	11	1,891	8,081	4.3	64
13.	Gerald Riggs[1]	8	1,788	7,465	4.2	52
14.	Mike Pruitt	11	1,844	7,378	4.0	51
15.	Marcus Allen[1]	8	1,781	7,275	4.1	63

1. Still active in 1990 season.

Scoring

Most points scored, lifetime—2,002, George Blanda, Chicago Bears, 1949–58; Baltimore, 1950; Houston, 1960–66; Oakland, 1967–75 (9tds, 943 pat, 335 fgs).

Most points, season—176, Paul Hornung, Green Bay, 1960 (15 td, 41 pat, 15 fg).

Most points, game—40, Ernie Nevers, Chicago Cardinals, 1929 (6 td, 4 pat).

Most points, per quarter—29, Don Hutson, Green Bay, 1945 (4 td, 5 pat).

Most touchdowns, lifetime—126, Jim Brown, Cleveland, 1957–65.

Most touchdowns, season—24, John Riggins, Washington, 1983.

Most touchdowns, game—6, Ernie Nevers, Chicago Cardinals, 1929; William Jones, Cleveland, 1951; Gale Sayers, Chicago Bears, 1965.

Most points after touchdown, lifetime—943, George Blanda, Chicago Bears, 1949–58; Baltimore, 1950; Houston, 1960–66; Oakland, 1967–75.

Most points after touchdown, game—9, Pat Harder, Chicago Cardinals, 1948; Bob Waterfield, Los Angeles, 1950; Charlie Gogolak, Washington, 1966.

Most consecutive points after touchdown—234, Tommy Davis, San Francisco, 1959–65.

Most points after touchdown, no misses, season—56, Danny Villanueva, Dallas, 1966.

Most field goals, lifetime—373, Jan Stenerud, Kansas City Chiefs, 1967–79; Green Bay Packers, 1980–84; Minnesota Vikings, 1985.

Most field goals, season—35, Ali Haji-Sheikh, N.Y. Giants, 1983.

Most field goals, game—7, Jim Bakken, St. Louis, 1967; and Rick Karlis, Minnesota, 1989.

Longest field goal—63 yards, Tom Dempsey, New Orleans, 1970.

Rushing

Most yards gained, lifetime—16,726, Walter Payton, Chicago Bears, 1975–1987.

Most yards gained, season—2,105, Eric Dickerson, Los Angeles, 1984.

Most yards gained, game—275, Walter Payton, Chicago, 1977.

Most touchdowns, lifetime—110, Walter Payton, Chicago, 1975–1987.

Most touchdowns, season—24, John Riggins, Washington, 1983.

Most touchdowns, game—6, Ernie Nevers, Chicago Cardinals, 1929.

Longest run from scrimmage—99 yards, Tony Dorsett, Dallas, 1982 (touchdown).

Passing

Most touchdown passes, lifetime—342, Fran Tarkenton, Minnesota, 1961–66, 72–78; New York Giants, 1967–71.

Most touchdown passes, season—48, Dan Marino, Miami, 1984.

Most touchdown passes, game—7, Sid Luckman, Chicago Bears, 1943; Adrian Burk, Philadelphia, 1954; George Blanda, Houston 1961; Y.A. Tittle, New York Giants, 1963; Joe Kapp, Minnesota, 1969.

Most consecutive games, touchdown passes—47, John Unitas, Baltimore.

Most consecutive passes attempted, none intercepted—294, Bart Starr, Green Bay, 1964–65.

Longest pass completion—99 yards, Frank Filchock (to Andy Farkas), Washington, 1939; George Izo (to Bob Mitchell), Washington, 1963; Karl Sweetan (to Pat Studstill), Detroit, 1966; Sonny Jurgensen (to Gerry Allen), Washington, 1968; Jim Plunkett (to Cliff Branch) L.A. Raiders, 1985; Ron Jaworski (to Mike Quick), Philadelphia, 1985.

Receiving

Most pass receptions, lifetime—819, Steve Largent, Seattle Seahawks, 1976–1989.

Most pass receptions, season—106, Art Monk, Washington, 1984.

Most pass receptions, game—18, Tom Fears, Los Angeles, 1950.

Most consecutive games, pass receptions—177, Steve Largent, 1976–1989.

Most yards gained, pass receptions, lifetime—13,089, Steve Largent, Seattle, 1976–1989.

Most yards gained receptions, season—1,746, Charley Hennigan, Houston, 1961.

Most yards gained receptions, game—336, Willie Anderson, Los Angeles Rams, Nov. 26, 1989, vs. New Orleans.

Most touchdown receptions, lifetime—100, Steve Largent, Seattle, 1976–1989.

Most touchdown pass receptions, season—22, Jerry Rice, San Francisco 49ers, 1987.

Most touchdown pass receptions, game—5, Bob Shaw, Chicago Cards, 1950 and Kellen Winslow, San Diego Chargers, 1981.

Most consecutive games, touchdown pass receptions—13, Jerry Rice, San Francisco 49ers, 1986–87.

Most pass interceptions, lifetime—81, Paul Krause, Washington, 1964–67; Minnesota, 1968–79.

Most pass interceptions, season—14, Richard (Night Train) Lane, Los Angeles, 1952.

Most pass interceptions, game—4, by 17 players.

Longest pass interception return—103 yards, Venice Glenn, San Diego, vs. Denver, Nov. 29, 1987.

Kicking

Longest punt—98 yards, Steve O'Neal, New York Jets, 1969.

Highest average punting, lifetime—45.16 yards, Sammy Baugh, Washington, 1937–52.

Longest punt return—98 yards, Gil LeFebvre, Cincinnati Reds, 1933; Charlie West, Minnesota, 1968; Dennis Morgan, Dallas, 1974.

Longest kick-off return—106 yards, Roy Green, St. Louis, 1979; Al Carmichael, Green Bay, 1956; Noland Smith, Kansas City, 1967.

Most punts lifetime—1,154, Dave Jennings, N.Y. Giants 1974–84, N.Y. Jets. 1985–87.

Passing

Most passes completed, lifetime—3,686, Fran Tarkenton, Minnesota, 1961–66, 72–78; New York Giants, 1967–71.

Most passes completed, season—378, Dan Marino, 1986.

Most passes completed, game—42, Richard Todd, New York Jets, 1980.

Most consecutive passes completed—22, Joe Montana, San Francisco, 1987.

Most yards gained, lifetime—47,003, Fran Tarkenton, Minnesota, 1961–66, 72–78; New York Giants, 1967–71.

Most yards gained, season—5,084, Dan Marino, Miami, 1984.

Most yards gained, game—554, Norm Van Brocklin, Los Angeles, 1951.

NFL GOVERNMENT

Commissioner's Office: Paul Tagliabue, Commissioner; Jay Moyer, Executive V.P./Counsel to Commissioner; Don Weiss, Executive Director; Joe Rhein, Director of Administration; John Schoemer, Treasurer; Jan Van Duser, Director of Operations; Joe Browne, Director of Communications; Jim Heffernan, Director of Public Relations; Val Pinchbeck, Jr., Director of Broadcasting; Nancy Dehar, Asst. Dir. of Broadcasting; Warren Welsh, Director of Security; Charles R. Jackson, Assistant Director of Security; Joel Bussert, Director of Player Personnel; Art McNally, Supervisor of Officials; Jack Reader, Assistant Supervisor of Officials; Jim Steeg, Director of Special Events; Susan McCann-Minogue, Asst. Dir. of Special Events; Bill Granholm, Director of Special Projects; Tom Sullivan, Controller; Dave Cornwell, Asst. Counsel/Dir. of Equal Employment; Mel Blount, Director of Player Relations.

American Football Conference: Lamar Hunt, President; Roger Goodell, Assistant to the President; Pete Abitante, Director of Information.

National Football Conference: Wellington Mara, President; James Noel, Assistant to the President; Dick Maxwell, Director of Information.

First U.S. Amateur Meets

The first U.S. amateur track and field championships were conducted by the New York Athletic Club in 1876. In 1877, the Winged Foot club held the initial amateur swimming championships and sponsored the first amateur boxing and wrestling championships in 1878.

BASKETBALL

Basketball may be the one sport whose exact origin is definitely known. In the winter of 1891–92, Dr. James Naismith, an instructor in the Y.M.C.A. Training College (now Springfield College) at Springfield, Mass., deliberately invented the game of basketball in order to provide indoor exercise and competition for the students between the closing of the football season and the opening of the baseball season. He affixed peach baskets overhead on the walls at opposite ends of the gymnasium and organized teams to play his new game in which the purpose was to toss an association (soccer) ball into one basket and prevent the opponents from tossing the ball into the other basket. The game is fundamentally the same today, though there have been improvements in equipment and some changes in rules.

Because Dr. Naismith had eighteen available players when he invented the game, the first rule was: "There shall be nine players on each side." Later the number of players became optional, depending upon the size of the available court, but the five-player standard was adopted when the game spread over the country. United States soldiers brought basketball to Europe in World War I, and it soon became a world-wide sport.

College Basketball

NATIONAL COLLEGIATE A.A. CHAMPIONS

1939	Oregon	1951	Kentucky	1963	Loyola (Chicago)	1981	Indiana
1940	Indiana	1952	Kansas	1964	U.C.L.A.	1982	North Carolina
1941	Wisconsin	1953	Indiana	1965	U.C.L.A.	1983	North Carolina State
1942	Stanford	1954	La Salle	1966	Texas Western	1984	Georgetown
1943	Wyoming	1955	San Francisco	1967–73	U.C.L.A.	1985	Villanova
1944	Utah	1956	San Francisco	1974	No. Carolina State	1986	Louisville
1945	Oklahoma A & M	1957	North Carolina	1975	U.C.L.A.	1987	Indiana
1946	Oklahoma A & M	1958	Kentucky	1976	Indiana	1988	Kansas
1947	Holy Cross	1959	California	1977	Marquette	1989	Michigan
1948	Kentucky	1960	Ohio State	1978	Kentucky	1990	Nevada–Las Vegas
1949	Kentucky	1961	Cincinnati	1979	Michigan State		
1950	C.C.N.Y.	1962	Cincinnati	1980	Louisville		

NATIONAL INVITATION TOURNAMENT (NIT) CHAMPIONS

1939	Long Island U.	1953	Seton Hall	1966	Brigham Young	1979	Indiana
1940	Colorado	1954	Holy Cross	1967	So. Illinois	1980	Virginia
1941	Long Island U.	1955	Duquesne	1968	Dayton	1981	Tulsa
1942	West Virginia	1956	Louisville	1969	Temple	1982	Bradley
1943–44	St. John's (N.Y.C.)	1957	Bradley	1970	Marquette	1983	Fresno State
1945	DePaul	1958	Xavier (Cincinnati)	1971	North Carolina	1984	Michigan
1946	Kentucky	1959	St. John's (N.Y.C.)	1972	Maryland	1985	U.C.L.A.
1947	Utah	1960	Bradley	1973	Virginia Tech	1986	Ohio State
1948	St. Louis	1961	Providence	1974	Purdue	1987	Southern Mississippi
1949	San Francisco	1962	Dayton	1975	Princeton	1988	Connecticut
1950	C.C.N.Y.	1963	Providence	1976	Kentucky	1989	St. John's
1951	Brigham Young	1964	Bradley	1977	St. Bonaventure	1990	Vanderbilt
1952	La Salle	1965	St. John's (N.Y.C.)	1978	Texas		

N.C.A.A. MAJOR COLLEGE INDIVIDUAL SCORING RECORDS

Single Season Averages

Player, Team	Year	G	FG	FT	Pts	Avg
Pete Maravich, Louisiana State	1969–70	31	522 [1]	337	1381 [1]	44.5 [1]
Pete Maravich	1968–69	26	433	282	1148	44.2
Pete Maravich	1967–68	26	432	274	1138	43.8
Frank Selvy, Furman	1953–54	29	427	355 [1]	1209	41.7
Johnny Neumann, Mississippi	1970–71	23	366	191	923	40.1
Freeman Williams, Portland State	1976–77	26	417	176	1010	38.8
Billy McGill, Utah	1961–62	26	394	221	1009	38.8
Calvin Murphy, Niagara	1967–68	24	337	242	916	38.2
Austin Carr, Notre Dame	1969–70	29	444	218	1106	38.1

1. Record.

N.C.A.A. CAREER SCORING TOTALS

Division I

Player, Team	Last year	G	FG	FT	Pts	Avg
Pete Maravich, Louisiana State	1970	83	1387 [1]	893 [1]	3667 [1]	44.2 [1]
Austin Carr, Notre Dame	1971	74	1017	526	2560	34.6
Oscar Robertson, Cincinnati	1960	88	1052	869	2973	33.8
Calvin Murphy, Niagara	1970	77	947	654	2548	33.1
Dwight Lamar [2]	1973	57	768	326	1862	32.7
Frank Selvy, Furman	1954	78	922	694	2538	32.5
Rick Mount, Purdue	1970	72	910	503	2323	32.3
Darrel Floyd, Furman	1956	71	868	545	2281	32.1
Nick Werkman, Seton Hall	1964	71	812	649	2273	32.0

1. Record. 2. Also played two seasons in college division.

Division II

Player, Team	Last year	G	FG	FT	Pts	Avg
Travis Grant, Kentucky State	1972	121	1760 [1]	525	4045 [1]	33.4 [1]
John Rinka, Kenyon	1970	99	1261	729	3251	32.8
Florindo Vierira, Quinnipiac	1957	69	761	741	2263	32.8
Willie Shaw, Lane	1964	76	960	459	2379	31.3
Mike Davis, Virginia Union	1969	89	1014	730	2758	31.0
Henry Logan, Western Carolina	1968	107	1263	764	3290	30.7
Willie Scott, Alabama State	1969	103	1277	601	3155	30.6
Gregg Northington, Alabama State	1972	75	894	403	2191	29.2
Bob Hopkins, Grambling	1956	126	1403	953	3759	29.8

1. Record.

TOP SINGLE-GAME SCORING MARKS

Player, Team (Opponent)	Yr	Pts	Player, Team (Opponent)	Yr	Pts
Selvy, Furman (Newberry)	1954	100 [1]	Floyd, Furman (Morehead)	1955	67
Williams, Portland State (Rocky Mtn.)	1978	81	Maravich, LSU (Tulane)	1969	66
Mlkvy, Temple (Wilkes)	1951	73	Handlan, W & L (Furman)	1951	66
Williams, Portland State (So. Oregon)	1977	71	Roberts, Oral Roberts (N.C. A&T)	1977	66
Maravich, LSU (Alabama)	1970	69	Williams, Portland State (Geo. Fox Coll.)	1978	66
Murphy, Niagara (Syracuse)	1969	68	Roberts, Oral Roberts (Oregon)	1977	65

1. Record.

MEN'S N.C.A.A. BASKETBALL CHAMPIONSHIPS—1990

DIVISION I
First Round—East
Connecticut 76, Boston University 52
California 65, Indiana 63
Clemson 49, Brigham Young 47
LaSalle 79, Southern Mississippi 63
St. John's 81, Temple 65
Duke 81, Richmond 46
UCLA 68, Alabama–Birmingham 56
Kansas 79, Robert Morris 71

First Round—Southeast
Michigan State 75, Murray State 71 (OT)
California–Santa Barbara 70, Houston 66
LSU 70, Villanova 63
Georgia Tech 99, East Tennessee State 83
Minnesota 64, Texas–El Paso 61 (OT)
Northern Iowa 74, Missouri 71
Virginia 75, Notre Dame 67
Syracuse 70, Coppin State 48

First Round—Midwest
Oklahoma 77, Towson State 68
North Carolina 83, Southwest Missouri State 70
Dayton 88, Illinois 86
Arkansas 68, Princeton 64
Xavier 87, Kansas State 79
Georgetown 70, Texas Southern 52
Texas 100, Georgia 88
Purdue 75, Northeast Louisiana 63

First Round—West
Nevada–Las Vegas 102, Arkansas–Little Rock 72
Ohio State 84, Providence 83 (OT)
Ball State 54, Oregon State 53
Louisville 78, Idaho 59
Loyola–Marymount 111, New Mexico State 92
Michigan 76, Illinois State 70
Alabama 71, Colorado State 54
Arizona 79, South Florida 67

Second Round—East
Connecticut 74, California 54
Clemson 79, LaSalle 75
Duke 76, St. John's 72
UCLA 71, Kansas 70

Second Round—Southeast
Michigan State 62, California–Santa Barbara 58
Georgia Tech 94, LSU 91
Minnesota 81, Northern Iowa 78
Syracuse 63, Virginia 61

Second Round—Midwest
North Carolina 79, Oklahoma 77
Arkansas 86, Dayton 84
Xavier 74, Georgetown 71
Texas 73, Purdue 72

Second Round—West
Nevada–Las Vegas 76, Ohio State 65
Ball State 62, Louisville 60
Loyola–Marymount 149, Michigan 115
Alabama 77, Arizona 55

Third Round—East
Connecticut 71, Clemson 70
Duke 90, UCLA 81

Third Round—Southeast
Georgia Tech 81, Michigan State 80 (OT)
Minnesota 82, Syracuse 75

Third round—Midwest
Arkansas 96, North Carolina 73
Texas 102, Xavier 89

Third Round—West
Loyola–Marymount 62, Alabama 60
Nevada–Las Vegas 69, Ball State 67

Regional Finals
East—Duke 79, Connecticut 78 (OT)
Southeast—Georgia Tech 93, Minnesota 91
Midwest—Arkansas 88, Texas 85
West—Nevada–Las Vegas 131, Loyola–Marymount 101

National Semifinals
(Saturday, March 31, 1990, at Denver, Colo.)
Duke 97, Arkansas 83
Nevada–Las Vegas 90, Georgia Tech 81

National Final
(Monday, April 2, 1990, at Denver, Colo.)
Nevada-Las Vegas 103, Duke 73

DIVISION II
Semifinals
Kentucky Wesleyan 101, North Dakota 92
Cal State Bakersfield 85, Morehouse 60

Championship
Kentucky Wesleyan 93, Cal State Bakersfield 79

DIVISION III
Semifinals
DePauw 82, Calvin 79
Rochester 86, Washington (Md.) 70

Championship
Rochester 43, DePauw 42

WOMEN'S N.C.A.A. BASKETBALL CHAMPIONSHIPS—1990

DIVISION I
First Round—East
Clemson 79, Manhattan 55
Penn St. 83, Florida St. 73
Maryland 100, Appalachian St. 71
Old Dominion 91, St. Joseph's (Pa.) 69

First Round—Mideast
South Carolina 93, Bowling Green 50
Vanderbilt 78, Rutgers 75
Tennessee Tech 77, Richmond 59
DePaul 73, Western Kentucky 63

First Round—Midwest
Northern Illinois 84, Texas Tech 63
Southern Mississippi 75, LSU 65
Ohio State 73, Southern Illinois 61
Michigan 77, Oklahoma 68

First Round—West
Mississippi 74, Utah 51
Arkansas 90, UCLA 80 (OT)
Long Beach State 87, California 84
Hawaii 83, Montana 78

Second Round—East
Providence 77, Maryland 75
Clemson 61, Connecticut 59
Tennessee 87, Old Dominion 68
Virginia 85, Penn St. 64

Second Round—Mideast
South Carolina 76, Northwestern 67
Vanderbilt 61, Iowa 56
Washington 77, De Paul 68
Auburn 73, Tennessee Tech 54

Second Round—Midwest
North Carolina St. 81, Michigan 64
Louisiana Tech 89, Southern Mississippi 70
Purdue 86, Northern Illinois 81
Texas 95, Ohio State 66

Second Round—West
S.F. Austin St. 78, Long Beach St. 62
Stanford 106, Hawaii 76
Mississippi 66, Nevada–Las Vegas 62
Arkansas 81, Georgia 70

Third Round—East
Tennessee 80, Clemson 62
Virginia 77, Providence 71

Third Round—Mideast
Washington 73, South Carolina 61
Auburn 89, Vanderbilt 67

Third Round—Midwest
Texas 72, North Carolina St. 63
Louisiana Tech 91, Purdue 47

Third Round—West
Arkansas 87, S.F. Austin St. 82
Stanford 78, Mississippi 65

Regional Finals
East—Virginia 79, Tennessee 75 (OT)
Mideast—Auburn 76, Washington 50
Midwest—Louisiana Tech 71, Texas 57
West—Stanford 114, Arkansas 87

National Semifinals
(Friday, March 30, 1990, at Knoxville, Tenn.)
Stanford 75, Virginia 66
Auburn 81, Louisiana Tech 69

National Championship
(Sunday, April 1, 1990, at Knoxville, Tenn.)
Stanford 88, Auburn 81

DIVISION II
Semifinals
Delta State 67, Cal Poly Pamona 53
Brentley 72, Oakland 68

Championship
Delta State 77, Brentley 44

DIVISION III
Semifinals
Hope 75, Gentre 62
St. John Fisher 77, Heidelberg 64

Championship
Hope 65, St. John Fisher 63

LEADING N.C.A.A. SCORERS—1989-1990
Division I

	FG	3-PT FG	FT	Pts	Avg
1. Bo Kimble, Loyola (Cal.)	404	92	231	1131	35.3
2. Kevin Bradshaw, U.S. Int'l	291	72	221	875	31.3
3. Dave Jamerson, Ohio	297	131	149	874	31.2
4. Alphonzo Ford, Miss. Val.	289	104	126	808	29.9
5. Steve Rogers, Alabama St.	286	46	213	831	29.7
6. Hank Gathers, Loyola (Cal.)	314	0	126	754	29.0
7. Darryl Brooks, Tennessee St.	258	95	79	690	28.8
8. Chris Jackson, L.S.U.	305	88	191	889	27.8
9. Dennis Scott, Georgia Tech	336	137	161	970	27.7
10. Mark Stevenson, Duquesne	297	34	160	788	27.2
11. Lionel Simmons, La Salle	335	31	146	847	26.5
12. Keith Gailes, Loyola (Ill.)	272	70	148	762	26.3
13. Kurk Lee, Towson St.	285	63	172	805	26.0
14. Gary Payton, Oregon St.	288	52	118	746	25.7
15. Bailey Alston, Liberty	266	41	141	714	25.5
16. Sydney Grider, S'western La.	251	131	106	739	25.5
17. Vernell Coles, Virginia Tech	280	67	158	785	25.3
18. Travis Mays, Texas	240	95	197	772	24.1
19. Gerald Glass, Mississippi	284	46	109	723	24.1
20. Tony Smith, Marquette	240	36	173	689	23.8
21. Tom Davis, Delaware St.	263	0	139	665	23.8
22. Jim McPhee, Gonzaga	242	29	149	662	23.6
23. John Taft, Marshall	204	51	125	584	23.4
24. Tharon Mayes, Florida St.	198	58	105	559	23.3
25. Rodney Monroe, N. Caro. St.	228	84	157	697	23.2

NATIONAL ASSOCIATION OF INTERCOLLEGIATE ATHLETICS—1990

MEN'S TOURNAMENT
Round of 16
Birmingham Southern 72, Southwestern (Texas) 68
Wisconsin–Eau Claire 92, Southern California College 59
Central Washington 92, Alderson–Broaddus 81
Pfeiffer 91, Indiana–Purdue at Indianapolis 86
South Carolina-Spartanburg 75, Grand Canyon 69
David Lipscomb 70, Central Arkansas 66
Oral Roberts 106, Columbia College (Mo.) 86
Georgetown (Ky.) 73, Minnesota–Duluth 72 (2OT)

Quarterfinals
Birmingham Southern 87, South Carolina–Spartanburg 80
Wisconsin–Eau Claire 84, Central Washington 57
David Lipscomb 125, Pfeiffer 83
Georgetown (Ky.) 80, Oral Roberts 78

Semifinals
Birmingham Southern 98, David Lipscomb 96
Wisconsin–Eau Claire 76, Georgetown (Ky.) 65

Championship
Birmingham Southern 88, Wisconsin–Eau Claire 80

WOMEN'S TOURNAMENT
Round of 16

St. Ambrose (Iowa) 97, Campbellsville (Ky.) 83
Central State (Ohio) 97, Wingate (N.C.) 77
Western New Mexico 72, Northern Montana 65
Southwestern Oklahoma 77, Georgian Court 54
Claflin (S.C.) 92, Charleston (W.Va.) 68
Simon–Fraser (BC) 79, Minnesota–Duluth 56
Wayland Baptist (Tex.) 86, David Lipscomb 74
Arkansas–Monticello 80, Aquinas 55

Quarterfinals

St. Ambrose 81, Central State 73
S.W. Okla. 76, Western New Mexico 42
Claflin 104, Simon Fraser 98 (OT)
Arkansas–Monticello 105, Wayland Baptist 67

Semifinals

Southwest Oklahoma 83, St. Ambrose 76
Arkansas–Monticello 93, Claflin (S.C.) 86

Championship

Southwest Oklahoma 82, Arkansas–Monticello 75

NATIONAL INVITATION TOURNAMENT (N.I.T.)—1990

Semifinals

(Monday, March 26, 1990, at Madison Square Garden, N.Y.)

St. Louis 80, New Mexico 73
Vanderbilt 75, Penn State 62

Championship

(Wednesday, March 28, 1990, at Madison Square Garden, N.Y.)

Vanderbilt 74, St. Louis 72

N.C.A.A. LEADING REBOUNDERS— 1989-1990

	Games	No.	Avg
1. Anthony Bonner, St. Louis	33	456	13.8
2. Eric McArthur, UC Santa Barb.	29	377	13.0
3. Tyrone Hill, Xavier (Ohio)	32	402	12.6
4. Lee Campbell, Southwest Mo. St.	29	363	12.5
5. Cedric Ceballos, Cal St. Fullerton	29	362	12.5
6. Hakim Shahid, South Fla.	31	383	12.4
7. Ron Draper, American	29	354	12.2
8. Derrick Coleman, Syracuse	33	398	12.1
9. Shaquille O'Neal, Louisiana St.	32	385	12.0
10. Clarence Weatherspoon, Southern M	32	371	11.6
11. Larry Johnson, Nevada-Las Vegas	40	457	11.4
12. Reggie Slater, Wyoming	29	328	11.3
13. Dale Davis, Clemson	35	395	11.3
14. Shaun Vandiver, Colorado	30	336	11.2
15. Popeye Jones, Murray St.	30	336	11.2
16. Steve Stevenson, Prairie View	27	302	11.2
17. Larry Stewart, Coppin St.	33	369	11.2
18. Loy Vaught, Michigan	31	346	11.2
19. Lionel Simmons, La Salle	32	356	11.1
20. Kenny Green, Rhode Island	26	284	10.9
21. Ian Lockhart, Tennessee	30	327	10.9
22. Hank Gathers, Loyola (Cal.)	26	281	10.8
23. Dikembe Mutombo, Georgetown	31	325	10.5
24. Alec Kessler, Georgia	29	300	10.3
25. Jerry Jones, Southern Ill.	33	341	10.3
26. Tim Jackson, Youngstown St.	28	289	10.3
27. Travis Williams, South Caro. St.	29	299	10.3
28. Demetrius Laffitte, U.S. Int'l	28	288	10.3
29. Steve Carney, Northeastern	23	236	10.3
30. Damon Lopez, Fordham	32	328	10.3

Professional Basketball

NATIONAL BASKETBALL ASSOCIATION CHAMPIONS

Source: Matt Winick, Director of Media Information, National Basketball Association.

The National Basketball Association was originally the Basketball Association of America. It took its current name in 1949 when it merged with the National Basketball League.

Season	Eastern Conference (W-L)	Western Conference (W-L)	Playoff Champions[1]
1946–47	Washington Capitols (49–11)	Chicago Stags (39–22)	Philadelphia Warriors
1947–48	Philadelphia Warriors (27–21)	St. Louis Bombers (29–19)	Baltimore Bullets
1948–49	Washington Capitols (38–22)	Rochester Royals (45–15)	Minneapolis Lakers
1949–50	Syracuse Nationals (51–13)	Indianapolis Olympians (39–25)	Minneapolis Lakers
1950–51	Philadelphia Warriors (40–26)	Minneapolis Lakers (44–24)	Rochester Royals
1951–52	Syracuse Nationals (40–26)	Rochester Royals (41–25)	Minneapolis Lakers
1952–53	New York Knickerbockers (47–23)	Minneapolis Lakers (48–22)	Minneapolis Lakers
1953–54	New York Knickerbockers (44–28)	Minneapolis Lakers (46–26)	Minneapolis Lakers
1954–55	Syracuse Nationals (43–29)	Ft. Wayne Pistons (43–29)	Syracuse Nationals
1955–56	Philadelphia Warriors (45–27)	Ft. Wayne Pistons (37–35)	Philadelphia Warriors
1956–57	Boston Celtics (44–28)	St. Louis Hawks (38–34)	Boston Celtics
1957–58	Boston Celtics (48–23)	St. Louis Hawks (41–31)	St. Louis Hawks
1958–59	Boston Celtics (52–20)	St. Louis Hawks (49–23)	Boston Celtics
1959–60	Boston Celtics (59–16)	St. Louis Hawks (46–29)	Boston Celtics
1960–61	Boston Celtics (57–22)	St. Louis Hawks (51–28)	Boston Celtics
1961–62	Boston Celtics (60–20)	Los Angeles Lakers (54–26)	Boston Celtics
1962–63	Boston Celtics (58–22)	Los Angeles Lakers (53–27)	Boston Celtics
1963–64	Boston Celtics (59–21)	San Francisco Warriors (48–32)	Boston Celtics
1964–65	Boston Celtics (62–18)	Los Angeles Lakers (49–31)	Boston Celtics
1965–66	Philadelphia 76ers (55–25)	Los Angeles Lakers (45–35)	Boston Celtics
1966–67	Philadelphia 76ers (68–13)	San Francisco Warriors (44–37)	Philadelphia 76ers
1967–68	Philadelphia 76ers (62–20)	St. Louis Hawks (56–26)	Boston Celtics
1968–69	Baltimore Bullets (57–25)	Los Angeles Lakers (55–27)	Boston Celtics
1969–70	New York Knickerbockers (60–22)	Atlanta Hawks (48–34)	New York Knicks
1970–71	Baltimore Bullets (42–40)	Milwaukee Bucks (66–16)	Milwaukee Bucks
1971–72	New York Knickerbockers (48–34)	Los Angeles Lakers (69–13)	Los Angeles Lakers
1972–73	New York Knickerbockers (57–25)	Los Angeles Lakers (60–22)	New York Knicks
1973–74	Boston Celtics (56–26)	Milwaukee Bucks (59–23)	Boston Celtics
1974–75	Washington Bullets (60–22)	Golden State Warriors (48–34)	Golden State Warriors
1975–76	Boston Celtics (54–28)	Phoenix Suns (42–40)	Boston Celtics

Season	Eastern Conference (W-L)	Western Conference (W-L)	Playoff Champions[1]
1976–77	Philadelphia 76ers (50–32)	Portland Trail Blazers (49–33)	Portland Trail Blazers
1977–78	Washington Bullets (44–38)	Seattle Super Sonics (47–35)	Washington Bullets
1978–79	Washington Bullets (54–28)	Seattle Super Sonics (52–30)	Seattle Super Sonics
1979–80	Philadelphia 76ers (59–23)	Los Angeles Lakers (60–22)	Los Angeles Lakers
1980–81	Boston Celtics (62–20)	Phoenix Suns (57–25)	Boston Celtics
1981–82	Boston Celtics (63–19)	Houston Rockets (46–36)	Los Angeles Lakers
1982–83	Philadelphia 76ers (65–17)	Los Angeles Lakers (58–24)	Philadelphia 76ers
1983–84	Boston Celtics (56–26)	Los Angeles Lakers (58–24)	Boston Celtics
1984–85	Boston Celtics (63–19)	Los Angeles Lakers (62–20)	Los Angeles Lakers
1985–86	Boston Celtics (67–15)	Houston Rockets (51–31)	Boston Celtics
1986–87	Boston Celtics (59–23)	Los Angeles Lakers (65-17)	Los Angeles Lakers
1987–88	Detroit Pistons (54–28)	Los Angeles Lakers (62–20)	Los Angeles Lakers
1988–89	Detroit Pistons (63–18)	Los Angeles Lakers (57–25)	Detroit Pistons
1989–90	Detroit Pistons (59–23)	Portland Trail Blazers (59–23)	Detroit Pistons

1. Playoffs may involve teams other than conference winners.

INDIVIDUAL N.B.A. SCORING CHAMPIONS

Season	Player, Team	G	FG	FT	Pts	Avg
1953–54	Neil Johnston, Philadelphia Warriors	72	591	577	1759	24.4
1954–55	Neil Johnston, Philadelphia Warriors	72	521	589	1631	22.7
1955–56	Bob Pettit, St. Louis Hawks	72	646	557	1849	25.7
1956–57	Paul Arizin, Philadelphia Warriors	71	613	591	1817	25.6
1957–58	George Yardley, Detroit Pistons	72	673	655	2001	27.8
1958–59	Bob Pettit, St. Louis Hawks	72	719	667	2105	29.2
1959–60	Wilt Chamberlain, Philadelphia Warriors	72	1065	577	2707	37.6
1960–61	Wilt Chamberlain, Philadelphia Warriors	79	1251	531	3033	38.4
1961–62	Wilt Chamberlain, Philadelphia Warriors	80	1597	835	4029	50.4
1962–63	Wilt Chamberlain, San Francisco Warriors	80	1463	660	3586	44.8
1963–64	Wilt Chamberlain, San Francisco Warriors	80	1204	540	2948	36.9
1964–65	Wilt Chamberlain, San Francisco Warriors-Phila. 76ers	73	1063	408	2534	34.7
1965–66	Wilt Chamberlain, Philadelphia 76ers	79	1074	501	2649	33.5
1966–67	Rick Barry, San Francisco Warriors	78	1011	753	2775	35.6
1967–68	Dave Bing, Detroit Pistons	79	835	472	2142	27.1
1968–69	Elvin Hayes, San Diego Rockets	82	930	467	2327	28.4
1969–70	Jerry West, Los Angeles Lakers	74	831	647	2309	31.2
1970–71	Lew Alcindor,[1] Milwaukee Bucks	82	1063	470	2596	31.7
1971–72	Kareem Abdul-Jabbar, Milwaukee Bucks	81	1159	504	2822	34.8
1972–73	Nate Archibald, Kansas City-Omaha Kings	80	1028	663	2719	34.0
1973–74	Bob McAdoo, Buffalo Braves	74	901	459	2261	30.8
1974–75	Bob McAdoo, Buffalo Braves	82	1095	641	2831	34.5
1975–76	Bob McAdoo, Buffalo Braves	78	934	559	2427	31.1
1976–77	Pete Maravich, New Orleans Jazz	73	886	501	2273	31.1
1977–78	George Gervin, San Antonio Spurs	82	864	504	2232	27.2
1978–79	George Gervin, San Antonio Spurs	80	947	471	2365	29.6
1979–80	George Gervin, San Antonio Spurs	78	1024	505	2585	33.1
1980–81	Adrian Dantley, Utah Jazz	80	909	632	2452	30.7
1981–82	George Gervin, San Antonio Spurs	79	993	555	2551	32.3
1982–83	Alex English, Denver Nuggets	82	959	406	2326	28.4
1983–84	Adrian Dantley, Utah Jazz	79	802	813	2418	30.6
1984–85	Bernard King, New York Knicks	55	691	426	1809	32.9
1985–86	Dominique Wilkins, Atlanta Hawks	78	888	527	2366	30.3
1986–87	Michael Jordan, Chicago Bulls[2]	82	1098	833	3041	37.1
1987–88	Michael Jordan, Chicago Bulls[3]	82	1069	723	2868	35.0
1988–89	Michael Jordan, Chicago Bulls[4]	81	966	674	2633	32.5
1989–90	Michael Jordan, Chicago Bulls[5]	82	1034	593	2753	33.6

1. (Kareem Abdul-Jabbar). 2. Also had 12 3-point field goals. 3. Also had 7 3-point field goals. 4. Also had 27 3-point field goals. 5. Also had 92 3-point field goals.

N.B.A. LIFETIME LEADERS

(Through 1989–1990 season)

Most Games Played

Kareem Abdul–Jabbar	1,560
Elvin Hayes	1,303
John Havlicek	1,270
Paul Silas	1,254
Hal Greer	1,122
Alex English	1,114
Dennis Johnson	1,100
Robert Parish	1,100
Moses Malone	1,082
Len Wilkens	1,077

Steals

Maurice Cheeks	2,066
Gus Williams	1,638
Magic Johnson	1,596
Julius Erving	1,508
Dennis Johnson	1,477

Isiah Thomas	1,477
Michael Ray Richardson	1,463
Lafayette Lever	1,455
Larry Bird	1,406
Randy Smith	1,403

BLOCKED SHOTS

Kareem Abdul–Jabbar	3,189
Mark Eaton	2,592
Wayne Rollins	2,374
George T. Johnson	2,082
Robert Parish	1,849
Elvin Hayes	1,771
Artis Gilmore	1,747
Akeem Olajuwon	1,577
Moses Malone	1,567
Caldwell Jones	1,517

FREE THROW PERCENTAGE
(1,200 free throws made, minimum)

	FTA	FTM	Pct
Rick Barry	4,243	3,818	.900
Calvin Murphy	3,864	3,445	.892
Larry Bird	4,126	3,647	.884
Bill Sharman	3,559	3,143	.883
Chris Mullin	1,928	1,695	.879
Kiki Vandeweghe	3,562	3,102	.871
Mike Newlin	3,456	3,005	.870
Jeff Malone	2,231	1,939	.869
John Long	2,051	1,765	.861
Fred Brown	2,211	1,896	.858

SCORING AVERAGE
(400 games or 10,000 points minimum)

	Games	Pts	Avg
Michael Jordan	427	14,016	32.8
Wilt Chamberlain	1045	31,419	30.1
Elgin Baylor	846	23,149	27.4
Jerry West	932	25,192	27.0
Bob Pettit	792	20,880	26.4
George Gervin	791	20,708	26.2
Dominique Wilkins	639	16,695	26.1

Oscar Robertson	1040	26,710	25.7
Larry Bird	792	19,719	24.9
Karl Malone	407	10,116	24.9

REBOUNDS

Wilt Chamberlain	23,924
Bill Russell	21,620
Kareem Abdul–Jabbar	17,440
Elvin Hayes	16,279
Moses Malone	14,483
Nate Thurmond	14,464
Walt Bellamy	14,241
Wes Unseld	13,769
Jerry Lucas	12,942
Bob Pettit	12,849

FIELD GOAL PERCENTAGE
(2,000 field goals made, minimum)

	FGA	FGM	Pct.
Artis Gilmore	9,570	5,732	.599
James Donaldson	4,494	2,614	.582
Charles Barkley	6,429	3,738	.581
Steve Johnson	4,902	2,807	.573
Darryl Dawkins	6,079	3,477	.572
Jeff Ruland	3,685	2,080	.564
Kevin McHale	10,139	5,705	.563
Kareem Abdul–Jabbar	28,307	15,837	.559
James Worthy	8,762	4,862	.555
Larry Nance	8,136	4,493	.552

ASSISTS

Oscar Robertson	9,887
Magic Johnson	8,932
Len Wilkens	7,211
Isiah Thomas	6,985
Bob Cousy	6,955
Guy Rodgers	6,917
Maurice Cheeks	6,665
Nate Archibald	6,476
John Lucas	6,454
Norm Nixon	6,386

N.B.A. MOST VALUABLE PLAYERS

1956	Bob Pettit	1971–72	Lew Alcindor (Kareem Abdul–Jabbar)	1981	Julius Erving, Philadelphia
1957	Bob Cousy			1982	Moses Malone, Houston
1958	Bill Russell	1973	Dave Cowens	1983	Moses Malone, Philadelphia
1959	Bob Pettit	1974	Kareem Abdul–Jabbar, Milwaukee	1984	Larry Bird, Boston
1960	Wilt Chamberlain			1985	Larry Bird, Boston
1961–63	Bill Russell	1975	Bob McAdoo, Buffalo	1986	Larry Bird, Boston
1964	Oscar Robertson	1976–77	Kareem Abdul–Jabbar, Los Angeles	1987	Earvin Johnson, Los Angeles
1965	Bill Russell			1988	Michael Jordan, Chicago
1966–68	Wilt Chamberlain	1978	Bill Walton, Portland	1989	Earvin Johnson, Los Angeles
1969	Wes Unseld	1979	Moses Malone, Houston	1990	Earvin Johnson, Los Angeles
1970	Willis Reed	1980	Kareem Abdul–Jabbar, Los Angeles		

N.B.A. TEAM RECORDS

Most points, game—186, Detroit vs. Denver, 3 overtimes, 1983
Most points, quarter—58, Buffalo vs. Boston, 1968
Most points, half—97, Atlanta vs. San Diego, 1970
Most points, overtime period—22, Detroit vs. Cleveland, 1973
Most field goals, game—74, Detroit, 1983
Most field goals, quarter—23, Boston, 1959; Buffalo, 1972
Most field goals, half—40, Boston, 1959; Syracuse, 1963; Atlanta, 1979
Most assists, game—53, Milwaukee, 1978
Most rebounds, game—109, Boston 1960
Most points, both teams, game—370

(Detroit 186, Denver 184) 3 overtimes, Denver, December 13, 1983
Most points, both teams, quarter—96 (Boston 52, Minneapolis 44), 1959; (Detroit 53, Cincinnati 43), 1972
Most points, both teams, half—170 (Philadelphia 90, Cincinnati 80), Philadelphia, 1971
Longest winning streak—33, Los Angeles, 1971–72
Longest losing streak—20, Philadelphia, 1973
Longest winning streak at home—36, Philadelphia, 1966–67
Most games won, season—69, Los Angeles, 1971–72
Most games lost, season—73, Philadelphia, 1972–73
Highest average points per game—126.5, Denver, 1981–82

N.B.A. INDIVIDUAL RECORDS

Most points, game—100, Wilt Chamberlain, Philadelphia vs. New York at Hershey, Pa., 1962
Most points, quarter—33, George Gervin, San Antonio, 1978
Most points, half—59, Wilt Chamberlain, Philadelphia, 1962
Most free throws, game—28, Wilt Chamberlain, Philadelphia, vs. New York at Hershey, Pa. 1962; 28, Adrian Dantley, Utah, vs. Houston, 1984

Most free throws, quarter—14, Rick Barry, San Francisco, 1966
Most free throws, half—19, Oscar Robertson, Cincinnati, 1964
Most field goals, game—36, Wilt Chamberlain, Philadelphia, 1962
Most consecutive field goals, game—18, Wilt Chamberlain, San Francisco, 1963; Wilt Chamberlain, Philadelphia, 1967
Most assists, game—29, Kevin Porter, New Jersey Nets, 1978
Most rebounds, game—55, Wilt Chamberlain, Philadelphia, 1963

NATIONAL BASKETBALL ASSOCIATION
FINAL STANDINGS OF THE CLUBS—1989–1990

EASTERN CONFERENCE
Atlantic Division

	W	L	Pct	Games behind
Philadelphia 76ers	53	29	.646	—
Boston Celtics	52	30	.634	1
New York Knicks	45	37	.549	8
Washington Bullets	31	51	.378	22
Miami Heat	18	64	.220	35
New Jersey Nets	17	65	.207	36

Central Division

	W	L	Pct	Games behind
Detroit Pistons	59	23	.720	—
Chicago Bulls	55	27	.671	4
Milwaukee Bucks	44	38	.547	15
Cleveland Cavaliers	42	40	.512	17
Indiana Pacers	42	40	.512	17
Atlanta Hawks	41	41	.500	18
Orlando Magic	18	64	.220	41

WESTERN CONFERENCE
Midwest Division

	W	L	Pct	Games behind
San Antonio Spurs	56	26	.683	—
Utah Jazz	55	27	.671	1
Dallas Mavericks	47	35	.573	9
Denver Nuggets	43	39	.524	13
Houston Rockets	41	41	.500	15
Minnesota Timberwolves	22	60	.268	34
Charlotte Hornets	19	63	.232	37

Pacific Division

	W	L	Pct	Games behind
Los Angeles Lakers	63	19	.768	—
Portland Trail Blazers	59	23	.720	4
Phoenix Suns	54	28	.659	9
Seattle SuperSonics	41	41	.500	22
Golden State Warriors	37	45	.451	26
Los Angeles Clippers	30	52	.366	33
Sacramento Kings	23	59	.280	40

N.B.A. PLAYOFFS—1990

EASTERN CONFERENCE
First Round

New York defeated Boston, 3 games to 2
Detroit defeated Indiana, 3 games to 0
Philadelphia defeated Cleveland, 3 games to 2
Chicago defeated Milwaukee, 3 games to 1

Semifinal Round

Chicago defeated Philadelphia, 4 games to 1
Detroit defeated New York, 4 games to 1

Conference Finals

Detroit defeated Chicago, 4 games to 3
  May 20—Detroit 86, Chicago 77
  May 22—Detroit 102, Chicago 93
  May 26—Chicago 107, Detroit 102
  May 28—Chicago 108, Detroit 101
  May 30—Detroit 97, Chicago 83
  June 1—Chicago 109, Detroit 91
  June 3—Detroit 93, Chicago 74

WESTERN CONFERENCE
First Round

Los Angeles Lakers defeated Houston, 3 games to 1
Phoenix defeated Utah, 3 games to 2
San Antonio defeated Denver, 3 games to 0
Portland defeated Dallas, 3 games to 0

Semifinal Round

Phoenix defeated Los Angeles Lakers, 4 games to 1
Portland defeated San Antonio, 4 games to 3

Conference Finals

Portland defeated Phoenix, 4 games to 2
  May 21—Portland 100, Phoenix 98
  May 23—Portland 108, Phoenix 107
  May 25—Phoenix 123, Portland 89
  May 27—Phoenix 119, Portland 107
  May 29—Portland 120, Phoenix 114
  May 31—Portland 112, Phoenix 109

CHAMPIONSHIP

Detroit defeated Portland, 4 games to 1
  June 5—Detroit 105, Portland 99
  June 7—Portland 106, Detroit 105 (OT)
  June 10—Detroit 121, Portland 106
  June 12—Detroit 112, Portland 109
  June 14—Detroit 92, Portland 90

LEADING SCORERS—1989–1990

	G	FG	FT	Pts	Avg
Jordan, Chi.	82	1034	593	2753	33.6
Malone, Utah	82	914	696	2540	31.0
Ewing, N.Y.	82	922	502	2347	28.6
Chambers, Phoe.	81	810	557	2201	27.2
Wilkins, Atl.	80	810	459	2138	26.7
Barkley, Phil.	79	706	557	1989	25.2
Mullin, G.S.	78	682	505	1956	25.1
Miller, Ind.	82	661	544	2016	24.6
Olajuwon, Hou.	82	806	382	1995	24.3
Robinson, S.A.	82	690	613	1993	24.3
Bird, Bos.	75	718	319	1820	24.3
Malone, Wash.	75	781	257	1820	24.3
Drexler, Port.	73	670	333	1703	23.3
Campbell, Minn.	82	723	448	1903	23.2
K. Johnson, Phoe.	74	578	501	1665	22.5
Cummings, S.A.	81	728	343	1818	22.4
King, Wash.	82	711	412	1837	22.4
Johnson, LAL	79	546	567	1765	22.3
Tisdale, Sac.	79	726	306	1758	22.3
Richmond, G.S.	78	640	406	1720	22.1
McDaniel, Sea.	69	611	244	1471	21.3
Smith, LAC	78	595	454	1645	21.1
Worthy, LAL	80	711	248	1685	21.1
McHale, Bos.	82	648	393	1712	20.9

STEALS LEADERS—1989–1990

(minimum 70 games or 125 steals)

	G	Stl	Avg
Jordan, Chi.	82	227	2.77
Stockton, Utah	78	207	2.65
Pippen, Chi.	82	211	2.57
Robertson, Mil.	81	207	2.56
Harper, Dall.	82	187	2.28
Corbin, Minn.	82	175	2.13
Lever, Den.	79	168	2.13
Olajuwon, Hou.	82	174	2.12
Conner, N.J.	82	172	2.10
Hardaway, G.S.	79	165	2.09
Bogues, Char.	81	166	2.05

ASSISTS LEADERS—1989–1990

(minimum 70 games or 400 assists)

	G	No.	Avg
Stockton, Utah	78	1134	14.5
Johnson, LAL	79	907	11.5
K. Johnson, Phoe.	74	846	11.4
Bogues, Char.	81	867	10.7
Grant, LAC	44	442	10.0
Thomas, Det.	81	765	9.4
Price, Clev.	73	666	9.1
Porter, Port.	80	726	9.1
Hardaway, G.S.	79	689	8.7
Walker, Wash.	81	652	8.0

BLOCKED-SHOTS LEADERS—1989–1990

(minimum 70 games or 100 blocked shots)

	G	No.	Avg
Olajuwon, Houston	82	376	4.59
Ewing, New York	82	327	3.99
Robinson, San Antonio	82	319	3.89
Bol, Golden State	75	238	3.17
Benjamin, Clippers	71	187	2.63
Eaton, Utah	82	201	2.45
Jones, Washington	81	197	2.43
West, Phoenix	82	184	2.24
Smits, Indiana	82	169	2.06
J. Williams, Cleveland	82	167	2.04

FIELD GOAL LEADERS—1989–1990

(minimum 300 FG made)

	FG	FGA	Pct
West, Phoe.	331	530	.625
Barkley, Phil.	706	1177	.600
Parish, Bos.	505	871	.580
Malone, Utah	914	1627	.562
Woolridge, LAL	306	550	.556
Ewing, N.Y.	922	1673	.551
McHale, Bos.	648	1181	.549
Thorpe, Hou.	547	998	.548
Worthy, LAL	711	1298	.548
Williams, Port.	413	754	.548

FREE-THROW LEADERS—1989–1990

(minimum 125 FT made)

	FTM	FTA	Pct
Bird, Boston	319	343	.930
E. Johnson, Phoenix	188	205	.917
Davis, Denver	207	227	.912
Dumars, Detroit	297	330	.900
McHale, Boston	393	440	.893
Porter, Portland	421	472	.892
Johnson, Lakers	567	637	.890
Mullin, Golden State	505	568	.889
Hawkins, Philadelphia	387	436	.888
Price, Cleveland	300	338	.888

REBOUND LEADERS—1989–1990

(minimum 70 games or 800 rebounds)

	G	Off	Def	Tot	Avg
Olajuwon, Hou.	82	299	850	1149	14.0
Robinson, S.A.	82	303	680	983	12.0
Barkley, Phil.	79	361	548	909	11.5
Malone, Utah	82	232	679	911	11.1
Ewing, N.Y.	82	235	658	893	10.9
Seikaly, Mia.	74	253	513	766	10.4
Parish, Bos.	79	259	537	796	10.1
Malone, Atl.	81	364	448	812	10.0
Cage, Sea.	82	306	515	821	10.0
Williams, Port.	82	250	550	800	9.8
Rodman, Det.	82	336	456	792	9.7
Laimbeer, Det.	81	166	614	780	9.6
Bird, Bos.	75	90	622	712	9.5
Lever, Den.	79	230	504	734	9.3
Benjamin, LAC	71	156	501	657	9.3
Thorpe, Hou.	82	258	476	734	9.0
West, Phoe.	82	212	516	728	8.9
Walker, Wash.	81	173	541	714	8.8
Green, LAL	82	262	450	712	8.7

3-POINT FIELD-GOAL LEADERS 1989–1990

(minimum 25 made)

	3FG	3FGA	Pct
Kerr, Clev.	73	144	.507
Hodges, Chi.	87	181	.481
Petrovic, Port.	34	74	.459
Sundvold, Mia.	44	100	.440
Scott, LAL	93	220	.423
Hawkins, Phil.	84	200	.420
Ehlo, Clev.	104	248	.419
Stockton, Utah	47	113	.416
Miller, Ind.	150	362	.414
Lever, Den.	36	87	.414

Sports Personalities

A name in parentheses is the original name or form of name. Localities are places of birth. Dates of birth appear as month/day/year. **Boldface** years in parentheses are dates of **(birth-death).** Information has been gathered from many sources, including the individuals themselves. However, the *Information Please Almanac* cannot guarantee the accuracy of every individual item.

Aaron, Hank (Henry) (baseball); Mobile, Ala., 2/5/1934
Aaron, Tommie (baseball); Mobile, Ala. **(1939–1984)**
Abdul-Jabbar, Kareem (Lewis Ferdinand Alcindor, Jr.) (basketball); New York City, 4/16/1947
Adderly, Herbert A. (football); Philadelphia, 6/8/1939
Affleck, Francis (auto racing) **(1951-1985)**
Alcindor, Lew. *See* Abdul-Jabbar
Ali, Muhammad (Cassius Clay) (boxing); Louisville, Ky., 1/18/1942
Allen, Dick (Richard Anthony) (baseball); Wampum, Pa., 3/8/1942
Allison, Bobby (Robert Arthur) (auto racing); Hueytown, Ala., 12/3/1937
Alston, Walter (baseball); Venice, Ohio **(1911-1984)**
Alworth, Lance (football); Houston, 8/3/1940
Ameche, Alan (football); Houston, Tex. **(1933-1988)**
Anderson, Donny (Gary Donny) (football); Brooklyn, N.Y., 4/3/1949
Anderson, Ken (football); Batavia, Ill., 2/15/1949
Anderson, Sparky (George) (baseball); Bridgewater, S.D., 2/22/1934
Andretti, Mario (auto racing); Montona, Trieste, Italy, 2/28/1940
Anthony, Earl (bowling); Kent, Wash., 4/27/1938
Appling, Luke (baseball); High Point, N.C., 4/2/1907
Arcaro, Eddie (George Edward) (jockey); Cincinnati, 2/19/1916
Ashe, Arthur (tennis); Richmond, Va., 7/10/1943
Austin, Tracy (tennis); Rolling Hills, Calif., 12/2/1962
Averill, Earl (baseball); Everett, Wash. **(1915–1983)**
Babashoff, Shirley (swimming); Whittier, Calif., 1/31/1957
Baer, Max (boxing); Omaha, Neb. **(1909-1959)**
Bakken, Jim (James Leroy) (football); Madison, Wis., 11/2/1940
Banks, Ernie (baseball); Dallas, 1/31/1931
Bannister, Roger (runner); Harrow, England, 3/24/1929
Barkley, Charles (basketball); Leeds, Ala., 2/20/1963
Barry, Rick (Richard) (basketball); Elizabeth, N.J., 3/28/1944
Bauer, Hank (Henry) (baseball); East St. Louis, Ill., 7/31/1922
Baugh, Sammy (football); Temple, Tex., 3/17/1914
Bayi, Filbert (runner); Karratu, Tanganyika, 6/23/1953
Baylor, Elgin (basketball); Washington, D.C., 9/16/1934
Beamon, Bob (long jumper); New York City, 8/2/1946
Becker, Boris (tennis); Leiman, W. Germany, 11/22/1967
Bee, Clair (basketball); Cleveland, Ohio **(1896–1983)**
Beliveau, Jean (hockey); Three Rivers, Quebec, Canada, 8/31/1931
Bell, Rickey (football); Inglewood, Calif. **(1949-1984)**
Beman, Deane (golf); Washington, D.C., 4/22/1938
Bench, Johnny (Johnny Lee) (baseball); Oklahoma City, 12/7/1947
Berg, Patty (Patricia Jane) (golf); Minneapolis, 2/13/1918
Berning, Susie Maxwell (golf); Pasadena, Calif., 7/22/1941
Berra, Yogi (Lawrence) (baseball); St. Louis, 5/12/1925
Biletnikoff, Frederick (football); Erie, Pa., 2/23/1943
Bing, Dave (basketball); Washington, D.C., 11/24/1943
Bird, Larry (basketball); French Lick, Ind., 12/7/1956
Blaik, Earl H. (football); Detroit, 2/15/1897
Blanda, George Frederick (football); Youngwood, Pa., 9/17/1927
Blue, Vida (baseball); Mansfield, La., 7/28/1949
Borg, Björn (tennis); Stockholm, 6/6/1956
Boros, Julius (golf); Fairfield, Conn., 3/3/1920
Bossy, Mike (hockey); Montreal, 1/22/1957
Boston, Ralph (long jumper); Laurel, Miss., 5/9/1939
Bradley, Bill (William Warren) (basketball); Crystal City, Mo., 7/28/1943
Bradshaw, Terry (football); Shreveport, La., 9/2/1948
Brathwaite, Chris (track); Eugene, Ore. **(1949-1984)**
Breedlove, Craig (Norman) (speed driving); Los Angeles, 3/23/1938
Brett, George (baseball); Glendale, W. Va., 5/15/1953
Brewer, James (Jim) (basketball); Merced, Calif. **(1937-1987)**
Brock, Louis Clark (baseball); El Dorado, Ark., 6/18/1939
Brown, Jimmy (football); St. Simon Island, Ga., 2/17/1936
Brown, Larry (football); Clairton, Pa., 9/19/1947
Brumel, Valeri (high jumper); Tolbuzino, Siberia, 4/14/1942
Bryant, Paul "Bear" (football); Tuscaloosa, Ala. **(1913–1983)**
Bryant, Rosalyn Evette (track); Chicago, 1/7/1956
Burton, Michael (swimming); Des Moines, Iowa, 7/3/1947
Butkus, Dick (Richard Marvin) (football); Chicago, 12/9/1942
Campanella, Roy (baseball); Homestead, Pa., 11/19/1921
Campbell, Earl (football); Tyler, Tex., 3/29/1955
Caponi, Donna Maria (golf); Detroit, 1/29/1945
Cappelletti, Gino (football); Keewatin, Minn., 3/26/1934
Carew, Rod (Rodney Cline) (baseball); Gatun, Panama, 10/1/1945

Carlos, John (sprinter); New York City, 6/5/1945
Carlton, Steven Norman (baseball); Miami, Fla., 12/22/1944
Carner, Joanne Gunderson (Mrs. Don) (golf); Kirkland, Wash., 3/4/1939
Casals, Rosemary (tennis); San Francisco, 9/16/1948
Casper, Billy (golf); San Diego, Calif., 6/24/1931
Caulkins, Tracy (swimming); Wimona, Minn., 1/11/63
Cauthen, Steve (jockey); Covington, Ky., 5/1/1960
Chamberlain, Wilt (Wilton) (basketball); Philadelphia, 8/21/1936
Chandler, Spud (baseball); Commerce, Ga. **(1907–1990)**
Chapot, Frank (equestrian); Camden, N.J., 2/24/1934
Chinaglia, Giorgio (soccer); Carrara, Italy, 1/24/1947
Clarke, Bobby (Robert Earle) (hockey); Flin Flon, Manitoba, Canada, 8/13/1949
Clay, Cassius. *See* Ali, Muhammad
Clemente, Roberto Walker (baseball); Carolina, Puerto Rico **(1934-1972)**
Cobb, Tyrus Raymond (Ty) (baseball); Narrows, Ga. **(1886-1961)**
Cochran, Barbara Ann (skiing); Claremont, N.H., 1/4/1951
Cochran, Marilyn (skiing); Burlington, Vt., 2/7/1950
Cochran, Robert (skiing); Claremont, N.H., 12/11/1951
Coe, Sebastian Newbold (track); London, England, 9/29/1956
Colavito, Rocky (Rocco Domenico) (baseball); New York City, 8/10/1933
Comaneci, Nadia (gymnast); Onesti, Romania, 11/12/1961
Conigliaro, Tony (baseball); Revere, Mass. **(1945–1990)**
Connors, Jimmy (James Scott) (tennis); East St. Louis, Ill., 9/2/1952
Cordero, Angel (jockey); Santurce, Puerto Rico, 5/8/1942
Cournoyer, Yvan Serge (hockey); Drummondville, Quebec, Canada, 11/22/1943
Court, Margaret Smith (tennis); Albury, New South Wales, Australia, 7/16/1942
Cousy, Bob (basketball); New York City, 8/9/1928
Crabbe, Buster (swimming); Scottsdale, Ariz. **(1908–1983)**
Crenshaw, Ben (golf); Austin, Tex., 1/11/1952
Cronin, Joe (baseball executive); San Francisco, **(1906–1984)**
Cruyff, Johan (soccer); Amsterdam, Netherlands, 4/25/47
Csonka, Larry (Lawrence Richard) (football); Stow, Ohio, 12/25/1946
Dancer, Stanley (harness racing); New Egypt, N.J., 7/25/1927
Dantley, Adrian (basketball); Washington, D.C., 2/28/1956
Dark, Alvin (baseball); Comanche, Okla., 1/7/1922
Davenport, Willie (track); Troy, Ala., 6/6/1943
Dawson, Leonard Ray (football); Alliance, Ohio, 6/20/1935
Dean, Dizzy (Jay Hanna) (baseball); Lucas, Ark. **(1911-1974)**
DeBusschere, Dave (basketball); Detroit, 10/16/1940
Delvecchio, Alex Peter (hockey); Fort William, Ontario, Canada, 12/4/1931
Demaret, Jim (golf); Houston **(1910-1983)**
Dempsey, Jack (William H.) (boxing); Manassa, Colo. **(1895-1983)**
DeVicenzo, Roberto (golf); Buenos Aires, 4/14/1923
Dibbs, Edward George (tennis); Brooklyn, New York, 2/23/1951
Dietz, James W. (rowing); New York, N.Y., 1/12/1949
DiMaggio, Joe (baseball); Martinez, Calif., 11/25/1914
Dionne, Marcel (hockey); Drummondville, Quebec, Canada, 8/3/1951
Dominguín, Luis Miguel (matador); Madrid, 12/9/1926
Dorsett, Tony (football); Rochester, Pa., 4/7/1954
Dryden, Kenneth (hockey); Hamilton, Ontario, Canada, 8/4/1947
Drysdale, Don (baseball); Van Nuys, Calif., 7/23/1936
Duran, Roberto (boxing); Panama City, 6/16/1951
Durocher, Leo (baseball); West Springfield, Mass., 7/27/1906
Durr, François (tennis); Algiers, Algeria, 12/25/1942
El Cordobés, (Manuel Benítez Pérez) (matador); Palma del Río, Córdoba, Spain, 5/4/1936(?)
Elder, Lee (golf); Dallas, 7/14/1934
Emerson, Roy (tennis); Kingsway, Australia, 11/3/1936
Ender, Kornelia (swimming); Plauen, East Germany, 10/25/1958
Erving, Julius (Dr. J) (basketball); Roosevelt, N.Y., 2/22/1950
Espinosa, Nino (baseball); Villa Altagracia, Dominican Republic **(1953-1988)**
Esposito, Phil (Philip Anthony) (hockey); Sault Ste. Marie, Ontario, Canada, 2/20/1942
Evans, Lee (runner); Mandena, Calif., 2/25/1947
Ewbank, Weeb (football); Richmond, Ind., 5/6/1907
Ewing, Patrick (basketball); Kingston, Jamaica, 8/5/1962
Feller, Robert (Bobby) (baseball); Van Meter, Iowa, 11/3/1918

Feuerbach, Allan Dean (track); Preston, Iowa, 1/12/1948
Finley, Charles O. (sportsman); Ensley, Ala., 2/22/1918
Fischer, Bobby (chess); Chicago, 3/9/1943
Fitzsimmons, Bob (Robert Prometheus) (boxing); Cornwall, England **(1862-1917)**
Fleming, Peggy Gale (ice skating); San Jose, Calif., 7/27/1948
Ford, Whitey (Edward) (baseball); New York City, 10/21/1928
Foreman, George (boxing); Marshall, Tex., 1/10/1949
Fosbury, Richard (high jumper); Portland, Ore., 3/6/1947
Fox, Nellie (Jacob Nelson) (baseball); St. Thomas, Pa. **(1927-1975)**
Foxx, James Emory (baseball); Sudlersville, Md., **(1907-1967)**
Foyt, A. J. (auto racing); Houston, 1/16/1935
Francis, Emile (hockey); North Battleford, Sask., 9/13/1926
Fratianne, Linda (figure skating); Los Angeles, 8/2/1960
Frazier, Joe (boxing); Beauford, S.C., 1/17/1944
Frazier, Walt (basketball); Atlanta, 3/29/1945
Frick, Ford C. (baseball); Wawaka, Ind., **(1894-1978)**
Furillo, Carl (baseball); Stony Creek Mills, Pa. **(1922–1989)**
Furniss, Bruce (swimming); Fresno, Calif., 5/27/1957
Gable, Dan (wrestling); Waterloo, Iowa, 10/25/1945
Gabriel, Roman (football); Wilmington, N.C., 8/5/1940
Gallagher, Michael Donald (skiing); Yonkers, N.Y., 10/3/1941
Garms, Debs (baseball); Glen Rose, Tex. **(1908-1984)**
Garvey, Steve (baseball); Tampa, Fla., 12/22/1948
Gehrig, Lou (Henry Louis) (baseball); New York City **(1903-1941)**
Gehringer, Charlie (baseball); Fowlerville, Mich., 5/11/1903
Geoffrion, Bernie (Boom Boom) (hockey); Montreal, 2/14/1931
Gerulaitis, Vitas (tennis); Brooklyn, N.Y., 7/26/1954
Giacomin, Ed (hockey); Sudbury, Ontario, Canada, 6/6/1939
Giamatti, A. Bartlett (baseball); South Hadley, Mass. **(1938–1989)**
Gibson, Bob (baseball); Omaha, Neb., 11/9/1935
Gifford, Frank (football); Santa Monica, Calif., 8/16/1930
Gilbert, Rod (Rodrique) (hockey); Montreal, 7/1/1941
Giles, Warren (baseball executive); Tiskilwa, Ill. **(1896–1979)**
Gilmore, Artis (basketball); Chipley, Fla., 9/21/1949
Glance, Harvey (track); Phenix City, Ala., 3/28/1957
Gonzalez, Pancho (tennis); Los Angeles, 5/9/1928
Goodell, Brian Stuart (swimming); Stockton, Calif., 4/2/1959
Gooden, Dwight (baseball); Tampa, Fla., 11/16/1964
Goodrich, Gail (basketball); Los Angeles, 4/23/1943
Goolagong Cawley, Evonne (tennis); Griffith, Australia, 7/31/1951
Gossage, Rich (Goose) (baseball); Colorado Springs, Colo., 4/5/1951
Gottfried, Brian (tennis); Baltimore, Md., 1/27/1952
Graf, Steffi (tennis); Mannheim, W. Germany, 6/14/1969
Graham, David (golf); Windson, Australia, 5/23/1946
Graham, Otto Everett (football); Waukegan, Ill., 12/6/1921
Grange, Red (Harold) (football); Forksville, Pa., 6/13/1904
Green, Hubert (golf); Birmingham, Ala., 12/28/1946
Greene, Charles E. (sprinter); Pine Bluff, Ark., 3/21/1945
Greene, Joe (Mean); (football); Temple, Tex., 9/24/1946
Gretzky, Wayne (hockey); Brantford, Ont., 1/26/1961
Griese, Bob (Robert Allen) (football); Evansville, Ind., 2/3/1945
Groebli, Werner (Mr. Frick) (ice skating); Basil, Switzerland, 4/21/1915
Grove, Lefty (Robert Moses) (baseball); Lonaconing, Md., **(1900-1975)**
Groza, Lou (football); Martins Ferry, Ohio, 1/25/1924
Guidry, Ronald Ames (baseball); Lafayette, La., 8/28/1950
Gunter, Nancy Richey (tennis); San Angelo, Tex., 8/23/1942
Halas, George (football); Chicago **(1895-1983)**
Hall, Gary (swimming); Fayetteville, N.C., 8/7/1951
Hamill, Dorothy (figure skating); Chicago, 1956(?)
Hamilton, Scott (figure skating); Bowling Green, Ohio, 8/28/1958
Hammond, Kathy (runner); Sacramento, Calif., 11/2/1951
Harris, Franco (football); Ft. Dix, N.J., 3/7/1950
Hartack, William, Jr. (jockey); Colver, Pa., 12/9/1932
Haughton, William (harness racing); Gloversville, N.Y. **(1923-1986)**
Havlicek, John (basketball); Martins Ferry, Ohio, 4/8/1940
Hayes, Elvin (basketball); Rayville, La., 11/17/1945
Hayes, Woody (football) Upper Arlington, Ohio **(1913-1987)**
Haynie, Sandra (golf); Fort Worth, 6/4/1943
Heiden, Eric (speed skating); Madison, Wis., 6/14/1958
Hencken, John (swimming); Culver City, Calif., 5/29/1954
Henderson, Rickey (baseball); Chicago, 12/25/1958
Henie, Sonja (ice skater); Oslo **(1912-1969)**
Herman, Floyd Caves (Babe) (baseball); Buffalo, N.Y. **(1903-1987)**
Hernandez, Keith (baseball); San Francisco, 10/20/1953
Hershiser, Orel (baseball); Buffalo, N.Y., 9/16/1958
Hickcox, Charles (swimming); Phoenix, Ariz., 2/6/1947
Hines, James (sprinter); Dumas, Ark., 9/10/1946
Hodges, Gil (baseball); Princeton, Ind. **(1924-1972)**
Hogan, Ben (golf); Dublin, Tex., 8/13/1912
Holmes, Larry (boxing); Cuthert, Ga., 11/3/1949
Hornsby, Rogers (baseball); Winters, Tex. **(1896-1963)**
Hornung, Paul (football); Louisville, Ky., 12/23/1935
Houk, Ralph (baseball); Lawrence, Kan., 8/9/1919

Howard, Elston (baseball); St. Louis **(1929-1980)**
Howe, Gordon (hockey); Floral, Sask., Canada, 3/31/1928
Howell, Jim Lee (football); Lonoke, Ark., 9/27/1914
Howser, Dick (baseball) Miami, Fla. **(1937-1987)**
Hubbell, Carl (baseball); Carthage, Mo., 6/22/1903
Huff, Sam (Robert Lee) (football); Morgantown, W. Va., 10/4/1934
Hull, Bobby (hockey); Point Anne, Ontario, Canada, 1/3/1939
Hunter, Jim (Catfish) (baseball); Hertford, N.C., 4/8/1946
Huntley, Joni (track); McMinnville, Ore., 8/4/1956
Hutson, Donald (football); Pine Bluff, Ark., 1/31/1913
Insko, Del (harness racing); Amboy, Minn., 7/10/1931
Irwin, Hale (golf); Joplin, Mo., 6/3/1945
Jackson, Reggie (baseball); Wyncote, Pa., 5/18/1946
Jeffries, James J. (boxing); Carroll, Ohio **(1875-1953)**
Jenkins, Ferguson Arthur (baseball); Chatham, Ontario, Canada, 12/13/1943
Jenner, (W.) Bruce (track); Mt. Kisco, N.Y., 10/28/1949
Jezek, Linda (swimming); Palo Alto, Calif., 3/10/1960
Johnson, Earvin (Magic) (basketball); E. Lansing, Mich., 8/14/1959
Johnson, Anthony (rowing); Washington, D.C., 11/16/1940
Johnson, Jack (John Arthur) (boxing); Galveston, Tex. **(1876-1946)**
Johnson, Rafer (decathlon); Hillsboro, Tex., 8/18/1935
Johnson, Wilham Julius (Judy) (baseball); Wilmington, Del. **(1899-1989)**
Jones, Deacon (David) (football); Eatonville, Fla., 12/9/1938
Jordan, Michael (basketball); Brooklyn, N.Y., 2/17/1963
Joyner, Florence Griffith (sprinter); Mojave Desert, Calif., 12/21/1959
Juantoreno, Alberto (track); Santiago, Cuba, 12/3/1951
Jurgensen, Sonny (football); Wilmington, N.C., 8/23/1934
Kaat, Jim (baseball); Zeeland, Mich., 11/7/1938
Kaline, Al (Albert) (baseball); Baltimore, 12/19/1934
Keino, Kipchoge (runner); Kapchemoiymo, Kenya, 1/?/1940
Kelly, Leroy (football); Philadelphia, 5/20/1942
Kelly, Red (Leonard Patrick) (hockey); Simcoe, Ontario, Canada, 7/9/1927
Killebrew, Harmon (baseball); Payette, Idaho, 6/29/1936
Killy, Jean-Claude (skiing); Saint-Cloud, France, 8/30/1943
Kilmer, Bill (William Orland) (football); Topeka, Kan., 9/5/1939
King, Billie Jean (Billie Jean Moffitt) (tennis); Long Beach, Calif., 11/22/1943
Kinsella, John (swimming); Oak Park, Ill., 8/26/1952
Kluszeewski, Ted (baseball); Argo, Ill. **(1924-1988)**
Kodes, Jan (tennis); Prague, 3/1/1946
Kolb, Claudia (swimming); Hayward, Calif., 12/19/1949
Koosman, Jerry Martin (baseball); Appleton, Minn., 12/23/1942
Korbut, Olga (gymnast); Grodno, Byelorussia, U.S.S.R., 5/16/1955
Koufax, Sandy (Sanford) (baseball); Brooklyn, N.Y., 12/30/1935
Kramer, Jack (tennis); Las Vegas, Nev., 8/1/1921
Kramer, Jerry (football); Jordan, Mont., 1/23/1936
Kuenn, Harvey (baseball); West Allis, Wis. **(1930-1988)**
Kuhn, Bowie Kent (baseball); Takoma Park, Md., 10/28/1926
Kwalik, Ted (Thaddeus John) (football); McKees Rocks, Pa., 4/15/1947
Lafleur, Guy Damien (hockey); Thurson, Quebec, Canada, 8/20/1951
Laird, Ronald (walker); Louisville, Ky., 5/31/1935
Lamonica, Daryle (football); Fresno, Calif., 7/17/1941
Landis, Kenesaw Mountain (1st baseball commissioner); Millville, Ohio **(1866-1944)**
Landry, Tom (football); Mission, Tex., 9/11/1924
Landy, John (runner); Australia, 4/4/1930
Larrieu, Francie (track); Palo Alto, Calif., 11/28/1952
Lasorda, Tom (baseball); Norristown, Pa., 9/22/1927
Laver, Rod (tennis); Rockhampton, Australia, 8/9/1938
Layne, Bobby (football) Lubbock, Texas **(1927-1986)**
Lemieux, Mario (hockey); Montreal, Que., Canada, 10/5/1965
Lendl, Ivan (tennis); Prague, 3/7/1960
Leonard, Benny (Benjamin Leiner) (boxing); New York City **(1896-1947)**
Leonard, Sugar Ray (boxing); Wilmington, N.C., 5/17/1956
Lewis, Carl (track); Willingboro, N.J., 7/1/1961
Linehan, Kim (swimming); Bronxville, N.Y., 12/11/1962
Liquori, Marty (runner); Montclair, N.J., 9/11/1949
Little, Floyd Douglas (football); New Haven, Conn., 7/4/1942
Little, Lou (football); Leominster, Mass., **(1893-1979)**
Littler, Gene (golf); La Jolla, Calif., 7/21/1930
Lloyd, Chris Evert (Christine Marie) (tennis); Fort Lauderdale, Fla., 12/21/1954
Lombardi, Vince (football); Brooklyn, N.Y. **(1913-1970)**
Longden, Johnny (horse racing); Wakefield, England, 2/14/1907
Lopez, Al (baseball); Tampa, Fla., 8/20/1908
Lopez, Nancy (golf); Torrance, Calif., 1/6/1957
Louis, Joe (Joe Louis Barrow) (boxing); Lafayette, Ala. **(1914-1981)**
Lynn, Frederic Michael (baseball); Chicago, Ill., 2/3/1952
Lynn, Janet (figure skating); Rockford, Ill., 4/6/1953

Mack, Connie (Cornelius Alexander McGillicuddy) (baseball executive); East Brookfield, Mass. **(1862-1956)**

Mackey, John (football); New York City, 9/24/1941

Mahovlich, Frank (Francis William) (hockey); Timmins, Ontario, Canada, 1/10/1938

Mahre, Phil (skiing); White Pass, Wash., 5/10/1957

Malone, Moses (basketball); Petersburg, Va. 3/23/1955

Mandlikova, Hana (tennis); Prague, Czechoslovakia, 2/1962

Mann, Carol (golf); Buffalo, N.Y., 2/3/1941

Manning, Madeline (runner); Cleveland, 1/11/1948

Mantle, Mickey Charles (baseball); Spavinaw, Okla., 10/20/1931

Maravich, Peter (Pistol Pete); Aliquippa, Pa. **(1948-1988)**

Marciano, Rocky (boxing); Brockton, Mass. **(1923-1969)**

Marichal, Juan (baseball); Laguna Verde, Montecristi, Dominican Republic, 10/20/1937

Maris, Roger (baseball); Hibbing, Minn. **(1934-1985)**

Martin, Billy (Alfred Manuel) (baseball); Berkeley, Calif., **(1928–1989)**

Martin, Rick (Richard Lionel) (hockey); Verdun, Quebec, Canada, 7/26/1951

Mathews, Ed (Edwin) (baseball); Texarkana, Tex., 10/13/1931

Matson, Randy (shot putter); Kilgore, Tex., 3/5/1945

Mays, Willie (baseball); Westfield, Ala., 5/6/1931

McAdoo, Bob (basketball); Greensboro, N.C., 9/25/1951

McCarthy, Joe (Joseph Vincent) (baseball); Philadelphia **(1887-1978)**

McCovey, Willie Lee (baseball); Mobile, Ala., 1/10/1938

McDonald, Lanny (hockey); Hanna, Alberta, Canada, 2/16/1953

McEnroe, John Patrick, Jr. (tennis); Wiesbaden, Germany, 2/16/1959

McGraw, John Joseph (baseball); Truxton, N.Y. **(1873-1934)**

McLain, Dennis (baseball); Chicago, 3/24/1944

McMillan, Kathy Laverne (track); Raeford, N.C., 11/7/1957

Merrill, Janice (track); New London, Conn., 6/18/1962

Meyer, Deborah (swimming); Haddonfield, N.J., 8/14/1952

Middlecoff, Cary (golf); Halls, Tenn., 1/6/1921

Mikita, Stan (hockey); Sokolce, Czechoslovakia, 5/20/1940

Milburn, Rodney, Jr. (hurdler); Opelousas, La., 5/18/1950

Miller, Johnny (golf); San Francisco, 4/29/1947

Montgomery, Jim (swimming); Madison, Wis., 1/24/1955

Moore, Archie (boxing); Benoit, Miss., 12/13/1916

Morgan, Joe Leonard (baseball); Bonham, Tex., 9/19/1943

Morrall, Earl (football); Muskegon, Mich., 5/17/1934

Morton, Craig L. (football); Flint, Mich., 2/5/1943

Mosconi, Willie (pocket billiards); Philadelphia, 6/27/1913

Moser, Annemarie. *See* Proell, Annemarie

Moses, Edward Corley (track); Dayton, Ohio, 8/31/1958

Mungo, Van Lingo (baseball); Pageland, S.C. **(1911-1985)**

Munson, Thurman (baseball); Akron, Ohio, **(1947-1979)**

Murphy, Calvin (basketball); Norwalk, Conn., 5/9/1948

Musial, Stan (baseball); Donora, Pa., 11/21/1920

Myers, Linda (archery); York, Pa., 6/19/1947

Naber, John (swimming); Evanston, Ill., 1/20/1956

Namath, Joe (Joseph William) (football); Beaver Falls, Pa., 5/31/1943

Nastase, Ilie (tennis); Bucharest, 7/19/1946

Navratilova, Martina (tennis); Prague, 10/18/1956

Nehemiah, Renaldo (track); Newark, N.J., 3/24/1959

Nelson, Cindy (skiing); Lutsen, Minn., 8/19/1955

Newcombe, John (tennis); Sydney, Australia, 5/23/1943

Niekro, Phil (baseball); Lansing, Ohio, 4/1/1939

Nicklaus, Jack (golf); Columbus, Ohio, 1/21/1940

Norman, Greg(ory) (golf); Mount Isa, Australia, 2/10/1955

North, Lowell (yachting); Springfield, Mo., 12/2/1929

Oerter, Al (discus thrower); New York City, 9/19/1936

Okker, Tom (tennis); Amsterdam, 2/22/1944

Oldfield, Barney (racing driver); Fulton County, Ohio **(1878-1946)**

Oliva, Tony (Pedro) (baseball); Pinar Del Rio, Cuba, 7/20/1940

Olsen, Merlin Jay (football); Logan, Utah, 9/15/1940

O'Malley, Walter (baseball executive); New York City **(1903–1979)**

Orantes, Manuel (tennis); Granada, Spain, 2/6/1949

Orr, Bobby (hockey); Parry Sound, Ontario, Canada, 3/20/1948

Ovett, Steve (track); Brighton, England, 10/9/1955

Owens, Jesse (track); Decatur, Ala. **(1914-1980)**

Pace, Darrell (archery); Cincinnati, 10/23/1956

Paige, Satchel (Leroy) (baseball); Mobile, Ala., **(1906-1982)**

Palmer, Arnold (golf); Latrobe, Pa., 9/10/1929

Palmer, James Alvin (baseball); New York City, 10/15/1945

Parent, Bernard Marcel (hockey); Montreal, 4/3/1945

Park, Brad (Douglas Bradford) (hockey); Toronto, Ontario, Canada, 7/6/1948

Parseghian, Ara (football); Akron, Ohio, 5/21/1923

Pasarell, Charles (tennis); San Juan, Puerto Rico, 2/12/1944

Patterson, Floyd (boxing); Waco, N.C., 1/4/1935

Peete, Calvin (golf); Detroit, Mich., 7/18/1943

Pelé (Edson Arantes do Nascimento) (soccer); Tres Coracoes, Brazil, 10/23/1940

Perry, Gaylord (baseball); Williamston, N.C., 9/15/1938

Perry, Jim (baseball); Williamston, N.C., 9/15/1938

Pettit, Bob (basketball); Baton Rouge, La., 12/12/1932

Petty, Richard Lee (auto racing); Randleman, N.C., 7/2/1937

Pincay, Laffit, Jr. (jockey); Panama City, Panama, 12/29/1946

Plager, Barclay (ice hockey); Kirkland Lake, Ontario **(1941-1988)**

Plante, Jacques (hockey); Shawinigan Falls, Quebec, Canada, 1/17/1929

Player, Gary (golf); Johannesburg, South Africa, 11/1/1935

Plunkett, Jim (football); San Jose, Calif., 12/5/1947

Potvin, Denis Charles (hockey); Hull, Quebec, Canada, 10/29/1953

Powell, Boog (John) (baseball); Lakeland, Fla., 8/17/1941

Prefontaine, Steve Roland (runner); Coos Bay, Ore. **(1951-1975)**

Prince, Bob (baseball announcer); Pittsburgh **(1917-1985)**

Proell, Annemarie Moser (Alpine skier); Kleinarl, Austria, 3/27/1953

Ralston, Dennis (tennis); Bakersfield, Calif., 7/27/1942

Rankin, Judy Torluemke (golf); St. Louis, Mo., 2/18/1945

Raschi, Vic (baseball); West Springfield, Mass. **(1919-1988)**

Ratelle, Jean (Joseph Gilbert Yvon Jean) (hockey); St. Jean, Quebec, Canada, 10/29/1953

Rawls, Betsy (Elizabeth Earle) (golf); Spartanburg, S.C., 5/4/1928

Reed, Willis (basketball); Hico, La., 6/25/1942

Reese, Pee Wee (Harold) (baseball); Ekron, Ky., 7/23/1919

Resch, Glenn "Chico" (hockey); Moose Jaw, Saskatchewan, Canada, 7/10/1948

Richard, Maurice (hockey); Montreal, 8/14/1924

Riessen, Martin (tennis); Hinsdale, Ill., 12/4/1941

Rigney, William (baseball); Alameda, Calif., 1/29/1918

Rizzuto, Phil (baseball); New York City, 9/25/1918

Roark, Helen Wills Moody (tennis); Centerville, Calif., 10/6/1906

Robertson, Oscar (basketball); Charlotte, Tenn., 11/24/1938

Robinson, Arnie (track); San Diego, Calif., 4/7/1948

Robinson, Brooks (baseball); Little Rock, Ark., 5/18/1937

Robinson, Frank (baseball); Beaumont, Tex., 8/31/1935

Robinson, Jackie (baseball); Cairo, Ga. **(1919-1972)**

Robinson, Larry Clark (hockey); Marvelville, Ontario, Canada, 6/2/1951

Robinson, (Sugar) Ray (boxing); Detroit **(1920-1989)**

Rockne, Knute Kenneth (football); Voss, Norway **(1888-1931)**

Rockwell, Martha (skiing); Providence, R.I., 4/26/1944

Rono, Harry (track); Kiptaragon, Kenya, 2/12/1952

Rooney, Art (football); Pittsburgh, Pa. **(1901-1988)**

Rose, Pete (Peter Edward) (baseball); Cincinnati, 4/14/1942

Rosenbloom, Maxie (boxing); New York City **(1904-1976)**

Rosewall, Ken (tennis); Sydney, Australia, 11/2/1934

Rote, Kyle (football); San Antonio, 10/27/1928

Roush, Edd (baseball); Oakland City, Ind. **(1893-1988)**

Rozelle, Pete (Alvin Ray) (commissioner of National Football League); South Gate, Calif., 3/1/1926

Rudolph, Wilma Glodean (sprinter); St. Bethlehem, Tenn., 6/23/1940

Russell, Bill (basketball); Monroe, La., 2/12/1934

Ruth, Babe (George Herman Ruth) (baseball); Baltimore **(1895-1948)**

Rutherford, Johnny (auto racing); Fort Worth, 3/12/1938

Ryan, Nolan (Lynn Nolan, Jr.) (baseball); Refugio, Tex., 1/31/1947

Ryon, Luann (archery); Long Beach, Calif., 1/13/1953

Ryun, Jim (runner); Wichita, Kan., 4/29/1947

Salazar, Alberto (track); Havana, 8/7/1958

Samuels, Howard (horse racing; soccer); New York City **(1920-1984)**

Santana, Manuel (Manuel Santana Martinez) (tennis); Chamartin, Spain, 5/10/1938

Sayers, Gale (football); Wichita, Kan., 5/30/1943

Schmidt, Mike (baseball); Dayton, Ohio, 9/27/1949

Schoendienst, Al (Albert) (baseball); Germantown, Ill., 2/2/1923

Schollander, Donald (swimming); Charlotte, N.C., 4/30/1946

Seagren, Bob (Robert Lloyd) (pole vaulter); Pomona, Calif., 10/17/1946

Seaver, Tom (baseball); Fresno, Calif., 11/17/1944

Seidler, Maren (track); Brooklyn, N.Y., 6/11/1962

Selke, Frank (ice hockey); Canada **(1893-1985)**

Sewell, Joe (baseball); Titus, Ala. **(1898-1990)**

Shepherd, Lee (auto racing) **(1945-1985)**

Shoemaker, Willie (jockey); Fabens, Tex., 8/19/1931

Shore, Eddie (ice hockey); Saskatchewan, Canada **(1902-1985)**

Shorter, Frank (runner); Munich, Germany, 10/31/1947

Shriver, Pam (tennis); Baltimore, 7/4/1962

Shula, Don (Donald Francis) (football); Grand River, Ohio, 1/4/1930

Silvester, Jay (discus thrower); Tremonton, Utah, 2/27/1937

Simpson, O. J. (Orenthal James) (football); San Francisco, 7/9/1947

Sims, Billy (football); St. Louis, 9/18/1955

Smith, Bubba (Charles Aaron) (football); Orange, Tex., 2/28/1945

Smith, Ronnie Ray (sprinter); Los Angeles, 3/28/1949

Smith, Stanley Roger (tennis); Pasadena, Calif., 12/14/1946

Smith, Tommie (sprinter); Clarksville, Tex., 6/5/1944

Smoke, Marcia Jones (canoeing); Oklahoma City, 7/18/1941

Snead, Sam (golf); Hot Springs, Va., 5/27/1912
Sneva, Tom (auto racing); Spokane, Wash., 6/1/1948
Snider, Duke (Edwin) (baseball); Los Angeles, 9/19/1926
Solomon, Harold (tennis); Washington, D.C., 9/17/1952
Spahn, Warren (baseball); Buffalo, N.Y., 4/23/1921
Speaker, Tristram (baseball); Hubbard City, Tex. **(1888-1958)**
Spencer, Brian (ice hockey); Fort St. James, British Columbia **(1949-1988)**
Spinks, Leon (boxing); St. Louis, 7/11/1953
Spitz, Mark (swimming); Modesto, Calif., 2/10/1950
Stabler, Kenneth (football); Foley, Ala., 12/25/1945
Stagg, Amos Alonzo (football); West Orange, N.J. **(1862-1965)**
Stargell, Willie (Wilver Dornell) (baseball); Earlsboro, Okla., 3/6/1941
Starr, Bart (football); Montgomery, Ala., 1/9/1934
Staub, Daniel (Rusty) (baseball); New Orleans, 4/4/1944
Staubach, Roger (football); Cincinnati, 2/5/1942
Steinkraus, William C. (equestrian); Cleveland, 10/12/1925
Stenerud, Jan (football); Fetsund, Norway, 11/26/1942
Stengel, Casey (Charles Dillon) (baseball); Kansas City, Mo. **(1891-1975)**
Stenmark, Ingemar (Alpine skier); Tarnaby, Sweden, 3/18/1956
Stockton, Richard LaClede (tennis); New York City, 2/18/1951
Stones, Dwight Edwin (track); Los Angeles, 12/6/1953
Strawberry, Darryl (baseball); Los Angeles, 3/12/1962
Sullivan, John Lawrence (boxing); Boston **(1858-1918)**
Sutton, Don (Donald Howard) (baseball); Clio, Ala., 4/2/1945
Swann, Lynn (football); Alcoa, Tenn., 3/7/1952
Tanner, Leonard Roscoe III (tennis); Chattanooga, Tenn., 10/15/1951
Tarkenton, Fran (Francis) (football); Richmond, Va., 2/3/1940
Tebbetts, Birdie (George R.) (baseball); Nashua, N.H., 11/10/1914
Theismann, Joe (football); New Brunswick, N.J., 9/9/1946
Thoeni, Gustavo (Alpine skier); Trafoi, Italy, 2/28/1951
Thomas, Isiah (basketball); Chicago, Ill., 4/30/1961
Thompson, David (basketball); Shelby, N.C., 7/13/1954
Thorpe, Jim (James Francis) (all-around athlete); nr. Prague, Okla. **(1888-1953)**
Tilden, William Tatem II (tennis); Philadelphia **(1893-1953)**
Tittle, Y. A. (Yelberton Abraham) (football); Marshall, Tex., 10/24/1926
Toomey, William (decathlon); Philadelphia, 1/10/1939
Trevino, Lee (golf); Dallas, 12/1/1939
Trottier, Bryan (hockey); Val Marie, Sask., Canada, 7/17/1956
Tunney, Gene (James J.) (boxing); New York City **(1898-1978)**
Tyus, Wyomia (runner); Griffin, Ga., 8/29/1945
Ueberroth, Peter (baseball); Evanston, Ill., 9/2/1937
Unitas, John (football); Pittsburgh, 5/7/1933
Unser, Al (auto racing); Albuquerque, N. Mex., 5/29/1939

Unser, Bobby (auto racing); Albuquerque N. Mex., 2/20/1934
Valenzuela, Fernando (baseball); Sonora, Mexico, 11/1/1960
Van Brocklin, Norm (football); Eagle Butte, S. Dak. **(1926-1983)**
Vilas, Guillermo (tennis); Mar del Plata, Argentina, 8/17/1952
Viola, Frank (baseball); Hempstead, N.Y., 4/19/1960
Viren, Lasse (track); Myrskyla, Finland, 7/12/1949
Wade, Virginia (tennis); Bournemouth, England, 7/10/1945
Wagner, Honus (John Peter Honus) (baseball); Carnegie, Pa. **(1867-1955)**
Waitz, Grete (Andersen) (running); Oslo, Norway, 10/1/1953
Wakefield, Dick (baseball); Chicago **(1921-1985)**
Walcott, Jersey Joe (Arnold Cream) (boxing); Merchantville, N.J., 1/31/1914
Walsh, Adam (football) **(1902-1985)**
Walton, Bill (basketball); La Mesa, Calif., 11/5/1952
Waterfield, Bob (football); Burbank, Calif. **(1921-1983)**
Watson, Martha Rae (track); Long Beach, Calif., 8/19/1946
Watson, Tom (golf); Kansas City, Mo., 9/4/1949
Weaver, Earl (baseball); St. Louis, 8/14/1930
Webster, Alex (football); Kearny, N.J., 4/19/1931
Weiskopf, Tom (golf); Massillon, Ohio, 11/9/1942
Weiss, George (baseball executive); New Haven, Conn. **(1895-1972)**
Weissmuller, Johnny (swimmer and actor); Windber, Pa. **(1904-1984)**
Weld, Philip (sailing); Cambridge, Mass. **(1915-1984)**
West, Jerry (basketball); Cheylan, W. Va., 5/28/1938
White, Willye B. (long jumper); Money, Miss., 1/1/1936
Whitworth, Kathy (golf); Monahans, Tex., 9/27/1939
Widing, Juha (ice hockey); Vancouver, Canada **(1948-1985)**
Wilkens, Mac Maurice (track); Eugene, Ore., 11/15/1950
Wilkins, Lennie (basketball); 11/25/1937
Wilkinson, Bud (football); Minneapolis, 4/23/1916
Williams, Del (football); New Orleans **(1945-1984)**
Williams, Dick (baseball); St. Louis, 5/7/1929
Williams, Ted (baseball); San Diego, Calif., 8/30/1918
Wills, Maury (baseball); Washington, D.C., 10/2/1932
Winfield, Dave (baseball); St. Paul, Minn., 10/3/1951
Wohlhuter, Richard C. (runner); Geneva, Ill. 12/23/1945
Wood, Joseph (Smokey) (baseball); Kansas City, Mo. **(1890-1985)**
Woodhead, Cynthia (swimming); Riverside, Calif., 2/7/1964
Wottle, David James (runner); Canton, Ohio, 8/7/1950
Wright, Mickey (Mary Kathryn) (golf); San Diego, Calif., 2/14/1935
Yarborough, Cale (William Caleb) (auto racing); Timmonsville, S.C., 3/27/1939
Yarbrough, Leeroy (auto racing); Jacksonville, Fla. **(1938-1984)**
Yastrzemski, Carl (baseball); Southampton, N.Y., 8/22/1939
Young, Cy (Denton True) (baseball); Gilmore, Ohio **(1867-1955)**
Young, Sheila (speed skater, bicycle racer); Detroit, 10/14/1950

Yachting

The word "yacht" is of Dutch origin and the first "yacht race" of record in the English language was a sailing contest from Greenwich to Gravesend and return in 1662 between a Dutch yacht and an English yacht designed and, at some part of the race, sailed by Charles II of England. The royal yacht won the contest.

The first yacht club was organized at Cork, Ireland, in 1720 under the name of the Cork Harbour Water Club, later changed to the Royal Cork Yacht Club. The Royal Yacht Squadron was organized at Cowes in 1812 and the name changed to the Royal Yacht Club in 1820. The New York Yacht Club was organized aboard the Stevens schooner "Gimcrack" on July 30, 1844, and a clubhouse erected at Elysian Fields, Hoboken, N.J., the following year.

Bowling

The game of bowling that is the favorite sport of millions in the United States is an indoor modification of the more ancient outdoor game. The outdoor game is prehistoric in origin and probably goes back to Primitive Man and round stones that were rolled at some target. It is believed that a game something like nine-pins was popular among the Dutch, Swiss, and Germans as long ago as 1200 A.D., at which time the game was played outdoors with an alley consisting of a single plank 12 to 18 inches wide along which was rolled a ball toward three rows of three pins each placed at the far end of the alley. When the first indoor alleys were built and how the game was modified from time to time are matters of dispute. Much of the confusion arises from a lack of certainty as to which game is meant, "bowls" or "bowling," one with a "jack" and the other with "pins," in historical passages.

It is supposed that the early settlers of New Amsterdam (New York City) being Dutch, they brought their two bowling games with them. About a century ago the game of nine-pins was flourishing in the United States but so corrupted by gambling on matches that it was barred by law in New York and Connecticut. Since the law specifically barred "nine-pins," it was eventually evaded by adding another pin and thus legally making it a new game. The genius who thought up that simple method of outwitting the law and putting a popular game in motion once more remained modestly anonymous. With the increase in the number of pins, the old diamond formation of nine-pins was abandoned for the triangle set-up of ten-pins that remains the rule to this day. Various organizations were formed to make rules for bowling and supervise competition in the United States but none was successful until the American Bowling Congress, organized Sept. 9, 1895, became the ruling body.

HOCKEY

Ice hockey, by birth and upbringing a Canadian game, is an offshoot of field hockey. Some historians say that the first ice hockey game was played in Montreal in December 1879 between two teams composed almost exclusively of McGill University students, but others assert that earlier hockey games took place in Kingston, Ontario, or Halifax, Nova Scotia. In the Montreal game of 1879, there were fifteen players on a side, who used an assortment of crude sticks to keep the puck in motion. Early rules allowed nine men on a side, but the number was reduced to seven in 1886 and later to six.

The first governing body of the sport was the Amateur Hockey Association of Canada, organized in 1887. In the winter of 1894–95, a group of college students from the United States visited Canada and saw hockey played. They became enthused over the game and introduced it as a winter sport when they returned home. The first profes-

sional league was the International Hockey League, which operated in northern Michigan in 1904–06.

Until 1910, professionals and amateurs were allowed to play together on "mixed teams," but this arrangement ended with the formation of the first "big league," the National Hockey Association, in eastern Canada in 1910. The Pacific Coast League was organized in 1911 for western Canadian hockey. The league included Seattle and later other American cities. The National Hockey League replaced the National Hockey Association in 1917. Boston, in 1924, was the first American city to join that circuit. The league expanded to include western cities in 1967. The Stanley Cup was competed for by "mixed teams" from 1894 to 1910, thereafter by professionals. It was awarded to the winner of the N.H.L. playoffs from 1926–67 and now to the league champion. The World Hockey Association was organized in October 1972 and was dissolved after the 1978–79 season when the N.H.L. absorbed four of the teams.

STANLEY CUP WINNERS

Emblematic of World Professional Championship; N.H.L. Championship after 1967

1894	Montreal A.A.A.	1924	Montreal Canadiens	1953	Montreal Canadiens
1895	Montreal Victorias	1925	Victoria Cougars	1954–55	Detroit Red Wings
1896	Winnipeg Victorias	1926	Montreal Maroons	1956–60	Montreal Canadiens
1897–99	Montreal Victorias	1927	Ottawa Senators	1961	Chicago Black Hawks
1900	Montreal Shamrocks	1928	N.Y. Rangers	1962–64	Toronto Maple Leafs
1901	Winnipeg Victorias	1929	Boston Bruins	1965–66	Montreal Canadiens
1902	Montreal A.A.A.	1930–31	Montreal Canadiens	1967	Toronto Maple Leafs
1903–05	Ottawa Silver Seven	1932	Toronto Maple Leafs	1968–69	Montreal Canadiens
1906	Montreal Wanderers	1933	N.Y. Rangers	1970	Boston Bruins
1907	Kenora Thistles[1]	1934	Chicago Black Hawks	1971	Montreal Canadiens
1907	Mont. Wanderers[2]	1935	Montreal Maroons	1972	Boston Bruins
1908	Montreal Wanderers	1936–37	Detroit Red Wings	1973	Montreal Canadiens
1909	Ottawa Senators	1938	Chicago Black Hawks	1974–75	Philadelphia Flyers
1910	Montreal Wanderers	1939	Boston Bruins	1976–79	Montreal Canadiens
1911	Ottawa Senators	1940	N.Y. Rangers	1980–83	New York Islanders
1912–13	Quebec Bulldogs	1941	Boston Bruins	1984	Edmonton Oilers
1914	Toronto	1942	Toronto Maple Leafs	1985	Edmonton Oilers
1915	Vancouver Millionaires	1943	Detroit Red Wings	1986	Montreal Canadiens
1916	Montreal Canadiens	1944	Montreal Canadiens	1987	Edmonton Oilers
1917	Seattle Metropolitans	1945	Toronto Maple Leafs	1988	Edmonton Oilers
1918	Toronto Arenas	1946	Montreal Canadiens	1989	Calgary Flames
1919	No champion	1947–49	Toronto Maple Leafs	1990	Edmonton Oilers
1920–21	Ottawa Senators	1950	Detroit Red Wings	1. January. 2. March.	
1922	Toronto St. Patricks	1951	Toronto Maple Leafs		
1923	Ottawa Senators	1952	Detroit Red Wings		

NATIONAL HOCKEY LEAGUE YEARLY TROPHY WINNERS

The Hart Trophy—Most Valuable Player

1924	Frank Nighbor, Ottawa	1941	Bill Cowley, Boston	1957–58	Gordon Howe, Detroit
1925	Billy Burch, Hamilton	1942	Tom Anderson, New York Americans	1959	Andy Bathgate, New York Rangers
1926	Nels Stewart, Montreal Maroons			1960	Gordon Howe, Detroit
1927	Herb Gardiner, Montreal Canadiens	1943	Bill Cowley, Boston	1961	Bernie Geoffrion, Montreal Canadiens
		1944	Babe Pratt, Toronto		
1928	Howie Morenz, Montreal Canadiens	1945	Elmer Lach, Montreal Canadiens	1962	Jacques Plante, Montreal Canadiens
		1946	Max Bentley, Chicago		
1929	Roy Worters, New York Americans	1947	Maurice Richard, Montreal Canadiens	1963	Gordon Howe, Detroit
1930	Nels Stewart, Montreal Maroons			1964	Jean Beliveau, Montreal Canadiens
1931–32	Howie Morenz, Montreal Canadiens	1948	Buddy O'Connor, New York Rangers	1965–66	Bobby Hull, Chicago
				1967–68	Stan Mikita, Chicago
1933	Eddie Shore, Boston	1949	Sid Abel, Detroit	1969	Phil Esposito, Boston
1934	Aurel Joliat, Montreal Canadiens	1950	Chuck Rayner, New York Rangers	1970–72	Bobby Orr, Boston
1935–36	Eddie Shore, Boston	1951	Milt Schmidt, Boston	1973	Bobby Clarke, Philadelphia
1937	Babe Siebert, Montreal Canadiens	1952–53	Gordon Howe, Detroit	1974	Phil Esposito, Boston
1938	Eddie Shore, Boston	1954	Al Rollins, Chicago	1975–76	Bobby Clarke, Philadelphia
1939	Toe Blake, Montreal Canadiens	1955	Ted Kennedy, Toronto	1977–78	Guy Lafleur, Montreal
1940	Ebbie Goodfellow, Detroit	1956	Jean Belveau, Montreal Canadiens	1979	Bryan Trottier, N.Y. Islanders

1980	Wayne Gretzky, Edmonton
1981	Wayne Gretzky, Edmonton
1982	Wayne Gretzky, Edmonton
1983	Wayne Gretzky, Edmonton
1984	Wayne Gretzky, Edmonton
1985	Wayne Gretzky, Edmonton
1986	Wayne Gretzky, Edmonton
1987	Wayne Gretzky, Edmonton
1988	Mario Lemieux, Pittsburgh
1989	Wayne Gretzky, Los Angeles
1990	Mark Messier, Edmonton

Vezina Trophy—Leading Goalkeeper

1956–60	Jacques Plante, Montreal
1961	Johnny Bower, Toronto
1962	Jacques Plante, Montreal
1963	Glenn Hall, Chicago
1964	Charlie Hodge, Montreal
1965	Terry Sawchuk—Johnny Bower, Toronto
1966	Lorne Worsley—Charlie Hodge, Montreal
1967	Glenn Hall—Denis DeJordy, Chicago
1968	Lorne Worsley—Rogatien Vachon, Montreal
1969	Glenn Hall—Jacques Plante, St. Louis
1970	Tony Esposito, Chicago
1971	Ed Giacomin—Gilles Villemure, New York
1972	Tony Esposito—Gary Smith, Chicago
1973	Ken Dryden, Montreal
1974	Bernie Parent, Philadelphia, and Tony Esposito, Chicago
1975	Bernie Parent, Philadelphia
1976	Ken Dryden, Montreal
1977–79	Ken Dryden—Michel Larocque, Montreal
1980	Bob Sauve—Don Edwards, Buffalo
1981	Richard Sevigny, Denis Herron and Michel Larocque, Montreal
1982	Billy Smith, New York Islanders
1983	Pete Peeters, Boston
1984	Tom Barrasso, Buffalo
1985	Pelle Lindbergh, Philadelphia
1986	John Vanbiesbrouck, New York Rangers
1987	Ron Hextall, Philadelphia
1988	Grant Fuhr, Edmonton
1989	Patrick Roy, Montreal
1990	Patrick Roy, Montreal

James Norris Trophy—Defenseman

1954	Red Kelly, Detroit
1955–58	Doug Harvey, Montreal
1959	Tom Johnson, Montreal
1960–62	Doug Harvey, Montreal, New York (62)
1963–65	Pierre Pilote, Chicago
1966	Jacques Laperriere, Montreal
1967	Harry Howell, New York
1968–75	Bobby Orr, Boston
1976	Denis Potvin, N.Y. Islanders
1977	Larry Robinson, Montreal
1978–79	Denis Potvin, N.Y. Islanders
1980	Larry Robinson, Montreal
1981	Randy Carlyle, Pittsburgh
1982	Doug Wilson, Chicago
1983–84	Rod Langway, Washington
1985	Paul Coffey, Edmonton
1986	Paul Coffey, Edmonton
1987	Ray Bourque, Boston
1988	Ray Bourque, Boston
1989	Chris Chelios, Montreal
1990	Ray Bourque, Boston

Lady Byng Trophy—Sportsmanship

1960	Don McKenney, Boston
1961	Red Kelly, Detroit
1962–63	Dave Keon, Toronto
1964	Ken Wharram, Chicago
1965	Bobby Hull, Chicago
1966	Alex Delvecchio, Detroit
1967–68	Stan Mikita, Chicago
1969	Alex Delvecchio, Detroit
1970	Phil Goyette, St. Louis
1971	John Bucyk, Boston
1972	Jean Ratelle, New York
1973	Gil Perreault, Buffalo
1974	John Bucyk, Boston
1975	Marcel Dionne, Detroit
1976	Jean Ratelle, N.Y. Rangers–Boston
1977	Marcel Dionne, Los Angeles
1978	Butch Goring, Los Angeles
1979	Bob MacMillan, Atlanta
1980	Wayne Gretzky, Edmonton
1981	Rick Kehoe, Pittsburgh
1982	Rick Middleton, Boston
1983–84	Mike Bossy, N.Y. Islanders
1985	Jari Kurri, Edmonton
1986	Mike Bossy, N.Y. Islanders
1987	Joe Mullen, Calgary
1988	Mats Naslund, Montreal
1989	Joe Mullen, Calgary
1990	Brett Hull, St. Louis

Calder Trophy—Rookie

1962	Bobby Rousseau, Montreal
1963	Kent Douglas, Toronto
1964	Jacques Laperriere, Montreal
1965	Roger Crozier, Detroit
1966	Brit Selby, Toronto
1967	Bobby Orr, Boston
1968	Derek Sanderson, Boston
1969	Danny Grant, Minnesota
1970	Tony Esposito, Chicago
1971	Gilbert Perreault, Buffalo
1972	Ken Dryden, Montreal
1973	Steve Vickers, New York Rangers
1974	Denis Potvin, N.Y. Islanders
1975	Eric Vail, Atlanta
1976	Bryan Trottier, N.Y. Islanders
1977	Willi Plett, Atlanta
1978	Mike Bossy, N.Y. Islanders
1979	Bobby Smith, Minnesota
1980	Ray Bourque, Boston
1981	Peter Stastny, Quebec
1982	Dale Hawerchuk, Winnipeg
1983	Steve Larmer, Chicago
1984	Tom Barrasso, Buffalo
1985	Mario Lemieux, Pittsburgh
1986	Gary Suter, Calgary
1987	Luc Robitaille, Los Angeles
1988	Joe Nieuwendyk, Calgary
1989	Brian Leetch, N.Y. Rangers
1990	Sergei Makarov, Calgary

Art Ross Trophy—Leading scorer

1955	Bernie Geoffrion, Montreal
1956	Jean Beliveau, Montreal
1957	Gordie Howe, Detroit
1958–59	Dickie Moore, Montreal
1960	Bobby Hull, Chicago
1961	Bernie Geoffrion, Montreal
1962	Bobby Hull, Chicago
1963	Gordie Howe, Detroit
1964–65	Stan Mikita, Chicago
1966	Bobby Hull, Chicago
1967–68	Stan Mikita, Chicago
1969	Phil Esposito, Boston
1970	Bobby Orr, Boston
1971–74	Phil Esposito, Boston
1975	Bobby Orr, Boston
1976–78	Guy Lafleur, Montreal
1979	Bryan Trottier, N.Y. Islanders
1980	Marcel Dionne, Los Angeles
1981–87	Wayne Gretzky, Edmonton
1988	Mario Lemieux, Pittsburgh
1989	Mario Lemieux, Pittsburgh
1990	Wayne Gretzky, Los Angeles

N.H.L. CHAMPIONS

Prince of Wales Trophy

1939	Boston
1940	Boston
1941	Boston
1942	New York
1943	Detroit
1944–47	Montreal
1948	Toronto
1948–55	Detroit
1956	Montreal
1957	Detroit
1958–62	Montreal
1963	Toronto
1964	Montreal
1965	Detroit
1966	Montreal
1967	Chicago

Eastern Division

1968–69	Montreal
1970	Chicago
1971	Boston
1972	Boston
1973	Montreal
1974	Boston

Prince of Wales Conference

1975	Buffalo
1976–79	Montreal
1980	Buffalo
1981	Montreal
1982	New York Islanders
1983	New York Islanders
1984	New York Islanders
1985	Philadelphia
1986	Montreal
1987	Philadelphia
1988	Boston
1989	Montreal
1990	Boston

CAMPBELL BOWL

Western Division

1968	Philadelphia
1969	St. Louis
1970	St. Louis
1971–73	Chicago
1974	Philadelphia

Clarence Campbell Conference

1975	Philadelphia
1976–77	Philadelphia
1978–79	N.Y. Islanders
1980	Philadelphia
1981	New York Islanders
1982	Edmonton
1983	Edmonton
1984	Edmonton
1985	Edmonton
1986	Calgary
1987	Edmonton
1988	Edmonton Oilers
1989	Calgary
1990	Edmonton

NATIONAL HOCKEY LEAGUE
Final Standing of the Clubs—1989–90

PRINCE OF WALES CONFERENCE
Patrick Division

	W	L	T	GF	GA	Pts
New York Rangers	36	31	13	279	267	85
New Jersey Devils	37	34	9	295	288	83
Washington Capitals	36	38	6	284	275	78
New York Islanders	31	38	11	281	288	73
Pittsburgh Penguins	32	40	8	318	359	72
Philadelphia Flyers	30	39	11	290	297	71

Adams Division

	W	L	T	GF	GA	Pts
Boston Bruins	46	25	9	289	232	101
Buffalo Sabres	45	27	8	286	248	98
Montreal Canadiens	41	28	11	288	234	93
Hartford Whalers	38	33	9	275	268	85
Quebec Nordiques	12	61	7	240	407	31

CLARENCE CAMPBELL CONFERENCE
Norris Division

	W	L	T	GF	GA	Pts
Chicago Black Hawks	41	33	6	316	294	88
St. Louis Blues	37	34	9	295	279	83
Toronto Maple Leafs	38	38	4	337	358	80
Minnesota North Stars	36	40	4	284	291	76
Detroit Red Wings	28	38	14	288	323	70

Smythe Division

	W	L	T	GF	GA	Pts
Calgary Flames	42	23	15	348	265	99
Edmonton Oilers	38	28	14	315	283	90
Winnipeg Jets	37	32	11	298	290	85
Los Angeles Kings	34	39	7	338	337	75
Vancouver Canucks	25	41	14	245	306	64

Stanley Cup Playoffs—1990

Division Semifinals
Patrick Division
Washington Capitals defeated New Jersey Devils, 4 games to 2
New York Rangers defeated New York Islanders, 4 games to 1

Adams Division
Montreal Canadiens defeated Buffalo Sabres, 4 games to 2
Boston Bruins defeated Hartford Whalers, 4 games to 3

Norris Division
Chicago Black Hawks defeated Minnesota North Stars, 4 games to 3
St. Louis Blues defeated Toronto Maple Leafs, 4 games to 1

Smythe Division
Los Angeles Kings defeated Calgary Flames, 4 games to 2
Edmonton Oilers defeated Winnipeg Jets, 4 games to 3

Division Finals
Patrick Division
Washington Capitals defeated New York Rangers, 4 games to 1

Adams Division
Boston Bruins defeated Montreal Canadiens, 4 games to 1

Norris Division
Chicago Black Hawks defeated St. Louis Blues, 4 games to 3

Smythe Division
Edmonton Oilers defeated Los Angeles Kings, 4 games to 0

CONFERENCE FINALS (League semifinals)
Prince of Wales Conference
Boston Bruins defeated Washington Capitals, 4 games to 0
(Home team in caps)
May 3—BOSTON 5, Washington 3
May 5—BOSTON 3, Washington 0
May 7—Boston 4, WASHINGTON 1
May 9—Boston 3, WASHINGTON 2

Clarence Campbell Conference
Edmonton Oilers defeated Chicago Black Hawks, 4 games to 2
(Home team in caps)
May 2—EDMONTON 5, Chicago 2
May 4—Chicago 4, EDMONTON 3
May 6—CHICAGO 5, Edmonton 1
May 8—Edmonton 4, CHICAGO 2
May 10—EDMONTON 4, Chicago 3
May 12—Edmonton 8, CHICAGO 4

Stanley Cup Championship Finals
Edmonton Oilers defeated Boston Bruins, 4 games to 1
(Home team in caps)
May 15—Edmonton 3, BOSTON 2 (3 OT)
May 18—Edmonton 7, BOSTON 2

May 20—Boston 2, EDMONTON 1
May 22—EDMONTON 5, Boston 1
May 24—Edmonton 4, Boston 1

N.H.L. LEADING GOALTENDERS—1989–90
(Minimum 1,300 minutes played)

	Min	GA	ShO	Avg
Patrick Roy, Montreal	3173	134	3	2.53
Mike Liut, Hart.-Wash.	2161	91	4	2.53
ReJean Lemelin, Boston	2310	108	2	2.81
Daren Puppa, Buffalo	3241	156	1	2.89
Andy Moog, Boston	2536	122	3	2.89
Mike Richter, Rangers	1320	66	0	3.00
Jacques Cloutier, Chicago	2178	112	2	3.09
Mike Vernon, Calgary	2795	146	0	3.13
Bob Essensa, Winnipeg	2035	107	1	3.15
Bill Ranford, Edmonton	3107	165	1	3.19
Jon Casey, Minnesota	3407	183	3	3.22
Don Beaupre, Washington	2793	150	2	3.22
Rick Wamsley, Calgary	1969	107	2	3.26
Clint Malarchuk, Buffalo	1596	89	0	3.35
John Vanbiesbrouck, NYR	2734	154	1	3.38
Mark Fitzpatrick, NYI	2653	150	3	3.39
Ken Wregget, Philadelphia	2961	169	0	3.42
Chris Terreri, New Jersey	1931	110	0	3.42
Kirk McLean, Vancouver	3739	216	0	3.47

Other NHL Awards—1990

Selke (Top defensive forward)—Rick Meagher, St. Louis Adams (Top coach)—Bob Murdoch, Winnipeg Masterson (Dedication to hockey)—Gord Kluzak, Boston King Clancy (humanitarian contributions)—Kevin Lowe, Edmonton Conn Smythe (Most valuable in playoffs)—Mark Messieri Edmonton

N.H.L. LEADING SCORERS—1989–90

	GP	G	A	Pts
Wayne Gretzky, Los Angeles	73	40	102	142
Mark Messier, Edmonton	79	45	84	129
Steve Yzerman, Detroit	79	62	65	127
Mario Lemieux, Pittsburgh	59	45	78	123
Brett Hull, St. Louis	80	72	41	113
Bernie Nicholls, L.A.-Rangers	79	39	73	112
Pierre Turgeon, Buffalo	80	40	66	106
Pat LaFontaine, Islanders	74	54	51	105
Paul Coffey, Pittsburgh	80	29	74	103
Joe Sakic, Quebec	80	39	63	102

Adam Oates, St. Louis	80	23	79	102	Marcel Dionne (2)	18	1,348	731	1040	1771
Luc Robitaille, Los Angeles	80	52	49	101	Phil Esposito (3)	18	1,282	717	873	1590
Ron Francis, Hartford	80	32	69	101	Stan Mikita (9)	22	1,394	541	926	1467
Brian Bellows, Minnesota	80	55	44	99	John Bucyk (7)	23	1,540	556	813	1369
Rick Tocchet, Philadelphia	75	37	59	96	Bryan Trottier[1]	15	1,123	500	853	1353
Gary Leeman, Toronto	80	51	44	95	Gilbert Perreault	17	1,191	512	814	1326
Joe Nieuwendyk, Calgary	79	45	50	95	Guy Lafleur (8)[1]	16	1,067	548	777	1325
Vincent Damphousse, Toronto	80	33	61	94	Alex Delvecchio	24	1,549	456	825	1,281
Jari Kurri, Edmonton	78	33	60	93	Jean Ratelle	21	1,281	491	776	1,267
Sam Neely, Boston	76	55	37	92	Norm Ullman	20	1,410	490	739	1,229
John Cullen, Pittsburgh	72	32	60	92	Jean Beliveau	20	1,125	507	712	1,219
Stephans Richer, Montreal	75	51	40	91	Bobby Clarke	15	1,144	358	852	1,210
Doug Gilmour, Calgary	78	24	67	91	Bobby Hull (5)	16	1,063	610	560	1,170
Steve Larmer, Chicago	80	31	59	90	Bernie Federko[1]	14	1,000	369	761	1,130
Al MacInnis, Calgary	79	28	62	90	Mike Bossy (6)	10	752	573	553	1,126
					Darryl Sittler	15	1,096	484	637	1,121
					Frank Mahovlich (10)	18	1,181	533	570	1,103
					Denis Potvin	15	1,060	310	742	1,052

N.H.L. CAREER SCORING LEADERS

(Listed in order of total points scored; figures in parentheses indicate Top 10 in goals scored.)

1. Still active in the N.H.L.

	Yrs	Games	G	A	Pts
Wayne Gretzky (4)[1]	11	847	677	1302	1979
Gordie Howe (1)	26	1,767	801	1049	1850

BOWLING

AMERICAN BOWLING CONGRESS CHAMPIONS

Year	Singles	All-events	Year	Singles	All-events
1959	Ed Lubanski	Ed Lubanski	1976	Mike Putzer	Jim Lindquist
1960	Paul Kulbaga	Vince Lucci	1977	Frank Gadaleto	Bud Debenham
1961	Lyle Spooner	Luke Karen	1978	Rich Mersek	Chris Cobus
1962	Andy Renaldo	Billy Young	1979	Rick Peters	Bob Basacchi
1963	Fred Delello	Bus Owalt	1980	Mike Eaton	Steve Fehr
1964	Jim Stefanich	Les Zikes, Jr.	1981	Rob Vital	Rod Toft
1965	Ken Roeth	Tom Hathaway	1982	Bruce Bohm	Rich Wonders
1966	Don Chapman	John Wilcox	1983	Rick Kendrick	Tony Cariello
1967	Frank Perry	Gary Lewis	1984	Bob Antczak and	Bob Goike
1968	Wayne Kowalski	Vince Mazzanti		Neal Young (tie)	
1969	Greg Campbell	Eddie Jackson	1985	Glen Harbison	Barry Asher
1970	Jake Yoder	Mike Berlin	1986	Jess Mackey	Ed Marazka
1971	Al Cohn	Al Cohn	1987	Terry Taylor	Ryan Schafer
1972	Bill Pointer	Mac Lowry	1988	Steve Hutkowski	Rick Steelsmith
1973	Ed Thompson	Ron Woolet	1989	Paul Tetreault	George Hall
1974	Gene Krause	Bob Hart	1990	Bob Hochrein	Mike Neumann
1975	Jim Setser	Bobby Meadows			

PROFESSIONAL BOWLERS ASSOCIATION

National Championship Tournament

1960	Don Carter	1969	Mike McGrath	1977	Tommy Hudson	1985	Mike Aulby
1961	Dave Soutar	1970	Mike McGrath	1978	Warren Nelson	1986	Tom Crites
1962	Carmen Salvino	1971	Mike Lemongello	1979	Mike Aulby	1987	Randy Pedersen
1963	Billy Hardwick	1972	Johnny Guenther	1980	Johnny Petraglia	1988	Brian Voss
1964	Bob Strampe	1973	Earl Anthony	1981	Earl Anthony	1989	Pete Weber
1965	Dave Davis	1974	Earl Anthony	1982	Earl Anthony	1990	Jim Pencak
1966	Wayne Zahn	1975	Earl Anthony	1983	Earl Anthony		
1967	Dave Davis	1976	Paul Colwell	1984	Bob Chamberlain		
1968	Wayne Zahn						

BOWLING PROPRIETORS' ASSOCIATION OF AMERICA—MEN

United States Open[1]

1971	Mike Lemongello	1976	Paul Moser	1981	Marshall Holman	1986	Steve Cook
1972	Don Johnson	1977	Johnny Petraglia	1982	Dave Husted	1987	Del Ballard
1973	Mike McGrath	1978	Nelson Burton, Jr.	1983	Gary Dickinson	1988	Pete Weber
1974	Larry Laub	1979	Joe Berardi	1984	Mark Roth	1989	Mike Aulby
1975	Steve Neff	1980	Steve Martin	1985	Marshall Holman	1990	Ron Palumbi, Jr.

1. Replaced All-Star tournament and is rolled as part of B.P.A. tour.

WOMEN'S INTERNATIONAL BOWLING CONGRESS CHAMPIONS

Year	Singles	All-events	Year	Singles	All-events
1959	Mae Bolt	Pat McBride	1976	Bev Shonk	Betty Morris
1960	Marge McDaniels	Judy Roberts	1977	Akiko Yamaga	Akiko Yamaga
1961	Elaine Newton	Evelyn Teal	1978	Mae Bolt	Annese Kelly
1962	Martha Hoffman	Flossie Argent	1979	Betty Morris	Betty Morris
1963	Dot Wilkinson	Helen Shablis	1980	Betty Morris	Cheryl Robinson
1964	Jean Havlish	Jean Havlish	1981	Virginia Norton	Virginia Norton
1965	Doris Rudell	Donna Zimmerman	1982	Gracie Freeman	Aleta Rzepecki
1966	Gloria Bouvia	Kate Helbig	1983	Aleta Rzepecki	Virginia Norton
1967	Gloria Paeth	Carol Miller	1984	Freida Gates	Shinobu Saitoh
1968	Norma Parks	Susie Reichley	1985	Polly Schwarzel	Aleta Sill
1969	Joan Bender	Helen Duval	1986	Dana Stewart	Robin Romeo
1970	Dorothy Fothergill	Dorothy Fothergill			Maria Lewis (tie)
1971	Mary Scruggs	Lorrie Nichols	1987	Regi Junak	Leanne Barrette
1972	D. D. Jacobson	Mildred Martorella	1988	Michelle Meyer-Welty	Lisa Wagner
1973	Bobby Buffaloe	Toni Calvery	1989	Lorraine Anderson	Nancy Fehn
1974	Shirley Garms	Judy C. Soutar	1990	Dana Miller-Mackie and	Carol Norman
1975	Barbara Leicht	Virginia Norton		Paula Carter	

WIBC QUEENS TOURNAMENT CHAMPIONS

1961	Janet Harman	1969	Ann Feigel	1977	Dana Stewart	1985	Aleta Sill
1962	Dorothy Wilkinson	1970	Mildred Martorella	1978	Loa Boxberger	1986	Cora Fiebig
1963	Irene Monterosso	1971	Mildred Martorella	1979	Donna Adamek	1987	Cathy Almeida
1964	D.D. Jacobson·	1972	Dorothy Fothergill	1980	Donna Adamek	1988	Wendy McPherson
1965	Betty Kuczynski	1973	Dorothy Fothergill	1981	Katsuko Sugimoto	1989	Carol Gianotti
1966	Judy Lee	1974	Judy Soutar	1982	Katsuko Sugimoto	1990	Patty Ann
1967	Mildred Martorella	1975	Cindy Powell	1983	Aleta Rzepecki		
1968	Phyllis Massey	1976	Pamela Buckner	1984	Kazue Inahashi		

BOWLING PROPRIETORS' ASSOCIATION OF AMERICA—WOMEN

United States Open

1971	Paula Carter	1976	Patty Costello (Pa.)	1981	Donna Adamek	1986	Wendy MacPherson
1972	Lorrie Nichols	1977	Betty Morris	1982	Shinobu Saitoh	1987	Carol Nurman
1973	Mildred Martorella	1978	Donna Adamek	1983	Dana Miller	1988	Lisa Wagner
1974	Pat Costello (Calif.)	1979	Diana Silva	1984	Karen Ellingsworth	1989	Robin Romeo
1975	Paula Carter	1980	Pat Costello (Calif.)	1985	Pat Mercatanti	1990	Dana Miller-Mackie

WOMEN'S INTERNATIONAL BOWLING CONGRESS TOURNAMENT—1990

(Tampa, Fla., April 5-July 4, 1990)

Open Division

Singles—Dana Miller-Mackie, Sydney, Australia, and Paula Carter, Miami 705
Doubles—Margi Melvin, New Castle, Del., and Ann Meconnahey, Bear, Del. 1,323
All Events—Carol Norman, Ardmore, Okla. 1,984
Team—R.A.T.'s Team, Lakeland, Fla. 2,985

Division I

Singles—Nancy Jones, Oklahoma City, Okla. 68.2
Doubles—Joann Anastasio and Cathie Cross, Augusta, Maine 1,204
All-Events—Bonnie Piszczek, Wauwatusa, Wis. 1,791
Team—Tie—Lucky Strikes, Savannah, Ga., and Just Them, Hampton, Va. 2,697

Division II

Singles—Denise Brockman, Cincinnati 642
Doubles—Anna Adams and Theresa Hruskocy, Whiting, Ind. 1,164
All-Events—Pamela Schmal, Winston-Salem, N.C. 1,667
Team—Bristol Five, Bristol, Va. 2,492.

AMERICAN BOWLING CONGRESS TOURNAMENT—1990

(Reno, Nev., Feb. 3-June 6, 1990)

Regular Division

Singles—Bob Hochrein, Dubuque, Iowa 791
Doubles—Mike Neumann and Bob Ujvari, Buffalo, N.Y. 1,448
All-Events—Mike Neumann, Buffalo, N.Y. 2,168
Team—Tie—Brunswick Rhinos, No. 1, Buffalo, N.Y., and State Farm-Lou Magic Agency, Detroit 3,201

Booster Division

Pro World Pro Shop, Milwaukee 2,934

PROFESSIONAL BOWLERS ASSOCIATION CHMAPIONSHIP—1990

Winner—Jim Pencak, Mayfield Heights, Ohio, defeated Chris Warren, Dallas, 223-214
Third place—Tom Crites, Tampa, Fla.
Fourth place—Doug Kent, Canandaigua, N.Y.
Fifth place—Amleto Moncelli, Venezuela

WIBC QUEENS TOURNAMENT—1990

(Tampa, Fla., May 13-17, 1990)

Winner—Patti Ann, Appleton, Wis., defeated Vesma Grinfelds, San Francisco, 267-169 in final.

Third place—Pat Costello, Lantana, Fla.
Fourth place—Chele Rutherford, Edgewood, Md.
Fifth place—Susan George, West Islip, N.Y.

SKIING

ALPINE WORLD CUP OVERALL WINNERS

Year	Men	Women	Team
1967	Jean-Claude Killy, France	Nancy Greene, Canada	France
1968	Jean-Claude Killy, France	Nancy Greene, Canada	France
1969	Karl Schranz, Austria	Gertrude Gabl, Austria	Austria
1970	Karl Schranz, Austria	Michel Jacot, France	France
1971	Gustavo Thoeni, Italy	Annemarie Proell, Austria	France
1972	Gustavo Thoeni, Italy	Annemarie Proell, Austria	France
1973	Gustavo Thoeni, Italy	Annemarie Proell Moser, Austria	Austria
1974	Piero Gros, Italy	Annemarie Proell Moser, Austria	Austria
1975	Gustavo Thoeni, Italy	Annemarie Proell Moser, Austria	Austria
1976	Ingemar Stenmark, Sweden	Rosi Mittermaier, West Germany	Austria
1977	Ingemar Stenmark, Sweden	Lise-Marie Morerod, Switzerland	Austria
1978	Ingemar Stenmark, Sweden	Hanni Wenzel, Liechtenstein	Austria
1979	Peter Luescher, Switzerland	Annemarie Proell Moser, Austria	Austria
1980	Andreas Wenzel, Liechtenstein	Hanni Wenzel, Liechtenstein	Liechtenstein
1981	Phil Mahre, United States	Marie-Theres Nadig, Switzerland	Switzerland
1982	Phil Mahre, United States	Erika Hess, Switzerland	Austria
1983	Phil Mahre, United States	Tamara McKinney, United States	
1984	Pirmin Zurbriggen, Switzerland	Erika Hess, Switzerland	
1985	Marc Girardelli, Luxembourg	Michela Figini, Switzerland	
1986	Marc Girardelli, Luxembourg	Maria Walliser, Switzerland	Switzerland
1987	Pirmin Zubriggen, Switzerland	Maria Walliser, Switzerland	Switzerland
1988	Pirmin Zubriggen, Switzerland	Michela Figini, Switzerland	Switzerland
1989	Marc Giradelli, Luxembourg	Vreni Schneider, Switzerland	Switzerland
1990	Pirmin Zubriggen, Switzerland	Petra Kronberger, Austria	Austria

ALPINE WORLD CUP—1990

Overall—Men

1. Pirmin Zubriggen, Switzerland — 357
2. Ole Kristian Furuseth, Norway — 234
3. Guenther Mader, Austria — 213
4. Armin Bittner, West Germany — 193
5. Helmut Hoeflehner, Austria — 174

Overall—Women

1. Petra Kronberger, Austria — 341
2. Anita Wachter, Austria — 300
3. Michaela Gerg, West Germany — 270
4. Maria Walliser, Switzerland — 227
5. Carole Merle, France — 198

Event Leaders—Men

Downhill—Helmut Hoeflehner, Austria — 166
  2. Atle Skaardal, Norway — 120
  3. Pirmin Zubriggen, Switzerland — 105
Best American finish—A.J. Kitt — 22
Slalom—Armin Bittner, West Germany — 150
  2. Ole Kristian Furuseth, Norway — 95
  3. Alberto Tomba, Italy — 95
Best American finish—Tiger Shaw — 18
Giant Slalom—Ole Kristian Furuseth, Norway — 96
  2. Guenther Mader, Austria — 96
  3. Hubert Strolz, Austria — 71
Best American finish—none
Super Giant Slalom—Pirmin Zubriggen, Switzerland — 98
  2. Guenther Mader, Austria — 71
  3. Lars-Boerje Eriksson, Sweden — 61
Best American finish—none

Event Leaders—Women

Downhill—Katrin Gutensohn-Knopf, West Germany — 110
  2. Petra Kronberger, Austria — 106
  3. Michaela Gerg, West Germany — 105
Best American finish—Hilary Lindh — 18
Slalom—Vreni Schneider, Switzerland — 125
  2. Claudia Strobl, Austria — 108
  3. Ida Ladstaetter, Austria — 98
Best American finish—Kristi Terzian — 32
Giant Slalom—Anita Wachter, Austria — 133
  2. Mateja Svet, Yugoslavia — 89
  3. Petra Kronberger, Austria — 85
Best American finish—Diann Roffe — 82
Super Giant Slalom—Carole Merle, France — 99
  2. Michaela Gerg, West Germany — 79
  3. Sigrid Wolf, Austria — 73
Best American finish—Diann Roffe — 29

UNITED STATES CHAMPIONSHIPS—1990

ALPINE
Men's Events

Downhill—Skip Merrick — 1:28.93
Slalom—Felix McGrath — 1:36.52
Giant Slalom—Tommy Moe — 2:28.10
Super Giant Slalom—A.J. Kitt — 1:29.83
Combined—Kyle Wieche — 60.56 points

Women's Events

Downhill—Lucie La Roche — 1:23.19
Slalom—Monique Pelletier — 1:27.89
Giant Slalom—Kristi Terzian — 2:35.99
Super Giant Slalom—Krista Schmidinger — 1:36.80
Combined—Julie Parisien — 59.95 points

NORDIC
Men's Cross Country

15 kilometers—Avdun Endestad	:45:33.9
30 kilometers—Avdun Endestad	1:28:12.5
50 kilometers—Avdun Endestad	2:34:28.7
4 × 5 kilometer relay—New England (Joe Galanes, Todd Boonstra, Brendan Sullivan, and John Golbe)	56:06.4

Women's Cross Country

10 kilometers—Nancy Fiddler	35:41.3
15 kilometers—Nancy Fiddler	:49:45.2
30 kilometers—Wendy Reeves	1:41:42.3
4×3 kilometer relay—New England (Wendy Reeves, Stacey Wooley, Laura Wilson, and Brenda White)	:37:49.6

NCAA RESULTS—1990

Men

Slalom—Chris Pedersen, Colorado	1:17.26
Giant Slalom—Einar Boehmer, Vermont	1:52.24
10K cross country—Luke Bodensteine, Utah	29:31.20
20K cross country—Tim Miller, Vermont	56:00.30

Women

Slalom—Anke Friedrich, Utah	1:25.04
Giant Slalom—Anke Friedrich, Utah	1:54.36
5K cross country—Laura Wilson, Vermont	:16:34.00
15K cross country—Laura Wilson, Vermont	:52:16.00

Team (men & women)
1. Vermont
2. Utah
3. Colorado
4. Wyoming
5. Dartmouth

WORLD CUP SKI JUMPING—1990

1. Ari Pekka Nikkola, Finland	287
2. Ernst Vettori, Austria	239
3. Andreas Felder, Austria	236
4. Dieter Thoma, West Germany	206
5. Frantisek Jez, Czechoslovakia	202

Ski Jumping
Nations Cup Standings

1. Austria	912
2. Czechoslovakia	506
3. Finland	502
4. West Germany	344
5. East Germany	233

WORLD CUP NORDIC COMBINED—1990

Final Standings

1. Klaus Sulzenbacher, Austria	164
2. Allar Levandi, Soviet Union	135
3. Knut Tore Apeland, Norway	99
4. Fred Borre Lundberg, Norway	94
5. Thomas Abratis, East Germany	84

Nordic Combined
Nations Cup Standings

1. Norway	521
2. Austria	405
3. Soviet Union	394
4. East Germany	275
5. France	176

WORLD CUP CROSS COUNTRY—1990

Final Women's Standings

1. Larissa Lazutina, Soviet Union	146
2. Elena Vialbe, Soviet Union	137
3. Trude Dybendahl, Norway	136
4. Svetlana Nagejkina, Soviet Union	134
5. Manuela DiCenta, Italy	126

Women's Cross-Country
Nations Cup Standings

1. Soviet Union	1167
2. Norway	759
3. Finland	441
4. Italy	412
5. Sweden	334

Women's Relays
1. Soviet Union	470
2. Norway	410
3. Finland	310
4. Sweden	270
5. East Germany	190

Final Men's Standings

1. Vegard Ulvang, Norway	145
2. Gunde Svan, Sweden	144
3. Bjoern Daehlie, Norway	118
4. Jochen Behle, West Germany	88
5. Christer Majbaeck, Sweden	86

Men's Cross-Country
Nations Cup Standings

1. Sweden	835
2. Norway	735
3. Soviet Union	470
4. Italy	363
5. Finland	234

Men's Relays
1. Sweden	370
2. Norway	330
3. Soviet Union	280
4. Italy	250
5. Finland	150

HISTORY OF SKIING IN THE UNITED STATES

Skis were devised for utility, to aid those who had to travel over snow. The Norwegians, Swedes, Lapps, and other inhabitants of northern lands used skis for many centuries before skiing became a sport. Emigrants from these countries brought skis to the United States with them. The first skier of record in the United States was a mailman by the name of "Snowshoe" Thompson, born and raised in Telemarken, Norway, who came to the United States and, beginning in 1850, used skis through 20 successive winters in carrying mail from Northern California to Carson Valley, Idaho.

Ski clubs sprang up over 100 years ago where there were Norwegian and Swedish settlers in Wisconsin and Minnesota and ski contests were held in that territory in 1886. On Feb. 21, 1904, at Ishpeming, Mich., a small group of skiers organized the National Ski Association. In 1961 it was renamed the United States Ski Association.

FISHING

SELECTED WORLD ALL-TACKLE FISHING RECORDS
Source: International Game Fish Association.

Caught with Rod and Reel in Fresh Water (as of July 12, 1990)

Species	lb-oz	Where caught	Year	Angler
Bass, Largemouth	22-4	Montgomery Lake, Ga.	1932	George W. Perry
Bass, Peacock	26-8	Mataveni River, Columbia	1982	Rod Neubert
Bass, Redeye	8-3	Flint River, Ga.	1977	David A. Hubbard
Bass, Rock	3-0	York River, Ontario	1974	Peter Gulgin
Bass, Smallmouth	11-15	Dale Hollow Lake, Ky.	1955	David L. Hayes
Bass, Spotted	9-4	Parris Lake, Calif.	1987	Steven West[1] & Gilbert Rowe
Bass, Striped	60-8	Anderson County, Tenn.	1988	Gary Everett Helms
Bass, Striped (landlocked)	66-0	O'Neill Forebay, Los Banos, Calif.	1988	Ted Furnish
Bass, White	6-13	Lake Orange, Orange, Va.	1989	Ronald L. Sprouse
Bass, Whiterock	24-3	Leesville Lake, Va.	1989	David Lambert
Bass, Yellow	2-4	Lake Monroe, Ind.	1977	Donald L. Stalker
Bluegill	4-12	Ketona Lake, Ala.	1950	T.S. Hudson
Bowfin	21-8	Florence, S.C.	1980	Robert L. Harmon
Buffalo, Bigmouth	70-5	Bussey Brake, Bastrop, La.	1980	Delbert Sisk
Buffalo, Smallmouth	68-8	Lake Hamilton, Ark.	1984	Jerry L. Dolezal
Bullhead, Black	8-0	Lake Waccabuc, N.Y.	1951	Kani Evans
Bullhead, Brown	5-8	Veal Pond, Ga.	1975	Jimmy Andrews
Burbot	18-4	Pickford, Mich.	1980	Tom Courtemanche
Carp	57-13	Potomac River, Wash., D.C.	1983	David Nikolow
Catfish, Blue	97-0	Missouri River, S.D.	1959	Edward B. Elliott
Catfish, Channel	58-0	Santee–Cooper Res., S.C.	1964	W.B. Whaley
Catfish, Flathead	98-0	Lewisville, Tex.	1986	William Stevens
Char, Arctic	32-9	Tree River, Canada	1981	Jeffery Ward
Crappie, Black	4-8	Kerr Lake, Va.	1981	L. Carl Herring, Jr.
Crappie, White	5-3	Enid Dam, Mississippi	1957	Fred L. Bright
Dolly Varden	12-0	Noatak River, Alaska	1987	Kenneth Alt
Drum, Freshwater	54-8	Nickajack Lake, Tenn.	1972	Benny E. Hull
Gar, Alligator	279	Rio Grande River, Tex.	1951	Bill Valverde
Gar, Longnose	50-5	Trinity River, Texas	1954	Townsend Miller
Gar, Shortnose	5-0	Vian, Okla.	1985	Buddy Croslin
Inconnu	38-2	Kobuk River, Alaska	1982	Mark L. Feldman
Muskellunge	69-15	St. Lawrence River, N.Y.	1957	Arthur Lawton
Muskellunge, Tiger	51-3	Lac-Vieux-Desert, Wisc.-Mich.	1919	John A. Knobla
Perch, White	4-12	Messalonskee Lake, Maine	1949	Mrs. Earl Small
Perch, Yellow	4-3	Bordentown, N.J.	1865	Dr. C.C. Abbot
Pickerel, Eastern Chain	9-6	Homerville, Ga.	1961	Baxley McQuaig, Jr.
Redhorse, Northern	3-11	Missouri River, S.D.	1977	Phillip Laumeyer
Redhorse, Silver	11-7	Plum Creek, Wisconsin	1985	Neal D.G. Long
Salmon, Atlantic	79-2	Tana River, Norway	1928	Henrik Henriksen
Salmon, Chinook	97-4	Kenai River, Alaska	1985	Les Anderson
Salmon, Chum	27-3	Raymond Cove, Alaska	1977	Robert A. Jahnke
Salmon, Coho	33-4	Pulaski, N.Y.	1989	Jerry Lifton
Salmon, Landlocked	22-8	Sebago Lake, Maine	1907	Edward Blakely
Salmon, Pink	12-9	Moose & Kenai Rivers, Alaska	1974	Steven Alan Lee
Salmon, Sockeye	15-3	Kenai River, Alaska	1987	Stan Roach
Shad, American	11-1	Delaware River, N.J.	1984	Charles J. Mower
Sturgeon	468-0	Benicia, Calif.	1983	Joey Pallotta III
Sturgeon, White	380-0	Snake River, Idaho	1973	Del Canty
Sunfish, Green	2-2	Stockton Lake, Missouri	1971	Paul M. Dilley
Sunfish, Redbreast	1-12	Suwannee River, Fla.	1984	Alvin Buchanan
Sunfish, Redear	4-10	Mill Pond, Fla.	1985	C.L. Windham
Tigerfish	61-11	Lake Tanganyika, Zambia	1984	Don Hunter
Trout, Brook	14-8	Nipigon River, Ontario	1916	Dr. W.J. Cook
Trout, Brown	35-15	Nahuel Huapi, Argentina	1952	Eugenio Cavaglia
Trout, Bull	32-0	Lake Pend Orielle, Idaho	1949	N.L. Higgins
Trout, Cutthroat	41-0	Pyramid Lake, Nev.	1925	John Skimmerhorn
Trout, Golden	11-0	Cook's Lake, Wyoming	1948	Charles S. Reed
Trout, Lake	65-0	Great Bear Lake, N.W.T., Canada	1970	Larry Daunis
Trout, Rainbow	42-2	Bell Island, Alaska	1970	David Robert White
Trout, Tiger	20-13	Lake Michigan, Wisc.	1978	Peter M. Friedland
Walleye	25-0	Old Hickory Lake, Tenn.	1960	Mabry Harper
Whitefish, Lake	14-6	Meaford, Ontario, Canada	1984	Dennis M. Laycock
Whitefish, Mountain	5-0	Athabasca River, Alberta, Canada	1963	Orville Welch
Whitefish, Round	6-0	Putahow River, Manitoba, Canada	1984	Allan J. Ristori

1. West and Rowe caught same size record spotted bass in 1987 in same location, Parris Lake, Calif. 3 months apart—West in Feb. and Rowe in April.

Caught With Rod and Reel in Salt Water (as of July 12, 1990)

Species	lb-oz	Where caught	Year	Angler
Albacore	88-2	Canary Islands	1977	Siegfried Dickemann
Amberjack	155-10	Challenger Bank, Bermuda	1981	Joseph Dawson
Barracuda	83	Lagos, Nigeria	1952	K. J. W. Hackett
Bass, Black Sea	9-8	Virginia Beach, Va.	1987	Joe Mizelle, Jr.
Bass, Giant Sea	563-8	Anacapa Island, Calif.	1968	J. D. McAdam, Jr.
Bass, Striped	78-8	Atlantic City, N.J.	1982	Albert R. McReynolds
Blackfish (Tautog)	21-8	Wachapreague, Virginia	1984	Tommy Wood
Bluefish	31-12	North Carolina	1972	James M. Hussey
Bonefish	19	Zululand, S. Africa	1962	Brian W. Batchelor
Bonito, Atlantic	18-4	Fayal Island, Azores	1984	D. Gama Higgs
Bonito, Pacific	23-8	Victoria, Mahe	1975	Mrs. Anne Cochain
Cobia	135-9	Shark Bay, Australia	1985	Peter Goulding
Cod, Atlantic	98-12	Isle of Shoals, N.H.	1969	Alphonse Bielevich
Cod, Pacific	30-0	Andrew Bay, Alaska	1984	Donald R. Vaughn
Conger	102-8	Plymouth, Devon, England	1983	Raymond Ewart Street
Dolphin	87	Papagallo Gulf, Costa Rica	1976	Manual Salazar
Drum, Black	113-1	Lewes, Del.	1975	G. M. Townsend
Drum, Red	94-2	Avon, North Carolina	1984	David G. Deuel
Flounder, Summer	22-7	Montauk, N.Y.	1975	Charles Nappi
Flounder, Winter	4-3	Perkins Cove, Maine	1989	Lisa Boughner
Haddock	9-15	Perkins Cove, Maine	1988	Jim Donohue
Halibut, Atlantic	255	Gloucester, Mass.	1989	Sonny Manley
Halibut, California	53-4	Santa Rosa Island, Calif.	1988	Russ Harmon
Hailbut, Pacific	350	Homer, Alaska	1982	Vern S. Foster
Jack, Crevalle	54-7	Port Michel, Gabon	1982	Thomas F. Gibson, Jr.
Jack, Horse-eye	24-8	Miami, Fla.	1982	Tito Schnau
Jack, Pacific Crevalle	24-0	Cabo San Lucas, Mexico	1987	Sharon Swanson
Jewfish	680	Fernandina Beach, Fla.	1961	Lynn Joyner
Lingcod	64-0	Elfin Cove, Alaska	1988	David Bauer
Mackerel, King	90	Key West, Florida	1976	Norton I. Thomton
Mackerel, Spanish	13-0	Ocracoke Inlet, N.C.	1987	Robert Cranton
Marlin, Atlantic Blue	1282	St. Thomas, Virgin Islands	1977	Larry Martin
Marlin, Black	1560	Cabo Blanco, Peru	1953	A. C. Glassel, Jr.
Marlin, Pacific Blue	1376	Kaaiwi Point, Kona, Hawaii	1982	Jay Wm. deBeaubien
Marlin, Striped	494	Tutukaka, New Zealand	1986	Bill Boniface
Marlin, White	181-14	Victoria, Brazil	1979	Evandro Luiz Coser
Permit	51-8	Lake Worth, Fla.	1978	William M. Kenney
Pollack	26-7	Salcombe, England	1984	Robert Perry
Pollack (Virens)	46-7	Brielle, N.J.	1975	John T. Holton
Pompano, African	41-8	Fort Lauderdale, Fla.	1979	Wayne Sommers
Sailfish, Atlantic	128-1	Luanda, Angola, Africa	1974	Harm Steyn
Sailfish, Pacific	221	Santa Cruz Is., Galapagos Is.	1947	C. W. Stewart
Seabass, White	83-12	San Felipe, Mexico	1953	L. C. Baumgardner
Shark, Blue	437	Catherine Bay, Australia	1976	Peter Hyde
Shark, Hammerhead	991	Sarasota, Fla.	1982	Allen Ogle
Shark, Mako	1115-0	Black River, Mauritius	1988	Patrick Guillanton
Shark, Porbeagle	465	Padstow, Cornwall, England	1976	Jorge Potier
Shark, Thresher	802	Tutukaka, New Zealand	1981	Dianne North
Shark, Tiger	1780	Cherry Grove, S.C.	1964	Walter Maxwell
Shark, White	2664	South Australia	1959	Alfred Dean
Snapper, Cubera	121-8	Cameron, La.	1982	Mike Hebert
Snook	53-10	Costa Rica	1978	Gilbert Ponzi
Spearfish	90-13	Madeira Island, Portugal	1980	Joseph Larkin
Swordfish	1182	Iquique, Chile	1953	L. E. Marron
Tanguigue	99	Scottburgh, Natal, South Africa	1982	Michael John Wilkinson
Tarpon	283	Lake Maracalbo, Venezuela	1956	M. Salazar
Trevally, Bigeye	15-0	Isla Coiba, Panama	1984	Sally S. Timms
Trevally, Giant	137-9	McKenzie State Park, Hawaii	1983	Roy K. Gushiken
Tuna, Atlantic Bigeye	375-8	Ocean City, Md.	1977	Cecil Browne
Tuna, Blackfin	42	Bermuda	1978	Alan J. Card (tie)
Tuna, Blackfin	42	Challenger Bank, Bermuda	1989	Gilbert C. Pearman (tie)
Tuna, Bluefin	1496	Nova Scotia, Canada	1979	Ken Fraser
Tuna, Dog-tooth	194	Kwan-Tall Island, Korea	1980	Kim Chul
Tuna, Longtail	79-2	Montague Island, Australia	1982	Tim Simpson
Tuna, Pacific Bigeye	435	Cobo Blanco, Peru	1957	R.V. A. Lee
Tuna, Skipjack	41-12	Black River, Mauritius	1982	Bruno de Ravel
Tuna, Southern Bluefin	348-5	Whakatane, New Zealand	1981	Rex Wood
Tuna, Yellowfin	388-12	Mexico	1977	Curt Wiesenmutter
Wahoo	149	Cat Cay, Bahamas	1962	John Pirovano
Weakfish	19-2	Jones Beach Inlet, N.Y.	1984	Dennis Roger Rooney
Yellowtail, California	78-0	Rocas Alijos, Mexico	1987	Richard Cresswell
Yellowtail, Southern	114-10	Tauranga, New Zealand	1984	Mike Godfrey

SPEED SKATING

U.S. OUTDOOR CHAMPIONS (LONG TRACK)

Men

1959–60	Ken Bartholomew	1983	Michael Ralston	1973	Nancy Class
1961	Ed Rudolph	1984	Michael Ralston	1974	Kris Garbe
1962	Floyd Bedbury	1985	Andy Gabel	1975	Nancy Swider
1963	Tom Gray	1986	Eric Klein	1976	Connie Carpenter
1964	Neil Blatchford	1987	Dave Paulicic	1977	Liz Crowe
1965–66	Rich Wurster	1988	Patrick Wentland	1978	Paula Class, Betsy Davis
1967	Mike Passarella	1989	Matt Trimble	1979	Gretchen Byrnes
1968–70	Peter Cefalu	1990	Andy Zak	1980	Shari Miller
1971	Jack Walters	**Women**		1981	Lisa Merrifield
1972	Barth Levy	1960	Mary Novak	1982	Lisa Merrifield
1973	Mike Woods	1961	Jean Ashworth	1983	Janet Hainstock
1974	Leigh Barczewski, Mike Passarella	1962	Jean Omelenchuk	1984	Janet Hainstock
		1963	Jean Ashworth	1985	Betsy Davis
1975	Rich Wurster	1964	Diane White	1986	Deb Perkins
1976	John Wurster	1965	Jean Omelenchuk	1987	Laura Zuckerman
1977	Jim Chapin	1966	Diane White	1988	Elise Brinich
1978	Bill Heinkel	1967	Jean Ashworth	1989	Liza Merrifield
1979	Erik Henriksen	1968	Helen Lutsch	1990	Jane Eickhoff
1980	Greg Oly	1969	Sally Blatchford		
1981	Tom Grannes	1970–71	Sheila Young		
1982	Greg Oly	1972	Ruth Moore, Nancy Thorne		

WORLD SPEED SKATING RECORDS

Men

Distance	Time	Skater	Place	Year
500m	0:36.45	Jens–Uwe Mey, East Germany	Calgary, Canada	1988
1000m	1:12.58	Pavel Pegov, Soviet Union	Medeo, U.S.S.R.	1983
1000m	1:12.58	Igor Zhelezovski	Heerenveea, The Netherlands	1989
1500m	1:52.50	Andre Hoffmann, East Germany	Calgary, Canada	1988
3000m	3:59.27	Leo Visser, Netherlands	Heerenveen, The Netherlands	1987
5000m	6:44.63	Tomas Gustafson, Sweden	Calgary, Canada	1988
10,000m	13:48:20	Tomas Gustafson, Sweden	Calgary, Canada	1988
All-around	160.807	Victor Shasherin, Soviet Union	Medeo, U.S.S.R.	1984

Women

Distance	Time	Skater	Place	Year
500m	0:39.10	Bonnie Blair, United States	Calgary, Canada	1988
1000m	1:17.65	Christa Rothenburger, E. Germany	Calgary, Canada	1988
1500m	2:00.68	Yvonne Van Gennip, Netherlands	Calgary, Canada	1988
3000m	4:11.94	Yvonne Van Gennip, Netherlands	Calgary, Canada	1988
5000m	7:14:13	Yvonne Van Gennip, Netherlands	Calgary, Canada	1988
All-around	171.760	Andrea Schone, East Germany	Medeo, U.S.S.R.	1984

U.S. INDOOR (SHORT TRACK) CHAMPIONS—1990

Men—Andy Gabel, Northbrook, Ill.
Women—Jane Eickhoff, Los Alamitos, Calif.
Intermediate men—Jeff Benjamin, Highland Park, Ill.
Intermediate women—Amy Peterson, Maplewood, Minn.
Junior boys—Casey Fitz Randolph, Verona, Wis.
Junior girls—Jessica Mills, Northfield, Ill.

WORLD SPRINT CHAMPIONSHIPS—1990

(Tromso, Norway, Feb. 24-25, 1990)

Men

(Two races in both 500m and 1000m. Overall winner on points)

500m—	Uwe Jens Mey, East Germany	0:37.65
	Uwe Jens Mey, East Germany	0:37.83
1000m—	Igor Zhelezouski, Soviet Union	1:16.84
	Alexander Klimov, Soviet Union	1:17.12
Overall—	Ki Tae Bae, South Korea	

Women

(Two races in both 500m and 1000m. Overall winner on points)

500m—	Angela Hauck, East Germany	0:41.37
	Angela Hauck, East Germany	0:41.66

1000m—	Christine Aaftink, The Netherlands	1:25.66
	Bonnie Blair, United States	1:24.90
Overall—	Angela Hauck, East Germany	

U.S. OUTDOOR (LONG TRACK) CHAMPIONS—1990

Men—Andy Zak, Minneapolis, Minn.
Women—Jane Eickhoff, Los Alamitos, Calif.
Intermediate men—Doug MacKenzie, Waukesha, Wis.
Intermediate women—Kim Strzykalski, Milwaukee, Wis.
Junior boys—Heath Haster, White Bear Lake, Minn.
Junior girls—Chris Witty, West Alice, Wis.

WORLD CHAMPIONSHIPS—1990

Men

(Insbrouck, Austria, Feb. 17-18, 1990)

Overall champion—Johann Olav Koss, Norway	164.099 pts.	
500m—Ki Tae Bae, South Korea	0:37.37	
1500m—Ben van de Burg, The Netherlands	1:56.23	
5000m—Bart Beldkamp, The Netherlands	6:56.82	

10,000m—Bart Beldkamp, The Netherlands	14:35.87	

500m—Seiko Hashimoto, Japan	0:40.22
1500m—Xiulo Wang, China	2:03.34
3000m—Jacqueline Boerner, East Germany	4:19.86
5000m—Heike Schalling, East Germany	7:28.37

Women

(Calgary, Alberta, Canada, Feb. 10-11, 1990)

Overall champion—Jacqueline Boerner, East Germany 171.634 pts

FIGURE SKATING

WORLD CHAMPIONS

Men

1960	Alain Giletti, France
1961	No competition
1962	Donald Jackson, Canada
1963	Don McPherson, Canada
1964	Manfred Schnelldorfer, West Germany
1965	Alain Calmat, France
1966-68	Emmerich Danzer, Austria
1969-70	Tim Wood, United States
1971-73	Ondrej Nepela, Czechoslovakia
1974	Jan Hoffman, East Germany
1975	Sergei Yolkov, U.S.S.R.
1976	John Curry, Britain
1977	Vladimir Kovalev, U.S.S.R.
1978	Charles Tickner, United States
1979	Vladimir Kovalev, U.S.S.R.
1980	Jan Hoffman, East Germany
1981	Scott Hamilton, United States

1982	Scott Hamilton, United States
1983	Scott Hamilton, United States
1984	Scott Hamilton, United States
1985	Alexandr Fadeev, U.S.S.R.
1986	Brian Boitano, United States
1987	Brian Orser, Canada
1988	Brian Boitano, United States
1989	Kurt Browning, Canada
1990	Kurt Browning, Canada

Women

1956-60	Carol Heiss, United States
1961	No competition
1962-64	Sjoukje Dijkstra, Netherlands
1965	Petra Burka, Canada
1966-68	Peggy Fleming, United States
1969-70	Gabriele Seyfert, East Germany
1971-72	Beatrix Schuba, Austria

1973	Karen Magnusson, Canada
1974	Christine Errath, East Germany
1975	Dianne de Leeuw, Netherlands
1976	Dorothy Hamill, United States
1977	Linda Fratianne, United States
1978	Anett Poetzsch, East Germany
1979	Linda Fratianne, United States
1980	Anett Poetzsch, East Germany
1981	Denise Beillmann, Switzerland
1982	Elaine Zayak, United States
1983	Rosalynn Sumners, United States
1984	Katarina Witt, East Germany
1985	Katarina Witt, East Germany
1986	Debi Thomas, United States
1987	Katarina Witt, East Germany
1988	Katarina Witt, East Germany
1989	Midori Ito, Japan
1990	Jill Trenary, United States

U.S. CHAMPIONS

Men

1946-52	Richard Button
1953-56	Hayes Jenkins
1957-60	David Jenkins
1961	Bradley Lord
1962	Monty Hoyt
1963	Tommy Liz
1964	Scott Allen
1965	Gary Visconti
1966	Scott Allen
1967	Gary Visconti
1968-70	Tim Wood
1971	John M. Petkevich
1972	Ken Shelley
1973-75	Gordon McKellen
1976	Terry Kubicka
1977-80	Charles Tickner

1981	Scott Hamilton
1982	Scott Hamilton
1983	Scott Hamilton
1984	Scott Hamilton
1985	Brian Boitano
1986	Brian Boitano
1987	Brian Boitano
1988	Brian Boitano
1989	Christopher Bowman
1990	Todd Eldredge

Women

1943-48	Gretchen Merrill
1949-50	Yvonne Sherman
1951	Sonya Klopfer
1952-56	Tenley Albright
1957-60	Carol Heiss

1961	Laurence Owen
1962	Barbara Roles Pursley
1963	Lorraine Hanlon
1964-68	Peggy Fleming
1969-73	Janet Lynn
1974-76	Dorothy Hamill
1977-80	Linda Fratianne
1981	Elaine Zayak
1982	Rosalynn Sumners
1983	Rosalynn Sumners
1984	Rosalynn Sumners
1985	Tiffany Chin
1986	Debi Thomas
1987	Jill Trenary
1988	Debi Thomas
1989	Jill Trenary
1990	Jill Trenary

WORLD CHAMPIONS—1990

(Halifax, Nova Scotia, Canada, March 6-11, 1990)

Men's singles—Kurt Browning, Canada
Women's singles—Jill Trenary, United States
Pairs—Ekaterina Gordeeva and Sergei Grinkov, Soviet Union
Dance—Marina Klimova and Sergei Pronomarenko, Soviet Union

UNITED STATES CHAMPIONSHIPS—1990

(Salt Lake City, Utah, Feb. 6-11, 1990)

Senior men—Todd Eldredge, Los Angeles Figure Skating Club
Senior women—Jill Trenary, Broadmoor Skating Club
Senior pairs—Kristi Yamaguchi and Rudi Galindo, St. Moritz Ice Skating Club
Senior dance—Susan Wynne, Broadmoor Skating Club, and Joseph Druar, Seattle Skating Club
Junior men—Scott Davis, Lakewood Skating Club
Junior women—Alice Sue Claeys, Braemar-City of Lakes Figure Skating Club
Junior pairs—Tristen Vega and Richard Alexander, Los Angeles Figure Skating Club

Junior dance—Beth Buhl, Seattle Skating Club and Neale Smull, Peninsula Figure Skating Club
Novice men—Michael Weiss, University of Delaware Figure Skating Club
Novice women—Natalie Thomas, Rocky Mountain Figure Skating Club

CURLING

United States Championships—1990

Men (Superior, Wis., March 4-10, 1990)—Seattle, Wash., Doug Jones, skip (defeated Minnesota, Craig Polski, skip, 6-4 in final)
Women (Superior, Wis., March 4-10, 1990)—Denver, Colo., Bev Behnke skip (defeated North Dakota, LaVonne Berg, skip, 6-2, in final)

World Championships—1990

Men (Winnipeg, Canada, March 23-31, 1990)—Canada, Ed Werenich, skip (defeated Scotland, David Smith, skip, 3-1 in final)
Women (Winnipeg, Canada, March 23-31, 1990)—Norway, Dordi Nordby, skip (defeated Scotland, Carolyn Hutchison, skip, 4-2 in final)

SWIMMING

WORLD RECORDS—MEN

(Through Sept. 17, 1990)
Approved by the International Swimming Federation (F.I.N.A.)
(F.I.N.A. discontinued acceptance of records in yards in 1968)
Source: United States Swim Team.

Distance	Record	Holder	Country	Date
Freestyle				
50 meters	0:21.81	Tom Jager	United States	March 24, 1990
100 meters	0:48.42	Matt Biondi	United States	August 9, 1988
200 meters	1:46.69	Georgio Lamberti	Italy	Aug. 15, 1989
400 meters	3:46.95	Uwe Dussler	East Germany	Sept. 23, 1988
800 meters	7:50.64	Vladimir Salnikov	Soviet Union	July 4, 1986
1,500 meters	14:54.76	Vladimir Salnikov	Soviet Union	Feb. 22, 1983
Backstroke				
100 meters	0:54.51	David Berkoff	United States	Sept. 24, 1988
200 meters	1:58.14	Igor Poliansky	Soviet Union	March 1, 1985
Breaststroke				
100 meters	1:01.49	Adrian Moorehouse	Great Britain	Jan. 25, 1990
200 meters	2:11.53	Mike Barrowman	United States	July 20, 1990
Butterfly				
100 meters	0:52.84	Pablo Morales	United States	June 23, 1986
200 meters	1:56.65	Michael Gross	West Germany	Aug. 10, 1985
Individual Medley				
200-meter individual medley	2:00.11	David Wharton	United States	Aug. 20, 1989
400-meter individual medley	4:15.42	Tamas Darnyi	Hungary	Sept. 21, 1988
Freestyle Relay				
400 meters	3:16.53	United States	National Team	Sept. 23, 1988
800-meters	7:12.51	United States	National Team	Sept. 21, 1988
Medley Relay				
400 meters	3:36.93	United States	National Team	Sept. 25, 1988

WORLD RECORDS—WOMEN

Distance	Record	Holder	Country	Date
Freestyle				
50 meters	0:24.98	Yang Wenyi	China	April 11, 1988
100 meters	0:54.73	Kristin Otto	East Germany	Aug. 19, 1986
200 meters	1:57.55	Heike Friedrich	East Germany	June 16, 1986
400 meters	4:03.85	Janet Evans	United States	Sept. 22, 1988
800 meters	8:16.22	Janet Evans	United States	Aug. 20, 1989
1,500 meters	15:52.10	Janet Evans	United States	March 26, 1988
Backstroke				
100 meters	1:00.59	Ina Kleber	East Germany	Aug. 24, 1984
200 meters	2:08.60	Betsy Mitchell	United States	June 27, 1986
Breaststroke				
100 meters	1:07.91	Silke Hoerner	East Germany	Aug. 21, 1987
200 meters	2:26.71	Silke Hoerner	East Germany	Sept. 21, 1988
Butterfly				
100 meters	0:57.93	Mary T. Meagher	United States	Aug. 16, 1981
200 meters	2:05.96	Mary T. Meagher	United States	Aug. 13, 1981
Individual Medley				
200 meters	2:11.73	Ute Geweniger	East Germany	July 4, 1981
400 meters	4:36.10	Petra Schneider	East Germany	Aug. 1, 1982

Freestyle Relay

400 meters	3:40.57	East German National Team	East Germany	Aug. 19, 1986
800 meters	7:55.47	East German National Team	East Germany	Aug. 18, 1987

Medley Relay

400 meters	4:03.69	East German National Team	East Germany	Aug. 24, 1984

AMERICAN SWIMMING RECORDS
(As of September 17, 1990)

Distance	Holder	Record	Date
MEN			
Freestyle			
50 meters	Tom Jager	0:21.81	March 24, 1990
100 meters	Matt Biondi	0:48.42	August 10, 1988
200 meters	Matt Biondi	1:47.72	August 15, 1989
400 meters	Matt Cetlinski	3:48.06	August 11, 1988
800 meters	Sean Killion	7:52.45	July 27, 1987
1500 meters	George DiCarlo	15:01.51	June 30, 1984
Backstroke			
100 meters	Dave Berkodd	0:54.51	September 24, 1988
200 meters	Rick Carey	1:58.86	June 27, 1984
Breaststroke			
100 meters	Steve Lundquist	1:01.65	July 29, 1984
200 meters	Mike Barrowman	2:11.53	July 20, 1990
Butterfly			
100 meters	Pablo Morales	0:52.84	June 23, 1986
200 meters	Melvin Stewart	1:57.05	July 21, 1990
Individual Medley			
200 meters	David Wharton	2:00.11	August 20, 1989
400 meters	Eric Namesnik	4:15.57	July 30, 1990
Freestyle Relay			
400 meters	US National Team	3:16.53	September 23, 1988
800 meters	US National Team	7:12.51	September 21, 1988
Medley Relay			
400 meters	US National Team	3:36.93	September 25, 1988

Distance	Holder	Record	Date
WOMEN			
Freestyle			
50 meters	Leigh Ann Fetter	0:24.98	August 13, 1988
100 meters	Dara Torres	0:53.30	March 25, 1988
200 meters	Cynthia Woodhead	1:58.23	September 3, 1979
400 meters	Janet Evans	4:03.85	September 22, 1988
800 meters	Janet Evans	8:16.22	August 20, 1989
1500 meters	Janet Evans	15:52.10	March 26, 1988
Backstroke			
100 meters	Betsy Mitchell	1:01.20	June 24, 1986
200 meters	Betsy Mitchell	2:08.60	June 27, 1986
Breaststroke			
100 meters	Tracey McFarlane	1:08.91	August 11, 1988
200 meters	Amy Shaw	2:29.58	August 16, 1987
Butterfly			
100 meters	Mary T. Meagher	0:57.93	August 16, 1981
200 meters	Mary T. Meagher	2:05.96	August 13, 1981
Individual Medley			
200 meters	Tracy Caulkins	2:12.64	August 3, 1984
400 meters	Janet Evans	4:37.76	September 19, 1988

Distance	Holder	Record	Date
Freestyle Relay			
400 meters	US National Team	3:43.43	August 26, 1978
	US National Team	3:43.43	July 31, 1984
800 meters	US National Team	8:02.12	August 17, 1986
Medley Relay			
400 meters	US National Team	4:06.94	July 23, 1990

U.S. SHORT COURSE CHAMPIONSHIPS

(Nashville, Tenn., March 19–23, 1990)

Men's Events

50-yard freestyle—Tom Jager	0:19.05
100-yard freestyle—Matt Biondi	0:42.30
200-yard freestyle—Michael Picotte	1:36.26
500-yard freestyle—Norbert Agh	4:20.27
1,000-yard freestyle—Eric Diehl	8:58.26
1,650-yard freestyle—Matt Hooper	15:05.17
100-yard backstroke—Eric Hansen	0:49.21
200-yard backstroke—Derek Weatherford	1:46.17
100-yard breaststroke—Nelson Diebel	0:53.84
200-yard breaststroke—Nelson Diebel	1:57.16
100-yard butterfly—Matt Biondi	0:46.33
200-yard butterfly—Brian Alderman	1:45.64
200-yard individual medley—Ron Karnaugh	1:46.00
400-yard individual medley—T. Darnyl	3:49.38
400-yard freestyle relay—Santa Clara	2:58.77
800-yard freestyle relay—Mission Viejo	6:35.40
400-yard medley relay—Longhorn Aquatic	3:16.14

Team champions—1. Longhorn Aquatic, 232
 2. Mission Viejo, 229
 3. Peddie, 160

Women's Events

50-yard freestyle—Nicole Haislett	0:22.80
100-yard freestyle—Nicole Haislett	0:48.83
200-yard freestyle—Nicole Haislett	1:45.59
500-yard freestyle—Jane Skillman	4:40.75
1,000-yard freestyle—Jane Skillman	9:30.35
1,650-yard freestyle—Jane Skillman	15:59.35
100-yard backstroke—Betsy Mitchell	0:54.86
200-yard backstroke—Jane Wagstaff	1:56.14
100-yard breaststroke—T. McFarlane	1:00.97
200-yard breaststroke—Mary Ellen Blanchard	2:10.13
100-yard butterfly—Jenny Thompson	0:54.03
200-yard butterfly—Summer Sanders	1:55.91
200-yard individual medley—Mary Ellen Blanchard	1:58.03
400-yard individual medley—Summer Sanders	4:09.79
400-yard freestyle relay—Longhorn Aquatic	3:20.84
800-yard freestyle relay—Longhorn Aquatic	7:18.59
400-yard medley relay—Longhorn Aquatic	3:39.78

Team champions—1. Longhorn Aquatic, 260
 2. Dynamo, 184
 3. Peddie, 180

Combined Team Champions—1. Longhorn Aquatic, 431
 2. Mission Viejo, 332
 3. Peddie, 284

U.S. LONG COURSE CHAMPIONSHIPS

(Austin, Texas, July 29—Aug. 3, 1990)

Men's Events

50-m freestyle—Tom Jager	0:22.26
100-m freestyle—Shaun Jordan	0:49.68
200-m freestyle—Troy Dalbey	1:48.69
400-m freestyle—Dan Jorgensen	3:49.80
800-m freestyle—Dan Jorgensen	7:59.97
1,500-m freestyle—Keith Frostad	15:14.52
100-m backstroke—Jeff Rouse	0:54.86
200-m backstroke—Jeff Rouse	2:00.13
100-m breaststroke—Eric Wunderlich	1:01.89

200-m breaststroke—Mike Barrowman	2:11.55
100-m butterfly—Mark Henderson	0:53.92
200-m butterfly—Melvin Stewart	1:57.43
200-m individual medley—David Wharton	2:01.33
400-m individual medley—Eric Namesnik	4:15.57

Women's Events

50-m freestyle—Jenny Thompson	0:25.90
100-m freestyle—Nicole Haislett	0:55.84
200-m freestyle—Janet Evans	2:00.27
400-m freestyle—Janet Evans	4:08.67
800-m freestyle—Janet Evans	8:24.32
1,500-m freestyle—Julie Kole	16:38.56
100-m backstroke—Jodi Wilson	1:02.52
200-m backstroke—Beth Barr	2:13.16
100-m breaststroke—Tori DeSilvia	1:10.09
200-m breaststroke—Mary Ellen Blanchard	2:32.18
100-m butterfly—Chrissy Ahmann–Leighton	1:00.47
200-m butterfly—Trina Radke	2:10.55
200-m individual medley—Summer Sanders	2:14.36
400-m individual medley—Erika Hansen	4:40.84

U.S. DIVING CHAMPIONSHIPS—1990

INDOOR

(Beaverton, Oregon, April 18-22, 1990)

Men's Events

1-meter—Mark Bradshaw, Ohio State	627.48
3-meter—Mark Bradshaw, Ohio State	691.65
Platform—Pat Evans, Stingray	600.10
Team—Ohio State	184

Women's Events

1-meter—Wendy Lucero, Kimball	481.77
3-meter—Krista Wilson, MST	514.50
10-meter—Wendy Lian Williams, MVN	435.39
Team—Kimball	138
Combined Team—Ohio State	299

OUTDOOR

(Dallas, Texas, August 14-19, 1990)

Men's Events

1-meter—Pat Evans, Cincinnati, Ohio	626.62
3-meter—Kent Furguson, Boca Raton, Fla.	653.70
Platform—Matt Scoggin, Austin, Tex.	643.29

Women's Events

1-meter—Krista Wilson, Dallas, Tex.	446.97
3-meter—Wendy Lucero, Aurora, Colo.	497.13
Platform—Wendy Lian Williams, Bridgeton, Mo.	411.27

Swimming History

The modern sport of swimming was developed in England during the 1800s. Contests using the breaststroke were held in London in 1837. A group of London swimming clubs met in 1869 and formed the London Swimming Association which later became the Amateur Swimming Association. The United States Amateur Athletic Union (AAU), formed in 1888, assumed supervision of swimming along with other sports.

BOXING

Whether it be called pugilism, prize fighting or boxing, there is no tracing "the Sweet Science" to any definite source. Tales of rivals exchanging blows for fun, fame or money go back to earliest recorded history and classical legend. There was a mixture of boxing and wrestling called the "pancratium" in the ancient Olympic Games and in such contests the rivals belabored one another with hands fortified with heavy leather wrappings that were sometimes studded with metal. More than one Olympic competitor lost his life at this brutal exercise.

There was little law or order in pugilism until Jack Broughton, one of the early champions of England, drew up a set of rules for the game in 1743. Broughton, called "the father of English box-

ing," also is credited with having invented boxing gloves. However, these gloves—or "mufflers" as they were called—were used only in teaching "the manly art of self-defense" or in training bouts. All professional championship fights were contested with "bare knuckles" until 1892, when John L. Sullivan lost the heavyweight championship of the world to James J. Corbett in New Orleans in a bout in which both contestants wore regulation gloves.

The Broughton rules were superseded by the London Prize Ring Rules of 1838. The 8th Marquis of Queensberry, with the help of John G. Chambers, put forward the "Queensberry Rules" in 1866, a code that called for gloved contests. Amateurs took quickly to the Queensberry Rules, the professionals slowly.

HISTORY OF WORLD HEAVYWEIGHT CHAMPIONSHIP FIGHTS

(Bouts in which a new champion was crowned)

Source: Nat Fleischer's Ring *Boxing Encyclopedia and Record Book*, published and copyrighted by The Ring Book Shop, Inc., 120 West 31st St., New York, N.Y. 10001.

Date	Where held	Winner, weight, age	Loser, weight, age	Rounds	Referee
Sept. 7, 1892	New Orleans, La.	James J. Corbett, 178 (26)	John L. Sullivan, 212 (33)	21	Prof. John Duffy
March 17, 1897	Carson City, Nev.	Bob Fitzsimmons, 167 (34)	James J. Corbett, 183 (30)	KO 14	George Siler
June 9, 1899	Coney Island, N.Y.	James J. Jeffries, 206 (24)[1]	Bob Fitzsimmons, 167 (37)	KO 11	George Siler
Feb. 23, 1906	Los Angeles	Tommy Burns, 180 (24)[2]	Marvin Hart, 188 (29)	20	James J. Jeffries
Dec. 26, 1908	Sydney, N.S.W.	Jack Johnson, 196 (30)	Tommy Burns, 176 (27)	KO 14	Hugh McIntosh
April 5, 1915	Havana, Cuba	Jess Willard, 230 (33)	Jack Johnson, 205 1/2 (37)	KO 26	Jack Welch
July 4, 1919	Toledo, Ohio	Jack Dempsey, 187 (24)	Jess Willard, 245 (37)	KO 3	Ollie Pecord
Sept. 23, 1926	Philadelphia	Gene Tunney, 189 (28)[3]	Jack Dempsey, 190 (31)	10	Pop Reilly
June 12, 1930	New York	Max Schmeling, 188 (24)	Jack Sharkey, 197 (27)	WF 4	Jim Crowley
June 21, 1932	Long Island City	Jack Sharkey, 205 (29)	Max Schmeling, 188 (26)	15	Gunboat Smith
June 29, 1933	Long Island City	Primo Carnera, 260 1/2 (26)	Jack Sharkey, 201 (30)	KO 6	Arthur Donovan
June 14, 1934	Long Island City	Max Baer, 209 1/2 (25)	Primo Carnera, 263 1/4 (27)	KO 11	Arthur Donovan
June 13, 1935	Long Island City	Jim Braddock, 193 3/4 (29)	Max Baer, 209 1/2 (26)	15	Jack McAvoy
June 22, 1937	Chicago	Joe Louis, 197 1/4 (23)	Jim Braddock, 197 (31)	KO 8	Tommy Thomas
June 22, 1949	Chicago	Ezzard Charles, 181 3/4 (27)[4]	Joe Walcott, 195 1/2 (35)	15	Davey Miller
Sept. 27, 1950	New York	Ezzard Charles, 184 1/2 (29)[5]	Joe Louis, 218 (36)	15	Mark Conn
July 18, 1951	Pittsburgh	Joe Walcott, 194 (37)	Ezzard Charles, 182 (30)	KO 7	Buck McTiernan
Sept. 23, 1952	Philadelphia	Rocky Marciano, 184 (29)[6]	Joe Walcott, 196 (38)	KO 13	Charley Daggert
Nov. 30, 1956	Chicago	Floyd Patterson, 182 1/4 (21)	Archie Moore, 187 3/4 (42)	KO 5	Frank Sikora
June 26, 1959	New York	Ingemar Johansson, 196 (26)	Floyd Patterson, 182 (24)	KO 3	Ruby Goldstein
June 20, 1960	New York	Floyd Patterson, 190 (25)	Ingemar Johansson, 194 3/4 (27)	KO 5	Arthur Mercante
Sept. 25, 1962	Chicago	Sonny Liston, 214 (28)	Floyd Patterson, 189 (27)	KO 1	Frank Sikora
Feb. 25, 1964	Miami Beach, Fla.	Cassius Clay, 210 (22)[7]	Sonny Liston, 218 (30)	KO 7	Barney Felix
March 4, 1968	New York	Joe Frazier, 204 1/2 (24)[8]	Buster Mathis, 243 1/2 (23)	KO 11	Arthur Mercante
April 27, 1968	Oakland, Calif.	Jimmy Ellis, 197 (28)[9]	Jerry Quarry, 195 (22)	15	Elmer Costa
Feb. 16, 1970	New York	Joe Frazier, 205 (26)[10]	Jimmy Ellis, 201 (29)	KO 5	Tony Perez
Jan. 22, 1973	Kingston, Jamaica	George Foreman, 217 1/2 (24)	Joe Frazier, 214 (29)	KO 2	Arthur Mercante
Oct. 30, 1974	Kinshasa, Zaire	Muhammad Ali, 216 1/2 (32)	George Foreman, 220 (26)	KO 8	Zack Clayton
Feb. 15, 1978	Las Vegas, Nev.	Leon Spinks, 197 (25)	Muhammad Ali, 224 1/2 (36)	15	Howard Buck
June 9, 1978	Las Vegas, Nev.	Larry Holmes, 212 (28)[11]	Ken Norton, 220 (32)	15	Mills Lans
Sept. 15, 1978	New Orleans	Muhammad Ali, 221 (36)[12]	Leon Spinks, 201 (25)	15	Lucien Joubert
Oct. 20, 1979	Pretoria, S. Africa	John Tate, 240 (24)[13]	Gerrie Coetzee, 222 (24)	15	Carlos Berrocal
March 31, 1980	Knoxville, Tenn.	Mike Weaver, 207 1/2 (27)	John Tate, 232 (25)	KO 15	Ernesto Magana Ansorena
Dec. 10, 1982	Las Vegas, Nev.	Michael Dokes, 216 (24)	Mike Weaver, 209 1/2 (30)	KO 1	Joey Curtis
Sept. 23, 1983	Richfield, Ohio	Gerrie Coetzee, 215 (28)	Michael Dokes, 217 (25)	KO 10	Tony Perez
March 9, 1984	Las Vegas, Nev.	Tim Witherspoon, 220 1/2 (26)[14]	Greg Page, 239 1/2 (25)	12	Mills Lane
August 31, 1984	Las Vegas, Nev.	Pinklon Thomas, 216 (26)	Tim Witherspoon, 217 (26)	12	Richard Steele
Nov. 9, 1984	Las Vegas, Nev.	Larry Holmes, 221 1/2 (35)[15]	James Smith 227 (31)	KO 12	Dave Pearl
Dec. 1, 1984	Sun City, S. Africa	Greg Page, 236 (25)[16]	Gerry Coetzee, 217 (29)	KO 8	unavailable
April 29, 1985	Buffalo, N.Y.	Tony Tubbs, 229 (26)[16]	Greg Page, 239 1/2 (26)	15	unavailable.
Sept. 21,1985	Las Vegas, Nev.	Michael Spinks, 200 (29)	Larry Holmes, 221 (35)	15	Carlos Padilla
Jan. 17, 1986	Atlanta, Ga.	Tim Witherspoon, 227 (28)	Tony Tubbs, 229 (27)	15	unavailable
Nov. 23, 1986	Las Vegas, Nev.	Mike Tyson, 217 (20)[17]	Trevor Berbick, 220 (29)	KO 2	unavailable
Dec. 12, 1986	New York, N.Y.	James Smith, 230 (33)[16]	Tim Witherspoon, 218 (29)	KO 1	unavailable
March 7, 1987	Las Vegas, Nev.	Mike Tyson, 217 (20)[16]	James Smith, 230 (33)	12	unavailable
Feb. 10, 1990	Tokyo	James "Buster" Douglas,[18] 231 1/2 (29)	Mike Tyson 220 (23)	KO 10	Octavio Meyrom

1. Jeffries retired as champion in March 1905. He named Marvin Hart and Jack Root as leading contenders and agreed to referee their fight in Reno, Nev., on July 3, 1905, with the stipulation that he would term the winner the champion. Hart, 190 (28), knocked out Root, 171 (29), in the 12th round. 2. Burns claimed the title after defeating Hart. 3. Tunney retired as champion after defeating Tom Heeney on July 26, 1928. 4. After Louis announced his retirement as champion on March 1, 1949, Charles won recognition from the National Boxing Association as champion by defeating Walcott. 5. Charles gained undisputed recognition as champion by defeating Louis, who came out of retirement. 6. Retired as Champion April 27, 1956. 7. The World Boxing Association later withdrew its recognition of Clay as champion and declared the winner of a bout between Ernie Terrell and Eddie Machen would gain its version of the title. Terrell, 199 (25), won a 15-round decision from Machen, 192 (32), in Chicago on March 5, 1965. Clay, 212 1/4 (25) and Terrell, 212 1/2 (27) met in Houston on Feb. 6, 1967, Clay winning a 15-round decision. 8. Winner recognized by New York, Massachusetts, Maine, Illinois, Texas and Pennsylvania to fill vacated title when Clay was stripped of championship for failing to accept U. S. Induction. 9. Bout was final of eight-man tournament to fill Clay's place and is recognized by World Boxing Association. 10. Bout settled controversy over title. 11. Holmes won World Boxing Council title after WBC had withdrawn recognition of Spinks, March 18, 1978, and awarded its title to Norton. WBC said Spinks had reneged on agreement to fight Norton 12. Ali regained World Boxing Association championship. 13. Tate won WBA title after Ali retired and left it vacant. 14. Tim Witherspoon and Greg Page fought for the WBC heavyweight title vacated by Larry Holmes, who could not come to agreement on a deal to fight Page, the No. 1 contender. Holmes declared he would fight under the banner of the International Boxing Federation. Several dates were set and postponed for fights between Holmes and Gerry Coetzee, the WBA champ, the latest being Nov. 16, 1984. 15. First fight under banner of International Boxing Federation. 16. New W.B.A. champion. 17. New W.B.C. champion. 18. New undisputed champion.

OTHER WORLD BOXING TITLEHOLDERS

(Through Aug. 1, 1990)

Light Heavyweight

1903	Jack Root, George Gardner	1968	Dick Tiger, Bob Foster	1981	Matthew Saad Muhammad
1903–05	Bob Fitzsimmons	1969–70	Bob Foster		(WBC), Eddie Mustafa
1905–12	Philadelphia Jack O'Brien[1]	1971	Vicente Rondon (WBA), Bob		Muhammad (WBA),
1912–16	Jack Dillon		Foster (WBC)		Michael Spinks (WBA),
1916–20	Battling Levinsky	1972–73	Bob Foster (WBA, WBC)		Dwight Braxton (WBC)
1920–22	Georges Carpentier	1974	John Conteh (WBA), Bob	1982	Dwight Braxton (WBC),
1923	Battling Siki		Foster (WBC)[1,4]		Michael Spinks (WBA)
1923–25	Mike McTigue	1975–76	Victor Galindez (WBA), John	1983	Michael Spinks (undisputed)
1925–26	Paul Berlenbach		Conteh (WBC)	1984	Michael Spinks (undisputed)
1926–27	Jack Delaney[2]	1977	Victor Galindez (WBA), John	1985	Michael Spinks (undisputed)[5]
1927	Mike McTigue		Conteh (WBC)[4], Miguel	1986	Marvin Johnson (WBA)
1927–29	Tommy Loughran		Cuello (WBC)		Dennis Andries (WBC)
1930	Jimmy Slattery	1978	Victor Galindez (WBA), Mike	1987	Thomas Hearns (WBC)
1930–34	Maxie Rosenbloom		Rossman (WBA), Miguel		Virgil Hill (WBA)
1934–35	Bob Olin		Cuello (WBC), Mate Parlov		Bobby Czyz (IBF)
1935–39	John Henry Lewis		(WBC), Marvin Johnson	1988	Charles Williams (IBF), Virgil Hill
1939	Melio Bettina		(WBC)		(WBA), Donny LaLonde
1939–41	Billy Conn[2]	1979	Mike Rossman (WBA), Victor		(WBC), Sugar Ray Leonard
1941	Anton Christoforidis (NBA)		Galindez (WBA), Marvin		(WBC)
1941–48	Gus Lesnevich		Johnson (WBC), Matthew	1989	Dennis Andries (WBC),
1948–50	Freddie Mills		(Franklin) Saad		Virgil Hill (WBA)
1950–52	Joey Maxim		Muhammad (WBC)		Charles Williams (IBF)
1952–61	Archie Moore[3]	1980	Matthew Saad Muhammad		Jeff Harding (WBC)
1961–63	Harold Johnson		(WBC), Marvin Johnson	1990	Virgil Hill (WBA)
1963–65	Willie Pastrano		(WBA), Eddie (Gregory)		Charles Williams (IBF)
1965–66	José Torres		Mustafa Muhammad		Jeff Harding (WBC)
1966–67	Dick Tiger		(WBA)		

1. Retired. 2. Abandoned title. 3. NBA withdrew recognition in 1961, New York Commission in 1962; recognized thereafter only by California and Europe. 4. WBC withdrew recognition. 5. Spinks relinquished title in 1985 to fight for heavyweight title.

Middleweight

			Freddy Steele, Al Hostak,	1962	Paul Pender[1]
1867–72	Tom Chandler		Solly Kreiger, Fred	1962–63	Dick Tiger
1872–81	George Rooke		Apostoli, Cerferino Garcia,	1963–65	Joey Giardello
1881–82	Mike Donovan[1]		Ken Overlin, Billy Soose,	1965–66	Dick Tiger
1884–91	Jack (Nonpareil) Dempsey		Tony Zale[4]	1966	Emile Griffith
1891–97	Bob Fitzsimmons[2]	1941–47	Tony Zale	1967	Nino Benvenuti, Emile Griffith
1908	Stanley Ketchel, Billy Papke	1947–48	Rocky Graziano	1968	Emile Griffith, Nino Benvenuti
1908–10	Stanley Ketchel[3]	1948	Tony Zale	1969	Nino Benvenuti
1913	Frank Klaus	1948–49	Marcel Cerdan	1970	Nino Benvenuti, Carlos Monzon
1913–14	George Chip	1949–51	Jake LaMotta		
1914–17	Al McCoy	1952	Ray Robinson, Randy Turpin	1971–73	Carlos Monzon
1917–20	Mike O'Dowd	1951–52	Ray Robinson[1]	1974–75	Carlos Monzon (WBA),
1920–23	Johnny Wilson	1953–55	Carl Olson		Rodrigo Valdez (WBC)
1923–26	Harry Greb	1955–57	Ray Robinson[5]	1976	Carlos Monzon (WBA, WBC),
1926	Tiger Flowers	1957	Gene Fullmer, Ray Robinson		Rodrigo Valdez (WBC)
1926–31	Mickey Walker[6]	1957–58	Carmen Basilio	1977	Carlos Monzon (WBA,
1931–41	Gorilla Jones, Ben Jeby,	1958–60	Ray Robinson[6]		WBC)[1], Rodrigo Valdez
	Marcel Thil, Lou Brouillard,	1960–61	Paul Pender[7]		(WBA, WBC)
	Vince Dundee, Teddy	1959–62	Gene Fullmer (NBA)	1978	Rodrigo Valdez, Hugo Corro
	Yarosz, Babe Risko,	1961–62	Terry Downes[1]	1979	Hugo Corro, Vito Antuofermo

1980	Vito Antuofermo, Alan Minter, Marvin Hagler	1988	Sumbu Kalambay (WBA), Thomas Hearns (WBC), Iran Barkley (WBC), Frank Tate (IBF), Michael Nunn (IBF), James Kinchen (NABF)	1989	Michael Nunn (IBF), Mike McCallum (WBA), Iran Barkley (WBC), Roberto Duran (WBC)
1981	Marvin Hagler			1990	Michael McCallum (WBA), Michael Nunn (IBF), Iran Barkley (WBC)
1982–86	Marvelous Marvin Hagler (undisputed)				
1987	Marvin Hagler (undisputed) Sugar Ray Leonard (undisputed)				

1. Retired. 2. Abandoned title. 3. Died. 4. National Boxing Association and New York Commission disagreed on champions. Those listed were accepted by one or the other until Zale gained world-wide recognition. 5. Ended retirement in 1954. 6. NBA withdrew recognition. 7. Recognized by New York, Massachusetts, and Europe.

Welterweight

1892–94	Mysterious Billy Smith	1940–41	Fritzie Zivic	1977–78	José Cuevas (WBA), Carlos Palomino (WBC)
1894–96	Tommy Ryan	1941–46	Freddie Cochrane	1979	José Cuevas (WBA), Carlos Palomino (WBC), Wilfredo Benitez (WBC)
1896	Kid McCoy[2]	1946	Marty Servo[1]		
1896– 1900	Mysterious Billy Smith	1946–51	Ray Robinson[2]		
		1951	Johnny Bratton (NBA)	1980	José Cuevas (WBA), Ray Leonard (WBC), Roberto Duran (WBC), Thomas Hearns (WBA)
1900	Rube Ferns	1951–54	Kid Gavilan		
1900–01	Matty Matthews	1954–55	Johnny Saxton		
1901	Ruby Ferns	1955	Tony DeMarco		
1901–04	Joe Walcott	1955–56	Carmen Basilio	1981	Ray Leonard (WBC), Thomas Hearns (WBA), Ray Leonard (WBC,WBA)
1904	Dixie Kid[2]	1956	Johnny Saxton		
1904–06	Joe Walcott	1956–57	Carmen Basilio[2]		
1906–07	Honey Mellody	1958	Virgil Akins	1982	Ray Leonard
1907	Mike (Twin) Sullivan[2]	1959–60	Don Jordan	1983–85	Donald Curry (WBA)
1915–19	Ted Lewis	1960–61	Benny (Kid) Paret	1983–85	Milton McCrory (WBC)
1919–22	Jack Britton	1961	Emile Griffith	1985–86	Donald Curry (undisputed)
1922–26	Mickey Walker	1961–62	Benny (Kid) Paret	1987	Mark Breland (WBA) Marlon Starling (WBA) Lloyd Honeychan (IBF)
1926–27	Pete Latzo	1962–63	Emile Griffith, Luis Rodriguez		
1927–29	Joe Dundee	1963–66	Emile Griffith[2]		
1929–30	Jackie Fields	1966–69	Curtis Cokes	1988	Marlon Starling (WBA), Tomas Molinares (WBA), Lloyd Honeyghan (WBC), Simon Brown (IBF)
1930	Young Jack Thompson	1969	Curtis Cokes, José Napoles		
1930–31	Tommy Freeman	1970	José Napoles, Billy Backus		
1931	Young Jack Thompson	1971	Billy Backus, José Napoles		
1931–32	Lou Brouillard	1972–74	José Napoles	1989	Mark Breland (WBA), Marlon Starling (WBC), Simon Brown (IBF)
1932–33	Jackie Fields	1975	José Napoles (WBA, WBC)[3], Angel Espada (WBA), John Stracey (WBC)		
1933	Young Corbett 3rd				
1933–34	Jimmy McLarnin, Barney Ross			1990	Mark Breland (WBA), Aaron Davis (WBA), Simon Brown (IBF), Marlon Starling (WBC)
1934–35	Jimmy McLarnin	1976	Angel Espada (WBA), José Cuevas (WBA), John Stracey (WBC), Carlos Palomino		
1935–38	Barney Ross				
1938–40	Henry Armstrong				

1. Retired. 2. Abandoned title. 3. WBA withdrew recognition.

Lightweight

1869–99	Kid Lavigne	1951–52	James Carter	1975	Roberto Duran (WBA), Guts Ishimatsu (WBC)
1899– 1902	Frank Erne	1952	Lauro Salas		
		1952–54	James Carter	1976	Roberto Duran (WBA), Guts Ishimatsu (WBC), Esteban De Jesus (WBC)
1902–08	Joe Gans	1954	Paddy DeMarco		
1908–10	Battling Nelson	1954–55	James Carter		
1910–12	Ad Wolgast	1955–56	Wallace Smith	1977	Roberto Duran (WBA), Esteban De Jesus (WBC)
1912–14	Willie Ritchie	1956–62	Joe Brown		
1914–17	Freddy Welsh	1962–65	Carlos Ortiz	1978	Roberto Duran (WBA, WBC)
1917–25	Benny Leonard[1]	1965	Ismael Laguna	1979	Roberto Duran[2], Jim Watt (WBC), Ernesto Espana (WBA)
1925	Jimmy Goodrich	1965–68	Carlos Ortiz		
1925–26	Rocky Kansas	1968	Teo Cruz		
1926–30	Sammy Mandell	1969	Teo Cruz, Mando Ramos	1980	Ernesto Espana (WBA), Hilmer Kenty (WBA), Jim Watt (WBC)
1930	Al Singer	1970	Mando Ramos, Ismael Laguna, Ken Buchanan		
1930–33	Tony Canzoneri				
1933–35	Barney Ross[2]	1971	Ken Buchanan (WBA), Mando Ramos (WBC), Pedro Carrasco (WBC)	1981	Hilmer Kenty (WBA), Sean O'Grady (WBA), James Watt (WBC), Alexis Arguello (WBC), Arturo Frias (WBA)
1935–36	Tony Canzoneri				
1936–38	Lou Ambers				
1938–39	Henry Armstrong	1972	Ken Buchanan (WBA), Roberto Duran (WBA), Pedro Carrasco (WBC), Mando Ramos (WBC), Chango Carmona (WBC), Rodolfo Gonzalez (WBC)		
1939–40	Lou Ambers			1982	Arturo Frias (WBA), Ray Mancini (WBA), Alexis Arguello (WBC)
1940–41	Lew Jenkins				
1941–42	Sammy Angott[1]				
1943–47	Beau Jack (N.Y.), Bob Montgomery (N.Y.), Sammy Angott (NBA), Juan Zurita (NBA), Ike Williams (NBA)	1973	Roberto Duran (WBA), Rodolfo Gonzalez (WBC)	1983	Edwin Rosario (WBC), Ray Mancini (WBA)
		1974	Roberto Duran (WBA), Rodolfo Gonzalez (WBC), Guts Ishimatsu (WBC)	1984	Edwin Rosario (WBC), Livingstone Bramble (WBA)
1947–51	Ike Williams			1985	Jose Luis Ramirez (WBC)

1. Retired. 2. Abandoned title.

	Hector Camacho (WBC)		Greg Haugen (IBF)	1989	Pernell Whitaker (IBF, WBC),
	Livingstone Bramble (WBA)	1988	Jose Luis Ramirez (WBC),		Edwin Rosario (WBA)
1986	Hector Camacho (WBC)		Julio Cesar Chavez (WBA),	1990	Pernell Whitaker (IBF, WBC),
	Livingstone Bramble (WBA)		Greg Haugen (IBF),		Juan Nazario (WBA)
	Jim Paul (IBF)		Julius Cesar Chavez (WBC &		
1987	Edwin Rosario (WBA)		WBA title unified)		
	Jose Luis Ramirez (WBC)				

Featherweight

1889	Dal Hawkins[1]		Sho Saijo (WBA)		Pedroza (WBA), Danny
1890	Billy Murphy	1969	Sho Saijo (WBA), Johnny		Lopez (WBC)
1892–			Famechon[3]	1979	Eusebio Pedroza (WBA),
1900	George Dixon	1970	Sho Saijo (WBA), Johnny		Danny Lopez (WBC)
1900–01	Terry McGovern		Famechon,[3] Vicente	1980	Eusebio Pedroza (WBA),
1901	Young Corbett[1]		Salvidar,[3] Kuniaki Shibata[3]		Danny Lopez (WBC),
1901–12	Abe Attell	1971	Sho Saijo (WBA), Antonio		Salvador Sanchez (WBC)
1912–23	Johnny Kilbane		Gomez (WBA), Kuniaki	1981	Eusebio Pedroza (WBA),
1923	Eugene Criqui		Shibata (WBC)		Salvador Sanchez (WBC)
1923–25	Johnny Dundee[1]	1972	Antonio Gomez (WBA),	1982	Eusebio Pedroza (WBA),
1925–27	Louis (Kid) Kaplan[1]		Ernesto Marcel (WBA),		Salvador Sanchez (WBC)[4]
1927–28	Benny Bass		Kuniaki Shibata (WBC),	1983	Juan Laporte (WBC),
1928	Tony Canzoneri		Clemente Sanchez (WBC),		Eusebio Pedroza (WBA)
1928–29	Andre Routis		José Legra (WBC)	1984	Wilfred Gomez (WBC),
1929–32	Battling Battalino[1]	1973	Ernesto Marcel (WBA), José		Eusebio Pedroza (WBA)
1932	Tommy Paul (NBA), Kid		Legra (WBC), Eder Jofre	1985	Eusebio Pedroza (WBA)
	Chocolate (N.Y.)		(WBC)		Barry McGuigan (WBA)
1933–36	Freddie Miller	1974	Ernesto Marcel (WBA)[2],		Azumah Nelson (WBC)
1936–37	Petey Sarron		Ruben Olivares (WBA),	1986	Barry McGuigan (WBA)
1937–38	Henry Armstrong[1]		Alexis Arguello (WBA),		Stevie Cruz (WBA)
1938–40	Joey Archibald		Eder Jofre (WBC), Bobby		Azumah Nelson (WBC)
1940–41	Harry Jefra, Joey Archibald		Chacon (WBC)	1987	Azumah Nelson (WBC)
1941–42	Chalky Wright	1975	Alexis Arguello (WBA),		Antonio Esparragoza (WBA)
1942–48	Willie Pep		Bobby Chacon (WBC),	1988	Calvin Grove (IBF),
1948–49	Sandy Saddler[2]		Ruben Olivares (WBC),		Jorge Paez (IBF),
1949–50	Willie Pep		David Kotey (WBC)		Antonio Esparragoza (WBA),
1950-57	Sandy Saddler	1976	Alexis Arguello (WBA),[2]		Jeff Fenech (WBC)
1957–59	Kid Bassey		David Kotey (WBC), Danny	1989	Jorge Paez (IBF),
1959–63	Davey Moore		Lopez (WBC)		Antonio Esparragoza (WBA),
1963–64	Sugar Ramos	1977	Rafael Ortega (WBA),		Jeff Fenech (WBC)
1964–67	Vicente Saldivar[2]		Danny Lopez (WBC)	1990	Marcos Villasana (WBC), Antonio
1968	Howard Winstone, José	1978	Rafael Ortega (WBA), Cecilio		Esparragoza (WBA), Jorge
	Legra,[3] Paul Rojas (WBA),		Lastra (WBA), Eusebio		Paez (IBF)

1. Abandoned title. 2. Retired. 3. Recognized in Europe, Mexico, and Orient. 4. Killed in auto accident.

Bantamweight

1890–92	George Dixon[1]	1937	Sixto Escobar, Harry Jeffra	1972	Ruben Olivares, Rafael
1894–99	Jimmy Barry[2]	1938	Harry Jeffra, Sixto Escobar		Herrera, Enrique Pinder
1899–		1939–40	Sixto Escobar[2]	1973	Enrique Pinder (WBA),
1900	Terry McGovern[1]	1940–42	Lou Salica		Romeo Anaya (WBA),
1901	Harry Harris[1]	1942–46	Manuel Ortiz		Arnold Taylor (WBA),
1902–03	Harry Forbes	1947	Manuel Ortiz, Harold Dade		Rodolfo Martinez (WBC),
1903–04	Frankie Neil	1948–50	Manuel Ortiz		Rafael Herrera
1904	Joe Bowker[1]	1950–52	Vic Toweel	1974	Arnold Taylor (WBA), Soo
1905–07	Jimmy Walsh[1]	1952–54	Jimmy Carruthers[2]		Hwan Hong (WBA), Rafael
1910–14	Johnny Coulon	1954–55	Robert Cohen		Herrera (WBC), Rodolfo
1914–17	Kid Williams	1956	Robert Cohen, Mario		Martinez (WBC)
1917–20	Pete Herman		D'Agata, Raul Macias	1975	Soo Hwan Hong (WBA),
1920	Joe Lynch		(NBA)		Alfonso Zamora (WBA),
1920–21	Joe Lynch, Pete Herman,	1957	Mario D'Agata, Alphonse		Rodolfo Martinez (WBC)
	Johnny Buff		Halimi	1976	Alfonso Zamora (WBA),
1922	Johnny Buff, Joe Lynch	1958–59	Alphonse Halimi		Rodolfo Martinez (WBC),
1923	Joe Lynch	1959–60	Jose Becerra[2]		Carlos Zarate (WBC)
1924	Joe Lynch, Abe Goldstein	1960–61	Alphonse Halimi[4]	1977	Alfonso Zamora (WBA),
1924	Abe Goldstein, Eddie	1961–62	Johnny Caldwell[4]		Jorge Lujan (WBA), Carlos
	(Cannonball) Martin	1961–65	Eder Jofre		Zarate (WBC)
1925	Eddie (Cannonball) Martin,	1965–68	Masahika (Fighting) Harada	1978	Jorge Lujan (WBA), Carlos
	Charlie (Phil) Rosenberg[3]	1968	Masahika (Fighting) Harada,		Zarate (WBC)
1927–28	Bud Taylor (NBA)[1]		Lionel Rose	1979	Jorge Lujan (WBA), Carlos
1929–34	Al Brown	1969	Lionel Rose, Ruben Olivares		Zarate (WBC), Lupe Pintor
1935	Al Brown, Baltazar Sangchili	1970	Ruben Olivares, Chucho		(WBC)
1936	Baltazar Sangchili, Tony		Castillo	1980	Jorge Lujan (WBA), Lupe
	Marino, Sixto Escobar	1971	Chucho Castillo, Ruben		Pintor (WBC), Julian Solis
			Olivares		

1. Abandoned title. 2. Retired. 3. Deprived of title for failing to make weight. 4. Recognized in Europe.

	(WBA), Jeff Chandler (WBA)		Daniel Zaragoza (WBC) Miguel Lora (WBC)	1989	Orlando Canizales (IBF) Jibaro Perez (WBC),
1981	Lupe Pintor (WBC), Jeff Chandler (WBA)	1986	Richard Sandoval (WBA) Bernardo Pinango (WBA)		Moon Sung-gil (WBA), Orlando Canizales (IBF)
1982	Lupe Pintor (WBC), Jeff Chandler (WBA)	1987	Jeff Fenech (IBF) Bernardo Pinango (WBA)		Kaokor Galaxy (WBA), Luis Espinosa (WBA)
1983	Jeff Chandler (WBA), Albert Dauila (WBC)		Takuya Muguruma (WBA) Miguel Lora (WBC)	1990	Orlando Canizales (IBF), Jibaro Perez (WBC),
1984	Richie Sandqual (WBA), Albert Dauila (WBC)	1988	Wilfred Vasquez (WBA), Jibaro Perez (WBC),		Luis Espinosa (WBA)
1985	Richard Sandoval (WBA)		Moon Sung-gil (WBA),		

Flyweight

1916–23	Jimmy Wilde		Masao Ohba (WBA)	1980	Luis Ibarra (WBA), Kim Tae Shik (WBA), Park
1923–25	Pancho Villa[1]	1971	Masao Ohba (WBA), Erbito Salavarria (WBC)		Chan-Hee (WBC), Shoji Oguma (WBC)
1925	Frankie Genaro				
1925–27	Fidel La Barba[2]	1972	Masao Ohba (WBA), Erbito Salavarria (WBA), Betulio Gonzalez (WBC), Venice Borkorsor (WBC)	1983	Frank Cedeno (WBC), Santos Lacia (WBA)
1927–31	Corporal Izzy Schwartz, Frankie Genaro, Emile (Spider) Pladner, Midget Wolgast, Young Perez[3]			1984	Koji Kobayashy (WBA), Gabriel Bernal (WBC), Santos Laciar (WBA)
1932–35	Jackie Brown	1973	Masao Ohba (WBA), Chartchai Chionoi (WBA), Venice Borkorsor (WBC), Betulio Gonzalez (WBC)	1985	Sot Chitlada (WBC) Santos Laciar (WBA)
1935–38	Bennie Lynch[4]				
1939	Peter Kane[4]				
1943–47	Jackie Paterson[1]	1974	Chartchai Chionoi (WBA), Susumu Hanagata (WBA), Betulio Gonzalez (WBC), Shoji Oguma (WBC)	1986	Hilario Zapata (WBA) Julio Cesar-Chevez (WBC)
1947–50	Rinty Monaghan[2]				
1950	Terry Allen			1987	Shin Hi Sop (IBF) Chang Ho Choi (IBF) Sot Chitlada (WBC)
1950–52	Dado Marino	1975	Susumu Hanagata (WBA), Erbito Salavarria (WBA), Shoji Oguma (WBC), Miguel Canto (WBC)		
1952–54	Yoshio Shirai			1988	Sot Chitlada (WBC), Kim Young Kang (WBC), Duke McKenzie (IBF), Fidel Bassa (WBA)
1954–60	Pascual Perez				
1960–62	Pone Kingpetch	1976	Erbito Salavarria (WBA), Alfonso Lopez (WBA), Guty Espadas (WBA), Miguel Canto (WBC)		
1962–63	Masahika (Fighting) Harada			1989	Kim Young-gang (WBC), Sot Chitlada (WBC), Lee Yol-woo (WBA), Duke McKenzie (IBF), Dave McAuley (IBF)
1963–64	Hiroyuki Ebihara				
1964–65	Pone Kingpetch	1977	Guty Espadas (WBA), Miguel Canto (WBC)		
1965–66	Salvatore Burrini				
1966	Walter McGown, Chartchai Chionoi	1978	Guty Espadas (WBA), Betulio Gonzalez (WBA), Miguel Canto (WBC)		Jesus Rojas (WBA)
1966–68	Charchai Chionoi			1990	Sot Chitlada (WBC), Kim Bong-Jung (WBA), Lee Yul-woo (WBA), Dave McAuley (IBF)
1969	Bernabe Villacampa, Efran Torres (WBA)	1979	Betulio Gonzalez (WBA), Miguel Canto (WBC), Park Chan-Hee (WBC)		
1970	Bernabe Villacampa, Chartchai Chionoi, Erbito Salavarria, Berkrerk Chartvanchai (WBA),				

1. Died. 2. Retired. 3. Claimants to NBA and New York Commission titles. 4. Abandoned title.

FENCING

World Champions—1990

Source: United States Fencing Association.

Men's epee—Thomas Gerull, West Germany
Men's foil—Phillippe Omnes, France
Men's sabre—Gyorgy Nebald, Hungary
Women's foil—Anja Fichto, West Germany
Women's epee—Taymi Chappe, Cuba
Men's foil team—Italy
Men's epee team—Italy
Men's sabre team—Soviet Union
Women's foil team—Italy
Women's epee team—West Germany

United States Champions—1990

Men's Foil

Division I—Michael Marx, Michigan City, Ind.
Division II—James Barin, Morristown, N.J.
Under-19—Ben Atkins, New York City

Men's Epee

Division I—Rob Stulo, San Antonio, Texas
Division II—William Spacy, Abilene, Texas
Under-19—Michael O'Donovan, San Francisco

Men's Sabre

Division I—Robert Cottingham, Orange, N.J.
Division II—Stephen Kovacs, Hampton, N.J.
Under 19—Stephen Kovacs, Hampton, N.J.

Women's Foil

Division I—Jennifer Yu, East Palo Alto, Calif.
Division II—Julianna Sikes, Dixon, Calif.
Under-19—Ann Marsh, Royal Oak, Mich.

Woman's Epee

Division I—Donna Stone, Belleville, N.J.
Division II—Wendy Bender, Seattle, Wash.
Under-19—Brooke Schneider, Northville, Mich.

Women's Sabre

Division II—Karen Dorren, Huntington Beach, Calif.

Team Champions

Men's foil team—New York Fencers Club, New York City
Men's epee team—U.S. Modern Pentathlon Association, San Antonio, Texas
Men's sabre team—New York Fencers Club
Women's foil team—New York Fencers Club
Women's epee team—Salle Auriol, Portland, Oregon

HORSE RACING

Ancient drawings on stone and bone prove that horse racing is at least 3000 years old, but Thoroughbred Racing is a modern development. Practically every thoroughbred in training today traces its registered ancestry back to one or more of three sires that arrived in England about 1728 from the Near East and became known, from the names of their owners, as the Byerly Turk, the Darley Arabian, and the Godolphin Arabian. The Jockey Club (English) was founded at Newmarket in 1750 or 1751 and became the custodian of the Stud Book as well as the court of last resort in deciding turf affairs.

Horse racing took place in this country before the Revolution, but the great lift to the breeding industry came with the importation in 1798, by Col. John Hoomes of Virginia, of Diomed, winner of the Epsom Derby of 1780. Diomed's lineal descendants included such famous stars of the American turf as American Eclipse and Lexington. From 1800 to the time of the Civil War there were race courses and breeding establishments plentifully scattered through Virginia, North Carolina, South Carolina, Tennessee, Kentucky, and Louisiana.

The oldest stake event in North America is the Queen's Plate, a Canadian fixture that was first run in the Province of Quebec in 1836. The oldest stake event in the United States is The Travers, which was first run at Saratoga in 1864. The gambling that goes with horse racing and trickery by jockeys, trainers, owners, and track officials caused attacks on the sport by reformers and a demand among horse racing enthusiasts for an honest and effective control of some kind, but nothing of lasting value to racing came of this until the formation in 1894 of The Jockey Club.

"TRIPLE CROWN" WINNERS IN THE UNITED STATES[1]
(Kentucky Derby, Preakness and Belmont Stakes)

Year	Horse	Owner	Year	Horse	Owner
1919	Sir Barton	J. K. L. Ross	1946	Assault	Robert J. Kleberg
1930	Gallant Fox	William Woodward	1948	Citation	Warren Wright
1935	Omaha	William Woodward	1973	Secretariat	Meadow Stable
1937	War Admiral	Samuel D. Riddle	1977	Seattle Slew	Karen Taylor
1941	Whirlaway	Warren Wright	1978	Affirmed	Louis Wolfson
1943	Count Fleet	Mrs. John Hertz			

KENTUCKY DERBY
Churchill Downs; 3-year-olds; 1 1/4 miles.

Year	Winner	Jockey	Wt.	Win val.	Year	Winner	Jockey	Wt.	Win val.
1875	Aristides	O. Lewis	100	$2,850	1909	Wintergreen	V. Powers	117	$4,850
1876	Vagrant	R. Swim	97	2,950	1910	Donau	F. Herbert	117	4,850
1877	Baden Baden	W. Walker	100	3,300	1911	Meridian	G. Archibald	117	4,850
1878	Day Star	J. Carter	100	4,050	1912	Worth	C. H. Shilling	117	4,850
1879	Lord Murphy	C. Schauer	100	3,550	1913	Donerail	R. Goose	117	5,475
1880	Fonso	G. Lewis	105	3,800	1914	Old Rosebud	J. McCabe	114	9,125
1881	Hindoo	J. McLaughlin	105	4,410	1915	Regret	J. Notler	112	11,450
1882	Apollo	B. Hurd	102	4,560	1916	George Smith	J. Loftus	117	9,750
1883	Leonatus	W. Donohue	105	3,760	1917	Omar Khayyam	C. Borel	117	16,600
1884	Buchanan	I. Murphy	110	3,990	1918	Exterminator	W. Knapp	114	14,700
1885	Joe Cotton	E. Henderson	110	4,630	1919	Sir Barton	J. Loftus	112 1/2	20,825
1886	Ben Ali	P. Duffy	118	4,890	1920	Paul Jones	T. Rice	126	30,375
1887	Montrose	I. Lewis	118	4,200	1921	Behave Yourself	C. Thompson	126	38,450
1888	Macbeth II	G. Covington	115	4,740	1922	Morvich	A. Johnson	126	46,775
1889	Spokane	T. Kiley	118	4,970	1923	Zev	E. Sande	126	53,600
1890	Riley	I. Murphy	118	5,460	1924	Black Gold	J. D. Mooney	126	52,775
1891	Kingman	I. Murphy	122	4,680	1925	Flying Ebony	E. Sande	126	52,950
1892	Azra	A. Clayton	122	4,230	1926	Bubbling Over	A. Johnson	126	50,075
1893	Lookout	E. Kunze	122	4,090	1927	Whiskery	L. McAtee	126	51,000
1894	Chant	F. Goodale	122	4,020	1928	Reigh Count	C. Lang	126	55,375
1895	Halma	J. Perkins	122	2,970	1929	Clyde Van Dusen	L. McAtee	126	53,950
1896	Ben Brush	W. Simms	117	4,850	1930	Gallant Fox	E. Sande	126	50,725
1897	Typhoon H	F. Garner	117	4,850	1931	Twenty Grand	C. Kurtsinger	126	48,725
1898	Plaudit	W. Simms	117	4,850	1932	Burgoo King	E. James	126	52,350
1899	Manuel	F. Taral	117	4,850	1933	Brokers Tip	D. Meade	126	48,925
1900	Lieut. Gibson	J. Boland	117	4,850	1934	Cavalcade	M. Garner	126	28,175
1901	His Eminence	J. Winkfield	117	4,850	1935	Omaha	W. Saunders	126	39,525
1902	Alan-a-Dale	J. Winkfield	117	4,850	1936	Bold Venture	I. Hanford	126	37,725
1903	Judge Himes	H. Booker	117	4,850	1937	War Admiral	C. Kurtsinger	126	52,050
1904	Elwood	F. Prior	117	4,850	1938	Lawrin	E. Arcaro	126	47,050
1905	Agile	J. Martin	122	4,850	1939	Johnstown	J. Stout	126	46,350
1906	Sir Huon	R. Troxler	117	4,850	1940	Gallahadion	C. Bierman	126	60,150
1907	Pink Star	A. Minder	117	4,850	1941	Whirlaway	E. Arcaro	126	61,275
1908	Stone Street	A. Pickens	117	4,850	1942	Shut Out	W. D. Wright	126	64,225

Year	Winner	Jockey	Wt.	Win val.	Year	Winner	Jockey	Wt.	Win val.
1943	Count Fleet	J. Longden	126	$ 60,725	1967	Proud Clarion	R. Ussery	126	$119,700
1944	Pensive	C. McCreary	126	64,675	1968	Forward Pass[1]	I. Valenzuela	126	122,600
1945	Hoop Jr.	E. Arcaro	126	64,850	1969	Majestic Prince	W. Hartack	126	113,200
1946	Assault	W. Mehrtens	126	96,400	1970	Dust Commander	M. Manganello	126	127,800
1947	Jet Pilot	E. Guerin	126	92,160	1971	Canonero II	G. Avila	126	145,500
1948	Citation	E. Arcaro	126	83,400	1972	Riva Ridge	R. Turcotte	126	140,300
1949	Ponde	S. Brooks	126	91,600	1973	Secretariat	R. Turcotte	126	155,050
1950	Middleground	W. Boland	126	92,650	1974	Cannonade	A. Cordero, Jr.	126	274,000
1951	Count Turf	C. McCreary	126	98,050	1975	Foolish Pleasure	J. Vasquez	126	209,600
1952	Hill Gail	E. Arcaro	126	96,300	1976	Bold Forbes	A. Cordero, Jr.	126	165,200
1953	Dark Star	H. Moreno	126	90,050	1977	Seattle Slew	J. Cruguet	126	214,700
1954	Determine	R. York	126	102,050	1978	Affirmed	S. Cauthen	126	186,900
1955	Swaps	W. Shoemaker	126	108,400	1979	Spectacular Bid	R. Franklin	126	228,650
1956	Needles	D. Erb	126	123,450	1980	Genuine Risk	J. Vasquez	126	250,550
1957	Iron Liege	W. Hartack	126	107,950	1981	Pleasant Colony	J. Velasquez	126	317,200
1958	Tim Tam	I. Valenzuela	126	116,400	1982	Gato del Sol	E. Delahoussaye	126	417,600
1959	Tomy Lee	W. Shoemaker	126	119,650	1983	Sunny's Halo	E. Delahoussaye	126	426,000
1960	Venetian Way	W. Hartack	126	114,850	1984	Swale	L. Pincay, Jr.	126	537,400
1961	Carry Back	J. Sellers	126	120,500	1985	Spend a Buck	A. Cordero, Jr.	126	406,800
1962	Decidedly	W. Hartack	126	119,650	1986	Ferdinand	W. Shoemaker	126	609,400
1963	Chateaugay	B. Baeza	126	108,900	1987	Alysheba	C. McCarron	126	618,600
1964	Northern Dancer	W. Hartack	126	114,300	1988	Winning Colors	Gary Stevens	126	611,200
1965	Lucky Debonair	W. Shoemaker	126	112,000	1989	Sunday Silence	Patrick Valenzuela	126	574,200
1966	Kauai King	D. Brumfield	126	120,500	1990	Unbridled	Craig Perret	126	581,000

1. Dancer's Image finished first but was disqualified after traces of drug were found in system.

PREAKNESS STAKES

Pimlico; 3-year-olds; 1 3/16 miles; first race 1873.

Year	Winner	Jockey	Wt.	Win Val.	Year	Winner	Jockey	Wt.	Win val.
1919	Sir Barton	J. Loftus	126	$24,500	1960	Bally Ache	R. Ussery	126	$121,000
1930	Gallant Fox	E. Sande	126	51,925	1961	Carry Back	J. Sellers	126	126,200
1931	Mate	G. Ellis	126	48,225	1962	Greek Money	J. Rotz	126	135,800
1932	Burgoo King	E. James	126	50,375	1963	Candy Spots	W. Shoemaker	126	127,500
1933	Head Play	C. Kurtsinger	126	26,850	1964	Northern Dancer	W. Hartack	126	124,200
1934	High Quest	R. Jones	126	25,175	1965	Tom Rolfe	R. Turcotte	126	128,100
1935	Omaha	W. Saunders	126	25,325	1966	Kauai King	D. Brumfield	126	129,000
1936	Bold Venture	G. Woolf	126	27,325	1967	Damascus	W. Shoemaker	126	141,500
1937	War Admiral	C. Kurtsinger	126	45,600	1968	Forward Pass	I. Valenzuela	126	142,700
1938	Dauber	M. Peters	126	51,875	1969	Majestic Prince	W. Hartack	126	129,500
1939	Challedon	G. Seabo	126	53,710	1970	Personality	E. Belmonte	126	151,300
1940	Bimelech	F.A. Smith	126	53,230	1971	Canonero II	G. Avila	126	137,400
1941	Whirlaway	E. Arcaro	126	49,365	1972	Bee Bee Bee	E. Nelson	126	135,300
1942	Alsab	B. James	126	58,175	1973	Secretariat	R. Turcotte	126	129,900
1943	Count Fleet	J. Longden	126	43,190	1974	Little Current	M. Rivera	126	156,000
1944	Pensive	C. McCreary	126	60,075	1975	Master Derby	D. McHargue	126	158,100
1945	Polynesian	W.D. Wright	126	66,170	1976	Elocutionist	J. Lively	126	129,700
1946	Assault	W. Mehrtens	126	96,620	1977	Seattle Slew	J. Cruguet	126	138,600
1947	Faultless	D. Dodson	126	98,005	1978	Affirmed	S. Cauthen	126	136,200
1948	Citation	E. Arcaro	126	91,870	1979	Spectacular Bid	R. Franklin	126	165,300
1949	Capot	T. Atkinson	126	79,985	1980	Codex	A. Cordero	126	180,600
1950	Hill Prince	E. Arcaro	126	56,115	1981	Pleasant Colony	J. Velasquez	126	270,800
1951	Bold	E. Arcaro	126	83,110	1982	Aloma's Ruler	J. Kaenel	126	209,900
1952	Blue Man	C. McCreary	126	86,135	1983	Deputed Testimony	D. Miller	126	251,200
1953	Native Dancer	E. Guerin	126	65,200	1984	Gate Dancer	A. Cordero	126	243,600
1954	Hasty Road	J. Adams	126	91,600	1985	Tank's Prospect	Pat Day	126	423,200
1955	Nashua	E. Arcaro	126	67,550	1986	Snow Chief	A. Solis	126	411,900
1956	Fabius	W. Hartack	126	84,250	1987	Alysheba	C. McCarron	126	421,100
1957	Bold Ruler	E. Arcaro	126	65,250	1988	Risen Star	E. Delahoussaye	126	413,700
1958	Tim Tam	I. Valenzuela	126	97,900	1989	Sunday Silence	P. Valenzuela	126	438,230
1959	Royal Orbit	W. Harmatz	126	136,200	1990	Summer Squall	Pat Day	126	445,900

BELMONT STAKES

Belmont Park; 3-year-olds; 1 1/2 miles.

Run at Jerome Park 1867 to 1890; at Morris Park 1890–94; at Belmont Park 1905–62; at Aqueduct 1963–67. Distance 1 5/8 miles prior to 1874; reduced to 1 1/2 miles, 1874; reduced to 1 1/4 miles, 1890; reduced to 1 1/8 miles, 1893; increased to 1 1/4 miles, 1895; increased to 1 3/8 miles, 1896; reduced to 1 1/4 miles in 1904; increased to 1 1/2 miles, 1926.

Year	Winner	Jockey	Wt.	Win val.	Year	Winner	Jockey	Wt.	Win val.
1919	Sir Barton	J. Loftus	126	$11,950	1930	Gallant Fox	E. Sande	126	66,040

Year	Winner	Jockey	Wt.	Win val.	Year	Winner	Jockey	Wt.	Win val.
1931	Twenty Grand	C. Kurtsinger	126	$58,770	1961	Sherluck	B. Baeza	126	$104,900
1932	Faireno	T. Malley	126	55,120	1962	Jaipur	W. Shoemaker	126	109,550
1933	Hurryoff	M. Garner	126	49,490	1963	Chateaugay	B. Baeza	126	101,700
1934	Peace Chance	W.D. Wright	126	43,410	1964	Quadrangle	M. Ycaza	126	110,850
1935	Omaha	W. Saunders	126	35,480	1965	Hail to All	J. Sellers	126	104,150
1936	Granville	J. Stout	126	29,800	1966	Amberoid	W. Boland	126	117,700
1937	War Admiral	C. Kurtsinger	126	38,020	1967	Damascus	W. Shoemaker	126	104,950
1938	Pasteurized	J. Stout	126	34,530	1968	Stage Door Johnny	H. Gustines	126	117,700
1939	Johnstown	J. Stout	126	37,020	1969	Arts and Letters	B. Baeza	126	104,050
1940	Bimelech	F.A. Smith	126	35,030	1970	High Echelon	J. Rotz	126	115,000
1941	Whirlaway	E. Arcaro	126	39,770	1971	Pass Catcher	R. Blum	126	97,710
1942	Shut Out	E. Arcaro	126	44,520	1972	Riva Ridge	R. Turcotte	126	93,540
1943	Count Fleet	J. Longden	126	35,340	1973	Secretariat	R. Turcotte	126	90,120
1944	Bounding Home	G.L. Smith	126	55,000	1974	Little Current	M. Rivera	126	101,970
1945	Pavot	E. Arcaro	126	56,675	1975	Avatar	W. Shoemaker	126	116,160
1946	Assault	W. Mehrtens	126	75,400	1976	Bold Forbes	A. Cordero, Jr.	126	117,000
1947	Phalanx	R. Donoso	126	78,900	1977	Seattle Slew	J. Cruguet	126	109,080
1948	Citation	E. Arcaro	126	77,700	1978	Affirmed	S. Cauthen	126	110,580
1949	Capot	T. Atkinson	126	60,900	1979	Coastal	R. Hernandez	126	161,400
1950	Middleground	W. Boland	126	61,350	1980	Temperence Hill	E. Maple	126	176,220
1951	Counterpoint	D. Gorman	126	82,000	1981	Summing	G. Martens	126	170,580
1952	One Count	E. Arcaro	126	82,400	1982	Conquistador Cielo	L. Pincay, Jr.	126	159,720
1953	Native Dancer	E. Guerin	126	82,500	1983	Caveat	L. Pincay, Jr.	126	215,100
1954	High Gun	E. Guerin	126	89,000	1984	Swale	L. Pincay, Jr.	126	310,020
1955	Nashua	E. Arcaro	126	83,700	1985	Creme Fraiche	Eddie Maple	126	307,740
1956	Needles	D. Erb	126	83,600	1986	Danzig Connection	C. McCarron	126	338,640
1957	Gallant Man	W. Shoemaker	126	77,300	1987	Bet Twice	C. Perret	126	329,160
1958	Cavan	P. Anderson	126	73,440	1988	Risen Star	E. Delahoussaye	126	303,720
1959	Sword Dancer	W. Shoemaker	126	93,525	1989	Easy Goer	P. Day	126	413,520
1960	Celtic Ash	W. Hartack	126	96,785	1990	Go And Go	Michael Kinane	126	411,600

TRIPLE CROWN RACES—1990

Kentucky Derby (Churchill Downs, Louisville, Ky., May 5, 1990). Gross purse: $756,000. Distance: 1 1/4 miles. Order of finish: 1. Unbridled (Perret), mutuel return: $23.60, $7.80, $5.80. 2. Summer Squall (Day), $3.80, $3.80. 3. Pleasant Tap (Desormeaux), $12. 4. Video Ranger (Hansen). 5. Silver Ending (McCarron). 6. Killer Diller (Bruin). 7. Land Rush (Cordero). 8. Mister Frisky (Stevens). 9. Thirty Six Red (Smith). 10. Power Lunch (Romero). 11. Real Cash (Solis). 12. Dr. Bobby A. (Santagata). 13. Pendleton Ridge (Pincay). 14. Burnt Hills (Valenzuela). 15. Fighting Fantasy (Sellers). Winner's purse: $581,000. Margin of victory: 3 1/2 lengths. Time of race: 2:02.00. Attendance: 128,257.

Preakness Stakes (Pimlico, Md., May 19, 1990). Gross purse: $686,000. Distance: 1 3/16 miles. Order of finish: 1. Summer Squall (Day), mutuel return: $6.80, $3.00, $2.60. 2. Unbridled (Perret), $3.00, $2.80. 3. Mister Frisky (Stevens), $3.40. 4. Mister Prospector (Olivares). 5. Fighting Notion (Delgado). 6. Land Rush (Cordero). 7. Kentucky Jazz (Desormeaux). 8. Baron de Vaux (Rocco). 9. J.R.'s Horizon (Johnston). Winner's purse: $445,900. Margin of victory: 2 1/4 lengths. Time of race: 1:53 3/5. Attendance: 86,531.

Belmont Stakes (Elmont, N.Y., June 9, 1990). Gross purse: $500,000. Distance: 1 1/2 miles. Order of finish: 1. Go and Go (Kinane), mutuel return: $17.00, $6.20, $4.80. 2. Thirty Six Red (Smith), $4.40, $4.20. 3. Baron de Vaux (Cruguet), $12.60. 4. Unbridled (Perret). 5. Yonder (Bailey). 6. Land Rush (Cordero). 7. Video Ranger (Santos). 8. Hawaiian Pass (Madrid). 9. Country Day (Antley). Winner's purse $411,600. Margin of victory: 8 1/4 lengths. Time of race: 2:27 1/5. Attendance: 50,123.

ECLIPSE AWARDS—1989

Horse of the Year	Sunday Silence
Two-year-old colt	Rhythm
Two-year-old filly	Go For Wand
Three-year-old colt	Sunday Silence
Three-year-old filly	Open Mind
Older male horse	Blushing John
Older filly or mare	Bayakoa
Male turf horse	Steinlen
Female turf horse	Brown Bess
Sprinter	Safely Kept
Steeplechaser	Highland Bud
Owner	Ogden Phipps
Trainer	Charlie Whittingham
Breeder	North Ridge Farm
Jockey	Kent Desormeaux
Apprentice Jockey	Michael Luzzi

RODEO

PROFESSIONAL RODEO COWBOY ASSOCIATION, ALL AROUND COWBOY

1953	Bill Linderman	1963–65	Dean Oliver	1976–79	Tom Ferguson	1986	Lewis Field
1954	Buck Rutherford	1966–70	Larry Mahan	1980	Paul Tierney	1987	Lewis Field
1955	Casey Tibbs	1971–72	Phil Lyne	1981	Jimmie Cooper	1988	Dave Appleton
1956–59	Jim Shoulders	1973	Larry Mahan	1982	Chris Lybbert	1989	Ty Murray[1]
1960	Harry Tompkins	1974	Tom Ferguson	1983	Roy Cooper		
1961	Benny Reynolds	1975	Leo Camarillo and	1984	Dee Pickett		
1962	Tom Nesmith		Tom Ferguson	1985	Lewis Field		

1. 1990 championship scheduled December 1990 after *Information Please Almanac* went to press.

TRACK AND FIELD

Running, jumping, hurdling and throwing weights—track and field sports, in other words—are as natural to young people as eating, drinking and breathing. Unorganized competition in this form of sport goes back beyond the Cave Man era. Organized competition begins with the first recorded Olympic Games in Greece, 776 B.C., when Coroebus of Elis won the only event on the program, a race of approximately 200 yards. The Olympic Games, with an ever-widening program of events, continued until "the glory that was Greece" had faded and "the grandeur that was Rome" was tarnished, and finally were abolished by decree of Emperor Theodosius I of Rome in A.D. 394. The Tailteann Games of Ireland are supposed to have antedated the first Olympic Games by some centuries, but we have no records of the specific events and winners thereof.

Professional contests of speed and strength were popular at all times and in many lands, but the widespread competition of amateur athletes in track and field sports is a comparatively modern development. The first organized amateur athletic meet of record was sponsored by the Royal Military Academy at Woolwich, England, in 1849. Oxford and Cambridge track and field rivalry began in 1864, and the English amateur championships were established in 1866. In the United States such organizations as the New York Athletic Club and the Olympic Club of San Francisco conducted track and field meets in the 1870s, and a few colleges joined to sponsor a meet in 1874. The success of the college meet led to the formation of the Intercollegiate Association of Amateur Athletes of America and the holding of an annual set of championship games beginning in 1876. The Amateur Athletic Union, organized in 1888, has been the ruling body in American amateur athletics since that time. In 1980, The Athletics Congress of the U.S.A. took over the governing of track and field from the A.A.U.

WORLD RECORDS—MEN

(Through Sept. 1, 1990)
Recognized by the International Athletic Federation.
The I.A.A.F. decided late in 1976 not to recognize records in yards except for the one-mile run.
The I.A.A.F. also requires automatic timing for all records for races of 400 meters or less.

Event	Record	Holder	Home Country	Where Made	Date
Running					
100 m	0:09.92	Carl Lewis	United States	Seoul, South Korea	Sept. 24, 1988
200 m	0:19.72	Pietro Mennea	Italy	Mexico City	Sept. 17, 1979
400 m	0:43.29	Butch Reynolds	United States	Indianapolis, Ind.	Aug. 17, 1988
800 m	1:41.8	Sebastian Coe	England	Florence, Italy	June 10, 1981
1,000 m	2:12.40	Sebastian Coe	England	Oslo, Norway	July 11, 1981
1,500 m	3:29.45	Said Aouita	Morocco	Berlin	August 23, 1985
1 mile	3:46.31	Steve Cram	Great Britain	Oslo	July 27, 1985
2,000 m	4:50.81	Said Aouita	Morocco	Paris	July 16, 1987
3,000 m	7:29.45	Said Aouita	Morocco	Cologne, W. Germany	Aug. 20, 1989
3,000 m steeplechase	8:05.35	Peter Koech	Kenya	Stockholm	July 3, 1989
5,000 m	12:58.39	Said Aouita	Morocco	Rome	July 22, 1987
10,000 m	27:08.23	Arturo Barrios	Mexico	Berlin	Aug. 18, 1989
25,000 m	1:13:55.8	Toshihiko Seko	Japan	Christchurch, N.Z.	March 22, 1981
30,000 m	1:29:18.8	Toshihiko Seko	Japan	Christchurch, N.Z.	March 22, 1981
20,000 m	57:24.2	Jos Hermans	Netherlands	Papandal, Neth.	May 1, 1976
1 hour	13 mi. 24 yd	Jos Hermans	Netherlands	Papandal, Neth.	May 1, 1976
Marathon	2:06.50	Belayneh Densimo	Ethiopia	Rotterdam	April 17, 1988
Walking					
20,000 m	1:18:39.9	Ernesto Canto	Mexico	Fana, Norway	May 5, 1984
2 hours	17 mi. 1,092 yd	Ralph Kowalsky	East Germany	East Berlin	March 28, 1982
30,000 m	2:06:27.0	Maurizio Damilano	Italy	Milanese, Italy	May 5, 1985
50,000 m	3:41.39	Raul Gonzales	Mexico	Bergen, Norway	May 25, 1979
Hurdles					
110 m	0:12.92	Roger Kingdom	United States	Berlin	Aug. 16, 1989
400 m	0:47.02	Edwin Moses	United States	Koblenz, W. Ger.	Aug. 31, 1983
Relay Races					
400 m (4×100)	0:37.83	Olympic Team	United States	Los Angeles, Ca.	Aug. 11, 1984
800 m (4×200)	1:19.38	Santa Monica Track Club	United States	Koblenz, W. Germany	Aug. 23, 1989
		(Danny Everett, Leroy Burrell, Floyd Heard, Carl Lewis)			
1,600 m (4×400)	2:56.16	National Team	United States	Mexico City	Oct. 20, 1968
		(Vince Matthews, Ron Freeman, Larry James, Lee Evans)			
1,600 m (4×400)	2:56.16	Olympic Team	United States	Seoul, South Korea	Oct. 1, 1988
3,200 m (4×800)	7:03.89	National Team	Britain	London	Aug. 30, 1982
		(Peter Elliot, Garry Cook, Steve Cram, Sebastian Coe)			

Field Events

High Jump	8 ft 0 in.	Javier Sotomayor	Cuba	San Juan, P.R.	July 29, 1989
Long jump	29 ft 2 1/2 in.	Bob Beamon	United States	Mexico City	Oct 18, 1968
Triple Jump	58 ft 11 1/2 in.	Willie Banks	Los Angeles, Calif.	Indianapolis	June 16, 1985
Pole vault	19 ft 10 1/2 in.	Sergey Bubka	U.S.S.R.	Niece, France	July 9, 1988
Shot-put	75 ft 10 1/4 in.	Randy Barnes	United States	Los Angeles	May 20, 1990
Discus throw	243 ft 0 in.	Juergen Schult	East Germany	Neubrandenburg	June 6, 1986
Hammer throw	284 ft 7 in.	Yuriy Syedikh	U.S.S.R.	Stuttgart	Aug. 28, 1986
Javelin throw	298 ft 6 in.	Steve Backley	Great Britain	London	July 20, 1990
Decathlon	8,798pts.	Jurgen Hingsen	W. Germany	Mannheim, W. Ger.	June 8–9, 1984

WORLD RECORDS—WOMEN

(Through Sept. 1, 1990—includes 1988 Summer Olympic Records)

Event	Record	Holder	Home Country	Where Made	Date
Running					
100 m	0:10.49	Florence Griffith-Joyner	United States	Indianapolis, Ind.	July 16, 1988
200 m	0:21.56	Florence Griffith-Joyner	United States	Seoul, South Korea	Oct. 1, 1988
400 m	0:47.60	Martina Koch	East Germany	Canberra	Oct. 6, 1985
800 m	1:53.28	Jarmila Kratochvilova	Czechoslovakia	Munich, W. Ger.	July 26, 1983
1,500 m	3:52.47	Tatyana Kazankina	U.S.S.R.	Zurich, Switz.	Aug. 13, 1980
1 mile	4:15.61	Paula Ivan	Romania	Nice, Italy	July 10, 1989
3,000 m	8:22.62	Tatyana Kazankina	U.S.S.R.	Moscow	Aug. 26, 1984
5,000 m	14:37.33	Ingrid Kristiansen	Norway	Stockholm	Aug. 5, 1986
10,000 m	30:13.74	Ingrid Kristiansen	Norway	Oslo	July 5, 1986
Marathon	2:21:06.0	Ingrid Kristiansen	Norway	London	April 21, 1985
Walking					
5,000 m	20:07.52	Beate Anders	East Germany	Rostock	June 23, 1990
10,000 m	41:46.21	Nadyezhda Ryashkina	Soviet Union	Seattle, Wash.	July 24, 1990
Hurdles					
100-m hurdles	0:12.25	Ginka Zagorcheva	Bulgaria	Greece	August 8, 1987
400 m	0:53.33	Maria Stepanova	U.S.S.R.	Stuttgart	Aug. 28, 1986
Relay Races					
400 m (4×100)	0:41.53	East Germany	E. Germany	Berlin, E. Ger.	July 31, 1983
800 m (4×200)	1:28.15	East Germany	E. Germany	Jena, E. Ger.	Aug. 9, 1980
1,600 m (4×400)	3:15.18	Soviet Union	Soviet Union	Seoul, South Korea	Oct. 1, 1988
3,200 m (4×800)	7:52.3	U.S.S.R.	U.S.S.R.	Podolsk, U.S.S.R.	Aug. 16, 1976
Field Events					
High jump	6 ft 10 1/4 in.	Stefka Kostadinova	Bulgaria	Rome	August 30, 1987
Long jump	24 ft 8 1/4 in.	Galina Chistyakova	Soviet Union	Leningrad	June 11, 1988
Triple jump	45 ft 5 1/4 in.	Sheila Hudson	United States	San Jose	June 26, 1987
Shot-put	74 ft 3 in.	Natalya Lisovskaya	U.S.S.R.	Moscow	June 7, 1987
Discus throw	252 ft 0 in.	Gabriele Reinsch	East Germany	Neubrandenburg, E. Germany	July 9, 1988
Javelin throw	262 ft 5 in.	Petra Felke	East Germany	Potsdam	Sept. 9, 1988
Heptathlon	7,291 pts	Jackie Joyner-Kersee	United States	Seoul, South Korea	Sept. 24, 1988

AMERICAN RECORDS—MEN

(Through Sept. 1, 1990)
Officially approved by The Athletics Congress.

Event	Record	Holder	Where Made	Date
Running				
100 m	0:09.92	Carl Lewis	Seoul, South Korea	Sept. 24, 1988
200 m	0:19.75	Carl Lewis	Indianapolis, Ind.	June 19, 1983
200 m	0:19.75	Jue De Loach	Seoul, South Korea	Sept. 28, 1988
400 m	0:43.29	Butch Reynolds	Indianapolis, Ind.	Aug. 17, 1988
800 m	1:42.60	Johnny Gray	Koblenz, W. Ger.	Aug. 29, 1985
1,000 m	2:13.9	Richard Wohlhuter	Oslo, Norway	July 30, 1974
1,500 m	3:29.77	Sydney Maree	Cologne, W. Ger.	Aug. 25, 1985
1 mile	3:47.69	Steve Scott	Oslo, Norway	July 7, 1982
2,000 m	4:54.71	Steve Scott	Ingelhem, W. Ger.	Aug. 31, 1982
3,000 m	7:35.84	Doug Padilla	Oslo, Norway	July 9, 1983
5,000 m	13:01.15	Sydney Maree	Oslo, Norway	July 27, 1985
10,000 m	27:20.56	Mark Nenow	Brussels	Sept. 5, 1986
20,000 m	58:15.0	Bill Rodgers	Boston, Mass.	Aug. 9, 1977
25,000 m	1:14:11.8	Bill Rodgers	Saratoga, Cal.	Feb. 21, 1979
30,000 m	1:31:49.0	Bill Rodgers	Saratoga, Cal.	Feb. 21, 1979

| 1 hour | 12 mi., 1351 yds | Bill Rodgers | Boston, Mass. | Aug. 9, 1977 |
| 3,000-m steeplechase | 8:09.17 | Henry Marsh | Koblenz, W. Ger. | Aug. 29, 1985 |

Hurdles

| 110 m | 0:12.92 | Roger Kingdom | Berlin | Aug. 16, 1989 |
| 400 m | 0:47.02 | Edwin Moses | Koblenz, W. Ger. | Aug. 31, 1983 |

Relay Races

400 m (4×100)	0:37.83	U.S. Olympic Team	Los Angeles, Cal.	Aug. 11, 1984
800 m (4×200)	1:20.26	Southern California	Tempe, Ariz.	May 27, 1978
1,600 m (4×400)	2:56.16	U.S. Olympic Team	Seoul, South Korea	Oct. 1, 1988
3,200 m (4×800)	7:06.50	Santa Monica Track Club	Walnut	Apr. 26, 1986

Field Events

High jump	7 ft 10 in.	Hollis Conway	Norman, Okla.	July 30, 1989
Long jump	29 ft 2 1/2 in.	Bob Beamon	Mexico City	Oct. 18, 1968
Triple jump	58 ft 11 1/2 in.	Willie Banks	Indianapolis, Ind.	June 16, 1985
Pole vault	19 ft 6 1/2 in.	Joe Dial	Norman	June 18, 1987
Shot-put	75 ft 10 1/4 in.	Randy Barnes	Los Angeles	May 20, 1990
Discus throw	237 ft 4 in.	Ben Plucknett	Stockholm, Swe.	July 7, 1981
Javelin throw	280 ft 1 in.	Tom Petranoff	Helsinki	July 7, 1986
Hammer throw	268 ft 8 in.	Judd Logan	University Park, Pa.	April 23, 1988
Decathlon	8,634 pts	Bruce Jenner	Montreal, Can.	July 29–30, 1976

AMERICAN RECORDS—WOMEN

(Through Sept. 1, 1990)

Event	Record	Holder	Where Made	Date

Running

100 m	0:10.49	Florence Griffith-Joyner	Indianapolis, Ind.	July 16, 1988
200 m	0:21.56	Florence Griffith-Joyner	Seoul, South Korea	Oct. 1, 1988
400 m	0:48.83	Valerie Brisco-Hooks	Los Angeles, Cal.	Aug. 6, 1984
800 m	1:56.90	Mary Decker Slaney	Bern	Aug. 16, 1985
1,500 m	3:57.12	Mary Decker Slaney	Stockholm, Swe.	July 26, 1983
1000 m	2:34.8	Mary Decker Slaney	Eugene, Ore.	July 4, 1985
1 mile	4:16.71	Mary Decker Slaney	Zurich	Aug. 21, 1985
3,000 m	8:29.69	Mary Decker Slaney	Cologne	Aug. 25, 1985
5,000 m	14:59.99	PattiSue Plummer	Stockholm	July 3, 1989
10,000 m	31:35.3	Mary Decker Slaney	Eugene, Ore.	July 16, 1982

Hurdles

| 100 m hurdles | 0:12.61 | Jackie Joyner-Kersee | San Jose, Calif. | May 28, 1988 |
| 400 m hurdles | 0:53.37 | Sandra Farmer-Patrick | New York | July 23, 1989 |

Relay Races

400 m (4×100)	0:41.61	U.S. National Team	Colorado Springs, Col.	July 3, 1983
800 m (4×200)	1:32.57	Louisiana State	Des Moines, Iowa	April 28, 1989
1,600 m (4×400)	3:15.51	U.S. Olympic Team	Seoul, South Korea	Oct. 1, 1988

Field Events

High jump	6 ft 8 in.	Louise Ritter	Austin, Tex.	July 9, 1988
Long jump	24 ft. 5 1/2 in.	Jackie Joyner-Kersee	Indianapolis	August 12, 1987
Triple jump	46 ft. 0 3/4 in.	Sheila Hudson	Durham, N.C.	June 2, 1990
Shot-put	66 ft. 2 1/2 in.	Ramon Pagel	San Diego, Calif.	June 25, 1988
Discus throw	216 ft 10 in.	Carol Cady	San Jose, Calif.	May 31, 1986
Javelin throw	227 ft 5 in.	Kate Schmidt	Furth, W. Ger.	Sept. 10, 1977
Heptathlon	7,291 pts	Jackie Joyner-Kersee	Seoul, South Korea	Sept. 23–24, 1988

HISTORY OF THE RECORD FOR THE MILE RUN

Time	Athlete	Country	Year	Location
4:36.5	Richard Webster	England	1865	England
4:29.0	William Chinnery	England	1868	England
4:28.8	Walter Gibbs	England	1868	England
4:26.0	Walter Slade	England	1874	England
4:24.5	Walter Slade	England	1875	London

4:23.2	Walter George	England	1880	London
4:21.4	Walter George	England	1882	London
4:18.4	Walter George	England	1884	Birmingham, England
4:18.2	Fred Bacon	Scotland	1894	Edinburgh, Scotland
4:17.0	Fred Bacon	Scotland	1895	London
4:15.6	Thomas Conneff	United States	1895	Travers Island, N.Y.
4:15.4	John Paul Jones	United States	1911	Cambridge, Mass.
4:14.4	John Paul Jones	United States	1913	Cambridge, Mass.
4:12.6	Norman Taber	United States	1915	Cambridge, Mass.
4:10.4	Paavo Nurmi	Finland	1923	Stockholm
4:09.2	Jules Ladoumegue	France	1931	Paris
4:07.6	Jack Lovelock	New Zealand	1933	Princeton, N.J.
4:06.8	Glenn Cunningham	United States	1934	Princeton, N.J.
4:06.4	Sydney Wooderson	England	1937	London
4:06.2	Gundar Hägg	Sweden	1942	Göteborg, Sweden
4:06.2	Arne Andersson	Sweden	1942	Stockholm
4:04.6	Gunder Hägg	Sweden	1942	Stockholm
4:02.6	Arne Andersson	Sweden	1943	Göteborg, Sweden
4:01.6	Arne Andersson	Sweden	1944	Malmö, Sweden
4:01.4	Gunder Hägg	Sweden	1945	Malmö, Sweden
3:59.4	Roger Bannister	England	1954	Oxford, England
3:58.0	John Landy	Australia	1954	Turku, Finland
3:57.2	Derek Ibbotson	England	1957	London
3:54.5	Herb Elliott	Australia	1958	Dublin
3:54.4	Peter Snell	New Zealand	1962	Wanganui, N.Z.
3:54.1	Peter Snell	New Zealand	1964	Auckland, N.Z.
3:53.6	Michel Jazy	France	1965	Rennes, France
3:51.3	Jim Ryun	United States	1966	Berkeley, Calif.
3:51.1	Jim Ryun	United States	1967	Bakersfield, Calif.
3:51.0	Filbert Bayi	Tanzania	1975	Kingston, Jamaica
3:49.4	John Walker	New Zealand	1975	Göteborg, Sweden
3:49.0	Sebastian Coe	England	1979	Oslo
3:48.8	Steve Ovett	England	1980	Oslo
3:48.53	Sebastian Coe	England	1981	Zurich, Switzerland
3:48.40	Steve Ovett	England	1981	Koblenz, W. Ger.
3:47.33	Sebastian Coe	England	1981	Brussels
3:46.31	Steve Cram	England	1985	Oslo

TOP TEN WORLD'S FASTEST OUTDOOR MILES

Time	Athlete	Country	Date	Location
3:46.31	Steve Cram	England	July 27, 1985	Oslo
3:47.33	Sebastian Coe	England	Aug. 28, 1981	Brussels
3:47.69	Steve Scott	United States	July 7, 1982	Oslo
3:47.79	Jose Gonzalez	Spain	July 27, 1985	Oslo
3:48.40	Steve Ovett	England	Aug. 26, 1981	Koblenz, W. Ger.
3:48.53	Sebastian Coe	England	Aug. 19, 1981	Zurich
3:48.53	Steve Scott	United States	June 26, 1982	Oslo
3:48.8	Steve Ovett	England	July 1, 1980	Oslo
3:48.83	Sydney Maree	United States	Sept. 9, 1981	Rieti, Italy
3:48.85	Sydney Maree[1]	United States	June 26, 1982	Oslo

1. Finished second. NOTE: Professional marks not included.

TOP TEN WORLD'S FASTEST INDOOR MILES

Time	Athlete	Country	Date	Location
3:49.78	Eamonn Coghlan	Ireland	Feb. 27, 1983	East Rutherford, N.J.
3:50.6	Eamonn Coghlan	Ireland	Feb. 20, 1981	San Diego
3:50.94	Marcus O'Sullivan	Ireland	Feb. 13, 1988	East Rutherford, N.J.
3:51.2	Ray Flynn[1]	Ireland	Feb. 27, 1983	East Rutherford, N.J.
3:51.66	Marcus O'Sullivan	Ireland	Feb. 10, 1989	East Rutherford, N.J.
3:51.8	Steve Scott[1]	United States	Feb. 20, 1981	San Diego
3:52.28	Steve Scott[2]	United States	Feb. 27, 1983	East Rutherford, N.J.
3:52:30	Frank O'Mara	Ireland	Feb. , 1986	New York
3:52.37	Eamonn Coughlan	Ireland	Feb. 9, 1985	East Rutherford, N.J.
3:52.40	Sydney Maree	United States	Feb. 9, 1985	East Rutherford, N.J.

1. Finished second. 2. Finished third.

TOP TEN POLE VAULT DISTANCES

(Figures from *Track & Field News.*)

Fiberglas Poles

1988	Sergey Bubka	19 ft 10 1/2 in.	1984	Thierry Vigneron	19 ft 4 3/4 in.
1987	Sergey Bubka	19 ft 9 1/4 in.	1984	Sergey Bubka	19 ft 4 1/4 in.
1986	Sergey Bubka	19 ft 8 1/2 in.	1984	Sergey Bubka	19 ft 3 1/2 in.
1985	Sergey Bubka	19 ft 8 1/4 in.	1984	Sergey Bubka	19 ft 2 1/4 in.
1984	Sergey Bubka	19 ft 5 3/4 in.	1989	Rodion Gataullin	19 ft 2 1/4 in.

THE ATHLETICS CONGRESS NATIONAL CHAMPIONSHIPS INDOOR—1990

(Madison Square Garden, New York, February 23, 1990)

Men's Events

(Running events in meters)

55 m—Brian Cooper, Florida Clippers	0:06.07
400 m—Michael Johnson, Baylor University	0:47.43
500 m—David Patrick, Flo Jo International	1:02.52
800 m—Ray Brown, Nike Atlantic Coast Club	1:47.52
Mile—Steve Scott, Asics Tiger Track Club	3:57.35
3000 m—Doug Padilla, Nike West	7:50.27
55 m hurdles—Anthony Dees, Florida Clippers	0:07.03
5000 m walk—Tim Barrett, Top Form Lions/Canada	19:42.90
4 × 400 m relay—Florida Clippers	3:12.70
4 × 800 m relay—Boston A.A.	7:40.03
High jump—Hollis Conway, Nike International	7 ft 8 1/2 in.
Pole vault—Istvan Bagyula, George Mason University	18 ft 8 1/2 in.
Long jump—Gordon McKee, San Marcos, Texas	26 ft 0 1/4 in.
Triple jump—Kenny Harrison, Accusplit Sports Club	55 ft 0 in.
Shot-put—Randy Barnes, Mazda Track Club	65 ft 6 in.
35-pound weight throw—Lance Deal, New York A.C.	78 ft 0 1/4 in.

Team—1. New York Athletic Club, 22 points
  2. Florida Clippers, 19
  3. Mazda Track Club, 10

Women's Events

(Running events in meters)

55 m—Michelle Finn, Atoms Track Club	0:06.61
200 m—Grace Jackson, Jamaica	0:23.53
400 m—Diane Dixon, Nike International	0:53.50
800 m—Joetta Clark, Nike South	2:04.32
Mile—Doina Melinte, Romania	4:27.62
3000 m—Lynn Jennings, Nike International	8:40.45
3000 m walk—Teresa Vaill, Natural Sport	12:53.17
4 × 400-meters relay—Atoms Track Club	3:48.96
High jump—Jan Wohlschlag, Nike International	6 ft 4 in.
Long jump—Jacinta Bartholomew, Atoms Track Club	21 ft 2 1/2 in.
Shot put—Ramona Pagel, Mazda Track Club	60 ft 4 1/4 in.
20-pound weight throw—Virginia Young, St. John's University	59 ft 11 3/4 in.

Team—1. Nike International, 26 points
  2. Atoms Track Club, 16 1/2
  3. Arizona State University, 8

THE ATHLETICS CONGRESS NATIONAL CHAMPIONSHIPS OUTDOOR

(June 14-16, 1990, Cerritos College, Norwalk, Calif.)

Men's Events

(Running events in meters)

100 m—Carl Lewis, Santa Monica Track Club	0:10.05
200 m—Michael Johnson, Florida Clippers	0:19.90
400 m—Steve Lewis, Santa Monica Track Club	0:44.75
800 m—Mark Everett, Nike International	1:45.01
1500 m—Joe Falcon, Asics Tiger Track Club	3:37.49
3000 m steeplechase—Brian Diemer, Nike International	8:24.79
5000 m—Doug Padilla, Nike West	13:41.85
10,000 m—Steve Plasencia, Nike West	28:11.41
110 m hurdles—Roger Kingdom, unattached	0:13.22
400 m hurdles—David Patrick, Flo-Jo International	0:48.79
20,000 m walk—Tim Lewis, Reebok Racing Club	1:27:28.00
High jump—Hollis Conway, Nike International	7 ft 8 3/4 in.
Pole vault—Earl Bell, Pacific Coast Club	18 ft 10 in.
Long jump—Michael Powell, Footlocker Slamfest	27 ft 1/2 in.
Triple jump—Kenny Harrison, Mizuno Track Club	56 ft 3 1/4 in.
Shot-put—Jim Doehring, Reebok Racing Club	69 ft 6 3/4 in.
Discus—Kamy Keshmiri, Reebok Racing Club	204 ft 5 in.
Hammer throw—Ken Flax, N.Y. Athletic Club	249 ft 6 in.
Javelin throw—Vince Labosky, University of Kansas	261 ft 3 in.
Decathlon—David Johnson, Nike International	8,600 points

Team—1. Santa Monica Track Club, 77
  2. Nike International, 71 1/4
  3. New York Athletic Club, 55 1/4

Women's Events

(Running events in meters)

100 m—Michelle Finn, Atoms Track Club	0:11.20
200 m—Grace Jackson, unattached	0:22.48
400 m—Maicel Malone, Nike Coast Track Club	0:51.23
800 m—Meredith Rainey, Atoms Track Club	2:00.70
1500 m—Suzy Favor, University of Wisconsin	4:13.47
3000 m—Lynn Jennings, Nike International	8:51.97
5000 m—Patti Sue Plumer, Nike International	15:45.67
10,000 m—Colette Murphy, Nike Indiana	32:20.92
100 m hurdles—LaVonna Martin, Reebok Running Club	:12.90
400 m hurdles—Janeene Vickers, World Class Athletic Club	0:54.80
10,000 m walk—Debbi Lawrence, Parkside Athletic Club	46:14.4
High jump—Yolanda Henry, Mazda Track Club	6 ft 5 in.
Long jump—Jackie Joyner-Kersee, McDonald's Track Club	23 ft 2 3/4 in.
Triple jump—Sheila Hudson, Mizuno Track Club	46 ft 2 in.
Shot-put—Connie Price, Nike North	60 ft 10 3/4 in.
Discus—Connie Price, Nike North	191 ft 6 in.
Javelin throw—Karin Smith, Nike Coast	206 ft 3 in.
Heptathlon—Cindy Greiner, Nike Coast	6,262 points

Team—1. Nike International, 79
  2. Nike Coast Track Club, 72
  3. Reebok Racing Club, 42

N.C.A.A. CHAMPIONSHIPS—1990

INDOOR

(Indianapolis, Ind., March 9-10, 1990)

Men's Events

55 m—Andre Cason, Texas	0:06.07
200 m—Michael Johnson, Baylor	0:20.72
400 m—Gabriel Luke, Rice	0:45.73
800 m—Mark Everett, Florida	1:47.45
Mile—Bob Whelan, Kentucky	3:58.77
3,000 m—Reuben Reina, Nebraska	7:56.62
5,000 m—Jonah Koech, Iowa State	13:37.94
55 m hurdles—Tony Li, Washington State	0:07.13
4 × 400 m relay—Baylor	3:06.49
4 × 800 m relay—Villanova	7:19.24
High jump—Brian Brown, Northwestern	7 ft 8 in.
Pole vault—Istvan Bagyula, George Mason	18 ft 6 1/2 in.
Long jump—Leroy Burrell, Houston	27 ft 0 in.
Triple jump—Edrick Floreal, Arkansas	54 ft 3 1/4 in.
Shot put—C.J. Hunter, Penn State	64 ft 4 1/4 in.
35-pound weight throw—Per Karlsson, Brigham Young	67 ft 9 3/4 in.
Team—1. Arkansas, 44 points	
2. Florida, 29 points	
3. Tie: Texas A&M & George Mason, 26 points	

Division II champion—St. Augustine, Raleigh, N.C.
Division III champion—Lincoln, University, Lincoln University, Pa.

Women's Events

55 m—Carlette Guidry, Texas	0:06.66
200 m—Carlette Guidry, Texas	0:23.28
400 m—Maicel Malone, Arizona State	0:51.97
800 m—Meredith Rainey, Harvard	2:02.77
Mile—Suzy Favor, Wisconsin	4:38.19
3,000 m—Suzy Favor, Wisconsin	9:02.30
5,000 m—Valerie McGovern, Kentucky	15:48.17
55 m hurdles—Lynda Tolbert, Arizona State	0:07:44
4 × 400 m relay—Texas	3:32.01
4 × 800 m relay—Villanova	8:31.95
High jump—Sissy Costner, Auburn	6 ft 2 in.
Long jump—Sheila Hudson, Cal-Berkeley	21 ft 9 1/2 in.
Triple jump—Sheila Hudson, Cal-Berkeley	45 ft 9 in.
Shotput—Tracie Millet, UCLA	51 ft 11 in.
Team—1. Texas, 50 points	
2. Wisconsin, 26	
3. Florida, 20 1/2	

Division II champion—Abilene Christian University, Abilene, Texas.
Division III champion—Christopher Newport College, Newport News, Va.

OUTDOOR

(Durham, N.C., May 30-June 2, 1990)

Men's Events

100 m—Leroy Burrell, Houston	0:09.94
200 m—Michael Johnson, Baylor	0:20.31
400 m—Steve Lewis, UCLA	0:45.19
800 m—Mark Everett, Florida	1:44.70
1500 m—Bob Kennedy, Indiana	3:40.42
3000 m—steeplechase—Mark Croghan, Ohio St.	8:36.19
5000 m—John Trautman, Georgetown	14:07.47
10,000 m—Shannon Butler, Montana St.	28:38.45
110 m hurdles—Chris Lancaster, Indiana St.	0:13.45
400 m hurdles—McClinton Neal, Texas-Arlington	0:49.23
400 m relay—Alabama	0:38.37

1,600 m relay—Baylor	3:01.86
High jump—Charles Austin, SW Texas State	7 ft 7 3/4 in.
Long jump—Llewellyn Starks, Louisiana St.	26 ft 5 3/4 in.
Triple jump—Edrick Floreal, Arkansas	56 ft 6 1/2 in.
Discus—Kamy Keshmiri, Nevada-Reno	207 ft 1 in.
Shot put—Dhane Collins, Arizona St.	66 ft 3 1/4 in.
Javelin—Patrik Boden, Texas	261 ft 10 in.
Hammer throw—Scott McGee, Oregon	217 ft 8 in.
Decathlon—Drew Fucci, SW Texas State	7,922 points
Team—1. Louisiana State, 44 points	
2. Arkansas, 36	
3. Baylor, 34	

DIVISION II—St. Augustine's College, Raleigh, N.C.
DIVISION III—Lincoln University, Lincoln University, Pa.

Women's Events

100 m—Esther Jones, Louisiana State	0:11.14
200 m—Esther Jones, Louisiana State	0:22.49
400 m—Maicel Malone, Arizona State	0:51.13
800 m—Suzy Favor, Wisconsin	1:59.11
1500 m—Suzy Favor, Wisconsin	4:08.26
3000 m—Sonia O'Sullivan, Villanova	8:56.27
5000 m—Valerie McGovern, Kentucky	15:45.72
10,000 m—Janet Haskin, Kansas State	33:49.72
100 m hurdles—Lynda Tolbert, Arizona State	0:12.84
400 m hurdles—Janeene Vickers, UCLA	0:55.40
400 m relay—Louisiana State	0:43.99
1600 m relay—Florida	3:30.41
High jump—Angie Bradburn, Texas	6 ft 2 3/4 in.
Triple jump—Sheila Hudson, Cal-Berkeley	46 ft 0 3/4 in.
Long jump—Sheila Hudson, Cal-Berkeley	22 ft 1 in.
Shot put—Tracie Millet, UCLA	53 ft 7 in.
Discus throw—Tracie Millet, UCLA	193 ft 9 in.
Javelin throw—Ashley Selman, Southern California	186 ft 3 in.
Heptathlon—Gea Johnson, Arizona State	6,132 points
Team—1. Louisiana State, 53 points	
2. UCLA, 46	
3. Wisconsin, 42	

DIVISION II—California Polytechnic University, San Luis Obispo, Calif.
DIVISION III—University of Wisconsin-Oshkosh, Oshkosh, Wisc.

U.S. CROSS COUNTRY CHAMPIONSHIPS

Golden Gate Park San Francisco, California November 25, 1989

Men—10,000 meters

1. Pat Porter (Athletics West), 32:08
2. Tim Hacker (Athletics West), 32:19
3. Robert Kempainen (Nike Boston), 32:33
4. Steve Plasencia (Athletics West), 32:36
5. Bill Reifsnyder (Unattached, Albuquerque, N.M.), 32:38

Women—6,000 meters

1. Lynn Jennings (Athletics West), 21:11
2. Elaine Van Blunk (Nike Running Room), 21:16
3. Gwyn Hardesty (Nike Boston), 21:29
4. Nan Doak-Davis (Athletics West), 21:33
5. Margaret Groos (Athletics West), 21:37

U.S. WOMEN'S MARATHON CHAMPIONSHIP

(Grandma's Marathon, Duluth, Minn., June 23, 1990)

1. Jane Welzel (Colorado), 2:33:25
2. Deborah Raunig (Montana), 2:34:34
3. Gordon Bloch (New York), 2:35:48
4. Janis Klecker (Minnesota), 2:40:08
5. Janice Ettle (Minnesota), 2:40:21

SPORTS ORGANIZATIONS AND BUREAUS

(Note: Addresses are subject to change)

Amateur Athletic Union of 'the U.S. 3400 West 86th St., P.O. Box 68207, Indianapolis, Ind. 46268-0207

Amateur Hockey Association of the U.S. Inc.; USA Hockey 2997 Broadmoor Valley Road, Colorado Springs, Colo. 80906

Amateur Softball Association. 2801 N.E. 50th St., Oklahoma City, Okla. 73111

American Amateur Racquetball Association. 815 North Weber St., Suite 101, Colorado Springs, Colo. 80903

American Association of Professional Baseball Clubs. P.O. Box 608, 3860 Broadway, Grove City, Ohio 43123

American Bowling Congress. 5301 South 76th St., Greendale, Wis. 53129-0500

American Hockey League. 425 Union St., Springfield, Mass. 01089

American Horse Shows Association. 220 E. 42nd St., New York, N.Y. 10017-5806

American Kennel Club Inc. 51 Madison Ave., New York, N.Y. 10010

American League (baseball). 350 Park Ave., New York, N.Y. 10022

American Sportcasters Association, The, 5 Beekman St., New York, N.Y. 10038

Athletics Congress/USA, The. 200 South Capital Ave., Suite 140, Indianapolis, Ind. 46225.

Baseball Hall of Fame. P.O. Box 590, Cooperstown, N.Y. 13326

Football Hall of Fame (college). Kings Island, Ohio 45034

(Big Ten) Conference (1896). 1111 Plaza Dr., Suite 600, Schaumburg, Ill. 60173-4990

International Game Fish Association. 3000 East Las Olas Blvd., Fort Lauderdale, Fla. 33316

International League of Professional Baseball Clubs, Inc. Box 608, Grove City, Ohio 43123

International Olympic Committee. Chateau de Vidy, 1007 Lausanne, Switzerland

International Tennis Hall of Fame. National Historic Landmark, Newport Casino, 194 Bellevue Ave., Newport, R.I. 02840

Little League Baseball. P.O. Box 3485 Williamsport, Pa. 17701

National Archery Association. 1750 E. Boulder St., Colorado Springs, Colo. 80909

National Association for Stock Car Auto Racing. P.O. Box 2875, Daytona Beach, Fla. 32115—2875

National Association of Intercollegiate Athletics. 1221 Baltimore St., Kansas City, Mo. 64105

National Baseball Congress. P.O. Box 1420, Wichita; Kan. 67201

National Collegiate Athletic Association. 6201 College Blvd., Overland Park, Kan. 66211—2422

National Duckpin Bowling Congress. 3703 Brownbrook Court, Randallstown, Md. 21133

National Field Archery Association. 31407 Outer I-10, Redlands, Calif. 92373

National Football Foundation. 1865 Palmer Ave., Larchmont, N.Y. 10538. See also: Football Hall of Fame (college)

National Football League. 410 Park Ave., New York, N.Y. 10022

National Hockey League. 1155 Metcalfe St., Suite 960, Montreal, Que., Canada H3B 2W2

National Horseshoe Pitchers Association. Box 278, Munroe Falls, Ohio 44262

National Hot Rod Association. P.O. Box 5555, Glendora, Calif. 91740

National Junior College Athletic Association. P.O. Box 7305, Colorado Springs, Colo. 80933—7305

National Rifle Association of America. 1600 Rhode Island Ave., N.W., Washington, D.C. 20036

National Shuffleboard Association. 3816 Norbrook Dr., Columbus, Ohio 43220

National Skeet Shooting Association. P.O. Box 680007, San Antonio, Tex. 78268-0007

New York Racing Association. P.O. Box 90, Jamaica, N.Y. 11417

New York State Athletic Commission (boxing and wrestling). 270 Broadway, New York, N.Y. 10007

North American Yacht Racing Union. See United States Yacht Racing Union

PGA TOUR, Inc., 112 TPC Blvd., Sawgrass, Ponte Vedra, Fla. 32082

Pro Football Hall of Fame. Canton, Ohio 44708

Roller Skating Associations. P.O. Box 81846, Lincoln, Neb. 68501

Thoroughbred Racing Assns. of N. America. 3000 Marcus Ave., Lake Success, N.Y. 11042

United States Amateur Confederation of Roller Skating. P.O. Box 6579 Lincoln, Neb. 68506

United States Auto Club. 4910 West 16th St., Speedway, Ind. 46224

United States Gymnastics Federation. 201 S. Capitol, Ste. 300, Indianapolis, Ind. 46225

United States-International Professional Shuffleboard 1901 S.W. 87th Terrace, Fort Lauderdale, Fla. 33324

U.S. Baseball Federation. 2160 Greenwood Ave., Trenton, N.J. 08609

U.S. Chess Federation. 186 Route 9W, New Windsor, N.Y. 12550

U.S. Cycling Federation. 1750 East Boulder St., Colorado Springs, Colo. 80909

U.S. Fencing Assn. 1750 E. Boulder St., Colorado Springs, Colo. 80909

U.S. Figure Skating Association. 20 First Street, Colorado Springs, Colo. 80906

U.S. Golf Association. Golf House, P.O. Box 708, Far Hills, N.J. 07931-0708

U.S. Handball Association. 930 N. Benton Ave., Tucson, Ariz. 85711

U.S. Olympic Committee. 1750 East Boulder Street, Colorado Springs, Colo. 80909

U.S. Orienteering Federation. Box 1444, Forest Park, Ga. 30051

U.S. Rowing Assn. Pan American Plaza, 201 S. Capitol Ave., Ste. 400, Indianapolis, Ind. 46225

U.S. Soccer Federation. 1750 East Boulder St., Colorado Springs, Colo. 80909—5791

U.S. Tennis Association. 1212 Avenue of the Americas, New York, N.Y. 10036

U.S. Trotting Association. 750 Michigan Ave., Columbus, Ohio 43215

U.S. Yacht Racing Union. P.O. Box 209, Goat Island, Newport, R.I. 02840

USA Amateur Boxing Federation. 1750 East Boulder St., Colorado Springs, Colo. 80909

U.S.A. Basketball. 1750 East Boulder St., Colorado Springs, Colo. 80909

Women's International Bowling Congress. 5301 S. 76th St., Greendale, Wis. 53129

TENNIS

Lawn tennis is a comparatively modern modification of the ancient game of court tennis. Major Walter Clopton Wingfield thought that something like court tennis might be played outdoors on lawns, and in December, 1873, at Nantclwyd, Wales, he introduced his new game under the name of *Sphairistike* at a lawn party. The game was a success and spread rapidly, but the name was a total failure and almost immediately disappeared when all the players and spectators began to refer to the new game as "lawn tennis." In the early part of 1874, a young lady named Mary Ewing Outerbridge returned from Bermuda to New York, bringing with her the implements and necessary equipment of the new game, which she had obtained from a British Army supply store in Bermuda. Miss Outerbridge and friends played the first game of lawn tennis in the United States on the grounds of the Staten Island Cricket and Baseball Club in the spring of 1874.

For a few years, the new game went along in haphazard fashion until about 1880, when standard measurements for the court and standard equipment within definite limits became the rule. In 1881, the U.S. Lawn Tennis Association (whose name was changed in 1975 to U.S. Tennis Association) was formed and conducted the first national championship at Newport, R.I. The international matches for the Davis Cup began with a series between the British and United States players on the courts of the Longwood Cricket Club, Chestnut Hill, Mass., in 1900, with the home players winning.

Professional tennis, which got its start in 1926 when the French star Suzanne Lenglen was paid $50,000 for a tour, received full recognition in 1968. Staid old Wimbledon, the London home of what are considered the world championships, let the pros compete. This decision ended a long controversy over open tennis and changed the format of the competition. The United States championships were also opened to the pros and the site of the event, long held at Forest Hills, N.Y., was shifted to the National Tennis Center in Flushing Meadows, N.Y., in 1978. Pro tours for men and women became worldwide in play that continued throughout the year.

DAVIS CUP CHAMPIONSHIPS

No matches in 1901, 1910, 1915–18, and 1940–45.

1900	United States 3, British Isles 0	1932	France 3, United States 2	1964	Australia 3, United States 2
1902	United States 3, British Isles 2	1933	Great Britain 3, France 2	1965	Australia 4, Spain 1
1903	British Isles 4, United States 1	1934	Great Britain 4, United States 1	1966	Australia 4, India 1
1904	British Isles 5, Belgium 0	1935	Great Britain 5, United States 0	1967	Australia 4, Spain 1
1905	British Isles 5, United States 0	1936	Great Britain 3, Australia 2	1968	United States 4, Australia 1
1906	British Isles 5, United States 0	1937	United States 4, Great Britain 1	1969	United States 5, Romania 0
1907	Australasia 3, British Isles 2	1938	United States 3, Australia 2	1970	United States 5, West Germany 0
1908	Australasia 3, United States 2	1939	Australia 3, United States 2	1971	United States 3, Romania 2
1909	Australasia 5, United States 0	1946	United States 5, Australia 0	1972	United States 3, Romania 2
1911	Australasia 5, United States 0	1947	United States 4, Australia 1	1973	Australia 5, United States 0
1912	British Isles 3, Australasia 2	1948	United States 5, Australia 0	1974	South Africa (Default by India)
1913	United States 3, British Isles 2	1949	United States 4, Australia 1	1975	Sweden 3, Czechoslovakia 2
1914	Australasia 3, United States 2	1950	Australia 4, United States 1	1976	Italy 4, Chile 1
1919	Australasia 4, British Isles 1	1951	Australia 3, United States 2	1977	Australia 3, Italy 1
1920	United States 5, Australasia 0	1952	Australia 4, United States 1	1978	United States 4, Britain 1
1921	United States 5, Japan 0	1953	Australia 3, United States 2	1979	United States 5, Italy 0
1922	United States 4, Australasia 1	1954	United States 3, Australia 2	1980	Czechoslovakia 3, Italy 2
1923	United States 4, Australasia 1	1955	Australia 5, United States 0	1981	United States 3, Argentina 1
1924	United States 5, Australasia 0	1956	Australia 5, United States 0	1982	United States 3, France 0
1925	United States 5, France 0	1957	Australia 3, United States 2	1983	Australia 3, Sweden 2
1926	United States 4, France 1	1958	United States 3, Australia 2	1984	Sweden 4, United States 1
1927	France 3, United States 2	1959	Australia 3, United States 2	1985	Sweden 3, West Germany 2
1928	France 4, United States 1	1960	Australia 4, Italy 1	1986	Australia 3, Sweden 2
1929	France 3, United States 2	1961	Australia 5, Italy 0	1987	Sweden 5, Austria 0
1930	France 4, United States 1	1962	Australia 5, Mexico 0	1988	West Germany 4, Sweden 1
1931	France 3, Great Britain 2	1963	United States 3, Australia 2	1989	West Germany 3, Sweden 2

FEDERATION CUP CHAMPIONSHIPS

World team competition for women conducted by International Lawn Tennis Federation.

1963	United States 2, Australia 1	1973	Australia 3, South Africa 0	1983	Czechoslovakia 2, West Germany 1
1964	Australia 2, United States 1	1974	Australia 2, United States 1	1984	Czechoslovakia 2, Australia 1
1965	Australia 2, United States 1	1975	Czechoslovakia 3, Australia 0	1985	Czechoslovakia 2, United States 1
1966	United States 3, West Germany 0	1976	United States 2, Australia 1	1986	United States 3, Czechoslovakia 0
1967	United States 2, Britain 0	1977	United States 2, Australia 1	1987	West Germany 2, United States 1[1]
1968	Australia 3, Netherlands 0	1978	United States 2, Australia 1	1988	Czechoslovakia 2, Soviet Union 1
1969	United States 2, Australia 1	1979	United States 3, Australia 0	1989	United States 3, Spain 0
1970	Australia 3, West Germany 0	1980	United States 3, Australia 0	1990	United States 2, Soviet Union 1
1971	Australia 3, Britain 0	1981	United States 3, Britain 0		
1972	South Africa 2, Britain 1	1982	United States 3, West Germany 0		

U.S. CHAMPIONS
Singles—Men

NATIONAL

						OPEN	
1881–87	Richard D. Sears	1919	William Johnston	1951–52	Frank Sedgman		
1888–89	Henry Slocum, Jr.	1920–25	Bill Tilden	1953	Tony Trabert	1968	Arthur Ashe
1890–92	Oliver S. Campbell	1926–27	Jean Rene Lacoste	1954	Vic Seixas	1969	Rod Laver
1893–94	Robert D. Wrenn	1928	Henri Cochet	1955	Tony Trabert	1970	Ken Rosewall
1895	Fred H. Hovey	1929	Bill Tilden	1956	Ken Rosewall	1971	Stan Smith
1896–97	Robert D. Wrenn	1930	John H. Doeg	1957	Mal Anderson	1972	Ilie Nastase
1898–		1931–32	Ellsworth Vines	1958	Ashley Cooper	1973	John Newcombe
1900	Malcolm Whitman	1933–34	Fred J. Perry	1959–60	Neale Fraser	1974	Jimmy Connors
1901–02	William A. Larned	1935	Wilmer L. Allison	1961	Roy Emerson	1975	Manuel Orantes
1903	Hugh L. Doherty	1936	Fred J. Perry	1962	Rod Laver	1976	Jimmy Connors
1904	Holcombe Ward	1937–38	Don Budge	1963	Rafael Osuna	1977	Guillermo Vilas
1905	Beals C. Wright	1939	Robert L. Riggs	1964	Roy Emerson	1978	Jimmy Connors
1906	William J. Clothier	1940	Donald McNeill	1965	Manuel Santana	1979	John McEnroe
1907–11	William A. Larned	1941	Robert L. Riggs	1966	Fred Stolle	1980–81	John McEnroe
1912–13	Maurice McLoughlin	1942	Fred Schroeder	1967	John Newcombe	1982	Jimmy Connors
		1943	Joseph Hunt	1968	Arthur Ashe	1983	Jimmy Connors
1914	R. N. Williams II	1944–45	Frank Parker	1969	Rod Laver	1984	John McEnroe
1915	William Johnston	1946–47	Jack Kramer			1985–87	Ivan Lendl
1916	R. N. William II	1948–49	Richard Gonzales			1988	Mats Wilander
1917–18	R. Lindley Murray[2]	1950	Arthur Larsen			1989	Boris Becker
						1990	Pete Sampras

Singles—Women

NATIONAL

						OPEN	
1887	Ellen F. Hansel	1906	Helen Homans	1938–40	Alice Marble	1968–69	Margaret Smith
1888–89	Bertha Townsend	1907	Evelyn Sears	1941	Sarah Palfrey		Court[3]
1890	Ellen C. Roosevelt	1908	Maud		Cooke		
1891–92	Mabel E. Cahill		Bargar–Wallach	1942–44	Pauline Betz	1968	Virginia Wade
1893	Aline M. Terry	1909–11	Hazel V.	1945	Sarah Cooke	1969–70	Margaret Court
1894	Helen R. Helwig		Hotchkiss	1946	Pauline Betz	1971–72	Billie Jean King
1895	Juliette P.	1912–14	Mary K. Browne	1947	Louise Brough	1973	Margaret Court
	Atkinson	1915–18	Molla Bjurstedt	1948–50	Margaret Osborne	1974	Billie Jean King
1896	Elisabeth H.	1919	Hazel Hotchkiss		duPont	1975–78	Chris Evert
	Moore		Wightman	1951–53	Maureen Connolly	1979	Tracy Austin
1897–98	Juliette P.	1920–22	Molla Bjurstedt	1954–55	Doris Hart	1980	Chris Evert-Lloyd
	Atkinson		Mallory	1956	Shirley Fry	1981	Tracy Austin
1899	Marion Jones	1923–25	Helen N. Wills	1957–58	Althea Gibson	1982	Chris Evert-Lloyd
1900	Myrtle McAteer	1926	Molla B. Mallory	1959	Maria Bueno	1983–84	Martina Navratilova
1901	Elisabeth H.	1927–29	Helen N. Wills	1960–61	Darlene Hard	1985	Hana Mandlikova
	Moore	1930	Betty Nuthall	1962	Margaret Smith	1986–87	Martina Navratilova
1902	Marion Jones	1931	Helen Wills Moody	1963–64	Maria Bueno	1988	Steffi Graf
1903	Elisabeth H. Moore	1932–35	Helen Jacobs	1965	Margaret Smith	1989	Steffi Graf
1904	May Sutton	1936	Alice Marble	1966	Maria Bueno	1990	Grabriela Sabatini
1905	Elisabeth H. Moore	1937	Anita Lizana	1967	Billie Jean King		

Doubles—Men

NATIONAL

1920	Bill Johnston-C. J. Griffin	1938	Don Budge-Gene Mako	1954	Vic Seixas-Tony Trabert
1921–22	Bill Tilden-Vincent Richards	1939	A. K. Quist-J. E. Bromwich	1955	Kosei Kamo-Atsushi Miyagi
1923	Bill Tilden-B. I. C. Norton	1940–41	Jack Kramer-F. R. Schroeder	1956	Lewis Hoad-Ken Rosewall
1924	H. O. Kinsey—R. G. Kinsey	1942	Gardnar Mulloy-Bill Talbert	1957	Ashley Cooper-Neale Fraser
1925–26	Vincent Richards—R. N. Williams	1943	Jack Kramer—Frank Parker	1958	Ham Richardson-Alex Olmedo
	II	1944	Don McNeill-Bob Falkenburg	1959–60	Neale Fraser-Roy Emerson
1927	Bill Tilden—Frank Hunter	1945	Gardnar Mulloy-Bill Talbert	1961	Chuck McKinley-Dennis Ralston
1928	G. M. Lott, Jr.-V. Hennessy	1946	Gardnar Mulloy-Bill Talbert	1962	Rafael Osuna-Antonio Palafox
1929–30	G. M. Lott, Jr.-J. H. Doeg	1947	Jack Kramer-Fred Schroeder	1963–64	Chuck McKinley-Dennis Ralston
1931	W. L. Allison-John Van Ryn	1948	Gardnar Mulloy-Bill Talbert	1965–66	Fred Stolle-Roy Emerson
1932	E. H. Vines, Jr.-Keith Gledh	1949	John Bromwich-William Sidwell	1967	John Newcombe-Tony Roche
1933–34	G. M. Lott, Jr.-L. R. Stoefen	1950	John Bromwich-Frank Sedgman	1968	Stan Smith-Bob Lutz[3]
1935	W. L. Allison-John Van Ryn	1951	Frank Sedgman-Ken McGregor	1969	Richard Crealy-Allan Stone[3]
1936	Don Budge-Gene Mako	1952	Vic Seixas-Mervyn Rose		
1937	G. von Cramm-H. Henkel	1953	Mervyn Rose-Rex Hartwig		

OPEN

1968	Stan Smith–Bob Lutz	1976	Marty Riessen–Tom Okker	1984	John Fitzgerald–Tomas Smid
1969	Fred Stolle–Ken Rosewall	1977	Frew McMillan–Bob Hewitt	1985	Ken Flach–Robert Seguso
1970	Nikki Pilic–Fred Barthes	1978	Bob Lutz–Stan Smith	1986	Andres Gomez–Slobodan Zivojinovic
1971	John Newcombe–Roger Taylor	1979	John McEnroe–Peter Fleming		
1972	Cliff Drysdale–Roger Taylor	1980	Stan Smith–Bob Lutz	1987	Stefan Edberg–Anders Jarryd
1973	John Newcombe–Owen Davidson	1981	John McEnroe–Peter Fleming	1988	Sergio Casal–Emilio Sanchez
1974	Bob Lutz–Stan Smith	1982	Kevin Curren–Steve Denton	1989	John McEnroe—Mark Woodforde
1975	Jimmy Connors–Ilie Nastase	1983	John McEnroe–Peter Fleming	1990	Pieter Aldrich–Danie Visser

1. Challenge round abandoned in 1912. 2. Patriotic Tournament in 1917. 3. With the inaugural of the Open Tournament in 1968, the United States Lawn Tennis Association held a national championship at Longwood, Chestnut Hill, Mass. which barred contract professionals in 1968 and 1969.

Doubles—Women

NATIONAL

1924	G. W. Wightman–Helen Wills	1951–54	Doris Hart–Shirley Fry	1971	Rosemary Casals–Judy Dalton
1925	Mary K. Browne–Helen Wills	1955–57	A. Louise Brough–Margaret O. duPont	1972	Francoise Durr–Betty Stove
1926	Elizabeth Ryan–Eleanor Goss			1973	Margaret Court–Virginia Wade
1927	L. A. Godfree–Ermyntrude Harvey	1958–59	Darlene Hard–Jeanne Arth	1974	Billie Jean King–Rosemary Casals
1928	Hazel Hotchkiss Wightman–Helen Wills	1960	Darlene Hard–Maria Bueno	1975	Margaret Court–Virginia Wade
		1961	Darlene Hard–Lesley Turner	1976	Linky Boshoff–Ilana Kloss
1929	Phoebe Watson–L. R. C. Michell	1962	Darlene Hard–Maria Bueno	1977	Martina Navratilova–Betty Stove
1930	Betty Nuthall–Sarah Palfrey	1963	Margaret Smith–Robyn Ebbern	1978	Billie Jean King–Martina Navratilova
1931	Betty Nuthall–E. B. Wittingstall	1964	Karen Hantze Susman–Billie Jean Moffitt		
1932	Helen Jacobs–Sarah Palfrey			1979	Betty Stove–Wendy Turnbull
1933	Betty Nuthall–Freda James	1965	Nancy Richey–Carole Caldwell Graebner	1980	Billie Jean King–Martina Navratilova
1934	Helen Jacobs–Sarah Palfrey				
1935	Helen Jacobs–Sarah Palfrey Fabyan	1966	Nancy Richey–Maria Bueno	1981	Kathy Jordan–Anne Smith
		1967	Billie Jean King–Rosemary Casals	1982	Rosemary Casals–Wendy Turnbull
1936	Marjorie G. Van Ryn–Carolin Babcock	1968	Margaret Court–Maria Bueno[3]	1983–84	Martina Navratilova–Pam Shriver
		1969	Margaret Court–Virginia Wade[3]	1985	Claudia Khode-Kilsch–Helena Sukova
1937–40	Sarah Palfrey Fabyan–Alice Marble				
1941	Sarah Palfrey Cooke–Margaret Osborne			1986–87	Martina Navratilova–Pam Shriver
				1988	Gigi Fernandez–Robin White
1942–47	A. Louise Brough–Margaret Osborne			1989	Hana Mandlikova–Martina Navratilova
		OPEN			
1948–50	A. Louise Brough–Margaret O. duPont	1968	Maria Bueno–Margaret Court	1990	Gigi Fernandez–Martina Navratilova
		1969	Darlene Hard–Francoise Durr		
		1970	Margaret Court–Judy Dalton		

1. Challenge round abandoned in 1912. 2. Patriotic Tournament in 1917. 3. With the inaugural of the Open Tournament in 1968, the United States Lawn Tennis Association held a national championship at Longwood, Chestnut Hill, Mass. which barred contract professionals in 1968 and 1969.

BRITISH (WIMBLEDON) CHAMPIONS

(Amateur from inception in 1877 through 1967)

Singles—Men

1908–09	Arthur Gore	1931	S. B. Wood	1954	Jaroslav Drobny	1973	Jan Kodes
1910–13	A. F. Wilding	1932	Ellsworth Vines	1955	Tony Trabert	1974	Jimmy Connors
1914	N. E. Brookes	1933	J. H. Crawford	1956–57	Lewis Hoad	1975	Arthur Ashe
1919	G. L. Patterson	1934–36	Fred Perry	1958	Ashley Cooper	1976–80	Bjorn Borg
1920–21	Bill Tilden	1937–38	Don Budge	1959	Alex Olmedo	1981	John McEnroe
1922	G. L. Patterson	1939	Robert L. Riggs	1960	Neale Fraser	1982	Jimmy Connors
1923	William Johnston	1946	Yvon Petra	1961–62	Rod Laver	1983–84	John McEnroe
1924	Jean Borotra	1947	Jack Kramer	1963	Chuck McKinley	1985–86	Boris Becker
1925	Rene Lacoste	1948	R. Falkenburg	1964–65	Roy Emerson	1987	Pat Cash
1926	Jean Borotra	1949	Fred Schroeder	1966	Manuel Santana	1988	Stefan Edberg
1927	Henri Cochet	1950	Budge Patty	1967	John Newcombe	1989	Boris Becker
1928	Rene Lacoste	1951	Richard Savitt	1968–69	Rod Laver	1990	Stefan Edberg
1929	Jean Cochet	1952	Frank Sedgman	1970–71	John Newcombe		
1930	Bill Tilden	1953	Vic Seixas	1972	Stan Smith		

Singles—Women

1919–23	Lenglen	1931	Frl. C. Aussen	1938	Helen Wills Moody	1952–54	Maureen Connolly
1924	Kathleen McKane	1932–33	Helen Wills Moody	1939	Alice Marble	1955	A. Louise Brough
1925	Lenglen	1934	D. E. Round	1946	Pauline M. Betz	1956	Shirley Fry
1926	Godfree	1935	Helen Wills Moody	1947	Margaret Osborne	1957–58	Althea Gibson
1927–29	Helen Wills	1936	Helen Jacobs	1948–50	A. Louise Brough	1959–60	Maria Bueno
1930	Helen Wills Moody	1937	D. E. Round	1951	Doris Hart	1961	Angela Mortimer

1962	Karen Susman	1969	Ann Jones	1976	Chris Evert	1982-87	Martina Navratilova
1963	Margaret Smith	1970	Margaret Court	1977	Virginia Wade	1988-89	Steffi Graf
1964	Maria Bueno	1971	Evonne Goolagong	1978-79	Martina Navratilova	1990	Martina Navratilova
1965	Margaret Smith	1972-73	Billie Jean King	1980	Evonne Goolagong		
1966-67	Billie Jean King	1974	Chris Evert		Cawley		
1968	Billie Jean King	1975	Billie Jean King	1981	Chris Evert-Lloyd		

Doubles—Men

1953	K. Rosewall–L. Hoad	1965	John Newcombe–Tony Roche	1979	Peter Fleming–John McEnroe
1954	R. Hartwig–M. Rose	1966	John Newcombe–Ken Fletcher	1980	Peter McNamara–Paul McNamee
1955	R. Hartwig–L. Hoad	1967	Bob Hewitt–Frew McMillan	1981	John McEnroe–Peter Fleming
1956	L. Hoad–K. Rosewall	1968-70	John Newcombe–Tony Roche	1982	Paul McNamee–Peter McNamara
1957	Gardnar Mulloy–Budge Patty	1971	Rod Laver–Roy Emerson	1983-84	John McEnroe–Peter Fleming
1958	Sven Davidson–Ulf Schmidt	1972	Bob Hewitt–Frew McMillan	1985	Heinz Gunthardt–Balazs Taroczy
1959	Roy Emerson–Neale Fraser	1973	Jimmy Connors–Ilie Nastase	1986	Joakim Nystrom–Mats Wilander
1960	Dennis Ralston–Rafael Osuna	1974	John Newcombe–Tony Roche	1987	Ken Flach–Robert Seguso
1961	Roy Emerson–Neale Fraser	1975	Vitas Gerulaitis–Sandy Mayer	1988	Ken Flach–Robert Seguso
1962	Fred Stolle–Bob Hewitt	1976	Brian Gottfried–Raul Ramirez	1989	John Fitzgerald–Anders Jarryd
1963	Rafael Osuna–Antonio Palafox	1977	Ross Case–Geoff Masters	1990	Rick Leach–Jim Pugh
1964	Fred Stolle–Bob Hewitt	1978	Fred McMillan–Bob Hewitt		

Doubles—Women

1956	Althea Gibson–Angela Buxton	1967-68	Billie Jean King–Rosemary Casals	1980	Kathy Jordan–Anne Smith
1957	Althea Gibson–Darlene Hard	1969	Margaret Court–Judy Tegart	1981	Martina Navratilova–Pam Shriver
1958	Althea Gibson–Maria Bueno	1970-71	Billie Jean King–Rosemary Casals	1982-84	Pam Shriver–Martina Navratilova
1959	Darlene Hard–Jeanne Arth	1972	Billie Jean King–Betty Stove	1985	Kathy Jordan–Elizabeth Smylie
1960	Darlene Hard–Maria Bueno	1973	Billie Jean King–Rosemary Casals	1986	Pam Shriver–Martina Navratilova
1961	Karen Hantze–Billie Jean Moffitt	1974	Evonne Goolagong–Peggy Michel	1987	Claudia Khode-Kilsch–Helena
1962	Karen Hantze Susman–Billie Jean	1975	Ann Kiyomura–Kazuko Sawamatsu		Sukova
	Moffitt	1976	Chris Evert–Martina Navratilova	1988	Steffi Graf–Gabriela Sabatini
1963	Darlene Hard–Maria Bueno	1977	Helen Cawley–JoAnne Russell	1989	Jana Novotna–Helena Sukova
1964	Margaret Smith–Les Turnerley	1978	Wendy Turnbull–Kerry Reid	1990	Jana Novotna–Helena Sukova
1965	Billie Jean Moffitt–Maria Bueno	1979	Billie Jean King–Martina Navra-		
1966	Nancy Richey–Maria Bueno		tilova		

UNITED STATES CHAMPIONS—1990

United States Open

(Flushing Meadow, Aug. 27-Sept. 9, 1990)

Men's singles—Pete Sampras, Rancho Palos Verdes, Calif., defeated Andre Agassi, Las Vegas, 6-4, 6-3, 6-2.

Women's singles—Gabriela Sabatini, Argentina, defeated Steffi Graff, West Germany, 6-2, 7-6 (7-4).

Men's doubles—Pieter Aldrich and Danie Visser, South Africa, defeated Paul Annacone, Bridgehampton, N.Y., and David Wheaton, Excelsior, Minn., 6-2, 7-6 (7-3), 6-2.

Womens doubles—Gigi Fernandez and Martina Navratilova, Aspen, Colo., defeated Jana Novotna and Helena Sukova, Czechoslovakia, 6-2, 6-4.

Mixed doubles—Elizabeth Smylie and Todd Woodbridge, Australia, defeated Natalia Zvereva, Soviet Union, and Jim Pugh, Rancho Palos Verdes, Calif., 6-4, 6-2.

Senior men's singles—Alex Mayer, Los Altos, Calif., defeated Tom Gulikson, Palm Coast, Fla., 6-4, 6-4.

Senior men's doubles—Tom Gulikson, Palm Coast, Fla., and Dick Stockton, Dallas, Texas, defeated Mark Edmondson, Australia, and Sherwood Stewart, The Woodlands, Texas, 6-7 (3-7), 7-6 (7-5), 6-4.

Senior women's doubles—Rose Casals, Sausalito, Calif., and Billie Jean King, New York, defeated Wendy Turnbull, Australia, and Virginia Wade, England, 2-6, 6-4, 6-3.

United States Hardcourts—Men

(Aug. 13-19, 1990, Indianapolis, Ind.)

Men's singles—Boris Becker, West Germany, defeated Peter Lundgren, Sweden, 6-3, 6-4.

Men's doubles—Scott Davis and David Pate, United States, defeated Grant Connell, United States, and Glenn Michibata, Canadas, 7-6, 7-6.

United States Hardcourts—Women

(March 26-April 2, 1990, San Antonio, Texas)

Women's singles—Monica Seles, Yugoslavia, defeated Katerina Maleeva, Bulgaria, 6-4, 6-3.

Women's doubles—Kathy Jordan, United States, and Elizabeth Smylie, Australia, defeated Robin White, United States and Gigi Fernandez, Puerto Rico, 7-5, 7-5.

U.S. Pro Championships

(July 30-Aug. 5, 1990, Brookline, Mass.)

Men's singles—Martin Jaite, Argentina, defeated Libor Nemecek, Czechoslovakia, 7-5, 6-2.

Men's doubles—Piet Norval, South Africa and Luke Jensen, South Africa, defeated Tim Mayotte and Bud Schulz, United States, 6-3, 7-6.

U.S. National Amateur Clay Court Championships

(July 9-15, Mount Lebanon, Pa.)

Men's singles—Woody Webb, Chapel Hill, N.C., defeated Ron Merger, Pittsburgh, Pa. 6-4, 6-7, 6-1.

Women's singles—Jennifer Rojohn, McKeesport, Pa., defeated Susan Klingenberg, Hampstead, Md., 5-7, 7-6, 7-5.

International Players Championships

(March 19-25, 1990, Key Biscayne, Fla.)

Men's singles—Andre Agassi, United States, defeated Stefan Edberg, Sweden, 6-1, 6-4, 0-6, 6-2.

Women's singles—Monica Seles, Yugoslavia, defeated Judith Wiesner, Australia, 6-1, 6-2.

Men's doubles—Jim Pugh and Rick Leach, United States, defeated Boris Becker, West Germany, and Cassio Motta, Brazil, 6-4, 3-6, 6-3.

Women's doubles—Jana Navotna and Helena Sukova, Czechoslovakia, defeated Robin White and Betsy Nagelsen, United States, 6-4, 6-3.

United States Pro Indoor

(Feb. 19-26, 1990, Philadelphia, Pa.)

Singles final—Peter Sampras, United States, defeated Andres Gomez, Ecuador, 7-6, 7-5, 6-2.

Doubles final—Rick Leach and Jim Pugh, United States, defeated Grant Connell, United States, and Glenn Michibata, Canada, 3-6, 6-4, 6-2.

OTHER 1990 CHAMPIONS

Australian Open

Men's singles—Ivan Lendl, Czechoslovakia, defeated Stefan Edberg, Sweden, 4-6, 7-6, 5-2 (injury default).

Women's singles—Steffi Graf, West Germany, defeated Mary Jo Fernandez, United States, 6-3, 6-4.

Men's doubles—Pieter Aldrich and Danie Visser, South Africa, defeated Grant Connell and Glenn Michibata, Canada, 6-4, 4-6, 6-1, 6-4.

Women's doubles—Jana Novotna and Helena Sukova, Czechoslovakia, defeated Patty Fendick and Mary Jo Fernandez, United States, 7-6, 7-6.

Wimbledon Open

Men's singles—Stefan Edberg, Sweden, defeated Boris Becker, West Germany, 6-2, 6-2, 3-6, 3-6, 6-4.

Women's singles—Martina Navratilova, United States, defeated Zina Garrison, United States, 6-4, 6-1.

Men's doubles—Rick Leach and Jim Pugh, United States, defeated Pieter Aldrich and Danie Visser, South Africa, 7-6, 7-6, 7-6.

Women's doubles—Jana Novotna and Helena Sukova, Czechoslovakia, defeated Kathy Jordan, United States, and Liz Smylie, Australia, 6-3, 6-4.

Mixed doubles—Rick Leach and Zina Garrison, United States, defeated John Fitzgerald and Liz Smylie, Australia, 7-5, 6-2.

French Open

Men's singles—Andres Gomez, Ecuador, defeated Andre Agassi, United States, 6-3, 2-6, 6-4, 6-4.

Women's singles—Monica Seles, Yugoslavia, defeated Steffi Graf, West Germany, 7-6, 6-4.

Men's doubles—Emilio Sanchez and Sergio Casal, Spain, defeated Goran Ivanisevic, Yugoslavia, and Petr Korda, Czechoslovakia, 7-5, 6-3.

Women's doubles—Jana Novotna and Helena Sukova, Czechoslovakia, defeated Larissa Savchenko and Natalia Zvereva, Soviet Union, 6-4, 7-5.

Mixed doubles—Jorge Lozano, Mexico, and Arantxa Sanchez, Spain, defeated Danie Visser, South Africa, and Nicole Provis, Australia, 7-6, 7-6.

DAVIS CUP RESULTS—1989

West Germany 3, Sweden 2 (at Stuttgart, West Germany, Dec. 15-17, 1989)

Singles—Boris Becker, West Germany, defeated Mats Wilander, Sweden, 6-2, 6-0, 6-2; Becker defeated Stefan Edberg, Sweden, 6-2, 6-2, 6-4; Edberg defeated Carl–Uwe Steeb, 6-2, 6-4; Wilander defeated Uwe–Steeb, 5-7, 7-6, 6-7, 6-2, 6-3.

Doubles—Becker and Eric Jelen, West Germany, defeated Anders Jarryd and Jan Gunnarsson, Sweden, 7-6, 6-4, 3-6, 6-7, 6-4.

MEN'S FINAL TENNIS EARNINGS—1990.

Men—1. Ivan Lendl (Czechoslovakia), $2,344,367. 2. Boris Becker (West Germany), $2,216,823. 3. Stefan Edberg (Sweden), $1,661,491. 4. John McEnroe, $946,023. 5. Brad Gilbert, $900,848. 6. Michael Chang, $682,130. 7. Aaron Krickstein, $582,651. 8. Alberto Mancini (Argentina), $510,430. 9. Anders Jarryd (Sweden), $485,873. 10. Andre Agassi, $478,901.

WOMEN'S FINAL TENNIS EARNINGS—1990

Women—1. Steffi Graf (West Germany), $1,963,905. 2. Martina Navratilova, $1,285,614. 3. Gabriela Sabatini (Argentina), $780,801. 4. Zina Garrison, $590,653. 5. Arantxa Sanchez (Spain), $549,098. 6. Helena Sukova, (Czechoslovakia), $431,579. 7. Jana Novotna (Czechoslovakia), $430,896. 8. Pam Shriver, $275,415. 9. Larisa Savchenko (Soviet Union), $250,122. 10. Natalia Zvereva (Soviet Union), $242,583.

COLLEGE SOCCER

(1989 NCAA PLAYOFFS)

DIVISION I
MEN

Quarterfinals

Rutgers 2, Vermont 1 (OT)
Santa Clara 2, UCLA 0
Virginia 1, South Carolina 0
Indiana 1, Howard 0

Semifinals

(at Rutgers University, New Brunswick, N.J., Dec. 2, 1989)

Virginia 3, Rutgers 0
Santa Clara 4, Indiana 2

Championship

(at Rutgers University, New Brunswick, N.J., Dec. 3, 1989)

Santa Clara 1, Virginia 1 (Tie), 4 Overtimes

WOMEN
Quarterfinals

North Carolina 9, Hartford 0
North Carolina St. 2, William & Mary 1
Santa Clara 2, UC–Santa Barbara 0

Colorado College 5, Massachusetts 2

Semifinals

(at N.C. State, Raleigh, N.C., Nov. 18, 1989)

North Carolina 2, North Carolina St. 0
Colorado 2, Santa Clara 0

Championship

(at N.C. State Raleigh, N.C., Nov. 19, 1989)

North Carolina 2, Colorado 0

ROWING

Rowing goes back so far in history that there is no possibility of tracing it to any particular aboriginal source. The oldest rowing race still on the calendar is the "Doggett's Coat and Badge" contest among professional watermen of the Thames (England) that began in 1715. The first Oxford-Cambridge race was held at Henley in 1829. Competitive rowing in the United States began with matches between boats rowed by professional oarsmen of the New York waterfront. They were oarsmen who rowed the small boats that plied as ferries from Manhattan Island to Brooklyn and return, or who rowed salesmen down the harbor to meet ships arriving from Europe. Since the first salesman to meet an incoming ship had some advantage over his rivals, there was keen competition in the bidding for fast boats and the best oarsmen. This gave rise to match races.

Amateur boat clubs sprang up in the United States between 1820 and 1830 and seven students of Yale joined together to purchase a four-oared lap-streak gig in 1843. The first Harvard-Yale race was held Aug. 3, 1852, on Lake Winnepesaukee, N.H. The first time an American college crew went abroad was in 1869 when Harvard challenged Oxford and was defeated on the Thames. There were early college rowing races on Lake Quinsigamond, near Worcester, Mass., and on Saratoga Lake, N.Y., but the Intercollegiate Rowing Association in 1895 settled on the Hudson, at Poughkeepsie, as the setting for the annual "Poughkeepsie Regatta." In 1950 the I.R.A. shifted its classic to Marietta, Ohio, and in 1952 it was moved to Syracuse, N.Y. The National Association of Amateur Oarsmen, organized in 1872, has conducted annual championship regattas since that time.

INTERCOLLEGIATE ROWING ASSOCIATION REGATTA

(Varsity Eight-Oared Shells)

Rowed at 4 miles, Poughkeepsie, N.Y., 1895–97, 1899–1916, 1925–32, 1934–41. Rowed at 3 miles, Saratoga, N.Y., 1898; Poughkeepsie, 1921–24, 1947–49; Syracuse, N.Y., 1952–1963, 1965–67. Rowed at 2,000 meters, Syracuse, N.Y., 1964 and from 1968 on. Rowed at 2 miles, Ithaca, N.Y., 1920; Marietta, Ohio, 1950–51. Suspended 1917–19, 1933, 1942–46.

Year	Time	First	Second	Year	Time	First	Second
1895	21:25	Columbia	Cornell	1948	14:06 2/5	Washington	California
1896	19:59	Cornell	Harvard	1949	14:42 3/5	California	Washington
1897	20:47 4/5	Cornell	Columbia	1950	8:07.5	Washington	California
1898	15:51 1/2	Pennsylvania	Cornell	1951	7:50.5	Wisconsin	Washington
1899	20:04	Pennsylvania	Wisconsin	1952	15:08.1	Navy	Princeton
1900	19:44 3/5	Pennsylvania	Wisconsin	1953	15:29.6	Navy	Cornell
1901	18:53 1/5	Cornell	Columbia	1954	16:04.4	Navy[1]	Cornell
1902	19:03 3/5	Cornell	Wisconsin	1955	15:49.9	Cornell	Pennsylvania
1903	18:57	Cornell	Georgetown	1956	16:22.4	Cornell	Navy
1904	20:22 3/5	Syracuse	Cornell	1957	15:26.6	Cornell	Pennsylvania
1905	20:29	Cornell	Syracuse	1958	17:12.1	Cornell	Navy
1906	19:36 4/5	Cornell	Pennsylvania	1959	18:01.7	Wisconsin	Syracuse
1907	20:02 2/5	Cornell	Columbia	1960	15:57	California	Navy
1908	19:24 1/5	Syracuse	Columbia	1961	16:49.2	California	Cornell
1909	19:02	Cornell	Columbia	1962	17:02.9	Cornell	Washington
1910	20:42 1/5	Cornell	Pennsylvania	1963	17:24	Cornell	Navy
1911	20:10 4/5	Cornell	Columbia	1964	6:31.1	California	Washington
1912	19:31 2/5	Cornell	Wisconsin	1965	16:51.3	Navy	Cornell
1913	19:28 3/5	Syracuse	Cornell	1966	16:03.4	Wisconsin	Navy
1914	19:37 4/5	Columbia	Pennsylvania	1967	16:13.9	Pennsylvania	Wisconsin
1915	19:36 3/5	Cornell	Stanford	1968	6:15.6	Pennsylvania	Washington
1916	20:15 2/5	Syracuse	Cornell	1969	6:30.4	Pennsylvania	Dartmouth
1920	11:02 3/5	Syracuse	Cornell	1970	6:39.3	Washington	Wisconsin
1921	14:07	Navy	California	1971	6:06	Cornell	Washington
1922	13:33 3/5	Navy	Washington	1972	6:22.6	Pennsylvania	Brown
1923	14:03 1/5	Washington	Navy	1973	6:21	Wisconsin	Brown
1924	15:02	Washington	Wisconsin	1974	6:33	Wisconsin	Mass. Inst. of Technology
1925	19:24 4/5	Navy	Washington				
1926	19:28 3/5	Washington	Navy	1975	6:08.2	Wisconsin	M.I.T.
1927	20:57	Columbia	Washington	1976	6:31	California	Princeton
1928	18:35 4/5	California	Columbia	1977	6:32.4	Cornell	Pennsylvania
1929	22:58	Columbia	Washington	1978	6:39.5	Syracuse	Brown
1930	21:42	Cornell	Syracuse	1979	6:26.4	Brown	Wisconsin
1931	18:54 1/5	Navy	Cornell	1980	6:46	Navy	Northeastern
1932	19:55	California	Cornell	1981	5:57.3	Cornell	Navy
1934	19:44	California	Washington	1982	5:57.5	Cornell	Princeton
1935	18:52	California	Cornell	1983	6:14.4	Brown	Navy
1936	19:09 3/5	Washington	California	1984	5:54.7	Navy	Pennsylvania
1937	18:33 3/5	Washington	Navy	1985	5:49.9	Princeton	Brown
1938	18:19	Navy	California	1986	5:50.2	Brown	Pennsylvania
1939	18:12 3/5	California	Washington	1987	6:02.9	Brown	Wisconsin
1940	22:42	Washington	Cornell	1988	6:14.0	Northeastern	Brown
1941	18:53 3/10	Washington	California	1989	5:56.0	Penn	Wisconsin
1947	13:59 1/5	Navy	Cornell	1990	5:55.5	Wisconsin	Pennsylvania

1. Disqualified.

HARNESS RACING

Oliver Wendell Holmes, the famous Autocrat of the Breakfast Table, wrote that the running horse was a gambling toy but the trotting horse was useful and, furthermore, "horse-racing is not a republican institution; horse-trotting is." Oliver Wendell Holmes was a born-and-bred New Englander, and New England was the nursery of the harness racing sport in America. Pacers and trotters were matters of local pride and prejudice in Colonial New England, and, shortly after the Revolution, the Messenger and Justin Morgan strains produced many winners in harness racing "matches" along the turnpikes of New York, Connecticut, Rhode Island, Massachusetts, Vermont, and New Hampshire.

There was English thoroughbred blood in Messenger and Justin Morgan, and, many years later, it was blended in Rysdyk's Hambletonian, foaled in 1849. Hambletonian was not particularly fast under harness but his descendants have had almost a monopoly of prizes, titles, and records in the harness racing game. Hambletonian was purchased as a foal with its dam for a total of $124 by William Rysdyk of Goshen, N.Y., and made a modest fortune for the purchaser.

Trotters and pacers often were raced under saddle in the old days, and, in fact, the custom still survives in some places in Europe. Dexter, the great trotter that lowered the mile record from 2:19 3/4 to 2:17 1/4 in 1867, was said to handle just as well under saddle as when pulling a sulky. But as sulkies were lightened in weight and improved in design, trotting under saddle became less common and finally faded out in this country.

WORLD RECORDS

Established in a Race or Against Time at One Mile *Source:* United States Trotting Association
(Through Sept. 1, 1990)

Trotting on Mile Track

	Record	Holder	Driver	Where Made	Year
All Age	1:52 1/5	Mack Lobell	John Campbell	Springfield, Ill.	1987
	1:52 4/5	Peace Corps	John Campbell	Du Quoin, Ill.	1989
	*1:54	Arndon	Del Miller	Lexington, Ky.	1982
	*1:55 1/4	Greyhound	Sep Palin	Lexington, Ky.	1938
2-year-old	*1:55	Noxie Hanover	Jim Simpson	Lexington, Ky.	1988
	1:55 3/5	Mack Lobell	John Campbell	Lexington, Ky.	1986
	1:57 2/5	I'm Impeccable	Dave Rankin	Lexington, Ky.	1989
3-year-old	1:52 1/5	Mack Lobell	John Campbell	Springfield, Ill.	1987
	1:52 4/5	Peace Corps	John Campbell	Du Quoin, Ill.	1989
	1:56	Nuclear Arsenal	Dave Magee	Springfield, Ill.	1989
4-year-old	1:53	Express Ride	Berndt Lindstedt	Lexington, Ky.	1987
	*1:55 2/5	Classical Way	John Simpson Jr.	Lexington, Ky.	1980
	1:56	Delray Lobell	John Campbell	East Rutherford, N.J.	1989
5-year-old and older	1:54 1/5	Napoletano	Stig Johansson	East Rutherford, N.J.	1989
	1:54 4/5	Kit Lobell	Berndt Lindstedt	East Rutherford, N.J.	1990
	1:55	Franconia	John Campbell	East Rutherford, N.J.	1987
	*1:55 1/4	Greyhound	Sep Palin	Lexington, Ky.	1938

Trotting on Five Eighths-Mile Track

	Record	Holder	Driver	Where Made	Year
All Age	1:54 1/5	Mack Lobell	John Campbell	Pompano Beach, Fla.	1987
2-year-old	1:57 3/5	Royal Troubador	Carl Allen	Pompano Beach, Fla.	1989
3-year-old	1:54 1/5	Mack Lobell	John Campbell	Pompano Beach, Fla.	1987
4-year-old	1:54 4/5	Mack Lobell	John Campbell	Solvalla, Sweden	1988
5-year-old and older	1:55	Minou Du Donjon	Olle Goop	Solvalla, Sweden	1985

Trotting on Half-Mile Track

	Record	Holder	Driver	Where Made	Year
All Age	1:56	Mack Lobell	John Campbell	Saratoga Springs, N.Y.	1988
2-year-old	1:58 1/5	Royal Troubador	Carl Allen	Delaware, Ohio	1989
3-year-old	1:56 4/5	Editor In Chief	John Campbell	Delaware, Ohio	1988
4-year-old	1:56	Mack Lobell	John Campbell	Saratoga Springs, N.Y.	1988
5-year-old and older	1:57 4/5	Lakewater Glory	Valery Tanishin	Northfield, Ohio	1989

Pacing on a Mile Track

	Record	Holder	Driver	Where Made	Year
All Age	*1:48 2/5	Matt's Scooter	Michel Lachance	Lexington, Ky.	1988
	*1:50 4/5	Fan Hanover	Glen Garnsey	Lexington, Ky.	1982
	1:51 1/5	Indian Alert	Jack Moiseyev	East Rutherford, N.J.	1988
2-year-old	1:52	L Dees Trish	Michel Lachance	Lexington, Ky.	1988
	1:52 1/5	Raque Bogart	Bill Fahy	Lexington, Ky.	1988
3-year-old	*1:48 2/5	Matt's Scooter	Michel Lachance	Lexington, Ky.	1988
	*1:51 2/5	Trini Hanover	Ron Waples	Springfield, Ill.	1987
	1:51 4/5	Indian Alert	Larry Noggle	Lexington, Ky.	1987
4-year-old	*1:49 2/5	Jaguar Spur	Dick Stillings	Lexington, Ky.	1988
	*1:50 4/5	Fan Hanover	Glen Garnsey	Lexington, Ky.	1982
	1:51 1/5	Indian Alert	Jack Moiseyev	East Rutherford, N.J.	1988
5-year-old and older	1:50 1/5	Ramblin' Storm	Michel Lachance	East Rutherford, N.J.	1988

Pacing on Five-Eighths-Mile Track

	Record	Holder	Driver	Where Made	Year
All Age	1:50 4/5	In the Pocket	John Campbell	Meadow Lands, Pa.	1990
2-year-old	1:53 2/5	Kentucky Spur	Dick Stillings	Pompano Beach, Fla.	1988
3-year-old	1:50 4/5	In the Pocket	John Campbell	Meadow Lands, Pa.	1990
	1:51 1/5	Goalie Jeff	Michel Lachance	Montreal, Canada	1989

4-year-old	1:51	Falcon Seelster	Tom Harmer	Meadow Lands, Pa.	1986
	1:51	Matt's Scooter	Michel Lachance	Campbellville, Ont., Cannada	1989
5-year-old and older	1:52 2/5	Ring of Light	James Morand	Laurel, Md.	1988

Pacing on a Half-Mile Track

All Age	1:51	Falcon Seelster	Tom Harmer	Delaware, Ohio	1985
2-year-old	1:54.3	OK Bye	John Campbell	Freehold, N.J.	1989
3-year-old	1:51	Falcon Seelster	Tom Harmer	Delaware, Ohio	1985
4-year-old	1:53 1/5	Falcon Seelster	Tom Harmer	Maywood, Ill.	1986
5-year-old and older	1:54 1/5	Port Stanley	John Reese	Maywood, Ill.	1988

*Set in a time trial.

HARNESS RACING RECORDS FOR THE MILE

Trotters			**Pacers**		
Time	**Trotter, age, driver**	**Year**	**Time**	**Pacer, age, driver**	**Year**
2:00	Lou Dillon, 5, Millard Sanders	1903	2:00 1/2	John R. Gentry, 7, W.J. Andrews	1896
1:58 1/2	Lou Dillon, 5, Millard Sanders	1903	1:59 1/4	Star Pointer, 8, D. McClary	1897
1:58	Uhlan, 8, Charles Tanner	1912	1:59	Dan Patch, 7, M. E. McHenry	1903
1:58	Peter Manning, 5, T. W. Murphy	1921	1:56 1/4	Dan Patch, 7, M. E. McHenry	1903
1:57 3/4	Peter Manning, 5, T. W. Murphy	1921	1:56	Dan Patch, 8, H. C. Hersey	1904
1:57	Peter Manning, 6, T. W. Murphy	1922	1:55	Billy Direct, 4, Vic Fleming	1938
1:56 3/4	Peter Manning, 6, T. W. Murphy	1922	1:55	Adios Harry, 4, Luther Lyons	1955
1:56 3/4	Greyhound, 5, Sep Palin	1937	1:54 3/5	Adios Butler, 4, Paige West	1960
1:56	Greyhound, 5, Sep Palin	1937	1:54	Bret Hanover, 4, Frank Ervin	1966
1:55 1/4	Greyhound, 6, Sep Palin	1938	1:53 3/5	Bret Hanover, 4, Frank Ervin	1966
1:54 4/5	Nevele Pride, 4, Stanley Dancer	1969	1:52	Steady Star, 4, Joe O'Brien	1971
1:54 4/5	Lindy's Crown, 4, Howard Beissinger	1980	1:49 1/5	Niatross, 3, Clint Galbraith	1980
1:54	Arndon, 3, Del Miller	1982	1:48 2/5	Matt's Scooter, 3, Michel Lachance	1989
1:52 1/5	Mack Lobell, 3, John Campbell	1987			

HISTORY OF TRADITIONAL HARNESS RACING STAKES

The Hambletonian

Three-year-old trotters. One mile. Guy McKinney won first race at Syracuse in 1926; held at Goshen, N.Y., 1930–1942, 1944–1956; at Yonkers, N.Y., 1943; at Du Quoin, Ill., 1957–1980. Since 1981, the race has been held at The Meadowlands in East Rutherford, N.J.

Year	Winner	Driver	Best time	Total purse
1967	Speedy Streak	Del Cameron	2:00	$ 122,650
1968	Nevele Pride	Stanley Dancer	1:59 2/5	116,190
1969	Lindy's Pride	Howard Beissinger	1:57 3/5	124,910
1970	Timothy T.	John Simpson, Jr.	1:58 2/5[1]	143,630
1971	Speedy Crown	Howard Beissinger	1:57 2/5	129,770
1972	Super Bowl	Stanley Dancer	1:56 2/5	119,090
1973	Flirth	Ralph Baldwin	1:57 1/5	144,710
1974	Christopher T	Billy Haughton	1:58 3/5	160,150
1975	Bonefish	Stanley Dancer	1:59[2]	232,192
1976	Steve Lobell	Billy Haughton	1:56 2/5	263,524
1977	Green Speed	Billy Haughton	1:55 3/5	284,131
1978	Speedy Somolli	Howard Beissinger	1:55[3]	241,280
1979	Legend Hanover	George Sholty	1:56 1/5	300,000
1980	Burgomeister	Billy Haughton	1:56 3/5	293,570
1981	Shiaway St. Pat	Ray Remmen	2:01 1/5[4]	838,000
1982	Speed Bowl	Tommy Haughton	1:56 4/5	875,750
1983	Duenna	Stanley Dancer	1:57 2/5	1,000,000
1984	Historic Free	Ben Webster	1:56 2/5	1,219,000
1985	Prakas	Bill O'Donnell	1:54 3/5	1,272,000
1986	Nuclear Kosmos	Ulf Thoresen	1:56	1,172,082
1987	Mack Lobell	John Campbell	1:53 3/5	1,046,300
1988	Armbro Goal	John Campbell	1:54 3/5	1,156,800
1989	Park Avenue Joe	Ron Wayples	1:55 3/5	1,131,000
1990	Embassy Lobell	Michel Lachance	1:56 1/5	1,346,000

1. By Formal Notice. 2. By Yankee Bambino. 3. By Speedy Somolli and Florida Pro. 4. By Super Juan.

Little Brown Jug

Three-year-old pacers. One Mile. Raced at Delaware County Fair Grounds, Delaware, Ohio.

Year	Winner	Driver	Best time	Total purse
1967	Best of All	Jim Hackett	1:59[1]	$ 84,778
1968	Rum Customer	Billy Haughton	1:59 3/5	104,226
1969	Laverne Hanover	Billy Haughton	2:00 2/5	109,731
1970	Most Happy Fella	Stanley Dancer	1:57 1/5	100,110
1971	Nansemond	Herve Filion	1:57 2/5	102,994
1972	Strike Out	Keith Waples	1:56 3/5	104,916

Year	Winner	Driver	Best time	Total purse
1973	Melvin's Woe	Joe O'Brien	1:57 3/5	120,000
1974	Ambro Omaha	Billy Haughton	1:57	132,630
1975	Seatrain	Ben Webster	1:57[2]	147,813
1976	Keystone Ore	Stanley Dancer	1:56 4/5[3]	153,799
1977	Governor Skipper	John Chapman	1:56 1/5	150,000
1978	Happy Escort	William Popfinger	1:55 2/5[4]	186,760
1979	Hot Hitter	Herve Filion	1:55 3/5	226,455
1980	Niatross	Clint Galbraith	1:54 4/5	207,361
1981	Fan Hanover	Glen Garnsey	1:56[5]	243,799
1982	Merger	John Campbell	1:56 3/5	328,900
1983	Ralph Hanover	Ron Waples	1:55 3/5	358,800
1984	Colt 46	Norman Boring	1:53 3/5	366,717
1985	Nihilator	Bill O'Donnell	1:52 1/5	350,730
1986	Barberry Spur	Bill O'Donnell	1:52 4/5	407,684
1987	Jaguar Spur	Richard Stillings	1:55 3/5	412,330
1988	B.J. Scoot	Michel Lachance	1:52 3/5	486,050
1989	Goalie Jeff	Michel Lachance	1:54 1/5	500,200
1990	Beach Towel	Ray Remmen	1:53 3/5	253,049

1. By Nardin's Byrd. 2. By Albert's Star. 3. By Armbro Ranger. 4. By Falcon Almahurst. 5. By Seahawk Hanover.

HARNESS HORSE OF THE YEAR

Chosen in poll conducted by United States Trotting Association in conjunction with the U.S. Harness Writers Assn.

1959	Bye Bye Byrd, Pacer	1970	Fresh Yankee, Trotter	1981	Fan Hanover, Pacer
1960	Adios Butler, Pacer	1971	Albatross, Pacer	1982	Cam Fella, Pacer
1961	Adios Butler, Pacer	1972	Albatross, Pacer	1983	Cam Fella, Pacer
1962	Su Mac Lad, Trotter	1973	Sir Dalrae, Pacer	1984	Fancy Crown, Trotter
1963	Speedy Scot, Trotter	1974	Delmonica Hanover, Trotter	1985	Nihilator, Trotter
1964	Bret Hanover, Pacer	1975	Savoir, Trotter	1986	Forrest Skipper
1965	Bret Hanover, Pacer	1976	Keystone Ore, Pacer	1987	Mack Lobell
1966	Bret Hanover, Pacer	1977	Green Speed, Trotter	1988	Mack Lobell
1967	Nevele Pride, Trotter	1978	Abercrombie, Pacer	1989	Matt's Scooter
1968	Nevele Pride, Trotter	1979	Niatross, Pacer		
1969	Nevele Pride, Trotter	1980	Niatross, Pacer		

WRESTLING

N.C.A.A. CHAMPIONSHIPS—1990

(March 22-24, 1990, College Park, Md.)

118 lb—Jack Griffin, Northwestern
126 lb—Terry Brands, Iowa
134 lb—Tom Brands, Iowa
142 lb—Joe Reynolds, Oklahoma
150 lb—Brian Dolph, Indiana
158 lb—Pat Smith, Oklahoma State
167 lb—Dan St. John, Arizona State
177 lb—Chris Barnes, Oklahoma State
190 lb—Matt Ruppel, Lehigh
Heavyweight—Kurt Angle, Clarion

Team Standings

1. Oklahoma State, 117.75 pts
2. Arizona State, 104.75 pts
3. Iowa, 102.75 pts

WORLD CUP—1989

105.5 lb (48 kg)—Jong-Shin Kim, Korea
114.5 lb (52 kg)—Vladimir Toguzov, Soviet Union
125.5 lb (57 kg)—Ruslan Karaev, Soviet Union
136.5 lb (62 kg)—Stepan Sarkisyan, Soviet Union
149.5 lb (68 kg)—Arsen Fadzaev, Soviet Union
163.0 lb (74 kg)—Gamat Khazamov, Soviet Union
180.5 lb (82 kg)—Rico Chaipparelli, United States
198.0 lb (90 kg)—Jim Scherr, United States
220.0 lb (100 kg)—Bill Scherr, United States
Unlimited—Bruce Baumgartner, United States

U.S.A. NATIONAL CHAMPIONSHIPS—1990

(April 20-22, 1990, Las Vegas, Nev.)

Freestyle

105.5 lb (48 kg)—Rob Eiter, Tempe, Ariz.
114.5 lb (52 kg)—Zeke Jones, Tempe, Ariz.
125.5 lb (57 kg)—Joe Melchiorre, Iowa City, Iowa
136.5 lb (62 kg)—John Smith, Stillwater, Okla.
149.5 lb (68 kg)—Nate Carr, Morgantown, W. Va.
163.0 lb (74 kg)—Rob Koll, Dryden, N.Y.
180.5 lb (82 kg)—Royce Alger, Iowa City, Iowa
198.0 lb (90 kg)—Chris Cambell, Fayetteville, N.Y.
220.0 lb (100 kg)—Bill Scherr, Colorado Springs, Colo.
Unlimited—Bruce Baumgartner, Cambridge Springs, Pa.

Greco-Roman

105.5 lb (48 kg)—Lewis Dorrance, Quantico, Va.
114.5 lb (52 kg)—Sam Henson, Charles City, Mo.
125.5 lb (57 kg)—Bam Pusteinik, Cedar Falls, Iowa
136.5 lb (62 kg)—Ike Anderson, Albany, N.Y.
149.5 lb (68 kg)—Andy Seras, Schenectady, N.Y.
163.0 lb (74 kg)—David Butler, San Diego, Calif.
180.5 lb (82 kg)—Derrick Waldroup, Fort Campbell, Ky.
198.0 lb (90 kg)—Randy Couture, Stillwater, Okla.
220.0 lb (100 kg)—Chris Tironi, Albany, N.Y.
Unlimited—Matt Ghaffari, Chander, Ariz.

GOLF

It may be that golf originated in Holland—historians believe it did—but certainly Scotland fostered the game and is famous for it. In fact, in 1457 the Scottish Parliament, disturbed because football and golf had lured young Scots from the more soldierly exercise of archery, passed an ordinance that "futeball and golf be utterly cryit doun and nocht usit." James I and Charles I of the royal line of Stuarts were golf enthusiasts, whereby the game came to be known as "the royal and ancient game of golf."

The golf balls used in the early games were leather-covered and stuffed with feathers. Clubs of all kinds were fashioned by hand to suit individual players. The great step in spreading the game came with the change from the feather ball to the guttapercha ball about 1850. In 1860, formal competition began with the establishment of an annual tournament for the British Open championship. There are records of "golf clubs" in the United States as far back as colonial days but no proof of actual play before John Reid and some friends laid out six holes on the Reid lawn in Yonkers, N.Y., in 1888 and played there with golf balls and clubs brought over from Scotland by Robert Lockhart. This group then formed the St. Andrews Golf Club of Yonkers, and golf was established in this country.

However, it remained a rather sedate and almost aristocratic pastime until a 20-year-old ex-caddy, Francis Ouimet of Boston, defeated two great British professionals, Harry Vardon and Ted Ray, in the United States Open championship at Brookline, Mass., in 1913. This feat put the game and Francis Ouimet on the front pages of the newspapers and stirred a wave of enthusiasm for the sport. The greatest feat so far in golf history is that of Robert Tyre Jones, Jr., of Atlanta, who won the British Open, the British Amateur, the U.S. Open, and the U.S. Amateur titles in one year, 1930.

THE MASTERS TOURNAMENT WINNERS

Augusta National Golf Club, Augusta, Ga.

Year	Winner	Score	Year	Winner	Score	Year	Winner	Score
1934	Horton Smith	284	1955	Cary Middlecoff	279	1974	Gary Player	278
1935	Gene Sarazen[1]	282	1956	Jack Burke	289	1975	Jack Nicklaus	276
1936	Horton Smith	285	1957	Doug Ford	283	1976	Ray Floyd	271
1937	Byron Nelson	283	1958	Arnold Palmer	284	1977	Tom Watson	276
1938	Henry Picard	285	1959	Art Wall, Jr.	284	1978	Gary Player	277
1939	Ralph Guldahl	279	1960	Arnold Palmer	282	1979	Fuzzy Zoeller[1]	280
1940	Jimmy Demaret	280	1961	Gary Player	280	1980	Severiano Ballesteros	275
1941	Craig Wood	280	1962	Arnold Palmer[1]	280	1981	Tom Watson	280
1942	Byron Nelson[1]	280	1963	Jack Nicklaus	286	1982	Craig Stadler[1]	284
1943–45	No Tournaments		1964	Arnold Palmer	276	1983	Severiano Ballesteros	280
1946	Herman Keiser	282	1965	Jack Nicklaus	271	1984	Ben Crenshaw	277
1947	Jimmy Demaret	281	1966	Jack Nicklaus[1]	288	1985	Bernhard Langer	282
1948	Claude Harmon	279	1967	Gay Brewer, Jr.	280	1986	Jack Nicklaus	279
1949	Sam Snead	282	1968	Bob Goalby	277	1987	Larry Mize[1]	285
1950	Jimmy Demaret	283	1969	George Archer	281	1988	Sandy Lyle	281
1951	Ben Hogan	280	1970	Billy Casper[1]	279	1989	Nick Faldo[1]	283
1952	Sam Snead	286	1971	Charles Coody	279	1990	Nick Faldo	278
1953	Ben Hogan	274	1972	Jack Nicklaus	286			
1954	Sam Snead[1]	289	1973	Tommy Aaron	283			

1. Winner in playoff.

U.S. OPEN CHAMPIONS

Year	Winner	Score	Where played	Year	Winner	Score	Where played
1895	Horace Rawlins	173	Newport	1919	Walter Hagen[2]	301	Brae Burn
1896	James Foulis	152	Shinnecock Hills	1920	Edward Ray	295	Inverness
1897	Joe Lloyd	162	Chicago	1921	Jim Barnes	289	Columbia
1898[3]	Fred Herd	328	Myopia	1922	Gene Sarazen	288	Skokie
1899	Willie Smith	315	Baltimore	1923	R. T. Jones, Jr.[1][2]	296	Inwood
1900	Harry Vardon	313	Chicago	1924	Cyril Walker	297	Oakland Hills
1901	Willie Anderson[1]	331	Myopia	1925	Willie Macfarlane[1]	291	Worcester
1902	Laurie Auchterlonie	307	Garden City	1926	R. T. Jones, Jr.[2]	293	Scioto
1903	Willie Anderson[1]	307	Baltusrol	1927	Tommy Armour[1]	301	Oakmont
1904	Willie Anderson	303	Glen View	1928	Johnny Farrell[1]	294	Olympia Fields
1905	Willie Anderson	314	Myopia	1929	R. T. Jones, Jr.[1][2]	294	Winged Foot
1906	Alex Smith	295	Onwentsia	1930	R. T. Jones, Jr.[2]	287	Interlachen
1907	Alex Ross	302	Philadelphia	1931	Billy Burke[1]	292	Inverness
1908	Fred McLeod[1]	322	Myopia	1932	Gene Sarazen	286	Fresh Meadow
1909	George Sargent	290	Englewood	1933	John Goodman[2]	287	North Shore
1910	Alex Smith[1]	298	Philadelphia	1934	Olin Dutra	293	Merion
1911	John McDermott[1]	307	Chicago	1935	Sam Parks, Jr.	299	Oakmont
1912	John McDermott	294	Buffalo	1936	Tony Manero	282	Baltusrol
1913	Francis Ouimet[1][2]	304	Brookline	1937	Ralph Guldahl	281	Oakland Hills
1914	Walter Hagen	290	Midlothian	1938	Ralph Guldahl	284	Cherry Hills
1915	Jerome D. Travers[2]	297	Baltusrol	1939	Byron Nelson[1]	284	Philadelphia
1916	Charles Evans, Jr.[2]	286	Minikahda	1940	Lawson Little[1]	287	Canterbury
1917–18	No tournaments[4]			1941	Craig Wood	284	Colonial

Year	Winner	Score	Where played	Year	Winner	Score	Where played
1942–45	No tournaments[5]			1969	Orville Moody	281	Champions G. C.
1946	Lloyd Mangrum[1]	284	Canterbury	1970	Tony Jacklin	281	Hazeltine
1947	Lew Worsham[1]	282	St. Louis	1971	Lee Trevino[1]	280	Merion
1948	Ben Hogan	276	Riviera	1972	Jack Nicklaus	290	Pebble Beach
1949	Cary Middlecoff	286	Medinah	1973	Johnny Miller	279	Oakmont
1950	Ben Hogan[1]	287	Merion	1974	Hale Irwin	287	Winged Foot
1951	Ben Hogan	287	Oakland Hills	1975	Lou Graham[1]	287	Medinah
1952	Julius Boros	281	Northwood	1976	Jerry Pate	277	Atlanta A.C.
1953	Ben Hogan	283	Oakmont	1977	Hubert Green	278	Southern Hills
1954	Ed Furgol	284	Baltusrol	1978	Andy North	285	Cherry Hills
1955	Jack Fleck[1]	287	Olympic	1979	Hale Irwin	284	Inverness
1956	Cary Middlecoff	281	Oak Hill	1980	Jack Nicklaus	272	Baltusrol
1957	Dick Mayer[1]	298	Inverness	1981	David Graham	273	Merion
1958	Tommy Bolt	283	Southern Hills	1982	Tom Watson	282	Pebble Beach
1959	Bill Casper, Jr.	282	Winged Foot	1983	Larry Nelson	280	Oakmont
1960	Arnold Palmer	280	Cherry Hills	1984	Fuzzy Zoeller[1]	276	Winged Foot
1961	Gene Littler	281	Oakland Hills	1985	Andy North	279	Oakland Hills
1962	Jack Nicklaus[1]	283	Oakmont	1986	Ray Floyd	279	Shinnecock Hills
1963	Julius Boros[1]	293	Country Club	1987	Scott Simpson	277	Olympic Golf Club
1964	Ken Venturi	278	Congressional				
1965	Gary Player[1]	282	Bellerive	1988	Curtis Strange[1]	278	The Country Club
1966	Bill Casper[1]	278	Olympic	1989	Curtis Strange	278	Oak Hill Country Club
1967	Jack Nicklaus	275	Baltusrol				
1968	Lee Trevino	275	Oak Hill	1990	Hale Irwin[1]	280	Medinah C.C.

1. Winner in playoff. 2. Amateur. 3. In 1898, competition was extended to 72 holes. 4. In 1917, Jock Hutchison, with a 292, won an Open Patriotic Tournament for the benefit of the American Red Cross at Whitemarsh Valley Country Club. 5. In 1942, Ben Hogan, with a 271 won a Hale American National Open Tournament for the benefit of the Navy Relief Society and USO at Ridgemoor Country Club.

U.S. AMATEUR CHAMPIONS

1895	Charles B. Macdonald	1923	Max R. Marston	1951	Billy Maxwell	1973[3]	Craig Stadler
1896–97	H. J. Whigham	1924–25	R. T. Jones, Jr.	1952	Jack Westland	1974	Jerry Pate
1898	Findlay S. Douglas	1926	George Von Elm	1953	Gene Littler	1975	Fred Ridley
1899	H. M. Harriman	1927–28	R. T. Jones, Jr.	1954	Arnold Palmer	1976	Bill Sander
1900–01	Walter J. Travis	1929	H. R. Johnston	1955–56	Harvie Ward	1977	John Fought
1902	Louis N. James	1930	R. T. Jones, Jr.	1957	Hillman Robbins	1978	John Cook
1903	Walter J. Travis	1931	Francis Ouimet	1958	Charles Coe	1979	Mark O'Meara
1904–05	H. Chandler Egan	1932	Ross Somerville	1959	Jack Nicklaus	1980	Hal Sutton
1906	Eben M. Byers	1933	G. T. Dunlap, Jr.	1960	Deane Beman	1981	Nathaniel Crosby
1907–08	Jerome D. Travers	1934–35	Lawson Little	1961	Jack Nicklaus	1982	Jay Sigel
1909	Robert A. Gardner	1936	John W. Fischer	1962	Labron Harris, Jr.	1983	Jay Sigel
1910	W. C. Fownes, Jr.	1937	John Goodman	1963	Deane Beman	1984	Scott Verplank
1911	Harold H. Hilton	1938	Willie Turnesa	1964	Bill Campbell	1985	Sam Randolph
1912–13	Jerome D. Travers	1939	Marvin H. Ward	1965[2]	Robert Murphy, Jr.	1986	Buddy Alexander
1914	Francis Ouimet	1940	R. D. Chapman	1966	Gary Cowan[1]	1987	Bill Mayfair
1915	Robert A. Gardner	1941	Marvin H. Ward	1967	Bob Dickson	1988	Eric Meeks
1916	Charles Evans, Jr.	1946	Ted Bishop	1968	Bruce Fleisher	1989	Chris Patton
1919	S. D. Herron	1947	Robert Riegel	1969	Steven Melnyk	1990	Phil Mickelson
1920	Charles Evans, Jr.	1948	Willie Turnesa	1970	Lanny Wadkins		
1921	Jesse P. Guilford	1949	Charles Coe	1971	Gary Cowan		
1922	Jess W. Sweetser	1950	Sam Urzetta	1972	Vinny Giles 3d		

1. Winner in playoff. 2. Tourney switched to medal play through 1972. 3. Return to match play.

U.S. P.G.A. CHAMPIONS

1916	Jim Barnes	1939	Henry Picard	1955	Doug Ford	1970	Dave Stockton
1919	Jim Barnes	1940	Byron Nelson	1956	Jack Burke, Jr.	1971	Jack Nicklaus
1920	Jock Hutchison	1941	Victor Ghezzi	1957	Lionel Hebert	1972	Gary Player
1921	Walter Hagen	1942	Sam Snead	1958[2]	Dow Finsterwald	1973	Jack Nicklaus
1922–23	Gene Sarazen	1944	Bob Hamilton	1959	Bob Rosburg	1974	Lee Trevino
1924–27	Walter Hagen	1945	Byron Nelson	1960	Jay Hebert	1975	Jack Nicklaus
1928–29	Leo Diegel	1946	Ben Hogan	1961	Jerry Barber[1]	1976	Dave Stockton
1930	Tommy Armour	1947	Jim Ferrier	1962	Gary Player	1977	Lanny Wadkins[1]
1931	Tom Creavy	1948	Ben Hogan	1963	Jack Nicklaus	1978	John Mahaffey
1932	Olin Dutra	1949	Sam Snead	1964	Bobby Nichols	1979	David Graham[1]
1933	Gene Sarazen	1950	Chandler Harper	1965	Dave Marr	1980	Jack Nicklaus
1934	Paul Runyan	1951	Sam Snead	1966	Al Geiberger	1981	Larry Nelson
1935	Johnny Revolta	1952	Jim Turnesa	1967	Don January[1]	1982	Ray Floyd
1936–37	Denny Shute	1953	Walter Burkemo	1968	Julius Boros	1983	Hal Sutton
1938	Paul Runyan	1954	Chick Harbert	1969	Ray Floyd	1984	Lee Trevino

1. Winner in playoff. 2. Switched to medal play.

1985	Hubert Green	1987	Larry Nelson	1989	Payne Stewart
1986	Bob Tway	1988	Jeff Sluman	1990	Mac Grady

U.S. WOMEN'S AMATEUR CHAMPIONS

1916	Alexa Stirling	1938	Patty Berg	1959	Barbara McIntire	1975	Beth Daniel
1919–20	Alexa Stirling	1939–40	Betty Jameson	1960	JoAnne Gunderson	1976	Donna Horton
1921	Marion Hollins	1941	Mrs. Frank Newell	1961	Anne Quast Decker	1977	Beth Daniel
1922	Glenna Collett	1946	Mildred Zaharias	1962	JoAnne Gunderson	1978	Cathy Sherk
1923	Edith Cummings	1947	Louise Suggs	1963	Anne Quast Welts	1979	Carolyn Hill
1924	Dorothy Campbell	1948	Grace Lenczyk	1964	Barbara McIntire	1980	Juli Inkster
	Hurd	1949	Mrs. D. G. Porter	1965	Jean Ashley	1981	Juli Inkster
1925	Glenna Collett	1950	Beverly Hanson	1966	JoAnne Gunderson	1982	Juli Inkster
1926	Helen Stetson	1951	Dorothy Kirby	1967	Lou Dill	1983	Joanne Pacillo
1927	Mrs. M. B. Horn	1952	Jacqueline Pung	1968	JoAnne G. Carner	1984	Deb Richard
1928–30	Glenna Collett	1953	Mary Lena Faulk	1969	Catherine LaCoste	1985	Michiko Hattori
1931	Helen Hicks	1954	Barbara Romack	1970	Martha Wilkinson	1986	Kay Cockerill
1932–34	Virginia Van Wie	1955	Patricia Lesser	1971	Laura Baugh	1987	Kay Cockerill
1935	Glenna Collett Vare	1956	Marlene Stewart	1972	Mary Ann Budke	1988	Pearl Sinn
1936	Pamela Barton	1957	JoAnne Gunderson	1973	Carol Semple	1989	Vicki Goetze
1937	Mrs. J. A. Page, Jr.	1958	Anne Quast	1974	Cynthia Hill	1990	Pat Hurst

U.S. WOMEN'S OPEN CHAMPIONS

Year	Winner	Score	Year	Winner	Score	Year	Winner	Score
1946	Patty Berg (match play)	—	1961	Mickey Wright	293	1976	JoAnne Carner[1]	292
1947	Betty Jameson	295	1962	Murle Lindstrom	301	1977	Hollis Stacy	292
1948	Mildred D. Zaharias	300	1963	Mary Mills	289	1978	Hollis Stacy	289
1949	Louise Suggs	291	1964	Mickey Wright[1]	290	1979	Jerilyn Britz	284
1950	Mildred D. Zaharias	291	1965	Carol Mann	290	1980	Amy Alcott	280
1951	Betsy Rawls	293	1966	Sandra Spuzich	297	1981	Pat Bradley	279
1952	Louise Suggs	284	1967	Catherine LaCoste[2]	294	1982	Janet Alex	283
1953	Betsy Rawls[1]	302	1968	Susie Berning	289	1983	Jan Stephenson	290
1954	Mildred D. Zaharias	291	1969	Donna Caponi	294	1984	Hollis Stacy	290
1955	Fay Crocker	299	1970	Donna Caponi	287	1985	Kathy Baker	280
1956	Katherine Cornelius[1]	302	1971	JoAnne Carner	288	1986	Jane Geddes[1]	287
1957	Betsy Rawls	299	1972	Susie Berning	299	1987	Laura Davies[1]	285
1958	Mickey Wright	290	1973	Susie Berning	290	1988	Liselotte Neumann	277
1959	Mickey Wright	287	1974	Sandra Haynie	295	1989	Betsy King	278
1960	Betsy Rawls	291	1975	Sandra Palmer	295	1990	Betsy King	284

1. Winner in playoff. 2. Amateur.

BRITISH OPEN CHAMPIONS

(First tournament, held in 1860, was won by Willie Park, Sr.)

Year	Winner	Score	Year	Winner	Score	Year	Winner	Score
1920	George Duncan	303	1948	Henry Cotton	283	1970	Jack Nicklaus[1]	283
1921	Jock Hutchison[1]	296	1949	Bobby Locke[1]	283	1971	Lee Trevino	278
1922	Walter Hagen	300	1950	Bobby Locke	279	1972	Lee Trevino	278
1923	A. G. Havers	295	1951	Max Faulkner	285	1973	Tom Weiskopf	276
1924	Walter Hagen	301	1952	Bobby Locke	287	1974	Gary Player	282
1925	Jim Barnes	300	1953	Ben Hogan	282	1975	Tom Watson[1]	279
1926	R. T. Jones, Jr.	291	1954	Peter Thomson	283	1976	Johnny Miller	279
1927	R. T. Jones, Jr.	285	1955	Peter Thomson	281	1977	Tom Watson	268
1928	Walter Hagen	292	1956	Peter Thomson	286	1978	Jack Nicklaus	281
1929	Walter Hagen	292	1957	Bobby Locke	279	1979	Severiano Ballesteros	283
1930	R. T. Jones, Jr.	291	1958	Peter Thomson[1]	278	1980	Tom Watson	271
1931	Tommy Armour	296	1959	Gary Player	284	1981	Bill Rogers	276
1932	Gene Sarazen	283	1960	Kel Nagle	278	1982	Tom Watson	284
1933	Denny Shute[1]	292	1961	Arnold Palmer	284	1983	Tom Watson	275
1934	Henry Cotton	283	1962	Arnold Palmer	276	1984	Severiano Ballesteros	276
1935	A. Perry	283	1963	Bob Charles[1]	277	1985	Sandy Lyle	282
1936	A. H. Padgham	287	1964	Tony Lema	279	1986	Greg Norman	280
1937	Henry Cotton	290	1965	Peter Thomson	285	1987	Nick Faldo	279
1938	R. A. Whitcombe	295	1966	Jack Nicklaus	282	1988	Seve Ballesteros	273
1939	R. Burton	290	1967	Roberto de Vicenzo	278	1989	Mark Calcavecchia	275
1940	Sam Snead	290	1968	Gary Player	289	1990	Nick Faldo	270
1947	Fred Daly	294	1969	Tony Jacklin	280			

1. Winner in playoff.

OTHER 1990 PGA TOUR WINNERS
(Through Aug. 20, 1990)

Spalding Pro-Am—Mark Calcavecchia (276)	$60,000
Tournament of Champions—Paul Azinger (272)	135,000
Tucson Open—Robert Gamez (270)	162,000
Bob Hope Classic—Peter Jacobson (329)	180,000
Phoenix Open—Tommy Armour III (267)	162,000
Pebble Beach National Pro-Am—Mark O'Meara (281)	180,000
Hawaiian Open—David Ishii (279)	180,000
Shearson Lehman Hutton Open—Dan Forsman (275)	162,000
Los Angeles Open—Fred Couples (266)	180,000
Doral-Ryder Open—Greg Norman (273)	252,000
Honda Classic—John Huston (282)	180,000
Tournament Players Championship—Jodie Mudd (278)	270,000
Nestle Invitational—Robert Gamez (274)	162,000
Insurance Open—Tony Sills (204)	180,000
Heritage Classic—Payne Stewart (276)	180,000
Greensboro Open—Steve Elkington (282)	225,000
USF&G Classic—David Frost (276)	180,000
Byron Nelson Classic—Payne Stewart (202)	180,000
Memorial—Greg Norman (216)	180,000
Colonial National—Ben Crenshaw (272)	180,000
Atlanta Classic—Wayne Levi (275)	180,000
Kemper Open—Gil Morgan (274)	180,000
Western Open—Wayne Levi (275)	180,000
Buick Classic—Hale Irwin (269)	180,000
Greater Hartford Open—Wayne Levi (267)	180,000
Busch Classic—Lanny Wadkins (266)	180,000
Bank of Boston Classic—Morris Hatalsky (275)	162,000
Buick Open—Chip Beck (272)	180,000
St. Jude Classic—Tom Kite (269)	180,000

OTHER 1990 LPGA TOUR WINNERS
(Through Aug. 20 1990)

Jamaica Classic—Patty Sheehan (212)	$135,000
Oldsmobile Classic—Pat Bradley (281)	45,000
Inverrary—Jane Crafter (209)	60,000
Hawaiian Open—Beth Daniel (210)	52,500
Kemper Open—Beth Daniel (283)	75,000
Desert Inn International—Maggie Will (214)	60,000
Tucson Open—Colleen Walker (276)	45,000
Turquoise Classic—Pat Bradley (280)	75,000
Dinah Shore—Betsy King (283)	90,000
Inamore Classic—Kris Monaghan (276)	45,000
Sara Lee Classic—Ayako Okamoto (210)	63,750
Crestar Classic—Dottie Mochrie (200)	52,500
Bradley International—Cindy Rarick (plus 25)	60,000
Corning Classic—Pat Bradley (274)	52,500
Lady Keystone Open—Cathy Gerring (208)	45,000
McDonalds Championship—Patty Sheehan (275)	97,500
Atlantic City Classic—Chris Johnson (275)	45,000
Rochester International—Patty Sheehan (271)	60,000
duMaurier Classic—Cathy Johnston (276)	90,000
Toledo Classic—Tina Purtzer (205)	48,750
Youngstown Classic—Beth Daniel (207)	60,000
LPGA Championship—Beth Daniel (280)	150,000
Stratton Mountain Classic—Cathy Gerring (281)	67,500
Big Apple Classic—Betsy King (273)	60,000

JAMES E. SULLIVAN MEMORIAL AWARD WINNERS
(Amateur Athlete of Year Chosen in Amateur Athletic Union Poll)

1930	Robert Tyre Jones, Jr.	Golf	1960	Rafer Johnson	Track and field
1931	Bernard E. Berlinger	Track and field	1961	Wilma Rudolph Ward	Track and field
1932	James A. Bausch	Track and field	1962	Jim Beatty	Track and field
1933	Glenn Cunningham	Track and field	1963	John Pennel	Track and field
1934	William R. Bonthron	Track and field	1964	Don Schollander	Swimming
1935	W. Lawson Little, Jr.	Golf	1965	Bill Bradley	Basketball
1936	Glenn Morris	Track and field	1966	Jim Ryun	Track and field
1937	J. Donald Budge	Tennis	1967	Randy Matson	Track and field
1938	Donald R. Lash	Track and field	1968	Debbie Meyer	Swimming
1939	Joseph W. Burk	Rowing	1969	Bill Toomey	Decathlon
1940	J. Gregory Rice	Track and field	1970	John Kinsella	Swimming
1941	Leslie MacMitchell	Track and field	1971	Mark Spitz	Swimming
1942	Cornelius Warmerdam	Track and field	1972	Frank Shorter	Marathon
1943	Bill L. Dodds	Track and field	1973	Bill Walton	Basketball
1944	Ann Curtis	Swimming	1974	Rick Wohlhuter	Track
1945	Felix (Doc) Blanchard	Football	1975	Tim Shaw	Swimming
1946	Y. Arnold Tucker	Football	1976	Bruce Jenner	Track and field
1947	John B. Kelly, Jr.	Rowing	1977	John Naber	Swimming
1948	Robert B. Mathias	Track and field	1978	Tracy Caulkins	Swimming
1949	Richard T. Button	Figure skating	1979	Kurt Thomas	Gymnastics
1950	Fred Wilt	Track and field	1980	Eric Heiden	Speed skating
1951	Robert E. Richards	Track and field	1981	Carl Lewis	Track and field
1952	Horace Ashenfelter	Track and field	1982	Mary Decker Tabb	Track and field
1953	Major Sammy Lee	Diving	1983	Edwin Moses	Track and field
1954	Malvin Whitfield	Track and field	1984	Greg Louganis	Diving
1955	Harrison Dillard	Track and field	1985	Joan Benoit–Samuelson	Marathon
1956	Patricia McCormick	Diving	1986	Jackie Joyner–Kersee	Heptathlon
1957	Bobby Jo Morrow	Track and Field	1987	Jim Abbott	Baseball
1958	Glenn Davis	Track and field	1988	Florence Griffith–Joyner	Track and field
1959	Parry O'Brien	Track and field	1989	Janet Evans	Swimming

SOCCER

WORLD CUP

1930 Uruguay	1950 Uruguay	1970 Brazil	1990 West Germany
1934 Italy	1954 West Germany	1974 West Germany	1994 To be held in United
1938 Italy	1958 Brazil	1978 Argentina	States
1942 No competition	1962 Brazil	1982 Italy	
1946 No competition	1966 England	1986 Argentina	

WORLD CUP—1990

SEMIFINALS

1. (at Naples, Italy, July 3, 1990)

Argentina 1, Italy 1 (Argentina wins, on 4-3 penalty kick shootout)

2. (at Turin, Italy, July 4, 1990)

West Germany 1, England 1 (West Germany wins, on 4-3 penalty kick shootout)

THIRD PLACE

(at Bari, Italy, July 7, 1990)

Italy 2, England 1

FINALS

(at Rome, Italy, July 8, 1990)

West Germany 1, Argentina 0

West Germany (Group D)	**Argentina (Group B)**
W. Germany 4, Yugoslavia 1	Cameroon 1, Argentina 0
W. Germany 5, United Arab Emirates 1	Argentina 2, Soviet Union 0
	Argentina 1, Romania 1 (tie)
W. Germany 1, Colombia 1 (tie)	Argentina 1, Brazil 0
West Germany 2, Netherlands 1	Argentina 0, Yugoslavia 0
West Germany 1, Czechoslovakia 0	(Argentina wins, 3-2, on a penalty shootout)
England (Group F)	**Italy (Group A)**
England 1, Ireland 1 (tie)	Italy 1, Austria 0
England 0, Netherlands 0 (tie)	Italy 1, United States 0
England 1, Egypt 0	Italy 2, Czechoslovakia 0
England 1, Belgium 0 (extra time)	Italy 2, Uruguay 0
England 3, Cameroon 2 (OT)	Italy 1, Ireland 0

WEST GERMANY WINS WORLD CUP ON A PENALTY KICK

Andreas Brehme's penalty kick in the 84th minute gave West Germany a 1-0 victory over Argentina in the World Cup championship game played in Rome, Italy. The championship was West Germany's third in the 60-year history of the event, tying that country for first in the all-time World Cup standings with Brazil.

West Germany dominated the final against an Argentine team crippled by injuries and the eventual expulsion of two players, which forced the defending champions to play with nine men at the end.

The shutout was the first in World Cup championship game history. Argentina had defeated West Germany, 3-2, in the 1986 World Cup championship game.

A crowd of 73,603 witnessed the championship, televised in America by Turner Network Television, a cable company.

The winning goal came with six minutes remaining in regulation. Midfielder Lothar Matthaeus passed the ball to forward Rudi Voeller. Voeller carried the ball into the box with Argentina's Roberto Sensini shadowing him. When Sensini reached in with his right leg, he was called for tripping Voeller, and West Germany was awarded the penalty kick.

Brehme was the choice to take it. He pushed the ball up, just inside the left post and just beyond the reach of Argentina's goalkeeper, Sergio Goycoechea.

The United States made a bit of World Cup history by qualifying for the first time since 1950. Though the U.S. went winless in the tournament's first round—losing to Czechoslovakia 5-1, Italy 1-0, and Austria 2-1—the experience gave the American team much-needed help in getting ready for its role as host of the 1994 World Cup.

UNITED STATES GAINS 1994 WORLD CUP

It was both fitting and a bit ironic that the Federation Internationale de Football Association picked July 4, 1989, to award the United States the 1994 World Cup competition.

The World Cup, arguably the No. 1 sports event in the world, thus comes to a country where soccer has struggled for a national foothold.

The 1990 World Cup was held in Italy, and 113 countries from around the world competed, including the United States.

The right to stage the World Cup is a prize the United States Soccer Federation had been seeking for many years. In 1983, the U.S. Federation bid for the 1986 tournament, but it was rejected by FIFA, which did not feel the necessary fan support existed in the United States.

What likely put the United States over the top was the total attendance of more than 1.4 million for soccer at the 1984 Summer Olympics in Los Angeles.

A new organization, World Cup USA 1994 was formed, with Paul Stiehl as director and financial backing from sponsors including Coca-Cola, Gillette, Anheuser-Busch, and American Express.

MAJOR INDOOR SOCCER LEAGUE—1990 FINAL STANDING

EASTERN DIVISION

	W	L	Pct	GB
Baltimore Blast	32	20	.615	—
Kansas City Comets	30	22	.577	2
Wichita Wings	25	26	.490	6 1/2
Cleveland Force	20	31	.392	11 1/2

WESTERN DIVISION

	W	L	Pct	GB
Dallas Mavericks	31	21	.596	—
San Diego Sockers	25	27	.481	6
St. Louis Spirit	24	28	.462	7
Tacoma Stars	20	32	.385	11

CHAMPIONSHIP PLAYOFFS

First Round

Kansas City Comets defeated Wichita Wings
San Siego Sockers defeated St. Louis

Semifinals

San Diego Sockers defeated Dallas Mavericks, 4 games to 2
Baltimore Blast defeated Kansas City Comets, 4 games to 2

Championship

San Diego Sockers defeated the Baltimore Blast, 4 games to 2, for fourth title
in five years and eighth in nine years

NORTH AMERICAN SOCCER LEAGUE CHAMPIONS

1968—Atlanta Chiefs
1969—Kansas City Stars
1970—Rochester Lancers
1971—Dallas Tornado
1972—New York Cosmos
1973—Philadelphia Atoms
1974—Los Angeles Aztecs
1975—Tampa Bay Rowdies
1976—Toronto Metro-Croatia
1977—New York Cosmos
1978—New York Cosmos
1979—Vancouver Whitecaps
1980—New York Cosmos
1981—Chicago Sting
1982—New York Cosmos
1983—Tulsa Roughnecks
1984—Chicago Sting

YACHTING

AMERICA'S CUP RECORD

First race in 1851 around Isle of Wight, Cowes, England. First defense and all others through 1920 held 30 miles off New York Bay. Races since 1930 held 30 miles off Newport, R.I. Conducted as one race only in 1851 and 1870; best four-of-seven basis, 1871; best two-of-three, 1876-1887; best three-of-five, 1893-1901; best four-of-seven, since 1930. Figures in parentheses indicate number of races won.

Year	Winner and owner	Loser and owner
1851	AMERICA (1), John C. Stevens, U.S.	AURORA, T. Le Marchant, England[1]
1870	MAGIC (1), Franklin Osgood, U.S.	CAMBRIA, James Ashbury, England[2]
1871	COLUMBIA (2), Franklin Osgood, U.S.[3] SAPPHO (2), William P. Douglas, U.S.	LIVONIA (1), James Ashbury, England
1876	MADELEINE (2), John S. Dickerson, U.S.	COUNTESS OF DUFFERIN, Chas. Gifford, Canada
1881	MISCHIEF (2), J. R. Busk, U.S.	ATALANTA, Alexander Cuthbert, Canada
1885	PURITAN (2), J. M. Forbes-Gen. Charles Paine, U.S.	GENESTA, Sir Richard Sutton, England
1886	MAYFLOWER (2), Gen. Charles Paine, U.S.	GALATEA, Lt. William Henn, England
1887	VOLUNTEER (2), Gen. Charles Paine, U.S.	THISTLE, James Bell et al., Scotland
1893	VIGILANT (3), C. Oliver Iselin et al., U.S.	VALKYRIE II, Lord Dunraven, England
1895	DEFENDER (3), C. O. Iselin-W. K. Vanderbilt-E. D. Morgan, U.S.	VALKYRIE III, Lord Dunraven-Lord Lonsdale-Lord Wolverton, England
1899	COLUMBIA (3), J. P. Morgan-C. O. Iselin, U.S.	SHAMROCK I, Sir Thomas Lipton, Ireland
1901	COLUMBIA (3), Edwin D. Morgan, U.S.	SHAMROCK II, Sir Thomas Lipton, Ireland
1903	RELIANCE (3), Cornelius Vanderbilt et al., U.S.	SHAMROCK III, Sir Thomas Lipton, Ireland
1920	RESOLUTE (3), Henry Walters et al., U.S.	SHAMROCK IV (2), Sir Thomas Lipton, Ireland
1930	ENTERPRISE (4), Harold S. Vanderbilt et al., U.S.	SHAMROCK V, Sir Thomas Lipton, Ireland
1934	RAINBOW (4), Harold S. Vanderbilt, U.S.	ENDEAVOUR (2), T. O. M. Sopwith, England
1937	RANGER (4), Harold S. Vanderbilt, U.S.	ENDEAVOUR II, T. O. M. Sopwith, England
1958	COLUMBIA (4), Henry Sears et al., U.S.	SCEPTRE, Hugh Goodson et al., England
1962	WEATHERLY (4), Henry D. Mercer et al., U.S.	GRETEL (1), Sir Frank Packer et al., Australia
1964	CONSTELLATION (4), New York Y.C. Syndicate, U.S.	SOVEREIGN (0), J. Anthony Bowden, England
1967	INTREPID (4), New York Y.C. Syndicate, U.S.	DAME PATTIE (0), Sydney (Aust.) Syndicate
1970	INTREPID (4), New York Y.C. Syndicate, U.S.	GRETEL II (1), Sydney (Aust.) Syndicate
1974	COURAGEOUS (4), New York, N.Y. Syndicate, U.S.	SOUTHERN CROSS (0), Sydney (Aust.) Syndicate
1977	COURAGEOUS (4), New York, N.Y. Syndicate, U.S.	AUSTRALIA (0), Sun City (Aust.) Syndicate
1980	FREEDOM (4), New York, N.Y. Syndicate, U.S.	AUSTRALIA (1), Alan Bond et al, Australia
1983	AUSTRALIA II (4) Alan Bond et al., Australia,	LIBERTY (3) New York, N.Y. Syndicate, U.S.
1987	STARS & STRIPES (4), Dennis Conner et al., United States	KOOKABURRA III (0), Iain Murray et al., Australia
1988[4]	NEW ZEALAND Michael Fay, et al., New Zealand	STARS & STRIPES, Dennis Conner, et al., United States

1. Fourteen British yachts started against America; Aurora finished second. 2. Cambria sailed against 23 U.S. yachts and finished tenth. 3. Columbia was disabled in the third race, after winning the first two; Sappho substituted and won the fourth and fifth. 4. Shortly after Dennis Conner and his 60-foot, twin-hulled catamaran easily defeated the challenge of the New Zealand, a 133-foot, single-hulled yacht in the waters off San Diego in early September 1988, a New York State Supreme Court judge ruled that the Americans did not live up to the America's Cup Deed of Gift, which means competing boats must be similar. The judge ruled that the Americans had an unfair advantage over the monohulled ship, and awarded the Cup to New Zealand. However, an Appeal awarded the Cup to the United States.

WEIGHTLIFTING

U.S. WEIGHTLIFTING FEDERATION
MEN'S NATIONAL CHAMPIONSHIPS

(Farmington Hills, Mich., May 4-6 1990)

	Snatch	C&J[1]	Total[2]
52 kg—Chris LeRoux	77.5	110.5	187.5
56 kg—Robert Gilsdorf	85.0	112.5	197.5
60 kg—Bryan Jacob	110.0	140.0	250.0
67.5 kg—Michael Jacques	120.0	145.0	265.0
75 kg—Michael Listro	127.5	165.0	292.5
82.5 kg—David Phillips	150.0	180.0	330.0
90 kg—Derrick Crass	152.5	192.5	345.0
100 kg—David Langon	152.5	185.0	337.5
110 kg—Richard Schultz	160.0	205.0	365.0
Over 110 kg—Jeffery Michels	160.0	200.0	360.0

WOMEN'S NATIONAL CHAMPIONSHIPS

(Farmington Hills, Mich., May 4-6, 1990)

	Snatch	C&J[1]	Total[2]
44 kg—Sibby Flowers	60.5	67.5	127.5
48 kg—Victoria Futch	62.5	75.0	137.5
52 kg—Thea Taylor	57.5	65.0	122.5
56 kg—Lynne Stoessel	67.5	87.5	155.0
60 kg—Giselle Shepatin	72.5	95.0	167.5
67.5 kg—Staphanie Zurek	67.5	85.0	152.5
75 kg—Le Ann Powers	65.0	82.5	147.5
82.5 kg—Mary Hyder	70.0	85.0	155.0
Over 82.5 kg—Stephanie Armitage-Johnson	77.5	92.5	170.0

1. Clean and jerk. 2. All results in kilograms.

AUTO RACING

INDIANAPOLIS 500

Year	Winner	Car	Time	mph	Second place
1911	Ray Harroun	Marmon	6:42:08	74.59	Ralph Mulford
1912	Joe Dawson	National	6:21:06	78.72	Teddy Tetzloff
1913	Jules Goux	Peugeot	6:35:05	75.93	Spencer Wishart
1914	René Thomas	Delage	6:03:45	82.47	Arthur Duray
1915	Ralph DePalma	Mercedes	5:33:55.51	89.84	Dario Resta
1916[1]	Dario Resta	Peugeot	3:34:17	84.00	Wilbur D'Alene
1919	Howard Wilcox	Peugeot	5:40:42.87	88.05	Eddie Hearne
1920	Gaston Chevrolet	Monroe	5:38:32	88.62	René Thomas
1921	Tommy Milton	Frontenac	5:34:44.65	89.62	Roscoe Sarles
1922	Jimmy Murphy	Murphy Special	5:17:30.79	94.48	Harry Hartz
1923	Tommy Milton	H. C. S. Special	5:29.50.17	90.95	Harry Hartz
1924	L. L. Corum–Joe Boyer	Dusenberg Special	5:05:23.51	98.23	Earl Cooper
1925	Peter DePaolo	Dusenberg Special	4:56:39.45	101.13	Dave Lewis
1926[2]	Frank Lockhart	Miller Special	4:10:14.95	95.904	Harry Hartz
1927	George Souders	Dusenberg Special	5:07:33.08	97.54	Earl DeVore
1928	Louis Meyer	Miller Special	5:01:33.75	99.48	Lou Moore
1929	Ray Keech	Simplex Special	5:07:25.42	97.58	Louis Meyer
1930	Billy Arnold	Miller–Hartz Special	4:58:39.72	100.448	Shorty Cantlon
1931	Louis Schneider	Bowes Special	5:10:27.93	96.629	Fred Frame
1932	Fred Frame	Miller–Hartz Special	4:48:03.79	104.144	Howard Wilcox
1933	Louis Meyer	Tydol Special	4:48:00.75	104.162	Wilbur Shaw
1934	Bill Cummings	Boyle Products Special	4:46:05.20	104.863	Mauri Rose
1935	Kelly Petillo	Gilmore Special	4:42:22.71	106.240	Wilbur Shaw
1936	Louis Meyer	Ring Free Special	4:35:03.39	109.069	Ted Horn
1937	Wilbur Shaw	Shaw–Gilmore Special	4:24:07.80	113.580	Ralph Hepburn
1938	Floyd Roberts	Burd Piston Ring Special	4:15:58.40	117.200	Wilbur Shaw
1939	Wilbur Shaw	Boyle Special	4:20:47.39	115.035	Jimmy Snyder
1940	Wilbur Shaw	Boyle Special	4:22:31.17	114.277	Rex Mays
1941	Floyd Davis–Mauri Rose	Noc–Out Hose Clamp Special	4:20:36.24	115.117	Rex Mays
1946	George Robson	Thorne Engineering Special	4:21:26.71	114.820	Jimmy Jackson
1947	Mauri Rose	Blue Crown Special	4:17:52.17	116.338	Bill Holland
1948	Mauri Rose	Blue Crown Special	4:10:23.33	119.814	Bill Holland
1949	Bill Holland	Blue Crown Special	4:07:15.97	121.327	Johnny Parsons
1950[3]	Johnnie Parsons	Wynn's Friction Proof Special	2:46:55.97	124.002	Bill Holland
1951	Lee Wallard	Belanger Special	3:57:38.05	126.244	Mike Nazaruk
1952	Troy Ruttman	Agajanian Special	3:52:41.88	128.922	Jim Rathmann
1953	Bill Vukovich	Fuel Injection Special	3:53:01.69	128.740	Art Cross
1954	Bill Vukovich	Fuel Injection Special	3:49:17.27	130.840	Jim Bryan
1955	Bob Sweikert	John Zink Special	3:53:59.13	128.209	Tony Bettenhausen
1956	Pat Flaherty	John Zink Special	3:53:28.84	128.490	Sam Hanks
1957	Sam Hanks	Belond Exhaust Special	3:41:14.25	135.601	Jim Rathmann
1958	Jimmy Bryan	Belond A–P Special	3:44:13.80	133.791	George Amick
1959	Rodger Ward	Leader Card 500 Roadster	3:40:49.20	135.857	Jim Rathmann
1960	Jim Rathmann	Ken–Paul Special	3:36:11.36	138.767	Rodger Ward
1961	A. J. Foyt	Bowes Special	3:35:37.49	139.130	Eddie Sachs
1962	Rodger Ward	Leader Card Special	3:33:50.33	140.293	Len Sutton
1963	Parnelli Jones	Agajanian Special	3:29:35.40	143.137	Jim Clark
1964	A. J. Foyt	Offenhauser Special	3:23:35.83	147.350	Rodger Ward
1965	Jim Clark	Lotus–Ford	3:19:05.34	150.686	Parnelli Jones
1966	Graham Hill	Lola–Ford	3:27:52.53	144.317	Jim Clark
1967[4]	A. J. Foyt	Coyote–Ford	3:18:24.22	151.207	Al Unser
1968	Bobby Unser	Eagle–Offenhauser	3:16:13.76	152.882	Dan Gurney
1969	Mario Andretti	STP Hawk–Ford	3:11:14.71	156.867	Dan Gurney
1970	Al Unser	P. J. Colt–Ford	3:12:37.04	155.749	Mark Donohue
1971	Al Unser	P. J. Colt–Ford	3:10:11.56	157.735	Peter Revson
1972	Mark Donohue	McLaren–Offenhauser	3:04:05.54	162.962	Al Unser
1973[5]	Gordon Johncock	Eagle–Offenhauser	2:05:26.59	159.036	Bill Vukovich
1974	Johnny Rutherford	McLaren–Offenhauser	3:09:10.06	158.589	Bobby Unser
1975[6]	Bobby Unser	Eagle–Offenhauser	2:54:55.08	149.213	Johnny Rutherford
1976[7]	Johnny Rutherford	McLaren–Offenhauser	1:42:52.48	148.725	A. J. Foyt
1977	A. J. Foyt	Coyote–Foyt	3:05:57.16	161.331	Tom Sneva
1978	Al Unser	Lola–Cosworth	3:05:54.99	161.363	Tom Sneva
1979	Rick Mears	Penske–Cosworth	3:08:27.97	158.899	A. J. Foyt
1980	Johnny Rutherford	Chaparral–Cosworth	3:29:59.56	142.862	Tom Sneva
1981[8]	Bobby Unser	Eagle–Offenhauser	3:35:41.78	139.029	Mario Andretti
1982	Gordon Johncock	Wildcat–Cosworth	3:05:09.14	162.029	Rick Mears
1983	Tom Sneva	March–Cosworth	3:05:03.06	162.117	Al Unser
1984	Rick Mears	March–Cosworth	3:03:21.00	162.962	Roberto Guerrero

1985	Danny Sullivan	March–Cosworth	3:16:06.069	152.982	Mario Andretti
1986	Bobby Rahal	March–Cosworth	2:55:43.48	170.722	Kevin Cogan
1987	Al Unser, Sr.	March–Cosworth	3:04:59.147	162.175	Roberto Guerrero
1988	Rick Mears	March–Cosworth	3:27:10.204	144.809	Emerson Fittipaldi
1989	Emerson Fittipaldi	P.C.–18 Chevrolet	2:59:01.04	167.581	Al Unser, Jr.
1990	Arie Luyendyk	Lola-T9000 Chevrolet	2:41:18.248	185.987	Bobby Rahal

1. 300 miles. 2. Race ended at 400 miles because of rain. 3. Race ended at 345 miles because of rain. 4. Race, postponed after 18 laps because of rain on May 30, was finished on May 31. 5. Race postponed May 28 and 29 was cut to 332.5 miles because of rain, May 30. 6. Race ended at 435 miles because of rain. 7. Race ended at 255 miles because of rain. 8. Andretti was awarded the victory the day after the race after Bobby Unser, whose car finished first, was penalized one lap and dropped from first place to second for passing other cars illegally under a yellow caution flag. Unser appealed the decision to the U.S. Auto Club and was upheld. A panel ruled the penalty was too severe and instead fined Unser $40,000, but restored the victory to him.

INDY CAR NATIONAL CHAMPIONS

1910	Ray Harroun	1926	Harry Hartz	1950	Henry Banks	1970	Al Unser
1911	Ralph Mulford	1927	Peter DePaolo	1951	Tony Bettenhausen	1971–72	Joe Leonard
1912	Ralph DePalma	1928–29	Louis Meyer	1952	Chuck Stevenson	1973	Roger McCluskey
1913	Earl Cooper	1930	Billy Arnold	1953	Sam Hanks	1974	Bobby Unser
1914	Ralph DePalma	1931	Louis Schneider	1954	Jimmy Bryan	1975	A. J. Foyt
1915	Earl Cooper	1932	Bob Carey	1955	Bob Sweikert	1976	Gordon Johncock
1916	Dario Resta	1933	Louis Meyer	1956–57	Jimmy Bryan	1977–78	Tom Sneva
1917	Earl Cooper	1934	Bill Cummings	1958	Tony Bettenhausen	1979	Rick Mears
1918	Ralph Mulford	1935	Kelly Petillo	1959	Rodger Ward	1980	Johnny Rutherford
1919	Howard Wilcox	1936	Mauri Rose	1960–61	A. J. Foyt	1981–82	Rick Mears
1920	Gaston Chevrolet	1937	Wilbur Shaw	1962	Rodger Ward	1983	Al Unser
1921	Tommy Milton	1938	Floyd Roberts	1963–64	A. J. Foyt	1984	Mario Andretti
1922	James Murphy	1939	Wilbur Shaw	1965–66	Mario Andretti	1985	Al Unser
1923	Eddie Hearne	1940–41	Rex Mays	1967	A. J. Foyt	1986–87	Bobby Rahal
1924	James Murphy	1946–48	Ted Horn	1968	Bobby Unser	1988	Danny Sullivan
1925	Peter DePaolo	1949	Johnnie Parsons	1969	Mario Andretti	1989	Emerson Fittipaldi

NOTE: There have been three sanctioning bodies for the series: the Automobile Association of America (1909-1955), the U.S. Auto Club (1956-1979), and the Championship Auto Racing Team (CART), 1979-present.

NATIONAL ASSOCIATION FOR STOCK CAR AUTO RACING (NASCAR) GRAND NATIONAL CHAMPIONS

1949	Red Byron	1960	Rex White	1971–72	Richard Petty	1984	Terry Labonte
1950	Bill Rexford	1961	Ned Jarrett	1973	Benny Parsons	1985	Darrell Waltrip
1951	Herb Thomas	1962–63	Joe Weatherly	1974–75	Richard Petty	1986	Dale Earnhardt
1952	Tim Flock	1964	Richard Petty	1976–78	Cale Yarborough	1987	Dale Earnhardt
1953	Herb Thomas	1965	Ned Jarrett	1979	Richard Petty	1988	Bill Elliott
1954	Lee Petty	1966	David Pearson	1980	Dale Earnhardt	1989	Rusty Wallace
1955	Tim Flock	1967	Richard Petty	1981	Darrell Waltrip		
1956–57	Buck Baker	1968–69	David Pearson	1982	Darrell Waltrip		
1958–59	Lee Petty	1970	Bobby Isaac	1983	Bobby Allison		

WORLD GRAND PRIX DRIVER CHAMPIONS

1950	Giuseppe Farina, Italy, Alfa Romeo	1970	Jochen Rindt, Austria, Lotus-Ford
1951	Juan Fangio, Argentina, Alfa Romeo	1971	Jackie Stewart, Scotland, Tyrrell-Ford
1952	Alberto Ascari, Italy, Ferrari	1972	Emerson Fittipaldi, Brazil, Lotus-Ford
1953	Alberto Ascari, Italy, Ferrari	1973	Jackie Stewart, Scotland, Tyrrell-Ford
1954	Juan Fangio, Argentina, Maserati, Mercedes-Benz	1974	Emerson Fittipaldi, Brazil, McLaren-Ford
1955	Juan Fangio, Argentina, Mercedes-Benz	1975	Niki Lauda, Austria, Ferrari
1956	Juan Fangio, Argentina, Lancia-Ferrari	1976	James Hunt, Britain, McLaren-Ford
1957	Juan Fangio, Argentina, Maserati	1977	Niki Lauda, Austria, Ferrari
1958	Mike Hawthorn, England, Ferrari	1978	Mario Andretti, Nazareth, Pa., Lotus
1959	Jack Brabham, Australia, Cooper	1979	Jody Scheckter, South Africa
1960	Jack Brabham, Australia, Cooper	1980	Alan Jones, Australia
1961	Phil Hill, United States, Ferrari	1981	Nelson Piquet, Brazil
1962	Graham Hill, England, BRM	1982	Kiki Rosberg, Finland
1963	Jim Clark, Scotland, Lotus-Ford	1983	Nelson Piquet, Brazil
1964	John Surtees, England, Ferrari	1984	Nikki Lauda, Austria
1965	Jim Clark, Scotland, Lotus-Ford	1985	Alain Prost, France
1966	Jack Brabham, Australia, Brabham-Repco	1986	Alain Prost, France
1967	Denis Hulme, New Zealand, Brabham-Repco	1987	Nelson Piquet, Brazil
1968	Graham Hill, England, Lotus-Ford	1988	Ayrton Senna, Brazil
1969	Jackie Stewart, Scotland, Matra-Ford	1989	Alain Prost, France

1989 NASCAR LEADING MONEY WINNERS

1.	Rusty Wallace	$2,247,950
2.	Dale Earnhardt	1,435,730
3.	Darrell Waltrip	1,313,079
4.	Ken Schrader	1,039,441
5.	Mark Martin	1,019,250
6.	Bill Elliott	854,570
7.	Terry Labonte	704,806
8.	Harry Gant	641,092
9.	Davey Allison	640,956
10.	Geoff Bodine	620,594

1989 WINSTON CUP POINT LEADERS

1.	Rusty Wallace	4176	11.	Davey Allison	3481
2.	Dale Earnhardt	4164	12.	Sterling Marlin	3422
3.	Mark Martin	4053	13.	Morgan Shepard	3403
4.	Darrell Waltrip	3971	14.	Alan Kulwicki	3236
5.	Ken Schrader	3786	15.	Dick Trickle	3203
6.	Bill Elliott	3774	16.	Bobby Hillin	3139
7.	Harry Gant	3610	17.	Rick Wilson	3119
8.	Ricky Rudd	3608	18.	Michael Waltrip	3057
9.	Geoff Bodine	3600	19.	Brett Bodine	3051
10.	Terry Labonte	3569	20.	Neil Bonnett	2995

TOP 25 1989 INDY CAR WORLD SERIES EARNINGS

Driver	Points	1989 Earnings	Driver	Points	1989 Earnings
1. Emerson Fittipaldi	196	$2,166,078	14. Kevin Cogan	18	$401,325
2. Al Unser, Jr.	136	1,247,571	15. Pancho Carter	18	382,976
3. Rick Mears	186	1,165,684	16. A.J. Foyt, Jr.	10	347,579
4. Michael Andretti	150	931,793	17. Bernard Jourdain	10	343,770
5. Teo Fabi	141	802,463	18. Didier Theys	9	304,541
6. Danny Sullivan	107	790,234	19. Randy Lewis	0	299,568
7. Mario Andretti	110	759,364	20. John Jones	14	291,423
8. Scott Pruett	101	712,096	21. Ludwig Heimrath, Jr.	4	244,928
9. Bobby Rahal	88	687,424	22. Dominic Dobson	10	223,456
10. Raul Boesel	68	662,821	23. Tom Sneva	3	219,554
11. Arie Luyendyk	75	541,445	24. Al Unser, Sr.	14	196,786
12. Scott Brayton	17	451,317	25. Roberto Guerrero	6	196,119
13. Derek Daly	25	410,279			

LACROSSE

NATIONAL INTERCOLLEGIATE CHAMPIONS

1946	Navy	1960	Navy	1976–77	Cornell		
1947–48	Johns Hopkins	1961	Army, Navy	1978–80	Johns Hopkins		
1949	Johns Hopkins, Navy	1962–66	Navy	1981	North Carolina		
1950	Johns Hopkins	1967	Johns Hopkins, Maryland, Navy	1982	North Carolina		
1951	Army, Princeton	1968	Johns Hopkins	1983	Syracuse		
1952	Virginia, R.P.I.	1969	Army, Johns Hopkins	1984	Johns Hopkins		
1953	Princeton	1970	Johns Hopkins, Navy, Virginia	1985	Johns Hopkins		
1954	Navy	1971[1]	Cornell	1986	North Carolina		
1955–56	Maryland	1972	Virginia	1987	Johns Hopkins		
1957	Johns Hopkins	1973	Maryland	1988	Syracuse		
1958	Army	1974	Johns Hopkins	1989	Syracuse		
1959	Army, Johns Hopkins, Maryland	1975	Maryland	1990	Syracuse		

1. First year of N.C.A.A. Championship Tournaments.

1990 N.C.A.A. LACROSSE

DIVISION I
Men's Championships
Quarterfinals

Syracuse 20, Brown 12
Yale 17, Princeton 8
North Carolina 18, Harvard 3
Loyola (Md) 19, Rutgers 10

Semifinals

Syracuse 21, North Carolina 10
Loyola (Md) 14, Yale 13 (2 OT)

Championship

(at Rutgers University, New Brunswick, N.J., May 28, 1990)
Syracuse 21, Loyola (Md) 9

Women's Championships
Semifinals

Harvard 13, Temple 7
Maryland 10, Loyola (Md) 5

Championship

(at Princeton University, Princeton, N.J. May 20, 1990)
Harvard 8, Maryland 7

BOBSLEDDING

WORLD CHAMPIONSHIPS—1990
World Four-Man Championships

(Feb. 11, 1990, St. Moritz, Switzerland)

1. Switzerland I	4:13.35
2. East Germany II	4:13.84
3. Austria	4:13.94
4. Switzerland II	4:14.07
5. East Germany I	4:14.60

Best United States finish—United States I – 13th – 4:16.70.

World Two-Man Championships

(Feb. 2, 1990, St. Moritz, Switzerland)

1. Switzerland I	4:19.30
2. East Germany II	4:20.30
3. East Germany I	4:20.58
4. Soviet Union I	4:20.72
5. West Germany I	4:21.23

Best United States finish—United States I – 12th – 4:23.13.

SOFTBALL

Source: Amateur Softball Association.

AMATEUR CHAMPIONS

1959	Aurora (Ill.) Sealmasters	1972	Raybestos Cardinals, Stratford, Conn.	
1960	Clearwater (Fla.) Bombers			
1961	Aurora (Ill.) Sealmasters	1973	Clearwater (Fla.) Bombers	
1962–63	Clearwater (Fla.) Bombers	1974	Santa Rosa (Calif.)	
1964	Burch Gage & Tool, Detroit	1975	Rising Sun Hotel, Reading, Pa.	
1965	Aurora (Ill.) Sealmasters	1976	Raybestos Cardinals, Stratford, Conn.	
1966	Clearwater (Fla.) Bombers			
1967	Aurora (Ill.) Sealmasters	1977	Billard Barbell, Reading, Pa.	
1968	Clearwater (Fla.) Bombers	1978	Reading, Pa.	
1969–70	Raybestos Cardinals, Stratford, Conn.	1979	Midland, Mich.	
		1980	Peterbilt Western, Seattle	
1971	Welty Way, Cedar Rapids, Iowa	1981	Archer Daniels Midland, Decatur, Ill.	

1982	Peterbilt Western, Seattle
1983	Franklin Cardinals, West Haven, Conn.
1984	California Coors Kings, Merced, Calif.
1985	Pay 'n Pak, Bellevue, Washington
1986	Pay 'n Pak, Bellevue, Washington
1987	Pay 'n Pak, Bellevue, Washington
1988	Trans-Aire, Elkhart, Ind.
1989	Penn Corp., Sioux City, Iowa
1990	Penn Corp., Sioux City, Iowa

ASA NATIONAL CHAMPIONS—1990

Adult Champions

Men's major fast pitch—Penn Corp., Sioux City, Iowa
Men's Masters 55-and-over—Cane Stables, Ft. Wright, Ky.
Men's Major 16-inch Slow Pitch—Pete's Hideway Whips, Chicago, Ill.
Men's Class A 16-inch Slow Pitch—Gamblers, Tinley Park, Ill.
Coed Slow Pitch—Steffe's Sports, Calestine, Ind.
Women's Major Fast Pitch—Raybestos Brakettes, Stratford, Conn.
Women's Class A Fast Pitch—Baldwin Saints, St. Louis, Mo.
Women's Class B Fast Pitch—Mavericks, Burbank, Calif.
Men's Class C Fast Pitch—First Bank Bucks, Santa Margarita, Calif.
Women's Class C Fast Pitch—Red Machine, Nashville, Tenn.
Men's Masters 40-and-over Fast Pitch—Townhouse, Sioux City, Iowa
Men's Major Modified Pitch—CBS, New York, N.Y.
Men's Major Slow Pitch—New Construction, Shelbyville, Ind.
Women's Major Slow Pitch—Spooks, Anoka, Minn.
Men's Class A Slow Pitch—Vernon's, Jacksonville, Fla.
Women's Class A Slow Pitch—Vernon's, Jacksonville, Fla.
Men's Super Slow Pitch—Steele's Silver Bullets, Grafton, Ohio
Men's Major Industrial Slow Pitch—Sikorsky Aircraft, Shelton, Conn.
Women's Major Industrial Slow Pitch—Shaw Industtries, Dalton, Ga.
Men's Class A Industrial Slow Pitch—Textron, Stratford, Conn.
Women's Class A Industrial Slow Pitch—Russell Athletic, Alexander City, Ala.
Men's Major Church Slow Pitch—Mt. Zion Methodist, Gadsden, Ala.
Women's Major Church Slow Pitch—Westside Baptist, Jasper, Ala.
Men's Class A Church Slow Pitch—First Baptist, Hendersonville, Ala.
Women's Class A Church Slow Pitch—Muskogee, OK First Baptist
Men's Masters 35-and-over Slow Pitch—Nothdurft Tool and Die, Mt. Clemens, Mich.
Men's Masters 40-and-over Slow Pitch—Interstate Battery, Angier, N.C.
Men's Masters 45-and-over Slow Pitch—Capitol Oil, Columbus, Ind.
Junior Men's Fast Pitch—Ruthon Rookies, Ruthon, Minn.
Men's Class B Fast Pitch—Reno Raiders, Reno, Nev.

Junior Champions

Girls' 16-and-under Slow Pitch—Lake Lytal Lazers, West Palm Beach, Fla.
Boys' 16-and-under Slow Pitch—Rudy's Tire Service, Tifton, Ga.
Girls' 18-and-under Slow Pitch—The Sting, Tacoma, Wash.
Girls' 12-and-under Fast Pitch—Bat Busters, Orange County, Calif.
Boys' 12-and-under Fast Pitch—California Quake, Westminster, Calif.
Girls' 14-and-under Fast Pitch—Crackerjacks, Santa Ana, Calif.
Boys' 14-and-under Fast Pitch—Rent To Own, Sioux Falls, S.D.
Girls' 16-and-under Fast Pitch—S. California Raiders, Valencia, Calif.
Boys' 16-and-under Fast Pitch—BIX, Sioux Falls, S.D.
Girls' 18-and-under Fast Pitch—Gordon's Panthers, LaPalma, Calif.
Boys' 18-and-under Fast Pitch—Kenrock Flyers, Rockford, Ill.
Girls' 12-and-under Slow Pitch—Pacers, Hollywood, Fla.
Boys' 12-and-under Slow Pitch—Maysville–Mason County, Maysville, Ky.
Girls' 14-and-under Slow Pitch—Thunder, Pembroke Pines, Fla.
Boys' 14-and-under Slow Pitch—Maysville Sports Shop, Maysville, Ky.
Boys' 18-and-under Slow Pitch—Royal Pharmacy Rangers, Tifton, Ga.

HANDBALL

U.S.H.A. NATIONAL FOUR-WALL CHAMPIONS

Singles

1960	Jimmy Jacobs
1961	John Sloan
1962–63	Oscar Obert
1964–65	Jimmy Jacobs
1966–67	Paul Haber
1968	Simon (Stuffy) Singer
1969–71	Paul Haber
1972	Fred Lewis
1973	Terry Muck
1974	Fred Lewis
1975	Jay Bilyeu
1976	Vern Roberts, Jr.
1977	Naty Alvarado
1978	Fred Lewis
1979	Naty Alvarado
1980	Naty Alvarado
1981	Fred Lewis

1. 10th time—American record.

1982	Naty Alvarado
1983	Naty Alvarado
1984	Naty Alvarado
1985	Naty Alvarado
1986	Naty Alvarado
1987	Naty Alvarado
1988	Naty Alvarado[1]
1989	Ponch Monreal
1990	Nat Alvarado

Doubles

1960	Jimmy Jacobs–Dick Weisman
1961	John Sloan–Vic Hershkowitz
1962–63	Jimmy Jacobs–Marty Decatur
1964	John Sloan–Phil Elbert
1965	Jimmy Jacobs–Marty Decatur
1966	Pete Tyson–Bob Lindsay
1967–68	Jimmy Jacobs–Marty Decatur
1969	Lou Kramberg–Lou Russo

1970	Karl and Ruby Obert
1971	Ray Neveau–Simie Fein
1972	Kent Fusselman–Al Drews
1973–74	Ray Neveau–Simie Fein
1975	Marty Decatur–Steve Lott
1976	Gary Rohrer–Dan O'Connor
1977	Skip McDowell–Matt Kelly
1978	Stuffy Singer–Marty Decatur
1979	Stuffy Singer–Marty Decatur
1980	Skip McDowell–Harry Robertson
1981	Tom Kopatich–Jack Roberts
1982	Naty Alvarado–Vern Roberts
1983	Naty Alvarado–Vern Roberts
1984	Naty Alvarado–Vern Roberts
1985	Naty Alvarado–Vern Roberts
1986–87	Jon Kemdler–Poncho Monreal
1988	Doug Glatt–Dennis Haynes
1989	Danny Bell–Charlie Kalil
1990	Doug Glatt–Rod Prince

BASEBALL

The popular tradition that baseball was invented by Abner Doubleday at Cooperstown, N.Y., in 1839 has been enshrined in the Hall of Fame and National Museum of Baseball erected in that town, but research has proved that a game called "Base Ball" was played in this country and England before 1839. The first team baseball as we know it was played at the Elysian Fields, Hoboken, N.J., on June 19, 1846, between the Knickerbockers and the New York Nine. The next fifty years saw a gradual growth of baseball and an improvement of equipment and playing skill.

Historians have it that the first pitcher to throw a curve was William A. (Candy) Cummings in 1867. The Cincinnati Red Stockings were the first all-professional team, and in 1869 they played 64 games without a loss. The standard ball of the same size and weight, still the rule, was adopted in 1872. The first catcher's mask was worn in 1875. The National League was organized in 1876. The first chest protector was worn in 1885. The three-strike rule was put on the books in 1887, and the four-ball ticket to first base was instituted in 1889. The pitching distance was lengthened to 60 feet 6 inches in 1893, and the rules have been modified only slightly since that time.

The American League, under the vigorous leadership of B. B. Johnson, became a major league in 1901. Judge Kenesaw Mountain Landis, by action of the two major leagues, became Commissioner of Baseball in 1921, and upon his death (1944), Albert B. Chandler, former United States Senator from Kentucky, was elected to that office (1945). Chandler failed to obtain a new contract and was succeeded by Ford C. Frick (1951), the National League president. Frick retired after the 1965 season, and William D. Eckert, a retired Air Force lieutenant general, was named to succeed him. Eckert resigned under pressure in December, 1968. Bowie Kuhn, a New York attorney, became interim commissioner for one year in February. His appointment was made permanent with two seven-year contracts until August 1983. In August 1983, Kuhn's contract was not renewed, and a search was begun for his successor. Peter Ueberroth was named new Commissioner and took office Oct. 1, 1984.

Ueberroth did not seek a new term in 1989 and was succeded by Bart Giamatti who died suddenly on Sept. 1, 1989. Francis T. Vincent, Jr., replaced him on Sept. 13, 1989.

MAJOR LEAGUE ALL-STAR GAME

Year	Date	Winning league and manager	Runs	Losing league and manager	Runs	Winning pitcher	Losing pitcher	Site	Paid attendance
1933	July 6	A.L. (Mack)	4	N.L. (McGraw)	2	Gomez	Hallahan	Chicago A.L.	47,595
1934	July 10	A.L. (Cronin)	9	N.L. (Terry)	7	Harder	Mungo	New York N.L.	48,363
1935	July 8	A.L. (Cochrane)	4	N.L. (Frisch)	1	Gomez	Walker	Cleveland A.L.	69,831
1936	July 7	N.L. (Grimm)	4	A.L. (McCarthy)	3	J. Dean	Grove	Boston N.L.	25,556
1937	July 7	A.L. (McCarthy)	8	N.L. (Terry)	3	Gomez	J. Dean	Washington A.L.	31,391
1938	July 6	N.L. (Terry)	4	A.L. (McCarthy)	1	Vander Meer	Gomez	Cincinnati N.L.	27,067
1939	July 11	A.L. (McCarthy)	3	N.L. (Hartnett)	1	Bridges	Lee	New York A.L.	62,892
1940	July 9	N.L. (McKechnie)	4	A.L. (Cronin)	0	Derringer	Ruffing	St. Louis N.L.	32,373
1941	July 8	A.L. (Baker)	7	N.L. (McKechnie)	5	E. Smith	Passeau	Detroit A.L.	54,674
1942	July 6	A.L. (McCarthy)	3	N.L. (Durocher)	1	Chandler	Cooper	New York A.L.	34,178
1943	July 13[1]	A.L. (McCarthy)	5	N.L. (Southworth)	3	Leonard	Cooper	Philadelphia A.L.	31,938
1944	July 11[1]	N.L. (Southworth)	7	A.L. (McCarthy)	1	Raffensberger	Hughson	Pittsburgh N.L.	29,589
1946	July 9	A.L. (O'Neill)	12	N.L. (Grimm)	0	Feller	Passeau	Boston A.L.	34,906
1947	July 8	A.L. (Cronin)	2	N.L. (Dyer)	1	Shea	Sain	Chicago N.L.	41,123
1948	July 13	A.L. (Harris)	5	N.L. (Durocher)	2	Raschi	Schmitz	St. Louis A.L.	34,009
1949	July 12	A.L. (Boudreau)	11	N.L. (Southworth)	7	Trucks	Newcombe	Brooklyn N.L.	32,577
1950	July 11	N.L. (Shotton)	4	A.L. (Stengel)	3[3]	Blackwell	Gray	Chicago A.L.	46,127
1951	July 10	N.L. (Sawyer)	8	A.L. (Stengel)	3	Maglie	Lopat	Detroit A.L.	52,075
1952	July 8	N.L. (Durocher)	3	A.L. (Stengel)	2[4]	Rush	Lemon	Philadelphia N.L.	32,785
1953	July 14	N.L. (Dressen)	5	A.L. (Stengel)	1	Spahn	Reynolds	Cincinnati N.L.	30,846
1954	July 13	A.L. (Stengel)	11	N.L. (Alston)	9	Stone	Conley	Cleveland A.L.	68,751
1955	July 12	N.L. (Durocher)	6	A.L. (Lopez)	5[5]	Conley	Sullivan	Milwaukee N.L.	45,643
1956	July 10	N.L. (Alston)	7	A.L. (Stengel)	3	Friend	Pierce	Washington A.L.	28,843
1957	July 9	A.L. (Stengel)	6	N.L. (Alston)	5	Bunning	Simmons	St. Louis N.L.	30,693
1958	July 8	A.L. (Stengel)	4	N.L. (Haney)	3	Wynn	Friend	Baltimore A.L.	48,829
1959[2]	July 7	N.L. (Haney)	5	A.L. (Stengel)	4	Antonelli	Ford	Pittsburgh A.L.	35,277
	Aug. 3	A.L. (Stengel)	5	N.L. (Haney)	3	Walker	Drysdale	Los Angeles N.L.	55,105
1960[2]	July 11	N.L. (Alston)	5	A.L. (Lopez)	3	Friend	Monbouquette	Kansas City A.L.	30,619
	July 13	N.L. (Alston)	6	A.L. (Lopez)	0	Law	Ford	New York A.L.	38,362
1961[2]	July 11	N.L. (Murtaugh)	5	A.L. (Richards)	4[6]	Miller	Wilhelm	San Francisco N.L.	44,115
	July 31	N.L. (Murtaugh)	1	A.L. (Richards)	1[7]	—	—	Boston A.L.	31,851
1962[2]	July 10	N.L. (Hutchinson)	3	A.L. (Houk)	1	Marichal	Pascual	Washington A.L.	45,480
	July 30	A.L. (Houk)	9	N.L. (Hutchinson)	4	Herbert	Mahaffey	Chicago N.L.	38,359
1963	July 9	N.L. (Dark)	5	A.L. (Houk)	3	Jackson	Bunning	Cleveland A.L.	44,160
1964	July 7	N.L. (Alston)	7	A.L. (Lopez)	4	Marichal	Radatz	New York N.L.	50,850
1965	July 13	N.L. (March)	6	A.L. (Lopez)	5	Koufax	McDowell	Minnesota N.L.	46,706
1966	July 12	N.L. (Alston)	2	A.L. (Mele)	1[6]	Perry	Rickert	St. Louis N.L.	49,926
1967	July 11	N.L. (Alston)	2	A.L. (Bauer)	1[8]	Drysdale	Hunter	Anaheim A.L.	46,309
1968	July 9	N.L. (Schoendienst)	1	A.L. (Williams)	0	Drysdale	Tiant	Houston N.L.	48,321
1969	July 23	N.L. (Schoendienst)	9	A.L. (M. Smith)	3	Carlton	Stottlemyre	Washington A.L.	45,259
1970	July 14	N.L. (Hodges)	5	A.L. (Weaver)	4	Osteen	Wright	Cincinnati N.L.	51,838
1971	July 13	A.L. (Weaver)	6	N.L. (Anderson)	4	Blue	Ellis	Detroit A.L.	53,559

1972 July 25	N.L. (Murtaugh)	4	A.L. (Weaver)	3[6]	McGraw	McNally	Atlanta N.L.	53,107
1973 July 24[1]	N.L. (Anderson)	7	A.L. (Williams)	1	Wise	Blyleven	Kansas City A.L.	40,849
1974 July 23[1]	N.L. (Berra)	7	A.L. (Williams)	2	Brett	Tiant	Pittsburgh N.L.	50,706
1975 July 15[1]	N.L. (Alston)	6	A.L. (Dark)	3	Matlack	Hunter	Milwaukee A.L.	51,540
1976 July 13	N.L. (Anderson)	7	A.L. (D. Johnson)	1	R. Jones	Fidrych	Philadelphia N.L.	63,974
1977 July 19[1]	N.L. (Anderson)	7	A.L. (Martin)	5	Sutton	Palmer	New York A.L.	56,683
1978 July 11[1]	N.L. (Lasorda)	7	A.L. (Martin)	3	Sutter	Gossage	San Diego N.L.	51,549
1979 July 17[1]	N.L. (Lasorda)	7	A.L. (Lemon)	6	Sutter	Kern	Seattle A.L.	58,905
1980 July 8[1]	N.L. (Tanner)	4	A.L. (Weaver)	2	Reuss	John	Los Angeles N.L.	56,088
1981 Aug. 9[1]	N.L. (Green)	5	A.L. (Frey)	4	Blue	Fingers	Cleveland* A.L.	72,086
1982 July 13[1]	N.L. (Lasorda)	4	A.L. (Martin)	1	Rogers	Eckersley	Montreal N.L.	59,057
1983 July 6[1]	A.L. (Kuenn)	13	N.L. (Herzog)	3	Steib	Soto	Chicago A.L.	43,801
1984 July 11[1]	N.L. (Owens)	3	A.L. (Altobelli)	1	Leg	Steib	San Francisco N.L.	57,756
1985 July 16[1]	N.L. (Williams)	6	A.L. (Anderson)	1	Hoyt	Morris	Minneapolis, A.L.	54,960
1986 July 15[1]	A.L. (Howser)	3	N.L. (Herzog)	2	Clemens	Gooden	Houston, N.L.	45,774
1987 July 14[1]	N.L. (Johnson)	2	A.L. (McNamara)	0	Smith	Howell	Oakland, A.L.	49,671
1988 July 12[1]	A.L. (Kelly)	2	N.L. (Herzog)	1	Viola	Gooden	Cincinnati, N.L	55,837
1989 July 11[1]	A.L. (LaRussa)	5	N.L. (Lasorda)	3	Ryan	Smoltz	California, A.L.	64,036
1990 July 10[1]	A.L. (LaRussa)	2	N.L. (Craig)	0	Saberhagen	Brantley	Chicago, N.L.	39,071

1. Night game. 2. Two games. 3. Fourteen innings. 4. Five innings, rain. 5. Twelve innings. 6. Ten innings. 7. Called because of rain after nine innings. 8. Fifteen innings. NOTE: No game in 1945. *Game was originally scheduled for July 14, but was put off because of players' strike.

NATIONAL BASEBALL HALL OF FAME

Cooperstown, N.Y.

Fielders

Member	Active years	Member	Active years	Member	Active years
Aaron, Henry (Hank)	1954–1976	Ewing, William	1880–1897	McGraw, John J.	1891–1906
Anson, Adrian (Cap)	1876–1897	Eyers, John	1902–1919	McCovey, Willie	1959–1980
Aparicio, Luis	1956–1973	Flick, Elmer	1898–1910	Medwick, Joseph	
Appling, Lucius (Luke)	1930–1950	Foxx, James	1925–1945	(Ducky)	1932–1948
Averill, H. Earl	1929–1941	Frisch, Frank	1919–1937	Mize, John (The Big Cat)	1936–1953
Baker, J. Frank		Gehrig, H. Louis (Lou)	1923–1939	Morgan, Joe	1963–1984
(Home Run)	1908–1922	Gehringer, Charles	1924–1942	Musial, Stanley	1941–1963
Bancroft, David	1915–1930	Gibson, Josh[1]	1929–1946	O'Rourke, James	1876–1894
Banks, Ernest	1953–1971	Goslin, Leon (Goose)	1921–1938	Ott, Melvin	1926–1947
Beckley, Jacob	1888–1907	Greenberg, Henry		Reese, Harold (Pee Wee)	1940–1958
Bell, James		(Hank)	1933–1947	Rice, Edgar (Sam)	1915–1934
(Cool Papa)[1]	1920–1947	Hafey, Charles (Chick)	1924–1937	Robinson, Brooks	1955–1977
Bench, John	1967–1983	Hamilton, William	1888–1901	Robinson, Frank	1956–1976
Berra, Lawrence (Yogi)	1946–1965	Hartnett, Charles		Robinson, Jack	1947–1956
Bottomley, James	1922–1937	(Gabby)	1922–1941	Robinson, Wilbert	1886–1902
Boudreau, Louis	1938–1952	Heilmann, Harry	1914–1932	Roush, Edd	1913–1931
Bresnahan, Roger	1897–1915	Herman, William	1931–1947	Ruth, George (Babe)	1914–1935
Brock, Lou	1961–1980	Hooper, Harry	1909–1925	Schalk, Raymond	1912–1929
Brouthers, Dennis	1879–1896	Hornsby, Rogers	1915–1937	Schoendienst, Red	1945–1963
Burkett, Jesse	1890–1905	Irvin, Monford (Monte)[1]	1939–1956	Sewell, Joseph	1920–1933
Campanella, Roy	1948–1957	Jackson, Travis	1922–1936	Simmons, Al	1924–1944
Carey, Max	1910–1929	Jennings, Hugh	1891–1918	Sisler, George	1915–1930
Chance, Frank	1898–1914	Johnson, William (Judy)[1]	1921–1937	Slaughter, Enos	1938–1959
Charleston, Oscar[1]	1915–1954	Kaline, Albert W.	1953–1974	Snider, Edwin D. (Duke)	1947–1964
Clarke, Fred	1894–1915	Keeler, William		Speaker, Tristram	1907–1928
Clemente, Roberto	1955–1972	(Wee Willie)	1892–1910	Stargell, Willie	1962–1982
Cobb, Tyrus	1905–1928	Kell, George	1943–1957	Terry, William	1923–1936
Cochrane, Gordon		Kelley, Joseph	1891–1908	Thompson, Samuel	1885–1906
(Mickey)	1925–1937	Kelly, George	1915–1932	Tinker, Joseph	1902–1916
Collins, Edward	1906–1930	Kelly, Michael (King)	1878–1893	Traynor, Harold (Pie)	1920–1937
Collins, James	1895–1908	Killebrew, Harmon	1954–1975	Vaughan, Arky	1932–1948
Comiskey, Charles	1882–1894	Kiner, Ralph	1946–1955	Wagner, John (Honus)	1897–1917
Combs, Earle	1924–1935	Klein, Charles H. (Chuck)	1928–1944	Wallace, Roderick	
Connor, Roger	1880–1897	Lajoie, Napoleon	1896–1916	(Bobby)	1894–1918
Crawford, Samuel	1899–1917	Leonard, Walter (Buck)[1]	1933–1955	Waner, Lloyd	1927–1945
Cronin, Joseph	1926–1945	Lindstrom, Frederick	1924–1936	Waner, Paul	1926–1945
Cuyler, Hazen (Kiki)	1921–1938	Lloyd, John Henry[1]	1905–1931	Ward, John (Monte)	1878–1894
Dandridge, Ray[1]	1933–1953	Lombardi, Ernie	1932–1947	Wheat, Zachariah	1909–1927
Delahanty, Edward	1888–1903	Mantle, Mickey	1951–1968	Williams, Billy	1959–1976
Dickey, William	1928–1946	Manush, Henry (Heinie)	1923–1939	Williams, Theodore	1939–1960
Dihigo, Martin[1]	1923–1945	Maranville, Walter (Rabbit)	1912–1935	Wilson, Lewis R. (Hack)	1923–1934
DiMaggio, Joseph	1936–1951	Matthews, Edwin	1952–1968	Yastrzemski, Carl	1961–1983
Doerr, Bobby	1937–1951	Mays, Willie	1951–1973	Youngs, Ross (Pep)	1917–1926
Duffy, Hugh	1888–1906	McCarthy, Thomas	1884–1896		

1. Negro League player selected by special committee.

Pitchers

Alexander, Grover	1911–1930	Grove, Robert (Lefty)	1925–1941	Plank, Edward	1901–1917
Bender, Charles (Chief)	1903–1925	Haines, Jesse	1918–1937	Radbourn, Charles	
Brown, Mordecai		Hoyt, Waite	1918–1938	(Hoss)	1880–1891
(3-Finger)	1903–1916	Hubbell, Carl	1928–1943	Rixey, Eppa	1912–1933
Chesbro, John	1899–1909	Hunter, Jim (Catfish)	1965–1979	Roberts, Robert (Robin)	1948–1966
Clarkson, John	1882–1894	Johnson, Walter	1907–1927	Ruffing, Charles (Red)	1924–1947
Coveleski, Stanley	1912–1928	Joss, Adrian	1902–1910	Rusie, Amos	1889–1901
Dean, Jerome (Dizzy)	1930–1947	Keefe, Timothy	1880–1893	Spahn, Warren	1942–1965
Drysdale, Don	1956–1969	Koufax, Sanford (Sandy)	1955–1966	Vance, Arthur (Dazzy)	1915–1935
Faber, Urban (Red)	1914–1933	Lemon, Robert	1946–1958	Waddell, George	1897–1910
Feller, Robert	1936–1956	Lyons, Theodore	1923–1946	Walsh, Edward	1904–1917
Ferrell, Rick	1929–1947	Marichal, Juan	1960–1975	Welch, Michael (Mickey)	1880–1892
Ford, Edward (Whitey)	1950–1967	Marquard, Richard		Wilhelm, Hoyt	1952–1972
Foster, Andrew (Rube)	1897–1926	(Rube)	1908–1924	Wynn, Early	1939–1963
Galvin, James (Pud)	1876–1892	Mathewson, Christopher	1900–1916	Young, Denton (Cy)	1890–1911
Gibson, Bob	1959–1975	McGinnity, Joseph	1899–1908		
Gomez, Vernon (Lefty)	1930–1943	Nichols, Charles (Kid)	1890–1906		
Griffith, Clark	1891–1914	Paige, Leroy (Satchel)[1]	1926–1965		
Grimes, Burleigh	1916–1934	Palmer, Jim	1965–1984		
		Pennock, Herbert	1912–1934		

Officials and Others

Alston, Walter[2]	Cummings, William A.[6]	Johnson, B. Bancroft[3]	Rickey, W. Branch[2][3]
Barrow, Edward[2][3]	Evans, William G.[5][3]	Klem, William[5]	Spalding, Albert G.[5]
Bulkeley, Morgan G.[3]	Frick, Ford C.[7][3]	Landis, Kenesaw M.[7]	Stengel, Charles D.[8]
Cartwright, Alexander[3]	Giles, Warren C.[3]	Lopez, Alfonso R.[8]	Weiss, George M.[3]
Chadwick, Henry[4]	Harridge, William[3]	Mack, Connie[2][3]	Wright, George[6]
Chandler, A.B.[7]	Harris, Stanley R.[8]	MacPhail, Leland S.[3]	Wright, Harry[6][2]
Conlan, John[3]	Hubbard, R. Calvin[5]	McCarthy, Joseph V.[2]	Yawkey, Thomas[3]
Connolly, Thomas[5]	Higgins, Miller J.[2]	McKechnie, William B.[2]	

1. Negro league player selected by special committee. 2. Manager. 3. Executive. 4. Writer-statistician. 5. Umpire. 6. Early player. 7. Commissioner. 8. Player-manager.

BASEBALL SUFFERS THROUGH TWO STRIKES AND A LOCKOUT

Major League baseball, endured a strike by players for the second time since 1981 in August 1985. Unlike the 1981 strike, which lasted seven weeks and canceled 713 games, this one was ended quickly. The players walked on Aug. 6, and were back on the field three days later.

While in 1981 the major issue was over compensation for free agent signings to the club losing players, the 1985 strike was primarily over the pension fund, and how much of the reported $1.1 billion the owners receive through network television agreements would go into the plan.

The players were seeking an increase of $45 million over the $15 million they'd been receiving under the contract signed in 1981. The owners were adamant in refusing such a large increase.

There were other matters at question, including the issue of arbitration. Under the 1981 agreement, a player with two years of major league service who couldn't come to terms with ownership could take his case to binding arbitration. The owners were looking to increase the number of years vested service required to three years, and pointed to substantial operating losses caused, in part, by large salaries granted by arbitrators and the increasing spiral of free agent salaries.

In the end, the players wound up with approximately $35 million for their pension fund, and the owners got their desired three years for arbitration, albeit the rule did not take effect until 1987.

The games canceled by the strike were rescheduled for later in the season, unlike the 1981 affair when far too many games were lost to be made up.

The 1981 strike settlement had been complicated by the decision to play a split season—awarding divisional championships to the teams in first place before the strike began, and starting a new second season to crown four additional champions. Those eight teams played off in a preliminary series. The survivors played for the league title and the right to move on to the World Series.

With the contract up at the end of the 1989 season, there was serious threat of another strike before the 1990 season. Instead, the owners locked the players out of spring training camps and the regular season was delayed a week in starting. Spring training was reduced to three weeks. A new three-year contract guaranteed baseball labor peace through 1992.

LIFETIME BATTING, PITCHING, AND BASE-RUNNING RECORDS

(An asterisk indicates active player)

Sources: Baseball Record Book, published and copyrighted by The Sporting News, St. Louis, Mo. 63166; *The Book of Baseball Records,* published and copyrighted by Seymour Siwoff, New York, N.Y. 10036; and *The Complete Handbook of Baseball,* published and copyrighted by New American Library, New York, N.Y. 10019. All records through 1989 unless noted.

(Records Through 1989)

Hits (3,000 or more)

Pete Rose	4,256
Ty Cobb	4,190
Henry Aaron	3,771
Stan Musial	3,630
Tris Speaker	3,515
Honus Wagner	3,430
Carl Yastrzemski	3,419
Eddie Collins	3,311
Willie Mays	3,283
Nap Lajoie	3,251
Paul Waner	3,152
Rod Carew	3,053
Lou Brock	3,023
Cap Anson	3,022
Al Kaline	3,007
Roberto Clemente	3,000

Earned Run Average

(Minimum 1,500 innings pitched)

Ed Walsh	1.82
Addie Joss	1.88
Joe Wood	2.03
Three Finger Brown	2.06
Christy Mathewson	2.13
Rube Waddell	2.16
Walter Johnson	2.17
Orvie Overall	2.23
Ed Ruelbach	2.28
Jim Scott	2.32
Ed Plank	2.34
Ed Cicotte	2.37
Ed Killian	2.38
Doc White	2.38
Nap Rucker	2.42
Jeff Tesreau	2.43
Chief Bender	2.46
Sam Leaver	2.47

Runs Scored

Ty Cobb	2,245
Henry Aaron	2,174
Babe Ruth	2,174
Pete Rose	2,165

Willie Mays	2,062
Stan Musial	1,949
Lou Gehrig	1,888
Tris Speaker	1,881
Mel Ott	1,859
Frank Robinson	1,829
Eddie Collins	1,816
Carl Yastrzemski	1,816
Ted Williams	1,798
Charlie Gehringer	1,774
Jimmie Foxx	1,751
Honus Wagner	1,740
Willie Keeler	1,720
Cap Anson	1,712
Jesse Burkett	1,708
Billy Hamilton	1,690
Mickey Mantle	1,677
John McPhee	1,674
George Van Haltren	1,650

Strikeouts, Pitching

Nolan Ryan**	5,076
Steve Carlton	4,136
Tom Seaver	3,640
Don Sutton	3,569
Bert Blyleven**	3,562
Gaylord Perry	3,534
Walter Johnson	3,509
Phil Niekro	3,342
Ferguson Jenkins	3,192
Bob Gibson	3,117
Jim Bunning	2,855
Mickey Lolich	2,832
Cy Young	2,819
Warren Spahn	2,583
Bob Feller	2,581
Tim Keefe	2,538
Christy Mathewson	2,505

**Active through 1989.

Home Runs (350 or More)

Henry Aaron	755
Babe Ruth	714
Willie Mays	660
Frank Robinson	586
Harmon Killebrew	573
Reggie Jackson	563

Mike Schmidt	548
Mickey Mantle	536
Jimmie Foxx	534
Ted Williams	521
Willie McCovey	521
Eddie Mathews	512
Ernie Banks	512
Mel Ott	511
Lou Gehrig	493
Stan Musial	475
Willie Stargell	475
Carl Yastrzemski	452
Dave Kingman	442
Billy Williams	426
Darrell Evans	414
Duke Snider	406
Al Kaline	399
Johnny Bench	389
Frank Howard	382
Jim Rice	382
Orlando Cepeda	379
Norm Cash	377
Rocky Colavito	374
Tony Perez	371
Gil Hodges	370
Ralph Kiner	369
Joe DiMaggio	361
Lee May	360
Johnny Mize	359
Yogi Berra	358
Dick Allen	351

Shutouts

Walter Johnson	110
Grover Alexander	90
Christy Mathewson	83
Cy Young	77
Ed Plank	64
Warren Spahn	63
Tom Seaver	60
Ed Walsh	58
Don Sutton	58
James Galvin	57
Bob Gibson	56
Steve Carlton	55

Bert Blyleven	55
Jim Palmer	53
Gaylord Perry	53
Juan Marichal	52

Strikeouts, Batting

Reggie Jackson	2,597
Willie Stargell	1,936
Mike Schmidt	1,883
Tony Perez	1,867
Dave Kingman	1,816
Bobby Bonds	1,757
Lou Brock	1,730
Mickey Mantle	1,710
Harmon Killebrew	1,699
Lee May	1,570
Darrell Evans	1,570
Dick Allen	1,566
Willie McCovey	1,550
Frank Robinson	1,532
Willie Mays	1,526

Bases on Balls

Babe Ruth	2,056
Ted Williams	2,019
Carl Yastrzemski	1,844
Mickey Mantle	1,734
Mel Ott	1,708
Eddie Yost	1,614
Darrell Evans	1,605
Stan Musial	1,599
Harmon Killebrew	1,559
Lou Gehrig	1,510
Mike Schmidt	1,507
Willie Mays	1,463
Jimmie Foxx	1,452
Eddie Mathews	1,444
Frank Robinson	1,426
Henry Aaron	1,402

BASEBALL'S PERFECTLY PITCHED GAMES[1]

(no opposing runner reached base)

John Richmond—Worcester vs. Cleveland (NL) June 12, 1880	(1-0)
John M. Ward—Providence vs. Buffalo (NL) June 17, 1880	(5-0)
Cy Young—Boston vs. Philadelphia (AL) May 5, 1904	(3-0)
Addie Joss—Cleveland vs. Chicago (AL) Oct. 2, 1908	(1-0)
Ernest Shore[2]—Boston vs. Washington (AL) June 23, 1917	(4-0)
Charles Robertson—Chicago vs. Detroit (AL) April 30, 1922	(2-0)
Don Larsen[3]—New York (AL) vs. Brooklyn (NL) Oct. 8, 1956	(2-0)
Jim Bunning—Philadelphia vs. New York (NL) June 21, 1964	(6-0)
Sandy Koufax—Los Angeles vs. Chicago (NL) Sept. 9, 1965	(1-0)
Jim Hunter—Oakland vs. Minnesota (AL) May 8, 1968	(4-0)
Len Barker—Cleveland vs. Toronto (AL) May 15, 1981	(3-0)
Mike Witt—California vs. Texas (AL) Sept. 30, 1984	(1-0)

1. Harvey Haddix, of Pittsburgh, pitched 12 perfect innings against Milwaukee (NL), May 26, 1959 but lost game in 13th on error and hit. 2. Shore, relief pitcher for Babe Ruth who walked first batter before being ejected by umpire, retired 26 batters who faced him and baserunner was out stealing. 3. World Series.

RECORD OF WORLD SERIES GAMES

(Through 1989)

Source: The Book of Baseball Records, published by Seymour Siwoff, New York City.

Figures in parentheses for winning pitchers (WP) and losing pitchers (LP) indicate the game number in the series.

1903—Boston A.L. 5 (Jimmy Collins); Pittsburgh N.L. 3 (Fred Clarke). WP—Bos.: Dinneen (2, 6, 8), Young (5, 7); Pitts.: Phillippe (1, 3, 4). LP—Bos.: Young (1), Hughes (3), Dinneen (4); Pitts.: Leever (2, 6), Kennedy (5), Phillippe (7, 8).

1904—No series.

1905—New York N.L. 4 (John J. McGraw); Philadelphia A.L. 1 (Connie Mack). WP—N.Y.: Mathewson (1, 3, 5); McGinnity (4); Phila.: Bender (2). LP—N.Y.: McGinnity (2); Phila.: Plank (1, 4), Coakley (3), Bender (5).

1906—Chicago A.L. 4 (Fielder Jones); Chicago N.L. 2 (Frank Chance). WP—Chi.: A.L.: Altrock (1), Walsh (3, 5), White (6); Chi.: N.L.: Reulbach (2), Brown (4). LP—Chi. A.L.: White (1, 4), Altrock. (4); Chi.: N.L.: Brown (1, 6), Pfeister (3, 5).

1907—Chicago N.L. 4 (Frank Chance); Detroit A.L. 0 (Hugh Jennings). First game tied 3–3, 12 innings. WP—Pfeister (2), Reulbach (3), Overall (4), Brown (5). LP—Mullin (2, 5), Siever (3), Donovan (4).

1908—Chicago N.L. 4 (Frank Chance); Detroit A.L. 1 (Hugh Jennings). WP—Chi.: Brown (1, 4), Overall (2, 5); Det.: Mullin (3). LP—Chi.: Pfeister (3); Det.: Summers (1, 4), Donovan (2, 5).

1909—Pittsburgh N.L. 4 (Fred Clarke); Detroit A.L. 3 (Hugh Jennings). WP—Pitts.: Adams (1, 5, 7), Maddox (3); Det.: Donovan (2), Mullin (4, 6). LP—Pitts.: Camnitz (2), Leifield (4), Willis (6); Det.: Mullin (1), Summers (3, 5), Donovan (7).

1910—Philadelphia A.L. 4 (Connie Mack); Chicago N.L. 1 (Frank Chance). WP—Phila.: Bender (1), Coombs (2, 3, 5); Chi.: Brown (4). LP—Phila.: Bender (4); Chi.: Overall (1), Brown (2, 5), McIntyre (3).

1911—Philadelphia A.L. 4 (Connie Mack); New York N.L. 2 (John J. McGraw). WP—Phila.: Plank (2), Coombs (3), Bender (4, 6); N.Y.: Mathewson (1), Crandall (3). LP—Phila.: Bender (1), Plank (5); N.Y.: Marquard (2), Mathewson (3, 4), Ames (6).

1912—Boston A.L. 4 (J. Garland Stahl); New York N.L. 3 (John J. McGraw). Second game tied, 6–6, 11 innings. WP—Bos.: Wood (1, 4, 8), Bedient (5); N.Y.: Marquard (3, 6), Tesreau (7). LP—Bos.: O'Brien (3, 6), Wood (7); N.Y.: Tesreau (1, 4), Mathewson (5, 8).

1913—Philadelphia A.L. 4 (Connie Mack); New York N.L. 1 (John J. McGraw). WP—Phila.: Bender (1, 4), Bush (3), Plank (5); N.Y.: Mathewson (2); LP—Phila.: Plank (2); N.Y.: Marquard (1), Tesreau (3), Demaree (4), Mathewson (5).

1914—Boston N.L. 4 (George Stallings); Philadelphia A.L. 0 (Connie Mack). WP—Rudolph (1, 4), James (2, 3). LP—Bender (1), Plank (2), Bush (3), Shawkey (4).

1915—Boston A.L. 4 (Bill Carrigan); Philadelphia N.L. 1 (Pat Moran). WP—Bos.: Foster (2, 5), Leonard (3), Shore (4); Phila.: Alexander (1). LP—Bos.: Shore (1); Phila.: Mayer (2), Alexander (3), Chalmers (4), Rixey (5).

1916—Boston A.L. 4 (Bill Carrigan); Brooklyn N.L. 1 (Wilbert Robinson). WP—Bos.: Shore (1, 5), Ruth (2), Leonard (4); Bklyn.: Coombs (3). LP—Bos.: Mays (3); Bklyn.: Marquard (1, 4), Smith (2), Pfeffer (5).

1917—Chicago A.L. 4 (Clarence Rowland); New York N.L. 2 (John J. McGraw). WP—Chi.: Cicotte (1), Faber (2, 5, 6); N.Y.: Benton (3), Schupp (4). LP—Chi.: Cicotte (3), Faber (4); N.Y.: Sallee (1, 5), Anderson (2), Benton (6).

1918—Boston A.L. 4 (Ed Barrow); Chicago N.L. 2 (Fred Mitchell). WP—Bos.: Ruth (1, 4), Mays (3, 6); Chi.: Tyler (2), Vaughn (5). LP—Bos.: Bush (2), Jones (5); Chi.: Vaughn (1, 3), Douglas (4), Tyler (6).

1919—Cincinnati N.L. 5 (Pat Moran); Chicago A.L. 3 (William Gleason). WP—Cin.: Ruether (1), Sallee (2), Ring (4), Eller (5, 8); Chi.: Kerr (3, 6), Cicotte (7). LP—Cin.: Fisher (3), Ring (6), Sallee (7); Chi.: Cicotte (1, 4), Williams (2, 5, 8).

1920—Cleveland A.L. 5 (Tris Speaker); Brooklyn N.L. 2 (Wilbert Robinson). WP—Cleve.: Coveleski (1, 4, 7), Bagby (5), Mails (6); Bklyn.: Grimes (2), Smith (3). LP—Cleve.: Bagby (2), Caldwell (3). Bklyn.: Marquard (1), Cadore (4), Grimes (5, 7), Smith (6).

1921—New York N.L. 5 (John J. McGraw); New York A.L. 3 (Miller Huggins). WP—N.Y. N.L.: Barnes (3, 6), Douglas (4, 7), Nehf (8); N.Y. A.L.: Mays (1), Hoyt (2, 5). LP—N.Y. N.L.: Nehf (2, 5), Douglas

(1). N.Y. A.L.: Quinn (3), Mays (4, 7), Shawkey (6), Hoyt (8).

1922—New York N.L. 4 (John J. McGraw); New York A.L. 0 (Miller Huggins). Second game tied 3–3, 10 innings. WP—Ryan (1), Scott (3), McQuillan (4), Nehf (5); LP—Bush (1, 5), Hoyt (3), Mays (4).

1923—New York A.L. 4 (Miller Huggins); New York N.L. 2 (John J. McGraw). WP—N.Y. A.L.: Pennock (2, 6), Shawkey (4), Bush (5); N.Y. N.L.: Ryan (1), Nehf (3). LP—N.Y. A.L.: Bush (1), Jones (3); N.Y. N.L.: McQuillan (2), Scott (4), Bentley (5), Nehf (6).

1924—Washington A.L. 4 (Bucky Harris); New York N.L. 3 (John J. McGraw). WP—Wash.: Zachary (2, 6), Mogridge (4), Johnson (7); N.Y.: Nehf (1), McQuillan (3), Bentley (5). LP—Wash.: Johnson (1, 5), Marberry (3); N.Y.: Bentley (2, 7), Barnes (4), Nehf (6).

1925—Pittsburgh N.L. 4 (Bill McKechnie); Washington A.L. 3 (Bucky Harris). WP—Pitts.: Aldridge (2, 5), Kremer (6, 7); Wash.: Johnson (1, 4), Ferguson (3). LP—Pitts.: Meadows (1), Kremer (3), Yde (4); Wash.: Coveleski (2, 5), Ferguson (6), Johnson (7).

1926—St. Louis N.L. 4 (Rogers Hornsby); New York A.L. 3 (Miller Huggins). WP—St. L.: Alexander (2, 6), Haines (3, 7); N.Y.: Pennock (1, 5), Hoyt (4). LP—St. L.: Sherdel (1, 5), Reinhart (4); N.Y.: Shocker (2), Ruether (3), Shawkey (6), Hoyt (7).

1927—New York A.L. 4 (Miller Huggins); Pittsburgh N.L. 0 (Donie Bush). WP—Hoyt (1), Pipgras (2), Pennock (3), Moore (4). LP—Kremer (1), Aldridge (2), Meadows (3), Miljus (4).

1928—New York A.L. 4 (Miller Huggins); St. Louis N.L. 0 (Bill McKechnie). WP—Hoyt (1, 4), Pipgras (2), Zachary (3). LP—Sherdel (1, 4), Alexander (2), Haines (3).

1929—Philadelphia A.L. 4 (Connie Mack); Chicago N.L. 1 (Joe McCarthy). WP—Phila.: Ehmke (1), Earnshaw (2), Rommel (4), Walberg (5); Chi.: Bush (3). LP—Phila.: Earnshaw (3) Chi.: Root (1), Malone (2, 5), Blake (4).

1930—Philadelphia A.L. 4 (Connie Mack); St. Louis N.L. 2 (Gabby Street). WP—Phila.: Grove (1, 5), Earnshaw (2, 6); St. L.: Hallahan (3), Haines (4). LP—Phila.: Walberg (3), Grove (4); St. L.: Grimes (1, 5), Rhem (2), Hallahan (6).

1931—St. Louis N.L. 4 (Gabby Street); Philadelphia A.L. 3 (Connie Mack). WP—St. L.: Hallahan (2, 5), Grimes (3, 7); Phila.: Grove (1, 6), Earnshaw (4). LP—St. L.: Derringer (1, 6), Johnson (4); Phila.: Earnshaw (2, 7), Grove (3), Hoyt (5).

1932—New York A.L. (Joe McCarthy); Chicago N.L. 0 (Charles Grimm). WP—Ruffing (1), Gomez (2), Pipgras (3), Moore (4). LP—Bush (1), Warneke (2), Root (3), May (4).

1933—New York N.L. 4 (Bill Terry); Washington A.L. 1 (Joe Cronin.). WP—N.Y.: Hubbell (1, 4), Schumacher (2), Luque (5); Wash.: Whitehill (3). LP—N.Y.: Fitzsimmons (3); Wash.: Stewart (1), Crowder (2), Weaver (4), Russell (5).

1934—St. Louis N.L. 4 (Frank Frisch); Detroit A.L. 3 (Mickey Cochrane). WP—St. L.: J. Dean (1, 7), P. Dean (3, 6); Det.: Rowe (2), Auker (4), Bridges (5). LP—St. L: W. Walker (2, 4), J. Dean (5); Det.: Crowder (1), Bridges (3), Rowe (6), Auker (7).

1935—Detroit A.L. 4 (Mickey Cochrane); Chicago N.L. 2 (Charles Grimm). WP—Det.: Bridges (2, 6), Rowe (3), Crowder (4); Chi.: Warneke (1, 5); LP—Det.: Rowe (1, 5), Chi.: Root (2), French (3, 6), Carleton (4).

1936—New York A.L. 4 (Joe McCarthy); New York N.L. 2 (Bill Terry). WP—N.Y. A.L.: Gomez (2, 6), Hadley (3), Pearson (4); N.Y. N.L.: Hubbell (1), Schumacher (5); LP—N.Y. A.L.: Ruffing (1), Malone (5); N.Y. N.L.: Schumacher (2), Fitzsimmons (3, 6), Hubbell (4).

1937—New York A.L. 4 (Joe McCarthy); New York N.L. 1 (Bill Terry). WP—N.Y. A.L.: Gomez (1, 5), Ruffing (2), Pearson (3); N.Y. N.L.: Hubbell (4). LP—N.Y. A.L.: Hadley (4); N.Y. N.L.: Hubbell (1), Melton (2, 5), Schumacher (3).

1938—New York A.L. 4 (Joe McCarthy); Chicago N.L. 0 (Gabby Hartnett). WP—Ruffing (1, 4), Gomez (2), Pearson (3) LP—Lee (1, 4), Dean (2), Bryant (3).

1939—New York A.L. 4 (Joe McCarthy); Cincinnati N.L. 0 (Bill McKechnie). WP—Ruffing (1), Pearson (2), Hadley (3), Murphy (4). LP—Derringer (1), Walters (2, 4), Thompson (3).

1940—Cincinnati N.L. 4 (Bill McKechnie); Detroit A.L. 3 (Del Baker).

WP—Cin.: Walters (2, 6), Derringer (4, 7); Det.: Newsom (1, 5), Bridges (3). LP—Cin.: Derringer (1), Turner (3), Thompson (5); Det.: Rowe (2, 6), Trout (4), Newsom (7).

1941—New York A.L. 4 (Joe McCarthy); Brooklyn N.L. 1 (Leo Durocher). WP—N.Y.: Ruffing (1), Russo (3), Murphy (4), Bonham (5); Bklyn: Wyatt (2). LP—N.Y.: Chandler (2); Bklyn: Davis (1), Casey (3, 4), Wyatt (5).

1942—St. Louis N.L. 4 (Billy Southworth); New York A.L. 1 (Joe McCarthy). WP—St. L.: Beazley (2, 5), White (3), Lanier (4); N.Y.: Ruffing (1). LP—St. L.: Cooper (1); N.Y.: Bonham (2), Chandler (3), Donald (4), Ruffing (5).

1943—New York A.L. 4 (Joe McCarthy); St. Louis N.L. 1 (Billy Southworth). WP—N.Y.: Chandler (1, 5), Borowy (3), Russo (4); St. L.: Cooper (2). LP—N.Y.: Bonham (2); St. L.: Lanier (1), Brazle (3), Brecheen (4), Cooper (5).

1944—St. Louis N.L. 4 (Billy Southworth); St. Louis A.L. 2 (Luke Sewell). WP—St. L. N.L.: Donnelly (2), Brecheen (4), Cooper (5), Lanier (6); St. L. A.L.: Galehouse (1), Kramer (3). LP—St. L. N.L.: Cooper (1), Wilks (3); St. L. A.L.: Muncrief (2), Jakucki (4), Galehouse (5), Potter (6).

1945—Detroit A.L. 4 (Steve O'Neill); Chicago N.L. 3 (Charles Grimm). WP—Det.: Trucks (2), Trout (4), Newhouser (5, 7); Chi.: Borowy (1, 6), Passeau (3). LP—Det.: Newhouser (1), Overmire (4), Trout (6); Chi.: Wyse (4), Prim (4), Borowy (5, 7).

1946—St. Louis N.L. 4 (Eddie Dyer); Boston A.L. 3 (Joe Cronin). WP—St. L.: Brecheen (2, 6, 7), Munger (4); Bos.: Johnson (1), Ferriss (3), Dobson (5). LP—St. L.: Pollet (1), Dickson (3), Brazle (5); Bos.: Harris (2, 6), Hughson (4), Klinger (7).

1947—New York A.L. 4 (Bucky Harris); Brooklyn N.L. 3 (Burt Shotton). WP—N.Y.: Shea (1, 5), Reynolds (2), Page (7); Bklyn.: Casey (3, 4), Branca (6). LP—N.Y.: Newsom (3), Bevens (4), Page (6); Bklyn.: Branca (1), Lombardi (2), Barney (5), Gregg (7).

1948—Cleveland A.L. 4 (Lou Boudreau); Boston N.L. 2 (Billy Southworth). WP—Cleve.: Lemon (2, 6), Bearden (3), Gromek (4); Bos.: Sain (1), Spahn (5). LP—Cleve.: Feller (1, 5); Bos.: Spahn (2), Bickford (3), Sain (4), Voiselle (6).

1949—New York A.L. 4 (Casey Stengel); Brooklyn N.L. 1 (Burt Shotton). WP—N.Y.: Reynolds (1), Page (3), Lopat (4), Raschi (5); Bklyn.: Roe (2). LP—N.Y.: Raschi (2); Bklyn.: Newcombe (1, 4), Branca (3), Barney (5).

1950—New York A.L. 4 (Casey Stengel); Philadelphia N.L. 0 (Eddie Sawyer). WP—Raschi (1), Reynolds (2), Ferrick (3), Ford (4). LP—Konstanty (1), Roberts (2), Meyer (3), Miller (4).

1951—New York A.L. 4 (Casey Stengel); New York N.L. 2 (Leo Durocher). WP—N.Y. A.L.: Lopat (2, 5), Reynolds (4), Raschi (6); N.Y. N.L.: Koslo (1), Hearn (3). LP—N.Y. A.L.: Reynolds (1), Raschi (3); N.Y. N.L.: Jansen (2, 5), Maglie (4), Koslo (6).

1952—New York A.L. 4 (Casey Stengel); Brooklyn N.L. 3 (Chuck Dressen). WP—N.Y.: Raschi (2, 6), Reynolds (4, 7); Bklyn.: Black (1), Roe (3), Erskine (5). LP—N.Y.: Reynolds (1), Lopat (3), Sain (5); Bklyn.: Erskine (2), Black (4, 7), Loes (6).

1953—New York A.L. 4 (Casey Stengel); Brooklyn N.L. 2 (Chuck Dressen). WP—N.Y.: Sain (1), Lopat (2), McDonald (5), Reynolds (6); Bklyn.: Erskine (3), Loes (4). LP—N.Y.: Raschi (3), Ford (4); Bklyn.: Labine (1, 6), Roe (2), Podres (5).

1954—New York N.L. 4 (Leo Durocher); Cleveland A.L. 0 (Al Lopez). WP—Grissom (1), Antonelli (2), Gomez (3), Liddle (4). LP—Lemon (1, 4), Wynn (2), Garcia (3).

1955—Brooklyn N.L. 4 (Walter Alston); New York A.L. 3 (Casey Stengel). WP—Bklyn.: Podres (3, 7), Labine (4), Craig (5); N.Y.: Ford (1, 6), Byrne (2). LP—Bklyn.: Newcombe (1), Loes (2), Spooner (6); N.Y.: Turley (3), Larsen (4), Grim (5), Byrne (7).

1956—New York A.L. 4 (Casey Stengel); Brooklyn N.L. 3 (Walter Alston). WP—N.Y.: Ford (3), Sturdivant (4), Larsen (5), Kucks (7); Bklyn.: Maglie (1), Bessent (2), Labine (6). LP—N.Y.: Ford (1), Morgan (2), Turley (6); Bklyn.: Craig (3), Erskine (4), Maglie (5), Newcombe (7).

1957—Milwaukee N.L. 4 (Fred Haney); New York A.L. 3 (Casey Stengel). WP—Mil.: Burdette (2, 5, 7), Spahn (4); N.Y.: Ford (1), Larsen (3), Turley (6). LP—Mil.: Spahn (1), Buhl (3), Johnson (6); N.Y.: Shantz (2), Grim (4), Ford (5), Larsen (7).

1958—New York A.L. 4 (Casey Stengel); Milwaukee N.L. 3 (Fred Haney). WP—N.Y.: Larsen (3), Turley (5, 7), Duren (6); Mil.: Spahn (1, 4), Burdette (2). LP—N.Y.: Duren (1), Turley (2), Ford (4); Mil.:

Rush (3), Burdette (5, 7), Spahn (6).

1959—Los Angeles N.L. 4 (Walter Alston); Chicago A.L. 2 (Al Lopez). WP—L.A.: Podres (2), Drysdale (3), Sherry (4, 6); Chi.: Wynn (1), Shaw (5). LP—L.A.: Craig (1), Koufax (5); Chi.: Shaw (2), Donovan (3), Staley (4), Wynn (6).

1960—Pittsburgh N.L. 4 (Danny Murtaugh); New York A.L. 3 (Casey Stengel). WP—Pitts.: Law (1, 4), Haddix (5, 7); N.Y.: Turley (2), Ford (3, 6). LP—Pitts.: Friend (2, 6), Mizell (3); N.Y.: Ditmar (1, 5), Terry (4, 7).

1961—New York A.L. 4 (Ralph Houk); Cincinnati N.L. 1 (Fred Hutchinson). WP—N.Y.: Ford (1, 4), Arroyo (3), Daley (5); Cin.: Jay (2). LP—N.Y.: Terry (2); Cin.: O'Toole (1, 4), Purkey (3), Jay (5).

1962—New York A.L. 4 (Ralph Houk); San Francisco N.L. 3 (Al Dark). WP—N.Y.: Ford (1), Stafford (3), Terry (5, 7); S.F. Sanford (2), Larsen (4), Pierce (6). LP—N.Y.: Terry (2), Coates (4), Ford (6); S.F.: O'Dell (1), Pierce (3), Sanford (5, 7).

1963—Los Angeles N.L. 4 (Walter Alston); New York A.L. 0 (Ralph Houk). WP—Koufax (1, 4), Podres (3), Drysdale (3). LP—Ford (1, 4), Downing (2), Bouton (3).

1964—St. Louis N.L. 4 (Johnny Keane); New York A.L. 3 (Yogi Berra). WP—St. L.: Sadecki (1), Craig (4), Gibson (5, 7); N.Y.: Stottlemyre (2), Bouton (3, 6). LP—St. L.: Gibson (2), Schultz (3), Simmons (6); N.Y.: Ford (1), Downing (4), Mikkelsen (5), Stottlemyre (7).

1965—Los Angeles N.L. 4 (Walter Alston); Minnesota A.L. 3 (Sam Mele). WP—L.A.: Osteen (3), Drysdale (4), Koufax (5, 7); Minn.: Grant (1, 6), Kaat (2). LP—L.A.: Drysdale (1), Koufax (2), Osteen (6); Minn.: Pascual (3), Grant (4), Kaat (5, 7).

1966—Baltimore A.L. 4 (Hank Bauer); Los Angeles N.L. 0 (Walter Alston). WP—Drabowsky (1), Palmer (2), Bunker (3), McNally (4). LP—Drysdale (1, 4), Koufax (2), Osteen (3).

1967—St. Louis N.L. 4 (Red Schoendienst); Boston A.L. 3 (Dick Williams). WP—St. L.: Gibson (1, 4, 7), Briles (3); Bos.: Lonborg (2, 5); Wyatt (6). LP—St. L.: Hughes (2), Carlton (5), Lamabe (6); Bos.: Santiago (1, 4), Bell (3), Lonborg (7).

1968—Detroit A.L. 4 (Mayo Smith); St. Louis N.L. 3 (Red Schoendienst). WP—Det.: Lolich (2, 5, 7), McLain (6); St. L.: Gibson (1, 4), Washburn (3), LP—Det.: McLain (1, 4), Wilson (3); St. L.: Briles (2), Hoerner (5), Washburn (6), Gibson (7).

1969—New York N.L. 4 (Gil Hodges); Baltimore A.L. 1 (Earl Weaver). WP—N.Y.: Koosman (2, 5), Gentry (3), Seaver (4); Balt.: Cuellar (1). LP—N.Y.: Seaver (1); Balt.: McNally (2), Palmer (3), Hall (4), Watt (5).

1970—Baltimore A.L. 4 (Earl Weaver); Cincinnati N.L. 1 (Sparky Anderson) 1. WP—Balt.: Palmer (1), Phoebus (2), McNally (3), Cuellar (5); Cin.: Carroll (4). LP—Cin.: Nolan (1), Wilcox (2), Cloninger (3), Merritt (5); Balt.: Watt (4).

1971—Pittsburgh N.L. 4 (Danny Murtaugh); Baltimore A.L. 3 (Earl Weaver). WP—Pitts.: Blass (3, 7), Kison (4), Briles (5); Balt.: McNally (1, 6), Palmer (2). LP—Pitts.: Ellis (1), R. Johnson (2), Miller (6); Balt.: Cuellar (3, 7), Watt (4) McNally (5).

1972—Oakland A.L. 4 (Dick Williams); Cincinnati N.L. (Sparky Anderson) 3. WP—Oakland: Holtzman (1), Hunter (2, 7), Fingers (4); Cincinnati: Billingham (3), Grimsley (5, 6). LP—Oakland: Odom (3), Fingers (5), Blue (6); Cincinnati: Nolan (1), Grimsley (2), Carroll (4), Borbon (7).

1973—Oakland A.L. 4 (Dick Williams); New York N.L. 3 (Yogi Berra). WP—Oakland: Holtzman (1, 7), Lindblad (3), Hunter (6). New York: McGraw (2), Matlack (4), Koosman (5). LP—Oakland: Fingers (2), Holtzman (4), Blue (5). New York: Matlack (1, 7) Parker (3), Seaver (6).

1974—Oakland A.L. 4 (Al Dark); Los Angeles N.L. 1 (Walter Alston). WP—Oakland: Fingers (1), Hunter (3), Holtzman (4), Odom (5). Los Angeles: Sutton (2). LP—Oakland: Blue (2), Los Angeles: Messersmith (1, 4), Downing (3), Marshall (5).

1975—Cincinnati N.L. 4 (Sparky Anderson); Boston A.L. 3 (Darrell Johnson). WP—Cincinnati: Eastwick (2, 3), Gullett (5), Carroll (7); Boston: Tiant (1, 4), Wise (6). LP—Cincinnati: Gullett (1), Norman (4), Darcy (6); Boston: Drago (5), Willoughby (3), Cleveland (5), Burton (7).

1976—Cincinnati N.L. 4 (Sparky Anderson); New York A.L. 0 (Billy Martin). WP—Gullett (1), Billingham (2), Zachry (3), Nolan (4). LP—Alexander (1), Hunter (2), Ellis (3), Figueroa (4).

1977—New York A.L. 4 (Billy Martin); Los Angeles N.L. 2 (Tom

Lasorda). WP—New York: Lyle (1), Torrez (3, 6), Guidry (4); Los Angeles: Hooton (2), Sutton (5). LP—New York: Hunter (2), Gullett (5); Los Angeles: Rhoden (1), John (3), Rau (4), Hooton (6).

1978—New York A.L. 4 (Bob Lemon), Los Angeles N.L. 2 (Tom Lasorda); WP—New York: Guidry (3), Gossage (4); Beattie (5), Hunter (6); Los Angeles: John (1), Hooton (2). LP—New York: Figueroa (1), Hunter (2); Los Angeles: Sutton (3, 6), Welch (4), Hooton (5).

1979—Pittsburgh N.L. 4 (Chuck Tanner), Baltimore A.L. 3 (Earl Weaver); WP—Pittsburgh: D. Robinson (2), Blyleven (5), Candelaria (6), Jackson (7); Baltimore: Flanagan (1), McGregor (3), Stoddard (4). LP—Pittsburgh: Kison (1), Candelaria (3), Tekulve (4); Baltimore: Stanhouse (2), Flanagan (5), Palmer (6), McGregor (7).

1980—Philadelphia N.L. 4 (Dallas Green), Kansas City A.L. 2 (Jim Frey); WP—Philadelphia: Walk (1), Carlton (2), McGraw (5), Carlton (6); Kansas City: Quisenberry (3), Leonard (4). LP—Philadelphia: McGraw (3), Christenson (4); Kansas City: Leonard (1), Quisenberry (2), Quisenberry (5), Gale (6).

1981—Los Angeles N.L. 4 (Tom Lasorda), New York A.L. 2 (Bob Lemon); WP—Los Angeles: Valenzuela (3), Howe (4), Reuss (5), Hooton (6); New York: Guidry (1), John (2). LP—Los Angeles: Reuss (1), Hooton (2); New York: Frazier (3), Frazier (4), Guidry (5), Frazier (6).

1982—St. Louis N.L. 4 (Whitey Herzog), Milwaukee A.L. 3 (Harvey Kuenn); WP—St. Louis: Sutter (2), Andujar (3), Stuper (6), Andujar (7). Milwaukee: Caldwell (1), Slaton (4), Caldwell (5). LP—St. Louis: Forsch (1), Bair (4), Forsch (5). Milwaukee: McClure (2), Vuckovich (3), Sutton (6), McClure (7).

1983—Baltimore A.L. 4 (Joe Altobelli), Philadelphia N.L. 1 (Paul Owens); WP—Baltimore: Boddicker (2), Palmer (3), Davis (4), McGregor (5). Philadelphia: Denny (1).

1984—Detroit A.L. 4 (Sparky Anderson), San Diego N.L. 1 (Dick Williams); WP—Det.: Morris (1,4), Wilcox (3), Lopez (5), San Diego: Hawkins (2). LP—Det.: Petry (2), San Diego: Thurmond (1), Lollar (3), Show (4), Hawkins (5).

1985—Kansas City A.L. 4 (Dick Howser), St. Louis N.L. 3 (Whitey Herzog); WP—KC: Saberhagen (3,7) Quisenberry (6), Jackson (5). St. Louis: Tudor (1,4) Dayley (2). LP—KC: Jackson (1), Leibrandt (2), Black (4); St. Louis: Andujar (3), Forsch (5), Worrell (6), Tudor (7).

1986—New York N.L. 4 (Dave Johnson); Boston A.L. (John McNamara) 3 WP—N.Y.—Ojeda (3), Darling (4), Aguilera (6), McDowell (7), Bos: Hurst (1), (5), Crawford (2). LP—N.Y. Darling (1), Gooden (2, 5).

1987—Minnesota. A.L. 4 (Tom Kelly); St. Louis N.L. (Whitey Herzog) 3. WP—Minn. Viola (1, 7), Blyleven (2), Schatzeder (6), St. Louis: Tudor (3), Forsch (4), Cox (5). LP—Minn. Berenguer (3), Viola (4), Blyleven (5); St. Louis: Magrane (1), Cox (2, 7), Tudor (6).

1988—Los Angeles N.L. 4 (Tommy Lasorda); Oakland A.L. (Tony LaRussa) 1. WP—Los Angeles: Hershiser (2, 5), Pena (1), Belcher (4); Oakland: Honeycutt (3). LP—Los Angeles: Howell (3); Oakland: Davis (2, 5), Eckersley (1), Stewart (4).

1989—Oakland, A.L. 4 (Tony LaRussa); San Francisco N.L. 0 (Roger Craig). WP—Oakland: Dave Stewart (1, 3), Mike Moore (2, 4). LP—San Francisco: Scott Garrelts (1, 3), Don Robinson (4), Rick Reuschel (2).

Before the World Series

Source: Information Please Sports Almanac, 1990 edition

The NL-American Assn. Series, 1882-90

When the National League met the American League for the first time in the 1903 World Series, it was not the N.L.'s first venture into post-season play.

From 1882-90, the N.L. pennant winner engaged in a championship series with the champion of the American Association. The Nationals won four of the eight series, lost once, and tied three times.

Year	Champion	Loser	Series	Year	Champion	Loser	Series
1882	Chicago (NL) & Cincinnati (AA)	—	1-1	1886	St. Louis (AA)	Chicago (NL)	4-2
				1887	Detroit (NL)	St. Louis (AA)	10-5
1883	No series			1888	New York (NL)	St. Louis (AA)	6-4
1884	Providence (NL)	New York (AA)	3-0	1889	New York (NL)	Brooklyn (AA)	6-3
1885	Chicago (NL) & St. Louis (AA)	—	3-3-1	1890	Brooklyn (NL) & Louisville (AA)	—	3-3-1

Early NL and AL Pennant Winners

The National League had been around 27 years before the 1903 World Series. The AL, however, was only in its third season when the two leagues met. The following lists account for the pennant winners in those pre-World Series years and in 1904 when the NL champion New York Giants refused to play Boston.

NL Pennant Winners, 1876-1902, '04

Year	Winner	Manager	Year	Winner	Manager	Year	Winner	Manager
1876	Chicago	Al Spalding	1885	Chicago	Cap Anson	1895	Baltimore	Ned Hanlon
1877	Boston	Harry Wright	1886	Chicago	Cap Anson	1896	Baltimore	Ned Hanlon
1878	Boston	Harry Wright	1887	Detroit	Bill Watkins	1897	Boston	Frank Selee
1879	Providence	George Wright	1888	New York	Jim Mutrie	1898	Boston	Frank Selee
1880	Chicago	Cap Anson	1889	New York	Jim Mutrie	1899	Brooklyn	Ned Hanlon
1881	Chicago	Cap Anson	1890	Brooklyn	Bill McGunnigle	1900	Brooklyn	Ned Hanlon
1882	Chicago	Cap Anson	1891	Boston	Frank Selee	1901	Pittsburgh	Fred Clarke
1883	Boston	John Morrill	1892	Boston	Frank Selee	1902	Pittsburgh	Fred Clarke
1884	Providence	Frank Bancroft	1893	Boston	Frank Selee	1904	New York	John McGraw
			1894	Baltimore	Ned Hanlon			

AL Pennant Winners, 1901-02, '04

Year	Winner	Manager	Year	Winner	Manager	Year	Winner	Manager
1901	Chicago	Clark Griffith	1902	Philadelphia	Connie Mack	1904	Boston	Jimmy Co...

WORLD SERIES CLUB STANDING
(Through 1989)

	Series	Won	Lost	Pct.		Series	Won	Lost	Pct.
Oakland (A)	5	4	1	.800	Kansas City (A)	2	1	1	.500
Pittsburgh (N)	7	5	2	.714	Detroit (A)	9	4	5	.444
New York (A)	33	22	11	.667	New York (N-Giants)	14	5	9	.357
Cleveland (A)	3	2	1	.667	Washington (A)	3	1	2	.333
New York (N-Mets)	3	2	1	.667	Philadelphia (N)	4	1	3	.250
Philadelphia (A)	8	5	3	.625	Chicago (N)	10	2	8	.200
St. Louis (N)	15	9	6	.600	Brooklyn (N)	9	1	8	.111
Boston (A)	9	5	4	.550	St. Louis (A)	1	0	1	.000
Los Angeles (N)	9	5	4	.550	San Francisco (N)	2	0	2	.000
Milwaukee (N)	2	1	1	.500	Milwaukee (A)	1	0	1	.000
Boston (A)	2	1	1	.500	San Diego (N)	1	0	1	.000
Chicago (A)	4	2	2	.500					
Cincinnati (N)	8	4	4	.500					
Baltimore (A)	6	3	3	.500					
Minnesota (A)	2	1	1	.500					

Recapitulation

	Won
American League	49
National League	35

LIFETIME WORLD SERIES RECORDS
(Through 1989)

Most hits—71, Yogi Berra, New York A.L., 1947, 1949–53, 1955–58, 1960–63.

Most runs—42, Mickey Mantle, New York A.L., 1951–53, 1955–58, 1960–64.

Most runs batted in—40, Mickey Mantle, New York A.L., 1951–53, 1955–58, 1960–64.

Most home runs—18, Mickey Mantle, New York A.L., 1951–53, 1955–58, 1960–64.

Most bases on balls—43, Mickey Mantle, New York A.L., 1951–53, 1955–58, 1960–64.

Most strikeouts—54, Mickey Mantle, New York A.L., 1951–53, 1955–58, 1960–64.

Most stolen bases—14, Eddie Collins, Philadelphia A.L. 1910–11, 13–14; Chicago A.L., 1917, 1919. Lou Brock, St. Louis N.L., 1964, 67–68.

Most victories, pitcher—10, Whitey Ford, New York A.L., 1950, 1953, 1955–58, 1960–64.

Most times member of winning team—10, Yogi Berra, New York A.L., 1947, 1949–53, 1956, 1958, 1961–62.

Most victories, no defeats—6, Vernon Gomez, New York A.L., 1932, 1936(2), 1937(2), 1938.

Most shutouts—4, Christy Mathewson, New York N.L., 1905 (3), 1913.

Most innings pitched—146, Whitey Ford, New York A.L., 1950, 1953, 1955–58, 1960–1964.

Most consecutive scoreless innings—33 2/3, Whitey Ford, New York A.L., 1960 (18), 1961 (14), 1962 (1 2/3).

Most strikeouts by pitcher—94, Whitey Ford, New York A.L., 1950, 1953, 1955–58, 1960–64.

SINGLE GAME AND SINGLE SERIES RECORDS
(Through 1989)

Most hits game—5, Paul Molitor, Milwaukee A.L., first game vs. St. Louis, N.L., 1982.

Most 4-hit games, series—2, Robin Yount, Milwaukee A.L., first and fifth games vs. St. Louis N.L., 1982.

Most hits inning—2, held by many players.

Most hits series—13 (7 games) Bobby Richardson, New York A.L., 1964; Lou Brock, St. Louis N.L., 1968; 12 (6 games) Billy Martin, New York A.L., 1953; 12 (8 games) Buck Herzog, New York N.L., 1912; Joe Jackson, Chicago A.L., 1919; 10 (4 games) Babe Ruth, New York A.L., 1928; 9 (5 games) held by 8 players.

Most home runs, series—5 (6 games) Reggie Jackson, New York A.L., 1977; 4 (7 games) Babe Ruth, New York A.L., 1926; Duke Snider, Brooklyn N.L., 1952, 1955; Hank Bauer, New York A.L., 1958; Gene Tenace, Oakland A.L., 1972; 4 (4 games) Lou Gehrig, New York A.L., 1928; 3 (6 games) Babe Ruth, New York A.L., 1923; Ted Kluszewski, Chicago A.L., 1959; 3 (5 games) Donn Clendenon, New York Mets N.L., 1969.

. home runs, game—3, Babe Ruth, New York A.L., 1926 and ²eggie Jackson, New York A.L., 1977.

 series—12 (6 games) Willie Wilson, Kansas City A.L., ames) Ed Mathews, Milwaukee N.L., 1958; Wayne rk N.L., 1973: 10 (8 games) George Kelly, New 9 (6 games) Jim Bottomley, St. Louis N.L., 1930;

9 (5 games) Carmelo Martinez, San Diego, N.L., 1984; Duke Snider, Brooklyn N.L., 1949; 7 (4 games) Bob Muesel, New York A.L., 1927.

Most stolen bases, game—3, Honus Wagner, Pittsburgh N.L., 1909; Willie Davis, Los Angeles N.L., 1965; Lou Brock, St. Louis N.L., 1967 and 1968.

Most strikeouts by pitcher, game—17, Bob Gibson, St. Louis N.L. 1968.

Most strikeouts by pitcher in succession—6, Horace Eller, Cincinnati N.L., 1919; Moe Drabowsky, Baltimore A.L., 1966.

Most strikeouts by pitcher, series—35 (7 games) Bob Gibson, St. Louis N.L., 1968; 28 (8 games) Bill Dinneen, Boston A.L., 1903; 23 (4 games) Sandy Koufax, Los Angeles, 1963; 20 (6 games) Chief Bender, Philadelphia A.L., 1911; 18 (5 games) Christy Mathewson, New York N.L., 1905.

Most bases on balls, series—11 (7 games) Babe Ruth, New York A.L., 1926; Gene Tenace, Oakland A.L., 1973; 9 (6 games) Willie Randolph, New York A.L., 1981; 7 (5 games) James Sheckard, Chicago N.L., 1910; Mickey Cochrane, Philadelphia A.L., 1929; Joe Gordon, New York A.L., 1941; 7 (4 games) Hank Thompson, New York N.L., 1954.

Most consecutive scoreless innings one series—27, Christy Mathewson, New York N.L., 1905.

AMERICAN LEAGUE HOME RUN CHAMPIONS

Year	Player, team	No.	Year	Player, team	No.	Year	Player, team	No.
1901	Nap Lajoie, Phila.	13	1932	Jimmy Foxx, Phila.	58	1964	Harmon Killebrew, Minn.	49
1902	Ralph Seybold, Phila.	16	1933	Jimmy Foxx, Phila.	48	1965	Tony Conigliaro, Bost.	32
1903	Buck Freeman, Bost.	13	1934	Lou Gehrig, N.Y.	49	1966	Frank Robinson, Balt.	49
1904	Harry Davis, Phila.	10	1935	Jimmy Foxx, Phila., and		1967	Carl Yastrzemski, Bost., and	
1905	Harry Davis, Phila.	8		Hank Greenberg, Det.	36		Harmon Killebrew, Minn.	44
1906	Harry Davis, Phila.	12	1936	Lou Gehrig, N.Y.	49	1968	Frank Howard, Wash.	44
1907	Harry Davis, Phila.	8	1937	Joe DiMaggio, N.Y.	46	1969	Harmon Killebrew, Minn.	49
1908	Sam Crawford, Det.	7	1938	Hank Greenberg, Det.	58	1970	Frank Howard, Wash.	44
1909	Ty Cobb, Det.	9	1939	Jimmy Foxx, Bost.	35	1971	Bill Melton, Chicago	33
1910	J. Garland Stahl, Bost.	10	1940	Hank Greenberg, Det.	41	1972	Dick Allen, Chicago	37
1911	Franklin Baker, Phila.	9	1941	Ted Williams, Bost.	37	1973	Reggie Jackson, Oak.	32
1912	Franklin Baker, Phila.	10	1942	Ted Williams, Bost.	36	1974	Dick Allen, Chicago	32
1913	Franklin Baker, Phila.	12	1943	Rudy York, Det.	34	1975	Reggie Jackson, Oak., and	
1914	Franklin Baker, Phila., and		1944	Nick Etten, N.Y.	22		George Scott, Mil.	36
	Sam Crawford, Det.	8	1945	Vern Stephens, St. L.	24	1976	Graig Nettles, N.Y.	32
1915	Robert Roth, Chi.-Cleve.	7	1946	Hank Greenberg, Det.	44	1977	Jim Rice, Boston	39
1916	Wally Pipp, N.Y.	12	1947	Ted Williams, Bost.	32	1978	Jim Rice, Boston	46
1917	Wally Pipp, N.Y.	9	1948	Joe DiMaggio, N.Y.	39	1979	Gorman Thomas, Milwaukee	45
1918	Babe Ruth, Bost., and		1949	Ted Williams, Bost.	43	1980	Reggie Jackson, N.Y., and	
	Clarence Walker, Phila.	11	1950	Al Rosen, Cleve.	37		Ben Oglivie, Mil.	41
1919	Babe Ruth, Bost.	29	1951	Gus Zernial, Chi.-Phila.	33	1981*	Tony Armas, Oak., Dwight	
1920	Babe Ruth, N.Y.	54	1952	Larry Doby, Cleve.	32		Evans, Bost., Bobby Grich,	
1921	Babe Ruth, N.Y.	59	1953	Al Rosen, Cleve.	43		Calif., and Eddie Murray,	
1922	Ken Williams, St. L.	39	1954	Larry Doby, Cleve.	32		Balt. (tie)	22
1923	Babe Ruth, N.Y.	41	1955	Mickey Mantle, N.Y.	37	1982	Gorman Thomas, Mil., and	
1924	Babe Ruth, N.Y.	46	1956	Mickey Mantle, N.Y.	52		Reggie Jackson, Calif.	39
1925	Bob Meusel, N.Y.	33	1957	Roy Sievers, Wash.	42	1983	Jim Rice, Boston	39
1926	Babe Ruth, N.Y.	47	1958	Mickey Mantle, N.Y.	42	1984	Tony Armas, Boston	43
1927	Babe Ruth, N.Y.	60	1959	Rocky Colavito, Cleve., and		1985	Darrell Evans, Detroit	40
1928	Babe Ruth, N.Y.	54		Harmon Killebrew, Wash.	42	1986	Jesse Barfield, Toronto	40
1929	Babe Ruth, N.Y.	46	1960	Mickey Mantle, N.Y.	40	1987	Mark McGwire, Oakland	49
1930	Babe Ruth, N.Y.	49	1961	Roger Maris, N.Y.	61	1988	Jose Canseco, Oakland	42
1931	Lou Gehrig, N.Y., and		1962	Harmon Killebrew, Minn.	48	1989	Fred McGriff, Toronto	36
	Babe Ruth, N.Y.	46	1963	Harmon Killebrew, Minn.	45	1990	Cecil Fielder, Detroit	51

AMERICAN LEAGUE BATTING CHAMPIONS

Year	Player, team	Avg	Year	Player, team	Avg	Year	Player, team	Avg.
1901	Nap Lajoie, Phila.	.422	1931	Al Simmons, Phila.	.390	1961	Norman Cash, Det.	.361
1902	Ed Delahanty, Wash.	.376	1932	Dale Alexander, Det.-Bost.	.367	1962	Pete Runnels, Bost.	.326
1903	Nap Lajoie, Cleve.	.355	1933	Jimmy Foxx, Phila.	.356	1963	Carl Yastrzemski, Bost.	.321
1904	Nap Lajoie, Cleve.	.381	1934	Lou Gehrig, N.Y.	.363	1964	Tony Oliva, Minn.	.323
1905	Elmer Flick, Cleve.	.306	1935	Buddy Myer, Wash.	.349	1965	Tony Oliva, Minn.	.321
1906	George Stone, St. L.	.358	1936	Luke Appling, Chi.	.388	1966	Frank Robinson, Balt.	.316
1907	Ty Cobb, Det.	.350	1937	Charley Gehringer, Det.	.371	1967	Carl Yastrzemski, Bost.	.326
1908	Ty Cobb, Det.	.324	1938	Jimmy Foxx, Bost.	.349	1968	Carl Yastrzemski, Bost.	.301
1909	Ty Cobb, Det.	.377	1939	Joe DiMaggio, N.Y.	.381	1969	Rod Carew, Minn.	.332
1910	Ty Cobb, Det.	.385	1940	Joe DiMaggio, N.Y.	.352	1970	Alex Johnson, Calif.	.329
1911	Ty Cobb, Det.	.420	1941	Ted Williams, Bost.	.406	1971	Tony Oliva, Minn.	.337
1912	Ty Cobb, Det.	.410	1942	Ted Williams, Bost.	.356	1972	Rod Carew, Minn.	.318
1913	Ty Cobb, Det.	.390	1943	Luke Appling, Chi.	.328	1973	Rod Carew, Minn.	.350
1914	Ty Cobb, Det.	.368	1944	Lou Boudreau, Cleve.	.327	1974	Rod Carew, Minn.	.364
1915	Ty Cobb, Det.	.369	1945	George Sternweiss, N.Y.	.309	1975	Rod Carew, Minn.	.359
1916	Tris Speaker, Cleve.	.386	1946	Mickey Vernon, Wash.	.353	1976	George Brett, Kansas City	.333
1917	Ty Cobb, Det.	.383	1947	Ted Williams, Bost.	.343	1977	Rod Carew, Minn.	.388
1918	Ty Cobb, Det.	.382	1948	Ted Williams, Bost.	.369	1978	Rod Carew, Minn.	.333
1919	Ty Cobb, Det.	.384	1949	George Kell, Det.	.343	1979	Fred Lynn, Boston	.333
1920	George Sisler, St. L.	.407	1950	Billy Goodman, Bost.	.354	1980	George Brett, Kansas City	.390
1921	Harry Heilmann, Det.	.394	1951	Ferris Fain, Phila.	.344	1981*	Carney Lansford, Bost.	.336
1922	George Sisler, St. L.	.420	1952	Ferris Fain, Phila.	.327	1982	Willie Wilson, Kansas City	.332
1923	Harry Heilmann, Det.	.403	1953	Mickey Vernon, Wash.	.337	1983	Wade Boggs, Boston	.361
1924	Babe Ruth, N.Y.	.378	1954	Bobby Avila, Cleve.	.341	1984	Don Mattingly, New York	.343
1925	Harry Heilmann, Det.	.393	1955	Al Kaline, Det.	.340	1985	Wade Boggs, Boston	.368
1926	Heinie Manush, Det.	.378	1956	Mickey Mantle, N.Y.	.353	1986	Wade Boggs, Boston	.357
1927	Harry Heilmann, Det.	.398	1957	Ted Williams, Bost.	.388	1987	Wade Boggs, Boston	.363
1928	Goose Goslin, Wash.	.379	1958	Ted Williams, Bost.	.328	1988	Wade Boggs, Boston	.366
1929	Lew Fonseca, Cleve.	.369	1959	Harvey Kuenn, Det.	.353	1989	Kirby Puckett, Minnesota	.339
1930	Al Simmons, Phila.	.381	1960	Pete Runnels, Bost.	.320	1990	George Brett, Kansas City	.32

*Split season because of player strike.

NATIONAL LEAGUE HOME RUN CHAMPIONS

Year	Player, team	No.	Year	Player, team	No.	Year	Player, team	No.
1876	George Hall, Phila. Athletics	5	1914	Cliff Cravath, Phila.	19	1950	Ralph Kiner, Pitts.	47
1877	George Shaffer, Louisville	3	1915	Cliff Cravath, Phila.	24	1951	Ralph Kiner, Pitts.	42
1878	Paul Hines, Providence	4	1916	Davis Robertson, N.Y., and		1952	Ralph Kiner, Pitts., and	
1879	Charles Jones, Bost.	9		Fred Williams, Chi.	12		Hank Sauer, Chi.	37
1880	James O'Rourke, Bost., and		1917	Davis Robertson, N.Y., and		1953	Ed Mathews, Mil.	47
	Harry Stovey, Worcester	6		Cliff Cravath, Phila.	12	1954	Ted Kluszewski, Cin.	49
1881	Dan Brouthers, Buffalo	8	1918	Cliff Cravath, Phila.	8	1955	Willie Mays, N.Y.	51
1882	George Wood, Det.	7	1919	Cliff Cravath, Phila.	12	1956	Duke Snider, Bklyn.	43
1883	William Ewing, N.Y.	10	1920	Cy Williams, Phila.	15	1957	Henry Aaron, Mil.	44
1884	Ed Williamson, Chi.	27	1921	George Kelly, N.Y.	23	1958	Ernie Banks, Chi.	47
1885	Abner Dalrymple, Chi.	11	1922	Rogers Hornsby, St. L.	42	1959	Ed Mathews, Mil.	46
1886	Arthur Richardson, Det.	11	1923	Cy Williams, Phila.	41	1960	Ernie Banks, Chi.	41
1887	Roger Connor, N.Y., and		1924	Jacques Fournier, Bklyn.	27	1961	Orlando Cepeda, San Fran.	46
	Wm. O'Brien, Wash.	17	1925	Rogers Hornsby, St. L.	39	1962	Willie Mays, San Fran.	49
1888	Roger Connor, N.Y.	14	1926	Hack Wilson, Chi.	21	1963	Henry Aaron, Mil., and	
1889	Sam Thompson, Phila.	20	1927	Hack Wilson, Chi., and			Willie McCovey, San Fran.	44
1890	Tom Burns, Bklyn. and			Cy Williams, Phila.	30	1964	Willie Mays, San Fran.	47
	Mike Tiernan, N.Y.	13	1928	Hack Wilson, Chi., and		1965	Willie Mays, San Fran.	52
1891	Harry Stovey, Bost., and			Jim Bottomley, St. L.	31	1966	Henry Aaron, Atlanta	44
	Mike Tiernan, N.Y.	16	1929	Chuck Klein, Phila.	43	1967	Henry Aaron, Atlanta	39
1892	Jim Holliday, Cin.	13	1930	Hack Wilson, Chi.	56	1968	Willie McCovey, San Fran.	36
1893	Ed Delahanty, Phila.	19	1931	Chuck Klein, Phila.	31	1969	Willie McCovey, San Fran.	45
1894	Hugh Duffy, Bost., and		1932	Chuck Klein, Phila., and		1970	Johnny Bench, Cin.	45
	Robert Lowe, Bost.	18		Mel Ott, N.Y.	38	1971	Willie Stargell, Pitts.	48
1895	Bill Joyce, Wash.	17	1933	Chuck Klein, Phila.	28	1972	Johnny Bench, Cin.	40
1896	Ed Delahanty, Phila., and		1934	Mel Ott, N.Y., and		1973	Willie Stargell, Pitts.	44
	Sam Thompson, Phila.	13		Rip Collins, St. L.	35	1974	Mike Schmidt, Phila.	36
1897	Nap Lajoie, Phila.	10	1935	Wally Berger, Bost.	34	1975	Mike Schmidt, Phila.	38
1898	James Colins, Bost.	14	1936	Mel Ott, N.Y.	33	1976	Mike Schmidt, Phila.	38
1899	John Freeman, Wash.	25	1937	Mel Ott, N.Y., and Joe		1977	George Foster, Cin.	52
1900	Herman Long, Bost.	12		Medwick, St. L.	31	1978	George Foster, Cin.	40
1901	Sam Crawford, Con.	16	1938	Mel Ott, N.Y.	36	1979	Dave Kingman, Chicago	48
1902	Tom Leach, Pitts.	6	1939	John Mize, St. L.	28	1980	Mike Schmidt, Phila.	48
1903	James Sheckard, Bklyn.	9	1940	John Mize, St. L.	43	1981*	Mike Schmidt, Phila.	31
1904	Harry Lumley, Bklyn.	9	1941	Dolph Camilli, Bklyn.	34	1982	Dave Kingman, N.Y.	37
1905	Fred Odwell, Cin.	9	1942	Mel Ott, N.Y.	30	1983	Mike Schmidt, Phila.	40
1906	Tim Jordan, Bklyn	12	1943	Bill Nicholson, Chi.	29	1984	Mike Schmidt, Phila. and	
1907	David Brain, Bost.	10	1944	Bill Nicholson, Chi.	33		Dale Murphy, Atlanta	36
1908	Tim Jordan, Bklyn.	12	1945	Tommy Holmes, Bost.	28	1985	Dale Murphy, Atlanta	37
1909	John Murray, N.Y.	7	1946	Ralph Kiner, Pitts.	23	1986	Mike Schmidt, Phila.	37
1910	Fred Beck, Bost., and		1947	Ralph Kiner, Pitts., and		1987	Andre Dawson, Chicago	49
	Frank Schulte, Chi.	10		John Mize, N.Y.	51	1988	Darryl Strawberry, N.Y.	39
1911	Frank Schulte, Chi.	21	1948	Ralph Kiner, Pitts., and		1989	Kevin Mitchell, San Francisco	47
1912	Henry Zimmerman, Chi.	14		John Mize, N.Y.	40	1990	Ryne Sandberg, Chicago	40
1913	Cliff Cravath, Phila.	19	1949	Ralph Kiner, Pitts.	54			

*Split season because of player strike.

NATIONAL LEAGUE BATTING CHAMPIONS

Year	Player, Team	Avg	Year	Player, Team	Avg	Year	Player, Team	Avg
1876	Roscoe Barnes, Chicago	.404	1894	Hugh Duffy, Boston	.438	1912	Henry Zimmerman, Chicago	.372
1877	Jim White, Boston	.385	1895	Jesse Burkett, Cleveland	.423	1913	Jake Daubert, Brooklyn	.350
1878	Abner Dalrymple, Mil.	.356	1896	Jesse Burkett, Cleveland	.410	1914	Jake Daubert, Brooklyn	.329
1879	Cap Anson, Chicago	.407	1897	Willie Keeler, Baltimore	.432	1915	Larry Doyle, New York	.320
1880	George Gore, Chicago	.365	1898	Willie Keeler, Baltimore	.379	1916	Hal Chase, Cincinnati	.339
1881	Cap Anson, Chicago	.399	1899	Ed Delahanty, Phila.	.408	1917	Edd Roush, Cincinnati	.341
1882	Dan Brouthers, Buffalo	.367	1900	Honus Wagner, Pittsburgh	.381	1918	Zack Wheat, Brooklyn	.335
1883	Dan Brouthers, Buffalo	.371	1901	Jesse Burkett, St. Louis	.382	1919	Edd Roush, Cincinnati	.321
1884	James O'Rourke, Buffalo	.350	1902	Clarence Beaumont, Pitts.	.357	1920	Rogers Hornsby, St. Louis	.370
1885	Roger Connor, N. Y.	.371	1903	Honus Wagner, Pittsburgh	.355	1921	Rogers Hornsby, St. Louis	.397
1886	King Kelly, Chicago	.388	1904	Honus Wagner, Pittsburgh	.349	1922	Rogers Hornsby, St. Louis	.401
1887	Cap Anson, Chicago	.421	1905	Cy Seymour, Cincinnati	.377	1923	Rogers Hornsby, St. Louis	.384
1888	Cap Anson, Chicago	.343	1906	Honus Wagner, Pittsburgh	.339	1924	Rogers Hornsby, St. Louis	.424
	Dan Brouthers, Boston	.373	1907	Honus Wagner, Pittsburgh	.350	1925	Rogers Hornsby, St. Louis	.403
	Glasscock, N. Y.	.336	1908	Honus Wagner, Pittsburgh	.354	1926	Gene Hargrave, Cincinnati	.353
	Hamilton, Phila.	.338	1909	Honus Wagner, Pittsburgh	.339	1927	Paul Waner; Pittsburgh	.380
	uthers, Bklyn., and		1910	Sherwood Magee,		1928	Rogers Hornsby, Boston	.387
	Childs, Cleve.	.335		Philadelphia	.331	1929	Lefty O'Doul, Phila.	.398
	Boston	.378	1911	Honus Wagner, Pittsburgh	.334	1930	Bill Terry, N.Y.	.401

Year	Player, Team	Avg	Year	Player, Team	Avg	Year	Player, Team	Avg
1931	Chick Hafey, St. Louis	.349	1951	Stan Musial, St. Louis	.355	1971	Joe Torre, St. Louis	.363
1932	Lefty O'Doul, Brooklyn	.368	1952	Stan Musial, St. Louis	.336	1972	Billy Williams, Chicago	.333
1933	Chuck Klein, Phila.	.368	1953	Carl Furillo, Brooklyn	.344	1973	Pete Rose, Cincinnati	.338
1934	Paul Waner, Pittsburgh	.362	1954	Willie Mays, N. Y.	.345	1974	Ralph Garr, Atlanta	.353
1935	Arky Vaughan, Pittsburgh	.385	1955	Richie Ashburn, Phila.	.338	1975	Bill Madlock, Chicago	.354
1936	Paul Waner, Pittsburgh	.373	1956	Henry Aaron, Mil.	.328	1976	Bill Madlock, Chicago	.339
1937	Joe Medwick, St. Louis	.374	1957	Stan Musial, St. Louis	.351	1977	Dave Parker, Pittsburgh	.338
1938	Ernie Lombardi, Cin.	.342	1958	Richie Ashburn, Phila.	.350	1978	Dave Parker, Pittsburgh	.334
1939	John Mize, St. Louis	.349	1959	Henry Aaron, Mil.	.355	1979	Keith Hernandez, St. Louis	.344
1940	Debs Garms, Pittsburgh	.355	1960	Dick Groat, Pittsburgh	.325	1980	Bill Buckner, Chicago	.324
1941	Pete Reiser, Brooklyn	.343	1961	Roberto Clemente, Pitts.	.351	1981*	Bill Madlock, Pittsburgh	.341
1942	Ernie Lombardi, Boston	.330	1962	Tommy Davis, L. A.	.346	1982	Al Oliver, Montreal	.331
1943	Stan Musial, St. Louis	.357	1963	Tommy Davis, L. A.	.326	1983	Bill Madlock, Pittsburgh	.323
1944	Dixie Walker, Brooklyn	.357	1964	Roberto Clemente, Pitts.	.339	1984	Tony Gwynn, San Diego	.351
1945	Phil Cavarretta, Chicago	.355	1965	Roberto Clemente, Pitts.	.329	1985	Willie McGee, St. Louis	.353
1946	Stan Musial, St. Louis	.365	1966	Matty Alou, Pittsburgh	.342	1986	Tim Raines, Montreal	.334
1947	Harry Walker, St. L.-Phila.	.363	1967	Roberto Clemente, Pitts.	.357	1987	Tony Gwynn, San Diego	.370
1948	Stan Musial, St. Louis	.376	1968	Pete Rose, Cincinnati	.335	1988	Tony Gwynn, San Diego	.313
1949	Jackie Robinson, Brooklyn	.342	1969	Pete Rose, Cincinnati	.348	1989	Tony Gwynn, San Diego	.336
1950	Stan Musial, St. Louis	.346	1970	Rico Carty, Atlanta	.366	1990	Willie McGee, St. Louis	.335

AMERICAN LEAGUE PENNANT WINNERS

Year	Club	Manager	Won	Lost	Pct	Year	Club	Manager	Won	Lost	Pct
1901	Chicago	Clark C. Griffith	83	53	.610	1947[1]	New York	Stanley R. Harris	97	57	.630
1902	Philadelphia	Connie Mack	83	53	.610	1948[1]	Cleveland	Lou Boudreau	97	58	.626
1903[1]	Boston	Jimmy Collins	91	47	.659	1949[1]	New York	Casey Stengel	97	57	.630
1904[2]	Boston	Jimmy Collins	95	59	.617	1950[1]	New York	Casey Stengel	98	56	.636
1905	Philadelphia	Connie Mack	92	56	.622	1951[1]	New York	Casey Stengel	98	56	.636
1906[1]	Chicago	Fielder A. Jones	93	58	.616	1952[1]	New York	Casey Stengel	95	59	.617
1907	Detroit	Hugh A. Jennings	92	58	.613	1953[1]	New York	Casey Stengel	99	52	.656
1908	Detroit	Hugh A. Jennings	90	63	.588	1954	Cleveland	Al Lopez	111	43	.721
1909	Detroit	Hugh A. Jennings	98	54	.645	1955	New York	Casey Stengel	96	58	.623
1910[1]	Philadelphia	Connie Mack	102	48	.680	1956[1]	New York	Casey Stengel	97	57	.630
1911[1]	Philadelphia	Connie Mack	101	50	.669	1957	New York	Casey Stengel	98	56	.636
1912[1]	Boston	J. Garland Stahl	105	47	.691	1958[1]	New York	Casey Stengel	92	62	.597
1913[1]	Philadelphia	Connie Mack	96	57	.627	1959	Chicago	Al Lopez	94	60	.610
1914	Philadelphia	Connie Mack	99	53	.651	1960	New York	Casey Stengel	97	57	.630
1915[1]	Boston	William F. Carrigan	101	50	.669	1961[1]	New York	Ralph Houk	109	53	.673
1916[1]	Boston	William F. Carrigan	91	63	.591	1962[1]	New York	Ralph Houk	96	66	.593
1917	Chicago	Clarence H. Rowland	100	54	.649	1963	New York	Ralph Houk	104	57	.646
1918[1]	Boston	Ed Barrow	75	51	.595	1964	New York	Yogi Berra	99	63	.611
1919	Chicago	William Gleason	88	52	.629	1965	Minnesota	Sam Mele	102	60	.630
1920[1]	Cleveland	Tris Speaker	98	56	.636	1966[1]	Baltimore	Hank Bauer	97	53	.606
1921	New York	Miller J. Huggins	98	55	.641	1967	Boston	Dick Williams	92	70	.568
1922	New York	Miller J. Huggins	94	60	.610	1968[1]	Detroit	Mayo Smith	103	59	.636
1923[1]	New York	Miller J. Huggins	98	54	.645	1969	Baltimore[3]	Earl Weaver	109	53	.673
1924[1]	Washington	Stanley R. Harris	92	62	.597	1970[1]	Baltimore[3]	Earl Weaver	108	54	.667
1925	Washington	Stanley R. Harris	96	55	.636	1971	Baltimore[4]	Earl Weaver	101	57	.639
1926	New York	Miller J. Huggins	91	63	.591	1972[1]	Oakland[5]	Dick Williams	93	62	.600
1927[1]	New York	Miller J. Huggins	110	44	.714	1973[1]	Oakland[6]	Dick Williams	94	68	.580
1928[1]	New York	Miller J. Huggins	101	53	.656	1974[1]	Oakland[6]	Alvin Dark	90	72	.556
1929[1]	Philadelphia	Connie Mack	104	46	.693	1975	Boston[6]	Darrell Johnson	95	65	.594
1930[1]	Philadelphia	Connie Mack	102	52	.662	1976	New York[7]	Billy Martin	97	62	.610
1931	Philadelphia	Connie Mack	107	45	.704	1977[1]	New York[7]	Billy Martin	100	62	.617
1932[1]	New York	Joseph V. McCarthy	107	47	.695	1978[1]	New York[7]	Billy Martin and Bob Lemon	100	63	.613
1933	Washington	Joseph E. Cronin	99	53	.651						
1934	Detroit	Gordon Cochrane	101	53	.656	1979	Baltimore[8]	Earl Weaver	102	57	.642
1935[1]	Detroit	Gordon Cochrane	93	58	.616	1980	Kansas City[9]	Jim Frey	97	65	.599
1936[1]	New York	Joseph V. McCarthy	102	51	.667	1981	New York[10]	Gene Michael-Bob			
1937[1]	New York	Joseph V. McCarthy	102	52	.662			Lemon	59	48	.551*
1938[1]	New York	Joseph V. McCarthy	99	53	.651	1982	Milwaukee[11]	Harvey Kuenn	95	67	.586
1939[1]	New York	Joseph V. McCarthy	106	45	.702	1983[1]	Baltimore[12]	Joe Altobelli	98	64	.605
1940	Detroit	Delmar D. Baker	90	64	.584	1984[1]	Detroit[13]	Sparky Anderson	104	58	.642
1941[1]	New York	Joseph V. McCarthy	101	53	.656	1985[1]	Kansas City[14]	Dick Howser	91	71	.562
1942	New York	Joseph V. McCarthy	103	51	.669	1986	Boston[11]	John McNamara	95	66	.590
1943[1]	New York	Joseph V. McCarthy	98	56	.636	1987	Minnesota[15]	Tom Kelly	85	77	.525
1944	St. Louis	Luke Sewell	89	65	.578	1988	Oakland[16]	Tony LaRussa	104	58	.642
1945[1]	Detroit	Steve O'Neill	88	65	.575	1989	Oakland[17]	Tony LaRussa	99	63	.611
1946	Boston	Joseph E. Cronin	104	50	.675	1990	Oakland[18]	Tony LaRussa	103	59	.636

*Split season because of player strike. 1. World Series winner. 2. No World Series. 3. Defeated Minnesota, Western Division winner, in playoff. 4. Defeated Oakland, Western Division Leader, in playoff. 5. Defeated Detroit, Eastern Division winner, in playoff. 6. Defeated Baltimore, Eastern Division winner, in playoff. 7. Defeated Kansas City, Western Division winner, in playoff. 8. Defeated California, Western Division winner, in playoff. 9. Defeated New York, Eastern Division winner, in playoff. 10. Defeated Oakland, Western Division winner, in playoff. 11. Defeated California, Western Division winner, in playoff. 12. Defeated Chicago, Western Division winner in playoff. 13. Defeated Kansas City, Western Division winner, in playoff. 14. Defeated Toronto, Eastern Division winner, in playoff. 15. Defeated Detroit, Eastern winner, in playoff. 16. Defeated Boston, Eastern division winner, in playoffs. 17. Defeated Toronto, Eastern Division winner, in playoffs. 18. Defeated Boston, Eastern Division winner, in playoffs.

NATIONAL LEAGUE PENNANT WINNERS

Year	Club	Manager	Won	Lost	Pct	Year	Club	Manager	Won	Lost	Pct
1876	Chicago	Albert G. Spalding	52	14	.788	1934	St. Louis[1]	Frank F. Frisch	95	58	.621
1877	Boston	Harry Wright	31	17	.646	1935	Chicago	Charles J. Grimm	100	54	.649
1878	Boston	Harry Wright	41	19	.683	1936	New York	William H. Terry	92	62	.597
1879	Providence	George Wright	55	23	.705	1937	New York	William H. Terry	95	57	.625
1880	Chicago	Adrian C. Anson	67	17	.798	1938	Chicago	Gabby Hartnett	89	63	.586
1881	Chicago	Adrian C. Anson	56	28	.667	1939	Cincinnati	William B. McKechnie	97	57	.630
1882	Chicago	Adrian C. Anson	55	29	.655	1940	Cincinnati[1]	William B. McKechnie	100	53	.654
1883	Boston	John F. Morrill	63	35	.643	1941	Brooklyn	Leo E. Durocher	100	54	.649
1884	Providence	Frank C. Bancroft	84	28	.750	1942	St. Louis[1]	William H. Southworth	106	48	.688
1885	Chicago	Adrian C. Anson	87	25	.777	1943	St. Louis	William H. Southworth	105	49	.682
1886	Chicago	Adrian C. Anson	90	34	.726	1944	St. Louis[1]	William H. Southworth	105	49	.682
1887	Detroit	W. H. Watkins	79	45	.637	1945	Chicago	Charles J. Grimm	98	56	.636
1888	New York	James J. Mutrie	84	47	.641	1946	St. Louis[1]	Edwin H. Dyer	98	58	.628
1889	New York	James J. Mutrie	83	43	.659	1947	Brooklyn	Burton E. Shotton	94	60	.610
1890	Brooklyn	William H. McGunnigle	86	43	.667	1948	Boston	William H. Southworth	91	62	.595
1891	Boston	Frank G. Selee	87	51	.630	1949	Brooklyn	Burton E. Shotton	97	57	.630
1892	Boston	Frank G. Selee	102	48	.680	1950	Philadelphia	Edwin M. Sawyer	91	63	.591
1893	Boston	Frank G. Selee	86	44	.662	1951	New York	Leo E. Durocher	98	59	.624
1894	Baltimore	Edward H. Hanlon	89	39	.695	1952	Brooklyn	Charles W. Dressen	96	57	.630
1895	Baltimore	Edward H. Hanlon	87	43	.669	1953	Brooklyn	Charles W. Dressen	105	49	.682
1896	Baltimore	Edward H. Hanlon	90	39	.698	1954	New York[1]	Leo E. Durocher	97	57	.630
1897	Boston	Frank G. Selee	93	39	.705	1955	Brooklyn[1]	Walter Alston	98	55	.641
1898	Boston	Frank G. Selee	102	47	.685	1956	Brooklyn	Walter Alston	93	61	.604
1899	Brooklyn	Edward H. Hanlon	88	42	.677	1957	Milwaukee[1]	Fred Haney	95	59	.617
1900	Brooklyn	Edward H. Hanlon	82	54	.603	1958	Milwaukee	Fred Haney	92	62	.597
1901	Pittsburgh	Fred C. Clarke	90	49	.647	1959	Los Angeles	Walter Alston	88	68	.564
1902	Pittsburgh	Fred C. Clarke	103	36	.741	1960	Pittsburgh[1]	Danny Murtaugh	95	59	.617
1903	Pittsburgh	Fred C. Clarke	91	49	.650	1961	Cincinnati	Fred Hutchinson	93	61	.604
1904	New York[2]	John J. McGraw	106	47	.693	1962	San Francisco	Alvin Dark	103	62	.624
1905	New York[1]	John J. McGraw	105	48	.686	1963	Los Angeles[1]	Walter Alston	99	63	.611
1906	Chicago	Frank L. Chance	116	36	.763	1964	St. Louis[1]	Johnny Keane	93	69	.574
1907	Chicago[1]	Frank L. Chance	107	45	.704	1965	Los Angeles[1]	Walter Alston	97	65	.599
1908	Chicago[1]	Frank L. Chance	99	55	.643	1966	Los Angeles	Walter Alston	95	67	.586
1909	Pittsburgh[1]	Fred C. Clarke	110	42	.724	1967	St. Louis[1]	Red Schoendienst	101	60	.627
1910	Chicago	Frank L. Chance	104	50	.675	1968	St. Louis	Red Schoendienst	97	65	.599
1911	New York	John J. McGraw	99	54	.647	1969	New York[1][3]	Gil Hodges	100	62	.617
1912	New York	John J. McGraw	103	48	.682	1970	Cincinnati[4]	Sparky Anderson	102	60	.630
1913	New York	John J. McGraw	101	51	.664	1971	Pittsburgh[1][5]	Danny Murtaugh	97	65	.599
1914	Boston[1]	George T. Stallings	94	59	.614	1972	Cincinnati[4]	Sparky Anderson	95	59	.617
1915	Philadelphia	Patrick J. Moran	90	62	.592	1973	New York[6]	Yogi Berra	82	79	.509
1916	Brooklyn	Wilbert Robinson	94	60	.610	1974	Los Angeles[4]	Walter Alston	102	60	.630
1917	New York	John J. McGraw	98	56	.636	1975	Cincinnati[1][4]	Sparky Anderson	108	54	.667
1918	Chicago	Fred L. Mitchell	84	45	.651	1976	Cincinnati[7][1]	Sparky Anderson	102	60	.630
1919	Cincinnati[1]	Patrick J. Moran	96	44	.686	1977	Los Angeles[7]	Tom Lasorda	98	64	.605
1920	Brooklyn	Wilbert Robinson	93	61	.604	1978	Los Angeles[7]	Tom Lasorda	95	67	.586
1921	New York[1]	John J. McGraw	94	59	.614	1979[1]	Pittsburgh[6]	Chuck Tanner	98	64	.605
1922	New York[1]	John J. McGraw	93	61	.604	1980[1]	Philadelphia[8]	Dallas Green	91	71	.562
1923	New York	John J. McGraw	95	58	.621	1981	Los Angeles[1][9]	Tom Lasorda	63	47	.573*
1924	New York	John J. McGraw	93	60	.608	1982[1]	St. Louis[3]	Whitey Herzog	92	70	.568
1925	Pittsburgh[1]	William B. McKechnie	95	58	.621	1983	Philadelphia[11]	Paul Owens	90	72	.556
1926	St. Louis[1]	Rogers Hornsby	89	65	.578	1984	San Diego[12]	Dick Williams	92	70	.568
1927	Pittsburgh	Donie Bush	94	60	.610	1985	St. Louis[11]	Whitey Herzog	101	61	.623
1928	St. Louis	William B. McKechnie	95	59	.617	1986	New York[8]	Dave Johnson	108	54	.667
1929	Chicago	Joseph V. McCarthy	98	54	.645	1987	St. Louis[5]	Whitey Herzog	95	67	.586
1930	St. Louis	Gabby Street	92	62	.597	1988	Los Angeles[10]	Tom Lasorda	94	67	.584
1931	St. Louis[1]	Gabby Street	101	53	.656	1989	San Francisco[12]	Roger Craig	92	70	.568
1932	Chicago	Charles J. Grimm	90	64	.584	1990	Cincinnati[4]	Lou Piniella	91	71	.562
1933	New York[1]	William H. Terry	91	61	.599						

*Split season because of player strike. 1. World Series winner. 2. No World Series. 3. Defeated Atlanta, Western Division winner, in playoff. 4. Defeated Pittsburgh, Eastern Division winner, in playoff. 5. Defeated San Francisco, Western Division winner, in playoff. 6. Defeated Cincinnati, Western Division winner, in playoff. 7. Defeated Philadelphia, Eastern Division winner, in playoff. 8. Defeated Houston, Western Division winner, in playoff. 9. Defeated Montreal, Eastern Division winner, in playoff. 10. Defeated New York, Eastern Division winner, in playoff. 11. Defeated Los Angeles, Western Division in playoff. 12. Defeated Chicago, Eastern Division champion in playoff.

MOST VALUABLE PLAYERS

(Baseball Writers Association selections)

American League

1931	Lefty Grove, Philadelphia
1932–33	Jimmy Foxx, Philadelphia
1934	Mickey Cochrane, Detroit
1935	Hank Greenberg, Detroit
1936	Lou Gehrig, New York
1937	Charlie Gehringer, Detroit
1938	Jimmy Foxx, Boston
1939	Joe DiMaggio, New York
1940	Hank Greenberg, Detroit
1941	Joe DiMaggio, New York
1942	Joe Gordon, New York
1943	Spurgeon Chandler, New York
1944–45	Hal Newhouser, Detroit
1946	Ted Williams, Boston
1947	Joe DiMaggio, New York
1948	Lou Boudreau, Cleveland
1949	Ted Williams, Boston
1950	Phil Rizzuto, New York
1951	Yogi Berra, New York
1952	Bobby Shantz, Philadelphia
1953	Al Rosen, Cleveland
1954–55	Yogi Berra, New York
1956–57	Mickey Mantle, New York
1958	Jackie Jensen, Boston
1959	Nellie Fox, Chicago
1960–61	Roger Maris, New York
1962	Mickey Mantle, New York
1963	Elston Howard, New York
1964	Brooks Robinson, Baltimore
1965	Zoilo Versalles, Minnesota
1966	Frank Robinson, Baltimore
1967	Carl Yastrzemski, Boston
1968	Dennis McLain, Detroit
1969	Harmon Killebrew, Minnesota
1970	John (Boog) Powell, Baltimore
1971	Vida Blue, Oakland
1972	Dick Allen, Chicago
1973	Reggie Jackson, Oakland
1974	Jeff Burroughs, Texas
1975	Fred Lynn, Boston
1976	Thurman Munson, New York
1977	Rod Carew, Minnesota
1978	Jim Rice, Boston
1979	Don Baylor, California
1980	George Brett, Kansas City
1981	Rollie Fingers, Milwaukee
1982	Robin Yount, Milwaukee
1983	Cal Ripken, Jr., Baltimore
1984	Willie Hernandez, Detroit
1985	Don Mattingly, New York
1986	Roger Clemens, Boston
1987	George Bell, Toronto
1988	Jose Canseco, Oakland
1989	Robin Yount, Milwaukee

National League

1931	Frank Frisch, St. Louis
1932	Chuck Klein, Philadelphia
1933	Carl Hubbell, New York
1934	Dizzy Dean, St. Louis
1935	Gabby Hartnett, Chicago
1936	Carl Hubbell, New York
1937	Joe Medwick, St. Louis
1938	Ernie Lombardi, Cincinnati
1939	Bucky Walters, Cincinnati
1940	Frank McCormick, Cincinnati
1941	Dolph Camilli, Brooklyn
1942	Mort Cooper, St. Louis
1943	Stan Musial, St. Louis
1944	Marty Marion, St. Louis
1945	Phil Cavarretta, Chicago
1946	Stan Musial, St. Louis
1947	Bob Elliott, Boston
1948	Stan Musial, St. Louis
1949	Jackie Robinson, Brooklyn
1950	Jim Konstanty, Philadelphia
1951	Roy Campanella, Brooklyn
1952	Hank Sauer, Chicago
1953	Roy Campanella, Brooklyn
1954	Willie Mays, New York
1955	Roy Campanella, Brooklyn
1956	Don Newcombe, Brooklyn
1957	Henry Aaron, Milwaukee
1958–59	Ernie Banks, Chicago
1960	Dick Groat, Pittsburgh
1961	Frank Robinson, Cincinnati
1962	Maury Wills, Los Angeles
1963	Sandy Koufax, Los Angeles
1964	Ken Boyer, St. Louis
1965	Willie Mays, San Francisco
1966	Roberto Clemente, Pittsburgh
1967	Orlando Cepeda, St. Louis
1968	Bob Gibson, St. Louis
1969	Willie McCovey, San Francisco
1970	Johnny Bench, Cincinnati
1971	Joe Torre, St. Louis
1972	Johnny Bench, Cincinnati
1973	Pete Rose, Cincinnati
1974	Steve Garvey, Los Angeles
1975–76	Joe Morgan, Cincinnati
1977	George Foster, Cincinnati
1978	Dave Parker, Pittsburgh
1979	Willie Stargell, Pittsburgh
1979	Keith Hernandez, St. Louis
1980	Mike Schmidt, Philadelphia
1981	Mike Schmidt, Philadelphia
1982	Dale Murphy, Atlanta
1983	Dale Murphy, Atlanta
1984	Ryne Sandberg, Chicago
1985	Willie McGee, St. Louis
1986	Mike Schmidt, Philadelphia
1987	Andre Dawson, Chicago
1988	Kirk Gibson, Los Angeles
1989	Kevin Mitchell, San Francisco

CY YOUNG AWARD

Year	Winner(s)
1956	Don Newcombe, Brooklyn N.L.
1957	Warren Spahn, Milwaukee N.L.
1958	Bob Turley, New York A.L.
1959	Early Wynn, Chicago A.L.
1960	Vernon Law, Pittsburgh, N.L.
1961	Whitey Ford, New York A.L.
1962	Don Drysdale, Los Angeles N.L.
1963	Sandy Koufax, Los Angeles N.L.
1964	Dean Chance, Los Angeles A.L.
1965	Sandy Koufax, Los Angeles N.L.
1966	Sandy Koufax, Los Angeles N.L.
1967	Jim Lonborg, Boston A.L.; Mike McCormick, San Francisco N.L.
1968	Dennis, McLain, Detroit A.L.; Bob Gibson, St. Louis N.L.
1969	Mike Cuellar, Baltimore, and Dennis McLain, Detroit, tied in A.L.; Tom Seaver, N.Y. N.L.
1970	Jim Perry, Minnesota A.L.; Bob Gibson, St. Louis N.L.
1971	Vida Blue, Oakland A.L.; Ferguson Jenkins, Chicago N.L.
1972	Gaylord Perry, Cleveland A.L.; Steve Carlton, Phila. N.L.
1973	Jim Palmer, Baltimore A.L.; Tom Seaver, New York N.L.
1974	Catfish Hunter, Oakland A.L.; Mike Marshall, Los Angeles N.L.
1975	Jim Palmer, Baltimore A.L.; Tom Seaver, New York N.L.
1976	Jim Palmer, Baltimore A.L.; Randy Jones, San Diego N.L.
1977	Sparky Lyle, N.Y., A.L.; Steve Carlton, Philadelphia N.L.
1978	Ron Guidry, N.Y., A.L.; Gaylord Perry, San Diego N.L.
1979	Mike Flanagan, Baltimore, A.L.; Bruce Sutter, Chicago, N.L.
1980	Steve Stone, Baltimore, A.L.; Steve Carlton, Philadelphia, N.L.
1981	Rollie Fingers, Milwaukee, A.L.; Fernando Valenzuela, Los Angeles, N.L.
1982	Pete Vuckovich, Milwaukee, A.L.; Steve Carlton, Philadelphia, N.L.
1983	LaMarr Hoyt, Chicago, A.L.; John Denny, Philadelphia, N.L.
1984	Willie Hernandez, Detroit, A.L.; Rick Sutcliffe, Chicago, N.L.
1985	Bret Saberhagen, A.L.; Dwight Gooden, N.L.
1986	Roger Clemens, A.L.; Mike Scott, N.L.
1987	Roger Clemens, A.L.; Steve Bedrosian, N.L.
1988	Frank Viola, A.L.; Orel Hershiser, N.L.
1989	Bret Saberhagen, A.L.; Mark Davis, N.L.

ROOKIE OF THE YEAR
(Baseball Writers Association selections)

American League

1949	Roy Sievers, St. Louis
1950	Walt Dropo, Boston
1951	Gil McDougald, New York
1952	Harry Byrd, Philadelphia
1953	Harvey Kuenn, Detroit
1954	Bob Grim, New York
1955	Herb Score, Cleveland
1956	Luis Aparicio, Chicago
1957	Tony Kubek, New York
1958	Albie Pearson, Washington
1959	Bob Allison, Washington
1960	Ron Hansen, Baltimore
1961	Don Schwall, Boston
1962	Tom Tresh, New York
1963	Gary Peters, Chicago
1964	Tony Oliva, Minnesota
1965	Curt Blefary, Baltimore
1966	Tommy Agee, Chicago
1967	Rod Carew, Minnesota
1968	Stan Bahnsen, New York
1969	Lou Piniella, Kansas City
1970	Thurman Munson, New York
1971	Chris Chambliss, Cleveland
1972	Carlton Fisk, Boston
1973	Alonzo Bumbry, Baltimore
1974	Mike Hargrove, Texas
1975	Fred Lynn, Boston
1976	Mark Fidrych, Detroit

1977	Eddie Murray, Baltimore
1978	Lou Whitaker, Detroit
1979	Alfredo Griffin, Toronto
1979	John Castino, Minnesota
1980	Joe Charboneau, Cleveland
1981	Dave Righetti, New York
1982	Cal Ripken, Jr., Baltimore
1983	Ron Kittle, Chicago
1984	Alvin Davis, Seattle
1985	Ozzie Guillen, Chicago
1986	Jose Canseco, Oakland
1987	Mark McGwire, Oakland
1988	Walter Weiss, Oakland
1989	Gregg Olson, Baltimore

National League

1949	Don Newcombe, Brooklyn
1950	Sam Jethroe, Boston
1951	Willie Mays, New York
1952	Joe Black, Brooklyn
1953	Jim Gilliam, Brooklyn
1954	Wally Moon, St. Louis
1955	Bill Virdon, St. Louis
1956	Frank Robinson, Cincinnati
1957	Jack Sanford, Philadelphia
1958	Orlando Cepeda, San Francisco
1959	Willie McCovey, San Francisco
1960	Frank Howard, Los Angeles
1961	Billy Williams, Chicago
1962	Ken Hubbs, Chicago

1963	Pete Rose, Cincinnati
1964	Richie Allen, Philadelphia
1965	Jim Lefebvre, Los Angeles
1966	Tommy Helms, Cincinnati
1967	Tom Seaver, New York
1968	Johnny Bench, Cincinnati
1969	Ted Sizemore, Los Angeles
1970	Carl Morton, Montreal
1971	Earl Williams, Atlanta
1972	Jon Matlack, New York
1973	Gary Matthews, San Francisco
1974	Bake McBride, St. Louis
1975	John Montefusco, San Francisco
1976	Pat Zachry, Cincinnati
1976	Bruce Metzger, San Diego
1977	Andre Dawson, Montreal
1978	Bob Horner, Atlanta
1979	Rick Sutcliffe, Los Angeles
1980	Steve Howe, Los Angeles
1981	Fernando Valenzuela, Los Angeles
1982	Steve Sax, Los Angeles
1983	Darryl Strawberry, New York
1984	Dwight Gooden, New York
1985	Vince Coleman, St. Louis
1986	Todd Worrell, St. Louis
1987	Benito Santiago, San Diego
1988	Chris Sabo, Cincinnati
1989	Jerome Walton, Chicago

MAJOR LEAGUE LIFETIME RECORDS
(Through 1990)

Leading Batters, by Average
(Minimum 10 major league seasons and 4,000 at bats)

	Years	At Bats	Hits	Avg
Ty Cobb	24	11,436	4,190	.366
Rogers Hornsby	23	8,173	2,930	.358
Joe Jackson	13	4,981	1,774	.356
Pete Browning	13	4,795	1,664	.347
Ed Delahanty	16	7,493	2,593	.346
Willie Keeler	19	8,570	2,955	.345
Billy Hamilton	14	6,262	2,157	.344
Ted Williams	19	7,706	2,654	.344
Tris Speaker	22	10,208	3,515	.344
Dan Brouthers	19	6,682	2,288	.342
Jesse Burkett	16	8,389	2,872	.342
Babe Ruth	22	8,399	2,873	.342
Harry Heilmann	17	7,787	2,660	.342
Bill Terry	14	6,428	2,193	.341
George Sisler	15	8,267	2,812	.340
Lou Gehrig	17	8,001	2,721	.340
Nap Lajoie	21	9,590	3,251	.339
Riggs Stephenson	14	4,508	1,515	.336
Al Simmons	20	8,761	2,927	.334
Cap Anson	22	9,067	3,022	.333
Paul Waner	20	9,459	3,152	.333
Eddie Collins	25	9,949	3,311	.333
Sam Thompson	15	5,972	1,984	.332
Stan Musial	22	10,972	3,630	.331
Heinie Manush	17	7,653	2,524	.330
Hugh Duffy	17	7,026	2,313	.329
Honus Wagner	21	10,427	3,430	.329
Rod Carew	19	9,315	3,053	.328

	Years	At Bats	Hits	Avg
Top O'Neill	10	4,254	1,389	.327
Jimmie Foxx	20	8,134	2,646	.325
Earle Combs	12	5,748	1,866	.325
Joe DiMaggio	13	6,821	2,214	.325

Leading Pitchers
(More than 250 career victories)

	Years	W	L	Pct
Cy Young	22	511	315	.619
Walter Johnson	21	416	279	.599
Christy Mathewson	17	374	187	.667
Grover Cleveland Alexander	20	373	208	.642
Warren Spahn	21	363	245	.597
James Galvin	15	361	309	.542
Kid Nichols	17	361	208	.634
Tim Keefe	14	341	224	.604
Steve Carlton	24	329	244	.574
John Clarkson	12	327	176	.650
Eddie Plank	17	325	193	.627
Don Sutton	24	324	256	.559
Phil Niekro	24	318	274	.537
Gaylord Perry	22	314	265	.542
Tom Seaver	20	311	205	.603
Mickey Welch	13	309	209	.597
Hoss Radbourne	21	308	191	.617
Nolan Ryan**	23	302	272	.526
Lefty Grove	20	300	141	.680
Early Wynn	23	300	244	.551

	Years	W	L	Pct		Years	W	L	Pct
Tommy John	27	288	231	.555	Bob Feller	18	266	162	.621
Robin Roberts	19	286	245	.539	Eppa Rixey	21	266	251	.515
Tony Mullane	14	286	213	.573	Gus Weyhing	14	266	229	.537
Ferguson Jenkins	19	284	226	.557	Jim McCormick	10	264	214	.562
Jim Kaat	25	283	236	.545	Ted Lyons	21	260	230	.531
Bert Blyleven**	21	279	238	.540	Red Faber	20	254	212	.545
Red Ruffing	22	273	225	.548	Carl Hubbell	16	253	154	.622
Burleigh Grimes	19	270	212	.560	Bob Gibson	17	251	174	.591
Jim Palmer	18	268	149	.643					

**Active through 1990.

MAJOR LEAGUE ALL-TIME PITCHING RECORDS

(Through 1990)

Most Games Won—511, Cy Young, Cleveland N.L., 1890–98, St. Louis N.L., 1899–1900, Boston A.L., 1901–08, Cleveland A.L., 1909–11, Boston N.L., 1911.

Most Games Won, Season—60, Hoss Radbourne, Providence N.L., 1884. (Since 1900—41, Jack Chesbro, New York A.L., 1904.)

Most Consecutive Games Won—24, Carl Hubbell, New York N.L., 1936 (16) and 1937 (8).

Most Consecutive Games Won, Season—19, Tim Keefe, New York N.L., 1888; Rube Marquard, New York N.L., 1912.

Most Years Won 20 or More Games—16, Cy Young, Cleveland N.L., 1891–98, St. Louis N.L., 1899–1900, Boston A.L., 1901–04, 1907–08.

Most Shutouts—113, Walter Johnson, Wash. A.L., 1907–27.

Most Shutouts, Season—16, Grover Alexander, Philadelphia N.L., 1916.

Most Consecutive Shutouts—6, Don Drysdale, Los Angeles, N.L., 1968.

Most Consecutive Scoreless Innings—59, Orel Hershiser, Los Angeles Dodgers, 1988.

Most Strikeouts—5,308, Nolan Ryan, New York N.L., California A.L., Houston N.L., 1968–1988 Texas, 1989-90 (still active).

Most Strikeouts, Season—505, Matthew Kilroy, Baltimore A.A., 1886. (Since 1900—383, Nolan Ryan, California, A.L., 1973.)

Most Strikeouts, Game—21, Tom Cheney, Washington A.L., 1962, 16 innings. Nine innings: 20, Roger Clemens, Boston, A.L., 1986; 19, Charles McSweeney, Providence N.L., 1884; Hugh Dailey, Chicago U.A., 1884. (Since 1900—19, Steve Carlton, St. Louis N.L. vs. New York, Sept. 15, 1969; Tom Seaver, New York N.L. vs. San Diego, April 22, 1970; Nolan Ryan, California A.L. vs. Boston, Aug. 12, 1974.)

Most Consecutive Strikeouts—10, Tom Seaver, New York N.L. vs. San Diego, April 22, 1970.

Most Games, Season—106, Mike Marshall, Los Angeles, N.L., 1974.

Most Complete Games, Season—74, William White, Cincinnati N.L., 1879. (Since 1900—48, Jack Chesbro, New York A.L., 1904.)

MAJOR LEAGUE INDIVIDUAL ALL-TIME RECORDS

(Through 1990)

Highest Batting Average—.442, James O'Neill, St. Louis, A.A., 1887; .438, Hugh Duffy, Boston, N.L., 1894 (Since 1900—.424, Rogers Hornsby, St. Louis, N.L., 1924; .422, Nap Lajoie, Phil., A.L., 1901)

Most Times at Bat—12,364, Henry Aaron, Milwaukee N.L., 1954–65; Atlanta N.L., 1966–74; Milwaukee A.L., 1975–76.

Most Years Batted .300 or Better—23, Ty Cobb, Detroit A.L., 1906–26, Philadelphia A.L., 1927–28.

Most hits—4,256, Pete Rose, Cincinnati 1963–79, Philadelphia 1980–83, Montreal 1984, Cincinnati 1984–86.

Most Hits, Season—257, George Sisler, St. Louis A.L., 1920.

Most Hits, Game (9 innings)—7, Wilbert Robinson, Baltimore N.L., 6 singles, 1 double, 1892. Rennie Stennett, Pittsburgh N.L., 4 singles, 2 doubles, 1 triple, 1975.

Most Hits, Game (extra innings)—9, John Burnett, Cleveland A.L., 18 innings, 7 singles, 2 doubles, 1932.

Most Hits in Succession—12, Mike Higgins, Boston A.L., in four games, 1938; Walt Dropo, Detroit A.L., in three games, 1952.

Most Consecutive Games Batted Safely—56, Joe DiMaggio, New York A.L., 1941.

Most Runs—2,244, Ty Cobb, Detroit A.L., 1905–26, Philadelphia A.L., 1927–28.

Most Runs, Season—196, William Hamilton, Philadelphia N.L., 1894. (Since 1900—177, Babe Ruth, New York A.L., 1921.)

Most Runs, Game—7, Guy Hecker, Louisville A.L., 1886. (Since 1900—6, by Mel Ott, New York N.L., 1934, 1944; Johnny Pesky, Boston, A.L., 1946; Frank Torre, Milwaukee N.L., 1957.)

Most Runs Batted in—2,297, Henry Aaron, Milwaukee N.L., 1954–1965; Atlanta N.L., 1966–74; Milwaukee A.L., 1975–76.

Most Runs Batted in, Season—190, Hack Wilson, Chicago N.L., 1930.

Most Runs Batted In, Game—12, Jim Bottomley, St. Louis N.L., 1924.

Most Home Runs—755, Henry Aaron, Milwaukee N.L., 1954–1965; Atlanta N.L., 1966–74; Milwaukee A.L., 1975–76.

Most Home Runs, Season—61, Roger Maris, New York A.L., 1961 (162-game season); 60, Babe Ruth, New York A.L., 1927 (154-game season)

Most Home Runs with Bases Filled—23, Lou Gehrig, New York A.L., 1927–39.

Most 2-Base Hits—793, Tris Speaker, Boston A.L., 1907–15, Cleveland A.L., 1916–26, Washington A.L., 1927, Philadelphia A.L., 1928.

Most 2-Base Hits, Season—67, Earl Webb, Boston A.L., 1931.

Most 2-base Hits, Game—4, by many.

Most 3-Base Hits—312, Sam Crawford, Cincinnati N.L., 1899–1902, Detroit A.L., 1903–17.

Most 3-Base Hits, Season—36, Owen Wilson, Pittsburgh N.L., 1912.

Most 3-Base Hits, Game—4, George Strief, Philadelphia A.A., 1885; William Joyce, New York N.L., 1897. (Since 1900—3, by many.)

Most Games Played—3,298, Henry Aaron, Milwaukee N.L., 1954–1965; Atlanta, N.L., 1966–74; Milwaukee A.L., 1975–76.

Most Consecutive Games Played—2,130, Lou Gehrig, New York A.L., 1925–39.

Most Bases on Balls—2,056, Babe Ruth, Boston A.L., 1914–19; New York A.L., 1920–34, Boston N.L., 1935.

Most Bases on Balls, Season—170, Babe Ruth, New York A.L., 1923.

Most bases on Balls, Game—6, Jimmy Foxx, Boston A.L., 1938.

Most Strikeouts, Season—189, Bobby Bonds, San Francisco N.L., 1970.

Most Strikeouts, Game (9 innings)—5, by many.

Most Strikeouts, Game (extra innings)—6, Carl Weilman, St. Louis A.L., 15 innings, 1913; Don Hoak, Chicago N.L., 17 innings, 1956; Fred Reichardt, California A.L., 17, innings, 1966; Billy Cowan, California A.L., 20, 1971; Cecil Cooper, Boston A.L., 15, 1974.

Most pinch—hits, lifetime—150, Manny Mota, S.F., 1962; Pitt., 1963–68; Montreal, 1969; L.A., 1969–80, N.L.

Most Pinch-hits, season—25, Jose Morales, Montreal N.L., 1976.

Most consecutive pinch-hits—9, Dave Philley, Phil., N.L., 1958 (8), 1959 (1).

Most pinch-hit home runs, lifetime—18, Gerald Lynch, Pitt.-Cin. N.L., 1957–66.

Most pinch-hit home runs, season—6, Johnny Frederick, Brooklyn, N.L., 1932.

Most stolen bases, lifetime (since 1900)—938, Lou Brock, Chicago N.L. 1961–64; St. Louis, N.L. 1964–79.*

Most stolen bases, season—156, Harry Stovey, Phil., A.A., 1888. Since 1900: 130, Rickey Henderson, Oak., A.L., 1982; 118, Lou Brock, St. Louis, N.L., 1974.

Most stolen bases, game—7, George Gore, Chicago N.L. 1881; William Hamilton, Philadelphia N.L. 1894. (Since 1900—6, Eddie Collins, Philadelphia A.L., 1912.)

Most time stealing home, lifetime—35, Ty Cobb, Detroit-Phil. A.L., 1905–28.

*Rickey Henderson of the Oakland Athletics comes into the 1991 season with 936 lifetime stolen bases, two off the major league record.

MAJOR LEAGUE BASEBALL EXPANDS PLAYOFFS TO BEST 4-OF-7

After 16 years of five-game league championship playoffs, baseball expanded to a seven-game format in 1985 for the purpose of reaping a reported additional $9 million in network television revenue.

An agreement was reached between management and players to expand the series for 1985. The decision immediately increased baseball's revenue from $20 to $29 million for the playoffs.

The formula for splitting that money was part of the agreement with the players which settled the Aug. 6–8 major league players strike.

The playoffs had been a best 3-of-5 affair since 1969, when divisional play was first initiated. The World Series remained a best 4-of-7 format.

MAJOR LEAGUE ATTENDANCE RECORDS

(Through 1990)

Single game—78,672, San Francisco at Los Angeles (N.L.), April 18, 1958. (At Memorial Coliseum.)

Doubleheader—84,587, New York at Cleveland (A.L.), Sept. 12, 1954.

Night—78,382, Chicago at Cleveland (A.L.), Aug. 20, 1948.

Season, home—3,608,881, Los Angeles (N.L.), 1982.

Season, road—2,461,240, New York (A.L.), 1980.

Season, league—29,848,782, American League, 1989.

Season, both leagues—55,174,745, 1989.

World Series, single game—92,706, Chicago (A.L.) at Los Angeles (N.L.), Oct. 6, 1959.

World Series, all games (6)—420,784, Chicago (A.L.) and Los Angeles (N.L.), 1959.

MOST HOME RUNS IN ONE SEASON

(45 or More)

HR	Player/Team	Year	HR	Player/Team	Year
61	Roger Maris, New York (AL)	1961	49	Andre Dawson, Chicago (NL)	1987
60	Babe Ruth, New York (AL)	1927	48	Jimmy Foxx, Philadelphia (AL)	1933
59	Babe Ruth, New York (AL)	1921	48	Harmon Killebrew, Minnesota (AL)	1962
58	Jimmy Foxx, Philadelphia (AL)	1932	48	Willie Stargell, Pittsburgh (NL)	1971
58	Hank Greenberg, Detroit (AL)	1938	48	Dave Kingman, Chicago (NL)	1979
56	Hack Wilson, Chicago (NL)	1930	48	Mike Schmidt, Philadelphia (NL)	1980
54	Babe Ruth, New York (AL)	1920	47	Babe Ruth, New York (AL)	1926
54	Babe Ruth, New York (AL)	1928	47	Ralph Kiner, Pittsburgh (NL)	1950
54	Ralph Kiner, Pittsburgh (NL)	1949	47	Ed Mathews, Milwaukee (NL)	1953
54	Mickey Mantle, New York (AL)	1961	47	Ernie Banks, Chicago (NL)	1958
52	Mickey Mantle, New York (AL)	1956	47	Willie Mays, San Francisco (NL)	1964
52	Willie Mays, San Francisco (NL)	1965	47	Henry Aaron, Atlanta (NL)	1971
52	George Foster, Cincinnati (NL)	1977	47	Reggie Jackson, Oakland (AL)	1969
51	Ralph Kiner, Pittsburgh (NL)	1947	47	George Bell, Toronto (AL)	1987
51	John Mize, New York (NL)	1947	47	Kevin Mitchell, San Francisco (NL)	1989
51	Willie Mays, New York (NL)	1955	46	Babe Ruth, New York (AL)	1924
51	Cecil Fielder (AL)	1990	46	Babe Ruth, New York, (AL)	1929
50	Jimmy Foxx, Boston (AL)	1938	46	Babe Ruth, New York (AL)	1931
49	Babe Ruth, New York (AL)	1930	46	Lou Gehrig, New York (AL)	1931
49	Lou Gehrig, New York (AL)	1934	46	Joe DiMaggio, New York (AL)	1937
49	Lou Gehrig, New York (AL)	1936	46	Ed Mathews, Milwaukee (NL)	1959
49	Ted Kluszewski, Cincinnati (NL)	1954	46	Orlando Cepeda, San Francisco (NL)	1961
49	Willie Mays, San Francisco (NL)	1962	46	Jim Rice, Boston (AL)	1978
49	Harmon Killebrew, Minnesota (AL)	1964	45	Harmon Killebrew, Minnesota (AL)	1963
49	Frank Robinson, Baltimore (AL)	1966	45	Willie McCovey, San Francisco (NL)	1969
49	Harmon Killebrew, Minnesota (AL)	1969	45	Johnny Bench, Cincinnati (NL)	1970
49	Mark McGwire, Oakland (AL)	1987	45	Gorman Thomas, Milwaukee (AL)	1979
			45	Henry Aaron, Milwaukee (NL)	1962

MAJOR LEAGUE BASEBALL—1990

AMERICAN LEAGUE
(Final Standing—1990)

EASTERN DIVISION

Team	W	L	Pct	GB
Boston Red Sox	88	74	.543	—
Toronto Blue Jays	86	76	.531	2
Detroit Tigers	79	83	.488	9
Cleveland Indians	77	85	.475	11
Baltimore Orioles	76	85	.472	11 1/2
Milwaukee Brewers	74	88	.457	14
New York Yankees	67	95	.414	21

WESTERN DIVISION

Team	W	L	Pct	GB
Oakland Athletics	103	59	.636	—
Chicago White Sox	94	68	.580	9
Texas Rangers	83	79	.512	20
California Angels	80	82	.494	23
Seattle Mariners	77	85	.475	26
Kansas City Royals	75	86	.466	27 1/2
Minnesota Twins	74	88	.457	29

AMERICAN LEAGUE LEADERS—1990

Batting—George Brett, Kansas City	.329
Runs—Rickey Henderson, Oakland	119
Hits—Rafael Palmeiro, Texas	191
Runs batted in—Cecil Fielder, Detroit	132
Triples—Tony Fernandez, Toronto	17
Doubles—George Brett, Kansas City	45
Home Runs—Cecil Fielder, Detroit	51
Stolen Bases—Rickey Henderson, Oakland	65
Total bases—Cecil Fielder, Detroit	339
Slugging percentage—Cecil Fielder, Detroit	.592
On-base percentage—Rickey Henderson, Oakland	.439

Pitching

Victories—Bob Welch, Oakland	27
Earned run average—Roger Clemens, Boston	1.93
Strikeouts—Nolan Ryan, Texas	232
Shutouts—Roger Clemens, Boston	4
Dave Stewart, Oakland (tie)	
Complete games—Dave Stewart, Oakland	11
Jack Morris, Detroit (tie)	
Saves—Bobby Thigpen, Chicago	57
Innings pitched—Dave Stewart, Oakland	267

AMERICAN LEAGUE AVERAGES—1990

Team Batting

	AB	R	H	HR	RBI	Pct
Boston	5516	699	1502	106	660	.272
Cleveland	5485	732	1465	110	675	.267
Kansas City	5488	707	1465	100	660	.267
Toronto	5589	767	1480	167	729	.265
Minnesota	5499	666	1458	100	625	.265
California	5570	690	1448	147	646	.260
Seattle	5474	640	1419	107	610	.259
Texas	5469	676	1417	110	641	.259
Detroit	5479	750	1418	172	714	.259
Chicago	5402	682	1393	106	637	.258
Milwaukee	5503	732	1409	128	680	.256
Oakland	5433	733	1381	164	693	.254
Baltimore	5410	669	1328	132	623	.245
New York	5483	603	1322	147	561	.241

Individual Batting
(300 or more at bats)

Player/Team	AB	R	H	HR	RBI	Pct
Polonia Cal	403	52	135	2	35	.335
Brett KC	544	82	179	14	87	.329

NATIONAL LEAGUE
(Final Standing—1990)

EASTERN DIVISION

Team	W	L	Pct	GB
Pittsburgh Pirates	95	67	.586	—
New York Mets	91	71	.562	4
Montreal Expos	85	77	.525	10
Chicago Cubs	77	85	.485	18
Philadelphia Phillies	77	85	.485	18
St. Louis Cardinals	70	92	.432	25

WESTERN DIVISION

Team	W	L	Pct	GB
Cincinnati Reds	91	71	.562	—
Los Angeles Dodgers	86	76	.531	5
San Francisco Giants	85	77	.525	6
Houston Astros	75	87	.463	16
San Diego Padres	75	87	.463	16
Atlanta Braves	65	97	.401	26

NATIONAL LEAGUE LEADERS—1990

Batting—Willie McGee, St. Louis	.335
Runs—Ryne Sandberg, Chicago	116
Hits—Brett Butler, San Francisco	192
Lenny Dykstra, Philadelphia (tie)	
Runs batted in—Matt Williams, San Francisco	122
Triples—Mariano Duncan, Cincinnati	11
Doubles—Gregg Jefferies, New York	40
Home Runs—Ryne Sandberg, Chicago	40
Stolen Bases—Vince Coleman, St. Louis	77
Total Bases—Ryne Sandberg, Chicago	344
Slugging percentage—Barry Bonds, Pittsburgh	.565
On-base percentage—Lenny Dykstra, Philadelphia	.418

Pitching

Victories—Doug Drabek, Pittsburgh	22
Earned run average—Danny Darwin, Houston	2.21
Strikeouts—David Cone, New York	233
Shutouts—Bruce Hurst, San Diego	4
Complete games—Ramon Martinez, Los Angeles	12
Saves—John Franco, New York	33
Innings pitched—Frank Viola, New York	249 2/3

Player	AB	R	H	HR	RBI	Pct
Mack Min	313	50	102	8	44	.326
Henderson Oak	489	119	159	28	61	.325
Palmeiro	598	72	191	14	89	.319
Trammell Det	559	71	170	14	89	.304
Boggs Bsn	619	89	187	6	63	.302
EMartinez Sea	487	71	147	11	49	.302
Daughrty Tex	310	36	93	6	47	.300
GrfyJr Sea	597	91	179	22	80	.300
McGriff Tor	557	91	167	35	88	.300
CJames Cle	528	62	158	12	70	.299
Puckett Min	551	82	164	12	80	.298
Greenwell Bsn	610	71	181	14	73	.297
Burks Bsn	588	89	174	21	89	.296
Franco Tex	582	96	172	11	69	.296
Harper Min	479	61	141	6	54	.294
Sheffield Mil	487	67	143	10	67	.294
Jacoby Cle	553	77	162	14	75	.293
BRipken Blt	406	48	118	3	38	.291
Alomar Cle	445	60	129	9	66	.290
WWilson KC	307	49	89	2	42	.290
DParker Mil	610	71	176	21	92	.289
JoReed Bsn	598	70	173	5	51	.289
Hrbek Min	492	61	141	22	79	.287
Quintana Bsn	512	56	147	7	67	.287

Individual Pitching
(6 or more decisions)

Player/Club	IP	H	BB	SO	W	L	ERA
Eckersley Oak	73	41	4	73	4	2	0.61
Nelson Oak	75	55	17	38	3	3	1.57
Thigpen Chi	89	60	32	68	4	6	1.83
Clemens Bsn	228	193	54	209	21	6	1.93
Farr KC	127	99	48	94	13	7	1.98
Arnsberg Tex	63	56	33	44	6	1	2.15
Henke Tor	75	58	19	75	2	4	2.17
Williamsn Blt	85	65	28	60	8	2	2.21
BJones Chi	74	62	33	45	11	4	2.31
Montgmry KC	94	81	34	94	6	5	2.39
Swift Sea	128	135	21	42	6	4	2.39
CFinley Cal	236	210	81	177	18	9	2.40
Olson Blt	74	57	31	74	6	5	2.42
McDonald Blt	119	88	35	65	8	5	2.43
DJones Cle	84	66	22	55	5	5	2.56
Stewart Oak	267	226	83	166	22	11	2.56
Plunk NY	73	58	43	67	6	3	2.72
Aguilera Min	65	55	19	61	5	3	2.76
Appier KC	186	179	54	127	12	8	2.76
Erickson Min	113	108	51	53	8	4	2.87
Comstock Sea	56	40	26	50	7	4	2.89
RRobinson Mil	148	158	37	57	12	5	2.91
Stieb Tor	209	179	64	125	18	6	2.93
Burns Oak	79	78	32	43	3	3	2.97
Gibson Det	97	99	44	56	5	4	3.05
Henneman Det	94	90	33	50	8	6	3.05

Team Pitching

	ERA	H	ER	BB	SO	ShO	SA
Oakland	3.18	1287	514	494	831	16	64
Chicago	3.61	1313	581	548	914	10	68
Seattle	3.69	1319	592	606	1064	7	41
Boston	3.72	1439	596	519	997	13	44
California	3.79	1482	613	544	944	13	42
Texas	3.83	1343	615	623	997	9	36
Toronto	3.84	1434	620	445	892	9	48
Kanss Cty	3.93	1449	621	560	1006	8	33
Baltimore	4.04	1445	644	537	776	5	43
Milwaukee	4.08	1558	655	469	771	13	42
Minnesota	4.12	1509	658	489	872	13	43
New York	4.21	1430	676	618	909	6	41
Cleveland	4.26	1491	676	518	860	10	47
Detroit	4.39	1401	697	661	856	12	45

NATIONAL LEAGUE AVERAGES—1990

Team Batting

	AB	R	H	HR	RBI	Pct
Cincinnati	5525	693	1466	125	644	.265
Chicago	5600	690	1475	136	649	.263
Los Angeles	5491	728	1436	129	669	.262
San Francisco	5573	719	1459	152	681	.262
Pittsburgh	5388	733	1395	138	693	.259
San Diego	5554	673	1429	123	628	.257
St. Louis	5462	599	1398	73	554	.256
New York	5504	775	1410	172	734	.256
Philadelphia	5535	646	1410	103	619	.255
Atlanta	5504	682	1377	162	636	.250
Montreal	5453	662	1363	114	607	.250
Houston	5379	573	1301	94	536	.242

Individual Batting
(300 or more at bats)

Player/Team	AB	R	H	HR	RBI	Pct
HMorris Cin	309	50	105	7	36	.340
McGee StL	501	76	168	3	62	.335
Murray LA	558	96	184	26	95	.330
Magadan NY	451	74	148	6	72	.328
Dykstra Phi	590	106	192	9	60	.325
Dawson Chi	529	72	164	27	100	.310
Butler SF	622	108	192	3	44	.309
Grace Chi	589	72	182	9	82	.309
Roberts SD	556	104	172	9	44	.309
TGwynn SD	573	79	177	4	72	.309
Duncan Cin	435	67	133	10	55	.306
Sandberg Chi	615	116	188	40	100	.306
LoSmith Atl	466	72	142	9	42	.305
LHarris LA	431	61	131	2	29	.304
Gant Atl	575	107	174	32	84	.303
Bonds Pit	519	104	156	33	114	.301
Larkin Cin	614	85	185	7	67	.301
Doran Cin	403	59	121	7	37	.300
Shrprsn LA	357	42	106	3	36	.297
Daniels LA	450	81	133	27	94	.296
Wallach Mon	626	69	185	21	98	.296
WClark SF	600	91	177	19	95	.295
Backman Pit	315	62	92	2	28	.292
Coleman StL	497	73	145	6	39	.292
Kruk Phi	443	52	129	7	67	.291
Mitchell SF	524	90	152	35	93	.290

Individual Pitching
(6 or more decisions)

Player/Team	IP	H	BB	SO	W	L	ERA
Brantley SF	87	77	33	61	5	3	1.56
Dibble Cin	98	62	34	136	8	3	1.74
Andersen Htn	74	61	24	68	5	2	1.95
Myers Cin	87	59	38	98	4	6	2.08
LeSmith StL	69	58	20	70	3	4	2.10
Frey Mon	56	44	29	29	8	2	2.10
Landrum Pit	72	69	21	39	7	3	2.13
JHowell LA	66	59	20	59	5	5	2.18
Darwin Htn	163	136	31	109	11	4	2.21
GHarris SD	117	92	49	97	8	8	2.30
DaSmith Htn	60	45	20	50	6	6	2.39
Tudor StL	146	120	30	63	12	4	2.40
Lefferts SD	79	67	22	60	7	5	2.52
Burke Mon	75	71	21	47	3	3	2.52
Franco NY	68	66	21	56	5	3	2.53
Tomlin Pit	78	62	12	42	4	4	2.55
ZSmith Pit	215	196	50	130	12	9	2.55
Whitson SD	229	215	47	127	14	9	2.60
Viola NY	250	227	60	182	20	12	2.67
Rijo Cin	197	151	78	152	14	8	2.70
Charlton Cin	154	131	70	117	12	9	2.74
Drabek Pit	231	190	56	131	22	6	2.76
Crews LA	107	98	24	76	4	5	2.77
Assnmchr Chi	103	90	36	95	7	2	2.80
Nabholz Mon	70	43	32	53	6	2	2.83
Gott LA	62	59	34	44	3	5	2.90

Team Pitching

	ERA	H	ER	BB	SO	ShO	SA
Montreal	3.37	1349	551	510	991	11	50
Cincinnati	3.39	1338	549	543	1029	12	50
Pittsburgh	3.40	1367	546	413	848	8	43
New York	3.42	1339	548	444	1217	14	41
Houston	3.61	1396	581	496	854	6	37
San Diego	3.68	1437	597	507	928	12	35
Los Angls	3.72	1364	596	478	1021	12	29
StLouis	3.87	1432	621	475	833	13	39
Philadelph	4.07	1381	655	651	840	7	35
Sn Frncsc	4.08	1477	655	553	788	6	45
Chicago	4.34	1510	695	572	877	7	42
Atlanta	4.58	1527	727	579	938	8	30

MAJOR LEAGUE BASEBALL—1990

AMERICAN LEAGUE PLAYOFFS—1990

1st game, Boston, Mass., Oct. 6, 1990

Oakland	000	000	117	— 9	13	0
Boston	000	100	000	— 1	5	1

Stewart, Eckersley; Clemens, Andersen, Bolton, Gray, Murphy.
Winner: Stewart. Loser: Andersen. Attendance: 35,192.

2nd game, Boston, Mass., Oct. 7, 1990

Oakland	000	100	102	— 4	13	1
Boston	001	000	000	— 1	6	0

Welch, Huneycutt, Eclersley; Kiecker, Harris, Andersen, Reardon.
Winner: Welch. Loser: Harris. Attendance: 35,070.

3rd game, Okland, Calif., Oct. 9, 1990

Boston	010	000	000	— 1	8	3
Oakland	000	202	00x	— 4	6	0

Boddicker; Moore, Nelson, Huneycutt, Eckersley.
Winner: Moore. Loser: Boddicker. Attendance: 49,026.

4th game, Oakland, Calif., Oct. 10, 1990

Boston	000	000	001	— 1	4	1
Oakland	030	000	000	— 3	6	0

Clemens, Bolton, Gray, Andersen; Stewart, Huneycutt.
Winner: Stewart. Loser: Clemens. Attendance: 49,052.

Oakland wins series, 4 games to 0.

NATIONAL LEAGUE PLAYOFFS—1990

1st game, Cincinnati, Ohio, Oct. 4, 1990

Pittsburgh	001	200	100	— 4	7	1
Cincinnati	300	000	000	— 3	5	0

Walk, Belinda, Patterson, Power; Rijo, Charlton, Dibble.
Winner: Walk. Loser: Charlton. Attendance: 55,700.

2nd game, Cincinnati, Ohio, Oct. 5, 1990

Pittsburgh	000	010	000	— 1	6	0
Cincinnati	100	010	000	— 2	5	0

Drabek, Browning, Dibble, Myers.
Winner: Browning. Loser: Drabek. Attendance: 54,456.

3rd game, Pittsburgh, Pa., Oct. 8, 1990

Cincinnati	020	030	001	— 6	13	1
Pittsbrugh	000	200	010	— 3	8	0

Jackson, Dibble, Charlton, Myers; Smith, Landrum, Smiley, Belinda.
Winner: Jackson. Loser: Smith. Attendance: 45,611.

4th game, Pittsburgh, Pa., Oct. 9, 1990

Cincinnati	000	200	201	— 5	10	1
Pittsburgh	100	100	010	— 3	8	0

Rijo, Myers, Dibble; Walk, Power.
Winner: Rijo. Loser: Wack. Attendance: 50,461.

5th game, Pittsburgh, Pa., Oct. 10, 1990

Cincinnati	100	000	010	— 2	7	0
Pittsburgh	200	100	000	— 3	6	1

Rajo, Mahlev, Scudder, Charlton; Drabek, Patterson.
Winner: Drabek. Loser: Rijo. Attendance: 48,221.

6th game, Cincinnati, Ohio, Oct. 12, 1990

Pittsburgh	000	010	000	— 1	1	3
Cincinnati	100	000	100	— 3	9	0

Power, Smith, Belinda, Landrum; Jackson, Charlton, Myers.
Winner: Charlton. Loser: Smith. Attendance: 56,079.

Cincinnati wins series, 4 games to 2.

WORLD SERIES—1990
Cincinnati Reds (NL) defeated Oakland Athletics (AL), 4 games to 0

1st Game—Cincinnati, Oct. 16

OAKLAND (A)	AB	R	H	RBI	CINCINNATI (N)	AB	R	H	RBI
R. Henderson, lf	5	0	3	0	Larkin, ss	4	1	0	0
McGee, cf	5	0	1	0	Hatcher, cf	3	3	3	1
Canseco, rf	2	0	0	0	O'Neill, rf	2	1	0	1
McGwire, 1b	3	0	0	0	Davis, lf	4	2	2	3
Lansford, 3b	4	0	2	0	Morris, 1b	4	0	1	0
Steinbach, c	4	0	1	0	Sabo, 3b	3	0	1	2
Randolph, 2b	4	0	1	0	Oliver, c	4	0	1	0
Gallego, ss	4	0	0	0	Duncan, 2b	3	0	1	0
Stewart, p	1	0	0	0	Rijo, p	3	0	1	0
Jennings, ph	1	0	1	0	Dibble, p	0	0	0	0
Burns, p	0	0	0	0	Benzinger, ph	1	0	0	0
Nelson, p	0	0	0	0	Myers, p	0	0	0	0
Hassey, ph	1	0	0	0					
Sanderson, p	0	0	0	0					
Eckersley, p	0	0	0	0					
D. Henderson, ph	1	0	0	0					
Totals	**35**	**0**	**9**	**0**	**Totals**	**31**	**7**	**10**	**7**

Oakland	000	000	000	— 0
Cincinnati	202	030	00x	— 7

E—Gallego. DP—Oakland 2, Cincinnati 1. LOB—Oakland 11, Cincinnati 6. 2B—R. Henderson 2, Hatcher 2. HR—Davis (1). SB—McGee (1), Landford (1).

Oakland	IP	H	R	ER	BB	SO
Stewart L, 0-1	4	3	4	4	4	3
Burns	2-3	4	3	3	1	0
Nelson	1 1-3	2	0	0	1	0
Sanderson	1	1	0	0	0	0
Eckersley	1	0	0	0	0	1
Cincinnati						
Rijo W, 1-0	7	7	0	0	2	5
Dibble	1	1	0	0	1	0
Myers	1	1	0	0	0	2

WP—Dibble. Tiime of Game—2:48. Attendance—55,830.

2nd Game—Cincinnati, Oct. 17

OAKLAND (A)	AB	R	H	RBI	CINCINNATI (N)	AB	R	H	RBI
R. Henderson, lf	4	1	1	0	Larkin, ss	5	1	3	0
Lansford, 3b	4	0	1	0	Hatcher, cf	4	2	4	1
Canseco, rf	5	1	1	2	O'Neill, rf	5	0	0	0
McGuire, 1b	4	1	2	0	Davis, lf	4	0	0	1
D. Henderson, cf	4	1	2	0	Morris, 1b	3	0	0	0
Steinbach, c	4	0	0	0	Braggs, rf	1	0	0	1
Randolph, 2b	4	0	0	0	Dibble, p	0	0	0	0
Hassey, c	4	0	2	1	Bates, ph	1	1	1	0
Bordick, ss	0	0	0	0	Sabo, 3b	5	0	3	0
Gallego, ss	4	0	1	1	Oliver, c	5	1	2	1
Baines, ph	1	0	0	0	Duncan, 2b	3	0	0	0
Eckersley, p	0	0	0	0	Jackson, p	1	0	0	0
Welch, p	3	0	0	0	Scudder, p	0	0	0	0
Honeycutt, p	0	0	0	0	Oester, ph	1	0	1	1
McGee, cf	0	0	0	0	Armstrong, p	0	0	0	0
					Winningham, ph	1	0	0	0
					Charlton, p	0	0	0	0
					Benzinger, 1b	1	0	0	0
Totals	**37**	**4**	**10**	**4**	**Totals**	**40**	**5**	**14**	**5**

Oakland	103	000	000 0	— 4
Cincinnati	200	100	010 1	— 5

One out when winning run scored.

E—Jackson, Oliver, Hassey, McGwire. DP—Cincinnati 1. LOB—Oakland 10, Cincinnati 10. 2B—Larkin, Hatcher 2, Oliver. 3B—Hatcher. HR—Canseco (1). SB—R. Henderson (1). S—Lansford, Welch. SF—Hassey.

	IP	H	R	ER	BB	SO
Oakland						
Welch,	7 1-3	9	4	4	2	2
Honeycutt	1 2-3	2	0	0	1	0
Eckersley L, 0-1	1-3	3	1	1	0	0
Cincinnati						
Jackson	2 2-3	6	4	3	2	0
Scudder	1 1-3	0	0	0	2	2
Armstrong	3	1	0	0	0	3
Charlton	1	1	0	0	0	0
Dibble W, 1-0	2	2	0	0	0	2

Time of Game—3:31. Attendance—55,832.

3rd Game—Oakland Oct. 19

CINCINNATI (N)	AB	H	R	RBI	OAKLAND (A)	AB	R	H	RBI
Larkin, ss	5	0,	2	1	R. Henderson lf	3	1	1	1
Hatcher, cf	5	1	2	1	Lansford, 3b	3	0	0	0
O'Neill, rf	3	1	1	0	Canseco, rf	4	0	0	0
Davis, lf	5	1	2	1	D. Henderson, cf	4	1	1	0
Morris, dh	4	0	0	1	Baines, lf	4	1	1	2
Sabo, 3b	4	2	2	3	McGwire, 1b	4	0	1	0
Benzinger, 1b	5	1	2	0	Steinbach, c	4	0	0	0
Oliver, c	5	1	2	1	Randolph, 2b	4	0	3	0
Duncan, 2b	4	1	1	1	Gallego, ss	2	0	0	0
					McGee, rf	1	0	0	0
					Bordick, ss	0	0	0	0
					Blankenship, ph	1	0	0	0
Totals	**40**	**8**	**14**	**8**	**Totals**	**34**	**3**	**7**	**3**

Cincinnati 017 000 000 — 8
Oakland 021 000 000 — 3

E—McGwire, Oliver. DP—Oakland 2. LOB—Cincinnati 9, Oakland 6. 2B—D. Henderson, Oliver. 3B—Larkin. HR—Sabo 2 (2), Baines (1), R. Henderson (1). SB—Duncan (1), O'Neill (1), R. Henderson (2), Randolph (1).

	IP	H	R	ER	BB	SO
Cincinnati						
Browning W, 1-0	6	6	3	3	2	2
Dibble	1 2-3	0	0	0	0	2
Myers	1 1-3	1	0	0	0	1
Oakland						
Moore L, 0-1	2 2-3	8	6	2	0	1
Sanderson	2-3	3	2	2	1	0
Klink	0	0	0	0	1	0
Nelson	3 2-3	1	0	0	1	0
Burns	1	1	0	0	1	0
Young	1	1	0	0	0	0

Klink pitched to 1 batter in the 4th. Browning pitched to 1 batter in the 7th. WP—Sanderson, Burns. Time of Game—3:01. Attendance—48,269.

4th Game—Oakland, Oct. 20

CINCINNATI (N)	AB	R	H	RBI	OAKLAND (A)	AB	R	H	RBI
Larkin, ss	3	1	1	0	R. Henderson, lf	3	0	0	0
Hatcher, cf	0	0	0	0	McGee, rf	4	1	1	0
Winningham, cf	3	1	2	0	D. Henderson, cf	4	0	0	0
O'Neill, rf	3	0	0	0	Baines, dh	2	0	0	0
Davis, lf	0	0	0	0	Canseco, ph	1	0	0	0
Braggs, lf	3	0	0	1	Lansford, 3b	4	0	1	1
Morris, dh	3	0	0	1	Quirk, c	3	0	0	0
Sabo, 3b	4	0	3	0	McGuire, 1b	3	0	0	0
Benzinger, 1b	4	0	0	0	Randolph, 2b	3	0	0	0
Oliver, c	4	0	1	0	Gallego, ss	1	0	0	0
Duncan, 2b	4	0	0	0	Hassey, ph	1	0	0	0
					Bordick, ss	0	0	0	0
Totals	**31**	**2**	**7**	**2**	**Totals**	**29**	**1**	**2**	**1**

Cincinnati 000 000 020 — 2
Oakland 100 000 000 — 1

E—Oliver, Stewart. DP—Oakland 1. LOB—Cincinnati 7, Oakland 4. 2B—McGee, Oliver, Sabo. SM—Gallego (1), R. Henderson (3). S—O'Neill. SF—Morris.

	IP	H	R	ER	BB	SO
Cincinnati						
Rijo W, 2-0	8 1-3	2	1	1	3	9
Myers S, 1	2-3	0	0	0	0	0
Oakland						
Stewart, L 0-2	9	7	2	1	2	2

HBP—Hatcher by Stewart. Time of Game—2:48. Attendance—48,613.

NOLAN RYAN BREAKS 5,000 STRIKEOUT MARK

Strikeout No. 5,000, as so many of the other 4,999 had before, came on a blazing fastball past Oakland Athletics outfielder Rickey Henderson on Tuesday night, Aug. 22, 1989, in Arlington, Texas.

Ryan, who had broken the 4,000 strikeout barrier for the first time in baseball history in 1985 (Danny Heep of the New York Mets was the victim then), was pitching for the Texas Rangers—his first year with that team.

Ryan first came into the Major Leagues with the New York Mets in 1966. He subsequently pitched for the California Angels and Houston Astros before signing with the Rangers as a free agent before the start of the 1989 season.

Ryan, who turns 43 in January 1990, announced in October that he would return for his 23rd year next season. In 1989 he went 16-10 with a league-leading 301 strikeouts. The previous season he had led the National League in strikeouts with 228.

Ryan also holds the record for most strikeouts in a season at 383, and has hurled five no-hitters. Five times during the 1989 season he took no-hitters into the seventh inning.

HENDERSON OF ATHLETICS SETS SINGLE-SEASON STOLEN BASE MARK

Rickey Henderson of the Oakland A's broke the major league record for stolen bases in one season on Aug. 27, 1982, at Milwaukee when he stole his 119th base in the third inning. The previous record of 118 was held by Lou Brock of St. Louis and was set in 1974. Henderson had broken the American League stolen-bases mark in 1980 when he surpassed Ty Cobb's record of 96, set in 1915. Henderson finished the 1980 season with 100 stolen bases. In 1982 he completed the season with 130. The major league record for career stolen bases in held by Brock with 938. Henderson was two short of that mark with 936 coming into the 1991 season.

VOLLEYBALL

1990 U.S. OPEN VOLLEYBALL CHAMPIONSHIPS

(May 16-20, Raleigh, N.C.)

Men's Open—Nike, Carson, Calif.
Women's Open—Plymouth Californians/I Dig, Hayward, Calif.
Men's Senior—Silverado, Burbank, Calif.
Women's Senior—Mavericks, Harbor City, Calif.
Men's Open Silver Division—Club Annapolis, Annapolis, Md.
Men's Open Bronze Division—Pasadena Volleyball Club, Pasadena, Texas
Women's Bronze Division—Sojourners, Birmingham, Ala.

Men's Masters Division—Rocky Mountain Masters, Denver, Colo.
Men's Silver Masters Division—NoDinks, Bellevue, Wash.
Men's Golden Masters Division—LNP, Fort Wayne, Ind.
Men's Open MVP—Bill Stetson
Women's Open MVP—Keba Phipps

NCAA CHAMPIONSHIPS

Men

Division I—University of Southern California

Women

Division I—California State University, Long Beach, Calif.
Division II—California State University, Bakersfield, Calif.
Division III—Washington University, St. Louis, Mo.

INDIVIDUAL WORLD SHOOTING RECORDS

(as ratified by the International Shooting Union—UIT)

MEN	SCORE	SHOOTER	PLACE	DATE
Free Rifle 50 m 3 × 40 shots	1283.4	Petr Kurka (Czech.)	Seoul, S Korea	Oct 1, 1987
Free Rifle 50 m 60 shots prone	704.9	Petr Kurka (Czech.)	Zürich, Switz.	Jun 2, 1987
	704.9	Goran Maksimovic (Yugo.)	Münich, W. Ger.	Oct 21, 1988
Air Rifle 10m 60 shots	699.2	Yuriy Fedkin (U.S.S.R.)	Zürich, Switz.	Jun 7, 1989
Free Pistol 50 m 60 shots	666	Igor Bassinskiy (U.S.S.R.)	Seoul, S. Korea	Sep 27, 1987
Rapid-Fire Pistol 25m 60 shots	698	Afanasiy Kuzmin (U.S.S.R.)	Seoul, S. Korea	Sep 23, 1988
Air Pistol 10m 60 shots	690.3	Sergey Pyzhyanov (U.S.S.R.)	Sarajevo, Yugo.	Apr 30, 1989
Running Game Target 50 m 30 + 30 shots	691	Sergey Luzov (U.S.S.R.)	Suhl, E. Ger.	Sep 7, 1986
	691	Nikolay Lapin (U.S.S.R.)	Lahti, Finland	Jul 25, 1987
WOMEN				
Standard Rifle 50m 3 × 20 shots	691.6	Vessela Letcheva (Bulg.)	Münich, W. Ger.	May 22, 1987
Air Rifle 10m 40 shots	504	Vessela Letcheva (Bulg.)	Suhl, E. Ger.	May 30, 1987
Sport Pistol 25m 60 shots	695	Nino Salukvadze (U.S.S.R.)	Seoul, S. Korea	Sep 28, 1987
Air Pistol 10m 40 shots	489.5	Jasna Sekaric (Yugo.)	Seoul, S. Korea	Sep 21, 1988
OPEN				
Trap 200 targets	224	Miroslav Bednarik (Czech.)	Suhl, E. Ger.	Sep 14, 1986
Skeet 200 targets	224	Matthew Dryke (U.S.)	Suhl, E. Ger.	Sep 8, 1986
	224	Luca Scribani (Italy)	Bologna, Italy	Jun 11, 1988
	224	Ribor Ole Rasmussen (Denmark)	Bologna, Italy	Jun 11, 1988

N.C.A.A. MEN'S GYMNASTICS CHAMPIONSHIPS—1990

(April 19-21, 1990, Minneapolis, Minn.)

	Pts
All-around—1. Mike Racanelli, Ohio State	114.750
2. John Roethlisberger, Minnesota	114.100
Pommel horse—1. Mark Sohn, Penn State	9.900
2. Christian Rohde, Arizona State	9.850
Still rings—1. Wayne Cowden, Penn State	9.900
2. Chainey Umphrey, UCLA	9.850
Vault—1. Brad Hayashi, UCLA	9.5125
2. Jim Endres, Oklahoma	9.4500
Parallel bars—1. Patrick Kirkey, Nebraska	9.725
2. Mark Warburton, Nebraska	9.675
Horizontal bar—1. Chris Waller, UCLA	9.975
2. Trent Dimas, Nebraska	9.900
Team standings: 1. Nebraska	287.400
2. Minnesota	287.300
3. UCLA	283.850

N.C.A.A. WOMEN'S GYMNASTICS CHAMPIONSHIPS—1990

(April 20-21, 1990, Corvallis, Oregon)

	Pts
All around—1. Dee Dee Foster, Alabama	39.300
2. Shelly Schaerrer, Utah	39.225
Vault—1. Michele Bryant, Nebraska	9.8500
2. Kristi Pinnick, Utah	9.8375

	Pts
Uneven bars—1. Marie Roethlisberger, Minnesota	9.875
2. (tie) Dee Dee Foster, Alabama; Shelly Schaerrer, Utah	9.850
Balance beam—1. Joy Selig, Oregon State	9.875
2. (tie) Dee Dee Foster, Alabama; Carol Ulrich, UCLA	9.825
Floor exercise—1. Joy Selig, Oregon State	9.900
2. (tie) Missy Marlowe, Utah; Shelly Schaerrer, Utah	9.850

History of the One-Mile Speed Mark

The first recorded effort for one mile was made in 1898 by Chasseloup-Laubat, driving a Jentaud, in France. His average speed was 39.23 m.p.h. This was increased to 65.79 in 1899 by Jenatzy, also in France. The first man to travel better than 100 m. p.h. was Bigolly, in 1904, at 103.56 m.p.h., followed by Baras, with 104.53 in the same year.

The first over 200 m.p.h. was Major H.O.D. Segrave, who drove at 203.790 in 1927 at Daytona, Florida.

In 1947, John Cobb of London became the first person to travel more than 400 m.p.h. on land. The Englishman accomplished the feat on Sept. 16 at Bonneville, Utah, while raising the world mile record to 394.196 m.p.h. and the world kilometer (. 62137 of a mile) mark to 398.825 m.p.h.

CHESS

WORLD CHAMPIONS

1894–1921	Emanuel Lasker, Germany
1921–27	Jose R. Capablanca, Cuba
1927–35	Alexander A. Alekhine, U.S.S.R.
1935–37	Dr. Max Euwe, Netherlands
1937–46	Alexander A. Alekhine, U.S.S.R.[1]
1948–57	Mikhail Botvinnik, U.S.S.R.
1957–58	Vassily Smyslov, U.S.S.R.
1958–60	Mikhail Botvinnik, U.S.S.R.
1960–61	Mikhail Tal, U.S.S.R.
1961–63	Mikhail Botvinnik, U.S.S.R.
1963–68	Tigran Petrosian, U.S.S.R.
1969–71	Boris Spassky, U.S.S.R.
1972–74	Bobby Fischer, Los Angeles
1975	Bobby Fischer[2], Anatoly Karpov, U.S.S.R.
1976–85	Anatoly Karpov, U.S.S.R.[3]
1985–90[4]	Gary Kasparov, U.S.S.R.

1. Alekhine, a French citizen, died while champion. 2. Relinquished title. 3. In 1978, Karpov defeated Viktor Korchnoi 6 games to 5. 4. Next World Championship scheduled for October, 1990, after *Information Please Almanac* went to press.

UNITED STATES CHAMPIONS

1909–36	Frank J. Marshall, New York
1936–44	Samuel Reshevsky, New York[1]
1944–46	Arnold S. Denker, New York
1946	Samuel Reshevsky, Boston
1948	Herman Steiner, Los Angeles
1951–52	Larry Evans, New York
1954–57	Arthur Bisguier, New York

1958–61	Bobby Fischer, Brooklyn, N.Y.
1962	Larry Evans, New York
1963–67	Bobby Fischer, New York
1968	Larry Evans, New York
1969–71	Samuel Reshevsky, Spring Valley, N.Y.
1972	Robert Byrne, Ossining, N.Y.
1973	Lubomir Kavelek, Washington; John Grefe, San Francisco
1974–77	Walter Browne, Berkeley, Calif.
1978–79	Lubomir Kavalek, New York
1980	Tie, Walter Browne, Berkeley, Calif. Larry Christiansen, Modesto, Calif. Larry Evans, Reno, Nev.
1981–82[2]	Tie, Walter Browne, Berkeley, Calif. Yasser Seirawan, Seattle, Wash.
1983	Tie, Walter Browne, Berkeley, Calif. Larry Christiansen, Los Angeles, Calif., Roman Dzindzichashvili, Corona, N.Y.
1984–85	Lev Alburt, New York City
1986	Yasser Seirawan, Seattle, Wash.
1987	Tie—Nick Defirmian, San Francisco, and Joel Benjamin, Brooklyn, N.Y.
1988	Michael Wilder, Princeton, N.J.
1989	Tie, Stuart Rachels, Birmingham, Ala. Yasser Seirawan, Seattle, Wash. Roman Dzindzichashvili, New York, N.Y.
1990	Lev Alburt, New York, N.Y.

1. In 1942, Isaac I. Kashdan of New York was co-champion for a while because of a tie with Reshevsky in that year's tournament. Reshevsky won the play-off. 2. Championship not contested in 1982.

GYMNASTICS

AMERICAN CUP CHAMPIONSHIPS—1990

(Fairfax, Va., March 3-4, 1990)

Men's Events

	Pts
All-around—1. Alexander Kolivanov, Soviet Union	57.65
2. (tie) Lance Ringnald, United States Ralf Buechner, East Germany	57.60
Floor exercise—1. Alexander Kolivanov, Soviet Union	9.75
2. (tie)—Lance Ringnald, United States Ralf Buechner, East Germany	9.65
Pommel horse—1. Kevin Davis, United States	9.65
2. Ralf Buechner, East Germany	9.60
Still rings—1. Alfonso Rodriguez, Spain	9.80
2. (tie) Lance Ringnald, United States Li Ge, China	9.65
Vault—1. Alexander Kolivanov, Soviet Union	9.75
2. Yutaka Aihara, Japan	9.60
Parallel bars—1. Li Ge, China	9.80
2. (tie) Lance Ringnald, United States Alexander Kolivanov, Soviet Union	9.70

Women's Events

	Pts
All-Around—1. Kim Zmeskai, United States	39.599
2. Natalia Kalinina, Soviet Union	39.450
Vault—1. Kim Zmeskai, United States	9.937
2. Natalia Kalinina, Soviet Union	9.875
Uneven bars—1. (tie) Kim Zmeskai, United States Sandy Woolsey, United States	9.887
Balance beam—1. (tie) Kim Zmeskai, United States Natalia Kalinina, Soviet Union	9.825
Floor exercise—1. Kim Zmeskai, United States	9.950
2. Natalia Kalinina, Soviet Union	9.925

UNITED STATES GYMNASTICS CHAMPIONSHIPS

(June 7-11, 1990, Denver, Colo.)

Men

(Top 12 all-around finishers qualified for U.S. national team)

	Pts
1. John Roethlisberger, Afton, Minn.	114.30
2. Chris Waller, Mount Prospect, Ill.	113.90
3. Lance Ringnald, Albuquerque, N.M.	113.78
4. Trent Dimas, Albuquerque, N.M.	113.74
5. Scott Keswick, Las Vegas, Nev.	113.16
6. Mark Warburton, Dunbarton, N.H.	113.02
7. Bill Roth, Mohegan Lake, N.Y.	112.58
8. Chainey Umphrey, Albuquerque, N.M.	112.26
9. Tom Schlesinger, Boulder, Colo.	112.10
10. Patrick Kirksey, Tucker, Ga.	112.06
11. Mike Racanelli, W. Babylon, N.Y.	112.02

Women

(Top 15 all-around finishers qualified for U.S. national team)

	Pts
1. Kim Zmeskai, Houston, Texas	77.420
2. Elizabeth Okino, Elmhurst, Ill.	77.000
3. Brandy Johnson, Altamonte Springs, Fla.	76.970
4. Erica Stokes, Olathe, Kan.	76.500
5. Sandy Woolsey, Tempe, Ariz.	76.460
6. Kim Kelly, King of Prussia, Pa.	76.050
7. Agina Simpkins, Bolingbrook, Ill.	75.950
8. Shannon Miller, Edmond, Okla.	75.880
9. Amy Scherr, Cincinnati, Ohio	75.860
10. Christy Henrich, Independence, Mo.	75.780
11. Chelle Stack, Birmingham, Ala.	75.720

STANDARD MEASUREMENTS IN SPORTS

BASEBALL

Home plate to pitcher's box: 60 feet 6 inches.
Plate to second base: 127 feet 3 3/8 inches.
Distance from base to base (home plate included): 90 feet.
Size of bases: 15 inches by 15 inches.
Pitcher's plate: 24 inches by 6 inches.
Batter's box: 4 feet by 6 feet.
Home plate: Five-sided, 17 inches by 8 1/2 inches by 8 1/2 inches by 12 inches by 12 inches, cut to a point at rear.
Home plate to backstop: Not less than 60 feet (recommended).
Weight of ball: Not less than 5 ounces nor more than 5 1/4 ounces.
Circumference of ball: Not less than 9 inches nor more than 9 1/4 inches.
Bat: Must be one piece of solid wood, round, not over 2 3/4 inches in diameter at thickest part, nor more than 42 inches in length.

BASKETBALL

(National Collegiate A.A. Men's Rules)

Playing court: College: 94 feet long by 50 feet wide (ideal dimensions). High School: 84 feet long by 50 feet wide (ideal inside dimensions).
Baskets: Rings 18 inches in inside diameter, with white cord 12-mesh nets, 15 to 18 inches in length. Each ring is made of metal, is not more than 5/8 of an inch in diameter, and is bright orange in color.
Height of basket: 10 feet (upper edge).
Weight of ball: Not less than 20 ounces nor more than 22.
Circumference of ball: Not greater than 30 inches and not less than 29 1/2.
Free-throw line: 15 feet from the face of the backboard, 2 inches wide.
Three-point field goal line: 19 feet, 9 inches from the center of the basket. In the National Basketball Association, the distance is 23 feet.

BOWLING

Lane dimensions: Overall length 62 feet 10 3/16 inches, measuring from foul line to pit (not including tail plank), with + or − 1/2 inch tolerance permitted. Foul line to center of No. 1 pinspot 60 feet, with + or − 1/2 inch tolerance permitted. Lane width, 41 1/2 inches with a tolerance of + or − 1/2 inch permitted. Approach, not less than 15 feet. Gutters, 9 5/16 inches wide with plus 3/16 inch or minus 5/16 inch tolerances permitted.
Ball: Circumference, not more than 27.002 inches. Weight, 16 pounds maximum.

BOXING

Ring: Professional matches take place in an area not less than 18 nor more than 24 feet square including apron. It is enclosed by four covered ropes, each not less than one inch in diameter. The floor has a 2-inch padding of Ensolite (or equivalent) underneath ring cover that extends at least 6 inches beyond the roped area in the case of elevated rings. For USA/ABF or amateur boxing, not less than 16 nor more than 20 feet square within the ropes. The floor must extend beyond the ring ropes not less than 2 feet. The ring posts shall be connected to the four ring ropes with the extension not shorter than 18 inches and must be properly padded.
Gloves: In professional fights, not less than 8-ounce gloves generally are used. USA/ABF, 10 ounces for boxers 106 pounds through

156 pounds; 12-ounce for boxers 165 pounds through 201+ pounds; for international competition, 8 ounces for lighter classes, 10 ounces for heavier divisions.
Headguards: Mandatory in amateur boxing.

FOOTBALL

(N.C.A.A.)

Length of field: 120 yards (including 10 yards of end zone at each end).
Width of field: 53 1/3 yards (160 feet).
Height of goal posts: At least 30 feet.
Height of crossbar: 10 feet.
Width of goal posts (above crossbar): 23 feet 4 inches, inside to inside, and not more than 24 feet, outside to outside.
Length of ball: 10 7/8 to 11 7/16 inches (long axis).
Circumference of ball: 20 3/4 to 21 1/4 inches (middle); 27 3/4 to 28 1/2 inches (long axis).

GOLF

Specifications of ball: Broadened to require that the ball be designed to perform as if it were spherically symmetrical. The weight of the ball shall not be greater than 1.620 ounces avoirdupois, and the size shall not be less than 1.680 inches in diameter.
Velocity of ball: Not greater than 250 feet per second when tested on U.S.G.A. apparatus, with 2 percent tolerance.
Hole: 4 1/4 inches in diameter and at least 4 inches deep.
Clubs: 14 is the maximum number permitted.
Overall distance standard: A brand of ball shall not exceed a distance of 280 yards plus 6% when tested on USGA apparatus under specified conditions, on an outdoor range at USGA Headquarters.

HOCKEY

Size of rink: 200 feet long by 85 feet wide surrounded by a wooden wall not less than 40 inches and not more than 48 inches above level of ice.
Size of goal: 6 feet wide by 4 feet in height.
Puck: 1 inch thick and 3 inches in diameter, made of vulcanized rubber; weight 5 1/2 to 6 ounces.
Length of stick: Not more than 60 inches from heel to end of shaft nor more than 12 1/2 inches from heel to end of blade. Blade should not be more than 3 inches in width but not less than 2 inches—except goal keeper's stick, which shall not exceed 3 1/2 inches in width except at the heel, where it must not exceed 4 1/2 inches, nor shall the goalkeeper's stick exceed 15 1/2 inches from the heel to the end of the blade.

TENNIS

Size of court: 120 feet long by 60 feet wide, with rectangle marked off at 78 feet long by 27 feet wide (singles) and 78 feet long by 36 feet wide (doubles).
Height of net: 3 feet in center, gradually rising to reach 3-foot 6-inch posts at a point 3 feet outside each side of court.
Ball: Shall be more than 2 1/2 inches and less than 2 5/8 inches in diameter and weigh more than 2 ounces and less than 2 1/16 ounces.
Service line: 21 feet from net.

BOXING—AMATEUR

NATIONAL GOLDEN GLOVES CHAMPIONSHIPS—1990

(May 7-12, 1990, Miami, Fla.)

106 lb—Russell Roberts, Louisiana
112 lb—Timmy Austin, Cincinnati
119 lb—Sandtanner Lewis, Miami
125 lb—Frank Sepulveda, Jr., Nevada

132 lb—Lamar Murphy, Miami
139 lb—Mark Lewis, Los Angeles
147 lb—Jesse Briseno, Michigan
156 lb—Ravea Springs, Cincinnati
165 lb—Frank Vassar, Nevada
178 lb—Jeremy Williams, Iowa
Heavyweight—Gregory Suttington, Kansas City
Super Heavyweight—Larry Donald, Cincinnati
Team title: Nevada defeated Cincinnati, 37-31 for championship

The Changing Face of Europe

By Arthur P. Reed, Jr.

Day by day, almost hour by hour, the face of Eastern and Central Europe changed during 1989 and through 1990 to a point unrecognizable earlier. By New Year's 1991 the Cold War was a memory, declared so officially in mid-1990 by President Bush and his fellow NATO leaders.

Nation after nation of the old Soviet bloc and other Communist states strove to turn their centralized economies around, throwing overboard the old lumbering mechanisms, and to adopt the free elections and other once-despised practices of capitalist democracy that had made the West such a model of material achievement.

The unification of the Germanys hurtled to its climax as 1990 drew on, perhaps the most stunning event of the European transformation. But affairs in the Soviet Union were likewise in the foreground as Mikhail Gorbachev strove to control the forces he had unleashed after becoming Soviet leader in 1985.

Germany. For the Germanys, the last step toward reunification was finally set for October 3, 1990, after extensive parliamentary maneuvering. All-national elections were scheduled for December 2—the first free balloting since Adolf Hitler was named chancellor in 1933. Meanwhile, negotiators sought to frame a second treaty reconciling the legal and political systems of the two states.

But de facto unification had come on July 2 with the economic merger. The West German mark became common currency and the official reunion ended the East's faltering 40-year effort to build a Communist state.

As a tangible symbol of approaching unity, leaders of both nations opened the Brandenburg Gate in the Berlin Wall December 22, 1989, with thousands celebrating the new pedestrian crossings. The Wall itself had been opened six weeks earlier, and crowds of East Germans had crossed to sample the bounty of the West.

The final barrier to unity toppled on July 16 when the Soviet Union and West Germany agreed that all the re-unified nation join the North Atlantic Treaty Organization.

One other thorny issue was resolved on July 17 when the East and West Germans promised to guarantee the postwar Polish border.

Months of unrest in East Germany had preceded the fall of the Communist regime in late 1989. Then the Communist leadership toppled in succession like pins in a bowling alley. In November, Erich Honecker was ousted as party leader after revelations of abuses. On December 5 Honecker and other former top officials were placed under house arrest as public fury mounted at revelations of corruption, abuses, and repression under the old regime.

Soviet Union. In the Soviet Union, the collapse of orthodox Communism continued at the pace that Gorbachev had set upon taking office in 1985, when he urged improvements in the economy.

With the coming of 1990 new problems confronted the innovative leader, caught up in tension between diehard conservatives and forces inspired by glasnost (openness), impatient with what they viewed as the slow pace of perestroika (restructuring).

The southern Republic of Azerbaijan erupted on January 14 in ethnic violence between the Azerbaijanis and Armenians. Some 11,000 Soviet troops and police consolidated control of the province, but seething unrest persisted with a heavy death toll.

Even more serious was the drive for independence by several important constituent republics of the Soviet Union, notably the Baltic states forcibly ceded to the Soviet Union in accords with Nazi Germany in 1940.

The tide of nationalism began rolling early in 1990. On March 11, Lithuania declared herself a sovereign state and named leaders of a non-Communist government to negotiate relations with Moscow. Finally, in an ultimatum on April 13, Gorbachev threatened to start cutting off Lithuania's supplies unless she recanted the declaration of independence. And on April 18 Soviet authorities completely severed the supply of crude oil. The next day the Kremlin cut off natural gas. Her supplies exhausted, Lithuania's only oil refinery shut down on April 23.

But on June 29 Lithuania agreed to suspend the independence declaration in exchange for negotiations and the lifting of the Soviet economic sanctions. The next day Moscow reopened the oil pipeline as the first concession.

On April 4, Gorbachev warned the Estonian President against following Lithuania's course, but on April 11 the Estonian Parliament voted to end all military service, a contentious issue.

Defying Gorbachev's warning, the Latvian parliament on May 4 declared a transition period leading to independence.

On May 14, President Gorbachev rejected the independence moves by the two republics, but left the door open for dialogue. However, the next day, crowds of anti-independence protesters stormed the parliamentary buildings in Latvia and Estonia.

In mid-July, the rich and important Ukraine, the second largest Soviet republic, declared its sovereignty and demanded a larger share of self-determination and natural resources, without, however, claiming full independence.

At the Kremlin the withering away of the Communist Party's once all-powerful status continued through the spring and later in 1990. On Feb. 7, the Party's Central Committee agreed to surrender the party's historic monopoly of power. Then, the 2,250-member Congress of Peoples Deputies approved broad new powers for Gorbachev through a popularly elected presidency (but without requiring him to face the voters himself). Gorbachev assumed the new post on March 15, and vowed to move the country more rapidly toward a market economy.

At the party's 28th Congress, Gorbachev was re-elected as the party's leader after routing hardliners with a spirited defense of his policies. He kept top posts in the separated party and government.

Romania. Romania, among the Communist nations of East Europe, saw perhaps the most dramatic, decisive, and violent overthrow of its dictator with the execution on Christmas Day 1989 of Nicolae Ceausescu and his wife, Elena, by his own army.

Popular unrest had erupted in Timisoara, in the west, in mid-December when demonstrators protected a clergyman who had promoted the rights of ethnic Hungarians. Security forces fired on thousands as the protest escalated with demands for freedom and a better life. On Dec. 21, security forces fired on demonstrators in Bucharest and the dictator was shouted down in attempting to address them.

On Dec. 22, the Army joined the protest movement. The Council of National Salvation announced that it had overthrown the Government.

As fierce fighting raged in the capital and other cities, Government forces captured the Ceausescus and executed them after secret trial by a military tribunal.

Ion Iliescu, 59, a former Communist official, became president. The Securitate, Ceausescu's feared internal police, was disbanded. The Council of National Salvation joined other political parties in a coalition. In May the former Communists of the renamed National Salvation Front won a smashing victory in Romania's first free election in half a century. By contrast, other Eastern European nations had generally ousted former Communists.

Poland. Poland, first of the former Soviet satellites to start on the road to democracy, coped with economic problems as 1990 wore on. The Solidarity movement, spark plug of reform, had shared power since August 1989 with the Communists, who had been crushed in the June elections. In September, Prime Minister Tadeusz Mazowiecki formed the first Eastern-bloc government not ruled by Communists.

By the end of the year, Mazowiecki and the Council of Ministers agreed to drastic economic changes in return for $4 billion in Western aid from the International Monetary Fund, to deal with a 900 percent inflation rate and reduce budget deficits while tolerating unemployment and poverty during a transition period.

In July, the Prime Minister dismissed the most prominent remaining Communists from his Cabinet, promising completely free elections for Parliament and the presidency. He also warned against civil disobedience actions threatening the Government's economic reform program.

Hungary. The Hungarian Communist Party—renamed Socialist—has suffered setbacks in a nation that already in 1989 had moved toward economic reforms and free elections. It thus attracted foreign aid.

In their first free election in 45 years, in March 1990, the voters split between the newly formed parties of the anti-Communist opposition, with the former Communists and other leftist parties behind. In this first-round parliamentary balloting, the Democratic Forum was the leader, followed by the Alliance of Free Democrats, which advocated a more rapid move from the post-World War II Communist rule.

In the April runoff, the Democratic Forum took a decisive lead. Its leader, Jozsef Antall, 58, became Prime Minister of a coalition that included two smaller parties. The first post-Communist Parliament in August chose as President of the nation Arpad Goncz, 68, a writer who had been imprisoned for political activity. All six parties, including the Socialists, supported him as sole candidate. He is a member of the Alliance of Free Democrats.

Czechoslovakia. Czechoslovakia was caught up in East Europe's storm in November 1989. On November 17, the police crushed an antigovernment rally by tens of thousands in Prague. As protesters denounced police brutality, opposition forces, with some Communist allies, marched into the new Civic Forum and demanded the resignation of the Communist leaders who had fostered the 1968 Soviet invasion. On Nov. 24, the Communist leadership, headed by Milos Jakes, resigned.

After some backing and filling, President Gustav Husak, Communist hardliner, also resigned. Alexander Dubceck, the party leader "disgraced" in the 1968 "Prague Spring," who had returned triumphantly to the capital, was elected chairman of Parliament on Dec. 28. The next day Parliament elected Vaclav Havel, the playwright and opposition leader, as the nation's President.

In June, Civic Forum and its sister party, Slovak Public Against Violence, won national and regional elections, taking 170 seats in the 300-seat Assembly. The discredited Communists won a surprising second place 13.6 percent of the vote, with 47 seats, smaller parties the rest.

Bulgaria. In Bulgaria, the Communist Party also surrendered its dominance in a constitutional change January 15, 1990, by the Sofia Parliament. The next month the Communist Government resigned after a stormy emergency meeting of the party that saw a heated power struggle over how far the party should go in revising its structure and policies. As a result the party named Andrei Lukanov, an advocate of change, as Prime Minister.

In June 1990 the Socialists, formerly the Communists, took an early lead in balloting for Parliament in the first free multiparty elections in 45 years. Early in July President Peter Mladenov resigned after accusations that he had ordered tanks to disperse antigovernment protests in the previous December. Thousands of Bulgarians cheered.

On August 1, the Parliament elected Zhelyu Zhelev, 59, who pledged economic reforms, as President. He is head of the Union of Democratic Forces, a coalition of 15 opposition parties.

Albania. Even Albania, isolated and doctrinaire, was buffeted by the winds of change. Early in 1990, the authorities imposed severe restrictions on the populace. Gunfire was reported as were emergency measures to contain unrest. But with spring, Albania began what its orthodox Communist leaders called "democratization" of social and economic institutions. In May, Albania announced far-reaching liberal policies, including freedom to travel abroad and restoration of the right to practice religion. The Communists, however—who had broken with the Soviet Union over opposition to Soviet liberal trends—indicated that the moves from orthodox Stalinism would be gradual. Popular unrest mounted as the year drew on.

Yugoslavia. Yugoslavia has since 1948 also not been part of the Soviet bloc, despite its official name of Socialist Federal Republic. Under Marshal Tito it followed a middle road of Communist economic control with some freedom in arts, travel, and individual enterprise. Early in 1990, the Yugoslav Communist Party voted to end its 45-year monopoly of power and allow other parties to compete in a new political system. □

Crisis in the Persian Gulf

By Arthur P. Reed, Jr.

The crisis in the Persian Gulf burst upon the world with frightening suddenness in August 1990 when powerful Iraq invaded its tiny neighbor, Kuwait.

It was the first major global explosion following the end of the Cold War, and it united the two superpowers in the common cause against aggression after decades of baleful confrontation. Further, it enlisted many Arab nations in opposing one of their own who had violated what most of the world considered the code of civilized conduct.

The U.N. Security Council revived the principle of collective security by approving moves to turn back the invasion, to stop Iraq's oil exports, and to reduce its supplies of essential goods by a massive blockade.

The rapport between the United States and the Soviet Union was evident in the "mini-summit" at Helsinki, Finland, on Sunday, September 9, between President Bush and Soviet President Gorbachev.

The two leaders pledged jointly to act "individually and in concert" to reverse Iraq's actions. They stated preference for a peaceful solution, but expressed determination to consider additional steps "consistent with the U.N. Charter." Gorbachev later told a questioner, however, that he had not agreed that military force might be necessary.

Their joint communiqué did hint at differences on actual steps to thwart Iraq's Saddam Hussein. Those differences included whether Soviet forces should join the international build-up to protect Saudi Arabia and the Soviet proposal for a linking of the crisis to a settlement of the Israeli-Palestinian dispute.

In an address to Congress and the nation on the following Tuesday, Bush emphasized that the United States would use force if necessary against Saddam Hussein, and would not let his own decisions be affected by compassion for American and other hostages trapped in Iraq and Kuwait, many used as "human shields."

The Gulf crisis, however, portended earth-shaking changes in the international alignment and the economies of most nations. For Bush and Gorbachev it meant a strengthening of bonds forged at earlier conferences into a new partnership of the superpowers that might go far beyond Iraq, Kuwait, and the wide problems of the region.

At home Bush won early wide bipartisan and public support despite misgivings on the left and a strangely divided right. In five weeks the U.S. had moved a massive force of troops, tanks, and airpower to the Gulf and set up a blockade of Iraqi ports.

The sharp jump in oil prices resulting from the crisis was viewed by economists as a threat to the U.S. economy. The control of Mideast oil was, in fact, a consideration in the international actions. The economists pointed to the indirect costs to business and consumers that might far surpass the direct expense of the military build-up and the rising cost of energy.

The Third World also began to feel severe shocks as hundreds of thousands of workers from Asia and elsewhere, fleeing from Iraq and Kuwait, flooded the squalid and pitiful refugee camps in Jordan.

Even the neutral states of Europe, long skittish about collective security commitments, moved toward involvement by condemning Iraq and sending money to Jordan and Turkey to aid the refugees.

The Arab nations were deeply divided about the invasion. Many supported the Arab League decision to send troops to join the forces protecting Saudi Arabia; others tended to favor Hussein.

In sum, the situation as 1990 drew on depended on many factors—what Hussein might do, the effectiveness of the international sanctions, and the strength of the anti-Iraq coalition. In Washington many officials felt that a lasting peace settlement must go further than forcing Iraq to disgorge Kuwait. It was imperative, they said, that an international move be taken to stamp out Hussein's potential for nuclear and chemical weapons destruction.

In the cat-and-mouse (or two-cat) game that continued into autumn, daily developments flashed by like episodes in a movie thriller. On one day President Bush taped an address, broadcast on Iraqi television, in which he told the people of that nation that their leaders had brought them to "the brink of war" with the West and the Arab world.

As the noose of international sanctions tightened, Hussein stepped up his bellicose rhetoric, saying that if the nation were "strangled," it would launch attacks on oil fields in Saudi Arabia and other Arab countries, and on Israel. Observers took this to be a threat of a pre-emptive strike.

But in Washington, internal tensions grew as the first shock of the crisis wore off. The Administration was accused by some in Congress of equivocation in its stance toward Iraq before the invasion. The U.S. Ambassador to Baghdad was reported to have assured the Iraqis that, while the U.S. was concerned about a build-up on the Kuwait border, it had no intention of intervening in what it viewed as an intra-Arab border dispute. The State Department and Secretary James A. Baker 3rd were particular targets of criticism in the Capitol.

The pre-invasion U.S. strategy had at least two rationales. One was the acceptance of a limited invasion of Kuwait, with concessions for Iraq from small conquests. Another was the desire for America to remain aloof in an effort to avoid inflaming the Arab world. But the consensus inside and out of the Administration was the Iraqis would not strike.

In a related Washington development, Defense Secretary Dick Cheney dismissed the Air Force Chief of Staff, Gen. Michael J. Dugan, for publicly revealing the Pentagon's contingency plans for a war with Iraq.

In the unfolding drama, the United Nations played a growing role following its original decision, moving toward including air traffic in an expanded embargo. And after the Iraqis had moved against French and other embassies in Kuwait, French President Francois Mitterand ordered thousands of troops and dozens of tanks and planes to join the growing U.N. force in the desert.

At home in the U.S., a patient populace welcomed returning refugees—mostly women and children, as able-bodied men were kept as human "shields" against attacks on Iraqi vital installations. And as reservists were called to duty and regulars sent overseas, the truncated families left behind tackled the problems of a new life. □

(Also *see* Current Events.)

What Happened in 1990

Highlights of the important events of the year from January to October 1990, organized month by month, in three categories for easy reference. The Countries of the World section (starting on page 152) covers specific international events, country by country.

JANUARY 1990

International

Romania Disbands Rebellious Police Force (Jan. 1): Abolishes Securitate, dreaded internal body. Former chief arrested when loyalty is questioned.

Two Nuns Slain in Nicaragua (Jan. 2): Gunmen ambush Roman Catholic workers' car in northeast. Third nun and American-born bishop are wounded. One slain nun also an American citizen.

Gen. Manuel Noriega Surrenders (Jan. 3): Fallen Panamanian leader taken by U.S. authorities as he leaves refuge in Vatican Embassy and is flown to Miami. (Jan. 4): Noriega arraigned in Federal Court in Miami on drug-trafficking charges. Refuses to enter plea.

Martial Law Lifted in Beijing (Jan. 10): U.S. announces easing of opposition to World Bank loans to China.

Gorbachev Visits Defiant Lithuania (Jan. 11-13): Bids republic stay in Soviet Union. Tells Communists he sees no "tragedy" in multi-party system.

U.S. Spy Captured by Moscow (Jan. 14): Soviet dooms "Donald F.," senior diplomat who passed defense secrets to American intelligence for almost 30 years. (Jan. 22): Spy identified as a senior Soviet officer, Lieut. Gen. Dmitri Fedorovich Polyakov.

Soviet Azerbaijan Erupts in Violence (Jan. 14): Mobs rampage and commit atrocities on Armenians. Many killed. (Jan. 15): Gorbachev issues emergency decree and orders troops and police to help contain hostilities between Azerbaijanis and Armenians. (Jan. 16): Soviet airlifts force of 11,000 to embattled regions. (Jan. 20): Troops claim control of Baku, capital. (Jan. 22): Azerbaijan Parliament demands removal of Soviet troops. (Jan. 23): Clashes go on as civil resistance mounts. Death toll at least 100. (Jan. 24): Troops arrest dozens of rebels, and break harbor blockade. About 12,000 members of families of Soviet forces evacuated for protection against anti-Russian attacks.

Bulgarian Communists Lose Leading Role (Jan. 15): Nation last of Soviet's East European allies in a halting transition to multiparty democracy.

Yugoslav Communists Halt Monopoly (Jan. 22): Vote to end 45 years of sole power and permit multiparty system.

Polish Communists Dissolve Party (Jan. 29): Members vote to form democratic, left-of-center grouping.

National

High Court Upsets Smoking Death Award (Jan. 5): Supreme bench overturns $400,000 verdict and orders new trial of family's suit in case of New Jersey woman who died of cancer. Broader claims reinstated.

Universities Lose Tenure Case (Jan. 9): Supreme Court rules unanimously against claim of academic freedom and orders disclosure of personnel files when discrimination is charged.

Justices Reaffirm Protection of Suspects (Jan. 10): Supreme Court, 5-4, upholds longstanding rule on exclusion from criminal trial of illegally obtained evidence.

Richard V. Secord Convicted (Jan. 24): Retired Air Force major general sentenced by U.S. judge to two years' probation for false statements to Congressional inquiry about role in Iran-Contra affair.

President's Veto of China Bill Upheld (Jan. 24): House, 390-25, hands Bush major setback by overwhelmingly reaffirming legislation protecting students in U.S. from deportation. (Jan. 25): Senate, 62-37, short of two-thirds majority, sustains veto after intense lobbying by President and top Administration officials.

President Submits Budget for 1991 (Jan. 29): Proposes revised plan for cutting capital gains taxes and more than two-dozen tax changes. Also seeks funds to expand child care, fight drugs, improve education, and plant trees.

Bush's State of the Union Address (Jan. 31): President calls for sharp reductions in Soviet and United States troops in Europe. Views collapse of Soviet empire as start of "new era in world's affairs." Adds education goals to domestic programs set forth in Budget Message.

General

Pittson Coal Strike Ended (Jan. 1): Company and union leaders resolve bitter nine-month tie-up in Appalachia. All 1,700 strikers and 4,000 sick and laid-off workers to vote on terms.

Shuttle Rescues Science Satellite (Jan. 9): Five astronauts aboard *Columbia* rocket into orbit at Cape Canaveral, Fla. Members of crew: Navy Capt. Daniel C. Brandenstein, 46, Vietnam war veteran, mission commander; Navy Lieut. Comdr. James D. Wetherbee, 36, pilot; and mission specialists: Dr. Bonnie J. Dunbar, 40, biomedical engineer, G. David Low, 33, engineer, and Marsha S. Ivins, 30, NASA engineer. (Jan. 12): Astronauts snare 11-ton science satellite, Long Duration Exposure Facility, in space nearly six years with test materials. (Jan. 20): *Columbia* lands safely at Edwards Air Force Base, Calif. Rescue mission called one of most successful.

A.T.& T. Service Disrupted (Jan. 15): Computer failure interrupts long-distance service for millions served by major national networks.

Department Store Chain in Bankruptcy (Jan. 15): U.S. retailing operations of Campeau Corporation of Canada file for court protection. Action will keep 258 department stores open across nation.

Washington Mayor Faces Drug Charge (Jan. 19): Marion S. Barry, Jr., 53, arraigned by U.S. after arrest on charge of using crack cocaine. His political career believed to be threatened.

Jetliner Crash Kills 72 (Jan. 25): Scores of 161 passengers injured as Avianca Airlines Boeing 707 from South America plunges to Long Island's North Shore in rain and fog. (Jan. 26): Federal investigators say plane may have run out of fuel.

FEBRUARY 1990

International

Romania's Ruling Body Shares Power (Feb. 1): Council of National Salvation bows to pressure from opposition forces and will join coalition.

Bulgarian Communist Government Resigns (Feb. 1): Party agrees to form cabinet on broad national basis. **(Feb. 3):** Communists, seeking popular support, name Andrei Lukanov, 50, economist, advocate of change, as Prime Minister. Orderly vote follows unrest.

Baltic Nations Aid Soviet Truce (Feb. 3): Separatist leaders of republics by-pass Kremlin and negotiate cease-fire in border violence between Azerbaijan and Armenia. Hostages to be exchanged.

Costa Rica Elects Peace Plan Critic (Feb. 4): Rafael Calderón, Jr., named to succeed President Oscar Arias Sánchez, whose proposals for Central America he had opposed. Arias party's candidate defeated.

Eight Israeli Tourists Killed in Egypt (Feb. 4): Seventeen wounded as armed assailants attack vehicle carrying academics and their wives on main highway east of Cairo. Palestinian extremists blamed.

Soviet Citizens Rally for Democracy (Feb. 4): More than 100,000 parade to Kremlin demanding that Communist Party surrender monopoly of power.

Nicaragua Vote Crushes Sandinistas (Feb. 5): Opposition candidate, Violeta Barrios de Chamorro, wins landslide victory over government of President Daniel Ortega Saavedra. **(Feb. 28):** Ortega declares cease-fire with U.S.-supported Contra rebels.

Soviet Communists Relinquish Power (Feb. 7): Leadership backs Gorbachev and agrees to creation of Western-style presidency and cabinet government. **(Feb. 8):** Leaders agree to endow Gorbachev with broad new Presidential powers, probably without election.

Hungary and Vatican Restore Ties (Feb. 9): Establish diplomatic relations after four-decade rupture.

South Africa Frees Nelson Mandela (Feb. 11): Black leader leaves prison after 27 1/2 years. Urges increased pressure against white minority government and urges other nations not to lift sanctions. Mandela sentenced to life imprisonment in 1964 for plotting to overthrow government and sabotage. **(Feb. 13):** Tens of thousands cheer Mandela as he returns to his home in Soweto.

Thousands Riot in Tadzhikistan (Feb. 12): Mob sets fire to cars, buses, and Communist headquarters in capital of Central Asian Soviet republic over rumors of favoritism to Armenian refugees in housing.

Four Powers Agree on German Unity (Feb. 13): World War II Allies frame outline for ending 45 years of division between East and West. Foreign ministers reach accord at three-day Ottawa conference.

Soviet Agrees to U.S. Troop Edge (Feb. 13): Abandons demand for equal levels in Europe and accepts Bush proposal that U.S. keep 30,000-man advantage.

Air Crash Kills 89 in India (Feb. 14): New Indian Airlines Airbus 320 hits reservoir at southern city of Bangalore. Fifty survivors taken to hospitals from fiery scene of crash.

Sweden's Government Resigns (Feb. 15): Prime Minister Ingvar Carlsson acts after his Social Democrats lose vote in Parliament on bill to resuscitate the economy. **(Feb. 26):** Parliament confirms Carlsson as Prime Minister after he revises proposals.

Regional Drug Cooperation Pledged (Feb. 15): Bush and three Andean leaders end Colombia conference without resolving major issues.

Japanese Voters Retain Ruling Party (Feb. 18): Return Liberal Democratic Party, in office 35 years, to power in elections to lower house of Parliament.

Moscow Bars Jewish Flights to Israel (Feb. 19): Soviet rejects Bush plea and bows to pressure by Arabs.

U.S. Welcomes Czech Leader (Feb. 20): Bush promises Vaclav Havel new trade benefits. **(Feb. 21):** Czech President addresses Congress, saying best way to help Eastern nations is to aid Soviet road to democracy.

Bush and German Chancellor Confer (Feb. 25): After two days of talks at Camp David, President and Kohl discount fears for economic, political, or military power of a reunited Germany.

Thousands Stage Protests in Soviet Union (Feb. 25): Throng streets in defiant call for share of power. Republic of Lithuania votes to end Communist rule.

Gorbachev Wins Bill on Presidency (Feb. 27): In angry session, Supreme Soviet gives initial approval to Gorbachev proposal to gain greater executive powers.

National

Iran-Contra Figure Fined $5,000 (Feb. 1): Albert A. Hakim, financial adviser on arms sales and other secret missions, placed on two years' probation by Federal Court. But he shares $1.7 million in proceeds from operations frozen in Swiss banks.

Bush Voids Sale of Company to China (Feb. 2): Cites national security law in nullifying transfer of Seattle company that manufactures airplane parts to military-related agency of Beijing Government.

Reagan Declines to Yield Diaries (Feb. 5): Refuses to turn over excerpts to John M. Poindexter for latter's use in Iran-Contra trial.

Accused U.S. Diplomat Dismissed (Feb. 7): State Department ousts Felix S. Bloch, under investigation of allegations of associating with Soviet spy.

Food Regulations Approved (Feb. 8): White House moves to halt proliferation of disease-prevention claims appearing on many food packages.

Justices Rule on Child-Abuse Cases (Feb. 20): Supreme Court, 7-2, upholds court orders for parents under supervision for previous child abuse to produce a child or disclose whereabouts.

Military Ban on Homosexuals Stands (Feb. 26): Supreme Court refuses to review longstanding policy.

High Court Backs Searches Abroad (Feb. 28): Justices, 5-4, rule Constitution does not bar U.S. agents without warrants from searches and seizures of property owned by foreigners in foreign countries.

General

Andy Rooney Suspended (Feb. 8): CBS News puts "60 Minutes" commentator on three-months' leave after complaints he had offended blacks and homosexuals.

"Junk Bond" Era Seems at End (Feb. 13): Drexel Burnham Lambert Inc. starts liquidation in rapid disintegration. Parent concern decides to file in bankruptcy.

Washington Mayor Indicted on Drug Counts (Feb. 15): U.S. grand jury accuses Marion S. Barry, Jr., 53, of possessing cocaine and lying about involvement with drugs.

Two-Month Coal Strike Ends (Feb. 20): United Mine Workers Union announces approval of agreement to end tie-up against the Pittston Coal Group.

Exxon Indicted in Alaska Oil Spill (Feb. 27): U.S. jury in Anchorage accuses corporation and shipping subsidiary on five criminal counts.

MARCH 1990

International

Mandela Heads African Congress (March 2): Elected deputy president to end leadership crisis resulting from illness of Oliver N. Tambo, 72, its president.

Military Rule Ends in Chile (March 11): Patricio Aylwin, Christian Democrat, installed as president to succeed controversial Gen. Augusto Pinochet.

Lithuania Proclaims Sovereignty (March 11): Parliament votes, 124-0, to be legally free of Soviet Union. Leaders of non-Communist Government named to negotiate future relations with Moscow.

Military Rule Ends in Haiti (March 12): Woman judge, Ertha Pascal-Trouillot, named provisional president after Lieut. Gen. Prosper Avril leaves on United States Air Force jet.

Israeli Coalition Collapses (March 13): Government breaks up over disagreement between Labor and Likud Party over whether to accept American plan for beginning Israeli-Palestinian peace talks. **(March 15):** Government dissolved over refusal of Prime Minister Yitzhak Shamir to accept terms suggested by U.S. for starting the peace negotiations.

Chemical Plant in Libya Burns (March 14): Fire reported in factory at Rabta, thought by United States to be producing poison gas. **(March 15):** U.S. officials say fire knocked plant out of operation indefinitely.

Iraq Hangs British Journalist (March 15): Defies calls for clemency to spare Iranian-born Farzad Bazoft, 31, who had been convicted of espionage.

Conservatives Win in East Germany (March 18): Coalition led by Christian Democrats scores surprising victory in first free election since 1933.

Soviet Communists Lose in Major Cities (March 19): Political opposition wins majorities in city councils of Moscow, Leningrad, and Kiev, and elects significant numbers of insurgents in republic parliaments.

Namibia Gains Independence (March 21): Ends 75 years under control by South Africa.

Albania Starts Program of Reforms (March 21): Hardline Communist nation opens "democratization" of social and economic institutions, joining East Europe's move to change policies.

Hungarian Voters Spurn Leftists (March 25): Split support between two anti-Communist parties in first free election for government in 45 years.

U.S. Missionary Slain in Lebanon (March 27): William Robinson shot at home in Israeli-designated "security Zone." Guerrillas say killing was to deter "establishment of Zionist settlements."

Six Held in Nuclear Smuggling (March 28): Arrested in London in what U.S. and British officials call scheme to send to Iraq electronic devices used to detonate nuclear weapons.

Soviet Stages Raids in Lithuania (March 30): Troops seize State Prosecutor's office and independent printing plant in actions against declaration of independence. President Bush appeals to Gorbachev for peaceful settlement of dispute.

Gorbachev Offers Talks to Lithuanians (March 31): Will open discussions if leaders agree to repeal declaration of independence. Warns against rejection.

London Rioters Protest New Head Tax (March 31): Scores injured in London as tens of thousands demonstrate against levy to replace real estate rates. Hundreds arrested.

National

Seabrook Nuclear Reactor Approved (March 1): Nuclear Regulatory Commission grants operating license to controversial project in New Hampshire.

Space Shuttle Lands After Secret Mission (March 4): *Atlantis* touches ground at Edwards Air Force Base, Calif., after four-and-a-half-day orbiting. Reported to have launched spy satellite over Soviet Union. Members of crew: Navy Capt. John O. Creighton, mission commander; Air Force Col. John H. Casper, pilot; mission specialists, Marine Lieut. Col. David C. Hilmers, Air Force Col. Richard M. Mullane, and Navy Lieut. Comdr. Pierre J. Thuot.

General

Earthquake Rocks Southern California (March 1): Damage assessed day after moderately strong temblor shakes buildings from Santa Barbara to Mexican border.

$50 Million for Negro College Fund (March 4): Walter H. Annenberg announces contribution to consortium.

Basketball Star Collapses and Dies (March 4): Hank Gathers, 23, victim of heart rhythm disturbance, suffers cardiac arrest as his Loyola Marymount team plays in championship game of West Coast Conference.

Gene Therapy Helps Children (March 7): National Institutes of Health panel approves treatment for victims suffering genetic disorder of immune system.

Record $3.6-Billion TV Deal (March 9): National Football League concludes four-year package for professional football coverage with $752-million agreement by NBC, last of a series.

Thieves Steal Boston Art Masterpieces (March 18): Loot Isabella Stewart Gardner Museum of 11 paintings, including works by Vermeer, Rembrandt, Degas, and Manet, and other priceless objects.

Baseball 32-Day Lockout Ends (March 19): Owners and players agree on four-year contract. Among provisions are salary arbitration and minimum major league salary increases from $68,000 to $100,000. Players union wins protection against collusion by owners against signing of free-agent players.

Long-Lost Tiny Primate Discovered (March 20): West German scientist photographs hairy-eared dwarf lemur in Madagascar, never before seen alive by scientists.

Bamboos Made to Flower in Laboratory (March 21): Scientists report advance for cultivation of one of world's most important food and timber crops.

New Use for Aspirin in Strokes (March 21): Daily doses found to reduce dramatically risk from heartbeat irregularity afflicting thousands.

Getty Museum Buys Van Gogh's "Irises" (March 21): West Coast institution acquires work from Australian industrialist for undisclosed sum.

Valdez Captain Convicted on Minor Charge (March 22): Joseph J. Hazelwood, 43, cleared of most serious counts in Alaskan oil spill, worst in U.S. history. **(March 23):** Captain sentenced to 1,000 hours of community service cleaning beaches and must pay Alaska $50,000.

Drug Found Useful in Spinal Injury (March 30): Federal researchers say steroid hormone can reduce paralysis and other disability in victims of serious injury.

Anti-Abortion Bill Blocked in Idaho (March 30): Gov. Cecil D. Andrus vetoes measure to outlaw about 95 percent of operations in state, with most restrictions of any state in the nation.

APRIL 1990

International

Japan to Lower Trade Barriers (April 5): Pledges to reduce obstacles confronting foreigners seeking to invest and do business in Japan.

Police and Army Fire on Nepal Demonstrators (April 6): At least nine of 200,000 marchers are killed and several hundred are wounded in Katmandu.

U.S. and Soviet End Three-Day Parley (April 6): Washington conference narrows differences over German unity but fails of progress on major arms issues.

Conservatives Win in Hungarian Run-Off (April 8): Democratic Forum takes decisive lead. **(April 9):** Forum leader, Jozsef Antall, 58, is Prime Minister of coalition including two smaller parties.

About 135 Killed in Fire on Danish Ferry (April 7): Hundreds flee to lifeboats in North Sea. **(April 8):** Norwegian police open arson investigation and check links with earlier ferry blazes.

Rightists Win Greek Election (April 8): New Democracy Party, led by Constantine Mitsotakis, 71, gets 150 of 300 seats in Parliament. **(April 9):** Party wins backing of independent rightists to secure one-vote parliamentary majority for first conservative government for Greece in nine years.

Bomb Kills Four British Soldiers (April 9): Irish terrorists attack two-vehicle army patrol on country road near Downpatrick, County Down.

Pepsico Signs Barter Deal With Soviet (April 9): In $3-billion agreement, U.S. corporation will exchange soft drink for ships and vodka.

Rightists Win in Greek Election (April 9): Victorious New Democracy Party backed by independent rightist leader for slim parliamentary majority.

Arab Militants Free Three Hostages (April 10): Release Frenchwoman, Belgian companion, and daughter, abducted two years previously on Mediterranean pleasure cruise, in French-Libyan deal.

Estonians Defy Moscow (April 12): Legislators vote to end military service in republic. Previously Gorbachev had warned Estonia against independence move.

East Germans Apologize for Nazi Crimes (April 12): As first democratic cabinet takes office, Government expresses willingness to pay reparations to Nazis' victims and to seek relations with Israel.

Soviet Cuts Off Supplies to Lithuania (April 13): Gorbachev warns republic to rescind strongest independence measures. **(April 18):** Moscow authorities cut off principal supply of crude oil. **(April 19):** Increasing sanctions, Soviet slashes supplies of natural gas. **(April 23):** Lithuania's only oil refiner forced to shut down. **(April 26):** France and West Germany urge Lithuania to suspend independence moves and seek negotiations with Moscow.

Soviet Admits Katyn Massacre (April 13): Gorbachev gives Polish President documents that Soviet leader says prove Soviet secret police killed thousands of Polish officers in forest in spring of 1940.

Two American Hostages Freed in Lebanon (April 22): Robert Polhill, 55, released in Beirut after three years as captive of pro-Iranian kidnappers. **(April 30):** Abductors free Frank Herbert Reed, 57, kidnapped nearly four years previously, after intercession by Iran and Syria.

Sandinista Rule Ends in Nicaragua (April 25): Violeta Barrios de Chamorro, 60, inaugurated as President to succeed Daniel Ortega Saavedra. She keeps his brother, Gen. Humberto Ortega Saavedra, as military leader.

National

Senate Confirms Thrifts Regulator (April 4): Approves T. Timothy Ryan, Jr., 44, a labor lawyer, to head bailout of insolvent savings and loan institutions.

Congress Votes for Bias-Crime Data (April 4): Sends Bush Administration an Administration-approved bill to require U.S. to collect statistics on crimes motivated by prejudice based on race, ethnic, or other factors.

John M. Poindexter Convicted (April 7): Former National Security Adviser, 53, guilty on five charges of deceiving and lying to Congress in effort to conceal Reagan Administration's actions in Iran-Contra affair.

President Bush Has "Early Glaucoma" (April 12): Physical check-up reveals condition in left eye with no loss of sight. It will be treated with drops.

Justices Restrict Right to Pornography (April 18): Supreme Court, 6-3, rules states can make it a crime to possess pornographic photographs of children.

High Court Backs Judges on Tax Power (April 18): Rules, 5-4, that Federal courts may order local governments to increase levies to remedy such constitutional violations as school segregation.

General

Heart Guide Program Dropped (April 2): American Heart Association cancels program to award seal of approval to healthful foods because of opposition from Government.

Kurt Masur Named New York Philharmonic Head (April 11): East German conductor, 62, to succeed Zubin Mehta.

Tuna Companies Spare Dolphins (April 12): Three major sellers agree to stop buying tuna caught with nets that also trap and kill dolphins.

Michael Milken Agrees to Guilty Plea (April 20): Financier, 43, behind "junk bonds" used to pay for big corporate takeovers will pay $600 million in fines in settling six criminal charges.

Earth Day 1990 Celebrated (April 22): Millions around world renew call to protect planet 20 years after birth of modern environmental movement.

China and Soviet Union to Cooperate (April 24): Sign 10-year economic and scientific agreement to focus on high-technology proficiency.

Telescope Carried Into Space (April 24): Shuttle *Discovery* orbited 381 miles high, with $1.5-billion Hubble Space Telescope to observe distant stars and galaxies with new comprehensive view of universe. Crew members: Air Force Col. Loren J. Shriver, 46, mission commander; Marine Col. Charles F. Bolden, Jr., 44, pilot, and mission specialists, Navy Capt. Bruce McCandless 2nd, 53; Dr. Steven A. Hawley, 39, and Dr. Kathryn D. Sullivan, 38. **(April 25):** Astronauts place Hubble in high orbit after trouble with solar power wing. **(April 27):** Telescope's wide front door opened to let in light from heavens. **(April 29):** *Discovery* lands safely at Edwards Air Force Base, Calif. Space agency acknowledges troubles with telescope are greater than expected.

Connecticut Makes Abortion a Right (April 27): Legislature completes action on bill, later signed by Governor, to assure woman's right in state even if Roe v. Wade decision is overturned.

Wisconsin Bans Genetically Engineered Drug (April 27): Legislation temporarily holds up sale or use of product to be given to dairy cows.

MAY 1990

International

May Day Marchers Jeer Gorbachev (May 1): President and Kremlin leaders amazed at shouting throngs of protesters following annual Red Square parade.

NATO Votes Transformation Measures (May 3): Brussels conference of foreign ministers agrees on proposals making military alliance more political.

South African Talks Achieve Gains (May 4): Government and African National Congress end three-day conference with progress toward full-scale negotiations on nation's future.

Loans for Poor Nations Increased (May 8): International Monetary Fund agrees on 50 percent increase, of $60 billion, to aid East Europe's economic policies and reduce third world debt.

Albania Relaxes Restrictions (May 9): Most hidebound Eastern Europe Communist nation announces freedom to travel abroad and to practice religion.

China Frees 211 Dissidents (May 10): Announces release of many who took part in 1989 democracy movement. Diplomats discern gesture to West.

Cyclone Kills More than 200 in India (May 12): Toll of homeless set at 3 million after worst storm in decade hits Andra Pradesh state. Cyclone battered at least 1,400 villages.

Gorbachev Bars Two Independence Moves (May 14): Charges Latvia and Estonia have no legal basis for separation from Soviet Union, but delays sanctions.

Independence Foes Riot in Baltic (May 15): Thousands of protesters storm Parliament buildings in Latvia and Estonia in largest demonstrations since republics began withdrawal moves.

Sandinistas Strike in Nicaragua (May 15): Civil servants ignore back-to-work order and confront new Chamorro Government with first serious crisis.

Independence for Lithuania Debated (May 16): Its Government agrees to suspend laws since declaration in attempt to have Gorbachev lift embargo. **(May 17):** Gorbachev meets Lithuanian Prime Minister. Agrees to begin talks if Republic lifts declaration of independence.

Two Germanys Sign Economic Pact (May 18): Ministers of East and West approve treaty to merge economies and make West German mark legal tender in both.

Palestinians Protest Slayings (May 20): Emotionally disturbed Israeli kills seven Arab day laborers in occupied Gaza Strip. In widespread Palestinian riots, seven are killed and 500 injured. **(May 21):** Angered Palestinians clash with Israeli security forces. Violence spreads from occupied territories to towns inside Israel.

Ex-Communists Sweep Romania Election (May 20): Ion Iliescu and National Salvation Front win smashing victory in nation's first free election in half a century. Observers report ballot fair.

Islamic Leader Slain in Kashmir (May 21): Maulvi Mohammed Farooq, 45, assassinated in state's capital of Srinagar. As 100,000 angry mourners follow body, police fire kills at least 30 and wounds 200.

Food Buying Panic in Soviet (May 25): Shoppers crowd stores around country to hoard supplies after Government plans sharp price increases. Athorities order restrictions in Moscow stores.

Foe of Drug Cartel Elected in Colombia (May 27): César Gaviria, 43, will be youngest President of this century. Attacked Colombia's drug-trafficking gangs.

Burmese Opposition Wins Landslide (May 28): Voters overwhelmingly reject military rule in first multiparty elections for nation (now Myanmar) in 30 years. Delay on new Government likely.

Twenty-Three Dead in Armenian Clashes (May 28): New casualties reported in fighting between Government troops and civilian bands as unrest simmers.

New Bank to Aid Eastern Europe (May 29): Forty-nation treaty establishes institution for reconstruction, with $12-billion lending fund.

Boris Yeltsin Elected Russian President (May 29): Foe of Gorbachev and Communist establishment named head of largest Soviet Republic with four-vote margin in third round of balloting.

Israel Repulses Arab Beach Attack (May 30): Troops kill four and capture 12 speedboat raiders. P.L.O. faction takes responsibility. **(May 31):** Yasir Arafat, P. L.O. chairman, denies P.L.O. involvement.

National

Oliver North's Notebooks Released (May 8): Reveal meeting with Bush shortly after Lieutenant Colonel lied to Congress about an Iran-Contra involvement. **(May 9):** Administration officials say meeting with then Vice President did not involve efforts to aid Nicaraguan Contras.

New Iran-Contra Inquiry Opened (May 18): U.S. grand jury expected to focus on activities of mid-level officials in Reagan Administration.

Navy Challenged on Blast Report (May 25): Government experts offer new evidence contradicting conclusion that 1989 explosion on battleship *Iowa* was an act of suicidal sabotage by young sailor.

General

Mormons Drop Some Secret Rituals (May 2): Eliminate parts of ceremonies viewed as offensive to women and members of other faiths.

A Wellesley Protest Over Mrs. Bush (May 3): Students "outraged" by selection of President's wife as commencement speaker. Feminism is the issue.

Computer Tamperer Sentenced (May 4): Robert Tappan Morris, 25, computer science student, gets three years' probation and $10,000 fine for disrupting nationwide network with "worm" software.

Yale University Gets $20-Million Gift (May 7): Bass family of Fort Worth, Tex., establishes Institute of Biospheric Studies that will greatly expand research into environmental issues.

Navy Destroyer Fire Kills One and Injures 12 (May 8): Blaze in boiler room of the *Conyngham* is worst sea accident since recent fleetwide safety review.

Poisoner of Texas Tree Convicted (May 10): Paul Stedman Cullen guilty of fatally damaging 500-year-old Treaty Oak at Austin.

Minnesota Rebuffs High Court (May 11): Expands human rights law to broaden rights of employees and subcontractors in discrimination cases.

Atomic Health Records Available (May 17): Energy Department to release secret data on 200,000 workers at weapons plants in eight states.

Paintings Bring Record Prices (May 19): Japanese industrialist identified as buyer of Van Gogh's "Portrait of Dr. Gachet" for $82.5 million and Renoir's "At the Moulin de la Galette" for $78.1 million at auctions in New York.

Space Telescope Opens Eye First Time (May 20): *Hubble* returns clear images from constellations in southern skies. Photographs a star cluster.

Universities Shed Tobacco Stocks (May 23): Harvard and City University of New York take action in protest against dangers of smoking.

New York Mets Dismiss Davey Johnson (May 29): Manager replaced by Bud Harrelson, third-base coach.

JUNE 1990

International

U.S. and Soviet Reach Accord at Summit (June 1): At second conference, in Washington, Bush and Gorbachev sign broad understanding, including cuts in nuclear arms and chemical weapons. Bush signs trade treaty sought by Soviet. (**June 4**): At San Francisco, Gorbachev ends U.S. visit with appeal for revised global alliances.

South Africa Lifts Emergency Decree (June 7): Ends four-year-old rules in all but one of four provinces. Regulations had been a major obstacle to negotiations with African National Congress.

Russian Republic Asserts Primacy (June 8): Its Parliament challenges Soviet authority.

New Right-Wing Israeli Government (June 8): Prime Minister Yitzhak Shamir assembles most conservative cabinet in nation's history. New regime committed to expanding Jewish settlements in occupied territories, likely to cause confrontation with U.S. (**June 11**): Israeli Parliament narrowly approves new government.

Ex-Communists Win in Bulgaria (June 10): Socialists take early lead in balloting for Parliament in first free multiparty elections in 45 years.

Rioting Flares in Bucharest (June 13): Troops reported to fire on antigovernment protesters. (**June 14**): Summoned by President, thousands of miners descend on capital and beat up suspected enemies of regime.

Islamic Party Sweeps Algeria (June 14): Final results show smashing victory for fundamentalists in municipal and provincial council elections.

Bush Cuts Off Talks with P.L.O. (June 20): Suspends 18-month discussions because of its failure to condemn terrorist attack on Israeli beach.

Iran Earthquake Toll Near 40,000 (June 21): Major temblor, measuring 7.3 on Richter scale, strikes heavily populated Caspian Sea region in northwest. Devastates scores of towns and villages and buries thousands in rubble of homes. Quake is Iran's worst in history. (**June 22**): Thousands dead and alive dug from wreckage. Global relief effort begins.

Canada Drops Accord on Quebec (June 22): Meech Lake agreement on constitutional changes to confer special station on province collapses after failure to win approval of all provinces.

Ninety-three Nations Agree to Protect Ozone (June 29): London accord calls for halting by end of century production of chemicals that would destroy the protective layer of earth's atmosphere.

Lithuania and Moscow Reach Accord (June 29): Lithuania agrees to suspend independence declaration for 100 days in exchange for negotiations and lifting of Soviet economic sanctions. (**June 30**): Soviet reopens oil pipeline as part of compromise.

National

Justices Approve School Bible Clubs (June 4): Supreme Court, 8-1, upholds Federal law requiring public high schools to allow religious and political groups equal status with others.

John M. Poindexter Sentenced (June 11): National Security Adviser under Reagan gets six months in prison for role in Iran-Contra affair.

High Court Upsets Flag-Burning Law (June 11): Justices, rule, 5-4, that legislation violates free-speech guarantees of the First Amendment.

Justices Approve Sobriety Checks (June 14): Supreme Court, 6-3, upholds constitutional right of police to stop motorists at roadsides and examine them for signs of intoxication.

Flash Floods Kill 16 in Ohio (June 19): Torrential thunderstorms send water surging through valley of Ohio River and into town of Shadyside.

House Blocks Flag Amendment (June 21): Votes 254 in favor of burning ban, 177 against, 34 short of two-thirds majority needed to propose constitutional change to prohibit desecration.

Spotted Owl Protected (June 22): U.S. agency declares Northwest bird an endangered species, with ancient forests, its habitat, to be protected. Area's logging industry threatened with loss of jobs.

Parental Notification in Abortions Upheld (June 25): Supreme Court, in two rulings, decides states may require teen-age girls to consult parents as long as state law provides for judicial hearing.

High Court Upholds "Right to Die" (June 25): Justices, 8-1, rule person whose wishes are clearly known can be cut off from life-extension treatment. Decision is a setback for Missouri family.

President Breaks With No-Tax Pledge (June 26): Says agreement with Congress to reduce ballooning budget deficit will require "tax revenue increases" despite "read my lips" vow. Seeks to break deadlock in talks with legislators.

High Court Backs Affirmative Action Programs (June 27): Justices, 5-4, uphold two Federal policies aimed at increasing minority ownership of broadcast licenses despite Administration opposition.

General

Doctor Helps Woman's Suicide (June 4): Jack Kevorkian connects victim of Alzheimer's disease with homemade device that she manipulates.

Californians Vote Tax Increase (June 5): Approve rise in gasoline levy and looser limit on state spending. Action comes a decade following state's revolt against taxes and spending.

Blasts Set Tanker Afire in Gulf (June 9): Explosions rock Norwegian vessel with more than 38 million gallons of crude oil aboard. Two crew members dead and two missing. Millions of gallons spilled and major environmental impact is feared.

Nelson Mandela Visits North America (June 17 et seq.**):** Highlights of trip: (**June 18**): Mandela appeals to Canadian Parliament to continue economic sanctions against South Africa. (**June 20**): Mandela starts eight-city U.S. visit. In New York, tens of thousands greet anti-apartheid leader emotionally. (**June 25**): Mandela tells President Bush he cannot rule out use of force to achieve racial equality. (**June 26**): In address to Congress, Mandela invoked names of American heroes as his inspiration. (**June 30**): Tour of U.S. ends at Oakland, Calif.

Two Blasts Hit Navy Destroyer (June 20): Intense fire sears aircraft carrier *Midway* off Japan. Sixteen crew members injured, two missing.

Heat Breaks Records in Southwest (June 27): Temperatures rise to 120s, slowing all activity. Heat kills several persons. Six firemen die battling many brush and forest fires.

Hubble Telescope Crippled (June 27): NASA reports major flaw in main light-gathering mirrors of $1.5-billion space project that is likely to curtail ability to probe depths of universe for several years. Rescue effort delayed.

Royal Wedding in Japan (June 29): Prince Aya, 24, Emperor Akihito's second son, marries commoner, Kiko Kawashima, 23, social psychology student.

NASA Grounds Shuttle Fleet (June 29): Suspends activity until engineers can repair elusive fuel leak.

JULY 1990

International

East Germans Convert Currency (July 1): Thousands line up to get West German marks in an official economic and social merger that marks end of the 40-year-old Communist state. Berlin subway system, severed in 1961, again links all city.

Death Toll 1,426 in Moslem Stampede (July 2): Pilgrims suffocated in crowded pedestrian tunnel leading to sacred city of Mecca.

Gorbachev Keeps Party Leadership (July 2): Fights to hold Communists together at 28th Congress. **(July 10):** He sweeps to re-election as party secretary after confronting hardliners with defense of his reforms. Heads off major split. **(July 12):** Boris N. Yeltsin, stormy political figure, quits party in a new blow to its once-monolithic power. **(July 13):** Leaders of Moscow and Leningrad City Councils quit party. Both champion free-market reforms. **(July 14):** Communists revamp Politburo to separate it from government. Gorbachev heads both as party General Secretary and President of Soviet Union.

West to Aid Four Eastern European Nations (July 4): Twenty-four leading industrial countries to expand economic relief program for Czechoslovakia, Bulgaria, Yugoslavia, and East Germany in addition to Poland and Hungary.

Western Alliance Ends Cold War (July 6): At London conference, Bush and other NATO leaders propose joint action with Moscow and East European nations and state "we are no longer adversaries." Promise new defensive strategy to make nuclear forces "truly weapons of last resort."

Houston Economic Conference Ends (July 11): Leaders of seven top industrial democracies proclaim goal of worldwide prosperity but fail to resolve major issues that had divided them.

Pact Ends Sandinista Protest (July 12): Nicaraguan Government and union agree on wage increases and other concessions to end 10-day walkout.

Thatcher Ally Quits in Cabinet Storm (July 14): Nicholas Ridley, 61, Minister of Trade and Industry, resigns in controversy over attack on European monetary union as "German racket." Peter Lilley, 46, a Treasury official, succeeds him.

Ukraine Declares Sovereignty (July 16): One of most important Soviet republics challenges Gorbachev Government to greater self-determination.

Soviet and Germany Agree on NATO (July 16): Gorbachev and Kohl announce decision on alliance for united Germany. Lift most other barriers to unification.

Germans Agree on Polish Border (July 17): East and West promise to guarantee postwar frontier.

U.S. Reverses Cambodia Policy (July 18): Withdraws recognition of guerrillas' coalition to block return to power of Khmer Rouge, a partner.

London Stock Exchange Bombed (July 20): No one hurt in blast after warning by Irish Republican Army allows for evacuation of 300 inside.

Bomb Kills Nun in Ulster (July 24): Three policemen also dead as car is blown up near Armagh in Northern Ireland. Irish Republican Army blamed.

New Archbishop of Canterbury Named (July 25): Bishop George Carey, 54, chosen as surprise successor to the retiring Robert Runcie.

I.R.A. Bomb Kills Tory Legislator (July 30): Ian Gow, 53, Conservative member of British Parliament, is latest victim of Irish Republican Army terrorists. He had been an outspoken opponent of it.

Gorbachev Accepts Economic Accord (July 31): Agrees with main rival, Boris N. Yeltsin, on move for liberal, market-oriented policies.

National

Congress Votes Rights for Disabled (July 13): Senate, 91-6, approves House-passed bill to bar discrimination against people with physical and mental disabilities. Bush "delighted," later signs it.

Justice William J. Brennan, Jr., Retires (July 20): Senior Supreme Court member, its leading liberal, is 84. He cites Court's "strenuous demands."

Oliver North's Convictions Overturned (July 20): U.S. Appeals Court casts doubt on entire Iran-Contra case against former Marine lieutenant colonel.

Bush Nominates New Justice (July 23): Picks David H. Souter, 50, of New Hampshire, a Federal Appeals Court judge, to replace Supreme Court Justice Brennan.

Senate Denounces Dave Durenberger (July 25): Disciplines Minnesota Republican for bringing it "dishonor and disrepute" through improper financial dealings and orders he pay restitution.

House Reprimands Rep. Barney Frank (July 26): Votes 408-18 to penalize Massachusetts Democrat for ethical breaches in relations with male prostitute.

General

Imelda Marcos Acquitted (July 2): Widow of former Philippine President, 61, cleared by U.S. jury in New York on charges of raiding her country's treasury and investing money in United States.

Radiation Danger in Northwest Revealed (July 11): U.S. Energy Department discloses illnesses, including cancer, caused by atomic weapons plant at Richland, Wash., in 1940s and 1950s.

Christian Science Couple Convicted (July 6): Boston judge orders 10 years' probation for parents guilty of manslaughter in death of son, 2, for relying on prayer instead of medical treatment for ailment.

Philippine Earthquake Toll Past 1,600 Dead (July 17): Main island rocked. School building collapses. Scores injured, hundreds trapped in debris. **(July 28):** Two rescued from rubble 11 days later.

Pete Rose Sentenced (July 19): Baseball's leading hitter gets five months in Federal institution for filing false income-tax returns.

"Golden Calf" Dug Up (July 24): Harvard archeologists unearth ancient object of worship in Canaanite ruins.

Exxon Valdez Captain Punished (July 25): Coast Guard suspends license of Joseph Hazelwood for nine months for conduct in Alaska oil spill.

U.S. Indicts Eastern Airlines (July 25): Charges company and nine managers ignored vital repairs and maintenance and falsified records.

Louisiana Governor Vetoes Abortion Bill (July 27): Buddy Roemer views as too restrictive a measure to limit procedures in cases of rape.

Gene Therapy Revolution Begins (July 31): U.S. panel approves experiments with two therapies to treat human disease by inserting new genes into cells. The diseases are cancer and an immune disorder.

Mistrial Ends Coast Molestation Case (July 27): California jury deadlocked in Raymond Buckey's retrial on charges of abusing three girls in McMartin school.

Mexican Guilty in Killing of U.S. Agent (July 31): U.S. jury convicts Rubén Zuno Arce, brother-in-law of former Mexican president, in torture and killing. He faces life in prison.

AUGUST 1990

International

Trinidad Gunmen Release Hostages (Aug. 1): Muslims surrender to police after five-day crisis. Free Prime Minister Arthur N.R. Robinson and others.

Iraqi Invasion Ignites Persian Gulf Crisis: Highlights (Aug. 2): Troops seize Kuwait's petroleum reserves and capital after talks break down over oil production and debt repayment. **(Aug. 3):** Iraqis maneuver for possible attack on Saudi Arabia. **(Aug. 4):** Iraqis fortify positions in Kuwait. Europeans embargo imports of Iraqi oil. **(Aug. 6):** U.N. Security Council orders sweeping trade and financial boycott of Iraq and Kuwait. **(Aug. 7):** Washington orders troops, planes, and armor to Saudi kingdom, discerning threat of invasion. Thousands of American troops deployed. **(Aug. 10):** Arab League votes to send troops to defend Saudis. **(Aug. 12):** Bush orders U.S. forces to block Iraqi oil exports and most imports. **(Aug. 17):** Administration decides on Reserve call-up **(Aug. 20):** Iraqis begin moving Americans and other non-Iraqis to strategic sites as human shields. **(Aug. 22):** U.S. and other nations defy Iraqi orders to close Kuwait embassies. Thousands of U.S. reservists face call. **(Aug. 25):** U.N. Security Council, 13-0, with two abstentions, gives U.S. and other nations right to enforce embargo by force. **(Aug. 28):** Iraq's President Saddam Hussein permits foreign women and children to leave. Bush actions get overwhelming support from members of Congress.

Romania Frees Student Leader (Aug. 3): Releases Marian Munteanu, 28, held six weeks after anti-Government rally. Beating protested worldwide.

Americans Evacuated From Liberia (Aug. 5); Marines fly to rescue after rebel leader is reported threatening to take foreigners prisoner.

Pakistan Government Overthrown (Aug. 6): Prime Minister Benazir Bhutto's regime dismissed by President on charges of corruption, nepotism, and other violations of "Constitution and the law."

Soviet Astronauts Back After Six Months (Aug. 9): Two return safely to Earth after mission on which they grew crystals for industry and survived space walk that nearly proved fatal.

South African Clashes Kill 140 Blacks (Aug. 15): Death toll heavy in three days of factional civil war across black townships.

More Than 500 Killed in South Africa (Aug. 23): Toll rises in ethnic enmity between Zulus and Xhosas in black townships east and west of Johannesburg. Bloodshed affects African National Congress policy in dealing with Zulu chief's movement. **(Aug. 27):** Tens of thousands stay away from work to commemorate deaths in factional clashes.

Irish Hostage Freed in Lebanon (Aug. 25): Abductors release Brian Keenan, 52, Belfast-born teacher of English, held four years.

Police Battle Bucharest Rioters (Aug. 26): Riot squads clash with youthful anti-Government demonstrators demanding overthrow of Romanian President Ion Iliescu, protesting deprivations.

Bulgarian Socialist Headquarters Stormed (Aug. 26): Rioters protest continued presence of Communist symbols in public places throughout country.

Blast Kills Yugoslav Coal Miners (Aug. 26): More than 170 feared dead as gas explosion rips through pit southwest of Belgrade. Many buried below surface.

Five U.N. Powers Agree on Cambodia (Aug. 28): Security Council members in accord on political settlement to end 20 years of civil war.

Rebels Kill 200 in Liberia (Aug. 31): Slay civilians of nations whose governments contributed to five-nation force sent to end civil war.

Germans Sign Reunification Treaty (Aug. 31): East and West agree on all aspects, including merger of legal and political systems and such specific questions as abortion and Berlin as capital.

National

Senate Bars Outside Speaking Fees (Aug. 2): Votes overwhelmingly for amendment that would also abolish political action committees.

Guam's Abortion Curbs Struck Down (Aug. 23): U.S. judge finds statute outlawing most operations violates rights guaranteed by Supreme Court in precedent-setting Roe v. Wade decision.

Pennsylvania Abortion Curbs Voided (Aug. 24): Federal judge rules several restrictive provisions violate constitutional rights established in landmark Roe v. Wade decision.

Congress Gets Medicare Fee Plan (Aug. 31): Model national system drafted to overhaul the system's chaotic reimbursement structure.

General

Drug Cures Chronic Hepatitis B (Aug. 1): Nationwide trial indicates synthetic interferon alpha-2b checks debilitating liver disease.

Tiny Error Found in Building of Hubble (Aug. 9): U.S. panel blames one-millimeter spacing error in optic device guiding mirror's construction for flaw in $1.5-billion space telescope.

Drug Case Abduction Ruled Illegal (Aug. 10): U.S. judge orders return to Mexico of Mexican doctor accused in torture slaying of U.S. agent.

Washington Mayor Guilty on One Count (Aug. 10): U.S. jury deadlocked on most serious charges. Convicts Marion S. Barry of drug possession.

Scientists Report Landmark Discovery (Aug. 12): Rival teams establish that universe contains no more than three fundamental types of matter.

Equity Reverses "Miss Saigon" Stand (Aug. 16): Actor's union votes to allow Jonathan Pryce, white Briton, to take role of Eurasian despite protests by Asian stage representatives in New York.

Three Guilty in Central Park Jogger Attack (Aug. 18): Black teen-agers convicted by New York jury of rape and assault, acquitted of murder attempt.

Three Pilots Guilty of Drunken Flying (Aug. 20): U.S. jury in Minneapolis finds former Northwest Airlines professionals guilty of operating jetliner under influence of alcohol in first test of new Federal statute.

Five Students Slain in Florida (Aug. 28): Widespread panic created by fear of serial killer.

Tornadoes Kill 25 in Midwest (Aug. 30): Touch down in Chicago area before National Weather Service issues warning. System's performance questioned.

Singer's Libel Award Overturned (Aug. 30): U.S. Appeals Court in San Francisco upsets $5.2-million verdict for Wayne Newton in suit over NBC news reports.

Paratrooper Acquitted in Panama Killing (Aug. 31): Military court clears Sgt. Roberto Bryan of charge he murdered unarmed man at invasion roadblock.

SEPTEMBER 1990

International

Two Germanys Reunited (Aug. 31): Representatives of East and West sign treaty on mechanics of reunification. **(Sept. 10):** Moscow and Bonn agree on how to share cost of Soviet military withdrawal from united nation. **(Sept. 12):** Four wartime Allies sign treaty relinquishing occupation rights in Germany. **(Sept. 20):** Lawmakers of East and West ratify treaty formally ending four decades of division and uniting both nations October 3.

A 500-Day Plan for Soviet Union (Sept. 1): Rivals Gorbachev and Yeltsin agree on dismantling of central economic controls and on move to free markets. Constitutional republics would gain autonomy.

The Persian Gulf Crisis—Highlights (Sept. 3): U.S. deploys combat aircraft in several Gulf nations to help defend Saudi Arabia. **(Sept. 9):** In Helsinki summit conference, Bush and Gorbachev pledge joint action to reverse Iraq's conquest of Kuwait. Bush drops opposition to Soviet involvement in Mideast peace talks. **(Sept. 10):** Arab League, stressing divisions, moves headquarters from Tunis back to Cairo. **(Sept. 14):** U.S. warship fires warning shot at Iraqi tanker in move to enforce embargo. **(Sept. 15):** French send troops, aircraft, and tanks to Saudi Arabia to protest Iraqi moves against diplomats. **(Sept. 16):** In talk broadcast in Iraq, Bush warns nation of "brink of war." **(Sept. 17):** Air Force Chief of Staff dismissed after revealing contingency plans for war on Iraq. **(Sept. 25):** Security Council votes embargo on air traffic with Iraq.

President of Liberia Slain (Sept. 9): Samuel K. Doe, 38, killed by rebel forces that captured him in gun battle. Mutilated body displayed.

Iraqis Barred From Olympic Games (Sept. 20): Asian nations order athletic teams out of Beijing mini-Olympics until troops are withdrawn from Kuwait.

Britain and Iran Resume Ties (Sept. 27): London satisfied that Teheran leaders will no longer encourage Muslims to kill British writer Salman Rushdie.

Sixteen Sentenced in Aquino Murder (Sept. 28): General and 15 soldiers get life in prison for killing seven years previously of Benigno S. Aquino, Jr., Philippine opposition leader.

World Leaders Act on Children (Sept. 30): U.N. World Summit for Children pledges international effort to save lives of millions who die before 5.

Soviet Accord With South Korea (Sept. 30): Nations establish partial diplomatic relations. Soviet also agrees to upgrade relations with Israel.

National

U.S. Banks Allowed to Trade Stocks (Sept. 20): Federal Reserve approves J.P. Morgan application, breaking down Depression-era restriction.

South African President in Washington (Sept. 24): F.W. de Klerk gets Bush assurance of effort to modify sanctions if conditions are met. **(Sept. 25):** De Klerk assures Congress he is determined to build U.S.-style democracy with "one man, one vote."

U.S. Releasing Oil Reserves (Sept. 26): President announces test sale of 5 million barrels. Sees "no justification" for mounting oil prices.

Clearing of Two Senators in S.&L. Inquiry Urged (Sept. 28): Special counsel recommends Senate Ethics Committee drop charges against John Glenn and John McCain.

Deficit-Cutting Plan Drafted (Sept. 30): Bush and Congressional leaders agree to major increases in taxes and reductions in domestic spending.

General

Miss America Receives Crown (Sept. 8): Marjorie Judith Vincent, a third-year law student at Duke University, becomes the 1991 title-holder. She is a native of Oak Park, Ill.

First Human Gene Therapy (Sept. 14): Girl, 4, gets blood transfusion in Maryland hospital to provide gene to relieve rare immune deficiency.

G.M. Labor Contract Reached (Sept. 17): Three-year tentative agreement with U.A.W. apparently breaks ground on job security for 300,000 hourly workers.

Savings and Loan Leader Indicted (Sept. 18): Charles M. Keating, Jr., charged with criminal fraud as symbol of industry's reckless investment style.

Atlanta Wins 1996 Summer Olympics (Sept. 18): Athens loses appeal for 100th anniversary.

Thirty Universities to Share Teaching Grant (Sept. 22): General Electric Foundation allots $2.1 million to attract women, blacks, American Indians, and Hispanics to careers in science and business.

Spacecraft Reports on Venus (Sept. 25): Scientists delighted as mapping by Magellan shows planet is active with volcanoes and other features.

Movie "X" Rating Replaced (Sept. 26): Hollywood creates "No Children" category (NC-17) for adult films.

Major Emmy Awards for TV, 1990

(September 16)

Drama series: *L.A. Law* (NBC)
  Actress: Patricia Wettig, *thirtysomething* (ABC)
  Actor: Peter Falk, *Columbo* (ABC)
  Supporting actress: Marg Helgenberger, *China Beach* (ABC)
  Supporting actor: Jimmy Smits, *L.A. Law* (NBC)
Comedy series: *Murphy Brown* (CBS)
  Actress: Candice Bergen, *Murphy Brown* (CBS)
  Actor: Ted Danson, *Cheers* (NBC)
  Supporting actress: Bebe Neuwirth, *Cheers* (NBC)
  Supporting actor: Alex Rocco, *The Famous Teddy Z* (CBS)
Variety, music or comedy series: *In Living Color* (Fox)
Variety, music or comedy special: *Sammy Davis Jr.'s 60th Anniversary Celebration* (ABC)
Mini-series: *Drug Wars: The Camarena Story* (NBC)
Drama-Comedy special (tie): *Hallmark Hall of Fame: Caroline?* (CBS); *AT&T Presents: The Incident* (CBS)
Actress in a Mini-series or special: Barbara Hershey, *A Killing in a Small Town* (CBS)
Actor in a Mini-series or special: Hume Cronyn, *Age-Old Friends* (HBO)
Supporting actress in a Mini-series or special: Eva Marie Saint, *People Like Us* (NBC)
Supporting actor in a Mini-series or special: Vincent Gardenia, *Age-Old Friends* (HBO)
Individual performance in a variety or music program: Tracey Ullman, *The Best of the Tracey Ullman Show* (Fox)
Governor's Award: Former ABC chairman Leonard Goldenson
Network totals: ABC 22, NBC 18, CBS 14, Fox 9, HBO 8

OCTOBER 1990
(Through October 23)

International

U.S. and Soviets Agree On New Arms Pact (Oct. 3): Secretary of State James A. Baker states that pending consultation with our allies, the U.S. agrees in principle on all remaining issues in the conventional-arms treaty talks, which have been going on since March 1989. It requires the Soviets to destroy thousands of tanks, artillery pieces, and armored vehicles in Europe.

Two Germanys Become One (Oct. 3): After 45 years Germany reunites in a midnight celebration of pealing bells national hymns, and the unfurling of the black, red, and gold flag of the Federal Republic of Germany in front of the Reichstag building in Berlin.

Mutinous Troops Seize Philippines Barracks (Oct 4): About 200 soldiers, led by Major Agapito Carbeno, take control of the Philippine Army headquarters in Butuan on the island of Mindanao. Rebels also advance toward Cagayan de Oro under Colonel Alexander Nobel. **(Oct. 5):** The rebellion in the two cities enters its second day but most of the country's armed forces remain loyal to President Corazon C. Aquino. **(Oct. 6):** Mutiny ends with the surrender of Colonel Nobel.

19 Arabs Die in Battle with Jerusalem Police (Oct. 8): An hourlong battle outside Al Aksa Mosque between Israeli Police and Arabs hurling rocks and bottles at Jews praying at the Western Wall leaves at least 19 Palestinians dead and 100 wounded. **(Oct 9):** The U.S. asks the U.N. Security Council to approve a resolution condemning Israel for excessive use of force in the incident. **(Oct 12):** Security Council votes unanimously to adopt a compromise resolution condemning Israel.

Lebanese General Ends Revolt (Oct 13): Gen. Michel Aoún, the leader of the Christian military forces opposing the Lebanese Government, surrenders after Syrian air the ground attacks force him to seek asylum in the French Embassy.

Christian Democrats Win Big in German Elections (Oct 14): Voters electing new state legislatures in what used to be East Germany give overwhelming support to Chancellor Helmut Kohl's Christian Democrats. Only in Bradenburg did the Social Democrats win out over the Christian Democrats.

A South Africa Color Bar Falls (Oct. 15): Racial discrimination becomes illegal in parks, swimming pools, libraries, toilets, and other publicly owned places across South Africa. However, the new integration does not apply to private establishments.

Gorbachev Offers Economic Plan (Oct. 16): He sends the Soviet Parliament a compromise economic reform plan that calls for dismantling the state's economic monopoly, but sets no timetable. **(Oct. 19):** Plan wins overwhelmingly in Parliament.

National

Senate Confirms Souter (Oct. 2); In an overwhelming vote, 90 to 9, David H. Souter becomes the Supreme Court's 105th Justice. **(Oct. 8):** Takes oath required by Constitution for all Federal employees in White House Ceremony. **(Oct. 9):** Assumes his seat on the bench after formal swearing in by Chief Justice William H. Rehnquist.

Deficit-Cutting Plan in Trouble (Oct. 2): President Bush appeals for public support in a TV address. **(Oct. 5):** Budget compromise fails in House. Congress approves stopgap spending legislation. **(Oct. 6):** President rejects it. Shuts down government ex-

cept for essential services. **(Oct. 9):** Stopgap legislation to end Federal shutdown passes both Houses and is approved by Bush. **(Oct. 10-22):** Impass over budget continues. **(Oct. 25):** Resolved.

Bush Vetoes Civil Rights Bill (Oct. 22): Saying that it would lead to quotas in employment, the President rejects a bill to expand job protection.

Bush Loses First Cabinet Member (Oct. 23): Elizabeth Dole resigns as Secretary of Labor to become the president of the American Red Cross.

General

Cincinnati Jury Acquits Museum in Obscenity Case (Oct. 5): After two hours of deliberation, the four-man, four-woman jury finds the Contemporary Arts Center and its director, Dennis Barrie, not guilty of obscenity charges stemming from an exhibition of photographs by Robert Mapplethorpe which was held in the spring.

Space Shuttle Discovery Takes Off (Oct. 6): After five months of delays in shuttle launchings, the *Discovery* rockets into orbit and dispatches the *Ulysses* spacecraft on its mission to explore the polar regions of the Sun

Leonard Bernstein Dies at 72 (Oct 14): His death follows by five days the announcement that he would retire from performing because of health problems.

White Supremacists Liable for Inciting Death (Oct. 22): A jury in Portland, Ore., finds a white supremacist group, the White Aryan Resistance, liable for intentionally inciting the 1988 beating death of an Ethiopian man and assesses $12.5 million in damages against the leaders, their organization, and two of the skinheads involved in the beating.

1990 Nobel Prize Winners

Peace: Mikhail S. Gorbachev (Russian) in recognition of his initiatives in promotion of international peace, including championing political change in Eastern Europe and helping to end the cold war.

Literature: Octavio Paz (Mexican), poet and essayist, "for impassioned writing with wide horizons, characterized by sensuous intelligence and humanistic integrity."

Medicine: Dr. Joseph E. Murray and Dr. E. Donnall Thomas (Americans) for their pioneering work in transplants. Dr. Murray, a surgeon at the Brigham and Women's Hospital in Boston, did the first kidney transplants. His work paved the way for other organ transplants. Dr. Thomas, of the Fred Hutchinson Cancer Research Center in Seattle, transplanted bone marrow from one person to another.

Economics: Harry M. Markowitz of Baruch College of the City University of New York, William F. Sharpe of Stanford University, and Merton H. Miller of the University of Chicago (all Americans) whose work provided new tools for weighing the risks and rewards of different investments and for valuing corporate stocks and bonds.

Physics: Dr. Richard E. Taylor (Canadian), a professor at Stanford University in California, and Dr. Jerome I. Friedman and Dr. Henry W. Kendall (Americans), both of the Massachusetts Institute of Technology, for their "breakthrough in our understanding of matter" which confirmed the reality of quarks.

Chemistry: Dr. Elias James Corey (American), a professor at Harvard University, for developing new ways to synthesize complex molecules ordinarily found in nature.

Deaths in 1989–1990
(As of September 1, 1990)

Ailey, Alvin, 58: choreographer, dancer, and director. Leader in popularizing modern dance and establishing black modern dance. Dec. 1, 1989.

Bailey, Pearl, 72: singer and entertainer with distinctive warm style. Appeared in star role on Broadway in all-black version of "Hello, Dolly!" Aug. 17, 1990.

Beckett, Samuel, 83: Irish playwright and novelist who charted new course in contemporary literature. "Waiting for Godot" became trail-blazing work in modern theater. Dec. 22, 1989.

Berlin, Irving, 101: songwriter, born in Russia, many of whose 1,500 compositions became American classics. Among them were "White Christmas," "God Bless America," and "Alexander's Ragtime Band." Sept. 22, 1989.

Bettelheim, Bruno, 86: psychoanalyst who was a pioneer in treating childhood emotional disturbances. March 13, 1990.

Bridges, Harry, 88: Australian-born, a leading figure in nation's twentieth century labor movement. Organized West Coast longshoremen in 1930s. March 30, 1990.

Callaghan, Morley, 87: Canadian writer famed throughout English-speaking world for hard-boiled style. Aug. 25, 1990.

Carney, Adm. Robert B., 95: retired Chief of Naval Operations and former commander-in-chief of North Atlantic Treaty Organization forces in Southern Europe. June 25, 1990.

Childs, Marquis W., 87: foreign correspondent and columnist for *St. Louis Dispatch* for 47 years. Author and winner of Pulitzer Prize for distinguished commentary. June 30, 1990.

Davis, Bette, 81: flamboyant Hollywood star who battled for good scripts. Won two Academy Awards. Top pictures included "Dangerous," "Jezebel," and "All About Eve." Oct. 6, 1989.

Davis, Sammy, Jr., 64: energetic singer, dancer, and actor. Was born in Harlem and grew up in vaudeville from age of 3. Never went to school and overcame obstacles to fame, breaking racial barriers. May 16, 1990.

de Hoffman, Frederic, 65: nuclear physicist who helped develop hydrogen bomb. Headed Salk Institute for Biological Studies for 18 years. Oct. 4, 1989.

Edgerton, Harold E. (Doc), 86: M.I.T. professor emeritus of electrical measurements. Invented electronic flash, which expanded scope of photography. Jan. 4, 1990.

Fain, Sammy, 87: songwriter for more than six decades. Wrote "I'll Be Seeing You," "That Old Feeling," and other popular songs. Dec. 6, 1989.

Faulk, John Henry, 76: Southern humorist and former radio comedian whose lawsuit broke blacklist on entertainment industry. April 8, 1990.

Forbes, Malcolm, 70: chairman and editor-in-chief of *Forbes* magazine. Multimillionaire whose pursuits included yachting, motorcycling, and ballooning. Feb. 24, 1990.

Franz Josef II, Prince of Liechtenstein, 83: head of state of tiny principality for half century in which it became one of richest nations. Nov. 13, 1989.

Elath, Eliahu, 86: journalist who championed Zionist cause and helped found state of Israel. Became in 1948 its first ambassador to U.S. June 21, 1990.

Gann, Paul, 77: co-author of Proposition 13, tax-cutting plan in California, and an advocate of AIDS testing and treatment. Sept. 11, 1989.

Garbo, Greta, 84: enigmatic and secretive Hollywood star of 1930s, known for classic beauty and emotional performances in such films as "Anna Christie" and "Grand Hotel." April 15, 1990.

Gardner, Ava, 67: world-famous movie actress who starred as worldly woman in such films as "One Touch of Venus," "The Snows of Kilimanjaro," "The Hucksters," and "Showboat." Jan. 25, 1990.

Gavin, Lieut. Gen. James M., 82: World War II Army commander, later a top Army administrator, diplomat, and a leading management consultant. Feb. 23, 1990.

Giamatti, Dr. A. Bartlett, 51: Renaissance scholar and former president of Yale University. Gave up academic career to become Commissioner of Baseball in 1989 after two years as president of National League. Aug. 31, 1989.

Gilford, Jack, 81: actor and comedian in plays, films, and television. Known for wit and buoyant manner. June 4, 1990.

Goddard, Paulette, 78: Hollywood star of 1930s, 40s, and 50s, known for comedy and melodrama roles. Married to Charles Chaplin and other famous stars. April 23, 1990.

Goldberg, Arthur J., 81: former Secretary of Labor, Associate Justice of Supreme Court, and U.S. Representative to United Nations. Known as human rights and labor advocate. Jan. 19, 1990.

Goulding, Ray, 68: half of Bob and Ray comedy team popular on radio and TV for four decades with low-key humor and gentle satire. March 24, 1990.

Graziano, Rocky (born Thomas Rocco Barbella), 71: former middleweight boxing champion. Life was subject of a movie. May 22, 1990.

Hagen, Dr. John P. 82: solar radio astronomer who in 1950s directed nation's first major space project. Aug. 26, 1990.

Halston (Roy Halston Frowick), 57: celebrated as a leading designer of women's clothes in 1970s. March 26, 1990.

Harrison, Sir Rex, 82: suave British actor with long career in theater and films. Won Tony in 1957 and Academy Award in 1964 for role as Henry Higgins in the musical "My Fair Lady." June 2, 1990.

Haynsworth, Clement F., Jr., 77: Federal judge whose nomination to Supreme Court in 1969 was rejected by Senate in battle with Nixon Administration. Nov. 22, 1989.

Henson, Jim, 53: award-winning creator of puppets, the "Muppets," with Kermit the Frog, Miss Piggy, and others that appeared in "Sesame Street," watched by millions of children. May 16, 1990.

Hoopes, Darlington, 93: longtime leader of Socialist Party, its candidate for President in 1952 and 1956. Sept. 25, 1989.

Horowitz, Vladimir, 86: eccentric and dazzling concert pianist whose power and virtuosity thrilled six decades of concert audiences. Nov. 5, 1989.

Horton, Myles, 84: founder of controversial Highlander Folk School in Tennessee, which taught leadership skills to blacks and whites in defiance of segregation. Feb. 19, 1990.

Ibarruri, Dolores (La Pasionaria), 93: President of Spanish Communist Party and fiery orator who was a heroine of nation's civil war. Nov. 12, 1989.

Jackson, Gordon, 66: British actor in many films. Known to thousands in Britain and U.S. as butler "Hudson" in popular "Upstairs, Downstairs" television series. Jan. 14, 1990.

Kelman, Rabbi Wolfe, 66: leader in Conservative Ju

daism for decades. Helped pave way for ordination of women. June 26, 1990.

Kreisky, Bruno, 79: Austria's longest-serving Chancellor, from 1970 to 1983. Consolidated neutral nation's prosperity. July 29, 1990.

Lockwood, Margaret, 73: British actress, one of most popular figures in films of late 1940s. July 15, 1990.

Lovestone, Jay, 91: controversial figure in labor movement, international affairs director of A.F.L.-C.I.O. Headed U.S. Communist Party in 1920s, then became staunch anti-Communist. March 7, 1990.

Luce, Claire, 85: actress who starred in 1920s Ziegfeld Follies and left musical stage for classical theater. Aug. 31, 1989.

Marcos, Ferdinand, 72: autocratic leader of Philippines for 20 years, who imposed martial law from 1972 to 1981. Overthrown by Government in 1986. Sept. 28, 1989.

Martin, Billy, 61: controversial five-time manager of Yankees. Had 1,258 victories and 1,068 losses in 16 seasons as major league manager. Dec. 25, 1989.

McCarthy, Mary, 77: a leading American writer with a long and prolific career as novelist, memoirist, journalist, and critic. In 1984 she won Edward MacDowell Medal for contributions to literature and National Medal for Literature. Oct. 25, 1989.

Medina, Harold R., 102: Federal judge for more than three decades. Known for presiding at New York trial of 11 Communist leaders in 1940s. March 14, 1990.

Menninger, Dr. Karl Augustus, 96: one of founders of Menninger clinic and a foremost U.S. practitioner and advocate of progressive psychiatry. July 18, 1990.

Middleton, Drew, 76: *New York Times* correspondent who covered World War II and postwar Europe. Chronicled major international affairs for nearly half a century. Jan. 10, 1990.

Mumford, Lewis, 94: city planner, cultural and political commentator, and writer on architecture. Fought large-scale public works he considered poorly planned. Awarded National Medal of Arts in 1986. Jan. 26, 1990.

Noyce, Robert N., 62: inventor of a tiny computer chip that revolutionized electronics industry. June 3, 1990.

Perls, Laura, 84: German psychiatrist, a founder of Gestalt school of psychotherapy, an eclectic borrowing from many sources. July 13, 1990.

Peter, Laurence J., 70: author who satirized climbers in corporations and other organizations. Formulated "Peter Principle," now part of language. Jan. 12, 1990.

Pimen, Patriarch, 79: head of Russian Orthodox Church from repressive Brezhnev years to new era of tolerance. Patriarch regarded as supporter of Kremlin line. May 3, 1990.

Powell, Michael, 84: British film director, screenwriter, and producer of quirky films, which included "Red Shoes." Feb. 19, 1990.

Quayle, Sir Anthony, 76: versatile British actor and director on stage and in television and films. Helped establish Stratford-on-Avon as major center of British theater. Oct. 20, 1989.

Raborn, William F., Jr., 84: retired Navy vice admiral. Led development of *Polaris* nuclear missile in 1950s. Later headed Central Intelligence Agency. March 7, 1990.

Rhodes, Erik, 84: stage, screen, and television actor who had memorable roles as a gigolo in Fred-Astaire-Ginger-Rogers musicals of 1930s. Feb. 17, 1990.

Roosevelt, Archibald B., 72: grandson of Theodore Roosevelt and former high official in Central Intelligence Agency. May 30, 1990.

Rose, Dr. Albert, 80: research scientist who converted optical images to electrical signs, leading way to television picture tube. July 26, 1990.

Rusk, Dr. Howard A., 88: pioneer in rehabilitation of physically disabled in United States and across world. Nov. 4, 1989.

Sakharov, Dr. Andrei D., 68: Soviet physicist, winner of Nobel Peace Prize in 1975. Human rights champion and long-time critic of Communist regime. Designed Soviet hydrogen bomb. Dec. 14, 1989.

Simenon, Georges, 86: Belgian novelist who became most widely published author of the century. Author of Inspector Maigret mysteries and other highly regarded works. Sept. 4, 1989.

Skinner, B. F., 86: leading American psychologist. As "behaviorist," he studied animal and human behavior with belief in its modification according to scientific principles. Aug. 18, 1990.

Stanwyck, Barbara, 82: star of such classic movies as "Stella Dallas," "The Lady Eve," and "Double Indemnity." Appeared in more than 80 films. Also starred in prize-winning television series "The Big Valley." Jan. 20, 1990.

Terry-Thomas (Thomas Terry Hoar Stevens), 78: British comedian and character actor known for gaptoothed grin and bristling moustache. Satirized all types of Briton in wide range of films. Jan. 8, 1990.

Thomson, Virgil, 92: American composer and music critic. Wrote two operas with Gertrude Stein texts. Center of intellectual life for 55 years. Sept. 30, 1989.

Van Heusen, Jimmy, 77: successful Hollywood composer of many popular songs, including "Moonlight Becomes You," "Sunday, Monday, and Always," and "Swingin' on a Star." Feb. 7, 1990.

Vaughan, Sara, 66: influential singer with powerful voice in performance of popular and jazz classics. April 3, 1990.

Wallace, Irving, 74: one of most popular and bestselling American authors. His 16 novels and 17 nonfiction works reported to have sold more than 120 million copies. June 29, 1990.

Wang, An, 70: founder of Wang Laboratories. Invented doughnut-shaped iron ring that preceded microchip in core of computer memory. March 24, 1990.

Warren, Robert Penn, 84: novelist and poet, author of "All the King's Men." Three-time winner of Pulitzer Prize and first Poet Laureate of United States. Sept. 15, 1989.

Wedemayer, Gen. Albert C., 92: renowned United States military planner and commander in World War II. His over-all war plan guided war effort after Japanese attack on Pearl Harbor. Dec. 17, 1989.

Weiss, Dr. Paul A., 91: biologist who won nation's highest science award, National Medal of Science, for pioneering work in theory of cellular development. Sept. 8, 1989.

White, Ryan, 18: Indiana youth dead of AIDS-related infection resulting from blood transfusion. Publicity about his rejection by school when he was 14 forced nation to pierce myths about disease. April 8, 1990.

Wilde, Cornel, 74: tall, dashing, and athletic actor starred in production of 1945 film "A Song to Remember," portrayal of Frederic Chopin. Oct. 16, 1989.

POSTAL REGULATIONS

Domestic Mail Service 1990

Rate Increases Proposed for 1991

On March 6, 1990, the U.S. Postal Service proposed an increase in all classes of mail. It would make the cost of a first-class stamp $.30 for the first ounce and $.23 for each additional ounce. A single postcard would go from $.15 to $.20 and express mail could rise from $8.75 to $9.75 for up to 8 ounces. A final decision on the increase will be made by the Postal Service Board of Governors in January 1991. The increase would start in February 1991.

First Class

First-class consists of letters and written and sealed matter. The rate is 25¢ for the first oz; 20¢ for each additional oz, or fraction of an oz, up to 12 oz. Pieces over 12 oz are subject to priority-mail (heavy pieces) rates. Single postcards, 15¢; double postcards, 30¢ (15¢ for each half). The post office sells prestamped single and double postal cards. Consult your postmaster for information on business-reply mail and presort rates.

The weight limit for first-class mail is 70 lb.

Weight	Rates
First oz	$ .25
Over 1 oz, but not over 2	.45
Over 2 oz, but not over 3	.65
Over 3 oz, but not over 4	.85
Over 4 oz, but not over 5	1.05
Over 5 oz, but not over 6	1.25
Over 6 oz, but not over 7	1.45
Over 7 oz, but not over 8	1.65
Over 8 oz, but not over 9	1.85
Over 9 oz, but not over 10	2.05
Over 10 oz, but not over 11	2.25
Over 11 oz, but not over 12	2.45
Over 12 oz, *see* Priority Mail	

Priority Mail (over 12 oz to 70 lb)

The zone rate applies to mailable matter over 12 oz of any class carried by air. Your local post office will supply free official zone tables appropriate to your location.

Airmail

First-class and priority mail receive airmail service.

Express Mail

Express Mail Service is available for any mailable article up to 70 lb in weight and 108 in. in combined length and girth. Flat rates: letter rate (up to 8 ounces), $8.75; up to 2 lb, $12.00; over 2 lb and up to 5 lb, $15.25; 6 to 70 pound rates vary by weight and distance (zones).

Articles received by 5 p.m. at a postal facility offering Express Mail Service will be delivered by 3 p.m. the next day or, if you prefer, your shipment can be picked up as early as 10 a.m. the next business day. Rates include Insurance, Shipment Receipt, and Record of Delivery at the destination post office.

Consult Postmaster for other Express Mail Services and rates.

The Postal Service will refund, upon application to originating office, the postage for any Express Mail shipments not meeting the service standard except for those delayed by strike or work stoppage.

Second Class

Second-class mail is used primarily by newspapers, magazines, and other periodicals with second-class mailing privileges. For copies mailed by the public, the rate is the applicable single piece third- or fourth-class rate.

Third Class (under 16 oz)

Third-class mail is used for circulars, books, printed matter, merchandise, seeds, cuttings, bulbs, roots, scions, and plants, and all other mailable matter not in first or second class. There are two rate structures for this class, a single-piece and a bulk rate.

Many community organizations, as well as businesses, find it economical to use this service. Because of the number of categories of third-class mail, you should consult your postmaster for the one best suited to your needs.

Third-Class, Single-Piece Rates

Weight	Rates	Weight	Rates
0 to 1 oz	$ .25	Over 8 to 10 oz	$ 1.20
Over 1 to 2 oz	.45	Over 10 to 12 oz	1.30
Over 2 to 3 oz	.65	Over 12 to 14 oz	1.40
Over 3 to 4 oz	.85	Over 14 but less	
Over 4 to 6 oz	1.00	than 16 oz	1.50
Over 6 to 8 oz	1.10		

Fourth Class (Parcel Post— 16 oz and over)

Fourth-class mail is used for merchandise, books, printed matter, and all other mailable matter not in first, second, or third class. Special fourth-class rates apply to books, library books, publications or records for the blind, and certain controlled-circulation publications.

Packages should be taken to your local post office, where the postage will be determined according to the weight of the package and the distance it is being sent. Information on weight and size limits for fourth-class mail may be obtained there.

Special Services

Registered Mail. When you use registered mail service, you are buying security—the safest way to send valuables. The full value of your mailing must be declared when mailed. You receive a receipt and the movement of your mail is controlled throughout the postal system. For an additional fee, a return receipt showing to whom, when, and where delivered may be obtained.

Fees for articles (in addition to postage)

Value			With insurance	Without insurance
$ 0.01	to	$ 100	$4.50	$4.40
100.01	to	500	4.85	4.70
500.01	to	1,000	5.25	5.05

For higher values, consult your postmaster.

Certified Mail. Certified mail service provides for a receipt to the sender and a record of delivery at the post office of address. No record is kept at the post office where mailed. It is handled in the ordinary mails and no insurance coverage is provided.
Fee in addition to postage, 85¢.

Return Receipts. Requested at time of mailing:
Showing to whom and date delivered	$ .90
Showing to whom, date, and address where delivered	1.20
Requested after mailing:	
Showing to whom and date delivered	5.00

C.O.D. Mail. Consult your postmaster for fees and conditions of mailing.

Insured Mail. Fees, in addition to postage, for coverage against loss or damage:

Liability		Fees
$ .01 to $50		$ .70
$ 50.01 to $100		1.50
$ 100.01 to $150		1.90
$ 150.01 to $200		2.20
$ 200.01 to $300		3.15
$ 300.01 to $400		4.30
$ 400.01 to $500		5.00

Special Delivery. The payment of the special-delivery fee entitles mail to the most expeditious transportation and delivery. The fee is in addition to the regular postage.

Weight/Fees

Class of mail	Not more than 2 lb	More than 2 lb but not more than 10 lb	More than 10 lb
First-class	$5.35	$5.75	$7.25
All other classes	5.65	6.50	8.10

Special Handling. Payment of the special-handling fee entitles third- and fourth-class matter to the most expeditious handling and transportation, but not special delivery. The fee is in addition to the regular postage.

Weight	Fees
Not more than 10 lb	$1.55
More than 10 lb	2.25

Money Orders. Money orders are used for the safe transmission of money.

Amount of money order			Fees
$ .01	to	$35	$ .75
$ 35.01	to	$700	1.00

Minimum Mail Sizes

All mail must be at least 0.007 in. thick and mail that is 1/4 in. or less in thickness must be at least 3 1/2 in. in height, at least 5 in. long, and rectangular in shape (except keys and identification devices). NOTE: Pieces greater than 1/4 in. thick can be mailed even if they measure less than 3 1/2 by 5 inches.

Adhesive Stamps Available

Purpose	Form	Denomination and prices
Ordinary postage	Single or sheet	1, 2, 3, 4, 5, 6, 7, 8, 9, 10, 11, 14, 15, 17, 18, 19, 20, 21, 22, 23, 25, 28, 30, 40, 45, 50, 65¢, $1, $2, $5, and $8.75.
	Books	20 at 25 cents ($5.00), 6 at 25 cents ($1.50), 12 at 25 cents ($3.00), Commemorative stamps, 20 at 25 cents ($5.00).
	Coil of 100	17, 20, 22, and 25¢ (dispenser and stamp affixer for use with these coils are also available).
	Coil of 500	1, 2, 3, 4, 5, 6, 9, 10, 11, 12, 14, 15, 17, 18, 20, 21, 22, 25¢ and $1.
	Coil of 3000	1, 2, 3, 4, 5, 6, 9, 10, 11, 12, 14, 15, 17, 18, 20, 21, 22, 25¢ and $1.
International airmail postage	Single or sheet	36 and 45¢

Note: Denominations listed are currently in stock. Others may be available until supplies are exhausted.

Non-Standard Mail

All first-class mail weighing one ounce or less and all single-piece rate third-class mail weighing one ounce or less is nonstandard (and subject to a 10¢ surcharge in addition to the applicable postage and fees) if any of the following dimensions are exceeded: length—11 1/2 inches; height—6 1/8 inches; thickness—1/4 inch, or the piece has a height to length (aspect) ratio which does not fall between 1 to 1.3 and 1 to 2.5 inclusive. (The aspect ratio is found by dividing the length by the height. If the answer is between 1.3 and 2.5 inclusive, the piece has a standard aspect ratio).

International Mail Service, 1990

Letters and Letter Packages

Items of mail containing personal handwritten or typewritten communications having the character of current correspondence must be sent as letters or letter packages. Unless prohibited by the country of destination, dutiable merchandise may be transmitted in packages prepaid at the letter rate of postage. Weight limit for all countries, 4 pounds. For rates, consult your local post office.

Post and Postal Cards

Canada	$0.21	All other—surface	$0.28
Mexico	$0.15	All other—air	$0.36

Aerogrammes—$0.39 each.

Canada and Mexico—Surface Rates

Letters and Letter Packages

Weight not over Lb	Oz	Canada	Mexico	Weight not over Lb	Oz	Canada	Mexico
0	1	$.30	$.25	0	11	2.50	2.25
0	2	.52	.45	0	12	2.72	2.45
0	3	.74	.65	1	0	3.08	3.25
0	4	.96	.85	1	8	3.70	4.05
0	5	1.18	1.05	2	0	4.32	4.85
0	6	1.40	1.25	2	8	4.94	5.65
0	7	1.62	1.45	3	0	5.56	6.45
0	8	1.84	1.65	3	8	6.18	7.25
0	9	2.06	1.85	4	0	6.80	8.05
0	10	2.28	2.05				

Weight Limit—4 Pounds*

Note: Mail paid at this rate receives First-Class service in the United States and air service in Canada and Mexico. *Registered letters to Canada may weigh up to 66 pounds. The rate for over 4 pounds to 66 pounds is $1.24 per pound or fraction of a pound.

Letters and Letter Packages— Airmail Rates

All Countries other than Canada & Mexico

Weight not over Oz	Rate	Weight not over Oz	Rate
0.5	$ 0.45	24.5	$20.70
1.0	0.90	25.0	21.12
1.5	1.35	25.5	21.54
2.0	1.80	26.0	21.96
2.5	2.22	26.5	22.38
3.0	2.64	27.0	22.80
3.5	3.06	27.5	23.22
4.0	3.48	28.0	23.64
4.5	3.90	28.5	24.06
5.0	4.32	29.0	24.48
5.5	4.74	29.5	24.90
6.0	5.16	30.0	25.32
6.5	5.58	30.5	25.74
7.0	6.00	31.0	26.16
7.5	6.42	31.5	26.58
8.0	6.84	32.0	27.00
8.5	7.26	33	27.42
9.0	7.68	34	27.84
9.5	8.10	35	28.26
10.0	8.52	36	28.68
10.5	8.94	37	29.10
11.0	9.36	38	29.52
11.5	9.78	39	29.94
12.0	10.20	40	30.36
12.5	10.62	41	30.78
13.0	11.04	42	31.20
13.5	11.46	43	31.62
14.0	11.88	44	32.04
14.5	12.30	45	32.46
15.0	12.72	46	32.88
15.5	13.14	47	33.30
16.0	13.56	48	33.72
16.5	13.98	49	34.14
17.0	14.40	50	34.56
17.5	14.82	51	34.98
18.0	15.24	52	35.40
18.5	15.66	53	35.82
19.0	16.08	54	36.24
19.5	16.50	55	36.66
20.0	16.92	56	37.08
20.5	17.34	57	37.50
21.0	17.76	58	37.92
21.5	18.18	59	38.34
22.0	18.60	60	38.76
22.5	19.02	61	39.18
23.0	19.44	62	39.60
23.5	19.86	63	40.02
24.0	20.28	64	40.44

Countries Other Than Canada and Mexico—Surface Rates

Letters and Letter Packages

Weight not over Lb	Oz	Rate	Weight not over Lb	Oz	Rate
0	1	0.40	0	11	3.80
0	2	0.63	0	12	3.80
0	3	0.86	1	0	3.80
0	4	1.09	1	8	5.20
0	5	1.32	2	0	6.60
0	6	1.55	2	8	7.60
0	7	1.78	3	0	8.60
0	8	2.01	3	8	9.60
0	9	3.80	4	0	10.60
0	10	3.80			

Weight limit—4 pounds.

International Surface Parcel Post

Other Than Canada

Weight through lb	Mexico, Central America, Caribbean Islands, Bahamas, Bermuda, St. Pierre and Miquelon	All other countries
2	$ 4.40 $1.40 each additional lb or fraction	$ 4.60 $1.50 each additional lb or fraction

Consult your postmaster for weight/size limits of individual countries.

For other international services and rates consult your local postmaster.

Canada Surface Parcel Post

Up to 2 lb $3.95, $1.20 for each additional lb up to the maximum weight of 66 lb. Minimum weight is 1 lb.

International Money Order Fees

This service available only to certain countries. Consult post office.

United Nations Stamps

United Nations stamps are issued in three different currencies, namely, U.S. dollars, Swiss francs, and Austrian schillings. Stamps in all three currencies are available at face value at each of the U.N. Postal Administration offices in New York, Geneva, and Vienna. They may be purchased over the counter, by mail, or by opening a Customer Deposit Account.

Mail orders for mint (unused) stamps and postal stationery may be sent to the U.N. Postal Administration in New York, Geneva, and Vienna. Write to: United Nations Postal Administration, P.O. Box 5900, Grand Central Station, New York, N.Y. 10017.

How to Complain About a Postal Problem

When you have a problem with your mail service, complete a Consumer Service Card which is available from letter carriers and at post offices. This will help your postmaster respond to your problem. If you wish to telephone a complaint, a postal employee will fill out the card for you.

The Consumer Advocate represents consumers at the top management level in the Postal Service. If your postal problems cannot be solved by your local post office, then write to the Consumer Advocate. His staff stands ready to serve you. Write to:

The Consumer Advocate, U.S. Postal Service, Washington, D.C. 20260-6320. Or phone: 1-202-268-2284.

The Mail Order Merchandise Rule

The mail order rule adopted by the Federal Trade Commission in October 1975 provides that when you order by mail:

You must receive the merchandise when the seller says you will.

If you are not promised delivery within a certain time period, the seller must ship the merchandise to you no later than 30 days after your order comes in.

If you don't receive it shortly after that 30-day period, you can cancel your order and get your money back.

How the Rule Works

The seller must notify you if the promised delivery date (or the 30-day limit) cannot be met. The seller must also tell you what the new shipping date will be and give you the option to cancel the order and receive a full refund or agree to the new shipping date. The seller must also give you a free way to send back your answer, such as a stamped envelope or a postage-paid postcard. *If you don't answer, it means that you agree to the shipping delay.*

The seller must tell you if the shipping delay is going to be more than 30 days. You then can agree to the delay or, if you do not agree, the seller must return your money by the end of the first 30 days of the delay.

If you cancel a prepaid order, the seller must mail you the refund within seven business days. Where there is a credit sale, the seller must adjust your account within one billing cycle.

It would be impossible, however, for one rule to apply uniformly to such a varied field as mail order merchandising. For example, the rule does not apply to mail order photo finishing, magazine subscriptions, and other serial deliveries (except for the initial shipment); to mail order seeds and growing plants; to COD orders; or to credit orders where the buyer's account is not charged prior to shipment of the merchandise.

Authorized 2-Letter State Abbreviations

When the Post Office instituted the ZIP Code for mail in 1963, it also drew up a list of two-letter abbreviations for the states which would gradually replace the traditional ones in use. Following is the official list, including the District of Columbia, Guam, Puerto Rico, and the Virgin Islands (note that only capital letters are used):

Alabama	AL	Kentucky	KY	Ohio	OH
Alaska	AK	Louisiana	LA	Oklahoma	OK
Arizona	AZ	Maine	ME	Oregon	OR
Arkansas	AR	Maryland	MD	Pennsylvania	PA
California	CA	Massachusetts	MA	Puerto Rico	PR
Colorado	CO	Michigan	MI	Rhode Island	RI
Connecticut	CT	Minnesota	MN	South Carolina	SC
Delaware	DE	Mississippi	MS	South Dakota	SD
Dist. of Columbia	DC	Missouri	MO	Tennessee	TN
Florida	FL	Montana	MT	Texas	TX
Georgia	GA	Nebraska	NE	Utah	UT
Guam	GU	Nevada	NV	Vermont	VT
Hawaii	HI	New Hampshire	NH	Virginia	VA
Idaho	ID	New Jersey	NJ	Virgin Islands	VI
Illinois	IL	New Mexico	NM	Washington	WA
Indiana	IN	New York	NY	West Virginia	WV
Iowa	IA	North Carolina	NC	Wisconsin	WI
Kansas	KS	North Dakota	ND	Wyoming	WY